# THE NEW
# ENGLISH BIBLE

## WITH THE APOCRYPHA

# THE BIBLE

## A NEW ENGLISH TRANSLATION

*Planned and Directed by Representatives of*

THE BAPTIST UNION OF GREAT BRITAIN AND IRELAND

THE CHURCH OF ENGLAND

THE CHURCH OF SCOTLAND

THE CONGREGATIONAL CHURCH IN ENGLAND AND WALES

THE COUNCIL OF CHURCHES FOR WALES

THE IRISH COUNCIL OF CHURCHES

THE LONDON YEARLY MEETING OF
THE SOCIETY OF FRIENDS

THE METHODIST CHURCH OF GREAT BRITAIN

THE PRESBYTERIAN CHURCH OF ENGLAND

THE BRITISH AND FOREIGN BIBLE SOCIETY

THE NATIONAL BIBLE SOCIETY OF SCOTLAND

*The publication of the books of the Apocrypha in this translation pre-
pared under the auspices of the Joint Committee on the New Translation
of the Bible does not imply that the bodies represented on the Joint Committee hold a common opinion upon the canonical status of these books*

# THE NEW ENGLISH BIBLE

## WITH THE APOCRYPHA

OXFORD UNIVERSITY PRESS
CAMBRIDGE UNIVERSITY PRESS
1970

*The New Testament*
*First edition* 1961
*Second edition* 1970

*The Old Testament and Apocrypha*
*First published* 1970

Library of Congress Catalogue Card Number: 61-16025

PRINTED IN THE UNITED STATES OF AMERICA

# PREFACE

## TO THE NEW ENGLISH BIBLE

IN MAY 1946 the General Assembly of the Church of Scotland received an overture from the Presbytery of Stirling and Dunblane, where it had been initiated by the Reverend G. S. Hendry, recommending that a translation of the Bible be made in the language of the present day, inasmuch as the language of the Authorized Version, already archaic when it was made, had now become even more definitely archaic and less generally understood. The General Assembly resolved to make an approach to other Churches, and, as a result, delegates of the Church of England, the Church of Scotland, and the Methodist, Baptist, and Congregational Churches met in conference in October. They recommended that the work should be undertaken; that a completely new translation should be made, rather than a revision, such as had earlier been contemplated by the University Presses of Oxford and Cambridge; and that the translators should be free to employ a contemporary idiom rather than reproduce the traditional 'biblical' English.

In January 1947 a second conference, held like the first in the Central Hall, Westminster, included representatives of the University Presses. At the request of this conference, the Churches named above appointed representatives to form the Joint Committee on the New Translation of the Bible. This Committee met for the first time in July of the same year. By January 1948, when its third meeting was held, invitations to be represented had been sent to the Presbyterian Church of England, the Society of Friends, the Churches in Wales, the Churches in Ireland, the British and Foreign Bible Society, and the National Bible Society of Scotland: these invitations were accepted. At a much later stage the hierarchies of the Roman Catholic Church in England and Scotland accepted an invitation to appoint representatives, and these attended as observers.

The Joint Committee provided for the actual work of translation from the original tongues by appointing three panels, to deal, respectively, with the Old Testament, the Apocrypha, and the New Testament. Their members were scholars drawn from various British universities, whom the Committee believed to be representative of competent biblical scholarship at the present time. Apprehending, however, that sound scholarship does not necessarily carry with it a delicate sense of English style, the Committee appointed a fourth panel, of trusted literary advisers, to whom all the work of the translating panels was to be submitted for scrutiny. It should be said that denominational considerations played no part in the appointment of the panels.

The Joint Committee issued general directions to the panels, in pursuance of the aims which the enterprise had in view. The translating panels adopted the following procedure. An individual was invited to submit a draft translation of a particular book, or group of books. Normally he would be a member of the panel concerned. Very occasionally a draft translation was invited from a scholar outside the panel, who was known to have worked specially on the book in question. The draft was circulated in typescript to members of the panel for their consideration. They then met together and discussed the draft round a table, verse by verse, sentence by sentence. Each member brought his view about the meaning of the original to the judgement of his fellows, and discussion went on until they reached a common mind. There are passages where, in the present state of our knowledge, no one could say with certainty which of two (or even more) possible meanings is intended. In such cases, after careful discussion, alternative meanings have been recorded in footnotes, but only where they seemed of sufficient importance. There is probably no member of a panel who has not found himself obliged to give up, perhaps with lingering regret, a cherished view about the meaning of this or that difficult passage, but in the end the panel accepted corporate responsibility for the interpretation set forth in the translation adopted.

The resultant draft was now remitted to the panel of literary advisers. They scrutinized it, once again, verse by verse, sentence by sentence, and took pains to secure, as best they could, the tone and level of language appropriate to the different kinds of writing to be found in the Bible, whether narrative, familiar discourse, argument, law, rhetoric or poetry. The translation thus amended was returned to the translating panel, who examined it to make sure that the meaning intended had not been in any way misunderstood. Passages of peculiar difficulty might on occasion pass repeatedly between the panels. The final form of the version was reached by agreement between the translators concerned and the literary advisers. It was then ready for submission to the Joint Committee.

Since January 1948 the Joint Committee has met regularly twice a year in the Jerusalem Chamber, Westminster Abbey, with four exceptions during 1954-5 when the Langham Room in the precincts of the Abbey was kindly made available. At these meetings the Committee has received reports on the progress of the work from the Conveners of the four panels, and its members have had in their hands typescripts of the books so far translated and revised. They have made such comments and given such advice or decisions as they judged to be necessary, and from time to time they have met members of the panels in conference.

Of the original members of the panels most have happily been able to stay with the work all through, though some have been lost, through death or otherwise, and their places have been filled by fresh appointments.

The Committee has warmly appreciated the courteous hospitality of the Dean of Westminster and of the Trustees of the Central Hall. We owe a great debt to the support and the experienced counsel of the University Presses of Oxford and Cambridge. We recognize gratefully the service rendered to the enterprise by the Reverend Dr. G. S. Hendry and the Reverend Professor J. K. S. Reid, who have successively held the office of Secretary to the Committee. To those who have borne special responsibility, as Chairmen of the Joint Committee, we owe more than could readily be told. Dr. J. W. Hunkin, Bishop of Truro, our first Chairman, brought to the work an exuberant vigour and initiative without which the formidable project might hardly have got off the ground at all. On his lamented death in 1950 he was succeeded by Dr. A. T. P. Williams, then Bishop of Durham and subsequently Bishop of Winchester, who for eighteen years guided our enterprise with judicious wisdom, tact, and benign firmness, but who to our sorrow died when the end of the task was in sight. To both of these we would put on record the gratitude of the Committee and of all engaged in the enterprise.

If we embarked on mentioning the names of those who have served on the various committees and panels, the list would be a long one; and if we mentioned some and not others, the selection would be an invidious one. There are, nevertheless, three names the omission of which would be utterly wrong. As Vice-Chairman and Director, Dr. C. H. Dodd has from start to finish given outstanding leadership and guidance to the project, bringing to the work scholarship, sensitivity, and an ever watchful eye. Professor Sir Godfrey Driver, Joint Director since 1965, has also brought to the work a wealth of knowledge and wisdom; to his enthusiasm, tenacity of purpose, and unflagging devotion the whole enterprise is greatly indebted. Professor W. D. McHardy, Deputy Director since 1968, has made an invaluable contribution particularly, but by no means exclusively, in the sphere of the Apocrypha. It is right that the names of these three scholars should always be associated with The New English Bible. Our debt to them is incalculably great.

DONALD EBOR:

*Chairman of the Joint Committee*

# CONTENTS

# CONTENTS

## THE APOCRYPHA

# CONTENTS

## THE NEW TESTAMENT

# CONTENTS

# THE
# OLD TESTAMENT

# INTRODUCTION

## TO THE OLD TESTAMENT

THE OLD TESTAMENT consists of a body of literature spread over a period extending from the twelfth to the second century B.C.; this literature is written in classical Hebrew, except some brief portions which are in Aramaic, a cognate or sister language (Ezra 4. 8—6. 18 and 7. 12-26, Jeremiah 10. 11, Daniel 2. 4—7. 28). No manuscripts of the Old Testament from the earlier part of this period have been preserved; indeed much of it must have been handed down by oral tradition from generation to generation. The impetus to collect, edit and make copies of the national literature may well have come from the disaster of 587/6 B.C., when the Babylonians captured and burnt Jerusalem and carried off many of its inhabitants into exile.

The earliest known Hebrew manuscripts containing any parts of the Old Testament are among the Scrolls (commonly called the Dead Sea Scrolls) found in caves at Qumran near the north-western end of the Dead Sea; they may be dated in the last two centuries B.C., though some may be a little earlier and others somewhat later. They include two copies of Isaiah, one complete and another badly damaged, a commentary containing most of the text of the first two chapters of Habakkuk, and fragments of every other Old Testament book, except Esther. The text which they present is to a large extent identical with that in our Hebrew Bibles.

In the second century A.D. or even earlier the Rabbis, the Jewish religious leaders, compiled a text from such manuscripts as had survived the destruction of Jerusalem in A.D. 70, and on this basis was established the traditional or Massoretic text, so called from the Hebrew word *massorah* 'tradition'. This text incorporated the mistakes of generations of copyists, and, in spite of the care bestowed on it, many errors of later copyists also found their way into it. The earliest surviving manuscripts of this text date from the ninth to eleventh centuries A.D.; and it is this text, as printed in R. Kittel's *Biblia Hebraica* (3rd edition, 1937), which has been used for the present translation.

The traditional text was originally written only in consonants, but in order to preserve what they regarded as the correct pronunciation of the words the Rabbis added vowel-signs to the text. Of the various systems of vowel-signs which were devised, that developed at Tiberias in the fifth to sixth centuries A.D. ultimately prevailed and is still used in our printed Bibles. The vowels are here represented by means of strokes and dots added to the consonantal text, and this method of vocalization made it possible for the Rabbis to indicate variant readings which they preferred, without meddling with the consonants: they put in the margin of their manuscript the consonants of the reading which they wished to adopt and added the vowel-signs of this reading to the consonants in the text which they were rejecting. The reader knew that he was to pronounce the consonants in the margin with the vowels in the text.

One variation of this convention is of special importance, inasmuch as it affects the divine name. This personal proper name, written with the consonants *YHWH*, was considered too sacred to be uttered; so the vowels for the words 'my Lord' or 'God' were added to the consonants *YHWH*, and the reader was warned by these vowels that he must substitute other consonants. This change having to be made so frequently, the Rabbis did not consider it necessary to put the consonants of the new reading in the margin. In course of time the true pronunciation of the divine name, probably *Yahweh*, passed into oblivion, and *YHWH* was read with the intruded vowels, the vowels of an entirely different word, namely 'my Lord' or 'God'. In late medieval times this mispronunciation became current as *Jehova*, and it was taken over as *Jehovah* by the Reformers in Protestant Bibles. The present translators have retained this incorrect but customary form in the text of passages where the name is explained with a note on its pronunciation (e.g. Exodus 3. 15) and in four place-names of which it forms a constituent element; elsewhere they have followed ancient translators in substituting 'LORD' or 'GOD', printed as here in capital letters, for the Hebrew name.

So much for the text of the Hebrew Old Testament as it lies before us; but it is certain that this does not always represent what was originally written. The translator must often go behind the traditional text to discover the writer's meaning. For this purpose he may have recourse first to the Scrolls; but these cover only a very small part of the Old Testament writings. Secondly he may have recourse to the Samaritan Pentateuch, which, though extant only in late manuscripts, the earliest being dated about the eleventh century A.D., may be somewhat earlier than the Scrolls and represents the text of the five books of the Law (Genesis to Deuteronomy) which the Samaritans took with them when they seceded from Judaism. It differs from the traditional Hebrew text in a considerable number of small and mostly unimportant points.

For further help the translator may turn to the ancient versions. Of these the earliest is the Old Testament in Greek, designed to meet the needs of Greek-speaking Jews in Egypt in the third and second centuries B.C. According to tradition the Pentateuch was translated by seventy-two elders, six from each of the twelve tribes of Israel, and so the Greek version of the Old Testament came to be called the Septuagint, from the Latin *septuaginta* 'seventy'. Clearly it is the work of a number of translators of unequal skill; their rendering is now literal, now paraphrastic, and now interpretative. Not infrequently it contains absurd mistranslations. Yet it is valuable for the recovery of the original Hebrew, because it is based on an underlying Hebrew text older than the Massoretic, and it often preserves the correct reading in passages where our Hebrew manuscripts are manifestly in error, or the true interpretation where this has been obscured in the traditional text. Its defects, however, were patent, and early in the

Christian era several scholars, Aquila, Symmachus and Theodotion, tried to improve on it; other scholars produced fresh recensions of it, among which the text associated with the name of Lucian is commonly included.

With the spread of Christianity across the Mediterranean world the need for a Latin version of the Scriptures arose, and a translation of the Septuagint was made by unknown translators. This, known as the Old Latin Version, of which only parts survive, was so unsatisfactory that towards the end of the fourth century A.D. Pope Damasus ordered Jerome to prepare a fresh Latin translation. The new version, commonly called the Vulgate, and produced with the help of Jewish scholars, is idiomatic and forceful, and, being made directly from the Hebrew text, is especially helpful in recovering the form and sense of that text.

As the knowledge of Hebrew died out among the Jews, the reading of the Scriptures in the synagogue had to be followed by a translation of the passages into Aramaic, the language which had supplanted Hebrew. Such renderings, known as Targums (Aramaic *targum*, 'translation'), tended to become traditional and stereotyped and finally were written down. Some of them contain pre-Christian material. There are Targums to every book of the Old Testament except Daniel, Ezra, and Nehemiah, but only one, on the Pentateuch, is a straightforward translation.

Between the first and third centuries A.D. a Syriac translation, known as the Peshitta (i.e. 'simple') Version, was made; some parts of it are more literal than others, and, though it agrees in the main with the Hebrew text, it bears traces of the influence of the Septuagint. Other versions in various languages appeared between the third and thirteenth centuries A.D., but they are of little value for the recovery and interpretation of the Hebrew text.

In spite of this wealth of ancient versions, and even when the earliest known form of the text has been established, many obscurities still remain in the Hebrew Scriptures. The classical Hebrew vocabulary as known today is small, with the consequence that the meaning of an unusually large number of words is uncertain or unknown. In such cases recourse may be had to the cognate languages. Already medieval scholars had begun to use the Arabic language for this purpose, and in later centuries Syriac and Ethiopic also were used. In more recent times scholars have had access to the vast literature in Babylonian, Assyrian, and kindred dialects which has been preserved on cuneiform tablets. Archaeology, too, has at times been helpful in clearing up an obscurity in the Hebrew text. But in the last resort, the translator may have to arrive at the sense of a word from the context alone, or he may even have to emend what is demonstrably faulty; such corrections of the text, except when only the vowels are affected, are recorded in the notes of the present translation.

The paragraphs in this translation are a modified form of those in the Authorized and Revised Versions, and the present translators have added headings to the main sections into which the text falls. Sometimes, for what seemed sufficient reasons, the order of the verses has been changed, as will be seen from the verse-numbering. Occasionally passages have been brought together if a common refrain or other evidence shows that they have been wrongly separated; such changes are recorded in the notes.

The headings of the Psalms, consisting partly of musical instructions, of which the meanings have mostly been lost, and partly of historical notices, deduced (sometimes incorrectly) from the individual Psalms, have been omitted; they are almost certainly not original. On the other hand, the designations of the speakers in the Song of Songs, though absent from the Hebrew text, have been introduced, with occasional corrections, from two manuscripts of the Septuagint.

A major difficulty in translating the Old Testament lies in the difference of time and place. Palestine differs greatly from the Western world in its physical aspects, in its plants, birds and beasts, its arts and crafts, as it did also in its social, administrative and religious, institutions, so that no English words exist to represent much about which the Old Testament speaks. The modern translator then must be content to use paraphrase or even to transliterate certain Hebrew words. The present translators have transliterated the Hebrew words for technical terms, where verbal exactness has seemed essential, while in other passages they have allowed themselves a paraphrase to bring out the general sense, where no technical problem requiring particularization is involved; but they have adopted such devices as rarely as possible.

Finally, the translators have endeavoured to avoid anachronisms and expressions reminiscent of foreign idioms. They have tried to keep their language as close to current usage as possible, while avoiding words and phrases likely soon to become obsolete. They have made every effort not only to make sense but also to offer renderings that will meet the needs of readers with no special knowledge of the background of the Old Testament.

G. R. D.

# GUIDE TO THE NOTES

The footnotes in this edition of the Old Testament serve (*a*) to give cross-references to parallel passages, chiefly in the historical books, (*b*) to indicate where verses or parts of verses have been transposed, (*c*) to give the meaning of proper names where it appears to be reflected in the context, (*d*) to give an alternative interpretation where the Hebrew is capable of such, and (*e*) to indicate places where the translators have adopted what seemed to them the most probable correction of the text where the Hebrew and the ancient versions cannot be convincingly translated as they stand.

Unless otherwise indicated by its wording, a note refers to the single word against which the reference is placed.

## ABBREVIATIONS, ETC.

### I. GENERAL

| | |
|---|---|
| *Aram.* | Aramaic (text or word) |
| *ch(s).* | chapter(s) |
| *cp.* | compare |
| *Heb.* | Hebrew (text or word) |
| *mng.* | meaning |
| *MS(S).* | manuscript(s) |
| *om.* | omit(s) |
| *or* | indicating an alternative interpretation |
| *poss.* | possible |
| *prob.* | probable |
| *rdg.* | reading |
| *Sept.* | Septuagint (Greek version of the Old Testament) |

| | |
|---|---|
| [. . .] | In the text itself square brackets are used to indicate words that are probably late additions to the Hebrew text. |

## II. BOOKS OF THE OLD TESTAMENT

| | | | |
|---|---|---|---|
| *Gen.* | Genesis | *Eccles.* | Ecclesiastes |
| *Exod.* | Exodus | *S. of S.* | Song of Songs |
| *Lev.* | Leviticus | *Isa.* | Isaiah |
| *Num.* | Numbers | *Jer.* | Jeremiah |
| *Deut.* | Deuteronomy | *Lam.* | Lamentations |
| *Josh.* | Joshua | *Ezek.* | Ezekiel |
| *Judg.* | Judges | *Dan.* | Daniel |
| *Ruth* | Ruth | *Hos.* | Hosea |
| *1 Sam.* | 1 Samuel | *Joel* | Joel |
| *2 Sam.* | 2 Samuel | *Amos* | Amos |
| *1 Kgs.* | 1 Kings | *Obad.* | Obadiah |
| *2 Kgs.* | 2 Kings | *Jonah* | Jonah |
| *1 Chr.* | 1 Chronicles | *Mic.* | Micah |
| *2 Chr.* | 2 Chronicles | *Nahum* | Nahum |
| *Ezra* | Ezra | *Hab.* | Habakkuk |
| *Neh.* | Nehemiah | *Zeph.* | Zephaniah |
| *Esther* | Esther | *Hag.* | Haggai |
| *Job* | Job | *Zech.* | Zechariah |
| *Ps(s).* | Psalm(s) | *Mal.* | Malachi |
| *Prov.* | Proverbs | | |

# MARGINAL NUMBERS

THE conventional verse divisions in the Old Testament are based on those in Hebrew manuscripts. Nevertheless any system of division into numbered verses is foreign to the spirit of this translation, which is intended to convey the meaning in natural English—the prose in paragraphs, the poetic passages in lines corresponding to the structure of the Hebrew.

For purposes of reference, and of comparison with other translations, verse numbers are placed in the margin opposite the line in which the first word belonging to the verse in question appears. Sometimes, however, successive verses are combined in a continuous translation, so that the precise point where a new verse begins cannot be fixed; in these cases the verse numbers, joined by a hyphen, are placed at the point where the passage begins.

# GENESIS

## The creation of the world

IN THE BEGINNING OF CREATION, when God made 1
heaven and earth,<sup>a</sup> the earth was without form and void, with darkness 2
over the face of the abyss, and a mighty wind that swept<sup>b</sup> over the
surface of the waters. God said, 'Let there be light', and there was light; 3
and God saw that the light was good, and he separated light from darkness. 4
He called the light day, and the darkness night. So evening came, and 5
morning came, the first day.

God said, 'Let there be a vault between the waters, to separate water 6
from water.' So God made the vault, and separated the water under the 7
vault from the water above it, and so it was; and God called the vault 8
heaven. Evening came, and morning came, a second day.

God said, 'Let the waters under heaven be gathered into one place, so 9
that dry land may appear'; and so it was. God called the dry land earth, 10
and the gathering of the waters he called seas; and God saw that it was
good. Then God said, 'Let the earth produce fresh growth, let there be 11
on the earth plants bearing seed, fruit-trees bearing fruit each with seed
according to its kind.' So it was; the earth yielded fresh growth, plants 12
bearing seed according to their kind and trees bearing fruit each with seed
according to its kind; and God saw that it was good. Evening came, and 13
morning came, a third day.

God said, 'Let there be lights in the vault of heaven to separate day from 14
night, and let them serve as signs both for festivals and for seasons and
years. Let them also shine in the vault of heaven to give light on earth.' So 15
it was; God made the two great lights, the greater to govern the day and 16
the lesser to govern the night; and with them he made the stars. God put 17
these lights in the vault of heaven to give light on earth, to govern day and 18
night, and to separate light from darkness; and God saw that it was good.
Evening came, and morning came, a fourth day. 19

God said, 'Let the waters teem with countless living creatures, and let 20
birds fly above the earth across the vault of heaven.' God then created the 21
great sea-monsters and all living creatures that move and swarm in the
waters, according to their kind, and every kind of bird; and God saw that
it was good. So he blessed them and said, 'Be fruitful and increase, fill the 22
waters of the seas; and let the birds increase on land.' Evening came, and 23
morning came, a fifth day.

God said, 'Let the earth bring forth living creatures, according to their 24
kind: cattle, reptiles, and wild animals, all according to their kind.' So it
was; God made wild animals, cattle, and all reptiles, each according to its 25

<sup>a</sup> Or In the beginning God created heaven and earth.     <sup>b</sup> Or and the spirit
of God hovering.

I

26 kind; and he saw that it was good. Then God said, 'Let us make man in our image and likeness to rule the fish in the sea, the birds of heaven, the cattle, all wild animals on earth, and all reptiles that crawl upon the earth.'
27 So God created man in his own image; in the image of God he created
28 him; male and female he created them. God blessed them and said to them, 'Be fruitful and increase, fill the earth and subdue it, rule over the fish in the sea, the birds of heaven, and every living thing that moves upon
29 the earth.' God also said, 'I give you all plants that bear seed everywhere on earth, and every tree bearing fruit which yields seed: they shall be yours
30 for food. All green plants I give for food to the wild animals, to all the birds of heaven, and to all reptiles on earth, every living creature.' So it was;
31 and God saw all that he had made, and it was very good. Evening came, and morning came, a sixth day.

2 Thus heaven and earth were completed with all their mighty throng.
2 On the sixth day God completed all the work he had been doing, and on
3 the seventh day he ceased from all his work. God blessed the seventh day and made it holy, because on that day he ceased from all the work he had set himself to do.
4 This is the story of the making of heaven and earth when they were created.

## The beginnings of history

5 WHEN THE LORD GOD MADE EARTH AND HEAVEN, there was neither shrub nor plant growing wild upon the earth, because the LORD God had sent no rain on the earth; nor was there any man to till the ground.
6 A flood*a* used to rise out of the earth and water all the surface of the ground.
7 Then the LORD God formed a man*b* from the dust of the ground*c* and breathed into his nostrils the breath of life. Thus the man became a living
8 creature. Then the LORD God planted a garden in Eden away to the east,
9 and there he put the man whom he had formed. The LORD God made trees spring from the ground, all trees pleasant to look at and good for food; and in the middle of the garden he set the tree of life and the tree of the knowledge of good and evil.
10 There was a river flowing from Eden to water the garden, and when it
11 left the garden it branched into four streams. The name of the first is Pishon; that is the river which encircles all the land of Havilah, where the
12 gold*d* is. The gold*d* of that land is good; bdellium*e* and cornelians are also
13 to be found there. The name of the second river is Gihon; this is the one
14 which encircles all the land of Cush. The name of the third is Tigris; this is the river which runs east of Asshur. The fourth river is the Euphrates.
15 The LORD God took the man and put him in the garden of Eden to till
16 it and care for it. He told the man, 'You may eat from every tree in the
17 garden, but not from the tree of the knowledge of good and evil; for on the
18 day that you eat from it, you will certainly die.' Then the LORD God said,

*a* Or mist.     *b* *Heb.* adam.     *c* *Heb.* adamah.     *d* Or frankincense.
*e* Or gum resin.

'It is not good for the man to be alone. I will provide a partner for him.'
So God formed out of the ground all the wild animals and all the birds of 19
heaven. He brought them to the man to see what he would call them, and
whatever the man called each living creature, that was its name. Thus the 20
man gave names to all cattle, to the birds of heaven, and to every wild
animal; but for the man himself no partner had yet been found. And so 21
the LORD God put the man into a trance, and while he slept, he took one
of his ribs and closed the flesh over the place. The LORD God then built 22
up the rib, which he had taken out of the man, into a woman. He brought
her to the man, and the man said: 23

'Now this, at last—
bone from my bones,
flesh from my flesh!—
this shall be called woman,*a*
for from man *b* was this taken.'

That is why a man leaves his father and mother and is united to his wife, 24
and the two become one flesh. Now they were both naked, the man and his 25
wife, but they had no feeling of shame towards one another.

THE SERPENT WAS MORE CRAFTY than any wild creature that the LORD 3
God had made. He said to the woman, 'Is it true that God has forbidden
you to eat from any tree in the garden?' The woman answered the serpent, 2
'We may eat the fruit of any tree in the garden, except for the tree in the 3
middle of the garden; God has forbidden us either to eat or to touch the
fruit of that; if we do, we shall die.' The serpent said, 'Of course you will 4
not die. God knows that as soon as you eat it, your eyes will be opened and 5
you will be like gods*c* knowing both good and evil.' When the woman saw 6
that the fruit of the tree was good to eat, and that it was pleasing to the eye
and tempting to contemplate, she took some and ate it. She also gave her
husband some and he ate it. Then the eyes of both of them were opened 7
and they discovered that they were naked; so they stitched fig-leaves
together and made themselves loincloths.

The man and his wife heard the sound of the LORD God walking in the 8
garden at the time of the evening breeze and hid from the LORD God
among the trees of the garden. But the LORD God called to the man and 9
said to him, 'Where are you?' He replied, 'I heard the sound as you were 10
walking in the garden, and I was afraid because I was naked, and I hid myself.' God answered, 'Who told you that you were naked? Have you eaten 11
from the tree which I forbade you?' The man said, 'The woman you gave 12
me for a companion, she gave me fruit from the tree and I ate it.' Then 13
the LORD God said to the woman, 'What is this that you have done?' The
woman said, 'The serpent tricked me, and I ate.' Then the LORD God said 14
to the serpent:

'Because you have done this you are accursed
more than all cattle and all wild creatures.

---

*a Heb.* ishshah.      *b Heb.* ish.      *c Or* God.

> On your belly you shall crawl, and dust you shall eat
> all the days of your life.
15  I will put enmity between you and the woman,
> between your brood and hers.
> They shall strike at your head,
> and you shall strike at their heel.'

16  To the woman he said:

> 'I will increase your labour and your groaning,
> and in labour you shall bear children.
> You shall be eager *a* for your husband,
> and he shall be your master.'

17  And to the man he said:

> 'Because you have listened to your wife
> and have eaten from the tree which I forbade you,
> accursed shall be the ground on your account.
> With labour you shall win your food from it
> all the days of your life.
18  It will grow thorns and thistles for you,
> none but wild plants for you to eat.
19  You shall gain your bread by the sweat of your brow
> until you return to the ground;
> for from it you were taken.
> Dust you are, to dust you shall return.'

20  The man called his wife Eve *b* because she was the mother of all who live.
21  The Lord God made tunics of skins for Adam and his wife and clothed
22  them. He said, 'The man has become like one of us, knowing good and
> evil; what if he now reaches out his hand and takes fruit from the tree of
23  life also, eats it and lives for ever?' So the Lord God drove him out of the
24  garden of Eden to till the ground from which he had been taken. He cast
> him out, and to the east of the garden of Eden he stationed the cherubim
> and a sword whirling and flashing to guard the way to the tree of life.

4  The man lay with his wife Eve, and she conceived and gave birth to Cain.
> She said, 'With the help of the Lord I have brought a man into being.'
2  Afterwards she had another child, his brother Abel. Abel was a shepherd
3  and Cain a tiller of the soil. The day came when Cain brought some of the
4  produce of the soil as a gift to the Lord; and Abel brought some of the
> first-born of his flock, the fat portions of them. *c* The Lord received Abel
5  and his gift with favour; but Cain and his gift he did not receive. Cain was
6  very angry and his face fell. Then the Lord said to Cain, 'Why are you so
> angry and cast down?

7  If you do well, you are accepted; *d*
> if not, sin is a demon crouching at the door.
> It shall be eager for you, and you will be mastered by it.' *e*

---

*a* Or feel an urge.    *b* *That is* Life.    *c* Or some of the first-born, that is the suck-
lings, of his flock.    *d* Or you hold your head up.    *e* Or but you must master it.

4

Cain said to his brother Abel, 'Let us go into the open country.' While 8
they were there, Cain attacked his brother Abel and murdered him. Then 9
the LORD said to Cain, 'Where is your brother Abel?' Cain answered, 'I
do not know. Am I my brother's keeper?' The LORD said, 'What have you 10
done? Hark! your brother's blood that has been shed is crying out to me
from the ground. Now you are accursed, and banished from*a* the ground 11
which has opened its mouth wide to receive your brother's blood, which
you have shed. When you till the ground, it will no longer yield you its 12
wealth. You shall be a vagrant and a wanderer on earth.' Cain said to the 13
LORD, 'My punishment is heavier than I can bear; thou hast driven me 14
today from the ground, and I must hide myself from thy presence. I shall
be a vagrant and a wanderer on earth, and anyone who meets me can kill
me.' The LORD answered him, 'No: if anyone kills Cain, Cain shall be 15
avenged sevenfold.' So the LORD put a mark on Cain, in order that anyone
meeting him should not kill him. Then Cain went out from the LORD's 16
presence and settled in the land of Nod *b c* to the east of Eden.

Then Cain lay with his wife; and she conceived and bore Enoch. Cain 17
was then building a city, which he named Enoch after his son. Enoch begot 18
Irad; Irad begot Mehujael; Mehujael begot Methushael; Methushael
begot Lamech.

Lamech married two wives, one named Adah and the other Zillah. Adah 19 20
bore Jabal who was the ancestor of herdsmen who live in tents; and his 21
brother's name was Jubal; he was the ancestor of those who play the harp
and pipe. Zillah, the other wife, bore Tubal-cain, the master of all copper- 22
smiths and blacksmiths, and Tubal-cain's sister was Naamah. Lamech said 23
to his wives:

> 'Adah and Zillah, listen to me;
> wives of Lamech, mark what I say:
> I kill a man for wounding me,
> a young man for a blow.
> Cain may be avenged seven times,                              24
> but Lamech seventy-seven.'

Adam lay with his wife again. She bore a son, and named him Seth,*d* 'for', 25
she said, 'God has granted me another son in place of Abel, because Cain
killed him.' Seth too had a son, whom he named Enosh. At that time men 26
began to invoke the LORD *e* by name.

THIS IS THE RECORD of the descendants of Adam. On the day when 5
God created man he made him in the likeness of God. He created them 2
male and female, and on the day when he created them, he blessed them
and called them man.

Adam was one hundred and thirty years old when he begot a son in his 3
likeness and image, and named him Seth. After the birth of Seth he lived 4

---

*a* and banished from: *or* more than (*cp. 3. 17*).     *b* *That is* Wandering.     *c* and
settled . . . Nod: *or* and he lived as a wanderer in the land.     *d* *That is* Granted.
*e* *This represents the Hebrew consonants* YHWH, *probably pronounced* Yahweh, *but
traditionally read as* Jehovah.

5 eight hundred years, and had other sons and daughters. He lived nine hundred and thirty years, and then he died.

6 7       Seth was one hundred and five years old when he begot Enosh. After the birth of Enosh he lived eight hundred and seven years, and had other 8 sons and daughters. He lived nine hundred and twelve years, and then he died.

9ᵃ 10     Enosh was ninety years old when he begot Kenan. After the birth of Kenan he lived eight hundred and fifteen years, and had other sons and 11 daughters. He lived nine hundred and five years, and then he died.

12 13     Kenan was seventy years old when he begot Mahalalel. After the birth of Mahalalel he lived eight hundred and forty years, and had other sons 14 and daughters. He lived nine hundred and ten years, and then he died.

15 16     Mahalalel was sixty-five years old when he begot Jared. After the birth of Jared he lived eight hundred and thirty years, and had other sons and 17 daughters. He lived eight hundred and ninety-five years, and then he died.

18      Jared was one hundred and sixty-two years old when he begot Enoch. 19 After the birth of Enoch he lived eight hundred years, and had other sons 20 and daughters. He lived nine hundred and sixty-two years, and then he died.

21 22     Enoch was sixty-five years old when he begot Methuselah. After the birth of Methuselah, Enoch walked with God for three hundred years, and 23 had other sons and daughters. He lived three hundred and sixty-five years. 24 Having walked with God, Enoch was seen no more, because God had taken him away.

25      Methuselah was one hundred and eighty-seven years old when he begot 26 Lamech. After the birth of Lamech he lived for seven hundred and eighty- 27 two years, and had other sons and daughters. He lived nine hundred and sixty-nine years, and then he died.

28      Lamech was one hundred and eighty-two years old when he begot a son. 29 He named him Noah, saying, 'This boy will bring us relief from our work, and from the hard labour that has come upon us because of the LORD's 30 curse upon the ground.' After the birth of Noah, he lived for five hundred 31 and ninety-five years, and had other sons and daughters. Lamech lived 32 seven hundred and seventy-seven years, and then he died. Noah was five hundred years old when he begot Shem, Ham and Japheth.

## The flood and the tower of Babel

6 WHEN MANKIND BEGAN TO INCREASE and to spread all over the
2 earth and daughters were born to them, the sons of the gods saw that the daughters of men were beautiful; so they took for themselves such 3 women as they chose. But the LORD said, 'My life-giving spirit shall not remain in man for ever; he for his part is mortal flesh: he shall live for a hundred and twenty years.'

4      In those days,ᵇ when the sons of the gods had intercourse with the

---

ᵃ *Verses 9–32: cp. I Chr. I. 2–4.*      ᵇ *Prob. rdg.; Heb. adds and also afterwards*
(*cp. Num. 13. 33*).

daughters of men and got children by them, the Nephilim *a* were on earth. They were the heroes of old, men of renown.

When the LORD saw that man had done much evil on earth and that his 5 thoughts and inclinations were always evil, he was sorry that he had made 6 man on earth, and he was grieved at heart. He said, 'This race of men whom 7 I have created, I will wipe them off the face of the earth—man and beast, reptiles and birds. I am sorry that I ever made them.' But Noah had won 8 the LORD's favour.

This is the story of Noah. Noah was a righteous man, the one blameless 9 man of his time; he walked with God. He had three sons, Shem, Ham and 10 Japheth. Now God saw that the whole world was corrupt *b* and full of 11 violence. In his sight the world had become corrupted, for all men had 12 lived corrupt lives on earth. God said to Noah, 'The loathsomeness *c* of all 13 mankind has become plain to me, for through them the earth is full of violence. I intend to destroy them, and the earth with them. Make yourself 14 an ark with ribs of cypress; cover it with reeds and coat it inside and out with pitch. This is to be its plan: the length of the ark shall be three hundred 15 cubits, its breadth fifty cubits, and its height thirty cubits. You shall make 16 a roof for the ark, giving it a fall of one cubit when complete; and put a door in the side of the ark, and build three decks, upper, middle, and lower. I intend to bring the waters of the flood over the earth to destroy every 17 human being under heaven that has the spirit of life; everything on earth shall perish. But with you I will make a covenant, and you shall go into the 18 ark, you and your sons, your wife and your sons' wives with you. And you 19 shall bring living creatures of every kind into the ark to keep them alive with you, two of each kind, a male and a female; two of every kind of bird, 20 beast, and reptile, shall come to you to be kept alive. See that you take and 21 store every kind of food that can be eaten; this shall be food for you and for them.' Exactly as God had commanded him, so Noah did.                    22

The LORD said to Noah, 'Go into the ark, you and all your household; 7 for I have seen that you alone are righteous before me in this generation. Take with you seven pairs, male and female, of all beasts that are ritually 2 clean, and one pair, male and female, of all beasts that are not clean; also 3 seven pairs, male and female, of every bird—to ensure that life continues on earth. In seven days' time I will send rain over the earth for forty days 4 and forty nights, and I will wipe off the face of the earth every living thing that I have made.' Noah did all that the LORD had commanded him. He 5 6 was six hundred years old when the waters of the flood came upon the earth.

And so, to escape the waters of the flood, Noah went into the ark with 7 his sons, his wife, and his sons' wives. And into the ark with Noah went one 8-9 pair, male and female, of all beasts, clean and unclean, of birds and of everything that crawls on the ground, two by two, as God had commanded. Towards the end of seven days the waters of the flood came upon the earth. 10 In the year when Noah was six hundred years old, on the seventeenth day 11 of the second month, on that very day, all the springs of the great abyss broke through, the windows of the sky were opened, and rain fell on the 12 earth for forty days and forty nights. On that very day Noah entered the 13

*a* Or giants.        *b* Or ripe for destruction.        *c* Or end.

ark with his sons, Shem, Ham and Japheth, his own wife, and his three
14 sons' wives. Wild animals of every kind, cattle of every kind, reptiles of
15 every kind that move upon the ground, and birds of every kind—all came
16 to Noah in the ark, two by two of all creatures that had life in them. Those
which came were one male and one female of all living things; they came
in as God had commanded Noah, and the LORD closed the door on him.
17 The flood continued upon the earth for forty days, and the waters swelled
18 and lifted up the ark so that it rose high above the ground. They swelled
and increased over the earth, and the ark floated on the surface of the waters.
19 More and more the waters increased over the earth until they covered all
20 the high mountains everywhere under heaven. The waters increased and
21 the mountains were covered to a depth of fifteen cubits. Every living creature that moves on earth perished, birds, cattle, wild animals, all reptiles,
22 and all mankind. Everything died that had the breath of life in its nostrils,
23 everything on dry land. God wiped out every living thing that existed on
earth, man and beast, reptile and bird; they were all wiped out over the
whole earth, and only Noah and his company in the ark survived.
24 When the waters had increased over the earth for a hundred and fifty
8 days, God thought of Noah and all the wild animals and the cattle with him
in the ark, and he made a wind pass over the earth, and the waters began
2 to subside. The springs of the abyss were stopped up, and so were the
3 windows of the sky; the downpour from the skies was checked. The water
gradually receded from the earth, and by the end of a hundred and fifty
4 days it had disappeared. On the seventeenth day of the seventh month the
5 ark grounded on a mountain in Ararat. The water continued to recede
until the tenth month, and on the first day of the tenth month the tops of
the mountains could be seen.
6 After forty days Noah opened the trap-door that he had made in the
7 ark, and released a raven to see whether the water had subsided, but the
bird continued flying to and fro until the water on the earth had dried up.
8 Noah waited for seven days,[a] and then he released a dove from the ark to
9 see whether the water on the earth had subsided further. But the dove
found no place where she could settle, and so she came back to him in the
ark, because there was water over the whole surface of the earth. Noah
10 stretched out his hand, caught her and took her into the ark. He waited
11 another seven days and again released the dove from the ark. She came
back to him towards evening with a newly plucked olive leaf in her beak.
Then Noah knew for certain that the water on the earth had subsided still
12 further. He waited yet another seven days and released the dove, but she
13 never came back. And so it came about that, on the first day of the first
month of his six hundred and first year, the water had dried up on the
earth, and Noah removed the hatch and looked out of the ark. The surface
of the ground was dry.
14 By the twenty-seventh day of the second month the whole earth was dry.
15 16 And God said to Noah, 'Come out of the ark, you and your wife, your sons
17 and their wives. Bring out every living creature that is with you, live things
of every kind, bird and beast and every reptile that moves on the ground,

[a] *Noah . . . days: prob. rdg., cp. verse 10; Heb. om.*

and let them swarm over the earth and be fruitful and increase there.' So 18
Noah came out with his sons, his wife, and his sons' wives. Every wild 19
animal, all cattle, every bird, and every reptile that moves on the ground,
came out of the ark by families. Then Noah built an altar to the LORD. He 20
took ritually clean beasts and birds of every kind, and offered whole-
offerings on the altar. When the LORD smelt the soothing odour, he said 21
within himself, 'Never again will I curse the ground because of man, however evil his inclinations may be from his youth upwards. I will never again
kill every living creature, as I have just done.

> While the earth lasts                                              22
> seedtime and harvest, cold and heat,
> summer and winter, day and night,
> shall never cease.'

GOD BLESSED NOAH and his sons and said to them, 'Be fruitful and in- 9
crease, and fill the earth. The fear and dread of you shall fall upon all wild 2
animals on earth, on all birds of heaven, on everything that moves upon
the ground and all fish in the sea; they are given into your hands. Every 3
creature that lives and moves shall be food for you; I give you them all, as
once I gave you all green plants. But you must not eat the flesh with the 4
life, which is the blood, still in it. And further, for your life-blood I will 5
demand satisfaction; from every animal I will require it, and from a man
also I will require satisfaction for the death of his fellow-man.

> He that sheds the blood of a man,                                  6
> for that man his blood shall be shed;
> for in the image of God
> has God made man.

But you must be fruitful and increase, swarm throughout the earth and 7
rule*a* over it.'

  God spoke to Noah and to his sons with him: 'I now make my covenant 8 9
with you and with your descendants after you, and with every living crea- 10
ture that is with you, all birds and cattle, all the wild animals with you on
earth, all that have come out of the ark. I will make my covenant with you: 11
never again shall all living creatures be destroyed by the waters of the flood,
never again shall there be a flood to lay waste the earth.'

  God said, 'This is the sign of the covenant which I establish between 12
myself and you and every living creature with you, to endless generations:

> My bow I set in the cloud,                                         13
> sign of the covenant
> between myself and earth.
> When I cloud the sky over the earth,                               14
> the bow shall be seen in the cloud.

Then will I remember the covenant which I have made between myself 15
and you and living things of every kind. Never again shall the waters become
a flood to destroy all living creatures. The bow shall be in the cloud; when 16

---

*a Prob. rdg., cp. 1. 28; Heb. increase.*

9

I see it, it will remind me of the everlasting covenant between God and
17 living things on earth of every kind.' God said to Noah, 'This is the sign
of the covenant which I make between myself and all that lives on earth.'
18     The sons of Noah who came out of the ark were Shem, Ham and Japheth;
19 Ham was the father of Canaan. These three were the sons of Noah, and
their descendants spread over the whole earth.
20 21     Noah, a man of the soil, began the planting of vineyards. He drank some
22 of the wine, became drunk and lay naked inside his tent. When Ham,
father of Canaan, saw his father naked, he told his two brothers outside.
23 So Shem and Japheth took a cloak, put it on their shoulders and walked
backwards, and so covered their father's naked body; their faces were
24 turned the other way, so that they did not see their father naked. When
Noah woke from his drunken sleep, he learnt what his youngest son had
25 done to him, and said:

> 'Cursed be Canaan,
> slave of slaves
> shall he be to his brothers.'

26 And he continued:

> 'Bless, O LORD,
> the tents of Shem; *a*
> may Canaan be his slave.
27    May God extend *b* Japheth's bounds,
> let him dwell in the tents of Shem,
> may Canaan be their slave.'

28 29 After the flood Noah lived for three hundred and fifty years, and he was
nine hundred and fifty years old when he died.
**10**     These are the descendants of the sons of Noah, Shem, Ham and Japheth,
the sons born to them after the flood.
2 *c*     The sons of Japheth: Gomer, Magog, Madai, Javan, *d* Tubal, Meshech
3 4 and Tiras. The sons of Gomer: Ashkenaz, Riphath and Togarmah. The
5 sons of Javan: Elishah, Tarshish, Kittim *e* and Rodanim. From these the
peoples of the coasts and islands separated into their own countries, each
with their own language, family by family, nation by nation.
6 *f* 7     The sons of Ham: Cush, Mizraim, *g* Put and Canaan. The sons of
Cush: Seba, Havilah, Sabtah, Raamah and Sabtecha. The sons of Raamah:
8 Sheba and Dedan. Cush was the father of Nimrod, who began to show
9 himself a man of might on earth; and he was a mighty hunter before the
LORD, as the saying goes, 'Like Nimrod, a mighty hunter before the LORD.'
10 His kingdom in the beginning consisted of Babel, Erech, and Accad, all
11 of them in the land of Shinar. From that land he migrated to Asshur and
12 built Nineveh, Rehoboth-Ir, Calah, and Resen, a great city between
13 *h* Nineveh and Calah. From Mizraim sprang the Lydians, Anamites,

---

*a* Bless . . . Shem: *prob. rdg.; Heb.* Blessed is the LORD the God of Shem.     *b Heb.*
japht.          *c Verses 2-4: cp. I Chr. I. 5-7.*          *d Or Greece.*          *e Or*
Tarshish of the Kittians.          *f Verses 6-8: cp. I Chr. I. 8-10.*          *g Or Egypt.*
*h Verses 13-18: cp. I Chr. I. 11-16.*

Lehabites, Naphtuhites, Pathrusites, Casluhites, and the Caphtorites, from  14
whom the Philistines were descended.

Canaan was the father of Sidon, who was his eldest son, and Heth,[a]  15
the Jebusites, the Amorites, the Girgashites, the Hivites, the Arkites, the  16 17
Sinites, the Arvadites, the Zemarites, and the Hamathites. Later the  18
Canaanites spread, and then the Canaanite border ran from Sidon towards  19
Gerar all the way to Gaza; then all the way to Sodom and Gomorrah,
Admah and Zeboyim as far as Lasha. These were the sons of Ham, by  20
families and languages with their countries and nations.

Sons were born also to Shem, elder brother of Japheth, the ancestor of  21
all the sons of Eber. The sons of Shem: Elam, Asshur, Arphaxad, Lud[b]  22[c]
and Aram. The sons of Aram: Uz, Hul, Gether and Mash. Arphaxad was  23 24
the father of Shelah, and Shelah the father of Eber. Eber had two sons: one  25
was named Peleg,[d] because in his time the earth was divided; and his
brother's name was Joktan. Joktan was the father of Almodad, Sheleph,  26
Hazarmoth, Jerah, Hadoram, Uzal, Diklah, Obal, Abimael, Sheba,  27 28
Ophir, Havilah and Jobab. All these were sons of Joktan. They lived in  29 30
the eastern hill-country, from Mesha all the way to Sephar. These were the  31
sons of Shem, by families and languages with their countries and nations.

These were the families of the sons of Noah according to their genea-  32
logies, nation by nation; and from them came the separate nations on earth
after the flood.

ONCE UPON A TIME all the world spoke a single language and used the  **11**
same[e] words. As men journeyed in the east, they came upon a plain in the  2
land of Shinar and settled there. They said to one another, 'Come, let us  3
make bricks and bake them hard'; they used bricks for stone and bitumen
for mortar. 'Come,' they said, 'let us build ourselves a city and a tower with  4
its top in the heavens, and make a name for ourselves; or we shall be dispersed all over the earth.' Then the LORD came down to see the city and  5
tower which mortal men had built, and he said, 'Here they are, one people  6
with a single language, and now they have started to do this; henceforward
nothing they have a mind to do will be beyond their reach. Come, let us  7
go down there and confuse their speech, so that they will not understand
what they say to one another.' So the LORD dispersed them from there all  8
over the earth, and they left off building the city. That is why it is called  9
Babel,[f] because the LORD there made a babble of the language of all the
world; from that place the LORD scattered men all over the face of the
earth.

This is the table of the descendants of Shem. Shem was a hundred  10[g]
years old when he begot Arphaxad, two years after the flood. After the  11
birth of Arphaxad he lived five hundred years, and had other sons and
daughters. Arphaxad was thirty-five years old when he begot Shelah. After  12 13
the birth of Shelah he lived four hundred and three years, and had other
sons and daughters.

---

[a] *Or* the Hittites.     [b] *Or* the Lydians.     [c] *Verses 22–29: cp. I Chr. 1. 17–23.*
[d] *That is* Division.     [e] *Or* used few.     [f] *That is* Babylon.     [g] *Verses*
*10–26: cp. I Chr. 1. 24–27.*

14 15     Shelah was thirty years old when he begot Eber. After the birth of Eber he lived four hundred and three years, and had other sons and daughters.

16 17     Eber was thirty-four years old when he begot Peleg. After the birth of Peleg he lived four hundred and thirty years, and had other sons and daughters.

18 19     Peleg was thirty years old when he begot Reu. After the birth of Reu he lived two hundred and nine years, and had other sons and daughters.

20 21     Reu was thirty-two years old when he begot Serug. After the birth of Serug he lived two hundred and seven years, and had other sons and daughters.

22 23     Serug was thirty years old when he begot Nahor. After the birth of Nahor he lived two hundred years, and had other sons and daughters.

24 25     Nahor was twenty-nine years old when he begot Terah. After the birth of Terah he lived a hundred and nineteen years, and had other sons and daughters.

26     Terah was seventy years old when he begot Abram, Nahor and Haran.

27     This is the table of the descendants of Terah. Terah was the father of

28 Abram, Nahor and Haran. Haran was the father of Lot. Haran died in the

29 presence of his father in the land of his birth, Ur of the Chaldees. Abram and Nahor married wives; Abram's wife was called Sarai, and Nahor's Milcah. She was Haran's daughter; and he was also the father of Milcah

30 31 and of Iscah. Sarai was barren; she had no child. Terah took his son Abram, his grandson Lot the son of Haran, and his daughter-in-law Sarai Abram's wife, and they set out from Ur of the Chaldees for the land of Canaan. But

32 when they reached Harran, they settled there. Terah was two hundred and five years old when he died in Harran.

## *Abraham and Isaac*

**12** THE LORD SAID TO ABRAM, 'Leave your own country, your kinsmen,
2   and your father's house, and go to a country that I will show you. I will make you into a great nation, I will bless you and make your name so great that it shall be used in blessings:

3          Those that bless you I will bless,
         those that curse you, I will execrate.
         All the families on earth
         will pray to be blessed as you are blessed.'

4 And so Abram set out as the LORD had bidden him, and Lot went with him.

5 Abram was seventy-five years old when he left Harran. He took his wife Sarai, his nephew Lot, all the property they had collected, and all the dependants they had acquired in Harran, and they started on their journey

6 to Canaan. When they arrived, Abram passed through the country to the sanctuary at Shechem, the terebinth-tree of Moreh. At that time the

7 Canaanites lived in this land. There the LORD appeared to Abram and said, 'I give this land to your descendants.' So Abram built an altar there to the

8 LORD who had appeared to him. Thence he went on to the hill-country

east of Bethel and pitched his tent between Bethel on the west and Ai on the east. There he built an altar to the LORD and invoked the LORD by name. Thus Abram journeyed by stages towards the Negeb. 9

There came a famine in the land, so severe that Abram went down to 10 Egypt to live there for a while. When he was approaching Egypt, he said 11 to his wife Sarai, 'I know very well that you are a beautiful woman, and 12 that when the Egyptians see you, they will say, "She is his wife"; then they will kill me but let you live. Tell them that you are my sister, so that 13 all may go well with me because of you and my life may be spared on your account.' When Abram arrived in Egypt, the Egyptians saw that she was 14 indeed very beautiful. Pharaoh's courtiers saw her and praised her to 15 Pharaoh, and she was taken into Pharaoh's household. He treated Abram 16 well because of her, and Abram came to possess sheep and cattle and asses, male and female slaves, she-asses, and camels. But the LORD struck 17 Pharaoh and his household with grave diseases on account of Abram's wife Sarai. Pharaoh summoned Abram and said to him, 'Why have you treated 18 me like this? Why did you not tell me that she is your wife? Why did you 19 say that she was your sister, so that I took her as a wife? Here she is: take her and be gone.' Then Pharaoh gave his men orders, and they sent Abram 20 away with his wife and all that he had.

Abram went up from Egypt into the Negeb, he and his wife and all that **13** he had, and Lot went with him. Abram was now very rich in cattle and in 2 silver and gold. From the Negeb he journeyed by stages to Bethel, to the 3 place between Bethel and Ai where he had pitched his tent in the beginning, where he had set up an altar on the first occasion and had invoked the LORD 4 by name. Now Lot was travelling with Abram, and he too possessed sheep 5 and cattle and tents. The land could not support them both together; for 6 their livestock were so numerous that they could not settle in the same district, and there were quarrels between Abram's herdsmen and Lot's. 7 The Canaanites and the Perizzites were then living in the land. So Abram 8 said to Lot, 'Let there be no quarrelling between us, between my herdsmen and yours; for we are close kinsmen. The whole country is there in front 9 of you; let us part company. If you go left, I will go right; if you go right, I will go left.' Lot looked up and saw how well-watered the whole Plain of 10 the Jordan was; all the way to Zoar it was like the Garden of the LORD, like the land of Egypt. This was before the LORD had destroyed Sodom and Gomorrah. So Lot chose all the Plain of the Jordan and took the road on 11 the east side. Thus they parted company. Abram settled in the land of 12 Canaan; but Lot settled among the cities of the Plain and pitched his tents near Sodom. Now the men of Sodom were wicked, great sinners against 13 the LORD.

After Lot and Abram had parted, the LORD said to Abram, 'Raise your 14 eyes and look into the distance from the place where you are, north and south, east and west. All the land you can see I will give to you and to your 15 descendants for ever. I will make your descendants countless as the dust 16 of the earth; if anyone could count the dust upon the ground, then he could count your descendants. Now go through the length and breadth 17 of the land, for I give it to you.' So Abram moved his tent and settled 18 by the terebinths of Mamre at Hebron; and there he built an altar to the LORD.

**14** IT WAS IN THE TIME OF AMRAPHEL king of Shinar, Arioch king of
2 Ellasar, Kedorlaomer king of Elam, and Tidal king of Goyim. They went to war against Bera king of Sodom, Birsha king of Gomorrah, Shinab king of Admah, Shemeber king of Zeboyim, and the king of Bela, that is Zoar.
3 These kings joined forces in the valley of Siddim, which is now the Dead
4 Sea. They had been subject to Kedorlaomer for twelve years, but in the
5 thirteenth year they rebelled. Then in the fourteenth year Kedorlaomer and his confederate kings came and defeated the Rephaim in Ashteroth-
6 karnaim, the Zuzim in Ham, the Emim in Shaveh-kiriathaim, and the Horites in the hill-country from Seir<sup>a</sup> as far as El-paran on the edge of the
7 wilderness. On their way back they came to En-mishpat, which is now Kadesh, and laid waste all the country of the Amalekites and also that of
8 the Amorites who lived in Hazazon-tamar. Then the kings of Sodom, Gomorrah, Admah, Zeboyim, and Bela, which is now Zoar, marched out
9 and drew up their forces against them in the valley of Siddim, against Kedorlaomer king of Elam, Tidal king of Goyim, Amraphel king of Shinar,
10 and Arioch king of Ellasar, four kings against five. Now the valley of Siddim was full of bitumen pits; and when the kings of Sodom and Gomorrah
11 fled, they fell into them, but the rest escaped to the hill-country. The four kings captured all the flocks and herds of Sodom and Gomorrah and all
12 their provisions, and went away. They also carried off Lot, Abram's
13 nephew, who was living in Sodom, and with him his flocks and herds. But a fugitive came and told Abram the Hebrew, who at that time was dwelling by the terebinths of Mamre the Amorite. This Mamre was the brother of
14 Eshcol and Aner, who were allies of Abram. When Abram heard that his kinsman had been taken prisoner, he mustered his retainers, men born in his household, three hundred and eighteen of them, and pursued as far as
15 Dan. Abram and his followers surrounded the enemy by night, attacked
16 them and pursued them as far as Hobah, north of Damascus; he then brought back all the flocks and herds and also his kinsman Lot with his
17 flocks and herds, together with the women and the other captives. On his return from this defeat of Kedorlaomer and his confederate kings, the king of Sodom came out to meet him in the valley of Shaveh, which is now the King's Valley.
18     Then Melchizedek king of Salem brought food and wine. He was priest
19 of God Most High, and he pronounced this blessing on Abram:

> 'Blessed be Abram
> by God Most High,
> creator<sup>b</sup> of heaven and earth.
20        And blessed be God Most High,
> who has delivered your enemies into your power.'

Abram gave him a tithe of all the booty.
21     The king of Sodom said to Abram, 'Give me the people, and you can

---

      *a Prob. rdg.; Heb.* in their hill-country, Seir.       *b Or* owner.

take the property'; but Abram said to the king of Sodom, 'I lift my hand 22
and swear by the LORD, God Most High, creator of heaven and earth: not 23
a thread or a shoe-string will I accept of anything that is yours. You shall
never say, "I made Abram rich." I will accept nothing but what the young 24
men have eaten and the share of the men who went with me. Aner, Eshcol,
and Mamre shall have their share.'

AFTER THIS the word of the LORD came to Abram in a vision. He said, **15**
'Do not be afraid, Abram, I am giving you a very great reward.'*a* Abram 2
replied, 'Lord GOD, what canst thou give me? I have no standing among
men, for the heir to my household is Eliezer of Damascus.' Abram con- 3
tinued, 'Thou hast given me no children, and so my heir must be a slave
born in my house.' Then came the word of the LORD to him: 'This man 4
shall not be your heir; your heir shall be a child of your own body.' He took 5
Abram outside and said, 'Look up into the sky, and count the stars if you
can. So many', he said, 'shall your descendants be.'

Abram put his faith in the LORD, and the LORD counted that faith to him 6
as righteousness; he said to him, 'I am the LORD who brought you out from 7
Ur of the Chaldees to give you this land to occupy.' Abram said, 'O Lord 8
GOD, how can I be sure that I shall occupy it?' The LORD answered, 'Bring 9
me a heifer three years old, a she-goat three years old, a ram three years old,
a turtle-dove, and a fledgling.' He brought him all these, halved the animals 10
down the middle and placed each piece opposite its corresponding piece,
but he did not halve the birds. When the birds of prey swooped down on 11
the carcasses, Abram scared them away. Then, as the sun was going down, 12
a trance came over Abram and great fear came upon him. The LORD said 13
to Abram, 'Know this for certain, that your descendants will be aliens
living in a land that is not theirs; they will be slaves, and will be held in
oppression there for four hundred years. But I will punish that nation 14
whose slaves they are, and after that they shall come out with great possessions. You yourself shall join your fathers in peace and be buried in a good 15
old age; and the fourth generation shall return here, for the Amorites will 16
not be ripe for punishment till then.' The sun went down and it was dusk, 17
and there appeared a smoking brazier and a flaming torch passing between
the divided pieces. That very day the LORD made a covenant with Abram, 18
and he said, 'To your descendants I give this land from the River of Egypt
to the Great River, the river Euphrates, the territory of the Kenites, 19
Kenizzites, Kadmonites, Hittites, Perizzites, Rephaim, Amorites, Canaan- 20 21
ites, Girgashites, Hivites, and Jebusites.'

Abram's wife Sarai had borne him no children. Now she had an Egyptian **16**
slave-girl whose name was Hagar, and she said to Abram, 'You see that 2
the LORD has not allowed me to bear a child. Take my slave-girl; perhaps
I shall found a family through her.' Abram agreed to what his wife said;
so Sarai, Abram's wife, brought her slave-girl, Hagar the Egyptian, 3
and gave her to her husband Abram as a wife.*b* When this happened
Abram had been in Canaan for ten years. He lay with Hagar and she 4

---

*a* I am giving . . . reward: *or* I am your shield, your very great reward.
*b* Or concubine.

conceived; and when she knew that she was with child, she despised her
5 mistress. Sarai said to Abram, 'I have been wronged and you must answer
for it. It was I who gave my slave-girl into your arms, but since she has
known that she is with child, she has despised me. May the LORD see justice
6 done between you and me.' Abram replied to Sarai, 'Your slave-girl is in
your hands; deal with her as you will.' So Sarai ill-treated her and she ran
away.
7     The angel of the LORD found her by a spring of water in the wilderness
8 on the way to Shur, and he said, 'Hagar, Sarai's slave-girl, where have you
come from and where are you going?' She answered, 'I am running away
9 from Sarai my mistress.' The angel of the LORD said to her, 'Go back to
10 your mistress and submit to her ill-treatment.' The angel also said, 'I will
11 make your descendants too many to be counted.' And the angel of the LORD
said to her:

> 'You are with child and will bear a son.
> You shall name him Ishmael,$^a$
> because the LORD has heard of your ill-treatment.
12   He shall be a man like the wild ass,
> his hand against every man
> and every man's hand against him;
> and he shall live at odds with$^b$ all his kinsmen.'

13 She called the LORD who was speaking to her by the name El-Roi,$^c$ for
14 she said, 'Have I indeed seen God and still live$^d$ after that vision?' That is
why men call the well Beer-lahai-roi;$^e$ it lies between Kadesh and Bered.
15 Hagar bore Abram a son, and he named the child she bore him Ishmael.
16 Abram was eighty-six years old when Hagar bore Ishmael.

**17**     When Abram was ninety-nine years old, the LORD appeared to him and
2 said, 'I am God Almighty. Live always in my presence and be perfect, so
that I may set my covenant between myself and you and multiply your
3 descendants.' Abram threw himself down on his face, and God spoke with
4 him and said, 'I make this covenant, and I make it with you: you shall be
5 the father of a host of nations. Your name shall no longer be Abram,$^f$ your
6 name shall be Abraham,$^g$ for I make you father of a host of nations. I will
make you exceedingly fruitful; I will make nations out of you, and kings
7 shall spring from you. I will fulfil my covenant between myself and you
and your descendants after you, generation after generation, an everlasting
8 covenant, to be your God, yours and your descendants' after you. As an
everlasting possession I will give you and your descendants after you the
land in which you now are aliens, all the land of Canaan, and I will be God
to your descendants.'
9     God said to Abraham, 'For your part, you must keep my covenant, you
10 and your descendants after you, generation by generation. This is how
you shall keep my covenant between myself and you and your descend-
11 ants after you: circumcise yourselves, every male among you. You shall

---

$^a$ *That is* God heard.      $^b$ *Or* live to the east of ...      $^c$ *That is* God of a vision.
$^d$ God and still live: *prob. rdg.; Heb.* hither.      $^e$ *That is* the Well of the Living
One of Vision.      $^f$ *That is* High Father.      $^g$ *That is* Father of a Multitude.

circumcise the flesh of your foreskin, and it shall be the sign of the covenant between us. Every male among you in every generation shall be circum- 12 cised on the eighth day, both those born in your house and any foreigner, not of your blood but bought with your money. Circumcise both those 13 born in your house and those bought with your money; thus shall my covenant be marked in your flesh as an everlasting covenant. Every 14 uncircumcised male, everyone who has not had the flesh of his foreskin circumcised, shall be cut off from the kin of his father. He has broken my covenant.'

God said to Abraham, 'As for Sarai your wife; you shall call her not 15 Sarai,*a* but Sarah.*b* I will bless her and give you a son by her. I will bless 16 her and she shall be the mother of nations; the kings of many people shall spring from her.' Abraham threw himself down on his face; he laughed 17 and said to himself, 'Can a son be born to a man who is a hundred years old? Can Sarah bear a son when she is ninety?' He said to God, 'If only 18 Ishmael might live under thy special care!' But God replied, 'No. Your 19 wife Sarah shall bear you a son, and you shall call him Isaac.*c* With him I will fulfil my covenant, an everlasting covenant with his descendants after him. I have heard your prayer for Ishmael. I have blessed him and will 20 make him fruitful. I will multiply his descendants; he shall be father of twelve princes, and I will raise a great nation from him. But my covenant 21 I will fulfil with Isaac, whom Sarah will bear to you at this season next year.' When he had finished talking with Abraham, God ascended and left him. 22

Then Abraham took Ishmael his son, everyone who had been born in 23 his household and everyone bought with money, every male in his household, and he circumcised them that very same day in the flesh of their foreskins as God had told him to do. Abraham was ninety-nine years old when 24 he circumcised the flesh of his foreskin. Ishmael was thirteen years old 25 when he was circumcised in the flesh of his foreskin. Both Abraham and 26 Ishmael were circumcised on the same day, and all the men of his house- 27 hold, born in the house or bought with money from foreigners, were circumcised with him.

THE LORD APPEARED TO ABRAHAM by the terebinths of Mamre. As **18** Abraham was sitting at the opening of his tent in the heat of the day, he 2 looked up and saw three men standing in front of him. When he saw them, he ran from the opening of his tent to meet them and bowed low to the ground. 'Sirs,' he said, 'if I have deserved your favour, do not pass by my 3 humble self without a visit. Let me send for some water so that you may 4 wash your feet and rest under a tree; and let me fetch a little food so that 5 you may refresh yourselves. Afterwards you may continue the journey which has brought you my way.' They said, 'Do by all means as you say.' So Abraham hurried into the tent to Sarah and said, 'Take three measures 6 of flour quickly, knead it and make some cakes.' Then Abraham ran to the 7 cattle, chose a fine tender calf and gave it to a servant, who hurriedly prepared it. He took curds and milk and the calf he had prepared, set it before 8 them, and waited on them himself under the tree while they ate. They 9

*a  That is* Mockery.　　*b  That is* Princess.　　*c  That is* He laughed.

10 asked him where Sarah his wife was, and he said, 'There, in the tent.' The
stranger said, 'About this time next year I will be sure to come back to you,
and Sarah your wife shall have a son.' Now Sarah was listening at the open-
11 ing of the tent, and he was close beside it. Both Abraham and Sarah had
12 grown very old, and Sarah was past the age of child-bearing. So Sarah
laughed to herself and said, 'I am past bearing children now that I am out
13 of my time, and my husband is old.' The LORD said to Abraham, 'Why
14 did Sarah laugh and say, "Shall I indeed bear a child when I am old?" Is
anything impossible for the LORD? In due season I will come back to you,
15 about this time next year, and Sarah shall have a son.' Sarah lied because
she was frightened, and denied that she had laughed; but he said, 'Yes,
you did laugh.'

16    The men set out and looked down towards Sodom, and Abraham went
17 with them to start them on their way. The LORD thought to himself, 'Shall
18 I conceal from Abraham what I intend to do? He will become a great and
powerful nation, and all nations on earth will pray to be blessed as he is
19 blessed. I have taken care of him on purpose that he may charge his sons
and family after him to conform to the way of the LORD and to do what is
20 right and just; thus I shall fulfil all that I have promised for him.' So the
LORD said, 'There is a great outcry over Sodom and Gomorrah; their sin
21 is very grave. I must go down and see whether their deeds warrant the out-
22 cry which has reached me. I am resolved to know the truth.' When the
men turned and went towards Sodom, Abraham remained standing before
23 the LORD. Abraham drew near him and said, 'Wilt thou really sweep away
24 good and bad together? Suppose there are fifty good men in the city; wilt
thou really sweep it away, and not pardon the place because of the fifty
25 good men? Far be it from thee to do this—to kill good and bad together;
for then the good would suffer with the bad. Far be it from thee. Shall not
26 the judge of all the earth do what is just?' The LORD said, 'If I find in the
city of Sodom fifty good men, I will pardon the whole place for their sake.'
27 Abraham replied, 'May I presume to speak to the Lord, dust and ashes
28 that I am: suppose there are five short of the fifty good men? Wilt thou
destroy the whole city for a mere five men?' He said, 'If I find forty-five
29 there I will not destroy it.' Abraham spoke again, 'Suppose forty can be
30 found there?'; and he said, 'For the sake of the forty I will not do it.' Then
Abraham said, 'Please do not be angry, O Lord, if I speak again: suppose
thirty can be found there?' He answered, 'If I find thirty there I will not
31 do it.' Abraham continued, 'May I presume to speak to the Lord: suppose
twenty can be found there?' He replied, 'For the sake of the twenty I will
32 not destroy it.' Abraham said, 'I pray thee not to be angry, O Lord, if I
speak just once more: suppose ten can be found there?' He said, 'For the
33 sake of the ten I will not destroy it.' When the LORD had finished talking
with Abraham, he left him, and Abraham returned home.

**19**    The two angels came to Sodom in the evening, and Lot was sitting in
the gateway of the city. When he saw them he rose to meet them and bowed
2 low with his face to the ground. He said, 'I pray you, sirs, turn aside to my
humble home, spend the night there and wash your feet; you can rise early
and continue your journey.' 'No,' they answered, 'we will spend the night

in the street.' But Lot was so insistent that they did turn aside and enter 3 his house. He prepared a meal for them, baking unleavened cakes, and they ate them. Before they lay down to sleep, the men of Sodom, both young 4 and old, surrounded the house—everyone without exception. They called 5 to Lot and asked him where the men were who had entered his house that night. 'Bring them out', they shouted, 'so that we can have intercourse with them.'

Lot went out into the doorway to them, closed the door behind him and 6 7 said, 'No, my friends, do not be so wicked. Look, I have two daughters, 8 both virgins; let me bring them out to you, and you can do what you like with them; but do not touch these men, because they have come under the shelter of my roof.' They said, 'Out of our way! This man has come and 9 settled here as an alien, and does he now take it upon himself to judge us? We will treat you worse than them.' They crowded in on the man Lot and pressed close to smash in the door. But the two men inside reached out, 10 pulled Lot in, and closed the door. Then they struck the men in the door- 11 way with blindness, both small and great, so that they could not find the door.

The two men said to Lot, 'Have you anyone else here, sons-in-law, sons, 12 or daughters, or any who belong to you in the city? Get them out of this place, because we are going to destroy it. The outcry against it has been so 13 great that the LORD has sent us to destroy it.' So Lot went out and spoke 14 to his intended sons-in-law.*ᵃ* He said, 'Be quick and leave this place; the LORD is going to destroy the city.' But they did not take him seriously.

As soon as it was dawn, the angels urged Lot to go, saying, 'Be quick, 15 take your wife and your two daughters who are here, or you will be swept away when the city is punished.' When he lingered, they took him by the 16 hand, with his wife and his daughters, and, because the LORD had spared him, led him on until he was outside the city. When they had brought them 17 out, they said, 'Flee for your lives; do not look back and do not stop any-where in the Plain. Flee to the hills or you will be swept away.' Lot replied, 18 'No, sirs. You have shown your servant favour and you have added to your 19 unfailing care for me by saving my life, but I cannot escape to the hills; I shall be overtaken by the disaster, and die. Look, here is a town, only a 20 small place, near enough for me to reach quickly. Let me escape to it—it is very small—and save my life.' He said to him, 'I grant your request: I 21 will not overthrow this town you speak of. But flee there quickly, because 22 I can do nothing until you are there.' That is why the place was called Zoar.*ᵇ* The sun had risen over the land as Lot entered Zoar; and then the 23 24 LORD rained down fire and brimstone from the skies on Sodom and Gomor-rah. He overthrew those cities and destroyed all the Plain, with everyone 25 living there and everything growing in the ground. But Lot's wife, behind 26 him, looked back, and she turned into a pillar of salt.

Next morning Abraham rose early and went to the place where he had 27 stood in the presence of the LORD. He looked down towards Sodom and 28 Gomorrah and all the wide extent of the Plain, and there he saw thick smoke rising high from the earth like the smoke of a lime-kiln. Thus, when God 29

*ᵃ Or* his sons-in-law, who had married his daughters.      *ᵇ That is* Small.

destroyed the cities of the Plain, he thought of Abraham and rescued Lot from the disaster, the overthrow of the cities where he had been living.

30 Lot went up from Zoar and settled in the hill-country with his two daughters, because he was afraid to stay in Zoar; he lived with his two
31 daughters in a cave. The elder daughter said to the younger, 'Our father is old and there is not a man in the country to come to us in the usual way.
32 Come now, let us make our father drink wine and then lie with him and in
33 this way keep the family alive through our father.' So that night they gave him wine to drink, and the elder daughter came and lay with him, and he
34 did not know when she lay down and when she got up. Next day the elder said to the younger, 'Last night I lay with my father. Let us give him wine to drink again tonight; then you go in and lie with him. So we shall keep
35 the family alive through our father.' So they gave their father wine to drink again that night, and the younger daughter went and lay with him, and he
36 did not know when she lay down and when she got up. In this way both
37 Lot's daughters came to be with child by their father. The elder daughter bore a son and called him Moab; he was the ancestor of the present Moab-
38 ites. The younger also bore a son, whom she called Ben-ammi; he was the ancestor of the present Ammonites.

20 ABRAHAM JOURNEYED BY STAGES from there into the Negeb, and
2 settled between Kadesh and Shur, living as an alien in Gerar. He said that Sarah his wife was his sister, and Abimelech king of Gerar sent and took
3 her. But God came to Abimelech in a dream by night and said, 'You shall die because of this woman whom you have taken. She is a married woman.'
4 Now Abimelech had not gone near her; and he said, 'Lord, wilt thou des-
5 troy an innocent people? Did he not tell me himself that she was his sister, and she herself said that he was her brother. It was with a clear conscience
6 and in all innocence that I did this.' God said to him in the dream, 'Yes: I know that you acted with a clear conscience. Moreover, it was I who held you back from committing a sin against me: that is why I did not let you
7 touch her. Send back the man's wife now; he is a prophet, and he will intercede on your behalf, and you shall live. But if you do not send her back,
8 I tell you that you are doomed to die, you and all that is yours.' So Abi-melech rose early in the morning, summoned all his servants and told them
9 the whole story; the men were terrified. Abimelech then summoned Abraham and said to him, 'Why have you treated us like this? What harm have I done to you that you should bring this great sin on me and my king-
10 dom? You have done a thing that ought not to be done.' And he asked
11 Abraham, 'What was your purpose in doing this?' Abraham answered, 'I said to myself, There can be no fear of God in this place, and they will kill
12 me for the sake of my wife. She is in fact my sister, she is my father's
13 daughter though not by the same mother; and she became my wife. When God set me wandering from my father's house, I said to her, "There is a duty towards me which you must loyally fulfil: wherever we go, you must
14 say that I am your brother."' Then Abimelech took sheep and cattle, and male and female slaves, gave them to Abraham, and returned his wife
15 Sarah to him. Abimelech said, 'My country lies before you; settle wherever

you please.' To Sarah he said, 'I have given your brother a thousand pieces 16
of silver, so that your own people may turn a blind eye on it all, and you will
be completely vindicated.' Then Abraham interceded with God, and God 17
healed Abimelech, his wife, and his slave-girls, and they bore children; for 18
the LORD had made every woman in Abimelech's household barren on
account of Abraham's wife Sarah.

The LORD showed favour to Sarah as he had promised, and made good **21**
what he had said about her. She conceived and bore a son to Abraham for 2
his old age, at the time which God had appointed. The son whom Sarah 3
bore to him, Abraham named Isaac.*ᵃ* When Isaac was eight days old 4
Abraham circumcised him, as God had commanded. Abraham was a 5
hundred years old when his son Isaac was born. Sarah said, 'God has given 6
me good reason to laugh, and everybody who hears will laugh with me.'
She said, 'Whoever would have told Abraham that Sarah would suckle 7
children? Yet I have borne him a son for his old age.' The boy grew and 8
was weaned, and on the day of his weaning Abraham gave a feast. Sarah 9
saw the son whom Hagar the Egyptian had borne to Abraham laughing at
him, and she said to Abraham, 'Drive out this slave-girl and her son; I 10
will not have this slave-girl's son sharing the inheritance with my son
Isaac.' Abraham was vexed at this on his son Ishmael's account, but God 11 12
said to him, 'Do not be vexed on account of the boy and the slave-girl. Do
what Sarah says, because you shall have descendants through Isaac. I will 13
make a great nation of the slave-girl's son too, because he is your own
child.'

Abraham rose early in the morning, took some food and a waterskin full 14
of water and gave it to Hagar; he set the child on her shoulder and sent her
away, and she went and wandered in the wilderness of Beersheba. When 15
the water in the skin was finished, she thrust the child under a bush, and 16
went and sat down some way off, about two bowshots away, for she said,
'How can I watch the child die?' So she sat some way off, weeping bitterly.
God heard the child crying, and the *ᵇ* angel of God called from heaven to 17
Hagar, 'What is the matter, Hagar? Do not be afraid: God has heard the
child crying where you laid him. Get to your feet, lift the child up and hold 18
him in your arms, because I will make of him a great nation.' Then God 19
opened her eyes and she saw a well full of water; she went to it, filled her
waterskin and gave the child a drink. God was with the child, and he grew 20-21
up and lived in the wilderness of Paran. He became an archer, and his
mother found him a wife from Egypt.

Now about that time Abimelech, with Phicol the commander of his army, 22
addressed Abraham in these terms: 'God is with you in all that you do. Now 23
swear an oath to me in the name of God, that you will not break faith with
me, my offspring, or my descendants. As I have kept faith with you, so
shall you keep faith with me and with the country where you have come to
live as an alien.' Abraham said, 'I swear.' It happened that Abraham had a 24 25
complaint against Abimelech about a well which Abimelech's men had
seized. Abimelech said, 'I do not know who did this. You never told me, 26
and I have heard nothing about it till now.' So Abraham took sheep and 27

ᵃ *That is* He laughed.      ᵇ *Or an.*

cattle and gave them to Abimelech; and the two of them made a pact.
28 29 Abraham set seven ewe-lambs apart, and when Abimelech asked him why
30 he had set these lambs apart, he said, 'Accept these from me in token that
31 I dug this well.' Therefore that place was called Beersheba,<sup>a</sup> because there
32 the two of them swore an oath. When they had made the pact at Beersheba,
Abimelech and Phicol the commander of his army returned at once to the
33 country of the Philistines, and Abraham planted a strip of ground<sup>b</sup> at
34 Beersheba. There he invoked the LORD, the everlasting God, by name, and
he lived as an alien in the country of the Philistines for many a year.

22 THE TIME CAME when God put Abraham to the test. 'Abraham', he
2 called, and Abraham replied, 'Here I am.' God said, 'Take your son Isaac,
your only son, whom you love, and go to the land of Moriah. There you
3 shall offer him as a sacrifice on one of the hills which I will show you.' So
Abraham rose early in the morning and saddled his ass, and he took with
him two of his men and his son Isaac; and he split the firewood for the sacri-
4 fice, and set out for the place of which God had spoken. On the third day
5 Abraham looked up and saw the place in the distance. He said to his men,
'Stay here with the ass while I and the boy go over there; and when we have
6 worshipped we will come back to you.' So Abraham took the wood for the
sacrifice and laid it on his son Isaac's shoulder; he himself carried the fire
7 and the knife, and the two of them went on together. Isaac said to Abraham,
'Father', and he answered, 'What is it, my son?' Isaac said, 'Here are the
8 fire and the wood, but where is the young beast for the sacrifice?' Abraham
answered, 'God will provide himself with a young beast for a sacrifice, my
9 son.' And the two of them went on together and came to the place of which
God had spoken. There Abraham built an altar and arranged the wood.
10 He bound his son Isaac and laid him on the altar on top of the wood. Then
11 he stretched out his hand and took the knife to kill his son; but the angel of
the LORD called to him from heaven, 'Abraham, Abraham.' He answered,
12 'Here I am.' The angel of the LORD said, 'Do not raise your hand against
the boy; do not touch him. Now I know that you are a God-fearing man.
13 You have not withheld from me your son, your only son.' Abraham looked
up, and there he saw a ram caught by its horns in a thicket. So he went and
14 took the ram and offered it as a sacrifice instead of his son. Abraham named
that place Jehovah-jireh;<sup>c</sup> and to this day the saying is: 'In the mountain of
15 the LORD it was provided.' Then the angel of the LORD called from heaven
16 a second time to Abraham, 'This is the word of the LORD: By my own self
I swear: inasmuch as you have done this and have not withheld your son,
17 your only son, I will bless you abundantly and greatly multiply your descendants until they are as numerous as the stars in the sky and the grains of
sand on the sea-shore. Your descendants shall possess the cities of their
18 enemies. All nations on earth shall pray to be blessed as your descendants
are blessed, and this because you have obeyed me.'
19    Abraham went back to his men, and together they returned to Beersheba;
and there Abraham remained.

<sup>a</sup> *That is* Well of Seven *and* Well of an Oath.          <sup>b</sup> *Or* planted a tamarisk.
<sup>c</sup> *That is* the LORD will provide.

After this Abraham was told, 'Milcah has borne sons to your brother 20
Nahor: Uz his first-born, then his brother Buz, and Kemuel father of 21
Aram, and Kesed, Hazo, Pildash, Jidlaph and Bethuel; and a daughter, 22 23
Rebecca, has been born to Bethuel.' These eight Milcah bore to Abraham's
brother Nahor. His concubine, whose name was Reumah, also bore him 24
sons: Tebah, Gaham, Tahash and Maacah.

Sarah lived for a hundred and twenty-seven years, and died in Kiriath- **23** 1 2
arba, which is Hebron, in Canaan. Abraham went in to mourn over Sarah
and to weep for her. At last he rose and left the presence of the dead. He 3
said to the Hittites, 'I am an alien and a settler among you. Give me land 4
enough for a burial-place, so that I can give my dead proper burial.' The 5
Hittites answered Abraham, 'Do, pray, listen to what we have to say, sir. 6
You are a mighty prince among us. Bury your dead in the best grave we
have. There is not one of us who will deny you his grave or hinder you from
burying your dead.' Abraham stood up and then bowed low to the Hittites, 7
the people of that country. He said to them, 'If you are willing to let me 8
give my dead proper burial, then listen to me and speak for me to Ephron
son of Zohar, asking him to give me the cave that belongs to him at Mach- 9
pelah, at the far end of his land. Let him give it to me for the full price, so
that I may take possession of it as a burial-place within your territory.'
Ephron the Hittite was sitting with the others, and he gave Abraham this 10
answer in the hearing of everyone as they came into the city gate: 'No, sir; 11
hear what I have to say. I will make you a gift of the land and I will also give
you the cave which is on it. In the presence of all my kinsmen I give it to
you; so bury your dead.' Abraham bowed low before the people of the 12
country and said to Ephron in their hearing, 'If you really mean it—but do 13
listen to me! I give you the price of the land: take it and I will bury my dead
there.' And Ephron answered, 'Do listen to me, sir: the land is worth four 14 15
hundred shekels of silver. But what is that between you and me? There
you may bury your dead.' Abraham came to an agreement with him and 16
weighed out the amount that Ephron had named in the hearing of the
Hittites, four hundred shekels of the standard recognized by merchants.
Thus the plot of land belonging to Ephron at Machpelah to the east of 17
Mamre, the plot, the cave that is on it, every tree on the plot, within the
whole area, became the legal possession of Abraham, in the presence of all 18
the Hittites as they came into the city gate. After this Abraham buried his 19
wife Sarah in the cave on the plot of land at Machpelah to the east of Mamre,
which is Hebron, in Canaan. Thus the plot and the cave on it became 20
Abraham's possession as a burial-place, by purchase from the Hittites.

By this time Abraham had become a very old man, and the Lord had **24**
blessed him in all that he did. Abraham said to his servant, who had been 2
long in his service and was in charge of all his possessions, 'Put your hand
under my thigh: I want you to swear by the Lord, the God of heaven and 3
earth, that you will not take a wife for my son from the women of the
Canaanites in whose land I dwell; you must go to my own country and to 4
my own kindred to find a wife for my son Isaac.' The servant said to him, 5
'What if the woman is unwilling to come with me to this country? Must I

6 in that event take your son back to the land from which you came?' Abra-
7 ham said to him, 'On no account are you to take my son back there. The
LORD the God of heaven who took me from my father's house and the land
of my birth, the LORD who swore to me that he would give this land to my
descendants—he will send his angel before you, and from there you shall
8 take a wife for my son. If the woman is unwilling to come with you, then
you will be released from your oath to me; but you must not take my son
9 back there.' So the servant put his hand under his master Abraham's thigh
and swore an oath in those terms.

10     The servant took ten camels from his master's herds, and also all kinds
of gifts from his master; he set out for Aram-naharaim[a] and arrived at the
11 city where Nahor lived. Towards evening, the time when the women come
out to draw water, he made the camels kneel down by the well outside the
12 city. He said, 'O LORD God of my master Abraham, give me good fortune
13 this day; keep faith with my master Abraham. Here I stand by the spring,
14 and the women of the city are coming out to draw water. Let it be like this:
I shall say to a girl, "Please lower your jar so that I may drink"; and if she
answers, "Drink, and I will water your camels also", that will be the girl
whom thou dost intend for thy servant Isaac. In this way I shall know that
thou hast kept faith with my master.'

15     Before he had finished praying silently, he saw Rebecca coming out with
her water-jug on her shoulder. She was the daughter of Bethuel son of
16 Milcah, the wife of Abraham's brother Nahor. The girl was very beautiful,
a virgin, who had had no intercourse with a man. She went down to the
17 spring, filled her jar and came up again. Abraham's servant hurried to
18 meet her and said, 'Give me a sip of water from your jar.' 'Drink, sir', she
answered, and at once lowered her jar on to her hand to let him drink.
19 When she had finished giving him a drink, she said, 'Now I will draw water
20 for your camels until they have had enough.' So she quickly emptied her
jar into the water-trough, hurried again to the well to draw water and
21 watered all the camels. The man was watching quietly to see whether or not
22 the LORD had made his journey successful. When the camels had finished
drinking, the man took a gold nose-ring weighing half a shekel, and two
23 bracelets for her wrists weighing ten shekels, also of gold, and said, 'Tell
me, please, whose daughter you are. Is there room in your father's house for
24 us to spend the night?' She answered, 'I am the daughter of Bethuel, the
25 son of Nahor and Milcah; and we have plenty of straw and fodder and also
26 room for you to spend the night.' So the man bowed down and prostrated
27 himself to the LORD. He said, 'Blessed be the LORD the God of my master
Abraham, who has not failed to keep faith and truth with my master; for
I have been guided by the LORD to the house of my master's kinsman.'

28     The girl ran to her mother's house and told them what had happened.
29-30 Now Rebecca had a brother named Laban; and, when he saw the nose-
ring, and also the bracelets on his sister's wrists, and heard his sister
Rebecca tell what the man had said to her, he ran out to the man at the
spring. When he came to him and found him still standing there by the
31 camels, he said, 'Come in, sir, whom the LORD has blessed. Why stay

          *a That is* Aram of Two Rivers.

outside? I have prepared the house, and there is room for the camels.' So 32
he brought the man into the house, unloaded the camels and provided straw
and fodder for them, and water for him and all his men to wash their feet.
Food was set before him, but he said, 'I will not eat until I have delivered 33
my message.' Laban said, 'Let us hear it.' He answered, 'I am the servant 34
of Abraham. The LORD has greatly blessed my master, and he has become a 35
man of power. The LORD has given him flocks and herds, silver and gold,
male and female slaves, camels and asses. My master's wife Sarah in her 36
old age bore him a son, to whom he has given all that he has. So my master 37
made me swear an oath, saying, "You shall not take a wife for my son from
the women of the Canaanites in whose land I dwell; but you shall go to my 38
father's house and to my family to find a wife for him." So I said to my 39
master, "What if the woman will not come with me?" He answered, "The 40
LORD, in whose presence I have lived, will send his angel with you and will
make your journey successful. You shall take a wife for my son from my
family and from my father's house; then you shall be released from the 41
charge I have laid upon you. But if, when you come to my family, they will
not give her to you, you shall still be released from the charge." So I came 42
to the spring today, and I said, "O LORD God of my master Abraham, if
thou wilt make my journey successful, let it be like this. Here I stand by 43
the spring. When a young woman comes out to draw water, I shall say to
her, 'Give me a little water to drink from your jar.' If she answers, 'Yes, 44
do drink, and I will draw water for your camels as well', she is the woman
whom the LORD intends for my master's son." Before I had finished pray- 45
ing silently, I saw Rebecca coming out with her water-jar on her shoulder.
She went down to the spring and drew some water, and I said to her,
"Please give me a drink." She quickly lowered her jar from her shoulder 46
and said, "Drink; and I will water your camels as well." So I drank, and
she also gave my camels water. I asked her whose daughter she was, and 47
she said, "I am the daughter of Bethuel, the son of Nahor and Milcah."
Then I put the ring in her nose and the bracelets on her wrists, and I 48
bowed low and prostrated myself before the LORD. I blessed the LORD the
God of my master Abraham, who had led me by the right road to take my
master's niece for his son. Now tell me if you will keep faith and truth with 49
my master. If not, say so, and I will turn elsewhere.'

Laban and Bethuel answered, 'This is from the LORD; we can say no- 50
thing for or against. Here is Rebecca herself; take her and go. She shall be 51
the wife of your master's son, as the LORD has decreed.' When Abraham's 52
servant heard what they said, he prostrated himself on the ground before
the LORD. Then he brought out gold and silver ornaments, and robes, and 53
gave them to Rebecca, and he gave costly gifts to her brother and her
mother. He and his men then ate and drank and spent the night there. 54
When they rose in the morning, he said, 'Give me leave to go back to my
master.' Her brother and her mother said, 'Let the girl stay with us for a 55
few days, say ten days, and then she shall go.' But he said to them, 'Do not 56
detain me, for the LORD has granted me success. Give me leave to return
to my master.' They said, 'Let us call the girl and see what she says.' They 57 58
called Rebecca and asked her if she would go with the man, and she said,

59 'Yes, I will go.' So they let their sister Rebecca and her nurse go with
60 Abraham's servant and his men. They blessed Rebecca and said to her:

> 'You are our sister, may you be the mother of myriads;
> may your sons possess the cities of their enemies.'

61 Then Rebecca and her companions mounted their camels at once and
followed the man. So the servant took Rebecca and went his way.
62 Isaac meanwhile had moved on as far as Beer-lahai-roi and was living in
63 the Negeb. One evening when he had gone out into the open country hoping
64 to meet them,*a* he looked up and saw camels approaching. When Rebecca
65 raised her eyes and saw Isaac, she slipped hastily from her camel, saying to
the servant, 'Who is that man walking across the open towards us?' The
servant answered, 'It is my master.' So she took her veil and covered her-
66 67 self. The servant related to Isaac all that had happened. Isaac conducted
her into the tent*b* and took her as his wife. So she became his wife, and he
loved her and was consoled for the death of his mother.

25 1*c* 2 ABRAHAM MARRIED ANOTHER WIFE, whose name was Keturah. She
3 bore him Zimran, Jokshan, Medan, Midian, Ishbak and Shuah. Jokshan
became the father of Sheba and Dedan. The sons of Dedan were Asshurim,
4 Letushim and Leummim, and the sons of Midian were Ephah, Epher,
Enoch, Abida and Eldaah. All these were descendants of Keturah.
5 6 Abraham had given all that he had to Isaac; and he had already in his
lifetime given presents to the sons of his concubines, and had sent them
7 away eastwards, to a land of the east, out of his son Isaac's way. Abraham
8 had lived for a hundred and seventy-five years when he breathed his last.
He died at a good old age, after a very long life, and was gathered to his
9 father's kin. His sons, Isaac and Ishmael, buried him in the cave at Mach-
10 pelah, on the land of Ephron son of Zohar the Hittite, east of Mamre, the
plot which Abraham had bought from the Hittites. There Abraham was
11 buried with his wife Sarah. After the death of Abraham, God blessed his
son Isaac, who settled close by Beer-lahai-roi.
12 This is the table of the descendants of Abraham's son Ishmael, whom
13*d* Hagar the Egyptian, Sarah's slave-girl, bore to him. These are the names
of the sons of Ishmael named in order of their birth: Nebaioth, Ishmael's
14 15 eldest son, then Kedar, Adbeel, Mibsam, Mishma, Dumah, Massa, Hadad,
16 Teman, Jetur, Naphish and Kedemah. These are the sons of Ishmael,
after whom their hamlets and encampments were named, twelve princes
17 according to their tribal groups. Ishmael had lived for a hundred and thirty-
seven years when he breathed his last. So he died and was gathered to his
18 father's kin. Ishmael's sons inhabited the land from Havilah to Shur, which
is east of Egypt on the way to Asshur, having settled to the east of his
brothers.

19 THIS IS THE TABLE of the descendants of Abraham's son Isaac. Isaac's
20 father was Abraham. When Isaac was forty years old he married Rebecca

---

*a* hoping . . . them: *or* to relieve himself.    *b* *Prob. rdg.; Heb. adds* Sarah his mother.
*c* *Verses 1–4: cp. 1 Chr. 1. 32, 33.*    *d* *Verses 13–16: cp. 1 Chr. 1. 29–31.*

the daughter of Bethuel the Aramaean from Paddan-aram and the sister
of Laban the Aramaean. Isaac appealed to the LORD on behalf of his wife  21
because she was barren; the LORD yielded to his entreaty, and Rebecca
conceived. The children pressed hard on each other in her womb, and she  22
said, 'If this is how it is with me, what does it mean?' So she went to seek
guidance of the LORD. The LORD said to her:  23

> 'Two nations in your womb.
> two peoples, going their own ways from birth!
> One shall be stronger than the other;
> the older shall be servant to the younger.'

When her time had come, there were indeed twins in her womb. The first  24 25
came out red, hairy all over like a hair-cloak, and they named him Esau.[a]
Immediately afterwards his brother was born with his hand grasping  26
Esau's heel, and they called him Jacob.[b] Isaac was sixty years old when
they were born. The boys grew up; and Esau became skilful in hunting,  27
a man of the open plains, but Jacob led a settled life and stayed among the
tents. Isaac favoured Esau because he kept him supplied with venison, but  28
Rebecca favoured Jacob. One day Jacob prepared a broth and when Esau  29
came in from the country, exhausted, he said to Jacob, 'I am exhausted;  30
let me swallow some of that red broth': this is why he was called Edom.[c]
Jacob said, 'Not till you sell me your rights as the first-born.' Esau replied,  31 32
'I am at death's door; what use is my birthright to me?' Jacob said, 'Not  33
till you swear!'; so he swore an oath and sold his birthright to Jacob. Then  34
Jacob gave Esau bread and the lentil broth, and he ate and drank and went
away without more ado. Thus Esau showed how little he valued his birthright.

There came a famine in the land—not the earlier famine in Abraham's  **26**
time—and Isaac went to Abimelech the Philistine king at Gerar. The  2
LORD appeared to Isaac and said, 'Do not go down to Egypt, but stay in
this country as I bid you. Stay in this country and I will be with you and  3
bless you, for to you and to your descendants I will give all these lands.
Thus shall I fulfil the oath which I swore to your father Abraham. I will  4
make your descendants as many as the stars in the sky; I will give them all
these lands, and all the nations of the earth will pray to be blessed as they
are blessed—all because Abraham obeyed me and kept my charge, my  5
commandments, my statutes, and my laws.' So Isaac lived in Gerar.  6

When the men of the place asked him about his wife, he told them that  7
she was his sister; he was afraid to say that Rebecca was his wife, in case
they killed him because of her; for she was very beautiful. When they had  8
been there for some considerable time, Abimelech the Philistine king
looked down from his window and saw Isaac and his wife Rebecca laughing
together. He summoned Isaac and said, 'So she is your wife, is she? What  9
made you say she was your sister?' Isaac answered, 'I thought I should be
killed because of her.' Abimelech said, 'Why have you treated us like this?  10
One of the people might easily have gone to bed with your wife, and then
you would have made us liable to retribution.' So Abimelech warned all  11

---

[a] *That is* Covering.　　　[b] *That is* He caught by the heel.　　　[c] *That is* Red.

the people, threatening that whoever touched this man or his wife would be put to death.

12 Isaac sowed seed in that land, and that year he reaped a hundredfold,
13 and the LORD blessed him. He became more and more powerful, until he
14 was very powerful indeed. He had flocks and herds and many slaves, so
15 that the Philistines were envious of him. They had stopped up all the wells dug by the slaves in the days of Isaac's father Abraham, and filled them with
18 earth. Isaac dug them again, all those wells dug in his father Abraham's time, and stopped up by the Philistines after his death, and he called them by the names which his father had given them.

16 Then Abimelech said to him, 'Go away from here; you are too strong for
17 us.' So Isaac left that place and encamped in the valley of Gerar, and stayed
19*a* there. Then Isaac's slaves dug in the valley and found a spring of running
20 water, but the shepherds of Gerar quarrelled with Isaac's shepherds, claiming the water as theirs. He called the well Esek,*b* because they made diffi-
21 culties for him. His men then dug another well, but the others quarrelled
22 with him over that also, so he called it Sitnah.*c* He moved on from there and dug another well, but there was no quarrel over that one, so he called it Rehoboth,*d* saying, 'Now the LORD has given us plenty of room and we shall be fruitful in the land.'

23 24 Isaac went up country from there to Beersheba. That same night the LORD appeared to him there and said, 'I am the God of your father Abraham. Fear nothing, for I am with you. I will bless you and give you many
25 descendants for the sake of Abraham my servant.' So Isaac built an altar there and invoked the LORD by name. Then he pitched his tent there, and
26 there also his slaves dug a well. Abimelech came to him from Gerar with
27 Ahuzzath his friend and Phicol the commander of his army. Isaac said to them, 'Why have you come here? You hate me and you sent me away.'
28 They answered, 'We have seen plainly that the LORD is with you, so we thought, "Let the two of us put each other to the oath and make a treaty
29 that will bind us." We have not attacked you, we have done you nothing but good, and we let you go away peaceably. Swear that you will do us no
30 harm, now that the LORD has blessed you.' So Isaac gave a feast and they
31 ate and drank. They rose early in the morning and exchanged oaths. Then
32 Isaac bade them farewell, and they parted from him in peace. The same day Isaac's slaves came and told him about a well that they had dug: 'We have
33 found water', they said. He named the well Shibah.*e* This is why the city is called Beersheba*f* to this day.

34 When Esau was forty years old he married Judith daughter of Beeri
35 the Hittite, and Basemath daughter of Elon the Hittite; this was a bitter grief to Isaac and Rebecca.

*a Verse 18 transposed to follow 15.*      *b That is* Difficulty.      *c That is* Enmity.
*d That is* Plenty of room.      *e That is* Oath.      *f That is* Well of an Oath.

## *Jacob and Esau*

WHEN ISAAC GREW OLD and his eyes became so dim that he could 27
not see, he called his elder son Esau and said to him, 'My son', and
he answered, 'Here I am.' Isaac said, 'Listen now: I am old and I do not 2
know when I may die. Take your hunting gear, your quiver and your bow, 3
and go out into the country and get me some venison. Then make me a 4
savoury dish of the kind I like, and bring it to me to eat so that I may give
you my blessing before I die.' Now Rebecca was listening as Isaac talked 5
to his son Esau. When Esau went off into the country to find some venison
and bring it home, she said to her son Jacob, 'I heard your father talking to 6
your brother Esau, and he said, "Bring me some venison and make it into 7
a savoury dish so that I may eat it and bless you in the presence of the LORD
before I die." Listen to me, my son, and do what I tell you. Go to the flock 8 9
and pick me out two fine young kids, and I will make them into a savoury
dish for your father, of the kind he likes. Then take them in to your father, 10
and he will eat them so that he may bless you before he dies.' Jacob said 11
to his mother Rebecca, 'But my brother Esau is a hairy man, and my skin
is smooth. Suppose my father feels me, he will know I am tricking him and 12
I shall bring a curse upon myself instead of a blessing.' His mother answered 13
him, 'Let the curse fall on me, my son, but do as I say; go and bring me the
kids.' So Jacob fetched them and brought them to his mother, who made 14
them into a savoury dish of the kind that his father liked. Then Rebecca 15
took her elder son's clothes, Esau's best clothes which she kept by her in
the house, and put them on her younger son Jacob. She put the goatskins 16
on his hands and on the smooth nape of his neck; and she handed her 17
son Jacob the savoury dish and the bread she had made. He came to his 18
father and said, 'Father.' He answered, 'Yes, my son; who are you?' Jacob 19
answered his father, 'I am Esau, your elder son. I have done as you told me.
Come, sit up and eat some of my venison, so that you may give me your
blessing.' Isaac said to his son, 'What is this that you found so quickly?', 20
and Jacob answered, 'It is what the LORD your God put in my way.' Isaac 21
then said to Jacob, 'Come close and let me feel you, my son, to see whether
you are really my son Esau.' When Jacob came close to his father, Isaac 22
felt him and said, 'The voice is Jacob's voice, but the hands are the hands
of Esau.' He did not recognize him because his hands were hairy like 23
Esau's, and that is why he blessed him. He said, 'Are you really my son 24
Esau?', and he answered, 'Yes.' Then Isaac said, 'Bring me some of your 25
venison to eat, my son, so that I may give you my blessing.' Then Jacob
brought it to him, and he ate it; he brought wine also, and he drank it.
Then his father Isaac said to him, 'Come near, my son, and kiss me.' So 26 27
he came near and kissed him, and when Isaac smelt the smell of his clothes,
he blessed him and said:

> 'Ah! The smell of my son is like the smell of open country
> blessed by the LORD.
> God give you dew from heaven 28
> and the richness of the earth,
> corn and new wine in plenty!

29    Peoples shall serve you,
      nations bow down to you.
        Be lord over your brothers;
      may your mother's sons bow down to you.
      A curse upon those who curse you;
      a blessing on those who bless you!'

30    Isaac finished blessing Jacob; and Jacob had scarcely left his father
31  Isaac's presence, when his brother Esau came in from his hunting. He too
    made a savoury dish and brought it to his father. He said, 'Come, father,
32  and eat some of my venison, so that you may give me your blessing.' His
    father Isaac said, 'Who are you?' He said, 'I am Esau, your elder son.'
33  Then Isaac became greatly agitated*a* and said, 'Then who was it that
    hunted and brought me venison? I ate it all before you came in and I
34  blessed him, and the blessing will stand.' When Esau heard what his father
35  said, he gave a loud and bitter cry and said, 'Bless me too, father.' But
    Isaac said, 'Your brother came treacherously and took away your blessing.'
36  Esau said, 'He is rightly called Jacob.*b* This is the second time he has sup-
    planted me. He took away my right as the first-born and now he has taken
37  away my blessing. Have you kept back any blessing for me?' Isaac answered,
    'I have made him lord over you, and I have given him all his brothers as
    slaves. I have bestowed upon him corn and new wine for his sustenance.
38  What is there left that I can do for you, my son?' Esau asked his father,
    'Had you then only one blessing, father? Bless me too, my father.' And
39  Esau cried bitterly. Then his father Isaac answered:

      'Your dwelling shall be far from the richness of the earth,
        far from the dew of heaven above.
40      By your sword shall you live,
        and you shall serve your brother;
        but the time will come when you grow restive
        and break off his yoke from your neck.'

41    Esau bore a grudge against Jacob because of the blessing which his father
    had given him, and he said to himself, 'The time of mourning for my father
42  will soon be here; then I will kill my brother Jacob.' When Rebecca was
    told what her elder son Esau was saying, she called her younger son Jacob,
43  and she said to him, 'Esau your brother is threatening to kill you. Now, my
44  son, listen to me. Slip away at once to my brother Laban in Harran. Stay
45  with him for a while until your brother's anger cools. When it has subsided
    and he forgets what you have done to him, I will send and fetch you back.
    Why should I lose you both in one day?'
46    Rebecca said to Isaac, 'I am weary to death of Hittite women! If Jacob
    marries a Hittite woman like those who live here, my life will not be worth
28  living.' Isaac called Jacob, blessed him and gave him instructions. He said,
2   'You must not marry one of these women of Canaan. Go at once to the
    house of Bethuel, your mother's father, in Paddan-aram, and there find
3   a wife, one of the daughters of Laban, your mother's brother. God Almighty

----

*a* Or incensed.        *b* That is He supplanted.

30

bless you, make you fruitful and increase your descendants until they become a host of nations. May he bestow on you and your offspring the 4 blessing of Abraham, and may you thus possess the country where you are now living, the land which God gave to Abraham!' So Isaac sent Jacob 5 away, and he went to Paddan-aram to Laban, son of Bethuel the Aramaean, and brother to Rebecca the mother of Jacob and Esau. Esau discovered 6 that Isaac had given Jacob his blessing and had sent him away to Paddan-aram to find a wife there; and that when he blessed him he had forbidden him to marry a woman of Canaan, and that Jacob had obeyed his father 7 and mother and gone to Paddan-aram. Then Esau, seeing that his father 8 disliked the women of Canaan, went to Ishmael, and, in addition to his 9 other wives, he married Mahalath sister of Nebaioth and daughter of Abraham's son Ishmael.

Jacob set out from Beersheba and went on his way towards Harran. He 10 11 came to a certain place and stopped there for the night, because the sun had set; and, taking one of the stones there, he made it a pillow for his head and lay down to sleep. He dreamt that he saw a ladder, which rested on the 12 ground with its top reaching to heaven, and angels of God were going up and down upon it. The LORD was standing beside him[a] and said, 'I am the 13 LORD, the God of your father Abraham and the God of Isaac. This land on which you are lying I will give to you and your descendants. They shall be 14 countless as the dust upon the earth, and you shall spread far and wide, to north and south, to east and west. All the families of the earth shall pray to be blessed as you and your descendants are blessed. I will be with you, and 15 I will protect you wherever you go and will bring you back to this land; for I will not leave you until I have done all that I have promised.' Jacob woke 16 from his sleep and said, 'Truly the LORD is in this place, and I did not know it.' Then he was afraid and said, 'How fearsome is this place! This is 17 no other than the house of God, this is the gate of heaven.' Jacob rose early 18 in the morning, took the stone on which he had laid his head, set it up as a sacred pillar and poured oil on the top of it. He named that place Beth-El;[b] but the earlier name of the city was Luz. 19

Thereupon Jacob made this vow: 'If God will be with me, if he will 20 protect me on my journey and give me food to eat and clothes to wear, and 21 I come back safely to my father's house, then the LORD shall be my God, and this stone which I have set up as a sacred pillar shall be a house of God. 22 And of all that thou givest me, I will without fail allot a tenth part to thee.'

JACOB CONTINUED HIS JOURNEY and came to the land of the eastern 29 tribes. There he saw a well in the open country and three flocks of sheep 2 lying beside it, because the flocks were watered from that well. Over its mouth was a huge stone, and all the herdsmen used to gather there and roll 3 it off the mouth of the well and water the flocks; then they would put it back in its place over the well. Jacob said to them, 'Where are you from, 4 my friends?' 'We are from Harran', they replied. He asked them if they 5 knew Laban the grandson of Nahor. They answered, 'Yes, we do.' 'Is he 6 well?' Jacob asked; and they answered, 'Yes, he is well, and here is his

[a] *Or* on it *or* by it.　　　[b] *That is* House of God.

7 daughter Rachel coming with the flock.' Jacob said, 'The sun is still high, and the time for folding the sheep has not yet come. Water the flocks and
8 then go and graze them.' But they replied, 'We cannot, until all the herdsmen have gathered together and the stone is rolled away from the mouth of
9 the well; then we can water our flocks.' While he was talking to them,
10 Rachel came up with her father's flock, for she was a shepherdess. When Jacob saw Rachel, the daughter of Laban his mother's brother, with Laban's flock, he stepped forward, rolled the stone off the mouth of the
11 well and watered Laban's sheep. He kissed Rachel, and was moved to
12 tears. He told her that he was her father's kinsman and Rebecca's son; so
13 she ran and told her father. When Laban heard the news of his sister's son Jacob, he ran to meet him, embraced him, kissed him warmly and welcomed
14 him to his home. Jacob told Laban everything, and Laban said, 'Yes, you are my own flesh and blood.' So Jacob stayed with him for a whole month.
15     Laban said to Jacob, 'Why should you work for me for nothing simply
16 because you are my kinsman? Tell me what your wages ought to be.' Now Laban had two daughters: the elder was called Leah, and the younger
17 18 Rachel. Leah was dull-eyed, but Rachel was graceful and beautiful. Jacob had fallen in love with Rachel and he said, 'I will work seven years for your
19 younger daughter Rachel.' Laban replied, 'It is better that I should give her
20 to you than to anyone else; stay with me.' So Jacob worked seven years for
21 Rachel, and they seemed like a few days because he loved her. Then Jacob said to Laban, 'I have served my time. Give me my wife so that we may
22 sleep together.' So Laban gathered all the men of the place together and
23 gave a feast. In the evening he took his daughter Leah and brought her to
24 Jacob, and Jacob slept with her. At the same time Laban gave his slave-
25 girl Zilpah to his daughter Leah. But when morning came, Jacob saw that it was Leah and said to Laban, 'What have you done to me? Did I not work
26 for Rachel? Why have you deceived me?' Laban answered, 'In our country
27 it is not right to give the younger sister in marriage before the elder. Go through with the seven days' feast for the elder, and the younger shall be
28 given you in return for a further seven years' work.' Jacob agreed, and completed the seven days for Leah.
29     Then Laban gave Jacob his daughter Rachel as wife; and he gave his
30 slave-girl Bilhah to serve his daughter Rachel. Jacob slept with Rachel also; he loved her rather than Leah, and he worked for Laban for a further seven
31 years. When the LORD saw that Leah was not loved, he granted her a child;
32 but Rachel was childless. Leah conceived and bore a son; and she called him Reuben,*a* for she said, 'The LORD has seen my humiliation; now my
33 husband will love me.' Again she conceived and bore a son and said, 'The LORD, hearing that I am not loved, has given me this child also'; and she
34 called him Simeon.*b* She conceived again and bore a son; and she said, 'Now that I have borne him three sons my husband and I will surely be
35 united.' So she called him Levi.*c* Once more she conceived and bore a son; and she said, 'Now I will praise the LORD'; therefore she named him Judah.*d* Then for a while she bore no more children.

*a That is* See, a son.     *b That is* Hearing.     *c That is* Union.
*d That is* Praise.

When Rachel found that she bore Jacob no children, she became jealous **30** of her sister and said to Jacob, 'Give me sons, or I shall die.' Jacob said 2 angrily to Rachel, 'Can I take the place of God, who has denied you children?' She said, 'Here is my slave-girl Bilhah. Lie with her, so that she may 3 bear sons to be laid upon my knees, and through her I too may build up a family.' So she gave him her slave-girl Bilhah as a wife, and Jacob lay with 4 her. Bilhah conceived and bore Jacob a son. Then Rachel said, 'God has 5 6 given judgement for me; he has indeed heard me and given me a son', so she named him Dan.*a* Rachel's slave-girl Bilhah again conceived and bore 7 Jacob another son. Rachel said, 'I have played a fine trick on my sister, 8 and it has succeeded'; so she named him Naphtali.*b* When Leah found 9 that she was bearing no more children, she took her slave-girl Zilpah and gave her to Jacob as a wife, and Zilpah bore Jacob a son. Leah said, 'Good 10 11 fortune has come', and she named him Gad.*c* Zilpah, Leah's slave-girl, 12 bore Jacob another son, and Leah said, 'Happiness has come, for young 13 women will call me happy.' So she named him Asher.*d*

In the time of wheat-harvest Reuben went out and found some man- 14 drakes in the open country and brought them to his mother Leah. Then Rachel asked Leah for some of her son's mandrakes, but Leah said, 'Is it 15 so small a thing to have taken away my husband, that you should take my son's mandrakes as well?' But Rachel said, 'Very well, let him sleep with you tonight in exchange for your son's mandrakes.' So when Jacob came 16 in from the country in the evening, Leah went out to meet him and said, 'You are to sleep with me tonight; I have hired you with my son's mandrakes.' That night he slept with her, and God heard Leah's prayer, and 17 she conceived and bore a fifth son. Leah said, 'God has rewarded me, 18 because I gave my slave-girl to my husband.' So she named him Issachar.*e* Leah again conceived and bore a sixth son. She said, 'God has endowed 19 20 me with a noble dowry. Now my husband will treat me in princely style, because I have borne him six sons.' So she named him Zebulun.*f* Later 21 she bore a daughter and named her Dinah. Then God thought of Rachel; 22 he heard her prayer and gave her a child; so she conceived and bore a 23 son and said, 'God has taken away my humiliation.' She named him 24 Joseph,*g* saying, 'May the LORD add another son!'

When Rachel had given birth to Joseph, Jacob said to Laban, 'Let me 25 go, for I wish to return to my own home and country. Give me my wives 26 and my children for whom I have served you, and I will go; for you know what service I have done for you.' Laban said to him, 'Let me have my say, 27 if you please. I have become prosperous and the LORD has blessed me for your sake. So now tell me what I owe you in wages, and I will give it you.' 28 Jacob answered, 'You must know how I have served you, and how your 29 herds have prospered under my care. You had only a few when I came, but 30 now they have increased beyond measure, and the LORD brought blessings to you wherever I went. But is it not time for me to provide for my family?' Laban said, 'Then what shall I give you?', but Jacob answered, 'Give me 31

*a That is* He has given judgement.          *b That is* Trickery.          *c That is* Good Fortune.          *d That is* Happy.          *e That is* Reward.          *f That is* Prince.
*g The name may mean either* He takes away *or* May he add.

nothing; I will mind your flocks *a* as before, if you will do what I suggest.
32 Today I will go over your flocks and pick out from them every black lamb, and all the brindled and the spotted goats, and they shall be my wages.
33 This is a fair offer, and it will be to my own disadvantage later on, when we come to settling my wages: every goat amongst mine that is not spotted or
34 brindled and every lamb that is not black will have been stolen.' Laban
35 said, 'Agreed; let it be as you have said.' But that day he removed the he-goats that were striped and brindled and all the spotted and brindled she-goats, all that had any white on them, and every ram that was black, and
36 he handed them over to his own sons. Then he put a distance of three days' journey between himself and Jacob, while Jacob was left tending those of
37 Laban's flocks that remained. Thereupon Jacob took fresh rods of white poplar, almond, and plane tree, and peeled off strips of bark, exposing the
38 white of the rods. Then he fixed the peeled rods upright in the troughs at the watering-places where the flocks came to drink; they faced the she-
39 goats that were on heat when they came to drink. They felt a longing for the rods and they gave birth to young that were striped and spotted and
40 brindled. As for the rams, Jacob divided them, and let the ewes run only with such of the rams in Laban's flock as were striped and black; and thus he bred separate flocks for himself, which he did not add to Laban's sheep.
41 As for the goats, whenever the more vigorous were on heat, he put the rods
42 in front of them at the troughs so that they would long for the rods; he did not put them there for the weaker goats. Thus the weaker came to be
43 Laban's and the stronger Jacob's. So Jacob increased in wealth more and more until he possessed great flocks, male and female slaves, camels, and asses.

31 JACOB LEARNT that Laban's sons were saying, 'Jacob has taken every-thing that was our father's, and all his wealth has come from our father's
2 property.' He also noticed that Laban was not so well disposed to him as
3 he had once been. Then the LORD said to Jacob, 'Go back to the land of
4 your fathers and to your kindred. I will be with you.' So Jacob sent to
5 fetch Rachel and Leah to his flocks out in the country and said to them, 'I see that your father is not as well disposed to me as once he was; yet the
6 God of my father has been with me. You know how I have served your
7 father to the best of my power, but he has cheated me and changed my
8 wages ten times over. Yet God did not let him do me any harm. If Laban said, "The spotted ones shall be your wages", then all the flock bore spotted young; and if he said, "The striped ones shall be your wages", then all the
9 flock bore striped young. God has taken away your father's property and
10 has given it to me. In the season when the flocks were on heat, I had a dream: I looked up and saw that the he-goats mounting the flock were striped and
11 spotted and dappled. The angel of God said to me in my dream, "Jacob",
12 and I replied, "Here I am", and he said, "Look up and see: all the he-goats mounting the flock are striped and spotted and dappled. I have seen
13 all that Laban is doing to you. I am the God who appeared to you at Bethel where you anointed a sacred pillar and where you made your vow. Now

*a Prob. rdg.; Heb. adds* I will watch.

leave this country at once and return to the land of your birth." ' Rachel 14
and Leah answered him, 'We no longer have any part or lot in our father's
house. Does he not look on us as foreigners, now that he has sold us and 15
spent on himself the whole of the money paid for us? But all the wealth 16
which God has saved from our father's clutches is ours and our children's.
Now do everything that God has said.' Jacob at once set his sons and his 17
wives on camels, and drove off all the herds and livestock which he had 18
acquired in Paddan-aram, to go to his father Isaac in Canaan.

When Laban the Aramaean had gone to shear his sheep, Rachel stole 19
her father's household gods, and Jacob deceived Laban, keeping his 20
departure secret. So Jacob ran away with all that he had, crossed the River 21
and made for the hill-country of Gilead. Three days later, when Laban 22
heard that Jacob had run away, he took his kinsmen with him, pursued 23
Jacob for seven days and caught up with him in the hill-country of Gilead.
But God came to Laban in a dream by night and said to him, 'Be careful 24
to say nothing to Jacob, either good or bad.'

When Laban overtook him, Jacob had pitched his tent in the hill- 25
country of Gilead, and Laban pitched his in the company of his kinsmen in
the same hill-country. Laban said to Jacob, 'What have you done? You 26
have deceived me and carried off my daughters as though they were captives taken in war. Why did you slip away secretly without telling me? I 27
would have set you on your way with songs and the music of tambourines
and harps. You did not even let me kiss my daughters and their children. 28
In this you were at fault. It is in my power to do you an injury, but yester- 29
day the God of your father spoke to me; he told me to be careful to say
nothing to you, either good or bad. I know that you went away because 30
you were homesick and pining for your father's house, but why did you
steal my gods?'

Jacob answered, 'I was afraid; I thought you would take your daughters 31
from me by force. Whoever is found in possession of your gods shall die 32
for it. Let our kinsmen here be witnesses: point out anything I have that
is yours, and take it back.' Jacob did not know that Rachel had stolen the
gods. So Laban went into Jacob's tent and Leah's tent and that of the two 33
slave-girls, but he found nothing. When he came out of Leah's tent he
went into Rachel's. Now she had taken the household gods and put them 34
in the camel-bag and was sitting on them. Laban went through everything
in the tent and found nothing. Rachel said to her father, 'Do not take it 35
amiss, sir, that I cannot rise in your presence: the common lot of woman
is upon me.' So for all his search Laban did not find his household gods.

Jacob was angry, and he expostulated with Laban, exclaiming, 'What 36
have I done wrong? What is my offence, that you have come after me in hot
pursuit and gone through all my possessions? Have you found anything 37
belonging to your household? If so, set it here in front of my kinsmen and
yours, and let them judge between the two of us. In all the twenty years 38
I have been with you, your ewes and she-goats have never miscarried; I
have not eaten the rams of your flocks; I have never brought to you the 39
body of any animal mangled by wild beasts, but I bore the loss myself; you
claimed compensation from me for anything stolen by day or by night.

40 This was the way of it: by day the heat consumed me and the frost by night,
41 and sleep deserted me. For twenty years I have been in your household. I
worked for you fourteen years to win your two daughters and six years for
42 your flocks, and you changed my wages ten times over. If the God of my
father, the God of Abraham and the Fear of Isaac, had not been with me,
you would have sent me away empty-handed. But God saw my labour and
my hardships, and last night he rebuked you.'
43 Laban answered Jacob, 'The daughters are my daughters, the children
are my children, the flocks are my flocks; all that you see is mine. But as
for my daughters, what can I do today about them and the children they
44 have borne? Come now, we will make an agreement, you and I, and let it
45 stand as a witness between us.' So Jacob chose a great stone and set it up-
46 right as a sacred pillar. Then he told his kinsmen to gather stones, and they
took them and built a cairn, and there beside the cairn they ate together.
47 48 Laban called it Jegar-sahadutha,*a* and Jacob called it Gal-ed.*b* Laban said,
'This cairn is witness today between you and me.' For this reason it was
49 named Gal-ed; it was also named Mizpah,*c* for Laban said, 'May the LORD
50 watch between you and me, when we are parted from each other's sight. If
you ill-treat my daughters or take other wives beside them when no one is
51 there to see, then God be witness between us.' Laban said further to Jacob,
52 'Here is this cairn, and here the pillar which I have set up between us. This
cairn is witness and the pillar is witness: I for my part will not pass beyond
this cairn to your side, and you for your part shall not pass beyond this
53 cairn and this pillar to my side to do an injury, otherwise the God of Abraham and the God of Nahor will judge between us.' And Jacob swore this
54 oath in the name of the Fear of Isaac his father. He slaughtered an animal
for sacrifice, there in the hill-country, and summoned his kinsmen to the
feast. So they ate together and spent the night there.
55 Laban rose early in the morning, kissed his daughters and their child-
32 ren, blessed them and went home again. Then Jacob continued his journey
2 and was met by angels of God. When he saw them, Jacob said, 'This is the
company of God', and he called that place Mahanaim.*d*
3 Jacob sent messengers on ahead to his brother Esau to the district of Seir
4 in the Edomite country, and this is what he told them to say to Esau, 'My
lord, your servant Jacob says, I have been living with Laban and have
5 stayed there till now. I have oxen, asses, and sheep, and male and female
slaves, and I have sent to tell you this, my lord, so that I may win your
6 favour.' The messengers returned to Jacob and said, 'We met your brother
7 Esau already on the way to meet you with four hundred men.' Jacob, much
afraid and distressed, divided the people with him, as well as the sheep,
8 cattle, and camels, into two companies, thinking that, if Esau should come
9 upon one company and destroy it, the other company would survive. Jacob
said, 'O God of my father Abraham, God of my father Isaac, O LORD at
whose bidding I came back to my own country and to my kindred, and
10 who didst promise me prosperity, I am not worthy of all the true and steadfast love which thou hast shown to me thy servant. When I crossed the

---

*a Aramaic for* Cairn of Witness.          *b Hebrew for* Cairn of Witness.
*c That is* Watch-tower.        *d That is* Two Companies.

Jordan, I had nothing but the staff in my hand; now I have two companies. Save me, I pray, from my brother Esau, for I am afraid that he may come 11 and destroy me, sparing neither mother nor child. But thou didst say, I will 12 prosper you and will make your descendants like the sand of the sea, which is beyond all counting.'

Jacob spent that night there; and as a present for his brother Esau he 13 chose from the herds he had with him two hundred she-goats, twenty he- 14 goats, two hundred ewes and twenty rams, thirty milch-camels with their 15 young, forty cows and ten young bulls, twenty she-asses and ten he-asses. He put each herd separately into the care of a servant and said to each, 'Go 16 on ahead of me, and leave gaps between the herds.' Then he gave these 17 instructions to the first: 'When my brother Esau meets you and asks you to whom you belong and where you are going and who owns these beasts you are driving, you are to say, "They belong to your servant Jacob; he 18 sends them as a present to my lord Esau, and he is behind us."' He gave 19 the same instructions to the second, to the third, and all the drovers, telling them to say the same thing to Esau when they met him. And they were to 20 add, 'Your servant Jacob is behind us'; for he thought, 'I will appease him with the present that I have sent on ahead, and afterwards, when I come into his presence, he will perhaps receive me kindly.' So Jacob's present 21 went on ahead of him, but he himself spent that night at Mahaneh.

During the night Jacob rose, took his two wives, his two slave-girls, and 22 his eleven sons, and crossed the ford of Jabbok. He took them and sent 23 them across the gorge with all that he had. So Jacob was left alone, and a 24 man wrestled with him there till$^a$ daybreak. When the man saw that he 25 could not throw Jacob, he struck him in the hollow of his thigh, so that Jacob's hip was dislocated as they wrestled. The man said, 'Let me go, 26 for day is breaking', but Jacob replied, 'I will not let you go unless you bless me.' He said to Jacob, 'What is your name?', and he answered, 'Jacob.' 27 The man said, 'Your name shall no longer be Jacob, but Israel,$^b$ because 28 you strove with God and with men, and prevailed.' Jacob said, 'Tell me, 29 I pray, your name.' He replied, 'Why do you ask my name?', but he gave him his blessing there. Jacob called the place Peniel,$^c$ 'because', he said, 30 'I have seen God face to face and my life is spared.' The sun rose as Jacob 31 passed through Penuel, limping because of his hip. This is why the Israel- 32 ites to this day do not eat the sinew of the nerve that runs in the hollow of the thigh; for the man had struck Jacob on that nerve in the hollow of the thigh.

Jacob raised his eyes and saw Esau coming towards him with four **33** hundred men; so he divided the children between Leah and Rachel and the two slave-girls. He put the slave-girls with their children in front, Leah 2 with her children next, and Rachel with Joseph last. He then went on 3 ahead of them, bowing low to the ground seven times as he approached his brother. Esau ran to meet him and embraced him; he threw his arms round 4 him and kissed him, and they wept. When Esau looked up and saw the 5 women and children, he said, 'Who are these with you?' Jacob replied, 'The children whom God has graciously given to your servant.' The 6

$^a$ Or at.    $^b$ *That is* God strove.    $^c$ *That is* Face of God (*elsewhere* Penuel).

7 slave-girls came near, each with her children, and they bowed low. Then Leah with her children came near and bowed low, and afterwards Joseph
8 and Rachel came near and bowed low also. Esau said, 'What was all that company of yours that I met?' And he answered, 'It was meant to win favour
9 with you, my lord.' Esau answered, 'I have more than enough. Keep what
10 is yours, my brother.' But Jacob said, 'On no account: if I have won your favour, then, I pray, accept this gift from me; for, you see, I come into your
11 presence as into that of a god, and you receive me favourably. Accept this gift which I bring you; for God has been gracious to me, and I have all I want.' So he urged him, and he accepted it.
12 13     Then Esau said, 'Let us set out, and I will go at your pace.' But Jacob answered him, 'You must know, my lord, that the children are small; the flocks and herds are suckling their young and I am concerned for them, and
14 if the men overdrive them for a single day, all my beasts will die. I beg you, my lord, to go on ahead, and I will go by easy stages at the pace of the children and of the livestock that I am driving, until I come to my lord in Seir.'
15 Esau said, 'Let me detail some of my own men to escort you', but he replied,
16 'Why should my lord be so kind to me?' That day Esau turned back towards
17 Seir, but Jacob set out for Succoth; and there he built himself a house and made shelters for his cattle. Therefore he named that place Succoth.*a*
18     On his journey from Paddan-aram, Jacob came safely to the city of
19 Shechem in Canaan and pitched his tent to the east of it. The strip of country where he had pitched his tent he bought from the sons of Hamor
20 father of Shechem for a hundred sheep.*b* There he set up an altar and called it El-Elohey-Israel.*c*

**34** DINAH, THE DAUGHTER WHOM LEAH HAD BORNE to Jacob, went out
2 to visit the women of the country, and Shechem, son of Hamor the Hivite the local prince, saw her; he took her, lay with her and dishonoured her.
3 But he remained true to Jacob's daughter Dinah; he loved the girl and
4 comforted her. So Shechem said to his father Hamor, 'Get me this girl for
5 a wife.' When Jacob heard that Shechem had violated his daughter Dinah, his sons were with the herds in the open country, so he said nothing until
6 they came home. Meanwhile Shechem's father Hamor came out to Jacob
7 to discuss it with him. When Jacob's sons came in from the country and heard, they were grieved and angry, because in lying with Jacob's daughter he had done what the Israelites held to be an outrage, an intolerable thing.
8 Hamor appealed to them in these terms: 'My son Shechem is in love with
9 this girl; I beg you to let him have her as his wife. Let us ally ourselves in marriage; you shall give us your daughters, and you shall take ours in
10 exchange. You must settle among us. The country is open to you; make
11 your home in it, move about freely and acquire land of your own.' And Shechem said to the girl's father and brothers, 'I am eager to win your
12 favour and I will give whatever you ask. Fix the bride-price and the gift as high as you like, and I will give whatever you ask; but you must give me the girl in marriage.'

*a That is* Shelters.                     *b Or* pieces of money (*cp. Josh.* 24. 32; *Job* 42. 11).
*c That is* God the God of Israel.

Jacob's sons gave a dishonest reply to Shechem and his father Hamor, 13
laying a trap for them because Shechem had violated their sister Dinah:
'We cannot do this,' they said; 'we cannot give our sister to a man who is 14
uncircumcised; for we look on that as a disgrace. There is one condition 15
on which we will consent: if you will follow our example and have every
male among you circumcised, we will give you our daughters and take 16
yours for ourselves. Then we can live among you, and we shall all become
one people. But if you refuse to listen to us and be circumcised, we will 17
take the girl and go away.' Their proposal pleased Hamor and his son 18
Shechem; and the young man, who was held in respect above anyone in 19
his father's house, did not hesitate to do what they had said, because his
heart was taken by Jacob's daughter.

So Hamor and Shechem went back to the city gate and addressed their 20
fellow-citizens: 'These men are friendly to us; let them live in our country 21
and move freely in it. The land has room enough for them. Let us marry
their daughters and give them ours. But these men will agree to live with 22
us and become one people on this one condition only: every male among
us must be circumcised as they have been. Will not their herds, their live- 23
stock, and all their chattels then be ours? We need only consent to their
condition, and then they are free to live with us.' All the able-bodied men 24
agreed with Hamor and Shechem, and every single one of them was circumcised, every able-bodied male. Then two days later, while they were still 25
in great pain, Jacob's two sons Simeon and Levi, full brothers to Dinah,
armed themselves with swords, boldly entered the city and killed every
male. They cut down Hamor and his son Shechem and took Dinah from 26
Shechem's house and went off with her. Then Jacob's other sons came in 27
over the dead bodies and plundered the city, to avenge their sister's dishonour. They seized flocks, cattle, asses, and everything, both inside the 28
city and outside in the open country; they also carried off all their posses- 29
sions, their dependants, and their women, and plundered everything in
the houses.

Jacob said to Simeon and Levi, 'You have brought trouble on me, you 30
have made my name stink among the people of the country, the Canaanites
and the Perizzites. My numbers are few; if they muster against me and
attack me, I shall be destroyed, I and my household with me.' They 31
answered, 'Is our sister to be treated as a common whore?'

GOD SAID TO JACOB, 'Go up to Bethel and settle there; build an altar 35
there to the God who appeared to you when you were running away from
your brother Esau.' So Jacob said to his household and to all who were 2
with him, 'Rid yourselves of the foreign gods which you have among you,
purify yourselves, and see your clothes are mended.*a* We are going to 3
Bethel, so that I can set up an altar there to the God who answered me in
the day of my distress, and who has been with me all the way that I have
come.' So they handed over to Jacob all the foreign gods in their posses- 4
sion and the rings from their ears, and he buried them under the terebinth-
tree near Shechem. Then they set out, and the cities round about were 5

---

*a Or* change your clothes.

panic-stricken, and the inhabitants dared not pursue the sons of Jacob.
6 Jacob and all the people with him came to Luz, that is Bethel, in Canaan.
7 There he built an altar, and he called the place El-bethel, because it was
there that God had revealed himself to him when he was running away from
8 his brother. Rebecca's nurse Deborah died and was buried under the oak
below Bethel, and he named it Allon-bakuth.[a]
9 God appeared again to Jacob when he came back from Paddan-aram and
10 blessed him. God said to him:

> 'Jacob is your name,
> but your name shall no longer be Jacob:
> Israel shall be your name.'

11 So he named him Israel. And God said to him:

> 'I am God Almighty.
> Be fruitful and increase as a nation;
> a host of nations shall come from you,
> and kings shall spring from your body.
12 The land which I gave to Abraham and Isaac I give to you;
> and to your descendants after you I give this land.'

13 14 God then left him, and Jacob erected a sacred pillar in the place where God
had spoken with him, a pillar of stone, and he offered a drink-offering over
15 it and poured oil on it. Jacob called the place where God had spoken with
him Bethel.
16 They set out from Bethel, and when there was still some distance to go
17 to Ephrathah, Rachel was in labour and her pains were severe. While her
pains were upon her, the midwife said, 'Do not be afraid, this is another
18 son for you.' Then with her last breath, as she was dying, she named him
19 Ben-oni,[b] but his father called him Benjamin.[c] So Rachel died and was
20 buried by the side of the road to Ephrathah, that is Bethlehem. Jacob set
up a sacred pillar over her grave; it is known to this day as the Pillar of
21 Rachel's Grave. Then Israel journeyed on and pitched his tent on the other
22 side of Migdal-eder. While Israel was living in that district, Reuben went
and lay with his father's concubine Bilhah, and Israel came to hear of it.
23 The sons of Jacob were twelve. The sons of Leah: Jacob's first-born
24 Reuben, then Simeon, Levi, Judah, Issachar and Zebulun. The sons of
25 Rachel: Joseph and Benjamin. The sons of Rachel's slave-girl Bilhah: Dan
26 and Naphtali. The sons of Leah's slave-girl Zilpah: Gad and Asher. These
27 were Jacob's sons, born to him in Paddan-aram. Jacob came to his father
Isaac at Mamre by Kiriath-arba, that is Hebron, where Abraham and Isaac
28 had dwelt. Isaac had lived for a hundred and eighty years when he breathed
29 his last. He died and was gathered to his father's kin at a very great age, and
his sons Esau and Jacob buried him.

36 1 2 THIS IS THE TABLE of the descendants of Esau: that is Edom. Esau took
Canaanite women in marriage, Adah daughter of Elon the Hittite and

---

[a] *That is* Oak of Weeping.       [b] *That is* Son of my ill luck.       [c] *That is* Son of
good luck *or* Son of the right hand.

Oholibamah daughter of Anah son of Zibeon the Horite,<sup>a</sup> and Basemath, 3
Ishmael's daughter, sister of Nebaioth.

Adah bore Eliphaz to Esau; Basemath bore Reuel, and Oholibamah bore 4<sup>b</sup> 5
Jeush, Jalam and Korah. These were Esau's sons, born to him in Canaan.
Esau took his wives, his sons and daughters and everyone in his household, 6
his herds, his cattle, and all the chattels that he had acquired in Canaan,
and went to the district of Seir out of the way of his brother Jacob, because 7
they had so much stock that they could not live together; the land where
they were staying could not support them because of their herds. So 8
Esau lived in the hill-country of Seir. Esau is Edom.

This is the table of the descendants of Esau father of the Edomites in 9
the hill-country of Seir.

These are the names of the sons of Esau: Eliphaz was the son of Esau's 10
wife Adah. Reuel was the son of Esau's wife Basemath. The sons of Eliphaz 11
were Teman, Omar, Zepho, Gatam and Kenaz. Timna was concubine to 12
Esau's son Eliphaz, and she bore Amalek to him. These are the descendants of Esau's wife Adah. These are the sons of Reuel: Nahath, Zerah, 13
Shammah and Mizzah. These were the descendants of Esau's wife Basemath. These were the sons of Esau's wife Oholibamah daughter of Anah 14
son of Zibeon. She bore him Jeush, Jalam and Korah.

These are the chiefs descended from Esau. The sons of Esau's eldest 15
son Eliphaz: chief Teman, chief Omar, chief Zepho, chief Kenaz, chief 16
Korah, chief Gatam, chief Amalek. These are the chiefs descended from
Eliphaz in Edom. These are the descendants of Adah.

These are the sons of Esau's son Reuel: chief Nahath, chief Zerah, chief 17
Shammah, chief Mizzah. These are the chiefs descended from Reuel in
Edom. These are the descendants of Esau's wife Basemath.

These are the sons of Esau's wife Oholibamah: chief Jeush, chief Jalam, 18
chief Korah. These are the chiefs born to Oholibamah daughter of Anah
wife of Esau.

These are the sons of Esau, that is Edom, and these are their chiefs. 19

These are the sons of Seir the Horite, the original inhabitants of the 20<sup>c</sup>
land: Lotan, Shobal, Zibeon, Anah, Dishon, Ezer and Dishan. These are 21
the chiefs of the Horites, the sons of Seir in Edom. The sons of Lotan were 22
Hori and Hemam, and Lotan had a sister named Timna.

These are the sons of Shobal: Alvan, Manahath, Ebal, Shepho and 23
Onam.

These are the sons of Zibeon: Aiah and Anah. This is the Anah who 24
found some mules in the wilderness while he was tending the asses of his
father Zibeon. These are the children of Anah: Dishon and Oholibamah 25
daughter of Anah.

These are the children of Dishon: Hemdan, Eshban, Ithran and Cheran. 26
These are the sons of Ezer: Bilhan, Zavan and Akan. These are the sons 27 28
of Dishan: Uz and Aran.

These are the chiefs descended from the Horites: chief Lotan, chief 29
Shobal, chief Zibeon, chief Anah, chief Dishon, chief Ezer, chief Dishan. 30

These are the chiefs that were descended from the Horites according to their clans in the district of Seir.

31ᵃ These are the kings who ruled over Edom before there were kings in
32 Israel: Bela son of Beor became king in Edom, and his city was named
33 Dinhabah; when he died, he was succeeded by Jobab son of Zerah of
34 35 Bozrah. When Jobab died, he was succeeded by Husham of Teman. When Husham died, he was succeeded by Hadad son of Bedad, who defeated
36 Midian in Moabite country. His city was named Avith. When Hadad died,
37 he was succeeded by Samlah of Masrekah. When Samlah died, he was
38 succeeded by Saul of Rehoboth on the River. When Saul died, he was suc-
39 ceeded by Baal-hanan son of Akbor. When Baal-hanan died, he was succeeded by Hadar.ᵇ His city was named Pau; his wife's name was Mehetabel daughter of Matred a woman of Me-zahab.ᶜ

40 These are the names of the chiefs descended from Esau, according to their families, their places, by name: chief Timna, chief Alvah, chief
41 42 Jetheth, chief Oholibamah, chief Elah, chief Pinon, chief Kenaz, chief
43 Teman, chief Mibzar, chief Magdiel, and chief Iram: all chiefs of Edom according to their settlements in the land which they possessed. (Esau is the father of the Edomites.)


## *Joseph in Egypt*

37 SO JACOB LIVED IN CANAAN, the country in which his father had
2 settled. And this is the story of the descendants of Jacob.

When Joseph was a boy of seventeen, he used to accompany his brothers, the sons of Bilhah and Zilpah, his father's wives, when they were in charge
3 of the flock; and he brought their father a bad report of them. Now Israel loved Joseph more than any other of his sons, because he was a child of his
4 old age, and he made him a long, sleeved robe. When his brothers saw that their father loved him more than any of them, they hated him and could not say a kind word to him.
5 Joseph had a dream; and when he told it to his brothers, they hated him
6 7 still more. He said to them, 'Listen to this dream I have had. We were in the field binding sheaves, and my sheaf rose on end and stood upright, and
8 your sheaves gathered round and bowed low before my sheaf.' His brothers answered him, 'Do you think you will one day be a king and lord it over us?'
9 and they hated him still more because of his dreams and what he said. He had another dream, which he told to his father and his brothers. He said, 'Listen: I have had another dream. The sun and moon and eleven stars
10 were bowing down to me.' When he told it to his father and his brothers, his father took him to task: 'What is this dream of yours?' he said. 'Must we come and bow low to the ground before you, I and your mother and
11 your brothers?' His brothers were jealous of him, but his father did not forget.
12 13 Joseph's brothers went to mind their father's flocks in Shechem. Israel

---

ᵃ *Verses 31–43: cp. 1 Chr. 1. 43–54.*       ᵇ *Or* Hadad; *cp. 1 Chr. 1. 50.*
ᶜ *Or* daughter of Mezahab.

said to him, 'Your brothers are minding the flocks in Shechem; come, I
will send you to them', and he said, 'I am ready.' He said to him, 'Go and 14
see if all is well with your brothers and the sheep, and bring me back word.'
So he sent off Joseph from the vale of Hebron and he came to Shechem. A 15
man met him wandering in the open country and asked him what he was
looking for. He replied, 'I am looking for my brothers. Tell me, please, 16
where they are minding the flocks.' The man said, 'They have gone away 17
from here; I heard them speak of going to Dothan.' So Joseph followed his
brothers and he found them in Dothan. They saw him in the distance, and 18
before he reached them, they plotted to kill him. They said to each other, 19
'Here comes that dreamer. Now is our chance; let us kill him and throw him 20
into one of these pits and say that a wild beast has devoured him. Then we
shall see what will come of his dreams.' When Reuben heard, he came to 21
his rescue, urging them not to take his life. 'Let us have no bloodshed', he 22
said. 'Throw him into this pit in the wilderness, but do him no bodily harm.'
He meant to save him from them so as to restore him to his father. When 23
Joseph came up to his brothers, they stripped him of the long, sleeved robe
which he was wearing, took him and threw him into the pit. The pit was 24
empty and had no water in it.

Then they sat down to eat some food and, looking up, they saw an 25
Ishmaelite caravan coming in from Gilead on the way down to Egypt, with
camels carrying gum tragacanth and balm and myrrh. Judah said to his 26
brothers, 'What shall we gain by killing our brother and concealing his
death? Why not sell him to the Ishmaelites? Let us do him no harm, for 27
he is our brother, our own flesh and blood'; and his brothers agreed with
him. Meanwhile some Midianite merchants passed by and drew Joseph 28
up out of the pit. They sold him for twenty pieces of silver to the Ishmaelites, and they brought Joseph to Egypt. When Reuben went back to the 29
pit, Joseph was not there. He rent his clothes and went back to his brothers 30
and said, 'The boy is not there. Where can I go?'

Joseph's brothers took his robe, killed a goat and dipped it in the goat's 31
blood. Then they tore the robe, the long, sleeved robe, brought it to their 32
father and said, 'Look what we have found. Do you recognize it? Is this
your son's robe or not?' Jacob did recognize it, and he replied, 'It is my 33
son's robe. A wild beast has devoured him. Joseph has been torn to pieces.'
Jacob rent his clothes, put on sackcloth and mourned his son for a long 34
time. His sons and daughters all tried to comfort him, but he refused to be 35
comforted. He said, 'I will go to my grave mourning for my son.' Thus
Joseph's father wept for him. Meanwhile the Midianites had sold Joseph 36
in Egypt to Potiphar, one of Pharaoh's eunuchs, the captain of the guard.[a]

ABOUT THAT TIME JUDAH LEFT HIS BROTHERS and went south and 38
pitched his tent in company with an Adullamite named Hirah. There he 2
saw Bathshua the daughter of a Canaanite and married her. He slept with
her, and she conceived and bore a son, whom she called Er. She conceived 3 4
again and bore a son whom she called Onan. Once more she conceived and 5
bore a son whom she called Shelah, and she ceased to bear children[b] when

---

[a] *Or* executioner.          [b] ceased . . . children: *or* was at Kezib.

c                            43

6 she had given birth to him. Judah found a wife for his eldest son Er; her
7 name was Tamar. But Judah's eldest son Er was wicked in the LORD's
8 sight, and the LORD took his life. Then Judah told Onan to sleep with his
brother's wife, to do his duty as the husband's brother and raise up issue
9 for his brother. But Onan knew that the issue would not be his; so whenever
he slept with his brother's wife, he spilled his seed on the ground so as not
10 to raise up issue for his brother. What he did was wicked in the LORD's
11 sight, and the LORD took his life. Judah said to his daughter-in-law Tamar,
'Remain as a widow in your father's house until my son Shelah grows up';
for he was afraid that he too would die like his brothers. So Tamar went
and stayed in her father's house.

12 Time passed, and Judah's wife Bathshua died. When he had finished
mourning, he and his friend Hirah the Adullamite went up to Timnath at
13 sheep-shearing. When Tamar was told that her father-in-law was on his
14 way to shear his sheep at Timnath, she took off her widow's weeds, veiled
her face, perfumed herself and sat where the road forks in two directions
on the way to Timnath. She did this because she knew that Shelah had
15 grown up and she had not been given to him as a wife. When Judah saw
16 her, he thought she was a prostitute, although she had veiled her face. He
turned to her where she sat by the roadside and said, 'Let me lie with you',
not knowing that she was his daughter-in-law. She said 'What will you
17 give me to lie with me?' He answered, 'I will send you a kid from my flock',
18 but she said, 'Will you give me a pledge until you send it?' He asked what
pledge he should give her, and she replied, 'Your seal and its cord, and the
staff which you hold in your hand.' So he gave them to her and lay with her,
19 and she conceived. She then rose and went home, took off her veil and
20 resumed her widow's weeds. Judah sent the kid by his friend the Adullamite in order to recover the pledge from the woman, but he could not find
21 her. He asked the men of that place, 'Where is that temple-prostitute, the
one who was sitting where the road forks?', but they answered, 'There is
22 no temple-prostitute here.' So he went back to Judah and told him that he
had not found her and that the men of the place had said there was no such
23 prostitute there. Judah said, 'Let her keep my pledge, or we shall get a
24 bad name. I did send a kid, but you could not find her.' About three months
later Judah was told that his daughter-in-law Tamar had behaved like a
common prostitute and through her wanton conduct was with child. Judah
25 said, 'Bring her out so that she may be burnt.' But when she was brought
out, she sent to her father-in-law and said, 'The father of my child is the
man to whom these things belong. See if you recognize whose they are,
26 the engraving on the seal, the pattern of the cord, and the staff.' Judah
recognized them and said, 'She is more in the right than I am, because I
did not give her to my son Shelah.' He did not have intercourse with her
27 28 again. When her time was come, there were twins in her womb, and while
she was in labour one of them put out a hand. The midwife took a scarlet
thread and fastened it round the wrist, saying, 'This one appeared first.'
29 No sooner had he drawn back his hand, than his brother came out and the
midwife said, 'What! you have broken out first!' So he was named Perez. *a*

*a That is* Breaking out.

Soon afterwards his brother was born with the scarlet thread on his wrist, 30
and he was named Zerah.*a*

WHEN JOSEPH WAS TAKEN DOWN TO EGYPT, he was bought by Poti- **39**
phar, one of Pharaoh's eunuchs, the captain of the guard, an Egyptian.
Potiphar bought him from the Ishmaelites who had brought him there.
The LORD was with Joseph and he prospered. He lived in the house of his 2
Egyptian master, who saw that the LORD was with him and was giving him 3
success in all that he undertook. Thus Joseph found favour with his master, 4
and he became his personal servant. Indeed, his master put him in charge of
his household and entrusted him with all that he had. From the time that 5
he put him in charge of his household and all his property, the LORD
blessed the Egyptian's household for Joseph's sake. The blessing of the
LORD was on all that was his in house and field. He left everything he 6
possessed in Joseph's care, and concerned himself with nothing but the
food he ate.

Now Joseph was handsome and good-looking, and a time came when his 7
master's wife took notice of him and said, 'Come and lie with me.' But he 8
refused and said to her, 'Think of my master. He does not know as much as
I do about his own house, and he has entrusted me with all he has. He has 9
given me authority in this house second only to his own, and has withheld
nothing from me except you, because you are his wife. How can I do anything so wicked, and sin against God?' She kept asking Joseph day after 10
day, but he refused to lie with her and be in her company. One day he came 11
into the house as usual to do his work, when none of the men of the household were there indoors. She caught him by his cloak, saying, 'Come and 12
lie with me', but he left the cloak in her hands and ran out of the house.
When she saw that he had left his cloak in her hands and had run out of the 13
house, she called out to the men of the household, 'Look at this! My 14
husband has brought in a Hebrew to make a mockery of us. He came in
here to lie with me, but I gave a loud scream. When he heard me scream and 15
call out, he left his cloak in my hand and ran off.' She kept his cloak with 16
her until his master came home, and then she repeated her tale. She said, 17
'That Hebrew slave whom you brought in to make a mockery of me, has
been here with me. But when I screamed for help and called out, he left 18
his cloak in my hands and ran off.' When Joseph's master heard his wife's 19
story of what his slave had done to her, he was furious. He took Joseph and 20
put him in the Round Tower, where the king's prisoners were kept;
and there he stayed in the Round Tower. But the LORD was with Joseph 21
and kept faith with him, so that he won the favour of the governor of the
Round Tower. He put Joseph in charge of all the prisoners in the tower and 22
of all their work. He ceased to concern himself with anything entrusted to 23
Joseph, because the LORD was with Joseph and gave him success in everything.

It happened later that the king's butler and his baker offended their **40**
master the king of Egypt. Pharaoh was angry with these two eunuchs, the 2
chief butler and the chief baker, and he put them in custody in the house of 3

*a* *That is* Redness.

45

the captain of the guard, in the Round Tower where Joseph was imprisoned.
4 The captain of the guard appointed Joseph as their attendant, and he
5 waited on them. One night, when they had been in prison for some time,
they both had dreams, each needing its own interpretation—the king of
Egypt's butler and his baker who were imprisoned in the Round Tower.
6 When Joseph came to them in the morning, he saw that they looked
7 dejected. So he asked these eunuchs, who were in custody with him in his
8 master's house, why they were so downcast that day. They replied, 'We
have each had a dream and there is no one to interpret it for us.' Joseph
said to them, 'Does not interpretation belong to God? Tell me your
9 dreams.' So the chief butler told Joseph his dream: 'In my dream', he said,
10 'there was a vine in front of me. On the vine there were three branches,
and as soon as it budded, it blossomed and its clusters ripened into grapes.
11 Now I had Pharaoh's cup in my hand, and I plucked the grapes, crushed
12 them into Pharaoh's cup and put the cup into Pharaoh's hand.' Joseph said
to him, 'This is the interpretation. The three branches are three days:
13 within three days Pharaoh will raise you and restore you to your post, and
then you will put the cup into Pharaoh's hand as you used to do when you
14 were his butler. But when things go well with you, if you think of me, keep
faith with me and bring my case to Pharaoh's notice and help me to get out
15 of this house. By force I was carried off*a* from the land of the Hebrews,
and I have done nothing here to deserve being put in this dungeon.'
16    When the chief baker saw that Joseph had given a favourable interpretation, he said to him, 'I too had a dream, and in my dream there were
17 three baskets of white bread on my head. In the top basket there was every
kind of food which the baker prepares for Pharaoh, and the birds were
18 eating out of the top basket on my head.' Joseph answered, 'This is the
19 interpretation. The three baskets are three days: within three days Pharaoh
will raise you and hang you up on a tree, and the birds of the air will eat
your flesh.'
20    The third day was Pharaoh's birthday and he gave a feast for all his
servants. He raised the chief butler and the chief baker in the presence of
21 his court. He restored the chief butler to his post, and the butler put the
22 cup into Pharaoh's hand; but he hanged the chief baker. All went as
23 Joseph had said in interpreting the dreams for them. Even so the chief
butler did not remember Joseph, but forgot him.
41    Nearly two years later Pharaoh had a dream: he was standing by the
2 Nile, and there came up from the river seven cows, sleek and fat, and they
3 grazed on the reeds. After them seven other cows came up from the river,
4 gaunt and lean, and stood on the river-bank beside the first cows. The cows
that were gaunt and lean devoured the cows that were sleek and fat. Then
5 Pharaoh woke up. He fell asleep again and had a second dream: he saw
6 seven ears of corn, full and ripe, growing on one stalk. Growing up after
7 them were seven other ears, thin and shrivelled by the east wind. The thin
ears swallowed up the ears that were full and ripe. Then Pharaoh woke up
8 and knew that it was a dream. When morning came, Pharaoh was troubled
in mind; so he summoned all the magicians and sages of Egypt. He told

*a* Or stolen.

them his dreams, but there was no one who could interpret them for him. Then Pharaoh's chief butler spoke up and said, 'It is time for me to recall 9 my faults. Once Pharaoh was angry with his servants, and he imprisoned 10 me and the chief baker in the house of the captain of the guard. One night 11 we both had dreams, each needing its own interpretation. We had with us 12 a young Hebrew, a slave of the captain of the guard, and we told him our dreams and he interpreted them for us, giving each man's dream its own interpretation. Each dream came true as it had been interpreted to us: I 13 was restored to my position, and he was hanged.'

Pharaoh thereupon sent for Joseph, and they hurriedly brought him out 14 of the dungeon. He shaved and changed his clothes, and came in to Pharaoh. Pharaoh said to him, 'I have had a dream, and no one can interpret it to 15 me. I have heard it said that you can understand and interpret dreams.' Joseph answered, 'Not I, but God, will answer for Pharaoh's welfare.' 16 Then Pharaoh said to Joseph, 'In my dream I was standing on the bank of 17 the Nile, and there came up from the river seven cows, fat and sleek, and 18 they grazed on the reeds. After them seven other cows came up that were 19 poor, very gaunt and lean; I have never seen such gaunt creatures in all Egypt. These lean, gaunt cows devoured the first cows, the fat ones. They 20 21 were swallowed up, but no one could have guessed that they were in the bellies of the others, which looked as gaunt as before. Then I woke up. After I had fallen asleep again, I saw in a dream seven ears of corn, full and 22 ripe, growing on one stalk. Growing up after them were seven other ears, 23 shrivelled, thin, and blighted by the east wind. The thin ears swallowed up 24 the seven ripe ears. When I told all this to the magicians, no one could explain it to me.'

Joseph said to Pharaoh, 'Pharaoh's dreams are one dream. God has 25 told Pharaoh what he is going to do. The seven good cows are seven years, 26 and the seven good ears of corn are seven years. It is all one dream. The 27 seven lean and gaunt cows that came up after them are seven years, and the empty ears of corn blighted by the east wind will be seven years of famine. It is as I have said to Pharaoh: God has let Pharaoh see what he is 28 going to do. There are to be seven years of great plenty throughout the 29 land. After them will come seven years of famine; all the years of plenty in 30 Egypt will be forgotten, and the famine will ruin the country. The good 31 years will not be remembered in the land because of the famine that follows; for it will be very severe. The doubling of Pharaoh's dream means 32 that God is already resolved to do this, and he will very soon put it into effect. Pharaoh should now look for a shrewd and intelligent man, and 33 put him in charge of the country. This is what Pharaoh should do: 34 appoint controllers over the land, and take one fifth of the produce of Egypt during the seven years of plenty. They should collect all this food 35 produced in the good years that are coming and put the corn under Pharaoh's control in store in the cities, and keep it under guard. This food 36 will be a reserve for the country against the seven years of famine which will come upon Egypt. Thus the country will not be devastated by the famine.'

The plan pleased Pharaoh and all his courtiers, and he said to them, 'Can 37 38

39 we find a man like this man, one who has the spirit of a god[a] in him?' He
said to Joseph, 'Since a god[b] has made all this known to you, there is no
40 one so shrewd and intelligent as you. You shall be in charge of my household, and all my people will depend on your every word. Only my royal
41 throne shall make me greater than you.' Pharaoh said to Joseph, 'I hereby
42 give you authority over the whole land of Egypt.' He took off his signet-ring
and put it on Joseph's finger, he had him dressed in fine linen, and hung a
43 gold chain round his neck. He mounted him in his viceroy's chariot and
men cried 'Make way!' before him. Thus Pharaoh made him ruler over all
44 Egypt and said to him, 'I am the Pharaoh. Without your consent no man
45 shall lift hand or foot throughout Egypt.' Pharaoh named him Zaphenath-
paneah, and he gave him as wife Asenath the daughter of Potiphera priest
of On. And Joseph's authority extended over the whole of Egypt.

46     Joseph was thirty years old when he entered the service of Pharaoh king
of Egypt. When he took his leave of the king, he made a tour of inspection
47 through the country. During the seven years of plenty there were abundant
48 harvests, and Joseph gathered all the food produced in Egypt during those
years and stored it in the cities, putting in each the food from the surround-
49 ing country. He stored the grain in huge quantities; it was like the sand of
the sea, so much that he stopped measuring: it was beyond all measure.

50     Before the years of famine came, two sons were born to Joseph by
51 Asenath the daughter of Potiphera priest of On. He named the elder
Manasseh,[c] 'for', he said, 'God has caused me to forget all my troubles and
52 my father's family.' He named the second Ephraim,[d] 'for', he said, 'God
53 has made me fruitful in the land of my hardships.' When the seven years
54 of plenty in Egypt came to an end, seven years of famine began, as Joseph
had foretold. There was famine in every country, but throughout Egypt
55 there was bread. So when the famine spread through all Egypt, the people
appealed to Pharaoh for bread, and he ordered them to go to Joseph and do
56 as he told them. In every region there was famine, and Joseph opened all
the granaries and sold corn to the Egyptians, for the famine was severe.
57 The whole world came to Egypt to buy corn from Joseph, so severe was
the famine everywhere.

**42** WHEN JACOB SAW that there was corn in Egypt, he said to his sons, 'Why
2 do you stand staring at each other? I have heard that there is corn in Egypt.
Go down and buy some so that we may keep ourselves alive and not starve.'
3 So Joseph's brothers, ten of them, went down to buy grain from Egypt,
4 but Jacob did not let Joseph's brother Benjamin go with them, for fear that
he might come to harm.

5     So the sons of Israel came down with everyone else to buy corn, because
6 of the famine in Canaan. Now Joseph was governor of all Egypt, and it was
he who sold the corn to all the people of the land. Joseph's brothers came
7 and bowed to the ground before him, and when he saw his brothers, he
recognized them but pretended not to know them and spoke harshly to
them. 'Where do you come from?' he asked. 'From Canaan,' they answered,
8 'to buy food.' Although Joseph had recognized his brothers, they did not

[a] *Or* of God.      [b] *Or* God.      [c] *That is* Causing to forget.      [d] *That is* Fruit.

recognize him. He remembered also the dreams he had had about them; 9
so he said to them, 'You are spies; you have come to spy out the weak
points in our defences.' They answered, 'No, sir: your servants have come 10
to buy food. We are all sons of one man. Your humble servants are honest 11
men, we are not spies.' 'No,' he insisted, 'it is to spy out our weaknesses that 12
you have come.' They answered him, 'Sir, there are twelve of us, all 13
brothers, sons of one man in Canaan. The youngest is still with our father,
and one has disappeared.' But Joseph said again to them, 'No, as I said 14
before, you are spies. This is how you shall be put to the proof: unless your 15
youngest brother comes here, by the life of Pharaoh, you shall not leave
this place. Send one of your number to bring your brother; the rest will 16
be kept in prison. Thus your story will be tested, and we shall see whether
you are telling the truth. If not, then, by the life of Pharaoh, you must be
spies.' So he kept them in prison for three days. 17
    On the third day Joseph said to the brothers, 'Do what I say and your 18
lives will be spared; for I am a God-fearing man: if you are honest men, 19
your brother there shall be kept in prison, and the rest of you shall take
corn for your hungry households and bring your youngest brother to me; 20
thus your words will be proved true, and you will not die.' *a*
    They said to one another, 'No doubt we deserve to be punished because 21
of our brother, whose suffering we saw; for when he pleaded with us we
refused to listen. That is why these sufferings have come upon us.' But 22
Reuben said, 'Did I not tell you not to do the boy a wrong? But you would
not listen, and his blood is on our heads, and we must pay.' They did not 23
know that Joseph understood, because he had used an interpreter. Joseph 24
turned away from them and wept. Then, turning back, he played a trick
on them. First he took Simeon and bound him before their eyes; then he 25
gave orders to fill their bags with grain, to return each man's silver, putting
it in his sack, and to give them supplies for the journey. All this was done;
and they loaded the corn on to their asses and went away. When they 26 27
stopped for the night, one of them opened his sack to give fodder to his ass,
and there he saw his silver at the top of the pack. He said to his brothers, 'My 28
silver has been returned to me, and here it is in my pack.' Bewildered and
trembling, they said to each other, 'What is this that God has done to us?'
    When they came to their father Jacob in Canaan, they told him all that 29
had happened to them. They said, 'The man who is lord of the country 30
spoke harshly to us and made out that we were spies. We said to him, "We 31
are honest men, we are not spies. There are twelve of us, all brothers, sons 32
of one father. One has disappeared, and the youngest is with our father in
Canaan." This man, the lord of the country, said to us, "This is how I shall 33
find out if you are honest men. Leave one of your brothers with me, take
food for your hungry households and go. Bring your youngest brother to 34
me, and I shall know that you are not spies, but honest men. Then I will
restore your brother to you, and you can move about the country freely."'
But on emptying their sacks, each of them found his silver inside, and when 35
they and their father saw the bundles of silver, they were afraid. Their 36
father Jacob said to them, 'You have robbed me of my children. Joseph has

*a Prob. rdg.; Heb. adds and they did so.*

disappeared; Simeon has disappeared; and now you are taking Benjamin.
37 Everything is against me.' Reuben said to his father, 'You may kill both
my sons if I do not bring him back to you. Put him in my charge, and I
38 shall bring him back.' But Jacob said, 'My son shall not go with you, for
his brother is dead and he alone is left. If he comes to any harm on the
journey, you will bring down my grey hairs in sorrow to the grave.'

**43** 1 2 The famine was still severe in the country. When they had used up the
corn they had brought from Egypt, their father said to them, 'Go back
3 and buy a little more corn for us to eat.' But Judah replied, 'The man
plainly warned us that we must not go into his presence unless our brother
4 was with us. If you let our brother go with us, we will go down and buy
5 food for you. But if you will not let him, we will not go; for the man said
to us, "You shall not come into my presence, unless your brother is with
6 you."' Israel said, 'Why have you treated me so badly? Why did you tell
7 the man that you had yet another brother?' They answered, 'He questioned
us closely about ourselves and our family: "Is your father still alive?" he
asked, "Have you a brother?", and we answered his questions. How could
we possibly know that he would tell us to bring our brother to Egypt?'
8 Judah said to his father Israel, 'Send the boy with me; then we can start at
once. By doing this we shall save our lives, ours, yours, and our dependants',
9 and none of us will starve. I will go surety for him and you may hold me
responsible. If I do not bring him back and restore him to you, you shall
10 hold me guilty all my life. If we had not wasted all this time, by now we
could have gone back twice over.'

11 Their father Israel said to them, 'If it must be so, then do this: take in
your baggage, as a gift for the man, some of the produce for which our
country is famous: a little balsam, a little honey, gum tragacanth, myrrh,
12 pistachio nuts, and almonds. Take double the amount of silver and restore
13 what was returned to you in your packs; perhaps it was a mistake. Take
14 your brother with you and go straight back to the man. May God Almighty
make him kindly disposed to you, and may he send back the one whom you
left behind, and Benjamin too. As for me, if I am bereaved, then I am
15 bereaved.' So they took the gift and double the amount of silver, and with
Benjamin they started at once for Egypt, where they presented themselves
to Joseph.

16 When Joseph saw Benjamin with them, he said to his steward, 'Bring
these men indoors, kill a beast and make dinner ready, for they will eat
17 with me at noon.' He did as Joseph told him and brought the men into the
18 house. When they came in they were afraid, for they thought, 'We have
been brought in here because of that affair of the silver which was replaced
in our packs the first time. He means to trump up some charge against us
19 and victimize us, seize our asses and make us his slaves.' So they approached
20 Joseph's steward and spoke to him at the door of the house. They said,
21 'Please listen, my lord. After our first visit to buy food, when we reached
the place where we were to spend the night, we opened our packs and each
of us found his silver in full weight at the top of his pack. We have brought
22 it back with us, and have added other silver to buy food. We do not know
23 who put the silver in our packs.' He answered, 'Set your minds at rest; do

not be afraid. It was your God, the God of your father, who hid treasure for you in your packs. I did receive the silver.' Then he brought Simeon out to them.

The steward brought them into Joseph's house and gave them water to 24 wash their feet, and provided fodder for their asses. They had their gifts 25 ready when Joseph arrived at noon, for they had heard that they were to eat there. When Joseph came into the house, they presented him with the 26 gifts which they had brought, bowing to the ground before him. He asked 27 them how they were and said, 'Is your father well, the old man of whom you spoke? Is he still alive?' They answered, 'Yes, my lord, our father is still 28 alive and well.' And they bowed low and prostrated themselves. Joseph 29 looked and saw his own mother's son, his brother Benjamin, and asked, 'Is this your youngest brother, of whom you told me?', and to Benjamin he said, 'May God be gracious to you, my son!' Joseph was overcome; his 30 feelings for his brother mastered him, and he was near to tears. So he went into the inner room and wept. Then he washed his face and came out; and, 31 holding back his feelings, he ordered the meal to be served. They served 32 him by himself, and the brothers by themselves, and the Egyptians who were at dinner were also served separately; for Egyptians hold it an abomination to eat with Hebrews. The brothers were seated in his presence, the 33 eldest first according to his age and so on down to the youngest: they looked at one another in astonishment. Joseph sent them each a portion from what 34 was before him, but Benjamin's was five times larger than any of the other portions. Thus they drank with him and all grew merry.

Joseph gave his steward this order: 'Fill the men's packs with as much **44** food as they can carry and put each man's silver at the top of his pack. And 2 put my goblet, my silver goblet, at the top of the youngest brother's pack with the silver for the corn.' He did as Joseph said. At daybreak the brothers 3 were allowed to take their asses and go on their journey; but before they 4 had gone very far from the city, Joseph said to his steward, 'Go after those men at once, and when you catch up with them, say, "Why have you repaid good with evil? Why have you stolen the silver goblet? It is the one from 5 which my lord drinks, and which he uses for divination. You have done a wicked thing."' When he caught up with them, he repeated all this to 6 them, but they replied, 'My lord, how can you say such things? No, sir, 7 God forbid that we should do any such thing! You remember the silver we 8 found at the top of our packs? We brought it back to you from Canaan. Why should we steal silver or gold from your master's house? If any one 9 of us is found with the goblet, he shall die; and, what is more, my lord, we will all become your slaves.' He said, 'Very well, then; I accept what you 10 say. The man in whose possession it is found shall be my slave, but the rest of you shall go free.' Each man quickly lowered his pack to the ground 11 and opened it. The steward searched them, beginning with the eldest and 12 finishing with the youngest, and the goblet was found in Benjamin's pack.

At this they rent their clothes; then each man loaded his ass and they 13 returned to the city. Joseph was still in the house when Judah and his 14 brothers came in. They threw themselves on the ground before him, and 15 Joseph said, 'What have you done? You might have known that a man like

51

16 myself would practise divination.' Judah said, 'What shall we say, my lord? What can we say to prove our innocence? God has found out our sin. Here we are, my lord, ready to be made your slaves, we ourselves as well as

17 the one who was found with the goblet.' Joseph answered, 'God forbid that I should do such a thing! The one who was found with the goblet shall become my slave, but the rest of you can go home to your father in peace.'

18 Then Judah went up to him and said, 'Please listen, my lord. Let me say a word to your lordship, I beg. Do not be angry with me, for you

19 are as great as Pharaoh. You, my lord, asked us whether we had a father or

20 a brother. We answered, "We have an aged father, and he has a young son born in his old age; this boy's full brother is dead and he alone is left of

21 his mother's children, he alone, and his father loves him." Your lordship

22 answered, "Bring him down to me so that I may set eyes on him." We told you, my lord, that the boy could not leave his father, and that his father

23 would die if he left him. But you answered, "Unless your youngest brother

24 comes here with you, you shall not enter my presence again." We went back

25 to your servant our father, and told him what your lordship had said. When

26 our father told us to go and buy food, we answered, "We cannot go down; for without our youngest brother we cannot enter the man's presence; but

27 if our brother is with us, we will go." Our father, my lord, then said to us,

28 "You know that my wife bore me two sons. One left me, and I said, 'He

29 must have been torn to pieces.' I have not seen him to this day. If you take this one from me as well, and he comes to any harm, then you will bring

30 down my grey hairs in trouble to the grave." Now, my lord, when I return to my father without the boy—and remember, his life is bound up with

31 the boy's—what will happen is this: he will see that the boy is not with us and will die, and your servants will have brought down our father's grey

32 hairs in sorrow to the grave. Indeed, my lord, it was I who went surety for the boy to my father. I said, "If I do not bring him back to you, then you

33 shall hold me guilty all my life." Now, my lord, let me remain in place of

34 the boy as your lordship's slave, and let him go with his brothers. How can I return to my father without the boy? I could not bear to see the misery which my father would suffer.'

**45** Joseph could no longer control his feelings in front of his attendants, and he called out, 'Let everyone leave my presence.' So there was nobody

2 present when Joseph made himself known to his brothers, but so loudly did he weep that the Egyptians and Pharaoh's household heard him.

3 Joseph said to his brothers, 'I am Joseph; can my father be still alive?' His brothers were so dumbfounded at finding themselves face to face with

4 Joseph that they could not answer. Then Joseph said to his brothers, 'Come closer', and so they came close. He said, 'I am your brother Joseph whom

5 you sold into Egypt. Now do not be distressed or take it amiss that you sold me into slavery here; it was God who sent me ahead of you to save

6 men's lives. For there have now been two years of famine in the country, and there will be another five years with neither ploughing nor harvest.

7 God sent me ahead of you to ensure that you will have descendants on

8 earth, and to preserve you all, a great band of survivors. So it was not you

who sent me here, but God, and he has made me a father *a* to Pharaoh, and
lord over all his household and ruler of all Egypt. Make haste and go back 9
to my father and give him this message from his son Joseph: "God has
made me lord of all Egypt. Come down to me; do not delay. You shall live 10
in the land of Goshen and be near me, you, your sons and your grandsons,
your flocks and herds and all that you have. I will take care of you there, 11
you and your household and all that you have, and see that you are not
reduced to poverty; there are still five years of famine to come." You can 12
see for yourselves, and so can my brother Benjamin, that it is Joseph himself who is speaking to you. Tell my father of all the honour which I enjoy 13
in Egypt, tell him all you have seen, and make haste to bring him down here.'
Then he threw his arms round his brother Benjamin and wept, and Ben- 14
jamin too embraced him weeping. He kissed all his brothers and wept over 15
them, and afterwards his brothers talked with him.

When the report that Joseph's brothers had come reached Pharaoh's 16
house, he and all his courtiers were pleased. Pharaoh said to Joseph, 'Say 17
to your brothers: "This is what you are to do. Load your beasts and go to
Canaan. Fetch your father and your households and bring them to me. I 18
will give you the best that there is in Egypt, and you shall enjoy the fat of
the land." You shall also tell them: "Take wagons from Egypt for your 19
dependants and your wives and fetch your father and come. Have no 20
regrets at leaving your possessions, for all the best that there is in Egypt is
yours." ' The sons of Israel did as they were told, and Joseph gave them 21
wagons, according to Pharaoh's orders, and food for the journey. He pro- 22
vided each of them with a change of clothing, but to Benjamin he gave three
hundred pieces of silver and five changes of clothing. Moreover he sent 23
his father ten asses carrying the best that there was in Egypt, and ten she-
asses loaded with grain, bread, and provisions for his journey. So he dis- 24
missed his brothers, telling them not to quarrel among themselves on the
road, and they set out. Thus they went up from Egypt and came to their 25
father Jacob in Canaan. There they gave him the news that Joseph was still 26
alive and that he was ruler of all Egypt. He was stunned and could not
believe it, but they told him all that Joseph had said; and when he saw the 27
wagons which Joseph had sent to take him away, his spirit revived. Israel 28
said, 'It is enough. Joseph my son is still alive; I will go and see him before
I die.'

SO ISRAEL SET OUT with all that he had and came to Beersheba where he **46**
offered sacrifices to the God of his father Isaac. God said to Israel in a 2
vision by night, 'Jacob, Jacob', and he answered, 'I am here.' God said, 'I 3
am God, the God of your father. Do not be afraid to go down to Egypt,
for there I will make you a great nation. I will go down with you to Egypt, 4
and I myself will bring you back again without fail; and Joseph shall close
your eyes.' So Jacob set out from Beersheba. Israel's sons conveyed their 5
father Jacob, their dependants, and their wives in the wagons which
Pharaoh had sent to carry them. They took the herds and the stock 6
which they had acquired in Canaan and came to Egypt, Jacob and all his

---

*a* *Or* counsellor.

7 descendants with him, his sons and their sons, his daughters and his sons'
daughters: he brought all his descendants to Egypt.

8*ᵃ*   These are the names of the Israelites who entered Egypt: Jacob and
9 his sons, as follows: Reuben, Jacob's eldest son. The sons of Reuben:
10 Enoch, Pallu, Hezron and Carmi. The sons of Simeon: Jemuel, Jamin,
Ohad, Jachin, Zohar, and Saul, who was the son of a Canaanite woman.
11 12 The sons of Levi: Gershon, Kohath and Merari. The sons of Judah: Er,
Onan, Shelah, Perez and Zerah; of these Er and Onan died in Canaan.
13 The sons of Perez were Hezron and Hamul. The sons of Issachar: Tola,
14 Pua, Iob and Shimron. The sons of Zebulun: Sered, Elon and Jahleel.
15 These are the sons of Leah whom she bore to Jacob in Paddan-aram, and
there was also his daughter Dinah. His sons and daughters numbered
thirty-three in all.

16   The sons of Gad: Ziphion, Haggi, Shuni, Ezbon, Eri, Arodi and Areli.
17 The sons of Asher: Imnah, Ishvah, Ishvi, Beriah, and their sister Serah.
18 The sons of Beriah: Heber and Malchiel. These are the descendants of
Zilpah whom Laban gave to his daughter Leah; sixteen in all, born to
Jacob.

19 20   The sons of Jacob's wife Rachel: Joseph and Benjamin. Manasseh and
Ephraim were born to Joseph in Egypt. Asenath daughter of Potiphera
21 priest of On bore them to him. The sons of Benjamin: Bela, Becher and
Ashbel; and the sons of Bela: Gera, Naaman, Ehi, Rosh, Muppim, Huppim
22 and Ard. These are the descendants of Rachel; fourteen in all, born to
Jacob.

23 24   The son*ᵇ* of Dan: Hushim. The sons of Naphtali: Jahzeel, Guni, Jezer
25 and Shillem. These are the descendants of Bilhah whom Laban gave to
his daughter Rachel; seven in all, born to Jacob.

26   The persons belonging to Jacob who came to Egypt, all his direct
27 descendants, not counting the wives of his sons, were sixty-six in all. Two
sons were born to Joseph in Egypt. Thus the house of Jacob numbered
seventy when it entered Egypt.

28   Judah was sent ahead that he might appear before Joseph in Goshen,
29 and so they entered Goshen. Joseph had his chariot made ready and went
up to meet his father Israel in Goshen. When they met, he threw his arms
30 round him and wept, and embraced him for a long time, weeping. Israel
said to Joseph, 'I have seen your face again, and you are still alive. Now I
31 am ready to die.' Joseph said to his brothers and to his father's household,
'I will go and tell Pharaoh; I will say to him, "My brothers and my father's
32 household who were in Canaan have come to me."' Now his brothers were
shepherds, men with their own flocks and herds, and they had brought
33 them with them, their flocks and herds and all that they possessed. So
Joseph said, 'When Pharaoh summons you and asks you what your
34 occupation is, you must say, "My lord, we have been herdsmen all our
lives, as our fathers were before us." You must say this if you are to settle
in the land of Goshen, because all shepherds are an abomination to the
Egyptians.'

*ᵃ Verses 8–25: cp. Exod. 6. 14–16; Num. 26. 5–50; 1 Chr. 4. 1, 24; 5. 3; 6. 1; 7. 1, 6,
13, 30; 8. 1–5.   ᵇ Prob. rdg.; Heb. sons.*

Joseph came and told Pharaoh, 'My father and my brothers have arrived 47
from Canaan, with their flocks and their cattle and all that they have, and
they are now in Goshen.' Then he chose five of his brothers and presented 2
them to Pharaoh, who asked them what their occupation was, and they 3
answered, 'My lord, we are shepherds, we and our fathers before us, and 4
we have come to stay in this land; for there is no pasture in Canaan for our
sheep, because the famine there is so severe. We beg you, my lord, to let us
settle now in Goshen.' Pharaoh said to Joseph, 'So your father and your 5
brothers have come to you. The land of Egypt is yours; settle them in the 6
best part of it. Let them live in Goshen, and if you know of any capable men
among them, make them chief herdsmen over my cattle.'

Then Joseph brought his father in and presented him to Pharaoh, and 7
Jacob gave Pharaoh his blessing. Pharaoh asked Jacob his age, and he 8 9
answered, 'The years of my earthly sojourn are one hundred and thirty;
hard years they have been and few, not equal to the years that my fathers
lived in their time.' Jacob then blessed Pharaoh and went out from his 10
presence. So Joseph settled his father and his brothers, and gave them 11
lands in Egypt, in the best part of the country, in the district of Rameses,
as Pharaoh had ordered. He supported his father, his brothers, and all his 12
father's household with all the food they needed.

There was no bread in the whole country, so very severe was the famine, 13
and Egypt and Canaan were laid low by it. Joseph collected all the silver in 14
Egypt and Canaan in return for the corn which the people bought, and
deposited it in Pharaoh's treasury. When all the silver in Egypt and Canaan 15
had been used up, the Egyptians came to Joseph and said, 'Give us bread,
or we shall die before your eyes. Our silver is all spent.' Joseph said, 'If your 16
silver is spent, give me your herds and I will give you bread in return.' So 17
they brought their herds to Joseph, who gave them bread in exchange for
their horses, their flocks of sheep and herds of cattle, and their asses. He
maintained them that year with bread in exchange for their herds. The year 18
came to an end, and the following year they came to him again and said,
'My lord, we cannot conceal it from you: our silver is all gone and our herds
of cattle are yours. Nothing is left for your lordship but our bodies and our
lands. Why should we perish before your eyes, we and our land as well? 19
Take us and our land in payment for bread, and we and our land alike will
be in bondage to Pharaoh. Give us seed-corn to keep us alive, or we shall
die and our land will become desert.' So Joseph bought all the land in 20
Egypt for Pharaoh, because the Egyptians sold all their fields, so severe
was the famine; the land became Pharaoh's. As for the people, Pharaoh 21
set them to work as slaves from one end of the territory of Egypt to the
other. But Joseph did not buy the land which belonged to the priests; they 22
had a fixed allowance from Pharaoh and lived on this, so that they had no
need to sell their land.

Joseph said to the people, 'Listen; I have today bought you and your 23
land for Pharaoh. Here is seed-corn for you. Sow the land, and give one 24
fifth of the crop to Pharaoh. Four fifths shall be yours to provide seed for
your fields and food for yourselves, your households, and your dependants.'
The people said, 'You have saved our lives. If it please your lordship, we 25

26 will be Pharaoh's slaves.' Joseph established it as a law in Egypt that one fifth should belong to Pharaoh, and this is still in force. It was only the priests' land that did not pass into Pharaoh's hands.

27 Thus Israel settled in Egypt, in Goshen; there they acquired land, and
28 were fruitful and increased greatly. Jacob stayed in Egypt for seventeen
29 years and lived to be a hundred and forty-seven years old. When the time of his death drew near, he summoned his son Joseph and said to him, 'If I may now claim this favour from you, put your hand under my thigh and swear by the LORD that you will deal loyally and truly with me and not bury
30 me in Egypt. When I die like my forefathers, you shall carry me from Egypt
31 and bury me in their grave.' He answered, 'I will do as you say'; but Jacob said, 'Swear it.' So he swore the oath, and Israel sank down over the end of the bed.

48 The time came when Joseph was told that his father was ill, so he took
2 with him his two sons, Manasseh and Ephraim. Jacob heard that his son Joseph was coming to him, and he summoned his strength and sat up on
3 the bed. Jacob said to Joseph, 'God Almighty appeared to me at Luz in
4 Canaan and blessed me. He said to me, "I will make you fruitful and increase your descendants until they become a host of nations. I will give this
5 land to your descendants after you as a perpetual possession." Now, your two sons, who were born to you in Egypt before I came here, shall be counted as my sons; Ephraim and Manasseh shall be mine as Reuben and
6 Simeon are. Any children born to you after them shall be counted as yours, but in respect of their tribal territory they shall be reckoned under their
7 elder brothers' names. As I was coming from Paddan-aram I was bereaved of Rachel your mother on the way, in Canaan, whilst there was still some distance to go to Ephrath, and I buried her there by the road to Ephrath, that is Bethlehem.'

8 9 When Israel saw Joseph's sons, he said, 'Who are these?' Joseph replied to his father, 'They are my sons whom God has given me here.' Israel said,
10 'Bring them to me, I beg you, so that I may take them on my knees.'*a* Now Israel's eyes were dim with age, and he could not see; so Joseph brought
11 the boys close to his father, and he kissed them and embraced them. He said to Joseph, 'I had not expected to see your face again, and now God has
12 granted me to see your sons also.' Joseph took them from his father's knees
13 and bowed to the ground. Then he took the two of them, Ephraim on his right at Israel's left and Manasseh on his left at Israel's right, and brought
14 them close to him. Israel stretched out his right hand and laid it on Ephraim's head, although he was the younger, and, crossing his hands,
15 laid his left hand on Manasseh's head; but Manasseh was the elder. He blessed Joseph and said:

> 'The God in whose presence my forefathers lived,
> my forefathers Abraham and Isaac,
> the God who has been my shepherd all my life until this day,
16 the angel who ransomed me from all misfortune,
> may he bless these boys;

*a Or* may bless them.

56

they shall be called by my name,
and by that of my forefathers, Abraham and Isaac;
may they grow into a great people on earth.'

When Joseph saw that his father was laying his right hand on Ephraim's 17
head, he was displeased; so he took hold of his father's hand to move it
from Ephraim's head to Manasseh's. He said, 'That is not right, my father. 18
This is the elder; lay your right hand on his head.' But his father refused; 19
he said, 'I know, my son, I know. He too shall become a people; he too
shall become great, but his younger brother shall be greater than he, and
his descendants shall be a whole nation in themselves.' That day he blessed 20
them and said:

'When a blessing is pronounced in Israel,
men shall use your names and say,
God make you like Ephraim and Manasseh',

thus setting Ephraim before Manasseh. Then Israel said to Joseph, 'I am 21
dying. God will be with you and will bring you back to the land of your
fathers. I give you one ridge of land more than your brothers: I took it from 22
the Amorites with my sword and my bow.'

JACOB SUMMONED HIS SONS and said, 'Come near, and I will tell you **49**
what will happen to you in days to come.

Gather round me and listen, you sons of Jacob; 2
listen to Israel your father.
Reuben, you are my first-born, 3
my strength and the first fruit of my vigour,
excelling in pride, excelling in might,
turbulent as a flood, you shall not excel; 4
because you climbed into your father's bed;
then you defiled his concubine's couch.
Simeon and Levi are brothers, 5
their spades became weapons of violence.
My soul shall not enter their council, 6
my heart shall not join their company;
for in their anger they killed men,
wantonly they hamstrung oxen.
A curse be on their anger because it was fierce; 7
a curse on their wrath because it was ruthless!
I will scatter them in Jacob,
I will disperse them in Israel.
Judah, your brothers shall praise you, 8
your hand is on the neck of your enemies.
Your father's sons shall do you homage.
Judah, you lion's whelp, 9
you have returned from the kill, my son,
and crouch and stretch like a lion;
and, like a lion,*a* who dare rouse you?
                    *a* *Or* lioness.

57

10 The sceptre shall not pass from Judah,
nor the staff from his descendants,
so long as tribute is brought to him
and the obedience of the nations is his.

11 To the vine he tethers his ass,
and the colt of his ass to the red vine;
he washes his cloak in wine,
his robes in the blood of grapes.

12 Darker than wine are his eyes,
his teeth whiter than milk.

13 Zebulun dwells by the sea-shore,
his shore is a haven for ships,
and his frontier rests on Sidon.

14 Issachar, a gelded ass
lying down in the cattle-pens,

15 saw that a settled home was good
and that the land was pleasant,
so he bent his back to the burden
and submitted to perpetual forced labour.

16 Dan—how insignificant his people,
lowly as any tribe in Israel! *a*

17 Let Dan be a viper on the road,
a horned snake on the path,
who bites the horse's fetlock
so that the rider tumbles backwards.

18 For thy salvation I wait in hope, O Lord.

19 Gad is raided by raiders,
and he raids them from the rear.

20 Asher shall have rich food as daily fare,
and provide dishes fit for a king.

21 Naphtali is a spreading terebinth
putting forth lovely boughs.

22 Joseph is a fruitful tree *b* by a spring
with branches climbing over the wall.

23 The archers savagely attacked him,
they shot at him and pressed him hard,

24 but their bow was splintered by the Eternal
and the sinews of their arms were torn apart
by the power of the Strong One of Jacob,
by the name of the Shepherd *c* of Israel,

25 by the God of your father—so may he help you,
by God Almighty—so may he bless you
with the blessings of heaven above,
the blessings of the deep that lurks below.

*a* Or Dan shall judge his people as one of the tribes of Israel. *b* Or a fruitful ben-tree. *c* Prob. rdg.; Heb. adds stone.

>The blessings of breast and womb
>and the blessings of your father are stronger                    26
>than the blessings of the everlasting pools<sup>a</sup>
>and the bounty of the eternal hills.
>They shall be on the head of Joseph,
>on the brow of the prince among<sup>b</sup> his brothers.
>Benjamin is a ravening wolf:                                      27
>in the morning he devours the prey,
>in the evening he snatches a share of the spoil.'

These, then, are the twelve tribes of Israel, and this is what their father 28 Jacob said to them, when he blessed them each in turn. He gave them 29 his last charge and said, 'I shall soon be gathered to my father's kin; bury me with my forefathers in the cave on the plot of land which belonged to Ephron the Hittite, that is the cave on the plot of land at 30 Machpelah east of Mamre in Canaan, the field which Abraham bought from Ephron the Hittite for a burial-place. There Abraham was buried 31 with his wife Sarah; there Isaac and his wife Rebecca were buried; and there I buried Leah. The land and the cave on it were bought from the 32 Hittites.' When Jacob had finished giving his last charge to his sons, he 33 drew his feet up on to the bed, breathed his last, and was gathered to his father's kin.

Then Joseph threw himself upon his father, weeping and kissing his **50** face. He ordered the physicians in his service to embalm his father Israel, 2 and they did so, finishing the task in forty days, which was the usual time 3 for embalming. The Egyptians mourned him for seventy days; and then, 4 when the days of mourning for Israel were over, Joseph approached members of Pharaoh's household and said, 'If I can count on your goodwill, then speak for me to Pharaoh; tell him that my father made me take an oath, 5 saying, "I am dying. Bury me in the grave that I bought<sup>c</sup> for myself in Canaan." Ask him to let me go up and bury my father, and afterwards I will return.' Pharaoh answered, 'Go and bury your father, as he has made 6 you swear to do.' So Joseph went to bury his father, accompanied by all 7 Pharaoh's courtiers, the elders of his household, and all the elders of Egypt, together with all Joseph's own household, his brothers, and his father's 8 household; only their dependants, with the flocks and herds, were left in Goshen. He took with him chariots and horsemen; they were a very great 9 company. When they came to the threshing-floor of Atad beside the river 10 Jordan, they raised a loud and bitter lament; and there Joseph observed seven days' mourning for his father. When the Canaanites who lived there 11 saw this mourning at the threshing-floor of Atad, they said, 'How bitterly the Egyptians are mourning!'; accordingly they named the place beside the Jordan Abel-mizraim.<sup>d</sup>

Thus Jacob's sons did what he had told them to do. They took him to 12 13 Canaan and buried him in the cave on the plot of land at Machpelah, the land which Abraham had bought as a burial-place from Ephron the Hittite,

---

<sup>a</sup> *Or* hills.          <sup>b</sup> the prince among: *or* the one cursed by.          <sup>c</sup> *Or* dug.
<sup>d</sup> *That is* Mourning (*or* Meadow) of Egypt.

14 to the east of Mamre. Then, after he had buried his father, Joseph returned to Egypt with his brothers and all who had gone up with him.

15 When their father was dead Joseph's brothers were afraid and said, 'What if Joseph should bear a grudge against us and pay us out for all the
16 harm that we did to him?' They therefore approached Joseph with these
17 words: 'In his last words to us before he died, your father gave us this message for you: "I ask you to forgive your brothers' crime and wickedness; I know they did you harm." So now forgive our crime, we beg; for we are servants of your father's God.' When they said this to him, Joseph wept.
18 His brothers also wept[a] and prostrated themselves before him; they said,
19 'You see, we are your slaves.' But Joseph said to them, 'Do not be afraid.
20 Am I in the place of God? You meant to do me harm; but God meant to bring good out of it by preserving the lives of many people, as we see today.
21 Do not be afraid. I will provide for you and your dependants.' Thus he comforted them and set their minds at rest.

22 Joseph remained in Egypt, he and his father's household. He lived there
23 to be a hundred and ten years old and saw Ephraim's children to the third generation; he also recognized as his the children of Manasseh's son
24 Machir. He said to his brothers, 'I am dying; but God will not fail to come to your aid and take you from here to the land which he promised on oath
25 to Abraham, Isaac and Jacob.' He made the sons of Israel take an oath, saying, 'When God thus comes to your aid, you must take my bones with
26 you from here.' So Joseph died at the age of a hundred and ten. He was embalmed and laid in a coffin in Egypt.

# EXODUS

## Israel enslaved in Egypt

1 THESE ARE THE NAMES of the Israelites who entered Egypt
2 with Jacob, each with his household: Reuben, Simeon, Levi and
3 4 Judah; Issachar, Zebulun and Benjamin; Dan and Naphtali, Gad
5 and Asher. There were seventy of them all told, all direct descendants of Jacob. Joseph was already in Egypt.
6 In course of time Joseph died, he and all his brothers and that whole
7 generation. Now the Israelites were fruitful and prolific; they increased in numbers and became very powerful,[b] so that the country was overrun by
8 them. Then a new king ascended the throne of Egypt, one who knew
9 nothing of Joseph. He said to his people, 'These Israelites have become
10 too many and too strong for us. We must take precautions to see that they do not increase any further; or we shall find that, if war breaks out, they will join the enemy and fight against us, and they will become masters of
11 the country.' So they were made to work in gangs with officers set over

*a Prob. rdg.; Heb.* came.          *b Or* numerous.

them, to break their spirit with heavy labour. This is how Pharaoh's store-cities, Pithom and Rameses, were built. But the more harshly they were 12 treated, the more their numbers increased beyond all bounds, until the Egyptians came to loathe the sight of them. So they treated their Israelite 13 slaves with ruthless severity, and made life bitter for them with cruel 14 servitude, setting them to work on clay and brick-making, and all sorts of work in the fields. In short they made ruthless use of them as slaves in every kind of hard labour.

Then the king of Egypt spoke to the Hebrew midwives, whose names 15 were Shiphrah and Puah. 'When you are attending the Hebrew women in 16 childbirth,' he told them, 'watch as the child is delivered and if it is a boy, kill him; if it is a girl, let her live.' But they were God-fearing women. They 17 did not do what the king of Egypt had told them to do, but let the boys live. So he summoned those Hebrew midwives and asked them why they had 18 done this and let the boys live. They told Pharaoh that Hebrew women 19 were not like Egyptian women. When they were in labour they gave birth before the midwife could get to them. So God made the midwives prosper, 20 and the people increased in numbers and in strength. God gave the mid- 21 wives homes and families of their own, because they feared him. Pharaoh 22 then ordered all his people to throw every new-born Hebrew boy into the Nile, but to let the girls live.

A descendant of Levi married a Levite woman who conceived and bore **2** 1 2 a son. When she saw what a fine child he was, she hid him for three months, but she could conceal him no longer. So she got a rush basket for him, made 3 it watertight with clay and tar, laid him in it, and put it among the reeds by the bank of the Nile. The child's sister took her stand at a distance to see 4 what would happen to him. Pharaoh's daughter came down to bathe in the 5 river, while her ladies-in-waiting walked along the bank. She noticed the basket among the reeds and sent her slave-girl for it. She took it from her and when she opened it, she saw the child. It was crying, and she was filled 6 with pity for it. 'Why,' she said, 'it is a little Hebrew boy.' Thereupon the 7 sister said to Pharaoh's daughter, 'Shall I go and fetch one of the Hebrew women as a wet-nurse to suckle the child for you?' Pharaoh's daughter told 8 her to go; so the girl went and called the baby's mother. Then Pharaoh's 9 daughter said to her, 'Here is the child, suckle him for me, and I will pay you for it myself.' So the woman took the child and suckled him. When the 10 child was old enough, she brought him to Pharaoh's daughter, who adopted him and called him Moses,<sup>a</sup> 'because', she said, 'I drew <sup>b</sup> him out of the water.'

ONE DAY WHEN MOSES WAS GROWN UP, he went out to his own kins- 11 men and saw them at their heavy labour. He saw an Egyptian strike one of his fellow-Hebrews. He looked this way and that, and, seeing there was 12 no one about, he struck the Egyptian down and hid his body in the sand. When he went out next day, two Hebrews were fighting together. He asked 13 the man who was in the wrong, 'Why are you striking him?' 'Who set you 14 up as an officer and judge over us?' the man replied. 'Do you mean to

<sup>a</sup> *Heb*. Mosheh.       <sup>b</sup> *Heb. verb* mashah.

murder me as you murdered the Egyptian?' Moses was alarmed. 'The
15 thing must have become known', he said to himself. When Pharaoh heard
of it, he tried to put Moses to death, but Moses made good his escape and
settled in the land of Midian.
16    Now the priest of Midian had seven daughters. One day as Moses sat
by a well, they came to draw water and filled the troughs to water their
17 father's sheep. Some shepherds came and drove them away; but Moses
18 got up, took the girls' part and watered their sheep himself. When the girls
came back to their father Reuel, he asked, 'How is it that you are back so
19 quickly today?' 'An Egyptian rescued us from the shepherds,' they
answered; 'and he even drew the water for us and watered the sheep.'
20 'But where is he then?' he said to his daughters. 'Why did you leave him
21 behind? Go and invite him to eat with us.' So it came about that Moses
agreed to live with the man, and he gave Moses his daughter Zipporah in
22 marriage. She bore him a son, and Moses called him Gershom, 'because',
he said, 'I have become an alien*a* living in a foreign land.'

23 YEARS PASSED, and the king of Egypt died, but the Israelites still groaned
in slavery. They cried out, and their appeal for rescue from their slavery
24 rose up to God. He heard their groaning, and remembered his covenant
25 with Abraham, Isaac and Jacob; he saw the plight of Israel, and he took
heed of it.
3    Moses was minding the flock of his father-in-law Jethro, priest of Midian.
He led the flock along the side of the wilderness and came to Horeb, the
2 mountain of God. There the angel of the LORD appeared to him in the
flame of a burning bush. Moses noticed that, although the bush was on
3 fire, it was not being burnt up; so he said to himself, 'I must go across to
4 see this wonderful sight. Why does not the bush burn away?' When the
LORD saw that Moses had turned aside to look, he called to him out of the
5 bush, 'Moses, Moses.' And Moses answered, 'Yes, I am here.' God said,
'Come no nearer; take off your sandals; the place where you are standing
6 is holy ground.' Then he said, 'I am the God of your forefathers, the God
of Abraham, the God of Isaac, the God of Jacob.' Moses covered his face,
for he was afraid to gaze on God.
7    The LORD said, 'I have indeed seen the misery of my people in Egypt.
I have heard their outcry against their slave-masters. I have taken heed of
8 their sufferings, and have come down to rescue them from the power of
Egypt, and to bring them up out of that country into a fine, broad land; it is
a land flowing with milk and honey, the home of Canaanites, Hittites,
9 Amorites, Perizzites, Hivites, and Jebusites. The outcry of the Israelites
has now reached me; yes, I have seen the brutality of the Egyptians towards
10 them. Come now; I will send you to Pharaoh and you shall bring my people
11 Israel out of Egypt.' 'But who am I,' Moses said to God, 'that I should go
12 to Pharaoh, and that I should bring the Israelites out of Egypt?' God
answered, 'I am*b* with you. This shall be the proof that it is I who have sent
you: when you have brought the people out of Egypt, you shall all worship
God here on this mountain.'

*a Heb.* ger.        *b Or* I will be; *Heb.* ehyeh.

Then Moses said to God, 'If I go to the Israelites and tell them that the 13
God of their forefathers has sent me to them, and they ask me his name,
what shall I say?' God answered, 'I AM; that is who I am.<sup>a</sup> Tell them that 14
I AM has sent you to them.' And God said further, 'You must tell the 15
Israelites this, that it is JEHOVAH<sup>b</sup> the God of their forefathers, the God of
Abraham, the God of Isaac, the God of Jacob, who has sent you to them.
This is my name for ever; this is my title in every generation. Go and 16
assemble the elders of Israel and tell them that JEHOVAH the God of their
forefathers, the God of Abraham, Isaac and Jacob, has appeared to you
and has said, "I have indeed turned my eyes towards you; I have marked
all that has been done to you in Egypt, and I am resolved to bring you up 17
out of your misery in Egypt, into the country of the Canaanites, Hittites,
Amorites, Perizzites, Hivites, and Jebusites, a land flowing with milk and
honey." They will listen to you, and then you and the elders of Israel must 18
go to the king of Egypt. Tell him, "It has happened that the LORD the
God of the Hebrews met us. So now give us leave to go a three days' journey into the wilderness to offer sacrifice to the LORD our God." I know well 19
that the king of Egypt will not give you leave unless he is compelled. I shall 20
then stretch out my hand and assail the Egyptians with all the miracles I
shall work among them. After that he will send you away. Further, I will 21
bring this people into such favour with the Egyptians that, when you go,
you will not go empty-handed. Every woman shall ask her neighbour or 22
any woman who lives in her house for jewellery of silver and gold and for
clothing. Load your sons and daughters with them, and plunder Egypt.'

Moses answered, 'But they will never believe me or listen to me; they **4**
will say, "The LORD did not appear to you." ' The LORD said, 'What have 2
you there in your hand?' 'A staff', Moses answered. The LORD said, 'Throw 3
it on the ground.' Moses threw it down and it turned into a snake. He ran
away from it, but the LORD said, 'Put your hand out and seize it by the tail.' 4
He did so and gripped it firmly, and it turned back into a staff in his hand.
'This is to convince the people that the LORD the God of their forefathers, 5
the God of Abraham, the God of Isaac, the God of Jacob, has appeared to
you.' Then the LORD said, 'Put your hand inside the fold of your cloak.' 6
He did so, and when he drew it out the skin was diseased, white as snow.
The LORD said, 'Put it back again', and he did so. When he drew it out this 7
time it was as healthy as the rest of his body. 'Now,' said the LORD, 'if they 8
do not believe you and do not accept the evidence of the first sign, they
may accept the evidence of the second. But if they are not convinced even 9
by these two signs, and will not accept what you say, then fetch some water
from the Nile and pour it out on the dry ground, and the water you take
from the Nile will turn to blood on the ground.'

But Moses said, 'O LORD, I have never been a man of ready speech, 10
never in my life, not even now that thou hast spoken to me; I am slow and
hesitant of speech.' The LORD said to him, 'Who is it that gives man speech? 11
Who makes him dumb or deaf? Who makes him clear-sighted or blind?
Is it not I, the LORD? Go now; I will help your speech and tell you what to 12

<sup>a</sup> I AM . . . I am: *or* I will be what I will be.      <sup>b</sup> *The Hebrew consonants are* YHWH,
*probably pronounced* Yahweh, *but traditionally read* Jehovah.

13 14 say.' But Moses still protested, 'No, Lord, send whom thou wilt.' At this
the LORD grew angry with Moses and said, 'Have you not a brother,
Aaron the Levite? He, I know, will do all the speaking. He is already on
15 his way out to meet you, and he will be glad indeed to see you. You shall
speak to him and put the words in his mouth; I will help both of you to
16 speak and tell you both what to do. He will do all the speaking to the people
for you, he will be the mouthpiece, and you will be the god he speaks for.
17 But take this staff, for with it you are to work the signs.'
18    At length Moses went back to Jethro his father-in-law and said, 'Let me
return to my kinsfolk in Egypt and see if they are still alive.' Jethro told
him to go and wished him well.

19 THE LORD SPOKE TO MOSES in Midian and said to him, 'Go back to
20 Egypt, for all those who wished to kill you are dead.' So Moses took his
wife and children, mounted them on an ass and set out for Egypt with the
21 staff of God in his hand. The LORD said to Moses, 'While you are on your
way back to Egypt, keep in mind all the portents I have given you power
to show. You shall display these before Pharaoh, but I will make him
22 obstinate and he will not let the people go. Then tell Pharaoh that these are
23 the words of the LORD: "Israel is my first-born son. I have told you to let
my son go, so that he may worship me. You have refused to let him go, so
I will kill your first-born son." '
24    During the journey, while they were encamped for the night, the LORD
25 met Moses, meaning to kill him, but Zipporah picked up a sharp flint, cut
off her son's foreskin, and touched him with it, saying, 'You are my blood-
26 bridegroom.' So the LORD let Moses alone. Then she said,*a* 'Blood-bride-
groom by circumcision.'
27    Meanwhile the LORD had ordered Aaron to go and meet Moses in the
wilderness. Aaron went and met him at the mountain of God, and he kissed
28 him. Then Moses told Aaron everything, the words the LORD had sent him
29 to say and the signs he had commanded him to perform. Moses and Aaron
30 went and assembled all the elders of Israel. Aaron told them everything
that the LORD had said to Moses; he performed the signs before the people,
31 and they were convinced. They heard that the LORD had shown his concern
for the Israelites and seen their misery; and they bowed themselves to the
ground in worship.
5    After this, Moses and Aaron came to Pharaoh and said, 'These are the
words of the LORD the God of Israel: "Let my people go so that they may
2 keep my pilgrim-feast in the wilderness." ' 'Who is the LORD,' asked
Pharaoh, 'that I should obey him and let Israel go? I care nothing for the
3 LORD: and I tell you I will not let Israel go.' They replied, 'It has happened
that the God of the Hebrews met us. So let us go three days' journey
into the wilderness to offer sacrifice to the LORD our God, or else he will
4 attack us with pestilence or sword.' But the king of Egypt said, 'Moses and
Aaron, what do you mean by distracting the people from their work? Back
5 to your labours! Your people already outnumber the native Egyptians; yet
you would have them stop working!'

*a Or* Therefore women say.

That very day Pharaoh ordered the people's overseers and their foremen 6
not to supply the people with the straw used in making bricks, as they had 7
done hitherto. 'Let them go and collect their own straw, but see that they 8
produce the same tally of bricks as before. On no account reduce it. They
are a lazy people, and that is why they are clamouring to go and offer
sacrifice to their god. Keep the men hard at work; let them attend to that 9
and take no notice of a pack of lies.' The overseers and foremen went out 10
and said to the people, 'Pharaoh's orders are that no more straw is to be
supplied. Go and get it for yourselves wherever you can find it; but there 11
will be no reduction in your daily task.' So the people scattered all over 12
Egypt to gather stubble for straw, while the overseers kept urging them on, 13
bidding them complete, day after day, the same quantity as when straw was
supplied. Then the Israelite foremen were flogged because they were held 14
responsible by Pharaoh's overseers, who asked them, 'Why did you not
complete the usual number of bricks yesterday or today?' So the foremen 15
came and appealed to Pharaoh: 'Why do you treat your servants like this?'
they said. 'We are given no straw, yet they keep on telling us to make 16
bricks. Here are we being flogged, but it is your people's fault.' But 17
Pharaoh replied, 'You are lazy, you are lazy. That is why you talk about
going to offer sacrifice to the LORD. Now go; get on with your work. You 18
will be given no straw, but you must produce the tally of bricks.' When they 19
were told that they must not let the daily tally of bricks fall short, the Israelite foremen saw that they were in trouble. As they came out from Pharaoh's 20
presence they found Moses and Aaron waiting to meet them, and said, 'May 21
this bring the LORD's judgement down upon you: you have made us stink
in the nostrils of Pharaoh and his subjects; you have put a sword in their
hands to kill us.'

Moses went back to the LORD, and said, 'Why, O Lord, hast thou brought 22
misfortune on this people? And why didst thou ever send me? Since I first 23
went to Pharaoh to speak in thy name he has heaped misfortune on my
people, and thou hast done nothing at all to rescue them.' The LORD **6**
answered, 'Now you shall see what I will do to Pharaoh. In the end Pharaoh
will let them go with a strong hand, nay, will drive them from his country
with an outstretched arm.'

God spoke to Moses and said, 'I am the LORD. I appeared to Abraham, 2 3
Isaac, and Jacob as God Almighty. But I did not let myself be known to
them by my name JEHOVAH.[a] Moreover, I made a covenant with them to 4
give them Canaan, the land where they settled for a time as foreigners. And 5
now I have heard the groaning of the Israelites, enslaved by the Egyptians,
and I have called my covenant to mind. Say therefore to the Israelites, "I 6
am the LORD. I will release you from your labours in Egypt. I will rescue
you from slavery there. I will redeem you with arm outstretched and with
mighty acts of judgement. I will adopt you as my people, and I will become 7
your God. You shall know that I, the LORD, am your God, the God who
releases you from your labours in Egypt. I will lead you to the land which I 8
swore with uplifted hand to give to Abraham, to Isaac and to Jacob. I will
give it you for your possession. I am the LORD."'

[a] *See note on 3. 15.*

9   Moses repeated these words to the Israelites, but they did not listen to him; they had become impatient because of their cruel slavery.

10 11   Then the LORD spoke to Moses and said, 'Go and tell Pharaoh king of
12   Egypt to set the Israelites free to leave his country.' Moses made answer in the presence of the LORD, 'If the Israelites do not listen to me, how will Pharaoh listen to such a halting speaker as I am?'

13   Thus the LORD spoke to Moses and Aaron and gave them their commission to the Israelites and to Pharaoh, namely that they should bring the Israelites out of Egypt.

14*a*   THESE WERE THE HEADS of fathers' families:
Sons of Reuben, Israel's eldest son: Enoch, Pallu, Hezron and Carmi; these were the families of Reuben.

15   Sons of Simeon: Jemuel, Jamin, Ohad, Jachin, Zohar, and Saul, who was the son of a Canaanite woman; these were the families of Simeon.

16   These were the names of the sons of Levi in order of seniority: Gershon, Kohath and Merari. Levi lived to be a hundred and thirty-seven.

17   Sons of Gershon, family by family: Libni and Shimei.

18   Sons of Kohath: Amram, Izhar, Hebron and Uzziel. Kohath lived to be a hundred and thirty-three.

19   Sons of Merari: Mahli and Mushi.

20   These were the families of Levi in order of seniority. Amram married his father's sister Jochebed, and she bore him Aaron and Moses. Amram lived to be a hundred and thirty-seven.

21   Sons of Izhar: Korah, Nepheg and Zichri.

22   Sons of Uzziel: Mishael, Elzaphan and Sithri.

23   Aaron married Elisheba, who was the daughter of Amminadab and the sister of Nahshon, and she bore him Nadab, Abihu, Eleazar and Ithamar.

24   Sons of Korah: Assir, Elkanah and Abiasaph; these were the Korahite families.

25   Eleazar son of Aaron married one of the daughters of Putiel, and she bore him Phinehas. These were the heads of the Levite families, family by family.

26   It was this Aaron, together with Moses, to whom the LORD said, 'Bring
27   the Israelites out of Egypt, mustered in their tribal hosts.' These were the men who told Pharaoh king of Egypt to let the Israelites leave Egypt. It was this same Moses and Aaron.

28 29   WHEN THE LORD SPOKE TO MOSES in Egypt he said, 'I am the LORD.
30   Tell Pharaoh king of Egypt all that I say to you.' Moses made answer in the presence of the LORD, 'I am a halting speaker; how will Pharaoh listen to
7   me?' The LORD answered Moses, 'See now, I have made you like a god for
2   Pharaoh, with your brother Aaron as your spokesman. You must tell your brother Aaron all I bid you say, and he will tell Pharaoh, and Pharaoh will
3   let the Israelites go out of his country; but I will make him stubborn. Then will I show sign after sign and portent after portent in the land of Egypt.
4   But Pharaoh will not listen to you, so I will assert my power in Egypt, and

*a Verses 14–16: cp. Gen. 46. 8–11; Num. 26. 5, 6, 12, 13.*

with mighty acts of judgement I will bring my people, the Israelites, out
of Egypt in their tribal hosts. When I put forth my power against the 5
Egyptians and bring the Israelites out from them, then Egypt will know
that I am the LORD.' So Moses and Aaron did exactly as the LORD had 6
commanded. At the time when they spoke to Pharaoh, Moses was eighty 7
years old and Aaron eighty-three.

The LORD said to Moses and Aaron, 'If Pharaoh demands some portent 8 9
from you, then you, Moses, must say to Aaron, "Take your staff and throw
it down in front of Pharaoh, and it will turn into a serpent." ' When Moses 10
and Aaron came to Pharaoh, they did as the LORD had told them. Aaron
threw down his staff in front of Pharaoh and his courtiers, and it turned into
a serpent. At this, Pharaoh summoned the wise men and the sorcerers, and 11
the Egyptian magicians too did the same thing by their spells. Every man 12
threw his staff down, and each staff turned into a serpent; but Aaron's
staff swallowed up theirs. Pharaoh, however, was obstinate; as the LORD 13
had foretold, he would not listen to Moses and Aaron.

Then the LORD said to Moses, 'Pharaoh is obdurate: he has refused to set 14
the people free. Go to him in the morning on his way out to the river. Stand 15
and wait on the bank of the Nile to meet him, and take with you the staff
that turned into a snake. Say this to him: "The LORD the God of the 16
Hebrews sent me to bid you let his people go in order to worship him in the
wilderness. So far you have not listened to his words; so now the LORD 17
says, 'By this you shall know that I am the LORD.' With this rod that I have
in my hand, I shall now strike the water in the Nile and it will be changed
into blood. The fish will die and the river will stink, and the Egyptians will 18
be unable to drink water from the Nile." ' The LORD then told Moses to 19
say to Aaron, 'Take your staff and stretch your hand out over the waters of
Egypt, its rivers and its streams, and over every pool and cistern, to turn
them into blood. There shall be blood throughout the whole of Egypt,
blood even in their wooden bowls and jars of stone.' So Moses and Aaron 20
did as the LORD had commanded. He lifted up his staff and struck the
water of the Nile in the sight of Pharaoh and his courtiers, and all the water
was changed into blood. The fish died and the river stank, and the Egyp- 21
tians could not drink water from the Nile. There was blood everywhere in
Egypt. But the Egyptian magicians did the same thing by their spells; and 22
still Pharaoh remained obstinate, as the LORD had foretold, and did not
listen to Moses and Aaron. He turned away, went into his house and dis- 23
missed the matter from his mind. Then the Egyptians all dug for drinking 24
water round about the river, because they could not drink from the waters
of the Nile itself. This lasted for seven days from the time when the LORD 25
struck the Nile.

The LORD then told Moses to go into Pharaoh's presence and say to him, 8
'These are the words of the LORD: "Let my people go in order to worship
me. If you refuse to let them go, I will plague the whole of your territory 2
with frogs. The Nile shall swarm with them. They shall come up from 3
the river into your house, into your bedroom and on to your bed, into
the houses of your courtiers and your people, into your ovens and your
kneading-troughs. The frogs shall clamber over you, your people, and your 4

5 courtiers." ' Then the LORD told Moses to say to Aaron, 'Take your staff in your hand and stretch it out over the rivers, streams, and pools, to bring
6 up frogs upon the land of Egypt.' So Aaron stretched out his hand over the
7 waters of Egypt, and the frogs came up and covered all the land. The magicians did the same thing by their spells: they too brought up frogs
8 upon the land of Egypt. Then Pharaoh summoned Moses and Aaron. 'Pray to the LORD', he said, 'to take the frogs away from me and my people, and
9 I will let the people go to sacrifice to the LORD.' Moses said, 'Of your royal favour, appoint a time when I may intercede for you and your courtiers and people, so that you and your houses may be rid of the frogs, and none
10 be left except in the Nile.' 'Tomorrow', Pharaoh said. 'It shall be as you say,' replied Moses, 'so that you may know there is no one like our God,
11 the LORD. The frogs shall depart from you, from your houses, your
12 courtiers, and your people: none shall be left except in the Nile.' Moses and Aaron left Pharaoh's presence, and Moses appealed to the LORD to remove
13 the frogs which he had brought on Pharaoh. The LORD did as Moses had asked, and in house and courtyard and in the open the frogs all perished.
14 15 They piled them into countless heaps and the land stank; but when Pharaoh found that he was given relief he became obdurate; as the LORD had foretold, he did not listen to Moses and Aaron.
16      The LORD then told Moses to say to Aaron, 'Stretch out your staff and strike the dust on the ground, and it will turn into maggots throughout the
17 land of Egypt', and they obeyed. Aaron stretched out his staff and struck the dust, and it turned into maggots on man and beast. All the dust turned
18 into maggots throughout the land of Egypt. The magicians tried to produce maggots in the same way by their spells, but they failed. The maggots were
19 everywhere, on man and beast. 'It is the finger of God', said the magicians to Pharaoh, but Pharaoh remained obstinate; as the LORD had foretold, he did not listen to them.
20      The LORD told Moses to rise early in the morning and stand in Pharaoh's path as he went out to the river and to say to him, 'These are the words of
21 the LORD: "Let my people go in order to worship me. If you do not let my people go, I will send swarms of flies upon you, your courtiers, your people, and your houses. The houses of the Egyptians shall be filled with
22 the swarms and so shall all the land they live in, but on that day I will make an exception of Goshen, the land where my people live: there shall be no swarms there. Thus you shall know that I, the LORD, am here in the land.
23 I will make a distinction between my people and yours. Tomorrow this
24 sign shall appear." ' The LORD did this; dense swarms of flies infested Pharaoh's house and those of his courtiers; throughout Egypt the land was
25 threatened with ruin by the swarms. Pharaoh summoned Moses and Aaron
26 and said to them, 'Go and sacrifice to your God, but in this country.' 'That we cannot do,' replied Moses, 'because the victim we shall sacrifice to the LORD our God is an abomination to the Egyptians. If the Egyptians see us
27 offer such an animal, will they not stone us to death? We must go a three days' journey into the wilderness to sacrifice to the LORD our God, as he
28 commands us.' 'I will let you go,' said Pharaoh, 'and you shall sacrifice to your God in the wilderness; only do not go far. Now intercede for me.'

Moses answered, 'As soon as I leave you I will intercede with the LORD. 29
Tomorrow the swarms will depart from Pharaoh, his courtiers, and his
people. Only let not Pharaoh trifle any more with the people by preventing
them from going to sacrifice to the LORD.' Then Moses left Pharaoh and 30
interceded with the LORD. The LORD did as Moses had said; he removed 31
the swarms from Pharaoh, his courtiers, and his people; not one was left.
But once again Pharaoh became obdurate and did not let the people go. 32

The LORD said to Moses, 'Go into Pharaoh's presence and say to him, **9**
"These are the words of the LORD the God of the Hebrews: 'Let my people
go in order to worship me.' If you refuse to let them go and still keep 2
your hold on them, the LORD will strike your grazing herds, your horses 3
and asses, your camels, cattle, and sheep with a terrible pestilence. But 4
the LORD will make a distinction between Israel's herds and those of the
Egyptians. Of all that belong to Israel not a single one shall die."' The 5
LORD fixed a time and said, 'Tomorrow I will do this throughout the land.'
The next day the LORD struck. All the herds of Egypt died, but from the 6
herds of the Israelites not one single beast died. Pharaoh inquired and was 7
told that not a beast from the herds of Israel had died; and yet he remained
obdurate and did not let the people go.

The LORD said to Moses and Aaron, 'Take handfuls of soot from a kiln. 8
Moses shall toss it into the air in Pharaoh's sight, and it will turn into a fine 9
dust over the whole of Egypt. All over Egypt it will become festering boils
on man and beast.' They took the soot from the kiln and stood before 10
Pharaoh. Moses tossed it into the air and it produced festering boils on
man and beast. The magicians were no match for Moses because of the 11
boils, which attacked them and all the Egyptians. But the LORD made 12
Pharaoh obstinate; as the LORD had foretold to Moses, he did not listen to
Moses and Aaron.

The LORD then told Moses to rise early in the morning, present himself 13
before Pharaoh, and say to him, 'These are the words of the LORD the God
of the Hebrews: "Let my people go in order to worship me. This time I 14
will strike home with all my plagues against you, your courtiers, and your
people, so that you may know that there is none like me in all the earth. By 15
now I could have stretched out my hand, and struck you and your people
with pestilence, and you would have vanished from the earth. I have let 16
you live only to show you my power and to spread my fame throughout the
land. Since you still obstruct my people and will not let them go, tomorrow 17 18
at this time I will send a violent hailstorm, such as has never been in Egypt
from its first beginnings until now. Send now and bring your herds under 19
cover, and everything you have out in the open field. If anything, whether
man or beast, which happens to be in the open, is not brought in, the hail
will fall on it, and it will die."' Those of Pharaoh's subjects who feared the 20
word of the LORD hurried their slaves and cattle into their houses. But those 21
who did not take to heart the word of the LORD left their slaves and cattle
in the open.

The LORD said to Moses, 'Stretch out your hand towards the sky to 22
bring down hail on the whole land of Egypt, on man and beast and every
growing thing throughout the land.' Moses stretched out his staff towards 23

the sky, and the LORD sent thunder and hail, with fire flashing down to the
24 ground. The LORD rained down hail on the land of Egypt, hail and fiery
flashes through the hail, so heavy that there had been nothing like it in all
25 Egypt from the time that Egypt became a nation. Throughout Egypt the
hail struck everything in the fields, both man and beast; it beat down every
26 growing thing and shattered every tree. Only in the land of Goshen, where
the Israelites lived, was there no hail.

27     Pharaoh sent and summoned Moses and Aaron. 'This time I have
sinned,' he said; 'the LORD is in the right; I and my people are in the wrong.
28 Intercede with the LORD, for we can bear no more of this thunder and hail.
29 I will let you go; you need wait no longer.' Moses said, 'When I leave the
city I will spread out my hands in prayer to the LORD. The thunder shall
cease, and there shall be no more hail, so that you may know that the earth
30 is the LORD's. But you and your subjects—I know that you do not yet fear
31 the LORD God.' (The flax and barley were destroyed because the barley was
32 in the ear and the flax in bud, but the wheat and spelt were not destroyed
33 because they come later.) Moses left Pharaoh's presence, went out of the
city and lifted up his hands to the LORD in prayer: the thunder and hail
34 ceased, and no more rain fell. When Pharaoh saw that the downpour, the
hail, and the thunder had ceased, he sinned again, he and his courtiers, and
35 became obdurate. So Pharaoh remained obstinate; as the LORD had foretold through Moses, he did not let the people go.

**10**     Then the LORD said to Moses, 'Go into Pharaoh's presence. I have made
him and his courtiers obdurate, so that I may show these my signs among
2 them, and so that you can tell your children and grandchildren the story:
how I made sport of the Egyptians, and what signs I showed among them.
3 Thus you will know that I am the LORD.' Moses and Aaron went in to
Pharaoh and said to him, 'These are the words of the LORD the God of the
Hebrews: "How long will you refuse to humble yourself before me? Let
4 my people go in order to worship me. If you refuse to let my people go,
5 tomorrow I will bring locusts into your country. They shall cover the face
of the land so that it cannot be seen. They shall eat up the last remnant left
you by the hail. They shall devour every tree that grows in your country-
6 side. Your houses and your courtiers' houses, every house in Egypt, shall
be full of them; your fathers never saw the like nor their fathers before
them; such a thing has not happened from their time until now." ' He turned
7 and left Pharaoh's presence. Pharaoh's courtiers said to him, 'How long
must we be caught in this man's toils? Let their menfolk go and worship
8 the LORD their God. Do you not know by now that Egypt is ruined?' So
Moses and Aaron were brought back to Pharaoh, and he said to them, 'You
9 may go and worship the LORD your God; but who exactly is to go?' 'All,'
said Moses, 'young and old, boys and girls, sheep and cattle; for we have
10 to keep the LORD's pilgrim-feast.' Pharaoh replied, 'Very well then; take
your dependants with you when you go; and the LORD be with you. But
11 beware, there is trouble in store for you. No, your menfolk may go and
worship the LORD, for that is all you asked.' So they were driven out from
Pharaoh's presence.

12     Then the LORD said to Moses, 'Stretch out your hand over Egypt so

that the locusts may come and invade the land and devour all the vegetation
in it, everything the hail has left.' Moses stretched out his staff over the  13
land of Egypt, and the LORD sent a wind roaring in from the east all that
day and all that night. When morning came, the east wind had brought the
locusts. They invaded the whole land of Egypt, and settled on all its terri-  14
tory in swarms so dense that the like of them had never been seen before,
nor ever will be again. They covered the surface of the whole land till it  15
was black with them. They devoured all the vegetation and all the fruit of
the trees that the hail had spared. There was no green left on tree or plant
throughout all Egypt. Pharaoh hastily summoned Moses and Aaron. 'I  16
have sinned against the LORD your God and against you', he said. 'Forgive  17
my sin, I pray, just this once. Intercede with the LORD your God and beg
him only to remove this deadly plague from me.' Moses left Pharaoh and  18
interceded with the LORD. The LORD changed the wind into a westerly *gale*,  19
which carried the locusts away and swept them into the Red Sea.*ᵃ* There
was not a single locust left in all the territory of Egypt. But the LORD made  20
Pharaoh obstinate, and he did not let the Israelites go.

Then the LORD said to Moses, 'Stretch out your hand towards the sky so  21
that there may be darkness over the land of Egypt, darkness that can be
felt.' Moses stretched out his hand towards the sky, and it became pitch  22
dark throughout the land of Egypt for three days. Men could not see one  23
another; for three days no one stirred from where he was. But there was no
darkness wherever the Israelites lived. Pharaoh summoned Moses. 'Go',  24
he said, 'and worship the LORD. Your dependants may go with you; but
your flocks and herds must be left with us.' But Moses said, 'No, you must  25
yourself supply us with animals for sacrifice and whole-offering to the
LORD our God; and our own flocks must go with us too—not a hoof must  26
be left behind. We may need animals from our own flocks to worship the
LORD our God; we ourselves cannot tell until we are there how we are to
worship the LORD.' The LORD made Pharaoh obstinate, and he refused to  27
let them go. 'Out! Pester me no more!' he said to Moses. 'Take care you do  28
not see my face again, for on the day you do, you die.' 'You are right,' said
Moses; 'I shall never see your face again.'

Then the LORD said to Moses, 'One last plague I will bring upon Pharaoh  11
and Egypt. After that he will let you go; he will send you packing, as a man
dismisses a rejected bride. Let the people be told that men and women alike  2
should ask their neighbours for jewellery of silver and gold.' The LORD  3
made the Egyptians well-disposed towards them, and, moreover, Moses
was a very great man in Egypt in the eyes of Pharaoh's courtiers and of
the people.

Moses then said, 'These are the words of the LORD: "At midnight I will  4
go out among the Egyptians. Every first-born creature in the land of  5
Egypt shall die: the first-born of Pharaoh who sits on his throne, the first-
born of the slave-girl at the handmill, and all the first-born of the cattle.
All Egypt will send up a great cry of anguish, a cry the like of which has  6
never been heard before, nor ever will be again. But among all Israel not  7
a dog's tongue shall be so much as scratched, no man or beast be hurt."

*ᵃ Or* the Sea of Reeds.

Thus you shall know that the LORD does make a distinction between Egypt
8 and Israel. Then all these courtiers of yours will come down to me, prostrate themselves and cry, "Go away, you and all the people who follow at
your heels." After that I will go away.' Then Moses left Pharaoh's presence
hot with anger.

9    The LORD said to Moses, 'Pharaoh will not listen to you; I will therefore
10 show still more portents in the land of Egypt.' All these portents had Moses
and Aaron shown in the presence of Pharaoh, and yet the LORD made him
obstinate, and he did not let the Israelites leave the country.

## The institution of the Passover

12 1 2   THE LORD SAID TO MOSES and Aaron in Egypt: This month is for you
3    the first of months; you shall make it the first month of the year. Speak
to the whole community of Israel and say to them: On the tenth day of
this month let each man take a lamb or a kid for his family, one for each
4 household, but if a household is too small for one lamb or one kid, then the
man and his nearest neighbour may take one between them. They shall
share the cost, taking into account both the number of persons and the
5 amount each of them eats. Your lamb or kid must be without blemish, a
6 yearling male. You may take equally a sheep or a goat. You must have
it in safe keeping until the fourteenth day of this month, and then all the
assembled community of Israel shall slaughter the victim between dusk
7 and dark. They must take some of the blood and smear it on the two door-
8 posts and on the lintel of every house in which they eat the lamb. On
that night they shall eat the flesh roast on the fire; they shall eat it with un-
9 leavened cakes and bitter herbs. You are not to eat any of it raw or even
10 boiled in water, but roasted, head, shins, and entrails. You shall not leave
any of it till morning; if anything is left over until morning, it must be
destroyed by fire.

11       This is the way in which you must eat it: you shall have your belt fastened,
your sandals on your feet and your staff in your hand, and you must eat in
12 urgent haste. It is the LORD's Passover. On that night I shall pass through
the land of Egypt and kill every first-born of man and beast. Thus will I
13 execute judgement, I the LORD, against all the gods of Egypt. And as for
you, the blood will be a sign on the houses in which you are: when I see the
blood I will pass over*a* you; the mortal blow shall not touch you, when I
strike the land of Egypt.

14       You shall keep this day as a day of remembrance, and make it a pilgrim-
feast, a festival of the LORD; you shall keep it generation after generation as
15 a rule for all time. For seven days you shall eat unleavened cakes. On the
very first day you shall rid your houses of leaven; from the first day to the
16 seventh anyone who eats leavened bread shall be outlawed from Israel. On
the first day there shall be a sacred assembly and on the seventh day there
shall be a sacred assembly: on these days no work shall be done, except
what must be done to provide food for everyone; and that will be allowed.

*a Or* stand guard over.

You shall observe these commandments because this was the very day on 17
which I brought you out of Egypt in your tribal hosts. You shall observe
this day from generation to generation as a rule for all time.

You shall eat unleavened cakes in the first month from the evening which 18
begins the fourteenth day until the evening which begins the twenty-first
day. For seven days no leaven may be found in your houses, for anyone who 19
eats anything fermented shall be outlawed from the community of Israel,
be he foreigner or native. You must eat nothing fermented. Wherever you 20
live you must eat your cakes unleavened.

Moses summoned all the elders of Israel and said to them, 'Go at once 21
and get sheep for your families and slaughter the Passover. Then take a 22
bunch of marjoram,*a* dip it in the blood in the basin*b* and smear some blood
from the basin*c* on the lintel and the two door-posts. Nobody may go out
through the door of his house till morning. The LORD will go through 23
Egypt and strike it, but when he sees the blood on the lintel and the two
door-posts, he will pass over that door and will not let the destroyer enter
your houses to strike you. You shall keep this as a rule for you and your 24
children for all time. When you enter the land which the LORD will give 25
you as he promised, you shall observe this rite. Then, when your children 26
ask you, "What is the meaning of this rite?" you shall say, "It is the LORD's 27
Passover, for he passed over the houses of the Israelites in Egypt when he
struck the Egyptians but spared our houses." ' The people bowed down
and prostrated themselves.

The Israelites went and did all that the LORD had commanded Moses and 28
Aaron; and by midnight the LORD had struck down every first-born in 29
Egypt, from the first-born of Pharaoh on his throne to the first-born of the
captive in the dungeon, and the first-born of cattle. Before night was over 30
Pharaoh rose, he and all his courtiers and all the Egyptians, and a great
cry of anguish went up, because not a house in Egypt was without its dead.
Pharaoh summoned Moses and Aaron while it was still night and said, 31
'Up with you! Be off, and leave my people, you and your Israelites. Go and
worship the LORD, as you ask; take your sheep and cattle, and go; and ask 32
God's blessing on me also.' The Egyptians urged on the people and hurried 33
them out of the country, 'or else', they said, 'we shall all be dead.' The 34
people picked up their dough before it was leavened, wrapped their
kneading-troughs in their cloaks, and slung them on their shoulders.
Meanwhile the Israelites had done as Moses had told them, asking the 35
Egyptians for jewellery of silver and gold and for clothing. As the LORD 36
had made the Egyptians well-disposed towards them, they let them have
what they asked; in this way they plundered the Egyptians.

## The exodus from Egypt

THE ISRAELITES SET OUT from Rameses on the way to Succoth, about 37
six hundred thousand men on foot, not counting dependants. And with 38
them too went a large company of every kind, and cattle in great numbers,

*a Or* hyssop.        *b Or* on the threshold.        *c Or* from the threshold.

39 both flocks and herds. The dough they had brought from Egypt they baked into unleavened cakes, because there was no leaven; for they had been driven out of Egypt and allowed no time even to get food ready for themselves.

40 The Israelites had been settled in Egypt for four hundred and thirty
41 years. At the end of four hundred and thirty years, on this very day, all the
42 tribes of the LORD came out of Egypt. This was a night of vigil as the LORD waited to bring them out of Egypt. It is the LORD's night; all Israelites keep their vigil generation after generation.

43 The LORD said to Moses and Aaron: These are the rules for the Passover.
44 No foreigner may partake of it; any bought slave may eat it if you have
45 46 circumcised him; no stranger or hired man may eat it. Each lamb must be eaten inside the one house, and you must not take any of the flesh outside
47 the house. You must not break a single bone of it. The whole community
48 of Israel shall keep this feast. If there are aliens living with you and they are to keep the Passover to the LORD, every male of them must be circumcised, and then he can take part; he shall rank as native-born. No one who
49 is uncircumcised may eat of it. The same law shall apply both to the native-born and to the alien who is living among you.

50 The Israelites did all that the LORD had commanded Moses and Aaron;
51 and on this very day the LORD brought the Israelites out of Egypt mustered in their tribal hosts.

13 1 2 The LORD spoke to Moses and said, 'Every first-born, the first birth of every womb among the Israelites, you must dedicate to me, both man and beast; it is mine.'

3 Then Moses said to the people, 'Remember this day, the day on which you have come out of Egypt, the land of slavery, because the LORD by the strength of his hand has brought you out. No leaven may be eaten this day,
4 5 for today, in the month of Abib, is the day of your exodus; and when the LORD has brought you into the country of the Canaanites, Hittites, Amorites, Hivites, and Jebusites, the land which he swore to your forefathers to give you, a land flowing with milk and honey, then you must observe
6 this rite in this same month. For seven days you shall eat unleavened cakes,
7 and on the seventh day there shall be a pilgrim-feast of the LORD. Only unleavened cakes shall be eaten during the seven days; nothing fermented
8 and no leaven shall be seen throughout your territory. On that day you shall tell your son, "This commemorates what the LORD did for me when
9 I came out of Egypt." You shall have the record of it as a sign upon your hand, and upon your forehead as a reminder, to make sure that the law of the LORD is always on your lips, because the LORD with a strong hand
10 brought you out of Egypt. This is a rule, and you shall keep it at the appointed time from year to year.

11 'When the LORD has brought you into the land of the Canaanites as he
12 swore to you and to your forefathers, and given it to you, you shall surrender to the LORD the first birth of every womb; and of all first-born offspring of your cattle the males belong to the LORD. Every first-born male
13 ass you may redeem with a kid or lamb, but if you do not redeem it, you must break its neck. Every first-born among your sons you must redeem.

When in time to come your son asks you what this means, you shall say to 14
him, "By the strength of his hand the LORD brought us out of Egypt, out
of the land of slavery. When Pharaoh proved stubborn and refused to let 15
us go, the LORD killed all the first-born in Egypt both man and beast. That
is why I sacrifice to the LORD the first birth of every womb if it is a male and
redeem every first-born of my sons. You shall have the record of it as a sign 16
upon your hand, and upon your forehead as a phylactery, because by the
strength of his hand the LORD brought us out of Egypt."'

NOW WHEN PHARAOH LET THE PEOPLE GO, God did not guide them 17
by the road towards the Philistines, although that was the shortest; for he
said, 'The people may change their minds when they see war before them,
and turn back to Egypt.' So God made them go round by way of the wilder- 18
ness towards the Red Sea; and the fifth generation of Israelites departed
from Egypt.

Moses took the bones of Joseph with him, because Joseph had exacted 19
an oath from the Israelites: 'Some day', he said, 'God will show his care
for you, and then, as you go, you must take my bones with you.'

They set out from Succoth and encamped at Etham on the edge of the 20
wilderness. And all the time the LORD went before them, by day a pillar 21
of cloud to guide them on their journey, by night a pillar of fire to give them
light, so that they could travel night and day. The pillar of cloud never left 22
its place in front of the people by day, nor the pillar of fire by night.

The LORD spoke to Moses and said, 'Speak to the Israelites: they are to **14** 1 2
turn back and encamp before Pi-hahiroth,*a* between Migdol and the sea
to the east of Baal-zephon; your camp shall be opposite, by the sea.
Pharaoh will then think that the Israelites are finding themselves in difficult 3
country, and are hemmed in by the wilderness. I will make Pharaoh ob- 4
stinate, and he will pursue them, so that I may win glory for myself at the
expense of Pharaoh and all his army; and the Egyptians shall know that I
am the LORD.' The Israelites did as they were bidden.

When the king of Egypt was told that the Israelites had slipped away, 5
he and his courtiers changed their minds completely, and said, 'What have
we done? We have let our Israelite slaves go free!' So Pharaoh put horses 6
to his chariot, and took his troops with him. He took six hundred picked 7
chariots and all the other chariots of Egypt, with a commander in each.
Then Pharaoh king of Egypt, made obstinate by the LORD, pursued the 8
Israelites as they marched defiantly away. The Egyptians, all Pharaoh's 9
chariots and horses, cavalry and infantry, pursued them and overtook
them encamped beside the sea by Pi-hahiroth to the east of Baal-zephon.
Pharaoh was almost upon them when the Israelites looked up and saw the 10
Egyptians close behind. In their terror they clamoured to the LORD for
help and said to Moses, 'Were there no graves in Egypt, that you should 11
have brought us here to die in the wilderness? See what you have done to
us by bringing us out of Egypt! Is not this just what we meant when we 12
said in Egypt, "Leave us alone; let us be slaves to the Egyptians"? We

*a Or where the desert tracks begin.*

would rather be slaves to the Egyptians than die here in the wilderness.'

13 'Have no fear,' Moses answered; 'stand firm and see the deliverance that the LORD will bring you this day; for as sure as you see the Egyptians now,

14 you will never see them again. The LORD will fight for you; so hold your peace.'

15 The LORD said to Moses, 'What is the meaning of this clamour? Tell the

16 Israelites to strike camp. And you shall raise high your staff, stretch out your hand over the sea and cleave it in two, so that the Israelites can pass

17 through the sea on dry ground. For my part I will make the Egyptians obstinate and they will come after you; thus will I win glory for myself at the expense of Pharaoh and his army, chariots and cavalry all together.

18 The Egyptians will know that I am the LORD when I win glory for myself at the expense of their Pharaoh, his chariots and cavalry.'

19 The angel of God, who had kept in front of the Israelites, moved away to the rear. The pillar of cloud moved from the front and took its place

20 behind them and so came between the Egyptians and the Israelites. And the cloud brought on darkness and early nightfall, so that contact was lost throughout the night.

21 Then Moses stretched out his hand over the sea, and the LORD drove the sea away all night with a strong east wind and turned the sea-bed into

22 dry land. The waters were torn apart, and the Israelites went through the sea on the dry ground, while the waters made a wall for them to right and

23 to left. The Egyptians went in pursuit of them far into the sea, all Pharaoh's

24 horse, his chariots, and his cavalry. In the morning watch the LORD looked down on the Egyptian army through the pillar of fire and cloud, and he

25 threw them into a panic. He clogged their chariot wheels and made them lumber along heavily, so that the Egyptians said, 'It is the LORD fighting

26 for Israel against Egypt; let us flee.' Then the LORD said to Moses, 'Stretch out your hand over the sea, and let the water flow back over the Egyptians,

27 their chariots and their cavalry.' So Moses stretched out his hand over the sea, and at daybreak the water returned to its accustomed place; but the Egyptians were in flight as it advanced, and the LORD swept them out into

28 the sea. The water flowed back and covered all Pharaoh's army, the chariots and the cavalry, which had pressed the pursuit into the sea. Not one man

29 was left alive. Meanwhile the Israelites had passed along the dry ground through the sea, with the water making a wall for them to right and to

30 left. That day the LORD saved Israel from the power of Egypt, and the

31 Israelites saw the Egyptians lying dead on the sea-shore. When Israel saw the great power which the LORD had put forth against Egypt, all the people feared the LORD, and they put their faith in him and in Moses his servant.

**15** Then Moses and the Israelites sang this song to the LORD:

> I will sing to the LORD, for he has risen up in triumph;
> the horse and his rider he has hurled into the sea.

2
> The LORD is my refuge and my defence,
> he has shown himself my deliverer.
> He is my God, and I will glorify him;
> he is my father's God, and I will exalt him.

The LORD is a warrior: the LORD is his name.                    3
The chariots of Pharaoh and his army                            4
he has cast into the sea;
the flower of his officers
are engulfed in the Red Sea.
The watery abyss has covered them,                              5
they sank into the depths like a stone.
Thy right hand, O LORD, is majestic in strength:               6
thy right hand, O LORD, shattered the enemy.
    In the fullness of thy triumph                           7
    thou didst cast the rebels down:
    thou didst let loose thy fury;
    it consumed them like chaff.
At the blast of thy anger the sea piled up:                     8
   the waters stood up like a bank:
   out at sea the great deep congealed.
The enemy said, 'I will pursue, I will overtake;                9
    I will divide the spoil,
    I will glut my appetite upon them;
    I will draw my sword,
    I will rid myself of them.'
Thou didst blow with thy blast; the sea covered them.          10
They sank like lead in the swelling waves.
    Who is like thee, O LORD, among the gods*a*?           11
    Who is like thee, majestic in holiness,
   worthy of awe and praise, who workest wonders?
    Thou didst stretch out thy right hand,                 12
    earth engulfed them.
In thy constant love thou hast led the people                 13
    whom thou didst ransom:
   thou hast guided them by thy strength
    to thy holy dwelling-place.
    Nations heard and trembled;                            14
   agony seized the dwellers in Philistia.
    Then the chieftains of Edom were dismayed,             15
   trembling seized the leaders of Moab,
all the inhabitants of Canaan were in turmoil;
   terror and dread fell upon them:                          16
through the might of thy arm they stayed stone-still,
    while thy people passed, O LORD,
while the people whom thou madest thy own*b* passed by.
Thou broughtest them in and didst plant them                  17
    in the mount that is thy possession,
   the dwelling-place, O LORD, of thy own making,
the sanctuary, O LORD, which thy own hands prepared.
    The LORD shall reign for ever and for ever.            18

    *a* Or in might.    *b* madest thy own: *or* didst create.

19 For Pharaoh's horse, both chariots and cavalry, went into the sea, and the LORD brought back the waters over them, but Israel had passed through
20 the sea on dry ground. And Miriam the prophetess, Aaron's sister, took up her tambourine, and all the women followed her, dancing to the sound
21 of tambourines; and Miriam sang them this refrain:

> Sing to the LORD, for he has risen up in triumph;
> the horse and his rider he has hurled into the sea.

22 MOSES LED ISRAEL FROM THE RED SEA out into the wilderness of Shur. For three days they travelled through the wilderness without finding water.
23 They came to Marah, but could not drink the Marah water because it was
24 bitter; that is why the place was called Marah. The people complained to
25 Moses and asked, 'What are we to drink?' Moses cried to the LORD, and the LORD showed him a log which he threw into the water, and then the water became sweet.

It was there that the LORD laid down a precept and rule of life; there he
26 put them to the test. He said, 'If only you will obey the LORD your God, if you will do what is right in his eyes, if you will listen to his commands and keep all his statutes, then I will never bring upon you any of the sufferings which I brought on the Egyptians; for I the LORD am your healer.'
27 They came to Elim, where there were twelve springs and seventy palm-trees, and there they encamped beside the water.

**16** The whole community of the Israelites set out from Elim and came into the wilderness of Sin, which lies between Elim and Sinai. This was on the fifteenth day of the second month after they had left Egypt.
2 3 The Israelites complained to Moses and Aaron in the wilderness and said, 'If only we had died at the LORD's hand in Egypt, where we sat round the fleshpots and had plenty of bread to eat! But you have brought us out
4 into this wilderness to let this whole assembly starve to death.' The LORD said to Moses, 'I will rain down bread from heaven for you. Each day the people shall go out and gather a day's supply, so that I can put them to
5 the test and see whether they will follow my instructions or not. But on the sixth day, when they prepare what they bring in, it shall be twice as much
6 as they have gathered on other days.' Moses and Aaron then said to all the Israelites, 'In the evening you will know that it was the LORD who brought
7 you out of Egypt, and in the morning you will see the glory of the LORD, because he has heeded your complaints against him; it is not against us
8 that you bring your complaints; we are nothing.' 'You shall know this', Moses said, 'when the LORD, in answer to your complaints, gives you flesh to eat in the evening, and in the morning bread in plenty. What are we? It is against the LORD that you bring your complaints, and not against us.'
9 Moses told Aaron to say to the whole community of Israel, 'Come into
10 the presence of the LORD, for he has heeded your complaints.' While Aaron was speaking to the community of the Israelites, they looked towards the wilderness, and there was the glory of the LORD appearing in the cloud.
11 12 The LORD spoke to Moses and said, 'I have heard the complaints of the Israelites. Say to them, "Between dusk and dark you will have flesh to eat

and in the morning bread in plenty. You shall know that I the LORD am
your God." '

That evening a flock of quails flew in and settled all over the camp, and 13
in the morning a fall of dew lay all around it. When the dew was gone, there 14
in the wilderness, fine flakes appeared, fine as hoar-frost on the ground.
When the Israelites saw it, they said to one another, 'What is that?', *a* be- 15
cause they did not know what it was. Moses said to them, 'That is the bread
which the LORD has given you to eat. This is the command the LORD has 16
given: "Each of you is to gather as much as he can eat: let every man take
an omer a head for every person in his tent." ' The Israelites did this, and 17
they gathered, some more, some less, but when they measured it by the 18
omer, those who had gathered more had not too much, and those who had
gathered less had not too little. Each had just as much as he could eat.
Moses said, 'No one may keep any of it till morning.' Some, however, did 19 20
not listen to Moses; they kept part of it till morning, and it became full of
maggots and stank, and Moses was angry with them. Each morning every 21
man gathered as much as he could eat, and when the sun grew hot, it melted
away. On the sixth day they gathered twice as much food, two omers each. 22
All the chiefs of the community came and told Moses. 'This', he answered, 23
'is what the LORD has said: "Tomorrow is a day of sacred rest, a sabbath
holy to the LORD." So bake what you want to bake now, and boil what you
want to boil; put aside what remains over and keep it safe till morning.'
So they put it aside till morning as Moses had commanded, and it did not 24
stink, nor did maggots appear in it. 'Eat it today,' said Moses, 'because today 25
is a sabbath of the LORD. Today you will find none outside. For six days 26
you may gather it, but on the seventh day, the sabbath, there will be none.'

Some of the people did go out to gather it on the seventh day, but they 27
found none. The LORD said to Moses, 'How long will you refuse to obey 28
my commands and instructions? The LORD has given you the sabbath, 29
and so he gives you two days' food every sixth day. Let each man stay
where he is; no one may stir from his home on the seventh day.' And the 30
people kept the sabbath on the seventh day.

Israel called the food manna; it was white, like coriander seed, and it 31
tasted like a wafer made with honey.

'This', said Moses, 'is the command which the LORD has given: "Take 32
a full omer of it to be kept for future generations, so that they may see the
bread with which I fed you in the wilderness when I brought you out of
Egypt." ' So Moses said to Aaron, 'Take a jar and fill it with an omer of 33
manna, and store it in the presence of the LORD to be kept for future generations.' Aaron did as the LORD had commanded Moses, and stored it before 34
the Testimony for safe keeping. The Israelites ate the manna for forty 35
years until they came to a land where they could settle; they ate it until
they came to the border of Canaan. (An omer is one tenth of an ephah.) 36

The whole community of Israel set out from the wilderness of Sin and **17**
travelled by stages as the LORD told them. They encamped at Rephidim,
where there was no water for the people to drink, and a dispute arose be- 2
tween them and Moses. When they said, 'Give us water to drink', Moses

---

*a* Heb. man-hu (*cp. verse 31*).

said, 'Why do you dispute with me? Why do you challenge the LORD?'
3 There the people became so thirsty that they raised an outcry against
Moses: 'Why have you brought us out of Egypt with our children and our
4 herds to let us all die of thirst?' Moses cried to the LORD, 'What shall I do
5 with these people? In a moment they will be stoning me.' The LORD
answered, 'Go forward ahead of the people; take with you some of the
6 elders of Israel and the staff with which you struck the Nile, and go. You
will find me waiting for you there, by a rock in Horeb. Strike the rock;
water will pour out of it, and the people shall drink.' Moses did this in the
7 sight of the elders of Israel. He named the place Massah *a* and Meribah, *b*
because the Israelites had disputed with him and challenged the LORD
with their question, 'Is the LORD in our midst or not?'

8 9     The Amalekites came and attacked Israel at Rephidim. Moses said to
Joshua, 'Pick your men, and march out tomorrow to fight for us against
Amalek; and I will take my stand on the hill-top with the staff of God in
10 my hand.' Joshua carried out his orders and fought against Amalek while
11 Moses, Aaron and Hur climbed to the top of the hill. Whenever Moses
raised his hands Israel had the advantage, and when he lowered his hands
12 Amalek had the advantage. But when his arms grew heavy they took a
stone and put it under him and, as he sat, Aaron and Hur held up his hands,
13 one on each side, so that his hands remained steady till sunset. Thus Joshua
defeated Amalek and put its people to the sword.

14     The LORD said to Moses, 'Record this in writing, and tell it to Joshua
in these words: "I am resolved to blot out all memory of Amalek from
15 16 under heaven."' Moses built an altar, and named it Jehovah-nissi and said,
'My oath upon it: the LORD is at war with Amalek generation after generation.'

18 JETHRO PRIEST OF MIDIAN, father-in-law of Moses, heard all that God
had done for Moses and Israel his people, and how the LORD had brought
2 Israel out of Egypt. When Moses had dismissed his wife Zipporah, Jethro
3 his father-in-law had received her and her two sons. The name of the one
was Gershom, 'for', said Moses, 'I have become an alien *c* living in a
4 foreign land'; the other's name was Eliezer, *d* 'for', he said, 'the God of
my father was my help and saved me from Pharaoh's sword.'
5     Jethro, Moses' father-in-law, now came to him with his sons and his
wife, to the wilderness where he was encamped at the mountain of God.
6 Moses was told, 'Here is Jethro, your father-in-law, coming to you with
7 your wife and her two sons.' Moses went out to meet his father-in-law,
bowed low to him and kissed him, and they greeted one another. When
8 they came into the tent Moses told him all that the LORD had done to
Pharaoh and to Egypt for Israel's sake, and about all their hardships on the
9 journey, and how the LORD had saved them. Jethro rejoiced at all the good
10-11 the LORD had done for Israel in saving them from the power of Egypt. He
said, 'Blessed be the LORD who has saved you from the power of Egypt and
of Pharaoh. Now I know that the LORD is the greatest of all gods, because

---

*a* *That is* Challenge.     *b* *That is* Dispute.     *c* *Cp. 2. 22.*
*d* *That is* God my help.

he has delivered the people from the power of the Egyptians who dealt so arrogantly with them.' Jethro, Moses' father-in-law, brought a whole- 12 offering and sacrifices for God; and Aaron and all the elders of Israel came and shared the meal with Jethro in the presence of God.

The next day Moses took his seat to settle disputes among the people, 13 and they were standing round him from morning till evening. When 14 Jethro saw all that he was doing for the people, he said, 'What are you doing for all these people? Why do you sit alone with all of them standing round you from morning till evening?' 'The people come to me', Moses 15 answered, 'to seek God's guidance. Whenever there is a dispute among 16 them, they come to me, and I decide between man and man. I declare the statutes and laws of God.' But his father-in-law said to Moses, 'This is not 17 the best way to do it. You will only wear yourself out and wear out all the 18 people who are here. The task is too heavy for you; you cannot do it by yourself. Now listen to me: take my advice, and God be with you. It is for 19 you to be the people's representative before God, and bring their disputes to him. You must instruct them in the statutes and laws, and teach them 20 how they must behave and what they must do. But you must yourself 21 search for capable, God-fearing men among all the people, honest and incorruptible men, and appoint them over the people as officers over units of a thousand, of a hundred, of fifty or of ten. They shall sit as a permanent 22 court for the people; they must refer difficult cases to you but decide simple cases themselves. In this way your burden will be lightened, and they will share it with you. If you do this, God will give you strength, and you will 23 be able to go on. And, moreover, this whole people will here and now regain peace and harmony.' Moses listened to his father-in-law and did all he had 24 suggested. He chose capable men from all Israel and appointed them 25 leaders of the people, officers over units of a thousand, of a hundred, of fifty or of ten. They sat as a permanent court, bringing the difficult cases 26 to Moses but deciding simple cases themselves. Moses set his father-in-law 27 on his way, and he went back to his own country.

## Israel at Mount Sinai

IN THE THIRD MONTH after Israel had left Egypt,[a] they came to the 19 wilderness of Sinai. They set out from Rephidim and entered the wilder- 2 ness of Sinai, where they encamped, pitching their tents opposite the mountain. Moses went up the mountain of God, and the LORD called to 3 him from the mountain and said, 'Speak thus to the house of Jacob, and tell this to the sons of Israel: You have seen with your own eyes what I 4 did to Egypt, and how I have carried you on eagles' wings and brought you here to me. If only you will now listen to me and keep my covenant, then 5 out of all peoples you shall become my special possession; for the whole earth is mine. You shall be my kingdom of priests, my holy nation. These 6 are the words you shall speak to the Israelites.'

> [a] *Prob. rdg.; Heb. adds* on this day.

7  Moses came and summoned the elders of the people and set before them
8  all these commands which the LORD had laid upon him. The people all
answered together, 'Whatever the LORD has said we will do.' Moses brought
9  this answer back to the LORD. The LORD said to Moses, 'I am now coming
to you in a thick cloud, so that I may speak to you in the hearing of the
people, and their faith in you may never fail.' Moses told the LORD what
10  the people had said, and the LORD said to him, 'Go to the people and hal-
11  low them today and tomorrow and make them wash their clothes. They
must be ready by the third day, because on the third day the LORD will
12  descend upon Mount Sinai in the sight of all the people. You must put
barriers round the mountain and say, "Take care not to go up the mountain
or even to touch the edge of it." Any man who touches the mountain must
13  be put to death. No hand shall touch him;<sup>a</sup> he shall be stoned or shot dead:<sup>b</sup>
neither man nor beast may live. But when the ram's horn sounds, they
14  may go up the mountain.' Moses came down from the mountain to the
15  people. He hallowed them and they washed their clothes. He said to the
16  people, 'Be ready by the third day; do not go near a woman.' On the third
day, when morning came, there were peals of thunder and flashes of
lightning, dense cloud on the mountain and a loud trumpet blast; the
people in the camp were all terrified.

17  Moses brought the people out from the camp to meet God, and they
18  took their stand at the foot of the mountain. Mount Sinai was all smoking
because the LORD had come down upon it in fire; the smoke went up like
19  the smoke of a kiln; all the people were terrified, and the sound of the
trumpet grew ever louder. Whenever Moses spoke, God answered him in
20  a peal of thunder.<sup>c</sup> The LORD came down upon the top of Mount Sinai
21  and summoned Moses to the mountain-top, and Moses went up. The LORD
said to Moses, 'Go down; warn the people solemnly that they must not
force their way through to the LORD to see him, or many of them will perish.
22  Even the priests, who have access to the LORD, must hallow themselves,
23  for fear that the LORD may break out against them.' Moses answered the
LORD, 'The people cannot come up Mount Sinai, because thou thyself
didst solemnly warn us to set a barrier to the mountain and so to keep it
24  holy.' The LORD therefore said to him, 'Go down; then come up and bring
Aaron with you, but let neither priests nor people force their way up to the
25  LORD, for fear that he may break out against them.' So Moses went down
to the people and spoke to them.

**20**  God spoke, and these were his words:

2  I am the LORD your God who brought you out of Egypt, out of the land
of slavery.

3  You shall have no other god<sup>d</sup> to set against me.

4  You shall not make a carved image for yourself nor the likeness of anything in the heavens above, or on the earth below, or in the waters under the
earth.

5  You shall not bow down to them or worship<sup>e</sup> them; for I, the LORD your
God, am a jealous god. I punish the children for the sins of the fathers to

_____
<sup>a</sup> _Or_ it.  <sup>b</sup> _Or_ hurled to his death.  <sup>c</sup> _in . . ._ thunder: _or_ by voice.
<sup>d</sup> _Or_ gods.  <sup>e</sup> _Or or be led to worship._

the third and fourth generations of those who hate me. But I keep faith 6
with thousands, with*ᵃ* those who love me and keep my commandments.

You shall not make wrong use of the name of the LORD your God; the 7
LORD will not leave unpunished the man who misuses his name.

Remember to keep the sabbath day holy. You have six days to labour and 8 9
do all your work. But the seventh day is a sabbath of the LORD your God; 10
that day you shall not do any work, you, your son or your daughter, your
slave or your slave-girl, your cattle or the alien within your gates; for in 11
six days the LORD made heaven and earth, the sea, and all that is in them,
and on the seventh day he rested. Therefore the LORD blessed the sabbath
day and declared it holy.

Honour your father and your mother, that you may live long in the land 12
which the LORD your God is giving you.

You shall not commit murder.                                              13
You shall not commit adultery.                                           14
You shall not steal.                                                     15
You shall not give false evidence against your neighbour.                16
You shall not covet your neighbour's house; you shall not covet your 17
neighbour's wife, his slave, his slave-girl, his ox, his ass, or anything that
belongs to him.

When all the people saw how it thundered and the lightning flashed, 18
when they heard the trumpet sound and saw the mountain smoking, they
trembled and stood at a distance. 'Speak to us yourself,' they said to Moses, 19
'and we will listen; but if God speaks to us we shall die.' Moses answered, 20
'Do not be afraid. God has come only to test you, so that the fear of him
may remain with you and keep you from sin.' So the people stood at a 21
distance, while Moses approached the dark cloud where God was.

THE LORD SAID TO MOSES, Say this to the Israelites: You know now 22
that I have spoken to you from heaven. You shall not make gods of silver 23
to be worshipped as well as me, nor shall you make yourselves gods of gold.
You shall make an altar of earth for me, and you shall sacrifice on it both 24
your whole-offerings and your shared-offerings, your sheep and your
cattle. Wherever I cause my name to be invoked, I will come to you and
bless you. If you make an altar of stones for me, you must not build it of 25
hewn stones, for if you use a chisel on it, you will profane it. You must 26
not mount up to my altar by steps, in case your private parts be exposed
on it.

These are the laws you shall set before them:                           **21**
When you buy a Hebrew slave, he shall be your slave for six years, but 2
in the seventh year he shall go free and pay nothing.

If he comes to you alone, he shall go away alone; but if he is married, 3
his wife shall go away with him.

If his master gives him a wife, and she bears him sons or daughters, the 4
woman and her children shall belong to her master, and the man shall go
away alone. But if the slave should say, 'I love my master, my wife, and 5
my children; I will not go free', then his master shall bring him to God: 6

*ᵃ* with . . . with: *or* for a thousand generations with . . .

he shall bring him to the door or the door-post, and his master shall pierce his ear with an awl, and the man shall be his slave for life.

7 When a man sells his daughter into slavery, she shall not go free as a
8 male slave may. If her master has not had intercourse with her and she does not please him, he shall let her be ransomed. He has treated her
9 unfairly and therefore has no right to sell her to strangers. If he assigns her
10 to his son, he shall allow her the rights of a daughter. If he takes another woman, he shall not deprive the first of meat, clothes, and conjugal rights.
11 If he does not provide her with these three things, she shall go free without any payment.

12 13 Whoever strikes another man and kills him shall be put to death. But if he did not act with intent, but they met by act of God, the slayer may
14 flee to a place which I will appoint for you. But if a man has the presumption to kill another by treachery, you shall take him even from my altar to be put to death.

15 Whoever strikes his father or mother shall be put to death.

16 Whoever kidnaps a man shall be put to death, whether he has sold him, or the man is found in his possession.

17 Whoever reviles his father or mother shall be put to death.

18 When men quarrel and one hits another with a stone or with a spade,*a*
19 and the man is not killed but takes to his bed; if he recovers so as to walk about outside with a stick, then the one who struck him has no liability, except that he shall pay for loss of time and shall see that he is cured.

20 When a man strikes his slave or his slave-girl with a stick and the slave
21 dies on the spot, he must be punished. But he shall not be punished if the slave survives for one day or two, because he is worth money to his master.

22 When, in the course of a brawl, a man knocks against a pregnant woman so that she has a miscarriage but suffers no further hurt, then the offender must pay whatever fine the woman's husband demands after assessment.

23 24 Wherever hurt is done, you shall give life for life, eye for eye, tooth for
25 tooth, hand for hand, foot for foot, burn for burn, bruise for bruise, wound for wound.

26 When a man strikes his slave or slave-girl in the eye and destroys it, he
27 shall let the slave go free in compensation for the eye. When he knocks out the tooth of a slave or a slave-girl, he shall let the slave go free in compensation for the tooth.

28 When an ox gores a man or a woman to death, the ox shall be stoned, and its flesh may not be eaten; the owner of the ox shall be free from liability.
29 If, however, the ox has for some time past been a vicious animal, and the owner has been duly warned but has not kept it under control, and the ox kills a man or a woman, then the ox shall be stoned, and the owner shall
30 be put to death as well. If, however, the penalty is commuted for a money payment, he shall pay in redemption of his life whatever is imposed upon
31 32 him. If the ox gores a son or a daughter, the same rule shall apply. If the ox gores a slave or slave-girl, its owner shall pay thirty shekels of silver to their master, and the ox shall be stoned.

33 When a man removes the cover of a well*b* or digs a well*b* and leaves it

*a Or* fist.        *b Or* cistern.

84

uncovered, then if an ox or an ass falls into it, the owner of the well shall 34
make good the loss. He shall repay the owner of the beast in silver, and the
dead beast shall be his.

When one man's ox butts another's and kills it, they shall sell the live 35
ox, share the price and also share the dead beast. But if it is known that the 36
ox has for some time past been vicious and the owner has not kept it under
control, he shall make good the loss, ox for ox, but the dead beast is his.

When a man steals an ox or a sheep and slaughters or sells it, he shall repay **22**
five beasts for the ox and four sheep for the sheep. He shall pay in full; 2-4[a]
if he has no means, he shall be sold to pay for the theft. But if the animal
is found alive in his possession, be it ox, ass, or sheep, he shall repay two.

If a burglar is caught in the act and is fatally injured, it is not murder;
but if he breaks in after sunrise and is fatally injured, then it is murder.

When a man burns off a field or a vineyard and lets the fire spread so that 5
it burns another man's field,[b] he shall make restitution from his own field
according to the yield expected; and if the whole field is laid waste, he
shall make restitution from the best part of his own field or vineyard.

When a fire starts and spreads to a heap of brushwood, so that sheaves, 6
or standing corn, or a whole field is destroyed, he who started the fire shall
make full restitution.

When one man gives another silver or chattels for safe keeping, and they 7
are stolen from that man's house, the thief, if he is found, shall restore
twofold. But if the thief is not found, the owner of the house shall appear 8
before God, to make a declaration that he has not touched his neighbour's
property. In every case of law-breaking involving an ox, an ass, or a sheep, 9
a cloak, or any lost property which may be claimed, each party shall bring
his case before God; he whom God declares to be in the wrong shall restore
twofold to his neighbour.

When a man gives an ass, an ox, a sheep or any beast into his neighbour's 10
keeping, and it dies or is injured or is carried off, there being no witness,
the neighbour shall swear by the LORD that he has not touched the man's 11
property. The owner shall accept this, and no restitution shall be made.
If it has been stolen from him, he shall make restitution to the owner. If 12 13
it has been mauled by a wild beast, he shall bring it in as evidence; he shall
not make restitution for what has been mauled.

When a man borrows a beast from his neighbour and it is injured or dies 14
while its owner is not with it, the borrower shall make full restitution; but 15
if the owner is with it, the borrower shall not make restitution. If it was
hired, only the hire shall be due.

When a man seduces a virgin who is not yet betrothed, he shall pay the 16
bride-price for her to be his wife. If her father refuses to give her to him, 17
the seducer shall pay in silver a sum equal to the bride-price for virgins.

You shall not allow a witch to live. 18

Whoever has unnatural connection with a beast shall be put to death. 19

Whoever sacrifices to any god but the LORD shall be put to death under 20
solemn ban.

---

[a] *Verses 2-4 rearranged thus: 3b, 4, 2, 3a.*          [b] *Or* When a man uses his field or
vineyard for grazing, and lets his beast loose, and it feeds in another man's field.

21    You shall not wrong an alien, or be hard upon him; you were yourselves
22 23 aliens in Egypt. You shall not ill-treat any widow or fatherless child. If
24 you do, be sure that I will listen if they appeal to me; my anger will be
roused and I will kill you with the sword; your own wives shall become
widows and your children fatherless.

25    If you advance money to any poor man amongst my people, you shall
not act like a money-lender: you must not exact interest in advance from
him.

26    If you take your neighbour's cloak in pawn, you shall return it to him
27 by sunset, because it is his only covering. It is the cloak in which he wraps
his body; in what else can he sleep? If he appeals to me, I will listen, for
I am full of compassion.

28    You shall not revile God, nor curse a chief of your own people.

29    You shall not hold back the first of your harvest, whether corn or wine.

30 You shall give me your first-born sons. You shall do the same with your
oxen and your sheep. They shall stay with the mother for seven days; on
the eighth day you shall give them to me.

31    You shall be holy to me: you shall not eat the flesh of anything in the
open country killed by beasts, but you shall throw it to the dogs.

**23**    You shall not spread a baseless rumour. You shall not make common
cause with a wicked man by giving malicious evidence.

2    You shall not be led into wrongdoing by the majority, nor, when you
give evidence in a lawsuit, shall you side with the majority to pervert
3 justice; nor shall you favour the poor man in his suit.

4    When you come upon your enemy's ox or ass straying, you shall take it
5 back to him. When you see the ass of someone who hates you lying helpless under its load, however unwilling you may be to help it, you must
give him a hand with it.

6 7    You shall not deprive the poor man of justice in his suit. Avoid all lies,
and do not cause the death of the innocent and the guiltless; for I the LORD
8 will never acquit the guilty. You shall not accept a bribe, for bribery makes
the discerning man blind and the just man give a crooked answer.

9    You shall not oppress the alien, for you know how it feels to be an alien;
you were aliens yourselves in Egypt.

10 11    For six years you may sow your land and gather its produce; but in the
seventh year you shall let it lie fallow and leave it alone. It shall provide
food for the poor of your people, and what they leave the wild animals
may eat. You shall do likewise with your vineyard and your olive-grove.

12    For six days you may do your work, but on the seventh day you shall
abstain from work, so that your ox and your ass may rest, and your home-
born slave and the alien may refresh themselves.

13    Be attentive to every word of mine. You shall not invoke other gods:
your lips shall not speak their names.

14 15    Three times a year you shall keep a pilgrim-feast to me. You shall celebrate the pilgrim-feast of Unleavened Bread for seven days; you shall eat
unleavened cakes as I have commanded you, at the appointed time in the
month of Abib, for in that month you came out of Egypt.

16    No one shall come into my presence empty-handed. You shall celebrate

the pilgrim-feast of Harvest, with the firstfruits of your work in sowing the land, and the pilgrim-feast of Ingathering at the end*ᵃ* of the year, when you bring in the fruits of all your work on the land. These three times a year 17 shall all your males come into the presence of the Lord GOD.

You shall not offer the blood of my sacrifice at the same time as anything 18 leavened.

The fat of my festal offering shall not remain overnight till morning.

You shall bring the choicest firstfruits of your soil to the house of the 19 LORD your God.

You shall not boil a kid in its mother's milk.

And now I send an angel before you to guard you on your way and to 20 bring you to the place I have prepared. Take heed of him and listen to his 21 voice. Do not defy him; he will not pardon your rebelliousness, for my authority rests in him. If you will only listen to his voice and do all I tell 22 you, then I will be an enemy to your enemies, and I will harass those who harass you. My angel will go before you and bring you to the Amorites, 23 the Hittites, the Perizzites, the Canaanites, the Hivites, and the Jebusites, and I will make an end of them. You are not to bow down to their gods, nor 24 worship them, nor observe their rites, but you shall tear down all their images and smash their sacred pillars. Worship the LORD your God, and 25 he will bless your bread and your water. I will take away all sickness out of your midst. None shall miscarry or be barren in your land. I will grant 26 you a full span of life.

I will send my terror before you and throw into confusion all the peoples 27 whom you find in your path. I will make all your enemies turn their backs. I will spread panic before you to drive out in front of you the Hivites, the 28 Canaanites and the Hittites. I will not drive them out all in one year, or the 29 land would become waste and the wild beasts too many for you. I will drive 30 them out little by little until your numbers have grown enough to take possession of the whole country. I will establish your frontiers from the 31 Red Sea to the sea of the Philistines, and from the wilderness to the River. I will give the inhabitants of the country into your power, and you shall drive them out before you. You shall make no covenant with them and their 32 gods. They shall not stay in your land for fear they make you sin against 33 me; for then you would worship their gods, and in this way you would be ensnared.

THEN HE SAID TO MOSES, 'Come up to the LORD, you and Aaron, **24** Nadab and Abihu, and seventy of the elders of Israel. While you are still at a distance, you are to bow down; and then Moses shall approach the 2 LORD by himself, but not the others. The people may not go up with him at all.'

Moses came and told the people all the words of the LORD, all his laws. 3 The whole people answered with one voice and said, 'We will do all that the LORD has told us.' Moses wrote down all the words of the LORD. He 4 rose early in the morning and built an altar at the foot of the mountain, and put up twelve sacred pillars, one for each of the twelve tribes of Israel. He 5

　　　　　　*ᵃ Or* beginning.

then sent the young men of Israel and they sacrificed bulls to the LORD
6 as whole-offerings and shared-offerings. Moses took half the blood and put
7 it in basins and the other half he flung against[a] the altar. Then he took the
book of the covenant and read it aloud for all the people to hear. They said,
8 'We will obey, and do all that the LORD has said.' Moses then took the blood
and flung it over the people, saying, 'This is the blood of the covenant which
the LORD has made with you on the terms of this book.'

9    Moses went up with Aaron, Nadab and Abihu, and seventy of the elders
10 of Israel, and they saw[b] the God of Israel. Under his feet there was, as it
11 were, a pavement of sapphire,[c] clear blue as the very heavens; but the
LORD did not stretch out his hand towards the leaders of Israel. They
12 stayed there before God;[d] they ate and they drank. The LORD said to
Moses, 'Come up to me on the mountain, stay there and let me give you
the tablets of stone, the law and the commandment, which I have written
13 down that you may teach them.' Moses arose with Joshua his assistant and
14 went up the mountain of God; he said to the elders, 'Wait for us here until
we come back to you. You have Aaron and Hur; if anyone has a dispute,
15 let him go to them.' So Moses went up the mountain and a cloud covered
16 it. The glory of the LORD rested upon Mount Sinai, and the cloud covered
the mountain for six days; on the seventh day he called to Moses out of
17 the cloud. The glory of the LORD looked to the Israelites like a devouring
18 fire on the mountain-top. Moses entered the cloud and went up the
mountain; there he stayed forty days and forty nights.

25 1 2   THE LORD SPOKE TO MOSES AND SAID: Tell the Israelites to set aside
a contribution for me; you shall accept whatever contribution each
3 man shall freely offer. This is what you shall accept: gold, silver, copper;
4 5 violet, purple, and scarlet yarn; fine linen and goats' hair; tanned rams'
6 skins, porpoise[e]-hides, and acacia-wood; oil for the lamp, balsam for the
7 anointing oil and for the fragrant incense; cornelian and other stones ready
8 for setting in the ephod and the breast-piece.[f] Make me a sanctuary, and
9 I will dwell among them. Make it exactly according to the design I show
you, the design for the Tabernacle and for all its furniture. This is how you
must make it:

10    Make an Ark, a chest of acacia-wood, two and a half cubits long, one
11 cubit and a half wide, and one cubit and a half high. Overlay it with pure
12 gold both inside and out, and put a band of gold all round it. Cast four gold
13 rings for it, and fasten them to its four feet, two rings on each side. Make
14 poles of acacia-wood and plate them with gold, and insert the poles in the
15 rings at the sides of the Ark to lift it. The poles shall remain in the rings of
16 the Ark and never be removed. Put into the Ark the Tokens of the Cove-
17 nant,[g] which I shall give you. Make a cover of pure gold, two and a half
18 cubits long and one cubit and a half wide. Make two gold cherubim of
19 beaten work at the ends of the cover, one at each end; make each cherub of

---

[a] *Or* upon.    [b] *Or* they were afraid of . . .    [c] *Or* lapis lazuli.    [d] *Or* They
saw God; and . . .    [e] *Strictly* sea-cow.    [f] *Or* pouch.    [g] Tokens of the
Covenant: *or* Testimony.

one piece with the cover. They shall be made with wings outspread and 20
pointing upwards, and shall screen the cover with their wings. They shall
be face to face, looking inwards over the cover. Put the cover above the 21
Ark, and put into the Ark the Tokens that I shall give you. It is there that 22
I shall meet you, and from above the cover, between the two cherubim
over the Ark of the Tokens, I shall deliver to you all my commands for the
Israelites.

Make a table of acacia-wood, two cubits long, one cubit wide, and one 23
cubit and a half high. Overlay it with pure gold, and put a band of gold all 24
round it. Make a rim round it a hand's breadth wide, and a gold band round 25
the rim. Make four gold rings for the table, and put the rings at the four 26
corners by the legs. The rings, which are to receive the poles for carrying 27
the table, must be adjacent to the rim. Make the poles of acacia-wood and 28
plate them with gold; they are to be used for carrying the table. Make its 29
dishes and saucers, and its flagons and bowls from which drink-offerings
may be poured: make them of pure gold. Put the Bread of the Presence*a* on 30
the table, to be always before me.

Make a lamp-stand of pure gold. The lamp-stand, stem and branches, 31
shall be of beaten work, its cups, both calyxes and petals, shall be of one
piece with it. There are to be six branches springing from its sides; three 32
branches of the lamp-stand shall spring from the one side and three
branches from the other side. There shall be three cups shaped like almond 33
blossoms, with calyx and petals, on the first branch, three cups shaped like
almond blossoms, with calyx and petals, on the next branch, and similarly
for all six branches springing from the lamp-stand. On the main stem of the 34
lamp-stand there are to be four cups shaped like almond blossoms, with
calyx and petals, and there shall be calyxes of one piece with it under the 35
six branches which spring from the lamp-stand, a single calyx under each
pair of branches. The calyxes and the branches are to be of one piece with 36
it, all a single piece of beaten work of pure gold. Make seven lamps for this 37
and mount them to shed light over the space in front of it. Its tongs and 38
firepans shall be of pure gold. The lamp-stand and all these fittings shall 39
be made from one talent of pure gold. See that you work to the design which 40
you were shown on the mountain.

Make the Tabernacle of ten hangings of finely woven linen, and violet, **26**
purple, and scarlet yarn, with cherubim worked on them, all made by a
seamster. The length of each hanging shall be twenty-eight cubits and the 2
breadth four cubits; all are to be of the same size. Five of the hangings shall 3
be joined together, and similarly the other five. Make violet loops along the 4
edge of the last hanging in each set, fifty for each set; they must be opposite 5
one another. Make fifty gold fasteners, join the hangings one to another 6
with them, and the Tabernacle will be a single whole.

Make hangings of goats' hair, eleven in all, to form a tent over the 7
Tabernacle; each hanging is to be thirty cubits long and four wide; all 8
eleven are to be of the same size. Join five of the hangings together, and 9
similarly the other six; then fold the sixth hanging double at the front of
the tent. Make fifty loops on the edge of the last hanging in the first set and 10

*a  Or* Shewbread.

11 make fifty loops on the joining edge of the second set. Make fifty bronze *a*
fasteners, insert them into the loops and join up the tent to make it a single
12 whole. The additional length of the tent hanging *b* is to fall over the back
13 of the Tabernacle. On each side there will be an additional cubit in the
length of the tent hangings; this shall fall over the two sides of the Taber-
14 nacle to cover it. Make for the tent a cover of tanned rams' skins and an
outer covering of porpoise-hides.

15 16    Make for the Tabernacle planks of acacia-wood as uprights, each plank
17 ten cubits long and a cubit and a half wide, and two tenons for each plank
joined to each other. You shall do the same for all the planks of the Taber-
18 nacle. Arrange the planks thus: twenty planks for the south side, facing
19 southwards, with forty silver sockets under them, two sockets under each
20 plank for its two tenons; and for the second or northern side of the Taber-
21 22 nacle, twenty planks, with forty silver sockets, two under each plank. Make
23 six planks for the far end of the Tabernacle on the west. Make two planks
24 for the corners of the Tabernacle at the far end; at the bottom they shall be
alike, and at the top, both alike, they shall fit into a single ring. Do the same
25 for both of them; they shall be for the two corners. There shall be eight
planks with their silver sockets, sixteen sockets in all, two sockets under
each plank severally.

26    Make bars of acacia-wood: five for the planks on the one side of the
27 Tabernacle, five for the planks on the other side and five for the planks on
28 the far end of the Tabernacle on the west. The middle bar is to run along
29 from end to end half-way up the planks. Overlay the planks with gold, make
30 rings of gold on them to hold the bars, and plate the bars with gold. Set up
the Tabernacle according to the design you were shown on the mountain.

31    Make a Veil of finely woven linen and violet, purple, and scarlet yarn,
32 with cherubim worked on it, all made by a seamster. Fasten it with hooks
of gold to four posts of acacia-wood overlaid with gold, standing in four
33 silver sockets. Hang the Veil below the fasteners and bring the Ark of the
Tokens inside the Veil. Thus the Veil will make a clear separation for you
34 between the Holy Place and the Holy of Holies. Place the cover over the
35 Ark of the Tokens in the Holy of Holies. Put the table outside the Veil and
the lamp-stand at the south side of the Tabernacle, opposite the table which
36 you shall put at the north side. For the entrance of the tent make a screen
37 of finely woven linen, embroidered with violet, purple, and scarlet. Make
five posts of acacia-wood for the screen and overlay them with gold; make
golden hooks for them and cast five bronze sockets for them.

27    Make the altar of acacia-wood; it shall be square, five cubits long by
2 five cubits broad and three cubits high. Let its horns at the four corners be
3 of one piece with it, and overlay it with bronze. Make for it pots to take away
the fat and the ashes, with shovels, tossing bowls, forks, and firepans, all
4 of bronze. Make a grating for it of bronze network, and fit four bronze rings
5 on the network at its four corners. Put it below the ledge of the altar, so that
6 the network comes half-way up the altar. Make poles of acacia-wood for
7 the altar and overlay them with bronze. They shall be inserted in the rings

*a Or* copper *and so throughout the description of the Tabernacle.*          *b Prob. rdg.; Heb.*
adds *half the hanging which remains over.*

at both sides of the altar to carry it. Leave the altar a hollow shell. As you 8
were shown on the mountain, so shall it be made.

Make the court of the Tabernacle. For the one side, the south side facing 9
southwards, the court shall have hangings of finely woven linen a hundred
cubits long, with twenty posts and twenty sockets of bronze; the hooks and 10
bands on the posts shall be of silver. Similarly all along the north side there 11
shall be hangings a hundred cubits long, with twenty posts and twenty
sockets of bronze; the hooks and bands on the posts shall be of silver. For 12
the breadth of the court, on the west side, there shall be hangings fifty
cubits long, with ten posts and ten sockets. On the east side, towards the 13
sunrise, which was fifty cubits, hangings shall extend fifteen cubits from 14
one corner, with three posts and three sockets, and hangings shall extend 15
fifteen cubits from the other corner, with three posts and three sockets. At 16
the gateway of the court, there shall be a screen twenty cubits long of finely
woven linen embroidered with violet, purple, and scarlet, with four posts
and four sockets. The posts all round the court shall have bands of silver, 17
with hooks of silver, and sockets of bronze. The length of the court shall be 18
a hundred cubits, and the breadth fifty, and the height five cubits, with
finely woven linen and bronze sockets throughout. All the equipment 19
needed for serving the Tabernacle, all its pegs and those of the court, shall
be of bronze.

You yourself are to command the Israelites to bring you pure oil of 20
pounded olives ready for the regular mounting of the lamp. In the Tent 21
of the Presence[a] outside the Veil that hides the Tokens, Aaron and his
sons shall keep the lamp in trim from dusk to dawn before the LORD.
This is a rule binding on their descendants among the Israelites for
all time.

You yourself are to summon to your presence your brother Aaron and **28**
his sons out of all the Israelites to serve as my priests: Aaron and his sons
Nadab and Abihu, Eleazar and Ithamar. For your brother Aaron make 2
sacred vestments, to give him dignity and grandeur. Tell all the craftsmen 3
whom I have endowed with skill to make the vestments for the consecration of Aaron as my priest. These are the vestments they shall make: a 4
breast-piece, an ephod, a mantle, a chequered tunic, a turban, and a sash.
They shall make sacred vestments for Aaron your brother and his sons to
wear when they serve as my priests, using gold; violet, purple, and scarlet 5
yarn; and fine linen.

The ephod shall be made of gold, and with violet, purple, and scarlet 6
yarn, and with finely woven linen worked by a seamster. It shall have two 7
shoulder-pieces joined back and front. The waist-band on it shall be of 8
the same workmanship and material as the fabric of the ephod, and shall
be of gold, with violet, purple, and scarlet yarn, and finely woven linen.
You shall take two cornelians and engrave on them the names of the sons 9
of Israel: six of their names on the one stone, and the six other names on 10
the second, all in order of seniority. With the skill of a craftsman, a seal- 11
cutter, you shall engrave the two stones with the names of the sons of
Israel; you shall set them in gold rosettes, and fasten them on the shoulders 12

[a] *Or* Tent of Meeting.

of the ephod, as reminders of the sons of Israel. Aaron shall bear their names on his two shoulders as a reminder before the LORD.

13 14 Make gold rosettes and two chains of pure gold worked into the form of
15 ropes, and fix them on the rosettes. Make the breast-piece of judgement; it shall be made, like the ephod, by a seamster in gold, with violet, purple,
16 and scarlet yarn, and finely woven linen. It shall be a square folded, a span
17 long and a span wide. Set in it four rows of precious stones: the first row,
18 sardin, chrysolite and green felspar; the second row, purple garnet, lapis
19 20 lazuli and jade; the third row, turquoise, agate and jasper; the fourth row,
21 topaz, cornelian and green jasper, all set in gold rosettes. The stones shall correspond to the twelve sons of Israel name by name; each stone shall bear the name of one of the twelve tribes engraved as on a seal.

22 23 Make for the breast-piece chains of pure gold worked into a rope. Make two gold rings, and fix them on the two upper corners of the breast-piece.
24 Fasten the two gold ropes to the two rings at those corners of the breast-
25 piece, and the other ends of the ropes to the two rosettes, thus binding the
26 breast-piece to the shoulder-pieces on the front of the ephod. Make two gold rings and put them at the two lower corners of the breast-piece on the
27 inner side next to the ephod. Make two gold rings and fix them on the two shoulder-pieces of the ephod, low down in front, along its seam above the
28 waist-band of the ephod. Then the breast-piece shall be bound by its rings to the rings of the ephod with violet braid, just above the waist-band of the ephod, so that the breast-piece will not be detached from the ephod.
29 Thus, when Aaron enters the Holy Place, he shall carry over his heart in the breast-piece of judgement the names of the sons of Israel, as a constant reminder before the LORD.
30 Finally, put the Urim and the Thummim into the breast-piece of judge-ment, and they will be over Aaron's heart when he enters the presence of the LORD. So shall Aaron bear these symbols of judgement upon the sons of Israel over his heart constantly before the LORD.

31 32 Make the mantle of the ephod a single piece of violet stuff. There shall be a hole for the head in the middle of it. All round the hole there shall be a
33 hem of woven work, with an oversewn edge, so that it cannot be torn. All round its skirts make pomegranates of violet, purple, and scarlet stuff, with
34 golden bells between them, a golden bell and a pomegranate alternately the
35 whole way round the skirts of the mantle. Aaron shall wear it when he ministers, and the sound of it shall be heard when he enters the Holy Place before the LORD and when he comes out; and so he shall not die.
36 Make a rosette of pure gold and engrave on it as on a seal, 'Holy to the
37 LORD'.*a* Fasten it on a violet braid and set it on the very front of the turban.
38 It shall be on Aaron's forehead; he has to bear the blame for shortcomings in the rites with which the Israelites offer their sacred gifts, and the rosette shall be always on his forehead so that they may be acceptable to the LORD.
39 Make the chequered tunic and the turban of fine linen, but the sash of
40 embroidered work. For Aaron's sons make tunics and sashes; and make tall
41 head-dresses to give them dignity and grandeur. With these invest your brother Aaron and his sons, anoint them, install them and consecrate

*a* as . . . LORD: *or* 'JEHOVAH' as on a seal in sacred characters.

them; so shall they serve me as priests. Make for them linen drawers 42
reaching to the thighs to cover their private parts; and Aaron and his sons 43
shall wear them when they enter the Tent of the Presence or approach the
altar to minister in the Holy Place. Thus they will not incur guilt and die.
This is a rule binding on him and his descendants for all time.

In consecrating them to be my priests this is the rite to be observed. Take **29**
a young bull and two rams without blemish. Take unleavened loaves, un- 2
leavened cakes mixed with oil, and unleavened wafers smeared with oil,
all made of wheaten flour; put them in a single basket and bring them in it. 3
Bring also the bull and the two rams. Bring Aaron and his sons to the 4
entrance of the Tent of the Presence, and wash them with water. Take the 5
vestments and invest Aaron with the tunic, the mantle of the ephod,
the ephod itself and the breast-piece, and fasten the ephod to him with its
waist-band. Set the turban on his head, and the symbol of holy dedication 6
on the turban. Take the anointing oil, pour it on his head and anoint him. 7
Then bring his sons forward, invest them with tunics, gird them with the 8 9
sashes and tie their tall head-dresses on them. They shall hold the priesthood by a rule binding for all time.

Next you shall install Aaron and his sons. Bring the bull to the front of the 10
Tent of the Presence, and they shall lay their hands on its head. Slaughter 11
the bull before the LORD at the entrance to the Tent of the Presence. Take 12
some of its blood, and put it with your finger on the horns of the altar. Pour
all the rest of it at the base of the altar. Then take the fat covering the entrails, 13
the long lobe of the liver, and the two kidneys with the fat upon them, and
burn it on the altar; but the flesh of the bull, and its skin and offal, you shall 14
destroy by fire outside the camp. It is a sin-offering.

Take one of the rams, and Aaron and his sons shall lay their hands on its 15
head. Then slaughter it, take its blood and fling it against the sides of the 16
altar. Cut the ram up; wash its entrails and its shins, lay them with the 17
pieces and the head, and burn the whole ram on the altar: it is a whole- 18
offering to the LORD; it is a soothing odour, a food-offering to the LORD.

Take the second ram, and let Aaron and his sons lay their hands on its 19
head. Then slaughter it, take some of its blood, and put it on the lobes of 20
the right ears of Aaron and his sons, and on their right thumbs and big toes.
Fling the rest of the blood against the sides of the altar. Take some of the 21
blood which is on the altar and some of the anointing oil, and sprinkle it on
Aaron and his vestments, and on his sons and their vestments. So shall he
and his vestments, and his sons and their vestments become holy. Take the 22
fat from the ram, the fat-tail, the fat covering the entrails, the long lobe of
the liver, the two kidneys with the fat upon them, and the right leg: for it is
a ram of installation. Take also one round loaf of bread, one cake cooked 23
with oil, and one wafer from the basket of unleavened bread that is before
the LORD. Set all these on the hands of Aaron and of his sons and present 24
them as a special gift before the LORD. Then take them out of their hands, 25
and burn them on the altar with the whole-offering for a soothing odour to
the LORD: it is a food-offering to the LORD. Take the breast of Aaron's ram 26
of installation, present it as a special gift before the LORD, and it shall be
your perquisite.

27  Hallow the breast of the special gift and the leg of the contribution, that
    which is presented and that which is set aside from the ram of installation,
28  that which is for Aaron and that which is for his sons; and they shall belong
    to Aaron and his sons, by a rule binding for all time, as a gift from the
    Israelites, for it is a contribution, set aside from their shared-offerings, their
    contribution to the LORD.
29  Aaron's sacred vestments shall be kept for the anointing and installation
30  of his sons after him. The priest appointed in his stead from among his
    sons, the one who enters *a* the Tent of the Presence to minister in the Holy
    Place, shall wear them for seven days.
31 32  Take the ram of installation, and boil its flesh in a sacred place; Aaron
    and his sons shall eat the ram's flesh and the bread left in the basket, at the
33  entrance to the Tent of the Presence. They shall eat the things with which
    expiation was made at their installation and their consecration. No un-
34  qualified person may eat them, for they are holy. If any of the flesh of the
    installation, or any of the bread, is left over till morning, you shall destroy
    it by fire; it shall not be eaten, for it is holy.
35  Do this with Aaron and his sons as I have commanded you, spending
    seven days over their installation.
36  Offer a bull daily, a sin-offering as expiation for sin; offer the sin-
    offering on the altar when you make expiation for it, and consecrate it by
37  anointing. For seven days you shall make expiation for the altar, and con-
    secrate it, and it shall be most holy. Whatever touches the altar shall be
    forfeit as sacred.
38  This is what you shall offer on the altar: two yearling rams regularly
39  every day. You shall offer the one ram at dawn, and the second between
40  dusk and dark, a tenth of an ephah of flour mixed with a quarter of a hin of
    pure oil of pounded olives, and a drink-offering of a quarter of a hin of wine
41  for the first ram. You shall offer the second ram between dusk and dark,
    and with it the same grain-offering and drink-offering as at dawn, for a
42  soothing odour: it is a food-offering to the LORD, a regular whole-offering
    in every generation; you shall make the offering at the entrance to the Tent
43  of the Presence before the LORD, where I meet you and speak to you. I
    shall meet the Israelites there, and the place will be hallowed by my glory.
44  I shall hallow the Tent of the Presence and the altar; and Aaron and his
45  sons I shall consecrate to serve me as priests. I shall dwell in the midst of
46  the Israelites, I shall become their God, and by my dwelling among them
    they will know that I am the LORD their God who brought them out of
    Egypt. I am the LORD their God.
30 1 2  Make an altar on which to burn incense; make it of acacia-wood. It shall
    be square, a cubit long by a cubit broad and two cubits high; the horns of
3   one piece with it. Overlay it with pure gold, the top, the sides all round, and
4   the horns; and put round it a band of gold. Make pairs of gold rings for it;
    put them under the band at the two corners on both sides to receive the
5   poles by which it is to be carried. Make the poles of acacia-wood and over-
6   lay them with gold. Put it before the Veil in front of the Ark of the Tokens
7   where I will meet you. On it Aaron shall burn fragrant incense; every

*a  Or* when he enters.

morning when he tends the lamps he shall burn the incense, and when he 8
mounts the lamps between dusk and dark, he shall burn the incense; so
there shall be a regular burning of incense before the LORD for all time.
You shall not offer on it any unauthorized incense, nor any whole-offering 9
or grain-offering; and you shall not pour a drink-offering over it. Aaron 10
shall make expiation with blood on its horns once a year; with blood from
the sin-offering of the yearly Expiation*a* he shall do this for all time. It is
most holy to the LORD.

The LORD spoke to Moses and said: When you number the Israelites 11 12
for the purpose of registration, each man shall give a ransom for his life
to the LORD, to avert plague among them during the registration. As each 13
man crosses over to those already counted he shall give half a shekel by the
sacred standard (twenty gerahs to the shekel) as a contribution to the LORD.
Everyone from twenty years old and upwards who has crossed over to those 14
already counted shall give a contribution to the LORD. The rich man shall 15
give no more than the half-shekel, and the poor man shall give no less, when
you give the contribution to the LORD to make expiation for your lives. The 16
money received from the Israelites for expiation you shall apply to the
service of the Tent of the Presence. The expiation for your lives shall be a
reminder of the Israelites to the LORD.

The LORD spoke to Moses and said: Make a bronze basin for ablution 17 18
with its stand of bronze; put it between the Tent of the Presence and the
altar, and fill it with water with which Aaron and his sons shall wash their 19
hands and feet. When they enter the Tent of the Presence they shall wash 20
with water, lest they die. So also when they approach the altar to minister,
to burn a food-offering to the LORD, they shall wash their hands and 21
feet, lest they die. It shall be a rule for all time binding on him and his
descendants in every generation.

The LORD spoke to Moses and said: You yourself shall take spices as 22 23
follows: five hundred shekels of sticks of myrrh, half that amount (two
hundred and fifty shekels) of fragrant cinnamon, two hundred and fifty
shekels of aromatic cane, five hundred shekels of cassia by the sacred 24
standard, and a hin of olive oil. From these prepare sacred anointing oil, 25
a perfume compounded by the perfumer's art. This shall be the sacred
anointing oil. Anoint with it the Tent of the Presence and the Ark of the 26
Tokens, the table and all its vessels, the lamp-stand and its fittings, the 27
altar of incense, the altar of whole-offering and all its vessels, the basin and 28
its stand. You shall consecrate them, and they shall be most holy; whatever 29
touches them shall be forfeit as sacred. Anoint Aaron and his sons, and 30
consecrate them to be my priests. Speak to the Israelites and say: This shall 31
be the holy anointing oil for my service in every generation. It shall not be 32
used for anointing the human body, and you must not prepare any oil like
it after the same prescription. It is holy, and you shall treat it as holy.
The man who compounds perfume like it, or who puts any of it on any 33
unqualified person, shall be cut off from his father's kin.

The LORD said to Moses, Take fragrant spices: gum resin,*b* aromatic 34
shell, galbanum; add pure frankincense to the spices in equal proportions.

---

*a Or* Atonement.          *b Or* mastic.

35 Make it into incense, perfume made by the perfumer's craft, salted and
36 pure, a holy thing. Pound some of it into fine powder, and put it in front of
the Tokens in the Tent of the Presence, where I shall meet you; you shall
37 treat it as most holy. The incense prepared according to this prescription
you shall not make for your own use. You shall treat it as holy to the LORD.
38 The man who makes any like it for his own pleasure shall be cut off from
his father's kin.

31 1 2 THE LORD SPOKE TO MOSES AND SAID, Mark this: I have specially
3 chosen Bezalel son of Uri, son of Hur, of the tribe of Judah. I have filled him
with divine spirit, making him skilful and ingenious, expert in every craft,
4 5 and a master of design, whether in gold, silver, copper, or cutting stones
6 to be set, or carving wood, for workmanship of every kind. Further, I have
appointed Aholiab*a* son of Ahisamach of the tribe of Dan to help him, and
I have endowed every skilled craftsman with the skill which he has. They
7 shall make everything that I have commanded you: the Tent of the Presence, the Ark for the Tokens, the cover over it, and all the furnishings of
8 the tent; the table and its vessels, the pure lamp-stand and all its fittings,
9 the altar of incense, the altar of whole-offering and all its vessels, the basin
10 and its stand; the stitched vestments, that is the sacred vestments for
Aaron the priest and the vestments for his sons when they minister as
11 priests, the anointing oil and the fragrant incense for the Holy Place. They
shall carry out all I have commanded you.

12 13     The LORD spoke to Moses and said, Speak to the Israelites, you yourself,
and say to them: Above all you shall observe my sabbaths, for the sabbath
is a sign between me and you in every generation that you may know that
14 I am the LORD who hallows you. You shall keep the sabbath, because it is
a holy day for you. If anyone profanes it he must be put to death. Anyone
15 who does work on it shall be cut off from his father's kin. Work may be
done on six days, but on the seventh day there is a sabbath of sacred rest,
holy to the LORD. Whoever does work on the sabbath day must be put to
16 death. The Israelites shall keep the sabbath, they shall keep it in every
17 generation as a covenant for ever. It is a sign for ever between me and the
Israelites, for in six days the LORD made the heavens and the earth, but on
the seventh day he ceased work and refreshed himself.
18     When he had finished speaking with Moses on Mount Sinai, the LORD
gave him the two tablets of the Tokens, tablets of stone written with the
finger of God.

32 WHEN THE PEOPLE SAW that Moses was so long in coming down from
the mountain, they confronted Aaron and said to him, 'Come, make us
gods to go ahead of us. As for this fellow Moses, who brought us up from
2 Egypt, we do not know what has become of him.' Aaron answered them,
'Strip the gold rings from the ears of your wives and daughters, and bring
3 them to me.' So all the people stripped themselves of their gold earrings
4 and brought them to Aaron. He took them out of their hands, cast the
metal in a mould, and made it into the image of a bull-calf. 'These', he

        *a Or* Oholiab.

said, 'are your gods, O Israel, that brought you up from Egypt.' Then Aaron 5
was afraid and built an altar in front of it and issued this proclamation,
'Tomorrow there is to be a pilgrim-feast to the LORD.' Next day the people 6
rose early, offered whole-offerings, and brought shared-offerings. After this
they sat down to eat and drink and then gave themselves up to revelry.
But the LORD said to Moses, 'Go down at once, for your people, the people 7
you brought up from Egypt, have done a disgraceful thing; so quickly have 8
they turned aside from the way I commanded them. They have made
themselves an image of a bull-calf, they have prostrated themselves before
it, sacrificed to it and said, "These are your gods, O Israel, that brought
you up from Egypt."' So the LORD said to Moses, 'I have considered this 9
people, and I see that they are a stubborn people. Now, let me alone to vent 10
my anger upon them, so that I may put an end to them and make a great
nation spring from you.' But Moses set himself to placate the LORD his 11
God: 'O LORD,' he said, 'why shouldst thou vent thy anger upon thy
people, whom thou didst bring out of Egypt with great power and a strong
hand? Why let the Egyptians say, "So he meant evil when he took them 12
out, to kill them in the mountains and wipe them off the face of the earth"?
Turn from thy anger, and think better of the evil thou dost intend against
thy people. Remember Abraham, Isaac and Israel, thy servants, to whom 13
thou didst swear by thy own self: "I will make your posterity countless as
the stars in the sky, and all this land, of which I have spoken, I will give to
them, and they shall possess it for ever."' So the LORD relented, and spared 14
his people the evil with which he had threatened them.

Moses turned and went down the mountain with the two tablets of the 15
Tokens in his hands, inscribed on both sides; on the front and on the back
they were inscribed. The tablets were the handiwork of God, and the 16
writing was God's writing, engraved on the tablets. Joshua, hearing the 17
uproar the people were making, said to Moses, 'Listen! There is fighting
in the camp.' Moses replied, 18

> 'This is not the clamour of warriors,
> nor the clamour of a defeated people;
> it is the sound of singing that I hear.'

As he approached the camp, Moses saw the bull-calf and the dancing, and 19
he was angry; he flung the tablets down, and they were shattered to pieces
at the foot of the mountain. Then he took the calf they had made and burnt 20
it; he ground it to powder, sprinkled it on water, and made the Israelites
drink it. He demanded of Aaron, 'What did this people do to you that you 21
should have brought such great guilt upon them?' Aaron replied, 'Do not 22
be angry, sir. The people were deeply troubled; that you well know. And 23
they said to me, "Make us gods to go ahead of us, because, as for this fellow
Moses, who brought us up from Egypt, we do not know what has become
of him." So I said to them, "Those of you who have any gold, strip it off." 24
They gave it me, I threw it in the fire, and out came this bull-calf.' Moses 25
saw that the people were out of control and that Aaron had laid them open
to the secret malice of their enemies. He took his place at the gate of the 26
camp and said, 'Who is on the LORD's side? Come here to me'; and the

27 Levites all rallied to him. He said to them, 'These are the words of the LORD the God of Israel: "Arm yourselves, each of you, with his sword. Go through the camp from gate to gate and back again. Each of you kill his
28 brother, his friend, his neighbour."' The Levites obeyed, and about three
29 thousand of the people died that day. Moses then said, 'Today you have consecrated yourselves to the LORD completely, because you have turned each against his own son and his own brother and so have this day brought a blessing upon yourselves.'

30   The next day Moses said to the people, 'You have committed a great sin. I shall now go up to the LORD; perhaps I may be able to secure pardon for
31 your sin.' So Moses returned to the LORD and said, 'O hear me! This people has committed a great sin: they have made themselves gods of gold.
32 If thou wilt forgive them, forgive. But if not, blot out my name, I pray,
33 from thy book which thou hast written.' The LORD answered Moses, 'It is the man who has sinned against me that I will blot out from my book.
34 But go now, lead the people to the place which I have told you of. My angel shall go ahead of you, but a day will come when I shall punish them
35 for their sin.' And the LORD smote the people for worshipping the bull-calf which Aaron had made.

**33** THE LORD SPOKE TO MOSES: 'Come, go up from here, you and the people you have brought up from Egypt, to the land which I swore to Abraham,
2 Isaac, and Jacob that I would give to their posterity. I will send an angel ahead of you, and will drive out the Canaanites, the Amorites and the
3 Hittites and the Perizzites, the Hivites and the Jebusites. I will bring you to a land flowing with milk and honey, but I will not journey in your company, for fear that I annihilate you on the way; for you are a stubborn
4 people.' When the people heard this harsh sentence they went about like
5 mourners, and no man put on his ornaments. The LORD said to Moses, 'Tell the Israelites, "You are a stubborn people: at any moment, if I journey in your company, I may annihilate you. Put away your ornaments
6 now, and I will determine what to do to you."' And so the Israelites stripped off their ornaments, and wore them no more from Mount Horeb onwards.
7   Moses used to take a*a* tent and pitch it at a distance outside the camp. He called it the Tent of the Presence, and everyone who sought the LORD
8 would go out to the Tent of the Presence outside the camp. Whenever Moses went out to the tent, all the people would rise and stand, each at the entrance to his tent, and follow Moses with their eyes until he entered the
9 tent. When Moses entered it, the pillar of cloud came down, and stayed at
10 the entrance to the tent while the LORD spoke with Moses. As soon as the people saw the pillar of cloud standing at the entrance to the tent, they
11 would all prostrate themselves, every man at the entrance to his tent. The LORD would speak with Moses face to face, as one man speaks to another. Then Moses would return to the camp, but his young assistant, Joshua son of Nun, never moved from inside the tent.
12   Moses said to the LORD, 'Thou bidst me lead this people up, but thou hast not told me whom thou wilt send with me. Thou hast said to me, "I

*a Or the.*

know you by name, and, further, you have found favour with me." If I 13
have indeed won thy favour, then teach me to know thy way, so that I can
know thee and continue in favour with thee, for this nation is thy own
people.' The LORD answered, 'I will go with you in person and set your 14
mind at rest.' Moses said to him, 'Indeed if thou dost not go in person, do 15
not send us up from here; for how can it ever be known that I and thy people 16
have found favour with thee, except by thy going with us? So shall we be
distinct, I and thy people, from all the peoples on earth.' The LORD said 17
to Moses, 'I will do this thing that you have asked, because you have found
favour with me, and I know you by name.'

And Moses prayed, 'Show me thy glory.' The LORD answered, 'I will 18 19
make all my goodness*a* pass before you, and I will pronounce in your
hearing the Name JEHOVAH. *b* I will be gracious to whom I will be gracious,
and I will have compassion on whom I will have compassion.' But he added, 20
'My face you cannot see, for no mortal man may see me and live.' The LORD 21
said, 'Here is a place beside me. Take your stand on the rock and when my 22
glory passes by, I will put you in a crevice of the rock and cover you with
my hand until I have passed by. Then I will take away my hand, and you 23
shall see my back, but my face shall not be seen.'

The LORD said to Moses, 'Cut two stone tablets like the first, and I will **34**
write on the tablets the words which were on the first tablets, which you
broke in pieces. Be ready by morning. Then in the morning go up Mount 2
Sinai; stand and wait for me there on the top. No man shall go up with you, 3
no man shall even be seen anywhere on the mountain, nor shall flocks or
herds graze within sight of that mountain.' So Moses cut two stone tablets 4
like the first, and he rose early in the morning and went up Mount Sinai
as the LORD had commanded him, taking the two stone tablets in his hands.
And the LORD came down in the cloud and took his place beside him and 5
pronounced the Name JEHOVAH. Then the LORD passed in front of him 6
and called aloud, 'JEHOVAH, the LORD, a god compassionate and gracious,
long-suffering, ever constant and true, maintaining constancy to thou- 7
sands, forgiving iniquity, rebellion, and sin, and not sweeping the guilty
clean away; but one who punishes sons and grandsons to the third and
fourth generation for the iniquity of their fathers!' Moses made haste, 8
bowed to the ground and prostrated himself. He said, 'If I have indeed won 9
thy favour, O Lord, then may the Lord go in our company. However stubborn a people they are, forgive our iniquity and our sin and take us as thy
own possession.'

The LORD said, Here and now I make a covenant. In full view of all 10
your people I will do such miracles as have never been performed in all
the world or in any nation. All the surrounding peoples shall see the work
of the LORD, for fearful is that which I will do for you. *c* Observe all I com- 11
mand you this day; and I for my part will drive out before you the Amorites
and the Canaanites and the Hittites and the Perizzites and the Hivites and
the Jebusites. Be careful not to make a covenant with the natives of the land 12
against which you are going, or they will prove a snare in your midst. No: 13

---

*a* Or character.   *b* *See note on 3. 15.*   *c* for fearful . . . for you: *or* (for he is to
be feared) which I will do for you.

you shall demolish their altars, smash their sacred pillars and cut down their
14 sacred poles. You shall not prostrate yourselves to any other god. For the
15 LORD's name is the Jealous God, and a jealous god he is. Be careful not to
make a covenant with the natives of the land, or, when they go wantonly
after their gods and sacrifice to them, you may be invited, any one of you,
16 to partake of their sacrifices, and marry your sons to their daughters, and
when their daughters go wantonly after their gods, they may lead your sons
astray too.

17 You shall not make yourselves gods of cast metal.

18 You shall observe the pilgrim-feast of Unleavened Bread: for seven days,
as I have commanded you, you shall eat unleavened cakes at the appointed
time, in the month of Abib, because in the month of Abib you went out
from Egypt.

19 Every first birth of the womb belongs to me, and the males of all your
20 herds, both cattle and sheep. You may buy back the first birth of an ass by
giving a sheep instead, but if you do not buy it, you must break its neck.
You shall buy back all the first-born of your sons, and no one shall come
into my presence empty-handed.

21 For six days you shall work, but on the seventh day you shall cease work;
even at ploughing time and harvest you shall cease work.

22 You shall observe the pilgrim-feast of Weeks, the firstfruits of the wheat
23 harvest, and the pilgrim-feast of Ingathering at the turn of the year. Three
times a year all your males shall come into the presence of the Lord, the
24 LORD the God of Israel; for after I have driven out the nations before you
and extended your frontiers, there will be no danger from covetous neighbours when you go up these three times to enter the presence of the LORD
your God.

25 You shall not offer the blood of my sacrifice at the same time as anything
leavened, nor shall any portion of the victim of the pilgrim-feast of Passover remain overnight till morning.

26 You shall bring the choicest firstfruits of your soil to the house of the
LORD your God.

You shall not boil a kid in its mother's milk.

27 The LORD said to Moses, 'Write these words down, because the cove-
28 nant I make with you and with Israel is in these words.' So Moses stayed
there with the LORD forty days and forty nights, neither eating nor drinking,
and wrote down the words of the covenant, the Ten Words,[a] on the tablets.

29 At length Moses came down from Mount Sinai with the two stone tablets
of the Tokens in his hands, and when he descended, he did not know that
the skin of his face shone because he had been speaking with the LORD.
30 When Aaron and the Israelites saw how the skin of Moses' face shone, they
31 were afraid to approach him. He called out to them, and Aaron and all the
32 chiefs in the congregation turned towards him. Moses spoke to them, and
afterwards all the Israelites drew near. He gave them all the commands
33 with which the LORD had charged him on Mount Sinai, and finished what
he had to say.

34 Then Moses put a veil over his face, and whenever he went in before the

a *Or* Ten Commandments.

LORD to speak with him, he removed the veil until he came out. Then he would go out and tell the Israelites all the commands he had received. Whenever the skin of Moses' face shone in the sight of the Israelites, he 35 would put the veil back over his face until he went in again to speak with the LORD.

M OSES CALLED THE WHOLE COMMUNITY of Israelites together and **35** thus addressed them: These are the LORD's commands to you: On 2 six days you may work, but the seventh you are to keep as a sabbath of sacred rest, holy to the LORD. Whoever works on that day shall be put to death. You are not even to light your fire at home on the sabbath day. 3

These words Moses spoke to all the community of Israelites: This is the 4 command the LORD has given: Each of you set aside a contribution to the 5 LORD. Let all who wish, bring a contribution to the LORD: gold, silver, copper; violet, purple, and scarlet yarn; fine linen and goats' hair; tanned 6 7 rams' skins, porpoise-hides, and acacia-wood; oil for the lamp, perfume for 8 the anointing oil and for the fragrant incense; cornelians and other stones 9 ready for setting in the ephod and the breast-piece. Let every craftsman 10 among you come and make everything the LORD has commanded. The 11 Tabernacle, its tent and covering, fasteners, planks, bars, posts, and sockets, the Ark and its poles, the cover and the Veil of the screen, the table, 12 13 its poles, and all its vessels, and the Bread of the Presence, the lamp- 14 stand for the light, its fittings, lamps and the lamp oil; the altar of incense 15 and its poles, the anointing oil, the fragrant incense, and the screen for the entrance of the Tabernacle, the altar of whole-offering, its bronze grating, 16 poles, and all appurtenances, the basin and its stand; the hangings of the 17 court, its posts and sockets, and the screen for the gateway of the court; the pegs of the Tabernacle and court and their cords, the stitched vest- 18 19 ments for ministering in the Holy Place, that is the sacred vestments for Aaron the priest and the vestments for his sons when they minister as priests.

The whole community of the Israelites went out from Moses' presence, 20 and everyone who was so minded brought of his own free will a contribu- 21 tion to the LORD for the making of the Tent of the Presence and all its service, and for the sacred vestments. Men and women alike came and 22 freely brought clasps, earrings, finger-rings, and pendants, gold ornaments of every kind, every one of them presenting a special gift of gold to the LORD. And every man brought what he possessed of violet, purple, and 23 scarlet yarn, fine linen and goats' hair, tanned rams' skins and porpoise-hides. Every man, setting aside a contribution of silver or copper, brought 24 it as a contribution to the LORD, and all who had acacia-wood suitable for any part of the work brought it. Every woman with the skill spun and 25 brought the violet, purple, and scarlet yarn, and fine linen. All the women 26 whose skill moved them spun the goats' hair. The chiefs brought cornelians 27 and other stones ready for setting in the ephod and the breast-piece, the 28 perfume and oil for the light, for the anointing oil, and for the fragrant incense. Every Israelite man and woman who was minded to bring offerings 29 to the Lord for all the work which he had commanded through Moses did so freely.

30 Moses said to the Israelites, 'Mark this: the Lord has specially chosen
31 Bezalel son of Uri, son of Hur, of the tribe of Judah. He has filled him with
32 divine spirit, making him skilful and ingenious, expert in every craft, and
33 a master of design, whether in gold, silver, and copper, or cutting precious
34 stones for setting, or carving wood, in every kind of design. He has inspired
both him and Aholiab son of Ahisamach of the tribe of Dan to instruct
35 workers and designers of every kind, engravers, seamsters, embroiderers
in violet, purple, and scarlet yarn and fine linen, and weavers, fully endow-
36 ing them with skill to execute all kinds of work. Bezalel and Aholiab shall
work exactly as the Lord has commanded, and so also shall every craftsman
whom the Lord has made skilful and ingenious in these matters, to know
how to execute every kind of work for the service of the sanctuary.'
2 Moses summoned Bezalel, Aholiab, and every craftsman to whom the
Lord had given skill and who was willing, to come forward and set to work.
3 They received from Moses every contribution which the Israelites had
brought for the work of the service of the sanctuary, but the people still
4 brought freewill offerings morning after morning, so that the craftsmen at
work on the sanctuary left what they were doing, every one of them, and
5 came to Moses and said, 'The people are bringing much more than we
6 need for doing the work which the Lord has commanded.' So Moses sent
word round the camp that no man or woman should prepare anything more
as a contribution for the sanctuary. So the people stopped bringing gifts;
7 what was there already was more than enough for all the work they had to do.
8 Then all the craftsmen among the workers made the Tabernacle of ten
hangings of finely woven linen, and violet, purple, and scarlet yarn, with
9 cherubim worked on them, all made by a seamster. The length of each
hanging was twenty-eight cubits and the breadth four cubits, all of the
10 same size. They joined five of the hangings together, and similarly the other
11 five. They made violet loops on the outer edge of the one set of hangings
12 and they did the same for the outer edge of the other set of hangings. They
made fifty loops for each hanging; they made also fifty loops for the end
13 hanging in the second set, the loops being opposite each other. They made
fifty gold fasteners, with which they joined the hangings one to another,
and the Tabernacle became a single whole.
14 They made hangings of goats' hair, eleven in all, to form a tent over the
15 Tabernacle; each hanging was thirty cubits long and four cubits wide, all
16 eleven of the same size. They joined five of the hangings together, and
17 similarly the other six. They made fifty loops on the edge of the outer
hanging in the first set and fifty loops on the joining edge of the second set,
18 and fifty bronze fasteners to join up the tent and make it a single whole.
19 They made for the tent a cover of tanned rams' skins and an outer covering
of porpoise-hides.
20 21 They made for the Tabernacle planks of acacia-wood as uprights, each
22 plank ten cubits long and a cubit and a half wide, and two tenons for each
plank joined to each other. They did the same for all the planks of the
23 Tabernacle. They arranged the planks thus: twenty planks for the south

side, facing southwards, with forty silver sockets under them, two sockets 24
under each plank for its two tenons; and for the second or northern side 25
of the Tabernacle twenty planks with forty silver sockets, two under each 26
plank. They made six planks for the far end of the Tabernacle on the west. 27
They made two planks for the corners of the Tabernacle at the far end; at 28 29
the bottom they were alike, and at the top, both alike, they fitted into a
single ring. They did the same for both of them at the two corners. There 30
were eight planks with their silver sockets, sixteen sockets in all, two sockets
under each plank.

They made bars of acacia-wood: five for the planks on the one side of 31
the Tabernacle, five bars for the planks on the second side of the Taber- 32
nacle, and five bars for the planks on the far end of the Tabernacle on the
west. They made the middle bar to run along from end to end half-way up 33
the frames. They overlaid the frames with gold, made rings of gold on them 34
to hold the bars and plated the bars with gold.

They made the Veil of finely woven linen and violet, purple, and scarlet 35
yarn, with cherubim worked on it, all made by a seamster. And they made 36
for it four posts of acacia-wood overlaid with gold, with gold hooks, and
cast four silver sockets for them. For the entrance of the tent a screen of 37
finely woven linen was made, embroidered with violet, purple, and scarlet,
and five posts of acacia-wood with their hooks. They overlaid the tops of 38
the posts and the bands round them with gold; the five sockets for them
were of bronze.

Bezalel then made the Ark, a chest of acacia-wood, two and a half cubits **37**
long, one cubit and a half wide, and one cubit and a half high. He overlaid 2
it with pure gold, both inside and out, and put a band of gold all round it.
He cast four gold rings to be on its four feet, two rings on each side of it. 3
He made poles of acacia-wood and plated them with gold, and inserted the 4 5
poles in the rings at the sides of the Ark to lift it. He made a cover of pure 6
gold, two and a half cubits long and one cubit and a half wide. He made 7
two gold cherubim of beaten work at the ends of the cover, one at each end; 8
he made each cherub of one piece with the cover. They had wings outspread 9
and pointing upwards, screening the cover with their wings; they stood
face to face, looking inwards over the cover.

He made the table of acacia-wood, two cubits long, one cubit wide, and 10
one cubit and a half high. He overlaid it with pure gold and put a band of 11
gold all round it. He made a rim round it a hand's breadth wide, and a gold 12
band round the rim. He cast four gold rings for it, and put the rings at the 13
four corners by the four legs. The rings, which were to receive the poles 14
for carrying the table, were close to the rim. These carrying-poles he made 15
of acacia-wood and plated them with gold. He made the vessels for the 16
table, its dishes and saucers, and its flagons and bowls from which drink-
offerings were to be poured; he made them of pure gold.

He made the lamp-stand of pure gold. The lamp-stand, stem, and 17
branches, were of beaten work, its cups, both calyxes and petals, were of
one piece with it. There were six branches springing from its sides; three 18
branches of the lamp-stand sprang from one side and three branches from
the other side. There were three cups shaped like almond blossoms, with 19

calyx and petals, on the first branch, three cups shaped like almond blossoms, with calyx and petals, on the next branch, and similarly for all six
20 branches springing from the lamp-stand. On the main stem of the lamp-
stand there were four cups shaped like almond blossoms, with calyx and
21 petals, and there were calyxes of one piece with it under the six branches
which sprang from the lamp-stand, a single calyx under each pair of
22 branches. The calyxes and the branches were of one piece with it, all a
23 single piece of beaten work of pure gold. He made its seven lamps, its tongs
24 and firepans of pure gold. The lamp-stand and all these fittings were made
from one talent of pure gold.

25 He made the altar of incense of acacia-wood, square, a cubit long by a
26 cubit broad and two cubits high, the horns of one piece with it. He overlaid it with pure gold, the top, the sides all round, and the horns, and he
27 put round it a band of gold. He made pairs of gold rings for it; he put them
under the band at the two corners on both sides to receive the poles by
28 which it was to be carried. He made the poles of acacia-wood and overlaid
them with gold.

29 He prepared the sacred anointing oil and the fragrant incense, pure,
compounded by the perfumer's art.

**38** He made the altar of whole-offering of acacia-wood, square, five cubits
2 long by five cubits broad and three cubits high. Its horns at the four corners
3 were of one piece with it, and he overlaid it with bronze. He made all the
vessels for the altar, its pots, shovels, tossing bowls, forks, and firepans,
4 all of bronze. He made for the altar a grating of bronze network under the
5 ledge, coming half-way up. He cast four rings for the four corners of the
6 bronze grating to receive the poles, and he made the poles of acacia-wood
7 and overlaid them with bronze. He inserted the poles in the rings at the
sides of the altar to carry it. He left the altar a hollow shell.

8 The basin and its stand of bronze he made out of the bronze mirrors of
the women who were on duty at the entrance to the Tent of the Presence.

9 He made the court. For the south side facing southwards the hangings
10 of the court were of finely woven linen a hundred cubits long, with twenty
posts and twenty sockets of bronze; the hooks and bands on the posts were
11 of silver. Along the north side there were hangings of a hundred cubits,
with twenty posts and twenty sockets of bronze; the hooks and bands on
12 the posts were of silver. On the west side there were hangings fifty cubits
long, with ten posts and ten sockets; the hooks and bands on the posts were
13 14-15 of silver. On the east side, towards the sunrise, fifty cubits, there were
hangings on either side of the gateway of the court; they extended fifteen
cubits to one corner, with their three posts and their three sockets, and
fifteen cubits to the second corner, with their three posts and their three
16 sockets. The hangings of the court all round were of finely woven linen.
17 The sockets for the posts were of bronze, the hooks and bands on the posts
of silver, the tops of them overlaid with silver, and all the posts of the court
18 were bound with silver. The screen at the gateway of the court was of finely
woven linen, embroidered with violet, purple, and scarlet, twenty cubits
19 long and five cubits high to correspond to the hangings of the court, with
four posts and four sockets of bronze, their hooks of silver, and the tops of

them and their bands overlaid with silver. All the pegs for the Tabernacle 20 and those for the court were of bronze.

These were the appointments of the Tabernacle, that is the Tabernacle 21 of the Tokens which was assigned by Moses to the charge of the Levites under Ithamar son of Aaron the priest. Bezalel son of Uri, son of Hur, of 22 the tribe of Judah made everything the LORD had commanded Moses. He 23 was assisted by Aholiab son of Ahisamach of the tribe of Dan, an engraver, a seamster, and an embroiderer in fine linen with violet, purple, and scarlet yarn.

The gold of the special gift used for the work of the sanctuary amounted 24 in all to twenty-nine talents seven hundred and thirty shekels, by the sacred standard. The silver contributed by the community when registered was 25 one hundred talents one thousand seven hundred and seventy-five shekels, by the sacred standard.

This amounted to a beka a head, that is half a shekel by the sacred 26 standard, for every man from twenty years old and upwards, who had been registered, a total of six hundred and three thousand five hundred and fifty men. The hundred talents of silver were for casting the sockets for the 27 sanctuary and for the Veil, a hundred sockets to a hundred talents, a talent to a socket. With the one thousand seven hundred and seventy-five shekels 28 he made hooks for the posts, overlaid the tops of the posts and put bands round them. The bronze of the special gift came to seventy talents two 29 thousand four hundred shekels; with this he made sockets for the entrance 30 to the Tent of the Presence, the bronze altar and its bronze grating, all the vessels for the altar, the sockets all round the court, the sockets for the posts 31 at the gateway of the court, all the pegs for the Tabernacle, and the pegs all round the court.

They used violet, purple, and scarlet yarn in making the stitched vest- **39** ments for ministering in the sanctuary and in making the sacred vestments for Aaron, as the LORD had commanded Moses.

They made the ephod of gold, with violet, purple, and scarlet yarn, and 2 finely woven linen. The gold was beaten into thin plates, cut and twisted 3 into braid to be worked in by a seamster with the violet, purple, and scarlet yarn, and fine linen. They made shoulder-pieces for it, joined back and 4 front. The waist-band on it was of the same workmanship and material as 5 the fabric of the ephod; it was gold, with violet, purple, and scarlet yarn, and finely woven linen, as the LORD commanded Moses.

They prepared the cornelians, fixed in gold rosettes, engraved by the 6 art of a seal-cutter with the names of the sons of Israel, and fastened them 7 on the shoulders of the ephod as reminders of the sons of Israel, as the LORD had commanded Moses.

They made the breast-piece; it was worked like the ephod by a seamster, 8 in gold, with violet, purple, and scarlet yarn, and finely woven linen. They 9 made the breast-piece square, folded, a span long and a span wide. They 10 set in it four rows of precious stones: the first row, sardin, chrysolite and green felspar; the second row, purple garnet, lapis lazuli and jade; the 11 12 third row, turquoise, agate and jasper; the fourth row, topaz, cornelian and 13 green jasper, all set in gold rosettes. The stones corresponded to the twelve 14

sons of Israel, name by name, each bearing the name of one of the twelve
15 tribes engraved as on a seal. They made for the breast-piece twisted cords
16 of pure gold worked into a rope. They made two gold rosettes and two
gold rings, and they fixed the two rings on the two corners of the breast-
17 piece. They fastened the two gold ropes to the two rings at those corners
18 of the breast-piece, and the other ends of the two ropes to the two rosettes,
19 thus binding them to the shoulder-pieces on the front of the ephod. They
made two gold rings and put them at the two corners of the breast-piece on
20 the inner side next to the ephod. They made two gold rings and fixed them
on the two shoulder-pieces of the ephod, low down and in front, close to its
21 seam above the waist-band on the ephod. They bound the breast-piece by
its rings to the rings of the ephod with a violet braid, just above the waist-
band on the ephod, so that the breast-piece would not become detached
22 from the ephod; so the LORD had commanded Moses. They made the
23 mantle of the ephod a single piece of woven violet stuff, with a hole in the
middle of it which had a hem round it, with an oversewn edge so that it
24 could not be torn. All round its skirts they made pomegranates of violet,
25 purple, and scarlet stuff, and finely woven linen. They made bells of pure
gold and put them all round the skirts of the mantle between the pome-
26 granates, a bell and a pomegranate alternately the whole way round the
skirts of the mantle, to be worn when ministering, as the LORD commanded
Moses.

27 They made the tunics of fine linen, woven work, for Aaron and his sons,
28 the turban of fine linen, the tall head-dresses and their bands all of fine
29 linen, the drawers of finely woven linen, and the sash of finely woven linen,
embroidered in violet, purple, and scarlet, as the LORD had commanded
Moses.

30 They made a rosette of pure gold as the symbol of their holy dedication
31 and inscribed on it as the engraving on a seal, 'Holy to the LORD', *a* and
they fastened on it a violet braid to fix it on the turban at the top, as the
LORD had commanded Moses.

32 Thus all the work of the Tabernacle of the Tent of the Presence was
completed, and the Israelites did everything exactly as the LORD had com-
33 manded Moses. They brought the Tabernacle to Moses, the tent and all
34 its furnishings, its fasteners, planks, bars, posts and sockets, the covering
of tanned rams' skins and the outer covering of porpoise-hides, the Veil of
35 36 the screen, the Ark of the Tokens and its poles, the cover, the table and its
37 vessels, and the Bread of the Presence, the pure lamp-stand with its lamps
38 in a row and all its fittings, and the lamp oil, the gold altar, the anointing
39 oil, the fragrant incense, and the screen at the entrance of the tent, the
bronze altar, the bronze grating attached to it, its poles and all its furnish-
40 ings, the basin and its stand, the hangings of the court, its posts and sockets,
the screen for the gateway of the court, its cords and pegs, and all the equip-
41 ment for the service of the Tabernacle for the Tent of the Presence, the
stitched vestments for ministering in the sanctuary, that is the sacred
vestments for Aaron the priest and the vestments for his sons when they
42 minister as priests. As the LORD had commanded Moses, so the Israelites

*a* on it . . . LORD: *or* 'JEHOVAH' on it in sacred characters as engraved on a seal.

carried out the whole work. Moses inspected all the work, and saw that 43 they had carried it out according to the command of the LORD; and he blessed them.

THE LORD SPOKE TO MOSES AND SAID: On the first day of the first 40 1 2 month you shall set up the Tabernacle, the Tent of the Presence. You 3 shall put the Ark of the Tokens in it and screen the Ark with the Veil. You 4 shall bring in the table and lay it; then you shall bring in the lamp-stand and mount its lamps. You shall then set the gold altar of incense in front 5 of the Ark of the Tokens and put the screen of the entrance of the Tabernacle in place. You shall put the altar of whole-offering in front of the 6 entrance of the Tabernacle, the Tent of the Presence. You shall put the 7 basin between the Tent of the Presence and the altar and put water in it. You shall set up the court all round and put in place the screen of the gate- 8 way of the court. You shall take the anointing oil and anoint the Taber- 9 nacle and everything in it; thus you shall consecrate it and all its furnishings, and it shall be holy. You shall anoint the altar of whole-offering and all its 10 vessels; thus shall you consecrate it, and it shall be most holy. You shall 11 anoint the basin and its stand and consecrate it. You shall bring Aaron 12 and his sons to the entrance of the Tent of the Presence and wash them with the water. Then you shall clothe Aaron with the sacred vestments, anoint 13 him and consecrate him; so shall he be my priest. You shall then bring 14 forward his sons, clothe them in tunics, anoint them as you anointed their 15 father, and they shall be my priests. Their anointing shall inaugurate a hereditary priesthood for all time.

Exactly as the LORD had commanded him, so Moses did. In the first 16 17 month of the second year, on the first day of that month, the Tabernacle was set up.

Moses set up the Tabernacle. He put the sockets in place, inserted the 18 planks, fixed the crossbars and set up the posts. He spread the tent over 19 the Tabernacle and fixed the covering of the tent above it, as the LORD had commanded him. He took the Tokens and put them in the Ark, in- 20 serted the poles in the Ark, and put the cover over the top of the Ark. He 21 brought the Ark into the Tabernacle, set up the Veil of the screen and so screened the Ark of the Tokens, as the LORD had commanded him. He put 22 the table in the Tent of the Presence on the north side of the Tabernacle outside the Veil and arranged bread on it before the LORD, as the LORD 23 had commanded him. He set the lamp-stand in the Tent of the Presence 24 opposite the table at the south side of the Tabernacle and mounted the 25 lamps before the LORD, as the LORD had commanded him. He set up the 26 gold altar in the Tent of the Presence in front of the Veil and burnt fra- 27 grant incense on it, as the LORD had commanded him. He set up the screen 28 at the entrance of the Tabernacle, fixed the altar of whole-offering at the 29 entrance of the Tabernacle, the Tent of the Presence, and offered on it whole-offerings and grain-offerings, as the LORD had commanded him. He set up the basin between the Tent of the Presence and the altar and 30 put water there for washing, and Moses and Aaron and his sons used to 31 wash their hands and feet when they entered the Tent of the Presence or 32

33 approached the altar, as the LORD had commanded Moses. He set up the
court all round the Tabernacle and the altar, and put a screen at the gateway of the court.

34 Thus Moses completed the work, and the cloud covered the Tent of the
35 Presence, and the glory of the LORD filled the Tabernacle. Moses was unable to enter the Tent of the Presence, because the cloud had settled on it
36 and the glory of the LORD filled the Tabernacle. At every stage of their
journey, when the cloud lifted from the Tabernacle, the Israelites broke
37 camp; but if the cloud did not lift from the Tabernacle, they did not break
38 camp until the day it lifted. For the cloud of the LORD hovered over the
Tabernacle by day, and there was fire in the cloud by night, and the
Israelites could see it at every stage of their journey.

# LEVITICUS

## *Laws concerning offerings and sacrifices*

1 THE LORD SUMMONED MOSES and spoke to him from
2 the Tent of the Presence, and said, Say this to the Israelites: When
any man among you presents an animal as an offering to the LORD,
the offering may be presented either from the herd or from the flock.

3 If his offering is a whole-offering from the cattle, he shall present a male
without blemish; he shall present it at the entrance to the Tent of the
4 Presence before the LORD so as to secure acceptance for himself. He shall
lay his hand on the head of the victim and it will be accepted on his behalf*a*
5 to make expiation for him. He shall slaughter the bull before the LORD,
and the Aaronite priests shall present the blood and fling it against the altar
6 all round at the entrance of the Tent of the Presence. He shall then flay
7 the victim and cut it up. The sons of Aaron the priest shall kindle a fire
8 on the altar and arrange wood on the fire. The Aaronite priests shall arrange
the pieces, including the head and the suet, on the wood on the altar-
9 fire, the entrails and shins shall be washed in water, and the priest shall
burn it all on the altar as a whole-offering, a food-offering of soothing odour
to the LORD.

10 If the man's whole-offering is from the flock, either from the rams or
11 from the goats, he shall present a male without blemish. He shall slaughter
it before the LORD at the north side of the altar, and the Aaronite priests
12 shall fling the blood against the altar all round. He shall cut it up, and the
priest shall arrange the pieces, together with the head and the suet, on the
13 wood on the altar-fire, the entrails and shins shall be washed in water, and
the priest shall present and burn it all on the altar: it is a whole-offering, a
food-offering of soothing odour to the LORD.

14 If a man's offering to the LORD is a whole-offering of birds, he shall

*a Or* by him (*the* LORD).

present turtle-doves or young pigeons as his offering. The priest shall 15
present it at the altar, and shall wrench off the head and burn it on the altar; and the blood shall be drained out against the side of the altar. He shall 16
take away the crop and its contents in one piece, and throw it to the east side of the altar where the ashes are. He shall tear it by its wings without 17
severing them completely, and shall burn it on the altar, on top of the wood of the altar-fire: it is a whole-offering, a food-offering of soothing odour to the LORD.

When any person presents a grain-offering to the LORD, his offering 2
shall be of flour. He shall pour oil on it and add frankincense to it. He shall 2
bring it to the Aaronite priests, one of whom shall scoop up a handful of the flour and oil with all the frankincense. The priest shall burn this as a token on the altar, a food-offering of soothing odour to the LORD. The 3
remainder of the grain-offering belongs to Aaron and his sons: it is most sacred, it is taken from the food-offerings of the LORD.

When you present as a grain-offering something baked in an oven, it 4
shall consist of unleavened cakes of flour mixed with oil and unleavened wafers smeared with oil. If your offering is a grain-offering cooked on a 5
griddle, it shall be an unleavened cake of flour mixed with oil. Crumble it 6
in pieces and pour oil on it. This is a grain-offering.

If your offering is a grain-offering cooked in a pan, it shall be made of 7
flour with oil. Bring an offering made up in this way to the LORD and 8
present it to the priest, who shall bring it to the altar; then he shall set aside 9
part of the grain-offering as a token and burn it on the altar, a food-offering of soothing odour to the LORD. The remainder of the grain-offering belongs 10
to Aaron and his sons: it is most sacred, it is taken from the food-offerings of the LORD.

No grain-offering which you present to the LORD shall be made of any- 11
thing that ferments; you shall not burn any leaven or any honey as a food-offering to the LORD. As for your offering of firstfruits, you shall present 12
them to the LORD, but they shall not be offered up at the altar as a soothing odour. Every offering of yours which is a grain-offering shall be salted; 13
you shall not fail to put the salt of your covenant with God on your grain-offering. Salt shall accompany all offerings.

If you present to the LORD a grain-offering of first-ripe grain, you must 14
present fresh corn roasted, crushed meal from fully ripened corn. You 15
shall add oil to it and put frankincense upon it. This is a grain-offering. The priest shall burn as its token some of the crushed meal, some of the 16
oil, and all the frankincense as a food-offering to the LORD.

If a man's offering is a shared-offering from the cattle, male or female, 3
he shall present it without blemish before the LORD. He shall lay his hand 2
on the head of the victim and slaughter it at the entrance to the Tent of the Presence. The Aaronite priests shall fling the blood against the altar all round. One of them shall present part of the shared-offering as a food- 3
offering to the LORD: he shall remove the fat covering the entrails and all the fat upon the entrails, the two kidneys with the fat on them be- 4
side the haunches, and the long lobe of the liver with the kidneys. The 5
Aaronites shall burn it on the altar on top of the whole-offering which

is upon the wood on the fire, a food-offering of soothing odour to the LORD.

6  If a man's offering as a shared-offering to the LORD is from the flock,
7 male or female, he shall present it without blemish. If he is presenting a
8 ram as his offering, he shall present it before the LORD, lay his hand on the
head of the victim and slaughter it in front of the Tent of the Presence. The
9 Aaronites shall then fling its blood against the altar all round. He shall
present part of the shared-offering as a food-offering to the LORD; he
shall remove its fat, the entire fat-tail cut off close by the spine, the fat
10 covering the entrails and all the fat upon the entrails, the two kidneys
with the fat on them beside the haunches, and the long lobe of the liver
11 with the kidneys. The priest shall burn it at the altar, as food offered to the
LORD.

12 13  If the man's offering is a goat, he shall present it before the LORD, lay
his hand on its head and slaughter it in front of the Tent of the Presence.
14 The Aaronites shall then fling its blood against the altar all round. He shall
present part of the victim as a food-offering to the LORD; he shall remove
15 the fat covering the entrails and all the fat upon the entrails, the two kidneys
with the fat on them beside the haunches, and the long lobe of the liver
16 with the kidneys. The priest shall burn this at the altar, as a food-offering
17 of soothing odour. All fat belongs to the LORD. This is a rule for all time
from generation to generation wherever you live: you shall not eat any fat
or any blood.

4 1 2  THE LORD SPOKE TO MOSES and said, Say this to the Israelites: These
are the rules for any man who inadvertently transgresses any of the commandments of the LORD and does anything prohibited by them:
3  If the anointed priest sins so as to bring guilt on the people, for the sin
he has committed he shall present to the LORD a young bull without blem-
4 ish as a sin-offering. He shall bring the bull to the entrance of the Tent of
the Presence before the LORD, lay his hand on its head and slaughter it
5 before the LORD. The anointed priest shall then take some of its blood and
6 bring it to the Tent of the Presence. He shall dip his finger in the blood and
sprinkle some of the blood in front of the sacred Veil seven times before
7 the LORD. The priest shall then put some of the blood before the LORD in
the Tent of the Presence on the horns of the altar where fragrant incense
is burnt, and he shall pour the rest of the bull's blood at the base of the altar
8 of whole-offering at the entrance of the Tent of the Presence. He shall set
aside all the fat from the bull of the sin-offering; he shall set aside the fat
9 covering the entrails and all the fat upon the entrails, the two kidneys with
the fat on them beside the haunches, and the long lobe of the liver with the
10 kidneys. It shall be set aside as the fat from the ox at the shared-offering is
set aside. The priest shall burn the pieces of fat on the altar of whole-
11 offering. But the skin of the bull and all its flesh, including head and shins,
12 its entrails and offal, the whole of it, he shall take away outside the camp
to a place ritually clean, where the ash-heap is, and destroy it on a wood-
fire on top of the ash-heap.
13  If the whole community of Israel sins inadvertently and the matter is

not known to the assembly, if they do what is forbidden in any commandment of the LORD and so incur guilt, then, when the sin they have com- 14
mitted is notified to them, the assembly shall present a young bull as a
sin-offering and shall bring it in front of the Tent of the Presence. The 15
elders of the community shall lay their hands on the victim's head before
the LORD, and it shall be slaughtered before the LORD. The anointed priest 16
shall then bring some of the blood to the Tent of the Presence, dip his 17
finger in it and sprinkle it in front of the Veil seven times before the LORD.
He shall put some of the blood on the horns of the altar before the LORD in 18
the Tent of the Presence and pour all the rest at the base of the altar of
whole-offering at the entrance of the Tent of the Presence. He shall then set 19
aside all the fat from the bull and burn it on the altar. He shall deal with this 20
bull as he deals with the bull of the sin-offering, and in this way the priest
shall make expiation for their guilt and they shall be forgiven. He shall take 21
the bull outside the camp and burn it as the other bull was burnt. This is
a sin-offering for the assembly.

　　When a man of standing sins by doing inadvertently what is forbidden in 22
any commandment of the LORD his God, thereby incurring guilt, and the 23
sin he has committed is made known to him, he shall bring as his offering
a he-goat without blemish. He shall lay his hand on the goat's head and 24
shall slaughter it before the LORD in the place where the whole-offering is
slaughtered. It is a sin-offering. The priest shall then take some of the 25
blood of the victim with his finger and put it on the horns of the altar of
whole-offering. He shall pour out the rest of the blood at the base of the
altar of whole-offering. He shall burn all the fat at the altar in the same way 26
as the fat of the shared-offering. Thus the priest shall make expiation for
that man's sin, and it shall be forgiven him.

　　If any person among the common people sins inadvertently and does 27
what is forbidden in any commandment of the LORD, thereby incurring
guilt, and the sin he has committed is made known to him, he shall bring 28
as his offering for the sin which he has committed a she-goat without
blemish. He shall lay his hand on the head of the victim and slaughter it in 29
the place where the whole-offering is slaughtered. The priest shall then take 30
some of its blood with his finger and put it on the horns of the altar of whole-
offering. All the rest of the blood he shall pour at the base of the altar. He 31
shall remove all its fat as the fat of the shared-offering is removed, and the
priest shall burn it on the altar as a soothing odour to the LORD. So the priest
shall make expiation for that person's guilt, and it shall be forgiven him.

　　If the man brings a sheep as his offering for sin, it shall be a ewe without 32
blemish. He shall lay his hand on the head of the victim and slaughter it as 33
a sin-offering in the place where the whole-offering is slaughtered. The 34
priest shall then take some of the blood of the victim with his finger and
put it on the horns of the altar of whole-offering. All the rest of the blood
he shall pour out at the base of the altar. He shall remove all the fat, as the 35
fat of the sheep is removed from the shared-offering. The priest shall burn
the pieces of fat at the altar on top of the food-offerings to the LORD, and
shall make expiation for the sin that the man has committed, and it shall
be forgiven him.

5 IF A PERSON HEARS a solemn adjuration to give evidence as a witness to something he has seen or heard and does not declare what he knows, he commits a sin and must accept responsibility.

2   If a person touches anything unclean, such as the dead body of an un-
3 clean animal, whether wild or domestic, or of an unclean reptile, or if he touches anything unclean in a man, whatever that uncleanness may be, and
4 it is concealed by him although he is aware of it, he shall incur guilt. Or if a person rashly utters an oath to do something evil or good, in any matter in which such a man may swear a rash oath, and it is concealed by him
5 although he is aware of it, he shall in either case incur guilt. Whenever a man incurs guilt in any of these cases and confesses how he has sinned
6 therein, he shall bring to the LORD, as his penalty for the sin that he has committed, a female of the flock, either a ewe or a she-goat, as a sin-offering, and the priest shall make expiation for him on account of his sin which he has committed, and he shall be pardoned.

7   But if he cannot afford as much as a young animal, he shall bring to the LORD for the sin he has committed two turtle-doves or two young pigeons,
8 one for a sin-offering and the other for a whole-offering. He shall bring them to the priest, and present first the one intended for the sin-offering.
9 He shall wrench its head back without severing it. He shall sprinkle some of the blood of the victim against the side of the altar, and what is left of the blood shall be drained out at the base of the altar: it is a sin-offering.
10 He shall deal with the second bird as a whole-offering according to custom, and the priest shall make expiation for the sin the man has committed, and it shall be forgiven him.

11   If the man cannot afford two turtle-doves or two young pigeons, for his sin he shall bring as his offering a tenth of an ephah of flour, as a sin-offering. He shall add no oil to it nor put frankincense on it, because it is a sin-
12 offering. He shall bring it to the priest, who shall scoop up a handful from it as a token and burn it on the altar on the food-offerings to the LORD: it
13 is a sin-offering. The priest shall make expiation for the sin the man has committed in any one of these cases, and it shall be forgiven him. The remainder belongs to the priest, as with the grain-offering.

14 15   The LORD spoke to Moses and said: When any person commits an offence by inadvertently defaulting in dues sacred to the LORD, he shall bring as his guilt-offering to the LORD a ram without blemish from the flock, the value to be determined by you in silver shekels according to the
16 sacred standard, for a guilt-offering; he shall make good his default in sacred dues, adding one fifth. He shall give it to the priest, who shall make expiation for his sin with the ram of the guilt-offering, and it shall be forgiven him.

17   If and when any person sins unwittingly and does what is forbidden by any commandment of the LORD, thereby incurring guilt, he must accept
18 responsibility. He shall bring to the priest as a guilt-offering a ram without blemish from the flock, valued by you, and the priest shall make expiation for the error into which he has unwittingly fallen, and it shall be forgiven
19 him. It is a guilt-offering; he has been guilty of an offence against the LORD.
6 1 2   The LORD spoke to Moses and said: When any person sins and commits

a grievous fault against the LORD, whether he lies to a fellow-countryman about a deposit or contract, or a theft, or wrongs him by extortion, or finds 3 lost property and then lies about it, and swears a false oath in regard to any sin of this sort that he commits—if he does this, thereby incurring guilt, 4 he shall restore what he has stolen or gained by extortion, or the deposit left with him or the lost property which he found, or anything at all con- 5 cerning which he swore a false oath. He shall make full restitution, adding one fifth to it, and give it back to the aggrieved party on the day when he offers his guilt-offering. He shall bring to the LORD as his guilt-offering a 6 ram without blemish from the flock, valued by you, as a guilt-offering. The 7 priest shall make expiation for his guilt before the LORD, and he shall be forgiven for any act which has brought guilt upon him.

THE LORD SPOKE TO MOSES and said, Give this command to Aaron and 8 9 his sons: This is the law of the whole-offering. The whole-offering shall remain on the altar-hearth all night till morning, and the altar-fire shall be kept burning there. Then the priest, having donned his linen robe and put 10 on linen drawers to cover himself, shall remove the ashes to which the fire reduces the whole-offering on the altar and put them beside the altar. He 11 shall then change into other garments and take the ashes outside the camp to a ritually clean place. The fire shall be kept burning on the altar; it shall 12 never go out. Every morning the priest shall have fresh wood burning thereon, arrange the whole-offering on it, and on top burn the fat from the shared-offerings. Fire shall always be kept burning on the altar; it shall not 13 go out.

This is the law of the grain-offering. The Aaronites shall present it before 14 the LORD in front of the altar. The priest shall set aside a handful of the 15 flour from it, with the oil of the grain-offering, and all the frankincense on it. He shall burn this token of it on the altar as a soothing odour to the LORD. The remainder Aaron and his sons shall eat. It shall be eaten in the 16 form of unleavened cakes and in a holy place. They shall eat it in the court of the Tent of the Presence. It shall not be baked with leaven. I have 17 allotted this to them as their share of my food-offerings. Like the sin-offering and the guilt-offering, it is most sacred. Any male descendant of 18 Aaron may eat it, as a due from the food-offerings to the LORD, for genera-tion after generation for all time. Whatever touches them is to be forfeit as sacred.

The LORD spoke to Moses and said: This is the offering which Aaron 19 20 and his sons shall present to the LORD:*a* one tenth of an ephah of flour, the usual grain-offering, half of it in the morning and half in the evening. It 21 shall be cooked with oil on a griddle; you shall bring it well-mixed, and so present it crumbled in small pieces as a grain-offering, a soothing odour to the LORD. The anointed priest in the line of Aaron shall offer it. This is a 22 rule binding for all time. It shall be burnt in sacrifice to the LORD as a complete offering. Every grain-offering of a priest shall be a complete 23 offering; it shall not be eaten.

The LORD spoke to Moses and said, Speak to Aaron and his sons in these 24 25

*a Prob. rdg.; Heb. adds* on the day when he is anointed.

words: This is the law of the sin-offering. The sin-offering shall be slaughtered before the LORD in the place where the whole-offering is slaughtered;
26 it is most sacred. The priest who officiates shall eat of the flesh; it shall be
27 eaten in a sacred place, in the court of the Tent of the Presence. Whatever
touches its flesh is to be forfeit as sacred. If any of the blood is splashed on
28 a garment, that shall be washed in a sacred place. An earthenware vessel
in which the sin-offering is boiled shall be smashed. If it has been boiled
29 in a copper vessel, that shall be scoured and rinsed with water. Any male
30 of priestly family may eat of this offering; it is most sacred. If, however,
part of the blood is brought to the Tent of the Presence to make expiation
in the holy place, the sin-offering shall not be eaten; it shall be destroyed
by fire.

7 1 2     This is the law of the guilt-offering: it is most sacred. The guilt-offering
shall be slaughtered in the place where the whole-offering is slaughtered,
3 and its blood shall be flung against the altar all round. The priest shall set
aside and present all the fat from it: the fat-tail and the fat covering the
4 entrails, the two kidneys with the fat on them beside the haunches, and
5 the long lobe of the liver with the kidneys. The priest shall burn these pieces
6 on the altar as a food-offering to the LORD; it is a guilt-offering. Any male
of priestly family may eat it. It shall be eaten in a sacred place; it is most
7 sacred. There is one law for both sin-offering and guilt-offering: they shall
8 belong to the priest who performs the rite of expiation. The skin of any
9 man's whole-offering shall belong to the priest who presents it. Every
grain-offering baked in an oven and everything that is cooked in a pan or
10 on a griddle shall belong to the priest who presents it. Every grain-offering,
whether mixed with oil or dry, shall be shared equally among all the
Aaronites.

11 12     This is the law of the shared-offering presented to the LORD. If a man
presents it as a thank-offering, then, in addition to the thank-offering, he
shall present unleavened cakes mixed with oil, wafers of unleavened flour
13 smeared with oil, and well-mixed flour and flat cakes mixed with oil. He
shall present flat cakes of leavened bread in addition to his shared thank-
14 offering. One part of every offering he shall present as a contribution for
the LORD: it shall belong to the priest who flings the blood of the shared-
15 offering against the altar. The flesh shall be eaten on the day of its presenta-
tion; none of it shall be put aside till morning.

16     If a man's sacrifice is a votive offering or a freewill offering, it may be
17 eaten on the day it is presented or on the next day. Any flesh left over on
18 the third day shall be destroyed by fire. If any flesh of his shared-offering
is eaten on the third day, the man who has presented it shall not be accepted.
It will not be counted to his credit, it shall be reckoned as tainted and the
19 person who eats any of it shall accept responsibility. No flesh which comes
into contact with anything unclean shall be eaten; it shall be destroyed by
fire.

20     The flesh may be eaten by anyone who is clean, but the person who,
while unclean, eats flesh from a shared-offering presented to the LORD
21 shall be cut off from his father's kin. When any person is contaminated by
contact with anything unclean, be it man, beast, or reptile, and then eats

any of the flesh from the shared-offerings presented to the LORD, that person shall be cut off from his father's kin.

The LORD spoke to Moses and said, Speak to the Israelites in these words: 22 23 You shall not eat the fat of any ox, sheep, or goat. The fat of an animal that 24 has died a natural death or has been mauled by wild beasts may be put to any other use, but you shall not eat it. Every man who eats fat from a beast 25 of which he has presented any part as a food-offering to the LORD shall be cut off from his father's kin.

You shall eat none of the blood, whether of bird or of beast, wherever you 26 may live. Every person who eats any of the blood shall be cut off from his 27 father's kin.

The LORD spoke to Moses and said, Speak to the Israelites in these 28 29 words: Whoever comes to present a shared-offering shall set aside part of it as an offering to the LORD. With his own hands he shall bring the food- 30 offerings to the LORD. He shall also bring the fat together with the breast which is to be presented as a special gift before the LORD; the priest shall 31 burn the fat on the altar, but the breast shall belong to Aaron and his descendants. You shall give the right hind-leg of your shared-offerings as 32 a contribution for the priest; it shall be the perquisite of the Aaronite who 33 presents the blood and the fat of the shared-offering. I have taken from the 34 Israelites the breast of the special gift and the leg of the contribution made out of the shared-offerings, and have given them as a due from the Israelites to Aaron the priest and his descendants for all time. This is the portion 35 prescribed for Aaron and his descendants out of the LORD's food-offerings, appointed on the day when they were presented as priests to the LORD; and on the day when they were anointed, the LORD commanded that these 36 prescribed portions should be given to them by the Israelites. This is a rule binding on their descendants for all time.

This, then, is the law of the whole-offering, the grain-offering, the sin- 37 offering, the guilt-offering, the installation-offerings, and the shared-offerings, with which the LORD charged Moses on Mount Sinai on the day 38 when he commanded the Israelites to present their offerings to the LORD in the wilderness of Sinai.

## The hallowing and installation of the priests

THE LORD SPOKE TO MOSES and said, 'Take Aaron and his sons with 8 1 2 him, the vestments, the anointing oil, the ox for a sin-offering, the two rams, and the basket of unleavened cakes, and assemble all the community 3 at the entrance to the Tent of the Presence.' Moses did as the LORD had 4 commanded him, and the community assembled at the entrance to the Tent of the Presence. He told the community that this was what the LORD 5 had commanded. He presented Aaron and his sons and washed them in 6 water. He invested Aaron with the tunic, girded him with the sash, robed 7 him with the mantle, put the ephod on him, tied it with its waist-band and fastened the ephod to him with the band. He put the breast-piece*a* on him 8

*a Or* pouch.

9 and set the Urim and Thummim in it. He then put the turban upon his head and set the gold rosette as a symbol of holy dedication on the front of
10 the turban, as the LORD had commanded him. Moses then took the anointing oil, anointed the Tabernacle and all that was within it and consecrated
11 them. He sprinkled some of the oil seven times on the altar, anointing the
12 altar, all its vessels, the basin and its stand, to consecrate them. He poured
13 some of the anointing oil on Aaron's head and so consecrated him. Moses then brought the sons of Aaron forward, invested them with tunics, girded them with sashes and tied their tall head-dresses on them, as the LORD had commanded him.

14 He then brought up the ox for the sin-offering; Aaron and his sons laid
15 their hands on its head, and he slaughtered it. Moses took some of the blood and put it with his finger on the horns round the altar. Thus he purified the altar, and when he had poured out the rest of the blood at the base of the
16 altar, he consecrated it by making expiation for it. He took all the fat upon the entrails, the long lobe of the liver, and the two kidneys with their fat,
17 and burnt them on the altar, but the ox, its skin, its flesh, and its offal, he destroyed by fire outside the camp, as the LORD had commanded him.
18 Moses then brought forward the ram of the whole-offering; Aaron and
19 his sons laid their hands on the ram's head, and he slaughtered it. Moses
20 flung its blood against the altar all round. He cut the ram up and burnt
21 the head, the pieces, and the suet. He washed the entrails and the shins in water and burnt the whole on the altar. This was a whole-offering, a food-offering of soothing odour to the LORD, as the LORD had commanded Moses.
22 Moses then brought forward the second ram, the ram for the installation
23 of priests. Aaron and his sons laid their hands upon its head, and he slaughtered it. Moses took some of its blood and put it on the lobe of Aaron's right ear, on his right thumb, and on the big toe of his right foot.
24 He then brought forward the sons of Aaron, put some of the blood on the lobes of their right ears, on their right thumbs, and on the big toes of their
25 right feet. He flung the rest of the blood against the altar all round; he took the fat, the fat-tail, the fat covering the entrails, the long lobe of the
26 liver, the two kidneys with their fat, and the right leg. Then from the basket of unleavened cakes before the LORD he took one unleavened cake, one cake of bread made with oil, and one wafer, and laid them on the fatty
27 parts and the right leg. He put the whole on the hands of Aaron and of his
28 sons, and he presented it as a special gift before the LORD. He took it from their hands and burnt it on the altar on top of the whole-offering. This was an installation-offering, it was a food-offering of soothing odour to the LORD.
29 Moses then took the breast and presented it as a special gift before the LORD; it was his portion of the ram of installation, as the LORD had com-
30 manded him. He took some of the anointing oil and some of the blood on the altar and sprinkled it on Aaron and his vestments, and on his sons and their vestments with him. Thus he consecrated Aaron and his vestments, and with him his sons and their vestments.
31 Moses said to Aaron and his sons, 'Boil the flesh of the ram at the entrance to the Tent of the Presence, and eat it there, together with the bread in the

installation-basket, in accordance with the command: "Aaron and his sons shall eat it." The remainder of the flesh and bread you shall destroy by fire. 32 You shall not leave the entrance to the Tent of the Presence for seven days, 33 until the day which completes the period of your installation, for it lasts seven days. What was done this day followed the LORD's command to 34 make expiation for you. You shall stay at the entrance to the Tent of the 35 Presence day and night for seven days, keeping vigil to the LORD, so that you do not die, for so I was commanded.'

Aaron and his sons did everything that the LORD had commanded 36 through Moses.

On the eighth day Moses summoned Aaron and his sons and the 9 Israelite elders. He said to Aaron, 'Take for yourself a bull-calf for a sin- 2 offering and a ram for a whole-offering, both without blemish, and present them before the LORD. Then bid the Israelites take a he-goat for a sin- 3 offering, a calf and a lamb, both yearlings without blemish, for a whole-offering, and a bull and a ram for shared-offerings to be sacrificed before the 4 LORD, together with a grain-offering mixed with oil. This day the LORD will appear to you.'

They brought what Moses had commanded to the front of the Tent of 5 the Presence, and all the community approached and stood before the LORD. Moses said, 'This is what the LORD has commanded you to do, so 6 that the glory of the LORD may appear to you. Come near to the altar,' he 7 said to Aaron; 'prepare your sin-offering and your whole-offering and make expiation for yourself and for your household. Then prepare the offering of the people and make expiation for them, as the LORD has commanded.'

So Aaron came near to the altar and slaughtered the calf, which was his 8 sin-offering. The sons of Aaron presented the blood to him, and he dipped 9 his finger in the blood and put it on the horns of the altar. The rest of the blood he poured out at the base of the altar. Part of the sin-offering, the 10 fat, the kidneys, and the long lobe of the liver, he burnt on the altar as the LORD had commanded Moses, but the flesh and the skin he destroyed 11 by fire outside the camp. Then he slaughtered the whole-offering; his sons 12 handed him the blood, and he flung it against the altar all round. They 13 handed him the pieces of the whole-offering and the head, and he burnt them on the altar. He washed the entrails and the shins and burnt them 14 on the altar, on top of the whole-offering.

He then brought forward the offering of the people. He took the he-goat, 15 the people's sin-offering, slaughtered it and performed the rite of the sin-offering as he had previously done for himself. He presented the whole- 16 offering and prepared it in the manner prescribed. He brought forward 17 the grain-offering, took a handful of it and burnt it on the altar, in addition to the morning whole-offering. He slaughtered the bull and the ram, the 18 shared-offerings of the people. His sons handed him the blood, and he flung it against the altar all round. But the fatty parts of the bull, the fat- 19 tail of the ram, the fat covering the entrails, and the two kidneys with the fat upon them, and the long lobe of the liver, all this fat they first put on 20 the breasts of the animals and then burnt it on the altar. Aaron presented 21 the breasts and the right leg as a special gift before the LORD, as Moses had commanded.

22 Then Aaron lifted up his hands towards the people and pronounced the blessing over them. He came down from performing the rites of the sin-
23 offering, the whole-offering, and the shared-offerings. Moses and Aaron entered the Tent of the Presence, and when they came out, they blessed the
24 people, and the glory of the LORD appeared to all the people. Fire came out from before the LORD and consumed the whole-offering and the fatty parts on the altar. All the people saw, and they shouted and fell on their faces.

10 NOW NADAB AND ABIHU, sons of Aaron, took their firepans, put fire in them, threw incense on the fire and presented before the LORD illicit fire
2 which he had not commanded. Fire came out from before the LORD and
3 destroyed them; and so they died in the presence of the LORD. Then Moses said to Aaron, 'This is what the LORD meant when he said: Among those who approach me, I must be treated as holy; in the presence of all the
4 people I must be given honour.' Aaron was dumbfounded. Moses sent for Mishael and Elzaphan, the sons of Aaron's uncle Uzziel, and said to them, 'Come and carry your cousins outside the camp away from the holy place.'
5 They came and carried them away in their tunics outside the camp, as
6 Moses had told them. Moses then said to Aaron and to his sons Eleazar and Ithamar, 'You shall not leave your hair dishevelled or tear your clothes in mourning, lest you die and the LORD be angry with the whole community. Your kinsmen, all the house of Israel, shall weep for the destruction by fire
7 which the LORD has kindled. You shall not leave the entrance to the Tent of the Presence lest you die, because the LORD's anointing oil is on you.' They did as Moses had said.

8 9 THE LORD SPOKE TO AARON and said: You and your sons with you shall not drink wine or strong drink when you are to enter the Tent of the Presence, lest you die. This is a rule binding on your descendants for all
10 time, to make a distinction between sacred and profane, between clean and
11 unclean, and to teach the Israelites all the decrees which the LORD has spoken to them through Moses.
12 Moses said to Aaron and his surviving sons Eleazar and Ithamar, 'Take what is left over of the grain-offering out of the food-offerings of the LORD,
13 and eat it without leaven beside the altar; it is most sacred. You shall eat it in a sacred place; it is your due and that of your sons out of the LORD's
14 food-offerings, for so I was commanded. You shall eat the breast of the special gift and the leg of the contribution in a clean place, you and your sons and daughters; for they have been given to you and your children as
15 your due out of the shared-offerings of the Israelites. The leg of the contribution and the breast of the special gift shall be brought, along with the food-offerings of fat, to be presented as a special gift before the LORD, and it shall belong to you and your children together, a due for all time; for so the LORD has commanded.'
16 Moses made searching inquiry about the goat of the sin-offering and found that it had been burnt. He was angry with Eleazar and Ithamar,

Aaron's surviving sons, and said, 'Why did you not eat the sin-offering in 17
the sacred place? It is most sacred. It was given to you to take away the
guilt of the community by making expiation for them before the LORD. If 18
the blood is not brought within the sacred precincts, you shall eat the sin-
offering there as I was commanded.' But Aaron replied to Moses, 'See, 19
they have today presented their sin-offering and their whole-offering before
the LORD, and this is what has befallen me; if I eat a sin-offering today, will
it be right in the eyes of the LORD?' When Moses heard this, he deemed it 20
right.

## Laws of purification and atonement

THE LORD SPOKE TO MOSES and Aaron and said, Speak to the Israel- 11 1 2
ites in these words: Of all animals on land these are the creatures you
may eat: you may eat any animal which has a parted foot or a cloven hoof 3
and also chews the cud; those which have only a cloven hoof or only chew 4
the cud you may not eat. These are: the camel, because it chews the cud
but has not a cloven hoof; you shall regard it as unclean; the rock-badger,*a* 5
because it chews the cud but has not a parted foot; you shall regard it as
unclean; the hare, because it chews the cud but has not a parted foot; you 6
shall regard it as unclean; the pig, because it has a parted foot and a cloven 7
hoof but does not chew the cud; you shall regard it as unclean. You shall 8
not eat their flesh or even touch their dead bodies; you shall regard them
as unclean.

Of creatures that live in water these you may eat: all those that have fins 9
and scales, whether in salt water or fresh; but all that have neither fins nor 10
scales, whether in salt or fresh water, including both small creatures in
shoals and larger creatures, you shall regard as vermin. They shall be 11
vermin to you; you shall not eat their flesh, and their dead bodies you shall
treat as those of vermin. Every creature in the water that has neither fins 12
nor scales shall be vermin to you.

These are the birds you shall regard as vermin, and for this reason they 13
shall not be eaten: the griffon-vulture,*b* the black vulture, and the bearded
vulture;*c* the kite and every kind of falcon; every kind of crow,*d* the desert- 14 15 16
owl, the short-eared owl, the long-eared owl, and every kind of hawk; the 17
tawny owl, the fisher-owl, and the screech-owl; the little owl, the horned 18
owl, the osprey, the stork,*e* every kind of cormorant, the hoopoe, and 19
the bat.

All teeming winged creatures that go on four legs shall be vermin to you, 20
except those which have legs jointed above their feet for leaping on the 21
ground. Of these you may eat every kind of great locust, every kind of long- 22
headed locust, every kind of green locust, and every kind of desert locust.
Every other teeming winged creature that has four legs you shall regard as 23
vermin; you would make yourselves unclean with them: whoever *f* touches 24
their dead bodies shall be unclean till evening. Whoever picks up their 25
dead bodies shall wash his clothes but remain unclean till evening.

*a Or* rock-rabbit.      *b Or* eagle.      *c Or* ossifrage.      *d Or* raven.
*e Or* heron.      *f Or* whatever.

26 You shall regard as unclean every animal which has a parted foot but has not a cloven hoof and does not chew the cud: whoever[a] touches them
27 shall be unclean. You shall regard as unclean all four-footed wild animals that go on flat paws; whoever[a] touches their dead bodies shall be unclean
28 till evening. Whoever takes up their dead bodies shall wash his clothes but remain unclean till evening. You shall regard them as unclean.
29 You shall regard these as unclean among creatures that teem on the ground: the mole-rat,[b] the jerboa, and every kind of thorn-tailed lizard;
30 the gecko, the sand-gecko, the wall-gecko, the great lizard, and the
31 chameleon. You shall regard these as unclean among teeming creatures; whoever[a] touches them when they are dead shall be unclean till evening.
32 Anything on which any of them falls when they are dead shall be unclean, any article of wood or garment or skin or sacking, any article in regular use; it shall be plunged into water but shall remain unclean till evening, when it
33 shall be clean. If any of these falls into an earthenware vessel, its contents
34 shall be unclean and it shall be smashed. Any food on which water from such a vessel is poured shall be unclean, and any drink in such a vessel shall
35 be unclean. Anything on which the dead body of such a creature falls shall be unclean; an oven or a stove shall be broken, for they are unclean and you
36 shall treat them as such; but a spring or a cistern where water collects shall remain clean, though whatever[c] touches the dead body shall be unclean.
37 When any of their dead bodies falls on seed intended for sowing, it remains
38 clean; but if the seed has been soaked in water and any dead body falls on it, you shall treat it as unclean.
39 When any animal allowed as food dies, all that touch the carcass shall be
40 unclean till evening. Whoever eats any of the carcass shall wash his clothes but remain unclean till evening; whoever takes up the carcass shall wash
41 his clothes and be unclean till evening. All creatures that teem on the ground
42 are vermin; they shall not be eaten. All creatures that teem on the ground, crawl on their bellies, go on all fours or have many legs, you shall not eat,
43 because they are vermin which contaminate. You shall not contaminate yourselves through any teeming creature. You shall not defile yourselves
44 with them and make yourselves unclean by them. For I am the LORD your God; you shall make yourselves holy and keep yourselves holy, because I am holy. You shall not defile yourselves with any teeming creature that
45 creeps on the ground. I am the LORD who brought you up from Egypt to become your God. You shall keep yourselves holy, because I am holy.
46 This, then, is the law concerning beast and bird, every living creature that swims in the water and every living creature that teems on the land.
47 It is to make a distinction between the unclean and the clean, between living creatures that may be eaten and living creatures that may not be eaten.

12 12 The LORD spoke to Moses and said, Speak to the Israelites in these words: When a woman conceives and bears a male child, she shall be unclean for seven days, as in the period of her impurity through menstruation.
3 On the eighth day, the child shall have the flesh of his foreskin circumcised.
4 The woman shall wait for thirty-three days because her blood requires

[a] *Or* whatever.　　[b] *Or* weasel.　　[c] *Or* whoever.

120

purification; she shall touch nothing that is holy, and shall not enter the sanctuary till her days of purification are completed. If she bears a female 5 child, she shall be unclean for fourteen days as for her menstruation and shall wait for sixty-six days because her blood requires purification. When 6 her days of purification are completed for a son or a daughter, she shall bring a yearling ram for a whole-offering and a young pigeon or a turtle-dove for a sin-offering to the priest at the entrance to the Tent of the Presence. He shall present it before the LORD and make expiation for her, 7 and she shall be clean from the issue of her blood. This is the law for the woman who bears a child, whether male or female. If she cannot afford a 8 ram, she shall bring two turtle-doves or two young pigeons, one for a whole-offering and the other for a sin-offering. The priest shall make expiation for her and she shall be clean.

The LORD spoke to Moses and Aaron and said: When any man has a 13 1 2 discoloration on the skin of his body, a pustule or inflammation, and it may develop into the sores of a malignant skin-disease, he shall be brought to the priest, either to Aaron or to one of his sons. The priest shall examine the 3 sore on the skin; if the hairs on the sore have turned white and it appears to be deeper than the skin, it shall be considered the sore of a malignant skin-disease, and the priest, after examination, shall pronounce him ritually unclean. But if the inflammation on his skin is white and seems no deeper 4 than the skin, and the hairs have not turned white, the priest shall isolate the affected person for seven days. If, when he examines him on the seventh 5 day, the sore remains as it was and has not spread in the skin, he shall keep him in isolation for another seven days. When the priest examines him again 6 on the seventh day, if the sore has faded and has not spread in the skin, the priest shall pronounce him ritually clean. It is only a scab; the man shall wash his clothes and so be clean. But if the scab spreads on the skin after 7 he has been to the priest to be pronounced ritually clean, the man shall show himself a second time to the priest. The priest shall examine him 8 again, and if it continues to spread, he shall pronounce him ritually unclean; it is a malignant skin-disease.

When anyone has the sores of a malignant skin-disease, he shall be 9 brought to the priest, and the priest shall examine him. If there is a white 10 mark on the skin, turning the hairs white, and an ulceration appears in the mark, it is a chronic skin-disease on the body, and the priest shall pronounce 11 him ritually unclean; there is no need for isolation because he is unclean already. If the skin-disease breaks out and covers the affected person from 12 head to foot as far as the priest can see, the priest shall examine him, and if 13 he finds the condition spread all over the body, he shall pronounce him ritually clean. It has all gone white; he is clean. But from the moment when 14 raw flesh appears, the man shall be considered unclean. When the priest 15 sees it, he shall pronounce him unclean. Raw flesh is to be considered unclean; it is a malignant skin-disease. On the other hand, when the raw 16 flesh heals and turns white, the man shall go to the priest, who shall examine 17 him, and if the sores have gone white, he shall pronounce him clean. He is ritually clean.

When a fester appears on the skin and heals up, but is followed by a 18 19

white mark or reddish-white inflammation on the site of the fester, the man
20 shall show himself to the priest. The priest shall examine him; if it seems
to be beneath the skin and the hairs have turned white, the priest shall
pronounce him ritually unclean. It is a malignant skin-disease which has
21 broken out on the site of the fester. But if the priest on examination finds
that it has no white hairs, is not beneath the skin and has faded, he shall
22 isolate him for seven days. If the affection has spread at all in the skin, then
the priest shall pronounce him unclean; for it is a malignant skin-disease.
23 But if the inflammation is no worse and has not spread, it is only the scar
of the fester, and the priest shall pronounce him ritually clean.

24 Again, in the case of a burn on the skin, if the raw spot left by the burn
25 becomes a reddish-white or white inflammation, the priest shall examine
it. If the hairs on the inflammation have turned white and it is deeper than
the skin, it is a malignant skin-disease which has broken out at the site of
the burn. The priest shall pronounce the man ritually unclean; it is a
26 malignant skin-disease. But if the priest on examination finds that there is
no white hair on the inflammation and it is not beneath the skin and has
27 faded, he shall keep him in isolation for seven days. When the priest
examines him on the seventh day, if the inflammation has spread at all in
the skin, the priest shall pronounce him unclean; it is a malignant skin-
28 disease. But if the inflammation is no worse, has not spread and has faded,
it is only a mark from the burn. The priest shall pronounce him ritually
clean because it is the scar of the burn.

29 30 When a man, or woman, has a sore on the head or chin, the priest shall
examine it; and if it seems deeper than the skin and the hair is yellow and
sparse, the priest shall pronounce him ritually unclean; it is a scurf, a
31 malignant skin-disease of the head or chin. But when the priest sees the
sore, if it appears to be no deeper than the skin and yet there is no yellow
hair on the place, the priest shall isolate the affected person for seven days.
32 He shall examine the sore on the seventh day: if the scurf has not spread
and there are no yellow hairs on it and it seems no deeper than the skin,
33 the man shall get himself shaved except for the scurfy part, and the priest
34 shall keep him in isolation for another seven days. The priest shall examine
it again on the seventh day, and if the scurf has not spread on the skin and
appears to be no deeper than the skin, the priest shall pronounce him clean.
35 The man shall wash his clothes and so be ritually clean. But if the scurf
36 spreads at all in the skin after the man has been pronounced clean, the priest
shall examine him again. If it has spread in the skin, the priest need not even
37 look for yellow hair; the man is unclean. If, however, the scurf remains as
it was but black hair has begun to grow on it, it has healed. The man is
ritually clean and the priest shall pronounce him so.

38 When a man, or woman, has inflamed patches on the skin and they are
39 white, the priest shall examine them. If they are white and fading, it is
dull-white leprosy that has broken out on the skin. The man is ritually
clean.

40 When a man's hair falls out from his head, he is bald behind but not
41 ritually unclean. If the hair falls out from the front of the scalp, he is
42 bald on the forehead but clean. But if on the bald patch behind or on the

forehead there is a reddish-white sore, it is a malignant skin-disease breaking out on those parts. The priest shall examine him, and if the 43 discoloured sore on the bald patch behind or on the forehead is reddish-white, similar in appearance to a malignant skin-disease on the body, the man 44 is suffering from such a disease; he is ritually unclean and the priest must not fail to pronounce him so. The symptoms are in this case on his head.

One who suffers from a malignant skin-disease shall wear his clothes 45 torn, leave his hair dishevelled, conceal his upper lip, and cry, 'Unclean, unclean.' So long as the sore persists, he shall be considered ritually unclean. 46 The man is unclean: he shall live apart and must stay outside the settlement.

When there is a stain of mould, whether in a garment of wool or linen, 47 or in the warp or weft of linen or wool, or in a skin or anything made of 48 skin; if the stain is greenish or reddish in the garment or skin, or in the 49 warp or weft, or in anything made of skin, it is a stain of mould which must be shown to the priest. The priest shall examine it and put the stained 50 material aside for seven days. On the seventh day he shall examine it again. 51 If the stain has spread in the garment, warp, weft, or skin, whatever the use of the skin, the stain is a rotting mould: it is ritually unclean. He shall 52 burn the garment or the warp or weft, whether wool or linen, or anything of skin which is stained; because it is a rotting mould, it must be destroyed by fire. But if the priest sees that the stain has not spread in the 53 garment, warp or weft, or anything made of skin, he shall give orders for 54 the stained material to be washed, and then he shall put it aside for another seven days. After it has been washed the priest shall examine the stain; if 55 it has not changed its appearance, although it has not spread, it is unclean and you shall destroy it by fire, whether the rot is on the right side or the wrong. If the priest examines it and finds the stain faded after being washed, 56 he shall tear it out of the garment, skin, warp, or weft. If, however, the stain 57 reappears in the garment, warp or weft, or in anything of skin, it is breaking out afresh and you shall destroy by fire whatever is stained. If you wash the 58 garment, warp, weft, or anything of skin and the stain disappears, it shall be washed a second time and then it shall be ritually clean.

This is the law concerning stain of mould in a garment of wool or linen, 59 in warp or weft, or in anything made of skin; by it they shall be pronounced clean or unclean.

THE LORD SPOKE TO MOSES and said: This is the law concerning a man 14 1 2 suffering from a malignant skin-disease. On the day when he is to be cleansed he shall be brought to the priest. The priest shall go outside the 3 camp and examine him. If the man is healed of his disease, then the priest 4 shall order two clean small birds to be brought alive for the man who is to be cleansed, together with cedar-wood, scarlet thread, and marjoram.*a* He 5 shall order one of the birds to be killed over an earthenware bowl containing fresh water. He shall then take the living bird and the cedar-wood, 6 scarlet thread, and marjoram and dip them and the living bird in the blood of the bird that has been killed over the fresh water. He shall sprinkle the 7 blood seven times on the man who is to be cleansed from his skin-disease

*a Or* hyssop.

and so cleanse him; the living bird he shall release to fly away over the open
8 country. The man to be cleansed shall wash his clothes, shave off all his
hair, bathe in water and so be ritually clean. He may then enter the camp
9 but must stay outside his tent for seven days. On the seventh day he shall
shave off all the hair on his head, his beard, and his eyebrows, and then
shave the rest of his hair, wash his clothes and bathe in water; then he shall
be ritually clean.
10     On the eighth day he shall bring two yearling rams and one yearling
ewe, all three without blemish, a grain-offering of three tenths of an ephah
11 of flour mixed with oil, and one log of oil. The officiating priest shall place
the man to be cleansed and his offerings before the LORD at the entrance
12 to the Tent of the Presence. He shall then take one of the rams and offer it
with the log of oil as a guilt-offering, presenting them as a special gift
13 before the LORD. The ram shall be slaughtered where the sin-offerings
and the whole-offerings are slaughtered, within the sacred precincts,
because the guilt-offering, like the sin-offering, belongs to the priest. It is
14 most sacred. The priest shall then take some of the blood of the guilt-
offering and put it on the lobe of the right ear of the man to be cleansed, and
15 on his right thumb and the big toe of his right foot. He shall next take the
16 log of oil and pour some of it on the palm of his own left hand, dip his right
forefinger into the oil on his left palm and sprinkle some of it with his
17 finger seven times before the LORD. He shall then put some of the oil
remaining on his palm on the lobe of the right ear of the man to be cleansed,
on his right thumb and on the big toe of his right foot, on top of the blood
18 of the guilt-offering. The remainder of the oil on the priest's palm shall be
put upon the head of the man to be cleansed, and thus the priest shall make
19 expiation for him before the LORD. The priest shall then perform the sin-
offering and make expiation for the uncleanness of the man who is to be
20 cleansed. After this he shall slaughter the whole-offering and offer it and
the grain-offering on the altar. Thus the priest shall make expiation for him,
and then he shall be clean.
21     If the man is poor and cannot afford these offerings, he shall bring one
young ram as a guilt-offering to be a special gift making expiation for him,
and a grain-offering of a tenth of an ephah of flour mixed with oil, and a log
22 of oil, also two turtle-doves or two young pigeons, whichever he can afford,
23 one for a sin-offering and the other for a whole-offering. He shall bring
them to the priest for his cleansing on the eighth day, at the entrance to the
24 Tent of the Presence before the LORD. The priest shall take the ram for the
guilt-offering and the log of oil, and shall present them as a special gift
25 before the LORD. The ram for the guilt-offering shall then be slaughtered,
and the priest shall take some of the blood of the guilt-offering, and put it
on the lobe of the right ear of the man to be cleansed and on his right thumb
26 and on the big toe of his right foot. He shall pour some of the oil on the
27 palm of his own left hand and sprinkle some of it with his right forefinger
28 seven times before the LORD. He shall then put some of the oil remaining on
his palm on the lobe of the right ear of the man to be cleansed, and on his
right thumb and on the big toe of his right foot exactly where the blood of
29 the guilt-offering was put. The remainder of the oil on the priest's palm

shall be put upon the head of the man to be cleansed to make expiation for him before the LORD. Of the birds which the man has been able to afford, 30 turtle-doves or young pigeons, whichever it may be, the priest shall deal 31 with one as a sin-offering and with the other as a whole-offering and shall make the grain-offering with them. Thus the priest shall make expiation before the LORD for the man who is to be cleansed. This is the law for the 32 man with a malignant skin-disease who cannot afford the regular offering for his cleansing.

The LORD spoke to Moses and Aaron and said: When you have entered 33 34 the land of Canaan which I give you to occupy, if I inflict a fungous infection upon a house in the land you have occupied, its owner shall come and 35 report to the priest that there appears to him to be a patch of infection in his house. The priest shall order the house to be cleared before he goes in 36 to examine the infection, or everything in it will become unclean. After this the priest shall go in to inspect the house. If on inspection he finds the 37 patch on the walls consists of greenish or reddish depressions, apparently going deeper than the surface, he shall go out of the house and, standing 38 at the entrance, shall put it in quarantine for seven days. On the seventh 39 day he shall come back and inspect the house, and if the patch has spread in the walls, he shall order the infected stones to be pulled out and thrown 40 away outside the city in an unclean place. He shall then have the house 41 scraped inside throughout, and all the daub*a* they have scraped off shall be tipped outside the city in an unclean place. They shall take fresh stones 42 to replace the others and replaster the house with fresh daub.

If the infection reappears in the house and spreads after the stones have 43 been pulled out and the house scraped and redaubed, the priest shall come 44 and inspect it. If the infection has spread in the house, it is a corrosive growth; the house is unclean. The house shall be demolished, stones, 45 timber, and daub, and it shall all be taken away outside the city to an unclean place. Anyone who has entered the house during the time it has been 46 in quarantine shall be unclean till evening. Anyone who has slept or eaten 47 a meal in the house shall wash his clothes. But if, when the priest goes 48 into the house and inspects it, he finds that the infection has not spread after the redaubing, then he shall pronounce the house ritually clean, because the infection has been cured.

In order to rid the house of impurity, he shall take two small birds, cedar- 49 wood, scarlet thread, and marjoram. He shall kill one of the birds over an 50 earthenware bowl containing fresh water. He shall then take the cedar- 51 wood, marjoram, and scarlet thread, together with the living bird, dip them in the blood of the bird that has been killed and in the fresh water, and sprinkle the house seven times. Thus he shall purify the house, using 52 the blood of the bird, the fresh water, the living bird, the cedar-wood, the marjoram, and the scarlet thread. He shall set the living bird free outside 53 the city to fly away over the open country, and make expiation for the house; and then it shall be clean.

This is the law for all malignant skin-diseases, and for scurf, for mould 54 55 in clothes and fungus in houses, for a discoloration of the skin, scab, and 56

*a Or* mud.

57 inflammation, to declare when these are pronounced unclean and when clean. This is the law for skin-disease, mould, and fungus.

15 1 2 THE LORD SPOKE TO MOSES and Aaron and said, Speak to the Israelites and say to them: When any man has a discharge from his body, the
3 discharge is ritually unclean. This is the law concerning the uncleanness
due to his discharge whether it continues or has been stopped; in either
case he is unclean.
4 Every bed on which the man with a discharge lies down shall be ritually
5 unclean, and everything on which he sits shall be unclean. Any man who
touches the bed shall wash his clothes, bathe in water and remain unclean
6 till evening. Whoever sits on anything on which the man with a discharge
has sat shall wash his clothes, bathe in water and remain unclean till even-
7 ing. Whoever touches the body of the man with a discharge shall wash his
8 clothes, bathe in water and remain unclean till evening. If the man spits on
one who is ritually clean, the latter shall wash his clothes, bathe in water
9 and remain unclean till evening. Everything on which the man sits when
10 riding shall be unclean. Whoever touches anything that has been under
him shall be unclean till evening, and whoever handles such things shall
11 wash his clothes, bathe in water and remain unclean till evening. Anyone
whom the man with a discharge touches without having rinsed his hands
in water shall wash his clothes, bathe in water and remain unclean till
12 evening. Any earthenware bowl touched by the man shall be smashed, and
every wooden bowl shall be rinsed with water.
13 When the man is cleansed from his discharge, he shall reckon seven days
to his cleansing, wash his clothes, bathe his body in fresh water and be
14 ritually clean. On the eighth day he shall obtain two turtle-doves or two
young pigeons and, coming before the LORD at the entrance to the Tent of
15 the Presence, shall give them to the priest. The priest shall deal with one
as a sin-offering and the other as a whole-offering, and shall make for him
before the LORD the expiation required by the discharge.
16 When a man has emitted semen, he shall bathe his whole body in water
17 and be unclean till evening. Every piece of clothing or skin on which there
18 is any semen shall be washed and remain unclean till evening. This applies
also to the woman with whom a man has had intercourse; they shall both
bathe themselves in water and remain unclean till evening.
19 When a woman has a discharge of blood, her impurity shall last for
20 seven days; anyone who touches her shall be unclean till evening. Every-
21 thing on which she lies or sits during her impurity shall be unclean. Anyone who touches her bed shall wash his clothes, bathe in water and remain
22 unclean till evening. Whoever touches anything on which she sits shall
23 wash his clothes, bathe in water and remain unclean till evening. If he is
on the bed or seat where she is sitting, by touching it he shall become un-
24 clean till evening. If a man goes so far as to have intercourse with her and
any of her discharge gets on to him, then he shall be unclean for seven days,
and every bed on which he lies down shall be unclean.
25 When a woman has a prolonged discharge of blood not at the time of
her menstruation, or when her discharge continues beyond the period of

menstruation, her impurity shall last all the time of her discharge; she shall be unclean as during the period of her menstruation. Any bed on which she 26 lies during the time of her discharge shall be like that which she used during menstruation, and everything on which she sits shall be unclean as in her menstrual uncleanness. Every person who touches them shall be unclean; 27 he shall wash his clothes, bathe in water and remain unclean till evening. If she is cleansed from her discharge, she shall reckon seven days and after 28 that she shall be ritually clean. On the eighth day she shall obtain two 29 turtle-doves or two young pigeons and bring them to the priest at the entrance to the Tent of the Presence. The priest shall deal with one as a 30 sin-offering and with the other as a whole-offering, and make for her before the LORD the expiation required by her unclean discharge.

In this way you shall warn the Israelites against uncleanness, in order 31 that they may not bring uncleanness upon the Tabernacle where I dwell among them, and so die.

This is the law for the man who has a discharge, or who has an emission 32 of semen and is thereby unclean, and for the woman who is suffering her 33 menstruation—for everyone, male or female, who has a discharge, and for the man who has intercourse with a woman who is unclean.

THE LORD SPOKE TO MOSES after the death of Aaron's two sons, who **16** died when they offered illicit fire before the LORD. He said to him: Tell 2 your brother Aaron that he must not enter the sanctuary within the Veil, in front of the cover over the Ark, except at the appointed time, on pain of death; for I appear in the cloud above the cover. When Aaron enters the 3 sanctuary, this is what he shall do. He shall bring a young bull for a sin-offering and a ram for a whole-offering. He shall wear a sacred linen tunic 4 and linen drawers to cover himself, and he shall put a linen sash round his waist and wind a linen turban round his head; all these are sacred vestments, and he shall bathe in water before putting them on. He shall take 5 from the community of the Israelites two he-goats for a sin-offering and a ram for a whole-offering. He shall present the bull as a sin-offering and 6 make expiation for himself and his household. Then he shall take the two 7 he-goats and set them before the LORD at the entrance to the Tent of the Presence. He shall cast lots over the two goats, one to be for the LORD and 8 the other for the Precipice.[a] He shall present the goat on which the lot 9 for the LORD has fallen and deal with it as a sin-offering; but the goat on 10 which the lot for the Precipice has fallen shall be made to stand alive before the LORD, for expiation to be made over it before it is driven away into the wilderness to the Precipice.

Aaron shall present his bull as a sin-offering, making expiation for him- 11 self and his household, and then slaughter the bull as a sin-offering. He 12 shall take a firepan full of glowing embers from the altar before the LORD, and two handfuls of powdered fragrant incense, and bring them within the Veil. He shall put the incense on the fire before the LORD, and the 13 cloud of incense will hide the cover over the Tokens so that he shall not die. He shall take some of the bull's blood and sprinkle it with his finger 14

*a   Or* for Azazel.

127

both on the surface of the cover, eastwards, and seven times in front of the cover.

15 He shall then slaughter the people's goat as a sin-offering, bring its blood within the Veil and do with its blood as he did with the bull's blood,
16 sprinkling it on the cover and in front of it. He shall make for the sanctuary the expiation required by the ritual uncleanness of the Israelites and their acts of rebellion, that is by all their sins; and he shall do the same for the Tent of the Presence, which dwells among them in the midst of all their
17 uncleanness. No other man shall be within the Tent of the Presence from the time when he enters the sanctuary to make expiation until he comes out, and he shall make expiation for himself, his household, and the whole assembly of Israel.

18 He shall then come out to the altar which is before the LORD and make expiation for it. He shall take some of the bull's blood and some of the
19 goat's blood and put it all over the horns of the altar; he shall sprinkle some of the blood on the altar with his finger seven times. So he shall purify it from all the uncleanness of the Israelites and hallow it.

20 When Aaron has finished making expiation for the sanctuary, for the Tent of the Presence, and for the altar, he shall bring forward the live goat.
21 He shall lay both his hands on its head and confess over it all the iniquities of the Israelites and all their acts of rebellion, that is all their sins; he shall lay them on the head of the goat and send it away into the wilderness in
22 charge of a man who is waiting ready. The goat shall carry all their iniquities upon itself into some barren waste and the man shall let it go, there in the wilderness.

23 Aaron shall then enter the Tent of the Presence, take off the linen clothes which he had put on when he entered the sanctuary, and leave them there.
24 He shall bathe in water in a consecrated place and put on his vestments; then he shall go out and perform his own whole-offering and that of the
25 people, thus making expiation for himself and for the people. He shall
26 burn the fat of the sin-offering upon the altar. The man who drove the goat away to the Precipice shall wash his clothes and bathe in water,
27 and not till then may he enter the camp. The two sin-offerings, the bull and the goat, the blood of which was brought within the Veil to make expiation in the sanctuary, shall be taken outside the camp and
28 destroyed by fire—skin, flesh, and offal. The man who burns them shall wash his clothes and bathe in water, and not till then may he enter the camp.

29 This shall become a rule binding on you for all time. On the tenth day of the seventh month you shall mortify yourselves; you shall do no work,
30 whether native Israelite or alien settler, because on this day expiation shall be made on your behalf to cleanse you, and so make you clean before the
31 LORD from all your sins. This is a sabbath of sacred rest for you, and you
32 shall mortify yourselves; it is a rule binding for all time. Expiation shall be made by the priest duly anointed and installed to serve in succession to his
33 father; he shall put on the sacred linen clothes and shall make expiation for the holy sanctuary, the Tent of the Presence, and the altar, on behalf of the
34 priests and the whole assembly of the people. This shall become a rule

binding on you for all time, to make for the Israelites once a year the expiation required by all their sins.

And Moses carried out the LORD's commands.

## The law of holiness

THE LORD SPOKE TO MOSES and said, Speak to Aaron, his sons, and 17 1 2 all the Israelites in these words: This is what the LORD has commanded. Any Israelite who slaughters an ox, a sheep, or a goat, either inside or 3 outside the camp, and does not bring it to the entrance of the Tent of the 4 Presence to present it as an offering to the LORD before the Tabernacle of the LORD shall be held guilty of bloodshed: that man has shed blood and shall be cut off from his people. The purpose is that the Israelites should 5 bring to the LORD the animals which they slaughter in the open country; they shall bring them to the priest at the entrance to the Tent of the Presence and sacrifice them as shared-offerings to the LORD. The priest 6 shall fling the blood against the altar of the LORD at the entrance to the Tent of the Presence, and burn the fat as a soothing odour to the LORD. They shall no longer sacrifice their slaughtered beasts to the demons*a* whom 7 they wantonly follow. This shall be a rule binding on them and their descendants for all time.

You shall say to them: Any Israelite or alien settled in Israel who offers 8 a whole-offering or a sacrifice and does not bring it to the entrance of the 9 Tent of the Presence to sacrifice it to the LORD shall be cut off from his father's kin.

If any Israelite or alien settled in Israel eats any blood, I will set my face 10 against the eater and cut him off from his people, because the life of a 11 creature is the blood, and I appoint it to make expiation on the altar for yourselves: it is the blood, that is the life, that makes expiation. Therefore 12 I have told the Israelites that neither you, nor any alien settled among you, shall eat blood.

Any Israelite or alien settled in Israel who hunts beasts or birds that may 13 lawfully be eaten shall drain out the blood and cover it with earth, because 14 the life of every living creature is the blood, and I have forbidden the Israelites to eat the blood of any creature, because the life of every creature is its blood: every man who eats it shall be cut off.

Every person, native or alien, who eats that which has died a natural 15 death or has been mauled by wild beasts shall wash his clothes and bathe in water, and remain ritually unclean till evening; then he shall be clean. If he does not wash his clothes and bathe his body, he must accept 16 responsibility.

THE LORD SPOKE TO MOSES and said, Speak to the Israelites in these 18 1 2 words: I am the LORD your God. You shall not do as they do in Egypt 3 where you once dwelt, nor shall you do as they do in the land of Canaan to which I am bringing you; you shall not conform to their institutions. You 4

*a Or* satyrs.

must keep my laws and conform to my institutions without fail: I am the
5 LORD your God. You shall observe my institutions and my laws: the man
who keeps them shall have life through them. I am the LORD.
6    No man shall approach a blood-relation for intercourse. I am the LORD.
7 You shall not bring shame on your father by intercourse with your mother:
8 she is your mother; you shall not bring shame upon her. You shall not have
intercourse with your father's wife: that is to bring shame upon your father.
9 You shall not have intercourse with your sister, your father's daughter, or
your mother's daughter, whether brought up in the family or in another
10 home; you shall not bring shame upon them. You shall not have intercourse with your son's daughter or your daughter's daughter: that is to
11 bring shame upon yourself. You shall not have intercourse with a daughter
of your father's wife, begotten by your father: she is your sister, and you
12 shall not bring shame upon her. You shall not have intercourse with your
13 father's sister: she is a blood-relation of your father. You shall not have
intercourse with your mother's sister: she is a blood-relation of your
14 mother. You shall not bring shame upon your father's brother by approach-
15 ing his wife: she is your aunt. You shall not have intercourse with your
daughter-in-law: she is your son's wife; you shall not bring shame upon her.
16 You shall not have intercourse with your brother's wife: that is to bring
17 shame upon him. You shall not have intercourse with both a woman and her
daughter, nor shall you take her son's daughter or her daughter's daughter to
have intercourse with them: they are her blood-relations, and such conduct
18 is lewdness. You shall not take a woman who is your wife's sister to make her
a rival-wife, and to have intercourse with her during her sister's lifetime.
19    You shall not approach a woman to have intercourse with her during
20 her period of menstruation. You shall not have sexual intercourse with the
wife of your fellow-countryman and so make yourself unclean with her.
21 You shall not surrender any of your children to Molech and thus profane
22 the name of your God: I am the LORD. You shall not lie with a man as with
23 a woman: that is an abomination. You shall not have sexual intercourse
with any beast to make yourself unclean with it, nor shall a woman submit
24 herself to intercourse with a beast: that is a violation of nature. You shall
not make yourselves unclean in any of these ways; for in these ways the
heathen, whom I am driving out before you, made themselves unclean.
25 This is how the land became unclean, and I punished it for its iniquity so
26 that it spewed out its inhabitants. You, unlike them, shall keep my laws
and my rules: none of you, whether natives or aliens settled among you,
27 shall do any of these abominable things. The people who were there before
28 you did these abominable things and the land became unclean. So the land
29 will not spew you out for making it unclean as it spewed them out; for
anyone who does any of these abominable things shall be cut off from his
30 people. Observe my charge, therefore, and follow none of the abominable
institutions customary before your time; do not make yourselves unclean
with them. I am the LORD your God.

19 1 2  THE LORD SPOKE TO MOSES and said, Speak to all the community of
the Israelites in these words: You shall be holy, because I, the LORD your

God, am holy. You shall revere, every man of you, his mother and his 3
father. You shall keep my sabbaths. I am the LORD your God. Do not 4
resort to idols; you shall not make gods of cast metal for yourselves. I am
the LORD your God.

When you sacrifice a shared-offering to the LORD, you shall slaughter it 5
so as to win acceptance for yourselves. It must be eaten on the day of your 6
sacrifice or the next day. Whatever is left over till the third day shall be
destroyed by fire; it is tainted, and if any of it is eaten on the third day, it 7
will not be acceptable. He who eats it must accept responsibility, because 8
he has profaned the holy-gift to the LORD: that person shall be cut off from
his father's kin.

When you reap the harvest of your land, you shall not reap right into the 9
edges of your field; neither shall you glean the loose ears of your crop; you 10
shall not completely strip your vineyard nor glean the fallen grapes. You
shall leave them for the poor and the alien. I am the LORD your God.

You shall not steal; you shall not cheat or deceive a fellow-countryman. 11
You shall not swear in my name with intent to deceive and thus profane 12
the name of your God. I am the LORD. You shall not oppress your neigh- 13
bour, nor rob him. You shall not keep back a hired man's wages till next
morning. You shall not treat the deaf with contempt, nor put an obstruc- 14
tion in the way of the blind. You shall fear your God. I am the LORD.

You shall not pervert justice, either by favouring the poor or by sub- 15
servience to the great. You shall judge your fellow-countryman with strict
justice. You shall not go about spreading slander among your father's kin, 16
nor take sides against your neighbour on a capital charge. I am the LORD.
You shall not nurse hatred against your brother. You shall reprove your 17
fellow-countryman frankly and so you will have no share in his guilt.[a] You 18
shall not seek revenge, or cherish anger towards your kinsfolk; you shall
love your neighbour as a man like yourself. I am the LORD.

You shall keep my rules. You shall not allow two different kinds of beast 19
to mate together. You shall not plant your field with two kinds of seed.
You shall not put on a garment woven with two kinds of yarn.

When a man has intercourse with a slave-girl who has been assigned to 20
another man and neither ransomed nor given her freedom, inquiry shall be
made. They shall not be put to death, because she has not been freed. The 21
man shall bring his guilt-offering, a ram, to the LORD to the entrance of
the Tent of the Presence, and with it the priest shall make expiation for him 22
before the LORD for his sin, and he shall be forgiven the sin he has committed.

When you enter the land, and plant any kind of tree for food, you shall 23
treat it as bearing forbidden fruit. For three years it shall be forbidden and
may not be eaten. In the fourth year all its fruit shall be a holy-gift to the 24
LORD, and this releases it for use. In the fifth year you may eat its fruit, and 25
thus the yield it gives you shall be increased. I am the LORD your God.

You shall not eat meat with the blood in it. You shall not practise 26
divination or soothsaying. You shall not round off your hair from side to 27
side, and you shall not shave the edge of your beards. You shall not gash 28

[a] *Or* and for that you will incur no blame.

yourselves in mourning for the dead; you shall not tattoo yourselves. I am the LORD.

29
30 Do not prostitute your daughter and so make her a whore; thus the land shall not play the prostitute and be full of lewdness. You shall keep my sabbaths, and revere my sanctuary. I am the LORD.

31 Do not resort to ghosts and spirits, nor make yourselves unclean by seeking them out. I am the LORD your God.

32 You shall rise in the presence of grey hairs, give honour to the aged, and fear your God. I am the LORD.

33 34 When an alien settles with you in your land, you shall not oppress him. He shall be treated as a native born among you, and you shall love him as a man like yourself, because you were aliens in Egypt. I am the LORD your God.

35
36
37 You shall not pervert justice in measurement of length, weight, or quantity. You shall have true scales, true weights, true measures dry and liquid. I am the LORD your God who brought you out of Egypt. You shall observe all my rules and laws and carry them out. I am the LORD.

**20** 1 2 The LORD spoke to Moses and said, Say to the Israelites: Any Israelite or alien settled in Israel who gives any of his children to Molech shall be

3 put to death: the common people shall stone him. I, for my part, set my face against that man and cut him off from his people, because he has given a child of his to Molech, thus making my sanctuary unclean and profaning

4
5 my holy name. If the common people connive at it when a man has given a child of his to Molech and do not put him to death, I will set my face against man and family, and both him and all who follow him in his wanton following after Molech,*a* I will cut off from their people.

6
7
8 I will set my face against the man who wantonly resorts to ghosts and spirits, and I will cut that person off from his people. Hallow yourselves and be holy, because I the LORD your God am holy. You shall keep my rules and obey them: I am the LORD who hallows you.

9 When any man reviles his father and his mother, he shall be put to death. He has reviled his father and his mother; his blood shall be on his own head.

10
11 If a man commits adultery with his neighbour's wife, both adulterer and adulteress shall be put to death. The man who has intercourse with his father's wife has brought shame on his father. They shall both be put to

12 death; their blood shall be on their own heads. If a man has intercourse with his daughter-in-law, they shall both be put to death. Their deed is a

13 violation of nature; their blood shall be on their own heads. If a man has intercourse with a man as with a woman, they both commit an abomination.

14 They shall be put to death; their blood shall be on their own heads. If a man takes both a woman and her mother, that is lewdness. Both he and they

15 shall be burnt; thus there shall be no lewdness in your midst. A man who has sexual intercourse with any beast shall be put to death, and you shall

16 kill the beast. If a woman approaches any animal to have intercourse with it, you shall kill both woman and beast. They shall be put to death; their

17 blood shall be on their own heads. If a man takes his sister, his father's daughter or his mother's daughter, and they see one another naked, it is a scandalous disgrace. They shall be cut off in the presence of their people.

*a* Or in his lusting after human sacrifice.

The man has had intercourse with his sister and he shall accept responsibility. If a man lies with a woman during her monthly period and brings 18 shame upon her, he has exposed her discharge and she has uncovered the source of her discharge; they shall both be cut off from their people. You 19 shall not have intercourse with your mother's sister or your father's sister: it is the exposure of a blood-relation. They shall accept responsibility. A 20 man who has intercourse with his uncle's wife has brought shame upon his uncle. They shall accept responsibility for their sin and shall be proscribed and put to death. If a man takes his brother's wife, it is impurity. He has 21 brought shame upon his brother; they shall be proscribed.

You shall keep all my rules and my laws and carry them out, that the 22 land into which I am bringing you to live may not spew you out. You shall 23 not conform to the institutions of the nations whom I am driving out before you: they did all these things and I abhorred them, and I told you 24 that you should occupy their land, and I would give you possession of it, a land flowing with milk and honey. I am the LORD your God: I have made a clear separation between you and the nations, and you shall make a clear 25 separation between clean beasts and unclean beasts and between unclean and clean birds. You shall not make yourselves vile through beast or bird or anything that creeps on the ground, for I have made a clear separation between them and you, declaring them unclean. You shall be holy to me, 26 because I the LORD am holy. I have made a clear separation between you and the heathen, that you may belong to me. Any man or woman among 27 you who calls up ghosts or spirits shall be put to death. The people shall stone them; their blood shall be on their own heads.

THE LORD SAID TO MOSES, Say to the priests, the sons of Aaron: A **21** priest shall not render himself unclean for the death of any of his kin except for a near blood-relation, that is for mother, father, son, daughter, 2 brother, or full sister who is unmarried and a virgin; nor shall he make 3 4 himself unclean for any married woman *a* among his father's kin, and so profane himself.

Priests shall not make bald patches on their heads as a sign of mourning, 5 nor cut the edges of their beards, nor gash their bodies. They shall be holy 6 to their God, and they shall not profane the name of their God, because they present the food-offerings of the LORD, the food of their God, and they shall be holy. A priest shall not marry a prostitute or a girl who has 7 lost her virginity, nor shall he marry a woman divorced from her husband; for he is holy to his God. You shall keep him holy because he presents the 8 food of your God; you shall regard him as holy because I the LORD, I who hallow them, am holy. When a priest's daughter profanes herself by becom- 9 ing a prostitute, she profanes her father. She shall be burnt to death.

The high priest, the one among his fellows who has had the anointing 10 oil poured on his head and has been consecrated to wear the vestments, shall neither leave his hair dishevelled nor tear his clothes. He shall not 11 enter the place where any man's dead body lies; not even for his father or his mother shall he render himself unclean. He shall not go out of the 12

*a* for any married woman: *prob. rdg.; Heb.* husband.

133

sanctuary for fear that he dishonour the sanctuary of his God, because the consecration of the anointing oil of his God is upon him. I am the LORD.

13 14 He shall marry a woman who is still a virgin. He shall not marry a widow, a divorced woman, a woman who has lost her virginity, or a prostitute, but

15 only a virgin from his father's kin; he shall not dishonour his descendants among his father's kin, for I am the LORD who hallows him.

16 17 The LORD spoke to Moses and said, Speak to Aaron in these words: No man among your descendants for all time who has any physical defect shall

18 come and present the food of his God. No man with a defect shall come,

19 whether a blind man, a lame man, a man stunted or overgrown, a man

20 deformed in foot or hand, or with mis-shapen brows or a film over his eye or a discharge from it, a man who has a scab or eruption or has had a testicle

21 ruptured. No descendant of Aaron the priest who has any defect in his body shall approach to present the food-offerings of the LORD; because

22 he has a defect he shall not approach to present the food of his God. He may eat the bread of God both from the holy-gifts and from the holiest

23 of holy-gifts, but he shall not come up to the Veil nor approach the altar, because he has a defect in his body. Thus he shall not profane my sanctuaries, because I am the LORD who hallows them.

24 Thus did Moses speak to Aaron and his sons and to all the Israelites.

22 1 2 The LORD spoke to Moses and said, Tell Aaron and his sons that they must be careful in the handling of the holy-gifts of the Israelites which they

3 hallow to me, lest they profane my holy name. I am the LORD. Say to them: Any man of your descent for all time who while unclean approaches the holy-gifts which the Israelites hallow to the LORD shall be cut off from my

4 presence. I am the LORD. No man descended from Aaron who suffers from a malignant skin-disease, or has a discharge, shall eat of the holy-gifts until he is cleansed. A man who touches anything which makes him unclean

5 or who has an emission of semen, a man who touches any vermin which

6 makes him unclean or any human being who makes him unclean: any person who touches such a thing shall be unclean till sunset and unless he

7 washes his body shall not eat of the holy-gifts. When the sun goes down, he shall be clean, and after that he may eat from the holy-gifts, because they

8 are his food. He shall not eat an animal that has died a natural death or has been mauled by wild beasts, thereby making himself unclean. I am the

9 LORD. The priests shall observe my charge, lest they make themselves guilty and die for profaning my name. I am the LORD who hallows them.

10 No unqualified person may eat any holy-gift; nor may a stranger lodging

11 with a priest or a hired man eat a holy-gift. A slave bought by a priest with his own money may do so, and slaves born in his household may also share

12 his food. When a priest's daughter marries an unqualified person, she shall

13 not eat any of the contributions of holy-gifts; but if she is widowed or divorced and is childless and comes back to her father's house as in her childhood, she shall share her father's food. No unqualified person may eat any of it.

14 When a man inadvertently eats a holy-gift, he shall make good the holy-

15 gift to the priest, adding a fifth to its value. The priests shall not profane

16 the holy-gifts of the Israelites which they set aside for the LORD; they shall

not let men eat their holy-gifts and so incur guilt and its penalty, because I am the LORD who hallows them.

The LORD spoke to Moses and said, Speak to Aaron and his sons and to all the Israelites in these words: When any man of the house of Israel or any alien in Israel presents, whether in fulfilment of a vow or for a freewill offering, such an offering as is presented to the LORD for a whole-offering so as to win acceptance for yourselves, it shall be a male without defect, of cattle, sheep, or goats. You shall not present anything which is defective, because it will not be acceptable on your behalf. When a man presents a shared-offering to the LORD, whether cattle or sheep, to fulfil a special*a* vow or as a freewill offering, if it is to be acceptable it must be perfect; there shall be no defect in it. You shall present to the LORD nothing blind, disabled, mutilated, with running sore, scab, or eruption, nor set any such creature on the altar as a food-offering to the LORD. If a bull or a sheep is overgrown or stunted, you may make of it a freewill offering, but it will not be acceptable in fulfilment of a vow. If its testicles have been crushed or bruised, torn or cut, you shall not present it to the LORD; this is forbidden in your land.

You shall not procure any such creature from a foreigner and present it as food for your God. Their deformity is inherent in them, a permanent defect, and they will not be acceptable on your behalf.

The LORD spoke to Moses and said: When a calf, a lamb, or a kid is born, it must not be taken from its mother for seven days. From the eighth day onwards it will be acceptable when offered as a food-offering to the LORD. You shall not slaughter a cow or sheep at the same time as its young. When you make a thank-offering to the LORD, you shall sacrifice it so as to win acceptance for yourselves; it shall be eaten that same day, and none be left till morning. I am the LORD.

You shall observe my commandments and perform them. I am the LORD. You shall not profane my holy name; I will be hallowed among the Israelites. I am the LORD who hallows you, who brought you out of Egypt to become your God. I am the LORD.

THE LORD SPOKE TO MOSES AND SAID, Speak to the Israelites in these words: These are the appointed seasons of the LORD, and you shall proclaim them as sacred assemblies; these are my appointed seasons. On six days work may be done, but every seventh day is a sabbath of sacred rest, a day of sacred assembly, on which you shall do no work. Wherever you live, it is the LORD's sabbath.

These are the appointed seasons of the LORD, the sacred assemblies which you shall proclaim in their appointed order. In the first month on the fourteenth day between dusk and dark is the LORD's Passover. On the fifteenth day of this month begins the LORD's pilgrim-feast of Unleavened Bread; for seven days you shall eat unleavened cakes. On the first day there shall be a sacred assembly; you shall not do your daily work. For seven days you shall present your food-offerings to the LORD. On the seventh day also there shall be a sacred assembly; you shall not do your daily work.

*a* fulfil a special: *or* discharge a . . .

9 10  The LORD spoke to Moses and said, Speak to the Israelites in these words: When you enter the land which I give you, and you reap its harvest,

11  you shall bring the first sheaf of your harvest to the priest. He shall present the sheaf as a special gift before the LORD on *a* the day after the sabbath, so

12  as to gain acceptance for yourselves. On the day you present the sheaf, you

13  shall prepare a perfect yearling ram for a whole-offering to the LORD, with the proper grain-offering, two tenths of an ephah of flour mixed with oil, as a food-offering to the LORD, of soothing odour, and also with the proper

14  drink-offering, a quarter of a hin of wine. You shall eat neither bread, nor grain, parched or fully ripened, during that day, the day on which you bring your God his offering; this is a rule binding on your descendants for all time wherever you live.

15  From the day after the sabbath, the day on which you bring your sheaf

16  as a special gift, you shall count seven full weeks. The day after the seventh sabbath will make fifty days, and then you shall present to the LORD a

17  grain-offering from the new crop. You shall bring from your homes two loaves as a special gift; they shall contain two tenths of an ephah of flour

18  and shall be baked with leaven. They are the LORD's firstfruits. In addition to the bread you shall present seven perfect yearling sheep, one young bull, and two rams. They shall be a whole-offering to the LORD with the proper grain-offering and the proper drink-offering, a food-offering of soothing

19  odour to the LORD. You shall also prepare one he-goat for a sin-offering

20  and two yearling sheep for a shared-offering, and the priest shall present them in addition to the bread of the firstfruits as a special gift before the

21  LORD. They shall be a holy-gift to the LORD for the priest. On that same day you shall proclaim a sacred assembly for yourselves; you shall not do your daily work. This is a rule binding on your descendants for all time wherever you live.

22  When you reap the harvest in your land, you shall not reap right into the edges of your field, neither shall you glean the fallen ears. You shall leave them for the poor and for the alien. I am the LORD your God.

23 24  The LORD spoke to Moses and said, Speak to the Israelites in these words: In the seventh month you shall keep the first day as a sacred rest, a day of

25  remembrance and acclamation, a day of sacred assembly. You shall not do your daily work; you shall present a food-offering to the LORD.

26 27  The LORD spoke to Moses and said: Further, the tenth day of this seventh month is the Day of Atonement. There shall be a sacred assembly;

28  you shall mortify yourselves and present a food-offering to the LORD. On that same day you shall do no work because it is a day of expiation, to make

29  expiation for you before the LORD your God. Therefore every person who does not mortify himself on that day shall be cut off from his father's kin.

30 31  I will extirpate any person who does any work on that day. You shall do no work; it is a rule binding on your descendants for all time wherever you

32  live. It is for you a sabbath of sacred rest, and you shall mortify yourselves. From the evening of the ninth day to the following evening you shall keep your sabbath-rest.

33 34  The LORD spoke to Moses and said, Speak to the Israelites in these

*a Or from.*

136

words: On the fifteenth day of this seventh month the LORD's pilgrim-feast of Tabernacles*ᵃ* begins, and it lasts for seven days. On the first day 35 there shall be a sacred assembly; you shall not do your daily work. For 36 seven days you shall present a food-offering to the LORD; and on the eighth day there shall be a sacred assembly, and you shall present a food-offering to the LORD. It is the closing ceremony; you shall not do your daily work.

These are the appointed seasons of the LORD which you shall proclaim 37 as sacred assemblies for presenting food-offerings to the LORD, whole-offerings and grain-offerings, shared-offerings and drink-offerings, each on its day, besides the LORD's sabbaths and all your gifts, your vows, and 38 your freewill offerings to the LORD.

Further, from the fifteenth day of the seventh month, when the harvest 39 has been gathered, you shall keep the LORD's pilgrim-feast for seven days. The first day is a sacred rest and so is the eighth day. On the first day you 40 shall take the fruit of citrus-trees, palm fronds, and leafy branches, and willows*ᵇ* from the riverside, and you shall rejoice before the LORD your God for seven days. You shall keep this as a pilgrim-feast in the LORD's 41 honour for seven days every year. It is a rule binding for all time on your descendants; in the seventh month you shall hold this pilgrim-feast. You 42 shall live in arbours for seven days, all who are native Israelites, so that 43 your descendants may be reminded how I made the Israelites live in arbours when I brought them out of Egypt. I am the LORD your God.

Thus Moses announced to the Israelites the appointed seasons of the 44 LORD.

THE LORD SPOKE TO MOSES and said: Command the Israelites to take 24 1 2 pure oil of pounded olives ready for the regular mounting of the lamp outside the Veil of the Tokens in the Tent of the Presence. Aaron shall 3 keep the lamp in trim regularly from dusk to dawn before the LORD: this is a rule binding on your descendants for all time. The lamps on the lamp- 4 stand, ritually clean, shall be regularly kept in trim by him before the LORD.

You shall take flour and bake it into twelve loaves, two tenths of an ephah 5 to each. You shall arrange them in two rows, six to a row on the table, 6 ritually clean, before the LORD. You shall sprinkle pure frankincense on 7 the rows, and this shall be a token of the bread, offered to the LORD as a food-offering. Sabbath after sabbath he shall arrange it regularly before 8 the LORD as a gift from the Israelites. This is a covenant for ever; it is the 9 privilege of Aaron and his sons, and they shall eat the bread in a holy place, because it is the holiest of holy-gifts. It is his due out of the food-offerings of the LORD for all time.

Now there was in the Israelite camp a man whose mother was an Israel- 10-11 ite and his father an Egyptian; his mother's name was Shelomith daughter of Dibri of the tribe of Dan; and he went out and became involved in a brawl with an Israelite of pure descent. He uttered the Holy Name in blasphemy, so they brought him to Moses; and they kept him in custody 12 until the LORD's will should be clearly made known to them.

The LORD spoke to Moses and said, Take the man who blasphemed out 13 14

*ᵃ Or* Booths *or* Arbours.　　　*ᵇ Or* poplars.

of the camp. Everyone who heard him shall put a hand*ᵃ* on his head, and
15 then all the community shall stone him to death. You shall say to the
Israelites: When any man whatever blasphemes his God, he shall accept
16 responsibility for his sin. Whoever utters the Name of the Lᴏʀᴅ shall be
put to death: all the community shall stone him; alien or native, if he utters
the Name, he shall be put to death.
17      When one man strikes another and kills him, he shall be put to death.
18 Whoever strikes a beast and kills it shall make restitution, life for life.
19 When one man injures and disfigures his fellow-countryman, it shall be
20 done to him as he has done; fracture for fracture, eye for eye, tooth for
tooth; the injury and disfigurement that he has inflicted upon another
shall in turn be inflicted upon him.
21      Whoever strikes a beast and kills it shall make restitution, but whoever
22 strikes a man and kills him shall be put to death. You shall have one penalty
for alien and native alike. For I am the Lᴏʀᴅ your God.
23      Thus did Moses speak to the Israelites, and they took the man who
blasphemed out of the camp and stoned him to death. The Israelites did
as the Lᴏʀᴅ had commanded Moses.

25 1 2 Tʜᴇ ʟᴏʀᴅ sᴘᴏᴋᴇ ᴛᴏ ᴍᴏsᴇs on Mount Sinai and said, Speak to the
Israelites in these words: When you enter the land which I give you, the
3 land shall keep sabbaths to the Lᴏʀᴅ. For six years you may sow your
4 fields and for six years prune your vineyards and gather the harvest, but
in the seventh year the land shall keep a sabbath of sacred rest, a sabbath
5 to the Lᴏʀᴅ. You shall not sow your field nor prune your vineyard. You
shall not harvest the crop that grows from fallen grain, nor gather in the
grapes from the unpruned vines. It shall be a year of sacred rest for the
6 land. Yet what the land itself produces in the sabbath year shall be food
for you, for your male and female slaves, for your hired man, and for the
7 stranger lodging under your roof, for your cattle and for the wild animals
in your country. Everything it produces may be used for food.
8      You shall count seven sabbaths of years, that is seven times seven years,
9 forty-nine years, and in the seventh month on the tenth day of the month,
on the Day of Atonement, you shall send the ram's horn round. You shall
10 send it through all your land to sound a blast, and so you shall hallow the
fiftieth year and proclaim liberation in the land for all its inhabitants. You
shall make this your year of jubilee. Every man of you shall return to his
11 patrimony, every man to his family. The fiftieth year shall be your jubilee.
You shall not sow, and you shall not harvest the self-sown crop, nor shall
12 you gather in the grapes from the unpruned vines, because it is a jubilee,
to be kept holy by you. You shall eat the produce direct from the land.
13      In this year of jubilee you shall return, every one of you, to his patri-
14 mony. When you sell or buy land amongst yourselves, neither party shall
15 drive a hard bargain. You shall pay your fellow-countryman according to
the number of years since the jubilee, and he shall sell to you according
16 to the number of annual crops. The more years there are to run, the higher
the price, the fewer the years, the lower, because he is selling you a series

*ᵃ Or their hands.*

of crops. You must not victimize one another, but you shall fear your God, 17
because I am the LORD your God. Observe my statutes, keep my judgements 18
and carry them out; and you shall live in the land in security. The land 19
shall yield its harvest; you shall eat your fill and live there secure. If you 20
ask what you are to eat during the seventh year, seeing that you will neither
sow nor gather the harvest, I will ordain my blessing for you in the sixth 21
year and the land shall produce a crop to carry over three years. When you 22
sow in the eighth year, you will still be eating from the earlier crop; you
shall eat the old until the new crop is gathered in the ninth year.

No land shall be sold outright, because the land is mine, and you are 23
coming into it as aliens and settlers. Throughout the whole land of your 24
patrimony, you shall allow land which has been sold to be redeemed.

When one of you is reduced to poverty and sells part of his patrimony, 25
his next-of-kin who has the duty of redemption shall come and redeem
what his kinsman has sold. When a man has no such next-of-kin and him- 26
self becomes able to afford its redemption, he shall take into account the 27
years since the sale and pay the purchaser the balance up to the jubilee.
Then he may return to his patrimony. But if the man cannot afford to buy 28
back the property, it shall remain in the hands of the purchaser till the year
of jubilee. It shall then revert to the original owner, and he shall return to
his patrimony.

When a man sells a dwelling-house in a walled town, he shall retain the 29
right of redemption till the end of the year of the sale; for a time he shall
have the right of redemption. If it is not redeemed before a full year is out, 30
the house in the walled town shall vest in perpetuity in the buyer and his
descendants; it shall not revert at the jubilee. Houses in unwalled hamlets 31
shall be treated as property in the open country: the right of redemption
shall hold good, and in any case the house shall revert at the jubilee.
Levites shall have the perpetual right to redeem houses of their own patri- 32
mony in towns belonging to them. If one of the Levites does not redeem his 33
house in such a town, then it shall still revert to him at the jubilee, because
the houses in Levite towns are their patrimony in Israel. The common land 34
surrounding their towns shall not be sold, because it is their property in
perpetuity.

When your brother-Israelite is reduced to poverty and cannot support 35
himself in the community, you shall assist him as you would an alien or a
stranger, and he shall live with you. You shall not charge him interest on 36
a loan, either by deducting it in advance from the capital sum, or by adding
it on repayment. You shall fear your God, and your brother shall live with
you; you shall not deduct interest when advancing him money nor add 37
interest to the payment due for food supplied on credit. I am the LORD 38
your God who brought you out of Egypt to give you the land of Canaan
and to become your God.

When your brother is reduced to poverty and sells himself to you, you 39
shall not use him to work for you as a slave. His status shall be that of a 40
hired man or a stranger lodging with you; he shall work for you until the
year of jubilee. He shall then leave your service, with his children, and go 41
back to his family and to his ancestral property: because they are my slaves 42

43 whom I brought out of Egypt, they shall not be sold as slaves are sold. You shall not drive him with ruthless severity, but you shall fear your God.
44 Such slaves as you have, male or female, shall come from the nations round
45 about you; from them you may buy slaves. You may also buy the children of those who have settled and lodge with you and such of their family as
46 are born in the land. These may become your property, and you may leave them to your sons after you; you may use them as slaves permanently. But your fellow-Israelites you shall not drive with ruthless severity.
47 When an alien or a stranger living with you becomes rich, and your brother becomes poor and sells himself to the alien or stranger or to a
48 member of some alien family, he shall have the right of redemption after
49 he has sold himself. One of his brothers may redeem him, or his uncle, his cousin, or any blood-relation of his family, or, if he can afford it, he may
50 redeem himself. He and his purchaser together shall reckon from the year when he sold himself to the year of jubilee, and the price shall be adjusted to the number of years. His period of service with his owner shall be
51 reckoned at the rate of a hired man. If there are still many years to run to the year of jubilee, he must repay for his redemption a proportionate
52 amount of the sum for which he sold himself; if there are few, he shall
53 reckon and repay accordingly. He shall have the status of a labourer hired from year to year, and you shall not let him be driven with ruthless severity
54 by his owner. If the man is not redeemed in the intervening years, he and
55 his children shall be released in the year of jubilee; for it is to me that the Israelites are slaves, my slaves whom I brought out of Egypt. I am the LORD your God.

26 YOU SHALL NOT MAKE IDOLS for yourselves; you shall not erect a carved image or a sacred pillar; you shall not put a figured stone on your land to
2 prostrate yourselves upon, because I am the LORD your God. You shall keep my sabbaths and revere my sanctuary. I am the LORD.
3 If you conform to my statutes, if you observe my commandments and
4 carry them out, I will give you rain at the proper time; the land shall yield
5 its produce and the trees of the country-side their fruit. Threshing shall last till vintage and vintage till sowing; you shall eat your fill and live
6 secure in your land. I will give peace in the land, and you shall lie down to sleep with no one to terrify you. I will rid your land of dangerous beasts
7 and it shall not be ravaged by war. You shall put your enemies to flight and
8 they shall fall in battle before you. Five of you shall pursue a hundred and a hundred of you ten thousand; so shall your enemies fall in battle before
9 you. I will look upon you with favour, I will make you fruitful and increase
10 your numbers: I will give my covenant with you its full effect. Your old harvest shall last you in store until you have to clear out the old to make
11 room for the new. I will establish my Tabernacle among you and will not
12 spurn you. I will walk to and fro among you; I will become your God and
13 you shall become my people. I am the LORD your God who brought you out of Egypt and let you be their slaves no longer; I broke the bars of your yoke and enabled you to walk upright.
14 But if you do not listen to me, if you fail to keep all these commandments

of mine, if you reject my statutes, if you spurn my judgements, and do not 15
obey all my commandments, but break my covenant, then be sure that this 16
is what I will do: I will bring upon you sudden terror, wasting disease,
recurrent fever, and plagues that dim the sight and cause the appetite to
fail. You shall sow your seed to no purpose, for your enemies shall eat the
crop. I will set my face against you, and you shall be routed by your enemies. 17
Those that hate you shall hound you on until you run when there is no
pursuit.

If after all this you do not listen to me, I will go on to punish you seven 18
times over for your sins. I will break down your stubborn pride. I will make 19
the sky above you like iron and the earth beneath you like bronze. Your 20
strength shall be spent in vain; your land shall not yield its produce nor the
trees of the land their fruit.

If you still defy me and refuse to listen, I will multiply your calamities 21
seven times, as your sins deserve. I will send wild beasts among you; they 22
shall tear your children from you, destroy your cattle and bring your numbers low; and your roads shall be deserted. If after all this you have not 23
learnt discipline but still defy me, I in turn will defy you and scourge you 24
seven times over for your sins. I will bring war in vengeance upon you, 25
vengeance irrevocable under covenant; you shall be herded into your
cities, I will send pestilence among you, and you shall be given over to the
enemy. I will cut short your daily bread until ten women can bake your 26
bread in a single oven; they shall dole it out by weight, and though you eat,
you shall not be satisfied.

If in spite of this you do not listen to me and still defy me, I will defy 27 28
you in anger, and I myself will punish you seven times over for your sins.
Instead of meat you shall eat your sons and your daughters. I will destroy 29 30
your hill-shrines and demolish your incense-altars. I will pile your rotting
carcasses on the rotting logs*a* that were your idols, and I will spurn you.
I will make your cities desolate and destroy your sanctuaries; the soothing 31
odour of your offerings I will not accept. I will destroy your land, and the 32
enemies who occupy it shall be appalled. I will scatter you among the 33
heathen, and I will pursue you with the naked sword; your land shall be
desolate and your cities heaps of rubble. Then, all the time that it lies 34
desolate, while you are in exile in the land of your enemies, your land shall
enjoy its sabbaths to the full. All the time of its desolation it shall have the 35
sabbath rest which it did not have when you lived there. And I will make 36
those of you who are left in the land of your enemies so ridden with fear
that, when a leaf flutters behind them in the wind, they shall run as if it
were the sword behind them; they shall fall with no one in pursuit. Though 37
no one pursues them they shall stumble over one another, as if the sword
were behind them, and there shall be no stand made against the enemy.
You shall meet your end among the heathen, and your enemies' land shall 38
swallow you up. Those who are left shall pine away in an enemy land under 39
their own iniquities; and with their fathers' iniquities upon them too, they
shall pine away as they did.

But though they confess their iniquity, their own and their fathers', 40

*a* rotting logs: *or* effigies.

141

41 their treachery, and even their defiance of me, I will defy them in my turn
   and carry them off into their enemies' land. Yet if then their stubborn
42 spirit is broken and they accept their punishment in full, I will remember
   my covenant with Jacob and my covenant with Isaac, yes, and my covenant
43 with Abraham, and I will remember the land. The land shall be rid of its
   people and enjoy in full its sabbaths while it lies desolate, and they shall
   pay in full the penalty because they rejected my judgements and spurned
44 my statutes. Yet even then, in their enemies' land, I shall not have rejected
   nor spurned them, bringing them to an end and so breaking my covenant
45 with them, because I am the LORD their God. I will remember on their
   behalf the covenant with the men of former times whom I brought out of
   Egypt in full sight of all the nations, that I might be their God. I am the
   LORD.
46      These are the statutes, the judgements, and the laws which the LORD
   established between himself and the Israelites on Mount Sinai through
   Moses.

27 1 2 THE LORD SPOKE TO MOSES and said, Speak to the Israelites in these
   words: When a man makes a special*a* vow to the LORD which requires
   3 your valuation of living persons, a male between twenty and sixty years old
   shall be valued at fifty silver shekels, that is shekels by the sacred standard.
   4 5 If it is a female, she shall be valued at thirty shekels. If the person is between
   five years old and twenty, the valuation shall be twenty shekels for a male
   6 and ten for a female. If the person is between a month and five years old,
   7 the valuation shall be five shekels for a male and three for a female. If the
   person is over sixty and a male, the valuation shall be fifteen shekels, but
   8 if a female, ten shekels. If the man is too poor to pay the amount of your
   valuation, the person shall be set before the priest, and the priest shall
   value him according to the sum which the man who makes the vow can
   afford: the priest shall make the valuation.
   9    If the vow concerns a beast such as may be offered as an offering to the
   10 LORD, then every gift shall be holy to the LORD. He shall not change it for
   another, or substitute good for bad or bad for good. But if a substitution is
   in fact made of one beast for another, then both the original beast and its
   11 substitute shall be holy to the LORD. If the vow concerns any unclean beast
   such as may not be offered as an offering to the LORD, then the animal shall
   12 be brought before the priest, and he shall value it whether good or bad. The
   13 priest's valuation shall be decisive; in case of redemption the payment shall
   be increased by one fifth.
   14    When a man dedicates his house as holy to the LORD, the priest shall
   value it whether good or bad, and the priest's valuation shall be decisive.
   15 If the donor redeems his house, he shall pay the amount of the valuation
   increased by one fifth, and the house shall be his.
   16    If a man dedicates to the LORD part of his ancestral land, you shall value
   it according to the amount of seed-corn it can carry, at the rate of fifty
   17 shekels of silver for a homer of barley seed. If he dedicates his land from
   18 the year of jubilee, it shall stand at your valuation; but if he dedicates it

*a* makes a special: *or* discharges a . . .

142

after the year of jubilee, the priest shall estimate the price in silver according to the number of years remaining till the next year of jubilee, and this shall be deducted from your valuation. If the man who dedicates his field 19 should redeem it, he shall pay the amount of your valuation in silver, increased by one fifth, and it shall be his. If he does not redeem it but sells 20 the land to another man, it shall no longer be redeemable; when the land 21 reverts at the year of jubilee, it shall be like land that has been devoted, holy to the LORD. It shall belong to the priest as his patrimony.

If a man dedicates to the LORD land which he has bought, land which 22 is not part of his ancestral land, the priest shall estimate the amount of 23 the value for the period until the year of jubilee, and the man shall give the amount fixed as at that day; it is holy to the LORD. At the year of jubilee the 24 land shall revert to the man from whom he bought it, whose patrimony it is. Every valuation you make shall be made by the sacred standard (twenty 25 gerahs to the shekel).

Notwithstanding, no man may dedicate to the LORD the first-born of a 26 beast which in any case has to be offered as a first-born, whether an ox or a sheep. It is the LORD's. If it is any unclean beast, he may redeem it at 27 your valuation and shall add one fifth; but if it is not redeemed, it shall be sold at your valuation. Notwithstanding, nothing which a man devotes to 28 the LORD irredeemably from his own property, whether man or beast or ancestral land, may be sold or redeemed. Everything so devoted is most holy to the LORD. No human being thus devoted may be redeemed, but he 29 shall be put to death.

Every tithe on land, whether from grain or from the fruit of a tree, 30 belongs to the LORD; it is holy to the LORD. If a man wishes to redeem any 31 of his tithe, he shall pay its value increased by one fifth. Every tenth creature 32 that passes under the counting rod shall be holy to the LORD; this applies to all tithes of cattle and sheep. There shall be no inquiry whether it is good 33 or bad, and no substitution. If any ·substitution is made, then both the tithe-animal and its substitute shall be forfeit as holy; it shall not be redeemed.

These are the commandments which the LORD gave Moses for the 34 Israelites on Mount Sinai.

# NUMBERS

*Israel in the wilderness of Sinai*

1 ON THE FIRST DAY OF THE SECOND MONTH in the second year after the Israelites came out of Egypt, the LORD spoke to Moses at the Tent of the Presence in the wilderness of
2 Sinai in these words: 'Number the whole community of Israel by families
3 in the father's line, recording the name of every male person aged twenty years and upwards fit for military service. You and Aaron are to make a
4 detailed list of them by their tribal hosts, and you shall have to assist you
5 one head of family from each tribe. These are their names:

of Reuben, Elizur son of Shedeur;
6 of Simeon, Shelumiel son of Zurishaddai;
7 of Judah, Nahshon son of Amminadab;
8 of Issachar, Nethaneel son of Zuar;
9 of Zebulun, Eliab son of Helon;
10 of Joseph: of Ephraim, Elishama son of Ammihud;
of Manasseh, Gamaliel son of Pedahzur;
11 of Benjamin, Abidan son of Gideoni;
12 of Dan, Ahiezer son of Ammishaddai;
13 of Asher, Pagiel son of Ocran;
14 of Gad, Eliasaph son of Reuel;
15 of Naphtali, Ahira son of Enan.'

16 These were the conveners of the whole community, chiefs of their fathers'
17 tribes and heads of Israelite clans. So Moses and Aaron took these men who
18 had been indicated by name. They summoned the whole community on the first day of the second month, and they registered their descent by families in the father's line, recording every male person aged twenty years
19 and upwards, as the LORD had told Moses to do. Thus it was that he drew up the detailed lists in the wilderness of Sinai:
20 The tribal list of Reuben, Israel's eldest son, by families in the father's line, with the name of every male person aged twenty years and upwards
21 fit for service, the number in the list of the tribe of Reuben being forty-six thousand five hundred.
22 The tribal list of Simeon, by families in the father's line, with the name
23 of every male person aged twenty years and upwards fit for service, the number in the list of the tribe of Simeon being fifty-nine thousand three hundred.
24 The tribal list of Gad, by families in the father's line, with the names
25 of all men aged twenty years and upwards fit for service, the number in the list of the tribe of Gad being forty-five thousand six hundred and fifty.

The tribal list of Judah, by families in the father's line, with the names of 26
all men aged twenty years and upwards fit for service, the number in the 27
list of the tribe of Judah being seventy-four thousand six hundred.

The tribal list of Issachar, by families in the father's line, with the names 28
of all men aged twenty years and upwards fit for service, the number in 29
the list of the tribe of Issachar being fifty-four thousand four hundred.

The tribal list of Zebulun, by families in the father's line, with the names 30
of all men aged twenty years and upwards fit for service, the number in the 31
list of the tribe of Zebulun being fifty-seven thousand four hundred.

The tribal lists of Joseph: that of Ephraim, by families in the father's 32
line, with the names of all men aged twenty years and upwards fit for
service, the number in the list of the tribe of Ephraim being forty thousand 33
five hundred; that of Manasseh, by families in the father's line, with the 34
names of all men aged twenty years and upwards fit for service, the num- 35
ber in the list of the tribe of Manasseh being thirty-two thousand two
hundred.

The tribal list of Benjamin, by families in the father's line, with the 36
names of all men aged twenty years and upwards fit for service, the number 37
in the list of the tribe of Benjamin being thirty-five thousand four hundred.

The tribal list of Dan, by families in the father's line, with the names of 38
all men aged twenty years and upwards fit for service, the number in the 39
list of the tribe of Dan being sixty-two thousand seven hundred.

The tribal list of Asher, by families in the father's line, with the names 40
of all men aged twenty years and upwards fit for service, the number in the 41
list of the tribe of Asher being forty-one thousand five hundred.

The tribal list of Naphtali, by families in the father's line, with the names 42
of all men aged twenty years and upwards fit for service, the number in the 43
list of the tribe of Naphtali being fifty-three thousand four hundred.

These were the numbers recorded in the detailed lists by Moses and 44
Aaron and the twelve chiefs of Israel, each representing one tribe and being
the head of a family. The total number of Israelites aged twenty years and 45
upwards fit for service, recorded in the lists of fathers' families, was six 46
hundred and three thousand five hundred and fifty. A list of the Levites 47
by their fathers' families was not made.

The LORD spoke to Moses and said, 'You shall not record the total 48 49
number of the Levites or make a detailed list of them among the Israelites.
You shall put the Levites in charge of the Tabernacle of the Tokens, with 50
its equipment and everything in it. They shall carry the Tabernacle and
all its equipment; they alone shall be its attendants and shall pitch their
tents round it. The Levites shall take the Tabernacle down when it is due 51
to move and shall put it up when it halts; any unqualified person who
comes near it shall be put to death. All other Israelites shall pitch their 52
tents, each tribal host in its proper camp and under its own standard. But 53
the Levites shall encamp round the Tabernacle of the Tokens, so that
divine wrath may not follow the whole community of Israel; the Tabernacle of the Tokens shall be in their keeping.'

The Israelites did exactly as the LORD had told Moses to do. 54

The LORD spoke to Moses and Aaron and said, 'The Israelites shall 2 1 2 encamp each under his own standard by the emblems of his father's family; they shall pitch their tents round the Tent of the Presence, facing it.

3 'In front of it, on the east, the division of Judah shall be stationed under the standard of its camp by tribal hosts. The chief of Judah shall be Nahshon
4 son of Amminadab. His host, with its members as detailed, numbers
5 seventy-four thousand six hundred men. Next to Judah the tribe of
6 Issachar shall be stationed. Its chief shall be Nethaneel son of Zuar; his host, with its members as detailed, numbers fifty-four thousand four
7 hundred. Then the tribe of Zebulun: its chief shall be Eliab son of Helon;
8 his host, with its members as detailed, numbers fifty-seven thousand four
9 hundred. The number listed in the camp of Judah, by hosts, is one hundred and eighty-six thousand four hundred. They shall be the first to march.

10 'To the south the division of Reuben shall be stationed under the standard of its camp by tribal hosts. The chief of Reuben shall be Elizur son
11 of Shedeur; his host, with its members as detailed, numbers forty-six
12 thousand five hundred. Next to him the tribe of Simeon shall be stationed.
13 Its chief shall be Shelumiel son of Zurishaddai; his host, with its members
14 as detailed, numbers fifty-nine thousand three hundred. Then the tribe
15 of Gad: its chief shall be Eliasaph son of Reuel; his host, with its members
16 as detailed, numbers forty-five thousand six hundred and fifty. The number listed in the camp of Reuben, by hosts, is one hundred and fifty-one thousand four hundred and fifty. They shall be the second to march.

17 'When the Tent of the Presence moves, the camp of the Levites shall keep its station in the centre of the other camps; they shall all move in the order of their encamping, each man in his proper place under his standard.

18 'To the west the division of Ephraim shall be stationed under the standard of its camp by tribal hosts. The chief of Ephraim shall be Elishama
19 son of Ammihud; his host, with its members as detailed, numbers
20 forty thousand five hundred. Next to him the tribe of Manasseh shall be
21 stationed. Its chief shall be Gamaliel son of Pedahzur; his host, with its
22 members as detailed, numbers thirty-two thousand two hundred. Then
23 the tribe of Benjamin: its chief shall be Abidan son of Gideoni; his host, with its members as detailed, numbers thirty-five thousand four hundred.
24 The number listed in the camp of Ephraim, by hosts, is one hundred and eight thousand one hundred. They shall be the third to march.

25 'To the north the division of Dan shall be stationed under the standard of its camp by tribal hosts. The chief of Dan shall be Ahiezer son of
26 Ammishaddai; his host, with its members as detailed, numbers sixty-two
27 thousand seven hundred. Next to him the tribe of Asher shall be stationed.
28 Its chief shall be Pagiel son of Ocran; his host, with its members as detailed,
29 numbers forty-one thousand five hundred. Then the tribe of Naphtali: its
30 chief shall be Ahira son of Enan; his host, with its members as detailed,
31 numbers fifty-three thousand four hundred. The number listed in the camp of Dan is a hundred and fifty-seven thousand six hundred. They shall march, under their standards, last.'

32 These were the Israelites listed by their fathers' families. The total number in the camp, recorded by tribal hosts, was six hundred and three thousand five hundred and fifty.

The Levites were not included in the detailed lists with their fellow- 33
Israelites, for so the LORD had commanded Moses. The Israelites did 34
exactly as the LORD had commanded Moses, pitching and breaking camp
standard by standard, each man according to his family in his father's line.

THESE WERE THE DESCENDANTS OF AARON and Moses at the time 3
when the LORD spoke to Moses on Mount Sinai. The names of the sons 2
of Aaron were Nadab the eldest, Abihu, Eleazar and Ithamar. These were 3
the names of Aaron's sons, the anointed priests who had been installed in
the priestly office. Nadab and Abihu fell dead before the LORD because they 4
had presented illicit fire before the LORD in the wilderness of Sinai. They
left no sons; Eleazar and Ithamar continued to perform the priestly office
in their father's presence.

The LORD spoke to Moses and said, 'Bring forward the tribe of Levi and 5 6
appoint them to serve Aaron the priest and to minister to him. They shall 7
be in attendance on him and on the whole community before the Tent of
the Presence, undertaking the service of the Tabernacle. They shall be in 8
charge of all the equipment in the Tent of the Presence, and be in attendance on the Israelites, undertaking the service of the Tabernacle. You shall 9
assign the Levites to Aaron and his sons as especially dedicated to him out
of all the Israelites. To Aaron and his line you shall commit the priestly 10
office and they shall perform its duties; any unqualified person who intrudes upon it shall be put to death.'

The LORD spoke to Moses and said, 'I take the Levites for myself out of 11 12
all the Israelites as a substitute for the eldest male child of every woman;
the Levites shall be mine. For every eldest child, if a boy, became mine 13
when I destroyed all the eldest sons in Egypt. So I have consecrated to
myself all the first-born in Israel, both man and beast. They shall be mine.
I am the LORD.'

The LORD spoke to Moses in the wilderness of Sinai and said, 'Make a 14 15
detailed list of all the Levites by their families in the father's line, every
male from the age of one month and upwards.'

Moses made a detailed list of them in accordance with the command 16
given him by the LORD. Now these were the names of the sons of Levi: 17

Gershon, Kohath and Merari.

Descendants of Gershon, by families: Libni and Shimei. 18

Descendants of Kohath, by families: Amram, Izhar, Hebron and 19
Uzziel.

Descendants of Merari, by families: Mahli and Mushi. 20

These were the families of Levi, by fathers' families:

Gershon: the family of Libni and the family of Shimei. These were the 21
families of Gershon, and the number of males in their list as detailed, from 22
the age of one month and upwards, was seven thousand five hundred. The 23
families of Gershon were stationed on the west, behind the Tabernacle.
Their chief was Eliasaph son of Lael, and in the service of the Tent of the 24 25
Presence they were in charge of the Tabernacle and its coverings, of the
screen at the entrance to the Tent of the Presence, the hangings of the court, 26

the screen at the entrance to the court all round the Tabernacle and the altar, and of all else needed for its maintenance.

27 Kohath: the family of Amram, the family of Izhar, the family of Heb-
28 ron, the family of Uzziel. These were the families of Kohath, and the number of males, from the age of one month and upwards, was eight
29 thousand six hundred. They were the guardians of the holy things. The families of Kohath were stationed on the south, at the side of the Taber-
30 31 nacle. Their chief was Elizaphan son of Uzziel; they were in charge of the Ark, the table, the lamp-stands and the altars, together with the sacred vessels used in their service, and the screen with everything needed for its
32 maintenance. The chief over all the chiefs of the Levites was Eleazar son of Aaron the priest, who was appointed overseer of those in charge of the sanctuary.

33 Merari: the family of Mahli, the family of Mushi. These were the
34 families of Merari, and the number of males in their list as detailed from
35 the age of one month and upwards was six thousand two hundred. Their chief was Zuriel son of Abihail; they were stationed on the north, at the
36 side of the Tabernacle. The Merarites were in charge of the planks, bars, posts, and sockets of the Tabernacle, together with its vessels and all the
37 equipment needed for its maintenance, the posts, sockets, pegs, and cords of the surrounding court.

38 In front of the Tabernacle on the east, Moses was stationed, with Aaron and his sons, in front of the Tent of the Presence eastwards. They were in charge of the sanctuary on behalf of the Israelites; any unqualified person who came near would be put to death.

39 The number of Levites recorded by Moses on the detailed list by families at the command of the LORD was twenty-two thousand males aged one month and upwards.

40 The LORD said to Moses, 'Make a detailed list of all the male first-born in Israel aged one month and upwards, and count the number of persons.
41 You shall reserve the Levites for me—I am the LORD—in substitution for the eldest sons of the Israelites, and in the same way the Levites' cattle in
42 substitution for the first-born cattle of the Israelites.' As the LORD had told
43 him to do, Moses made a list of all the eldest sons of the Israelites, and the total number of first-born males recorded by name in the register, aged one month and upwards, was twenty-two thousand two hundred and seventy-three.

44 45 The LORD spoke to Moses and said, 'Take the Levites as a substitute for all the eldest sons in Israel and the cattle of the Levites as a substitute
46 for their cattle. The Levites shall be mine. I am the LORD. The eldest sons in Israel will outnumber the Levites by two hundred and seventy-three.
47 This remainder must be ransomed, and you shall accept five shekels for each of them, taking the sacred shekel and reckoning twenty gerahs to the
48 shekel; you shall give the money with which they are ransomed to Aaron and his sons.'

49 Moses took the money paid as ransom for those who remained over when
50 the substitution of Levites was complete. The amount received was one thousand three hundred and sixty-five shekels of silver by the sacred

standard. In accordance with what the LORD had said, he gave the money 51
to Aaron and his sons, doing what the LORD had told him to do.

The LORD spoke to Moses and Aaron and said, 'Among the Levites, **4** 1 2
make a count of the descendants of Kohath between the ages of thirty and 3
fifty, by families in the father's line, comprising everyone who comes to
take duty in the service of the Tent of the Presence.

'This is the service to be rendered by the Kohathites in the Tent of the 4
Presence; it is most sacred. When the camp is due to move, Aaron and his 5
sons shall come and take down the Veil of the screen and cover the Ark of
the Tokens with it; over this they shall put a covering of porpoise-hide *a* 6
and over that again a violet cloth all of one piece; they shall then put its
poles in place. Over the Table of the Presence they shall spread a violet 7
cloth and lay on it the dishes, saucers, and flagons, and the bowls for drink-
offerings; the Bread regularly presented shall also lie upon it; then they 8
shall spread over them a scarlet cloth and over that a covering of porpoise-
hide, and put the poles in place. They shall take a violet cloth and cover 9
the lamp-stand, its lamps, tongs, firepans, and all the containers for the
oil used in its service; they shall put it with all its equipment in a sheet of 10
porpoise-hide slung from a pole. Over the gold altar they shall spread a 11
violet cloth, cover it with a porpoise-hide covering, and put its poles in
place. They shall take all the articles used for the service of the sanctuary, 12
put them on a violet cloth, cover them with a porpoise-hide covering, and
sling them from a pole. They shall clear the altar of the fat and ashes, spread 13
a purple cloth over it, and then lay on it all the equipment used in its service, 14
the firepans, forks, shovels, tossing-bowls, and all the equipment of the
altar, spread a covering of porpoise-hide over it and put the poles in place.
Once Aaron and his sons have finished covering the sanctuary and all the 15
sacred equipment, when the camp is due to move, the Kohathites shall
come to carry it; they must not touch it on pain of death. All these things
are the load to be carried by the Kohathites, the things connected with the
Tent of the Presence. Eleazar son of Aaron the priest shall have charge of 16
the lamp-oil, the fragrant incense, the regular grain-offering, and the
anointing oil, with the general oversight of the whole Tabernacle and its
contents, the sanctuary and its equipment.'

The LORD spoke to Moses and Aaron and said, 'You must not let the 17 18
families of Kohath be extirpated, and lost to the tribe of Levi. If they are 19
to live and not die when they approach the most holy things, this is what
you must do: Aaron and his sons shall come and set each man to his
appointed task and to his load, and the Kohathites themselves shall not 20
enter to cast even a passing glance on the sanctuary, on pain of death.'

The LORD spoke to Moses and said, 'Number the Gershonites by 21 22
families in the father's line. Make a detailed list of all those between the 23
ages of thirty and fifty who come on duty to perform service in the Tent
of the Presence.

'This is the service to be rendered by the Gershonite families, comprising 24
their general duty and their loads. They shall carry the hangings of the 25
Tabernacle, the Tent of the Presence, its covering, that is the covering of

*a Strictly* hide of sea-cow.

porpoise-hide which is over it, the screen at the entrance to the Tent of
26 the Presence, the hangings of the court, the screen at the entrance to the
court surrounding the Tabernacle and the altar, their cords and all the
equipment for their service; and they shall perform all the tasks connected
27 with them. These are the acts of service they shall render. All the service
of the Gershonites, their loads and their other duties, shall be directed by
Aaron and his sons; you shall assign them the loads for which they shall be
28 responsible. This is the service assigned to the Gershonite families in
connection with the Tent of the Presence; Ithamar son of Aaron shall be
in charge of them.
29 'You shall make a detailed list of the Merarites by families in the father's
30 line, all those between the ages of thirty and fifty, who come on duty to
perform service in the Tent of the Presence.
31 'These are the loads for which they shall be responsible in virtue of their
service in the Tent of the Presence: the planks of the Tabernacle with its
32 bars, posts, and sockets, the posts of the surrounding court with their
sockets, pegs, and cords, and all that is needed for the maintenance of them;
you shall assign to each man by name the load for which he is responsible.
33 These are the duties of the Merarite families in virtue of their service in
the Tent of the Presence. Ithamar son of Aaron the priest shall be in charge
of them.'
34 Moses and Aaron and the chiefs of the community made a detailed list
35 of the Kohathites by families in the father's line, taking all between the
ages of thirty and fifty who came on duty to perform service in the Tent
36 of the Presence. The number recorded by families in the detailed lists was
37 two thousand seven hundred and fifty. This was the total number in the
detailed lists of the Kohathite families who did duty in the Tent of the
Presence; they were recorded by Moses and Aaron as the LORD had told
them to do through Moses.
38-39 The Gershonites between the ages of thirty and fifty, who came on duty
for service in the Tent of the Presence, were recorded in detailed lists by
40 families in the father's line. Their number, by families in the father's line,
41 was two thousand six hundred and thirty. This was the total recorded in
the lists of the Gershonite families who came on duty in the Tent of the
Presence, and were recorded by Moses and Aaron as the LORD had told
them to do.
42-43 The families of Merari, between the ages of thirty and fifty, who came
on duty to perform service in the Tent of the Presence, were recorded
44 in detailed lists by families in the father's line. Their number by families
45 was three thousand two hundred. These were recorded in the Merarite
families by Moses and Aaron as the LORD had told them to do through
Moses.
46 Thus Moses and Aaron and the chiefs of Israel made a detailed list of all
47 the Levites by families in the father's line, between the ages of thirty and
fifty years; these were all who came to perform their various duties and
48 carry their loads in the service of the Tent of the Presence. Their number
49 was eight thousand five hundred and eighty. They were recorded one
by one by Moses at the command of the LORD, according to their

general duty and the loads they carried.<sup>a</sup> For so the LORD had told Moses to do.

THE LORD SPOKE TO MOSES and said: Command the Israelites to expel **5** 1 2 from the camp everyone who suffers from a malignant skin-disease or a discharge, and everyone ritually unclean from contact with a corpse. You 3 shall put them outside the camp, both male and female, so that they will not defile your camps in which I dwell among you. The Israelites did this: 4 they put them outside the camp. As the LORD had said when he spoke to Moses, so the Israelites did.

The LORD spoke to Moses and said, Say to the Israelites: When anyone, 5 6 man or woman, wrongs another and thereby breaks faith with the LORD, that person has incurred guilt which demands reparation. He shall confess 7 the sin he has committed, make restitution in full with the addition of one fifth, and give it to the man to whom compensation is due. If there is no 8 next-of-kin to whom compensation can be paid, the compensation payable in that case shall be the LORD's, for the use of the priest, in addition to the ram of expiation with which the priest makes expiation for him.

Every contribution made by way of holy-gift which the Israelites bring 9 to the priest shall be the priest's. The priest shall have the holy-gifts which 10 a man gives; whatever is given to him shall be his.

The LORD spoke to Moses and said, Speak to the Israelites in these 11 12 words: When a married woman goes astray, is unfaithful to her husband, and has sexual intercourse with another man, and this happens without 13 the husband's knowledge, and the crime is undetected, because, though she has been defiled, there is no direct evidence against her and she was not caught in the act, but when in such a case a fit of jealousy comes over 14 the husband which causes him to suspect his wife, she being in fact defiled; or when, on the other hand, a fit of jealousy comes over a husband which causes him to suspect his wife, when she is not in fact defiled; then in either 15 case, the husband shall bring his wife to the priest together with the prescribed offering for her, a tenth of an ephah of barley meal. He shall not pour oil on it nor put frankincense on it, because it is a grain-offering for jealousy, a grain-offering of protestation conveying an imputation of guilt. The priest shall bring her forward and set her before the LORD. He shall 16 17 take clean<sup>b</sup> water in an earthenware vessel, and shall take dust from the floor of the Tabernacle and add it to the water. He shall set the woman 18 before the LORD, uncover her head, and place the grain-offering of protestation in her hands; it is a grain-offering for jealousy. The priest shall hold in his own hand the water of contention which brings out the truth. He shall then put the woman on oath and say to her, 'If no man has had 19 intercourse with you, if you have not gone astray and let yourself become defiled while owing obedience to your husband, then may your innocence be established by the water of contention which brings out the truth. But 20 if, while owing him obedience, you have gone astray and let yourself become defiled, if any man other than your husband has had intercourse with you' (the priest shall here put the woman on oath with an adjuration, 21

<sup>a</sup> *Prob. rdg.; Heb. adds* and his registered ones.          <sup>b</sup> *Or* holy.

and shall continue), 'may the LORD make an example of you among your people in adjurations and in swearing of oaths by bringing upon you mis-
22 carriage and untimely birth; and this water that brings out the truth shall enter your body, bringing upon you miscarriage and untimely birth.' The
23 woman shall respond, 'Amen, Amen.' The priest shall write these curses
24 on a scroll and wash them off into the water of contention; he shall make the woman drink the water that brings out the truth, and the water shall
25 enter her body. The priest shall take the grain-offering for jealousy from the woman's hand, present it as a special gift before the LORD, and offer it
26 at the altar. He shall take a handful from the grain-offering by way of token, and burn it at the altar; after this he shall make the woman drink the water.
27 If she has let herself become defiled and has been unfaithful to her husband, then when the priest makes her drink the water that brings out the truth and the water has entered her body, she will suffer a miscarriage or un-timely birth, and her name will become an example in adjuration among
28 her kin. But if the woman has not let herself become defiled and is pure, then her innocence is established and she will bear her child.

29 Such is the law for cases of jealousy, where a woman, owing obedience
30 to her husband, goes astray and lets herself become defiled, or where a fit of jealousy comes over a man which causes him to suspect his wife. He shall set her before the LORD, and the priest shall deal with her as this law
31 prescribes. No guilt will attach to the husband, but the woman shall bear the penalty of her guilt.

6 1 2 The LORD spoke to Moses and said, Speak to the Israelites in these words: When anyone, man or woman, makes a special*a* vow dedicating
3 himself to the LORD as a Nazirite,*b* he shall abstain from wine and strong drink. These he shall not drink, nor anything made from the juice of grapes;
4 nor shall he eat grapes, fresh or dried. During the whole term of his vow he shall eat nothing that comes from the vine, nothing whatever, shoot or
5 berry. During the whole term of his vow no razor shall touch his head; he shall let his hair grow long and plait it until he has completed the term of
6 his dedication: he shall keep himself holy to the LORD. During the whole
7 term of his vow he shall not go near a corpse, not even when his father or mother, brother or sister, dies; he shall not make himself ritually unclean
8 for them, because the Nazirite vow to his God is on his head. He shall keep himself holy to the LORD during the whole term of his Nazirite vow.

9 If someone suddenly falls dead by his side touching him and thereby making his hair, which has been dedicated, ritually unclean, he shall shave
10 his head seven days later, on the day appointed for his ritual cleansing. On the eighth day he shall bring two turtle-doves or two young pigeons to the
11 priest at the entrance to the Tent of the Presence. The priest shall offer one as a sin-offering and the other as a whole-offering and shall make expiation for him for the sin he has incurred through contact with the dead body;
12 and he shall consecrate his head afresh on that day. The man shall re-dedicate himself to the LORD for the term of his vow and bring a yearling ram as a guilt-offering. The previous period shall not be reckoned, because the hair which he dedicated became unclean.

*a* makes a special: *or* performs a . . .      *b* *That is* separated one *or* dedicated one.

The law for the Nazirite, when the term of his dedication is completed, 13 shall be this. He shall be brought to the entrance to the Tent of the Presence and shall present his offering to the LORD: one yearling ram without blemish 14 as a whole-offering, one yearling ewe without blemish as a sin-offering, one ram without blemish as a shared-offering, and a basket of cakes made of 15 flour mixed with oil, and of wafers smeared with oil, both unleavened, together with the proper grain-offerings and drink-offerings. The priest 16 shall present all these before the LORD and offer the man's sin-offering and whole-offering; the ram he shall offer as a shared-offering to the 17 LORD, together with the basket of unleavened cakes and the proper grain-offering and drink-offering. The Nazirite shall shave his head at the 18 entrance to the Tent of the Presence, take the hair which had been dedicated and put it on the fire where the shared-offering is burning. The priest shall 19 take the shoulder of the ram, after boiling it, and take also one unleavened cake from the basket and one unleavened wafer, and put them on the palms of the Nazirite's hands, his hair which had been dedicated having been shaved. The priest shall then present them as a special gift before the LORD; 20 these, together with the breast of the special gift and the leg of the contribution, are holy and belong to the priest. When this has been done, the Nazirite is again free to drink wine.

Such is the law for the Nazirite who has made his vow. Such is the 21 offering he must make to the LORD for his dedication, apart from anything else that he can afford. He must carry out his vow in full according to the law governing his dedication.

The LORD spoke to Moses and said, Speak to Aaron and his sons in these 22 23 words: These are the words with which you shall bless the Israelites:

> The LORD bless you and watch over you; 24
> the LORD make his face shine upon*a* you 25
> and be gracious to you;
> the LORD look kindly on you and give you peace. 26

They shall pronounce my name over the Israelites, and I will bless them. 27

ON THE DAY THAT MOSES COMPLETED the setting up of the Taber- 7 nacle, he anointed and consecrated it; he also anointed and consecrated its equipment, and the altar and its vessels. The chief men of Israel, heads 2 of families—that is the chiefs of the tribes, who had assisted in preparing the detailed lists—came forward and brought their offering before the 3 LORD, six covered wagons and twelve oxen, one wagon from every two chiefs and from each one an ox.*b* These they brought forward before the Tabernacle; and the LORD spoke to Moses and said, 'Accept these from 4 5 them: they shall be used for the service of the Tent of the Presence. Assign them to the Levites as their several duties require.'

So Moses accepted the wagons and oxen and assigned them to the 6 Levites. He gave two wagons and four oxen to the Gershonites as required 7 for their service; four wagons and eight oxen to the Merarites as required 8 for their service, in charge of Ithamar the son of Aaron the priest. He gave 9

---

*a* Or to.    *b* Or a bull.

none to the Kohathites because the service laid upon them was that of the holy things: these they had to carry themselves on their shoulders.

10 When the altar was anointed, the chiefs brought their gift for its dedica-
11 tion and presented their offering before it. The LORD said to Moses, 'Let the chiefs present their offering for the dedication of the altar one by one, on consecutive days.'

12 The chief who presented his offering on the first day was Nahshon son
13 of Amminadab of the tribe of Judah. His offering was one silver dish weighing a hundred and thirty shekels by the sacred standard and one silver tossing-bowl weighing seventy, both full of flour mixed with oil as a grain-
14 15 offering; one saucer weighing ten gold shekels, full of incense; one young
16 bull, one full-grown ram, and one yearling ram, as a whole-offering; one
17 he-goat as a sin-offering; and two bulls, five full-grown rams, five he-goats, and five yearling rams, as a shared-offering. This was the offering of Nahshon son of Amminadab.

18 On the second day Nethaneel son of Zuar, chief of Issachar, brought his
19 offering. He brought one silver dish weighing a hundred and thirty shekels by the sacred standard and one silver tossing-bowl weighing seventy, both
20 full of flour mixed with oil as a grain-offering; one saucer weighing ten
21 gold shekels, full of incense; one young bull, one full-grown ram, and one
22 23 yearling ram, as a whole-offering; one he-goat as a sin-offering; and two bulls, five full-grown rams, five he-goats, and five yearling rams, as a shared-offering. This was the offering of Nethaneel son of Zuar.

24 On the third day the chief of the Zebulunites, Eliab son of Helon, came.
25 His offering was one silver dish weighing a hundred and thirty shekels by the sacred standard and one silver tossing-bowl weighing seventy, both full
26 of flour mixed with oil as a grain-offering; one saucer weighing ten gold
27 shekels, full of incense; one young bull, one full-grown ram, and one year-
28 29 ling ram, as a whole-offering; one he-goat as a sin-offering; and two bulls, five full-grown rams, five he-goats, and five yearling rams, as a shared-offering. This was the offering of Eliab son of Helon.

30 On the fourth day the chief of the Reubenites, Elizur son of Shedeur,
31 came. His offering was one silver dish weighing a hundred and thirty shekels by the sacred standard and one silver tossing-bowl weighing
32 seventy, both full of flour mixed with oil as a grain-offering; one saucer
33 weighing ten gold shekels, full of incense; one young bull, one full-grown
34 ram, and one yearling ram, as a whole-offering; one he-goat as a sin-offer-
35 ing; and two bulls, five full-grown rams, five he-goats, and five yearling rams, as a shared-offering. This was the offering of Elizur son of Shedeur.

36 On the fifth day the chief of the Simeonites, Shelumiel son of Zurishad-
37 dai, came. His offering was one silver dish weighing a hundred and thirty shekels by the sacred standard and one silver tossing-bowl weighing
38 seventy, both full of flour mixed with oil as a grain-offering; one saucer
39 weighing ten gold shekels, full of incense; one young bull, one full-grown
40 ram, and one yearling ram, as a whole-offering; one he-goat as a sin-
41 offering; and two bulls, five full-grown rams, five he-goats, and five year-ling rams, as a shared-offering. This was the offering of Shelumiel son of Zurishaddai.

On the sixth day the chief of the Gadites, Eliasaph son of Reuel, came. 42
His offering was one silver dish weighing a hundred and thirty shekels by 43
the sacred standard and one silver tossing-bowl weighing seventy, both
full of flour mixed with oil as a grain-offering; one saucer weighing ten 44
gold shekels, full of incense; one young bull, one full-grown ram, and one 45
yearling ram, as a whole-offering; one he-goat as a sin-offering; and two 46 47
bulls, five full-grown rams, five he-goats, and five yearling rams, as a
shared-offering. This was the offering of Eliasaph son of Reuel.

On the seventh day the chief of the Ephraimites, Elishama son of 48
Ammihud, came. His offering was one silver dish weighing a hundred and 49
thirty shekels by the sacred standard and one silver tossing-bowl weighing
seventy, both full of flour mixed with oil as a grain-offering; one saucer 50
weighing ten gold shekels, full of incense; one young bull, one full-grown 51
ram, and one yearling ram, as a whole-offering; one he-goat as a sin- 52
offering; and two bulls, five full-grown rams, five he-goats, and five year- 53
ling rams, as a shared-offering. This was the offering of Elishama son of
Ammihud.

On the eighth day the chief of the Manassites, Gamaliel son of Pedahzur, 54
came. His offering was one silver dish weighing a hundred and thirty 55
shekels by the sacred standard and one silver tossing-bowl weighing
seventy, both full of flour mixed with oil as a grain-offering; one saucer 56
weighing ten gold shekels, full of incense; one young bull, one full-grown 57
ram, and one yearling ram, as a whole-offering; one he-goat as a sin-offering; 58
and two bulls, five full-grown rams, five he-goats, and five yearling rams, 59
as a shared-offering. This was the offering of Gamaliel son of Pedahzur.

On the ninth day the chief of the Benjamites, Abidan son of Gideoni, 60
came. His offering was one silver dish weighing a hundred and thirty 61
shekels by the sacred standard and one silver tossing-bowl weighing
seventy, both full of flour mixed with oil as a grain-offering; one saucer 62
weighing ten gold shekels, full of incense; one young bull, one full-grown 63
ram, and one yearling ram, as a whole-offering; one he-goat as a sin- 64
offering; and two bulls, five full-grown rams, five he-goats, and five year- 65
ling rams, as a shared-offering. This was the offering of Abidan son of
Gideoni.

On the tenth day the chief of the Danites, Ahiezer son of Ammishaddai, 66
came. His offering was one silver dish weighing a hundred and thirty 67
shekels by the sacred standard and one silver tossing-bowl weighing
seventy, both full of flour mixed with oil as a grain-offering; one saucer 68
weighing ten gold shekels, full of incense; one young bull, one full-grown 69
ram, and one yearling ram, as a whole-offering; one he-goat as a sin- 70
offering; and two bulls, five full-grown rams, five he-goats, and five year- 71
ling rams, as a shared-offering. This was the offering of Ahiezer son of
Ammishaddai.

On the eleventh day the chief of the Asherites, Pagiel son of Ocran, came. 72
His offering was one silver dish weighing a hundred and thirty shekels by 73
the sacred standard and one silver tossing-bowl weighing seventy, both
full of flour mixed with oil as a grain-offering; one saucer weighing ten 74
gold shekels, full of incense; one young bull, one full-grown ram, and one 75

76 77  yearling ram, as a whole-offering; one he-goat as a sin-offering; and two bulls, five full-grown rams, five he-goats, and five yearling rams, as a shared-offering. This was the offering of Pagiel son of Ocran.

78  On the twelfth day the chief of the Naphtalites, Ahira son of Enan, came.

79  His offering was one silver dish weighing a hundred and thirty shekels by the sacred standard and one silver tossing-bowl weighing seventy, both

80  full of flour mixed with oil as a grain-offering; one saucer weighing ten

81  gold shekels, full of incense; one young bull, one full-grown ram, and one

82 83  yearling ram, as a whole-offering; one he-goat as a sin-offering; and two bulls, five full-grown rams, five he-goats, and five yearling rams, as a shared-offering. This was the offering of Ahira son of Enan.

84  This was the gift from the chiefs of Israel for the dedication of the altar when it was anointed: twelve silver dishes, twelve silver tossing-bowls, and

85  twelve golden saucers; each silver dish weighed a hundred and thirty shekels, each silver tossing-bowl seventy shekels. The total weight of the silver vessels was two thousand four hundred shekels by the sacred stan-

86  dard. There were twelve golden saucers full of incense, ten shekels each by the sacred standard: the total weight of the gold of the saucers was a

87  hundred and twenty shekels. The number of beasts for the whole-offering was twelve bulls, twelve full-grown rams, and twelve yearling rams, with the prescribed grain-offerings, and twelve he-goats for the sin-offering.

88  The number of beasts for the shared-offering was twenty-four bulls, sixty full-grown rams, sixty he-goats, and sixty yearling rams. This was the gift

89  for the dedication of the altar when it was anointed. And when Moses entered the Tent of the Presence to speak with God, he heard the Voice speaking from above the cover over the Ark of the Tokens from between the two cherubim: the Voice spoke to him.

8 1 2  The LORD spoke to Moses and said, 'Speak to Aaron in these words: "When you mount the seven lamps, see that they shed their light forwards

3  in front of the lamp-stand."' Aaron did this: he mounted the lamps, so as to shed light forwards in front of the lamp-stand, as the LORD had in-

4  structed Moses. The lamp-stand was made of beaten-work in gold, as well as the stem and the petals. Moses made it to match the pattern which the LORD had shown him.

5 6  The LORD spoke to Moses and said: Take the Levites apart from the

7  rest of the Israelites and cleanse them ritually. This is what you shall do to cleanse them. Sprinkle lustral water over them; they shall then shave

8  their whole bodies, wash their clothes, and so be cleansed. Next, they shall take a young bull as a whole-offering *a* with its prescribed grain-offering, flour mixed with oil; and you shall take a second young bull as a sin-

9  offering. Bring the Levites before the Tent of the Presence and call the

10  whole community of Israelites together. Bring the Levites before the LORD,

11  and let the Israelites lay their hands on their heads. Aaron shall present the Levites before the LORD as a special gift from the Israelites, and they shall

12  be dedicated to the service of the LORD. The Levites shall lay their hands on the heads of the bulls; one bull shall be offered as a sin-offering and the other as a whole-offering to the LORD, to make expiation for the Levites.

*a* as a whole-offering: *prob. rdg.; Heb. om.*

Then you shall set the Levites before Aaron and his sons, presenting them 13
to the LORD as a special gift. You shall thus separate the Levites from the 14
rest of the Israelites, and they shall be mine.

After this, the Levites shall enter the Tent of the Presence to serve in it, 15
ritually cleansed and presented as a special gift; for they are given and 16
dedicated to me, out of all the Israelites. I have accepted them as mine in
place of all that comes first from the womb, every first child among the
Israelites; for every first-born male creature, man or beast, among the 17
Israelites is mine. On the day when I struck down every first-born creature
in Egypt, I hallowed all the first-born of the Israelites to myself, and I 18
have accepted the Levites in their place. I have given the Levites to Aaron 19
and his sons, dedicated among the Israelites to perform the service of the
Israelites in the Tent of the Presence and to make expiation for them, and
then no calamity will befall them when they come close to the sanctuary.

Moses and Aaron and the whole community of Israelites carried out all 20
the commands the LORD had given to Moses for the dedication of the
Levites. The Levites purified themselves of sin and washed their clothes, 21
and Aaron presented them as a special gift before the LORD and made
expiation for them, to cleanse them. Then at last they went in to perform 22
their service in the Tent of the Presence, before Aaron and his sons. Thus
the commands the LORD had given to Moses concerning the Levites were
all carried out.

The LORD spoke to Moses and said: Touching the Levites: they shall 23 24
begin their active work in the service of the Tent of the Presence at the
age of twenty-five. At the age of fifty a Levite shall retire from regular 25
service and shall serve no longer. He may continue to assist his colleagues 26
in attendance in the Tent of the Presence but shall perform no regular
service. This is how you shall arrange the attendance of the Levites.

In the first month of the second year after they came out of Egypt, the 9
LORD spoke to Moses in the wilderness of Sinai and said, 'Let the Israel- 2
ites prepare the Passover at the time appointed for it. This shall be between 3
dusk and dark on the fourteenth day of this month, and you shall keep it
at this appointed time, observing every rule and custom proper to it.' So 4
Moses told the Israelites to prepare the Passover, and they prepared it on 5
the fourteenth day of the first month, between dusk and dark, in the
wilderness of Sinai. The Israelites did exactly as the LORD had instructed
Moses.

It happened that some men were ritually unclean through contact with 6
a corpse and so could not keep the Passover on the right day. They came
before Moses and Aaron that same day and said, 'We are unclean through 7
contact with a corpse. Must we therefore be debarred from presenting the
LORD's offering at its appointed time with the rest of the Israelites?' Moses 8
answered, 'Wait, and let me hear what commands the LORD has for you.'

The LORD spoke to Moses and said, Tell the Israelites: If any one of 9 10
you or of your descendants is ritually unclean through contact with a
corpse, or if he is away on a long journey, he shall keep a Passover to the
LORD none the less. But in that case he shall prepare the victim in the 11
second month, between dusk and dark on the fourteenth day. It shall be

12 eaten with unleavened cakes and bitter herbs; nothing shall be left over
13 till morning, and no bone of it shall be broken. The Passover shall be kept
exactly as the law prescribes. The man who, being ritually clean and
not absent on a journey, neglects to keep the Passover, shall be cut off
from his father's kin, because he has not presented the LORD's offering at
its appointed time. That man shall accept responsibility for his sin.
14 When an alien is settled among you, he also shall keep the Passover to
the LORD, observing every rule and custom proper to it. The same law is
binding on you all, alien and native alike.

## *The journey from Sinai to Edom*

15 ON THE DAY WHEN THEY SET UP THE TABERNACLE, that is the Tent
of the Tokens, cloud covered it, and in the evening a brightness like
16 fire appeared over it till morning. So it continued: the cloud covered it by
17 day and a brightness like fire by night. Whenever the cloud lifted from
the tent, the Israelites struck camp, and at the place where the cloud
18 settled, there they pitched their camp. At the command of the LORD they
struck camp, and at the command of the LORD they encamped again, and
19 continued in camp as long as the cloud rested over the Tabernacle. When
the cloud stayed long over the Tabernacle, the Israelites remained in
20 attendance on the LORD and did not move on; and it was the same when
the cloud continued over the Tabernacle only a few days: at the command
of the LORD they remained in camp, and at the command of the LORD they
21 struck camp. There were also times when the cloud continued only from
evening till morning, and in the morning, when the cloud lifted, they moved
on. Whether by day or by night, they moved as soon as the cloud lifted.
22 Whether it was for a day or two, for a month or a year, whenever the cloud
stayed long over the Tabernacle, the Israelites remained where they were
23 and did not move on; they did so only when the cloud lifted. At the command of the LORD they encamped, and at his command they struck camp.
At the LORD's command, given through Moses, they remained in attendance on the LORD.

**10** 1 2    The LORD spoke to Moses and said: Make two trumpets of beaten silver
and use them for summoning the community and for breaking camp.
3 When both are sounded, the whole community shall muster before you
4 at the entrance to the Tent of the Presence. If a single trumpet is sounded,
5 the chiefs who are heads of the Israelite clans shall muster. When you give
the signal for a shout, those encamped on the east side are to move off.
6 When the signal is given for a second shout those encamped to the south
7 are to move off. A signal to shout is the signal to move off. When you con-
8 vene the assembly, you shall sound a trumpet but not raise a shout. This
sounding of the trumpets is the duty of the Aaronite priests and shall be a
rule binding for all time on your descendants.
9 When you go into battle against an invader and you are hard pressed
by him, you shall raise a cheer when the trumpets sound, and this will
serve as a reminder of you before the LORD your God and you will be

delivered from your enemies. On your festal days and at your appointed 10
seasons and on the first day of every month, you shall sound the trumpets
over your whole-offerings and your shared-offerings, and the trumpets
shall be a reminder on your behalf before the LORD your God. I am the
LORD your God.

In the second year, on the twentieth day of the second month, the cloud 11
lifted from the Tabernacle of the Tokens, and the Israelites moved by 12
stages from the wilderness of Sinai, until the cloud came to rest in the
wilderness of Paran. The first time that they broke camp at the command 13
of the LORD given through Moses, the standard of the division of Judah 14
moved off first with its tribal hosts: the host of Judah under Nahshon son
of Amminadab, the host of Issachar under Nethaneel son of Zuar, and the 15 16
host of Zebulun under Eliab son of Helon. Then the Tabernacle was taken 17
down, and its bearers, the sons of Gershon and Merari, moved off.

Secondly, the standard of the division of Reuben moved off with its 18
tribal hosts: the host of Reuben under Elizur son of Shedeur, the host of 19
Simeon under Shelumiel son of Zurishaddai, and the host of Gad under 20
Eliasaph son of Reuel. The Kohathites, the bearers of the holy things, 21
moved off next, and on their arrival found the Tabernacle set up.

Thirdly, the standard of the division of Ephraim moved off with its 22
tribal hosts: the host of Ephraim under Elishama son of Ammihud, the 23
host of Manasseh under Gamaliel son of Pedahzur, and the host of Ben- 24
jamin under Abidan son of Gideoni.

Lastly, the standard of the division of Dan, the rearguard of all the 25
divisions, moved off with its tribal hosts: the host of Dan under Ahiezer
son of Ammishaddai, the host of Asher under Pagiel son of Ocran, and the 26 27
host of Naphtali under Ahira son of Enan.

This was the order of march for the Israelites, mustered in their hosts, 28
and in this order they broke camp.

And Moses said to Hobab son of Reuel the Midianite, his brother-in- 29
law, 'We are setting out for the place which the LORD promised to give us.
Come with us, and we will deal generously with you, for the LORD has
given an assurance of good fortune for Israel.' But he replied, 'No, I will 30
not; I would rather go to my own country and my own people.' Moses 31
said, 'Do not desert us, I beg you; for you know where we ought to camp
in the wilderness, and you will be our guide. If you will go with us, then 32
all the good fortune with which the LORD favours us we will share
with you.'

Then they moved off from the mountain of the LORD and journeyed for 33
three days, and the Ark of the Covenant of the LORD kept a day's journey
ahead of them to find them a place to rest. The cloud of the LORD hung 34
over them by day when they moved camp. Whenever the Ark began to 35
move, Moses said,

> 'Up, LORD, and may thy enemies be scattered
> and those that hate thee flee before thee.'

When it halted, he said,                                           36

> 'Rest, LORD of the countless thousands of Israel.'

**11** There came a time when the people complained to the LORD of their hardships. When he heard, he became angry and fire from the LORD broke
2 out among them, and was raging at one end of the camp, when the people appealed to Moses. He interceded with the LORD, and the fire died down.
3 Then they named that place Taberah,*a* because the fire of the LORD had burned among them there.

4 Now there was a mixed company of strangers who had joined the Israelites. These people began to be greedy for better things, and the Israelites themselves wept once again and cried, 'Will no one give us meat?
5 Think of it! In Egypt we had fish for the asking, cucumbers and water-
6 melons, leeks and onions and garlic. Now our throats are parched; there
7 is nothing wherever we look except this manna.' (The manna looked like
8 coriander seed, the colour of gum resin. The people went about collecting it, ground it up in hand-mills or pounded it in mortars, then boiled it in
9 the pot and made it into cakes. It tasted like butter-cakes. When dew fell on
10 the camp at night, the manna fell with it.) Moses heard the people wailing, all of them in their families at the opening of their tents. Then the LORD
11 became very angry, and Moses was troubled. He said to the LORD, 'Why hast thou brought trouble on thy servant? How have I displeased the LORD
12 that I am burdened with the care of this whole people? Am I their mother? Have I brought them into the world, and am I called upon to carry them in my bosom, like a nurse with her babies, to the land promised by thee on
13 oath to their fathers? Where am I to find meat to give them all? They
14 pester me with their wailing and their "Give us meat to eat." This whole
15 people is a burden too heavy for me; I cannot carry it alone. If that is thy purpose for me, then kill me outright. But if I have won thy favour, let me suffer this trouble at thy hands *b* no longer.'

16 The LORD answered Moses, 'Assemble seventy elders from Israel, men known to you as elders and officers in the community; bring them to me at
17 the Tent of the Presence, and there let them take their stand with you. I will come down and speak with you there. I will take back part of that same spirit which has been conferred on you and confer it on them, and they will share with you the burden of taking care for the people; then you will
18 not have to bear it alone. And to the people you shall say this: "Hallow yourselves in readiness for tomorrow; you shall have meat to eat. You wailed in the LORD's hearing; you said, 'Will no one give us meat? In Egypt we lived well.' The LORD will give you meat and you shall eat it.
19 20 Not for one day only, nor for two days, nor five, nor ten, nor twenty, but for a whole month you shall eat it until it comes out at your nostrils and makes you sick; because you have rejected the LORD who dwells in your midst, wailing in his presence and saying, 'Why did we ever come out of Egypt?' "'

21 Moses replied, 'Here am I with six hundred thousand men on the march around me, and thou dost promise them meat to eat for a whole month.
22 How can the sheep and oxen be slaughtered that would be enough for them?
23 If all the fish in the sea could be caught, would they be enough?' The LORD

*a That is* Burning.    *b* this trouble ... hands: *prob. original rdg., altered in Heb.* *to* my trouble.

said to Moses, 'Is there a limit to the power of the LORD? You will see this very day whether or not my words come true.'

Moses came out and told the people what the LORD had said. He assem- 24
bled seventy men from the elders of the people and stationed them round the Tent. Then the LORD descended in the cloud and spoke to him. He 25
took back part of that same spirit which he had conferred on Moses and conferred it on the seventy elders; as the spirit alighted on them, they fell into a prophetic ecstasy, for the first and only time.

Now two men named Eldad and Medad, who had been enrolled with the 26
seventy, were left behind in the camp. But, though they had not gone out to the Tent, the spirit alighted on them none the less, and they fell into an ecstasy there in the camp. A young man ran and told Moses that Eldad and 27
Medad were in an ecstasy in the camp, whereupon Joshua son of Nun, who 28
had served with Moses since he was a boy, broke in, 'My lord Moses, stop them!' But Moses said to him, 'Are you jealous on my account? I wish that 29
all the LORD's people were prophets and that the LORD would confer his spirit on them all!' And Moses rejoined the camp with the elders of Israel. 30

Then a wind from the LORD sprang up; it drove quails in from the west, 31
and they were flying all round the camp for the distance of a day's journey, three feet above the ground. The people were busy gathering quails all 32
that day, all night, and all next day, and even the man who got least gathered ten homers. They spread them out to dry all about the camp. But the meat 33
was scarcely between their teeth, and they had not so much as bitten it, when the LORD's anger broke out against the people and he struck them with a deadly plague. That place was called Kibroth-hattaavah[a] because 34
there they buried the people who had been greedy for meat.

From Kibroth-hattaavah the Israelites went on to Hazeroth, and while 35
they were at Hazeroth, Miriam and Aaron began to speak against Moses. **12**
They blamed him for his Cushite wife (for he had married a Cushite woman), and they said, 'Is Moses the only one with[b] whom the LORD has 2
spoken? Has he not spoken with[b] us as well?' Moses was in fact a man of 3
great humility, the most humble man on earth. But the LORD heard them and suddenly he said to Moses, Aaron and Miriam, 'Go out all three of 4
you to the Tent of the Presence.' So the three went out, and the LORD 5
descended in a pillar of cloud; he stood at the entrance to the tent and summoned Aaron and Miriam. The two of them went forward, and he said, 6

'Listen to my words.
If he[c] were your prophet and nothing more,
  I would make myself known to him in a vision,
  I would speak with him in a dream.
But my servant Moses is not such a prophet;          7
he alone is faithful[d] of all my household.
  With him I speak face to face,                      8
  openly and not in riddles.
He shall see the very form of the LORD.
How do you dare speak against my servant Moses?'

[a] *That is* the Graves of Greed.      [b] *Or by.*      [c] *Prob. rdg.; Heb.* the LORD.
[d] *Or to be trusted.*

161

9 Thus the anger of the LORD was roused against them, and he left them;
10 and as the cloud moved from the tent, there was Miriam, her skin diseased and white as snow. Aaron turned towards her and saw her skin diseased.
11 Then he said to Moses, 'Pray, my lord, do not make us pay the penalty of
12 sin, foolish and wicked though we have been. Let her not be like something still-born, whose flesh is half eaten away when it comes from the womb.'
13 14 So Moses cried, 'Not this, O LORD! Heal her, I pray.' The LORD replied, 'Suppose her father had spat in her face, would she not have to remain in disgrace for seven days? Let her be kept for seven days in confinement
15 outside the camp and then be brought back.' So Miriam was kept outside for seven days, and the people did not strike camp until she was brought
16 back. After this they set out from Hazeroth and pitched camp in the wilderness of Paran.

13 1 2 THE LORD SPOKE TO MOSES and said, 'Send men out to explore the land of Canaan which I am giving to the Israelites; from each of their fathers'
3 tribes send one man, and let him be a man of high rank.' So Moses sent them from the wilderness of Paran at the command of the LORD, all of
4 them leading men among the Israelites. These were their names:

from the tribe of Reuben, Shammua son of Zaccur;
5 from the tribe of Simeon, Shaphat son of Hori;
6 from the tribe of Judah, Caleb son of Jephunneh;
7 from the tribe of Issachar, Igal son of Joseph;
8 from the tribe of Ephraim, Hoshea son of Nun;
9 from the tribe of Benjamin, Palti son of Raphu;
10 from the tribe of Zebulun, Gaddiel son of Sodi;
11 from the tribe of Joseph (that is from the tribe of Manasseh), Gaddi son of Susi;
12 from the tribe of Dan, Ammiel son of Gemalli;
13 from the tribe of Asher, Sethur son of Michael;
14 from the tribe of Naphtali, Nahbi son of Vophsi;
15 from the tribe of Gad, Geuel son of Machi.

16 These are the names of the men whom Moses sent to explore the land. But Moses called the son of Nun Joshua, not Hoshea.
17 When Moses sent them to explore the land of Canaan, he said to them,
18 'Make your way up by the Negeb, and go on into the hill-country. See what the land is like, and whether the people who live there are strong or
19 weak, few or many. See whether it is easy or difficult country in which they live, and whether the cities in which they live are weakly defended or
20 well fortified; is the land fertile or barren, and does it grow trees or not? Go boldly in and take some of its fruit.' It was the season when the first grapes were ripe.
21 They went up and explored the country from the wilderness of Zin as
22 far as Rehob by Lebo-hamath. They went up by the Negeb and came to Hebron, where Ahiman, Sheshai and Talmai, the descendants of Anak, [a]
23 were living. (Hebron was built seven years before Zoan in Egypt.) They

*a* descendants of Anak: *or* tall men.

came to the gorge of Eshcol,*ᵃ* and there they cut a branch with a single
bunch of grapes, and they carried it on a pole two at a time; they also
picked pomegranates and figs. It was from the bunch of grapes which the 24
Israelites cut there that that place was named the gorge of Eshcol. After 25
forty days they returned from exploring the country, and came back to 26
Moses and Aaron and the whole community of Israelites at Kadesh in the
wilderness of Paran. They made their report to them and to the whole
community, and showed them the fruit of the country. And this was the 27
story they told Moses: 'We made our way into the land to which you sent
us. It is flowing with milk and honey, and here is the fruit it grows; but its 28
inhabitants are sturdy, and the cities are very strongly fortified; indeed,
we saw there the descendants of Anak. We also saw the Amalekites who 29
live in the Negeb, Hittites, Jebusites, and Amorites who live in the hill-
country, and the Canaanites who live by the sea and along the Jordan.'

Then Caleb called for silence before Moses and said, 'Let us go up at 30
once and occupy the country; we are well able to conquer it.' But the men 31
who had gone with him said, 'No, we cannot attack these people; they are
stronger than we are.' Thus their report to the Israelites about the land 32
which they had explored was discouraging: 'The country we explored',
they said, 'will swallow up any who go to live in it. All the people we saw
there are men of gigantic size. When we set eyes on the Nephilim*ᵇ* (the 33
sons of Anak*ᶜ* belong to the Nephilim) we felt no bigger than grasshoppers;
and that is how we looked to them.'

Then the whole Israelite community cried out in dismay; all night long **14**
they wept. One and all they made complaints against Moses and Aaron: 'If 2
only we had died in Egypt or in the wilderness!' they said. 'Far happier if
we had! Why should the LORD bring us to this land, to die in battle and 3
leave our wives and our dependants to become the spoils of war? To go
back to Egypt would be better than this.' And they began to talk of choos- 4
ing someone to lead them back.

Then Moses and Aaron flung themselves on the ground before the 5
assembled community of the Israelites, and two of those who had explored 6
the land, Joshua son of Nun and Caleb son of Jephunneh, rent their clothes
and addressed the whole community: 'The country we penetrated and 7
explored', they said, 'is very good land indeed. If the LORD is pleased with 8
us, he will bring us into this land which flows with milk and honey, and
give it to us. But you must not rebel against the LORD. You need not fear 9
the people of the land; for there we shall find food. They have lost the
protection that they had: the LORD is with us. You have nothing to fear
from them.' But by way of answer the assembled Israelites threatened to 10
stone them, when suddenly the glory of the LORD appeared to them all in
the Tent of the Presence.

Then the LORD said to Moses, 'How much longer will this people treat 11
me with contempt? How much longer will they refuse to trust me in spite
of all the signs I have shown among them? I will strike them with pestilence. 12
I will deny them their heritage, and you and your descendants I will make
into a nation greater and more numerous than they.' But Moses answered 13

*ᵃ* Eshcol: *that is* Bunch of Grapes.     *ᵇ* *Or* giants.     *ᶜ* sons of Anak: *or* tall men.

the LORD, 'What if the Egyptians hear of it? It was thou who didst bring
14 this people out of Egypt by thy strength. What if they tell the inhabitants
of this land? They too have heard of thee, LORD, that thou art with this
people, and art seen face to face, that thy cloud stays over them, and thou
goest before them in a pillar of cloud by day and in a pillar of fire by night.
15 If then thou dost put them all to death at one blow, the nations who have
16 heard these tales of thee will say, "The LORD could not bring this people
into the land which he promised them by oath; and so he destroyed them
in the wilderness."

17 'Now let the LORD's might be shown in its greatness, true to thy pro-
18 clamation of thyself—"The LORD, long-suffering, ever constant, who forgives iniquity and rebellion, and punishes sons to the third and fourth
generation for the iniquity of their fathers, though he does not sweep them
19 clean away." Thou hast borne with this people from Egypt all the way here;
forgive their iniquity, I beseech thee, as befits thy great and constant love.'

20 21 The LORD said, 'Your prayer is answered; I pardon them. But as I live,
22-23 in very truth the glory of the LORD shall fill the earth. Not one of all those
who have seen my glory and the signs which I wrought in Egypt and in the
wilderness shall see the country which I promised on oath to their fathers.
Ten times they have challenged me and not obeyed my voice. None of
24-25 those who have flouted me shall see this land. But my servant Caleb showed
a different spirit: he followed me with his whole heart. Because of this, I
will bring him into the land in which he has already set foot, the territory
of the Amalekites and the Canaanites who dwell in the Vale, and put his
descendants in possession of it. Tomorrow you must turn back and set
out for the wilderness by way of the Red Sea.'*a*

26 27 The LORD spoke to Moses and Aaron and said, 'How long must I tolerate*b* the complaints of this wicked community? I have heard the Israelites
28 making complaints against me. Tell them that this is the very word of the
LORD: As I live, I will bring home to you the words I have heard you utter.
29 Here in this wilderness your bones shall lie, every man of you on the
register from twenty years old and upwards, because you have made these
30 complaints against me. Not one of you shall enter the land which I swore
with uplifted hand should be your home, except only Caleb son of Jephun-
31 neh and Joshua son of Nun. As for your dependants, those dependants who,
you said, would become the spoils of war, I will bring them in to the land
32 you have rejected, and they shall enjoy it. But as for the rest of you, your
33 bones shall lie in this wilderness; your sons shall be wanderers in the
wilderness forty years, paying the penalty of your wanton disloyalty till
34 the last man of you dies there. Forty days you spent exploring the country,
and forty years you shall spend—a year for each day—paying the penalty
35 of your iniquities. You shall know what it means to have me against you.*c* I,
the LORD, have spoken. This I swear to do to all this wicked community
who have combined against me. There shall be an end of them here in this
36 wilderness; here they shall die.' But the men whom Moses had sent to
explore the land, and who came back and by their report set all the com-
37 munity complaining against him, died of the plague before the LORD; they

*a* Or the Sea of Reeds.   *b* must I tolerate: *prob. rdg.; Heb.* for.   *c* Or to thwart me.

died of the plague because they had made a bad report. Of those who went 38
to explore the land, Joshua son of Nun and Caleb son of Jephunneh alone
remained alive.

When Moses reported the LORD's words to all the Israelites, the people 39
were plunged in grief. They set out early next morning and made for the 40
heights of the hill-country, saying, 'Look, we are on our way up to the
place the LORD spoke of. We admit that we have been wrong.' But Moses 41
replied, 'Must you persist in disobeying the LORD's command? No good
will come of this. Go no further; you will not have the LORD with you, and 42
your enemies will defeat you. For in front of you are the Amalekites and 43
Canaanites, and you will die by the sword, because you have ceased to
follow the LORD, and he will no longer be with you.' But they went reck- 44
lessly on their way towards the heights of the hill-country, though neither
the Ark of the Covenant of the LORD nor Moses moved with them out of
the camp; and the Amalekites and Canaanites from those hills came down 45
and fell upon them, and crushed them at Hormah.

THE LORD SPOKE TO MOSES and said, Speak to the Israelites in these **15** 1 2
words: When you enter the land where you are to live, the land I am giving
you, you will make food-offerings to the LORD; they may be whole-offer- 3
ings or any sacrifice made in fulfilment of a special*a* vow or by way of freewill offering or at one of the appointed seasons. When you thus make an
offering of soothing odour from herd or flock to the LORD, the man who 4
offers, in presenting it, shall add a grain-offering of a tenth of an ephah of
flour mixed with a quarter of a hin of oil. You shall also add to the whole- 5
offering or shared-offering a quarter of a hin of wine as a drink-offering
with each lamb sacrificed.

If the animal is a ram, the grain-offering shall be two tenths of an ephah 6
of flour mixed with a third of a hin of oil, and the wine for the drink- 7
offering shall be a third of a hin; in this way you will make an offering of
soothing odour to the LORD.

When you offer to the LORD a young bull, whether as a whole-offering 8
or as a sacrifice to fulfil a special*b* vow, or as a shared-offering, you shall 9
add a grain-offering of three tenths of an ephah of flour mixed with half
a hin of oil, and for the drink-offering, half a hin of wine; the whole will 10
thus be a food-offering of soothing odour to the LORD. This is what must 11
be done in each case, for every bull or ram, lamb or kid, whatever the 12
number of each that you offer. Every native Israelite shall observe these 13
rules in each case when he offers a food-offering of soothing odour to the
LORD.

When an alien residing with you or permanently settled among you 14
offers a food-offering of soothing odour to the LORD, he shall do as you do.
There is one and the same rule for you and for the resident alien, a rule 15
binding for all time on your descendants; you and the alien are alike before
the LORD. There shall be one law and one custom for you and for the alien 16
residing with you.

*a* in fulfilment of a special: *or* to discharge a . . .
*b* fulfil a special: *or* discharge a . . .

17 18   The LORD spoke to Moses and said, Speak to the Israelites in these words:
19 After you have entered the land into which I am bringing you, whenever you eat the bread of the country, you shall set aside a contribution for the
20 LORD. You shall set aside a cake made of your first kneading of dough, as
21 you set aside the contribution from the threshing-floor. You must give a contribution to the LORD from your first kneading of dough; this rule is binding on your descendants.

22   When through inadvertence you omit to carry out any of these com-
23 mands which the LORD gave to Moses—any command whatever that the LORD gave you through Moses on that first day and thereafter and made
24 binding on your descendants—if it be done inadvertently, unnoticed by the community, then the whole community shall offer one young bull as a whole-offering, a soothing odour to the LORD, with its proper grain-offering and drink-offering according to custom; and they shall add one
25 he-goat as a sin-offering. The priest shall make expiation for the whole community of Israelites, and they shall be forgiven. The omission was inadvertent; and they have brought their offering, a food-offering to the LORD; they have made their sin-offering before the LORD for their in-
26 advertence; the whole community of Israelites and the aliens residing among you shall be forgiven. The inadvertence was shared by the whole people.

27   If any individual sins inadvertently, he shall present a yearling she-goat
28 as a sin-offering, and the priest shall make expiation before the LORD for
29 the said individual, and he shall be forgiven. For anyone who sins in-advertently, there shall be one law for all, whether native Israelite or
30 resident alien. But the person who sins presumptuously, native or alien,
31 insults the LORD. He shall be cut off from his people, because he has brought the word of the LORD into contempt and violated his command. That person shall be wholly cut off; the guilt shall be on his head alone.

32   During the time that the Israelites were in the wilderness, a man was
33 found gathering sticks on the sabbath day. Those who had caught him in
34 the act brought him to Moses and Aaron and all the community, and they kept him in custody, because it was not clearly known what was to be done
35 with him. The LORD said to Moses, 'The man must be put to death; he
36 must be stoned by all the community outside the camp.' So they took him outside the camp and all stoned him to death, as the LORD had commanded Moses.

37 38   The LORD spoke to Moses and said, Speak to the Israelites in these words: You must make tassels like flowers on the corners of your garments, you and your children's children. Into this tassel you shall work a violet
39 thread, and whenever you see this in the tassel, you shall remember all the LORD's commands and obey them, and not go your own wanton ways,
40 led astray by your own eyes and hearts. This token is to ensure that you remember all my commands and obey them, and keep yourselves holy, consecrated to your God.
41   I am the LORD your God who brought you out of Egypt to become your God. I am the LORD your God.

NOW KORAH SON OF IZHAR, son of Kohath, son of Levi, with the Reuben- **16**
ites Dathan and Abiram sons of Eliab and On son of Peleth, challenged the 2
authority of Moses. With them in their revolt were two hundred and fifty
Israelites, all men of rank in the community, conveners of assembly and
men of good standing. They confronted Moses and Aaron and said to them, 3
'You take too much upon yourselves. Every member of the community is
holy and the LORD is among them all. Why do you set yourselves up above
the assembly of the LORD?' When Moses heard this, he prostrated himself, 4
and he said to Korah and all his company, 'Tomorrow morning the LORD 5
shall declare who is his, who is holy and may present offerings to him. The
man whom the LORD chooses shall present them. This is what you must 6
do, you, Korah, and all your company: you must take censers and put fire 7
in them, and then place incense on them before the LORD tomorrow. The
man whom the LORD then chooses is the man who is holy. You take too
much upon yourselves, you sons of Levi.'

Moses said to Korah, 'Now listen, you sons of Levi. Is it not enough for 8 9
you that the God of Israel has set you apart from the community of Israel,
bringing you near him to maintain the service of the Tabernacle of the
LORD and to stand before the community as their ministers? He has 10
brought you near him and your brother Levites with you; now you seek
the priesthood as well. That is why you and all your company have com- 11
bined together against the LORD. What is Aaron that you should make these
complaints against him?'

Moses sent to fetch Dathan and Abiram sons of Eliab, but they answered, 12
'We are not coming. Is it a small thing that you have brought us away from 13
a land flowing with milk and honey to let us die in the wilderness? Must
you also set yourself up as prince over us? What is more, you have not 14
brought us into a land flowing with milk and honey, nor have you given us
fields and vineyards to inherit. Do you think you can hoodwink men like
us? We are not coming.' This answer made Moses very angry, and he said 15
to the LORD, 'Take no notice of their murmuring. I have not taken from
them so much as a single ass; I have done no wrong to any of them.'

Moses said to Korah, 'Present yourselves before the LORD tomorrow, 16
you and all your company, you and they and Aaron. Each man of you is to 17
take his censer and put incense on it. Then you shall present them before
the LORD with their two hundred and fifty censers, and you and Aaron
shall also bring your censers.' So each man took his censer and put fire in 18
it and placed incense on it; Moses and Aaron took their stand at the entrance
to the Tent of the Presence, and Korah gathered his whole company 19
together and faced them at the entrance to the Tent of the Presence.

Then the glory of the LORD appeared to the whole community. And the 20
LORD spoke to Moses and Aaron and said, 'Stand apart from this company, 21
so that I may make an end of them in a single instant.' But they prostrated 22
themselves and said, 'O God, God of the spirits of all mankind, if one man
sins, wilt thou be angry with the whole community?' But the LORD said 23
to Moses, 'Tell them to stand back from the dwellings of Korah, Dathan 24
and Abiram.'

So Moses rose and went to Dathan and Abiram, and the elders of Israel 25

26 followed him. He said to the whole community, 'Stand well away from the tents of these wicked men; touch nothing of theirs, or you will be swept
27 away because of all their sins.' So they moved away from the places occupied by Korah, Dathan and Abiram. Now Dathan and Abiram, holding themselves erect, had come out to the entrance of their tents with their
28 wives, their sons, and their dependants. Then Moses said, 'This shall prove to you that it is the LORD who sent me to do all these things, and it was not
29 my own heart that prompted me. If these men die a natural death and share
30 the common fate of man, then the LORD has not sent me; but if the LORD makes a great chasm, and the ground opens its mouth and swallows them and all that is theirs, and they go down alive to Sheol, then you will know that these men have held the LORD in contempt.'

31 32   Hardly had Moses spoken when the ground beneath them split; the earth opened its mouth and swallowed them and their homes—all the
33 followers of Korah and all their property. They went down alive into Sheol with all that they had; the earth closed over them, and they vanished from
34 the assembly. At their cries all the Israelites round them fled, shouting,
35 'Look to yourselves! the earth will swallow us up.' Meanwhile fire had come out from the LORD and burnt up the two hundred and fifty men who were presenting the incense.

36 37   Then the LORD spoke to Moses and said, 'Bid Eleazar son of Aaron the priest set aside the censers from the burnt remains, and scatter the fire
38 from them far and wide, because they are holy. And the censers of these men who sinned at the cost of their lives you shall make into beaten plates to cover the altar; they are holy, because they have been presented before
39 the LORD. Let them be a sign to the Israelites.' So Eleazar the priest took the bronze*a* censers which the victims of the fire had presented, and they
40 were beaten into plates to make a covering for the altar, as a reminder to the Israelites that no person unqualified, not descended from Aaron, should come forward to burn incense before the LORD, or his fate would be that of Korah and his company. All this was done as the LORD commanded Eleazar through Moses.

41   Next day all the community of the Israelites raised complaints against Moses and Aaron and taxed them with causing the death of some of the
42 LORD's people. As they gathered against Moses and Aaron, they turned towards the Tent of the Presence and saw that the cloud covered it, and
43 the glory of the LORD appeared. Moses and Aaron came to the front of the
44 Tent of the Presence, and the LORD spoke to Moses and Aaron and said,
45 'Stand well clear of this community, so that in a single instant I may make
46 an end of them.' Then they prostrated themselves, and Moses said to Aaron, 'Take your censer, put fire from the altar in it, set incense on it, and go with it quickly to the assembled community to make expiation for them. Wrath has gone forth already from the presence of the LORD. The plague
47 has begun.' So Aaron took his censer, as Moses had said, ran into the midst of the assembly and found that the plague had begun among the people.
48 He put incense on the censer and made expiation for the people, stand-
49 ing between the dead and the living, and the plague stopped. ·Fourteen

*a Or copper.*

168

thousand seven hundred died of it, in addition to those who had died for
the offence of Korah. When Aaron came back to Moses at the entrance to 50
the Tent of the Presence, the plague had stopped.

The LORD spoke to Moses and said, 'Speak to the Israelites and tell 17 1 2
them to give you a staff for each tribe, one from every tribal chief, twelve in
all, and write each man's name on his staff. On Levi's staff write the name 3
of Aaron, for there shall be one staff for each head of a tribe. You shall put 4
them all in the Tent of the Presence before the Tokens, where I meet you,
and the staff of the man I choose shall sprout. I will rid myself of the com- 5
plaints of these Israelites, who keep on complaining against you.'

Moses thereupon spoke to the Israelites, and each of their chiefs handed 6
him a staff, each of them one for his tribe, twelve in all, and Aaron's staff
among them. Moses put them before the LORD in the Tent of the Tokens, 7
and next day when he entered the tent, he found that Aaron's staff, the 8
staff for the tribe of Levi, had sprouted. Indeed, it had sprouted, blossomed, and produced ripe almonds. Moses then brought out the staffs 9
from before the LORD and showed them to all the Israelites; they saw for
themselves, and each man took his own staff. The LORD said to Moses, 10
'Put back Aaron's staff in front of the Tokens to be kept as a warning to all
rebels, so that you may rid me once and for all of their complaints, and then
they shall not die.' Moses did this; as the LORD had commanded him, so 11
he did.

The Israelites said to Moses, 'This is the end of us! We perish, one and 12
all! Every single person who goes near the Tabernacle of the LORD dies. 13
Is this to be our final end?'

THE LORD SAID TO AARON: You and your sons, together with the 18
members of your father's tribe, shall be fully answerable for the sanctuary.
You and your sons alone shall be answerable for your priestly office; but 2
you shall admit your kinsmen of Levi, your father's tribe, to be attached
to you and assist you while you and your sons are before the Tent of the
Tokens. They shall be in attendance on you and fulfil all the duties of the 3
Tent, but shall not go near the holy vessels and the altar, or they will die
and you with them. They shall be attached to you and be responsible for 4
the maintenance of the Tent of the Presence in every detail; no unqualified
person shall come near you. You yourselves shall be responsible for the 5
sanctuary and the altar, so that wrath may no more fall on the Israelites.
I have myself taken the Levites your kinsmen out of all the Israelites as a 6
gift for you, given to the LORD for the maintenance of the Tent of the
Presence. But only you and your sons may fulfil the duties of your priestly 7
office that concern the altar or lie within the Veil. This duty is yours; I
bestow on you this gift of priestly service. The unqualified person who
intrudes on it shall be put to death.

The LORD said to Aaron: I, the LORD, commit to your control the con- 8
tributions made to me, that is all the holy-gifts of the Israelites. I give them
to you and to your sons for your allotted portion due to you in perpetuity.
Out of the most holy gifts kept back from the altar-fire this part shall 9
belong to you: every offering, whether grain-offering, sin-offering, or

10 guilt-offering, rendered to me as a most holy gift, belongs to you and to your sons. You shall eat it as befits most holy gifts; every male may eat it. You shall regard it as holy.

11 This also is yours: the contribution from all such of their gifts as are presented as special gifts by the Israelites. I give them to you and to your sons and daughters with you as a due in perpetuity. Every person in your household who is ritually clean may eat them.

12 I give you all the choicest of the oil, the choicest of the new wine and the
13 corn, the firstfruits which are given to the LORD. The first-ripe fruits of all produce in the land which are brought to the LORD shall be yours. Every-one in your household who is clean may eat them.

14 Everything in Israel which has been devoted to God shall be yours.

15 All the first-born of man or beast which are brought to the LORD shall be yours. Notwithstanding, you must accept payment in redemption of
16 any first-born of man and of unclean beasts: at the end of one month you shall redeem it at the fixed price of five shekels of silver by the sacred
17 standard (twenty gerahs to the shekel). You must not, however, allow the redemption of the first-born of a cow, sheep, or goat; they are holy. You shall fling their blood against the altar and burn their fat in sacrifice as a
18 food-offering of soothing odour to the LORD; their flesh shall be yours, as are the breast of the special gift and the right leg.

19 All the contributions from holy-gifts, which the Israelites set aside for the LORD, I give to you and to your sons and daughters with you as a due in perpetuity. This is a perpetual covenant of salt before the LORD with you and your descendants also.

20 The LORD said to Aaron: You shall have no patrimony in the land of Israel, no holding among them; I am your holding in Israel, I am your patrimony.

21 To the Levites I give every tithe in Israel to be their patrimony, in return for the service they render in maintaining the Tent of the Presence.
22 In order that the Israelites may not henceforth approach the Tent and thus
23 incur the penalty of death, the Levites alone shall perform the service of the Tent, and they shall accept the full responsibility for it. This rule is binding on your descendants for all time. They shall have no patrimony
24 among the Israelites, because I give them as their patrimony the tithe which the Israelites set aside as a contribution to the LORD. Therefore I say to them: You shall have no patrimony among the Israelites.

25 26 The LORD spoke to Moses and said, Speak to the Levites in these words: When you receive from the Israelites the tithe which I give you from them as your patrimony, you shall set aside from it the contribution to the LORD,
27 a tithe of the tithe. Your contribution shall count for you as if it were corn
28 from the threshing-floor and juice from the vat. In this way you too shall set aside the contribution due to the LORD out of all tithes which you receive from the Israelites and shall give the LORD's contribution to Aaron
29 the priest. Out of all the gifts you receive you shall set aside the contribu-tion due to the LORD; and the gift which you hallow[a] must be taken from the choicest of them.

*a* you hallow: *prob. rdg.; Heb. obscure.*

You shall say to the Levites: When you have set aside the choicest part 30
of your portion, the remainder shall count for you as the produce of the
threshing-floor and the winepress, and you may eat it anywhere, you and 31
your households. It is your payment for service in the Tent of the Presence.
When you have set aside its choicest part, you will incur no penalty in 32
respect of it, and you will not be profaning the holy-gifts of the Israelites;
so you will not die.

THE LORD SPOKE TO MOSES and Aaron and said: This is a law and a 19 1 2
statute which the LORD has ordained. Tell the Israelites to bring you a red
cow without blemish or defect, which has never borne the yoke. You shall 3
give it to Eleazar the priest, and it shall be taken outside the camp and
slaughtered*a* to the east of it. Eleazar the priest shall take some of the blood 4
on his finger and sprinkle it seven times towards the front of the Tent of
the Presence. The cow shall be burnt in his sight, skin, flesh, and blood, 5
together with the offal. The priest shall then take cedar-wood, marjoram, 6
and scarlet thread, and throw them into the heart of the fire in which the
cow is burning. He shall wash his clothes and bathe his body in water; 7
after which he may enter the camp, but he remains ritually unclean till
sunset. The man who burnt the cow shall wash his clothes and bathe 8
his body in water, but he also remains unclean till sunset. Then a man 9
who is clean shall collect the ashes of the cow and deposit them outside
the camp in a clean place. They shall be reserved for use by the Israelite
community in the water of ritual purification; for the cow is a sin-offering.
The man who collected the ashes of the cow shall wash his clothes, but he 10
remains unclean till sunset. This rule shall be binding for all time on the
Israelites and on the alien who is living with them.
Whoever touches a corpse shall be ritually unclean for seven days. He 11 12
shall get himself purified with the water of ritual purification on the third
day and on the seventh day, and then he shall be clean. If he is not purified
both on the third day and on the seventh, he shall not be clean. Everyone 13
who touches a corpse, that is the body of a man who has died, and does not
purify himself, defiles the Tabernacle of the LORD. That person shall be
cut off from Israel. The water of purification has not been flung over him;
he remains unclean, and his impurity is still upon him.
When a man dies in a tent, this is the law: everyone who goes into the 14
tent and everyone who was inside the tent shall be ritually unclean for seven
days, and every open vessel which has no covering tied over it shall also 15
be unclean. In the open, anyone who touches a man killed with a weapon 16
or one who has died naturally, or who touches a human bone or a grave,
shall be unclean for seven days. For such uncleanness, they shall take some 17
of the ash from the burnt mass of the sin-offering and add fresh water to
it in a vessel. Then a man who is clean shall take marjoram, dip it in the 18
water, and sprinkle the tent with all the vessels in it and all the people who
were there, or the man who has touched a human bone, a corpse (whether
the man was killed or died naturally), or a grave. The man who is clean 19
shall sprinkle the unclean man on the third day and on the seventh; on the

*a* Or he shall take it outside the camp and slaughter it . . .

seventh day he shall purify him; then the man shall wash his clothes and
20 bathe in water, and at sunset he shall be clean. If a man who is unclean
does not get himself purified, that person shall be cut off from the assembly,
because he has defiled the sanctuary of the LORD. The water of purification
21 has not been flung over him: he is unclean. This rule shall be binding on
you for all time. The man who sprinkles the water of purification shall also
wash his clothes, and whoever touches the water shall be unclean till sun-
22 set. Whatever the unclean man touches shall be unclean, and any person
who touches that shall be unclean till sunset.

20 IN THE FIRST MONTH the whole community of Israel reached the wilderness of Zin and stayed some time at Kadesh; there Miriam died and was
buried.
2 There was no water for the community; so they gathered against Moses
3 and Aaron. The people disputed with Moses and said, 'If only we had
4 perished when our brothers perished in the presence of the LORD! Why
have you brought the assembly of the LORD into this wilderness for us and
5 our beasts to die here? Why did you fetch us up from Egypt to bring us to
this vile place, where nothing will grow, neither corn nor figs, vines nor
6 pomegranates? There is not even any water to drink.' Moses and Aaron
came forward in front of the assembly to the entrance of the Tent of the
Presence. There they fell prostrate, and the glory of the LORD appeared
to them.
7 8 The LORD spoke to Moses and said, 'Take a *a* staff, and then with Aaron
your brother assemble all the community, and, in front of them all, speak
to the rock and it will yield its water. Thus you will produce water for the
9 community out of the rock, for them and their beasts to drink.' Moses left
10 the presence of the LORD with the staff, as he had commanded him. Then
he and Aaron gathered the assembly together in front of the rock, and he
said to them, 'Listen to me, you rebels. Must we get water out of this rock
11 for you?' Moses raised his hand and struck the rock twice with his staff.
12 Water gushed out in abundance and they all drank, men and beasts. But
the LORD said to Moses and Aaron, 'You did not trust me so far as to uphold my holiness in the sight of the Israelites; therefore you shall not lead
13 this assembly into the land which I promised to give them.' Such were the
waters of Meribah,*b* where the people disputed with the LORD and through
which his holiness was upheld.

## The approach to the promised land

14 FROM KADESH MOSES SENT ENVOYS to the king of Edom: 'This is a
message from your brother Israel. You know all the hardships we have
15 encountered, how our fathers went down to Egypt, and we lived there for
16 many years. The Egyptians ill-treated us and our fathers before us, and
we cried to the LORD for help. He listened to us and sent an angel, and he
brought us out of Egypt; and now we are here at Kadesh, a town on your

*a* Or the.    *b* *That is* Dispute.

frontier. Grant us passage through your country. We will not trespass on 17
field or vineyard, or drink from your wells. We will keep to the king's highway; we will not turn off to right or left until we have crossed your territory.' But the Edomites answered, 'You shall not cross our land. If you 18
do, we will march out and attack you in force.' The Israelites said, 'But we 19
will keep to the main road. If we and our flocks drink your water, we will
pay you for it; we will simply cross your land on foot.' But the Edomites 20
said, 'No, you shall not', and took the field against them with a large army
in full strength. Thus the Edomites refused to allow Israel to cross their 21
frontier, and Israel went a different way to avoid a conflict.

The whole community of Israel set out from Kadesh and came to Mount 22
Hor. At Mount Hor, near the frontier of Edom, the LORD said to Moses 23
and Aaron, 'Aaron shall be gathered to his father's kin. He shall not enter 24
the land which I promised to give the Israelites, because over the waters
of Meribah you rebelled against my command. Take Aaron and his son 25
Eleazar, and go up Mount Hor. Strip Aaron of his robes and invest Eleazar 26
his son with them, for Aaron shall be taken from you: he shall die there.'
Moses did as the LORD had commanded him: they went up Mount Hor 27
in sight of the whole community, and Moses stripped Aaron of his robes 28
and invested his son Eleazar with them. There Aaron died on the mountain-
top, and Moses and Eleazar came down from the mountain. So the whole 29
community saw that Aaron had died, and all Israel mourned him for thirty
days.

When the Canaanite king of Arad who lived in the Negeb heard that **21**
the Israelites were coming by way of Atharim, he attacked them and took
some of them prisoners. Israel thereupon made a vow to the LORD and 2
said, 'If thou wilt deliver this people into my power, I will destroy their
cities.' The LORD listened to Israel and delivered the Canaanites into their 3
power. Israel destroyed them and their cities and called the place Hormah. *a*

Then they left Mount Hor by way of the Red Sea to march round the 4
flank of Edom. But on the way they grew impatient and spoke against God 5
and Moses. 'Why have you brought us up from Egypt', they said, 'to die
in the desert where there is neither food nor water? We are heartily sick
of this miserable fare.' Then the LORD sent poisonous snakes among the 6
people, and they bit the Israelites so that many of them died. The people 7
came to Moses and said, 'We sinned when we spoke against the LORD and
you. Plead with the LORD to rid us of the snakes.' Moses therefore pleaded
with the LORD for the people; and the LORD told Moses to make a serpent *b* 8
of bronze and erect it as a standard, so that anyone who had been bitten
could look at it and recover. So Moses made a bronze serpent and erected 9
it as a standard, so that when a snake had bitten a man, he could look at
the bronze serpent and recover.

The Israelites went on and encamped at Oboth. They moved on from 10 11
Oboth and encamped at Iye-abarim in the wilderness on the eastern
frontier of Moab. From there they moved and encamped by the gorge of 12
the Zared. They moved on from the Zared and encamped by the farther 13
side of the Arnon in the wilderness which extends into Amorite territory,

*a That is* Destruction.     *b Or* snake.

for the Arnon was the Moabite frontier; it lies between Moab and the

14 Amorites. That is why the Book of the Wars of the LORD speaks of Vaheb [a] in Suphah and the gorges:

15 　　　Arnon and the watershed of the gorges
　　　　that falls away towards the dwellings at Ar
　　　　and slopes towards the frontier of Moab.

16 From there they moved on to Beer: [b] this is the water-hole where the LORD
17 said to Moses, 'Gather the people together and I will give them water.' It was then that Israel sang this song:

　　　　Well up, spring water! Greet it with song,
18 　　　the spring unearthed by the princes,
　　　　laid open by the leaders of the people
　　　　with sceptre and with mace,
　　　　a gift from the wilderness.

19 And they proceeded from Beer [c] to Nahaliel, and from Nahaliel to Bamoth;
20 then from Bamoth to the valley in the Moabite country below the summit of Pisgah overlooking the desert.

21 22 Then Israel sent envoys to the Amorite king Sihon and said, 'Grant us passage through your country. We will not trespass on field or vineyard, nor will we drink from your wells. We will travel by the king's highway till
23 we have crossed your territory.' But Sihon would not grant Israel passage through his territory; he mustered all his people and came out against Israel in the wilderness. He advanced as far as Jahaz and attacked Israel,
24 but Israel put them to the sword, giving no quarter, and occupied their land from the Arnon to the Jabbok, the territory of the Ammonites, where
25 the country became difficult. So Israel took all these Amorite cities and
26 settled in them, that is in Heshbon and all its dependent villages. Heshbon was the capital of the Amorite king Sihon, who had fought against the former king of Moab and taken from him all his territory as far as the Arnon.
27 Therefore the bards say:

　　　　Come to Heshbon, come!
　　　Let us see the city of Sihon rebuilt and restored!
28 　　　For fire blazed out from Heshbon,
　　　　and flames from Sihon's city.
　　　　It devoured Ar of Moab,
　　　　and swept the high ground at Arnon head.

29 　　　　Woe to you, Moab;
　　　　it is the end of you, you people of Kemosh.
　　　　He has made his sons fugitives
　　　　and his daughters the prisoners of Sihon the Amorite king.
30 　　　From Heshbon to Dibon their very embers are burnt out
　　　　　and they are extinct,
　　　　while the fire spreads onward to Medeba.

31 Thus Israel occupied the territory of the Amorites.

---

*a Name meaning Watershed.*　　　*b Name meaning Water-hole.*　　　*c Prob. rdg.;*
*Heb. from a gift.*

Moses then sent men to explore Jazer; the Israelites captured it together 32
with its dependent villages and drove out the Amorites living there. Then 33
they turned and advanced along the road to Bashan. Og king of Bashan,
with all his people, took the field against them at Edrei. The LORD said to 34
Moses, 'Do not be afraid of him. I have delivered him into your hands, with
all his people and his land. Deal with him as you dealt with Sihon the
Amorite king who lived in Heshbon.' So they put him to the sword with his 35
sons and all his people, until there was no survivor left, and they occupied
his land.

## Israel in the plains of Moab

THE ISRAELITES WENT FORWARD and encamped in the lowlands of 22
Moab on the farther side of the Jordan from Jericho.

Balak son of Zippor saw what Israel had done to the Amorites, and 2 3
Moab was in terror of the people because there were so many of them. The
Moabites were sick with fear at the sight of them; and they said to the 4
elders of Midian, 'This horde will soon lick up everything round us as a
bull crops the spring grass.' Balak son of Zippor was at that time king of
Moab. He sent a deputation to summon Balaam son of Beor, who was at 5
Pethor by the Euphrates in the land of the Amavites, with this message,
'Look, an entire nation has come out of Egypt; they cover the face of the
country and are settling at my very door. Come at once and lay a curse on 6
them, because they are too many for me; then I may be able to defeat them
and drive them from the country. I know that those whom you bless are
blessed, and those whom you curse are cursed.'

The elders of Moab and Midian took the fees for augury with them, and 7
they came to Balaam and told him what Balak had said. 'Spend this night 8
here,' he said, 'and I will give you whatever answer the LORD gives to me.'
So the Moabite chiefs stayed with Balaam. God came to Balaam and asked 9
him, 'Who are these men with you?' Balaam replied, 'Balak son of Zippor 10
king of Moab has sent them to me and he says, "Look, a people newly come 11
out of Egypt is covering the face of the country. Come at once and denounce
them for me; then I may be able to fight them and drive them away."' God 12
said to Balaam, 'You are not to go with them or curse the people, because
they are to be blessed.'*a* So Balaam rose in the morning and said to Balak's 13
chiefs, 'Go back to your own country; the LORD has refused to let me go
with you.' Then the Moabite chiefs took their leave and went back to Balak, 14
and told him that Balaam had refused to come with them; whereupon 15
Balak sent a second and larger embassy of higher rank than the first. They 16
came to Balaam and told him, 'This is the message from Balak son of
Zippor: "Let nothing stand in the way of your coming. I will confer great 17
honour upon you; I will do whatever you ask me. But you must come and
denounce this people for me."' Balaam gave this answer to Balak's mes- 18
sengers: 'Even if Balak were to give me all the silver and gold in his house,
I could not disobey the command of the LORD my God in anything, small

*a Or* are blessed.

19 or great. But stay here for this night, as the others did, that I may learn
20 what more the LORD has to say to me.' During the night God came to
Balaam and said to him, 'If these men have come to summon you, then
21 rise and go with them, but do only what I tell you.' So in the morning
Balaam rose, saddled his ass and went with the Moabite chiefs.

22 But God was angry because Balaam was going, and as he came riding on
his ass, accompanied by his two servants, the angel of the LORD took his
23 stand in the road to bar his way. When the ass saw the angel standing in the
road with his sword drawn, she turned off the road into the fields, and
24 Balaam beat the ass to bring her back on to the road. Then the angel of the
LORD stood where the road ran through a hollow, with fenced vineyards
25 on either side. The ass saw the angel and, crushing herself against the wall,
26 crushed Balaam's foot against it, and he beat her again. The angel of the
LORD moved on further and stood in a narrow place where there was no
27 room to turn either to right or left. When the ass saw the angel, she lay
down under Balaam. At that Balaam lost his temper and beat the ass with
28 his stick. The LORD then made the ass speak, and she said to Balaam, 'What
29 have I done? This is the third time you have beaten me.' Balaam answered
the ass, 'You have been making a fool of me. If I had had a sword here, I
30 should have killed you on the spot.' But the ass answered, 'Am I not still
the ass which you have ridden all your life? Have I ever taken such a liberty
31 with you before?' He said, 'No.' Then the LORD opened Balaam's eyes:
he saw the angel of the LORD standing in the road with his sword drawn,
32 and he bowed down and fell flat on his face before him. The angel said to
him, 'What do you mean by beating your ass three times like this? I came
33 out to bar your way but you made straight for me, and three times your ass
saw me and turned aside. If she had not turned aside, I should by now have
34 killed you and spared her.' Balaam replied to the angel of the LORD, 'I have
done wrong. I did not know that you stood in the road confronting me.
35 But now, if my journey displeases you, I am ready to go back.' The angel
of the LORD said to Balaam, 'Go on with these men; but say only what I
tell you.' So Balaam went on with Balak's chiefs.

36 When Balak heard that Balaam was coming, he came out to meet him as
37 far as Ar of Moab by the Arnon on his frontier. Balak said to Balaam, 'Did
I not send time and again to summon you? Why did you not come? Did
38 you think that I could not do you honour?' Balaam replied, 'I have come,
as you see. But now that I am here, what power have I of myself to say
anything? Whatever the word God puts into my mouth, that is what I
39 40 will say.' So Balaam went with Balak till they came to Kiriath-huzoth, and
Balak slaughtered cattle and sheep and sent them to Balaam and to the
chiefs who were with him.

41 In the morning Balak took Balaam and led him up to the Heights of
23 Baal, from where he could see the full extent of the Israelite host. Then
Balaam said to Balak, 'Build me here seven altars and prepare for me seven
2 bulls and seven rams.' Balak did as he asked and offered a bull and a ram
3-4 on each altar. Then he said to him, 'I have prepared the seven altars, and
I have offered the bull and the ram on each altar.' Balaam said to Balak,
'Take your stand beside your sacrifice, and let me go off by myself. It may

happen that the LORD will meet me. Whatever he reveals to me, I will tell
you.' So he went forthwith, and God met him. The LORD put words into 5
Balaam's mouth and said, 'Go back to Balak, and speak as I tell you.' So 6
he went back, and found Balak standing by his sacrifice, and with him all
the Moabite chiefs. And Balaam uttered his oracle: 7

> From Aram,*a* from the mountains of the east,
> Balak king of Moab has brought me:
> 'Come, lay a curse for me on Jacob,
> come, execrate Israel.'
> How can I denounce whom God has not denounced? 8
> How can I execrate whom the LORD has not execrated?
> From the rocky heights I see them, 9
> I watch them from the rounded hills.
> I see a people that dwells alone,
> that has not made itself one with the nations.
> Who can count the host *b* of Jacob 10
> or number the hordes *c* of Israel?
> Let me die as men die who are righteous,
> grant that my end may be as theirs!

Then Balak said to Balaam, 'What is this you have done? I sent for you 11
to denounce my enemies, and what you have done is to bless them.' But 12
he replied, 'Must I not keep to the words that the LORD puts into my
mouth?'

Balak then said to him, 'Come with me now to another place from which 13
you will see them, though not the full extent of them; you will not see them
all. Denounce them for me from there.' So he took him to the Field of the 14
Watchers *d* on the summit of Pisgah, where he built seven altars and offered
a bull and a ram on each altar. Balaam said to Balak, 'Take your stand beside 15
your sacrifice, and I will meet God over there.' The LORD met Balaam and 16
put words into his mouth, and said, 'Go back to Balak, and speak as I tell
you.' So he went back, and found him standing beside his sacrifice, with 17
the Moabite chiefs. Balak asked what the LORD had said, and Balaam 18
uttered his oracle:

> Up, Balak, and listen:
> hear what I am charged to say, son of Zippor.
> God is not a mortal that he should lie, 19
> not a man that he should change his mind. *e*
> Has he not spoken, and will he not make it good?
> What he has proclaimed, he will surely fulfil.
> I have received command to bless; 20
> I will bless and I cannot gainsay it.
> He has discovered no iniquity in Jacob 21
> and has seen no mischief in Israel. *f*

*a Or* Syria.    *b Or* dust.    *c Or* quarter *or* sands.
*d Or* Field of Zophim.    *e Or* feel regret.    *f Or* None can discover
calamity in Jacob nor see trouble in Israel.

> The LORD their God is with them,
> acclaimed among them as king. [a]

22
> What its curving horns are to the wild ox,
> God is to them, who brought them out of Egypt.

23
> Surely there is no divination in [b] Jacob,
> and no augury in [b] Israel;
> now is the time to say of Jacob
> and of Israel, 'See what God has wrought!'

24
> Behold a people rearing up like a lioness,
> rampant like a lion;
> he will not couch till he devours the prey
> and drinks the blood of the slain.

25  Then Balak said to Balaam, 'You will not denounce them; then at least do not
26  bless them'; and he answered, 'Did I not warn you that I must do all the
27  LORD tells me?' Balak replied, 'Come, let me take you to another place; per-
28  haps God will be pleased to let you denounce them for me from there.' So he
29  took Balaam to the summit of Peor overlooking Jeshimon, and Balaam told
    him to build seven altars for him there and prepare seven bulls and seven rams.
30  Balak did as Balaam had said, and he offered a bull and a ram on each altar.

**24**  But now that Balaam knew that the LORD wished him to bless Israel, he
    did not go and resort to divination as before. He turned towards the desert;
2  and as he looked, he saw Israel encamped tribe by tribe. The spirit of God
3  came upon him, and he uttered his oracle:

> The very word of Balaam son of Beor,
> the very word of the man whose sight is clear,

4
> the very word of him who hears the words of God,
> who with staring eyes sees in a trance
> the vision from the Almighty:

5
>     how goodly are your tents, O Jacob,
> your dwelling-places, Israel,

6
> like long rows of palms,
> like gardens by a river,
> like lign-aloes planted by the LORD,
> like cedars beside the water!

7
> The water in his vessels shall overflow,
> and his seed shall be like great waters
> so that his king may be taller than Agag,
> and his kingdom lifted high.

8
> What its curving horns are to the wild ox,
> God is to him, who brought him out of Egypt;
> he shall devour his adversaries the nations,
> crunch their bones, and smash their limbs in pieces.

9
> When he reclines he couches like a lion,
> like a lioness, and no one dares rouse him.
> Blessed be they that bless you,
> and they that curse you be accursed!

[a] *Or* royal care is bestowed on them.      [b] *Or* against.

At that Balak was very angry with Balaam, beat his hands together and 10
said, 'I summoned you to denounce my enemies, and three times you have
persisted in blessing them. Off with you to your own place! I promised to 11
confer great honour upon you, but now the LORD has kept this honour from
you.' Balaam answered, 'But I told your own messengers whom you sent: 12
"If Balak gives me all the silver and gold in his house, I cannot disobey the 13
command of the LORD by doing anything of my own will, good or bad.
What the LORD speaks to me, that is what I will say." Now I am going to 14
my own people; but first, I will warn you what this people will do to yours
in the days to come.' So he uttered his oracle: 15

> The very word of Balaam son of Beor,
> the very word of the man whose sight is clear,
> the very word of him who hears the words of God, 16
> who shares the knowledge of the Most High,
> who with staring eyes sees in a trance
> the vision from the Almighty:
> I see him, but not now; 17
> I behold him, but not near:
> a star shall come forth out of Jacob,
> a comet arise from Israel.
> He shall smite the squadrons*a* of Moab,
> and beat down all the sons of strife.
> Edom shall be his by conquest 18
> and Seir, his enemy, shall be his.
> Israel shall do valiant deeds;
> Jacob shall trample them down, 19
> the last survivor from Ar shall he destroy.

He saw Amalek and uttered his oracle: 20

> First of all the nations was Amalek,
> but his end shall be utter destruction.

He saw the Kenites and uttered his oracle: 21

> Your refuge, though it seems secure,
> your nest, though set on the mountain crag,
> is doomed to burning, O Cain. 22
> How long must you dwell there in my sight?

He uttered his oracle: 23

> Ah, who are these assembling in the north,
> invaders from the region of Kittim? 24
> They will lay waste Assyria; they will lay Eber waste:
> he too shall perish utterly.

Then Balaam arose and returned home, and Balak also went on his way. 25

WHEN THE ISRAELITES WERE IN SHITTIM, the people began to have **25**
intercourse with Moabite women, who invited them to the sacrifices 2
offered to their gods; and they ate the sacrificial food and prostrated

---

*a* *Or* heads.

3 themselves before the gods of Moab. The Israelites joined in the worship
4 of the Baal of Peor, and the LORD was angry with them. He said to Moses,
'Take all the leaders of the people and hurl them down to their death before
the LORD in the full light of day, that the fury of his anger may turn away
5 from Israel.' So Moses said to the judges of Israel, 'Put to death, each one
of you, those of his tribe who have joined in the worship of the Baal of Peor.'
6   One of the Israelites brought a Midianite woman into his family in open
defiance of Moses and all the community of Israel, while they were weep-
7 ing by the entrance of the Tent of the Presence. Phinehas son of Eleazar,
son of Aaron the priest, saw him. He stepped out from the crowd and took
8 up a spear, and he went into the inner room after the Israelite and trans-
fixed the two of them, the Israelite and the woman, pinning them together.
Thus the plague which had attacked the Israelites was brought to a stop;
9 but twenty-four thousand had already died.
10 11   The LORD spoke to Moses and said, 'Phinehas son of Eleazar, son of
Aaron the priest, has turned my wrath away from the Israelites; he displayed among them the same jealous anger that moved me, and therefore
12 in my jealousy I did not exterminate the Israelites. Tell him that I hereby
13 grant him my covenant of security of tenure. He and his descendants after
him shall enjoy the priesthood under a covenant for all time, because he
14 showed his zeal for his God and made expiation for the Israelites.' The
name of the Israelite struck down with the Midianite woman was Zimri
15 son of Salu, a chief in a Simeonite family, and the Midianite woman's
name was Cozbi daughter of Zur, who was the head of a group of fathers'
families in Midian.
16 17–18   The LORD spoke to Moses and said, 'Make the Midianites suffer as they
made you suffer with their crafty tricks, and strike them down; their
craftiness was your undoing at Peor and in the affair of Cozbi their sister,
the daughter of a Midianite chief, who was struck down at the time of the
plague that followed Peor.'

19 26 1 AFTER THE PLAGUE the LORD said to Moses and Eleazar the priest, son
2 of Aaron, 'Number the whole community of Israel by fathers' families,
recording everyone in Israel aged twenty years and upwards fit for military
3 service.' Moses and Eleazar collected them in the lowlands of Moab by
4 the Jordan near Jericho,*a* all who were twenty years of age and upwards,
as the LORD had commanded Moses.
    These were the Israelites who came out of Egypt:
5 *b*   Reubenites (Reuben was Israel's eldest son): Enoch, the Enochite
6 family; Pallu, the Palluite family; Hezron, the Hezronite family; Carmi,
7 the Carmite family. These were the Reubenite families; the number in
8 their detailed list was forty-three thousand seven hundred and thirty. Son
9 of Pallu: Eliab. Sons of Eliab: Nemuel, Dathan and Abiram. These were
the same Dathan and Abiram, conveners of the community, who defied
Moses and Aaron and joined the company of Korah in defying the LORD.
10 Then the earth opened its mouth and swallowed them up with Korah, and

*a Prob. rdg.; Heb. adds* saying.     *b Verses 5–50: cp. Gen. 46. 8–25; Exod. 6. 14, 15;
1 Chr. chs. 4–8.*

so their company died, while fire burnt up the two hundred and fifty men, and they became a warning sign. The Korahites, however, did not die. 11

Simeonites, by their families: Nemuel, the Nemuelite family; Jamin, 12 the Jaminite family; Jachin, the Jachinite family; Zerah, the Zarhite 13 family; Saul, the Saulite family. These were the Simeonite families; the 14 number in their detailed list was twenty-two thousand two hundred.

Gadites, by their families: Zephon, the Zephonite family; Haggi, the 15 Haggite family; Shuni, the Shunite family; Ozni, the Oznite family; Eri, 16 the Erite family; Arod, the Arodite family; Areli, the Arelite family. These 17 18 were the Gadite families; the number in their detailed list was forty thousand five hundred.

The sons of Judah were Er, Onan, Shelah, Perez and Zerah; Er and 19 Onan died in Canaan. Judahites, by their families: Shelah, the Shelanite 20 family; Perez, the Perezite family; Zerah, the Zarhite family. Perezites: 21 Hezron, the Hezronite family; Hamul, the Hamulite family. These were 22 the families of Judah; the number in their detailed list was seventy-six thousand five hundred.

Issacharites, by their families: Tola, the Tolaite family; Pua, the Puite 23 family; Jashub, the Jashubite family; Shimron, the Shimronite family. 24 These were the families of Issachar; the number in their detailed list was 25 sixty-four thousand three hundred.

Zebulunites, by their families: Sered, the Sardite family; Elon, the 26 Elonite family; Jahleel, the Jahleelite family. These were the Zebulun- 27 ite families; the number in their detailed list was sixty thousand five hundred.

Josephites, by their families: Manasseh and Ephraim. Manassites: 28 29 Machir, the Machirite family. Machir was the father of Gilead: Gilead, the Gileadite family. Gileadites: Jeezer, the Jeezerite family; Helek, the 30 Helekite family; Asriel, the Asrielite family; Shechem, the Shechemite 31 family; Shemida, the Shemidaite family; Hepher, the Hepherite family. 32 Zelophehad son of Hepher had no sons, only daughters; their names were 33 Mahlah, Noah, Hoglah, Milcah and Tirzah. These were the families of 34 Manasseh; the number in their detailed list was fifty-two thousand seven hundred.

Ephraimites, by their families: Shuthelah, the Shuthalhite family; 35 Becher, the Bachrite family; Tahan, the Tahanite family. Shuthalhites: 36 Eran, the Eranite family. These were the Ephraimite families; the number 37 in their detailed list was thirty-two thousand five hundred. These were the Josephites, by families.

Benjamites, by their families: Bela, the Belaite family; Ashbel, the 38 Ashbelite family; Ahiram, the Ahiramite family; Shupham, the Shupham- 39 ite family; Hupham, the Huphamite family. Belaites: Ard and Naaman. 40 Ard, the Ardite family; Naaman, the Naamite family. These were the 41 Benjamite families; the number in their detailed list was forty-five thousand six hundred.

Danites, by their families: Shuham, the Shuhamite family. These were 42 the families of Dan by their families; the number in the detailed list of the 43 Shuhamite family was sixty-four thousand four hundred.

44 Asherites, by their families: Imna, the Imnite family; Ishvi, the Ishvite
45 family; Beriah, the Beriite family. Beriite families: Heber, the Heberite
46 family; Malchiel, the Malchielite family. The daughter of Asher was named
47 Serah. These were the Asherite families; the number in their detailed list
was fifty-three thousand four hundred.

48 Naphtalites, by their families: Jahzeel, the Jahzeelite family; Guni, the
49 Gunite family; Jezer, the Jezerite family; Shillem, the Shillemite family.
50 These were the Naphtalite families by their families; the number in their
detailed list was forty-five thousand four hundred.

51 The total in the Israelite lists was six hundred and one thousand seven
hundred and thirty.

52 53 The LORD spoke to Moses and said, 'The land shall be apportioned
54 among these tribes according to the number of names recorded. To the
larger group you shall give a larger property and to the smaller a smaller;
a property shall be given to each in proportion to its size as shown in the
55 detailed lists. The land, however, shall be apportioned by lot; the lots shall
56 be cast for the properties by families in the father's line. Properties shall
be apportioned by lot between the larger families and the smaller.'

57 The detailed lists of Levi, by families: Gershon, the Gershonite family;
Kohath, the Kohathite family; Merari, the Merarite family.

58 These were the families of Levi: the Libnite, Hebronite, Mahlite,
Mushite, and Korahite families.

59 Kohath was the father of Amram; Amram's wife was named Jochebed
daughter of Levi, born to him in Egypt. She bore to Amram Aaron, Moses,
60 and their sister Miriam. Aaron's sons were Nadab, Abihu, Eleazar and
61 Ithamar. Nadab and Abihu died because they presented illicit fire before
the LORD.

62 In the detailed lists of Levi the number of males, aged one month and
upwards, was twenty-three thousand. They were recorded separately from
the other Israelites because no property was allotted to them among the
Israelites.

63 These were the detailed lists prepared by Moses and Eleazar the priest
when they numbered the Israelites in the lowlands of Moab by the Jordan
64 near Jericho. Among them there was not a single one of the Israelites whom
65 Moses and Aaron the priest had recorded in the wilderness of Sinai; for
the LORD had said they should all die in the wilderness. None of them was
still living except Caleb son of Jephunneh and Joshua son of Nun.

**27** A claim was presented by the daughters of Zelophehad son of Hepher,
son of Gilead, son of Machir, son of Manasseh, son of Joseph. Their
2 names were Mahlah, Noah, Hoglah, Milcah and Tirzah. They appeared
at the entrance of the Tent of the Presence before Moses, Eleazar the priest,
3 the chiefs, and all the community, and spoke as follows: 'Our father died
in the wilderness. He was not among the company of Korah which combined together against the LORD; he died for his own sin and left no sons.
4 Is it right that, because he had no son, our father's name should disappear
from his family? Give us our property on the same footing as our father's
brothers.'

5 6 So Moses brought their case before the LORD, and the LORD spoke to

Moses and said, 'The claim of the daughters of Zelophehad is good. You 7
must allow them to inherit on the same footing as their father's brothers.
Let their father's patrimony pass to them. Then say this to the Israelites: 8
"When a man dies leaving no son, his patrimony shall pass to his daughter.
If he has no daughter, you shall give it to his brothers. If he has no brothers, 9 10
you shall give it to his father's brothers. If his father had no brothers, then 11
you shall give possession to the nearest survivor in his family, and he shall
inherit. This shall be a legal precedent for the Israelites, as the LORD has
commanded Moses."'

The LORD said to Moses, 'Go up this mountain, Mount Abarim, and 12
look out over the land which I have given to the Israelites. Then, when 13
you have looked out over it, you shall be gathered to your father's kin like
your brother Aaron; for you and Aaron disobeyed my command when the 14
community disputed with me in the wilderness of Zin: you did not uphold
my holiness before them at the waters.' These were the waters of Meribah-
by-Kadesh in the wilderness of Zin.

Then Moses said, 'Let the LORD, the God of the spirits of all mankind, 15 16
appoint a man over the community to go out and come in at their head, to 17
lead them out and bring them home, so that the community of the LORD
may not be like sheep without a shepherd.' The LORD answered Moses, 18
'Take Joshua son of Nun, a man endowed with spirit; lay your hand on
him and set him before Eleazar the priest and all the community. Give him 19
his commission in their presence, and delegate some of your authority to 20
him, so that all the community of the Israelites may obey him. He must 21
appear before Eleazar the priest, who will obtain a decision for him by
consulting the Urim before the LORD; at his word they shall go out and
shall come home, both Joshua and the whole community of the Israelites.'

Moses did as the LORD had commanded him. He took Joshua, presented 22
him to Eleazar the priest and the whole community, laid his hands on him 23
and gave him his commission, as the LORD had instructed him.

THE LORD SPOKE TO MOSES and said, Give this command to the Israel- 28 1 2
ites: See that you present my offerings, the food for the food-offering of
soothing odour, to me at the appointed time.

Tell them: This is the food-offering which you shall present to the 3
LORD: the regular daily whole-offering of two yearling rams without
blemish. One you shall sacrifice in the morning and the second between 4
dusk and dark. The grain-offering shall be a tenth of an ephah of flour 5
mixed with a quarter of a hin of oil of pounded olives. (This was the regular 6
whole-offering made at Mount Sinai, a soothing odour, a food-offering to
the LORD.) The wine for the proper drink-offering shall be a quarter of a 7
hin to each ram; you are to pour out this strong drink in the holy place as
an offering to the LORD. You shall sacrifice the second ram between dusk 8
and dark, with the same grain-offering as at the morning sacrifice and with
the proper drink-offering; it is a food-offering of soothing odour to the
LORD.

For the sabbath day: two yearling rams without blemish, a grain- 9
offering of two tenths of an ephah of flour mixed with oil, and the proper

10  drink-offering. This whole-offering, presented every sabbath, is in addition to the regular whole-offering and the proper drink-offering.

11  On the first day of every month you shall present a whole-offering to the LORD, consisting of two young bulls, one ram and seven yearling rams

12  without blemish. The grain-offering shall be three tenths of flour mixed with oil for each bull, two tenths of flour mixed with oil for the full-grown

13  ram, and one tenth of flour mixed with oil for each young ram. This is a

14  whole-offering, a food-offering of soothing odour to the LORD. The proper drink-offering shall be half a hin of wine for each bull, a third for the full-grown ram and a quarter for each young ram. This is the whole-offering

15  to be made, month by month, throughout the year. Further, one he-goat shall be sacrificed as a sin-offering to the LORD, in addition to the regular whole-offering and the proper drink-offering.

16  The Passover of the LORD shall be held on the fourteenth day of the

17  first month, and on the fifteenth day there shall be a pilgrim-feast; for seven

18  days you must eat only unleavened cakes. On the first day there shall be a

19  sacred assembly; you shall not do your daily work. As a food-offering, a whole-offering to the LORD, you shall present two young bulls, one ram,

20  and seven yearling rams, all without blemish. You shall offer the proper grain-offerings of flour mixed with oil, three tenths for each bull, two

21 22  tenths for the ram, and one tenth for each of the seven young rams; and as

23  a sin-offering, one he-goat to make expiation for you. All these you shall offer in addition to the morning whole-offering, which is the regular

24  sacrifice. You shall repeat this daily till the seventh day, presenting food as a food-offering of soothing odour to the LORD, in addition to the regu-

25  lar whole-offering and the proper drink-offering. On the seventh day there shall be a sacred assembly; you shall not do your daily work.

26  On the day of Firstfruits, when you bring to the LORD your grain-offering from the new crop at your Feast of Weeks, there shall be a sacred

27  assembly; you shall not do your daily work. You shall bring a whole-offering as a soothing odour to the LORD: two young bulls, one full-grown

28  ram, and seven yearling rams. The proper grain-offering shall be of flour

29  mixed with oil, three tenths for each bull, two tenths for the one ram, and

30  a tenth for each of the seven young rams, and there shall be one he-

31  goat as a sin-offering to make expiation for you; they shall all be without blemish. All these you shall offer in addition to the regular whole-offering with the proper grain-offering and drink-offering.

**29**  On the first day of the seventh month there shall be a sacred assembly;

2  you shall not do your daily work. It shall be a day of acclamation. You shall sacrifice a whole-offering as a soothing odour to the LORD: one young

3  bull, one full-grown ram, and seven yearling rams, without blemish. Their proper grain-offering shall be of flour mixed with oil, three tenths for the

4  bull, two tenths for the one ram, and one tenth for each of the seven young

5  rams, and there shall be one he-goat as a sin-offering to make expiation for

6  you. This is in addition to the monthly whole-offering and the regular whole-offering with their proper grain-offerings and drink-offerings according to custom; it is a food-offering of soothing odour to the LORD.

7  On the tenth day of this seventh month there shall be a sacred assembly,

and you shall mortify yourselves; you shall not do any work. You shall 8
bring a whole-offering to the LORD as a soothing odour: one young bull,
one full-grown ram, and seven yearling rams; they shall all be without
blemish. The proper grain-offering shall be of flour mixed with oil, three 9
tenths for the bull, two tenths for the one ram, and one tenth for each of the 10
seven young rams, and there shall be one he-goat as a sin-offering, in addi- 11
tion to the expiatory sin-offering and the regular whole-offering, with the
proper grain-offering and drink-offering.

On the fifteenth day of the seventh month there shall be a sacred assem- 12
bly. You shall not do your daily work, but shall keep a pilgrim-feast to the
LORD for seven days. As a whole-offering, a food-offering of soothing 13
odour to the LORD, you shall bring thirteen young bulls, two full-grown
rams, and fourteen yearling rams; they shall all be without blemish. The 14
proper grain-offering shall be of flour mixed with oil, three tenths for each
of the thirteen bulls, two tenths for each of the two rams, and one tenth for 15
each of the fourteen young rams, and there shall be one he-goat as a sin- 16
offering, in addition to the regular whole-offering with the proper grain-
offering and drink-offering.

On the second day: twelve young bulls, two full-grown rams, and four- 17
teen yearling rams, without blemish, together with the proper grain- 18
offerings and drink-offerings for bulls, full-grown rams, and young rams,
as prescribed according to their number, and there shall be one he-goat 19
as a sin-offering, in addition to the regular whole-offering with the proper
grain-offering and drink-offering.

On the third day: eleven bulls, two full-grown rams, and fourteen 20
yearling rams, without blemish, together with the proper grain-offerings 21
and drink-offerings for bulls, full-grown rams, and young rams, as prescribed according to their number, and there shall be one he-goat as a 22
sin-offering, in addition to the regular whole-offering, with the proper
grain-offering and drink-offering.

On the fourth day: ten bulls, two full-grown rams, and fourteen yearling 23
rams, without blemish, together with the proper grain-offerings and drink- 24
offerings for bulls, full-grown rams, and young rams, as prescribed according to their number, and there shall be one he-goat as a sin-offering, in 25
addition to the regular whole-offering with the proper grain-offering and
drink-offering.

On the fifth day: nine bulls, two full-grown rams, and fourteen yearling 26
rams, without blemish, together with the proper grain-offerings and drink- 27
offerings for bulls, full-grown rams, and young rams, as prescribed according to their number, and there shall be one he-goat as a sin-offering, in 28
addition to the regular whole-offering with the proper grain-offering and
drink-offering.

On the sixth day: eight bulls, two full-grown rams, and fourteen yearling 29
rams, without blemish, together with the proper grain-offerings and drink- 30
offerings for bulls, full-grown rams, and young rams, as prescribed according to their number, and there shall be one he-goat as a sin-offering, in 31
addition to the regular whole-offering with the proper grain-offering and
drink-offering.

32 On the seventh day: seven bulls, two full-grown rams, and fourteen
33 yearling rams, without blemish, together with the proper grain-offerings
   and drink-offerings for bulls, full-grown rams, and young rams, as pre-
34 scribed according to their number, and there shall be one he-goat as a
   sin-offering, in addition to the regular whole-offering with the proper
   grain-offering and drink-offering.

35 The eighth day you shall keep as a closing ceremony; you shall not do
36 your daily work. As a whole-offering, a food-offering of soothing odour to
   the LORD, you shall bring one bull, one full-grown ram, and seven yearling
37 rams, without blemish, together with the proper grain-offerings and drink-
   offerings for bulls, full-grown rams, and young rams, as prescribed accord-
38 ing to their number, and there shall be one he-goat as a sin-offering, in
   addition to the regular whole-offering with the proper grain-offering and
   drink-offering.

39 These are the sacrifices which you shall offer to the LORD at the appointed seasons, in addition to the votive offerings, the freewill offerings,
   the whole-offerings, the grain-offerings, the drink-offerings, and the
   shared-offerings.

40 Moses told the Israelites exactly what the LORD had commanded
   him.

**30** THEN MOSES SPOKE to the heads of the Israelite tribes and said, This is
2 the LORD's command: When a man makes a vow to the LORD or swears
  an oath and so puts himself under a binding obligation, he must not break
3 his word. Every word he has spoken, he must make good. When a woman,
  still young and living in her father's house, makes a vow to the LORD or
4 puts herself under a binding obligation, if her father hears of it and keeps
5 silence, then any such vow or obligation shall be valid. But if her father
  disallows it when he hears of it, none of her vows or obligations shall be
6 valid; the LORD will absolve her, because her father has disallowed it. If
  the woman is married when she is under a vow or a binding obligation
7 rashly uttered, then if her husband hears of it and keeps silence when he
  hears, her vow or obligation by which she has bound herself shall be valid.
8 If, however, her husband disallows it when he hears of it and repudiates
  the vow which she has taken upon herself or the rash utterance with which
9 she has bound herself, then the LORD will absolve her. Every vow by which
10 a widow or a divorced woman has bound herself shall be valid. But if it is
   in her husband's house that a woman makes a vow or puts herself under a
11 binding obligation by an oath, and her husband, hearing of it, keeps silence
   and does not disallow it, then every vow and obligation under which she
12 has put herself shall be valid; but if her husband clearly repudiates them
   when he hears of them, then nothing that she has uttered, whether vow or
   obligation, shall be valid. Her husband has repudiated them, and the LORD
   will absolve her.

13 The husband can confirm or repudiate any vow or oath by which a
14 woman binds herself to mortification. If he maintains silence day after day,
   he thereby confirms every vow or obligation under which she has put herself: he confirms them, because he kept silence at the time when he heard

them. If he repudiates them some time after he has heard them, he shall be  15
responsible for her default.

Such are the decrees which the LORD gave to Moses concerning a husband  16
and his wife and a father and his daughter, still young and living in her
father's house.

THE LORD SPOKE TO MOSES and said, 'You are to exact vengeance for  **31** 1 2
Israel on the Midianites and then you will be gathered to your father's kin.'

Then Moses spoke to the people in these words: 'Let some men among  3
you be drafted for active service. They shall fall upon Midian and exact
vengeance in the LORD's name. You shall send out a thousand men from  4
each of the tribes of Israel.' So the men were called up from the clans of  5
Israel, a thousand from each tribe, twelve thousand in all, drafted for active
service. Moses sent out this force, a thousand from each tribe, with  6
Phinehas son of Eleazar the priest, who was in charge of the holy vessels
and of the trumpets to give the signal for the battle-cry. They made war  7
on Midian as the LORD had commanded Moses, and slew all the men. In  8
addition to those slain in battle they killed the kings of Midian—Evi,
Rekem, Zur, Hur, and Reba, the five kings of Midian—and they put to
death also Balaam son of Beor. The Israelites took captive the Midianite  9
women and their dependants, and carried off all their beasts, their flocks,
and their property. They burnt all their cities, in which they had settled,  10
and all their encampments. They took all the spoil and plunder, both  11
man and beast, and brought them—captives, plunder, and spoil—to Moses  12
and Eleazar the priest and to all the community of the Israelites, to the
camp in the lowlands of Moab by the Jordan at Jericho.

Moses and Eleazar the priest and all the leaders of the community went  13
to meet them outside the camp. Moses spoke angrily to the officers of the  14
army, the commanders of units of a thousand and of a hundred, who were
returning from the campaign: 'Have you spared all the women?' he said.  15
'Remember, it was they who, on Balaam's departure, set about seducing  16
the Israelites into disloyalty to the LORD that day at Peor, so that the
plague struck the community of the LORD. Now kill every male dependant,  17
and kill every woman who has had intercourse with a man, but spare for  18
yourselves every woman among them who has not had intercourse. You  19
yourselves, every one of you who has taken life and every one who has
touched the dead, must remain outside the camp for seven days. Purify
yourselves and your captives on the third day and on the seventh day, and  20
purify also every piece of clothing, every article made of skin, everything
woven of goat's hair, and everything made of wood.'

Eleazar the priest said to the soldiers returning from battle, 'This is a  21
law and statute which the LORD has ordained through Moses. Anything  22-23
which will stand fire, whether gold, silver, copper, iron, tin, or lead, you
shall pass through fire and then it will be clean. Other things shall be
purified by the water of ritual purification; whatever cannot stand fire shall
be passed through the water. On the seventh day you shall wash your  24
clothes, and then be clean; after this you may re-enter the camp.'

The LORD spoke to Moses and said, 'Count all that has been captured,  25 26

man or beast, you and Eleazar the priest and the heads of families in the
27 community, and divide it equally between the fighting men who went on
28 the campaign and the whole community. You shall levy a tax for the LORD:
from the combatants it shall be one out of every five hundred, whether
29 men, cattle, asses, or sheep, to be taken out of their share and given to
30 Eleazar the priest as a contribution for the LORD. Out of the share of the
Israelites it shall be one out of every fifty taken, whether man or beast,
cattle, asses, or sheep, to be given to the Levites who are in charge of the
LORD's Tabernacle.'

31   Moses and Eleazar the priest did as the LORD had commanded Moses.
32 These were the spoils, over and above the plunder taken by the fighting
33 men: six hundred and seventy-five thousand sheep, seventy-two thousand
34 35 cattle, sixty-one thousand asses; and of persons, thirty-two thousand girls
who had had no intercourse with a man.

36   The half-share of those who took part in the campaign was thus three
37 hundred and thirty-seven thousand five hundred sheep, the tax for the
38 LORD from these being six hundred and seventy-five; thirty-six thousand
39 cattle, the tax being seventy-two; thirty thousand five hundred asses, the
40 tax being sixty-one; and sixteen thousand persons, the tax being thirty-
41 two. Moses gave Eleazar the priest the tax levied for the LORD, as the LORD
had commanded him.

42-43   The share of the community, being the half-share for the Israelites
which Moses divided off from that of the combatants, was three hundred
44 and thirty-seven thousand five hundred sheep, thirty-six thousand cattle,
45 46 47 thirty thousand five hundred asses, and sixteen thousand persons. Moses
took one out of every fifty, whether man or beast, from the half-share of the
Israelites, and gave it to the Levites who were in charge of the LORD's
Tabernacle, as the LORD had commanded him.

48   Then the officers who had commanded the forces on the campaign, the
49 commanders of units of a thousand and of a hundred, came to Moses and
said to him, 'Sir, we have checked the roll of the fighting men who were
50 under our command, and not one of them is missing. So we have brought
the gold ornaments, the armlets, bracelets, finger-rings, earrings, and
pendants that each man has found, to offer them before the LORD as a
ransom for our lives.'

51   Moses and Eleazar the priest received this gold from the commanders
52 of units of a thousand and of a hundred, all of it craftsman's work, and the
gold thus levied as a contribution to the LORD weighed sixteen thousand
53 seven hundred and fifty shekels; for every man in the army had taken
54 plunder. So Moses and Eleazar the priest received the gold from the commanders of units of a thousand and of a hundred, and brought it to the
Tent of the Presence that the LORD might remember Israel.

32   Now the Reubenites and the Gadites had large and very numerous
flocks, and when they saw that the land of Jazer and Gilead was good
2 grazing country, they came and said to Moses and Eleazar the priest and
3 to the leaders of the community, 'Ataroth, Dibon, Jazer, Nimrah, Heshbon,
4 Elealeh, Sebam, Nebo, and Beon, the region which the LORD has subdued
before the advance of the Israelite community, is grazing country, and our

flocks are our livelihood. If', they said, 'we have found favour with you, 5
sir, then let this country be given to us as our possession, and do not make
us cross the Jordan.' Moses replied to the Gadites and the Reubenites, 6
'Are your kinsmen to go into battle while you stay here? How dare you dis- 7
courage the Israelites from crossing over to the land which the LORD has
given them? This is what your fathers did when I sent them out from 8
Kadesh-barnea to view the land. They went up as far as the gorge of 9
Eshcol and viewed the land, and on their return so discouraged the Israelites that they would not enter the land which the LORD had given them.
The LORD became angry that day, and he solemnly swore: "Because they 10 11
have not followed me with their whole heart, none of the men who came
out of Egypt, from twenty years old and upwards, shall see the land which
I promised on oath to Abraham, Isaac and Jacob." This meant all except 12
Caleb son of Jephunneh the Kenizzite and Joshua son of Nun, who followed the LORD with their whole heart. The LORD became angry with 13
Israel, and he made them wander in the wilderness for forty years until
that whole generation was dead which had done what was wrong in his
eyes. And now you are following in your fathers' footsteps, a fresh brood 14
of sinful men to fire the LORD's anger once more against Israel; for if you 15
refuse to follow him, he will again abandon this whole people in the wilderness and you will be the cause of their destruction.'

Presently they came forward with this offer: 'We will build folds for our 16
sheep here and towns for our dependants. Then we can be drafted as a 17
fighting force to go at the head of the Israelites until we have brought them
to the lands that will be theirs. Meanwhile our dependants can live in the
walled towns, safe from the people of the country. We will not return 18
until every Israelite is settled in possession of his patrimony; we will claim 19
no share of the land with them over the Jordan and beyond, because our
patrimony has already been allotted to us east of the Jordan.' Moses 20
answered, 'If you stand by your promise, if in the presence of the LORD
you are drafted for battle, and the whole draft crosses the Jordan in front of 21
the LORD and remains there until the LORD has driven out his enemies, and 22
the land falls before him, then you may come back and be quit of your
obligation to the LORD and to Israel; and this land shall be your possession
in the sight of the LORD. But I warn you, if you fail to do all this, you will 23
have sinned against the LORD, and your sin will find you out. So build 24
towns for your dependants and folds for your sheep; but carry out your
promise.'

The Gadites and Reubenites answered Moses, 'Sir, we are your servants 25
and will do as you command. Our dependants and wives, our flocks and 26
all our beasts shall remain here in the cities of Gilead; but we, all who have 27
been drafted for active service with the LORD, will cross the river and fight,
according to your command.'

Accordingly Moses gave these instructions to Eleazar the priest and 28
Joshua son of Nun and to the heads of the families in the Israelite tribes:
'If the Gadites and Reubenites, all who have been drafted for battle before 29
the LORD, cross the Jordan with you, and if the land falls into your hands,
then you shall give them Gilead for their possession. But if, thus drafted, 30

they fail to cross with you, then they shall acquire land alongside you in
31 Canaan.' The Gadites and Reubenites said in response, 'Sir, the LORD
32 has spoken, and we will obey. Once we have been drafted, we will cross
over before the LORD into Canaan; then we shall have our patrimony here
beyond the Jordan.'

33  So to the Gadites, the Reubenites, and half the tribe of Manasseh son
of Joseph, Moses gave the kingdoms of Sihon king of the Amorites and
Og king of Bashan, the whole land with its towns and the country round
34 35 them. The Gadites built Dibon, Ataroth, Aroer, Atroth-shophan, Jazer,
36 Jogbehah, Beth-nimrah, and Beth-haran, all of them walled towns with
37 folds for their sheep. The Reubenites built Heshbon, Elealeh, Kiriathaim,
38 Nebo, Baal-meon (whose name was changed), and Sibmah; these were the
39 names they gave to the towns they built. The sons of Machir son of Manas-
40 seh invaded Gilead, took it and drove out the Amorite inhabitants; Moses
then assigned Gilead to Machir son of Manasseh, and he made his home
41 there. Jair son of Manasseh attacked and took the tent-villages of Ham *a*
42 and called them Havvoth-jair. *b* Nobah attacked and took Kenath and its
villages and gave it his own name, Nobah.

33  THESE ARE THE STAGES in the journey of the Israelites, when they were
2 led by Moses and Aaron in their tribal hosts out of Egypt. Moses recorded
their starting-points stage by stage as the LORD commanded him. These
are their stages from one starting-point to the next:

3  The Israelites left Rameses on the fifteenth day of the first month, the
day after the Passover; they marched out defiantly in full view of all the
4 Egyptians, while the Egyptians were burying all the first-born struck down
by the LORD as a judgement on their gods.

5  The Israelites left Rameses and encamped at Succoth.
6  They left Succoth and encamped at Etham on the edge of the wilderness.
7  They left Etham, turned back near Pi-hahiroth *c* on the east of Baal-
zephon, and encamped before Migdol.
8  They left Pi-hahiroth, passed through the Sea into the wilderness,
marched for three days through the wilderness of Etham, and encamped
at Marah.
9  They left Marah and came to Elim, where there were twelve springs of
water and seventy palm-trees, and encamped there.
10  They left Elim and encamped by the Red Sea.
11  They left the Red Sea and encamped in the wilderness of Sin.
12  They left the wilderness of Sin and encamped at Dophkah.
13  They left Dophkah and encamped at Alush.
14  They left Alush and encamped at Rephidim, where there was no water
for the people to drink.
15  They left Rephidim and encamped in the wilderness of Sinai.
16  They left the wilderness of Sinai and encamped at Kibroth-hattaavah.
17  They left Kibroth-hattaavah and encamped at Hazeroth.
18  They left Hazeroth and encamped at Rithmah.

*a Prob. rdg.; Heb. their tent-villages.*          *b That is Tent-villages of Jair.*
*c See Exod. 14. 2.*

They left Rithmah and encamped at Rimmon-parez.  19
They left Rimmon-parez and encamped at Libnah.  20
They left Libnah and encamped at Rissah.  21
They left Rissah and encamped at Kehelathah.  22
They left Kehelathah and encamped at Mount Shapher.  23
They left Mount Shapher and encamped at Haradah.  24
They left Haradah and encamped at Makheloth.  25
They left Makheloth and encamped at Tahath.  26
They left Tahath and encamped at Tarah.  27
They left Tarah and encamped at Mithcah.  28
They left Mithcah and encamped at Hashmonah.  29
They left Hashmonah and encamped at Moseroth.  30
They left Moseroth and encamped at Bene-jaakan.  31
They left Bene-jaakan and encamped at Hor-haggidgad.  32
They left Hor-haggidgad and encamped at Jotbathah.  33
They left Jotbathah and encamped at Ebronah.*a*  34
They left Ebronah and encamped at Ezion-geber.  35
They left Ezion-geber and encamped in the wilderness of Zin, that is of  36
Kadesh.

They left Kadesh and encamped on Mount Hor on the frontier of Edom.  37
Aaron the priest went up Mount Hor at the command of the LORD and  38
there he died, on the first day of the fifth month in the fortieth year after
the Israelites came out of Egypt; he was a hundred and twenty-three years  39
old when he died there.

The Canaanite king of Arad, who lived in the Canaanite Negeb, heard  40
that the Israelites were coming.

They left Mount Hor and encamped at Zalmonah.  41
They left Zalmonah and encamped at Punon.  42
They left Punon and encamped at Oboth.  43
They left Oboth and encamped at Iye-abarim on the frontier of Moab.  44
They left Iyim and encamped at Dibon-gad.  45
They left Dibon-gad and encamped at Almon-diblathaim.  46
They left Almon-diblathaim and encamped in the mountains of Abarim  47
east of Nebo.

They left the mountains of Abarim and encamped in the lowlands of  48
Moab by the Jordan near Jericho. Their camp beside the Jordan extended  49
from Beth-jeshimoth to Abel-shittim in the lowlands of Moab. In the  50
lowlands of Moab by the Jordan near Jericho the LORD spoke to Moses and
said, Speak to the Israelites in these words: You will soon be crossing the  51
Jordan to enter Canaan. You must drive out all its inhabitants as you  52
advance, destroy all their carved figures and their images of cast metal,
and lay their hill-shrines in ruins. You must take possession of the land  53
and settle there, for to you I have given the land to occupy. You must divide  54
it by lot among your families, each taking its own territory, the large family
a large territory and the small family a small. It shall be assigned to them
according to the fall of the lot, each tribe and family taking its own territory.
If you do not drive out the inhabitants of the land as you advance, any  55

*a Or* Abronah.

whom you leave in possession will become like a barbed hook in your eye and a thorn in your side. They shall continually dispute your possession
56 of the land, and what I meant to do to them I will do to you.

34 1 2 The LORD spoke to Moses and said, Give these instructions to the Israelites: Soon you will be entering Canaan. This is the land assigned to you as a perpetual patrimony, the land of Canaan thus defined by its
3 frontiers. Your southern border shall start from the wilderness of Zin, where it marches with Edom, and run southwards from the end of the
4 Dead Sea on its eastern side. It shall then turn from the south up the ascent of Akrabbim and pass by Zin, and its southern limit shall be Kadesh-
5 barnea. It shall proceed by Hazar-addar to Azmon and from Azmon turn
6 towards the Torrent of Egypt, and its limit shall be the sea. Your western frontier shall be the Great Sea and the seaboard; this shall be your frontier
7 to the west. This shall be your northern frontier: you shall draw a line from
8 the Great Sea to Mount Hor and from Mount Hor to Lebo-hamath, and
9 the limit of the frontier shall be Zedad. From there it shall run to Ziphron, and its limit shall be Hazar-enan; this shall be your frontier to the north.
10 11 To the east you shall draw a line from Hazar-enan to Shepham; it shall run down from Shepham to Riblah east of Ain, continuing until it strikes the
12 ridge east of the sea of Kinnereth. The frontier shall then run down to the Jordan and its limit shall be the Dead Sea. The land defined by these frontiers shall be your land.
13 Moses gave these instructions to the Israelites: This is the land which you shall assign by lot, each taking your own territory; it is the land which
14 the LORD has ordered to be given to nine tribes and a half tribe. For the Reubenites, the Gadites, and the half tribe of Manasseh have already
15 occupied their territories, family by family. These two and a half tribes have received their territory here beyond the Jordan, east of Jericho, towards the sunrise.
16 17 The LORD spoke to Moses and said, These are the men who shall assign
18 the land for you: Eleazar the priest and Joshua son of Nun. You shall also
19 take one chief from each tribe to assign the land. These are their names:
from the tribe of Judah: Caleb son of Jephunneh;
20 from the tribe of Simeon: Samuel son of Ammihud;
21 from the tribe of Benjamin: Elidad son of Kislon;
22 from the tribe of Dan: the chief Bukki son of Jogli;
23 from the Josephites: from Manasseh, the chief Hanniel son of Ephod;
24 and from Ephraim, the chief Kemuel son of Shiphtan;
25 from Zebulun: the chief Elizaphan son of Parnach;
26 from Issachar: the chief Paltiel son of Azzan;
27 from Asher: the chief Ahihud son of Shelomi;
28 from Naphtali: the chief Pedahel son of Ammihud.
29 These were the men whom the LORD appointed to assign the territories in the land of Canaan.

35 THE LORD SPOKE TO MOSES in the lowlands of Moab by the Jordan near
2 Jericho and said: Tell the Israelites to set aside towns in their patrimony as homes for the Levites, and give them also the common land surrounding

the towns. They shall live in the towns, and keep their beasts, their herds, 3
and all their livestock on the common land. The land of the towns which 4
you give the Levites shall extend from the centre of the town outwards for
a thousand cubits in each direction. Starting from the town the eastern 5
boundary shall measure two thousand cubits, the southern two thousand,
the western two thousand, and the northern two thousand, with the town
in the centre. They shall have this as the common land adjoining their
towns.

When you give the Levites their towns, six of them shall be cities of 6
refuge, in which the homicide may take sanctuary; and you shall give them
forty-two other towns. The total number of towns to be given to the 7
Levites, each with its common land, is forty-eight. When you set aside 8
these towns out of the territory of the Israelites, you shall allot more from
the larger tribe and less from the smaller; each tribe shall give towns to the
Levites in proportion to the patrimony assigned to it.

The LORD spoke to Moses and said, Speak to the Israelites in these 9 10
words: You are crossing the Jordan to the land of Canaan. You shall 11
designate certain cities to be places of refuge, in which the homicide who
has killed a man by accident may take sanctuary. These cities shall be 12
places of refuge from the vengeance of the dead man's next-of-kin, so
that the homicide shall not be put to death without standing his trial before
the community. The cities appointed as places of refuge shall be six in 13
number, three east of the Jordan and three in Canaan. These six cities 14 15
shall be places of refuge, so that any man who has taken life inadvertently,
whether he be Israelite, resident alien, or temporary settler, may take
sanctuary in one of them.

If the man strikes his victim with anything made of iron and he dies, 16
then he is a murderer: the murderer must be put to death. If a man has a 17
stone in his hand capable of causing death and strikes another man and he
dies, he is a murderer: the murderer must be put to death. If a man has a 18
wooden thing in his hand capable of causing death, and strikes another man
and he dies, he is a murderer: the murderer must be put to death. The dead 19
man's next-of-kin shall put the murderer to death; he shall put him to death
because he had attacked his victim. If the homicide sets upon a man openly 20
of malice aforethought or aims a missile at him of set purpose and he dies,
or if in enmity he falls upon him with his bare hands and he dies, then the 21
assailant must be put to death; he is a murderer. His next-of-kin shall put
the murderer to death because he had attacked his victim.

If he attacks a man on the spur of the moment, not being his enemy, or 22
hurls a missile at him not of set purpose, or if without looking he throws a 23
stone capable of causing death and it hits a man, then if the man dies,
provided he was not the man's enemy and was not harming him of set
purpose, the community shall judge between the striker and the next-of- 24
kin according to these rules. The community shall protect the homicide 25
from the vengeance of the kinsman and take him back to the city of refuge
where he had taken sanctuary. He must stay there till the death of the duly
anointed high priest. If the homicide ever goes beyond the boundaries of 26
the city where he has taken sanctuary, and the next-of-kin finds him outside 27

28 and kills him, then the next-of-kin shall not be guilty of murder. The homicide must remain in the city of refuge till the death of the high priest;
29 after the death of the high priest he may go back to his property. These shall be legal precedents for you for all time wherever you live.
30 The homicide shall be put to death as a murderer only on the testimony of witnesses; the testimony of a single witness shall not be enough to bring
31 him to his death. You shall not accept payment for the life of a homicide
32 guilty of a capital offence; he must be put to death. You shall not accept a payment from a man who has taken sanctuary in a city of refuge, allowing
33 him to go back before the death of the high priest and live at large. You shall not defile your land by bloodshed. Blood defiles the land, and expiation cannot be made on behalf of the land for blood shed on it except by the
34 blood of the man that shed it. You shall not make the land which you inhabit unclean, the land in which I dwell; for I, the LORD, dwell among the Israelites.

36 THE HEADS OF THE FATHERS' FAMILIES OF GILEAD son of Machir, son of Manasseh, one of the families of the sons of Joseph, approached Moses and the chiefs, heads of families in Israel, and addressed them.
2 'Sir,' they said, 'the LORD commanded you to distribute the land by lot to the Israelites, and you were also commanded to give the patrimony of our
3 brother Zelophehad to his daughters. Now if any of them shall be married to a husband from another Israelite tribe, her patrimony will be lost to the patrimony of our fathers and be added to that of the tribe into which she is
4 married, and so part of our allotted patrimony will be lost. Then, when the jubilee year comes round in Israel, her patrimony would be added to the patrimony of the tribe into which she is married, and it would be permanently lost to the patrimony of our fathers' tribe.'
5 So Moses, instructed by the LORD, gave the Israelites this ruling: 'The
6 tribe of the sons of Joseph is right. This is the LORD's command for the daughters of Zelophehad: They may marry whom they please, but only
7 within a family of their father's tribe. No patrimony in Israel shall pass from
8 tribe to tribe, but every Israelite shall retain his father's patrimony. Any woman of an Israelite tribe who is an heiress may marry a man from any family in her father's tribe. Thus the Israelites shall retain each one the
9 patrimony of his forefathers. No patrimony shall pass from one tribe to another, but every tribe in Israel shall retain its own patrimony.'
10 The daughters of Zelophehad acted in accordance with the LORD's
11 command to Moses; Mahlah, Tirzah, Hoglah, Milcah and Noah, the
12 daughters of Zelophehad, married sons of their father's brothers. They married within the families of the sons of Manasseh son of Joseph, and their patrimony remained with the tribe of their father's family.
13 These are the commandments and the decrees which the LORD issued to the Israelites through Moses in the lowlands of Moab by the Jordan near Jericho.

# DEUTERONOMY

## Primary charge of Moses to the people

THESE ARE THE WORDS THAT MOSES SPOKE to all 1
Israel in Transjordan, in the wilderness, that is to say in the Arabah
opposite Suph, between Paran on the one side and Tophel, Laban,
Hazeroth, and Dizahab on the other. (The journey from Horeb through the 2
hill-country of Seir to Kadesh-barnea takes eleven days.)
On the first day of the eleventh month of the fortieth year, after the 3-4
defeat of Sihon king of the Amorites who ruled in Heshbon, and the defeat
at Edrei of Og king of Bashan who ruled in Ashtaroth, Moses repeated to
the Israelites all the commands that the LORD had given him for them. It 5
was in Transjordan, in Moab, that Moses resolved to promulgate this law.
These were his words: The LORD our God spoke to us at Horeb and said, 6
'You have stayed on this mountain long enough; go now, make for the 7
hill-country of the Amorites, and pass on to all their neighbours in the
Arabah, in the hill-country, in the Shephelah, in the Negeb, and on
the coast, in short, all Canaan and the Lebanon as far as the great river, the
Euphrates. I have laid the land open before you; go in and occupy it, 8
the land which the LORD swore to give to your forefathers Abraham, Isaac
and Jacob, and to their descendants after them.'
At that time I said to you, 'You are a burden too heavy for me to carry 9
unaided. The LORD your God has increased you so that today you are as 10
numerous as the stars in the sky. May the LORD the God of your fathers 11
increase your number a thousand times and may he bless you as he promised. How can I bear unaided the heavy burden you are to me, and put 12
up with your complaints? Choose men of wisdom, understanding, and 13
repute for each of your tribes, and I will set them in authority over you.'
Your answer was, 'What you have told us to do is right.' So I took men of 14 15
wisdom and repute and set them in authority over you, some as commanders
over units of a thousand, of a hundred, of fifty or of ten, and others as
officers, for each of your tribes. And at that time I gave your judges this 16
command: 'You are to hear the cases that arise among your kinsmen and
judge fairly between man and man, whether fellow-countryman or resident
alien. You must be impartial and listen to high and low alike: have no fear 17
of man, for judgement belongs to God. If any case is too difficult for you,
bring it before me and I will hear it.' At the same time I instructed you in 18
all these duties.
Then we set out from Horeb, in obedience to the orders of the LORD 19
our God, and marched through that vast and terrible wilderness, as you
found it to be, on the way to the hill-country of the Amorites; and so we
came to Kadesh-barnea. Then I said to you, 'You have reached the 20

21 hill-country of the Amorites which the LORD our God is giving us. The LORD your God has indeed now laid the land open before you. Go forward and occupy it in fulfilment of the promise which the LORD the God of your

22 fathers made you; do not be discouraged or afraid.' But you all came to me and said, 'Let us send men ahead to spy out the country and report back

23 to us about the route we should take and the cities we shall find.' I approved

24 this plan and picked twelve of you, one from each tribe. They set out and made their way up into the hill-country as far as the gorge of Eshcol,

25 which they explored. They took samples of the fruit of the country and brought them back to us, and made their report: 'It is a rich land that the LORD our God is giving us.'

26 But you refused to go up and rebelled against the command of the LORD

27 your God. You muttered treason in your tents and said, 'It was because the LORD hated us that he brought us out of Egypt to hand us over to the

28 Amorites to be wiped out. What shall we find up there? Our kinsmen have discouraged us by their report of a people bigger and taller than we are, and of great cities with fortifications towering to the sky. And they told us they saw there the descendants of the Anakim.'*a*

29 Then I said to you, 'You must not dread them nor be afraid of them.

30 The LORD your God who goes at your head will fight for you and he will

31 do again what you saw him do for you in Egypt and in the wilderness. You saw there how the LORD your God carried you all the way to this place,

32 as a father carries his son.' In spite of this you did not trust the LORD your

33 God, who went ahead on the journey to find a place for your camp. He went in fire by night to show you the way you should take, and in a cloud by day.

34 When the LORD heard your complaints, he was indignant and solemnly

35 swore: 'Not one of these men, this wicked generation, shall see the rich

36 land which I swore to give your forefathers, except Caleb son of Jephunneh. He shall see it, and to him and his descendants I will give the land on which

37 he has set foot, because he followed the LORD with his whole heart.' On your account the LORD was angry with me also and said, 'You yourself

38 shall never enter it, but Joshua son of Nun, who is in attendance on you, shall enter it. Encourage him, for he shall put Israel in possession of that

39 land. Your dependants who, you thought, would become spoils of war, and your children who do not yet know good and evil, they shall enter;

40 I will give it to them, and they shall occupy it. You must turn back and set out for the wilderness by way of the Red Sea.'*b*

41 You answered me, 'We have sinned against the LORD; we will now go up and attack just as the LORD our God commanded us.' And each of you fastened on his weapons, thinking it an easy thing to invade the hill-

42 country. But the LORD said to me, 'Tell them not to go up and not to fight;

43 for I will not be with them, and their enemies will defeat them.' And I told you this, but you did not listen; you rebelled against the LORD's command

44 and defiantly went up to the hill-country. The Amorites living in the hills came out against you and like bees they chased you; they crushed you at

45 Hormah in Seir. Then you came back and wept before the LORD, but he

*a* the descendants . . . Anakim: *or* the tall men.      *b Or* the Sea of Reeds.

would not hear you or listen to you. That is why you remained in Kadesh 46
as long as you did.

So we turned and set out for the wilderness by way of the Red Sea as 2
the LORD had told me we must do, and we spent many days marching
round the hill-country of Seir. Then the LORD said to me, 'You have been 2 3
long enough marching round these hills; turn towards the north. And give 4
the people this charge: "You are about to go through the territory of your
kinsmen the descendants of Esau who live in Seir. Although they are
afraid of you, be on your guard and do not provoke them; for I shall not 5
give you any of their land, not so much as a foot's-breadth: I have given
the hill-country of Seir to Esau as a possession. You may purchase food 6
from them for silver, and eat it, and you may buy*a* water to drink." ' The 7
LORD your God has blessed you in everything you have undertaken; he
has watched your journey through this great wilderness; these forty years
the LORD your God has been with you and you have gone short of nothing.
So we went on past our kinsmen, the descendants of Esau who live in Seir, 8
and along the road of the Arabah which comes from Elath and Ezion-
geber, and we turned and followed the road to the wilderness of Moab.
There the LORD said to me, 'Do not harass the Moabites nor provoke them 9
to battle, for I will not give you any of their land as a possession. I have
given Ar to the descendants of Lot as a possession.' (The Emim once lived 10
there—a great and numerous people, as tall as the Anakim. The Rephaim 11
also were reckoned as Anakim; but the Moabites called them Emim. The 12
Horites lived in Seir at one time, but the descendants of Esau occupied their
territory: they destroyed them as they advanced and then settled in the land
instead of them, just as Israel did in their own territory which the LORD
gave them.) 'Come now, cross the gorge of the Zared.' So we went across. 13
The journey from Kadesh-barnea to the crossing of the Zared took us 14
thirty-eight years, until the whole generation of fighting men had passed
away as the LORD had sworn that they would. The LORD's hand was raised 15
against them, and he rooted them out of the camp to the last man.

When the last of the fighting men among the people had died, the LORD 16 17
spoke to me, 'Today', he said, 'you are to cross by Ar*b* which lies on the 18
frontier of Moab, and when you reach the territory of the Ammonites, you 19
must not harass them or provoke them to battle, for I will not give you any
Ammonite land as a possession; I have assigned it to the descendants of
Lot.' (This also is reckoned as the territory of the Rephaim, who lived there 20
at one time; but the Ammonites called them Zamzummim. They were a 21
great and numerous people, as tall as the Anakim, but the LORD destroyed
them as the Ammonites advanced and occupied their territory instead of
them, just as he had done for the descendants of Esau who lived in Seir. As 22
they advanced, he destroyed the Horites so that they occupied their territory and took possession instead of them: so it is to this day. It was 23
Caphtorites from Caphtor who destroyed the Avvim who lived in the
hamlets near Gaza, and settled in the land instead of them.) 'Come, set out 24
on your journey and cross the gorge of the Arnon, for I have put Sihon the
Amorite, king of Heshbon, and his territory into your hands. Begin to

*a* Or dig for.　　　*b* by Ar: or the gully.

25 occupy it and provoke him to battle. Today I will begin to put the fear and dread of you upon all the peoples under heaven; if they so much as hear a rumour of you, they will quake and tremble before you.'

26 Then I sent messengers from the wilderness of Kedemoth to Sihon king
27 of Heshbon with these peaceful overtures: 'Grant us passage through your country by the highway: we will keep to the highway, trespassing neither
28 to right nor to left, and we will pay you the full price for the food we eat
29 and the water we drink. The descendants of Esau who live in Seir granted us passage, and so did the Moabites who live in Ar. We will simply pass through your land on foot, until we cross the Jordan to the land which
30 the LORD our God is giving us.' But Sihon king of Heshbon refused to grant us passage; for the LORD your God had made him stubborn and obstinate, in order that he and his land might become subject to you, as it
31 still is. So the LORD said to me, 'Come, I have begun to deliver Sihon and
32 his territory into your hands. Begin now to occupy his land.' Then Sihon
33 with all his people came out to meet us in battle at Jahaz, and the LORD our God delivered him into our hands; we killed him with his sons and all
34 his people. We captured all his cities at that time and put to death everyone
35 in the cities, men, women, and dependants; we left no survivor. We took
36 the cattle as booty and plundered the cities we captured. From Aroer on the edge of the gorge of the Arnon and the level land of the gorge, as far as Gilead, no city walls were too lofty for us; the LORD our God laid them all
37 open to us. But you avoided the territory of the Ammonites, both the parts along the gorge of the Jabbok and their cities in the hills, thus fulfilling all that the LORD our God had commanded.

3 Next we turned and advanced along the road to Bashan. Og king of
2 Bashan, with all his people, came out against us at Edrei. The LORD said to me, 'Do not be afraid of him, for I have delivered him into your hands, with all his people and his land. Deal with him as you dealt with Sihon the
3 king of the Amorites who lived in Heshbon.' So the LORD our God also delivered Og king of Bashan into our hands, with all his people. We
4 slaughtered them and left no survivor, and at the same time we captured all his cities; there was not a single town that we did not take from them. In all we took sixty cities, the whole region of Argob, the kingdom of Og
5 in Bashan; all these were fortified cities with high walls, gates, and bars,
6 apart from a great many open settlements. Thus we put to death all the men, women, and dependants in every city, as we did to Sihon king of
7 Heshbon. All the cattle and the spoil from the cities we took as booty for ourselves.

8 At that time we took from these two Amorite kings in Transjordan the
9 territory that runs from the gorge of the Arnon to Mount Hermon (the
10 mountain that the Sidonians call Sirion and the Amorites Senir), all the cities of the tableland, and the whole of Gilead and Bashan as far as
11 Salcah and Edrei, cities in the kingdom of Og in Bashan. (Only Og king of Bashan remained as the sole survivor of the Rephaim. His sarcophagus of basalt*a* was nearly fourteen feet long and six feet wide, and it may still be seen in the Ammonite city of Rabbah.)

*a Or* iron.

At that time, when we occupied this territory, I assigned to the Reuben- 12
ites and Gadites the land beyond Aroer on the gorge of the Arnon and half
the hill-country of Gilead with its towns. The rest of Gilead and the whole 13
of Bashan the kingdom of Og, all the region of Argob, I assigned to half
the tribe of Manasseh. (All Bashan used to be called the land of the
Rephaim. Jair son of Manasseh took all the region of Argob as far as the 14
Geshurite and Maacathite border. There are tent-villages in Bashan still
called by his name, Havvoth-jair.*a*) To Machir I assigned Gilead, and to 15 16
the Reubenites and the Gadites I assigned land from Gilead to the gorge of
the Arnon, that is to the middle of the gorge; and its territory ran *bc* to the
gorge of the Jabbok, the Ammonite frontier, and included the Arabah, 17
with the Jordan and adjacent land, from Kinnereth to the Sea of the
Arabah, that is the Dead Sea, below the watershed of Pisgah on the east.
At that time I gave you this command: 'The LORD your God has given 18
you this land to occupy; let all your fighting men be drafted and cross at
the head of their fellow-Israelites. Only your wives and dependants and 19
your livestock—I know you have much livestock—shall stay in the towns
I have given you. This you shall do until the LORD gives your kinsmen 20
security as he has given it to you, and until they too occupy the land which
the LORD your God is giving them on the other side of the Jordan; then you
may return to the possession which I have given you, every man to his own.'

At that time also I gave Joshua this charge: 'You have seen with your 21
own eyes all that the LORD your God has done to these two kings; he will
do the same to all the kingdoms into which you will cross over. Do not be 22
afraid of them, for the LORD your God himself will fight for you.'

At that same time I pleaded with the LORD, 'O Lord GOD, thou hast 23 24
begun to show to thy servant thy greatness and thy strong hand: what god
is there in heaven or on earth who can match thy works and mighty deeds?
Let me cross over and see that rich land which lies beyond the Jordan, and 25
the fine hill-country and the Lebanon.' But because of you the LORD 26
brushed me aside and would not listen. 'Enough!' he answered. 'Say no
more about this. Go to the top of Pisgah and look west and north, south and 27
east; look well at what you see, for you shall not cross this river Jordan.
Give Joshua his commission, encourage him and strengthen him; for he 28
will lead this people across, and he will put them in possession of the land
you see before you.'

So we remained in the valley opposite Beth-peor. 29

NOW, ISRAEL, LISTEN to the statutes and laws which I am teaching you, 4
and obey them; then you will live, and go in and occupy the land which
the LORD the God of your fathers is giving you. You must not add any- 2
thing to my charge, nor take anything away from it. You must carry out all
the commandments of the LORD your God which I lay upon you.

You saw with your own eyes what the LORD did at Baal-peor; the LORD 3
your God destroyed among you every man who went over to the Baal of

---

*a* *That is* Tent-villages of Jair.     *b* that is . . . ran: *or* including the bed of the gorge
and the adjacent strip of land . . .     *c* and its territory ran: *prob. rdg.; Heb.* and
territory and . . .

4 5 Peor, but you who held fast to the LORD your God are all alive today. I
have taught you statutes and laws, as the LORD my God commanded me;
6 these you must duly keep when you enter the land and occupy it. You
must observe them carefully, and thereby you will display your wisdom
and understanding to other peoples. When they hear about these statutes,
they will say, 'What a wise and understanding people this great nation is!'
7 What great nation has a god*a* close at hand as the LORD our God is close to
8 us whenever we call to him? What great nation is there whose statutes and
9 laws are just, as is all this law which I am setting before you today? But
take good care: be on the watch not to forget the things that you have seen
with your own eyes, and do not let them pass from your minds as long as
10 you live, but teach them to your sons and to your sons' sons. You must
never forget that day when you stood before the LORD your God at Horeb,
and the LORD said to me, 'Assemble the people before me; I will make
them hear my words and they shall learn to fear me all their lives on earth,
11 and they shall teach their sons to do so.' Then you came near and stood at
the foot of the mountain. The mountain was ablaze with fire to the very
12 skies: there was darkness, cloud, and thick mist. When the LORD spoke to
you from the fire you heard a voice speaking, but you saw no figure; there
13 was only a voice. He announced the terms of his covenant to you, bidding
you observe the Ten Words,*b* and he wrote them on two tablets of stone.
14 At that time the LORD charged me to teach you statutes and laws which you
should observe in the land into which you are passing to occupy it.
15 On the day when the LORD spoke to you out of the fire on Horeb, you
16 saw no figure of any kind; so take good care not to fall into the degrading
practice of making figures carved in relief, in the form of a man or a woman,
17 18 or of any animal on earth or bird that flies in the air, or of any reptile on the
19 ground or fish in the waters under the earth. Nor must you raise your eyes
to the heavens and look up to the sun, the moon, and the stars, all the host
of heaven, and be led on to bow down to them and worship them; the LORD
your God assigned these for the worship of*c* the various peoples under
20 heaven. But you are the people whom the LORD brought out of Egypt,
from the smelting-furnace, and took for his own possession, as you are
21 to this day. The LORD was angry with me on your account and swore that
I should not cross the Jordan nor enter the rich land which the LORD your
22 God is giving you for your possession. I shall die in this country; I shall
not cross the Jordan, but you are about to cross and occupy that rich land.
23 Be careful not to forget the covenant which the LORD your God made with
you, and do not make yourselves a carved figure of anything which the
24 LORD your God has forbidden. For the LORD your God is a devouring fire,
a jealous god.
25 When you have children and grandchildren and grow old in the land,
if you then fall into the degrading practice of making any kind of carved
figure, doing what is wrong in the eyes of the LORD your God and provok-
26 ing him to anger, I summon heaven and earth to witness against you this
day: you will soon vanish from the land which you are to occupy after

*a* *Or* gods.     *b* *Or* Ten Commandments.     *c* assigned . . . worship of: *or*
created these for.

crossing the Jordan. You will not live long in it; you will be swept away. The LORD will disperse you among the peoples, and you will be left few in 27 number among the nations to which the LORD will lead you. There you 28 will worship gods made by human hands out of wood and stone, gods that can neither see nor hear, neither eat nor smell. But if from there you seek 29 the LORD your God, you will find him, if indeed you search with all your heart and soul. When you are in distress and all these things come upon 30 you, you will in days to come turn back to the LORD your God and obey him. The LORD your God is a merciful god; he will never fail you nor 31 destroy you, nor will he forget the covenant guaranteed by oath with your forefathers.

Search into days gone by, long before your time, beginning at the day 32 when God created man on earth; search from one end of heaven to the other, and ask if any deed as mighty as this has been seen or heard. Did 33 any people ever hear the voice of God speaking out of the fire, as you heard it, and remain alive? Or did ever a god attempt to come and take a 34 nation for himself away from another nation, with a challenge, and with signs, portents, and wars, with a strong hand and an outstretched arm, and with great deeds of terror, as the LORD your God did for you in Egypt in the sight of you all? You have had sure proof that the LORD is God; 35 there is no other. From heaven he let you hear his voice for your instruction, 36 and on earth he let you see his great fire, and out of the fire you heard his words. Because he loved your fathers and chose their children after them, 37 he in his own person brought you out of Egypt by his great strength, so 38 that he might drive out before you nations greater and more powerful than you and bring you in to give you their land in possession as it is today. This 39 day, then, be sure and take to heart that the LORD is God in heaven above and on earth below; there is no other. You shall keep his statutes and his 40 commandments which I give you today; then all will be well with you and with your children after you, and you will live long in the land which the LORD your God is giving you for all time.

Then Moses set apart three cities in the east, in Transjordan, to be places 41 42 of refuge for the homicide who kills a man without intent, with no previous enmity between them. If he takes sanctuary in one of these cities his life shall be safe. The cities were: Bezer-in-the-Wilderness on the tableland 43 for the Reubenites, Ramoth in Gilead for the Gadites, and Golan in Bashan for the Manassites.

This is the law which Moses laid down for the Israelites. These are the 44 45 precepts, the statutes, and the laws which Moses proclaimed to the Israelites, when they came out of Egypt and were in Transjordan in the valley 46 opposite Beth-peor in the land of Sihon king of the Amorites who lived in Heshbon. Moses and the Israelites had defeated him when they came out of Egypt and had occupied his territory and the territory of Og king of 47 Bashan, the two Amorite kings in the east, in Transjordan. The territory 48 ran from Aroer on the gorge of the Arnon to Mount Sirion, that is Hermon; and all the Arabah on the east, in Transjordan, as far as the Sea of the Arabah 49 below the watershed of Pisgah.

Moses summoned all Israel and said to them: Listen, O Israel, to the 5

statutes and the laws which I proclaim in your hearing today. Learn them
2 and be careful to observe them. The LORD our God made a covenant with
3 us at Horeb. It was not with our forefathers that the LORD made this cove-
4 nant, but with us, all of us who are alive and are here this day. The LORD
5 spoke with you face to face on the mountain out of the fire. I stood between
the LORD and you at that time to report the words of the LORD; for you were
afraid of the fire and did not go up the mountain. And the LORD said:

6     I am the LORD your God who brought you out of Egypt, out of the land
of slavery.

7     You shall have no other god*a* to set against me.

8     You shall not make a carved image for yourself nor the likeness of anything in the heavens above, or on the earth below, or in the waters under
the earth.

9     You shall not bow down to them or worship*b* them; for I, the LORD your
God, am a jealous god. I punish the children for the sins of the fathers to
10 the third and fourth generations of those who hate me. But I keep faith
with thousands, with*c* those who love me and keep my commandments.

11     You shall not make wrong use of the name of the LORD your God; the
LORD will not leave unpunished the man who misuses his name.

12     Keep the sabbath day holy as the LORD your God commanded you.
13 14 You have six days to labour and do all your work. But the seventh day is a
sabbath of the LORD your God; that day you shall not do any work, neither
you, your son or your daughter, your slave or your slave-girl, your ox,
your ass, or any of your cattle, nor the alien within your gates, so that your
15 slaves and slave-girls may rest as you do. Remember that you were slaves
in Egypt and the LORD your God brought you out with a strong hand and
an outstretched arm, and for that reason the LORD your God commanded
you to keep the sabbath day.

16     Honour your father and your mother, as the LORD your God commanded
you, so that you may live long, and that it may be well with you in the land
which the LORD your God is giving you.

17     You shall not commit murder.

18     You shall not commit adultery.

19     You shall not steal.

20     You shall not give false evidence against your neighbour.

21     You shall not covet your neighbour's wife; you shall not set your heart
on your neighbour's house, his land, his slave, his slave-girl, his ox, his
ass, or on anything that belongs to him.

22     These Commandments the LORD spoke in a great voice to your whole
assembly on the mountain out of the fire, the cloud, and the thick mist;
then he said no more. He wrote them on two tablets of stone and gave them
23 to me. When you heard the voice out of the darkness, while the mountain
was ablaze with fire, all the heads of your tribes and the elders came to me
24 and said, 'The LORD our God has shown us his glory and his greatness,
and we have heard his voice out of the fire: today we have seen that God
25 may speak with men and they may still live. Why should we now risk

*a Or* gods.          *b Or* or be led to worship . . .          *c* with . . . with: *or* for a
thousand generations with . . .

death? for this great fire will devour us. If we hear the voice of the LORD
our God again, we shall die. Is there any mortal man who has heard the 26
voice of the living God speaking out of the fire, as we have, and has lived?
You shall go near and listen to all that the LORD our God says, and report 27
to us all that the LORD our God has said to you; we will listen and obey.'

When the LORD heard these words which you spoke to me, he said, 'I 28
have heard what this people has said to you; every word they have spoken
is right. Would that they always had such a heart to fear me and to observe 29
all my commandments, so that all might be well with them and their
children for ever! Go, and tell them to return to their tents, but you your- 30 31
self stand here beside me, and I will set forth to you all the commandments,
the statutes and laws which you shall teach them to observe in the land
which I am giving them to occupy.'

You shall be careful to do as the LORD your God has commanded you; 32
do not turn from it to right or to left. You must conform to all the LORD 33
your God commands you, if you would live and prosper and remain long
in the land you are to occupy.

These are the commandments, statutes, and laws which the LORD your 6
God commanded me to teach you to observe in the land into which you
are passing to occupy it, a land flowing with milk and honey, so that you 2
may fear the LORD your God and keep all his statutes and commandments
which I am giving you, both you, your sons, and your descendants all your
lives, and so that you may live long. If you listen, O Israel, and are careful 3
to observe them, you will prosper and increase greatly as the LORD the
God of your fathers promised you.

Hear, O Israel, the LORD*ᵃ* is our God, one LORD, and you must love the 4 5
LORD your God with all your heart and soul and strength. These com- 6
mandments which I give you this day are to be kept in your heart; you 7
shall repeat them to your sons, and speak of them indoors and out of doors,
when you lie down and when you rise. Bind them as a sign on the hand and 8
wear them as a phylactery on the forehead; write them up on the door- 9
posts of your houses and on your gates.

The LORD your God will bring you into the land which he swore to your 10
forefathers Abraham, Isaac and Jacob that he would give you, a land of
great and fine cities which you did not build, houses full of good things 11
which you did not provide, rock-hewn cisterns which you did not hew,
and vineyards and olive-groves which you did not plant. When you eat
your fill there, be careful not to forget the LORD who brought you out of 12
Egypt, out of the land of slavery. You shall fear the LORD your God, serve 13
him alone and take your oaths in his name. You must not follow other gods, 14
gods of the nations that are around you; if you do, the LORD your God who 15
is in your midst will be angry with you, and he will sweep you away off the
face of the earth, for the LORD your God is a jealous god.

You must not challenge the LORD your God as you challenged him at 16
Massah.*ᵇ* You must diligently keep the commandments of the LORD your 17
God as well as the precepts and statutes which he gave you. You must do 18
what is right and good in the LORD's eyes so that all may go well with you,

---

*ᵃ See note on Exod. 3. 15.*      *ᵇ That is* Challenge.

H                              203

and you may enter and occupy the rich land which the LORD promised by
19  oath to your forefathers; then you shall drive out all your enemies before
you, as the LORD promised.
20    When your son asks you in time to come, 'What is the meaning of the
21  precepts, statutes, and laws which the LORD our God gave you?', you shall
say to him, 'We were Pharaoh's slaves in Egypt, and the LORD brought us
22  out of Egypt with his strong hand, sending great disasters, signs, and portents against the Egyptians and against Pharaoh and all his family, as we
23  saw for ourselves. But he led us out from there to bring us into the land and
24  give it to us as he had promised to our forefathers. The LORD commanded
us to observe all these statutes and to fear the LORD our God; it will be for
25  our own good at all times, and he will continue to preserve our lives. It
will be counted to our credit if we keep all these commandments in the
sight of the LORD our God, as he has bidden us.'

7  WHEN THE LORD YOUR GOD BRINGS YOU into the land which you are
entering to occupy and drives out many nations before you—Hittites,
Girgashites, Amorites, Canaanites, Perizzites, Hivites, and Jebusites,
2  seven nations more numerous and powerful than you—when the LORD
your God delivers them into your power and you defeat them, you must
put them to death. You must not make a treaty with them or spare them.
3  You must not intermarry with them, neither giving your daughters to
4  their sons nor taking their daughters for your sons; if you do, they will
draw your sons away from the LORD*a* and make them worship other gods.
5  Then the LORD will be angry with you and will quickly destroy you. But
this is what you must do to them: pull down their altars, break their sacred
6  pillars, hack down their sacred poles and destroy their idols by fire, for you
are a people holy to the LORD your God; the LORD your God chose you out
of all nations on earth to be his special possession.
7    It was not because you were more numerous than any other nation that
the LORD cared for you and chose you, for you were the smallest of all
8  nations; it was because the LORD loved you and stood by his oath to your
forefathers, that he brought you out with his strong hand and redeemed
you from the land of slavery, from the power of Pharaoh king of Egypt.
9  Know then that the LORD your God is God, the faithful God; with those
who love him and keep his commandments he keeps covenant and faith
10  for a thousand generations, but those who defy him and show their hatred
for him he repays with destruction: he will not be slow to requite any who
so hate him.
11    You are to observe these commandments, statutes, and laws which I give
you this day, and keep them.
12    If you listen to these laws and are careful to observe them, then the LORD
your God will observe the sworn covenant he made with your forefathers
13  and will keep faith with you. He will love you, bless you and cause you to
increase. He will bless the fruit of your body and the fruit of your land, your
corn and new wine and oil, the offspring of your herds, and of your lamb-
14  ing flocks, in the land which he swore to your forefathers to give you. You

*a Prob. rdg.; Heb.* me.

shall be blessed above every other nation; neither among your people nor among your cattle shall there be impotent male or barren female. The LORD 15 will take away all sickness from you; he will not bring upon you any of the foul diseases of Egypt which you know so well, but will bring them upon all your enemies. You shall devour all the nations which the LORD your 16 God is giving over to you. Spare none of them, and do not worship their gods; that is the snare which awaits you.

You may say to yourselves, 'These nations outnumber us, how can we 17 drive them out?' But you need have no fear of them; only remember what 18 the LORD your God did to Pharaoh and to the whole of Egypt, the great 19 challenge which you yourselves witnessed, the signs and portents, the strong hand and the outstretched arm by which the LORD your God brought you out. He will deal thus with all the nations of whom you are afraid. He 20 will also spread panic among them until all who are left or have gone into hiding perish before you. Be in no dread of them, for the LORD your God 21 is in your midst, a great and terrible god. He will drive out these nations 22 before you little by little. You will not be able to exterminate them quickly, for fear the wild beasts become too numerous for you. The LORD your God 23 will deliver these nations over to you and will throw them into great panic in the hour of their destruction. He will put their kings into your hands, 24 and you shall wipe out their name from under heaven. When you destroy them, no man will be able to withstand you. Their idols you shall destroy 25 by fire; you must not covet the silver and gold on them and take it for yourselves, or you will be ensnared by it; for these things are abominable to the LORD your God. You must not introduce any abominable idol 26 into your houses and thus bring yourselves under solemn ban along with it. You shall hold it loathsome and abominable, for it is forbidden under the ban.

You must carefully observe everything that I command you this day so 8 that you may live and increase and may enter and occupy the land which the LORD promised to your forefathers upon oath. You must remember all 2 that road by which the LORD your God has led you these forty years in the wilderness to humble you, to test you and to discover whether or no it was in your heart to keep his commandments. He humbled you and made you 3 hungry; then he fed you on manna which neither you nor your fathers had known before, to teach you that man cannot live on bread alone but lives by every word that comes from the mouth of the LORD. The clothes on 4 your backs did not wear out nor did your feet swell all these forty years. Take this lesson to heart: that the LORD your God was disciplining you as 5 a father disciplines his son; and keep the commandments of the LORD your 6 God, conforming to his ways and fearing him. For the LORD your God is 7 bringing you to a rich land, a land of streams, of springs and underground waters gushing out in hill and valley, a land of wheat and barley, of vines, 8 fig-trees, and pomegranates, a land of olives, oil, and honey. It is a land 9 where you will never live in poverty nor want for anything, a land whose stones are iron-ore and from whose hills you will dig copper. You will have 10 plenty to eat and will bless the LORD your God for the rich land that he has given you.

11 Take care not to forget the LORD your God and do not fail to keep his
12 commandments, laws, and statutes which I give you this day. When you
13 have plenty to eat and live in fine houses of your own building, when your
herds and flocks increase, and your silver and gold and all your possessions
14 increase too, do not become proud and forget the LORD your God who
15 brought you out of Egypt, out of the land of slavery; he led you through the
vast and terrible wilderness infested with poisonous snakes and scorpions,
a thirsty, waterless land, where he caused water to flow from the hard rock;
16 he fed you in the wilderness on manna which your fathers did not know, to
17 humble you and test you, and in the end to make you prosper. Nor must
you say to yourselves, 'My own strength and energy have gained me this
18 wealth', but remember the LORD your God; it is he that gives you strength
to become prosperous, so fulfilling the covenant guaranteed by oath with
your forefathers, as he is doing now.
19 If you forget the LORD your God and adhere to other gods, worshipping
them and bowing down to them, I give you a solemn warning this day that
20 you will certainly be destroyed. You will be destroyed because of your disobedience to the LORD your God, as surely as were the nations whom the
LORD destroyed at your coming.

**9** Listen, O Israel; this day you will cross the Jordan to occupy the
territory of nations greater and more powerful than you, and great cities
2 with walls towering to the sky. They are great and tall people, the descendants of the Anakim, of whom you know, for you have heard it said, 'Who
3 can withstand the sons of Anak?' Know then this day that it is the LORD
your God himself who goes at your head as a devouring fire; he will subdue
them and destroy them at your approach; you shall drive them out and
overwhelm them, as he promised you.
4 When the LORD your God drives them out before you, do not say to
yourselves, 'It is because of my own merit that the LORD has brought me in
5 to occupy this land.' It is not because of your merit or your integrity that
you are entering their land to occupy it; it is because of the wickedness of
these nations that the LORD your God is driving them out before you, and
to fulfil the promise which the LORD made to your forefathers, Abraham,
Isaac and Jacob.
6 Know then that it is not because of any merit of yours that the LORD
your God is giving you this rich land to occupy; indeed, you are a stubborn
7 people. Remember and never forget, how you angered the LORD your God
in the wilderness: from the day when you left Egypt until you came to this
8 place you have defied the LORD. In Horeb you roused the LORD's anger,
9 and the LORD in his wrath was on the point of destroying you. When I
went up the mountain to receive the tablets of stone, the tablets of the
covenant which the LORD made with you, I remained on the mountain
10 forty days and forty nights without food or drink. Then the LORD gave me
the two tablets of stone written with the finger of God, and upon them
were all the words the LORD spoke to you out of the fire, upon the mountain
11 on the day of the assembly. At the end of forty days and forty nights the
12 LORD gave me the two tablets of stone, the tablets of the covenant, and said
to me, 'Make haste down from the mountain because your people whom

you brought out of Egypt have done a disgraceful thing. They have already turned aside from the way which I told them to follow and have cast for themselves an image of metal.'

Then the LORD said to me, 'I have considered this people and I find 13 them a stubborn people. Let me be, and I will destroy them and blot out 14 their name from under heaven; and of you alone I will make a nation more powerful and numerous than they.' So I turned and went down the moun- 15 tain, and it was ablaze; and I had the two tablets of the covenant in my hands. When I saw that you had sinned against the LORD your God and 16 had cast for yourselves an image of a bull-calf, and had already turned aside from the way the LORD had told you to follow, I took the two tablets 17 and flung them down and shattered them in the sight of you all. Then once 18 again I lay prostrate before the LORD, forty days and forty nights without food or drink, on account of all the sins that you had committed, and because you had done what was wrong in the eyes of the LORD and provoked him to anger. I dreaded the LORD's anger and his wrath which threatened 19 to destroy you; and once again the LORD listened to me. The LORD was 20 greatly incensed with Aaron also and would have killed him; so I prayed for him as well at that same time. I took the calf, that sinful thing that you 21 had made, and burnt it and pounded it, grinding it until it was as fine as dust; then I flung its dust into the torrent that flowed down the mountain. You also roused the LORD's anger at Taberah, and at Massah, and at 22 Kibroth-hattaavah. Again, when the LORD sent you from Kadesh-barnea 23 with orders to advance and occupy the land which he was giving you, you defied the LORD your God and did not trust him or obey him. You were 24 defiant from the day that the LORD first knew you. Forty days and forty 25 nights I lay prostrate before the LORD because he had threatened to destroy you, and I prayed to the LORD and said, 'O Lord GOD, do not destroy thy 26 people, thy own possession, whom thou didst redeem by thy great power and bring out of Egypt by thy strong hand. Remember thy servants, 27 Abraham, Isaac and Jacob, and overlook the stubbornness of this people, their wickedness and their sin; otherwise the people in the land out of 28 which thou didst lead us will say, "It is because the LORD was not able to bring them into the land which he promised them and because he hated them, that he has led them out to kill them in the wilderness." But they are 29 thy people, thy own possession, whom thou didst bring out by thy great strength and by thy outstretched arm.'

AT THAT TIME THE LORD SAID to me, 'Cut two tablets of stone like the **10** first, and make also a wooden chest, an Ark. Come to me on the mountain, and I will write on the tablets the words that were on the first tablets which 2 you broke in pieces, and you shall put them into the Ark.' So I made the 3 Ark of acacia-wood and cut two tablets of stone like the first, and went up the mountain taking the tablets with me. Then in the same writing as 4 before, the LORD wrote down the Ten Words[a] which he had spoken to you out of the fire, upon the mountain on the day of the assembly, and the LORD gave them to me. I turned and came down the mountain, and I put 5

*a Or* Ten Commandments.

the tablets in the Ark that I had made, as the LORD had commanded me, and there they have remained ever since.

6*a* (The Israelites journeyed by stages from Beeroth-bene-jaakan to Moserah. There Aaron died and was buried; and his son Eleazar succeeded him in

7 the priesthood. From there they came to Gudgodah and from Gudgodah

8 to Jotbathah, a land of many ravines. At that time the LORD set apart the tribe of Levi to carry the Ark of the Covenant of the LORD, to attend on the LORD and minister to him, and to give the blessing in his name, as they

9 have done to this day. That is why the Levites have no holding or patrimony with their kinsmen; the LORD is their patrimony, as he promised them.)

10 I stayed on the mountain forty days and forty nights, as I did before, and once again the LORD listened to me; he consented not to destroy you.

11 The LORD said to me, 'Set out now at the head of the people so that they may enter and occupy the land which I swore to give to their forefathers.'

12 What then, O Israel, does the LORD your God ask of you? Only to fear the LORD your God, to conform to all his ways, to love him and to serve

13 him with all your heart and soul. This you will do by keeping the commandments of the LORD and his statutes which I give you this day for your good.

14 To the LORD your God belong heaven itself, the highest heaven, the earth

15 and everything in it; yet the LORD cared for your forefathers in his love for them and chose their descendants after them. Out of all nations you were

16 his chosen people as you are this day. So now you must circumcise the

17 foreskin of your hearts and not be stubborn any more, for the LORD your God is God of gods and Lord of lords, the great, mighty, and terrible God.

18 He is no respecter of persons and is not to be bribed; he secures justice for widows and orphans, and loves the alien who lives among you, giving

19 him food and clothing. You too must love the alien, for you once lived as

20 aliens in Egypt. You must fear the LORD your God, serve him, hold fast

21 to him and take your oaths in his name. He is your praise, your God who has done for you these great and terrible things which you have seen with

22 your own eyes. When your forefathers went down into Egypt they were only seventy strong, but now the LORD your God has made you countless as the stars in the sky.

11 You shall love the LORD your God and keep for all time the charge he

2 laid upon you, the statutes, the laws, and the commandments. This day you know the discipline of the LORD, though your children who have neither known nor experienced it do not; you know his greatness, his

3 strong hand and outstretched arm, the signs he worked and his acts in

4 Egypt against Pharaoh the king and his country, and all that he did to the Egyptian army, its horses and chariots, when he caused the waters of the Red Sea to flow over them as they pursued you. In this way the LORD

5 destroyed them, and so things remain to this day. You know what he did

6 for you in the wilderness as you journeyed to this place, and what he did to Dathan and Abiram sons of Eliab, son of Reuben, when the earth opened its mouth and swallowed them in the sight of all Israel, together with their

*a* *Verses 6, 7 : cp. Num. 33. 31, 32.*

households and their tents and every living thing in their company. With 7
your own eyes you have seen the mighty work that the LORD did.

You shall observe all that I command you this day, so that you may have 8
strength to enter and occupy the land into which you are crossing, and so 9
that you may live long in the land which the LORD swore to your forefathers
to give them and their descendants, a land flowing with milk and honey.
The land which you are entering to occupy is not like the land of Egypt 10
from which you have come, where, after sowing your seed, you irrigated it
by foot like a vegetable garden. But the land into which you are crossing 11
to occupy is a land of mountains and valleys watered by the rain of heaven.
It is a land which the LORD your God tends<sup>a</sup> and on which his eye rests 12
from year's end to year's end. If you pay heed to the commandments which 13
I give you this day, and love the LORD your God and serve him with all
your heart and soul, then I will send rain for your land in season, both 14
autumn and spring rains, and you will gather your corn and new wine and
oil, and I will provide pasture in the fields for your cattle: you shall eat 15
your fill. Take good care not to be led astray in your hearts nor to turn 16
aside and serve other gods and prostrate yourselves to them, or the LORD 17
will become angry with you: he will shut up the skies and there will be no
rain, your ground will not yield its harvest, and you will soon vanish from
the rich land which the LORD is giving you. You shall take these words of 18
mine to heart and keep them in mind; you shall bind them as a sign on the
hand and wear them as a phylactery on the forehead. Teach them to your 19
children, and speak of them indoors and out of doors, when you lie down
and when you rise. Write them up on the door-posts of your houses and 20
on your gates. Then you will live long, you and your children, in the land 21
which the LORD swore to your forefathers to give them, for as long as the
heavens are above the earth.

If you diligently keep all these commandments that I now charge you 22
to observe, by loving the LORD your God, by conforming to his ways and
by holding fast to him, the LORD will drive out all these nations before you 23
and you shall occupy the territory of nations greater and more powerful
than you. Every place where you set the soles of your feet shall be yours. 24
Your borders shall run from the wilderness to<sup>b</sup> the Lebanon and from the
River, the river Euphrates, to the western sea. No man will be able to 25
withstand you; the LORD your God will put the fear and dread of you upon
the whole land on which you set foot, as he promised you. Understand that 26
this day I offer you the choice of a blessing and a curse. The blessing will 27
come if you listen to the commandments of the LORD your God which I
give you this day, and the curse if you do not listen to the commandments 28
of the LORD your God but turn aside from the way that I command you
this day and follow other gods whom you do not know.

When the LORD your God brings you into the land which you are enter- 29
ing to occupy, there on Mount Gerizim you shall pronounce the blessing
and on Mount Ebal the curse. (These mountains are on the other side of 30
the Jordan, close to Gilgal beside the terebinth of Moreh, beyond the road

<sup>a</sup> which . . . tends: *or* whose soil the LORD your God has made firm.
<sup>b</sup> *Prob. rdg.; Heb.* and.

to the west which lies in the territory of the Canaanites of the Arabah.)
31 You are about to cross the Jordan to enter and occupy the land which the
32 LORD your God is giving you; you shall occupy it and settle in it, and you
shall be careful to observe all the statutes and laws which I set before you
this day.

## God's laws delivered by Moses

12 THESE ARE THE STATUTES AND LAWS that you shall be careful to
observe in the land which the LORD the God of your fathers is giving
2 you to occupy as long as you live on earth. You shall demolish all the
sanctuaries where the nations whose place you are taking worship their
3 gods, on mountain-tops and hills and under every spreading tree. You shall
pull down their altars and break their sacred pillars, burn their sacred poles
and hack down the idols of their gods and thus blot out the name of them
from that place.
4    You shall not follow such practices in the worship of the LORD your God,
5 but you shall resort to the place which the LORD your God will choose out
of all your tribes to receive his Name that it may dwell there. There you
6 shall come and bring your whole-offerings and sacrifices, your tithes and
contributions, your vows and freewill offerings, and the first-born of your
7 herds and flocks. There you shall eat before the LORD your God; so you
shall find joy in whatever you undertake, you and your families, because
the LORD your God has blessed you.
8    You shall not act as we act here today, each of us doing what he pleases,
9 for till now you have not reached the place of rest, the patrimony which
10 the LORD your God is giving you. You shall cross the Jordan and settle in
the land which the LORD your God allots you as your patrimony; he will
grant you peace from all your enemies on every side, and you will live in
11 security. Then you shall bring everything that I command you to the place
which the LORD your God will choose as a dwelling for his Name—your
whole-offerings and sacrifices, your tithes and contributions, and all the
12 choice gifts that you have vowed to the LORD. You shall rejoice before the
LORD your God with your sons and daughters, your male and female
slaves, and the Levites who live in your settlements because they have no
holding or patrimony among you.
13    See that you do not offer your whole-offerings in any place at random,
14 but offer them only at the place which the LORD will choose in one of your
15 tribes, and there you must do all I command you. On the other hand, you
may freely kill for food in all your settlements, as the LORD your God blesses
you. Clean and unclean alike may eat it, as they would eat the meat of
16 gazelle or buck. But on no account must you eat the blood; pour it out on
17 the ground like water. In all your settlements you may not eat any of the
tithe of your corn and new wine and oil, or any of the first-born of your
cattle and sheep, or any of the gifts that you vow, or any of your freewill
18 offerings and contributions; but you shall eat it before the LORD your God
in the place that the LORD your God will choose—you, your sons and

daughters, your male and female slaves, and the Levites in your settlements; so you shall find joy before the LORD your God in all that you undertake. Be careful not to neglect the Levites in your land as long as 19 you live.

When the LORD your God extends your boundaries, as he has promised 20 you, and you say to yourselves, 'I would like to eat meat', because you have a craving for it, then you may freely eat it. If the place that the LORD your 21 God will choose to receive his Name is far away, then you may slaughter a beast from the herds or flocks which the LORD has given you and freely eat it in your own settlements as I command you. You may eat it as you 22 would the meat of gazelle or buck; both clean and unclean alike may eat it. But you must strictly refrain from eating the blood, because the blood is 23 the life; you must not eat the life with the flesh. You must not eat it, you 24 must pour it out on the ground like water. If you do not eat it, all will be 25 well with you and your children after you; for you will be doing what is right in the eyes of the LORD. But such holy-gifts as you may have and the 26 gifts you have vowed, you must bring to the place which the LORD will choose. You must present your whole-offerings, both the flesh and the 27 blood, on the altar of the LORD your God; but of your shared-offerings you shall eat the flesh, while the blood is to be poured on the altar of the LORD your God. See that you listen and do all that I command you, and 28 then it will go well with you and your children after you for ever; for you will be doing what is good and right in the eyes of the LORD your God.

When the LORD your God exterminates, as you advance, the nations 29 whose country you are entering to occupy, you shall take their place and settle in their land. After they have been destroyed, take care that you are 30 not ensnared into their ways. Do not inquire about their gods and say, 'How do these nations worship their gods? I too will do the same.' You 31 must not do for the LORD your God what they do, for all that they do for their gods is hateful and abominable to the LORD. As sacrifices for their gods they even burn their sons and their daughters.

See that you observe everything I command you: you must not add 32 anything to it, nor take anything away from it.

When a prophet or dreamer appears among you and offers you a sign 13 or a portent and calls on you to follow other gods whom you have not known 2 and worship them, even if the sign or portent should come true, do not 3 listen to the words of that prophet or that dreamer. God is testing you through him to discover whether you love the LORD your God with all your heart and soul. You must follow the LORD your God and fear him; 4 you must keep his commandments and obey him, serve him and hold fast to him. That prophet or that dreamer shall be put to death, for he has 5 preached rebellion against the LORD your God who brought you out of Egypt and redeemed you from that land of slavery; he has tried to lead you astray from the path which the LORD your God commanded you to take. You must rid yourselves of this wickedness.

If your brother, your father's son or your mother's son, or your son or 6 daughter, or the wife of your bosom or your dearest friend should entice you secretly to go and worship other gods—gods whom neither you nor

7 your fathers have known, gods of the people round about you, near or far,
8 at one end of the land or the other—then you shall not consent or listen.
9 You shall have no pity on him, you shall not spare him nor shield him, you shall put him to death; your own hand shall be the first to be raised against
10 him and then all the people shall follow. You shall stone him to death, because he tried to lead you astray from the LORD your God who brought
11 you out of Egypt, out of the land of slavery. All Israel shall hear of it and be afraid; never again will anything as wicked as this be done among you.
12-13 When you hear that miscreants have appeared in any of the cities which the LORD your God is giving you to occupy, and have led its inhabitants astray by calling on them to serve other gods whom you have not known,
14 then you shall investigate the matter carefully. If, after diligent examination, the report proves to be true and it is shown that this abominable thing has
15 been done among you, you shall put the inhabitants of that city to the sword; you shall lay the city under solemn ban together with everything
16 in it. You shall gather all its goods into the square and burn both city and goods as a complete offering to the LORD your God; and it shall remain a
17 mound of ruins, never to be rebuilt. Let nothing out of all that has been laid under the ban be found in your possession, so that the LORD may turn from his anger and show you compassion; and in his compassion he will
18 increase you as he swore to your forefathers, provided that you obey the LORD your God and keep all his commandments which I give you this day, doing only what is right in the eyes of the LORD your God.

**14** YOU ARE THE SONS OF THE LORD your God: you shall not gash your-
2 selves nor shave your forelocks in mourning for the dead. You are a people holy to the LORD your God, and the LORD has chosen you out of all peoples on earth to be his special possession.
3 4 You shall not eat any abominable thing. These are the animals you may
5 eat: ox, sheep, goat, buck, gazelle, roebuck, wild-goat, white-rumped deer,
6 long-horned antelope, and rock-goat. You may eat any animal which has
7 a parted foot or a cloven hoof and also chews the cud; those which only chew the cud or only have a parted or cloven hoof you may not eat. These are: the camel, the hare, and the rock-badger, *a* because they chew the cud
8 but do not have cloven hoofs; and the pig, because it has a cloven hoof but does not chew the cud, you shall regard as unclean. You shall not eat their flesh or even touch their dead
9 carcasses. Of creatures that live in water you may eat all those that have
10 fins and scales, but you may not eat any that have neither fins nor scales;
11 12 you shall regard them as unclean. You may eat all clean birds. These are the birds you may not eat: the griffon-vulture, *b* the black vulture, the
13 14 bearded vulture, *c* the kite, every kind of falcon, every kind of crow, *d*
15 the desert-owl, the short-eared owl, the long-eared owl, every kind of
16 17 hawk, the tawny owl, the screech-owl, the little owl, the horned owl, the
18 osprey, the fisher-owl, the stork, *e* every kind of cormorant, the hoopoe, and the bat.

*a* Or rock-rabbit.   *b* Or eagle.   *c* Or ossifrage.   *d* Or raven.
*e* Or heron.

All teeming winged creatures you shall regard as unclean; they may not 19
be eaten. You may eat every clean insect. 20

You shall not eat anything that has died a natural death. You shall give 21
it to the aliens who live in your settlements, and they may eat it, or you may
sell it to a foreigner; for you are a people holy to the LORD your God.

You shall not boil a kid in its mother's milk.

Year by year you shall set aside a tithe of all the produce of your seed, 22
of everything that grows on the land. You shall eat it in the presence of the 23
LORD your God in the place which he will choose as a dwelling for his
Name—the tithe of your corn and new wine and oil, and the first-born of
your cattle and sheep, so that for all time you may learn to fear the LORD
your God. When the LORD your God has blessed you with prosperity, and 24
the place which he will choose to receive his Name is far from you and the
journey too great for you to be able to carry your tithe, then you may 25
exchange it for silver. You shall tie up the silver and take it with you to the
place which the LORD your God will choose. There you shall spend it as 26
you will on cattle or sheep, wine or strong drink, or whatever you desire;
you shall consume it there with rejoicing, both you and your family, in the
presence of the LORD your God. You must not neglect the Levites who live 27
in your settlements; for they have no holding or patrimony among you.

At the end of every third year you shall bring out all the tithe of your 28
produce for that year and leave it in your settlements so that the Levites, 29
who have no holding or patrimony among you, and the aliens, orphans,
and widows in your settlements may come and eat their fill. If you do this
the LORD your God will bless you in everything to which you set your hand.

At the end of every seventh year you shall make a remission of debts. **15**
This is how the remission shall be made: everyone who holds a pledge shall 2
remit the pledge of anyone indebted to him. He shall not press a fellow-
countryman for repayment, for the LORD's year of remission has been
declared.[a] You may press foreigners; but if it is a fellow-countryman that 3
holds anything of yours, you must remit all claim upon it. There will 4-5
never be any poor among you if only you obey the LORD your God by carefully keeping these commandments which I lay upon you this day; for
the LORD your God will bless you with great prosperity in the land which
he is giving you to occupy as your patrimony. When the LORD your God 6
blesses you, as he promised, you will lend to men of many nations, but you
yourselves will not borrow; you will rule many nations, but they will not
rule you.

When one of your fellow-countrymen in any of your settlements in the 7
land which the LORD your God is giving you becomes poor, do not be
hard-hearted or close-fisted with your countryman in his need. Be open- 8
handed towards him and lend him on pledge as much as he needs. See that 9
you do not harbour iniquitous thoughts when you find that the seventh
year, the year of remission, is near, and look askance at your needy countryman and give him nothing. If you do, he will appeal to the LORD against
you, and you will be found guilty of sin. Give freely to him and do not 10
begrudge him your bounty, because it is for this very bounty that the LORD

---

[a] *Or* has come.

11 your God will bless you in everything that you do or undertake. The poor will always be with you in the land, and for that reason I command you to be open-handed with your countrymen, both poor and distressed, in your own land.

12 When a fellow-Hebrew, man or woman, sells himself to you as a slave, he shall serve you for six years and in the seventh year you shall set him 13 14 free. But when you set him free, do not let him go empty-handed. Give to him lavishly from your flock, from your threshing-floor and your wine-press. Be generous to him, because the LORD your God has blessed you.

18 Do not take it amiss when you have to set him free, for his six years' service to you has been worth twice *a* the wage of a hired man. Then the LORD your 15 God will bless you in everything you do. Remember that you were slaves in Egypt and the LORD your God redeemed you; that is why I am giving you this command today.

16 If, however, a slave is content to be with you and says, 'I will not leave 17 you, I love you and your family', then you shall take an awl and pierce through his ear to the door, and he will be your slave for life. You shall treat a slave-girl in the same way.

19*b* You shall dedicate to the LORD your God every male first-born of your herds and flocks. You shall not plough with the first-born of your cattle, 20 nor shall you shear the first-born of your sheep. Year by year you and your family shall eat them in the presence of the LORD your God, in the place 21 which the LORD will choose. If any animal is defective, if it is lame or blind, or has any other serious defect, you must not sacrifice it to the LORD your 22 God. Eat it in your settlements; both clean and unclean alike may eat it as 23 they would the meat of gazelle or buck. But you must not eat the blood; pour it out on the ground like water.

16 OBSERVE THE MONTH OF ABIB and keep the Passover to the LORD your God, for it was in that month that the LORD your God brought you out 2 of Egypt by night. You shall slaughter a lamb, a kid, or a calf as a Passover victim to the LORD your God in the place which he will choose as a dwelling 3 for his Name. You shall eat nothing leavened with it. For seven days you shall eat unleavened cakes, the bread of affliction. In urgent haste you came out of Egypt, and thus as long as you live you shall commemorate the day 4 of your coming out of Egypt. No leaven shall be seen in all your territory for seven days, nor shall any of the flesh which you have slaughtered in the 5 evening of the first day remain overnight till morning. You may not slaughter the Passover victim in any of the settlements which the LORD 6 your God is giving you, but only in the place which he will choose as a dwelling for his Name; you shall slaughter the Passover victim in the 7 evening as the sun goes down, the time of your coming out of Egypt. You shall boil it and eat it in the place which the LORD your God will choose, 8 and then next morning you shall turn and go to your tents. For six days you shall eat unleavened cakes, and on the seventh day there shall be a closing ceremony in honour of the LORD your God; you shall do no work. 9 Seven weeks shall be counted: start counting the seven weeks from the

*a* worth twice: *or* equivalent to.          *b Verse 18 transposed to follow verse 14.*

time when the sickle is put to the standing corn; then you shall keep the 10
pilgrim-feast of Weeks to the LORD your God and offer a freewill offering
in proportion to the blessing that the LORD your God has given you. You 11
shall rejoice before the LORD your God, with your sons and daughters,
your male and female slaves, the Levites who live in your settlements, and
the aliens, orphans, and widows among you. You shall rejoice in the place
which the LORD your God will choose as a dwelling for his Name and 12
remember that you were slaves in Egypt. You shall keep and observe all
these statutes.

You shall keep the pilgrim-feast of Tabernacles *a* for seven days, when 13
you bring in the produce from your threshing-floor and winepress. You 14
shall rejoice in your feast, with your sons and daughters, your male and
female slaves, the Levites, aliens, orphans, and widows who live in your
settlements. For seven days you shall keep this feast to the LORD your God 15
in the place which he will choose, when the LORD your God gives you his
blessing in all your harvest and in all your work; you shall keep the feast
with joy.

Three times a year all your males shall come into the presence of the 16
LORD your God in the place which he will choose: at the pilgrim-feasts of
Unleavened Bread, of Weeks, and of Tabernacles. No one shall come into
the presence of the LORD empty-handed. Each of you shall bring such a 17
gift as he can in proportion to the blessing which the LORD your God has
given you.

You shall appoint for yourselves judges and officers, tribe by tribe, in 18
every settlement which the LORD your God is giving you, and they shall
dispense true justice to the people. You shall not pervert the course of 19
justice or show favour, nor shall you accept a bribe; for bribery makes the
wise man blind and the just man give a crooked answer. Justice, and justice 20
alone, you shall pursue, so that you may live and occupy the land which
the LORD your God is giving you.

You shall not plant any kind of tree as a sacred pole beside the altar of 21
the LORD your God which you shall build. You shall not set up a sacred 22
pillar, for the LORD your God hates them.

You shall not sacrifice to the LORD your God a bull or sheep that has any **17**
defect or serious blemish, for that would be abominable to the LORD your
God.

If so be that, in any one of the settlements which the LORD your God is 2
giving you, a man or woman is found among you who does what is wrong
in the eyes of the LORD your God, by breaking his covenant and going to 3
worship other gods and prostrating himself before them or before the sun
and moon and all the host of heaven—a thing that I have forbidden—then, 4
if it is reported to you or you hear of it, make thorough inquiry. If the report
proves to be true, and it is shown that this abominable thing has been done
in Israel, then bring the man or woman who has done this wicked deed to 5
the city gate and stone him to death. Sentence of death shall be carried 6
out on the testimony of two or of three witnesses: no one shall be put to
death on the testimony of a single witness. The first stones shall be thrown 7

*a* Or Booths or Arbours.

by the witnesses and then all the people shall follow; thus you shall rid yourselves of this wickedness.

8 When the issue in any lawsuit is beyond your competence, whether it be a case of blood against blood, plea against plea, or blow against blow, that is disputed in your courts, then go up without delay to the place which the

9 LORD your God will choose. There you must go to the levitical priests or to the judge then in office; seek their guidance, and they will pronounce the

10 sentence. You shall act on the pronouncement which they make from the place which the LORD will choose. See that you carry out all their instruc-

11 tions. Act on the instruction which they give you, or on the precedent that they cite; do not swerve from what they tell you, either to right or to left.

12 Anyone who presumes to reject the decision either of the priest who ministers there to the LORD your God, or of the judge, shall die; thus you

13 will rid Israel of wickedness. Then all the people will hear of it and be afraid, and will never again show such presumption.

14 When you come into the land which the LORD your God is giving you, and occupy it and settle in it, and you then say, 'Let us appoint over us a

15 king, as all the surrounding nations do', you shall appoint as king the man whom the LORD your God will choose. You shall appoint over you a man of your own race; you must not appoint a foreigner, one who is not of your

16 own race. He shall not acquire many horses, nor, to add to his horses, shall he cause the people to go back to Egypt, for this is what the LORD said to

17 you, 'You shall never go back that way.' He shall not acquire many wives and so be led astray; nor shall he acquire great quantities of silver and gold

18 for himself. When he has ascended the throne of the kingdom, he shall make a copy of this law in a book at the dictation of the levitical priests.

19 He shall keep it by him and read from it all his life, so that he may learn to fear the LORD his God and keep all the words of this law and observe

20 these statutes. In this way he shall not become prouder than his fellow-countrymen, nor shall he turn from these commandments to right or to left; then he and his sons will reign long over his kingdom in Israel.

**18** The levitical priests, the whole tribe of Levi, shall have no holding or patrimony in Israel; they shall eat the food-offerings of the LORD, their

2 patrimony. They shall have no patrimony among their fellow-countrymen; the LORD is their patrimony, as he promised them.

3 This shall be the customary due of the priests from those of the people who offer sacrifice, whether a bull or a sheep: the shoulders, the cheeks,

4 and the stomach shall be given to the priest. You shall give him also the firstfruits of your corn and new wine and oil, and the first fleeces at the

5 shearing of your flocks. For it was he whom the LORD your God chose from all your tribes to attend on the LORD and to minister in the name of the LORD, both he and his sons for all time.

6 When a Levite comes from any settlement in Israel where he may be lodging to the place which the LORD will choose, if he comes in the eager-

7 ness of his heart and ministers in the name of the LORD his God, like all

8 his fellow-Levites who attend on the LORD there, he shall have an equal share of food with them, besides what he may inherit from his father's family.

When you come into the land which the LORD your God is giving you,    9
do not learn to imitate the abominable customs of those other nations. Let   10
no one be found among you who makes his son or daughter pass through
fire, no augur or soothsayer or diviner or sorcerer, no one who casts spells   11
or traffics with ghosts and spirits, and no necromancer. Those who do   12
these things are abominable to the LORD, and it is because of these abominable practices that the LORD your God is driving them out before you. You   13
shall be whole-hearted in your service of the LORD your God.

These nations whose place you are taking listen to soothsayers and   14
augurs, but the LORD your God does not permit you to do this. The LORD   15
your God will raise up a prophet from among you like myself, and you
shall listen to him. All this follows from your request to the LORD your   16
God on Horeb on the day of the assembly. There you said, 'Let us not hear
again the voice of the LORD our God, nor see this great fire again, or we
shall die.' Then the LORD said to me, 'What they have said is right. I will   17 18
raise up for them a prophet like you, one of their own race, and I will put
my words into his mouth. He shall convey all my commands to them, and   19
if anyone does not listen to the words which he will speak in my name I will
require satisfaction from him. But the prophet who presumes to utter in   20
my name what I have not commanded him or who speaks in the name of
other gods—that prophet shall die.' If you ask yourselves, 'How shall we   21
recognize a word that the LORD has not uttered?', this is the answer: When   22
the word spoken by the prophet in the name of the LORD is not fulfilled
and does not come true, it is not a word spoken by the LORD. The prophet
has spoken presumptuously; do not hold him *a* in awe.

WHEN THE LORD YOUR GOD EXTERMINATES the nations whose land   **19**
he is giving you, and you take their place and settle in their cities and
houses, you shall set apart three cities in the land which he is giving you   2
to occupy. Divide into three districts the territory which the LORD your   3
God is giving you as patrimony, and determine where each city shall lie.
These shall be places in which homicides may take sanctuary.

This is the kind of homicide who may take sanctuary there and save his   4
life: the man who strikes another without intent and with no previous
enmity between them; for instance, the man who goes into a wood with   5
his mate to fell trees, and, when cutting a tree, he relaxes his grip on the
axe,*b* the head glances off the tree, hits the other man and kills him. The
homicide may take sanctuary in any one of these cities, and his life shall be
safe. Otherwise, when the dead man's next-of-kin who had the duty of   6
vengeance pursued him in the heat of passion, he might overtake him if
the distance were great, and take his life, although the homicide was not
liable to the death-penalty because there had been no previous enmity on
his part. That is why I command you to set apart three cities.   7

If the LORD your God extends your boundaries, as he swore to your fore-   8
fathers, and gives you the whole land which he promised to them, because   9
you keep all the commandments that I am laying down today and carry
them out by loving the LORD your God and by conforming to his ways for

___
*a* Or it.    *b* when . . . axe: *or* as he swings the axe to cut a tree.

10 all time, then you shall add three more cities of refuge to these three. Let no innocent blood be shed in the land which the LORD your God is giving you as your patrimony, or blood-guilt will fall on you.

11 When one man is the enemy of another, and he lies in wait for him, attacks him and strikes him a blow so that he dies, and then takes sanctuary
12 in one of these cities, the elders of his own city shall send to fetch him; they
13 shall hand him over to the next-of-kin, and he shall die. You shall show him no mercy, but shall rid Israel of the guilt of innocent blood; then all will be well with you.

14 Do not move your neighbour's boundary stone, fixed by the men of former times in the patrimony which you shall occupy in the land the LORD your God gives you for your possession.

15 A single witness may not give evidence against a man in the matter of any crime or sin which he commits: a charge must be established on the evidence of two or of three witnesses.

16 When a malicious witness comes forward to give false evidence against
17 a man, and the two disputants stand before the LORD, before the priests
18 and the judges then in office, if, after careful examination by the judges, he be proved to be a false witness giving false evidence against his fellow,
19 you shall treat him as he intended to treat his fellow, and thus rid your-
20 selves of this wickedness. The rest of the people when they hear of it will be afraid: never again will anything as wicked as this be done among you.
21 You shall show no mercy: life for life, eye for eye, tooth for tooth, hand for hand, foot for foot.

20 WHEN YOU TAKE THE FIELD against an enemy and are faced by horses and chariots and an army greater than yours, do not be afraid of them; for the LORD your God, who brought you out of Egypt, will be with you.
2 When you are about to join battle, the priest shall come forward and
3 address the army in these words: 'Hear, O Israel, this day you are joining battle with the enemy; do not lose heart, or be afraid, or give way to panic
4 in face of them; for the LORD your God will go with you to fight your
5 enemy for you and give you the victory.' Then the officers shall address the army in these words: 'Any man who has built a new house and has not dedicated it shall go back to his house; or he may die in battle and another
6 man dedicate it. Any man who has planted a vineyard and has not begun to use it shall go back home; or he may die in battle and another man use
7 it. Any man who has pledged himself to take a woman in marriage and has not taken her shall go back home; or he may die in battle and another man
8 take her.' The officers shall further address the army: 'Any man who is afraid and has lost heart shall go back home; or his comrades will be dis-
9 couraged as he is.' When these officers have finished addressing the army, commanders shall be appointed to lead it.
10 11 When you advance on a city to attack it, make an offer of peace. If the city accepts the offer and opens its gates to you, then all the people in it
12 shall be put to forced labour and shall serve you. If it does not make peace
13 with you but offers battle, you shall besiege it, and the LORD your God will
14 deliver it into your hands. You shall put all its males to the sword, but you

may take the women, the dependants, and the cattle for yourselves, and plunder everything else in the city. You may enjoy the use of the spoil of your enemies which the LORD your God gives you. That is what you shall 15 do to cities at a great distance, as opposed to those which belong to nations near at hand. In the cities of these nations whose land the LORD your God 16 is giving you as a patrimony, you shall not leave any creature alive. You 17 shall annihilate them—Hittites, Amorites, Canaanites, Perizzites, Hivites, Jebusites—as the LORD your God commanded you, so that they may not 18 teach you to imitate all the abominable things that they have done for their gods and so cause you to sin against the LORD your God.

When you are at war, and lay siege to a city for a long time in order to 19 take it, do not destroy its trees by taking the axe to them, for they provide you with food; you shall not cut them down. The trees of the field are not men that you should besiege them. But you may destroy or cut down any 20 trees that you know do not yield food, and use them in siege-works against the city that is at war with you, until it falls.

When a dead body is found lying in open country, in the land which the **21** LORD your God is giving you to occupy, and it is not known who struck the blow, your elders and your judges shall come out and measure the 2 distance to the surrounding towns to find which is nearest. The elders of 3 that town shall take a heifer that has never been mated*a* or worn a yoke, and bring it down to a ravine where there is a stream that never runs dry 4 and the ground is never tilled or sown, and there in the ravine they shall break its neck. The priests, the sons of Levi, shall then come forward; for 5 the LORD your God has chosen them to minister to him and to bless in the name of the LORD, and their voice shall be decisive in all cases of dispute and assault. Then all the elders of the town nearest to the dead body shall 6 wash their hands over the heifer whose neck has been broken in the ravine. They shall solemnly declare: 'Our hands did not shed this blood, nor did 7 we witness the bloodshed. Accept expiation, O LORD, for thy people 8 Israel whom thou hast redeemed, and do not let the guilt of innocent blood rest upon thy people Israel: let this bloodshed be expiated on their behalf.' Thus, by doing what is right in the eyes of the LORD, you shall rid yourselves 9 of the guilt of innocent blood.

When you wage war against your enemy and the LORD your God 10 delivers them into your hands and you take some of them captive, then if 11 you see a comely woman among the captives and take a liking to her, you may marry her. You shall bring her into your house, where she shall shave 12 her head, pare her nails, and discard the clothes which she had when 13 captured. Then she shall stay in your house and mourn for her father and mother for a full month. After that you may have intercourse with her; you shall be her husband and she your wife. But if you no longer find her 14 pleasing, let her go free. You must not sell her, nor treat her harshly, since you have had your will with her.

When a man has two wives, one loved and the other unloved, if they 15 both bear him sons, and the son of the unloved wife is the elder, then, when 16 the day comes for him to divide his property among his sons, he shall not

*a* *Prob. rdg.; Heb.* put to work.

17 treat the son of the loved wife as his first-born in contempt of his true first-born, the son of the unloved wife. He shall recognize the rights of his first-born, the son of the unloved wife, and give him a double share of all that he possesses; for he was the firstfruits of his manhood, and the right of the first-born is his.

18 When a man has a son who is disobedient and out of control, and will not obey his father or his mother, or pay attention when they punish
19 him, then his father and mother shall take hold of him and bring him out
20 to the elders of the town, at the town gate. They shall say to the elders of the town, 'This son of ours is disobedient and out of control; he will not
21 obey us, he is a wastrel and a drunkard.' Then all the men of the town shall stone him to death, and you will thereby rid yourselves of this wickedness. All Israel will hear of it and be afraid.

22 When a man is convicted of a capital offence and is put to death, you
23 shall hang him on a gibbet; but his body shall not remain on the gibbet overnight; you shall bury it on the same day, for a hanged man is offensive[a] in the sight of God. You shall not pollute the land which the LORD your God is giving you as your patrimony.

22 WHEN YOU SEE A FELLOW-COUNTRYMAN'S OX or sheep straying, do
2 not ignore it but take it back to him. If the owner is not a near neighbour and you do not know who he is, take the animal into your own house and
3 keep it with you until he claims it, and then give it back to him. Do the same with his ass or his cloak or anything else that your fellow-countryman has lost, if you find it. You may not ignore it.

4 When you see your fellow-countryman's ass or ox lying on the road, do not ignore it; you must help him to lift it to its feet again.

5 No woman shall wear an article of man's clothing, nor shall a man put on woman's dress; for those who do these things are abominable to the LORD your God.

6 When you come across a bird's nest by the road, in a tree or on the ground, with fledglings or eggs in it and the mother-bird on the nest, do
7 not take both mother and young. Let the mother-bird go free, and take only the young; then you will prosper and live long.

8 When you build a new house, put a parapet along the roof, or you will bring the guilt of bloodshed on your house if anyone should fall from it.

9 You shall not sow your vineyard with a second crop, or the full yield will be forfeit, both the yield of the seed you sow and the fruit of the vine-yard.

10 You shall not plough with an ox and an ass yoked together.

11 You shall not wear clothes woven with two kinds of yarn, wool and flax together.

12 You shall make twisted tassels on the four corners of your cloaks which you wrap round you.

13 When a man takes a wife and after having intercourse with her turns
14 against her and brings trumped-up charges against her, giving her a bad name and saying, 'I took this woman and slept with her and did not find

*a Or* accursed.

proof of virginity in her', then the girl's father and mother shall take the 15
proof of her virginity to the elders of the town, at the town gate. The girl's 16
father shall say to the elders, 'I gave my daughter in marriage to this man,
and he has turned against her. He has trumped up a charge and said, "I 17
have not found proofs of virginity in your daughter." Here are the proofs.'
They shall then spread the garment before the elders of the town. The 18
elders shall take the man and punish him: they shall fine him a hundred 19
pieces of silver because he has given a bad name to a virgin of Israel, and
hand them to the girl's father. She shall be his wife: he is not free to divorce
her all his life long. If, on the other hand, the accusation is true and no 20
proof of the girl's virginity is found, then they shall bring her out to the 21
door of her father's house and the men of her town shall stone her to death.
She has committed an outrage in Israel by playing the prostitute in her
father's house: you shall rid yourselves of this wickedness.

When a man is discovered lying with a married woman, they shall both 22
die, the woman as well as the man who lay with her: you shall rid Israel
of this wickedness.

When a virgin is pledged in marriage to a man and another man comes 23
upon her in the town and lies with her, you shall bring both of them out to 24
the gate of that town and stone them to death; the girl because, although in
the town, she did not cry for help, and the man because he dishonoured
another man's wife: you shall rid yourselves of this wickedness. If the man 25
comes upon such a girl in the country and rapes her, then the man alone
shall die because he lay with her. You shall do nothing to the girl, she has 26
done nothing worthy of death: this deed is like that of a man who attacks
another and murders him, for the man came upon her in the country and, 27
though the girl cried for help, there was no one to rescue her.

When a man comes upon a virgin who is not pledged in marriage and 28
forces her to lie with him, and they are discovered, then the man who lies 29
with her shall give the girl's father fifty pieces of silver, and she shall be
his wife because he has dishonoured her. He is not free to divorce her all
his life long.

A man shall not take his father's wife: he shall not bring shame on his 30
father.

No man whose testicles have been crushed or whose organ has been **23**
severed shall become a member of the assembly of the LORD.

No descendant of an irregular union, even down to the tenth generation, 2
shall become a member of the assembly of the LORD.

No Ammonite or Moabite, even down to the tenth generation, shall 3
become a member of the assembly of the LORD. They shall never become
members of the assembly of the LORD, because they did not meet you with 4
food and water on your way out of Egypt, and because they hired Balaam
son of Beor from Pethor in Aram-naharaim*a* to revile you. The LORD 5
your God refused to listen to Balaam and turned his denunciation into a
blessing, because the LORD your God loved you. You shall never seek their 6
welfare or their good all your life long.

You shall not regard an Edomite as an abomination, for he is your own 7

*a   That is* Aram of Two Rivers.

8 kin; nor an Egyptian, for you were aliens in his land. The third generation of children born to them may become members of the assembly of the LORD.

9 When you are encamped against an enemy, you shall be careful to avoid
10 any foulness. When one of your number is unclean because of an emission of seed at night, he must go outside the camp; he may not come within it.
11 Towards evening he shall wash himself in water, and at sunset he may come
12 back into the camp. You shall have a sign outside the camp showing where
13 you can withdraw. With your equipment you will have a trowel, and when you squat outside, you shall scrape a hole with it and then turn and cover
14 your excrement. For the LORD your God goes about in your camp, to keep you safe and to hand over your enemies as you advance, and your camp must be kept holy for fear that he should see something indecent and go with you no further.

15 You shall not surrender to his master a slave who has taken refuge with
16 you. Let him stay with you anywhere he chooses in any one of your settlements, wherever suits him best; you shall not force him.

17 No Israelite woman shall become a temple-prostitute, and no Israelite man shall prostitute himself in this way.

18 You shall not allow a common prostitute's fee, or the pay of a male prostitute, to be brought into the house of the LORD your God in fulfilment of any vow, for both of them are abominable to the LORD your God.

19 You shall not charge interest on anything you lend to a fellow-countryman, money or food or anything else on which interest can be
20 charged. You may charge interest on a loan to a foreigner but not on a loan to a fellow-countryman, for then the LORD your God will bless you in all you undertake in the land which you are entering to occupy.

21 When you make a vow to the LORD your God, do not put off its fulfilment; otherwise the LORD your God will require satisfaction of you and you will
22 be guilty of sin. If you choose not to make a vow, you will not be guilty of
23 sin; but if you voluntarily make a vow to the LORD your God, mind what you say and do what you have promised.

24 When you go into another man's vineyard, you may eat as many grapes as you wish to satisfy your hunger, but you may not put any into your basket.

25 When you go into another man's standing corn, you may pluck ears to rub in your hands, but you may not put a sickle to his standing corn.

**24** When a man has married a wife, but she does not win his favour because he finds something shameful in her, and he writes her a note of divorce,
2 gives it to her and dismisses her; and suppose after leaving his house she
3 goes off to become the wife of another man, and this next husband turns against her and writes her a note of divorce which he gives her and dis-
4 misses her, or dies after making her his wife—then in that case her first husband who dismissed her is not free to take her back to be his wife again after she has become for him unclean. This is abominable to the LORD; you must not bring sin upon the land which the LORD your God is giving you as your patrimony.

5 When a man is newly married, he shall not be liable for military service

or any other public duty. He shall remain at home exempt from service for one year and enjoy the wife he has taken.

No man shall take millstones, or even the upper one alone, in pledge; 6 that would be taking a life in pledge.

When a man is found to have kidnapped a fellow-countryman, an Israel- 7 ite, and to have treated him harshly and sold him, he shall die: you shall rid yourselves of this wickedness.

Be careful how you act in all cases of malignant skin-disease; be careful 8 to observe all that the levitical priests tell you; I gave them my commands which you must obey. Remember what the LORD your God did to Miriam, 9 on your way out of Egypt.

When you make a loan to another man, do not enter his house to take a 10 pledge from him. Wait outside, and the man whose creditor you are shall 11 bring the pledge out to you. If he is a poor man, you shall not sleep in the 12 cloak he has pledged. Give it back to him at sunset so that he may sleep in 13 it and bless you; then it will be counted to your credit in the sight of the LORD your God.

You shall not keep back the wages of a man who is poor and needy, 14 whether a fellow-countryman or an alien living in your country in one of your settlements. Pay him his wages on the same day before sunset, for 15 he is poor and his heart is set on them: he may appeal to the LORD against you, and you will be guilty of sin.

Fathers shall not be put to death for their children, nor children for 16 their fathers; a man shall be put to death only for his own sin.

You shall not deprive aliens and orphans of justice nor take a widow's 17 cloak in pledge. Remember that you were slaves in Egypt and the LORD 18 your God redeemed you from there; that is why I command you to do this.

When you reap the harvest in your field and forget a swathe, do not go 19 back to pick it up; it shall be left for the alien, the orphan, and the widow, in order that the LORD your God may bless you in all that you undertake.

When you beat your olive-trees, do not strip them afterwards; what is 20 left shall be for the alien, the orphan, and the widow.

When you gather the grapes from your vineyard, do not glean after- 21 wards; what is left shall be for the alien, the orphan, and the widow. Remember that you were slaves in Egypt; that is why I command you to 22 do this.

When two men go to law and present themselves for judgement, the **25** judges shall try the case; they shall acquit the innocent and condemn the guilty. If the guilty man is sentenced to be flogged, the judge shall cause him 2 to lie down and be beaten in his presence; the number of strokes shall correspond to the gravity of the offence. They may give him forty strokes, 3 but not more; otherwise, if they go further and exceed this number, your fellow-countryman will have been publicly degraded.

You shall not muzzle an ox while it is treading out the corn. 4

When brothers live together and one of them dies without leaving a son, 5 his widow shall not marry outside the family. Her husband's brother shall have intercourse with her; he shall take her in marriage and do his duty by her as her husband's brother. The first son she bears shall perpetuate the 6

7 dead brother's name so that it may not be blotted out from Israel. But if the man is unwilling to take his brother's wife, she shall go to the elders at the town gate and say, 'My husband's brother refuses to perpetuate his 8 brother's name in Israel; he will not do his duty by me.' At this the elders of the town shall summon him and reason with him. If he still stands his 9 ground and says, 'I will not take her', his brother's widow shall go up to him in the presence of the elders; she shall pull his sandal off his foot and spit in his face and declare: 'Thus we requite the man who will not build 10 up his brother's family.' His family shall be known in Israel as the House of the Unsandalled Man.

11 When two men are fighting and the wife of one of them comes near to drag her husband clear of his opponent, if she puts out her hand and 12 catches hold of the man's genitals, you shall cut off her hand and show her no mercy.

13 You shall not have unequal weights in your bag, one heavy, the other 14 light. You shall not have unequal measures in your house, one large, the 15 other small. You shall have true and correct weights and true and correct measures, so that you may live long in the land which the LORD your God 16 is giving you. All who commit these offences, all who deal dishonestly, are abominable to the LORD.

17 Remember what the Amalekites did to you on your way out of Egypt, 18 how they met you on the road when you were faint and weary and cut off your rear, which was lagging behind exhausted: they showed no fear of 19 God. When the LORD your God gives you peace from your enemies on every side, in the land which he is giving you to occupy as your patrimony, you shall not fail to blot out the memory of the Amalekites from under heaven.

26 WHEN YOU COME INTO THE LAND which the LORD your God is giving 2 you to occupy as your patrimony and settle in it, you shall take the first-fruits of all the produce of the soil, which you gather in from the land which the LORD your God is giving you, and put them in a basket. Then you shall go to the place which the LORD your God will choose as a dwelling for his 3 Name and come to the priest, whoever he shall be in those days. You shall say to him, 'I declare this day to the LORD your God that I have entered 4 the land which the LORD swore to our forefathers to give us.' The priest shall take the basket from your hand and set it down before the altar of the 5 LORD your God. Then you shall solemnly recite before the LORD your God: 'My father was a homeless *a* Aramaean who went down to Egypt with a small company and lived there until they became a great, powerful, and 6 numerous nation. But the Egyptians ill-treated us, humiliated us and im-7 posed cruel slavery upon us. Then we cried to the LORD the God of our fathers for help, and he listened to us and saw our humiliation, our hard-8 ship and distress; and so the LORD brought us out of Egypt with a strong hand and outstretched arm, with terrifying deeds, and with signs and 9 portents. He brought us to this place and gave us this land, a land flowing 10 with milk and honey. And now I have brought the firstfruits of the soil

*a Or* wandering.

which thou, O Lord, hast given me.' You shall then set the basket before
the Lord your God and bow down in worship before him. You shall all  11
rejoice, you and the Levites and the aliens living among you, for all the
good things which the Lord your God has given to you and to your family.

When you have finished taking a tithe of your produce in the third year,  12
the tithe-year, you shall give it to the Levites and to the aliens, the orphans,
and the widows. They shall eat it in your settlements and be well fed. Then  13
you shall declare before the Lord your God: 'I have rid my house of the
tithe that was holy to thee and given it to the Levites, to the aliens, the
orphans, and the widows, according to all the commandments which thou
didst lay upon me. I have not broken or forgotten any of thy commandments. I have not eaten any of the tithe while in mourning, nor have I rid  14
myself of it for unclean purposes, nor offered any of it to *a* the dead. I have
obeyed the Lord my God: I have done all that thou didst command me.
Look down from heaven, thy holy dwelling-place, and bless thy people  15
Israel and the ground which thou hast given to us as thou didst swear to
our forefathers, a land flowing with milk and honey.'

This day the Lord your God commands you to keep these statutes and  16
laws: be careful to observe them with all your heart and soul. You have  17
recognized the Lord this day as your God; you are to conform to his ways,
to keep his statutes, his commandments, and his laws, and to obey him.
The Lord has recognized you this day as his special possession, as he  18
promised you, and to keep his commandments; he will raise you high  19
above all the nations which he has made, to bring him praise and fame and
glory, and to be a people holy to the Lord your God, according to his
promise.

## Concluding charge of Moses to the people

MOSES, WITH THE ELDERS OF ISRAEL, gave the people this charge:  27
'Keep all the commandments that I lay upon you this day. On the  2
day that you cross the Jordan to the land which the Lord your God is
giving you, you shall set up great stones and plaster them over. You shall  3
inscribe on them all the words of this law, when you have crossed over to
enter the land which the Lord your God is giving you, a land flowing with
milk and honey, as the Lord the God of your fathers promised you. When  4
you have crossed the Jordan you shall set up these stones on Mount Ebal,
as I command you this day, and cover them with plaster. You shall build  5
an altar there to the Lord your God: it shall be an altar of stones on which
you shall use no tool of iron. You shall build the altar of the Lord your  6
God with blocks of undressed stone, and you shall offer whole-offerings
upon it to the Lord your God. You shall slaughter shared-offerings and  7
eat them there, and rejoice before the Lord your God. You shall inscribe  8
on the stones all the words of this law, engraving them with care.'

Moses and the levitical priests spoke to all Israel, 'Be silent, Israel, and  9
listen; this day you have become a people belonging to the Lord your God.

*a Or for.*

225

10 Obey the LORD your God, and observe his commandments and statutes which I lay upon you this day.'

11 12    That day Moses gave the people this command: 'Those who shall stand for the blessing of the people on Mount Gerizim when you have crossed the Jordan are these: Simeon, Levi, Judah, Issachar, Joseph, and Benjamin.

13 Those who shall stand on Mount Ebal for the curse are these: Reuben, Gad, Asher, Zebulun, Dan, and Naphtali.'

14    The Levites, in the hearing of all Israel, shall intone these words:

15 'A curse upon the man who carves an idol or casts an image, anything abominable to the LORD that craftsmen make, and sets it up in secret': the people shall all respond and say, 'Amen.'

16 'A curse upon him who slights his father or his mother': the people shall all say, 'Amen.'

17 'A curse upon him who moves his neighbour's boundary stone': the people shall all say, 'Amen.'

18 'A curse upon him who misdirects a blind man': the people shall all say, 'Amen.'

19 'A curse upon him who withholds justice from the alien, the orphan, and the widow': the people shall all say, 'Amen.'

20 'A curse upon him who lies with his father's wife, for he brings shame upon his father': the people shall all say, 'Amen.'

21 'A curse upon him who lies with any animal': the people shall all say, 'Amen.'

22 'A curse upon him who lies with his sister, his father's daughter or his mother's daughter': the people shall all say, 'Amen.'

23 'A curse upon him who lies with his wife's mother': the people shall all say, 'Amen.'

24 'A curse upon him who strikes another man in secret': the people shall all say, 'Amen.'

25 'A curse upon him who takes reward to kill a man with whom he has no feud': the people shall all say, 'Amen.'

26 'A curse upon any man who does not fulfil this law by doing all that it prescribes': the people shall all say, 'Amen.'

28 IF YOU WILL OBEY THE LORD your God by diligently observing all his commandments which I lay upon you this day, then the LORD your

2 God will raise you high above all nations of the earth, and all these blessings shall come to you and light upon you, because you obey the LORD your God:

3 A blessing on you in the city; a blessing on you in the country.

4 A blessing on the fruit of your body, the fruit of your land and of your cattle, the offspring of your herds and of your lambing flocks.

5 A blessing on your basket and your kneading-trough.

6 A blessing on you as you come in; and a blessing on you as you go out.

7 May the LORD deliver up the enemies who attack you and let them be put to rout before you. Though they come out against you by one way, they shall flee before you by seven ways.

8 May the LORD grant you a blessing in your granaries and in all your

labours; may the LORD your God bless you in the land which he is giving you.

The LORD will set you up as his own holy people, as he swore to you, if 9 you keep the commandments of the LORD your God and conform to his ways. Then all people on earth shall see that the LORD has named you as 10 his very own, and they shall go in fear of you. The LORD will make you 11 prosper greatly in the fruit of your body and of your cattle, and in the fruit of the ground in the land which he swore to your forefathers to give you. May the LORD open the heavens for you, his rich treasure house, to give 12 rain upon your land at the proper time and bless everything to which you turn your hand. You shall lend to many nations, but you shall not borrow; the LORD will make you the head and not the tail: you shall be always at the 13 top and never at the bottom, when you listen to the commandments of the LORD your God, which I give you this day to keep and to fulfil. You shall 14 turn neither to the right nor to the left from all the things which I command you this day nor shall you follow after and worship other gods.

BUT IF YOU DO NOT OBEY the LORD your God by diligently observing 15 all his commandments and statutes which I lay upon you this day, then all these maledictions shall come to you and light upon you:

A curse upon you in the city; a curse upon you in the country. 16

A curse upon your basket and your kneading-trough. 17

A curse upon the fruit of your body, the fruit of your land, the offspring 18 of your herds and of your lambing flocks.

A curse upon you as you come in; and a curse upon you as you go out. 19

May the LORD send upon you starvation, burning thirst, and dysentery,<sup>a</sup> 20 whatever you are about, until you are destroyed and quickly perish for your evil doings, because you have forsaken me.

May the LORD cause pestilence to haunt you until he has exterminated 21 you out of the land which you are entering to occupy; may the LORD 22 afflict you with wasting disease and recurrent fever, ague and eruptions; with drought, black blight and red; and may these plague you until you perish. May the skies above you be bronze, and the earth beneath you iron. 23 May the LORD turn the rain upon your country into fine sand, and may dust 24 come down upon you from the sky until you are blotted out.

May the LORD put you to rout before the enemy. Though you go out 25 against them by one way, you shall flee before them by seven ways. May you be repugnant to all the kingdoms on earth. May your bodies become 26 food for the birds of the air and the wild beasts, with no man to scare them away.

May the LORD strike you with Egyptian boils and with tumours, scabs, 27 and itches, for which you will find no cure. May the LORD strike you with 28 madness, blindness, and bewilderment; so that you will grope about in 29 broad daylight, just as a blind man gropes in darkness, and you will fail to find your way. You will also be oppressed and robbed, day in, day out, with no one to save you. A woman will be pledged to you, but another 30 shall ravish her; you will build a house but not live in it; you will plant a

<sup>a</sup> *Or* cursing, confusion, and rebuke.

31 vineyard but not enjoy its fruit. Your ox will be slaughtered before your eyes, but you will not eat any of it; and before your eyes your ass will be stolen and will not come back to you; your sheep will be given to the enemy,

32 and there will be no one to recover them. Your sons and daughters will be given to another people while you look on; your eyes will strain after them

33 all day long, and you will be powerless. A nation whom you do not know shall eat the fruit of your land and all your toil, and your lot will be nothing

34 35 but brutal oppression. The sights you see will drive you mad. May the LORD strike you on knee and leg with malignant boils for which you will find no cure; they will spread from the sole of your foot to the crown of

36 your head. May the LORD give you up, you and the king whom you have appointed, to a nation whom neither you nor your fathers have known, and

37 there you will worship other gods, gods of wood and stone. You will become a horror, a byword, and an object-lesson to all the peoples amongst whom the LORD disperses you.

38 You will carry out seed for your fields in plenty, but you will harvest

39 little; for the locusts will devour it. You will plant vineyards and cultivate them, but you will not drink the wine or gather the grapes; for the grub

40 will eat them. You will have olive-trees all over your territory, but you will

41 not anoint yourselves with their oil; for your olives will drop off. You will bear sons and daughters, but they will not remain yours because they will be

42 taken into captivity. All your trees and the fruit of the ground will be

43 infested with the mole-cricket. The alien who lives with you will raise

44 himself higher and higher, and you will sink lower and lower. He will lend to you but you will not lend to him: he will be the head and you the tail.

45 All these maledictions will come upon you; they will pursue you and overtake you until you are destroyed because you did not obey the LORD your God by keeping the commandments and statutes which he gave you.

46 They shall be a sign and a portent to you and your descendants for ever,

47 because you did not serve the LORD your God with joy and with a glad

48 heart for all your blessings. Then in hunger and thirst, in nakedness and extreme want, you shall serve your enemies whom the LORD will send against you, and they will put a yoke of iron on your neck when they have

49 subdued you. May the LORD raise against you a nation from afar, from the other end of the earth, who will swoop upon you like a vulture, a nation

50 whose language you will not understand, a nation of grim aspect with no

51 reverence for age and no pity for the young. They will devour the young of your cattle and the fruit of your land, when you have been subdued. They will leave you neither corn, nor new wine nor oil, neither the offspring of your herds nor of your lambing flocks, until you are annihilated.

52 They will besiege you in all your cities until they bring down your lofty impregnable walls, those city walls throughout your land in which you trust. They will besiege you within all your cities, throughout the land

53 which the LORD your God has given you. Then you will eat your own children, the flesh of your sons and daughters whom the LORD your God has given you, because of the dire straits to which you will be reduced

54 when your enemy besieges you. The pampered, delicate man will not share with his brother, or the wife of his bosom, or his own remaining children,

any of the meat which he is eating, the flesh of his own children. He is left 55
with nothing else because of the dire straits to which you will be reduced
when your enemy besieges you within your cities. The pampered, delicate 56
woman, the woman who has never even tried to put a foot to the ground,
so delicate and pampered she is, will not share with her own husband or
her son or her daughter the afterbirth which she expels, or any boy or girl 57
that she may bear. She will herself eat them secretly in her extreme want,
because of the dire straits to which you will be reduced when your enemy
besieges you within your cities.

If you do not observe and fulfil all the law written down in this book, if 58
you do not revere this honoured and dreaded name, this name 'the LORD[a]
your God', then the LORD will strike you and your descendants with 59
unimaginable plagues, malignant and persistent, and with sickness,
persistent and severe. He will bring upon you once again all the diseases of 60
Egypt which you dread, and they will cling to you. The LORD will bring 61
upon you sickness and plague of every kind not written down in this book
of the law, until you are destroyed. Then you who were countless as the 62
stars in the sky will be left few in number, because you did not obey the
LORD your God. Just as the LORD took delight in you, prospering and 63
increasing you, so now it will be his delight to destroy and exterminate you,
and you will be uprooted from the land which you are entering to occupy.
The LORD will scatter you among all peoples from one end of the earth to 64
the other, and there you will worship other gods whom neither you have
known nor your forefathers, gods of wood and stone. Among those nations 65
you will find no peace, no rest for the sole of your foot. Then the LORD
will give you an unquiet mind, dim eyes, and failing appetite. Your life 66
will hang continually in suspense, fear will beset you night and day, and
you will find no security all your life long. Every morning you will say, 67
'Would God it were evening!', and every evening, 'Would God it were
morning!', for the fear that lives in your heart and the sights that you see.
The LORD will bring you sorrowing back to Egypt by that very road of 68
which I said to you, 'You shall not see that road again'; and there you will
offer to sell yourselves to your enemies as slaves and slave-girls, but there
will be no buyer.

These are the words of the covenant which the LORD commanded Moses **29**
to make with the Israelites in Moab, in addition to the covenant which he
made with them on Horeb.

MOSES SUMMONED ALL THE ISRAELITES and said to them: 'You 2
have seen with your own eyes all that the LORD did in Egypt to Pharaoh,
to all his servants, and to the whole land, the great challenge which you 3
yourselves witnessed, those great signs and portents, but to this day the 4
LORD has not given you a mind to learn, or eyes to see, or ears to hear. I 5
led you for forty years in the wilderness; your clothes did not wear out on
you, nor did your sandals wear out and fall off your feet; you ate no bread 6
and drank no wine or strong drink, in order that you might learn that I am
the LORD your God. You came to this place where Sihon king of Heshbon 7

[a] *See note on Exod. 3. 15.*

8 and Og king of Bashan came to attack us, and we defeated them. We took
their land and gave it as patrimony to the Reubenites, the Gadites, and
9 half the tribe of Manasseh. You shall observe the provisions of this covenant and keep them so that you may be successful in all you do.

10   'You all stand here today before the Lord your God, tribal chiefs,
11 elders, and officers, all the men of Israel, with your dependants, your
wives, the aliens who live in your camp—all of them, from those who chop
12 wood to those who draw water—and you are ready to accept the oath and
enter into the covenant which the Lord your God is making with you
13 today. The covenant is to constitute you his people this day, and he will
be your God, as he promised you and as he swore to your forefathers,
14 Abraham, Isaac and Jacob. It is not with you alone that I am making this
15 covenant and this oath, but with all those who stand here with us today
before the Lord our God and also with those who are not here with us
16 today. For you know how we lived in Egypt and how we and you, as we
17 passed through the nations, saw their loathsome idols and the false gods
18 they had, the gods of wood and stone, of silver and gold. If there should be
among you a man or woman, family or tribe, who is moved today to turn
from the Lord our God and to go worshipping the gods of those nations—
if there is among you such a root from which springs gall and wormwood,
19 then when he hears the terms of this oath, he may inwardly flatter himself
and think, "All will be well with me even if I follow the promptings of my
20 stubborn heart"; but this will bring everything to ruin. The Lord will not
be willing to forgive him; for then his anger and resentment will overwhelm
this man, and the denunciations prescribed in this book will fall heavily
21 on him, and the Lord will blot out his name from under heaven. The
Lord will single him out from all the tribes of Israel for disaster to fall upon
him, according to the oath required by the covenant and prescribed in this
book of the law.

22   'The next generation, your sons who follow you and the foreigners who
come from distant countries, will see the plagues of this land and the
23 ulcers which the Lord has brought upon its people, the whole land burnt
up with brimstone and salt, so that it cannot be sown, or yield herb or green
plant. It will be as desolate as were Sodom and Gomorrah, Admah and
24 Zeboyim, when the Lord overthrew them in his anger and rage. Then
they, and all the nations with them, will ask, "Why has the Lord so
afflicted this land? Why has there been this great outburst of wrath?"
25 The answer will be: "Because they forsook the covenant of the Lord the
God of their fathers which he made with them when he brought them out
26 of Egypt. They began to worship other gods and to bow down to them,
gods whom they had not known and whom the Lord had not assigned to
27 them. The anger of the Lord was roused against that land, so that he
28 brought upon it all the maledictions written in this book. The Lord uprooted them from their soil in anger, in wrath and great fury, and banished
them to another land, where they are to this day."

29   'There are things hidden, and they belong to the Lord our God, but
what is revealed belongs to us and our children for ever; it is for us to
observe all that is prescribed in this law.

'When these things have befallen you, the blessing and the curse of **30** which I have offered you the choice, if you and your sons take them to heart there in all the countries to which the LORD your God has banished you, if you turn back to him and obey him heart and soul in all that I command **2** you this day, then the LORD your God will show you compassion and **3** restore your fortunes. He will gather you again from all the countries to which he has scattered you. Even though he were to banish you to the four **4** corners of the world, the LORD your God will gather you from there, from there he will fetch you home. The LORD your God will bring you into the **5** land which your forefathers occupied, and you will occupy it again; then he will bring you prosperity and make you more numerous than your forefathers were. The LORD your God will circumcise *a* your hearts and the **6** hearts of your descendants, so that you will love him with all your heart and soul and you will live. Then the LORD your God will turn all these **7** denunciations against your enemies and the foes who persecute you. You **8** will then again obey the LORD and keep all his commandments which I give you this day. The LORD your God will make you more than prosperous **9-10** in all that you do, in the fruit of your body and of your cattle and in the fruits of the earth; for, when you obey the LORD your God by keeping his commandments and statutes, as they are written in this book of the law, and when you turn back to the LORD your God with all your heart and soul, he will again rejoice over you and be good to you, as he rejoiced over your forefathers.

'The commandment that I lay on you this day is not too difficult for you, **11** it is not too remote. It is not in heaven, that you should say, "Who will go **12** up to heaven for us to fetch it and tell it to us, so that we can keep it?" Nor is it beyond the sea, that you should say, "Who will cross the sea for **13** us to fetch it and tell it to us, so that we can keep it?" It is a thing very **14** near to you, upon your lips and in your heart ready to be kept.

'Today I offer you the choice of life and good, or death and evil. If you **15 16** obey the commandments of the LORD your God which I give you this day, by loving the LORD your God, by conforming to his ways and by keeping his commandments, statutes, and laws, then you will live and increase, and the LORD your God will bless you in the land which you are entering to occupy. But if your heart turns away and you do not listen and you are led **17** on to bow down to other gods and worship them, I tell you this day that **18** you will perish; you will not live long in the land which you will enter to occupy after crossing the Jordan. I summon heaven and earth to witness **19** against you this day: I offer you the choice of life or death, blessing or curse. Choose life and then you and your descendants will live; love the **20** LORD your God, obey him and hold fast to him: that is life for you and length of days in the land which the LORD swore to give to your forefathers, Abraham, Isaac and Jacob.'

Moses finished speaking these words to all Israel, and then he said, 'I **31 1 2** am now a hundred and twenty years old, and I can no longer move about as I please; and the LORD has told me that I may not cross the Jordan. The **3** LORD your God will cross over at your head and destroy these nations before

*a* Or incline.

your advance, and you shall occupy their lands; and, as he directed, Joshua
4 will lead you across. The LORD will do to these nations as he did to Sihon
and Og, kings of the Amorites, and to their lands; he will destroy them.
5 The LORD will deliver them into your power, and you shall do to them as I
6 commanded you. Be strong, be resolute; you must not dread them or be
afraid, for the LORD your God himself goes with you; he will not fail you
or forsake you.'

7 Moses summoned Joshua and said to him in the presence of all Israel,
'Be strong, be resolute; for it is you who are to lead this people into the
land which the LORD swore to give their forefathers, and you are to bring
8 them into possession of it. The LORD himself goes at your head; he will
be with you; he will not fail you or forsake you. Do not be discouraged or
afraid.'

9 Moses wrote down this law and gave it to the priests, the sons of Levi,
who carried the Ark of the Covenant of the LORD, and to all the elders of
10 Israel. Moses gave them this command: 'At the end of every seven years,
at the appointed time for the year of remission, at the pilgrim-feast of
11 Tabernacles, when all Israel comes to enter the presence of the LORD your
God in the place which he will choose, you shall read this law publicly in
12 the hearing of all Israel. Assemble the people, men, women, and dependants,
together with the aliens who live in your settlements, so that they may listen,
and learn to fear the LORD your God and observe all these laws with care.
13 Their children, too, who do not know them, shall hear them, and learn to
fear the LORD your God all their lives in the land which you will occupy
after crossing the Jordan.'

## *Joshua appointed successor to Moses*

14 THE LORD SAID TO MOSES, 'The time of your death is drawing near;
call Joshua, and then come and stand in the Tent of the Presence so
that I may give him his commission.' So Moses and Joshua went and took
15 their stand in the Tent of the Presence; and the LORD appeared in the tent
in a pillar of cloud, and the pillar of cloud stood at the entrance of the tent.
16 The LORD said to Moses, 'You are about to die like your forefathers,
and this people, when they come into the land and live among foreigners,
will go wantonly after their gods; they will abandon me and break the
17 covenant which I have made with them. Then my anger will be roused
against them, and I will abandon them and hide my face from them. They
will be an easy prey, and many terrible disasters will come upon them.
They will say on that day, "These disasters have come because our God is
18 not among us." On that day I will hide my face because of all the evil they
have done in turning to other gods.
19 'Now write down this rule of life[a] and teach it to the Israelites; make
20 them repeat it, so that it may be on record against them. When I have
brought them into the land which I swore to give to their forefathers, a
land flowing with milk and honey, and they have plenty to eat and grow

*a* rule of life: *or* song.

fat, they will turn to other gods and worship them, they will spurn me
and break my covenant; and many calamities and disasters will follow. 21
Then this rule of life will confront them as a record, for it will not be
forgotten by their descendants. For even before I bring them into the
land which I swore to give them, I know which way their thoughts incline
already.'

That day Moses wrote down this rule of life and taught it to the Israelites. 22
The LORD*a* gave Joshua son of Nun his commission in these words: 'Be 23
strong, be resolute; for you shall bring the Israelites into the land which
I swore to give them, and I will be with you.'

When Moses had finished writing down these laws in a book, from begin- 24
ning to end, he gave this command to the Levites who carried the Ark of 25
the Covenant of the LORD: 'Take this book of the law and put it beside the 26
Ark of the Covenant of the LORD your God to be a witness against you. For 27
I know how defiant and stubborn you are; even during my lifetime you
have defied the LORD; how much more, then, will you do so when I am
dead? Assemble all the elders of your tribes and your officers; I will say 28
all these things in their hearing and will summon heaven and earth to
witness against them. For I know that after my death you will take 29
to degrading practices and turn aside from the way which I told you to
follow, and in days to come disaster will come upon you, because you are
doing what is wrong in the eyes of the LORD and so provoking him to
anger.'

## Two historical poems

MOSES RECITED THIS SONG from begining to end in the hearing 30
of the whole assembly of Israel:

> Give ear to what I say, O heavens,                                    **32**
> earth, listen to my words;
> my teaching shall fall like drops of rain,                             2
> my words shall distil like dew,
> like fine rain upon the grass
> and like the showers on young plants.
>
> When I call aloud the name of the LORD,*b*                             3
> you shall respond, 'Great is our God,
> the creator*c* whose work is perfect,                                  4
> and all his ways are just,
> a faithful god, who does no wrong,
> righteous and true is He!'
>
> Perverse and crooked generation                                       5
> whose faults have proved you no children of his,
> is this how you repay the LORD,                                        6
> you brutish and stupid people?

---

*a Prob. rdg.; Heb.* He.        *b Or the name* JEHOVAH.        *c Or* rock.

Is he not your father who formed you?
Did he not make you and establish you?

7 Remember the days of old,
think of the generations long ago;
ask your father to recount it
and your elders to tell you the tale.

8 When the Most High parcelled out the nations,
when he dispersed all mankind,
he laid down the boundaries of every people
according to the number of the sons of God;

9 but the LORD's share was his own people,
Jacob was his allotted portion.

10 He found him in a desert land,
in a waste and howling void.
He protected and trained him,
he guarded him as the apple of his eye,

11 as an eagle watches over its nest,
hovers above its young,
spreads its pinions and takes them up,
and carries them upon its wings.

12 The LORD alone led him,
no alien god at his side.

13 He made him ride on the heights of the earth
and fed him on the harvest of the fields;
he satisfied him with honey from the crags
and oil from the flinty rock,

14 curds from the cattle, milk from the ewes,
the fat of lambs' kidneys,
of rams, the breed of Bashan, and of goats,
with the finest flour of wheat;
and he drank wine from the blood of the grape.

15 Jacob ate and was well fed,
Jeshurun grew fat and unruly,*a*
he grew fat, he grew bloated and sleek.
He forsook God who made him
and dishonoured the Rock of his salvation.

16 They roused his jealousy with foreign gods
and provoked him with abominable practices.

17 They sacrificed to foreign demons that are no gods,
gods who were strangers to them;
they took up with new gods from their neighbours,
gods whom your fathers did not acknowledge.

18 You forsook the creator *b* who begot you
and cared nothing for God who brought you to birth.

19 The LORD saw and spurned them;
his own sons and daughters provoked him.

*a* Or *and kicked.*      *b* Or *rock.*

'I will hide my face from them,' he said;   20
'let me see what their end will be,
for they are a mutinous generation,
sons who are not to be trusted.
They roused my jealousy with a god of no account,  21
with their false gods they provoked me;
so I will rouse their jealousy with a people of no account,
with a brutish nation I will provoke them.
For fire is kindled by my anger,   22
it burns to the depths of Sheol;
it devours earth and its harvest
and sets fire to the very roots of the mountains.
I will heap on them one disaster after another,  23
I will use up all my arrows on them:
pangs of hunger, ravages of plague,  24
and bitter pestilence.
I will harry them with the fangs of wild beasts
and the poison of creatures that crawl in the dust.
The sword will make orphans in the streets  25
and widows in their own homes;
it will take toll of young man and maid,
of babes in arms and old men.
I had resolved to strike them down  26
and to destroy all memory of them,
but I feared that I should be provoked by their foes, 27
that their enemies would take the credit
and say, "It was not the LORD,
it was we who raised the hand that did this."'

They are a nation that lacks good counsel,  28
devoid of understanding.
If only they had the wisdom to understand this 29
and give thought to their end!
How could one man pursue a thousand of them, 30
how could two put ten thousand to flight,
if their Rock had not sold them to their enemies,
if the LORD had not handed them over?
For the enemy have no Rock like ours,  31
in themselves they are mere fools.
Their vines are vines of Sodom,  32
grown on the terraces of Gomorrah;
their grapes are poisonous,
the clusters bitter to the taste.
Their wine is the venom of serpents,  33
the cruel poison of asps;
all this I have in reserve,  34
sealed up in my storehouses
till the day of punishment and vengeance,  35

I      

till the moment when they slip and fall;
for the day of their downfall is near,
their doom is fast approaching.

36 The LORD will give his people justice
and have compassion on his servants;
for he will see that their strength is gone:
alone, or defended by his clan, no one is left.

37 He will say, 'Where are your gods,
the rock in which you sought shelter,

38 the gods who ate the fat of your sacrifices
and drank the wine of your drink-offerings?
Let them rise to help you!
Let them give you shelter!

39 See now that I, I am He,
and there is no god beside me:
I put to death and I keep alive,
I wound and I heal;
there is no rescue from my grasp.

40 I lift my hand to heaven
and swear: As I live for ever,

41 when I have whetted my flashing sword,
when I have set my hand to judgement,
then I will punish my adversaries
and take vengeance on my enemies.

42 I will make my arrows drunk with blood,
my sword shall devour flesh,
blood of slain and captives,
the heads of the enemy princes.'

43 Rejoice with him, you heavens,
bow down, all you gods, before him;
for he will avenge the blood of his sons
and take vengeance on his adversaries;
he will punish those who hate him
and make expiation for his people's land.

44 This is the song that Moses came and recited in the hearing of the
people, he and Joshua son of Nun.

45 46 Moses finished speaking to all Israel, and then he said, 'Take to heart
all these warnings which I solemnly give you this day: command your

47 children to be careful to observe all the words of this law. For you they
are no empty words; they are your very life, and by them you shall live
long in the land which you are to occupy after crossing the Jordan.'

48 49 That same day the LORD spoke to Moses and said, 'Go up this mount
Abarim, Mount Nebo in Moab, to the east of Jericho, and look out over
the land of Canaan that I am giving to the Israelites for their possession.

50 On this mountain you shall die and be gathered to your father's kin, just
as Aaron your brother died on Mount Hor and was gathered to his father's

51 kin. This is because both of you were unfaithful to me at the waters of

Meribah-by-Kadesh in the wilderness of Zin, when you did not uphold my holiness among the Israelites. You shall see the land from a distance 52 but you may not enter the land I am giving to the Israelites.'

THIS IS THE BLESSING that Moses the man of God pronounced upon 33 the Israelites before his death:

> The LORD came from Sinai     2
> and shone forth from Seir.
> He showed himself from Mount Paran,
> and with him were myriads of holy ones *a*
> streaming along at his right hand.
> > Truly he loves his people     3
> > and blesses his saints.*b*
> > They sit at his feet
> > and receive his instruction,
> > , the law which Moses laid upon us,     4
> as a possession for the assembly of Jacob.
> Then a king arose*c* in Jeshurun,     5
> when the chiefs of the people were assembled
> together with all the tribes of Israel.

Of Reuben he said: *d*     6

> May Reuben live and not die out,
> but may he be few in number.

And of Judah he said this:     7

> Hear, O LORD, the cry of Judah
> and join him to his people,
> thou whose hands fight for him,
> who art his helper against his foes.

Of Levi he said:     8

> Thou didst give thy Thummim to Levi,
> thy Urim to thy loyal servant
> whom thou didst prove at Massah,
> for whom thou didst plead at the waters of Meribah,
> who said of his parents, I do not know them,     9
> who did not acknowledge his brothers,
> nor recognize his children.
> They observe thy word
> and keep thy covenant;
> they teach thy precepts to Jacob,     10
> thy law to Israel.
> They offer thee the smoke of sacrifice
> and offerings on thy altar.

*a* and with . . . holy ones: *prob. rdg.; Heb.* and he came from myriads of holiness.
*b Or* holy ones.     *c Or* Then there was a king . . .     *d Of* Reuben he said:
*prob. rdg.; Heb. om.*

11       Bless all his powers,<sup>a</sup> O LORD,
and accept the work of his hands.
Strike his adversaries hip and thigh,
and may his enemies rise no more.

12  Of Benjamin he said:

      The LORD's beloved dwells in security,
the High God<sup>b</sup> shields him all the day long,
and he dwells under his protection.

13  Of Joseph he said:

      The LORD's blessing is on his land
with precious fruit watered from heaven above
and from the deep that lurks below,
14     with precious fruit ripened by the sun,
precious fruit, the produce of the months,
15     with all good things from the ancient mountains,
the precious fruit of the everlasting hills,
16     the precious fruits of earth and all its store,
by the favour of him who dwells in the burning bush.
This shall rest<sup>c</sup> upon the head of Joseph,
on the brow of him who was prince among<sup>d</sup> his brothers.
17     In majesty he shall be like a first-born ox,
his horns those of a wild ox
with which he will gore nations
and drive<sup>e</sup> them to the ends of earth.
Such will be the myriads of Ephraim,
and such the thousands of Manasseh.

18  Of Zebulun he said:

      Rejoice, Zebulun, when you sally forth,
rejoice in your tents, Issachar.
19     They shall summon nations to the mountain,
there they will offer true sacrifices,
for they shall suck the abundance of the seas
and draw out<sup>f</sup> the hidden wealth of the sand.

20  Of Gad he said:

      Blessed be Gad, in his wide domain;
he couches like a lion
tearing an arm or a scalp.
21     He chose the best for himself,
for to him was allotted a ruler's portion,
when the chiefs of the people were assembled together.
He did what the LORD deemed right,
observing his ordinances for Israel.

---

*a Or* skill.   *b* the High God: *prob. rdg.; Heb.* upon him.   *c Prob. rdg., cp. Gen.*
*49. 26; Heb. has an unintelligible form.*   *d* him . . . among: *or* the one cursed by.
*e* and drive: *prob. rdg.; Heb.* together.   *f* draw out: *prob. rdg.; Heb. obscure.*

Of Dan he said:     22

> Dan is a lion's cub
> springing out from Bashan.

Of Naphtali he said:     23

> Naphtali is richly favoured
> and full of the blessings of the LORD;
> his patrimony stretches to the sea and southward.

Of Asher he said:     24

> Asher is most blest of sons,
> may he be the favourite among *a* his brothers
> and bathe his feet in oil.
> May your bolts be of iron and bronze,     25
> and your strength last as long as you live.

> There is none like the God of Jeshurun     26
> who rides the heavens to your help,
> riding the clouds in his glory,
> who humbled the gods of old
> and subdued *b* the ancient powers;     27
> who drove out the enemy before you
> and gave the word to destroy.
> Israel lives in security,     28
> the tribes of Jacob by themselves,
> in a land of corn and wine *c*
> where the skies drip with dew.
> Happy are you, people of Israel, peerless, set free;     29
> the LORD is the shield that guards you,
> the Blessed One is your glorious sword.
> Your enemies come cringing to you,
> and you shall trample their bodies under foot.

## The death of Moses

THEN MOSES WENT UP from the lowlands of Moab to Mount Nebo, 34 to the top of Pisgah, eastwards from Jericho, and the LORD showed him the whole land: Gilead as far as Dan; the whole of Naphtali; the 2 territory of Ephraim and Manasseh, and all Judah as far as the western sea; the Negeb and the Plain; the valley of Jericho, the Vale of Palm Trees, 3 as far as Zoar. The LORD said to him, 'This is the land which I swore to 4 Abraham, Isaac and Jacob that I would give to their descendants. I have let you see it with your own eyes, but you shall not cross over into it.'

There in the land of Moab Moses the servant of the LORD died, as the 5 LORD had said. He was buried in a valley in Moab opposite Beth-peor, but 6 to this day no one knows his burial-place. Moses was a hundred and twenty 7

---

*a* Or of.     *b* *Prob. rdg.; Heb.* under.     *c* Or new wine

years old when he died; his sight was not dimmed nor had his vigour failed.
8 The Israelites wept for Moses in the lowlands of Moab for thirty days;
9 then the time of mourning for Moses was ended. And Joshua son of Nun
was filled with the spirit of wisdom, for Moses had laid his hands on him,
and the Israelites listened to him and did what the LORD had commanded
Moses.

10   There has never yet risen in Israel a prophet like Moses, whom the LORD
11 knew face to face: remember all the signs and portents which the LORD
sent him to show in Egypt to Pharaoh and all his servants and the whole
12 land; remember the strong hand of Moses and the terrible deeds which he
did in the sight of all Israel.

# THE BOOK OF
# JOSHUA

## *Israel's entry into the promised land*

AFTER THE DEATH OF MOSES the servant of the LORD, 1 the LORD said to Joshua son of Nun, his assistant, 'My servant 2 Moses is dead; now it is for you to cross the Jordan, you and this whole people of Israel, to the land which I am giving them. Every place 3 where you set foot is yours: I have given it to you, as I promised Moses. From the desert and the Lebanon to the great river, the river Euphrates, and 4 across all the Hittite country westwards to the Great Sea,*a* all this shall be your land. No one will ever be able to stand against you: as I was with 5 Moses, so will I be with you; I will not fail you or forsake you. Be strong, 6 be resolute; it is you who are to put this people in possession of the land which I swore to give to their fathers. Only be strong and resolute; observe 7 diligently all the law which my servant Moses has given you. You must not turn from it to right or left, if you would prosper wherever you go. This book of the law must ever be on your lips; you must keep it in mind 8 day and night so that you may diligently observe all that is written in it. Then you will prosper and be successful in all that you do. This is my 9 command: be strong, be resolute; do not be fearful or dismayed, for the LORD your God is with you wherever you go.' Then Joshua told the officers 10 to pass through the camp and give this order to the people: 'Get food ready 11 to take with you; for within three days you will be crossing the Jordan to occupy the country which the LORD your God is giving you to possess.' To the Reubenites, the Gadites, and the half tribe of Manasseh, Joshua 12 said, 'Remember the command which Moses the servant of the LORD 13 gave you when he said, "The LORD your God will grant you security here and will give you this territory." Your wives and dependants and your 14 herds may stay east of the Jordan in the territory which Moses has given you, but for yourselves, all the warriors among you must cross over as a fighting force at the head of your kinsmen. You must help them, until the 15 LORD grants them security like you and they too take possession of the land which the LORD your God is giving them. You may then return to the land which is your own possession, the territory which Moses the servant of the LORD has given you east of the Jordan.' They answered Joshua, 'What- 16 ever you tell us, we will do; wherever you send us, we will go. As we obeyed 17 Moses, so will we obey you; and may the LORD your God be with you as he was with Moses! Whoever rebels against your authority, and fails to carry 18 out all your orders, shall be put to death. Only be strong and resolute.'

---

*a* Or the Mediterranean Sea.

**2** Joshua son of Nun sent two spies out from Shittim secretly with orders to reconnoitre the country. The two men came to Jericho and went to the house of a prostitute named Rahab, and spent the night there. It was reported to the king of Jericho that some Israelites had arrived that night to explore the country. So the king sent to Rahab and said, 'Bring out the men who have come to you and are now in your house; they are here to explore the whole country.' The woman, who had taken the two men and hidden them,*a* replied, 'Yes, the men did come to me, but I did not know where they came from; and when it was time to shut the gate at nightfall, they had gone. I do not know where they were going, but if you hurry after them, you will catch them up.' In fact, she had taken them up on to the roof and concealed them among the stalks of flax which she had laid out there in rows. The messengers went in pursuit of them down the road to the fords of the Jordan, and the gate was closed as soon as they had gone out. The men had not yet settled down, when Rahab came up to them on the roof and said to them, 'I know that the LORD has given this land to you, that terror of you has descended upon us all, and that because of you the whole country is panic-stricken. For we have heard how the LORD dried up the water of the Red Sea *b* before you when you came out of Egypt, and what you did to Sihon and Og, the two Amorite kings beyond the Jordan, whom you put to death. When we heard this, our courage failed us; your coming has left no spirit in any of us; for the LORD your God is God in heaven above and on earth below. Swear to me now by the LORD that you will keep faith with my family, as I have kept faith with you. Give me a token of good faith; promise that you will spare the lives of my father and mother, my brothers and sisters and all who belong to them, and save us from death.' The men replied, 'Our lives for yours, so long as you do not betray our business. When the LORD gives us the country, we will deal honestly and faithfully by you.' She then let them down through an opening by a rope; for the house where she lived was on an angle of the wall. 'Take to the hills,' she said, 'or the pursuers will come upon you. Hide yourselves there for three days until they come back, and then go on your way.' The men warned her that they would be released from the oath she had made them take unless she did what they told her. 'When we enter the land,' they said, 'you must fasten this strand of scarlet cord in the opening through which you have lowered us, and get everybody together here in the house, your father and mother, your brothers and all your family. If anybody goes out of doors into the street, his blood shall be on his own head; we shall be quit of the oath. But if a hand is laid on anyone who stays indoors with you, his blood shall be on our heads. Remember too that, if you betray our business, then we shall be quit of the oath you have made us take.' She replied, 'It shall be as you say', and sent them away. They set off, and she fastened the strand of scarlet cord in the opening. The men made their way into the hills and stayed there three days until the pursuers returned. They had searched all along the road, but had not found them. *c* The two men

---

*a Prob. rdg.; Heb.* him.    *b Or* the Sea of Reeds.    *c* three days ... found them: *or* three days while the pursuers scoured the land and searched all along the road, but did not find them.

then turned and came down from the hills, crossed the river and returned
to Joshua son of Nun. They told him all that had happened to them and   24
said to him, 'The LORD has put the whole country into our hands, and now
all its people are panic-stricken at our approach.'

Joshua rose early in the morning, and he and all the Israelites set out   3
from Shittim and came to the Jordan, where they encamped before crossing
the river. At the end of three days the officers passed through the camp,   2
and gave this order to the people: 'When you see the Ark of the Covenant   3
of the LORD your God being carried forward by the levitical priests, then
you too shall leave your positions and set out. Follow it, but do not go   4
close to it; keep some distance behind, about a thousand yards. This will
show you the way you are to go, for you have not travelled this way before.'
Joshua then said to the people, 'Hallow yourselves, for tomorrow the LORD   5
will do a great miracle among you.' To the priests he said, 'Lift up the Ark   6
of the Covenant and pass in front of the people.' So they lifted up the Ark
of the Covenant and went in front of the people. Then the LORD said to   7
Joshua, 'Today I will begin to make you stand high in the eyes of all
Israel, and they shall know that I will be with you as I was with Moses.
Give orders to the priests who carry the Ark of the Covenant, and tell them   8
that when they come to the edge of the waters of the Jordan, they are to
take their stand in the river.'

Then Joshua said to the Israelites, 'Come here and listen to the words   9
of the LORD your God. By this you shall know that the living God is among   10
you and that he will drive out before you the Canaanites, the Hittites, the
Hivites, the Perizzites, the Girgashites, the Amorites, and the Jebusites:
the Ark of the Covenant of the LORD,*[a]* the lord of all the earth, is to cross   11
the Jordan at your head. Choose twelve men from the tribes of Israel, one   12
man from each tribe. When the priests carrying the Ark of the LORD, the   13
lord of all the earth, set foot in the waters of the Jordan, then the waters of
the Jordan will be cut off; the water coming down from upstream will
stand piled up like a bank.' So the people set out from their tents to cross   14
the Jordan, with the priests in front of them carrying the Ark of the Covenant. Now the Jordan is in full flood in all its reaches throughout the time   15
of harvest. When the priests reached the Jordan and dipped their feet in
the water at the edge, the water coming down from upstream was brought   16
to a standstill; it piled up like a bank for a long way back, as far as Adam,
a town near Zarethan. The waters coming down to the Sea of the Arabah,
the Dead Sea, were completely cut off, and the people crossed over opposite
Jericho. The priests carrying the Ark of the Covenant of the LORD stood   17
firm on the dry bed in the middle of the Jordan; and all Israel passed over
on dry ground until the whole nation had crossed the river.

WHEN THE WHOLE NATION HAD FINISHED CROSSING the Jordan,   4
the LORD said to Joshua, 'Take twelve men from the people, one from each   2
tribe, and order them to lift up twelve stones from this place, out of the   3
middle of the Jordan, where the feet of the priests stood firm. They are to
carry them across and set them down in the camp where you spend the
        *[a]* of the LORD: *prob. rdg., cp. verse 17; Heb. om.*

4 night.' Joshua summoned the twelve men whom he had chosen out of the
5 Israelites, one man from each tribe, and said to them, 'Cross over in front
of the Ark of the LORD your God as far as the middle of the Jordan, and let
each of you take a stone and hoist it on his shoulder, one for each of the
6 tribes of Israel. These stones are to stand as a memorial among you; and
7 in days to come, when your children ask you what these stones mean, you
shall tell them how the waters of the Jordan were cut off before the Ark of
the Covenant of the LORD when it crossed the Jordan. Thus these stones
8 will always be a reminder to the Israelites.' The Israelites did as Joshua had
commanded: they lifted up twelve stones from the middle of the Jordan,
as the LORD had instructed Joshua, one for each of the tribes of Israel,
carried them across to the camp and set them down there.
9    Joshua set up twelve stones in the middle of the Jordan at the place
where the priests stood who carried the Ark of the Covenant, and there
10 they are to this day. The priests carrying the Ark remained standing in the
middle of the Jordan until every command which the LORD had told Joshua
to give to the people was fulfilled, and the people had made good speed
11 across. When all the people had finished crossing, then the Ark of the LORD
12 crossed, and the priests with it.ᵃ At the head of the Israelites, there crossed
over the Reubenites, the Gadites, and the half tribe of Manasseh, as a
13 fighting force, as Moses had told them to do; about forty thousand strong,
drafted for active service, they crossed over to the lowlands of Jericho in
the presence of the LORD to do battle.
14    That day the LORD made Joshua stand very high in the eyes of all Israel,
and the people revered him, as they had revered Moses all his life.
15 16    The LORD said to Joshua, 'Command the priests carrying the Ark of the
17 Tokens to come up from the Jordan.' So Joshua commanded the priests
18 to come up from the Jordan; and when the priests carrying the Ark of the
Covenant of the LORD came up from the river-bed, they had no sooner set
foot on dry land than the waters of the Jordan came back to their place and
19 filled up all its reaches as before. On the tenth day of the first month the
people came up out of the Jordan and camped in Gilgal in the district east
20 of Jericho, and there Joshua set up the twelve stones which they had taken
21 from the Jordan. He said to the Israelites, 'In days to come, when your
22 descendants ask their fathers what these stones mean, you shall explain
23 that the Jordan was dry when Israel crossed over, and that the LORD your
God dried up the waters of the Jordan in front of you until you had gone
across, just as the LORD your God did at the Red Sea when he dried it up
24 for us until we had crossed. Thus all people on earth will know how strong
is the hand of the LORD; and thus they will stand in awe of the LORD your
God for ever.'
5    When all the Amorite kings to the west of the Jordan and all the Canaanite kings by the sea-coast heard that the LORD had dried up the waters before
the advance of the Israelites until they had crossed, their courage melted
away and there was no more spirit left in them for fear of the Israelites.
2    At that time the LORD said to Joshua, 'Make knives of flint, seat yourself,
3 and make Israel a circumcised people again.' Joshua thereupon made knives

ᵃ *Prob. rdg.; Heb. adds* before the people.

244

of flint and circumcised the Israelites at Gibeath-haaraloth. [a] This is why 4
Joshua circumcised them: all the males who came out of Egypt, all the
fighting men, had died in the wilderness on the journey from Egypt. The 5
people who came out of Egypt had all been circumcised, but not those who
had been born in the wilderness during the journey. For the Israelites 6
travelled in the wilderness for forty years, until the whole nation, all the
fighting men among them, had passed away, all who came out of Egypt
and had disobeyed the voice of the LORD. The LORD swore that he would
not allow any of these to see the land which he had sworn to their fathers
to give us, a land flowing with milk and honey. So it was their sons, whom 7
he had raised up in their place, that Joshua circumcised; they were uncircumcised because they had not been circumcised on the journey. When 8
the circumcision of the whole nation was complete, they stayed where they
were in camp until they had recovered. The LORD then said to Joshua, 9
'Today I have rolled away from you the reproaches of the Egyptians.'
Therefore the place is called Gilgal [b] to this very day.

The Israelites encamped in Gilgal, and at sunset on the fourteenth day 10
of the month they kept the Passover in the lowlands of Jericho. On the day 11
after the Passover, they ate their unleavened cakes and parched grain, and
that day it was the produce of the country. It was from that day, when they 12
first ate the produce of the country, that the manna ceased. The Israelites
received no more manna; and that year they ate what had grown in the
land of Canaan.

When Joshua came near Jericho he looked up and saw a man standing in 13
front of him with a drawn sword in his hand. Joshua went up to him and
said, 'Are you for us or for our enemies?' And the man said to him, 'I am 14
here as captain of the army of the LORD.' Joshua fell down before him, face
to the ground, and said, 'What have you to say to your servant, my lord?'
The captain of the LORD's army said to him, 'Take off your sandals; the 15
place where you are standing is holy'; and Joshua did so.

JERICHO WAS BOLTED AND BARRED against the Israelites; no one went 6
out, no one came in. The LORD said to Joshua, 'Look, I have delivered 2
Jericho and her king [c] into your hands. You shall march round the city with 3
all your fighting men, making the circuit of it once, for six days running.
Seven priests shall go in front of the Ark carrying seven trumpets made 4
from rams' horns. On the seventh day you shall march round the city
seven times and the priests shall blow their trumpets. At the blast of the 5
rams' horns, when you hear the trumpet sound, the whole army shall raise
a great shout; the wall of the city will collapse and the army shall advance,
every man straight ahead.' So Joshua son of Nun summoned the priests 6
and gave them their orders: 'Take up the Ark of the Covenant; let seven
priests with seven trumpets of ram's horn go in front of the Ark of the
LORD.' Then he said to the army, 'March on and make the circuit of the 7
city, and let the men drafted from the two and a half tribes go in front of
the Ark of the LORD.' When Joshua had spoken to the army, the seven 8

[a] *That is* the Hill of Foreskins.     [b] *That is* Rolling Stones.     [c] *Prob. rdg.;*
Heb. *adds* the fighting men.

priests carrying the seven trumpets of ram's horn before the LORD passed
on and blew the trumpets, with the Ark of the Covenant of the LORD
9 following them. The drafted men marched in front of the priests who blew
the trumpets, and the rearguard followed the Ark, the trumpets sounding
10 as they marched. But Joshua ordered the army not to shout, or to raise their
voices or utter a word, till the day came when he would tell them to shout;
11 then they were to give a loud shout. Thus he caused the Ark of the LORD
to go round the city, making the circuit of it once, and then they went back
12 to the camp and spent the night there. Joshua rose early in the morning and
13 the priests took up the Ark of the LORD. The seven priests carrying the
seven trumpets of ram's horn went marching in front of the Ark of the
LORD, blowing the trumpets as they went, with the drafted men in front
of them and the rearguard following the Ark of the LORD, the trumpets
14 sounding as they marched. They marched round the city once on the
15 second day and returned to the camp; this they did for six days. But on the
seventh day they rose at dawn and marched seven times round the city in
the same way; that was the only day on which they marched round seven
16 times. The seventh time the priests blew the trumpets and Joshua said to
17 the army, 'Shout! The LORD has given you the city. The city shall be under
solemn ban: everything in it belongs to the LORD. No one is to be spared
except the prostitute Rahab and everyone who is with her in the house,
18 because she hid the men whom we sent. And you must beware of coveting
anything that is forbidden under the ban; you must take none of it for
yourselves; this would put the Israelite camp itself under the ban and
19 bring trouble on it. All the silver and gold, all the vessels of copper and iron,
shall be holy; they belong to the LORD and they must go into the LORD's
20 treasury.' So they blew the trumpets, and when the army heard the
trumpet sound, they raised a great shout, and down fell the walls. The
21 army advanced on the city, every man straight ahead, and took it. Under
the ban they destroyed everything in the city; they put everyone to
the sword, men and women, young and old, and also cattle, sheep, and
asses.
22      But the two men who had been sent out as spies were told by Joshua to
go into the prostitute's house and bring out her and all who belonged to
23 her, as they had sworn to do. So the young men went and brought out
Rahab, her father and mother, her brothers and all who belonged to her.
They brought out the whole family and left them outside the Israelite
24 camp. They then set fire to the city and everything in it, except that they
deposited the silver and gold and the vessels of copper and iron in the
25 treasury of the LORD's house. Thus Joshua spared the lives of Rahab the
prostitute, her household and all who belonged to her, because she had
hidden the men whom Joshua had sent to Jericho as spies; she and her
26 family settled permanently among the Israelites. It was then that Joshua
laid this curse on Jericho:

> May the LORD's curse light on the man who comes forward
>      to rebuild this city of Jericho:
> the laying of its foundations shall cost him his eldest son,
> the setting up of its gates shall cost him his youngest.

Thus the LORD was with Joshua, and his fame spread throughout the 27 country.

But the Israelites defied the ban: Achan son of Carmi, son of Zabdi, son 7 of Zerah, of the tribe of Judah, took some of the forbidden things, and the LORD was angry with the Israelites.

Joshua sent men from Jericho with orders to go up to Ai, near Beth-2 aven, east of Bethel, and see how the land lay; so the men went up and explored Ai. They returned to Joshua and reported that there was no need 3 for the whole army to move: 'Let some two or three thousand men go forward to attack Ai. Do not make the whole army toil up there; the population is small.' And so about three thousand men went up, but they turned 4 tail before the men of Ai, who killed some thirty-six of them; they chased 5 them all the way from the gate to the Quarries*a* and killed them on the pass. At this the courage of the people melted and flowed away like water. Joshua and the elders of Israel rent their clothes and flung themselves face 6 downwards to the ground; they lay before the Ark of the LORD till evening and threw dust on their heads. Joshua said, 'Alas, O Lord GOD, why didst 7 thou bring this people across the Jordan only to hand us over to the Amorites to be destroyed? If only we had been content to settle on the other side of the Jordan! I beseech thee, O Lord; what can I say, now that 8 Israel has been routed by the enemy? When the Canaanites and all the 9 natives of the country hear of this, they will come swarming around us and wipe us off the face of the earth. What wilt thou do then for the honour of thy great name?'

The LORD said to Joshua, 'Stand up; why lie prostrate on your face? 10 Israel has sinned: they have broken the covenant which I laid upon them, 11 by taking forbidden things for themselves. They have stolen them, and concealed it by mingling them with their own possessions. That is why the 12 Israelites cannot stand against their enemies: they are put to flight because they have brought themselves under the ban. Unless they destroy every single thing among them that is forbidden under the ban, I will be with them no longer. Stand up; you must hallow the people; tell them they must 13 hallow themselves for tomorrow. Tell them, These are the words of the LORD the God of Israel: You have forbidden things among you, Israel; you cannot stand against your enemies until you have rid yourselves of them. In the morning come forward tribe by tribe, and the tribe which the 14 LORD chooses shall come forward clan by clan; the clan which the LORD chooses shall come forward family by family; and the family which the LORD chooses shall come forward man by man. The man who is chosen as 15 the harbourer of forbidden things shall be burnt, he and all that is his, because he has broken the covenant of the LORD and committed outrage in Israel.' Early in the morning Joshua rose and brought Israel forward tribe 16 by tribe, and the tribe of Judah was chosen. He brought forward the clans 17 of Judah, and the clan of Zerah was chosen; then the clan of Zerah family by family, and the family of Zabdi was chosen. He brought that family 18 forward man by man, and Achan son of Carmi, son of Zabdi, son of Zerah, of the tribe of Judah, was chosen. Then Joshua said to Achan, 'My 19

*a Or to Shebarim.*

20 son, give honour to the LORD the God of Israel and make your confession to him: tell me what you have done, hide nothing from me.' Achan answered Joshua, 'I confess, I have sinned against the LORD the God of Israel. This
21 is what I did: among the booty I caught sight of a fine mantle from Shinar, two hundred shekels of silver, and a bar of gold weighing fifty shekels. I coveted them and I took them. You will find them hidden in the ground
22 inside my tent, with the silver underneath.' So Joshua sent messengers, who ran to the tent, and there was the stuff *a* hidden in the tent with the
23 silver underneath. They took the things from the tent, brought them to
24 Joshua and all the Israelites, and spread them out before the LORD. Then Joshua took Achan son of Zerah, with the silver, the mantle, and the bar of gold, together with his sons and daughters, his oxen, his asses, and his sheep, his tent, and everything he had, and he and all Israel brought them
25 up to the Vale of Achor. *b* Joshua said, 'What trouble you have brought on us! Now the LORD will bring trouble on you.' Then all the Israelites stoned
26 him to death; and they raised a great pile of stones over him, which remains to this day. So the LORD's anger was abated. That is why to this day that place is called the Vale of Achor.

8 THE LORD SAID TO JOSHUA, 'Do not be fearful or dismayed; take the whole army and attack Ai. I deliver the king of Ai into your hands, him
2 and his people, his city and his country. Deal with Ai and her king as you dealt with Jericho and her king; but you may keep for yourselves the cattle and any other spoil that you may take. Set an ambush for the city to the
3 west of it.' So Joshua and all the army prepared for the assault on Ai. He
4 chose thirty thousand fighting men and dispatched them by night, with these orders: 'Lie in ambush to the west of the city, not far from it, and all
5 of you hold yourselves in readiness. I myself will approach the city with the rest of the army, and when the enemy come out to meet us as they did
6 last time, we shall take to flight before them. Then they will come out and pursue us until we have drawn them away from the city, thinking that we
7 have taken to flight as we did last time. While we are in flight, come out from your ambush and occupy the city; the LORD your God will deliver it
8 into your hands. When you have taken it, set it on fire. Thus you will do
9 what the LORD commands. These are your orders.' So Joshua sent them off, and they went to the place of ambush and waited between Bethel and Ai to the west of Ai, while Joshua spent the night with the army.
10     Early in the morning Joshua rose, mustered the army and marched
11 against Ai, he himself and the elders of Israel at its head. All the armed forces with him marched on until they came within sight of the city. They
12 encamped north of Ai, with the valley between them and the city; but Joshua took some five thousand men and set them in ambush between
14 Bethel and Ai to the west of the city. *c* When the king of Ai saw them, he and the citizens rose with all speed that morning and marched out to do battle against Israel; he did not know that there was an ambush set for him

---

*a Or* the mantle.      *b That is* Trouble.      *c So Sept.; Heb. adds* (13) So the army pitched camp to the north of the city, and the rearguard to the west, while Joshua went that night into the valley.

to the west of the city. Joshua and all the Israelites made as if they were 15
routed by them and fled towards the wilderness, and all the people in the 16
city were called out in pursuit. So they pursued Joshua and were drawn
away from the city. Not a man was left in Ai; they had all gone out 17
in pursuit of the Israelites and during the pursuit had left the city
undefended.

Then the LORD said to Joshua, 'Point towards Ai with the dagger you 18
are holding, for I will deliver the city into your hands.' So Joshua pointed
with his dagger towards Ai. At his signal, the men in ambush rose quickly 19
from their places and, entering the city at a run, took it and promptly set fire
to it. The men of Ai looked back and saw the smoke from the city already 20
going up to the sky; they were powerless to make their escape in any direction, and the Israelites who had feigned flight towards the wilderness turned
on their pursuers. For when Joshua and all the Israelites saw that the 21
ambush had seized the city and that smoke was already going up from it,
they turned and fell upon the men of Ai. Those who had come out to meet 22
the Israelites were now hemmed in with Israelites on both sides of them,
and the Israelites cut them down until there was not a single survivor, nor
had any escaped. The king of Ai was taken alive and brought to Joshua. 23
When the Israelites had cut down to the last man all the citizens of Ai who 24
were in the open country or in the wilderness to which they had pursued
them, and the massacre was complete, they all turned back to Ai and put it
to the sword. The number who were killed that day, men and women, was 25
twelve thousand, the whole population of Ai. Joshua held out his dagger 26
and did not draw back his hand until he had put to death all who lived in
Ai; but the Israelites kept for themselves the cattle and any other spoil that 27
they took, following the word of the LORD spoken to Joshua. So Joshua 28
burnt Ai to the ground, and left it the desolate ruined mound it remains to
this day. He hanged the king of Ai on a tree and left him there till sunset; 29
and when the sun had set, he gave the order and they cut him down and
flung down his body at the entrance of the city gate. Over the body they
raised a great pile of stones, which is there to this day.

At that time Joshua built an altar to the LORD the God of Israel on Mount 30
Ebal. The altar was of blocks of undressed stone on which no tool of iron 31
had been used, following the commands given to the Israelites by Moses the
servant of the LORD, as is described in the book of the law of Moses. At the
altar they offered whole-offerings to the LORD, and slaughtered shared-
offerings. There in the presence of the Israelites he engraved on blocks *a* of 32
stone a copy of the law of Moses. And all Israel, elders, officers, and judges, 33
took their stand on either side of the Ark, facing the levitical priests who
carried the Ark of the Covenant of the LORD—all Israel, native and alien
alike. Half of them stood facing Mount Gerizim and half facing Mount
Ebal, to fulfil the command of Moses the servant of the LORD that the
blessing should be pronounced first. Then Joshua recited the whole of the 34
blessing and the cursing word by word, as they are written in the book of
the law. There was not a single word of all that Moses had commanded 35
which he did not read aloud before the whole congregation of Israel,

*a* Or *on the blocks.*

including the women and dependants and the aliens resident in their company.

9 When the news of these happenings reached all the kings west of the Jordan, in the hill-country, the Shephelah, and all the coast of the Great Sea running up to the Lebanon, the kings of the Hittites, Amorites,

2 Canaanites, Perizzites, Hivites, and Jebusites agreed to join forces and fight against Joshua and Israel.

3 When the inhabitants of Gibeon heard how Joshua had dealt with

4 Jericho and Ai, they adopted a ruse of their own. They went and disguised themselves, with old sacking for their asses, old wine-skins split and

5 mended, old and patched sandals for their feet, old clothing to wear, and by

6 way of provisions nothing but dry and mouldy bread. They came to Joshua in the camp at Gilgal and said to him and the Israelites, 'We have come from

7 a distant country to ask you now to grant us a treaty.' The Israelites said to the Hivites, 'But maybe you live in our neighbourhood: if so, how can we

8 grant you a treaty?' They said to Joshua, 'We are your slaves.' Joshua asked

9 them who they were and where they came from. 'Sir,' they replied, 'our country is very far away, and we have come because of the renown of the LORD your God. We have heard of his fame, of all that he did to Egypt,

10 and to the two Amorite kings east of the Jordan, Sihon king of Heshbon

11 and Og king of Bashan who lived at Ashtaroth. Our elders and all the people of our country told us to take provisions for the journey and come

12 to meet you, and say, "We are your slaves; please grant us a treaty." Look at our bread; it was hot from the oven when we packed it at home on the

13 day we came away. Now it is dry and mouldy. Look at the wine-skins; they were new when we filled them, and now they are all split; look at our clothes

14 and our sandals, worn out by the long journey.' The chief men of the community accepted some of their provisions, and did not at first seek guidance

15 from the LORD. So Joshua received them peaceably and granted them a treaty, promising to spare their lives, and the chiefs pledged their faith to them on oath.

16 Within three days of granting them the treaty, the Israelites learnt that

17 they were in fact neighbours and lived near by. So the Israelites set out and on the third day they reached their cities; these were Gibeon, Kephirah,

18 Beeroth, and Kiriath-jearim. The Israelites did not slaughter them, because of the oath which the chief men of the community had sworn to them by the LORD the God of Israel, but the people were all indignant with their

19 chiefs. The chiefs all replied to the assembled people, 'But we swore an oath to them by the LORD the God of Israel; we cannot touch them now.

20 What we will do is this: we will spare their lives so that the oath which we

21 swore to them may bring no harm upon us. But though their lives must be spared, they shall be set to chop wood and draw water for the com-

22 munity.' The people agreed to do as their chiefs had said. Joshua summoned the Gibeonites and said, 'Why did you play this trick on us? You told us

23 that you live a long way off, when you are near neighbours. There is a curse upon you for this: for all time you shall provide us with slaves, to

24 chop wood and draw water for the house of my God.' They answered Joshua, 'We were told, sir, that the LORD your God had commanded Moses

his servant to give you the whole country and to exterminate all its inhabitants; so because of you we were in terror of our lives, and that is why we did this. We are in your power: do with us whatever you think right and proper.' What he did was this: he saved them from death at the hands of the Israelites, and they did not kill them; but thenceforward he set them to chop wood and draw water for the community and for the altar of the LORD. And to this day they do it at the place which the LORD chose. 25 26 27

When Adoni-zedek king of Jerusalem heard that Joshua had captured **10** Ai and destroyed it (for Joshua had dealt with Ai and her king as he had dealt with Jericho and her king), and that the inhabitants of Gibeon had made their peace with Israel and were living among them, he was greatly 2 alarmed; for Gibeon was a large place, like a royal city: it was larger than Ai, and its men were all good fighters. So Adoni-zedek king of Jerusalem 3 sent to Hoham king of Hebron, Piram king of Jarmuth, Japhia king of Lachish, and Debir king of Eglon, and said, 'Come up and help me, and 4 we will attack the Gibeonites, because they have made their peace with Joshua and the Israelites.' So the five Amorite kings, the kings of Jerusalem, 5 Hebron, Jarmuth, Lachish, and Eglon, joined forces and advanced to take up their positions for the attack on Gibeon. But the men of Gibeon sent 6 this message to Joshua in the camp at Gilgal: 'We are your slaves, do not abandon us, come quickly to our relief. All the Amorite kings in the hill-country have joined forces against us; come and help us.' So Joshua went 7 up from Gilgal with all his forces and all his fighting men. The LORD said 8 to Joshua, 'Do not be afraid of them; I have delivered them into your hands, and not a man will be able to stand against you.' Joshua came upon them 9 suddenly, after marching all night from Gilgal. The LORD threw them into 10 confusion before the Israelites, and Joshua defeated them utterly in Gibeon; he pursued them down the pass of Beth-horon and kept up the slaughter as far as Azekah and Makkedah. As they were fleeing from Israel down the 11 pass, the LORD hurled great hailstones at them out of the sky all the way to Azekah: more died from the hailstones than the Israelites slew by the sword.

On that day when the LORD delivered the Amorites into the hands of 12 Israel, Joshua spoke with the LORD, and he said in the presence of Israel:

> Stand still, O Sun, in Gibeon;
> stand, Moon, in the Vale of Aijalon.

So the sun stood still and the moon halted until a nation had taken vengeance 13 on its enemies, as indeed is written in the Book of Jashar.[a] The sun stayed in mid heaven and made no haste to set for almost a whole day. Never 14 before or since has there been such a day as this day on which the LORD listened to the voice of a man; for the LORD fought for Israel. So Joshua 15 and all the Israelites returned to the camp at Gilgal.

The five kings fled and hid themselves in a cave at Makkedah, and 16 17 Joshua was told that they had been found hidden in this cave. Joshua 18 replied, 'Roll some great stones to the mouth of the cave and post men there to keep watch over the kings. But you must not stay; keep up the 19

[a] Or the Book of the Upright.

pursuit, attack your enemies from the rear and do not let them reach their
20 cities; the LORD your God has delivered them into your hands.' When
Joshua and the Israelites had finished the work of slaughter and all had
been put to the sword—except a few survivors who escaped and entered
21 the fortified cities—the whole army rejoined Joshua at Makkedah in peace;
not a man of the Israelites suffered so much as a scratch on his tongue.
22 Then Joshua said, 'Open the mouth of the cave, and bring me out those
23 five kings.' They did so; they brought the five kings out of the cave, the
24 kings of Jerusalem, Hebron, Jarmuth, Lachish, and Eglon. When they
had brought them to Joshua, he summoned all the Israelites and said to
the commanders of the troops who had served with him, 'Come forward
and put your feet on the necks of these kings.' So they came forward and
25 put their feet on their necks. Joshua said to them, 'Do not be fearful or
dismayed; be strong and resolute; for the LORD will do this to every enemy
26 you fight against.' And he struck down the kings and slew them; then he
hung their bodies on five trees, where they remained hanging till evening.
27 At sunset, on Joshua's orders they took them down from the trees and
threw them into the cave in which they had hidden; they piled great stones
against its mouth, and there the stones are to this day.*a*

28    On that same day, Joshua captured Makkedah and put both king and
people to the sword, destroying both them and every living thing in the
city. He left no survivor, and he dealt with the king of Makkedah as he
29 had dealt with the king of Jericho. Then Joshua and all the Israelites
30 marched on from Makkedah to Libnah and attacked it. The LORD delivered the city and its king to the Israelites, and they put its people and
every living thing in it to the sword; they left no survivor there, and dealt
31 with its king as they had dealt with the king of Jericho. From Libnah
Joshua and all the Israelites marched on to Lachish, took up their positions
32 and attacked it. The LORD delivered Lachish into their hands; they took
it on the second day and put every living thing in it to the sword, as they
had done at Libnah.

33    Meanwhile Horam king of Gezer had advanced to the relief of Lachish;
but Joshua struck them down, both king and people, and not a man of
34 them survived. Then Joshua and all the Israelites marched on from Lachish
35 to Eglon, took up their positions and attacked it; that same day they captured it and put its inhabitants to the sword, destroying every living thing
36 in it as they had done at Lachish. From Eglon Joshua and all the Israelites
37 advanced to Hebron and attacked it. They captured it and put its king to
the sword together with every living thing in it and in all its villages; as at
38 Eglon, he left no survivor, destroying it and every living thing in it. Then
Joshua and all the Israelites wheeled round towards Debir and attacked it.
39 They captured the city with its king, and all its villages, put them to the
sword and destroyed every living thing; they left no survivor. They dealt
with Debir and its king as they had dealt with Hebron and with Libnah
and its king.

40    So Joshua massacred the population of the whole region—the hill-
country, the Negeb, the Shephelah, the watersheds—and all their kings.

*a* and there . . . day: *or* on this very day.

He left no survivor, destroying everything that drew breath, as the LORD the God of Israel had commanded. Joshua carried the slaughter from 41 Kadesh-barnea to Gaza, over the whole land of Goshen and as far as Gibeon. All these kings he captured at the same time, and their country 42 with them, for the LORD the God of Israel fought for Israel. And Joshua 43 returned with all the Israelites to the camp at Gilgal.

When Jabin king of Hazor heard of all this, he sent to Jobab king of 11 Madon, to the kings of Shimron and Akshaph, to the northern kings in the 2 hill-country, in the Arabah opposite Kinnereth, in the Shephelah, and in the district of Dor on the west, the Canaanites to the east and the west, the 3 Amorites, Hittites, Perizzites, and Jebusites in the hill-country, and the Hivites below Hermon in the land of Mizpah. They took the field with all 4 their forces, a great horde countless as the grains of sand on the sea-shore, among them a great number of horses and chariots. All these kings made 5 common cause, and came and encamped at the waters of Merom to fight against Israel. The LORD said to Joshua, 'Do not be afraid of them, for at 6 this time tomorrow I shall deliver them to Israel all dead men; you shall hamstring their horses and burn their chariots.' So Joshua and his army 7 surprised them by the waters of Merom and fell upon them. The LORD 8 delivered them into the hands of Israel; they struck them down and pursued them as far as Greater Sidon, Misrephoth on the west, and the Vale of Mizpah on the east. They struck them down until not a man was left alive. Joshua dealt with them as the LORD had commanded: he hamstrung their 9 horses and burnt their chariots.

At this point Joshua turned his forces against Hazor, formerly the head 10 of all these kingdoms. He captured the city and put its king to death with the sword. They killed every living thing in it and wiped them all out; they 11 spared nothing that drew breath, and Hazor itself they destroyed by fire. So Joshua captured these kings and their cities and put them to the sword, 12 destroying them all, as Moses the servant of the LORD had commanded. The cities whose ruined mounds are still standing were not burnt by the 13 Israelites; it was Hazor alone that Joshua burnt. The Israelites plundered 14 all these cities and kept for themselves the cattle and any other spoil they took; but they put every living soul to the sword until they had destroyed every one; they did not leave alive any one that drew breath. The LORD 15 laid his commands on his servant Moses, and Moses laid these same commands on Joshua, and Joshua carried them out. Not one of the commands laid on Moses by the LORD did he leave unfulfilled.

And so Joshua took the whole country, the hill-country, all the Negeb, 16 all the land of Goshen, the Shephelah, the Arabah, and the Israelite hill-country with the adjoining lowlands. His conquests extended from the 17 bare mountain which leads up to Seir as far as Baal-gad in the Vale of Lebanon under Mount Hermon. He took prisoner all their kings, struck them down and put them to death. It was a long war that he fought 18 against all these kingdoms. Except for the Hivites who lived in Gibeon, 19 not one of their cities came to terms with the Israelites; all were taken by storm. It was the LORD's purpose that they should offer an obstin- 20 ate resistance to the Israelites in battle, and that thus they should be annihilated without mercy and utterly destroyed,[a] as the LORD had commanded Moses.

21 It was then that Joshua proceeded to wipe out the Anakim from the hill-country, from Hebron, Debir, Anab, all the hill-country of Judah and

22 all the hill-country of Israel, destroying both them and their cities. No Anakim were left in the land taken by the Israelites; they survived only in Gaza, Gath, and Ashdod.

23 Thus Joshua took the whole country, fulfilling all the commands that the LORD had laid on Moses; he assigned it as Israel's patrimony, allotting to each tribe its share; and the land was at peace.

12 These are the names of the kings of the land whom the Israelites slew, and whose territory they occupied beyond the Jordan towards the sunrise from the gorge of the Arnon as far as Mount Hermon and all the Arabah

2 on the east. Sihon the Amorite king who lived in Heshbon: his rule extended from Aroer, which is on the edge of the gorge of the Arnon, along the middle of the gorge and over half Gilead as far as the gorge of the Jabbok,

3 the Ammonite frontier; along the Arabah as far as the eastern side of the Sea of Kinnereth and as far as the eastern side of the Sea of the Arabah, the Dead Sea, by the road to Beth-jeshimoth and from Teman under the

4 watershed of Pisgah. Og king of Bashan, one of the survivors of the Reph-

5 aim, who lived in Ashtaroth and Edrei: he ruled over Mount Hermon, Salcah, all Bashan as far as the Geshurite and Maacathite borders, and half

6 Gilead as far as the boundary of Sihon king of Heshbon. Moses the servant of the LORD put them to death, he and the Israelites, and he gave their land to the Reubenites, the Gadites, and half the tribe of Manasseh, as their possession.

7 These are the names of the kings whom Joshua and the Israelites put to death beyond the Jordan to the west, from Baal-gad in the Vale of Lebanon as far as the bare mountain that leads up to Seir. Joshua gave their land to the Israelite tribes to be their possession according to their allotted shares,

8 in the hill-country, the Shephelah, the Arabah, the watersheds, the wilderness, and the Negeb; lands of the Hittites, Amorites, Canaanites, Perizzites,

9 Hivites, and Jebusites. The king of Jericho; the king of Ai which is beside

10 11 Bethel; the king of Jerusalem; the king of Hebron; the king of Jarmuth;

12 13 the king of Lachish; the king of Eglon; the king of Gezer; the king of

14 15 Debir; the king of Geder; the king of Hormah; the king of Arad; the king

16 of Libnah; the king of Adullam; the king of Makkedah; the king of Bethel;

17 18 the king of Tappuah; the king of Hepher; the king of Aphek; the king of

19 20 Aphek[b]-in-Sharon; the king of Madon; the king of Hazor; the king

21 of Shimron-meron; the king of Akshaph; the king of Taanach; the king

22 23 of Megiddo; the king of Kedesh; the king of Jokneam-in-Carmel; the

24 king of Dor in the district of Dor; the king of Gaiam-in-Galilee; the king of Tirzah: thirty-one kings in all, one of each town.

---

[a] offer . . . destroyed: or obstinately engage the Israelites in battle so that they should annihilate them without mercy, only that he might destroy them . . .     [b] of Aphek: *prob. rdg.; Heb. om.*

## The division of the land among the tribes

B Y THIS TIME JOSHUA HAD BECOME VERY OLD, and the LORD said 13
to him, 'You are now a very old man, and much of the country remains
to be occupied. The country which remains is this: all the districts of the 2
Philistines and all the Geshurite country (this is reckoned as Canaanite 3
territory from Shihor to the east of Egypt as far north as Ekron; and it
belongs to the five lords of the Philistines, those of Gaza, Ashdod, Ashkelon,
Gath, and Ekron); all the districts of the Avvim on the south; all the 4
Canaanite country from the low-lying land which belongs to the Sidonians
as far as Aphek, the Amorite frontier; the land of the Gebalites and all the 5
Lebanon to the east from Baal-gad under Mount Hermon as far as Lebo-
hamath. I will drive out in favour of the Israelites all the inhabitants of the 6
hill-country from the Lebanon as far as Misrephoth on the west, and all
the Sidonians. In the mean time you are to allot all this to the Israelites for
their patrimony, as I have commanded you. Distribute this land now to the 7
nine tribes and half the tribe of Manasseh for their patrimony.' For half 8
the tribe of Manasseh and *a* with them the Reubenites and the Gadites
had each taken their patrimony which Moses gave them east of the Jordan,
as Moses the servant of the LORD had ordained. It started from Aroer 9
which is by the edge of the gorge of the Arnon, and the level land half-way
along the gorge, and included all the tableland from Medeba as far as
Dibon; all the cities of Sihon, the Amorite king who ruled in Heshbon, as 10
far as the Ammonite frontier; and it also included Gilead and the Geshurite 11
and Maacathite territory, and all Mount Hermon and the whole of Bashan
as far as Salcah, all the kingdom of Og which he ruled from both Ashtaroth 12
and Edrei in Bashan. He was a survivor of the remnant of the Rephaim,
but Moses put them both to death and occupied their lands. But the 13
Israelites did not drive out the Geshurites and the Maacathites; the
Geshurites and the Maacathites live among the Israelites to this day.
The tribe of Levi, however, received no patrimony; the LORD the God of 14
Israel is their patrimony, as he promised them.
So Moses allotted territory to the tribe of the Reubenites family by 15
family. Their territory started from Aroer which is by the edge of the gorge 16
of the Arnon, and the level land half-way along the gorge, and included all
the tableland as far as Medeba; Heshbon and all its cities on the tableland, 17
Dibon, Bamoth-baal, Beth-baal-meon, Jahaz, Kedemoth, Mephaath, 18
Kiriathaim, Sibmah, Zereth-shahar on the hill in the Vale, Beth-peor, the 19 20
watershed of Pisgah, and Beth-jeshimoth, all the cities of the tableland, all 21
the kingdom of Sihon the Amorite king who ruled in Heshbon, whom
Moses put to death together with the princes of Midian, Evi, Rekem, Zur,
Hur, and Reba, the vassals of Sihon who dwelt in the country. Balaam son 22
of Beor, who practised augury, was among those whom the Israelites put
to the sword. The boundary of the Reubenites was the Jordan and the 23
adjacent land: this is the patrimony of the Reubenites family by family,
both the cities and their hamlets.
Moses allotted territory to the Gadites family by family. Their territory 24 25

*a* For half . . . Manasseh and: *prob. rdg.; Heb. om.*

26 was Jazer, all the cities of Gilead and half the Ammonite country as far as Aroer which is east of Rabbah. It reached from Heshbon as far as Ramoth-mizpeh and Betonim, and from Mahanaim as far as the boundary of Lo-

27 debar; it included in the valley Beth-haram, Beth-nimrah, Succoth, and Zaphon, the rest of the kingdom of Sihon king of Heshbon. The boundary was the Jordan and the adjacent land as far as the end of the Sea of Kinnereth

28 east of the Jordan. This is the patrimony of the Gadites family by family, both the cities and their hamlets.

29 Moses allotted territory to the half tribe of Manasseh: it was for half the

30 tribe of the Manassites family by family. Their territory ran from Mahanaim and included all Bashan, all the kingdom of Og king of Bashan and all

31 Havvoth-jair in Bashan—sixty cities. Half Gilead, and Ashtaroth and Edrei the royal cities of Og in Bashan, belong to the sons of Machir son of Manasseh on behalf of half the Machirites family by family.

32 These are the territories which Moses allotted to the tribes as their

33 patrimonies in the lowlands of Moab east of the Jordan. But to the tribe of Levi he gave no patrimony: the LORD the God of Israel is their patrimony, as he promised them.

14 Now follow the possessions which the Israelites acquired in the land of Canaan, as Eleazar the priest, Joshua son of Nun, and the heads of the

2 families of the Israelite tribes allotted them. They were assigned by lot, following the LORD's command given through Moses, to the nine and a

3 half tribes. To two and a half tribes Moses had given patrimonies beyond

4 the Jordan; but he gave none to the Levites as he did to the others. The tribe of Joseph formed the two tribes of Manasseh and Ephraim. The Levites were given no share in the land, only cities to dwell in, with their

5 common land for flocks and herds. So the Israelites, following the LORD's command given to Moses, assigned the land.

6 Now the tribe of Judah had come to Joshua in Gilgal, and Caleb son of Jephunneh the Kenizzite said to him, 'You remember what the LORD said

7 to Moses the man of God concerning you and me at Kadesh-barnea. I was forty years old when Moses the servant of the LORD sent me from there to

8 explore the land, and I brought back an honest report. The others who went with me discouraged the people, but I loyally carried out the purpose of

9 the LORD my God. Moses swore an oath that day and said, "The land on which you have set foot shall be your patrimony and your sons' after you as a possession for ever; for you have loyally carried out the purpose of the

10 LORD my God." Well, the LORD has spared my life as he promised; it is now forty-five years since he made this promise to Moses, at the time when Israel was journeying in the wilderness. Today I am eighty-five years old.

11 I am still as strong as I was on the day when Moses sent me out; I am as fit

12 now for war as I was then and am ready to take the field again. Give me today this hill-country which the LORD then promised me. You heard on that day that the Anakim were there and their cities were large and well fortified. Perhaps the LORD will be with me and I shall dispossess them as

13 he promised.' Joshua blessed Caleb and gave him Hebron for his patri-

14 mony, and that is why Hebron remains to this day in the patrimony of Caleb son of Jephunneh the Kenizzite. It is because he loyally carried out

the purpose of the LORD the God of Israel. Formerly the name of Hebron 15
was Kiriath-arba. This Arba was the chief man of the Anakim. And the
land was at peace.

This is the territory allotted to the tribe of the sons of Judah family by 15
family. It started from the Edomite frontier at the wilderness of Zin and
ran as far as the Negeb at its southern end, and it had a common border 2
with the Negeb at the end of the Dead Sea, where an inlet of water bends
towards the Negeb. It continued from the south by the ascent of Akrabbim, 3
passed by Zin, went up from the south of Kadesh-barnea, passed by Hezron,
went on to Addar and turned round to Karka. It then passed along to 4
Azmon, reached the Torrent of Egypt, and its limit was the sea. This was
their southern boundary.

The eastern boundary is the Dead Sea as far as the mouth of the Jordan 5
and the adjacent land northwards from the inlet of the sea, at the mouth of
the Jordan. The boundary goes up to Beth-hoglah; it passes north of 6
Beth-arabah and thence to the stone of Bohan son of Reuben, thence to 7
Debir from the Vale of Achor, and then turns north to the districts *a* in
front of the ascent of Adummim south of the gorge. The boundary then
passes the waters of En-shemesh and the limit there is En-rogel. It then 8
goes up by the Valley of Ben-hinnom to the southern slope of the Jebusites
(that is Jerusalem). Thence it goes up to the top of the hill which faces the
Valley of Hinnom on the west; this is at the northern end of the Vale of
Rephaim. The boundary then bends round from the top of the hill to the 9
spring of the waters of Nephtoah, runs round to the cities of Mount
Ephron and round to Baalah, that is Kiriath-jearim. It then continues 10
westwards from Baalah to Mount Seir, passes on to the north side of the
slope of Mount Jearim, that is Kesalon, down to Beth-shemesh and on to
Timnah. The boundary then goes north to the slope of Ekron, bends round 11
to Shikkeron, crosses to Mount Baalah and reaches Jabneel; its limit is the
sea. The western boundary is the Great Sea and the land adjacent. This is 12
the whole circuit of the boundary of the tribe of Judah family by family.

Caleb son of Jephunneh received his share of the land within the tribe 13
of Judah as the LORD had said to Joshua. It was Kiriath-arba, that is
Hebron. This Arba was the ancestor of the Anakim. Caleb drove out the 14
three Anakim: these were Sheshai, Ahiman and Talmai, descendants of
Anak. From there he attacked the inhabitants of Debir; the name of Debir 15
was formerly Kiriath-sepher. Caleb announced that whoever should 16
attack Kiriath-sepher and capture it would receive his daughter Achsah in
marriage. Othniel, son of Caleb's brother Kenaz, captured it, and Caleb 17
gave him his daughter Achsah. When she came to him, he incited her to 18
ask her father for a piece of land. As she sat on the ass, she broke wind, and
Caleb asked her, 'What did you mean by that?' She replied, 'I want a 19
favour from you. You have put me in this dry Negeb; you must give me
pools of water as well.' So Caleb gave her the upper pool and the lower pool.

This is the patrimony of the tribe of the sons of Judah family by family. 20
These are the cities belonging to the tribe of Judah, the full count. By the 21
Edomite frontier in the Negeb: Kabzeel, Eder, Jagur, Kinah, Dimonah, 22

---

*a* *Prob. rdg., cp. 18. 17; Heb. to Gilgal.*

23 24 25 Ararah,[a] Kedesh, Hazor, Ithnan, Ziph, Telem, Bealoth, Hazor-hadattah,
26 27 Kerioth-hezron, Amam, Shema, Moladah, Hazar-gaddah, Heshmon,
28 29 Beth-pelet, Hazar-shual, Beersheba and its villages, Baalah, Iyim, Ezem,
30 31 32 Eltolad, Kesil, Hormah, Ziklag, Madmannah, Sansannah, Lebaoth, Shilhim, Ain, and Rimmon: in all, twenty-nine cities with their hamlets.
33 34 In the Shephelah: Eshtaol, Zorah, Ashnah, Zanoah, En-gannim,
35 36 Tappuah, Enam, Jarmuth, Adullam, Socoh, Azekah, Shaaraim, Adithaim, Gederah, namely both parts of Gederah: fourteen cities with their hamlets.
37 38 39 Zenan, Hadashah, Migdal-gad, Dilan, Mizpeh, Joktheel, Lachish, Boz-
40 41 kath, Eglon, Cabbon, Lahmas, Kithlish, Gederoth, Beth-dagon, Naamah,
42 and Makkedah: sixteen cities with their hamlets. Libnah, Ether, Ashan,
43 44 Jiphtah, Ashnah, Nezib, Keilah, Achzib, and Mareshah: nine cities with
45 46 their hamlets. Ekron, with its villages and hamlets, and from Ekron west-
47 wards, all the cities near Ashdod and their hamlets. Ashdod with its villages and hamlets, Gaza with its villages and hamlets as far as the Torrent of Egypt and the Great Sea and the land adjacent.
48 49 In the hill-country: Shamir, Jattir, Socoh, Dannah, Kiriath-sannah,
50 51 that is Debir, Anab, Eshtemoh, Anim, Goshen, Holon, and Giloh: eleven
52 53 cities in all with their hamlets. Arab, Dumah, Eshan, Janim, Beth-
54 tappuah, Aphek,[b] Humtah, Kiriath-arba, that is Hebron, and Zior: nine
55 56 cities in all with their hamlets. Maon, Carmel, Ziph, Juttah, Jezreel,
57 Jokdeam, Zanoah, Cain, Gibeah, and Timnah: ten cities in all with their
58 59 hamlets. Halhul, Beth-zur, Gedor, Maarath, Beth-anoth, and Eltekon: six cities in all with their hamlets. Tekoa, Ephrathah, that is Bethlehem, Peor, Etam, Culom, Tatam, Sores, Carem, Gallim, Baither, and Manach:
60 eleven cities in all with their hamlets. Kiriath-baal, that is Kiriath-jearim, and Rabbah: two cities with their hamlets.
61 62 In the wilderness: Beth-arabah, Middin, Secacah, Nibshan, Ir-melach, and En-gedi: six cities with their hamlets.
63 At Jerusalem, the men of Judah were unable to drive out the Jebusites who lived there, and to this day Jebusites and men of Judah live together in Jerusalem.

**16** This is the lot that fell to the sons of Joseph: the boundary runs from the Jordan at Jericho, east of the waters of Jericho by the wilderness, and goes
2 up from Jericho into the hill-country to Bethel. It runs on from Bethel to
3 Luz and crosses the Archite border at Ataroth.[c] Westwards it descends to the boundary of the Japhletites as far as the boundary of Lower Beth-
4 horon and Gezer; its limit is the sea. Here Manasseh and Ephraim the sons of Joseph received their patrimony.
5 This was the boundary of the Ephraimites family by family: their
6 eastern boundary ran from Ataroth-addar up to Upper Beth-horon. It continued westwards to Michmethath on the north, going round by the
7 east of Taanath-shiloh and passing by it on the east of Janoah. It descends from Janoah to Ataroth and Naarath, touches Jericho and continues to the
8 Jordan, and from Tappuah it goes westwards by the gorge of Kanah; and its limit is the sea. This is the patrimony of the tribe of Ephraim family by

---

[a] *Prob. rdg.; Heb.* Adadah.     [b] *Or* Aphekah.     [c] Ataroth-addar *in 16. 5; 18. 13.*

family. There were also cities reserved for the Ephraimites within the 9
patrimony of the Manassites, each of these cities with its hamlets. They 10
did not however drive out the Canaanites who dwelt in Gezer; the Canaanites have lived among the Ephraimites to the present day but have been
subject to forced labour in perpetuity.

This is the territory allotted to the tribe of Manasseh, Joseph's eldest 17
son. Machir was Manasseh's eldest son and father of Gilead, a fighting
man; Gilead and Bashan were allotted to him.

The rest of the Manassites family by family were the sons of Abiezer, 2
the sons of Helek, the sons of Asriel, the sons of Shechem, the sons of
Hepher, and the sons of Shemida; these were the male offspring of Manasseh son of Joseph family by family.

Zelophehad son of Hepher, son of Gilead, son of Machir, son of Manas- 3
seh, had no sons but only daughters: their names were Mahlah, Noah,
Hoglah, Milcah and Tirzah. They presented themselves before Eleazar 4
the priest and Joshua son of Nun, and before the chiefs, and they said, 'The
LORD commanded Moses to allow us to inherit on the same footing as our
kinsmen.' They were therefore given a patrimony on the same footing as
their father's brothers according to the commandment of the LORD.

There fell to Manasseh's lot ten shares, apart from the country of Gilead 5
and Bashan beyond the Jordan, because Manasseh's daughters had re- 6
ceived a patrimony on the same footing as his sons. The country of Gilead
belonged to the rest of Manasseh's sons. The boundary of Manasseh 7
reached from Asher as far as Michmethath, which is to the east of Shechem,
and thence southwards towards Jashub by *a* En-tappuah. The territory of 8
Tappuah belonged to Manasseh, but Tappuah itself was on the border of
Manasseh and belonged to Ephraim. The boundary then followed the 9
gorge of Kanah to the south of the gorge (these cities *b* belong to Ephraim,
although they lie among the cities of Manasseh), the boundary of Manasseh
being on the north of the gorge; its limit was the sea. The southern side 10
belonged to Ephraim and the northern to Manasseh, and their boundary
was the sea. They marched with Asher on the north and Issachar on the
east. But in Issachar and Asher, Manasseh possessed Beth-shean and its 11
villages, Ibleam and its villages, the inhabitants of Dor and its villages, the
inhabitants of En-dor and its villages, the inhabitants of Taanach and its
villages, and the inhabitants of Megiddo and its villages. (The third is the
district of Dor.*c*) The Manassites were unable to occupy these cities; 12
the Canaanites maintained their hold on that part of the country. When 13
the Israelites grew stronger, they put the Canaanites to forced labour, but
they did not drive them out.

The sons of Joseph appealed to Joshua and said, 'Why have you given 14
us only one lot and one share as our patrimony? We are a numerous people;
so far the LORD has blessed us.' Joshua replied, 'If you are so numerous, 15
go up into the forest in the territory of the Perizzites and the Rephaim and
clear it for yourselves. You are their near neighbours *d* in the hill-country

*a* Jashub by: *prob. rdg.; Heb.* the inhabitants of.      *b* these cities: *prob. rdg.;*
*Heb. obscure.*     *c* The third . . . Dor: *prob. rdg.; Heb.* The three districts.     *d* You
are . . . neighbours: *prob. rdg.; Heb. obscure.*

16 of Ephraim.' The sons of Joseph said, 'The hill-country is not enough for us; besides, all the Canaanites have chariots of iron, those who inhabit the valley beside Beth-shean and its villages and also those in the Vale of

17 Jezreel.' Joshua replied to the tribes of Joseph, that is Ephraim and Manasseh: 'You are a numerous people with great resources. You shall not have

18 one lot only. The hill-country is yours. It is forest land; clear it and it shall be yours to its furthest limits. The Canaanites may be powerful and equipped with chariots of iron, but you will be able to drive them out.'

**18** THE WHOLE COMMUNITY OF THE ISRAELITES met together at Shiloh and established the Tent of the Presence there. The country now lay sub-

2 dued at their feet, but there remained seven tribes among the Israelites who had not yet taken possession of the patrimonies which would fall to

3 them. Joshua therefore said to them, 'How much longer will you neglect to take possession of the land which the LORD the God of your fathers has

4 given you? Appoint three men from each tribe whom I may send out to travel through the whole country. They shall make a register showing the

5 patrimony suitable for each tribe, and come back to me, and then it can be shared out among you in seven portions. Judah shall retain his boundary

6 in the south, and the house of Joseph their boundary in the north. You shall register the land in seven portions, bring the lists here, and I will cast

7 lots for you in the presence of the LORD our God. Levi has no share among you, because his share is the priesthood of the LORD; and Gad, Reuben, and the half tribe of Manasseh have each taken possession of their patrimony east of the Jordan, which Moses the servant of the LORD gave them.'

8 So the men set out on their journeys. Joshua ordered the emissaries to survey the country: 'Go through the whole country,' he said, 'survey it and return to me, and I will cast lots for you here before the LORD in

9 Shiloh.' So the men went and passed through the country; they registered it on a scroll, city by city, in seven portions, and came to Joshua in the

10 camp at Shiloh. Joshua cast lots for them in Shiloh before the LORD, and distributed the land there to the Israelites in their proper shares.

11    This is the lot which fell to the tribe of the Benjamites family by family. The territory allotted to them lay between the territory of Judah and

12 Joseph. Their boundary at its northern corner starts from the Jordan; it goes up the slope on the north side of Jericho, continuing westwards into

13 the hill-country, and its limit there is the wilderness of Beth-aven. From there it runs on to Luz, to the southern slope of Luz, that is Bethel, and down to Ataroth-addar over the hill-country south of Lower Beth-horon.

14 The boundary then bends round at the west corner southwards from the hill-country above Beth-horon, and its limit is Kiriath-baal, that is

15 Kiriath-jearim, a city of Judah. This is the western side. The southern side starts from the edge of Kiriath-jearim and ends *a* at the spring of the

16 waters of Nephtoah. It goes down to the edge of the hill to the east of the Valley of Ben-hinnom, north of the Vale of Rephaim, down the Valley of

17 Hinnom, to the southern slope of the Jebusites and so to En-rogel. It then bends round north and comes out at En-shemesh, goes on to the districts

*a Prob. rdg.; Heb. adds* westwards and ends . . .

in front of the ascent of Adummim and thence down to the Stone of
Bohan son of Reuben. It passes to the northern side of the slope facing the  18
Arabah and goes down to the Arabah, passing the northern slope of Beth-  19
hoglah, and its limit is the northern inlet of the Dead Sea, at the southern
mouth of the Jordan. This forms the southern boundary. The Jordan is  20
the boundary on the east side. This is the patrimony of the Benjamites, the
complete circuit of their boundaries family by family.

The cities belonging to the tribe of the Benjamites family by family are:  21
Jericho, Beth-hoglah, Emek-keziz, Beth-arabah, Zemaraim, Bethel,  22
Avvim, Parah, Ophrah, Kephar-ammoni, Ophni, and Geba: twelve cities  23 24
in all with their hamlets. Gibeon, Ramah, Beeroth, Mizpah, Kephirah,  25 26
Mozah, Rekem, Irpeel, Taralah, Zela, Eleph, Jebus, that is Jerusalem,  27 28
Gibeah, and Kiriath-jearim: fourteen cities in all with their hamlets. This
is the patrimony of the Benjamites family by family.

The second lot cast was for Simeon, the tribe of the Simeonites family **19**
by family. Their patrimony was included in that of Judah. For their patri-  2
mony they had Beersheba,[a] Moladah, Hazar-shual, Balah, Ezem, Eltolad,  3 4
Bethul, Hormah, Ziklag, Beth-marcaboth, Hazar-susah, Beth-lebaoth,  5 6
and Sharuhen: in all, thirteen cities and their hamlets. They had Ain,  7
Rimmon, Ether, and Ashan: four cities and their hamlets, all the hamlets  8
round these cities as far as Baalath-beer, Ramath-negeb. This was the
patrimony of the tribe of Simeon family by family. The patrimony of the  9
Simeonites was part of the land allotted to the men of Judah, because their
share was larger than they needed. The Simeonites therefore had their
patrimony within the territory of Judah.

The third lot fell to the Zebulunites family by family. The boundary of  10
their patrimony extended to Shadud.[b] Their boundary went up westwards  11
as far as Maralah and touched Dabbesheth and the gorge east of Jokneam.
It turned back from Shadud eastwards towards the sunrise up to the border  12
of Kisloth-tabor, on to Daberath and up to Japhia. From there it crossed  13
eastwards towards the sunrise to Gath-hepher, to Ittah-kazin, out to
Rimmon, and bent round[c] to Neah. The northern boundary went round  14
to Hannathon, and its limits were the Valley of Jiphtah-el, Kattath,  15
Nahalal, Shimron, Idalah, and Bethlehem: twelve cities in all with their
hamlets. These cities and their hamlets were the patrimony of Zebulun  16
family by family.

The fourth lot cast was for the sons of Issachar family by family. Their  17 18
boundary included Jezreel, Kesulloth, Shunem, Hapharaim, Shion,  19
Anaharath, Rabbith, Kishion, Ebez, Remeth, En-gannim, En-haddah,  20 21
and Beth-pazzez. The boundary touched Tabor, Shahazumah, and Beth-  22
shemesh, and its limit was the Jordan: sixteen cities with their hamlets.
This was the patrimony of the tribe of the sons of Issachar family by family,  23
both cities and hamlets.

The fifth lot cast was for the tribe of the Asherites family by family.  24
Their boundary included Helkath, Hali, Beten, Akshaph, Alammelech,  25 26
Amad, and Mishal; it touched Carmel on the west and the swamp of

---

[a] *Prob. rdg., cp. I Chr. 4. 28; Heb. adds and Sheba.*      [b] *Prob. rdg.; Heb. Sarid*
*(similarly in verse 12).*    [c] *and bent round: prob. rdg.; Heb. which stretched.*

27 Libnath. It then turned back towards the east to Beth-dagon, touched
Zebulun and the Valley of Jiphtah-el on the north at Beth-emek and Neiel,
28 and reached Cabul on its northern side, and Abdon, Rehob, Hammon, and
29 Kanah as far as Greater Sidon. The boundary turned at Ramah, going as
far as the fortress city of Tyre, and then back again to Hosah, and its limits
30 to the west were Mehalbeh, Achzib, Acco,ᵃ Aphek, and Rehob: twenty-
31 two cities in all with their hamlets. This was the patrimony of the tribe of
Asher family by family, these cities and their hamlets.
32 33    The sixth lot cast was for the sons of Naphtali family by family. Their
boundary started from Heleph and from Elon-bezaanannim and ran past
Adami-nekeb and Jabneel as far as Lakkum, and its limit was the Jordan.
34 The boundary turned back westwards to Aznoth-tabor and from there on
to Hukok. It touched Zebulun on the south, Asher on the west, and the
35 low-lying land by the Jordan on the east. Their fortified cities were Ziddim,
36 37 Zer, Hammath, Rakkath, Kinnereth, Adamah, Ramah, Hazor, Kedesh,
38 Edrei, En-hazor, Iron, Migdal-el, Horem, Beth-anath, and Beth-shemesh:
39 nineteen cities with their hamlets. This was the patrimony of the tribe of
Naphtali family by family, both cities and hamlets.
40    The seventh lot cast was for the tribe of the sons of Dan family by
41 family. The boundary of their patrimony was Zorah, Eshtaol, Ir-shemesh,
42 43 44 Shaalabbin, Aijalon, Jithlah, Elon, Timnah, Ekron, Eltekeh, Gibbethon,
45 46 Baalath, Jehud, Bene-berak, Gath-rimmon; and on the west Jarkon was
47 the boundary opposite Joppa. But the Danites, when they lost this territory,
marched against Leshem, attacked it and captured it. They put its people
to the sword, occupied it and settled in it; and they renamed the place Dan
48 after their ancestor Dan. This was the patrimony of the tribe of the sons
of Dan family by family, these cities and their hamlets.
49    So the Israelites finished allocating the land and marking out its frontiers; and they gave Joshua son of Nun a patrimony within their territory.
50 They followed the commands of the LORD and gave him the city for which
he asked, Timnath-serah in the hill-country of Ephraim, and he rebuilt
the city and settled in it.
51    These are the patrimonies which Eleazar the priest and Joshua son of
Nun and the heads of families assigned by lot to the Israelite tribes at
Shiloh before the LORD at the entrance of the Tent of the Presence. Thus
they completed the distribution of the land.

20 1 2    THE LORD SPOKE TO JOSHUA and commanded him to say this to the
Israelites: 'You must now appoint your cities of refuge, of which I spoke
3 to you through Moses. They are to be places where the homicide, the man
who kills another inadvertently without intent, may take sanctuary. You
shall single them out as cities of refuge from the vengeance of the dead
4 man's next-of-kin. When a man takes sanctuary in one of these cities, he
shall halt at the entrance of the city gate and state his case in the hearing of
the elders of that city; if they admit him into the city, they shall grant him
5 a place where he may live as one of themselves. When the next-of-kin
comes in pursuit, they shall not surrender him: he struck down his fellow

ᵃ Mehalbeh . . . Acco: *prob. rdg.*; *Heb.* from the district of Achzib and Ummah.

without intent and had not previously been at enmity with him. The 6
homicide may stay in that city until he stands trial before the community.
On the death of the ruling high priest, he may return to the city and home
from which he has fled.' They dedicated Kedesh in Galilee in the hill- 7
country of Naphtali, Shechem in the hill-country of Ephraim, and Kiriath-
arba, that is Hebron, in the hill-country of Judah. Across the Jordan 8
eastwards from Jericho they appointed these cities: from the tribe of
Reuben, Bezer-in-the-wilderness on the tableland, from the tribe of Gad,
Ramoth in Gilead, and from the tribe of Manasseh, Golan in Bashan. These 9
were the appointed cities where any Israelite or any alien residing among
them might take sanctuary. They were intended for any man who killed
another inadvertently, to ensure that no one should die at the hand of the
next-of-kin until he had stood his trial before the community.

   The heads of the Levite families approached Eleazar the priest and 21
Joshua son of Nun and the heads of the families of the tribes of Israel.
They came before them at Shiloh in the land of Canaan and said, 'The 2
LORD gave his command through Moses that we were to receive cities to
live in, together with the common land belonging to them for our cattle.'
The Israelites therefore gave part of their patrimony to the Levites, the 3
following cities with their common land, according to the command of the
LORD.

   This is the territory allotted to the Kohathite family: those Levites who 4
were descended from Aaron the priest received thirteen cities chosen by
lot from the tribes of Judah, Simeon, and Benjamin; the rest of the Kohath- 5
ites were allotted family by family *a* ten cities from the tribes of Ephraim,
Dan, and half Manasseh.

   The Gershonites were allotted family by family thirteen cities from the 6
tribes of Issachar, Asher, Naphtali, and the half tribe of Manasseh in
Bashan.

   The Merarites were allotted family by family twelve cities from the 7
tribes of Reuben, Gad, and Zebulun.

   So the Israelites gave the Levites these cities with their common land, 8
allocating them by lot as the LORD had commanded through Moses.

   The Israelites designated the following cities out of the tribes of Judah 9
and Simeon for those sons of Aaron who were of the Kohathite families of 10
the Levites, because their lot came out first. They gave them Kiriath-arba 11
(Arba was the father of Anak), that is Hebron, in the hill-country of Judah,
and the common land round it, but they gave the open country near the 12
city, and its hamlets, to Caleb son of Jephunneh as his patrimony.

   To the sons of Aaron the priest they gave Hebron, a city of refuge for 13*b*
the homicide, Libnah, Jattir, Eshtemoa, Holon, Debir, Ashan, *c* Juttah, 14 15 16
and Beth-shemesh, each with its common land: nine cities from these two
tribes. They also gave cities from the tribe of Benjamin, Gibeon, Geba, 17
Anathoth, and Almon, each with its common land: four cities. The number 18 19
of the cities with their common land given to the sons of Aaron the priest
was thirteen.

---

*a* family by family: *prob. rdg.; Heb.* from the families (*similarly in verse 6*).     *b* Verses
*13–39: cp. 1 Chr. 6. 57–81.*     *c* Prob. rdg., cp. 1 Chr. 6. 59; Heb. Ain.

20 The cities which the rest of the Kohathite families of the Levites re-
21 ceived by lot were from the tribe of Ephraim. They gave them Shechem, a
city of refuge for the homicide, in the hill-country of Ephraim, Gezer,
22 23 Kibzaim, and Beth-horon, each with its common land: four cities. From
24 the tribe of Dan, they gave them Eltekeh, Gibbethon, Aijalon, and Gath-
25 rimmon, each with its common land: four cities. From the half tribe of
Manasseh, they gave them Taanach and Gath-rimmon, each with its
26 common land: two cities. The number of the cities belonging to the rest of
the Kohathite families with their common land was ten.

27 The Gershonite families of the Levites received, out of the share of the
half tribe of Manasseh, Golan in Bashan, a city of refuge for the homicide,
28 and Be-ashtaroth,*a* each with its common land: two cities. From the tribe
29 of Issachar they received Kishon, Daberah, Jarmuth, and En-gannim,
30 each with its common land: four cities. From the tribe of Asher they
31 received Mishal, Abdon, Helkath, and Rehob, each with its common land:
32 four cities. From the tribe of Naphtali they received Kedesh in Galilee, a
city of refuge for the homicide, Hammoth-dor, and Kartan, each with its
33 common land: three cities. The number of the cities of the Gershonite
families with their common land was thirteen.

34 From the tribe of Zebulun the rest of the Merarite families of the Levites
35 received Jokneam, Kartah, Rimmon,*b* and Nahalal, each with its common
36 land: four cities. East of the Jordan at Jericho, from the tribe of Reuben
they were given Bezer-in-the-wilderness on the tableland, a city of refuge
37 for the homicide, Jahaz, Kedemoth, and Mephaath, each with its common
38 land: four cities. From the tribe of Gad they received Ramoth in Gilead,
39 a city of refuge for the homicide, Mahanaim, Heshbon, and Jazer, each
40 with its common land: four cities in all. Twelve cities in all fell by lot to the
rest of the Merarite families of the Levites.

41 The cities of the Levites within the Israelite patrimonies numbered
42 forty-eight in all, with their common land. Each city had its common land
round it, and it was the same for all of them.

43 Thus the LORD gave Israel all the land which he had sworn to give to
44 their forefathers; they occupied it and settled in it. The LORD gave them
security on every side as he had sworn to their forefathers. Of all their
enemies not a man could withstand them; the LORD delivered all their
45 enemies into their hands. Not a word of the LORD's promises to the house
of Israel went unfulfilled; they all came true.

22 AT THAT TIME JOSHUA SUMMONED THE REUBENITES, the Gadites,
2 and the half tribe of Manasseh, and said to them, 'You have observed all
the commands of Moses the servant of the LORD, and you have obeyed me
3 in all the commands that I too have laid upon you. All this time you have
not deserted your brothers; up to this day you have diligently observed
4 the charge laid on you by the LORD your God. And now that the LORD
your God has given your brothers security as he promised them, you may
turn now and go to your homes in your own land, the land which Moses

*a Prob. rdg.; Heb.* Be-ashtarah.      *b Prob. rdg., cp. 19. 13; 1 Chr. 6. 77; Heb.*
Dimnah.

the servant of the LORD gave you east of the Jordan. But take good care to keep the commands and the law which Moses the servant of the LORD gave you: to love the LORD your God; to conform to his ways; to observe his commandments; to hold fast to him; to serve him with your whole heart and soul.' Joshua blessed them and dismissed them; and they went to their homes. He sent them home with his blessing, and with these words: 'Go to your homes richly laden, with great herds, with silver and gold, copper and iron, and with large stores of clothing. See that you share with your kinsmen the spoil you have taken from your enemies.'

Moses had given territory to one half of the tribe of Manasseh in Bashan, and Joshua gave territory to the other half west of the Jordan among their kinsmen.

So the Reubenites, the Gadites, and the half tribe of Manasseh left the rest of the Israelites and went from Shiloh in Canaan on their way into Gilead, the land which belonged to them according to the decree of the LORD given through Moses. When these tribes came to Geliloth by the Jordan,[a] they built a great altar there by the river for all to see. The Israelites heard that the Reubenites, the Gadites, and the half tribe of Manasseh had built the altar facing the land of Canaan, at Geliloth by the Jordan opposite the Israelite side. When the news reached them, all the community of the Israelites assembled at Shiloh to advance against them with a display of force. At the same time the Israelites sent Phinehas son of Eleazar the priest into the land of Gilead, to the Reubenites, the Gadites, and the half tribe of Manasseh, and ten leading men with him, one from each of the tribes of Israel, each of them the head of a household among the clans of Israel. They came to the Reubenites, the Gadites, and the half tribe of Manasseh in the land of Gilead, and remonstrated with them in these words: 'We speak for the whole community of the LORD. What is this treachery you have committed against the God of Israel? Are you ceasing to follow the LORD and building your own altar this day in defiance of the LORD? Remember our offence at Peor, for which a plague fell upon the community of the LORD; to this day we have not been purified from it. Was that offence so slight that you dare cease to follow the LORD today? If you defy the LORD today, then tomorrow he will be angry with the whole community of Israel. If the land you have taken is unclean, then cross over to the LORD's own land, where the Tabernacle of the LORD now rests, and take a share of it with us; but do not defy the LORD and involve us in your defiance by building an altar of your own apart from the altar of the LORD our God. Remember the treachery of Achan son of Zerah, who defied the ban and the whole community of Israel suffered for it. He was not the only one who paid for that sin with his life.'

Then the Reubenites, the Gadites, and the half tribe of Manasseh remonstrated with the heads of the clans of Israel: 'The LORD the God of gods, the LORD the God of gods, he knows, and Israel must know: if this had been an act of defiance or treachery against the LORD, you could not save us today. If we had built ourselves an altar meaning to forsake the LORD, or had offered whole-offerings and grain-offerings upon it, or had

[a] *Prob. rdg.; Heb. adds* which was in Canaan.

presented shared-offerings, the LORD himself would exact punishment.
24 The truth is that we have done this for fear that the day may come when
your sons will say to ours, "What have you to do with the LORD, the God
25 of Israel? The LORD put the Jordan as a boundary between our sons and
your sons. You have no share in the LORD, you men of Reuben and Gad."
26 Thus your sons will prevent our sons from going in awe of the LORD. So
we resolved to set ourselves to build an altar, not for whole-offerings and
27 sacrifices, but as a witness between us and you, and between our descendants after us. Thus we shall be able to do service before the LORD, as we do
now, with our whole-offerings, our sacrifices, and our shared-offerings;
and your sons will never be able to say to our sons that they have no
28 share in the LORD. And we thought, if ever they do say this to us and our
descendants, we will point to this copy of the altar of the LORD which we
have made, not for whole-offerings and not for sacrifices, but as a witness
29 between us and you. God forbid that we should defy the LORD and forsake
him this day by building another altar for whole-offerings, grain-offerings,
and sacrifices, in addition to the altar of the LORD our God which stands in
front of his Tabernacle.'
30     When Phinehas the priest and the leaders of the community, the heads
of the Israelite clans, who were with him, heard what the Reubenites, the
31 Gadites, and the Manassites said, they were satisfied. Phinehas son of
Eleazar the priest said to the Reubenites, Gadites, and Manassites, 'We
know now that the LORD is in our midst today; you have not acted treacherously against the LORD, and thus you have preserved all Israel from punish-
32 ment at his hand.' Then Phinehas son of Eleazar the priest and the leaders
left the Reubenites and the Gadites in Gilead and reported to the Israelites
33 in Canaan. The Israelites were satisfied, and they blessed God and thought
34 no more of attacking Reuben and Gad and ravaging their land. The
Reubenites and Gadites said, 'The altar is a witness between us that the
LORD is God', and they named it 'Witness'.

## *Joshua's farewell and death*

23 A LONG TIME HAD PASSED since the LORD had given Israel security
from all the enemies who surrounded them, and Joshua was now a
2 very old man. He summoned all Israel, their elders and heads of families,
their judges and officers, and said to them, 'I have become a very old man.
3 You have seen for yourselves all that the LORD our God has done to these
peoples for your sake; it was the LORD God himself who fought for you.
4 I have allotted you your patrimony tribe by tribe, the land of all the peoples
that I have wiped out and of all these that remain between the Jordan and
5 the Great Sea which lies towards the setting sun. The LORD your God himself drove them out for your sake; he drove them out to make room for
you, and you occupied their land, as the LORD your God had promised
6 you. Be resolute therefore: observe and perform everything written in the
7 book of the law of Moses, without swerving to right or to left. You must
not associate with the peoples that are left among you; you must not call

upon their gods by name, nor *a* swear by them nor prostrate yourselves in worship before them. You must hold fast to the LORD your God as you have done down to this day. For your sake the LORD has driven out great and mighty nations; to this day not a man of them has withstood you. One of you can put to flight a thousand, because the LORD your God fights for you, as he promised. Be on your guard then, love the LORD your God, for *b* if you do turn away and attach yourselves to the peoples that still remain among you, and intermarry with them and associate with them and they with you, then be sure that the LORD will not continue to drive those peoples out to make room for you. They will be snares to entrap you, whips for your backs and barbed hooks in your eyes, until you vanish from the good land which the LORD your God has given you. And now I am going the way of all mankind. You know in your heart of hearts that nothing that the LORD your God has promised you has failed to come true, every word of it. But the same LORD God who has kept his word to you to such good effect can equally bring every kind of evil on you, until he has rooted you out from this good land which he has given you. If you break the covenant which the LORD your God has prescribed and prostrate yourselves in worship before other gods, then the LORD will be angry with you and you will quickly vanish from the good land he has given you.'

Joshua assembled all the tribes of Israel at Shechem. He summoned the **24** elders of Israel, the heads of families, the judges and officers; and they presented themselves before God. Joshua then said this to all the people: 'This is the word of the LORD the God of Israel: "Long ago your fore-fathers, Terah and his sons Abraham and Nahor, lived beside the Euphrates, and they worshipped other gods. I took your father Abraham from beside the Euphrates and led him through the length and breadth of Canaan. I gave him many descendants: I gave him Isaac, and to Isaac I gave Jacob and Esau. I put Esau in possession of the hill-country of Seir, but Jacob and his sons went down to Egypt. I sent Moses and Aaron, and I struck the Egyptians with plagues—you know well what I did among them—and after that I brought you out; I brought your fathers out of Egypt and you came to the Red Sea. The Egyptians sent their chariots and cavalry to pursue your fathers to the sea. But when they appealed to the LORD, he put a screen of darkness between you and the Egyptians, and brought the sea down on them and it covered them; you saw for yourselves what I did to Egypt. For a long time you lived in the wilderness. Then I brought you into the land of the Amorites who lived east of the Jordan; they fought against you, but I delivered them into your hands; you took possession of their country and I destroyed them for your sake. The king of Moab, Balak son of Zippor, took the field against Israel. He sent for Balaam son of Beor to lay a curse on you, but I would not listen to him. Instead of that he blessed you; and so I saved you from the power of Balak. Then you crossed the Jordan and came to Jericho. The citizens of Jericho fought against you, *c*

8
9
10
11 12
13
14
15
16

2
3
4
5
6
7
8
9
10
11

---

*a* you must not call . . . nor: *or* the name of their gods shall not be your boast, nor must you . . . 　　　*b* Be on . . . for: *or* Take very good care to love the LORD your God, but . . . 　　　*c* *Prob. rdg.; Heb. adds* Amorites, Perizzites, Canaanites, Hittites, Girgashites, Hivites, and Jebusites.

12 but I delivered them into your hands. I spread panic before you, and it was this, not your sword or your bow, that drove out the two kings of the
13 Amorites. I gave you land on which you had not laboured, cities which you had never built; you have lived in those cities and you eat the produce of vineyards and olive-groves which you did not plant."
14    'Hold the LORD in awe then, and worship him in loyalty and truth. Banish the gods whom your fathers worshipped beside the Euphrates and
15 in Egypt, and worship the LORD. But if it does not please you to worship the LORD, choose here and now whom you will worship: the gods whom your forefathers worshipped beside the Euphrates, or the gods of the Amorites in whose land you are living. But I and my family, we will
16 worship the LORD.' The people answered, 'God forbid that we should for-
17 sake the LORD to worship other gods, for it was the LORD our God who brought us and our fathers up from Egypt, that land of slavery; it was he who displayed those great signs before our eyes and guarded us on all our
18 wanderings among the many peoples through whose lands we passed. The LORD drove out before us the Amorites and all the peoples who lived in
19 that country. We too will worship the LORD; he is our God.' Joshua answered the people, 'You cannot worship the LORD. He is a holy god, a
20 jealous god, and he will not forgive your rebellion and your sins. If you forsake the LORD and worship foreign gods, he will turn and bring adversity upon you and, although he once brought you prosperity, he will make
21 an end of you.' The people said to Joshua, 'No; we will worship the LORD.'
22 He said to them, 'You are witnesses against yourselves that you have chosen the LORD and will worship him.' 'Yes,' they answered, 'we are witnesses.'
23 He said to them, 'Then here and now banish the foreign gods that are
24 among you, and turn your hearts to the LORD the God of Israel.' The people said to Joshua, 'The LORD our God we will worship and his voice
25 we will obey.' So Joshua made a covenant that day with*a* the people; he
26 drew up a statute and an ordinance for them in Shechem and wrote its terms in the book of the law of God. He took a great stone and set it up there under
27 the terebinth*b* in the sanctuary of the LORD, and said to all the people, 'This stone is a witness against us; for it has heard all the words which the LORD has spoken to us. If you renounce your God, it shall be a witness against
28 you.' Then Joshua dismissed the people, each man to his patrimony.
29    After these things, Joshua son of Nun the servant of the LORD died; he
30 was a hundred and ten years old. They buried him within the border of his own patrimony in Timnath-serah in the hill-country of Ephraim to the
31 north of Mount Gaash. Israel served the LORD during the lifetime of Joshua and of the elders who outlived him and who well knew all that the LORD had done for Israel.
32    The bones of Joseph, which the Israelites had brought up from Egypt, were buried in Shechem, in the plot of land which Jacob had bought from the sons of Hamor father of Shechem for a hundred sheep;*c* and they passed
33 into the patrimony of the house of Joseph. Eleazar son of Aaron died and was buried in the hill which had been given to Phinehas his son in the hill-country of Ephraim.

*a Or* for.        *b Or* pole.        *c Or* pieces of money (*cp. Gen. 33. 19; Job 42. 11*).

# THE BOOK OF
# JUDGES

## The conquest of Canaan completed

AFTER THE DEATH OF JOSHUA the Israelites inquired of 1
the LORD which tribe should attack the Canaanites first. The LORD 2
answered, 'Judah shall attack. I hereby deliver the country into
his power.' Judah said to his brother Simeon, 'Go forward with me into 3
my allotted territory, and let us do battle with the Canaanites; then I in
turn will go with you into your territory.' So Simeon went with him; then 4
Judah advanced to the attack, and the LORD delivered the Canaanites and
Perizzites into their hands. They slaughtered ten thousand of them at
Bezek. There they came upon Adoni-bezek, engaged him in battle and 5
defeated the Canaanites and Perizzites. Adoni-bezek fled, but they pursued 6
him, took him prisoner and cut off his thumbs and his great toes. Adoni- 7
bezek said, 'I once had seventy kings whose thumbs and great toes were cut
off picking up the scraps from under my table. What I have done God has
done to me.' He was brought to Jerusalem and died there.

The men of Judah made an assault on Jerusalem and captured it, put its 8
people to the sword and set fire to the city. Then they turned south to 9
fight the Canaanites of the hill-country, the Negeb, and the Shephelah.
Judah attacked the Canaanites in Hebron, formerly called Kiriath-arba, 10
and defeated Sheshai, Ahiman and Talmai. From there they marched 11
against the inhabitants of Debir, formerly called Kiriath-sepher. Caleb 12
said, 'Whoever attacks Kiriath-sepher and captures it, to him I will give
my daughter Achsah in marriage.' Othniel, son of Caleb's younger 13
brother Kenaz, captured it, and Caleb gave him his daughter Achsah.
When she came to him, he incited her to ask her father for a piece of land. 14
As she sat on the ass, she broke wind, and Caleb said, 'What did you mean
by that?' She replied, 'I want to ask a favour of you. You have put me in 15
this dry Negeb; you must give me pools of water as well.' So Caleb gave
her the upper pool and the lower pool.

The descendants of Moses' father-in-law, the Kenite, went up with the 16
men of Judah from the Vale of Palm Trees to the wilderness of Judah
which is in the Negeb of Arad and settled among the Amalekites. Judah 17
then accompanied his brother Simeon, attacked the Canaanites in Zephath
and destroyed it; hence the city was called Hormah.[a] Judah took Gaza, 18
Ashkelon, and Ekron, and the territory of each. The LORD was with Judah 19
and they occupied the hill-country, but they could not drive out the inhabitants of the Vale because they had chariots of iron. Hebron was given 20

[a] *That is* Destruction.

to Caleb as Moses had directed, and he drove out the three sons of Anak.

21 But the Benjamites did not drive out the Jebusites of Jerusalem; and the Jebusites have lived on in Jerusalem with the Benjamites till the present day.

22 23 The tribes of Joseph attacked Bethel, and the LORD was with them. They
24 sent spies to Bethel, formerly called Luz. These spies saw a man coming out of the city and said to him, 'Show us how to enter the city, and we will
25 see that you come to no harm.' So he showed them how to enter, and they
26 put the city to the sword, but let the man and his family go free. He went into Hittite country, built a city and named it Luz, which is still its name today.

27 Manasseh did not drive out the inhabitants of Beth-shean with its villages, nor of Taanach, Dor, Ibleam, and Megiddo, with the villages of
28 each of them; the Canaanites held their ground in that region. Later, when Israel became strong, they put them to forced labour, but they never completely drove them out.

29 Ephraim did not drive out the Canaanites who lived in Gezer, but the Canaanites lived among them there.

30 Zebulun did not drive out the inhabitants of Kitron and Nahalol, but the Canaanites lived among them and were put to forced labour.

31 Asher did not drive out the inhabitants of Acco and Sidon, of Ahlab,
32 Achzib, Helbah, Aphik and Rehob. Thus the Asherites lived among the Canaanite inhabitants and did not drive them out.

33 Naphtali did not drive out the inhabitants of Beth-shemesh and of Beth-anath, but lived among the Canaanite inhabitants and put the inhabitants of Beth-shemesh and Beth-anath to forced labour.

34 The Amorites pressed the Danites back into the hill-country and did
35 not allow them to come down into the Vale. The Amorites held their ground in Mount Heres and in Aijalon and Shaalbim, but the tribes of Joseph increased their pressure on them until they reduced them to forced labour.

36 The boundary of the Edomites ran from the ascent of Akrabbim, upwards from Sela.

2 The angel of the LORD came up from Gilgal to Bokim, and said, 'I brought*a* you up out of Egypt and into the country which I vowed I would give to your forefathers. I said, I will never break my covenant with you,
2 and you in turn must make no covenant with the inhabitants of the country; you must pull down their altars. But you did not obey me, and look what
3 you have done! So I said, I will not drive them out before you; they will
4 decoy you, and their gods will shut you fast in the trap.' When the angel of
5 the LORD said this to the Israelites, they all wept and wailed, and so the place was called Bokim;*b* and they offered sacrifices there to the LORD.

---

*a* *Prob. rdg.; Heb.* I will bring.     *b* *That is* Weepers.

## Israel under the judges

JOSHUA DISMISSED THE PEOPLE, and the Israelites went off to occupy 6 the country, each man to his allotted portion. As long as Joshua was 7 alive and the elders who survived him—everyone, that is, who had witnessed the whole great work which the LORD had done for Israel—the people worshipped the LORD. At the age of a hundred and ten Joshua son of 8 Nun, the servant of the LORD, died, and they buried him within the border 9 of his own property in Timnath-heres north of Mount Gaash in the hill-country of Ephraim. Of that whole generation, all were gathered to their 10 forefathers, and another generation followed who did not acknowledge the LORD and did not know what he had done for Israel. Then the Israelites 11 did what was wrong in the eyes of the LORD, and worshipped the Baalim.*a* They forsook the LORD, their fathers' God who had brought them out of 12 Egypt, and went after other gods, gods of the races among whom they lived; they bowed down before them and provoked the LORD to anger; they forsook the LORD and worshipped the Baal and the Ashtaroth.*b* The 13 14 LORD in his anger made them the prey of bands of raiders and plunderers; he sold them to their enemies all around them, and they could no longer make a stand. Every time they went out to battle the LORD brought 15 disaster upon them, as he had said when he gave them his solemn warning, and they were in dire straits.

The LORD set judges over them, who rescued them from the marauding 16 bands. Yet they did not listen even to these judges, but turned wantonly 17 to worship other gods and bowed down before them; all too soon they abandoned the path of obedience to the LORD's commands which their forefathers had followed. They did not obey the LORD. Whenever the LORD 18 set up a judge over them, he was with that judge, and kept them safe from their enemies so long as he lived. The LORD would relent as often as he heard them groaning under oppression and ill-treatment. But as soon as 19 the judge was dead, they would relapse into deeper corruption than their forefathers and give their allegiance to other gods, worshipping them and bowing down before them. They gave up none of their evil practices and their wilful ways. And the LORD was angry with Israel and said, 'This 20 nation has broken the covenant which I laid upon their forefathers and has not obeyed me, and now, of all the nations which Joshua left at his 21 death, I will not drive out to make room for them one single man. By their 22 means I will test Israel, to see whether or not they will keep strictly to the way of the LORD as their forefathers did.' So the LORD left those nations 23 alone and made no haste to drive them out or give them into Joshua's hands.

These are the nations which the LORD left as a means of testing all the 3 Israelites who had not taken part in the battles for Canaan, his purpose 2 being to teach succeeding generations of Israel, or those at least who had not learnt in former times, how to make war. These were: the five lords of 3 the Philistines, all the Canaanites, the Sidonians, and the Hivites who lived in Mount Lebanon from Mount Baal-hermon as far as Lebo-hamath.

*a* The Baalim *were Canaanite deities.*   *b* The Ashtaroth *were Canaanite deities.*

4 His purpose also was to test whether the Israelites would obey the com-
5 mands which the LORD had given to their forefathers through Moses. Thus
the Israelites lived among the Canaanites, the Hittites, the Amorites, the
6 Perizzites, the Hivites, and the Jebusites. They took their daughters in
marriage and gave their own daughters to their sons; and they worshipped
their gods.

7    The Israelites did what was wrong in the eyes of the LORD; they forgot
8 the LORD their God and worshipped the Baalim and the Asheroth.*a* The
LORD was angry with Israel and he sold them to Cushan-rishathaim, king
9 of Aram-naharaim,*b* who kept them in subjection for eight years. Then
the Israelites cried to the LORD for help and he raised up a man to deliver
them, Othniel son of Caleb's younger brother Kenaz, and he set them
10 free. The spirit of the LORD came upon him and he became judge over
Israel. He took the field, and the LORD delivered Cushan-rishathaim king
11 of Aram into his hands; Othniel was too strong for him. Thus the land was
at peace for forty years until Othniel son of Kenaz died.

12    Once again the Israelites did what was wrong in the eyes of the LORD,
13 and because of this he roused Eglon king of Moab against Israel. Eglon
mustered the Ammonites and the Amalekites, advanced to attack Israel
14 and took possession of the Vale of Palm Trees. The Israelites were subject
15 to Eglon king of Moab for eighteen years. When they cried to the LORD
for help, he raised up a man to deliver them, Ehud son of Gera the Benjamite, who was left-handed. The Israelites sent him to pay their tribute
16 to Eglon king of Moab. Ehud made himself a two-edged sword, only
fifteen inches long, which he fastened on his right side under his clothes,
17 and he brought the tribute to Eglon king of Moab. Eglon was a very fat
18 man. When Ehud had finished presenting the tribute, he sent on the men
19 who had carried it, and he himself turned back from the Carved Stones at
Gilgal. 'My lord king,' he said, 'I have a word for you in private.' Eglon
20 called for silence and dismissed all his attendants. Ehud then came up to
him as he sat in the roof-chamber of his summer palace and said, 'I have
21 a word from God for you.' So Eglon rose from his seat, and Ehud reached
with his left hand, drew the sword from his right side and drove it into his
22 belly. The hilt went in after the blade and the fat closed over the blade;
23 he did not draw the sword out but left it protruding behind. Ehud went
24 out to the porch, shut the doors on him and fastened them. When he had
gone away, Eglon's servants came and, finding the doors fastened, they
said, 'He must be relieving himself in the closet of his summer palace.'
25 They waited until they were ashamed to delay any longer, and still he did
not open the doors of the roof-chamber. So they took the key and opened
26 the doors; and there was their master lying on the floor dead. While they
had been waiting, Ehud made his escape; he passed the Carved Stones and
27 escaped to Seirah. When he arrived there, he sounded the trumpet in the
hill-country of Ephraim, and the Israelites came down from the hills with
28 him at their head. He said to them, 'Follow me, for the LORD has delivered
your enemy the Moabites into your hands.' Down they came after him,
and they seized the fords of the Jordan against the Moabites and allowed

*a  Plural of* Asherah, *the name of a Canaanite goddess.*      *b  That is* Aram of Two Rivers.

no man to cross. They killed that day some ten thousand Moabites, all of 29
them men of substance and all fighting men; not one escaped. Thus Moab 30
on that day became subject to Israel, and the land was at peace for eighty
years.

After Ehud there was Shamgar of Beth-anath.*ᵃ* He killed six hundred 31
Philistines with an ox-goad, and he too delivered Israel.

After Ehud's death the Israelites once again did what was wrong in the 4
eyes of the LORD, so he sold them to Jabin the Canaanite king, who ruled 2
in Hazor. The commander of his forces was Sisera, who lived in Harosheth-
of-the-Gentiles. The Israelites cried to the LORD for help, because Sisera 3
had nine hundred chariots of iron and had oppressed Israel harshly for
twenty years. At that time Deborah wife of Lappidoth,*ᵇ* a prophetess, was 4
judge in Israel. It was her custom to sit beneath the Palm-tree of Deborah 5
between Ramah and Bethel in the hill-country of Ephraim, and the
Israelites went up to her for justice. She sent for Barak son of Abinoam 6
from Kedesh in Naphtali and said to him, 'These are the commands of
the LORD the God of Israel: "Go and draw ten thousand men from Naphtali
and Zebulun and bring them with you to Mount Tabor, and I will draw 7
Sisera, Jabin's commander, to the Torrent of Kishon with his chariots and
all his rabble, and there I will deliver them into your hands."' Barak 8
answered her, 'If you go with me, I will go; but if you will not go, neither
will I.' 'Certainly I will go with you,' she said, 'but this venture will bring 9
you no glory, because the LORD will leave Sisera to fall into the hands of a
woman.' So Deborah rose and went with Barak to Kedesh. Barak sum- 10
moned Zebulun and Naphtali to Kedesh and marched up with ten thousand men, and Deborah went with him.

Now Heber the Kenite had parted company with the Kenites, the 11
descendants of Hobab, Moses' brother-in-law, and he had pitched his
tent at Elon-bezaanannim near Kedesh.

Word was brought to Sisera that Barak son of Abinoam had gone up to 12
Mount Tabor; so he summoned all his chariots, nine hundred chariots of 13
iron, and his troops, from Harosheth-of-the-Gentiles to the Torrent of
Kishon. Then Deborah said to Barak, 'Up! This day the LORD gives 14
Sisera into your hands. Already the LORD has gone out to battle before
you.' So Barak came charging down from Mount Tabor with ten thousand
men at his back. The LORD put Sisera to rout with all his chariots and his 15
army before Barak's onslaught; but Sisera himself dismounted from his
chariot and fled on foot. Barak pursued the chariots and the army as far 16
as Harosheth, and the whole army was put to the sword and perished; not
a man was left alive. Meanwhile Sisera fled on foot to the tent of Jael wife 17
of Heber the Kenite, because Jabin king of Hazor and the household of
Heber the Kenite were at peace. Jael came out to meet Sisera and said to 18
him, 'Come in here, my lord, come in; do not be afraid.' So he went into
the tent, and she covered him with a rug. He said to her, 'Give me some 19
water to drink; I am thirsty.' She opened a skin full of milk, gave him a
drink and covered him up again. He said to her, 'Stand at the tent door, 20
and if anybody comes and asks if someone is here, say No.' But Jael, 21

*ᵃ* of Beth-anath: *or* son of Anath.        *ᵇ* wife of Lappidoth: *or* a spirited woman.

Heber's wife, took a tent-peg, picked up a hammer, crept up to him, and drove the peg into his skull as he lay sound asleep. His brains oozed out
22 on the ground, his limbs twitched, and he died. When Barak came up in pursuit of Sisera, Jael went out to meet him and said to him, 'Come, I will show you the man you are looking for.' He went in with her, and there
23 was Sisera lying dead with the tent-peg in his skull. That day God gave
24 victory to the Israelites over Jabin king of Canaan, and they pressed home their attacks upon that king of Canaan until they had made an end of him.

5    That day Deborah and Barak son of Abinoam sang this song:

2    For the leaders, the leaders<sup>a</sup> in Israel,
for the people who answered the call,
bless ye the LORD.

3    Hear me, you kings; princes, give ear;
I will sing, I will sing to the LORD.
I will raise a psalm to the LORD the God of Israel.

4    O LORD, at thy setting forth from Seir,
when thou camest marching out of the plains of Edom,
earth trembled; heaven quaked;
the clouds streamed down in torrents.

5    Mountains shook in fear before the LORD, the lord of Sinai,
before the LORD, the God of Israel.

6    In the days of Shamgar of Beth-anath,<sup>b</sup>
in the days of Jael, caravans plied no longer;
men who had followed the high roads
went round by devious paths.

7    Champions there were none,
none left in Israel,
until I,<sup>c</sup> Deborah, arose,
arose, a mother in Israel.

8    They chose new gods,
they consorted with demons.<sup>d</sup>
Not a shield, not a lance was to be seen
in the forty thousand of Israel.

9    Be proud at heart, you marshals of Israel;
you among the people that answered the call,
bless ye the LORD.

10    You that ride your tawny she-asses,
that sit on saddle-cloths,
and you that take the road afoot,
     ponder this well.

11    Hark, the sound of the players striking up
in the places where the women draw water!
It is the victories of the LORD that they commemorate there,
his triumphs as the champion of Israel.

---

<sup>a</sup> *Or* For those who had flowing locks.          <sup>b</sup> of Beth-anath: *or* son of Anath.
<sup>c</sup> *Or* you.     <sup>d</sup> *Or* satyrs.

Down to the gates came the LORD's people:
　'Rouse, rouse yourself, Deborah,　　　　　　　　　　　12
　rouse yourself, lead out the host.
　Up, Barak! Take prisoners in plenty,
　son of Abinoam.'
Then down marched the column*a* and its chieftains,　　　13
the people of the LORD marched down *b* like warriors.
The men of Ephraim showed a brave front in the vale,　　14
crying, 'With you, Benjamin! Your clansmen are here!'
From Machir down came the marshals,
from Zebulun the bearers of the musterer's staff.
Issachar joined with Deborah in the uprising, *c*　　　　15
Issachar stood by Barak;
down into the valley they rushed.
But Reuben, he was split into factions,
great were their heart-searchings.
What made you linger by the cattle-pens　　　　　　　16
to listen to the shrill calling of the shepherds? *d*
Gilead stayed beyond Jordan;　　　　　　　　　　　17
and Dan, why did he tarry by the ships?
Asher lingered by the sea-shore,
by its creeks he stayed.
The people of Zebulun risked their very lives,　　　　　18
so did Naphtali on the heights of the battlefield.

Kings came, they fought;　　　　　　　　　　　　　19
then fought the kings of Canaan
at Taanach by the waters of Megiddo;
no plunder of silver did they take.
The stars fought from heaven,　　　　　　　　　　　20
the stars in their courses fought against Sisera.
The Torrent of Kishon swept him away,　　　　　　　21
the Torrent barred his flight, the Torrent of Kishon;
　march on in might, my soul!
Then hammered the hooves of his horses,　　　　　　22
his chargers galloped, galloped away.
A curse on Meroz, said the angel of the LORD;　　　　23
a curse, a curse on its inhabitants,
because they brought no help to the LORD,
no help to the LORD and the fighting men.
Blest above women be Jael,　　　　　　　　　　　　24
the wife of Heber the Kenite;
blest above all women in the tents.
He asked for water: she gave him milk,　　　　　　　25
she offered him curds in a bowl fit for a chieftain.

---

*a* *Prob. rdg.; Heb.* survivor.　　*b* *Prob. rdg.; Heb. adds* to me.　　*c* in the uprising:
*prob. rdg.; Heb.* my officers.　　*d* *Prob. rdg.; Heb. adds* Reuben was split into factions,
great were their heart-searchings.

26       She stretched out her hand for the tent-peg,
      her right hand to hammer the weary.
      With the hammer she struck Sisera, she crushed his head;
      she struck and his brains ebbed out.

27       At her feet he sank down, he fell, he lay;
      at her feet he sank down and fell.
      Where he sank down, there he fell, done to death.

28       The mother of Sisera peered through the lattice,
      through the window she peered and shrilly cried,
      'Why are his chariots so long coming?
      Why is the clatter of his chariots so long delayed?'

29       The wisest of her princesses answered her,
      yes, she found her own answer:

30       'They must be finding spoil, taking their shares,
      a wench to each man, two wenches,
      booty of dyed stuffs for Sisera,
      booty of dyed stuffs,
      dyed stuff, and striped, two lengths of striped stuff—
      to grace the victor's neck.'

31       So perish all thine enemies, O LORD;
      but let all who love thee be like the sun rising in strength.

The land was at peace for forty years.

**6** THE ISRAELITES DID WHAT WAS WRONG in the eyes of the LORD and
2 he delivered them into the hands of Midian for seven years. The Midianites were too strong for Israel, and the Israelites were forced to find them-
3 selves hollow places in the mountains, and caves and strongholds. If the
Israelites had sown their seed, the Midianites and the Amalekites and other
4 eastern tribes would come up and attack Israel. They then pitched their
camps in the country and destroyed the crops as far as the outskirts of
5 Gaza, leaving nothing to support life in Israel, sheep or ox or ass. They
came up with their herds and their tents, like a swarm of locusts; they and
their camels were past counting. They had come into the land for its
6 growing crop,*a* and so the Israelites were brought to destitution by the
7 Midianites, and they cried to the LORD for help. When the Israelites cried
8 to the LORD because of what they had suffered from the Midianites, he
sent them a prophet who said to them, 'These are the words of the LORD
9 the God of Israel: I brought you up from Egypt, that land of slavery. I
delivered you from the Egyptians and from all your oppressors. I drove
10 them out before you and gave you their lands. I said to you, "I am the
LORD your God: do not stand in awe of the gods of the Amorites in whose
country you are settling." But you did not listen to me.'
11     Now the angel of the LORD came and sat under the terebinth at Ophrah
which belonged to Joash the Abiezrite. His son Gideon was threshing
wheat in the winepress, so that he might get it away quickly from the

*a* for its growing crop: *or* and laid it waste.

Midianites. The angel of the LORD showed himself to Gideon and said, 12 'You are a brave man, and the LORD is with you.' Gideon said, 'But pray, 13 my lord, if the LORD really is with us, why has all this happened to us? What has become of all those wonderful deeds of his, of which we have heard from our fathers, when they told us how the LORD brought us out of Egypt? But now the LORD has cast us off and delivered us into the power of the Midianites.' The LORD turned to him and said, 'Go and use 14 this strength of yours to free Israel from the power of the Midianites. It is I that send you.' Gideon said, 'Pray, my lord, how can I save Israel? 15 Look at my clan: it is the weakest in Manasseh, and I am the least in my father's family.' The LORD answered, 'I will be with you, and you shall lay 16 low all Midian as one man.' He replied, 'If I stand so well with you, give 17 me a sign that it is you who speak to me. Please do not leave this place until 18 I come with my gift and lay it before you.' He answered, 'I will stay until you come back.' So Gideon went in, prepared a kid and made an ephah of 19 flour into unleavened cakes. He put the meat in a basket, poured the broth into a pot and brought it out to him under the terebinth. As he approached, the angel of God said to him, 'Take the meat and the cakes, and put them 20 here on the rock and pour out the broth', and he did so. Then the angel of 21 the LORD reached out the staff in his hand and touched the meat and the cakes with the tip of it. Fire sprang up from the rock and consumed the meat and the cakes; and the angel of the LORD was no more to be seen. Then Gideon knew that it was the angel of the LORD and said, 'Alas, Lord 22 GOD! Then it is true: I have seen the angel of the LORD face to face.' But 23 the LORD said to him, 'Peace be with you; do not be afraid, you shall not die.' So Gideon built an altar there to the LORD and named it Jehovah- 24 shalom.*a* It stands to this day at Ophrah-of-the-Abiezrites.

That night the LORD said to Gideon, 'Take a young bull of your father's, 25 the yearling bull,*b* tear down the altar of Baal which belongs to your father and cut down the sacred pole which stands beside*c* it. Then build an altar 26 of the proper pattern*d* to the LORD your God on the top of this earthwork; *e* take the yearling bull and offer it as a whole-offering with the wood of the sacred pole that you cut down.' So Gideon took ten of his servants and did 27 as the LORD had told him. He was afraid of his father's family and his fellow-citizens, and so he did it by night, and not by day. When the citizens 28 rose early in the morning, they found the altar of Baal overturned and the sacred pole which had stood beside it cut down and the yearling bull offered up as a whole-offering on the altar which he had built. They asked 29 each other who had done it, and, after searching inquiries, were told that it was Gideon son of Joash. So the citizens said to Joash, 'Bring out your 30 son. He has overturned the altar of Baal and cut down the sacred pole beside it, and he must die.' But as they crowded round him Joash retorted, 31 'Are you pleading Baal's cause then? Do you think that it is for you to save him? Whoever pleads his cause shall be put to death at dawn. If Baal is a god, and someone has torn down his altar, let him take up his own cause.'

*a* *That is* the LORD is peace.     *b* the yearling bull: *prob. rdg.; Heb.* the second bull, seven years old.     *c* *Or* on.     *d* of . . . pattern: *or* with the stones in rows. *e* *Or* stronghold *or* refuge.

32 That day Joash named Gideon Jerubbaal,*a* saying, 'Let Baal plead his cause against this man, for he has torn down his altar.'

33 All the Midianites, the Amalekites, and the eastern tribes joined forces,
34 crossed the river and camped in the Vale of Jezreel. Then the spirit of the LORD took possession of Gideon; he sounded the trumpet and the Abi-
35 ezrites were called out to follow him. He sent messengers all through Manasseh; and they too were called out. He sent messengers to Asher, Zebulun,
36 and Naphtali, and they came up to meet the others. Gideon said to God, 'If
37 thou wilt deliver Israel through me as thou hast promised—now, look, I am putting a fleece of wool on the threshing-floor. If there is dew only on the fleece and all the ground is dry, then I shall be sure that thou wilt
38 deliver Israel through me, as thou hast promised.' And that is what happened. He rose early next day and wrung out the fleece, and he squeezed
39 enough dew from it to fill a bowl with water. Gideon then said to God, 'Do not be angry with me, but give me leave to speak once again. Let me, I pray thee, make one more test with the fleece. This time let the fleece
40 alone be dry, and all the ground be covered with dew.' God let it be so that night: the fleece alone was dry, and on all the ground there was dew.

7 Jerubbaal, that is Gideon, and all the people with him rose early and pitched camp at En-harod;*b* the Midianite camp was in the vale to the
2 north of the hill of Moreh. The LORD said to Gideon, 'The people with you are more than I need to deliver Midian into their hands: Israel will claim the glory for themselves and say that it is their own strength that has given
3 them the victory. Now make a proclamation for all the people to hear, that anyone who is scared or frightened is to leave Mount Galud*c* at once and go back home.' Twenty-two thousand of them went, and ten thousand
4 were left. The LORD then said to Gideon, 'There are still too many. Bring them down to the water, and I will separate them for you there. When I say to you, "This man shall go with you", he shall go; and if I say, "This
5 man shall not go with you", he shall not go.' So Gideon brought the people down to the water and the LORD said to him, 'Make every man who laps the water with his tongue like a dog stand on one side, and on the other
6 every man who goes down on his knees and drinks.' The number of those who lapped was three hundred, and all the rest went down on their knees
7 to drink, putting their hands to their mouths. The LORD said to Gideon, 'With the three hundred men who lapped I will save you and deliver
8 Midian into your hands, and all the rest may go home.' So Gideon sent all these Israelites home, but he kept the three hundred, and they took with them the jars*d* and the trumpets which the people had. The Midianite camp was below him in the vale.

9 That night the LORD said to him, 'Go down at once and attack the camp,
10 for I have delivered it into your hands. If you are afraid to do so, then go
11 down first with your servant Purah and listen to what they are saying. That will give you courage to go down and attack the camp.' So he and his servant Purah went down to the part of the camp where the fighting men
12 lay. Now the Midianites, the Amalekites, and the eastern tribes were so

---

*a* *That is* Let Baal plead.          *b* *That is* Spring of Fright.          *c* *Prob. rdg.; Heb.* Mount Gilead.          *d* *Prob. rdg.; Heb.* provisions.

many that they lay there in the valley like a swarm of locusts; there was no counting their camels; in number they were like grains of sand on the seashore. When Gideon came close, there was a man telling his companion a 13 dream. He said, 'I dreamt that I saw a hard, stale barley-cake rolling over and over through the Midianite camp; it came to a tent, hit it*a* and turned it upside down, and the tent collapsed.' The other answered, 'Depend upon 14 it, this is the sword of Gideon son of Joash the Israelite. God has delivered Midian and the whole army into his hands.' When Gideon heard the story 15 of the dream and its interpretation, he prostrated himself. Then he went back to the Israelite camp and said, 'Up! The LORD has delivered the camp of the Midianites into your hands.' He divided the three hundred men into 16 three companies, and gave every man a trumpet and an empty jar with a torch inside it. Then he said to them, 'Watch me: when I come to the 17 edge of the camp, do exactly as I do. When I and my men blow our trum- 18 pets, you too all round the camp will blow your trumpets, and shout, "For the LORD and for Gideon!"'

Gideon and the hundred men who were with him reached the outskirts 19 of the camp at the beginning of the middle watch; the sentries had just been posted. They blew their trumpets and smashed their jars. The three 20 companies all blew their trumpets and smashed their jars, then grasped the torches in their left hands and the trumpets in their right, and shouted, 'A sword for the LORD and for Gideon!' Every man stood where he was, 21 all round the camp, and the whole camp leapt up in a panic and fled. The 22 three hundred blew their trumpets, and throughout the camp the LORD set every man against his neighbour. The army fled as far as Beth-shittah in Zererah, as far as the ridge of Abel-meholah by Tabbath. The Israelites 23 from Naphtali and Asher and all Manasseh were called out and they pursued the Midianites. Gideon sent men through all the hill-country of 24 Ephraim with this message: 'Come down and cut off the Midianites. Hold the fords of the Jordan against them as far as Beth-barah.' So all the Ephraimites were called out and they held the fords of the Jordan as far as Beth-barah. They captured the two Midianite princes, Oreb and Zeeb. 25 Oreb they killed at the Rock of Oreb, and Zeeb by the Winepress of Zeeb, and they kept up the pursuit of the Midianites; afterwards they brought the heads of Oreb and Zeeb across the Jordan to Gideon.

The men of Ephraim said to Gideon, 'Why have you treated us like **8** this? Why did you not summon us when you went to fight Midian?'; and they reproached him violently. But he said to them, 'What have I done 2 compared with you? Are not Ephraim's gleanings better than the whole vintage of Abiezer? God has delivered Oreb and Zeeb, the princes of 3 Midian, into your hands. What have I done compared with you?' At these words of his, their anger died down.

Gideon came to the Jordan, and he and his three hundred men crossed 4 over to continue the pursuit, weary though they were. He said to the men 5 of Succoth, 'Will you give these men of mine some bread, for they are weary, and I am pursuing Zebah and Zalmunna, the kings of Midian?' But the chief men of Succoth replied, 'Are Zebah and Zalmunna already 6

*a Prob. rdg.; Heb. adds and it fell.*

7 in your hands, that we should give your army bread?' Gideon said, 'For that, when the LORD delivers Zebah and Zalmunna into my hands, I will

8 thresh your bodies with desert thorns and briars.' He went on from there to Penuel and made the same request; the men of Penuel answered like

9 the men of Succoth. He said to the men of Penuel, 'When I return safely, I will pull down your castle.'

10 Zebah and Zalmunna were in Karkor with their army of fifteen thousand men. These were all that remained of the whole host of the eastern tribes;

11 a hundred and twenty thousand armed men had fallen in battle. Gideon advanced along the track used by the tent-dwellers east of Nobah and Jogbehah, and his attack caught the army when they were off their guard.

12 Zebah and Zalmunna fled; but he went in pursuit of these Midianite kings and captured them both; and their whole army melted away.

13 As Gideon son of Joash was returning from the battle by the Ascent of

14 Heres, he caught a young man from Succoth. He questioned him, and one by one he numbered off the names of the rulers of Succoth and its elders,

15 seventy-seven in all. Gideon then came to the men of Succoth and said, 'Here are Zebah and Zalmunna, about whom you taunted me. "Are Zebah and Zalmunna", you said, "already in your hands, that we should give

16 your weary men bread?"' Then he took the elders of the city and he dis-

17 ciplined those men of Succoth with desert thorns and briars. He also pulled

18 down the castle of Penuel and put the men of the city to death. Then he said to Zebah and Zalmunna, 'What of the men you killed in Tabor?' They answered, 'They were like you, every one had the look of a king's

19 son.' 'They were my brothers,' he said, 'my mother's sons. I swear by the

20 LORD, if you had let them live I would not have killed you'; and he said to his eldest son Jether, 'Up with you, and kill them.' But he was still only a

21 lad, and did not draw his sword, because he was afraid. So Zebah and Zalmunna said, 'Rise up yourself and dispatch us, for you have a man's strength.' So Gideon rose and killed them both, and he took the crescents from the necks of their camels.

22 After this the Israelites said to Gideon, 'You have saved us from the Midianites; now you be our ruler, you and your son and your grandson.'

23 Gideon replied, 'I will not rule over you, nor shall my son; the LORD will

24 rule over you.' Then he said, 'I have a request to make: will every one of you give me the earrings from his booty?'—for the enemy wore golden

25 earrings, being Ishmaelites. They said, 'Of course, we will give them.' So a cloak was spread out and every man threw on to it the golden earrings

26 from his booty. The earrings for which he asked weighed seventeen hundred shekels of gold; this was in addition to the crescents and pendants and the purple cloaks worn by the Midianite kings, not counting the chains on the

27 necks of their camels. Gideon made it into an ephod and he set it up in his own city of Ophrah. All the Israelites turned wantonly to its worship, and it became a trap to catch Gideon and his household.

28 Thus the Midianites were subdued by the Israelites; they could no longer hold up their heads. For forty years the land was at peace, all the

29 lifetime of Gideon, that is Jerubbaal son of Joash; and he retired to his

30 own home. Gideon had seventy sons, his own offspring, for he had many

wives. He had a concubine who lived in Shechem, and she also bore him 31
a son, whom he named Abimelech. Gideon son of Joash died at a ripe old 32
age and was buried in his father's grave at Ophrah-of-the-Abiezrites.
After his death, the Israelites again went wantonly to the worship of the 33
Baalim and made Baal-berith their god. They forgot the LORD their God 34
who had delivered them from their enemies on every side, and did not 35
show to the family of Jerubbaal, that is Gideon, the loyalty that was due to
them for all the good he had done for Israel.

ABIMELECH SON OF JERUBBAAL went to Shechem to his mother's 9
brothers, and spoke with them and with all the clan of his mother's family.
'I beg you,' he said, 'whisper a word in the ears of the chief citizens of 2
Shechem. Ask them which is better for them: that seventy men, all the
sons of Jerubbaal, should rule over them, or one man. Tell them to remember that I am their own flesh and blood.' So his mother's brothers 3
repeated all this to each of them on his behalf; and they were moved to
come over to Abimelech's side, because, as they said, he was their brother.
They gave him seventy pieces of silver from the temple of Baal-berith, and 4
with these he hired idle and reckless men, who followed him. He came to 5
his father's house in Ophrah and butchered his seventy brothers, the sons
of Jerubbaal, on a single stone block, all but Jotham the youngest, who
survived because he had hidden himself. Then all the citizens of Shechem 6
and all Beth-millo came together and made Abimelech king beside the old
propped-up terebinth at Shechem.

When this was reported to Jotham, he went and stood on the summit of 7
Mount Gerizim. He cried at the top of his voice: 'Listen to me, you
citizens of Shechem, and may God listen to you:

'Once upon a time the trees came to anoint a king, and they said to the 8
olive-tree: Be king over us. But the olive-tree answered: What, leave my 9
rich oil by which gods and men are honoured, to come and hold sway over
the trees?

'So the trees said to the fig-tree: Then will you come and be king over 10
us? But the fig-tree answered: What, leave my good fruit and all its sweet- 11
ness, to come and hold sway over the trees?

'So the trees said to the vine: Then will you come and be king over us? 12
But the vine answered: What, leave my new wine which gladdens gods and 13
men, to come and hold sway over the trees?

'Then all the trees said to the thorn-bush: Will you then be king over 14
us? And the thorn said to the trees: If you really mean to anoint me as your 15
king, then come under the protection of my shadow; if not, fire shall come
out of the thorn and burn up the cedars of Lebanon.'

Then Jotham said, 'Now, have you acted fairly and honestly in making 16
Abimelech king? Have you done the right thing by Jerubbaal and his
household? Have you given my father his due—who fought for you, and 17
threw himself into the forefront of the battle and delivered you from the
Midianites? Today you have risen against my father's family, butchered 18
his seventy sons on a single stone block, and made Abimelech, the son of
his slave-girl, king over the citizens of Shechem because he is your brother.

19 In this day's work have you acted fairly and honestly by Jerubbaal and his
20 family? If so, I wish you joy in Abimelech and wish him joy in you! If not,
may fire come out of Abimelech and burn up the citizens of Shechem and
all Beth-millo; may fire also come out from the citizens of Shechem and
21 Beth-millo and burn up Abimelech.' After which Jotham slipped away
and made his escape; he came to Beer, and there he settled out of reach of
his brother Abimelech.

22 23   After Abimelech had been prince over Israel for three years, God sent
an evil spirit to make a breach between Abimelech and the citizens of
24 Shechem, and they played him false. This was done on purpose, so that
the violent murder of the seventy sons of Jerubbaal might recoil on their
brother Abimelech who did the murder and on the citizens of Shechem
25 who encouraged him to do it. The citizens of Shechem set men to lie in
wait for him on the hill-tops, but they robbed all who passed that way, and
so the news reached Abimelech.

26   Now Gaal son of Ebed came with his kinsmen to Shechem, and the
27 citizens of Shechem transferred their allegiance to him. They went out
into the country-side, picked the early grapes in their vineyards, trod them
in the winepress and held festival. They went into the temple of their god,
28 where they ate and drank and reviled Abimelech. 'Who is Abimelech,' said
Gaal son of Ebed, 'and who are the Shechemites, that we should be his
subjects? Have not this son of Jerubbaal and his lieutenant Zebul been
subjects of the men of Hamor the father of Shechem? Why indeed should
29 we be subject to him? If only this people were in my charge I should know
how to get rid of Abimelech! I would say to him, "Get your men together,
30 and come out and fight." ' When Zebul the governor of the city heard what
31 Gaal son of Ebed said, he was very angry. He resorted to a ruse and sent
messengers to Abimelech to say, 'Gaal son of Ebed and his kinsmen have
32 come to Shechem and are turning the city against you. Get up now in the
night, you and the people with you, and lie in wait in the open country.
33 Then be up in the morning at sunrise, and advance rapidly against the city.
When he and his people come out, do to him what the situation demands.'
34 So Abimelech and his people rose in the night, and lay in wait to attack
35 Shechem, in four companies. Gaal son of Ebed came out and stood in the
entrance of the city gate, and Abimelech and his people rose from their
36 hiding-place. Gaal saw them and said to Zebul, 'There are people coming
down from the tops of the hills', but Zebul replied, 'What you see is the
37 shadow of the hills, looking like men.' Once more Gaal said, 'There are
people coming down from the central ridge of the hills, and one company
38 is coming along the road of the Soothsayers' Terebinth.' Then Zebul said
to him, 'Where are your brave words now? You said, "Who is Abimelech
that we should be subject to him?" Are not these the people you despised?
39 Go out and fight him.' Gaal led the citizens of Shechem out and attacked
40 Abimelech, but Abimelech routed him and he fled. The ground was
41 strewn with corpses all the way to the entrance of the gate. Abimelech
established himself in Arumah, and Zebul drove away Gaal and his kinsmen and allowed them no place in Shechem.
42   Next day the people came out into the open, and this was reported to

Abimelech. He on his side took his supporters, divided them into three 43 companies and lay in wait in the open country; and when he saw the people coming out of the city, he rose and attacked them. Abimelech and the 44 company with him advanced rapidly and took up position at the entrance of the city gate, while the other two companies advanced against all those who were in the open and struck them down. Abimelech kept up the attack 45 on the city all that day and captured it; he killed the people in it, pulled the city down and sowed the site with salt. When the occupants of the castle 46 of Shechem heard of this, they went into the great hall *a* of the temple of El-berith. It was reported to Abimelech that all the occupants of the castle 47 of Shechem had collected together. So he and his people went up Mount 48 Zalmon carrying axes; there he cut brushwood, and took it and hoisted it on his shoulder. He said to his men, 'You see what I am doing; be quick and do the same.' So each man cut brushwood; then they followed Abi- 49 melech and laid the brushwood against the hall, and burnt it over their heads. Thus all the occupants of the castle of Shechem died, about a thousand men and women.

Abimelech then went to Thebez, besieged it and took it. There was a 50 51 strong castle in the middle of the city, and all the citizens, men and women, took refuge there. They shut themselves in and went on to the roof. Abimelech came up to the castle and attacked it. As he approached the 52 entrance to the castle to set fire to it, a woman threw a millstone down on 53 his head and fractured his skull. He called hurriedly to his young armour- 54 bearer and said, 'Draw your sword and dispatch me, or men will say of me: A woman killed him.' So the young man ran him through and he died. When the Israelites saw that Abimelech was dead, they all went back to 55 their homes. It was thus that God requited the crime which Abimelech 56 had committed against his father by the murder of his seventy brothers, and brought all the wickedness of the men of Shechem on their own heads. 57 The curse of Jotham son of Jerubbaal came home to them.

After Abimelech, Tola son of Pua, son of Dodo, a man of Issachar who 10 lived in Shamir in the hill-country of Ephraim, came in his turn to deliver Israel. He was judge over Israel for twenty-three years, and when he died 2 he was buried in Shamir.

After him came Jair the Gileadite; he was judge over Israel for twenty- 3 two years. He had thirty sons, who rode thirty asses; they had thirty towns 4 in the land of Gilead, which to this day are called Havvoth-jair.*b* When 5 Jair died, he was buried in Kamon.

Once more the Israelites did what was wrong in the eyes of the LORD, 6 worshipping the Baalim and the Ashtaroth, the deities of Aram and of Sidon and of Moab, of the Ammonites and of the Philistines. They forsook the LORD and did not worship him. The LORD was angry with Israel, and 7 he sold them to the Philistines and the Ammonites, who *c* for eighteen 8 years harassed and oppressed the Israelites who lived beyond the Jordan in the Amorite country in Gilead. Then the Ammonites crossed the Jordan 9 to attack Judah, Benjamin, and Ephraim, so that Israel was in great dis- tress. The Israelites cried to the LORD for help and said, 'We have sinned 10

*a Or* vault.      *b That is* Tent-villages of Jair.      *c Prob. rdg.; Heb. adds* in that year.

11 against thee; we have forsaken our God and worshipped the Baalim.' And
the LORD said to the Israelites, 'The Egyptians, the Amorites, the Ammon-
12 ites, the Philistines; the Sidonians too and the Amalekites and the Midianites—all these oppressed you and you cried to me for help; and did not I
13 deliver you? But you forsook me and worshipped other gods; therefore I
14 will deliver you no more. Go and cry for help to the gods you have chosen,
15 and let them save you in the day of your distress.' But the Israelites said
to the LORD, 'We have sinned. Deal with us as thou wilt; only save us this
16 day, we implore thee.' They banished the foreign gods and worshipped the
LORD; and he could endure no longer to see the plight of Israel.

17     Then the Ammonites were called to arms, and they encamped in Gilead,
18 while the Israelites assembled and encamped in Mizpah. The people of
Gilead and their chief men said to one another, 'If any man will strike the
first blow at the Ammonites, he shall be lord over the inhabitants of Gilead.'

**11**     Jephthah the Gileadite was a great warrior; he was the son of Gilead by
2 a prostitute. But Gilead had a wife who bore him several sons, and when
they grew up they drove Jephthah away; they said to him, 'You have no
3 inheritance in our father's house; you are another woman's son.' So
Jephthah, to escape his brothers, went away and settled in the land of Tob,
and swept up a number of idle men who followed him.

4 5     The time came when the Ammonites made war on Israel, and when the
fighting began, the elders of Gilead went to fetch Jephthah from the land
6 of Tob. They said to him, 'Come and be our commander so that we can
7 fight the Ammonites.' But Jephthah said to the elders of Gilead, 'You drove
me from my father's house in hatred. Why come to me now when you are
8 in trouble?' 'It is because of that', they replied, 'that we have turned to you
now. Come with us and fight the Ammonites, and become lord over all the
9 inhabitants of Gilead.' Jephthah said to them, 'If you ask me back to fight
the Ammonites and if the LORD delivers them into my hands, then I will
10 be your lord.' The elders of Gilead said again to Jephthah, 'We swear by
the LORD, who shall be witness between us, that we will do what you say.'
11 Jephthah then went with the elders of Gilead, and the people made him
their lord and commander. And at Mizpah, in the presence of the LORD,
Jephthah repeated all that he had said.

12     Jephthah sent a mission to the king of Ammon to ask what quarrel he
13 had with them that made him invade their country. The king gave Jephthah's men this answer: 'When the Israelites came up from Egypt, they
took our land from the Arnon as far as the Jabbok and the Jordan. Give us
14 back these lands in peace.' Jephthah sent a second mission to the king of
15 Ammon, and they said, 'This is Jephthah's answer: Israel did not take
16 either the Moabite country or the Ammonite country. When they came up
from Egypt, the Israelites passed through the wilderness to the Red Sea[a]
17 and came to Kadesh. They then sent envoys to the king of Edom asking
him to grant them passage through his country, but the king of Edom would
not hear of it. They sent also to the king of Moab, but he was not willing;
18 so Israel remained in Kadesh. They then passed through the wilderness,
skirting Edom and Moab, and kept to the east of Moab. They encamped

---

*a  Or the Sea of Reeds.*

beside the Arnon, but they did not enter Moabite territory, because the
Arnon is the frontier of Moab. Israel then sent envoys to the king of the   19
Amorites, Sihon king of Heshbon, asking him to give them free passage
through his country to their destination. But Sihon would not grant Israel   20
free passage through his territory; he mustered all his people, encamped
in Jahaz and fought Israel. But the LORD the God of Israel delivered Sihon   21
and all his people into the hands of Israel; they defeated them and occupied
all the territory of the Amorites in that region. They took all the Amorite   22
territory from the Arnon to the Jabbok and from the wilderness to the
Jordan. The LORD the God of Israel drove out the Amorites for the benefit   23
of his people Israel. And do you now propose to take their place? It is for   24
you to possess whatever Kemosh your god gives you; and all that the LORD
our God gave us as we advanced is ours. For that matter, are you any better   25
than Balak son of Zippor, king of Moab? Did he ever quarrel with Israel or
attack them? For three hundred years Israelites have lived in Heshbon and   26
its dependent villages, in Aroer and its villages, and in all the towns by the
Arnon. Why did you not oust *a* them during all that time? We have done you   27
no wrong; it is you who are doing us wrong by attacking us. The LORD who
is judge will judge this day between the Israelites and the Ammonites.'
But the king of the Ammonites would not listen to the message which   28
Jephthah had sent him.

   Then the spirit of the LORD came upon Jephthah and he passed through   29
Gilead and Manasseh, by Mizpeh of Gilead, and from Mizpeh over to the
Ammonites. Jephthah made this vow to the LORD: 'If thou wilt deliver the   30
Ammonites into my hands, then the first creature that comes out of the door   31
of my house to meet me when I return from them in peace shall be the
LORD's; I will offer that as a whole-offering.' So Jephthah crossed over to   32
attack the Ammonites, and the LORD delivered them into his hands. He   33
routed them with great slaughter all the way from Aroer to Minnith, taking
twenty towns, and as far as Abel-keramim. Thus Israel crushed Ammon.
But when Jephthah came to his house in Mizpah, who should come out to   34
meet him with tambourines and dances but his daughter, and she his only
child; he had no other, neither son nor daughter. When he saw her, he rent   35
his clothes and said, 'Alas, my daughter, you have broken my heart, such
trouble you have brought upon me. I have made a vow to the LORD and I
cannot go back.' She replied, 'Father, you have made a vow to the LORD;   36
do to me what you have solemnly vowed, since the LORD has avenged you
on the Ammonites, your enemies. But, father, grant me this one favour.   37
For two months let me be, that I may roam *b* the hills with my companions
and mourn that I must die a virgin.' 'Go', he said, and he let her depart for   38
two months. She went with her companions and mourned her virginity on
the hills. At the end of two months she came back to her father, and he   39
fulfilled the vow he had made; she died a virgin. It became a tradition that   40
the daughters of Israel should go year by year and commemorate the fate
of Jephthah's daughter, four days in every year.

   The Ephraimites mustered their forces and crossed over to Zaphon. **12**
They said to Jephthah, 'Why did you march against the Ammonites and

   *a Or* recover.        *b Or* that I may go down country to . . .

not summon us to go with you? We will burn your house over your head.'
2 Jephthah answered, 'I and my people had a feud with the Ammonites, and
had I appealed to you for help, you would not have saved us *a* from them.
3 When I saw that we were not to look for help from you, I took my life in
my hands and marched against the Ammonites, and the LORD delivered
4 them into my power. Why then do you attack me today?' Jephthah then
mustered all the men of Gilead and fought Ephraim, and the Gileadites
5 defeated them. The Gileadites seized the fords of the Jordan and held
them against Ephraim. When any Ephraimite who had escaped begged
leave to cross, the men of Gilead asked him, 'Are you an Ephraimite?',
6 and if he said, 'No', they would retort, 'Say Shibboleth.' He would say
'Sibboleth', and because he could not pronounce the word properly, they
seized him and killed him at the fords of the Jordan. At that time forty-two
thousand men of Ephraim lost their lives.

7    Jephthah was judge over Israel for six years; when he died he was
8 buried in his own city in Gilead. After him Ibzan of Bethlehem was judge
9 over Israel. He had thirty sons and thirty daughters. He gave away the
thirty daughters in marriage and brought in thirty girls for his sons. He
10 was judge over Israel for seven years, and when he died he was buried in
Bethlehem.

11    After him Elon the Zebulunite was judge over Israel for ten years.
12 13 When he died, he was buried in Aijalon in the land of Zebulun. Next
14 Abdon son of Hillel the Pirathonite was judge over Israel. He had forty
sons and thirty grandsons, who rode each on his own ass. He was judge
15 over Israel for eight years; and when he died he was buried in Pirathon in
the land of Ephraim on the hill of the Amalekite.


## Israel oppressed by the Philistines

13 O NCE MORE THE ISRAELITES DID WHAT WAS WRONG in the eyes
of the LORD, and he delivered them into the hands of the Philistines
for forty years.
2    There was a man from Zorah of the tribe of Dan whose name was
3 Manoah and whose wife was barren and childless. The angel of the LORD
appeared to her and said, 'You are barren and have no child, but you shall
4 conceive and give birth to a son. Now you must do as I say: be careful to
5 drink no wine or strong drink, and to eat no forbidden food; you will
conceive and give birth to a son, and no razor shall touch his head, for the
boy is to be a Nazirite consecrated to God from the day of his birth. He
will strike the first blow to deliver Israel from the power of the Philistines.'
6 The woman went and told her husband; she said to him, 'A man of God
came to me; his appearance was that of an *b* angel of God, most terrible to
7 see. I did not ask him where he came from nor did he tell me his name. He
said to me, "You shall conceive and give birth to a son. From this time
onwards drink no wine or strong drink and eat no forbidden food, for the

*a* and had I . . . saved us: *or* I did appeal to you for help, but you would not save us . . .
*b* *Or* the.

boy is to be a Nazirite consecrated to God from his birth to the day of his death." ' Manoah prayed to the LORD, 'If it please thee, O LORD, let the 8 man of God whom thou didst send come again to tell us what we are to do with the boy who is to be born.' God heard Manoah's prayer, and the angel 9 of God came again to the woman, who was sitting in the fields; her husband was not with her. The woman ran quickly and said to him, 'The man who 10 came to me the other day has appeared to me again.' Manoah went with 11 her at once and approached the man and said, 'Was it you who talked with my wife?' He said, 'Yes, it was I.' 'Now when your words come true,' 12 Manoah said, 'what kind of boy will he be and what will he do?' The angel 13 of the LORD answered him, 'Your wife must be careful to do all that I told her: she must not taste anything that comes from the vine. She must 14 drink no wine or strong drink, and she must eat no forbidden food. She must do what I say.' Manoah said to the angel of the LORD, 'May we urge 15 you to stay? Let us prepare a kid for you.' The angel of the LORD replied, 16 'Though you urge me to stay, I will not eat your food; but prepare a whole-offering if you will, and offer that to the LORD.' Manoah did not perceive that he was the angel of the LORD and said to him, 'What is your name? 17 For we shall want to honour you when your words come true.' The angel 18 of the LORD said to him, 'How can you ask my name? It is a name of wonder.' Manoah took a kid with the proper grain-offering, and offered it 19 on the rock to the LORD, to him whose works are full of wonder. And while Manoah and his wife were watching, the flame went up from the altar 20 towards heaven, and the angel of the LORD went up in the flame; and seeing this, Manoah and his wife fell on their faces. The angel of the LORD did 21 not appear again to Manoah and his wife; and Manoah knew that he was the angel of the LORD. He said to his wife, 'We are doomed to die, we have 22 seen God',*a* but she replied, 'If the LORD had wanted to kill us, he would 23 not have accepted a whole-offering and a grain-offering at our hands; he would not now have let us see and hear all this.' The woman gave birth to 24-25 a son and named him Samson. The boy grew up in Mahaneh-dan between Zorah and Eshtaol, and the LORD blessed him, and the spirit of the LORD began to drive him hard.

    Samson went down to Timnath, and there he saw a woman, one of the **14** Philistines. When he came back, he told his father and mother that he had 2 seen a Philistine woman in Timnath and asked them to get her for him as his wife. His father and mother said to him, 'Is there no woman among 3 your cousins or in all our own people? Must you go and marry one of the uncircumcised Philistines?' But Samson said to his father, 'Get her for me, because she pleases me.' His father and mother did not know that the 4 LORD was at work in this, seeking an opportunity against the Philistines, who at that time were masters of Israel.

    Samson*b* went down to Timnath and, when he reached the vineyards 5 there, a young lion came at him growling. The spirit of the LORD suddenly 6 seized him and, having no weapon in his hand, he tore the lion in pieces as if it were a kid. He did not tell his parents what he had done. Then he went 7 down and spoke to the woman, and she pleased him. After a time he went 8

*a Or* a god.     *b Prob. rdg.; Heb. adds* and his father and mother.

9 down again to take her to wife; he turned aside to look at the carcass of the lion, and he saw a swarm of bees in it, and honey. He scraped the honey into his hands and went on, eating as he went. When he came to his father and mother, he gave them some and they ate it; but he did not tell them that
10 he had scraped the honey out of the lion's carcass. His father went down to see the woman, and Samson gave a feast there as the custom of young men
11 was. When the people saw him, they brought thirty young men to be his
12 escort. Samson said to them, 'Let me ask you a riddle. If you can guess it during the seven days of the feast, I will give you thirty lengths of linen and
13 thirty changes of clothing; but if you cannot guess the answer, then you shall give me thirty lengths of linen and thirty changes of clothing.' 'Tell
14 us your riddle,' they said; 'let us hear it.' So he said to them:

Out of the eater came something to eat;
out of the strong came something sweet.

15 At the end of three days they had failed to guess the riddle. On the fourth day they said to Samson's wife, 'Coax your husband and make him tell you the riddle, or we shall burn you and your father's house. Did you
16 invite us here to beggar us?' So Samson's wife wept over him and said, 'You do not love me, you only hate me. You have asked my kinsfolk a riddle and you have not told it to me.' He said to her, 'I have not told it
17 even to my father and mother; and am I to tell you?' But she wept over him every day until the seven feast days were ended, and on the seventh day, because she pestered him, he told her, and she told the riddle to her
18 kinsfolk. So that same day the men of the city said to Samson before he entered the bridal chamber: *a*

What is sweeter than honey?
What is stronger than a lion?

and he replied, 'If you had not ploughed with my heifer, you would not
19 have found out my riddle.' Then the spirit of the LORD suddenly seized him. He went down to Ashkelon and there he killed thirty men, took their belts and gave their clothes to the men who had answered his riddle; but
20 he was very angry and went off to his father's house. And Samson's wife was given in marriage to the friend who had been his groomsman.

**15** After a while, during the time of wheat harvest, Samson went to visit his wife, taking a kid as a present for her. He said, 'I am going to my wife
2 in our bridal chamber', but her father would not let him in. He said, 'I was sure that you hated her, so I gave her in marriage to your groomsman. Her
3 young sister is better than she—take her instead.' But Samson said, 'This time I will settle my score with the Philistines; I will do them some real
4 harm.' So he went and caught three hundred jackals and got some torches; he tied the jackals tail to tail and fastened a torch between each pair of tails.
5 He then set the torches alight and turned the jackals loose in the standing corn of the Philistines. He burnt up standing corn and stooks as well,
6 vineyards and olive groves. The Philistines said, 'Who has done this?' They were told that it was Samson, because the Timnite, his father-in-law, had

---

*a* he entered . . . chamber: *prob. rdg.; Heb.* the sun went down.

taken his wife and given her to his groomsman. So the Philistines came and
burnt her and her father. Samson said, 'If you do things like this, I swear 7
I will be revenged upon you before I have done.' He smote them hip and 8
thigh with great slaughter; and after that he went down to live in a cave in
the Rock of Etam.

The Philistines came up and pitched camp in Judah, and overran Lehi. 9
The men of Judah said, 'Why have you attacked us?' They answered, 'We 10
have come to take Samson prisoner and serve him as he served us.' So 11
three thousand men from Judah went down to the cave in the Rock of
Etam. They said to Samson, 'Surely you know that the Philistines are our
masters? Now see what you have brought upon us.' He answered, 'I only
served them as they had served me.' They said to him, 'We have come down 12
to bind you and hand you over to the Philistines.' 'Then you must swear
to me', he said, 'that you will not set upon me yourselves.' They answered, 13
'No; we will only bind you and hand you over to them, we will not kill you.'
So they bound him with two new ropes and brought him up from the cave
in the Rock. He came to Lehi, and when they met him, the Philistines 14
shouted in triumph; but the spirit of the LORD suddenly seized him, the
ropes on his arms became like burnt tow and his bonds melted away. He 15
found the jaw-bone of an ass, all raw, and picked it up and slew a thousand
men. He made this saying: 16

> With the jaw-bone of an ass *a* I have flayed them like asses; *b*
> with the jaw-bone of an ass I have slain a thousand men.

When he had said his say, he threw away the jaw-bone; and he called that 17
place Ramath-lehi.*c* He began to feel very thirsty and cried aloud to the 18
LORD, 'Thou hast let me, thy servant, win this great victory, and must I
now die of thirst and fall into the hands of the uncircumcised?' God split 19
open the Hollow of Lehi and water came out of it. Samson drank, his
strength returned and he revived. This is why the spring in Lehi is called
En-hakkore*d* to this day.

Samson was judge over Israel for twenty years in the days of the 20
Philistines.

Samson went to Gaza, and there he saw a prostitute and went in to **16**
spend the night with her. The people of Gaza heard that Samson had come, 2
and they surrounded him and lay in wait for him all that night at the city
gate. During the night, however, they took no action, saying to themselves,
'When day breaks we shall kill him.' Samson lay in bed till midnight; and 3
when midnight came he rose, seized hold of the doors of the city gate and
the two posts, pulled them out, bar and all, hoisted them on to his shoulders
and carried them to the top of the hill east of Hebron.

After this Samson fell in love with a woman named Delilah, who lived 4
in the valley of Sorek. The lords of the Philistines went up country to see 5
her and said, 'Coax him and find out what gives him his great strength,
and how we can master him, bind him and so hold him captive; then we

---

*a* ass: *Heb.* hamor.          *b* I have . . . asses: *or* I have reddened them blood-red, *or* I
have heaped them in heaps; *Heb.* hamor himmartim.          *c* *That is* Jaw-bone Hill.
*d* *That is* the Crier's Spring.

6 will each give you eleven hundred pieces of silver.' So Delilah said to
Samson, 'Tell me what gives you your great strength, and how you can be
7 bound and held captive.' Samson replied, 'If they bind me with seven
fresh bowstrings not yet dry, then I shall become as weak as any other man.'
8 So the lords of the Philistines brought her seven fresh bowstrings not yet
9 dry, and she bound him with them. She had men already hidden in the
inner room, and she cried, 'The Philistines are upon you, Samson!' But
he snapped the bowstrings as a strand of tow snaps when it feels the fire,
10 and his strength was not tamed. Delilah said to Samson, 'I see you have
made a fool of me and told me lies. Tell me this time how you can be
11 bound.' He said to her, 'If you bind me tightly with new ropes that have
12 never been used, then I shall become as weak as any other man.' So
Delilah took new ropes and bound him with them. Then she cried, 'The
Philistines are upon you, Samson!', while the men waited hidden in the
13 inner room. He snapped the ropes off his arms like pack-thread. Delilah
said to him, 'You are still making a fool of me and have told me lies. Tell
me: how can you be bound?' He said, 'Take the seven loose locks of my
hair and weave them into the warp, and then drive them tight with the
beater; and I shall become as weak as any other man.' So she lulled him to
14 sleep, wove the seven loose locks of his hair into the warp, and drove them
tight with the beater, and cried, 'The Philistines are upon you, Samson!'
15 He woke from sleep and pulled away the warp and the loom with it.[a] She
said to him, 'How can you say you love me when you do not confide in me?
This is the third time you have made a fool of me and have not told me
16 what gives you your great strength.' She so pestered him with these words
17 day after day, pressing him hard and wearying him to death, that he told
her his secret. 'No razor has touched my head,' he said, 'because I am a
Nazirite, consecrated to God from the day of my birth. If my head were
shaved, then my strength would leave me, and I should become as weak as
18 any other man.' Delilah saw that he had told her his secret; so she sent to
the lords of the Philistines and said, 'Come up at once, he has told me his
secret.' So the lords of the Philistines came up and brought the money
19 with them. She lulled him to sleep on her knees, summoned a man and he
shaved the seven locks of his hair for her. She began to take him captive
20 and his strength left him. Then she cried, 'The Philistines are upon you,
Samson!' He woke from his sleep and said, 'I will go out as usual and shake
21 myself'; he did not know that the LORD had left him. The Philistines
seized him, gouged out his eyes and brought him down to Gaza. There
they bound him with fetters of bronze, and he was set to grinding corn in
22 the prison. But his hair, after it had been shaved, began to grow again.
23   The lords of the Philistines assembled together to offer a great sacrifice
to their god Dagon and to rejoice before him. They said, 'Our god has
24 delivered Samson our enemy into our hands.' The people, when they saw
him, praised their god, chanting:

> Our god has delivered our enemy into our hands,
> the scourge of our land who piled it with our dead.

[a] *the warp ... with it: prob. rdg.; Heb. adds an unintelligible word.*

When they grew merry, they said, 'Call Samson, and let him fight to make 25
sport for us.' So they summoned Samson from prison and he made sport
before them all. They stood him between the pillars, and Samson said to 26
the boy who held his hand, 'Put me where I can feel the pillars which support the temple, so that I may lean against them.' The temple was full of 27
men and women, and all the lords of the Philistines were there, and there
were about three thousand men and women on the roof watching Samson
as he fought. Samson called on the LORD and said, 'Remember me, O 28
Lord GOD, remember me: give me strength only this once, O God, and let
me at one stroke be avenged on the Philistines for my two eyes.' He put 29
his arms round the two central pillars which supported the temple, his
right arm round one and his left round the other, and braced himself and 30
said, 'Let me die with the Philistines.' Then Samson leaned forward with
all his might, and the temple fell on the lords and on all the people who were
in it. So the dead whom he killed at his death were more than those he had
killed in his life. His brothers and all his father's family came down, carried 31
him up to the grave of his father Manoah between Zorah and Eshtaol and
buried him there. He had been judge over Israel for twenty years.

## *Years of lawlessness*

THERE WAS ONCE A MAN NAMED MICAH from the hill-country of 17
Ephraim. He said to his mother, 'You remember the eleven hundred 2
pieces of silver which were taken from you, and how you called down a
curse on the thief in my hearing? I have the money; I took it and now I
will give it back to you.'*a* His mother said, 'May the LORD bless you, my
son.' So he gave the eleven hundred pieces of silver back to his mother, 3
and she said, 'I now solemnly dedicate this money of mine to the LORD for
the benefit of my son, to make a carved idol and a cast image.' He returned 4
the money to his mother, and she took two hundred pieces of silver and
handed them to a silversmith, who made them into an idol and an image,
which stood in Micah's house.

This man Micah had a shrine, and he made an ephod and teraphim*b* 5
and installed one of his sons to be his priest. In those days there was no 6
king in Israel and every man did what was right in his own eyes. Now 7
there was a young man from Bethlehem in Judah, from the clan of Judah,
a Levite named Ben-gershom.*c* He had left the city of Bethlehem to go 8
and find somewhere to live. On his way he came to Micah's house in the
hill-country of Ephraim. Micah said to him, 'Where have you come from?' 9
He replied, 'I am a Levite from Bethlehem in Judah, and I am looking for
somewhere to live.' Micah said to him, 'Stay with me and be priest and 10
father to me. I will give you ten pieces of silver a year, and provide you with
food and clothes.' The Levite agreed to stay with the man and was treated 11
as one of his own sons. Micah installed the Levite, and the young man 12
became his priest and a member of his household. Micah said, 'Now I 13

*a* and now . . . you: *transposed from verse 3.*　　　*b* Or household gods.　　　*c* named
Ben-gershom: *prob. rdg., cp. 18. 30; Heb.* he lodged there.

know that the LORD will make me prosper, because I have a Levite for my priest.'

18    In those days there was no king in Israel and the tribe of the Danites was looking for territory to occupy, because they had not so far come into

2   possession of the territory allotted to them among the tribes of Israel. The Danites therefore sent out five fighting men of their clan from Zorah and Eshtaol to prospect, with instructions to go and explore the land. They came to Micah's house in the hill-country of Ephraim and spent the night

3   there. While they were there, they recognized the speech of the young Levite; they turned there and then and said to him, 'Who brought you

4   here? What are you doing? What is your business here?' He said, 'This is

5   all Micah's doing: he has hired me and I have become his priest.' They said to him, 'Then inquire of God on our behalf whether our mission will

6   be successful.' The priest replied, 'Go in peace. Your mission is in the

7   LORD's hands.' The five men went on their way and came to Laish. There they found the inhabitants living a carefree life, in the same way as the Sidonians, a quiet, carefree folk, with no hereditary king to keep the country under his thumb.*ᵃ* They were a long way from the Sidonians, and

8   had no contact with the Aramaeans. So the five men went back to Zorah

9   and Eshtaol, and when their kinsmen asked their news, they said, 'Come and attack them. It is an excellent country that we have seen. Will you hang back and do nothing about it? Start off now and take possession of the land.

10  When you get there, you will find a people living a carefree life in a wide expanse of open country. God has delivered it into your hands, a place where there is no lack of anything on earth.'

11     And so six hundred armed men from the clan of the Danites set out from

12  Zorah and Eshtaol. They went up country and encamped in Kiriath-jearim in Judah: this is why that place to this day is called Mahaneh-dan;*ᵇ*

13  it lies west of Kiriath-jearim. From there they passed on to the hill-country

14  of Ephraim and came to Micah's house. The five men who had been to explore the country round Laish spoke up and said to their kinsmen, 'Do you know that in one of these houses there are now an ephod and teraphim,

15  an idol and an image? Now consider what you had best do.' So they turned

16  aside to Micah's house and greeted him. The six hundred armed Danites

17  took their stand at the entrance of the gate, and the five men who had gone to explore the country went indoors to take the idol and the image, ephod and teraphim, while the priest was standing at the entrance with the six

18  hundred armed men. The five men entered Micah's house and took the idol and the image, ephod and teraphim.*ᶜ* The priest asked them what they

19  were doing, but they said to him, 'Be quiet; not a word. Come with us and be our priest and father. Which is better, to be priest in the household of

20  one man or to be priest to a whole tribe and clan in Israel?' This pleased the priest; so he took the ephod and teraphim, the idol and the image, and

21  joined the company. They turned and went off, putting the dependants,

22  the herds, and the valuables in front. The Danites had gone some distance

---

*ᵃ* with no . . . thumb: *prob. rdg.; Heb.* and none humiliating anything in the land with inherited authority.      *ᵇ* *That is* the Camp of Dan.      *ᶜ* *Prob. rdg.; Heb.* the idol of the ephod, and teraphim and image.

from Micah's house, when his neighbours were called out in pursuit and caught up with them. They shouted after them, and the Danites turned 23 round and said to Micah, 'What is the matter with you? Why have you come after us?' He said, 'You have taken my gods which I made for myself, 24 you have taken the priest, and you have gone off and left me nothing. How dare you say, "What is the matter with you?" ' The Danites said to him, 25 'Do not shout at us. We are desperate men and if we fall upon you it will be the death of yourself and your family.' With that the Danites went on 26 their way and Micah, seeing that they were too strong for him, turned and went home.

Thus they carried off the priest and the things Micah had made for 27 himself, and attacked Laish, whose people were quiet and carefree. They put them to the sword and set fire to their city. There was no one to save 28 them, for the city was a long way from Sidon and they had no contact with the Aramaeans,*a* although the city was in the vale near Beth-rehob. They rebuilt the city and settled in it, naming it Dan after the name of their fore- 29 father Dan, a son of Israel; but its original name was Laish. The Danites 30 set up the idol, and Jonathan son of Gershom, son of Moses, and his sons were priests to the tribe of Dan until the people went into exile. (They set 31 up for themselves the idol which Micah had made, and it was there as long as the house of God was at Shiloh.)

IN THOSE DAYS when no king ruled in Israel, a Levite was living in the 19 heart of the hill-country of Ephraim. He had taken himself a concubine from Bethlehem in Judah. In a fit of anger she had left him and had gone 2 to her father's house in Bethlehem in Judah. When she had been there four months, her husband set out after her with his servant and two asses to 3 appeal to her and bring her back. She brought him in to the house of her father, who welcomed him when he saw him. His father-in-law, the girl's 4 father, pressed him and he stayed with him three days, and they were well entertained during their visit. On the fourth day, they rose early in the 5 morning, and he prepared to leave, but the girl's father said to his son-in-law, 'Have something to eat first, before you go.' So the two of them sat 6 down and ate and drank together. The girl's father said to the man, 'Why not spend the night and enjoy yourself?' When he rose to go, his father-in- 7 law urged him to stay, and again he stayed for the night. He rose early in 8 the morning on the fifth day to depart, but the girl's father said, 'Have something to eat first.' So they lingered till late afternoon, eating and drinking together. Then the man stood up to go with his concubine and 9 servant, but his father-in-law said, 'See how the day wears on towards sunset. Spend the night here and enjoy yourself, and then rise early to-morrow and set out for home.' But the man would not stay the night; he 10 rose and left. He had reached a point opposite Jebus, that is Jerusalem, with his two laden asses and his concubine, and when they were close to 11 Jebus, the weather grew wild and stormy, and the young man said to his master, 'Come now, let us turn into this Jebusite town and spend the night there.' But his master said to him, 'No, not into a strange town where the 12

*a Prob. rdg., cp. verse 7; Heb. men.*

13 people are not Israelites; let us go on to Gibeah. Come, we will go and find
14 some other place, and spend the night in Gibeah or Ramah.' So they went
   on until sunset overtook them; they were then near Gibeah which belongs
15 to Benjamin. They turned in to spend the night there, and went and sat
   down in the open street of the town; but nobody took them into his house
   for the night.
16   Meanwhile an old man was coming home in the evening from his work
   in the fields. He was from the hill-country of Ephraim, but he lived in
17 Gibeah, where the people were Benjamites. He looked up, saw the traveller in the open street of the town, and asked him where he was going and
18 where he came from. He answered, 'We are travelling from Bethlehem in
   Judah to the heart of the hill-country of Ephraim. I come from there; I
   have been to Bethlehem in Judah and I am going home, but nobody has
19 taken me into his house. I have straw and provender for the asses, food and
   wine for myself, the girl, and the young man; we have all we need, sir.'
20 The old man said, 'You are welcome, I will supply all your wants; you
21 must not spend the night in the street.' So he took him inside and provided
22 fodder for the asses; they washed their feet, and ate and drank. While they
   were enjoying themselves, some of the worst scoundrels in the town surrounded the house, hurling themselves against the door and shouting to
   the old man who owned the house, 'Bring out the man who has gone into
23 your house, for us to have intercourse with him.' The owner of the house
   went outside to them and said, 'No, my friends, do nothing so wicked. This
24 man is my guest; do not commit this outrage. Here is my daughter, a
   virgin;*a* let me bring her*b* out to you. Rape her*b* and do to her*b* what you
25 please; but you shall not commit such an outrage against this man.' But
   the men refused to listen to him, so the Levite took hold of his concubine
   and thrust her outside for them. They assaulted her and abused her all
26 night till the morning, and when dawn broke, they let her go. The girl
   came at daybreak and fell down at the entrance of the man's house where
27 her master was, and lay there until it was light. Her master rose in the
   morning and opened the door of the house to set out on his journey, and
   there was his concubine lying at the door with her hands on the threshold.
28 He said to her, 'Get up and let us be off'; but there was no answer. So he
29 lifted her on to his ass and set off for home. When he arrived there, he
   picked up a knife, and he took hold of his concubine and cut her up limb
   by limb into twelve pieces; and he sent them through the length and
30 breadth of Israel. He told the men he sent with them to say to every
   Israelite, 'Has the like of this happened or been seen from the time the
   Israelites came up from Egypt till today? Consider this among yourselves
   and speak your minds.' So everyone who saw them said, 'No such thing
   has ever happened or been seen before.'

**20** All the Israelites, the whole community from Dan to Beersheba and out
   of Gilead also, left their homes as one man and assembled before the LORD
 2 at Mizpah. The leaders of the people and all the tribes of Israel presented
   themselves in the general assembly of the people of God, four hundred
 3 thousand foot-soldiers armed with swords; and the Benjamites heard that

   *a Prob. rdg.; Heb. adds and his concubine.*       *b Prob. rdg.; Heb. them.*

the Israelites had gone up to Mizpah. The Israelites asked how this wicked
thing had come about, and the Levite, to whom the murdered woman 4
belonged, answered, 'I and my concubine came to Gibeah in Benjamin to
spend the night there. The citizens of Gibeah rose against me that night 5
and surrounded the house where I was, intending to kill me; and they raped
my concubine and she died. I took her and cut her in pieces, and sent them 6
through the length and breadth of Israel, because of the filthy outrage they
had committed in Israel. Now it is for you, the whole of Israel, to say here 7
and now what you think ought to be done.' All the people rose to their feet 8
as one man and said, 'Not one of us shall go back to his tent, not one shall
return home. This is what we will now do to Gibeah. We will draw lots for 9
the attack: and we will take ten men out of every hundred in all the tribes 10
of Israel, a hundred out of every thousand, and a thousand out of every
ten thousand, to collect provisions from the people for those who have taken
the field against Gibeah in Benjamin to avenge the outrage committed in
Israel.' Thus all the Israelites to a man were massed against the town. 11

The tribes of Israel sent men all through the tribe of Benjamin saying, 12
'What is this wicked thing which has happened in your midst? Hand over 13
to us those scoundrels in Gibeah, and we will put them to death and purge
Israel of this wickedness.' But the Benjamites refused to listen to their
fellow-Israelites. They flocked from their cities to Gibeah to go to war with 14
the Israelites, and that day they mustered out of their cities twenty-six 15
thousand men armed with swords. There were also seven hundred picked
men from Gibeah, left-handed men, who could sling a stone and not miss 16
by a hair's breadth. The Israelites, without Benjamin, numbered four 17
hundred thousand men armed with swords, every one a fighting man. The 18
Israelites at once moved on to Bethel, and there they sought an oracle from
God, asking, 'Which of us shall attack Benjamin first?', and the LORD's
answer was, 'Judah shall attack first.' So the Israelites set out at dawn and 19
encamped opposite Gibeah. They advanced to do battle with Benjamin 20
and drew up their forces before the town. The Benjamites made a sally 21
from Gibeah and left twenty-two thousand of Israel dead on the field that
day. The Israelites went up to Bethel,*a* lamented before the LORD until 23*b*
evening and inquired whether they should again attack their brother
Benjamin. The LORD said, 'Yes, attack him.' Then the Israelites took fresh 22
courage and again formed up on the same ground as the first day. So the 24
second day they advanced against the Benjamites, who sallied out from 25
Gibeah to meet them and laid another eighteen thousand armed men low.
The Israelites, the whole people, went back to Bethel, where they sat before 26
the LORD lamenting and fasting until evening, and they offered whole-
offerings and shared-offerings before the LORD. In those days the Ark of 27
the Covenant of God was there, and Phinehas son of Eleazar, son of 28
Aaron, served before the LORD.*c* The Israelites inquired of the LORD and
said, 'Shall we again march out to battle against Benjamin our brother or
shall we desist?' The LORD answered, 'Attack him: tomorrow I will deliver
him into your hands.' Israel then posted men in ambush all round Gibeah. 29

---

*a* to Bethel: *prob. rdg., cp. verses 18, 26; Heb. om.*      *b Verses 22 and 23 transposed.*
*c* Or before the Ark.

30 On the third day the Israelites advanced against the Benjamites and
31 drew up their forces at Gibeah as they had before; and the Benjamites
sallied out to meet the army. They were drawn away from the town and
began the attack as before by killing a few Israelites, about thirty,[a] on the
highways which led across open country, one to Bethel and the other to
32 Gibeah. They thought they were defeating them once again, but the
Israelites had planned a retreat to draw them away from the town out on to
33 the highways. Meanwhile the main body of Israelites left their positions
and re-formed in Baal-tamar, while those in ambush, ten thousand picked
men all told, burst out from their position in the neighbourhood of Gibeah
34 and came in on the east of the town. There was soon heavy fighting; yet
35 the Benjamites did not suspect the disaster that was threatening them. So
the LORD put Benjamin to flight before Israel, and on that day the Israelites
killed twenty-five thousand one hundred Benjamites, all armed men.
36 The men of Benjamin now saw that they had been defeated, for all that
the Israelites, trusting in the ambush which they had set by Gibeah, had
37 given way before them. The men in ambush made a sudden dash on
Gibeah, fell on the town from all sides and put all the inhabitants to the
38 sword. The agreed signal between the Israelites and those in ambush[b] was
39 to be a column of smoke sent up from the town. The Israelites then faced
about in the battle; and Benjamin began to cut down the Israelites, killing
about thirty of them,[c] in the belief that they were defeating them as they
40 had done in the first encounter. As the column of smoke began to go up
from the town, the Benjamites looked back and thought the whole town
41 was going up in flames. When the Israelites faced about, the Benjamites
42 saw that disaster had overtaken them and were seized with panic. They
turned and fled before the Israelites in the direction of the wilderness, but
the fighting caught up with them and soon those from the town were
43 among them, cutting them down. They hemmed in the Benjamites, pursuing them without respite,[d] and overtook them at a point to the east of
44 Gibeah. Eighteen thousand of the Benjamites fell, all of them fighting
45 men. The survivors turned and fled into the wilderness towards the Rock
of Rimmon. The Israelites picked off the stragglers on the roads, five thousand of them, and chased them until they had cut down and killed two
46 thousand more. Twenty-five thousand armed men of Benjamin fell in battle
47 that day, all fighting men. The six hundred who survived turned and fled
into the wilderness as far as the Rock of Rimmon, and there they remained
48 for four months. The Israelites then turned back to deal with the Benjamites, and put to the sword the people in the towns and the cattle, every
creature that they found; they also set fire to every town within their reach.

21 In Mizpah the Israelites had bound themselves by oath that none of
2 them would marry his daughter to a Benjamite. The people now came to
Bethel and remained there in God's presence till sunset, raising their voices
3 in loud lamentation. They said, 'O LORD God of Israel, why has it happened
4 in Israel that one tribe should this day be lost to Israel?' Next day the

[a] *Or* about thirty wounded men.          [b] *Prob. rdg.; Heb. adds an unintelligible word.*
[c] to cut ... them: *or* to kill about thirty wounded men among the Israelites.          [d] *without*
*respite: or* from Nohah.

people rose early, built an altar there and offered whole-offerings and shared-offerings. At that the Israelites asked themselves whether among all 5 the tribes of Israel there was anyone who did not go up to the assembly before the LORD; for under the terms of the great oath anyone who had not gone up to the LORD at Mizpah was to be put to death. And the Israelites 6 felt remorse over their brother Benjamin, because, as they said, 'This day Israel has lost one whole tribe.' So they asked, 'What shall we do for wives 7 for those who are left? We have sworn to the LORD not to give any of our daughters to them in marriage. Is there anyone in all the tribes of Israel 8 who did not go up to the LORD at Mizpah?' Now it happened that no one from Jabesh-gilead had come to the camp for the assembly; so when they 9 held a roll-call of the people, they found that no inhabitant of Jabesh-gilead was present. Thereupon the community sent off twelve thousand 10 fighting men with orders to go and put the inhabitants of Jabesh-gilead to the sword, men, women, and dependants. 'This is what you shall do,' they 11 said: 'put to death every male person, and every woman who has had intercourse with a man, but spare any who are virgins.' This they did. Among 12 the inhabitants of Jabesh-gilead they found four hundred young women who were virgins and had not had intercourse with a man, and they brought them to the camp at Shiloh in Canaan. Then the whole community sent 13 messengers to the Benjamites at the Rock of Rimmon to parley with them, and peace was proclaimed. At this the Benjamites came back, and were 14 given those of the women of Jabesh-gilead who had been spared; but these were not enough.

The people were still full of remorse over Benjamin because the LORD 15 had made this gap in the tribes of Israel, and the elders of the community 16 said, 'What shall we do for wives for the rest? All the women in Benjamin have been massacred.' They said, 'Heirs there must be for the remnant 17 of Benjamin who have escaped! Then Israel will not see one of its tribes blotted out. We cannot give them our own daughters in marriage because 18 we have sworn that there shall be a curse on the man who gives a wife to a Benjamite.' Then they bethought themselves of the pilgrimage in honour 19 of the LORD, made every year to Shiloh, the place which lies to the north of Bethel, on the east side of the highway from Bethel to Shechem and to the south of Lebonah. They said to the Benjamites, 'Go and hide in the vine- 20 yards and keep watch. When the girls of Shiloh come out to dance, sally 21 out of the vineyards, and each of you seize one of them for his wife; then make your way home to the land of Benjamin. Then, if their fathers or 22 brothers come and complain to you, say to them, "Let us keep them with your approval, for none of us has captured a wife in battle. Had you offered them to us, the guilt would be yours."'

All this the Benjamites did. They carried off as many wives as they 23 needed, snatching them as they danced; then they went their way and returned to their patrimony, rebuilt their cities and settled in them. The 24 Israelites also dispersed by tribes and families, and every man went back to his own patrimony.

In those days there was no king in Israel and every man did what was 25 right in his own eyes.

# RUTH

## *Naomi and Ruth*

1 ONG AGO, IN THE TIME OF THE JUDGES, there was a
famine in the land, and a man from Bethlehem in Judah went to
2 live in the Moabite country with his wife and his two sons. The man's
name was Elimelech, his wife's name was Naomi, and the names of his two
sons Mahlon and Chilion. They were Ephrathites from Bethlehem in
Judah. They arrived in the Moabite country and there they stayed.
3 Elimelech Naomi's husband died, so that she was left with her two sons.
4 These sons married Moabite women, one of whom was called Orpah and
5 the other Ruth. They had lived there about ten years, when both Mahlon
and Chilion died, so that the woman was bereaved of her two sons as well
6 as of her husband. Thereupon she set out with her two daughters-in-law
to return home, because she had heard while still in the Moabite country
7 that the LORD had cared for his people and given them food. So with her
two daughters-in-law she left the place where she had been living, and took
8 the road home to Judah. Then Naomi said to her two daughters-in-law,
'Go back, both of you, to your mothers' homes. May the LORD keep faith
9 with you, as you have kept faith with the dead and with me; and may he
grant each of you security in the home of a new husband.' She kissed them
10 and they wept aloud. Then they said to her, 'We will return with you to
11 your own people.' But Naomi said, 'Go back, my daughters. Why should
you go with me? Am I likely to bear any more sons to be husbands for you?
12 Go back, my daughters, go. I am too old to marry again. But even if I could
say that I had hope of a child, if I were to marry this night and if I were to
13 bear sons, would you then wait until they grew up? Would you then refrain
from marrying? No, no, my daughters, my lot is more bitter than yours,
14 because the LORD has been against me.' At this they wept again. Then
Orpah kissed her mother-in-law and returned to her people, but Ruth
clung to her.
15 'You see,' said Naomi, 'your sister-in-law has gone back to her people
16 and her gods;*a* go back with her.' 'Do not urge me to go back and desert
you', Ruth answered. 'Where you go, I will go, and where you stay, I will
17 stay. Your people shall be my people, and your God my God. Where you
die, I will die, and there I will be buried. I swear a solemn oath before the
18 LORD your God: nothing but*b* death shall divide us.' When Naomi saw
19 that Ruth was determined to go with her, she said no more, and the two
of them went on until they came to Bethlehem. When they arrived in
Bethlehem, the whole town was in great excitement about them, and the
20 women said, 'Can this be Naomi?' 'Do not call me Naomi,'*c* she said, 'call

---

*a* Or god.     *b* I swear . . . nothing but: or The LORD your God do so to me and
more if . . .     *c* That is Pleasure.

me Mara,[a] for it is a bitter lot that the Almighty has sent me. I went away　21
full, and the LORD has brought me back empty. Why do you call me Naomi?
The LORD has pronounced against me; the Almighty has brought disaster
on me.' This is how Naomi's daughter-in-law, Ruth the Moabitess,　22
returned with her from the Moabite country. The barley harvest was
beginning when they arrived in Bethlehem.

## Ruth and Boaz

NOW NAOMI HAD A KINSMAN on her husband's side, a well-to-do　2
man of the family of Elimelech; his name was Boaz. Ruth the　2
Moabitess said to Naomi, 'May I go out to the cornfields and glean behind
anyone who will grant me that favour?' 'Yes, go, my daughter', she replied.
So Ruth went gleaning in the fields behind the reapers. As it happened,　3
she was in that strip of the fields which belonged to Boaz of Elimelech's
family, and there was Boaz coming out from Bethlehem. He greeted the　4
reapers, saying, 'The LORD be with you'; and they replied, 'The LORD
bless you.' Then he asked his servant in charge of the reapers, 'Whose girl　5
is this?' 'She is a Moabite girl', the servant answered, 'who has just come　6
back with Naomi from the Moabite country. She asked if she might glean　7
and gather among the swathes behind the reapers. She came and has been
on her feet with hardly a moment's rest[b] from daybreak till now.' Then　8
Boaz said to Ruth, 'Listen to me, my daughter: do not go and glean in any
other field, and do not look any further, but keep close to my girls. Watch　9
where the men reap, and follow the gleaners; I have given them orders not
to molest you. If you are thirsty, go and drink from the jars the men have
filled.' She fell prostrate before him and said, 'Why are you so kind as to　10
take notice of me when I am only a foreigner?' Boaz answered, 'They have　11
told me all that you have done for your mother-in-law since your husband's
death, how you left your father and mother and the land of your birth, and
came to a people you did not know before. The LORD reward your deed;　12
may the LORD the God of Israel, under whose wings you have come to
take refuge, give you all that you deserve.' 'Indeed, sir,' she said, 'you have　13
eased my mind and spoken kindly to me; may I ask you as a favour not to
treat me only as one of your slave-girls?'[c] When meal-time came round,　14
Boaz said to her, 'Come here and have something to eat, and dip your
bread into the sour wine.' So she sat beside the reapers, and he passed her
some roasted grain. She ate all she wanted and still had some left over.
When she got up to glean, Boaz gave the men orders. 'She', he said, 'may　15
glean even among the sheaves; do not scold her. Or you may even pull out　16
some corn from the bundles and leave it for her to glean, without reproving
her.'

So Ruth gleaned in the field till evening, and when she beat out what she　17
had gleaned, it came to about a bushel of barley. She took it up and went　18
into the town, and her mother-in-law saw how much she had gleaned.

[a] *That is* Bitter.　　　[b] *Prob. rdg.; Heb. adds* in the house.　　　[c] may I . . . slave-
girls?: *or* if you please, treat me as one of your slave-girls.

Then Ruth brought out what she had saved from her meal and gave it to
19 her. Her mother-in-law asked her, 'Where did you glean today? Which
way did you go? Blessings on the man who kindly took notice of you.' So
she told her mother-in-law whom she had been working with. 'The man
20 with whom I worked today', she said, 'is called Boaz.' 'Blessings on him
from the LORD', said Naomi. 'The LORD has kept faith with the living and
21 the dead. For this man is related to us and is our next-of-kin.' 'And what
is more,' said Ruth the Moabitess, 'he told me to stay close to his men until
22 they had finished all his harvest.' 'It is best for you, my daughter,' Naomi
answered, 'to go out with his girls; let no one catch you in another field.'
23 So she kept close to his girls, gleaning with them till the end of both barley
and wheat harvests; but she lived with her mother-in-law.

3 One day Ruth's mother-in-law Naomi said to her, 'My daughter, I want
2 to see you happily settled. Now there is our kinsman Boaz; you were with
3 his girls. Tonight he is winnowing barley at his threshing-floor. Wash and
anoint yourself, put on your cloak and go down to the threshing-floor, but
do not make yourself known to the man until he has finished eating and
4 drinking. But when he lies down, take note of the place where he lies.
Then go in, turn back the covering at his feet and lie down. He will tell
5 6 you what to do.' 'I will do whatever you tell me', Ruth answered. So she
went down to the threshing-floor and did exactly as her mother-in-law
7 had told her. When Boaz had eaten and drunk, he felt at peace with the
world and went to lie down at the far end of the heap of grain. She came in
8 quietly, turned back the covering at his feet and lay down. About midnight
something disturbed the man as he slept; he turned over and, lo and behold,
9 there was a woman lying at his feet. 'Who are you?' he asked. 'I am your
servant, Ruth', she replied. 'Now spread your skirt over your servant,
10 because you are my next-of-kin.' He said, 'The LORD has blessed you, my
daughter. This last proof of your loyalty is greater than the first; you have
11 not sought after any young man, rich or poor. Set your mind at rest, my
daughter. I will do whatever you ask; for, as the whole neighbourhood
12 knows, you are a capable woman. Are you sure that I am the next-of-kin?
13 There is a kinsman even closer than I. Spend the night here and then in
the morning, if he is willing to act as your next-of-kin, well and good; but
if he is not willing, I will do so; I swear it by the LORD. Now lie down till
14 morning.' So she lay at his feet till morning, but rose before one man could
recognize another; and he said, 'It must not be known that a woman has
15 been to the threshing-floor.' Then he said, 'Bring me the cloak you have
on, and hold it out.' So she held it out, and he put in six measures of barley
16 and lifted it on her back, and she went to the town. When she came to her
mother-in-law, Naomi asked, 'How did things go with you, my daughter?'
17 Ruth told her all that the man had done for her. 'He gave me these six measures of barley,' she said; 'he would not let me come home to my mother-in-
18 law empty-handed.' Naomi answered, 'Wait, my daughter, until you see
what will come of it. He will not rest until he has settled the matter today.'

4 Now Boaz had gone up to the city gate, and was sitting there; and, after
a time, the next-of-kin of whom he had spoken passed by. 'Here,' he cried,
2 calling him by name, 'come and sit down.' He came and sat down. Then

Boaz stopped ten elders of the town, and asked them to sit there, and they
did so. Then he said to the next-of-kin, 'You will remember the strip of 3
field that belonged to our brother Elimelech. Naomi has returned from
the Moabite country and is selling it. I promised to open the matter with 4
you, to ask you to acquire it in the presence of those who sit here, in the
presence of the elders of my people. If you are going to do your duty as
next-of-kin, then do so, but if not, someone must do it. So tell me, and then
I shall know; for I come after you as next-of-kin.' He answered, 'I will act
as next-of-kin.' Then Boaz said, 'On the day when you acquire the field 5
from Naomi, you also acquire Ruth the Moabitess, the dead man's wife,
so as to perpetuate the name of the dead man with his patrimony.' There- 6
upon the next-of-kin said, 'I cannot act myself, for I should risk losing my
own patrimony. You must therefore do my duty as next-of-kin. I cannot
act.'

Now in those old days, when property was redeemed or exchanged, it 7
was the custom for a man to pull off his sandal and give it to the other
party. This was the form of attestation in Israel. So the next-of-kin said to 8
Boaz, 'Acquire it for yourself', and pulled off his sandal. Then Boaz 9
declared to the elders and all the people, 'You are witnesses today that I
have acquired from Naomi all that belonged to Elimelech and all that
belonged to Mahlon and Chilion; and, further, that I have myself acquired 10
Ruth the Moabitess, wife of Mahlon, to be my wife, to perpetuate the name
of the deceased with his patrimony, so that his name may not be missing
among his kindred and at the gate of his native place. You are witnesses
this day.' Then the elders and all who were at the gate said, 'We are wit- 11
nesses. May the LORD make this woman, who has come to your home, like
Rachel and Leah, the two who built up the house of Israel. May you do
great things in Ephrathah and keep a name alive in Bethlehem. May your 12
house be like the house of Perez, whom Tamar bore to Judah, through the
offspring the LORD will give you by this girl.'

So Boaz took Ruth and made her his wife. When they came together, 13
the LORD caused her to conceive and she bore Boaz a son. Then the women 14
said to Naomi, 'Blessed be the LORD today, for he has not left you without
a next-of-kin. May the dead man's name be kept alive in Israel. The child 15
will give you new life and cherish you in your old age; for your daughter-
in-law who loves you, who has proved better to you than seven sons, has
borne him.' Naomi took the child and laid him in her lap and became his 16
nurse. Her neighbours gave him a name: 'Naomi has a son,' they said; 'we 17
will call him Obed.' He was the father of Jesse, the father of David.

THIS IS THE GENEALOGY OF PEREZ: Perez was the father of Hezron, 18
Hezron of Ram, Ram of Amminadab, Amminadab of Nahshon, Nahshon of 19 20
Salmon, Salmon of Boaz, Boaz of Obed, Obed of Jesse, and Jesse of David. 21 22

# THE FIRST BOOK OF
# SAMUEL

*The birth and call of Samuel*

1 THERE WAS A MAN FROM RAMATHAIM, a Zuphite
from the hill-country of Ephraim, named Elkanah son of Jeroham,
2 son of Elihu, son of Tohu, son of Zuph an Ephraimite; and he had
two wives named Hannah and Peninnah. Peninnah had children, but
3 Hannah was childless. This man used to go up from his own town every
year to worship and to offer sacrifice to the LORD of Hosts in Shiloh. There
4 Eli's two sons, Hophni and Phinehas, were priests of the LORD. On the
day when Elkanah sacrificed, he gave several shares of the meat to his wife
5 Peninnah with all her sons and daughters; but, although he loved Hannah,
he gave her only one share, because the LORD had not granted her children.
6 Further, Hannah's rival used to torment her and humiliate her because
7 she had no children. Year after year this happened when they went up to
the house of the LORD; her rival used to torment her. Once when she was
8 in tears and would not eat, her husband Elkanah said to her, 'Hannah, why
are you crying and eating nothing? Why are you so miserable? Am I not
9-10 more to you than ten sons?' After they had finished eating and drinking
at the sacrifice at Shiloh, Hannah rose in deep distress, and stood before
the LORD and prayed to him, weeping bitterly. Meanwhile Eli the priest
11 was sitting on his seat beside the door of the temple of the LORD. Hannah
made a vow in these words: 'O LORD of Hosts, if thou wilt deign to take
notice of my trouble and remember me, if thou wilt not forget me but
grant me offspring, then I will give the child to the LORD for his whole life,
12 and no razor shall ever touch his head.' For a long time she went on praying
13 before the LORD, while Eli watched her lips. Hannah was praying silently;
but, although her voice could not be heard, her lips were moving and Eli
14 took her for a drunken woman. He said to her, 'Enough of this drunken
15 behaviour! Go away till the wine has worn off.' 'No, sir,' she answered,
'I am a sober person, I have drunk no wine or strong drink, and I have
16 been pouring out my heart before the LORD. Do not think me so degraded,
sir; all this time I have been speaking out of the fullness of my grief and
17 misery.' 'Go in peace,' said Eli, 'and may the God of Israel answer the
18 prayer you have made to him.' Hannah said, 'May I be worthy of your
kindness.' And she went away and took something to eat, no longer down-
19 cast. Next morning they were up early and, after prostrating themselves
before the LORD, returned to their own home at Ramah. Elkanah had
20 intercourse with his wife Hannah, and the LORD remembered her. She
conceived, and in due time bore a son, whom she named Samuel, 'because',
she said, 'I asked the LORD for him.'

Elkanah, with his whole household, went up to make the annual sacrifice 21
to the LORD and to redeem his vow. Hannah did not go with them, but said 22
to her husband, 'When the child is weaned I will come up with him to
enter the presence of the LORD, and he shall*a* stay there always.' Her 23
husband Elkanah said to her, 'Do what you think best; stay at home until
you have weaned him. Only, may the LORD indeed see your vow fulfilled.'
So the woman stayed and nursed her son until she had weaned him; and 24
when she had weaned him, she took him up with her. She took also a bull
three years old, an ephah of meal, and a flagon of wine, and she brought
him, child as he was, into the house of the LORD at Shiloh. They slaughtered 25
the bull, and brought the boy to Eli. Hannah said to him, 'Sir, as sure as 26
you live, I am the woman who stood near you here praying to the LORD.
It was this boy that I prayed for and the LORD has given me what I asked. 27
What I asked I have received; and now I lend him to the LORD; for his 28
whole life he is lent to the LORD.' And they prostrated themselves there
before the LORD.

Then Hannah offered this prayer:                                          2

My heart rejoices in the LORD,
in the LORD I now hold my head high;
my mouth is full of derision of my foes,
exultant because thou hast saved me.
  There is none except thee,
   none so holy as the LORD,                               2
    no rock like our God.
Cease your proud boasting,
let no word of arrogance pass your lips;                                  3
for the LORD is a god of all knowledge:
he governs all that men do.

Strong men stand in mute*b* dismay
but those who faltered put on new strength.                              4
Those who had plenty sell themselves for a crust,
and the hungry grow strong again.                                        5
The barren woman has seven children,
and the mother of many sons is left to languish.

The LORD kills and he gives life,
he sends down to Sheol, he can bring the dead up again.                 6
The LORD makes a man poor, he makes him rich,
he brings down and he raises up.                                         7
He lifts the weak out of the dust
and raises the poor from the dunghill;                                   8
to give them a place among the great,
to set them in seats of honour.

For the foundations of the earth are the LORD's,
he has built the world upon them.

---

*a* come up . . . he shall: *or* bring him up, and he shall come into the presence of the LORD
and . . .    *b* in mute: *prob. rdg.; Heb. obscure.*

9 He will guard the footsteps of his saints,
while the wicked sink into silence and gloom;
not by mere strength shall a man prevail.

10 Those that stand against the Lord will be terrified
when the High God*ᵃ* thunders out of heaven.
The Lord is judge even to the ends of the earth,
he will give strength to his king
and raise high the head of his anointed prince.

11 Then Elkanah went to Ramah with his household, but the boy remained behind in the service of the Lord under Eli the priest.

12 13 Now Eli's sons were scoundrels and had no regard for the Lord. The custom of the priests in their dealings with the people was this: when a man offered a sacrifice, the priest's servant would come while the flesh

14 was stewing and would thrust a three-pronged fork into the cauldron or pan or kettle or pot; and the priest would take whatever the fork brought out. This should have been their practice whenever Israelites came to

15 sacrifice at Shiloh; but now under Eli's sons, even before the fat was burnt, the priest's servant came and said to the man who was sacrificing, 'Give me meat to roast for the priest; he will not accept what has been already stewed,

16 only raw meat.' And if the man answered 'Let them burn the fat first, and then take what you want', he said, 'No, give it to me now, or I will take it

17 by force.' The young men's sin was very great in the Lord's sight; for they brought the Lord's sacrifice into general contempt.

18 Samuel continued in the service of the Lord, a mere boy with a linen

19 ephod fastened round him. Every year his mother made him a little cloak and took it to him when she went up with her husband to offer the annual

20 sacrifice. Eli would give his blessing to Elkanah and his wife and say, 'The Lord grant you children by this woman in place of the one for which you asked him.'*ᵇ* Then they went home again.

21 The Lord showed his care for Hannah, and she conceived and gave birth to three sons and two daughters; meanwhile the boy Samuel grew up in the presence of the Lord.

22 Eli, now a very old man, had heard how his sons were treating all the Israelites, and how they lay with the women who were serving at the

23 entrance to the Tent of the Presence. So he said to them, 'Why do you do

24 such things? I hear from all the people how wickedly you behave. Have done with it, my sons; for it is no good report that I hear spreading among

25 the Lord's people. If a man sins against another man, God will intervene; but if a man sins against the Lord, who can intercede for him?' For all this, they did not listen to their father's rebuke, for the Lord meant that they

26 should die. But the young Samuel, as he grew up, commended himself to the Lord and to men.

27 Now a man of God came to Eli and said, 'This is the word of the Lord: You know that I revealed myself to your forefather when he and his family

28 were in Egypt in slavery in the house of Pharaoh. You know that I chose

---

*ᵃ* the High God: *prob. rdg.; Heb.* upon him.      *ᵇ* for which . . . him: *or* which you lent him.

him from all the tribes of Israel to be my priest, to mount the steps of my altar, to burn sacrifices and to carry*a* the ephod before me; and that I assigned all the food-offerings of the Israelites to your family. Why then 29 do you show disrespect for my sacrifices and the offerings which I have ordained? What makes you resent them? Why do you honour your sons more than me by letting them batten on the choicest offerings of my people Israel? The LORD's word was, "I promise that your house and your 30 father's house shall serve before me for all time"; but now his word is, "I will have no such thing: I will honour those who honour me, and those who despise me shall meet with contempt. The time is coming when I will 31 lop off every limb of your own and of your father's family, so that no man in your house shall come to old age. You will even resent*b* the prosperity I 32 give to Israel; never again shall there be an old man in your house. If I 33 allow any to survive to serve my altar, his eyes will grow dim and his appetite fail, his issue will be weaklings and die off. The fate of your two 34 sons shall be a sign to you: Hophni and Phinehas shall both die on the same day. I will appoint for myself a priest who will be faithful, who will do 35 what I have in my mind and in my heart. I will establish his family to serve in perpetual succession before my anointed king. Any of your family 36 that still live will come and bow humbly before him to beg a fee, a piece of silver and a loaf, and will ask for a turn of priestly duty to earn a crust of bread." '

So the child Samuel was in the LORD's service under his master Eli. Now 3 in those days the word of the LORD was seldom heard, and no vision was granted. But one night Eli, whose eyes were dim and his sight failing, was 2 lying down in his usual place, while Samuel slept in the temple of the LORD 3 where the Ark of God was. Before the lamp of God had gone out, the LORD 4 called him, and Samuel answered, 'Here I am', and ran to Eli saying, 'You 5 called me: here I am.' 'No, I did not call you,' said Eli; 'lie down again.' So he went and lay down. The LORD called Samuel again, and he got up 6 and went to Eli. 'Here I am,' he said; 'surely you called me.' 'I did not call, my son,' he answered; 'lie down again.' Now Samuel had not yet come to 7 know the LORD, and the word of the LORD had not been disclosed to him. When the LORD called him for the third time, he again went to Eli and said, 8 'Here I am; you did call me.' Then Eli understood that it was the LORD calling the child; he told Samuel to go and lie down and said, 'If he calls 9 again, say, "Speak, LORD; thy servant hears thee." ' So Samuel went and lay down in his place.

The LORD came and stood there, and called, 'Samuel, Samuel', as before. 10 Samuel answered, 'Speak; thy servant hears thee.' The LORD said, 'Soon 11 I shall do something in Israel which will ring in the ears of all who hear it. When that day comes I will make good every word I have spoken against 12 Eli and his family from beginning to end. You are to*c* tell him that my 13 judgement on his house shall stand for ever because*d* he knew of his sons' blasphemies against God*e* and did not rebuke them. Therefore I have 14

---

*a Or* wear.      *b* You . . . resent: *prob. rdg.; Heb. obscure.*      *c Prob. rdg.; Heb.* I will.      *d* because: *prob. rdg.; Heb.* in guilt.      *e* against God: *prob. original reading, altered in Heb. to* to them.

sworn to the family of Eli that their abuse of sacrifices and offerings shall never be expiated.'

15 Samuel lay down till morning and then opened the doors of the house
16 of the LORD, but he was afraid to tell Eli about the vision. Eli called
17 Samuel: 'Samuel, my son', he said; and he answered, 'Here I am.' Eli asked, 'What did the LORD say to you? Do not hide it from me. God forgive
18 you if you hide one word of all that he said to you.' Then Samuel told him everything and hid nothing. Eli said, 'The LORD must do what is good in his eyes.'
19 As Samuel grew up, the LORD was with him, and none of his words
20 went unfulfilled. From Dan to Beersheba, all Israel recognized that
21 Samuel was confirmed as a prophet of the LORD. So the LORD continued to appear in Shiloh, because he had revealed himself there to Samuel.[a]

## The struggle with the Philistines

4 SO SAMUEL'S WORD HAD AUTHORITY throughout Israel. And the time came when the Philistines mustered for battle against Israel, and the Israelites went out to meet them. The Israelites encamped at Eben-
2 ezer and the Philistines at Aphek. The Philistines drew up their lines facing the Israelites, and when they joined battle the Israelites were routed
3 by the Philistines, who killed about four thousand men on the field. When the army got back to the camp, the elders of Israel asked, 'Why did the LORD let us be routed today by the Philistines? Let us fetch the Ark of the Covenant of the LORD from Shiloh to go with us and deliver us from the
4 power of our enemies.' So the people sent to Shiloh and fetched the Ark of the Covenant of the LORD of Hosts, who is enthroned upon the cherubim;
5 Eli's two sons, Hophni and Phinehas, were there with the Ark. When the Ark came into the camp all the Israelites greeted it with a great shout, and
6 the earth rang with the shouting. The Philistines heard the noise and asked, 'What is this great shouting in the camp of the Hebrews?' When
7 they knew that the Ark of the LORD had come into the camp, they were afraid and cried, 'A god has come into the camp. We are lost! No such
8 thing has ever happened before. We are utterly lost! Who can deliver us from the power of these mighty gods? These are the very gods who broke
9 the Egyptians and crushed them in the wilderness. Courage, Philistines, and act like men, or you will become slaves to the Hebrews as they were
10 yours. Be men, and fight!' The Philistines then gave battle, and the Israelites were defeated and fled to their homes. It was a great defeat, and thirty
11 thousand Israelite foot-soldiers perished. The Ark of God was taken, and Eli's two sons, Hophni and Phinehas, were killed.
12 A Benjamite ran from the battlefield and reached Shiloh on the same
13 day, his clothes rent and dust on his head. When he arrived Eli was sitting on a seat by the road to Mizpah, for he was deeply troubled about the Ark of God. The man entered the city with his news, and all the people cried
14 out in horror. When Eli heard it, he asked, 'What does this uproar mean?'

[a] *Prob. rdg.; Heb. adds* according to the word of the LORD.

The man hurried to Eli and told him. Eli was ninety-eight years old and 15
sat staring with sightless eyes; so the man said to him, 'I am the man who 16
has just arrived from the battle; this very day I have escaped from the field.'
Eli asked, 'What is the news, my son?' The runner answered, 'The 17
Israelites have fled from the Philistines; utter panic has struck the army;
your two sons, Hophni and Phinehas, are killed, and the Ark of God is
taken.' At the mention of the Ark of God, Eli fell backwards from his seat 18
by the gate and broke his neck, for he was old and heavy. So he died; he
had been judge over Israel for forty years. His daughter-in-law, the wife 19
of Phinehas, was with child and near her time, and when she heard of the
capture of the Ark and the deaths of her father-in-law and her husband,
her labour suddenly began and she crouched down and was delivered.
As she lay dying, the women who attended her said, 'Do not be afraid; 20
you have a son.' But she did not answer or heed what they said. Then they 21
named the boy Ichabod,*a* saying, 'Glory has departed from Israel' (in
allusion to the capture of the Ark of God and the death of her father-in-
law and her husband); 'Glory has departed from Israel,' they said, 'because 22
the Ark of God is taken.'

After the Philistines had captured the Ark of God, they brought it 5
from Eben-ezer to Ashdod; and there they carried it into the temple of 2
Dagon and set it beside Dagon himself. When the people of Ashdod rose 3
next morning, there was Dagon fallen face downwards before the Ark of
the LORD; so they took him and put him back in his place. Next morning 4
when they rose, Dagon had again fallen face downwards before the Ark
of the LORD, with his head and his two hands lying broken off beside his
platform; only Dagon's body remained on it. This is why from that day 5
to this the priests of Dagon and all who enter the temple of Dagon at Ashdod
do not set foot upon Dagon's platform.

Then the LORD laid a heavy hand upon the people of Ashdod; he threw 6
them into distress and plagued them with tumours, and their territory
swarmed with rats.*b* There was death and destruction all through the city.
When the men of Ashdod saw this, they said, 'The Ark of the God of 7
Israel shall not stay here, for he has laid a heavy hand upon us and upon
Dagon our god.' So they sent and called all the Philistine princes together 8
to ask what should be done with the Ark. They said, 'Let the Ark of the
God of Israel be taken across to Gath.' They took it there, and after its 9
arrival the hand of the LORD caused great havoc in the city; he plagued
everybody, high and low alike, with the tumours which broke out. Then 10
they sent the Ark of God on to Ekron. When the Ark reached Ekron, the
people cried, 'They have brought the Ark of the God of Israel over to us,
to kill us and our families.' So they summoned all the Philistine princes and 11
said, 'Send the Ark of the God of Israel away; let it go back to its own place,
or it will be the death of us all.' There was death and destruction all through
the city; for the hand of God lay heavy upon it. Even those who did not die 12
were plagued with tumours; the cry of the city went up to heaven.

When the Ark of the LORD had been in their territory for seven months, 6
the Philistines summoned the priests and soothsayers and asked, 'What 2

*a That is* No-glory.    *b Or* mice.

shall we do with the Ark of the LORD? Tell us how we ought to send it
3 back to its own place.' They answered, 'If you send the Ark of the God of
Israel back, do not let it go without a gift, but send it back with a gift for
him by way of indemnity; then you will be healed and restored to favour;
4 there is no reason why his hand should not be lifted from you.' When they
were asked, 'What gift shall we send back to him?', they answered, 'Send
five tumours modelled in gold and five gold rats, one for each of the
Philistine princes, for the same plague afflicted all of you and your princes.
5 Make models of your tumours and of the rats which are ravaging the land,
and give honour to the God of Israel; perhaps he will relax the pressure of
6 his hand on you, on your god, and on your land. Why should you be stubborn like Pharaoh and the Egyptians? Remember how this god made
7 sport of them until they let Israel go. Now make a new wagon ready with
two milch-cows which have never been yoked; harness the cows to the
wagon, and take their calves from them and drive them back to their stalls.
8 Then take the Ark of the LORD and put it on the wagon, place in a casket,
beside it, the gold offerings that you are sending to him as an indemnity,
9 and let it go where it will. Watch it: if it goes up towards its own territory
to Beth-shemesh, then it is the LORD who has done us this great injury;
but if not, then we shall know that his hand has not touched us, but we
have been the victims of chance.'
10 The men did this. They took two milch-cows and harnessed them to a
11 wagon, shutting up their calves in the stall, and they placed the Ark of the
LORD on the wagon together with the casket, the gold rats, and the models
12 of their haemorrhoids. Then the cows went straight in the direction of
Beth-shemesh; they kept to the same road, lowing as they went and turning
neither right nor left, while the Philistine princes followed them as far as
13 the territory of Beth-shemesh. Now the people of Beth-shemesh were
harvesting their wheat in the Vale, and when they looked up and saw the
14 Ark they rejoiced at the sight of it. The wagon came to the farm of Joshua
of Beth-shemesh and halted there. Close by stood a great stone; so they
chopped up the wood of the wagon and offered the cows as a whole-
15 offering to the LORD. Then the Levites lifted down the Ark of the LORD
and the casket containing the gold offerings, and laid them on the great
stone; and the men of Beth-shemesh offered whole-offerings and shared-
16 offerings that day to the LORD. The five princes of the Philistines watched
all this, and returned to Ekron the same day.
17 These golden haemorrhoids which the Philistines sent back as a gift of
indemnity to the LORD were for Ashdod, Gaza, Ashkelon, Gath, and
18 Ekron, one for each city. The gold rats were for all the towns of the Philistines governed by the five princes, both fortified towns and open settlements. The great stone where they deposited the Ark of the LORD stands
witness on the farm of Joshua of Beth-shemesh to this very day.
19 But the sons of Jeconiah did not rejoice with the rest of the men of
Beth-shemesh when they welcomed the Ark of the LORD, and he struck
down seventy of them. The people mourned because the LORD had struck
20 them so heavy a blow, and the men of Beth-shemesh said, 'No one is safe
in the presence of the LORD, this holy God. To whom can we send it, to

be rid of him?' So they sent this message to the inhabitants of Kiriath- 21
jearim: 'The Philistines have returned the Ark of the LORD; come down
and take charge of it.' Then the men of Kiriath-jearim came and took the 7
Ark of the LORD away; they brought it into the house of Abinadab on the
hill and consecrated his son Eleazar as its custodian.

## Samuel judge over Israel

S O FOR A LONG WHILE the Ark was housed in Kiriath-jearim; and 2
after some time, twenty years later, there was a movement throughout
Israel to follow the LORD. So Samuel addressed these words to the whole 3
nation: 'If your return to the LORD is whole-hearted, banish the foreign
gods and the Ashtaroth from your shrines; turn to the LORD with heart
and mind, and worship him alone, and he will deliver you from the Philistines.' The Israelites then banished the Baalim and the Ashtaroth, and 4
worshipped the LORD alone.

Samuel summoned all Israel to an assembly at Mizpah, so that he might 5
intercede with the LORD for them. When they had assembled there, they 6
drew water and poured it out before the LORD and fasted all day, confessing
that they had sinned against the LORD. It was at Mizpah that Samuel acted
as judge over Israel.

When the Philistines heard that the Israelites had assembled at Mizpah, 7
their princes marched against them. The Israelites heard that the Philistines were advancing, and they were afraid. They said to Samuel, 'Do 8
not cease to pray for us to the LORD our God to save us from the power of
the Philistines.' Thereupon Samuel took a sucking lamb, offered it up 9
complete as a whole-offering and prayed aloud to the LORD on behalf of
Israel; and the LORD answered his prayer. As Samuel was offering the 10
sacrifice and the Philistines were advancing to battle with the Israelites,
the LORD thundered loud and long over the Philistines and threw them into
confusion. They fled in panic before the Israelites, who set out from Mizpah 11
in pursuit and kept up the slaughter of the Philistines till they reached a
point below Beth-car. There Samuel took a stone and set it up as a monu- 12
ment between Mizpah and Jeshanah,*a* naming it Eben-ezer,*b* 'for to this
point', he said, 'the LORD has helped us.' Thus the Philistines were sub- 13
dued and no longer encroached on the territory of Israel; and the hand
of the LORD was against them as long as Samuel lived. The cities they had 14
captured were restored to Israel, and from Ekron to Gath the borderland
was freed from their control. Between Israel and the Amorites peace was
maintained. Samuel acted as judge in Israel as long as he lived, and every 15 16
year went on circuit to Bethel and Gilgal and Mizpah; he dispensed justice
at all these places, returning always to Ramah. That was his home and 17
the place from which he governed Israel, and there he built an altar to
the LORD.

---

*a* *Prob. rdg. (cp. 2 Chr. 13. 19); Heb. the tooth.*    *b* *That is Stone of Help.*

## *Saul anointed king*

8 WHEN SAMUEL GREW OLD, he appointed his sons to be judges in
2    Israel. The eldest son was named Joel and the second Abiah; they
3 acted as judges in Beersheba. His sons did not follow in their father's
footsteps but were intent on their own profit, taking bribes and perverting
4 the course of justice. So all the elders of Israel met, and came to Samuel
5 at Ramah and said to him, 'You are now old and your sons do not follow
6 in your footsteps; appoint us a king to govern us, like other nations.' But
their request for a king to govern them displeased Samuel, and he prayed
7 to the LORD. The LORD answered Samuel, 'Listen to the people and all
that they are saying; they have not rejected you, it is I whom they have
8 rejected, I whom they will not have to be their king. They are now doing
to you just what they have done to me since I brought them up from Egypt:
9 they have forsaken me and worshipped other gods. Hear what they have
to say now, but give them a solemn warning and tell them what sort of king
10 will govern them.' Samuel told the people who were asking him for a king
11 all that the LORD had said to him. 'This will be the sort of king who will
govern you', he said. 'He will take your sons and make them serve in his
chariots and with his cavalry, and will make them run before his chariot.
12 Some he will appoint officers over units of a thousand and units of fifty.
Others will plough his fields and reap his harvest; others again will make
13 weapons of war and equipment for mounted troops. He will take your
14 daughters for perfumers, cooks, and confectioners, and will seize the best
of your cornfields, vineyards, and olive-yards, and give them to his lackeys.
15 He will take a tenth of your grain and your vintage to give to his eunuchs
16 and lackeys. Your slaves, both men and women, and the best of your cattle
17 and your asses he will seize and put to his own use. He will take a tenth of
18 your flocks, and you yourselves will become his slaves. When that day
comes, you will cry out against the king whom you have chosen; but it
19 will be too late, the LORD will not answer you.' The people refused to listen
20 to Samuel; 'No,' they said, 'we will have a king over us; then we shall be
like other nations, with a king to govern us, to lead us out to war and fight
21 our battles.' So Samuel, when he had heard what the people said, told the
22 LORD; and he answered, 'Take them at their word and appoint them a
king.' Samuel then dismissed all the men of Israel to their homes.
9    There was a man from the district of Benjamin, whose name was Kish
son of Abiel, son of Zeror, son of Bechorath, son of Aphiah a Benjamite.
2 He was a man of substance, and had a son named Saul, a young man in
his prime; there was no better man among the Israelites than he. He was
a head taller than any of his fellows.
3    One day some asses belonging to Saul's father Kish had strayed, so he
said to his son Saul, 'Take one of the servants with you, and go and look
4 for the asses.' They crossed the hill-country of Ephraim and went through
the district of Shalisha but did not find them; they passed through the
district of Shaalim but they were not there; they passed through the
5 district of Benjamin but again did not find them. When they had entered
the district of Zuph, Saul said to the servant with him, 'Come, we ought to

turn back, or my father will stop thinking about the asses and begin to
worry about us.' The servant answered, 'There is a man of God in the city 6
here, who has a great reputation, because everything he says comes true.
Suppose we go there; he may tell us something about this errand of ours.'
Saul said, 'If we do go, what shall we offer him? There is no food left in 7
our packs and we have no present for the man of God, nothing at all.' The 8
servant answered him again, 'Wait! I have here a quarter-shekel of silver.
I can give that to the man, to tell us what we should do.' Saul said, 'Good! 10*a*
let us go to him.' So they went to the city where the man of God was. (In 9
days gone by in Israel, when a man wished to consult God, he would say,
'Let us go to the seer.' For what is nowadays called a prophet used to be
called a seer.) As they were going up the hill to the city they met some girls 11
coming out to draw water and asked, 'Shall we find the seer there?' 'Yes,' 12
they said, 'the seer is ahead of you now; he has just *b* arrived in the city
because there is a feast at the hill-shrine today. As you enter the city you 13
will meet him before he goes up to the shrine to eat; the people will not
start until he comes, for he has to bless the sacrifice before the company
can eat. Go up now, and you will find him at once.' So they went up to the 14
city, and just as they were going in, there was Samuel coming towards them
on his way up to the shrine.

Now the day before Saul came, the LORD had disclosed his intention to 15
Samuel in these words: 'At this same time tomorrow I will send you a man 16
from the land of Benjamin. Anoint him prince over my people Israel, and
then he shall deliver my people from the Philistines. I have seen the
sufferings of my people and their cry has reached my ears.' The moment 17
Saul appeared the LORD said to Samuel, 'Here is the man of whom I
spoke to you. This man shall rule my people.' Saul came up to Samuel in 18
the gateway and said, 'Would you tell me where the seer lives?' Samuel 19
replied, 'I am the seer. Go on ahead of me to the hill-shrine and you shall
eat with me today; in the morning I will set you on your way, after telling
you what you have on your mind. Trouble yourself no more about the 20
asses lost three days ago, for they have been found. But what is it that all
Israel is wanting? It is you and your ancestral house.' 'But I am a Benjamite,' 21
said Saul, 'from the smallest of the tribes of Israel, and my family is the
least important of all the families of the tribe of Benjamin. Why do you
say this to me?' Samuel then brought Saul and his servant into the dining- 22
hall and gave them a place at the head of the company, which numbered
about thirty. Then he said to the cook, 'Bring the portion that I gave you 23
and told you to put on one side.' So the cook took up the whole haunch 24
and leg and put it before Saul; and Samuel said, 'Here is the portion of
meat *c* kept for you. Eat it: it has been reserved for you at this feast to
which I have invited the people.' So Saul dined with Samuel that day, and 25
when they came down from the hill-shrine to the city a bed was spread on
the roof for Saul, and he stayed there that night. At dawn Samuel called 26
to Saul on the roof, 'Get up, and I will set you on your way.' When Saul

---

*a* *Verses 9 and 10 transposed.*          *b* the seer . . . just: *prob. rdg.; Heb.* he is ahead of
you, hurry now, for he has today . . .          *c* the portion of meat: *prob. rdg.; Heb.* what
is left over.

27 rose, he and Samuel went out together into the street. As they came to the end of the town, Samuel said to Saul, 'Tell the boy to go on.' He did so, and then Samuel said, 'Stay here a moment, and I will tell you the word of God.'

**10** Samuel took a flask of oil and poured it over Saul's head, and he kissed him and said, 'The LORD anoints you prince over his people Israel; you shall rule the people of the LORD and deliver them from the enemies round about them. You shall have a sign that the LORD has anointed you prince
2 to govern his inheritance: when you leave me today, you will meet two men by the tomb of Rachel at Zelzah in the territory of Benjamin. They will tell you that the asses you are looking for have been found and that your father is concerned for them no longer; he is anxious about you and says
3 again and again, "What shall I do about my son?" From there go across country as far as the terebinth of Tabor, where three men going up to Bethel to worship God will meet you. One of them will be carrying three
4 kids, the second three loaves, and the third a flagon of wine. They will greet you and will offer you two loaves, which you will accept from them.
5 Then when you reach the Hill of God, where the Philistine governor *a* resides, you will meet a company of prophets coming down from the hill-shrine, led by lute, harp, fife, and drum, and filled with prophetic rapture.
6 Then the spirit of the LORD will suddenly take possession of you, and you
7 too will be rapt like a prophet and become another man. When these signs
8 happen, do whatever the occasion demands; God will be with you. You shall go down to Gilgal ahead of me, and I will come to you to sacrifice whole-offerings and shared-offerings. Wait seven days until I join you;
9 then I will tell you what to do.' As Saul turned to leave Samuel, God gave
10 him a new heart. On that same day all these signs happened. When they reached the Hill there was a company of prophets coming to meet him, and the spirit of God suddenly took possession of him, so that he too was filled
11 with prophetic rapture. When people who had known him previously saw that he was rapt like the prophets, they said to one another, 'What can
12 have happened to the son of Kish? Is Saul also among the prophets?' One of the men of that place said, 'And whose sons are they?' Hence the pro-
13 verb, 'Is Saul also among the prophets?' When the prophetic rapture had
14 passed, he went home. *b* Saul's uncle said to him and the boy, 'Where have you been?' Saul answered, 'To look for the asses, and when we could not
15 find them, we went to Samuel.' His uncle said, 'Tell me what Samuel said.'
16 'He told us that the asses had been found', said Saul; but he did not repeat what Samuel had said about his being king.
17 Meanwhile Samuel summoned the Israelites to the LORD at Mizpah
18 and said to the people, 'This is the word of the LORD the God of Israel: I brought Israel up from Egypt; I delivered you from the Egyptians and
19 from all the kingdoms that oppressed you; but today you have rejected your God who saved you from all your misery and distress; you have said, "No, set up a king over us." Now therefore take up your positions before
20 the LORD tribe by tribe and clan by clan.' Samuel then presented all the
21 tribes of Israel, and Benjamin was picked by lot. Then he presented the

*a* Or garrison.   *b* Prob. rdg.; Heb. to the hill-shrine.

tribe of Benjamin, family by family, and the family of Matri was picked. Then he presented the family of Matri, man by man, and Saul son of Kish was picked; but when they looked for him he could not be found. They 22 went on to ask the LORD, 'Will the man be coming back?' The LORD answered, 'There he is, hiding among the baggage.' So someone ran and 23 fetched him out, and as he took his stand among the people, he was a head taller than anyone else. Samuel said to the people, 'Look at the man whom 24 the LORD has chosen; there is no one like him in this whole nation.' They all acclaimed him, shouting, 'Long live the king!' Samuel then explained 25 to the people the nature of a king, and made a written record of it on a scroll which he deposited before the LORD; he then dismissed them to their homes. Saul too went home to Gibeah, and with him went some fighting 26 men whose hearts God had moved. But there were scoundrels who said, 27 'How can this fellow deliver us?' They thought nothing of him and brought him no gifts.

About a month later Nahash the Ammonite attacked and besieged **11** Jabesh-gilead. The men of Jabesh said to Nahash, 'Come to terms with us and we will be your subjects.' Nahash answered them, 'On one con- 2 dition only will I come to terms with you: that I gouge out your right eyes and bring disgrace on Israel.' The elders of Jabesh-gilead then said, 'Give 3 us seven days' respite to send messengers throughout Israel and then, if no one relieves us, we will surrender to you.' When the messengers came 4 to Gibeah, where Saul lived, and delivered their message, all the people broke into lamentation. Saul was just coming from the field driving in the 5 oxen, and asked why the people were lamenting; and they repeated what the men of Jabesh had said. When Saul heard this, the spirit of God 6 suddenly seized him. In his anger he took a pair of oxen and cut them in 7 pieces, and sent messengers with the pieces all through Israel to proclaim that the same would be done to the oxen of any man who did not follow Saul and Samuel into battle. The fear of the LORD fell upon the people and they came out, to a man. Saul mustered them in Bezek; there were three 8 hundred thousand men from Israel and thirty thousand from Judah. He said to the men who brought the message, 'Tell the men of Jabesh- 9 gilead, "Victory will be yours tomorrow by the time the sun is hot." ' The men of Jabesh heard what the messengers reported and took heart; and 10 they said to Nahash, 'Tomorrow we will surrender to you, and then you may deal with us as you think fit.' Next day Saul drew up his men in three 11 columns; they forced their way right into the enemy camp during the morning watch and massacred the Ammonites while the day grew hot, after which the survivors scattered until no two men were left together.

Then the people said to Samuel, 'Who said that Saul should not reign 12 over us? Hand the men over to us to be put to death.' But Saul said, 'No 13 man shall be put to death on a day when the LORD has won such a victory in Israel.' Samuel said to the people, 'Let us now go to Gilgal and there 14 renew our allegiance to the kingdom.' So they all went to Gilgal and 15 invested Saul there as king in the presence of the LORD, sacrificing shared-offerings before the LORD; and Saul and all the Israelites celebrated the occasion with great joy.

12  THEN SAMUEL THUS ADDRESSED the assembled Israelites: 'I have
2   listened to your request and installed a king to rule over you. And the king
    is now your leader, while I am old and white-haired and my sons are with
3   you; but I have been your leader ever since I was a child. Here I am. Lay
    your complaints against me in the presence of the LORD and of his anointed
    king. Whose ox have I taken, whose ass have I taken? Whom have I
    wronged, whom have I oppressed? From whom have I taken a bribe, to
4   turn a blind eye? Tell me, and I will make restitution.' They answered,
    'You have not wronged us, you have not oppressed us; you have not taken
5   anything from any man.' Samuel then said to them, 'This day the LORD
    is witness among you, his anointed king is witness, that you have found
6   my hands empty.' They said, 'He is witness.' Samuel said to the people,
    'Yes, the LORD is witness, the LORD who gave you Moses and Aaron and
7   brought your fathers out of Egypt. Now stand up, and here in the presence
    of the LORD I will put the case against you and recite all the victories which
8   he has won for you and for your fathers. After Jacob and his sons had come
    down to Egypt and the Egyptians had made them suffer, your fathers cried
    to the LORD for help, and he sent Moses and Aaron, who brought them out
9   of Egypt and settled them in this place. But they forgot the LORD their
    God, and he abandoned them to Sisera, commander-in-chief of Jabin
    king of Hazor, to the Philistines, and to the king of Moab, and they had to
10  fight against them. Then your fathers cried to the LORD for help: "We
    have sinned, we have forsaken the LORD and we have worshipped the
    Baalim and the Ashtaroth. But now, if thou wilt deliver us from our
11  enemies, we will worship thee." So the LORD sent Jerubbaal and Barak,
    Jephthah and Samson, and delivered you from your enemies on every
    side; and you lived in peace and quiet.
12      'Then, when you saw Nahash king of the Ammonites coming against
    you, although the LORD your God was your king, you said to me, "No, let
13  us have a king to rule over us." Now, here is the king you asked for; you
14  chose him, and the LORD has set a king over you. If you will revere the LORD
    and give true and loyal service, if you do not rebel against his commands,
    and if you and the king who reigns over you are faithful to the LORD your
15  God, well and good; but if you do not obey the LORD, and if you rebel
    against his commands, then he will set his face against you and against
    your king.
16      'Stand still, and see the great wonder which the LORD will do before your
17  eyes. It is now wheat harvest; when I call upon the LORD and he sends
    thunder and rain, you will see and know how wicked it was in the LORD's
18  eyes for you to ask for a king.' So Samuel called upon the LORD and he
    sent thunder and rain that day; and all the people were in great fear of the
19  LORD and of Samuel. They said to Samuel, 'Pray for us your servants to
    the LORD your God, to save us from death; for we have added to all our
20  other sins the great wickedness of asking for a king.' Samuel said to the
    people, 'Do not be afraid; although you have been so wicked, do not give
21  up the worship of the LORD, but serve him with all your heart. Give up
    the worship of false gods which can neither help nor save, because they
22  are false. For his name's sake the LORD will not cast you off, because he

has resolved to make you his own people. As for me, God forbid that I  23
should sin against the LORD and cease to pray for you. I will show you what
is right and good: to revere the LORD and worship him faithfully with all  24
your heart. Consider what great things he has done for you; but if you per-  25
sist in wickedness, you shall be swept away, you and your king.'

Saul was fifty years[a] old when he became king, and he reigned over  **13**
Israel for twenty-two[b] years. He picked three thousand men from Israel,  2
two thousand to be with him in Michmash and the hill-country of Bethel
and a thousand to be with Jonathan in Gibeah of Benjamin; and he sent
the rest of the people home.

Jonathan killed the Philistine governor[c] in Geba, and the news spread  3
among the Philistines that the Hebrews were in revolt.[d] Saul sounded
the trumpet all through the land; and when the Israelites all heard that  4
Saul had killed a Philistine governor and that the name of Israel stank
among the Philistines, they answered the call to arms and came to join
Saul at Gilgal.[e] The Philistines mustered to attack Israel; they had thirty  5
thousand chariots and six thousand horse, with infantry as countless as
sand on the sea-shore. They went up and camped at Michmash, to the east
of Beth-aven. The Israelites found themselves in sore straits, for the army  6
was hard pressed, so they hid themselves in caves and holes and among the
rocks, in pits and cisterns. Some of them crossed the Jordan into the  7
district of Gad and Gilead, but Saul remained at Gilgal, and all the people
at his back were in alarm.[f] He waited seven days for his meeting with  8
Samuel, but Samuel did not come to Gilgal; so the people began to drift
away from Saul. He said therefore, 'Bring me the whole-offering and the  9
shared-offerings', and he offered up the whole-offering. Saul had just  10
finished the sacrifice, when Samuel arrived, and he went out to greet him.
Samuel said, 'What have you done?', and Saul answered, 'I saw that the  11
people were drifting away from me, and you yourself had not come as
you had promised, and the Philistines were assembling at Michmash; and  12
I thought, "The Philistines will now move against me at Gilgal, and I
have not placated the LORD"; so I felt compelled to make the whole-
offering myself.' Samuel said to Saul, 'You have behaved foolishly. You  13
have not kept the command laid on you by the LORD your God; if you had,
he would have established your dynasty over Israel for all time. But now  14
your line will not endure; the LORD will seek a man after his own heart, and
will appoint him prince over his people, because you have not kept the
LORD's command.'

Samuel left Gilgal without more ado and went on his way. The rest of  15
the people followed Saul, as he moved from Gilgal towards the enemy.
At Gibeah of Benjamin he mustered the people who were with him; they
were about six hundred men. Saul and his son Jonathan and the men they  16
had with them took up their quarters in Gibeah of Benjamin, while the
Philistines were encamped in Michmash. Raiding parties went out from  17

---

[a] *fifty years: prob. rdg.; Heb.* a year.          [b] *Prob. rdg.; Heb.* two.          [c] *Or* garrison.
[d] *that . . . revolt: prob. rdg.; Heb. has* saying, Let the Hebrews hear *after* through the
land.          [e] *they answered . . . Gilgal: or* they were summoned to follow Saul to Gilgal.
[f] *but Saul . . . in alarm: or* but Saul was still at Gilgal, and all the army joined him there.

the Philistine camp in three directions. One party turned towards Ophrah
18 in the district of Shual, another towards Beth-horon, and the third towards
the range of hills overlooking the valley of Zeboim and the wilderness
beyond.
19 No blacksmith was to be found in the whole of Israel, for the Philistines
were determined to prevent the Hebrews from making swords and spears.
20 The Israelites had to go down to the Philistines for their ploughshares,
21 mattocks, axes, and sickles to be sharpened. The charge was two-thirds of
a shekel for ploughshares and mattocks, and one-third of a shekel for
22 sharpening the axes and setting the goads.*a* So when war broke out none
of the followers of Saul and Jonathan had either sword or spear; only Saul
and Jonathan carried arms.
23 Now the Philistines had posted a force to hold the pass of Michmash;
**14** and one day Saul's son Jonathan said to his armour-bearer, 'Come, let us
go over to the Philistine post beyond that ridge'; but he did not tell his
2 father. Saul, at the time, had his tent under the pomegranate-tree at
Migron on the outskirts of Gibeah; and he had about six hundred men
3 with him. The ephod was carried by Ahijah son of Ahitub, Ichabod's
brother, son of Phinehas son of Eli, the priest of the LORD at Shiloh.
4 Nobody knew that Jonathan had gone. On either side of the pass through
which Jonathan tried to make his way over to the Philistine post stood two
5 sharp columns of rock, called Bozez*b* and Seneh; *c* one of them was on the
north towards Michmash, and the other on the south towards Geba.
6 Jonathan said to his armour-bearer, 'Now we will visit the post of those
uncircumcised rascals. Perhaps the LORD will take a hand in it, and if he
will, nothing can stop him. He can bring us safe through, whether we are
7 few or many.' The young man answered, 'Do what you will, go forward;
8 I am with you whatever you do.' 'Good!' said Jonathan, 'we will cross over
9 and let them see us. If they say, "Stay where you are till we come to you",
10 then we will stay where we are and not go up to them. But if they say,
"Come up to us", we will go up; this will be the sign that the LORD has put
11 them into our power.' So they showed themselves to the Philistines, and
the Philistines said, 'Look! Hebrews coming out of the holes where they
12 have been hiding!' And they called across to Jonathan and the young man,
'Come up to us; we have something to show you.' Jonathan said to the
young man, 'Come on, the LORD has put them into the power of Israel.'
13 Jonathan climbed up on hands and feet, and the young man followed him.
The Philistines fell in front of Jonathan, and the young man, coming
14 behind him, dispatched them. In that first attack Jonathan and his armour-
bearer killed about twenty of them, like men cutting a furrow across a
15 half-acre field. Terror spread through the army in the field and through
the whole people; the men at the post and the raiding parties were terrified;
the very earth quaked, and there was panic.
16 Saul's men on the watch in Gibeah of Benjamin saw the mob of Philis-
17 tines surging to and fro in confusion; so he ordered the people to call the
roll and find out who was missing; and they called the roll and found that

*a* one-third . . . the goads: *prob. rdg.; Heb. obscure.* *b* *That is* Shining. *c* *That is* Bramble-bush.

Jonathan and his armour-bearer were absent. Saul said to Ahijah, 'Bring 18
forward the ephod', for it was he who carried the ephod at that time before
Israel. But while Saul was still speaking, the confusion in the Philistine 19
camp was increasing more and more, and he said to the priest, 'Hold your
hand.' Then Saul and all his men with shouting made for the battlefield, 20
where they found the enemy fighting one another in complete disorder.
The Hebrews who up to now had been under the Philistines, and had been 21
with them in camp, changed sides and joined the Israelites under Saul and
Jonathan. All the Israelites in hiding in the hill-country of Ephraim heard 22
that the Philistines were in flight, and they also joined in and set off in hot
pursuit. The LORD delivered Israel that day, and the fighting passed on 23
beyond Beth-aven.

Now the Israelites on that day had been driven to exhaustion. Saul had 24
adjured the people in these words: 'A curse be on the man who eats any
food before nightfall until I have taken vengeance on my enemies.' So no
one ate any food. Now there was honeycomb*a* in the country-side; but 25 26
when his men came upon it, dripping with honey though it was, not one
of them put his hand to his mouth for fear of the oath. But Jonathan had 27
not heard his father lay this solemn prohibition on the people, and he
stretched out the stick that was in his hand, dipped the end of it in the
honeycomb, put it to his mouth and was refreshed. One of the people said 28
to him, 'Your father solemnly forbade this; he said, "A curse on the man
who eats food today!"' Now the men were faint with hunger. Jonathan 29
said, 'My father has done the people nothing but harm; see how I am
refreshed by this mere taste of honey. How much better if the people had 30
eaten today whatever they took from their enemies by way of spoil! Then
there would indeed have been a great slaughter of Philistines.'

They defeated the Philistines that day, and pursued them from Mich- 31
mash to Aijalon. But the people were so faint with hunger that they turned 32
to plunder and seized sheep, cattle, and bullocks; they slaughtered them
on the bare ground, and ate the meat with the blood in it. Someone told 33
Saul that the people were sinning against the LORD by eating their meat with
the blood in it. 'This is treason!' cried Saul. 'Roll a great stone here at
once.' He then said, 'Go about among the people and tell them to bring 34
their oxen and sheep, and let each man slaughter his here and eat it; and
so they will not sin against the LORD by eating meat with the blood in it.'
So as night fell each man came, driving his own ox, and slaughtered it
there. Thus Saul came to build an altar to the LORD, and this was the first 35
altar to the LORD that Saul built.

Saul said, 'Let us go down and make a night attack on the Philistines 36
and harry them till daylight; we will not spare a man of them.' The people
answered, 'Do what you think best', but the priest said, 'Let us first consult
God.' So Saul inquired of God, 'Shall I pursue the Philistines? Wilt 37
thou put them into Israel's power?'; but this time he received no answer.
So he said, 'Let all the leaders of the people come forward and let us find 38
out where the sin lies this day. As the LORD lives, the deliverer of Israel, 39

---

*a* Now . . . honeycomb: *prob. rdg.*; *Heb.* All the land went into the forest, and there was
honey.

even if it lies in my son Jonathan, he shall die.' Not a soul answered him.
40 Then he said to the Israelites, 'All of you stand on one side, and I and my
son Jonathan will stand on the other.' The people answered, 'Do what you
41 think best.' Saul said to the LORD the God of Israel, 'Why hast thou not
answered thy servant today? If this guilt lie in me or in my son Jonathan,
O LORD God of Israel, let the lot be Urim; if it lie in thy people Israel,
let it be Thummim.' Jonathan and Saul were taken, and the people were
42 cleared. Then Saul said, 'Cast lots between me and my son Jonathan';
43 and Jonathan was taken. Saul said to Jonathan, 'Tell me what you have
done.' Jonathan told him, 'True, I did taste a little honey on the tip of my
44 stick. Here I am; I am ready to die.' Then Saul swore a great oath that
45 Jonathan should die. But the people said to Saul, 'Shall Jonathan die,
Jonathan who has won this great victory in Israel? God forbid! As the
LORD lives, not a hair of his head shall fall to the ground, for he has been
at work with God today.' So the people ransomed Jonathan and he did not
46 die. Saul broke off the pursuit of the Philistines because they had made their
way home.
47 When Saul had made his throne secure in Israel, he fought against his
enemies on every side, the Moabites, the Ammonites, the Edomites, the
king of Zobah, and the Philistines; and wherever he turned he was success-
48 ful.*a* He displayed his strength by defeating the Amalekites and freeing
Israel from hostile raids.
49 Saul's sons were: Jonathan, Ishyo and Malchishua. These were the
50 names of his two daughters: Merab the elder and Michal the younger. His
wife was Ahinoam daughter of Ahimaaz, and his commander-in-chief
51 was Abner son of his uncle Ner; Kish, Saul's father, and Ner, Abner's
father, were sons*b* of Abiel.
52 There was bitter warfare with the Philistines throughout Saul's lifetime;
any strong man and any brave man that he found he took into his own
service.
15 Samuel said to Saul, 'The LORD sent me to anoint you king over his
2 people Israel. Now listen to the voice of the LORD. This is the very word of
the LORD of Hosts: "I am resolved to punish the Amalekites for what they
3 did to Israel, how they attacked them on their way up from Egypt." Go
now and fall upon the Amalekites and destroy them, and put their property
under ban. Spare no one; put them all to death, men and women, children
4 and babes in arms, herds and flocks, camels and asses.' Thereupon Saul
called out the levy and mustered them in Telaim. There were two hundred
5 thousand foot-soldiers and another ten thousand from Judah.*c* He came
6 to the Amalekite city and halted for a time in the gorge. Meanwhile he sent
word to the Kenites to leave the Amalekites and come down, 'or', he said,
'I shall destroy you as well as them; but you were friendly to Israel when
7 they came up from Egypt.' So the Kenites left the Amalekites. Then Saul
cut the Amalekites to pieces, all the way from Havilah to Shur on the borders
8 of Egypt. Agag the king of the Amalekites he took alive, but he destroyed
9 all the people, putting them to the sword. Saul and his army spared Agag

---

*a Or* he found ample provision.    *b Prob. rdg.; Heb.* son.    *c Prob. rdg.; Heb.*
ten thousand with the men of Judah.

and the best of the sheep and cattle, the fat beasts and the lambs and everything worth keeping; they were unwilling to destroy them, but anything
that was useless and of no value they destroyed.

Then the word of the LORD came to Samuel: 'I repent of having made 10 11
Saul king, for he has turned his back on me and has not obeyed my commands.' Samuel was angry; all night he cried aloud to the LORD. Early 12
next morning he went to meet Saul, but was told that he had gone to
Carmel; Saul had set up a monument for himself there, and had then
turned and gone down to Gilgal. There Samuel found him, and Saul 13
greeted him with the words, 'The LORD's blessing upon you! I have
obeyed the LORD's commands.' But Samuel said, 'What then is this bleat- 14
ing of sheep in my ears? Why do I hear the lowing of cattle?' Saul answered, 15
'The people have taken them from the Amalekites. These are what they
spared, the best of the sheep and cattle, to sacrifice to the LORD your God.
The rest we completely destroyed.' Samuel said to Saul, 'Let be, and I will 16
tell you what the LORD said to me last night.' 'Tell me', said Saul. So 17
Samuel went on, 'Time was when you thought little of yourself, but now
you are head of the tribes of Israel, and the LORD has anointed you king
over Israel. The LORD sent you with strict instructions to destroy that 18
wicked nation, the Amalekites; you were to fight against them until you
had wiped them out. Why then did you not obey the LORD? Why did you 19
pounce upon the spoil and do what was wrong in the eyes of the LORD?'
Saul answered Samuel, 'But I did obey the LORD; I went where the LORD 20
sent me, and I have brought back Agag king of the Amalekites. The rest
of them I destroyed. Out of the spoil the people took sheep and oxen, the 21
choicest of the animals laid under ban, to sacrifice to the LORD your God
at Gilgal.' Samuel then said: 22

> Does the LORD desire offerings and sacrifices
>   as he desires obedience?
> Obedience is better than sacrifice,
>   and to listen to him than the fat of rams.
> Defiance of him is sinful as witchcraft,
>   yielding to men*a* as evil as*b* idolatry.*c* 23
> Because you have rejected the word of the LORD,
>   the LORD has rejected you as king.

Saul said to Samuel, 'I have sinned. I have ignored the LORD's com- 24
mand and your orders: I was afraid of the people and deferred to them.
But now forgive my sin, I implore you, and come back with me, and I will 25
make my submission before the LORD.' Samuel answered, 'I will not come 26
back with you; you have rejected the word of the LORD and therefore the
LORD has rejected you as king over Israel.' He turned to go, but Saul caught 27
the edge of his cloak and it tore. And Samuel said to him, 'The LORD has 28
torn the kingdom of Israel from your hand today and will give it to another,
a better man than you. God who is the Splendour of Israel does not deceive 29
or change his mind; he is not a man that he should change his mind.' Saul 30

---

*a* yielding to men: *or* arrogance *or* obstinacy.  *b* as evil as: *prob. rdg.; Heb.* evil
and . . .  *c Or* household gods; *Heb.* teraphim.

said, 'I have sinned; but honour me this once before the elders of my people and before Israel and come back with me, and I will make my submission
31 to the LORD your God.' So Samuel went back with Saul, and Saul made
32 his submission to the LORD. Then Samuel said, 'Bring Agag king of the Amalekites.' So Agag came to him with faltering step and said, 'Surely the
33 bitterness of death has passed.' Samuel said, 'Your sword has made women childless, and your mother of all women shall be childless too.' Then Samuel hewed Agag in pieces before the LORD at Gilgal.
34 35 Saul went to his own home at Gibeah, and Samuel went to Ramah; and he never saw Saul again to his dying day, but he mourned for him, because the LORD had repented of having made him king over Israel.

## Saul and David

16 THE LORD SAID TO SAMUEL, 'How long will you mourn for Saul because I have rejected him as king over Israel? Fill your horn with oil and take it with you; I am sending you to Jesse of Bethlehem; for I
2 have chosen myself a king among his sons.' Samuel answered, 'How can I go? Saul will hear of it and kill me.' 'Take a heifer with you,' said the
3 LORD; 'say you have come to offer a sacrifice to the LORD, and invite Jesse to the sacrifice; then I will let you know what you must do. You shall
4 anoint for me the man whom I show you.' Samuel did as the LORD had told him, and went to Bethlehem. The elders of the city came in haste to
5 meet him, saying, 'Why have you come? Is all well?' 'All is well,' said Samuel; 'I have come to sacrifice to the LORD. Hallow yourselves and come with me to the sacrifice.' He himself hallowed Jesse and his sons and
6 invited them to the sacrifice also. They came, and when Samuel saw Eliab
7 he thought, 'Here, before the LORD, is his anointed king.' But the LORD said to him, 'Take no account of it if he is handsome and tall; I reject him. The LORD does not see as man sees; men judge by appearances but the
8 LORD judges by the heart.' Then Jesse called Abinadab and made him pass before Samuel, but he said, 'No, the LORD has not chosen this one.'
9 Then he presented Shammah, and Samuel said, 'Nor has the LORD chosen
10 him.' Seven of his sons Jesse presented to Samuel, but he said, 'The LORD
11 has not chosen any of these.' Then Samuel asked, 'Are these all?' Jesse answered, 'There is still the youngest, but he is looking after the sheep.' Samuel said to Jesse, 'Send and fetch him; we will not sit down until he
12 comes.' So he sent and fetched him. He was handsome, with ruddy cheeks and bright eyes.[a] The LORD said, 'Rise and anoint him: this is the man.'
13 Samuel took the horn of oil and anointed him in the presence of his brothers. Then the spirit of the LORD came upon David and was with him from that day onwards. And Samuel set out on his way back to Ramah.
14 The spirit of the LORD had forsaken Saul, and at times an evil spirit
15 from the LORD would seize him suddenly. His servants said to him, 'You
16 see, sir, how an evil spirit from God seizes you; why do you not command your servants here to go and find some man who can play the harp?—then,

*a* and bright eyes: *prob. rdg.; Heb. obscure.*

when an evil spirit from God comes on you, he can play and you will recover.' Saul said to his servants, 'Find me a man who can play well and bring him to me.' One of his attendants said, 'I have seen a son of Jesse of Bethlehem who can play; he is a brave man and a good fighter, wise in speech and handsome, and the LORD is with him.' Saul therefore sent messengers to Jesse and asked him to send him his son David, who was with the sheep. Jesse took a homer of bread, a skin of wine, and a kid, and sent them to Saul by his son David. David came to Saul and entered his service; and Saul loved him dearly, and he became his armour-bearer. So Saul sent word to Jesse: 'Let David stay in my service, for I am pleased with him.' And whenever a spirit from God came upon Saul, David would take his harp and play on it, so that Saul found relief; he recovered and the evil spirit left him alone.

The Philistines collected their forces for war and massed at Socoh in Judah; they camped between Socoh and Azekah at Ephes-dammim. Saul and the Israelites also massed, and camped in the Vale of Elah. They drew up their lines facing the Philistines, the Philistines occupying a position on one hill and the Israelites on another, with a valley between them. A champion came out from the Philistine camp, a man named Goliath, from Gath; he was over nine feet in height. He had a bronze helmet on his head, and he wore plate-armour of bronze, weighing five thousand shekels. On his legs were bronze greaves, and one of his weapons was a dagger of bronze. The shaft of his spear was like a weaver's beam, and its head, which was of iron, weighed six hundred shekels; and his shield-bearer marched ahead of him. The champion stood and shouted to the ranks of Israel, 'Why do you come out to do battle, you slaves of Saul? I am the Philistine champion; choose your man to meet me. If he can kill me in fair fight, we will become your slaves; but if I prove too strong for him and kill him, you shall be our slaves and serve us. Here and now I defy the ranks of Israel. Give me a man,' said the Philistine, 'and we will fight it out.' When Saul and the Israelites heard what the Philistine said, they were shaken and dismayed.

David was the son of an Ephrathite<sup>a</sup> called Jesse, who had eight sons. By Saul's time he had become a feeble old man, and his three eldest sons had followed Saul to the war. The eldest was called Eliab, the next Abinadab, and the third Shammah; David was the youngest. The three eldest followed Saul, while David used to go to Saul's camp and back to Bethlehem to mind his father's flocks. Morning and evening for forty days the Philistine came forward and took up his position. Then one day Jesse said to his son David, 'Take your brothers an ephah of this parched grain and these ten loaves of bread, and run with them to the camp. These ten cream-cheeses are for you to take to the commanding officer. See if your brothers are well and bring back some token from them.' Saul and the brothers and all the Israelites were in the Vale of Elah, fighting the Philistines. Early next morning David left someone in charge of the sheep, set out on his errand and went as Jesse had told him. He reached the lines just as the army was going out to

<sup>a</sup> *Prob. rdg.; Heb. adds* Is this the man from Bethlehem in Judah?

21 take up position and was raising the war-cry. The Israelites and the
22 Philistines drew up their ranks opposite each other. David left his things
   in charge of the quartermaster, ran to the line and went up to his brothers
23 to greet them. While he was talking to them the Philistine champion,
   Goliath, came out from the Philistine ranks and issued his challenge in the
24 same words as before; and David heard him. When the Israelites saw the
25 man they ran from him in fear. 'Look at this man who comes out day after
   day to defy Israel', they said. 'The king is to give a rich reward to the man
   who kills him; he will give him his daughter in marriage too and will
26 exempt his family from service due in Israel.' Then David turned to his
   neighbours and said, 'What is to be done for the man who kills this Philistine and wipes out our disgrace? And who is he, an uncircumcised Philis-
27 tine, to defy the army of the living God?' The people told him how the
28 matter stood and what was to be done for the man who killed him. His
   elder brother Eliab overheard David talking with the men and grew angry.
   'What are you doing here?' he asked. 'And who have you left to look after
   those few sheep in the wilderness? I know you, you impudent young
29 rascal; you have only come to see the fighting.' David answered, 'What
30 have I done now? I only asked a question.' And he turned away from him
   to someone else and repeated his question, but everybody gave him the
   same answer.
31     What David had said was overheard and reported to Saul, who sent for
32 him. David said to him, 'Do not lose heart, sir. I will go and fight this
33 Philistine.' Saul answered, 'You cannot go and fight with this Philistine;
34 you are only a lad, and he has been a fighting man all his life.' David said
   to Saul, 'Sir, I am my father's shepherd; when a lion or bear comes and
35 carries off a sheep from the flock, I go after it and attack it and rescue the
   victim from its jaws. Then if it turns on me, I seize it by the beard and batter
36 it to death. Lions I have killed and bears, and this uncircumcised Philistine will fare no better than they; he has defied the army of the living God.
37 The LORD who saved me from the lion and the bear will save me from this
38 Philistine.' 'Go then,' said Saul; 'and the LORD will be with you.' He put
   his own tunic on David, placed a bronze helmet on his head and gave him
39 a coat of mail to wear; he then fastened his sword on David over his tunic.
   But David hesitated, because he had not tried them. 'I
   cannot go with these, because I have not tried them.' So he took them off.
40 Then he picked up his stick, chose five smooth stones from the brook and
   put them in a shepherd's bag which served as his pouch. He walked out to
   meet the Philistine with his sling in his hand.
41     The Philistine came on towards David, with his shield-bearer marching
42 ahead; and he looked David up and down and had nothing but contempt
43 for this handsome lad with his ruddy cheeks and bright eyes.[a] He said to
   David, 'Am I a dog that you come out against me with sticks?' And he
44 swore at him in the name of his god. 'Come on,' he said, 'and I will give
45 your flesh to the birds and the beasts.' David answered, 'You have come
   against me with sword and spear and dagger, but I have come against you
   in the name of the LORD of Hosts, the God of the army of Israel which you

---

[a] handsome . . . bright eyes: *prob. rdg.; Heb. obscure.*

have defied. The LORD will put you into my power this day; I will kill you 46
and cut your head off and leave your carcass and the carcasses of the
Philistines to the birds and the wild beasts; all the world shall know that
there is a God in Israel. All those who are gathered here shall see that the 47
LORD saves neither by sword nor spear; the battle is the LORD's, and he
will put you all into our power.'

When the Philistine began moving towards him again, David ran quickly 48
to engage him. He put his hand into his bag, took out a stone, slung it, and 49
struck the Philistine on the forehead. The stone sank into his forehead, and
he fell flat on his face on the ground. So David proved the victor with his 50
sling and stone; he struck Goliath down and gave him a mortal wound,
though he had no sword. Then he ran to the Philistine and stood over him, 51
and grasping his sword, he drew it out of the scabbard, dispatched him and
cut off his head. The Philistines, when they saw that their hero was dead,
turned and ran. The men of Israel and Judah at once raised the war-cry 52
and hotly pursued them all the way to Gath and even to the gates of Ekron.
The road that runs to Shaarim, Gath, and Ekron was strewn with their
dead. On their return from the pursuit of the Philistines, the Israelites 53
plundered their camp. David took Goliath's head and carried it to Jerusa- 54
lem, leaving his weapons in his tent.

Saul had said to Abner his commander-in-chief, when he saw David 55
going out against the Philistine, 'That boy there, Abner, whose son is he?'
'By your life, your majesty,' said Abner, 'I do not know.' The king said 56
to Abner, 'Go and find out whose son the lad is.' When David came back 57
after killing the Philistine, Abner took him and presented him to Saul
with the Philistine's head still in his hand. Saul asked him, 'Whose son 58
are you, young man?', and David answered, 'I am the son of your servant
Jesse of Bethlehem.'

That same day, when Saul had finished talking with David, he kept him **18** 1-2
and would not let him return any more to his father's house, for he saw that
Jonathan had given his heart to David and had grown to love him as
himself. So Jonathan and David made a solemn compact because each 3
loved the other as dearly as himself. And Jonathan stripped off the cloak 4
he was wearing and his tunic, and gave them to David, together with his
sword, his bow, and his belt. David succeeded so well in every venture on 5
which Saul sent him that he was given a command in the army, and his
promotion pleased the ordinary people, and even pleased Saul's officers.

At the home-coming of the army when David returned from the 6
slaughter of the Philistines, the women came out from all the cities of
Israel to look on, and the dancers came out to meet King Saul with tambourines, singing, and dancing. The women as they made merry sang to 7
one another:

> Saul made havoc among thousands
> but David among tens of thousands.

Saul was furious, and the words rankled. He said, 'They have given David 8
tens of thousands and me only thousands; what more can they do but
make him king?' From that day forward Saul kept a jealous eye on David. 9

10 Next day an evil spirit from God seized upon Saul; he fell into a frenzy *a*
in the house, and David played the harp to him as he had before. Saul had
11 his spear in his hand, and he hurled it at David, meaning to pin him to the
12 wall; but twice David swerved aside. After this Saul was afraid of David,
13 because he saw that the LORD had forsaken him and was with David. He
therefore removed David from his household and appointed him to the
14 command of a thousand men. David led his men into action, and succeeded
15 in everything that he undertook, because the LORD was with him. When
16 Saul saw how successful he was, he was more afraid of him than ever; all
Israel and Judah loved him because he took the field at their head.

17 Saul said to David, 'Here is my elder daughter Merab; I will give her
to you in marriage, but in return you must serve me valiantly and fight the
LORD's battles.' For Saul meant David to meet his end at the hands of the
18 Philistines and not himself. David answered Saul, 'Who am I and what
are my father's people, my kinsfolk, in Israel, that I should become the
19 king's son-in-law?' However, when the time came for Saul's daughter
Merab to be married to David, she had already been given to Adriel of
20 Meholah. But Michal, Saul's other daughter, fell in love with David, and
21 when Saul was told of this, he saw that it suited his plans. He said to himself, 'I will give her to him; let her be the bait that lures him to his death
at the hands of the Philistines.' So Saul proposed a second time to make
22 David his son-in-law, and ordered his courtiers to say to David privately,
'The king is well disposed to you and you are dear to us all; now is the time
23 for you to marry into the king's family.' When Saul's people spoke in this
way to David, he said to them, 'Do you think that marrying the king's
daughter is a matter of so little consequence that a poor man of no con-
24 sequence, like myself, can do it?' Saul's courtiers reported what David
25 had said, and he replied, 'Tell David this: all the king wants as the bride-
price is the foreskins of a hundred Philistines, by way of vengeance on his
enemies.' Saul was counting on David's death at the hands of the Philis-
26 tines. The courtiers told David what Saul had said, and marriage with
the king's daughter on these terms pleased him well. Before the appointed
27 time, David went out with his men and slew two hundred Philistines; he
brought their foreskins and counted them out to the king in order to be
accepted as his son-in-law. So Saul married his daughter Michal to David.
28 He saw clearly that the LORD was with David, and knew that Michal his
29 daughter had fallen in love with him; and so he grew more and more afraid
of David and was his enemy for the rest of his life.

30 The Philistine officers used to come out to offer single combat; and
whenever they did, David had more success against them than all the rest
of Saul's men, and he won a great name for himself.

**19** SAUL SPOKE TO JONATHAN his son and all his household about killing
2 David. But Jonathan was devoted to David and told him that his father
Saul was looking for an opportunity to kill him. 'Be on your guard to-
3 morrow morning,' he said; 'conceal yourself, and remain in hiding. Then
I will come out and join my father in the open country where you are and

*a Or fell into prophetic rapture.*

speak to him about you, and if I discover anything I will tell you.' Jonathan   4
spoke up for David to his father Saul and said to him, 'Sir, do not wrong
your servant David; he has not wronged you; his conduct towards you has
been beyond reproach. Did he not take his life in his hands when he killed   5
the Philistine, and the LORD won a great victory for Israel? You saw it, you
shared in the rejoicing; why should you wrong an innocent man and put
David to death without cause?' Saul listened to Jonathan and swore   6
solemnly by the LORD that David should not be put to death. So Jonathan   7
called David and told him all this; then he brought him to Saul, and he
was in attendance on the king as before.

War broke out again, and David attacked the Philistines and dealt them   8
such a blow that they ran before him.

An evil spirit from the LORD came upon Saul as he was sitting in the   9
house with his spear in his hand; and David was playing the harp. Saul   10
tried to pin David to the wall with the spear, but he avoided the king's
thrust so that Saul drove the spear into the wall. David escaped and got
safely away. That night Saul sent servants to keep watch on David's house,   11
intending to kill him in the morning, but David's wife Michal warned him
to get away that night, 'or tomorrow', she said, 'you will be a dead man.'
She let David down through a window and he slipped away and escaped.   12
Michal took their household gods and put them on the bed; at its head she   13
laid a goat's-hair rug and covered it all with a cloak. When the men arrived   14
to arrest David she told them he was ill. Saul sent them back to see David   15
for themselves. 'Bring him to me, bed and all,' he said, 'and I will kill him.'
When they came, there were the household gods on the bed and the goat's-   16
hair rug at its head. Then Saul said to Michal, 'Why have you played this   17
trick on me and let my enemy get safe away?' And Michal answered, 'He
said to me, "Help me to escape or I will kill you."'

Meanwhile David made good his escape and came to Samuel at Ramah,   18
and told him how Saul had treated him. Then he and Samuel went to
Naioth and stayed there. Saul was told that David was there, and he sent   19 20
a party of men to seize him. When they saw the company of prophets in
rapture, with Samuel standing at their head, the spirit of God came upon
them and they fell into prophetic rapture. When this was reported to Saul   21
he sent another party. These also fell into a rapture, and when he sent more
men a third time, they did the same. Saul himself then set out for Ramah   22
and came to the great cistern in Secu. He asked where Samuel and David
were and was told that they were at Naioth in Ramah. On his way there the   23
spirit of God came upon him too and he went on, in a rapture as he went,
till he came to Naioth in Ramah. There too stripped off his clothes and   24
like the rest fell into a rapture before Samuel and lay down naked all that
day and all that night. That is why men say, 'Is Saul also among the
prophets?'

Then David made his escape from Naioth in Ramah and came to   **20**
Jonathan. 'What have I done?' he asked. 'What is my offence? What does
your father think I have done wrong, that he seeks my life?' Jonathan   2
answered him, 'God forbid! There is no thought of putting you to death.
I am sure my father will not do anything whatever without telling me. Why

3 should my father hide such a thing from me? I cannot believe it!' David said, 'I am ready to swear to it: your father has said to himself, "Jonathan must not know this or he will resent it", because he knows that you have a high regard for me. As the LORD lives, your life upon it, there is only a step
4 between me and death.' Jonathan said to David, 'What do you want me to
5 do for you?' David answered, 'It is new moon tomorrow, and I ought to dine with the king. Let me go and lie hidden in the fields until the third
6 evening. If your father happens to miss me, then say, "David asked me for leave to pay a rapid visit to his home in Bethlehem, for it is the annual
7 sacrifice there for the whole family." If he says, "Well and good", that will be a good sign for me; but if he flies into a rage, you will know that he is set
8 on doing me wrong. My lord, keep faith with me; for you and I have entered into a solemn compact before the LORD. Kill me yourself if I am guilty.
9 Why let me fall into your father's hands?' 'God forbid!' cried Jonathan.
10 'If I find my father set on doing you wrong I will tell you.' David answered
11 Jonathan, 'How will you let me know if he answers harshly?' Jonathan said,
12 'Come with me into the fields.' So they went together into the fields, and Jonathan said to David, 'I promise you, David, in the sight of the LORD the God of Israel, this time tomorrow I will sound my father for the third
13 time and, if he is well disposed to you, I will send and let you know. If my father means mischief, the LORD do the same to me and more, if I do not let you know and get you safely away. The LORD be with you as he has been
14 with my father! I know that as long as I live you will show me faithful
15 friendship, as the LORD requires; and if I should die, you will continue loyal to my family for ever. When the LORD rids the earth of all David's
16 enemies, may the LORD call him to account if he and his house are no longer
17 my friends.' Jonathan pledged himself afresh to David because of his love
18 for him, for he loved him as himself. Then he said to him, 'Tomorrow is
19 the new moon, and you will be missed when your place is empty. So go down at nightfall for the third time to the place where you hid on the
20 evening of the feast and stay by the mound there. Then I will shoot three
21 arrows towards it, as though I were aiming at a mark. Then I will send my boy to find the arrows. If I say to him, "Look, the arrows are on this side of you, pick them up", then you can come out of hiding. You will be quite
22 safe, I swear it; for there will be nothing amiss. But if I say to the lad, "Look, the arrows are on the other side of you, further on", then the LORD
23 has said that you must go; the LORD stand witness between us for ever to the pledges we have exchanged.'
24 So David hid in the fields. The new moon came, the dinner was prepared,
25 and the king sat down to eat. Saul took his customary seat by the wall, and Abner sat beside him; Jonathan too was present, but David's place was
26 empty. That day Saul said nothing, for he thought that David was absent
27 by some chance, perhaps because he was ritually unclean. But on the second day, the day after the new moon, David's place was still empty, and Saul said to his son Jonathan, 'Why has not the son of Jesse come to the feast,
28 either yesterday or today?' Jonathan answered Saul, 'David asked permis-
29 sion to go to Bethlehem. He asked my leave and said, "Our family is hold-ing a sacrifice in the town and my brother himself has ordered me to be

there. Now, if you have any regard for me, let me slip away to see my brothers." That is why he has not come to dine with the king.' Saul was 30 angry with Jonathan, 'You son of a crooked and unfaithful mother! You have made friends with the son of Jesse only to bring shame on yourself and dishonour on your mother; I see how it will be. As long as Jesse's son 31 remains alive on earth, neither you nor your crown will be safe. Send at once and fetch him; he deserves to die.' Jonathan answered his father, 32 'Deserves to die! Why? What has he done?' At that, Saul picked up his 33 spear and threatened to kill him; and he knew that his father was bent on David's death. Jonathan left the table in a rage and ate nothing on the 34 second day of the festival; for he was indignant on David's behalf because his father had humiliated him.

Next morning, Jonathan went out into the fields to meet David at the 35 appointed time, taking a young boy with him. He said to the boy, 'Run and 36 find the arrows; I am going to shoot.' The boy ran on, and he shot the arrows over his head. When the boy reached the place where Jonathan's 37 arrows had fallen, Jonathan called out after him, 'Look, the arrows are beyond you. Hurry! No time to lose! Make haste!' The boy gathered up 38 the arrows and brought them to his master; but only Jonathan and David 39 knew what this meant; the boy knew nothing. Jonathan handed his weapons 40 to the boy and told him to take them back to the city. When the boy had 41 gone, David got up from behind the mound and bowed humbly three times. Then they kissed one another and shed tears together, until David's grief was even greater than Jonathan's. Jonathan said to David, 'Go in 42 safety; we have pledged each other in the name of the LORD who is witness for ever between you and me and between your descendants and mine.'

David went off at once, while Jonathan returned to the city. David made **21** his way to the priest Ahimelech at Nob, who hurried out to meet him and said, 'Why have you come alone and no one with you?' David answered 2 Ahimelech, 'I am under orders from the king: I was to let no one know about the mission on which he was sending me or what these orders were. When I took leave of my men I told them to meet me in such and such a place. Now, what have you got by you? Let me have five loaves, or as many 3 as you can find.' The priest answered David, 'I have no ordinary bread 4 available. There is only the sacred bread; but have the young men kept themselves from women?' David answered the priest, 'Women have been 5 denied us hitherto, when I have been on campaign, even an ordinary campaign, and the young men's bodies have remained holy; and how much more will they be holy today?' So, as there was no other bread there, the 6 priest gave him the sacred bread, the Bread of the Presence, which had just been taken from the presence of the LORD to be replaced by freshly baked bread on the day that the old was removed. One of Saul's servants 7 happened to be there that day, detained before the LORD; his name was Doeg the Edomite, and he was the strongest of all Saul's herdsmen. David 8 said to Ahimelech, 'Have you a spear or sword here at hand? I have no sword or other weapon with me, because the king's business was urgent.' The priest answered, 'There is the sword of Goliath the Philistine whom 9 you slew in the Vale of Elah; it is wrapped up in a cloak behind the ephod.

If you wish to take that, take it; there is no other weapon here.' David said, 'There is no sword like it; give it to me.'

10 That day, David went on his way, eluding Saul, and came to Achish
11 king of Gath. The servants of Achish said to him, 'Surely this is David, the king of his country, the man of whom they sang as they danced:

> Saul made havoc among thousands
> but David among tens of thousands.'

12 These words were not lost on David, and he became very much afraid of
13 Achish king of Gath. So he altered his behaviour in public and acted like a lunatic in front of them all, scrabbling on the double doors of the city gate
14 and dribbling down his beard. Achish said to his servants, 'The man is
15 mad! Why bring him to me? Am I short of madmen that you bring this one to plague me? Must I have this fellow in my house?'

22 DAVID MADE HIS ESCAPE and went from there to the cave of Adullam. When his brothers and all his family heard that he was there, they joined
2 him. Men in any kind of distress or in debt or with a grievance gathered round him, about four hundred in number, and he became their chief.
3 From there David went to Mizpeh in Moab and said to the king of Moab, 'Let my father and mother come and take shelter with you until I know
4 what God will do for me.' So he left them at the court of the king of Moab, and they stayed there as long as David was in his stronghold.
5 The prophet Gad said to David, 'You must not stay in your stronghold;
6 go at once into Judah.' So David went as far as the forest of Hareth. News that David and his men had been seen reached Saul while he was in Gibeah, sitting under the tamarisk-tree on the hill-top with his spear in
7 his hand and all his retainers standing about him. He said to them, 'Listen to me, you Benjamites: do you expect the son of Jesse to give you all fields and vineyards, or make you all officers over units of a thousand and a
8 hundred? Is that why you have all conspired against me? Not one of you told me when my son made a compact with the son of Jesse; none of you spared a thought for me or told me that my son had set my own servant against me, who is lying in wait for me now.'
9 Then Doeg the Edomite, who was standing with the servants of Saul, spoke: 'I saw the son of Jesse coming to Nob, to Ahimelech son of Ahitub.
10 Ahimelech consulted the LORD on his behalf, then gave him food and
11 handed over to him the sword of Goliath the Philistine.' The king sent for Ahimelech the priest and his family, who were priests at Nob, and they
12 all came into his presence. Saul said, 'Now listen, you son of Ahitub', and
13 the man answered, 'Yes, my lord?' Then Saul said to him, 'Why have you and the son of Jesse plotted against me? You gave him food and the sword too, and consulted God on his behalf; and now he has risen against me and
14 is at this moment lying in wait for me.' 'And who among all your servants', answered Ahimelech, 'is like David, a man to be trusted, the king's son-in-law, appointed to your staff and holding an honourable place in your
15 household? Have I on this occasion done something profane in consulting God on his behalf? God forbid! I trust that my lord the king will not accuse

me or my family; for I know nothing whatever about it.' But the king said, 16
'Ahimelech, you must die, you and all your family.' He then turned to the 17
bodyguard attending him and said, 'Go and kill the priests of the LORD;
for they are in league with David, and, though they knew that he was a
fugitive, they did not tell me.' The king's men, however, were unwilling
to raise a hand against the priests of the LORD. The king therefore said to 18
Doeg the Edomite, 'You, Doeg, go and fall upon the priests'; so Doeg went
and fell upon the priests, killing that day with his own hand eighty-five
men who could carry the ephod. He put to the sword every living thing in 19
Nob, the city of priests: men and women, children and babes in arms, oxen,
asses, and sheep. One son of Ahimelech named Abiathar made his escape 20
and joined David. He told David how Saul had killed the priests of the 21
LORD. Then David said to him, 'When Doeg the Edomite was there that 22
day, I knew that he would inform Saul. I have gambled with the lives of all
your father's family. Stay here with me, have no fear; he who seeks your 23
life seeks mine, and you will be safe with me.'

The Philistines were fighting against Keilah and plundering the 23
threshing-floors; and when David heard this, he consulted the LORD and 2
asked whether he should go and attack the Philistines. The LORD answered,
'Go, attack them, and relieve Keilah.' But David's men said to him, 'As 3
we are now, we have enough to fear from Judah. How much worse if we
challenge the Philistine forces at Keilah!' David consulted the LORD once 4
again and the LORD answered him, 'Go to Keilah; I will give the Philistines into your hands.' So David and his men went to Keilah and fought 5
the Philistines; they carried off their cattle, inflicted a heavy defeat on them
and relieved the inhabitants. Abiathar son of Ahimelech made good his 6
escape and joined David at Keilah, bringing the ephod with him. Saul was 7
told that David had entered Keilah, and he said, 'God has put him into
my hands; for he has walked into a trap by entering a walled town with
gates and bars.' He called out the levy to march on Keilah and besiege David 8
and his men. When David learnt how Saul planned his undoing, he told 9
Abiathar the priest to bring the ephod, and then he prayed, 'O LORD God 10
of Israel, I thy servant have heard news that Saul intends to come to Keilah
and destroy the city because of me. Will the citizens of Keilah surrender me 11
to him? Will Saul come as I have heard? O LORD God of Israel, I pray
thee, tell thy servant.' The LORD answered, 'He will come.' Then David 12
asked, 'Will the citizens of Keilah surrender me and my men to Saul?',
and the LORD answered, 'They will.' Then David left Keilah at once with 13
his men, who numbered about six hundred, and moved about from place
to place. When the news reached Saul that David had escaped from Keilah,
he made no further move.

While David was living in the fastnesses of the wilderness of Ziph, in 14
the hill-country, Saul searched for him day after day, but God did not put
him into his power. David well knew that Saul had come out to seek his 15
life; and while he was at Horesh in the wilderness of Ziph, Saul's son 16
Jonathan came to him there and gave him fresh courage in God's name:
'Do not be afraid,' he said; 'my father's hand shall not touch you. You will 17
become king of Israel and I shall hold rank after you; and my father knows

18 it.' The two of them made a solemn compact before the LORD; then David
19 remained in Horesh and Jonathan went home. While Saul was at Gibeah
the Ziphites brought him this news: 'David, we hear, is in hiding among
us in the fastnesses of Horesh on the hill of Hachilah, south of Jeshimon.
20 Come down, your majesty, come whenever you will, and we are able to
21 surrender him to you.' Saul said, 'The LORD has indeed blessed you; you
22 have saved me a world of trouble. Go now and make further inquiry, and
find out exactly where he is and who saw him there. They tell me that he
23 by himself is crafty enough to outwit me. Find out which of his hiding-
places he is using; then come back to me at such and such a place, and I
will go along with you. So long as he stays in this country, I will hunt him
24 down, if I have to go through all the clans of Judah one by one.' They set
out for Ziph without delay, ahead of Saul; David and his men were in the
25 wilderness of Maon in the Arabah to the south of Jeshimon. Saul set off
with his men to look for him; but David got wind of it and went down to a
refuge in the rocks, and there he stayed in the wilderness of Maon. Hearing
26 of this, Saul went into the wilderness after him; he was on one side of the
hill, David and his men on the other. While David and his men were
trying desperately to get away and Saul and his followers were closing in
27 for the capture, a runner brought a message to Saul: 'Come at once! the
28 Philistines are harrying the land.' So Saul called off the pursuit and turned
back to face the Philistines. This is why that place is called the Dividing
29 Rock. David went up from there and lived in the fastnesses of En-gedi.

24    When Saul returned from the pursuit of the Philistines, he learnt that
2 David was in the wilderness of En-gedi. So he took three thousand men
picked from the whole of Israel and went in search of David and his men
3 to the east of the Rocks of the Wild Goats. There beside the road were
some sheepfolds, and near by was a cave, at the far end of which David and
his men were sitting concealed. Saul came to the cave and went in to relieve
4-7*a* himself. His men said to David, 'The day has come: the LORD has put your
enemy into your hands, as he promised he would, and you may do what you
please with him.' David said to his men, 'God forbid that I should harm
my master, the LORD's anointed, or lift a finger against him; he is the LORD's
anointed.' So David reproved his men severely and would not let them
attack Saul. He himself got up stealthily and cut off a piece of Saul's cloak;
but when he had cut it off, his conscience smote him. Saul rose, left the
8 cave and went on his way; whereupon David also came out of the cave and
called after Saul, 'My lord the king!' When Saul looked round, David
9 prostrated himself in obeisance and said to him, 'Why do you listen when
10 they say that David is out to do you harm? Today you can see for yourself
that the LORD put you into my power in the cave; I had a mind to kill you,
but no, I spared your life and said, "I cannot lift a finger against my master,
11 for he is the LORD's anointed." Look, my dear lord, look at this piece of
your cloak in my hand. I cut it off, but I did not kill you; this will show you
that I have no thought of violence or treachery against you, and that I have
12 done you no wrong; yet you are resolved to take my life. May the LORD
judge between us! but though he may take vengeance on you for my sake,

*a Verses 4–7 are re-arranged thus: 4a, 6, 7a, 4b, 5, 7b.*

I will never lift my hand against you; "One wrong begets another", as   13
the old saying goes, yet I will never lift my hand against you. Who has the   14
king of Israel come out against? What are you pursuing? A dead dog, a
mere flea. The LORD will be judge and decide between us; let him look into   15
my cause, he will plead for me and will acquit me.'

When David had finished speaking, Saul said, 'Is that you, David my   16
son?', and he wept. Then he said, 'The right is on your side, not mine;   17
you have treated me so well, I have treated you so badly. Your goodness to   18
me this day has passed all bounds: the LORD put me at your mercy but you
did not kill me. Not often does a man find his enemy and let him go safely   19
on his way; so may the LORD reward you well for what you have done for
me today! I know now for certain that you will become king, and that the   20
kingdom of Israel will flourish under your rule. Swear to me by the LORD   21
then that you will not exterminate my descendants and blot out my name
from my father's house.' David swore an oath to Saul; and Saul went back   22
to his home, while David and his men went up to their fastness.

SAMUEL DIED, and all Israel came together to mourn for him, and he   **25**
was buried in his house in Ramah. Afterwards David went down to the
wilderness of Paran.

There was a man at Carmel in Maon, who had great influence and owned   2
three thousand sheep and a thousand goats; and he was shearing his flocks
in Carmel. His name was Nabal and his wife's name Abigail; she was a   3
beautiful and intelligent woman, but her husband, a Calebite, was surly
and mean. David heard in the wilderness that Nabal was shearing his   4
flocks, and sent ten of his men, saying to them, 'Go up to Carmel, find   5
Nabal and give him my greetings. You are to say, "All good wishes for the   6
year ahead! Prosperity to yourself, your household, and all that is yours!
I hear that you are shearing. Your shepherds have been with us lately and   7
we did not molest them; nothing of theirs was missing all the time they
were in Carmel. Ask your own people and they will tell you. Receive my   8
men kindly, for this is an auspicious day with us, and give what you can to
David your son and your servant."' David's servants came and delivered   9
this message to Nabal in David's name. When they paused, Nabal answered,   10
'Who is David? Who is this son of Jesse? In these days every slave who
breaks away from his master sets himself up as a chief.[a] Am I to take my   11
food and my wine and the meat I have provided for my shearers and give
it to men who come from I know not where?' David's men turned and   12
made their way back to him and told him all this. He said to his men,   13
'Buckle on your swords, all of you.' So they buckled on their swords and
followed David, four hundred of them, while two hundred stayed behind
with the baggage.

One of the young men said to Abigail, Nabal's wife, 'David sent mes-   14
sengers from the wilderness to ask our master politely for a present, and
he flew out[b] at them. The men have been very good to us and have not   15
molested us, nor did we miss anything all the time we were going about

---

[a] *Or* In these days there are many slaves who break away from their master.
[b] flew out: *or* screamed.

16 with them in the open country. They were as good as a wall round us, night
17 and day, while we were minding the flocks. Think carefully what you had
better do, for it is certain ruin for our master and his whole family; he is
18 such a good-for-nothing that it is no good talking to him.' So Abigail
hastily collected two hundred loaves and two skins of wine, five sheep
ready dressed, five measures of parched grain, a hundred bunches of
19 raisins, and two hundred cakes of dried figs, and loaded them on asses, but
told her husband nothing about it. Then she said to her servants, 'Go on
20 ahead, I will follow you.' As she made her way on her ass, hidden by the
hill, there were David and his men coming down towards her, and she met
21 them. David had said, 'It was a waste of time to protect this fellow's property in the wilderness so well that nothing of his was missing. He has
22 repaid me evil for good.' David swore a great oath: 'God do the same to
me and more if I leave him a single mother's son alive by morning!'
23     When Abigail saw David she dismounted in haste and prostrated herself
24 before him, bowing low to the ground at his feet, and said, 'Let me take
the blame, my lord, but allow me, your humble servant, to speak out and
25 let my lord give me a hearing. How can you take any notice of this good-
for-nothing? He is just what his name Nabal means: "Churl" is his name,
and churlish his behaviour. I did not myself, sir, see the men you sent.
26 And now, sir, the LORD has restrained you from bloodshed and from giving
vent to your anger. As the LORD lives, your life upon it, your enemies and
27 all who want to see you ruined will be like Nabal. Here is the present which
I, your humble servant, have brought; give it to the young men under
28 your command. Forgive me, my lord, if I am presuming; for the LORD
will establish your family for ever, because you have fought his wars. No
29 calamity shall overtake you as long as you live. If any man sets out to pursue
you and take your life, the LORD your God will wrap your life up and put
it with his own treasure, but the lives of your enemies he will hurl away like
30 stones from a sling. When the LORD has made good all his promises to you,
31 and has made you ruler of Israel, there will be no reason why you should
stumble or your courage falter because you have shed innocent blood or
given way to your anger. Then when the LORD makes all you do prosper,
32 you will remember me, your servant.' David said to Abigail, 'Blessed is
33 the LORD the God of Israel who has sent you today to meet me. A blessing
on your good sense, a blessing on you because you have saved me today
34 from the guilt of bloodshed and from giving way to my anger. For I swear
by the life of the LORD the God of Israel who has kept me from doing you
wrong: if you had not come at once to meet me, not a man of Nabal's
household, not a single mother's son, would have been left alive by morn-
35 ing.' Then David took from her what she had brought him and said, 'Go
home in peace, I have listened to you and I grant your request.'
36     On her return she found Nabal holding a banquet in his house, a banquet
fit for a king. He grew merry and became very drunk, so drunk that his wife
37 said nothing to him, trivial or serious, till daybreak. In the morning, when
the wine had worn off, she told him everything, and he had a seizure and
38 lay there like a stone. Ten days later the LORD struck him again and he
39 died. When David heard that Nabal was dead he said, 'Blessed be the LORD,

who has himself punished Nabal for his insult, and has kept me his servant from doing wrong. The LORD has made Nabal's wrongdoing recoil on his own head.' David then sent to make proposals that Abigail should become his wife. And his servants came to Abigail at Carmel and said to her, 'David 40 has sent us to fetch you to be his wife.' She rose and prostrated herself with 41 her face to the ground, and said, 'I am his slave to command, I would wash the feet of my lord's servants.' So Abigail made her preparations with all 42 speed and, with her five maids in attendance, accompanied by David's messengers, rode away on an ass; and she became David's wife. David had 43 also married Ahinoam of Jezreel; both these women became his wives. Saul meanwhile had given his daughter Michal, David's wife, to Palti son 44 of Laish from Gallim.

THE ZIPHITES CAME TO SAUL at Gibeah to report that David was in 26 hiding on the hill of Hachilah overlooking Jeshimon. Saul went down at 2 once to the wilderness of Ziph, taking with him three thousand picked men, to search for David there. He encamped beside the road on the hill 3 of Hachilah overlooking Jeshimon, while David was still in the wilderness. As soon as David knew that Saul had come to the wilderness in pursuit of him, he sent out scouts and found that Saul had reached such and such a 4 place. Without delay, he went to the place where Saul had pitched his 5 camp and observed where Saul and Abner son of Ner, the commander-in-chief, were lying. Saul lay within the lines with his troops encamped in a circle round him. David turned to Ahimelech the Hittite and Abishai son 6 of Zeruiah, Joab's brother, and said, 'Who will venture with me into the camp, to go to Saul?' Abishai answered, 'I will.' David and Abishai 7 entered the camp at night and found Saul lying asleep within the lines with his spear thrust into the ground by his head. Abner and the army were lying all round him. Abishai said to David, 'God has put your enemy into 8 your power today; let me strike him and pin him to the ground with one thrust of the spear; I shall not have to strike twice.' David said to him, 'Do 9 him no harm; who has ever lifted a finger against the LORD's anointed and gone unpunished? As the LORD lives,' went on David, 'the LORD will 10 strike him down; either his time will come and he will die, or he will go down to battle and meet his end. God forbid that I should lift a finger 11 against the LORD's anointed! But now let us take the spear which is by his head, and the water-jar, and go.' So David took the spear and the water- 12 jar from beside Saul's head and they went. The whole camp was asleep; no one saw him, no one knew anything, no one even woke up. A heavy sleep sent by the LORD had fallen on them.

Then David crossed over to the other side and stood on the top of a hill 13 a long way off; there was no little distance between them. David shouted 14 across to the army and hailed Abner, 'Answer me, Abner!' He answered, 'Who are you to shout to the king?' David said to Abner, 'Do you call 15 yourself a man? Is there anyone like you in Israel? Why, then, did you not keep watch over your lord the king, when someone came to harm your lord the king? This was not well done. As the LORD lives, you deserve to die, all 16 of you, because you have not kept watch over your master the LORD's anointed. Look! Where are the king's spear and the water-jar that were by his head?'

17 Saul recognized David's voice and said, 'Is that you, David my son?'
18 'Yes, sir, it is', said David. 'Why must your majesty pursue me? What have
19 I done? What mischief am I plotting? Listen, my lord, to what I have to say. If it is the LORD who has set you against me, may an offering be acceptable to him; but if it is men, a curse on them in the LORD's name; for they have ousted me today from my share in the LORD's inheritance and
20 have banished me to serve other gods! Do not let my blood be shed on foreign soil, far from the presence of the LORD, just because the king of Israel came out to look for a flea, as one might hunt a partridge over the
21 hills.' Saul answered, 'I have done wrong; come back, David my son. You have held my life precious this day, and I will never harm you again. I have
22 been a fool, I have been sadly in the wrong.' David answered, 'Here is the
23 king's spear; let one of your men come across and fetch it. The LORD who rewards uprightness and loyalty will reward the man into whose power he put you today, when I refused to lift a finger against the LORD's anointed.
24 As I held your life precious today, so may the LORD hold mine precious and
25 deliver me from every distress.' Then Saul said to David, 'A blessing is on you, David my son. You will do great things and be victorious.' So David went on his way and Saul returned home.

27 David thought, 'One of these days I shall be killed by Saul. The best thing for me to do will be to escape into Philistine territory; then Saul will lose all further hope of finding me anywhere in Israel, search as he may, and
2 I shall escape his clutches.' So David and his six hundred men crossed the
3 frontier forthwith to Achish son of Maoch king of Gath. David settled in Gath with Achish, taking with him his men and their families and his two
4 wives, Ahinoam of Jezreel and Abigail of Carmel, Nabal's widow. Saul was told that David had escaped to Gath, and he gave up the search.
5 David said to Achish, 'If I stand well in your opinion, grant me a place in one of your country towns where I may settle. Why should I remain in the
6 royal city with your majesty?' Achish granted him Ziklag on that day: that is why Ziklag still belongs to the kings of Judah.

7 8 David spent a year and four months in Philistine country. He and his men would sally out and raid the Geshurites, the Gizrites, and the Amalekites, for it was they who inhabited the country from Telaim[a] all the way
9 to Shur and Egypt. When David raided the country he left no one alive, man or woman; he took flocks and herds, asses and camels, and clothes too,
10 and then came back again to Achish. When Achish asked, 'Where was your raid today?', David would answer, 'The Negeb of Judah' or 'The Negeb
11 of the Jerahmeelites' or 'The Negeb of the Kenites'. Neither man nor woman did David bring back alive to Gath, for fear that they should denounce him and his men for what they had done. This was his practice
12 as long as he remained with the Philistines. Achish trusted David, thinking that he had won such a bad name among his own people the Israelites that he would remain his subject all his life.

*a* from Telaim: *prob. rdg.; Heb.* from of old.

## Saul and his sons killed

IN THOSE DAYS THE PHILISTINES MUSTERED their army for an attack 28 on Israel. Achish said to David, 'You know that you and your men must take the field with me.' David answered Achish, 'Good, you will 2 learn what your servant can do.' And Achish said to David, 'I will make you my bodyguard for life.'

By this time Samuel was dead, and all Israel had mourned for him and 3 buried him in Ramah, his own city; and Saul had banished from the land all who trafficked with ghosts and spirits. The Philistines mustered and 4 encamped at Shunem, and Saul gathered all the Israelites and encamped on Gilboa; and when Saul saw the Philistine force, fear struck him to the 5 heart. He inquired of the LORD, but the LORD did not answer him, whether 6 by dreams or by Urim or by prophets. So he said to his servants, 'Find me a 7 woman who has a familiar spirit, and I will go and inquire through her.' His servants told him that there was such a woman at En-dor. Saul put on 8 different clothes and went in disguise with two of his men. He came to the woman by night and said, 'Tell me my fortunes by consulting the dead, and call up the man I name to you.' But the woman answered, 'Surely you 9 know what Saul has done, how he has made away with those who call up ghosts and spirits; why do you press me to do what will lead to my death?' Saul swore her an oath: 'As the LORD lives, no harm shall come to you for 10 this.' The woman asked whom she should call up, and Saul answered, 11 'Samuel.' When the woman saw Samuel appear, she shrieked and said to 12 Saul, 'Why have you deceived me? You are Saul!' The king said to her, 13 'Do not be afraid. What do you see?' The woman answered, 'I see a ghostly form coming up from the earth.' 'What is it like?' he asked; she answered, 14 'Like an old man coming up, wrapped in a cloak.' Then Saul knew it was Samuel, and he bowed low with his face to the ground, and prostrated himself. Samuel said to Saul, 'Why have you disturbed me and brought 15 me up?' Saul answered, 'I am in great trouble; the Philistines are pressing me and God has turned away; he no longer answers me through prophets or through dreams, and I have summoned you to tell me what I should do.' Samuel said, 'Why do you ask me, now that the LORD has turned from you 16 and become your adversary? He has done what he foretold through me. 17 He has torn the kingdom from your hand and given it to another man, to David. You have not obeyed the LORD, or executed the judgement of his 18 fury against the Amalekites; that is why he has done this to you today. For the same reason the LORD will let your people Israel fall into the hands 19 of the Philistines and, what is more, tomorrow you and your sons shall be with me. Yes, indeed, the LORD will give the Israelite army into the hands of the Philistines.' Saul was overcome and fell his full length to the ground, 20 terrified by Samuel's words. He had no strength left, for he had eaten nothing all day and all night.

The woman went to Saul and saw that he was much disturbed, and she 21 said to him, 'I listened to what you said and I risked my life to obey you. Now listen to me: let me set before you a little food to give you strength for 22 your journey.' But he refused to eat anything. When his servants joined the 23

woman in pressing him, he yielded, rose from the ground and sat on the
24 couch. The woman had a fatted calf at home, which she quickly slaughtered.
25 She took some meal, kneaded it and baked unleavened cakes, which she
set before Saul and his servants. They ate the food and departed that same
night.

29 The Philistines mustered all their troops at Aphek, while the Israelites
2 encamped at En-harod*a* in Jezreel. The Philistine princes were advancing
with their troops in units of a hundred and a thousand; David and his men
3 were in the rear of the column with Achish. The Philistine commanders
asked, 'Why are those Hebrews there?' Achish answered, 'This is David,
the servant of Saul king of Israel who has been with me now for a year or
more. I have had no fault to find in him ever since he came over to me.'
4 The Philistine commanders were indignant and said to Achish, 'Send the
man back to the town which you allotted to him. He shall not fight side by
side with us, or he may turn traitor in the battle. What better way to buy
5 his master's favour, than at the price of our lives? This is that David of
whom they sang, as they danced:

> Saul made havoc among thousands
> but David among tens of thousands.'

6 Achish summoned David and said to him, 'As the LORD lives, you are
an upright man and your service with my troops has well satisfied me. I
have had no fault to find with you ever since you joined me, but the other
7 princes are not willing to accept you. Now go home in peace, and you will
8 then be doing nothing that they can regard as wrong.' David protested,
'What have I done, or what fault have you found in me from the day I
first entered your service till now, that I should not come and fight against
9 the enemies of my lord the king?' Achish answered David, 'I agree that
you have been as true to me as an angel of God, but the Philistine com-
10 manders insist that you shall not fight alongside them. Now rise early in
the morning with those of your lord's subjects who have followed you, and
go to the town which I allotted to you; harbour no evil thoughts, for I am
11 well satisfied with you. Rise early and start as soon as it is light.' So David
and his men rose early to start that morning on their way back to the land
of the Philistines, while the Philistines went on to Jezreel.

30 On the third day David and his men reached Ziklag. Now the Amalekites
2 had made a raid into the Negeb, attacked Ziklag and set fire to it; they had
carried off all the women, high and low, without putting one of them to
3 death. These they drove with them and continued their march. When
David and his men approached the town, they found it destroyed by fire,
4 and their wives, their sons, and their daughters carried off. David and the
5 people with him wept aloud until they could weep no more. David's two
wives, Ahinoam of Jezreel and Abigail widow of Nabal of Carmel, were
6 among the captives. David was in a desperate position because the people,
embittered by the loss of their sons and daughters, threatened to stone him.
7 So David sought strength in the LORD his God. He told Abiathar the priest,
son of Ahimelech, to bring the ephod. When Abiathar had brought the

---

*a Prob. rdg.; Heb. at the spring.*

ephod, David inquired of the LORD, 'Shall I pursue these raiders? and   8
shall I overtake them?' The answer came, 'Pursue them: you will overtake
them and rescue everyone.' So David and his six hundred men set out and   9
reached the ravine of Besor.*ᵃ* Two hundred of them who were too weary to   10
cross the ravine stayed behind, and David with four hundred pressed on
in pursuit.

In the open country they came across an Egyptian and took him to   11
David. They gave him food to eat and water to drink, also a lump of dried   12
figs and two bunches of raisins. When he had eaten these he revived; for
he had had nothing to eat or drink for three days and nights. David asked   13
him, 'Whose slave are you? and where have you come from?' 'I am an
Egyptian boy,' he answered, 'the slave of an Amalekite, but my master left
me behind because I fell ill three days ago. We had raided the Negeb of the   14
Kerethites, part of Judah, and the Negeb of Caleb; we also set fire to
Ziklag.' David asked, 'Can you guide me to this band?' 'Swear to me by   15
God', he answered, 'that you will not put me to death or hand me back to
my master, and I will guide you to them.' So he led him down, and there   16
they were scattered everywhere, eating and drinking and celebrating the
capture of the great mass of spoil taken from Philistine and Judaean
territory.

David attacked from dawn till dusk and continued till next day; only   17
four hundred young men mounted on camels made good their escape.
David rescued all those whom the Amalekites had taken, including his   18
two wives. No one was missing, high or low, sons or daughters, and none   19
of the spoil, nor anything they had taken for themselves: David recovered
everything. They took all the flocks and herds, drove the cattle before   20
him*ᵇ* and said, 'This is David's spoil.' When David returned to the two   21
hundred men who had been too weak to follow him and whom he had left
behind at the ravine of Besor, they came forward to meet him and his men.
David greeted them all, inquiring how things were with them. But some   22
of those who had gone with David, worthless men and scoundrels, broke
in and said, 'These men did not go with us; we will not allot them any of
the spoil that we have retrieved, except that each of them may take his own
wife and children and then go.' 'That you shall never do,' said David,   23
'considering what the LORD has given us, and how he has kept us safe and
given the raiding party into our hands. Who could agree with what you   24
propose? Those who stayed with the stores shall have the same share as
those who went into battle. They shall share and share alike.' From   25
that time onwards, this has been the established custom in Israel down to
this day.

When David reached Ziklag, he sent some of the spoil to the elders of   26
Judah and to his friends, with this message: 'This is a present for you out
of the spoil taken from the LORD's enemies.' He sent to those in Bethuel,   27
in Ramoth-negeb, in Jattir, in Ararah,*ᶜ* in Siphmoth, in Eshtemoa, in   28 29
Rachal, in the cities of the Jerahmeelites, in the cities of the Kenites, in   30

---

*ᵃ* *Prob. rdg.; Heb. adds* those who were left over remained.     *ᵇ* They took . . . before
him: *prob. rdg.; Heb.* David took all the flocks and herds; they drove before that cattle.
*ᶜ* *Prob. rdg.; Heb.* Aroer.

31 Hormah, in Borashan, in Athak, in Hebron, and in all the places over which he and his men had ranged.

31 1<sup>a</sup> The Philistines fought a battle against Israel, and the men of Israel were 2 routed, leaving their dead on Mount Gilboa. The Philistines hotly pursued Saul and his sons and killed the three sons, Jonathan, Abinadab and 3 Malchishua. The battle went hard for Saul, for some archers came upon 4 him and he was wounded in the belly by the archers. So he said to his armour-bearer, 'Draw your sword and run me through, so that these uncircumcised brutes may not come and taunt me and make sport of me.' But the armour-bearer refused, he dared not; whereupon Saul took his 5 own sword and fell on it. When the armour-bearer saw that Saul was dead, 6 he too fell on his sword and died with him. Thus they all died together on that day, Saul, his three sons, and his armour-bearer, as well as his men. 7 And all the Israelites in the district of the Vale and of the Jordan, when they saw that the other Israelites had fled and that Saul and his sons had perished, fled likewise, abandoning their cities, and the Philistines went in and occupied them.

8 Next day, when the Philistines came to strip the slain, they found Saul 9 and his three sons lying dead on Mount Gilboa. They cut off his head and stripped him of his weapons; then they sent messengers through the length and breadth of their land to take the good news to idols and people 10 alike. They deposited his armour in the temple of Ashtoreth and nailed his 11 body on the wall of Beth-shan. When the inhabitants of Jabesh-gilead 12 heard what the Philistines had done to Saul, the bravest of them journeyed together all night long and recovered the bodies of Saul and his sons from the wall of Beth-shan; they brought them back to Jabesh and anointed 13 them there with spices. Then they took their bones and buried them under the tamarisk-tree in Jabesh, and fasted for seven days.

# THE SECOND BOOK OF

# SAMUEL

## David's rule at Hebron

1 WHEN DAVID RETURNED from his victory over the 2 Amalekites, he spent two days in Ziklag. And on the third day after Saul's death a man came from the army with his clothes rent and dust on his head. When he came into David's presence he fell to 3 the ground in obeisance, and David asked him where he had come from. 4 He answered, 'I have escaped from the army of Israel.' And David said to him, 'What news? Tell me.' 'The army has been driven from the field,' he answered, 'and many have fallen in battle. Saul and Jonathan his son 5 are dead.' David said to the young man who brought the news, 'How do

*a Verses 1–13: cp. 1 Chr. 10. 1–12.*

338

you know that Saul and Jonathan are dead?' The man answered, 'It so  6
happened that I was on Mount Gilboa and saw Saul leaning on his spear
with the chariots and horsemen closing in upon him. He turned round and,  7
seeing me, called to me. I said, "What is it, sir?" He asked who I was, and  8
I said, "An Amalekite." Then he said to me, "Come and stand over me  9
and dispatch me. I still live, but the throes of death have seized me." So I  10
stood over him and gave him the death-blow; for I knew that, broken as
he was, he could not live. Then I took the crown from his head and the
armlet from his arm, and I have brought them here to you, sir.' At that  11
David caught at his clothes and rent them, and so did all the men with him.
They beat their breasts and wept, because Saul and Jonathan his son and  12
the people of the LORD, the house of Israel, had fallen in battle; and they
fasted till evening. David said to the young man who brought the news,  13
'Where do you come from?', and he answered, 'I am the son of an alien,
an Amalekite.' 'How is it', said David, 'that you were not afraid to raise your  14
hand to slay the LORD's anointed?' And he summoned one of his own  15
young men and ordered him to fall upon the man. So the young man struck
him down and killed him; and David said, 'Your blood be on your own  16
head; for out of your own mouth you condemned yourself when you said,
"I killed the LORD's anointed."'

David made this lament over Saul and Jonathan his son; and he ordered  17 18
that this dirge over them should be taught to the people of Judah. It was
written down and may be found in the Book of Jashar: *a*

> O prince of Israel, laid low in death!
>> How are the men of war fallen!           19
>
> Tell it not in Gath,                      20
> proclaim it not in the streets of Ashkelon,
>> lest the Philistine women rejoice,
>> lest the daughters of the uncircumcised exult.
>
> Hills of Gilboa, let no dew or rain fall on you,
>> no showers on the uplands *b*!           21
> For there the shields of the warriors lie tarnished,
>> and the shield of Saul, no longer bright with oil.
> The bow of Jonathan never held back       22
> from the breast of the foeman, from the blood of the slain;
> the sword of Saul never returned
>> empty to the scabbard.
>
> Delightful and dearly loved were Saul and Jonathan;  23
>> in life, in death, they were not parted.
> They were swifter than eagles,
>> stronger than lions.
>
> Weep for Saul, O daughters of Israel!     24
>> who clothed you in scarlet and rich embroideries,
>> who spangled your dress with jewels of gold.

*a* Or the Book of the Upright.        *b* showers on the uplands: *prob. rdg.; Heb.* fields
of offerings.

25  How are the men of war fallen, fallen on the field!
    O Jonathan, laid low in death!

26  I grieve for you, Jonathan my brother;
    dear and delightful you were to me;
    your love for me was wonderful,
    surpassing the love of women.

27  Fallen, fallen are the men of war;
    and their armour left on the field.

2   After this David inquired of the LORD, 'Shall I go up into one of the
    cities of Judah?' The LORD answered, 'Go.' David asked, 'To which city?',
2   and the answer came, 'To Hebron.' So David went to Hebron with his
    two wives, Ahinoam of Jezreel and Abigail widow of Nabal of Carmel.
3   David also brought the men who had joined him, with their families, and
4   they settled in the city *a* of Hebron. The men of Judah came, and there they
    anointed David king over the house of Judah.
    Word came to David that the men of Jabesh-gilead had buried Saul,
5   and he sent them this message: 'The LORD bless you because you kept
6   faith with Saul your lord and buried him. For this may the LORD keep faith
    and truth with you, and I for my part will show you favour too, because
7   you have done this. Be strong, be valiant, now that Saul your lord is dead,
    and the people of Judah have anointed me to be king over them.'
8   Meanwhile Saul's commander-in-chief, Abner son of Ner, had taken
9   Saul's son Ishbosheth, brought him across the Jordan to Mahanaim, and
    made him king over Gilead, the Asherites, Jezreel, Ephraim, and Benjamin,
10  and all Israel. Ishbosheth was forty years old when he became king over
    Israel, and he reigned two years. The tribe of Judah, however, followed
11  David. David's rule over Judah in Hebron lasted seven years and a half.
12  Abner son of Ner, with the troops of Saul's son Ishbosheth, marched
13  out from Mahanaim to Gibeon, and Joab son of Zeruiah marched out with
    David's troops from Hebron. They met at the pool of Gibeon and took up
    their positions one on one side of the pool and the other on the other side.
14  Abner said to Joab, 'Let the young men come forward and join in single
15  combat before us.' Joab answered, 'Yes, let them.' So they came up, one
    by one, and took their places, twelve for Benjamin and for Ishbosheth and
16  twelve from David's men. Each man seized his opponent by the head and
    thrust his sword into his side; and thus they fell together. That is why
    that place, which lies in Gibeon, was called the Field of Blades.
17  There ensued a fierce battle that day, and Abner and the men of Israel
18  were defeated by David's troops. All three sons of Zeruiah were there,
    Joab, Abishai and Asahel. Asahel, who was swift as a gazelle on the plains,
19  ran straight after Abner, swerving neither to right nor left in his pursuit.
20  Abner turned and asked, 'Is it you, Asahel?' Asahel answered, 'It is.'
21  Abner said, 'Turn aside to right or left, tackle one of the young men and
    win his belt for yourself.' But Asahel would not abandon the pursuit.
22  Abner again urged him to give it up. 'Why should I kill you?' he said. 'How
23  could I look Joab your brother in the face?' When he still refused to turn

*a Prob. rdg.; Heb.* cities.

aside, Abner struck him in the belly with a back-thrust of his spear[a] so that the spear came out behind him, and he fell dead in his tracks. All who came to the place where Asahel lay dead stopped there. But Joab and Ab-  24 ishai kept up the pursuit of Abner, until, at sunset, they reached the hill of Ammah, opposite Giah on the road leading to the pastures of Gibeon. The Benjamites rallied to Abner and, forming themselves into a single  25 company, took up their stand on the top of the hill of Ammah.[b] Abner  26 called to Joab, 'Must the slaughter go on for ever? Can you not see that it will be all the more bitter in the end? Will you never recall the people from the pursuit of their kinsmen?' Joab answered, 'As God lives, if you had  27 not spoken, the people would not have given up the pursuit till morning.' Then Joab sounded the trumpet, and all the people abandoned the pursuit  28 of the men of Israel and the fighting ceased. Abner and his men moved  29 along the Arabah all that night, crossed the Jordan and went on all the morning till they reached Mahanaim. When Joab returned from the  30 pursuit of Abner, he assembled his troops and found that, besides Asahel, nineteen of David's men were missing. David's forces had routed the Ben-  31 jamites and the followers of Abner, killing three hundred and sixty of them. They took up Asahel and buried him in his father's tomb at Bethlehem.  32 Joab and his men marched all night, and as day broke they reached Hebron.

THE WAR BETWEEN THE HOUSES of Saul and David was long drawn  3 out, David growing steadily stronger while the house of Saul became weaker and weaker.

Sons were born to David at Hebron. His eldest was Amnon, whose  2[c] mother was Ahinoam of Jezreel; his second Chileab, whose mother was  3 Abigail widow of Nabal of Carmel; the third Absalom, whose mother was Maacah daughter of Talmai king of Geshur; the fourth Adonijah,  4 whose mother was Haggith; the fifth Shephatiah, whose mother was Abital; and the sixth Ithream, whose mother was David's wife Eglah.  5 These were all born to David at Hebron.

As the war between the houses of Saul and David went on, Abner made  6 his position gradually stronger in the house of Saul. Now Saul had had  7 a concubine named Rizpah daughter of Aiah. Ishbosheth asked Abner, 'Why have you slept with my father's concubine?' Abner was very angry  8 at this and exclaimed, 'Am I a baboon in the pay of Judah? Up to now I have been loyal to the house of your father Saul, to his brothers and friends, and I have not betrayed you into David's hands; yet you choose this moment to charge me with disloyalty over this woman. But now, so help me  9 God, I will do all I can to bring about what the LORD swore to do for David: I will set to work to bring down the house of Saul and to put David on the  10 throne over Israel and Judah from Dan to Beersheba.' Ishbosheth could  11 not say another word; he was too much afraid of Abner. Then Abner, seek-  12 ing to make friends where he could, instead of going to David himself sent envoys with this message: 'Let us come to terms, and I will do all I can to bring the whole of Israel over to you.' David sent answer: 'Good, I will  13

[a] a back-thrust of his spear: *prob. rdg.; Heb. obscure.*  [b] the hill of Ammah: *prob. rdg., cp. verse 24; Heb.* a single hill.  [c] *Verses 2–5: cp. 1 Chr. 3. 1–4.*

come to terms with you, but on this one condition, that you do not come into
14 my presence without bringing Saul's daughter Michal to me.' David also
sent messengers to Saul's son Ishbosheth with the demand: 'Hand over
to me my wife Michal to whom I was betrothed at the price of a hundred
15 Philistine foreskins.' Thereupon Ishbosheth sent and took her away from
16 her husband, Paltiel son of Laish. Paltiel followed her as far as Bahurim,
weeping all the way, until Abner ordered him to go back home, and he went.

17 Abner now approached the elders of Israel and said, 'For some time
18 past you have wanted David for your king; now is the time to act, for this
is the word of the LORD about David: "By the hand of my servant David
I will deliver my people Israel from the Philistines and from all their
19 enemies."' Abner spoke also to the Benjamites and then went on to report
to David at Hebron all that the Israelites and the Benjamites had agreed.
20 When Abner was admitted to David's presence, there were twenty men
21 with him and David gave a feast for them all. Then Abner said to David,
'I shall now go and bring the whole of Israel over to your majesty, and they
shall make a covenant with you. Then you will be king over a realm after
your own heart.' David dismissed Abner, granting him safe conduct.

22 David's men and Joab returned from a raid bringing a great deal of
plunder with them, and by this time Abner, after his dismissal, was no
23 longer with David in Hebron. So when Joab and his raiding party arrived,
they were greeted with the news that Abner son of Ner had been with the
24 king and had departed under safe conduct. Joab went in to the king and
said, 'What have you done? Here you have had Abner with you. How
25 could you let him go? He has got clean away! You know Abner son of Ner:
he came meaning to deceive you, to learn all about your movements and
26 to find out what you are doing.' When he left David's presence, Joab sent
messengers after Abner and they brought him back from the Pool of Sirah;
27 but David knew nothing of all this. On Abner's return to Hebron, Joab
drew him aside in the gateway, as though to speak privately with him, and
there, in revenge for his brother Asahel, he stabbed him in the belly, and he
28 died. When David heard the news he said, 'I and my realm are for ever
29 innocent in the sight of the LORD of the blood of Abner son of Ner. May it
recoil upon the head of Joab and upon all his family! May the house of
Joab never be free from running sore or foul disease, nor lack a son fit
30 only to ply the distaff or doomed to die by the sword or beg his bread!' So
Joab and Abishai his brother slew Abner because he had killed their brother
31 Asahel in battle at Gibeon. Then David ordered Joab and all the people
with him to rend their clothes, put on sackcloth and beat their breasts for
32 Abner, and the king himself walked behind the bier. They buried Abner
in Hebron and the king wept aloud at the tomb, while all the people wept
33 with him. The king made this lament for Abner:

> Must Abner die so base a death?
34 > Your hands were not bound,
> your feet not thrust into fetters;
> you fell as one who falls at a ruffian's hands.

And the people wept for him again.

They came to persuade David to eat something; but it was still day and 35
he swore, 'So help me God! I will not touch food of any kind before sunset.'
The people took note of this and approved; indeed, everything the king 36
did pleased them. Everyone throughout Israel knew on that day that the 37
king had had no hand in the murder of Abner son of Ner. The king said 38
to his servants, 'Do you not know that a warrior, a great man, has fallen
this day in Israel? King though I am, I feel weak and powerless in face of 39
these ruthless sons of Zeruiah; they are too much for me; the LORD will
requite the wrongdoer as he deserves.'

When Saul's son Ishbosheth heard that Abner had been killed in Hebron, 4
his courage failed him and all Israel was dismayed. Now Ishbosheth had<sup>a</sup> 2
two officers, who were captains of raiding parties, and whose names were
Baanah and Rechab; they were Benjamites, sons of Rimmon of Beeroth,
Beeroth being reckoned part of Benjamin; but the Beerothites had fled to 3
Gittaim, where they have lived ever since.

(Saul's son Jonathan had a son lame in both feet. He was five years old 4
when word of the death of Saul and Jonathan came from Jezreel. His nurse
had picked him up and fled, but in her hurry to get away he fell and was
crippled. His name was Mephibosheth.)

Rechab and Baanah, the sons of Rimmon of Beeroth, came to the house 5
of Ishbosheth in the heat of the day and went in, while he was taking his
midday rest. Now the door-keeper had been sifting wheat, but she had 6
grown drowsy and fallen asleep, so Rechab and his brother Baanah crept in,
found their way to the room where he was asleep on the bed, and struck 7
him dead. They cut off his head and took it with them, and, making their
way along the Arabah all night, came to Hebron. They brought Ish- 8
bosheth's head to David at Hebron and said to the king, 'Here is the head
of Ishbosheth son of Saul, your enemy, who sought your life. The LORD
has avenged your majesty today on Saul and on his family.' David answered 9
Rechab and his brother Baanah, the sons of Rimmon of Beeroth, with an
oath: 'As the LORD lives, who has rescued me from all my troubles! I 10
seized the man who brought me word that Saul was dead and thought it
good news; I killed him in Ziklag, and that was how I rewarded him for
his news. How much more when ruffians have killed an innocent man on 11
his bed in his own house? Am I not to take vengeance on you now for the
blood you have shed, and rid the earth of you?' David gave the word, and 12
the young men killed them; they cut off their hands and feet and hung
them up beside the pool in Hebron, but the head of Ishbosheth they took
and buried in Abner's tomb at Hebron.

## David king in Jerusalem

NOW ALL THE TRIBES OF ISRAEL came to David at Hebron and said 5 1<sup>b</sup>
to him, 'We are your own flesh and blood. In the past, while Saul was 2
still king over us, you led the forces of Israel to war and you brought them
home again. And the LORD said to you, "You shall be shepherd of my

<sup>a</sup> had: *prob. rdg.; Heb. om.* <sup>b</sup> *Verses 1–3, 6–10: cp. 1 Chr. 11. 1–9.*

3 people Israel; you shall be their prince.'' All the elders of Israel came to the king at Hebron; there David made a covenant with them before the

4 LORD, and they anointed David king over Israel. David came to the throne

5 at the age of thirty and reigned for forty years. In Hebron he had ruled over Judah for seven years and a half, and for thirty-three years he reigned in Jerusalem over Israel and Judah together.

6 The king and his men went to Jerusalem to attack the Jebusites, whose land it was. The Jebusites said to David, 'Never shall you come in here; not till you have disposed of the blind and the lame', meaning that David

7 should never come in. None the less David did capture the stronghold of

8 Zion, and it is now known as the City of David. David said on that day, 'Everyone who would kill a Jebusite, let him use his grappling-iron to reach the lame and the blind, David's bitter enemies.' That is why they say, 'No blind or lame man shall come into the LORD's house.'

9 David took up his residence in the stronghold and called it the City of David. He built the city *a* round it, starting at the Millo and working

10 inwards. So David steadily grew stronger, for the LORD the God of Hosts was with him.

11*b* Hiram king of Tyre sent an embassy to David; he sent cedar logs, and

12 with them carpenters and stonemasons, who built David a house. David knew by now that the LORD had confirmed him as king over Israel and had made his royal power stand higher for the sake of his people Israel.

13 After he had moved from Hebron he took more concubines and wives

14*c* from Jerusalem; and more sons and daughters were born to him. These are the names of the children born to him in Jerusalem: Shammua,

15 16 Shobab, Nathan, Solomon, Ibhar, Elishua, Nepheg, Japhia, Elishama, Eliada and Eliphelet.

17 When the Philistines learnt that David had been anointed king over Israel, they came up in force to seek him out. David, hearing of this, took

18 refuge in the stronghold. The Philistines had come and overrun the Vale

19 of Rephaim. So David inquired of the LORD, 'If I attack the Philistines, wilt thou deliver them into my hands?' And the LORD answered, 'Go, I

20 will deliver the Philistines into your hands.' So he went up and attacked them at Baal-perazim and defeated them there. 'The LORD has broken through my enemies' lines,' David said, 'as a river breaks its banks.' That

21 is why the place was named Baal-perazim.*d* The Philistines left their idols behind them there, and David and his men carried them off.

22 The Philistines made another attack and overran the Vale of Rephaim.

23 David inquired of the LORD, who said, 'Do not attack now but wheel round

24 and take them in the rear opposite the aspens. As soon as you hear a rustling sound in the tree-tops, then act at once; for the LORD will have gone out

25 before you to defeat the Philistine army.' David did as the LORD had commanded, and drove the Philistines in flight all the way from Geba to Gezer.

6 After that David again summoned the picked men of Israel, thirty

---

*a* the city: *prob. rdg., cp. I Chr. II. 8; Heb. om.*    *b* Verses *11-25: cp. I Chr. 14. 1-16.*    *c* Verses *14-16: cp. I Chr. 3. 5-8; 14. 4-7.*    *d* That is Baal of Break-through.

thousand in all, and went with the whole army to Baalath-judah*a* to fetch 2*b*
the Ark of God which bears the name of the LORD of Hosts, who is enthroned upon the cherubim. They mounted the Ark of God on a new cart 3
and conveyed it from the house of Abinadab on the hill, with Uzzah and
Ahio, sons of Abinadab, guiding the cart. They took it with the Ark of God 4
upon it from Abinadab's house on the hill, with Ahio walking in front.
David and all Israel danced for joy before the LORD without restraint to the 5
sound of singing,*c* of harps and lutes, of tambourines and castanets and
cymbals. But when they came to a certain threshing-floor, the oxen 6
stumbled, and Uzzah reached out to the Ark of God and took hold of it.
The LORD was angry with Uzzah and struck him down there for his rash 7
act. So he died there beside the Ark of God. David was vexed because the 8
LORD's anger had broken out upon Uzzah, and he called the place Perez-
uzzah,*d* the name it still bears. David was afraid of the LORD that day and 9
said, 'How can I harbour the Ark of the LORD after this?' He felt he could 10
not take the Ark of the LORD with him to the City of David, but turned
aside and carried it to the house of Obed-edom the Gittite. Thus the Ark 11
of the LORD remained at Obed-edom's house for three months, and the
LORD blessed Obed-edom and all his family.

When they told David that the LORD had blessed Obed-edom's family 12*e*
and all that was his because of the Ark of God, he went and brought up
the Ark of God from the house of Obed-edom to the City of David with
much rejoicing. When the bearers of the Ark of the LORD had gone six 13
steps he sacrificed an ox and a buffalo. David, wearing a linen ephod, 14
danced without restraint before the LORD. He and all the Israelites brought 15
up the Ark of the LORD with shouting and blowing of trumpets. But as the 16
Ark of the LORD was entering the City of David, Saul's daughter Michal
looked down through a window and saw King David leaping and capering
before the LORD, and she despised him in her heart. When they had brought 17
in the Ark of the LORD, they put it in its place inside the tent that David had
pitched for it, and David offered whole-offerings and shared-offerings
before the LORD. After David had completed these sacrifices, he blessed the 18
people in the name of the LORD of Hosts and gave food to all the people, a flat 19
loaf of bread, a portion of meat, and a cake of raisins, to every man and woman
in the whole gathering of the Israelites. Then all the people went home.
When David returned to greet his household, Michal, Saul's daughter, 20
came out to meet him and said, 'What a glorious day for the king of Israel,
when he exposed his person in the sight of his servants' slave-girls like any
empty-headed fool!' David answered Michal, 'But it was done in the 21
presence of the LORD, who chose me instead of your father and his family
and appointed me prince over Israel, the people of the LORD. Before the
LORD I will dance for joy, yes, and I will earn yet more disgrace and lower 22
myself still more in your eyes. But those girls of whom you speak, they will
honour me for it.' Michal, Saul's daughter, had no child to her dying day. 23

*a* to Baalath-judah: *prob. rdg., cp. 1 Chr. 13. 6; Heb.* from the lords of Judah.      *b Verses
2-11: cp. 1 Chr. 13. 6-14.*      *c* without . . . singing: *prob. rdg., cp. 1 Chr. 13.
8; Heb.* to the beating of batons.      *d That is* Outbreak on Uzzah.      *e Verses
12-19: cp. 1 Chr. 15. 25—16. 3.*

**7** 1[a]  As soon as the king was established in his house and the LORD had given
2  him security from his enemies on all sides, he said to Nathan the prophet,
'Here I live in a house of cedar, while the Ark of God is housed in curtains.'
3  Nathan answered the king, 'Very well, do whatever you have in mind, for
4  the LORD is with you.' But that night the word of the LORD came to Nathan:
5  'Go and say to David my servant, "This is the word of the LORD: Are you
6  the man to build me a house to dwell in? Down to this day I have never
dwelt in a house since I brought Israel up from Egypt; I made my journey
7  in a tent and a tabernacle. Wherever I journeyed with Israel, did I ever ask
any of the judges [b] whom I appointed shepherds of my people Israel why
8  they had not built me a house of cedar?" Then say this to my servant David:
"This is the word of the LORD of Hosts: I took you from the pastures, and
9  from following the sheep, to be prince over my people Israel. I have been
with you wherever you have gone, and have destroyed all the enemies in
your path. I will make you a great name among the great ones of the earth.
10  I will assign a place for my people Israel; there I will plant them, and they
shall dwell in their own land. They shall be disturbed no more, never again
11  shall wicked men oppress them as they did in the past, ever since the time
when I appointed judges over Israel my people; and I will give you peace
from all your enemies. The LORD has told you that he would build up your
12  royal house. When your life ends and you rest with your forefathers, I
will set up one of your family, one of your own children, to succeed you
13  and I will establish his kingdom. It is he shall build a house in honour of
14  my name, and I will establish his royal throne for ever. I will be his father,
and he shall be my son. When he does wrong, I will punish him as any
15  father might, and not spare the rod. My love will never be withdrawn from
16  him as I withdrew it from Saul, whom I removed from your path. Your
family shall be established and your kingdom shall stand for all time in my
sight, and your throne shall be established for ever."'
17  Nathan recounted to David all that had been said to him and all that
18  had been revealed. Then King David went into the presence of the LORD
and took his place there and said, 'What am I, Lord GOD, and what is my
19  family, that thou hast brought me thus far? It was a small thing in thy
sight to have planned for thy servant's house in days long past. But such,
20  O Lord GOD, is the lot of a man embarked on a high career. [c] And now
what more can I say? for well thou knowest thy servant David, O Lord
21  GOD. Thou hast made good thy word; it was thy purpose to spread thy
22  servant's fame, and so thou hast raised me to this greatness. Great indeed
art thou, O Lord GOD; we have never heard of one like thee; there is no
23  god but thee. And thy people Israel, to whom can they be compared? Is
there any other nation on earth whom thou, O God, hast set out to redeem
from slavery to be thy people? Any other for whom thou hast done great
and terrible things to win fame for thyself? Any other whom thou hast
redeemed for thyself from Egypt by driving out other nations and their
24  gods to make way for them? Thou hast established thy people Israel as
25  thy own for ever, and thou, O LORD, hast become their God. But now,

---

[a] *Verses 1–29: cp. 1 Chr. 17. 1–27.*          [b] *Prob. rdg., cp. 1 Chr. 17. 6; Heb.* tribes.
[c] embarked on a high career: *prob. rdg., cp. 1 Chr. 17. 17; Heb. om.*

LORD God, perform what thou hast promised for thy servant and his
house, and for all time; make good what thou hast said. May thy fame be 26
great for evermore and let men say, "The LORD of Hosts is God over Israel."
So shall the house of thy servant David be established before thee. O LORD 27
of Hosts, God of Israel, thou hast shown me thy purpose, in saying to thy
servant, "I will build up your house"; and therefore I have made bold to
offer this prayer to thee. Thou, O Lord GOD, art God; thou hast made these 28
noble promises to thy servant, and thy promises come true; be pleased now 29
to bless thy servant's house that it may continue always before thee; thou,
O Lord GOD, hast promised, and thy blessing shall rest upon thy servant's
house for evermore.'

After this David defeated the Philistines and conquered them, and took 8 1 *a*
from them Metheg-ha-ammah. He defeated the Moabites, and he made 2
them lie along the ground and measured them off with a length of cord; for
every two lengths that were to be put to death one full length was spared.
The Moabites became subject to him and paid him tribute. David also 3
defeated Hadadezer the Rehobite, king of Zobah, who was on his way to
re-erect his monument of victory by *b* the river Euphrates. From him 4
David captured seventeen hundred horse and twenty thousand foot; he
hamstrung all the chariot-horses, except a hundred which he retained.
When the Aramaeans of Damascus came to the help of Hadadezer king of 5
Zobah, David destroyed twenty-two thousand of them, and established 6
garrisons among these Aramaeans; they became subject to him and paid
him tribute. Thus the LORD gave David victory wherever he went. David 7
took the gold quivers borne by Hadadezer's servants and brought them to
Jerusalem; and he also took a great quantity of bronze *c* from Hadadezer's 8
cities, Betah and Berothai.

When Toi king of Hamath heard that David had defeated the entire 9
army of Hadadezer, he sent his son Joram to King David to greet him and 10
to congratulate him on defeating Hadadezer in battle (for Hadadezer had
been at war with Toi); and he brought with him vessels of silver, gold,
and copper, which King David dedicated to the LORD. He dedicated 11
also the silver and gold taken from all the nations he had subdued, from 12
Edom and Moab, from the Ammonites, the Philistines, and Amalek,
as well as part of the spoil taken from Hadadezer the Rehobite, king of
Zobah.

David made a great name for himself by the slaughter of eighteen 13
thousand Edomites in the Valley of Salt, and on returning he stationed 14
garrisons throughout Edom, and all the Edomites were subject to him.
Thus the LORD gave victory to David wherever he went.

David ruled over the whole of Israel and maintained law and justice 15 *d*
among all his people. Joab son of Zeruiah was in command of the army; 16
Jehoshaphat son of Ahilud was secretary of state; Zadok and Abiathar son 17
of Ahimelech, son of Ahitub, *e* were priests; Seraiah was adjutant-general;

*a* *Verses 1–14: cp. 1 Chr. 18. 1–13.*       *b* re-erect . . . victory by: *or* recover control of
the crossings of . . .       *c* *Or* copper.       *d* *Verses 15–18: cp. 20. 23–26; 1 Kgs. 4.
2–6; 1 Chr. 18. 14–17.*       *e* and Abiathar . . . Ahitub: *prob. rdg., cp. 1 Sam. 22. 11,
20; 2 Sam. 20. 25; Heb.* son of Ahitub and Ahimelech son of Abiathar.

18 Benaiah son of Jehoiada commanded the Kerethite and Pelethite guards. David's sons were priests.

9 David asked, 'Is any member of Saul's family left, to whom I can show
2 true kindness for Jonathan's sake?' There was a servant of Saul's family named Ziba; and he was summoned to David. The king asked, 'Are you
3 Ziba?', and he answered, 'Your servant, sir.' So the king said, 'Is no member of Saul's family still alive to whom I may show the kindness that God requires?' 'Yes,' said Ziba, 'there is a son of Jonathan still alive; he is a
4 cripple, lame in both feet.' 'Where is he?' said the king, and Ziba answered, 'He is staying with Machir son of Ammiel in Lo-debar.'

5 So the king sent and fetched him from Lo-debar, from the house of
6 Machir son of Ammiel, and when Mephibosheth, son of Jonathan and Saul's grandson, entered David's presence, he prostrated himself and did obeisance. David said to him, 'Mephibosheth', and he answered, 'Your
7 servant, sir.' Then David said, 'Do not be afraid; I mean to show you kindness for your father Jonathan's sake, and I will give you back the whole estate of your grandfather Saul; you shall have a place for yourself at my
8 table.' So Mephibosheth prostrated himself again and said, 'Who am I
9 that you should spare a thought for a dead dog like me?' Then David summoned Saul's servant Ziba to his presence and said to him, 'I assign to your master's grandson all the property that belonged to Saul and his
10 family. You and your sons and your slaves must cultivate the land and bring in the harvest to provide for your master's household, but Mephibosheth your master's grandson shall have a place at my table.' This man
11 Ziba had fifteen sons and twenty slaves. Then Ziba answered the king, 'I will do all that your majesty commands.' So Mephibosheth took his
12 place in the royal household like one of the king's sons. He had a young son, named Mica; and the members of Ziba's household were all Mephi-
13 bosheth's servants, while Mephibosheth lived in Jerusalem and had his regular place at the king's table, crippled as he was in both feet.

10 1*a* Some time afterwards the king of the Ammonites died and was succeeded
2 by his son Hanun. David said, 'I must keep up the same loyal friendship with Hanun son of Nahash as his father showed me', and he sent a mission to condole with him on the death of his father. But when David's envoys
3 entered the country of the Ammonites, the Ammonite princes said to Hanun their lord, 'Do you suppose David means to do honour to your father when he sends you his condolences? These men of his are spies
4 whom he has sent to find out how to overthrow the city.' So Hanun took David's servants, and he shaved off half their beards, cut off half their
5 garments up to the buttocks, and dismissed them. When David heard how they had been treated, he sent to meet them, for they were deeply humiliated, and ordered them to wait in Jericho and not to return until
6 their beards had grown again. The Ammonites knew that they had fallen into bad odour with David, so they hired the Aramaeans of Beth-rehob and of Zobah to come to their help with twenty thousand infantry; they also hired the king of Maacah with a thousand men, and twelve thousand men
7 from Tob. When David heard of it, he sent out Joab and all the fighting

*a Verses 1-19: cp. 1 Chr. 19. 1-19.*

men. The Ammonites came and took up their position at the entrance to the 8
city, while the Aramaeans of Zobah and of Rehob and the men of Tob
and Maacah took up theirs in the open country. When Joab saw that he was 9
threatened both front and rear, he detailed some picked Israelite troops
and drew them up facing the Aramaeans. The rest of his forces he put under 10
his brother Abishai, who took up a position facing the Ammonites. 'If 11
the Aramaeans prove too strong for me,' he said, 'you must come to my
relief; and if the Ammonites prove too strong for you, I will come to yours.
Courage! Let us fight bravely for our people and for the cities *a* of our God. 12
And the LORD's will be done.' But when Joab and his men came to close 13
quarters with the Aramaeans, they put them to flight; and when the 14
Ammonites saw them in flight, they too fled before Abishai and entered the
city. Then Joab returned from the battle against the Ammonites and came
to Jerusalem. The Aramaeans saw that they had been worsted by Israel; 15
but they rallied their forces, and Hadadezer sent to summon other Ara- 16
maeans from the Great Bend of the Euphrates, and they advanced to
Helam under Shobach, commander of Hadadezer's army. Their move- 17
ment was reported to David, who immediately mustered all the forces of
Israel, crossed the Jordan and advanced to meet them at Helam. There the
Aramaeans took up positions facing David and engaged him, but were put 18
to flight by Israel. David slew seven hundred Aramaeans in chariots and
forty thousand horsemen, mortally wounding Shobach, who died on the
field. When all the vassal kings of Hadadezer saw that they had been 19
worsted by Israel, they sued for peace and submitted to the Israelites. The
Aramaeans never dared help the Ammonites again.

AT THE TURN OF THE YEAR, when kings take the field, David sent Joab 11
out with his other officers and all the Israelite forces, and they ravaged
Ammon and laid siege to Rabbah, while David remained in Jerusalem.
One evening David got up from his couch and, as he walked about on the 2
roof of the palace, he saw from there a woman bathing, and she was very
beautiful. He sent to inquire who she was, and the answer came, 'It must 3
be Bathsheba daughter of Eliam and wife of Uriah the Hittite.' So he sent 4
messengers to fetch her, and when she came to him, he had intercourse with
her; though she was still being purified after her period, and then she went
home. She conceived, and sent word to David that she was pregnant. David 5 6
ordered Joab to send Uriah the Hittite to him. So Joab sent him to David,
and when he arrived, David asked him for news of Joab and the troops and 7
how the campaign was going; and then said to him, 'Go down to your house 8
and wash your feet after your journey.' As he left the palace, a present from
the king followed him. But Uriah did not return to his house; he lay down 9
by the palace gate with the king's slaves. David heard that Uriah had not 10
gone home, and said to him, 'You have had a long journey, why did you
not go home?' Uriah answered David, 'Israel and Judah are under canvas, *b* 11
and so is the Ark, and my lord Joab and your majesty's officers are camping
in the open; how can I go home to eat and drink and to sleep with my wife?
By your life, I cannot do this!' David then said to Uriah, 'Stay here another 12

*a* Or altars.      *b* under canvas: or at Succoth.

day, and tomorrow I will let you go.' So Uriah stayed in Jerusalem that
13 day. The next day David invited him to eat and drink with him and made
him drunk. But in the evening Uriah went out to lie down in his blanket *a*
among the king's slaves and did not go home.
14     The following morning David wrote a letter to Joab and sent Uriah with
15 it. He wrote in the letter, 'Put Uriah opposite the enemy where the fighting
16 is fiercest and then fall back, and leave him to meet his death.' Joab had
been watching the city, and he stationed Uriah at a point where he knew
17 they would put up a stout fight. The men of the city sallied out and engaged
Joab, and some of David's guards fell; Uriah the Hittite was also killed.
18 19 Joab sent David a dispatch with all the news of the battle and gave the
messenger these instructions: 'When you have finished your report to the
20 king, if he is angry and asks, "Why did you go so near the city during
the fight? You must have known there would be shooting from the wall.
21 Remember who killed Abimelech son of Jerubbesheth. It was a woman
who threw down an upper millstone on to him from the wall of Thebez
and killed him! Why did you go so near the wall?"—if he asks this, then
tell him, "Your servant Uriah the Hittite also is dead."'
22     So the messenger set out and, when he came to David, he made his report
as Joab had instructed. David was angry with Joab and said to the messenger, 'Why did you go so near the city during the fight? You must have
known you would be struck down from the wall. Remember who killed
Abimelech son of Jerubbesheth. Was it not a woman who threw down an
upper millstone on to him from the wall of Thebez and killed him? Why
23 did you go near the wall?' He answered, 'The enemy massed against us
and sallied out into the open; we pressed them back as far as the gateway.
24 There the archers shot down at us from the wall and some of your majesty's
25 men fell; and your servant Uriah the Hittite is dead.' David said to the
man, 'Give Joab this message: "Do not let this distress you—there is no
knowing where the sword will strike; press home your attack on the city,
and you will take it and raze it to the ground"; and tell him to take heart.'
26     When Uriah's wife heard that her husband was dead, she mourned for
27 him; and when the period of mourning was over, David sent for her and
brought her into his house. She became his wife and bore him a son. But
what David had done was wrong in the eyes of the LORD.

**12**     The LORD sent Nathan the prophet to David, and when he entered his
presence, he said to him, 'There were once two men in the same city, one
2 3 rich and the other poor. The rich man had large flocks and herds, but the
poor man had nothing of his own except one little ewe lamb. He reared
it himself, and it grew up in his home with his own sons. It ate from his
dish, drank from his cup and nestled in his arms; it was like a daughter to
4 him. One day a traveller came to the rich man's house, and he, too mean to
take something from his own flocks and herds to serve to his guest, took
5 the poor man's lamb and served up that.' David was very angry, and burst
6 out, 'As the LORD lives, the man who did this deserves to die! He shall pay
for the lamb four times over, because he has done this and shown no pity.'
7 Then Nathan said to David, 'You are the man. This is the word of the LORD

*a* in his blanket: *or* on his pallet.

the God of Israel to you: "I anointed you king over Israel, I rescued you
from the power of Saul, I gave you your master's daughter *a* and his wives  8
to be your own, I gave you the daughters of Israel and Judah; and, had this
not been enough, I would have added other favours as great. Why then  9
have you flouted the word of the LORD by doing what is wrong in my eyes?
You have struck down Uriah the Hittite with the sword; the man himself
you murdered by the sword of the Ammonites, and you have stolen his
wife. Now, therefore, since you have despised me and taken the wife of  10
Uriah the Hittite to be your own wife, your family shall never again have
rest from the sword." This is the word of the LORD: "I will bring trouble  11
upon you from within your own family; I will take your wives and give
them to another man before your eyes, and he will lie with them in broad
daylight. What you did was done in secret; but I will do this in the light of  12
day for all Israel to see." ' David said to Nathan, 'I have sinned against the  13
LORD.' Nathan answered him, 'The LORD has laid on another the consequences of your sin: you shall not die, but, because in this you have  14
shown your contempt for the LORD, *b* the boy that will be born to you shall
die.'

When Nathan had gone home, the LORD struck the boy whom Uriah's  15
wife had borne to David, and he was very ill. David prayed to God for  16
the child; he fasted and went in and spent the night fasting, lying on the
ground. The older men of his household tried to get him to rise from the  17
ground, but he refused and would eat no food with them. On the seventh  18
day the boy died, and David's servants were afraid to tell him. 'While the
boy was alive,' they said, 'we spoke to him, and he did not listen to us; how
can we now tell him that the boy is dead? He may do something desperate.'
But David saw his servants whispering among themselves and guessed  19
that the boy was dead. He asked, 'Is the boy dead?', and they answered,
'He is dead.' Then David rose from the ground, washed and anointed  20
himself, and put on fresh clothes; he entered the house of the LORD and
prostrated himself there. Then he went home, asked for food to be brought,
and when it was ready, he ate it. His servants asked him, 'What is this?  21
While the boy lived you fasted and wept for him, but now that he is dead
you rise up and eat.' He answered, 'While the boy was still alive I fasted  22
and wept, thinking, "It may be that the LORD will be gracious to me, and
the boy may live." But now that he is dead, why should I fast? Can I  23
bring him back again? I shall go to him; he will not come back to me.'
David consoled Bathsheba his wife; he went to her and had intercourse  24
with her, and she gave birth to a son and called him Solomon. And because
the LORD loved him, he sent word through Nathan the prophet that for  25
the LORD's sake he should be given the name Jedidiah. *c*

Joab attacked the Ammonite city of Rabbah and took the King's Pool.  26*d*
He sent messengers to David with this report: 'I have attacked Rabbah and  27
have taken the pool. You had better muster the rest of the army yourself,  28
besiege the city and take it; otherwise I shall take the city and the name to
be proclaimed over it will be mine.' David accordingly mustered his whole  29

*a* *Prob. rdg.; Heb.* house.       *b* the LORD: *prob. rdg.; Heb.* the enemies of the LORD.
*c* *That is* Beloved of the LORD.       *d* *Verses 26–31 : cp. 1 Chr. 20. 1–3.*

30 forces, marched to Rabbah, attacked it and took it. He took the crown from
the head of Milcom, which weighed a talent of gold and was set with a
precious stone, and this he placed on his own head. He also removed a
31 great quantity of booty from the city; he took its inhabitants and set them
to work with saws and other iron tools, sharp and toothed, and made them
work in the brick-kilns. David did this to all the cities of the Ammonites;
then he and all his people returned to Jerusalem.

## *Absalom's rebellion and other conflicts*

**13** Now David's son Absalom had a beautiful sister named Tamar,
2 and Amnon, another of David's sons, fell in love with her. Amnon was
so distressed that he fell sick with love for his half-sister; for he thought it
3 an impossible thing to approach her since she was a virgin. But he had a
friend named Jonadab, son of David's brother Shimeah, who was a very
4 shrewd man. He said to Amnon, 'Why are you so low-spirited morning
after morning, my lord? Will you not tell me?' So Amnon told him that
5 he was in love with Tamar, his brother Absalom's sister. Jonadab said to
him, 'Take to your bed and pretend to be ill. When your father comes to
visit you, say to him, "Please let my sister Tamar come and give me my
food. Let her prepare it in front of me, so that I may watch her and then
6 take it from her own hands."' So Amnon lay down and pretended to be
ill. When the king came to visit him, he said, 'Sir, let my sister Tamar come
and make a few cakes in front of me, and serve them to me with her own
7 hands.' So David sent a message to Tamar in the palace: 'Go to your
8 brother Amnon's quarters and prepare a meal for him.' Tamar came to
her brother and found him lying down; she took some dough and kneaded
9 it, made the cakes in front of him and baked them. Then she took the pan
and turned them out before him. But Amnon refused to eat and ordered
10 everyone out of the room. When they had all left, he said to Tamar, 'Bring
the food over to the recess so that I may eat from your own hands.' Tamar
took the cakes she had made and brought them to Amnon in the recess.
11 But when she offered them to him, he caught hold of her and said, 'Come
12 to bed with me, sister.' But she answered, 'No, brother, do not dishonour
13 me, we do not do such things in Israel; do not behave like a beast. Where
could I go and hide my disgrace?—and you would sink as low as any beast
in Israel. Why not speak to the king for me? He will not refuse you leave
14 to marry me.' He would not listen, but overpowered her, dishonoured her
and raped her.
15 Then Amnon was filled with utter hatred for her; his hatred was stronger
16 than the love he had felt, and he said to her, 'Get up and go.' She answered,
'No. It is wicked to send me away. This is harder to bear than all you have
17 done to me.' He would not listen to her, but summoned the boy who
attended him and said, 'Get rid of this woman, put her out and bolt the
18 door after her.' She had on a long, sleeved robe, the usual dress of unmarried princesses; and the boy turned her out and bolted the door.
19 Tamar threw ashes over her head, rent the long, sleeved robe that she was

wearing, put her hands on her head and went away, sobbing as she went. Her brother Absalom asked her, 'Has your brother Amnon been with you? 20 Keep this to yourself, he is your brother; do not take it to heart.' So Tamar remained in her brother Absalom's house, desolate. When King David 21 heard the whole story he was very angry; but he would not hurt Amnon because he was his eldest son and he loved him. Absalom did not speak a 22 single word to Amnon, friendly or unfriendly; he hated him for having dishonoured his sister Tamar.

Two years later Absalom invited all the king's sons to his sheep-shearing 23 at Baal-hazor, near Ephron. *a* He approached the king and said, 'Sir, I am 24 shearing; will your majesty and your servants come?' The king answered, 25 'No, my son, we must not all come and be a burden to you.' Absalom pressed him, but David was still unwilling to go and dismissed him with his blessing. But Absalom said, 'If you cannot, may my brother Amnon 26 come with us?' 'Why should he go with you?' the king asked; but Absalom 27 pressed him again, so he let Amnon and all the other princes go with him.

Then Absalom prepared a feast fit for a king. He gave his servants these 28 orders: 'Bide your time, and when Amnon is merry with wine I shall say to you, "Strike." Then kill Amnon. You have nothing to fear, these are my orders; be bold and resolute.' Absalom's servants did as he had told 29 them, whereupon all the king's sons mounted their mules in haste and set off for home.

While they were on their way, a rumour reached David that Absalom 30 had murdered all the royal princes and that not one was left alive. The king 31 stood up and rent his clothes and then threw himself on the ground; all his servants were standing round him with their clothes rent. Then 32 Jonadab, son of David's brother Shimeah, said, 'Your majesty must not think that they have killed all the young princes; only Amnon is dead; Absalom has looked black ever since Amnon ravished his sister Tamar. Your majesty must not pay attention to a mere rumour that all the princes 33 are dead; only Amnon is dead.'

Absalom made good his escape. Meanwhile the sentry looked up and 34 saw a crowd of people coming down the hill from the direction of Horon-aim. *b* He came and reported to the king, 'I see men coming down the hill from Horonaim.' Then Jonadab said to the king, 'Here come the royal 35 princes, just as I said they would.' As he finished speaking, the princes 36 came in and broke into loud lamentations; the king and all his servants also wept bitterly.

But Absalom went to take refuge with Talmai son of Ammihur king of 37 Geshur; and for a long while the king mourned for Amnon. Absalom, 38 having escaped to Geshur, stayed there for three years; and David's heart 39 went out to him with longing, for he became reconciled to the death of Amnon.

Joab son of Zeruiah saw that the king's heart was set on Absalom, so he **14** 1 2 sent to Tekoah and fetched a wise woman. He said to her, 'Pretend to be a mourner; put on mourning, go without anointing yourself, and behave like a bereaved woman who has been long in mourning. Then go to the 3

---

*a* *Prob. rdg.; Heb.* Ephraim.     *b* *Prob. rdg.; Heb.* from a road behind him.

king and repeat what I tell you.' He then told her exactly what she was to say.

4 When the woman from Tekoah came into the king's presence, she threw herself, face downwards, on the ground and did obeisance, and cried,
5 'Help, your majesty!' The king asked, 'What is it?' She answered, 'O sir,
6 I am a widow; my husband is dead. I had two sons; they came to blows out in the country where there was no one to part them, and one of them struck
7 the other and killed him. Now, sir, the kinsmen have risen against me and they all cry, "Hand over the man who has killed his brother, so that we can put him to death for taking his brother's life, and so cut off the succession." If they do this, they will stamp out my last live ember and leave my husband
8 no name and no descendant upon earth.' 'Go home,' said the king to the
9 woman, 'and I will settle your case.' But the woman continued, 'The guilt be on me, your majesty, and on my father's house; let the king and his
10 throne be blameless.' The king said, 'If anyone says anything more to you,
11 bring him to me and he shall never molest you again.' Then the woman went on, 'Let your majesty call upon the LORD your God, to prevent his kinsmen bound to vengeance from doing their worst and destroying my son.' The king swore, 'As the LORD lives, not a hair of your son's head shall fall to the ground.'
12 The woman then said, 'May I add one word more, your majesty?' 'Say
13 on', said the king. So she continued, 'How then could it enter your head to do this same wrong to God's people? Out of your own mouth, your majesty, you condemn yourself: you have refused to bring back the man
14 you have banished. We shall all die; we shall be like water that is spilt on the ground and lost; but God will spare the man who does not set himself
15 to keep the outlaw in banishment. I came to say this to your majesty be- cause the people have threatened me. I thought, "If I can only speak to the
16 king, perhaps he will attend to my case; for he will listen, and he will save me from the man who is seeking to cut off me and my son together from
17 Israel, God's own possession." I thought too that the words of my lord the king would be a comfort to me; for your majesty is like the angel of God and can decide between right and wrong. The LORD your God be with
18 you!' Then the king said to the woman, 'Tell me no lies: I shall now ask you
19 a question.' 'Speak on, your majesty', she said. So he asked, 'Is the hand of Joab behind you in all this?' 'Your life upon it, sir!' she answered; 'when your majesty asks a question, there is no way round it, right or left. Yes, your servant Joab did prompt me; it was he who put the whole story
20 into my mouth. He did it to give a new turn to this affair. Your majesty is as wise as the angel of God and knows all that goes on in the land.'
21 The king said to Joab, 'You have my consent; go and fetch back the
22 young man Absalom.' Then Joab humbly prostrated himself, took leave of the king with a blessing and said, 'Now I know that I have found favour
23 with your majesty, because you have granted my humble petition.' Joab
24 went at once to Geshur and brought Absalom to Jerusalem, but the king said, 'Let him go to his own quarters; he shall not come into my presence.' So Absalom went to his own quarters and did not enter the king's presence.
25 No one in all Israel was so greatly admired for his beauty as Absalom;

he was without flaw from the crown of his head to the sole of his foot. His 26
hair, when he cut his hair (as he had to do every year, for he found it heavy),
weighed two hundred shekels by the royal standard. Three sons were born 27
to Absalom, and a daughter named Tamar, who was a very beautiful
woman.

Absalom remained in Jerusalem for two whole years without entering 28
the king's presence. He summoned Joab to send a message by him to the 29
king, but Joab refused to come; he sent for him a second time, but he still
refused. Then Absalom said to his servants, 'You know that Joab has a 30
field next to mine with barley growing in it; go and set fire to it.' So
Absalom's servants set fire to the field. Joab promptly came to Absalom 31
in his own quarters and said to him, 'Why have your servants set fire to my
field?' Absalom answered Joab, 'I had sent for you to come here, so that 32
I could ask you to give the king this message from me: "Why did I leave
Geshur? It would be better for me if I were still there. Let me now come
into your majesty's presence and, if I have done any wrong, put me to
death."' When Joab went to the king and told him, he summoned Absalom, 33
who came and prostrated himself humbly before the king; and he greeted
Absalom with a kiss.

AFTER THIS, ABSALOM PROVIDED himself with a chariot and horses 15
and an escort of fifty men. He made it a practice to rise early and stand 2
beside the road which runs through the city gate. He would hail every man
who had a case to bring before the king for judgement and would ask him
what city he came from. When he answered, 'I come, sir, from such and
such a tribe of Israel', Absalom would say to him, 'I can see that you have 3
a very good case, but you will get no hearing from the king.' And he would 4
add, 'If only I were appointed judge in the land, it would be my business
to see that everyone who brought a suit or a claim got justice from me.'
Whenever a man approached to prostrate himself, Absalom would stretch 5
out his hand, take hold of him and kiss him. By behaving like this to every 6
Israelite who sought the king's justice, Absalom stole the affections of the
Israelites.

At the end of four years, Absalom said to the king, 'May I have leave 7
now to go to Hebron to fulfil a vow there that I made to the LORD? For 8
when I lived in Geshur, in Aram, I made this vow: "If the LORD brings
me back to Jerusalem, I will become a worshipper of the LORD in Hebron."'
The king answered, 'Certainly you may go'; so he set off for Hebron at 9
once. Absalom sent runners through all the tribes of Israel with this 10
message: 'As soon as you hear the sound of the trumpet, then say, "Absalom
is king in Hebron."' Two hundred men accompanied Absalom from 11
Jerusalem; they were invited and went in all innocence, knowing nothing
of the affair. Absalom also sent to summon Ahithophel the Gilonite, 12
David's counsellor, from Giloh his city, where he was offering the customary sacrifices. The conspiracy gathered strength, and Absalom's supporters
increased in number.

When news reached David that the men of Israel had transferred their 13
allegiance to Absalom, he said to those who were with him in Jerusalem, 14

'We must get away at once; or there will be no escape from Absalom for any of us. Make haste, or else he will soon be upon us and bring disaster 15 on us, showing no mercy to anyone in the city.' The king's servants said to him, 'As your majesty thinks best; we are ready.'

16 When the king departed, all his household followed him except ten 17 concubines, whom he left in charge of the palace. At the Far House the 18 king and all the people who were with him halted. His own servants then stood *a* beside him, while the Kerethite and Pelethite guards and Ittai *b* 19 with the six hundred Gittites under him marched past the king. The king said to Ittai the Gittite, 'Are you here too? Why are you coming with us? Go back and stay with the new king, for you are a foreigner and, what is 20 more, an exile from your own country. You came only yesterday, and today must you be compelled to share my wanderings? I do not know where I am going. Go back home and take your countrymen with you; and may 21 the LORD ever be your steadfast friend.' Ittai swore to the king, 'As the LORD lives, your life upon it, wherever you may be, in life or in death, I, 22 your servant, will be there.' David said to Ittai, 'It is well, march on!' So Ittai the Gittite marched on with his whole company and all the depend- 23 ants who were with him. The whole country-side re-echoed with their weeping. And the king remained standing *c* while all the people crossed the gorge of the Kidron before him, by way of the olive-tree in the wilderness. *d*

24 Zadok also was there with all the Levites; they were carrying the Ark of the Covenant of God, which they set down beside Abiathar *e* until all 25 the people had passed out of the city. But the king said to Zadok, 'Take the Ark of God back to the city. If I find favour with the LORD, he will bring 26 me back and will let me see the Ark and its dwelling-place again. But if he says he does not want me, then here I am; let him do what he pleases 27 with me.' The king went on to say to Zadok the priest, 'Can you make good use of your eyes? You may safely go back to the city, you and Abiathar, *f* and take with you the two young men, Ahimaaz your son and Abiathar's 28 son Jonathan. Do not forget: I will linger at the Fords of the Wilderness 29 until you can send word to me.' Then Zadok and Abiathar took the Ark of God back to Jerusalem and stayed there.

30 David wept as he went up the slope of the Mount of Olives; he was bare-headed and went bare-foot. The people with him all had their heads un- 31 covered and wept as they went. David had been told that Ahithophel was among the conspirators with Absalom, and he prayed, 'Frustrate, O LORD, the counsel of Ahithophel.'

32 As David was approaching the top of the ridge where it was the custom to prostrate oneself to God, Hushai the Archite was there to meet him with 33 his tunic rent and earth on his head. David said to him, 'If you come with 34 me you will only be a hindrance; but you can help me to frustrate Ahitho-phel's plans if you go back to the city and say to Absalom, "I will be your majesty's servant; up to now I have been your father's servant, and now

---

*a* *Prob. rdg.; Heb.* passed.     *b* and Ittai: *prob. rdg.; Heb. om.*     *c* *Prob. rdg.;* *Heb.* passing.     *d* by way . . . wilderness: *prob. rdg.; Heb. obscure.*     *e* beside Abiathar: *prob. rdg.; Heb.* and Abiathar went up.     *f* you and Abiathar: *prob. rdg.,* cp. *verse* 29*; Heb. om.*

I will be yours." You will have with you, as you know, the priests Zadok 35
and Abiathar; tell them everything that you hear in the king's household.
They have with them Zadok's son Ahimaaz and Abiathar's son Jonathan, 36
and through them you may pass on to me everything you hear.' So Hushai, 37
David's friend, came to the city as Absalom was entering Jerusalem.

When David had moved on a little from the top of the ridge, he was met 16
by Ziba the servant of Mephibosheth, who had with him a pair of asses
saddled and loaded with two hundred loaves, a hundred clusters of raisins,
a hundred bunches of summer fruit, and a flagon of wine. The king said 2
to him, 'What are you doing with these?' Ziba answered, 'The asses are
for the king's family to ride on, the bread and the summer fruit are for the
servants to eat, and the wine for anyone who becomes exhausted in the
wilderness.' The king asked, 'Where is your master's grandson?' 'He is 3
staying in Jerusalem,' said Ziba, 'for he thought that the Israelites might
now restore to him his grandfather's throne.' The king said to Ziba, 'You 4
shall have everything that belongs to Mephibosheth.' Ziba said, 'I am your
humble servant, sir; may I continue to stand well with you.'

As King David approached Bahurim, a man of Saul's family, whose 5
name was Shimei son of Gera, came out, cursing as he came. He showered 6
stones right and left on David and on all the king's servants and on everyone, soldiers and people alike. This is what Shimei said as he cursed him: 7
'Get out, get out, you scoundrel! you man of blood! The LORD has taken 8
vengeance on you for the blood of the house of Saul whose throne you stole,
and he has given the kingdom to your son Absalom. You murderer, see
how your crimes have overtaken you!'

Then Abishai son of Zeruiah said to the king, 'Why let this dead dog 9
curse your majesty? I will go across and knock off his head.' But the king 10
said, 'What has this to do with you, you sons of Zeruiah? If he curses and
if the LORD has told him to curse David, who can question it?' David said 11
to Abishai and to all his servants, 'If my son, my own son, is out to kill me,
who can wonder at this Benjamite? Let him be, let him curse; for the LORD
has told him to do it. But perhaps the LORD will mark my sufferings and 12
bestow a blessing on me in place of the curse laid on me this day.' David 13
and his men continued on their way, and Shimei moved along the ridge
of the hill parallel to David's path, cursing as he went and hurling stones
across the valley at him and kicking up the dust. When the king and all the 14
people with him reached the Jordan, they were worn out; and they refreshed
themselves there.

By now Absalom and all his Israelites had reached Jerusalem, and 15
Ahithophel with him. When Hushai the Archite, David's friend, met 16
Absalom he said to him, 'Long live the king! Long live the king!' But 17
Absalom retorted, 'Is this your loyalty to your friend? Why did you not go
with him?' Hushai answered Absalom, 'Because I mean to attach myself 18
to the man chosen by the LORD, by this people, and by all the men of Israel,
and with him I will remain. After all, whom ought I to serve? Should I not 19
serve the son? I will serve you as I have served your father.' Then Absalom 20
said to Ahithophel, 'Give us your advice: how shall we act?' Ahithophel 21
answered, 'Have intercourse with your father's concubines whom he left

357

in charge of the palace. Then all Israel will come to hear that you have given great cause of offence to your father, and this will confirm the resolution
22 of your followers.' So they set up a tent for Absalom on the roof, and he
23 lay with his father's concubines in the sight of all Israel. In those days a man would seek counsel of Ahithophel as readily as he might make an inquiry of the word of God; that was how Ahithophel's counsel was esteemed by David and Absalom.

17 Ahithophel said to Absalom, 'Let me pick twelve thousand men, and I
2 will pursue David tonight. I shall overtake him when he is tired and dispirited; I will cut him off from his people and they will all scatter; and I
3 shall kill no one but the king. I will bring all the people over to you as a bride is brought to her husband. It is only one man's life that you are seek-
4 ing; the rest of the people will be unharmed.' Absalom and all the elders
5 of Israel approved of Ahithophel's advice; but Absalom said, 'Summon
6 Hushai the Archite and let us hear what he too has to say.' Hushai came, and Absalom told him all that Ahithophel had said and asked him, 'Shall we do what he says? If not, say what you think.'

7 Hushai said to Absalom, 'For once the counsel that Ahithophel has given
8 is not good. You know', he went on, 'that your father and the men with him are hardened warriors and savage as a bear in the wilds robbed of her cubs. Your father is an old campaigner and will not spend the night with the
9 main body; even now he will be lying hidden in a pit or in some such place. Then if any of your men are killed at the outset, anyone who hears the news
10 will say, "Disaster has overtaken the followers of Absalom." The courage of the most resolute and lion-hearted will melt away, for all Israel knows
11 that your father is a man of war and has determined men with him. My advice is this. Wait until the whole of Israel, from Dan to Beersheba, is gathered about you, countless as grains of sand on the sea-shore, and then
12 you shall march with them in person. Then we shall come upon him some-where, wherever he may be, and descend on him like dew falling on the
13 ground, and not a man of his family or of his followers will be left alive. If he retreats into a city, all Israel will bring ropes to that city, and we will
14 drag it into a ravine until not a stone can be found on the site.' Absalom and all the men of Israel said, 'Hushai the Archite gives us better advice than Ahithophel.' It was the LORD's purpose to frustrate Ahithophel's good advice and so bring disaster upon Absalom.

15 Hushai told Zadok and Abiathar the priests all the advice that Ahithophel
16 had given to Absalom and the elders of Israel, and also his own. 'Now send quickly to David,' he said, 'and warn him not to spend the night at the Fords of the Wilderness but to cross the river at once, before a blow can
17 be struck at the king and his followers.' Jonathan and Ahimaaz were waiting at En-rogel, and a servant girl would go and tell them what happened and they would pass it on to King David; for they could not risk
18 being seen entering the city. But this time a lad saw them and told Absalom; so the two of them hurried to the house of a man in Bahurim. He had a pit
19 in his courtyard, and they climbed down into it. The man's wife took a covering, spread it over the mouth of the pit and strewed grain over it,
20 and no one was any the wiser. Absalom's servants came to the house and

asked the woman, 'Where are Ahimaaz and Jonathan?' She answered, 'They went beyond the pool.' The men searched but could not find them; so they went back to Jerusalem. When they had gone the two climbed out 21 of the pit and went off to report to King David and said, 'Over the water at once, make haste!', and they told him Ahithophel's plan against him. So 22 David and all his company began at once to cross the Jordan; by daybreak there was not one who had not reached the other bank.

When Ahithophel saw that his advice had not been taken he saddled his 23 ass, went straight home to his own city, gave his last instructions to his household, and hanged himself. So he died and was buried in his father's grave.

By the time that Absalom had crossed the Jordan with the Israelites, 24 David was already at Mahanaim. Absalom had appointed Amasa as 25 commander-in-chief instead of Joab; he was the son of a man named Ithra, an Ishmaelite, by Abigal daughter of Nahash and sister to Joab's mother Zeruiah. The Israelites and Absalom camped in the district of Gilead. 26 When David came to Mahanaim, he was met by Shobi son of Nahash 27 from the Ammonite town Rabbah, Machir son of Ammiel from Lo-debar, and Barzillai the Gileadite from Rogelim, bringing mattresses and blankets, 28 bowls and jugs.*a* They brought also wheat and barley, meal and parched 29 grain, beans and lentils, honey and curds, sheep and fat cattle, and offered them to David and his people to eat, knowing that the people must be hungry and thirsty and weary in the wilderness.

David mustered the people who were with him, and appointed officers **18** over units of a thousand and a hundred. Then he divided the army in three, 2 one division under the command of Joab, one under Joab's brother Abishai son of Zeruiah, and the third under Ittai the Gittite. The king announced to the army that he was coming out himself with them to battle. But they said, 'No, you must not come out; if we turn and run, no 3 one will take any notice, nor will they, even if half of us are killed; but you are worth ten thousand of us, and it would be better now for you to remain in the city in support.' 'I will do what you think best', answered the king; 4 and he then stood beside the gate, and the army marched past in their units of a thousand and a hundred. The king gave orders to Joab, Abishai, 5 and Ittai: 'Deal gently with the young man Absalom for my sake.' The whole army heard the king giving all his officers this order to spare Absalom.

The army took the field against the Israelites and the battle was fought 6 in the forest of Ephron.*b* There the Israelites were routed before the 7 onslaught of David's men; so great was the rout that twenty thousand men fell that day. The fighting spread over the whole country-side, and the 8 forest took toll of more people that day than the sword.

Now some of David's men caught sight of Absalom. He was riding a 9 mule and, as it passed beneath a great oak,*c* his head was caught in its boughs; he found himself in mid air and the mule went on from under him. One of the men who saw it went and told Joab, 'I saw Absalom hanging 10 from an oak.' While the man was telling him, Joab broke in, 'You saw him? 11

*a* bringing . . . jugs: *prob. rdg.; Heb.* a couch, bowls and a potter's vessel.      *b Prob. rdg.; Heb.* Ephraim.     *c Or* terebinth.

Why did you not strike him to the ground then and there? I would have
12 given you ten pieces of silver and a belt.' The man answered, 'If you were
to put in my hands a thousand pieces of silver, I would not lift a finger
against the king's son; for we all heard the king giving orders to you and
Abishai and Ittai that whoever finds himself near the young man Absalom
13 must take great care of him. If I had dealt him a treacherous blow, the king
14 would soon have known, and you would have kept well out of it.' 'That is a
lie!' said Joab. 'I will make a start and show you.' *a* So he picked up three
stout sticks and drove them against Absalom's chest while he was held
15 fast in the tree and still alive. Then ten young men who were Joab's
16 armour-bearers closed in on Absalom, struck at him and killed him. Joab
sounded the trumpet, and the army came back from the pursuit of Israel
17 because he had called it off. They took Absalom's body and flung it into
a great pit in the forest, and raised over it a huge pile of stones. The Israelites
all fled to their homes.

18 The pillar in the King's Vale had been set up by Absalom in his lifetime,
for he said, 'I have no son to carry on my name.' He had named the pillar
after himself; and to this day it is called Absalom's Monument.

19 Ahimaaz son of Zadok said, 'Let me run and take the news to the king
20 that the LORD has avenged him and delivered him from his enemies.' But
Joab replied, 'This is no day for you to be the bearer of news. Another day
you may have news to carry, but not today, because the king's son is dead.'
21 Joab told a Cushite to go and report to the king what he had seen. The
22 Cushite bowed low before Joab and set off running. Ahimaaz pleaded again
with Joab, 'Come what may,' he said, 'let me run after the Cushite.' 'Why
should you, my son?' asked Joab. 'You will get no reward for your news.'
23 'Come what may,' he said, 'I will run.' 'Go, then', said Joab. So Ahimaaz
ran by the road through the Plain of the Jordan and outstripped the Cushite.

24 David was sitting between the two gates when the watchman went up
to the roof of the gatehouse by the wall and, looking out, saw a man running
25 alone. The watchman called to the king and told him. 'If he is alone,' said
26 the king, 'then he has news.' The man came nearer and nearer. Then the
watchman saw another man running. He called down to the gate-keeper
and said, 'Look, there is another man running alone.' The king said, 'He
27 too brings news.' The watchman said, 'I see by the way he runs that the
first runner is Ahimaaz son of Zadok.' The king said, 'He is a good fellow
28 and shall earn the reward for good news.' Ahimaaz called out to the king,
'All is well!' He bowed low before him and said, 'Blessed be the LORD
your God who has given into your hands the men who rebelled against
29 your majesty.' The king asked, 'Is all well with the young man Absalom?'
Ahimaaz answered, 'Sir, your servant Joab sent me,*b* I saw a great com-
30 motion, but I did not know what had happened.' The king told him
31 to stand on one side; so he turned aside and stood there. Then the Cushite came in and said, 'Good news, your majesty! The LORD has avenged
32 you this day on all those who rebelled against you.' The king said to
the Cushite, 'Is all well with the young man Absalom?' The Cushite

*a* I will . . . show you: *or* I can waste no more time on you like this.    *b* Sir . . . sent
me: *prob. rdg.; Heb.* At the sending of Joab the king's servant and your servant.

answered, 'May all the king's enemies and all rebels who would do you harm be as that young man is.' The king was deeply moved and went up 33 to the roof-chamber over the gate and wept, crying out as he went, 'O, my son! Absalom my son, my son Absalom! If only I had died instead of you! O Absalom, my son, my son.'

Joab was told that the king was weeping and mourning for Absalom; 19 and that day victory was turned to mourning for the whole army, because 2 they heard how the king grieved for his son; they stole into the city like 3 men ashamed to show their faces after a defeat in battle. The king hid his 4 face and cried aloud, 'My son Absalom; O Absalom, my son, my son.' But Joab came into the king's quarters and said to him, 'You have put to 5 shame this day all your servants, who have saved you and your sons and daughters, your wives and your concubines. You love those that hate you 6 and hate those that love you; you have made us feel, officers and men alike, that we are nothing to you; for it is plain that if Absalom were still alive and all of us dead, you would be content. Now go at once and give your 7 servants some encouragement; if you refuse, I swear by the LORD that not a man will stay with you tonight, and that would be a worse disaster than any you have suffered since your earliest days.' Then the king rose and took 8 his seat in the gate; and when the army was told that the king was sitting in the gate, they all appeared before him.

## Various events of David's reign

MEANWHILE THE ISRAELITES had all scattered to their homes. Throughout all the tribes of Israel people were discussing it among 9 themselves and saying, 'The king has saved us from our enemies and freed us from the power of the Philistines, and now he has fled the country because of Absalom. But Absalom, whom we anointed king, has fallen in 10 battle; so now why have we no plans for bringing the king back?'

What all Israel was saying came to the king's ears.[a] So he sent word to 11 Zadok and Abiathar the priests: 'Ask the elders of Judah why they should be the last to bring the king back to his palace. Tell them, "You are my 12 brothers, my flesh and my blood; why are you last to bring me back?" And 13 tell Amasa, "You are my own flesh and blood. You shall be my commander-in-chief, so help me God, for the rest of your life in place of Joab."' David's message won all hearts in Judah, and they sent to the king, urging 14 him to return with all his men.

So the king came back to the Jordan; and the men of Judah came to 15 Gilgal to meet him and escort him across the river. Shimei son of Gera the 16 Benjamite from Bahurim hastened down among the men of Judah to meet King David with a thousand men from Benjamin; Ziba was there too, the 17 servant of Saul's family, with his fifteen sons and twenty servants. They rushed into the Jordan under the king's eyes and crossed to and fro con- 18 veying his household in order to win his favour. Shimei son of Gera,

[a] What . . . ears: *prob. rdg.; Heb. has these words after* back to his palace *and adds to* his palace.

19 when he had crossed the river, fell down before the king and said to him,
'I beg your majesty not to remember how disgracefully your servant
behaved when your majesty left Jerusalem; do not hold it against me or take
20 it to heart. For I humbly acknowledge that I did wrong, and today I am
the first of all the house of Joseph to come down to meet your majesty.'
21 But Abishai son of Zeruiah objected, 'Ought not Shimei to be put to death
22 because he cursed the LORD's anointed prince?' David answered, 'What
right have you, you sons of Zeruiah, to oppose me today? Why should any
man be put to death this day in Israel? I know now that I am king of Israel.'
23 Then the king said to Shimei, 'You shall not die', and confirmed it with an
oath.

24     Saul's grandson Mephibosheth also went down to meet the king. He had
not dressed his feet, combed his beard or washed his clothes, from the day
25 the king went out until he returned victorious. When he came from Jerusalem to meet the king, David said to him, 'Why did you not go with me,
26 Mephibosheth?' He answered, 'Sir, my servant deceived me; I did intend
27 to harness my ass and ride with the king (for I am lame), but his stories set
your majesty against me. Your majesty is like the angel of God; you must
28 do what you think right. My father's whole family, one and all, deserved
to die at your majesty's hands, but you gave me, your servant, my place at
29 your table. What further favour can I expect of the king?' The king
answered, 'You have said enough. My decision is that you and Ziba are to
30 share the estate.' Mephibosheth said, 'Let him have it all, now that your
majesty has come home victorious.'

31     Barzillai the Gileadite too had come down from Rogelim, and he went
32 as far as the Jordan with the king to send him on his way. Now Barzillai
was very old, eighty years of age; it was he who had provided for the king
33 while he was at Mahanaim, for he was a man of high standing. The king
said to Barzillai, 'Cross over with me and I will provide for your old age in
34 my household in Jerusalem.' Barzillai answered, 'Your servant is far too
35 old to go up with your majesty to Jerusalem. I am already eighty; and I
cannot tell good from bad. I cannot taste what I eat or drink; I cannot hear
the voices of men and women singing. Why should I be a burden any
36 longer on your majesty? Your servant will attend the king for a short way
across the Jordan; and why should the king reward me so handsomely?
37 Let me go back and end my days in my own city near the grave of my father
and mother. Here is my son Kimham; let him cross over with your majesty,
38 and do for him what you think best.' The king answered, 'Kimham shall
cross with me and I will do for him whatever you think best; and I will do
for you whatever you ask.'

39     All the people crossed the Jordan while the king waited. The king then
kissed Barzillai and gave him his blessing. Barzillai went back to his own
40 home; the king crossed over to Gilgal, Kimham with him. All the people
of Judah escorted the king over the river, and so did half the people of
Israel.

41     The men of Israel came to the king in a body and said, 'Why should our
brothers of Judah have got possession of the king's person by joining King
David's own men and then escorting him and his household across the

Jordan?' The men of Judah replied, 'Because his majesty is our near kins- 42
man. Why should you resent it? Have we eaten at the king's expense? Have
we received any gifts?' The men of Israel answered, 'We have ten times 43
your interest in the king and, what is more, we are senior to you; why do
you disparage us? Were we not the first to speak of bringing the king back?'
The men of Judah used language even fiercer than the men of Israel.

There happened to be a man there, a scoundrel named Sheba son of **20**
Bichri, a man of Benjamin. He blew the trumpet and cried out:

> What share have we in David?
> We have no lot in the son of Jesse.
> Away to your homes, O Israel.

The men of Israel all left David, to follow Sheba son of Bichri, but the men 2
of Judah stood by their king and followed him from the Jordan to Jerusalem.

When David came home to Jerusalem he took the ten concubines whom 3
he had left in charge of the palace and put them under guard; he maintained
them but did not have intercourse with them. They were kept in confinement to the day of their death, widowed in the prime of life.

The king said to Amasa, 'Call up the men of Judah and appear before 4
me again in three days' time.' So Amasa went to call up the men of Judah, 5
but it took longer than the time fixed by the king. David said to Abishai, 6
'Sheba son of Bichri will give us more trouble than Absalom; take the
royal bodyguard and follow him closely. If he has occupied some fortified
cities, he may escape us.' Abishai was followed by Joab *a* with the Kerethite 7
and Pelethite guards and all the fighting men; they left Jerusalem in
pursuit of Sheba son of Bichri. When they reached the great stone in 8
Gibeon, Amasa came towards them. Joab was wearing his tunic and over
it a belt supporting a sword in its scabbard. He came forward, concealing
his treachery, and said to Amasa, 'I hope you are well, my brother', and with 9
his right hand he grasped Amasa's beard to kiss him. Amasa was not on his 10
guard against the sword in Joab's hand. Joab struck him with it in the
belly and his entrails poured out to the ground; he did not strike a second
blow, for Amasa was dead. Joab and his brother Abishai went on in pursuit of Sheba son of Bichri. One of Joab's young men stood over Amasa 11
and called out, 'Follow Joab, all who are for Joab and for David!' Amasa's 12
body lay soaked in blood in the middle of the road, and when the man
saw how all the people stopped, he rolled him off the road into the field
and threw a cloak over him; for everyone who came by saw the body
and stopped. When he had been dragged from the road, they all went on 13
after Joab in pursuit of Sheba son of Bichri.

Sheba passed through all the tribes of Israel until he came to Abel-beth- 14
maacah,*b* and all the clan of Bichri *c* rallied to him and followed him into
the city. Joab's forces came up and besieged him in Abel-beth-maacah, 15
raised a siege-ramp against it and began undermining the wall to bring it
down. Then a wise woman stood on the rampart *d* and called from the city, 16

---

*a* Abishai . . . Joab: *prob. rdg.; Heb.* Some men of Joab followed him.     *b Prob. rdg.,*
*cp. verse 15; Heb.* Abel and Beth-maacah.     *c Prob. rdg.; Heb.* Beri.     *d* stood . . .
rampart: *transposed from verse 15.*

17 'Listen, listen! Tell Joab to step forward and let me speak with him.' So
he came forward and the woman said, 'Are you Joab?' He answered, 'I am.'
'Listen to what I have to say, sir', she went on, to which he replied, 'I am
18 listening.' 'In the old days', she said, 'there was a saying, "Go to Abel for
19 the answer", and that settled the matter. My city is known to be one of the
most peaceable and loyal *a* in Israel; she is like a watchful mother in Israel,
and you are seeking to kill her. Would you destroy the LORD's own posses-
20 sion?' Joab answered, 'God forbid, far be it from me to ruin or destroy!
21 That is not our aim; but a man from the hill-country of Ephraim named
Sheba son of Bichri has raised a revolt against King David; surrender this
one man, and I will retire from the city.' The woman said to Joab, 'His
22 head shall be thrown to you over the wall.' Then the woman withdrew, and
her wisdom won over the assembled people; they cut off Sheba's head and
threw it to Joab. Then he sounded the trumpet and the whole army left
the city and dispersed to their homes, while Joab went back to the king in
Jerusalem.

23 *b*     Joab was in command of the army, *c* and Benaiah son of Jehoiada com-
24 manded the Kerethite and Pelethite guards. Adoram was in charge of the
25 forced levy, and Jehoshaphat son of Ahilud was secretary of state. Sheva
26 was adjutant-general, and Zadok and Abiathar were priests; Ira the Jairite
was David's priest.

21 IN DAVID'S REIGN there was a famine that lasted year after year for three
years. So David consulted the LORD, and he answered, 'Blood-guilt rests
2 on Saul and on his family because he put the Gibeonites to death.' (The
Gibeonites were not of Israelite descent; they were a remnant of Amorite
stock whom the Israelites had sworn that they would spare. Saul, however,
had sought to exterminate them in his zeal for Israel and Judah.) King
3 David summoned the Gibeonites, therefore, and said to them, 'What can
be done for you? How can I make expiation, so that you may have cause to
4 bless the LORD's own people?' The Gibeonites answered, 'Our feud with
Saul and his family cannot be settled in silver and gold, and there is no one
man in Israel whose death would content us.' 'Then what do you want me
5 to do for you?' asked David. They answered, 'Let us make an end of the
6 man who caused our undoing and ruined us, so that he shall never again
have his place within the borders of Israel. Hand over to us seven of that
man's sons, and we will hurl them down to their death before *d* the LORD
in Gibeah of Saul, the LORD's chosen king.' The king agreed to hand them
7 over, but he spared Mephibosheth son of Jonathan, son of Saul, because of
the oath that had been taken in the LORD's name by David and Saul's son
8 Jonathan. The king then took the two sons whom Rizpah daughter of Aiah
had borne to Saul, Armoni and Mephibosheth, and the five sons whom
Merab, Saul's daughter, had borne to Adriel son of Barzillai of Meholah.
9 He handed them over to the Gibeonites, and they flung them down from
the mountain before the LORD; the seven of them fell together. They were

---

*a* My city . . . loyal: *prob. rdg.; Heb.* I am the requited ones of the loyal ones.
*b* *Verses 23–26: cp. 8. 16–18; 1 Kgs. 4. 2–6; 1 Chr. 18. 15–17.*       *c* *Prob. rdg.,*
*cp. 8. 16; Heb. adds* Israel.      *d* Or for.

put to death in the first days of harvest at the beginning of the barley harvest.
Rizpah daughter of Aiah took sackcloth and spread it out as a bed for her- 10
self on the rock, from the beginning of harvest until the rains came and
fell from heaven upon the bodies. She allowed no bird to set upon them by
day nor any wild beast by night. When David was told what Rizpah 11
daughter of Aiah the concubine of Saul had done, he went and took the 12
bones of Saul and his son Jonathan from the citizens of Jabesh-gilead, who
had stolen them from the public square at Beth-shan, where the Philistines
had hung them on the day they defeated Saul at Gilboa. He removed the 13
bones of Saul and Jonathan from there and gathered up the bones of the
men who had been hurled to death. They buried the bones of Saul and his 14
son Jonathan in the territory of Benjamin at Zela, in the grave of his father
Kish. Everything was done as the king ordered, and thereafter the LORD
was willing to accept prayers offered for the country.

Once again war broke out between the Philistines and Israel. David and 15
his men went down to the battle, but as he fought with the Philistines he fell
exhausted. Then Benob, one of the race of the Rephaim, whose bronze 16
spear weighed three hundred shekels*a* and who wore a belt of honour, took
David prisoner and was about to kill him. But Abishai son of Zeruiah came 17
to David's help, struck the Philistine down and killed him. Then David's
officers took an oath that he should never again go out with them to war,
for fear that the lamp of Israel might be extinguished.

Some time later war with the Philistines broke out again in Gob: it was 18*b*
then that Sibbechai of Hushah killed Saph, a descendant of the Rephaim.
In another war with the Philistines in Gob, Elhanan son of Jair *c* of Bethle- 19
hem killed Goliath of Gath, whose spear had a shaft like a weaver's beam.
In yet another war in Gath there appeared a giant with six fingers on each 20
hand and six toes on each foot, twenty-four in all. He too was descended
from the Rephaim; and, when he defied Israel, Jonathan son of David's 21
brother Shimeai killed him. These four giants were the descendants of the 22
Rephaim in Gath, and they all fell at the hands of David and his men.

THESE ARE THE WORDS OF THE SONG David sang to the LORD on the 22 1
day when the LORD delivered him from the power of all his enemies and
from the power of Saul:

> The LORD is my stronghold, my fortress and my champion,      2*d*
> my God, my rock where I find safety;      3
> my shield, my mountain fastness, my strong tower,
> my refuge, my deliverer, who saves me from violence.
> I will call on the LORD to whom all praise is due,      4
> and I shall be delivered from my enemies.
> When the waves of death swept round me,      5
> and torrents of destruction overtook me,
> the bonds of Sheol tightened about me,      6
> the snares of death were set to catch me;

---

*a* shekels: *prob. rdg.; Heb.* weight.     *b* *Verses 18–22: cp. 1 Chr. 20. 4–7.*     *c* Jair:
*prob. rdg., cp. 1 Chr. 20. 5; Heb.* Jaare-oregim.     *d* *Verses 2–51: cp. Ps. 18. 2–50.*

| 7 | then in anguish of heart I cried to the LORD, |
|   | I called for help to my God; |
|   | he heard me from his temple, |
|   | and my cry rang in his ears. |
| 8 | The earth heaved and quaked, |
|   | heaven's foundations shook; |
|   | they heaved, because he was angry. |
| 9 | Smoke rose from his nostrils, |
|   | devouring fire came out of his mouth, |
|   | glowing coals and searing heat. |
| 10 | He swept the skies aside as he descended, |
|   | thick darkness lay under his feet. |
| 11 | He rode on a cherub, he flew through the air; |
|   | he swooped *a* on the wings of the wind. |
| 12 | He curtained himself in darkness |
|   | and made dense vapour his canopy. |
| 13 | Thick clouds came out of the radiance before him; |
|   | glowing coals burned brightly. |
| 14 | The LORD thundered from the heavens |
|   | and the voice of the Most High spoke out. |
| 15 | He loosed his arrows, he sped them far and wide, |
|   | his lightning shafts, and sent them echoing. |
| 16 | The channels of the sea-bed were revealed, |
|   | the foundations of earth laid bare |
|   | at the LORD's rebuke, |
|   | at the blast of the breath of his nostrils. |
| 17 | He reached down from the height and took me, |
|   | he drew me out of mighty waters, |
| 18 | he rescued me from my enemies, strong as they were, |
|   | from my foes when they grew too powerful for me. |
| 19 | They confronted me in the hour of my peril, |
|   | but the LORD was my buttress. |
| 20 | He brought me out into an open place, |
|   | he rescued me because he delighted in me. |
| 21 | The LORD rewarded me as my righteousness deserved; |
|   | my hands were clean, and he requited me. |
| 22 | For I have followed the ways of the LORD |
|   | and have not turned wickedly from my God; |
| 23 | all his laws are before my eyes, |
|   | I have not failed to follow his decrees. |
| 24 | In his sight I was blameless |
|   | and kept myself from wilful sin; |
| 25 | the LORD requited me as my righteousness deserved |
|   | and my purity in his eyes. |
| 26 | With the loyal thou showest thyself loyal |
|   | and with the blameless man blameless. |

*a Prob. rdg., cp. Ps. 18. 10; Heb. was seen.*

With the savage man thou showest thyself savage,    27
and *a* tortuous with the perverse.
Thou deliverest humble folk,    28
thou lookest with contempt upon the proud.
Thou, LORD, art my lamp,    29
and the LORD will lighten my darkness.
With thy help I leap over a bank,    30
by God's aid I spring over a wall.

The way of God is perfect,    31
the LORD's word has stood the test;
he is the shield of all who take refuge in him.
What god is there but the LORD?    32
What rock but our God?—
the God who girds me *b* with strength    33
and makes my way blameless, *c*
who makes me swift as a hind    34
and sets me secure on the mountains;
who trains my hands for battle,    35
and my arms aim an arrow tipped with bronze.

Thou hast given me the shield of thy salvation,    36
in thy providence thou makest me great.
Thou givest me room for my steps,    37
my feet have not faltered.
I pursue my enemies and destroy them,    38
I do not return until I have made an end of them.
I make an end of them, I strike them down;    39
they rise no more, they fall beneath my feet.
Thou dost arm me with strength for the battle    40
and dost subdue my foes before me.
Thou settest *d* my foot on my enemies' necks,    41
and I bring to nothing those that hate me.
They cry out *e* and there is no one to help them,    42
they cry to the LORD and he does not answer.
I will pound them fine as dust on the ground,    43
like mud in the streets will I trample them. *f*
Thou dost deliver me from the clamour of the people,    44
and makest me master of the nations.
A people I never knew shall be my subjects.
Foreigners shall come cringing to me;    45
as soon as they hear tell of me, they shall obey me.
Foreigners shall be brought captive to me,    46
and come limping from their strongholds.

*a* With the savage . . . savage, and: *or* With the pure thou showest thyself pure, but . . .
*b* who girds me: *prob. rdg., cp. Ps. 18. 32; Heb.* my refuge *or* my strength.    *c* and
makes . . . blameless: *prob. rdg., cp. Ps. 18. 32; Heb. unintelligible.*    *d Prob. rdg.,*
*cp. Ps. 18. 40; Heb. unintelligible.*    *e* cry out: *prob. rdg., cp. Ps. 18. 41; Heb.* look.
*f Prob. rdg., cp. Ps. 18. 42; Heb. adds* will I stamp them down.

·47
> The LORD lives, blessed is my rock,
> high above all is God my rock and safe refuge.

48
> O God, who grantest me vengeance,
> who dost subdue peoples under me,

49
> who dost snatch me from my foes and set me over my enemies,
> thou dost deliver me from violent men.

50
> Therefore, LORD, I will praise thee among the nations
> and sing psalms to thy name,

51
> to one who gives his king great victories
> and in all his acts keeps faith with his anointed king,
> with David and his descendants for ever.

**23**   These are the last words of David:

> The very word of David son of Jesse,
> the very word of the man whom the High God raised up,
> the anointed prince of the God of Jacob,
> and the singer of Israel's psalms:

2
> the spirit of the LORD has spoken through me,
> and his word is on my lips.

3
> The God of Israel spoke,
> the Rock of Israel spoke of me:
> 'He who rules men in justice,
> who rules in the fear of God,

4
> is like the light of morning at sunrise,
> a morning that is cloudless after rain
> and makes the grass sparkle from the earth.'

5
> Surely, surely my house is true to God;
> for he has made a pact with me for all time,
> its terms spelled out and faithfully kept,
> my whole salvation, all my *a* delight.

6
> But the ungodly put forth no shoots,
> they are all like briars tossed aside;
> none dare put out his hand to pick them up,

7
> none touch them but *b* with tool of iron or of wood;
> they are fit only for burning in the fire. *c*

8*d*   THESE ARE THE NAMES OF DAVID'S HEROES. First came Ishbosheth the Hachmonite,*e* chief of the three; it was he who brandished his spear *f*
9   over eight hundred dead, all slain at one time. Next to him was Eleazar son of Dodo the Ahohite,*g* one of the heroic three. He was with David at Pas-dammim where the Philistines*h* had gathered for battle. When the

---

*a Prob. rdg.; Heb. om.*      *b but: prob. rdg.; Heb. he shall be filled.*      *c Prob. rdg.;*
*Heb. adds in sitting.*      *d Verses 8–39: cp. 1 Chr. 11. 10–41.*      *e Prob. rdg.; Heb.*
*Josheb-basshebeth a Tahchemonite.*      *f who . . . spear: prob. rdg., cp. 1 Chr. 11. 11;*
*Heb. unintelligible.*      *g the Ahohite: prob. rdg., cp. 1 Chr. 11. 12; Heb. son of Ahohi.*
*h He was . . . Philistines: prob. rdg., cp. 1 Chr. 11. 13; Heb. With David when they*
*taunted them among the Philistines.*

Israelites fell back, he stood his ground and rained blows on the Philistines 10
until, from sheer weariness, his hand stuck fast to his sword; and so the
LORD brought about a great victory that day. Afterwards the people rallied
behind him, but it was only to strip the dead. Next to him was Shammah son 11
of Agee a Hararite. The Philistines had gathered at Lehi, where there was a
field with a fine crop of lentils; and, when the Philistines put the people to
flight, he stood his ground in the field, saved it *a* and defeated them. So 12
the LORD again brought about a great victory.

Three of the thirty went down towards the beginning of harvest to join 13
David at the cave of Adullam, while a band of Philistines was encamped in
the Vale of Rephaim. At that time David was in the stronghold and a Philis- 14
tine garrison held Bethlehem. One day a longing came over David, and he 15
exclaimed, 'If only I could have a drink of water from the well *b* by the gate
of Bethlehem!' At this the heroic three made their way through the 16
Philistine lines and drew water from the well by the gate of Bethlehem and
brought it to David. But David refused to drink it; he poured it out to the
LORD and said, 'God forbid that I should do such a thing! Can I drink *c* 17
the blood of these men who risked their lives for it?' So he would not
drink it. Such were the exploits of the heroic three.

Abishai the brother of Joab son of Zeruiah was chief of the thirty. He 18
once brandished his spear over three hundred dead, and he was famous
among the thirty. Some think he even surpassed the rest of the thirty *d* in 19
reputation, and he became their captain, but he did not rival the three.
Benaiah son of Jehoiada, from Kabzeel, was a hero of many exploits. It 20
was he who smote the two champions of Moab, and who went down into
a pit and killed a lion on a snowy day. It was he who also killed the Egyptian, 21
a man of striking appearance armed with a spear: he went to meet him
with a club, snatched the spear out of the Egyptian's hand and killed him
with his own weapon. Such were the exploits of Benaiah son of Jehoiada, 22
famous among the heroic thirty. *d* He was more famous than the rest of the 23
thirty, but he did not rival the three. David appointed him to his household.

Asahel the brother of Joab was one of the thirty, and Elhanan son of 24
Dodo from Bethlehem; Shammah from Harod, and Elika from Harod; 25
Helez from Beth-pelet, *e* and Ira son of Ikkesh from Tekoa; Abiezer from 26 27
Anathoth, and Mebunnai from Hushah; Zalmon the Ahohite, and Maharai 28
from Netophah; Heled son of Baanah from Netophah, and Ittai son of 29
Ribai from Gibeah of Benjamin; Benaiah from Pirathon, and Hiddai 30
from the ravines of Gaash; Abi-albon from Beth-arabah, *f* and Azmoth 31
from Bahurim; *g* Eliahba from Shaalbon, and Hashem the Gizonite; 32
Jonathan son of *h* Shammah the Hararite, and Ahiam son of Sharar the 33
Hararite; *i* Eliphelet son of Ahasbai son of the Maacathite, and Eliam son 34
of Ahithophel the Gilonite; Hezrai from Carmel, and Paarai the Arbite; 35

---

*a* saved it: *or* cleared it of the Philistines. *b* *Or* cistern. *c* I drink: *prob. rdg.*,
*cp. 1 Chr. 11. 19; Heb. om.* *d* *Prob. rdg.; Heb.* three. *e* *Prob. rdg., cp. Josh. 15.*
*27; Heb.* from Pelet. *f* *Prob. rdg., cp. Josh. 18. 22; Heb.* from Arabah. *g* *Prob.*
*rdg., cp. 1 Chr. 11. 33; Heb.* from Barhum. *h* Hashem . . . son of: *prob. rdg., cp.*
*1 Chr. 11. 34; Heb.* the sons of Jashen, Jonathan. *i* *Prob. rdg., cp. 1 Chr. 11. 35;*
*Heb.* Ararite.

36 37 Igal son of Nathan from Zobah, and Bani the Gadite; Zelek the Ammonite,
38 and Naharai from Beeroth, armour-bearer to Joab son of Zeruiah; Ira the
39 Ithrite, Gareb the Ithrite, and Uriah the Hittite: there were thirty-seven
in all.

24 1*a* ONCE AGAIN THE ISRAELITES felt the LORD's anger, when he incited
David against them and gave him orders that Israel and Judah should
2 be counted. So he instructed Joab and the officers of the army*b* with him
to go round all the tribes of Israel, from Dan to Beersheba, and make a
3 record of the people and report the number to him. Joab answered, 'Even
if the LORD your God should increase the people a hundredfold and your
majesty should live to see it, what pleasure would that give your majesty?'
4 But Joab and the officers were overruled by the king and they left his
5 presence in order to count the people. They crossed the Jordan and began
at Aroer and the level land of the gorge, proceeding towards Gad*c* and
6 Jazer. They came to Gilead and to the land of the Hittites, to Kadesh,
7 and then to Dan and Iyyon*d* and so round towards Sidon. They went as
far as the walled city of Tyre and all the towns of the Hivites and Canaan-
8 ites, and then went on to the Negeb of Judah at Beersheba. They covered
the whole country and arrived back at Jerusalem after nine months and
9 twenty days. Joab reported to the king the total number of people: the
number of able-bodied men, capable of bearing arms, was eight hundred
thousand in Israel and five hundred thousand in Judah.
10 After he had counted the people David's conscience smote him, and
he said to the LORD, 'I have done a very wicked thing: I pray thee, LORD,
11 remove thy servant's guilt, for I have been very foolish.' He rose next
morning, and meanwhile the command of the LORD had come to the
12 prophet Gad, David's seer, to go and speak to David: 'This is the word of
the LORD: I have three things in store for you; choose one and I will bring
13 it upon you.' So Gad came to David and repeated this to him and said, 'Is
it to be three years of famine in your land, or three months of flight with
the enemy at your heels, or three days of pestilence in your land? Consider
14 carefully what answer I am to take back to him who sent me.' Thereupon
David said to Gad, 'I am in a desperate plight; let us fall into the hands of
the LORD, for his mercy is great; and let me not fall into the hands of men.'
15 So the LORD sent a pestilence throughout Israel from morning till the hour
of dinner, and from Dan to Beersheba seventy thousand of the people died.
16 Then the angel stretched out his arm towards Jerusalem to destroy it; but
the LORD repented of the evil and said to the angel who was destroying the
people, 'Enough! Stay your hand.' At that moment the angel of the LORD
was standing by the threshing-floor of Araunah the Jebusite.
17 When David saw the angel who was striking down the people, he said to
the LORD, 'It is I who have done wrong, the sin is mine; but these poor
sheep, what have they done? Let thy hand fall upon me and upon my

---

*a* Verses 1–25: cp. 1 Chr. 21. 1–27.  *b* Joab . . . army: *prob. rdg., cp. 1 Chr. 21. 2;*
Heb. Joab the officer of the army.  *c* began at . . . Gad: *prob. rdg.; Heb. encamped
in Aroer on the right of the level land of the gorge Gad.*  *d* Prob. rdg., cp. 1 Kgs. 15.
20; Heb. Yaan.

family.' That same day Gad came to David and said to him, 'Go and set 18
up an altar to the LORD on the threshing-floor of Araunah the Jebusite.'
David did what Gad told him to do, and went up as the LORD had com- 19
manded. When Araunah looked down and saw the king and his servants 20
coming over towards him, he went out, prostrated himself low before the
king and said, 'Why has your majesty come to visit his servant?' David 21
answered, 'To buy the threshing-floor from you to build an altar to the
LORD, so that the plague which has attacked the people may be stopped.'
Araunah answered David, 'I beg your majesty to take it and sacrifice what 22
you think fit. I have here the oxen for a whole-offering, and their harness
and the threshing-sledges for the fuel.' Araunah*ᵃ* gave it all to the king 23
for his own use and said to him, 'May the LORD your God accept you.'
But the king said to Araunah, 'No, I will buy it from you; I will not offer 24
to the LORD my God whole-offerings that have cost me nothing.' So
David bought the threshing-floor and the oxen for fifty shekels of silver.
He built an altar to the LORD there and offered whole-offerings and shared- 25
offerings. Then the LORD yielded to his prayer for the land; and the plague
in Israel stopped.

*ᵃ Prob. rdg.; Heb. adds* the king.

# THE FIRST BOOK OF
# KINGS

## The death of David and accession of Solomon

1  **K**ING DAVID WAS NOW A VERY OLD MAN and, though
2  they wrapped clothes round him, he could not keep warm. So
his household said to him, 'Let us find a young virgin for your
majesty, to attend you and take care of you; and let her lie in your bosom,
3  sir, and make you warm.' So they searched all over Israel for a beautiful
maiden and found Abishag, a Shunammite, and brought her to the king.
4  She was a very beautiful girl, and she took care of the king and waited on
him, but he had no intercourse with her.

5  Now Adonijah, whose mother was Haggith, was boasting that he was
to be king; and he had already provided himself with chariots and horse-
6  men*a* and fifty outrunners. Never in his life had his father corrected
him or asked why he behaved as he did. He was a very handsome man, too,
7  and was next in age to Absalom. He talked with Joab son of Zeruiah and
8  with Abiathar the priest, and they gave him their strong support; but
Zadok the priest, Benaiah son of Jehoiada, Nathan the prophet, Shimei,
9  Rei, and David's bodyguard of heroes, did not take his side. Adonijah
then held a sacrifice of sheep, oxen, and buffaloes at the stone Zoheleth
beside En-rogel, and he invited all his royal brothers and all those
10  officers of the household who were of the tribe of Judah. But he did
not invite Nathan the prophet, Benaiah and the bodyguard, or Solomon
his brother.

11  Then Nathan said to Bathsheba, the mother of Solomon, 'Have you not
heard that Adonijah son of Haggith has become king, all unknown to our
12  lord David? Now come, let me advise you what to do for your own safety
13  and for the safety of your son Solomon. Go in and see King David and say
to him, "Did not your majesty swear to me, your servant, that my son
Solomon should succeed you as king; that it was he who should sit on
14  your throne? Why then has Adonijah become king?" Then while you
are still speaking there with the king, I will follow you in and tell the whole
story.'

15  So Bathsheba went to the king in his private chamber; he was now very
16  old, and Abishag the Shunammite was waiting on him. Bathsheba bowed
before the king and prostrated herself. 'What do you want?' said the king.
17  She answered, 'My lord, you swore to me your servant, by the LORD your
God, that my son Solomon should succeed you as king, and that he should
18  sit on your throne. But now, here is Adonijah become king, all unknown to

*a Or* a chariot and horses.

your majesty. He has sacrificed great numbers of oxen, buffaloes, and 19
sheep, and has invited to the feast all the king's sons, and Abiathar the
priest, and Joab the commander-in-chief, but he has not invited your
servant Solomon. And now, your majesty, all Israel is looking to you to 20
announce who is to succeed you on the throne. Otherwise, when you, 21
sir, rest with your forefathers, my son Solomon and I shall be treated as
criminals.' She was still speaking to the king when Nathan the prophet 22
arrived. The king was told that Nathan was there; he came into the king's 23
presence and prostrated himself with his face to the ground. 'My lord,' he 24
said, 'your majesty must, I suppose, have declared that Adonijah should
succeed you and that he should sit on your throne. He has today gone 25
down and sacrificed great numbers of oxen, buffaloes, and sheep, and has
invited to the feast all the king's sons, Joab the commander-in-chief, and
Abiathar the priest; and at this very moment they are eating and drinking
in his presence and shouting, "Long live King Adonijah!" But he has not 26
invited me your servant, Zadok the priest, Benaiah son of Jehoiada, or
your servant Solomon. Has this been done by your majesty's authority, 27
while we *a* your servants have not been told who should succeed you on
the throne?' Thereupon King David said, 'Call Bathsheba', and she came 28
into the king's presence and stood before him. Then the king swore an oath 29
to her: 'As the LORD lives, who has delivered me from all my troubles: I 30
swore by the LORD the God of Israel that Solomon your son should succeed
me and that he should sit on my throne, and this day I give effect to my
oath.' Bathsheba bowed low to the king and prostrated herself; and she 31
said, 'May my lord King David live for ever!'

Then King David said, 'Call Zadok the priest, Nathan the prophet, and 32
Benaiah son of Jehoiada.' They came into the king's presence and he gave 33
them these orders: 'Take the officers of the household with you; mount
my son Solomon on the king's mule and escort him down to Gihon. There 34
Zadok the priest and Nathan the prophet shall anoint him king over Israel.
Sound the trumpet and shout, "Long live King Solomon!" Then escort 35
him home again, and he shall come and sit on my throne and reign in my
place; for he is the man that I have appointed prince over Israel and Judah.'
Benaiah son of Jehoiada answered the king, 'It shall be done. And may the 36
LORD, the God of my lord the king, confirm it! As the LORD has been with 37
your majesty, so may he be with Solomon; may he make his throne even
greater than the throne of my lord King David.' So Zadok the priest, 38
Nathan the prophet, and Benaiah son of Jehoiada, together with the
Kerethite and Pelethite guards, went down and mounted Solomon on
King David's mule and escorted him to Gihon. Zadok the priest took the 39
horn of oil from the Tent of the LORD and anointed Solomon; they sounded
the trumpet and all the people shouted, 'Long live King Solomon!' Then 40
all the people escorted him home in procession, with great rejoicing and
playing of pipes, so that the very earth split with the noise.

Adonijah and his guests had finished their banquet when the noise 41
reached their ears. Joab, hearing the sound of the trumpet, exclaimed,

*a* Has this . . . while we: *or* If this has been done by your majesty's authority, then
we . . .

42 'What is all this uproar in the city? What has happened?' While he was still speaking, Jonathan son of Abiathar the priest arrived. 'Come in', said
43 Adonijah. 'You are an honourable man and bring good news.' 'Far otherwise,' Jonathan replied; 'our lord King David has made Solomon king
44 and has sent with him Zadok the priest, Nathan the prophet, and Benaiah son of Jehoiada, together with the Kerethite and Pelethite guards; they
45 have mounted him on the king's mule, and Zadok the priest and Nathan the prophet have anointed him king at Gihon, and they have now escorted him home rejoicing, and the city is in an uproar. That was the noise you
46 heard. More than that, Solomon has taken his seat on the royal throne.
47 Yes, and the officers of the household have been to greet our lord King David with these words: "May your God make the name of Solomon your son more famous than your own and his throne even greater than yours",
48 and the king bowed upon his couch. What is more, he said this: "Blessed be the LORD the God of Israel who has set a successor on my throne this
49 day while I am still alive to see it." ' Then Adonijah's guests all rose in
50 panic and scattered. Adonijah himself, in fear of Solomon, sprang up and
51 went to the altar and caught hold of its horns. Then a message was sent to Solomon: 'Adonijah is afraid of King Solomon; he has taken hold of the horns of the altar and has said, "Let King Solomon first swear to me that
52 he will not put his servant to the sword." ' Solomon said, 'If he proves himself a man of worth, not a hair of his head shall fall to the ground; but
53 if he is found to be troublesome, he shall die.' Then King Solomon sent and had him brought down from the altar; he came in and prostrated himself before the king, and Solomon ordered him home.

2 When the time of David's death drew near, he gave this last charge to
2 his son Solomon: 'I am going the way of all the earth. Be strong and show
3 yourself a man. Fulfil your duty to the LORD your God; conform to his ways, observe his statutes and his commandments, his judgements and his solemn precepts, as they are written in the law of Moses, so that you
4 may prosper in whatever you do and whichever way you turn, and that the LORD may fulfil this promise that he made about me: "If your descendants take care to walk faithfully in my sight with all their heart and with all their soul, you shall never lack a successor on the throne of Israel."
5 You know how Joab son of Zeruiah treated me and what he did to two commanders-in-chief in Israel, Abner son of Ner and Amasa son of Jether. He killed them both, breaking the peace by bloody acts of war; and with that blood he stained the belt about my waist and the sandals on my
6 feet. Do as your wisdom prompts you, and do not let his grey hairs go
7 down to the grave in peace. Show constant friendship to the family of Barzillai of Gilead; let them have their place at your table; they befriended
8 me when I was a fugitive from your brother Absalom. Do not forget Shimei son of Gera, the Benjamite from Bahurim, who cursed me bitterly the day I went to Mahanaim. True, he came down to meet me at the
9 Jordan, and I swore by the LORD that I would not put him to death. But you do not need to let him go unpunished now; you are a wise man and will know how to deal with him; bring down his grey hairs in blood to the grave.'

So David rested with his forefathers and was buried in the city of David, 10
having reigned over Israel for forty years, seven in Hebron and thirty- 11
three in Jerusalem; and Solomon succeeded his father David as king and 12
was firmly established on the throne.

## The reign of Solomon

THEN ADONIJAH SON OF HAGGITH came to Bathsheba, the mother 13
of Solomon. 'Do you come as a friend?' she asked. 'As a friend,' he
answered; 'I have something to say to you.' 'Tell me', she said. 'You 14 15
know', he went on, 'that the throne was mine and that all Israel was looking to me to be king; but I was passed over and the throne has gone to my
brother; it was his by the LORD's will. And now I have one request to make 16
of you; do not refuse me.' 'What is it?' she said. He answered, 'Will you 17
ask King Solomon (he will never refuse you) to give me Abishag the
Shunammite in marriage?' 'Very well,' said Bathsheba, 'I will speak for 18
you to the king.' So Bathsheba went in to King Solomon to speak for 19
Adonijah. The king rose to meet her and kissed her, and seated himself on
his throne. A throne was set for the king's mother and she sat at his right
hand. Then she said, 'I have one small request to make of you; do not 20
refuse me.' 'What is it, mother?' he replied; 'I will not refuse you.' 'It is 21
this, that Abishag the Shunammite should be given to your brother Adonijah in marriage.' At that Solomon answered his mother, 'Why do you 22
ask for Abishag the Shunammite as wife for Adonijah? you might as well
ask for the throne, for he is my elder brother and has both Abiathar the
priest and Joab son of Zeruiah on his side.' Then King Solomon swore 23
by the LORD: 'So help me God, Adonijah shall pay for this with his life.
As the LORD lives, who has established me and set me on the throne of 24
David my father and has founded a house for me as he promised, this
very day Adonijah shall be put to death!' Thereupon King Solomon 25
gave Benaiah son of Jehoiada his orders, and he struck him down and
he died.

Abiathar the priest was told by the king to go off to Anathoth to his own 26
estate. 'You deserve to die,' he said, 'but in spite of this day's work I shall
not put you to death, for you carried the Ark of the Lord GOD before my
father David, and you shared in all the hardships that he endured.' So 27
Solomon dismissed Abiathar from his office as priest of the LORD, and so
fulfilled the sentence that the LORD had pronounced against the house of
Eli in Shiloh.

News of all this reached Joab, and he fled to the Tent of the LORD and 28
caught hold of the horns of the altar; for he had sided with Adonijah,
though not with Absalom. When King Solomon learnt that Joab had fled 29
to the Tent of the LORD and that he was by the altar, he sent Benaiah son of
Jehoiada with orders to strike him down. Benaiah came to the Tent of the 30
LORD and ordered Joab in the king's name to come away; but he said, 'No;
I will die here.' Benaiah reported Joab's answer to the king, and the king 31
said, 'Let him have his way; strike him down and bury him, and so rid me

32 and my father's house of the guilt for the blood that he wantonly shed. The LORD will hold him responsible for his own death, because he struck down two innocent men who were better men than he, Abner son of Ner, commander of the army of Israel, and Amasa son of Jether, commander of the army of Judah, and ran them through with the sword, without my father

33 David's knowledge. The guilt of their blood shall recoil on Joab and his descendants for all time; but David and his descendants, his house and

34 his throne, will enjoy perpetual prosperity from the LORD.' So Benaiah son of Jehoiada went up to the altar and struck Joab down and killed him,

35 and he was buried in his house on the edge of the wilderness. Thereafter the king appointed Benaiah son of Jehoiada to command the army in his place, and installed Zadok the priest in place of Abiathar.

36 Next the king sent for Shimei and said to him, 'Build yourself a house in Jerusalem and stay there; you are not to leave the city for any other place.

37 If ever you leave it and cross the gorge of the Kidron, you shall die; make

38 no mistake about that. Your blood will be on your own head.' And Shimei said to the king, 'I accept your sentence; I will do as your majesty com-

39 mands.' So for a long time Shimei remained in Jerusalem; but three years later two of his slaves ran away to Achish son of Maacah, king of Gath.

40 When Shimei heard that his slaves were in Gath, he immediately saddled his ass and went there to Achish in search of his slaves; he came to Gath

41 and returned with them. When King Solomon was told that Shimei had

42 gone from Jerusalem to Gath and back, he sent for him and said, 'Did I not require you to swear by the LORD? Did I not give you this solemn warning: "If ever you leave this city for any other place, you shall die; make no mistake about it"? And you said, "I accept your sentence; I

43 obey." Why then have you not kept the oath which you swore by the LORD,

44 and the order which I gave you? Shimei, you know in your own heart all the mischief you did to my father David; the LORD is now making that

45 mischief recoil on your own head. But King Solomon is blessed and the

46 throne of David will be secure before the LORD for all time.' The king then gave orders to Benaiah son of Jehoiada, and he went out and struck Shimei down; and he died. Thus Solomon's royal power was securely established.

3 Solomon allied himself to Pharaoh king of Egypt by marrying his daughter. He brought her to the City of David, until he had finished building his own house and the house of the LORD and the wall round

2 Jerusalem. The people however continued to sacrifice at the hill-shrines, for till then no house had been built in honour of the name of the LORD.

3 Solomon himself loved the LORD, conforming to the precepts laid down by his father David; but he too slaughtered and burnt sacrifices at the hill-shrines.

4 Now King Solomon went to Gibeon to offer a sacrifice, for that was the chief hill-shrine, and he used to offer a thousand whole-offerings on its

5[a] altar. There that night the LORD God appeared to him in a dream and said,

6 'What shall I give you? Tell me.' And Solomon answered, 'Thou didst show great and constant love to thy servant David my father, because he

[a] *Verses 5–14: cp. 2 Chr. 1. 7–12.*

walked before thee in loyalty, righteousness, and integrity of heart; and
thou hast maintained this great and constant love towards him and hast
now given him a son to succeed him on the throne. Now, O LORD my God, 7
thou hast made thy servant king in place of my father David, though I am
a mere child, unskilled in leadership. And I am here in the midst of thy 8
people, the people of thy choice, too many to be numbered or counted.
Give thy servant, therefore, a heart with skill to listen, so that he may 9
govern thy people justly and distinguish good from evil. For who is equal
to the task of governing this great people of thine?' The Lord was well 10
pleased that Solomon had asked for this, and he said to him, 'Because you 11
have asked for this, and not for long life for yourself, or for wealth, or for
the lives of your enemies, but have asked for discernment in administering
justice, I grant your request; I give you a heart so wise and so understand- 12
ing that there has been none like you before your time nor will be after you.
I give you furthermore those things for which you did not ask, such wealth 13
and honour*a* as no king of your time can match. And if you conform to 14
my ways and observe my ordinances and commandments, as your father
David did, I will give you long life.' Then he awoke, and knew it was a 15
dream.

Solomon came to Jerusalem and stood before the Ark of the Covenant
of the Lord; there he sacrificed whole-offerings and brought shared-
offerings, and gave a feast to all his household.

Then there came into the king's presence two women who were pro- 16
stitutes and stood before him. The first said, 'My lord, this woman and I 17
share the same house, and I gave birth to a child when she was there with
me. On the third day after my baby was born she too gave birth to a child. 18
We were quite alone; no one else was with us in the house; only the two
of us were there. During the night this woman's child died because she 19
overlaid it, and she got up in the middle of the night, took my baby from 20
my side while I, your servant, was asleep, and laid it in her bosom, putting
her dead child in mine. When I got up in the morning to feed my baby, I 21
found him dead; but when I looked at him closely, I found that it was not
the child that I had borne.' The other woman broke in, 'No; the living 22
child is mine; yours is the dead one', while the first retorted, 'No; the dead
child is yours; mine is the living one.' So they went on arguing in the king's
presence. The king thought to himself, 'One of them says, "This is my 23
child, the living one; yours is the dead one." The other says, "No; it is your
child that is dead and mine that is alive." ' Then he said, 'Fetch me a sword.' 24
They brought in a sword and the king gave the order: 'Cut the living child 25
in two and give half to one and half to the other.' At this the woman who 26
was the mother of the living child, moved with love for her child, said to
the king, 'Oh! sir, let her have the baby; whatever you do, do not kill it.'
The other said, 'Let neither of us have it; cut it in two.' Thereupon the 27
king gave judgement: 'Give the living baby to the first woman; do not kill
it. She is its mother.' When Israel heard the judgement which the king had 28
given, they all stood in awe of him; for they saw that he had the wisdom of
God within him to administer justice.

*a Or riches.*

**4** 1 2*ᵃ* KING SOLOMON REIGNED OVER ISRAEL. His officers were as follows:

In charge of the calendar:*ᵇ* Azariah son of Zadok the priest.

3 Adjutant-general:*ᶜ* Ahijah son*ᵈ* of Shisha.
Secretary of state: Jehoshaphat son of Ahilud.

4 Commander of the army: Benaiah son of Jehoiada.
Priests: Zadok and Abiathar.

5 Superintendent of the regional governors: Azariah son of Nathan.
King's Friend: Zabud son of Nathan.

6 Comptroller of the household: Ahishar.
Superintendent of the forced levy: Adoniram son of Abda.

7 Solomon had twelve regional governors over Israel and they supplied the food for the king and the royal household, each being responsible for 8 one month's provision in the year. These were their names:

Ben-hur in the hill-country of Ephraim.

9 Ben-dekar in Makaz, Shaalbim, Beth-shemesh, Elon, and Beth-hanan.

10 Ben-hesed in Aruboth; he had charge also of Socoh and all the land of Hepher.

11 Ben-abinadab, who had married Solomon's daughter Taphath, in all the district of Dor.

12 Baana son of Ahilud in Taanach and Megiddo, all Beth-shean as far as Abel-meholah beside Zartanah, and from Beth-shean below Jezreel as far as Jokmeam.

13 Ben-geber in Ramoth-gilead, including the tent-villages of Jair son of Manasseh in Gilead and the region of Argob in Bashan, sixty large walled cities with gate-bars of bronze.

14 Ahinadab son of Iddo in Mahanaim.

15 Ahimaaz in Naphtali; he also had married a daughter of Solomon, Basmath.

16 Baanah son of Hushai in Asher and Aloth.

17 Jehoshaphat son of Paruah in Issachar.

18 Shimei son of Elah in Benjamin.

19 Geber son of Uri in Gilead, the land of Sihon king of the Amorites and of Og king of Bashan.
In addition, one governor over all the governors*ᵉ* in the land.

20 The people of Judah and Israel were countless as the sands of the sea; 21 they ate and they drank, and enjoyed life. Solomon ruled over all the kingdoms from the river Euphrates to Philistia and as far as the frontier of Egypt; they paid tribute and were subject to him all his life.

22 Solomon's provision for one day was thirty kor of flour and sixty kor 23 of meal, ten fat oxen and twenty oxen from the pastures and a hundred 24 sheep, as well as stags, gazelles, roebucks, and fattened fowl. For he was paramount over all the land west of the Euphrates from Tiphsah to Gaza, 25 ruling all the kings west of the river; and he enjoyed peace on all sides. All

*ᵃ Verses 2–6: cp. 2 Sam. 8. 16–18; 20. 23–26; 1 Chr. 18. 15–17.* *ᵇ In . . . calendar: prob. rdg.; Heb. Elihoreph.* *ᶜ Prob. rdg., cp. 1 Chr. 18. 16; Heb. Adjutants-general.* *ᵈ Prob. rdg.; Heb. sons.* *ᵉ over . . . governors: prob. rdg.; Heb. om.*

through his reign Judah and Israel continued at peace, every man under his own vine and fig-tree, from Dan to Beersheba.

Solomon had forty thousand chariot-horses in his stables and twelve 26 thousand cavalry horses.

The regional governors, each for a month in turn, supplied provisions 27 for King Solomon and for all who came to his table; they never fell short in their deliveries. They provided also barley and straw, each according to 28 his duty, for the horses and chariot-horses where it was required.

And God gave Solomon depth of wisdom and insight, and under- 29 standing as wide as the sand on the sea-shore, so that Solomon's wisdom 30 surpassed that of all the men of the east and of all Egypt. For he was wiser 31 than any man, wiser than Ethan the Ezrahite, and Heman, Kalcol, and Darda, the sons of Mahol; his fame spread among all the surrounding nations. He uttered three thousand proverbs, and his songs numbered a 32 thousand and five. He discoursed of trees, from the cedar of Lebanon down 33 to the marjoram that grows out of the wall, of beasts and birds, of reptiles and fishes. Men of all races came to listen to the wisdom of Solomon, and 34 from all the kings of the earth who had heard of his wisdom he received gifts.

WHEN HIRAM KING OF TYRE heard that Solomon had been anointed 5 king in his father's place, he sent envoys to him, because he had always been a friend of David. Solomon sent this answer to Hiram: 'You know 2ᵃ 3 that my father David could not build a house in honour of the name of the LORD his God, because he was surrounded by armed nations until the LORD made them subject to him. But now on every side the LORD my God 4 has given me peace; there is no one to oppose me, I fear no attack. So I 5 propose to build a house in honour of the name of the LORD my God, following the promise given by the LORD to my father David: "Your son whom I shall set on the throne in your place will build the house in honour of my name." If therefore you will now give orders that cedars be 6 felled and brought from Lebanon, my men will work with yours, and I will pay you for your men whatever sum you fix; for, as you know, we have none so skilled at felling timber as your Sidonians.'

When Hiram received Solomon's message, he was greatly pleased and 7 said, 'Blessed be the LORD today who has given David a wise son to rule over this great people.' And he sent this reply to Solomon: 'I have received 8 your message. In this matter of timber, both cedar and pine, I will do all you wish. My men shall bring down the logs from Lebanon to the sea and 9 I will make them up into rafts to be floated to the place you appoint; I will have them broken up there and you can remove them. You, on your part, will meet my wishes if you provide the food for my household.' So Hiram 10 kept Solomon supplied with all the cedar and pine that he wanted, and 11 Solomon supplied Hiram with twenty thousand kor of wheat as food for his household and twenty kor of oil of pounded olives; Solomon gave this yearly to Hiram. (The LORD had given Solomon wisdom as he had 12 promised him; there was peace between Hiram and Solomon and they

ᵃ *Verses 2-11 : cp. 2 Chr. 2. 3-16.*

13 concluded an alliance.) King Solomon raised a forced levy from the whole
14 of Israel amounting to thirty thousand men. He sent them to Lebanon in
monthly relays of ten thousand, so that the men spent one month in
Lebanon and two at home; Adoniram was superintendent of the whole
15 levy. Solomon had also seventy thousand hauliers and eighty thousand
16 quarrymen, apart from the three thousand three hundred foremen in
17 charge of the work who superintended the labourers. By the king's orders
they quarried huge, massive blocks for laying the foundation of the LORD's
18 house in hewn stone. Solomon's and Hiram's builders and the Gebalites
shaped the blocks and prepared both timber and stone for the building of
the house.

6 1ᵃ    It was in the four hundred and eightieth year after the Israelites had
come out of Egypt, in the fourth year of Solomon's reign over Israel, in
the second month of that year, the month of Ziv, that he began to build
the house of the LORD.

2    The house which King Solomon built for the LORD was sixty cubits
3 long by twenty cubits broad, and its height was thirty cubits. The vestibule
in front of the sanctuary was twenty cubits long, spanning the whole
breadth of the house, while it projected ten cubits in front of the house;
4 5 and he furnished the house with embrasures. Then he built a terrace
against its wall round both the sanctuary and the inner shrine. He made
6 arcades all round: the lowest arcade was five cubits in depth, the middle
six, and the highest seven; for he made rebates all round the outside of
the main wall so that the bearer beams might not be set into the walls.
7 In the building of the house, only blocks of undressed stone direct from
the quarry were used; no hammer or axe or any iron tool whatever was
heard in the house while it was being built.
8    The entrance to the lowest arcade was in the right-hand corner of the
house; there was access by a spiral stairway from that to the middle arcade,
9-10 and from the middle arcade to the highest. So he built the house and finished
it, having constructed the terrace five cubits high against the whole
building, braced the house with struts of cedar and roofed it with beams
and coffering of cedar.
11 12    Then the word of the LORD came to Solomon, saying, 'As for this house
which you are building, if you are obedient to my ordinances and conform
to my precepts and loyally observe all my commands, then I will fulfil my
13 promise to you, the promise I gave to your father David, and I will dwell
among the Israelites and never forsake my people Israel.'
14 15    So Solomon built the LORD's house and finished it. He lined the inner
walls of the house with cedar boards, covering the interior from floor to
16 rafters with wood; the floor he laid with boards of pine. In the innermost
part of the house he partitioned off a space of twenty cubits with cedar
boards from floor to rafters and made of it an inner shrine, to be the Most
17 18 Holy Place. The sanctuary in front of this was forty cubits long. The cedar
inside the house was carved with open flowers and gourds; all was cedar,
no stone was left visible.
19    He prepared an inner shrine in the furthest recesses of the house to

ᵃ *Verses 1–3: cp. 2 Chr. 3. 2–4.*

receive the Ark of the Covenant of the LORD. This inner shrine was twenty 20 cubits square and it stood twenty cubits high; he overlaid it with red gold and made an altar of cedar. And Solomon overlaid the inside of the house 21 with red gold and drew a Veil*a* with golden chains across in front of the inner shrine.*b* The whole house he overlaid with gold until it was all 22 covered; and the whole of the altar by the inner shrine he overlaid with gold.

In the inner shrine he made two cherubim of wild olive, each ten cubits 23*c* high. Each wing of the cherubim was five cubits long, and from wing-tip 24 to wing-tip was ten cubits. Similarly the second cherub measured ten 25 cubits; the two cherubim were alike in size and shape, and each ten cubits 26 high. He put the cherubim within the shrine at the furthest recesses and 27 their wings were outspread, so that a wing of the one cherub touched the wall on one side and a wing of the other touched the wall on the other side, and their other wings met in the middle; and he overlaid the cherubim 28 with gold.

Round all the walls of the house he carved figures of cherubim, palm- 29 trees, and open flowers, both in the inner chamber and in the outer. The 30 floor of the house he overlaid with gold, both in the inner chamber and in the outer. At the entrance to the inner shrine he made a double door of 31 wild olive; the pilasters and the*d* door-posts were pentagonal. The doors 32 were of wild olive, and he carved cherubim, palms, and open flowers on them, overlaying them with gold and hammering the gold upon the cherubim and the palms. Similarly for the doorway of the sanctuary he 33 made a square frame of wild olive and a double door of pine, each leaf 34 having two swivel-pins. On them he carved cherubim, palms, and open 35 flowers, overlaying them evenly with gold over the carving.

He built the inner court with three courses of dressed stone and one 36 course of lengths of cedar.

In the fourth year of Solomon's reign the foundation of the house of 37 the LORD was laid, in the month of Ziv; and in the eleventh year, in the 38 month of Bul, which is the eighth month, the house was finished in all its details according to the specification. It had taken seven years to build.

Solomon had been engaged on his building for thirteen years by the 7 time he had finished it. He built the House of the Forest of Lebanon, a 2 hundred cubits long, fifty broad, and thirty high, constructed of four rows of cedar columns, over which were laid lengths of cedar. It had a cedar roof, 3 extending over the beams, which rested on the columns, fifteen in each row; and the number of the beams was forty-five. There were three rows of 4 window-frames, and the windows corresponded to each other at three levels. All the doorways and the windows had square frames, and window 5 corresponded to window at three levels.

He made also the colonnade, fifty cubits long and thirty broad,*e* with 6 a cornice above.

He built the Hall of Judgement, the hall containing the throne where he 7 was to give judgement; this was panelled in cedar from floor to rafters.

*a* a Veil: *prob. rdg.; Heb. om.*      *b* *Prob. rdg.; Heb. adds* and overlaid it with gold.
*c* *Verses 23–28*: cp. 2 Chr. 3. *10–13.*      *d* and the: *prob. rdg.; Heb. om.*      *e* *Prob. rdg.; Heb. adds* and a colonnade and pillars in front of them.

8 His own house where he was to reside, in a court set back from the colonnade, and the house he made for Pharaoh's daughter whom he had married, were constructed like the hall.

9 All these were made of heavy blocks of stone, hewn to measure and trimmed with the saw on the inner and outer sides, from foundation to 10 coping and from the court of the house*a* as far as the great court. At the base were heavy stones, massive blocks, some ten and some eight cubits 11 12 in size, and above were heavy stones dressed to measure, and cedar. The great court had three courses of dressed stone all around and a course of lengths of cedar; so had the inner court of the house of the LORD, and so had the vestibule of the house.

13 14 King Solomon fetched from Tyre Hiram, the son of a widow of the tribe of Naphtali. His father, a native of Tyre, had been a worker in bronze, and he himself was a man of great skill and ingenuity, versed in every kind of craftsmanship in bronze. Hiram came to King Solomon and executed all his works.

15*b* He cast in a mould the two bronze pillars. One stood eighteen cubits high and it took a cord twelve cubits long to go round it; it was hollow, and 16 the metal was four fingers thick.*c* The second pillar was the same. He made two capitals of solid copper to set on the tops of the pillars, each capital five 17 cubits high. He made two bands of ornamental network, in festoons of chain-work, for the capitals on the tops of the pillars, a band of network 18 for each capital. Then he made pomegranates in two rows all round on top of the ornamental network of the one pillar; he did the same with the 19 other capital. (The capitals at the tops of the pillars in the vestibule were 20 shaped like lilies and were four cubits high.) Upon the capitals at the tops of the two pillars, immediately above the cushion, which was beyond the network upwards, were two hundred pomegranates in rows all round on 21 the two capitals.*d* Then he erected the pillars at the vestibule of the sanctuary. When he had erected the pillar on the right side, he named it Jachin; *e* 22 and when he had erected the one on the left side, he named it Boaz.*f* On the tops of the pillars was lily-work. Thus the work of the pillars was finished.

23*g* He then made the Sea of cast metal; it was round in shape, the diameter from rim to rim being ten cubits; it stood five cubits high, and it took a line 24 thirty cubits long to go round it. All round the Sea on the outside under its rim, completely surrounding the thirty*h* cubits of its circumference, were 25 two rows of gourds, cast in one piece with the Sea itself. It was mounted on twelve oxen, three facing north, three west, three south, and three east, 26 their hind quarters turned inwards; the Sea rested on top of them. Its thickness was a hand-breadth; its rim was made like that of a cup, shaped like the calyx of a lily; it held two thousand bath of water.

27 He also made the ten trolleys of bronze; each trolley was four cubits long, 28 four wide, and three high. This was the construction of the trolleys. They

---

*a Prob. rdg., cp. verse 12; Heb. from outside.*   *b Verses 15–21: cp. 2 Chr. 3. 15–17.*
*c it was ... thick: prob. rdg., cp. Jer. 52. 21; Heb. om.*   *d the two capitals: prob. rdg.; Heb. the second capital.*   *e Or Jachun, meaning It shall stand.*   *f Or Booz, meaning In strength.*   *g Verses 23–26: cp. 2 Chr. 4. 2–5.*   *h Prob. rdg.; Heb. ten.*

had panels set in frames; on these panels were portrayed lions, oxen, and  29
cherubim, and similarly on the frames. Above and below the lions, oxen,
and cherubim[a] were fillets of hammered work of spiral design. Each  30
trolley had four bronze wheels with axles of bronze; it also had four
flanges and handles beneath the laver, and these handles were of cast
metal with a spiral design on their sides. The opening for the basin was set  31
within a crown which projected one cubit; the opening was round with
a level edge,[b] and it had decorations in relief. (The panels of the trolleys
were square, not round.) The four wheels were beneath the panels, and  32
the wheel-forks were made in one piece with the trolleys; the height of
each wheel was a cubit and a half. The wheels were constructed like those  33
of a chariot, their axles, hubs, spokes, and felloes being all of cast metal.
The four handles were at the four corners of each trolley, of one piece with  34
the trolley. At the top of the trolley there was a circular band half a cubit  35
high; the struts and panels on[c] the trolley were of one piece with it. On  36
the plates, that is on the panels,[d] he carved cherubim, lions, and palm-
trees, wherever there was a blank space, with spiral work all round it.
This is how the ten trolleys were made; all of them were cast alike, having  37
the same size and the same shape.

He then made ten bronze basins, each holding forty bath and measuring  38
four cubits; there was a basin for each of the ten trolleys. He put five  39
trolleys on the right side of the house and five on the left side; and he put
the Sea in the south-east corner of it.

Hiram made also the pots, the shovels, and the tossing-bowls. So he  40[e]
finished all the work which he had undertaken for King Solomon on the
house of the LORD: the two pillars; the two bowl-shaped capitals on the  41
tops of the pillars; the two ornamental networks to cover the two bowl-
shaped capitals on the tops of the pillars; the four hundred pomegranates  42
for the two networks, two rows of pomegranates for each network, to cover
the bowl-shaped capitals on the two pillars; the ten trolleys and the ten  43
basins on the trolleys; the one Sea and the twelve oxen which supported  44
it; the pots, the shovels, and the tossing-bowls—all these objects in the  45
house of the LORD which Hiram made for King Solomon being of bronze,
burnished work. In the Plain of the Jordan the king cast them, in the  46
foundry between Succoth and Zarethan.

Solomon put all these objects in their places; so great was the quantity  47
of bronze used in their making that the weight of it was beyond all reckoning. He made also all the furnishings for the house of the LORD: the golden  48
altar and the golden table upon which was set the Bread of the Presence;
the lamp-stands of red gold, five on the right side and five on the left side  49
of the inner shrine; the flowers, lamps, and tongs, of gold; the cups,  50
snuffers, tossing-bowls, saucers, and firepans, of red gold; and the panels
for the doors of the inner sanctuary, the Most Holy Place, and for the doors
of the house,[f] of gold.

When all the work which King Solomon did for the house of the LORD  51

[a] *and cherubim: prob. rdg.; Heb. om.*    [b] *Prob. rdg.; Heb. adds* a cubit and a half (*cp.*
*verse 32*).    [c] *Prob. rdg.; Heb. adds* the head of.    [d] *Prob. rdg.; Heb. adds* its struts.
[e] *Verses 40–51: cp. 2 Chr. 4. 11—5. 1.*    [f] *Prob. rdg.; Heb. adds* for the temple.

was completed, he brought in the sacred treasures of his father David, the silver, the gold, and the vessels, and deposited them in the storehouses of the house of the LORD.

8 1[a] THEN SOLOMON SUMMONED THE ELDERS of Israel, all the heads of the tribes who were chiefs of families in Israel, to assemble in Jerusalem, in order to bring up the Ark of the Covenant of the LORD from the City of

2 David, which is called Zion. All the men of Israel assembled in King Solomon's presence at the pilgrim-feast in the month Ethanim, the

3 seventh month. When the elders of Israel had all come, the priests took

4 the Ark of the LORD and carried it up with the Tent of the Presence and all the sacred furnishings of the Tent: it was the priests and the Levites

5 together who carried them up. King Solomon and the whole congregation of Israel, assembled with him before the Ark, sacrificed sheep and oxen

6 in numbers past counting or reckoning. Then the priests brought in the Ark of the Covenant of the LORD to its place, the inner shrine of the house,

7 the Most Holy Place, beneath the wings of the cherubim. The cherubim spread their wings over the place of the Ark; they formed a screen above

8 the Ark and its poles. The poles projected, and their ends could be seen from the Holy Place immediately in front of the inner shrine, but from

9 nowhere else outside; they are there to this day. There was nothing inside the Ark but the two tablets of stone which Moses had deposited there at Horeb, the tablets of the covenant which the LORD made with the Israelites when they left Egypt.

10 Then the priests came out of the Holy Place, since the cloud was filling

11 the house of the LORD, and they could not continue to minister because of

12[b] it, for the glory of the LORD filled his house. And Solomon said:

> O LORD who hast set the sun in heaven,
>> but hast chosen to dwell in thick darkness,
13 >here have I built thee a lofty house,
>> a habitation for thee to occupy for ever.

14 And as they stood waiting, the king turned round and blessed all the

15 assembly of Israel in these words: 'Blessed be the LORD the God of Israel who spoke directly to my father David and has himself fulfilled his pro-

16 mise. For he said, "From the day when I brought my people Israel out of Egypt, I chose no city out of all the tribes of Israel where I should build a house for my Name to be there, but I chose David to be over my people

17 Israel." My father David had in mind to build a house in honour of the

18 name of the LORD the God of Israel, but the LORD said to him, "You purposed to build a house in honour of my name; and your purpose was

19 good. Nevertheless, you shall not build it; but the son who is to be born to

20 you, he shall build the house in honour of my name." The LORD has now fulfilled his promise: I have succeeded my father David and taken his place on the throne of Israel, as the LORD promised; and I have built the

21 house in honour of the name of the LORD the God of Israel. I have assigned

*a Verses 1–9: cp. 2 Chr. 5. 2–10.*    *b Verses 12–50: cp. 2 Chr. 6. 1–39.*

therein a place for the Ark containing the Covenant of the LORD, which he made with our forefathers when he brought them out of Egypt.'

Then Solomon, standing in front of the altar of the LORD in the presence 22 of the whole assembly of Israel, spread out his hands towards heaven and said, 'O LORD God of Israel, there is no god like thee in heaven above or 23 on earth beneath, keeping covenant with thy servants and showing them constant love while they continue faithful to thee in heart and soul. Thou 24 hast kept thy promise to thy servant David my father; by thy deeds this day thou hast fulfilled what thou didst say to him in words. Now therefore, 25 O LORD God of Israel, keep this promise of thine to thy servant David my father: "You shall never want for a man appointed by me to sit on the throne of Israel, if only your sons look to their ways and walk before me as you have walked before me." And now, O God of Israel, let the words 26 which thou didst speak to thy servant David my father be confirmed.

'But can God indeed dwell on earth? Heaven itself, the highest heaven, 27 cannot contain thee; how much less this house that I have built! Yet 28 attend to the prayer and the supplication of thy servant, O LORD my God, listen to the cry and the prayer which thy servant utters this day, that thine 29 eyes may ever be upon this house night and day, this place of which thou didst say, "My Name shall be there"; so mayest thou hear thy servant when he prays towards this place. Hear the supplication of thy servant and 30 of thy people Israel when they pray towards this place. Hear thou in heaven thy dwelling and, when thou hearest, forgive.

'When a man wrongs his neighbour and he is adjured to take an oath, 31 and the adjuration is made before thy altar in this house, then do thou hear 32 in heaven and act: be thou thy servants' judge, condemning the guilty man and bringing his deeds upon his own head, acquitting the innocent and rewarding him as his innocence may deserve.

'When thy people Israel are defeated by an enemy because they have 33 sinned against thee, and they turn back to thee, confessing thy name and making their prayer and supplication to thee in this house, do thou hear 34 in heaven; forgive the sin of thy people Israel and restore them to the land which thou gavest to their forefathers.

'When the heavens are shut up and there is no rain because thy servant 35 and thy people Israel have sinned against thee, and when they pray towards this place, confessing thy name and forsaking their sin when they feel thy punishment, do thou hear in heaven and forgive their sin; so mayest 36 thou teach them the good way which they should follow; and grant rain to thy land which thou hast given to thy people as their own possession.

'If there is famine in the land, or pestilence, or black blight or red, or 37 locusts new-sloughed or fully grown; or if their enemies besiege them in any of their cities; or if plague or sickness befall them, then hear the prayer 38 or supplication of every man among thy people Israel, as each one, prompted by the remorse of his own heart, spreads out his hands towards this house: hear it in heaven thy dwelling and forgive, and act. And, as thou knowest 39 a man's heart, reward him according to his deeds, for thou alone knowest the hearts of all men; and so they will fear thee all their lives in the land 40 thou gavest to our forefathers.

385

41 'The foreigner too, the man who does not belong to thy people Israel,
42 but has come from a distant land because of thy fame (for men shall hear
of thy great fame and thy strong hand and arm outstretched), when he
43 comes and prays towards this house, hear in heaven thy dwelling and
respond to the call which the foreigner makes to thee, so that like thy
people Israel all peoples of the earth may know thy fame and fear thee, and
learn that this house which I have built bears thy name.

44 'When thy people go to war with an enemy, wherever thou dost send
them, when they pray to the LORD, turning towards this city which thou
hast chosen and towards this house which I have built in honour of thy
45 name, do thou in heaven hear their prayer and supplication, and grant
them justice.

46 'Should they sin against thee (and what man is free from sin?) and
shouldst thou in thy anger give them over to an enemy, who carries them
47 captive to his own land, far or near; if in the land of their captivity they
learn their lesson and make supplication again to thee in that land and say,
48 "We have sinned and acted perversely and wickedly", if they turn back to
thee with heart and soul in the land of their captors, and pray to thee,
turning towards their land which thou gavest to their forefathers and
towards this city which thou didst choose and this house which I have
49 built in honour of thy name; then in heaven thy dwelling do thou hear
50 their prayer and supplication, and grant them justice. Forgive thy people
their sins and transgressions against thee; put pity for them in their
51 captors' hearts. For they are thy possession, thy people whom thou didst
52 bring out of Egypt, from the smelting-furnace, and so thine eyes are ever
open to the entreaty of thy servant and of thy people Israel, and thou dost
53 hear whenever they call to thee. Thou thyself hast singled them out from
all the peoples of the earth to be thy possession; so thou didst promise
through thy servant Moses when thou didst bring our forefathers from
Egypt, O Lord GOD.'

54 When Solomon had finished this prayer and supplication to the LORD,
he rose from before the altar of the LORD, where he had been kneeling with
55 his hands spread out to heaven, stood up and in a loud voice blessed the
56 whole assembly of Israel: 'Blessed be the LORD who has given his people
Israel rest, as he promised: not one of the promises he made through his
57 servant Moses has failed. The LORD our God be with us as he was with
58 our forefathers; may he never leave us nor forsake us. May he turn our
hearts towards him, that we may conform to all his ways, observing his
commandments, statutes, and judgements, as he commanded our fore-
59 fathers. And may the words of my supplication to the LORD be with the
LORD our God day and night, that, as the need arises day by day, he may
60 grant justice to his servant and justice to his people Israel. So all the
61 peoples of the earth will know that the LORD is God, he and no other, and
you will be perfect in loyalty to the LORD our God as you are this day,
conforming to his statutes and observing his commandments.'

62 When the king and all Israel came to offer sacrifices before the LORD,
63 Solomon offered as shared-offerings to the LORD twenty-two thousand
oxen and a hundred and twenty thousand sheep; thus it was that the king

and the Israelites dedicated the house of the LORD. On that day also the  64 <sup>a</sup>
king consecrated the centre of the court which lay in front <sup>b</sup> of the house of
the LORD; there he offered the whole-offering, the grain-offering, and the
fat portions of the shared-offerings, because the bronze altar which stood
before the LORD was too small to take them all, the whole-offering, the
grain-offering, and the fat portions of the shared-offerings.

So Solomon and all Israel with him, a great assembly from Lebo-  65
hamath to the Torrent of Egypt, celebrated the pilgrim-feast at that time
before the LORD our God for seven days. On the eighth day he dismissed  66
the people; and they blessed the king, and went home happy and glad at
heart for all the prosperity granted by the LORD to his servant David and
to his people Israel.

WHEN SOLOMON HAD FINISHED the house of the LORD and the royal  9 1 <sup>c</sup>
palace and all the plans for building on which he had set his heart, the LORD  2
appeared to him a second time, as he had appeared to him at Gibeon. The  3
LORD said to him, 'I have heard the prayer and supplication which you
have offered me; I have consecrated this house which you have built, to
receive my Name for all time, and my eyes and my heart shall be fixed on
it for ever. And if you, on your part, live in my sight as your father David  4
lived, in integrity and uprightness, doing all I command you and observing
my statutes and my judgements, then I will establish your royal throne  5
over Israel for ever, as I promised your father David when I said, "You
shall never want for a man upon the throne of Israel." But if you or your  6
sons turn back from following me and do not observe my commandments
and my statutes which I have set before you, and if you go and serve other
gods and prostrate yourselves before them, then I will cut off Israel from  7
the land which I gave them; I will renounce this house which I have consecrated in honour of my name, and Israel shall become a byword and an
object lesson among all peoples. And this house will become a ruin; every  8
passer-by will be appalled and gasp at the sight of it; and they will ask,
"Why has the LORD so treated this land and this house?" The answer will  9
be, "Because they forsook the LORD their God, who brought their forefathers out of Egypt, and clung to other gods, prostrating themselves
before them and serving them; that is why the LORD has brought this great
evil on them." '

Solomon had taken twenty years to build the two houses, the house of  10 <sup>d</sup>
the LORD and the royal palace. Hiram king of Tyre had supplied him with  11
all the timber, both cedar and pine, and all the gold, that he desired, and
King Solomon gave Hiram twenty cities in the land of Galilee. But when  12
Hiram went from Tyre to inspect the cities which Solomon had given him,
they did not satisfy him, and he said, 'What kind of cities are these you have  13
given me, my brother?' And so he called them the Land of Cabul,<sup>e</sup> the
name they still bear. Hiram sent a hundred and twenty talents of gold to  14
the king.

This is the record of the forced labour which King Solomon conscripted  15

<sup>a</sup> *Verses 64–66 : cp. 2 Chr. 7. 7–10.*     <sup>b</sup> *Or to the east.*     <sup>c</sup> *Verses 1–9 : cp. 2 Chr. 7.*
*11–22.*     <sup>d</sup> *Verses 10–28 : cp. 2 Chr. 8. 1–18.*     <sup>e</sup> *That is Sterile Land.*

to build the house of the Lord, his own palace, the Millo, the wall of
16 Jerusalem, and Hazor, Megiddo, and Gezer. Gezer had been attacked and
captured by Pharaoh king of Egypt, who had burnt it to the ground, put
its Canaanite inhabitants to death, and given it as a marriage gift to his
17 daughter, Solomon's wife; and Solomon rebuilt it. He also built Lower
18 19 Beth-horon, Baalath, and Tamar in the wilderness, as well as all his store-
cities, and the towns where he quartered his chariots and horses; and he
carried out all his cherished plans for building in Jerusalem, in the Lebanon,
20 and throughout his whole dominion. All the survivors of the Amorites,
Hittites, Perizzites, Hivites, and Jebusites, who did not belong to Israel—
21 that is their descendants who survived in the land, wherever the Israelites
had been unable to annihilate them—were employed by Solomon on
22 perpetual forced labour, as they still are. But Solomon put none of the
Israelites to forced labour; they were his fighting men,[a] his captains and
23 lieutenants, and the commanders of his chariots and of his cavalry. The
number of officers in charge of the foremen over Solomon's work was five
hundred and fifty; these superintended the people engaged on the work.
24    Then Solomon brought Pharaoh's daughter up from the City of David
to her own house which he had built for her; later on he built the Millo.
25    Three times a year Solomon used to offer whole-offerings and shared-
offerings on the altar which he had built to the Lord, making smoke-
offerings before the Lord. So he completed the house.
26    King Solomon built a fleet of ships at Ezion-geber, near Eloth[b] on the
27 shore of the Red Sea,[c] in Edom. Hiram sent men of his own to serve with
28 the fleet, experienced seamen, to work with Solomon's men; and they went
to Ophir and brought back four hundred and twenty talents of gold, which
they delivered to King Solomon.

10 1[d] The queen of sheba heard of Solomon's fame[e] and came to test him
2 with hard questions. She arrived in Jerusalem with a very large retinue,
camels laden with spices, gold in great quantity, and precious stones. When
3 she came to Solomon, she told him everything she had in her mind, and
Solomon answered all her questions; not one of them was too abstruse for
4 the king to answer. When the queen of Sheba saw all the wisdom of Sol-
5 omon, the house which he had built, the food on his table, the courtiers
sitting round him, and his attendants standing behind in their livery, his
cupbearers, and the whole-offerings which he used to offer in the house of
6 the Lord, there was no more spirit left in her. Then she said to the king,
'The report which I heard in my own country about you and your wisdom
7 was true, but I did not believe it until I came and saw for myself. Indeed
I was not told half of it; your wisdom and your prosperity go far beyond
8 the report which I had of them. Happy are your wives, happy these courtiers
9 of yours who wait on you every day and hear your wisdom! Blessed be the
Lord your God who has delighted in you and has set you on the throne of
Israel; because he loves Israel for ever, he has made you their king to

---

[a] *Prob. rdg.; Heb. adds* and his servants.     [b] *Or* Elath.     [c] *Or the* Sea of Reeds.
[d] *Verses 1–25: cp. 2 Chr. 9. 1–24.*     [e] *Prob. rdg., cp. 2 Chr. 9. 1; Heb. adds* to the
name of the Lord.

maintain law and justice.' Then she gave the king a hundred and twenty 10 talents of gold, spices in great abundance, and precious stones. Never again came such a quantity of spices as the queen of Sheba gave to King Solomon.

Besides all this, Hiram's fleet of ships, which had brought gold from 11 Ophir, brought in also from Ophir cargoes of almug wood and precious stones. The king used the wood to make stools for the house of the LORD 12 and for the royal palace, as well as harps and lutes for the singers. No such almug wood has ever been imported or even seen since that time.

And King Solomon gave the queen of Sheba all she desired, whatever 13 she asked, in addition to all that he gave her of his royal bounty. So she departed and returned with her retinue to her own land.

Now the weight of gold which Solomon received yearly was six hundred 14 and sixty-six talents, in addition to the tolls levied by the customs officers 15 and profits on foreign trade, and the tribute of *a* the kings of Arabia and the regional governors.

King Solomon made two hundred shields of beaten gold, and six hundred 16 shekels of gold went to the making of each one; he also made three hundred 17 bucklers of beaten gold, and three minas of gold went to the making of each buckler. The king put these into the House of the Forest of Lebanon.

The king also made a great throne of ivory and overlaid it with fine gold. 18 Six steps led up to the throne; at the back of the throne there was the head 19 of a calf. There were arms on each side of the seat, with a lion standing beside each of them, and twelve lions stood on the six steps, one at either end 20 of each step. Nothing like it had ever been made for any monarch. All Sol- 21 omon's drinking vessels were of gold, and all the plate in the House of the Forest of Lebanon was of red gold; no silver was used, for it was reckoned of no value in the days of Solomon. The king had a fleet of merchantmen 22 at sea with Hiram's fleet; once every three years this fleet of merchantmen came home, bringing gold and silver, ivory, apes and monkeys.

Thus King Solomon outdid all the kings of the earth in wealth and 23 wisdom, and all the world courted him, to hear the wisdom which God 24 had put in his heart. Each brought his gift with him, vessels of silver and 25 gold, garments, perfumes and spices, horses and mules, so much year by year.

And Solomon got together many chariots and horses; he had fourteen 26 *b* hundred chariots and twelve thousand horses, and he stabled some in the chariot-towns and kept others at hand in Jerusalem. The king made silver 27 as common in Jerusalem as stones, and cedar as plentiful as sycomore-fig in the Shephelah. Horses were imported from Egypt and Coa for Solomon; 28 the royal merchants obtained them from Coa by purchase. Chariots were 29 imported from Egypt for six hundred silver shekels each, and horses for a hundred and fifty; in the same way the merchants obtained them for export from all the kings of the Hittites and the kings of Aram.

King Solomon was a lover of women, and besides Pharaoh's daughter 11 he married many foreign women, Moabite, Ammonite, Edomite, Sidonian, and Hittite, from the nations with whom the LORD had forbidden the 2

*a* and the tribute of: *prob. rdg.; Heb.* and all.     *b Verses 26–29: cp. 2 Chr. 1. 14–17; 9. 25–28.*

Israelites to intermarry, 'because', he said, 'they will entice you to serve
3 their gods.' But Solomon was devoted to them and loved them dearly. He
had seven hundred wives, who were princesses, and three hundred con-
4 cubines, and they turned his heart from the truth. When he grew old, his
wives turned his heart to follow other gods, and he did not remain wholly
5 loyal to the LORD his God as his father David had been. He followed
Ashtoreth, goddess of the Sidonians, and Milcom, the loathsome god of
6 the Ammonites. Thus Solomon did what was wrong in the eyes of the
7 LORD, and was not loyal to the LORD like his father David. He built a
hill-shrine for Kemosh, the loathsome god of Moab, on the height to the
east of Jerusalem, and for Molech, the loathsome god of the Ammonites.
8 Thus he did for the gods to which all his foreign wives burnt offerings and
9 made sacrifices. The LORD was angry with Solomon because his heart had
turned away from the LORD the God of Israel, who had appeared to him
10 twice and had strictly commanded him not to follow other gods; but he
11 disobeyed the LORD's command. The LORD therefore said to Solomon,
'Because you have done this and have not kept my covenant and my
statutes as I commanded you, I will tear the kingdom from you and give
12 it to your servant. Nevertheless, for the sake of your father David I will
13 not do this in your day; I will tear it out of your son's hand. Even so not
the whole kingdom; I will leave him one tribe for the sake of my servant
David and for the sake of Jerusalem, my chosen city.'
14 Then the LORD raised up an adversary for Solomon, Hadad the Edomite,
15 of the royal house of Edom. At the time when David reduced Edom, his
commander-in-chief Joab had destroyed every male in the country when
16 he went into it to bury the slain. He and the armies of Israel remained there
17 for six months, until he had destroyed every male in Edom. Then Hadad,
who was still a boy, fled the country with some of his father's Edomite
18 servants, intending to enter Egypt. They set out from Midian, made their
way to Paran and, taking some men from there, came to Pharaoh king of
Egypt, who assigned Hadad a house and maintenance and made him a
19 grant of land. Hadad found great favour with Pharaoh, who gave him in
20 marriage a sister of Queen Tahpenes his wife. She bore him his son
Genubath; Tahpenes weaned the child in Pharaoh's house, and he lived
21 there along with Pharaoh's children. When Hadad heard in Egypt that
David rested with his forefathers and that his commander-in-chief Joab
was also dead, he said to Pharaoh, 'Let me go so that I may return to my
22 own country.' 'What is it that you find wanting in my country', said
Pharaoh, 'that you want to go back to your own?' 'Nothing,' said Hadad,
25 'but do, pray, let me go.' He remained an adversary for Israel all through
Solomon's reign. This is the harm that Hadad caused: he maintained a
stranglehold on Israel and became king of Edom.
23 Then God raised up another adversary against Solomon, Rezon son of
24 Eliada, who had fled from his master Hadadezer king of Zobah. He gathered
men about him and became a captain of freebooters, who came to Damascus
and occupied it; he became king there.
26ᵃ Jeroboam son of Nebat, one of Solomon's courtiers, an Ephrathite from

ᵃ *Verse 25 transposed to follow verse 22.*

Zeredah, whose widowed mother was named Zeruah, rebelled against the
king. And this is the story of his rebellion. Solomon had built the Millo and 27
closed the breach in the wall of the city of his father David. Now this 28
Jeroboam was a man of great energy; and Solomon, seeing how the young
man worked, had put him in charge of all the labour-gangs in the tribal
district of Joseph. On one occasion Jeroboam had left Jerusalem, and the 29
prophet Ahijah from Shiloh met him on the road. The prophet was wrapped
in a new cloak, and the two of them were alone in the open country. Then 30
Ahijah took hold of the new cloak he was wearing, tore it into twelve pieces
and said to Jeroboam, 'Take ten pieces, for this is the word of the LORD 31
the God of Israel: "I am going to tear the kingdom from the hand of
Solomon and give you ten tribes. But one tribe will remain his, for the sake 32
of my servant David and for the sake of Jerusalem, the city I have chosen
out of all the tribes of Israel. I have done this because Solomon has for- 33
saken me; he has prostrated himself before Ashtoreth goddess of the
Sidonians, Kemosh god of Moab, and Milcom god of the Ammonites,
and has not conformed to my ways. He has not done what is right in my
eyes or observed my statutes and judgements as David his father did.
Nevertheless I will not take the whole kingdom from him, but will maintain 34
his rule as long as he lives, for the sake of my chosen servant David, who
did observe my commandments and statutes. But I will take the kingdom, 35
that is the ten tribes, from his son and give it to you. One tribe I will give 36
to his son, that my servant David may always have a flame burning before
me in Jerusalem, the city which I chose to receive my Name. But I will 37
appoint you to rule over all that you can desire, and to be king over Israel.
If you pay heed to all my commands, if you conform to my ways and do 38
what is right in my eyes, observing my statutes and commandments as my
servant David did, then I will be with you. I will establish your family for
ever as I did for David; I will give Israel to you, and punish David's 39
descendants as they have deserved, but not for ever."'

After this Solomon sought to kill Jeroboam, but he fled to King Shishak 40
in Egypt and remained there till Solomon's death.

The other acts and events of Solomon's reign, and all his wisdom, are 41ᵃ
recorded in the annals of Solomon. The reign of King Solomon in Jerusalem 42
over the whole of Israel lasted forty years. Then he rested with his fore- 43
fathers and was buried in the city of David his father, and he was succeeded
by his son Rehoboam.

## The divided kingdom

Rᴇʜᴏʙᴏᴀᴍ ᴡᴇɴᴛ ᴛᴏ sʜᴇᴄʜᴇᴍ, for all Israel had gone there to make 12 1ᵇ
him king. When Jeroboam son of Nebat, who was still in Egypt, heard 2
of it, he remained there, having taken refuge there to escape King Solomon.
They now recalled him, and he and all the assembly of Israel came to 3
Rehoboam and said, 'Your father laid a cruel yoke upon us; but if you will 4
now lighten the cruel slavery he imposed on us and the heavy yoke he laid

ᵃ *Verses 41–43: cp. 2 Chr. 9. 29–31.* ᵇ *Verses 1–19: cp. 2 Chr. 10. 1–19.*

5 on us, we will serve you.' 'Give me three days,' he said, 'and come back
6 again.' So the people went away. King Rehoboam then consulted the
elders who had been in attendance on his father Solomon while he lived:
7 'What answer do you advise me to give to this people?' And they said, 'If
today you are willing to serve this people, show yourself their servant now
8 and speak kindly to them, and they will be your servants ever after.' But
he rejected the advice which the elders gave him. He next consulted those
9 who had grown up with him, the young men in attendance, and asked
them, 'What answer do you advise me to give to this people's request that
10 I should lighten the yoke which my father laid on them?' The young men
replied, 'Give this answer to the people who say that your father made
their yoke heavy and ask you to lighten it; tell them: "My little finger is
11 thicker than my father's loins. My father laid a heavy yoke on you; I will
make it heavier. My father used the whip on you; but I will use the lash."'
12 Jeroboam and the people all came back to Rehoboam on the third day, as
13 the king had ordered. And the king gave them a harsh answer. He rejected
14 the advice which the elders had given him and spoke to the people as the
young men had advised: 'My father made your yoke heavy; I will make it
15 heavier. My father used the whip on you; but I will use the lash.' So the
king would not listen to the people; for the LORD had given this turn to the
affair, in order that the word he had spoken by Ahijah of Shiloh to Jeroboam
son of Nebat might be fulfilled.
16 When all Israel saw that the king would not listen to them, they answered:

> What share have we in David?
> We have no lot in the son of Jesse.
> Away to your homes, O Israel;
> now see to your own house, David.

17 So Israel went to their homes, and Rehoboam ruled over those Israelites
who lived in the cities of Judah.
18     Then King Rehoboam sent out Adoram, the commander of the forced
levies, but the Israelites stoned him to death; thereupon King Reho-
19 boam mounted his chariot in haste and fled to Jerusalem. From that day
to this, the whole of Israel has been in rebellion against the house of
David.
20     When the men of Israel heard that Jeroboam had returned, they sent
and called him to the assembly and made him king over the whole of
Israel. The tribe of Judah alone followed the house of David.
21*a*     When Rehoboam reached Jerusalem, he assembled all the house of
Judah, the tribe of Benjamin also, a hundred and eighty thousand chosen
22 warriors, to fight against the house of Israel and recover his kingdom. But
23 the word of God came to Shemaiah the man of God: 'Say to Rehoboam
son of Solomon, king of Judah, and to the house of Judah and to Benjamin
24 and the rest of the people, "This is the word of the LORD: You shall not
go up to make war on your kinsmen the Israelites. Return to your homes,
for this is my will."' So they listened to the word of the LORD and returned
home, as the LORD had told them.

*a Verses 21-24: cp. 2 Chr. 11. 1-4.*

THEN JEROBOAM REBUILT SHECHEM in the hill-country of Ephraim  25
and took up residence there; from there he went out and built Penuel. 'As  26
things now stand,' he said to himself, 'the kingdom will revert to the house
of David. If this people go up to sacrifice in the house of the LORD in  27
Jerusalem, it will revive their allegiance to their lord Rehoboam king of
Judah, and they will kill me and return to King Rehoboam.' After giving  28
thought to the matter he made two calves of gold and said to the people,
'It is too much trouble for you to go up to Jerusalem; here are your gods,
Israel, that brought you up from Egypt.' One he set up at Bethel and the  29
other he put at Dan, and this thing became a sin in Israel; the people went  30
to Bethel to worship the one, and all the way to Dan to worship the other.
He set up shrines on the hill-tops also and appointed priests from every  31
class of the people, who did not belong to the Levites. He instituted a  32
pilgrim-feast on the fifteenth day of the eighth month like that in Judah,
and he offered sacrifices upon the altar. This he did at Bethel, sacrificing
to the calves that he had made and compelling the priests of the hill-
shrines, which he had set up, to serve at Bethel. So he went up to the altar  33
that he had made at Bethel on the fifteenth day of the eighth month; there,
in a month of his own choosing, he instituted for the Israelites a pilgrim-
feast and himself went up to the altar to burn the sacrifice.

As Jeroboam stood by the altar to burn the sacrifice, a man of God from  **13**
Judah, moved by the word of the LORD, appeared at Bethel. He inveighed  2
against the altar in the LORD's name, crying out, 'O altar, altar! This is the
word of the LORD: "Listen! A child shall be born to the house of David,
named Josiah. He will sacrifice upon you the priests of the hill-shrines
who make offerings upon you, and he will burn human bones upon you."'
He gave a sign the same day: 'This is the sign which the LORD has ordained:  3
This altar will be rent in pieces and the ashes upon it will be spilt.' When  4
King Jeroboam heard the sentence which the man of God pronounced
against the altar at Bethel, he pointed to him from the altar and said,
'Seize that man!' Immediately the hand which he had pointed at him
became paralysed, so that he could not draw it back. The altar too was rent  5
in pieces and the ashes were spilt, in fulfilment of the sign that the man of
God had given at the LORD's command. The king appealed to the man of  6
God to pacify the LORD his God and pray for him that his hand might be
restored. The man of God did as he asked; his hand was restored and
became as it had been before. Then the king said to the man of God, 'Come  7
home and take refreshment at my table, and let me give you a present.' But  8
the man of God answered, 'If you were to give me half your house, I would
not enter it with you: I will eat and drink nothing in this place, for the  9
LORD's command to me was to eat and drink nothing, and not to go back
by the way I came.' So he went back another way; he did not return by the  10
road he had taken to Bethel.

At that time there was an aged prophet living in Bethel. His sons came  11
and recounted to him all that the man of God had done in Bethel that day;
they also told their father what he had said to the king. Their father said to  12
them, 'Which road did he take?' They pointed out the road taken by the
man of God who had come from Judah. He said to his sons, 'Saddle an  13

14 ass for me.' They saddled the ass, and he mounted it and went after the man of God. He found him seated under a terebinth and said to him, 'Are you the man of God who came from Judah?' And he said, 'Yes, I am.'

15 16 'Come home and eat with me', said the prophet. 'I cannot go back with you or enter your house,' said the other; 'I can neither eat nor drink with

17 you in this place, for it was told me by the word of the LORD: "You shall eat and drink nothing there, nor shall you go back the way you came."'

18 And the old man said to him, 'I also am a prophet, as you are; and an angel commanded me by the word of the LORD to bring you home with me to

19 eat and drink with me.' He was lying; but the man of Judah went back

20 with him and ate and drank in his house. While they were still seated at table the word of the LORD came to the prophet who had brought him back,

21 and he cried out to the man of God from Judah, 'This is the word of the LORD: "You have defied the word of the LORD your God and have not

22 obeyed his command; you have come back to eat and to drink in the place where he forbade it; therefore your body shall not be laid in the grave of your forefathers."'

23 After they had eaten and drunk, he saddled an ass for the prophet whom

24 he had brought back. As he went on his way a lion met him and killed him, and his body was left lying in the road, with the ass and the lion both

25 standing beside it. Some passers-by saw the body lying in the road and the lion standing beside it, and they brought the news to the city where the old

26 prophet lived. When the prophet who had caused him to break his journey heard it, he said, 'It is the man of God who defied the word of the LORD. The LORD has given him to the lion, and it has broken his neck and killed

27 him in fulfilment of the word of the LORD.' He told his sons to saddle an

28 ass and, when they had saddled it, he set out and found the body lying in the road with the ass and the lion standing beside it; the lion had neither

29 devoured the body nor broken the back of the ass. Then the prophet lifted the body of the man of God, laid it on the ass and brought it back to his

30 own city to mourn over it and bury it. He laid the body in his own grave

31 and they mourned for him, saying, 'My brother, my brother!' After burying him, he said to his sons, 'When I die, bury me in the grave where the

32 man of God lies buried; lay my bones beside his; for the sentence which he pronounced at the LORD's command against the altar in Bethel and all the hill-shrines of Samaria shall be carried out.'

33 After this Jeroboam still did not abandon his evil ways but went on appointing priests for the hill-shrines from all classes of the people; any man who offered himself he would consecrate to be priest of a hill-shrine.

34 By doing this he brought guilt upon his own house and doomed it to utter destruction.

14 1 2 At that time Jeroboam's son Abijah fell ill, and Jeroboam said to his wife, 'Come now, disguise yourself so that people may not be able to recognize you as my wife, and go to Shiloh. Ahijah the prophet is there, the man who

3 said I was to be king over this people. Take with you ten loaves, some raisins, and a flask of syrup, and go to him; he will tell you what will happen to the

4 child.' Jeroboam's wife did so; she set off at once for Shiloh and came to Ahijah's house. Now Ahijah could not see, for his eyes were fixed in the

blindness of old age, and the LORD had said to him, 'The wife of Jeroboam  5
is on her way to consult you about her son, who is ill; you shall give her
such and such an answer.' When she came in, concealing who she was, and  6
Ahijah heard her footsteps at the door, he said, 'Come in, wife of Jeroboam.
Why conceal who you are? I have heavy news for you. Go and tell Jeroboam:  7
"This is the word of the LORD the God of Israel: I raised you out of the
people and appointed you prince over my people Israel; I tore away the  8
kingdom from the house of David and gave it to you; but you have not
been like my servant David, who kept my commands and followed me
with his whole heart, doing only what was right in my eyes. You have out-  9
done all your predecessors in wickedness; you have provoked me to anger
by making for yourself other gods and images of cast metal; and you have
turned your back on me. For this I will bring disaster on the house of  10
Jeroboam and I will destroy them all, every mother's son, whether still
under the protection of the family or not, and I will sweep away the house
of Jeroboam in Israel, as a man sweeps up dung until none is left. Those  11
of that house who die in the city shall be food for the dogs, and those
who die in the country shall be food for the birds. It is the word of the
LORD."

'You must go home now; the moment you set foot in the city, the child  12
will die. All Israel will mourn for him and bury him; he alone of all Jero-  13
boam's family will have proper burial, because in him alone could the LORD
the God of Israel find anything good. Then the LORD will set up a king  14
over Israel who shall put an end to the house of Jeroboam. This first; and
what next? The LORD will strike Israel, till it trembles like a reed in the  15
water; he will uproot its people from this good land which he gave to their
forefathers and scatter them beyond the Euphrates, because they have
made their sacred poles and provoked the LORD's anger. And he will  16
abandon Israel for the sins that Jeroboam has committed and has led
Israel to commit.' Jeroboam's wife went home at once to Tirzah and, as  17
she crossed the threshold of the house, the boy died. They buried him, and  18
all Israel mourned over him; and thus the word of the LORD was fulfilled
which he had spoken through his servant Ahijah the prophet.

The other events of Jeroboam's reign, in war and peace, are recorded in  19
the annals of the kings of Israel. He reigned twenty-two years; then he  20
rested with his forefathers and was succeeded by his son Nadab.

IN JUDAH REHOBOAM SON OF SOLOMON had become king. He was  21
forty-one years old when he came to the throne, and he reigned for seventeen years in Jerusalem, the city which the LORD had chosen out of all the
tribes of Israel to receive his Name. Rehoboam's mother was a woman of
Ammon called Naamah. Judah did what was wrong in the eyes of the LORD,  22
rousing his jealous indignation by the sins they committed, beyond anything that their forefathers had done. They erected hill-shrines, sacred  ‹23
pillars, and sacred poles, on every high hill and under every spreading tree.
Worse still, all over the country there were male prostitutes attached to the  24
shrines, and the people adopted all the abominable practices of the nations
whom the LORD had dispossessed in favour of Israel.

O                                          395

25<sup>a</sup> In the fifth year of Rehoboam's reign Shishak king of Egypt attacked
26 Jerusalem. He removed the treasures of the house of the LORD and of the
royal palace, and seized everything, including all the shields of gold that
27 Solomon had made. King Rehoboam replaced them with bronze shields
and entrusted them to the officers of the escort who guarded the entrance
28 of the royal palace. Whenever the king entered the house of the LORD,
the escort carried them; afterwards they returned them to the guard-
room.

29<sup>b</sup> The other acts and events of Rehoboam's reign are recorded in the annals
30 of the kings of Judah. There was continual fighting between him and
31 Jeroboam. He rested with his forefathers and was buried with them in the
city of David. (His mother was a woman of Ammon, whose name was
Naamah.) He was succeeded by his son Abijam.

**15** In the eighteenth year of the reign of Jeroboam son of Nebat, Abijam
2 became king of Judah. He reigned in Jerusalem for three years; his mother
3 was Maacah granddaughter of Abishalom. All the sins that his father had
committed before him he committed too, nor was he faithful to the LORD
4 his God as his ancestor David had been. But for David's sake the LORD
his God gave him a flame to burn in Jerusalem, by establishing his dynasty
5 and making Jerusalem secure, because David had done what was right in
the eyes of the LORD and had not disobeyed any of his commandments all
7 his life, except in the matter of Uriah the Hittite.<sup>c</sup> The other acts and
events of Abijam's reign are recorded in the annals of the kings of Judah.
8 There was fighting between Abijam and Jeroboam. And Abijam rested
with his forefathers and was buried in the city of David; and he was
succeeded by his son Asa.

9 In the twentieth year of Jeroboam king of Israel, Asa became king of
10 Judah. He reigned in Jerusalem for forty-one years; his grandmother was
11 Maacah granddaughter of Abishalom. Asa did what was right in the eyes
12 of the LORD, like his ancestor David. He expelled from the land the male
prostitutes attached to the shrines and did away with all the idols which
13<sup>d</sup> his predecessors had made. He even deprived his own grandmother
Maacah of her rank as queen mother because she had an obscene object
made for the worship of Asherah; Asa cut it down and burnt it in the gorge
14 of the Kidron. Although the hill-shrines were allowed to remain, Asa
15 himself remained faithful to the LORD all his life. He brought into the house
of the LORD all his father's votive offerings and his own, gold and silver
and sacred vessels.

16 17<sup>e</sup> Asa was at war with Baasha king of Israel all through their reigns. Baasha
king of Israel invaded Judah and fortified Ramah to cut off all access to
18 Asa king of Judah. So Asa took all the gold and silver that remained in the
treasuries of the house of the LORD and of the royal palace, and sent his
servants with them to Ben-hadad son of Tabrimmon, son of Hezion, king
19 of Aram, whose capital was Damascus, with instructions to say, 'There is
an alliance between us, as there was between our fathers. I now send you

---

<sup>a</sup> *Verses 25-28 : cp. 2 Chr. 12. 9-11.* <sup>b</sup> *Verses 29-31 : cp. 2 Chr. 12. 13-16.* <sup>c</sup> *Prob.
rdg.; Heb. adds* (6) There was war between Rehoboam and Jeroboam all his days (*cp.
14. 30*). <sup>d</sup> *Verses 13-15 : cp. 2 Chr. 15. 16-18.* <sup>e</sup> *Verses 17-22 : cp. 2 Chr. 16. 1-6.*

this present of silver and gold; break off your alliance with Baasha king of Israel, so that he may abandon his campaign against me.' Ben-hadad 20 listened willingly to King Asa; he ordered the commanders of his armies to move against the cities of Israel, and they attacked Iyyon, Dan, Abel-beth-maacah, and that part of Kinnereth which marches with the land of Naphtali. When Baasha heard of it, he stopped fortifying Ramah and fell 21 back on Tirzah. Then King Asa issued a proclamation requiring every 22 man in Judah to join in removing the stones of Ramah and the timbers with which Baasha had fortified it; no one was exempted; and he used them to fortify Geba of Benjamin and Mizpah.

All the other events of Asa's reign, his exploits and his achievements, 23$^a$ and the cities he built, are recorded in the annals of the kings of Judah. But in his old age his feet were crippled by disease. He rested with his 24 forefathers and was buried with them in the city of his ancestor David; and he was succeeded by his son Jehoshaphat.

Nadab son of Jeroboam became king of Israel in the second year of Asa 25 king of Judah, and he reigned for two years. He did what was wrong in the 26 eyes of the LORD and followed in his father's footsteps, repeating the sin which he had led Israel to commit. Baasha son of Ahijah, of the house of 27 Issachar, conspired against him and attacked him at Gibbethon, a Philistine city, which Nadab was besieging with all his forces. And Baasha slew 28 him and usurped the throne in the third year of Asa king of Judah. As soon 29 as he became king, he struck down all the family of Jeroboam, destroying every living soul and leaving not one survivor. Thus the word of the LORD was fulfilled which he spoke through his servant Ahijah the Shilonite. This 30 happened because of the sins of Jeroboam and the sins which he led Israel to commit, and because he had provoked the anger of the LORD the God of Israel. The other events of Nadab's reign and all his acts are recorded in 31 the annals of the kings of Israel. Asa was at war with Baasha king of Israel 32 all through their reigns.

In the third year of Asa king of Judah, Baasha son of Ahijah became king 33 of all Israel in Tirzah and reigned twenty-four years. He did what was 34 wrong in the eyes of the LORD and followed in Jeroboam's footsteps, repeating the sin which he had led Israel to commit. Then the word of the 16 LORD came to Jehu son of Hanani concerning Baasha: 'I raised you from 2 the dust and made you a prince over my people Israel, but you have followed in the footsteps of Jeroboam and have led my people Israel into sin, and have provoked me to anger with their sins. Therefore I will sweep 3 away Baasha and his house and will deal with it as I dealt with the house of Jeroboam son of Nebat. Those of Baasha's family who die in the city shall 4 be food for the dogs, and those who die in the country shall be food for the birds.' The other events of Baasha's reign, his achievements and his 5 exploits, are recorded in the annals of the kings of Israel. Baasha rested 6 with his forefathers and was buried in Tirzah; and he was succeeded by his son Elah. Moreover the word of the LORD concerning Baasha and his 7 family came through the prophet Jehu son of Hanani, because of all the wrong that he had done in the eyes of the LORD, thereby provoking his

$^a$ *Verses 23, 24: cp. 2 Chr. 16. 11–14.*

anger: because he had not only sinned like the house of Jeroboam, but had also brought destruction upon it.

8 In the twenty-sixth year of Asa king of Judah, Elah son of Baasha be-
9 came king of Israel and he reigned in Tirzah two years. Zimri, who was in his service commanding half the chariotry, plotted against him. The king was in Tirzah drinking himself drunk in the house of Arza, comptroller
10 of the household there, when Zimri broke in and attacked him, assassinated him and made himself king. This took place in the twenty-seventh
11 year of Asa king of Judah. As soon as he had become king and was enthroned, he struck down all the family of Baasha and left not a single
12 mother's son alive, kinsman or friend. He destroyed the whole family of Baasha, and thus fulfilled the word of the LORD concerning Baasha, spoken
13 through the prophet Jehu. This was what came of all the sins which Baasha and his son Elah had committed and the sins into which they had led Israel, provoking the anger of the LORD the God of Israel with their worth-
14 less idols. The other events and acts of Elah's reign are recorded in the annals of the kings of Israel.

15 In the twenty-seventh year of Asa king of Judah, Zimri reigned in Tirzah for seven days. At the time the army was investing the Philistine
16 city of Gibbethon. When the Israelite troops in the field heard of Zimri's conspiracy and the murder of the king, there and then in the camp they
17 made their commander Omri king of Israel by common consent. Then Omri and his whole force withdrew from Gibbethon and laid siege to
18 Tirzah. Zimri, as soon as he saw that the city had fallen, retreated to the keep of the royal palace, set the whole of it on fire over his head and so
19 perished. This was what came of the sin he had committed by doing what was wrong in the eyes of the LORD and following in the footsteps of Jero-
20 boam, repeating the sin into which he had led Israel. The other events of Zimri's reign, and his conspiracy, are recorded in the annals of the kings of Israel.

21 Thereafter the people of Israel were split into two factions: one supported Tibni son of Ginath, determined to make him king; the other
22 supported Omri. Omri's party proved the stronger; Tibni lost his life and Omri became king.

23 It was in the thirty-first year of Asa king of Judah that Omri became king
24 of Israel and he reigned twelve years, six of them in Tirzah. He bought the hill of Samaria from Shemer for two talents of silver and built a city on it
25 which he named Samaria after Shemer the owner of the hill. Omri did what was wrong in the eyes of the LORD; he outdid all his predecessors in
26 wickedness. He followed in the footsteps of Jeroboam son of Nebat, repeating the sins which he had led Israel to commit, so that they provoked
27 the anger of the LORD their God with their worthless idols. The other events of Omri's reign, and his exploits, are recorded in the annals of the
28 kings of Israel. So Omri rested with his forefathers and was buried in Samaria; and he was succeeded by his son Ahab.

## Ahab and Elijah

AHAB SON OF OMRI BECAME KING of Israel in the thirty-eighth 29 year of Asa king of Judah, and he reigned over Israel in Samaria for twenty-two years. He did more that was wrong in the eyes of the LORD than 30 all his predecessors. As if it were not enough for him to follow the sinful 31 ways of Jeroboam son of Nebat, he contracted a marriage with Jezebel daughter of Ethbaal king of Sidon, and went and worshipped Baal; he prostrated himself before him and erected an altar to him in the temple of 32 Baal which he built in Samaria. He also set up a sacred pole; indeed he did 33 more to provoke the anger of the LORD the God of Israel than all the kings of Israel before him. In his days Hiel of Bethel rebuilt Jericho; laying its 34 foundations cost him his eldest son Abiram, and the setting up of its gates cost him Segub his youngest son. Thus was fulfilled what the LORD had spoken through Joshua son of Nun.

Elijah the Tishbite, of Tishbe in Gilead, said to Ahab, 'I swear by the 17 life of the LORD the God of Israel, whose servant I am, that there shall be neither dew nor rain these coming years unless I give the word.' Then the 2 word of the LORD came to him: 'Leave this place and turn eastwards; and 3 go into hiding in the ravine of Kerith east of the Jordan. You shall drink 4 from the stream, and I have commanded the ravens to feed you there.' He 5 did as the LORD had told him: he went and stayed in the ravine of Kerith east of the Jordan, and the ravens brought him bread and meat morning 6 and evening, and he drank from the stream. After a while the stream dried 7 up, for there had been no rain in the land. Then the word of the LORD 8 came to him: 'Go now to Zarephath, a village of Sidon, and stay there; 9 I have commanded a widow there to feed you.' So he went off to Zarephath. 10 When he reached the entrance to the village, he saw a widow gathering sticks, and he called to her and said, 'Please bring me a little water in a pitcher to drink.' As she went to fetch it, he called after her, 'Bring me, 11 please, a piece of bread as well.' But she said, 'As the LORD your God lives, 12 I have no food to sustain me except a handful of flour in a jar and a little oil in a flask. Here I am, gathering two or three sticks to go and cook something for my son and myself before we die.' 'Never fear,' said Elijah; 'go and do 13 as you say; but first make me a small cake from what you have and bring it out to me; and after that make something for your son and yourself. For 14 this is the word of the LORD the God of Israel: "The jar of flour shall not give out nor the flask of oil fail, until the LORD sends rain on the land."' She went and did as Elijah had said, and there was food for him and for 15 her and her family for a long time. The jar of flour did not give out nor did 16 the flask of oil fail, as the word of the LORD foretold through Elijah.

Afterwards the son of this woman, the mistress of the house, fell ill and 17 grew worse and worse, until at last his breathing ceased. Then she said to 18 Elijah, 'What made you interfere, you man of God? You came here to bring my sins to light and kill my son!' 'Give me your son', he said. He 19 took the boy from her arms and carried him up to the roof-chamber where his lodging was, and laid him on his own bed. Then he called out to the 20 LORD, 'O LORD my God, is this thy care for the widow with whom I lodge,

21 that thou hast been so cruel to her son?' Then he breathed deeply *a* upon the child three times and called on the LORD, 'O LORD my God, let the breath of
22 life, I pray, return to the body of this child.' The LORD listened to Elijah's cry, and the breath of life returned to the child's body, and he revived;
23 Elijah lifted him up and took him down from the roof into the house, gave
24 him to his mother and said, 'Look, your son is alive.' Then she said to Elijah, 'Now I know for certain that you are a man of God and that the word of the LORD on your lips is truth.'

18 Time went by, and in the third year the word of the LORD came to Elijah: 'Go and show yourself to Ahab, and I will send rain upon the land.'
2 So he went to show himself to Ahab. At this time the famine in Samaria
3 was at its height, and Ahab summoned Obadiah, the comptroller of his
4 household, a devout worshipper of the LORD. When Jezebel massacred the prophets of the LORD, he had taken a hundred of them and hidden them in caves, fifty by fifty, giving them food and drink to keep them alive.
5 Ahab said to Obadiah, 'Let us go through the land, both of us, to every spring and gully; if we can find enough grass we may keep the horses and
6 mules alive and lose none of our cattle.' They divided the land between them for their survey, Ahab going one way by himself and Obadiah another.

7 As Obadiah was on his way, Elijah met him. Obadiah recognized him and
8 fell prostrate before him and said, 'Can it be you, my lord Elijah?' 'Yes,'
9 he said, 'it is I; go and tell your master that Elijah is here.' 'What wrong have I done?' said Obadiah. 'Why should you give me into Ahab's hands?
10 He will put me to death. As the LORD your God lives, there is no nation or kingdom to which my master has not sent in search of you. If they said, "He is not here", he made that kingdom or nation swear on oath that they
11 could not find you. Yet now you say, "Go and tell your master that Elijah
12 is here." What will happen? As soon as I leave you, the spirit of the LORD will carry you away, who knows where? I shall go and tell Ahab, and when he fails to find you, he will kill me. Yet I have been a worshipper of the
13 LORD from boyhood. Have you not been told, my lord, what I did when Jezebel put the LORD's prophets to death, how I hid a hundred of them in
14 caves, fifty by fifty, and kept them alive with food and drink? And now you
15 say, "Go and tell your master that Elijah is here"! He will kill me.' Elijah answered, 'As the LORD of Hosts lives, whose servant I am, I swear that I
16 will show myself to him this very day.' So Obadiah went to find Ahab and gave him the message, and Ahab went to meet Elijah.

17 As soon as Ahab saw Elijah, he said to him, 'Is it you, you troubler of
18 Israel?' 'It is not I who have troubled Israel,' he replied, 'but you and your father's family, by forsaking the commandments of the LORD and
19 following Baal. But now, send and summon all Israel to meet me on Mount Carmel, and the four hundred and fifty prophets of Baal with them and the four hundred prophets of the goddess Asherah, who are Jezebel's pen-
20 sioners.' So Ahab sent out to all the Israelites and assembled the prophets
21 on Mount Carmel. Elijah stepped forward and said to the people, 'How long will you sit on the fence? If the LORD is God, follow him; but if Baal,

*a Or* stretched himself.

then follow him.' Not a word did they answer. Then Elijah said to the 22
people, 'I am the only prophet of the LORD still left, but there are four
hundred and fifty prophets of Baal. Bring two bulls; let them choose one 23
for themselves, cut it up and lay it on the wood without setting fire to it,
and I will prepare the other and lay it on the wood without setting fire to it.
You shall invoke your god by name and I will invoke the LORD by name; 24
and the god who answers by fire, he is God.' And all the people shouted
their approval.

Then Elijah said to the prophets of Baal, 'Choose one of the bulls and 25
offer it first, for there are more of you; invoke your god by name, but do
not set fire to the wood.' So they took the bull provided for them and 26
offered it, and they invoked Baal by name from morning until noon,
crying, 'Baal, Baal, answer us'; but there was no sound, no answer. They
danced wildly beside the altar they had set up. At midday Elijah mocked 27
them: 'Call louder, for he is a god; it may be he is deep in thought, or
engaged, or on a journey; or he may have gone to sleep and must be woken
up.' They cried still louder and, as was their custom, gashed themselves 28
with swords and spears until the blood ran. All afternoon they raved and 29
ranted till the hour of the regular sacrifice, but still there was no sound, no
answer, no sign of attention.

Then Elijah said to all the people, 'Come here to me.' They all came, 30
and he repaired the altar of the LORD which had been torn down. He took 31
twelve stones, one for each tribe of the sons of Jacob, the man named
Israel by the word of the LORD. With these stones he built an altar in the 32
name of the LORD; he dug a trench round it big enough to hold two
measures of seed; he arranged the wood, cut up the bull and laid it on the 33
wood. Then he said, 'Fill four jars with water and pour it on the whole- 34
offering and on the wood.' They did so, and he said, 'Do it again.' They did
it again, and he said, 'Do it a third time.' They did it a third time, and the 35
water ran all round the altar and even filled the trench. At the hour of the 36
regular sacrifice the prophet Elijah came forward and said, 'LORD God of
Abraham, of Isaac, and of Israel, let it be known today that thou art God
in Israel and that I am thy servant and have done all these things at thy
command. Answer me, O LORD, answer me and let this people know that 37
thou, LORD, art God and that it is thou that hast caused them to be back-
sliders.'<sup>a</sup> Then the fire of the LORD fell. It consumed the whole-offering, 38
the wood, the stones, and the earth, and licked up the water in the trench.
When all the people saw it, they fell prostrate and cried, 'The LORD is 39
God, the LORD is God.' Then Elijah said to them, 'Seize the prophets of 40
Baal; let not one of them escape.' They seized them, and Elijah took them
down to the Kishon and slaughtered them there in the valley.

Elijah said to Ahab, 'Go back now, eat and drink, for I hear the sound 41
of coming rain.' He did so, while Elijah himself climbed to the crest of 42
Carmel. There he crouched on the ground with his face between his
knees. He said to his servant, 'Go and look out to the west.' He went and 43
looked; 'There is nothing to see', he said. Seven times Elijah ordered him
back, and seven times he went. The seventh time he said, 'I see a cloud no 44

<sup>a</sup> *Or* thou that dost bring them back to their allegiance.

bigger than a man's hand, coming up from the west.' 'Now go', said
Elijah, 'and tell Ahab to harness his chariot and be off, or the rain will
45 stop him.' Meanwhile the sky had grown black with clouds, the wind rose,
and heavy rain began to fall. Ahab mounted his chariot and set off for
46 Jezreel; but the power of the LORD had come upon Elijah: he tucked up
his robe and ran before Ahab all the way to Jezreel.

**19** Ahab told Jezebel all that Elijah had done and how he had put all the
2 prophets to death with the sword. Jezebel then sent a messenger to Elijah
to say, 'The gods do the same to me and more, unless by this time to-
3 morrow I have taken your life as you took theirs.' He was afraid and fled
for his life. When he reached Beersheba in Judah, he left his servant there
4 and himself went a day's journey into the wilderness. He came upon a
broom-bush, and sat down under it and prayed for death: 'It is enough,'
he said; 'now, LORD, take my life, for I am no better than my fathers before
5 me.' He lay down under the bush and, while he slept, an angel touched
6 him and said, 'Rise and eat.' He looked, and there at his head was a cake
baked on hot stones, and a pitcher of water. He ate and drank and lay down
7 again. The angel of the LORD came again and touched him a second time,
8 saying, 'Rise and eat; the journey is too much for you.' He rose and ate and
drank and, sustained by this food, he went on for forty days and forty
9 nights to Horeb, the mount of God. He entered a cave and there he spent
the night.

Suddenly the word of the LORD came to him: 'Why are you here,
10 Elijah?' 'Because of my great zeal for the LORD the God of Hosts', he said.
'The people of Israel have forsaken thy covenant, torn down thy altars
and put thy prophets to death with the sword. I alone am left, and they
11 seek to take my life.' The answer came: 'Go and stand on the mount before
the LORD.' For the LORD was passing by: a great and strong wind came
rending mountains and shattering rocks before him, but the LORD was not
in the wind; and after the wind there was an earthquake, but the LORD
12 was not in the earthquake; and after the earthquake fire, but the LORD
13 was not in the fire; and after the fire a low murmuring sound. When
Elijah heard it, he muffled his face in his cloak and went out and stood at
the entrance of the cave. Then there came a voice: 'Why are you here,
14 Elijah?' 'Because of my great zeal for the LORD the God of Hosts', he said.
'The people of Israel have forsaken thy covenant, torn down thy altars
and put thy prophets to death with the sword. I alone am left, and they
seek to take my life.'

15 The LORD said to him, 'Go back by way of the wilderness of Damascus,
16 enter the city and anoint Hazael to be king of Aram; anoint Jehu son[a] of
Nimshi to be king of Israel, and Elisha son of Shaphat of Abel-meholah
17 to be prophet in your place. Anyone who escapes the sword of Hazael Jehu
18 will slay, and anyone who escapes the sword of Jehu Elisha will slay. But
I will leave seven thousand in Israel, all who have not bent the knee to Baal,
all whose lips have not kissed him.'

19 Elijah departed and found Elisha son of Shaphat ploughing; there were
twelve pair of oxen ahead of him, and he himself was with the last of them.

[a] *Or* grandson (*cp. 2 Kgs. 9. 2*).

As Elijah passed, he threw his cloak over him, and Elisha, leaving his oxen, 20
ran after Elijah and said, 'Let me kiss my father and mother goodbye, and
then I will follow you.' 'Go back,' he replied; 'what have I done to prevent
you?' He followed him no further but went home, took his pair of oxen, 21
slaughtered them and burnt the wooden gear to cook the flesh, which he
gave to the people to eat. Then he followed Elijah and became his disciple.

BEN-HADAD KING OF ARAM, having mustered all his forces, and taking **20**
with him thirty-two kings with their horses and chariots, marched against
Samaria to take it by siege or assault. He sent envoys into the city to Ahab 2
king of Israel to say, 'Hear what Ben-hadad says: Your silver and gold are 3
mine, your wives and your splendid sons are mine.'[a] The king of Israel 4
answered, 'As you say, my lord king, I am yours and all that I have.' The 5
envoys came again and said, 'Hear what Ben-hadad says: I demand that
you hand over your silver and gold, your wives and your sons. This time 6
tomorrow I will send my servants to search your house and your subjects'
houses and to take possession of everything you prize, and remove it.' The 7
king of Israel then summoned all the elders of the land and said, 'You see
this? The man is plainly picking a quarrel; for I did not demur when he
sent to claim my wives and my sons, my silver and gold.' All the elders and 8
all the people answered, 'Do not listen to him; you must not consent.' So 9
he gave this reply to Ben-hadad's envoys: 'Say to my lord the king: I
accepted your majesty's demands on the first occasion; but what you now
ask I cannot do.' The envoys went away and reported to their master, and 10
Ben-hadad sent back word: 'The gods do the same to me and more, if there
is enough dust in Samaria to provide a handful for each of my men.' The 11
king of Israel made reply, 'Remind him of the saying: "The lame must
not think himself a match for the nimble."' This message reached Ben- 12
hadad while he and the kings were drinking in their quarters.[b] At once he
ordered his men to attack the city, and they did so.

Meanwhile a prophet had come to Ahab king of Israel and said to him, 13
'This is the word of the LORD: "You see this great rabble? Today I will
give it into your hands and you shall know that I am the LORD."' 'Whom will 14
you use for that?' asked Ahab. 'The young men who serve the district
officers', was the answer. 'Who will draw up the line of battle?' asked the
king. 'You', said the prophet. Then Ahab called up these young men, two 15
hundred and thirty-two all told, and behind them the people of Israel,
seven thousand in all. They went out at midday, while Ben-hadad and his 16
allies, those thirty-two kings, were drinking themselves drunk in their
quarters.[b] The young men sallied out first, and word was sent to Ben- 17
hadad that a party had come out of Samaria. 'If they have come out for 18
peace,' he said, 'take them alive; if for battle, take them alive.'

So out of the city the young men went, and the army behind them; each 19 20
struck down his man, and the Aramaeans fled. The Israelites pursued them,
but Ben-hadad king of Aram escaped on horseback with some of the
cavalry. Then the king of Israel advanced and captured the horses and 21
chariots, inflicting a heavy defeat on the Aramaeans.

[a] *Or* are your wives and your sons any good to me?  [b] *in their quarters: or* at Succoth.

22     Then the prophet came to the king of Israel and said to him, 'Build up your forces; you know what you must do. At the turn of the year the king
23 of Aram will renew the attack.' But the king of Aram's ministers gave him this advice: 'Their gods are gods of the hills; that is why they defeated us. Let us fight them in the plain; and then we shall have the upper hand.
24 What you must do is to relieve the kings of their command and appoint
25 other officers in their place. Raise another army like the one you have lost. Bring your cavalry and chariots up to their former strength, and then let us fight them in the plain, and we shall have the upper hand.' He listened to their advice and acted on it.

26     At the turn of the year Ben-hadad mustered the Aramaeans and advanced
27 to Aphek to attack Israel. The Israelites too were mustered and formed into companies, and then went out to meet them and encamped opposite them. They seemed no better than a pair of new-born kids, while the Aramaeans
28 covered the country-side. The man of God came to the king of Israel and said, 'This is the word of the LORD: The Aramaeans may think that the LORD is a god of the hills and not a god of the valleys; but I will give all this great rabble into your hands and you shall know that I am the LORD.'
29     They lay in camp opposite one another for seven days; on the seventh day battle was joined and the Israelites destroyed a hundred thousand of
30 the Aramaean infantry in one day. The survivors fled to Aphek, into the citadel, and the city wall fell upon the twenty-seven thousand men who were left. Ben-hadad took refuge in the citadel, retreating into an inner room;
31 and his attendants said to him, 'Listen; we have heard that the kings of Israel are men to be trusted. Let us therefore put sackcloth round our waists and wind rough cord round our heads and go out to the king of
32 Israel. It may be that he will spare your life.' So they fastened on the sackcloth and the cord, and went to the king of Israel and said, 'Your servant Ben-hadad pleads for his life.' 'My royal cousin,' he said, 'is he still
33 alive?' The men, taking the word for a favourable omen, caught it up at once and said, 'Your cousin, yes, Ben-hadad.' 'Go and fetch him', he said.
34 Then Ben-hadad came out and Ahab invited him into his chariot. And Ben-hadad said to him, 'I will restore the cities which my father took from your father, and you may establish for yourself a trading quarter in Damascus, as my father did in Samaria.' 'On these terms', said Ahab, 'I will let you go.' So he granted him a treaty and let him go.

35     One of a company of prophets, at the command of the LORD, ordered a
36 certain man to strike him, but the man refused. 'Because you have not obeyed the LORD,' said the prophet, 'when you leave me, a lion will attack
37 you.' When the man left, a lion did meet him and attacked him. The prophet fell in with another man and ordered him to strike him. He struck and
38 wounded him. Then the prophet went off, with a bandage over his eyes,
39 and thus disguised waited by the wayside for the king. As the king was passing, he called out to him, 'Sir, I went into the thick of the battle, and a soldier came over to me with a prisoner and said, "Take charge of this fellow. If by any chance he gets away, your life shall be forfeit, or you shall
40 pay a talent of silver." As I was busy with one thing and another, sir, he disappeared.' The king of Israel said to him, 'You deserve to die.' And he

said to the king of Israel,[a] 'You have passed sentence on yourself.' Then he 41
tore the bandage from his eyes, and the king of Israel saw that he was one
of the prophets. And he said to the king, 'This is the word of the LORD: 42
"Because you let that man go when I had put him under a ban, your life
shall be forefeit for his life, your people for his people."' The king of 43
Israel went home sullen and angry and entered Samaria.

NABOTH OF JEZREEL HAD A VINEYARD near the palace of Ahab king 21
of Samaria. One day Ahab made a proposal to Naboth: 'Your vineyard is 2
close to my palace; let me have it for a garden; I will give you a better
vineyard in exchange for it or, if you prefer, its value in silver.' But Naboth 3
answered, 'The LORD forbid that I should let you have land which has
always been in my family.' So Ahab went home sullen and angry because 4
Naboth would not let him have his ancestral land. He lay down on his bed,
covered his face and refused to eat. His wife Jezebel came in to him and 5
said, 'What makes you so sullen and why do you refuse to eat?' He told 6
her, 'I proposed to Naboth of Jezreel that he should let me have his vineyard at its value or, if he liked, in exchange for another; but he would not
let me have the vineyard.' 'Are you or are you not king in Israel?' said 7
Jezebel. 'Come, eat and take heart; I will make you a gift of the vineyard
of Naboth of Jezreel.' So she wrote a letter in Ahab's name, sealed it with 8
his seal and sent it to the elders and notables of Naboth's city, who sat in
council with him. She wrote: 'Proclaim a fast and give Naboth the seat of 9
honour among the people. And see that two scoundrels are seated opposite 10
him to charge him with cursing God and the king, then take him out and
stone him to death.' So the elders and notables of Naboth's city, who sat 11
with him in council, carried out the instructions Jezebel had sent them in
her letter: they proclaimed a fast and gave Naboth the seat of honour, and 12 13
these two scoundrels came in, sat opposite him and charged him publicly
with cursing God and the king. Then they took him outside the city and
stoned him, and sent word to Jezebel that Naboth had been stoned to 14
death.

As soon as Jezebel heard that Naboth had been stoned and was dead, 15
she said to Ahab, 'Get up and take possession of the vineyard which Naboth
refused to sell you, for he is no longer alive; Naboth of Jezreel is dead.'
When Ahab heard that Naboth was dead, he got up and went to the vine- 16
yard to take possession. Then the word of the LORD came to Elijah the 17
Tishbite: 'Go down at once to Ahab king of Israel, who is in Samaria; you 18
will find him in Naboth's vineyard, where he has gone to take possession.
Say to him, "This is the word of the LORD: Have you killed your man, and 19
taken his land as well?" Say to him, "This is the word of the LORD: Where
dogs licked the blood of Naboth, there dogs shall lick your blood."' Ahab 20
said to Elijah, 'Have you found me, my enemy?' 'I have found you', he
said, 'because you have sold yourself to do what is wrong in the eyes of the
LORD. I will bring[b] disaster upon you; I will sweep you away and destroy 21
every mother's son of the house of Ahab in Israel, whether under protection

---

[a] You deserve . . . Israel: *prob. rdg.; Heb. om.*          [b] he said, . . . bring: *or* he said.
'Because you . . . LORD, I am bringing . . .

22 of the family or not. And I will deal with your house as I did with the house of Jeroboam son of Nebat and of Baasha son of Ahijah, because you have
23 provoked my anger and led Israel into sin.' And the LORD went on to say
24 of Jezebel, 'Jezebel shall be eaten by dogs by the rampart of Jezreel. Of the house of Ahab, those who die in the city shall be food for the dogs, and
25 those who die in the country shall be food for the birds.' (Never was a man who sold himself to do what is wrong in the LORD's eyes as Ahab did, and
26 all at the prompting of Jezebel his wife. He committed gross abominations in going after false gods, doing everything that the Amorites did, whom the
27 LORD had dispossessed in favour of Israel.) When Ahab heard this, he rent his clothes, put on sackcloth and fasted; he lay down in his sackcloth
28 and went about muttering to himself. Then the word of the LORD came to
29 Elijah the Tishbite: 'Have you seen how Ahab has humbled himself before me? Because he has thus humbled himself, I will not bring disaster upon his house in his own lifetime, but in his son's.'

22 FOR THREE YEARS THERE WAS NO WAR between the Aramaeans and
2ᵃ the Israelites, but in the third year Jehoshaphat king of Judah went down
3 to visit the king of Israel. The latter said to his courtiers, 'You know that Ramoth-gilead belongs to us, and yet we do nothing to recover it from the
4 king of Aram.' He said to Jehoshaphat, 'Will you join me in attacking Ramoth-gilead?' Jehoshaphat said to the king of Israel, 'What is mine is
5 yours: myself, my people, and my horses.' Then Jehoshaphat said to the
6 king of Israel, 'First let us seek counsel from the LORD.' The king of Israel assembled the prophets, some four hundred of them, and asked them, 'Shall I attack Ramoth-gilead or shall I refrain?' 'Attack,' they answered;
7 'the Lord will deliver it into your hands.' Jehoshaphat asked, 'Is there no other prophet of the LORD here through whom we may seek guidance?'
8 'There is one more', the king of Israel answered, 'through whom we may seek guidance of the LORD, but I hate the man, because he prophesies no good for me; never anything but evil. His name is Micaiah son of Imlah.' Jehoshaphat exclaimed, 'My lord king, let no such word pass your lips!'
9 So the king of Israel called one of his eunuchs and told him to fetch Micaiah son of Imlah with all speed.
10 The king of Israel and Jehoshaphat king of Judah were seated on their thrones, in shining armour, at the entrance to the gate of Samaria, and all
11 the prophets were prophesying before them. One of them, Zedekiah son of Kenaanah, made himself horns of iron and said, 'This is the word of the LORD: "With horns like these you shall gore the Aramaeans and make an
12 end of them."' In the same vein all the prophets prophesied, 'Attack Ramoth-gilead and win the day; the LORD will deliver it into your hands.'
13 The messenger sent to fetch Micaiah told him that the prophets had with one voice given the king a favourable answer. 'And mind you agree with
14 them', he added. 'As the LORD lives,' said Micaiah, 'I will say only what the LORD tells me to say.'
15 When Micaiah came into the king's presence, the king said to him, 'Micaiah, shall we attack Ramoth-gilead or shall we refrain?' 'Attack and

ᵃ *Verses 2–35: cp. 2 Chr. 18. 2–34.*

win the day,' he said; 'the LORD will deliver it into your hands.' 'How 16
often must I adjure you', said the king, 'to tell me nothing but the truth
in the name of the LORD?' Then Micaiah said, 'I saw all Israel scattered on 17
the mountains, like sheep without a shepherd; and I heard the LORD say,
"They have no master, let them go home in peace."' The king of Israel 18
said to Jehoshaphat, 'Did I not tell you that he never prophesies good for
me, nothing but evil?' Micaiah went on, 'Listen now to the word of the 19
LORD. I saw the LORD seated on his throne, with all the host of heaven in
attendance on his right and on his left. The LORD said, "Who will entice 20
Ahab to attack and fall on*ᵃ* Ramoth-gilead?" One said one thing and one
said another; then a spirit came forward and stood before the LORD and 21
said, "I will entice him." "How?" said the LORD. "I will go out", he said, 22
"and be a lying spirit in the mouth of all his prophets." "You shall entice
him," said the LORD, "and you shall succeed; go and do it." You see, then, 23
how the LORD has put a lying spirit in the mouth of all these prophets of
yours, because he has decreed disaster for you.' Then Zedekiah son of 24
Kenaanah came up to Micaiah and struck him in the face: 'And how did
the spirit of the LORD pass from me to speak to you?' he said. Micaiah 25
answered, 'That you will find out on the day when you run into an inner
room to hide yourself.' Then the king of Israel ordered Micaiah to be 26
arrested and committed to the custody of Amon the governor of the city
and Joash the king's son.*ᵇ* 'Lock this fellow up', he said, 'and give him 27
prison diet of bread and water until I come home in safety.' Micaiah 28
retorted, 'If you do return in safety, the LORD has not spoken by me.'

So the king of Israel and Jehoshaphat king of Judah marched on Ramoth- 29
gilead, and the king of Israel said to Jehoshaphat, 'I will disguise myself 30
to go into battle, but you shall wear your royal robes.' So he went into
battle in disguise. Now the king of Aram had commanded the thirty-two 31
captains of his chariots not to engage all and sundry but the king of Israel
alone. When the captains saw Jehoshaphat, they thought he was the king 32
of Israel and turned to attack him. But Jehoshaphat cried out and, when the 33
captains saw that he was not the king of Israel, they broke off the attack on
him. But one man drew his bow at random and hit the king of Israel where 34
the breastplate joins the plates of the armour. So he said to his driver,
'Wheel round and take me out of the line; I am wounded.' When the day's 35
fighting reached its height, the king was facing the Aramaeans propped up
in his chariot, and the blood from his wound flowed down upon the floor
of the chariot; and in the evening he died. At sunset the herald went 36
through the ranks, crying, 'Every man to his city, every man to his country.'
Thus died the king. He was brought to Samaria and they buried him there. 37
The chariot was swilled out at the pool of Samaria, and the dogs licked up 38
the blood, and the prostitutes washed themselves in it, in fulfilment of the
word the LORD had spoken.

Now the other acts and events of Ahab's reign, the ivory house and all 39
the cities he built, are recorded in the annals of the kings of Israel. So 40
Ahab rested with his forefathers and was succeeded by his son Ahaziah.

Jehoshaphat son of Asa had become king of Judah in the fourth year of 41*ᶜ*

---

*ᵃ Or at.*     *ᵇ son: or deputy.*     *ᶜ Verses 41–43: cp. 2 Chr. 20. 31–33.*

42 Ahab king of Israel. He was thirty-five years old when he came to the throne, and he reigned in Jerusalem for twenty-five years; his mother was
43 Azubah daughter of Shilhi. He followed in the footsteps of Asa his father and did not swerve from them; he did what was right in the eyes of the LORD. But the hill-shrines were allowed to remain; the people continued
44 to slaughter and burn sacrifices there. Jehoshaphat remained at peace with
45 the king of Israel. The other events of Jehoshaphat's reign, his exploits
46 and his wars, are recorded in the annals of the kings of Judah. But he did away with such of the male prostitutes attached to the shrines as were still left over from the days of Asa his father.
47 48 There was no king in Edom, only*a* a viceroy of Jehoshaphat; he built merchantmen to sail to Ophir for gold, but they never made the journey
49 because they were wrecked at Ezion-geber. Ahaziah son of Ahab proposed to Jehoshaphat that his own men should go to sea with his; but Jehoshaphat would not consent.
50 Jehoshaphat rested with his forefathers and was buried with them in the city of David his father, and was succeeded by his son Joram.
51 Ahaziah son of Ahab became king of Israel in Samaria in the seventeenth year of Jehoshaphat king of Judah, and reigned over Israel for two years.
52 He did what was wrong in the eyes of the LORD, following in the footsteps of his father and mother and in those of Jeroboam son of Nebat, who had
53 led Israel into sin. He served Baal and worshipped him, and provoked the anger of the LORD the God of Israel, as his father had done.

# THE SECOND BOOK OF
# KINGS

## *Elisha and the end of the house of Ahab*

1 AFTER AHAB'S DEATH Moab rebelled against Israel.
2 Ahaziah fell through a latticed window in his roof-chamber in Samaria and injured himself; he sent messengers to inquire of Baal-
3 zebub the god of Ekron whether he would recover from his illness. The angel of the LORD ordered Elijah the Tishbite to go and meet the messengers of the king of Samaria and say to them, 'Is there no god in Israel,
4 that you go to inquire of Baal-zebub the god of Ekron? This is the word of the LORD to your master: "You shall not rise from the bed where you are
5 lying; you will die."' Then Elijah departed. The messengers went back
6 to the king. When asked why they had returned, they answered that a man had come to meet them and had ordered them to return and say to the king who had sent them, 'This is the word of the LORD: "Is there no god in Israel, that you send to inquire of Baal-zebub the god of Ekron? In consequence, you shall not rise from the bed where you are lying; you will

*a only: prob. rdg.; Heb. om.*

die." ' The king asked them what kind of man it was who had met them and 7
said this. 'A hairy man', they answered, 'with a leather apron round his 8
waist.' 'It is Elijah the Tishbite', said the king.

Then the king sent a captain to him with his company of fifty. He went 9
up and found the prophet sitting on a hill-top and said to him, 'Man of
God, the king orders you to come down.' Elijah answered the captain, 'If 10
I am a man of God, may fire fall from heaven and consume you and your
company!' Fire fell from heaven and consumed the officer and his fifty
men. The king sent another captain of fifty with his company, and he went 11
up and said to the prophet, 'Man of God, this is the king's command: Come
down at once.' Elijah answered, 'If I am a man of God, may fire fall from 12
heaven and consume you and your company!' God's fire fell from heaven
and consumed the man and his company. The king sent the captain of a 13
third company with his fifty men, and this third captain went up the hill
to Elijah and knelt down before him and pleaded with him: 'Man of God,
consider me and these fifty servants of yours, and set some value on our
lives. Fire fell from heaven and consumed the other two captains of fifty 14
and their companies; but let my life have some value in your eyes.' The 15
angel of the LORD said to Elijah, 'Go down with him. Do not be afraid.'
So he rose and went down with him to the king, and he said, 'This is the 16
word of the LORD: "You have sent to inquire of Baal-zebub the god of
Ekron, and therefore you shall not rise from the bed where you are lying;
you will die." ' The word of the LORD which Elijah had spoken was ful- 17
filled, and Ahaziah died; and because he had no son, his brother Jehoram
succeeded him in the second year of Joram son of Jehoshaphat king of
Judah.

The other events of Ahaziah's reign are recorded in the annals of the 18
kings of Israel.

The time came when the LORD would take Elijah up to heaven in a **2**
whirlwind. Elijah and Elisha left Gilgal, and Elijah said to Elisha, 'Stay 2
here; for the LORD has sent me to Bethel.' But Elisha said, 'As the LORD
lives, your life upon it, I will not leave you.' So they went down country
to Bethel. There a company of prophets came out to Elisha and said to 3
him, 'Do you know that the LORD is going to take your lord and master
from you today?' 'I do know,' he replied; 'say no more.' Then Elijah said 4
to him, 'Stay here, Elisha; for the LORD has sent me to Jericho.' But he
replied, 'As the LORD lives, your life upon it, I will not leave you.' So they
went to Jericho. There a company of prophets came up to Elisha and said 5
to him, 'Do you know that the LORD is going to take your lord and master
from you today?' 'I do know,' he said; 'say no more.' Then Elijah said to 6
him, 'Stay here; for the LORD has sent me to the Jordan.' The other
replied, 'As the LORD lives, your life upon it, I will not leave you.' So the
two of them went on.

Fifty of the prophets followed them, and stood watching from a distance 7
as the two of them stopped by the Jordan. Elijah took his cloak, rolled it up 8
and struck the water with it. The water divided to right and left, and they
both crossed over on dry ground. While they were crossing, Elijah said to 9
Elisha, 'Tell me what I can do for you before I am taken from you.' Elisha

10 said, 'Let me inherit a double share of your spirit.' 'You have asked a hard thing', said Elijah. 'If you see me taken from you, may your wish be
11 granted; if you do not, it shall not be granted.' They went on, talking as they went, and suddenly there appeared chariots of fire and horses of fire, which separated them one from the other, and Elijah was carried up in the
12 whirlwind to heaven. When Elisha saw it, he cried, 'My father, my father, the chariots and the horsemen of Israel!', and he saw him no more. Then
13 he took hold of his mantle and rent it in two, and he picked up the cloak which had fallen from Elijah, and came back and stood on the bank of the
14 Jordan. There he too struck the water with Elijah's cloak and said, 'Where is the LORD the God of Elijah?' When he struck the water, it was again
15 divided to right and left, and he crossed over. The prophets from Jericho, who were watching, saw him and said, 'The spirit of Elijah has settled on
16 Elisha.' So they came to meet him, and fell on their faces before him and said, 'Your servants have fifty stalwart men. Let them go and search for your master; perhaps the spirit of the LORD has lifted him up and cast him on some mountain or into some valley.' But he said, 'No, you must not
17 send them.' They pressed him, however, until he had not the heart to refuse. So they sent out the fifty men but, though they searched for three
18 days, they did not find him. When they came back to Elisha, who had remained at Jericho, he said to them, 'Did I not tell you not to go?'
19 The people of the city said to Elisha, 'You can see how pleasantly our city is situated, but the water is polluted and the country is troubled with
20 miscarriages.' He said, 'Fetch me a new bowl and put some salt in it.' When
21 they had fetched it, he went out to the spring and, throwing the salt into it, he said, 'This is the word of the LORD: "I purify this water. It shall cause
22 no more death or miscarriage." ' The water has remained pure till this day, in fulfilment of Elisha's word.
23 He went up from there to Bethel and, as he was on his way, some small boys came out of the city and jeered at him, saying, 'Get along with you,
24 bald head, get along.' He turned round and looked at them and he cursed them in the name of the LORD; and two she-bears came out of a wood and
25 mauled forty-two of them. From there he went on to Mount Carmel, and thence back to Samaria.
3 In the eighteenth year of Jehoshaphat king of Judah, Jehoram son of Ahab became king of Israel in Samaria, and he reigned for twelve years.
2 He did what was wrong in the eyes of the LORD, though not as his father and his mother had done; he did remove the sacred pillar of the Baal
3 which his father had made. Yet he persisted in the sins into which Jeroboam son of Nebat had led Israel, and did not give them up.
4 Mesha king of Moab was a sheep-breeder, and he used to supply the king of Israel regularly with the wool of a hundred thousand lambs and a
5 hundred thousand rams. When Ahab died, the king of Moab rebelled
6 against the king of Israel. Then King Jehoram came from Samaria and
7 mustered all Israel. He also sent this message to Jehoshaphat king of Judah: 'The king of Moab has rebelled against me. Will you join me in attacking Moab?' 'I will,' he replied; 'what is mine is yours: myself, my
8 people, and my horses.' 'From which direction shall we attack?' Jehoram

asked. 'Through the wilderness of Edom', replied the other. So the king 9
of Israel set out with the king of Judah and the king of Edom. When they
had been seven days on the march, they had no water left for the army or
the pack-animals. Then the king of Israel said, 'Alas, the LORD has brought 10
together three kings, only to put us at the mercy of the Moabites.' But 11
Jehoshaphat said, 'Is there not a prophet of the LORD here through whom
we may seek guidance of the LORD?' One of the officers of the king of Israel
answered, 'Elisha son of Shaphat is here, the man who poured water on
Elijah's hands.' 'The word of the LORD is with him', said Jehoshaphat. So 12
the king of Israel and Jehoshaphat and the king of Edom went down to
Elisha. Elisha said to the king of Israel, 'Why do you come to me? Go to 13
the prophets of your father and your mother.' But the king of Israel said
to him, 'No; the LORD has called us three kings out to put us at the mercy of
the Moabites.' 'As the LORD of Hosts lives, whom I serve,' said Elisha, 'I 14
would not spare a look or a glance for you, if it were not for my regard for
Jehoshaphat king of Judah. But now, fetch me a minstrel.' They fetched a 15
minstrel, and while he was playing, the power of the LORD came upon
Elisha and he said, 'This is the word of the LORD: "Pools will form all over 16
this ravine." The LORD has decreed that you shall see neither wind nor 17
rain, yet this ravine shall be filled with water for you and your army and
your pack-animals to drink. But that is a mere trifle in the sight of the LORD; 18
what he will also do, is to put Moab at your mercy. You will raze to the 19
ground every fortified town and every noble city; you will cut down all
their fine trees; you will stop up all the springs of water; and you will spoil
every good piece of land by littering it with stones.' In the morning at the 20
hour of the regular sacrifice they saw water flowing in from the direction
of Edom, and the land was flooded.

Meanwhile all Moab had heard that the kings had come up to fight against 21
them, and every man, young and old, who could carry arms, was called out
and stationed on the frontier. When they got up next morning and the sun 22
had risen over the water, the Moabites saw the water in front of them red
like blood and cried out, 'It is blood. The kings must have quarrelled and 23
attacked one another. Now to the plunder, Moab!' When they came to the 24
Israelite camp, the Israelites turned out and attacked them and drove the
Moabites headlong in flight, and themselves entered the land of Moab,
destroying as they went. They razed the cities to the ground; they littered 25
every good piece of land with stones, each man casting one stone on to it;
they stopped up every spring of water; they cut down all their fine trees;
and they harried Moab until only in Kir-hareseth were any buildings left
standing, and even this city the slingers surrounded and attacked.

When the king of Moab saw that the war had gone against him, he took 26
seven hundred men with him, armed with swords, to cut a way through to
the king of Aram, but they failed in the attempt. Then he took his eldest 27
son, who would have succeeded him, and offered him as a whole-offering
upon the city wall. The Israelites were filled with such consternation at
this sight,[a] that they struck camp and returned to their own land.

The wife of a member of a company of prophets appealed to Elisha. **4**

---

[a] The Israelites . . . sight: *or* There was such great anger against the Israelites . . .

'My husband, your servant, has died', she said. 'You know that he was a man who feared the LORD; but a creditor has come to take away my two
2 boys as his slaves.' Elisha said to her, 'How can I help you? Tell me what you have in the house.' 'Nothing at all', she answered, 'except a flask of
3 oil.' 'Go out then', he said, 'and borrow vessels from all your neighbours;
4 get as many empty ones as you can. Then, when you come home, shut yourself in with your sons, pour from the flask into all these vessels and, as
5 they are filled, set them aside.' She left him and shut herself in with her
6 sons. As they brought her the vessels she filled them. When they were all full, she said to one of her sons, 'Bring me another.' 'There is not one left',
7 he said. Then the flow of oil ceased. She came out and told the man of God, and he said, 'Go and sell the oil and redeem your boys who are being taken as pledges,*a* and you and they can live on what is left.'
8     It happened once that Elisha went over to Shunem. There was a great lady there who pressed him to accept her hospitality, and so, whenever he
9 came that way, he stopped to take food there. One day she said to her husband, 'I know that this man who comes here regularly is a holy man of
10 God. Why not build up the wall to make him a little roof-chamber, and put in it a bed, a table, a seat, and a lamp, and let him stay there whenever
11 he comes to us?' Once when he arrived and went to this roof-chamber and
12 lay down to rest, he said to Gehazi, his servant, 'Call this Shunammite
13 woman.' He called her and, when she appeared before the prophet, he said to his servant, 'Say to her, "You have taken all this trouble for us. What can I do for you? Shall I speak for you to the king or to the com-mander-in-chief?"' But she replied, 'I am content where I am, among my
14 own people.' He said, 'Then what can be done for her?' Gehazi said,
15 'There is only this: she has no child and her husband is old.' 'Call her
16 back', Elisha said. When she was called, she appeared in the doorway, and he said, 'In due season, this time next year, you shall have a son in your arms.' But she said, 'No, no, my lord, you are a man of God and would not
17 lie to your servant.' Next year in due season the woman conceived and bore a son, as Elisha had foretold.
18     When the child was old enough, he went out one day to the reapers where
19 his father was. All of a sudden he cried out to his father, 'O my head, my
20 head!' His father told a servant to carry him to his mother. He brought him to his mother; the boy sat on her lap till midday, and then he died.
21 She went up and laid him on the bed of the man of God, shut the door and
22 went out. She called her husband and said, 'Send me one of the servants and a she-ass, I must go to the man of God as fast as I can, and come straight
23 back.' 'Why go to him today?' he asked. 'It is neither new moon nor
24 sabbath.'*b* 'Never mind that', she answered. When the ass was saddled, she said to her servant, 'Lead on and do not slacken pace unless I tell you.'
25 So she set out and came to the man of God on Mount Carmel. The man of God spied her in the distance and said to Gehazi, his servant, 'That is the
26 Shunammite woman coming. Run and meet her, and ask, "Is all well with you? Is all well with your husband? Is all well with the boy?"' She
27 answered, 'All is well.' When she reached the man of God on the hill, she

*a* redeem . . . pledges: *or* pay off your debt.          *b* *Or* full moon.

clutched his feet. Gehazi came forward to push her away, but the man of God said, 'Let her alone; she is in great distress, and the LORD has concealed it from me and not told me.' 'My lord,' she said, 'did I ask for a 28 son? Did I not beg you not to raise my hopes and then dash them?' Then 29 he turned to Gehazi: 'Hitch up your cloak; take my staff with you and run. If you meet anyone on the way, do not stop to greet him; if anyone greets you, do not answer him. Lay my staff on the boy's face.' But the mother 30 cried, 'As the LORD lives, your life upon it, I will not leave you.' So he got up and followed her. *a*

Gehazi went on ahead of them and laid the staff on the boy's face, but 31 there was no sound and no sign of life. So he went back to meet Elisha and told him that the boy had not roused. When Elisha entered the house, there 32 was the boy dead, on the bed where he had been laid. He went into the room, 33 shut the door on the two of them and prayed to the LORD. Then, getting 34 on to the bed, he lay upon the child, put his mouth to the child's mouth, his eyes to his eyes and his hands to his hands; and, as he pressed *b* upon him, the child's body grew warm. Elisha got up and walked once up and 35 down the room; then, getting on to the bed again, he pressed *b* upon him and breathed into him *c* seven times; and the boy opened his eyes. The 36 prophet summoned Gehazi and said, 'Call this Shunammite woman.' She answered his call and the prophet said, 'Take your child.' She came in and 37 fell prostrate before him. Then she took up her son and went out.

Elisha returned to Gilgal at a time when there was a famine in the land. 38 One day, when a group of prophets was sitting at his feet, he said to his servant, 'Set the big pot on the fire and prepare some broth for the company.' One of them went out into the fields to gather herbs and found a 39 wild vine, and filled the skirt of his garment with bitter-apples. *d* He came back and sliced them into the pot, not knowing what they were. They 40 poured it out for the men to eat, but, when they tasted it, they cried out, 'Man of God, there is death in the pot', and they could not eat it. The 41 prophet said, 'Fetch some meal.' He threw it into the pot and said, 'Now pour out for the men to eat.' This time there was no harm in the pot.

A man came from Baal-shalisha, bringing the man of God some of the 42 new season's bread, twenty barley loaves, and fresh ripe ears of corn. *e* Elisha said, 'Give this to the people to eat.' But his disciple protested, 'I 43 cannot set this before a hundred men.' Still he repeated, 'Give it to the people to eat; for this is the word of the LORD: "They will eat and there will be some left over."' So he set it before them, and they ate and left 44 some over, as the LORD had said.

NAAMAN, COMMANDER of the king of Aram's army, was a great man 5 highly esteemed by his master, because by his means the LORD had given victory to Aram; but he was a leper. *f* On one of their raids the Aramaeans 2 brought back as a captive from the land of Israel a little girl, who became a servant to Naaman's wife. She said to her mistress, 'If only my master 3

---

*a Or* went with her.     *b Prob. rdg.; Heb.* crouched.     *c* and breathed into him:
*or* and the boy sneezed.     *d Or* poisonous wild gourds.     *e* fresh . . . corn: *prob.*
*rdg.; Heb. unintelligible.*     *f* he was a leper: *or* his skin was diseased.

could meet the prophet who lives in Samaria, he would get rid of the
4 disease for him.' Naaman went in and reported to his master word for
5 word what the girl from the land of Israel had said. 'Very well, you may
go,' said the king of Aram, 'and I will send a letter to the king of Israel.'
So Naaman went, taking with him ten talents of silver, six thousand shekels
6 of gold, and ten changes of clothing. He delivered the letter to the king of
Israel, which read thus: 'This letter is to inform you that I am sending to
7 you my servant Naaman, and I beg you to rid you of his disease.' When
the king of Israel read the letter, he rent his clothes and said, 'Am I a god *a*
to kill and to make alive, that this fellow sends to me to cure a man of his
8 disease? Surely you must see that he is picking a quarrel with me.' When
Elisha, the man of God, heard how the king of Israel had rent his clothes,
he sent to him saying, 'Why did you rend your clothes? Let the man come
9 to me, and he will know that there is a prophet in Israel.' So Naaman came
with his horses and chariots and stood at the entrance to Elisha's house.
10 Elisha sent out a messenger to say to him, 'If you will go and wash seven
times in the Jordan, your flesh will be restored and you will be clean.'
11 Naaman was furious and went away, saying, 'I thought he would at least
have come out and stood, and invoked the LORD his God by name, waved
12 his hand over the place and so rid me of the disease. Are not Abana and
Pharpar, rivers of Damascus, better than all the waters of Israel? Can I
13 not wash in them and be clean?' So he turned and went off in a rage. But
his servants came up to him and said, 'If the prophet had bidden you do
something difficult, would you not do it? How much more then, if he tells
14 you to wash and be clean?' So he went down and dipped himself in the
Jordan seven times as the man of God had told him, and his flesh was
restored as a little child's, and he was clean.
15    Then he and his retinue went back to the man of God and stood before
him; and he said, 'Now I know that there is no god anywhere on earth
except in Israel. Will you accept a token of gratitude from your servant?'
16 'As the LORD lives, whom I serve,' said the prophet, 'I will accept nothing.'
17 He was pressed to accept, but he refused. 'Then if you will not,' said
Naaman, 'let me, sir, have two mules' load of earth. For I will no longer
18 offer whole-offering or sacrifice to any god but the LORD. In this one matter
only may the LORD pardon me: when my master goes to the temple of
Rimmon to worship, leaning on my arm, and I worship in the temple of
19 Rimmon when he worships there, for this let the LORD pardon me.' And
Elisha bade him farewell.
20    Naaman had gone only a short distance on his way, when Gehazi, the
servant of Elisha the man of God, said to himself, 'What? Has my master let
this Aramaean, Naaman, go scot-free, and not accepted what he brought?
21 As the LORD lives, I will run after him and get something from him.' So
Gehazi hurried after Naaman. When Naaman saw him running after him,
he jumped down from his chariot to meet him and said, 'Is anything
22 wrong?' 'Nothing,' said Gehazi, 'but my master sent me to say that two
young men of the company of prophets from the hill-country of Ephraim
have just arrived. Could you provide them with a talent of silver and two

*a* *Or* Am I God.

changes of clothing?' Naaman said, 'By all means; take two talents.' He 23
pressed*ᵃ* him to take them; so he tied up the two talents of silver in two
bags, and the two changes of clothing, and gave them to his two servants,
and they walked ahead carrying them. When Gehazi came to the citadel*ᵇ* 24
he took them from the two servants, deposited them in the house and dismissed the men; and they departed. When he went in and stood before 25
his master, Elisha said, 'Where have you been, Gehazi?' 'Nowhere', said
Gehazi. But he said to him, 'Was I not with you in spirit when the man 26
turned back from his chariot to meet you? Is it not true that you have the
money? You may buy gardens with it,*ᶜ ᵈ* and olive-trees and vineyards,
sheep and oxen, slaves and slave-girls; but the disease of Naaman will 27
fasten on you and on your descendants for ever.' Gehazi left his presence,
his skin diseased, white as snow.

A COMPANY OF PROPHETS said to Elisha, 'You can see that this place 6
where our community is living, under you as its head, is too small for us.
Let us go to the Jordan and each fetch a log, and make ourselves a place to 2
live in.' The prophet agreed. Then one of them said, 'Please, sir, come with 3
us.' 'I will', he said, and he went with them. When they reached the 4
Jordan, they began cutting down trees; but it chanced that, as one man was 5
felling a trunk, the head of his axe flew off into the water. 'Oh, master!'
he exclaimed, 'it was a borrowed one.' 'Where did it fall?' asked the man 6
of God. When he was shown the place, he cut off a piece of wood and threw
it in and made the iron float. Then he said, 'There you are, lift it out.' So 7
he stretched out his hand and took it.

Once, when the king of Aram was making war on Israel, he held a con- 8
ference with his staff at which he said, 'I mean to attack in such and such a
direction.' But the man of God warned the king of Israel: 'Take care to 9
avoid this place, for the Aramaeans are going down that way.' So the king 10
of Israel sent to the place about which the man of God had given him this
warning; and the king took special precautions every time he found himself near that place. The king of Aram was greatly perturbed at this and, 11
summoning his staff, he said to them, 'Tell me, one of you, who has betrayed us to the king of Israel?' 'None of us, my lord king,' said one of his 12
staff; 'but Elisha, the prophet in Israel, tells the king of Israel the very
words you speak in your bedchamber.' 'Go and find out where he is,' said 13
the king, 'and I will send and seize him.' He was told that the prophet was
at Dothan, and he sent a strong force there with horses and chariots. They 14
came by night and surrounded the city.

When the disciple of the man of God rose early in the morning and went 15
out, he saw a force with horses and chariots surrounding the city. 'Oh,
master,' he said, 'which way are we to turn?' He answered, 'Do not be 16
afraid, for those who are on our side are more than those on theirs.' Then 17
Elisha offered this prayer: 'O LORD, open his eyes and let him see.' And
the LORD opened the young man's eyes, and he saw the hills covered with
horses and chariots of fire all round Elisha. As they came down towards 18

*ᵃ Prob. rdg.; Heb.* broke out on.     *ᵇ Or* hill.     *ᶜ* gardens with it: *prob. rdg.; Heb.*
garments.     *ᵈ* Is it not . . . with it: *or* Was it a time to get the money and to get garments?

him, Elisha prayed to the LORD: 'Strike this host, I pray thee, with blind-
19 ness'; and he struck them blind as Elisha had asked. Then Elisha said
to them, 'You are on the wrong road; this is not the city. Follow me and
I will lead you to the man you are looking for.' And he led them to Sama-
20 ria. As soon as they had entered Samaria, Elisha prayed, 'O LORD, open
the eyes of these men and let them see again.' And he opened their eyes
21 and they saw that they were inside Samaria. When the king of Israel
22 saw them, he said to Elisha, 'My father, am I to destroy them?' 'No, you
must not do that', he answered. 'You may destroy*a* those whom you have
taken prisoner with your own sword and bow, but as for these men, give
them food and water, and let them eat and drink, and then go back to their
23 master.' So he prepared a great feast for them, and they ate and drank and
then went back to their master. And Aramaean raids on Israel ceased.
24   But later, Ben-hadad king of Aram called up his entire army and marched
25 to the siege of Samaria. The city was near starvation, and they besieged it
so closely that a donkey's head was sold for eighty shekels of silver, and a
26 quarter of a kab of locust-beans for five shekels. One day, as the king of
Israel was walking along the city wall, a woman called to him, 'Help, my
27 lord king!' He said, 'If the LORD will not bring you help, where can I find
28 any for you? From threshing-floor or from winepress? What is your
trouble?' She replied, 'This woman said to me, "Give up your child for
29 us to eat today, and we will eat mine tomorrow." So we cooked my son
and ate him; but when I said to her the next day, "Now give up your child
30 for us to eat", she had hidden him.' When he heard the woman's story, the
king rent his clothes. He was walking along the wall at the time, and when
the people looked, they saw that he had sackcloth underneath, next to his
31 skin. Then he said, 'The LORD do the same to me and more, if the head of
Elisha son of Shaphat stays on his shoulders today.'
32   Elisha was sitting at home, the elders with him. The king had dispatched
one of his retinue but, before the messenger arrived, Elisha said to the
elders, 'See how this son of a murderer has sent to behead me! Take care,
when the messenger comes, to shut the door and hold it fast against him.
33 Can you not hear his master following on his heels?' While he was still
speaking, the king*b* arrived and said, 'Look at our plight! This is the
7 LORD's doing. Why should I wait any longer for him to help us?' But
Elisha answered, 'Hear this word of the LORD: By this time tomorrow a
shekel will buy a measure of flour or two measures of barley in the gateway
2 of Samaria.' Then the lieutenant on whose arm the king leaned said to the
man of God, 'Even if the LORD were to open windows in the sky, such a
thing could not happen!' He answered, 'You will see it with your own eyes,
but none of it will you eat.'
3   At the city gate were four lepers.*c* They said to one another, 'Why
4 should we stay here and wait for death? If we say we will go into the city,
there is famine there, and we shall die; if we say we will stay here, we shall
die just the same. Well then, let us go to the camp of the Aramaeans and
give ourselves up: if they spare us, we shall live; if they put us to death,

---

*a Prob. rdg.; Heb.* Would you destroy.      *b Prob. rdg.; Heb.* messenger.      *c Or* men
suffering from skin-disease.

we can but die.' And so in the twilight they set out for the Aramaean camp; 5
but when they reached the outskirts, they found no one there; for the 6
Lord had caused the Aramaean army to hear a sound like that of chariots
and horses and of a great host, so that the word went round: 'The king of
Israel has hired the kings of the Hittites and the kings of Egypt to attack
us.' They had fled at once in the twilight, abandoning their tents, their 7
horses and asses, and leaving the camp as it stood, while they fled for their
lives. When the four men came to the outskirts of the camp, they went into 8
a tent and ate and drank and looted silver and gold and clothing, and made
off and hid them. Then they came back, went into another tent and rifled
it, and made off and hid the loot. Then they said to one another, 'What we 9
are doing is not right. This is a day of good news and we are keeping it to
ourselves. If we wait till morning, we shall be held to blame. We must go
now and give the news to the king's household.' So they came and called 10
to the watch at the city gate and described how they had gone to the
Aramaean camp and found not a single man in it and had heard no sound:
nothing but horses and asses tethered, and the tents left as they were. Then 11
the watch called out and gave the news to the king's household in the
palace. The king rose in the night and said to his staff, 'I will tell you what 12
the Aramaeans have done. They know that we are starving, and they have
left their camp to go and hide in the open country, expecting us to come
out, and then they can take us alive and enter the city.' One of his staff said, 13
'Send out a party of men with some of the horses that are left; if they live,
they will be as well off as all the other Israelites who are still left; if they
die,*a* they will be no worse off than all those who have already perished.
Let them go and see what has happened.' So they picked two mounted 14
men, and the king dispatched them in the track of the Aramaean army
with the order to go and find out what had happened. They followed as 15
far as the Jordan and found the whole road littered with clothing and
equipment which the Aramaeans had flung aside in their haste. The messengers returned and reported this to the king. Then the people went out 16
and plundered the Aramaean camp, and a measure of flour was sold for a
shekel and two measures of barley for a shekel, so that the word of the
Lord came true. Now the king had appointed the lieutenant on whose 17
arm he leaned to take charge of the gate, and the people trampled him to
death there, just as the man of God had foretold when the king visited him.
For when the man of God said to the king, 'By this time tomorrow a shekel 18
will buy two measures of barley or one measure of flour in the gateway of
Samaria', the lieutenant had answered, 'Even if the Lord were to open 19
windows in the sky, such a thing could not happen!' And the man of God
had said, 'You will see it with your own eyes, but none of it will you eat.'
And this is just what happened to him: the people trampled him to death 20
at the gate.

Elisha said to the woman whose son he had restored to life, 'Go away at **8**
once with your household and find lodging where you can, for the Lord
has decreed a seven years' famine and it has already come upon the land.'
The woman acted at once on the word of the man of God and went away 2

*a* if they live . . . if they die: *prob. rdg.; Heb. obscure.*

417

with her household; and she stayed in the Philistine country for seven years.
3 When she came back at the end of the seven years, she sought an audience
4 of the king to appeal for the return of her house and land. Now the king was
questioning Gehazi, the servant of the man of God, about all the great
5 things Elisha had done; and, as he was describing to the king how he had
brought the dead to life, the selfsame woman began appealing to the king
for her house and her land. 'My lord king,' said Gehazi, 'this is the very
6 woman, and this is her son whom Elisha brought to life.' The king asked
the woman about it, and she told him. Then he entrusted the case to a
eunuch and ordered him to restore all her property to her, with all the
revenues from her land from the time she left the country till that day.

7 Elisha came to Damascus, at a time when Ben-hadad king of Aram was
8 ill; and when he was told that the man of God had arrived, he bade Hazael
take a gift with him and go to the man of God and inquire of the LORD
9 through him whether he would recover from his illness. Hazael went,
taking with him as a gift all kinds of wares of Damascus, forty camel-
loads. When he came into the prophet's presence, he said, 'Your son Ben-
hadad king of Aram has sent me to you to ask whether he will recover from
10 his illness.' 'Go and tell him that he will recover,' he answered; 'but the
11 LORD has revealed to me that in fact he will die.' The man of God stood
there with set face like a man stunned, until he could bear it no longer;
12 then he wept. 'Why do you weep, my lord?' said Hazael. He answered,
'Because I know the harm you will do to the Israelites: you will set their
fortresses on fire and put their young men to the sword; you will dash their
13 children to the ground and you will rip open their pregnant women.' But
Hazael said, 'But I am a dog, a mere nobody; how can I do this great thing?'
Elisha answered, 'The LORD has revealed to me that you will be king of
14 Aram.' Hazael left Elisha and returned to his master, who asked him what
15 Elisha had said. 'He told me that you would recover', he replied. But the
next day he took a blanket and, after dipping it in water, laid it over the
king's face, and he died; and Hazael succeeded him.

16 In the fifth year of Jehoram son of Ahab king of Israel, Joram son of
17ᵃ Jehoshaphat king of Judah became king. He was thirty-two years old when
18 he came to the throne, and he reigned in Jerusalem for eight years. He
followed the practices of the kings of Israel as the house of Ahab had done,
for he had married Ahab's daughter; and he did what was wrong in the
19 eyes of the LORD. But for his servant David's sake the LORD was unwilling
to destroy Judah, since he had promised to give him and his sons a flame,
to burn for all time.

20 During his reign Edom revolted against Judah and set up its own king.
21 Joram crossed over to Zair with all his chariots. He and his chariot-
commanders set out by night, but they were surrounded by the Edomites
22 and defeated,ᵇ whereupon the people fled to their tents. So Edom has
remained independent of Judah to this day; Libnah also revolted at the
23 same time. The other acts and events of Joram's reign are recorded in
24 the annals of the kings of Judah. So Joram rested with his forefathers

---

ᵃ *Verses 17-22: cp. 2 Chr. 21. 5-10.*          ᵇ and defeated: *prob. rdg.; Heb.* and he
defeated Edom.

and was buried with them in the city of David, and his son Ahaziah succeeded him.

In the twelfth year of Jehoram son of Ahab king of Israel, Ahaziah son 25[a] of Joram king of Judah became king. Ahaziah was twenty-two years old 26 when he came to the throne, and he reigned in Jerusalem for one year; his mother was Athaliah granddaughter of Omri king of Israel. He followed 27 the practices of the house of Ahab and did what was wrong in the eyes of the LORD like the house of Ahab, for he was connected with that house by marriage. He allied himself with Jehoram son of Ahab to fight against 28 Hazael king of Aram at Ramoth-gilead; but King Jehoram was wounded by the Aramaeans, and returned to Jezreel to recover from the wounds 29 which were inflicted on him at Ramoth in battle with Hazael king of Aram; and because of his illness Ahaziah son of Joram king of Judah went down to Jezreel to visit him.

ELISHA THE PROPHET SUMMONED one of the company of prophets 9 and said to him, 'Hitch up your cloak, take this flask of oil with you and go to Ramoth-gilead. When you arrive, you will find Jehu son of Jehosha- 2 phat, son of Nimshi; go in and call him aside from his fellow-officers, and lead him through to an inner room. Then take the flask and pour the oil 3 on his head and say, "This is the word of the LORD: I anoint you king over Israel"; then open the door and flee for your life.' So the young prophet 4 went to Ramoth-gilead. When he arrived, he found the officers sitting 5 together and said, 'Sir, I have a word for you.' 'For which of us?' asked Jehu. 'For you, sir', he said. He rose and went into the house, and the 6 prophet poured the oil on his head, saying, 'This is the word of the LORD the God of Israel: "I anoint you king over Israel, the people of the LORD. You shall strike down the house of Ahab your master, and I will take 7 vengeance on Jezebel for the blood of my servants the prophets and for the blood of all the LORD's servants. All the house of Ahab shall perish and I 8 will destroy every mother's son of his house in Israel, whether under the protection of the family or not. And I will make the house of Ahab like the 9 house of Jeroboam son of Nebat and the house of Baasha son of Ahijah. Jezebel shall be devoured by dogs in the plot of ground at Jezreel and 10 no one will bury her." ' Then he opened the door and fled. When Jehu 11 rejoined the king's officers, they said to him, 'Is all well? What did this crazy fellow want with you?' 'You know him and the way his thoughts run', he said. 'Nonsense!' they replied; 'tell us what happened.' 'I will tell 12 you exactly what he said: "This is the word of the LORD: I anoint you king over Israel." ' They snatched up their cloaks and spread them under him 13 on the stones [b] of the steps, and sounded the trumpet and shouted, 'Jehu is king.'

Then Jehu son of Jehoshaphat, son of Nimshi, laid his plans against 14 Jehoram, while Jehoram and the Israelites were defending Ramoth-gilead against Hazael king of Aram. King Jehoram had returned to Jezreel to 15 recover from the wounds inflicted on him by the Aramaeans when he fought against Hazael king of Aram. Jehu said to them, 'If you are on my side, see

[a] *Verses 25–29: cp. 2 Chr. 22. 1–6.*     [b] *Prob. rdg.; Heb. obscure.*

16 that no one escapes from the city to tell the news in Jezreel.' He mounted his chariot and drove to Jezreel, for Jehoram was laid up there, and Ahaziah king of Judah had gone down to visit him.

17 The watchman standing on the watch-tower in Jezreel saw Jehu and his troop approaching and called out, 'I see a troop of men.' Then Jehoram
18 said, 'Fetch a horseman and send to find out if they come peaceably.' The horseman went to meet him and said, 'The king asks, "Is it peace?"' Jehu said, 'Peace? What is peace to you? Fall in behind me.' Thereupon the watchman reported, 'The messenger has met them but he is not coming
19 back.' A second horseman was sent; when he met them, he also said, 'The king asks, "Is it peace?"' 'Peace?' said Jehu. 'What is peace to you? Fall
20 in behind me.' Then the watchman reported, 'He has met them but he is not coming back. The driving is like the driving of Jehu son<sup>a</sup> of Nimshi,
21 for he drives furiously.' 'Harness my chariot', said Jehoram. They harnessed it, and Jehoram king of Israel and Ahaziah king of Judah went out each in his own chariot to meet Jehu, and met him by the plot of Naboth of
22 Jezreel. When Jehoram saw Jehu, he said, 'Is it peace, Jehu?' But he replied, 'Do you call it peace while your mother Jezebel keeps up her
23 obscene idol-worship and monstrous sorceries?' Jehoram wheeled about
24 and fled, crying out to Ahaziah, 'Treachery, Ahaziah!' Jehu seized his bow and shot Jehoram between the shoulders; the arrow pierced his heart
25 and he sank down in his chariot. Then Jehu said to Bidkar, his lieutenant, 'Pick him up and throw him into the plot of land belonging to Naboth of Jezreel; remember how, when you and I were riding side by side behind
26 Ahab his father, the LORD pronounced this sentence against him: "It is the very word of the LORD: as surely as I saw yesterday the blood of Naboth and the blood of his sons, I will requite you in this plot." So pick him up
27 and throw him into it and thus fulfil the word of the LORD.' When Ahaziah king of Judah saw this, he fled by the road to Beth-haggan. Jehu went after him and said, 'Make sure of him too.' They shot him down in his chariot on the road up the valley <sup>b</sup> near Ibleam, but he escaped to Megiddo and died
28 there. His servants conveyed his body to Jerusalem and buried him in his tomb with his forefathers in the city of David.

29 In the eleventh year of Jehoram son of Ahab, Ahaziah became king over Judah.

30 Jehu came to Jezreel. Now Jezebel had heard what had happened; she had painted her eyes and dressed her hair, and she stood looking down from
31 a window. As Jehu entered the gate, she said, 'Is it peace, you Zimri, you
32 murderer of your master?' He looked up at the window and said, 'Who is
33 on my side, who?' Two or three eunuchs looked out, and he said, 'Throw her down.' They threw her down, and some of her blood splashed on to
34 the wall and the horses, which trampled her underfoot. Then he went in and ate and drank. 'See to this accursed woman', he said, 'and bury her;
35 for she is a king's daughter.' But when they went to bury her they found
36 nothing of her but the skull, the feet, and the palms of the hands; and they went back and told him. Jehu said, 'It is the word of the LORD which his servant Elijah the Tishbite spoke, when he said, "In the plot of ground at

    <sup>a</sup> *Or* grandson (*cp. verse 2*).     <sup>b</sup> the valley: *prob. rdg.; Heb.* to Gur.

Jezreel the dogs shall devour the flesh of Jezebel, and Jezebel's corpse shall 37
lie like dung upon the ground in the plot at Jezreel so that no one will be
able to say: This is Jezebel." '

Now seventy sons of Ahab were left in Samaria. Jehu therefore sent a **10**
letter to Samaria, to the elders, the rulers of the city, and to the tutors of
Ahab's children, in which he wrote: 'Now, when this letter reaches you, 2
since you have in your care your master's family as well as his chariots and
horses, fortified cities and weapons, choose the best and the most suitable 3
of your master's family, set him on his father's throne, and fight for your
master's house.' They were panic-stricken and said, 'The two kings could 4
not stand against him; what hope is there that we can?' Therefore the 5
comptroller of the household and the governor of the city, with the elders
and the tutors, sent this message to Jehu: 'We are your servants. Whatever
you tell us we will do; but we will not make anyone king. Do as you think
fit.' Then he wrote them a second letter: 'If you are on my side and will 6
obey my orders, then bring the heads of your master's sons to me at
Jezreel by this time tomorrow.' Now the royal princes, seventy in all, were
with the nobles of the city who were bringing them up. When the letter 7
reached them, they took the royal princes and killed all seventy; they put
their heads in baskets and sent them to Jehu in Jezreel. When the mes- 8
senger came to him and reported that they had brought the heads of the
royal princes, he ordered them to be put in two heaps and left at the
entrance of the city gate till morning. In the morning he went out, stood 9
there and said to all the people, 'You are fair judges. If I conspired against
my master and killed him, who put all these to death? Be sure then that 10
every word which the LORD has spoken against the house of Ahab shall
be fulfilled, and that the LORD has now done what he spoke through his
servant Elijah.' So Jehu put to death all who were left of the house of Ahab 11
in Jezreel, as well as all his nobles, his close friends, and his priests, until
he had left not one survivor.

Then he set out for Samaria, and on the way there, when he had reached 12
a shepherds' shelter,[a] he came upon the kinsmen of Ahaziah king of 13
Judah and said, 'Who are you?' 'We are kinsmen of Ahaziah,' they replied;
'and we have come down to greet the families of the king and of the queen
mother.' 'Take them alive', he said. So they took them alive; then they 14
slew them and flung them into the pit that was there, forty-two of them;
they did not leave a single survivor.

When he had left that place, he found Jehonadab son of Rechab coming 15
to meet him. He greeted him and said, 'Are you with me heart and soul, as
I am with you?' 'I am', said Jehonadab. 'Then if you are,' said Jehu, 'give
me your hand.' He gave him his hand and Jehu helped him up into his
chariot. 'Come with me,' he said, 'and you will see my zeal for the LORD.' 16
So he took him with him in his chariot. When he came to Samaria, he put 17
to death all of Ahab's house who were left there and so blotted it out, in
fulfilment of the word which the LORD had spoken to Elijah. Then Jehu 18
called all the people together and said to them, 'Ahab served the Baal a
little; Jehu will serve him much. Now, summon all the prophets of Baal, 19

---

[a] a shepherds' shelter: *or* Beth-eker of the Shepherds.

all his ministers and priests; not one must be missing. For I am holding a great sacrifice to Baal, and no one who is missing from it shall live.' In this
20 way Jehu outwitted the ministers of Baal in order to destroy them. So
21 Jehu said, 'Let a sacred ceremony for Baal be held.' They did so, and Jehu himself sent word throughout Israel, and all the ministers of Baal came; there was not a man left who did not come. They went into the temple of
22 Baal and it was filled from end to end. Then he said to the person who had charge of the wardrobe, 'Bring out robes for all the ministers of Baal'; and
23 he brought them out. Then Jehu and Jehonadab son of Rechab went into the temple of Baal and said to the ministers of Baal, 'Look carefully and make sure that there are no servants of the LORD here with you, but only
24 the ministers of Baal.' Then they went in to offer sacrifices and whole-offerings. Now Jehu had stationed eighty men outside and said to them, 'I am putting these men in your charge, and any man who lets one escape
25 shall answer for it with his life.' When he had finished offering the whole-offering, Jehu ordered the guards and the lieutenants to go and cut them all down, and let not one of them escape; so they slew them without quarter. The escort and the lieutenants then rushed into the keep of the temple of
26 Baal and brought out the sacred pole[a] from the temple of Baal and burnt it;
27 and they pulled down the sacred pillar of the Baal and the temple itself and
28 made a privy of it—as it is today. Thus Jehu stamped out the worship of
29 Baal in Israel. He did not however abandon the sins of Jeroboam son of Nebat who led Israel into sin, but he maintained the worship of the golden calves of Bethel and Dan.
30    Then the LORD said to Jehu, 'You have done well what is right in my eyes and have done to the house of Ahab all that it was in my mind to do. Therefore your sons to the fourth generation shall sit on the throne of
31 Israel.' But Jehu was not careful to follow the law of the LORD the God of Israel with all his heart; he did not abandon the sins of Jeroboam who led Israel into sin.
32    In those days the LORD began to work havoc on Israel, and Hazael struck
33 at them in every corner of their territory eastwards from the Jordan: all the land of Gilead, Gad, Reuben, and Manasseh, from Aroer which is by the gorge of the Arnon, including Gilead and Bashan.
34    The other events of Jehu's reign, his achievements and his exploits, are
35 recorded in the annals of the kings of Israel. So Jehu rested with his fore-fathers and was buried in Samaria; and he was succeeded by his son
36 Jehoahaz. Jehu reigned over Israel in Samaria for twenty-eight years.

## Kings of Israel and Judah

11 1[b]  AS SOON AS ATHALIAH mother of Ahaziah saw that her son was dead,
2       she set out to destroy all the royal line. But Jehosheba daughter of King Joram, sister of Ahaziah, took Ahaziah's son Joash and stole him away from among the princes who were being murdered; she put[c] him

---

[a] *Prob. rdg.; Heb.* sacred pillars.     [b] *Verses 1–20: cp. 2 Chr. 22. 10—23. 21.*
[c] she put: *prob. rdg., cp. 2 Chr. 22. 11; Heb. om.*

and his nurse in a bedchamber where he was hidden from Athaliah and
was not put to death. He remained concealed with her in the house of the 3
LORD for six years, while Athaliah ruled the country. In the seventh year 4
Jehoiada sent for the captains of units of a hundred, both of the Carites
and of the guards, and he brought them into the house of the LORD; he
made an agreement with them and put them on their oath in the house of
the LORD, and showed them the king's son, and gave them the following 5
orders: 'One third of you who are on duty on the sabbath are to be on
guard in the palace; the rest of you are to be on special duty in the house of 6
the LORD, one third at the Sur Gate and the other third at the gate with*a*
the outrunners. Your two companies who are off duty on the sabbath shall 7
be on duty for the king in the house of the LORD. So you shall be on guard 8
round the king, each man with his arms at the ready, and anyone who
comes near the ranks is to be put to death; you must be with the king
wherever he goes.'

The captains carried out the orders of Jehoiada the priest to the letter. 9
Each took his men, both those who came on duty on the sabbath and those
who came off, and came to Jehoiada. The priest handed out to the captains 10
King David's spears and shields, which were in the house of the LORD.
Then the guards took up their stations, each man carrying his arms at the 11
ready, from corner to corner of the house to north and south,*b* surrounding
the king. Then he brought out the king's son, put the crown on his head, 12
handed him the warrant and anointed him king. The people clapped their
hands and shouted, 'Long live the king.' When Athaliah heard the noise 13
made by the guards and the people, she came into the house of the LORD
where the people were and found the king standing, as was the custom, 14
on the dais,*c* amidst outbursts of song and fanfares of trumpets in his
honour, and all the populace rejoicing and blowing trumpets. Then
Athaliah rent her clothes and cried, 'Treason! Treason!' Jehoiada the 15
priest gave orders to the captains in command of the troops: 'Bring her
outside the precincts and put to the sword anyone in attendance on her';
for the priest said, 'She shall not be put to death in the house of the LORD.'
So they laid hands on her and took her out by the entry for horses to the 16
royal palace, and there she was put to death.

Then Jehoiada made a covenant between the LORD and the king and 17
people that they should be the LORD's people, and also between the king
and the people. And all the people went into the temple of Baal and pulled 18
it down; they smashed to pieces its altars and images, and they slew Mattan
the priest of Baal before the altars. Then Jehoiada set a watch over the house
of the LORD; he took the captains of units of a hundred, the Carites and the 19
guards and all the people, and they escorted the king from the house of the
LORD through the Gate of the Guards to the royal palace, and seated him
on the royal throne. The whole people rejoiced and the city was tranquil. 20
That is how Athaliah was put to the sword in the royal palace.

Joash was seven years old when he became king. In the seventh year of 21*d* **12** 1
Jehu, Joash became king, and he reigned in Jerusalem for forty years; his

*a* Or behind.    *b* Prob. rdg.; Heb. adds of the altar and the house.    *c* Or by the
pillar.    *d* 11. 21—12. 15: cp. 2 Chr. 24. 1-14.

2 mother was Zibiah of Beersheba. He did what was right in the eyes of the
3 LORD all his days, as Jehoiada the priest had taught him. The hill-shrines,
however, were allowed to remain; the people still continued to sacrifice
and make smoke-offerings there.

4 Then Joash ordered the priests to take all the silver brought as holy-
gifts into the house of the LORD, the silver for which each man was assessed,[a]
the silver for the persons assessed under his name, and any silver which
5 any man brought voluntarily to the house of the LORD. He ordered the
priests, also, each to make a contribution from his own funds, and to repair
6 the house wherever it was found necessary. But in the twenty-third year
of the reign of Joash the priests had still not carried out the repairs to the
7 house. King Joash summoned Jehoiada the priest and the other priests and
said to them, 'Why are you not repairing the house? Henceforth you need
8 not contribute from your own funds for the repair of the house.' So the
priests agreed neither to receive money from the people nor to undertake
9 the repairs of the house. Then Jehoiada the priest took a chest and bored a
hole in the lid and put it beside the altar on the right side going into the
house of the LORD, and the priests on duty at the entrance put in it all the
10 money brought into the house of the LORD. And whenever they saw that
the chest was well filled, the king's secretary and the high priest came and
melted down the silver found in the house of the LORD and weighed it.
11 When it had been checked, they gave the silver to the foremen over the
work in the house of the LORD and they paid the carpenters and the builders
12 working on the temple and the masons and the stone-cutters; they used it
also to buy timber and hewn stone for the repairs and for all other expenses
13 connected with them. They did not use the silver brought into the house
of the LORD to make silver cups, snuffers, tossing-bowls, trumpets, or
14 any gold or silver vessels; but they paid it to the workmen and used it for
15 the repairs. No account was demanded from the foremen to whom the
money was given for the payment of the workmen, for they were acting on
16 trust. Money from guilt-offerings and sin-offerings was not brought into
the house of the LORD: it belonged to the priests.

17 Then Hazael king of Aram came up and attacked Gath and took it; and
18 he moved on against Jerusalem. But Joash king of Judah took all the holy-
gifts that Jehoshaphat, Joram, and Ahaziah his forefathers, kings of Judah,
had dedicated, and his own holy-gifts, and all the gold that was found in
the treasuries of the house of the LORD and in the royal palace, and sent
them to Hazael king of Aram; and he withdrew from Jerusalem.

19 The other acts and events of the reign of Joash are recorded in the annals
20[b] of the kings of Judah. His servants revolted against him and struck him
21 down in the house of Millo on the descent to Silla. It was his servants
Jozachar son of Shimeath and Jehozabad son of Shomer who struck the
fatal blow; and he was buried with his forefathers in the city of David. He
was succeeded by his son Amaziah.

**13** In the twenty-third year of Joash son of Ahaziah king of Judah, Jehoahaz
son of Jehu became king over Israel in Samaria and he reigned seventeen

---

[a] *the silver . . . assessed: prob. rdg.; Heb. obscure.*      [b] *Verses 20, 21 : cp. 2 Chr. 24.
25–27.*

years. He did what was wrong in the eyes of the LORD and continued the 2
sinful practices of Jeroboam son of Nebat who led Israel into sin, and did
not give them up. So the LORD was roused to anger against Israel and he 3
made them subject for some years to Hazael king of Aram and Ben-hadad
son of Hazael. Then Jehoahaz sought to placate the LORD, and the LORD 4
heard his prayer, for he saw how the king of Aram oppressed Israel. The 5
LORD appointed a deliverer for Israel, who rescued them from the power
of Aram, and the Israelites settled down again in their own homes. But 6
they did not give up the sinful practices of the house of Jeroboam who led
Israel into sin, but continued in them; the goddess Asherah*ᵃ* remained in
Samaria. Hazael had left Jehoahaz no armed force except fifty horsemen, 7
ten chariots, and ten thousand infantry; all the rest the king of Aram had
destroyed and made like dust under foot.

The other events of the reign of Jehoahaz, and all his achievements and 8
his exploits, are recorded in the annals of the kings of Israel. So Jehoahaz 9
rested with his forefathers and was buried in Samaria; and he was succeeded by his son Jehoash.

In the thirty-ninth year of Joash king of Judah, Jehoash son of Jehoahaz 10
became king over Israel in Samaria and reigned sixteen years. He did what 11
was wrong in the eyes of the LORD; he did not give up any of the sinful
practices of Jeroboam son of Nebat who led Israel into sin, but continued
in them. The other events of the reign of Jehoash, all his achievements, his 12
exploits and his war with Amaziah king of Judah, are recorded in the annals
of the kings of Israel. So Jehoash rested with his forefathers and was buried 13
in Samaria with the kings of Israel, and Jeroboam sat upon his throne.

Elisha fell ill and lay on his deathbed, and Jehoash king of Israel went 14
down to him and wept over him and said, 'My father! My father, the
chariots and the horsemen of Israel!' 'Take bow and arrows', said Elisha, 15
and he took bow and arrows. 'Put your hand to the bow', said the prophet. 16
He did so, and Elisha laid his hands on those of the king. Then he said, 17
'Open the window toward the east'; he opened it and Elisha told him to
shoot, and he shot. Then the prophet said, 'An arrow for the LORD's
victory, an arrow for victory over Aram! You will defeat Aram utterly at
Aphek'; and he added, 'Now take up your arrows.' When the king had 18
taken them, Elisha said, 'Strike the ground with them.' He struck three
times and stopped. The man of God was furious with him and said, 'You 19
should have struck five or six times; then you would have defeated Aram
utterly; as it is, you will strike Aram three times and no more.'

Then Elisha died and was buried. 20

Year by year Moabite raiders used to invade the land. Once some men 21
were burying a dead man when they caught sight of the raiders. They
threw the body into the grave of Elisha and made off; when the body
touched the prophet's bones, the man came to life and rose to his feet.

All through the reign of Jehoahaz, Hazael king of Aram oppressed Israel. 22
But the LORD was gracious and took pity on them; because of his covenant 23
with Abraham, Isaac, and Jacob, he looked on them with favour and was
unwilling to destroy them; nor has he even yet banished them from his

---

*ᵃ* the goddess Asherah: *or* the sacred pole.

24 sight. When Hazael king of Aram died and was succeeded by his son Ben-
25 hadad, Jehoash son of Jehoahaz recaptured the cities which Ben-hadad
had taken in war from Jehoahaz his father; three times Jehoash defeated
him and recovered the cities of Israel.

**14** 1[a]   In the second year of Jehoash son of Jehoahaz king of Israel, Amaziah
2 son of Joash king of Judah succeeded his father. He was twenty-five years
old when he came to the throne, and he reigned in Jerusalem for twenty-
3 nine years; his mother was Jehoaddin of Jerusalem. He did what was right
in the eyes of the LORD, yet not as his forefather David had done; he
4 followed his father Joash in everything. The hill-shrines were allowed to
5 remain; the people continued to slaughter and burn sacrifices there. When
the royal power was firmly in his grasp, he put to death those of his servants
6 who had murdered the king his father; but he spared the murderers'
children in obedience to the LORD's command written in the law of Moses:
'Fathers shall not be put to death for their children, nor children for their
7 fathers; a man shall be put to death only for his own sin.' He defeated ten
thousand Edomites in the Valley of Salt and captured Sela; he gave it the
name Joktheel, which it still bears.

8[b]   Then Amaziah sent messengers to Jehoash son of Jehoahaz, son of
9 Jehu, king of Israel, to propose a meeting. But Jehoash king of Israel sent
this answer to Amaziah king of Judah: 'A thistle in Lebanon sent to a
cedar in Lebanon to say, "Give your daughter in marriage to my son." But
10 a wild beast in Lebanon, passing by, trampled on the thistle. You have
defeated Edom, it is true; and it has gone to your head. Stay at home and
enjoy your triumph. Why should you involve yourself in disaster and bring
yourself to the ground, and Judah with you?'

11   But Amaziah would not listen; so Jehoash king of Israel marched out,
and he and Amaziah king of Judah met one another at Beth-shemesh in
12 Judah. The men of Judah were routed by Israel and fled to their homes.
13 But Jehoash king of Israel captured Amaziah king of Judah, son of Joash,
son of Ahaziah, at Beth-shemesh. He went to Jerusalem and broke down
the city wall from the Gate of Ephraim to the Corner Gate, a distance of
14 four hundred cubits. He also took all the gold and silver and all the vessels
found in the house of the LORD and in the treasuries of the royal palace,
as well as hostages, and returned to Samaria.

15   The other events of the reign of Jehoash, and all his achievements, his
exploits and his wars with Amaziah king of Judah, are recorded in the
16 annals of the kings of Israel. So Jehoash rested with his forefathers and
was buried in Samaria with the kings of Israel; and he was succeeded by
his son Jeroboam.

17[c]   Amaziah son of Joash, king of Judah, outlived Jehoash son of Jehoahaz,
18 king of Israel, by fifteen years. The other events of Amaziah's reign are
19 recorded in the annals of the kings of Judah. A conspiracy was formed
against him in Jerusalem and he fled to Lachish; but they sent after him
20 to Lachish and put him to death there. Then his body was conveyed on
horseback to Jerusalem, and there he was buried with his forefathers in the

---

[a] *Verses 1–6: cp. 2 Chr. 25. 1–4.*   [b] *Verses 8–14: cp. 2 Chr. 25. 17–24.*   [c] *Verses 17–22: cp. 2 Chr. 25. 25—26. 2.*

city of David. The people of Judah took Azariah, now sixteen years old, 21
and made him king in succession to his father Amaziah. It was he who 22
built Elath and restored it to Judah after the king rested with his forefathers.

In the fifteenth year of Amaziah son of Joash king of Judah, Jeroboam 23
son of Jehoash king of Israel became king in Samaria and reigned for
forty-one years. He did what was wrong in the eyes of the LORD; he did 24
not give up the sinful practices of Jeroboam son of Nebat who led Israel
into sin. He re-established the frontiers of Israel from Lebo-hamath to the 25
Sea of the Arabah, in fulfilment of the word of the LORD the God of Israel
spoken by his servant the prophet Jonah son of Amittai, of Gath-hepher.
For the LORD had seen how bitterly Israel had suffered; no one was safe, 26
whether under the protection of his family or not, and Israel was left
defenceless. But the LORD had made no threat to blot out the name of 27
Israel under heaven, and he saved them through Jeroboam son of Jehoash.
The other events of Jeroboam's reign, and all his achievements, his ex- 28
ploits, the wars he fought and how he recovered Damascus and Hamath
in Jaudi for *a* Israel, are recorded in the annals of the kings of Israel. So 29
Jeroboam rested with his forefathers the kings of Israel; and he was
succeeded by his son Zechariah.

In the twenty-seventh year of Jeroboam king of Israel, Azariah *b* son of **15**
Amaziah king of Judah became king. He was sixteen years old when he 2*c*
came to the throne, and he reigned in Jerusalem for fifty-two years; his
mother was Jecoliah of Jerusalem. He did what was right in the eyes of 3
the LORD, as Amaziah his father had done. But the hill-shrines were allowed 4
to remain; the people still continued to slaughter and burn sacrifices there.
The LORD struck the king with leprosy,*d* which he had till the day of his 5*e*
death; he was relieved of all duties and lived in his own house, while his
son Jotham was comptroller of the household and regent. The other acts 6
and events of Azariah's reign are recorded in the annals of the kings of
Judah. So he rested with his forefathers and was buried with them in the 7
city of David; and he was succeeded by his son Jotham.

In the thirty-eighth year of Azariah king of Judah, Zechariah son of 8
Jeroboam became king over Israel in Samaria and reigned six months. He 9
did what was wrong in the eyes of the LORD, as his forefathers had done;
he did not give up the sinful practices of Jeroboam son of Nebat who led
Israel into sin. Shallum son of Jabesh formed a conspiracy against him, 10
attacked him in Ibleam, killed him and usurped the throne. The other 11
events of Zechariah's reign are recorded in the annals of the kings of
Israel. Thus the word of the LORD spoken to Jehu was fulfilled: 'Your sons 12
to the fourth generation shall sit on the throne of Israel.'

Shallum son of Jabesh became king in the thirty-ninth year of Uzziah 13
king of Judah, and he reigned one full month in Samaria. Then Menahem 14
son of Gadi came up from Tirzah to Samaria, attacked Shallum son of
Jabesh there, killed him and usurped the throne. The other events of 15

---

*a* in Jaudi for: *prob. rdg.; Heb.* to Judah in.          *b* Uzziah *in verses 13, 30, 32, 34.*
*c* *Verses 2, 3 : cp. 2 Chr. 26. 3, 4.*          *d* *Or* a skin-disease.          *e* *Verses 5–7 : cp.*
*2 Chr. 26. 21–23.*

Shallum's reign and the conspiracy that he formed are recorded in the annals of the kings of Israel.

16   Then Menahem, starting out from Tirzah, destroyed Tappuah and everything in it and ravaged its territory; he ravaged it because it had not opened its gates to him, and he ripped open all the pregnant women.

17   In the thirty-ninth year of Azariah king of Judah, Menahem son of Gadi
18 became king over Israel and he reigned in Samaria for ten years. He did what was wrong in the eyes of the LORD; he did not give up the sinful
19 practices of Jeroboam son of Nebat who led Israel into sin. In his days Pul king of Assyria invaded the country, and Menahem gave him a thousand talents of silver to obtain his help in strengthening his hold on the kingdom.
20 Menahem laid a levy on all the men of wealth in Israel, and each had to give the king of Assyria fifty silver shekels. Then the king of Assyria withdrew
21 without occupying the country. The other acts and events of Menahem's
22 reign are recorded in the annals of the kings of Israel. So Menahem rested with his forefathers; and he was succeeded by his son Pekahiah.

23   In the fiftieth year of Azariah king of Judah, Pekahiah son of Menahem
24 became king over Israel in Samaria and reigned for two years. He did what was wrong in the eyes of the LORD; he did not give up the sinful practices
25 of Jeroboam son of Nebat who led Israel into sin. Pekah son of Remaliah, his lieutenant, formed a conspiracy against him and, with the help of fifty Gileadites, attacked him in Samaria in the citadel of the royal palace,[a]
26 killed him and usurped the throne. The other acts and events of Pekahiah's reign are recorded in the annals of the kings of Israel.

27   In the fifty-second year of Azariah king of Judah, Pekah son of Remaliah
28 became king over Israel in Samaria and reigned for twenty years. He did what was wrong in the eyes of the LORD; he did not give up the sinful
29 practices of Jeroboam son of Nebat who led Israel into sin. In the days of Pekah king of Israel, Tiglath-pileser king of Assyria came and seized Iyyon, Abel-beth-maacah, Janoah, Kedesh, Hazor, Gilead, and Galilee,
30 with all the land of Naphtali, and deported the people to Assyria. Then Hoshea son of Elah formed a conspiracy against Pekah son of Remaliah, attacked him, killed him and usurped the throne in the twentieth year of
31 Jotham son of Uzziah. The other acts and events of Pekah's reign are recorded in the annals of the kings of Israel.

32   In the second year of Pekah son of Remaliah king of Israel, Jotham son
33b of Uzziah king of Judah became king. He was twenty-five years old when he came to the throne, and he reigned in Jerusalem for sixteen years; his
34 mother was Jerusha daughter of Zadok. He did what was right in the eyes
35 of the LORD, as his father Uzziah had done; but the hill-shrines were allowed to remain and the people continued to slaughter and burn sacrifices there. It was he who constructed the upper gate of the house of the LORD.
36 The other acts and events of Jotham's reign are recorded in the annals of
37 the kings of Judah. In those days the LORD began to make Rezin king of
38 Aram and Pekah son of Remaliah attack Judah. And Jotham rested with his forefathers and was buried with them in the city of David his forefather; and he was succeeded by his son Ahaz.

[a] *Prob. rdg.; Heb. adds* Argob and Arieh.      [b] *Verses 33–35: cp. 2 Chr. 27. 1–3.*

## Downfall of the northern kingdom

IN THE SEVENTEENTH YEAR OF PEKAH son of Remaliah, Ahaz son **16** of Jotham king of Judah became king. Ahaz was twenty years old when **2** *a* he came to the throne, and he reigned in Jerusalem for sixteen years. He did not do what was right in the eyes of the LORD his God like his fore- father David, but followed in the footsteps of the kings of Israel; he even **3** passed his son through the fire, adopting the abominable practice of the nations whom the LORD had dispossessed in favour of the Israelites. He **4** slaughtered and burnt sacrifices at the hill-shrines and on the hill-tops and under every spreading tree.

Then Rezin king of Aram and Pekah son of Remaliah king of Israel **5** attacked Jerusalem and besieged Ahaz but could not bring him to battle. At that time the king of Edom *b* recovered Elath and drove the Judaeans **6** out of it; so the Edomites entered the city and have occupied it to this day. Ahaz sent messengers to Tiglath-pileser king of Assyria to say, 'I am your **7** servant and your son. Come and save me from the king of Aram and from the king of Israel who are attacking me.' Ahaz took the silver and gold found **8** in the house of the LORD and in the treasuries of the royal palace and sent them to the king of Assyria as a bribe. The king of Assyria listened to him; **9** he advanced on Damascus, captured it, deported its inhabitants to Kir and put Rezin to death.

When King Ahaz went to meet Tiglath-pileser king of Assyria at **10** Damascus, he saw there an altar of which he sent a sketch and a detailed plan to Uriah the priest. Accordingly, Uriah built an altar, following all the **11** instructions that the king had sent him from Damascus, and had it ready against the king's return. When the king returned from Damascus he saw **12** the altar, approached it and mounted the steps; there he burnt his whole- **13** offering and his grain-offering and poured out his drink-offering, and he flung the blood of his shared-offerings against it. The bronze altar that was **14** before the LORD he removed from the front of the house, from between this altar and the house of the LORD, and put it on the north side of this altar. Then King Ahaz gave these instructions to Uriah the priest: 'Burn on the **15** great altar the morning whole-offering and the evening grain-offering, and the king's whole-offering and his grain-offering, and the whole-offering of all the people of the land, their grain-offering and their drink-offerings, and fling against it all the blood of the sacrifices. But the bronze altar shall be mine, to offer morning sacrifice.' Uriah the priest did all that the king **16** told him. Then King Ahaz broke up the trolleys and removed the panels, **17** and he took down the basin and the Sea of bronze from the oxen which supported it and put it on a stone base. In the house of the LORD he **18** turned round the structure they had erected for use on the sabbath, and the outer gate for the king, to satisfy the king of Assyria. The other acts **19** *c* and events of the reign of Ahaz are recorded in the annals of the kings of Judah. So Ahaz rested with his forefathers and was buried with them in the **20** city of David; and he was succeeded by his son Hezekiah.

*a* *Verses 2–4: cp. 2 Chr. 28. 1–4.*     *b* the king of Edom: *prob. rdg.; Heb.* Rezin king of Aram.     *c* *Verses 19, 20: cp. 2 Chr. 28. 26, 27.*

**17** In the twelfth year of Ahaz king of Judah, Hoshea son of Elah became
2 king over Israel in Samaria and reigned nine years. He did what was wrong
in the eyes of the LORD, but not as the previous kings of Israel had done.
3 Shalmaneser king of Assyria made war upon him and Hoshea became
4 tributary to him. But when the king of Assyria discovered that Hoshea was
being disloyal to him, sending messengers to the king of Egypt at So,[a] and
withholding the tribute which he had been paying year by year, the king of
5 Assyria arrested him and put him in prison. Then he invaded the whole
6 country and, reaching Samaria, besieged it for three years. In the ninth
year of Hoshea he captured Samaria and deported its people to Assyria and
settled them in Halah and on the Habor, the river of Gozan, and in the
cities of Media.
7      All this happened to the Israelites because they had sinned against the
LORD their God who brought them up from Egypt, from the rule of
8 Pharaoh king of Egypt; they paid homage to other gods and observed the
laws and customs of the nations whom the LORD had dispossessed before
9 them and uttered blasphemies against the LORD their God; they built hill-
shrines for themselves in all their settlements, from watch-tower to fortified
10 city, and set up sacred pillars and sacred poles on every high hill and under
11 every spreading tree, and burnt sacrifices at all the hill-shrines there, as
the nations did whom the LORD had displaced before them. By this wicked-
12 ness of theirs they provoked the LORD's anger. They worshipped idols, a
13 thing which the LORD had forbidden them to do. Still the LORD solemnly
charged Israel and Judah by every prophet and seer, saying, 'Give up your
evil ways; keep my commandments and statutes given in the law which I
enjoined on your forefathers and delivered to you through my servants the
14 prophets.' They would not listen, however, but were as stubborn and rebellious as their forefathers had been, who refused to put their trust in the
15 LORD their God; they rejected his statutes and the covenant which he had
made with their forefathers and the solemn warnings which he had given
to them; they followed worthless idols and became worthless themselves;
they imitated the nations round about them, a thing which the LORD had
16 forbidden them to do. Forsaking every commandment of the LORD their
God, they made themselves images of cast metal, two calves, and also a
sacred pole; they prostrated themselves to all the host of heaven and wor-
17 shipped the Baal, and they made their sons and daughters pass through
the fire. They practised augury and divination; they sold themselves to do
what was wrong in the eyes of the LORD and so provoked his anger.
18      Thus it was that the LORD was incensed against Israel and banished them
19 from his presence; only the tribe of Judah was left. Even Judah did not
keep the commandments of the LORD their God but followed the practices
20 adopted by Israel; so the LORD rejected the whole race of Israel and
punished them and gave them over to plunderers and finally flung them
21 out of his sight. When he tore Israel from the house of David, they made
Jeroboam son of Nebat king, who seduced Israel from their allegiance to
22 the LORD and led them into grave sin. The Israelites persisted in all the
23 sins that Jeroboam had committed and did not give them up, until finally

*a to the king of Egypt at So: prob. rdg.; Heb. to So king of Egypt.*

the LORD banished the Israelites from his presence, as he had threatened through his servants the prophets, and they were carried into exile from their own land to Assyria; and there they are to this day.

Then the king of Assyria brought people from Babylon, Cuthah, Avva, 24 Hamath, and Sepharvaim, and settled them in the cities of Samaria in place of the Israelites; so they occupied Samaria and lived in its cities. In 25 the early years of their settlement they did not pay homage to the LORD; and the LORD sent lions among them, and the lions preyed upon them. The king was told that the deported peoples whom he had settled in the 26 cities of Samaria did not know the established usage of the god of the country, and that he had sent lions among them which were preying upon them because they did not know this. The king of Assyria, therefore, gave 27 orders that one of the priests deported from Samaria should be sent back to live there and teach the people the usage of the god of the country. So 28 one of the deported priests came and lived at Bethel, and taught them how they should pay their homage to the LORD. But each of the nations made 29 its own god, and they set them up within*a* the hill-shrines which the Samaritans had made, each nation in its own settlements. Succoth-benoth 30 was worshipped by the men of Babylon, Nergal by the men of Cuth, Ashima by the men of Hamath, Nibhaz and Tartak by the Avvites; and the 31 Sepharvites burnt their children as offerings to Adrammelech and Anam-melech, the gods of Sepharvaim. While still paying homage to the LORD, 32 they appointed people from every class to act as priests of the hill-shrines and they resorted to them there. They paid homage to the LORD while at 33 the same time they served their own gods, according to the custom of the nations from which they had been carried into exile.

They keep up these old practices to this day; they do not pay homage to 34 the LORD, for they do not keep his*b* statutes and his*b* judgements, the law and commandment, which he enjoined upon the descendants of Jacob whom he named Israel. When the LORD made a covenant with them, he 35 gave them this commandment: 'You shall not pay homage to other gods or bow down to them or serve them or sacrifice to them, but you shall pay 36 homage to the LORD who brought you up from Egypt with great power and with outstretched arm; to him you shall bow down, to him you shall offer sacrifice. You shall faithfully keep the statutes, the judgements, the law, 37 and the commandments which he wrote for you, and you shall not pay homage to other gods. You shall not forget the covenant which I made 38 with you; you shall not pay homage to other gods. But to the LORD your 39 God you shall pay homage, and he will preserve you from all your enemies.' However, they would not listen but continued their former practices. 40 While these nations paid homage to the LORD they continued to serve their 41 images, and their children and their children's children have maintained the practice of their forefathers to this day.

IN THE THIRD YEAR OF HOSHEA son of Elah king of Israel, Hezekiah 18 1*c* son of Ahaz king of Judah became king. He was twenty-five years old when 2 he came to the throne, and he reigned in Jerusalem for twenty-nine years;

*a* Or in niches at.     *b* Prob. rdg.; Heb. their.     *c* Verses 1–3: cp. 2 Chr. 29. 1, 2.

3 his mother was Abi daughter of Zechariah. He did what was right in the
4 eyes of the LORD, as David his forefather had done. It was he who suppressed the hill-shrines, smashed the sacred pillars, cut down every
sacred pole and broke up the bronze serpent that Moses had made; for up
to that time the Israelites had been burning sacrifices to it; they called it
5 Nehushtan. He put his trust in the LORD the God of Israel; there was
nobody like him among all the kings of Judah who succeeded him or among
6 those who had gone before him. He remained loyal to the LORD and did
not fail in his allegiance to him, and he kept the commandments which the
7 LORD had given to Moses. So the LORD was with him and he prospered in
all that he undertook; he rebelled against the king of Assyria and was no
8 longer subject to him. He conquered the Philistine country as far as Gaza
and its boundaries, alike the watch-tower and the fortified city.

9    In the fourth year of Hezekiah's reign (that was the seventh year of
Hoshea son of Elah king of Israel) Shalmaneser king of Assyria made an
10 attack on Samaria, invested it and captured it after a siege of three years;
it was in the sixth year of Hezekiah (the ninth year of Hoshea king of Israel)
11 that Samaria was captured. The king of Assyria deported the Israelites to
Assyria and settled them in Halah and on the Habor, the river of Gozan,
12 and in the cities of Media, because they did not obey the LORD their God
but violated his covenant and every commandment that Moses the servant
of the LORD had given them; they would not listen and they would not
obey.

13ᵃ    In the fourteenth year of the reign of Hezekiah, Sennacherib king of
14 Assyria attacked and took all the fortified cities of Judah. Hezekiah king
of Judah sent a message to the king of Assyria at Lachish: 'I have done
wrong; withdraw from my land, and I will pay any penalty you impose
upon me.' So the king of Assyria laid on Hezekiah king of Judah a penalty
15 of three hundred talents of silver and thirty talents of gold; and Hezekiah
gave him all the silver found in the house of the LORD and in the treasuries
16 of the royal palace. At that time Hezekiah broke up the doors of the temple
of the LORD and the door-frames which he himself had plated, and gave
them to the king of Assyria.

17    From Lachish the king of Assyria sent the commander-in-chief, the
chief eunuch, and the chief officer ᵇ with a strong force to King Hezekiah
at Jerusalem, and they went up and came to Jerusalem and halted by the
conduit of the Upper Pool on the causeway which leads to the Fuller's
18 Field. When they called for the king, Eliakim son of Hilkiah, the comptroller
of the household, came out to them, with Shebna the adjutant-general and
19 Joah son of Asaph, the secretary of state. The chief officer said to them,
'Tell Hezekiah that this is the message of the Great King, the king of
20 Assyria: "What ground have you for this confidence of yours? Do you
think fine words can take the place of skill and numbers? On whom then
21 do you rely for support in your rebellion against me? On Egypt? Egypt is
a splintered cane that will run into a man's hand and pierce it if he leans
on it. That is what Pharaoh king of Egypt proves to all who rely on him.

ᵃ *Verses 13–37: cp. Isa. 36. 1–22; 2 Chr. 32. 1–19.*          ᵇ the commander-in-chief,
the chief eunuch, and the chief officer: *or* Tartan, Rab-saris, and Rab-shakeh.

And if you tell me that you are relying on the LORD your God, is he not 22
the god whose hill-shrines and altars Hezekiah has suppressed, telling
Judah and Jerusalem that they must prostrate themselves before this altar
in Jerusalem?"

'Now, make a bargain with my master the king of Assyria: I will give 23
you two thousand horses if you can find riders for them. Will you reject 24
the authority of even the least of my master's servants and rely on Egypt
for chariots and horsemen? Do you think that I have come to attack this 25
place and destroy it without the consent of the LORD? No; the LORD
himself said to me, "Attack this land and destroy it."'

Eliakim son of Hilkiah, Shebna, and Joah said to the chief officer, 26
'Please speak to us in Aramaic, for we understand it; do not speak Hebrew
to us within earshot of the people on the city wall.' The chief officer 27
answered, 'Is it to your master and to you that my master has sent me to
say this? Is it not to the people sitting on the wall who, like you, will have
to eat their own dung and drink their own urine?' Then he stood and 28
shouted in Hebrew, 'Hear the message of the Great King, the king of
Assyria. These are the king's words: "Do not be taken in by Hezekiah. He 29
cannot save you from me. Do not let him persuade you to rely on the LORD, 30
and tell you that the LORD will save you and that this city will never be
surrendered to the king of Assyria." Do not listen to Hezekiah; these are 31
the words of the king of Assyria: "Make peace with me. Come out to me,
and then you shall each eat the fruit of his own vine and his own fig-tree,
and drink the water of his own cistern, until I come and take you to a land 32
like your own, a land of grain and new wine, of corn and vineyards, of olives,
fine oil, and honey—life for you all, instead of death. Do not listen to
Hezekiah; he will only mislead you by telling you that the LORD will save
you. Did the god of any of these nations ever save his land from the king of 33
Assyria? Where are the gods of Hamath and Arpad? Where are the gods of 34
Sepharvaim, Hena, and Ivvah? Where are the gods of Samaria? Did they
save Samaria from me? Among all the gods of the nations is there one who 35
saved his land from me? And how is the LORD to save Jerusalem?"'

The people were silent and answered not a word, for the king had given 36
orders that no one was to answer him. Eliakim son of Hilkiah, comptroller 37
of the household, Shebna the adjutant-general, and Joah son of Asaph,
secretary of state, came to Hezekiah with their clothes rent and reported
what the chief officer had said.

When King Hezekiah heard their report, he rent his clothes and wrapped **19** 1[a]
himself in sackcloth, and went into the house of the LORD. He sent Eliakim 2
comptroller of the household, Shebna the adjutant-general, and the senior
priests, all covered in sackcloth, to the prophet Isaiah son of Amoz, to 3
give him this message from the king: 'This day is a day of trouble for us, a
day of reproof and contempt. We are like a woman who has no strength to
bear the child that is coming to the birth. It may be that the LORD your 4
God heard all the words of the chief officer whom his master the king of
Assyria sent to taunt the living God, and will confute what he, the LORD
your God, heard. Offer a prayer for those who still survive.' King Hezekiah's 5

---

[a] *Verses 1–37: cp. Isa. 37. 1–38; 2 Chr. 32. 20–22.*

6 servants came to Isaiah, and he told them to say this to their master: 'This
is the word of the LORD: "Do not be alarmed at what you heard when the
7 lackeys of the king of Assyria blasphemed me. I will put a spirit in him and
he shall hear a rumour and withdraw to his own country; and there I will
make him fall by the sword." '

8 So the chief officer withdrew. He heard that the king of Assyria had
9 left Lachish, and he found him attacking Libnah. But when the king learnt
that Tirhakah king of Cush was on the way to make war on him, he sent
10 messengers again to Hezekiah king of Judah, to say to him, 'How can you
be deluded by your god on whom you rely when he promises that Jerusalem
11 shall not fall into the hands of the king of Assyria? Surely you have heard
what the kings of Assyria have done to all countries, exterminating their
12 people; can you then hope to escape? Did their gods save the nations which
my forefathers destroyed, Gozan, Harran, Rezeph, and the people of Beth-
13 eden living in Telassar? Where are the kings of Hamath, of Arpad, and of
Lahir, Sepharvaim, Hena, and Ivvah?'

14 Hezekiah took the letter from the messengers and read it; then he went
15 up into the house of the LORD, spread it out before the LORD and offered
this prayer: 'O LORD God of Israel, enthroned on the cherubim, thou
alone art God of all the kingdoms of the earth; thou hast made heaven and
16 earth. Turn thy ear to me, O LORD, and listen; open thine eyes, O LORD,
and see; hear the message that Sennacherib has sent to taunt the living God.
17 It is true, O LORD, that the kings of Assyria have ravaged the nations and
18 their lands, that they have consigned their gods to the fire and destroyed
them; for they were no gods but the work of men's hands, mere wood
19 and stone. But now, O LORD our God, save us from his power, so that
all the kingdoms of the earth may know that thou, O LORD, alone art
God.'

20 Isaiah son of Amoz sent to Hezekiah and said, 'This is the word of the
LORD the God of Israel: I have heard your prayer to me concerning
21 Sennacherib king of Assyria. This is the word which the LORD has spoken
concerning him:

The virgin daughter of Zion disdains you,
    she laughs you to scorn;
the daughter of Jerusalem tosses her head
    as you retreat.
22      Whom have you taunted and blasphemed?
    Against whom have you clamoured,
casting haughty glances at the Holy One of Israel?
23      You have sent your messengers to taunt the Lord,
    and said:
I have mounted my chariot and done mighty deeds:
I have gone high up in the mountains,
    into the recesses of Lebanon.
I have cut down its tallest cedars,
    the best of its pines,
I have reached its farthest corners,
    forest and meadow.

> I have dug wells 24
> and drunk the waters of a foreign land,
> and with the soles of my feet I have dried up
> all the streams of Egypt.

> Have you not heard long ago? 25
> I did it all.
> In days gone by I planned it
> and now I have brought it about,
> making fortified cities tumble down
> into heaps of rubble.*a*
> Their citizens, shorn of strength, 26
> disheartened and ashamed,
> were but as plants in the field, as green herbs,
> as grass on the roof-tops blasted before the east wind.*b*
> I know your rising up*c* and your sitting down, 27
> your going out and your coming in.
> The frenzy of your rage against me*d* and your arrogance 28
> have come to my ears.
> I will put a ring in your nose
> and a hook in your lips,
> and I will take you back by the road
> on which you have come.

This shall be the sign for you: this year you shall eat shed grain and in the 29 second year what is self-sown; but in the third year sow and reap, plant vineyards and eat their fruit. The survivors left in Judah shall strike fresh 30 root under ground and yield fruit above ground, for a remnant shall come 31 out of Jerusalem and survivors from Mount Zion. The zeal of the LORD will perform this. 'Therefore, this is the word of the LORD concerning the king of Assyria: 32

> He shall not enter this city
> nor shoot an arrow there,
> he shall not advance against it with shield
> nor cast up a siege-ramp against it.
> By the way on which he came he shall go back; 33
> this city he shall not enter.
> This is the very word of the LORD.
> I will shield this city to deliver it, 34
> for my own sake and for the sake of my servant David.'

That night the angel of the LORD went out and struck down a hundred 35 and eighty-five thousand men in the Assyrian camp; when morning dawned, they all lay dead. So Sennacherib king of Assyria broke camp, went back 36 to Nineveh and stayed there. One day, while he was worshipping in the 37 temple of his god Nisroch, Adrammelech and Sharezer his sons murdered

---

*a* heaps of rubble: *prob. rdg., cp. Isa. 37. 26; Heb. obscure.*    *b* the east wind: *prob. rdg., cp. Isa. 37. 27; Heb. it is mature.*    *c* your rising up: *prob. rdg., cp. Isa. 37. 28; Heb. om.*    *d Prob. rdg., cp. Isa. 37. 29; Heb. repeats* the frenzy of your rage against me.

him and escaped to the land of Ararat. He was succeeded by his son Esarhaddon.

**20** 1[a]    At this time Hezekiah fell dangerously ill and the prophet Isaiah son of Amoz came to him and said, 'This is the word of the LORD: Give your last instructions to your household, for you are a dying man and will not

2 recover.' Hezekiah turned his face to the wall and offered this prayer to

3 the LORD: 'O LORD, remember how I have lived before thee, faithful and loyal in thy service, always doing what was good in thine eyes.' And he

4 wept bitterly. But before Isaiah had left the citadel, the word of the LORD

5 came to him: 'Go back and say to Hezekiah, the prince of my people: "This is the word of the LORD the God of your father David: I have heard your prayer and seen your tears; I will heal you and on the third day you

6 shall go up to the house of the LORD. I will add fifteen years to your life and deliver you and this city from the king of Assyria, and I will protect

7 this city for my own sake and for my servant David's sake."' Then Isaiah told them to apply a fig-plaster; so they made one and applied it to the

8 boil, and he recovered. Then Hezekiah asked Isaiah what sign the LORD would give him that he would be cured and would go up into the house of

9 the LORD on the third day. And Isaiah said, 'This shall be your sign from the LORD that he will do what he has promised; shall the shadow go for-

10 ward ten steps or back ten steps?' Hezekiah answered, 'It is an easy thing for the shadow to move forward ten steps; rather let it go back ten steps.'

11 Isaiah the prophet called to the LORD, and he made the shadow go back ten steps where it had advanced down the stairway of Ahaz.

12[b]    At this time Merodach-baladan son of Baladan king of Babylon sent envoys with a gift to Hezekiah; for he had heard that he had been ill.

13 Hezekiah welcomed them and showed them all his treasury, silver and gold, spices and fragrant oil, his armoury and everything to be found among his treasures; there was nothing in his house and in all his realm

14 that Hezekiah did not show them. Then the prophet Isaiah came to King Hezekiah and asked him, 'What did these men say and where have they come from?' 'They have come from a far-off country,' Hezekiah answered,

15 'from Babylon.' Then Isaiah asked, 'What did they see in your house?' 'They saw everything,' Hezekiah replied; 'there was nothing among my

16 treasures that I did not show them.' Then Isaiah said to Hezekiah, 'Hear

17 the word of the LORD: The time is coming, says the LORD, when everything in your house, and all that your forefathers have amassed till the present day,

18 will be carried away to Babylon; not a thing shall be left. And some of the sons who will be born to you, sons of your own begetting, shall be taken and

19 shall be made eunuchs in the palace of the king of Babylon.' Hezekiah answered, 'The word of the LORD which you have spoken is good'; thinking to himself that peace and security would last out his lifetime.

20    The other events of Hezekiah's reign, his exploits, and how he made the pool and the conduit and brought water into the city, are recorded in

21 the annals of the kings of Judah. So Hezekiah rested with his forefathers and was succeeded by his son Manasseh.

*a Verses 1–11: cp. Isa. 38. 1–8, 21, 22.*       *b Verses 12–19: cp. Isa. 39. 1–8.*

## The last kings of Judah

MANASSEH WAS TWELVE YEARS OLD when he came to the throne, 21 1[a] and he reigned in Jerusalem for fifty-five years; his mother was Hephzi-bah. He did what was wrong in the eyes of the LORD, in following 2 the abominable practices of the nations which the LORD had dispossessed in favour of the Israelites. He rebuilt the hill-shrines which his father 3 Hezekiah had destroyed, he erected altars to the Baal and made a sacred pole as Ahab king of Israel had done, and prostrated himself before all the host of heaven and worshipped them. He built altars in the house of the 4 LORD, that house of which the LORD had said, 'Jerusalem shall receive my Name.' He built altars for all the host of heaven in the two courts of the 5 house of the LORD; he made his son pass through the fire, he practised sooth- 6 saying and divination, and dealt with ghosts and spirits. He did much wrong in the eyes of the LORD and provoked his anger; and the image that 7 he had made of the goddess Asherah he put in the house, the place of which the LORD had said to David and Solomon his son, 'This house and Jeru-salem, which I chose out of all the tribes of Israel, shall receive my Name for all time. I will not again make Israel outcasts from the land which I gave 8 to their forefathers, if only they will be careful to observe all my commands and all the law that my servant Moses gave them.' But they did not obey, 9 and Manasseh misled them into wickedness far worse than that of the nations which the LORD had exterminated in favour of the Israelites.

Then the LORD spoke through his servants the prophets: 'Because 10 11 Manasseh king of Judah has done these abominable things, outdoing the Amorites before him in wickedness, and because he has led Judah into sin with his idols, this is the word of the LORD the God of Israel: I will bring 12 disaster on Jerusalem and Judah, disaster which will ring in the ears of all who hear of it. I will mark down every stone of Jerusalem with the plumb- 13 line of Samaria and the plummet of the house of Ahab; I will wipe away Jerusalem as when a man wipes his plate and turns it upside down, and I 14 will cast off what is left of my people, my own possession, and hand them over to their enemies. They shall be plundered and fall a prey to all their enemies; for they have done what is wrong in my eyes and have 15 provoked my anger from the day their forefathers left Egypt up to the present day. And this Manasseh shed so much innocent blood that he 16 filled Jerusalem full to the brim, not to mention the sin into which he led Judah by doing what is wrong in my eyes.' The other events and acts of 17 Manasseh's reign, and the sin that he committed, are recorded in the annals of the kings of Judah. So Manasseh rested with his forefathers and 18 was buried in the garden-tomb of his family, in the garden of Uzza; he was succeeded by his son Amon.

Amon was twenty-two years old when he came to the throne, and he 19[b] reigned in Jerusalem for two years; his mother was Meshullemeth daughter of Haruz of Jotbah. He did what was wrong in the eyes of the LORD as his 20 father Manasseh had done. He followed in his father's footsteps and served 21 the idols that his father had served and prostrated himself before them. He 22

[a] Verses 1-9: cp. 2 Chr. 33. 1-9.   [b] Verses 19-24: cp. 2 Chr. 33. 21-25.

forsook the LORD the God of his fathers and did not conform to his ways.

23 King Amon's courtiers conspired against him and murdered him in his
24 house; but the people of the land killed all the conspirators and made his
25 son Josiah king in his place. The other events of Amon's reign are recorded
26 in the annals of the kings of Judah. He was buried in his grave in the garden of Uzza; he was succeeded by his son Josiah.

22 1ᵃ Josiah was eight years old when he came to the throne, and he reigned in Jerusalem for thirty-one years; his mother was Jedidah daughter of
2 Adaiah of Bozkath. He did what was right in the eyes of the LORD; he followed closely in the footsteps of his forefather David, swerving neither right nor left.

3ᵇ In the eighteenth year of his reign Josiah sent Shaphan son of Azaliah,
4 son of Meshullam, the adjutant-general, to the house of the LORD. 'Go to the high priest Hilkiah,' he said, 'and tell him to melt down the silver that has been brought into the house of the LORD, which those on duty at the
5 entrance have received from the people, and to hand it over to the foremen in the house of the LORD, to pay the workmen who are carrying out repairs
6 in it, the carpenters, builders, and masons, and to purchase timber and
7 hewn stones for its repair. They are not to be asked to account for the
8 money that has been given them; they are acting on trust.' The high priest Hilkiah told Shaphan the adjutant-general that he had discovered the book of the law in the house of the LORD, and he gave it to him, and Shaphan
9 read it. Then Shaphan came to report to the king and told him that his servants had melted down the silver in the house of the LORD and handed
10 it over to the foremen there. Then Shaphan the adjutant-general told the king that the high priest Hilkiah had given him a book, and he read it out
11 in the king's presence. When the king heard what was in the book of the
12 law, he rent his clothes, and ordered the priest Hilkiah, Ahikam son of Shaphan, Akbor son of Micaiah, Shaphan the adjutant-general, and
13 Asaiah the king's attendant, to go and seek guidance of the LORD for himself, for the people, and for all Judah, about what was written in this book that had been discovered. 'Great is the wrath of the LORD', he said, 'that has been kindled against us, because our forefathers did not obey the commands in this book and do all that is laid upon us.'

14 So Hilkiah the priest, Ahikam, Akbor, Shaphan, and Asaiah went to Huldah the prophetess, wife of Shallum son of Tikvah, son of Harhas, the keeper of the wardrobe, and consulted her at her home in the second
15 quarter of Jerusalem. 'This is the word of the LORD the God of Israel,' she
16 answered: 'Say to the man who sent you to me, "This is the word of the LORD: I am bringing disaster on this place and its inhabitants as foretold
17 in the book which the king of Judah has read, because they have forsaken me and burnt sacrifices to other gods, provoking my anger with all the idols they have made with their own hands; therefore, my wrath is kindled
18 against this place and will not be quenched." This is what you shall say to the king of Judah who sent you to seek guidance of the LORD: "This is the
19 word of the LORD the God of Israel: You have listened to my words and shown a willing heart, you humbled yourself before the LORD when you

ᵃ *Verses 1, 2: cp. 2 Chr. 34. 1, 2.* ᵇ *Verses 3–20: cp. 2 Chr. 34. 8–28.*

heard me say that this place and its inhabitants would become objects of loathing and scorn, you rent your clothes and wept before me. Because of all this, I for my part have heard you. This is the very word of the LORD. Therefore, I will gather you to your forefathers, and you will be gathered 20 to your grave in peace; you will not live to see all the disaster which I am bringing upon this place." ' So they brought back word to the king.

Then the king sent and called all the elders of Judah and Jerusalem **23** 1*ᵃ* together, and went up to the house of the LORD; he took with him the men 2 of Judah and the inhabitants of Jerusalem, the priests and the prophets, the whole population, high and low. There he read out to them all the book of the covenant discovered in the house of the LORD; and then, standing 3 on the dais,*ᵇ* the king made a covenant before the LORD to obey him and keep his commandments, his testimonies, and his statutes, with all his heart and soul, and so fulfil the terms of the covenant written in this book. And all the people pledged themselves to the covenant.

Next, the king ordered the high priest Hilkiah, the deputy high priest,*ᶜ* 4 and those on duty at the entrance, to remove from the house of the LORD all the objects made for Baal and Asherah and all the host of heaven; he burnt these outside Jerusalem, in the open country by the Kidron, and carried the ashes to Bethel. He suppressed the heathen priests whom the 5 kings of Judah had appointed to burn sacrifices at the hill-shrines in the cities of Judah and in the neighbourhood of Jerusalem, as well as those who burnt sacrifices to Baal, to the sun and moon and planets and all the host of heaven. He took the symbol of Asherah*ᵈ* from the house of the LORD to 6 the gorge of the Kidron outside Jerusalem, burnt it there and pounded it to dust, which was then scattered over the common burial-ground. He 7 also pulled down the houses of the male prostitutes attached to the house of the LORD, where the women wove vestments in honour of Asherah.

He brought in all the priests from the cities of Judah and desecrated the 8 hill-shrines where they had burnt sacrifices, from Geba to Beersheba, and dismantled the hill-shrines of the demons*ᵉ* in front of the gate of Joshua, the governor of the city, to the left of the city gate. These priests, however, 9 never came up to the altar of the LORD in Jerusalem but used to eat un-leavened bread with the priests of their clan. He desecrated Topheth in the 10 Valley of Ben-hinnom, so that no one might make his son or daughter pass through the fire in honour of Molech.*ᶠ* He destroyed the horses that the 11 kings of Judah had set up in honour of the sun at the entrance to the house of the LORD, beside the room of Nathan-melek the eunuch in the colon-nade, and he burnt the chariots of the sun. He pulled down the altars made 12 by the kings of Judah on the roof by the upper chamber of Ahaz and the altars made by Manasseh in the two courts of the house of the LORD; he pounded them to dust and threw it into the gorge of the Kidron. Also, on 13 the east of Jerusalem, to the south of the Mount of Olives, the king dese-crated the hill-shrines which Solomon the king of Israel had built for Ashtoreth the loathsome goddess of the Sidonians, and for Kemosh the

---

*ᵃ Verses 1–3: cp. 2 Chr. 34. 29–32.*　　*ᵇ Or by the pillar.*　　*ᶜ Prob. rdg.; Heb. priests.*
*ᵈ symbol of Asherah: or sacred pole.*　　*ᵉ Or satyrs.*　　*ᶠ in honour of Molech: or for an offering.*

loathsome god of Moab, and for Milcom the abominable god of the Ammon-
14 ites; he broke down the sacred pillars and cut down the sacred poles and
filled the places where they had stood with human bones.
15     At Bethel he dismantled the altar by*a* the hill-shrine made by Jeroboam
son of Nebat who led Israel into sin, together with the hill-shrine itself;
he broke its stones in pieces, crushed them to dust and burnt the sacred
16 pole. When Josiah set eyes on the graves which were there on the hill, he
sent and took the bones from them and burnt them on the altar to desecrate
it, thus fulfilling the word of the LORD announced by the man of God
when Jeroboam stood by the altar at the feast. But when he caught sight
17 of the grave of the man of God who had foretold these things, he asked,
'What is that monument I see there?' The people of the city answered,
'The grave of the man of God who came from Judah and foretold all that
18 you have done to the altar at Bethel.' 'Leave it alone,' he said; 'let no one
disturb his bones.' So they spared his bones and also those of the prophet
19 who came from Samaria. Further, Josiah suppressed all the hill-shrines
in the cities of Samaria, which the kings of Israel had set up and thereby
provoked the LORD's anger, and he did to them what he had done at
20 Bethel. He slaughtered on the altars all the priests of the hill-shrines who
were there, and he burnt human bones upon them. Then he went back to
Jerusalem.
21     The king ordered all the people to keep the Passover to the LORD their
22 God, as this book of the covenant prescribed; no such Passover had been
kept either when the judges were ruling Israel or during the times of the
23 kings of Israel and Judah. But in the eighteenth year of Josiah's reign this
24 Passover was kept to the LORD in Jerusalem. Further, Josiah got rid of all
who called up ghosts and spirits, of all household gods and idols and all
the loathsome objects seen in the land of Judah and in Jerusalem, so that he
might fulfil the requirements of the law written in the book which the
25 priest Hilkiah had discovered in the house of the LORD. No king before
him had turned to the LORD as he did, with all his heart and soul and
strength, following the whole law of Moses; nor did any king like him
appear again.
26     Yet the LORD did not abate his fierce anger; it still burned against Judah
27 because of all the provocation which Manasseh had given him. 'Judah also
I will banish from my presence', he declared, 'as I banished Israel; and I
will cast off this city of Jerusalem which once I chose, and the house where
I promised that my Name should be.'
28     The other events and acts of Josiah's reign are recorded in the annals of
29 the kings of Judah. It was in his reign that Pharaoh Necho king of Egypt
set out for the river Euphrates to help the king of Assyria. King Josiah
went to meet him; and when they met at Megiddo, Pharaoh Necho slew
30*b* him. His attendants conveyed his body in a chariot from Megiddo to
Jerusalem and buried him in his own burial place. Then the people of the
land took Josiah's son Jehoahaz and anointed him king in place of his
father.
31     Jehoahaz was twenty-three years old when he came to the throne, and
       *a Prob. rdg.; Heb. om.*     *b Verses 30–34: cp. 2 Chr. 36. 1–4.*

he reigned in Jerusalem for three months; his mother was Hamutal
daughter of Jeremiah of Libnah. He did what was wrong in the eyes of the 32
LORD, as his forefathers had done. Pharaoh Necho removed him from the 33
throne*a* in Jerusalem, and imposed on the land a fine of a hundred talents
of silver and one talent of gold. Pharaoh Necho made Josiah's son Eliakim 34
king in place of his father and changed his name to Jehoiakim. He took
Jehoahaz and brought him to Egypt, where he died. Jehoiakim paid the 35
silver and gold to Pharaoh, taxing the country to meet Pharaoh's demands;
he exacted it from the people, from every man according to his assessment,
so that he could pay Pharaoh Necho.

Jehoiakim was twenty-five years old when he came to the throne, and 36
he reigned in Jerusalem for eleven years; his mother was Zebidah daughter
of Pedaiah of Rumah. He did what was wrong in the eyes of the LORD, as 37
his forefathers had done. During his reign Nebuchadnezzar king of **24**
Babylon took the field, and Jehoiakim became his vassal; but three years
later he broke with him and revolted. The LORD launched against him 2
raiding-parties of Chaldaeans, Aramaeans, Moabites, and Ammonites,
letting them range through Judah and ravage it, as the LORD had foretold
through his servants the prophets. All this happened to Judah in fulfilment 3
of the LORD's purpose to banish them from his presence, because of all
the sin that Manasseh had committed and because of the innocent blood 4
that he had shed; he had drenched Jerusalem with innocent blood, and
the LORD would not forgive him. The other events and acts of Jehoiakim's 5
reign are recorded in the annals of the kings of Judah. He rested with his 6
forefathers, and was succeeded by his son Jehoiachin. The king of Egypt 7
did not leave his own land again, because the king of Babylon had stripped
him of all his possessions, from the Torrent of Egypt to the river Euphrates.

## *Downfall of the southern kingdom*

JEHOIACHIN WAS EIGHTEEN YEARS OLD when he came to the throne, 8*b*
and he reigned in Jerusalem for three months; his mother was Nehushta
daughter of Elnathan of Jerusalem. He did what was wrong in the eyes of 9
the LORD, as his father had done. At that time the troops of Nebuchad- 10
nezzar king of Babylon advanced on Jerusalem and besieged the city.
Nebuchadnezzar arrived while his troops were besieging it, and Jehoiachin 11 12
king of Judah, his mother, his courtiers, his officers, and his eunuchs, all
surrendered to the king of Babylon. The king of Babylon, now in the
eighth year of his reign, took him prisoner; and, as the LORD had foretold, 13
he carried off all the treasures of the house of the LORD and of the royal
palace and broke up all the vessels of gold which Solomon king of Israel
had made for the temple of the LORD. He carried the people of Jerusalem 14
into exile, the officers and the fighting men, ten thousand in number,
together with all the craftsmen and smiths; only the weakest class of people
were left. He deported Jehoiachin to Babylon; he also took into exile from 15

*a* removed . . . throne: *prob. rdg., cp. 2 Chr. 36. 3; Heb.* bound him at Riblah in the land
of Hamath when he was king . . .        *b Verses 8–17: cp. 2 Chr. 36. 9, 10.*

Jerusalem to Babylon the king's mother and his wives, his eunuchs and
16 the foremost men of the land. He also deported to Babylon all the men of
substance, seven thousand in number, and a thousand craftsmen and
17 smiths, all of them able-bodied men and skilled armourers. He made
Mattaniah, uncle of Jehoiachin, king in his place and changed his name to
Zedekiah.
18*a* Zedekiah was twenty-one years old when he came to the throne, and he
reigned in Jerusalem for eleven years; his mother was Hamutal daughter
19 of Jeremiah of Libnah. He did what was wrong in the eyes of the LORD, as
20 Jehoiakim had done. Jerusalem and Judah so angered the LORD that in the
end he banished them from his sight; and Zedekiah rebelled against the
king of Babylon.

25 1*b* In the ninth year of his reign, in the tenth month, on the tenth day of the
month, Nebuchadnezzar king of Babylon advanced with all his army
against Jerusalem, invested it and erected watch-towers against it on every
2 3 side; the siege lasted till the eleventh year of King Zedekiah. In the fourth
month of that year,*c* on the ninth day of the month, when famine was
4 severe in the city and there was no food for the common people, the city
was thrown open. When Zedekiah king of Judah saw this,*d* he and all his
armed escort left the city and fled by night through the gate called Between
the Two Walls, near the king's garden. They escaped towards the Arabah,
5 although the Chaldaeans were surrounding the city. But the Chaldaean
army pursued the king and overtook him in the lowlands of Jericho; and
6 all his company was dispersed. The king was seized and brought before the
7 king of Babylon at Riblah, where he pleaded his case before him. Zedekiah's
sons were slain before his eyes; then his eyes were put out, and he was
brought to Babylon in fetters of bronze.
8 In the fifth month, on the seventh day of the month, in the nineteenth
year of Nebuchadnezzar king of Babylon, Nebuzaradan, captain of the
9 king's bodyguard, came to Jerusalem and set fire to the house of the LORD
and the royal palace; all the houses in the city, including the mansion of
10 Gedaliah,*e* were burnt down. The Chaldaean forces with the captain of
11 the guard pulled down the walls all round Jerusalem. Nebuzaradan captain
of the guard deported the rest of the people left in the city, those who had
12 deserted to the king of Babylon and any remaining artisans.*f* He left only
the weakest class of people to be vine-dressers and labourers.
13 The Chaldaeans broke up the pillars of bronze in the house of the LORD,
14 the trolleys, and the Sea of bronze, and took the metal to Babylon. They
took also the pots, shovels, snuffers, saucers, and all the vessels of bronze
15 used in the service of the temple. The captain of the guard took away the
precious metal, whether gold or silver, of which the firepans and the
16 tossing-bowls were made. The bronze of the two pillars, the one Sea, and
the trolleys, which Solomon had made for the house of the LORD, was

---

*a* *24. 18—25. 21 : cp. Jer. 52. 1-27.*      *b* *Verses 1-12 : cp. Jer. 39. 1-10; verses
1-17 : cp. 2 Chr. 36. 17-20.*      *c* *In ... year: prob. rdg., cp. Jer. 52. 6; Heb. om.*
*d* *When ... this: prob. rdg., cp. Jer. 39. 4; Heb. om.*      *e* *Gedaliah: prob. rdg.;
Heb. a great man.*      *f* *any remaining artisans: prob. rdg., cp. Jer. 52. 15; Heb.
the remaining crowd.*

beyond weighing. The one pillar was eighteen cubits high and its capital 17
was bronze; the capital was three cubits high, and a decoration of network
and pomegranates ran all round it, wholly of bronze. The other pillar,
with its network, was exactly like it.

The captain of the guard took Seraiah the chief priest and Zephaniah 18
the deputy chief priest and the three on duty at the entrance; he took also 19
from the city a eunuch who was in charge of the fighting men, five of those
with right of access to the king who were still in the city, the adjutant-
general*a* whose duty was to muster the people for war, and sixty men of
the people who were still there. These Nebuzaradan captain of the guard 20
brought to the king of Babylon at Riblah. There, in the land of Hamath, 21
the king of Babylon had them flogged and put to death. So Judah went into
exile from their own land.

Nebuchadnezzar king of Babylon appointed Gedaliah son of Ahikam, 22
son of Shaphan, governor over the few people whom he had left in Judah.
When the captains of the armed bands and their men heard that the king 23
of Babylon had appointed Gedaliah governor, they all came to him at
Mizpah: Ishmael son of Nethaniah, Johanan son of Kareah, Seraiah son
of Tanhumeth of Netophah, and Jaazaniah of Beth-maacah. Then Gedaliah 24
gave them and their men this assurance: 'Have no fear of the Chaldaean
officers. Settle down in the land and serve the king of Babylon; and then
all will be well with you.' But in the seventh month Ishmael son of Nethan- 25
iah, son of Elishama, who was a member of the royal house, came with ten
men and murdered Gedaliah and the Jews and Chaldaeans who were with
him at Mizpah. Thereupon all the people, high and low, and the captains 26
of the armed bands, fled to Egypt for fear of the Chaldaeans.

In the thirty-seventh year of the exile of Jehoiachin king of Judah, on 27*b*
the twenty-seventh day of the twelfth month, Evil-merodach*c* king of
Babylon in the year of his accession showed favour to Jehoiachin king
of Judah. He brought him out of prison, treated him kindly and gave him 28
a seat at table above the kings with him in Babylon. So Jehoiachin dis- 29
carded his prison clothes and lived as a pensioner of the king for the rest
of his life. For his maintenance, a regular daily allowance was given him 30
by the king as long as he lived.

*a* *Prob. rdg.; Heb. adds* commander-in-chief.        *b* *Verses 27–30: cp. Jer. 52. 31–34.*
*c* *Or* Ewil-marduk.

# THE FIRST BOOK OF THE
# CHRONICLES

## *Genealogies from Adam to Saul*

1 2[a] 3 ADAM, SETH, ENOSH, Kenan, Mahalalel, Jared, Enoch, Methu-
4 selah, Lamech, Noah.
The sons of Noah: Shem, Ham and Japheth.
5[b] The sons of Japheth: Gomer, Magog, Madai, Javan,[c] Tubal, Meshech
6 7 and Tiras. The sons of Gomer: Ashkenaz, Diphath and Togarmah. The
sons of Javan: Elishah, Tarshish, Kittim[d] and Rodanim.
8[e] 9 The sons of Ham: Cush, Mizraim,[f] Put and Canaan. The sons of Cush:
Seba, Havilah, Sabta, Raama and Sabtecha. The sons of Raama: Sheba
10 and Dedan. Cush was the father of Nimrod, who began to show himself a
11[g] man of might on earth. From Mizraim sprang the Lydians, Anamites,
12 Lehabites, Naphtuhites, Pathrusites, Casluhites, and the Caphtorites,
from whom the Philistines were descended.
13 14 Canaan was the father of Sidon, who was his eldest son, and Heth,[h] the
15 Jebusites, the Amorites, the Girgashites, the Hivites, the Arkites, the
16 Sinites, the Arvadites, the Zemarites, and the Hamathites.
17[i] The sons of Shem: Elam, Asshur, Arphaxad, Lud[j] and Aram. The sons
18 of Aram: Uz, Hul, Gether and Mash. Arphaxad was the father of Shelah,
19 and Shelah the father of Eber. Eber had two sons: one was named Peleg,[k]
because in his time the earth was divided, and his brother's name was
20 Joktan. Joktan was the father of Almodad, Sheleph, Hazarmoth, Jerah,
21 22 23 Hadoram, Uzal, Diklah, Ebal,[l] Abimael, Sheba, Ophir, Havilah and
Jobab. All these were sons of Joktan.
24[m] 25 26 The line of[n] Shem: Arphaxad, Shelah, Eber, Peleg, Reu, Serug, Nahor,
27 28 Terah, Abram, also known as Abraham, whose sons were Isaac and
Ishmael.
29[o] The sons of[p] Ishmael in the order of their birth: Nebaioth the eldest,
30 then Kedar, Adbeel, Mibsam, Mishma, Dumah, Massa, Hadad, Teman,
31 Jetur, Naphish and Kedemah. These were Ishmael's sons.
32[q] The sons of Keturah, Abraham's concubine: she bore him Zimran,
Jokshan, Medan, Midian, Ishbak and Shuah. The sons of Jokshan: Sheba
33 and Dedan. The sons of Midian: Ephah, Epher, Enoch, Abida and Eldaah.
All these were descendants of Keturah.

[a] *Verses 2–4: cp. Gen.* 5. 9–32. [b] *Verses 5–7: cp. Gen.* 10. 2–4. [c] *Or* Greece. [d] *Or* Tarshish of the Kittians. [e] *Verses 8–10: cp. Gen.* 10. 6–8. [f] *Or* Egypt. [g] *Verses 11–16: cp. Gen.* 10. 13–18. [h] *Or* the Hittites. [i] *Verses 17–23: cp. Gen.* 10. 22–29. [j] *Or* the Lydians. [k] *That is* Division. [l] *Or* Obal, *cp. Gen.* 10. 28. [m] *Verses 24–27: cp. Gen.* 11. 10–26. [n] The line of: *prob. rdg.; Heb. om.* [o] *Verses 29–31: cp. Gen.* 25. 13–16. [p] The sons of: *prob. rdg., cp. Gen.* 25. 13; *Heb. om.* [q] *Verses 32, 33: cp. Gen.* 25. 1–4.

Abraham was the father of Isaac, and Isaac's sons were Esau and Israel. 34
The sons of Esau: Eliphaz, Reuel, Jeush, Jalam and Korah. The sons of 35*a* 36
Eliphaz: Teman, Omar, Zephi, Gatam, Kenaz, Timna and Amalek. The 37
sons of Reuel: Nahath, Zerah, Shammah and Mizzah.

The sons of Seir: Lotan, Shobal, Zibeon, Anah, Dishon, Ezer and 38*b*
Dishan. The sons of Lotan: Hori and Homam; and Lotan had a sister 39
named Timna. The sons of Shobal: Alvan, Manahath, Ebal, Shephi and 40
Onam. The sons of Zibeon: Aiah and Anah. The son*c* of Anah: Dishon. 41
The sons of Dishon: Amram, Eshban, Ithran and Cheran. The sons of 42
Ezer: Bilhan, Zavan and Akan. The sons of Dishan: Uz and Aran.

These are the kings who ruled over Edom before there were kings in 43*d*
Israel: Bela son of Beor, whose city was named Dinhabah. When he died, 44
he was succeeded by Jobab son of Zerah of Bozrah. When Jobab died, he 45
was succeeded by Husham of Teman. When Husham died, he was suc- 46
ceeded by Hadad son of Bedad, who defeated Midian in Moabite country.
His city was named Avith. When Hadad died, he was succeeded by Samlah 47
of Masrekah. When Samlah died, he was succeeded by Saul of Rehoboth 48
on the River. When Saul died, he was succeeded by Baal-hanan son of 49
Akbor. When Baal-hanan died, he was succeeded by Hadad. His city was 50
named Pai; his wife's name was Mehetabel daughter of Matred a woman of
Me-zahab.*e*

After Hadad died the chiefs in Edom were: chief Timna, chief Aliah, 51
chief Jetheth, chief Oholibamah, chief Elah, chief Pinon, chief Kenaz, chief 52 53
Teman, chief Mibzar, chief Magdiel and chief Iram. These were the chiefs 54
of Edom.

These were the sons of Israel: Reuben, Simeon, Levi, Judah, Issachar, **2**
Zebulun, Dan, Joseph, Benjamin, Naphtali, Gad and Asher. 2

The sons of Judah: Er, Onan and Shelah; the mother of these three was 3
a Canaanite woman, Bathshua.*f* Er, Judah's eldest son, displeased the
LORD and the LORD slew him. Then Tamar, Judah's daughter-in-law, 4
bore him Perez and Zerah, making in all five sons of Judah. The sons of 5
Perez: Hezron and Hamul. The sons of Zerah: Zimri, Ethan, Heman, 6
Calcol and Darda, five in all. The son of Zimri: Carmi.*g* The son of Carmi: 7
Achar, who troubled Israel by his violation of the sacred ban. The son of 8
Ethan: Azariah. The sons of Hezron: Jerahmeel, Ram and Caleb. Ram 9 10
was the father of Amminadab, Amminadab father of Nahshon prince of
Judah. Nahshon was the father of Salma, Salma father of Boaz, Boaz 11 12
father of Obed, Obed father of Jesse. The eldest son of Jesse was Eliab, 13
the second Abinadab, the third Shimea, the fourth Nethaneel, the fifth 14
Raddai, the sixth Ozem, the seventh David; their sisters were Zeruiah 15 16
and Abigail. The sons of Zeruiah: Abishai, Joab and Asahel, three in all.
Abigail was the mother of Amasa; his father was Jether the Ishmaelite. 17

Caleb son of Hezron had Jerioth by Azubah his wife;*h* these were her 18

---

*a* *Verses 35–37: cp. Gen. 36. 4, 5, 9–13.*　　　　*b* *Verses 38–42: cp. Gen. 36. 20–28.*
*c* *Prob. rdg.; Heb.* sons; *the same correction is made in several other places in chs. 1–9.*
*d* *Verses 43–54: cp. Gen. 36. 31–43.*　　*e* *Or* daughter of Mezahab.　　*f* Bathshua: *or*
daughter of Shua.　　　　*g* The son . . . Carmi: *prob. rdg. (cp. Josh. 7. 1, 18); Heb. om.*
*h* his wife: *prob. rdg.; Heb.* a woman and.

19 sons: Jesher, Shobab and Ardon. When Azubah died, Caleb married
20 Ephrath, who bore him Hur. Hur was the father of Uri, and Uri father of
21 Bezalel. Later, Hezron, then sixty years of age, had intercourse with the
daughter of Machir father of Gilead, having married her, and she bore
22 Segub. Segub was the father of Jair, who had twenty-three cities in Gilead.
23 Geshur and Aram took from them Havvoth-jair, and Kenath and its
dependent villages, a total of sixty towns. All these were descendants of
24 Machir father of Gilead. After the death of Hezron, Caleb had intercourse
with Ephrathah and she bore him Ashhur the founder of Tekoa.

25      The sons of Jerahmeel eldest son of Hezron by*a* Ahijah were Ram the
26 eldest, Bunah, Oren and Ozem. Jerahmeel had another wife, whose name
27 was Atarah; she was the mother of Onam. The sons of Ram eldest son of
28 Jerahmeel: Maaz, Jamin and Eker. The sons of Onam: Shammai and Jada.
29 The sons of Shammai: Nadab and Abishur. The name of Abishur's wife
30 was Abihail; she bore him Ahban and Molid. The sons of Nadab: Seled
31 and Ephraim; Seled died without children. Ephraim's son was Ishi, Ishi's
32 son Sheshan, Sheshan's son Ahlai. The sons of Jada brother of Shammai:
33 Jether and Jonathan; Jether died without children. The sons of Jonathan:
Peleth and Zaza. These were the descendants of Jerahmeel.

34      Sheshan had daughters but no sons. He had an Egyptian servant named
35 Jarha; he gave his daughter in marriage to this Jarha, and she bore him
36 37 Attai. Attai was the father of Nathan, Nathan father of Zabad, Zabad
38 father of Ephlal, Ephlal father of Obed, Obed father of Jehu, Jehu father
39 40 of Azariah, Azariah father of Helez, Helez father of Elasah, Elasah father
41 of Sisamai, Sisamai father of Shallum, Shallum father of Jekamiah, and
Jekamiah father of Elishama.

42      The sons of Caleb brother of Jerahmeel: Mesha the eldest, founder of
43 Ziph, and*b* Mareshah founder of Hebron. The sons of Hebron: Korah,
44 Tappuah, Rekem and Shema. Shema was the father of Raham father of
45 Jorkoam, and Rekem was the father of Shammai. The son of Shammai was
46 Maon, and Maon was the founder of Beth-zur. Ephah, Caleb's concubine,
was the mother of Haran, Moza and Gazez; Haran was the father of Gazez.
47 The sons of Jahdai: Regem, Jotham, Geshan, Pelet, Ephah and Shaaph.
48 49 Maacah, Caleb's concubine, was the mother of Sheber and Tirhanah; she
bore also Shaaph founder of Madmannah, and Sheva founder of Machbe-
nah and Gibea. Caleb also had a daughter named Achsah.

50      The descendants of Caleb: the sons of Hur, the eldest son of Ephrathah:
51 Shobal the founder of Kiriath-jearim, Salma the founder of Bethlehem,
52 and Hareph the founder of Beth-gader. Shobal the founder of Kiriath-
jearim was the father of Reaiah*c* and the ancestor of half the Manahethites.*d*
53 The clans of Kiriath-jearim: Ithrites, Puhites, Shumathites, and
Mishraites, from whom were descended the Zareathites and the Eshtaulites.
54 The descendants of Salma: Bethlehem, the Netophathites, Ataroth,
Beth-joab, half the Manahethites, and the Zorites.
55 The clans of Sophrites*e* living at Jabez: Tirathites, Shimeathites, and

*a* by: *prob. rdg.; Heb. om.*      *b* *Prob. rdg.; Heb. adds* the sons of.      *c* *Prob. rdg.,*
*cp. 4. 2; Heb.* the seer.      *d* *Prob. rdg., cp. verse 54; Heb.* Menuhoth.      *e* *Or*
secretaries.

Suchathites. These were Kenites who were connected by marriage with the ancestor of the Rechabites.

These were the sons of David, born at Hebron: the eldest Amnon, 3 1[a] whose mother was Ahinoam of Jezreel; the second Daniel, whose mother was Abigail of Carmel; the third Absalom, whose mother was Maacah 2 daughter of Talmai king of Geshur; the fourth Adonijah, whose mother was Haggith; the fifth Shephatiah, whose mother was Abital; the sixth 3 Ithream, whose mother was David's wife Eglah. These six were born at 4 Hebron, where David reigned seven years and six months. In Jerusalem he reigned thirty-three years, and there the following sons were born to 5[b] him: Shimea, Shobab, Nathan and Solomon; these four were sons of Bathsheba daughter of Ammiel. There were nine others: Ibhar, Elishama, 6 Eliphelet, Nogah, Nepheg, Japhia, Elishama, Eliada and Eliphelet. These 7 8 9 were all the sons of David, with their sister Tamar, in addition to his sons by concubines.

Solomon's son was Rehoboam, his son Abia, his son Asa, his son 10 Jehoshaphat, his son Joram, his son Ahaziah, his son Joash, his son Amazi- 11 12 ah, his son Azariah, his son Jotham, his son Ahaz, his son Hezekiah, his 13 son Manasseh, his son Amon, and his son Josiah. The sons of Josiah: the 14 15 eldest was Johanan, the second Jehoiakim, the third Zedekiah, the fourth Shallum. The sons of Jehoiakim: Jeconiah and Zedekiah. The sons of 16 17 Jeconiah, a prisoner:[c] Shealtiel, Malchiram, Pedaiah, Shenazzar, Jekami- 18 ah, Hoshama and Nedabiah. The sons of Pedaiah: Zerubbabel and 19 Shimei. The sons of Zerubbabel: Meshullam and Hananiah; they had a sister, Shelomith. There were five others: Hashubah, Ohel, Berechiah, 20 Hasadiah and Jushab-hesed. The sons of Hananiah: Pelatiah and Isaiah; 21 his son was Rephaiah, his son Arnan, his son Obadiah, his son Shecaniah. The sons of Shecaniah: Shemaiah,[d] Hattush, Igeal, Bariah, Neariah and 22 Shaphat, six in all. The sons of Neariah: Elioenai, Hezekiah and Azrikam, 23 three in all. The sons of Elioenai: Hodaiah, Eliashib, Pelaiah, Akkub, 24 Johanan, Dalaiah and Anani, seven in all.

The sons of Judah: Perez, Hezron, Carmi, Hur and Shobal. Reaiah son 4 1 2 of Shobal was the father of Jahath, Jahath father of Ahumai and Lahad. These were the clans of the Zorathites.

The sons of Etam: Jezreel, Ishma, Idbash, Penuel the founder of Gedor, 3-4 and Ezer the founder of Hushah; they had a sister named Hazelelponi. These were the sons of Hur: Ephrathah the eldest, the founder of Bethlehem.

Ashhur the founder of Tekoa had two wives, Helah and Naarah. 5 Naarah bore him Ahuzam, Hepher, Temeni and Haahashtari.[e] These 6 were the sons of Naarah. The sons of Helah: Zereth, Jezoar, Ethnan and 7 Coz. Coz was the father of Anub and Zobebah and the clans of Aharhel 8 son of Harum.

Jabez ranked higher than his brothers; his mother called him Jabez 9 because, as she said, she had borne him in pain. Jabez called upon the God 10

[a] *Verses 1-4: cp. 2 Sam. 3. 2-5.*     [b] *Verses 5-8: cp. 14. 4-7; 2 Sam. 5. 14-16.*
[c] Jeconiah, a prisoner: *or* Jeconiah: Assir, ...     [d] *Prob. rdg.; Heb. adds* and the sons of Shemaiah.     [e] Temeni and Haahashtari: *or* the Temanite and the Ahashtarite.

of Israel and said, 'I pray thee, bless me and grant me wide territories. May thy hand be with me, and do me no harm, I pray thee, and let me be free from pain'; and God granted his petition.

11 Kelub brother of Shuah was the father of Mehir the father of Eshton.
12 Eshton was the father of Beth-rapha, Paseah, and Tehinnah father of Ir-nahash. These were the men of Rechah.

13 The sons of Kenaz: Othniel and Seraiah. The sons of Othniel: Hathath and Meonothai.
14 Meonothai was the father of Ophrah.

Seraiah was the father of Joab founder of Ge-harashim,*a* for they were craftsmen.

15 The sons of Caleb son of Jephunneh: Iru, Elah and Naam. The son of Elah: Kenaz.

16 The sons of Jehaleleel: Ziph and Ziphah, Tiria and Asareel.

17-18 The sons of Ezra: Jether, Mered, Epher and Jalon. These were the sons of Bithiah daughter of Pharaoh, whom Mered had married; she conceived and gave birth to*b* Miriam, Shammai and Ishbah founder of Eshtemoa. His Jewish wife was the mother of Jered founder of Gedor, Heber founder
19 of Soco, and Jekuthiel founder of Zanoah. The sons of his*c* wife Hodiah sister of Naham were Daliah father of Keilah the Garmite, and Eshtemoa the Maacathite.

20 The sons of Shimon: Amnon, Rinnah, Ben-hanan and Tilon.

The sons of Ishi: Zoheth and Ben-zoheth.

21 The sons of Shelah son of Judah: Er founder of Lecah, Laadah founder of Mareshah, the clans of the guild of linen-workers at Ashbea,
22 Jokim, the men of Kozeba, Joash, and Saraph who fell out with Moab
23 and came back to Bethlehem.*d* (The records are ancient.) They were the potters, and those who lived at Netaim and Gederah were there on the king's service.

24 25 The sons of Simeon: Nemuel, Jamin, Jarib, Zerah, Saul, his son Shal-
26 lum, his son Mibsam and his son Mishma. The sons of Mishma: his son
27 Hamuel, his son Zaccur and his son Shimei. Shimei had sixteen sons and six daughters, but others of his family had fewer children, and the clan as
28 a whole did not increase as much as the tribe of Judah. They lived at
29 30 Beersheba, Moladah, Hazar-shual, Bilhah, Ezem, Tolad, Bethuel,
31 Hormah, Ziklag, Beth-marcaboth, Hazar-susim, Beth-birei, and Shaaraim.
32 These were their cities until David came to the throne. Their settlements *e*
33 were Etam, Ain, Rimmon, Tochen, and Ashan, five cities in all. They had also hamlets round these cities as far as Baal. These were the places where they lived.

34 The names on their register were: Meshobab, Jamlech, Joshah son of
35 36 Amaziah, Joel, Jehu son of Josibiah, son of Seraiah, son of Asiel, Elioenai,
37 Jaakobah, Jeshohaiah, Asaiah, Adiel, Jesimiel, Benaiah, Ziza son of
38 Shiphi, son of Allon, son of Jedaiah, son of Shimri, son of Shemaiah, whose names are recorded as princes in their clans, and their families had greatly

---

*a* Or *the Valley of Craftsmen.*　　*b* and gave birth to: *prob. rdg.; Heb. om.*　　*c* his: *prob. rdg.; Heb. om.*　　*d* and came ... Bethlehem: *prob. rdg.; Heb. unintelligible.*
*e Prob. rdg.; Heb.* hamlets.

increased. They then went from the approaches to Gedor east of the valley 39
in search of pasture for their flocks. They found rich and good pasture in a 40
wide stretch of open country where everything was quiet and peaceful;
before then it had been occupied by Hamites. During the reign of Hezekiah 41
king of Judah these whose names are written above came and destroyed
the tribes of Ham*a* and the Meunites whom they found there. They
annihilated them so that no trace of them has remained to this day; and
they occupied the land in their place, for there was pasture for their flocks.
Of their number five hundred Simeonites invaded the hill-country of Seir, 42
led by Pelatiah, Neariah, Rephaiah, and Uzziel, the sons of Ishi. They 43
destroyed all who were left of the surviving Amalekites; and they live there
still.

The sons of Reuben, the eldest of Israel's sons. (He was, in fact, the 5
first son born, but because he had committed incest with a wife of his
father's the rank of the eldest was transferred to the sons of Joseph,
Israel's son, who, however, could not be registered as the eldest son. Judah 2
held the leading place among his brothers because he fathered a ruler,
and the rank of the eldest was his, not*b* Joseph's.) The sons of Reuben, the 3
eldest of Israel's sons: Enoch, Pallu, Hezron and Carmi. The sons of Joel: 4
his son Shemaiah, his son Gog, his son Shimei, his son Micah, his son 5
Reaia, his son Baal, his son Beerah, whom Tiglath-pileser king of Assyria 6
carried away into exile; he was a prince of the Reubenites. His kinsmen, 7
family by family, as registered in their tribal lists: Jeiel the chief, Zechariah,
Bela son of Azaz, son of Shema, son of Joel. They lived in Aroer, and their 8
lands stretched as far as Nebo and Baal-meon. Eastwards they occupied 9
territory as far as the edge of the desert which stretches from the river
Euphrates, for they had large numbers of cattle in Gilead. During Saul's 10
reign they made war on the Hagarites, whom they conquered, occupying
their encampments over all the country east of Gilead.

Adjoining them were the Gadites, occupying the district of Bashan as 11
far as Salcah: Joel the chief; second in rank, Shapham; then Jaanai and 12
Shaphat in Bashan. Their fellow-tribesmen belonged to the families of 13
Michael, Meshullam, Sheba, Jorai, Jachan, Zia and Heber, seven in all.
These were the sons of Abihail son of Huri, son of Jaroah, son of Gilead, 14
son of Michael, son of Jeshishai, son of Jahdo, son of Buz. Ahi son of 15
Abdiel, son of Guni, was head of their family; they lived in Gilead, in 16
Bashan and its villages, in all the common land of Sharon as far as it
stretched. These registers were all compiled in the reigns of Jotham king 17
of Judah and Jeroboam king of Israel.

The sons of Reuben, Gad, and half the tribe of Manasseh: of their 18
fighting men armed with shield and sword, their archers and their
battle-trained soldiers, forty-four thousand seven hundred and sixty
were ready for active service. They made war on the Hagarites, Jetur, 19
Nephish, and Nodab. They were given help against them, for they cried 20
to their God for help in the battle, and because they trusted him he listened
to their prayer, and the Hagarites and all their allies surrendered to

*a* the tribes of Ham: *prob. rdg., cp. verse 40; Heb.* their tribes.          *b* his, not: *prob.
rdg.; Heb. om.*

21 them.*a* They drove off their cattle, fifty thousand camels, two hundred
and fifty thousand sheep, and two thousand asses, and they took a hundred
22 thousand captives. Many had been killed, for the war was of God's making,
and they occupied the land instead of them until the exile.

23 Half the tribe of Manasseh lived in the land from Bashan to Baal-
hermon, Senir, and Mount Hermon, and were numerous also in Lebanon.
24 The heads of their families were: Epher, Ishi, Eliel, Azriel, Jeremiah,
Hodaviah, and Jahdiel, all men of ability and repute, heads of their
25 families. But they sinned against the God of their fathers, and turned
wantonly to worship the gods of the peoples whom God had destroyed
26 before them. So the God of Israel stirred up Pul king of Assyria, that is
Tiglath-pileser king of Assyria, and he carried into exile Reuben, Gad,
and half the tribe of Manasseh. He took them to Halah, Habor, Hara, and
the river Gozan, where they are to this day.

6 1 2 THE SONS OF LEVI: Gershon,*b* Kohath and Merari. The sons of Kohath:
3 Amram, Izhar, Hebron and Uzziel. The children of Amram: Aaron,
Moses and Miriam. The sons of Aaron: Nadab, Abihu, Eleazar and
4*c* Ithamar. Eleazar was the father of Phinehas, Phinehas father of Abishua,
5 6 Abishua father of Bukki, Bukki father of Uzzi, Uzzi father of Zerahiah,
7 Zerahiah father of Meraioth, Meraioth father of Amariah, Amariah father
8 9 of Ahitub, Ahitub father of Zadok, Zadok father of Ahimaaz, Ahimaaz
10 father of Azariah, Azariah father of Johanan, and Johanan father of
Azariah, the priest who officiated in the LORD's house which Solomon
11 built at Jerusalem. Azariah was the father of Amariah, Amariah father of
12 13 Ahitub, Ahitub father of Zadok, Zadok father of Shallum, Shallum father
14 of Hilkiah, Hilkiah father of Azariah, Azariah father of Seraiah, and
15 Seraiah father of Jehozadak. Jehozadak went into exile when the LORD
sent Judah and Jerusalem into exile under Nebuchadnezzar.

16*d* 17 The sons of Levi: Gershom, Kohath and Merari. The sons of Gershom.
18 Libni and Shimei. The sons of Kohath: Amram, Izhar, Hebron and
19 Uzziel. The sons of Merari: Mahli and Mushi. The clans of Levi, family
20*e* 21 by family: Gershom: his son Libni, his son Jahath, his son Zimmah, his
22*f* son Joah, his son Iddo, his son Zerah, his son Jeaterai. The sons of Kohath:
23 his son Amminadab, his son Korah, his son Assir, his son Elkanah, his
24 son Ebiasaph, his son Assir, his son Tahath, his son Uriel, his son Uzziah,
25 26 his son Saul. The sons of Elkanah: Amasai and Ahimoth, his son Elkanah,
27 his son Zophai, his son Nahath, his son Eliab, his son Jeroham, his son
28 29 Elkanah. The sons of Samuel: Joel the eldest and Abiah the second. The
sons of Merari: his son Mahli, his son Libni, his son Shimei, his son Uzza,
30 his son Shimea, his son Haggiah, his son Asaiah.

31 These are the men whom David appointed to take charge of the music
32 in the house of the LORD when the Ark should be deposited there. They

---

*a* They were . . . surrendered to them: *or* They attacked them boldly, and the Hagarites
and all their allies surrendered to them, for they cried . . . to their prayer.    *b* Gershom
*in verses 16 and 17.*    *c* *Verses 4–8: cp. verses 50–53.*    *d* *Verses 16–19:*
*cp. Exod. 6. 16–19.*    *e* *Verses 20, 21: cp. verses 41–43.*    *f* *Verses 22–28:*
*cp. verses 33–38.*

performed their musical duties before the Tent of the Presence until Solomon built the house of the LORD in Jerusalem, and took their regular turns of duty there. The following, with their descendants, took this duty. 33 Of the line of Kohath: Heman the musician, son of Joel, son of Samuel, son of Elkanah, son of Jeroham, son of Eliel, son of Toah, son of Zuph, 34 35 son of Elkanah, son of Mahath, son of Amasai, son of Elkanah, son of 36 Joel, son of Azariah, son of Zephaniah, son of Tahath, son of Assir, son 37 of Ebiasaph, son of Korah, son of Izhar, son of Kohath, son of Levi, son of 38 Israel. Heman's colleague Asaph stood at his right hand. He was the son 39 of Berachiah, son of Shimea, son of Michael, son of Baaseiah, son of 40 Malchiah, son of Ethni, son of Zerah, son of Adaiah, son of Ethan, son of 41*a* 42 Zimmah, son of Shimei, son of Jahath, son of Gershom, son of Levi. On 43 44 their left stood their colleague of the line of Merari: Ethan son of Kishi, son of Abdi, son of Malluch, son of Hashabiah, son of Amaziah, son of 45 Hilkiah, son of Amzi, son of Bani, son of Shamer, son of Mahli, son of 46 47 Mushi, son of Merari, son of Levi. Their kinsmen the Levites were dedi- 48 cated to all the service of the Tabernacle, the house of God.

But it was Aaron and his descendants who burnt the sacrifices on the 49 altar of whole-offering and the altar of incense, in fulfilment of all the duties connected with the most sacred gifts, and to make expiation for Israel, exactly as Moses the servant of God had commanded. The sons of 50*b* Aaron: his son Eleazar, his son Phinehas, his son Abishua, his son Bukki, 51 his son Uzzi, his son Zerahiah, his son Meraioth, his son Amariah, his 52 son Ahitub, his son Zadok, his son Ahimaaz. 53

These are their settlements in encampments in the districts assigned to 54 the descendants of Aaron, to the clan of Kohath, for it was to them that the lot had fallen: they gave them Hebron in Judah, with the common land 55 round it, but they assigned to Caleb son of Jephunneh the open country 56 belonging to the town and its hamlets. They gave to the sons of Aaron: 57*c* Hebron the city*d* of refuge, Libnah, Jattir, Eshtemoa, Hilen, Debir, 58 Ashan, and Beth-shemesh, each with its common land. And from the tribe 59 60 of Benjamin: Geba, Alemeth, and Anathoth, each with its common land, making thirteen cities in all by their clans.

They gave to the remaining clans of the sons of Kohath ten cities by lot 61 from the half tribe of Manasseh. To the sons of Gershom according to 62 their clans they gave thirteen cities from the tribes of Issachar, Asher, Naphtali, and Manasseh in Bashan. To the sons of Merari according to 63 their clans they gave by lot twelve cities from the tribes of Reuben, Gad, and Zebulun. Israel gave these cities, each with its common land, to the 64 Levites. (The cities mentioned above, from the tribes of Judah, Simeon, 65 and Benjamin, were assigned by lot.)

Some of the clans of Kohath had cities allotted*e* to them. They gave 66 67 them the city*f* of refuge, Shechem in the hill-country of Ephraim, Gezer, Jokmeam, Beth-horon, Aijalon, and Gath-rimmon, each with its common 68 69

---

*a* *Verses 41–43: cp. verses 20, 21.*     *b* *Verses 50–53: cp. verses 4–8.*     *c* *Verses 57–81: cp. Josh. 21. 13–39.*     *d* *Prob. rdg., cp. Josh. 21. 13; Heb.* cities.     *e* allotted: *prob. rdg., cp. Josh. 21. 20; Heb.* of their frontier.     *f* *Prob. rdg., cp. Josh. 21. 21; Heb.* cities.

70 land. From the half tribe of Manasseh, Aner and Bileam, each with its common land, were given to the rest of the clans of Kohath.

71 To the sons of Gershom they gave from the half tribe of Manasseh:
72 Golan in Bashan, and Ashtaroth, each with its common land. From the
73 tribe of Issachar: Kedesh, Daberath, Ramoth, and Anem, each with its
74 75 common land. From the tribe of Asher: Mashal, Abdon, Hukok, and
76 Rehob, each with its common land. From the tribe of Naphtali: Kedesh in Galilee, Hammon, and Kiriathaim, each with its common land.

77 To the rest of the sons of Merari they gave from the tribe of Zebulun:
78 Rimmon and Tabor, each with its common land. On the east of Jordan, opposite Jericho, from the tribe of Reuben: Bezer-in-the-wilderness,
79 80 Jahzah, Kedemoth, and Mephaath, each with its common land. From the
81 tribe of Gad: Ramoth in Gilead, Mahanaim, Heshbon, and Jazer, each with its common land.

7 1<sup>a</sup> 2 The sons of Issachar: Tola, Pua, Jashub and Shimron, four. The sons of Tola: Uzzi, Rephaiah, Jeriel, Jahmai, Jibsam, and Samuel, all able men and heads of families by paternal descent from Tola according to their tribal lists; their number in David's time was twenty-two thousand six
3 hundred. The son of Uzzi: Izrahiah. The sons of Izrahiah: Michael,
4 Obadiah, Joel and Isshiah, making a total of five, all of them chiefs. In addition there were bands of fighting men recorded by families according to the tribal lists to the number of thirty-six thousand, for they had many
5 wives and children. Their fellow-tribesmen in all the clans of Issachar were able men, eighty-seven thousand; every one of them was registered.

6 7 The sons of Benjamin: Bela, Becher and Jediael, three. The sons of Bela: Ezbon, Uzzi, Uzziel, Jerimoth and Iri, five. They were heads of their families and able men; the number registered was twenty-two
8 thousand and thirty-four. The sons of Becher: Zemira, Joash, Eliezer, Elioenai, Omri, Jeremoth, Abiah, Anathoth and Alemeth; all these were
9 sons of Becher according to their tribal lists, heads of their families and able men; and the number registered was twenty thousand two hundred.
10 The son of Jediael: Bilhan. The sons of Bilhan: Jeush, Benjamin, Ehud,
11 Kenaanah, Zethan, Tarshish and Ahishahar. All these were descendants of Jediael, heads of<sup>b</sup> families and able men. The number was seventeen thousand two hundred men, fit for active service in war.

12 The sons of Dan:<sup>c</sup> Hushim and the sons of Aher.<sup>d</sup>

13 The sons of Naphtali: Jahziel, Guni, Jezer, Shallum. These were sons of Bilhah.

14<sup>e</sup> The sons of Manasseh,<sup>f</sup> born of his concubine, an Aramaean: Machir
15 father of Gilead. Machir married a woman whose name was<sup>g</sup> Maacah. The second son was named Zelophehad, and Zelophehad had daughters.
16 Maacah wife of Machir had a son whom she named Peresh. His brother's
17 name was Sheresh, and his sons were Ulam and Rakem. The son of Ulam:

*a Verses 1, 6, 13, 30 and 8. 1–5: cp. Gen. 46. 13, 17, 21–24.*     *b Prob. rdg.; Heb. to the heads of.*     *c The sons of Dan: prob. rdg., cp. Gen. 46. 23; Heb. And Shuppim and Huppim, the sons of Ir.*     *d Or another.*     *e Verses 14–19: cp. Num. 26. 29–33.*     *f Prob. rdg.; Heb. adds Asriel.*     *g whose name was: prob. rdg.; Heb. to Huppim and Shuppim, and his sister's name was . . .*

Bedan. These were the sons of Gilead son of Machir, son of Manasseh.
His sister Hammoleketh was the mother of Ishhod, Abiezer and Mahalah.   18
The sons of Shemida: Ahian, Shechem, Likhi and Aniam.   19
   The sons of Ephraim: Shuthelah, his son Bered, his son Tahath, his   20
son Eladah, his son Tahath, his son Zabad, his son Shuthelah. Ephraim's   21
other sons Ezer and Elead were killed by the native Gittites when they
came down to lift their cattle. Their father Ephraim long mourned for   22
them, and his kinsmen came to comfort him. Then he had intercourse with   23
his wife; she conceived and had a son whom he named Beriah (because
disaster*a* had come on his family). He had a daughter named Sherah; she   24
built Lower and Upper Beth-horon and Uzzen-sherah. He also had a son   25
named Rephah; his son was Resheph, his son Telah, his son Tahan, his   26
son Laadan, his son Ammihud, his son Elishama, his son Nun, his son   27
Joshua.
   Their lands and settlements were: Bethel and its dependent villages, to   28
the east Naaran, to the west Gezer, Shechem, and Gaza, with their villages.
In the possession of Manasseh were Beth-shean, Taanach, Megiddo, and   29
Dor, with their villages. In all of these lived the descendants of Joseph the
son of Israel.
   The sons of Asher: Imnah, Ishvah, Ishvi and Beriah, together with their   30
sister Serah. The sons of Beriah: Heber and Malchiel father of Birzavith.   31
Heber was the father of Japhlet, Shomer, Hotham, and their sister Shua.   32
The sons of Japhlet: Pasach, Bimhal and Ashvath. These were the sons of   33
Japhlet. The sons of Shomer: Ahi, Rohgah, Jehubbah and Aram. The sons   34 35
of his brother Hotham:*b* Zophah, Imna, Shelesh and Amal. The sons of   36
Zophah: Suah, Harnepher, Shual, Beri, Imrah, Bezer, Hod, Shamma,   37
Shilshah, Ithran and Beera. The sons of Jether: Jephunneh, Pispah and   38
Ara. The sons of Ulla: Arah, Haniel and Rezia. All these were descendants   39 40
of Asher, heads of families, picked men of ability, leading princes. They
were enrolled among the fighting troops; the total number was twenty-six
thousand men.
   The sons of Benjamin were: the eldest Bela, the second Ashbel, the third   **8**
Aharah, the fourth Nohah and the fifth Rapha. The sons of Bela: Addar,   2 3
Gera father of Ehud,*c* Abishua, Naaman, Ahoah, Gera, Shephuphan and   4 5
Huram. These were the sons of Ehud, heads of families living in Geba,   6
who were removed to Manahath: Naaman, Ahiah, and Gera—he it was   7
who removed them. He was the father of Uzza and Ahihud. Shaharaim   8
had sons born to him in Moabite country, after putting away his wives
Mahasham and Baara. By his wife Hodesh he had Jobab, Zibia, Mesha,   9
Malcham, Jeuz, Shachia and Mirmah. These were his sons, heads of fami-   10
lies. By Mahasham he had had Abitub and Elpaal. The sons of Elpaal:   11 12
Eber, Misham, Shamed who built Ono and Lod with its villages, also Beriah   13
and Shema who were heads of families living in Aijalon, having expelled the
inhabitants of Gath. Ahio, Shashak, Jeremoth, Zebadiah, Arad, Ader,   14 15
Michael, Ispah, and Joha were sons of Beriah; Zebadiah, Meshullam,   16 17
Hezeki, Heber, Ishmerai, Jezliah, and Jobab were sons of Elpaal; Jakim,   18 19

*a Heb.* beraah.     *b Prob. rdg., cp. verse 32; Heb.* Helem.     *c* father of Ehud:
*prob. rdg., cp. Judg. 3. 15; Heb.* Abihud.

453

20 21 Zichri, Zabdi, Elienai, Zilthai, Eliel, Adaiah, Beraiah, and Shimrath were
22 23 24 sons of Shimei; Ishpan, Heber, Eliel, Abdon, Zichri, Hanan, Hananiah,
25 26 Elam, Antothiah, Iphedeiah, and Penuel were sons of Shashak; Sham-
27 sherai, Shehariah, Athaliah, Jaresiah, Eliah, and Zichri were sons of
28 Jeroham. These were enrolled in the tribal lists as heads of families, chiefs
living in Jerusalem.
29*ª* Jehiel founder of Gibeon lived at Gibeon; his wife's name was Maacah.
30 31 His eldest son was Abdon, followed by Zur, Kish, Baal, Nadab, Gedor,
32 Ahio, Zacher and Mikloth. Mikloth was the father of Shimeah; they lived
alongside their kinsmen in Jerusalem.
33 Ner was the father of Kish, Kish father of Saul, Saul father of Jonathan,
34 Malchishua, Abinadab and Eshbaal. Jonathan's son· was Meribbaal, and
35 he was the father of Micah. The sons of Micah: Pithon, Melech, Tarea
36 and Ahaz. Ahaz was the father of Jehoaddah, Jehoaddah father of Alemeth,
37 Azmoth and Zimri. Zimri was the father of Moza, and Moza father of
38 Binea; his son was Raphah, his son Elasah, and his son Azel. Azel had six
sons, whose names were Azrikam, Bocheru, Ishmael, Sheariah, Obadiah
39 and Hanan. All these were sons of Azel. The sons of his brother Eshek:
40 the eldest Ulam, the second Jeush, the third Eliphelet. The sons of Ulam
were able men, archers, and had many sons and grandsons, a hundred and
fifty. All these were descendants of Benjamin.

## *The restored community*

9 **SO ALL ISRAEL WERE REGISTERED** and recorded in the book of the
kings of Israel; but Judah for their sins were carried away to exile
2*ᵇ* in Babylon. The first to occupy their ancestral land in their cities were
3 lay Israelites, priests, Levites, and temple-servitors. Jerusalem was
occupied partly by Judahites, partly by Benjamites, and partly by men of
4 Ephraim and Manasseh. Judahites:*ᶜ* Uthai son of Ammihud, son of
Omri, son of Imri, son of Bani, a descendant of Perez son of Judah.
5 6 Shelanites: Asaiah the eldest and his sons. The sons of Zerah: Jeuel and
7 six hundred and ninety of their kinsmen. Benjamites: Sallu son of Meshul-
8 lam, son of Hodaviah, son of Hassenuah, Ibneiah son of Jeroham, Elah
son of Uzzi, son of Micri, Meshullam son of Shephatiah, son of Reuel, son
9 of Ibniah, and their recorded kinsmen numbering nine hundred and
fifty-six, all heads of families.
10 11 Priests: Jedaiah, Jehoiarib, Jachin, Azariah son of Hilkiah, son of
Meshullam, son of Zadok, son of Meraioth, son of Ahitub, the officer in
12 charge of the house of God, Adaiah son of Jeroham, son of Pashhur, son
of Malchiah, Maasai son of Adiel, son of Jahzerah, son of Meshullam, son
13 of Meshillemith, son of Immer, and their colleagues, heads of families
numbering one thousand seven hundred and sixty, men of substance and
fit for the work connected with the service of the house of God.
14 Levites: Shemaiah son of Hasshub, son of Azrikam, son of Hashabiah,

*ª Verses 29–38: cp. 9. 35–44.*     *ᵇ Verses 2–22: cp. Neh. 11. 3–22.*     *ᶜ Prob. rdg.;*
*Heb. om.*

454

a descendant of Merari, Bakbakkar, Heresh, Galal, Mattaniah son of 15
Mica, son of Zichri, son of Asaph, Obadiah son of Shemaiah, son of Galal, 16
son of Jeduthun, and Berechiah son of Asa, son of Elkanah, who lived in
the hamlets of the Netophathites.

The door-keepers were Shallum, Akkub, Talmon, and Ahiman; their 17
brother Shallum was the chief. Until then they had all been door-keepers 18
in the quarters of the Levites at the king's gate, on the east. Shallum son 19
of Kore, son of Ebiasaph, son of Korah, and his kinsmen of the Korahite
family were responsible for service as guards of the thresholds of the
Tabernacle; their ancestors had performed the duty of guarding the
entrances to the camp of the LORD. Phinehas son of Eleazar had been their 20
overseer in the past—the LORD be with him! Zechariah son of Meshelemiah 21
was the door-keeper of the Tent of the Presence. Those picked to be door- 22
keepers numbered two hundred and twelve in all, registered in their
hamlets. David and Samuel the seer had installed them because they were
trustworthy. They and their sons had charge, by watches, of the gates of 23
the house, the tent-dwelling of the LORD. The door-keepers were to be on 24
four sides, east, west, north, and south. Their kinsmen from their hamlets 25
had to come on duty with them for seven days at a time in turn. The four 26
principal door-keepers were chosen for their trustworthiness; they were
Levites and had charge of the rooms and the stores in the house of God.
They always slept in the precincts of the house of God (for the watch was 27
their duty) and they had charge of the key for opening the gates every
morning. Some of them had charge of the vessels used in the service of the 28
temple, keeping count of them as they were brought in and taken out.
Some of them were detailed to take charge of the furniture and all the 29
sacred vessels, the flour, the wine, the oil, the incense, and the spices.

Some of the priests compounded the ointment for the spices. Mat- 30 31
tithiah the Levite, the eldest son of Shallum the Korahite, was in charge of
the preparation of the wafers because he was trustworthy. Some of their 32
Kohathite kinsmen were in charge of setting out the rows of the Bread of
the Presence every sabbath.

These, the musicians, heads of Levite families, were lodged in rooms 33
set apart for them, because they were liable for duty by day and by night.

These are the heads of Levite families, chiefs according to their tribal 34
lists, living in Jerusalem.

Jehiel founder of Gibeon lived at Gibeon; his wife's name was Maacah, 35*a*
and his sons were Abdon the eldest, Zur, Kish, Baal, Ner, Nadab, Gedor, 36 37
Ahio, Zechariah and Mikloth. Mikloth was the father of Shimeam; they 38
lived alongside their kinsmen in Jerusalem.*b* Ner was the father of Kish, 39
Kish father of Saul, Saul father of Jonathan, Malchishua, Abinadab and
Eshbaal. The son of Jonathan was Meribbaal, and Meribbaal was the 40
father of Micah. The sons of Micah: Pithon, Melech, Tahrea and Ahaz. 41
Ahaz was the father of Jarah, Jarah father of Alemeth, Azmoth, and Zimri; 42
Zimri father of Moza, and Moza father of Binea; his son was Rephaiah, his 43
son Elasah, his son Azel. Azel had six sons, whose names were Azrikam, Bo- 44
cheru, Ishmael, Sheariah, Obadiah and Hanan. These were the sons of Azel.

*a* *Verses 35–44: cp. 8. 29–38.*      *b* *Prob. rdg.; Heb. adds* with their kinsmen.

## The death of Saul

**10** ¹ᵃ THE PHILISTINES FOUGHT A BATTLE against Israel, and the men ² of Israel were routed, leaving their dead on Mount Gilboa. The Philistines hotly pursued Saul and his sons and killed the three sons, ³ Jonathan, Abinadab and Malchishua. The battle went hard for Saul, for ⁴ some archers came upon him and he was wounded by them. So he said to his armour-bearer, 'Draw your sword and run me through, so that these uncircumcised brutes may not come and make sport of me.' But the armour-bearer refused, he dared not; whereupon Saul took his own sword ⁵ and fell on it. When the armour-bearer saw that Saul was dead, he too fell ⁶ on his sword and died. Thus Saul died and his three sons; his whole house ⁷ perished at one and the same time. And all the Israelites in the Vale, when they saw that their army had fled and that Saul and his sons had perished, fled likewise, abandoning their cities, and the Philistines went in and occupied them.

⁸ Next day, when the Philistines came to strip the slain, they found Saul ⁹ and his sons lying dead on Mount Gilboa. They stripped him, cut off his head and took away his armour; then they sent messengers through the length and breadth of their land to take the good news to idols and people ¹⁰ alike. They deposited his armour in the temple of their god,ᵇ and nailed ¹¹ up his skull in the temple of Dagon. When the people of Jabesh-gilead ¹² heard all that the Philistines had done to Saul, the bravest of them set out together to recover the bodies of Saul and his sons; they brought them back to Jabesh and buried their bones under the oak-tree there, and fasted ¹³ for seven days. Thus Saul paid with his life for his unfaithfulness: he had disobeyed the word of the LORD and had resorted to ghosts for guidance. ¹⁴ He had not sought guidance of the LORD, who therefore destroyed him and transferred the kingdom to David son of Jesse.

## David king over Israel

**11** ¹ᶜ THEN ALL ISRAEL ASSEMBLED at Hebron to wait upon David. 'We ² are your own flesh and blood', they said. 'In the past, while Saul was still king, you led the forces of Israel to war, and you brought them home again. And the LORD your God said to you, "You shall be shepherd of my ³ people Israel, you shall be their prince."' All the elders of Israel came to the king at Hebron; there David made a covenant with them before the LORD, and they anointed David king over Israel, as the LORD had said through the lips of Samuel.

⁴ Then David and all Israel went to Jerusalem (that is Jebus, where the ⁵ Jebusites, the inhabitants of the land, lived). The people of Jebus said to David, 'Never shall you come in here'; none the less David did capture ⁶ the stronghold of Zion, and it is now known as the City of David. David said, 'The first man to kill a Jebusite shall become a commander or an

---

ᵃ *Verses 1–12: cp. 1 Sam. 31. 1–13.*     ᵇ *Or gods.*     ᶜ *Verses 1–9: cp. 2 Sam. 5.*
*1–3, 6–10.*

officer', and the first man to go up was Joab son of Zeruiah; so he was given the command.

David took up his residence in the stronghold: that is why they called it 7 the City of David. He built the city round it, starting at the Millo and 8 including its neighbourhood, while Joab reconstructed the rest of the city. So David steadily grew stronger, for the LORD of Hosts was with him. 9

Of David's heroes these were the chief, men who lent their full strength 10<sup>a</sup> to his government and, with all Israel, joined in making him king; such was the LORD's decree for Israel. First came Jashoboam the Hachmonite, chief 11 of the three; he it was who brandished his spear over three hundred, all slain at one time. Next to him was Eleazar son of Dodo the Ahohite, one of 12 the heroic three. He was with David at Pas-dammim where the Philistines 13 had gathered for battle in a field carrying a good crop of barley; and when the people had fled from the Philistines he stood his ground in the field, 14 saved it<sup>b</sup> and defeated them. So the LORD brought about a great victory.

Three of the thirty chiefs went down to the rock to join David at the 15 cave of Adullam, while the Philistines were encamped in the Vale of Rephaim. At that time David was in the stronghold, and a Philistine 16 garrison held Bethlehem. One day a longing came over David, and he 17 exclaimed, 'If only I could have a drink of water from the well<sup>c</sup> by the gate of Bethlehem!' At this the three made their way through the Philistine 18 lines and drew water from the well by the gate of Bethlehem, and brought it to David. But David refused to drink it; he poured it out to the LORD and said, 'God forbid that I should do such a thing! Can I drink the blood 19 of these men? They have brought it at the risk of their lives.' So he would not drink it. Such were the exploits of the heroic three.

Abishai the brother of Joab was chief of the thirty. He once brandished 20 his spear over three hundred dead, and he was famous among the thirty. He held higher rank than the rest of the thirty and became their captain, 21 but he did not rival the three. Benaiah son of Jehoiada, from Kabzeel, was 22 a hero of many exploits. It was he who smote the two champions of Moab, and who went down into a pit and killed a lion on a snowy day. It was he 23 who also killed the Egyptian, a giant seven and a half feet high armed with a spear as big as the beam of a loom; he went to meet him with a club, snatched the spear out of the Egyptian's hand and killed him with his own weapon. Such were the exploits of Benaiah son of Jehoiada, famous among 24 the heroic thirty.<sup>d</sup> He was more famous than the rest of the thirty, but did 25 not rival the three. David appointed him to his household.

These were his valiant heroes: Asahel the brother of Joab, and Elhanan 26 son of Dodo from Bethlehem; Shammoth from Harod,<sup>e</sup> and Helez from 27 a place unknown; Ira son of Ikkesh from Tekoa, and Abiezer from Ana- 28 thoth; Sibbecai from Hushah, and Ilai the Ahohite; Maharai from Neto- 29 30 phah, and Heled son of Baanah from Netophah; Ithai son of Ribai from 31 Gibeah of Benjamin, and Benaiah from Pirathon; Hurai from the ravines 32 of Gaash, and Abiel from Beth-arabah; Azmoth from Bahurim, and 33

---

<sup>a</sup> *Verses 10–41: cp. 2 Sam. 23. 8–39.*      <sup>b</sup> *saved it: or cleared it of the Philistines.*
<sup>c</sup> *Or cistern.*      <sup>d</sup> *Prob. rdg.; Heb. three.*      <sup>e</sup> *Prob. rdg., cp. 2 Sam. 23. 25; Heb.* *Haror.*

34 Eliahba from Shaalbon; Hashem the Gizonite, and Jonathan son of Shage
35 the Hararite; Ahiam son of Sacar the Hararite, and Eliphal son of Ur;
36 37 Hepher from Mecherah, and Ahijah from a place unknown; Hezro from
38 Carmel, and Naarai son of Ezbai; Joel the brother of Nathan, and Mibhar
39 the son of Haggeri; Zelek the Ammonite, and Naharai from Beeroth,
40 armour-bearer to Joab son of Zeruiah; Ira the Ithrite, and Gareb the
41 42 Ithrite; Uriah the Hittite, and Zabad son of Ahlai. Adina son of Shiza the
43 Reubenite, a chief of the Reubenites, was over these thirty. Also Hanan
44 son of Maacah, and Joshaphat the Mithnite; Uzzia from Ashtaroth, Shama
45 and Jeiel the sons of Hotham from Aroer; Jediael son of Shimri, and Joha
46 his brother, the Tizite; Eliel the Mahavite, and Jeribai and Joshaviah sons
47 of Elnaam, and Ithmah the Moabite; Eliel, Obed, and Jasiel, from Zobah. *a*

12   These are the men who joined David at Ziklag while he was banned from
the presence of Saul son of Kish. They ranked among the warriors valiant
2 in battle. They carried bows and could sling stones or shoot arrows with
3 the left hand or the right; they were Benjamites, kinsmen of Saul. The
foremost were Ahiezer and Joash, the sons of Shemaah the Gibeathite;
Jeziel and Pelet, men of Beth-azmoth; Berachah and Jehu of Anathoth;
4 Ishmaiah the Gibeonite, a hero among the thirty and a chief among them;
5 Jeremiah, Jahaziel, Johanan, and Josabad of Gederah; Eluzai, Jerimoth,
6 Bealiah, Shemariah, and Shephatiah the Haruphite; Elkanah, Isshiah,
7 Azareel, Joezer, Jashobeam, the Korahites; and Joelah and Zebadiah sons
of Jeroham, of Gedor.

8   Some Gadites also joined David at the stronghold in the wilderness,
valiant men trained for war, who could handle the heavy shield and spear,
9 grim as lions and swift as gazelles on the hills. Ezer was their chief, Obadiah
10 the second, Eliab the third; Mishmannah the fourth and Jeremiah the
11 12 fifth; Attai the sixth and Eliel the seventh; Johanan the eighth and Elzabad
13 14 the ninth; Jeremiah the tenth and Machbanai the eleventh. These were
chiefs of the Gadites in the army, the least of them a match for a hundred,
15 the greatest a match for a thousand. These were the men who in the first
month crossed the Jordan, which was in full flood in all its reaches, and
wrought havoc in the valleys, east and west.

16   Some men of Benjamin and Judah came to David at the stronghold.
17 David went out to them and said, 'If you come as friends to help me, join
me and welcome; but if you come to betray me to my enemies, innocent
though I am of any crime of violence, may the God of our fathers see and
18 judge.' At that a spirit took possession of Amasai, the chief of the thirty,
and he said:

> We are on your side, David!
> We are with you, son of Jesse!
> Greetings, greetings to you
> and greetings to your ally!
> For your God is your ally.

So David welcomed them and attached them to the columns of his raiding
parties.

*a* from Zobah: *prob. rdg.; Heb. obscure.*

Some men of Manasseh had deserted to David when he went with the 19
Philistines to war against Saul, though he did not, in fact, fight on the side
of the Philistines. Their princes brusquely dismissed him, saying to
themselves that he would desert them for his master Saul, and that would
cost them their heads. The men of Manasseh who deserted to him when 20
he went to Ziklag were these: Adnah, Jozabad, Jediael, Michael, Jozabad,
Elihu, and Zilthai, each commanding his thousand in Manasseh. It was 21
they who stood valiantly by David against the raiders, for they were all
good fighters, and they were given commands in his forces. From day to 22
day men came in to help David, until he had gathered an immense army.

These are the numbers of the armed bands which joined David at 23
Hebron to transfer Saul's sovereignty to him, as the Lord had said: men 24
of Judah, bearing heavy shield and spear, six thousand eight hundred,
drafted for active service; of Simeon, fighting men drafted for active service, 25
seven thousand one hundred; of Levi, four thousand six hundred, together 26 27
with Jehoiada prince of the house of Aaron and three thousand seven hundred men, and Zadok a valiant fighter, with twenty-two officers of his own 28
clan; of Benjamin, Saul's kinsmen, three thousand, though most of them 29
had hitherto remained loyal to the house of Saul; of Ephraim, twenty 30
thousand eight hundred, fighting men, famous in their own clans; of the 31
half tribe of Manasseh, eighteen thousand, who had been nominated to
come and make David king; of Issachar, whose tribesmen were skilled in 32
reading the signs of the times to discover what course Israel should follow,
two hundred chiefs, with all their kinsmen under their command; of 33
Zebulun, fifty thousand troops well-drilled for battle, armed with every
kind of weapon, bold and single-minded; of Naphtali, a thousand officers 34
with thirty-seven thousand men bearing heavy shield and spear; of the 35
Danites, twenty-eight thousand six hundred well-drilled for battle; of 36
Asher, forty thousand troops well-drilled for battle; of the Reubenites and 37
the Gadites and the half tribe of Manasseh east of Jordan, a hundred and
twenty thousand, armed with every kind of weapon.

All these warriors, bold men in battle, came to Hebron, loyally deter- 38
mined to make David king over the whole of Israel; the rest of Israel, too,
had but one thought, to make him king. They spent three days there with 39
David, eating and drinking, for their kinsmen made provision for them.
Their neighbours also round about, as far away as Issachar, Zebulun, and 40
Naphtali, brought food on asses and camels, on mules and oxen, supplies
of meal, fig-cakes, raisin-cakes, wine and oil, oxen and sheep, in plenty;
for there was rejoicing in Israel.

David consulted the officers over units of a thousand and a 13
hundred on every matter brought forward. Then he said to the whole 2
assembly of Israel, 'If you approve, and if the Lord our God opens a way,
let us*a* send to our kinsmen who have stayed behind, in all the districts of
Israel, and also to the priests and Levites in the cities where they have
common lands, bidding them join us. Let us fetch the Ark of our God, for 3

---

*a* and if . . . let us: *or* and if it is from the Lord our God, let us seize the opportunity
and . . .

4 while Saul lived we never resorted to it.' The whole assembly resolved to do this; the entire nation approved it.

5 So David assembled all Israel from the Shihor in Egypt to Lebo-hamath,
6ᵃ in order to fetch the Ark of God from Kiriath-jearim. Then David and all Israel went up to Baalah, to Kiriath-jearim, which belonged to Judah, to fetch the Ark of God, the LORD enthroned upon the cherubim, the Ark
7 which bore his name.ᵇ And they conveyed the Ark of God on a new cart
8 from the house of Abinadab, with Uzza and Ahio guiding the cart. David and all Israel danced for joy before God without restraint to the sound of singing, of harps and lutes, of tambourines, and cymbals and trumpets.
9 But when they came to the threshing-floor of Kidon, the oxen stumbled,
10 and Uzza put out his hand to hold the Ark. The LORD was angry with Uzza and struck him down because he had put out his hand to the Ark.
11 So he died there before God. David was vexed because the LORD's anger had broken out upon Uzza, and he called the place Perez-uzza,ᶜ the name
12 it still bears. David was afraid of God that day and said, 'How can I harbour
13 the Ark of God after this?' So he did not take the Ark with him into the City of David, but turned aside and carried it to the house of Obed-edom
14 the Gittite. Thus the Ark of God remained beside the house of Obed-edom, in its tent,ᵈ for three months, and the LORD blessed the family of Obed-edom and all that he had.

**14** 1ᵉ Hiram king of Tyre sent an embassy to David; he sent cedar logs, and
2 masons and carpenters with them to build him a house. David knew by now that the LORD had confirmed him as king over Israel and had made his royal power stand higher for the sake of his people Israel.

3 David married more wives in Jerusalem, and more sons and daughters
4ᶠ were born to him. These are the names of the children born to him in
5 Jerusalem: Shammua, Shobab, Nathan, Solomon, Ibhar, Elishua, Elpelet,
6 7 Nogah, Nepheg, Japhia, Elishama, Beeliada and Eliphelet.

8 When the Philistines learnt that David had been anointed king over the whole of Israel, they came up in force to seek him out. David, hearing of
9 this, went out to face them. Now the Philistines had come and raided the
10 Vale of Rephaim. So David inquired of God, 'If I attack the Philistines, wilt thou deliver them into my hands?' And the LORD answered, 'Go; I
11 will deliver them into your hands.' So he went up and attacked them at Baal-perazim and defeated them there. 'God has used me to break through my enemies' lines,' David said, 'as a river breaks its banks'; that is why the
12 place was named Baal-perazim.ᵍ The Philistines left their gods behind them there, and by David's orders these were burnt.

13 14 The Philistines made another raid on the Vale. Again David inquired of God, and God said to him, 'No, you must go up towards their rear; wheel round without making contact andʰ come upon them opposite the
15 aspens. Then, as soon as you hear a rustling sound in the tree-tops, you

---

*a Verses 6–14: cp. 2 Sam. 6. 2–11.*          *b which bore his name: prob. rdg.; Heb. obscure.*          *c That is Outbreak on Uzza.*          *d Or in his tent.*          *e Verses 1–16: cp. 2 Sam. 5. 11–25.*          *f Verses 4–7: cp. 3. 5–8.*          *g That is Baal of Break-through.*          *h No . . . contact and: or Do not go up to the attack; withdraw from them and then . . .*

shall give battle, for God will have gone out before you to defeat the
Philistine army.' David did as God commanded, and they drove the 16
Philistine army in flight all the way from Gibeon to Gezer. So David's 17
fame spread through every land, and the LORD inspired all nations with
dread of him.

DAVID BUILT HIMSELF QUARTERS in the City of David, and prepared 15
a place for the Ark of God and pitched a tent for it. Then he decreed that 2
only Levites should carry the Ark of God, since they had been chosen by
the LORD to carry it and to serve him *a* for ever. Next David assembled all 3
Israel at Jerusalem, to bring up the Ark of the LORD to the place he had
prepared for it. He gathered together the sons of Aaron and the Levites: 4
of the sons of Kohath, Uriel the chief with a hundred and twenty of his 5
kinsmen; of the sons of Merari, Asaiah the chief with two hundred and 6
twenty of his kinsmen; of the sons of Gershom, Joel the chief with a 7
hundred and thirty of his kinsmen; of the sons of Elizaphan, Shemaiah 8
the chief with two hundred of his kinsmen; of the sons of Hebron, Eliel the 9
chief with eighty of his kinsmen; of the sons of Uzziel, Amminadab the 10
chief with a hundred and twelve of his kinsmen. And David summoned 11
Zadok and Abiathar the priests, together with the Levites, Uriel, Asaiah,
Joel, Shemaiah, Eliel, and Amminadab, and said to them, 'You who are 12
heads of families of the Levites, hallow yourselves, you and your kinsmen,
and bring up the Ark of the LORD the God of Israel to the place which I
have prepared for it. It was because you were not present the first time, 13
that the LORD our God broke out upon us. For we had not sought his
guidance as we should have done.' So the priests and the Levites hallowed 14
themselves to bring up the Ark of the LORD the God of Israel, and the 15
Levites carried the Ark of God, bearing it on their shoulders with poles as
Moses had prescribed at the command of the LORD.

David also ordered the chiefs of the Levites to install as musicians those 16
of their kinsmen who were players skilled in making joyful music on their
instruments, lutes and harps and cymbals. So the Levites installed Heman 17
son of Joel and, from his kinsmen, Asaph son of Berechiah; and from their
kinsmen the Merarites, Ethan son of Kushaiah, together with their kins- 18
men of the second degree, Zechariah, Jaaziel, Shemiramoth, Jehiel, Unni,
Eliab, Benaiah, Maaseiah, Mattithiah, Eliphelehu, and Mikneiah, and the
door-keepers Obed-edom and Jeiel. They installed the musicians Heman, 19
Asaph, and Ethan to sound the cymbals of bronze; Zechariah, Jaaziel, 20
Shemiramoth, Jehiel, Unni, Eliab, Maaseiah, and Benaiah to play on
lutes; *b* Mattithiah, Eliphelehu, Mikneiah, Obed-edom, Jeiel, and Azaziah 21
to play on harps. *c* Kenaniah, officer of the Levites, was precentor in charge 22
of the music because of his proficiency. Berechiah and Elkanah were door- 23
keepers for the Ark, while the priests Shebaniah, Jehoshaphat, Nethaneel, 24
Amasai, Zechariah, Benaiah, and Eliezer sounded the trumpets before
the Ark of God; and Obed-edom and Jehiah also were door-keepers for
the Ark.

*a* Or it.    *b* *Prob. rdg.; Heb. adds* al alamoth, *possibly a musical term.*    *c* *Prob. rdg.;*
*Heb. adds* al hashsheminith lenasseah, *possibly musical terms.*

25<sup>a</sup> Then David and the elders of Israel and the captains of units of a thousand went to bring up the Ark of the Covenant of the LORD with much
26 rejoicing from the house of Obed-edom. Because God had helped the Levites who carried the Ark of the Covenant of the LORD, they sacrificed seven bulls and seven rams.
27 Now David and all the Levites who carried the Ark, and the musicians, and Kenaniah the precentor,<sup>b</sup> were arrayed in robes of fine linen; and
28 David had on a linen ephod. All Israel escorted the Ark of the Covenant of the LORD with shouts of acclamation, blowing on horns and trumpets,
29 clashing cymbals and playing on lutes and harps. But as the Ark of the Covenant of the LORD was entering the city of David, Saul's daughter Michal looked down through a window and saw King David dancing and making merry, and she despised him in her heart.

16 1<sup>c</sup> When they had brought in the Ark of God, they put it inside the tent that David had pitched for it, and they offered whole-offerings and shared-
2 offerings before God. After David had completed these sacrifices, he
3 blessed the people in the name of the LORD and gave food, a loaf of bread, a portion of meat, and a cake of raisins, to each Israelite, man or woman.
4 He appointed certain Levites to serve before the Ark of the LORD, to repeat the Name, to confess and to praise the LORD the God of Israel.
5 Their leader was Asaph; second to him was Zechariah; then came Jaaziel,<sup>d</sup> Shemiramoth, Jehiel, Mattithiah, Eliab, Benaiah, Obed-edom, and Jeiel,
6 with lutes and harps, Asaph, who sounded the cymbals; and Benaiah and Jahaziel the priests, who blew the trumpets before the Ark of the Covenant
7 of God continuously throughout that day. It was then that David first ordained the offering of thanks to the LORD by Asaph and his kinsmen:

8<sup>e</sup>  Give the LORD thanks and invoke him by name,
      make his deeds known in the world around.
9    Pay him honour with song and psalm
      and think upon all his wonders.
10   Exult in his hallowed name;
      let those who seek the LORD be joyful in heart.
11   Turn to the LORD, your strength,<sup>f</sup>
      seek his presence always.
12   Remember the wonders that he has wrought,
      his portents and the judgements he has given,
13   O offspring of Israel his servants, O chosen sons of Jacob.

14   He is the LORD our God;
      his judgements fill the earth.
15   He called to mind his covenant from long ago,<sup>g</sup>
      the promise he extended to a thousand generations—
16      the covenant made with Abraham,
         his oath given to Isaac,

---

*a  Verses 25–29: cp. 2 Sam. 6. 12–16.*   *b  the precentor: prob. rdg.; Heb. obscure.*
*c  Verses 1–3: cp. 2 Sam. 6. 17–19.*   *d  Prob. rdg., cp. 15. 18, 20; Heb. Jeiel.*
*e  Verses 8–22: cp. Ps. 105. 1–15.*   *f  your strength: or the symbol of his strength;*
*lit. and his strength.*   *g  from long ago: or for ever.*

the decree by which he bound himself for Jacob,      17
his everlasting covenant with Israel:
'I will give you the land of Canaan', he said,      18
    'to be your possession, your patrimony.'
    A small company it was,      19
few in number, strangers in that land,
roaming from nation to nation,      20
from one kingdom to another;
but he let no man ill-treat them,      21
for their sake he admonished kings:
    'Touch not my anointed servants,      22
    do my prophets no harm.'

Sing to the LORD, all men on earth,      23[a]
proclaim his triumph day by day.
Declare his glory among the nations,      24
    his marvellous deeds among all peoples.
Great is the LORD and worthy of all praise;      25
he is more to be feared than all gods.
For the gods of the nations are idols every one;      26
but the LORD made the heavens.
Majesty and splendour attend him,      27
might and joy are in his dwelling.

Ascribe to the LORD, you families of nations,      28
ascribe to the LORD glory and might;
    ascribe to the LORD the glory due to his name,      29
bring a gift and come before him.
    Bow down to the LORD in the splendour of holiness,[b]
    and dance in his honour, all men on earth.      30
    He has fixed the earth firm, immovable.
Let the heavens rejoice and the earth exult,      31
let men declare among the nations, 'The LORD is king.'
    Let the sea roar and all the creatures in it,      32
    let the fields exult and all that is in them;
    then let the trees of the forest shout for joy      33
    before the LORD when he comes to judge the earth.

It is good to give thanks to the LORD,      34[c]
    for his love endures for ever.
Cry, 'Deliver us, O God our saviour,      35[d]
gather us in and save us from the nations
    that we may give thanks to thy holy name
    and make thy praise our pride.'

Blessed be the LORD the God of Israel      36
    from everlasting to everlasting.

And all the people said 'Amen' and 'Praise the LORD.'

[a] *Verses 23–33: cp. Ps. 96. 1–13.*      [b] *Or in holy vestments.*      [c] *Verse 34:*
*cp. Ps. 107. 1.*      [d] *Verses 35, 36: cp. Ps. 106. 47, 48.*

37 David left Asaph and his kinsmen there before the Ark of the Covenant of the LORD, to perform regular service before the Ark as each day's duty
38 required; as door-keepers he left Obed-edom son of Jeduthun, and Hosah.
39 (Obed-edom and his kinsmen were sixty-eight in number.) He left Zadok the priest and his kinsmen the priests before the Tabernacle of the LORD
40 at the hill-shrine in Gibeon, to make offerings there to the LORD upon the altar of whole-offering regularly morning and evening, exactly as it is
41 written in the law enjoined by the LORD upon Israel. With them he left Heman and Jeduthun and the other men chosen and nominated to give
42 thanks to the LORD, 'for his love endures for ever.' They had trumpets and cymbals for the players, and the instruments used for sacred song. The sons of Jeduthun kept the gate.
43 So all the people went home, and David returned to greet his household.

17 1ᵃ As soon as David was established in his house, he said to Nathan the prophet, 'Here I live in a house of cedar, while the Ark of the Covenant
2 of the LORD is housed in curtains.' Nathan answered David, 'Do whatever
3 you have in mind, for God is with you.' But that night the word of God
4 came to Nathan: 'Go and say to David my servant, "This is the word of
5 the LORD: It is not you who shall build me a house to dwell in. Down to this day I have never dwelt in a house since I brought Israel up from
6 Egypt; I lived in a tent and a tabernacle.ᵇ Wherever I journeyed with Israel, did I ever ask any of the judges whom I appointed shepherds of my
7 people why they had not built me a house of cedar?" Then say this to my servant David: "This is the word of the LORD of Hosts: I took you from the pastures, and from following the sheep, to be prince over my people
8 Israel. I have been with you wherever you have gone, and have destroyed all the enemies in your path. I will make you as famous as the great ones
9 of the earth. I will assign a place for my people Israel; there I will plant them, and they shall dwell in their own land. They shall be disturbed no
10 more, never again shall wicked men wear them down as they did from the time when I first appointed judges over Israel my people, and I will sub-
11 due all your enemies. But I will make you great and the LORD shall build up your royal house. When your life ends and you go to join your fore-
12 fathers, I will set up one of your family, one of your own sons, to succeed you, and I will establish his kingdom. It is he shall build me a house, and
13 I will establish his throne for all time. I will be his father, and he shall be my son. I will never withdraw my love from him as I withdrew it from your
14 predecessor. But I will give him a sure place in my house and kingdom for all time, and his throne shall be established for ever."'
15 Nathan recounted to David all that had been said to him and all that
16 had been revealed. Then King David went into the presence of the LORD and took his place there and said, 'What am I, LORD God, and what is my
17 family, that thou hast brought me thus far? It was a small thing in thy sight, O God, to have planned for thy servant's house in days long past, and now thou lookest upon me as a man already embarked on a high

ᵃ *Verses 1–27: cp. 2 Sam. 7. 1–29.* ᵇ I lived . . . tabernacle: *prob. rdg.; Heb.* I have been from tent to tent and from a tabernacle.

career, O LORD God. What more can David say to thee of the honour thou 18
hast done thy servant, well though thou knowest him? For the sake of thy 19
servant, LORD, and according to thy purpose, thou hast brought me to all
this greatness. O LORD, we have never heard of one like thee; there is no 20
god but thee. And thy people Israel, to whom can they be compared? Is 21
there any other nation on earth whom God has gone out to redeem from
slavery, to make them his people? Thou hast won a name for thyself by
great and terrible deeds, driving out nations before thy people whom thou
didst redeem from Egypt. Thou hast made thy people Israel thy own for 22
ever, and thou, O LORD, hast become their God. But now, LORD, let what 23
thou hast promised for thy servant and his house stand fast for all time;
make good what thou hast said. Let it stand fast, that thy fame may be 24
great for ever, and let men say, "The LORD of Hosts, the God of Israel, is
Israel's God." So shall the house of thy servant David be established before
thee. Thou, my God, hast shown me thy purpose to build up thy servant's 25
house; therefore I have been able to pray before thee. Thou, O LORD, art 26
God, and thou hast made these noble promises to thy servant; thou hast 27
been pleased to bless thy servant's house, that it may continue always
before thee; thou it is who hast blessed it, and it shall be blessed for
ever.'

After this David defeated the Philistines and conquered them, and took **18** 1[a]
from them Gath with its villages; he defeated the Moabites, and they 2
became subject to him and paid him tribute. He also defeated Hadadezer 3
king of Zobah-hamath, who was on his way to set up a monument of victory
by the river Euphrates. From him David captured a thousand chariots, 4
seven thousand horsemen and twenty thousand foot; he hamstrung all the
chariot-horses, except a hundred which he retained. When the Aramaeans 5
of Damascus came to the help of Hadadezer king of Zobah, David destroyed
twenty-two thousand of them, and established garrisons among these 6
Aramaeans; they became subject to him and paid him tribute. Thus the
LORD gave David victory wherever he went. David took the gold quivers 7
borne by Hadadezer's servants and brought them to Jerusalem. He also 8
took a great quantity of bronze[b] from Hadadezer's cities, Tibhath and
Kun; from this Solomon made the Sea of bronze,[b] the pillars, and the
bronze[b] vessels.

When Tou king of Hamath heard that David had defeated the entire 9
army of Hadadezer king of Zobah, he sent his son Hadoram to King David 10
to greet him and to congratulate him on defeating Hadadezer in battle (for
Hadadezer had been at war with Tou); and he brought with him vessels of
gold, silver, and copper, which King David dedicated to the LORD. He 11
dedicated also the silver and the gold which he had carried away from all
the other nations, from Edom and Moab, from the Ammonites and the
Philistines, and from Amalek.

Edom was defeated by Abishai son of Zeruiah, who destroyed eighteen 12
thousand of them in the Valley of Salt and stationed garrisons in the 13
country. All the Edomites now became subject to David. Thus the LORD
gave victory to David wherever he went.

[a] *Verses 1–13: cp. 2 Sam. 8. 1–14.*     [b] *Or* copper.

14*a* David ruled over the whole of Israel and maintained law and justice
15 among all his people. Joab son of Zeruiah was in command of the army;
16 Jehoshaphat son of Ahilud was secretary of state; Zadok and Abiathar
son of Ahimelech, son of Ahitub,*b* were priests; Shavsha was adjutant-
17 general; Benaiah son of Jehoiada commanded the Kerethite and Pelethite
guards. The eldest sons of David were in attendance on the king.

19 1*c* Some time afterwards Nahash king of the Ammonites died and was
2 succeeded by his son. David said, 'I must keep up the same loyal friendship with Hanun son of Nahash as his father showed me', and he sent a
mission to condole with him on the death of his father. But when David's
3 envoys entered the country of the Ammonites to condole with Hanun, the
Ammonite princes said to Hanun, 'Do you suppose David means to do
honour to your father when he sends you his condolences? These men of
his are spies whom he has sent to find out how to overthrow the country.'
4 So Hanun took David's servants, and he shaved them, cut off half their
5 garments up to the hips, and dismissed them. When David heard how they
had been treated, he sent to meet them, for they were deeply humiliated,
and ordered them to wait in Jericho and not to return until their beards
6 had grown again. The Ammonites knew that they had brought themselves
into bad odour with David, so Hanun and the Ammonites sent a thousand
talents of silver to hire chariots and horsemen from Aram-naharaim,*d*
7 Maacah, and Aram-zobah.*e* They hired thirty-two thousand chariots and
the king of Maacah and his people, who came and encamped before
Medeba, while the Ammonites came from their cities and mustered for
8 battle. When David heard of it, he sent out Joab and all the fighting men.
9 The Ammonites came and took up their position at the entrance to the
10 city, while the allied kings took up theirs in the open country. When Joab
saw that he was threatened both front and rear, he detailed some picked
11 Israelite troops and drew them up facing the Aramaeans. The rest of his
forces he put under his brother Abishai, who took up a position facing the
12 Ammonites. 'If the Aramaeans prove too strong for me,' he said, 'you must
come to my relief; and if the Ammonites prove too strong for you, I will
13 relieve you. Courage! Let us fight bravely for our people and for the cities *f*
14 of our God. And the LORD's will be done.' But when Joab and his men came
15 to close quarters with the Aramaeans, they put them to flight; and when the
Ammonites saw them in flight, they too fled before his brother Abishai and
16 entered the city. Then Joab came to Jerusalem. The Aramaeans saw that
they had been worsted by Israel, and they sent messengers to summon other
Aramaeans from the Great Bend of the Euphrates under Shophach, com-
17 mander of Hadadezer's army. Their movement was reported to David,
who immediately mustered all the forces of Israel, crossed the Jordan and
advanced against them and took up battle positions. The Aramaeans like-
18 wise took up positions facing David and engaged him, but were put to
flight by Israel. David slew seven thousand Aramaeans in chariots and

---

*a Verses 14–17: cp. 2 Sam. 8. 15–18; 20. 23–26; 1 Kgs. 4. 2–4.* *b and Abiathar . . .
Ahitub: prob. rdg., cp. 2 Sam. 8. 17; Heb. son of Ahitub and Abimelech son of Abiathar.*
*c Verses 1–19: cp. 2 Sam. 10. 1–19.* *d That is Aram of Two Rivers.* *e Maacah,
and Aram-zobah: prob. rdg.; Heb. Aram-maacah, and Zobah.* *f Or altars.*

forty thousand infantry, killing Shophach the commander of the army.
When Hadadezer's men saw that they had been worsted by Israel, they 19
sued for peace and submitted to David. The Aramaeans were never again
willing to give support to the Ammonites.

AT THE TURN OF THE YEAR, when kings take the field, Joab led the army 20 1*a*
out and ravaged the Ammonite country. He came to Rabbah and laid siege
to it, while David remained in Jerusalem; he reduced the city and razed it
to the ground. David took the crown from the head of Milcom and found 2
that it weighed a talent of gold and was set with a precious stone, and this
he placed on his own head. He also removed a great quantity of booty from
the city; he took its inhabitants and set them to work with saws and other 3
iron tools, sharp and toothed. David did this to all the cities of the Ammonites; then he and all his people returned to Jerusalem.

Some time later war with the Philistines broke out in Gezer; it was then 4*b*
that Sibbechai of Hushah killed Sippai, a descendant of the Rephaim, and
the Philistines were reduced to submission. In another war with the 5
Philistines, Elhanan son of Jair killed Lahmi brother of Goliath of Gath,
whose spear had a shaft like a weaver's beam. In yet another war in Gath, 6
there appeared a giant with six fingers on each hand and six toes on each
foot, twenty-four in all; he too was descended from the Rephaim, and, 7
when he defied Israel, Jonathan son of David's brother Shimea killed him.
These giants were the descendants of the Rephaim in Gath, and they all 8
fell at the hands of David and his men.

NOW SATAN, SETTING HIMSELF AGAINST ISRAEL, incited David 21 1*c*
to count the people. So he instructed Joab and his public officers to go 2
out and number Israel, from Beersheba to Dan, and to report the number
to him. Joab answered, 'Even if the LORD should increase his people a 3
hundredfold, would not your majesty still be king and all the people your
slaves? Why should your majesty want to do this? It will only bring guilt
on Israel.' But Joab was overruled by the king; he set out and went up and 4
down the whole country. He then came to Jerusalem and reported to 5
David the numbers recorded: those capable of bearing arms were one
million one hundred thousand in Israel, and four hundred and seventy
thousand in Judah. Levi and Benjamin were not counted by Joab, so deep 6
was his repugnance against the king's order.

God was displeased with all this and proceeded to punish Israel. David 7 8
said to God, 'I have done a very wicked thing: I pray thee remove thy
servant's guilt, for I have been very foolish.' And the LORD said to Gad, 9
David's seer, 'Go and tell David, "This is the word of the LORD: I have 10
three things to offer you; choose one of them and I will bring it upon you."'
So Gad came to David and said to him, 'This is the word of the LORD: 11
"Make your choice: three years of famine, three months of harrying by your 12
foes and close pursuit by the sword of your enemy, or three days of the
LORD's own sword, bringing pestilence throughout the country, and the

---

*a* Verses 1-3: cp. 2 Sam. 12. 26-31.     *b* Verses 4-7: cp. 2 Sam. 21. 18-22.
*c* Verses 1-27: cp. 2 Sam. 24. 1-25.

LORD's angel working destruction in all the territory of Israel." Consider
13 now what answer I am to take back to him who sent me.' Thereupon David
said to Gad, 'I am in a desperate plight; let me fall into the hands of the
LORD, for his mercy is very great; and let me not fall into the hands of man.'
14 So the LORD sent a pestilence throughout Israel, and seventy thousand men
15 of Israel died. And God sent an angel to Jerusalem to destroy it; but, as he
was destroying it, the LORD saw and repented of the evil, and said to the
destroying angel at the moment when he was standing beside the threshing-
floor of Ornan the Jebusite, 'Enough! Stay your hand.'
16 When David looked up and saw the angel of the LORD standing between
earth and heaven, with his sword drawn in his hand and stretched out over
Jerusalem, he and the elders, clothed in sackcloth, fell prostrate to the
17 ground; and David said to God, 'It was I who gave the order to count the
people. It was I who sinned, I, the shepherd,*a* who did wrong. But these
poor sheep, what have they done? O LORD my God, let thy hand fall upon
me and upon my family, but check this plague on the people.'*b*
18 The angel of the LORD, speaking through the lips of Gad, commanded
David to go to the threshing-floor of Ornan the Jebusite and to set up there
19 an altar to the LORD. David went up as Gad had bidden him in the LORD's
20 name. Ornan's four sons who were with him hid themselves, but he was
21 busy threshing his wheat when he turned and saw the angel. As David
approached, Ornan looked up and, seeing the king, came out from the
22 threshing-floor and prostrated himself before him. David said to Ornan,
'Let me have the site of the threshing-floor that I may build on it an altar
to the LORD; sell it me at the full price, that the plague which has attacked
23 my people may be stopped.' Ornan answered David, 'Take it and let your
majesty do as he thinks fit; see, here are the oxen for whole-offerings, the
threshing-sledges for the fuel, and the wheat for the grain-offering; I give
24 you everything.' But King David said to Ornan, 'No, I will pay the full
price; I will not present to the LORD what is yours, or offer a whole-offering
25 which has cost me nothing.' So David gave Ornan six hundred shekels of
26 gold for the site, and built an altar to the LORD there; on this he offered
whole-offerings and shared-offerings, and called upon the LORD, who
answered him with fire falling from heaven on the altar of whole-offering.
27 Then, at the LORD's command, the angel sheathed his sword.
28 It was when David saw that the LORD had answered him at the threshing-
29 floor of Ornan the Jebusite that he offered sacrifice there. The tabernacle
of the LORD and the altar of whole-offering which Moses had made in the
30 wilderness were then at the hill-shrine in Gibeon; but David had been
unable to go there and seek God's guidance, so shocked and shaken was he
**22** at the sight of the angel's sword. Then David said, 'This is to be the house
of the LORD God, and this is to be an altar of whole-offering for Israel.'

---

*a* I, the shepherd: *prob. rdg.; Heb.* doing wrong.     *b* check . . . people: *prob. rdg.;*
*Heb.* among thy people, not for a plague.

## The temple and its organization

D AVID NOW GAVE ORDERS to assemble the aliens resident in Israel, 2 and he set them as masons to dress hewn stones and to build the house of God. He laid in a great store of iron to make nails and clamps for the 3 doors, more bronze than could be weighed and cedar-wood without limit; 4 the men of Sidon and Tyre brought David an ample supply of cedar. David said, 'My son Solomon is a boy of tender years, and the house that 5 is to be built to the LORD must be exceedingly magnificent, renowned and celebrated in every land; therefore I must make preparations for it myself.' So David made abundant preparation before his death.

He sent for Solomon his son and charged him to build a house for the 6 LORD the God of Israel. 'Solomon, my son,' he said, 'I had intended to 7 build a house in honour of the name of the LORD my God; but the LORD 8 forbade me and said, "You have shed much blood in my sight and waged great wars; for this reason you shall not build a house in honour of my name. But you shall have a son who shall be a man of peace; I will give him 9 *a* peace from all his enemies on every side; his name shall be Solomon, 'Man of Peace', and I will grant peace and quiet to Israel in his days. He 10 shall build a house in honour of my name; he shall be my son and I will be a father to him, and I will establish the throne of his sovereignty over Israel for ever." Now, Solomon my son, the LORD be with you! May you 11 prosper and build the house of the LORD your God, as he promised you should. But may the LORD grant you wisdom and discretion, so that when 12 he gives you authority in Israel you may keep the law of the LORD your God. You will prosper only if you are careful to observe the decrees and 13 ordinances which the LORD enjoined upon Moses for Israel; be strong and resolute, neither faint-hearted nor dismayed.

'In spite of all my troubles, I have here ready for the house of the LORD 14 a hundred thousand talents of gold and a million talents of silver, with great quantities of bronze and iron, more than can be weighed; timber and stone, too, I have got ready; and you may add to them. Besides, you have 15 a large force of workmen, masons, sculptors, and carpenters, and countless men skilled in work of every kind, in gold and silver, bronze and iron. So 16 now to work, and the LORD be with you!'

David ordered all the officers of Israel to help Solomon his son: 'Is not 17 18 the LORD your God with you? Will he not give you peace on every side? For he has given the inhabitants of the land into my power, and they will be subject to the LORD and his people. Devote yourselves, therefore, heart 19 and soul, to seeking guidance of the LORD your God, and set about building his sanctuary, so that the Ark of the Covenant of the LORD and God's holy vessels may be brought into a house built in honour of his name.'

David was now an old man, weighed down with years, and he appointed **23** Solomon his son king over Israel. He gathered together all the officers of 2 Israel, the priests, and the Levites. The Levites were enrolled from the age 3 of thirty upwards, their males being thirty-eight thousand in all. Of these, 4 twenty-four thousand were to be responsible for the maintenance and

*a* Verse 9: cp. 1 Kgs. 5. 4.

service of the house of the LORD, six thousand to act as officers and magis-
5 trates, four thousand to be door-keepers, and four thousand to praise the
LORD on the musical instruments which David had made for the service
6 of praise. David organized them in divisions, called after Gershon, Kohath,
and Merari, the sons of Levi.

7 8    The sons of Gershon: Laadan and Shimei. The sons of Laadan: Jehiel
9 the chief, Zetham and Joel, three.[a] These were the heads of the families
10 grouped under Laadan. The sons of Shimei: Jahath, Ziza, Jeush and
11 Beriah, four. Jahath was the chief and Ziza the second, but Jeush and
Beriah, having few children, were reckoned for duty as a single family.

12 13    The sons of Kohath: Amram, Izhar, Hebron and Uzziel, four. The sons
of Amram: Aaron and Moses. Aaron was set apart, he and his sons in
perpetuity, to dedicate the most holy gifts,[b] to burn sacrifices before the
14 LORD, to serve him, and to give the blessing in his name for ever, but
15 the sons of Moses, the man of God, were to keep the name of Levite. The
16 sons of Moses: Gershom and Eliezer. The sons of Gershom: Shubael the
17 chief. The sons of Eliezer: Rehabiah the chief. Eliezer had no other sons,
18 but Rehabiah had very many. The sons of Izhar: Shelomoth the chief.
19 The sons of Hebron: Jeriah the chief, Amariah the second, Jahaziel the
20 third and Jekameam the fourth. The sons of Uzziel: Micah the chief and
Isshiah the second.

21    The sons of Merari: Mahli and Mushi. The sons of Mahli: Eleazar and
22 Kish. When Eleazar died, he left daughters but no sons, and their cousins,
23 the sons of Kish, married them. The sons of Mushi: Mahli, Eder and
Jeremoth, three.

24    Such were the Levites, grouped by families in the father's line whose
heads were entered in the detailed list; they performed duties in the
25 service of the house of the LORD, from the age of twenty upwards. For
David said, 'The LORD the God of Israel has given his people peace and
26 has made his abode in Jerusalem for ever. The Levites will no longer have
27 to carry the Tabernacle or any of the vessels for its service.' By these last
words of David the Levites were enrolled from the age of twenty upwards.
28 Their duty was to help the sons of Aaron in the service of the house of the
LORD: they were responsible for the care of the courts and the rooms, for
the cleansing of all holy things, and the general service of the house of God;
29 for the rows of the Bread of the Presence, the flour for the grain-offerings,
unleavened wafers, cakes baked on the griddle, and pastry, and for the
30 weights and measures. They were to be on duty continually before the
31 LORD every morning and evening, giving thanks and praise to him, and
at every offering of whole-offerings to the LORD, on sabbaths, new moons
32 and at the appointed seasons, according to their prescribed number. The
Levites were to have charge of the Tent of the Presence and of the sanctuary,
but the sons of Aaron their kinsmen were charged with the service of
worship in the house of the LORD.

**24**    The divisions of the sons of Aaron: his sons were Nadab and Abihu,
2 Eleazar and Ithamar. Nadab and Abihu died before their father, leaving

---

[a] *Prob. rdg.; Heb. adds* The sons of Shimei: Shelomith, Haziel and Haran, three.
[b] to dedicate ... gifts: *or* to be hallowed as most holy.

no sons; therefore Eleazar and Ithamar held the office of priest. David, 3
acting with Zadok of the sons of Eleazar and with Ahimelech of the sons
of Ithamar, organized them in divisions for the discharge of the duties of
their office. The male heads of families proved to be more numerous in the 4
line of Eleazar than in that of Ithamar, so that sixteen heads of families
were grouped under the line of Eleazar and eight under that of Ithamar.
He organized them by drawing lots among them, for there were sacred 5
officers*a* and officers of God in the line of Eleazar and in that of Ithamar.
Shemaiah the clerk, a Levite, son of Nethaneel, wrote down the names in 6
the presence of the king, the officers, Zadok the priest, and Ahimelech son
of Abiathar, and of the heads of the priestly and levitical families, one
priestly family being taken from the line of Eleazar and one from that of
Ithamar. The first lot fell to Jehoiarib, the second to Jedaiah, the third to 7 8
Harim, the fourth to Seorim, the fifth to Malchiah, the sixth to Mijamin, 9
the seventh to Hakkoz, the eighth to Abiah, the ninth to Jeshua, the tenth 10 11
to Shecaniah, the eleventh to Eliashib, the twelfth to Jakim, the thirteenth 12 13
to Huppah, the fourteenth to Jeshebeab, the fifteenth to Bilgah, the six- 14
teenth to Immer, the seventeenth to Hezir, the eighteenth to Aphses, the 15 16
nineteenth to Pethahiah, the twentieth to Jehezekel, the twenty-first to 17
Jachin, the twenty-second to Gamul, the twenty-third to Delaiah, and the 18
twenty-fourth to Maaziah. This was their order of duty for the discharge 19
of their service when they entered the house of the LORD, according to the
rule prescribed for them by their ancestor Aaron, who had received his
instructions from the LORD the God of Israel.

Of the remaining Levites: of the sons of Amram: Shubael. Of the sons 20
of Shubael: Jehdeiah. Of Rehabiah: Isshiah, the chief of Rehabiah's sons. 21
Of the line of Izhar: Shelomoth. Of the sons of Shelomoth: Jahath. The 22 23
sons of Hebron: Jeriah the chief, Amariah the second, Jahaziel the third
and Jekameam the fourth. The sons of Uzziel: Micah. Of the sons of 24
Micah: Shamir; Micah's brother: Isshiah. Of the sons of Isshiah: Zechari- 25
ah. The sons of Merari: Mahli and Mushi and also*b* Jaaziah his son. The 26 27
sons of Merari: of Jaaziah: Beno, Shoham, Zaccur and Ibri. Of Mahli: 28
Eleazar, who had no sons; of Kish: the sons of Kish: Jerahmeel; and the 29 30
sons of Mushi: Mahli, Eder and Jerimoth. These were the Levites by
families. These also, side by side with their kinsmen the sons of Aaron, 31
cast lots in the presence of King David, Zadok, Ahimelech, and the heads
of the priestly and levitical families, the senior and junior houses casting
lots side by side.

David and his chief officers assigned special duties to the sons of Asaph, **25**
of Heman, and of Jeduthun, leaders in inspired prophecy to the accompaniment of harps, lutes, and cymbals; the number of the men who performed this work in the temple was as follows. Of the sons of Asaph: 2
Zaccur, Joseph, Nethaniah and Asarelah; these were under Asaph, a
leader in inspired prophecy under the king. Of the sons of Jeduthun: 3
Gedaliah, Izri,*c* Isaiah, Shimei, Hashabiah, Mattithiah, these six under
their father Jeduthun, a leader in inspired prophecy to the accompaniment

---

*a* sacred officers: *or* officers of the sanctuary.     *b* and also: *prob. rdg.; Heb.* the sons of.
*c* *Prob. rdg., cp. verse 11; Heb.* Zeri.

4 of the harp, giving thanks and praise to the LORD. Of the sons of Heman:
Bukkiah, Mattaniah, Uzziel, Shubael, Jerimoth, Hananiah, Hanani,
Eliathah, Giddalti, Romamti-ezer, Joshbekashah, Mallothi, Hothir, and
5 Mahazioth; all these were sons of Heman the king's seer, given to him
through the promises of God for his greater glory. God had given Heman
6 fourteen sons and three daughters, and they all served under their father
for the singing in the house of the LORD; they took part in the service of
the house of God, with cymbals, lutes, and harps, while Asaph, Jeduthun,
7 and Heman were under the king. Reckoned with their kinsmen, trained
singers of the LORD, they brought the total number of skilled musicians up
8 to two hundred and eighty-eight. They cast lots for their duties, young
and old, master-singer and apprentice side by side.

9     The first lot fell*a* to Joseph: he and his brothers and his sons, twelve. *b*
10 The second to Gedaliah: he and his brothers and his sons, twelve. The third
11 to Zaccur: his sons and his brothers, twelve. The fourth to Izri: his sons
12 and his brothers, twelve. The fifth to Nethaniah: his sons and his brothers,
13 14 'twelve. The sixth to Bukkiah: his sons and his brothers, twelve. The
15 seventh to Asarelah: his sons and his brothers, twelve. The eighth to
16 Isaiah: his sons and his brothers, twelve. The ninth to Mattaniah: his sons
17 and his brothers, twelve. The tenth to Shimei: his sons and his brothers,
18 19 twelve. The eleventh to Azareel: his sons and his brothers, twelve. The
20 twelfth to Hashabiah: his sons and his brothers, twelve. The thirteenth
21 to Shubael: his sons and his brothers, twelve. The fourteenth to Mat-
22 tithiah: his sons and his brothers, twelve. The fifteenth to Jeremoth: his
23 sons and his brothers, twelve. The sixteenth to Hananiah: his sons and
24 his brothers, twelve. The seventeenth to Joshbekashah: his sons and his
25 brothers, twelve. The eighteenth to Hanani: his sons and his brothers,
26 twelve. The nineteenth to Mallothi: his sons and his brothers, twelve.
27 28 The twentieth to Eliathah: his sons and his brothers, twelve. The twenty-
29 first to Hothir: his sons and his brothers, twelve. The twenty-second to
30 Giddalti: his sons and his brothers, twelve. The twenty-third to Mahazioth:
31 his sons and his brothers, twelve. The twenty-fourth to Romamti-ezer:
his sons and his brothers, twelve.

**26**     The divisions of the door-keepers: Korahites: Meshelemiah son of
2 Kore, son of Ebiasaph.*c* Sons of Meshelemiah: Zechariah the eldest,
3 Jediael the second, Zebediah the third, Jathniel the fourth, Elam the fifth,
4 Jehohanan the sixth, Elioenai the seventh. Sons of Obed-edom: Shemaiah
the eldest, Jehozabad the second, Joah the third, Sacar the fourth, Neth-
5 aneel the fifth, Ammiel the sixth, Issachar the seventh, Peulthai the eighth
6 (for God had blessed him). Shemaiah, his son, was the father of sons who
7 had authority in their family, for they were men of great ability. Sons of
Shemaiah: Othni, Rephael, Obed, Elzabad and his brothers Elihu and
8 Semachiah, men of ability. All these belonged to the family of Obed-edom;
they, their sons and brothers, were men of ability, fit for service in the
9 temple; total: sixty-two. Sons and brothers of Meshelemiah, all men of abil-
10 ity, eighteen. Sons of Hosah, a Merarite: Shimri the chief (he was not the

*a Prob. rdg.; Heb. adds* to Asaph.     *b* he . . . twelve: *prob. rdg.; Heb. om.*     *c* son
of Ebiasaph: *prob. rdg.; Heb.* from the sons of Asaph.

eldest, but his father had made him chief), Hilkiah the second, Tebaliah the 11
third, Zechariah the fourth. Total of Hosah's sons and brothers: thirteen.

The male heads of families constituted the divisions of the door-keepers; 12
their duty was to serve in the house of the LORD side by side with their
kinsmen. Young and old, family by family, they cast lots for the gates. The 13 14
lot for the east gate fell to Shelemiah; then lots were cast for his son
Zechariah, a prudent counsellor, and he was allotted the north gate. To 15
Obed-edom was allotted the south gate, and the gatehouse to his sons.
Hosah*a* was allotted the west gate, together with the Shallecheth gate on 16
the ascending causeway. Guard corresponded to guard. Six Levites were 17
on duty daily on the east side, four on the north and four on the south, and
two at each gatehouse; at the western colonnade there were four at the 18
causeway and two at the colonnade itself. These were the divisions of the 19
door-keepers, Korahites and Merarites.

Fellow-Levites were in charge of the stores of the house of God and of the 20
stores of sacred gifts. Of the children of Laadan, descendants of the Ger- 21
shonite line through Laadan, heads of families in the group of Laadan the
Gershonite, Jehiel and*b* his brothers Zetham and Joel were in charge of the 22
stores of the house of the LORD. Of the families of Amram, Izhar, Hebron 23
and Uzziel, Shubael son of Gershom, son of Moses, was overseer of the 24
stores. The line of Eliezer his brother: his son Rehabiah, his son Isaiah, 25
his son Joram, his son Zichri, and his son Shelomoth. This Shelomoth and 26
his kinsmen were in charge of all the stores of the sacred gifts dedicated by
David the king, the heads of families, the officers over units of a thousand
and a hundred, and other officers of the army. They had dedicated some 27
of the spoils taken in the wars for the upkeep of the house of the LORD.
Everything which Samuel the seer, Saul son of Kish, Abner son of Ner, 28
and Joab son of Zeruiah had dedicated, in short every sacred gift, was
under the charge of Shelomoth and his kinsmen. Of the family of Izhar, 29
Kenaniah and his sons acted as clerks and magistrates in the secular affairs
of Israel. Of the family of Hebron, Hashabiah and his kinsmen, men of 30
ability to the number of seventeen hundred, had the oversight of Israel
west of the Jordan, both in the work of the LORD and in the service of the
king. Also of the family of Hebron, Jeriah was the chief. (In the fortieth 31
year of David's reign search was made in the family histories of the Hebron-
ites, and men of great ability were found among them at Jazer in Gilead.)
His kinsmen, all men of ability, two thousand seven hundred of them, 32
heads of families, were charged by King David with the oversight of the
Reubenites, the Gadites, and the half tribe of Manasseh, in religious and
civil affairs alike.

THE NUMBER OF THE ISRAELITES—that is to say, of the heads of fami- 27
lies, the officers over units of a thousand and a hundred, and the clerks
who had their share in the king's service in the various divisions which took
monthly turns of duty throughout the year—was twenty-four thousand in
each division.

*a* Hosah: *prob. rdg.; Heb.* Shuppim and Hosah.     *b* Jehiel and: *prob. rdg.; Heb.*
Jehieli. The sons of Jehieli . . .

2    First, Jashobeam son of Zabdiel commanded the division for the first
3    month with twenty-four thousand in his division; a member of the house
4    of Perez, he was chief officer of the temple staff for the first month. Eleazar
son of *a* Dodai the Ahohite commanded the division for the second month
5    with twenty-four thousand in his division. Third, Benaiah son of Jehoiada
the chief priest, commander of the army, was the officer for the third month
6    with twenty-four thousand in his division (he was the Benaiah who was
one of the thirty warriors and was a chief among the thirty); but his son
7    Ammizabad commanded his division. Fourth, Asahel, the brother of
Joab, was the officer commanding for the fourth month with twenty-four
8    thousand in his division; and his successor was Zebediah his son. Fifth,
Shamhuth the Zerahite *b* was the officer commanding for the fifth month
9    with twenty-four thousand in his division. Sixth, Ira son of Ikkesh, a man
of Tekoa, was the officer commanding for the sixth month with twenty-
10   four thousand in his division. Seventh, Helez an Ephraimite, from a
place unknown, was the officer commanding for the seventh month with
11   twenty-four thousand in his division. Eighth, Sibbecai the Hushathite,
of the family of Zerah, was the officer commanding for the eighth month
12   with twenty-four thousand in his division. Ninth, Abiezer, from Anathoth
in Benjamin, was the officer commanding for the ninth month with twenty-
13   four thousand in his division. Tenth, Maharai the Netophathite, of the
family of Zerah, was the officer commanding for the tenth month with
14   twenty-four thousand in his division. Eleventh, Benaiah the Pirathonite,
from Ephraim, was the officer commanding for the eleventh month with
15   twenty-four thousand in his division. Twelfth, Heldai the Netophathite,
of the family of Othniel, was the officer commanding for the twelfth month
with twenty-four thousand in his division.

16   The following were the principal officers in charge of the tribes of
Israel: of Reuben, Eliezer son of Zichri; of Simeon, Shephatiah son of
17 18 Maacah; of Levi, Hashabiah son of Kemuel; of Aaron, Zadok; of Judah,
19   Elihu a kinsman of David; of Issachar, Omri son of Michael; of Zebulun,
20   Ishmaiah son of Obadiah; of Naphtali, Jerimoth son of Azriel; of Ephraim,
Hoshea son of Azaziah; of the half tribe of Manasseh, Joel son of Pedaiah;
21   of the half of Manasseh in Gilead, Iddo son of Zechariah; of Benjamin,
22   Jaasiel son of Abner; of Dan, Azareel son of Jeroham. These were the
officers in charge of the tribes of Israel.

23   David took no census of those under twenty years of age, for the LORD
had promised to make the Israelites as many as the stars in the heavens.
24   Joab son of Zeruiah did begin to take a census but he did not finish it;
this brought harm upon Israel, and the census was not entered in the
chronicle of King David's reign.

25   Azmoth son of Adiel was in charge of the king's stores; Jonathan son of
Uzziah was in charge of the stores in the country, in the cities, in the
26   villages and in the fortresses. Ezri son of Kelub had oversight of the workers
27   on the land; Shimei of Ramah was in charge of the vine-dressers, while
Zabdi of Shephem had charge of the produce of the vineyards for the

*a* Eleazar son of: *prob. rdg., cp. 11. 12; Heb. om.*          *b* the Zerahite: *prob. rdg.; Heb.*
the Izrah.

wine-cellars. Baal-hanan the Gederite supervised the wild olives and the 28
sycomore-figs in the Shephelah; Joash was in charge of the oil-stores.
Shitrai of Sharon was in charge of the herds grazing in Sharon, Shaphat son 29
of Adlai of the herds in the vales. Obil the Ishmaelite was in charge of the 30
camels, Jehdeiah the Meronothite of the asses. Jaziz the Hagerite was in 31
charge of the flocks. All these were the officers in charge of King David's
possessions. David's favourite nephew Jonathan, a counsellor, a discreet 32
and learned man, and Jehiel the Hachmonite, were tutors to the king's sons.
Ahithophel was a king's counsellor; Hushai the Archite was the King's 33
Friend. Ahithophel was succeeded by Jehoiada son of Benaiah, and 34
Abiathar. Joab was commander of the army.

DAVID ASSEMBLED AT JERUSALEM all the officers of Israel, the officers **28**
over the tribes, over the divisions engaged in the king's service, over the
units of a thousand and a hundred, and those in charge of all the property
and the cattle of the king and of his sons, as well as the eunuchs, the heroes
and all the men of ability. Then King David rose to his feet and said, 'Hear 2
me, kinsmen and people. I had in mind to build a house as a resting-place
for the Ark of the Covenant of the LORD which might serve as a footstool
for the feet of our God, and I made preparations to build it. But God said 3
to me, "You shall not build a house in honour of my name, for you have
been a fighting man and you have shed blood." Nevertheless, the LORD 4
the God of Israel chose me out of all my father's family to be king over
Israel in perpetuity; for it was Judah that he chose as ruling tribe, and, out
of the house of Judah, my father's family; and among my father's sons it
was I whom he was pleased to make king over all Israel. And out of all 5
my sons—for the LORD gave me many sons—he chose Solomon to sit
upon the throne of the LORD's sovereignty over Israel; and he said to me, 6
"It is Solomon your son who shall build my house and my courts, for I
have chosen him to be a son to me and I will be a father to him. I will 7
establish his sovereignty in perpetuity, if only he steadfastly obeys my
commandments and my laws as they are now obeyed." Now therefore, in 8
the presence of all Israel, the assembly of the LORD, and within the hearing
of our God, I bid you all study carefully the commandments of the LORD
your God, that you may possess this good land and hand it down as an
inheritance for all time to your children after you. And you, Solomon my 9
son, acknowledge your father's God and serve him with whole heart and
willing mind, for the LORD searches all hearts and discerns every invention
of men's thoughts. If you search for him, he will let you find him, but if you
forsake him, he will cast you off for ever. Remember, then, that the LORD 10
has chosen you to build a house for a sanctuary: be steadfast and do it.'

David gave Solomon his son the plan of the porch of the temple *a* and 11
its buildings, strong-rooms, roof-chambers and inner courts, and the
shrine of expiation; *b* also the plans of all he had in mind for the courts of 12
the house of the LORD and for all the rooms around it, for the stores of
God's house and for the stores of the sacred gifts, for the divisions of the 13

*a* of the temple: *prob. rdg.; Heb. om.*     *b* the shrine . . . expiation: *or* the place for
the Ark with its cover.

priests and the Levites, for all the work connected with the service of the
14 house of the LORD and for all the vessels used in its service. He prescribed
the weight of gold for all the gold vessels[a] used in the various services, and
the weight of silver[b] for all the silver vessels used in the various services;
15 and the weight of gold for the gold lamp-stands and their lamps; and the
weight of silver for the silver lamp-stands, the weight required for each
16 lamp-stand and its lamps according to the use of each; and the weight of
gold for each of the tables for the rows of the Bread of the Presence, and
17 of silver for the silver tables. He prescribed also the weight of pure gold
for the forks, tossing-bowls and cups, the weight of gold for each of the
18 golden dishes and of silver[b] for each of the silver dishes; the weight also
of refined gold for the altar of incense, and of gold for the model of the
chariot, that is the cherubim with their wings outspread to screen the Ark
19 of the Covenant of the LORD. 'All this was drafted by the LORD's own hand,'
said David; 'my part was to consider the detailed working out of the plan.'
20    Then David said to Solomon his son, 'Be steadfast and resolute and do
it; be neither faint-hearted nor dismayed, for the LORD God, my God, will
be with you; he will neither fail you nor forsake you, until you have finished
21 all the work needed for the service of the house of the LORD. Here are the
divisions of the priests and the Levites, ready for all the service of the house
of God. In all the work you will have the help of every willing craftsman for
any task; and the officers and all the people will be entirely at your
command.'

29    King David then said to the whole assembly, 'My son Solomon is the
one chosen by God, Solomon alone, a boy of tender years; and this is a
2 great work, for it is a palace not for man but for the LORD God. Now to the
best of my strength I have made ready for the house of my God gold for
the gold work, silver for the silver, bronze for the bronze, iron for the iron,
and wood for the woodwork, together with cornelian and other gems for
setting, stones for mosaic work, precious stones of every sort, and marble
3 in plenty. Further, because I delight in the house of my God, I give my
own private store of gold and silver for the house of my God—over and
4 above all the store which I have collected for the sanctuary—namely three
thousand talents of gold, gold from Ophir, and seven thousand talents of
5 fine silver for overlaying the walls of the buildings, for providing gold for
the gold work, silver for the silver, and for any work to be done by skilled
craftsmen. Now who is willing to give with open hand to the LORD today?'
6    Then the heads of families, the officers administering the tribes of
Israel, the officers over units of a thousand and a hundred, and the officers
7 in charge of the king's service, responded willingly and gave for the work
of the house of God five thousand talents of gold, ten thousand darics,
ten thousand talents of silver, eighteen thousand talents of bronze, and a
8 hundred thousand talents of iron. Further, those who possessed precious
stones gave them to the treasury of the house of the LORD, into the charge
9 of Jehiel the Gershonite. The people rejoiced at this willing response,
because in the loyalty of their hearts they had given willingly to the LORD;
10 King David also was full of joy, and he blessed the LORD in the presence of

[a] *for . . . vessels: prob. rdg.; Heb. for gold.*     [b] *of silver: prob. rdg.; Heb. om.*

all the assembly and said, 'Blessed art thou, LORD God of our father Israel, from of old and for ever. Thine, O LORD, is the greatness, the power, the 11 glory, the splendour, and the majesty; for everything in heaven and on earth is thine;[a] thine, O LORD, is the sovereignty, and thou art exalted over all as head. Wealth and honour come from thee; thou rulest over all; 12 might and power are of thy disposing; thine it is to give power and strength to all. And now, we give thee thanks, our God, and praise thy glorious 13 name.

'But what am I, and what is my people, that we should be able to give 14 willingly like this? For everything comes from thee, and it is only of thy gifts that we give to thee. We are aliens before thee and settlers, as were all 15 our fathers; our days on earth are like a shadow, we have no abiding place. O LORD our God, from thee comes all this wealth that we have laid up to 16 build a house in honour of thy holy name, and everything is thine. I know, 17 O my God, that thou dost test the heart and that plain honesty pleases thee; with an honest heart I have given all these gifts willingly, and have rejoiced now to see thy people here present give willingly to thee. O LORD 18 God of Abraham, Isaac and Israel our fathers, maintain this purpose for ever in thy people's thoughts and direct their hearts toward thyself. Grant 19 that Solomon my son may loyally keep thy commandments, thy solemn charge, and thy statutes, that he may fulfil them all and build the palace for which I have prepared.'

Then, turning to the whole assembly, David said, 'Now bless the LORD 20 your God.' So all the assembly blessed the LORD the God of their fathers, bowing low and prostrating themselves before the LORD and the king. The 21 next day they sacrificed to the LORD and offered whole-offerings to him, a thousand oxen, a thousand rams, a thousand lambs, with the prescribed drink-offerings, and abundant sacrifices for all Israel. So they ate and drank 22 before the LORD that day with great rejoicing. They then appointed Solomon, David's son, king a second time and anointed him as the LORD's prince, and Zadok as priest. So Solomon sat on the LORD's throne as king 23 in place of his father David, and he prospered and all Israel obeyed him. All the officers and the warriors, as well as all the sons of King David, 24 swore fealty to King Solomon. The LORD made Solomon stand very high 25 in the eyes of all Israel, and bestowed upon him sovereignty such as no king in Israel had had before him.

David son of Jesse had ruled over the whole of Israel, and the length of 26 27 his reign over Israel was forty years; he ruled for seven years in Hebron, and for thirty-three in Jerusalem. He died in ripe old age, full of years, 28 wealth, and honour; and Solomon his son ruled in his place. The events 29 of King David's reign from first to last are recorded in the books of Samuel the seer, of Nathan the prophet, and of Gad the seer, with a full account 30 of his reign, his prowess, and of the times through which he and Israel and all the kingdoms of the world had passed.

[a] is thine: *prob. rdg.; Heb. om.*

# THE SECOND BOOK OF THE
# CHRONICLES

### *The reign of Solomon and dedication of the temple*

1 KING SOLOMON, DAVID'S SON, strengthened his hold on the kingdom, for the LORD his God was with him and made him very great.

2 Solomon spoke to all Israel, to the officers over units of a thousand and of a hundred, the judges and all the leading men of Israel, the heads of

3 families; and he, together with all the assembled people, went to the hill-shrine at Gibeon; for the Tent of God's Presence, which Moses the

4 LORD's servant had made in the wilderness, was there. (But David had brought up the Ark of God from Kiriath-jearim to the place which he had

5 prepared for it, for he had pitched a tent for it in Jerusalem.) The altar of bronze also, which Bezalel son of Uri, son of Hur, had made, was there in front of the Tabernacle of the LORD; and Solomon and the assembly

6 resorted to it.*a* There Solomon went up to the altar of bronze before the LORD in the Tent of the Presence and offered on it a thousand whole-

7*b* offerings. That night God appeared to Solomon and said, 'What shall I

8 give you? Tell me.' Solomon answered, 'Thou didst show great and constant love to David my father and thou hast made me king in his place.

9 Now, O LORD God, let thy word to David my father be confirmed, for thou hast made me king over a people as numerous as the dust on the earth.

10 Give me now wisdom and knowledge, that I may lead this people; for who

11 is fit to govern this great people of thine?' God answered Solomon, 'Because this is what you desire, because you have not asked for wealth or possessions or honour *c* or the lives of your enemies or even long life for yourself, but have asked for wisdom and knowledge to govern my

12 people over whom I have made you king, wisdom and knowledge are given to you; I shall also give you wealth and possessions and honour *c* such as

13 no king has had before you and none shall have after you.' Then Solomon returned from the hill-shrine at Gibeon, from before the Tent of the Presence, to Jerusalem and ruled over Israel.

14*d* Solomon got together many chariots and horses; he had fourteen hundred chariots and twelve thousand horses, and he stabled some in the chariot-

15 towns and kept others at hand in Jerusalem. The king made silver and gold as common in Jerusalem as stones, and cedar as plentiful as sycomore-fig

16 in the Shephelah. Horses were imported from Egypt and Coa for Solomon;

17 the royal merchants obtained them from Coa by purchase. Chariots were

---

*a* resorted to it: *or* worshipped him.          *b* *Verses 7–12: cp. I Kgs. 3. 5–14.*
*c* Or riches.          *d* *Verses 14–17: cp. 9. 25–28; I Kgs. 10. 26–29.*

imported from Egypt for six hundred silver shekels each, and horses for a hundred and fifty; in the same way the merchants obtained them for export from all the kings of the Hittites and the kings of Aram.

Solomon resolved to build a house in honour of the name of the LORD, **2** and a royal palace for himself. He engaged seventy thousand hauliers and **2** eighty thousand quarrymen, and three thousand six hundred men to superintend them. Then Solomon sent this message to Huram king of **3**<sup>*a*</sup> Tyre: 'You were so good as to send my father David cedar-wood to build his royal residence. Now I am about to build a house in honour of the **4** name of the LORD my God and to consecrate it to him, so that I may burn fragrant incense in it before him, and present the rows of the Bread of the Presence regularly, and whole-offerings morning and evening, on the sabbaths and the new moons and the appointed festivals of the LORD our God; for this is a duty laid upon Israel for ever. The house I am about to build will **5** be a great house, because our God is greater than all gods. But who is able to **6** build him a house when heaven itself, the highest heaven, cannot contain him? And who am I that I should build him a house, except that I may burn sacrifices before him? Send me then a skilled craftsman, a man able **7** to work in gold and silver, copper<sup>*b*</sup> and iron, and in purple, crimson, and violet yarn, who is also an expert engraver and will work with my skilled workmen in Judah and in Jerusalem who were provided by David my father. Send me also cedar, pine, and algum timber from Lebanon, for I **8** know that your men are expert at felling the trees of Lebanon; my men will work with yours to get an ample supply of timber ready for me, for the **9** house which I shall build will be great and wonderful. I will supply pro- **10** visions for your servants, the woodmen who fell the trees: twenty thousand kor of wheat and twenty thousand kor of barley, with twenty thousand bath of wine and twenty thousand bath of oil.'

Huram king of Tyre sent this answer by letter to Solomon: 'It is because **11** of the love which the LORD has for his people that he has made you king over them.' The letter went on to say, 'Blessed is the LORD the God of **12** Israel, maker of heaven and earth, who has given to King David a wise son, endowed with intelligence and understanding, to build a house for the LORD and a royal palace for himself. I now send you a skilful and **13** experienced craftsman, master Huram. He is the son of a Danite woman, **14** his father a Tyrian; he is an experienced worker in gold and silver, copper<sup>*b*</sup> and iron, stone and wood, as well as in purple, violet, and crimson yarn, and in fine linen; he is also a trained engraver who will be able to work with your own skilled craftsmen and those of my lord David your father, to any design submitted to him. Now then, let my lord send his **15** servants the wheat and the barley, the oil and the wine, which he promised; we will fell all the timber in Lebanon that you need and float it as rafts **16** to the roadstead at Joppa, and you will convey it from there up to Jerusalem.'

Solomon took a census of all the aliens resident in Israel, similar to the **17** census which David his father had taken; these were found to be a hundred and fifty-three thousand six hundred. He made seventy thousand of them **18**

<sup>*a*</sup> *Verses 3–16: cp. I Kgs. 5. 2–11.*      <sup>*b*</sup> *Or* bronze.

hauliers and eighty thousand quarrymen, and three thousand six hundred superintendents to make the people work.

3   Then Solomon began to build the house of the LORD in Jerusalem on Mount Moriah, where the LORD had appeared to his father David, on the site which David had prepared on the threshing-floor of Ornan the

2ᵃ  Jebusite. He began to build in the second month of the fourth year of his

3   reign. These are the foundations which Solomon laid for building the house of God: the length, according to the old standard of measurement,

4   was sixty cubits and the breadth twenty. The vestibule in front of the house ᵇ was twenty cubits long, spanning the whole breadth of the house, and its

5   height was twenty; on the inside he overlaid it with pure gold. He panelled the large chamber with pine, covered it with fine gold and carved on it

6   palm-trees and chain-work. He adorned the house with precious stones for

7   decoration, and the gold he used was from Parvaim. He covered the whole house with gold, its rafters and frames, its walls and doors; and he carved cherubim on the walls.

8   He made the Most Holy Place twenty cubits long, corresponding to the breadth of the house, and twenty cubits broad. He covered it all with six

9   hundred talents of fine gold, and the weight of the nails was fifty shekels of gold. He also covered the upper chambers with gold.

10ᶜ  In the Most Holy Place he carved two images of cherubim and overlaid

11  them with gold. The total span of the wings of the cherubim was twenty cubits. A wing of the one cherub extended five cubits to reach the wall of the house, while its other wing reached out five cubits to meet a wing of the

12  other cherub. Similarly, a wing of the second cherub extended five cubits to reach the other wall of the house, while its other wing met a wing of the

13  first cherub. The wings of these cherubim extended twenty cubits; they

14  stood with their feet on the ground, facing the outer chamber. He made the Veil of violet, purple, and crimson yarn, and fine linen, and embroidered cherubim on it.

15ᵈ  In front of the house he erected two pillars eighteen cubits high, with an

16  architrave five cubits high on top of each. He made chain-work like a necklaceᵉ and set it round the tops of the pillars, and he carved a hundred

17  pomegranates and set them in the chain-work. He erected the two pillars in front of the temple, one on the right and one on the left; the one on the right he named Jachin ᶠ and the one on the left Boaz.ᵍ

4   He then made an altar of bronze, twenty cubits long, twenty cubits

2ʰ  broad, and ten cubits high. He also made the Sea of cast metal; it was round in shape, the diameter from rim to rim being ten cubits; it stood five cubits

3   high, and it took a line thirty cubits long to go round it. Under the Sea, on every side, completely surrounding the thirty ⁱ cubits of its circumference, were what looked like gourds, ʲ two rows of them, cast in one piece

4   with the Sea itself. It was mounted on twelve oxen, three facing north,

ᵃ *Verses 2–4: cp. 1 Kgs. 6. 1–3.*     ᵇ house: *prob. rdg.; Heb.* length.     ᶜ *Verses 10–13: cp. 1 Kgs. 6. 23–28.*     ᵈ *Verses 15–17: cp. 1 Kgs. 7. 15–21.*     ᵉ necklace: *prob. rdg.; Heb.* obscure.     ᶠ *Or* Jachun, *meaning* It shall stand.     ᵍ *Or* Booz, *meaning* In strength.     ʰ *Verses 2–5: cp. 1 Kgs. 7. 23–26.*     ⁱ *Prob. rdg.; Heb.* ten.     ʲ *Prob. rdg., cp. 1 Kgs. 7. 24; Heb.* oxen.

three west, three south, and three east, their hind quarters turned inwards; the Sea rested on top of them. Its thickness was a hand-breadth; its rim 5 was made like that of a cup, shaped like the calyx of a lily; when full it held three thousand bath. He also made ten basins for washing, setting 6 five on the left side and five on the right; in these they rinsed everything used for the whole-offering. The Sea was made for the priests to wash in.

He made ten golden lamp-stands in the prescribed manner and set them 7 in the temple, five on the right side and five on the left. He also made ten 8 tables and placed them in the temple, five on the right and five on the left; and he made a hundred golden tossing-bowls. He made the court of the 9 priests and the great precinct and the doors for it, and overlaid the doors of both with copper; he put the Sea at the right side, at the south-east 10 corner of the temple.

Huram made the pots, the shovels, and the tossing-bowls. So he finished 11[a] the work which he had undertaken for King Solomon on the house of God. The two pillars; the two bowl-shaped capitals [b] on the tops of the pillars; 12 the two ornamental networks to cover the two bowl-shaped capitals on the tops of the pillars; the four hundred pomegranates for the two networks, 13 two rows of pomegranates for each network, to cover the two bowl-shaped capitals on the two[c] pillars; the ten[d] trolleys and the ten[d] basins on the 14 trolleys; the one Sea and the twelve oxen which supported it; the pots, the 15 16 shovels, and the tossing-bowls[e]—all these[f] objects master Huram made of bronze, burnished work for King Solomon for the house of the LORD. In the Plain of the Jordan the king cast them, in the foundry between 17 Succoth and Zeredah. Solomon made great quantities of all these objects; 18 the weight of the copper[g] used was beyond reckoning.

Solomon made also all the furnishings for the house of God: the golden 19 altar, the tables upon which was set the Bread of the Presence, the lamp- 20 stands of red gold whose lamps burned before the inner shrine in the prescribed manner, the flowers and lamps and tongs of solid gold, 21 the snuffers, tossing-bowls, saucers, and firepans of red gold, and, at the 22 entrance to the house, the inner doors leading to the Most Holy Place and those leading to the sanctuary, of gold.

When all the work which Solomon did for the house of the LORD was 5 completed, he brought in the sacred treasures of his father David, the silver, the gold, and the vessels, and deposited them in the storehouses of the house of God.

THEN SOLOMON SUMMONED THE ELDERS of Israel, and all the heads 2[h] of the tribes who were chiefs of families in Israel, to assemble in Jerusalem, in order to bring up the Ark of the Covenant of the LORD from the City of David, which is called Zion. All the men of Israel assembled in the king's 3

---

[a] 4. 11—5. 1: cp. 1 Kgs. 7. 40-51.      [b] bowl-shaped capitals: prob. rdg., cp. 1 Kgs. 7. 41; Heb. the bowls and the capitals.      [c] two: prob. rdg., cp. 1 Kgs. 7. 42; Heb. surface of the.      [d] the ten: prob. rdg., cp. 1 Kgs. 7. 43; Heb. he made the . . . [e] tossing-bowls: prob. rdg., cp. 1 Kgs. 7. 45; Heb. forks.      [f] Prob. rdg., cp. 1 Kgs. 7. 45; Heb. their.      [g] Or bronze.      [h] Verses 2-10: cp. 1 Kgs. 8. 1-9.

4 presence at the pilgrim-feast in the seventh month. When the elders of
5 Israel had all come, the Levites took the Ark and carried it up with the
Tent of the Presence and all the sacred furnishings of the Tent: it was the
6 priests and the Levites together who carried them up. King Solomon and
the whole congregation of Israel, assembled with him before the Ark, sacri-
7 ficed sheep and oxen in numbers past counting or reckoning. Then the
priests brought in the Ark of the Covenant of the LORD to its place,
the inner shrine of the house, the Most Holy Place, beneath the wings of
8 the cherubim. The cherubim spread their wings over the place of the Ark,
9 and formed a covering above the Ark and its poles. The poles projected,
and their ends could be seen from the Holy Place immediately in front of
the inner shrine, but from nowhere else outside; they are there to this day.
10 There was nothing inside the Ark but the two tablets which Moses had
put there at Horeb, the tablets of the covenant *a* which the LORD made with
the Israelites when they left Egypt.
11     Now when the priests came out of the Holy Place (for all the priests who
were present had hallowed themselves without keeping to their divisions),
12 all the levitical singers, Asaph, Heman, and Jeduthun, their sons and their
kinsmen, clothed in fine linen, stood with cymbals, lutes, and harps, to
the east of the altar, together with a hundred and twenty priests who blew
13 trumpets. Now the trumpeters and the singers joined in unison to sound
forth praise and thanksgiving to the LORD, and the song was raised with
trumpets, cymbals, and musical instruments, in praise of the LORD,
because 'that *b* is good, for his love endures for ever'; and the house was
14 filled with the cloud of the glory of the LORD. The priests could not continue to minister because of the cloud, for the glory of the LORD filled the
**6** 1*c* house of God. Then Solomon said:

O LORD who hast chosen to dwell in thick darkness,
2          here have I built thee a lofty house,
a habitation for thee to occupy for ever.

3     And as they stood waiting, the king turned round and blessed all the
4 assembly of Israel in these words: 'Blessed be the LORD the God of Israel
who spoke directly to my father David and has himself fulfilled his promise.
5 For he said, "From the day when I brought my people out of Egypt, I
chose no city out of all the tribes of Israel where I should build a house for
my Name to be there, nor did I choose any man to be prince over my
6 people Israel. But I chose Jerusalem for my Name to be there, and I chose
7 David to be over my people Israel." My father David had in mind to build
8 a house in honour of the name of the LORD the God of Israel, but the LORD
said to him, "You purposed to build a house in honour of my name; and
9 your purpose was good. Nevertheless, you shall not build it; but the son
who is to be born to you, he shall build the house in honour of my name."
10 The LORD has now fulfilled his promise: I have succeeded my father
David and taken his place on the throne of Israel, as the LORD promised;
and I have built the house in honour of the name of the LORD the God of

*a* the tablets of the covenant: *prob. rdg., cp. 1 Kgs. 8. 9; Heb. om.*          *b* Or he.
*c* *Verses 1–39: cp. 1 Kgs. 8. 12–50.*

Israel. I have installed there the Ark containing the covenant of the LORD 11
which he made with Israel.'

Then Solomon, standing in front of the altar of the LORD, in the presence 12
of the whole assembly of Israel, spread out his hands. He had made a 13
bronze*a* platform, five cubits long, five cubits broad, and three cubits
high, and had placed it in the centre of the precinct. He mounted it and
knelt down in the presence of the assembly, and, spreading out his hands
towards heaven, he said, 'O LORD God of Israel, there is no god like thee in 14
heaven or on earth, keeping covenant with thy servants and showing them
constant love while they continue faithful to thee in heart and soul. Thou 15
hast kept thy promise to thy servant David my father; by thy deeds this
day thou hast fulfilled what thou didst say to him in words. Now, therefore, 16
O LORD God of Israel, keep this promise of thine to thy servant David my
father: "You shall never want for a man appointed by me to sit on the
throne of Israel, if only your sons look to their ways and conform to my
law, as you have done in my sight." And now, O LORD God of Israel, let 17
the word which thou didst speak to thy servant David be confirmed.

'But can God indeed dwell with man on the earth? Heaven itself, the 18
highest heaven, cannot contain thee; how much less this house that I have
built! Yet attend to the prayer and the supplication of thy servant, O LORD 19
my God; listen to the cry and the prayer which thy servant utters before
thee, that thine eyes may ever be upon this house day and night, this place 20
of which thou didst say, "It shall receive my Name"; so mayest thou hear
thy servant when he prays towards this place. Hear thou the supplications 21
of thy servant and of thy people Israel when they pray towards this place.
Hear from heaven thy dwelling and, when thou hearest, forgive.

'When a man wrongs his neighbour and he is adjured to take an oath, 22
and the adjuration is made before thy altar in this house, then do thou hear 23
from heaven and act: be thou thy servants' judge, requiting the guilty man
and bringing his deeds upon his own head, acquitting the innocent and
rewarding him as his innocence may deserve.

'When thy people Israel are defeated by an enemy because they have 24
sinned against thee, and they turn back to thee, confessing thy name and
making their prayer and supplication before thee in this house, do thou 25
hear from heaven; forgive the sin of thy people Israel and restore them to
the land which thou gavest to them and to their forefathers.

'When the heavens are shut up and there is no rain, because thy servant 26
and thy people Israel have sinned against thee, and when they pray towards
this place, confessing thy name and forsaking their sin when they feel thy
punishment, do thou hear in heaven and forgive their sin; so mayest thou 27
teach them the good way which they should follow, and grant rain to thy
land which thou hast given to thy people as their own possession.

'If there is famine in the land, or pestilence, or black blight or red, or 28
locusts new-sloughed or fully grown, or if their enemies besiege them in
any*b* of their cities, or if plague or sickness befall them, then hear the 29
prayer or supplication of every man among thy people Israel, as each one,
prompted by his own suffering and misery, spreads out his hands towards

*a* Or copper.          *b* in any: *prob. rdg.; Heb.* in the land.

30 this house; hear it from heaven thy dwelling and forgive. And, as thou knowest a man's heart, reward him according to his deeds, for thou alone
31 knowest the hearts of all men; and so they will fear and obey thee all their lives in the land thou gavest to our forefathers.
32 'The foreigner too, the man who does not belong to thy people Israel, but has come from a distant land because of thy great fame and thy strong hand and arm outstretched, when he comes and prays towards this house,
33 hear from heaven thy dwelling and respond to the call which the foreigner makes to thee, so that like thy people Israel all peoples of the earth may know thy fame and fear thee, and learn that this house which I have built bears thy name.
34 'When thy people go to war with their enemies, wherever thou dost send them, and they pray to thee, turning towards this city which thou hast chosen and towards this house which I have built in honour of thy name,
35 do thou from heaven hear their prayer and supplication, and grant them justice.
36 'Should they sin against thee (and what man is free from sin?) and shouldst thou in thy anger give them over to an enemy, who carries them
37 captive to a land far or near; if in the land of their captivity they learn their lesson and turn back and make supplication to thee in that land and say, "We
38 have sinned and acted perversely and wickedly", if they turn back to thee with heart and soul in the land of their captivity to which they have been taken, and pray, turning towards their land which thou gavest to their forefathers and towards this city which thou didst choose and this house which
39 I have built in honour of thy name; then from heaven thy dwelling do thou hear their prayer and supplications and grant them justice. Forgive their
40 people their sins against thee. Now, O my God, let thine eyes be open and
41 thy ears attentive to the prayer made in this place. Arise now, O LORD God, and come to thy place of rest, thou and the Ark of thy might. Let thy priests, O LORD God, be clothed with salvation and thy saints rejoice in
42 prosperity. O LORD God, reject not thy anointed prince; remember thy servant David's loyal service.' *a*
7 When Solomon had finished this prayer, fire came down from heaven and consumed the whole-offering and the sacrifices, while the glory of the
2 LORD filled the house. The priests were unable to enter the house of the
3 LORD because the glory of the LORD had filled it. All the Israelites were watching as the fire came down with the glory of the LORD on the house, and where they stood on the paved court they bowed low to the ground and worshipped and gave thanks to the LORD, because 'that *b* is good, for his love endures for ever.'
4 5 Then the king and all the people offered sacrifice before the LORD. King Solomon offered a sacrifice of twenty-two thousand oxen and a hundred and twenty thousand sheep; in this way the king and all the people dedi-
6 cated the house of God. The priests stood at their appointed posts; so too the Levites with their musical instruments for the LORD's service, which King David had made for giving thanks to the LORD—'for his love endures for ever'—whenever he rendered praise with their help; opposite them,

*a* thy servant . . . service: *or* thy constant love for David thy servant.       *b* *Or* he.

the priests sounded their trumpets; and all the Israelites were standing there.

Then Solomon consecrated the centre of the court which lay in front[a] 7[b] of the house of the LORD; there he offered the whole-offerings and the fat portions of the shared-offerings, because the bronze altar which he had made could not take the whole-offering, the grain-offering, and the fat portions. So Solomon and all Israel with him, a very great assembly from 8 Lebo-hamath to the Torrent of Egypt, celebrated the pilgrim-feast at that time for seven days. On the eighth day they held a closing ceremony; for 9 they had celebrated the dedication of the altar for seven days; the pilgrim-feast lasted seven days. On the twenty-third day of the seventh month he 10 sent the people to their homes, happy and glad at heart for all the prosperity granted by the LORD to David and Solomon and to his people Israel.

When Solomon had finished the house of the LORD and the royal palace 11 and had successfully carried out all that he had planned for the house of the LORD and the palace, the LORD appeared to him by night and said, 'I 12 have heard your prayer and I have chosen this place to be my place of sacrifice. When I shut up the heavens and there is no rain, or command 13 the locusts to consume the land, or send a pestilence against my people, if my people whom I have named my own submit and pray to me and seek 14 me and turn back from their evil ways, I will hear from heaven and forgive their sins and heal their land. Now my eyes will be open and my ears 15 attentive to the prayers which are made in this place. I have chosen and 16 consecrated this house, that my Name may be there for all time and my eyes and my heart be fixed on it for ever. And if you, on your part, live in 17 my sight as your father David lived, doing all I command you, and observing my statutes and my judgements, then I will establish your royal throne, 18 as I promised by a covenant granted to your father David when I said, "You shall never want for a man to rule over Israel." But if you turn away 19 and forsake my statutes and my commandments which I have set before you, and if you go and serve other gods and prostrate yourselves before them, then I will uproot you from my land which I gave you, I will reject 20 this house which I have consecrated in honour of my name, and make it a byword and an object-lesson among all peoples. And this house will 21 become a ruin; every passer-by will be appalled at the sight of it, and they will ask, "Why has the LORD so treated this land and this house?" The 22 answer will be, "Because they forsook the LORD the God of their fathers, who brought them out of Egypt, and clung to other gods, prostrating themselves before them and serving them; that is why the LORD has brought this great evil on them."'

Solomon had taken twenty years to build the house of the LORD and his 8 1[c] own palace, and he rebuilt the cities which Huram had given him and 2 settled Israelites in them. He went to Hamath-zobah and seized it, and 3 4 rebuilt Tadmor in the wilderness and all the store-cities which he had built in Hamath. He also built Upper Beth-horon and Lower Beth-horon 5 as fortified cities with walls and barred gates, and Baalath, as well as all 6

---

[a] *Or to the east.*      [b] *Verses 7–22 : cp. 1 Kgs. 8. 64—9. 9.*      [c] *Verses 1–18 : cp. 1 Kgs. 9. 10–28.*

his store-cities, and all the towns where he quartered his chariots and horses; and he carried out all his cherished plans for building in Jerusalem,

7 in the Lebanon, and throughout his whole dominion. All the survivors of the Hittites, Amorites, Perizzites, Hivites, and Jebusites, who did not

8 belong to Israel—that is their descendants who survived in the land, wherever the Israelites had been unable to exterminate them—were

9 employed by Solomon on forced labour, as they still are. He put none of the Israelites to forced labour for his public works; they were his fighting men, his captains and lieutenants, and the commanders of his chariots

10 and of his cavalry. These were King Solomon's officers, two hundred and fifty of them, in charge of the foremen who superintended the people.

11 Solomon brought Pharaoh's daughter up from the City of David to the house he had built for her, for he said, 'No wife of mine shall live in the house of David king of Israel, because this place which the Ark of ·the LORD has entered is*ª* holy.'

12 Then Solomon offered whole-offerings to the LORD on the altar which

13 he had built to the east of the vestibule, according to what was required for each day, making offerings according to the law of Moses for the sabbaths, the new moons, and the three annual appointed feasts—the pilgrim-feasts

14 of Unleavened Bread, of Weeks, and of Tabernacles.*ᵇ* Following the practice of his father David, he drew up the roster of service for the priests and that for the Levites for leading the praise and for waiting upon the priests, as each day required, and that for the door-keepers at each gate;

15 for such was the instruction which David the man of God had given. The instructions which David had given concerning the priests and the Levites and concerning the treasuries were not forgotten.

16 By this time all Solomon's work was achieved, from the foundation of the house of the LORD to its completion; the house of the LORD was

17 perfect. Then Solomon went to Ezion-geber and to Eloth on the coast of

18 Edom, and Huram sent ships under the command of his own officers and manned by crews of experienced seamen; and these, in company with Solomon's servants, went to Ophir and brought back four hundred and fifty talents of gold, which they delivered to King Solomon.

**9** 1*ᶜ* THE QUEEN OF SHEBA HEARD of Solomon's fame and came to test him with hard questions. She arrived in Jerusalem with a very large retinue, camels laden with spices, gold in abundance, and precious stones. When

2 she came to Solomon, she told him everything she had in her mind, and Solomon answered all her questions; not one of them was too abstruse for

3 him to answer. When the queen of Sheba saw the wisdom of Solomon, the

4 house which he had built, the food on his table, the courtiers sitting round him, his attendants and his cupbearers in their livery standing behind, and the stairs by which he went up to the house of the LORD, there was no

5 more spirit left in her. Then she said to the king, 'The report which I

6 heard in my own country about you and your wisdom was true, but I did not believe what they told me until I came and saw for myself. Indeed, I

---

*ª* this place which . . . is: *prob. rdg.; Heb.* those which . . . are.      *ᵇ Or* Booths.
*ᶜ Verses 1–24: cp. 1 Kgs. 10. 1–25.*

was not told half of the greatness of your wisdom; you surpass the report
which I had of you. Happy are your wives, happy these courtiers of yours 7
who wait on you every day and hear your wisdom! Blessed be the LORD 8
your God who has delighted in you and has set you on his throne as his
king; because in his love your God has elected Israel to make it endure for
ever, he has made you king over it to maintain law and justice.' Then she 9
gave the king a hundred and twenty talents of gold, spices in great abundance, and precious stones. There had never been any spices to equal
those which the queen of Sheba gave to King Solomon.

Besides all this, the servants of Huram and of Solomon, who had 10
brought gold from Ophir, brought also cargoes of algum wood and precious
stones. The king used the wood to make stands for the house of the LORD 11
and for the royal palace, as well as harps and lutes for the singers. The
like of them had never before been seen in the land of Judah.

King Solomon gave the queen of Sheba all she desired, whatever she 12
asked, besides his gifts in return for *a* what she had brought him. Then she
departed and returned with her retinue to her own land.

Now the weight of gold which Solomon received yearly was six hundred 13
and sixty-six talents, in addition to the tolls levied on merchants and on 14
traders who imported goods; all the kings of Arabia and the regional
governors also*b* brought gold and silver to the king.

King Solomon made two hundred shields of beaten gold, and six hundred 15
shekels of gold went to the making of each one; he also made three hundred 16
bucklers of beaten gold, and three hundred shekels of gold went to the
making of each buckler. The king put these into the House of the Forest
of Lebanon.

The king also made a great throne of ivory and overlaid it with pure 17
gold. Six steps and a footstool for the throne were all encased in gold. 18
There were arms on each side of the seat, with a lion standing beside each
of them, and twelve lions stood on the six steps, one at either end of each 19
step. Nothing like it had ever been made for any monarch. All Solomon's 20
drinking vessels were of gold, and all the plate in the House of the Forest
of Lebanon was of red gold; silver was reckoned of no value in the days of
Solomon. The king had a fleet of ships plying to Tarshish with Huram's 21
men; once every three years this fleet of merchantmen came home,
bringing gold and silver, ivory, apes, and monkeys.

Thus King Solomon outdid all the kings of the earth in wealth and 22
wisdom, and all the kings of the earth courted him, to hear the wisdom 23
which God had put in his heart. Each brought his gift with him, vessels of 24
silver and gold, garments, perfumes and spices, horses and mules, so much
year by year.

Solomon had standing for four thousand horses and chariots, and twelve 25*c*
thousand cavalry horses, and he stabled some in the chariot-towns and
kept others at hand in Jerusalem. He ruled over all the kings from the 26
Euphrates to the land of the Philistines and the border of Egypt. He made 27

---

*a* his gifts ... for: *prob. rdg.; Heb. om.*     *b* all ... also: *or* and on all the kings of
Arabia and the regional governors who ...     *c* *Verses 25-28: cp. I. 14-17; I Kgs. 10.*
26-29.

28 silver as common in Jerusalem as stones, and cedar as plentiful as sycomore-fig in the Shephelah. Horses were imported from Egypt and from all countries for Solomon.

29[a] The rest of the acts of Solomon's reign, from first to last, are recorded in the history of Nathan the prophet, in the prophecy of Ahijah of Shiloh, and in the visions of Iddo the seer concerning Jeroboam son of Nebat.

30 31 Solomon ruled in Jerusalem over the whole of Israel for forty years. Then he rested with his forefathers and was buried in the city of David his father, and he was succeeded by his son Rehoboam.

## The kings of Judah from Rehoboam to Ahaz

10 1[b] REHOBOAM WENT TO SHECHEM, for all Israel had gone there to make
2 him king. When Jeroboam son of Nebat heard of it in Egypt, where
3 he had taken refuge to escape Solomon, he returned from Egypt. They
4 now recalled him, and he and all Israel came to Rehoboam and said, 'Your father laid a cruel yoke upon us; but if you will now lighten the cruel slavery he imposed on us and the heavy yoke he laid on us, we will serve
5 you.' 'Give me three days,' he said, 'and come back again.' So the people
6 went away. King Rehoboam then consulted the elders who had been in attendance on his father Solomon while he lived: 'What answer do you
7 advise me to give to this people?' And they said, 'If you show yourself well-disposed to this people and gratify them by speaking kindly to them,
8 they will be your servants ever after.' But he rejected the advice which the elders gave him. He next consulted those who had grown up with him, the
9 young men in attendance, and asked them, 'What answer do you advise me to give to this people's request that I should lighten the yoke which my
10 father laid on them?' The young men replied, 'Give this answer to the people who say that your father made their yoke heavy and ask you to
11 lighten it; tell them: "My little finger is thicker than my father's loins. My father laid a heavy yoke on you; I will make it heavier. My father used the
12 whip on you; but I will use the lash."' Jeroboam and the people all came
13 back to Rehoboam on the third day, as the king had ordered. And the king gave them a harsh answer. He rejected the advice which the elders had given
14 him and spoke to the people as the young men had advised: 'My father made your yoke heavy; I will make it heavier. My father used the whip on
15 you; but I will use the lash.' So the king would not listen to the people; for the LORD had given this turn to the affair, in order that the word he had spoken by Ahijah of Shiloh to Jeroboam son of Nebat might be fulfilled.
16 When all Israel saw[c] that the king would not listen to them, they answered:

> What share have we in David?
> We have no lot in the son of Jesse.
> Away to your homes, O Israel;
> now see to your own house, David.

---

[a] *Verses 29–31: cp. I Kgs. 11. 41–43.*     [b] *Verses 1–19: cp. I Kgs. 12. 1–19.*     [c] *saw: prob. rdg., cp. I Kgs. 12. 16; Heb. om.*

So all Israel went to their homes, and Rehoboam ruled over those Israelites 17 who lived in the cities of Judah.

Then King Rehoboam sent out Hadoram, the commander of the forced 18 levies, but the Israelites stoned him to death; whereupon King Rehoboam mounted his chariot in haste and fled to Jerusalem. From that day to this, 19 Israel has been in rebellion against the house of David.

When Rehoboam reached Jerusalem, he assembled the tribes of Judah **11** 1[a] and Benjamin, a hundred and eighty thousand chosen warriors, to fight against Israel and recover his kingdom. But the word of the LORD came to 2 Shemaiah the man of God: 'Say to Rehoboam son of Solomon, king of 3 Judah, and to all the Israelites in Judah and Benjamin, "This is the word 4 of the LORD: You shall not go up to make war on your kinsmen. Return to your homes, for this is my will."' So they listened to the word of the LORD and abandoned their campaign against Jeroboam.

Rehoboam resided in Jerusalem and built up the defences of certain 5 cities in Judah. The cities in Judah and Benjamin which he fortified were 6 Bethlehem, Etam, Tekoa, Beth-zur, Soco, Adullam, Gath, Mareshah, 7 8 Ziph, Adoraim, Lachish, Azekah, Zorah, Aijalon, and Hebron. He 9 10 11 strengthened the fortifications of these fortified cities, and put governors in them, as well as supplies of food, oil, and wine. Also he stored shields 12 and spears in every one of the cities, and strengthened their fortifications. Thus he retained possession of Judah and Benjamin.

Now the priests and the Levites throughout the whole of Israel resorted 13 to Rehoboam from all their territories; for the Levites had left all their 14 common land and their own patrimony and had gone to Judah and Jerusalem, because Jeroboam and his successors rejected their services as priests of the LORD, and he appointed his own priests for the hill-shrines, 15 for the demons,[b] and for the calves which he had made. Those, from all 16 the tribes of Israel, who were resolved to seek the LORD the God of Israel followed the Levites to Jerusalem to sacrifice to the LORD the God of their fathers. So they strengthened the kingdom of Judah and for three years 17 made Rehoboam son of Solomon secure, because he followed the example of David and Solomon during that time.

Rehoboam married Mahalath, whose father was Jerimoth son of David 18 and whose mother was Abihail daughter of Eliab son of Jesse. His sons 19 by her were: Jeush, Shemariah and Zaham. Next he married Maacah 20 granddaughter of Absalom, who bore him Abijah, Attai, Ziza and Shelomith. Of all his wives and concubines, Rehoboam loved Maacah most; 21 he had in all eighteen wives and sixty concubines and became the father of twenty-eight sons and sixty daughters. He appointed Abijah son of 22 Maacah chief among his brothers, making him crown prince and planning to make him his successor on the throne. He showed discretion in detailing 23 his sons to take charge of all the fortified cities throughout the whole territory of Judah and Benjamin; he also made generous provision for them and procured them[c] wives.

When the kingdom of Rehoboam was on a firm footing and he became **12**

---

[a] *Verses 1-4: cp. 1 Kgs. 12. 21-24.*    [b] *Or* satyrs.    [c] procured them: *prob. rdg.;* Heb. asked for a multitude of . . .

2 strong, he forsook the law of the LORD, he and all Israel with him. In the
fifth year of Rehoboam's reign, because of this disloyalty to the LORD,
3 Shishak king of Egypt attacked Jerusalem with twelve hundred chariots
and sixty thousand horsemen, and brought with him from Egypt an
4 innumerable following of Libyans, Sukkites, and Cushites.*a* He captured
5 the fortified cities of Judah and reached Jerusalem. Then Shemaiah the
prophet came to Rehoboam and the leading men of Judah, who had
assembled in Jerusalem before the advance of Shishak, and said to them,
'This is the word of the LORD: You have abandoned me; therefore I now
6 abandon you to Shishak.' The princes of Israel and the king submitted and
7 said, 'The LORD is just.' When the LORD saw that they had submitted,
there came from him this word to Shemaiah: 'Because they have submitted I will not destroy them, I will let them barely escape; my wrath
8 shall not be poured out on Jerusalem by means of Shishak, but they shall
become his servants; then they will know the difference between serving
9*b* me and serving the rulers of other countries.' Shishak king of Egypt in his
attack on Jerusalem removed the treasures of the house of the LORD and
of the royal palace. He seized everything, including the shields of gold that
10 Solomon had made. King Rehoboam replaced them with bronze shields
and entrusted them to the officers of the escort who guarded the entrance
11 of the royal palace. Whenever the king entered the house of the LORD, the
escort entered, carrying the shields; afterwards they returned them to the
12 guard-room. Because Rehoboam submitted, the LORD's wrath was
averted from him, and he was not utterly destroyed; Judah enjoyed
prosperity.
13*c*    Thus King Rehoboam increased his power in Jerusalem. He was forty-
one years old when he came to the throne, and he reigned for seventeen
years in Jerusalem, the city which the LORD had chosen out of all the tribes
of Israel as the place to receive his Name. Rehoboam's mother was a
14 woman of Ammon called Naamah. He did what was wrong, he did not
15 make a practice of seeking guidance of the LORD. The events of Rehoboam's
reign, from first to last, are recorded in the histories of Shemaiah the
prophet and Iddo the seer.*d* There was continual fighting between
16 Rehoboam and Jeroboam. He rested with his forefathers and was buried
in the city of David; and he was succeeded by his son Abijah.

13 IN THE EIGHTEENTH YEAR of King Jeroboam's reign Abijah became
2 king of Judah. He reigned in Jerusalem for three years; his mother was
Maacah daughter of Uriel of Gibeah. There was fighting between Abijah
3 and Jeroboam. Abijah drew up his army of four hundred thousand picked
troops in order of battle, while Jeroboam formed up against him with
4 eight hundred thousand picked troops. Abijah took up position on the
slopes of Mount Zemaraim in the hill-country of Ephraim and called out,
5 'Hear me, Jeroboam and all Israel: Ought you not to know that the LORD
the God of Israel gave the kingship over Israel to David and his descend-
6 ants in perpetuity by a covenant of salt? Yet Jeroboam son of Nebat, the

---

*a* Or Nubians.   *b* *Verses 9–11 : cp. 1 Kgs. 14. 25–28.*   *c* *Verses 13–16 : cp.*
*1 Kgs. 14. 29–31.*   *d* *Prob. rdg.; Heb. adds* to be enrolled by genealogy.

servant of Solomon son of David, rose in rebellion against his lord, and ₇
certain worthless scoundrels gathered round him, who stubbornly opposed
Solomon's son Rehoboam when he was young and inexperienced, and he
was no match for them. Now you propose to match yourselves against the ₈
kingdom of the LORD as ruled by David's sons, you and your mob of
supporters and the golden calves which Jeroboam has made to be your
gods. Have you not dismissed from office the Aaronites, priests of the ₉
LORD, and the Levites, and followed the practice of other lands in appointing priests? Now, if any man comes for consecration with an offering of a
young bull and seven rams, you accept him as a priest to a god that is no
god. But as for us, the LORD is our God and we have not forsaken him; we ₁₀
have Aaronites as priests ministering to the LORD with the Levites, duly
discharging their office. Morning and evening, these burn whole-offerings ₁₁
and fragrant incense to the LORD and offer the Bread of the Presence
arranged in rows on a table ritually clean; they also kindle the lamps on
the golden lamp-stand every evening. Thus we do indeed keep the charge
of the LORD our God, whereas you have forsaken him. God is with us at ₁₂
our head, and his priests stand there with trumpets to signal the battle-cry
against you. Men of Israel, do not fight the LORD the God of your fathers;
you will have no success.'

Jeroboam sent a detachment of his troops to go round and lay an ambush ₁₃
in the rear, so that his main body faced Judah while the ambush lay behind
them. The men of Judah turned to find that they were engaged front and ₁₄
rear. Then they cried to the LORD for help. The priests sounded their
trumpets, and the men of Judah raised a shout, and when they did so, God ₁₅
put Jeroboam and all Israel to rout before Abijah and Judah. The Israelites ₁₆
fled before the men of Judah, and God delivered them into their power. So ₁₇
Abijah and his men defeated them with very heavy losses, and five hundred
thousand picked Israelites fell in the battle. After this, the Israelites were ₁₈
reduced to submission, and Judah prevailed because they relied on the
LORD the God of their fathers. Abijah followed up his victory over Jero- ₁₉
boam and captured from him the cities of Bethel, Jeshanah, and Ephron,
with their villages. Jeroboam did not regain his power during the days of ₂₀
Abijah; finally the LORD struck him down and he died.

But Abijah established his position; he married fourteen wives and ₂₁
became the father of twenty-two sons and sixteen daughters. The other ₂₂
events of Abijah's reign, both what he said and what he did, are recorded
in the story of the prophet Iddo. Abijah rested with his forefathers and **14**
was buried in the city of David; and he was succeeded on the throne by his
son Asa. In his days the land was at peace for ten years.

Asa did what was good and right in the eyes of the LORD his God. He ₂ ₃
suppressed the foreign altars and the hill-shrines, smashed the sacred
pillars and hacked down the sacred poles, and ordered Judah to seek ₄
guidance of the LORD the God of their fathers and to keep the law and the
commandments. He also suppressed the hill-shrines and the incense- ₅
altars in all the cities, and the kingdom was at peace under him. He built ₆
fortified cities in Judah, for the land was at peace. He had no war to fight
during those years, because the LORD had given him security. He said to ₇

the men of Judah, 'Let us build these cities and fortify them, with walls round them, and towers and barred gates. The land still lies open before us. Because we have sought guidance of the LORD our God, he has sought us and given us security on every side.' So they built and prospered.

8 Asa had an army equipped with shields and spears; three hundred thousand men came from Judah, and two hundred and eighty thousand from Benjamin, shield-bearers and archers; all were valiant warriors.
9 Zerah the Cushite came out against them with an army a million strong
10 and three hundred chariots. When he reached Mareshah, Asa came out to meet him and they took up position in the valley of Zephathah at Mareshah.
11 Asa called upon the LORD his God and said, 'There is none like thee, O LORD, to help men, whether strong or weak; help us, O LORD our God, for on thee we rely and in thy name we have come out against this horde.
12 O LORD, thou art our God, how can man vie with thee?' So the LORD gave
13 Asa and Judah victory over the Cushites and they fled, and Asa and his men pursued them as far as Gerar. The Cushites broke before the LORD and his army, and many of them fell mortally wounded; and Judah carried
14 off great loads of spoil. They destroyed all the cities around Gerar, for the LORD had struck the people with panic; and they plundered the cities,
15 finding rich spoil in them all. They also killed the herdsmen and seized many sheep and camels, and then they returned to Jerusalem.

**15** 1 2 The spirit of God came upon Azariah son of Oded, and he went out to meet Asa and said to him, 'Hear me, Asa and all Judah and Benjamin. The LORD is with you when you are with him; if you look for him, he will let
3 himself be found; if you forsake him, he will forsake you. For a long time Israel was without the true God, without a priest to interpret the law and
4 without law.*ᵃ* But when, in their distress, they turned to the LORD the God
5 of Israel and sought him, he let himself be found by them. At those times there was no safety for people as they went about their business; the inhabitants of every land had their fill of trouble; there was ruin on every
6 side, nation at odds with nation, city with city, for God harassed them with
7 every kind of distress. But now you must be strong and not let your courage
8 fail; for your work will be rewarded.' When Asa heard these words,*ᵇ* he resolutely suppressed the loathsome idols in all Judah and Benjamin and in the cities which he had captured in the hill-country of Ephraim; and he repaired the altar of the LORD which stood before the vestibule of the
9 LORD's house.*ᶜ* Then he assembled all Judah and Benjamin and all who had come from Ephraim, Manasseh, and Simeon to reside among them; for great numbers had come over to him from Israel, when they saw that
10 the LORD his God was with him. So they assembled at Jerusalem in the
11 third month of the fifteenth year of Asa's reign, and that day they sacrificed to the LORD seven hundred oxen and seven thousand sheep from the spoil
12 which they had brought. And they entered into a covenant to seek guidance
13 of the LORD the God of their fathers with all their heart and soul; all who would not seek the LORD the God of Israel were to be put to death, young
14 and old, men and women alike. Then they bound themselves by an oath

---

*ᵃ without law: or* without the law.          *ᵇ Prob. rdg.; Heb. adds* and the prophecy, Oded the prophet.          *ᶜ house: prob. rdg.; Heb. om.*

to the LORD, with loud shouts of acclamation while trumpets and horns sounded; and all Judah rejoiced at the oath, because they had bound 15 themselves with all their heart and had sought him earnestly, and he had let himself be found by them. So the LORD gave them security on every side. King Asa also deprived Maacah his grandmother of her rank as 16<sup>a</sup> queen mother because she had an obscene object made for the worship of Asherah; Asa cut it down, ground it to powder and burnt it in the gorge of the Kidron. Although the hill-shrines were allowed to remain in Israel, 17 Asa himself remained faithful all his life. He brought into the house of 18 God all his father's votive offerings and his own, gold and silver and sacred vessels. And there was no more war until the thirty-fifth year of Asa's 19 reign.

In the thirty-sixth year of the reign of Asa, Baasha king of Israel invaded **16** 1<sup>b</sup> Judah and fortified Ramah to cut off all access to Asa king of Judah. So 2 Asa brought out silver and gold from the treasuries of the house of the LORD and the royal palace, and sent this request to Ben-hadad king of Aram, whose capital was Damascus: 'There is an alliance between us, as 3 there was between our fathers. I now send you herewith silver and gold; break off your alliance with Baasha king of Israel, so that he may abandon his campaign against me.' Ben-hadad listened willingly to King Asa 4 and ordered the commanders of his armies to move against the cities of Israel, and they attacked Iyyon, Dan, Abel-mayim, and all the store-cities of Naphtali. When Baasha heard of it, he ceased fortifying Ramah 5 and stopped all work on it. Then King Asa took with him all the men 6 of Judah and they carried away the stones of Ramah and the timbers with which Baasha had fortified it; and he used them to fortify Geba and Mizpah.

At that time the seer Hanani came to Asa king of Judah and said to him, 7 'Because you relied on the king of Aram and not on the LORD your God, the army of the king of Israel has escaped. The Cushites and the Libyans, 8 were they not a great army with a vast number of chariots and horsemen? Yet, because you relied on the LORD, he delivered them into your power. The eyes of the LORD range through the whole earth, to bring aid and 9 comfort to those whose hearts are loyal to him. You have acted foolishly in this affair; you will have wars from now on.' Asa was angry with the 10 seer and put him in the stocks; for these words of his had made the king very indignant. At the same time he treated some of the people with great brutality.

The events of Asa's reign, from first to last, are recorded in the annals 11<sup>c</sup> of the kings of Judah and Israel. In the thirty-ninth year of his reign Asa 12 became gravely affected with gangrene in his feet; he did not seek guidance of the LORD but resorted to physicians. He rested with his forefathers, 13 in the forty-first year of his reign, and was buried in the tomb which he 14 had bought<sup>d</sup> for himself in the city of David, being laid on a bier<sup>e</sup> which had been heaped with all kinds of spices skilfully compounded; and they kindled a great fire in his honour.

<sup>a</sup> *Verses 16–18: cp. 1 Kgs. 15. 13–15.*     <sup>b</sup> *Verses 1–6: cp. 1 Kgs. 15. 17–22.*
<sup>c</sup> *Verses 11–14: cp. 1 Kgs. 15. 23, 24.*     <sup>d</sup> *Or dug.*     <sup>e</sup> *Or in a niche.*

**17** ASA WAS SUCCEEDED BY HIS SON JEHOSHAPHAT, who determined
2 to resist Israel by force. He posted troops in all the fortified cities of Judah
and stationed officers *a* throughout Judah and in the cities of Ephraim
3 which his father Asa had captured. The LORD was with Jehoshaphat, for
he followed the example his father had set in his early years and did not
4 resort to the Baalim; he sought guidance of the God of his father and
5 obeyed his commandments and did not follow the practices of Israel. So
the LORD established the kingdom under his rule, and all Judah brought
6 him gifts, and his wealth and fame *b* became very great. He took pride in
the service of the LORD; he also suppressed the hill-shrines and the sacred
poles in Judah.
7     In the third year of his reign he sent his officers, Ben-hayil, Obadiah,
8 Zechariah, Nethaneel, and Micaiah, to teach in the cities of Judah, together with the Levites, Shemaiah, Nethaniah, Zebadiah, Asahel, Shemiramoth, Jehonathan, Adonijah, Tobiah, and Tob-adonijah, *c* accompanied
9 by the priests Elishama and Jehoram. They taught in Judah, having with
them the book of the law of the LORD; they went round the cities of Judah,
teaching the people.
10     So the dread of the LORD fell upon all the rulers of the lands surrounding
11 Judah, and they did not make war on Jehoshaphat. Certain Philistines
brought a gift, a great quantity of silver, to Jehoshaphat; the Arabs too
brought him seven thousand seven hundred rams and seven thousand
12 seven hundred he-goats. Jehoshaphat became ever more powerful and
13 built fortresses and store-cities in Judah; and he had much work on hand
in the cities of Judah. He had regular, seasoned troops in Jerusalem,
14 enrolled according to their clans in this way: of Judah, the officers over
units of a thousand: Adnah the commander, together with three hundred
15 thousand seasoned troops; and next to him the commander Johanan, with
16 two hundred and eighty thousand; and next to him Amasiah son of
Zichri, who had volunteered for the service of the LORD, with two hundred
17 thousand seasoned troops; and of Benjamin: an experienced soldier
Eliada, with two hundred thousand men armed with bows and shields;
18 next to him Jehozabad, with a hundred and eighty thousand fully-armed
19 men. These were the men who served the king, apart from those whom
the king had posted in the fortified cities throughout Judah.

**18**     When Jehoshaphat had become very wealthy and famous, *d* he allied
2 *e* himself with Ahab by marriage. Some years afterwards he went down to
visit Ahab in Samaria, and Ahab slaughtered many sheep and oxen for
3 him and his retinue, and incited him to attack Ramoth-gilead. What Ahab
king of Israel said to Jehoshaphat king of Judah was this: 'Will you join
me in attacking Ramoth-gilead?' And he answered, 'What is mine is yours,
4 myself and my people; I will join with you in the war.' Then Jehoshaphat
5 said to the king of Israel, 'First let us seek counsel from the LORD.' The
king of Israel assembled the prophets, some four hundred of them, and
asked them, 'Shall I attack Ramoth-gilead or shall I refrain?' 'Attack,'
6 they answered; 'God will deliver it into your hands.' Jehoshaphat asked,

*a Or garrisons.    b Or riches.    c Prob. rdg.; Heb. adds the Levites.    d Or rich.
e Verses 2–34: cp. 1 Kgs. 22. 2–35.*

'Is there no other prophet of the LORD here through whom we may seek guidance?' 'There is one more', the king of Israel answered, 'through whom 7 we may seek guidance of the LORD, but I hate the man, because he never prophesies any good for me; never anything but evil. His name is Micaiah son of Imla.' Jehoshaphat exclaimed, 'My lord king, let no such word pass your lips!' So the king of Israel called one of his eunuchs and told him to 8 fetch Micaiah son of Imla with all speed.

The king of Israel and Jehoshaphat king of Judah were seated on their 9 thrones, clothed in their royal robes and in shining armour, at the entrance to the gate of Samaria, and all the prophets were prophesying before them. One of them, Zedekiah son of Kenaanah, made himself horns of iron and 10 said, 'This is the word of the LORD: "With horns like these you shall gore the Aramaeans and make an end of them."' In the same vein all the pro- 11 phets prophesied, 'Attack Ramoth-gilead and win the day; the LORD will deliver it into your hands.' The messenger sent to fetch Micaiah told him 12 that the prophets had with one voice given the king a favourable answer. 'And mind you agree with them', he added. 'As the LORD lives,' said 13 Micaiah, 'I will say only what my God tells me to say.'

When Micaiah came into the king's presence, the king said to him, 14 'Micaiah, shall I attack Ramoth-gilead or shall I refrain?' 'Attack and win the day,' he said, 'and it will fall into your hands.' 'How often must I 15 adjure you', said the king, 'to tell me nothing but the truth in the name of the LORD?' Then Micaiah said, 'I saw all Israel scattered on the mountains, 16 like sheep without a shepherd; and I heard the LORD say, "They have no master; let them go home in peace."' The king of Israel said to Jehoshaphat, 17 'Did I not tell you that he never prophesies good for me, nothing but evil?' Micaiah went on, 'Listen now to the word of the LORD: I saw the LORD 18 seated on his throne, with all the host of heaven in attendance on his right and on his left. The LORD said, "Who will entice Ahab to attack and fall on *a* 19 Ramoth-gilead?" One said one thing and one said another; then a spirit 20 came forward and stood before the LORD and said, "I will entice him." "How?" said the LORD. "I will go out", he said, "and be a lying spirit in 21 the mouth of all his prophets." "You shall entice him," said the LORD, "and you shall succeed; go and do it." You see, then, how the LORD has 22 put a lying spirit in the mouth of all these prophets of yours, because he has decreed disaster for you.' Then Zedekiah son of Kenaanah came up to 23 Micaiah and struck him in the face: 'And how did the spirit of the LORD pass from me to speak to you?' he said. Micaiah answered, 'That you will 24 find out on the day when you run into an inner room to hide yourself.' Then the king of Israel ordered Micaiah to be arrested and committed to 25 the custody of Amon the governor of the city and Joash the king's son. *b* 'Lock this fellow up', he said, 'and give him prison diet of bread and water 26 until I come home in safety.' Micaiah retorted, 'If you do return in safety, 27 the LORD has not spoken by me.' *c*

So the king of Israel and Jehoshaphat king of Judah marched on Ramoth- 28 gilead, and the king of Israel said to Jehoshaphat, 'I will disguise myself 29

*a* Or at.　　*b* son: or deputy.　　*c* Prob. rdg.; Heb. adds and he said, 'Listen, peoples, all together.'

to go into battle, but you shall wear your royal robes.' So he went into battle
30  in disguise. Now the king of Aram had commanded the captains of his
31  chariots not to engage all and sundry but the king of Israel alone. When
the captains saw Jehoshaphat, they thought he was the king of Israel and
wheeled to attack him. But Jehoshaphat cried out, and the LORD came to
32  his help; and God drew them away from him. When the captains saw that
33  he was not the king of Israel, they broke off the attack on him. But one
man drew his bow at random and hit the king of Israel where the breastplate joins the plates of the armour. So he said to his driver, 'Wheel round
34  and take me out of the line; I am wounded.' When the day's fighting reached
its height, the king of Israel was facing the Aramaeans, propped up in his
chariot; he remained so till evening, and at sunset he died.

**19**   As Jehoshaphat king of Judah returned in safety to his home in Jeru-
2  salem, Jehu son of Hanani, the seer, went out to meet him and said, 'Do
you take delight in helping the wicked and befriending the enemies of the
3  LORD? The LORD will make you suffer for this. Yet there is some good in
you, for you have swept away the sacred poles from the land and have made
a practice of seeking guidance of God.'

4     Jehoshaphat had his residence in Jerusalem, but he went out again
among his people from Beersheba to the hill-country of Ephraim and
5  brought them back to the LORD the God of their fathers. He appointed
6  judges throughout the land, one in each of the fortified cities of Judah,
7  and said to them, 'Be careful what you do; you are there as judges, to please
not man but the LORD, who is with you when you pass sentence. Let the
dread of the LORD be upon you, then; take care what you do, for the LORD
our God will not tolerate injustice, partiality, or bribery.'

8     In Jerusalem Jehoshaphat appointed some of the Levites and priests
and some heads of families by paternal descent in Israel to administer the
law of the LORD and to arbitrate in lawsuits among the inhabitants[a] of
9  the city, and he gave them these instructions: 'You must always act in the
10  fear of the LORD, faithfully and with singleness of mind. In every suit
which comes before you from your kinsmen, in whatever city they live,
whether cases of bloodshed or offences against the law or the commandments, against statutes or regulations, you shall warn them to commit no
offence against the LORD; otherwise you and your kinsmen will suffer for
11  it. If you act thus, you will be free of all offence. Your authority in all
matters which concern the LORD is Amariah the chief priest, and in those
which concern the king it is Zebediah son of Ishmael, the prince of the
house of Judah; the Levites are your officers. Be strong and resolute, and
may the LORD be on the side of the good!'

**20**   It happened some time afterwards that the Moabites, the Ammonites,
2  and some of the Meunites made war on Jehoshaphat. News was brought
to him that a great horde of them was attacking him from beyond the Dead
Sea, from Edom, and was already at Hazazon-tamar, which is En-gedi.
3  Jehoshaphat in his alarm resolved to seek guidance of the LORD and pro-
4  claimed a fast for all Judah. Judah gathered together to ask counsel of the
5  LORD; from every city of the land they came to consult him. Jehoshaphat

---

[a]  *in . . . inhabitants: prob. rdg.; Heb. obscure.*

stood up in the assembly of Judah and Jerusalem in the house of the LORD, in front of the New Court, and said, 'O LORD God of our fathers, art not thou God in heaven? Thou rulest over all the kingdoms of the nations; in thy hand are strength and power, and there is none who can withstand thee. Didst not thou, O God our God, dispossess the inhabitants of this land in favour of thy people Israel, and give it for ever to the descendants of Abraham thy friend? So they lived in it and have built a sanctuary in it in honour of thy name and said, "Should evil come upon us, war or flood,ᵃ pestilence or famine, we will stand before this house and before thee, for in this house is thy Name, and we will cry to thee in our distress and thou wilt hear and save." Thou didst not allow Israel, when they came out of Egypt, to enter the land of the Ammonites, the Moabites, and the people of the hill-country of Seir, so they turned aside and left them alone and did not destroy them. Now see how these people repay us: they are coming to drive us out of thy possession which thou didst give to us. Judge them, O God our God, for we have no strength to face this great horde which is invading our land; we know not what we ought to do; we lift our eyes to thee.'

So all Judah stood there before the LORD, with their dependants, their wives and their children. Then, in the midst of the assembly, the spirit of the LORD came upon Jahaziel son of Zechariah, son of Benaiah, son of Jeiel, son of Mattaniah, a Levite of the line of Asaph, and he said, 'Attend, all Judah, all inhabitants of Jerusalem, and King Jehoshaphat; this is the word of the LORD to you: "Have no fear; do not be dismayed by this great horde, for the battle is in God's hands, not yours. Go down to meet them tomorrow; they will come up by the Ascent of Ziz. You will find them at the end of the valley, east of the wilderness of Jeruel. It is not you who will fight this battle; stand firm and wait, and you will see the deliverance worked by the LORD: he is on your side, O Judah and Jerusalem. Do not fear or be dismayed; go out tomorrow to face them; for the LORD is on your side." ' Jehoshaphat bowed his face to the ground, and all Judah and the inhabitants of Jerusalem fell down before the LORD to make obeisance to him. Then the Levites of the lines of Kohath and Korah stood up and praised the LORD the God of Israel with a mighty shout.

So they rose early in the morning and went out to the wilderness of Tekoa; and, as they were starting, Jehoshaphat took his stand and said, 'Hear me, O Judah and inhabitants of Jerusalem: hold firmly to your faith in the LORD your God and you will be upheld; have faith in his prophets and you will prosper.' After consulting with the people, he appointed men to sing to the LORD and praise the splendour of his holinessᵇ as they went before the armed troops, and they sang:

> Give thanks to the LORD,
>     for his love endures for ever.

As soon as their loud shouts of praise were heard, the LORD deluded the Ammonites and Moabites and the men of the hill-country of Seir, who

---

ᵃ *Prob. rdg.; Heb.* judgement.     ᵇ *Or* singers in sacred vestments to praise the LORD.

23 were invading Judah, and they were defeated. It turned out that the Ammonites and Moabites had taken up a position against the men of the hill-country of Seir, and set themselves to annihilate and destroy them; and when they had exterminated the men of Seir, they savagely attacked

24 one another. So when Judah came to the watch-tower in the wilderness and looked towards the enemy horde, there they were all lying dead upon

25 the ground; none had escaped. When Jehoshaphat and his men came to collect the booty, they found a large number of cattle, goods, clothing, and precious things, which they plundered until they could carry away no more. They spent three days collecting the booty, there was so much of it.

26 On the fourth day they assembled in the Valley of Berakah,<sup>a</sup> the name that

27 it bears to this day because they blessed the LORD there. Then all the men of Judah and Jerusalem, with Jehoshaphat at their head, returned home to the city in triumph; for the LORD had given them cause to triumph over

28 their enemies. They entered Jerusalem with lutes, harps, and trumpets

29 playing, and went into the house of the LORD. So the dread of God fell upon the rulers of every country, when they heard that the LORD had

30 fought against the enemies of Israel; and the realm of Jehoshaphat was at peace, God giving him security on all sides.

31<sup>b</sup>    Thus Jehoshaphat reigned over Judah. He was thirty-five years old when he came to the throne, and he reigned in Jerusalem for twenty-five

32 years; his mother was Azubah daughter of Shilhi. He followed in the footsteps of Asa his father and did not swerve from them; he did what was

33 right in the eyes of the LORD. But the hill-shrines were allowed to remain,

34 and the people did not set their hearts upon the God of their fathers. The other events of Jehoshaphat's reign, from first to last, are recorded in the history of Jehu son of Hanani, which is included in the annals of the kings of Israel.

35    Later Jehoshaphat king of Judah allied himself with Ahaziah king of

36 Israel; he did wrong in joining with him to build ships for trade with

37 Tarshish; these were built in Ezion-geber. But Eliezer son of Dodavahu of Mareshah denounced Jehoshaphat with this prophecy: 'Because you have joined with Ahaziah, the LORD will bring your work to nothing.' So the ships were wrecked and could not make the voyage to Tarshish.

21 JEHOSHAPHAT RESTED WITH HIS FOREFATHERS and was buried with

2 them in the city of David. He was succeeded by his son Joram, whose brothers were Azariah, Jehiel, Zechariah, Azariah, Michael, and Shephatiah, sons of Jehoshaphat. All of them were sons of Jehoshaphat king of

3 Judah, and their father gave them many gifts, silver and gold and other costly things, as well as fortified cities in Judah; but the kingship he gave to Joram because he was the eldest.

4    When Joram was firmly established on his father's throne, he put to

5<sup>c</sup> the sword all his brothers and also some of the princes of Israel. He was thirty-two years old when he came to the throne, and he reigned in Jeru-

6 salem for eight years. He followed the practices of the kings of Israel as

<sup>a</sup> *That is* Valley of Blessing.     <sup>b</sup> *Verses 31–33: cp. 1 Kgs. 22. 41–43.*     <sup>c</sup> *Verses 5–10: cp. 2 Kgs. 8. 17–22.*

the house of Ahab had done, for he had married Ahab's daughter; and he did what was wrong in the eyes of the LORD. But for the sake of the covenant 7 which he had made with David, the LORD was unwilling to destroy the house of David, since he had promised to give him and his sons a flame, to burn for all time.

During his reign Edom revolted against Judah and set up its own king. 8 Joram, with his commanders and all his chariots, advanced into Edom. 9 He and his chariot-commanders set out by night, but they were surrounded by the Edomites and defeated.ᵃ So Edom has remained independent of 10 Judah to this day. Libnah revolted against him at the same time, because he had forsaken the LORD the God of his fathers, and because he had built 11 hill-shrines in the hill-country of Judah and had seduced the inhabitants of Jerusalem into idolatrous practices and corrupted Judah.

A letter reached Joram from Elijah the prophet, which ran thus: 'This 12 is the word of the LORD the God of David your father: "You have not followed in the footsteps of Jehoshaphat your father and of Asa king of Judah, but have followed the kings of Israel and have seduced Judah and 13 the inhabitants of Jerusalem, as the house of Ahab did; and you have put to death your own brothers, sons of your father's house, men better than yourself. Because of all this, the LORD is about to strike a heavy blow at 14 your people, your children, your wives, and all your possessions, and you 15 yourself will suffer from a chronic disease of the bowels, until they prolapse and become severely ulcerated."' Then the LORD aroused against Joram 16 the anger of the Philistines and of the Arabs who live near the Cushites, and they invaded Judah and made their way right through it, carrying 17 off all the property which they found in the king's palace, as well as his sons and wives; not a son was left to him except the youngest, Jehoahaz. It was after all this that the LORD struck down the king with an incurable 18 disease of the bowels. It continued for some time, and towards the end of 19 the second year the disease caused his bowels to prolapse, and the painful ulceration brought on his death. But his people kindled no fire in his honour as they had done for his fathers. He was thirty-two years old when 20 he became king, and he reigned in Jerusalem for eight years. His passing went unsung, and he was buried in the city of David, but not in the burial-place of the kings.

Then the inhabitants of Jerusalem made Ahaziah, his youngest son, 22 1ᵇ king in his place, for the raiders who had joined the Arabs in the campaign had killed all the elder sons. So Ahaziah son of Joram became king of Judah. He was forty-two years old when he came to the throne, and he 2 reigned in Jerusalem for one year; his mother was Athaliah granddaughter of Omri. He too followed the practices of the house of Ahab, for his mother 3 was his counsellor in wickedness. He did what was wrong in the eyes of the 4 LORD like the house of Ahab, for they had been his counsellors after his father's death, to his undoing. He followed their counsel also in the 5 alliance he made with Jehoram son of Ahab king of Israel, to fight against Hazael king of Aram at Ramoth-gilead. But Jehoram was wounded by the

ᵃ *and defeated: prob. rdg.; Heb.* and he defeated them.     ᵇ *Verses 1–6: cp.*
2 *Kgs.* 8. 25–29.

6   Aramaeans, and returned to Jezreel to recover from the wounds which were inflicted on him at Ramoth in battle with Hazael king of Aram.

7   Because of Jehoram's illness Ahaziah son of Joram king of Judah went down to Jezreel to visit him. It was God's will that the visit of Ahaziah to Jehoram should be the occasion of his downfall. During the visit he went out with Jehoram to meet Jehu son of Nimshi, whom the LORD had

8   anointed to bring the house of Ahab to an end. So it came about that Jehu, who was then at variance with the house of Ahab, found the officers of Judah and the kinsmen of Ahaziah who were his attendants, and killed

9   them. Then he searched out Ahaziah himself, and his men captured him in Samaria, where he had gone into hiding. They brought him to Jehu and put him to death; they gave him burial, for they said, 'He was a son of Jehoshaphat who sought the guidance of the LORD with his whole heart.' Then the house of Ahaziah had no one strong enough to rule.

10<sup>a</sup>   As soon as Athaliah mother of Ahaziah saw that her son was dead, she

11   set out to extirpate the royal line of the house of Judah. But Jehosheba daughter of King Joram took Ahaziah's son Joash and stole him away from among the princes who were being murdered; she put him and his nurse in a bedchamber. Thus Jehosheba, daughter of King Joram and wife of Jehoiada the priest, because she was Ahaziah's sister, hid Joash from

12   Athaliah so that she did not put him to death. He remained concealed with them in the house of God for six years, while Athaliah ruled the country.

23   In the seventh year Jehoiada felt himself strong enough to make an agreement with Azariah son of Jeroham, Ishmael son of Jehohanan, Azariah son of Obed, Maaseiah son of Adaiah, and Elishaphat son of

2   Zichri, all captains of units of a hundred. They went all through Judah and gathered to Jerusalem the Levites from the cities of Judah and the heads

3   of clans in Israel, and they came to Jerusalem. All the assembly made a compact with the king in the house of God, and Jehoiada said to them, 'Here is the king's son! He shall be king, as the LORD promised that the

4   sons of David should be. This is what you must do: a third of you, priests and Levites, as you come on duty on the sabbath, are to be on guard at the

5   threshold gates, another third are to be in the royal palace, and another third are to be at the Foundation Gate, while all the people will be in the

6   courts of the house of the LORD. Let no one enter the house of the LORD except the priests and the attendant Levites; they may enter, for they are

7   holy, but all the people shall continue to keep the LORD's charge. The Levites shall mount guard round the king, each with his weapons at the ready; anyone who tries to enter the house is to be put to death. They shall stay with the king wherever he goes.'

8   The Levites and all Judah carried out the orders of Jehoiada the priest to the letter. Each captain took his men, both those who came on duty on the sabbath and those who came off, for Jehoiada the priest had not

9   released the outgoing divisions. And Jehoiada the priest handed out to the captains King David's spears, shields, and bucklers, which were in the

10   house of God; and he posted all the people, each man carrying his weapon

<hr>

*a  22. 10—23. 21 : cp. 2 Kgs. 11. 1–20.*

at the ready, from corner to corner of the house to north and south,<sup>a</sup> surrounding the king. Then they brought out the king's son, put the crown 11 on his head, handed him the warrant and proclaimed him king, and Jehoiada and his sons anointed him; and a shout went up: 'Long live the king.' When Athaliah heard the noise of the people as they ran about 12 cheering for the king, she came into the house of the LORD where the people were and found the king standing on the dais<sup>b</sup> at the entrance, amidst 13 outbursts of song and fanfares of trumpets in his honour; all the populace were rejoicing and blowing trumpets, and singers with musical instruments were leading the celebrations. Athaliah rent her clothes and cried, 'Treason! Treason!' Jehoiada the priest gave orders to<sup>c</sup> the captains in 14 command of the troops: 'Bring her outside the precincts and let anyone in attendance on her be put to the sword'; for the priest said, 'Do not kill her in the house of the LORD.' So they laid hands on her and took her to 15 the royal palace and killed her there at the passage to the Horse Gate.

Then Jehoiada made a covenant between the LORD<sup>d</sup> and the whole 16 people and the king, that they should be the LORD's people. And all the 17 people went into the temple of Baal and pulled it down; they smashed its altars and images, and they slew Mattan the priest of Baal before the altars. Then Jehoiada committed the supervision of the house of the LORD to the 18 charge of the priests and the Levites whom David had allocated to the house of the LORD, to offer whole-offerings to the LORD as prescribed in the law of Moses, with the singing and rejoicing as handed down from David. He stationed the door-keepers at the gates of the house of the LORD, 19 to prevent anyone entering who was in any way unclean. Then he took the 20 captains of units of a hundred, the nobles, and the governors of the people, and all the people of the land, and they escorted the king from the house of the LORD through the Upper Gate to the royal palace, and seated him on the royal throne. The whole people rejoiced and the city was tranquil. 21 That is how Athaliah was put to the sword.

Joash was seven years old when he became king, and he reigned in **24** 1<sup>e</sup> Jerusalem for forty years; his mother was Zibiah of Beersheba. He did 2 what was right in the eyes of the LORD as long as Jehoiada the priest was alive. Jehoiada chose him two wives, and he had a family of sons and 3 daughters.

Some time after this, Joash decided to repair the house of the LORD. So 4 5 he assembled the priests and the Levites and said to them, 'Go through the cities of Judah and collect the annual tax from all the Israelites for the restoration of the house of your God, and do it quickly.' But the Levites did not act quickly. The king then called for Jehoiada the chief priest and 6 said to him, 'Why have you not required the Levites to bring in from Judah and Jerusalem the tax imposed by Moses the servant of the LORD and by the assembly of Israel for the Tent of the Tokens?' For the wicked Athaliah 7 and her adherents had broken into the house of God and had devoted all

<sup>a</sup> *Prob. rdg.; Heb. adds of the altar and the house.*     <sup>b</sup> *Prob. rdg., cp. 2 Kgs. 11. 14; Heb. by his pillar.*     <sup>c</sup> *gave orders to: prob. rdg., cp. 2 Kgs. 11. 15; Heb. brought out.* <sup>d</sup> *the LORD: prob. rdg., cp. 2 Kgs. 11. 17; Heb. him.*     <sup>e</sup> *Verses 1–14: cp. 2 Kgs. 11. 21—12. 15.*

8 its holy things to the service of the Baalim. So the king ordered them to
9 make a chest and to put it outside the gate of the house of the LORD; and
proclamation was made throughout Judah and Jerusalem that the people
should bring to the LORD the tax imposed on Israel in the wilderness by
10 Moses the servant of God. And all the leaders and all the people gladly
11 brought their taxes and cast them into the chest until it was full. Whenever the chest was brought to the king's officers by the Levites and they
saw that it was well filled, the king's secretary and the chief priest's officer
would come to empty it, after which it was carried back to its place. This
12 they did daily, and they collected a great sum of money. The king and
Jehoiada gave it to those responsible for carrying out the work in the house
of the LORD, and they hired masons and carpenters to do the repairs, as
13 well as craftsmen in iron and copper*a* to restore the house. So the workmen
proceeded with their task and the new work progressed under their hands;
they restored the house of God according to its original design and
14 strengthened it. When they had finished, they brought what was left of
the money to the king and to Jehoiada, and it was made into vessels for the
house of the LORD, both for service and for sacrificing, saucers and other
vessels of gold and silver. While Jehoiada lived, whole-offerings were
offered in the house of the LORD continually.
15 Jehoiada, now old and weighed down with years, died at the age of a
16 hundred and thirty and was buried with the kings in the city of David,
because he had done good in Israel and served God and his house.
17 After the death of Jehoiada the leading men of Judah came and made
18 obeisance to the king. He listened to them, and they forsook the house of
the LORD the God of their fathers and worshipped sacred poles and idols.
19 And Judah and Jerusalem suffered for this wickedness. But the LORD sent
prophets to bring them back to himself, prophets who denounced them
20 and were not heeded. Then the spirit of God took possession of Zechariah
son of Jehoiada the priest, and he stood looking down on the people and
said to them, 'This is the word of God: "Why do you disobey the commands
of the LORD and court disaster? Because you have forsaken the LORD, he
21 has forsaken you."' But they made common cause against him, and on
orders from the king they stoned him to death in the court of the house of
22 the LORD. King Joash did not remember the loyalty of Zechariah's father
Jehoiada but killed his son, who said as he was dying, 'May the LORD see
this and exact the penalty.'
23 At the turn of the year an Aramaean army advanced against Joash; they
invaded Judah and Jerusalem and massacred all the officers, so that the
army ceased to exist, and sent all their spoil to the king of Damascus.
24 Although the Aramaeans had invaded with a small force, the LORD
delivered a very great army into their hands, because the people had forsaken the LORD the God of their fathers; and Joash suffered just punishment.
25*b* When the Aramaeans had withdrawn, leaving the king severely wounded,
his servants conspired against him to avenge the death of the son of
Jehoiada the priest; and they killed him on his bed. Thus he died and was

*a* Or bronze.  *b* Verses 25–27: cp. 2 Kgs. 12. 20, 21.

buried in the city of David, but not in the burial-place of the kings. The 26
conspirators were Zabad son of Shimeath an Ammonite woman and
Jehozabad son of Shimrith a Moabite woman. His children, the many 27
oracles about him, and his reconstruction of the house of God are all on
record in the story given in the annals of the kings. He was succeeded by
his son Amaziah.

AMAZIAH WAS TWENTY-FIVE YEARS OLD when he came to the throne, 25 1*a*
and he reigned in Jerusalem for twenty-nine years; his mother was
Jehoaddan of Jerusalem. He did what was right in the eyes of the LORD, 2
but not whole-heartedly. When the royal power was firmly in his grasp, 3
he put to death those of his servants who had murdered the king his father;
but he spared their children, in obedience to the LORD's command written 4
in the law of Moses: 'Fathers shall not die for their children, nor children
for their fathers; a man shall die only for his own sin.'

Then Amaziah assembled the men of Judah and drew them up by 5
families, all Judah and Benjamin as well, under officers over units of a
thousand and a hundred. He mustered those of twenty years old and
upwards and found their number to be three hundred thousand, all
picked troops ready for service, able to handle spear and shield. He also 6
hired a hundred thousand seasoned troops from Israel for a hundred talents
of silver. But a man of God came to him and said, 'My lord king, do not let 7
the Israelite army march with you; the LORD is not with Israel—all these
Ephraimites! For, if you make these people *b* your allies in the war, God will 8
overthrow you in battle; he has power to help or to overthrow.' Then Ama- 9
ziah said to the man of God, 'What am I to do about the hundred talents
which I have spent on the Israelite army?' The man of God answered, 'It
is in the LORD's power to give you much more than that.' So Amaziah 10
detached the troops which had come to him from Ephraim and sent them
home; that infuriated them against Judah and they went home in a rage.

Then Amaziah took heart and led his men to the Valley of Salt and there 11
killed ten thousand men of Seir. The men of Judah captured another ten 12
thousand men alive, brought them to the top of a cliff *c* and hurled them
over so that they were all dashed to pieces. Meanwhile the troops which 13
Amaziah had sent home without allowing them to take part in the battle
raided the cities of Judah from Samaria to Beth-horon, massacred three
thousand people in them and carried off quantities of booty.

After Amaziah had returned from the defeat of the Edomites, he brought 14
the gods of the people of Seir and, setting them up as his own gods, worshipped them and burnt sacrifices to them. The LORD was angry with 15
Amaziah for this and sent a prophet who said to him, 'Why have you resorted to gods who could not save their own people from you?' But while 16
he was speaking, the king said to him, 'Have we appointed you counsellor
to the king? Stop! Why risk your life?' The prophet did stop, but first he
said, 'I know that God has determined to destroy you because you have
done this and have not listened to my counsel.'

*a* *Verses 1–4: cp. 2 Kgs. 14. 1–6.*     *b* these people: *prob. rdg.; Heb. obscure.*
*c* a cliff: *or* Sela.

17<sup>a</sup> Then Amaziah king of Judah, after consultation, sent messengers to Jehoash son of Jehoahaz, son of Jehu, king of Israel, to propose a meeting.

18 But Jehoash king of Israel sent this answer to Amaziah king of Judah: 'A thistle in Lebanon sent to a cedar in Lebanon to say, "Give your daughter in marriage to my son." But a wild beast in Lebanon, passing by, trampled

19 on the thistle. You have defeated Edom, you say, but it has gone to your head. Enjoy your glory at home and stay there. Why should you involve yourself in disaster and bring yourself to the ground, and Judah with you?'

20 But Amaziah would not listen; and this was God's doing in order to give Judah into the power of Jehoash, because they had resorted to the gods of

21 Edom. So Jehoash king of Israel marched out, and he and Amaziah king

22 of Judah met one another at Beth-shemesh in Judah. The men of Judah

23 were routed by Israel and fled to their homes. But Jehoash king of Israel captured Amaziah king of Judah, son of Joash, son of Jehoahaz, at Beth-shemesh, and brought him to Jerusalem. There he broke down the city wall from the Gate of Ephraim to the Corner Gate, a distance of four

24 hundred cubits; he also took *b* all the gold and silver and all the vessels found in the house of God, in the care of Obed-edom, and the treasures of the royal palace, as well as hostages, and returned to Samaria.

25<sup>c</sup> Amaziah son of Joash, king of Judah, outlived Jehoash son of Jehoahaz,

26 king of Israel, by fifteen years. The other events of Amaziah's reign, from first to last, are recorded in the annals of the kings of Judah and Israel.

27 From the time when he turned away from the LORD, there was conspiracy against him in Jerusalem and he fled to Lachish; but they sent after him

28 to Lachish and put him to death there. Then his body was conveyed on horseback to Jerusalem, and there he was buried with his forefathers in the city of David.

**26** All the people of Judah took Uzziah, now sixteen years old, and made

2 him king in succession to his father Amaziah. It was he who built Eloth and restored it to Judah after the king rested with his forefathers.

3<sup>d</sup> Uzziah was sixteen years old when he came to the throne, and he reigned in Jerusalem for fifty-two years; his mother was Jecoliah of Jerusalem.

4 He did what was right in the eyes of the LORD, as Amaziah his father had

5 done. He set himself to seek the guidance of God in the days of Zechariah, who instructed him in the fear of God; as long as he sought guidance of the LORD, God caused him to prosper.

6 He took the field against the Philistines and broke down the walls of Gath, Jabneh, and Ashdod; and he built cities in the territory of Ashdod

7 and among the Philistines. God aided him against them, against the Arabs

8 who lived in Gur-baal, and against the Meunites. The Ammonites brought gifts to Uzziah and his fame spread to the borders of Egypt, for he had

9 become very powerful. Besides, he built towers in Jerusalem at the Corner

10 Gate, at the Valley Gate, and at the escarpment, and fortified them. He built other towers in the wilderness and dug many cisterns, for he had large herds of cattle both in the Shephelah and in the plain. He also had

---

*a Verses 17–24: cp. 2 Kgs. 14. 8–14.*     *b he also took: prob. rdg., cp. 2 Kgs. 14. 14; Heb. om.*     *c 25. 25—26. 2: cp. 2 Kgs. 14. 17–22.*     *d Verses 3, 4: cp. 2 Kgs. 15. 2, 3.*

farmers and vine-dressers in the hill-country and in the fertile lands, for he loved the soil.

Uzziah had an army of soldiers trained and ready for service, grouped 11 according to the census made by Jeiel the adjutant-general and Maaseiah the clerk under the direction of Hananiah, one of the king's commanders. The total number of heads of families which supplied seasoned warriors 12 was two thousand six hundred. Under their command was an army of 13 three hundred and seven thousand five hundred, a powerful fighting force to aid the king against his enemies. Uzziah prepared for the whole army 14 shields, spears, helmets, coats of mail, bows, and*a* sling-stones. In Jeru- 15 salem he had machines designed by engineers for use upon towers and bastions, made to discharge arrows and large stones. His fame spread far and wide, for he was so wonderfully gifted that he became very powerful.

But when he grew powerful his pride led to his own undoing:*b* he 16 offended against the LORD his God by entering the temple of the LORD to burn incense on the altar of incense. Azariah the priest and eighty others 17 of the LORD's priests, courageous men, went in after King Uzziah, con- 18 fronted him and said, 'It is not for you, Uzziah, to burn incense to the LORD, but for the Aaronite priests who have been consecrated for that office. Leave the sanctuary; for you have offended, and that will certainly bring you no honour from the LORD God.' The king, who had a censer in 19 his hand ready to burn incense, was indignant; and because of his indigna- tion at the priests, leprosy broke out on his forehead in the presence of the priests, there in the house of the LORD, beside the altar of incense. When 20 Azariah the chief priest and the other priests looked towards him, they saw that he had leprosy on his forehead and they hurried him out of the temple, and indeed he himself hastened to leave, because the LORD had struck him with the disease. And King Uzziah remained a leper till the day of his 21*c* death; he lived in his own house as a leper, relieved of all duties and excluded from the house of the LORD, while his son Jotham was comptroller of the household and regent. The other events of Uzziah's reign, from first 22 to last, are recorded by the prophet Isaiah son of Amoz. So he rested with 23 his forefathers and was buried in a burial-ground, but not that of the kings; for they said, 'He is a leper'; and he was succeeded by his son Jotham.

Jotham was twenty-five years old when he came to the throne, and he **27** 1*d* reigned in Jerusalem for sixteen years; his mother was Jerushah daughter of Zadok. He did what was right in the eyes of the LORD, as his father 2 Uzziah had done, but unlike him he did not enter the temple of the LORD; the people, however, continued their corrupt practices. He constructed 3 the upper gate of the house of the LORD and built extensively on the wall at Ophel. He built cities in the hill-country of Judah, and forts and towers 4 on the wooded hills. He made war on the king of the Ammonites and 5 defeated him; and that year the Ammonites gave him a hundred talents of silver, ten thousand kor of wheat and ten thousand of barley. They paid him the same tribute in the second and third years. Jotham became very 6

---

*a* *Prob. rdg.; Heb. adds for.*    *b* *his pride . . . undoing: or* he became so proud that he acted corruptly.    *c* *Verses 21–23: cp. 2 Kgs. 15. 5–7.*    *d* *Verses 1–3: cp. 2 Kgs. 15. 33–35.*

powerful because he maintained a steady course of obedience to the LORD
7 his God. The other events of Jotham's reign, all that he did in war and in
8 peace, are recorded in the annals of the kings of Israel and Judah. He was
twenty-five years old when he came to the throne, and he reigned in
9 Jerusalem for sixteen years. He rested with his forefathers and was buried
in the city of David; and he was succeeded by his son Ahaz.

28 1ᵃ AHAZ WAS TWENTY YEARS OLD when he came to the throne, and he
reigned in Jerusalem for sixteen years. He did not do what was right in the
2 eyes of the LORD like his forefather David, but followed in the footsteps of
3 the kings of Israel, and cast metal images for the Baalim. He also burnt
sacrifices in the Valley of Ben-hinnom; he even burnt his sons in the fire
according to the abominable practice of the nations whom the LORD had
4 dispossessed in favour of the Israelites. He slaughtered and burnt sacrifices
at the hill-shrines and on the hill-tops and under every spreading tree.

5    The LORD his God let him suffer at the hands of the king of Aram, and
the Aramaeans defeated him, took many captives and brought them to
Damascus; he was also made to suffer at the hands of the king of Israel,
6 who inflicted a severe defeat on him. This was Pekah son of Remaliah, who
killed in one day a hundred and twenty thousand men of Judah, seasoned
7 troops, because they had forsaken the LORD the God of their fathers. And
Zichri, an Ephraimite hero, killed Maaseiah the king's son ᵇ and Azrikam
the comptroller of the household and Elkanah the king's chief minister.
8 The Israelites took captive from their kinsmen two hundred thousand
women and children; they also took a large amount of booty and brought
it to Samaria.

9    A prophet of the LORD was there, Oded by name; he went out to meet
the army as it returned to Samaria and said to them, 'It is because the
LORD the God of your fathers is angry with Judah that he has given them
into your power; and you have massacred them in a rage that has towered
10 up to heaven. Now you propose to force the people of Judah and Jerusalem,
male and female, into slavery. Are not you also guilty men before the LORD
11 your God? Now, listen to me. Send back those you have taken captive from
12 your kinsmen, for the anger of the LORD is roused against you.' Next, some
Ephraimite chiefs, Azariah son of Jehohanan, Berechiah son of Meshillemoth, Hezekiahᶜ son of Shallum, and Amasa son of Hadlai, met those who
13 were returning from the war and said to them, 'You must not bring these
captives into our country; what you are proposing would make us guilty
before the LORD and add to our sins and transgressions. We are guilty
14 enough already, and there is fierce anger against Israel.' So the armed men
left the captives and the spoil with the officers and the assembled people.
15 The captives were put in charge of men nominated for this duty, who
found clothes from the spoil for all who were naked. They clothed them
and shod them, gave them food and drink, and anointed them; those who
were tottering from exhaustion they conveyed on the backs of asses, and
so brought them to their kinsmen in Jericho, in the Vale of Palm Trees.
Then they themselves returned to Samaria.

ᵃ *Verses 1–4: cp. 2 Kgs. 16. 2–4.*    ᵇ son: *or* deputy.    ᶜ *Or* Jehizkiah.

At that time King Ahaz sent to the king of Assyria for help. The Edom- 16 17
ites had invaded again and defeated Judah and taken away prisoners; and 18
the Philistines had raided the cities of the Shephelah and of the Negeb of
Judah and had captured Beth-shemesh, Aijalon, and Gederoth, as well as
Soco, Timnah, and Gimzo with their villages, and occupied them. The 19
LORD had reduced Judah to submission because of Ahaz king of Judah;
for his actions in Judah had been unbridled and he had been grossly unfaithful to the LORD. Then Tiglath-pileser king of Assyria marched against 20
him and, so far from assisting him, pressed him hard. Ahaz stripped the 21
house of the LORD, the king's palace and the houses of his officers, and gave
the plunder to the king of Assyria; but all to no purpose.

This King Ahaz, when hard pressed, became more and more unfaithful 22
to the LORD; he sacrificed to the gods of Damascus who had defeated him 23
and said, 'The gods of the kings of Aram helped them; I will sacrifice to
them so that they may help me.' But in fact they caused his downfall and
that of all Israel. Then Ahaz gathered together the vessels of the house of 24
God and broke them up, and shut the doors of the house of the LORD; he
made himself altars at every corner in Jerusalem, and at every single city 25
of Judah he made hill-shrines to burn sacrifices to other gods and provoked
the anger of the LORD the God of his fathers.

The other acts and all the events of his reign, from first to last, are 26*a*
recorded in the annals of the kings of Judah and Israel. So Ahaz rested with 27
his forefathers and was buried in the city of Jerusalem, but was not given
burial with the kings of Judah. He was succeeded by his son Hezekiah.

## *The kings of Judah from Hezekiah to the exile*

HEZEKIAH WAS TWENTY-FIVE YEARS OLD when he came to the 29 1*b*
throne, and he reigned in Jerusalem for twenty-nine years; his
mother was Abijah daughter of Zechariah. He did what was right in the 2
eyes of the LORD, as David his forefather had done.

In the first year of his reign, in the first month, he opened the gates of 3
the house of the LORD and repaired them. He brought in the priests and 4
the Levites and gathered them together in the square on the east side, and 5
said to them, 'Levites, listen to me. Hallow yourselves now, hallow the
house of the LORD the God of your fathers, and remove the pollution from
the sanctuary. For our forefathers were unfaithful and did what was wrong 6
in the eyes of the LORD our God: they forsook him, they would have nothing
to do with his dwelling-place, they turned their backs on it. They shut the 7
doors of the porch and extinguished the lamps, they ceased to burn incense
and offer whole-offerings in the sanctuary to the God of Israel. Therefore 8
the anger of the LORD fell upon Judah and Jerusalem and he made them
repugnant, an object of horror and derision, as you see for yourselves.
Hence it is that our fathers have fallen by the sword, our sons and daughters 9
and our wives are in captivity. Now I intend that we should pledge our- 10
selves to the LORD the God of Israel, in order that his anger may be averted

*a Verses 26, 27: cp. 2 Kgs. 16. 19, 20.*    *b Verses 1, 2: cp. 2 Kgs. 18. 1–3.*

11 from us. So, my sons, let no time be lost; for the LORD has chosen you to serve him and to minister to him, to be his ministers and to burn sacrifices.'

12 Then the Levites set to work—Mahath son of Amasai and Joel son of Azariah of the family of Kohath; of the family of Merari, Kish son of Abdi and Azariah son of Jehalelel; of the family of Gershon, Joah son of Zim-

13 mah and Eden son of Joah; of the family of Elizaphan, Shimri and Jeiel;

14 of the family of Asaph, Zechariah and Mattaniah; of the family of Heman, Jehiel and Shimei; and of the family of Jeduthun, Shemaiah and Uzziel.

15 They assembled their kinsmen and hallowed themselves, and then went in, as the king had instructed them at the LORD's command, to purify the

16 house of the LORD. The priests went inside to purify the house of the LORD; they removed all the pollution which they found in the temple into the court of the house of the LORD, and the Levites took it from them and

17 carried it outside to the gorge of the Kidron. They began the rites on the first day of the first month, and on the eighth day they reached the porch; then for eight days they consecrated the house of the LORD, and on the

18 sixteenth day of the first month they finished. Then they went into the palace and said to King Hezekiah, 'We have purified the whole of the house of the LORD, the altar of whole-offering with all its vessels, and the table

19 for the Bread of the Presence arranged in rows with all its vessels; and we have put in order and consecrated all the vessels which King Ahaz cast aside during his reign, when he was unfaithful. They are now in place before the altar of the LORD.'

20 Then King Hezekiah rose early, assembled the officers of the city and

21 went up to the house of the LORD. They brought seven bulls, seven rams, and seven lambs for the whole-offering,[a] and seven he-goats as a sin-offering for the kingdom, for the sanctuary, and for Judah; these he com-

22 manded the priests of Aaron's line to offer on the altar of the LORD. So the bulls were slaughtered, and the priests took their blood and flung it against the altar; the rams were slaughtered, and their blood was flung against the altar; the lambs were slaughtered, and their blood was flung against

23 the altar. Then the he-goats for the sin-offering were brought before the

24 king and the assembly, who laid their hands on them; and the priests slaughtered them and used their blood as a sin-offering on the altar to make expiation for all Israel. For the king had commanded that the whole-offering and the sin-offering should be made for all Israel.

25 He posted the Levites in the house of the LORD with cymbals, lutes, and harps, according to the rule prescribed by David, by Gad the king's seer and Nathan the prophet; for this rule had come from the LORD through

26 his prophets. The Levites stood ready with the instruments of David, and

27 the priests with the trumpets. Hezekiah gave the order that the whole-offering should be offered on the altar. At the moment when the whole-offering began, the song to the LORD began too, with the trumpets, led by

28 the instruments of David king of Israel. The whole assembly prostrated themselves, the singers sang and the trumpeters sounded; all this con-

29 tinued until the whole-offering was complete. When the offering was

[a] for the whole-offering: *prob. rdg.; Heb. om.*

complete, the king and all his company bowed down and prostrated themselves. And King Hezekiah and his officers commanded the Levites to 30 praise the LORD in the words of David and of Asaph the seer. So they praised him most joyfully and bowed down and prostrated themselves.

Then Hezekiah said, 'You have now given to the LORD with open hands; 31 approach with your sacrifices and thank-offerings for the house of the LORD.' So the assembly brought sacrifices and thank-offerings; and every man of willing spirit brought whole-offerings. The number of whole- 32 offerings which the assembly brought was seventy bulls, a hundred rams, and two hundred lambs; all these made a whole-offering to the LORD. And 33 the consecrated offerings were six hundred bulls and three thousand sheep. But the priests were too few and could not flay all the whole-offerings; so 34 their colleagues the Levites helped them until the work was completed and all the priests had hallowed themselves—for the Levites had been more scrupulous than the priests in hallowing themselves. There were 35 indeed whole-offerings in abundance, besides the fat of the shared-offerings and the drink-offerings for the whole-offerings. In this way the service of the house of the LORD was restored; and Hezekiah and all the 36 people rejoiced over what God had done for the people and because it had come about so suddenly.

Then Hezekiah sent word to all Israel and Judah, and also wrote letters **30** to Ephraim and Manasseh, inviting them to come to the house of the LORD in Jerusalem to keep the Passover of the LORD the God of Israel. The king 2 and his officers and all the assembly in Jerusalem had agreed to keep the Passover in the second month, but they had not been able to keep it at that 3 time, because not enough priests had hallowed themselves and the people had not assembled in Jerusalem. The proposal was acceptable to the king 4 and the whole assembly. So they resolved to make a proclamation through- 5 out all Israel, from Beersheba to Dan, that the people should come to Jerusalem to keep the Passover of the LORD the God of Israel. Never before had so many kept it according to the prescribed form. Couriers went 6 throughout all Israel and Judah with letters from the king and his officers, proclaiming the royal command: 'Turn back, men of Israel, to the LORD the God of Abraham, Isaac, and Israel, so that he may turn back to those of you who escaped capture by the kings of Assyria. Do not be like your 7 forefathers and your kinsmen, who were unfaithful to the LORD the God of their fathers, so that he made them an object of horror, as you yourselves saw. Do not be stubborn as your forefathers were; submit yourselves to 8 the LORD and enter his sanctuary which he has sanctified for ever, and worship the LORD your God, so that his anger may be averted from you. For when you turn back to the LORD, your kinsmen and your children will 9 win compassion from their captors and return to this land. The LORD your God is gracious and compassionate, and he will not turn away from you if you turn back to him.'

So the couriers passed from city to city through the land of Ephraim and 10 Manasseh and as far as Zebulun, but they were treated with scorn and ridicule. However, a few men of Asher, Manasseh, and Zebulun submitted 11 and came to Jerusalem. Further, the hand of God moved the people in 12

Judah with one accord to carry out what the king and his officers had ordered at the LORD's command.

13 Many people, a very great assembly, came together in Jerusalem to
14 keep the pilgrim-feast of Unleavened Bread in the second month. They began by removing the altars in Jerusalem; they removed the altars for
15 burning sacrifices and threw them into the gorge of the Kidron. They killed the passover lamb on the fourteenth day of the second month; and the priests and the Levites were bitterly ashamed. They hallowed
16 themselves and brought whole-offerings to the house of the LORD. They took their accustomed places, according to the direction laid down for them in the law of Moses the man of God; the priests flung against the
17 altar the blood which they received from the Levites. But many in the assembly had not hallowed themselves; therefore the Levites had to kill the passover lamb for every one who was unclean, in order to hallow him
18 to the LORD. For a majority of the people, many from Ephraim, Manasseh, Issachar, and Zebulun, had not kept themselves ritually clean, and therefore kept the Passover irregularly. But Hezekiah prayed for them, saying,
19 'May the good LORD grant pardon to every one who makes a practice of seeking guidance of God, the LORD the God of his fathers, even if he has
20 not observed the rules for the purification of the sanctuary.' The LORD
21 heard Hezekiah and healed the people. And the Israelites who were present in Jerusalem kept the feast of Unleavened Bread for seven days with great rejoicing, and the Levites and the priests praised the LORD every day with
22 unrestrained fervour.[a] Hezekiah spoke encouragingly to all the Levites who had shown true understanding in the service of the LORD. So they spent the seven days of the festival sacrificing shared-offerings and making confession to[b] the LORD the God of their fathers.

23 Then the whole assembly agreed to keep the feast for another seven days;
24 so they kept it for another seven days with general rejoicing. For Hezekiah king of Judah set aside for the assembly a thousand bulls and seven thousand sheep, and his officers set aside for the assembly a thousand bulls and ten
25 thousand sheep; and priests hallowed themselves in great numbers. So the whole assembly of Judah, including the priests and the Levites, rejoiced, together with all the assembly which came out of Israel, and the
26 resident aliens from Israel and those who lived in Judah. There was great rejoicing in Jerusalem, the like of which had not been known there since
27 the days of Solomon son of David king of Israel. Then the priests and the Levites stood to bless the people; the LORD listened to their cry, and their prayer came to God's holy dwelling-place in heaven.

31 When this was over, all the Israelites present went out to the cities of Judah and smashed the sacred pillars, hacked down the sacred poles and broke up the hill-shrines and the altars throughout Judah and Benjamin, Ephraim and Manasseh, until they had made an end of them. That done, the Israelites returned, each to his own patrimony in his own city.

2 Then Hezekiah installed the priests and the Levites in office, division by division, allotting to each priest or Levite his own particular duty, for

---

[a] with unrestrained fervour: *prob. rdg.; Heb.* with powerful instruments.    [b] making confession to: *or* confessing.

whole-offerings or shared-offerings, to give thanks or to sing praise, or to serve in the gates of the several quarters in the LORD's house.

The king provided from his own resources, as the share due from him, 3 the whole-offerings for both morning and evening, and for sabbaths, new moons, and appointed seasons, as prescribed in the law of the LORD. He 4 ordered the people living in Jerusalem to provide the share due from the priests and the Levites, so that they might devote themselves entirely to the law of the LORD. As soon as the king's order was issued to the Israelites, 5 they gave generously from the firstfruits of their corn and new wine, oil and honey, all the produce of their land; they brought a full tithe of everything. The Israelites and the Judaeans living in the cities of Judah also 6 brought a tithe of cattle and sheep, and a tithe of all produce as offerings dedicated to the LORD their God, and they stacked the produce in heaps. They began to deposit the heaps in the third month and completed them 7 in the seventh. When Hezekiah and his officers came and saw the heaps, 8 they blessed the LORD and his people Israel. Hezekiah asked the priests 9 and the Levites about these heaps, and Azariah the chief priest, who was 10 of the line of Zadok, answered, 'From the time when the people began to bring their contribution into the house of the LORD, they have had enough to eat, enough and to spare; indeed, the LORD has so greatly blessed them that they have this great store left over.'

Then Hezekiah ordered store-rooms to be prepared in the house of the 11 LORD, and this was done; and the people honestly brought in their con- 12 tributions, the tithe, and their dedicated gifts. The overseer in charge of them was Conaniah the Levite, with Shimei his brother as his deputy; Jehiel, Azaziah, Nahath, Asahel, Jerimoth, Jozabad, Eliel, Ismachiah, 13 Mahath, and Benaiah were appointed by King Hezekiah and Azariah, the chief overseer of the house of God, to assist Conaniah and Shimei his brother. And Kore son of Imnah the Levite, keeper of the East Gate, was 14 in charge of the freewill offerings to God, to apportion the contributions made to the LORD and the most sacred offerings. Eden, Miniamin, Jeshua, 15 Shemaiah, Amariah, and Shecaniah in the priestly cities assisted him in the fair distribution of portions to their kinsmen, young and old *a* alike, by divisions. Irrespective of their registration, shares were distributed to 16 all males three years of age and upwards who entered the house of the LORD to take their daily part in the service, according to their divisions, as their office demanded. The priests were registered by families, the Levites from 17 twenty years of age and upwards by their offices in their divisions. They 18 were registered with all their dependants, their wives, their sons, and their daughters, the whole company of them, because in virtue of their permanent standing they had to keep themselves duly hallowed. As for the 19 priests of Aaron's line in the common lands attached to their cities, in every city men were nominated to distribute portions to every male among the priests and to every one who was registered with the Levites.

Such was the action taken by Hezekiah throughout Judah; he did what 20 was good and right and loyal in the sight of the LORD his God. Whatever 21 he undertook in the service of the house of God and in obedience to the

*a* *Or* high and low.

law and the commandment to seek guidance of his God, he did with all his heart, and he prospered.

**32** 1 After these events and this example of loyal conduct, Sennacherib king of Assyria invaded Judah and encamped against the fortified cities, believ-
2 ing that he could attach them to himself. When Hezekiah saw that he had
3 come and was determined to attack Jerusalem, he consulted his civil and military officers about blocking up the springs outside the city; and they
4 encouraged him. They gathered together a large number of people and blocked up all the springs and the stream which flowed through the land. 'Why', they said, 'should Assyrian kings come here and find plenty of
5 water?' Then the king acted boldly; he made good every breach in the city wall and erected towers on it; he built another wall outside it and strengthened the Millo of the city of David; he also collected a great
6 quantity of weapons and shields. He appointed military commanders over the people and assembled them in the square by the city gate and spoke
7 encouragingly to them in these words: 'Be strong; be brave. Do not let the king of Assyria or the rabble he has brought with him strike terror or
8 panic into your hearts. We have more on our side than he has. He has human strength; but we have the LORD our God to help us and to fight our battles.' So spoke Hezekiah king of Judah, and the people were buoyed up by his words.

9 After this, Sennacherib king of Assyria, while he and his high command were at Lachish, sent envoys to Jerusalem to deliver this message to
10 Hezekiah king of Judah and to all the Judaeans in Jerusalem: 'Sennacherib king of Assyria says, "What gives you confidence to stay in Jerusalem under
11 siege? Hezekiah is misleading you into risking death by famine or thirst where you are, when he tells you that the LORD your God will save you
12 from the grip of the Assyrian king. Was it not Hezekiah himself who suppressed the LORD's hill-shrines and altars and told the people of Judah and Jerusalem that they must prostrate themselves before one altar only and
13 burn sacrifices there? You know very well what I and my forefathers have done to all the peoples of the lands. Were the gods of these nations able to
14 save their lands from me? Not one of the gods of these nations, which my forefathers exterminated, was able to save his people from me. Much less
15 will your god save you! How, then, can Hezekiah deceive you or mislead you like this? How can you believe him, for no god of any nation or kingdom has been able to save his people from me or my forefathers? Much less will your gods save you!"'

16 The envoys of Sennacherib spoke still more against the LORD God and
17 against his servant Hezekiah. And the king himself wrote a letter to defy the LORD the God of Israel, in these terms: 'Just as the gods of other nations could not save their people from me, so the god of Hezekiah will
18 not save his people from me.' Then they shouted in Hebrew at the top of their voices at the people of Jerusalem on the wall, to strike them with fear
19 and terror, hoping thus to capture the city. They described the god *b* of Jerusalem as being like the gods of the other peoples of the earth—things made by the hands of men.

*a Verses 1–19: cp. 2 Kgs. 18. 13–37; Isa. 36. 1–22.*      *b Or gods.*

In this plight King Hezekiah and the prophet Isaiah son of Amoz cried 20 *a*
to heaven in prayer. So the LORD sent an angel who cut down all the fighting 21
men, as well as the leaders and the commanders, in the camp of the king
of Assyria, so that he went home disgraced to his own land. When he
entered the temple of his god, certain of his own sons struck him down
with their swords.

Thus the LORD saved Hezekiah and the inhabitants of Jerusalem from 22
Sennacherib king of Assyria and all their enemies; and he gave them respite
on every side. Many people brought to Jerusalem offerings for the LORD 23
and costly gifts for Hezekiah king of Judah. From then on he was held in
high honour by all the nations.

About this time Hezekiah fell dangerously ill and prayed to the LORD; 24
the LORD said, 'I will heal you', *b* and granted him a sign. But, being a 25
proud man, he was not grateful for the good done to him, and Judah and
Jerusalem suffered for it. Then, proud as he was, Hezekiah submitted, 26
and the people of Jerusalem with him, and the LORD's anger did not fall
on them again in Hezekiah's time.

Hezekiah enjoyed great wealth and fame. *c* He built for himself treasuries 27
for silver and gold, precious stones and spices, shields and other costly
things; and barns for the harvests of corn, new wine, and oil; and stalls for 28
every kind of cattle, as well as sheepfolds. He amassed *d* a great many 29
flocks and herds; God had indeed given him vast riches. It was this same 30
Hezekiah who blocked the upper outflow of the waters of Gihon and
directed them downwards and westwards to the city of David. In fact,
Hezekiah was successful in everything he attempted, even in the affair of 31
the envoys sent by the king *e* of Babylon—the envoys who came to inquire
about the portent which had been seen in the land at the time when God
left him to himself, to test him and to discover all that was in his heart.

The other events of Hezekiah's reign, and his works of piety, are re- 32
corded in the vision of the prophet Isaiah son of Amoz and in the annals of
the kings of Judah and Israel. So Hezekiah rested with his forefathers and 33
was buried in the uppermost of the graves of David's sons; all Judah and
the people of Jerusalem paid him honour when he died, and he was
succeeded by his son Manasseh.

MANASSEH WAS TWELVE YEARS OLD when he came to the throne, and 33 1 *f*
he reigned in Jerusalem for fifty-five years. He did what was wrong in the 2
eyes of the LORD, in following the abominable practices of the nations
which the LORD had dispossessed in favour of the Israelites. He rebuilt the 3
hill-shrines which his father Hezekiah had dismantled, he erected altars
to the Baalim and made sacred poles, he prostrated himself before all
the host of heaven and worshipped them. He built altars in the house of the 4
LORD, that house of which the LORD had said, 'In Jerusalem shall my Name
be for ever.' He built altars for all the host of heaven in the two courts of the 5
house of the LORD; he made his sons pass through the fire in the Valley 6

---

*a* Verses 20–22: cp. 2 Kgs. 19. 1–37; Isa. 37. 1–38.     *b* I will heal you: *prob. rdg.*,
cp. 2 Kgs. 20. 5; Heb. om.     *c* Or riches.     *d* Prob. rdg.; Heb. adds cities.
*e* Prob. rdg., cp. 2 Kgs. 20. 12; Heb. officers.     *f* Verses 1–9: cp. 2 Kgs. 21. 1–9.

of Ben-hinnom, he practised soothsaying, divination, and sorcery, and dealt with ghosts and spirits. He did much wrong in the eyes of the LORD

7 and provoked his anger; and the image that he had had carved in relief he put in the house of God, the place of which God had said to David and Solomon his son, 'This house and Jerusalem, which I chose out of all the

8 tribes of Israel, shall receive my Name for all time. I will not again displace Israel from the land which I assigned to their forefathers, if only they will be careful to observe all that I commanded them through Moses, all

9 the law, the statutes, and the rules.' But Manasseh misled Judah and the inhabitants of Jerusalem into wickedness far worse than that of the nations which the LORD had exterminated in favour of the Israelites.

10   The LORD spoke to Manasseh and to his people, but they paid no heed.

11 So the LORD brought against them the commanders of the army of the king of Assyria; they captured Manasseh with spiked weapons, and bound

12 him with fetters, and brought him to Babylon. In his distress he prayed to the LORD his God and sought to placate him, and made his humble sub-

13 mission before the God of his fathers. He prayed, and God accepted his petition and heard his supplication. He brought him back to Jerusalem and restored him to the throne; and thus Manasseh learnt that the LORD was God.

14   After this he built an outer wall for the city of David, west of Gihon in the gorge, and extended it to the entrance by the Fish Gate, enclosing Ophel; and he raised it to a great height. He also put military commanders

15 in all the fortified cities of Judah. He removed the foreign gods and the carved image from the house of the LORD and all the altars which he had built on the temple mount and in Jerusalem, and threw them out of the

16 city. Moreover, he repaired the altar of the LORD and sacrificed at it shared-offerings and thank-offerings, and commanded Judah to serve the LORD

17 the God of Israel. But the people still continued to sacrifice at the hill-shrines, though only to the LORD their God.

18   The rest of the acts of Manasseh, his prayer to his God, and the discourses of the seers who spoke to him in the name of the LORD the God of

19 Israel, are recorded in the chronicles of the kings of Israel. His prayer and the answer he received to it, and all his sin and unfaithfulness, and the places where he built hill-shrines and set up sacred poles and carved idols,

20 before he submitted, are recorded in the chronicles of the seers. So Manasseh rested with his forefathers and was buried in the garden-tomb of*a* his family; he was succeeded by his son Amon.

21*b*   Amon was twenty-two years old when he came to the throne, and he

22 reigned in Jerusalem for two years. He did what was wrong in the eyes of the LORD as his father Manasseh had done. He sacrificed to all the images

23 that his father Manasseh had made, and worshipped them. He was not submissive before the LORD like his father Manasseh; his guilt was much

24 greater. His courtiers conspired against him and murdered him in his

25 house; but the people of the land killed all the conspirators and made his son Josiah king in his place.

*a* the garden-tomb of: *prob. rdg., cp. 2 Kgs. 21. 18; Heb. om.*     *b Verses 21–25: cp. 2 Kgs. 21. 19–24.*

JOSIAH WAS EIGHT YEARS OLD when he came to the throne, and he **34** 1<sup>a</sup>
reigned in Jerusalem for thirty-one years. He did what was right in the 2
eyes of the LORD; he followed in the footsteps of his forefather David,
swerving neither right nor left. In the eighth year of his reign, when he was 3
still a boy, he began to seek guidance of the God of his forefather David;
and in the twelfth year he began to purge Judah and Jerusalem of the hill-
shrines and the sacred poles, and the carved idols and the images of metal.
He saw to it that the altars for the Baalim were destroyed and he hacked 4
down the incense-altars which stood above them; he broke in pieces the
sacred poles and the carved and metal images, grinding them to powder
and scattering it on the graves of those who had sacrificed to them. He also 5
burnt the bones of the priests on their altars and purged Judah and Jerusalem. In the cities of Manasseh, Ephraim, and Simeon, and as far as 6
Naphtali, he burnt down their houses wherever he found them; he de- 7
stroyed the altars and the sacred poles, ground the idols to powder, and
hacked down the incense-altars throughout the land of Israel. Then he
returned to Jerusalem.

In the eighteenth year of his reign, after he had purified the land and 8<sup>b</sup>
the house, he sent Shaphan son of Azaliah and Maaseiah the governor of
the city and Joah son of Joahaz the secretary of state to repair the house
of the LORD his God. They came to Hilkiah the high priest and gave him 9
the silver that had been brought to the house of God, the silver which the
Levites, on duty at the threshold, had gathered from Manasseh, Ephraim,
and all the rest of Israel, as well as from Judah and Benjamin and the
inhabitants of Jerusalem. It was then handed over to the foremen in 10
charge of the work in the house of the LORD, and these men, working in the
house, used it for repairing and strengthening the fabric; they gave it also 11
to the carpenters and builders to buy hewn stone, and timber for rafters
and beams, for the buildings which the kings of Judah had allowed to fall
into ruin. The men did their work honestly under the direction of Jahath 12-13
and Obadiah, Levites of the line of Merari, and Zechariah and Meshullam,
members of the family of Kohath. These also had control of the porters
and directed the workmen of every trade. The Levites were all skilled
musicians, and some of them were secretaries, clerks, or door-keepers.
When they fetched the silver which had been brought to the house of the 14
LORD, the priest Hilkiah discovered the book of the law of the LORD which
had been given through Moses. Then Hilkiah told Shaphan the adjutant- 15
general, 'I have discovered the book of the law in the house of the LORD.'
Hilkiah gave the book to Shaphan, and he brought it to the king and reported 16
to him: 'Your servants are doing all that was entrusted to them. They have 17
melted down the silver in the house of the LORD and have handed it over
to the foremen and the workmen.' Shaphan the adjutant-general also told 18
the king that the priest Hilkiah had given him a book; and he read it out
in the king's presence. When the king heard what was in the book of the 19
law, he rent his clothes, and ordered Hilkiah, Ahikam son of Shaphan, 20
Abdon son of Micah, Shaphan the adjutant-general, and Asaiah the king's
attendant, to go and seek guidance of the LORD, for himself and for all who 21

<sup>a</sup> *Verses 1, 2: cp. 2 Kgs. 22. 1, 2.*     <sup>b</sup> *Verses 8–32: cp. 2 Kgs. 22. 3—23. 3.*

still remained in Israel and Judah, about the contents of the book that had been discovered. 'Great is the wrath of the LORD,' he said, 'and it has been poured out upon us because our forefathers did not observe the command of the LORD and do all that is written in this book.'

22 So Hilkiah and those whom the king had instructed went to Huldah the prophetess, wife of Shallum son of Tikvah,*a* son of Hasrah, the keeper of the wardrobe, and consulted her at her home in the second quarter of
23 Jerusalem. 'This is the word of the LORD the God of Israel,' she answered:
24 'Say to the man who sent you to me, "This is the word of the LORD: I am bringing disaster on this place and its inhabitants, fulfilling all the imprecations recorded in the book which was read in the presence of the king of
25 Judah, because they have forsaken me and burnt sacrifices to other gods, provoking my anger with all the idols they have made with their own hands; therefore my wrath is poured out upon this place and will not be quenched."
26 This is what you shall say to the king of Judah who sent you to seek guidance of the LORD: "This is the word of the LORD the God of Israel: You
27 have listened to my words and shown a willing heart, you humbled yourself before God when you heard what I said about this place and its inhabitants; you humbled yourself and rent your clothes and wept before me. Because of all this,*b* I for my part have heard you. This is the very word
28 of the LORD. Therefore, I will gather you to your forefathers, and you will be gathered to your grave in peace; you will not live to see all the disaster which I am bringing upon this place and upon its inhabitants."' So they brought back word to the king.

29 Then the king sent and called all the elders of Judah and Jerusalem
30 together, and went up to the house of the LORD; he took with him all the men of Judah and the inhabitants of Jerusalem, the priests and the Levites, the whole population, high and low. There he read them the whole book
31 of the covenant discovered in the house of the LORD; and then, standing on the dais, the king made a covenant before the LORD to obey him and keep his commandments, his testimonies, and his statutes, with all his heart and soul, and so fulfil the terms of the covenant written in this book.
32 Then he swore an oath with all who were present in Jerusalem to keep the covenant.*c* Thereafter the inhabitants of Jerusalem did obey the covenant
33 of God, the God of their fathers. Josiah removed all abominable things from all the territories of the Israelites, so that everyone living in Israel might serve the LORD his God. As long as he lived they did not fail in their allegiance to the LORD the God of their fathers.

35 Josiah kept a Passover to the LORD in Jerusalem, and the passover lamb
2 was killed on the fourteenth day of the first month. He appointed the priests to their offices and encouraged them to perform the service of the
3 house of the LORD. He said to the Levites, the teachers of Israel, who were dedicated to the LORD, 'Put the holy Ark in the house which Solomon son of David king of Israel built; it is not to be carried about on your shoulders.
4 Now is the time to serve the LORD your God and his people Israel: prepare yourselves by families according to your divisions, following the written

---

*a* *Prob. rdg., cp. 2 Kgs. 22. 14; Heb.* Tokhath.      *b* Because of all this: *prob. rdg.;*
*Heb. om.*      *c* to keep the covenant: *prob. rdg., cp. 2 Kgs. 23. 3; Heb.* and Benjamin.

instructions of David king of Israel and those of Solomon his son; and 5 stand in the Holy Place as representatives of the family groups of the lay people, your brothers, one division of Levites to each family group. Kill 6 the passover lamb and hallow yourselves and prepare for your brothers to fulfil the word of the LORD given through Moses.'

Josiah contributed on behalf of all the lay people present thirty thousand 7 small cattle, that is young rams and goats, for the Passover, in addition to three thousand bulls; all these were from the king's own resources. And 8 his officers contributed willingly for the people, the priests, and the Levites. Hilkiah, Zechariah, and Jehiel, the chief officers of the house of God, gave on behalf of the priests two thousand six hundred small cattle for the Passover, in addition to three hundred bulls. And Conaniah, Shemaiah 9 and Nethaneel his brothers, and Hashabiah, Jeiel, and Jozabad, the chiefs of the Levites, gave on behalf of the Levites for the Passover five thousand small cattle in addition to five hundred bulls.

When the service had been arranged, the priests stood in their places 10 and the Levites in their divisions, according to the king's command. They 11 killed the passover victim, and the priests flung the blood against the altar as the Levites flayed the animals. Then they removed the fat flesh,*a* which 12 they allocated to the people by groups of families for them to offer to the LORD, as prescribed in the book of Moses; and so with the bulls. They 13 cooked the passover victim over the fire according to custom, and boiled the holy offerings in pots, cauldrons, and pans, and served them quickly to all the people. After that they made the necessary preparations for 14 themselves and the priests, because the priests of Aaron's line were engaged till nightfall in offering whole-offerings and the fat portions; so the Levites made the necessary preparations for themselves and for the priests of Aaron's line. The singers, the sons of Asaph, were in their places according 15 to the rules laid down by David and by Asaph, Heman, and Jeduthun, the king's seers. The door-keepers stood, each at his gate; there was no need for them to leave their posts, because their kinsmen the Levites had made the preparations for them.

In this manner all the service of the LORD was arranged that day, to keep 16 the Passover and to offer whole-offerings on the altar of the LORD, accord- ing to the command of King Josiah. The people of Israel who were present 17 kept the Passover at that time and the pilgrim-feast of Unleavened Bread for seven days. No Passover like it had been kept in Israel since the days 18 of the prophet Samuel; none of the kings of Israel had ever kept such a Passover as Josiah kept, with the priests and Levites and all Judah and Israel who were present and the inhabitants of Jerusalem. In the eighteenth 19 year of Josiah's reign this Passover was kept.

After Josiah had thus organized all the service of the house, Necho 20 king of Egypt marched up to attack Carchemish on the Euphrates; and Josiah went out to confront him. But Necho sent envoys to him, saying, 21 'What do you want with me, king of Judah? I have no quarrel with you today, only with those with whom I am at war. God has purposed to speed me on my way, and God is on my side; do not stand in his way, or he will

*a* fat flesh: *or* whole-offering.

22 destroy you.' Josiah would not be deflected from his purpose but insisted on fighting; he refused to listen to Necho's words spoken at God's com-
23 mand, and he sallied out to join battle in the vale of Megiddo. The archers shot at him; he was severely wounded and told his bodyguard to carry him
24 off. They lifted him out of his chariot and carried him in his viceroy's chariot to Jerusalem. There he died and was buried among the tombs of
25 his ancestors, and all Judah and Jerusalem mourned for him. Jeremiah also made a lament for Josiah; and to this day the minstrels, both men and women, commemorate Josiah in their lamentations. Such laments have become traditional in Israel, and they are found in the written collections.
26 The other events of Josiah's reign, and his works of piety, all performed
27 in accordance with what is laid down in the law of the LORD, and his acts, from first to last, are recorded in the annals of the kings of Israel and Judah.

36 1*a* THE PEOPLE OF THE LAND took Josiah's son Jehoahaz and made him
2 king in place of his father in Jerusalem. He was twenty-three years old when he came to the throne, and he reigned in Jerusalem for three months.
3 Then Necho king of Egypt deposed him and fined the country a hundred
4 talents of silver and one talent of gold, and made his brother Eliakim king over Judah and Jerusalem in his place, changing his name to Jehoiakim;
5 he also carried away his brother Jehoahaz to Egypt. Jehoiakim was twenty-five years old when he came to the throne, and he reigned in Jerusalem for
6 eleven years. He did what was wrong in the eyes of the LORD his God. So Nebuchadnezzar king of Babylon marched against him and put him in
7 fetters and took him to Babylon. He also removed to Babylon some of the vessels of the house of the LORD and put them into his own palace there.
8 The other events of Jehoiakim's reign, including the abominations he committed, and everything of which he was held guilty, are recorded in the annals of the kings of Israel and Judah. He was succeeded by his son Jehoiachin.
9*b* Jehoiachin was eight years old when he came to the throne, and he reigned in Jerusalem for three months and ten days. He did what was
10 wrong in the eyes of the LORD. At the turn of the year King Nebuchadnezzar sent and brought him to Babylon, together with the choicest vessels of the house of the LORD, and made his father's brother Zedekiah king over Judah and Jerusalem.
11 Zedekiah was twenty-one years old when he came to the throne, and he
12 reigned in Jerusalem for eleven years. He did what was wrong in the eyes of the LORD his God; he did not defer to the guidance of the prophet
13 Jeremiah, the spokesman of the LORD. He also rebelled against King Nebuchadnezzar, who had laid on him a solemn oath of allegiance. He was obstinate and stubborn and refused to return to the LORD the God of
14 Israel. All the chiefs of Judah and the priests and the people became more and more unfaithful, following all the abominable practices of the other nations; and they defiled the house of the LORD which he had hallowed in
15 Jerusalem. The LORD God of their fathers had warned them betimes

*a Verses 1–4: cp. 2 Kgs. 23. 30–34.*   *b Verses 9, 10: cp. 2 Kgs. 24. 8–17.*

through his messengers, for he took pity on his people and on his dwelling-
place; but they never ceased to deride his messengers, scorn his words and　16
scoff at his prophets, until the anger of the LORD burst out against his
people and could not be appeased. So he brought against them the king of　17[a]
the Chaldaeans, who put their young men to the sword in the sanctuary
and spared neither young man nor maiden, neither the old nor the weak;
God gave them all into his power. And he brought all the vessels of the　18
house of God, great and small, and the treasures of the house of the LORD
and of the king and his officers—all these he brought to Babylon. And they　19
burnt down the house of God, razed the city wall of Jerusalem and burnt
down all its stately mansions and all their precious possessions until everything was destroyed. Those who escaped the sword he took captive to　20
Babylon, and they became slaves to him and his sons until the sovereignty
passed to the Persians, while the land of Israel ran the full term of its　21
sabbaths. All the time that it lay desolate it kept the sabbath rest, to complete seventy years in fulfilment of the word of the LORD by the prophet
Jeremiah.

Now in the first year of Cyrus king of Persia, so that the word of the LORD　22[b]
spoken through Jeremiah might be fulfilled, the LORD stirred up the heart
of Cyrus king of Persia; and he issued a proclamation throughout his kingdom, both by word of mouth and in writing, to this effect:

This is the word of Cyrus king of Persia: The LORD the God of heaven　23
has given me all the kingdoms of the earth, and he himself has charged
me to build him a house at Jerusalem in Judah. To every man of his
people now among you I say, the LORD his God be[c] with him, and let
him go up.

# THE BOOK OF

# EZRA

## *The return of the exiles to Jerusalem*

NOW IN THE FIRST YEAR OF CYRUS king of Persia,　1
so that the word of the LORD spoken through Jeremiah might be
fulfilled, the LORD stirred up the heart of Cyrus king of Persia;
and he issued a proclamation throughout his kingdom, both by word of
mouth and in writing, to this effect:

This is the word of Cyrus king of Persia: The LORD the God of heaven　2
has given me all the kingdoms of the earth, and he himself has charged
me to build him a house at Jerusalem in Judah. To every man of his　3

---

[a] *Verses 17-20: cp. 2 Kgs. 25. 1-17.*　　　　[b] *Verses 22, 23: cp. Ezra 1. 1-3.*
[c] be: *prob. rdg., cp. Ezra 1. 3; Heb. om.*

people now among you I say, God be with him, and let him go up to Jerusalem in Judah, and rebuild the house of the LORD the God of
4 Israel, the God whose city is Jerusalem. And every remaining Jew, wherever he may be living, may claim aid from his neighbours in that place, silver and gold, goods*a* and cattle, in addition to the voluntary offerings for the house of God in Jerusalem.

5 Thereupon the heads of families of Judah and Benjamin, and the priests and the Levites, answered the summons, all whom God had moved to go
6 up to rebuild the house of the LORD in Jerusalem. Their neighbours all assisted them with gifts of every kind, silver*b* and gold, goods*a* and cattle and valuable gifts in abundance,*c* in addition to any voluntary service.
7 Moreover, Cyrus king of Persia produced the vessels of the house of the LORD which Nebuchadnezzar had removed from Jerusalem and placed in
8 the temple of his god; and he handed them over into the charge of Mithredath the treasurer, who made an inventory of them for Sheshbazzar the
9 ruler of Judah. This was the list: thirty gold basins, a thousand silver basins,
10 twenty-nine vessels of various kinds, thirty golden bowls, four hundred
11 and ten silver bowls of various types, and a thousand other vessels. The vessels of gold and silver amounted in all to five thousand four hundred; and Sheshbazzar took them all up to Jerusalem, when the exiles were brought back from Babylon.

2 1*d* Of the captives whom Nebuchadnezzar king of Babylon had taken into exile in Babylon, these were the people of the province who returned to
2 Jerusalem and Judah, each to his own city, led by Zerubbabel, Jeshua,*e* Nehemiah, Seraiah, Reelaiah, Mordecai, Bilshan, Mispar, Bigvai, Rehum and Baanah.
3 The roll of the men of the people of Israel: the family of Parosh, two
4 thousand one hundred and seventy-two; the family of Shephatiah, three
5 hundred and seventy-two; the family of Arah, seven hundred and seventy-
6 five; the family of Pahath-moab, namely the families of Jeshua and*f* Joab,
7 two thousand eight hundred and twelve; the family of Elam, one thousand
8 two hundred and fifty-four; the family of Zattu, nine hundred and forty-
9 10 five; the family of Zaccai, seven hundred and sixty; the family of Bani, six
11 hundred and forty-two; the family of Bebai, six hundred and twenty-three;
12 13 the family of Azgad, one thousand two hundred and twenty-two; the
14 family of Adonikam, six hundred and sixty-six; the family of Bigvai, two
15 thousand and fifty-six; the family of Adin, four hundred and fifty-four;
16 17 the family of Ater, namely that of Hezekiah, ninety-eight; the family of
18 Bezai, three hundred and twenty-three; the family of Jorah, one hundred
19 20 and twelve; the family of Hashum, two hundred and twenty-three; the
21 family of Gibbar, ninety-five. The men*g* of Bethlehem, one hundred and
22 23 twenty-three; the men of Netophah, fifty-six; the men of Anathoth, one
24 25 hundred and twenty-eight; the men of Beth-azmoth,*h* forty-two; the men

*a* Or pack-animals.     *b* with gifts . . . silver: *prob. rdg., cp. 1 Esdras 2. 9; Heb.* with vessels of silver.     *c* in abundance: *prob. rdg., cp. 1 Esdras 2. 9; Heb.* apart. *d* Verses 1–70: cp. Neh. 7. 6–73.     *e* Or Joshua (cp. Hag. 1. 1).     *f* and: *prob. rdg., cp. Neh. 7. 11; Heb. om.*     *g* Prob. rdg., cp. Neh. 7. 26; Heb.* family.     *h* Prob. rdg., cp. Neh. 7. 28; Heb.* the family of Azmoth.

of Kiriath-jearim,[a] Kephirah, and Beeroth, seven hundred and forty-
three; the men[b] of Ramah and Geba, six hundred and twenty-one; the    26 27
men of Michmas, one hundred and twenty-two; the men of Bethel and Ai,    28
two hundred and twenty-three; the men[c] of Nebo, fifty-two; the men of   29 30
Magbish, one hundred and fifty-six; the men of the other Elam, one        31
thousand two hundred and fifty-four; the men of Harim, three hundred      32
and twenty; the men of Lod, Hadid, and Ono, seven hundred and twenty-     33
five; the men of Jericho, three hundred and forty-five; the men of Senaah, 34 35
three thousand six hundred and thirty.

Priests: the family of Jedaiah, of the line of Jeshua, nine hundred and   36
seventy-three; the family of Immer, one thousand and fifty-two; the       37 38
family of Pashhur, one thousand two hundred and forty-seven; the family   39
of Harim, one thousand and seventeen.

Levites: the families of Jeshua and Kadmiel, of the line of Hodaviah,     40
seventy-four. Singers: the family of Asaph, one hundred and twenty-eight. 41
The guild of door-keepers: the family of Shallum, the family of Ater, the 42
family of Talmon, the family of Akkub, the family of Hatita, and the family
of Shobai, one hundred and thirty-nine in all.

Temple-servitors: the family of Ziha, the family of Hasupha, the family   43
of Tabbaoth, the family of Keros, the family of Siaha, the family of Padon, 44
the family of Lebanah, the family of Hagabah, the family of Akkub, the    45 46
family of Hagab, the family of Shamlai,[d] the family of Hanan, the family 47
of Giddel, the family of Gahar, the family of Reaiah, the family of Rezin, 48
the family of Nekoda, the family of Gazzam, the family of Uzza, the family 49
of Paseah, the family of Besai, the family of Asnah, the family of the     50
Meunim,[e] the family of the Nephusim,[f] the family of Bakbuk, the family 51
of Hakupha, the family of Harhur, the family of Bazluth, the family of    52
Mehida, the family of Harsha, the family of Barkos, the family of Sisera, 53
the family of Temah, the family of Neziah, and the family of Hatipha.     54

Descendants of Solomon's servants: the family of Sotaí, the family of     55
Hassophereth, the family of Peruda, the family of Jaalah, the family of   56
Darkon, the family of Giddel, the family of Shephatiah, the family of Hattil, 57
the family of Pochereth-hazzebaim, and the family of Ami.

The temple-servitors and the descendants of Solomon's servants           58
amounted to three hundred and ninety-two in all.

The following were those who returned from Tel-melah, Tel-harsha,         59
Kerub, Addan, and Immer, but could not establish their father's family
nor whether by descent they belonged to Israel: the family of Delaiah, the 60
family of Tobiah, and the family of Nekoda, six hundred and fifty-two.
Also of the priests: the family of Hobaiah, the family of Hakkoz, and the 61
family of Barzillai who had married a daughter of Barzillai the Gileadite
and went by his[g] name. These searched for their names among those       62
enrolled in the genealogies, but they could not be found; they were disqualified for the priesthood as unclean, and the governor forbade them to 63

---

[a] *Prob. rdg., cp. Neh. 7. 29; Heb.* the family of Kiriath-arim.          [b] *Prob. rdg.,*
*cp. Neh. 7. 30; Heb.* family.          [c] *Prob. rdg.; Heb.* family (*also in verses 30–35*).
[d] *Or* Shalmai (*cp. Neh. 7. 48*).     [e] *Or* Meinim.     [f] *Or* Nephisim.     [g] *Prob. rdg.,*
*cp. I Esdras 5. 38; Heb.* their.

partake of the most sacred food until there should be a priest able to consult the Urim and the Thummim.

64   The whole assembled people numbered forty-two thousand three
65   hundred and sixty, apart from their slaves, male and female, of whom there were seven thousand three hundred and thirty-seven; and they had two
66   hundred singers, men and women. Their horses numbered seven hundred
67   and thirty-six, their mules two hundred and forty-five, their camels four hundred and thirty-five, and their asses six thousand seven hundred and twenty.
68   When they came to the house of the LORD in Jerusalem, some of the heads of families volunteered to rebuild the house of God on its original
69   site. According to their resources they gave for the fabric fund a total of sixty-one thousand drachmas of gold, five thousand minas of silver, and one hundred priestly robes.
70   The priests, the Levites, and some of the people lived in Jerusalem and its suburbs;*a* the singers, the door-keepers, and temple-servitors,*b* and all other Israelites, lived in their own towns.

## Worship restored and the temple rebuilt

3    WHEN THE SEVENTH MONTH CAME, the Israelites now being settled
2    in their towns, the people assembled as one man in Jerusalem. Then Jeshua son of Jozadak and his fellow-priests, and Zerubbabel son of Shealtiel and his kinsmen, set to work and built the altar of the God of Israel, in order to offer upon it whole-offerings as prescribed in the law of Moses
3    the man of God. They put the altar in place first, because they lived in fear of the foreign population; and they offered upon it whole-offerings
4    to the LORD, both morning and evening offerings. They kept the pilgrim-feast of Tabernacles*c* as ordained, and offered whole-offerings every day
5    in the number prescribed for each day, and, in addition to these, the regular whole-offerings and the offerings for sabbaths,*d* for new moons and for all the sacred seasons appointed by the LORD, and all voluntary offerings
6    brought to the LORD. The offering of whole-offerings began from the first day of the seventh month, although the foundation of the temple of the
7    LORD had not yet been laid. They gave money for the masons and carpenters, and food and drink and oil for the Sidonians and the Tyrians to fetch cedar-wood from the Lebanon to the roadstead at Joppa, by licence from Cyrus king of Persia.
8    In the second year after their return to the house of God in Jerusalem, and in the second month, Zerubbabel son of Shealtiel and Jeshua son of Jozadak started work, aided by all their fellow-Israelites, the priests and the Levites and all who had returned from captivity to Jerusalem. They appointed Levites from the age of twenty years and upwards to supervise
9    the work of the house of the LORD. Jeshua with his sons and his kinsmen,

---

*a* in Jerusalem and its suburbs: *prob. rdg., cp. 1 Esdras 5. 46; Heb. om.*          *b* Prob.
*rdg.; Heb. adds in their towns.*          *c* Or Booths.          *d* for sabbaths: *prob. rdg.,
cp. 1 Esdras 5. 52; Heb. om.*

Kadmiel, Binnui, and Hodaviah,[a] together assumed control of those responsible for the work on the house of God.[b]

When the builders had laid the foundation of the temple of the LORD, 10 the priests in their robes took their places with their trumpets, and the Levites, the sons of Asaph, with their cymbals, to praise the LORD in the manner prescribed by David king of Israel; and they chanted praises and 11 thanksgiving to the LORD, singing, 'It is good to give thanks to the LORD,[c] for his love towards Israel endures for ever.' All the people raised a great shout of praise to the LORD because the foundation of the house of the LORD had been laid. But many of the priests and Levites and heads of 12 families, who were old enough to have seen the former house, wept and wailed aloud when they saw the foundation of this house laid, while many others shouted for joy at the top of their voice. The people could not dis- 13 tinguish the sound of the shout of joy from that of the weeping and wailing, so great was the shout which the people were raising, and the sound could be heard a long way off.

When the enemies of Judah and Benjamin heard that the returned exiles **4** were building a temple to the LORD the God of Israel, they approached 2 Zerubbabel and Jeshua[d] and the heads of families and said to them, 'Let us join you in building, for like you we seek your God, and we have been sacrificing to him ever since the days of Esarhaddon king of Assyria, who brought us here.' But Zerubbabel and Jeshua and the rest of the heads of 3 families in Israel said to them, 'The house which we are building for our God is no concern of yours. We alone will build it for the LORD the God of Israel, as his majesty Cyrus king of Persia commanded us.'

Then the people of the land caused the Jews to lose heart and made them 4 afraid to continue building; and in order to defeat their purpose they 5 bribed officials at court to act against them. This continued throughout the reign of Cyrus and into the reign of Darius king of Persia.

At the beginning of the reign of Ahasuerus, the people of the land 6 brought a charge in writing against the inhabitants of Judah and Jerusalem.

And in the days of Artaxerxes king of Persia, with the agreement of 7 Mithredath, Tabeel and all his colleagues wrote to him; the letter was written in Aramaic and read aloud in Aramaic.

Rehum the high commissioner and Shimshai the secretary wrote a 8[e] letter to King Artaxerxes concerning Jerusalem in the following terms:

> From Rehum the high commissioner, Shimshai the secretary, and all 9 their colleagues, the judges, the commissioners, the overseers, and chief officers, the men of Erech and Babylon, and the Elamites in Susa, and the 10 other peoples whom the great and renowned Asnappar[f] deported and settled in the city of Samaria and in the rest of the province of Beyond-Euphrates.

---

[a] Binnui, and Hodaviah: *prob. rdg.; Heb.* and his sons the family of Judah.          [b] *Prob.* *rdg.; Heb. adds* the family of Henadad, their family and their kinsmen the Levites. [c] to give thanks to the LORD: *prob. rdg., cp. Ps. 106. 1; Heb. om.*          [d] and Jeshua: *prob. rdg., cp. 1 Esdras 5. 68; Heb. om.*          [e] *From 4. 8 to 6. 18 the text is in Aramaic.* [f] *Or* Osnappar.

11   Here follows the text of their letter:

To King Artaxerxes from his servants, the men of the province of Beyond-Euphrates:

12   Be it known to Your Majesty that the Jews who left you and came to these parts have reached Jerusalem and are rebuilding that wicked and rebellious city; they have surveyed<sup>a</sup> the foundations and are completing

13   the walls. Be it known to Your Majesty that, if their city is rebuilt and the walls are completed, they will pay neither general levy, nor poll-tax,

14   nor land-tax, and in the end<sup>b</sup> they will harm the monarchy. Now, because we eat the king's salt and it is not right that we should witness the king's dishonour, therefore we have sent to inform Your Majesty,

15   in order that search may be made in the annals of your predecessors. You will discover by searching through the annals that this has been a rebellious city, harmful to the monarchy and its provinces, and that sedition has long been rife within its walls. That is why the city was laid waste.

16   We submit to Your Majesty that, if it is rebuilt and its walls are completed, the result will be that you will have no more footing in the province of Beyond-Euphrates.

17   The king sent this answer:

To Rehum the high commissioner, Shimshai the secretary, and all your colleagues resident in Samaria and in the rest of the province of

18   Beyond-Euphrates, greeting. The letter which you sent to me has now

19   been read clearly in my presence. I have given orders and search has been made, and it has been found that the city in question has a long history of revolt against the monarchy, and that rebellion and sedition

20   have been rife in it. Powerful kings have ruled in Jerusalem, exercising authority over the whole province of Beyond-Euphrates, and general

21   levy, poll-tax, and land-tax have been paid to them. Therefore, issue orders that these men must desist. This city is not to be rebuilt until a

22   decree to that effect is issued by me. See that you do not neglect your duty in this matter, lest more damage and harm be done to the monarchy.

23   When the text of the letter from King Artaxerxes was read before Rehum the high commissioner, Shimshai the secretary, and their colleagues, they

24   hurried to Jerusalem and forcibly compelled the Jews to stop work. From then onwards the work on the house of God in Jerusalem stopped; and it remained at a standstill till the second year of the reign of Darius king of Persia.

5    But the prophets Haggai<sup>c</sup> and Zechariah grandson of Iddo upbraided the Jews in Judah and Jerusalem, prophesying in the name of the God of

2    Israel. Then Zerubbabel son of Shealtiel and Jeshua son of Jozadak at once began to rebuild the house of God in Jerusalem, and the prophets of

3    God were with them and supported them. Tattenai, governor of the province of Beyond-Euphrates, Shethar-bozenai, and their colleagues promptly came to them and said, 'Who issued a decree permitting you to

4    rebuild this house and complete its furnishings?' They also asked them

---

<sup>a</sup> have surveyed: *prob. rdg.; Aram.* are surveying.       <sup>b</sup> in the end: *or* certainly.
<sup>c</sup> *Prob. rdg., cp. 1 Esdras 6. 1; Aram. adds* the prophet.

for the names of the men engaged in the building. But the elders of the 5
Jews were under God's watchful eye, and they were not prevented from
continuing the work, until such time as a report should reach Darius and
a royal letter should be received in answer.

Here follows the text of the letter sent by Tattenai, governor of the 6
province of Beyond-Euphrates, Shethar-bozenai, and his colleagues, the
inspectors in the province of Beyond-Euphrates, to King Darius. This is 7
the written report that they sent:

> To King Darius, all greetings. Be it known to Your Majesty that we 8
> went to the province of Judah and found the house of the great God
> being rebuilt by the Jewish elders,*a* with massive stones and timbers
> laid in the walls. The work was being done thoroughly and was making
> good progress under their direction. We asked these elders who had 9
> issued a decree for the rebuilding of this house and the completion of
> the furnishings. We also asked them for their names, so that we might 10
> make a list of the leaders for your information. This was their reply: 'We 11
> are the servants of the God of heaven and earth, and we are rebuilding
> the house originally built many years ago; a great king of Israel built it
> and completed it. But because our forefathers provoked the anger of the 12
> God of heaven, he put them into the power of Nebuchadnezzar the
> Chaldaean, king of Babylon, who pulled down this house and carried
> the people captive to Babylon. However, Cyrus king of Babylon in the 13
> first year of his reign issued a decree that this house of God should be
> rebuilt. Moreover, there were gold and silver vessels of the house of God, 14
> which Nebuchadnezzar had taken from the temple in Jerusalem and put
> in the temple in Babylon; and these King Cyrus took out of the temple
> in Babylon. He gave them to a man named Sheshbazzar, whom he had
> appointed governor, and said to him, "Take these vessels; go and restore 15
> them to the temple in Jerusalem, and let the house of God there be
> rebuilt on its original site." Then this Sheshbazzar came and laid the 16
> foundation of the house of God in Jerusalem; and from that time until
> now the rebuilding has continued, but it is not yet finished.' Now, there- 17
> fore, if it please Your Majesty, let search be made in the royal archives
> in Babylon, to discover whether a decree was issued by King Cyrus for
> the rebuilding of this house of God in Jerusalem. Then let the king send
> us his wishes in the matter.

Then King Darius issued an order, and search was made in the archives **6**
where the treasures were deposited in Babylon. But it was in Ecbatana, 2
in the royal residence in the province of Media, that a scroll was found, on
which was written the following memorandum:

> In the first year of King Cyrus, the king issued this decree concerning 3
> the house of God in Jerusalem: Let the house be rebuilt as a place where
> sacrifices are offered and fire-offerings brought. Its height shall be sixty
> cubits and its breadth sixty cubits, with three courses of massive stones 4
> and one*b* course of timber, the cost to be defrayed from the royal

---

*a* by . . . elders: *prob. rdg., cp. 1 Esdras 6. 8; Aram. om.*       *b* *Prob. rdg., cp.*
*1 Esdras 6. 25; Aram. a new.*

5 treasury. Also the gold and silver vessels of the house of God, which Nebuchadnezzar took out of the temple in Jerusalem and brought to Babylon, shall be restored; they shall all be taken back to the temple in Jerusalem, and restored each to its place in the house of God.

6 Then King Darius issued this order:[a]

Now, Tattenai, governor of the province of Beyond-Euphrates, Shethar-bozenai, and your colleagues, the inspectors in the province of
7 Beyond-Euphrates, you are to keep away from the place, and to leave the governor of the Jews and their elders free to rebuild this house of
8 God; let them rebuild it on its original site. I also issue an order prescribing what you are to do for these elders of the Jews, so that the said house of God may be rebuilt. Their expenses are to be defrayed in full from the royal funds accruing from the taxes of the province of Beyond-
9 Euphrates, so that the work may not be brought to a standstill. And let them have daily without fail whatever they want, young bulls, rams, or lambs as whole-offerings for the God of heaven, or wheat, salt, wine, or
10 oil, as the priests in Jerusalem demand, so that they may offer soothing sacrifices to the God of heaven, and pray for the life of the king and his
11 sons. Furthermore, I decree that, if any man tampers with this edict, a beam shall be pulled out of his house and he shall be fastened erect to
12 it and flogged; and, in addition, his house shall be forfeit.[b] And may the God who made that place a dwelling for his Name overthrow any king or people that shall presume to tamper with this edict or to destroy this house of God in Jerusalem. I Darius have issued a decree; it is to be carried out to the letter.

13 Then Tattenai, governor of the province of Beyond-Euphrates, Shethar-bozenai, and their colleagues carried out to the letter the instructions which
14 King Darius had sent them, and the elders of the Jews went on with the rebuilding. As a result of the prophecies of Haggai the prophet and Zechariah grandson of Iddo they had good success and finished the rebuilding as commanded by the God of Israel and according to the decrees
15 of Cyrus and Darius;[c] and the house was completed on the twenty-third[d] day of the month Adar, in the sixth year of King Darius.

16 Then the people of Israel, the priests and the Levites and all the other exiles who had returned, celebrated the dedication of the house of God
17 with great rejoicing. For its dedication they offered one hundred bulls, two hundred rams, and four hundred lambs, and as a sin-offering for all Israel twelve he-goats, corresponding to the number of the tribes of Israel.
18 And they re-established the priests in their groups and the Levites in their divisions for the service of God in Jerusalem, as prescribed in the book of Moses.

19 On the fourteenth day of the first month the exiles who had returned
20 kept the Passover. The priests and the Levites, one and all, had purified themselves; all of them were ritually clean, and they killed the passover

[a] Then ... order: *prob. rdg., cp. 1 Esdras 6. 27; Aram. om.*       [b] *Or* made into a dunghill (*mng. of Aram. word uncertain*).       [c] *Prob. rdg.; Aram. adds* and Artaxerxes king of Persia.       [d] *Prob. rdg., cp. 1 Esdras 7. 5; Aram. third.*

lamb for all the exiles who had returned, for their fellow-priests and for themselves. It was eaten by the Israelites who had come back from exile 21 and by all who had separated themselves from the peoples of the land and their uncleanness and sought the LORD the God of Israel. And they kept 22 the pilgrim-feast of Unleavened Bread for seven days with rejoicing; for the LORD had given them cause for joy by changing the disposition of the king of Assyria towards them, so that he encouraged them in the work of the house of God, the God of Israel.

## *Ezra's mission to Jerusalem*

NOW AFTER THESE EVENTS, in the reign of Artaxerxes king of Persia, 7 there came up from Babylon one Ezra son of Seraiah, son of Azariah, son of Hilkiah, son of Shallum, son of Zadok, son *a* of Ahitub, son of 2 3 Amariah, son of Azariah, son of Meraioth, son of Zerahiah, son of Uzzi, 4 son of Bukki, son of Abishua, son of Phinehas, son of Eleazar, son of Aaron 5 the chief priest. He was a scribe *b* learned in the law of Moses which the 6 LORD the God of Israel had given them; and the king granted him all that he asked, for the hand of the LORD his God was upon him. In the seventh 7 year of King Artaxerxes, other Israelites, priests, Levites, singers, door-keepers, and temple-servitors went up with him to Jerusalem; and they 8 reached Jerusalem in the fifth month, in the seventh year of the king. On 9 the first day of the first month Ezra fixed the day for departure from Babylon, and on the first day of the fifth month he arrived at Jerusalem, for the gracious hand of his God was upon him. For Ezra had devoted himself to 10 the study and observance of the law of the LORD and to teaching statute and ordinance in Israel.

This is a copy of the royal letter which King Artaxerxes had given to 11 Ezra the priest and scribe, a scribe versed in questions concerning the commandments and the statutes of the LORD laid upon Israel:

Artaxerxes, king of kings, to Ezra the priest and scribe learned in the 12 *c* law of the God of heaven:

This is my decision. I hereby issue a decree that any of the people of 13 Israel or of its priests or Levites in my kingdom who volunteer to go to Jerusalem may go with you. You are sent by the king and his seven 14 counsellors to find out how things stand in Judah and Jerusalem with regard to the law of your God with which you are entrusted. You are 15 also to convey the silver and gold which the king and his counsellors have freely offered to the God of Israel whose dwelling is in Jerusalem, together with any silver and gold that you may find throughout the 16 province of Babylon, and the voluntary offerings of the people and of the priests which they freely offer for the house of their God in Jerusalem. In pursuance of this decree you shall use the money solely for the 17 purchase of bulls, rams, and lambs, and the proper grain-offerings and drink-offerings, to be offered on the altar in the house of your God in

*a* Or grandson.　　　*b* Or doctor of the law.　　　*c* *The text of verses 12–26 is in Aramaic.*

18  Jerusalem. Further, should any silver and gold be left over, you and your colleagues may use it at your discretion according to the will of your
19  God. The vessels which have been given you for the service of the house
20  of your God you shall hand over to the God of Jerusalem; and if anything else should be required for the house of your God, which it may fall to you to provide, you may provide it out of the king's treasury.

21     And I, King Artaxerxes, issue an order to all treasurers in the province of Beyond-Euphrates that whatever is demanded of you by Ezra the priest, a scribe learned in the law of the God of heaven, is to be supplied
22  exactly, up to a hundred talents of silver, a hundred kor of wheat, a hundred bath of wine, a hundred bath of oil, and salt without reckoning.
23  Whatever is demanded by the God of heaven, let it be diligently carried out for the house of the God of heaven; otherwise wrath may fall upon
24  the realm of the king and his sons. We also make known to you that you have no authority to impose general levy, poll-tax, or land-tax on any of the priests, Levites, musicians, door-keepers, temple-servitors, or other servants of this house of God.

25     And you, Ezra, in accordance with the wisdom of your God with which you are entrusted, are to appoint arbitrators and judges to judge all your people in the province of Beyond-Euphrates, all who acknowledge the laws of your God;[a] and you and they are to instruct those who
26  do not acknowledge them. Whoever will not obey the law of your God and the law of the king, let judgement be rigorously executed upon him, be it death, banishment, confiscation of property, or imprisonment.

27     Then Ezra said,[b] 'Blessed be the LORD the God of our fathers who has prompted the king thus to add glory to the house of the LORD in Jerusalem,
28  and has made the king and his counsellors and all his high officers well disposed towards me!'
    So, knowing that the hand of the LORD my God was upon me, I took courage and assembled leading men out of Israel to go up with me.

**8**    These are the heads of families, as registered, family by family, of those
2  who went up with me from Babylon in the reign of King Artaxerxes: of the family of Phinehas, Gershom; of the family of Ithamar, Daniel; of the
3  family of David, Hattush son of[c] Shecaniah; of the family of Parosh,
4  Zechariah, and with him a hundred and fifty males in the register; of the family of Pahath-moab, Elihoenai son of Zerahiah, and with him two
5  hundred males; of the family of Zattu,[d] Shecaniah son of Jahaziel, and
6  with him three hundred males; of the family of Adin, Ebed son of Jonathan,
7  and with him fifty males; of the family of Elam, Isaiah son of Athaliah,
8  and with him seventy males; of the family of Shephatiah, Zebadiah son of
9  Michael, and with him eighty males; of the family of Joab, Obadiah son
10  of Jehiel, and with him two hundred and eighteen males; of the family of Bani,[e] Shelomith son of Josiphiah, and with him a hundred and sixty males;

---

[a] to judge . . . your God: *or* all of them versed in the laws of your God, to judge all the people in the province of Beyond-Euphrates.      [b] Then Ezra said: *prob. rdg., cp.*
*1 Esdras 8. 25; Heb. om.*      [c] son of: *prob. rdg.; Heb.* of the family of.      [d] of Zattu:
*prob. rdg., cp. 1 Esdras 8. 32; Heb. om.*      [e] of Bani: *prob. rdg., cp. 1 Esdras 8. 36;
Heb. om.*

of the family of Bebai, Zechariah son of Bebai, and with him twenty-eight 11
males; of the family of Azgad, Johanan son of Hakkatan, and with him a hun- 12
dred and ten males. The last were the family of Adonikam, and these were 13
their names: Eliphelet, Jeiel, and Shemaiah, and with them sixty males;
and the family of Bigvai, Uthai and Zabbud, and with them seventy males. 14

I assembled them by the river which flows toward Ahava; and we en- 15
camped there three days. When I reviewed the people and the priests, I
found no Levite there. So I sent Eliezer, Ariel, Shemaiah, Elnathan, Jarib, 16
Elnathan, Nathan, Zechariah, and Meshullam, prominent men, and
Joiarib and Elnathan, men of discretion, with instructions to go to Iddo, 17
the chief man of the settlement at Casiphia; and I gave them a message for
him and his kinsmen, the temple-servitors there, asking for servitors for
the house of our God to be sent to us. And, because the gracious hand of 18
our God was upon us, they let us have Sherebiah, a man of discretion, of
the family of Mahli son of Levi, son of Israel, together with his sons and
kinsmen, eighteen men; also Hashabiah, together with Isaiah of the family 19
of Merari, his kinsmen and their sons, twenty men; besides two hundred 20
and twenty temple-servitors (this was an order instituted by David and his
officers to assist the Levites). These were all indicated by name.

Then I proclaimed a fast there by the river Ahava, so that we might 21
mortify ourselves before our God and ask from him a safe journey for ourselves, our dependants, and all our possessions. For I was ashamed to ask 22
the king for an escort of soldiers and horsemen to help us against enemies
on the way, because we had said to the king, 'The hand of our God is upon
all who seek him, working their good; but his fierce anger is on all who
forsake him.' So we fasted and asked our God for a safe journey, and he 23
answered our prayer.

Then I separated twelve of the chiefs of the priests, together with*a* 24
Sherebiah and Hashabiah and ten of their kinsmen, and handed over to 25
them the silver and gold and the vessels which had been set aside by the
king, his counsellors and his officers and all the Israelites who were present,
as their contribution to the house of our God. I handed over to them six 26
hundred and fifty talents of silver, a hundred silver vessels weighing two
talents, a hundred talents of gold, twenty golden bowls worth a thousand 27
drachmas, and two vessels of a fine red copper,*b* precious as gold. And I 28
said to the men, 'You are dedicated to the LORD, and the vessels too are
sacred; the silver and gold are a voluntary offering to the LORD the God of
your fathers. Watch over them and guard them, until you hand them over 29
in the presence of the chiefs of the priests and the Levites and the heads
of families of Israel in Jerusalem, in the rooms of the house of the LORD.'

So the priests and Levites received the consignment of silver and gold 30
and vessels, to be taken to the house of our God in Jerusalem; and on the 31
twelfth day of the first month we left the river Ahava bound for Jerusalem.
The hand of our God was upon us, and he saved us from enemy attack and
from ambush on the way. When we arrived at Jerusalem, we rested for 32
three days. And on the fourth day the silver and gold and the vessels were 33
deposited in the house of our God in the charge of Meremoth son of Uriah

*a* together with: *prob. rdg., cp. 1 Esdras 8. 54; Heb. om.*     *b* red copper: *or* orichalc.

the priest, who had with him Eleazar son of Phinehas, and they had with
them the Levites Jozabad son of Jeshua and Noadiah son of Binnui.
34 Everything was checked as it was handed over, and at the same time a
35 written record was made of the whole consignment. Then those who had
come home from captivity, the exiles who had returned, offered as whole-
offerings to the God of Israel twelve bulls for all Israel, ninety-six rams
and seventy-two[a] lambs, with twelve he-goats as a sin-offering; all these
36 were offered as a whole-offering to the LORD. They also delivered the king's
commission to the royal satraps and governors in the province of Beyond-
Euphrates; and these gave support to the people and the house of God.

9    When all this had been done, some of the leaders approached me and
said, 'The people of Israel, including priests and Levites, have not kept
themselves apart from the foreign population and from the abominable
practices of the Canaanites, the Hittites, the Perizzites, the Jebusites, the
2 Ammonites, the Moabites, the Egyptians, and the Amorites. They have
taken women of these nations as wives for themselves and their sons, so
that the holy race has become mixed with the foreign population; and the
3 leaders and magistrates have been the chief offenders.' When I heard this
news, I rent my robe and mantle, and tore my hair and my beard, and I sat
4 dumbfounded; and all who went in fear of the words of the God of Israel
rallied to me because of the offence of these exiles. I sat there dumbfounded
till the evening sacrifice.
5    Then, at the evening sacrifice, I rose from my humiliation and, in my
rent robe and mantle, I knelt down and spread out my hands to the LORD
6 my God and said, 'O my God, I am humiliated, I am ashamed to lift my
face to thee, my God; for we are sunk in our iniquities, and our guilt is so
7 great that it reaches high heaven. From the days of our fathers down to this
present day our guilt has been great. For our iniquities we, our kings, and
our priests have been subject to death, captivity, pillage, and shameful
humiliation at the hands of foreign kings, and such is our present plight.
8 But now, for a brief moment, the LORD our God has been gracious to us,
leaving us some survivors and giving us a foothold in his holy place. He
has brought light to our eyes again and given us some chance to renew our
9 lives in our slavery. For slaves we are; nevertheless, our God has not forsaken us in our slavery, but has made the kings of Persia so well disposed
towards us as to give us the means of renewal, so that we may repair
the house of our God and rebuild its ruins, and to give us a wall of defence
10 in[b] Judah and Jerusalem. Now, O our God, what are we to say after this?
11 For we have neglected the commands which thou gavest through thy
servants the prophets, when thou saidst, "The land which you are entering
and will possess is a polluted land, polluted by the foreign population with
their abominable practices, which have made it unclean from end to end.
12 Therefore, do not give your daughters in marriage to their sons, and do not
marry your sons to their daughters, and never seek their welfare or prosperity. Thus you will be strong and enjoy the good things of the land, and
13 pass it on to your children as an everlasting possession." Now, after all

---

[a] *Prob. rdg., cp. I Esdras 8. 65; Heb.* seventy-seven.          [b] *Or* thereby giving us a
wall of defence for . . .

that we have suffered for our evil deeds and for our great guilt—although
thou, our God, hast punished us less than our iniquities deserved and hast
allowed us to survive as now we do—shall we again disobey thy commands   14
and join in marriage with peoples who indulge in such abominable practices? Would not thy anger against us be unrelenting, until no remnant,
no survivor was left? O LORD God of Israel, thou art righteous; now as   15
before, we are only a remnant that has survived. Look upon us, guilty as
we are in thy sight; for because of our guilt none of us can stand in thy
presence.'

While Ezra was praying and making confession, prostrate in tears before   **10**
the house of God, a very great crowd of Israelites assembled round him,
men, women, and children, and they all wept bitterly. Then Shecaniah son   2
of Jehiel, one of the family of Elam, spoke up and said to Ezra, 'We have
committed an offence against our God in marrying foreign wives, daughters
of the foreign population. But in spite of this, there is still hope for Israel.
Now, therefore, let us pledge ourselves to our God to dismiss all these   3
women and their brood, according to your advice, my lord, and the
advice of those who go in fear of the command of our God; and let us act as
the law prescribes. Up now, the task is yours, and we will support you.   4
Take courage and act.'

Ezra stood up and made the chiefs of the priests, the Levites, and all the   5
Israelites swear to do as had been said; and they took the oath. Then Ezra   6
left his place in front of the house of God and went to the room of Jehohanan
grandson of Eliashib and lodged[a] there; he neither ate bread nor drank
water, for he was mourning for the offence committed by the exiles who
had returned. Next, there was issued throughout Judah and Jerusalem a   7
proclamation that all the exiles should assemble in Jerusalem, and that if   8
anyone did not arrive within three days, it should be within the discretion
of the chief officers and the elders to confiscate all his property and to
exclude him from the community of the exiles. So all the men of Judah and   9
Benjamin assembled in Jerusalem within the three days; and on the twentieth day of the ninth month the people all sat in the forecourt of the house
of God, trembling with apprehension and shivering in the heavy rain.
Ezra the priest stood up and said, 'You have committed an offence in   10
marrying foreign wives and have added to Israel's guilt. Make your con-   11
fession now to the LORD the God of your fathers and do his will, and
separate yourselves from the foreign population and from your foreign
wives.' Then all the assembled people shouted in reply, 'Yes; we must do   12
what you say. But there is a great crowd of us here, and it is the rainy   13
season; we cannot go on standing out here in the open. Besides, this business will not be finished in one day or even two, because we have committed
so grave an offence in this matter. Let our leading men act for the whole   14
assembly, and let all in our cities who have married foreign women present
themselves at appointed times, each man with the elders and judges of his
own city, until God's anger against us on this account is averted.' Only   15
Jonathan son of Asahel and Jahzeiah son of Tikvah, supported by Meshullam and Shabbethai the Levite, opposed this.

[a] *Prob. rdg., cp. 1 Esdras 9. 2; Heb. went.*

16   So the exiles acted as agreed, and Ezra the priest selected *a* certain men,
heads of households representing their families, all of them designated by
name. They began their formal inquiry into the matter on the first day of
17   the tenth month, and by the first day of the first month they had finished
their inquiry into all the marriages with foreign women.
18   Among the members of priestly families who had married foreign
women were found Maaseiah, Eliezer, Jarib, and Gedaliah of the family of
19   Jeshua son of Jozadak and his brothers. They pledged themselves to dismiss their wives, and they brought a ram from the flock as a guilt-offering
20 21   for their sins. Of the family of Immer: Hanani and Zebadiah. Of the family
22   of Harim: Maaseiah, Elijah, Shemaiah, Jehiel and Uzziah. Of the family
of Pashhur: Elioenai, Maaseiah, Ishmael, Nethaneel, Jozabad and Elasah.
23   Of the Levites: Jozabad, Shimei, Kelaiah (that is Kelita), Pethahiah,
24   Judah and Eliezer. Of the singers: Eliashib. Of the door-keepers: Shallum,
Telem and Uri.
25   And of Israel: of the family of Parosh: Ramiah, Izziah, Malchiah,
26   Mijamin, Eleazar, Malchiah and Benaiah. Of the family of Elam: Mat-
27   taniah, Zechariah, Jehiel, Abdi, Jeremoth and Elijah. Of the family of
28   Zattu: Elioenai, Eliashib, Mattaniah, Jeremoth, Zabad and Aziza. Of the
29   family of Bebai: Jehohanan, Hananiah, Zabbai and Athlai. Of the family
30   of Bani: Meshullam, Malluch, Adaiah, Jashub, Sheal and Jeremoth. Of
the family of Pahath-moab: Adna, Kelal, Benaiah, Maaseiah, Mattaniah,
31   Bezalel, Binnui and Manasseh. Of the family of Harim: Eliezer, Isshijah,
32 33   Malchiah, Shemaiah, Simeon, Benjamin, Malluch and Shemariah. Of the
family of Hashum: Mattenai, Mattattah, Zabad, Eliphelet, Jeremai,
34   Manasseh and Shimei. Of the family of Bani: Maadai, Amram and Uel,
35 36 37   Benaiah, Bedeiah and Keluhi, Vaniah, Meremoth, Eliashib, Mattaniah,
38 39   Mattenai and Jaasau. Of the family of *b* Binnui: Shimei, Shelemiah,
40 41   Nathan and Adaiah, Maknadebai, Shashai and Sharai, Azareel, Shelemiah
42 43   and Shemariah, Shallum, Amariah and Joseph. Of the family of Nebo:
44   Jeiel, Mattithiah, Zabad, Zebina, Jaddai, Joel and Benaiah. All these had
married foreign women, and they dismissed them, together with their
children.*c*

*a* and Ezra the priest selected: *prob. rdg., cp. 1 Esdras 9. 16; Heb. obscure.*     *b* Of the
family of: *prob. rdg., cp. 1 Esdras 9. 34; Heb.* and Bani and.          *c* and they . . .
children: *prob. rdg., cp. 1 Esdras 9. 36; Heb.* and some of them were women; and they
had borne sons.

# THE BOOK OF
# NEHEMIAH

## *Nehemiah's commission*

T HE NARRATIVE OF NEHEMIAH son of Hacaliah. 1
In the month Kislev in the twentieth year, when I was in Susa
the capital city, it happened that one of my brothers, Hanani, arrived 2
with some others from Judah; and I asked them about Jerusalem and about
the Jews, the families still remaining of those who survived the captivity.
They told me that those still remaining in the province who had survived 3
the captivity were facing great trouble and reproach; the wall of Jerusalem
was broken down and the gates had been destroyed by fire. When I heard 4
this news, I sat down and wept; I mourned for some days, fasting and
praying to the God of heaven. This was my prayer: 'O LORD God of heaven, 5
O great and terrible God who faithfully keepest covenant with those who
love thee and observe thy commandments, let thy ear be attentive and 6
thine eyes open, to hear my humble prayer which I make to thee day and
night on behalf of thy servants the sons of Israel. I confess the sins which
we Israelites have all committed against thee, and of which I and my father's
house are also guilty. We have wronged thee and have not observed the 7
commandments, statutes, and rules which thou didst enjoin upon thy
servant Moses. Remember what thou didst impress upon him in these 8
words: "If you are unfaithful, I will disperse you among the nations; but 9
if you return to me and observe my commandments and fulfil them, I will
gather your children who have been scattered to the ends of the earth and
will bring them home to the place which I have chosen as a dwelling for my
Name." They are thy servants and thy people, whom thou hast redeemed 10
with thy great might and thy strong hand. O Lord, let thy ear be attentive 11
to my humble prayer, and to the prayer of thy servants who delight to
revere thy name. Grant me good success this day, and put it into this
man's heart to show me kindness.'

Now I was the king's cupbearer, and one day, in the month Nisan, in the 2
twentieth year of King Artaxerxes, when his wine was ready, I took it up
and handed it to the king, and as I stood before him I was feeling very
unhappy. He said to me, 'Why do you look so unhappy? You are not ill; 2
it can be nothing but unhappiness.' I was much afraid and answered, 'The 3
king will live for ever. But how can I help looking unhappy when the city
where my forefathers are buried lies waste and its gates are burnt?' 'What 4
are you asking of me?' said the king. I prayed to the God of heaven, and 5
then I answered, 'If it please your majesty, and if I enjoy your favour, I
beg you to send me to Judah, to the city where my forefathers are buried,
so that I may rebuild it.' The king, with the queen consort sitting beside 6

him, asked me, 'How long will the journey last, and when will you return?'
Then the king approved the request and let me go, and I told him how long
7 I should be. Then I said to the king, 'If it please your majesty, let letters be
given me for the governors in the province of Beyond-Euphrates with
8 orders to grant me all the help I need for my journey to Judah. Let me have
also a letter for Asaph, the keeper of your royal forests, instructing him to
supply me with timber to make beams for the gates of the citadel, which
adjoins the palace, and for the city wall, and for the palace which I shall
occupy.' The king granted my requests, for the gracious hand of my God
9 was upon me. I came in due course to the governors in the province of
Beyond-Euphrates and presented to them the king's letters; the king had
10 given me an escort of army officers with cavalry. But when Sanballat the
Horonite and the slave Tobiah, an Ammonite, heard this, they were much
vexed that someone should have come to promote the interests of the
Israelites.

## The walls of Jerusalem rebuilt

11 12  WHEN I ARRIVED IN JERUSALEM, I waited three days. Then I set
out by night, taking a few men with me; but I told no one what my
God was prompting me to do for Jerusalem. I had no beast with me except
13 the one on which I myself rode. I went out by night through the Valley
Gate towards the Dragon Spring and the Dung Gate, and I inspected the
places where the walls of Jerusalem had been broken down and her gates
14 burnt. Then I passed on to the Fountain Gate and the King's Pool; but
15 there was no room for me to ride through. I went up the valley in the night
and inspected the city wall; then I re-entered the city by the Valley Gate.
16 So I arrived back without the magistrates knowing where I had been or
what I was doing. I had not yet told the Jews, the priests, the nobles, the
magistrates, or any of those who would be responsible for the work.
17    Then I said to them, 'You see our wretched plight. Jerusalem lies in
ruins, its gates destroyed by fire. Come, let us rebuild the wall of Jerusalem
18 and be rid of the reproach.' I told them how the gracious hand of my God
had been upon me and also what the king had said to me. They replied,
'Let us start the rebuilding.' So they set about the work vigorously and to
good purpose.
19    But when Sanballat the Horonite, Tobiah the Ammonite slave, and
Geshem the Arab heard of it, they jeered at us, asking contemptuously,
20 'What is this you are doing? Is this a rebellion against the king?' But I
answered them, 'The God of heaven will give us success. We, his servants
are making a start with the rebuilding. You have no stake, or claim, or
traditional right in Jerusalem.'
3    Eliashib the high priest and his fellow-priests started work and rebuilt
the Sheep Gate. They laid its beams *a* and set its doors in place; they carried
the work as far as the Tower of the Hundred, as far as the Tower of Hananel,

_____
*a* laid its beams: *prob. rdg.; Heb.* consecrated it.

and consecrated it. Next to Eliashib the men of Jericho worked; and next 2
to them Zaccur son of Imri.

The Fish Gate was built by the sons of Hassenaah; they laid its tie- 3
beams and set its doors in place with their bolts and bars. Next to them 4
Meremoth son of Uriah, son of Hakkoz, repaired his section; next to them
Meshullam son of Berechiah, son of Meshezabel; next to them Zadok son
of Baana did the repairs; and next again the men of Tekoa did the repairs, 5
but their nobles would not demean themselves to serve their governor.

The Jeshanah Gate*a* was repaired by Joiada son of Paseah and Meshul- 6
lam son of Besodeiah; they laid its tie-beams and set its doors in place with
their bolts and bars. Next to them Melatiah the Gibeonite and Jadon the 7
Meronothite, the men of Gibeon and Mizpah, did the repairs as far as the
seat of the governor of the province of Beyond-Euphrates. Next to them 8
Uzziel son of Harhaiah, a goldsmith, did the repairs, and next Hananiah,
a perfumer; they reconstructed Jerusalem as far as the Broad Wall. Next 9
to them Rephaiah son of Hur, ruler of half the district of Jerusalem, did
the repairs. Next to them Jedaiah son of Harumaph did the repairs opposite 10
his own house; and next Hattush son of Hashabniah. Malchiah son of 11
Harim and Hasshub son of Pahath-moab repaired a second section including the Tower of the Ovens.*b* Next to them Shallum son of Hallohesh, ruler 12
of half the district of Jerusalem, did the repairs with the help of his
daughters.

The Valley Gate was repaired by Hanun and the inhabitants of Zanoah; 13
they rebuilt it and set its doors in place with their bolts and bars, and they
repaired a thousand cubits of the wall as far as the Dung Gate. The Dung 14
Gate itself was repaired by Malchiah son of Rechab, ruler of the district
of Beth-hakkerem; he rebuilt*c* it and set its doors in place with their bolts
and bars. The Fountain Gate was repaired by Shallun son of Col-hozeh, 15
ruler of the district of Mizpah; he rebuilt*c* it and roofed it and set its doors
in place with their bolts and bars; and he built the wall of the Pool of
Shelah next to the king's garden and onwards as far as the steps leading
down from the City of David.

After him Nehemiah son of Azbuk, ruler of half the district of Beth-zur, 16
did the repairs as far as a point opposite the burial-place of David, as far
as the artificial pool and the House of the Heroes.*d* After him the Levites 17
did the repairs: Rehum son of Bani and next to him Hashabiah, ruler of
half the district of Keilah, did the repairs for his district. After him their 18
kinsmen did the repairs: Binnui son of Henadad, ruler of half the district
of Keilah; next to him Ezer son of Jeshua, ruler of Mizpah, repaired a 19
second section opposite the point at which the ascent meets the escarpment; after him Baruch son of Zabbai repaired a second section, from the 20
escarpment to the door of the house of Eliashib the high priest. After him 21
Meremoth son of Uriah, son of Hakkoz, repaired a second section, from
the door of the house of Eliashib to the end of the house of Eliashib.

After him the priests of the neighbourhood of Jerusalem did the repairs. 22
Next Benjamin and Hasshub did the repairs opposite their own house; 23

*a* The Jeshanah Gate: *or* The gate of the Old City.    *b Or* Furnaces.    *c Prob. rdg.;*
*Heb.* he will rebuild.     *d Or* and the barracks.

and next Azariah son of Maaseiah, son of Ananiah, did the repairs beside
24 his house. After him Binnui son of Henadad repaired a second section,
25 from the house of Azariah as far as the escarpment and the corner. Palal
son of Uzai worked opposite the escarpment and the upper tower which
projects from the king's house and belongs to the court of the guard. After
26 him Pedaiah son of Parosh[a] worked as far as a point on the east opposite
27 the Water Gate and the projecting tower. Next the men of Tekoa repaired
a second section, from a point opposite the great projecting tower as far as
the wall of Ophel.

28 Above the Horse Gate the priests did the repairs opposite their own
29 houses. After them Zadok son of Immer did the repairs opposite his own
house; after him Shemaiah son of Shecaniah, the keeper of the East Gate,
30 did the repairs. After him Hananiah son of Shelemiah and Hanun, sixth
son of Zalaph, repaired a second section. After him Meshullam son of
31 Berechiah did the repairs opposite his room. After him Malchiah, a goldsmith, did the repairs as far as the house of the temple-servitors and the
merchants, opposite the Mustering Gate, as far as the roof-chamber at
32 the corner. Between the roof-chamber at the corner and the Sheep Gate
the goldsmiths and merchants did the repairs.

4 WHEN SANBALLAT HEARD that we were rebuilding the wall, he was very
2 indignant; in his anger he jeered at the Jews and said in front of his companions and of the garrison in Samaria, 'What do these feeble Jews think
they are doing? Do they mean to reconstruct the place? Do they hope to
offer sacrifice and finish the work in a day? Can they make stones again out
3 of heaps of rubble, and burnt at that?' Tobiah the Ammonite, who was
beside him, said, 'Whatever it is they are building, if a fox climbs up their
stone walls, it will break them down.'

4 Hear us, our God, for they treat us with contempt. Turn back their
reproach upon their own heads and let them become objects of contempt
5 in a land of captivity. Do not condone their guilt or let their sin be struck
off the record, for they have openly provoked the builders.

6 We built up the wall until it was continuous all round up to half its
7 height; and the people worked with a will. But when Sanballat and Tobiah,
the Arabs and Ammonites and Ashdodites, heard that the new work on
the walls of Jerusalem had made progress and that the filling of the breaches
8 had begun, they were very angry; and they all banded together to come and
9 attack Jerusalem and to create confusion. So we prayed to our God, and
posted a guard day and night against them.

10 But the men of Judah said, 'The labourers' strength has failed, and there
is too much rubble; we shall never be able to rebuild the wall by ourselves.'
11 And our adversaries said, 'Before they know it or see anything, we shall be
12 upon them and kill them, and so put an end to the work.' When the Jews
who lived among them came in to the city, they warned us many times
that they would gather from every place where they lived to attack us,
13 and that they would station themselves on the lowest levels below the wall,
on patches of open ground. Accordingly I posted my people by families,

[a] *Prob. rdg.; Heb. adds* and the temple-servitors lodged on Ophel (*cp. 11. 21*).

armed with swords, spears, and bows. Then I surveyed the position  14
and at once addressed the nobles, the magistrates, and all the people.
'Do not be afraid of them', I said. 'Remember the Lord, great and terrible,
and fight for your brothers, your sons and daughters, your wives and
your homes.' Our enemies heard that everything was known to us, and  15
that God had frustrated their plans; and we all returned to our work on
the wall.

From that day forward half the men under me were engaged in the  16
actual building, while the other half stood by holding their spears, shields,
and bows, and wearing coats of mail; and officers supervised all the people
of Judah who were engaged on the wall. The porters carrying the loads had  17
one hand on the load and a weapon in the other. The builders had their  18
swords attached to their belts as they built; the trumpeter was beside me.
I addressed the nobles, the magistrates, and all the people: 'The work is  19
great and covers much ground', I said. 'We are isolated on the wall, each
man at some distance from his neighbour. Wherever the trumpet sounds,  20
rally to us there, and our God will fight for us.' So we continued with the  21
work, half the men holding the spears, from daybreak until the stars came
out. At the same time I had said to the people, 'Let every man and his  22
servant pass the night in Jerusalem, to act as a guard for us by night and a
working party by day.' So neither I nor my kinsmen nor the men under  23
me nor my bodyguard ever took off our clothes, each keeping his right hand
on*[a]* his weapon.

THERE CAME A TIME when the common people, both men and women,  5
raised a great outcry against their fellow-Jews. Some complained that they  2
were giving their sons and daughters as pledges*[b]* for food to keep themselves alive; others that they were mortgaging their fields, vineyards, and  3
houses to buy corn in the famine; others again that they were borrowing  4
money on their fields and vineyards to pay the king's tax. 'But', they said,  5
'our bodily needs are the same as other people's, our children are as good as
theirs; yet here we are, forcing our sons and daughters to become slaves.
Some of our daughters are already enslaved, and there is nothing we can
do, because our fields and vineyards now belong to others.' I was very  6
angry when I heard their outcry and the story they told. I mastered my  7
feelings and reasoned with the nobles and the magistrates. I said to them,
'You are holding your fellow-Jews as pledges for debt.' I rebuked them
severely and said, 'As far as we have been able, we have bought back our  8
fellow-Jews who had been sold to other nations; but you are now selling
your own fellow-countrymen, and they will have to be bought back by us!'
They were silent and had not a word to say. I went on, 'What you are doing  9
is wrong. You ought to live so much in the fear of God that you are above
reproach in the eyes of the nations who are our enemies. Speaking for  10
myself, I and my kinsmen and the men under me are advancing them money
and corn. Let us give up this taking of persons as pledges for debt. Give  11
back today to your debtors their fields and vineyards, their olive-groves

*[a]* keeping his right hand on: *prob. rdg.; Heb. obscure.*     *[b]* that they . . . as pledges:
*prob. rdg.; Heb.* that they, their sons and daughters were many.

and houses, as well as the income*a* in money, and in corn, new wine, and
12 oil.' 'We will give them back', they promised, 'and exact nothing more.
We will do what you say.' So, summoning the priests, I put the offenders
13 on oath to do as they had promised. Then I shook out the fold of my robe
and said, 'So may God shake out from his house and from his property
every man who does not fulfil this promise. May he be shaken out like this
and emptied!' And all the assembled people said 'Amen' and praised the
LORD. And they did as they had promised.

14    Moreover, from the time when I was appointed governor in the land of
Judah, from the twentieth to the thirty-second year of King Artaxerxes,
a period of twelve years, neither I nor my kinsmen drew the governor's
15 allowance of food. Former governors had laid a heavy burden on the
people, exacting from them a daily toll*b* of bread and wine to the value of
forty shekels of silver. Further, the men under them had tyrannized over
16 the people; but, for fear of God, I did not behave like this. I also put all my
energy into the work on this wall, and I acquired no land; and all my men
17 were gathered there for the work. Also I had as guests at my table a hundred
and fifty Jews, including the magistrates, as well as men who came to us
18 from the surrounding nations. The provision which had to be made each
day was an ox and six prime sheep; fowls also were prepared for me, and
every ten days skins of wine in abundance. Yet, in spite of all this, I did
not draw the governor's allowance, because the people were so heavily bur-
19 dened. Remember for my good, O God, all that I have done for this people.

6    When the news came to Sanballat, Tobiah, Geshem the Arab, and the
rest of our enemies, that I had rebuilt the wall and that not a single breach
2 remained in it, although I had not yet set up the doors in the gates, Sanballat
.  and Geshem sent me an invitation to come and confer with them at
Hakkephirim in the plain of Ono; this was a ruse on their part to do me
3 harm. So I sent messengers to them with this reply: 'I have important
work on my hands at the moment; I cannot come down. Why should the
4 work be brought to a standstill while I leave it and come down to you?' They
sent me a similar invitation four times, and each time I gave them the same
5 answer. On a fifth occasion Sanballat made a similar approach, but this
6 time his messenger came with an open letter. It ran as follows: 'It is
reported among the nations—and Gashmu*c* confirms it—that you and the
Jews are plotting rebellion, and it is for this reason that you are rebuilding
7 the wall, and—so the report goes—that you yourself want to be king. You
are also said to have put up prophets to proclaim in Jerusalem that Judah
has a king, meaning yourself. The king will certainly hear of this. So come
8 at once and let us talk the matter over.' Here is the reply I sent: 'No such
thing as you allege has taken place; you have made up the whole story.'
9 They were all trying to intimidate us, in the hope that we should then relax
our efforts and that the work would never be finished. So I applied myself
to it with greater energy.

10    One day I went to the house of Shemaiah son of Delaiah, son of Mehetabel, for he was confined to his house. He said, 'Let us meet in the house of

---

*a* Prob. rdg.; Heb. hundredth.          *b* a daily toll: prob. rdg.; Heb. obscure.
*c* Geshem in 2. 19 and 6. 1, 2.

God, within the sanctuary, and let us shut the doors, for they are coming
to kill you—they are coming to kill you by night.' But I said, 'Should a  11
man like me run away? And can a man like me go into the sanctuary and
survive*ᵃ*? I will not go in.' Then it dawned on me: God had not sent him.  12
His prophecy aimed at harming me, and Tobiah and Sanballat had bribed
him to utter it. He had been bribed to frighten me into compliance and into  13
committing sin; then they could give me a bad name and discredit me.
Remember Tobiah and Sanballat, O God, for what they have done, and  14
also the prophetess Noadiah and all the other prophets who have tried to
intimidate me.

On the twenty-fifth day of the month Elul the wall was finished; it had  15
taken fifty-two days. When our enemies heard of it, and all the surrounding  16
nations saw it,*ᵇ* they thought it a very wonderful achievement,*ᶜ* and they
recognized that this work had been accomplished by the help of our God.
All this time the nobles in Judah were sending many letters to Tobiah,  17
and receiving replies from him. For many in Judah were in league with  18
him, because he was a son-in-law of Shecaniah son of Arah, and his son
Jehohanan had married a daughter of Meshullam son of Berechiah. They  19
were always praising*ᵈ* him in my presence and repeating to him what I
said. Tobiah also wrote to me to intimidate me.

NOW WHEN THE WALL HAD BEEN REBUILT, and I had set the doors  7
in place and the gate-keepers*ᵉ* had been appointed, I gave the charge of  2
Jerusalem to my brother Hanani, and to Hananiah, the governor of the
citadel, for he was trustworthy and God-fearing above other men. And I  3
said to them, 'The entrances to Jerusalem are not to be left open during
the heat of the day; the gates must be kept shut and barred while the gate-
keepers are standing at ease. Appoint guards from among the inhabitants
of Jerusalem, some on sentry-duty and others posted in front of their own
homes.'

The city was large and spacious; there were few people in it and no  4
houses had yet been rebuilt. Then God prompted me to assemble the  5
nobles, the magistrates, and the people, to be enrolled family by family.
And I found the book of the genealogies of those who had been the first
to come back. This is what I found written in it: Of the captives whom  6*ᶠ*
Nebuchadnezzar king of Babylon had taken into exile, these are the people
of the province who have returned to Jerusalem and Judah, each to his
own town, led by Zerubbabel, Jeshua,*ᵍ* Nehemiah, Azariah, Raamiah,  7
Nahamani, Mordecai, Bilshan, Mispereth, Bigvai, Nehum and Baanah.
The roll of the men of the people of Israel: the family of Parosh, two  8
thousand one hundred and seventy-two; the family of Shephatiah, three  9
hundred and seventy-two; the family of Arah, six hundred and fifty-two;  10
the family of Pahath-moab, namely the families of Jeshua and Joab, two  11
thousand eight hundred and eighteen; the family of Elam, one thousand  12

---

*ᵃ* and survive: *or* to save his life.     *ᵇ* *Or* were afraid.     *ᶜ* they thought . . . achievement: *prob. rdg.; Heb.* they fell very much in their own eyes.     *ᵈ* *Or* repeating rumours
about . . .     *ᵉ* *Prob. rdg.; Heb. adds* the singers and the Levites.     *ᶠ* *Verses 6–73:*
*cp. Ezra 2. 1–70.*     *ᵍ* *Or* Joshua (*cp. Hag. 1. 1*).

13 two hundred and fifty-four; the family of Zattu, eight hundred and forty-
14 15 five; the family of Zaccai, seven hundred and sixty; the family of Binnui,
16 six hundred and forty-eight; the family of Bebai, six hundred and twenty-
17 eight; the family of Azgad, two thousand three hundred and twenty-two;
18 19 the family of Adonikam, six hundred and sixty-seven; the family of Bigvai,
20 two thousand and sixty-seven; the family of Adin, six hundred and fifty-
21 22 five; the family of Ater, namely that of Hezekiah, ninety-eight; the family
23 of Hashum, three hundred and twenty-eight; the family of Bezai, three
24 hundred and twenty-four; the family of Harif, one hundred and twelve;
25 26 the family of Gibeon, ninety-five. The men of Bethlehem and Netophah,
27 one hundred and eighty-eight; the men of Anathoth, one hundred and
28 29 twenty-eight; the men of Beth-azmoth, forty-two; the men of Kiriath-
30 jearim, Kephirah, and Beeroth, seven hundred and forty-three; the men
31 of Ramah and Geba, six hundred and twenty-one; the men of Michmas,
32 one hundred and twenty-two; the men of Bethel and Ai, one hundred and
33 34 twenty-three; the men of $^a$ Nebo, fifty-two; the men $^b$ of the other Elam,
35 one thousand two hundred and fifty-four; the men of Harim, three hundred
36 37 and twenty; the men of Jericho, three hundred and forty-five; the men of
38 Lod, Hadid, and Ono, seven hundred and twenty-one; the men of Senaah,
three thousand nine hundred and thirty.

39     Priests: the family of Jedaiah, of the line of Jeshua, nine hundred and
40 41 seventy-three; the family of Immer, one thousand and fifty-two; the
42 family of Pashhur, one thousand two hundred and forty-seven; the family
of Harim, one thousand and seventeen.

43     Levites: the families of Jeshua and$^c$ Kadmiel, of the line of Hodvah,
44 seventy-four. Singers: the family of Asaph, one hundred and forty-eight.
45 Door-keepers: the family of Shallum, the family of Ater, the family of
Talmon, the family of Akkub, the family of Hatita, and the family of
Shobai, one hundred and thirty-eight in all.

46     Temple-servitors: the family of Ziha, the family of Hasupha, the family
47 of Tabbaoth, the family of Keros, the family of Sia, the family of Padon,
48 49 the family of Lebanah, the family of Hagabah, the family of Shalmai, the
50 family of Hanan, the family of Giddel, the family of Gahar, the family of
51 Reaiah, the family of Rezin, the family of Nekoda, the family of Gazzam,
52 the family of Uzza, the family of Paseah, the family of Besai, the family of
53 the Meunim, the family of the Nephishesim,$^d$ the family of Bakbuk, the
54 family of Hakupha, the family of Harhur, the family of Bazlith,$^e$ the
55 family of Mehida, the family of Harsha, the family of Barkos, the family of
56 Sisera, the family of Temah, the family of Neziah, and the family of Hatipha.

57     Descendants of Solomon's servants: the family of Sotai, the family of
58 Sophereth, the family of Perida, the family of Jaalah, the family of Darkon,
59 the family of Giddel, the family of Shephatiah, the family of Hattil, the
family of Pochereth-hazzebaim, and the family of Amon.

60     The temple-servitors and the descendants of Solomon's servants
amounted to three hundred and ninety-two in all.

$^a$ *Prob. rdg., cp. Ezra 2. 29; Heb. adds* the other.     $^b$ *Prob. rdg.; Heb.* family (*also
in verses 35–38*).    $^c$ and: *prob. rdg., cp. Ezra 2. 40; Heb.* to.    $^d$ *Or* Nephusheim.
$^e$ *Or* Bazluth (*cp. Ezra 2. 52*).

The following were those who returned from Tel-melah, Tel-harsha, 61
Kerub, Addon, and Immer, but could not establish their father's family
nor whether by descent they belonged to Israel: the family of Delaiah, the 62
family of Tobiah, the family of Nekoda, six hundred and forty-two. Also 63
of the priests: the family of Hobaiah, the family of Hakkoz, and the family
of Barzillai who had married a daughter of Barzillai the Gileadite and went
by his*a* name. These searched for their names among those enrolled in the 64
genealogies, but they could not be found; they were disqualified for the
priesthood as unclean, and the governor forbade them to partake of 65
the most sacred food until there should be a priest able to consult the Urim
and the Thummim.

The whole assembled people numbered forty-two thousand three 66
hundred and sixty, apart from their slaves, male and female, of whom there 67
were seven thousand three hundred and thirty-seven; and they had two
hundred and forty-five singers, men and women. Their horses numbered 68
seven hundred and thirty-six, their mules two hundred and forty-five,
their camels four hundred and thirty-five, and their asses six thousand seven 69
hundred and twenty.

Some of the heads of families gave contributions for the work. The 70
governor gave to the treasury a thousand drachmas of gold, fifty tossing-
bowls, and five hundred and thirty priestly robes. Some of the heads of 71
families gave for the fabric fund twenty thousand drachmas of gold and
two thousand two hundred minas of silver. What the rest of the people gave 72
was twenty thousand drachmas of gold, two thousand minas of silver, and
sixty-seven priestly robes.

The priests, the Levites, and some of the people lived in Jerusalem and 73
its suburbs;*b* the door-keepers, the singers, the temple-servitors, and all
other Israelites, lived in their own towns.

## The law read by Ezra and the covenant renewed

WHEN THE SEVENTH MONTH CAME, and the Israelites were now
settled in their towns, the people assembled as one man in the 8
square in front of the Water Gate, and Ezra the scribe*c* was asked to bring
the book of the law of Moses, which the LORD had enjoined upon Israel.
On the first day of the seventh month, Ezra the priest brought the law 2
before the assembly, every man and woman, and all who were capable of
understanding what they heard.*d* He read from it, facing the square in 3
front of the Water Gate, from early morning till noon, in the presence of
the men and the women, and those who could understand;*e* all the people
listened attentively to the book of the law. Ezra the scribe stood on a wooden 4
platform made for the purpose,*f* and beside him stood Mattithiah, Shema,
Anaiah, Uriah, Hilkiah, and Maaseiah on his right hand; and on his left

*a* Prob. rdg., cp. 1 Esdras 5. 38; Heb. their.   *b* in Jerusalem and its suburbs: *prob.*
*rdg., cp. 1 Esdras 5. 46; Heb. om.*   *c* Or doctor of the law.   *d* were capable . . .
heard: *or* would teach them to understand.   *e* could understand: *or* were to
instruct.   *f* Or for the address.

Pedaiah, Mishael, Malchiah, Hashum, Hashbaddanah, Zechariah and
5 Meshullam. Ezra opened the book in the sight of all the people, for he was
6 standing above them; and when he opened it, they all stood. Ezra blessed
the LORD, the great God, and all the people raised their hands and answered,
'Amen, Amen'; and they bowed their heads and prostrated themselves
7 humbly before the LORD. Jeshua, Bani, Sherebiah, Jamin, Akkub, Shabbethai, Hodiah, Maaseiah, Kelita, Azariah, Jozabad, Hanan, Pelaiah,
the Levites,*a* expounded the law to the people while they remained in their
8 places. They read from the book of the law of God clearly, made its sense
plain and gave instruction in what was read.
9      Then Nehemiah the governor and Ezra the priest and scribe, and the
Levites who instructed the people, said to them all, 'This day is holy to
the LORD your God; do not mourn or weep.' For all the people had been
10 weeping while they listened to the words of the law. Then he said to them,
'You may go now; refresh yourselves with rich food and sweet drinks, and
send a share to all who cannot provide for themselves; for this day is holy
to our Lord. Let there be no sadness, for joy in the LORD is your strength.'
11 The Levites silenced the people, saying, 'Be quiet, for this day is holy;
12 let there be no sadness.' So all the people went away to eat and to drink, to
send shares to others and to celebrate the day with great rejoicing, because
they had understood what had been explained to them.
13      On the second day the heads of families of the whole people, with the
priests and the Levites, assembled before Ezra the scribe to study the law.
14 And they found written in the law that the LORD had given commandment
through Moses that the Israelites should live in arbours *b* during the feast
15 of the seventh month, and that they should make proclamation throughout
all their cities and in Jerusalem: 'Go out into the hills and fetch branches
of olive and wild olive, myrtle and palm, and other leafy boughs to make
16 arbours, as prescribed.' So the people went out and fetched them and made
arbours for themselves, each on his own roof, and in their courts and in the
courts of the house of God, and in the square at the Water Gate and the
17 square at the Ephraim Gate. And the whole community of those who had
returned from the captivity made arbours and lived in them, a thing that
the Israelites had not done from the days of Joshua son of Nun to that day;
18 and there was very great rejoicing. And day by day, from the first day to
the last, the book of the law of God was read. They kept the feast for seven
days, and on the eighth day there was a closing ceremony, according to
the rule.

9  ON THE TWENTY-FOURTH DAY of this month the Israelites assembled
2 for a fast, clothed in sackcloth and with earth on their heads. Those who
were of Israelite descent separated themselves from all the foreigners; they
took their places and confessed their sins and the iniquities of their fore-
3 fathers. Then they stood up in their places, and the book of the law of the
LORD their God was read for one fourth of the day, and for another fourth
4 they confessed and did obeisance to the LORD their God. Upon the steps
assigned to the Levites stood Jeshua, Bani, Kadmiel, Shebaniah, Bunni,

*a* Prob. rdg.; Heb. and the Levites.        *b* Or tabernacles or booths.

Sherebiah, Bani, and Kenani, and they cried aloud to the LORD their God. Then the Levites, Jeshua, Kadmiel, Bani, Hashabniah, Sherebiah, Hodiah, 5 Shebaniah, and Pethahiah, said, 'Stand up and bless the LORD your God, saying: From everlasting to everlasting thy glorious name is blessed *a* and exalted above all blessing and praise. Thou alone art the LORD; thou hast 6 made heaven, the highest heaven with all its host, the earth and all that is on it, the seas and all that is in them. Thou preservest all of them, and the host of heaven worships thee. Thou art the LORD, the God who chose 7 Abram and brought him out of Ur of the Chaldees and named him Abraham. Thou didst find him faithful to thee and didst make a covenant 8 with him to give to him and to his descendants the land of the Canaanites, the Hittites, the Amorites, the Perizzites, the Jebusites, and the Girgashites; and thou didst fulfil thy promise, for thou art just.

'And thou didst see the misery of our forefathers in Egypt and didst hear 9 their cry for help at the Red Sea,*b* and didst work signs and portents 10 against Pharaoh, all his courtiers and all the people of his land, knowing how arrogantly they treated our forefathers, and thou didst win for thyself a name that lives on to this day. Thou didst tear the sea apart before them 11 so that they went through the middle of it on dry ground; but thou didst cast their pursuers into the depths, like a stone cast into turbulent waters. Thou didst guide them by a pillar of cloud in the day-time and by a pillar 12 of fire at night to give them light on the road by which they travelled. Thou 13 didst descend upon Mount Sinai and speak with them from heaven, and give them right judgements and true laws, and statutes and commandments which were good, and thou didst make known to them thy holy 14 sabbath and give them commandments, statutes, and laws through thy servant Moses. Thou gavest them bread from heaven to stay their hunger 15 and thou broughtest water out from a rock for them to quench their thirst, and thou didst bid them enter and take possession of the land which thou hadst solemnly sworn to give them. But they, our forefathers, were arro- 16 gant and stubborn, and disobeyed thy commandments. They refused to 17 obey and did not remember the miracles which thou didst accomplish among them; they remained stubborn, and they appointed a man to lead them back to slavery in Egypt. But thou art a forgiving god, gracious and compassionate, long-suffering and ever constant, and thou didst not forsake them. Even when they made the image of a bull-calf in metal and said, 18 "This is your god who brought you up from Egypt", and were guilty of great blasphemies, thou in thy great compassion didst not forsake them in 19 the wilderness. The pillar of cloud did not fail to guide them on their journey by day nor the pillar of fire by night to give them light on the road by which they travelled. Thou gavest thy good spirit to instruct them; thy 20 manna thou didst not withhold from them, and thou gavest them water to quench their thirst. Forty years long thou didst sustain them in the wilder- 21 ness, and they lacked nothing; their clothes did not wear out and their feet were not swollen.

'Thou gavest them kingdoms and peoples, allotting these to them as 22

*a* thy glorious name is blessed: *prob. rdg.*; *Heb.* and let them bless thy glorious name.
*b* Or the Sea of Reeds.

spoils of war. Thus they took possession of the land of Sihon king of
23 Heshbon and the land of Og king of Bashan. Thou didst multiply their
descendants so that they became countless as the stars in the sky, bringing
them into the land which thou didst promise to give to their forefathers
24 as their possession. When their descendants entered the land and took
possession of it, thou didst subdue before them the Canaanites who
inhabited it and gavest these, kings and peoples alike, into their hands to
25 do with them whatever they wished. They captured fortified cities and a
fertile land and took possession of houses full of all good things, rock-
hewn cisterns, vineyards, olive-trees, and fruit-trees in abundance; so
they ate and were satisfied and grew fat and found delight in thy great
26 goodness. But they were defiant and rebelled against thee; they turned
their backs on thy law and killed thy prophets, who solemnly warned them
27 to return to thee, and they were guilty of great blasphemies. Because of
this thou didst hand them over to their enemies who oppressed them. But
when, in the time of their oppression, they cried to thee for help, thou
heardest them from heaven and in thy great compassion didst send them
28 saviours to save them from their enemies. But when they had had a respite,
they once more did what was wrong in thine eyes; and thou didst abandon
them to their enemies who held them in subjection. But again they cried
to thee for help, and many times over thou heardest them from heaven and
29 in thy compassion didst save them. Thou didst solemnly warn them to
return to thy law, but they grew arrogant and did not heed thy commandments; they sinned against thy ordinances, which bring life to him who
keeps them. Stubbornly they turned away in mulish obstinacy and would
30 not obey. Many years thou wast patient with them and didst warn them by
thy spirit through thy prophets; but they would not listen. Therefore thou
31 didst hand them over to foreign peoples. Yet in thy great compassion thou
didst not make an end of them nor forsake them; for thou art a gracious and
compassionate god.

32    'Now therefore, our God, thou great and mighty and terrible God, who
faithfully keepest covenant, do not make light of the hardships that have
befallen us—our kings, our princes, our priests, our prophets, our forefathers, and all thy people—from the days of the kings of Assyria to this
33 day. In all that has befallen us thou hast been just, thou hast kept faith,
34 but we have done wrong. Our kings, our princes, our priests, and our forefathers did not keep thy law nor heed thy commandments and the warnings
35 which thou gavest them. Even under their own kings, while they were
enjoying the great prosperity which thou gavest them and the broad and
fertile land which thou didst bestow upon them, they did not serve thee;
36 they did not abandon their evil ways. Today we are slaves, slaves here in
the land which thou gavest to our forefathers so that they might eat its
37 fruits and enjoy its good things. All its produce now goes to the kings
whom thou hast set over us because of our sins. They have power over our
bodies, and they do as they please with our beasts, while we are in dire
distress.

38    'Because of all this we make a binding declaration in writing, and our
princes, our Levites, and our priests witness the sealing.

'Those who witness the sealing are Nehemiah the governor, son of **10**
Hacaliah, Zedekiah, Seraiah, Azariah, Jeremiah, Pashhur, Amariah, 2 3
Malchiah, Hattush, Shebaniah, Malluch, Harim, Meremoth, Obadiah, 4 5
Daniel, Ginnethon, Baruch, Meshullam, Abiah, Mijamin, Maaziah, 6 7 8
Bilgai, Shemaiah; these are the priests. The Levites: Jeshua[a] son of 9
Azaniah, Binnui of the family of Henadad, Kadmiel; and their brethren, .10
Shebaniah, Hodiah,[b] Kelita, Pelaiah, Hanan, Mica, Rehob, Hashabiah, 11
Zaccur, Sherebiah, Shebaniah, Hodiah, Bani, Beninu. The chiefs of the 12 13 14
people: Parosh, Pahath-moab, Elam, Zattu, Bani, Bunni, Azgad, Bebai, 15
Adonijah, Bigvai, Adin, Ater, Hezekiah, Azzur, Hodiah, Hashum, Bezai, 16 17 18
Hariph, Anathoth, Nebai,[c] Magpiash, Meshullam, Hezir, Meshezabel, 19 20 21
Zadok, Jaddua, Pelatiah, Hanan, Anaiah, Hoshea, Hananiah, Hasshub, 22 23
Hallohesh, Pilha, Shobek, Rehum, Hashabnah, Maaseiah, Ahiah, Hanan, 24 25 26
Anan, Malluch, Harim, Baanah. 27

'The rest of the people, the priests, the Levites, the door-keepers, the 28
singers, the temple-servitors, with their wives, their sons, and their
daughters, all who are capable of understanding, all who for the sake of the
law of God have kept themselves apart from the foreign population, join 29
with the leading brethren,[d] when the oath is put to them, in swearing to
obey God's law given by Moses the servant of God, and to observe and
fulfil all the commandments of the LORD our Lord, his rules and his
statutes.

'We will not give our daughters in marriage to the foreign population or 30
take their daughters for our sons. If on the sabbath these people bring in 31
merchandise, especially corn, for sale, we will not buy from them on the
sabbath or on any holy day. We will forgo the crops of the seventh year
and release every person still held as a pledge for debt.

'We hereby undertake the duty of giving yearly the third of a shekel for 32
the service of the house of our God, for the Bread of the Presence, the 33
regular grain-offering and whole-offering, the sabbaths, the new moons,
the appointed seasons, the holy-gifts, and the sin-offerings to make expiation
on behalf of Israel, and for all else that has to be done in the house of our
God. We, the priests, the Levites, and the people, have cast lots for the 34
wood-offering, so that it may be brought into the house of our God by
each family in turn, at appointed times, year by year, to burn upon the
altar of the LORD our God, as prescribed in the law. We undertake to bring 35
the firstfruits of our land and the firstfruits of every fruit-tree, year by
year, to the house of the LORD; also to bring to the house of our God, to the 36
priests who minister in the house of our God, the first-born of our sons and
of our cattle, as prescribed in the law, and the first-born of our herds and
of our flocks; and to bring to the priests the first kneading of our dough, 37
and the first of the fruit of every tree, of the new wine and of the oil, to the
store-rooms in the house of our God; and to bring to the Levites the tithes
from our land, for it is the Levites who collect the tithes in all our farming
villages. The Aaronite priest shall be with the Levites when they collect 38
the tithes; and the Levites shall bring up one tenth of the tithes to the

[a] *Prob. rdg.; Heb.* and Jeshua.     [b] *Or, with Ezra 2. 40,* Hodaviah.     [c] *Or* Nobai.
[d] the leading brethren: *prob. rdg.; Heb.* their brethren, their leading men.

39 house of our God, to the appropriate rooms in the storehouse. For the Israelites and the Levites shall bring the contribution of corn, new wine, and oil to the rooms where the vessels of the sanctuary are kept, and where the ministering priests, the door-keepers, and the singers are lodged. We will not neglect the house of our God.'

11 THE LEADERS OF THE PEOPLE settled in Jerusalem; and the rest of the people cast lots to bring one in every ten to live in Jerusalem, the holy city,

2 while the remaining nine lived in other towns. And the people were grateful to all those who volunteered to live in Jerusalem.

3 These are the chiefs of the province who lived in Jerusalem; but, in the towns of Judah, other Israelites, priests, Levites, temple-servitors, and descendants of Solomon's servants lived on their own property, in their

4 own towns. Some members of the tribes of Judah and Benjamin lived in Jerusalem. Of Judah: Athaiah son of Uzziah, son of Zechariah, son of

6 Amariah, son of Shephatiah, son of Mahalalel of the family of Perez, all of whose family, to the number of four hundred and sixty-eight men of sub-

5 stance, lived in Jerusalem; and Maaseiah son of Baruch, son of Col-hozeh, son of Hazaiah, son of Adaiah, son of Joiarib, son of Zechariah of the Shelanite family.

7 These were the Benjamites: Sallu son of Meshullam, son of Joed, son of Pedaiah, son of Kolaiah, son of Maaseiah, son of Ithiel, son of Isaiah,

8 and his kinsmen Gabbai and Sallai, nine hundred and twenty-eight in all.

9 Joel son of Zichri was their overseer, and Judah son of Hassenuah was second over the city.*[a]*

10 11 Of the priests: Jedaiah son of Joiarib, son of*[b]* Seraiah, son of Hilkiah, son of Meshullam, son of Zadok, son of Meraioth, son of Ahitub, super-

12 visor of the house of God, and his*[c]* brethren responsible for the work in the temple, eight hundred and twenty-two in all; and Adaiah son of Jeroham, son of Pelaliah, son of Amzi, son of Zechariah, son of Pashhur,

13 son of Malchiah, and his brethren, heads of fathers' houses, two hundred and forty-two in all; and Amasai*[d]* son of Azarel, son of Ahzai, son of

14 Meshillemoth, son of Immer, and his brethren, men of substance, a hundred and twenty-eight in all; their overseer was Zabdiel son of Haggedolim.

15 And of the Levites: Shemaiah son of Hasshub, son of Azrikam, son of

16 Hashabiah, son of Bunni; and Shabbethai and Jozabad of the chiefs of the Levites, who had charge of the external business of the house of God;

17 and Mattaniah son of Micah, son of Zabdi, son of Asaph, who as precentor led the prayer of thanksgiving, and Bakbukiah who held the second place among his brethren; and Abda son of Shammua, son of Galal, son of

18 Jeduthun. The number of Levites in the holy city was two hundred and eighty-four in all.

19 The gate-keepers who kept guard at the gates were Akkub, Talmon, and

20 their brethren, a hundred and seventy-two. The rest of the Israelites*[e]* were

*[a]* second over the city: *or* over the second quarter of the city.    *[b]* son of: *prob. rdg.; Heb. obscure.*    *[c] Prob. rdg.; Heb.* their.    *[d] Prob. rdg.; Heb.* Amashsai.
*[e] Prob. rdg.; Heb. adds* the levitical priests.

in all the towns of Judah, each man on his own inherited property. But the 21
temple-servitors lodged on Ophel, and Ziha and Gishpa were in charge of
them.

The overseer of the Levites in Jerusalem was Uzzi son of Bani, son of 22
Hashabiah, son of Mattaniah, son of Mica, of the family of Asaph the
singers, for the supervision of the business of the house of God. For they 23
were under the king's orders, and there was obligatory duty for the singers
every day. Pethahiah son of Meshezabel, of the family of Zerah son of 24
Judah, was the king's adviser on all matters affecting the people.

As for the hamlets with their surrounding fields: some of the men of 25
Judah lived in Kiriath-arba and its villages, in Dibon and its villages, and
in Jekabzeel and its hamlets, in Jeshua, Moladah, and Bethpelet, in Hazar- 26 27
shual, and in Beersheba and its villages, in Ziklag and in Meconah and its 28
villages, in Enrimmon, Zorah, and Jarmuth, in Zanoah, Adullam, and their 29 30
hamlets, in Lachish and its fields and Azekah and its villages. Thus they
occupied the country from Beersheba to the Valley of Hinnom.

The men of Benjamin lived in*ᵃ* Geba, Michmash, Aiah, and Bethel with 31
its villages, in Anathoth, Nob, and Ananiah, in Hazor, Ramah, and Git- 32 33
taim, in Hadid, Zeboim, and Neballat, in Lod, Ono, and*ᵇ* Ge-harashim.*ᶜ* 34 35
And certain divisions of the Levites in Judah were attached to Benjamin. 36

These are the priests and the Levites who came back with Zerubbabel 12
son of Shealtiel, and Jeshua:*ᵈ* Seraiah, Jeremiah, Ezra, Amariah, Malluch, 2
Hattush, Shecaniah, Rehum, Meremoth, Iddo, Ginnethon, Abiah, 3 4
Mijamin, Maadiah, Bilgah, Shemaiah, Joiarib, Jedaiah, Sallu, Amok, 5 6 7
Hilkiah, Jedaiah. These were the chiefs of the priests and of their brethren
in the days of Jeshua.

And the Levites: Jeshua, Binnui, Kadmiel, Sherebiah, Judah, and Mat- 8
taniah, who with his brethren was in charge of the songs of thanksgiving.
And Bakbukiah and Unni their brethren stood opposite them in the 9
service. And Jeshua was the father of Joiakim, Joiakim the father of 10
Eliashib, Eliashib of Joiada, Joiada the father of Jonathan, and Jonathan 11
the father of Jaddua. And in the days of Joiakim the priests who were heads 12
of families were: of Seraiah, Meraiah; of Jeremiah, Hananiah; of Ezra, 13
Meshullam; of Amariah, Jehohanan; of Malluch,*ᵉ* Jonathan; of Shebaniah, 14
Joseph; of Harim, Adna; of Meraioth, Helkai; of Iddo, Zechariah; of 15 16
Ginnethon, Meshullam; of Abiah, Zichri; of Miniamin*ᶠ*; of Moadiah, 17
Piltai; of Bilgah, Shammua; of Shemaiah, Jehonathan; of Joiarib, Mat- 18 19
tenai; of Jedaiah, Uzzi; of Sallu,*ᵍ* Kallai; of Amok, Eber; of Hilkiah, 20 21
Hashabiah; of Jedaiah, Nethaneel.

*ʰ*The heads of the priestly families*ⁱ* in the days of Eliashib, Joiada, 22
Johanan, and Jaddua were recorded down to the reign of Darius the
Persian. The heads of the levitical families were recorded in the annals 23
only down to the days of Johanan the grandson of Eliashib. And the chiefs 24

---

*ᵃ Prob. rdg.; Heb. from.* *ᵇ and: prob. rdg.; Heb. om.* *ᶜ Or and the Valley of*
Woods *or and the Valley of Craftsmen.* *ᵈ Or Joshua.* *ᵉ Prob. rdg.; Heb. Malluchi,*
*or Melichu.* *ᶠ A name is missing here.* *ᵍ Prob. rdg., cp. verse 7; Heb. Sallai.*
*ʰ Prob. rdg.; Heb. prefixes The Levites.* *ⁱ heads ... families: prob. rdg.; Heb.*
heads of the families and the priests.

of the Levites: Hashabiah, Sherebiah, Jeshua, Binnui,[a] Kadmiel, with their brethren in the other turn of duty, to praise and to give thanks, according to the commandment of David the man of God, turn by turn.

25 Mattaniah, Bakbukiah, Obadiah, Meshullam, Talmon, and Akkub were
26 gate-keepers standing guard at the gatehouses. This was the arrangement in the days of Joiakim son of Jeshua, son of Jozadak, and in the days of Nehemiah the governor and of Ezra the priest and scribe.

27    At the dedication of the wall of Jerusalem they sought out the Levites in all their settlements, and brought them to Jerusalem to celebrate the dedication with[b] rejoicing, with thanksgiving and song, to the accompani-
28 ment of cymbals, lutes, and harps. And the Levites,[c] the singers, were assembled from the district round Jerusalem and from the hamlets of the
29 Netophathites; also from Beth-gilgal and from the region of Geba and Beth-azmoth;[d] for the singers had built themselves hamlets in the neigh-
30 bourhood of Jerusalem. The priests and the Levites purified themselves;
31 and they purified the people, the gates, and the wall. Then I brought the leading men of Judah up on to the city wall, and appointed two great choirs to give thanks. One went in procession[e] to the right, going along the wall
32 to the Dung Gate; and after it went Hoshaiah with half the leading men of
33 34 Judah, and Azariah, Ezra, Meshullam, Judah, Benjamin, Shemaiah, and
35 Jeremiah; and certain of the priests with trumpets: Zechariah son of Jonathan, son of Shemaiah, son of Mattanaiah, son of Micaiah, son of
36 Zaccur, son of Asaph, and his kinsmen, Shemaiah, Azarel, Milalai, Gilalai, Maai, Nethaneel, Judah, and Hanani, with the musical instru-
37 ments of David the man of God; and Ezra the scribe led them. They went past the Fountain Gate and thence straight forward by the steps up to the City of David, by the ascent to the city wall, past the house of David, and
38 on to the Water Gate on the east. The other thanksgiving choir went to the left,[f] and I followed it with half the leading men of[g] the people, continuing
39 along the wall, past the Tower of the Ovens[h] to the Broad Wall, and past the Ephraim Gate, and over the Jeshanah Gate,[i] and over the Fish Gate, taking in the Tower of Hananel and the Tower of the Hundred, as far as
40 the Sheep Gate; and they halted at the Gate of the Guardhouse. So the two thanksgiving choirs took their place in the house of God, and I and
41 half the magistrates with me; and the priests Eliakim, Maaseiah, Miniamin,
42 Micaiah, Elioenai, Zechariah, and Hananiah, with trumpets; and Maaseiah, Shemaiah, Eleazar, Uzzi, Jehohanan, Malchiah, Elam, and Ezer. The
43 singers, led by Izrahiah, raised their voices. A great sacrifice was celebrated that day, and they all rejoiced because God had given them great cause for rejoicing; the women and children rejoiced with them. And the rejoicing in Jerusalem was heard a long way off.

44    On that day men were appointed to take charge of the store-rooms for the contributions, the firstfruits, and the tithes, to gather in the portions

---

[a] Jeshua, Binnui: *prob. rdg.; Heb.* and Jeshua son of.          [b] *Prob. rdg.; Heb.* and.
[c] the Levites: *prob. rdg.; Heb.* the sons of.          [d] Beth-azmoth: *prob. rdg., cp. 7. 28;*
*Heb.* Azmoth.          [e] One ... procession: *prob. rdg.; Heb.* Processions.          [f] to the
left: *prob. rdg.; Heb.* to the front.          [g] the leading men of: *prob. rdg.; Heb. om.*
[h] Or Furnaces.          [i] the Jeshanah Gate: *or* the gate of the Old City.

required by the law for the priests and Levites according to the extent of the farmlands round the towns; for all Judah was full of rejoicing at the ministry of the priests and Levites. And they performed the service of their 45 God and the service of purification, as did the singers and the door-keepers, according to the rules laid down by David and his son Solomon. For it was 46 in the days of David that Asaph took the lead as chief of the singers and director*a* of praise and thanksgiving to God. And in the days of Zerubbabel 47 and of Nehemiah all Israel gave the portions for the singers and the door-keepers as each day required; and they set apart the portion for the Levites, and the Levites set apart the portion for the Aaronites.

## *Nehemiah's reforms*

O N THAT DAY AT THE PUBLIC READING from the book of Moses, 13 it was found to be laid down that no Ammonite or Moabite should ever enter the assembly of God, because they did not meet the Israelites 2 with food and water but hired Balaam to curse them, though our God turned the curse into a blessing. When the people heard the law, they 3 separated from Israel all who were of mixed blood.

But before this, Eliashib the priest, who was appointed over the store- 4 rooms of the house of our God, and who was connected by marriage with Tobiah, had provided for his use a large room where formerly they had 5 kept the grain-offering, the incense, the temple vessels, the tithes of corn, new wine, and oil prescribed for the Levites, singers, and door-keepers, and the contributions for the priests. All this time I was not in Jerusalem 6 because, in the thirty-second year of Artaxerxes king of Babylon, I had gone to the king. Some time later, I asked permission from him and returned 7 to Jerusalem. There I discovered the wicked thing that Eliashib had done for Tobiah's sake in providing him with a room in the courts of the house of God. I was greatly displeased and threw all Tobiah's belongings out of 8 the room. Then I gave orders that the room should be purified, and that 9 the vessels of the house of God, with the grain-offering and incense, should be put back into it.

I also learnt that the Levites had not been given their portions; both they 10 and the singers, who were responsible for their respective duties, had made off to their farms. So I remonstrated with the magistrates and said, 'Why 11 is the house of God deserted?' And I recalled the men and restored them to their places. Then all Judah brought the tithes of corn, new wine, and 12 oil into the storehouses; and I put in charge of them Shelemiah the priest, 13 Zadok the accountant, and Pedaiah a Levite, with Hanan son of Zaccur, son of Mattaniah, as their assistant, for they were considered trustworthy men; their duty was the distribution of their shares to their brethren. Remember this, O God, to my credit, and do not wipe out of thy memory 14 the devotion which I have shown in the house of my God and in his service.

In those days I saw men in Judah treading winepresses on the sabbath, 15 collecting quantities of produce and piling it on asses—wine, grapes, figs,

*a Prob. rdg.; Heb. song.*

and every kind of load, which they brought into Jerusalem on the sabbath;
16 and I protested to them about selling food on that day. Tyrians living in
Jerusalem also brought in fish and all kinds of merchandise and sold them
17 on the sabbath to the people of Judah, even in Jerusalem. Then I complained to the nobles of Judah and said to them, 'How dare you profane
18 the sabbath in this wicked way? Is not this just what your fathers did, so
that our God has brought all this evil on us and on this city? Now you are
19 bringing more wrath upon Israel by profaning the sabbath.' When the
entrances to Jerusalem had been cleared in preparation for the sabbath, I
gave orders that the gates should be shut and not opened until after the
sabbath. And I appointed some of the men under me to have charge of the
20 gates so that no load might enter on the sabbath. Then on one or two
occasions the merchants and all kinds of traders camped just outside
21 Jerusalem, but I cautioned them. 'Why are you camping in front of the
city wall?' I asked. 'If you do it again, I will take action against you.' After
22 that they did not come on the sabbath again. And I commanded the
Levites who were to purify themselves and take up duty as guards at the
gates, to ensure that the sabbath was kept holy. Remember this also to my
credit, O God, and spare me in thy great love.

23    In those days also I saw that some Jews had married women from Ashdod,
24 Ammon, and Moab. Half their children spoke the language of Ashdod or
25 of the other peoples and could not speak the language of the Jews. I argued
with them and reviled them, I beat them and tore out their hair; and I
made them swear in the name of God: 'We will not marry our daughters
to their sons, or take any of their daughters in marriage for our sons or for
26 ourselves.' 'Was it not for such women', I said, 'that King Solomon of
Israel sinned? Among all the nations there was no king like him; he was
loved by his God, and God made him king over all Israel; nevertheless
27 even he was led by foreign women into sin. Are we then to follow your
example and commit this grave offence, breaking faith with our God by
marrying foreign women?'

28    Now one of the sons of Joiada son of Eliashib the high priest had married
a daughter of Sanballat the Horonite; therefore I drove him out of my
29 presence. Remember, O God, to their shame that they have defiled the
priesthood and the covenant of the priests *a* and the Levites.

30    Thus I purified them from everything foreign, and I made the Levites
31 and the priests resume the duties of their office; I also made provision for
the wood-offering, at appointed times, and for the firstfruits. Remember
me for my good, O God.

*a Or* priesthood.

# ESTHER

## Esther chosen as queen by the Persian king

THE EVENTS HERE RELATED happened in the days of 1
Ahasuerus, the Ahasuerus who ruled from India to Ethiopia, a hundred and twenty-seven provinces. At this time he sat on his royal 2
throne in Susa the capital city. In the third year of his reign he gave a 3
banquet for all his officers and his courtiers; and when his army of Persians
and Medes, with his nobles and provincial governors, were in attendance,
he displayed the wealth of his kingdom and the pomp and splendour of his 4
majesty for many days, a hundred and eighty in all. When these days were 5
over, the king gave a banquet for all the people present in Susa the capital
city, both high and low; it was held in the garden court of the royal pavilion
and lasted seven days. There were white curtains and violet hangings 6
fastened to silver rings with bands of fine linen and purple;[a] there were
alabaster pillars and couches of gold and silver set on a mosaic pavement of
malachite and alabaster, of mother-of-pearl and turquoise. Wine was 7
served in golden cups of various patterns: the king's wine flowed freely as
befitted a king, and the law of the drinking was that there should be no 8
compulsion, for the king had laid it down that all the stewards of his palace
should respect each man's wishes. In addition, Queen Vashti gave a 9
banquet for the women in the royal apartments of King Ahasuerus.

On the seventh day, when he was merry with wine, the king ordered 10
Mehuman, Biztha, Harbona, Bigtha, Abagtha, Zethar, and Carcas, the
seven eunuchs who were in attendance on the king's person, to bring Queen 11
Vashti before him wearing her royal crown, in order to display her beauty
to the people and the officers; for she was indeed a beautiful woman. But 12
Queen Vashti refused to come in answer to the royal command conveyed
by the eunuchs. This greatly incensed the king, and he grew hot with
anger.

Then the king conferred with his wise men versed in misdemeanours;[b] 13
for it was his royal custom to consult all who were versed in law and religion,
those closest to him being Carshena, Shethar, Admatha, Tarshish, Meres, 14
Marsena, and Memucan, the seven princes of Persia and Media who had
access to the king and held first place in the kingdom. He asked them, 15
'What does the law require to be done with Queen Vashti for disobeying
the command of King Ahasuerus brought to her by the eunuchs?' Then 16
Memucan made answer before the king and the princes: 'Queen Vashti
has done wrong, and not to the king alone, but also to all the officers and to
all the peoples in all the provinces of King Ahasuerus. Every woman will 17
come to know what the queen has done, and this will make them treat their
husbands with contempt; they will say, "King Ahasuerus ordered Queen

[a] bands . . . purple: *or* white and purple cords.     [b] *Or* times.

551

18 Vashti to be brought before him and she did not come." The great ladies of Persia and Media, who have heard of the queen's conduct, will tell all the king's officers about this day, and there will be endless disrespect and
19 insolence! If it please your majesty, let a royal decree go out from you and let it be inscribed in the laws of the Persians and Medes, never to be revoked, that Vashti shall not again appear before King Ahasuerus; and let the king give her place as queen to another woman who is more worthy
20 of it than she. Thus when this royal edict is heard through the length and breadth of the kingdom, all women will give honour to their husbands,
21 high and low alike.' Memucan's advice pleased the king and the princes,
22 and the king did as he had proposed. Letters were sent to all the royal provinces, to every province in its own script and to every people in their own language, in order that each man might be master in his own house and control all his own womenfolk.[a]

2 Later, when the anger of King Ahasuerus had died down, he remembered
2 Vashti and what she had done and what had been decreed against her. So the king's attendants said, 'Let beautiful young virgins be sought out for
3 your majesty; and let your majesty appoint commissioners in all the provinces of your kingdom to bring all these beautiful young virgins into the women's quarters in Susa the capital city. Let them be committed to the care of Hegai, the king's eunuch in charge of the women, and let cosmetics
4 be provided for them; and let the one who is most acceptable to the king become queen in place of Vashti.' This idea pleased the king and he acted on it.
5 Now there was in Susa the capital city a Jew named Mordecai son of
6 Jair, son of Shimei, son of Kish, a Benjamite; he had been carried into exile from Jerusalem among those whom Nebuchadnezzar king of Babylon
7 had carried away with Jeconiah king of Judah. He had a foster-child Hadassah, that is Esther, his uncle's daughter, who had neither father nor mother. She was a beautiful and charming girl, and after the death of her
8 father and mother Mordecai had adopted her as his own daughter. When the king's order and his edict were published, and many girls were brought to Susa the capital city to be committed to the care of Hegai, Esther too was taken to the king's palace to be entrusted to Hegai, who had charge
9 of the women. She attracted his notice and received his special favour: he readily provided her with her cosmetics and her allowance of food, and also with seven picked maids from the king's palace, and he gave her and her maids privileges in the women's quarters.
10 Esther had not disclosed her race or her family, because Mordecai had
11 forbidden her to do so. Every day Mordecai passed along by the forecourt of the women's quarters to learn how Esther was faring and what was happening to her.
12 The full period of preparation prescribed for the women was twelve months, six months with oil and myrrh and six months with perfumes and cosmetics. When the period was complete, each girl's turn came to go to
13 King Ahasuerus, and she was allowed to take with her whatever she asked,
14 when she went from the women's quarters to the king's palace. She went

[a] *and control . . . womenfolk:* prob. rdg.; *Heb.* and speak in his own language.

into the palace in the evening and returned in the morning to another part
of the women's quarters, to be under the care of Shaashgaz, the king's
eunuch in charge of the concubines. She did not again go to the king unless
he expressed a wish for her; then she was summoned by name.

When the turn came for Esther, daughter of Abihail the uncle of 15
Mordecai her adoptive father, to go to the king, she asked for nothing to
take with her except what was advised by Hegai, the king's eunuch in
charge of the women; and Esther charmed all who saw her. When she was 16
taken to King Ahasuerus in the royal palace, in the seventh year of his
reign, in the tenth month, that is the month Tebeth, the king loved her 17
more than any of his other women and treated her with greater favour and
kindness than the rest of the virgins. He put a royal crown on her head and
made her queen in place of Vashti. Then the king gave a great banquet for 18
all his officers and courtiers, a banquet in honour of Esther. He also proclaimed a holiday*a* throughout the provinces and distributed gifts worthy
of a king.

Mordecai was in attendance at court; on his instructions Esther had 19 20
not disclosed her family or her race, she had done what Mordecai told her,
as she did when she was his ward. One day when Mordecai was in attend- 21
ance at court, Bigthan and Teresh, two of the king's eunuchs, keepers of
the threshold, who were disaffected, were plotting to lay hands on King
Ahasuerus. This became known to Mordecai, who told Queen Esther; and 22
she told the king, mentioning Mordecai by name. The affair was investi- 23
gated and the report confirmed; the two men were hanged on the gallows.
All this was recorded in the royal chronicle in the presence of the king.

## *Haman's plot against the Jews*

AFTER THIS, KING AHASUERUS promoted Haman son of Hammedatha 3
the Agagite, advancing him and giving him precedence above all his
fellow-officers. So the king's attendants at court all bowed down to Haman 2
and did obeisance, for so the king had commanded; but Mordecai did not
bow down to him or do obeisance. Then the attendants at court said to 3
Mordecai, 'Why do you flout his majesty's command?' Day by day they 4
challenged him, but he refused to listen to them; so they informed Haman,
in order to discover if Mordecai's refusal would be tolerated, for he had
told them that he was a Jew. When Haman saw that Mordecai was not 5
bowing down to him or doing obeisance, he was infuriated. On learning 6
who Mordecai's people were, he scorned to lay hands on him alone, and
looked for a way to destroy all the Jews throughout the whole kingdom of
Ahasuerus, Mordecai and all his race.

In the twelfth year of King Ahasuerus, in the first month, Nisan, they 7
cast lots, Pur as it is called, in the presence of Haman, taking day by day
and month by month, and the lot fell on the thirteenth day of the twelfth
month,*b* the month Adar. Then Haman said to King Ahasuerus, 'There is 8

*a* *Or* an amnesty.          *b* and the lot . . . twelfth month: *prob. rdg., cp. verse 13; Heb.*
the twelfth.

a certain people, dispersed among the many peoples in all the provinces of your kingdom, who keep themselves apart. Their laws are different from those of every other people; they do not keep your majesty's laws. It does
9 not befit your majesty to tolerate them. If it please your majesty, let an order be made in writing for their destruction; and I will pay ten thousand talents of silver to your majesty's officials, to be deposited in the royal
10 treasury.' So the king took the signet-ring from his hand and gave it to
11 Haman son of Hammedatha the Agagite, the enemy of the Jews; and he said to him, 'The money and the people are yours; deal with them as you wish.'

12 On the thirteenth day of the first month the king's secretaries were summoned and, in accordance with Haman's instructions, a writ was issued to the king's satraps and the governor of every province, and to the officers over each separate people: for each province in its own script and for each people in their own language. It was drawn up in the name of King
13 Ahasuerus and sealed with the king's signet. Thus letters were sent by courier to all the king's provinces with orders to destroy, slay, and exterminate all Jews, young and old, women and children, in one day, the thirteenth day of the twelfth month, the month Adar, and to plunder their
14 possessions. A copy of the writ was to be issued as a decree in every province and to be published to all the peoples, so that they might be ready for
15 that day. The couriers were dispatched post-haste at the king's command, and the decree was issued in Susa the capital city. The king and Haman sat down to drink; but the city of Susa was thrown into confusion.

4 When Mordecai learnt all that had been done, he rent his clothes, put on sackcloth and ashes, and went through the city crying loudly and bitterly.
2 He came within sight of the palace gate, because no one clothed with sack-
3 cloth was allowed to pass through the gate. In every province reached by the royal command and decree there was great mourning among the Jews, with fasting and weeping and beating of the breast. Most of them made
4 their beds of sackcloth and ashes. When Queen Esther's maids and eunuchs came and told her, she was distraught, and sent garments for Mordecai, so that they might take off the sackcloth and clothe him with them; but he
5 would not accept them. Then Esther summoned Hathach, one of the king's eunuchs who had been appointed to wait upon her, and ordered him to
6 find out from Mordecai what the trouble was and what it meant. Hathach
7 went to Mordecai in the city square in front of the palace gate, and Mordecai told him all that had happened to him and how much money Haman had offered to pay into the royal treasury for the destruction of the Jews.
8 He also gave him a copy of the writ for their destruction issued in Susa, so that he might show it to Esther and tell her about it, bidding her go to
9 the king to plead for his favour and entreat him for her people. Hathach
10 went and told Esther what Mordecai had said, and she sent him back with
11 this message: 'All the king's courtiers and the people of the provinces are aware that if any person, man or woman, enters the king's presence in the inner court unbidden, there is one law only: that person shall be put to death, unless the king stretches out to him the golden sceptre; then and then only shall he live. It is now thirty days since I myself was called to go

to the king.' But when they told Mordecai what Esther had said, he bade 12 13
them go back to her and say, 'Do not imagine that you alone of all the Jews
will escape because you are in the royal palace. If you remain silent at such 14
a time as this, relief and deliverance for the Jews will appear from another
quarter, but you and your father's family will perish. Who knows whether
it is not for such a time as this that you have come to royal estate?' Esther 15
gave them this answer to take back to Mordecai: 'Go and assemble all the 16
Jews to be found in Susa and fast for me; take neither food nor drink for
three days, night or day, and I and my maids will fast as you do. After that
I will go to the king, although it is against the law; and if I perish, I perish.'
So Mordecai went away and did exactly as Esther had bidden him. 17

On the third day Esther put on her royal robes and stood in the inner 5
court of the king's palace, facing the palace itself; the king was seated on
his royal throne in the palace, facing the entrance. When the king caught 2
sight of Queen Esther standing in the court, she won his favour and he
stretched out to her the golden sceptre which he was holding. Thereupon
Esther approached and touched the head of the sceptre. Then the king said 3
to her, 'What is it, Queen Esther? Whatever you ask of me, up to half my
kingdom, shall be given to you.' 'If it please your majesty,' said Esther, 4
'will you come today, sire, and Haman with you, to a banquet which I have
made ready for you?' The king gave orders that Haman should be fetched 5
quickly, so that Esther's wish might be fulfilled; and the king and Haman
went to the banquet which she had prepared. Over the wine the king said 6
to Esther, 'Whatever you ask of me shall be given to you. Whatever you
request of me, up to half my kingdom, it shall be done.' Esther said in 7
answer, 'What I ask and request of you is this. If I have won your majesty's 8
favour, and if it please you, sire, to give me what I ask and to grant my
request, will your majesty and Haman come tomorrow to the banquet
which I shall prepare for you both? Tomorrow I will do as your majesty·
has said.'

So Haman went away that day in good spirits and well pleased with 9
himself. But when he saw Mordecai in attendance at court and how he did
not rise nor defer to him, he was filled with rage; but he kept control of 10
himself and went home. Then he sent for his friends and his wife Zeresh
and held forth to them about the splendour of his wealth and his many 11
sons, and how the king had promoted him and advanced him above the
other officers and courtiers. 'That is not all,' said Haman; 'Queen Esther 12
invited no one but myself to accompany the king to the banquet which she
had prepared; and she has invited me again tomorrow with the king. Yet 13
all this means nothing to me so long as I see that Jew Mordecai in attendance
at court.' Then his wife Zeresh and all his friends said to him, 'Let a gallows 14
seventy-five feet high be set up, and recommend to the king in the morning to have Mordecai hanged upon it. Then go with the king to the banquet
in good spirits.' Haman thought this an excellent plan, and he set up the
gallows.

## *Haman's downfall and Mordecai's triumph*

**6** THAT NIGHT SLEEP ELUDED THE KING, so he ordered the chronicle
**2** of daily events to be brought; and it was read to him. Therein was
recorded that Mordecai had given information about Bigthana and Teresh,
the two royal eunuchs among the keepers of the threshold who had plotted
**3** to lay hands on King Ahasuerus. Whereupon the king said, 'What honour
or dignity has been conferred on Mordecai for this?' The king's courtiers
who were in attendance told him that nothing had been done for Mordecai.
**4** The king asked, 'Who is that in the court?' Now Haman had just entered
the outer court of the palace to recommend to the king that Mordecai should
**5** be hanged on the gallows which he had prepared for him. The king's
servants answered, 'It is Haman standing there'; and the king bade him
**6** enter. He came in, and the king said to him, 'What should be done for the
man whom the king wishes to honour?' Haman said to himself, 'Whom
**7** would the king wish to honour more than me?' And he said to the king,
**8** 'For the man whom the king wishes to honour, let there be brought royal
robes which the king himself wears, and a horse which the king rides, with
**9** a royal crown upon its head. And let the robes and the horse be delivered
to one of the king's most honourable officers, and let him attire the man
whom the king wishes to honour and lead him mounted on the horse
through the city square, calling out as he goes: "See what is done for the
**10** man whom the king wishes to honour."' Then the king said to Haman,
'Fetch the robes and the horse at once, as you have said, and do all this for
Mordecai the Jew who is in attendance at court. Leave nothing undone of
**11** all that you have said.' So Haman took the robes and the horse, attired
Mordecai, and led him mounted through the city square, calling out as he
went: 'See what is done for the man whom the king wishes to honour.'
**12** Then Mordecai returned to court and Haman hurried off home mourn-
**13** ing, with head uncovered. He told his wife Zeresh and all his friends
everything that had happened to him. And this was the reply of his friends
and his wife Zeresh: 'If Mordecai, in face of whom your fortunes begin to
fall, belongs to the Jewish race, you will not get the better of him; he will
see your utter downfall.'
**14** While they were still talking with Haman, the king's eunuchs arrived
and hurried him away to the banquet which Esther had prepared.
**7 1 2** So the king and Haman went to dine with Queen Esther. Again on that
second day, over the wine, the king said, 'Whatever you ask of me will be
given to you, Queen Esther. Whatever you request of me, up to half my
**3** kingdom, it shall be done.' Queen Esther answered, 'If I have found favour
with your majesty, and if it please your majesty, my request and petition is
**4** that my own life and the lives of my people may be spared. For we have been
sold, I and my people, to be destroyed, slain, and exterminated. If it had
been a matter of selling us, men and women alike, into slavery, I should
have kept silence; for then our plight would not be such as to injure the
**5** king's interests.' Then King Ahasuerus said to Queen Esther, 'Who is he,
**6** and where is he, who has presumed to do such a thing as this?' 'An adversary and an enemy,' said Esther, 'this wicked Haman.' At that Haman was

dumbfounded in the presence of the king and the queen. The king rose 7
from the banquet in a rage and went to the garden of the pavilion, while
Haman remained where he was, to plead for his life with Queen Esther;
for he saw that in the king's mind his fate was determined. When the king 8
returned from the garden to the banqueting hall, Haman had flung himself
across the couch on which Esther was reclining. The king exclaimed, 'Will
he even assault the queen here in my presence?' No sooner had the words
left the king's mouth than Haman hid his face in despair.*a* Then Harbona, 9
one of the eunuchs in attendance on the king, said, 'At Haman's house
stands the gallows, seventy-five feet high, which he himself has prepared
for Mordecai, who once served the king well.' 'Hang Haman on it', said
the king. So they hanged him on the gallows that he himself had prepared 10
for Mordecai. After that the king's rage abated.

On that day King Ahasuerus gave Queen Esther the house of Haman, 8
enemy of the Jews; and Mordecai came into the king's presence, for Esther
had told him how he was related to her. Then the king took off his signet- 2
ring, which he had taken back from Haman, and gave it to Mordecai. And
Esther put Mordecai in charge of Haman's house.

Once again Esther spoke before the king, falling at his feet in tears and 3
pleading with him to avert the calamity planned by Haman the Agagite
and to frustrate his plot against the Jews. The king stretched out the golden 4
sceptre to Esther, and she rose and stood before the king, and said, 'May 5
it please your majesty: if I have found favour with you, and if the proposal
seems right to your majesty and I have won your approval, let a writ be
issued to recall the letters which Haman son of Hammedatha the Agagite
wrote in pursuance of his plan to destroy the Jews in all the royal provinces.
For how can I bear to see the calamity which is coming upon my race? Or 6
how can I bear to see the destruction of my family?' Then King Ahasuerus 7
said to Queen Esther and to Mordecai the Jew, 'I have given Haman's house
to Esther, and he has been hanged on the gallows, because he threatened the
lives of the Jews. Now you shall issue a writ concerning the Jews in my 8
name, in whatever terms you think fit, and seal it with the royal signet; for
an order written in the name of the king and sealed with the royal signet
cannot be revoked.'

And so, on the twenty-third day of the third month, the month Sivan, 9
the king's secretaries were summoned; and a writ was issued to the Jews,
exactly as Mordecai directed, and to the satraps, the governors, and the
officers in the provinces from India to Ethiopia, a hundred and twenty-
seven provinces, for each province in its own script and for each people in
their own language, and also for the Jews in their own script and language.
The writ was drawn up in the name of King Ahasuerus and sealed with the 10
royal signet, and letters were sent by mounted couriers riding on horses
from the royal stables. By these letters the king granted permission to the 11
Jews in every city to unite and defend themselves, and to destroy, slay, and
exterminate the whole strength of any people or province which might
attack them, women and children too, and to plunder their possessions,
throughout all the provinces of King Ahasuerus, in one day, the thirteenth 12

*a* Haman . . . despair: *prob. rdg.; Heb.* they covered Haman's face.

13 day of the twelfth month, the month Adar. A copy of the writ was to be issued as a decree in every province and published to all peoples, and the Jews were to be ready for that day, the day of vengeance on their enemies.

14 So the couriers, mounted on their royal horses, were dispatched post-haste at the king's urgent command; and the decree was issued also in Susa the capital city.

15 Mordecai left the king's presence in royal robes of violet and white, wearing a great golden crown and a cloak of fine linen and purple, and all

16 the city of Susa shouted for joy. For the Jews there was light and joy,

17 gladness and honour. In every province and every city reached by the royal command and decree, there was joy and gladness for the Jews, feasting and holiday. And many of the peoples of the land professed themselves Jews, because fear of the Jews had seized them.

9 ON THE THIRTEENTH DAY of the twelfth month, the month Adar, the time came for the king's command and his edict to be carried out. The very day on which the enemies of the Jews had hoped to gain the upper hand over them was to become the day when the Jews should gain the upper

2 hand over those who hated them. On that day the Jews united in their cities in all the provinces of King Ahasuerus to fall upon those who had planned their ruin. No one could resist them, because fear of them had

3 seized all peoples. All the officers of the provinces, the satraps and the governors, and all the royal officials, aided the Jews, because fear of

4 Mordecai had seized them. Mordecai had become a great personage in the royal palace; his fame had spread throughout all the provinces as the power

5 of the man grew steadily greater. So the Jews put their enemies to the sword, with great slaughter and destruction; they worked their will on

6 those who hated them. In Susa, the capital city, the Jews killed five hundred

7 men and destroyed them; and they killed also Parshandatha, Dalphon and

8 9 Aspatha, Poratha, Adalia and Aridatha, Parmashta, Arisai, Aridai and

10 Vaizatha, the ten sons of Haman son of Hammedatha, the enemy of the Jews; but they did not touch the plunder.

11 That day when the number of those killed in Susa the capital city came to

12 the notice of the king, he said to Queen Esther, 'In Susa, the capital city, the Jews have killed and destroyed five hundred men and the ten sons of Haman. What have they done in the rest of the king's provinces? Whatever you ask further will be given to you; whatever more you seek shall be done.'

13 Esther answered him, 'If it please your majesty, let tomorrow be granted to the Jews in Susa to do according to the edict for today; and let the bodies

14 of Haman's ten sons be hung up on the gallows.' The king gave orders for this to be done; the edict was issued in Susa and Haman's ten sons were

15 hung up on the gallows. The Jews in Susa united again on the fourteenth day of the month Adar and killed three hundred men in Susa; but they did not touch the plunder.

16 The rest of the Jews in the king's provinces had united to defend themselves; they took vengeance on[a] their enemies by killing seventy-five thousand of those who hated them; but they did not touch the plunder.

[a] *Prob. rdg.; Heb.* got respite from.

This was on the thirteenth day of the month Adar, and they rested on the 17
fourteenth day and made that a day of feasting and joy. The Jews in Susa 18
had united on the thirteenth and fourteenth days of the month, and rested
on the fifteenth day and made that a day of feasting and joy. This is why 19
isolated Jews who live in remote villages keep the fourteenth day of the
month Adar in joy and feasting, as a holiday on which they send presents
of food to one another.

Then Mordecai set these things on record and sent letters to all the Jews 20
in all the provinces of King Ahasuerus, far and near, binding them to keep 21
the fourteenth and fifteenth days of the month Adar, year by year, as the 22
days on which the Jews obtained relief from their enemies and as the month
which was changed for them from sorrow into joy, from a time of mourning
to a holiday. They were to keep them as days of feasting and joy, days for
sending presents of food to one another and gifts to the poor.

So the Jews undertook to continue the practice that they had begun in 23
accordance with Mordecai's letter. This they did because Haman son of 24
Hammedatha the Agagite, the enemy of all the Jews, had plotted to destroy
the Jews and had cast lots, Pur as it is called, with intent to crush and
destroy them. But when the matter came before the king, he issued written 25
orders that the wicked plot which Haman had devised against the Jews
should recoil on his own head, and that he and his sons should be hanged on
the gallows. Therefore, these days were named Purim after the word Pur. 26
Accordingly, because of all that was written in this letter, because of all they
had seen and experienced in this affair, the Jews resolved and undertook, 27
on behalf of themselves, their descendants, and all who should join them,
that they would without fail keep these two days as a yearly festival in the
prescribed manner and at the appointed time; that these days should be re- 28
membered and kept, generation after generation, in every family, province,
and city, that the days of Purim should always be observed among the Jews,
and that the memory of them should never cease among their descendants.

Queen Esther daughter of Abihail gave full authority in writing to *a* 29
Mordecai the Jew, to confirm this second letter about Purim. Letters 30
wishing peace and security were sent to all the Jews in the hundred and
twenty-seven provinces of King Ahasuerus, making the observance of 31
these days of Purim at their appointed time binding on them, as Mordecai
the Jew *b* had prescribed. In the same way they had prescribed regulations
for fasts and lamentations for themselves and their descendants. The com- 32
mand of Esther confirmed these regulations for Purim, and the record is
preserved in writing.

King Ahasuerus imposed forced labour on the land and the coasts and **10**
islands. All the king's acts of authority and power, and the dignities which 2
he conferred on Mordecai, are written in the annals of the kings of Media
and Persia. For Mordecai the Jew was second only to King Ahasuerus; he 3
was a great man among the Jews and was popular with the mass of his
countrymen, for he sought the good of his people and promoted the welfare
of all their descendants. *c*

*a Prob. rdg.; Heb. and.*     *b Prob. rdg.; Heb. adds and Queen Esther.*     *c Or and*
was in friendly relations with all his race.

# THE BOOK OF
# JOB

*Prologue*

1 THERE LIVED IN THE LAND OF UZ a man of blameless
and upright life named Job, who feared God and set his face against
2 3 wrongdoing. He had seven sons and three daughters; and he owned
seven thousand sheep and three thousand camels, five hundred yoke of
oxen and five hundred asses, with a large number of slaves. Thus Job was
the greatest man in all the East.

4 Now his sons used to foregather and give, each in turn, a feast in his
own house; and they used to send and invite their three sisters to eat and
5 drink with them. Then, when a round of feasts was finished, Job sent for
his children and sanctified them, rising early in the morning and sacrificing
a whole-offering for each of them; for he thought that they might somehow
have sinned against God and committed blasphemy in their hearts. This
he always did.

6 The day came when the members of the court of heaven took their
places in the presence of the LORD, and Satan*a* was there among them.
7 The LORD asked him where he had been. 'Ranging over the earth', he said,
8 'from end to end.' Then the LORD asked Satan, 'Have you considered my
servant Job? You will find no one like him on earth, a man of blameless
and upright life, who fears God and sets his face against wrongdoing.'
9 Satan answered the LORD, 'Has not Job good reason to be God-fearing?
10 Have you not hedged him round on every side with your protection,
him and his family and all his possessions? Whatever he does you have
11 blessed, and his herds have increased beyond measure. But stretch out your
hand and touch all that he has, and then he will curse you to your face.'
12 Then the LORD said to Satan, 'So be it. All that he has is in your hands;
only Job himself you must not touch.' And Satan left the LORD's presence.

13 When the day came that Job's sons and daughters were eating and drink-
14 ing in the eldest brother's house, a messenger came running to Job and
15 said, 'The oxen were ploughing and the asses were grazing near them, when
the Sabaeans swooped down and carried them off, after putting the herds-
16 men to the sword; and I am the only one to escape and tell the tale.' While
he was still speaking, another messenger arrived and said, 'God's fire
flashed from heaven. It struck the sheep and the shepherds and burnt them
17 up; and I am the only one to escape and tell the tale.' While he was still
speaking, another arrived and said, 'The Chaldaeans, three bands of them,
have made a raid on the camels and carried them off, after putting the drivers

*a Or* the adversary.

560

to the sword; and I am the only one to escape and tell the tale.' While this 18
man was speaking, yet another arrived and said, 'Your sons and daughters
were eating and drinking in the eldest brother's house, when suddenly a 19
whirlwind swept across from the desert and struck the four corners of the
house, and it fell on the young people and killed them; and I am the only
one to escape and tell the tale.' At this Job stood up and rent his cloak; then 20
he shaved his head and fell prostrate on the ground, saying: 21

> Naked I came from the womb,
> naked I shall return whence I came.
> The LORD gives and the LORD takes away;
> blessed be the name of the LORD.

Throughout all this Job did not sin; he did not charge God with unreason. 22
Once again the day came when the members of the court of heaven took **2**
their places in the presence of the LORD, and Satan was there among them.
The LORD asked him where he had been. 'Ranging over the earth', he said, 2
'from end to end.' Then the LORD asked Satan, 'Have you considered my 3
servant Job? You will find no one like him on earth, a man of blameless and
upright life, who fears God and sets his face against wrongdoing. You
incited me to ruin him without a cause, but his integrity is still unshaken.'
Satan answered the LORD, 'Skin for skin! There is nothing the man will 4
grudge to save himself. But stretch out your hand and touch his bone and 5
his flesh, and see if he will not curse you to your face.'

Then the LORD said to Satan, 'So be it. He is in your hands; but spare 6
his life.' And Satan left the LORD's presence, and he smote Job with running 7
sores from head to foot, so that he took a piece of a broken pot to scratch 8
himself as he sat among the ashes. Then his wife said to him, 'Are you still 9
unshaken in your integrity? Curse God and die!' But he answered, 'You 10
talk as any wicked fool of a woman might talk. If we accept good from God,
shall we not accept evil?' Throughout all this, Job did not utter one sinful
word.

When Job's three friends, Eliphaz of Teman, Bildad of Shuah, and 11
Zophar of Naamah, heard of all these calamities which had overtaken him,
they left their homes and arranged to come and condole with him and
comfort him. But when they first saw him from a distance, they did not 12
recognize him; and they wept aloud, rent their cloaks and tossed dust into
the air over their heads. For seven days and seven nights they sat beside 13
him on the ground, and none of them said a word to him; for they saw that
his suffering was very great.

## *Job's complaint to God*

After this Job broke silence and cursed the day of his birth: 3 1-2

> Perish the day when I was born 3
> and the night which said, 'A man is conceived'!
> May that day turn to darkness; may God above not look for it, 4
> nor light of dawn shine on it.

5    May blackness sully it, and murk and gloom,
     cloud smother that day, swift darkness eclipse its sun.
6    Blind darkness swallow up that night;
     count it not among the days of the year,
     reckon it not in the cycle of the months.
7    That night, may it be barren for ever,
     no cry of joy be heard in it.
8    Cursed be it by those whose magic binds even the monster of the deep,
     who are ready to tame Leviathan himself with spells.
9    May no star shine out in its twilight;
     may it wait for a dawn that never comes,
     nor ever see the eyelids of the morning,
10   because it did not shut the doors of the womb that bore me
     and keep trouble away from my sight.
11   Why was I not still-born,
     why did I not die when I came out of the womb?
12   Why was I ever laid on my mother's knees
     or put to suck at her breasts?
16   Why was I not hidden like an untimely birth,
     like an infant that has not lived to see the light?
13   For then I should be lying in the quiet grave,
     asleep in death, at rest,
14   with kings and their ministers
     who built themselves palaces,
15   with princes rich in gold
     who filled their houses with silver.
17 *a*   There the wicked man chafes no more,
     there the tired labourer rests;
18   the captive too finds peace there
     and hears no taskmaster's voice;
19   high and low are there,
     even the slave, free from his master.

20   Why should the sufferer be born to see the light?
     Why is life given to men who find it so bitter?
21   They wait for death but it does not come,
     they seek it more eagerly than *b* hidden treasure.
22   They are glad when they reach the tomb,
     and when they come to the grave they exult.
23   Why should a man be born to wander blindly,
     hedged in by God on every side?
24   My sighing is all my food,
     and groans pour from me in a torrent.
25   Every terror that haunted me has caught up with me,
     and all that I feared has come upon me.
26   There is no peace of mind nor quiet for me;
     I chafe in torment and have no rest.

     *a  Verse 16 transposed to follow verse 12.      b  Or seek it among . . .*

## *First cycle of speeches*

Then Eliphaz the Temanite began: 4

If one ventures to speak with you, will you lose patience? 2
For who could hold his tongue any longer?
Think how once you encouraged those who faltered, 3
how you braced feeble arms,
how a word from you upheld the stumblers 4
and put strength into weak knees.
But now that adversity comes upon you, you lose patience; 5
it touches you, and you are unmanned.
Is your religion no comfort to you? 6
Does your blameless life give you no hope?
For consider, what innocent man has ever perished? 7
Where have you seen the upright destroyed?
This I know, that those who plough mischief and sow trouble 8
reap as they have sown;
they perish at the blast of God 9
and are shrivelled by the breath of his nostrils.

The roar of the lion, the whimpering of his cubs, fall silent; 10
the teeth of the young lions are broken;
the lion perishes for lack of prey 11
and the whelps of the lioness are abandoned.

A word stole into my ears, 12
and they caught the whisper of it;
in the anxious visions of the night, 13
when a man sinks into deepest sleep,
terror seized me and shuddering; 14
the trembling of my body frightened me.
A wind brushed my face 15
and made the hairs bristle on my flesh;
and a figure stood there whose shape I could not discern, 16
an apparition loomed before me,
and I heard the sound of a low voice:
'Can mortal man be more righteous than God, 17
or the creature purer than his Maker?
If God mistrusts his own servants 18
and finds his messengers at fault,
how much more those that dwell in houses whose walls are clay, 19
whose foundations are dust,
which can be crushed like a bird's nest
or torn down between dawn and dark, 20
how much more shall such men perish outright and unheeded,
*a* die, without ever finding wisdom?' 21

*a Prob. rdg.; transposing* Their rich possessions are snatched from them *to follow 5. 4.*

5   Call if you will; is there any to answer you?
     To which of the holy ones will you turn?

2   The fool is destroyed by his own angry passions,
     and the end of childish resentment is death.

3   I have seen it for myself: a fool uprooted,
     his home in sudden ruin about him,[a]

4   his children past help,
     browbeaten in court with none to save them.

5   [b]Their rich possessions are snatched from them;
     what they have harvested others hungrily devour;
     the stronger man seizes it from the panniers,
     panting, thirsting for their wealth.

6   Mischief does not grow out of the soil
     nor trouble spring from the earth;

7   man is born to trouble,
     as surely as birds fly[c] upwards.

8   For my part, I would make my petition to God
     and lay my cause before him,

9   who does great and unsearchable things,
     marvels without number.

10  He gives rain to the earth
     and sends water on the fields;

11  he raises the lowly to the heights,
     the mourners are uplifted by victory;

12  he frustrates the plots of the crafty,
     and they win no success,

13  he traps the cunning in their craftiness,
     and the schemers' plans are thrown into confusion.

14  In the daylight they run into darkness,
     and grope at midday as though it were night.

15  He saves the destitute from their greed,
     and the needy from the grip of the strong;

16  so the poor hope again,
     and the unjust are sickened.

17  Happy the man whom God rebukes!
     therefore do not reject the discipline of the Almighty.

18  For, though he wounds, he will bind up;
     the hands that smite will heal.

19  You may meet disaster six times, and he will save you;
     seven times, and no harm shall touch you.

20  In time of famine he will save you from death,
     in battle from the sword.

21  You will be shielded from the lash of slander,[d]
     and when violence comes you need not fear.

---

[a] ruin about him: *prob. rdg.; Heb. obscure.*   [b] *Line transposed from 4. 21.*
[c] *Or as sparks shoot.*   [d] *from . . . slander: or when slander is rife.*

You will laugh at violence and starvation 22
and have no need to fear wild beasts;
for you have a covenant with the stones to spare your fields, 23
and the weeds have been constrained to leave you at peace.
You will know that all is well with your household, 24
you will look round your home and find nothing amiss;
you will know, too, that your descendants will be many 25
and your offspring like grass, thick upon the earth.
You will come in sturdy old age to the grave 26
as sheaves come in due season to the threshing-floor.

We have inquired into all this, and so it is; 27
this we have heard, and you may know it for the truth.

Then Job answered: **6**

O that the grounds for my resentment might be weighed, 2
and my misfortunes set with them on the scales!
For they would outweigh the sands of the sea: 3
what wonder if my words are wild? *a*
The arrows of the Almighty find their mark in me, 4
and their poison soaks into my spirit;
God's onslaughts wear me away.
Does the wild ass bray when he has grass 5
or the ox low when he has fodder?
Can a man eat tasteless food unseasoned with salt, 6
or find any flavour in the juice of mallows?
Food that should nourish me sticks in my throat, 7
and my bowels rumble with an echoing sound.

O that I might have my request, 8
that God would grant what I hope for:
that he would be pleased to crush me, 9
to snatch me away with his hand and cut me off!
For that would bring me relief, 10
and in the face of unsparing anguish I would leap for joy. *b*
Have I the strength to wait? 11
What end have I to expect, that I should be patient?
Is my strength the strength of stone, 12
or is my flesh bronze?
Oh how shall I find help within myself? 13
The power to aid myself is put out of my reach.

Devotion is due from his friends 14
to one who despairs and loses faith in the Almighty;
but my brothers have been treacherous as a mountain stream, 15
like the channels of streams that run dry,

---

*a* what . . . wild?: *or therefore words fail me.* *b* *Prob. rdg.; Heb. adds* I have not
denied the words of the Holy One.

16   which turn dark with ice
or are hidden with piled-up snow;

17   or they vanish the moment they are in spate,
dwindle in the heat and are gone.

18   Then the caravans, winding hither and thither,
go up into the wilderness and perish;<sup>a</sup>

19   the caravans of Tema look for their waters,
travelling merchants of Sheba hope for them;

20   but they are disappointed, for all their confidence,
they reach them only to be balked.

21   So treacherous have you now been to me:<sup>b</sup>
you felt dismay and were afraid.

22   Did I ever say, 'Give me this or that;
open your purses to save my life;

23   rescue me from my enemy;
ransom me out of the hands of ruthless men'?

24   Tell me plainly, and I will listen in silence;
show me where I have erred.

25   How harsh are the words of the upright man!
What do the arguments of wise men<sup>c</sup> prove?

26   Do you mean to argue about words
or to sift the utterance of a man past hope?

27   Would you assail an orphan<sup>d</sup>?
Would you hurl yourselves on a friend?

28   So now, I beg you, turn and look at me:
am I likely to lie to your faces?

29   Think again, let me have no more injustice;
think again, for my integrity is in question.

30   Do I ever give voice to injustice?
Does my sense not warn me when my words are wild?

**7**   Has not man hard service on earth,
and are not his days like those of a hired labourer,

2   like those of a slave longing for the shade
or a servant kept waiting for his wages?

3   So months of futility are my portion,
troubled nights are my lot.

4   When I lie down, I think,
'When will it be day that I may rise?'
When the evening grows long and I lie down,
I do nothing but toss till morning twilight.

5   My body is infested with worms,
and scabs cover my skin.<sup>e</sup>

6   My days are swifter than a shuttle <sup>f</sup>
and come to an end as the thread runs out. <sup>g</sup>

---

[a] *Or* and are lost.    [b] So . . . to me: *prob. rdg.; Heb. obscure.*    [c] wise men:
*prob. rdg.; Heb. unintelligible.*    [d] *Or* a blameless man.    [e] *Prob. rdg.; Heb. adds* it
is cracked and discharging.    [f] *Or* a fleeting odour.    [g] as . . . out: *or* without hope.

Remember, my life is but a breath of wind; 7
I shall never again see good days.
Thou wilt behold me no more with a seeing eye; 8
under thy very eyes I shall disappear.
As clouds break up and disperse, 9
so he that goes down to Sheol never comes back;
he never returns home again, 10
and his place will know him no more.[a]

But I will not hold my peace; 11
I will speak out in the distress of my mind
and complain in the bitterness of my soul.
Am I the monster of the deep, am I the sea-serpent, 12
that thou settest a watch over me?
When I think that my bed will comfort me, 13
that sleep will relieve my complaining,
thou dost terrify me with dreams 14
and affright me with visions.
I would rather be choked outright; 15
I would prefer death to all my sufferings.
I am in despair, I would not go on living; 16
leave me alone, for my life is but a vapour.
What is man that thou makest much of him 17
and turnest thy thoughts towards him,
only to punish him morning by morning 18
or to test him every hour of the day?
Wilt thou not look away from me for an instant? 19
Wilt thou not let me be while I swallow my spittle?
If I have sinned, how do I injure thee, 20
thou watcher of the hearts of men?
Why hast thou made me thy butt,
and why have I become thy target?
Why dost thou not pardon my offence 21
and take away my guilt?
But now I shall lie down in the grave;
seek me, and I shall not be.

Then Bildad the Shuhite began: **8**

How long will you say such things, 2
the long-winded ramblings of an old man?
Does God pervert judgement? 3
Does the Almighty pervert justice?
Your sons sinned against him, 4
so he left them to be victims of their own iniquity.
If only you will seek God betimes 5
and plead for the favour of the Almighty,

[a] *Or* and he will not be noticed any more in his place.

6   if you are innocent and upright,
then indeed will he watch over you
and see your just intent fulfilled.

7   Then, though your beginnings were humble,
your end will be great.

8   Inquire now of older generations
and consider the experience of their fathers;

9   for we ourselves are of yesterday and are transient;
our days on earth are a shadow.

10   Will not they speak to you and teach you
and pour out the wisdom of their hearts?

11   Can rushes grow where there is no marsh?
Can reeds flourish without water?

12   While they are still in flower and not ready to cut, *a*
they wither earlier than *b* any green plant.

13   Such is the fate of all who forget God;
the godless man's life-thread breaks off;

14   his confidence is gossamer,
and the ground of his trust a spider's web.

15   He leans against his house but it does not stand;
he clutches at it but it does not hold firm.

16   His is the lush growth of a plant in the sun,
pushing out shoots over the garden;

17   but its roots become entangled in a stony patch
and run against a bed of rock.

18   Then someone uproots it from its place,
which *c* disowns it and says, 'I have never known you.'

19   That is how its life withers away,
and other plants spring up from the earth.

20   Be sure, God will not spurn the blameless man,
nor will he grasp the hand of the wrongdoer.

21   He will yet fill your mouth with laughter,
and shouts of joy will be on your lips;

22   your enemies shall be wrapped in confusion,
and the tents of the wicked shall vanish away.

**9**  Then Job answered:

2   Indeed this I know for the truth,
that no man can win his case against God.

3   If a man chooses to argue with him,
God will not answer one question in a thousand. *d*

4   He is wise, he is powerful;
what man has stubbornly resisted him and survived?

---

*a* and . . . cut: *or* they are surely cut.     *b* *Or* wither like . . .     *c* *Or* and.
*d* If a man . . . thousand: *or* If God is pleased to argue with him, man cannot answer one
question in a thousand.

It is God who moves mountains, giving them no rest, 5
turning them over in his wrath;
who makes the earth start from its place 6
so that its pillars are convulsed;
who commands the sun's orb not to rise 7
and shuts up the stars under his seal;
who by himself spread out the heavens 8
and trod on the sea-monster's back; <sup>a</sup>
who made Aldebaran and Orion, 9
the Pleiades and the circle of the southern stars;
who does great and unsearchable things, 10
marvels without number.

He passes by me, and I do not see him; 11
he moves on his way undiscerned by me;
if he hurries on, who can bring him back? 12
Who will ask him what he does?
God does not turn back his wrath; 13
the partisans of Rahab lie prostrate at his feet.
How much less can I answer him 14
or find words to dispute with him?
Though I am right, I get no answer, 15
though I plead with my accuser for mercy.
If I summoned him to court and he responded, 16
I do not believe that he would listen to my plea—
for he bears hard upon me for a trifle 17
and rains blows on me without cause;
he leaves me no respite to recover my breath 18
but fills me with bitter thoughts.
If the appeal is to force, see how strong he is; 19
if to justice, who can compel him to give me a hearing?
Though I am right, he condemns me out of my own mouth; 20
though I am blameless, he twists my words.
Blameless, I say; of myself 21
I reck nothing, I hold my life cheap.
But it is all one; therefore I say, 22
'He destroys blameless and wicked alike.'
When a sudden flood brings death, 23
he mocks the plight of the innocent.
The land is given over to the power of the wicked, 24
and the eyes of its judges are blindfold. <sup>b</sup>

My days have been swifter than a runner, 25
they have slipped away and seen no prosperity;
they have raced by like reed-built skiffs, 26
swift as vultures swooping on carrion.

---

<sup>a</sup> *Or* on the crests of the waves.     <sup>b</sup> *Prob. rdg.; Heb. adds* if not he, then who?

27  If I think, 'I will forget my griefs,
    I will show a cheerful face and smile',
28  I tremble in every nerve;[a]
    I know that thou wilt not hold me innocent.
29  If I am to be accounted guilty,
    why do I labour in vain?
30  Though I wash myself with soap
    or cleanse my hands with lye,
31  thou wilt thrust me into the mud
    and my clothes will make me loathsome.

32  He is not a man as I am, that I can answer him
    or that we can confront one another in court.
33  If only there were one to arbitrate between us
    and impose his authority on us both,
34  so that God might take his rod from my back,
    and terror of him might not come on me suddenly.
35  I would then speak without fear of him;
    for I know I am not what I am thought to be.

10  I am sickened of life;
    I will give free rein to my griefs,
    I will speak out in bitterness of soul.
2   I will say to God, 'Do not condemn me,
    but tell me the ground of thy complaint against me.
3   Dost thou find any advantage in oppression,
    in spurning the fruit of all thy labour
    and smiling on the policy of wicked men?
4   Hast thou eyes of flesh
    or dost thou see as mortal man sees?
5   Are thy days as those of a mortal
    or thy years as the life of a man,
6   that thou lookest for guilt in me
    and dost seek in me for sin,
7   though thou knowest that I am guiltless
    and have none to save me from thee?

8   'Thy hands gave me shape and made me;
    and dost thou at once turn and destroy me?
9   Remember that thou didst knead me like clay;
    and wouldst thou turn me back into dust?
10  Didst thou not pour me out like milk
    and curdle me like cheese,
11  clothe me with skin and flesh
    and knit me together with bones and sinews?
12  Thou hast given me life and continuing favour,
    and thy providence has watched over my spirit.

[a] *Or* I am afraid of all that I must suffer.

Yet this was the secret purpose of thy heart,     13
and I know that this was thy intent:
that, if I sinned, thou wouldst be watching me     14
and wouldst not acquit me of my guilt.
If I indeed am wicked, the worse for me!     15
If I am righteous, even so I may lift up my head; *a*
if I am proud as a lion, thou dost hunt me down     16
and dost confront me again with marvellous power;
thou dost renew thy onslaught upon me,     17
and with mounting anger against me
bringest fresh forces to the attack.
Why didst thou bring me out of the womb?     18
O that I had ended there and no eye had seen me,
that I had been carried from the womb to the grave     19
and were as though I had not been born.
Is not my life short and fleeting?     20
Let me be, that I may be happy for a moment,
before I depart to a land of gloom,     21
a land of deep darkness, never to return,
a land of gathering shadows, of deepening darkness,     22
lit by no ray of light,*b* dark *c* upon dark.'

Then Zophar the Naamathite began:     **11**

Should this spate of words not be answered?     2
Must a man of ready tongue be always right?
Is your endless talk to reduce men to silence?     3
Are you to talk nonsense and no one rebuke you?
You claim that your opinions are sound;     4
you say to God, 'I am spotless in thy sight.'
But if only he would speak     5
and open his lips to talk with you,
and expound to you the secrets of wisdom,     6
for wonderful are its effects!
[Know then that God exacts from you less than your sin deserves.]
Can you fathom the mystery of God,     7
can you fathom the perfection of the Almighty?
It is higher than heaven; you can do nothing.     8
It is deeper than Sheol; you can know nothing.
Its measure is longer than the earth     9
and broader than the sea.
If he passes by, he may keep secret his passing;     10
if he proclaims it, who can turn him back?
He surely knows which men are false,     11
and when he sees iniquity, does he not take note of it? *d*

---

*a Prob. rdg.; Heb. adds* filled with shame and steeped in my affliction.     *b* lit . . .
light: *or* a place of disorder.     *c Prob. rdg.; Heb. obscure.*     *d* does . . . of it?:
*or* he does not stand aloof.

12   Can a fool grow wise?
    can a wild ass's foal be born a man?

13   If only you had directed your heart rightly
    and spread out your hands to pray to him!

14   If you have wrongdoing in hand, thrust it away;
    let no iniquity make its home with you.

15   Then you could hold up your head without fault,
    a man of iron, knowing no fear.

16   Then you will forget your trouble;
    you will remember it only as flood-waters that have passed;

17   life will be lasting, bright as noonday,
    and darkness will be turned to morning.

18   You will be confident, because there is hope;
    sure of protection, you will lie down in confidence; [a]

19   great men will seek your favour.

20   Blindness will fall on the wicked;
    the ways of escape are closed to them,
    and their hope is despair.

**12**  Then Job answered:

2   No doubt you are perfect men [b]
    and absolute wisdom is yours!

3   But I have sense as well as you;
    in nothing do I fall short of you;
    what gifts indeed have you that others have not?

4   Yet I am a laughing-stock to my friend—
    a laughing-stock, though I am innocent and blameless,
    one that called upon God, and he answered. [c]

5   Prosperity and ease look down on misfortune,
    on the blow that fells the man who is already reeling,

6   while the marauders' tents are left undisturbed
    and those who provoke God live safe and sound. [d]

7   Go and ask the cattle,
    ask the birds of the air to inform you,

8   or tell the creatures that crawl to teach you,
    and the fishes of the sea to give you instruction.

9   Who cannot learn from all these
    that the LORD's own hand has done this?

11 [e]  (Does not the ear test what is spoken
    as the palate savours food?

12   There is wisdom, remember, in age,
    and long life brings understanding.)

---

[a] *Prob. rdg.; Heb. adds* and you will lie down unafraid.
doubt you are people.    [c] *Or* and he afflicted me.
*adds* He brings it in full measure to whom he will (*cp. 21. 17*).
*posed to follow verse 12.*

[b] *Prob. rdg.; Heb.* No
[d] *Prob. rdg.; Heb.*
[e] *Verse 10 trans-*

In God's hand are the souls of all that live,                    10
the spirits of all human kind.
Wisdom and might are his,                                        13
with him are firmness and understanding.
If he pulls down, there is no rebuilding;                        14
if he imprisons, there is no release.
If he holds up the waters, there is drought;                     15
if he lets them go, they turn the land upside down.
Strength and success belong to him,                             16
deceived and deceiver are his to use.
He makes counsellors behave like idiots                         17
and drives judges mad;
he looses the bonds imposed by kings                            18
and removes the girdle of office from their waists;
he makes priests behave like idiots                             19
and overthrows men long in office;
those who are trusted he strikes dumb,                          20
he takes away the judgement of old men;
he heaps scorn on princes                                       21
and abates the arrogance of nobles.
He leads peoples astray and destroys them,                      23*a*
he lays them low, and there they lie.
He takes away their wisdom from the rulers of the nations       24
and leaves them wandering in a pathless wilderness;
they grope in the darkness without light                        25
and are left to wander like a drunkard.
He uncovers mysteries deep in obscurity                         22
and into thick darkness he brings light.

All this I have seen with my own eyes,                         **13**
with my own ears I have heard it, and understood it.
What you know, I also know;                                      2
in nothing do I fall short of you.
But for my part I would speak with the Almighty                 3
and am ready to argue with God,
while you like fools are smearing truth with your falsehoods,   4
stitching a patchwork of lies, one and all.
Ah, if you would only be silent                                 5
and let silence be your wisdom!
Now listen to my arguments                                      6
and attend while I put my case.
Is it on God's behalf that you speak so wickedly,               7
or in his defence that you allege what is false?
Must you take God's part,                                        8
or put his case for him?
Will all be well when he examines you?                          9
Will you quibble with him as you quibble with a man?

*a Verse 22 transposed to follow verse 25.*

573

10 He will most surely expose you
 if you take his part by falsely accusing me.
11 Will not God's majesty strike you with dread,
 and terror of him overwhelm you?
12 Your pompous talk is dust and ashes,
 your defences will crumble like clay.
13 Be silent, leave me to speak my mind,
 and let what may come upon me!
14 I will put my neck in the noose
 and take my life in my hands.
15 If he would slay me, I should not hesitate;
 I should still argue my cause to his face.
16 This at least assures my success,
 that no godless man may appear before him.
17 Listen then, listen to my words,
 and give a hearing to my exposition.
18 Be sure of this: once I have stated my case
 I know that I shall be acquitted.
19 Who is there that can argue so forcibly with me
 that he could reduce me straightway to silence and death?

20 Grant me these two conditions only,
 and then I will not hide myself out of thy sight:
21 take thy heavy hand clean away from me
 and let not the fear of thee strike me with dread.
22 Then summon me, and I will answer;
 or I will speak first, and do thou answer me.
23 How many iniquities and sins are laid to my charge?
 let me know my offences and my sin.
24 Why dost thou hide thy face
 and treat me as thy enemy?
25 Wilt thou chase a driven leaf,
 wilt thou pursue dry chaff,
26 prescribing punishment for me
 and making me heir to the iniquities of my youth,
27 putting my feet in the stocks *a*
 and setting a slave-mark on the arches of my feet? *b*

**14** Man born of woman is short-lived and full of disquiet.
2 He blossoms like a flower and then he withers;
 he slips away like a shadow and does not stay;
 *c* he is like a wine-skin that perishes
 or a garment that moths have eaten.
3 Dost thou fix thine eyes on such a creature,
 and wilt thou bring him into court to confront thee? *d*

---

*a Prob. rdg.; Heb. adds* keeping a close watch on all I do.    *b Prob. rdg.; Heb. adds*
*verse 28,* he is like ... have eaten, *now transposed to follow 14. 2.*    *c* he is like ...
have eaten: *13. 28 transposed here.*    *d So one Heb. MS.; others add* (4) Who can
produce pure out of unclean? No one.

The days of his life are determined, 5
and the number of his months is known to thee;
thou hast laid down a limit, which he cannot pass.
Look away from him therefore and leave him alone 6
counting the hours day by day like a hired labourer.

If a tree is cut down, 7
there is hope that it will sprout again
and fresh shoots will not fail.
Though its roots grow old in the earth, 8
and its stump is dying in the ground,
if it scents water it may break into bud 9
and make new growth like a young plant.
But a man dies, and he disappears; *a* 10
man comes to his end, and where is he?
As the waters of a lake dwindle, 11
or as a river shrinks and runs dry,
so mortal man lies down, never to rise 12
until the very sky splits open.
If a man dies, can he live again? *b*
He shall never be roused from his sleep.
If only thou wouldst hide me in Sheol 13
and conceal me till thy anger turns aside,
if thou wouldst fix a limit for my time there, and then remember me!
*c* Then I would not lose hope, however long my service, 14
waiting for my relief to come.
Thou wouldst summon me, and I would answer thee; 15
thou wouldst long to see the creature thou hast made.
But now thou dost count every step I take, 16
watching all my course.
Every offence of mine is stored in thy bag; 17
thou dost keep my iniquity under seal.
Yet as a falling mountain-side is swept away, 18
and a rock is dislodged from its place,
as water wears away stones, 19
and a rain-storm scours the soil from the land,
so thou hast wiped out the hope of frail man;
thou dost overpower him finally, and he is gone; 20
his face is changed, and he is banished from thy sight.
His flesh upon him becomes black, 22 *d*
and his life-blood dries up within him. *e*
His sons rise to honour, and he sees nothing of it; 21
they sink into obscurity, and he knows it not.

*a* Or *and is powerless.* *b* *Line transposed from beginning of verse 14.* *c* *See note on verse 12.* *d* *Verses 21 and 22 transposed.* *e* His flesh . . . within him: *or His own kin, maybe, regret him, and his slaves mourn his loss.*

## *Second cycle of speeches*

15  Then Eliphaz the Temanite answered:

2  Would a man of sense give vent to such foolish notions
and answer with a bellyful of wind?

3  Would he bandy useless words
and arguments so unprofitable?

4  Why! you even banish the fear of God from your mind,
usurping the sole right to speak in his presence;

5  your iniquity dictates what you say,
and deceit is the language of your choice.

6  You are condemned out of your own mouth, not by me;
your own lips give evidence against you.

7  Were you born first of mankind?
were you brought forth before the hills?

8  Do you listen in God's secret council
or usurp all wisdom for yourself alone?

9  What do you know that we do not know?
What insight have you that we do not share?

10  We have age and white hairs in our company,
men older than your father.

11  Does not the consolation of God suffice you,
a word whispered quietly in your ear?

12  What makes you so bold at heart,
and why do your eyes flash,

13  that you vent your anger on God
and pour out such a torrent of words?

14  What is frail man that he should be innocent,
or any child of woman that he should be justified?

15  If God puts no trust in his holy ones,
and the heavens are not innocent in his sight,

16  how much less so is man, who is loathsome and rotten
and laps up evil like water!

17  I will tell you, if only you will listen,
and I will describe what I have seen

18  [what has been handed down by wise men
and was not concealed from them by their fathers;

19  to them alone the land was given,
and no foreigner settled among them]:

20  the wicked are racked with anxiety all their days,
the ruthless man for all the years in store for him.

21  The noise of the hunter's scare rings in his ears,
and in time of peace the raider falls on him;

22  he cannot hope to escape from dark death;
he is marked down for the sword;

he is flung out as food for vultures;                           23
such a man knows that his destruction is certain.
Suddenly a black day comes upon him,                           24
distress and anxiety overwhelm him
[like a king ready for battle];
for he has lifted his hand against God                           25
and is pitting himself against the Almighty,
charging him head down,                           26
with the full weight of his bossed shield.

Heavy though his jowl is and gross,                           27
and though his sides bulge with fat,
the city where he lives will lie in ruins,                           28
his house will be deserted;
it will soon become a heap of rubble.
He will no longer be rich, his wealth will not last,                           29
and he will strike no root in the earth; *a*
scorching heat will shrivel his shoots,                           30
and his blossom will be shaken off by the wind.
He deceives himself, trusting in his high rank,                           31
for all his dealings will come to nothing.
His palm-trees will wither unseasonably,                           32
and his branches will not spread;
he will be like a vine that sheds its unripe grapes,                           33
like an olive-tree that drops its blossom.
For the godless, one and all, are barren,                           34
and their homes, enriched by bribery, are destroyed by fire;
they conceive mischief and give birth to trouble,                           35
and the child of their womb is deceit.

Then Job answered:                           **16**

I have heard such things often before,                           2
you who make trouble, all of you, with every breath,
saying, 'Will this windbag never have done?                           3
What makes him so stubborn in argument?'
If you and I were to change places,                           4
I could talk like you;
how I could harangue you
and wag my head at you!
But no, I would speak words of encouragement,                           5
and then my condolences would flow in streams.
If I speak, my pain is not eased;                           6
if I am silent, it does not leave me.
Meanwhile, my friend wearies me with false sympathy;                           7
they tear me to pieces, he and his *b* fellows.                           8
He has come forward to give evidence against me;

*a Prob. rdg.; Heb. adds* he will not escape from darkness.                    *b Prob. rdg.; Heb.* my.

the liar testifies against me to my face,
9    in his wrath he wears me down, his hatred is plain to see;
he grinds his teeth at me.

My enemies look daggers at me,
10   they bare their teeth to rend me,
they slash my cheeks with knives;
they are all in league against me.
11   God has left me at the mercy of malefactors
and cast me into the clutches of wicked men.
12   I was at ease, but he set upon me and mauled me,
seized me by the neck and worried me.
He set me up as his target;
13   his arrows rained upon me from every side;
pitiless, he cut deep into my vitals,
he spilt my gall on the ground.
14   He made breach after breach in my defences;
he fell upon me like a fighting man.

15   I stitched sackcloth together to cover my body
and I buried my forelock in the dust;
16   my cheeks were flushed with weeping
and dark shadows were round my eyes,
17   yet my hands were free from violence
and my prayer was sincere.

18   O earth, cover not my blood
and let my cry for justice find no rest!
19   For look! my witness is in heaven;
there is one on high ready to answer for me.
20   My appeal will come before God,
while my eyes turn again and again to him.
21   If only there were one to arbitrate between man and God,
as between a man and his neighbour!
22   For there are but few years to come
before I take the road from which I shall not return.

17   My mind is distraught, my days are numbered,
and the grave is waiting for me.
2    Wherever I turn, men taunt me,
and my day is darkened by their sneers.
3    Be thou my surety with thyself,
for who else can pledge himself for me?
4    Thou wilt not let those men triumph,
whose minds thou hast sunk in ignorance;
5    if such a man denounces his friends to their ruin,
his sons' eyes shall grow dim.

6    I am held up as a byword in every land,
a portent for all to see;

my eyes are dim with grief,    7
my limbs wasted to a shadow.
Honest men are bewildered at this,    8
and the innocent are indignant at my plight.
In spite of all, the righteous man maintains his course,    9
and he whose hands are clean grows strong again.

But come on, one and all, try again!    10
I shall not find a wise man among you.

My days die away like an echo;    11
my heart-strings<sup>a</sup> are snapped.
Day is turned into night,    12
and morning<sup>b</sup> light is darkened before me.
If I measure Sheol for my house,    13
if I spread my couch in the darkness,
if I call the grave my father    14
and the worm my mother or my sister,
where, then, will my hope be,    15
and who will take account of my piety?
I cannot take them down to Sheol with me,    16
nor can they descend with me into the earth.

Then Bildad the Shuhite answered:    **18**

How soon will you bridle<sup>c</sup> your tongue?    2
Do but think, and then we will talk.
What do you mean by treating us as cattle?    3
Are we nothing but brute beasts to you?<sup>d</sup>
Is the earth to be deserted to prove you right,    4
or the rocks to be moved from their place?

No, it is the wicked whose light is extinguished,    5
from whose fire no flame will rekindle;
the light fades in his tent,    6
and his lamp dies down and fails him.
In his iniquity his steps totter,    7
and his disobedience trips him up;
he rushes headlong into a net    8
and steps through the hurdle that covers a pit;
his heel is caught in a snare,    9
the noose grips him tight;
a cord lies hidden in the ground for him    10
and a trap in the path.
The terrors of death suddenly beset him    11
and make him piss over his feet.

---

<sup>a</sup> *Prob. rdg.; Heb.* the desires of my heart.      <sup>b</sup> morning: *prob. rdg.; Heb.* near.
<sup>c</sup> bridle: *prob. rdg.; Heb. unintelligible.*      <sup>d</sup> *Prob. rdg.; Heb. adds* rending himself
in his anger.

12   For all his vigour he is paralysed with fear;
     strong as he is, disaster awaits him.

13   Disease eats away his skin,
     Death's eldest child devours his limbs.

14   He is torn from the safety of his home,
     and Death's terrors escort him to their king. [a]

15   Magic herbs lie strewn about his tent,
     and his home is sprinkled with sulphur to protect it.

16   His roots beneath dry up,
     and above, his branches wither.

17   His memory vanishes from the face of the earth
     and he leaves no name in the world.

18   He is driven from light into darkness
     and banished from the land of the living.

19   He leaves no issue or offspring among his people,
     no survivor in his earthly home;

20   in the west men hear of his doom and are appalled;
     in the east they shudder with horror.

21   Such is the fate of the dwellings of evildoers,
     and of the homes of those who care nothing for God.

**19** Then Job answered:

2   How long will you exhaust me
     and pulverize me with words?

3   Time and time again you have insulted me
     and shamelessly done me wrong.

4   If in fact I had erred,
     the error would still be mine.

5   But if indeed you lord it over me
     and try to justify the reproaches levelled at me,

6   I tell you, God himself has put me in the wrong,
     he has drawn the net round me.

7   If I cry 'Murder!' no one answers;
     if I appeal for help, I get no justice.

8   He has walled in my path so that I cannot break away,
     and he has hedged in the road before me.

9   He has stripped me of all honour
     and has taken the crown from my head.

10   On every side he beats me down and I am gone;
     he has pulled up my tent-rope [b] like a tree.

11   His anger is hot against me
     and he counts me his enemy.

12   His raiders gather in force [c]
     and encamp about my tent.

[a] *Or* and you conduct him to the king of terrors.    [b] *Or* he has uprooted my hope.
[c] *Prob. rdg.; Heb. adds* they raise an earthwork against me.

My brothers hold aloof from me,
my friends are utterly estranged from me;    13
my kinsmen and intimates fall away,
my retainers have forgotten me;    14-15
my slave-girls treat me as a stranger,
I have become an alien in their eyes.
I summon my slave, but he does not answer,
though I entreat him as a favour.    16
My breath is noisome to my wife,
and I stink in the nostrils of my own family.    17
Mere children despise me
and, when I rise, turn their backs on me;    18
my intimate companions loathe me,
and those whom I love have turned against me.    19
My bones stick out through my skin,*a*
and I gnaw my under-lip with my teeth.    20

Pity me, pity me, you that are my friends;
for the hand of God has touched me.    21
Why do you pursue me as God pursues me?
Have you not had your teeth in me long enough?    22
O that my words might be inscribed,
O that they might be engraved in an inscription,    23
cut with an iron tool and filled with lead
to be a witness*b* in hard rock!    24
But in my heart I know that my vindicator lives
and that he will rise last to speak in court;    25
and I shall discern my witness standing at my side*c*
and see my defending counsel, even God himself,    26
whom I shall see with my own eyes,
I myself and no other.    27

My heart failed me when you said,
'What a train of disaster he has brought on himself!    28
The root of the trouble lies in him.'
Beware of the sword that points at you,
the sword that sweeps away all iniquity;    29
then you will know that there is a judge.*d*

Then Zophar the Naamathite answered:    **20**

My distress of mind forces me to reply,
and this is why*e* I hasten to speak:    2
I have heard arguments that are a reproach to me,
a spirit beyond my understanding gives me the answers.    3

---

*a Prob. rdg.; Heb. adds and my flesh.*    *b to . . . witness: or for ever.*
witness . . . side: *prob. rdg.; Heb. unintelligible.*    *d Or* judgement.    *c my*
why: *prob. rdg.; Heb. obscure.*    *e this is*

4    Surely you know that this has been so since time began,
     since man was first set on the earth:

5    the triumph of the wicked is short-lived,
     the glee of the godless lasts but a moment?

6    Though he stands high as heaven,
     and his head touches the clouds,

7    he will be swept utterly away like his own dung,
     and all that saw him will say, 'Where is he?'

8    He will fly away like a dream and be lost,
     driven off like a vision of the night;

9    the eye which glimpsed him shall do so no more
     and shall never again see him in his place.

11ᵃ   The youth and strength which filled his bones
     shall lie with him in the dust.

10   His sons will pay court to the poor,
     and theirᵇ hands will give back his wealth.

12   Though evil tastes sweet in his mouth,
     and he savours it, rolling it round his tongue,

13   though he lingers over it and will not let it go,
     and holds it back on his palate,

14   yet his food turns in his stomach,
     changing to asps' venom within him.

15   He gulps down wealth, then vomits it up,
     or God makes him discharge it.

16   He sucks the poison of asps,
     and the tongue of the viper kills him.

17   Not for him to swill down rivers of creamᶜ
     or torrents of honey and curds;

18   he must give back his gains without swallowing them,
     and spew up his profit undigested;

19   for he has hounded and harassed the poor,
     he has seized houses which he did not build.

20   Because his appetite gave him no rest,
     and he cannot escape his own desires,

21   nothing is left for him to eat,
     and so his well-being does not last;

22   with every need satisfied his troubles begin,
     and the full force of hardship strikes him.

23   God vents his anger upon him
     and rains on him cruel blows.

24   He is wounded by weapons of iron
     and pierced by a bronze-tipped arrow;

25   out at his back the point comes,
     the gleaming tip from his gall-bladder.

26   Darkness unrelieved awaits him,
     a fire that needs no fanning will consume him.

ᵃ *Verses 10 and 11 transposed.*          ᵇ *Prob. rdg.; Heb.* his.          ᶜ rivers of cream:
*prob. rdg.; Heb. obscure.*

[Woe betide any survivor in his tent!]
The heavens will lay bare his guilt, 27
and earth will rise up to condemn him.
A flood will sweep away his house, 28
rushing waters on the day of wrath.
Such is God's reward for the wicked man 29
and the lot appointed for the rebel[a] by God.

Then Job answered: **21**

Listen to me, do but listen, 2
and let that be the comfort you offer me.
Bear with me while I have my say; 3
when I have finished, you may mock.
May not I too voice[b] my thoughts? 4
Have not I as good cause to be impatient?
Look at my plight, and be aghast; 5
clap your hand to your mouth.
When I stop to think, I am filled with horror, 6
and my whole body is convulsed.

Why do the wicked enjoy long life, 7
hale in old age, and great and powerful?
They live to see their children settled, 8
their kinsfolk and descendants flourishing;
their families are secure and safe; 9
the rod of God's justice does not reach them.
Their bull mounts and fails not of its purpose; 10
their cow calves and does not miscarry.
Their children like lambs run out to play, 11
and their little ones skip and dance;
they rejoice with tambourine and harp 12
and make merry to the sound of the flute.
Their lives close in prosperity, 13
and they go down to Sheol in peace.
To God they say, 'Leave us alone; 14
we do not want to know your ways.
What is the Almighty that we should worship him, 15
or what should we gain by seeking his favour?'

Is not the prosperity of the wicked in their own hands? 16
Are not their purposes very different from God's[c]?
How often is the lamp of the wicked snuffed out, 17
and how often does their ruin come upon them?
How often does God in his anger deal out suffering,
bringing it in full measure to whom he will?[d]

---

[a] the rebel: *prob. rdg.; Heb.* his word.   [b] May . . . voice: *prob. rdg.; Heb. obscure.*
[c] God's: *prob. rdg.; Heb.* mine.   [d] *Line transposed from 12. 6.*

18  How often is that man like a wisp of straw before the wind,
    like chaff which the storm-wind whirls away?

19  You say, 'The trouble he has earned, God will keep for his
       sons';
    no, let him be paid for it in full and be punished.

20  Let his own eyes see damnation come upon him,
    and the wrath of the Almighty be the cup he drinks.

21  What joy shall he have in his children after him,
    if his very months and days are numbered?

22  Can any man teach God,
    God who judges even those in heaven above?


23  One man, I tell you, dies crowned with success,
    lapped in security and comfort,

24  his loins full of vigour
    and the marrow juicy in his bones;

25  another dies in bitterness of soul
    and never tastes prosperity;

26  side by side they are laid in earth,
    and worms are the shroud of both.


27  I know well what you are thinking
    and the arguments you are marshalling against me;

28  I know you will ask, 'Where is the great man's home now,
    what has become of the home of the wicked?'

29  Have you never questioned travellers?
    Can you not learn from the signs they offer,

30  that the wicked is spared when disaster comes
    and conveyed to safety before the day of wrath?

31  No one denounces his conduct to his face,
    no one requites him for what he has done.

32-33  When he is carried to the grave,
    all the world escorts him, before and behind;
    the dust of earth is sweet to him,
    and thousands keep watch at his tomb.

34  How futile, then, is the comfort you offer me!
    How false your answers ring!


## Third cycle of speeches

22  Then Eliphaz the Temanite answered:

2   Can man be any benefit to God?
    Can even a wise man benefit him?

3   Is it an asset to the Almighty if you are righteous?
    Does he gain if your conduct is perfect?

Do not think that he reproves you because you are pious,    4
that on this count he brings you to trial.
No: it is because you are a very wicked man,                5
and your depravity passes all bounds.
Without due cause you take a brother in pledge,            6
you strip men of their clothes and leave them naked.
When a man is weary, you give him no water to drink       7
and you refuse bread to the hungry.
Is the earth, then, the preserve of the strong            8
and a domain for the favoured few?
Widows you have sent away empty-handed,                   9
orphans you have struck defenceless.
No wonder that there are pitfalls in your path,           10
that scares are set to fill you with sudden fear.
The light is turned into darkness, and you cannot see;    11
the flood-waters cover you.
Surely God is at the zenith of the heavens                12
and looks down on all the stars, high as they are.
But you say, 'What does God know?                         13
Can he see through thick darkness to judge?
His eyes cannot pierce the curtain of the clouds          14
as he walks to and fro on the vault of heaven.'
Consider the course of the wicked man,                    15
the path the miscreant treads:
see how they are carried off before their time,           16
their very foundation flowing away like a river;
these men said to God, 'Leave us alone;                   17
what can the Almighty do to us?'
Yet it was he that filled their houses with good things,  18
although their purposes and his were very different.
The righteous see their fate and exult,                   19
the innocent make game of them;
for their riches are swept away,                          20
and the profusion of their wealth is destroyed by fire.

Come to terms with God and you will prosper;              21
that is the way to mend your fortune.
Take instruction from his mouth                           22
and store his words in your heart.
If you come back to the Almighty in true sincerity,       23
if you banish wrongdoing from your home,
if you treat your precious metal as dust *a*              24
and the gold of Ophir as stones from the river-bed,
then the Almighty himself will be your precious metal;    25
he will be your silver in double measure.
Then, with sure trust in *b* the Almighty,                26
you will raise your face to God;

*a* *Prob. rdg.; Heb.* if you put your precious metal on dust.   *b* with . . . in: *or* delighting in.

27    you will pray to him, and he will hear you,
      and you will have cause to fulfil your vows.
28    In all your designs you will succeed,
      and light will shine on your path;
29    but God brings down the pride of the haughty *a*
      and keeps safe the man of modest looks.
30    He will deliver the innocent, *b*
      and you will be delivered, because your hands are clean.


23  Then Job answered:

2     My thoughts today are resentful,
      for God's hand is heavy on me in my trouble.
3     If only I knew how to find him,
      how to enter his court,
4     I would state my case before him
      and set out my arguments in full;
5     then I should learn what answer he would give
      and find out what he had to say.
6     Would he exert his great power to browbeat me?
      No; God himself would never bring a charge against me.
7     There the upright are vindicated before him,
      and I shall win from my judge an absolute discharge.
8     If I go forward, *c* he is not there;
      if backward, *d* I cannot find him;
9     when I turn *e* left, *f* I do not descry him;
      I face right, *g* but I see him not.
10    But he knows me in action or at rest;
      when he tests me, I prove to be gold.
11    My feet have kept to the path he has set me,
      I have followed his way and not turned from it.
12    I do not ignore the commands that come from his lips,
      I have stored in my heart what he says.
13    He decides, *h* and who can turn him from his purpose?
      He does what his own heart desires.
14    What he determines, that he carries out;
      his mind is full of plans like these.
15    Therefore I am fearful of meeting him;
      when I think about him, *i* I am afraid;
16    it is God who makes me faint-hearted
      and the Almighty who fills me with fear,
17    yet I am not reduced to silence by the darkness
      nor *j* by the mystery which hides him.

---

*a* but . . . haughty: *prob. rdg.; Heb.* obscure.          *b* *Prob. rdg.; Heb.* the not innocent.
*c* *Or* east.     *d* *Or* west.     *e* *Prob. rdg.; Heb.* he turns.     *f* *Or* north.     *g* *Or* south.
*h* He decides: *prob. rdg.; Heb.* He in one.          *i* when . . . him: *or* I stand aloof.
*j* yet I am not . . . nor: *or* indeed I am . . . and . . .

<sup>a</sup> The day of reckoning is no secret to the Almighty,    **24**
though those who know him have no hint of its date.
Wicked men move boundary-stones    2
and carry away flocks and their shepherds.
In the field they reap what is not theirs,    6<sup>b</sup>
and filch the late grapes from the rich<sup>c</sup> man's vineyard.
They drive off the orphan's ass    3
and lead away the widow's ox with a rope.
They snatch the fatherless infant from the breast    9
and take the poor man's child in pledge.
They jostle the poor out of the way;    4
the destitute huddle together, hiding from them.
The poor rise early like the wild ass,    5
when it scours the wilderness for food;
but though they work till nightfall,<sup>d</sup>
their children go hungry.<sup>e</sup>
Naked and bare they pass the night;    7
in the cold they have nothing to cover them.
They are drenched by rain-storms from the hills    8
and hug the rock, their only shelter.
Naked and bare they go about their work,    10
and hungry they carry the sheaves;
they press the oil in the shade where two walls meet,    11
they tread the winepress but themselves go thirsty.
Far from the city, they groan like dying men,    12
and like wounded men they cry out;
but God pays no heed to their prayer.
Some there are who rebel against the light of day,    13
who know nothing of its ways
and do not linger in the paths of light.
The murderer rises before daylight    14
to kill some miserable wretch.<sup>f</sup>
The seducer watches eagerly for twilight,    15
thinking, 'No eye will catch sight of me.'
The thief prowls<sup>g</sup> by night,<sup>h</sup>
his face covered with a mask,
and in the darkness breaks into houses    16
which he has marked down in the day.
One and all,<sup>i</sup> they are strangers to the daylight,
but dark night is morning to them;    17
and in the welter of night they are at home.
Such men are scum on the surface of the water;    18
their fields have a bad name throughout the land,
and no labourer will go near their vineyards.

19 As drought and heat make away with snow,
so the waters of Sheol<sup>a</sup> make away with the sinner.

20 The womb forgets him, the worm sucks him dry;
he will not be remembered ever after. <sup>b</sup>

21 He may have wronged the barren childless woman
and been no help to the widow;

22 yet God in his strength carries off even the mighty;
they may rise, but they have no firm hope of life.

23 He lulls them into security and confidence;
but his eyes are fixed on their ways.

24 For a moment they rise to the heights, but are soon gone;
iniquity is snapped like a stick.<sup>c</sup>
They are laid low and wilt like a mallow-flower;
they droop like an ear of corn on the stalk.

25 If this is not so, who will prove me wrong
and make nonsense of my argument?

**25** Then Bildad the Shuhite answered:

2 Authority and awe rest with him
who has established peace in his realm on high.

3 His squadrons are without number;
at whom will they not spring from ambush?

4 How then can a man be justified in God's sight,
or one born of woman be innocent?

5 If the circling moon is found wanting,
and the stars are not innocent in his eyes,

6 much more so man who is but a maggot,
mortal man who is only a worm.

**26** Then Job answered:

2 What help you have given to the man without resource,
what deliverance you have brought to the powerless!

3 What counsel you offer to a man at his wit's end,
what sound advice to the foolish!

4 Who has prompted you to say such things,
and whose spirit is expressed in your speech?

5 In the underworld the shades writhe in fear,
the waters and all that live in them are struck with terror. <sup>d</sup>

6 Sheol is laid bare,
and Abaddon uncovered before him.

7 God spreads the canopy of the sky over chaos
and suspends earth in the void.

8 He keeps the waters penned in dense cloud-masses,
and the clouds do not burst open under their weight.

---

*a* snow ... Sheol: *prob. rdg.; Heb.* snow-water, Sheol.      *b Prob. rdg.; Heb. here adds* iniquity is snapped like a stick *(see note on verse 24).*      *c Line transposed from end of verse 20.*     *d* are struck with terror: *prob. rdg.; Heb. om.*

He covers the face of the full moon,[a]                                9
unrolling his clouds across it.
He has fixed the horizon on the surface of the waters              10
at the farthest limit of light and darkness.
The pillars of heaven quake                                        11
and are aghast at his rebuke.
With his strong arm he cleft the sea-monster,                      12
and struck down the Rahab by his skill.
At his breath the skies are clear,                                 13
and his hand breaks the twisting[b] sea-serpent.
These are but the fringe of his power;                             14
and how faint the whisper that we hear of him!
[Who could fathom the thunder of his might?]

Then Job resumed his discourse:                                    **27**

I swear by God, who has denied me justice,                         2
and by the Almighty, who has filled me with bitterness:
so long as there is any life left in me                            3
and God's breath is in my nostrils,
no untrue word shall pass my lips                                  4
and my tongue shall utter no falsehood.
God forbid that I should allow you to be right;                    5
till death, I will not abandon my claim to innocence.
I will maintain the rightness of my cause, I will never give up;   6
so long as I live, I will not change.

May my enemy meet the fate of the wicked,                          7
and my antagonist the doom of the wrongdoer!
What hope has a godless man, when he is cut off,[c]                8
when God takes away his life?
Will God listen to his cry                                         9
when trouble overtakes him?
Will he trust himself to the Almighty                              10
and call upon God at all times?

I will teach you what is in God's power,                           11
I will not conceal the purpose of the Almighty.
If all of you have seen these things,                              12
why then do you talk such empty nonsense?

This is the lot prescribed by God for the wicked,                  13
and the ruthless man's reward from the Almighty.
He may have many sons, but they will fall by the sword,            14
and his offspring will go hungry;
the survivors will be brought to the grave by pestilence,          15
and no widows will weep for them.

[a] *Or* He overlays the surface of his throne.     [b] *Or* primeval.     [c] *Or* What
is a godless man's thread of life when it is cut . . .

16  He may heap up silver like dirt
    and get himself piles of clothes;
17  he may get them, but the righteous will wear them,
    and his silver will be shared among the innocent.
18  The house he builds is flimsy as a bird's nest
    or a shelter put up by a watchman.
19  He may lie down rich one day, but never again;
    he opens his eyes and all is gone.
20  Disaster overtakes him like a flood,
    and a storm snatches him away in the night;
21  the east wind lifts him up and he is gone;
    it whirls him far from home;
22  it flings itself on him without mercy,
    and he is battered and buffeted by its force;
23  it snaps its fingers at him
    and whistles over him wherever he may be.

## God's unfathomable wisdom

28  There are mines for silver
    and places where men refine gold;
2   where iron is won from the earth
    and copper smelted from the ore;
3   the end of the seam lies in darkness,
    and it is followed to its farthest limit.[a]
4   Strangers cut the galleries;[b]
    they are forgotten as they drive forward far from men.[c]
5   While corn is springing from the earth above,
    what lies beneath is raked over like a fire,
6   and out of its rocks comes lapis lazuli,
    dusted with flecks of gold.
7   No bird of prey knows the way there,
    and the falcon's keen eye cannot descry it;
8   proud beasts do not set foot on it,
    and no serpent comes that way.
9   Man sets his hand to the granite rock
    and lays bare the roots of the mountains;
10  he cuts galleries in the rocks,
    and gems of every kind meet his eye;
11  he dams up the sources of the streams
    and brings the hidden riches of the earth to light.
12  But where can wisdom be found?
    And where is the source of understanding?
13  No man knows the way to it;
    it is not found in the land of living men.

[a] *Prob. rdg.; Heb. adds* stones of darkness and deep darkness.   [b] Strangers . . . galleries:
*prob. rdg.; Heb. obscure.*        [c] *Prob. rdg.; Heb. adds* languishing without foothold.

The depths of ocean say, 'It is not in us',    14
and the sea says, 'It is not with me.'
Red gold cannot buy it,    15
nor can its price be weighed out in silver;
it cannot be set in the scales against gold of Ophir,    16
against precious cornelian or lapis lazuli;
gold and crystal are not to be matched with it,    17
no work in fine gold can be bartered for it;
black coral and alabaster are not worth mention,    18
and a parcel of wisdom fetches more than red coral;
topaz *a* from Ethiopia is not to be matched with it,    19
it cannot be set in the scales against pure gold.
Where then does wisdom come from,    20
and where is the source of understanding?
No creature on earth can see it,    21
and it is hidden from the birds of the air.
Destruction and death say,    22
'We know of it only by report.'
But God understands the way to it,    23
he alone knows its source;
for he can see to the ends of the earth    24
and he surveys everything under heaven.
When he made a counterpoise for the wind    25
and measured out the waters in proportion,
when he laid down a limit for the rain    26
and a path for the thunderstorm,
even then he saw wisdom and took stock of it,    27
he considered it and fathomed its very depths.
And he said to man:    28
     The fear of the Lord is wisdom,
     and to turn from evil is understanding.

## *Job's final survey of his case*

Then Job resumed his discourse:    **29**

   If I could only go back to the old days,    2
   to the time when God was watching over me,
   when his lamp shone above my head,    3
   and by its light I walked through the darkness!
   If I could be as in the days of my prime,    4
   when God protected my home,
   while the Almighty was still there at my side,    5
   and my servants stood round me,
   while my path flowed with milk,    6
   and the rocks streamed oil!

       *a* Or chrysolite.

7   If I went through the gate out of the town
    to take my seat in the public square,
8   young men saw me and kept out of sight;
    old men rose to their feet,
9   men in authority broke off their talk
    and put their hands to their lips;
10  the voices of the nobles died away,
    and every man held his tongue.
21 *a*  They listened to me expectantly
    and waited in silence for my opinion.
22  When I had spoken, no one spoke again;
    my words fell gently on them;
23  they waited for them as for rain
    and drank them in like showers in spring.
24  When I smiled on them, they took heart;
    when my face lit up, they lost their gloomy looks.
25  I presided over them, planning their course,
    like a king encamped with his troops. *b*

11  Whoever heard of me spoke in my favour,
    and those who saw me bore witness to my merit,
12  how I saved the poor man when he called for help
    and the orphan who had no protector.
13  The man threatened with ruin blessed me,
    and I made the widow's heart sing for joy.
14  I put on righteousness as a garment and it clothed me;
    justice, like a cloak or a turban, wrapped me round.
15  I was eyes to the blind
    and feet to the lame;
16  I was a father to the needy,
    and I took up the stranger's cause.
17  I broke the fangs of the miscreant
    and rescued the prey from his teeth.
18  I thought, 'I shall die with my powers unimpaired
    and my days uncounted as the grains of sand, *c*
19  with my roots spreading out to the water
    and the dew lying on my branches,
20  with the bow always new in my grasp
    and the arrow ever ready to my hand.' *d*

30  But now I am laughed to scorn
    by men of a younger generation,
    men whose fathers I would have disdained
    to put with the dogs who kept my flock.
2   What use were their strong arms to me,
    since their sturdy vigour had wasted away?

---

*a Verses 21–25 transposed to this point.*   *b Prob. rdg.; Heb. adds as when one*
comforts mourners.   *c Or as those of the phoenix.*   *d Verses 21–25 transposed*
*to follow verse 10.*

They gnawed roots<sup>a</sup> in the desert,    3
gaunt with want and hunger,<sup>b</sup>
they plucked saltwort and wormwood    4
and root of broom<sup>c</sup> for their food.
Driven out from the society of men,<sup>d</sup>    5
pursued like thieves with hue and cry,
they lived in gullies and ravines,    6
holes in the earth and rocky clefts;
they howled like beasts among the bushes,    7
huddled together beneath the scrub,
vile base-born wretches,    8
hounded from the haunts of men.
Now I have become the target of their taunts,    9
my name is a byword among them.
They loathe me, they shrink from me,    10
they dare to spit in my face.
They run wild and savage<sup>e</sup> me;    11
at sight of me they throw off all restraint.
On my right flank they attack in a mob;<sup>f</sup>    12
they raise their siege-ramps against me,
they tear down my crumbling defences to my undoing,    13
and scramble up against me unhindered;
they burst in through the gaping breach;    14
at the moment of the crash they come rolling in.
Terror upon terror overwhelms me,    15
it sweeps away my resolution like the wind,
and my hope of victory vanishes like a cloud.
So now my soul is in turmoil within me,    16
and misery has me daily in its grip.
By night pain pierces my very bones,    17
and there is ceaseless throbbing in my veins;
my garments are all bespattered with my phlegm,    18
which chokes me like the collar of a shirt.
God himself<sup>g</sup> has flung me down in the mud,    19
no better than dust or ashes.

I call for thy help, but thou dost not answer;    20
I stand up to plead, but thou sittest aloof;
thou hast turned cruelly against me    21
and with thy strong hand pursuest me in hatred;
thou dost snatch me up and set me astride the wind,    22
and the tempest<sup>h</sup> tosses me up and down.
I know that thou wilt hand me over to death,    23
to the place appointed for all mortal men.

<sup>a</sup> roots: *prob. rdg.; Heb. om.*      <sup>b</sup> *Prob. rdg.; Heb. adds* yesterday waste and derelict
land.    <sup>c</sup> root of broom: *probably* fungus on broom root.    <sup>d</sup> the society of men: *prob.
rdg.; Heb. obscure.*    <sup>e</sup> They run ... savage: *prob. rdg.; Heb.* He runs ... savages.
<sup>f</sup> *Prob. rdg.; Heb. adds* they let loose my feet.    <sup>g</sup> God himself: *prob. rdg.; Heb. om.*
<sup>h</sup> the tempest: *prob. rdg.; Heb. unintelligible.*

24   Yet no beggar held out his hand
     but was relieved<sup>a</sup> by me in his distress.

25   Did I not weep for the man whose life was hard?
     Did not my heart grieve for the poor?

26   Evil has come though I expected good;
     I looked for light but there came darkness.

27   My bowels are in ferment and know no peace;
     days of misery stretch out before me.

28   I go about dejected and friendless;
     I rise in the assembly, only to appeal for help.

29   The wolf is now my brother,
     the owls of the desert have become my companions.

30   My blackened skin peels off,
     and my body is scorched by the heat.

31   My harp has been tuned for a dirge,
     my flute to the voice of those who weep.

**31**  2<sup>b</sup>  What is the lot prescribed by God above,
     the reward from the Almighty on high?

3   Is not ruin prescribed for the miscreant
     and calamity for the wrongdoer?

4   Yet does not God himself see my ways
     and count my every step?

5   I swear I have had no dealings with falsehood
     and have not embarked on a course of deceit.

1   I have come to terms with my eyes,
     never to take notice of a girl.

6   Let God weigh me in the scales of justice,
     and he will know that I am innocent!

7   If my steps have wandered from the way,
     if my heart has followed my eyes,
     or any dirt stuck to my hands,

8   may another eat what I sow,
     and may my crops be pulled up by the roots!

9   If my heart has been enticed by a woman
     or I have lain in wait at my neighbour's door,

10   may my wife be another man's slave,
     and may other men enjoy her.

11   [But that is a wicked act, an offence before the law;

12   it would be a consuming and destructive fire,
     raging<sup>c</sup> among my crops.]

13   If I have ever rejected the plea of my slave
     or of my slave-girl, when they brought their complaint to me,

14   what shall I do if God appears?
     What shall I answer if he intervenes?

15   Did not he who made me in the womb make them?

<sup>a</sup> *was relieved: prob. rdg.; Heb. unintelligible.*     <sup>b</sup> *Verse 1 transposed to follow verse 5.*
<sup>c</sup> *Prob. rdg.; Heb. uprooting.*

Did not the same God create us in the belly?
If I have withheld their needs from the poor                    16
or let the widow's eye grow dim with tears,
if I have eaten my crust alone,                    17
and the orphan has not shared it with me—
the orphan who from boyhood honoured me like a father,                    18
whom I guided from the day of his<sup>a</sup> birth—
if I have seen anyone perish for lack of clothing,                    19
or a poor man with nothing to cover him,
if his body had no cause to bless me,                    20
because he was not kept warm with a fleece from my flock,
if I have raised<sup>b</sup> my hand against the innocent,<sup>c</sup>                    21
knowing that men would side with me in court,
then may my shoulder-blade be torn from my shoulder,                    22
my arm be wrenched out of its socket!
But the terror of God was heavy upon me,<sup>d</sup>                    23
and for fear of his majesty I could do none of these things.
If I have put my faith in gold                    24
and my trust in the gold of Nubia,
if I have rejoiced in my great wealth                    25
and in the increase of riches;
if I ever looked on the sun in splendour                    26
or the moon moving in her glory,
and was led astray in my secret heart                    27
and raised my hand in homage;
this would have been an offence before the law,                    28
for I should have been unfaithful to God on high.
If my land has cried out in reproach at me,                    38<sup>e</sup>
and its furrows have joined in weeping,
if I have eaten its produce without payment                    39
and have disappointed my creditors,
may thistles spring up instead of wheat,                    40
and weeds instead of barley!

Have I rejoiced at the ruin of the man that hated me                    29
or been filled with malice when trouble overtook him,
even though I did not allow my tongue to sin                    30
by demanding his life with a curse?
Have the men of my household never said,                    31
'Let none of us speak ill of him!
No stranger has spent the night in the street'?                    32
For I have kept open house for the traveller.
Have I ever concealed my misdeeds as men do,                    33
keeping my guilt to myself,
because I feared the gossip of the town                    34
or dreaded the scorn of my fellow-citizens?

---

<sup>a</sup> *Prob. rdg.; Heb.* my.     <sup>b</sup> *Or* waved.     <sup>c</sup> *Or* orphan.     <sup>d</sup> *Prob. rdg.; Heb.* A fear towards me is a disaster from God.     <sup>e</sup> *Verses 38–40 transposed (but see note c, page 596).*

35  Let me but call a witness in my defence!
    Let the Almighty state his case against me!
    If my accuser had written out his indictment,
    I would not keep silence and remain indoors.*a*
36  No! I would flaunt it on my shoulder
    and wear it like a crown on my head;
37  I would plead the whole record of my life
    and present that in court as my defence.*b*

Job's speeches are finished.*c*


## Speeches of Elihu

**32** So these three men gave up answering Job; for he continued to think him-
2  self righteous. Then Elihu son of Barakel the Buzite, of the family of Ram,
   grew angry; angry because Job had made himself out more righteous than
3  God,*d* and angry with the three friends because they had found no answer
4  to Job and had let God appear wrong.*e* Now Elihu had hung back while
5  they were talking with Job because they were older than he; but, when he
6  saw that the three had no answer, he could no longer contain his anger. So
   Elihu son of Barakel the Buzite began to speak:

    I am young in years,
    and you are old;
    that is why I held back and shrank
    from displaying my knowledge in front of you.
7   I said to myself, 'Let age speak,
    and length of years expound wisdom.'
8   But the spirit of God himself is in man,
    and the breath of the Almighty gives him understanding;
9   it is not only the old who are wise
    or the aged who understand what is right.
10  Therefore I say: Listen to me;
    I too will display my knowledge.
11  Look, I have been waiting upon your words,
    listening for the conclusions of your thoughts,
    while you sought for phrases;
12  I have been giving thought to your conclusions,
    but not one of you refutes Job or answers his arguments.
13  Take care then not to claim that you have found wisdom;
    God will rebut him, not man.
14  I will not string*f* words together like you*g*
    or answer him as you have done.

---

*a* *Line transposed from verse 34.*      *b* *Verses 38–40 transposed to follow verse 28 (but*
*see note c).*      *c* *The last line of verse 40 retained here.*      *d* *Or* had justified himself
with God.      *e* *Prob. original rdg., altered in Heb. to* and had not proved Job wrong.
*f* *Prob. rdg.; Heb.* He has not strung.      *g* *Prob. rdg.; Heb.* towards me.

If these men are confounded and no longer answer,                    15
if words fail them,
am I to wait because they do not speak,                               16
because they stand there and no longer answer?
I, too, have a furrow to plough;                                      17
I will express my opinion;
for I am bursting with words,                                         18
a bellyful of wind gripes me.
My stomach is distended as if with wine,                             19
bulging like a blacksmith's bellows;
I must speak to find relief,                                          20
I must open my mouth and answer;
I will show no favour to anyone,                                      21
I will flatter no one, God or man; *a*
for I cannot use flattering titles,                                   22
or my Maker would soon do away with me.

Come now, Job, listen to my words                                    **33**
and attend carefully to everything I say.
Look, I am ready to answer;                                           2
the words are on the tip of my tongue.
My heart assures me that I speak with knowledge,                     3
and that my lips speak with sincerity.
For the spirit of God made me,                                       4
and the breath of the Almighty gave me life.
Answer me if you can,                                                5
marshal your arguments and confront me.
In God's sight *b* I am just what you are;                           6
I too am only a handful of clay.
Fear of me need not abash you,                                       7
nor any pressure from me overawe you.
You have said your say and I heard you;                              8
I have listened to the sound of your words:
'I am innocent', you said, 'and free from offence,                   9
blameless and without guilt.
Yet God finds occasions to put me in the wrong                       10
and counts me his enemy;
he puts my feet in the stocks                                        11
and keeps a close watch on all I do.'

Well, this is my answer: You are wrong.                              12
God is greater than man;
why then plead your case with him?                                   13
for no one can answer his arguments.
Indeed, once God has spoken                                          14
he does not speak a second time to confirm it.

---

*a* *Prob. rdg.; Heb.* I will not flatter man.      *b* In God's sight: *or* In strength.

15    In dreams, in visions of the night,
      when deepest sleep falls upon men,
16    while they sleep on their beds, God makes them listen,
      and his correction strikes them with terror.
17    To turn a man from reckless conduct,
      to check the pride<sup>a</sup> of mortal man,
18    at the edge of the pit he holds him back alive
      and stops him from crossing the river of death.
19    Or again, man learns his lesson on a bed of pain,
      tormented by a ceaseless ague in his bones;
20    he turns from his food with loathing
      and has no relish for the choicest meats;
21    his flesh hangs loose upon him,
      his bones are loosened and out of joint,
22    his soul draws near to the pit,
      his life to the ministers of death.
23    Yet if an angel, one of thousands, stands by him,
      a mediator between him and God,
      to expound what he has done right
      and to secure mortal man his due; <sup>b</sup>
24    if he speaks in the man's favour and says, 'Reprieve him,
      let him not go down to the pit, I have the price of his release';
25    then that man will grow sturdier<sup>c</sup> than he was in youth,
      he will return to the days of his prime.
26    If he entreats God to show him favour,
      to let him see his face and shout for joy; <sup>d</sup>
27    if he declares before all men, 'I have sinned,
      turned right into wrong and thought nothing of it';
28    then he saves himself from going down to the pit,
      he lives and sees the light.
29    All these things God may do to a man,
      again and yet again,
30    bringing him back from the pit
      to enjoy the full light of life.

31    Listen, Job, and attend to me;
      be silent, and I myself will speak.
32    If you have any arguments, answer me;
      speak, and I would gladly find you proved right;
33    but if you have none, listen to me:
      keep silence, and I will teach you wisdom.

34 Then Elihu went on to say:
2     Mark my words, you wise men;
      you men of long experience, listen to me;
3     for the ear tests what is spoken
      as the palate savours food.

<sup>a</sup> the pride: *prob. rdg.; Heb. obscure.*     <sup>b</sup> *Line transposed from verse 26.*     <sup>c</sup> will
grow sturdier: *prob. rdg.; Heb. unintelligible.*     <sup>d</sup> *See note on verse 23.*

Let us then examine for ourselves what is right;                    4
let us together establish the true good.
Job has said, 'I am innocent,                                       5
but God has deprived me of justice,
he has falsified my case;                                           6
my state is desperate, yet I have done no wrong.'
Was there ever a man like Job                                      7
with his thirst for irreverent talk,
choosing bad company to share his journeys,                         8
a fellow-traveller with wicked men?
For he says that it brings a man no profit                          9
to find favour with God.
But listen to me, you men of good sense.                            10
    Far be it from God to do evil
     or the Almighty to play false!
For he pays a man according to his work                             11
and sees that he gets what his conduct deserves.
The truth is, God does no wrong,                                    12
the Almighty does not pervert justice.
Who committed the earth to his keeping?                             13
Who but he established the whole world?
If he were to turn his thoughts inwards                             14
and recall his life-giving spirit,
all that lives would perish on the instant,                         15
and man return again to dust.


Now Job, if you have the wit, consider this;                        16
listen to the words I speak.
Can it be that a hater of justice holds the reins?                  17
Do you disparage a sovereign whose rule is so fair,
who will say to a prince, 'You scoundrel',                          18
and call his magnates blackguards to their faces;
who does not show special favour to those in office                 19
and thinks no more of rich than of poor?
All alike are God's creatures,
who may die in a moment, in the middle of the night;                20
at his touch the rich are no more,
and the mighty vanish though no hand is laid on them.
His eyes are on the ways of men,                                    21
and he sees every step they take,
there is nowhere so dark, so deep in shadow,                        22
that wrongdoers may hide from him.
Therefore he repudiates all that they do;                           25
he turns on them in the night, and they are crushed.
There are no appointed days for men                                 23
to appear before God for judgement.
He holds no inquiry, but breaks the powerful                        24
and sets up others in their place.

26<sup>a</sup>  For their crimes he strikes them down<sup>b</sup>
    and makes them disgorge their bloated wealth,<sup>c</sup>

27  because they have ceased to obey him
    and pay no heed to his ways.

28  Then the cry of the poor reaches his ears,
    and he hears the cry of the distressed.

29-30  [Even if he is silent, who can condemn him?
    If he looks away, who can find fault?
    What though he makes a godless man king
    over a stubborn nation and all its people?]

31  But suppose you were to say to God,
    'I have overstepped the mark; I will do no more<sup>d</sup> mischief.

32  Vile wretch that I am, be thou my guide;
    whatever wrong I have done, I will do wrong no more.'

33  Will he, at these words, condone your rejection of him?
    It is for you to decide, not me:
    but what can you answer?

34  Men of good sense will say,
    any intelligent hearer will tell me,

35  'Job talks with no knowledge,
    and there is no sense in what he says.

36  If only Job could be put to the test once and for all
    for answers that are meant to make mischief!

37  He is a sinner and a rebel as well<sup>e</sup>
    with his endless ranting against God.'

**35**  Then Elihu went on to say:

2  Do you think that this is a sound plea
    or maintain that you are in the right against God?—

3  if you say, 'What would be the advantage to me?
    how much should I gain from sinning?'

4  I will bring arguments myself against you,
    you and your three friends.

5  Look up at the sky and then consider,
    observe the rain-clouds towering above you.

6  How does it touch him if you have sinned?
    However many your misdeeds, what does it mean to him?

7  If you do right, what good do you bring him,
    or what does he gain from you?

8  Your wickedness touches only men, such as you are;
    the right that you do affects none but mortal man.

9  Men will cry out beneath the burdens of oppression
    and call for help against the power of the great;

---

<sup>a</sup> *Verse 25 transposed to follow verse 22.*      <sup>b</sup> *he strikes them down: prob. rdg.; Heb. om.*
<sup>c</sup> *Or and chastises them where people see.*         <sup>d</sup> *more: prob. rdg.; Heb. obscure.*
<sup>e</sup> *Prob. rdg.; Heb. adds* between us it is enough.

but none of them asks, 'Where is God my Maker     10
who gives protection by night,
who grants us more knowledge than the beasts of the earth     11
and makes us wiser than the birds of the air?'
So, when they cry out, he does not answer,     12
because they are self-willed and proud.
All to no purpose! God does not listen,     13
the Almighty does not see.

The worse for you when you say, 'He does not see me'!     14
Humble yourself*a* in his presence and wait for his word.
But now, because God does not grow angry and punish     15
and because he lets folly pass unheeded,
Job gives vent to windy nonsense     16
and makes a parade of empty words.

Then Elihu went on to say:     **36**

Be patient a little longer, and let me enlighten you;     2
there is still something more to be said on God's side.
I will search far and wide to support my conclusions,     3
as I defend the justice of my Maker.
There are no flaws in my reasoning;     4
before you stands one whose conclusions are sound.

God,*b* I say, repudiates the high and*c* mighty     5
and does not let the wicked prosper,     6
but allows the just claims of the poor and suffering;
he does not deprive the sufferer of his due.*d*     7
Look at kings on their thrones:
when God gives them sovereign power, they grow arrogant.
Next you may see them loaded with fetters,     8
held fast in captives' chains:
he denounces their conduct to them,     9
showing how insolence and tyranny was their offence;
his warnings sound in their ears     10
and summon them to turn back from their evil courses.
If they listen to him, they spend*e* their days in prosperity     11
and their years in comfort.
But, if they do not listen, they die, their lesson unlearnt,     12
and cross the river of death.
Proud men rage against him     13
and do not cry to him for help when caught in his toils;
so they die in their prime,     14
like male prostitutes,*f* worn out.*g*

---

*a* Humble yourself: *prob. rdg.; Heb.* Judge.     *b Prob. rdg.; Heb. adds* a mighty one
and not.     *c* and: *prob. rdg.; Heb. om.*     *d* deprive . . . due: *or* withdraw his
gaze from the righteous.     *e Prob. rdg.; Heb. adds* they end.     *f Cp. Deut. 23. 17.*
*g* worn out: *prob. rdg.; Heb. unintelligible.*

15    Those who suffer he rescues through suffering
      and teaches them by the discipline of affliction.

16    Beware, if you are tempted to exchange hardship for comfort, *a*
      for unlimited plenty spread before you, and a generous table;
17    if you eat your fill of a rich man's fare
      when you are occupied with the business of the law,
18    do not be led astray by lavish gifts of wine
      and do not let bribery warp your judgement.
19    Will that wealth of yours, however great, avail you,
      or all the resources of your high position?
21 *b*   Take care not to turn to mischief;
      for that is why you are tried by affliction.

20    Have no fear if in the breathless terrors of the night
      you see nations vanish where they stand.
22    God towers in majesty above us;
      who wields such sovereign power as he?
23    Who has prescribed his course for him?
      Who has said to him, 'Thou hast done wrong'?
24    Remember then to sing the praises of his work,
      as men have always sung them.
25    All men stand back from *c* him;
      the race of mortals look on from afar.
26    Consider; God is so great that we cannot know him;
      the number of his years is beyond reckoning.
27    He draws up drops of water from the sea *d*
      and distils rain from the mist he has made;
28    the rain-clouds pour down in torrents, *e*
      they descend in showers on mankind;
31    thus he sustains the nations
      and gives them food in plenty.
29    Can any man read the secret of the sailing clouds,
      spread like a carpet under *f* his pavilion?
30    See how he unrolls the mist across the waters,
      and its streamers *g* cover the sea.
32 *h*   He charges the thunderbolts with flame
      and launches them straight *i* at the mark;
33    in his anger he calls up the tempest,
      and the thunder is the herald of its coming. *j*

**37**    This too makes my heart beat wildly
      and start from its place.
2    Listen, listen to the thunder of God's voice
      and the rumbling of his utterance.

---

*a* for comfort: *prob. rdg.; Heb. om.*    *b* Verses 20 and 21 transposed.    *c* Or gaze at.
*d* from the sea: *prob. rdg.; Heb. om.*    *e* in torrents: *prob. rdg.; Heb.* which.    *f* spread
... under: *prob. rdg.; Heb.* crashing noises.      *g* its streamers: *prob. rdg.; Heb.* the
roots of.    *h* Verse 31 transposed to follow verse 28.    *i* and ... straight: *prob. rdg.; Heb.*
and gives orders concerning it.    *j* in his anger ... coming: *prob. rdg.; Heb. obscure.*

Under the vault of heaven he lets it roll,
and his lightning reaches the ends of the earth;  3
there follows a sound of roaring
as he thunders with the voice of majesty.*a*  4
God's voice is marvellous in its working;*b*  5
he does great deeds that pass our knowledge.
For he says to the snow, 'Fall to earth',  6
and to the rainstorms, 'Be fierce.'
And when his voice is heard,
the floods of rain pour down unchecked.*c*
He shuts every man fast indoors,*d*  7
and all men whom he has made must stand idle;
the beasts withdraw into their lairs  8
and take refuge in their dens.
The hurricane bursts from its prison,  9
and the rain-winds bring bitter cold;
at the breath of God the ice-sheet is formed,  10
and the wide waters are frozen hard as iron.
He gives the dense clouds their load of moisture,  11
and the clouds spread his mist abroad,
as they travel round in their courses,  12
steered by his guiding hand
to do his bidding
all over the habitable world.*e*

Listen, Job, to this argument;  14
stand still, and consider God's wonderful works.
Do you know how God assigns them their tasks,  15
how he sends light flashing from his clouds?
Do you know why the clouds hang poised overhead,  16
a wonderful work of his consummate skill,
sweating there in your stifling clothes,  17
when the earth lies sultry under the south wind?
Can you beat out the vault of the skies, as he does,  18
hard as a mirror of cast metal?
Teach us then what to say to him;  19
for all is dark, and we cannot marshal our thoughts.
Can any man dictate to God when he is *f* to speak?  20
or command him to make proclamation?
At one moment the light is not seen,  21
it is overcast with clouds and rain;
then the wind passes by and clears them away,
and a golden glow comes from the north.*g*  22

---

*a See note on verse 6.* *b Prob. rdg.; Heb. thundering.* *c And when . . . unchecked: prob. rdg.; some words in these lines transposed from verse 4.* *d indoors: prob. rdg.; Heb. obscure.* *e Prob. rdg.; Heb. adds (13) whether he makes him attain the rod, or his earth, or constant love.* *f Prob. rdg.; Heb. I am.* *g Prob. rdg.; Heb. adds this refers to God, terrible in majesty.*

23  But the Almighty we cannot find; his power is beyond our ken,
and his righteousness not slow to do justice.

24  Therefore mortal men pay him reverence,
and all who are wise look to him.


## God's answer and Job's submission

38  Then the LORD answered Job out of the tempest:

2  Who is this whose ignorant words
cloud my design in darkness?

3  Brace yourself and stand up like a man;
I will ask questions, and you shall answer.

4  Where were you when I laid the earth's foundations?
Tell me, if you know and understand.

5  Who settled its dimensions? Surely you should know.
Who stretched his measuring-line over it?

6  On what do its supporting pillars rest?
Who set its corner-stone in place,

7  when the morning stars sang together
and all the sons of God shouted aloud?

8  Who watched over the birth of the sea, *a*
when it burst in flood from the womb?—

9  when I wrapped it in a blanket of cloud
and cradled it in fog,

10  when I established its bounds,
fixing its doors and bars in place,

11  and said, 'Thus far shall you come and no farther,
and here your surging waves shall halt.' *b*

12  In all your life have you ever called up the dawn
or shown the morning its place?

13  Have you taught it to grasp the fringes of the earth
and shake the Dog-star from its place;

14  to bring up the horizon in relief as clay under a seal,
until all things stand out like the folds of a cloak,

15  when the light of the Dog-star is dimmed
and the stars of the Navigator's Line go out one by one?

16  Have you descended to the springs of the sea
or walked in the unfathomable deep?

17  Have the gates of death been revealed to you?
Have you ever seen the door-keepers of the place of darkness?

18  Have you comprehended the vast expanse of the world?
Come, tell me all this, if you know.

19  Which is the way to the home of light
and where does darkness dwell?

*a* Who . . . sea: *prob. rdg.; Heb.* And he held back the sea with two doors.    *b Prob.*
*rdg.; Heb.* here one shall set on your surging waves.

And can you then take each to its appointed bound      20
and escort it on its homeward path?
Doubtless you know all this; for you were born already,      21
so long is the span of your life!

Have you visited the storehouse of the snow      22
or seen the arsenal where hail is stored,
which I have kept ready for the day of calamity,      23
for war and for the hour of battle?
By what paths is the heat spread abroad      24
or the east wind carried far and wide over the earth?
Who has cut channels for the downpour      25
and cleared a passage for the thunderstorm,
for rain to fall on land where no man lives      26
and on the deserted wilderness,
clothing lands waste and derelict with green      27
and making grass grow on thirsty ground*ᵃ*?
Has the rain a father?      28
Who sired the drops of dew?
Whose womb gave birth to the ice,      29
and who was the mother of the frost from heaven,
which lays a stony cover over the waters      30
and freezes the expanse of ocean?
Can you bind the cluster of the Pleiades      31
or loose Orion's belt?
Can you bring out the signs of the zodiac in their season      32
or guide Aldebaran and its train?
Did you proclaim the rules that govern the heavens,      33
or determine the laws of nature on earth?
Can you command the dense clouds      34
to cover you with their weight of waters?
If you bid lightning speed on its way,      35
will it say to you, 'I am ready'?
Who put wisdom in depths of darkness      36
and veiled understanding in secrecy *ᵇ*?
Who is wise enough to marshal the rain-clouds      37
and empty the cisterns of heaven,
when the dusty soil sets hard as iron,      38
and the clods of earth cling together?
Do you hunt her prey for the lioness      39
and satisfy the hunger of young lions,
as they crouch in the lair      40
or lie in wait in the covert?
Who provides the raven with its quarry      41
when its fledglings croak *ᶜ* for lack of food?

---

*ᵃ* thirsty ground: *prob. rdg.; Heb.* source.     *ᵇ* secrecy: *prob. rdg.; Heb. word unknown.*
*ᶜ* *Prob. rdg.; Heb. adds* they cry to God.

39   Do you know when the mountain-goats are born
     or attend the wild doe when she is in labour?

2    Do you count the months that they carry their young
     or know the time of their delivery,

3    when they crouch down to open their wombs
     and bring their offspring to the birth,

4    when the fawns grow and thrive in the open forest,
     and go forth and do not return?

5    Who has let the wild ass of Syria range at will
     and given the wild ass of Arabia its freedom?—

6    whose home I have made in the wilderness
     and its lair in the saltings;

7    it disdains the noise of the city
     and is deaf to the driver's shouting;

8    it roams the hills as its pasture
     and searches for anything green.

9    Does the wild ox consent to serve you,
     does it spend the night in your stall?

10   Can you harness its strength *a* with ropes,
     or will it harrow the furrows *a* after you?

11   Can you depend on it, strong as it is,
     or leave your labour to it?

12   Do you trust it to come back
     and bring home your grain to the threshing-floor?

13   The wings of the ostrich are stunted; *b*
     *c* her pinions and plumage are so scanty *d*

14   that she abandons her eggs to the ground,
     letting them be kept warm by the sand.

15   She forgets that a foot may crush them,
     or a wild beast trample on them;

16   she treats her chicks heartlessly as if they were not hers,
     not caring if her labour is wasted

17   (for God has denied her wisdom
     and left her without sense),

18   while like a cock she struts over the uplands,
     scorning both horse and rider.

19   Did you give the horse his strength?
     Did you clothe his neck with a mane?

20   Do you make him quiver like a locust's wings,
     when his shrill neighing strikes terror?

21   He shows his mettle as he paws and prances;
     he charges the armoured line with all his might.

22   He scorns alarms and knows no dismay;
     he does not flinch before the sword.

---

*a* *Prob. rdg.; Heb. transposes* strength *and* furrows.
*Heb. unintelligible.*    *c* *Prob. rdg.; Heb. prefixes* if.    *b* are stunted: *prob. rdg.;*    *d* *Prob. rdg.; Heb.* godly
*or* stork.

The quiver rattles at his side,
the spear and sabre flash.     23
Trembling with eagerness, he devours the ground
and cannot be held in when he hears the horn;     24
at the blast of the horn he cries 'Aha!'
and from afar he scents the battle.<sup>a</sup>     25
Does your skill teach the hawk to use its pinions
and spread its wings towards the south?     26
Do you instruct the vulture to fly high
and build its nest aloft?     27
It dwells among the rocks and there it lodges;
its station is a crevice in the rock;     28
from there it searches for food,
keenly scanning the distance,     29
that its brood may be gorged with blood;
and where the slain are, there the vulture is.     30
Can you pull out the whale<sup>b</sup> with a gaff
or can you slip a noose round its tongue?     **41** 1<sup>c</sup>
Can you pass a cord through its nose
or put a hook through its jaw?     2
Will it plead with you for mercy
or beg its life with soft words?     3
Will it enter into an agreement with you
to become your slave for life?     4
Will you toy with it as with a bird
or keep it on a string like a song-bird for your maidens?     5
Do trading-partners haggle over it
or merchants share it out?     6

Then the L ORD said to Job:     **40**

Is it for a man who disputes with the Almighty to be stubborn?
Should he that argues with God answer back?     2

And Job answered the L ORD:     3

What reply can I give thee, I who carry no weight?
I put my finger to my lips.     4
I have spoken once and now will not answer again;
twice have I spoken, and I will do so no more.     5

Then the L ORD answered Job out of the tempest:     6

Brace yourself and stand up like a man;
I will ask questions, and you shall answer.     7
Dare you deny that I am just
or put me in the wrong that you may be right?     8

---

<sup>a</sup> *Prob. rdg.; Heb. adds* the thunder of the captains and the shouting.     <sup>b</sup> *Or* Leviathan.
<sup>c</sup> *41. 1–6 (in Heb. 40. 25–30) transposed to this point.*

9       Have you an arm like God's arm,
        can you thunder with a voice like his?

10      Deck yourself out, if you can, in pride and dignity,
        array yourself in pomp and splendour;

11      unleash the fury of your wrath,
        look upon the proud man and humble him;

12      look upon every proud man and bring him low,
        throw down the wicked where they stand;

13      hide them in the dust together,
        and shroud them in an unknown grave.

14      Then I in my turn will acknowledge
        that your own right hand can save you.

15      Consider the chief of the beasts, the crocodile,*a*
        who devours cattle as if they were grass:*b*

16      what strength is in his loins!
        what power in the muscles of his belly!

17      His tail is rigid as*c* a cedar,
        the sinews of his flanks are closely knit,

18      his bones are tubes of bronze,
        and his limbs like bars of iron.

19      He is the chief of God's works,
        made to be a tyrant over his peers;*d*

20      for he takes*e* the cattle of the hills for his prey
        and in his jaws he crunches all wild beasts.

21      There under the thorny lotus he lies,
        hidden in the reeds and the marsh;

22      the lotus conceals him in its shadow,
        the poplars of the stream surround him.

23      If the river is in spate, he is not scared,
        he sprawls at his ease though the stream is in flood.

24      Can a man blind*f* his eyes and take him
        or pierce his nose with the teeth of a trap?

**41** 7*g*  Can you fill his skin with harpoons
        or his head with fish-hooks?

8       If ever you lift your hand against him,
        think of the struggle that awaits you, and let be.

9       No, such a man is in desperate case,
        hurled headlong at the very sight of him.

10      How fierce he is when he is roused!
        Who is there to stand up to him?

11      Who has ever attacked him*h* unscathed?
        Not a man*i* under the wide heaven.

[a] chief . . . crocodile: *prob. rdg.; Heb.* beasts (behemoth) which I have made with you.
[b] cattle . . . grass: *prob. rdg.; Heb.* grass like cattle.     [c] *Or* He bends his tail like . . .
[d] *Prob. rdg.; Heb.* his sword.     [e] *Prob. rdg.; Heb.* they take.     [f] Can a man blind:
*prob. rdg.; Heb. obscure.*     [g] *Verses 1–6 transposed to follow 39. 30.*     [h] *Prob. rdg.;
Heb.* me.     [i] *Prob. rdg.; Heb.* He is mine.

| | |
|---|---|
| I will not pass over in silence his limbs, | 12 |
| his prowess and the grace of his proportions. | |
| Who has ever undone his outer garment | 13 |
| or penetrated his doublet of hide? | |
| Who has ever opened the portals of his face? | 14 |
| for there is terror in his arching teeth. | |
| His back<sup>a</sup> is row upon row of shields, | 15 |
| enclosed in a wall <sup>b</sup> of flints; | |
| one presses so close on the other | 16 |
| that air cannot pass between them, | |
| each so firmly clamped to its neighbour | 17 |
| that they hold and cannot spring apart. | |
| His sneezing sends out sprays of light, | 18 |
| and his eyes gleam like the shimmer of dawn. | |
| Firebrands shoot from his mouth, | 19 |
| and sparks come streaming out; | |
| his nostrils pour forth smoke | 20 |
| like a cauldron on a fire blown to full heat. | |
| His breath sets burning coals ablaze, | 21 |
| and flames flash from his mouth. | |
| Strength is lodged in his neck, | 22 |
| and untiring energy dances ahead of him. | |
| Close knit is his underbelly, | 23 |
| no pressure will make it yield. | |
| His heart is firm as a rock, | 24 |
| firm as the nether millstone. | |
| When he raises himself, strong men<sup>c</sup> take fright, | 25 |
| bewildered at the lashings of his tail. | |
| Sword or spear, dagger or javelin, | 26 |
| if they touch him, they have no effect. | |
| Iron he counts as straw, | 27 |
| and bronze as rotting wood. | |
| No arrow can pierce him, | 28 |
| and for him sling-stones are turned into chaff; | |
| to him a club is a mere reed, | 29 |
| and he laughs at the swish of the sabre. | |
| Armoured beneath with jagged sherds, | 30 |
| he sprawls on the mud like a threshing-sledge. | |
| He makes the deep water boil like a cauldron, | 31 |
| he whips up the lake like ointment in a mixing-bowl. | |
| He leaves a shining trail behind him, | 32 |
| and the great river is like white hair in his wake. | |
| He has no equal on earth; | 33 |
| for he is made quite without fear. | |
| He looks down on all creatures, even the highest; | 34 |
| he is king over all proud beasts. | |

---

<sup>a</sup> *Prob. rdg.; Heb.* pride.      <sup>b</sup> *Prob. rdg.; Heb.* seal.      <sup>c</sup> strong men: *or* leaders *or* gods.

**42** Then Job answered the LORD:

2    I know that thou canst do all things
     and that no purpose is beyond thee.
3    But I have spoken of great things which I have not understood,
     things too wonderful for me to know. *a*
5    I knew of thee then only by report,
     but now I see thee with my own eyes.
6    Therefore I melt away; *b*
     I repent in dust and ashes.

## *Epilogue*

7   When the LORD had finished speaking to Job, he said to Eliphaz the Teman-
    ite, 'I am angry with you and your two friends, because you have not spoken
8   as you ought about me, as my servant Job has done. So now take seven bulls
    and seven rams, go to my servant Job and offer a whole-offering for your-
    selves, and he will intercede for you; I will surely show him favour by not
    being harsh with you because you have not spoken as you ought about me,
9   as he has done.' Then Eliphaz the Temanite and Bildad the Shuhite and
    Zophar the Naamathite went and carried out the LORD's command, and
    the LORD showed favour to Job when he had interceded for his friends.
10  So the LORD restored Job's fortunes and doubled all his possessions.
11      Then all Job's brothers and sisters and his former acquaintance came
    and feasted with him in his home, and they consoled and comforted him for
    all the misfortunes which the LORD had brought on him; and each of them
12  gave him a sheep *c* and a gold ring. Furthermore, the LORD blessed the
    end of Job's life more than the beginning; and he had fourteen thousand
    head of small cattle and six thousand camels, a thousand yoke of oxen and
13 14 as many she-asses. He had seven *d* sons and three daughters; and he named
    his eldest daughter Jemimah, the second Keziah and the third Keren-
15  happuch. There were no women in all the world so beautiful as Job's
    daughters; and their father gave them an inheritance with their brothers.
16      Thereafter Job lived another hundred and forty years, he saw his sons
17  and his grandsons to four generations, and died at a very great age.

---

*a* *Prob. rdg.; Heb. adds* (4) O listen, and let me speak; I will ask questions, and you shall
answer.     *b* *Or* despise myself.     *c* *Or* piece of money.     *d* *Or* fourteen.

# PSALMS

## BOOK 1

### 1

Happy is the man                                            1
  who does not take the wicked for his guide
  nor walk the road that sinners tread
  nor take his seat among the scornful;
  the law of the LORD is his delight,                    2
the law his meditation night and day.
    He is like a tree                                3
  planted beside a watercourse,
  which yields its fruit in season
    and its leaf never withers:
  in all that he does he prospers.
Wicked men are not like this;                               4
  they are like chaff driven by the wind.
So when judgement comes the wicked shall not stand firm,    5
nor shall sinners stand in the assembly of the righteous.
  The LORD watches over the way of the righteous,       6
    but the way of the wicked is doomed.

### 2

  Why are the nations in turmoil?                       1
  Why do the peoples hatch their futile plots?
    The kings of the earth stand ready,           2
  and the rulers conspire together
  against the LORD and his anointed king.
  'Let us break their fetters,' they cry,               3
  'let us throw off their chains!'
  The Lord who sits enthroned in heaven                 4
    laughs them to scorn;
then he rebukes them in anger,                              5
  he threatens them in his wrath.
  Of me he says, 'I have enthroned my king              6
  on Zion my holy mountain.'
  I will repeat the LORD's decree:                      7
'You are my son,' he said;
  'this day I become your father.
  Ask of me what you will:                              8
  I will give you nations as your inheritance,
  the ends of the earth as your possession.

9    You shall break them with a rod of iron,
    you shall shatter them like a clay pot.'
10   Be mindful then, you kings;
    learn your lesson, rulers of the earth:
11-12   worship the LORD with reverence;
    tremble, and kiss the king,[a]
lest the LORD be angry and you are struck down in mid course;
    for his anger flares up in a moment.
      Happy are all who find refuge in him.

## 3

1    LORD, how my enemies have multiplied!
    Many rise up against me,
2    many there are who say of me,
    'God will not bring him victory.'
3    But thou, LORD, art a shield to cover me:
    thou art my glory, and thou dost raise my head high.
4    I cry aloud to the LORD,
    and he answers me from his holy mountain.
5    I lie down and sleep,
    and I wake again, for the LORD upholds me.
6    I will not fear the nations in their myriads
    who set on me from all sides.

7    Rise up, LORD; save me, O my God.
    Thou dost strike all my foes across the face
      and breakest the teeth of the wicked.
8        Thine is the victory, O LORD,
    and may[b] thy blessing rest upon thy people.

## 4

1    Answer me when I call, O God, maintainer of my right,
    I was hard pressed, and thou didst set me at large;
    be gracious to me now and hear my prayer.
2    Mortal men, how long will you pay me not honour but dishonour,
    or set your heart on trifles and run after lies?
3    Know that the LORD has shown me[c] his marvellous love;
    the LORD hears when I call to him.
4        However angry your hearts, do not do wrong;
    though you lie abed resentful,[d] do not break silence:
5    pay your due of sacrifice, and trust in the LORD.

6    There are many who say, 'If only we might be prosperous again!
    But the light of thy presence has fled from us, O LORD.'

---

[a] tremble . . . king: *prob. rdg.; lit.* tremble and kiss the mighty one; *Heb. obscure.*
[b] Thine . . . and may: *or* O LORD of salvation, may . . .          [c] *Prob. rdg.; Heb.* him.
[d] lie abed resentful: *prob. rdg.; Heb.* say on your beds.

Yet in my heart thou hast put more happiness                    7
than they enjoyed when there was corn and wine in plenty.
Now I will lie down in peace, and sleep;                         8
for thou alone, O LORD, makest me live unafraid.

### 5

Listen to my words, O LORD,                                      1
   consider my inmost thoughts;
heed my cry for help, my king and my God.                       2
In the morning, when I say my prayers,                          3
   thou wilt hear me.
I set out my morning sacrifice*a*
   and watch for thee, O LORD.
For thou art not a God who welcomes wickedness;                 4
   evil can be no guest of thine.*b*
   There is no place for arrogance before thee;                 5
   thou hatest evildoers,
   thou makest an end of all liars.                             6

The LORD detests traitors and men of blood.
But I, through thy great love, may come into thy house,         7
and bow low toward thy holy temple in awe of thee.
   Lead me, LORD, in thy righteousness,                         8
      because my enemies are on the watch;
   give me a straight path to follow.
   There is no trusting what they say,                          9
      they are nothing but wind.
   Their throats are an open*c* sepulchre;
   smooth talk runs off their tongues.
   Bring ruin on them, O God;                                   10
   let them fall by their own devices.
   Cast them out, after all their rebellions,
   for they have defied thee.
   But let all who take refuge in thee rejoice,                 11
   let them for ever break into shouts of joy;
   shelter those who love thy name,
   that they may exult in thee.
For thou, O LORD, wilt bless the righteous;                     12
   thou wilt hedge him round with favour as with a shield.

### 6

O LORD, do not condemn me in thy anger,                         1
   do not punish me in thy fury.
Be merciful to me, O LORD, for I am weak;                       2
   heal me, my very bones are shaken;

---

*a* *Or* plea.    *b* who welcomes ... thine: *or* who protects a wicked man; an evil man cannot be thy guest.    *c* *Or* inscribed.

3    my soul quivers in dismay.
    And thou, O LORD—how long?

4   Come back, O LORD; set my soul free,
     deliver me for thy love's sake.

5    None talk of thee among the dead;
    who praises thee in Sheol?

6     I am wearied with groaning;
    all night long my pillow is wet with tears,
    I soak my bed with weeping.

7    Grief dims my eyes;
     they are worn out with all my woes.

8    Away from me, all you evildoers,
    for the LORD has heard the sound of my weeping.

9    The LORD has heard my entreaty;
    the LORD will accept my prayer.

10   All my enemies shall be confounded and dismayed;
    they shall turn away in sudden confusion.

## 7

1    O LORD my God, in thee I find refuge;
     save me, rescue me from my pursuers,

2     before they tear at my throat like a lion
     and carry me off beyond hope of rescue.

3    O LORD my God, if I have done any of these things—
     if I have stained my hands with guilt,

4     if I have repaid a friend evil for good
     or set free an enemy who attacked me without cause,

5   may my adversary come after me and overtake me,
     trample my life to the ground
     and lay my honour in the dust!

6     Arise, O LORD, in thy anger,
     rouse thyself in wrath against my foes.
   Awake, my God who hast ordered that justice be done;

7     let the peoples assemble around thee,
     and take thou thy seat on high above them.

8     O LORD, thou who dost pass sentence on the nations,
     O LORD, judge me as my righteousness deserves,
     for I am clearly innocent.

9    Let wicked men do no more harm,
    establish the reign of righteousness,[a]
    thou who examinest both heart and mind,
     thou righteous God.

10    God, the High God, is my shield
     who saves men of honest heart.

  [a] the reign of righteousness: *or* the cause of the righteous.

God is a just judge,                                                    11
every day he requites the raging enemy.

He sharpens his sword,                                                  12
strings his bow and makes it ready.
He has prepared his deadly shafts                                      13
and tipped his arrows with fire.
But the enemy is in labour with iniquity;                              14
he conceives mischief, and his brood is lies.
He has made a pit and dug it deep,                                     15
and he himself shall fall into the hole that he has made.
His mischief shall recoil upon himself,                                16
and his violence fall on his own head.

I will praise the LORD for his righteousness                           17
and sing a psalm to the name of the LORD Most High.

## 8

O LORD our sovereign,                                                   1
how glorious is thy name in all the earth!
Thy majesty is praised high as the heavens.
Out of the mouths of babes, of infants at the breast,                  2
    thou hast rebuked*a* the mighty,
silencing enmity and vengeance to teach thy foes a lesson.
When I look up at thy heavens, the work of thy fingers,                3
    the moon and the stars set in their place by thee,
what is man that thou shouldst remember him,                           4
    mortal man that thou shouldst care for him?
Yet thou hast made him little less than a god,                         5
crowning him with glory and honour.
Thou makest him master over all thy creatures;                         6
thou hast put everything under his feet:
all sheep and oxen, all the wild beasts,                                7
    the birds in the air and the fish in the sea,                      8
    and all that moves along the paths of ocean.
    O LORD our sovereign,                                              9
how glorious is thy name in all the earth!

## 9-10

I will praise thee, O LORD, with all my heart,                         1
    I will tell the story of thy marvellous acts.
I will rejoice and exult in thee,                                      2
I will praise thy name in psalms, O thou Most High,
    when my enemies turn back,                                         3
when they fall headlong and perish at thy appearing;

*a Prob. rdg.; Heb. founded.*

4    for thou hast upheld my right and my cause,
    seated on thy throne, thou righteous judge.
5    Thou hast rebuked the nations and overwhelmed the ungodly,
    thou hast blotted out their name for all time.
6    The strongholds of the enemy are thrown down for evermore;
    thou hast laid their cities in ruins, all memory of them is lost.
7    The LORD thunders,*a* he sits enthroned for ever:
    he has set up his throne, his judgement-seat.
8    He it is who will judge the world with justice
    and try the cause of the peoples fairly.
9    So may the LORD be a tower of strength for the oppressed,
    a tower of strength in time of need,
10   that those who acknowledge thy name may trust in thee;
    for thou, LORD, dost not forsake those who seek thee.
11   Sing psalms to the LORD who dwells in Zion,
    proclaim his deeds among the nations.
12   For the Avenger of blood has remembered men's desire,
    and has not forgotten the cry of the poor.

13   Have pity on me, O LORD; look upon my affliction,
    thou who hast lifted me up*b* and caught me back from the gates of death,
14   that I may repeat all thy praise
and exult at this deliverance in the gates of Zion's city.

15   The nations have plunged into a pit of their own making;
    their own feet are entangled in the net which they hid.
16   Now the LORD makes himself known. Justice is done:
    the wicked man is trapped in his own devices.
17   They rush blindly down to Sheol, the wicked,
    all the nations who are heedless of God.
18   But the poor shall not always be unheeded
    nor the hope of the destitute be always vain.
19   Arise, LORD, give man no chance to boast his strength;
    summon the nations before thee for judgement.
20   Strike them with fear, O LORD,
let the nations know that they are but men.
**10**  Why stand so far off, LORD,
    hiding thyself in time of need?
2    The wicked man in his pride hunts down the poor:
    may his crafty schemes be his own undoing!
3    The wicked man is obsessed with his own desires,
    and in his greed gives wickedness his blessing;
4    arrogant as he is, he scorns the LORD
    and leaves no place for God in all his schemes.
5    His ways are always devious;
    thy judgements are beyond his grasp,*c*
    and he scoffs at all restraint.

*a* thunders: *prob. rdg.; Heb. unintelligible.*    *b* thou . . . me up: *prob. rdg.; Heb. from*
those who hate me.    *c* beyond his grasp: *prob. rdg.; Heb. on high before him.*

He says to himself, 'I shall never be shaken;                      6
  no misfortune can check my course.' *a*
His mouth is full of lies and violence;                            7
  mischief and trouble lurk under his tongue.
  He lies in ambush in the villages                           8
  and murders innocent men by stealth.
  He is watching *b* intently for some poor wretch;
he seizes him and drags him away in his net;                       9
he crouches stealthily, like a lion in its lair
  crouching to seize its victim;
  the good man *c* is struck down and sinks to the ground,    10
  and poor wretches fall into his toils.
He says to himself, 'God has forgotten;                            11
he has hidden his face and has seen nothing.'

Arise, Lord, set *d* thy hand to the task;                         12
  do not forget the poor, O God.
Why, O God, has the wicked man rejected thee                       13
  and said to himself that thou dost not care?
Thou seest that mischief and trouble are his companions,           14
  thou takest the matter into thy own hands.
  The poor victim commits himself to thee;
fatherless, he finds in thee his helper.
  Break the power of wickedness and wrong;                    15
  hunt out all wickedness until thou canst find no more.

The Lord is king for ever and ever;                                16
  the nations have vanished from his land.
  Thou hast heard the lament of the humble, O Lord,           17
  and art attentive to their heart's desire,
  bringing justice to the orphan and the downtrodden          18
that fear may never drive men from their homes again.

## 11

In the Lord I have found my refuge; why do you say to me,          1
  'Flee to the mountains like a bird;
see how the wicked string their bows                               2
  and fit the arrow to the string,
  to shoot down honest men out of the darkness'?
When foundations are undermined, what can the good man do?         3
    The Lord is in his holy temple,                    4
  the Lord's throne is in heaven.
His eye is upon mankind, he takes their measure at a glance.
The Lord weighs just and unjust                                    5
  and hates with all his soul the lover of violence.

*a* my course: *prob. rdg.; Heb.* which.　　*b* *Prob. rdg.; Heb.* storing up.　　*c* the good
man: *prob. rdg.; Heb. om.*　　*d* *Or* who settest.

6 He shall rain down red-hot coals upon the wicked;
  brimstone and scorching winds shall be the cup they drink.
7 For the LORD is just and loves just dealing;
  his face is turned towards the upright man.

## 12

1 Help, LORD, for loyalty is no more;
  good faith between man and man is over.
2 One man lies to another:
 they talk with smooth lip and double heart.
3  May the LORD make an end of such smooth lips
  and the tongue that talks so boastfully!
4  They said, 'Our tongue can win the day.
 Words are our ally; who can master us?'
5 'For the ruin of the poor, for the groans of the needy,
 now I will arise,' says the LORD,
  'I will place him in the safety for which he longs.'

6  The words of the LORD are pure words:
  silver refined in a crucible,
  gold *a* seven times purified.
7  Do thou, LORD, protect us
  and guard us from a profligate and evil generation. *b*
8  The wicked flaunt themselves on every side,
   while profligacy stands high among mankind.

## 13

1 How long, O LORD, wilt thou quite forget me?
 How long wilt thou hide thy face from me?
2 How long must I suffer anguish in my soul,
  grief in my heart, day and night?
 How long shall my enemy lord it over me?
3 Look now and answer me, O LORD my God.
 Give light to my eyes lest I sleep the sleep of death,
4  lest my adversary say, 'I have overthrown him',
  and my enemies rejoice at my downfall.
5 But for my part I trust in thy true love.
 My heart shall rejoice, for thou hast set me free.
6 I will sing to the LORD, who has granted all my desire.

## 14

1*c* The impious fool says in his heart,
  'There is no God.'
 How vile men are, how depraved and loathsome;
  not one does anything good!

---

*a* gold: *prob. rdg.; Heb.* to the earth.  *b* a profligate and evil generation: *prob. rdg.;*
*Heb.* the generation which is for ever.  *c* *Verses 1–7 : cp. Ps. 53. 1–6.*

The L<small>ORD</small> looks down from heaven      2
   on all mankind
to see if any act wisely,
   if any seek out God.
But all are disloyal, all are rotten to the core;      3
   not one does anything good,
   no, not even one.

   Shall they not rue it,      4
all evildoers who devour my people
   as men devour bread,
   and never call upon the L<small>ORD</small>?
There they were in dire alarm;      5
for God was in the brotherhood of the godly.
   The resistance of their victim was too much for them,      6
   because the L<small>ORD</small> was his refuge.
If only Israel's deliverance might come out of Zion!      7
   When the L<small>ORD</small> restores his people's fortunes,
let Jacob rejoice, let Israel be glad.

## 15

O L<small>ORD</small>, who may lodge in thy tabernacle?      1
Who may dwell on thy holy mountain?
The man of blameless life, who does what is right      2
and speaks the truth from his heart;
   who has no malice on his tongue,      3
who never wrongs a friend
and tells no tales against his neighbour;
the man who shows his scorn for the worthless      4
and honours all who fear the L<small>ORD</small>;
who swears to his own hurt and does not retract;
who does not put his money out to usury      5
and takes no bribe against an innocent man.
He who does these things shall never be brought low.

## 16

Keep me, O God, for in thee have I found refuge.      1
   I have said to the L<small>ORD</small>,      2
'Thou, Lord, art my felicity.'
The gods whom earth holds sacred are all worthless,      3
and cursed are all who make them their delight;<sup>*a*</sup>
those who run after them<sup>*b*</sup> find trouble without end.      4
I will not offer them libations of blood
nor take their names upon my lips.
Thou, L<small>ORD</small>, my allotted portion, thou my cup,      5
thou dost enlarge my boundaries:

---

<sup>*a*</sup> are all worthless . . . delight: *prob. rdg.; Heb. obscure.*     <sup>*b*</sup> after them: *prob. rdg.;*
*Heb. obscure.*

6      the lines fall for me in pleasant places,
        indeed I am well content with my inheritance.

7      I will bless the LORD who has given me counsel:
        in the night-time wisdom comes to me in my inward parts.

8      I have set the LORD continually before me:
        with him *a* at my right hand I cannot be shaken.

9      Therefore my heart exults
          and my spirit rejoices,
        my body too rests unafraid;

10      for thou wilt not abandon me to Sheol
        nor suffer thy faithful servant to see the pit.

11      Thou wilt show me the path of life;
        in thy presence is the fullness of joy,
        in thy right hand pleasures for evermore.

## 17

1      Hear, LORD, my plea for justice,
        give my cry a hearing,
        listen to my prayer,
        for it is innocent of all deceit.

2      Let judgement in my cause issue from thy lips,
        let thine eyes be fixed on justice.

3      Thou hast tested my heart and watched me all night long;
        thou hast assayed me and found in me no mind to evil.

4      I will not speak of the deeds of men;
        I have taken good note of all thy sayings.

5      I have not strayed from the course of duty;
        I have followed thy path and never stumbled.

6      I call upon thee, O God, for thou wilt answer me.
        Bend down thy ear to me, listen to my words.

7      Show me how marvellous thy true love can be,
        who with thy hand dost save
          all who seek sanctuary from their enemies.

8      Keep me like the apple of thine eye;
        hide me in the shadow of thy wings

9      from the wicked who obstruct me,
        from deadly foes who throng round me.

10      They have stifled all compassion;
        their mouths are full of pride;

11      they press me hard, *b* now they hem me in,
        on the watch to bring me to the ground.

12      The enemy is like a lion eager for prey,
        like a young lion crouching in ambush.

13      Arise, LORD, meet him face to face and bring him down.

---

*a* with him: *prob. rdg.;* Heb. *om.*      *b* they press me hard: *prob. rdg.;* Heb. our footsteps.

Save my life from the wicked;
   make an end of them *a* with thy sword.                    14
With thy hand, O Lord, make an end of them; *a*
thrust them out of this world in the prime of their life,
gorged as they are with thy good things,
   blest with many sons
and leaving their children wealth in plenty.
But my plea is just: I shall see thy face,                    15
   and be blest with a vision of thee when I awake.


# 18

   I love thee, O Lord my strength.                    1
The Lord is my stronghold, my fortress and my champion,    2 *b*
my God, my rock where I find safety,
my shield, my mountain refuge, my strong tower.
I will call on the Lord to whom all praise is due,         3
and I shall be delivered from my enemies.
When the bonds of death held me fast,                      4
destructive torrents overtook me,
the bonds of Sheol tightened round me,                     5
the snares of death were set to catch me;
then in anguish of heart I cried to the Lord,             6
I called for help to my God;
he heard me from his temple,
and my cry reached his ears.
The earth heaved and quaked,                               7
the foundations of the mountains shook;
they heaved, because he was angry.
Smoke rose from his nostrils,                              8
devouring fire came out of his mouth,
glowing coals and searing heat.
He swept the skies aside as he descended,                 9
thick darkness lay under his feet.
He rode on a cherub, he flew through the air;            10
he swooped on the wings of the wind.
He made darkness around him his hiding-place             11
and dense *c* vapour his canopy. *d*
Thick clouds came out of the radiance before him,        12
hailstones and glowing coals.
The Lord thundered from the heavens                       13
and the voice of the Most High spoke out. *e*
. He loosed his arrows, he sped them far and wide,       14
he shot forth lightning shafts and sent them echoing.

---

*a* make an end of them: *prob. rdg.; Heb. unintelligible.*    *b Verses 2–50 : cp. 2 Sam.*
*22. 2–51.*    *c Prob. rdg., cp. 2 Sam. 22. 12; Heb.* dark.    *d Prob. rdg.;*
*Heb. adds* thick clouds.    *e Prob. rdg.; Heb. adds* hailstones and glowing coals.

| | |
|---|---|
| 15 | The channels of the sea-bed were revealed, |
| | the foundations of earth laid bare |
| | at the LORD's rebuke, |
| | at the blast of the breath of his *a* nostrils. |
| 16 | He reached down from the height and took me, |
| | he drew me out of mighty waters, |
| 17 | he rescued me from my enemies, strong as they were, |
| | from my foes when they grew too powerful for me. |
| 18 | They confronted me in the hour of my peril, |
| | but the LORD was my buttress. |
| 19 | He brought me out into an open place, |
| | he rescued me because he delighted in me. |
| 20 | The LORD rewarded me as my righteousness deserved; |
| | my hands were clean, and he requited me. |
| 21 | For I have followed the ways of the LORD |
| | and have not turned wickedly from my God; |
| 22 | all his laws are before my eyes, |
| | I have not failed to follow his decrees. |
| 23 | In his sight I was blameless |
| | and kept myself from wilful sin; |
| 24 | the LORD requited me as my righteousness deserved |
| | and the purity of my life in his eyes. |
| | |
| 25 | With the loyal thou showest thyself loyal |
| | and with the blameless man blameless. |
| 26 | With the savage man thou showest thyself savage, |
| | and *b* tortuous with the perverse. |
| 27 | Thou deliverest humble folk, |
| | and bringest proud looks down to earth. |
| 28 | Thou, LORD, dost make my lamp burn bright, |
| | and my God will lighten my darkness. |
| 29 | With thy help I leap over a bank, |
| | by God's aid I spring over a wall. |
| | |
| 30 | The way of God is perfect, |
| | the LORD's word has stood the test; |
| | he is the shield of all who take refuge in him. |
| 31 | What god is there but the LORD? |
| | What rock but our God?— |
| 32 | the God who girds me with strength |
| | and makes my way blameless, |
| 33 | who makes me swift as a hind |
| | and sets me secure on the mountains; |
| 34 | who trains my hands for battle, |
| | and my arms aim an arrow tipped with bronze. |

---

*a* *Prob. rdg.; Heb.* thy.  *b* With the savage . . . savage, and: *or* With the pure thou showest thyself pure, but . . .

Thou hast given me the shield of thy salvation,                        35
thy hand sustains me, thy providence makes me great.
Thou givest me room for my steps,                                      36
my feet have not faltered.
I pursue my enemies and overtake them,                                 37
I do not return until I have made an end of them.
I strike them down and they will never rise again;                     38
they fall beneath my feet.
Thou dost arm me with strength for the battle                          39
and dost subdue my foes before me.
Thou settest my foot on my enemies' necks,                             40
and I bring to nothing those that hate me.
They cry out and there is no one to help them,                         41
they cry to the LORD and he does not answer.
I will pound them fine as dust before the wind,                        42
like mud in the streets will I trample them. *a*
Thou dost deliver me from the clamour of the people,                   43
and makest me master of the nations.
A people I never knew shall be my subjects;
as soon as they hear tell of me, they shall obey me,                   44
and foreigners shall come cringing to me.
Foreigners shall be brought captive to me,                             45
and emerge from their strongholds.

The LORD lives, blessed is my rock,                                    46
high above all is God who saves me.

O God, who grantest me vengeance,                                      47
who layest nations prostrate at my feet,
who dost rescue me from my foes and set me over my enemies,            48
thou dost deliver me from violent men.
Therefore, LORD, I will praise thee among the nations                  49
and sing psalms to thy name,
to one who gives his king great victories                              50
and in all his acts keeps faith with his anointed king,
with David and his descendants for ever.


# 19

The heavens tell out the glory of God,                                 1
the vault of heaven reveals his handiwork.
One day speaks to another,                                             2
night with night shares its knowledge,
and this without speech or language                                    3
or sound of any voice.
Their music goes out through all the earth,                            4
their words reach to the end of the world.

*a* Prob. rdg., cp. 2 Sam. 22. 43; Heb. will I empty them out.

In them a tent is fixed for the sun,
5   who comes out like a bridegroom from his wedding canopy,
rejoicing like a strong man to run his race.

6          His rising is at one end of the heavens,
his circuit touches their farthest ends;
and nothing is hidden from his heat.

7      The law of the LORD is perfect and revives the soul.
The LORD's instruction never fails,
and makes the simple wise.

8   The precepts of the LORD are right and rejoice the heart.
The commandment of the LORD shines clear
and gives light to the eyes.

9      The fear of the LORD is pure and abides for ever.
The LORD's decrees are true and righteous every one,

10  more to be desired than gold, pure gold in plenty,
sweeter than syrup or honey from the comb.

11   It is these that give thy servant warning,
and he who keeps them wins a great reward.

12          Who is aware of his unwitting sins?
Cleanse me of any secret fault.

13      Hold back thy servant also from sins of self-will,
lest they get the better of me.
Then I shall be blameless
and innocent of any great transgression.

14  May all that I say and think be acceptable to thee,
O LORD, my rock and my redeemer!

## 20

1      May the LORD answer you in the hour of trouble!
The name of Jacob's God be your tower of strength,

2   give you help from the sanctuary
and send you support from Zion!

3          May he remember all your offerings
and look with favour on your rich sacrifices,

4   give you your heart's desire
and grant success to all your plans!

5          Let us sing aloud in praise of your victory,
let us do homage to the name of our God!
The LORD grant all you ask!

6          Now I know
that the LORD has given victory to his anointed king:
he will answer him from his holy heaven
with the victorious might of his right hand.

7   Some boast of chariots and some of horses,
but our boast is the name of the LORD our God.

They totter and fall,        8
but we rise up and are full of courage.
O Lord, save the king,        9
    and answer us in the hour of our calling.

## 21

The king rejoices in thy might, O Lord:      1
    well may he exult in thy victory,
    for thou hast given him his heart's desire    2
      and hast not refused him what he asked.
  Thou dost welcome him with blessings and prosperity    3
  and set a crown of fine gold upon his head.
He asked of thee life, and thou didst give it him,    4
    length of days for ever and ever.
    Thy salvation has brought him great glory;    5
thou dost invest him with majesty and honour,
    for thou bestowest blessings on him for evermore    6
  and dost make him glad with joy in thy presence.
    The king puts his trust in the Lord;    7
    the loving care of the Most High holds him unshaken.

    Your hand shall reach all your enemies:    8
your right hand shall reach those who hate you;
    at your coming you shall plunge them into a fiery furnace;    9
    the Lord in his anger will strike them down,
      and fire shall consume them.
    It will exterminate their offspring from the earth    10
    and rid mankind of their posterity.
    For they have aimed wicked blows at you,    11
they have plotted mischief but could not prevail;
    but you will catch them round the shoulders    12
and will aim with your bow-strings at their faces.

    Be exalted, O Lord, in thy might;    13
we will sing a psalm of praise to thy power.

## 22

My God, my God, why hast thou forsaken me    1
    and art so far from saving me, from heeding my groans?
O my God, I cry in the day-time but thou dost not answer,    2
    in the night I cry but get no respite.
  And yet thou art enthroned in holiness,    3
    thou art he whose praises Israel sings.
  In thee our fathers put their trust;    4
    they trusted, and thou didst rescue them.
  Unto thee they cried and were delivered;    5
    in thee they trusted and were not put to shame.

6  But I am a worm, not a man,
   abused by all men, scorned by the people.

7  All who see me jeer at me,
make mouths at me and wag their heads:

8  'He threw himself on the LORD for rescue;
let the LORD deliver him, for he holds him dear!'

9  But thou art he who drew me from the womb,
   who laid me at my mother's breast.

10  Upon thee was I cast at birth;
from my mother's womb thou hast been my God.

11  Be not far from me,
for trouble is near, and I have no helper.

12  A herd of bulls surrounds me,
   great bulls of Bashan beset me.

13  Ravening and roaring lions
open their mouths wide against me.

14  My strength drains away like water
and all my bones are loose.
My heart has turned to wax and melts within me.

15  My mouth*a* is dry as a potsherd,
and my tongue sticks to my jaw;
   I am laid*b* low in the dust of death.

16  The huntsmen are all about me;
   a band of ruffians rings me round,
and they have hacked off*c* my hands and my feet.

17  I tell my tale of misery,
while they look on and gloat.

18  They share out my garments among them
and cast lots for my clothes.

19  But do not remain so far away, O LORD;
O my help, hasten to my aid.

20  Deliver my very self from the sword,
   my precious life from the axe.

21  Save me from the lion's mouth,
   my poor body*d* from the horns of the wild ox.

22  I will declare thy fame to my brethren;
   I will praise thee in the midst of the assembly.

23  Praise him, you who fear the LORD;
   all you sons of Jacob, do him honour;
stand in awe of him, all sons of Israel.

24  For he has not scorned the downtrodden,
   nor shrunk in loathing from his plight,
nor hidden his face from him,
but gave heed to him when he cried out.

---

*a* *Prob. rdg.; Heb.* My strength.     *b* I am laid: *prob. rdg.; Heb.* thou wilt lay me.
*c* and they have hacked off: *prob. rdg.; Heb.* like a lion.     *d* my poor body: *prob. rdg.; Heb.* thou hast answered me.

Thou dost inspire my praise in the full assembly; 25
  and I will pay my vows before all who fear thee.
Let the humble eat and be satisfied. 26
Let those who seek the LORD praise him
  and be in good heart for ever.
Let all the ends of the earth remember and turn again to the 27
    LORD;
let all the families of the nations bow down before him.
  For kingly power belongs to the LORD, 28
  and dominion over the nations is his.
How can those buried in the earth do him homage, 29
how can those who go down to the grave bow before him?
  But I shall live for his sake,
  my posterity*a* shall serve him. 30
This shall be told of the Lord to future generations;
  and they shall justify him, 31
  declaring to a people yet unborn
  that this was his doing.

## 23

The LORD is my shepherd; I shall want nothing. 1
  He makes me lie down in green pastures, 2
and leads me beside the waters of peace;
  he renews life within me, 3
and for his name's sake guides me in the right path.
Even though I walk through a valley dark as death 4
I fear no evil, for thou art with me,
thy staff and thy crook are my comfort.

Thou spreadest a table for me in the sight of my enemies; 5
  thou hast richly bathed my head with oil,
  and my cup runs over.
Goodness and love unfailing, these will follow me 6
  all the days of my life,
  and I shall dwell in the house of the LORD
  my whole life long.

## 24

The earth is the LORD's and all that is in it, 1
  the world and those who dwell therein.
For it was he who founded it upon the seas 2
  and planted it firm upon the waters beneath.

Who may go up the mountain of the LORD? 3
And who may stand in his holy place?

    *a* But I . . . posterity: *prob. rdg.; Heb. obscure.*

4   He who has clean hands and a pure heart,
    who has not set his mind on falsehood,
     and has not committed perjury.

5   He shall receive a blessing from the LORD,
    and justice from God his saviour.

6   Such is the fortune of those who seek him,
    who seek the face of the God of Jacob.

7   Lift up your heads, you gates,
    lift yourselves up, you everlasting doors,
  that the king of glory may come in.

8   Who is the king of glory?
   The LORD strong and mighty,
   the LORD mighty in battle.

9   Lift up your heads, you gates,
    lift them up, you everlasting doors,
   that the king of glory may come in.

10   Who then is the king of glory?
   The king of glory is the LORD of Hosts.

## 25

1  Unto thee, O LORD my God, I lift up my heart.

2  In thee I trust: do not put me to shame,
   let not my enemies exult over me.

3  No man who hopes in thee is put to shame;
  but shame comes to all who break faith without cause.

4   Make thy paths known to me, O LORD;
   teach me thy ways.

5  Lead me in thy truth and teach me;
   thou art God my saviour.
  For thee I have waited all the day long,
   for the coming of thy goodness, LORD. <sup>*a*</sup>

6  Remember, LORD, thy tender care and thy love unfailing,
   shown from ages past.

7  Do not remember the sins and offences of my youth,
  but remember me in thy unfailing love.

8  The LORD is good and upright;
 therefore he teaches sinners the way they should go.

9  He guides the humble man in doing right,
  he teaches the humble his ways.

10  All the ways of the LORD are loving and sure
   to men who keep his covenant and his charge.

11  For the honour of thy name, O LORD,
  forgive my wickedness, great as it is.

12  If there is any man who fears the LORD,
  he shall be shown the path that he should choose;

*a* for the coming . . . LORD: *transposed from end of verse 7.*

he shall enjoy lasting prosperity, 13
and his children after him shall inherit the land.
    The Lord confides his purposes to those who fear him, 14
    and his covenant is theirs to know.
My eyes are ever on the Lord, 15
who alone can free my feet from the net.

Turn to me and show me thy favour, 16
for I am lonely and oppressed.
    Relieve the sorrows of my heart 17
    and bring me out of my distress.
Look at my misery and my trouble 18
    and forgive me every sin.
Look at my enemies, see how many they are 19
    and how violent their hatred for me.
Defend me and deliver me, 20
do not put me to shame when I take refuge in thee.
Let integrity and uprightness protect me, 21
    for I have waited for thee, O Lord.
O God, redeem Israel from all his sorrows. 22

## 26

    Give me justice, O Lord, 1
for I have lived my life without reproach,
and put unfaltering trust in the Lord.
Test me, O Lord, and try me; 2
put my heart and mind to the proof.
For thy constant love is before my eyes, 3
    and I live in thy truth.
I have not sat among worthless men, 4
    nor do I mix with hypocrites;
    I hate the company of evildoers 5
    and will not sit among the ungodly.
I wash my hands in innocence 6
to join in procession round thy altar, O Lord,
singing of thy marvellous acts, 7
    recounting them all with thankful voice.
O Lord, I love the beauty of thy house, 8
    the place where thy glory dwells.
Do not sweep me away with sinners, 9
nor cast me out with men who thirst for blood,
    whose fingers are active in mischief, 10
and their hands are full of bribes.
But I live my life without reproach; 11
redeem me, O Lord, and show me thy favour.
When once my feet are planted on firm ground, 12
I will bless the Lord in the full assembly.

## 27

1　The Lord is my light and my salvation;
　　whom should I fear?
　The Lord is the refuge of my life;
　　of whom then should I go in dread?

2　When evildoers close in on me to devour me,
　　it is my enemies, my assailants,
　　who stumble and fall.

3　If an army should encamp against me,
　　my heart would feel no fear;
　if armed men should fall upon me,
　even then I should be undismayed.

4　One thing I ask of the Lord,
　　one thing I seek:
　　that I may be constant in the house of the Lord
　　all the days of my life,
　　to gaze upon the beauty of the Lord
　　and to seek him*ᵃ* in his temple.

5　For he will keep me safe beneath his roof
　　in the day of misfortune;
　he will hide me under the cover of his tent;
　he will raise me beyond reach of distress.

6　Now I can raise my head high
　　above the enemy all about me;
　so will I acclaim him with sacrifice before his tent
　　and sing a psalm of praise to the Lord.

7　Hear, O Lord, when I call aloud;
　　show me favour and answer me.

8　'Come,' my heart has said,
　　'seek his face.'*ᵇ*
　I will seek thy face, O Lord;

9　do not hide it from me,
　nor in thy anger turn away thy servant,
　　whose help thou hast been;
　do not cast me off or forsake me, O God my saviour.

10　Though my father and my mother forsake me,
　　the Lord will take me into his care.

11–12　Teach me thy way, O Lord;
　do not give me up to the greed of my enemies;
　lead me by a level path
　　to escape my watchful foes;
　liars stand up to give evidence against me,
　　breathing malice.

---

*ᵃ Or* and to pay my morning worship.　　*ᵇ* seek his face: *prob. rdg.; Heb.* seek ye my face.

Well I know that I shall see the goodness of the Lord       13
  in the land of the living.

Wait for the Lord; be strong, take courage,                14
  and wait for the Lord.

## 28

To thee, O Lord, I call;                                   1
O my Rock, be not deaf to my cry,
  lest, if thou answer me with silence,
I become like those who go down to the abyss.
  Hear my cry for mercy                                2
    when I call to thee for help,
  when I lift my hands to thy holy shrine.
Do not drag me away with the ungodly, with evildoers,      3
who speak civilly to neighbours, with malice in their hearts.
Reward them for their works, their evil deeds;             4
  reward them for what their hands have done;
  give them their deserts.
Because they pay no heed to the works of the Lord          5
  or to what his hands have done,
    may he tear them down and never build them up!

  Blessed be the Lord,                                 6
for he has heard my cry for mercy.
The Lord is my strength, my shield,                        7
  in him my heart trusts;
so I am sustained, and my heart leaps for joy,
  and I praise him with my whole body.*a*
The Lord is strength to his people,                        8
a safe refuge for his anointed king.

O save thy people and bless thy own,                       9
  shepherd them, carry them for ever.

## 29

Ascribe to the Lord, you gods,                             1
ascribe to the Lord glory and might.
  Ascribe to the Lord the glory due to his name;       2
  bow down to the Lord in the splendour of holiness.*b*
    The God of glory thunders:                       3
    the voice of the Lord echoes over the waters,
    the Lord is over the mighty waters.
    The voice of the Lord is power.                   4
    The voice of the Lord is majesty.

*a* with my whole body: *prob. rdg.; Heb.* from my song.    *b* the splendour of holiness: *or* holy vestments.

5    The voice of the LORD breaks the cedars,
    the LORD splinters the cedars of Lebanon.
6    He makes Lebanon skip like a calf,
    Sirion like a young wild ox.
7    The voice of the LORD makes flames of fire burst forth,
8    the voice of the LORD makes the wilderness writhe in travail;
    the LORD makes the wilderness of Kadesh writhe.
9    The voice of the LORD makes the hinds calve
    and brings kids early to birth;
and in his temple all cry, 'Glory!'
10   The LORD is king above *a* the flood,
    the LORD has taken his royal seat as king for ever.
11   The LORD will give strength to his people;
    the LORD will bless his people with peace.

## 30

1    I will exalt thee, O LORD;
    thou hast lifted me up
    and hast not let my enemies make merry over me.
2    O LORD my God, I cried to thee and thou didst heal me.
3    O LORD, thou hast brought me up from Sheol
    and saved my life as I was sinking into the abyss. *b*
4    Sing a psalm to the LORD, all you his loyal servants,
    and give thanks to his holy name.
5    In his anger is disquiet, in his favour there is life.
    Tears may linger at nightfall,
      but joy comes in the morning.
6    Carefree as I was, I had said,
    'I can never be shaken.'
7    But, LORD, it was thy will to shake my mountain refuge;
    thou didst hide thy face, and I was struck with dismay.
8    I called unto thee, O LORD,
    and I pleaded with thee, Lord, for mercy:
9    'What profit in my death if I go down into the pit?
Can the dust confess thee or proclaim thy truth?
10   Hear, O LORD, and be gracious to me;
    LORD, be my helper.'
11   Thou hast turned my laments into dancing;
    thou hast stripped off my sackcloth and clothed me with joy,
12   that my spirit may sing psalms to thee and never cease.
I will confess thee for ever, O LORD my God.

---

*a Or* since.      *b* and saved . . . abyss: *or* and rescued me alive from among those who go down to the abyss.

## 31

With thee, O Lord, I have sought shelter,       1
   let me never be put to shame.
   Deliver me in thy righteousness;
bow down and hear me,          2
   come quickly to my rescue;
be thou my rock of refuge,
   a stronghold to keep me safe.
Thou art to me both rock and stronghold;      3
lead me and guide me for the honour of thy name.
Set me free from the net men have hidden for me;    4
   thou art my refuge,
into thy keeping I commit my spirit.        5
Thou hast redeemed me, O Lord thou God of truth.
   Thou hatest all who worship useless idols,    6
   but I put my trust in the Lord.
I will rejoice and be glad in thy unfailing love;    7
   for thou hast seen my affliction
   and hast cared for me in my distress.
Thou hast not abandoned me to the power of the enemy   8
but hast set me free to range at will.
Be gracious to me, O Lord, for I am in distress,    9
and my eyes are dimmed with grief.ᵃ
My life is worn away with sorrow        10
   and my years with sighing;
strong as I am, I stumble under my load of misery;
   there is disease in all my bones.
I have such enemies that all men scorn me;ᵇ     11
   my neighbours find me a burden,
   my friends shudder at me;
when they see me in the street they turn quickly away.
I am forgotten, like a dead man out of mind;     12
I have come to be like something lost.
For I hear many men whispering       13
   threats from every side,
in league against me as they are
and plotting to take my life.
But, Lord, I put my trust in thee;       14
I say, 'Thou art my God.'
   My fortunes are in thy hand;       15
rescue me from my enemies and those who persecute me.
Make thy face shine upon thy servant;      16
   save me in thy unfailing love.
   O Lord, do not put me to shame when I call upon thee;   17
let the wicked be ashamed, let them sink into Sheol.

---

ᵃ *Prob. rdg.; Heb. adds* my soul and my body.      ᵇ I have . . . scorn me: *or* I am
scorned by all my enemies.

18
>Strike dumb the lying lips
>>which speak with contempt against the righteous
>>>in pride and arrogance.

19
>How great is thy goodness,
>>stored up for those who fear thee,
>made manifest before the eyes of men
>>for all who turn to thee for shelter.

20
>Thou wilt hide them under the cover of thy presence
>>from men in league together;
>>thou keepest them beneath thy roof,
>>>safe from contentious men.

21
>Blessed be the LORD,
>>who worked a miracle of unfailing love for me
>>>when I was in sore straits.[a]

22
>In sudden alarm I said,
>>'I am shut out from thy sight.'
>But thou didst hear my cry for mercy
>>when I called to thee for help.

23
>Love the LORD, all you his loyal servants.
>The LORD protects the faithful
>>but pays the arrogant in full.

24
>Be strong and take courage,
>>all you whose hope is in the LORD.

## 32

1
>Happy the man whose disobedience is forgiven,
>>whose sin is put away!

2
>Happy is a man when the LORD lays no guilt to his account,
>>and in his spirit there is no deceit.

3
>While I refused to speak, my body wasted away
>>with moaning all day long.

4
>For day and night
>thy hand was heavy upon me,
>>the sap in me dried up as in summer drought.

5
>Then I declared my sin, I did not conceal my guilt.
>I said, 'With sorrow I will confess
>>my disobedience to the LORD';
>>then thou didst remit the penalty of my sin.

6
>So every faithful heart shall pray to thee
>>in the hour of anxiety,[b] when great floods threaten.
>Thou art a refuge for me from distress
>>so that it cannot touch me;[c]

*a* when . . . straits: *prob. rdg.; Heb.* like a city besieged.      *b* of anxiety: *prob. rdg.;*
*Heb. unintelligible.*      *c Prob. rdg.; Heb.* him.

thou dost guard me<sup>a</sup> and enfold me in salvation     7
    beyond all reach of harm.<sup>b</sup>

I will teach you, and guide you in the way you should go.     8
    I will keep you under my eye.
Do not behave like horse or mule, unreasoning creatures,     9
whose course must be checked with bit and bridle.
    Many are the torments of the ungodly;     10
but unfailing love enfolds him who trusts in the LORD.
Rejoice in the LORD and be glad, you righteous men,     11
    and sing aloud, all men of upright heart.

# 33

Shout for joy before the LORD, you who are righteous;     1
praise comes well from the upright.
Give thanks to the LORD on the harp;     2
sing him psalms to the ten-stringed lute.
Sing to him a new song;     3
strike up with all your art and shout in triumph.
    The word of the LORD holds true,     4
    and all his work endures.
The LORD loves righteousness and justice,     5
his love unfailing fills the earth.
The LORD's word made the heavens,     6
all the host of heaven was made at his command.
He gathered the sea like water in a goatskin;     7
he laid up the deep in his store-chambers.
Let the whole world fear the LORD     8
and all men on earth stand in awe of him.
For he spoke, and it was;     9
he commanded, and it stood firm.
The LORD brings the plans of nations to nothing;     10
    he frustrates the counsel of the peoples.
But the LORD's own plans shall stand for ever,     11
and his counsel endure for all generations.
Happy is the nation whose God is the LORD,     12
the people he has chosen for his own possession.
The LORD looks out from heaven,     13
he sees the whole race of men;
he surveys from his dwelling-place     14
    all the inhabitants of earth.
It is he who fashions the hearts of all men alike,     15
    who discerns all that they do.
A king is not saved by a great army,     16
nor a warrior delivered by great strength.

<sup>a</sup> *Prob. rdg.; Heb. adds an unintelligible word.*      <sup>b</sup> beyond . . . harm: *transposed from end of verse 9.*

17     A man cannot trust his horse to save him,
        nor can it deliver him for all its strength.

18     The Lord's eyes are turned towards those who fear him,
        towards those who hope for his unfailing love

19     to deliver them from death,
        to keep them alive in famine.

20     We have waited eagerly for the Lord;
        he is our help and our shield.

21         For in him our hearts are glad,
        because we have trusted in his holy name.

22     Let thy unfailing love, O Lord, rest upon us,
        as we have put our hope in thee.

## 34

1     I will bless the Lord continually;
        his praise shall be always on my lips.

2     In the Lord I will glory;
        the humble shall hear and be glad.

3     O glorify the Lord with me,
        and let us exalt his name together.

4     I sought the Lord's help and he answered me;
        he set me free from all my terrors.

5     Look towards him and shine with joy;
        no longer hang your heads in shame.

6     Here was a poor wretch who cried to the Lord;
        he heard him and saved him from all his troubles.

7     The angel of the Lord is on guard
        round those who fear him, and rescues them.

8     Taste, then, and see that the Lord is good.
        Happy the man who finds refuge in him!

9     Fear the Lord, all you his holy people;
        for those who fear him lack nothing.

10     Unbelievers suffer want and go hungry,
        but those who seek the Lord lack no good thing.

11     Come, my children, listen to me:
        I will teach you the fear of the Lord.

12     Which of you delights in life
        and desires a long life to enjoy all good things?

13     Then keep your tongue from evil
        and your lips from uttering lies;

14     turn from evil and do good,
        seek peace and pursue it.

15     The eyes of the Lord are upon the righteous,
        and his ears are open to their cries.

16     The Lord sets his face against evildoers
        to blot out their memory from the earth.

When men cry for help, the LORD hears them     17
and sets them free from all their troubles.
The LORD is close to those whose courage is broken     18
and he saves those whose spirit is crushed.
The good man's misfortunes may be many,     19
the LORD delivers him out of them all.
     He guards every bone of his body,     20
and not one of them is broken.
Their own misdeeds are death to the wicked,     21
     and those who hate the righteous are brought to ruin.

The LORD ransoms the lives of his servants,     22
and none who seek refuge in him are brought to ruin.

# 35

Strive, O LORD, with those who strive against me;     1
     fight against those who fight me.
Grasp shield and buckler,     2
     and rise up to help me.
Uncover the spear and bar the way     3
against my pursuers.
Let me hear thee declare,
     'I am your salvation.'
Shame and disgrace be on those who seek my life;     4
and may those who plan to hurt me retreat in dismay!
     May they be like chaff before the wind,     5
     driven by the angel of the LORD!
Let their way be dark and slippery     6
     as the angel of the LORD pursues them!
For unprovoked they have hidden a net*a* for me,     7
unprovoked they have dug a pit to trap me.
May destruction unforeseen come on him;     8
may the net which he hid catch him;
may he crash headlong into it!
Then I shall rejoice in the LORD     9
     and delight in his salvation.
     My very bones cry out,     10
     'LORD, who is like thee?—
thou saviour of the poor from those too strong for them,
the poor and wretched from those who prey on them.'
     Malicious witnesses step forward;     11
     they question me on matters of which I know nothing.
They return me evil for good,     12
     lying in wait*b* to take my life.
And yet when they were sick, I put on sackcloth,     13
     I mortified myself with fasting.

*a* *Prob. rdg., transposing* a pit *from this line to follow* have dug.     *b* lying in wait:
*prob. rdg.; Heb.* bereavement.

When my prayer came back unanswered,
14       I walked with head bowed in grief as if for a brother;
as one in sorrow for his mother I lay prostrate in mourning.

15       But when I stumbled, they crowded round rejoicing,
     they crowded about me;
   nameless ruffians[a] jeered at me
     and nothing would stop them.

16       When I slipped, brutes who would mock even a hunchback
     ground their teeth at me.

17       O Lord, how long wilt thou look on
     at those who hate me for no reason[b]?
   Rescue me out of their cruel grasp,
     save my precious life from the unbelievers.

18       Then I will praise thee before a great assembly,
I will extol thee where many people meet.

19       Let no treacherous enemy gloat over me
     nor leer at me in triumph.[c]

20       No friendly greeting do they give
     to peaceable folk.
   They invent lie upon lie,
21       they open their mouths at me:
     'Hurrah!' they shout in their joy,
     feasting their eyes on me.

22       Thou hast seen all this, O Lord, do not keep silence;
O Lord, be not far from me.

23       Awake, bestir thyself, to do me justice,
     to plead my cause, my Lord and my God.

24       Judge me, O Lord my God, as thou art true;
     do not let them gloat over me.

25       Do not let them say to themselves, 'Hurrah!
     We have swallowed him up at one gulp.'

26       Let them all be disgraced and dismayed
     who rejoice at my fall;
   let them be covered with shame and dishonour
     who glory over me.

27       But let all who would see me righted shout for joy,
     let them cry continually,
     'All glory to the Lord
   who would see his servant thrive!'

28       So shall I talk of thy justice
     and of thy praise all the day long.

## 36

1       Deep in his heart, sin whispers to the wicked man
who cherishes no fear of God.

[a] nameless ruffians: *or* ruffians who give me no rest.    [b] *Line transposed from verse 19.*
[c] *See note on verse 17.*

For he flatters himself in his own opinion 2
and, when he is found out, he does not mend his ways. *a*
All that he says is mischievous and false; 3
he has turned his back on wisdom;
in his bed he plots how best to do mischief.
So set is he on his wrong courses 4
that he rejects nothing evil.
But thy unfailing love, O LORD, reaches to heaven, 5
thy faithfulness to the skies.
Thy righteousness is like the lofty mountains, 6
thy judgements are like the great abyss;
O LORD, who savest man and beast,
how precious is thy unfailing love! 7
Gods and men seek refuge in the shadow of thy wings.
They are filled with the rich plenty of thy house, 8
and thou givest them water from the flowing stream of thy
delights;
for with thee is the fountain of life, 9
and in thy light we are bathed with light.
Maintain thy love unfailing over those who know thee, 10
and thy justice toward men of honest heart.
Let not the foot of pride come near me, 11
no wicked hand disturb me.
There they lie, the evildoers, 12
they are hurled down and cannot rise.

## 37

Do not strive to outdo the evildoers 1
or emulate those who do wrong.
For like grass they soon wither, 2
and fade like the green of spring.
Trust in the LORD and do good; 3
settle in the land and find safe pasture.
Depend upon the LORD, 4
and he will grant you your heart's desire.
Commit your life to the LORD; 5
trust in him and he will act.
He will make your righteousness shine clear as the day 6
and the justice of your cause like the sun at noon.
Wait quietly for the LORD, be patient till he comes; 7
do not strive to outdo the successful
nor envy him who gains his ends.
Be angry no more, have done with wrath; 8
strive not to outdo in evildoing.
For evildoers will be destroyed, 9
but they who hope in the LORD shall possess the land.

*a* he does . . . ways: *prob. rdg.; Heb. unintelligible.*

10     A little while, and the wicked will be no more;  
      look well, and you will find their place is empty.

11     But the humble shall possess the land  
      and enjoy untold prosperity.

12     The wicked mutter against the righteous man  
      and grind their teeth at the sight of him;

13     the Lord shall laugh at them,  
      for he sees that their time is coming.

14     The wicked have drawn their swords  
      and strung their bows  
    to bring low the poor and needy  
      and to slaughter honest men.

15     Their swords shall pierce their own hearts  
      and their bows be broken.

16     Better is the little which the righteous has  
      than the great wealth of the wicked.

17     For the strong arm of the wicked shall be broken,  
      but the LORD upholds the righteous.

18     The LORD knows each day of the good man's life,  
      and his inheritance shall last for ever.

19     When times are bad, he shall not be distressed,  
      and in days of famine he shall have enough.

20     But the wicked shall perish,  
    and their children shall beg their bread. [a]  
    The enemies of the LORD, like fuel in a furnace, [b]  
      are consumed in smoke.

21     The wicked man borrows and does not pay back,  
      but the righteous is a generous giver.

22     All whom the LORD has blessed shall possess the land,  
      and all who are cursed by him shall be destroyed.

23     It is the LORD who directs a man's steps,  
      he holds him firm and watches over his path.

24     Though he may fall, he will not go headlong,  
      for the LORD grasps him by the hand.

25     I have been young and am now grown old,  
      and never have I seen a righteous man forsaken. [c]

26     Day in, day out, he lends generously,  
      and his children become a blessing.

27     Turn from evil and do good,  
      and live at peace for ever;

28     for the LORD is a lover of justice  
      and will not forsake his loyal servants.  
    The lawless are banished for ever  
      and the children of the wicked destroyed.

29     The righteous shall possess the land  
      and shall live there at peace for ever.

---

[a] *Line transposed from verse 25.*     [b] like . . . furnace: *prob. rdg.; Heb.* like the worth of rams.     [c] *See note on verse 20.*

The righteous man utters words of wisdom                              30
and justice is always on his lips.
   The law of his God is in his heart,                              31
   his steps do not falter.
The wicked watch for the righteous man                              32
   and seek to take his life;
but the LORD will not leave him in their power                              33
   nor let him be condemned before his judges.
Wait for the LORD and hold to his way;                              34
   he will keep you*a* safe from wicked men*b*
and will raise you to be master of the land.
When the wicked are destroyed, you shall be there to see.
   I have watched a wicked man at his work,                              35
   rank as a spreading tree in its native soil.
   I passed by one day, and he was gone;                              36
   I searched for him, but he could not be found.
Now look at the good man, watch him who is honest,                              37
   for the man of peace leaves descendants;
but transgressors are wiped out one and all,                              38
   and the descendants of the wicked are destroyed.
Deliverance for the righteous comes from the LORD,                              39
   their refuge in time of trouble.
The LORD will help them and deliver them; *c*                              40
he will save them because they seek shelter with him.

## 38

O LORD, do not rebuke me in thy anger,                              1
   nor punish me in thy wrath.
For thou hast aimed thy arrows*d* at me,                              2
   and thy hand weighs heavy upon me.
Thy indignation has left no part of my body unscarred;                              3
there is no health in my whole frame because of my sin.
For my iniquities have poured over my head;                              4
they are a load heavier than I can bear.
My wounds fester and stink because of my folly.                              5
I am bowed down and utterly prostrate.                              6
All day long I go about as if in mourning,
for my loins burn with fever,                              7
   and there is no wholesome flesh in me.
All battered and benumbed,                              8
   I groan aloud in my heart's longing.
O Lord, all my lament lies open before thee                              9
and my sighing is no secret to thee.
My heart beats fast, my strength has ebbed away,                              10
   and the light has gone out of my eyes.

*a* *Prob. rdg.; Heb.* them.     *b* he will . . . wicked men: *transposed from verse 40.*
*c* *See note on verse 34.*   *d* thou . . . arrows: *prob. rdg.; Heb.* thy arrows have come down.

11 My friends and my companions shun me in my sickness,
and my kinsfolk keep far away.

12 Those who wish me dead defame me,
those who mean to injure me spread cruel gossip
and mutter slanders all day long.

13 But I am deaf, I do not listen;
I am like a dumb man who cannot open his mouth.

14 I behave like a man who cannot hear
and whose tongue offers no defence.

15 On thee, O LORD, I fix my hope;
thou wilt answer, O Lord my God.

16 I said, 'Let them never rejoice over me
who exult when my foot slips.'

17 I am indeed prone to stumble,
and suffering is never far away.

18 I make no secret of my iniquity
and am anxious at the thought of my sin.

19 But many are my enemies, all without cause,*a*
and many those who hate me wrongfully.

20 Those who repay good with evil
oppose me because my purpose is good.

21 But, LORD, do not thou forsake me;
keep not far from me, my God.

22 Hasten to my help, O Lord my salvation.

## 39

1 I said: I will keep close watch over myself
that all I say may be free from sin.
I will keep a muzzle on my mouth,
so long as wicked men confront me.

2 In dumb silence I held my peace.
So my agony was quickened,

3 and my heart burned within me.
My mind wandered as the fever grew,
and I began to speak:

4 LORD, let me know my end
and the number of my days;
tell me how short my life must be.

5 I know thou hast made my days a mere span long,
and my whole life is nothing in thy sight.
Man, though he stands upright, is but a puff of wind,

6 he moves like a phantom;
the riches*b* he piles up are no more than vapour,
he does not know who will enjoy them.

7 And now, Lord, what do I wait for?
My hope is in thee.

*a* all . . . cause: *prob. rdg.; Heb.* living.　　*b* the riches: *prob. rdg.; Heb.* they murmur.

Deliver me from all who do me wrong,                    8
  make me no longer the butt of fools.
I am dumb, I will not open my mouth,                    9
  because it is thy doing.
Plague me no more;                                     10
I am exhausted by thy blows.
When thou dost rebuke a man to punish his sin,         11
  all his charm festers and drains away;
    indeed man is only a puff of wind.
Hear my prayer, O LORD;                                12
    listen to my cry,
hold not thy peace at my tears;
for I find shelter with thee,
I am thy guest, as all my fathers were.
Frown on me no more and let me smile again,            13
before I go away and cease to be.

## 40

I waited, waited for the LORD,                          1
he bent down to me and heard my cry.
He brought me up out of the muddy pit,                  2
  out of the mire and the clay;
he set my feet on a rock
  and gave me a firm footing;
and on my lips he put a new song,                       3
  a song of praise to our God.
Many when they see will be filled with awe
  and will learn to trust in the LORD:
  happy is the man                                4
who makes the LORD his trust,
and does not look to brutal and treacherous men.
Great things thou hast done,                            5
  O LORD my God;
thy wonderful purposes are all for our good;
  none can compare with thee;
I would proclaim them and speak of them,
  but they are more than I can tell.
If thou hadst desired sacrifice and offering           6
  thou wouldst have given me ears to hear.
If thou hadst asked for whole-offering and sin-offering
  I would have said, 'Here I am.'[a]               7
My desire is to do thy will, O God,                     8
  and thy law is in my heart.
In the great assembly I have proclaimed what is right,  9
  I do not hold back my words,
    as thou knowest, O LORD.

---

[a] *Prob. rdg.; Heb. adds* in a scroll of a book it is prescribed for me.

10　　　I have not kept thy goodness hidden in my heart;
　　　I have proclaimed thy faithfulness and saving power,
　　　　and not concealed thy unfailing love and truth
　　　　　from the great assembly.

11　　　Thou, O LORD, dost not withhold
　　　　thy tender care from me;
　　　thy unfailing love and truth for ever guard me.

12　　　For misfortunes beyond counting
　　　　press on me from all sides;
　　　　my iniquities have overtaken me,
　　　　and my sight fails;
　　　they are more than the hairs of my head,
　　　　and my courage forsakes me.

13*ᵃ*　　Show me favour, O LORD, and save me;
　　　　hasten to help me, O LORD.

14　　　Let those who seek to take my life
　　　　be put to shame and dismayed one and all;
　　　let all who love to hurt me shrink back disgraced;

15　　　let those who cry 'Hurrah!' at my downfall
　　　　be horrified at their reward of shame.

16　　　But let all those who seek thee
　　　　be jubilant and rejoice in thee;
　　　and let those who long for thy saving help ever cry,
　　　　'All glory to the LORD!'

17　　　But I am poor and needy;
　　　　O Lord, think of me.*ᵇ*
　　　Thou art my help and my salvation;
　　　　O my God, make no delay.

# 41

1　　　Happy the man who has a concern for the helpless!
　　　The LORD will save him in time of trouble.

2　　　The LORD protects him and gives him life,
　　　　making him secure in the land;
　　　the LORD never leaves him*ᶜ* to the greed of his enemies.

3　　　He nurses him on his sick-bed;
　　　he turns his bed when he is ill.

4　　　But I said, 'LORD, be gracious to me;
　　　heal me, for I have sinned against thee.'

5　　　'His case is desperate,' my enemies say;
　　　'when will he die, and his line become extinct?'

6　　　All who visit me speak from an empty heart,
　　　　alert to gather bad news;
　　　then they go out to spread it abroad.

---

*ᵃ* *Verses 13–17: cp. Ps. 70. 1–5.*　　　*ᵇ* O Lord . . . me: *prob. rdg.; Heb.* may the Lord think of me.　　*ᶜ* never leaves him: *prob. rdg.; Heb.* do thou not give him up . . .

All who hate me whisper together about me     7
and love to make the worst of everything:
   'An evil spell is cast upon him;     8
he is laid on his bed, and will rise no more.'
Even the friend whom I trusted, who ate at my table, *a*     9
   exults over my misfortune.
O Lord, be gracious and restore me,     10
   that I may pay them out to the full. *b*
Then I shall know that thou delightest in me     11
   and that my enemy will not triumph over me.
But I am upheld by thee because of my innocence;     12
   thou keepest me for ever in thy sight.

   Blessed be the Lord, the God of Israel,     13
     from everlasting to everlasting.
           Amen, Amen.

# BOOK 2

## 42-43

As a hind longs for the running streams,     1
so do I long for thee, O God.
With my whole being I thirst for God, the living God.     2
When shall I come to God and appear in his presence?
Day and night, tears are my food;     3
'Where is your God?' they ask me all day long.
As I pour out my soul in distress, I call to mind     4
how I marched in the ranks of the great to the house of God,
among exultant shouts of praise, the clamour of the pilgrims.
   How deep I am sunk in misery,     5
     groaning in my distress:
   yet I will wait for God;
   I will praise him continually,
     my deliverer, my God.
I am sunk in misery, therefore will I remember thee,     6
   though from the Hermons and the springs of Jordan,
     and from the hill of Mizar,
deep calls to deep in the roar of thy cataracts,     7
and all thy waves, all thy breakers, pass over me.
   The Lord makes his unfailing love shine forth *c*     8
     alike by day and night;
   his praise on my lips is a prayer
     to the God of my life.

---

*a* who . . . table: *or* slanders me.       *b* to the full: *transposed from end of verse 9.*
*c* makes . . . forth: *or* entrusts me to his unfailing love.

9     I will say to God my rock, 'Why hast thou forgotten me?'
    Why must I go like a mourner because my foes oppress me?

10     My enemies taunt me, jeering *a* at my misfortunes;
    'Where is your God?' they ask me all day long.

11         How deep I am sunk in misery,
        groaning in my distress:
        yet I will wait for God;
        I will praise him continually,
        my deliverer, my God.

**43**    Plead my cause and give me judgement against an impious race;
    save me from malignant men and liars, O God.

2     Thou, O God, art my refuge; why hast thou rejected me?
    Why must I go like a mourner because my foes oppress me?

3     Send forth thy light and thy truth to be my guide
    and lead me to thy holy hill, to thy tabernacle,

4     then shall I come to the altar of God, the God of my joy,
    and praise thee on the harp, O God, thou God of my delight.

5         How deep I am sunk in misery,
        groaning in my distress:
        yet I will wait for God;
        I will praise him continually,
        my deliverer, my God.

## 44

1         O God, we have heard for ourselves,
        our fathers have told us
    all the deeds which thou didst in their days,

2     all the work of thy hand in days of old.
    Thou didst plant them in the land and drive the nations out,
    thou didst make them strike root, breaking up the peoples;

3     it was not our fathers' swords won them the land,
    nor their arm that gave them the victory,
        but thy right hand and thy arm
        and the light of thy presence; such was thy favour to them.

4     Thou art my king and my God;
    at thy bidding Jacob is victorious.

5     By thy help we will throw back our enemies,
    in thy name we will trample down our adversaries.

6     I will not trust in my bow,
    nor will my sword win me the victory;

7     for thou dost deliver us from our foes
    and put all our enemies to shame.

8     In God have we gloried all day long,
    and we will praise thy name for ever.

9     But now thou hast rejected and humbled us
    and dost no longer lead our armies into battle.

*a* jeering: *prob. rdg.; Heb. obscure.*

Thou hast hurled us back before the enemy,  10
and our foes plunder us as they will.
Thou hast given us up to be butchered like sheep  11
and hast scattered us among the nations.
Thou hast sold thy people for next to nothing  12
and had no profit from the sale.
Thou hast exposed us to the taunts of our neighbours,  13
to the mockery and contempt of all around.
Thou hast made us a byword among the nations,  14
and the peoples shake their heads at us;
so my disgrace confronts me all day long,  15
and I am covered with shame
at the shouts of those who taunt and abuse me  16
as the enemy takes his revenge.
All this has befallen us, but we do not forget thee  17
and have not betrayed thy covenant;
we have not gone back on our purpose,  18
nor have our feet strayed from thy path.
Yet thou hast crushed us as the sea-serpent was crushed  19
and covered us with the darkness of death.
If we had forgotten the name of our God  20
and spread our hands in prayer to any other,
would not God find this out,  21
for he knows the secrets of the heart?
Because of thee we are done to death all day long,  22
and are treated as sheep for slaughter.
Bestir thyself, Lord; why dost thou sleep?  23
Awake, do not reject us for ever.
Why dost thou hide thy face,  24
heedless of our misery and our sufferings?
For we sink down to the dust  25
and lie prone on the earth.
Arise and come to our help;  26
for thy love's sake set us free.

## 45

My heart is stirred by a noble theme,  1
in a king's honour I utter the song I have made,
and my tongue runs like the pen of an expert scribe.

You surpass all mankind in beauty,  2
your lips are moulded in grace,
so you are blessed by God for ever.
With your sword ready at your side, warrior king,  3
your limbs resplendent *a* in their royal armour,  4
ride on to execute true sentence and just judgement.

*a* your limbs resplendent: *prob. rdg.; Heb.* and in your pomp prosper.

Your right hand shall show you a scene of terror:
5    your sharp arrows flying, nations beneath your feet,
        the courage of the king's foes melting away! [a]

6    Your throne is like God's throne, eternal,
        your royal sceptre a sceptre of righteousness.
7    You have loved right and hated wrong;
        so God, your God, has anointed you
            above your fellows with oil, the token of joy.
8    Your robes are all fragrant with myrrh and powder of aloes,
            and the music of strings greets you
                from a palace panelled with ivory.
9    A princess takes her place among the noblest of your women,
        a royal lady at your side in gold of Ophir.

10       Listen, my daughter, hear my words
            and consider them:
        forget your own people and your father's house;
11       and, when the king desires your beauty,
            remember that he is your lord.
12       Do him obeisance, daughter of Tyre,
        and the richest in the land will court you with gifts.

13       In the palace honour awaits her; [b]
            she is a king's daughter,
14          arrayed in cloth-of-gold richly embroidered.
        Virgins shall follow her into the presence of the king;
            her companions shall be brought to her,
15       escorted with the noise of revels and rejoicing
            as they enter the king's palace.

16       You shall have sons, O king, in place of your forefathers
            and will make them rulers over all the land. [c]
17       I will declare your fame to all generations;
        therefore the nations will praise you for ever and ever.


# 46

1    God is our shelter and our refuge,
        a timely help in trouble;
2    so we are not afraid when the earth heaves
        and the mountains are hurled into the sea,
3        when its waters seethe in tumult
        and the mountains quake before his majesty.
4    There is a river whose streams gladden the city of God, [d]
        which the Most High has made his holy dwelling;

---

[a] *the courage . . . away: prob. rdg.; Heb. obscure.*      [b] *honour awaits her: prob. rdg.;*
*Heb. all honoured.*      [c] *over all the land: or in all the earth.*      [d] *the city of God:*
*or a wondrous city.*

God is in that city; she will not be overthrown,　　5
and he will help her at the break of day.
Nations are in tumult, kingdoms hurled down;　　6
when he thunders, the earth surges like the sea.
The Lord of Hosts is with us,　　7
the God of Jacob our high stronghold.

Come and see what the Lord has done,　　8
the devastation he has brought upon earth,
from end to end of the earth he stamps out war:　　9
he breaks the bow, he snaps the spear
and burns the shield in the fire.

Let be then: learn that I am God,　　10
high over the nations, high above earth.
The Lord of Hosts is with us,　　11
the God of Jacob our high stronghold.

# 47

Clap your hands, all you nations;　　1
acclaim our God with shouts of joy.
How fearful is the Lord Most High,　　2
great sovereign over all the earth!
He lays the nations prostrate beneath us,　　3
he lays peoples under our feet;
he chose our patrimony for us,　　4
the pride of Jacob whom he loved.

God has gone up with shouts of acclamation,　　5
the Lord has gone up with a fanfare of trumpets.
Praise God,[a] praise him with psalms;　　6
praise our king, praise him with psalms.
God is king of all the earth;　　7
sing psalms with all your art.
God reigns over the nations,　　8
God is seated on his holy throne.
The princes of the nations assemble　　9
with the families of Abraham's line;[b]
for the mighty ones of earth belong to God,
and he is raised above them all.

# 48

The Lord is great and worthy of our praise　　1
in the city of our God, upon his holy hill.

---

[a] Praise God: *or* Praise, you gods.　　[b] the families of Abraham's line: *prob. rdg.*;
*Heb.* the God of Abraham.

2          Fair and lofty, the joy of the whole earth
             is Zion's hill, like the farthest reaches of the north, [a]
             the hill of the great King's city.

3      In her palaces God is known for a tower of strength.
4          See how the kings all gather round her,
             marching on in company.

5      They are struck with amazement when they see her,
             they are filled with alarm and panic;

6      they are seized with trembling,
             they toss in pain like a woman in labour,

7          like the ships of Tarshish
             when an east wind wrecks them.

8      All we had heard we saw with our own eyes
             in the city of the LORD of Hosts,
             in the city of our God,
             the city which God plants firm for evermore.

9      O God, we re-enact the story of thy true love
             within thy temple;

10     the praise thy name deserves, O God,
             is heard at earth's farthest bounds.
      Thy hand is charged with justice,
             and the hill of Zion rejoices,
11     Judah's daughter-cities exult
             in thy judgements.

12     Make the round of Zion in procession,
             count the number of her towers,

13     take good note of her ramparts,
             pass her palaces in review,
      that you may tell generations yet to come:

14          Such is God,
      our God for ever and ever;
             he shall be our guide eternally.

## 49

1      Hear this, all you nations;
      listen, all who inhabit this world,

2      all mankind, every living man,
      rich and poor alike;

3      for the words that I speak are wise,
             my thoughtful heart is full of understanding.

4      I will set my ear to catch the moral of the story
      and tell on the harp how I read the riddle;

5      why should I be afraid in evil times,
      beset by the wickedness of treacherous foes,

[a] *Or of Zaphon.*

who trust in their riches 6
and boast of their great wealth?
Alas! no man can ever ransom himself 7
nor pay God the price of that release;
his ransom would cost too much, 8
for ever beyond his power to pay,
the ransom that would let him live on always 9
and never see the pit of death.

But remember this:*<sup>a</sup>* wise men must die; 10
stupid men, brutish men, all perish.*<sup>b</sup>*
The grave is their eternal home, 11
their dwelling for all time to come;
they may give their own names to estates,
but they must leave their riches to others.*<sup>c</sup>*
For men are like oxen whose life cannot last, 12
they are like cattle whose time is short.
Such is the fate of foolish men 13
and of all who seek to please them:
like sheep they run headlong into Sheol, the land of 14
Death;
he is their shepherd and urges them on;
their flesh must rot away *<sup>d</sup>*
and their bodies be wasted by Sheol,
stripped of all honour.
But God will ransom my life, 15
he will take me from the power of Sheol.
Do not envy a man when he grows rich, 16
when the wealth of his family increases;
for he will take nothing when he dies, 17
and his wealth will not go with him.
Though in his lifetime he counts himself happy 18
and men praise him in his*<sup>e</sup>* prosperity,
he*<sup>f</sup>* will go to join the company of his forefathers 19
who will never again see the light.
For men are like oxen whose life cannot last, 20
they are like cattle whose time is short.

## 50

God, the Lord God, has spoken 1
and summoned the world from the rising to the setting sun.
God shines out from Zion, perfect in beauty. 2

---

*<sup>a</sup> But remember this: prob. rdg.; Heb. But he will remember this.*     *<sup>b</sup> Line transposed from here to follow verse 11.*     *<sup>c</sup> Line transposed from verse 10.*     *<sup>d</sup> and urges ... rot away: prob. rdg.; Heb. obscure.*     *<sup>e</sup> him ... his: prob. rdg.; Heb. you ... your.*     *<sup>f</sup> he: prob. rdg.; Heb. you.*

3    Our God is coming and will not keep silence:
     consuming fire runs before him
     and wreathes him closely round.<sup>a</sup>
4    He summons heaven on high and earth
     to the judgement of his people:
5    'Gather to me my loyal servants,
     all who by sacrifice have made a covenant with me.'
6    The heavens proclaim his justice,
     for God himself is the judge.

7    Listen, my people, and I will speak;
     I will bear witness against you, O Israel:
     I am God, your God,
8    shall I not<sup>b</sup> find fault with your sacrifices,
     though<sup>c</sup> your offerings are before me always?
9    I need take no young bull from your house,
         no he-goat from your folds;
10   for all the beasts of the forest are mine
         and the cattle in thousands on my hills.
11   I know every bird on those hills,
     the teeming life of the fields is my care.
12   If I were hungry, I would not tell you,
     for the world and all that is in it are mine.
13       Shall I eat the flesh of your bulls
         or drink the blood of he-goats?
14   Offer to God the sacrifice of thanksgiving
     and pay your vows to the Most High.
15       If you call upon me in time of trouble,
         I will come to your rescue, and you shall honour me.

16       God's word to the wicked man is this:
         What right have you to recite my laws
         and make so free with the words of my covenant,
17       you who hate correction
         and turn your back when I am speaking?
18   If you meet a thief, you choose him as your friend;
         you make common cause with adulterers;
19   you charge your mouth with wickedness
     and harness your tongue to slander.
20   You are for ever talking against your brother,
     stabbing your own mother's son in the back.
21   All this you have done, and shall I keep silence?
     You thought that I was another like yourself,
     but point by point I will rebuke you to your face.
22   Think well on this, you who forget God,
     or I will tear you in pieces and no one shall save you.

---

<sup>a</sup> and wreathes him closely round: *or* and rages round him.          <sup>b</sup> *Or* I will not.
<sup>c</sup> *Or* for.

He who offers a sacrifice of thanksgiving                        23
does me due honour,
and to him who follows my way *a*
I will show the salvation of God.

## 51

Be gracious to me, O God, in thy true love;                       1
in the fullness of thy mercy blot out my misdeeds.

Wash away all my guilt                                            2
    and cleanse me from my sin.
For well I know my misdeeds,                                      3
and my sins confront me all the day long.
Against thee, thee only, I have sinned                            4
and done what displeases thee,
so that thou mayest be proved right in thy charge
    and just in passing sentence.

In iniquity I was brought to birth                               5
and my mother conceived me in sin;
yet, though thou hast hidden the truth in darkness,              6
through this mystery thou dost teach me wisdom.
Take hyssop *b* and sprinkle me, that I may be clean;            7
wash me, that I may become whiter than snow;
let me hear the sounds of joy and gladness,                      8
let the bones dance which thou hast broken.
Turn away thy face from my sins                                  9
    and blot out all my guilt.

Create a pure heart in me, O God,                               10
    and give me a new and steadfast spirit;
        do not drive me from thy presence                       11
    or take thy holy spirit from me;
    revive in me the joy of thy deliverance                     12
        and grant me a willing spirit to uphold me.

I will teach transgressors the ways that lead to thee,          13
and sinners shall return to thee again.
O LORD God, my deliverer, save me from bloodshed, *c*           14
and I will sing the praises of thy justice.
Open my lips, O Lord,                                           15
that my mouth may proclaim thy praise.
Thou hast no delight in sacrifice;                              16
if I brought thee an offering, thou wouldst not accept it.
My sacrifice, O God, is a broken spirit;                        17
a wounded heart, O God, thou wilt not despise.

*a* him who follows my way: *prob. rdg.; Heb.* him who puts a way.     *b Or* marjoram.
*c Or* from punishment by death.

18      Let it be thy pleasure to do good to Zion,
          to build anew the walls of Jerusalem.
19      Then only shalt thou delight in the appointed sacrifices; [a]
          then shall young bulls be offered on thy altar.

## 52

1-2     Why make your wickedness your boast, you man of might,
          forging wild lies all day against God's loyal servant?
        Your slanderous tongue is sharp as a razor.
3           You love evil and not good,
              falsehood, not speaking the truth;
4       cruel gossip you love and slanderous talk.
5           So may God [b] pull you down to the ground,
              sweep you away, leave you ruined and homeless,
                uprooted from the land of the living.
6           The righteous will look on, awestruck,
              and laugh at his plight:
7             'This is the man', they say,
              'who does not make God his refuge,
            but trusts in his great wealth
              and takes refuge in wild lies.'
8       But I am like a spreading olive-tree in God's house;
          for I trust in God's true love for ever and ever.
9       I will praise thee for ever for what thou hast done,
          and glorify thy name among thy loyal servants;
            for that is good.

## 53

1 [c]    The impious fool says in his heart,
            'There is no God.'
        How vile men are, how depraved and loathsome;
            not one does anything good!
2       God looks down from heaven
            on all mankind
        to see if any act wisely,
            if any seek out God.
3       But all are unfaithful, all are rotten to the core;
            not one does anything good,
            no, not even one.

4             Shall they not rue it,
            these evildoers who devour my people
              as men devour bread,
              and never call upon God?

---

[a] *Prob. rdg.; Heb. adds* a whole-offering and one wholly consumed.      [b] *Or* So God
will.      [c] *Verses 1-6: cp. Ps. 14. 1-7.*

There they were in dire alarm 5
when God scattered them.
The crimes of the godless were frustrated;[a]
for God had rejected them.
If only Israel's deliverance might come out of Zion! 6
When God restores his people's fortunes,
let Jacob rejoice, let Israel be glad.

## 54

Save me, O God, by the power of thy name, 1
and vindicate me through thy might.
O God, hear my prayer, 2
listen to my supplication.
Insolent men rise to attack me, 3
ruthless men seek my life;
they give no thought to God.

But God is my helper, 4
the Lord the mainstay of my life.
May their own malice recoil on my watchful foes; 5
silence them by thy truth, O LORD.
I will offer thee a willing sacrifice 6
and praise thy name, for that is good;
God has rescued me from every trouble, 7
and I look on my enemies' downfall with delight.

## 55

Listen, O God, to my pleading, 1
do not hide thyself when I pray.
Hear me and answer, 2
for my cares give me no peace.
I am panic-stricken at the shouts of my enemies, 3
at the shrill clamour of the wicked;
for they heap trouble on me
and they revile me in their anger.
My heart is torn with anguish 4
and the terrors of death come upon me.
Fear and trembling overwhelm me 5
and I shudder from head to foot.
[b]Oh that I had the wings of a dove 6
to fly away and be at rest!
I should escape far away 7
and find a refuge in the wilderness;

[a] The crimes . . . frustrated: *prob. rdg.; Heb. obscure.*   [b] *Prob. rdg.; Heb. prefixes* And I said.

8      soon I should find myself a sanctuary
           from wind and storm,
9      from the blasts of calumny, O Lord,
           from my enemies' contentious tongues.
       I have seen violence and strife in the city;
10         day and night they encircle it,
               all along its walls;
           it is filled with trouble and mischief,
11             alive with rumour and scandal,
           and its public square is never free
               from violence and spite.
12     It was no enemy that taunted me,
           or I should have avoided him;
       no adversary that treated me with scorn,
           or I should have kept out of his way.
13     It was you, a man of my own sort,
           my comrade, my own dear friend,
14-15  with whom I kept pleasant company
           in the house of God.

       May death strike them,
       and may they *a* perish in confusion,
       may they go down alive into Sheol;
           for their homes are haunts of evil!

16     But I will call upon God;
           the Lord will save me.
17     Evening and morning and at noon
           I nurse my woes, and groan.
18     He has heard my cry, he rescued me
           and gave me back my peace,
       when they beset me like archers, *b*
           massing against me,
19     like Ishmael and the desert tribes
           and those who dwell in the East,
       who have no respect for an oath
           nor any fear of God.
20     Such men do violence to those at peace with them
           and break their promised word;
21     their speech is smoother than butter
           but their thoughts are of war;
       their words are slippery as oil
           but sharp as drawn swords.

22     Commit your fortunes to the Lord,
           and he will sustain you;
       he will never let the righteous be shaken.

*a Prob. rdg.; Heb.* we.          *b* when . . . archers: *prob. rdg.; Heb. obscure.*

Cast them, O God, into the pit of destruction;       23
    bloodthirsty and treacherous,
  they shall not live out half their days;
  but I will put my trust in thee.

## 56

Be gracious to me, O God, for the enemy persecute me,    1
  my assailants harass me all day long.
All the day long my watchful foes persecute me;     2
  countless are those who assail me.
Appear on high *a* in my day of fear;         3
  I put my trust in thee.
With God to help me I will shout defiance,      4
  in God I trust and shall not be afraid;
  what can mortal men do to me?
All day long abuse of me is their only theme,      5
    all their thoughts are hostile.
In malice they are on the look-out, and watch for me,   6
    they dog my footsteps;
but, while they lie in wait for me,
it is they who will not *b* escape.          7
O God, in thy anger bring ruin on the nations.

Enter my lament in thy book, *c*         8
  store every tear in thy flask. *d*
Then my enemies will turn back         9
    on the day when I call upon thee; *e*
for this I know, that God is on my side,
with God to help me I will shout defiance. *f*     10
In God I trust and shall not be afraid;       11
  what can man do to me?
I have bound myself with vows to thee, O God,     12
  and will redeem them with due thank-offerings;
for thou hast rescued me from death *g*      13
  to walk in thy presence, in the light of life.

## 57

Be gracious to me, O God, be gracious;       1
  for I have made thee my refuge.
I will take refuge in the shadow of thy wings
    until the storms are past.

---

*a* Appear on high: *prob. rdg.; Heb.* Height.      *b* it is . . . not: *prob. rdg.; Heb. for* iniquity.    *c* Enter . . . book: *prob. rdg.; Heb. obscure.*    *d Prob. rdg.; Heb. adds* is it not in thy book?     *e* Enter . . . thee: *or* Thou hast entered my lament in thy book, my tears are put in thy flask. Then my enemies turned back, when I called upon thee. *f Prob. rdg.; Heb. adds* With the LORD to help me I will shout defiance.     *g Prob. rdg.; Heb. adds* is it not my feet from stumbling (*cp. Ps. 116. 8*).

2    I will call upon God Most High,
     on God who fulfils his purpose for me.
3    He will send his truth and his love that never fails,
     he will send from heaven and save me.
     God himself will frustrate my persecutors;
4    for I lie down among lions, man-eaters,
     whose teeth are spears and arrows
     and whose tongues are sharp swords.
5    Show thyself, O God, high above the heavens;
     let thy glory shine over all the earth.
6    Men have prepared a net to catch me as I walk,
     but I bow my head to escape from it;
    they have dug a pit in my path
     but have fallen into it themselves.

7[a]   My heart is steadfast, O God,
     my heart is steadfast.
    I will sing and raise a psalm;
8     awake, my spirit,
    awake, lute and harp,
     I will awake at dawn of day.[b]
9    I will confess thee, O Lord, among the peoples,
     among the nations I will raise a psalm to thee,
10   for thy unfailing love is wide as the heavens
     and thy truth reaches to the skies.
11   Show thyself, O God, high above the heavens;
     let thy glory shine over all the earth.

## 58

1    Answer, you rulers:[c] are your judgements just?
    Do you decide impartially between man and man?
2     Never! Your hearts devise all kinds of wickedness
    and survey the violence that you have done on earth.

3    Wicked men, from birth they have taken to devious ways;
    liars, no sooner born than they go astray,
4    venomous with the venom of serpents,
    of the deaf asp which stops its ears
5    and will not listen to the sound of the charmer,
     however skilful his spells may be.

6    O God, break the teeth in their mouths.
    Break, O Lord, the jaws of the unbelievers.[d]

---

[a] *Verses 7–11: cp. Ps. 108. 1–5.*  [b] at dawn of day: *or* the dawn.  [c] *Or* you
gods.  [d] the jaws of the unbelievers: *or* the lions' fangs.

May they melt, may they vanish like water,     7
may they wither like trodden grass,<sup>*a*</sup>
    like an abortive birth which melts away     8
    or a still-born child which never sees<sup>*b*</sup> the sun!
All unawares, may they be rooted up like<sup>*c*</sup> a thorn-bush,     9
    like weeds which a man angrily<sup>*d*</sup> clears away!

The righteous shall rejoice that he has seen vengeance done     10
    and shall wash his feet in the blood of the wicked,
      and men shall say,     11
    'There is after all a reward for the righteous;
after all, there is a God that judges on earth.'


# 59

Rescue me from my enemies, O my God,     1
be my tower of strength against all who assail me,
    rescue me from these evildoers,     2
    deliver me from men of blood.
Savage men lie in wait for me,     3
they lie in ambush ready to attack me;
for no fault or guilt of mine, O LORD,
innocent as I am, they run to take post against me.     4-5
But thou, LORD God of Hosts, Israel's God,
    do thou bestir thyself at my call, and look:
    awake, and punish all the nations.
    Have no mercy on villains and traitors,
    who run wild at nightfall like dogs,     6
    snarling and prowling round the city,
    wandering to and fro in search of food,     15<sup>*e*</sup>
    and howling if they are not satisfied.
    From their mouths comes a stream of nonsense;     7
    'But who will hear?' they murmur.
But thou, O LORD, dost laugh at them,     8
    and deride all the nations.
O my strength,<sup>*f*</sup> to thee I turn in the night-watches;     9
    for thou, O God, art my strong tower.
My God, in his true love, shall be my champion;     10
with God's help, I shall gloat over my watchful foes.
Wilt thou not kill them, lest my people forget?     11
Scatter them by thy might and bring them to ruin.
    Deliver them,<sup>*g*</sup> O Lord, to be destroyed     12
    by their own sinful words;
    let what they have spoken entrap them in their pride.

---

<sup>*a*</sup> like trodden grass: *prob. rdg.; Heb. obscure.*       <sup>*b*</sup> sees: *prob. rdg.; Heb.* they see.
<sup>*c*</sup> may they be rooted up like: *prob. rdg.; Heb.* your pots.       <sup>*d*</sup> angrily: *prob. rdg.;*
*Heb.* like anger.       <sup>*e*</sup> *Verse transposed.*       <sup>*f*</sup> *Or* refuge.       <sup>*g*</sup> Deliver them: *prob.*
*rdg.; Heb.* Our shield.

Let them be cut off for their cursing and falsehood;
13         bring them to an end in thy wrath,
and they will be no more;
then they will know that God is ruler in Jacob,
even to earth's farthest limits. *a b*

16        But I will sing of thy strength,
and celebrate thy love when morning comes;
for thou hast been my strong tower
and a sure retreat in days of trouble.

17        O thou my strength, I will raise a psalm to thee;
for thou, O God, art my strong tower.

## 60

1        O God, thou hast cast us off and broken us;
thou hast been angry and rebuked us cruelly.

2        Thou hast made the land quake and torn it open;
it gives way and crumbles into pieces.

3        Thou hast made thy people drunk with a bitter draught,
thou hast given us wine that makes us stagger.

4        But thou hast given a warning to those who fear thee,
to make their escape before the sentence falls.

5 *c*     Deliver those that are dear to thee;
save them with thy right hand, and answer.

6        God has spoken from his sanctuary: *d*
'I will go up now and measure out Shechem;
I will divide the valley of Succoth into plots;

7        Gilead and Manasseh are mine;
Ephraim is my helmet, Judah my sceptre;

8        Moab is my wash-bowl, I fling my shoes at Edom;
Philistia is the target of my anger.'

9        Who can bring me to the fortified city,
who can guide me to Edom,

10       since thou, O God, hast abandoned us
and goest not forth with our armies?

11       Grant us help against the enemy,
for deliverance by man is a vain hope.

12       With God's help we shall do valiantly,
and God himself will tread our enemies under foot.

---

*a Prob. rdg.; Heb. adds* (14) who run wild at nightfall like dogs, snarling and prowling
round the city (*cp. verse 6*).    *b Verse 15 transposed to follow verse 6.*    *c Verses
5–12: cp. Ps. 108. 6–13.*    *d* from his sanctuary: *or* in his holiness.

# 61

| | |
|---|---|
| Hear my cry, O God, listen to my prayer. | 1 |
| From the end of the earth I call to thee with fainting heart; | 2 |
| lift me up and set me upon a rock. | |
| For thou hast been my shelter, | 3 |
| a tower for refuge from the enemy. | |
| In thy tent will I make my home for ever | 4 |
| and find my shelter under the cover of thy wings. | |
| For thou, O God, hast heard my vows | 5 |
| and granted the wish*a* of all who revere thy name. | |

To the king's life add length of days,     6
    year upon year for many generations;
    may he dwell in God's presence for ever,     7
    may true and constant love preserve him.

So will I ever sing psalms in honour of thy name     8
    as I fulfil my vows day after day.

# 62

Truly my heart waits silently for God;     1
    my deliverance comes from him.
In truth he is my rock of deliverance,     2
    my tower of strength, so that I stand unshaken.
    How long will you assail a man with your threats,     3
    all battering on a leaning wall?
In truth men plan to topple him from his height,     4
    and stamp on the fallen stones.*b*
    With their lips they bless him, the hypocrites,
    but revile him in their hearts.
Truly my heart waits silently for God;     5
    my hope of deliverance comes from him.
In truth he is my rock of deliverance,     6
    my tower of strength, so that I am unshaken.
    My deliverance and my honour depend upon God,     7
    God who is my rock of refuge and my shelter.
    Trust always in God, my people,     8
pour out your hearts before him;
    God is our shelter.

In very truth men are a puff of wind,     9
    all men are faithless;
put them in the balance and they can only rise,
    all of them lighter than wind.

---

*a* *Prob. rdg.; Heb.* the inheritance.       *b* the fallen stones: *transposed from end of verse 3.*

10                Put no trust in extortion,
                   do not be proud of stolen goods;
           though wealth breeds wealth, set not your heart on it.

11                One thing God has spoken,
                   two things I have learnt:
               'Power belongs to God'

12                and 'True love, O Lord, is thine';
           thou dost requite a man for his deeds.

## 63

1                O God, thou art my God, I seek thee early
                   with a heart that thirsts for thee
                   and a body wasted with longing for thee,
           like a dry and thirsty land that has no water.

2                So longing, I come before thee in the sanctuary
                   to look upon thy power and glory.

3                Thy true love is better than life;
                   therefore I will sing thy praises.

4                And so I bless thee all my life
                   and in thy name lift my hands in prayer.

5            I am satisfied as with a rich and sumptuous feast
                   and wake the echoes with thy praise.

6                When I call thee to mind upon my bed
                   and think on thee in the watches of the night,

7                remembering how thou hast been my help
                   and that I am safe in the shadow of thy wings,

8                then I humbly follow thee with all my heart,
                   and thy right hand is my support.

9                Those who seek my life, bent on evil,
                   shall sink into the depths of the earth;

10                they shall be given over to the sword;
                   they shall be carrion for jackals.

11                The king shall rejoice in God,
                   and whoever swears by God's name shall exult;
                   the voice of falsehood shall be silenced.

## 64

1                Hear me, O God, hear my lament;
                   keep me safe from the threats of the enemy.

2                    Hide me from the factions of the wicked,
                   from the turbulent mob of evildoers,

3                who sharpen their tongues like swords
                 and wing their cruel words like arrows, [a]

4                to shoot down the innocent from cover,
                 shooting suddenly, themselves unseen.

[a] and wing . . . arrows: *prob. rdg.*; *Heb.* they tread their arrow a cruel word.

They boldly<sup>a</sup> hide their snares,     5
    sure that none will see them;
they hatch their secret plans<sup>b</sup> with skill and cunning,     6
with evil<sup>c</sup> purpose and deep design.
    But God with his arrow shoots them down,     7
    and sudden is their overthrow.

    They may repeat their wicked tales,<sup>d</sup>     8
    but their mischievous tongues<sup>e</sup> are their undoing.
All who see their fate take fright at it,
    every man is afraid;     9
    'This is God's work', they declare;
    they learn their lesson from what he has done.
The righteous rejoice and seek refuge in the LORD     10
    and all the upright exult.

# 65

We owe thee praise, O God, in Zion;     1–2
thou hearest prayer, vows shall be paid to thee.
All men shall lay their guilt before thee:     3
    our sins are too heavy for us;
    only thou canst blot them out.
Happy is the man of thy choice, whom thou dost bring     4
    to dwell in thy courts;
    let us enjoy the blessing of thy house,
        thy holy temple.
By deeds of terror answer us with victory,     5
    O God of our deliverance,
in whom men trust from the ends of the earth
    and far-off seas;
    thou art girded with strength,     6
and by thy might dost fix the mountains in their place,
dost calm the rage of the seas and their raging waves.<sup>f</sup>     7
    The dwellers at the ends of the earth     8
    hold thy signs in awe;
thou makest morning and evening sing aloud in triumph.

Thou dost visit the earth and give it abundance,     9
    as often as thou dost enrich it
with the waters of heaven, brimming in their channels,
    providing rain<sup>g</sup> for men.
    For this is thy provision for it,
watering its furrows, levelling its ridges,     10
softening it with showers and blessing its growth.

---

<sup>a</sup> *See first note on verse 8.*     <sup>b</sup> their secret plans: *prob. rdg.; Heb. unintelligible.*
<sup>c</sup> evil: *prob. rdg.; Heb.* man.     <sup>d</sup> They . . . tales: *transposed from after* boldly *in
verse 5.*     <sup>e</sup> their mischievous tongues: *prob. rdg.; Heb.* against them their tongues.
<sup>f</sup> *Prob. rdg.; Heb. adds* and tumult of people.     <sup>g</sup> *Or* corn.

11        Thou dost crown the year with thy good gifts
        and the palm-trees drip with sweet juice;
12           the pastures in the wild are rich with blessing
        and the hills wreathed in happiness,
13        the meadows are clothed with sheep
        and the valleys mantled in corn,
           so that they shout, they break into song.

# 66

1        Acclaim our God, all men on earth;
2           let psalms declare the glory of his name,
        make glorious his praise.
3       Say unto God, 'How fearful are thy works!
       Thy foes cower before the greatness of thy strength.
4       All men on earth fall prostrate in thy presence,
       and sing to thee, sing psalms in honour of thy name.'
5        Come and see all that God has done,
        tremendous in his dealings with mankind.
6        He turned the waters into dry land
        so that his people passed through the sea on foot;
        there did we rejoice in him. *a*

7        He rules for ever by his power,
        his eye rests on the nations;
        let no rebel rise in defiance.

8        Bless our God, all nations;
           let his praise be heard far and near.
9        He set us in the land of the living;
        he keeps our feet from stumbling.
10          For thou, O God, hast put us to the proof
        and refined us like silver.
11          Thou hast caught us in a net,
        thou hast bound our bodies fast;
12       thou hast let men ride over our heads.
       We went through fire and water,
          but thou hast brought us out into liberty.

13       I will bring sacrifices into thy temple
       and fulfil my vows to thee,
14       vows which I made with my own lips
       and swore with my own mouth when in distress.
15       I will offer thee fat beasts as sacrifices
         and burn rams as a savoury offering;
       I will make ready oxen and he-goats.

16       Come, listen, all who fear God,
       and I will tell you all that he has done for me;

*a* there . . . him: *or* where we see this, we will rejoice in him.

I lifted up my voice in prayer,                              17
    his high praise was on my lips.
If I had cherished evil thoughts,                            18
    the Lord would not have heard me;
but in truth God has heard                                   19
    and given heed to my prayer.
Blessed is God                                               20
who has not withdrawn his love and care from me.

## 67

God be gracious to us and bless us,                          1
God make his face shine upon us,
    that his ways may be known on earth                      2
    and his saving power among all the nations.
Let the peoples praise thee, O God;                          3
let all peoples praise thee.
Let all nations rejoice and shout in triumph;               4
    for thou dost judge the peoples with justice
    and guidest the nations of the earth.
Let the peoples praise thee, O God;                          5
let all peoples praise thee.
The earth has given its increase                             6
and God, our God, will bless us.

God grant us his blessing,                                   7
that all the ends of the earth may fear him.

## 68

God arises and his enemies are scattered;                    1
    those who hate him flee before him,
    driven away like smoke in the wind;                      2
    like wax melting at the fire,
    the wicked perish at the presence of God.
But the righteous are joyful, they exult before God,         3
    they are jubilant and shout for joy.

Sing the praises of God, raise a psalm to his name,          4
    extol him who rides over the desert plains. <sup>a</sup>
Be joyful <sup>b</sup> and exult before him,
    father of the fatherless, the widow's champion—         5
    God in his holy dwelling-place.
God gives the friendless a home                              6
    and brings out the prisoner safe and sound;
but rebels must live in the scorching desert.

---

<sup>a</sup> over the desert plains: *or* on the plains.     <sup>b</sup> Be joyful: *prob. rdg.*; *Heb.* In the
LORD is his name.

7     O God, when thou didst go forth before thy people,
          marching across the wilderness,

8     earth trembled, the very heavens quaked
      before God the lord of Sinai, before God the God of Israel.

9     Of thy bounty, O God, thou dost refresh with rain
          thy own land in its weariness,
          the land which thou thyself didst provide,

10        where thy own people made their home,
      which thou, O God, in thy goodness providest for the poor.

11–13  The Lord proclaims good news:[a]
      'Kings with their armies have fled headlong.'
      O mighty host, will you linger among the sheepfolds
          while the women in your tents divide the spoil—
          an image of a dove, its wings sheathed in silver
          and its pinions in yellow gold—

14        while the Almighty scatters kings far and wide
          like snowflakes falling on Zalmon?

15    The hill of Bashan is a hill of God indeed,
          a hill of many peaks is Bashan's hill.

16    But, O hill of many peaks, why gaze in envy
      at the hill where the LORD delights to dwell,
      where the LORD himself will live for ever?

17        Twice ten thousand were God's chariots, thousands upon
              thousands,
      when the Lord came in holiness from Sinai.[b]

18    Thou didst go up to thy lofty home with captives in thy train,
          having received tribute from men;
      in the presence of the LORD God no rebel could live.

19        Blessed is the Lord:
          he carries us day by day,
              God our salvation.

20    Our God is a God who saves us,
      in the LORD God's hand lies escape from death.[c]

21    God himself will smite[d] the head of his enemies,
          those proud sinners with their flowing locks.

22    The Lord says, 'I will return from the Dragon,[e]
          I will return from the depths of the sea,

23    that you may dabble your feet in blood,
          while the tongues of your dogs are eager[f] for it.'

24        Thy procession, O God, comes into view,
          the procession of my God and King into the sanctuary:

---

[a] proclaims good news: *or* gives the word, women bearing good news.   [b] came . . .
from Sinai: *prob. rdg.; Heb. obscure.*   [c] in the LORD God's hand . . . death: *or*
death is expelled by the LORD God.   [d] will smite: *or* smites.   [e] the Dragon:
*or* Bashan.   [f] are eager: *prob. rdg.; Heb.* from enemies.

at its head the singers, next come minstrels, 25
  girls among them playing on tambourines.
  In the great concourse they bless God, 26
  all Israel assembled *a* bless the LORD.
There is the little tribe of Benjamin leading them, 27
  there the company of Judah's princes,
  the princes of Zebulun and of Naphtali.

O God, in virtue of thy power *b*— 28
  that godlike power which has acted for us—
command kings to bring gifts to thee 29
  for the honour of thy temple in Jerusalem.
Rebuke those wild beasts of the reeds, that herd of bulls, 30
  the bull-calf warriors of the nations; *c*
scatter these nations which revel in war;
  make them bring tribute from Egypt, 31
  precious stones and silver from Pathros; *d*
let Nubia stretch out *e* her hands to God.

All you kingdoms of the world, sing praises to God, 32
  sing psalms to the Lord,
  to him who rides on the heavens, the ancient heavens. 33
Hark! he speaks in the mighty thunder.
Ascribe all might to God, Israel's High God, 34
  Israel's pride and might throned in the skies.
  Terrible is God as he comes from his sanctuary; 35
  he is Israel's own God,
who gives to his people might and abundant power.

  Blessed be God.

# 69

  Save me, O God; 1
  for the waters have risen up to my neck.
I sink in muddy depths and have no foothold; 2
I am swept into deep water, and the flood carries me away.
I am wearied with crying out, my throat is sore, 3
my eyes grow dim as I wait for God to help me.
  Those who hate me without reason 4
  are more than the hairs of my head;
they outnumber my hairs, those who accuse me falsely.
How can I give back what I have not stolen?
O God, thou knowest how foolish I am, 5
  and my guilty deeds are not hidden from thee.

---

*a* assembled: *prob. rdg.; Heb. obscure.*      *b* O God ... power: *prob. rdg.; Heb.*
Your God your power.      *c See first note on verse 31.*      *d* precious ... Pathros:
*prob. rdg., transposed from verse 30 and slightly altered.*      *e* stretch out: *prob. rdg.;*
*Heb. obscure.*

6 Let none of those who look to thee be shamed on my account,
  O Lord God of Hosts;
 let none who seek thee be humbled through my fault,
  O God of Israel.

7 For in thy service I have suffered reproach;
 I dare not show my face for shame.

8 I have become a stranger to my brothers,
  an alien to my own mother's sons;

9 bitter enemies of thy temple tear me in pieces;[a]
 those who reproach thee reproach me.

10 I have broken my spirit with fasting,
 only to lay myself open to many reproaches.

11 I have made sackcloth my clothing
 and have become a byword among them.

12 Those who sit by the town gate talk about me;
 drunkards sing songs about me in their cups.

13 But I lift up this prayer to thee, O Lord:
 accept me[b] now in thy great love,
 answer me with thy sure deliverance, O God.

14 Rescue me from the mire, do not let me sink;
 let me be rescued from the muddy depths,[c]

15  so that no flood may carry me away,
  no abyss swallow me up,
  no deep close over me.

16 Answer me, O Lord, in the goodness of thy unfailing love,
 turn towards me in thy great affection.

17 I am thy servant, do not hide thy face from me.
 Make haste to answer me, for I am in distress.

18 Come near to me and redeem me;
 ransom me, for I have many enemies.

19 Thou knowest what reproaches I bear,
 all my anguish is seen by thee.

20 Reproach has broken my heart,
 my shame and my dishonour[d] are past hope;
 I looked for consolation and received none,
  for comfort and did not find any.

21 They put poison in my food
 and gave me vinegar when I was thirsty.

22 May their own table be a snare to them
 and their sacred feasts lure them to their ruin;

23 may their eyes be darkened so that they do not see,
 let a continual ague shake their loins.

24 Pour out thine indignation upon them
 and let thy burning anger overtake them.

---

[a] bitter ... pieces: *or* zeal for thy temple has eaten me up (*cp. John 2. 17*).   [b] *Prob. rdg.; Heb.* acceptance.   [c] from ... depths: *prob. rdg.; Heb.* from my haters and from the depths.   [d] my shame and my dishonour: *transposed from after* reproaches *in verse 19.*

May their settlements be desolate, 25
and no one living in their tents;
for they pursue him whom thou hast struck down 26
and multiply the torments of those whom thou hast wounded.
Give them the punishment their sin deserves;*a* 27
exclude them from thy righteous mercy;
let them be blotted out from the book of life 28
and not be enrolled among the righteous.

But by thy saving power, O God, lift me high 29
above my pain and my distress,
then I will praise God's name in song 30
and glorify him with thanksgiving;
that will please the LORD more than the offering of a bull, 31
a young bull with horn and cloven hoof.

See and rejoice, you humble folk, 32
take heart, you seekers after God;
for the LORD listens to the poor 33
and does not despise those bound to his service.
Let sky and earth praise him, 34
the seas and all that move in them,
for God will deliver Zion 35-36
and rebuild the cities of Judah.
His servants' children shall inherit them;
they shall dwell there in their own possession
and all who love his name shall live in them.

# 70

Show me favour,*b* O God, and save me; 1*c*
hasten to help me, O LORD.
Let all who seek my life be brought to shame and dismay, 2
let all who love to hurt me shrink back disgraced;
let those who cry 'Hurrah!' at my downfall 3
turn back at the shame they incur,
but let all who seek thee 4
be jubilant and rejoice in thee,
and let those who long for thy saving help ever cry,
'All glory to God!'

But I am poor and needy; 5
O God, hasten to my aid.
Thou art my help, my salvation;
O LORD, make no delay.

---

*a* Give them . . . deserves: *or* Add punishment to punishment. *b* Show me favour:
*prob. rdg., cp. Ps. 40. 13; Heb. om.* *c* *Verses 1–5: cp. Ps. 40. 13–17.*

# 71

1 In thee, O Lord, I have taken refuge;
  never let me be put to shame.
2 As thou art righteous rescue me and save my life;
  hear me and set me free,
3 be a rock of refuge for me,
  where I may ever find safety at thy call;
    for thou art my towering crag and stronghold.
4 O God, keep my life safe from the wicked,
    from the clutches of unjust and cruel men.

5 Thou art my hope, O Lord,
  my trust, O Lord, since boyhood.
6 From birth I have leaned upon thee,
  my protector since I left<sup>a</sup> my mother's womb.<sup>b</sup>
7 To many I seem a solemn warning;
  but I have thee for my strong refuge.
8 My mouth shall be full of thy praises,
    I shall tell of thy splendour all day long.
9 Do not cast me off when old age comes,
    nor forsake me when my strength fails,
10 when my enemies' rancour bursts upon me<sup>c</sup>
   and those who watch me whisper together,
11 saying, 'God has forsaken him;
   after him! seize him; no one will rescue him.'
12 O God, do not stand aloof from me;
   O my God, hasten to my help.
13 Let all my traducers be shamed and dishonoured,
   let all who seek my hurt be covered with scorn.
14 But I will wait in continual hope,
   I will praise thee again and yet again;
15   all day long thy righteousness,
     thy saving acts, shall be upon my lips.
   Thou shalt ever be the theme of my praise,<sup>d</sup>
   although I have not the skill of a poet.
16 I will begin with a tale of great deeds, O Lord God,
   and sing of thy righteousness, thine alone.
17 O God, thou hast taught me from boyhood,
   all my life I have proclaimed thy marvellous works;
18 and now that I am old and my hairs are grey,
     forsake me not, O God,
   when I extol thy mighty arm to future generations,
19   thy power and righteousness, O God, to highest heaven;
     for thou hast done great things.
   Who is like thee, O God?

---

<sup>a</sup> *my . . . left: or who didst bring me out from.*     <sup>b</sup> *See note on verse 15.*
<sup>c</sup> *enemies' . . . me: prob. rdg.; Heb. enemies say of me.*     <sup>d</sup> *Line transposed from verse 6.*

Thou hast made me pass through bitter and deep distress,          20
    yet dost revive me once again
and lift me again from earth's watery depths.
Restore me to honour, turn and comfort me,                        21
    then I will praise thee on the lute                          22
      for thy faithfulness, O God;
  I will sing psalms to thee with the harp,
    thou Holy One of Israel;
      songs of joy shall be on my lips;                     23
I will sing thee psalms, because thou hast redeemed me.
All day long my tongue shall tell of thy righteousness;           24
  shame and disgrace await those who seek my hurt.

# 72

O God, endow the king with thy own justice,                       1
    and give thy righteousness to a king's son,
  that he may judge thy people rightly                           2
    and deal out justice to the poor and suffering.
May hills and mountains afford thy people                         3
  peace and prosperity in righteousness.
  He shall give judgement for the suffering                     4
  and help those of the people that are needy;
  he shall crush the oppressor.
  He shall live as long as the sun endures,                     5
  long as the moon, age after age.
He shall be like rain falling on early crops,                     6
  like showers watering *a* the earth.
In his days righteousness shall flourish,                         7
prosperity abound until the moon is no more.
May he hold sway from sea to sea,                                 8
from the River to the ends of the earth.
Ethiopians shall crouch low before him;                          9
his enemies shall lick the dust.
The kings of Tarshish and the islands shall bring gifts,          10
the kings of Sheba and Seba shall present their tribute,
  and all kings shall pay him homage,                           11
  all nations shall serve him.
For he shall rescue the needy from their rich oppressors,         12
  the distressed who have no protector.
  May he have pity on the needy and the poor,                   13
    deliver the poor from death;
  may he redeem them from oppression and violence              14
  and may their blood be precious in his eyes.

  May the king live long                                        15
    and receive gifts of gold *b* from Sheba;

---

*a* like showers watering: *prob. rdg.; Heb. unintelligible.*    *b* Or frankincense.

　　　　prayer be made for him continually,
　　　　　　blessings be his all the day long.
16　　　May there be abundance of corn in the land,
　　　　　　growing in plenty to the tops of the hills;
　　　　may the crops flourish like Lebanon,
　　　　　　and the sheaves *a* be numberless as blades of grass.
17　　　Long may the king's name endure,
　　　　　　may it live for ever like the sun;
　　　　so shall all peoples pray to be blessed as he was,
　　　　　　all nations tell of his happiness.

18　　　Blessed be the Lord God, the God of Israel,
　　　　who alone does marvellous things;
19　　　blessed be his glorious name for ever,
　　　　and may his glory fill all the earth.
　　　　　　　　　　Amen, Amen.

20　　　Here end the prayers of David son of Jesse.

## BOOK 3

## 73

1　　　How good God is to the upright! *b*
　　　　How good to those who are pure in heart!

2　　　　My feet had almost slipped,
　　　　　　my foothold had all but given way,
3　　　　because the boasts of sinners roused my envy
　　　　　　when I saw how they prosper.
4　　　　No pain, no suffering is theirs;
　　　　　　they are sleek and sound in limb;
5　　　　they are not plunged in trouble as other men are,
　　　　　　nor do they suffer the torments of mortal men.
6　　　　Therefore pride is their collar of jewels
　　　　　　and violence the robe that wraps them round.
7　　　　Their eyes gleam through folds of fat;
　　　　　　while vain fancies pass through their minds.
8　　　　Their talk is all sneers and malice;
　　　　　　scornfully they spread their calumnies.
9　　　　Their slanders reach up to heaven,
　　　　　　while their tongues ply to and fro on earth.
10　　　And so my people follow their lead *c*
　　　　　　and find nothing to blame in them, *d*
11　　　even though they say, 'What does God know?
　　　　　　The Most High neither knows nor cares.'

*a* the sheaves: *prob. rdg.; Heb.* from a city.　　　*b* How . . . upright: *prob. rdg.; Heb.*
How good it is to Israel!　　*c* their lead: *prob. rdg.; Heb.* hither.　　*d* and find . . .
in them: *prob. rdg.; Heb. obscure.*

So wicked men talk, yet still they prosper,                    12
and rogues<sup>a</sup> amass great wealth.

So it was all in vain that I kept my heart pure               13
and washed my hands in innocence.
For all day long I suffer torment                             14
and am punished every morning.
Yet had I let myself talk on in this fashion,                 15
I should have betrayed the family of God.
So I set myself to think this out                             16
but I found it too hard for me,
until I went into God's sacred courts;                        17
there I saw clearly what their end would be.

How often thou dost set them on slippery ground              18
and drive them headlong into ruin!
Then in a moment how dreadful their end,                     19
cut off root and branch by death with all its terrors,
like a dream when a man rouses himself, O Lord,              20
like images in sleep which are dismissed on waking!

When my heart was embittered                                 21
I felt the pangs of envy,
I would not understand, so brutish was I,                    22
I was a mere beast in thy sight, O God.
Yet I am always with thee,                                   23
thou holdest my right hand;
thou dost guide me by thy counsel                            24
and afterwards wilt receive me with glory.
Whom have I in heaven but thee?                              25
And having thee,<sup>b</sup> I desire nothing else on earth.
Though heart and body fail,                                   26
yet God is my possession for ever.
They who are far from thee are lost;                         27
thou dost destroy all who wantonly forsake thee.
But my chief good is to be near thee, O God;                 28
I have chosen thee, Lord GOD, to be my refuge.<sup>c</sup>

## 74

Why hast thou cast us off, O God? Is it for ever?            1
Why art thou so stern, so angry with the sheep of thy flock?
Remember the assembly of thy people,                         2
taken long since for thy own,<sup>d</sup>
and Mount Zion, which was thy home.

---

<sup>a</sup> yet . . . rogues: *prob. rdg.; Heb.* those at ease for ever.     <sup>b</sup> *Or* And compared
with thee.     <sup>c</sup> *Prob. rdg.; Heb. adds* to tell all thy works.     <sup>d</sup> *Prob. rdg.; Heb.*
*adds* thou didst redeem the tribe of thy possession.

3      Now at last[a] restore what was ruined beyond repair,
      the wreck that the foe has made of thy sanctuary.

4        The shouts of thy enemies filled the holy place,[b]
        they planted their standards there as tokens of victory.

5        They brought it crashing down,[c]
          like woodmen plying their axes in the forest;

6        they ripped the carvings clean out,
        they smashed them with hatchet and pick.

7        They set fire to thy sanctuary,
        tore down and polluted the shrine sacred to thy name.

8      They said to themselves, 'We will sweep them away',
        and all over the land they burnt God's holy places.[d]

9      We cannot see what lies before us,[e] we have no prophet now;
      we have no one who knows how long this is to last.

10     How long, O God, will the enemy taunt thee?
     Will the adversary pour scorn on thy name for ever?

11       Why dost thou hold back thy hand,
       why keep thy right hand within thy bosom?

12       But thou, O God, thou king from of old,
         thou mighty conqueror all the world over,

13     by thy power thou didst cleave the sea-monster in two
        and break the sea-serpent's heads above the waters;

14        thou didst crush Leviathan's many heads
        and throw him to the sharks[f] for food.

15     Thou didst open channels for spring and torrent;
        thou didst dry up rivers never known to fail.

16     The day is thine, and the night is thine also,
     thou didst ordain the light of moon and sun;

17       thou hast fixed all the regions of the earth;
     summer and winter, thou didst create them both.

18     Remember, O LORD, the taunts of the enemy,
     the scorn a savage nation pours on thy name.

19     Cast not to the beasts the soul that confesses thee;
        forget not for ever the sufferings of thy servants.

20     Look upon thy creatures:[g] they are filled with hatred,
        and earth is the haunt of violence.

21       Let not the oppressed be shamed and turned away;
     let the poor and the downtrodden praise thy name.

22     Rise up, O God, maintain thy own cause;
        remember how brutal men taunt thee all day long.

23     Ignore no longer the cries of thy assailants,
     the mounting clamour of those who defy thee.

---

[a] Now at last: *prob. rdg.*; *Heb.* Thy steps.     [b] the holy place: *or* thy meeting place.
[c] They . . . down: *prob. rdg.*; *Heb. unintelligible.*    [d] holy places: *or* meeting places.
[e] what . . . us: *prob. rdg.*; *Heb.* our signs.     [f] to the sharks: *prob. rdg.*; *Heb.* to a
people, desert-dwellers.     [g] thy creatures: *prob. rdg.*; *Heb.* the covenant, because.

## 75

We give thee thanks, O God, we give thee thanks;                    1
   thy name is brought very near to us
   in the story of thy wonderful deeds.

   I seize the appointed time                                                        2
   and then I judge mankind with justice.
   When the earth rocks, with all who live on it,                      3
   I make its pillars firm.
   To the boastful I say, 'Boast no more',                                 4
   and to the wicked, 'Do not toss your proud horns:
   toss not your horns against high heaven                            5
   nor speak arrogantly against your Creator.'
   No power from the east nor from the west,                        6
   no power from the wilderness, can raise a man up.
      For God is judge;                                                      7
he puts one man down and raises up another.
   The LORD holds a cup in his hand,                                    8
and the wine foams in it, hot with spice;
he offers it to every man for drink,
and all the wicked on earth must drain it to the dregs.
   But I will glorify him for ever;                                            9
   I will sing praises to the God of Jacob.

   I will break off the horns of the wicked,                            10
   but the horns of the righteous shall be lifted high.

## 76

   In Judah God is known,                                                    1
   his name is great in Israel;
   his tent is pitched in Salem,                                              2
   in Zion his battle-quarters are set up.*a*
   He has broken the flashing arrows,                                    3
   shield and sword and weapons of war.

   Thou art terrible, O Lord, and mighty:                               4
   men that lust for plunder stand aghast,                              5
   the boldest swoon away,
   and the strongest cannot lift a hand.
      At thy rebuke, O God of Jacob,                               6
   rider and horse fall senseless.
   Terrible art thou, O Lord;                                                  7
   who can stand in thy presence when thou art angry?
   Thou didst give sentence out of heaven;                          8
   the earth was afraid and kept silence.

   *a* are set up: *prob. rdg.; Heb.* thither (*at beginning of verse 3*).

9   O God, at thy rising<sup>a</sup> in judgement
    to deliver all humble men on the earth,
10   for all her fury Edom shall confess thee,
    and the remnant left in Hamath shall dance in worship.

11   Make vows to the LORD your God, and pay them duly;
    let the peoples all around him bring their tribute; <sup>b</sup>
12   for he breaks the spirit of princes,
    he is the terror of the kings on earth.


# 77

1    I cried aloud to God,
   I cried to God, and he heard me.
2   In the day of my distress I sought the Lord,
   and by night I lifted<sup>c</sup> my outspread hands in prayer.
   I lay sweating and nothing would cool me;
   I refused all comfort.
3   When I called God to mind, I groaned;
   as I lay thinking, darkness came over my spirit.
4   My eyelids were tightly closed;
   I was dazed and I could not speak.
5   My thoughts went back to times long past,
    I remembered forgotten years;
6   all night long I was in deep distress,
   as I lay thinking, my spirit was sunk in despair.

7   Will the Lord reject us for evermore
    and never again show favour?
8   Has his unfailing love now failed us utterly,
   must his promise time and again be unfulfilled?
9   Has God forgotten to be gracious,
   has he in anger withheld his mercies?
10   'Has his right hand', I said, 'lost its grasp?
   Does it hang powerless,<sup>d</sup> the arm of the Most High?'

11   But then, O LORD, I call to mind thy deeds;<sup>e</sup>
   I recall thy wonderful acts in times gone by.
12    I meditate upon thy works
    and muse on all that thou hast done.
13   O God, thy way is holy;
   what god is so great as our God?
14   Thou art the God who workest miracles;
   thou hast shown the nations thy power.

---

<sup>a</sup> O God . . . rising: *prob. rdg.; Heb.* When God rises.  <sup>b</sup> *Prob. rdg.; Heb. adds* for
the terror (*cp. verse 12*).  <sup>c</sup> I lifted: *prob. rdg.; Heb. om.*  <sup>d</sup> lost . . . powerless:
*prob. rdg.; Heb. unintelligible.*  <sup>e</sup> *Prob. rdg.; Heb.* then I call to mind the deeds
of the LORD, for.

With thy strong arm thou didst redeem thy people,      15
     the sons of Jacob and Joseph.

The waters saw thee, O God,      16
     they saw thee and writhed in anguish;
     the ocean was troubled to its depths.
The clouds poured water, the skies thundered,      17
     thy arrows flashed hither and thither.
The sound of thy thunder was in the whirlwind, *a*      18
     thy lightnings lit up the world,
     earth shook and quaked.
Thy path was through the sea, thy way through mighty      19
       waters,
     and no man marked thy footsteps.
Thou didst guide thy people like a flock of sheep,      20
     under the hand of Moses and Aaron.

## 78

Mark my teaching, O my people,      1
listen to the words I am to speak.
I will tell you a story with a meaning,      2
I will expound the riddle of things past,
things that we have heard and know,      3
and our fathers have repeated to us.
From their sons we will not hide      4
the praises of the LORD and his might
nor the wonderful acts he has performed;
then they shall repeat them to the next generation.
He laid on Jacob a solemn charge      5
and established a law in Israel,
which he commanded our fathers
     to teach their sons,
that it might be known to a future generation,      6
     to children yet unborn,
and these would repeat it to their sons in turn.
He charged them to put their trust in God,      7
to hold his great acts ever in mind
     and to keep all his commandments;
not to do as their fathers did,      8
a disobedient and rebellious race,
a generation with no firm purpose,
with hearts not fixed steadfastly on God.

The men of Ephraim, bowmen all and marksmen,      9
     turned and ran in the hour of battle.

*a*   *Or* in the chariot-wheels.

| | |
|---|---|
| 10 | They had not kept God's covenant<br>and had refused to live by his law; |
| 11 | they forgot all that he had done<br>and the wonderful acts which he had shown them. |

| | |
|---|---|
| 12 | He did wonders in their fathers' sight<br>in the land of Egypt, the country of Zoan: |
| 13 | he divided the sea and took them through it,<br>making the water stand up like banks on either side. |
| 14 | He led them with a cloud by day<br>and all night long with a glowing fire. |
| 15 | He cleft the rock in the wilderness<br>and gave them water to drink, abundant as the sea; |
| 16 | he brought streams out of the cliff<br>and made water run down like rivers. |
| 17 | But they sinned against him yet again:<br>in the desert they defied the Most High, |
| 18 | they tried God's patience wilfully,<br>demanding food to satisfy their hunger. |
| 19 | They vented their grievance against God and said,<br>'Can God spread a table in the wilderness?' |
| 20 | When he struck a rock, water gushed out<br>until the gullies overflowed;<br>they said, 'Can he give bread as well,<br>can he provide meat for his people?' |
| 21 | When he heard this, the Lord was filled with fury:<br>fire raged against Jacob,<br>anger blazed up against Israel, |
| 22 | because they put no trust in God<br>and had no faith in his power to save. |
| 23 | Then he gave orders to the skies above<br>and threw open heaven's doors, |
| 24 | he rained down manna for them to eat<br>and gave them the grain of heaven. |
| 25 | So men ate the bread of angels;<br>he sent them food to their heart's desire. |
| 26 | He let loose the east wind from heaven<br>and drove the south wind by his power; |
| 27 | he rained meat like a dust-storm upon them,<br>flying birds like the sand of the sea-shore, |
| 28 | which he made settle all over the camp<br>round the tents where they lived. |
| 29 | So the people ate and were well filled,<br>for he had given them what they craved. |
| 30 | Yet they did not abandon their complaints[a]<br>even while the food was in their mouths. |
| 31 | Then the anger of God blazed up against them; |

[a] *Or* craving.

he spread death among their stoutest men
and brought the young men of Israel to the ground.

In spite of all, they persisted in their sin 32
and had no faith in his wonderful acts.
So in one moment he snuffed out their lives 33
and ended their years in calamity.
When he struck them, they began to seek him, 34
they would turn and look eagerly for God;
they remembered that God was their Creator, 35
that God Most High was their deliverer.
But still they beguiled him with words 36
and deceived him with fine speeches;
they were not loyal to him in their hearts 37
nor were they faithful to his covenant.
Yet he wiped out their guilt 38
and did not smother his own*a* natural affection;
often he restrained his wrath
and did not rouse his anger to its height.
He remembered that they were only mortal men, 39
who pass by like a wind and never return.

How often they rebelled against him in the wilderness 40
and grieved him in the desert!
Again and again they tried God's patience 41
and provoked the Holy One of Israel.
They did not remember his prowess 42
on the day when he saved them from the enemy,
how he set his signs in Egypt, 43
his portents in the land of Zoan.
He turned their streams into blood, 44
and they could not drink the running water.
He sent swarms of flies which devoured them, 45
and frogs which brought devastation;
he gave their harvest over to locusts 46
and their produce to the grubs;
he killed their vines with hailstones 47
and their figs with torrents of rain;
he abandoned their cattle to the plague 48
and their beasts to the arrows of pestilence.
He loosed upon them the violence of his anger, 49
wrath and enmity and rage,
launching those messengers of evil
to open a way for his fury. 50-51
He struck down all the first-born in Egypt,
the flower of their manhood in the tents of Ham,
not shielding their lives from death
but abandoning their bodies to the plague.

*a* his own: *prob. rdg.; Heb. om.*

| 52 | But he led out his own people like sheep |
| | and guided them like a flock in the wilderness. |
| 53 | He led them in safety and they were not afraid, |
| | and the sea closed over their enemies. |
| 54 | He brought them to his holy mountain, |
| | the hill which his right hand had won; |
| 55 | he drove out nations before them, |
| | he allotted their lands to Israel as a possession |
| | and settled his tribes in their dwellings. |
| 56 | Yet they tried God's patience and rebelled against him; |
| | they did not keep the commands of the Most High; |
| 57 | they were renegades, traitors like their fathers, |
| | they changed, they went slack like a bow. |
| 58 | They provoked him to anger with their hill-shrines |
| | and roused his jealousy with their carved images. |
| 59 | When God heard this, he put them out of mind |
| | and utterly rejected Israel. |
| 60 | He forsook his home at Shiloh, |
| | the tabernacle in which he dwelt among men; |
| 61 | he surrendered the symbol of his strength into captivity |
| | and his pride into enemy hands; |
| 62 | he gave his people over to the sword |
| | and put his own possession out of mind. |
| 63 | Fire devoured his young men, |
| | and his maidens could raise no lament for them; |
| 64 | his priests fell by the sword, |
| | and his widows could not weep. |
| 65 | Then the Lord awoke as a sleeper awakes, |
| | like a warrior heated with wine; |
| 66 | he struck his foes in the back parts |
| | and brought perpetual shame upon them. |
| 67 | He despised the clan of Joseph |
| | and did not choose the tribe of Ephraim; |
| 68 | he chose the tribe of Judah |
| | and Mount Zion which he loved; |
| 69 | he built his sanctuary high as the heavens, |
| | founded like the earth to last for ever. |
| 70 | He chose David to be his servant |
| | and took him from the sheepfolds; |
| 71 | he brought him from minding the ewes |
| | to be the shepherd of his people Jacob; [a] |
| 72 | and he shepherded them in singleness of heart |
| | and guided them with skilful hand. |

[a] *Prob. rdg.; Heb. adds* and Israel his possession.

## 79

O God, the heathen have set foot in thy domain,  1
    defiled thy holy temple
and laid Jerusalem in ruins.
    They have thrown out the dead bodies of thy servants  2
        to feed the birds of the air;
    they have made thy loyal servants carrion for wild beasts.
Their blood is spilled all round Jerusalem like water,  3
    and there they lie unburied.
    We suffer the contempt of our neighbours,  4
the gibes and mockery of all around us.

How long, O LORD, wilt thou be roused to such fury?  5
    Must thy jealousy rage like a fire?
Pour out thy wrath over nations which do not know thee  6
and over kingdoms which do not invoke thee by name;
see how they have devoured Jacob and laid waste his homesteads.  7
    Do not remember against us the guilt of past generations  8
    but let thy compassion come swiftly to meet us,
        we have been brought so low.

Help us, O God our saviour, for the honour of thy name;  9
    for thy name's sake deliver us and wipe out our sins.
Why should the nations ask, 'Where is their God?'  10
    Let thy vengeance for the bloody slaughter of thy servants
fall on those nations before our very eyes.

Let the groaning of the captives reach thy presence  11
    and in thy great might set free death's prisoners.
As for the contempt our neighbours pour on thee, O Lord,  12
    turn it back sevenfold on their own heads.
    Then we thy people, the flock which thou dost shepherd,  13
    will give thee thanks for ever
and repeat thy praise to every generation.

## 80

Hear us, O shepherd of Israel,  1
who leadest Joseph like a flock of sheep.
    Show thyself, thou that art throned on the cherubim,
    to Ephraim and to Benjamin.  2
    Rouse thy victorious might from slumber, *a*
    come to our rescue.
    Restore us, O God,  3
and make thy face shine upon us that we may be saved.
    O LORD God of Hosts,  4
how long wilt thou resist thy people's prayer?

      *a* from slumber: *prob. rdg.; Heb.* and Manasseh.

5　Thou hast made sorrow their daily bread
and tears of threefold grief their drink.

6　Thou hast humbled us before our neighbours,
and our enemies mock us to their hearts' content.

7　O God of Hosts, restore us;
make thy face shine upon us that we may be saved.

8　Thou didst bring a vine out of Egypt;
thou didst drive out nations and plant it;

9　thou didst clear the ground before it,
so that it made good roots and filled the land.

10　The mountains were covered with its shade,
and its branches were like those of mighty cedars.

11　It put out boughs all the way to the Sea
and its shoots as far as the River.

12　Why hast thou broken down the wall round it
so that every passer-by can pluck its fruit?

13　The wild boar from the thickets gnaws it,
and swarming insects from the fields feed on it.

14　O God of Hosts, once more look down from heaven,
take thought for this vine and tend it,

15　this stock that thy right hand has planted. [a]

16　Let them that set fire to it or cut it down
perish before thy angry face.

17　Let thy hand rest upon the man at thy right side,
the man whom thou hast made strong for thy service.

18　We have not turned back from thee,
so grant us new life, and we will invoke thee by name.

19　LORD God of Hosts, restore us;
make thy face shine upon us that we may be saved.

# 81

1　Sing out in praise of God our refuge, [b]
acclaim the God of Jacob.

2　Take pipe and tabor,
take tuneful harp and lute.

3　Blow the horn for the new month,
for the full moon on the day of our pilgrim-feast.

4　This is a law for Israel,
an ordinance of the God of Jacob,

5　laid as a solemn charge on Joseph
when he came out of Egypt. [c]

6　When I lifted the load from his shoulders,
his hands let go the builder's basket.

[a] *Prob. rdg.; Heb. adds* and on the son whom thou hast made strong for thy service
(*cp. verse 17*). 　[b] *Or* strength. 　[c] *Prob. rdg.; Heb. adds* I hear an unfamiliar
language.

When you cried to me in distress, I rescued you;     7
    unseen, I answered you in thunder.
I tested you at the waters of Meribah,
where I opened your mouths and filled them.*a*
I fed Israel*b* with the finest wheat-flour     16*c*
and satisfied him with honey from the rocks.
Listen, my people, while I give you a solemn charge—     8
do but listen to me, O Israel:
you shall have no strange god     9
nor bow down to any foreign god;
I am the LORD your God     10
    who brought you up from Egypt.*d*
But my people did not listen to my words     11
and Israel would have none of me;
    so I sent them off, stubborn as they were,     12
    to follow their own devices.

If my people would but listen to me,     13
if Israel would only conform to my ways,
I would soon bring their enemies to their knees     14
and lay a heavy hand upon their persecutors.
Let those who hate them*e* come cringing to them,     15
and meet with everlasting troubles.*f*

## 82

God takes his stand in the court of heaven     1
    to deliver judgement among the gods themselves.

How long will you judge unjustly     2
    and show favour to the wicked?
You ought to give judgement for the weak and the orphan,     3
    and see right done to the destitute and downtrodden,
you ought to rescue the weak and the poor,     4
    and save them from the clutches of wicked men.
    But you know nothing, you understand nothing,     5
    you walk in the dark
    while earth's foundations are giving way.
This is my sentence: Gods you may be,     6
    sons all of you of a high god,*g*
yet you shall die as men die;*h*     7
princes fall, every one of them, and so shall you.

Arise, O God, and judge the earth;     8
    for thou dost pass all nations through thy sieve.

---

*a* *Line transposed from end of verse 10.*    *b* I fed Israel: *prob. rdg.; Heb.* He fed him.
*c* *Verse transposed.*    *d* *See note on verse 7.*    *e* those . . . them: *prob. rdg.; Heb.*
those who hate the LORD.    *f* *Verse 16 transposed to follow verse 7.*    *g* *Or of the*
*Most High.*    *h* *Or as Adam died.*

## 83

1 Rest not, O God;
  O God, be neither silent nor still,
2 for thy enemies are making a tumult,
  and those that hate thee carry their heads high.
3 They devise cunning schemes against thy people
  and conspire against those thou hast made thy treasure:
4 'Come, away with them,' they cry,
  'let them be a nation no longer,
  let Israel's name be remembered no more.'
5 With one mind they have agreed together
  to make a league against thee:
6 the families of Edom, the Ishmaelites,
  Moabites and Hagarenes,
7 Gebal, Ammon and Amalek,
  Philistia and the citizens of Tyre,
8 Asshur too their ally,
  all of them lending aid to the descendants of Lot.
9 Deal with them as with Sisera,
  as with Jabin by the torrent of Kishon,
10 who fell vanquished as Midian[a] fell at En-harod,[b]
   and were spread on the battlefield like dung.
11 Make their princes like Oreb and Zeeb,
   make all their nobles like Zebah and Zalmunna;
12 for they said, 'We will seize for ourselves
   all the pastures of God's people.'
13 Scatter them, O God, like thistledown,
   like chaff before the wind.
14 Like fire raging through the forest
   or flames which blaze across the hills,
15 hunt them down with thy tempest,
   and dismay them with thy storm-wind.
16 Heap shame upon their heads, O LORD,
   until they confess the greatness of thy name.
17 Let them be abashed, and live in perpetual dismay;
   let them feel their shame and perish.
18 So let them learn that thou alone art LORD,
   God Most High over all the earth.

## 84

1 How dear is thy dwelling-place,
    thou LORD of Hosts!
2 I pine, I faint with longing
    for the courts of the LORD's temple;

---

[a] as Midian: *transposed from previous verse.*   [b] En-harod: *prob. rdg., cp. Judg. 7. 1;*
*Heb.* Endor.

my whole being cries out with joy
  to the living God.
Even the sparrow finds a home, 3
  and the swallow has her nest,
where she rears her brood beside thy altars,
  O LORD of Hosts, my King and my God.
Happy are those who dwell in thy house; 4
  they never cease from praising thee.
Happy the men whose refuge is in thee, 5
  whose hearts are set on the pilgrim ways *a*!
As they pass through the thirsty valley 6
  they find water from a spring;
and the LORD provides even men who lose their way
  with pools to quench their thirst. *b*
So they pass on from outer wall to inner, 7
  and the God of gods shows himself in Zion.

O LORD God of Hosts, hear my prayer; 8
  listen, O God of Jacob.
O God, look upon our lord the king 9
  and accept thy anointed prince with favour.

Better one day in thy courts 10
  than a thousand days at home;
better to linger by the threshold of God's house
  than to live in the dwellings of the wicked.
The LORD God is a battlement and a shield; 11
  grace and honour are his to give.
The LORD will hold back no good thing
  from those whose life is blameless.

  O LORD of Hosts, 12
happy the man who trusts in thee!

## 85

LORD, thou hast been gracious to thy land 1
  and turned the tide of Jacob's fortunes.
Thou hast forgiven the guilt of thy people 2
  and put away all their sins.
Thou hast taken back all thy anger 3
  and turned from thy bitter wrath.

Turn back to us, O God our saviour, 4
  and cancel thy displeasure.
Wilt thou be angry with us for ever? 5
  Must thy wrath last for all generations?

*a* are set . . . ways: *or high praises fill.*    *b* they find . . . thirst: *prob. rdg.; Heb.*
*obscure.*

6      Wilt thou not give us new life
         that thy people may rejoice in thee?
7      O Lord, show us thy true love
         and grant us thy deliverance.

8      Let me hear the words of the Lord:
         are they not [a] words of peace,
            peace to his people and his loyal servants
         and to all who turn and trust in him?
9      Deliverance is near to those who worship him,
            so that glory may dwell in our land.
10     Love and fidelity have come together;
         justice and peace join hands.
11     Fidelity springs up from earth
         and justice looks down from heaven.
12     The Lord will add prosperity,
         and our land shall yield its harvest.
13     Justice shall go in front of him
         and the path before his feet shall be peace. [b]

# 86

1      Turn to me, Lord, and answer;
         I am downtrodden and poor.
2      Guard me, for I am constant and true;
         save thy servant who puts his trust in thee.
3      O Lord my God, [c] show me thy favour;
         I call to thee all day long.
4      Fill thy servant's heart with joy, O Lord,
         for I lift up my heart to thee.
5      Thou, O Lord, art kind and forgiving,
         full of true love for all who cry to thee.
6      Listen, O Lord, to my prayer
         and hear my pleading.
7      In the day of my distress I call on thee;
         for thou wilt answer me.

8      Among the gods not one is like thee, O Lord,
         no deeds are like thine.
9      All the nations thou hast made, O Lord, will come,
         will bow down before thee and honour thy name;
10     for thou art great, thy works are wonderful,
         thou alone art God.

11     Guide me, O Lord,
         that I may be true to thee and follow thy path;

---

[a] of the Lord: are they not: *prob. rdg.; Heb.* of God the Lord.     [b] and the path . . .
peace: *prob. rdg.; Heb.* so that he may put his feet to the way.     [c] my God: *trans-posed from previous verse.*

    let me be one in heart
    with those who revere thy name.
I will praise thee, O Lord my God, with all my heart     12
    and honour thy name for ever.
    For thy true love stands high above me;     13
thou hast rescued my soul from the depths of Sheol.
O God, proud men attack me;     14
    a mob of ruffians seek my life
      and give no thought to thee.
Thou, Lord, art God, compassionate and gracious,     15
    forbearing, ever constant and true.
    Turn towards me and show me thy favour;     16
    grant thy slave protection
      and rescue thy slave-girl's son.
Give me proof of thy kindness;     17
    let those who hate thee see to their shame
that thou, O Lord, hast been my help and comfort.

## 87 *a*

    The Lord loves the gates of Zion     1-2
      more than all the dwellings of Jacob;
      her *b* foundations are laid upon holy hills,
    and he has made her his home. *c*     4-5
I will count Egypt and Babylon among my friends;
Philistine, Tyrian and Nubian shall be *d* there;
    and Zion shall be called a mother
    in whom men of every race are born.
    The Lord shall write against each in the roll of nations:     6
    'This one was born in her.'
Singers and dancers alike all chant *e* your praises,     7
proclaiming glorious things of you, O city of God.     3

## 88

    O Lord, my God, by day I call for help, *f*     1
    by night I cry aloud in thy presence.
    Let my prayer come before thee,     2
    hear my loud lament;
    for I have had my fill of woes,     3
    and they have brought me to the threshold of Sheol.

---

*a The text of this psalm is disordered, and several verses have been re-arranged.*   *b Prob.*
*rdg.; Heb.* his.   *c* his home: *prob. rdg.; Heb.* most high.   *d Prob. rdg.; Heb. adds*
this one was born (*cp. verse 6*).   *e* all chant: *prob. rdg.; Heb.* all my springs.
*f* I call for help: *prob. rdg.; Heb.* my deliverance.

4    I am numbered with those who go down to the abyss
     and have become like a man beyond help,

5     like a man who lies dead *a*
     or the slain who sleep in the grave,
    whom thou rememberest no more
    because they are cut off from thy care.

6     Thou hast plunged me into the lowest abyss,
     in dark places, in the depths.

7    Thy wrath rises against me,
    thou hast turned on me the full force of thy anger. *b*

8    Thou hast taken all my friends far from me,
    and made me loathsome to them.
     I am in prison and cannot escape;

9    my eyes are failing and dim with anguish.
    I have called upon thee, O LORD, every day
    and spread out my hands in prayer to thee.

10    Dost thou work wonders for the dead?
    Shall their company rise up and praise thee?

11    Will they speak of thy faithful love in the grave,
     of thy sure help in the place of Destruction?

12    Will thy wonders be known in the dark,
     thy victories in the land of oblivion?

13    But, LORD, I cry to thee,
     my prayer comes before thee in the morning.

14    Why hast thou cast me off, O LORD,
     why dost thou hide thy face from me?

15    I have suffered from boyhood and come near to death;
     I have borne thy terrors, I cower beneath thy blows.

16    Thy burning fury has swept over me,
     thy onslaughts have put me to silence;

17    all the day long they surge round me like a flood,
     they engulf me in a moment.

18    Thou hast taken lover and friend far from me,
     and parted me from my companions.

## 89

1    I will sing the story of thy love, O LORD, for ever;
    I will proclaim thy faithfulness to all generations.

2    Thy true love is firm as the ancient earth, *c*
    thy faithfulness fixed as the heavens.

5 *d*   The heavens praise thy wonders, O LORD,
    and the council of the holy ones exalts thy faithfulness.

---

*a* who lies dead: *prob. rdg.; Heb. obscure.*  *b* anger: *or* waves.  *c* Thy . . .
earth: *prob. rdg.; Heb.* Thou hast said for ever true love shall be made firm. *d Verses
3 and 4 transposed to follow* servants *in verse 19.*

In the skies who is there like the LORD,          6
    who like the LORD in the court of heaven,
      like God who is dreaded among the assembled holy ones,      7
      great and terrible above all who stand about him?
O LORD God of Hosts, who is like thee?          8
Thy strength*ᵃ* and faithfulness, O LORD, surround thee.
    Thou rulest the surging sea,          9
    calming the turmoil*ᵇ* of its waves.
Thou didst crush the monster Rahab with a mortal blow      10
    and scatter thy enemies with thy strong arm.
Thine are the heavens, the earth is thine also;      11
the world with all that is in it is of thy foundation.
Thou didst create Zaphon and Amanus;*ᶜ*      12
Tabor and Hermon echo thy name.
    Strength of arm and valour are thine;      13
thy hand is mighty, thy right hand lifted high;
    thy throne is built upon righteousness and justice,      14
true love and faithfulness herald thy coming.

    Happy the people who have learnt to acclaim thee,      15
    who walk, O LORD, in the light of thy presence!
In thy name they shall rejoice all day long;      16
    thy righteousness shall lift them up.
Thou art thyself the strength in which they glory;      17
    through thy favour we hold our heads high.
    The LORD, he is our shield;      18
    the Holy One of Israel, he is our king.

    Then didst thou announce in a vision      19
and declare to thy faithful servants:
    I have made a covenant with him I have chosen,      3
    I have sworn to my servant David:
'I will establish your posterity for ever,      4
I will make your throne endure for all generations.'
I have endowed a warrior with princely gifts,
so that the youth I have chosen towers over his people.
I have discovered David my servant;      20
    I have anointed him with my holy oil.
My hand shall be ready to help him      21
    and my arm to give him strength.
No enemy shall strike at him      22
    and no rebel bring him low;
I will shatter his foes before him      23
    and vanquish those who hate him.
My faithfulness and true love shall be with him      24
and through my name he shall hold his head high.

---

*ᵃ* Thy strength: *prob. rdg.; Heb. obscure.*          *ᵇ* turmoil: *prob. rdg.; Heb. obscure.*
*ᶜ* Amanus: *prob. rdg.; Heb.* right hand *or* south.

25            I will extend his rule over the Sea
                and his dominion as far as the River.

26            He will say to me, 'Thou art my father,
                my God, my rock and my safe refuge.'

27            And I will name him my first-born,
                highest among the kings of the earth.

28            I will maintain my love for him for ever
                and be faithful in my covenant with him.

29            I will establish his posterity for ever
                and his throne as long as the heavens endure.

30            If his sons forsake my law
                and do not conform to my judgements,

31               if they renounce my statutes
                and do not observe my commands,

32            I will punish their disobedience with the rod
                and their iniquity with lashes.

33            Yet I will not deprive him of my true love
                nor let my faithfulness prove false;

34               I will not renounce my covenant
                nor change my promised purpose.

35            I have sworn by my holiness once and for all,
                I will not break my word to David:

36            his posterity shall continue for ever,
                his throne before me like the sun;

37               it shall be sure for ever as the moon's return,
                faithful so long as the skies remain.*a*

38            Yet thou hast rejected thy anointed king,
                thou hast spurned him and raged against him,*b*

39            thou hast denounced the covenant with thy servant,
                defiled his crown and flung it to the ground.

40            Thou hast breached his walls
                and laid his fortresses in ruin;

41            all who pass by plunder him,
                and he suffers the taunts of his neighbours.

42               Thou hast increased the power of his enemies
                and brought joy to all his foes;

43               thou hast let his sharp sword be driven back
                and left him without help in the battle.

44               Thou hast put an end to his glorious rule*c*
                and hurled his throne to the ground;

45            thou hast cut short the days of his youth and vigour
                and covered him with shame.

46            How long, O LORD, wilt thou hide thyself from sight?
                How long must thy wrath blaze like fire?

---

*a* so long . . . remain: *prob. rdg.*; *Heb.* a witness in the skies.    *b* raged against him:
*or* put him out of mind.    *c* his glorious rule: *prob. rdg.*; *Heb.* from his purity.

Remember that I shall not live for ever; *a*                    47
hast thou created man in vain?
What man shall live and not see death                    48
or save himself from the power of Sheol?
Where are those former acts of thy love, O Lord,                    49
those faithful promises given to David?
Remember, O Lord, the taunts hurled at thy servant,                    50
how I have borne in my heart the calumnies of the nations; *b*
so have thy enemies taunted us, O LORD,                    51
taunted the successors of thy anointed king.

Blessed is the LORD for ever.                    52
        Amen, Amen.

## BOOK 4

## 90

Lord, thou hast been our refuge                    1
   from generation to generation.
Before the mountains were brought forth,                    2
or earth and world were born in travail,
from age to age everlasting thou art God.
   Thou turnest man back into dust;                    3
   'Turn back,' thou sayest, 'you sons of men';
for in thy sight a thousand years are as yesterday;                    4
a night-watch passes, and thou hast cut them off;                    5
they are like a dream at daybreak,
they fade like grass which springs up *c* with the morning                    6
but when evening comes is parched and withered.
So we are brought to an end by thy anger                    7
   and silenced by thy wrath.
   Thou dost lay bare our iniquities before thee                    8
   and our lusts in the full light of thy presence.
All our days go by under the shadow of thy wrath;                    9
our years die away like a murmur.
Seventy years is the span of our life,                    10
   eighty if our strength holds; *d*
the hurrying years are labour and sorrow,
so quickly they pass and are forgotten.
Who feels the power of thy anger,                    11
who feels thy wrath like those that fear thee?
Teach us to order our days rightly,                    12
   that we may enter the gate of wisdom.

*a* live for ever: *prob. rdg.; Heb. obscure.*        *b* the calumnies . . . nations: *prob. rdg.;*
*Heb.* all of many peoples.        *c Prob. rdg.; Heb. adds* and passes away.        *d Or* eighty
at the most.

13    How long, O LORD?
      Relent, and take pity on thy servants.
14    Satisfy us with thy love when morning breaks,
      that we may sing for joy and be glad all our days.
15    Repay us days of gladness for our days of suffering,
      for the years thou hast humbled us.
16    Show thy servants thy deeds
      and their children thy majesty.
17    May all delightful things be ours, O Lord our God;
      establish firmly all we do.

## 91

1     You that live in the shelter of the Most High
      and lodge under the shadow of the Almighty,
2     who say, 'The LORD is my safe retreat,
      my God the fastness in which I trust';
3         he himself will snatch you away
          from fowler's snare or raging tempest.
4     He will cover you with his pinions,
          and you shall find safety beneath his wings;
5     you shall not fear the hunters' trap by night
      or the arrow that flies by day,
6     the pestilence that stalks in darkness
      or the plague raging at noonday.
7     A thousand may fall at your side,
          ten thousand close at hand,
          but you it shall not touch;
          his truth*a* will be your shield and your rampart.*b*
8     With your own eyes you shall see all this;
          you shall watch the punishment of the wicked.
9     For you, the LORD is a*c* safe retreat;
      you have made the Most High your refuge.
10    No disaster shall befall you,
      no calamity shall come upon your home.
11    For he has charged his angels
          to guard you wherever you go,
12        to lift you on their hands
      for fear you should strike your foot against a stone.
13    You shall step on asp and cobra,
      you shall tread safely on snake and serpent.

14    Because his love is set on me, I will deliver him;
      I will lift him beyond danger, for he knows me by my name.
15        When he calls upon me, I will answer;
      I will be with him in time of trouble;
          I will rescue him and bring him to honour.

---

*a Or his arm.*      *b his truth . . . rampart: transposed from end of verse 4.*
*c Prob. rdg.; Heb. my.*

I will satisfy him with long life                               16
to enjoy the fullness of my salvation.

## 92

O LORD, it is good to give thee thanks,                          1
to sing psalms to thy name, O Most High,
to declare thy love in the morning                               2
    and thy constancy every night,
    to the music of a ten-stringed lute,                         3
    to the sounding chords of the harp.
Thy acts, O LORD, fill me with exultation;                       4
    I shout in triumph at thy mighty deeds.
How great are thy deeds, O LORD!                                 5
How fathomless thy thoughts!

He who does not know this is a brute,                            6
a fool is he who does not understand this:
that though the wicked grow like grass                           7
and every evildoer prospers,
    they will be destroyed for ever.
While thou, LORD, dost reign on high eternally,                  8
    thy foes will surely perish,                                 9
    all evildoers will be scattered.

I lift my head high, like a wild ox tossing its horn;            10
    I am anointed richly with oil.
    I gloat over all who speak ill of me,                        11
I listen for the downfall of my cruel foes.
    The righteous flourish like a palm-tree,                     12
    they grow tall as a cedar on Lebanon;
        planted as they are in the house of the LORD,            13
        they flourish in the courts of our God,
    vigorous in old age like trees full of sap,                  14
        luxuriant, wide-spreading,
    eager to declare that the LORD is just,                      15
    the LORD my rock,*a* in whom there is no unrighteousness.

## 93

The LORD is king; he is clothed in majesty;                      1
the LORD clothes himself with might and fastens on his belt of wrath.

Thou hast fixed the earth immovable and firm,
    thy throne firm from of old;                                 2
    from all eternity thou art God.
O LORD, the ocean lifts up, the ocean lifts up its clamour;      3
    the ocean lifts up*b* its pounding waves.

*a* Or creator.      *b* the ocean lifts up: *or* let the ocean lift up.

4     The LORD on high is mightier far
      than the noise of great waters,
      mightier than the breakers of the sea.

5     Thy law stands firm, and holiness is the beauty of thy temple,
      while time shall last, O LORD.

## 94

1     O LORD, thou God of vengeance,
      thou God of vengeance, show thyself.
2     Rise up, judge of the earth;
      punish the arrogant as they deserve.
3     How long shall the wicked, O LORD,
      how long shall the wicked exult?
4     Evildoers are full of bluster,
      boasting and swaggering;
5     they beat down thy people, O LORD,
      and oppress thy chosen nation;
6     they murder the widow and the stranger
      and do the fatherless to death;
7     they say, 'The LORD does not see,
      the God of Jacob pays no heed.'
8     Pay heed yourselves, most brutish of the people;
      you fools, when will you be wise?
9     Does he that planted the ear not hear,
      he that moulded the eye not see?
10    Shall not he that instructs the nations correct them?
      The teacher of mankind, has he no*a* knowledge?
11    The LORD knows the thoughts of man,
      that they are but a puff of wind.

12    Happy the man whom thou dost instruct, O LORD,
      and teach out of thy law,
13    giving him respite from adversity
      until a pit is dug for the wicked.
14    The LORD will not abandon his people
      nor forsake his chosen nation;
15    for righteousness still informs his judgement,*b*
      and all upright men follow it.

16    Who is on my side against these sinful men?
      Who will stand up for me against these evildoers?
17    If the LORD had not been my helper,
      I should soon have slept in the silent grave.
18    When I felt that my foot was slipping,
      thy love, O LORD, held me up.

---

*a* no: *prob. rdg.; Heb. om.*     *b* for . . . judgement: *prob. rdg.; Heb.* for judgement
will return as far as righteousness.

Anxious thoughts may fill my heart,                                    19
but thy presence is my joy and my consolation.
Shall sanctimonious calumny call thee partner,                         20
or he that contrives a mischief under cover of law?
For they put the righteous on trial*a* for his life                    21
and condemn to death innocent men.
But the LORD has been my strong tower,                                 22
and God my rock of refuge;
our God requites the wicked for their injustice,                       23
the LORD puts them to silence for their misdeeds.

### 95

Come! Let us raise a joyful song to the LORD,                          1
a shout of triumph to the Rock of our salvation.
Let us come into his presence with thanksgiving,                       2
and sing him psalms of triumph.
For the LORD is a great God,                                           3
a great king over all gods;
the farthest places of the earth are in his hands,                     4
and the folds of the hills are his;
the sea is his, he made it;                                            5
the dry land fashioned by his hands is his.
Come! Let us throw ourselves at his feet in homage,                    6
let us kneel before the LORD who made us;
for he is our God,                                                     7
we are his people, we the flock he shepherds.
You shall know*b* his power today
if you will listen to his voice.

Do not grow stubborn, as you were at Meribah,*c*                       8
as at the time of Massah*d* in the wilderness,
when your forefathers challenged me,                                   9
tested me and saw for themselves all that I did.
For forty years I was indignant                                        10
with that generation, and I said:
They are a people whose hearts are astray,
and they will not discern my ways.
As I swore in my anger:                                                11
They shall never enter my rest.

### 96

Sing a new song to the LORD;                                           1*e*
sing to the LORD, all men on earth.

---

*a* they put . . . trial: *prob. rdg.; Heb.* they cut the righteous.     *b* You shall know:
*prob. rdg.; Heb. om.*     *c That is* Dispute.     *d That is* Challenge.     *e Verses
1-13: cp. 1 Chr. 16. 23-33.*

2          Sing to the LORD and bless his name,
               proclaim his triumph day by day.
3          Declare his glory among the nations,
               his marvellous deeds among all peoples.
4          Great is the LORD and worthy of all praise;
               he is more to be feared than all gods.
5          For the gods of the nations are idols every one;
               but the LORD made the heavens.
6          Majesty and splendour attend him,
               might and beauty are in his sanctuary.

7          Ascribe to the LORD, you families of nations,
           ascribe to the LORD glory and might;
8              ascribe to the LORD the glory due to his name,
           bring a gift and come into his courts.
9          Bow down to the LORD in the splendour of holiness, *a*
               and dance in his honour, all men on earth.
10         Declare among the nations, 'The LORD is king.
               He has fixed the earth firm, immovable;
               he will judge the peoples justly.'
11         Let the heavens rejoice and the earth exult,
               let the sea roar and all the creatures in it,
12             let the fields exult and all that is in them;
               then let all the trees of the forest shout for joy
13         before the LORD when he comes to judge the earth.
               He will judge the earth with righteousness
               and the peoples in good faith.

## 97

1          The LORD is king, let the earth be glad,
               let coasts and islands all rejoice.
2          Cloud and mist enfold him,
                   righteousness and justice
                   are the foundation of his throne.
3          Fire goes before him
               and burns up his enemies all around.
4          The world is lit up beneath his lightning-flash;
               the earth sees it and writhes in pain.
5          The mountains melt like wax as the LORD approaches,
               the Lord of all the earth.
6          The heavens proclaim his righteousness,
               and all peoples see his glory.
7          Let all who worship images, who vaunt their idols,
                   be put to shame;
               bow down, all gods, *b* before him.

*a* the splendour of holiness: *or* holy vestments.          *b* bow . . . gods: *or* all gods
bow down . . .

Zion heard and rejoiced, the cities of Judah were glad 8
  at thy judgements, O LORD.
For thou, LORD, art most high over all the earth, 9
  far exalted above all gods.

The LORD loves*a* those who hate evil; 10
  he keeps his loyal servants safe
  and rescues them from the wicked.
A harvest of light is sown for the righteous, 11
  and joy for all good men.
You that are righteous, rejoice in the LORD 12
  and praise his holy name.

## 98

Sing a new song to the LORD, 1
  for he has done marvellous deeds;
his right hand and holy arm have won him victory.
  The LORD has made his victory known; 2
  he has displayed his righteousness to all the nations.
    He has remembered his constancy, 3
    his love for the house of Israel.
All the ends of the earth have seen
    the victory of our God.

Acclaim the LORD, all men on earth, 4
  break into songs of joy, sing psalms.
Sing psalms in the LORD's honour with the harp, 5
  with the harp and with the music of the psaltery.
    With trumpet and echoing horn 6
  acclaim the presence of the LORD our king.
Let the sea roar and all its creatures, 7
    the world and those who dwell in it.
Let the rivers clap their hands, 8
  let the hills sing aloud together
before the LORD; for he comes 9
    to judge the earth.
He will judge the world with righteousness
    and the peoples in justice.

## 99

The LORD is king, the peoples are perturbed; 1
he is throned on the cherubim, earth quivers.
  The LORD is great in Zion; 2
  he is exalted above all the peoples.

---

*a* The LORD loves: *prob. rdg.; Heb.* Lovers of the LORD.

3    They extol his *a* name as great and terrible;
4    he is holy, he is mighty,
        a king who loves justice.

     Thou hast established justice and equity;
     thou hast dealt righteously in Jacob.
5        Exalt the LORD our God,
            bow down before his footstool;
            he is holy.

6        Moses and Aaron among his priests,
            and Samuel among those who call on his name,
     called to the LORD, and he answered.
7        He spoke to them in a pillar of cloud;
     they followed his teaching and kept the law he gave them.
8        Thou, O LORD our God, thou didst answer them;
     thou wast a God who forgave all their misdeeds
            and held them innocent.
9        Exalt the LORD our God,
            bow down towards his holy hill;
            for the LORD our God is holy.

## 100

1        Acclaim the LORD, all men on earth,
2            worship the LORD in gladness;
     enter his presence with songs of exultation.
3        Know that the LORD is God;
     he has made us and we are his own,
            his people, the flock which he shepherds.
4        Enter his gates with thanksgiving
            and his courts with praise.
     Give thanks to him and bless his name;
5        for the LORD is good and his love is everlasting,
            his constancy endures to all generations.

## 101

1        I sing of loyalty and justice;
     I will raise a psalm to thee, O LORD.*b*

2        I will follow a wise and blameless course,
     whatever may befall me.*c*
     I will go about my house in purity of heart.
3        I will set before myself no sordid aim;
     I will hate disloyalty, I will have none of it.

---

*a* *Prob. rdg.; Heb.* thy.        *b* I sing ... O LORD: *or* I will follow a course of justice
and loyalty; I will hold thee in awe, O LORD.        *c* whatever may befall me: *prob.
rdg.; Heb.* when comest thou to me?

I will reject all crooked thoughts;        4
     I will have no dealings with evil.
I will silence those who spread tales behind mens' backs,    5
I will not sit at table with proud, pompous men,
I will choose the most loyal for my companions;     6
my servants shall be men whose lives are blameless.
No scandal-monger shall live in my household;      7
no liar shall set himself up where I can see him.
Morning after morning I will put all wicked men to silence    8
and will rid the LORD's city of all evildoers.

## 102

LORD, hear my prayer             1
and let my cry for help reach thee.
Hide not thy face from me         2
when I am in distress.
Listen to my prayer
and, when I call, answer me soon;
for my days vanish like smoke,        3
my body is burnt up as in an oven.
I am stricken, withered like grass;      4
I cannot find the strength to eat.
Wasted away,[a] I groan aloud       5
and my skin hangs on my bones.
I am like a desert-owl in the wilderness,     6
an owl that lives among ruins.
Thin and meagre, I wail in solitude,     7
like a bird that flutters on the roof-top.
My enemies insult me all the day long;     8
mad with rage, they conspire against me.
I have eaten ashes for bread        9
and mingled tears with my drink.
    In thy wrath and fury         10
     thou hast taken me up and flung me aside.
My days decline as the shadows lengthen,     11
and like grass I wither away.

But thou, LORD, art enthroned for ever     12
and thy fame shall be known to all generations.
Thou wilt arise and have mercy on Zion;     13
for the time is come[b] to pity her.
Her very stones are dear to thy servants,     14
and even her dust moves them with pity.
Then shall the nations revere thy name, O LORD,    15
and all the kings of the earth thy glory,

---

    [a] Wasted away: *transposed from previous verse.*
    [b] *Prob. rdg.; Heb. adds* season.

16     when the LORD builds up Zion again
      and shows himself in his glory.

17     He turns to hear the prayer of the destitute
      and does not scorn them when they pray.

18     This shall be written down for future generations,
    and a people yet unborn shall praise the LORD.

19     The LORD looks down from his sanctuary on high,
      from heaven he surveys the earth

20         to listen to the groaning of the prisoners
      and set free men under sentence of death;

21     so shall the LORD's name be on men's lips in Zion
      and his praise shall be told in Jerusalem,

22     when peoples are assembled together,
    peoples and kingdoms, to serve the LORD.

23     My strength is broken in mid course;
24     the time allotted me is short.
      Snatch me not away before half my days are done,
      for thy years last through all generations.

25     Long ago thou didst lay the foundations of the earth,
      and the heavens were thy handiwork.

26     They shall pass away, but thou endurest;
      like clothes they shall all grow old;
        thou shalt cast them off like a cloak,
        and they shall vanish;

27     but thou art the same and thy years shall have no end;
28         thy servants' children shall continue,
    and their posterity shall be established in thy presence.

## 103

1     Bless the LORD, my soul;
      my innermost heart, bless his holy name.

2     Bless the LORD, my soul,
      and forget none of his benefits.

3       He pardons all my guilt
      and heals all my suffering.

4     He rescues me from the pit of death
    and surrounds me with constant love,
      with tender affection;

5     he contents me with all good in the prime of life,
    and my youth is ever new like an eagle's.

6     The LORD is righteous in his acts;
      he brings justice to all who have been wronged.

7     He taught Moses to know his way
      and showed the Israelites what he could do.

8     The LORD is compassionate and gracious,
      long-suffering and for ever constant;

he will not always be the accuser                           9
 or nurse his anger for all time.
He has not treated us as our sins deserve                   10
or requited us for our misdeeds.
For as the heaven stands high above the earth,             11
so his strong love stands high over all who fear him.
 Far as east is from west,                            12
so far has he put our offences away from us.
 As a father has compassion on his children,         13
so has the LORD compassion on all who fear him.
For he knows how we were made,                             14
he knows full well that we are dust.

Man's days are like the grass;                             15
he blossoms like the flowers of the field:
a wind passes over them, and they cease to be,             16
and their place knows them no more.
But the LORD's love never fails those who fear him;        17
 his righteousness never fails their sons and their grandsons
who listen to his voice *a* and keep his covenant,         18
 who remember his commandments and obey them.

The LORD has established his throne in heaven,             19
his kingly power over the whole world.
Bless the LORD, all his angels,                            20
 creatures of might who do his bidding.
Bless the LORD, all his hosts,                             21
 his ministers who serve his will.
Bless the LORD, all created things,                        22
 in every place where he has dominion.

Bless the LORD, my soul.

## 104

Bless the LORD, my soul:                                    1
O LORD my God, thou art great indeed,
clothed in majesty and splendour,
and wrapped in a robe of light.                             2
Thou hast spread out the heavens like a tent
and on their waters laid the beams of thy pavilion;        3
who takest the clouds for thy chariot,
riding on the wings of the wind;
who makest the winds thy messengers                        4
and flames of fire thy servants;
thou didst fix the earth on its foundation                 5
so that it never can be shaken;

 *a* who listen to his voice: *transposed from end of verse 20.*

| | |
|---|---|
| 6 | the deep overspread it like a cloak, |
| | and the waters lay above the mountains. |
| 7 | At thy rebuke they ran, |
| | at the sound of thy thunder they rushed away, |
| 8 | flowing over the hills, |
| | pouring down into the valleys |
| | to the place appointed for them. |
| 9 | Thou didst fix a boundary which they might not pass; |
| | they shall not return to cover the earth. |
| 10 | Thou dost make springs break out in the gullies, |
| | so that their water runs between the hills. |
| 11 | The wild beasts all drink from them, |
| | the wild asses quench their thirst; |
| 12 | the birds of the air nest on their banks |
| | and sing among the leaves. |
| 13 | From thy high pavilion thou dost water the hills; |
| | the earth is enriched by thy provision. |
| 14 | Thou makest grass grow for the cattle |
| | and green things for those who toil for man, |
| | bringing bread out of the earth |
| 15 | and wine to gladden men's hearts, |
| | oil to make their faces shine |
| | and bread to sustain their strength. |
| 16 | The trees of the LORD are green and leafy, |
| | the cedars of Lebanon which he planted; |
| 17 | the birds build their nests in them, |
| | the stork makes her home in their tops.*a* |
| 18 | High hills are the haunt of the mountain-goat, |
| | and boulders a refuge for the rock-badger. |
| 19 | Thou hast made the moon to measure the year |
| | and taught the sun where to set. |
| 20 | When thou makest darkness and it is night, |
| | all the beasts of the forest come forth; |
| 21 | the young lions roar for prey, |
| | seeking their food from God. |
| 22 | When thou makest the sun rise, they slink away |
| | and go to rest in their lairs; |
| 23 | but man comes out to his work |
| | and to his labours until evening. |
| 24 | Countless are the things thou hast made, O LORD. |
| | Thou hast made all by thy wisdom; |
| | and the earth is full of thy creatures, |
| 25 | beasts great and small. |

*a* in their tops: *prob. rdg.; Heb.* the pine-trees.

Here is the great immeasurable sea,
   in which move creatures beyond number.
Here ships sail to and fro,                                    26
here is Leviathan whom thou hast made thy plaything.*a*

   All of them look expectantly to thee                   27
   to give them their food at the proper time;
   what thou givest them they gather up;                  28
   when thou openest thy hand, they eat their fill.
   Then thou hidest thy face, and they are restless and troubled;   29
   when thou takest away their breath, they fail
   [and they return to the dust from which they came];
but when thou breathest into them, they recover;              30
   thou givest new life to the earth.

   May the glory of the LORD stand for ever              31
   and may he rejoice in his works!
   When he looks at the earth, it quakes;                32
   when he touches the hills, they pour forth smoke.

   I will sing to the LORD as long as I live,           33
   all my life I will sing psalms to my God.
   May my meditation please the LORD,                   34
   as I show my joy in him!
   Away with all sinners from the earth                 35
   and may the wicked be no more!

Bless the LORD, my soul.

   O praise the LORD.

## 105

Give the LORD thanks and invoke him by name,                 1*b*
   make his deeds known in the world around.
Pay him honour with song and psalm                           2
   and think upon all his wonders.
Exult in his hallowed name;                                  3
   let those who seek the LORD be joyful in heart.
   Turn to the LORD, your strength,                     4
   seek his presence always.
   Remember the wonders that he has wrought,            5
   his portents and the judgements he has given,
O offspring of Abraham his servant, O chosen sons of Jacob.  6

   He is the LORD our God;                              7
   his judgements fill the earth.

---

*a* thy plaything: *or* that it may sport in it.    *b* *Verses 1–15: cp. 1 Chr. 16. 8–22.*

8   He called to mind his covenant from long ago,<sup>a</sup>
    the promise he extended to a thousand generations—
9       the covenant made with Abraham,
        his oath given to Isaac,
10  the decree by which he bound himself for Jacob,
    his everlasting covenant with Israel:
11  'I will give you the land of Canaan', he said,
        'to be your possession, your patrimony.'
12      A small company it was,
    few in number, strangers in that land,
13  roaming from nation to nation,
    from one kingdom to another;
14  but he let no one ill-treat them,
    for their sake he admonished kings:
15      'Touch not my anointed servants,
        do my prophets no harm.'

16  He called down famine on the land
    and cut short their daily bread.
17  But he had sent on a man before them,
    Joseph, who was sold into slavery;
18  he was kept a prisoner with fetters on his feet
    and an iron collar clamped on his neck.
19  He was tested by the LORD's command
    until what he foretold came true.
20  Then the king sent and set him free,
        the ruler of nations released him;
21  he made him master of his household
        and ruler over all his possessions,
22  to correct his officers at will
        and teach his counsellors wisdom.
23  Then Israel too went down into Egypt
    and Jacob came to live in the land of Ham.
24  There God made his people very fruitful,
        he made them stronger than their enemies,
25  whose hearts he turned to hatred of his people
        and double-dealing with his servants.
26  He sent his servant Moses
    and Aaron whom he had chosen.
27  They were his mouthpiece to announce his signs,
        his portents in the land of Ham.
28  He sent darkness, and all was dark,
    but still they resisted his commands.
29  He turned their waters into blood
        and killed all their fish.
30  Their country swarmed with frogs,
        even their princes' inner chambers.

<sup>a</sup>  from long ago: *or* for ever.

At his command came swarms of flies      31
    and maggots the whole land through.
He changed their rain into hail      32
    and flashed fire over their country.
He blasted their vines and their fig-trees      33
    and splintered the trees throughout the land.
At his command came locusts,      34
    hoppers past all number,
they consumed every green thing in the land,      35
    consumed all the produce of the soil.
Then he struck down all the first-born in Egypt,      36
    the firstfruits of their manhood;
he led Israel out, laden with silver and gold,      37
    and among all their tribes no man fell.
The Egyptians were glad when they went,      38
    for fear of Israel had taken hold of them.
He spread a cloud as a screen,      39
    and fire to light up the night.
They asked, and he sent them quails,      40
    he gave them bread from heaven in plenty.
He opened a rock and water gushed out,      41
    a river flowing in a parched land;
for he had remembered his solemn promise      42
    given to his servant Abraham.
So he led out his people rejoicing,      43
    his chosen ones in triumph.
He gave them the lands of heathen nations      44
and they took possession where others had toiled,
    so that they might keep his statutes      45
    and obey his laws.

O praise the LORD.

## 106

O praise the LORD.      1

It is good to give thanks to the LORD;
    for his love endures for ever.
Who will tell of the LORD's mighty acts      2
    and make his praises heard?
    Happy are they who act justly      3
    and do right at all times!
Remember me, LORD, when thou showest favour to thy people,      4
    look upon me when thou savest them,
    that I may see the prosperity of thy chosen,      5
rejoice in thy nation's joy and exult with thy own people.

We have sinned like our forefathers,      6
we have erred and done wrong.

| 7  | Our fathers in Egypt took no account of thy marvels, |
|    | they did not remember thy many acts of faithful love, |
|    | but in spite of all*a* they rebelled by the Red Sea.*b* |
| 8  | Yet the LORD delivered them for his name's sake |
|    | and so made known his mighty power. |
| 9  | He rebuked the Red Sea and it dried up, |
|    | he led his people through the deeps as through the wilderness. |
| 10 | So he delivered them from those who hated them, |
|    | and claimed them back from the enemy's hand. |
| 11 | The waters closed over their adversaries, |
|    | not one of them survived. |
| 12 | Then they believed his promises and sang praises to him. |
|    | |
| 13 | But they quickly forgot all he had done |
|    | and would not wait to hear his counsel; |
| 14 | their greed was insatiable in the wilderness, |
|    | they tried God's patience in the desert. |
| 15 | He gave them what they asked |
|    | but sent a wasting sickness among them. *c* |
|    | |
| 16 | They were envious of Moses in the camp, |
|    | and of Aaron, who was consecrated to the LORD. |
| 17 | The earth opened and swallowed Dathan, |
|    | it closed over the company of Abiram; |
| 18 | fire raged through their company, |
|    | the wicked perished in flames. |
|    | |
| 19 | At Horeb they made a calf |
|    | and bowed down to an image; |
| 20 | they exchanged their Glory*d* |
|    | for the image of a bull that feeds on grass. |
| 21 | They forgot God their deliverer, |
|    | who had done great deeds in Egypt, |
| 22 | marvels in the land of Ham, |
|    | terrible things at the Red Sea. |
| 23 | So his purpose was to destroy them, |
|    | but Moses, the man he had chosen, |
|    | threw himself into the breach |
|    | to turn back his wrath lest it destroy them. |
|    | |
| 24 | They made light of the pleasant land, |
|    | disbelieving his promise; |
| 25 | they muttered treason in their tents |
|    | and would not obey the LORD. |
| 26 | So with uplifted hand he swore |
|    | to strike them down in the wilderness, |

*a* in spite of all: *prob. rdg.; Heb. obscure.*     *b* *Or* the Sea of Reeds.     *c* among them: *or* in their throats.     *d* their Glory: *or* the glory of God (*cp. Jer. 2. 11; Romans 1. 23*).

to scatter their descendants among the nations 27
and disperse them throughout the world.

They joined in worshipping the Baal of Peor 28
and ate meat sacrificed to lifeless gods.
Their deeds provoked the LORD to anger, 29
and plague broke out amongst them;
but Phinehas stood up and interceded, 30
so the plague was stopped.
This was counted to him as righteousness 31
throughout all generations for ever.

They roused the LORD to anger at the waters of Meribah, 32
and Moses suffered because of them;
for they had embittered his spirit 33
and he had spoken rashly.

They did not destroy the peoples round about, 34
as the LORD had commanded them to do,
but they mingled with the nations, 35
learning their ways;
they worshipped their idols 36
and were ensnared by them.
Their sons and their daughters 37
they sacrificed to foreign demons;
they shed innocent blood, 38
the blood of sons and daughters
offered to the gods of Canaan,
and the land was polluted with blood.
Thus they defiled themselves by their conduct 39
and they followed their lusts and broke faith with God.
Then the LORD grew angry with his people 40
and loathed them, his own chosen nation;
so he gave them into the hands of the nations, 41
and they were ruled by their foes;
their enemies oppressed them 42
and made them subject to their power.
Many times he came to their rescue, 43
but they were disobedient and rebellious still.*a*
And yet, when he heard them wail and cry aloud, 44
he looked with pity on their distress;
he called to mind his covenant with them 45
and, in his boundless love, relented;
he roused compassion for them 46
in the hearts of all their captors.

*a Prob. rdg.; Heb. adds* and were brought low by their guilt.

47        Deliver us, O LORD our God,
         and gather us in from among the nations
         that we may give thanks to thy holy name
         and make thy praise our pride.

48        Blessed be the LORD the God of Israel
         from everlasting to everlasting;
         and let all the people say 'Amen.'

       O praise the LORD.

# BOOK 5

## 107

1        It is good to give thanks to the LORD,
         for his love endures for ever.
2        So let them say who were redeemed by the LORD,
         redeemed by him from the power of the enemy
3          and gathered out of every land,
       from east and west, from north and south.

4        Some lost their way in desert wastes;
         they found no road to a city to live in;
5          hungry and thirsty,
         their spirit sank within them.
6        So they cried to the LORD in their trouble,
         and he rescued them from their distress;
7        he led them by a straight and easy way
         until they came to a city to live in.
8        Let them thank the LORD for his enduring love
         and for the marvellous things he has done for men:
9        he has satisfied the thirsty
         and filled the hungry with good things.

10       Some sat in darkness, dark as death,
         prisoners bound fast in iron,
11       because they had rebelled against God's commands
         and flouted the purpose of the Most High.
12       Their spirit was subdued by hard labour;
         they stumbled and fell with none to help them.
13       So they cried to the LORD in their trouble,
         and he saved them from their distress;
14       he brought them out of darkness, dark as death,
         and broke their chains.
15       Let them thank the LORD for his enduring love
         and for the marvellous things he has done for men:

he has shattered doors of bronze,                                16
    bars of iron he has snapped in two.

Some were fools, they took to rebellious ways,                   17
    and for their transgression they suffered punishment.
They sickened at the sight of food                               18
    and drew near to the very gates of death.
So they cried to the LORD in their trouble,                      19
    and he saved them from their distress;
he sent his word to heal them                                    20
    and bring them alive out of the pit of death.*a*
Let them thank the LORD for his enduring love                    21
    and for the marvellous things he has done for men.
Let them offer sacrifices of thanksgiving                        22
    and recite his deeds with shouts of joy.

Others there are who go to sea in ships                          23
    and make their living on the wide waters.
These men have seen the acts of the LORD                         24
    and his marvellous doings in the deep.
At his command the storm-wind rose                               25
    and lifted the waves high.
Carried up to heaven, plunged down to the depths,                26
    tossed to and fro in peril,
they reeled and staggered like drunken men,                      27
    and their seamanship was all in vain.
So they cried to the LORD in their trouble,                      28
    and he brought them out of their distress.
The storm sank to a murmur                                       29
    and the waves of the sea were stilled.
They were glad then that all was calm,                           30
    as he guided them to the harbour they desired.
Let them thank the LORD for his enduring love                    31
    and for the marvellous things he has done for men.
Let them exalt him in the assembly of the people                 32
    and praise him in the council of the elders.

He turns rivers into desert                                      33
    and springs of water into thirsty ground;
he turns fruitful land into salt waste,                          34
    because the men who dwell there are so wicked.
Desert he changes into standing pools,                           35
    and parched land into springs of water.
There he gives the hungry a home,                                36
    and they build themselves a city to live in;
they sow fields and plant vineyards                              37
    and reap a fruitful harvest.

    *a* alive . . . death: *prob. rdg.; Heb.* from their corruption.

38   He blesses them and their numbers increase,
  and he does not let their herds lose strength.
39   Tyrants[a] lose their strength and are brought low
  in the grip of misfortune and sorrow;
40   he brings princes into contempt
  and leaves them wandering in a trackless waste.
41   But the poor man he lifts clear of his troubles
  and makes families increase like flocks of sheep.
42   The upright see it and are glad,
  while evildoers are filled with disgust.
43   Let the wise man lay these things to heart,
  and ponder the record of the LORD's enduring love.

## 108

1[b]  My heart is steadfast, O God,
  my heart is steadfast.
 I will sing and raise a psalm;
  awake,[c] my spirit,
2  awake, lute and harp,
  I will awake at dawn of day.[d]
3 I will confess thee, O LORD, among the peoples,
  among the nations I will raise a psalm to thee;
4 for thy unfailing love is wider than the heavens
  and thy truth reaches to the skies.
5 Show thyself, O God, high above the heavens;
  let thy glory shine over all the earth.
6[e]  Deliver those that are dear to thee;
  save with thy right hand and answer.

7 God has spoken from his sanctuary:[f]
  'I will go up now and measure out Shechem;
  I will divide the valley of Succoth into plots;
8 Gilead and Manasseh are mine;
 Ephraim is my helmet, Judah my sceptre;
9 Moab is my wash-bowl, I fling my shoes at Edom;
  Philistia is the target of my anger.'

10   Who can bring me to the impregnable city,
  who can guide me to Edom,
11   since thou, O God, hast abandoned us
  and goest not forth with our armies?
12   Grant us help against the enemy,
  for deliverance by man is a vain hope.
13   With God's help we shall do valiantly,
  and God himself will tread our enemies under foot.

## 109

O God of my praise, be silent no longer,                                          1
    for wicked men heap calumnies upon me.                     2
They have lied to my face
    and ringed me round with words of hate.                     3
They have attacked me without a cause*a*
    and accused me though I have done nothing unseemly.*b*       4
They have repaid me evil for good                                                 5
    and hatred in return for my love.
They say, 'Put up some rascal to denounce him,                                    6
    an accuser to stand at his right side.'
But when judgement is given, that rascal will be exposed                          7
    and his follies accounted a sin.
May his days be few;                                                              8
    may his hoarded wealth*c* fall to another!
May his children be fatherless,                                                   9
    his wife a widow!
May his children be vagabonds and beggars,                                        10
    driven from their homes!
May the money-lender distrain on all his goods                                    11
    and strangers seize his earnings!
May none remain loyal to him,                                                     12
    and none have mercy on his fatherless children!
May his line be doomed to extinction,                                             13
    may their name be wiped out within a generation!
May the sins of his forefathers be remembered                                     14
    and his mother's wickedness never be wiped out!
May they remain on record before the LORD,                                        15
    but may he extinguish their name from the earth!
For that man never set himself                                                    16
    to be loyal to his friend
but persecuted the downtrodden and the poor
    and hounded the broken-hearted to their death.
Curses he loved: may the curse fall on him!                                       17
He took no pleasure in blessing: may no blessing be his!
He clothed himself in cursing like a garment:                                     18
may it seep into his body like water
    and into his bones like oil!
May it wrap him round like the clothes he puts on,                                19
    like the belt which he wears every day!
May the LORD so requite my accusers                                               20
    and those who speak evil against me!

But thou, O LORD God,                                                             21
    deal with me as befits thy honour;

---

*a Prob. rdg.; Heb. adds* in return for my love.    *b* though . . . unseemly: *prob. rdg.;*
*Heb. obscure.*    *c* hoarded wealth: *or* charge, *cp. Acts 1. 20.*

in the goodness of thy unfailing love deliver me,
22 for I am downtrodden and poor,
and my heart within me is distracted.
23 I fade like a passing shadow,
I am shaken off like a locust.
24 My knees are weak with fasting
and my flesh wastes away, so meagre is my fare.
25 I have become the victim of their taunts;
when they see me they toss their heads.
26 Help me, O LORD my God;
save me, by thy unfailing love,
27 that men may know this is thy doing
and thou alone, O LORD, hast done it.
28 They may curse, but thou dost bless;
may my opponents be put to shame,
but may thy servant rejoice!
29 May my accusers be clothed with dishonour,
wrapped in their shame as in a cloak!
30 I will lift up my voice to extol the LORD,
and before a great company I will praise him.
31 For he stands at the poor man's right side
to save him from his adversaries. *a*

# 110

1 The LORD said to my lord,
'You shall sit *b* at my right hand
when *c* I make your enemies the footstool under your feet.'
2 When the LORD from Zion hands you the sceptre, the symbol of your power,
march forth through the ranks of *d* your enemies.
3 At birth *e* you were endowed with princely gifts
and *f* resplendent *g* in holiness.
You have shone with the dew of youth since your mother bore you.
4 The LORD has sworn and will not change his purpose:
'You are a priest for ever,
in the succession of Melchizedek.'
5 The Lord at your right hand
has broken kings in the day of his anger.
6 So the king in his majesty, *h* sovereign of a mighty land,
will punish nations; *i*
7 he will drink from the torrent beside the path
and therefore will hold his head high.

*a* Prob. rdg.; *Heb.* his judges.    *b* You shall sit: *or* Sit.    *c* Or until *or* while.
*d* Or reign in the midst of.    *e* At birth: *or* On the day of your power.    *f* you
were . . . and: *or* your people offered themselves willingly; *mng. of Heb. uncertain.*    *g* Or
apparelled.    *h* So . . . majesty: *poss. rdg.; Heb.* full of corpses, he crushed.
*i* So . . . nations: *or* He shall punish the nations—heaps of corpses, broken heads—over
a wide expanse.

# 111

O praise the LORD. 1

With all my heart will I praise the LORD
in the company of good men, in the whole congregation.
Great are the doings of the LORD; 2
all men study them for their delight.
His acts are full of majesty and splendour; 3
righteousness is his for ever.
He has won a name by his marvellous deeds; 4
the LORD is gracious and compassionate.
He gives food to those who fear him, 5
he keeps his covenant always in mind.
He showed his people what his strength could do, 6
bestowing on them the lands of other nations.
His works are truth and justice; 7
his precepts all stand on firm foundations,
strongly based to endure for ever, 8
their fabric goodness and truth.
He sent and redeemed his people; 9
he decreed that his covenant should always endure.
Holy is his name, inspiring awe.
The fear of the LORD is the beginning *a* of wisdom, 10
and they who live by it grow in understanding.
Praise will be his for ever.

# 112

O praise the LORD. 1

Happy is the man who fears the LORD
and finds great joy in his commandments.
His descendants shall be the mightiest in the land, 2
a blessed generation of good men.
His house shall be full of wealth and riches; 3
righteousness shall be his for ever.
He is gracious, compassionate, good, 4
a beacon in darkness for honest men.
It is right for a man to be gracious in his lending, 5
to order his affairs with judgement.
Nothing shall ever shake him; 6
his goodness shall be remembered for all time.
Bad news shall have no terrors for him, 7
because his heart is steadfast, trusting in the LORD.
His confidence is strongly based, he will have no fear; 8
and in the end he will gloat over his enemies.

*a* *Or* chief part.

9          He gives freely to the poor;
              righteousness shall be his for ever;
              in honour he carries his head high.
10         The wicked man shall see it with rising anger
              and grind his teeth in despair;
              the hopes of wicked men shall come to nothing.


## 113

1              O praise the LORD.

              Praise the LORD, you that are his servants,
                 praise the name of the LORD.
2              Blessed be the name of the LORD
                 now and evermore.
3              From the rising of the sun to its setting
                 may the LORD's name be praised.
4              High is the LORD above all nations,
                 his glory above the heavens.
5-6            There is none like the LORD our God
                 in heaven or on earth,
              who sets his throne so high
                 but deigns to look down so low;
7              who lifts the weak out of the dust
                 and raises the poor from the dunghill,
8              giving them a place among princes,
                 among the princes of his people;
9              who makes the woman in a childless house
                 a happy mother of children.*a*


## 114

1              O praise the LORD.*b*

              When Israel came out of Egypt,
                 Jacob from a people of outlandish speech,
2              Judah became his sanctuary,
                 Israel his dominion.
3              The sea looked and ran away;
                 Jordan turned back.
4              The mountains skipped like rams,
                 the hills like young sheep.
5              What was it, sea? Why did you run?
                 Jordan, why did you turn back?
6              Why, mountains, did you skip like rams,
                 and you, hills, like young sheep?

*a*  O praise the LORD *transposed to the beginning of Ps. 114.*          *b  See note*
*on Ps. 113. 9.*

Dance, O earth, at the presence of the Lord,   7
    at the presence of the God of Jacob,
who turned the rock into a pool of water,   8
    the granite cliff into a fountain.


# 115

Not to us, O LORD, not to us,   1
    but to thy name ascribe the glory,
    for thy true love and for thy constancy.

Why do the nations ask,   2
    'Where then is their God?'
Our God is in high heaven;   3
    he does whatever pleases him.
Their idols are silver and gold,   4
    made by the hands of men.
They have mouths that cannot speak,   5
    and eyes that cannot see;
they have ears that cannot hear,   6
    nostrils, and cannot smell;
with their hands they cannot feel,   7
    with their feet they cannot walk,
    and no sound comes from their throats.
Their makers grow to be like them,   8
    and so do all who trust in them.

But Israel trusts in the LORD;   9
    he is their helper and their shield.
The house of Aaron trusts in the LORD;   10
    he is their helper and their shield.
Those who fear the LORD trust in the LORD;   11
    he is their helper and their shield.
The LORD remembers us, and he will bless us;   12
    he will bless the house of Israel,
    he will bless the house of Aaron.
The LORD will bless all who fear him,   13
    high and low alike.

May the LORD give you increase,   14
    both you and your sons.
You are blessed by the LORD,   15
    the LORD who made heaven and earth.
The heavens, they are the LORD's;   16
    the earth he has given to all mankind.
It is not the dead who praise the LORD,   17
    not those who go down into silence;

18      but we, the living, bless the LORD,
            now and for evermore.

        O praise the LORD.

# 116

1       I love the LORD, for he has heard me
            and listens to my prayer;
2       for he has given me a hearing
            whenever I have cried to him.
3       The cords of death bound me,
            Sheol held me in its grip.
        Anguish and torment held me fast;
4           so I invoked the LORD by name,
        'Deliver me, O LORD, I beseech thee;
            for I am thy slave.' *a*
5       Gracious is the LORD and righteous,
            our God is full of compassion.
6       The LORD preserves the simple-hearted;
            I was brought low and he saved me.
7       Be at rest once more, my heart,
            for the LORD has showered gifts upon you.
8       He has rescued me from death
            and my feet from stumbling.
9       I will walk in the presence of the LORD
            in the land of the living.

10      I was sure that I should be swept away,
            and my distress was bitter.
11      In panic I cried,
            'How faithless all men are!'
12      How can I repay the LORD
            for all his gifts to me?
13      I will take in my hands the cup of salvation
            and invoke the LORD by name.
14      I will pay my vows to the LORD
            in the presence of all his people.
15      A precious thing in the LORD's sight
            is the death of those who die faithful to him.
16      *b* I am thy slave, thy slave-girl's son;
            thou hast undone the bonds that bound me.
17      To thee will I bring a thank-offering
            and invoke the LORD by name.
18      I will pay my vows to the LORD
            in the presence of all his people,

---

*a* for . . . slave: *transposed from the beginning of verse 16; Heb. adds* O LORD.
*b* *Prob. rdg.; Heb. prefixes* For I am thy slave, O LORD; *see note on verse 4.*

in the courts of the LORD's house,⠀⠀⠀⠀⠀⠀⠀⠀⠀19
⠀⠀in the midst of you, Jerusalem.

⠀O praise the LORD.

## 117

Praise the LORD, all nations,⠀⠀⠀⠀⠀⠀⠀⠀⠀1
⠀⠀extol him, all you peoples;
for his love protecting us is strong,⠀⠀⠀⠀⠀2
⠀⠀the LORD's constancy is everlasting.

⠀O praise the LORD.

## 118

It is good to give thanks to the LORD,⠀⠀⠀⠀1
⠀⠀for his love endures for ever.
Declare it, house of Israel:⠀⠀⠀⠀⠀⠀⠀⠀2
⠀⠀his love endures for ever.
Declare it, house of Aaron:⠀⠀⠀⠀⠀⠀⠀⠀3
⠀⠀his love endures for ever.
Declare it, you that fear the LORD:⠀⠀⠀⠀4
⠀⠀his love endures for ever.
When in my distress I called to the LORD,⠀⠀5
⠀⠀his answer was to set me free.
The LORD is on my side, I have no fear;⠀⠀6
⠀⠀what can man do to me?
The LORD is on my side, he is my helper,⠀⠀7
⠀⠀and I shall gloat over my enemies.
It is better to find refuge in the LORD⠀⠀⠀8
⠀⠀than to trust in men.
It is better to find refuge in the LORD⠀⠀⠀9
⠀⠀than to trust in princes.
All nations surround me,⠀⠀⠀⠀⠀⠀⠀⠀10
⠀⠀but in the LORD's name I will drive them away.
They surround me on this side and on that,⠀⠀11
⠀⠀but in the LORD's name I will drive them away.
They surround me like bees at the honey;⠀⠀12
⠀⠀they attack me, as fire attacks brushwood,
⠀⠀but in the LORD's name I will drive them away.
They thrust hard against me so that I nearly fall;⠀13
⠀⠀but the LORD has helped me.
The LORD is my refuge and defence,⠀⠀⠀⠀14
⠀⠀and he has become my deliverer.
Hark! Shouts of deliverance⠀⠀⠀⠀⠀⠀15
⠀⠀in the camp of the victors[a]!

⠀⠀⠀⠀⠀[a] *Or* righteous.

> With his right hand the LORD does mighty deeds,
> 16      the right hand of the LORD raises up.
> 17   I shall not die but live
>      to proclaim the works of the LORD.
> 18   The LORD did indeed chasten me,
>      but he did not surrender me to Death.
>
> 19   Open to me the gates of victory; [a]
>      I will enter by them and praise the LORD.
> 20   This is the gate of the LORD;
>      the victors [b] shall make their entry through it.
> 21   I will praise thee, for thou hast answered me
>      and hast become my deliverer.
> 22   The stone which the builders rejected
>      has become the chief corner-stone.
> 23   This is the LORD's doing;
>      it is marvellous in our eyes.
> 24   This is the day on which the LORD has acted: [c]
>      let us exult and rejoice in it.
> 25   We pray thee, O LORD, deliver us;
>      we pray thee, O LORD, send us prosperity.
> 26   Blessed in the name of the LORD are all who come;
>      we bless you from the house of the LORD.
> 27   The LORD is God; he has given light to us,
>      the ordered line of pilgrims by the horns of the altar.
> 28   Thou art my God and I will praise thee;
>      my God, I will exalt thee.
> 29   It is good to give thanks to the LORD,
>      for his love endures for ever.

# 119

> 1   Happy are they whose life is blameless,
>      who conform to the law of the LORD.
> 2   Happy are they who obey his instruction,
>      who set their heart on finding him;
> 3   who have done no wrong
>      and have lived according to his will.
> 4   Thou, Lord, hast laid down thy precepts
>      for men to keep them faithfully.
> 5   If only I might hold a steady course,
>      keeping thy statutes!
> 6   I shall never be put to shame
>      if I fix my eyes on thy commandments.
> 7   I will praise thee in sincerity of heart
>      as I learn thy just decrees.

[a] *Or* righteousness.      [b] *Or* righteous.      [c] *Or* which the LORD has made.

Thy statutes will I keep faithfully; 8
　O do not leave me forsaken.

How shall a young man steer an honest course? 9
　By holding to thy word.
With all my heart I strive to find thee; 10
　let me not stray from thy commandments.
I treasure thy promise in my heart, 11
　for fear that I might sin against thee.
Blessed art thou, O LORD; 12
　teach me thy statutes.
I say them over, one by one, 13
　the decrees that thou hast proclaimed.
I have found more joy along the path of thy instruction 14
　than in any kind of wealth.
I will meditate on thy precepts 15
　and keep thy paths ever before my eyes.
In thy statutes I find continual delight; 16
　I will not forget thy word.

Grant this to me, thy servant: let me live 17
　and, living, keep thy word.
Take the veil from my eyes, that I may see 18
　the marvels that spring from thy law.
I am but a stranger here on earth,[a] 19
　do not hide thy commandments from me.
My heart pines with longing 20
　day and night for thy decrees.
The proud have felt thy rebuke; 21
　cursed are those who turn from thy commandments.
Set me free from scorn and insult, 22
　for I have obeyed thy instruction.
The powers that be sit scheming together against me; 23
　but I, thy servant, will study thy statutes.
Thy instruction is my continual delight; 24
　I turn to it for counsel.

I lie prone in the dust; 25
　grant me life according to thy word.
I tell thee all I have done and thou dost answer me; 26
　teach me thy statutes.
Show me the way set out in thy precepts, 27
　and I will meditate on thy wonders.
I cannot rest for misery; 28
　renew my strength in accordance with thy word.
Keep falsehood far from me 29
　and grant me the grace of living by thy law.

　　　　　*a Or in the land.*

30   I have chosen the path of truth
        and have set thy decrees before me.
31   I hold fast to thy instruction;
        O LORD, let me not be put to shame.
32   I will run the course set out in thy commandments,
        for they gladden my heart.

33   Teach me, O LORD, the way set out in thy statutes,
        and in keeping them I shall find my reward.
34   Give me the insight to obey thy law
        and to keep it with all my heart;
35   make me walk in the path of thy commandments,
        for that is my desire.
36   Dispose my heart toward thy instruction
        and not toward ill-gotten gains;
37   turn away my eyes from all that is vile,
        grant me life by thy word.
38   Fulfil thy promise for thy servant,
        the promise made to those who fear thee.
39   Turn away the censure which I dread,
        for thy decrees are good.
40   How I long for thy precepts!
        In thy righteousness grant me life.

41   Thy love never fails; let it light on me, O LORD,
        and thy deliverance, for that was thy promise;
42   then I shall have my answer to the man who taunts me,
        because I trust in thy word.
43   Rob me not of my power to speak the truth,
        for I put my hope in thy decrees.
44   I will heed thy law continually,
        for ever and ever;
45   I walk in freedom wherever I will,
        because I have studied thy precepts.
46   I will speak of thy instruction before kings
        and will not be ashamed;
47   in thy commandments I find continuing delight;
        I love them with all my heart.
48   I will welcome thy commandments *a*
        and will meditate on thy statutes.

49   Remember the word spoken to me, thy servant,
        on which thou hast taught me to fix my hope.
50   In time of trouble my consolation is this,
        that thy promise has given me life.
51   Proud men treat me with insolent scorn,
        but I do not swerve from thy law.

*a   Prob. rdg.; Heb. adds which I love.*

I have cherished thy decrees all my life long, 52
    and in them I find consolation, O Lord.
Gusts of anger seize me as I think of evil men 53
    who forsake thy law.
Thy statutes are the theme of my song*a* 54
    wherever I make my home.
In the night I remember thy name, O Lord, 55
    and dwell upon thy law.
This is true of me, 56
    that I have kept thy precepts.

Thou, Lord, art all I have; 57
    I have promised to keep thy word.
With all my heart I have tried to please thee; 58
    fulfil thy promise and be gracious to me.
I have thought much about the course of my life 59
    and always turned back to thy instruction;
I have never delayed but always made haste 60
    to keep thy commandments.
Bands of evil men close round me, 61
    but I do not forget thy law.
At midnight I rise to give thee thanks 62
    for the justice of thy decrees.
I keep company with all who fear thee, 63
    with all who follow thy precepts.
The earth is full of thy never-failing love; 64
    O Lord, teach me thy statutes.

Thou hast shown thy servant much kindness, 65
    fulfilling thy word, O Lord.
Give me insight, give me knowledge, 66
    for I put my trust in thy commandments.
I went astray before I was punished; 67
    but now I pay heed to thy promise.
Thou art good and thou doest good; 68
    teach me thy statutes.
Proud men blacken my name with lies, 69
    yet I follow thy precepts with all my heart;
their hearts are thick and gross; 70
    but I continually delight in thy law.
How good it is for me to have been punished, 71
    to school me in thy statutes!
The law thou hast ordained means more to me 72
    than a fortune in gold and silver.

Thy hands moulded me and made me what I am; 73
    show me how I may learn thy commandments.

*a* the theme of my song: *or* wonderful to me.

74 Let all who fear thee be glad when they see me,
  because I hope for the fulfilment of thy word.
75 I know, O LORD, that thy decrees are just
  and even in punishing thou keepest faith with me.
76 Let thy never-failing love console me,
  as thou hast promised me, thy servant.
77 Extend thy compassion to me, that I may live;
  for thy law is my continual delight.
78 Put the proud to shame, for with their lies they wrong me;
  but I will meditate on thy precepts.
79 Let all who fear thee turn to me,
  all who cherish thy instruction.
80 Let me give my whole heart to thy statutes,
  so that I am not put to shame.

81 I long with all my heart for thy deliverance,
  hoping for the fulfilment of thy word;
82 my sight grows dim with looking for thy promise
  and still I cry, 'When wilt thou comfort me?'
83 Though I shrivel like a wine-skin in the smoke,
  I do not forget thy statutes.
84 How long has thy servant to wait
  for thee to fulfil thy decree against my persecutors?
85 Proud men who flout thy law
  spread tales about me.
86 Help me, for they hound me with their lies,
  but thy commandments all stand for ever.
87 They had almost swept me from the earth,
  but I did not forsake thy precepts;
88 grant me life, as thy love is unchanging,
  that I may follow all thy instruction.

89 Eternal is thy word, O LORD,
  planted firm in heaven.
90 Thy promise*a* endures for all time,
  stable as the earth which thou hast fixed.
91 This day, as ever, thy decrees stand fast;
  for all things serve thee.
92 If thy law had not been my continual delight,
  I should have perished in all my troubles;
93 never will I forget thy precepts,
  for through them thou hast given me life.
94 I am thine; O save me,
  for I have pondered thy precepts.
95 Evil men lie in wait to destroy me;
  but I will give thought to thy instruction.

*a Prob. rdg.; Heb.* Thy constancy.

I see that all things come to an end,
    but thy commandment has no limit. 96

O how I love thy law!
    It is my study all day long. 97
Thy commandments are mine for ever;
    through them I am wiser than my enemies. 98
I have more insight than all my teachers,
    for thy instruction is my study; 99
I have more wisdom than the old,
    because I have kept thy precepts. 100
I set no foot on any evil path
    in my obedience to thy word; 101
I do not swerve from thy decrees,
    for thou thyself hast been my teacher. 102
How sweet is thy promise in my mouth,
    sweeter on my tongue than honey! 103
From thy precepts I learn wisdom;
    therefore I hate the paths of falsehood. 104

Thy word is a lamp to guide my feet
    and a light on my path; 105
I have bound myself by oath and solemn vow
    to keep thy just decrees. 106
I am cruelly afflicted;
    O LORD, revive me and make good thy word. 107
Accept, O LORD, the willing tribute of my lips
    and teach me thy decrees. 108
Every day I take my life in my hands,
    yet I never forget thy law. 109
Evil men have set traps for me,
    but I do not stray from thy precepts. 110
Thy instruction is my everlasting inheritance;
    it is the joy of my heart. 111
I am resolved to fulfil thy statutes;
    they are a reward that never fails. 112

I hate men who are not single-minded,
    but I love thy law. 113
Thou art my shield and hiding-place;
    I hope for the fulfilment of thy word. 114
Go, you evildoers, and leave me to myself,
    that I may keep the commandments of my God. 115
Support me as thou hast promised, that I may live;
    do not disappoint my hope. 116
Sustain me, that I may see deliverance;
    so shall I always be occupied with thy statutes. 117
Thou dost reject those who stray from thy statutes,
    for their talk is all malice and lies. 118

| | |
|---|---|
| 119 | In thy sight all the wicked on earth are scum; |
| | therefore I love thy instruction. |
| 120 | The dread of thee makes my flesh creep, |
| | and I stand in awe of thy decrees. |
| | |
| 121 | I have done what is just and right; |
| | thou wilt not abandon me to my oppressors. |
| 122 | Stand surety for the welfare of thy servant; |
| | let not the proud oppress me.*a* |
| 123 | My sight grows dim with looking for thy deliverance |
| | and waiting for thy righteous promise. |
| 124 | In all thy dealings with me, LORD, show thy true love |
| | and teach me thy statutes. |
| 125 | I am thy servant; give me insight |
| | to understand thy instruction. |
| 126 | It is time to act, O LORD; |
| | for men have broken thy law. |
| 127 | Truly I love thy commandments |
| | more than the finest gold. |
| 128 | It is by thy precepts that I find the right way; |
| | I hate the paths of falsehood. |
| | |
| 129 | Thy instruction is wonderful; |
| | therefore I gladly keep it. |
| 130 | Thy word is revealed, and all is light; |
| | it gives understanding even to the untaught. |
| 131 | I pant, I thirst, |
| | longing for thy commandments. |
| 132 | Turn to me and be gracious, |
| | as thou hast decreed for those who love thy name. |
| 133 | Make my step firm according to thy promise, |
| | and let no wrong have the mastery over me. |
| 134 | Set me free from man's oppression, |
| | that I may observe thy precepts. |
| 135 | Let thy face shine upon thy servant |
| | and teach me thy statutes. |
| 136 | My eyes stream with tears |
| | because men do not heed thy law. |
| | |
| 137 | How just thou art, O LORD! |
| | How straight and true are thy decrees! |
| 138 | How just is the instruction thou givest! |
| | It is fixed firm and sure. |
| 139 | I am speechless with resentment, |
| | for my enemies have forgotten thy words. |
| 140 | Thy promise has been tested through and through, |
| | and thy servant loves it. |

*a* oppress me: *or* charge me falsely.

I may be despised and of little account,                                    141
   but I do not forget thy precepts.
Thy justice is an everlasting justice,                                       142
   and thy law is truth.
Though I am oppressed by trouble and anxiety,                               143
   thy commandments are my continual delight.
Thy instruction is ever just;                                                144
   give me understanding that I may live.

I call with my whole heart; answer me, LORD.                               145
   I will keep thy statutes.
I call to thee; O save me                                                    146
   that I may heed thy instruction.
I rise before dawn and cry for help;                                        147
   I hope for the fulfilment of thy word.
Before the midnight watch also my eyes are open                            148
   for meditation on thy promise.
Hear me, as thy love is unchanging,                                         149
   and give me life, O LORD, by thy decree.
My pursuers in their malice are close behind me,                           150
   but they are far from thy law.
Yet thou art near, O LORD,                                                   151
   and all thy commandments are true.
I have long known from thy instruction                                      152
   that thou hast given it eternal foundations.

See in what trouble I am and set me free,                                   153
   for I do not forget thy law.
Be thou my advocate and win release for me;                                154
   true to thy promise, give me life.
Such deliverance is beyond the reach of wicked men,                        155
   because they do not ponder thy statutes.
Great is thy compassion, O LORD;                                            156
   grant me life by thy decree.
Many are my persecutors and enemies,                                        157
   but I have not swerved from thy instruction.
I was cut to the quick when I saw traitors                                  158
   who had no regard for thy promise.
See how I love thy precepts, O LORD!                                        159
   Grant me life, as thy love is unchanging.
Thy word is founded in truth,                                               160
   and thy just decrees are everlasting.

The powers that be persecute me without cause,                             161
   yet my heart thrills at thy word.
I am jubilant over thy promise,                                             162
   like a man carrying off much booty.
Falsehood I detest and loathe,                                              163
   but I love thy law.

164 Seven times a day I praise thee
for the justice of thy decrees.
165 Peace is the reward of those who love thy law;
no pitfalls beset their path.
166 I hope for thy deliverance, O LORD,
and I fulfil thy commandments;
167 gladly I heed thy instruction
and love it greatly.
168 I heed thy precepts and thy instruction,
for all my life lies open before thee.

169 Let my cry of joy reach thee, O LORD;
give me understanding of thy word.
170 Let my supplication reach thee;
be true to thy promise and save me.
171 Let thy praise pour from my lips,
because thou teachest me thy statutes;
172 let the music of thy promises be on my tongue,
for thy commandments are justice itself.
173 Let thy hand be prompt to help me,
for I have chosen thy precepts;
174 I long for thy deliverance, O LORD,
and thy law is my continual delight.
175 Let me live and I will praise thee;
let thy decrees be my support.
176 I have strayed like a lost sheep;
come, search for thy servant,
for I have not forgotten thy commandments.

## 120

1 I called to the LORD in my distress,
and he answered me.
2 'O LORD,' I cried, 'save me from lying lips
and from the tongue of slander.'
3 What has he in store for you, slanderous tongue?
What more has he for you?
4 Nothing but a warrior's sharp arrows
or red-hot charcoal.
5 Hard is my lot, exiled in Meshech,
dwelling by the tents of Kedar.
6 All the time that I dwelt
among men who hated peace,
7 I sought peace; but whenever I spoke of it,
they were for war.

## 121

If I lift up my eyes to the hills,                                    1
  where shall I find help?
Help comes only from the LORD,                                        2
  maker of heaven and earth.
How could he let your foot stumble?                                   3
  How could he, your guardian, sleep?
The guardian of Israel                                               4
  never slumbers, never sleeps.
The LORD is your guardian,                                           5
  your defence at your right hand;
the sun will not strike you by day                                   6
  nor the moon by night.
The LORD will guard you against all evil;                            7
  he will guard you, body and soul.
The LORD will guard your going and your coming,                      8
  now and for evermore.

## 122

I rejoiced when they said to me,                                     1
  'Let us go to the house of the LORD.'
Now we stand within your gates,                                      2
  O Jerusalem:
Jerusalem that is built to be a city                                 3
  where people come together in unity;
to which the tribes resort, the tribes of the LORD,                  4
  to give thanks to the LORD himself,
  the bounden duty of Israel.
For in her are set the thrones of justice,                           5
  the thrones of the house of David.
Pray for the peace of Jerusalem:                                     6
  'May those who love you prosper;
peace be within your ramparts                                        7
  and prosperity in your palaces.'
For the sake of these my brothers and my friends,                    8
  I will say, 'Peace be within you.'
For the sake of the house of the LORD our God                        9
  I will pray for your good.

## 123

I lift my eyes to thee                                               1
  whose throne is in heaven.
As the eyes of a slave follow his master's hand                      2
  or the eyes of a slave-girl her mistress,
  so our eyes are turned to the LORD our God
  waiting for kindness from him.

3    Deal kindly with us, O LORD, deal kindly,
         for we have suffered insult enough;
4    too long have we had to suffer
         the insults of the wealthy,
         the scorn of proud men.

## 124

1    If the LORD had not been on our side,
         Israel may now say,
2    if the LORD had not been on our side
         when they assailed us,
3    they would have swallowed us alive
         when their anger was roused against us.
4    The waters would have carried us away
         and the torrent swept over us;
5    over us would have swept
         the seething waters.
6    Blessed be the LORD, who did not leave us
         to be the prey between their teeth.
7    We have escaped like a bird
         from the fowler's trap;
         the trap broke, and so we escaped.
8    Our help is in the name of the LORD,
         maker of heaven and earth.

## 125

1    Those who trust in the LORD are like Mount Zion,
         which cannot be shaken but stands fast for ever.
2    As the hills enfold Jerusalem,
         so the LORD enfolds his people, now and evermore.
3    The sceptre of wickedness shall surely find no home
         in the land allotted to the righteous,
         so that the righteous shall not set
         their hands to injustice.
4    Do good, O LORD, to those who are good
         and to those who are upright in heart.
5        But those who turn aside into crooked ways,
         may the LORD destroy them, as he destroys all evildoers!

     Peace be upon Israel!

## 126

1    When the LORD turned the tide of Zion's fortune,
         we were like men who had found new health.[a]

         [a] like . . . health: *or* like dreamers.

Our mouths were full of laughter 2
    and our tongues sang aloud for joy.
Then word went round among the nations,
    'The LORD has done great things for them.'
GREAT things indeed the LORD then did for us, 3
    and we rejoiced.

Turn once again our fortune, LORD, 4
    as streams return in the dry south.
Those who sow in tears 5
    shall reap with songs of joy.
A man may go out weeping, 6
    carrying his bag of seed;
but he will come back with songs of joy,
    carrying home his sheaves.

## 127

Unless the LORD builds the house, 1
    its builders will have toiled in vain.
Unless the LORD keeps watch over a city,
    in vain the watchman stands on guard.
In vain you rise up early 2
    and go late to rest,
toiling for the bread you eat;
    he supplies the need of those he loves.[a]
Sons are a gift from the LORD 3
    and children a reward from him.
Like arrows in the hand of a fighting man 4
    are the sons of a man's youth.
Happy is the man 5
    who has his quiver full of them;
such men shall not be put to shame
    when they confront their enemies in court.

## 128

Happy are all who fear the LORD, 1
    who live according to his will.
You shall eat the fruit of your own labours, 2
    you shall be happy and you shall prosper.
Your wife shall be like a fruitful vine 3
    in the heart of your house;
your sons shall be like olive-shoots
    round about your table.
This is the blessing in store for the man 4
    who fears the LORD.

[a] *Prob. rdg.; Heb. adds an unintelligible word.*

5    May the Lord bless you from Zion;
        may you share the prosperity of Jerusalem
all the days of your life,
6        and live to see your children's children!

    Peace be upon Israel!

## 129

1    Often since I was young have men attacked me—
        let Israel now say—
2    often since I was young have men attacked me,
        but never have they prevailed.
3    They scored my back with scourges,
        like ploughmen driving long furrows.
4    Yet the Lord in his justice
        has cut me loose from the bonds of the wicked.
5    Let all enemies of Zion
        be thrown back in shame;
6    let them be like grass growing on the roof,
        which withers before it can shoot,
7    which will never fill a mower's hand
        nor yield an armful for the harvester,
8    so that passers-by will never say to them,
        'The blessing of the Lord be upon you!
        We bless you in the name of the Lord.'

## 130

1    Out of the depths have I called to thee, O Lord;
2        Lord, hear my cry.
    Let thy ears be attentive
        to my plea for mercy.
3    If thou, Lord, shouldest keep account of sins,
        who, O Lord, could hold up his head?
4    But in thee is forgiveness,
        and therefore thou art revered.
5    I wait for the Lord with all my soul,
        I hope for the fulfilment of his word.
6    My soul waits[a] for the Lord
        more eagerly than watchmen for the morning.
    Like men who watch for the morning,
7        O Israel, look for the Lord.
    For in the Lord is love unfailing,
        and great is his power to set men free.
8    He alone will set Israel free
        from all their sins.

      *a*  waits: *transposed from after* the Lord *in verse 5.*

# 131

O Lord, my heart is not proud,　　　　　　　　　　1
　nor are my eyes haughty;
I do not busy myself with great matters
　or things too marvellous for me.
No; I submit myself, I account myself lowly,　　　2
　as a weaned child clinging to its mother.ᵃ
O Israel, look for the Lord　　　　　　　　　　　3
　now and evermore.

# 132

O Lord, remember David　　　　　　　　　　　　1
　in the time of his adversity,
how he swore to the Lord　　　　　　　　　　　　2
　and made a vow to the Mighty One of Jacob:
'I will not enter my house　　　　　　　　　　　3
　nor will I mount my bed,
I will not close my eyes in sleep　　　　　　　　4
　or my eyelids in slumber,
until I find a sanctuary for the Lord,　　　　　　5
　a dwelling for the Mighty One of Jacob.'
We heard of it in Ephrathah;　　　　　　　　　　6
　we came upon it in the region of Jaar.
Let us enter his dwelling,　　　　　　　　　　　7
　let us fall in worship at his footstool.
Arise, O Lord, and come to thy resting-place,　　8
　thou and the ark of thy power.
Let thy priests be clothed in righteousness　　　9
　and let thy loyal servants shout for joy.
For thy servant David's sake　　　　　　　　　　10
　reject not thy anointed king.
The Lord swore to David　　　　　　　　　　　11
　an oath which he will not break:
'A prince of your own line
　will I set upon your throne.
If your sons keep my covenant　　　　　　　　　12
　and heed the teaching that I give them,
their sons in turn for all time
　shall sit upon your throne.'
For the Lord has chosen Zion　　　　　　　　　13
　and desired it for his home:
'This is my resting-place for ever;　　　　　　　14
　here will I make my home, for such is my desire.

ᵃ *Prob. rdg.; Heb. adds* as a weaned child clinging to me.

15   I will richly bless her destitute <sup>a</sup>
    and satisfy her needy with bread.

16   With salvation will I clothe her priests;
    her loyal servants shall shout for joy.

17   There will I renew the line of David's house
    and light a lamp for my anointed king;

18   his enemies will I clothe with shame,
    but on his head shall be a shining crown.'

## 133

1   How good it is and how pleasant
    for brothers to live<sup>b</sup> together!

2   It is fragrant as oil poured upon the head
    and falling over the beard,
  Aaron's beard, when the oil runs down
    over the collar of his vestments.

3   It is like the dew of Hermon falling
    upon the hills of Zion.
  There the LORD bestows his blessing,
    life for evermore.

## 134

1   Come, bless the LORD,
    all you servants of the LORD,
  who stand night after night
    in the house of the LORD.

2   Lift up your hands in the sanctuary
    and bless the LORD.

3   The LORD, maker of heaven and earth,
    bless you from Zion!

## 135

1   O praise the LORD.

  Praise the name of the LORD;
    praise him, you servants of the LORD,

2   who stand in the house of the LORD,
    in the temple courts of our God.

3   Praise the LORD, for that is good;
    honour his name with psalms, for that is pleasant.

4   The LORD has chosen Jacob to be his own
    and Israel as his special treasure.

5   I know that the LORD is great,
    that our Lord is above all gods.

<sup>a</sup> her destitute: *prob. rdg.; Heb.* her provisions.      <sup>b</sup> *Or* to worship.

Whatever the LORD pleases,                    6
   that he does, in heaven and on earth,
   in the sea, in the depths of ocean.
He brings up the mist from the ends of the earth,       7
he opens rifts[a] for the rain,
and brings the wind out of his storehouses.
He struck down all the first-born in Egypt,          8
   both man and beast.
In Egypt he sent signs and portents             9
   against Pharaoh and all his subjects.
He struck down mighty nations              10
   and slew great kings,
Sihon king of the Amorites, Og the king of Bashan,    11
   and all the princes of Canaan,
and gave their land to Israel,                12
   to Israel his people as their patrimony.
O LORD, thy name endures for ever;           13
thy renown, O LORD, shall last for all generations.
The LORD will give his people justice          14
   and have compassion on his servants.
The gods of the nations are idols of silver and gold,    15
   made by the hands of men.
They have mouths that cannot speak          16
   and eyes that cannot see;
they have ears that do not hear,            17
   and there is no breath in their nostrils.[b]
Their makers grow like them,               18
   and so do all who trust in them.
O house of Israel, bless the LORD;           19
   O house of Aaron, bless the LORD.
O house of Levi, bless the LORD;            20
   you who fear the LORD, bless the LORD.
Blessed from Zion be the LORD              21
   who dwells in Jerusalem.

   O praise the LORD.

# 136

It is good to give thanks to the LORD,          1
   for his love endures for ever.
Give thanks to the God of gods;            2
   his love endures for ever.
Give thanks to the Lord of lords;           3
   his love endures for ever.
Alone he works great marvels;             4
   his love endures for ever.

[a] *Prob. rdg.; Heb.* lightnings.       [b] *Prob. rdg.; Heb.* mouths.

| | |
|---|---|
| 5 | In wisdom he made the heavens; |
| | his love endures for ever. |
| 6 | He laid the earth upon the waters; |
| | his love endures for ever. |
| 7 | He made the great lights, |
| | his love endures for ever, |
| 8 | the sun to rule by day, |
| | his love endures for ever, |
| 9 | the moon and the stars to rule by night; |
| | his love endures for ever. |
| 10 | He struck down the first-born of the Egyptians, |
| | his love endures for ever, |
| 11 | and brought Israel from among them; |
| | his love endures for ever. |
| 12 | With strong hand and outstretched arm, |
| | his love endures for ever, |
| 13 | he divided the Red Sea in two, |
| | his love endures for ever, |
| 14 | and made Israel pass through it, |
| | his love endures for ever; |
| 15 | but Pharaoh and his host he swept into the sea; |
| | his love endures for ever. |
| 16 | He led his people through the wilderness; |
| | his love endures for ever. |
| 17 | He struck down great kings; |
| | his love endures for ever. |
| 18 | He slew mighty kings, |
| | his love endures for ever, |
| 19 | Sihon king of the Amorites, |
| | his love endures for ever, |
| 20 | and Og the king of Bashan; |
| | his love endures for ever. |
| 21 | He gave their land to Israel, |
| | his love endures for ever, |
| 22 | to Israel his servant as their patrimony; |
| | his love endures for ever. |
| 23 | He remembered us when we were cast down, |
| | his love endures for ever, |
| 24 | and rescued us from our enemies; |
| | his love endures for ever. |
| 25 | He gives food to all his creatures; |
| | his love endures for ever. |
| 26 | Give thanks to the God of heaven, |
| | for his love endures for ever. |

## 137

By the rivers of Babylon we sat down and wept     1
  when we remembered Zion.
There on the willow-trees *a*                      2
  we hung up our harps,
for there those who carried us off                 3
  demanded music and singing,
and our captors called on us to be merry:
  'Sing us one of the songs of Zion.'
How could we sing the LORD's song                  4
  in a foreign land?

If I forget you, O Jerusalem,                      5
  let my right hand wither away;
let my tongue cling to the roof of my mouth        6
  if I do not remember you,
if I do not set Jerusalem
  above my highest joy.
Remember, O LORD, against the people of Edom       7
  the day of Jerusalem's fall,
when they said, 'Down with it, down with it,
  down to its very foundations!'
O Babylon, Babylon the destroyer,                  8
  happy the man who repays you
  for all that you did to us!
Happy is he who shall seize your children          9
  and dash them against the rock.

## 138

I will praise thee, O LORD, with all my heart;     1
  boldly, O God, will I sing psalms to thee. *b*
I will bow down towards thy holy temple,           2
for thy love and faithfulness I will praise thy name;
for thou hast made thy promise wide as the heavens.
When I called to thee thou didst answer me         3
  and make me bold and valiant-hearted.
Let all the kings of the earth praise *c* thee, O LORD,   4
  when they hear the words thou hast spoken;
and let them sing of *d* the LORD's ways,          5
  for great is the glory of the LORD.
For the LORD, high as he is, cares for the lowly,  6
  and from afar he humbles the proud.
Though I walk among foes thou dost preserve my life,   7
  exerting thy power against the rage of my enemies,
  and with thy right hand thou savest me.

*a* Or poplars.      *b* boldly . . . thee: *or* I will sing psalms to thee before the gods.
*c* Or confess.      *d* Or walk in.

8        The LORD will accomplish his purpose for me.
          Thy true love, O LORD, endures for ever;
          leave not thy work unfinished.

## 139

1     LORD, thou hast examined me and knowest me.
2     Thou knowest all, whether I sit down or rise up;
        thou hast discerned my thoughts from afar.
3     Thou hast traced my journey and my resting places,
        and art familiar with all my paths.
4     For there is not a word on my tongue
        but thou, LORD, knowest them all.[a]
5     Thou hast kept close guard before me and behind
        and hast spread thy hand over me.
6     Such knowledge is beyond my understanding,
        so high that I cannot reach it.
7     Where can I escape from thy spirit?
        Where can I flee from thy presence?
8     If I climb up to heaven, thou art there;
        if I make my bed in Sheol, again I find thee.
9     If I take my flight to the frontiers of the morning
        or dwell at the limit of the western sea,
10    even there thy hand will meet me
        and thy right hand will hold me fast.
11    If I say, 'Surely darkness will steal over me,
        night will close around me',
12    darkness is no darkness for thee
        and night is luminous as day;
        to thee both dark and light are one.

13    Thou it was who didst fashion my inward parts;
        thou didst knit me together in my mother's womb.
14    I will praise thee, for thou dost fill me with awe;
        wonderful thou art, and wonderful thy works.
        Thou knowest me through and through:
15        my body is no mystery to thee,
        how I was secretly kneaded into shape
        and patterned in the depths of the earth.
16    Thou didst see my limbs unformed in the womb,
        and in thy book they are all recorded;
        day by day they were fashioned,
        not one of them was late in growing.[b]
17    How deep I find thy thoughts, O God,
        how inexhaustible their themes!

[a] *For . . . them all:* or *If there is any offence on my tongue, thou, LORD, knowest it all.*
[b] *was late in growing: prob. rdg.; Heb. om.*

Can I count them? They outnumber the grains of sand;          18
  to finish the count, my years must equal thine.

O God, if only thou wouldst slay the wicked!                  19
If those men of blood would but leave me in peace—
those who provoke thee with deliberate evil                   20
  and rise in vicious rebellion against thee!
How I hate them, O LORD, that hate thee!                      21
I am cut to the quick when they oppose thee;
I hate them with undying hatred;                              22
  I hold them all my enemies.

Examine me, O God, and know my thoughts;                      23
  test me, and understand my misgivings.
Watch lest I follow any path that grieves thee;               24
  guide me in the ancient*a* ways.

## 140

Rescue me, O LORD, from evil men;                             1
  keep me safe from violent men,
whose heads are full of wicked schemes,                       2
  who stir up contention day after day.
Their tongues are sharp as serpents' fangs;                   3
  on their lips is spiders' poison.
Guard me, O LORD, from wicked men;                            4
  keep me safe from violent men,
  who plan to thrust me out of the way.
Arrogant men set hidden traps for me,                         5
  rogues spread their nets
  and lay snares for me along the path.
I said, 'O LORD, thou art my God;                             6
  O LORD, hear my plea for mercy.
O LORD God, stronghold of my safety,                          7
thou hast shielded my head in the day of battle.
Frustrate, O LORD, their designs against me;                  8-9
  never let the wicked gain their purpose.
If any of those at my table rise against me,
  let their own conspiracies be their undoing.
Let burning coals be tipped upon them;                        10
  let them be plunged into the miry depths,
  never to rise again.
Slander shall find no home in the land;                       11
evil and violence shall be hounded to destruction.'

I know that the LORD will give their due to the needy        12
  and justice to the downtrodden.

*a Or* everlasting.

13    Righteous men will surely give thanks to thy name;
      the upright will worship in thy presence.


## 141

1     O LORD, I call to thee, come quickly to my aid;
      listen to my cry when I call to thee.
2     Let my prayer be like incense duly set before thee
      and my raised hands like the evening sacrifice.
3     Set a guard, O LORD, over my mouth;
      keep watch at the door of my lips.
4     Turn not my heart to sinful thoughts
      nor to any pursuit of evil courses.
      The evildoers appal me; *a*
      not for me the delights of their table.
5     I would rather be buffeted by the righteous
      and reproved by good men.
      My head shall not be anointed with the oil of wicked men,
      for that would make me a party to their crimes.
6     They shall founder on the rock of justice
      and shall learn how acceptable my words are.
7     Their bones shall be scattered at the mouth of Sheol,
      like splinters of wood or stone on the ground.
8     But my eyes are fixed on thee, O LORD God;
      thou art my refuge; leave me not unprotected.
9     Keep me from the trap which they have set for me,
      from the snares of evildoers.
10    Let the wicked fall into their own nets,
      whilst I pass in safety, all alone.


## 142

1     I cry aloud to the LORD;
      to the LORD I plead aloud for mercy.
2     I pour out my complaint before him
      and tell over my troubles in his presence.
3     When my spirit is faint within me,
      thou art there to watch over my steps.
      In the path that I should take
      they have hidden a snare.
4     I look to my right hand,
      I find no friend by my side;
      no way of escape is in sight,
      no one comes to rescue me.
5     I cry to thee, O LORD,
      and say, 'Thou art my refuge;

      *a* appal me: *prob. rdg.; Heb.* with men.

thou art all I have
　　in the land of the living.
Give me a hearing when I cry,                        6
　　for I am brought very low;
save me from my pursuers,
　　for they are too strong for me.
Set me free from my prison,                          7
　　so that I may praise thy name.'
The righteous shall crown me with garlands,[a]
　　when thou givest me my due reward.

## 143

LORD, hear my prayer;                                1
be true to thyself, and listen to my pleading;
　　then in thy righteousness answer me.
Bring not thy servant to trial before thee;          2
against thee no man on earth can be right.
An enemy has hunted me down,                         3
　　has ground my living body under foot
and plunged me into darkness like a man long dead,
so that my spirit fails me                           4
　　and my heart is dazed with despair.
I dwell upon the years long past,                    5
　　upon the memory of all that thou hast done;
　　the wonders of thy creation fill my mind.
To thee I lift my outspread hands,                   6
　　athirst for thee in a thirsty land.
LORD, make haste to answer,                          7
　　for my spirit faints.
Do not hide thy face from me
or I shall be like those who go down to the abyss.
In the morning let me know thy true love;            8
　　I have put my trust in thee.
Show me the way that I must take;
　　to thee I offer all my heart.
Deliver me, LORD, from my enemies,                   9
　　for with thee have I sought refuge.
Teach me to do thy will, for thou art my God;        10
in thy gracious kindness, show me the level road.
Keep me safe, O LORD, for the honour of thy name     11
and, as thou art just, release me from my distress.
In thy love for me, reduce my enemies to silence     12
and bring destruction on all who oppress me;
　　for I am thy servant.

　　[a] crown me with garlands: *or* crowd round me.

# 144

1 Blessed is the L<small>ORD</small>, my rock,<br>
who trains my hands for war,<br>
my fingers for battle;<br>
2 my help that never fails, my fortress,<br>
my strong tower and my refuge,<br>
my shield in which I trust,<br>
he who puts nations under my feet.

3 O L<small>ORD</small>, what is man that thou carest for him?<br>
What is mankind? Why give a thought to them?<br>
4 Man is no more than a puff of wind,<br>
his days a passing shadow.<br>
5 If thou, L<small>ORD</small>, but tilt the heavens, down they come;<br>
touch the mountains, and they smoke.<br>
6 Shoot forth thy lightning flashes, far and wide,<br>
and send thy arrows whistling.<br>
7 Stretch out thy hands from on high to rescue me<br>
and snatch me from great waters.<sup>a</sup>

9 I will sing a new song to thee, O God,<br>
psalms to the music of a ten-stringed lute.<br>
10 O God who gavest victory to kings<br>
and deliverance to thy servant David,<br>
rescue me from the cruel sword;<br>
11 snatch me from the power of foreign foes,<br>
whose every word is false<br>
and all their oaths are perjury.

12 Happy<sup>b</sup> are we whose sons in their early prime<br>
stand like tall towers,<br>
our daughters like sculptured pillars<br>
at the corners of a palace.<br>
13 Our barns are full and furnish plentiful provision;<br>
our sheep bear lambs in thousands upon thousands;<br>
14 the oxen in our fields are fat and sleek;<br>
there is no miscarriage or untimely birth,<br>
no cries of distress in our public places.<br>
15 Happy are the people in such a case as ours;<br>
happy the people who have the L<small>ORD</small> for their God.

# 145

1 I will extol thee, O God my king,<br>
and bless thy name for ever and ever.<br>
2 Every day will I bless thee<br>
and praise thy name for ever and ever.

---

<sup>a</sup> *Prob. rdg.; Heb. adds* from the power of foreign foes, (8) whose every word is false and all their oaths are perjury (*cp. verse 11*).    <sup>b</sup> *Prob. rdg.; Heb.* Who.

Great is the LORD and worthy of all praise;     3
  his greatness is unfathomable.
One generation shall commend thy works to another     4
  and set forth thy mighty deeds.
My theme shall be thy marvellous works,     5
  the glorious splendour of thy majesty.
Men shall declare thy mighty acts with awe     6
  and tell of thy great deeds.
They shall recite the story of thy abounding goodness     7
  and sing of thy righteousness with joy.

The LORD is gracious and compassionate,     8
  forbearing, and constant in his love.
The LORD is good to all men,     9
and his tender care rests upon all his creatures.

All thy creatures praise thee, LORD,     10
  and thy servants bless thee.
They talk of the glory of thy kingdom     11
  and tell of thy might,
they proclaim to their fellows how mighty are thy deeds,     12
  how glorious the majesty of thy kingdom.
Thy kingdom is an everlasting kingdom,     13
and thy dominion stands for all generations.

In all his promises the LORD keeps faith,     14
  he is unchanging in all his works;
the LORD holds up those who stumble
  and straightens backs which are bent.
The eyes of all are lifted to thee in hope,     15
and thou givest them their food when it is due;
with open and bountiful hand     16
thou givest what they desire*a* to every living creature.
The LORD is righteous in all his ways,     17
  unchanging in all that he does;
very near is the LORD to those who call to him,     18
  who call to him in singleness of heart.
He fulfils their desire if only they fear him;     19
  he hears their cry and saves them.
The LORD watches over all who love him     20
  but sends the wicked to their doom.
My tongue shall speak out the praises of the LORD,     21
  and all creatures shall bless his holy name
  for ever and ever.

*a* they desire: *or* thou wilt.

# 146

1       O praise the LORD.

        Praise the LORD, my soul.
2       As long as I live I will praise the LORD;
            I will sing psalms to my God all my life long.
3       Put no faith in princes,
            in any man, who has no power to save.
4           He breathes his last breath,
            he returns to the dust;
        and in that same hour all his thinking ends.

5       Happy the man whose helper is the God of Jacob,
            whose hopes are in the LORD his God,
6       maker of heaven and earth,
            the sea, and all that is in them;
        who serves wrongdoers as he has sworn
7           and deals out justice to the oppressed.
        The LORD feeds the hungry
            and sets the prisoner free.
8       The LORD restores sight to the blind
            and straightens backs which are bent;
        the LORD loves the righteous
9           and watches over the stranger;
        the LORD gives heart to the orphan and widow
        but turns the course of the wicked to their ruin.
10      The LORD shall reign for ever,
            thy God, O Zion, for all generations.

        O praise the LORD.

# 147

1       O praise the LORD.

        How good it is to sing psalms to our God!
            How pleasant to praise him!
2       The LORD is rebuilding Jerusalem;
        he gathers in the scattered sons of Israel.
3       It is he who heals the broken in spirit
            and binds up their wounds,
4       he who numbers the stars one by one
            and names them one and all.
5       Mighty is our Lord and great his power,
            and his wisdom beyond all telling.
6       The LORD gives new heart to the humble
            and brings evildoers down to the dust.
7       Sing to the LORD a song of thanksgiving,
        sing psalms to the harp in honour of our God.

He veils the sky in clouds                                          8
   and prepares rain for the earth;
he clothes the hills with grass
   and green plants for the use of man.
He gives the cattle their food                                      9
and the young ravens all that they gather.
The LORD sets no store by the strength of a horse                  10
   and takes no pleasure in a runner's legs;
his pleasure is in those who fear him,                             11
   who wait for his true love.

Sing to the LORD, Jerusalem;                                       12
   O Zion, praise your God,
for he has put new bars in your gates;                             13
   he has blessed your children within them.
He has brought peace to your realm                                14
   and given you fine wheat in plenty.
He sends his command to the ends of the earth,                    15
   and his word runs swiftly.
He showers down snow, white as wool,                              16
   and sprinkles hoar-frost thick as ashes;
crystals of ice he scatters like bread-crumbs;                    17
he sends the cold, and the water stands frozen,
he utters his word, and the ice is melted;                        18
   he blows with his wind and the waters flow.
To Jacob he makes his word known,                                 19
   his statutes and decrees to Israel;
he has not done this for any other nation,                        20
   nor taught them his decrees.

O praise the LORD.

# 148

O praise the LORD.                                                 1

Praise the LORD out of heaven;
   praise him in the heights.
Praise him, all his angels;                                        2
   praise him, all his host.
Praise him, sun and moon;                                          3
   praise him, all you shining stars;
praise him, heaven of heavens,                                     4
   and you waters above the heavens.
Let them all praise the name of the LORD,                         5
for he spoke the word and they were created;
he established them for ever and ever                             6
by an ordinance which shall never pass away.

743

7 Praise the LORD from the earth,
    you water-spouts and ocean depths;
8 fire and hail, snow and ice,
    gales of wind obeying his voice;
9 all mountains and hills;
    all fruit-trees and all cedars;
10 wild beasts and cattle,
    creeping things and winged birds;
11 kings and all earthly rulers,
    princes and judges over the whole earth;
12 young men and maidens,
    old men and young together.
13 Let all praise the name of the LORD,
    for his name is high above all others,
    and his majesty above earth and heaven;
14 he has exalted his people in the pride of power
    and crowned with praise his loyal servants,
        all Israel, the people nearest him.

O praise the LORD.


# 149

1 O praise the LORD.

Sing to the LORD a new song,
    sing his praise in the assembly of the faithful;
2 let Israel rejoice in his maker
    and the sons of Zion exult in their king.
3 Let them praise his name in the dance,
    and sing him psalms with tambourine and harp.
4 For the LORD accepts the service of his people;
    he crowns his humble folk with victory.
5 Let his faithful servants exult in triumph;
    let them shout for joy as they kneel before him.
6 Let the high praises of God be on their lips
    and a two-edged sword in their hand,
7 to wreak vengeance on the nations
    and to chastise the heathen;
8 to load their kings with chains
    and put their nobles in irons;
9 to execute the judgement decreed against them—
    this is the glory of all his faithful servants.

O praise the LORD.

# 150

O praise the LORD.                                                    1

O praise God in his holy place,
praise him in the vault of heaven, the vault of his power;
praise him for his mighty works,                                     2
    praise him for his immeasurable greatness.
Praise him with fanfares on the trumpet,                             3
    praise him upon lute and harp;
praise him with tambourines and dancing,                             4
    praise him with flute and strings;
praise him with the clash of cymbals,                                5
    praise him with triumphant cymbals;
let everything that has breath praise the LORD!                      6

    O praise the LORD.

# PROVERBS

## *Advice to the reader*

1 The proverbs of Solomon son of David, king of Israel,
2     by which men will come to wisdom and instruction
    and will understand words that bring understanding,
3     and by which they will gain a well-instructed intelligence,
    righteousness, justice, and probity.
4     The simple will be endowed with shrewdness
    and the young with knowledge and prudence.
5     If the wise man listens, he will increase his learning,
    and the man of understanding will acquire skill
6     to understand proverbs and parables,
    the sayings of wise men and their riddles.

7     The fear of the Lord is the beginning[a] of knowledge,
    but fools scorn wisdom and discipline.

8     Attend, my son, to your father's instruction
    and do not reject the teaching of your mother;
9     for they are a garland of grace on your head
    and a chain of honour round your neck.

10 11 My son, bad men may tempt you[b] and say,
    'Come with us; let us lie in wait for someone's blood;
    let us waylay[c] an innocent man who has done us no harm.
12     Like Sheol we will swallow them alive;
    though blameless, they shall be like men who go down to the abyss.
13     We shall take rich treasure of every sort
    and fill our homes with booty;
14     throw in your lot with us,
    and we will have a common purse.'
15     My son, do not go along with them,
    keep clear of their ways;
16     they hasten hot-foot into crime,
    impatient to shed blood.

17     In vain is a net spread wide
    if any bird that flies can see it.

18     These men lie in wait for their own blood
    and waylay[c] no one but themselves.

---

[a] *Or* chief part.  [b] *Prob. rdg.; Heb. adds* do not come, *or, with some MSS.,* do not consent.  [c] *Prob. rdg.; Heb.* store up.

This is the fate<sup>a</sup> of men eager for ill-gotten gain:     19
it robs those who get it of their lives.

Wisdom cries aloud in the open air,     20
   she raises her voice in public places;
   she calls at the top of the busy street     21
and proclaims at the open gates of the city:
   'Simple fools, how long will you be content with your simplicity?<sup>b</sup>     22
If only you would respond to my reproof,     23
   I would give you my counsel
and teach you my precepts.
But because you refused to listen when I called,     24
   because no one attended when I stretched out my hand,
   because you spurned all my advice     25
and would have nothing to do with my reproof,
   I in my turn will laugh at your doom     26
and deride you when terror comes upon you,
   when terror comes upon you like a hurricane     27
and your doom descends like a whirlwind.<sup>c</sup>
Insolent men delight in their insolence;
   stupid men hate knowledge.<sup>d</sup>
When they call upon me, I will not answer them;     28
   when they search for me, they shall not find me.
Because they hate knowledge     29
   and have not chosen to fear the LORD,
   because they have not accepted my counsel     30
and have spurned all my reproof,
   they shall eat the fruits of their behaviour     31
and have a surfeit of their own devices;
   for the simpleton turns a deaf ear and comes to grief,     32
and the stupid are ruined by their own complacency.
But whoever listens to me shall live without a care,     33
   undisturbed by fear of misfortune.'

My son, if you take my words to heart     **2**
   and lay up my commands in your mind,
   giving your attention to wisdom     2
and your mind to understanding,
   if you summon discernment to your aid     3
and invoke understanding,
   if you seek her out like silver     4
and dig for her like buried treasure,
   then you will understand the fear of the LORD     5
and attain to the knowledge of God;
   for the LORD bestows wisdom     6
and teaches knowledge and understanding.

---

<sup>a</sup> This . . . fate: *prob. rdg.; Heb.* Such are the courses.      <sup>b</sup> *The rest of verse 22*
*transposed to follow verse 27.*     <sup>c</sup> *Prob. rdg.; Heb. adds* when anguish and distress
come upon you.     <sup>d</sup> Insolent . . . knowledge: *transposed from end of verse 22.*

7  Out of his store he endows the upright with ability
   as a shield for those who live blameless lives;
8  for he guards the course of justice
   and keeps watch over the way of his loyal servants.

9  Then you will understand what is right and just
   and keep *a* only to the good man's path;
10 for wisdom will sink into your mind,
   and knowledge will be your heart's delight.
11 Prudence will keep watch over you,
   understanding will guard you,
12 it will save you from evil ways
   and from men whose talk is subversive,
13 who forsake the honest course
   to walk in ways of darkness,
14 who rejoice in doing evil
   and exult in evil and subversive acts,
15 whose own ways are crooked,
   whose tracks are devious.
16 It will save you from the adulteress,
   from the loose woman with her seductive words,
17 who forsakes the teaching of her childhood
   and has forgotten the covenant of her God;
18 for her path *b* runs downhill towards death,
   and her course is set for the land of the dead.
19 No one who resorts to her *c* finds his way back
   or regains the path to life.

20 See then that you follow the footsteps of good men
   and keep to the course of the righteous;
21 for the upright shall dwell on earth
   and blameless men remain there;
22 but the wicked shall be uprooted from it
      and traitors weeded out.

3  My son, do not forget my teaching,
   but guard my commands in your heart;
2  for long life and years in plenty
   will they bring you, and prosperity as well.
3  Let your good faith and loyalty never fail,
   but bind them about your neck.
4  Thus will you win favour and success
   in the sight of God and man.

5  Put all your trust in the LORD
   and do not rely on your own understanding.

---

*a* keep: *prob. rdg.; Heb.* uprightness.   *b Prob. rdg.; Heb.* house.   *c* resorts to
her: *or* takes to them.

Think of him in all your ways, 6
and he will smooth your path.
Do not think how wise you are, 7
but fear the LORD and turn from evil.
Let that be the medicine to keep you in health, 8
the liniment for your limbs.
Honour the LORD with your wealth 9
as the first charge on all your earnings;
then your granaries will be filled with corn *a* 10
and your vats bursting with new wine.
My son, do not spurn the LORD's correction 11
or take offence at his reproof;
for those whom he loves the LORD reproves, 12
and he punishes a favourite son.

Happy he who has found wisdom, 13
and the man who has acquired understanding;
for wisdom is more profitable than silver, 14
and the gain she brings is better than gold.
She is more precious than red coral, 15
and all your jewels are no match for her.
Long life is in her right hand, 16
in her left hand are riches and honour.
Her ways are pleasant ways 17
and all her paths lead to prosperity.
She is a staff of life to all who grasp her, 18
and those who hold her fast are safe.

In wisdom the LORD founded the earth 19
and by understanding he set the heavens in their place;
by his knowledge the depths burst forth 20
and the clouds dropped dew.

My son, keep watch over your ability and prudence, 21
do not let them slip from sight;
they shall be a charm hung about your neck 22
and an ornament on your breast.
Then you will go your way without a care, 23
and your feet will not stumble.
When you sit, you need have no fear; 24
when you lie down, your sleep will be pleasant.
Do not be afraid when fools are frightened 25
or when ruin comes upon the wicked;
for the LORD will be at your side, 26
and he will keep your feet clear of the trap.
Refuse no man any favour that you owe him 27
when it lies in your power to pay it.

*a* with corn: *or* to overflowing.

28    Do not say to your friend, 'Come back again;
      you shall have it tomorrow'—when you have it already.
29    Plot no evil against your friend,
      your unsuspecting neighbour.
30    Do not pick a quarrel with a man for no reason,
      if he has not done you a bad turn.
31    Do not emulate a lawless man,
      do not choose to follow his footsteps;
32    for one who is not straight is detestable to the LORD,
      but upright men are in God's confidence.
33    The LORD's curse rests on the house of the evildoer,
      while he blesses the home of the righteous.
34    Though God himself meets the arrogant with arrogance,
      yet he bestows his favour on the meek.*a*
35    Wise men are adorned with*b* honour,
      but the coat*c* on a fool's back is contempt.

4  Listen, my sons, to a father's instruction,
      consider attentively how to gain understanding;
2     for it is sound learning I give you;
      so do not forsake my teaching.
3     I too have been a father's son,
      tender in years, my mother's only child.
4     He taught me and said to me:
      Hold fast to my words with all your heart,
      keep my commands and you will have life.
5     Do not forget or turn a deaf ear to what I say.

7     The first thing*d* is to acquire wisdom;
      gain understanding though it cost you all you have.
6     Do not forsake her, and she will keep you safe;
      love her, and she will guard you;
8     cherish her, and she will lift you high;
      if only you embrace her, she will bring you to honour.
9     She will set a garland of grace on your head
      and bestow on you a crown of glory.

10    Listen, my son, take my words to heart,
      and the years of your life shall be multiplied.
11    I will guide you in the paths of wisdom
      and lead you in honest ways.
12    As you walk you will not slip,
      and, if you run, nothing will bring you down.
13    Cling to instruction and never let it go;
      observe it well, for it is your life.
14    Do not take to the course of the wicked
      or follow the way of evil men;

---

*a Or* wretched.      *b* are adorned with: *prob. rdg.; Heb.* shall inherit.      *c* the coat:
*prob. rdg.; Heb. obscure.*      *d Prob. rdg.; Heb. adds* wisdom.

do not set foot on it, but avoid it;  15
turn aside and go on your way.
For they cannot sleep unless they have done some wrong;  16
unless they have been someone's downfall they lose their sleep.
The bread they eat is the fruit of crime  17
and they drink wine got by violence.
The course of the righteous is like morning light,  18
growing brighter till it is broad day;
but the ways of the wicked are like darkness at night,  19
and they do not know what has been their downfall.

My son, attend to my speech,  20
pay heed to my words;
do not let them slip out of your mind,  21
keep them close in your heart;
for they are life to him who finds them,  22
and health to his whole body.
Guard your heart more than any treasure,  23
for it is the source of all life.
Keep your mouth from crooked speech  24
and your lips from deceitful talk.
Let your eyes look straight before you,  25
fix your gaze upon what lies ahead.
Look out for the path that your feet must take,  26
and your ways will be secure.
Swerve neither to right nor left,  27
and keep clear of every evil thing.

My son, attend to my wisdom  **5**
and listen to my good counsel,
so that you may observe proper prudence  2
and your speech be informed with knowledge.
For though the lips of an adulteress drip honey  3
and her tongue is smoother than oil,
yet in the end she is more bitter than wormwood,  4
and sharp as a two-edged sword.
Her feet go downwards on the path to death,  5
her course is set for Sheol.
She does not watch for the road that leads to life;  6
her course turns this way and that, and what does she care? *a*

Now, my son, listen to me  7
and do not ignore what I say:
keep well away from her  8
and do not go near the door of her house;
or you will lose your dignity in the eyes of others  9
and your honour before strangers;

---

*a* what ... care?: *or* she is restless.

10   strangers will batten on your wealth,
and your hard-won gains pass to another man's family.

11   The end will be that you will starve,
you will shrink to mere skin and bones.

12   Then you will say, 'Why did I hate correction
and set my heart against reproof?

13   I did not listen to the voice of my teachers
or pay attention to my masters.

14   I soon earned *a* a bad name
and was despised in the public assembly.'

15   Drink water from your own cistern
and running water from your own spring;

16   do not let your *b* well overflow into the road,
your runnels of water pour into the street;

17   let them be yours alone,
not shared with strangers.

18   Let your fountain, the wife of your youth,
be blessed, rejoice in her,

19   a lovely doe, a graceful hind, let her be your companion;
you will at all times be bathed in her love,
and her love will continually wrap you round.
Wherever you turn, she will guide you;
when you lie in bed, she will watch over you,
and when you wake she will talk with you. *c*

20   Why, my son, are you wrapped up in the love of an adulteress?
Why do you embrace a loose woman?

21   For a man's ways are always in the LORD's sight
who watches for every path that he must take.

22   The wicked man is caught in his own iniquities
and held fast in the toils of his own sin;

23   he will perish for want of discipline,
wrapped in the shroud of his boundless folly.

**6** My son, if you pledge yourself to another man
and stand surety for a stranger,

2   if you are caught by your promise,
trapped by some promise you have made,

3   do what I now tell you
and save yourself, my son:
when you fall into another man's power,
bestir yourself, go and pester the man,

4   give yourself no rest,
allow yourself no sleep.

5   Save yourself like a gazelle from the toils,
like a bird from the grasp of the fowler.

---

*a*  *Or* I almost earned.     *b*  do not let your: *prob. rdg.; Heb.* shall your.
*c*  Wherever . . . with you: *transposed from ch. 6 (verse 22).*

Go to the ant, you sluggard,                                              6
watch her ways and get wisdom.
She has no overseer,                                                      7
no governor or ruler;
but in summer she prepares her store of food                             8
and lays in her supplies at harvest.
How long, you sluggard, will you lie abed?                               9
When will you rouse yourself from sleep?
A little sleep, a little slumber,                                        10
a little folding of the hands in rest,
and poverty will come upon you like a robber,                            11
want like a ruffian.

A scoundrel, a mischievous man, is he                                    12
who prowls about with crooked talk—
   a wink of the eye,
   a touch with the foot,                                  13
   a sign with the fingers.
Subversion is the evil that he is plotting,                              14
he stirs up quarrels all the time.
Down comes disaster suddenly upon him;                                   15
suddenly he is broken beyond all remedy.

Six things the LORD hates,                                               16
  seven things are detestable to him:
  a proud eye, a false tongue,                                  17
  hands that shed innocent blood,
  a heart that forges thoughts of mischief,                     18
  and feet that run swiftly to do evil,
  a false witness telling a pack of lies,                       19
  and one who stirs up quarrels between brothers.

My son, observe your father's commands                                  20
  and do not reject the teaching of your mother;
wear them always next your heart                                        21
  and bind them close about your neck;
for a command is a lamp, and teaching a light,                          23[a]
reproof and correction point the way of life,
to keep you from the wife of another man,                               24
from the seductive tongue of the loose woman.
Do not desire her beauty in your heart                                  25
or let her glance provoke you;
for a prostitute can be had for the price of a loaf,                    26
but a married woman is out for bigger game.

Can a man kindle fire in his bosom                                      27
without burning his clothes?

    [a] *Verse 22 transposed to follow* wrap you round *in 5. 19.*

28  If a man walks on hot coals,
    will his feet not be scorched?
29  So is he who sleeps with his neighbour's wife;
    no one can touch such a woman and go free.
30  Is not a thief contemptible when he steals
    to satisfy his appetite, even if he is hungry?
31  And, if he is caught, must he not pay seven times over
    and surrender all that his house contains?
32  So one who commits adultery is a senseless fool:
    he dishonours the woman and ruins himself;
33  he will get nothing but blows and contumely
    and will never live down the disgrace;
34  for a husband's anger is a jealous anger
    and in the day of vengeance he will show no mercy;
35  compensation will not buy his forgiveness; *a*
    no bribe, however large, will purchase his connivance.

7   My son, keep my words,
    store up my commands in your mind.
2   Keep my commands if you would live,
    and treasure my teaching as the apple of your eye.
3   Wear them like a ring on your finger;
    write them on the tablet of your memory.
4   Call Wisdom your sister,
    greet Understanding as a familiar friend;
5   then they will save you from the adulteress,
    from the loose woman with her seductive words.

6   I glanced *b* out of the window of my house,
    I looked down through the lattice,
7   and I saw among simple youths,
    there amongst the boys I noticed
    a lad, a foolish lad,
8   passing along the street, at the corner,
    stepping out in the direction of her house
9   at twilight, as the day faded,
    at dusk as the night grew dark;
10  suddenly a woman came to meet him,
    dressed like a prostitute, full of wiles,
11  flighty and inconstant,
    a woman never content to stay at home,
12  lying in wait at every corner,
    now in the street, now in the public squares.
13  She caught hold of him and kissed him;
    brazenly she accosted him and said,
14  'I have had a sacrifice, an offering, to make
    and I have paid my vows today;

*a* compensation . . . forgiveness: *prob. rdg.; Heb. obscure.*
*rdg.; Heb. om.*

*b* I glanced: *prob.*

that is why I have come out to meet you,                          15
to watch for you and find you.
I have spread coverings on my bed                                 16
of coloured linen from Egypt.
I have sprinkled my bed with myrrh,                               17
my clothes *a* with aloes and cassia.
Come! Let us drown ourselves in pleasure,                        18
let us spend a whole night of love;
for the man of the house is away,                                19
he has gone on a long journey,
he has taken a bag of silver with him;                           20
until the moon is full he will not be home.'
Persuasively she led him on,                                     21
she pressed him with seductive words.
Like a simple fool he followed her,                             22
like an ox on its way to the slaughter-house,
like an antelope bounding into the noose,
like a bird hurrying into the trap;                             23
he did not know that he was risking his life
until the arrow pierced his vitals.

But now, my son, listen to me,                                  24
attend to what I say.
Do not let your heart entice you into her ways,                 25
do not stray down her paths;
many has she pierced and laid low,                              26
and her victims are without number.
Her house is the entrance to Sheol,                             27
    which leads down to the halls of death.

## Wisdom and folly contrasted

Hear how Wisdom lifts her voice                                  **8**
and Understanding cries out.
She stands at the cross-roads,                                   2
by the wayside, at the top of the hill;
beside the gate, at the entrance to the city,                   3
at the entry by the open gate she calls aloud:
'Men, it is to you I call,                                       4
I appeal to every man:
understand, you simple fools, what it is to be shrewd;          5
you stupid people, understand what sense means.
Listen! For I will speak clearly,                               6
you will have plain speech from me;
for I speak nothing but truth                                   7
and my lips detest wicked talk.

*a* my clothes: *prob. rdg.; Heb. om.*

8  All that I say is right,
   not a word is twisted or crooked.
9  All is straightforward to him who can understand,
   all is plain to the man who has knowledge.
10 Accept instruction and not silver,
   knowledge rather than pure gold;
11 for wisdom is better than red coral,
   no jewels can match her.
12 I am Wisdom, I bestow shrewdness
   and show the way to knowledge and prudence.
13 *a* Pride, presumption, evil courses,
   subversive talk, all these I hate.
14 I have force, I also have ability;
   understanding and power are mine.
15 Through me kings are sovereign
   and governors make just laws.
16 Through me princes act like princes,
   from me all rulers on earth derive their nobility.
17 Those who love me I love,
   those who search for me find me.
18 In my hands are riches and honour,
   boundless wealth and the rewards of virtue.
19 My harvest is better than gold, fine gold,
   and my revenue better than pure silver.
20 I follow the course of virtue,
   my path is the path of justice;
21 I endow with riches those who love me
       and I will fill their treasuries.

22 'The LORD created me the beginning of his works,
   before all else that he made, long ago.
23 Alone, I was fashioned in times long past,
   at the beginning, long before earth itself.
24 When there was yet no ocean I was born,
   no springs brimming with water.
25 Before the mountains were settled in their place,
   long before the hills I was born,
26 when as yet he had made neither land nor lake
   nor the first clod *b* of earth.
27 When he set the heavens in their place I was there,
   when he girdled the ocean with the horizon,
28 when he fixed the canopy of clouds overhead
   and set the springs of ocean firm in their place,
29 when he prescribed its limits for the sea *c*
   and knit together earth's foundations.

---

*a* *Prob. rdg.; Heb. prefixes* The fear of the LORD is to hate evil.     *b* the first clod:
or the sum of the clods.     *c* *Prob. rdg.; Heb. adds* and the water shall not disobey
his command.

Then I was at his side each day,                                         30
his darling and delight,
playing in his presence continually,
playing on the earth, when he had finished it,                           31
while my delight was in mankind.

'Now, my sons, listen to me,                                             32-33
listen to instruction and grow wise, do not reject it.
Happy is the man who keeps to my ways,
happy the man who listens to me,                                         34
watching daily at my threshold
with his eyes on the doorway;
for he who finds me finds life                                           35
and wins favour with the LORD,
while he who finds me not, hurts himself,                                36
and all who hate me are in love with death.'

Wisdom has built her house,                                              **9**
she has hewn her seven pillars;
she has killed a beast and spiced her wine,                              2
and she has spread her table.
She has sent out her maidens to proclaim                                 3
from the highest part of the town,
'Come in, you simpletons.'                                               4
She says also to the fool,
'Come, dine with me                                                      5
and taste the wine that I have spiced.
Cease to be silly, and you will live,                                    6
you will grow in understanding.'

Correct an insolent man, and be sneered at for your pains;              7
correct a bad man, and you will put yourself in the wrong.
Do not correct the insolent or they will hate you;                       8
correct a wise man, and he will be your friend.
Lecture a wise man, and he will grow wiser;                              9
teach a righteous man, and his learning will increase.

The first step to wisdom is the fear of the LORD,                        10
and knowledge of the Holy One is understanding;
for through me your days will be multiplied                              11
and years will be added to your life.
If you are wise, it will be to your own advantage;                       12
if you are haughty, you alone are to blame.
The Lady Stupidity is a flighty creature;                                13
the simpleton, she cares for nothing.
She sits at the door of her house,                                       14
on a seat in the highest part of the town,
to invite the passers-by indoors                                         15
as they hurry on their way:
'Come in, you simpletons', she says.                                     16

She says also to the fool,

17 'Stolen water is sweet
and bread got by stealth tastes good.'

18 Little does he know that death lurks there,
that her guests are in the depths of Sheol.

## *A collection of wise sayings*

**10** The proverbs of Solomon:

A wise son brings joy to his father;
a foolish son is his mother's bane.

2 Ill-gotten wealth brings no profit;
uprightness is a safeguard against death.

3 The LORD does not let the righteous go hungry,[a]
but he disappoints the cravings[b] of the wicked.

4 Idle hands make a man poor;
busy hands grow rich.

5 A thoughtful son puts by in summer;
a son who sleeps at harvest is a disgrace.

6 Blessings are showered on the righteous;
the wicked are choked by their own violence.

7 The righteous are remembered in blessings;
the name of the wicked turns rotten.

8 A wise man takes a command to heart;
a foolish talker comes to grief.

9 A blameless life makes for security;
crooked ways bring a man down.

10 To wink at a fault causes trouble;
a frank rebuke leads to peace.

11 The words of good men are a fountain of life;
the wicked are choked by their own violence.

12 Hate is always picking a quarrel,
but love turns a blind eye to every fault.

13 The man of understanding has wisdom on his lips;
a rod is in store for the back of the fool.

14 Wise men lay up knowledge;
when a fool speaks, ruin is near.

15 A rich man's wealth is his strong city,
but poverty is the undoing of the helpless.

16 The good man's labour is his livelihood;
the wicked man's earnings bring him to a bad end.

17 Correction is the high road to life;
neglect reproof and you miss the way.

18 There is no spite in a just man's talk;
it is the stupid who are fluent with calumny.

19 When men talk too much, sin is never far away;

<hr>

[a] *Or* be afraid.     [b] *Or* the clamour.

common sense holds its tongue.
A good man's tongue is pure silver;  20
the heart of the wicked is trash.
The lips of a good man teach many,  21
but fools perish for want of sense.
The blessing of the LORD brings riches  22
and he sends no sorrow with them.
Lewdness is sport for the stupid;  23
wisdom a delight to men of understanding.
The fears of the wicked will overtake them;  24
the desire of the righteous will be granted.
When the whirlwind has passed by, the wicked are gone;  25
the foundations of the righteous are eternal.
Like vinegar on the teeth or smoke in the eyes,  26
so is the lazy servant to his master.
The fear of the LORD brings length of days;  27
the years of the wicked are few.
The hope of the righteous blossoms;  28
the expectation of the wicked withers away.
The way of the LORD gives refuge to the honest man,  29
but dismays those who do evil.
The righteous man will never be shaken;  30
the wicked shall not remain on earth.
Wisdom flows from the mouth of the righteous;  31
the subversive tongue will be rooted out.
The righteous man can suit his words to the occasion;  32
the wicked know only subversive talk.

False scales are the LORD's abomination;  **11**
correct weights are dear to his heart.
When presumption comes in, in comes contempt,  2
but wisdom goes with sagacity.
Honesty is a guide to the upright,  3
but rogues are balked by their own perversity.
Wealth is worth nothing in the day of wrath,  4
but uprightness is a safeguard against death.
By uprightness the blameless keep their course,  5
but the wicked are brought down by their wickedness.
Uprightness saves the righteous,  6
but rogues are trapped in their own greed.
When a man dies, his thread of life ends,  7
and with it ends the hope of affluence.
A righteous man is rescued from disaster,  8
and the wicked man plunges into it.
By his words a godless man tries to ruin others,  9
but they are saved when the righteous plead for them.
A city rejoices in the prosperity of the righteous;  10
there is jubilation when the wicked perish.

11    By the blessing of the upright a city is built up;
      the words of the wicked tear it down.

12    A man without sense despises others,
      but a man of understanding holds his peace.

13    A gossip gives away secrets,
      but a trusty man keeps his own counsel.

14    For want of skilful strategy an army is lost;
      victory is the fruit of long planning.

15    Give a pledge for a stranger and know no peace;
      refuse to stand surety and be safe.

16    Grace in a woman wins honour,
      but she who hates virtue makes a home for dishonour.
      Be timid in business and come to beggary;
      be bold and make a fortune.

17    Loyalty brings its own reward;
      a cruel man makes trouble for his kin.

18    A wicked man earns a fallacious *a* profit;
      he who sows goodness reaps a sure reward. *b*

19    A man set on righteousness finds life,
      but the pursuit of evil leads to death.

20    The LORD detests the crooked heart,
      but honesty is dear to him.

21    Depend upon it: an evil man shall not escape punishment;
      the righteous and all their offspring shall go free.

22    Like a gold ring in a pig's snout
      is a beautiful woman without good sense.

23    The righteous desire only what is good;
      the hope of the wicked comes to nothing.

24    A man may spend freely and yet grow richer;
      another is sparing beyond measure, yet ends in poverty.

25    A generous man grows fat and prosperous,
      and he who refreshes others will himself be refreshed.

26    He who withholds his grain is cursed by the people,
      but he who sells his corn is blessed.

27    He who eagerly seeks what is good finds much favour,
      but if a man pursues evil it turns upon him.

28    Whoever relies on his wealth is riding for a fall,
      but the righteous flourish like the green leaf.

29    He who brings trouble on his family inherits the wind,
      and a fool becomes slave to a wise man.

30    The fruit of righteousness is a tree of life,
      but violence means the taking away of life.

31    If the righteous in the land get their deserts,
      how much more the wicked man and the sinner!

12    He who loves correction loves knowledge;
      he who hates reproof is a mere brute.

---

*a* Or fraudulent.        *b* a sure reward: *or* the reward of honesty.

A good man earns favour from the LORD; 2
the schemer is condemned.
No man can establish himself by wickedness, 3
but good men have roots that cannot be dislodged.
A capable wife is her husband's crown; 4
one who disgraces him is like rot in his bones.
The purposes of the righteous are lawful; 5
the designs of the wicked are full of deceit.
The wicked are destroyed[a] by their own words; 6
the words of the good man are his salvation.
Once the wicked are down, that is the end of them, 7
but the good man's line continues.
A man is commended for his intelligence, 8
but a warped mind is despised.
It is better to be modest[b] and earn one's living 9
than to be conceited[c] and go hungry.
A righteous man cares for his beast, 10
but a wicked man is cruel at heart.
He who tills his land has enough to eat, 11
but to follow idle pursuits is foolishness.
The stronghold of the wicked crumbles like clay,[d] 12
but the righteous take lasting root.
The wicked man is trapped by his own falsehoods, 13
but the righteous comes safe through trouble.
One man wins success by his words; 14
another gets his due reward by the work of his hands.
A fool thinks that he is always right; 15
wise is the man who listens to advice.
A fool shows his ill humour at once; 16
a clever man slighted conceals his feelings.
An honest speaker comes out with the truth, 17
but the false witness is full of deceit.
Gossip can be sharp as a sword, 18
but the tongue of the wise heals.
Truth spoken stands firm for ever, 19
but lies live only for a moment.
Those who plot evil delude themselves, 20
but there is joy for those who seek the common good.
No mischief will befall the righteous, 21
but wicked men get their fill of adversity.
The LORD detests a liar 22
but delights in the honest man.
A clever man conceals his knowledge, 23
but a stupid man broadcasts his folly.
Diligence brings a man to power, 24
but laziness to forced labour.

[a] *Prob. rdg.; Heb.* are an ambush for blood.    [b] *Or* scorned.    [c] *Or* honoured.
[d] *Prob. rdg.; Heb.* A wicked man covets a stronghold of crumbling earth.

25 An anxious heart dispirits a man,
   and a kind word fills him with joy.
26 A righteous man recoils from evil,[a]
   but the wicked take a path that leads them astray.
27 The lazy hunter puts up no game,
   but the industrious man reaps a rich harvest.[b]
28 The way of honesty leads to life,
   but there is a well-worn path to death.

13 A wise man sees the reason for his father's correction;
   an arrogant man will not listen to rebuke.
2 A good man enjoys the fruit of righteousness,
   but violence is meat and drink for the treacherous.
3 He who minds his words preserves his life;
   he who talks too much comes to grief.
4 A lazy man is torn by appetite unsatisfied,
   but the diligent grow fat and prosperous.
5 The righteous hate falsehood;
   the doings of the wicked are foul and deceitful.
6 To do right is the protection of an honest man,
   but wickedness brings sinners to grief.[c]
7 One man pretends to be rich, although he has nothing;
   another has great wealth but goes in rags.[d]
8 A rich man must buy himself off,
   but a poor man is immune from threats.
9 The light of the righteous burns brightly;
   the embers of the wicked will be put out.
10 A brainless fool causes strife by his presumption;
   wisdom is found among friends in council.
11 Wealth quickly come by dwindles away,
   but if it comes little by little, it multiplies.
12 Hope deferred makes the heart sick;
   a wish come true is a staff of life.
13 To despise a word of advice is to ask for trouble;
   mind what you are told, and you will be rewarded.
14 A wise man's teaching is a fountain of life
   for one who would escape the snares of death.
15 Good intelligence wins favour,
   but treachery leads to disaster.
16 A clever man is wise and conceals everything,
   but the stupid parade their folly.
17 An evil messenger causes trouble,[e]
   but a trusty envoy makes all go well again.
18 To refuse correction brings poverty and contempt;
   one who takes a reproof to heart comes to honour.

---

[a] recoils from evil: *prob. rdg.; Heb.* let him spy out his friend.  [b] but . . . harvest: *prob. rdg.; Heb. obscure.*  [c] brings . . . grief: *or* plays havoc with a man.
[d] One man . . . rags: *or* One man may grow rich though he has nothing; another may grow poor though he has great wealth.  [e] causes trouble: *or* is unsuccessful.

Lust indulged sickens a man;*ᵃ*     19
stupid people loathe to mend their ways.
Walk with the wise and be wise;     20
mix with the stupid and be misled.
Ill fortune follows the sinner close behind,     21
but good rewards the righteous.
A good man leaves an inheritance to his descendants,     22
but the sinner's hoard passes to the righteous.
Untilled land might yield food enough for the poor,     23
but even that may be lost through injustice.
A father who spares the rod hates his son,     24
but one who loves him keeps him in order.
A righteous man eats his fill,     25
    but the wicked go hungry.

The wisest women build up their homes;     **14**
the foolish pull them down with their own hands.
A straightforward man fears the LORD;     2
the double-dealer scorns him.
The speech of a fool is a rod for his back;*ᵇ*     3
a wise man's words are his safeguard.
Where there are no oxen the barn is empty,     4
but the strength of a great ox ensures rich crops.
A truthful witness is no liar;     5
a false witness tells a pack of lies.
A conceited man seeks wisdom, yet finds none;     6
to one of understanding, knowledge comes easily.
Avoid a stupid man,     7
you will hear not a word of sense from him.
A clever man has the wit to find the right way;     8
the folly of stupid men misleads them.
A fool is too arrogant to make amends;     9
upright men know what reconciliation means.
The heart knows its own bitterness,     10
and a stranger has no part in its joy.
The house of the wicked will be torn down,     11
but the home of the upright flourishes.
A road may seem straightforward to a man,     12
yet may end as the way to death.
Even in laughter the heart may grieve,     13
and mirth may end in sorrow.
The renegade reaps the fruit of his conduct,     14
a good man the fruit of his own achievements.
A simple man believes every word he hears;     15
a clever man understands the need for proof.
A wise man is cautious and turns his back on evil;     16

*ᵃ* Lust . . . a man: *or* Desire fulfilled is pleasant to the appetite.     *ᵇ* his back: *prob.*
*rdg.; Heb.* pride.

the stupid is heedless and falls headlong.

17 Impatience runs into folly;
distinction comes by careful thought. *a*

18 The simple wear the trappings of folly;
the clever are crowned with knowledge.

19 Evil men cringe before the good,
wicked men at the righteous man's door.

20 A poor man is odious even to his friend;
the rich have friends in plenty.

21 He who despises a hungry man does wrong,
but he who is generous to the poor is happy.

22 Do not those who intend evil go astray,
while those with good intentions are loyal and faithful?

23 The pains of toil bring gain,
but mere talk brings nothing but poverty.

24 Insight is the crown of the wise;
folly the chief ornament of the stupid.

25 A truthful witness saves life;
the false accuser utters nothing but lies.

26 A strong man who trusts in the fear of the LORD
will be a refuge for his sons.

27 The fear of the LORD is the fountain of life
for the man who would escape the snares of death.

28 Many subjects make a famous king;
with none to rule, a prince is ruined.

29 To be patient shows great understanding;
quick temper is the height of folly.

30 A tranquil mind puts flesh on a man,
but passion rots his bones.

31 He who oppresses *b* the poor insults his Maker;
he who is generous to the needy honours him.

32 An evil man is brought down by his wickedness;
the upright man is secure in his own honesty.

33 Wisdom is at home in a discerning mind,
but is ill at ease in the heart of a fool.

34 Righteousness raises a people to honour;
to do wrong is a disgrace to any nation.

35 A king shows favour to an intelligent servant,
but his displeasure strikes down those who fail him.

15 A soft answer turns away anger,
but a sharp word makes tempers hot.

2 A wise man's tongue spreads knowledge;
stupid men talk nonsense.

3 The eyes of the LORD are everywhere,
surveying evil and good men alike.

*a* distinction . . . thought: *prob. rdg.; Heb.* a man of careful thought is hated.
*b* *Or* slanders.

A soothing word is a staff of life,     4
but a mischievous tongue breaks the spirit.
A fool spurns his father's correction,     5
but to take a reproof to heart shows good sense.
In the righteous man's house there is ample wealth;     6
the gains of the wicked bring trouble.
The lips of a wise man promote knowledge;     7
the hearts of the stupid are dishonest.
The wicked man's sacrifice is abominable to the LORD;     8
the good man's prayer is his delight.
The conduct of the wicked is abominable to the LORD,     9
but he loves the seeker after righteousness.
A man who leaves the main road resents correction,     10
and he who hates reproof will die.
Sheol and Abaddon lie open before the LORD,     11
how much more the hearts of men!
The conceited man does not take kindly to reproof     12
and he will not consult the wise.
A merry heart makes a cheerful face;     13
heartache crushes the spirit.
A discerning mind seeks knowledge,     14
but the stupid man feeds on folly.
In the life of the downtrodden every day is wretched,     15
but to have a glad heart is a perpetual feast.
Better a pittance with the fear of the LORD     16
than great treasure and trouble in its train.
Better a dish of vegetables if love go with it     17
than a fat ox eaten in hatred.
Bad temper provokes a quarrel,     18
but patience heals discords.
The path of the sluggard is a tangle of weeds,     19
but the road of the diligent is a highway.
A wise son brings joy to his father;     20
a young fool despises his mother.
Folly may amuse the empty-headed;     21
a man of understanding makes straight for his goal.
Schemes lightly made come to nothing,     22
but with long planning they succeed.
A man may be pleased with his own retort;     23
how much better is a word in season!
For men of intelligence the path of life leads upwards     24
and keeps them clear of Sheol below.
The LORD pulls down the proud man's home     25
but fixes the widow's boundary-stones.
A bad man's thoughts are the LORD's abomination,     26
but the words of the pure are a delight. [a]

[a] the words . . . delight: *or* gracious words are pure.

27　A grasping man brings trouble on his family,
　　but he who spurns a bribe will enjoy long life.

28　The righteous think before they answer;
　　a bad man's ready tongue is full of mischief.

29　The LORD stands aloof from the wicked,
　　he listens to the righteous man's prayer.

30　A bright look brings joy to the heart,
　　and good news warms a man's marrow.

31　Whoever listens to wholesome reproof
　　shall enjoy the society of the wise.

32　He who refuses correction is his own worst enemy,
　　but he who listens to reproof learns sense.

33　The fear of the LORD is a training in wisdom,
　　and the way to honour is humility.

**16**　A man may order his thoughts,
　　but the LORD inspires the words he utters.

2　A man's whole conduct may be pure in his own eyes,
　　but the LORD fixes a standard for the spirit of man.

3　Commit to the LORD all that you do,
　　and your plans will be fulfilled.

4　The LORD has made each thing for its own end;
　　he made even the wicked for a day of disaster.

5　Proud men, one and all, are abominable to the LORD;
　　depend upon it: they will not escape punishment.

6　Guilt is wiped out by faith and loyalty,
　　and the fear of the LORD makes men turn from evil.

7　When the LORD is pleased with a man and his ways,
　　he makes even his enemies live at peace with him.

8　Better a pittance honestly earned
　　than great gains ill gotten.

9　Man plans his journey by his own wit,
　　but it is the LORD who guides his steps.

10　The king's mouth is an oracle,
　　he cannot err when he passes sentence.

11　Scales*a* and balances*b* are the LORD's concern;
　　all the weights in the bag are his business.

12　Wickedness is abhorrent to kings,
　　for a throne rests firm on righteousness.

13　Honest speech is the desire of kings,
　　they love a man who speaks the truth.

14　A king's anger is a messenger of death,
　　and a wise man will appease it.

15　In the light of the king's countenance is life,
　　his favour is like a rain-cloud in the spring.

16　How much better than gold it is to gain wisdom,
　　and to gain discernment is better than pure silver.

*a* Or Pointer.　　*b* *Prob. rdg.; Heb.* balances of justice.

To turn from evil is the highway of the upright;          17
watch your step and save your life.
Pride comes before disaster,          18
and arrogance before a fall.
Better sit humbly with those in need          19
than divide the spoil with the proud.
The shrewd man of business will succeed well,          20
but the happy man is he who trusts in the LORD.
The sensible man seeks advice from the wise,          21
he drinks it in and increases his knowledge. *a*
Intelligence is a fountain of life to its possessors,          22
but a fool is punished by his own folly.
The wise man's mind guides his speech,          23
and what his lips impart increases learning. *b*
Kind words are like dripping honey,          24
sweetness on the tongue and health for the body.
A road may seem straightforward to a man,          25
yet may end as the way to death.
The labourer's appetite is always plaguing him,          26
his hunger spurs him on.
A scoundrel repeats evil gossip;          27
it is like a scorching fire on his lips.
Disaffection stirs up quarrels,          28
and tale-bearing breaks up friendship.
A man of violence draws others on          29
and leads them into lawless ways.
The man who narrows his eyes is disaffected at heart,          30
and a close-lipped man is bent on mischief.
Grey hair is a crown of glory,          31
and it is won by a virtuous life.
Better be slow to anger than a fighter,          32
better govern one's temper than capture a city.
The lots may be cast into the lap,          33
but the issue depends wholly on the LORD.

Better a dry crust and concord with it          **17**
than a house full of feasting and strife.
A wise slave may give orders to a disappointing son          2
and share the inheritance with the brothers.
The melting-pot is for silver and the crucible for gold,          3
but it is the LORD who assays the hearts of men.
A rogue gives a ready ear to mischievous talk,          4
and a liar listens to slander.
A man who sneers at the poor insults his Maker,          5
and he who gloats over another's ruin will answer for it.
Grandchildren are the crown of old age,          6

*a* he drinks . . . knowledge: *or* and he whose speech is persuasive increases learning.
*b* and what . . . learning: *or* and increases the learning of his utterance.

and sons are proud of their fathers.

7 Fine talk is out of place in a boor,
how much more is falsehood in the noble!

8 He who offers a bribe finds it work like a charm,
he prospers in all he undertakes.

9 He who conceals another's offence seeks his goodwill,
but he who harps on something breaks up friendship.

10 A reproof is felt by a man of discernment
more than a hundred blows by a stupid man.

11 An evil man is set only on disobedience,
but a messenger without mercy will be sent against him.

12 Better face a she-bear robbed of her cubs
than a stupid man in his folly.

13 If a man repays evil for good,
evil will never quit his house.

14 Stealing water starts a quarrel;
drop a dispute before you bare your teeth.

15 To acquit the wicked and condemn the righteous,
both are abominable in the LORD's sight.

16 What use is money in the hands of a stupid man?
Can he buy wisdom if he has no sense?

17 A friend is a loving companion at all times,
and a brother is born to share troubles.

18 A man is without sense who gives a guarantee
and surrenders himself to another as surety.

19 He who loves strife loves sin.
He who builds a lofty entrance invites thieves.

20 A crooked heart will come to no good,
and a mischievous tongue will end in disaster.

21 A stupid man is the bane of his parent,
and his father has no joy in a boorish son.

22 A merry heart makes a cheerful countenance,
but low spirits sap a man's strength.

23 A wicked man accepts a bribe under his cloak
to pervert the course of justice.

24 Wisdom is never out of sight of a discerning man,
but a stupid man's eyes are roving everywhere.

25 A stupid son exasperates his father
and is a bitter sorrow to the mother who bore him.

26 Again, to punish the righteous is not good
and it is wrong to inflict blows on men of noble mind.

27 Experience uses few words;
discernment keeps a cool head.

28 Even a fool, if he holds his peace, is thought wise;
keep your mouth shut and show your good sense.

**18** The man who holds aloof seeks every pretext
to bare his teeth in scorn at competent people.

The foolish have no interest in seeking to understand,    2
but prefer to display their wit.
When wickedness comes in, in comes contempt;    3
with loss of honour comes reproach.
The words of a man's mouth are a gushing torrent,    4
but deep is the water in the well of wisdom.*a*
It is not good to show favour to the wicked    5
or to deprive the righteous of justice.
When the stupid man talks, contention follows;    6
his words provoke blows.
The stupid man's tongue is his undoing;    7
his lips put his life in jeopardy.
A gossip's whispers are savoury morsels,    8
gulped down into the inner man.
Again, the lazy worker is own brother    9
to the man who enjoys destruction.
The name of the Lord is a tower of strength,    10
where the righteous may run for refuge.
A rich man's wealth is his strong city,    11
a towering wall, so he supposes.
Before disaster comes, a man is proud,    12
but the way to honour is humility.
To answer a question before you have heard it out    13
is both stupid and insulting.
A man's spirit may sustain him in sickness,    14
but if the spirit is wounded, who can mend it?
Knowledge comes to the discerning mind;    15
the wise ear listens to get knowledge.
A gift opens the door to the giver    16
and gains access to the great.
In a lawsuit the first speaker seems right,    17
until another steps forward and cross-questions him.
Cast lots, and settle a quarrel,    18
and so keep litigants apart.
A reluctant brother is more unyielding than a fortress,    19
and quarrels are stubborn as the bars of a castle.
A man may live by the fruit of his tongue,    20
his lips may earn him a livelihood.
The tongue has power of life and death;    21
make friends with it and enjoy its fruits.
Find a wife, and you find a good thing;    22
so you will earn the favour of the Lord.
The poor man speaks in a tone of entreaty,    23
and the rich man gives a harsh answer.
Some companions are good only for idle talk,    24
but a friend may stick closer than a brother.

---

*a* The words . . . wisdom: *prob. rdg., inverting phrases.*

**19** Better be poor and above reproach
than rich and crooked in speech.

2 Again, desire without knowledge is not good;
the man in a hurry misses the way.

3 A man's own folly wrecks his life,
and then he bears a grudge against the LORD.

4 Wealth makes many friends,
but a man without means loses the friend he has.

5 A false witness will not escape punishment,
and one who utters nothing but lies will not go free.

6 Many curry favour with the great;
a lavish giver has the world for his friend.

7 A poor man's brothers all dislike him,
how much more is he shunned by his friends!
Practice in evil makes the perfect scoundrel;
the man who talks too much meets his deserts.

8 To learn sense is true self-love;
cherish discernment and make sure of success.

9 A false witness will not escape punishment,
and one who utters nothing but lies will perish.

10 A fool at the helm is out of place,
how much worse a slave in command of men of rank!

11 To be patient shows intelligence;
to overlook faults is a man's glory.

12 A king's rage is like a lion's roar,
his favour like dew on the grass.

13 A stupid son is a calamity to his father;
a nagging wife is like water dripping endlessly.

14 Home and wealth may come down from ancestors,
but an intelligent wife is a gift from the LORD.

15 Laziness is the undoing of the worthless;
idlers must starve.

16 To keep the commandments keeps a man safe,
but scorning the way of the LORD brings death.

17 He who is generous to the poor lends to the LORD;
he will repay him in full measure.

18 Chastise your son while there is hope for him,
but be careful not to flog him to death.

19 A man's ill temper brings its own punishment;
try to save him, and you make matters worse.

20 Listen to advice and accept instruction,
and you will die a wise man.

21 A man's heart may be full of schemes,
but the LORD's purpose will prevail.

22 Greed is a disgrace to a man;
better be a poor man than a liar.

23 The fear of the LORD is life;
he who is full of it will rest untouched by evil.

The sluggard plunges his hand in the dish 24
but will not so much as lift it to his mouth.
Strike an arrogant man, and he resents it like a fool; 25
reprove an understanding man, and he understands what you mean.
He who talks his father down vexes his mother; 26
he is a son to bring shame and disgrace on them.
A son who ceases to accept correction 27
is sure to turn his back on the teachings of knowledge.
A rascally witness perverts justice, 28
and the talk of the wicked fosters mischief.
There is a rod in pickle for the arrogant, 29
and blows ready for the stupid man's back.

Wine is an insolent fellow, and strong drink makes an uproar; **20**
no one addicted to their company grows wise.
A king's threat is like a lion's roar; 2
one who ignores it is his own worst enemy.
To draw back from a dispute is honourable; 3
it is the fool who bares his teeth.
The sluggard who does not plough in autumn 4
goes begging at harvest and gets nothing.
Counsel in another's heart is like deep water, 5
but a discerning man will draw it up.
Many a man protests his loyalty, 6
but where will you find one to keep faith?
If a man leads a good and upright life, 7
happy are the sons who come after him!
A king seated on the judgement-throne 8
has an eye to sift all that is evil.
Who can say, 'I have a clear conscience; 9
I am purged from my sin'?
A double standard in weights and measures 10
is an abomination to the LORD.
Again, a young man is known by his actions, 11
whether his conduct is innocent or guilty.*a*
The ear that hears, the eye that sees, 12
the LORD made them both.
Love sleep, and you will end in poverty; 13
keep your eyes open, and you will eat your fill.
'A bad bargain!' says the buyer to the seller, 14
but off he goes to brag about it.
There is gold in plenty and coral too, 15
but a wise word is a rare jewel.
Take a man's garment when he pledges his word for a stranger 16
and hold that as a pledge for the unknown person.
Bread got by fraud tastes good, 17
but afterwards it fills the mouth with grit.

*a Prob. rdg.; Heb. upright.*

18 Care is the secret of good planning;
    wars are won by skilful strategy.

19 A gossip will betray secrets;<sup>a</sup>
    have nothing to do with a tattler.

20 If a man reviles father and mother,
    his lamp will go out when darkness comes.

21 If you begin by piling up property in haste,
    it will bring you no blessing in the end.

22 Do not think to repay evil for evil,
    wait for the LORD to deliver you.

23 A double standard in weights is an abomination to the LORD,
    and false scales are not good in his sight.

24 It is the LORD who directs a man's steps;
    how can mortal man understand the road he travels?

25 It is dangerous to dedicate a gift rashly
    or to make a vow and have second thoughts.

26 A wise king sifts out the wicked
    and turns back for them the wheel of fortune.

27 The LORD shines into a man's very soul,
    searching out his inmost being.

28 A king's guards are loyalty and good faith,
    his throne is upheld by righteousness.

29 The glory of young men is their strength,
    the dignity of old men their grey hairs.

30 A good beating purges the mind,
    and blows chasten the inmost being.

**21** The king's heart is under the LORD's hand;
    like runnels of water, he turns it wherever he will.

2 A man may think that he is always right,
    but the LORD fixes a standard for the heart.

3 Do what is right and just;
    that is more pleasing to the LORD than sacrifice.

4 Haughty looks and a proud heart—
    these sins mark a wicked man.

5 Forethought and diligence are sure of profit;
    the man in a hurry is as sure of poverty.

6 He who makes a fortune by telling lies
    runs needlessly into the toils of death.

7 The wicked are caught up in their own violence,
    because they refuse to do what is just.

8 The criminal's conduct is tortuous;
    straight dealing is a sign of integrity.

9 Better to live in a corner of the house-top
    than have a nagging wife and a brawling household.

10 The wicked man is set on evil;
    he has no pity to spare for his friend.

<sup>a</sup> *Or* He who betrays secrets is a gossip.

The simple man is made wise when he sees the insolent punished,    11
and learns his lesson when the wise man prospers.
The just God *a* makes the wicked man's home childless; *b*    12
he overturns the wicked and ruins them.
If a man shuts his ears to the cry of the helpless,    13
he will cry for help himself and not be heard.
A gift in secret placates an angry man;    14
a bribe slipped under the cloak pacifies great wrath.
When justice is done, all good men rejoice,    15
but it brings ruin to evildoers.
A man who takes leave of common sense    16
comes to rest in the company of the dead.
Love pleasure and you will beg your bread;    17
a man who loves wine and oil will never grow rich.
The wicked man serves as a ransom for the righteous,    18
so does a traitor for the upright.
Better to live alone in the desert    19
than with a nagging and ill-tempered wife.
The wise man has his home full of fine and costly treasures;    20
the stupid man is a mere spendthrift.
Persevere in right conduct and loyalty    21
and you shall find life and honour.
A wise man climbs into a city full of armed men    22
and undermines its strength and its confidence.
Keep a guard over your lips and tongue    23
and keep yourself out of trouble.
The conceited man is haughty, his name is insolence;    24
conceit and impatience are in all he does.
The sluggard's cravings will be the death of him,    25
because his hands refuse to work;
all day long his cravings go unsatisfied,    26
while the righteous man gives without stint.
The wicked man's sacrifice is an abomination to the LORD;    27
how much more when he offers it with vileness at heart!
A lying witness will perish,    28
but he whose words ring true will leave children behind him.
A wicked man puts a bold face on it,    29
whereas the upright man secures his line of retreat.
Face to face with the LORD,    30
wisdom, understanding, counsel go for nothing.
A horse may be made ready for the day of battle,    31
but victory comes from the LORD.

A good name is more to be desired than great riches;    **22**
esteem is better than silver or gold.
Rich and poor have this in common:    2

---

*a* Or The just man.    *b* makes . . . childless: *prob. rdg.; Heb.* considers the wicked
man's home.

the LORD made them both.

3 A shrewd man sees trouble coming and lies low;
the simple walk into it and pay the penalty.

4 The fruit of humility is the fear of God
with riches and honour and life.

5 The crooked man's path is set with snares and pitfalls;
the cautious man will steer clear of them.

6 Start a boy on the right road,
and even in old age he will not leave it.

7 The rich lord it over the poor;
the borrower becomes the lender's slave.

8 The man who sows injustice reaps trouble,
and the end of his work will be the rod. *a*

9 The kindly man will be blessed,
for he shares his food with the poor.

10 Drive out the insolent man, and strife goes with him;
if he sits on the bench, he makes a mockery of justice.

11 The LORD loves a sincere man;
but you will make a king your friend with your fine phrases.

12 The LORD keeps watch over every claim at law,
and overturns the scoundrel's case.

13 The sluggard protests, 'There's a lion outside;
I shall get myself killed in the street.'

14 The words of an adulteress are like a deep pit;
those whom the LORD has cursed will fall into it.

15 Folly is deep-rooted in the heart of a boy;
a good beating will drive it right out of him.

16 Oppression of the poor may bring gain to a man,
but giving to the rich leads only to penury.

## *Thirty wise sayings*

17 The sayings of the wise:

Pay heed and listen to my words,
open your mind to the knowledge I impart;

18 to keep them in your heart will be a pleasure,
and then you will always have them ready on your lips.

19 I would have you trust in the LORD
and so I tell you these things this day for your own good.

20 Here I have written out for you thirty sayings,
full of knowledge and wise advice,

21 to impart to you a knowledge of the truth,
that you may take back a true report *b* to him who sent you.

22 Never rob a helpless man because he is helpless,
nor ill-treat a poor wretch in court;

*a* the rod: *or* the threshing.          *b* *Prob. rdg.; Heb. adds* words of truth.

for the LORD will take up their cause                              23
and rob him who robs them of their livelihood.
Never make friends with an angry man                               24
nor keep company with a bad-tempered one;
be careful not to learn his ways,                                  25
or you will find yourself caught in a trap.
Never be one to give guarantees,                                   26
or to pledge yourself as surety for another;
for if you cannot pay, beware:                                     27
your bed will be taken from under you.
Do not move the ancient boundary-stone                             28
which your forefathers set up.
You see a man skilful at his craft:                                29
he will serve kings, he will not serve common men.

When you sit down to eat with a ruling prince,                     **23**
be sure to keep your mind on what is before you,
and if you are a greedy man,                                        2
cut your throat first.
Do not be greedy for his dainties,                                  3
for they are not what they seem.
Do not slave to get wealth; *a*                                     4
be a sensible man, and give up.
Before you can look round, it will be gone;                         5
it will surely grow wings
like an eagle, like a bird in the sky.
Do not go to dinner with a miser, *b*                               6
do not be greedy for his dainties;
for they will stick in your *c* throat like a hair.                7
He will bid you eat and drink,
but his heart is not with you;
you will bring up the mouthful you have eaten,                      8
and your winning words will have been wasted.

Hold your tongue in the hearing of a stupid man;                    9
for he will despise your words of wisdom.
Do not move the ancient boundary-stone                             10
or encroach on the land of orphans:
they have a powerful guardian                                      11
who will take up their cause against you.
Apply your mind to instruction                                     12
and open your ears to knowledge when it speaks.
Do not withhold discipline from a boy;                             13
take the stick to him, and save him from death.
If you take the stick to him yourself,                             14
you will preserve him from the jaws of death.

---

*a* to get wealth: *or* for an invitation to a feast.          *b* *Or* a man with an evil eye.
*c* *Prob. rdg.; Heb.* his.

15 My son, if you are wise at heart,
   my heart in its turn will be glad;
16 I shall rejoice with all my soul
   when you speak plain truth.

17 Do not try to emulate sinners;
   envy only those who fear the LORD day by day;
18 do this, and you may look forward to the future,
   and your thread of life will not be cut short.

19 Listen, my son, listen, and become wise;
   set your mind on the right course.
20 Do not keep company with drunkards
   or those who are greedy for the fleshpots;
21 for drink and greed will end in poverty,
   and drunken stupor goes in rags.

22 Listen to your father, who gave you life,
   and do not despise your mother when she is old.
23 Buy truth, never sell it;
   buy wisdom, instruction, and understanding.
24 A good man's father will rejoice
   and he who has a wise son will delight in him.
25 Give your father and your mother cause for delight,
   let her who bore you rejoice.

26 My son, mark my words,
   and accept my guidance with a will.
27 A prostitute is a deep pit,
   a loose woman a narrow well;
28 she lies in wait like a robber
   and betrays her husband with man after man.

29 Whose is the misery? whose the remorse?
   Whose are the quarrels and the anxiety?
   Who gets the bruises without knowing why?
   Whose eyes are bloodshot?
30 Those who linger late over their wine,
   those who are always trying some new spiced liquor.
31 Do not gulp down the wine, the strong red wine,
   when the droplets form on the side of the cup; [a]
32 in the end it will bite like a snake
   and sting like a cobra.
33 Then your eyes see strange sights,
   your wits and your speech are confused;
34 you become like a man tossing out at sea,
   like one who clings to [b] the top of the rigging;

---

[a] *Prob. rdg.; Heb. adds* it runs smoothly to and fro.
*Heb.* lies on.

[b] clings to: *prob. rdg.;*

you say, 'If it lays me flat, what do I care?                          35
If it brings me to the ground, what of it?
As soon as I wake up,
I shall turn to it again.'

Do not emulate wicked men                                              **24**
or long to make friends with them;
for violence is all they think of,                                      2
and all they say means mischief.

Wisdom builds the house,                                                3
good judgement makes it secure,
knowledge furnishes the rooms                                           4
with all the precious and pleasant things that wealth can buy.

Wisdom prevails over strength,                                          5
knowledge over brute force;
for wars are won by skilful strategy,                                   6
and victory is the fruit of long planning.

Wisdom is too high for a fool;                                          7
he dare not open his mouth in court.

A man who is bent on mischief                                           8
gets a name for intrigue;
the intrigues of foolish men misfire,                                   9
and the insolent man is odious to his fellows.

If your strength fails on a lucky*a* day,                              10
how helpless will you be on a day of disaster!

When you see a man being dragged to be killed, go to his rescue,       11
and save those being hurried away to their death.
If you say, 'But I do not know this man',                              12
God, who fixes a standard for the heart, will take note.
God who watches you—be sure he will know;
he will requite every man for what he does.

Eat honey, my son, for it is good,                                     13
and the honeycomb so sweet upon the tongue.
Make wisdom too your own;                                              14
if you find it, you may look forward to the future,
and your thread of life will not be cut short.

Do not lie in wait like a felon at the good man's house,              15
or raid his farm.
Though the good man may fall seven times, he is soon up again,         16
but the rascal is brought down by misfortune.
Do not rejoice when your enemy falls,                                  17
do not gloat when he is brought down;

*a* lucky: *prob. rdg.; Heb. om.*

18    or the LORD will see and be displeased with you,
and he will cease to be angry with him.

19    Do not vie with evildoers
or emulate the wicked;
20    for wicked men have no future to look forward to;
their embers will be put out.

21    My son, fear the LORD and grow rich,
but have nothing to do with men of rank,
22    they will bring about disaster without warning;
who knows what ruin such men may cause*ᵃ*?

23  More sayings of wise men:

Partiality in dispensing justice is not good.
24    A judge who pronounces a guilty man innocent
is cursed by all nations, all peoples execrate him;
25    but for those who convict the guilty all will go well,
they will be blessed with prosperity.
26    A straightforward answer
is as good as a kiss of friendship.

27    First put all in order out of doors
and make everything ready on the land;
then establish your house and home.

28    Do not be a witness against your neighbour without good reason
nor misrepresent him in your evidence.
29    Do not say,
'I will do to him what he has done to me;
I will requite him for what he has done.'

30    I passed by the field of an idle man,
by the vineyard of a man with no sense.
31    I looked, and it was all dried up,
it was overgrown with thistles
and covered with weeds,
and the stones of its walls had been torn down.
32    I saw and I took good note,
I considered and learnt the lesson:
33    a little sleep, a little slumber,
a little folding of the hands in rest,
34    and poverty will come upon you like a robber,
want like a ruffian.

*ᵃ* they . . . cause: *or* they will come to sudden disaster; who knows what the ruin of such men will be.

## *Other collections of wise sayings*

More proverbs of Solomon transcribed by the men of Hezekiah king of **25**
Judah:

The glory of God is to keep things hidden    2
but the glory of kings is to fathom them.
The heavens for height, the earth*ᵃ* for depth:    3
unfathomable is the heart of a king.
Rid silver of its impurities,    4
then it may go to*ᵇ* the silversmith;
rid the king's presence of wicked men,    5
and his throne will rest firmly on righteousness.
Do not put yourself forward in the king's presence    6
or take your place among the great;
for it is better that he should say to you, 'Come up here',    7
than move you down to make room for a nobleman.
Be in no hurry to tell everyone what you have seen,    8
or it will end in bitter reproaches from your friend.
Argue your own case with your neighbour,    9
but do not reveal another man's secrets,
or he will reproach you when he hears of it    10
and your indiscretion will then be beyond recall.
Like apples of gold set in silver filigree    11
is a word spoken in season.
Like a golden earring or a necklace of Nubian gold    12
is a wise man whose reproof finds attentive ears.
Like the coolness of snow in harvest    13
is a trusty messenger to those who send him. *ᶜ*
Like clouds and wind that bring no rain    14
is the man who boasts of gifts he never gives.
A prince may be persuaded by patience,    15
and a soft tongue may break down solid bone. *ᵈ*
If you find honey, eat only what you need,    16
too much of it will make you sick;
be sparing in visits to your neighbour's house,    17
if he sees too much of you, he will dislike you.
Like a club or a sword or a sharp arrow    18
is a false witness who denounces his friend.
Like a tooth decayed or a foot limping    19
is a traitor relied on in the day of trouble.
Like one who dresses*ᵉ* a wound with vinegar,    20
so is the sweetest of singers to the heavy-hearted.
If your enemy is hungry, give him bread to eat;    21
if he is thirsty, give him water to drink;

---

*ᵃ* *Or* the underworld.    *ᵇ* then it may go to: *or* and it will come out bright for.
*ᶜ* *Prob. rdg.; Heb. adds* refreshing his master.    *ᵈ* solid bone: *or* authority.
*ᵉ* *Prob. rdg.; Heb. adds* a garment on a cold day.

22  so you will heap glowing coals on his head,
    and the LORD will reward you.
23  As the north wind holds back the rain,
    so an angry glance holds back slander.
24  Better to live in a corner of the house-top
    than have a nagging wife and a brawling household.
25  Like cold water to the throat when it is dry
    is good news from a distant land.
26  Like a muddied spring or a tainted well
    is a righteous man who gives way to a wicked one.
27  A surfeit of honey is bad for a man,
    and the quest for honour is burdensome.
28  Like a city that has burst out of its confining walls *a*
    is a man who cannot control his temper.

**26**  Like snow in summer or rain at harvest,
    honour is unseasonable in a stupid man.
2   Like a fluttering sparrow or a darting swallow,
    groundless abuse gets nowhere.
3   The whip for a horse, the bridle for an ass,
    the rod for the back of a fool!
4   Do not answer a stupid man in the language of his folly,
    or you will grow like him;
5   answer a stupid man as his folly deserves,
    or he will think himself a wise man.
6   He who sends a fool on an errand
    cuts his own leg off and displays the stump.
7   A proverb in the mouth of stupid men
    dangles helpless as a lame man's legs.
8   Like one who gets the stone caught in his sling
    is he who bestows honour on a fool.
9   Like a thorn that pierces a drunkard's hand
    is a proverb in a stupid man's mouth.
10  Like an archer who shoots at any passer-by *b*
    is one who hires a stupid man or a drunkard.
11  Like a dog returning to its vomit
    is a stupid man who repeats his folly.
12  Do you see that man who thinks himself so wise?
    There is more hope for a fool than for him.
13  The sluggard protests, 'There is a lion *c* in the highway,
    a lion at large in the streets.'
14  A door turns on its hinges,
    a sluggard on his bed.
15  A sluggard plunges his hand in the dish
    but is too lazy to lift it to his mouth.
16  A sluggard is wiser in his own eyes

---

*a* Or *that is breached and left unwalled.*     *b* passer-by: *transposed from end of verse.*
*c* Or snake.

than seven men who answer sensibly.
Like a man who seizes a passing cur by the ears     17
is he who meddles in another's quarrel.
A man who deceives another     19[a]
and then says, 'It was only a joke',
is like a madman shooting at random     18
his deadly darts and arrows.
For lack of fuel a fire dies down     20
and for want of a tale-bearer a quarrel subsides.
Like bellows for the coal and fuel for the fire     21
is a quarrelsome man for kindling strife.
A gossip's whispers are savoury morsels     22
gulped down into the inner man.
Glib speech that covers a spiteful heart     23
is like glaze spread on earthenware.
With his lips an enemy may speak you fair     24
but inwardly he harbours deceit;
when his words are gracious, do not trust him,     25
for seven abominations fill his heart;
he may cloak his enmity in dissimulation,     26
but his wickedness is shown up before the assembly.
If he digs a pit, he will fall into it;     27
if he rolls a stone, it will roll back upon him.
A lying tongue makes innocence seem guilty,     28
and smooth words conceal their sting.

Do not flatter yourself about tomorrow,     **27**
for you never know what a day will bring forth.
Let flattery come from a stranger, not from yourself,     2
from the lips of an outsider and not from your own.
Stone is a burden and sand a dead weight,     3
but to be vexed by a fool is more burdensome than either.
Wrath is cruel and anger is a deluge;     4
but who can stand up to jealousy?
Open reproof is better     5
than love concealed.
The blows a friend gives are well meant,     6
but the kisses of an enemy are perfidious.
A man full-fed refuses honey,     7
but even bitter food tastes sweet to a hungry man.
Like a bird that strays far from its nest     8
is a man far from his home.
Oil and perfume bring joy to the heart,     9
but cares torment a man's very soul.
Do not neglect your own friend or your father's; [b]     10
a neighbour at hand is better than a brother far away.

---

[a] *Verses 18 and 19 transposed.*     [b] *Prob. rdg.; Heb. adds* or how should you enter
your brother's house in the day of your ruin?

11    Be wise, my son, then you will bring joy to my heart,
       and I shall be able to forestall my critics.

12    A shrewd man sees trouble coming and lies low;
       the simple walk into it and pay the penalty.

13    Take a man's garment when he pledges his word for a stranger
       and hold that as a pledge for the unknown person.

14    If one man greets another too heartily,
       he may give great offence.

15    Endless dripping on a rainy day—
       that is what a nagging wife is like.

16    As well try to control the wind as to control her!
       As well try to pick up oil in one's fingers!

17    As iron sharpens iron,
       so one man sharpens the wits of another.

18    He who guards the fig-tree will eat its fruit,
       and he who watches his master's interests will come to honour.

19    As face answers face reflected in the water,
       so one man's heart answers another's.

20    Sheol and Abaddon are insatiable;
       a man's eyes too are never satisfied.

21    The melting-pot is for silver and the crucible for gold,
       but praise is the test of character.

22    Pound a fool with pestle and mortar,*a*
       his folly will never be knocked out of him.

23    Be careful to know your own sheep
       and take good care of your flocks;

24    for possessions do not last for ever,
       nor will a crown endure to endless generations.

25    The grass disappears, new shoots are seen
       and the green growth on the hills is gathered in;

26    the lambs clothe you,
       the he-goats are worth the price of a field,

27    while the goats' milk is enough for your food
       and nourishment for your maidens.

**28**    The wicked man runs away with no one in pursuit,
       but the righteous is like a young lion in repose.

2    It is the fault of a violent man that quarrels start,
       but they are settled by a man of discernment.

3    A tyrant oppressing the poor
       is like driving rain which ruins the crop.

4    The lawless praise wicked men;
       the law-abiding contend with them.

5    Bad men do not know what justice is,
       but those who seek the LORD know everything good.

6    Better be poor and above reproach
       than rich and crooked.

*a* *Prob. rdg.; Heb. adds* with groats.

A discerning son observes the law, 7
but one who keeps riotous company wounds his father.
He who grows rich by lending at discount or at interest 8
is saving for another who will be generous to the poor.
If a man turns a deaf ear to the law, 9
even his prayers are an abomination.
He who tempts the upright into evil courses 10
will himself fall into the pit he has dug.
The honest shall inherit a fortune,
but the wicked shall inherit nothing.
The rich man may think himself wise, 11
but a poor man of discernment sees through him.
When the just are in power, there are great celebrations,*a* 12
but when the wicked come to the top, others are downtrodden.
Conceal your faults, and you will not prosper; 13
confess and give them up, and you will find mercy.
Happy the man who is scrupulous in conduct, 14
but he who hardens his heart falls into misfortune.
Like a starving lion or a thirsty bear 15
is a wicked man ruling a helpless people.
The man who is stupid and grasping will perish, 16
but he who hates ill-gotten gain will live long.
A man charged with bloodshed 17
will jump into a well to escape arrest.
Whoever leads an honest life will be safe, 18
but a rogue will fail, one way or another.
One who cultivates his land has plenty to eat; 19
idle pursuits lead to poverty.
A man of steady character will enjoy many blessings, 20
but one in a hurry to grow rich will not go unpunished.
To show favour is not good; 21
but men will do wrong for a mere crust of bread.
The miser*b* is in a hurry to grow rich, 22
never dreaming that want will overtake him.
Take a man to task and in the end win more thanks 23
than the man with a flattering tongue.
To rob your father or mother and say you do no wrong 24
is no better than wanton destruction.
A self-important*c* man provokes quarrels, 25
but he who trusts in the LORD grows fat and prosperous.
It is plain stupidity to trust in one's own wits, 26
but he who walks the path of wisdom will come safely through.
He who gives to the poor will never want, 27
but he who turns a blind eye gets nothing but curses.
When the wicked come to the top, others are pulled down;*d* 28
but, when they perish, the righteous come into power.

*a* *Or* there is great pageantry.    *b* *Or* The man with the evil eye.    *c* *Or* grasping.
*d* are pulled down: *or* hide themselves.

**29** A man who is still stubborn after much reproof
    will suddenly be broken past mending.

2  When the righteous are in power the people rejoice,
    but they groan when the wicked hold office.

3  A lover of wisdom brings joy to his father,
    but one who keeps company with harlots squanders his wealth.

4  By just government a king gives his country stability,
    but by forced contributions he reduces it to ruin.

5  A man who flatters his neighbour
    is spreading a net for his feet.

6  An evil man is ensnared by his sin, *a*
    but a righteous man lives and flourishes.

7  The righteous man is concerned for the cause of the helpless,
    but the wicked understand no such concern.

8  Arrogance can inflame a city,
    but wisdom averts the people's anger.

9  If a wise man goes to law with a fool,
    he will meet abuse or derision, but get no remedy.

10 Men who have tasted blood hate an honest man,
    but the upright set much store by his life.

11 A stupid man gives free rein to his anger;
    a wise man waits and lets it grow cool.

12 If a prince listens to falsehood,
    all his servants will be wicked.

13 Poor man and oppressor have this in common:
    what happiness each has comes from the LORD.

14 A king who steadfastly deals out justice to the weak
    will be secure for ever on his throne.

15 Rod and reprimand impart wisdom,
    but a boy who runs wild brings shame on his mother.

16 When the wicked are in power, sin is in power,
    but the righteous will gloat over their downfall.

17 Correct your son, and he will be a comfort to you
    and bring you delights of every kind.

18 Where there is no one in authority, *b* the people break loose,
    but a guardian of the law keeps them on the straight path.

19 Mere words will not keep a slave in order;
    he may understand, but he will not respond.

20 When you see someone over-eager to speak, *c*
    there will be more hope for a fool than for him.

21 Pamper a slave from boyhood,
    and in the end he will prove ungrateful.

22 A man prone to anger provokes a quarrel
    and a hot-head is always doing wrong.

23 Pride will bring a man low;
    a man lowly in spirit wins honour.

---

*a* An evil . . . sin: *or* When an evil man steps out a trap awaits him.     *b* *Or* no vision.
*c* *Or* someone hasty in business.

He who goes shares with a thief is his own enemy:     24
he hears himself put on oath and dare not give evidence.
A man's fears will prove a snare to him,     25
but he who trusts in the LORD has a high tower of refuge.
Many seek audience of a prince,     26
but in every case the LORD decides.
The righteous cannot abide an unjust man,     27
nor the wicked a man whose conduct is upright.

Sayings of Agur son of Jakeh from Massa:[a]     **30**

This is the great man's very word: I am weary, O God,
I am weary and worn out;
I am a dumb brute, scarcely a man,     2
without a man's powers of understanding;
I have not learnt wisdom     3
nor have I received knowledge from the Holy One.
Who has ever gone up to heaven and come down again?     4
Who has cupped the wind in the hollow of his hands?
Who has bound up the waters in the fold of his garment?
Who has fixed the boundaries of the earth?
What is his name or his son's name, if you know it?

God's every promise has stood the test:     5
he is a shield to all who seek refuge with him.
Add nothing to his words,     6
or he will expose you for a liar.
Two things I ask of thee;     7
do not withhold them from me before I die.
Put fraud and lying far from me;     8
give me neither poverty nor wealth,
provide me only with the food I need.
If I have too much, I shall deny thee     9
and say, 'Who is the LORD?'
If I am reduced to poverty, I shall steal
and blacken the name of my God.

Never disparage a slave to his master,     10
or he will speak ill of you, and you will pay for it.

There is a sort of people who defame their fathers     11
and do not speak well of their own mothers;
a sort who are pure in their own eyes     12
and yet are not cleansed of their filth;
a sort—how haughty are their looks,     13
how disdainful their glances!
A sort whose teeth are swords,     14
their jaws are set with knives,

----

[a] *from Massa: prob. rdg. (cp. 31. 1); Heb.* the oracle.

they eat the wretched out of the country
and the needy out of house and home. [a]

15    The leech has two daughters;
'Give', says one, and 'Give', says the other.

Three things there are which will never be satisfied,
four which never say, 'Enough!'
16    The grave and a barren womb, [b]
a land thirsty for water
and fire that never says, 'Enough!'

17    The eye that mocks a father or scorns a mother's old age [c]
will be plucked out by magpies
or eaten by the vulture's young.

18   Three things there are which are too wonderful for me,
four which I do not understand:
19    the way of a vulture in the sky,
the way of a serpent on the rock,
the way of a ship out at sea,
and the way of a man with a girl.

20    The way of an unfaithful wife is this:
she eats, then she wipes her mouth
and says, 'I have done no harm.'

21   At three things the earth shakes,
four things it cannot bear:
22    a slave turned king,
a churl gorging himself,
23    a woman unloved when she is married,
and a slave-girl displacing her mistress.

24   Four things there are which are smallest on earth
yet wise beyond the wisest:
25    ants, a people with no strength,
yet they prepare their store of food in the summer;
26    rock-badgers, a feeble folk,
yet they make their home among the rocks;
27    locusts, which have no king,
yet they all sally forth in detachments;
28    the lizard, which can be grasped in the hand,
yet is found in the palaces of kings.

29   Three things there are which are stately in their stride,
four which are stately as they move:
30    the lion, a hero among beasts,
which will not turn tail for anyone;

[a] house and home: *prob. rdg.; Heb.* man.    [b] *Or* a woman's desire.    [c] old age:
*prob. rdg.; Heb. unintelligible.*

the strutting cock and the he-goat;                                     31
and a king going forth to lead his army. *a*

If you are churlish and arrogant                                       32
and fond of filthy talk, hold your tongue;
for wringing out the milk produces curd                                33
and wringing the nose produces blood,
so provocation leads to strife.

Sayings of Lemuel king of Massa, which his mother taught him:     **31**

What, O my son, what shall I say to you,                               2
you, the child of my womb and answer to my prayers?
Do not give the vigour of your manhood to women                       3
nor consort with those who make eyes at *b* kings.
It is not for kings, O Lemuel, not for kings to drink wine            4
nor for princes to crave strong drink;
if they drink, they will forget rights and customs                    5
and twist the law against their wretched victims.
Give strong drink to the desperate                                    6
and wine to the embittered;
such men will drink and forget their poverty                          7
and remember their trouble no longer.
Open your mouth and speak up for the dumb,                            8
against the suit of any that oppose them;
open your mouth and pronounce just sentence                           9
and give judgement for the wretched and the poor.

## A capable wife

Who can find a capable wife?                                          10
Her worth is far beyond coral.
Her husband's whole trust is in her,                                  11
and children are not lacking.
She repays him with good, not evil,                                   12
all her life long.
She chooses wool and flax                                            13
and toils at her work.
Like a ship laden with merchandise,                                  14
she brings home food from far off.
She rises while it is still night                                    15
and sets meat before her household. *c*
After careful thought she buys a field                               16
and plants a vineyard out of her earnings.

---

*a* going forth to lead his army: *prob. rdg.; Heb. unintelligible.*       *b* who make eyes
at: *prob. rdg.; Heb. unintelligible.*       *c* *Prob. rdg.; Heb. adds* and a prescribed portion
for her maidens.

17  She sets about her duties with vigour
    and braces herself for the work.
18  She sees that her business goes well,
    and never puts out her lamp at night.
19  She holds the distaff in her hand,
    and her fingers grasp the spindle.
20  She is open-handed to the wretched
    and generous to the poor.
21  She has no fear for her household when it snows,
    for they are wrapped in two cloaks.
22  She makes her own coverings,
    and clothing of fine linen and purple.
23  Her husband is well known in the city gate
    when he takes his seat with the elders of the land.
24  She weaves linen and sells it,
    and supplies merchants with their sashes.
25  She is clothed in dignity and power
    and can afford to laugh at tomorrow.
26  When she opens her mouth, it is to speak wisely,
    and loyalty is the theme of her teaching.
27  She keeps her eye on the doings of her household
    and does not eat the bread of idleness.
28  Her sons with one accord call her happy;
    her husband too, and he sings her praises:
29  'Many a woman shows how capable she is; *a*
    but you excel them all.'
30  Charm is a delusion and beauty fleeting;
    it is the God-fearing woman who is honoured.
31  Extol her for the fruit of all her toil,
    and let her labours bring her honour in the city gate.

# ECCLESIASTES

## The emptiness of all endeavour

1  THE WORDS OF THE SPEAKER, the son of David, king in
   Jerusalem.
2  Emptiness, emptiness, says the Speaker, emptiness, all is empty.
3  What does man gain from all his labour and his toil here under the sun?
4  Generations come and generations go, while the earth endures for ever.
5  The sun rises and the sun goes down; back it returns to its place *b* and
6  rises there again. The wind blows south, the wind blows north, round and
7  round it goes and returns full circle. All streams run into the sea, yet the

---

*a* Or Many daughters show how capable they are.          *b* back . . . place: *prob. rdg.;*
*Heb.* to its place panting.

sea never overflows; back to the place from which the streams ran they return to run again.

All things are wearisome;*a* no man can speak of them all. Is not the eye 8 surfeited with seeing, and the ear sated with hearing? What has happened 9 will happen again, and what has been done will be done again, and there is nothing new under the sun. Is there anything of which one can say, 10 'Look, this is new'? No, it has already existed, long ago before our time. The men of old are not remembered, and those who follow will not be 11 remembered by those who follow them.

I, the Speaker, ruled as king over Israel in Jerusalem; and in wisdom I 12 13 applied my mind to study and explore all that is done under heaven. It is a sorry business that God has given men to busy themselves with. I have 14 seen all the deeds that are done here under the sun; they are all emptiness and chasing the wind. What is crooked cannot become straight; what is 15 not there cannot be counted. I said to myself, 'I have amassed great wisdom 16 more than all my predecessors on the throne in Jerusalem; I have become familiar with wisdom and knowledge.' So I applied my mind to under- 17 stand wisdom and knowledge, madness and folly, and I came to see that this too is chasing the wind. For in much wisdom is much vexation, and 18 the more a man knows, the more he has to suffer.

I said to myself, 'Come, I will plunge into pleasures and enjoy myself'; **2** but this too was emptiness. Of laughter I said, 'It is madness!' And of 2 pleasure, 'What is the good of that?' So I sought to stimulate myself with 3 wine, in the hope of finding out what was good for men to do under heaven throughout the brief span of their lives. But my mind was guided by wis- dom, not blinded by*b* folly.

I undertook great works; I built myself houses and planted vineyards; 4 I made myself gardens and parks and planted all kinds of fruit-trees in 5 them; I made myself pools of water to irrigate a grove of growing trees; 6 I bought slaves, male and female, and I had my home-born slaves as well; 7 I had possessions, more cattle and flocks than any of my predecessors in Jerusalem; I amassed silver and gold also, the treasure of kings and pro- 8 vinces; I acquired singers, men and women, and all that man delights in.*c* I was great, greater than all my predecessors in Jerusalem; and my wisdom 9 stood me in good stead. Whatever my eyes coveted, I refused them nothing, 10 nor did I deny myself any pleasure. Yes indeed, I got pleasure from all my labour, and for all my labour this was my reward. Then I turned and 11 reviewed all my handiwork, all my labour and toil, and I saw that every- thing was emptiness and chasing the wind, of no profit under the sun.

I set myself to look at wisdom and at madness and folly.*d* Then I per- 12 13 ceived that wisdom is more profitable than folly, as light is more profitable than darkness: the wise man has eyes in his head, but the fool walks in the 14 dark. Yet I saw also that one and the same fate overtakes them both. So I 15 said to myself, 'I too shall suffer the fate of the fool. To what purpose have I been wise? What *e* is the profit of it? Even this', I said to myself, 'is

---

*a Prob. rdg.; Heb.* weary.          *b* not blinded by: *prob. rdg.; Heb.* to grasp.
*c Prob. rdg.; Heb. adds two unintelligible words.*          *d The rest of verse 12 transposed to follow verse 18.*          *e Prob. rdg.; Heb.* Then.

16 emptiness. The wise man is remembered no longer than the fool, for, as
the passing days multiply,[a] all will be forgotten. Alas, wise man and fool
17 die the same death!' So I came to hate life, since everything that was done
here under the sun was a trouble to me; for all is emptiness and chasing the
18 wind. So I came to hate all my labour and toil here under the sun, since I
should have to leave its fruits to my successor. What sort of a man will he
19 be who succeeds me, who inherits what others have acquired?[b] Who knows
whether he will be a wise man or a fool? Yet he will be master of all the
fruits of my labour and skill here under the sun. This too is emptiness.
20    Then I turned and gave myself up to despair, reflecting upon all my
21 labour and toil here under the sun. For anyone who toils with wisdom,
knowledge, and skill must leave it all to a man who has spent no labour on
22 it. This too is emptiness and utterly wrong. What reward has a man for all
23 his labour, his scheming, and his toil here under the sun? All his life long
his business is pain and vexation to him; even at night his mind knows no
24 rest. This too is emptiness. There is nothing better for a man to do than to
eat and drink and enjoy himself in return for his labours. And yet I saw
25 that this comes from the hand of God. For without him who can enjoy his
26 food, or who can be anxious? God gives wisdom and knowledge and joy
to the man who pleases him, while to the sinner is given the trouble of
gathering and amassing wealth only to hand it over to someone else who
pleases God. This too is emptiness and chasing the wind.

3 FOR EVERYTHING ITS SEASON, and for every activity under heaven its
time:

2              a time to be born and a time to die;
              a time to plant and a time to uproot;
3              a time to kill and a time to heal;
              a time to pull down and a time to build up;
4              a time to weep and a time to laugh;
              a time for mourning and a time for dancing;
5              a time to scatter stones and a time to gather them;
              a time to embrace and a time to refrain from embracing;
6              a time to seek and a time to lose;
              a time to keep and a time to throw away;
7              a time to tear and a time to mend;
              a time for silence and a time for speech;
8              a time to love and a time to hate;
              a time for war and a time for peace.

9 10    What profit does one who works get from all his labour? I have seen
11 the business that God has given men to keep them busy. He has made
everything to suit its time; moreover he has given men a sense of time past
and future, but no comprehension of God's work from beginning to end.
12 I know that there is nothing good for man[c] except to be happy and live
13 the best life he can while he is alive. Moreover, that a man should eat and

---

[a] for . . . multiply: *prob. rdg.; Heb.* because already.        [b] What sort . . . acquired:
*see note on verse 12.*      [c] for man: *prob. rdg., cp. 2. 24; Heb.* in them.

drink and enjoy himself, in return for all his labours, is a gift of God. I 14
know that whatever God does lasts for ever; to add to it or subtract from it
is impossible. And he has done it all in such a way that men must feel awe
in his presence. Whatever is has been already,*ᵃ* and whatever is to come has 15
been already, and God summons each event back in its turn. Moreover I 16
saw here under the sun that, where justice ought to be, there was wickedness, and where righteousness ought to be, there was wickedness. I said to 17
myself, 'God will judge the just man and the wicked equally; every activity
and *ᵇ* every purpose has its proper time.' I said to myself, 'In dealing with 18
men it is God's purpose *ᶜ* to test them and to see what they truly are.*ᵈ* For 19
man is a creature of chance and the beasts are creatures of chance, and one
mischance awaits them all: death comes to both alike. They all draw the
same breath. Men have no advantage over beasts; for everything is emptiness. All go to the same place: all came from the dust, and to the dust all 20
return. Who knows whether the spirit *ᵉ* of man goes upward or whether 21
the spirit *ᵉ* of the beast goes downward to the earth?' So I saw that there is 22
nothing better than that a man should enjoy his work, since that is his lot.
For who can bring him through to see what will happen next?

Again, I considered all the acts of oppression here under the sun; I saw **4**
the tears of the oppressed, and I saw that there was no one to comfort them.
Strength was on the side of their oppressors, and there was no one to avenge
them. I counted the dead happy because they were dead, happier than the 2
living who are still in life. More fortunate than either I reckoned the man 3
yet unborn, who had not witnessed the wicked deeds done here under the
sun. I considered all toil and all achievement and saw that it comes from 4
rivalry between man and man. This too is emptiness and chasing the wind.
The fool folds his arms and wastes away. Better one hand full and peace of 5 6
mind, than both fists full and toil that is chasing the wind.

Here again, I saw emptiness under the sun: a lonely man without a 7 8
friend, without son or brother, toiling endlessly yet never satisfied with his
wealth—'For whom', he asks, 'am I toiling and denying myself the good
things of life?' This too is emptiness, a sorry business. Two are better 9
than one; they receive a good reward for their toil, because, if one falls, the 10
other *ᶠ* can help his companion up again; but alas for the man who falls
alone with no partner to help him up. And, if two lie side by side, they keep 11
each other warm; but how can one keep warm by himself? If a man is 12
alone, an assailant may overpower him, but two can resist; and a cord of
three strands is not quickly snapped.

Better a young man poor and wise than a king old and foolish who will 13
listen to advice no longer. A man who leaves prison may well come to be 14
king, though born a pauper in his future kingdom. But I have studied all 15
life here under the sun, and I saw his place taken by yet another young man,
and no limit set to the number of the subjects whose master he became. 16
And he in turn will be no hero to those who come after him. This too is
emptiness and chasing the wind.

*ᵃ* *Or* Whatever has been already is.     *ᵇ* *Prob. rdg.; Heb.* and upon.     *ᶜ* it is God's
purpose: *prob. rdg.; Heb. obscure.*          *ᵈ* *Prob. rdg.; Heb.* adds they to them.
*ᵉ* *Or* breath.          *ᶠ* if one falls, the other: *prob. rdg.; Heb. obscure.*

5 Go carefully when you visit the house of God. Better draw near in
2 obedience than offer the sacrifice of fools, who sin without a thought. Do
not rush into speech, let there be no hasty utterance in God's presence.
3 God is in heaven, you are on earth; so let your words be few. The sensible
man has much business on his hands; the fool talks and it is so much chatter.
4 When you make a vow to God, do not be slow to pay it, for he has no use for
5 fools; pay whatever you vow. Better not vow at all than vow and fail to pay.
6 Do not let your tongue lead you into sin, and then say before the angel of
God that it was a mistake; or God will be angry at your words, and all your
7 achievements will be brought to nothing.[a] You must fear God.
8 If you witness in some province the oppression of the poor and the
denial of right and justice, do not be surprised at what goes on, for every
official has a higher one set over him, and the highest[b] keeps watch over
9 them all. The best thing for a country is a king whose[c] own lands are well
tilled.
10 The man who loves money can never have enough, and the man who is
in love with great wealth enjoys no return from it. This too is emptiness.
11 When riches multiply, so do those who live off them; and what advantage
12 has the owner, except to look at them? Sweet is the sleep of the labourer
whether he eats little or much; but the rich man owns too much and cannot
13 sleep. There is a singular evil here under the sun which I have seen: a man
14 hoards wealth to his own hurt, and then that wealth is lost through an
15 unlucky venture, and the owner's son left with nothing. As he came from
the womb of mother earth, so must he return, naked as he came; all his
16 toil produces nothing which he can take away with him. This too is a
singular evil: exactly as he came, so shall he go, and what profit does he
17 get when his labour is all for the wind? What is more, all his days are overshadowed; gnawing anxiety and great vexation are his lot, sickness[d] and
18 resentment. What I have seen is this: that it is good and proper for a man
to eat and drink and enjoy himself in return for his labours here under the
19 sun, throughout the brief span of life which God has allotted him. Moreover, it is a gift of God that every man to whom he has granted wealth and
riches and the power to enjoy them should accept his lot and rejoice in his
20 labour. He will not dwell overmuch upon the passing years; for God fills
his[e] time with joy of heart.
6 Here is an evil under the sun which I have seen, and it weighs heavy
2 upon men. Consider the man to whom God grants wealth, riches, and substance,[f] and who lacks nothing that he has set his heart on: if God has not
given him the power to enjoy these things, but a stranger enjoys them
3 instead, that is emptiness and a grave disorder. A man may have a hundred
children and live a long life; but however many his days may be, if he does
not get satisfaction from the good things of life and in the end receives no
4 burial, then I maintain that the still-born child is in better case than he. Its
coming is an empty thing, it departs into darkness, and in darkness its

---

[a] *Prob. rdg.; Heb. adds* for in a multitude of dreams and empty things and many words.
[b] for every . . . the highest: *or though every . . . over him, the Highest . . .*  [c] whose:
*prob. rdg.; Heb.* for.  [d] sickness: *prob. rdg.; Heb.* and his sickness.  [e] his: *prob.
rdg.; Heb. om.*  [f] *Or honour.*

name is hidden; it has never seen the sun or known anything,[a] yet its state 5
is better than his. What if a man should live a thousand years twice over, 6
and never prosper? Do not both go to one place?

The end of all man's toil is but to fill his belly, yet his appetite is never 7
satisfied. What advantage then in facing life has the wise man over the fool, 8
or the poor man for all his experience? It is better to be satisfied with what 9
is before your eyes than give rein to desire; this too is emptiness and chasing the wind. Whatever has already existed has been given a name, its 10
nature is known; a man cannot contend with what is stronger than he. The 11
more words one uses the greater is the emptiness of it all; and where is the
advantage to a man? For who can know what is good for a man in this life, 12
this brief span of empty existence through which he passes like a shadow?
Who can tell a man what is to happen next here under the sun?

## Wisdom and folly compared

A GOOD NAME SMELLS SWEETER than the finest ointment, and the 7
day of death is better than the day of birth. Better to visit the house of 2
mourning than the house of feasting; for to be mourned is the lot of every
man, and the living should take this to heart. Grief is better than laughter: 3
a sad face may go with a cheerful heart. Wise men's thoughts are at home 4
in the house of mourning, but a fool's thoughts in the house of mirth. It is 5
better to listen to a wise man's rebuke than to the praise of fools. For the 6
laughter of a fool is like the crackling of thorns under a pot. This too is
emptiness. Slander drives a wise man crazy and breaks a strong man's[b] 7
spirit. Better the end of anything than its beginning; better patience than 8
pride. Do not be quick to show resentment; for resentment is nursed by 9
fools. Do not ask why the old days were better than these; for that is a 10
foolish question. Wisdom is better than possessions and an advantage to 11
all who see the sun. Better have wisdom behind you than money; wisdom 12
profits men by giving life to those who know her.

Consider God's handiwork; who can straighten what he has made 13
crooked? When things go well, be glad; but when things go ill, consider 14
this: God has set the one alongside the other in such a way that no one can
find out what is to happen next.[c] In my empty existence I have seen it all, 15
from a righteous man perishing in his righteousness to a wicked man
growing old in his wickedness. Do not be over-righteous and do not be 16
over-wise. Why make yourself a laughing-stock? Do not be over-wicked 17
and do not be a fool. Why should you die before your time? It is good to 18
hold on to the one thing and not lose hold of the other; for a man who fears
God will succeed both ways. Wisdom makes the wise man stronger than 19
the ten rulers of a city. The world contains no man so righteous that he can 20
do right always and never do wrong.[d] Moreover, do not pay attention to 21
everything men say, or you may hear your servant disparage you; for you 22

[a] Or it.    [b] strong man's: *prob. rdg.; Heb.* obscure.    [c] find out . . . next: *or*
hold him responsible.          [d] can do . . . wrong: *or* prospers without ever making
a mistake.

23 know very well how many times you yourself have disparaged others. All
this I have put to the test of wisdom. I said, 'I am resolved to be wise', but
24 wisdom was beyond my grasp—whatever has happened lies beyond our
grasp, deep down, deeper than man can fathom.
25 I went on to reflect, I set my mind *a* to inquire and search for wisdom and
for the reason in things, only to discover that it is folly to be wicked and
26 madness to act like a fool. The wiles of a woman I find mightier *b* than
death; her heart is a trap to catch you and her arms are fetters. The man
27 who is pleasing to God may escape her, but she will catch a sinner. 'See,'
says the Speaker, 'this is what I have found, reasoning things out one by
28 one, after searching long without success: I have found one man in a
thousand worth the name, but I have not found one woman among them
29 all. This alone I have found, that God, when he made man, made him
straightforward, but man invents endless subtleties of his own.'

8   Who is wise enough for all this? Who knows the meaning of anything?
2 Wisdom lights up a man's face, but grim looks make a man hated. *c* Do as
the king commands you, and if you have to swear by God, do not be
3 precipitate. Leave the king's presence and do not persist in a thing which
4 displeases him; he does what he chooses. For the king's word carries
5 authority. Who can question what he does? Whoever obeys a command
will come to no harm. A wise man knows in his heart the right time and
6 method for action. There is a time and a method for every enterprise,
7 although man is greatly troubled by ignorance of the future; who can tell
8 him what it will bring? It is not in man's power to restrain the wind, *d*
and no one has power over the day of death. In war no one can lay aside
9 his arms, no wealth will save its possessor. All this I have seen, having
applied my mind to everything done under the sun. There was a time when
10 one man had power over another and could make him suffer. It was then
that I saw wicked men approaching and even entering *e* the holy place;
and they went about the city priding themselves on having done right. This
11 too is emptiness. It is because sentence upon a wicked act is not promptly
12 carried out that men do evil so boldly. A sinner may do wrong *f* and live to
old age, yet I know that it will be well with those who fear God: their fear
13 of him ensures this, but it will not be well with a wicked man nor will he
14 live long; the man who does not fear God is a mere shadow. There is an
empty thing found on earth: when the just man gets what is due to the
unjust, and the unjust what is due to the just. I maintain that this too is
15 emptiness. So I commend enjoyment, since there is nothing good for a
man to do here under the sun but to eat and drink and enjoy himself; this
is all that will remain with him to reward his toil throughout the span of
16 life which God grants him here under the sun. I applied my mind to acquire
wisdom and to observe the business which goes on upon earth, when man
17 never closes an eye in sleep day or night; and always I perceived that God
has so ordered it that man should not be able to discover what is happening
here under the sun. However hard a man may try, he will not find out; the

---

*a Prob. rdg.; Heb. adds* to know and.     *b Or* more bitter.     *c* make . . . hated:
*prob. rdg.; Heb. obscure.*     *d Or* to retain the breath of life.     *e* approaching . . .
entering: *prob. rdg.; Heb. obscure.*     *f Prob. rdg.; Heb. adds an unintelligible word.*

wise man may think that he knows, but he will be unable to find the truth of it.

I applied my mind to all this, and I understood that the righteous and 9 the wise and all their doings are under God's control; but is it love or hatred? No man knows. Everything that confronts him, everything is empty, since 2 one and the same fate befalls every one, just and unjust alike, good and bad, clean and unclean, the man who offers sacrifice and the man who does not. Good man and sinner fare alike, the man who can take an oath and the man who dares not. This is what is wrong in all that is done here under the sun: 3 that one and the same fate befalls every man. The hearts of men are full of evil; madness fills their hearts all through their lives, and after that they go down to join the dead. But for a man who is counted among the living 4 there is still hope: remember, a live dog is better than a dead lion. True, 5 the living know that they will die; but the dead know nothing. There are no more rewards for them; they are utterly forgotten. For them love, hate, 6 ambition,[a] all are now over. Never again will they have any part in what is done here under the sun.

Go to it then, eat your food and enjoy it, and drink your wine with a 7 cheerful heart; for already God has accepted what you have done. Always 8 be dressed in white and never fail to anoint your head. Enjoy life with a 9 woman you love all the days of your allotted span here under the sun, empty as they are;[b] for that is your lot while you live and labour here under the sun. Whatever task lies to your hand, do it with all your might; because 10 in Sheol, for which you are bound, there is neither doing nor thinking, neither understanding nor wisdom. One more thing I have observed here 11 under the sun: speed does not win the race nor strength the battle. Bread does not belong to the wise, nor wealth to the intelligent, nor success to the skilful; time and chance govern all. Moreover, no man knows when his 12 hour will come; like fish caught in a net, like a bird taken in a snare, so men are trapped when bad times come suddenly.

This too is an example of wisdom as I have observed it here under the 13 sun, and notable I find it. There was a small town with few inhabitants, and 14 a great king came to attack it; he besieged it and constructed great siege-works against it. There was in it a poor wise man, and he alone might have 15 saved the town by his wisdom, but no one remembered that poor wise man. 'Surely', I said to myself, 'wisdom is better than strength.' But the poor 16 man's wisdom was despised, and his words went unheeded. A wise man 17 who speaks his mind calmly is more to be heeded than a commander shouting orders among fools. Wisdom is better than weapons of war, and 18 one mistake can undo many things done well.

Dead flies make the perfumer's sweet ointment turn rancid and ferment; 10 so can a little folly make wisdom lose its worth. The mind of the wise man 2 faces right, but the mind of the fool faces left. Even when he walks along 3 the road, the fool shows no sense and calls everyone else[c] a fool. If your 4 ruler breaks out in anger against you, do not resign your post; submission makes amends for great mistakes. There is an evil that I have observed 5

---

[a] *Or* passion.          [b] *Prob. rdg.; Heb. adds* all your days, empty as they are.
[c] calls everyone else: *or* tells everyone he is.

6 here under the sun, an error for which a ruler is responsible: the fool given
7 high office, but *a* the great and the rich in humble posts. I have seen slaves
8 on horseback and men of high rank going on foot like slaves. The man who
digs a pit may fall into it, and he who pulls down a wall may be bitten by a
9 snake. The man who quarries stones may strain himself, and the wood-
10 cutter runs a risk of injury. When the axe is blunt and has not first *b* been
sharpened, then one must use more force; the wise man has a better chance
11 of success. If a snake bites before it is charmed, the snake-charmer loses
his fee.

12 A wise man's words win him favour, but a fool's tongue is his undoing.
13 14 He begins by talking nonsense and ends in mischief run mad. The fool
talks on and on; but no man knows what is coming, and who can tell him
15 what will come after that? The fool wearies himself to death *c* with all his
labour, for he does not know the way to town.

16 Woe betide the land when a slave has become its king, and its princes
17 feast in the morning. Happy the land when its king is nobly born, and its
princes feast at the right time of day, with self-control, and not as drunkards.
18 If the owner is negligent the rafters collapse, and if he is idle the house
19 crumbles away. The table has its pleasures, and wine makes a cheerful
20 life; and money is behind it all. Do not speak ill of the king in your ease, or
of a rich man in your bedroom; for a bird may carry your voice, and a
winged messenger may repeat what you say.

**11** 1 2 Send your grain across the seas, and in time you will get a return. Divide
your merchandise among seven ventures, eight maybe, since you do not
3 know what disasters may occur on earth. *d* If the clouds are heavy with rain,
they will discharge it on the earth; whether a tree falls south or north, it
4 must lie as it falls. He who watches the wind will never sow, and he who
5 keeps an eye on the clouds will never reap. You do not know how a pregnant
woman comes to have a body and a living spirit in her womb; nor do you
6 know how God, the maker of all things, works. In the morning sow your
seed betimes, and do not stop work until evening, for you do not know
whether this or that sowing will be successful, or whether both alike will
do well.

## Advice to a young man

7 THE LIGHT OF DAY IS SWEET, and pleasant to the eye is the sight
8 of the sun; if a man lives for many years, he should rejoice in all of
them. But let him remember that the days of darkness will be many.
9 Everything that is to come will be emptiness. Delight in your boyhood,
young man, make the most of the days of your youth; let your heart
and your eyes show you the way; but remember that for all these things
10 God will call you to account. Banish discontent from your mind, and
shake off the troubles of the body; boyhood and the prime of life are mere
emptiness.

*a* but: *prob. rdg.; Heb. om.*    *b* first: *prob. rdg.; Heb.* face.    *c* fool . . . death:
*prob. rdg.; Heb. obscure.*    *d* *Or* on land.

Remember your Creator in the days of your youth, before the time of **12**
trouble comes and the years draw near when you will say, 'I see no purpose
in them.'<sup>a</sup> Remember him before the sun and the light of day give place 2
to darkness, before the moon and the stars grow dim, and the clouds return
with the rain—when the guardians of the house tremble, and the strong 3
men stoop, when the women grinding the meal cease work because they
are few, and those who look through the windows look no longer, when 4
the street-doors are shut, when the noise of the mill is low, when the chirp-
ing of the sparrow grows faint <sup>b</sup> and the song-birds fall silent;<sup>c</sup> when men 5
are afraid of a steep place and the street is full of terrors, when the blossom
whitens on the almond-tree and the locust's paunch is swollen and caper-
buds have no more zest. For man goes to his everlasting home, and the
mourners go about the streets. Remember him before the silver cord is 6
snapped <sup>d</sup> and the golden bowl is broken, before the pitcher is shattered at
the spring and the wheel broken at the well, before the dust returns to the 7
earth as it began and the spirit<sup>e</sup> returns to God who gave it. Emptiness, 8
emptiness, says the Speaker, all is empty.

So the Speaker, in his wisdom, continued to teach the people what he 9
knew. He turned over many maxims in his mind and sought how best to
set them out. He chose his words to give pleasure, but what he wrote was 10
the honest truth. The sayings of the wise are sharp as goads, like nails 11
driven home; they lead the assembled people, for they come from one
shepherd. One further warning, my son: the use of books is endless, and 12
much study is wearisome.

This is the end of the matter: you have heard it all. Fear God and obey 13
his commands; there is no more to man than this. For God brings every- 14
thing we do to judgement, and every secret, whether good or bad.

# THE SONG OF SONGS

*Bride <sup>f</sup>*

| | |
|---|---|
| I will sing the song of all songs to Solomon | 1 |
| that he may <sup>g</sup> smother me with kisses. | 2 |
| | |
| Your love is more fragrant than wine, | |
| fragrant is <sup>h</sup> the scent of your perfume, | 3 |
| and your name like perfume poured out; <sup>i</sup> | |
| for this the maidens love you. | |
| Take me with you, and we will run together; | 4 |
| bring me into your chamber, O king. | |

<sup>a</sup> *Or* I have no pleasure in them.　　　　　<sup>b</sup> grows faint: *prob. rdg.; Heb. obscure.*
<sup>c</sup> *Prob. rdg.; Heb.* sink low.　　　　　<sup>d</sup> is snapped: *prob. rdg.; Heb. unintelligible.*
<sup>e</sup> *Or* breath.　　　<sup>f</sup> *The Hebrew text implies, by its pronouns, different speakers, but does
not indicate them; they are given, however, in two MSS. of Sept.*　　　<sup>g</sup> I will . . . that
he may: *or* The song of all songs which was Solomon's; may he . . .　　　<sup>h</sup> *Or* more
fragrant than.　　　<sup>i</sup> poured out: *prob. rdg.; Heb. word uncertain.*

*Companions*
>Let us rejoice and be glad for you;
>let us praise your love more than wine,
>>and your caresses more than any song.

*Bride*

5
>I am dark but lovely, daughters of Jerusalem,
>>like the tents of Kedar
>>or the tent-curtains of Shalmah.

6
>Do not look down on me; a little dark I may be
>>because I am scorched by the sun.
>My mother's sons were displeased with me,
>they sent me to watch over the vineyards;
>so I did not watch over my own vineyard.

7
Tell me, my true love,
>>where you mind your flocks,
>where you rest them at midday,
>that I may not be left picking lice
>>as I sit among your companions' herds.

*Bridegroom*

8
>If you yourself do not know,
>>O fairest of women,
>go, follow the tracks of the sheep
and mind your kids by the shepherds' huts.

9
>I would compare you, my dearest,
>>to Pharaoh's chariot-horses.

10
>Your cheeks are lovely between plaited tresses,
>>your neck with its jewelled chains.

*Companions*

11
>We will make you braided plaits of gold
>>set with beads of silver.

*Bride*

12
>While the king reclines on his couch,
>my spikenard gives forth its scent.

13
>My beloved is for me a bunch of myrrh
>>as he lies on my breast,

14
>my beloved is for me a cluster of henna-blossom
>>from the vineyards of En-gedi.

*Bridegroom*

15
>How beautiful you are, my dearest,
>>O how beautiful,
>>>your eyes are like doves!

*Bride*
> How beautiful you are, O my love,                    16
> and how pleasant!

*Bridegroom*
> Our couch is shaded with branches;
> the beams of our house are of cedar,                    17
> our ceilings are all of fir.

*Bride*
> I am an asphodel in Sharon,                    2
> a lily growing in the valley.

*Bridegroom*
> No, a lily among thorns                    2
> is my dearest among girls.

*Bride*
> Like an apricot-tree among the trees of the wood,                    3
> so is my beloved among boys.
> To sit in its shadow was my delight,
> and its fruit was sweet to my taste.
> He took me into the wine-garden                    4
> and gave me loving glances.
> He refreshed me with raisins, he revived me with apricots;                    5
> for I was faint with love.
> His left arm was under my head, his right arm was round me.                    6

*Bridegroom*
> I charge you, daughters of Jerusalem,                    7
> by the spirits and the goddesses *a* of the field:
> Do not rouse her, do not disturb my love
> until she is ready. *b*

*Bride*
> Hark! My beloved! Here he comes,                    8
> bounding over the mountains, leaping over the hills.
> My beloved is like a gazelle                    9
> or a young wild goat:
> there he stands outside our wall,
> peeping in at the windows, glancing through the lattice.
>
> My beloved answered, he said to me:                    10
> Rise up, my darling;
> my fairest, come away.

---

*a* by . . . goddesses: *or* by the gazelles and the hinds.          *b* until . . . ready: *or* while
she is resting.

11         For now the winter is past,
        the rains are over and gone;
12         the flowers appear in the country-side;
        the time is coming when the birds will sing,
        and the turtle-dove's cooing will be heard in our land;
13         when the green figs will ripen on the fig-trees
        and the vines *a* give forth their fragrance.
        Rise up, my darling;
        my fairest, come away.

*Bridegroom*

14         My dove, that hides in holes in the cliffs
        or in crannies on the high ledges,
        let me see your face, let me hear your voice;
        for your voice is pleasant, your face is lovely.

*Companions*

15         Catch for us the jackals, the little jackals, *b*
        that spoil our vineyards, when the vines are in flower.

*Bride*

16         My beloved is mine and I am his;
        he delights in the lilies.
17         While the day is cool and the shadows are dispersing,
        turn, my beloved, and show yourself
        a gazelle or a young wild goat
        on the hills where cinnamon grows. *c*

3         Night after night on my bed
        I have sought my true love;
        I have sought him but not found him,
        I have called him but he has not answered.
2         I said, 'I will rise and go the rounds of the city,
        through the streets and the squares,
        seeking my true love.'
        I sought him but I did not find him,
        I called him but he did not answer.
3         The watchmen, going the rounds of the city, met me,
        and I asked, 'Have you seen my true love?'
4         Scarcely had I left them behind me
        when I met my true love.
        I seized him and would not let him go
        until I had brought him to my mother's house,
        to the room of her who conceived me.

*a Prob. rdg.; Heb. adds* blossom.    *b Or* fruit-bats.    *c* on . . . grows: *or* on the
rugged hills *or* on the hills of Bether.

**Bridegroom**

> I charge you, daughters of Jerusalem,                                                    5
> by the spirits and the goddesses <sup>a</sup> of the field:
> Do not rouse her, do not disturb my love
>     until she is ready. <sup>b</sup>

**Companions**

> What is this coming up from the wilderness                                               6
>     like a column of smoke
>     from burning myrrh or frankincense,
>     from all the powdered spices that merchants bring?
> Look; it is Solomon carried in his litter;                                               7
> sixty of Israel's chosen warriors
>     are his escort,
>     all of them skilled swordsmen,                                                       8
>     all trained to handle arms,
> each with his sword ready at his side
>     to ward off the demon of the night.

> The palanquin which King Solomon had made for himself                                    9
>     was of wood from Lebanon.
> Its poles he had made of silver,                                                         10
>     its head-rest of gold;
>     its seat was of purple stuff,
> and its lining was of leather.

> Come out, daughters of Jerusalem;                                                        11
> you daughters of Zion, come out and welcome King Solomon,
>     wearing the crown with which his mother has crowned him,
>     on his wedding day, on his day of joy.

**Bridegroom**

> How beautiful you are, my dearest, how beautiful!                                        **4**
> Your eyes behind your veil are like doves,
> your hair like a flock of goats streaming down Mount Gilead.
>     Your teeth are like a flock of ewes just shorn                                        2
>         which have come up fresh from the dipping;
> each ewe has twins and none has cast a lamb.
>     Your lips are like a scarlet thread,                                                  3
>         and your words are delightful; <sup>c</sup>
>     your parted lips behind your veil
>         are like a pomegranate cut open.
>     Your neck is like David's tower,                                                      4
>         which is built with winding courses;
>     a thousand bucklers hang upon it,
>         and all are warriors' shields.

---

<sup>a</sup> by . . . goddesses: *or* by the gazelles and the hinds.     <sup>b</sup> until . . . ready: *or* while
she is resting.     <sup>c</sup> *Or* and your mouth is lovely.

5    Your two breasts are like two fawns,
     twin fawns of a gazelle. [a]
6    While the day is cool and the shadows are dispersing,
     I will go to the mountains of myrrh
     and to the hills of frankincense.
7    You are beautiful, my dearest,
     beautiful without a flaw.

8   Come from Lebanon, my bride;
    come with me from Lebanon.
    Hurry down from the top of Amana,
     from Senir's top and Hermon's,
     from the lions' lairs, and the hills the leopards haunt.

9    You have stolen my heart,[b] my sister,
     you have stolen it,[c] my bride,
     with one of your eyes, with one jewel of your necklace.
10   How beautiful are your breasts, my sister, my bride!
     Your love is more fragrant than wine,
     and your perfumes sweeter than any spices.
11    Your lips drop sweetness like the honeycomb, my bride,
     syrup and milk are under your tongue,
     and your dress has the scent of Lebanon.
13[d]    Your two cheeks[e] are an orchard of pomegranates,
     an orchard full of rare fruits: [f]
14  spikenard and saffron, sweet-cane and cinnamon
    with every incense-bearing tree,
     myrrh and aloes
    with all the choicest spices.
12    My sister, my bride, is a garden close-locked,
  a garden close-locked, a fountain sealed.

*Bride*
15   The fountain in my garden[g] is a spring of running water
     pouring down from Lebanon.
16   Awake, north wind, and come, south wind;
   blow upon my garden that its perfumes may pour forth,
    that my beloved may come to his garden
     and enjoy its rare fruits.

*Bridegroom*
5    I have come to my garden, my sister and bride,
    and have plucked my myrrh with my spices;
    I have eaten my honey and my syrup,
    I have drunk my wine and my milk.

[a] *Prob. rdg.; Heb. adds* which delight in the lilies.   [b] stolen my heart: *or* put
heart into me.  [c] stolen it: *or* put heart into me.  [d] *Verse 12 transposed to
follow verse 14.*  [e] Your two cheeks: *prob. rdg.; Heb.* Your shoots.  [f] *Prob. rdg.;
Heb. adds* henna with spikenard.  [g] my garden: *prob. rdg.; Heb.* gardens.

    Eat, friends, and drink,
      until you are drunk with love.

*Bride*

    I sleep but my heart is awake.      2
    Listen! My beloved is knocking:

'Open to me, my sister, my dearest,
    my dove, my perfect one;
for my head is drenched with dew,
    my locks with the moisture of the night.'

'I have stripped off my dress; must I put it on again?  3
I have washed my feet; must I soil them again?'

When my beloved slipped his hand through the latch-hole,  4
    my bowels stirred within me.
When I arose to open for my beloved,  5
    my hands dripped with myrrh;
the liquid myrrh from my fingers
    ran over the knobs of the bolt.
    With my own hands I opened to my love,  6
    but my love had turned away and gone by;
    my heart sank when he turned his back.
    I sought him but I did not find him,
    I called him but he did not answer.
The watchmen, going the rounds of the city, met me;  7
    they struck me and wounded me;
the watchmen on the walls took away my cloak.
    I charge you, daughters of Jerusalem,  8
if you find my beloved, will you not tell him *a*
    that I am faint with love?

*Companions*

    What is your beloved more than any other,  9
      O fairest of women?
    What is your beloved more than any other,
      that you give us this charge?

*Bride*

    My beloved is fair and ruddy,  10
      a paragon among ten thousand.
    His head is gold, finest gold;  11
      his locks are like palm-fronds. *b*
His eyes are like doves beside brooks of water,  12
    splashed by the milky water
    as they sit where it is drawn.

*a* will you . . . him: *or* what will you tell him?    *b Prob. rdg.; Heb. adds* black as the raven.

13 His cheeks are like beds of spices or chests full of perfumes;
his lips are lilies, and drop liquid myrrh;
14 his hands are golden rods set in topaz;
his belly a plaque of ivory overlaid with lapis lazuli.
15 His legs are pillars of marble in sockets of finest gold;
his aspect is like Lebanon, noble as cedars.
16 His whispers are*a* sweetness itself, wholly desirable.
Such is my beloved, such is my darling,
daughters of Jerusalem.

*Companions*

6 Where has your beloved gone,
O fairest of women?
Which way did your beloved go,
that we may help you to seek him?

*Bride*

2 My beloved has gone down to his garden,
to the beds where balsam grows,
to delight in the garden*b* and to pick the lilies.
3 I am my beloved's, and my beloved is mine,
he who delights in the lilies.

*Bridegroom*

4 You are beautiful, my dearest, as Tirzah,
lovely as Jerusalem.*c*
5 Turn your eyes away from me;
they dazzle me.
Your hair is like a flock of goats streaming down Mount Gilead;
6 your teeth are like a flock of ewes come up fresh from the dipping,
each ewe has twins and none has cast a lamb.
7 Your parted lips behind your veil
are like a pomegranate cut open.
8 There may be sixty princesses,
eighty concubines, and young women past counting,
9 but there is one alone, my dove, my perfect one,
her mother's only child,
devoted to the mother who bore her;
young girls see her and call her happy,
princesses and concubines praise her.
10 Who is this that looks out like the dawn,
beautiful as the moon, bright as the sun,
majestic as the starry heavens?

11 I went down to a garden of nut-trees
to look at the rushes by the stream,

---

*a Or His nature is.*   *b Prob. rdg.; Heb. gardens.*   *c Prob. rdg.; Heb. adds*
majestic as the starry heavens (*see verse 10*).

    to see if the vine had budded
    or the pomegranates were in flower.
    I did not know myself;        12
    she made me feel more than a prince
    reigning over the myriads [a] of his people.

*Companions*

    Come back, come back, Shulammite maiden,      13
    come back, that we may gaze upon you.

*Bridegroom*

    How you love to gaze on the Shulammite maiden,
      as she moves between the lines of dancers!

How beautiful are your sandalled feet, O prince's daughter!    7
    The curves of your thighs are like jewels,
      the work of a skilled craftsman.
      Your navel is a rounded goblet      2
      that never shall want for spiced wine.
      Your belly is a heap of wheat
      fenced in by lilies.
    Your two breasts are like two fawns,      3
      twin fawns of a gazelle.
    Your neck is like a tower of ivory.      4
    Your eyes are the pools in Heshbon,
      beside the gate of the crowded city. [b]
    Your nose is like towering Lebanon
      that looks towards Damascus.
    You carry your head like Carmel;      5
      the flowing hair on your head is lustrous black,
      your tresses are braided with ribbons.
      How beautiful, how entrancing you are,      6
      my loved one, daughter of delights!
    You are stately as a palm-tree,      7
      and your breasts are the clusters of dates.
    I said, 'I will climb up into the palm      8
      to grasp its fronds.'
May I find your breasts like clusters of grapes on the vine,
      the scent of your breath like apricots,
    and your whispers like spiced wine      9
    flowing smoothly to welcome my caresses,
    gliding down through lips and teeth.

*Bride*

    I am my beloved's, his longing is all for me.      10
    Come, my beloved, let us go out into the fields      11
      to lie among the henna-bushes;

[a] *Prob. rdg.; Heb.* chariots.      [b] *Or* the gate of Beth-rabbim.

12    let us go early to the vineyards
   and see if the vine has budded or its blossom opened,
    if the pomegranates are in flower.
   There will I give you my love,
13   when the mandrakes give their perfume,
   and all rare fruits are ready at our door,
   fruits new and old
   which I have in store for you, my love.

8    If only you were my own true brother
   that sucked my mother's breasts!
   Then, if I found you outside, I would kiss you,
    and no man would despise me.
2   I would lead you to the room of the mother who bore me,
  bring you to her house for you to embrace me;[a]
   I would give you mulled wine to drink
   and the fresh juice of pomegranates,
3   your [b] left arm under my head and your [b] right arm round me.

*Bridegroom*

4   I charge you, daughters of Jerusalem:
   Do not rouse her, do not disturb my love
    until she is ready.[c]

*Companions*

5   Who is this coming up from the wilderness
   leaning on her beloved?

*Bridegroom*

    Under the apricot-trees I roused you,
   there where your mother was in labour with you,
   there where she who bore you was in labour.
6   Wear me as a seal upon your heart,
    as a seal upon your arm;
   for love is strong as death,
   passion cruel as the grave;
    it blazes up like blazing fire,
   fiercer than any flame.
7   Many waters cannot quench love,
    no flood can sweep it away;
   if a man were to offer for love
   the whole wealth of his house,
   it would be utterly scorned.

*Companions*

8   We have a little sister
   who has no breasts;

---

[a] for you to embrace me: *or* to teach me how to love you.   [b] *Prob. rdg.; Heb.* his.
[c] until . . . ready: *or* while she is resting.

what shall we do for our sister
when she is asked in marriage?
If she is a wall,                                    9
we will build on it a silver parapet,
but *a* if she is a door,
we will close it up with planks of cedar.

*Bride*

I am a wall and my breasts are like towers;         10
so in his eyes I am as one who brings contentment.
Solomon has a vineyard at Baal-hamon;               11
he has let out his vineyard to guardians,
and each is to bring for its fruit
a thousand pieces of silver.
But my vineyard is mine to give;                    12
the thousand pieces are yours, O Solomon,
and the guardians of the fruit shall have two hundred.

*Bridegroom*

My bride, you who sit in my garden,                 13
what is it that my friends *b* are listening to?
Let me also hear your voice.

*Bride*

Come into the open, my beloved,                     14
and show yourself like a gazelle or a young wild goat
on the spice-bearing mountains.

*a Or* and.    *b* my garden . . . friends: *prob. rdg.; Heb.* the gardens, friends.

# THE BOOK OF THE PROPHET
# ISAIAH

### *Judah arraigned*

1 THE VISION RECEIVED BY ISAIAH son of Amoz concerning Judah and Jerusalem during the reigns of Uzziah, Jotham, Ahaz, and Hezekiah, kings of Judah.

2     Hark you heavens, and earth give ear,
      for the LORD has spoken:
    I have sons whom I reared and brought up,
    but they have rebelled against me.
3     The ox knows its owner
      and the ass its master's stall;
    but Israel, my own people,
    has no knowledge, no discernment.

4     O sinful nation, people loaded with iniquity,
    race of evildoers, wanton destructive children
      who have deserted the LORD,
      spurned the Holy One of Israel
      and turned your backs on him.
5     Where can you still be struck
      if you will be disloyal still?
    Your head is covered with sores,
    your body diseased;
6     from head to foot there is not a sound spot in you—
    nothing but bruises and weals and raw wounds
      which have not felt compress or bandage
      or soothing oil.
7     Your country is desolate, your cities lie in ashes.
    Strangers devour your land before your eyes;
      it is desolate as Sodom*a* in its overthrow.
8       Only Zion is left,
    like a watchman's shelter in a vineyard,
    a shed in a field of cucumbers,
      a city well guarded.
9     If the LORD of Hosts had not left us a remnant,
      we should soon have been like Sodom,
      no better than Gomorrah.

---

*a* Sodom: *prob. rdg.; Heb.* strangers.

Hear the word of the LORD, you rulers of Sodom;       10
attend, you people of Gomorrah, to the instruction of our God:
    Your countless sacrifices, what are they to me?       11
       says the LORD.
    I am sated with whole-offerings of rams
       and the fat of buffaloes;
    I have no desire for the blood of bulls,
       of sheep and of he-goats.
    Whenever you come to enter my presence—       12–13
    who asked you for this?
    No more shall you trample my courts.
       The offer of your gifts is useless,
    the reek of sacrifice is abhorrent to me.
    New moons and sabbaths and assemblies,
    sacred seasons and ceremonies, I cannot endure.
I cannot tolerate your new moons and your festivals;       14
    they have become a burden to me,
       and I can put up with them no longer.
       When you lift your hands outspread in prayer,       15
    I will hide my eyes from you.
    Though you offer countless prayers,
       I will not listen.
    There is blood on your hands;
       wash yourselves and be clean.       16
    Put away the evil of your deeds,
       away out of my sight.
Cease to do evil and learn to do right,       17
pursue justice and champion the oppressed;
give the orphan his rights, plead the widow's cause.

    Come now, let us argue it out,       18
       says the LORD.
    Though your sins are scarlet,
       they may become white as snow;
       though they are dyed crimson,
       they may yet be like wool.
       Obey with a will,       19
and you shall eat the best that earth yields;
       but, if you refuse and rebel,       20
       locust-beans shall be your only food.[a]
    The LORD himself has spoken.

How the faithful city has played the whore,       21
once the home of justice where righteousness dwelt—
       but now murderers!
    Your silver has turned into base metal       22
    and your liquor is diluted with water.

[a] locust-beans . . . food: *or, with Scroll,* you shall be eaten by the sword.

23 Your very rulers are rebels, confederate with thieves;
  every man of them loves a bribe
   and itches for a gift;
   they do not give the orphan his rights,
  and the widow's cause never comes before them.

24 This therefore is the word of the Lord, the LORD of Hosts, the Mighty One of Israel:

  Enough! I will secure a respite from my foes
   and take vengeance on my enemies.
25  Once again I will act against you
  to refine away your base metal as with potash
   and purge all your impurities;
26  I will again make your judges what once they were
   and your counsellors like those of old.
  Then at length you shall be called
  the home of righteousness, the faithful city.
27   Justice shall redeem Zion
   and righteousness her repentant people.
28  Rebels and sinners shall be broken together
  and those who forsake the LORD shall cease to be.
29  For the sacred oaks in which you delighted shall fail you,
  the garden-shrines of your fancy shall disappoint you.
30  You shall be like a terebinth whose leaves have withered,
   like a garden without water;
31   the strongest tree[a] shall become like tow,
   and what is made of it[b] shall go up in sparks,
  and the two shall burst into flames together
   with no one to quench them.

**2** This is the word which Isaiah son of Amoz received in a vision concerning Judah and Jerusalem.

2[c]  In days to come
  the mountain of the LORD's house
  shall be set over all other mountains,
   lifted high above the hills.
  All the nations shall come streaming to it,
3  and many peoples shall come and say,
  'Come, let us climb up on to the mountain of the LORD,
   to the house of the God of Jacob,
   that he may teach us his ways
   and we may walk in his paths.'
  For instruction issues from Zion,
   and out of Jerusalem comes the word of the LORD;
4   he will be judge between nations,
  arbiter among many peoples.

---

   [a] *Or* the strong man.  [b] *Or* what he makes.
   [c] *Verses 2–4: cp. Mic. 4. 1–3.*

They shall beat their swords into mattocks
    and their spears into pruning-knives; *a*
nation shall not lift sword against nation
    nor ever again be trained for war.

O people of Jacob, come,          5
    let us walk in the light of the LORD.
Thou hast abandoned thy people the house of Jacob;    6
    for they are crowded with traders *b*
    and barbarians like the Philistines,
    and with the children of foreigners everywhere.
Their land is filled with silver and gold,    7
    and there is no end to their treasure;
their land is filled with horses,
    and there is no end to their chariots;
their land is filled with idols,    8
and they bow down to the work of their own hands,
to what their fingers have made.
Mankind shall be brought low,    9
all men shall be humbled;
and how can they raise themselves? *c*
Get you into the rocks and hide yourselves in the ground    10
from the dread of the LORD and the splendour of his majesty.
Man's proud eyes shall be humbled,    11
    the loftiness of men brought low,
and the LORD alone shall be exalted
    on that day.

For the LORD of Hosts has a day of doom waiting    12
    for all that is proud and lofty,
    for all that is high and lifted up,
for all the cedars of Lebanon, lofty and high,    13
    and for all the oaks of Bashan,
for all lofty mountains and for all high hills,    14
for every high tower and for every sheer wall,    15
for all ships of Tarshish and all the dhows of Arabia.    16
    Then man's pride shall be brought low,    17
    and the loftiness of man shall be humbled,
and the LORD alone shall be exalted
    on that day,
while the idols shall pass away utterly.    18
Get you into caves in the rocks    19
    and crevices in the ground
from the dread of the LORD and the splendour of his majesty,
    when he rises to inspire the earth with fear.
On that day a man shall fling away    20

---

*a* They shall beat . . . pruning-knives: *cp. Joel 3. 9–12.*    *b Or* hawkers.
*c Prob. rdg.; Heb.* and do not forgive them.

his idols of silver and his idols of gold
  which he has made for himself to worship;
he shall fling them to the dung-beetles and the bats,
21 and creep into clefts in the rocks and crannies in the cliffs
from the dread of the LORD and the splendour of his majesty,
  when he rises to inspire the earth with fear.
22 Have no more to do with man, for what is he worth?
  He is no more than the breath in his nostrils.

3     Be warned: the Lord, the LORD of Hosts,
      is stripping Jerusalem and Judah
        of every prop and stay,*a*
2          warrior and soldier,
      judge and prophet, diviner and elder,
3        captains of companies and men of rank,
        counsellor, magician, and cunning enchanter.
4        Then I will appoint mere boys to be their captains,
        who shall govern as the fancy takes them;
5          the people shall deal harshly
      each man with his fellow and with his neighbour;
        children shall break out against their elders,
        and nobodies against men of substance.
6      If a man takes hold of his brother in his father's house,
      saying, 'You have a cloak, you shall be our chief;
        our stricken family shall be under you',
7      he will cry out that day and say,
        'I will not be your master;
        there is neither bread nor cloak in my house,
        and you shall not make me head of the clan.'

8      Jerusalem is stricken and Judah fallen
        because they have spoken and acted against the LORD,
          rebelling against the glance of his glorious eye.
9        The look on their faces testifies against them;
        like Sodom they proclaim their sins
          and do not conceal them.*b*
      Woe upon them! they have earned their own disaster.
10       Happy*c* the righteous man! all goes well with him,
        for such men enjoy the fruit of their actions.
11       Woe betide the wicked! with him all goes ill,
        for he reaps the reward that he has earned.
12       Money-lenders strip my people bare,
        and usurers lord it over them.
      O my people! your guides lead you astray
        and confuse the path that you should take.

---

*a Prob. rdg.; Heb. adds* all stay of bread and all stay of water.      *b* like ... them:
*or* and their sins, like those of Sodom, denounce them; they do not deny them.      *c Prob.*
*rdg.; Heb.* Say.

The LORD comes forward to argue his case                  13
and stands to judge his people.
The LORD opens the indictment                             14
against the elders of his people and their officers:
You have ravaged the vineyard,
and the spoils of the poor are in your houses.
Is it nothing to you that you crush my people             15
and grind the faces of the poor?
This is the very word of the Lord, the LORD of Hosts.

Then the LORD said:                                       16
Because the women of Zion hold themselves high
and walk with necks outstretched and wanton glances,
moving with mincing gait
and jingling feet,
the Lord will give the women of Zion bald heads,          17
the LORD will strip the hair from their foreheads.

In that day the Lord will take away all finery: anklets, discs, crescents,   18
pendants, bangles, coronets, head-bands, armlets, necklaces, lockets,    19 20
charms, signets, nose-rings, fine dresses, mantles, cloaks, flounced skirts,   21 22
scarves of gauze, kerchiefs of linen, turbans, and flowing veils.        23

So instead of perfume you shall have the stench of decay,    24
and a rope in place of a girdle,
baldness instead of hair elegantly coiled,
a loin-cloth of sacking instead of a mantle,
and branding instead of beauty.
Your men shall fall by the sword,                         25
and your warriors in battle;
then Zion's gates shall mourn and lament,                 26
and she shall sit on the ground stripped bare.

Then on that day                                          **4**
seven women shall take hold of one man and say,
'We will eat our own bread and wear our own clothes
if only we may be called by your name;
take away our disgrace.'

On that day the plant that the LORD has grown             2
shall become glorious in its beauty,
and the fruit of the land shall be
the pride and splendour
of the survivors of Israel.

Then those who are left in Zion, who remain in Jerusalem, every one   3
enrolled in the book of life, shall be called holy. If the Lord washes away   4
the filth of the women of Zion and cleanses Jerusalem from the blood that
is in it by a spirit of judgement, a consuming spirit, then over every build-   5
ing on Mount Zion and on all her places of assembly the LORD will create
a cloud of smoke by day and a bright flame of fire by night; for glory shall

6 be spread over all as a covering and a canopy, a shade from the heat by
day, a refuge and a shelter from rain and tempest.

5         I will sing for my beloved
           my love-song about his vineyard:
        My beloved had a vineyard
           high up on a fertile hill-side.
2         He trenched it and cleared it of stones
           and planted it with red vines;
      he built a watch-tower in the middle
      and then hewed out a winepress in it.
      He looked for it to yield grapes,
           but it yielded wild grapes.
3         Now, you who live in Jerusalem,
           and you men of Judah,
      judge between me and my vineyard.
4         What more could have been done for my vineyard
        that I did not do in it?
    Why, when I looked for it to yield grapes,
           did it yield wild grapes?
5         Now listen while I tell you
        what I will do to my vineyard:
    I will take away its fences and let it be burnt,
    I will break down its walls and let it be trampled underfoot,
6            and so I will leave it derelict;
      it shall be neither pruned nor hoed,
      but shall grow thorns and briars.
        Then I will command the clouds
        to send no more rain upon it.
7     The vineyard of the Lord of Hosts is Israel,
        and the men of Judah are the plant he cherished.
    He looked for justice and found it denied,
        for righteousness but heard cries of distress.

8     Shame on you! you who add house to house
        and join field to field,
        until not an acre remains,
    and you are left to dwell alone in the land.
9         The Lord of Hosts has sworn[a] in my hearing:
    Many houses shall go to ruin,
    fine large houses shall be uninhabited.
10     Five acres of vineyard shall yield only a gallon,
    and ten bushels of seed return only a peck.
11     Shame on you! you who rise early in the morning
        to go in pursuit of liquor
    and draw out the evening inflamed with wine,
12         at whose feasts there are harp and lute,
        tabor and pipe and wine,

*a* has sworn: *prob. rdg.; Heb. om.*

who have no eyes for the work of the LORD,
    and never see the things that he has done.
Therefore my people are dwindling away       13
    all unawares;
    the nobles are starving to death,
and the common folk die of thirst.
Therefore Sheol gapes with straining throat     14
and has opened her measureless jaws:
    down go nobility and common people,
    their noisy bustling mob.*a*
Mankind is brought low, men are humbled,     15
    humbled are haughty looks.
But the LORD of Hosts sits high in judgement,     16
and by righteousness the holy God shows himself holy.
Young rams shall feed where fat bullocks once pastured,     17
and kids shall graze broad acres where cattle grew fat.*b*
Shame on you! you who drag wickedness along like a tethered sheep  18
    and sin like a heifer on a rope,
    who say, 'Let the LORD make haste,     19
    let him speed up his work for us to see it,
    let the purpose of the Holy One of Israel
    be soon fulfilled, so that we may know it.'
Shame on you! you who call evil good and good evil,     20
who turn darkness into light and light into darkness,
who make bitter sweet and sweet bitter.
    Shame on you! you who are wise in your own eyes     21
    and prudent in your own esteem.
Shame on you! you mighty topers, valiant mixers of drink,     22
    who for a bribe acquit the guilty     23
    and deny justice to those in the right.

So he will hoist a signal to a nation far away,     26*c*
    he will whistle to call them from the end of the earth;
    and see, they come, speedy and swift;
    none is weary, not one of them stumbles,     27
        not one slumbers or sleeps.
None has his belt loose about his waist
    or a broken thong to his sandals.
Their arrows are sharpened and their bows all strung,     28
    their horses' hooves flash like shooting stars,
        their chariot-wheels are like the whirlwind.
Their growling is the growling of a lioness,     29
    they growl like young lions,
which roar as they seize the prey
    and carry it beyond reach of rescue.

---

*a* nobility . . . mob: *or* nobility, common people and noisy mob, and are restless there.
*b* Young . . . grew fat: *prob. rdg.; Heb. unintelligible.*     *c Verses 24 and 25 transposed to follow 10. 4.*

30        They shall roar over it on that day
           like the roaring of the sea.
       If a man looks over the earth, behold, darkness closing in,
          and the light darkened on the hill-tops[a]!

## *The call of Isaiah*

6 IN THE YEAR OF KING UZZIAH'S DEATH I saw the Lord seated on a
2 throne, high and exalted, and the skirt of his robe filled the temple. About
him were attendant seraphim, and each had six wings; one pair covered
3 his face and one pair his feet, and one pair was spread in flight. They were
calling ceaselessly to one another,

      Holy, holy, holy is the LORD of Hosts:
        the whole earth is full of his glory.

4 And, as each one called, the threshold shook to its foundations, while the
5 house was filled with smoke. Then I cried,

      Woe is me! I am lost,
        for I am a man of unclean lips
      and I dwell among a people of unclean lips;
        yet with these eyes I have seen the King, the LORD of Hosts.

6 Then one of the seraphim flew to me carrying in his hand a glowing coal
7 which he had taken from the altar with a pair of tongs. He touched my
mouth with it and said,

      See, this has touched your lips;
        your iniquity is removed,
        and your sin is wiped away.

8 Then I heard the Lord saying, Whom shall I send? Who will go for me?
9 And I answered, Here am I; send me. He said, Go and tell this people:

      You may listen and listen, but you will not understand.[b]
      You may look and look again, but you will never know.[c]
10       This people's wits are dulled,
     their ears are deafened and their eyes blinded,
        so that they cannot see with their eyes
        nor listen with their ears
        nor understand with their wits,
      so that they may turn and be healed.

11 Then I asked, How long, O Lord? And he answered,

      Until cities fall in ruins and are deserted,
        houses are left without people,
      and the land goes to ruin and lies waste,
12       until the LORD has sent all mankind far away,
        and the whole country is one vast desolation.

[a] hill-tops: *or* clouds.     [b] *Or* but how will you understand?     [c] *Or* but how
will you know?

Even if a tenth part of its people remain there,                    13
they too will be exterminated
[like an oak or a terebinth,
a sacred pole thrown out from its place in a hill-shrine*a*].

## Prophecies during the Syro-Ephraimite war

WHILE AHAZ SON OF JOTHAM and grandson of Uzziah was king of 7
Judah, Rezin king of Aram with Pekah son of Remaliah, king of
Israel, marched on Jerusalem, but could not force a battle. When the house 2
of David heard that the Aramaeans had come to terms with the Ephraimites,
king and people were shaken like forest trees in the wind. Then the LORD 3
said to Isaiah, Go out with your son Shear-jashub*b* to meet Ahaz at the
end of the conduit of the Upper Pool by the causeway leading to the Fuller's
Field, and say to him, Be on your guard, keep calm; do not be frightened 4
or unmanned by these two smouldering stumps of firewood, because Rezin
and his Aramaeans with Remaliah's son are burning with rage. The 5
Aramaeans with Ephraim and Remaliah's son have laid their plans against
you, saying, Let us invade Judah and break her spirit;*c* let us make her 6
join with us, and set the son of Tabeal on the throne. Therefore the Lord 7
GOD has said:

This shall not happen now, and never shall,
for all that the chief city of Aram is Damascus,                    8
and Rezin is the chief of Damascus;
within sixty-five years
Ephraim shall cease to be a nation,
for all that Samaria is the chief city of Ephraim,                    9
and Remaliah's son the chief of Samaria.
Have firm faith, or you will not stand firm.

Once again the LORD spoke to Ahaz and said, Ask the LORD your God 10 11
for a sign, from lowest Sheol or from highest heaven. But Ahaz said, No, 12
I will not put the LORD to the test by asking for a sign. Then the answer 13
came: Listen, house of David. Are you not content to wear out men's
patience? Must you also wear out the patience of my God? Therefore the 14
Lord himself shall give you a sign: A young woman is with child, and she
will bear a son, and will*d* call him Immanuel.*e* By the time that he has learnt 15
to reject evil and choose good, he will be eating curds and honey;*f* before 16
that child has learnt to reject evil and choose good, desolation will come
upon the land before whose two kings you cower now. The LORD will bring 17
on you, your people, and your house, a time the like of which has not been
seen since Ephraim broke away from Judah.*g*
On that day the LORD will whistle for the fly from the distant streams of 18
Egypt and for the bee from Assyria. They shall all come and settle in the 19

*a* a sacred pole . . . hill-shrine: *prob. rdg.; Heb. obscure.*        *b* *That is* A remnant
shall return.    *c* *Or* and parley with her.    *d* *Or* you will.    *e* *That is* God
is with us.    *f* he will . . . honey: *or* curds and honey will be eaten.    *g* *Prob. rdg.;*
*Heb. adds* the king of Assyria.

precipitous ravines and in the clefts of the rock; camel-thorn and stink-
20 wood shall be black with them. On that day the Lord shall shave the head
and body with a razor hired on the banks of the Euphrates,[a] and it shall
21 remove the beard as well. On that day a man shall save alive a young cow
22 and two ewes; and he shall get so much milk that he eats curds; for all who
23 are left in the land shall eat curds and honey. On that day every place where
there used to be a thousand vines worth a thousand pieces of silver shall be
24 given over to thorns and briars. A man shall go there only to hunt with bow
25 and arrows, for thorns and briars cover the whole land; and no one who
fears thorns and briars shall set foot on any of those hills once worked with
the hoe. Oxen shall be turned loose on them, and sheep shall trample them.

**8**     The LORD said to me, Take a large tablet and write on it in common
2 writing,[b] Maher-shalal-hash-baz;[c] and fetch Uriah the priest and Zech-
3 ariah son of Jeberechiah for me as trustworthy witnesses. Then I lay with
the prophetess, and she conceived and bore a son; and the LORD said to
4 me, Call him Maher-shalal-hash-baz. Before the boy can say Father or
Mother, the wealth of Damascus and the spoils of Samaria shall be carried
off and presented to the king of Assyria.

5     Once again the LORD said to me:

6         Because this nation has rejected
         the waters of Shiloah, which run so softly and gently,[d]
7         therefore the Lord will bring up against it
         the strong, flooding waters of the Euphrates,
         the king of Assyria and all his glory;
         it shall run up all its channels
         and overflow all its banks;
8         it shall sweep through Judah in a flood,
         pouring over it and rising shoulder-high.
         The whole expanse of the land shall be filled,
         so wide he spreads his wings; for God is with us.[e]
9         Take note, you nations, and be dismayed.
         Listen, all you distant parts of the earth:
         you may arm yourselves but will be dismayed;
         you may arm yourselves but will be dismayed.
10        Make your plans, but they will be foiled,
         propose what you please, but it shall not stand;
         for God is with us.[e]

11     These were the words of the LORD to me, for his hand was strong
upon me; and he warned me not to follow[f] the ways of this people:
12 You shall not say 'too hard' of everything that this people calls hard;
13 you shall neither dread nor fear that which they fear. It is the LORD of
Hosts whom you must count 'hard';[g] he it is whom you must fear and
14 dread. He shall become your 'hardship',[g] a boulder and a rock which

---

[a] *Prob. rdg.; Heb. adds* with the king of Assyria.      [b] in common writing: *or* with
an ordinary stylus.     [c] *That is* Speed-spoil-hasten-plunder.     [d] *Prob. rdg.; Heb.
adds* Rezin and the son of Remaliah.      [e] God is with us: *Heb.* Immanuel.
[f] *Or* and he turned me from following . . .      [g] 'hard' *and* 'hardship': *prob. rdg.;
Heb. unintelligible in this context.*

the two houses of Israel shall run against and over which they shall stumble, a trap and a snare to those who live in Jerusalem; and many shall stumble over them, many shall fall and be broken, many shall be snared and caught.    15

> Fasten up the message,      16
> seal the oracle with my teaching;<sup>a</sup>
>    and I will wait for the LORD      17
>    who hides his face from the house of Jacob;
>    I will watch for him.
> See, I and the sons whom the LORD has given me      18
>    are to be signs and portents in Israel,
> sent by the LORD of Hosts who dwells on Mount Zion.
>    But men will say to you,      19
>    'Seek guidance of ghosts and familiar spirits
>      who squeak and gibber;
>    a nation may surely seek guidance of its gods,
>    of the dead on behalf of the living,
>      for an oracle or a message?'
> They will surely say some such thing as this;      20
>    but what they say is futile.
> So despondency and fear will come over them,
>    and then, when they are afraid and fearful,      21
>    they will turn against their king and their gods.
> Then, whether they turn their gaze upwards or look down,      22
>    everywhere is distress and darkness inescapable,
>    constraint and gloom that cannot be avoided;
> for there is no escape for an oppressed people.      **9**

For, while the first invader has dealt lightly with the land of Zebulun and the land of Naphtali, the second has dealt heavily with Galilee of the Nations on the road beyond Jordan to the sea.

> The people who walked in darkness      2
> have seen a great light:
> light has dawned upon them,
>    dwellers in a land as dark as death.
> Thou hast increased their joy and<sup>b</sup> given them great gladness;      3
> they rejoice in thy presence as men rejoice at harvest,
> or as they are glad when they share out the spoil;
>    for thou hast shattered the yoke that burdened them,      4
>      the collar that lay heavy on their shoulders,
>    the driver's goad, as on the day of Midian's defeat.
> All the boots of trampling soldiers      5
>    and the garments fouled with blood
> shall become a burning mass, fuel for fire.
> For a boy has been born for us, a son given to us      6
>    to bear the symbol of dominion on his shoulder;

---

<sup>a</sup> *Or* among my disciples.          <sup>b</sup> their joy and: *prob. rdg.; Heb.* the nation, not.

and he shall be called
in purpose wonderful, in battle God-like,
Father for all time,[a] Prince of peace.

7 Great shall the dominion be,
and boundless the peace
bestowed on David's throne and on his kingdom,
to establish it and sustain it
with justice and righteousness
from now and for evermore.
The zeal of the LORD of Hosts shall do this.


## Prophecies addressed to Israel

8 The Lord has sent forth his word against Jacob
and it shall fall on Israel;

9 all the people shall be humbled,
Ephraim and the dwellers in Samaria,
though in their pride and arrogance they say,

10 The bricks are fallen, but we will build in hewn stone;
the sycomores are hacked down,
but we will use cedars instead.

11 The LORD has raised their foes[b] high against them
and spurred on their enemies,

12 Aramaeans from the east and Philistines from the west,
and they have swallowed Israel in one mouthful.
For all this his anger has not turned back,
and his hand is stretched out still.

13 Yet the people did not come back to him who struck them,
or seek guidance of the LORD of Hosts;

14 therefore on one day the LORD cut off from Israel
head and tail, palm and reed.[c]

16 This people's guides have led them astray;
those who should have been guided are in confusion.

17 Therefore the Lord showed no mercy to their young men,
no tenderness to their orphans and widows;
all were godless and evildoers,
every one speaking profanity.
For all this his anger has not turned back,
and his hand is stretched out still.

18 Wicked men have been set ablaze like a fire
fed with briars and thorns,
kindled in the forest thickets;
they are wrapped in a murky pall of smoke.

[a] *Or* of a wide realm.      [b] their foes: *prob. rdg.; Heb.* the foes of Rezin.
[c] *Prob. rdg.; Heb. adds* (15) The aged and honoured are the head, and the prophet who
gives false instruction is the tail.

The land is scorched by the fury of the LORD of Hosts,     19
    and the people have become fuel for the fire. [a]
On the right, one man eats his fill but yet is hungry;     20
    on the left, another devours but is not satisfied;
    each feeds on his own children's flesh,
    and neither spares his own brother. [b]
[c] For all this his anger has not turned back,     21
    and his hand is stretched out still.

Shame on you! you who make unjust laws     **10**
    and publish burdensome decrees,
    depriving the poor of justice,     2
    robbing the weakest of my people of their rights,
despoiling the widow and plundering the orphan.
    What will you do when called to account,     3
    when ruin from afar confronts you?
    To whom will you flee for help
    and where will you leave your children,
    so that they do not cower before the gaoler     4
      or fall by the executioner's hand?
    For all this his anger has not turned back,
    and his hand is stretched out still.

So, as tongues of fire lick up the stubble     [24[d]]
    and the heat of the flame dies down,
    their root shall moulder away,
    and their shoots vanish like dust;
for they have spurned the instruction of the LORD of Hosts
and have rejected the word of the Holy One of Israel.
So the anger of the LORD is roused against his people,     [25[d]]
he has stretched out his hand against them and struck them down;
      the mountains trembled,
    and their corpses lay like offal in the streets.
    For all this his anger has not turned back,
    and his hand is stretched out still.

The Assyrian! He is the rod that I wield in my anger,     5
    and the staff of my wrath is in his hand. [e]
I send him against a godless nation,     6
I bid him march against a people who rouse my wrath,
to spoil and plunder at will
    and trample them down like mud in the streets.
But this man's purpose is lawless,     7
    lawless are the plans in his mind;

---

[a] *See note on verse 20.*     [b] *and neither . . . brother:* transposed from end of verse 19.
[c] *Prob. rdg.; Heb. prefixes* Manasseh devours Ephraim, and Ephraim Manasseh; together they are against Judah.     [d] *These are verses 24 and 25 of ch. 5, transposed to this point.*     [e] *and . . . hand: prob. rdg.; Heb. obscure.*

for his thought is only to destroy
and to wipe out nation after nation.

8   'Are not my officers all kings?' he says;
9   'see how Calno has suffered the fate of Carchemish.
Is not Hamath like Arpad, and Samaria like Damascus?
10   Before now I have found kingdoms full of idols,
with more images than Jerusalem and Samaria,
11   and now, what I have done to Samaria and her worthless gods,
I will do also to Jerusalem and her idols.'

12   When the Lord has finished all that he means to do on Mount Zion and
in Jerusalem, he will punish the king of Assyria for this fruit of his pride
13   and for his arrogance and vainglory, because he said:

By my own might I have acted
and in my own wisdom I have laid my schemes;
I have removed the frontiers of nations
and plundered their treasures,
like a bull I have trampled on their inhabitants.
14   My hand has found its way to the wealth of nations,
and, as a man takes the eggs from a deserted nest,
so have I taken every land;
not a wing fluttered,
not a beak gaped, no chirp was heard.

15   Shall the axe set itself up against the hewer,
or the saw claim mastery over the sawyer,
as if a stick were to brandish him who wields it,
or a staff of wood to wield one who is not wood?

16   Therefore the Lord, the Lord of Hosts, will send disease
on his sturdy frame, from head to toe,*a*
and within his flesh*b* a fever like fire shall burn.
17   The light of Israel shall become a fire
and his Holy One a flame,
which in one day shall burn up and consume
his thorns and his briars;
18   the glory of forest and meadow shall be destroyed
as when a man falls in a fit;
19   and the remnant of trees in the forest shall be so few
that a child may count them one by one.

20   On that day the remnant of Israel, the survivors of Jacob, shall cease to
lean on him that proved their destroyer, but shall loyally lean on the Lord,
the Holy One of Israel.

21   A remnant shall turn again, a remnant of Jacob,
to God their champion.

---

*a* from . . . toe: *transposed from verse 18.*      *b* within his flesh: *or in his strong*
body.

Your people, Israel, may be many as the sands of the sea,                22
    but only a remnant shall turn again,
the instrument of final destruction,
    justice in full flood; *a*
for the Lord, the LORD of Hosts, will bring final destruction                23
    upon all the earth.

Therefore these are the words of the Lord, the LORD of Hosts: My 24
people who live in Zion, you must not be afraid of the Assyrians, though
they beat you with their rod and lift their staff against you as the Egyptians
did; for soon, very soon, my anger will come to an end, and my wrath will 25
all be spent.*b* Then the LORD of Hosts will brandish his whip over them as 26
he did when he struck Midian at the Rock of Oreb, and will lift his staff
against the River as he did against Egypt.

On that day                27
the burden they laid on your shoulder shall be removed
and their yoke shall be broken from your neck.
An invader from Rimmon*c* has come to Aiath,                28
    has passed by Migron,
and left his baggage-train at Michmash;
    he has passed by Maabarah                29
and camped for the night at Geba.
Ramah is anxious, Gibeah of Saul is in panic.
    Raise a shrill cry, Bath-gallim;                30
hear it, Laish, and answer her, Anathoth:
'Madmenah is in flight; take refuge, people of Gebim.'                31
Today he is due to pitch his camp in Nob;                32
    he gives the signal to advance
against the mount of the daughter of Zion,
    the hill of Jerusalem.

Look, the Lord, the LORD of Hosts,                33
    cleaves the trees with a flash of lightning,
the tallest are hewn down, the lofty laid low,
    the heart of the forest is felled with the axe,                34
and Lebanon with its noble trees has fallen.
Then a shoot shall grow from the stock of Jesse,                **11**
    and a branch shall spring from his roots.
The spirit of the LORD shall rest upon him,                2
    a spirit of wisdom and understanding,
a spirit of counsel*d* and power,
    a spirit of knowledge and the fear of the LORD.*e*
He shall not judge by what he sees                3
    nor decide by what he hears;

---

*a* the instrument . . . flood: *or* wasting with sickness, yet overflowing with righteousness.
*b* will . . . spent: *prob. rdg.; Heb. obscure.*                *c* and their yoke . . . Rimmon: *prob.*
*rdg.; Heb.* and their yoke from upon your neck, and a yoke shall be broken because of oil.
He . . .                *d Or* force.                *e Prob. rdg.; Heb. adds* and his delight shall be in the
fear of the LORD.

4        he shall judge the poor with justice
          and defend the humble in the land with equity;
          his mouth shall be a rod to strike down the ruthless, [a]
          and with a word he shall slay the wicked.

5       Round his waist he shall wear the belt of justice,
          and good faith shall be the girdle round his body.

6       Then the wolf shall live with the sheep,
          and the leopard lie down with the kid;
     the calf and the young lion shall grow up together,
     and a little child shall lead them;

7       the cow and the bear shall be friends,
          and their young shall lie down together.
     The lion shall eat straw like cattle;

8       the infant shall play over the hole of the cobra,
          and the young child dance over the viper's nest.

9       They shall not hurt or destroy in all my holy mountain;
          for as the waters fill the sea,
     so shall the land be filled with the knowledge of the LORD.

10      On that day a scion from the root of Jesse
          shall be set up as a signal to the peoples;
          the nations shall rally to it,
          and its resting-place shall be glorious.

11     On that day the Lord will make his power more glorious by recovering the remnant of his people, those who are still left, from Assyria and Egypt, from Pathros, from Cush and Elam, from Shinar, Hamath and the islands of the sea.

12     Then he will raise a signal to the nations
          and gather together those driven out of Israel;
          he will assemble Judah's scattered people
          from the four corners of the earth.

13     Ephraim's jealousy shall vanish,
          and Judah's enmity shall be done away.
     Ephraim shall not be jealous of Judah,
          nor Judah the enemy of Ephraim.

14     They shall swoop down on the Philistine flank in the west
          and together they shall plunder the tribes of the east;
          Edom and Moab shall be within their grasp,
          and Ammon shall obey them.

15     The LORD will divide the tongue of the Egyptian sea
          and wave his hand over the River
            to bring a scorching wind;
          he shall split it into seven channels
          and let men go across dry-shod.

16     So there shall be a causeway for the remnant of his people,
          for the remnant rescued from Assyria,
     as there was for Israel when they came up out of Egypt.

               [a] *Prob. rdg.; Heb.* land.

You shall say on that day:       **12**
  I will praise thee, O LORD,
  though thou hast been angry with me;
  thy anger has turned back,
  and thou hast comforted me.
God is indeed my deliverer.      2
  I am confident and unafraid;
for the LORD is my refuge and defence
  and has shown himself my deliverer.
And so you shall draw water with joy    3
  from the springs of deliverance.

You shall all say on that day:     4
Give thanks to the LORD and invoke him by name,
  make his deeds known in the world around;
  declare that his name is supreme.
Sing psalms to the LORD, for he has triumphed,    5
  and this must be made known in all the world.
Cry out, shout aloud, you that dwell in Zion,    6
for the Holy One of Israel is among you in majesty.

## *Prophecies relating to foreign nations*

BABYLON: AN ORACLE which Isaiah son of Amoz received in a **13**
vision.

Raise the standard on a windy height,    2
roar out your summons,
beckon with arm upraised to the advance,
  draw your swords, you nobles.
I have given my warriors their orders    3
and summoned my fighting men to launch my anger;
  they are eager for my triumph.
Hark, a tumult in the mountains, the sound of a vast multitude;    4
hark, the roar of kingdoms, of nations gathering!
The LORD of Hosts is mustering a host for war,
men from a far country, from beyond the horizon.    5
  It is the LORD with the weapons of his wrath
  coming to lay the whole land waste.
Howl, for the Day of the LORD is at hand;    6
it comes, a mighty blow from Almighty God.
Thereat shall every hand hang limp,    7
every man's courage shall melt away,
  his stomach hollow with fear;    8
anguish shall grip them, like a woman in labour.
One man shall look aghast at another,
  and their faces shall burn with shame.
The Day of the LORD is coming indeed,    9
  that cruel day of wrath and fury,

> to make the land a desolation
> and exterminate its wicked people.

10 The stars of heaven in their constellations shall give no light,
> the sun shall be darkened at its rising,
> and the moon refuse to shine.

11 I will bring disaster upon the world
> and their due punishment upon the wicked.
>> I will check the pride of the haughty
>> and bring low the arrogance of ruthless men.

12 I will make men scarcer than fine gold,
> rarer than gold of Ophir.

13 Then the heavens shall shudder,*a*
> and the earth shall be shaken from its place
> at the fury of the LORD of Hosts, on the day of his anger.

14 Then, like a gazelle before the hunter
>> or a flock with no man to round it up,
> each man will go back to his own people,
> every one will flee to his own land.

15 All who are found will be stabbed,
> all who are taken will fall by the sword;

16 their infants will be dashed to the ground before their eyes,
> their houses rifled and their wives ravished.

17 I will stir up against them the Medes,
> who care nothing for silver and are not tempted by gold,*b*

18 who have no pity on little children
> and spare no mother's son;

19 and Babylon, fairest of kingdoms,
>> proud beauty of the Chaldaeans,
> shall be like Sodom and Gomorrah
>> when God overthrew them.

20 Never again shall she be inhabited,
> no man shall dwell in her through all the ages;
> there no Arab shall pitch his tent,
> no shepherds fold their flocks.

21 There marmots shall have their lairs,
> and porcupines shall overrun her houses;
> there desert owls shall dwell,
> and there he-goats shall gambol;

22 jackals shall occupy her mansions,*c*
> and wolves her gorgeous palaces.
> Her time draws very near,
> and her days have not long to run.

**14** The LORD will show compassion for Jacob and will once again make
Israel his choice. He will settle them on their own soil, and strangers will
2 come to join them and attach themselves to Jacob. Many nations shall

---

*a Prob. rdg.; Heb.* Then I will make the heavens shudder.       *b Prob. rdg.; Heb.*
*adds* bows shall dash young men to the ground.       *c Prob. rdg.; Heb.* her widows.

escort Israel to her place, and she shall employ them as slaves and slave-girls on the land of the LORD; she shall take her captors captive and rule over her task-masters.

When the LORD gives you relief from your pain and your fears and from 3 the cruel slavery laid upon you, you will take up this song of derision over 4 the king of Babylon:

See how the oppressor has met his end and his frenzy ceased!
The LORD has broken the rod of the wicked,                             5
    the sceptre of the ruler
who struck down peoples in his rage                                    6
    with unerring blows,
who crushed nations in anger
and persecuted them unceasingly.
The whole world has rest and is at peace;                             7
    it breaks into cries of joy.
The pines themselves and the cedars of Lebanon exult over you:        8
    Since you have been laid low, they say,
    no man comes up to fell us.

Sheol below was all astir                                            9
    to meet you at your coming;
she roused the ancient dead to meet you,
    all who had been leaders on earth;
she made all who had been kings of the nations
    rise from their thrones.
One and all they greet you with these words:                         10
    So you too are weak as we are,
    and have become one of us!
Your pride and all the music of your lutes                            11
    have been brought down to Sheol;*a*
maggots are the pallet beneath you,
    and worms your coverlet.

How you have fallen from heaven, bright morning star,                12
felled to the earth, sprawling helpless across the nations!
You thought in your own mind,                                        13
    I will scale the heavens;
I will set my throne high above the stars of God,
I will sit on the mountain where the gods meet
    in the far recesses of the north.
I will rise high above the cloud-banks                               14
    and make myself like the Most High.
Yet you shall be brought down to Sheol,                              15
    to the depths of the abyss.
Those who see you will stare at you,                                 16
    they will look at you and ponder:

*a Or* Your pride has been brought down to Sheol to the crowding throng of your dead.

Is this, they will say, the man who shook the earth,
  who made kingdoms quake,
17    who turned the world into a desert
  and laid its cities in ruins,
who never let his prisoners go free to their homes,
18    the kings of every land?
Now they lie all of them in honour,
  each in his last home.
19    But you have been flung out unburied,
  mere loathsome carrion,
a companion to the slain pierced by the sword
who have gone down to the stony abyss.
  And you, a corpse trampled underfoot,
20    shall not share burial with them,
for you have ruined your land and slaughtered your people.
Such a brood of evildoers shall never be seen again.
21    Make the shambles ready for his sons
  butchered for their fathers' sin;
they shall not rise up and possess the world
nor cover the face of the earth with cities.

22    I will rise against them, says the LORD of Hosts; I will destroy the name
of Babylon and what remains of her, her offspring and posterity, says the
23  LORD; I will make her a haunt of the bustard, a waste of fen, and sweep
her with the besom of destruction. This is the very word of the LORD of
Hosts.

24    The LORD of Hosts has sworn:
In very truth, as I planned, so shall it be;
  as I designed, so shall it fall out:
25    I will break the Assyrian in my own land
  and trample him underfoot upon my mountains;
his yoke shall be lifted from you,
  his burden taken from your shoulders.
26    This is the plan prepared for the whole earth,
this the hand stretched out over all the nations.
27    For the LORD of Hosts has prepared his plan:
  who shall frustrate it?
His is the hand stretched out, and who shall turn it back?

28    In the year that King Ahaz died this oracle came from God:

29    Let none of you rejoice, you Philistines,
  because the rod that chastised you is broken;
for a viper shall be born of a snake as a plant from the root,
  and its fruit shall be a flying serpent.
30    But the poor shall graze their flocks in my meadows,
  and the destitute shall lie down in peace;
but the offspring of your roots I will kill by starvation,
  and put the remnant of you to death.

Howl in the gate, cry for help in the city,                                31
    let all Philistia be in turmoil;
    for a great enemy is coming from the north,
      not a man straying from his ranks.
What answer is there for the envoys of the nation?                          32
This, that the LORD has fixed Zion in her place,
    and the afflicted among his people shall take refuge there.

Moab: an oracle.                                    15

On the night when Ar is sacked, Moab meets her doom;
on the night when Kir is sacked, Moab meets her doom.
The people of Dibon go up*ᵃ* to the hill-shrines to weep;                   2
Moab howls over Nebo and over Medeba.
The hair is torn from every head, and every beard shaved off.
    In the streets men go clothed with sackcloth,                    3
      they cry out on the roofs;
    in the public squares every man howls,
      weeping as he goes through them.
    Heshbon and Elealeh cry for help,                                4
    their voices are heard as far as Jahaz.
    Thus Moab's stoutest warriors become cowards,
    and her courage ebbs away.
    My heart cries out for Moab,                                      5
    whose nobles have fled*ᵇ* as far as Zoar.*ᶜ*
On the ascent to Luhith men go up weeping;
on the road to Horonaim there are cries of 'Disaster!'
The waters of Nimrim are desolate indeed;                                  6
the grass is parched, the herbage dead,
    not a green thing is left;
and so the people carry off across the gorge of the Arabim                 7
    their hard-earned wealth and all their savings.
The cry for help echoes round the frontiers of Moab,                       8
their howling reaches Eglaim and Beer-elim.
    The waters of Dimon already run with blood;                      9
    yet I have more troubles in store for Dimon,
      for I have a vision*ᵈ* of the survivors of Moab,
    of the remnant of Admah.
The rulers of the country send a present of lambs                      16
    from Sela in the wilderness
    to the hill of the daughter of Zion;
the daughters of Moab at the fords of the Arnon                             2
shall be like fluttering birds, like scattered nestlings.
'Take up our cause with all your might;                                    3
let your shadow shield us at high noon, dark as night.

---

*ᵃ* The people . . . go up: *prob. rdg.; Heb.* He has gone up to the house and Dibon.
*ᵇ* have fled: *prob. rdg.; Heb. om.*          *ᶜ Prob. rdg.; Heb. adds* Eglath Shelishiya.
*ᵈ* I have a vision: *prob. rdg.; Heb.* a lion.

Shelter the homeless, do not betray the fugitive;
4  let the homeless people of Moab find refuge with you;
  hide them from the despoiler.'

When extortion has done its work and the looting is over,
  when the heel of the oppressor has vanished from the land,
5  a throne shall be set up in mutual trust in David's tent,
   and on it there shall sit a true judge,
  one who seeks justice and is swift to do right.

6   We have heard tell of Moab's pride, how great it is,
   we have heard of his pride, his overweening pride;
    his talk is full of lies.
7   For this all Moab shall howl;
   Moab shall howl indeed;
  he *a* shall mourn for the prosperous farmers of Kir-hareseth,
    utterly ruined;
8    the orchards of Heshbon,
    the vines of Sibmah languish,
  though their red grapes once laid low the lords of the nations,
   though they reached as far as Jazer
   and trailed out to the wilderness,
  though their branches spread abroad and crossed the sea.
9  Therefore I will weep for Sibmah's vines as I weep for Jazer.
  I will drench you with my tears, Heshbon and Elealeh;
   for over your summer-fruits and your harvest
    the shouts of the harvesters are ended.
10  Joy and gladness shall be banished from the meadows,
  no more shall men shout and sing in the vineyards,
   no more shall they tread wine in the winepresses;
   I have silenced the shouting of the harvesters.
11   Therefore my heart throbs
    like a harp for Moab,
  and my very soul for Kir-hareseth. *b*
12   When Moab comes to worship
   and wearies himself at the hill-shrines,
  when he enters his sanctuary to pray,
   he will gain nothing.

13 14  These are the words which the LORD spoke long ago about Moab; and
now he says, In three years, as a hired labourer counts them off, the glory
of Moab shall become contemptible for all his vast numbers; a handful
shall be left and those of no account.

17        Damascus: an oracle.

Damascus shall be a city no longer,
  she shall be but a heap of ruins.

   *a Prob. rdg.; Heb.* you.    *b Prob. rdg.; Heb.* Kir-hares.

For ever desolate, flocks shall have her for their own,          2
    and lie there undisturbed.
No longer shall Ephraim boast a fortified city,          3
    or Damascus a kingdom;
the remnant of Aram and the glory of Israel, their fate is one.
This is the very word of the LORD of Hosts.

On that day Jacob's weight shall dwindle          4
    and the fat on his limbs waste away,
as when the harvester gathers up the standing corn          5
    and reaps the ears in armfuls,
or as when a man gleans the ears in the Vale of Rephaim,
    or as when one beats an olive-tree          6
    and only gleanings are left on it,
two or three berries on the top of a branch,
    four or five on the boughs of the fruiting tree.
This is the very word of the LORD the God of Israel.

On that day men shall look to their Maker and turn their eyes to the   7
Holy One of Israel; they shall not look to the altars made by their own   8
hands nor to anything that their fingers have made, sacred poles or incense-
altars.

On that day their strong cities shall be deserted like the cities of the   9
Hivites and the Amorites, which they abandoned when Israel came in;
all shall be desolate.

For you forgot the God who delivered you,          10
    and did not remember the rock, your stronghold.
Plant then, if you will, your gardens in honour of Adonis,
    strike your cuttings for a foreign god;
protect your gardens on the day you plant them,          11
    and next day make the seed sprout.
But the crop will be scorched when wasting disease comes
    in the day of incurable pain.

Listen! it is the thunder of many peoples,          12
they thunder with the thunder of the sea.
Listen! it is the roar of nations
roaring with the roar of mighty waters.
When he rebukes them, away they fly,          13
driven like chaff on the hills before the wind,
    like thistledown before the storm.
At evening all is confusion,          14
    and before morning they are gone.
Such is the fate of our plunderers,
    the lot of those who despoil us.

There is a land of sailing ships,          **18**
a land beyond the rivers of Cush
which sends its envoys by the Nile,          2
journeying on the waters in vessels of reed.

> Go, swift messengers,
> go to a people tall and smooth-skinned,
> to a people dreaded near and far,
> a nation strong and proud,
> whose land is scoured by rivers.

3     All you who dwell in the world, inhabitants of earth,
> shall see when the signal is hoisted on the mountains
> and shall hear when the trumpet sounds.

4   These were the words of the LORD to me:

> From my dwelling-place I will look quietly down
> when the heat shimmers in the summer sun,
> when the dew is heavy at harvest time.

5     Before the vintage, when the budding is over
> and the flower ripens into a berry,
> the shoots shall be cut down with knives,
> the branches struck off and cleared away.

6     All shall be left to birds of prey on the hills
> and to beasts of the earth;
> in summer the birds shall make their home there,
> in winter every beast of the earth.

7     At that time tribute shall be brought to the LORD of Hosts from a people tall and smooth-skinned, dreaded near and far, a nation strong and proud, whose land is scoured by rivers. They shall bring it to Mount Zion, the place where men invoke the name of the LORD of Hosts.

**19**                       Egypt: an oracle.

> See how the LORD comes riding swiftly upon a cloud,
> he shall descend upon Egypt;
> the idols of Egypt quail before him,
> Egypt's courage melts within her.

2     I will set Egyptian against Egyptian,
> and they shall fight one against another,
> neighbour against neighbour,
> city against city and kingdom against kingdom.

3     Egypt's spirit shall sink within her,
> and I will throw her counsels into confusion.
> They may resort to idols and oracle-mongers,
> to ghosts and spirits,

4     but I will hand Egypt over to a hard master,
> and a cruel king shall rule over them.
> This is the very word of the Lord, the LORD of Hosts.

5     The waters of the Nile shall drain away,
> the river shall be parched and run dry;

6       its channels shall stink,
> the streams of Egypt shall be parched and dry up;
> reeds and rushes shall wither away;

the lotus too beside the Nile [a]  7
and all that is sown along the Nile shall dry up,
    shall be blown away and vanish.
The fishermen shall groan and lament,  8
all who cast their hooks into the Nile
and those who spread nets on the water shall lose heart.
    The flax-dressers shall hang their heads,  9
    the women carding and the weavers shall grow pale,
    Egypt's spinners shall be downcast,  10
    and all her artisans sick at heart.

Fools that you are, you princes of Zoan!  11
Wisest of Pharaoh's counsellors you may be,
    but stupid counsellors you are.
    How can you say to Pharaoh,
'I am the heir of wise men and spring from ancient kings'?
    Where are your wise men, Pharaoh,  12
    to teach you and make known to you
what the LORD of Hosts has planned for Egypt?
Zoan's princes are fools, the princes of Noph are dupes;  13
    the chieftains of her clans have led Egypt astray.
    The LORD has infused into them  14
        a spirit that warps their judgement;
    they make Egypt miss her way in all she does,
    as a drunkard will miss his footing as he vomits.
There shall be nothing in Egypt that any man can do,  15
head or tail, palm or rush.

When that day comes the Egyptians shall become weak as women; they  16
shall fear and tremble when they see the LORD of Hosts raise his hand
against them, as raise it he will. The land of Judah shall strike terror into  17
Egypt; its very name shall cause dismay, because of the plans that the LORD
of Hosts has laid against them.

When that day comes there shall be five cities in Egypt speaking the  18
language of Canaan and swearing allegiance to the LORD of Hosts, and one
of them shall be called the City of the Sun.[b]

When that day comes there shall be an altar to the LORD in the heart of  19
Egypt, and a sacred pillar set up for the LORD upon her frontier. It shall  20
stand as a token and a reminder to the LORD of Hosts in Egypt, so that
when they appeal to him against their oppressors, he may send a deliverer
to champion their cause, and he shall rescue them. The LORD will make  21
himself known to the Egyptians; on that day they shall acknowledge the
LORD and do him service with sacrifice and grain-offering, make vows to
him and pay them. The LORD will strike down Egypt, healing as he  22
strikes; then they will turn back to him and he will hear their prayers and
heal them.

When that day comes there shall be a highway between Egypt and  23

---

[a] *Prob. rdg.; Heb. adds* on the mouth of the Nile.    [b] the City of the Sun: *or*
Heliopolis.

Assyria; Assyrians shall come to Egypt and Egyptians to Assyria; then
Egyptians shall worship with*a* Assyrians.

24  When that day comes Israel shall rank with Egypt and Assyria, those
25  three, and shall be a blessing in the centre of the world. So the LORD of
Hosts will bless them: A blessing be upon Egypt my people, upon Assyria
the work of my hands, and upon Israel my possession.

**20**  SARGON KING OF ASSYRIA SENT his commander-in-chief*b* to Ashdod,
2  and he took it by storm. At that time the LORD said to Isaiah son of Amoz,
Come, strip the sackcloth from your waist and take your sandals off. He did
3  so, and went about naked and barefoot. The LORD said, My servant Isaiah
has gone naked and barefoot for three years as a sign and a warning to
4  Egypt and Cush; just so shall the king of Assyria lead the captives of
Egypt and the exiles of Cush naked and barefoot, their buttocks shame-
5  fully exposed, young and old alike. All men shall be dismayed, their hopes
6  in Cush and their pride in Egypt humbled. On that day those who dwell
along this coast will say, So much for all our hopes on which we relied for
help and deliverance from the king of Assyria; what escape have we now?

**21**                    A wilderness: an oracle.

Rough weather, advancing like a storm in the south,
coming from the wilderness, from a land of terror!
2           Grim is the vision shown to me:
the traitor betrayed, the spoiler himself despoiled.
Up, Elam; up, Medes, to the siege,
           no time for weariness!
3    At this my limbs writhe in anguish,
I am gripped by pangs like a woman in labour.
I am distraught past hearing, dazed past seeing,
4    my mind reels, sudden convulsions seize me.

The cool twilight I longed for has become a terror:
5    the banquet is set out, the rugs are spread;
           they are eating and drinking—
rise, princes, burnish your shields.
6           For these were the words of the Lord to me:
           Go, post a watchman to report what he sees.
7           He sees chariots, two-horsed chariots,
           riders on asses, riders on camels.
           He is alert, alert, always on the alert.
8           Then the look-out cried:
All day long I stand on the Lord's watch-tower
and night after night I keep my station.
9    See, there come men in a chariot, a two-horsed chariot.
           And a voice calls back:
           Fallen, fallen is Babylon,
and all the images of her gods lie shattered on the ground.

           *a* Or shall be slaves to.      *b* Or sent Tartan.

O my people, 10
once trodden out and winnowed on the threshing-floor,
　what I have heard from the LORD of Hosts,
　from the God of Israel, I have told you.

Dumah: an oracle. 11

One calls to me from Seir:
Watchman, what is left of the night?
Watchman, what is left?
　The watchman answered: 12
Morning comes, and also night. [a]
Ask if you must; then come back again.

With the Arabs: an oracle. 13

You caravans of Dedan, that camp in the scrub with the Arabs,
　bring water to meet the thirsty. 14
You dwellers in Tema, meet the fugitives with food,
　for they flee from the sword, the sharp edge of the sword, 15
　from the bent bow, and from the press of battle.
For these are the words of the Lord to me: Within a year, as a hired 16
labourer counts off the years, all the glory of Kedar shall come to an end;
few shall be the bows left to the warriors of Kedar. 17
The LORD the God of Israel has spoken.

The Valley of Vision:[b] an oracle. 22

Tell me, what is amiss
　that you have all climbed on to the roofs,
O city full of tumult, town in ferment 2
　and filled with uproar,
whose slain were not slain with the sword
　and did not die in battle?
Your commanders are all in flight, 3
huddled together out of bowshot;
all your stoutest warriors are huddled together,
　they have taken to their heels.
Then I said, Turn your eyes away from me; 4
　leave me to weep in misery.
Do not thrust consolation on me
　for the ruin of my own people.

For the Lord, the LORD of Hosts, has ordained a day of tumult, a day of 5
trampling and turmoil in the Valley of Vision,[b] rousing cries for help that
echo among the mountains.

Elam took up his quiver, 6
horses were harnessed to the chariots of Aram,[c]
Kir took the cover from his shield.

[a] and also night: *or* and the night is full spent.　　[b] *Or* of Calamity.
[c] *Prob. rdg.; Heb.* man.

835

7      Your fairest valleys were overrun by chariots and horsemen,
       the gates were hard beset,
8           the heart of Judah's defence was laid open.

   On that day you looked to the weapons stored in the House of the Forest;
9  you filled all the many pools in the City of David, collecting water from
10 the Lower Pool.*a* Then you surveyed the houses in Jerusalem, tearing some
11 down to make the wall inaccessible, and between the two walls you made
   a cistern for the Waters of the Old Pool;
       but you did not look to the Maker of it all
       or consider him who fashioned it long ago.

12     On that day the Lord, the LORD of Hosts,
       called for weeping and beating the breast,
       for shaving the head and putting on sackcloth;
13     but instead there was joy and merry-making,
       slaughtering of cattle and killing of sheep,
       eating of meat and drinking of wine, as you thought,
       Let us eat and drink; for tomorrow we die.

14 The LORD of Hosts has revealed himself to me; in my hearing he swore:

       Your wickedness shall never be purged
       until you die.
       This is the word of the Lord, the LORD of Hosts.

15 These were the words of the Lord, the LORD of Hosts:

       Go to this steward,
       to Shebna, comptroller of the household, and say:
16     What right, what business, have you here,
       that you have dug yourself a grave here,
       cutting out your grave on a height
       and carving yourself a resting-place in the rock?
17     The LORD will shake you out,
       shake you as a garment*b* is shaken out
       to rid it of lice;
18     then he will bundle you tightly and throw you
       like a ball into a great wide land.
       There you shall die,
       and there shall lie your chariot of honour,
       an object of contempt to your master's household.
19     I will remove you from office and drive you from your post.

20 21  On that day I will send for my servant Eliakim son of Hilkiah; I will
   invest him with your robe, gird him with your sash; and hand over your
   authority to him. He shall be a father to the inhabitants of Jerusalem and
22 the people of Judah. I will lay the key of the house of David on his shoulder;
   what he opens no man shall shut, and what he shuts no man shall open.

---

*a* you filled . . . Lower Pool: *or* you took note of the cracks, many as they were, in the wall
of the City of David, and you collected water from the Lower Pool.       *b* *Prob. rdg.;*
*Heb.* man.

He shall be a seat of honour for his father's family; I will fasten him firmly 23
in place like a peg. On him shall hang all the weight of the family, down to 24
the lowest dregs—all the little vessels, both bowls and pots. On that day, 25
says the LORD of Hosts, the peg which was firmly fastened in its place shall
be removed; it shall be hacked out and shall fall, and the load of things
hanging on it shall be destroyed. The LORD has spoken.

Tyre: an oracle.     **23**

The ships of Tarshish howl, for the harbour is sacked;
the port of entry from Kittim is swept away.
> The people of the sea-coast, the merchants of Sidon, wail, 2-3
> people whose agents cross the great waters,
>> whose harvest*a* is the grain of the Shihor
>> and their revenue the trade of nations.

Sidon, the sea-fortress,*b* cries in her disappointment,*c* 4
I no longer feel the anguish of labour or bear children;
I have no young sons to rear, no daughters to bring up.
> When the news is confirmed in Egypt 5
> her people sway in anguish at the fate of Tyre.
> Make your way to Tarshish, they say, 6
> howl, you who dwell by the sea-coast.
> Is this your busy city, ancient in story, 7

on whose voyages you were carried to settle far away?

Whose plan was this against Tyre, the city of battlements, 8
> whose merchants were princes
> and her traders the most honoured men on earth?

The LORD of Hosts planned it to prick every noble's pride 9
> and bring all the most honoured men on earth into contempt.
> Take to the tillage of your fields, you people of Tarshish; 10
> for your market*d* is lost.

The LORD has stretched out his hand over the sea 11
> and shaken kingdoms,

he has given his command to destroy the marts of Canaan;
and he has said, You shall busy yourselves no more, 12
> you, the sorely oppressed virgin city of Sidon.
> Though you arise and cross over to Kittim,
> even there you shall find no rest.

Look at this land, the destined home of ships*e*! The Chaldaeans*f* 13
erected their*g* siege-towers, dismantled its palaces and laid it in ruins.

> Howl, you ships of Tarshish; 14
> for your haven is sacked.

---

*a* whose harvest: *prob. rdg.; Heb.* the harvest of the Nile.     *b* the sea-fortress:
*prob. rdg.; Heb.* the sea, sea-fortress, saying.     *c* in her disappointment: *prob.
rdg.; Heb.* be disappointed.     *d* *Prob. rdg.; Heb.* girdle.     *e* *Or* marmots.
*f* *Prob. rdg.; Heb. adds* this was the people; it was not Assyria.     *g* *Prob. rdg.;*
*Heb.* his.

15 From that day Tyre shall be forgotten for seventy years, the span of one
king's life. At the end of the seventy years her plight shall be that of the
harlot in the song:

16     Take your harp, go round the city,
      poor forgotten harlot;
    touch the strings sweetly, sing all your songs,
      make men remember you again.

17 At the end of seventy years, the LORD will turn again to Tyre; she shall go
18 back to her old trade and hire herself out to every kingdom on earth. The
profits of her trading will be dedicated to the LORD; they shall not be
hoarded or stored up, but shall be given to those who worship the LORD,
to purchase food in plenty and fine attire.

## The LORD's judgement on the earth

24     Beware, the LORD will empty the earth,
    split it open and turn it upside down,
      and scatter its inhabitants.

2     Then it will be the same for priest and people,
    the same for master and slave, mistress and slave-girl,
      seller and buyer,
    borrower and lender, debtor and creditor.

3     The earth is emptied clean away
      and stripped clean bare.
    For this is the word that the LORD has spoken.

4     The earth dries up and withers,
    the whole world withers and grows sick;
      the earth's high places sicken,

5     and earth itself is desecrated by the feet of those who live in it,
    because they have broken the laws, disobeyed the statutes
      and violated the eternal covenant.

6     For this a curse has devoured the earth
      and its inhabitants stand aghast.
    For this those who inhabit the earth dwindle
    and only a few men are left.

7     The new wine dries up, the vines sicken,
    and all the revellers turn to sorrow.

8     Silent the merry beat of tambourines,
      hushed the shouts of revelry,
      the merry harp is silent.

9     No one shall drink wine to the sound of song;
    the liquor will be bitter to the man who drinks it.

10     The city of chaos is a broken city,
    every house barred, that no one may enter.

11     Men call for wine in the streets;
      all revelry is darkened,
      and mirth is banished from the land.

Desolation alone is left in the city 12
and the gate is broken into pieces.
So shall it be in all the world, in every nation, 13
as when an olive-tree is beaten and stripped,
as when the vintage is ended.

Men raise their voices and cry aloud, 14
they shout in the west,<sup>a</sup> so great is the LORD's majesty.
Therefore let the LORD be glorified in the regions of the east, 15
and the name of the LORD the God of Israel
in the coasts and islands of the west.

From the ends of the earth we have heard them sing, 16
How lovely is righteousness!
But I thought, Villainy, villainy!
Woe to the traitors and their treachery!
Traitors double-dyed they are indeed!
The hunter's scare, the pit, and the trap 17
threaten all who dwell in the land;
if a man runs from the rattle of the scare 18
he will fall into the pit;
if he climbs out of the pit
he will be caught in the trap.
When the windows of heaven above are opened
and earth's foundations shake,
the earth is utterly shattered, 19
it is convulsed and reels wildly.
The earth reels to and fro like a drunken man 20
and sways like a watchman's shelter;
the sins of men weigh heavy upon it,
and it falls to rise no more.

On that day the LORD will punish 21
the host of heaven in heaven, and on earth the kings of the earth,
herded together, close packed like prisoners in a dungeon; 22
shut up in gaol, after a long time they shall be punished.
The moon shall grow pale and the sun hide its face in shame; 23
for the LORD of Hosts has become king
on Mount Zion and in Jerusalem,
and shows his glory before their elders.


## The deliverance and ingathering of Judah

O LORD, thou art my God; 25
I will exalt thee and praise thy name;
for thou hast accomplished a wonderful purpose,
certain and sure, from of old.

<sup>a</sup> in the west: *or* more loudly than the sea.

2       For thou hast turned cities into heaps of ruin,
        and fortified towns into rubble;
        every mansion in the cities is swept away,
          never to be rebuilt.
3       For this a cruel nation holds thee in honour,
        the cities of ruthless nations fear thee.
4       Truly thou hast been a refuge to the poor,
        a refuge to the needy in his trouble,
    shelter from the tempest and shade from the heat.
        For the blast of the ruthless is like an icy storm
5          or a scorching drought;
        thou subduest the roar of the foe,[a]
        and the song of the ruthless dies away.

6       On this mountain the LORD of Hosts will prepare
        a banquet of rich fare for all the peoples,
        a banquet of wines well matured and richest fare,
          well-matured wines strained clear.
7       On this mountain the LORD will swallow up
        that veil that shrouds all the peoples,
        the pall thrown over all the nations;
8        he will swallow up death for ever.
    Then the Lord GOD will wipe away the tears
        from every face
    and remove the reproach of his people from the whole earth.
    The LORD has spoken.

9       On that day men will say,
        See, this is our God
        for whom we have waited to deliver us;
        this is the LORD for whom we have waited;
        let us rejoice and exult in his deliverance.
10      For the hand of the LORD will rest on this mountain,
        but Moab shall be trampled under his feet
        as straw is trampled into a midden.
11      In it Moab shall spread out his hands
        as a swimmer spreads his hands to swim,
    but he shall sink his pride with every stroke of his hands.
12      The LORD has thrown down the high defences of your walls,
        has levelled them to the earth
        and brought them down to the dust.

**26**    On that day this song shall be sung in Judah:

        We have a strong city
      whose walls and ramparts are our deliverance.
2       Open the gates to let a righteous nation in,
        a nation that keeps faith.

       [a] *Prob. rdg.; Heb. adds* heat in the shadow of a cloud.

Thou dost keep in peace men of constant mind,                    3
    in peace because they trust in thee.
  Trust in the LORD for ever;                    4
for the LORD himself is an everlasting rock.
He has brought low all who dwell high in a towering city;                    5
  he levels it to the ground and lays it in the dust,
that the oppressed and the poor may tread it underfoot.                    6
  The path of the righteous is level,                    7
and thou markest out the right way for the upright.
We too look to the path prescribed in thy laws, O LORD;                    8
    thy name and thy memory are our heart's desire.
  With all my heart I long for thee in the night,                    9
  I seek thee eagerly when dawn breaks;
for, when thy laws prevail in the land,
  the inhabitants of the world learn justice.
The wicked are destroyed, they have never learnt justice;                    10
    corrupt in a land of honest ways,
  they do not regard the majesty of the LORD.

  O LORD, thy hand is lifted high,                    11
but the bitter enemies of thy people do not see it; [a]
  let the fire of thy enmity destroy them.
O LORD, thou wilt bestow prosperity on us;                    12
for in truth all our works are thy doing.
    O LORD our God,                    13
other lords than thou have been our masters,
but thee alone do we invoke by name.
    The dead will not live again,                    14
    those long in their graves will not rise;
to this end thou hast punished them and destroyed them,
    and made all memory of them perish.
Thou hast enlarged the nation, O LORD,                    15
enlarged it and won thyself honour,
thou hast extended all the frontiers of the land.
In our distress, O LORD, we [b] sought thee out,                    16
chastened by the mere whisper of thy rebuke.
As a woman with child, when her time is near,                    17
is in labour and cries out in her pains,
so were we in thy presence, O LORD.
    We have been with child, we have been in labour,                    18
    but have brought forth wind.
  We have won no success for the land,
  and no one will be born to inhabit the world.
But thy dead live, their bodies will rise again.                    19
They that sleep in the earth will awake and shout for joy;
  for thy dew is a dew of sparkling light,
and the earth will bring those long dead to birth again.

[a] *Prob. rdg.; Heb. adds* let them see and be ashamed.          [b] *Prob. rdg.; Heb.* they.

20  Go, my people, enter your rooms
    and shut your doors behind you;
    withdraw for a brief while, until wrath has gone by.

21  For see, the LORD is coming from his place
    to punish the inhabitants of the earth for their sins;
    then the earth shall uncover her blood-stains
    and hide her slain no more.

**27**  On that day the LORD will punish
    with his cruel sword, his mighty and powerful sword,
    Leviathan that twisting*ᵃ* sea-serpent,
    that writhing serpent Leviathan,
    and slay the monster of the deep.

2  On that day sing to the pleasant vineyard,
3    I the LORD am its keeper,
    moment by moment I water it for fear its green leaves fail.
    Night and day I tend it,
4      but I get no wine;
    I would as soon have briars and thorns,
    then I would wage war upon it and burn it all up,
5  unless it grasps me as its refuge and makes peace with me—
    unless it makes peace with me.

6  In time to come Jacob's offspring shall take root
    and Israel shall bud and blossom,
    and they shall fill the whole earth with fruit.

7  Has God struck him down as he struck others down?
    Has the slayer been slain as he slew others?
8-10*ᵇ*  This then purges Jacob's iniquity,
    this*ᶜ* has removed his sin:
    that he grinds all altar stones to powder like chalk;
    no sacred poles and incense-altars are left standing.

    The fortified city is left solitary,
    and his quarrel with her ends in brushing her away,*ᵈ*
    removing her by a cruel blast when the east wind blows;
    it is a homestead stripped bare, deserted like a wilderness;
    there the calf grazes and there lies down,
      and crops every twig.
11  Its boughs snap off when they grow dry,
    and women come and light their fires with them.
    For they are a people without sense;
    therefore their maker will show them no mercy,
    he who formed them will show them no favour.

---

*ᵃ Or primeval.*     *ᵇ Verses 8-10 re-arranged thus: 9, 10a, 8, 10b.*     *ᶜ Prob. rdg.;*
*Heb. adds all fruit.*     *ᵈ Prob. rdg.; Heb. adds by dismissing her.*

On that day the LORD will beat out the grain,                    12
from the streams of the Euphrates to the Torrent of Egypt;
but you Israelites will be gleaned
    one by one.

On that day                                                     13
a blast shall be blown on a great trumpet,
    and those who are lost in Assyria
and those dispersed in Egypt will come in
and worship the LORD on the holy mountain, in Jerusalem.

## *Assyria and Judah*

Oh, the proud garlands of the drunkards of Ephraim              **28**
and the flowering sprays, so lovely in their beauty,
on the heads of revellers dripping with perfumes,
    overcome with wine!
See, the Lord has one at his bidding, mighty and strong,         2
    whom he sets to work with violence against the land,
like a sweeping storm of hail, like a destroying tempest,
like a torrent of water in overwhelming flood.
    The proud garlands of Ephraim's drunkards                    3
        shall be trampled underfoot,
    and the flowering sprays, so lovely in their beauty          4
        on the heads dripping with perfumes,
    shall be like early figs ripe before summer;
    he who sees them plucks them,
        and their bloom is gone while they lie in his hand.
On that day the LORD of Hosts shall be a lovely garland,         5
    a beautiful diadem for the remnant of his people,
a spirit of justice for one who presides in a court of justice,  6
and of valour for*a* those who repel the enemy at the gate.

These too are addicted to wine,                                  7
    clamouring in their cups:
priest and prophet are addicted to strong drink
    and bemused with wine;
clamouring in their cups, confirmed topers,*b*
    hiccuping in drunken stupor;
every table is covered with vomit,                               8
    filth that leaves no clean spot.
Who is it that the prophet hopes to teach,                       9
to whom will what they hear make sense?

---

*a* for: *prob. rdg.; Heb. om.*          *b* These too . . . topers: *or* These too lose their way
through wine and are set wandering by strong drink: priest and prophet lose their way
through strong drink and are fuddled with wine; are set wandering by strong drink,
lose their way through tippling.

Are they babes newly weaned, just taken from the breast?

10 It is all harsh cries and raucous shouts,
   'A little more here, a little there!'

11 So it will be with barbarous speech and strange tongue
   that this people will hear God speaking,

12 this people to whom he once said,
   'This is true rest; let the exhausted have rest.
   This is repose', and they refused to listen.

13 Now to them the word of the LORD will be
   harsh cries and raucous shouts,
   'A little more here, a little there!'—
   and so, as they walk, they will stumble backwards,
   they will be injured, trapped and caught.

14 Listen then to the word of the LORD, you arrogant men
   who rule this people in Jerusalem.

15 You say, 'We have made a treaty with Death
   and signed a pact with Sheol:
   so that, when the raging flood sweeps by, it shall not touch us;
   for we have taken refuge in lies
   and sheltered behind falsehood.'

16 These then are the words of the Lord GOD:
   Look, I am laying a stone in Zion, a block of granite,
   a precious corner-stone for a firm foundation;
   he who has faith shall not waver.

17 I will use justice as a plumb-line
   and righteousness as a plummet;
   hail shall sweep away your refuge of lies,
   and flood-waters carry away your shelter.

18 Then your treaty with Death shall be annulled
   and your pact with Sheol shall not stand;
   the raging waters will sweep by,
   and you will be like land swept by the flood.

19 As often as it sweeps by, it will take you;
   morning after morning it will sweep by,
   day and night.
   The very thought of such tidings
   will bring nothing but dismay;

20 for 'The bed is too short for a man to stretch,
   and the blanket too narrow to cover him.'

21 But the LORD shall arise as he rose on Mount Perazim
   and storm with rage as he did in the Vale of Gibeon
   to do what he must do—how strange a deed!
   to perform his work—how outlandish a work!

22 But now have done with your arrogance,
   lest your bonds grow tighter;
   for I have heard destruction decreed
   by the Lord GOD of Hosts for the whole land.

Listen and hear what I say, 23
attend and hear my words.
Will the ploughman continually plough for the sowing, 24
breaking his ground and harrowing it?
Does he not, once he has levelled it, 25
broadcast the dill and scatter the cummin?
Does he not plant the wheat in rows
with barley*a* and spelt along the edge?
Does not his God instruct him and train him aright? 26
Dill is not threshed with a sledge, 27
and the cartwheel is not rolled over cummin;
dill is beaten with a rod,
and cummin with a flail.
Corn is crushed, but not to the uttermost, 28
not with a final crushing;
his cartwheels rumble over it and break it up,
but they do not grind it fine.
This message, too, comes from the LORD of Hosts, 29
whose purposes are wonderful
and his power great.

Alas for Ariel! Ariel, **29**
the city where David encamped.
Add year to year,
let the pilgrim-feasts run their round,
and I will bring Ariel to sore straits,
when there shall be moaning and lamentation. 2
I will make her my Ariel indeed, my fiery altar.
I will throw my army round you like a wall; 3
I will set a ring of outposts all round you
and erect siege-works against you.
You shall be brought low, you will speak out of the ground 4
and your words will issue from the earth;
your voice will come like a ghost's from the ground,
and your words will squeak out of the earth.
Yet the horde of your enemies shall crumble into dust, 5
the horde of ruthless foes shall fly like chaff.
Then suddenly, all in an instant,
punishment shall come from the LORD of Hosts 6
with thunder and earthquake and a great noise,
with storm and tempest and a flame of devouring fire;
and the horde of all the nations warring against Ariel, 7
all their baggage-trains and siege-works,
and all her oppressors themselves,
shall fade as a dream, a vision of the night.
Like a starving man who dreams 8
and thinks that he is eating,

*a Prob. rdg.; Heb. adds an unintelligible word.*

but wakes up to find himself empty,
or a thirsty man who dreams
and thinks that he is drinking,
but wakes up to find himself thirsty and dry,
so shall the horde of all the nations be
that war against Mount Zion.

9    Loiter and be dazed, enjoy yourselves and be blinded,
be drunk but not with wine, reel but not with strong drink;
10   for the LORD has poured upon you a spirit of deep stupor;
he has closed your eyes, the prophets,
and muffled your heads, the seers.

11   All prophetic vision has become for you like a sealed book. Give such a
book to one who can read and say, 'Come, read this'; he will answer,
12   'I cannot', because it is sealed. Give it to one who cannot read and say,
'Come, read this'; he will answer, 'I cannot read.'
13   Then the Lord said:

Because this people approach me with their mouths
and honour me with their lips
while their hearts are far from me,
and their religion is but a precept of men, learnt by rote,
14   therefore I will yet again shock this people,
adding shock to shock:
the wisdom of their wise men shall vanish
and the discernment of the discerning shall be lost.

15   Shame upon those who seek to hide their purpose
too deep for the LORD to see,
and who, when their deeds are done in the dark,
say, 'Who sees us? Who knows of us?'
16   How you turn things upside down,
as if the potter ranked no higher than the clay!
Shall the thing made say of its maker, 'He did not make me'?
Shall the pot say of the potter, 'He has no skill'?
17   The time is but short
before Lebanon goes back to grassland
and the grassland is no better than scrub.

18   On that day deaf men shall hear
when a book is read,
and the eyes of the blind shall see
out of impenetrable darkness.
19   The lowly shall once again rejoice in the LORD,
and the poorest of men exult in the Holy One of Israel.
20   The ruthless shall be no more, the arrogant shall cease to be;
those who are quick to see mischief,
21   those who charge others with a sin
or lay traps for him who brings the wrongdoer into court

or by falsehood deny justice to the righteous—
all these shall be exterminated.

Therefore these are the words of the Lord the God of the house of  22
Jacob, the God who ransomed Abraham:

This is no time for Jacob to be shamed,
no time for his face to grow pale;
for his descendants will hallow my name                              23
when they see what I have done in their nation.
They will hallow the Holy One of Jacob
and hold the God of Israel in awe;
those whose minds are confused will gain understanding,              24
and the obstinate will receive instruction.

Oh, rebel sons! says the Lord,                                       **30**
you make plans, but not of my devising,
you weave schemes, but not inspired by me,
piling sin upon sin;
you hurry down to Egypt without consulting me,                        2
to seek protection under Pharaoh's shelter
and take refuge under Egypt's wing.
Pharaoh's protection will bring you disappointment                    3
and refuge under Egypt's wing humiliation;
for, though his officers are at Zoan                                   4
and his envoys reach as far as Hanes,
all are left in sorry plight by that unprofitable nation,             5
no help they find, no profit, only disappointment and disgrace.

The Beasts of the South: an oracle.                                   6

Through a land of hardship and distress
the tribes of lioness and roaring lion,
sand-viper and venomous flying serpent,
carry their wealth on the backs of asses
and their treasures on camels' humps
to an unprofitable people.
Vain and worthless is the help of Egypt;                              7
therefore have I given her this name,
Rahab Quelled.
Now come and write it on a tablet,                                    8
engrave it as an inscription before their eyes,
that it may be there in future days,
a testimony for all time.
For they are a race of rebels, disloyal sons,                         9
sons who will not listen to the Lord's instruction;
they say to the seers, 'You shall not see',                          10
and to the visionaries, 'You shall have no true visions;
give us smooth words and seductive visions.

11          Turn aside, leave the straight path,
          and rid us for ever of the Holy One of Israel.'

12  These are the words of the Holy One of Israel:
          Because you have rejected this warning
          and trust in devious and dishonest practices,
          resting on them for support,
13        therefore you shall find this iniquity will be
          like a crack running down
          a high wall, which bulges
          and suddenly, all in an instant, comes crashing down,
14        as an earthen jar is broken with a crash,
          mercilessly shattered,
          so that not a shard is found among the fragments
          to take fire from the glowing embers,
          or to scoop up water from a pool.

15  These are the words of the Lord GOD the Holy One of Israel:
          Come back, keep peace, and you will be safe;
          in stillness and in staying quiet, there lies your strength.
16        But you would have none of it; you said, No,
          we will take horse and flee;
          therefore you shall be put to flight:
          We will ride apace;
          therefore swift shall be the pace of your pursuers.
17        When a thousand flee at the challenge of one,
          you shall all flee at the challenge of five, until you are left
          like a pole on a mountain-top, a signal post on a hill.
18        Yet the LORD is waiting to show you his favour,
          yet he yearns to have pity on you;
          for the LORD is a God of justice.
          Happy are all who wait for him!

19     O people of Zion who dwell in Jerusalem, you shall weep no more. The
LORD will show you favour and answer you when he hears your cry for
20  help. The Lord may give you bread of adversity and water of affliction,
but he who teaches you shall no longer be hidden out of sight, but with
21  your own eyes you shall see him always. If you stray from the road to right
or left you shall hear with your own ears a voice behind you saying, This
22  is the way; follow it. You will reject, as things unclean, your silvered
images and your idols sheathed in gold; you will loathe them like a foul
23  discharge and call them ordure.*ª* The Lord will give you rain for the seed
you sow, and as the produce of your soil he will give you heavy crops of
corn in plenty. When that day comes the cattle shall graze in broad pastures;
24  the oxen and asses that work your land shall be fed with well-seasoned
25  fodder, winnowed with shovel and fork. On each high mountain and each
lofty hill shall be streams of running water, on the day of massacre when the
26  highest in the land fall. The moon shall shine with a brightness like the

        *ª* call them ordure: *or* say to them, Be off.

sun's, and the sun with seven times his wonted brightness, seven days'
light in one, on the day when the LORD binds up the broken limbs of his
people and heals their wounds.

See, the name of the LORD comes from afar,                27
  his anger blazing and his doom heavy.
His lips are charged with wrath
  and his tongue is a devouring fire.
His breath is like a torrent in spate,                  28
  rising neck-high,
a yoke to force the nations to their ruin,
a bit in the mouth to guide the peoples astray.
But for you there shall be songs,                       29
  as on a night of sacred pilgrimage,
your hearts glad, as the hearts of men who walk to the sound of the pipe
on their way to the LORD's hill, to the rock of Israel.
Then the LORD shall make his voice heard in majesty     30
and show his arm sweeping down in fierce anger
  with devouring flames of fire,
with cloudburst and tempests of rain and hailstones;
  for at the voice of the LORD Assyria's heart fails her,   31
  as she feels the stroke of his rod.
Tambourines and harps and shaking sistrums              32
  shall keep time
  with every stroke of his rod,
of the chastisement which the LORD inflicts on her.
Long ago was Topheth made ready,*a*                     33
  made deep and broad,
  its fire-pit a blazing mass of logs,
and the breath of the LORD like a stream of brimstone
  blazing in it.

Shame upon those who go down to Egypt for help      **31**
  and rely on horses,
putting their trust in chariots many in number
  and in horsemen in their thousands,
but do not look to the Holy One of Israel
  or seek guidance of the LORD!
Yet the LORD too in his wisdom can bring about trouble   2
  and he does not take back his words;
he will rise up against the league of evildoers,
  against all who help those who do wrong.
The Egyptians are men, not God,*b*                       3
  their horses are flesh, not spirit;
and, when the LORD stretches out his hand,
the helper will stumble and he who is helped will fall,
  and they will all vanish together.

  *a Prob. rdg.; Heb. adds* is that prepared also for the king?    *b Or* gods.

4    This is what the Lord has said to me:

>      As a lion or a young lion growls over its prey
>      when the muster of shepherds is called out against it,
>           and is not scared at their noise
>           or cowed by their clamour,
>      so shall the Lord of Hosts come down to do battle
>      for Mount Zion and her high summit.

5          Thus the Lord of Hosts, like a bird hovering over its young,
>      will be a shield over Jerusalem;
>           he will shield her and deliver her,
>           standing over her and delivering her.

6      O Israel, come back to him whom you have so deeply offended,
7          for on that day when you spurn, one and all,
>      the idols of silver and the idols of gold
>      which your own sinful hands have made,

8      Assyria shall fall by the sword, but by no sword of man;
>      a sword that no man wields shall devour him.
>      He shall flee before the sword,
>      and his young warriors shall be put to forced labour,

9          his officers shall be helpless from terror
>      and his captains too dismayed to flee.
>           This is the very word of the Lord
>      whose fire blazes in Zion,
>      and whose furnace is set up in Jerusalem.

32     Behold, a king shall reign in righteousness
>      and his rulers rule with justice,

2          and a man shall be a refuge from the wind
>           and a shelter from the tempest,
>           or like runnels of water in dry ground,
>      like the shadow of a great rock in a thirsty land.

3          The eyes that can see will not be clouded,
>      and the ears that can hear will listen;

4          the anxious heart will understand and know,
>      and the man who stammers will at once speak plain.

5      The scoundrel will no longer be thought noble,
>      nor the villain called a prince;

6          for the scoundrel will speak like a scoundrel
>      and will hatch evil in his heart;
>           he is an impostor in all his actions,
>           and in his words a liar even to the Lord;
>           he starves the hungry of their food
>           and refuses drink to the thirsty.

7          The villain's ways are villainous
>      and he devises infamous plans
>      to ruin the poor with his lies
>      and deny justice to the needy.

But the man of noble mind forms noble designs    8
and stands firm in his nobility.

You women that live at ease, stand up    9
    and hear what I have to say.
You young women without a care, mark my words.
You have no cares now, but when the year is out, you will tremble,   10
for the vintage will be over and no produce gathered in.
    You who are now at ease, be anxious;    11
    tremble, you who have no cares.
    Strip yourselves bare;
    put a cloth round your waists
    and beat your breasts    12
for the pleasant fields and fruitful vines.
On the soil of my people shall spring up thorns and briars,   13
in every happy home and in the busy town,
for the palace is forsaken and the crowded streets deserted;   14
citadel*a* and watch-tower are turned into open heath,
the joy of wild asses ever after and pasture for the flocks,
until a spirit from on high is lavished upon us.   15
    Then the wilderness will become grassland
    and grassland will be cheap as scrub;
    then justice shall make its home in the wilderness,   16
    and righteousness dwell in the grassland;
    when righteousness shall yield peace   17
and its fruit be quietness and confidence for ever.
    Then my people shall live in a tranquil country,   18
dwelling in peace, in houses full of ease;
    it will be cool on the slopes of the forest then,   19
    and cities shall lie peaceful in the plain.
    Happy shall you be, sowing every man by the water-side,   20
      and letting ox and ass run free.

Ah! you destroyer, yourself undestroyed,    **33**
    betrayer still unbetrayed,
    when you cease to destroy you will be destroyed,
    after all your betrayals, you will be betrayed yourself.

O Lord, show us thy favour; we hope in thee.    2
    Uphold us every morning,
    save us when troubles come.
    At the roar of the thunder the peoples flee,   3
    at thy rumbling nations are scattered;
their spoil is swept up as if young locusts had swept it,   4
    like a swarm of locusts men swarm upon it.

The Lord is supreme, for he dwells on high;    5
if you fill Zion with justice and with righteousness,

       *a* Or hill; *Heb.* Ophel.

6          then he will be the mainstay of the age: [a]
wisdom and knowledge are the assurance of salvation;
    the fear of the LORD is her [b] treasure.

7          Hark, how the valiant cry aloud for help,
    and those sent to sue for peace weep bitterly!
8          The highways are deserted, no travellers tread the roads.
Covenants are broken, treaties are flouted;
    man is of no account.
9          The land is parched and wilting,
    Lebanon is eaten away and crumbling;
Sharon has become a desert,
    Bashan and Carmel are stripped bare.
10        Now, says the LORD, I will rise up.
Now I will exalt myself, now lift myself up.
11        What you conceive and bring to birth is chaff and stubble;
    a wind like fire shall devour you.
12        Whole nations shall be heaps of white ash,
or like thorns cut down and set on fire.
13        You who dwell far away, hear what I have done;
    acknowledge my might, you who are near.
14        In Zion sinners quake with terror,
    the godless are seized with trembling and ask,
Can any of us live with a devouring fire?
Can any live in endless burning?
15        The man who lives an upright life and speaks the truth,
    who scorns to enrich himself by extortion,
who snaps his fingers at a bribe,
    who stops his ears to hear nothing of bloodshed,
    who closes his eyes to the sight of evil—
16        that is the man who shall dwell on the heights,
    his refuge a fastness in the cliffs,
his bread secure and his water never failing.

17        Your eyes shall see a king in his splendour
    and will look upon a land of far distances.
18        You will call to mind what once you feared:
'Where then is he that counted, where is he that weighed,
    where is he that counted the treasures?'
19        You will no longer see that barbarous people,
    that people whose speech was so hard to catch,
    whose stuttering speech you could not understand.

20        Look upon Zion, city of our solemn feasts,
    let your eyes rest on Jerusalem,
a land of comfort, a tent that shall never be shifted,
    whose pegs shall never be pulled up,
    not one of its ropes cast loose.

[a] the age: *prob. rdg.; Heb.* your times.    [b] *Prob. rdg.; Heb.* his.

There we have the LORD's majesty;[a]                                    21
it will be a place[b] of rivers and broad streams;
but[c] no galleys shall be rowed there,
no stately ship sail by.
For the LORD our judge, the LORD our law-giver,                        22
the LORD our king—he himself will save us.
[Men may say, Your rigging is slack;                                   23
it will not hold the mast firm in its socket,
    nor can the sails be spread.]
Then the blind man shall have a full share of the spoil
and the lame shall take part in the pillage;
no man who dwells there shall say, 'I am sick';                        24
and the sins of the people who live there shall be pardoned.


## Edom and Israel

Approach, you nations, to listen,                                      **34**
    and attend, you peoples;
    let the earth listen and everything in it,
the world and all that it yields;
for the LORD's anger is turned against all the nations                 2
    and his wrath against all the host of them:
he gives them over to slaughter and destruction.
    Their slain shall be flung out,                                    3
    the stench shall rise from their corpses,
and the mountains shall stream with their blood.
All the host of heaven shall crumble into nothing,                     4
    the heavens shall be rolled up like a scroll,
    and the starry host fade away,
as the leaf withers from the vine
    and the ripening fruit from the fig-tree;
for the sword of the LORD[d] appears in heaven.                        5
See how it descends in judgement on Edom,
on the people whom he dooms[e] to destruction.
The LORD has a sword steeped in blood,                                 6
    it is gorged with fat,
the fat of rams' kidneys, and the blood of lambs and goats;
    for he has a sacrifice in Bozrah,
    a great slaughter in Edom.
Wild oxen shall come down and buffaloes[f] with them,                  7
    bull and bison together,
and the land shall drink deep of blood
    and the soil be sated with fat.
For the LORD has a day of vengeance,                                   8

[a] Or threshing-floor.          [b] it . . . place: or instead.          [c] Or and.
[d] the sword of the LORD: prob. rdg.; Heb. my sword.     [e] Prob. rdg.; Heb. I doom.
[f] and buffaloes: prob. rdg.; Heb. om.

the champion of Zion has a year when he will requite.
9     Edom's torrents shall be turned into pitch
    and its soil into brimstone,
and the land shall become blazing pitch,
10     which night and day shall never be quenched,
    and its smoke shall go up for ever.
From generation to generation it shall lie waste,
    and no man shall pass through it ever again.
11     Horned owl and bustard shall make their home in it,
    screech-owl and raven shall haunt it.
He has stretched across it a measuring-line of chaos,
12     and its frontiers shall be a jumble of stones.
No king shall be acclaimed there,
    and all its princes shall come to nought.
13     Thorns shall sprout in its palaces;
    nettles and briars shall cover its walled towns.
It shall be rough land fit for wolves, a haunt of desert-owls.
14     Marmots shall consort with jackals,
    and he-goat shall encounter he-goat.
There too the nightjar shall rest
    and find herself a place for repose.
15     There the sand-partridge shall make her nest,
    lay her eggs and hatch them
    and gather her brood under her wings;
    there shall the kites gather,
        one after another.
16   Consult the book of the LORD and read it:
    not one of these shall be lacking,
        not one miss its fellow,
    for with his own mouth he has ordered it
    and with his own breath he has brought them together.
17   He it is who has allotted each its place,
    and his hand has measured out their portions;
    they shall occupy it for ever
    and dwell there from generation to generation.

35     Let the wilderness and the thirsty land be glad,
    let the desert rejoice and burst into flower.
2     Let it flower with fields of asphodel,
    let it rejoice and shout for joy.
The glory of Lebanon is given to it,
    the splendour too of Carmel and Sharon;
these shall see the glory of the LORD, the splendour of our God.
3     Strengthen the feeble arms,
    steady the tottering knees;
4   say to the anxious, Be strong and fear not.
See, your God comes with vengeance,
    with dread retribution he comes to save you.

Then shall blind men's eyes be opened,                    5
  and the ears of the deaf unstopped.
Then shall the lame man leap like a deer,                 6
  and the tongue of the dumb shout aloud;
for water springs up in the wilderness,
  and torrents flow in dry land.
The mirage becomes a pool,                                7
  the thirsty land bubbling springs;
instead of reeds and rushes, grass shall grow
  in the rough land where wolves now lurk.
And there shall be a causeway there                       8
  which shall be called the Way of Holiness,
  and the unclean shall not pass along it;
it shall become a pilgrim's way,<sup>*a*</sup>
  no fool shall trespass on it.
No lion shall come there,                                 9
  no savage beast climb on to it;
  not one shall be found there.
By it those he has ransomed shall return
  and the LORD's redeemed come home;                      10
they shall enter Zion with shouts of triumph,
  crowned with everlasting gladness.
Gladness and joy shall be their escort,
  and suffering and weariness shall flee away.


## *Jerusalem delivered from Sennacherib*

IN THE FOURTEENTH YEAR of the reign of Hezekiah, Sennacherib king **36** 1<sup>*b*</sup>
of Assyria attacked and took all the fortified cities of Judah. From Lachish 2
he sent the chief officer<sup>*c*</sup> with a strong force to King Hezekiah at Jerusalem; and he halted by the conduit of the Upper Pool on the causeway
which leads to the Fuller's Field. There Eliakim son of Hilkiah, the comp- 3
troller of the household, came out to him, with Shebna the adjutant-general
and Joah son of Asaph, the secretary of state. The chief officer said to 4
them, 'Tell Hezekiah that this is the message of the Great King, the king
of Assyria: "What ground have you for this confidence of yours? Do you 5
think fine words can take the place of skill and numbers? On whom then
do you rely for support in your rebellion against me? On Egypt? Egypt 6
is a splintered cane that will run into a man's hand and pierce it if he leans
on it. That is what Pharaoh king of Egypt proves to all who rely on him.
And if you tell me that you are relying on the LORD your God, is he not the 7
god whose hill-shrines and altars Hezekiah has suppressed, telling Judah
and Jerusalem that they must prostrate themselves before this altar alone?"
  'Now, make a bargain with my master the king of Assyria: I will give 8
you two thousand horses if you can find riders for them. Will you reject 9

<sup>*a*</sup> a pilgrim's way: *prob. rdg.; Heb. unintelligible.*         <sup>*b*</sup> *Verses 1-22 : cp. 2 Kgs.*
*18. 13-37; 2 Chr. 32. 1-19.*         <sup>*c*</sup> *Or sent Rab-shakeh.*

the authority of even the least of my master's servants and rely on Egypt
10 for chariots and horsemen? Do you think that I have come to attack this
land and destroy it without the consent of the LORD? No; the LORD himself
said to me, "Attack this land and destroy it."'
11     Eliakim, Shebna, and Joah said to the chief officer, 'Please speak to us
in Aramaic, for we understand it; do not speak Hebrew to us within earshot
12 of the people on the city wall.' The chief officer answered, 'Is it to your
master and to you that my master has sent me to say this? Is it not to the
people sitting on the wall who, like you, will have to eat their own dung
13 and drink their own urine?' Then he stood and shouted in Hebrew, 'Hear
14 the message of the Great King, the king of Assyria. These are the king's
15 words: "Do not be taken in by Hezekiah. He cannot save you. Do not let
him persuade you to rely on the LORD, and tell you that the LORD will save
you and that this city will never be surrendered to the king of Assyria."
16 Do not listen to Hezekiah; these are the words of the king of Assyria:
"Make peace with me. Come out to me, and then you shall each eat the
fruit of his own vine and his own fig-tree, and drink the water of his own
17 cistern, until I come and take you to a land like your own, a land of grain
18 and new wine, of corn and vineyards. Beware lest Hezekiah mislead you
by telling you that the LORD will save you. Did the god of any of these
19 nations save his land from the king of Assyria? Where are the gods of
Hamath and Arpad? Where are the gods of Sepharvaim? Where are the
20 gods of Samaria? Did they save Samaria from me? Among all the gods of
these nations is there one who saved his land from me? And how is the
LORD to save Jerusalem?"'
21     The people were silent and answered not a word, for the king had given
22 orders that no one was to answer him. Eliakim son of Hilkiah, comptroller
of the household, Shebna the adjutant-general, and Joah son of Asaph,
secretary of state, came to Hezekiah with their clothes rent and reported
what the chief officer had said.
37 1[a]     When King Hezekiah heard their report, he rent his clothes and wrapped
2 himself in sackcloth, and went into the house of the LORD. He sent Eliakim
comptroller of the household, Shebna the adjutant-general, and the senior
3 priests, all covered in sackcloth, to the prophet Isaiah son of Amoz, to
give him this message from the king: 'This day is a day of trouble for us,
a day of reproof and contempt. We are like a woman who has no strength
4 to bear the child that is coming to the birth. It may be that the LORD your
God heard the words of the chief officer whom his master the king of
Assyria sent to taunt the living God, and will confute what he, the LORD
5 your God, heard. Offer a prayer for those who still survive.' King Hezekiah's
6 servants came to Isaiah, and he told them to say this to their master: 'This
is the word of the LORD: "Do not be alarmed at what you heard when the
7 lackeys of the king of Assyria blasphemed me. I will put a spirit in him, and
he shall hear a rumour and withdraw to his own country; and there I will
make him fall by the sword."'
8     So the chief officer withdrew. He heard that the king of Assyria had
9 left Lachish, and he found him attacking Libnah. But when the king learnt

[a] *Verses 1–38: cp. 2 Kgs. 19. 1–37; 2 Chr. 32. 20–22.*

that Tirhakah king of Cush was on the way to make war on him, he sent
messengers again*ᵃ* to Hezekiah king of Judah, to say to him, 'How can   10
you be deluded by your god on whom you rely when he promises that
Jerusalem shall not fall into the hands of the king of Assyria? Surely you   11
have heard what the kings of Assyria have done to all countries, exterminating their people; can you then hope to escape? Did their gods save   12
the nations which my forefathers destroyed, Gozan, Harran, Rezeph, and
the people of Beth-eden living in Telassar? Where are the kings of Hamath,   13
of Arpad, and of Lahir, Sepharvaim, Hena, and Ivvah?'

Hezekiah took the letter from the messengers and read it; then he went   14
up into the house of the LORD, spread it out before the LORD and offered   15
this prayer: 'O LORD of Hosts, God of Israel, enthroned on the cherubim,   16
thou alone art God of all the kingdoms of the earth; thou hast made heaven
and earth. Turn thy ear to me, O LORD, and listen; open thine eyes, O LORD,   17
and see; hear the message that Sennacherib has sent to taunt the living God.
It is true, O LORD, that the kings of Assyria have laid waste every country,   18
that they have consigned their gods to the fire and destroyed them; for   19
they were no gods but the work of men's hands, mere wood and stone. But   20
now, O LORD our God, save us from his power, so that all the kingdoms of
the earth may know that thou, O LORD, alone art God.'

Isaiah son of Amoz sent to Hezekiah and said, 'This is the word of   21
the LORD the God of Israel: I have heard your prayer to me concerning
Sennacherib king of Assyria. This is the word which the LORD has spoken   22
concerning him:

> The virgin daughter of Zion disdains you,
>     she laughs you to scorn;
> the daughter of Jerusalem tosses her head
>     as you retreat.
> Whom have you taunted and blasphemed?          23
>     Against whom have you clamoured,
> casting haughty glances at the Holy One of Israel?
> You have sent your servants to taunt the Lord,          24
>     and said:
> With my countless chariots I have gone up
> high in the mountains, into the recesses of Lebanon.
> I have cut down its tallest cedars,
>     the best of its pines,
> I have reached its highest limit of forest and meadow.*ᵇ*
> I have dug wells          25
> and drunk the waters of a foreign land,
> and with the soles of my feet I have dried up
>     all the streams of Egypt.
>
> Have you not heard long ago?          26
>     I did it all.

---

*ᵃ* again: *prob. rdg., cp. 2 Kgs. 19. 9; Heb.* and he heard.          *ᵇ* and meadow: *prob.*
*rdg.; Heb.* its meadow.

In days gone by I planned it
and now I have brought it about,
making fortified cities tumble down
into heaps of rubble.

27     Their citizens, shorn of strength,
disheartened and ashamed,
were but as plants in the field, as green herbs,
as grass on the roof-tops blasted before the east wind.

28     I know your rising up and your sitting down,
your going out and your coming in.

29     The frenzy of your rage against me and your arrogance
have come to my ears.
I will put a ring in your nose
and a hook in your lips,
and I will take you back by the road
on which you have come.

30   This shall be the sign for you: this year you shall eat shed grain and in the
second year what is self-sown; but in the third year sow and reap, plant
31   vineyards and eat their fruit. The survivors left in Judah shall strike fresh
32   root under ground and yield fruit above ground, for a remnant shall come
out of Jerusalem and survivors from Mount Zion. The zeal of the LORD
of Hosts will perform this.

33   'Therefore, this is the word of the LORD concerning the king of Assyria:

He shall not enter this city
nor shoot an arrow there,
he shall not advance against it with shield
nor cast up a siege-ramp against it.

34     By the way on which he came he shall go back;
this city he shall not enter.
This is the very word of the LORD.

35     I will shield this city to deliver it,
for my own sake and for the sake of my servant David.'

36   The angel of the LORD went out and struck down a hundred and eighty-
five thousand men in the Assyrian camp; when morning dawned, they
37   all lay dead. So Sennacherib king of Assyria broke camp, went back to
38   Nineveh and stayed there. One day, while he was worshipping in the temple
of his god Nisroch, Adrammelech and Sharezer his sons murdered him
and escaped to the land of Ararat. He was succeeded by his son Esarhaddon.

38 1*a*    At this time Hezekiah fell dangerously ill and the prophet Isaiah son
of Amoz came to him and said, 'This is the word of the LORD: Give your
last instructions to your household, for you are a dying man and will not
2   recover.' Hezekiah turned his face to the wall and offered this prayer to
3   the LORD: 'O LORD, remember how I have lived before thee, faithful and
loyal in thy service, always doing what was good in thine eyes.' And he
4 5   wept bitterly. Then the word of the LORD came to Isaiah: 'Go and say to
Hezekiah: "This is the word of the LORD the God of your father David:

*a  Verses 1–8, 21, 22 : cp. 2 Kgs. 20. 1–11.*

I have heard your prayer and seen your tears; I will add fifteen years to
your life. I will deliver you and this city from the king of Assyria and will  6
protect this city." ' Then Isaiah told them to apply a fig-plaster; so they  21[a]
made one and applied it to the boil, and he recovered. Then Hezekiah said,  22
'By what sign shall I know that I shall go up into the house of the LORD?'
And Isaiah said,[b] 'This shall be your sign from the LORD that he will do  7
what he has promised. Watch the shadow cast by the sun on the stairway  8
of Ahaz: I will bring backwards ten steps the shadow which has gone down
on the stairway.' And the sun went back ten steps on the stairway down
which it had gone.

A poem of Hezekiah king of Judah after his recovery from his illness, as  9
it was written down:

> I thought: In the prime of life I must pass away;                          10
> for the rest of my years I am consigned to the gates of Sheol.
> I said: I shall no longer see the LORD                                     11
>     in the land of the living;
> never again, like those who live in the world,
>     shall I look on a man.
> My dwelling is taken from me,                                              12
>     pulled up like a shepherd's tent;
> thou hast cut short my life like a weaver
> who severs the web from the thrum.
> From morning to night thou tormentest me,
>     then I am racked with pain till the morning.                           13
> All my bones are broken, as a lion would break them;
> from morning to night thou tormentest me.
> I twitter as if I were a swallow,                                          14
> I moan like a dove.
> My eyes falter as I look up to the heights;
> O Lord, pay heed, stand surety for me.
> How can I complain, what can I say to the LORD                             15
>     when he himself has done this?
> I wander to and fro all my life long
>     in the bitterness of my soul.
> Yet, O Lord, my soul shall live with thee;                                 16
>     do thou give my spirit rest.[c]
> Restore me and give me life.
> Bitterness had indeed been my lot in place of prosperity;                  17
> but thou by thy love hast brought me back
>     from the pit of destruction;
> for thou hast cast all my sins behind thee.
> Sheol cannot confess thee,                                                 18
> Death cannot praise thee,
> nor can they who go down to the abyss
>     hope for thy truth.

---

[a] *Verses 21, 22 transposed.*     [b] And Isaiah said: *prob. rdg., cp. 2 Kgs. 20. 9; Heb. om.*
[c] Yet . . . rest: *prob. rdg.; Heb. unintelligible.*

19      The living, the living alone can confess thee
            as I do this day,
        as a father makes thy truth known, O God, to his sons.
20      The LORD is at hand to save me;
            so let us sound the music of our praises
        all our life long in the house of the LORD.*a*

**39** 1*b*  At this time Merodach-baladan son of Baladan king of Babylon sent envoys with a gift to Hezekiah; for he had heard that he had been ill and 2 was well again. Hezekiah welcomed them and showed them all his treasury, silver and gold, spices and fragrant oil, his entire armoury and everything to be found among his treasures; there was nothing in his house and in all 3 his realm that Hezekiah did not show them. Then the prophet Isaiah came to King Hezekiah and asked him, 'What did these men say and where have they come from?' 'They have come from a far-off country,' Hezekiah 4 answered, 'from Babylon.' Then Isaiah asked, 'What did they see in your house?' 'They saw everything,' Hezekiah replied; 'there was nothing among 5 my treasures that I did not show them.' Then Isaiah said to Hezekiah, 6 'Hear the word of the LORD of Hosts: The time is coming, says the LORD, when everything in your house, and all that your forefathers have amassed till the present day, will be carried away to Babylon; not a thing shall be 7 left. And some of the sons who will be born to you, sons of your own begetting, shall be taken and shall be made eunuchs in the palace of the 8 king of Babylon.' Hezekiah answered, 'The word of the LORD which you have spoken is good'; thinking to himself that peace and security would last out his lifetime.

## News of the returning exiles

**40**      Comfort, comfort my people;*c*
            —it is the voice of your God;
2          speak tenderly to Jerusalem *d*
            and tell her this,
        that she has fulfilled her term of bondage,
            that her penalty is paid;
        she has received at the LORD's hand
            double*e* measure for all her sins.

3          There is a voice that cries:
        Prepare a road for the LORD through the wilderness,
        clear a highway across the desert for our God.
4          Every valley shall be lifted up,
        every mountain and hill brought down;
            rugged places shall be made smooth
            and mountain-ranges become a plain.

---

*a* *Verses 21, 22 transposed to follow verse 6.*      *b* *Verses 1–8: cp. 2 Kgs. 20. 12–19.*
*c* Comfort . . . people: *or* Comfort, O my people, comfort.      *d* speak . . . Jerusalem: *or* bid Jerusalem be of good heart.      *e* double: *or* full.

Thus shall the glory of the LORD be revealed,      5
and all mankind together shall see it;
for the LORD himself has spoken.

A voice says, 'Cry',      6
and another asks, 'What shall I cry?'
'That all mankind is grass,
they last no longer than a flower of the field.
The grass withers, the flower fades,      7
when the breath of *a* the LORD blows upon them; *b*
the grass withers, the flowers fade,      8
but the word of our God endures for evermore.'

You who bring Zion good news,*c* up with you to the mountain-top; 9
lift up your voice and shout,
you who bring good news to Jerusalem, *d*
lift it up fearlessly;
cry to the cities of Judah, 'Your God is here.'
Here is the Lord GOD coming in might,      10
coming to rule with his right arm.
His recompense comes with him,
he carries his reward before him.
He will tend his flock like a shepherd      11
and gather them together with his arm;
he will carry the lambs in his bosom
and lead the ewes to water.

## *Israel delivered and redeemed*

Who has gauged the waters in the palm of his hand,      12
or with its span set limits to the heavens?
Who has held all the soil of earth in a bushel,
or weighed the mountains on a balance
and the hills on a pair of scales?
Who has set limits to the spirit of the LORD?      13
What counsellor stood at his side to instruct him?
With whom did he confer to gain discernment?      14
Who taught him how to do justice
or gave him lessons in wisdom?
Why, to him nations are but drops from a bucket,      15
no more than moisture on the scales;
coasts and islands weigh as light as specks of dust.
All Lebanon does not yield wood enough for fuel      16
or beasts enough for a sacrifice.

*a* the breath of: *or* a wind from.      *b* *Prob. rdg.; Heb. adds* surely the people are grass.
*c* You . . . news: *or* O Zion, bringer of good news.      *d* you . . . Jerusalem: *or*
O Jerusalem, bringer of good news.

17          All nations dwindle to nothing before him,
            he reckons them mere nothings, less than nought.

18          What likeness will you find for God
            or what form to resemble his?
19          Is it an image which a craftsman sets up,
            and a goldsmith covers with plate
            and fits with studs of silver as a costly gift?
20          Or is it mulberry-wood that will not rot which a man chooses,
            seeking out a skilful craftsman for it,
            to mount an image that will not fall?

[6<sup>*a*</sup>]     Each workman helps the others,
            each man encourages his fellow.
[7<sup>*a*</sup>]     The craftsman urges on the goldsmith,
            the gilder urges the man who beats the anvil,
            he declares the soldering to be sound;
            he fastens the image with nails
            so that it will not fall down.

21          Do you not know, have you not heard,
            were you not told long ago,
            have you not perceived ever since the world began,
22          that God sits throned on the vaulted roof of earth,
                whose inhabitants are like grasshoppers<sup>*b*</sup>?
            He stretches out the skies like a curtain,
            he spreads them out like a tent to live in;
23          he reduces the great to nothing
            and makes all earth's princes less than nothing.
24          Scarcely are they planted, scarcely sown,
            scarcely have they taken root in the earth,
                before he blows upon them and they wither away,
                and a whirlwind carries them off like chaff.
25          To whom then will you liken me,
                whom set up as my equal?
            asks the Holy One.
26          Lift up your eyes to the heavens;
            consider who created it all,
            led out their host one by one
            and called them all by their names;
                through his great might, his might and power,
                not one is missing.
27          Why do you complain, O Jacob,
                and you, Israel, why do you say,
            'My plight is hidden from the Lord
            and my cause has passed out of God's notice'?

---

<sup>*a*</sup> *These are verses 6 and 7 of ch. 41, transposed to this point.*          <sup>*b*</sup> *Or* locusts.

Do you not know, have you not heard?      28
The LORD, the everlasting God, creator of the wide world,
    grows neither weary nor faint;
    no man can fathom his understanding.
He gives vigour to the weary,      29
    new strength to the exhausted.
Young men may grow weary and faint,      30
    even in their prime they may stumble and fall;
but those who look to the LORD will win new strength,      31
    they will grow wings like eagles;
they will run and not be weary,
    they will march on and never grow faint.

Keep silence before me, all you coasts and islands;      **41**
    let the peoples come to meet me.*a*
Let them come near, then let them speak;
    we will meet at the place of judgement, I and they.
Tell me, who raised up that one from the east,      2
    one greeted by victory wherever he goes?
Who is it that puts nations into his power
    and makes kings go down before him,*b*
he scatters them with his sword like dust
    and with his bow like chaff before the wind;
he puts them to flight and passes on unscathed,      3
    swifter than any traveller on foot?
Whose work is this, I ask, who has brought it to pass?      4
Who has summoned the generations from the beginning?
It is I, the LORD, I am the first,
    and to the last of them I am He.
Coasts and islands saw it and were afraid,      5
    the world trembled from end to end.*c*

But you, Israel my servant,      8*d*
you, Jacob whom I have chosen,
    race of Abraham my friend,
I have taken you up,      9
have fetched you from the ends of the earth,
    and summoned you from its farthest corners,
I have called you my servant,
have chosen you and not cast you off:
fear nothing, for I am with you;      10
    be not afraid, for I am your God.
I strengthen you, I help you,
    I support you with my victorious right hand.

---

*a* come to meet me: *prob. rdg., transposing, with slight change, from end of verse 5; Heb.*
win new strength (*repeated from 40. 31*).      *b* before him: *prob. rdg.; Heb. om.*
*c* *See note on verse 1.*      *d* *Verses 6 and 7 transposed to follow 40. 20.*

11      Now shall all who defy you
        be disappointed and put to shame;
        all who set themselves against you
        shall be as nothing; they shall vanish.
12      You will look for your assailants but not find them;
        all who take up arms against you
        shall be as nothing, nothing at all.
13      For I, the LORD your God,
        take you by the right hand;
        I say to you, Do not fear;
        it is I who help you,
14      fear not, Jacob you worm and Israel poor louse.
        It is I who help you, says the LORD,
            your ransomer, the Holy One of Israel.
15      See, I will make of you a sharp threshing-sledge,
            new and studded with teeth;
        you shall thresh the mountains and crush them
        and reduce the hills to chaff;
16      you shall winnow them, the wind shall carry them away
        and a great gale shall scatter them.
        Then shall you rejoice in the LORD
            and glory in the Holy One of Israel.

17      The wretched and the poor look for water and find none,
            their tongues are parched with thirst;
        but I the LORD will give them an answer,
        I, the God of Israel, will not forsake them.
18      I will open rivers among the sand-dunes
            and wells in the valleys;
        I will turn the wilderness into pools
        and dry land into springs of water;
19      I will plant cedars in the wastes,
        and acacia and myrtle and wild olive;
        the pine shall grow on the barren heath
        side by side with fir and box,
20      that men may see and know,
        may once for all give heed and understand
        that the LORD himself has done this,
            that the Holy One of Israel has performed it.

21      Come, open your plea, says the LORD,
        present your case, says Jacob's King;
22          let them come forward, these idols,
            let them foretell the future.
        Let them declare the meaning of past events
            that we may give our minds to it;
        let them predict things that are to be
            that we may know their outcome.
23          Declare what will happen hereafter;

then we shall know you are gods.
Do what you can, good or ill,
anything that may grip us with fear and awe.
You cannot! You are sprung from nothing,                          24
your works are rotten;
whoever chooses you is vile as you are.
I roused one from the north, and he obeyed;                       25
I called one from the east, summoned him in<sup>a</sup> my name,
he marches over viceroys as if they were mud,
like a potter treading his clay.
Tell us, who declared this from the beginning, that we might know it,   26
or told us beforehand so that we could say, 'He was right'?
Not one declared, not one foretold,
not one heard a sound from you.
Here is one who will speak first as advocate for Zion,            27
here I appoint defending counsel for Jerusalem;
but from the other side no advocate steps forward                 28
and, when I look, there is no one there.
I ask a question and no one answers;
see what empty things they are!                                   29
    Nothing that they do has any worth,
their effigies are wind, mere nothings.

Here is my servant, whom I uphold,                                **42**
my chosen one in whom I delight,
I have bestowed my spirit upon him,
and he will make justice shine on the nations.
He will not call out or lift his voice high,                      2
or<sup>b</sup> make himself heard in the open street.
He will not break a bruised reed,                                 3
or snuff out a smouldering wick;
he will make justice shine on every race,<sup>c</sup>
never faltering, never breaking down,<sup>d</sup>                 4
he will plant justice on earth,
while coasts and islands wait for his teaching.

Thus speaks the LORD who is God,                                  5
he who created the skies and stretched them out,
who fashioned the earth and all that grows in it,
who gave breath to its people,
    the breath of life to all who walk upon it:
I, the LORD, have called you with righteous purpose              6
    and taken you by the hand;
    I have formed you, and appointed you
    to be a light<sup>e</sup> to all peoples,
    a beacon for the nations,

<sup>a</sup> summoned him in: *or* who will call on.         <sup>b</sup> He will not . . . *or*: *or* In very truth
he will call out and lift his voice high, and . . .        <sup>c</sup> on every race: *or* in truth.
<sup>d</sup> never faltering . . . down: *or* he will neither rebuke nor wound.      <sup>e</sup> *Or* a covenant.

7    to open eyes that are blind,
     to bring captives out of prison,
       out of the dungeons where they lie in darkness.
8    I am the LORD; the LORD*ᵃ* is my name;
     I will not give my glory to another god,
       nor my praise to any idol.
9    See how the first prophecies have come to pass,
     and now I declare new things;
     before they break from the bud I announce them to you.

10   Sing a new song to the LORD,
       sing his praise throughout the earth,
       you that sail the sea, and all sea-creatures,
       and you that inhabit the coasts and islands.
11   Let the wilderness and its towns rejoice,
       and the villages of the tribe of Kedar.
     Let those who live in Sela shout for joy
       and cry out from the hill-tops.
12   You coasts and islands, all uplift his praises;
       let all ascribe glory to the LORD.
13   The LORD will go forth as a warrior,
       he will rouse the frenzy of battle like a hero;
       he will shout, he will raise the battle-cry
       and triumph over his foes.
14   Long have I lain still,
       I kept silence and held myself in check;
       now I will cry like a woman in labour,
       whimpering, panting and gasping.
15   I will lay waste mountains and hills
       and shrivel all their green herbs;
       I will turn rivers into desert wastes *ᵇ*
       and dry up all the pools.
16   Then will I lead blind men on their way *ᶜ*
       and guide them by paths they do not know;
     I will turn darkness into light before them
       and straighten their twisting roads.
     All this I will do and leave nothing undone.
17       Those who trust in an image,
     those who take idols for their gods
     turn tail in bitter shame.

18       Hear now, you that are deaf;
       you blind men, look and see:
19       yet who is blind but my servant,
       who so deaf as the messenger whom I send?
     Who so blind as the one who holds my commission,
       so deaf as the servant of the LORD?

---

*ᵃ* the LORD: *or* He.          *ᵇ* desert wastes: *prob. rdg.; Heb.* coasts and islands.
*ᶜ* *Prob. rdg.; Heb. adds* which they do not know.

You have seen much but remembered little,                    20
your ears are wide open but nothing is heard.
It pleased the LORD, for the furtherance of his justice,      21
to make his law a law of surpassing majesty;
yet here is a people plundered and taken as prey,            22
all of them ensnared, trapped in holes,
   lost to sight in dungeons,
carried off as spoil without hope of rescue,
as plunder with no one to say, 'Give it back.'
Hear this, all of you who will,                              23
listen henceforward and give me a hearing:
who gave away Jacob for plunder,                             24
   who gave Israel away for spoil?
Was it not the LORD? They sinned against him,
they would not follow his ways
   and refused obedience to his law;
so in his anger he poured out upon Jacob                     25
his wrath and the fury of battle.
It wrapped him in flames, yet still he did not learn the lesson,
scorched him, yet he did not lay it to heart.

But now this is the word of the LORD,                        **43**
the word of your creator, O Jacob,
   of him who fashioned you, Israel:
Have no fear; for I have paid your ransom;
I have called you by name and you are my own.
When you pass through deep waters, I am with you,            2
   when you pass through rivers,
   they will not sweep you away;
walk through fire and you will not be scorched,
through flames and they will not burn you.
For I am the LORD your God,                                  3
   the Holy One of Israel, your deliverer;
for your ransom I give Egypt,
Nubia and Seba are your price.
You are more precious to me than the Assyrians,             4
   you are honoured and I have loved you,
I would give the Edomites in exchange for you,
and the Leummim for your life.

Have no fear; for I am with you;                             5
I will bring your children from the east
   and gather you all from the west.
I will say to the north, 'Give them up',                     6
   and to the south, 'Do not hold them back.
Bring my sons and daughters from afar,
   bring them from the ends of the earth;
bring every one who is called by my name,                   7

all whom I have created, whom I have formed,
all whom I have made for my glory.'

8     Bring out this people,
a people who have eyes but are blind,
who have ears but are deaf.

9 All the nations are gathered together
and the peoples assembled.
Who amongst them can expound this thing
and interpret for us all that has gone before?
Let them produce witnesses to prove their case,
or let them listen and say, 'That is the truth.'

10 My witnesses, says the LORD, are you, my servants,
you whom I have chosen
to know me and put your faith in me
and understand that I am He.
Before me there was no god fashioned
nor ever shall be after me.

11 I am the LORD, I myself,
and none but I can deliver.

12 I myself have made it known in full, and declared it,
I and no alien god amongst you,
and you are my witnesses, says the LORD.

13 I am God; from this very day I am He.
What my hand holds, none can snatch away;
what I do, none can undo.

14 Thus says the LORD your ransomer, the Holy One of Israel:
For your sakes I have sent to Babylon;
I will lay the Chaldaeans prostrate as they flee,
and their cry of triumph will turn to groaning.

15 I am the LORD, your Holy One,
your creator, Israel, and your King.

16 Thus says the LORD,
who opened a way in the sea
and a path through mighty waters,

17 who drew on chariot and horse to their destruction,
a whole army, men of valour;
there they lay, never to rise again;
they were crushed, snuffed out like a wick:

18     Cease to dwell on days gone by
and to brood over past history.

19     Here and now I will do a new thing;
this moment it will break from the bud.
Can you not perceive it?
I will make a way even through the wilderness
and paths in the barren desert;

20 the wild beasts shall do me honour,
the wolf and the ostrich;

for I will provide water in the wilderness
  and rivers in the barren desert,
  where my chosen people may drink.
I have formed this people for myself
  and they shall proclaim my praises.
Yet you did not call upon me, O Jacob;           22
much less did you weary yourself in my service, O Israel.
You did not bring me sheep as whole-offerings      23
  or honour me with sacrifices;
    I asked you for no burdensome offerings
    and wearied you with no demands for incense.
You did not buy me sweet-cane with your money     24
  or glut me with the fat of your sacrifices;
  rather you burdened me with your sins
    and wearied me with your iniquities.
I alone, I am He,                           25
  who for his own sake wipes out your transgressions,
  who will remember your sins no more.
Cite me by name, let us argue it out;           26
  set forth your pleading and justify yourselves.
Your first father transgressed,             27
  your spokesmen rebelled against me,
  and your princes profaned my sanctuary;      28
so I sent Jacob to his doom
  and left Israel to execration.

Hear me now, Jacob my servant,          **44**
  hear me, my chosen Israel.
Thus says the LORD your maker,           2
  your helper, who fashioned you from birth:
have no fear, Jacob my servant,
  Jeshurun whom I have chosen,
for I will pour down rain on a thirsty land,      3
  showers on the dry ground.
I will pour out my spirit on your offspring
  and my blessing on your children.
They shall spring up like a green tamarisk,      4
  like poplars by a flowing stream.
This man shall say, 'I am the LORD's man',      5
  that one shall call himself a son of Jacob,
another shall write the LORD's name on his hand
  and shall add the name of Israel to his own.

Thus says the LORD, Israel's King,          6
  the LORD of Hosts, his ransomer:
I am the first and I am the last,
  and there is no god but me.
Who is like me? Let him stand up,          7
  let him declare himself and speak and show me his evidence,

1S  let him announce beforehand<sup>a</sup> things to come,
let him<sup>b</sup> declare what is yet to happen.
Take heart, do not be afraid.
Did I not foretell this long ago?
I declared it, and you are my witnesses.
Is there any god beside me,
or any creator, even one that I do not know?
Those who make idols are less than nothing;
all their cherished images profit nobody;
their worshippers are blind,
sheer ignorance makes fools of them.

10 If a man makes a god or casts an image,
his labour is wasted.

11 Why! its votaries show their folly;
the craftsmen too are but men.
Let them all gather together and confront me,
all will be afraid and look the fools they are.

12 The blacksmith sharpens a graving tool and hammers out his work <sup>c</sup> hot from the coals and shapes it with his strong arm; when he grows hungry
13 his strength fails, if he has no water to drink he tires. The woodworker draws his line taut and marks out a figure with a scriber; he planes the wood and measures it with callipers, and he carves it to the shape of a man, comely as the human form, to be set up presently in a house.<sup>d</sup>
14 A man plants a cedar and the rain makes it grow, so that later on he will have cedars to cut down; or he chooses an ilex or an oak to raise a stout
15 tree for himself in the forest. It becomes fuel for his fire: some of it he takes and warms himself, some he kindles and bakes bread on it, and some he makes into a god and prostrates himself, shaping it into an idol and
16 bowing down before it. The one half of it he burns in the fire and on this he roasts meat, so that he may eat his roast and be satisfied; he also warms himself at it and he says, 'Good! I can feel the heat, I am growing warm.'
17 Then what is left of the wood he makes into a god by carving it into shape; he bows down to it and prostrates himself and prays to it, saying, 'Save me;
18 for thou art my god.' Such people neither know nor understand, their eyes
19 made too blind to see, their minds too narrow to discern. Such a man will not use his reason, he has neither the wit nor the sense to say, 'Half of it I have burnt, yes, and used its embers to bake bread; I have roasted meat on them too and eaten it; but the rest of it I turn into this abominable thing
20 and so I am worshipping a log of wood.' He feeds on ashes indeed! His own deluded mind has misled him, he cannot recollect himself so far as to say, 'Why! this thing in my hand is a sham.'

21 Remember all this, Jacob,
remember, Israel, for you are my servant,
I have fashioned you, and you are to serve me;

<sup>a</sup> let him announce beforehand: *prob. rdg.; Heb.* since my appointing an ancient people and . . .    <sup>b</sup> *Prob. rdg.; Heb.* them.    <sup>c</sup> his work: *prob. rdg.; Heb.* he works.
<sup>d</sup> *Or* a shrine.

you shall not forget me, Israel.
I have swept away your sins like a dissolving mist,
    and your transgressions are dispersed like clouds;
turn back to me; for I have ransomed you.
Shout in triumph, you heavens, for it is the LORD's doing;
    cry out for joy, you lowest depths of the earth;
break into songs of triumph, you mountains,
    you forest and all your trees;
for the LORD has ransomed Jacob
    and made Israel his masterpiece.

Thus says the LORD, your ransomer,          24
    who fashioned you from birth:
I am the LORD who made all things,
    by myself I stretched out the skies,
alone I hammered out the floor of the earth.
I frustrate false prophets and their signs       25
    and make fools of diviners;
I reverse what wise men say
    and make nonsense of their wisdom.
I make my servants' prophecies come true     26
    and give effect to my messengers' designs.
    I say of Jerusalem,
    'She shall be inhabited once more',
and of the cities of Judah, 'They shall be rebuilt;
    all their ruins I will restore.'
I say to the deep waters, 'Be dried up;       27
    I will make your streams run dry.'
I say to Cyrus, 'You shall be my shepherd     28
    to carry out all my purpose,
so that Jerusalem may be rebuilt
    and the foundations of the temple may be laid.'

Thus says the LORD to Cyrus his anointed,     **45**
    Cyrus whom he has taken by the hand
to subdue nations before him
    and undo the might of kings;
before whom gates shall be opened
    and no doors be shut:
I will go before you       2
    and level the swelling hills;
    I will break down gates of bronze
    and hack through iron bars.
I will give you treasures from dark vaults,     3
    hoarded in secret places,
that you may know that I am the LORD,
    Israel's God who calls you by name.

r the sake of Jacob my servant and Israel my chosen
I have called you by name
and given you your title, though you have not known me.
I am the LORD, there is no other;
there is no god beside me.

I will strengthen you though you have not known me,
so that men from the rising and the setting sun
may know that there is none but I:
I am the LORD, there is no other;

7    I make the light, I create darkness,
author alike of prosperity and trouble.
I, the LORD, do all these things.


8    Rain righteousness, you heavens,
let the skies above pour down;
let the earth open to receive it,
that it may bear the fruit of salvation
with righteousness in blossom at its side.
All this I, the LORD, have created.


9    Will the pot contend*a* with the potter,
or the earthenware *b* with the hand that shapes it?
Will the clay ask the potter what he is making?
or his *c* handiwork say to him, 'You have no skill'?
10   Will the babe say*d* to his father, 'What are you begetting?',
or to his mother, 'What are you bringing to birth?'
11   Thus says the LORD, Israel's Holy One, his maker:
Would you dare question me concerning my children,
or instruct me in my handiwork?
12   I alone, I made the earth
and created man upon it;
I, with my own hands, stretched out the heavens
and caused all their host to shine.
13   I alone have roused this man in righteousness,
and I will smooth his path before him;
he shall rebuild my city
and let my exiles go free—
not for a price nor for a bribe,
says the LORD of Hosts.


14   Thus says the LORD:
Toilers of Egypt and Nubian merchants
and Sabaeans bearing tribute *e*
shall come into your power and be your slaves,
shall come and march behind you in chains;

---

*a* Will . . . contend: *prob. rdg.; Heb.* Ho! he has contended.    *b* *Or* shard.
*c* *Prob. rdg.; Heb.* your.    *d* Will . . . say: *prob. rdg.; Heb.* Ho! you that say.
*e* bearing tribute: *or* men of stature.

they shall bow down before you in supplication, saying,
'Surely God is among you and there is no other,
   no other god.
How then canst thou be a god that hidest thyself,       15
   O God of Israel, the deliverer?'

Those who defy him are confounded and brought to shame,   16
those who make idols perish in confusion.
   But Israel has been delivered by the LORD,       17
   delivered for all time to come;
they shall not be confounded or put to shame for all eternity.

Thus says the LORD, the creator of the heavens,       18
   he who is God,
who made the earth and fashioned it
   and himself fixed it fast,
who created it no empty void,
   but made it for a place to dwell in:
I am the LORD, there is no other.
I do not speak in secret, in realms of darkness,       19
   I do not say to the sons of Jacob,
      'Look for me in the empty void.'
I the LORD speak what is right, declare what is just.
   Gather together, come, draw near,       20
      all you survivors of the nations,
   you fools, who carry your wooden idols in procession
   and pray to a god that cannot save you.
Come forward and urge your case, consult together:    21
   who foretold this in days of old,
      who stated it long ago?
Was it not I the LORD?
There is no god but me;
there is no god other than I, victorious and able to save.
   Look to me and be saved,       22
      you peoples from all corners of the earth;
   for I am God, there is no other.
   By my life I have sworn,       23
I have given a promise of victory,
   a promise that will not be broken,
that to me every knee shall bend
   and by me every tongue shall swear.
In the LORD alone, men shall say,       24
   are victory and might;
   and all who defy him
shall stand ashamed in his presence,
   but all the sons of Israel shall stand victorious    25
      and find their glory in the LORD.

**46** Bel has crouched down, Nebo has stooped low:
their images, once carried in your processions,
have been loaded on to beasts and cattle,
a burden for the weary creatures;
2     they stoop and they crouch;
not for them to bring the burden to safety;
the gods themselves go into captivity.
3     Listen to me, house of Jacob
and all the remnant of the house of Israel,
a load on me from your birth, carried by me from the womb:
4     till you grow old I am He,
and when white hairs come, I will carry you still;
I have made you and I will bear the burden,
I will carry you and bring you to safety.
5     To whom will you liken me? Who is my equal?
With whom can you compare me? Where is my like?
6     Those who squander their bags of gold
and weigh out their silver with a balance
hire a goldsmith to fashion them into a god;
then they worship it and fall prostrate before it;
7     they hoist it shoulder-high and carry it home;
they set it down on its base;
there it must stand, it cannot stir from its place.
Let a man cry to it as he will, it never answers him;
it cannot deliver him from his troubles.

8     Remember this, you rebels,
consider it well, and abandon hope,
9     remember all that happened long ago;
for I am God, there is no other,
I am God, and there is no one like me;
10    I reveal the end from the beginning,
from ancient times I reveal what is to be;
I say, 'My purpose shall take effect,
I will accomplish all that I please.'
11    I summon a bird of prey[a] from the east,
one from a distant land to fulfil my purpose.
Mark this; I have spoken, and I will bring it about,
I have a plan to carry out, and carry it out I will.
12    Listen to me, all you stubborn hearts,
for whom victory is far off:
13    I bring my victory near, it is not far off,
and my deliverance shall not be delayed;
I will grant deliverance in Zion
and give my glory to Israel.[b]

[a] a bird of prey: *or* a massed host.
[b] and give my glory to Israel: *or* for Israel my glory.

Down with you, sit in the dust,                                        47
virgin daughter of Babylon.
Down from your throne, sit on the ground,
daughter of the Chaldaeans;
never again shall men call you
soft-skinned and delicate.
Take up the millstone, grind meal, uncover your tresses;        2
strip off your skirt, bare your thighs, wade through rivers,
so that your nakedness may be plain to see                       3
and your shame exposed.
I will take vengeance, I will treat with none of you,
says the Holy One of Israel, our ransomer,                       4
whose name is the LORD of Hosts.

Sit silent,                                                        5
be off into the shadows, daughter of the Chaldaeans;
for never again shall men call you
queen of many kingdoms.
When I was angry with my people,                                  6
I dishonoured my own possession
and gave them into your power.
You showed them no mercy,
you made your yoke weigh heavy on the aged.
You said then, 'I shall reign a queen for ever',                 7
while*a* you gave no thought to this
and did not consider how it would end.
Now therefore listen to this,                                     8
you lover of luxury, carefree on your throne.
You say to yourself,
'I am, and who but I?
No widow's weeds for me, no deaths of children.'
Yet suddenly, in a single day,                                    9
these two things shall come upon you;
they shall both come upon you in full measure:*b*
children's deaths and widowhood,
for all your monstrous sorceries, your countless spells.
Secure in your wicked ways you thought, 'No one is looking.'     10
Your wisdom betrayed you, omniscient as you were,
and you said to yourself,
'I am, and who but I?'
Therefore evil shall come upon you,                              11
and you will not know how to master it;
disaster shall befall you,
and you will not be able to charm it away;
ruin all unforeseen
shall come suddenly upon you.

---

*a* for ever', while: *or* of a wide realm, for all time'; but.
*b* in full measure: *or* at random.

12    Persist in your spells and your monstrous sorceries,<sup>a</sup>
         maybe you can get help from them,
            maybe you will yet inspire awe.
13    But no! in spite of your many wiles you are powerless.
      Let your astrologers, your star-gazers
      who foretell your future month by month,
            persist, and save you!
14    But look, they are gone like chaff;
            fire burns them up;
      they cannot snatch themselves from the flames;
            this is no glowing coal to warm them,
      no fire for them to sit by.
15    So much for your magicians
      with whom you have trafficked all your life:
      they have stumbled off, each his own way,
            and there is no one to save you.

**48**    Hear this, you house of Jacob,
            you who are called by the name of Israel,
            you who spring from the seed of Judah;
      who swear by the name of the LORD
      and boast in the God of Israel,
            but not in honesty or sincerity,
2     although you call yourselves citizens of a holy city
            and lean for support on the God of Israel;
            his name is the LORD of Hosts.
3     Long ago I announced what would first happen,
      I revealed it with my own mouth;
      suddenly I acted and it came about.
4     I knew that you were stubborn,
            your neck stiff as iron, your brow like bronze,
5     therefore I told you of these things long ago,
      and declared them before they came about,
      so that you could not say, 'This was my idol's doing;
      my image, the god that I fashioned, he ordained them.'
6     You have heard what I said; consider it well,
      and you must admit the truth of it.
      Now I show you new things,
            hidden things which you did not know before.
7     They were not created long ago, but in this very hour;
      you had never heard of them before today.
      You cannot say, 'I know them already.'
8     You neither heard nor knew,
      long ago your ears were closed;
      for I knew that you were untrustworthy, treacherous,
      a notorious rebel from your birth.

---

<sup>a</sup> *Prob. rdg.; Heb. adds* with which you have trafficked all your life (*cp. verse 15*).

For the sake of my own name I was patient,<sup>*a*</sup>  9
rather than destroy you I held myself in check.
See how I tested you, not as silver is tested,  10
but in the furnace of affliction; there I purified you.
For my honour, for my own honour I did it;  11
let them disparage my past triumphs<sup>*b*</sup> if they will:
I will not give my glory to any other god.

Hear me, Jacob,  12
and Israel whom I called:
I am He; I am the first,
I am the last also.
With my own hands I founded the earth,  13
with my right hand I formed the expanse of sky;
when I summoned them,
they sprang at once into being.
Assemble, all of you, and listen to me;  14
which of you has declared what is coming,
that he whom I love shall wreak my<sup>*c*</sup> will on Babylon
and the Chaldaeans shall be scattered?
I, I myself, have spoken, I have called him,  15
I have made him appear, and wherever he goes he shall prosper.
Draw near to me and hear this:  16
from the beginning I have never spoken in secret;
from the moment of its first happening I was there.<sup>*d*</sup>

Thus says the LORD your ransomer, the Holy One of Israel:  17
I am the LORD your God:
I teach you for your own advantage
and lead you in the way you must go.
If only you had listened to my commands,  18
your prosperity would have rolled on like a river in flood
and your just success like the waves of the sea;
in number your children would have been like the sand  19
and your descendants countless as its grains;
their name would never be erased or blotted from my sight.
Come out of Babylon, hasten away from the Chaldaeans;  20
proclaim it with loud songs of triumph,
crying the news to the ends of the earth;
tell them, 'The LORD has ransomed his servant Jacob.'
Though he led them through desert places they suffered no thirst,  21
for them he made water run from the rock,
for them he cleft the rock and streams gushed forth.

There is no peace for the wicked,  22
says the LORD.

---

<sup>*a*</sup> *See note on verse 11.*     <sup>*b*</sup> my past triumphs: *transposed from verse 9.*     <sup>*c*</sup> *Or* his.
<sup>*d*</sup> *Prob. rdg.; Heb. adds* and now the Lord GOD has sent me, and his spirit.

## Israel a light to the nations

**49** Listen to me, you coasts and islands,
pay heed, you peoples far away:
from birth the LORD called me,
he named me from my mother's womb.

2 He made my tongue his sharp sword
and concealed me under cover of his hand;
he made me a polished arrow
and hid me out of sight in his quiver.

3 He said to me, 'You are my servant,
Israel through whom I shall win glory';
so I rose to honour in the LORD's sight
and my God became my strength.*a*

4 Once I said, 'I have laboured in vain;
I have spent my strength for nothing, to no purpose';
yet in truth my cause is with the LORD
and my reward is in God's hands.

5 And now the LORD who formed me in the womb to be his servant,
to bring Jacob back to him
that Israel should be gathered to him,*b*
now the LORD calls me again:*c*

6 it is too slight a task for you, as my servant,
to restore the tribes of Jacob,
to bring back the descendants of Israel:
I will make you a light to the nations,
to be my salvation*d* to earth's farthest bounds.

7 Thus says the Holy One, the LORD who ransoms Israel,
to one who thinks little of himself,
whom every nation abhors,
the slave of tyrants:
When they see you kings shall rise,
princes shall rise and bow down,
because of the LORD who is faithful,
because of the Holy One of Israel who has chosen you.

8 Thus says the LORD:
In the hour of my favour I answered you,
and I helped you on the day of deliverance,*e*
putting the land to rights
and sharing out afresh its desolate fields;

9 I said to the prisoners, 'Go free',
and to those in darkness, 'Come out and be seen.'

---

*a* so I rose ... strength: *transposed from end of verse 5.*     *b* be gathered to him:
*or* not be swept away.     *c* *See note on verse 3.*     *d* to be my salvation: *or* that
my salvation may reach.     *e* *Prob. rdg.; Heb. adds* I have formed you, and
appointed you to be a light to all peoples (*cp. 42. 6*).

They shall find pasture in the desert sands<sup>a</sup>
and grazing on all the dunes.
   They shall neither hunger nor thirst,                    10
no scorching heat or sun shall distress them;
   for one who loves them shall lead them
   and take them to water at bubbling springs.
I will make every hill a path                    11
   and build embankments for my highways.
See, they come; some from far away,                    12
these from the north and these from the west
   and those from the land of Syene.
Shout for joy, you heavens, rejoice, O earth,                    13
   you mountains, break into songs of triumph,
   for the LORD has comforted his people
   and has had pity on his own in their distress.


   But Zion says,                    14
'The LORD has forsaken me; my God has forgotten me.'
   Can a woman forget the infant at her breast,                    15
   or a loving mother the child of her womb?
Even these forget, yet I will not forget you.
   Your walls are always before my eyes,                    16
   I have engraved them on the palms of my hands.
Those who are to rebuild you make better speed                    17
   than those who pulled you down,
while those who laid you waste depart.
Raise your eyes and look around you:                    18
see how they assemble, how they are flocking back to you.
   By my life I, the LORD, swear it,
you shall wear them proudly as your jewels,
   and adorn yourself with them like a bride;
I did indeed make you waste and desolate,                    19
   I razed you to the ground,
but your boundaries<sup>b</sup> shall now be too narrow
   for your inhabitants—
   and those who laid you in ruins are far away.
The children born in your bereavement shall yet say in your hearing,    20
'This place is too narrow; make room for me to live in.'
   Then you will say to yourself,                    21
'All these children, how did I come by them,
bereaved and barren as I was?
Who reared them
when I was left alone, left by myself;
where did I get them all?'

---

<sup>a</sup> desert sands: *prob. rdg.; Heb.* ways.    <sup>b</sup> I did . . . boundaries: *or* your wasted
and desolate land, your ruined countryside.

22         The Lord GOD says,
Now is the time: I will beckon to the nations
    and hoist a signal to the peoples,
    and they shall bring your sons in their arms
    and carry your daughters on their shoulders;

23         kings shall be your foster-fathers
    and their princesses shall be your nurses.
They shall bow to the earth before you
    and lick the dust from your feet;
and you shall know that I am the LORD
and that none who look to me will be disappointed.

24         Can his prey be taken from the strong man,
    or the captive be rescued from the ruthless?

25           And the LORD answers,
The captive shall be taken even from the strong,
    and the prey of the ruthless shall be rescued;
I will contend with all who contend against you
    and save your children from them.

26         I will force your oppressors to feed on their own flesh
and make them drunk with their own blood as if with fresh wine,
    and all mankind shall know
    that it is I, the LORD, who save you,
    I your ransomer, the Mighty One of Jacob.

**50**         The LORD says,
Is there anywhere a deed of divorce
    by which I have put your mother away?
    Was there some creditor of mine
    to whom I sold you?
No; it was through your own wickedness that you were sold
    and for your own misconduct that your mother was put away.

2         Why, then, did I find no one when I came?
    Why, when I called, did no one answer?
Did you think my arm too short to redeem,
    did you think I had no power to save?
Not so. By my rebuke I dried up the sea
    and turned rivers into desert;
    their fish perished for lack of water
    and died on the thirsty ground;

3         I clothed the skies in mourning
and covered them with sackcloth.

4         The Lord GOD has given me
    the tongue of a teacher
    and skill to console the weary
    with a word in the morning;
    he sharpened my hearing
that I might listen like one who is taught.

The Lord GOD opened my ears                                  5
and I did not disobey or turn back in defiance.
I offered my back to the lash,                               6
    and let my beard be plucked from my chin,
I did not hide my face from spitting and insult;
    but the Lord GOD stands by to help me;                   7
therefore no insult can wound me.
I have set my face like flint,
    for I know that I shall not be put to shame,
    because one who will clear my name is at my side.        8
Who dare argue against me? Let us confront one another.
Who will dispute my cause? Let him come forward.
The Lord GOD will help me;                                   9
    who then can prove me guilty?
They will all wear out like a garment,
    the moths will eat them up.

Which of you fears the LORD and obeys his servant's commands?   10
The man who walks in dark places with no light,
yet trusts in the name of the LORD and leans on his God.
    But you who kindle a fire and set fire-brands alight,    11
    go, walk into your own fire
    and among the fire-brands you have set ablaze.
    This is your fate at my hands:
    you shall lie down in torment.

Listen to me, all who follow the right and seek the LORD:     **51**
    look to the rock from which you were hewn,
        to the quarry from which you were dug;
    look to your father Abraham                               2
        and to Sarah who gave you birth:
when I called him he was but one,
    I blessed him and made him many.
The LORD has indeed comforted Zion,                          3
    comforted all her ruined homes,
turning her wilderness into an Eden,
    her thirsty plains into a garden of the LORD.
Joy and gladness shall be found in her,
    thanksgiving and melody.
Pay heed to me, my people,                                   4
and hear me, O my nation;
    for my law shall shine forth
and I will flash the light of my judgement over the nations.
My victory is near, my deliverance has gone *a* forth        5
    and my arm shall rule the nations;
for me coasts and islands shall wait
    and they shall look to me for protection.

*a  Or* shone.

881

6     Lift your eyes to the heavens,
look at the earth beneath:
the heavens grow murky as smoke;
the earth wears into tatters like a garment,
and those who live on it die like maggots;
but my deliverance is everlasting
and my saving power shall never wane.

7     Listen to me, my people who know what is right,
you who lay my law to heart:
do not fear the taunts of men,
let no reproaches dismay you;
8     for the grub will devour them like a garment
and the moth as if they were wool,
but my saving power shall last for ever
and my deliverance to all generations.

9     Awake, awake, put on your strength, O arm of the LORD,
awake as you did long ago, in days gone by.
Was it not you
who hacked the Rahab in pieces and ran the dragon through?
10     Was it not you
who dried up the sea, the waters of the great abyss,
and made the ocean depths a path for the ransomed?
11     So the LORD's people shall come back, set free,
and enter Zion with shouts of triumph,
crowned with everlasting joy;
joy and gladness shall overtake them as they come,
and sorrow and sighing shall flee away.
12     I, I myself, am he that comforts you.
Why then fear man, man who must die,
man frail as grass?
13     Why have you forgotten the LORD your maker,
who stretched out the skies and founded the earth?
Why are you continually afraid, all the day long,
why dread the fury of oppressors ready to destroy you?
Where is that fury?
14     He that cowers under it shall soon stand upright and not die,
he shall soon reap the early crop and not lack bread.

15   I am the LORD your God, the LORD of Hosts is my name. I cleft the sea
16 and its waves roared, that I might fix the heavens in place and form the
earth and say to Zion, 'You are my people.' I have put my words in your
mouth and kept you safe under the shelter of my hand.

17     Awake, awake; rise up, Jerusalem.
You have drunk from the LORD's hand
the cup of his wrath,
drained to its dregs the bowl of drunkenness;

of all the sons you have borne there is not one to guide you,             18
of all you have reared, not one to take you by the hand.
   These two disasters have overtaken you;                  19
    who can console you?—
havoc and ruin, famine and the sword;
    who can comfort you?
   Your sons are in stupor, they lie at the head of every street,    20
    like antelopes caught in the net,
    glutted with the wrath of the LORD,
    the rebuke of your God.
Therefore listen to this, in your affliction,                            21
    drunk that you are, but not with wine:
thus says the LORD, your Lord and your God,                              22
    who will plead his people's cause:
   Look, I take from your hand
    the cup of drunkenness;
you shall never again drink from the bowl of my wrath,
   I will give it instead to your tormentors and oppressors,          23
those who said to you, 'Lie down and we will walk over you';
   and you made your backs like the ground beneath them,
   like a roadway for passers-by.

Awake, awake, put on your strength, O Zion,                              **52**
put on your loveliest garments, holy city of Jerusalem;
for never shall the uncircumcised and the unclean enter you again.
Rise up, captive Jerusalem, shake off the dust;                          2
   loose your neck from the collar that binds it,
   O captive daughter of Zion.

   The LORD says, You were sold but no price was paid, and without pay- 3
ment you shall be ransomed. The Lord GOD says, At the beginning my 4
people went down into Egypt to live there, and at the end it was the
Assyrians who oppressed them; but now what do I find here? says the 5
LORD. My people carried off and no price paid, their rulers derided,
and my name reviled all day long, says the LORD. But on that day my 6
people shall know my name; they shall know that it is I who speak; here
I am.

   How lovely on the mountains are the feet of the herald              7
who comes to proclaim prosperity and bring good news,
   the news of deliverance,
calling to Zion, 'Your God is king.'
Hark, your watchmen raise their voices                                   8
   and shout together in triumph;
   for with their own eyes they shall see
   the LORD returning in pity to Zion.
   Break forth together in shouts of triumph,                       9
    you ruins of Jerusalem;
   for the LORD has taken pity on his people
    and has ransomed Jerusalem.

10     The LORD has bared his holy arm
           in the sight of all nations,
       and the whole world from end to end
           shall see the deliverance of our God.

11     Away from Babylon; come out, come out,
           touch nothing unclean.
       Come out from Babylon, keep yourselves pure,
           you who carry the vessels of the LORD.

12     But you shall not come out in urgent haste
           nor leave like fugitives;
       for the LORD will march at your head,
           your rearguard will be Israel's God.


13     Behold, my servant shall prosper,
       he shall be lifted up, exalted to the heights.


14     Time was when many *a* were aghast at you, my people; *b*
15     so now many nations *c* recoil at sight of him,
       and kings curl their lips in disgust.
       For they see what they had never been told
       and things unheard before fill their thoughts.


53         Who could have believed what we have heard,
       and to whom has the power of the LORD been revealed?

2      He grew up before the LORD like a young plant
           whose roots are in parched ground;
       he had no beauty, no majesty to draw our eyes,
           no grace to make us delight in him;
       his form, disfigured, lost all the likeness of a man,
           his beauty changed beyond human semblance. *d*

3      He was despised, he shrank from the sight of men,
           tormented and humbled by suffering;
       we despised him, we held him of no account,
           a thing from which men turn away their eyes.

4      Yet on himself he bore our sufferings,
           our torments he endured,
       while we counted him smitten by God,
           struck down by disease and misery;

5      but he was pierced for our transgressions,
           tortured for our iniquities;
       the chastisement he bore is health for us
           and by his scourging we are healed.

6      We had all strayed like sheep,
           each of us had gone his own way;
       but the LORD laid upon him
           the guilt of us all.

*a Or* the great.     *b See note on 53. 2.*     *c Or* great nations.     *d* his form . . .
semblance: *transposed from end of 52. 14.*

He was afflicted, he submitted to be struck down                7
    and did not open his mouth;
he was led like a sheep to the slaughter,
like a ewe that is dumb before the shearers.*a*
Without protection, without justice,*b* he was taken away;        8
    and who gave a thought to his fate,
    how he was cut off from the world of living men,
stricken to the death for my people's transgression?
He was assigned a grave with the wicked,                          9
a burial-place among the refuse of mankind,
    though he had done no violence
    and spoken no word of treachery.
Yet the LORD took thought for his tortured servant               10
and healed him who had made himself*c* a sacrifice for sin;
so shall he enjoy long life and see his children's children,
    and in his hand the LORD's cause shall prosper.
After all his pains he shall be bathed in light,                 11
after his disgrace he shall be fully vindicated;
    so shall he, my servant, vindicate many,
    himself bearing the penalty of their guilt.
Therefore I will allot him a portion with the great,             12
    and he shall share the spoil with the mighty,
because he exposed himself to face death *d*
    and was reckoned among transgressors,
because he bore the sin of many
    and interceded for their transgressions.

Sing aloud, O barren woman who never bore a child,               **54**
break into cries of joy, you who have never been in labour;
for the deserted wife has more sons than she who lives in wedlock,
    says the LORD.
Enlarge the limits of your home,                                  2
    spread wide the curtains of your tent;
let out its ropes to the full
    and drive the pegs home;
for you shall break out of your confines right and left,          3
your descendants shall dispossess wide regions,*e*
and re-people cities now desolate.
Fear not; you shall not be put to shame,                          4
you shall suffer no insult, have no cause to blush.
It is time to forget the shame of your younger days
and remember no more the reproach of your widowhood;
for your husband is your maker, whose name is the LORD of Hosts;  5
    your ransomer is the Holy One of Israel
    who is called God of all the earth.

*a Prob. rdg.; Heb. adds* and he would not open his mouth.     *b* Without protection,
without justice: *or* After arrest and sentence.      *c* healed . . . himself: *prob. rdg.;*
*Heb.* he made sick, if you make.      *d Or* because he poured out his life to the death.
*e* wide regions: *or* the nations.

6     The LORD has acknowledged you a wife again,
        once deserted and heart-broken,
      your God has called you a bride still young
        though once rejected.
7     On the impulse of a moment I forsook you,
      but with tender affection I will bring you home again.
8         In sudden anger
      I hid my face from you for a moment;
      but now have I pitied you with a love which never fails,
        says the LORD who ransoms you.
9     These days recall for me the days of Noah:
      as I swore that the waters of Noah's flood
      should never again pour over the earth,
        so now I swear to you
      never again to be angry with you or reproach you.
10    Though the mountains move and the hills shake,
      my love shall be immovable and never fail,
        and my covenant of peace shall not be shaken.
      So says the LORD who takes pity on you.

11        O storm-battered city, distressed and disconsolate,
      now I will set your stones in the finest mortar
        and your foundations in lapis lazuli;
12    I will make your battlements of red jasper*a*
        and your gates of garnet;*b*
        all your boundary-stones shall be jewels.
13        Your masons shall all be instructed by the LORD,
        and your sons shall enjoy great prosperity;
14        and in triumph*c* shall you be restored.
      You shall be free from oppression and have no fears,
      free from terror, and it shall not come near you;
15    should any attack you, it will not be my doing,
      the aggressor, whoever he be, shall perish for his attempt.
16    It was I who created the smith
        to fan the coals in the furnace
        and forge weapons each for its purpose,
      and I who created the destroyer to lay waste;
17    but now no weapon made to harm you shall prevail,
      and you shall rebut every charge brought against you.
        Such is the fortune of the servants of the LORD;
        their vindication comes from me.
      This is the very word of the LORD.

55    Come, all who are thirsty, come, fetch water;
      come, you who have no food, buy corn and eat;
      come and buy, not for money, not for a price.*d*

---

*a* Or carbuncle.        *b* Or firestone.        *c* Or in righteousness.
*d* Prob. rdg.; Heb. adds wine and milk.

Why spend money and get what is not bread, 2
    why give the price of your labour and go unsatisfied?
Only listen to me and you will have good food to eat,
    and you will enjoy the fat of the land.
Come to me and listen to my words, 3
    hear me, and you shall have life:
I will make a covenant with you, this time for ever,
to love you faithfully as I loved David.
I made him a witness to all races, 4
    a prince and instructor of peoples;
and you in turn shall summon nations you do not know, 5
and nations that do not know you shall come running to you,
    because the LORD your God,
    the Holy One of Israel, has glorified you.

Inquire of the LORD while he is present, 6
call upon him when he is close at hand.
Let the wicked abandon their ways 7
    and evil men their thoughts:
let them return to the LORD, who will have pity on them,
    return to our God, for he will freely forgive.
For my thoughts are not your thoughts, 8
    and your ways are not my ways.
    This is the very word of the LORD.
For as the heavens are higher than the earth, 9
so are my ways higher than your ways
    and my thoughts than your thoughts;
and as the rain and the snow come down from heaven 10
and do not return until they have watered the earth,
    making it blossom and bear fruit,
and give seed for sowing and bread to eat,
so shall the word which comes from my mouth prevail; 11
    it shall not return to me fruitless
without accomplishing my purpose
    or succeeding in the task I gave it.
    You shall indeed go out with joy 12
    and be led forth in peace.
Before you mountains and hills shall break into cries of joy,
and all the trees of the wild shall clap their hands,
    pine-trees shall shoot up in place of camel-thorn, 13
    myrtles instead of briars;
    all this shall win the LORD a great name,
    imperishable, a sign for all time.

## *Warnings to keep the moral law*

**56** These are the words of the LORD:
Maintain justice, do the right;
for my deliverance is close at hand,
 and my righteousness will show itself victorious.
2 Happy is the man who follows these precepts,
happy the mortal who holds them fast,
 who keeps the sabbath undefiled,
 who refrains from all wrong-doing!
3 The foreigner who has given his allegiance to the LORD must not say,
'The LORD will keep me separate from his people for ever';
 and the eunuch must not say,
 'I am nothing but a barren tree.'
4 For these are the words of the LORD:
The eunuchs who keep my sabbaths,
who choose to do my will and hold fast to my covenant,
5 shall receive from me something better than sons and daughters,
a memorial and a name in my own house and within my walls;
 I will give them an everlasting name,
 a name imperishable for all time.
6 So too with the foreigners who give their allegiance to me, the LORD,
 to minister to me and love my name
 and to become my servants,
 all who keep the sabbath undefiled
 and hold fast to my covenant:
7 them will I bring to my holy hill
 and give them joy in my house of prayer.
Their offerings and sacrifices shall be acceptable on my altar;
 for my house shall be called
 a house of prayer for all nations.
8 This is the very word of the Lord GOD,
 who brings home the outcasts of Israel:
I will yet bring home all that remain to be brought in.

9 Come, beasts of the plain, beasts of the forest,
 come, eat your fill,
10 for Israel's watchmen are blind, all of them unaware.
They are all dumb dogs who cannot bark,
 stretched on the ground, dreaming, lovers of sleep,
11 greedy dogs that can never have enough.
They are shepherds who understand nothing,
 absent each of them on his own pursuits,
 each intent on his own gain wherever he can find it.
12 'Come,' says each of them, 'let me fetch wine,
 strong drink, and we will drain it down;
 let us make tomorrow like today,
 or greater far!'

The righteous perish,                                           57
  and no one takes it to heart;
men of good faith are swept away, but no one cares,
the righteous are swept away before the onset of evil,
    but they enter into peace;                               2
    they have run a straight course
    and rest in their last beds.

Come, stand forth, you sons of a soothsayer.                     3
You spawn of an adulterer and a harlot,
    who is the target of your jests?                         4
  Against whom do you open your mouths
    and wag your tongues,
children of sin that you are, spawn of a lie,
    burning with lust under the terebinths,                  5
      under every spreading tree,
    and sacrificing children in the gorges,
      under the rocky clefts?
    And you, woman,                                          6
  your place is with the creatures of the gorge;
    that is where you belong.
  To them you have dared to pour a libation
    and present an offering of grain.*a*
On a high mountain-top                                           7
  you have made your bed;
there too you have gone up to offer sacrifice.
In spite of all this am I to relent?*b*
Beside door and door-post you have put up your sign.            8
  Deserting me, you have stripped and lain down
    on the wide bed which you have made,
  and you drove bargains with men
    for the pleasure of sleeping together,
  and you have committed countless acts of fornication
    in the heat of your lust.
You drenched your tresses in oil                                9
  blended with many perfumes;
you sent out your procurers far and wide
  even down to the gates of Sheol.
Worn out by your unending excesses,                             10
  even so you never said, 'I am past hope.'
  You earned a livelihood
  and so you had no anxiety.
Whom do you fear so much, that you should be false,            11
that you never remembered me or gave me a thought?
Did I not hold my peace and seem not to see
  while you showed no fear of me?

---

*a* *See note on verse 7.*      *b* *Line transposed from end of verse 6.*

12          Now I will denounce your conduct
                 that you think so righteous.
13          These idols of yours shall not help when you cry;
                 no idol shall save you.
            The wind shall carry them off, one and all,
                 a puff of air shall blow them away;
            but he who makes me his refuge shall possess the earth
                 and inherit my holy hill.

14              Then a voice shall be heard:
            Build up a highway, build it and clear the track,
                 sweep away all that blocks my people's path.
15          Thus speaks the high and exalted one,
            whose name is holy, who lives for ever:
                 I dwell in a high and holy place
                     with him who is broken and humble in spirit,
                     to revive the spirit of the humble,
                     to revive the courage of the broken.
16          I will not be always accusing,
            I will not continually nurse my wrath.
            For a breath of life passed out from me,
                 and by my own act I created living creatures.
17          For a time I was angry at the guilt of Israel;
                 I smote him in my anger and withdrew my favour.
            But he ran wild and went his wilful way.
18              Then I considered his ways,
                 I cured him and gave him relief,
            and I brought him comfort in full measure,
19              brought peace to those who mourned for him,
                 by the words that issue from my lips,
            peace for all men, both near and far,
                 and so I cured him, says the LORD.
20          But the wicked are like a troubled sea,
                 a sea that cannot rest,
            whose troubled waters cast up mud and filth.

21              There is no peace for the wicked,
                 says the LORD.

58          Shout aloud without restraint;
            lift up your voice like a trumpet.
            Call my people to account for their transgression
                 and the house of Jacob for their sins,
2           although they ask counsel of me day by day
                 and say they delight in knowing my ways,
            although, like nations which have acted rightly
                 and not forsaken the just laws of their gods,
            they ask me for righteous laws
                 and say they delight in approaching God.

Why do we fast, if thou dost not see it?　　　　　3
Why mortify ourselves, if thou payest no heed?
Since you serve your own interest only on your fast-day
　　and make all your men work the harder,
since your fasting leads only to wrangling and strife　　4
　　and dealing vicious blows with the fist,
on such a day you are keeping no fast
　　that will carry your cry to heaven.
Is it a fast like this that I require,　　　　　5
　　a day of mortification such as this,
　　that a man should bow his head like a bulrush
　　and make his bed on sackcloth and ashes?
Is this what you call a fast,
　　a day acceptable to the LORD?
Is not this what I require of you as a fast:　　　6
　　to loose the fetters of injustice,
　　to untie the knots of the yoke,
　　　　to snap every yoke
　　and set free those who have been crushed?
Is it not sharing your food with the hungry,　　　7
taking the homeless poor into your house,
　　clothing the naked when you meet them
　　and never evading a duty to your kinsfolk?
Then shall your light break forth like the dawn　　8
and soon you will grow healthy like a wound newly healed;
　　your own righteousness shall be your vanguard
　　　and the glory of the LORD your rearguard.
Then, if you call, the LORD will answer;　　　9
　　if you cry to him, he will say, 'Here I am.'
　　If you cease to pervert justice,
to point the accusing finger and lay false charges,
　　if you feed the hungry from your own plenty　　10
　　　and satisfy the needs of the wretched,
　　then your light will rise like dawn out of darkness
　　　and your dusk be like noonday;
　　the LORD will be your guide continually　　11
　　and will satisfy your needs in the shimmering heat;
　　　he will give you strength of limb;
　　you will be like a well-watered garden,
like a spring whose waters never fail.
The ancient ruins will be restored by your own kindred　　12
　　and you will build once more on ancestral foundations;
you shall be called Rebuilder of broken walls,
　　Restorer of houses in ruins.

If you cease to tread the sabbath underfoot,　　13
and keep my holy day free from your own affairs,
　　if you call the sabbath a day of joy

and the LORD's holy day a day to be honoured,
if you honour it by not plying your trade,
not seeking your own interest
or attending to your own affairs,
14 then you shall find your joy in the LORD,
and I will set you riding on the heights of the earth,
and your father Jacob's patrimony shall be yours to enjoy;
the LORD himself has spoken it.

59 The LORD's arm is not so short that he cannot save
nor his ear too dull to hear;
2 it is your iniquities that raise a barrier
between you and your God,
because of your sins he has hidden his face
so that he does not hear you.
3 Your hands are stained with blood
and your fingers with crime;
your lips speak lies
and your tongues utter injustice.
4 No man sues with just cause,
no man goes honestly to law;
all trust in empty words, all tell lies,
conceive mischief and give birth to trouble.
5 They hatch snakes' eggs, they weave cobwebs;
eat their eggs and you will die,
for rotten eggs hatch only rottenness.
6 As for their webs, they will never make cloth,
no one can use them for clothing;
their works breed trouble
and their hands are busy with deeds of violence.
7 They rush headlong into crime
in furious haste to shed innocent blood;
their schemes are schemes of mischief
and leave a trail of ruin and devastation.
8 They do not know the way to peace,
no justice guides their steps;
all the paths they follow are crooked;
no one who walks in them enjoys true peace.

9 Therefore justice is far away from us,
right does not reach us;
we look for light but all is darkness,
for the light of dawn, but we walk in deep gloom.
10 We grope like blind men along a wall,
feeling our way like men without eyes;
we stumble at noonday as if it were twilight,
like dead men in the ghostly underworld.
11 We growl like bears,
like doves we moan incessantly,

waiting for justice, and there is none;
for deliverance, but it is still far away.

Our acts of rebellion against thee are past counting          12
and our sins bear witness against us;
we remember our many rebellions, we know well our guilt:
we have rebelled and broken faith with the LORD,            13
we have relapsed and forsaken our God;
we have conceived lies in our hearts and repeated them
in slanderous and treacherous words.
Justice is rebuffed and flouted                              14
while righteousness stands aloof;
truth stumbles in the market-place
and honesty is kept out of court,
so truth is lost to sight,                                   15
and whoever shuns evil is thought a madman.

The LORD saw, and in his eyes it was an evil thing,
that there was no justice;
he saw that there was no man to help
and was outraged that no one intervened;                     16
so his own arm brought him victory
and his own integrity upheld him.
He put on integrity as a coat of mail                        17
and the helmet of salvation on his head;
he put on garments of vengeance
and wrapped himself in a cloak of jealous anger.
High God of retribution that he is,                          18
he pays in full measure,
wreaking his anger on his foes, retribution on his enemies.
So from the west men shall fear his name,
fear his glory from the rising of the sun;                   19
for it shall come like a shining river,
the spirit of the LORD hovering over it,
come as the ransomer of Zion                                 20
and of all in Jacob who repent of their rebellion.
This is the very word of the LORD.

This, says the LORD, is my covenant, which I make with them: My  21
spirit which rests on you and my words which I have put into your mouth
shall never fail you from generation to generation of your descendants from
now onward for ever. The LORD has said it.

## *Promise of the new Jerusalem*

**60** Arise, Jerusalem,
rise clothed in light; your light has come
and the glory of the LORD shines over you.

2 For, though darkness covers the earth
and dark night the nations,
the LORD shall shine upon you
and over you shall his glory appear;

3 and the nations shall march towards your light
and their kings to your sunrise.

4 Lift up your eyes and look all around:
they flock together, all of them, and come to you;
your sons also shall come from afar,
your daughters walking beside them leading the way.

5 Then shall you see, and shine with joy,
then your heart shall thrill with pride:
the riches of the sea shall be lavished upon you
and you shall possess the wealth of nations.

6 Camels in droves shall cover the land,
dromedaries of Midian and Ephah,
all coming from Sheba
laden with golden spice*a* and frankincense,
heralds of the LORD's praise.

7 All Kedar's flocks shall be gathered for you,
rams of Nebaioth shall serve your need,
acceptable offerings on my altar,
and glory shall be added to glory in my temple.

8 Who are these that sail along like clouds,
that fly like doves to their dovecotes?

9 They are vessels assembling from the coasts and islands,
ships from Tarshish leading the convoy;
they bring your sons from afar,
their gold and their silver with them,
to the honour of the LORD your God,
the Holy One of Israel;
for he has made you glorious.

10 Foreigners shall rebuild your walls
and their kings shall be your servants;
for though in my wrath I struck you down,
now I have shown you pity and favour.

11 Your gates shall be open continually,
they shall never be shut day or night,
that through them may be brought the wealth of nations
and their kings under escort.

*a* golden spice: *or* gold.

For the nation or kingdom which refuses to serve you shall perish, and   12
wide regions shall be laid utterly waste.

    The wealth of Lebanon shall come to you,           13
pine, fir,[a] and boxwood,[b] all together,
    to bring glory to my holy sanctuary,
    to honour the place where my feet rest.
The sons of your oppressors shall come forward to do homage,    14
all who reviled you shall bow low at your feet;
    they shall call you the City of the LORD,
    the Zion of the Holy One of Israel.

    No longer will you be deserted,
    a wife hated and unvisited;[c]          15
    I will make you an eternal pride
    and a never-ending joy.
    You shall suck the milk of nations          16
    and be suckled at the breasts of kings.
So you shall know that I the LORD am your deliverer,
    your ransomer the Mighty One of Jacob.

    For bronze[d] I will bring you gold
    and for iron I will bring silver,          17
bronze[d] for timber and iron for stone;
    and I will make your government be peace
    and righteousness rule over you.
The sound of violence shall be heard no longer in your land,    18
    or ruin and devastation within your borders;
    but you shall call your walls Deliverance
    and your gates Praise.

    The sun shall no longer be your light by day,
nor the moon shine on you when evening falls;    19
    the LORD shall be your everlasting light,
    your God shall be your glory.
    Never again shall your sun set          20
    nor your moon withdraw her light;
but the LORD shall be your everlasting light
    and the days of your mourning shall be ended.

    Your people shall all be righteous
    and shall for ever possess the land,          21
    a shoot of my own planting,
    a work of my own hands to bring me glory.
    The few shall become ten thousand,
    the little nation great.          22
    I am the LORD;
soon, in the fullness of time, I will bring this to pass.

[a] *Or* elm.    [b] *Or* cypress.    [c] *Or* divorced and unmated.    [d] *Or* copper.

**61**
The spirit of the Lord GOD is upon me
because the LORD has anointed me;
he has sent me to bring good news to the humble,
to bind up the broken-hearted,
to proclaim liberty to captives
and release to those in prison;

2
to proclaim a year of the LORD's favour
and a day of the vengeance of our God;
to comfort all who mourn,<sup>a</sup>

3
to give them garlands instead of ashes,
oil of gladness instead of mourners' tears,
a garment of splendour for the heavy heart.
They shall be called Trees of Righteousness,
planted by the LORD for his glory.

4
Ancient ruins shall be rebuilt
and sites long desolate restored;
they shall repair the ruined cities
and restore what has long lain desolate.

5
Foreigners shall serve as shepherds of your flocks,
and aliens shall till your land and tend your vines;

6
but you shall be called priests of the LORD
and be named ministers of our God;
you shall enjoy the wealth of other nations
and be furnished<sup>b</sup> with their riches.

7
And so, because shame in double measure
and jeers and insults<sup>c</sup> have been my people's lot,
they shall receive in their own land a double measure of
wealth,
and everlasting joy shall be theirs.

8
For I, the LORD, love justice
and hate robbery and wrong-doing;
I will grant them a sure reward
and make an everlasting covenant with them;

9
their posterity will be renowned among the nations
and their offspring among the peoples;
all who see them will acknowledge in them
a race whom the LORD has blessed.

10
Let me rejoice in the LORD with all my heart,
let me exult in my God;
for he has robed me in salvation as a garment
and clothed me in integrity as a cloak,
like a bridegroom with his priestly garland,
or a bride decked in her jewels.

11
For, as the earth puts forth her blossom
or bushes in the garden burst into flower,

---

<sup>a</sup> *Prob. rdg.; Heb. adds* to appoint to Zion's mourners.    <sup>b</sup> be furnished: *prob. rdg.;*
*Heb. unintelligible.*    <sup>c</sup> and insults: *prob. rdg.; Heb.* they shout in triumph.

so shall the Lord GOD make righteousness and praise
blossom before all the nations.

For Zion's sake I will not keep silence,                    62
for Jerusalem's sake I will speak out,
until her right shines forth like the sunrise,
her deliverance like a blazing torch,
until the nations see the triumph of your right            2
and all kings see your glory.
Then you shall be called by a new name
which the LORD shall pronounce with his own lips;
you will be a glorious crown in the LORD's hand,
a kingly diadem in the hand of your God.                   3
No more shall men call you Forsaken,
no more shall your land be called Desolate,                4
but you shall be named Hephzi-bah*a*
and your land Beulah;*b*
for the LORD delights in you
and to him your land is wedded.
For, as a young man weds a maiden,
so you shall wed him who rebuilds you,                     5
and your God shall rejoice over you
as a bridegroom rejoices over the bride.
I have posted watchmen on your walls, Jerusalem,           6
who shall not keep silence day or night:
'You who invoke the LORD's name,
take no rest, give him no rest
until he makes Jerusalem                                    7
a theme of endless praise on earth.'

The LORD has sworn with raised right hand and mighty arm:  8
Never again will I give your grain to feed your foes
or let foreigners drink the new wine
for which you have toiled;
but those who bring in the corn shall eat and praise the LORD, 9
and those who gather the grapes shall drink in my holy courts.

Go out of the gates, go out,                               10
prepare a road for my people;
build a highway, build it up,
clear away the boulders;
raise a signal to the peoples.
This is the LORD's proclamation                            11
to earth's farthest bounds:
Tell the daughter of Zion,
Behold, your deliverance has come.
His recompense comes with him;
he carries his reward before him;

---

*a* *That is* My delight is in her.    *b* *That is* Wedded.

12        and they shall be called a Holy People,
          the Ransomed of the LORD,
        a People long-sought, a City not forsaken.

63        'Who is this coming from Edom,
          coming from Bozrah, his garments stained red?
          Under his clothes his muscles stand out,
            and he strides, stooping in his might.'
          It is I, who announce that right has won the day,
            I, who am strong to save.
2         'Why is your clothing all red,
        like the garments of one who treads grapes in the vat?'
3         I have trodden the winepress alone;
          no man, no nation was with me.
          I trod them down in my rage,
          I trampled them in my fury;
        and their life-blood spurted over my garments
          and stained all my clothing.
4         For I resolved on a day of vengeance;
          the year for ransoming my own had come.
5         I looked for a helper but found no one,
          I was amazed that there was no one to support me;
        yet my own arm brought me victory,
          alone my anger supported me.
6         I stamped on nations in my fury,
          I pierced them in my rage
        and let their life-blood run out upon the ground.

7         I will recount the LORD's acts of unfailing love
          and the LORD's praises as High God,
          all that the LORD has done for us
          and his great goodness to the house of Israel,
          all that he has done for them in his tenderness
          and by his many acts of love.
8         He said, 'Surely they are my people,
          my sons who will not play me false';
9         and he became their deliverer in all their troubles.
        It was no envoy, no angel, but he himself that delivered them;
        he himself ransomed them by his love and pity,
          lifted them up and carried them
          through all the years gone by.
10        Yet they rebelled and grieved his holy spirit;
          only then was he changed into their enemy
          and himself fought against them.
11        Then men remembered days long past
          and him who drew out*a* his people:

*a That is Moses whose name resembles the Heb. verb meaning draw out, cp. Exod. 2. 10
and the note there.*

Where is he who brought them up from the Nile
with the shepherd[a] of his flock?
Where is he who put within him
his holy spirit,
who made his glorious power march 12
at the right hand of Moses,
dividing the waters before them,
to win for himself an everlasting name,
causing them to go through the depths 13
sure-footed as horses in the wilderness,
like cattle moving down into a valley without stumbling, 14
guided by the spirit of the LORD?
So didst thou lead thy people
to win thyself a glorious name.

Look down from heaven and behold 15
from the heights where thou dwellest holy and glorious.
Where is thy zeal, thy valour,
thy burning and tender love?
Stand not aloof;[b] for thou art our father, 16
though Abraham does not know us nor Israel acknowledge us.
Thou, LORD, art our father;
thy name is our Ransomer[c] from of old.
Why, LORD, dost thou let us wander from thy ways 17
and harden our hearts until we cease to fear thee?
turn again for the sake of thy servants,
the tribes of thy patrimony.
Why have wicked men trodden down thy sanctuary,[d] 18
why have our enemies trampled on thy shrine?
We have long been reckoned as beyond thy sway, 19
as if we had not been named thy own.

Why didst thou not rend the heavens and come down, **64**
and make the mountains shudder before thee
as when fire blazes up in brushwood
or fire makes water boil? 2
then would thy name be known to thy enemies
and nations tremble at thy coming.
When thou didst terrible things that we did not look for, 3
the mountains shuddered before thee.
Never has ear heard[e] or eye seen 4
any other god taking the part of those who wait for him.
Thou dost welcome him who rejoices to do what is right, 5
who remembers thee in thy ways.
Though thou wast angry, yet we sinned,
in spite of it we have done evil from of old,

---

[a] *Or* shepherds.  [b] *Stand not aloof: prob. rdg.; Heb. obscure in context.*  [c] *Or* our
Kinsman.  [d] *Why . . . sanctuary: prob. rdg.; Heb.* For a little while they possessed
thy holy people.  [e] *Never . . . heard: prob. rdg.; Heb.* They have never heard or listened.

6    we all became like a man who is unclean
     and all our righteous deeds like a filthy rag;
        we have all withered*a* like leaves
        and our iniquities sweep us away like the wind.
7          There is no one who invokes thee by name
        or rouses himself to cling to thee;
        for thou hast hidden thy face from us
        and abandoned us to our iniquities.
8       But now, LORD, thou art our father;
        we are the clay, thou the potter,
           and all of us are thy handiwork.
9       Do not be angry beyond measure, O LORD,
        and do not remember iniquity for ever;
        look on us all, look on thy people.
10      Thy holy cities are a wilderness,
     Zion a wilderness, Jerusalem desolate;
11         our sanctuary, holy and glorious,
           where our fathers praised thee,
        has been burnt to the ground
        and all that we cherish is a ruin.
12      After this, O LORD, wilt thou hold back,
        wilt thou keep silence and punish us beyond measure?

65    I was there to be sought by a people who did not ask,
        to be found by men who did not seek me.
        I said, 'Here am I, here am I',
        to a nation that did not invoke me by name.
2        I spread out my hands all day
           appealing to an unruly people
        who went their evil way,
           following their own devices,
3          a people who provoked me
           continually to my face,
     offering sacrifice in gardens, burning incense on brick
           altars,
4    crouching among graves, keeping vigil all night long,
     eating swine's flesh, their cauldrons full of a tainted brew.
5       'Stay where you are,' they cry,
        'do not dare touch me; for I am too sacred for you.'
        Such people are a smouldering fire,
        smoking in my nostrils all day long.
6    All is on record before me; I will not keep silence;
7          I will repay*b* your iniquities,
        yours and your fathers', all at once, says the LORD,
        because they burnt incense*c* on the mountains
           and defied me on the hills;

---

*a* have all withered: *or* are all carried away.          *b* *Prob. rdg., transposing* and then
pay *to follow* reward.          *c* *Or* sacrifices.

I will first measure out their reward
and then pay them in full.

These are the words of the LORD:              8
As there is new wine in a cluster of grapes
and men say, 'Do not destroy it; there is a blessing in it',
  so will I do for my servants' sake:
I will not destroy the whole nation.
I will give Jacob children to come after him       9
and Judah heirs who shall possess my mountains;
  my chosen shall inherit them
and my servants shall live there.
Flocks shall range over Sharon,           10
  and the Vale of Achor be a pasture for cattle;
  they shall belong to my people who seek me.
But you that forsake the LORD and forget my holy    11
  mountain,
who spread a table for the god of Fate,
and fill bowls of spiced wine in honour of Fortune,
I will deliver you to your fate, to execution,      12
and you shall all bend the neck to the sword,
  because I called and you did not answer,
  I spoke and you did not listen;
and you did what was wrong in my eyes
and you chose what was against my will.
Therefore these are the words of the Lord GOD:    13
My servants shall eat but you shall starve;
my servants shall drink but you shall go thirsty;
my servants shall rejoice but you shall be put to shame;
  my servants shall shout in triumph
  in the gladness of their hearts,         14
  but you shall cry from sorrow
  and wail from anguish of spirit;
your name shall be used as an oath by my chosen,
  and the Lord GOD shall give you over to death;   15
  but his servants he shall call by another name.
He who invokes a blessing on himself in the land   16
  shall do so by the God whose name is Amen,
and he who utters an oath in the land
  shall do so by the God of Amen;
  the former troubles are forgotten
  and they are hidden from my sight.
  For behold, I create
new heavens and a new earth.         17
  Former things shall no more be remembered
  nor shall they be called to mind.
  Rejoice and be filled with delight,
  you boundless realms which I create;     18

for I create Jerusalem to be a delight
and her people a joy;

19 I will take delight in Jerusalem and rejoice in my people;
weeping and cries for help
shall never again be heard in her.

20 There no child shall ever again die an infant,
no old man fail to live out his life;
every boy shall live his hundred years before he dies,
whoever falls short of a hundred shall be despised.*a*

21 Men shall build houses and live to inhabit them,
plant vineyards and eat their fruit;

22 they shall not build for others to inhabit
nor plant for others to eat.
My people shall live the long life of a tree,
and my chosen shall enjoy the fruit of their labour.

23 They shall not toil in vain or raise children for misfortune.
For they are the offspring of the blessed of the LORD
and their issue after them;

24 before they call to me, I will answer,
and while they are still speaking I will listen.

25 The wolf and the lamb shall feed together
and the lion shall eat straw like cattle.*b*
They shall not hurt or destroy in all my holy mountain,
says the LORD.

66 These are the words of the LORD:
Heaven is my throne and earth my footstool.
Where will you build a house for me,
where shall my resting-place be?

2 All these are of my own making
and all these are mine.
This is the very word of the LORD.

The man I look to is a man down-trodden and distressed,
one who reveres my words.

3 But to sacrifice an ox or to*c* kill a man,
slaughter a sheep or break a dog's neck,
offer grain or offer pigs' blood,
burn incense as a token and worship an idol—
all these are the chosen practices of men
who*d* revel in their own loathsome rites.

4 I too will practise those wanton rites of theirs
and bring down on them the very things they dread;
for I called and no one answered,
I spoke and no one listened.

---

*a* Or cursed.     *b* Prob. rdg.; Heb. adds and the food of the snake shall be dust.
*c* to sacrifice an ox or to: or those who sacrifice an ox and . . .     *d* are the chosen
practices of men who: or have chosen their own devices and . . .

They did what was wrong in my eyes
and chose practices not to my liking.

Hear the word of the LORD, you who revere his word:                5
   Your fellow-countrymen who hate you,
     who spurn you because you bear my name, have said,
    'Let the LORD show his glory,
     then we shall see you rejoice';
    but they shall be put to shame.
That roar from the city, that uproar in the temple,               6
is the sound of the LORD dealing retribution to his foes.

Shall a woman bear a child without pains?
give birth to a son before the onset of labour?                   7
   Who has heard of anything like this?
   Who has seen any such thing?                              8
Shall a country be born after one day's labour,
shall a nation be brought to birth all in a moment?
But Zion, at the onset of her pangs, bore her sons.
   Shall I bring to the point of birth and not deliver?
    the LORD says;                                         9
   shall I who deliver close the womb?
    your God has spoken.

Rejoice with Jerusalem and exult in her,
   all you who love her;                                     10
  share her joy with all your heart,
   all you who mourn over her.
Then you may suck and be fed from the breasts that give comfort,  11
delighting in her plentiful milk.
   For thus says the LORD:
I will send peace flowing over her like a river,                  12
and the wealth of nations like a stream in flood;
    it shall suckle you,
    and you shall be carried in their arms
    and dandled on their knees.
  As a mother comforts her son,
   so will I myself comfort you,                             13
    and you shall find comfort in Jerusalem.
  This you shall see and be glad at heart,
   your limbs shall be as fresh as grass in spring;         14
the LORD shall make his power known among his servants
   and his indignation felt among his foes.
For see, the LORD is coming in fire,
   with his chariots like a whirlwind,                       15
  to strike home with his furious anger
   and with the flaming fire of his reproof.
The LORD will judge by fire,
   with fire he will test all living men,                    16

and many will be slain by the LORD;

17 those who hallow and purify themselves in garden-rites,
one after another in a magic ring,
those who eat the flesh of pigs and rats<sup>a</sup> and all vile vermin,
shall meet their end, one and all,
says the LORD,

18 for I know their deeds and their thoughts.

Then I myself will come to gather all nations and races,
and they shall come and see my glory;

19 and I will perform a sign among them.
I will spare some of them and send them to the nations,
to Tarshish, Put, and Lud,<sup>b</sup>
to Meshek, Rosh,<sup>c</sup> Tubal, and Javan,<sup>d</sup>
distant coasts and islands which have never yet heard of me
and have not seen my glory;
these shall announce that glory among the nations.

20 From every nation they shall bring your countrymen
on horses, in chariots and wagons,
on mules and dromedaries,
as an offering to the LORD,
on my holy mountain Jerusalem,
says the LORD,
as the Israelites bring offerings
in pure vessels to the LORD's house;

21 and some of them I will take for priests, for Levites,
says the LORD.

22 For, as the new heavens and the new earth
which I am making shall endure in my sight,
says the LORD,
so shall your race and your name endure;

23 and month by month at the new moon,
week by week on the sabbath,
all mankind shall come to bow down before me,
says the LORD;

24 and they shall come out and see
the dead bodies of those who have rebelled against me;
their worm shall not die nor their fire be quenched,
and they shall be abhorred by all mankind.

---

<sup>a</sup> *Or* jerboas.    <sup>b</sup> *Or* Lydia.    <sup>c</sup> Meshek, Rosh: *prob. rdg.*; *Heb.* those who
draw the bow.    <sup>d</sup> *Or* Greece.

# THE BOOK OF THE PROPHET
# JEREMIAH

THE WORDS OF JEREMIAH son of Hilkiah, one of the priests 1
at Anathoth in Benjamin. The word of the LORD came to him in the 2
thirteenth year of the reign of Josiah son of Amon, king of Judah;
also during the reign of Jehoiakim son of Josiah, king of Judah, until the 3
eleventh year of Zedekiah son of Josiah, king of Judah, was completed.
In the fifth month the people of Jerusalem were carried away into exile.

## Jeremiah's call and two visions

THE WORD OF THE LORD CAME TO ME: 'Before I formed you in the 4 5
womb I knew you for my own; before you were born I consecrated you,
I appointed you a prophet to the nations.' 'Ah! Lord GOD,' I answered, 6
'I do not know how to speak; I am only a child.' But the LORD said, 'Do 7
not call yourself a child; for you shall go to whatever people I send you
and say whatever I tell you to say. Fear none of them, for I am with you 8
and will keep you safe.' This was the very word of the LORD. Then the 9
LORD stretched out his hand and touched my mouth, and said to me, 'I
put my words into your mouth. This day I give you authority over nations 10
and over kingdoms, to pull down and to uproot, to destroy and to demolish,
to build and to plant.'

The word of the LORD came to me: 'What is it that you see, Jeremiah?' 11
'An almond in early bloom',*a* I answered. 'You are right,' said the LORD to 12
me, 'for I am early on the watch*b* to carry out my purpose.' The word of 13
the LORD came to me a second time: 'What is it that you see?' 'A cauldron',
I said, 'on a fire, fanned by the wind; it is tilted away from the north.'
The LORD said:

14

From the north disaster shall flare up
against all who live in this land;
for now I summon all peoples and kingdoms of the north, 15
says the LORD.
Their kings shall come and each shall set up his throne
before the gates of Jerusalem,
against her walls on every side,
and against all the cities of Judah.
I will state my case against my people 16
for all the wrong they have done in forsaking me,
in burning sacrifices to other gods,
worshipping the work of their own hands.

*a* Heb. shaked.　　*b* Heb. shoked.

17 Brace yourself, Jeremiah;
   stand up and speak to them.
   Tell them everything I bid you,
   do not let your spirit break at sight of them,
   or I will break you before their eyes.

18 This day I make you a fortified city,
   a pillar of iron, a wall of bronze,
   to stand fast against the whole land,
   against the kings and princes of Judah,
   its priests and its people.

19 They will make war on you but shall not overcome you,
   for I am with you and will keep you safe.
   This is the very word of the LORD.


## Exhortations to Israel and Judah

2 1 2 THE WORD OF THE LORD CAME TO ME: Go, make a proclamation that
       all Jerusalem shall hear: These are the words of the LORD:

   I remember the unfailing devotion of your youth,
      the love of your bridal days,
   when you followed me in the wilderness,
      through a land unsown.
3    Israel then was holy to the LORD,
      the firstfruits of his harvest;
   no one who devoured her went unpunished,
   evil always overtook them.
      This is the very word of the LORD.

4 Listen to the word of the LORD, people of Jacob, families of Israel, one
5 and all. These are the words of the LORD:

   What fault did your forefathers find in me,
      that they wandered far from me,
   pursuing empty phantoms and themselves becoming empty;
6    that they did not ask, 'Where is the LORD,
      who brought us up from Egypt,
      and led us through the wilderness,
   through a country of deserts and shifting sands,
   a country barren and ill-omened, where no man ever trod,
      no man made his home?'
7    I brought you into a fruitful land
      to enjoy its fruit and the goodness of it;
   but when you entered upon it you defiled it
      and made the home I gave you loathsome.
8    The priests no longer asked, 'Where is the LORD?'
   Those who handled the law had no thought of me,
      the shepherds of the people rebelled against me;

the prophets prophesied in the name of Baal
and followed gods powerless to help.
Therefore I will bring a charge against you once more,     9
   says the LORD,
against you and against your descendants.
   Cross to the coasts and islands of Kittim and see,     10
   send to Kedar and consider well,
   see whether there has been anything like this:
has a nation ever changed its gods,     11
   although they were no gods?
But my people have exchanged their Glory
   for a god altogether powerless.
   Stand aghast at this, you heavens,     12
   tremble in utter despair,
     says the LORD.
Two sins have my people committed:     13
   they have forsaken me,
   a spring of living water,
and they have hewn out for themselves cisterns,
cracked cisterns that can hold no water.


Is Israel a slave? Was he born in slavery?     14
If not, why has he been despoiled?
Why do lions roar and growl at him?     15
Why has his land been laid waste,
why are his cities razed to the ground and abandoned?
Men of Noph and Tahpanhes     16
   will break your heads.
Is it not your desertion of the LORD your God     17
  that brings all this upon you?
And now, why should you make off to Egypt     18
  to drink the waters of the Shihor?
Or why make off to Assyria
  to drink the waters of the River?
It is your own wickedness that will punish you,     19
  your own apostasy that will condemn you.
See for yourselves how bitter a thing it is and how evil,
to forsake the LORD your God and revere me no longer.
   This is the very word of the Lord GOD of Hosts.
Ages ago you broke your yoke and snapped your traces,     20
   crying, 'I will not be your slave';
   and you sprawled in promiscuous vice
   on all the hill-tops, under every spreading tree.
I planted you as a choice red vine,     21
   true stock all of you,
yet now you are turned into a vine
   debased and worthless!
The stain of your sin is still there and I see it,     22

> though you wash with soda and do not stint the soap.
> This is the very word of the Lord GOD.

23    How can you say, 'I am not polluted, not I!
> I have not followed the Baalim'?
> Look how you conducted yourself in the valley;
> remember what you have done.
> You have been like a she-camel,
> twisting and turning as she runs,

24    rushing alone into *a* the wilderness,
> snuffing the wind in her lust;
> who can restrain her in her heat?
> No one need tire himself out in pursuit of her;
> she is easily found at mating time.

25    Why not save your feet from stony ground
> and your throats from thirst?
> But you said, 'No; I am desperate.
> I love foreign gods and I must go after them.'

26    As a thief is ashamed when he is found out,
> so the people of Israel feel ashamed,
> they, their kings, their princes,
> their priests and their prophets;

27    they say 'You are our father' to a block of wood
> and cry 'Mother' to a stone.
> But on me they have turned their backs
> and averted their faces from me.
> And now on the day of disaster they say,
> 'Rise up and save us.'

28    Where are they, those gods you made for yourselves?
> Let them come and save you in the day of disaster.
> For you, Judah, have as many gods as you have towns. *b*

29       The LORD answers,
> Why argue your case with me?
> You are rebels, every one of you.

30    In vain I struck down your sons,
> the lesson was not learnt;
> still your own sword devoured your prophets
> like a ravening lion.

31    *c* Have I shown myself inhospitable to Israel
> like some wilderness or waterless land?
> Why do my people say, 'We have broken away;
> we will never come back to thee'?

32      Will a girl forget her finery
> or a bride her ribbons?
> Yet my people have forgotten me
> over and over again.

---

*a* rushing alone into: *prob. rdg.; Heb.* a wild-ass taught in.    *b* towns: *or* blood-spattered altars.    *c Prob. rdg.; Heb. prefixes* You, O generation, see the word of the LORD.

How well you pick your way in search of lovers!               33
Why! even the worst of women can learn from you.
Yes, and there is blood on the corners of your robe—          34
the life-blood of the innocent poor.
    You did not get it by housebreaking
    but by your sacrifices under every oak.
You say, 'I am innocent;                                       35
surely his anger has passed away.'
But I will challenge your claim
    to have done no sin.
Why do you so lightly change your course?                     36
Egypt will fail you as Assyria did;
    you shall go out from here,                                37
        each of you with his hands above his head,
    for the LORD repudiates those in whom you trusted,
    and from them you shall gain nothing.

If a man puts away his wife                                    3
    and she leaves him,
and if she then becomes another's,
    may he go back to her again?
Is not that woman defiled,
    a forbidden thing?
You have played the harlot with many lovers;
    can you come back to me?
    says the LORD.
Look up to the high bare places and see:                      2
    where have you not been ravished?
You sat by the wayside to catch lovers,
    like an Arab lurking in the desert,
and defiled the land
    with your fornication and your wickedness.
Therefore the showers were withheld                           3
    and the spring rain failed.
But yours was a harlot's brow,
    and you were resolved to show no shame.
Not so long since, you called me 'Father,                     4
    dear friend of my youth',
thinking, 'Will he be angry for ever?                         5
    Will he rage eternally?'
This is how you spoke; you have done evil
    and gone unchallenged.

In the reign of King Josiah, the LORD said to me, Do you see what   6
apostate Israel did? She went up to every hill-top and under every spreading tree, and there she played the whore. Even after she had done all this,   7
I said to her, Come back to me, but she would not. That faithless woman,
her sister Judah, saw it all; she saw too that I had put apostate Israel away   8
and given her a note of divorce because she had committed adultery. Yet

that faithless woman, her sister Judah, was not afraid; she too has gone and
9 played the whore. She defiled the land with her thoughtless harlotry and
10 her adulterous worship of stone and wood. In spite of all this that faithless
woman, her sister Judah, has not come back to me in good faith, but only
in pretence. This is the very word of the LORD.
11 The LORD said to me, Apostate Israel is less to blame than that faithless
12 woman Judah. Go and proclaim this message to the north:

> Come back to me, apostate Israel,
>     says the LORD,
> I will no longer frown on you.
> For my love is unfailing, says the LORD,
>     I will not be angry for ever.
> 13 Only you must acknowledge your wrongdoing,
>     confess your rebellion against the LORD your God.
> Confess your promiscuous traffic with foreign gods
> under every spreading tree,
>     confess that you have not obeyed me.
> This is the very word of the LORD.

14 Come back to me, apostate children, says the LORD, for I am patient
with you, and I will take you, one from a city and two from a clan, and bring
15 you to Zion. There will I give you shepherds after my own heart, and they
16 shall lead you with knowledge and understanding. In those days, when
you have increased and become fruitful in the land, says the LORD, men
shall speak no more of the Ark of the Covenant of the LORD; they shall not
17 think of it nor remember it nor resort to it; it will be needed no more. At
that time Jerusalem shall be called the Throne of the LORD. All nations
shall gather in Jerusalem to honour the LORD's name; never again shall
18 they follow the promptings of their evil and stubborn hearts. In those days
Judah shall join Israel, and together they shall come from a northern land
into the land I gave their fathers as their patrimony.

> 19 I said, How gladly would I treat you as a son,
>     giving you a pleasant land,
>         a patrimony fairer than that of any nation!
> I said, You shall call me Father
>     and never cease to follow me.
> 20 But like a woman who is unfaithful to her lover,
>     so you, Israel, were unfaithful to me.
>     This is the very word of the LORD.
> 21 Hark, a sound of weeping on the bare places,
>     Israel's people pleading for mercy!
> For they have taken to crooked ways
>     and ignored the LORD their God.
> 22 Come back to me, wayward[a] sons;
>     I will heal your apostasy.

*a Or apostate.*

O LORD, we come! We come to thee;
for thou art our God.
There is no help in worship on the hill-tops,                23
    no help from clamour on the heights;
truly in the LORD our God
    is Israel's only salvation.
From our early days                                          24
Baal, god of shame, has devoured
    the fruits of our fathers' labours,
their flocks and herds, their sons and daughters.
Let us lie down in shame, wrapped round by our dishonour,   25
for we have sinned against the LORD our God,
    both we and our fathers,
    from our early days till now,
and we have not obeyed the LORD our God.

If you will but come back, O Israel,                         **4**
if you will but come back to me, says the LORD,
if you will banish your loathsome idols from my sight,
    and stray no more,
    if you swear by the life of the LORD,                2
    in truth, in justice and uprightness,
then shall the nations pray to be blessed like you *a*
    and in you *a* shall they boast.
These are the words of the LORD to the men of Judah and Jerusalem:   3
Break up your fallow ground,
    do not sow among thorns,
circumcise yourselves to the service of the LORD,           4
    circumcise your hearts,
    men of Judah and dwellers in Jerusalem,
lest the fire of my fury blaze up and burn unquenched,
    because of your evil doings.
Tell this in Judah,                                          5
    proclaim it in Jerusalem,
blow the trumpet throughout the land,
    sound the muster,
give the command, Stand to!—and let us fall back
    on the fortified cities.
Raise the signal—To Zion!                                    6
    make for safety, lose no time,
for I bring disaster out of the north,
    and dire destruction.
A lion has come out from his lair,                           7
    the destroyer of nations;
he has struck his tents, he has broken camp,
    to harry your land
and lay your cities waste and unpeopled.

*a* Prob. rdg.; Heb. him.

8     Well may you put on sackcloth,
      beat the breast and wail,
     for the anger of the LORD
      is not averted from us.

9     On that day, says the LORD,
     the hearts of the king and his officers shall fail them,
     priests shall be struck with horror and prophets dumbfounded.

10     And I said, O Lord GOD, thou surely didst deceive this people and Jerusalem in saying, 'You shall have peace', while the sword is at our throats.

11     At that time this people and Jerusalem shall be told:

     A scorching wind from the high bare places in the wilderness
      sweeps down upon my people,
     no breeze for winnowing or for cleansing;

12     a wind too strong for these
      will come at my bidding,
     and now I will state my case against them.

13     Like clouds the enemy advances
      with a whirlwind of chariots;
     his horses are swifter than eagles—
      alas, we are overwhelmed!

14     O Jerusalem, wash the wrongdoing from your heart
      and you may yet be saved;
     how long will you cherish
      your evil schemes?

15     Hark, a runner from Dan,
      tidings of evil from Mount Ephraim!

16     Tell all this to the nations,
      proclaim the doom of Jerusalem:
     hordes of invaders come from a distant land,
     howling against the cities of Judah.

17     Their pickets are closing in all round her,
      because she has rebelled against me.
     This is the very word of the LORD.

18     Your own ways, your own deeds
     have brought all this upon you;
     this is your punishment,
     and all this comes of your rebellion.[a]

19     Oh, the writhing of my bowels
      and the throbbing of my heart!
     I cannot keep silence.
     I hear the sound of the trumpet,
      the sound of the battle-cry.

20     Crash upon crash,
      the land goes down in ruin,

[a] your rebellion: *prob. rdg.*; *Heb. obscure.*

　　my tents are thrown down,
　　　　their coverings torn to shreds.
　　How long must I see the standard raised　　　　21
　　　　and hear the trumpet call?
　　My people are fools, they know nothing of me;　　22
　　silly children, with no understanding,
　　they are clever only in wrongdoing,
　　　　and of doing right they know nothing.

　　I saw the earth, and it was without form and void;　　23
　　　　the heavens, and their light was gone.
　　I saw the mountains, and they reeled;　　　　24
　　　　all the hills rocked to and fro.
　　I saw, and there was no man,　　　　25
　　　　and the very birds had taken flight.
　　I saw, and the farm-land was wilderness,　　26
　　　　and the towns all razed to the ground,
　　before the LORD in his anger.
　　　　These are the words of the LORD:　　27
　　The whole land shall be desolate,
　　　　though I will not make an end of it.
　　Therefore the earth will mourn　　　　28
　　and the heavens above turn black.
　　For I have made known my purpose;
　　I will not relent or change my mind.

　　At the sound of the horsemen and archers　　29
　　　　the whole country is in flight;
　　they creep into caves, they hide in thickets,
　　　　they scramble up the crags.
　　Every town is forsaken,
　　　　no one dwells there.

　　And you, what are you doing?　　　　30
　　When you dress yourself in scarlet,
　　　　deck yourself out with golden ornaments,
　　and make your eyes big with antimony,
　　　　you are beautifying yourself to no purpose.
　　Your lovers spurn you
　　　　and are out for your life.
　　I hear a sound as of a woman in labour,　　31
　　　　the sharp cry of one bearing her first child.
　　It is Zion, gasping for breath,
　　　　clenching her fists.
　　Ah me! I am weary,
　　　　weary of slaughter.

　　Go up and down the streets of Jerusalem　　5
　　　　and see for yourselves;
　　search her wide squares:

can you find any man who acts justly,
who seeks the truth,
that I may forgive that city?

2   Men may swear by the life of the LORD,
but they only perjure themselves.

3   O LORD, are thine eyes not set upon the truth?
Thou didst strike them down,
but they took no heed;
didst pierce them to the heart,
but they refused to learn.
They set their faces harder than flint
and refused to come back.

4   I said, 'After all, these are the poor,
these are stupid folk,
who do not know the way of the LORD,
the ordinances of their God.

5   I will go to the great
and speak with them;
for they will know the way of the LORD,
the ordinances of their God.'
But they too have broken the yoke
and snapped their traces.

6   Therefore a lion out of the scrub shall strike them down,
a wolf from the plains shall ravage them;
a leopard shall prowl about their cities
and maul any who venture out.
For their rebellious deeds are many,
their apostasies past counting.

7   How can I forgive you for all this?
Your sons have forsaken me and sworn by gods
that are no gods.
I gave them all they needed, yet they preferred adultery,
and haunted the brothels;

8   each neighs after another man's wife,
like a well-fed and lusty stallion.

9   Shall I not punish them for this?
the LORD asks.
Shall I not take vengeance
on such a people?

10   Go along her rows of vines and slash them,
yet do not make an end of them.
Hack away her green branches,
for they are not the LORD's.

11   Faithless are Israel and Judah,
both faithless to me.
This is the very word of the LORD.

12   They have denied the LORD,
saying, 'He does not exist.

No evil shall come upon us;
we shall never see sword or famine.
The prophets will prove mere wind,　　　　　　　13
the word not in them.'

And so, because you talk in this way, these are the words of the LORD　14
the God of Hosts to me:

I will make my words a fire in your mouth;
and it shall burn up this people like brushwood.

I bring against you, Israel, a nation from afar,　　　　　15
an ancient people established long ago,
says the LORD.
A people whose language you do not know,
whose speech you will not understand;
they are all mighty warriors,　　　　　　　　　16
their jaws are a grave, wide open,
to devour your harvest and your bread,　　　　　17
to devour your sons and your daughters,
to devour your flocks and your herds,
to devour your vines and your fig-trees.
They shall batter down the cities in which you trust,*a*
walled though they are.

But in those days, the LORD declares, I will still not make an end of you.　18
When you ask, 'Why has the LORD our God done all this to us?' I shall　19
answer, 'As you have forsaken me and served alien gods in your own land,
so shall you serve foreigners*b* in a land that is not yours.'

Tell this to the people of Jacob,　　　　　　　20
proclaim it in Judah:
Listen, you foolish and senseless people,　　　　21
who have eyes and see nothing,
ears and hear nothing.
Have you no fear of me? says the LORD;　　　　22
will you not shiver before me,
before me, who made the shivering sand to bound the sea,
a barrier it never can pass?
Its waves heave and toss but they are powerless;
roar as they may, they cannot pass.
But this people has a rebellious and defiant heart,　　　23
rebels they have been and now they are clean gone.
They did not say to themselves,　　　　　　24
'Let us fear the LORD our God,
who gives us the rains of autumn
and spring showers in their turn,
who brings us unfailingly
fixed seasons of harvest.'

---

*a* *Prob. rdg.; Heb. adds* with the sword.　　　*b* *Or* foreign gods.

25
But your wrongdoing has upset nature's order,
and your sins have kept from you her kindly gifts.

26
For among my people there are wicked men,
who lay snares like a fowler's net [a]
and set deadly traps to catch men.

27
Their houses are full of fraud,
as a cage is full of birds.
They grow rich and grand,

28
bloated and rancorous;
their thoughts are all of evil,
and they refuse to do justice,
the claims of the orphan they do not put right
nor do they grant justice to the poor.

29
Shall I not punish them for this?
says the LORD;
shall I not take vengeance
on such a people?

30
An appalling thing, an outrage,
has appeared in this land:

31
prophets prophesy lies and priests go hand in hand with them,
and my people love to have it so.
How will you fare at the end of it all?

6
Save yourselves, men of Benjamin,
come out of Jerusalem,
blow the trumpet in Tekoa,
fire the beacon on Beth-hakkerem,
for calamity looms from the north
and great disaster.

2
Zion, delightful and lovely:
her end is near—

3
she to whom the shepherds come
and bring their flocks with them.
There they pitch their tents all round her,
each grazing his own strip of pasture.

4
Declare war solemnly against her;
come, let us attack her at noon.
Too late! the day declines
and the shadows lengthen.

5
Come then, let us attack her by night
and destroy her palaces.

6
These are the words of the LORD of Hosts:
Cut down the trees of Jerusalem
and raise siege-ramps against her,
the city whose name is Licence,
oppression is rampant in her.

[a] who ... net: *prob. rdg.; Heb. unintelligible.*

As a well keeps its water fresh,　　　　　　　　　　7
so she keeps her evil fresh.
Violence and outrage echo in her streets;
sickness and wounds stare me in the face.
　Learn your lesson, Jerusalem,　　　　　　　　　8
lest my love for you be torn from my heart,
　and I leave you desolate,
　a land where no one can live.
These are the words of the Lord of Hosts:　　　　9
　Glean the remnant of Israel
　　like a vine,
pass your hand like a vintager one last time
　over the branches.
　To whom can I address myself,　　　　　　　　10
　to whom give solemn warning? Who will hear me?
Their ears are uncircumcised;
　they cannot listen;
they treat the Lord's word as a reproach;
　they show no concern with it.
But I am full of the anger of the Lord,　　　　　11
　I cannot hold it in.
I must pour it out on the children in the street
and on the young men in their gangs.
Man and wife alike shall be caught in it,
　the greybeard and the very old.
Their houses shall be turned over to others,　　　12
their fields and their women alike.
　For I will raise my hand, says the Lord,
against the people of the country.
For all, high and low,　　　　　　　　　　　　13
　are out for ill-gotten gain;
prophets and priests are frauds,
　every one of them;
they dress my people's wound, but skin-deep only,　14
　with their saying, 'All is well.'
All well? Nothing is well!
Are they ashamed when they practise their abominations?　15
　Ashamed? Not they!
They can never be put out of countenance.
Therefore they shall fall with a great crash,*a*
and be brought to the ground on the day of my reckoning.
　The Lord has said it.

　These are the words of the Lord: Stop at the cross-roads; look for　16
the ancient paths; ask, 'Where is the way that leads to what is good?'
Then take that way, and you will find rest for yourselves. But they said,
'We will not.' Then I will appoint watchmen to direct you; listen for their　17

*a* with a great crash: *or* where they fall *or* among the fallen.

18 trumpet-call. But they said, 'We will not.' Therefore hear, you nations, and
19 take note, all you who witness it, of the plight of this people. Listen, O
earth, I bring ruin on them, the harvest of all their scheming; for they have
20 given no thought to my words and have spurned my instruction. What
good is it to me if frankincense is brought from Sheba and fragrant spices
from distant lands? I will not accept your whole-offerings, your sacrifices
21 do not please me. Therefore these are the words of the LORD:

I will set obstacles before this people
    which shall bring them to the ground;
fathers and sons, friends and neighbours
    shall all perish together.

22 These are the words of the LORD:

See, a people is coming from a northern land,
    a great nation rouses itself from earth's farthest corners.
23      They come with bow and sabre, cruel men and pitiless,
    bestriding their horses, they sound like the thunder of the sea,
    they are like men arrayed for battle against you, Zion.
24          We have heard tell of them
                and our hands hang limp,
    agony grips us, the anguish of a woman in labour.
25          Do not go out into the country,
                do not walk by the high road;
            for the foe, sword in hand,
                is a terror let loose.
26      Daughter of my people, wrap yourself in sackcloth,
            sprinkle ashes over yourself, wail bitterly,
        as one who mourns an only son;
            in an instant shall the marauder be upon us.

27          I have appointed you an assayer of my people;
        you will know how to test them and will assay their conduct;
28              arch-rebels all of them,
            mischief-makers, corrupt to a man.
29      The bellows puff and blow, the furnace glows;
                in vain does the refiner smelt the ore,
            lead, copper and iron*a* are not separated out.
30      Call them spurious silver;
                for the LORD has spurned them.


## *False religion and its punishment*

7 1 2  THIS WORD CAME FROM THE LORD to Jeremiah. Stand at the gate of
    the LORD's house and there make your proclamation: Listen to the
words of the LORD, all you men of Judah who come in through these gates
3 to worship him. These are the words of the LORD of Hosts the God of

---

*a* copper and iron: *transposed from after* mischief-makers *in verse 28.*

Israel: Mend your ways and your doings, that I may let you live in this
place. You keep saying, 'This place*a* is the temple of the LORD, the temple  4
of the LORD, the temple of the LORD!' This catchword of yours is a lie;
put no trust in it. Mend your ways and your doings, deal fairly with one  5
another, do not oppress the alien, the orphan, and the widow, shed no  6
innocent blood in this place, do not run after other gods to your own ruin.
Then will I let you live in this place, in the land which I gave long ago to  7
your forefathers for all time. You gain nothing by putting your trust in  8
this lie. You steal, you murder, you commit adultery and perjury, you  9
burn sacrifices to Baal, you run after other gods whom you have not known;
then you come and stand before me in this house, which bears my name, and  10
say, 'We are safe'; safe, you think, to indulge in all these abominations. Do  11
you think that this house, this house which bears my name, is a robbers'
cave? I myself have seen all this, says the LORD. Go to my shrine at Shiloh,  12
which once I made a dwelling for my Name, and see what I did to it because
of the wickedness of my people Israel. And now you have done all these  13
things, says the LORD; though I took pains to speak to you, you did not
listen, and though I called, you gave no answer. Therefore what I did to  14
Shiloh I will do to this house which bears my name, the house in which
you put your trust, the place I gave to you and your forefathers; I will  15
fling you away out of my sight, as I flung away all your kinsfolk, the whole
brood of Ephraim.

Offer up no prayer, Jeremiah, for this people, raise no plea or prayer on  16
their behalf, and do not intercede with me; for I will not listen to you.
Do you not see what is going on in the cities of Judah and in the streets of  17
Jerusalem? Children are gathering wood, fathers lighting fires, women  18
kneading dough to make crescent-cakes in honour of the queen of heaven;
and drink-offerings are poured out to other gods than me—all to provoke
and hurt me. But is it I, says the LORD, whom they hurt? No; it is them-  19
selves, covering their own selves with shame. Therefore, says the Lord GOD,  20
my anger and my fury shall fall on this place, on man and beast, on trees
and crops, and it shall burn unquenched.

These are the words of the LORD of Hosts the God of Israel: Add whole-  21
offerings to sacrifices and eat the flesh if you will. But when I brought your  22
forefathers out of Egypt, I gave them no commands about whole-offering
and sacrifice; I said not a word about them. What I did command them  23
was this: If you obey me, I will be your God and you shall be my people.
You must conform to all my commands, if you would prosper. But they  24
did not listen; they paid no heed, and persisted in disobedience with evil
and stubborn hearts; they looked backwards and not forwards, from the  25
day when your forefathers left Egypt until now. I took pains to send to
them all my servants the prophets; they did not listen to me, they paid no  26
heed, but were obstinate and proved even more wicked than their forefathers. When you tell them this, they will not listen to you; if you call them,  27
they will not answer. Then you shall say to them, This is the nation that  28
did not obey the LORD its God nor accept correction; truth has perished,
it is heard no more on their lips.

*a* This place: *prob. rdg.; Heb.* Those.

29        O Jerusalem, cut off your hair,
       the symbol of your dedication, and throw it away;
       raise up a lament on the high bare places.

For the LORD has spurned the generation which has roused his wrath, and
30 has abandoned them. For the men of Judah have done what is wrong in my
eyes, says the LORD. They have defiled with their loathsome idols the house
31 that bears my name, they have built a shrine of Topheth in the Valley of
Ben-hinnom, at which to burn their sons and daughters; that was no
32 command of mine, nor did it ever enter my thought. Therefore a time is
coming, says the LORD, when it shall no longer be called Topheth or the
Valley of Ben-hinnom, but the Valley of Slaughter; for the dead shall be
33 buried in Topheth because there is no room elsewhere. So the bodies of
this people shall become food for the birds of the air and the wild beasts,
34 and there will be no one to scare them away. From the cities of Judah and
the streets of Jerusalem I will banish all sounds of joy and gladness, the
voice of the bridegroom and the bride; for the land shall become desert.

**8**    At that time, says the LORD, men shall bring out from their graves the
bones of the kings of Judah, of the officers, priests, and prophets, and of
2 all who lived in Jerusalem. They shall expose them to the sun, the moon,
and all the host of heaven, whom they loved and served and adored, to
whom they resorted and bowed in worship. Those bones shall not be
3 gathered up nor buried but shall become dung on the ground. All the
survivors of this wicked race, wherever I have banished them, would rather
die than live. This is the very word of the LORD of Hosts.

4    You shall say to them, These are the words of the LORD:

       If men fall, can they not also rise?
       If a man breaks away, can he not return?
5        Then why are this people so wayward,
       incurable in their waywardness?
       Why have they clung to their treachery
       and refused to return to their obedience?
6        I have listened to them
       and heard not one word of truth,
       not one sinner crying remorsefully,
       'Oh, what have I done?'
       Each one breaks away [a] in headlong career
       as a war-horse plunges in battle.

7        The stork in the sky
       knows the time to migrate,
       the dove and the swift and the wryneck
       know the season of return;
       but my people do not know the ordinances of the LORD.
8        How can you say, 'We are wise,
       we have the law of the LORD',
       when scribes with their lying pens
       have falsified it?

       *a* breaks away: *or* is wayward.

The wise are put to shame, they are dismayed and have lost their wits.   9
  They have spurned the word of the LORD,
    and what sort of wisdom is theirs?
Therefore will I give their wives to other men   10
  and their lands to new owners.
  For all, high and low,
    are out for ill-gotten gain;
  prophets and priests are frauds,
    every one of them;
  they dress my people's wound, but skin-deep only,   11
    with their saying, 'All is well.'
  All well? Nothing is well!
  Are they ashamed when they practise their abominations?   12
  Ashamed? Not they!
    They can never be put out of countenance.
Therefore they shall fall with a great crash,*a*
and be brought to the ground on the day of my reckoning.
  The LORD has said it.
  I would gather their harvest, says the LORD,   13
  but there are no grapes on the vine,
  no figs on the fig-tree;
    even their leaves are withered.
Why do we sit idle? Up, all of you together,   14
let us go into our walled cities and there meet our doom.
  For the LORD our God has struck us down,
  he has given us a draught of bitter poison;
    for we have sinned against the LORD.
  Can we hope to prosper when nothing goes well?   15
  Can we hope for respite when the terror falls suddenly?
  The snorting of his horses is heard from Dan;   16
at the neighing of his stallions the whole land trembles.
The enemy come; they devour the land and all its store,
  city and citizens alike.
Beware, I am sending snakes against you,   17
  vipers, such as no man can charm,
    and they shall bite you.
  This is the very word of the LORD.

How can I bear my sorrow?*b*   18
  I am sick at heart.
Hark, the cry of my people   19
  from a distant land:
  'Is the LORD not in Zion?
    Is her King no longer there?'
  Why do they provoke me with their images
  and foreign gods?

---

*a* with a great crash: *or* where they fall *or* among the fallen.   *b* How . . . sorrow?:
*prob. rdg.; Heb. unintelligible.*

20      Harvest is past, summer is over,
            and we are not saved.
21      I am wounded at the sight of my people's wound;
        I go like a mourner, overcome with horror.
22      Is there no balm in Gilead,
            no physician there?
        Why has no new skin grown over their wound?

9       Would that my head were all water,
            my eyes a fountain of tears,
        that I might weep day and night
            for my people's dead!

2       Oh that I could find in the wilderness a shelter by the wayside,
        that I might leave my people and depart!
            Adulterers are they all, a mob of traitors.
3           The tongue is their weapon, a bow ready bent.
        Lying, not truth, is master in the land.
        They run from one sin to another,
            and for me they care nothing.
        This is the very word of the LORD.

4       Be on your guard, each man against his friend;
            put no trust even in a brother.
        Brother supplants brother,*a*
            and friend slanders friend.
5       They make game of their friends
            but never speak the truth;
        they have trained their tongues to lies;
            deep in their sin, they cannot retrace their steps.
6       Wrong follows wrong, deceit follows deceit;
            they refuse to acknowledge me.
        This is the very word of the LORD.
7       Therefore these are the words of the LORD of Hosts:
        I am their refiner and will assay them.
        How can I disregard my people?
8       Their tongue is a cruel arrow,
            their mouths speak lies.
        One speaks amicably to another,
            while inwardly he plans a trap for him.
9       Shall I not punish them for this?
            says the LORD;
        shall I not take vengeance
            on such a people?

10      Over the mountains will I raise weeping and wailing,
            and over the desert pastures will I chant a dirge.

*a* Brother supplants brother: *or* Every brother is a supplanter like Jacob (*cp. Gen.*
*27. 35 and note*).

> They are scorched and untrodden,
>   they hear no lowing of cattle;
> birds of the air and beasts have fled and are gone.

> I will make Jerusalem a heap of ruins, a haunt of wolves,   11
> and the cities of Judah an unpeopled waste.

What man is wise enough to understand this, to understand what the 12
LORD has said and to proclaim it? Why has the land become a dead land, scorched like the desert and untrodden? The LORD said, It is because they 13 forsook my law which I set before them; they neither obeyed me nor conformed to it. They followed the promptings of their own stubborn hearts, 14 they followed the Baalim as their forefathers had taught them. Therefore 15 these are the words of the LORD of Hosts the God of Israel: I will feed this people with wormwood and give them bitter poison to drink. I will scatter 16 them among nations whom neither they nor their forefathers have known; I will harry them with the sword until I have made an end of them. These are the words of the LORD of Hosts:   17

> Summon the wailing women to come,
>   send for the women skilled in keening
> to come quickly and raise a lament for us,   18
>   that our eyes may run with tears
>   and our eyelids be wet with weeping.
> Hark, hark, lamentation is heard in Zion:   19
>   How fearful is our ruin! How great our shame!
> We have left our lands, our houses have been pulled down.
>   Listen, you women, to the words of the LORD,   20
>   that your ears may catch what he says.
>   Teach your daughters the lament,
>   let them teach one another this dirge:
> Death has climbed in through our windows,   21
>   it has entered our palaces,
>   it sweeps off the children in the open air
>   and drives young men from the streets.

This is the word of the LORD:   22
> The corpses of men shall fall and lie like dung in the fields,
>   like swathes behind the reaper, but no one shall gather them.

These are the words of the LORD:   23
> Let not the wise man boast of his wisdom
>   nor the valiant of his valour;
> let not the rich man boast of his riches;
>   but if any man would boast, let him boast of this,   24
>   that he understands and knows me.
> For I am the LORD, I show unfailing love,
>   I do justice and right upon the earth;
>   for on these I have set my heart.
>   This is the very word of the LORD.

25  The time is coming, says the LORD, when I will punish all the circum-
26  cised, Egypt and Judah, Edom and Ammon, Moab, and all who haunt the
fringes of the desert;[a] for all alike, the nations and Israel, are uncircumcised
in heart.

**10**  Listen, Israel, to this word that the LORD has spoken against you:

2       Do not fall into the ways of the nations,
            do not be awed by signs in the heavens;
            it is the nations who go in awe of these.
3       For the carved images of the nations are a sham,
            they are nothing but timber cut from the forest,
            worked with his chisel by a craftsman;
4       he adorns it with silver and gold,
        fastening them on with hammer and nails
            so that they do not fall apart.
5       They can no more speak than a scarecrow in a plot of cucumbers;
            they must be carried, for they cannot walk.
        Do not be afraid of them: they can do no harm,
            and they have no power to do good.
6       Where can one be found like thee, O LORD?
        Great thou art and great the might of thy name.
7       Who shall not fear thee, king of the nations?
            for fear is thy fitting tribute.
        Where among the wisest of the nations and all their royalty
            can one be found like thee?
8       They are fools and blockheads one and all,
            learning their nonsense from a log of wood.
9       The beaten silver is brought from Tarshish
            and the gold from Ophir;
        all are the work of craftsmen and goldsmiths.
        They are draped in violet and purple,
            all the work of skilled men.
10      But the LORD is God in truth,
            a living god, an eternal king.
        The earth quakes under his wrath,
            nations cannot endure his fury.

11  [You shall say this to them: The gods who did not make heaven and earth
shall perish from the earth and from under these heavens.]

12[b]     God made the earth by his power,
            fixed the world in place by his wisdom,
            unfurled the skies by his understanding.
13      At the thunder of his voice the waters in heaven are amazed;[c]
            he brings up the mist from the ends of the earth,
            he opens rifts[d] for the rain
            and brings the wind out of his storehouses.

---

[a] who ... desert: or the dwellers in the desert who clip the hair on their temples.    [b] *Verses*
*12-16 : cp. 51. 15-19.*    [c] At the thunder ... amazed: *prob. rdg.; Heb.* At the sound
of his giving tumult of waters in heaven.    [d] rifts: *prob. rdg.; Heb.* lightnings.

All men are brutish and ignorant;　　　　　　　　14
every goldsmith is discredited by his idol;
for the figures he casts are a sham,
there is no breath in them.
They are worth nothing, mere mockeries,　　　　　15
which perish when their day of reckoning comes.
God, Jacob's creator, is not like these;　　　　　16
　for he is the maker of all.
　Israel is the people he claims as his own;
　the LORD of Hosts is his name.

Put your goods together and carry them out of the country,　17
　living as you are under siege.
For these are the words of the LORD:　　　　　18
　This time I will uproot
the whole population of the land,
and I will press them hard and squeeze them dry.

　O the pain of my wounds!　　　　　　　　19
　Cruel are the blows I suffer.
But this is my plight, I said, and I must endure it.
My home is ruined, my tent-ropes all severed,　　　20
　my sons have left me and are gone,
　there is no one to pitch my tent again,
　　no one to put up its curtains.
　　The shepherds of the people are mere brutes;　　21
　they never consult the LORD,
　　and so they do not prosper,
and all their flocks at pasture are scattered.

Hark, a rumour comes flying,　　　　　　　22
　then a mounting uproar from the land of the north,
an army to make Judah's cities desolate, a haunt of wolves.
　I know, O LORD,　　　　　　　　23
　that man's ways are not of his own choosing;
　nor is it for a man to determine his course in life.
Correct us, O LORD, but with justice, not in anger,　24
　lest thou bring us almost to nothing.
Pour out thy fury on nations　　　　　　　25
　that have not acknowledged thee,
on tribes that have not invoked thee by name;
for they have devoured Jacob and made an end of him
　and have left his home a waste.

## Warnings and punishment

11 1 2 THE WORD WHICH CAME TO JEREMIAH from the LORD: Listen to the terms of this covenant and repeat them to the men of Judah and the
3 inhabitants of Jerusalem. Tell them, These are the words of the LORD the God of Israel: A curse on the man who does not observe the terms of this
4 covenant by which I bound your forefathers when I brought them out of Egypt, from the smelting-furnace. I said, If you obey me and do all that I
5 tell you, you shall become my people and I will become your God. And I will thus make good the oath I swore to your forefathers, that I would give them a land flowing with milk and honey, the land you now possess.
6 I answered, 'Amen, LORD.' Then the LORD said: Proclaim all these terms in the cities of Judah and in the streets of Jerusalem. Say, Listen to the
7 terms of this covenant and carry them out. I have protested to your forefathers since I brought them out of Egypt, till this day; I took pains to
8 warn them: Obey me, I said. But they did not obey; they paid no attention to me, but each followed the promptings of his own stubborn and wicked heart. So I brought on them all the penalties laid down in this covenant by which I had bound them, whose terms they did not observe.

9 The LORD said to me, The men of Judah and the inhabitants of Jeru-
10 salem have entered into a conspiracy: they have gone back to the sins of their earliest forefathers and refused to listen to me. They have followed other gods and worshipped them; Israel and Judah have broken the
11 covenant which I made with their fathers. Therefore these are the words of the LORD: I now bring on them disaster from which they cannot escape;
12 though they cry to me for help I will not listen. The inhabitants of the cities of Judah and of Jerusalem may go and cry for help to the gods to whom they have burnt sacrifices; they will not save them in the hour of disaster.
13 For you, Judah, have as many gods as you have towns; you have set up as
14 many altars to burn sacrifices to Baal as there are streets in Jerusalem. So offer up no prayer for this people; raise no cry or prayer on their behalf, for I will not listen when they call to me in the hour of disaster.

15     What right has my beloved in my house
      with her shameless ways?
    Can the flesh of fat offerings on the altar
      ward off the disaster that threatens you?
16     Once the LORD called you an olive-tree,
      leafy and fair;
    but now with a great roaring noise
      you will feel sharp anguish; *a*
    fire sets its leaves alight
      and consumes *b* its branches.

17 The LORD of Hosts who planted you has threatened you with disaster, because of the harm Israel and Judah brought on themselves when they provoked me to anger by burning sacrifices to Baal.

*a* you will feel sharp anguish: *transposed from end of verse 15.*      *b* consumes: *prob. rdg.; Heb.* they consume.

It was the LORD who showed me, and so I knew; he opened my eyes to  18
what they were doing. I had been like a sheep led obedient to the slaughter;  19
I did not know that they were hatching plots against me and saying, 'Let
us cut down the tree while the sap is in it; let us destroy him out of the
living, so that his very name shall be forgotten.'

> O LORD of Hosts who art a righteous judge,                           20
>> testing the heart and mind,
>> I have committed my cause to thee;
>> let me see thy vengeance upon them.

Therefore these are the words of the LORD about the men of Anathoth who  21
seek to take my life, and say, 'Prophesy no more in the name of the LORD
or we will kill you'—these are his words: I will punish them: their young  22
men shall die by the sword, their sons and daughters shall die by famine.
Not one of them shall survive; for in the year of their reckoning I will  23
bring ruin on the men of Anathoth.

> O LORD, I will dispute with thee, for thou art just;             **12**
>> yes, I will plead my case before thee.
> Why do the wicked prosper
>> and traitors live at ease?
>> Thou hast planted them and their roots strike deep,               2
>> they grow up and bear fruit.
>> Thou art ever on their lips,
>>> yet far from their hearts.
> But thou knowest me, O LORD, thou seest me;                       3
>> thou dost test my devotion to thyself.
> Drag them away like sheep to the shambles;
>> set them apart for the day of slaughter.

>> How long must the country lie parched                            4
>> and its green grass wither?
> No birds and beasts are left, because its people are so wicked,
> because they say, 'God will not see what we are doing.'

> If you have raced with men and the runners have worn you down,    5
>> how then can you hope to vie with horses?
>> If you fall headlong in easy country,
>> how will you fare in Jordan's dense thickets?
> All men, your brothers and kinsmen, are traitors to you,          6
>> they are in full cry after you;
> trust them not, for all the fine words they give you.

>> I have forsaken the house of Israel,                             7
>> I have cast off my own people.
> I have given my beloved into the power of her foes.
> My own people have turned on me like a lion from the scrub,       8
> roaring against me; therefore I hate them.
>> Is this land of mine a hyena's lair,                             9
>> with birds of prey hovering all around it?
> Come, you wild beasts; come, all of you, flock to the feast.

10     Many shepherds have ravaged my vineyard
        and trampled down my field,
    they have made my pleasant field a desolate wilderness,
11     made it a waste land, waste and waterless, to my sorrow.
    The whole land is waste, and no one cares.

12   Plunderers have swarmed across the high bare places in the wilderness,
a sword of the LORD devouring the land from end to end; no creature can
find peace.

13     Men sow wheat and reap thistles;
        they sift but get no grain.
    They are disappointed of their[a] harvest
    because of the anger of the LORD.

14     These are the words of the LORD about all those evil neighbours who are
laying hands on the land which I gave to my people Israel as their patri-
16[b] mony: I will uproot them from that[c] soil. Yet, if they will learn the ways
of my people, swearing by my name, 'By the life of the LORD', as they
taught my people to swear by the Baal, they shall form families among my
17 people. But if they will not listen, I will uproot that people, uproot and
15 destroy them. Also I will uproot Judah from among them; but after I
have uprooted them, I will have pity on them again and will bring each
man back to his patrimony and his land. This is the very word of the LORD.

**13**     These were the words of the LORD to me: Go and buy yourself a linen
2 girdle and put it round your waist, but do not let it come near water. So
3 I bought it as the LORD had told me and put it round my waist. The LORD
4 spoke to me a second time: Take the girdle which you bought and put round
your waist; go at once to Perath and hide it in a crevice among the rocks.
5 6 So I went and hid the girdle at[d] Perath, as the LORD had told me. After
a long time the LORD said to me: Go at once to Perath and fetch back the
7 girdle which I told you to hide there. So I went to Perath and looked for
the place where I had hidden it, but when I picked it up, I saw that it was
8 9 spoilt, and no good for anything. Again the LORD spoke to me and these
were his words: Thus will I spoil the gross pride of Judah, the gross pride
10 of Jerusalem. This wicked nation has refused to listen to my words; they
have followed other gods, serving them and bowing down to them. So it
11 shall be[e] like this girdle, no good for anything. For, just as a girdle is
bound close to a man's waist, so I bound all Israel and all Judah to myself,
says the LORD, so that they should become my people to win a name for
me, and praise and glory; but they did not listen.

12     You shall say this to them: These are the words of the LORD the God of
Israel: Wine-jars should be filled with wine. They will answer, 'We know
13 quite well that wine-jars should be filled with wine.' Then you shall say
to them, These are the words of the LORD: I will fill all the inhabitants of
this land with wine until they are drunk—kings of David's line who sit on
14 his throne, priests, prophets, and all who live in Jerusalem. I will dash them

---

[a] *Prob. rdg.; Heb.* your.         [b] *The rest of verse 14 and verse 15 transposed to follow*
destroy them *in verse 17.*     [c] *Prob. rdg.; Heb.* their.     [d] *Or by.*     [e] *Prob.*
*rdg.; Heb.* And let it be.

to pieces one against another, fathers and sons alike, says the LORD, I will
show them no compassion or pity or tenderness; nor refrain from destroying them.<sup>a</sup>

> Hear and attend. Be not too proud to listen,                    15
>     for it is the LORD who speaks.
> Ascribe glory to the LORD your God                               16
>     before the darkness falls,
> before your feet stumble
>     on the twilit hill-sides,
> before he turns the light you look for
>     to deep gloom and thick darkness.
> If in those depths of gloom you will not listen,                 17
> then for very anguish I can only weep and shed tears,<sup>b</sup>
> my eyes must stream with tears;
>     for the LORD's flock is carried away into captivity.
> Say to the king and the queen mother:<sup>c</sup>               18
>     Down, take a humble seat,
> for your proud crowns are fallen from your heads.
> Your cities in the Negeb are besieged,                           19
> and no one can relieve them;
> all Judah has been swept into exile,
>     swept clean away.
> Lift up your eyes and see                                        20
>     those who are coming from the north.
> Where is the flock that was entrusted to you,
>     the flock you were so proud of?
> What will you say when you suffer                                21
>     because your leaders<sup>d</sup> cannot be found,
> though it was you who trained them
>     to be your head?
> Will not pangs seize you,
>     like the pangs of a woman in labour,
>         when you wonder,                                         22
> 'Why has this come upon me?'
> For your many sins your skirts are torn off you,
>     your limbs uncovered.
>
> Can the Nubian change his skin,                                  23
>     or the leopard its spots?
> And you? Can you do good,
>     you who are schooled in evil?
> Therefore I will scatter you<sup>e</sup> like chaff            24
>     driven by the desert wind.
> This is your lot, the portion of the rebel,                      25
>     measured out by me, says the LORD,

---

<sup>a</sup> nor refrain . . . them: *or* so corrupt are they.     <sup>b</sup> If . . . shed tears: *or* If you will
not listen to this, for very anguish I must weep in secret.              <sup>c</sup> *Or* queen.
<sup>d</sup> leaders: *transposed from next line.*     <sup>e</sup> *Prob. rdg.; Heb.* them.

because you have forsaken me
and trusted in false gods.

26      So I myself have stripped off your skirts
and laid bare your shame.

27      Your adulteries, your lustful neighing,
your wanton lewdness, are an offence to me.[a]
On the hills and in the open country
I have seen your foul deeds.
Alas, Jerusalem, unclean that you are!
How long, how long will you delay?[b]

**14**   This came to Jeremiah as the word of the LORD concerning the drought:

2       Judah droops, her cities languish,
her men sink to the ground;
Jerusalem's cry goes up.

3       Their flock-masters send their boys for water;
they come to the pools but find no water there.
Back they go, with empty vessels;

4       the produce[c] of the land has failed,
because there is no rain.
The farmers' hopes are wrecked,
they uncover their heads for grief.

5       The hind calves in the open country
and forsakes her young
because there is no grass;

6       for lack of herbage, wild asses stand on the high bare places
and snuff the wind for moisture,
as wolves do, and their eyes begin to fail.

7       Though our sins testify against us,
yet act,[d] O LORD, for thy own name's sake.
Our disloyalties indeed are many; we have sinned against thee.

8       O hope of Israel, their saviour in time of trouble,
must thou be a stranger in the land,
a traveller pitching his tent for a night?

9       Must thou be like a man suddenly overcome,
like a man powerless to save himself?
Thou art in our midst, O LORD,
and thou hast named us thine; do not forsake us.

10      The LORD speaks thus of this people: They love to stray from my ways,
they wander where they will. Therefore he has no more pleasure in them;

11      he remembers their guilt now, and punishes their sins. Then the LORD

12      said to me, Do not pray for the well-being of this people. When they fast, I
will not listen to their cry; when they sacrifice whole-offering and grain-
offering, I will not accept them. I will make an end of them with sword,
with famine and pestilence. But I said, O Lord GOD, the prophets tell them

13      that they shall see no sword and suffer no famine; for thou wilt give them

---

[a] *an offence to me* (*Heb.* you): *transposed from verse 26.*      [b] *How . . . delay?: prob.
rdg.; Heb. unintelligible.*      [c] *the produce: prob. rdg.; Heb. obscure.*      [d] *Or turn away.*

lasting prosperity in this place. The LORD answered me, The prophets 14
are prophesying lies in my name. I have not sent them; I have given them
no charge; I have not spoken to them. The prophets offer them false
visions, worthless augury, and their own deluding fancies. Therefore these 15
are the words of the LORD about the prophets who, though not sent by me,
prophesy in my name and say that neither sword nor famine shall touch
this land: By sword and by famine shall those prophets meet their end.
The people to whom they prophesy shall be flung out into the streets of 16
Jerusalem, victims of famine and sword; they, their wives, their sons, and
their daughters, with no one to bury them: I will pour down upon them the
evil they deserve.

> So this is what you shall say to them:                    17
> Let my eyes stream with tears,
> ceaselessly, day and night.
> For the virgin daughter of my people
> has been broken in pieces,
> struck by a cruel blow.
> If I go out into the country,                    18
> I see men slain by the sword;
> if I enter the city, I see the ravages of famine;
> prophet and priest alike
> go begging round the land and are never at rest.
> Hast thou spurned Judah utterly?                    19
> Dost thou loathe Zion?
> Why hast thou wounded us, and there is no remedy;
> why let us hope for better days, and we find nothing good,
> for a time of healing, and all is disaster?
> We acknowledge our wickedness,                    20
> the guilt of our forefathers;
> O LORD, we have sinned against thee.
> Do not despise the place where thy name dwells                    21
> nor bring contempt on the throne of thy glory.
> Remember thy covenant with us and do not make it void.
> Can any of the false gods of the nations give rain?                    22
> Or do the heavens send showers of themselves?
> Art thou not God, O LORD,
> that we may hope in thee?
> It is thou only who doest*a* all these things.

The LORD said to me, Even if Moses and Samuel stood before me, I 15
would not be moved to pity this people. Banish them from my presence;
let them be gone. When they ask where they are to go, you shall say to them, 2
These are the words of the LORD:

> Those who are for death shall go to their death,
> and those for the sword to the sword;
> those who are for famine to famine,
> and those for captivity to captivity.

*a Or* madest.

3    Four kinds of doom do I ordain for them, says the LORD: the sword to
kill, dogs to tear, birds of prey from the skies and beasts from their lairs
4 to devour and destroy. I will make them repugnant to all the kingdoms
of the earth, because of the crimes of Manasseh son of Hezekiah, king of
Judah, in Jerusalem.

5        Who will take pity on you, Jerusalem,
         who will offer you consolation?
       Who will turn aside to wish you well?
6      You cast me off, says the LORD,
         you turned your backs on me.
       So I stretched out my hand and ruined you;
         I was weary of relenting.
7        I winnowed them and scattered them
         through the cities of the land;
       I brought bereavement on them, I destroyed my people,
         for they would not abandon their ways.
8        I made widows among them more in number
         than the sands of the sea;
       I brought upon them a horde of raiders *a*
         to plunder at high noon.
       I made the terror of invasion fall upon them
         all in a moment.
9        The mother of seven sons grew faint,
         she sank into a swoon;
       her light was quenched while it was yet day;
         she was left humbled and shamed.
       All the remnant I gave to perish by the sword
         at the hand of their enemies.
       This is the very word of the LORD.

## Confessions and addresses

10        Alas, alas, my mother, that you ever gave me birth!
       a man doomed to strife, with the whole world against me.
       I have borrowed from no one, I have lent to no one,
         yet all men abuse me.
11 The LORD answered,

       But I will greatly strengthen you;
       in time of distress and in time of disaster
       I will bring the enemy to your feet.
12      Can iron break steel from the north?*b*
15        LORD, thou knowest;
       remember me, LORD, and come to visit me,
       take vengeance for me on my persecutors.

*a* I brought . . . raiders: *prob. rdg.; Heb. obscure.*   *b* *Prob. rdg.; Heb. adds* and bronze.
*Heb. also adds* (13) I will give away your wealth as spoil, and your treasure for no payment,
because of your sin throughout your country. (14) I will make your enemies pass through a
land you do not know; for my anger is a blazing fire and it shall burn for ever (*cp. 17. 3, 4*).

Be patient with me and take me not away,
see what reproaches I endure for thy sake.
I have to suffer those who despise thy words,                    16
but thy word is joy and happiness to me,
for thou hast named me thine,
O LORD, God of Hosts.
I have never kept company with any gang of roisterers,          17
or made merry with them;
because I felt thy hand upon me I have sat alone;
for thou hast filled me with indignation.
Why then is my pain unending,                                   18
my wound desperate and incurable?
Thou art to me like a brook that is not to be trusted,
whose waters fail.

This was the LORD's answer:                                     19
If you will turn back to me, I will take you back
and you shall stand before me.
If you choose noble utterance and reject the base,
you shall be my spokesman.
This people will turn again to you,
but you will not turn to them.
To withstand them I will make you impregnable,                  20
a wall of bronze.
They will attack you but they will not prevail,
for I am with you to deliver you
and save you, says the LORD;
I will deliver you from the wicked,                             21
I will rescue you from the ruthless.

The word of the LORD came to me: You shall not marry a wife; you **16** 1 2
shall have neither son nor daughter in this place. For these are the words 3
of the LORD concerning sons and daughters born in this place, the mothers
who bear them and the fathers who beget them in this land: When men 4
die, struck down by deadly ulcers, there shall be no wailing for them and
no burial; they shall be like dung lying upon the ground. When men
perish by sword or famine, their corpses shall become food for birds and
for beasts.

For these are the words of the LORD: Enter no house where there is a 5
mourning-feast; do not go in to wail or to bring comfort, for I have withdrawn my peace from this people, says the LORD, my love and affection.
High and low shall die in this land, but there shall be no burial, no wailing 6
for them; no one shall gash himself, or shave his head. No one shall give 7
the mourner a portion of bread to console him for the dead, nor give him
the cup of consolation, even for his father or mother. Nor shall you enter 8
a house where there is feasting, to sit eating and drinking there. For these 9
are the words of the LORD of Hosts, the God of Israel: In your own days,
in the sight of you all, and in this very place, I will silence all sounds of
joy and gladness, and the voice of bridegroom and bride.

10 When you tell this people all these things they will ask you, 'Why has the LORD decreed that this great disaster is to come upon us? What wrong have we done? What sin have we committed against the LORD our God?'

11 You shall answer, Because your forefathers forsook me, says the LORD, and followed other gods, serving them and bowing down to them. They forsook

12 me and did not keep my law. And you yourselves have done worse than your forefathers; for each of you follows the promptings of his wicked and

13 stubborn heart instead of obeying me. So I will fling you headlong out of this land into a country unknown to you and to your forefathers; there you

14 can serve other gods day and night, for I will show you no favour. Therefore, says the LORD, the time is coming when men shall no longer swear,

15 'By the life of the LORD who brought the Israelites up from Egypt', but, 'By the life of the LORD who brought the Israelites back from a northern land and from all the lands to which he had dispersed them'; and I will bring them back to the soil which I gave to their forefathers.

16 I will send for many fishermen, says the LORD, and they shall fish for them. After that I will send for many hunters, and they shall hunt them

17 out from every mountain and hill and from the crevices in the rocks. For my eyes are on all their ways; they are not hidden from my sight, nor is

18 their wrongdoing concealed from me. I will first make them pay in full*a* for the wrong they have done and the sin they have committed by defiling with the dead lumber of their idols the land which belongs to me, and by filling it with their abominations.

19         O LORD, my strength and my stronghold,
           my refuge in time of trouble,
       to thee shall the nations come
           from the ends of the earth and say,
       Our forefathers inherited only a sham,
           an idol vain and useless.

20        Can man make gods for himself?
           They would be no gods.

21        Therefore I am teaching them,
       once for all will I teach them
           my power and my might,
       and they shall learn that my name is the LORD.

**17** The sin of Judah is recorded with an iron tool, engraved on the tablet of their heart with a point of adamant and carved on the horns of their

2 altars to bear witness against them.*b* Their altars and their sacred poles

3 stand by every spreading tree, on the heights and the hills in the mountain country. I will give away your wealth as spoil, and all your treasure for no

4 payment,*c* because of your*d* sin throughout your country. You will lose possession*e* of the patrimony which I gave you. I will make you serve your enemies as slaves in a land you do not know; for my anger is a blazing fire*f* and it shall burn for ever.

*a* in full: *or* double.    *b* to bear . . . them: *prob. rdg.; Heb.* as their sons remember.
*c* for no payment: *prob. rdg., cp. 15. 13; Heb.* your hill-shrines.    *d* your: *prob. rdg.,*
*cp. 15. 13; Heb. om.*    *e* You . . . possession: *prob. rdg.; Heb.* obscure.    *f* for . . .
fire: *prob. rdg., cp. 15. 14; Heb.* for you have kindled a fire in my anger.

These are the words of the LORD:                                    5

   A curse on the man who trusts in man
     and leans for support on human kind,
     while his heart is far from the LORD!
   He shall be like a juniper in the desert;                    6
     when good comes he shall not see it.
   He shall dwell among the rocks in the wilderness,
     in a salt land where no man can live.
Blessed is the man who trusts in the LORD,                          7
   and rests his confidence upon him.
He shall be like a tree planted by the waterside,                   8
   that stretches its roots along the stream.
When the heat comes it has nothing to fear;
   its spreading foliage stays green.
   In a year of drought it feels no care,
     and does not cease to bear fruit.

   The heart is the most deceitful of all things,               9
desperately sick;[a] who can fathom it?
   I, the LORD, search the mind                                 10
     and test the heart,
   requiting man for his conduct,
     and as his deeds deserve.
   Like a partridge which gathers into its nest                 11
     eggs which it has not laid,
   so is the man who amasses wealth unjustly.
   Before his days are half done he must leave it,
     and prove but a fool at the last.

   O throne of glory, exalted from the beginning,               12
     the place of our sanctuary,
     O LORD on whom Israel's hope is fixed,                    13
     all who reject thee shall be put to shame;
   all in this land who forsake thee shall be humbled,[b]
for they have rejected the fountain of living water.[c]
Heal me, O LORD, and I shall be healed,                             14
   save me and I shall be saved;
   for thou art my praise.
They say to me, 'Where is the word of the LORD?                     15
   Let it come if it can!'
It is not the thought of disaster that makes me press after thee;   16
   never did I desire this day of despair.
   Thou knowest all that has passed my lips;
     it was approved by thee.
   Do not become a terror to me;                                17
     thou art my only refuge on the day of disaster.

---

[a] the most . . . sick: *or* too deceitful for any man.   [b] humbled: *prob. rdg.; Heb.*
written.   [c] *Prob. rdg.; Heb. adds* the LORD.

18      May my persecutors be foiled, not I;
        may they be terrified, not I.
        Bring on them the day of disaster;
        destroy them, destroy them utterly.

19      These were the words of the LORD to me: Go and stand in the Benjamin *a*
Gate, through which the kings of Judah go in and out, and in all the gates
20  of Jerusalem. Say, Hear the words of the LORD, you princes of Judah,
all you men of Judah, and all you inhabitants of Jerusalem who come
21  in through these gates. These are the words of the LORD: Observe this with
care, that you do not carry any load on the sabbath or bring it through the
22  gates of Jerusalem. You shall not bring any load out of your houses or do
any work on the sabbath, but you shall keep the sabbath day holy as I
23  commanded your forefathers. Yet they did not obey or pay attention, but
24  obstinately refused to hear or learn their lesson. Now if you will obey me,
says the LORD, and refrain from bringing any load through the gates of
this city on the sabbath, and keep that day holy by doing no work on it,
25  then kings shall come through the gates of this city, kings *b* who shall sit
on David's throne. They shall come riding in chariots or on horseback,
escorted by their captains, by the men of Judah and the inhabitants of
26  Jerusalem; and this city shall be inhabited for ever. People shall come from
the cities of Judah, the country round Jerusalem, the land of Benjamin,
the Shephelah, the hill-country and the Negeb, bringing whole-offerings,
sacrifices, grain-offerings, and frankincense, bringing also thank-offerings
27  to the house of the LORD. But if you do not obey me by keeping the sabbath
day holy and by not carrying any load as you come through the gates of
Jerusalem on the sabbath, then I will set fire to those gates; it shall consume
the palaces of Jerusalem and shall not be put out.

18 1 2     These are the words which came to Jeremiah from the LORD: Go down
at once to the potter's house, and there I will tell you what I have to say.
3   So I went down to the potter's house and found him working at the wheel.
4   Now and then a vessel he was making out of the clay would be spoilt in his
hands, and then he would start again and mould it into another vessel to
5 6   his liking. Then the word of the LORD came to me: Can I not deal with you,
Israel, says the LORD, as the potter deals with his clay? You are clay in my
7   hands like the clay in his, O house of Israel. At any moment I may threaten
8   to uproot a nation or a kingdom, to pull it down and destroy it. But if the
nation which I have threatened turns back from its wicked ways, then I
9   shall think better of the evil I had in mind to bring on it. Or at any moment
10  I may decide to build or to plant a nation or a kingdom. But if it does evil
in my sight and does not obey me, I shall think better of the good I had in
11  mind for it. Go now and tell the men of Judah and the inhabitants of Jerusalem that these are the words of the LORD: I am the potter; I am preparing
evil for you and perfecting my designs against you. Turn back, every one
12  of you, from his evil course; mend your ways and your doings. But they
answer, 'Things are past hope. We will do as we like, and each of us will

---

*a* Benjamin: *prob. rdg.; Heb.* sons of the people.       *b* *Prob. rdg.; Heb. adds and*
officers.

follow the promptings of his own wicked and stubborn heart.' Therefore 13
these are the words of the LORD:

> Inquire among the nations: who ever heard the like of this?
> The virgin Israel has done a thing most horrible.
> Will the snow cease to fall on the rocky slopes of Lebanon?     14
> Will the cool rain streaming in torrents ever fail?
> No, but my people have forgotten me;      15
> > they burn sacrifices to a mere idol,
> > so they stumble in their paths, the ancient ways,
> > and they take to byways and unmade roads;
> > their own land they lay waste,      16
> > and men will jeer at it for ever in contempt.
> All who go by will be horror-struck and shake their heads.
> > Like a wind from the east      17
> I will scatter them before their enemies.
> > In the hour of their downfall
> I will turn my back towards them and not my face.

'Come, let us decide what to do with Jeremiah', men say. 'There will 18
still be priests to guide us, still wise men to advise, still prophets to proclaim
the word. Come, let us invent some charges against him; let us pay no
attention to his message.'

> But do thou, O LORD, pay attention,      19
> > and hear what my opponents are saying against me.
> Is good to be repaid with evil? *ᵃ*      20
> Remember how I stood before thee,
> pleading on their behalf
> to avert thy wrath from them.
> Therefore give their sons over to famine,      21
> > leave them at the mercy of the sword.
> Let their women be childless and widowed,
> > let death carry off their men,
> let their young men be cut down in battle.
> Bring raiders upon them without warning,      22
> and let screams of terror ring out from their houses.
> For they have dug a pit to catch me
> and have hidden snares for my feet.
> Well thou knowest, O LORD,      23
> all their murderous plots against me.
> > Do not blot out their wrongdoing
> or annul their sin;
> when they are brought stumbling into thy presence,
> deal with them on the day of thy anger.

These are the words of the LORD: Go and buy an earthenware jar. **19**
Then take with you some of the elders of the people and of the priests,
and go out to the Valley of Ben-hinnom, on which the Gate of the Pot- 2
sherds opens, and there proclaim what I tell you. Say, Hear the word of 3

*ᵃ Prob. rdg.; Heb. adds* they have dug a pit for me (*cp. verse 22*).

the LORD, you princes of Judah and inhabitants of Jerusalem. These are the words of the LORD of Hosts the God of Israel: I will bring on this place

4 a disaster which shall ring in the ears of all who hear of it. For they have forsaken me, and treated this place as if it were not mine, burning sacrifices to other gods whom neither they nor their fathers nor the kings of Judah

5 have known, and filling this place with the blood of the innocent. They have built shrines to Baal, where they burn their sons as whole-offerings to Baal. It was no command of mine; I never spoke of it; it never entered my

6 thought. Therefore, says the LORD, the time is coming when this place shall no longer be called Topheth or the Valley of Ben-hinnom, but the

7 Valley of Slaughter. In this place I will shatter the plans of Judah and Jerusalem as a jar is shattered; I will make the people fall by the sword before their enemies, at the hands of those who would kill them, and I will

8 give their corpses to the birds and beasts to devour. I will make this city a scene of horror and contempt, so that every passer-by will be horror-

9 struck and jeer in contempt at the sight of its wounds. I will compel men to eat the flesh of their sons and their daughters; they shall devour one another's flesh in the dire straits to which their enemies and those who

10 would kill them will reduce them in the siege. Then you must shatter the

11 jar before the eyes of the men who have come with you and say to them, These are the words of the LORD of Hosts: Thus will I shatter this people and this city as one shatters an earthen vessel so that it cannot be mended, and the dead shall be buried in Topheth because there is no room elsewhere

12 to bury them. This is what I will do to this place, says the LORD, and to

13 those who live there: I will make this city like Topheth. Because of their defilement, the houses of Jerusalem and those of the kings of Judah shall be like Topheth, every one of the houses on whose roofs men have burnt sacrifices to the host of heaven and poured drink-offerings to other gods.

14 Jeremiah came in from Topheth, where the LORD had sent him to pro-phesy, and stood in the court of the LORD's house. He said to all the people,

15 These are the words of the LORD of Hosts the God of Israel: I am bringing on this city and on all its blood-spattered altars every disaster with which I have threatened it, for its people have remained obstinate and refused to listen to me.

20 When Pashhur son of Immer the priest, the chief officer in the house

2 of the LORD, heard Jeremiah prophesying these things, he had him flogged<sup>a</sup> and put him into the stocks at the Upper Gate of Benjamin, in the house of

3 the LORD. The next morning he released him, and Jeremiah said to him,

4 The LORD has called you not Pashhur but Magor-missabib.<sup>b</sup> For these are the words of the LORD: I will make you a terror to yourself and to all your friends; they shall fall by the sword of the enemy before your very eyes. I will hand over all Judah to the king of Babylon, and he will deport

5 them to Babylon and put them to the sword. I will give all this city's store of wealth and riches and all the treasures of the kings of Judah to their enemies; they shall seize them as spoil and carry them off to Babylon.

6 You, Pashhur, and all your household shall go into captivity and come to Babylon. There shall you die and there shall you be buried, you and all your friends to whom you have been a false prophet.

---

<sup>a</sup> had him flogged: *or* struck him.   <sup>b</sup> *That is* Terror let loose.

O Lord, thou hast duped me, and I have been thy dupe;    7
    thou hast outwitted me and hast prevailed.
I have been made a laughing-stock all the day long,
    everyone mocks me.
Whenever I speak I must needs cry out    8
    and proclaim violence and destruction.
I am reproached and mocked all the time
    for uttering the word of the Lord.
Whenever I said, 'I will call him to mind no more,    9
    nor speak in his name again',
then his word was imprisoned in my body,
    like a fire blazing in my heart,
and I was weary with holding it under,
    and could endure no more.
     For I heard many whispering, *a*    10
    'Denounce him! we will denounce him.'
All my friends were on the watch for a false step,
    saying, 'Perhaps he may be tricked, then we can catch him
     and take our revenge.'
But the Lord is on my side, strong and ruthless,    11
    therefore my persecutors shall stumble and fall powerless.
Bitter shall be their abasement when they fail,
    and their shame shall long be remembered.
O Lord of Hosts, thou dost test the righteous    12
    and search the depths of the heart;
    to thee have I committed my cause,
    let me see thee take vengeance on them.
Sing to the Lord, praise the Lord;    13
    for he rescues the poor from those who would do them wrong.

A curse on the day when I was born!    14
    Be it for ever unblessed,
    the day when my mother bore me!
A curse on the man who brought word to my father,    15
    'A child is born to you, a son',
    and gladdened his heart!
That man shall fare like the cities    16
    which the Lord overthrew without mercy.
He shall hear cries of alarm in the morning
    and uproar at noon,
because death did not claim me before birth,    17
    and my mother did not become my grave,
    her womb great with me for ever.
Why did I come forth from the womb    18
    to know only sorrow and toil,
    to end my days in shame?

---

*a*   *Prob. rdg.; Heb. adds* Terror let loose.

## Kings and prophets denounced

**21** THE WORD WHICH CAME FROM THE LORD to Jeremiah when King Zedekiah sent to him Pashhur son of Malchiah and Zephaniah the
2 priest, son of Maaseiah, with this request: 'Nebuchadrezzar king of Babylon is making war on us; inquire of the LORD on our behalf. Perhaps the LORD will perform a miracle as he has done in past times, so that
3 Nebuchadrezzar may raise the siege.' But Jeremiah answered them, Tell
4 Zedekiah, these are the words of the LORD the God of Israel: I will turn back upon you your own weapons with which you are fighting the king of Babylon and the Chaldaeans besieging you outside the wall; and I will
5 bring them into the heart of this city. I myself will fight against you in burning rage and great fury, with an outstretched hand and a strong arm.
6 I will strike down those who live in this city, men and cattle alike; they
7 shall die of a great pestilence. After that, says the LORD, I will take Zedekiah king of Judah, his courtiers and the people, all in this city who survive pestilence, sword, and famine, and hand them over to Nebuchadrezzar the king of Babylon, to their enemies and those who would kill them. He shall put them to the sword and shall show no pity, no mercy or compassion.
8    You shall say further to this people, These are the words of the LORD: I offer you now a choice between the way of life and the way of death.
9 Whoever remains in this city shall die by sword, by famine, or by pestilence, but whoever goes out to surrender to the Chaldaeans, who are now besieging you, shall survive; he shall take home his life, and nothing more.
10 I have set my face against this city, meaning to do them harm, not good, says the LORD. It shall be handed over to the king of Babylon, and he shall burn it to the ground.

11            To the royal house of Judah.
              Listen to the word of the LORD:
12            O house of David, these are the words of the LORD:
              Administer justice betimes,
              rescue the victim from his oppressor,
          lest the fire of my fury blaze up and burn unquenched
              because of your evil doings.

13            The LORD says,
          I am against you who lie in the valley,
              you, the rock in the plain,
          you who say, 'Who can come down upon us?
              Who can penetrate our lairs?'
14            I will punish you as you deserve,
                  says the LORD,
          I will kindle fire on the heathland around you,
          and it shall consume everything round about.

**22**    These were the words of the LORD: Go down to the house of the king of
2 Judah and say this: Listen to the words of the LORD, O king of Judah, you who sit on David's throne, you and your courtiers and your people who

come in at these gates. These are the words of the LORD: Deal justly and 3
fairly, rescue the victim from his oppressor, do not ill-treat or do violence
to the alien, the orphan or the widow, do not shed innocent blood in this
place. If you obey, and only if you obey, kings who sit on David's throne shall 4
yet come riding through these gates in chariots and on horses, with their
retinue of courtiers and people. But if you do not listen to my words, then 5
by myself I swear, says the LORD, this house shall become a desolate ruin.
For these are the words of the LORD about the royal house of Judah: 6

> Though you are dear to me as Gilead
> or as the heights of Lebanon,
> I swear that I will make you a wilderness,
> a land of unpeopled cities.
> I will dedicate an armed host to fight against you, 7
> a ravening horde;
> they shall cut your choicest cedars down
> and fling them on the fire.

Men of many nations shall pass by this city and say to one another, 8
'Why has the LORD done this to such a great city?' The answer will be, 9
'Because they forsook their covenant with the LORD their God; they
worshipped other gods and served them.'

> Weep not for the dead nor brood over his loss. 10
> Weep rather for him who has gone away,
> for he shall never return,
> never again see the land of his birth.

For these are the words of the LORD concerning Shallum son of Josiah, 11
king of Judah, who succeeded his father on the throne and has gone away:
He shall never return; he shall die in the place of his exile and never see 12
this land again.

> Shame on the man who builds his house by unjust means 13
> and completes its roof-chambers by fraud,
> making his countrymen work without payment,
> giving them no wage for their labour!
> Shame on the man who says, 'I will build a spacious house 14
> with airy roof-chambers,
> set windows in it, panel it with cedar
> and paint it with vermilion'!
> If your cedar is more splendid, 15
> does that prove you a king?
> Think of your father: he ate and drank,
> dealt justly and fairly; all went well with him.
> He dispensed justice to the lowly and poor; *a* 16
> did not this show he knew me? says the LORD.
> But you have no eyes, no thought for anything but gain, 17
> set only on the innocent blood you can shed,
> on cruel acts of tyranny.

*a* *Prob. rdg.; Heb. adds* all went well (*repeated from verse 15*).

18    Therefore these are the words of the LORD concerning Jehoiakim son
of Josiah, king of Judah:

> For him no mourner shall say, 'Alas, brother, dear brother!'
> no one say, 'Alas, lord and master!'

19    He shall be buried like a dead ass,
>         dragged along and flung out
>         beyond the gates of Jerusalem.

20    Get up into Lebanon and cry aloud,
>         make your voice heard in Bashan,
> cry aloud from Abarim, for all who befriend you are broken.

21    I spoke to you in your days of prosperous ease,
>         but you said, 'I will not listen.'
> This is how you behaved since your youth;
>         never have you obeyed me.

22    The wind shall carry away all your friends,*a*
> your lovers shall depart into exile.
> Then you will be put to shame and abashed
>         for all your evil deeds.*b*

23    You dwellers in Lebanon, who make your nests among the
>              cedars,
> how you will groan when the pains come upon you,
>         like the pangs of a woman in labour!

24    By my life, says the LORD, Coniah son of Jehoiakim, king of Judah,
shall be the signet-ring on my right hand no longer. Yes, Coniah, I will
25   pull you off. I will hand you over to those who seek your life, to those
you fear, to Nebuchadrezzar king of Babylon and to the Chaldaeans.
26   I will fling you headlong, you and the mother who gave you birth, into
another land, a land where you were not born; and there shall you both
27   die. They shall never come back to their own land, the land for which
they long.
28    This man, Coniah, then, is he a mere puppet, contemptible and broken,
only a thing unwanted? Why else are he and his children flung out headlong and hurled into a country they do not know?
29 30  O land, land, land, hear the words of the LORD: These are the words
of the LORD: Write this man down as stripped of all honour, one who in
his own life shall not prosper, nor shall he leave descendants to sit in
prosperity on David's throne or rule again in Judah.

**23**    Shame on the shepherds who let the sheep of my flock scatter and be
2    lost! says the LORD. Therefore these are the words of the LORD the God
of Israel about the shepherds who tend my people: You have scattered
and dispersed my flock. You have not watched over them; but I am
3    watching you to punish you for your evil doings, says the LORD. I will
myself gather the remnant of my sheep from all the lands to which I
have dispersed them. I will bring them back to their homes, and they
4    shall be fruitful and increase. I will appoint shepherds to tend them;

---

*a Or* shepherds.          *b Or* calamities.

they shall never again know fear or dismay or punishment. This is the
very word of the LORD.

> The days are now coming, says the LORD,     5
>    when I will make a righteous Branch spring from David's line,
>      a king who shall rule wisely,
>   maintaining law and justice in the land.
>     In his days Judah shall be kept safe,     6
>    and Israel shall live undisturbed.
>     This is the name to be given to him:
>      The LORD is our Righteousness.

Therefore the days are coming, says the LORD, when men shall no longer 7
swear, 'By the life of the LORD who brought Israel up from Egypt', but, 8
'By the life of the LORD who brought the descendants of the Israelites back
from a northern land and from all the lands to which he had dispersed them,
to live again on their own soil.'

On the prophets.     9

> Deep within me my heart is broken,
>   there is no strength in my bones;
> because of the LORD, because of his dread words
>   I have become like a drunken man,
>   like a man overcome with wine.
> For the land is full of adulterers,     10
> and because of them the earth lies parched,
>    the wild pastures have dried up.
> The course that they run is evil,
>    and their powers are misused.
> For prophet and priest alike are godless;     11
> I have come upon the evil they are doing even in my own house.
>    This is the very word of the LORD.

> Therefore the path shall turn slippery beneath their feet;     12
> they shall be dispersed in the dark and shall fall there.
> For I will bring disaster on them when their day of reckoning comes.
>    This is the very word of the LORD.
>   I found the prophets of Samaria men of no sense:     13
> they prophesied in Baal's name and led my people Israel astray.
> In the prophets of Jerusalem I see a thing most horrible:     14
>   adulterers and hypocrites that they are,
>     they encourage evildoers,
>   so that no man turns back from his sin;
> to me all her inhabitants are like Sodom and Gomorrah.

These then are the words of the LORD of Hosts concerning the prophets: 15

> I will give them wormwood to eat
>   and a bitter poison to drink;
>    for a godless spirit has spread over all the land
>    from the prophets of Jerusalem.

16 These are the words of the LORD of Hosts:

> Do not listen to what the prophets say,
> who buoy you up with false hopes;
> the vision they report springs from their own imagination,
> it is not from the mouth of the LORD.

17 They say to those who spurn the word of the LORD,
> 'Prosperity shall be yours';
> and to all who follow the promptings of their own stubborn heart they say,
> 'No disaster shall befall you.'

18 But which of them has stood in the council of the LORD,
> seen him and heard his word?
> Which of them has listened to his word and obeyed?

19 See what a scorching wind has gone out from the LORD,
> a furious whirlwind;
> it whirls round the heads of the wicked.

20 The LORD's anger is not to be turned aside,
> until he has accomplished and fulfilled his deep designs.
> In days to come you will fully understand.

21 I did not send these prophets, yet they went in haste;
> I did not speak to them, yet they prophesied.

22 If they have stood in my council,
> let them proclaim my words to my people
> and turn them from their evil course and their evil doings.

23 Am I a god only near at hand, not far away?

24 Can a man hide in any secret place and I not see him?
> Do I not fill heaven and earth?
> This is the very word of the LORD.

25 I have heard what the prophets say, the prophets who speak lies in my
26 name and cry, 'I have had a dream, a dream!' How long will it be till they
change their tune, these prophets who prophesy lies and give voice to
27 their own inventions? By these dreams which they tell one another these
men think they will make my people forget my name, as their fathers
28 forgot my name for the name of*a* Baal. If a prophet has a dream, let him
tell his dream; if he has my word, let him speak my word in truth. What
29 has chaff to do with grain? says the LORD. Do not my words scorch*b* like
30 fire? says the LORD. Are they not like a hammer that splinters rock? I am
against the prophets, says the LORD, who steal my words from one another
31 for their own use. I am against the prophets, says the LORD, who concoct
32 words of their own and then say, 'This is his very word.' I am against the
prophets, says the LORD, who dream lies and retail them, misleading my
people with wild and reckless falsehoods. It was not I who sent them or
commissioned them, and they will do this people no good. This is the
very word of the LORD.

33 When you are asked by this people or by a prophet or priest what the
burden of the LORD's message is, you shall answer, You are his burden,
34 and I shall throw you down, says the LORD. If prophet or priest or layman

---

*a* for the name of: *or* by their worship of.          *b* scorch: *prob. rdg.; Heb.* thus.

uses the term 'the LORD's burden', I will punish that man and his family.
The form of words you shall use in speaking amongst yourselves is: 'What  35
answer has the LORD given?' or, 'What has the LORD said?' You shall  36
never again mention 'the burden of the LORD'; that is reserved for the
man to whom he entrusts his message. If you do, you will make nonsense
of the words of the living God, the LORD of Hosts our God. This is the  37
form you shall use in speaking to a prophet: 'What answer has the LORD
given?' or, 'What has the LORD said?' But to any of you who do say, 'the  38
burden of the LORD', the LORD speaks thus: Because you say, 'the burden
of the LORD', though I sent to tell you not to say it, therefore I myself will  39
carry you like a burden and throw you down, casting out of my sight both
you and the city which I gave to you and to your forefathers. I will inflict  40
on you endless reproach, endless shame which shall never be forgotten.

## *Two visions*

THIS IS WHAT THE LORD SHOWED ME: I saw two baskets of figs set  24
out in front of the sanctuary of the LORD. This was after Nebuchadrezzar king of Babylon had deported from Jerusalem Jeconiah son of Jehoiakim, king of Judah, with the officers of Judah, the craftsmen and the
smiths,[a] and taken them to Babylon. In one basket the figs were very good,  2
like the figs that are first ripe; in the other the figs were very bad, so bad
that they were not fit to eat. The LORD said to me, 'What are you looking  3
at, Jeremiah?' 'Figs,' I answered, 'the good very good, and the bad so bad
that they are not fit to eat.' Then this word came to me from the LORD:  4
These are the words of the LORD the God of Israel: I count the exiles of  5
Judah whom I sent away from this place to the land of the Chaldaeans as
good as these good figs. I will look upon them meaning to do them good,  6
and I will restore them to their land; I will build them up and not pull them
down, plant them and not uproot them. I will give them the wit to know  7
me, for I am the LORD; they shall become my people and I will become
their God, for they will come back to me with all their heart. But Zedekiah  8
king of Judah, his officers and the survivors of Jerusalem, whether they
remain in this land or live in Egypt—all these I will treat as bad figs, says
the LORD, so bad that they are not fit to eat. I will make them repugnant to  9
all the kingdoms of the earth, a reproach, a by-word, an object-lesson and
a thing of ridicule wherever I drive them. I will send against them sword,  10
famine, and pestilence until they have vanished from the land which I
gave to them and to their forefathers.

This came to Jeremiah as the word concerning all the people of Judah  25
in the fourth year of Jehoiakim son of Josiah, king of Judah (that is the
first year of Nebuchadrezzar king of Babylon). This is what the prophet  2
Jeremiah said to all Judah and all the inhabitants of Jerusalem: For  3
twenty-three years, from the thirteenth year of Josiah son of Amon, king
of Judah, to the present day, I have been receiving the words of the LORD
and taking pains to speak to you, but you have not listened. The LORD has  4

---

[a] the smiths: *or* the harem.

5 taken pains to send you his servants the prophets, but you have not listened or shown any inclination to listen. If each of you will turn from his wicked ways and evil courses, he has said, then you shall for ever live on the soil

6 which the LORD gave to you and to your forefathers. You must not follow other gods, serving and worshipping them, nor must you provoke me to anger with the idols your hands have made; then I will not do you harm.

7 But you did not listen to me, says the LORD; you provoked me to anger with the idols your hands had made and so brought harm upon yourselves.

8 Therefore these are the words of the LORD of Hosts: Because you have

9 not listened to my words, I will summon all the tribes of the north, says the LORD: I will send for my servant Nebuchadrezzar king of Babylon. I will bring them against this land and all its inhabitants and all these nations round it; I will exterminate them and make them a thing of horror

10 and derision, a scandal for ever. I will silence all sounds of joy and gladness among them, the voices of bridegroom and bride, and the sound of

11 the handmill; I will quench the light of every lamp. For seventy years this whole country shall be a scandal and a horror; these nations shall be in

12 subjection to the king of Babylon. When those seventy years are completed, I will punish the king of Babylon and his people, says the LORD, for all their misdeeds and make the land of the Chaldaeans a waste for ever.

13 I will bring upon that country all I have said, all that is written in this book,

14 all that Jeremiah has prophesied against these peoples. They will be the victims*a* of mighty nations and great kings, and thus I will repay them for their actions and their deeds.

15 These were the words of the LORD the God of Israel to me: Take from my hand this cup of fiery wine and make all the nations to whom I send

16 you drink it. When they have drunk it they will vomit and go mad; such

17 is the sword which I am sending among them. Then I took the cup from the LORD's hand, gave it to all the nations to whom he sent me and made

18 them drink it: to Jerusalem, the cities of Judah, its kings and officers, making them a scandal, a thing of horror and derision and an object of

19 ridicule, as they still are: to Pharaoh king of Egypt, his courtiers, his

20 officers, all his people, and all his rabble of followers, all the kings of the land of Uz, all the kings of the Philistines: to Ashkelon, Gaza, Ekron, and

21 22 the remnant of Ashdod: also to Edom, Moab, and the Ammonites, all the kings of Tyre, all the kings of Sidon, and the kings of the coasts and islands:

23 24 to Dedan, Tema, Buz, and all who roam the fringes of the desert,*b* all the

25 kings of Arabia living in the wilderness, all the kings of Zamri, all the kings

26 of Elam, and all the kings of the Medes, all the kings of the north, neighbours or far apart, and all the kingdoms on the face of the earth. Last of all

27 the king of Sheshak*c* shall drink. You shall say to them, These are the words of the LORD of Hosts the God of Israel: Drink this, get drunk and be sick; fall, to rise no more, before the sword which I am sending among

28 you. If they refuse to take the cup from you and to drink, say to them, These

29 are the words of the LORD of Hosts: You must and shall drink. I will first punish the city which bears my name; do you think that you can be exempt?

*a* They ... victims: *prob. rdg.; Heb.* They were the victims.       *b* who roam ...
desert: *or* who clip the hair on their temples.       *c* *A name for Babylon.*

No, you cannot be exempt, for I am invoking the sword against all that inhabit the earth. This is the very word of the LORD of Hosts.

Prophesy to them and tell them all I have said:    30

> The LORD roars from Zion on high
> and thunders from his holy dwelling-place.
> Yes, he roars across the heavens, his home;
> an echo comes back like the shout of men treading grapes.
> The great noise reaches to the ends of the earth    31
> and all its inhabitants.
> For the LORD brings a charge against the nations,
> he goes to law with all mankind
> and has handed the wicked over to the sword.
> This is the very word of the LORD.

> These are the words of the LORD of Hosts:    32
> Ruin spreads from nation to nation,
> a mighty tempest is blowing up from the ends of the earth.

In that day those whom the LORD has slain shall lie like dung on the 33 ground from one end of the earth to the other; no one shall wail for them, they shall not be taken up and buried.

> Howl, shepherds, cry aloud,
>    34
> sprinkle yourselves with ashes, you masters of the flock.
> It is your turn to go to the slaughter,
> and you shall fall like fine rams.
> The shepherds shall have nowhere to flee,    35
> the flockmasters no way of escape.
> Hark, the shepherds cry out, the flockmasters howl,    36
> for the LORD is ravaging their pasture,
> and their peaceful homesteads lie in ruins beneath his anger.    37
> They flee like a young lion abandoning his lair,    38
> for their land has become a waste,
> wasted by the cruel sword and by his anger.

## *Jerusalem laid under a curse*

A<small>T THE BEGINNING OF THE REIGN</small> of Jehoiakim son of Josiah, king 26 of Judah, this word came to Jeremiah from the LORD: These are the 2 words of the LORD: Stand in the court of the LORD's house and speak to the inhabitants of all the cities of Judah who come to worship there. You shall tell them everything that I command you to say to them, keeping nothing back. Perhaps they may listen, and every man may turn back 3 from his evil courses. Then I will relent, and give up my purpose to bring disaster on them for their evil deeds. You shall say to them, These are 4 the words of the LORD: If you do not obey me, if you do not follow the law I have set before you, and listen to the words of my servants the prophets, 5 the prophets whom I have taken pains to send to you, but you have never listened to them, then I will make this house like Shiloh and this city an 6 object of ridicule to all nations on earth.

7 The priests, the prophets, and all the people heard Jeremiah say this
8 in the LORD's house and, when he came to the end of what the LORD had
commanded him to say to them, priests, prophets, and people seized him
9 and threatened him with death. 'Why', they demanded, 'have you prophesied in the LORD's name that this house shall become like Shiloh and
this city waste and uninhabited?' The people all gathered against Jeremiah
10 in the LORD's house. The officers of Judah heard what was happening, and
they went up from the royal palace to the LORD's house and took their
11 places there at the entrance of the new gate. Then the priests and the
prophets said to the officers and all the people, 'Condemn this fellow to
death. He has prophesied against this city: you have heard it with your own
12 ears.' Then Jeremiah said to the officers and the people, 'The LORD sent me
13 to prophesy against this house and this city all that you have heard. If you
now mend your ways and your doings and obey the LORD your God, then
he may relent and revoke the disaster with which he has threatened you.
14 But I am in your hands; do with me whatever you think right and proper.
15 Only you may be certain that, if you put me to death, you and this city and
all who live in it will be guilty of murdering an innocent man; for in very
truth the LORD has sent me to you to say all this in your hearing.'

16 Then the officers and all the people said to the priests and the prophets,
'This man ought not to be condemned to death, for he has spoken to us in
17 the name of the LORD our God.' Some of the elders of the land also stood
18 up and said to the assembled people, 'In the time of Hezekiah king of
Judah, Micah of Moresheth was prophesying and said to all the people
of Judah: "These are the words of the LORD of Hosts:

> Zion shall become a ploughed field,
> Jerusalem a heap of ruins,
> and the temple-hill rough heath."

19 Did King Hezekiah and all Judah put him to death? Did not the king show
reverence for the LORD and seek to placate him? Then the LORD relented
and revoked the disaster with which he had threatened them. Are we to
bring great disaster on ourselves?'

20 There was another man who prophesied in the name of the LORD, Uriah
son of Shemaiah, from Kiriath-jearim. He also prophesied against this
21 city and this land, just as Jeremiah had done. King Jehoiakim with all his
officers and his bodyguard heard what he said and sought to put him to
22 death. When Uriah heard of it, he was afraid and fled to Egypt. King
23 Jehoiakim sent Elnathan son of Akbor with others to fetch Uriah from
Egypt, and they brought him to the king. He had him put to death by the
24 sword, and his body flung into the burial-place of the common people. But
Ahikam son of Shaphan used his influence on Jeremiah's behalf to save
him from death at the hands of the people.

## A rising against Nebuchadrezzar checked

A T THE BEGINNING OF THE REIGN of Zedekiah son of Josiah, king of 27
Judah, this word came from the LORD to Jeremiah: These are the 2
words of the LORD to me: Take the cords and bars of a yoke and put them
on your neck. Then send to the kings of Edom, Moab, Ammon, Tyre, and 3
Sidon by the envoys who have come from them to Zedekiah king of Judah
in Jerusalem, and give them the following message for their masters: 4
These are the words of the LORD of Hosts the God of Israel: Say to your
masters: I made the earth with my great strength and with outstretched 5
arm, I made man and beast on the face of the earth, and I give it to whom
I see fit. I now give all these lands to my servant Nebuchadrezzar king 6
of Babylon, and I give him also all the beasts of the field to serve him.
All nations shall serve him, and his son and his grandson, until the 7
destined hour of his own land comes, and then mighty nations and
great kings shall use him as they please. If any nation or kingdom will 8
not serve Nebuchadrezzar king of Babylon or submit to his yoke, I will
punish them with sword, famine, and pestilence, says the LORD, until
I leave them entirely in his power. Therefore do not listen to your pro- 9
phets, your diviners, your wise women, your soothsayers, and your
sorcerers when they tell you not to serve the king of Babylon. They are 10
prophesying falsely to you; and so you will be carried far from your
own land, and I shall banish you and you will perish. But if any nation 11
submits to the yoke of the king of Babylon and serves him, I will leave
them on their own soil, says the LORD; they shall cultivate it and live
there.

I have said all this to Zedekiah king of Judah: If you will submit to the 12
yoke of the king of Babylon and serve him and his people, then you shall
save your lives. Why should you and your people die by sword, famine, and 13
pestilence, the fate with which the LORD has threatened any nation which
does not serve the king of Babylon? Do not listen to the prophets who tell 14
you not to become subject to the king of Babylon; they are prophesying
falsely to you. I have not sent them, says the LORD; they are prophesying 15
falsely in my name, and so I shall banish you and you will perish, you and
these prophets who prophesy to you.

I said to the priests and all the people, These are the words of the 16
LORD: Do not listen to your prophets who tell you that the vessels of
the LORD's house will very soon be brought back from Babylon; they
are only prophesying falsely to you. Do not listen to them; serve the 17
king of Babylon, and save your lives. Why should this city become a
ruin? If they are prophets, and if they have the word of the LORD, let 18
them intercede with the LORD of Hosts to grant that the vessels still
left in the LORD's house, in the royal palace, and in Jerusalem, may not
be carried off to Babylon. For these are the words of the LORD of Hosts 19
concerning the pillars, the sea, the trolleys, and all the other vessels still
left in this city, which Nebuchadrezzar king of Babylon did not take 20
when he deported Jeconiah son of Jehoiakim, king of Judah, from

Jerusalem to Babylon, together with all the nobles of Judah and Jerusalem.
21 These indeed are the words of the LORD of Hosts the God of Israel concerning the vessels still left in the LORD's house, in the royal palace, and
22 in Jerusalem: They shall be taken to Babylon and stay there until I recall them, says the LORD; then I will bring them back and restore them to this place.

28 That same year,*a* in the fifth month of the first*b* year of the reign of Zedekiah king of Judah, Hananiah son of Azzur, the prophet from Gibeon, said to me in the house of the LORD, in the presence of the priests and all
2 the people, 'These are the words of the LORD of Hosts the God of Israel:
3 I have broken the yoke of the king of Babylon. Within two years I will bring back to this place all the vessels of the LORD's house which Nebuchadrezzar king of Babylon took from here and carried off to Babylon.
4 I will also bring back to this place, says the LORD, Jeconiah son of Jehoiakim, king of Judah, and all the exiles of Judah who went to Babylon; for I will
5 break the yoke of the king of Babylon.' The prophet Jeremiah said to Hananiah the prophet in the presence of the priests and all the people
6 standing in the LORD's house: 'May it be so! May the LORD indeed do this: may he fulfil all that you have prophesied, by bringing back the vessels of
7 the LORD's house and all the exiles from Babylon to this place! Only hear
8 what I have to say to you and to all the people: the prophets who preceded you and me from earliest times have foretold war, famine, and pestilence
9 for many lands and for great kingdoms. If a prophet foretells prosperity, when his words come true it will be known that the LORD has sent him.'
10 Then the prophet Hananiah took the yoke from the neck of the prophet
11 Jeremiah and broke it, saying before all the people, 'These are the words of the LORD: Thus will I break the yoke of Nebuchadrezzar king of Babylon; I will break it off the necks of all nations within two years';*c* and the
12 prophet Jeremiah went his way. After Hananiah had broken the yoke which had been on Jeremiah's neck, the word of the LORD came to Jeremiah:
13 Go and say to Hananiah, These are the words of the LORD: You have
14 broken bars of wood; in their place you shall get bars of iron. For these are the words of the LORD of Hosts the God of Israel: I have put a yoke of iron on the necks of all these nations, making them serve Nebuchadrezzar king of Babylon. They shall serve him, and I have given him even the beasts of
15 the field. Then Jeremiah said to Hananiah, 'Listen, Hananiah. The LORD has not sent you, and you have led this nation to trust in false prophecies.
16 Therefore these are the words of the LORD: Beware, I will remove you from the face of the earth; you shall die within the year, because you have
17 preached rebellion against the LORD.' The prophet Hananiah died that same year, in the seventh month.

29 Jeremiah sent a letter from Jerusalem to the remaining elders among the exiles, to the priests and prophets, and to all the people whom Nebu-
2 chadrezzar had deported from Jerusalem to Babylon, after King Jeconiah had left Jerusalem with the queen mother and the eunuchs, the officers of

*a Prob. rdg.; Heb. adds at the beginning of the reign.* *b Prob. rdg.; Heb. fourth.*
*c within two years: or while there are still two full years to run.*

Judah and Jerusalem, the craftsmen and the smiths.*a* The prophet en- 3
trusted the letter to Elasah son of Shaphan and Gemariah son of Hilkiah,
whom Zedekiah king of Judah had sent to Babylon to King Nebuchadrezzar. This is what he wrote: These are the words of the LORD of Hosts the 4
God of Israel: To all the exiles whom I have carried off from Jerusalem to
Babylon: Build houses and live in them; plant gardens and eat their pro- 5
duce. Marry wives and beget sons and daughters; take wives for your sons 6
and give your daughters to husbands, so that they may bear sons and
daughters and you may increase there and not dwindle away. Seek the 7
welfare of any city to which I have carried you off, and pray to the LORD
for it; on its welfare your welfare will depend. For these are the words of 8
the LORD of Hosts the God of Israel: Do not be deceived by the prophets
or the diviners among you, and do not listen to the wise women whom you
set to dream dreams. They prophesy falsely to you in my name; I did not 9
send them. This is the very word of the LORD.

These are the words of the LORD: When a full seventy years has passed 10
over Babylon, I will take up your cause and fulfil the promise of good things
I made you, by bringing you back to this place. I alone know my purpose 11
for you, says the LORD: prosperity and not misfortune, and a long line of
children after you. If you invoke me and pray to me, I will listen to you: 12
when you seek me, you shall find me; if you search with all your heart, I 13 14
will let you find me, says the LORD. I will restore your fortunes and gather
you again from all the nations and all the places to which I have banished
you, says the LORD, and bring you back to the place from which I have
carried you into exile.

You say that the LORD has raised up prophets for you in Babylon. These 15 16
are the words of the LORD concerning the king who sits on the throne of
David and all the people who live in this city, your fellow-countrymen who
have not gone into exile with you. These are the words of the LORD of 17
Hosts: I bring upon them sword, famine, and pestilence, and make them
like rotten figs, too bad to be eaten. I pursue them with sword, famine, 18
and pestilence, and make them repugnant to all the kingdoms of the earth,
an object of execration and horror, of derision and reproach, among all
the nations to which I have banished them. Just as they did not listen to 19
my words, says the LORD, when I took pains to send them my servants the
prophets, so you did not listen, says the LORD. But now, you exiles whom 20
I have sent from Jerusalem to Babylon, listen to the words of the LORD.
These are the words of the LORD of Hosts the God of Israel concerning 21
Ahab son of Kolaiah and Zedekiah son of Maaseiah, who prophesy falsely
to you in my name. I will hand them over to Nebuchadrezzar king of
Babylon, and he will put them to death before your eyes. Their names shall 22
be used by all the exiles of Judah in Babylon when they curse a man; they
shall say, May the LORD treat you like Zedekiah and Ahab, whom the king
of Babylon roasted in the fire! For their conduct in Israel was an outrage: 23
they committed adultery with other men's wives, and without my authority
prophesied in my name, and what they prophesied was false. I know; I
can testify. This is the very word of the LORD.

*a* the smiths: *or* the harem.

24 25 To Shemaiah the Nehelamite.[a] These are the words of the LORD of Hosts the God of Israel: You have sent a letter in your own name to

26 Zephaniah son of Maaseiah the priest, in which you say: 'The LORD has appointed you to be priest in place of Jehoiada the priest, and it is your duty, as officer in charge of the LORD's house, to put every madman who

27 sets up as a prophet into the stocks and the pillory. Why, then, have you not reprimanded Jeremiah of Anathoth, who poses as a prophet before

28 you? On the strength of this he has sent to us in Babylon and said, "Your exile will be long; build houses and live in them, plant gardens and eat

29 their produce."' Zephaniah the priest read this letter to Jeremiah the

30 31 prophet, and the word of the LORD came to Jeremiah: Send and tell all the exiles that these are the words of the LORD concerning Shemaiah the Nehelamite: Because Shemaiah has prophesied to you, though I did not

32 send him, and has led you to trust in false prophecies, these are now the words of the LORD: I will punish Shemaiah and his children. He shall have no one to take his place in this nation and enjoy the prosperity which I will bestow on my people, says the LORD, because he has preached rebellion against me.

## *Hopes for the restoration of Jerusalem*

30 1 2 THE WORD WHICH CAME TO JEREMIAH from the LORD. These are the words of the LORD the God of Israel: Write in a book all that I

3 have said to you, for this is the very word of the LORD: The time is coming when I will restore the fortunes of my people Israel and Judah, says the LORD, and bring them back to the land which I gave to their forefathers; and it shall be their possession.

4 5 This is what the LORD has said to Israel and Judah. These are the words of the LORD:

You shall hear a cry of terror, of fear without relief.

6 Ask and see: can a man bear a child?
Why then do I see every man
gripping his sides like a woman in labour,
every face changed, all turned pale?

7 Awful is that day:
when has there been its like?
A time of anguish for Jacob,
yet he shall come through it safely.

8 In that day, says the LORD of Hosts, I will break their yoke off their necks and snap their cords; foreigners shall no longer use them as they

9 please; they shall serve the LORD their God and David their king, whom I will raise up for them.

10 And you, Jacob my servant, have no fear;
despair not, O Israel, says the LORD.

---

*a Prob. rdg.; Heb. adds* you shall say, saying.

For I will bring you back safe from afar
and your offspring from the land where they are captives;
and Jacob shall be at rest once more,
    prosperous and unafraid.
For I am with you and will save you, says the LORD.    11
   I will make an end of all the nations
   amongst whom I have scattered you,
but I will not make an end of you;
   though I punish you as you deserve,
   I will not sweep you clean away.

For these are the words of the LORD to Zion:    12
   Your injury is past healing,
   cruel was the blow you suffered.
   There can be no*a* remedy for your sore,    13
   the new skin cannot grow.
   All your lovers have forgotten you;    14
   they look for you no longer.
   I have struck you down
as an enemy strikes, and punished you cruelly;
for your wickedness is great and your sins are many.
   Why complain of your injury,    15
   that your sore cannot be healed?*b*
   I have done this to you,
because your wickedness is great and your sins are many.

Yet all who devoured you shall themselves be devoured,    16
all your oppressors shall go into captivity.
   Those who plunder you shall be plundered,
   and those who despoil you I will give up to be spoiled.
   I will cause the new skin to grow    17
   and heal your wounds, says the LORD,
   although men call you the Outcast,
     Zion, nobody's friend.

These are the words of the LORD:    18
   Watch; I will restore the fortunes of Jacob's clans
   and show my love for all his dwellings.
   Every city shall be rebuilt on its mound of ruins,
   every mansion shall have its familiar household.
   From them praise shall be heard    19
   and sounds of merrymaking.
I will increase them, they shall not diminish,
I will raise them to honour, they shall no longer be despised.
   Their sons shall be what they once were,    20
   and their community shall be established in my sight.
   I will punish all their oppressors;

*a* *Prob. rdg.; Heb. adds* one judging your case.     *b* Why ... healed?: *or* Cry not
for help in your injury. Your sore cannot be healed.

21     a ruler shall appear, one of themselves,
    a governor shall arise from their own number.
    I will myself bring him*a* near and so he*b* shall approach me;
for no one ventures of himself to approach me,
    says the LORD.

22     So you shall be my people,
    and I will be your God.

23     See what a scorching wind has gone out from the LORD,
    a sweeping whirlwind.
    It whirls round the heads of the wicked;

24     the LORD's anger is not to be turned aside,
till he has finished and achieved his heart's desire.
In days to come you will understand.

31   At that time, says the LORD, I will become God of all the families of
2 Israel, and they shall become my people. These are the words of the
LORD:

    A people that survived the sword
    found favour in the wilderness;
    Israel journeyed to find rest;

3     long ago*c* the LORD appeared to them:
I have dearly loved you from of old,
and still I maintain my unfailing care for you.

4     I will build you up again, O virgin Israel,
    and you shall be rebuilt.
    Again you shall adorn yourself with jingles,
    and go forth with the merry throng of dancers.

5     Again you shall plant vineyards on the hills of Samaria,
    vineyards which those who planted them defiled;

6     for a day will come when the watchmen on Ephraim's hills cry out,
    Come, let us go up to Zion, to the LORD our God.

7 For these are the words of the LORD:

    Break into shouts of joy for Jacob's sake,
    lead the nations, crying loud and clear,
    sing out your praises and say,
    The LORD has saved his people,
    and preserved a remnant of Israel.

8     See how I bring them from the land of the north;
    I will gather them from the ends of the earth,
    their blind and lame among them,
    women with child and women in labour,
    a great company.

9     They come home, weeping as they come,
    but I will comfort them and be their escort.
    I will lead them to flowing streams;
they shall not stumble, their path will be so smooth.

*a Or* them.     *b Or* they.     *c* long ago: *or* from afar.

For I have become a father to Israel,
and Ephraim is my eldest son.

Listen to the word of the LORD, you nations,    10
announce it, make it known to coasts and islands far away:
   He who scattered Israel shall gather them again
and watch over them as a shepherd watches his flock.
For the LORD has ransomed Jacob    11
and redeemed him from a foe too strong for him.
They shall come with shouts of joy to Zion's height,    12
shining with happiness at the bounty of the LORD,
the corn, the new wine, and the oil,
   the young of flock and herd.
They shall become like a watered garden
and they shall never want again.
Then shall the girl show her joy in the dance,    13
   young men and old shall rejoice;
I will turn their mourning into gladness,
I will relent and give them joy to outdo their sorrow.
I will satisfy the priests with the fat of the land    14
and fill my people with my bounty.
   This is the very word of the LORD.

These are the words of the LORD:    15
   Hark, lamentation is heard in Ramah, and bitter weeping,
   Rachel weeping for her sons.
   She refuses to be comforted: they are no more.

These are the words of the LORD:    16
   Cease your loud weeping,
     shed no more tears;
   for there shall be a reward for your toil,
     they shall return from the land of the enemy.
   You shall leave descendants after you; *a*    17
   your sons shall return to their own land.
I listened; Ephraim was rocking in his grief:    18
'Thou hast trained me to the yoke like an unbroken calf,
   and now I am trained;
   restore me, let me return,
for thou, LORD, art my God.
Though I broke loose I have repented:    19
now that I am tamed I beat my breast;
   in shame and remorse
I reproach myself for the sins of my youth.'
Is Ephraim still my dear son,
a child in whom I delight?    20
   As often as I turn my back on him
I still remember him;

*a* You shall . . . you: *or* There shall be hope for your posterity.

955

and so my heart yearns for him,
    I am filled with tenderness towards him.
      This is the very word of the LORD.

21     Build cairns to mark your way,
set up sign-posts;
    make sure of the road,
      the path which you will tread.
      Come back, virgin Israel,
    come back to your cities.

22     How long will you twist and turn, my wayward child?
For the LORD has created a new thing in the earth:
    a woman turned into a man.

23    These are the words of the LORD of Hosts the God of Israel: Once more shall these words be heard in the land of Judah and in her cities, when I restore their fortunes:

    The LORD bless you,
    the LORD, your true goal,*a* your holy mountain.

24     Ploughmen and shepherds who wander with their flocks
    shall live together there.*b*

25     For I have given deep draughts to the thirsty,
    and satisfied those who were faint with hunger.

26 Thereupon I woke and looked about me, and my dream*c* had been pleasant.

27    The time is coming, says the LORD, when I will sow Israel and Judah
28 with the seed of man and the seed of cattle. As I watched over them with intent to pull down and to uproot, to demolish and destroy and harm, so now will I watch over them to build and to plant. This is the very word of the LORD.

29    In those days it shall no longer be said,

    'The fathers have eaten sour grapes
      and the children's teeth are set on edge';

30 for a man shall die for his own wrongdoing; the man who eats sour grapes shall have his own teeth set on edge.

31    The time is coming, says the LORD, when I will make a new covenant
32 with Israel and Judah. It will not be like the covenant I made with their forefathers when I took them by the hand and led them out of Egypt. Although they broke my covenant, I was patient with them, says the LORD.
33 But this is the covenant which I will make with Israel after those days, says the LORD; I will set my law within them and write it on their hearts; I will
34 become their God and they shall become my people. No longer need they teach one another to know the LORD; all of them, high and low alike, shall know me, says the LORD, for I will forgive their wrongdoing and remember their sin no more.

35    These are the words of the LORD, who gave the sun for a light by day

*a* the LORD . . . goal: *or* O home of righteousness.     *b* *Prob. rdg.; Heb. adds* Judah
and all his cities.    *c* *Or* sleep.

and the moon and stars for a light by night, who cleft the sea and its waves roared; the LORD of Hosts is his name:

> If this fixed order could vanish out of my sight,        36
>     says the LORD,
> then the race of Israel too could cease for evermore
>     to be a nation in my sight.

These are the words of the LORD: If any man could measure the heaven 37 above or fathom the depths of the earth beneath, then I could spurn the whole race of Israel because of all they have done. This is the very word of the LORD.

The time is coming, says the LORD, when the city shall be rebuilt in the 38 LORD's honour from the Tower of Hananel to the Corner Gate. The 39 measuring line shall then be laid straight out over the hill of Gareb and round Goath.[a] All the valley and every field as far as the gorge of the 40 Kidron to the corner by the Horse Gate eastwards shall be holy to the LORD. It shall never again be pulled down or demolished.

The word which came to Jeremiah from the LORD in the tenth year of 32 Zedekiah king of Judah (the eighteenth year of Nebuchadrezzar). At that 2 time the forces of the Babylonian king were besieging Jerusalem, and the prophet Jeremiah was imprisoned in the court of the guard-house attached to the royal palace. Zedekiah king of Judah had imprisoned him 3 after demanding what he meant by this prophecy: 'These are the words of the LORD: I will deliver this city into the hands of the king of Babylon, and he shall take it. Zedekiah king of Judah will not escape from the Chal- 4 daeans but will be surrendered to the king of Babylon; he will speak with him face to face and see him with his own eyes. Zedekiah will be taken to 5 Babylon and will remain there until I turn my thoughts to him, says the LORD. However much you fight against the Chaldaeans you will have no success.'

Jeremiah said, The word of the LORD came to me: Hanamel son of your 6 7 uncle Shallum is coming to see you and will say, 'Buy my field at Anathoth; you have the right of redemption, as next of kin, to buy it.' As the LORD 8 had foretold, my cousin Hanamel came to the court of the guard-house and said, 'Buy my field at Anathoth in Benjamin. You have the right of redemption and possession as next of kin; buy it.' I knew that this was the LORD's message; so I bought the field at Anathoth from my cousin Hanamel and 9 weighed out the price, seventeen shekels of silver. I signed and sealed the 10 deed and had it witnessed; then I weighed out the money on the scales. I took my copies of the deed of purchase, both the sealed and the unsealed, 11 and gave them to Baruch son of Neriah, son of Mahseiah, in the presence 12 of Hanamel my cousin, of the witnesses whose names were on the deed of purchase, and of the Judaeans sitting in the court of the guard-house. In 13 the presence of them all I gave my instructions to Baruch: These are the 14 words of the LORD of Hosts the God of Israel: Take these copies of the deed of purchase, the sealed and the unsealed, and deposit them in an earthenware jar so that they may be preserved for a long time. For these 15

---

[a] *Or* Goah.

are the words of the LORD of Hosts the God of Israel: The time will come when houses, fields, and vineyards will again be bought and sold in this

16 land. After I had given the deed of purchase to Baruch son of Neriah, I

17 prayed to the LORD: O Lord GOD, thou hast made the heavens and the earth by thy great strength and with thy outstretched arm; nothing is

18 impossible for thee. Thou keepest faith with thousands and thou dost requite the sins of fathers on to the heads of their sons. O great and mighty

19 God whose name is the LORD of Hosts, great are thy purposes and mighty thy actions. Thine eyes watch all the ways of men, and thou rewardest

20 each according to his ways and as his deeds deserve. Thou didst work signs and portents in Egypt and hast continued them to this day, both in Israel and amongst all men, and hast won for thyself a name that lives on

21 to this day. Thou didst bring thy people Israel out of Egypt with signs and portents, with a strong hand and an outstretched arm, and with terrible

22 power. Thou didst give them this land which thou didst promise with an

23 oath to their forefathers, a land flowing with milk and honey. They came and took possession of it, but they did not obey thee or follow thy law, they disobeyed all thy commands; and so thou hast brought this disaster upon

24 them. Look at the siege-ramps, the men who are advancing to take the city, and the city given over to its assailants from Chaldaea, the victim of sword, famine, and pestilence. The word thou hast spoken is fulfilled and

25 thou dost see it. And yet thou hast bidden me buy the field, O Lord GOD, and have the deed witnessed, even though the city is given to the Chaldaeans.

26 27 These are the words of the LORD to Jeremiah: I am the LORD, the God of

28 all flesh; is anything impossible for me? Therefore these are the words of the LORD: I will deliver this city into the hands of the Chaldaeans and

29 of Nebuchadrezzar king of Babylon, and he shall take it. The Chaldaeans who are fighting against this city will enter it, set it on fire and burn it down, with the houses on whose roofs sacrifices have been burnt to Baal and drink-offerings poured out to other gods, by which I was provoked to anger.

30 From their earliest days Israel and Judah have been doing what is wrong

31 in my eyes, provoking me to anger by their actions, says the LORD. For this city has so roused my anger and my fury, from the time it was built down

32 to this day, that I would rid myself of it. Israel and Judah, their kings, officers, priests, prophets, and everyone living in Jerusalem and Judah

33 have provoked me to anger by their wrongdoing. They have turned their backs on me and averted their faces; though I took pains to teach them,

34 they would not hear or learn their lesson. They set up their loathsome idols

35 in the house which bears my name and so defiled it. They built shrines to Baal in the Valley of Ben-hinnom, to surrender their sons and daughters to Molech. It was no command of mine, nor did it ever enter my thought to do this abominable thing and lead Judah into sin.

36 Now, therefore, these are the words of the LORD the God of Israel to this city of which you say, 'It is being given over to the king of Babylon,

37 with sword, famine, and pestilence': I will gather them from all the lands to which I banished them in my anger, rage, and fury, and I will bring

them back to this place and let them dwell there undisturbed. They shall 38
become my people and I will become their God. I will give them one heart 39
and one way of life so that they shall fear me at all times, for their own good
and the good of their children after them. I will enter into an eternal 40
covenant with them, to follow them unfailingly with my bounty; I will
fill their hearts with fear of me, and so they will not turn away from me.
I will rejoice over them, rejoice to do them good, and faithfully with all 41
my heart and soul I will plant them in this land. For these are the words 42
of the LORD: As I brought on this people such great disaster, so will I
bring them all the prosperity which I now promise them. Fields shall 43
again be bought and sold in this land of which you now say, 'It is desolate,
without man or beast; it is given over to the Chaldaeans.' Fields shall be 44
bought and sold, deeds signed, sealed, and witnessed, in Benjamin, in the
neighbourhood of Jerusalem, in the cities of Judah, of the hill-country, of
the Shephelah, and of the Negeb; for I will restore their fortunes. This is
the very word of the LORD.

The word of the LORD came to Jeremiah a second time while he was still 33
imprisoned in the court of the guard-house: These are the words of the 2
LORD who made the earth, who formed it and established it; the LORD is
his name: If you call to me I will answer you, and tell you great and 3
mysterious things which you do not understand. These are the words of 4
the LORD the God of Israel concerning the houses in this city and the royal
palace, which are to be razed to the ground, concerning siege-ramp and
sword, and attackers*a* who fill the houses with the corpses of those whom 5
he struck down in his furious rage: I hid my face from this city because of
their wicked ways, but now I will bring her healing; I will heal and cure 6
Judah and Israel, and will let my people see an age of peace and security.
I will restore their fortunes and build them again as once they were. I will 7 8
cleanse them of all the wickedness and sin that they have committed; I
will forgive all the evil deeds they have done in rebellion against me. This 9
city will win me a name*b* and praise and glory before all the nations on
earth, when they hear of all the blessings I bestow on her; and they shall
be moved and filled with awe because of the blessings and the peace which
I have brought upon her.

These are the words of the LORD: You say of this place, 'It is in ruins, 10
and neither man nor beast lives in the cities of Judah or in the streets of
Jerusalem. It is all a waste, inhabited by neither man nor beast.' Yet in
this place shall be heard once again the sounds of joy and gladness, the 11
voice of the bridegroom and the bride; here too shall be heard voices
shouting, 'Praise the LORD of Hosts, for he is good, for his love endures
for ever', as they offer praise and thanksgiving in the house of the LORD.
For I will restore the fortunes of the land as once they were. This is the
word of the LORD.

These are the words of the LORD of Hosts: In this place and in all its 12
cities, now ruined and inhabited by neither man nor beast, there shall
once more be a refuge where shepherds may fold their flocks. In the cities 13
of the hill-country, of the Shephelah, of the Negeb, in Benjamin, in the

---

*a Prob. rdg.; Heb. adds* the Chaldaeans.          *b Prob. rdg.; Heb. adds* of joy.

neighbourhood of Jerusalem and the cities of Judah, flocks will once more pass under the shepherd's hand as he counts them. This is the word of the LORD.

14 Wait, says the LORD, the days are coming when I will bestow on Israel
15 and Judah all the blessings I have promised them. In those days, at that time, I will make a righteous Branch of David spring up; he shall maintain
16 law and justice in the land. In those days Judah shall be kept safe and Jerusalem shall live undisturbed; and this shall be her name: The LORD is our Righteousness.

17 For these are the words of the LORD: David will never lack a successor
18 on the throne of Israel, nor will the levitical priests lack a man who shall come before me continually to present whole-offerings, to burn grain-offerings and to make other offerings.

19 20 This word came from the LORD to Jeremiah: These are the words of the LORD: If the law that I made for the day and the night could be annulled
21 so that they fell out of their proper order, then my covenant with my servant David could be annulled so that none of his line should sit upon his throne; so also could my covenant with the levitical priests who minister
22 to me. Like the innumerable host of heaven or the countless sands of the sea, I will increase the descendants of my servant David and the Levites who minister to me.

23 24 The word of the LORD came to Jeremiah: Have you not observed how this people have said, 'It is the two families whom he chose that the LORD has spurned'? So others will despise my people and no longer regard them
25 as a nation. These are the words of the LORD: If I had not made my law
26 for day and night nor established a fixed order in heaven and earth, then I would spurn the descendants of Jacob and of my servant David, and would not take any of David's line to be rulers over the descendants of Abraham, Isaac and Jacob. But now I will restore their fortunes and have compassion upon them.

## Events under Jehoiakim and Zedekiah

34 THE WORD WHICH CAME TO JEREMIAH from the LORD when Nebu-chadrezzar king of Babylon and his army, with all his vassal kingdoms
2 and nations, were fighting against Jerusalem and all her towns: These are the words of the LORD the God of Israel: Go and say to Zedekiah king of Judah, These are the words of the LORD: I will give this city into the
3 hands of the king of Babylon and he will burn it down. You shall not escape, you will be captured and handed over to him. You will see him face to
4 face, and he will speak to you in person; and you shall go to Babylon. But listen to the LORD's word to you, Zedekiah king of Judah. This is his word:
5 You shall not die by the sword; you will die a peaceful death, and they will kindle fires in your honour like the fires kindled in former times for the kings your ancestors who preceded you. 'Alas, my lord!' they will say as they beat their breasts in mourning for you. This I have spoken. This
6 is the very word of the LORD. The prophet Jeremiah repeated all this to

Zedekiah king of Judah in Jerusalem when the army of the king of Babylon 7
was attacking Jerusalem and the remaining cities of Judah, namely
Lachish and Azekah. These were the only fortified cities left in Judah.

The word that came to Jeremiah from the LORD after Zedekiah had 8
made a covenant with all the people in Jerusalem to proclaim an act of
freedom for the slaves. All who had Hebrew slaves, male or female, were 9
to set them free; they were not to keep their fellow Judaeans in servitude.
All the officers and people, having made this covenant to set free their 10
slaves, both male and female, and not to keep them in servitude any longer,
fulfilled its terms and let them go. Afterwards, however, they changed their 11
minds and forced back again into slavery the men and women whom they
had freed. Then this word came from the LORD to Jeremiah: These are 12 13
the words of the LORD the God of Israel: I made a covenant with your
forefathers on the day that I brought them out of Egypt, out of the land of
slavery. These were its terms: 'Within seven years each of you shall set free 14
any Hebrew who has sold himself to you as a slave and has served you
for six years; you shall set him free.' Your forefathers did not listen to me
or obey me. You, on the contrary, recently proclaimed an act of freedom 15
for the slaves and made a covenant in my presence, in the house that bears
my name, and so have done what is right in my eyes. But you too have 16
profaned my name. You have all taken back the slaves you had set free and
you have forced them, both male and female, to be your slaves again.
Therefore these are the words of the LORD: After you had proclaimed an 17
act of freedom, a deliverance for your kinsmen and your neighbours, you
did not obey me; so I will proclaim a deliverance for you, says the LORD,
a deliverance over to sword, to pestilence, and to famine, and I will make
you repugnant to all the kingdoms of the earth. You have disregarded my 18
covenant and have not fulfilled the terms to which you yourselves had
agreed; so I will make you like the calf of the covenant when they cut it
into two and passed between the pieces. Those who passed between the 19
pieces of the calf were the officers of Judah and Jerusalem, the eunuchs
and priests and all the people of the land. I will give them up to their 20
enemies who seek their lives, and their bodies shall be food for birds of
prey and wild beasts. I will deliver Zedekiah king of Judah and his officers 21
to their enemies who seek their lives and to the army of the king of Babylon,
which is now raising the siege. I will give the command, says the LORD, 22
and will bring them back to this city. They shall attack it and take it and
burn it down, and I will make the cities of Judah desolate and unpeopled.

The word which came to Jeremiah from the LORD in the days of Jehoia- 35
kim son of Josiah, king of Judah: Go and speak to the Rechabites, bring 2
them to one of the rooms in the house of the LORD and offer them wine to
drink. So I fetched Jaazaniah son of Jeremiah, son of Habaziniah, with his 3
brothers and all his sons and all the family of the Rechabites. I brought 4
them into the house of the LORD to the room of the sons of Hanan son
of Igdaliah, the man of God; this adjoins the officers' room above that of
Maaseiah son of Shallum, the keeper of the threshold. I set bowls full of 5
wine and drinking-cups before the Rechabites and invited them to drink
wine; but they said, 'We will not drink wine, for our forefather Jonadab 6

son of Rechab laid this command on us: "You shall never drink wine,
7 neither you nor your children. You shall not build houses or sow seed or plant vineyards; you shall have none of these things. Instead, you shall remain tent-dwellers all your lives, so that you may live long in the land
8 where you are sojourners." We have honoured all the commands of our forefather Jonadab son of Rechab and have drunk no wine all our lives,
9 neither we nor our wives, nor our sons, nor our daughters. We have not built houses to live in, nor have we possessed vineyards or sown fields.
10 We have lived in tents, obeying and observing all the commands of our
11 forefather Jonadab. But when Nebuchadrezzar king of Babylon invaded the land we said, "Come, let us go to Jerusalem before the advancing Chaldaean and Aramaean armies." And we have stayed in Jerusalem.'
12 13 Then the word of the LORD came to Jeremiah: These are the words of the LORD of Hosts the God of Israel: Go and say to the men of Judah and the inhabitants of Jerusalem, You must accept correction and obey my
14 words, says the LORD. The command of Jonadab son of Rechab to his descendants not to drink wine has been honoured; they have not drunk wine to this day, for they have obeyed their ancestor's command. But I have taken especial pains to warn you and yet you have not obeyed me.
15 I sent my servants the prophets especially to say to you, 'Turn back every one of you from his evil course, mend your ways and cease to follow other gods and worship them; then you shall remain on the land that I have given to you and to your forefathers.' Yet you did not obey or listen to me.
16 The sons of Jonadab son of Rechab have honoured their ancestor's com-
17 mand laid on them, but this people have not listened to me. Therefore, these are the words of the LORD the God of Hosts, the God of Israel: Because they did not listen when I spoke to them, nor answer when I called them, I will bring upon Judah and upon all the inhabitants of Jerusalem
18 the disaster with which I threatened them. To the Rechabites Jeremiah said, These are the words of the LORD of Hosts the God of Israel: Because you have kept the command of Jonadab your ancestor and obeyed all his
19 instructions and carried out all that he told you to do, therefore these are the words of the LORD of Hosts the God of Israel: Jonadab son of Rechab shall not want a descendant to stand before me for all time.

36 IN THE FOURTH YEAR OF JEHOIAKIM son of Josiah, king of Judah,
2 this word came to Jeremiah from the LORD: Take a scroll and write on it every word that I have spoken to you about Jerusalem and Judah and all the nations, from the day that I first spoke to you in the reign of Josiah
3 down to the present day. Perhaps the house of Judah will be warned of the calamity that I am planning to bring on them, and every man will abandon
4 his evil course; then I will forgive their wrongdoing and their sin. So Jeremiah called Baruch son of Neriah, and he wrote on the scroll at Jere-
5 miah's dictation all the words which the LORD had spoken to him. He gave Baruch this instruction: 'I am prevented from going to the LORD's house.
6 You must go there in my place on a fast-day and read the words of the LORD in the hearing of the people from the scroll you have written at my dictation. You shall read them in the hearing of all the men of Judah who come in

from their cities. Then perhaps they will present a petition to the LORD 7
and every man will abandon his evil course; for the LORD has spoken
against this people in great anger and wrath.' Baruch son of Neriah did all 8
that the prophet Jeremiah had told him to do, and read the words of the
LORD in the LORD's house out of the book.

In the ninth month of the fifth year of the reign of Jehoiakim son of 9
Josiah, king of Judah, all the people in Jerusalem and all who came there
from the cities of Judah proclaimed a fast before the LORD. Then Baruch 10
read Jeremiah's words in the house of the LORD out of the book in the
hearing of all the people; he read them from the room of Gemariah son
of the adjutant-general Shaphan in the upper court at the entrance to the
new gate of the LORD's house. Micaiah son of Gemariah, son of Shaphan, 11
heard all the words of the LORD out of the book and went down to the 12
palace, to the adjutant-general's room where all the officers were gathered
—Elishama the adjutant-general, Delaiah son of Shemaiah, Elnathan son
of Akbor, Gemariah son of Shaphan, Zedekiah son of Hananiah and all the
other officers. There Micaiah repeated all the words he had heard when 13
Baruch read out of the book in the people's hearing. Then the officers sent 14
Jehudi son of Nethaniah, son of Shelemiah, son of Cushi, to Baruch with
this message: 'Come here and bring the scroll from which you read in the
people's hearing.' So Baruch son of Neriah brought the scroll to them, and 15
they said, 'Sit down and*ᵃ* read it to us.' When they heard what he read, 16
they turned to each other trembling and said, 'We must report this to the
king.' They asked Baruch to tell them how he had come to write all this. 17
He said to them, 'Jeremiah dictated every word of it to me, and I wrote it 18
down in ink in the book.' The officers said to Baruch, 'You and Jeremiah 19
must go into hiding so that no one may know where you are.' When they 20
had deposited the scroll in the room of Elishama the adjutant-general, they
went to the court and reported everything to the king.

The king sent Jehudi to fetch the scroll. When he had fetched it from the 21
room of Elishama the adjutant-general, he read it to the king and to all the
officers in attendance. It was the ninth month of the year, and the king was 22
sitting in his winter apartments with a fire burning in a brazier in front of
him. When Jehudi had read three or four columns of the scroll, the king 23
cut them off with a penknife and threw them into the fire in the brazier.
He went on doing so until the whole scroll had been thrown on the fire.
Neither the king nor any of his courtiers who heard these words showed 24
any fear or rent their clothes; and though Elnathan, Delaiah, and Gemariah 25
begged the king not to burn the scroll, he would not listen to them. The 26
king then ordered Jerahmeel, a royal prince,*ᵇ* Seraiah son of Azriel, and
Shelemiah son of Abdeel to fetch the scribe Baruch and the prophet
Jeremiah; but the LORD had hidden them.

After the king had burnt the scroll with all that Baruch had written on 27
it at Jeremiah's dictation, the word of the LORD came to Jeremiah: Now 28
take another scroll and write on it all the words that were on the first scroll
which Jehoiakim king of Judah burnt. You shall say to Jehoiakim king of 29
Judah, These are the words of the LORD: You burnt this scroll and said,

---

*ᵃ* Sit down and: *or* This time.          *ᵇ* a royal prince: *or* the king's deputy.

Why have you written here that the king of Babylon shall come and destroy
30 this land and exterminate both men and beasts? Therefore these are the
words of the LORD about Jehoiakim king of Judah: He shall have no one to
succeed him on the throne of David, and his dead body shall be exposed
31 to scorching heat by day and frost by night. I will punish him and also
his offspring and his courtiers for their wickedness, and I will bring down
on them and on the inhabitants of Jerusalem and on the men of Judah all
the calamities with which I threatened them, and to which they turned a
32 deaf ear. Then Jeremiah took another scroll and gave it to the scribe Baruch
son of Neriah, who wrote on it at Jeremiah's dictation all the words of the
book which Jehoiakim king of Judah had burnt; and much else was added
to the same effect.

**37** King Zedekiah son of Josiah was set on the throne of Judah by Nebuchadrezzar king of Babylon, in succession to Coniah son of Jehoiakim.
2 Neither he nor his courtiers nor the people of the land listened to the words
which the LORD spoke through the prophet Jeremiah.

3 King Zedekiah sent Jehucal son of Shelemiah and the priest Zephaniah
son of Maaseiah to the prophet Jeremiah to say to him, 'Pray for us to the
4 LORD our God.' At the time Jeremiah was free to come and go among the
5 people; he had not yet been thrown into prison. Meanwhile, Pharaoh's
army had marched out of Egypt, and when the Chaldaeans who were
6 besieging Jerusalem heard of it they raised the siege. Then this word came
7 from the LORD to the prophet Jeremiah: These are the words of the LORD
the God of Israel: Say to the king of Judah who sent you to consult me,
Pharaoh's army which marched out to help you is on its way back to Egypt,
8 its own land, and the Chaldaeans will return to the attack. They will cap-
9 ture this city and burn it to the ground. These are the words of the LORD:
Do not deceive yourselves, do not imagine that the Chaldaeans will go away
10 and leave you alone. They will not go; for even if you defeated the whole
Chaldaean force with which you are now fighting, and only the wounded
were left lying in their tents, they would rise and burn down the city.

11 When the Chaldaean army had raised the siege of Jerusalem because of
12 the advance of Pharaoh's army, Jeremiah was on the point of leaving
Jerusalem to go into Benjamite territory and take possession of his patri-
13 mony in the presence of the people there. Irijah son of Shelemiah, son of
Hananiah, the officer of the guard, was in the Benjamin Gate when Jeremiah reached it, and he arrested the prophet, accusing him of going over
14 to the Chaldaeans. 'It is a lie,' said Jeremiah; 'I am not going over to the
Chaldaeans.' Irijah would not listen to him but arrested him and brought
15 him before the officers. The officers were indignant with Jeremiah; they
flogged him and imprisoned him in the house of Jonathan the scribe, which
16 they had converted into a prison; for Jeremiah had been put into a vaulted
pit beneath the house, and here he remained for a long time.

17 King Zedekiah had Jeremiah brought to him and consulted him privately
in the palace, asking him if there was a word from the LORD. 'Indeed there
is,' said Jeremiah; 'you shall fall into the hands of the king of Babylon.'
18 Then Jeremiah said to King Zedekiah, 'What wrong have I done to you
or your courtiers or this people? Why have you thrown me into prison?

Where are your prophets who prophesied that the king of Babylon would 19
not attack you or your country? I pray you now, my lord king, give me a 20
hearing and let my petition be presented: do not send me back to the house
of Jonathan the scribe, or I shall die there.' Then King Zedekiah gave the 21
order and Jeremiah was committed to the court of the guard-house and
was granted a daily ration of one loaf from the Street of the Bakers, until
the bread in the city was all gone. So Jeremiah remained in the court of
the guard-house.

Shephatiah son of Mattan, Gedaliah son of Pashhur, Jucal son of 38
Shelemiah, and Pashhur son of Malchiah heard what Jeremiah was saying
to all the people: These are the words of the LORD: Whoever remains in 2
this city shall die by sword, by famine, or by pestilence, but whoever goes
out to surrender to the Chaldaeans shall survive; he shall survive, he shall
take home his life and nothing more. These are the words of the LORD: 3
This city will fall into the hands of the king of Babylon's army, and they
will capture it. Then the officers said to the king, 'The man must be put 4
to death. By talking in this way he is discouraging the soldiers and the rest
of the people left in the city. He is pursuing not the people's welfare but
their ruin.' King Zedekiah said, 'He is in your hands; the king is powerless 5
against you.' So they took Jeremiah and threw him into the pit,ᵃ in the 6
court of the guard-house, letting him down with ropes. There was no water
in the pit, only mud, and Jeremiah sank in the mud. Now Ebed-melech 7-8
the Cushite, a eunuch, who was in the palace, heard that they had thrown
Jeremiah into the pit and went to tell the king, who was seated in the
Benjamin Gate. 'Your majesty,' he said, 'these men have shown great 9
wickedness in their treatment of the prophet Jeremiah. They have thrown
him into the pit, and when there is no more bread in the city he will die of
hunger where he lies.' Thereupon the king told Ebed-melech the Cushite 10
to take three men with him and hoist Jeremiah out of the pit before he died.
So Ebed-melech went to the palace with the men and took some tattered, 11
cast-off clothes from the wardrobeᵇ and let them down with ropes to
Jeremiah in the pit. Ebed-melech the Cushite said to Jeremiah, 'Put these 12
old clothes under your armpits to ease the ropes.' Jeremiah did this, and 13
they pulled him up out of the pit with the ropes; and he remained in the
court of the guard-house.

King Zedekiah had the prophet Jeremiah brought to him by the third 14
entrance to the LORD's house and said to him, 'I want to ask you something;
hide nothing from me.' Jeremiah answered, 'If I speak out, you will 15
certainly put me to death; if I offer you any advice, you will not take it.'
But King Zedekiah swore to Jeremiah privately, 'By the life of the LORD 16
who gave us our lives, I will not put you to death, nor will I hand you over
to these men who are seeking to take your life.' Jeremiah said to Zedekiah, 17
'These are the words of the LORD the God of Hosts, the God of Israel: If
you go out and surrender to the officers of the king of Babylon, you shall
live and this city shall not be burnt down; you and your family shall live.
But if you do not surrender to the officers of the king of Babylon, the city 18

ᵃ *Prob. rdg.; Heb. adds* Malchiah son (*or* deputy) of the king.          ᵇ the wardrobe:
*prob. rdg.; Heb.* underneath the treasury.

19 shall fall into the hands of the Chaldaeans, and they shall burn it down, and you will not escape them.' King Zedekiah said to Jeremiah, 'I am afraid of the Judaeans who have gone over to the enemy. I fear the Chaldaeans will
20 give me up to them and I shall be roughly handled.' Jeremiah answered, 'They will not give you up. If you obey the LORD in everything I tell you,
21 all will be well with you and you shall live. But if you refuse to go out and
22 surrender, this is what the LORD has shown me: all the women left in the king of Judah's palace will be led out to the officers of the king of Babylon and they will say:

> Your own friends have misled you
> and have been too strong for you;
> they have let your feet sink in the mud
> and have turned away and left you.

23 All your women and children will be led out to the Chaldaeans, and you will not escape; you will be seized by the king of Babylon and this city will
24 be burnt down.' Zedekiah said to Jeremiah, 'Let no one know about this,
25 and you shall not be put to death. If the officers hear that I have been speaking with you and they come to you and say, "Tell us what you said to the king and what he said to you; hide nothing from us, and we will not put
26 you to death", then answer, "I was presenting a petition to the king not to
27 send me back to the house of Jonathan to die there."' The officers all came to Jeremiah and questioned him, and he said to them just what the king had told him to say; so their talk came to an end and they were none
28 the wiser. Jeremiah remained in the court of the guard-house till the day Jerusalem fell.

39 1a IN THE TENTH MONTH OF THE NINTH YEAR of the reign of Zedekiah king of Judah, Nebuchadrezzar advanced with all his army against Jeru-
2 salem, and they laid siege to it. In the fourth month of the eleventh year
3 of Zedekiah, on the ninth day of the month, the city was thrown open. All the officers of the king of Babylon came in and took their seats in the middle gate: Nergalsarezer of Simmagir, Nebusarsekim*b* the chief eunuch,*c* Nergalsarezer the commander of the frontier troops,*d* and all the other
4 officers of the king of Babylon. When Zedekiah king of Judah saw them, he and all his armed escort left the city and fled by night by way of the king's garden through the gate called Between the Two Walls. They
5 escaped towards the Arabah, but the Chaldaean army pursued them and overtook Zedekiah in the lowlands of Jericho. The king was seized and brought before Nebuchadrezzar king of Babylon at Riblah in the land of
6 Hamath, and he pleaded his case before him. The king of Babylon slew Zedekiah's sons before his eyes at Riblah; he also put to death the nobles
7 of Judah. Then Zedekiah's eyes were put out, and he was bound in fetters
8 of bronze to be brought to Babylon. The Chaldaeans burnt the royal palace and the house of the LORD and the houses*e* of the people, and pulled down

---

*a Verses 1–10: cp. 52. 4–16 and 2 Kgs. 25. 1–12.*        *b Probably a different form of* Nebushazban *(verse 13).*        *c the chief eunuch: or Rab-saris.*        *d the commander . . . troops: or Rab-mag.*        *e of the LORD and the houses: prob. rdg.; Heb. om.*

the walls of Jerusalem. Nebuzaradan captain of the bodyguard deported 9 to Babylon the rest of the people left in the city, those who had deserted to him and any remaining artisans.*a* At the same time the captain of the guard 10 left behind the weakest class of the people, those who owned nothing at all, and made them vine-dressers and labourers.

Nebuchadrezzar king of Babylon sent orders about Jeremiah to Nebu- 11 zaradan captain of the guard. 'Take him,' he said; 'take special care of 12 him, and do him no harm of any kind, but do for him whatever he says.' So Nebuzaradan captain of the guard sent Nebushazban the chief eunuch, 13 Nergalsarezer the commander of the frontier troops, and all the chief officers of the king of Babylon, and they fetched Jeremiah from the court 14 of the guard-house and handed him over to Gedaliah son of Ahikam, son of Shaphan, to take him out to the Residence. So he stayed with his own people.

The word of the LORD had come to Jeremiah while he was under arrest 15 in the court of the guard-house: Go and say to Ebed-melech the Cushite, 16 These are the words of the LORD of Hosts the God of Israel: I will make good the words I have spoken against this city, foretelling ruin and not prosperity, and when that day comes you will be there to see it. But I will 17 preserve you on that day, says the LORD, and you shall not be handed over to the men you fear. I will keep you safe and you shall not fall a victim to 18 the sword; because you trusted in me you shall escape, you shall take home your life and nothing more. This is the very word of the LORD.

## *Jeremiah after the capture of Jerusalem*

THE WORD WHICH CAME FROM THE LORD concerning Jeremiah: 40 Nebuzaradan captain of the guard had taken him in chains to Ramah along with the other exiles from Jerusalem and Judah who were being deported to Babylon; and there he set him free, and took it upon himself 2 to say to Jeremiah, 'The LORD your God threatened this place with disaster, and has duly carried out his threat that this should happen to all of you 3 because you have sinned against the LORD and not obeyed him. But as 4 for you, Jeremiah, today I remove the fetters from your wrists. Come with me to Babylon if you wish, and I will take special care of you; but if you prefer not to come, well and good. The whole country lies before you; go wherever you think best.' Jeremiah had not yet answered when Nebu- 5 zaradan went on,*b* 'Go back to Gedaliah son of Ahikam, son of Shaphan, whom the king of Babylon has appointed governor of the cities of Judah, and stay with him openly; or else go wherever you choose.' Then the captain of the guard granted him an allowance of food, and gave him a present, and so took leave of him. Jeremiah then came to Gedaliah son of Ahikam 6 at Mizpah and stayed with him among the people left in the land.

When all the captains of the armed bands in the country-side and their 7 men heard that the king of Babylon had appointed Gedaliah son of Ahikam

---

*a* artisans: *prob. rdg., cp. 52. 15; Heb.* people who were left.     *b* Jeremiah . . . went on: *prob. rdg.; Heb. unintelligible in context.*

governor of the land, and had put him in charge of the weakest class of the population, men, women, and children, who had not been deported to
8 Babylon, they came to him at Mizpah; Ishmael son of Nethaniah came, and Johanan and Jonathan sons of Kareah, Seraiah son of Tanhumeth, the sons of Ephai*a* from Netophah, and Jezaniah of Beth-maacah, with their
9 men. Gedaliah son of Ahikam, son of Shaphan, gave them all this assurance: 'Have no fear of the Chaldaean officers. Settle down in the land and
10 serve the king of Babylon; and then all will be well with you. I am to stay in Mizpah and attend upon the Chaldaeans whenever they come, and you are to gather in the summer-fruits, wine, and oil, store them in jars, and
11 settle in the towns you have taken over.' The Judaeans also, in Moab, Ammon, Edom and other countries, heard that the king of Babylon had left a remnant in Judah and that he had set over them Gedaliah son of
12 Ahikam, son of Shaphan. The Judaeans, therefore, from all the places where they were scattered, came back to Judah and presented themselves before Gedaliah at Mizpah; and they gathered in a considerable store of fruit and wine.

13 Johanan son of Kareah and all the captains of the armed bands from the
14 country-side came to Gedaliah at Mizpah and said to him, 'Do you know that Baalis king of the Ammonites has sent Ishmael son of Nethaniah to
15 assassinate you?' But Gedaliah son of Ahikam did not believe them. Then Johanan son of Kareah said in private to Gedaliah, 'Let me go, unknown to anyone else, and kill Ishmael son of Nethaniah. Why allow him to assassinate you, and so let all the Judaeans who have rallied round you be
16 scattered and the remnant of Judah lost?' Gedaliah son of Ahikam answered him, 'Do no such thing. Your story about Ishmael is a lie.'

41 In the seventh month Ishmael son of Nethaniah, son of Elishama, who was a member of the royal house, came with ten men to Gedaliah son of
2 Ahikam at Mizpah. While they were at table with him there, Ishmael son of Nethaniah and the ten men with him rose to their feet and assassinated Gedaliah son of Ahikam, son of Shaphan, whom the king of Babylon had
3 appointed governor of the land. They also murdered the Judaeans with
4 him in Mizpah and the Chaldaeans who happened to be there. The second day after the murder of Gedaliah, while it was not yet common knowledge,
5 there came eighty men from Shechem, Shiloh, and Samaria. They had shaved off their beards, their clothes were rent and their bodies gashed, and they were carrying grain-offerings and frankincense to take to the
6 house of the LORD. Ishmael son of Nethaniah came out weeping from Mizpah to meet them and, when he met them, he said, 'Come to Gedaliah
7 son of Ahikam.' But as soon as they reached the centre of the town, Ishmael son of Nethaniah and his men murdered them and threw their bodies into
8 a pit, all except ten of them who said to Ishmael, 'Do not kill us, for we have a secret hoard in the country, wheat and barley, oil and honey.' So he held
9 his hand and did not kill them with the others. The pit into which he threw the bodies of those whose death he had caused by using Gedaliah's name was the pit which King Asa had made when threatened by Baasha king
10 of Israel; and the dead bodies filled it. He rounded up the rest of the

*a* Or Ophai.

people in Mizpah, that is the king's daughters and all who remained in Mizpah when Nebuzaradan captain of the guard appointed Gedaliah son of Ahikam governor; and with these he set out to cross over into Ammon. When Johanan son of Kareah and all the captains of the armed bands heard 11 of the crimes committed by Ishmael son of Nethaniah, they took all the 12 men they had and went to attack him. They found him by the greal pool in Gibeon. The people with Ishmael were glad when they saw Johanan 13 son of Kareah and the captains of the armed bands with him; and all whom 14 Ishmael had taken prisoner at Mizpah turned and joined Johanan son of Kareah. But Ishmael son of Nethaniah escaped from Johanan with eight 15 men, and they made their way to the Ammonites.

Johanan son of Kareah and all the captains of the armed bands took from 16 Mizpah the survivors whom he had rescued from Ishmael son of Nethaniah after the murder of Gedaliah son of Ahikam—men, armed and unarmed, women, children, and eunuchs, whom he had brought back from Gibeon. They started out and broke their journey at Kimham's holding near 17 Bethlehem, on their way into Egypt to escape the Chaldaeans. They were 18 afraid because Ishmael son of Nethaniah had assassinated Gedaliah son of Ahikam, whom the king of Babylon had appointed governor of the country.

All the captains of the armed bands, including Johanan son of Kareah 42 and Azariah son of Hoshaiah, together with the people, high and low, came to the prophet Jeremiah and said to him, 'May our petition be 2 acceptable to you: Pray to the LORD your God on our behalf and on behalf of this remnant; for, as you see for yourself, only a few of us remain out of many. Pray that the LORD your God may tell us which way we ought to go 3 and what we ought to do.' Then the prophet Jeremiah said to them, 'I have 4 heard your request and will pray to the LORD your God as you desire, and whatever answer the LORD gives I will tell you; I will keep nothing back.' They said to Jeremiah, 'May the LORD be a true and faithful witness against 5 us if we do not keep our oath! We swear that we will do whatever the LORD your God sends you to tell us. Whether we like it or not, we will obey the 6 LORD our God to whom we send you, in order that it may be well with us; we will obey the LORD our God.'

Within ten days the word of the LORD came to Jeremiah; so he summoned 7 8 Johanan son of Kareah, all the captains of the armed bands with him, and all the people, both high and low. He said to them, These are the words of 9 the LORD the God of Israel, to whom you sent me to present your petition: If you will stay in this land, then I will build you up and not pull you down, 10 I will plant you and not uproot you; I grieve for the disaster which I have brought upon you. Do not be afraid of the king of Babylon whom you now 11 fear. Do not be afraid of him, says the LORD; for I am with you, to save you and deliver you from his power. I will show you compassion, and he too 12 will have compassion on you; he will let you stay on your own soil. But it 13 may be that you will disobey the LORD your God and say, 'We will not stay in this land. No, we will go to Egypt, where we shall see no sign of war, 14 never hear the sound of the trumpet, and not starve for want of bread; and there we will live.' Then hear the word of the LORD, you remnant of Judah. 15

These are the words of the LORD of Hosts the God of Israel: If you are
16 bent on going to Egypt, if you do settle there, then the sword you fear will
overtake you in Egypt, and the famine you dread will still be with you,
17 even in Egypt, and there you will die. All the men who are bent on going
to Egypt and settling there will die by sword, by famine, or by pestilence;
not one shall escape or survive the calamity which I will bring upon them.
18 These are the words of the LORD of Hosts the God of Israel: As my anger
and my wrath were poured out upon the inhabitants of Jerusalem, so will
my wrath be poured out upon you when you go to Egypt; you will become
an object of execration and horror, of ridicule and reproach; you will
19 never see this place again. To you, then, remnant of Judah, the LORD says,
Do not go to Egypt. Make no mistake, I can bear witness against you this
20 day. You deceived yourselves when you sent me to the LORD your God and
said, 'Pray for us to the LORD our God; tell us all that the LORD our God
21 says and we will do it.' I have told you everything today; but you have not
22 obeyed the LORD your God in what he sent me to tell you. So now be sure
of this: you will die by sword, by famine, and by pestilence in the place
where you desire to go and make your home.

43 When Jeremiah had finished reciting to the people all that the LORD
2 their God had sent him to say, Azariah son of Hoshaiah and Johanan son
of Kareah and their party had the effrontery to say to*a* Jeremiah, 'You are
lying; the LORD our God has not sent you to forbid us to go and make our
3 home in Egypt. Baruch son of Neriah has incited you against us in order
to put us in the power of the Chaldaeans, so that they may kill us or deport
4 us to Babylon.' Johanan son of Kareah and the captains of the armed bands
5 and all the people refused to obey the LORD and stay in Judah. So Johanan
son of Kareah and the captains collected the remnant of Judah, all who had
returned from the countries among which they had been scattered to
6 make their home in Judah—men, women and children, including the
king's daughters, all the people whom Nebuzaradan captain of the guard
had left with Gedaliah son of Ahikam, son of Shaphan, as well as the pro-
7 phet Jeremiah and Baruch son of Neriah; these all went to Egypt and came
to Tahpanhes, disobeying the LORD.

8 9 The word of the LORD came to Jeremiah at Tahpanhes: Take some large
stones and set them in cement in the pavement at the entrance to Pharaoh's
10 palace in Tahpanhes. Let the Judaeans see you do it and say to them, These
are the words of the LORD of Hosts the God of Israel: I will send for my
servant Nebuchadrezzar king of Babylon, and he will place his throne on
11 these stones that I have set there, and spread his canopy over them. He
will then proceed to strike Egypt down, killing those doomed to death,
taking captive those who are for captivity, and putting to the sword those
12 who are for the sword. He will set fire to the temples of the Egyptian gods,
burning the buildings and carrying the gods into captivity. He will scour
the land of Egypt as a shepherd scours his clothes to rid them of lice. He
13 will leave Egypt with his purpose achieved. He will smash the sacred
pillars of Beth-shemesh in Egypt and burn down the temples of the
Egyptian gods.

*a* to say to: *or* to say: It is being said to.

The word that came to Jeremiah for all the Judaeans who were living in **44**
Egypt, in Migdol, Tahpanhes, Noph, and the district of Pathros: These 2
are the words of the LORD of Hosts the God of Israel: You have seen the
calamity that I brought upon Jerusalem and all the cities of Judah: today
they are laid waste and left uninhabited, all because of the wickedness of 3
those who provoked me to anger by going after other gods, gods unknown
to them, by burning sacrifices to them. It was you and your fathers who
did this. I took pains to send all my servants the prophets to you with this 4
warning: 'Do not do this abominable thing which I hate.' But your fathers 5
would not listen; they paid no heed. They did not give up their wickedness
or cease to burn sacrifices to other gods; so my anger and wrath raged like 6
a fire through the cities of Judah and the streets of Jerusalem, and they
became the desolate ruin that they are today.

Now these are the words of the LORD the God of Hosts, the God of 7
Israel: Why bring so great a disaster upon yourselves? Why bring destruction upon Judaeans, men and women, children and babes, and leave
yourselves without a survivor? This is what comes of your provoking me 8
by all your idolatry in burning sacrifices to other gods in Egypt where you
have made your home. You will destroy yourselves and become an object
of ridicule and reproach to all the nations of the earth. Have you forgotten 9
all the wickedness committed by your forefathers, by the kings of Judah
and their wives, by yourselves and your wives in the land of Judah and in
the streets of Jerusalem? To this day you have shown no remorse, no 10
reverence; you have not conformed to the law and the statutes which I
set before you and your forefathers. These, therefore, are the words of the 11
LORD of Hosts the God of Israel: I have made up my mind to bring calamity
upon you and exterminate the people of Judah. I will deal with the rem- 12
nant of Judah who were bent on going to make their home in Egypt; in
Egypt they shall all meet their end. Some shall fall by the sword, others
will meet their end by famine. High and low alike will die by sword or by
famine and will be an object of execration and horror, of ridicule and reproach. I will punish those who live in Egypt as I punished those in 13
Jerusalem, by sword, famine, and pestilence. Those who had remained in 14
Judah came to make their home in Egypt, confident that they would
return and live once more in Judah. But they shall not return;*a* not one of
them shall survive, not one escape.

Then all the men who knew that their wives were burning sacrifices to 15
other gods and the crowds of women standing by*b* answered Jeremiah,
'We will not listen to what you tell us in the name of the LORD. We intend 16 17
to fulfil all the promises by which we have bound ourselves: we will burn
sacrifices to the queen of heaven and pour drink-offerings to her as we used
to do, we and our fathers, our kings and our princes, in the cities of Judah
and in the streets of Jerusalem. We then had food in plenty and were
content; no calamity touched us. But from the time we left off burning 18
sacrifices to the queen of heaven and pouring drink-offerings to her, we
have been in great want, and in the end we have fallen victims to sword and

*a Prob. rdg.; Heb. adds* except fugitives.     *b Prob. rdg.; Heb. adds* and all the people
who lived in Egypt, in Pathros.

19 famine.' And the women said, 'When we burnt sacrifices to the queen of heaven and poured drink-offerings to her, our husbands knew full well that we were making crescent-cakes marked with her image and pouring
20 drink-offerings to her.' When Jeremiah received this answer from these
21 men and women and all the people, he said, 'The LORD did not forget those sacrifices which you and your fathers, your kings and princes and the people of the land burnt in the cities of Judah and in the streets of Jeru-
22 salem, and they mounted up in his mind until he could no longer tolerate them, so wicked were your deeds and so abominable the things you did. Your land became a desolate waste, an object of horror and ridicule, with
23 no inhabitants, as it still is. This calamity has come upon you because you burnt these sacrifices and sinned against the LORD and did not obey the LORD or conform to his laws, statutes, and teachings.'

24 Jeremiah further said to all the people and to the women, Listen to the
25 word of the LORD, all you from Judah who live in Egypt. These are the words of the LORD of Hosts the God of Israel: You women have made your actions match your words. 'We will carry out our vows', you said, 'to burn sacrifices to the queen of heaven and to pour drink-offerings to her.' Well
26 then, fulfil your vows by all means, and make your words good. But listen to the word of the LORD, all you from Judah who live in Egypt. I have sworn by my great name, says the LORD, that my name shall never again be on the lips of the men of Judah; they shall no longer swear in Egypt, 'By the life of
27 the Lord GOD.' I am on the watch to bring you evil and not good, and all the men of Judah who are in Egypt shall meet their end by sword and by
28 famine until not one is left.[a] It is then that all the survivors of Judah who have made their home in Egypt shall know whose word prevails, theirs or mine.

29 This is the sign I give you, says the LORD, that I intend to punish you in this place, so that you may learn that my words against you will prevail
30 to bring evil upon you: These are the words of the LORD: I will hand over Pharaoh Hophra king of Egypt to his enemies and to those who seek his life, just as I handed over Zedekiah king of Judah to his enemy Nebu-chadrezzar king of Babylon who was seeking to take his life.

45 THE WORD WHICH THE PROPHET JEREMIAH SPOKE to Baruch son of Neriah when he wrote these words in a book at Jeremiah's dictation in
2 the fourth year of Jehoiakim son of Josiah, king of Judah: These are the
3 words of the LORD the God of Israel concerning you, Baruch: You said, 'Woe is me, for the LORD has added grief to all my trials. I have worn my-
4 self out with my labours and have had no respite.' This is what you shall say to Baruch, These are the words of the LORD: What I have built, I demolish; what I have planted, I uproot. So it will be with the whole earth.
5 You seek great things for yourself. Leave off seeking them; for I will bring disaster upon all mankind, says the LORD, and I will let you live wherever you go, but you shall save your life and nothing more.

[a] *Prob. rdg.; Heb. adds* Few will escape the sword in Egypt to return to Judah.

## Prophecies against the nations

T HIS CAME TO THE PROPHET JEREMIAH as the word of the LORD **46**
concerning the nations.

Of Egypt: concerning the army of Pharaoh Necho king of Egypt at 2
Carchemish on the river Euphrates, which Nebuchadrezzar king of
Babylon defeated in the fourth year of Jehoiakim son of Josiah, king of
Judah.

Hold shield and buckler ready 3
and advance to battle;
harness the horses, let the riders mount; 4
form up, your helmets on, your lances burnished;
on with your coats of mail!
But now, what sight is this? 5
They are broken and routed,
their warriors beaten down;
they have turned to flight and do not look behind them.
Terror let loose!
This is the very word of the LORD.

Can the swift escape, can the warrior save himself? 6
In the north, by the river Euphrates,
they stumble and fall.

Who is this rising like the Nile, 7
like its streams turbulent in flood?
Egypt is rising like the Nile, 8
like its streams turbulent in flood.

He<sup>a</sup> says:

I will rise and cover the earth,
I will destroy both city and people.

Charge, horsemen! On, you flashing chariots, on! 9
Forward, the warriors,
Cushites and men of Put carrying shields,
Lydians grasping their bent bows!
This is the day of the Lord, the GOD of Hosts, 10
a day of vengeance, vengeance on his enemies;
the sword shall devour and be sated,
drunk with their blood.
For the GOD of Hosts, the Lord, holds sacrifice
in a northern land, by the river Euphrates.
Go up into Gilead and fetch balm, 11
O virgin people of Egypt.
You have tried many remedies, all in vain;
no skin shall grow over your wounds.

<sup>a</sup> Or It.

12 　　The nations have heard your cry,
　　　　and the earth echoes with your screams;
　　　　　warrior stumbles against warrior
　　　　　and both fall together.

13 　The word which the LORD spoke to the prophet Jeremiah when Nebuchadrezzar king of Babylon was coming to harry the land of Egypt:

14 　　Announce it in Egypt, proclaim it in Migdol,
　　　　proclaim it in Noph and Tahpanhes.
　　　　Say, Stand to! Be ready!
　　　　for a sword devours all around you.

15 　　Why does Apis flee, why does your bull-god not *a* stand fast?
　　　　The LORD has thrust him out.

16 　　The rabble of Egypt stumbles and falls,
　　　　　man against man;
　　　　each says, 'Quick, back to our people,
　　　to the land of our birth, far from the cruel sword!'

17 　　Give Pharaoh of Egypt the title King Bombast,
　　　　the man who missed his moment.

18 　　By my life, says the King
　　　　whose name is the LORD of Hosts,
　　　　one shall come mighty as Tabor among the hills,
　　　　　as Carmel by the sea.

19 　　Make ready your baggage for exile,
　　　　　you native people of Egypt;
　　　　for Noph shall become a waste,
　　　　　ruined and unpeopled.

20 　　Egypt was a lovely heifer,
　　　　but a gadfly from the north descended on her.

21 　　The mercenaries in her land were like stall-fed calves;
　　　　but they too turned and fled,
　　　　　not one of them stood his ground.
　　　　The hour of their downfall has come upon them,
　　　　　their day of reckoning.

22 　　Hark, she is hissing like a snake,
　　　　　for the enemy has come in all his force.
　　　　They fall upon her with axes
　　　　　like woodcutters at their work.

23 　　They cut down her forest, says the LORD,
　　　　　and it flaunts itself no more;
　　　　for they are many as locusts and past counting.

24 　　The Egyptians are put to shame, enslaved to a northern race.

25 　　The LORD of Hosts the God of Israel has spoken:
　　　　I will punish Amon god of No, *b*
　　　　Egypt with her gods and her princes,
　　　　Pharaoh and all who trust in him.

*a* Why does Apis . . . not: *or* Why is your bull-god routed, why does he not . . .
*b* *Prob. rdg.; Heb. adds* and Pharaoh.

I will deliver them to those bent on their destruction, 26
to Nebuchadrezzar king of Babylon and his troops;
yet in after time the land shall be peopled as of old.
 This is the very word of the LORD.

But you, Jacob my servant, have no fear, 27
 despair not, O Israel;
for I will bring you back safe from afar
 and your offspring from the land where they are captives;
and Jacob shall be at rest once more,
  prosperous and unafraid.
O Jacob my servant, have no fear, 28
says the LORD; for I am with you.
 I will make an end of all the nations
  amongst whom I have banished you;
 but I will not make an end of you;
  though I punish you as you deserve,
  I will not sweep you clean away.

This came to the prophet Jeremiah as the word of the LORD concerning 47
the Philistines before Pharaoh's harrying of Gaza: The LORD has spoken: 2
 See how waters are rising from the north
 and swelling to a torrent in spate,
 flooding the land and all that is in it,
  cities and all who live in them.
  Men shall shriek in alarm
 and all who live in the land shall howl.
 Hark, the pounding of his chargers' hooves, 3
 the rattle of his chariots and their rumbling wheels!
 Fathers spare no thought for their children;
  their hands hang powerless,
because the day is upon them when Philistia will be despoiled, 4
and Tyre and Sidon destroyed to the last defender;
 for the LORD will despoil the Philistines,
  that remnant of the isle of Caphtor.
Gaza is shorn bare, Ashkelon ruined. 5
 Poor remnant of their strength,
 how long will you gash yourselves and cry:
 Ah, sword in the hand of the LORD, 6
  how long will it be before you rest?
Sheathe yourself, rest and be quiet.
How can it rest? for the LORD has given it work to do 7
 against Ashkelon and the plain by the sea;
 there he has assigned the sword its task.

Of Moab. The LORD of Hosts the God of Israel has spoken: 48
 Alas for Nebo! it is laid waste;
 Kiriathaim is put to shame and captured,

Misgab reduced to shame and dismay;
2      Moab is renowned no longer.
In Heshbon they plot evil against her:
Come, destroy her, and leave her no longer a nation.
And you who live in Madmen shall be struck down,
your people pursued by the sword.
3      Hark to the cries of anguish from Horonaim:
great havoc and disaster!
4      Moab is broken.
Their cries are heard as far as Zoar.
5      On the ascent of Luhith
men go up weeping bitterly;
on the descent of Horonaim
cries of 'Disaster!' are heard.
6      Flee, flee for your lives
like a sand-grouse in the wilderness.
7      Because you have trusted in your defences and your arsenals,
you too will be captured,
and Kemosh will go into exile,
his priests and his captains with him;
8      and a spoiler shall descend on every city.
No city shall escape,
valley and tableland will be laid waste and plundered;
the LORD has spoken.

9      Let a warning flash to Moab,[a]
for she shall be laid in ruins[b]
and her cities shall become waste places
with no inhabitant.
10      A curse on him who is slack in doing the LORD's work!
A curse on him who withholds his sword from bloodshed!

11      All his life long, Moab has lain undisturbed
like wine settled on its lees,
not emptied from vessel to vessel;
he has not gone into exile.
Therefore the taste of him is unaltered,
and the flavour stays unchanged.
12      Therefore the days are coming, says the LORD,
when I will send men to tilt the jars; they shall tilt them
and empty his vessels and smash his jars;
13      and Moab shall be betrayed by Kemosh,
as Israel was betrayed by Bethel,
a god in whom he trusted.

14      How can you say, 'We are warriors
and men valiant in battle'?

[a] Let . . . Moab: *or* Doom Moab to become saltings.      [b] laid in ruins: *prob. rdg.;*
*Heb. obscure.*

> The spoiler of Moab and her cities has come up,                    15
> and the flower of her army goes down to the slaughter.

This is the very word of the King whose name is the LORD of Hosts.

> The downfall of Moab is near at hand,                    16
> disaster rushes swiftly upon him.
> Grieve for him, all you his neighbours                    17
> and all you who acknowledge him,
> and say, 'Alas! The commander's staff is broken,
> broken is the baton of honour.'
> Come down from your place of honour,                    18
> sit on the thirsty ground, you natives of Dibon;
> for the spoiler of Moab has come upon you
> and destroyed your citadels.
> You that live in Aroer, stand on the roadside and watch,                    19
> ask the fugitives, the man running, the woman escaping,
> ask them, 'What has happened?'

> Moab is reduced to shame and dismay:                    20
> howl and shriek,
> proclaim by the Arnon that Moab is despoiled,

and that judgement has come to the tableland, to Holon and Jahazah,    21
Mephaath and Dibon, Nebo and Beth-diblathaim and Kiriathaim, Beth-    22 23
gamul, Beth-meon, Kirioth and Bozrah, and to all the cities of Moab far    24
and near.

> Moab's horn is hacked off                    25
> and his strong arm is broken,
> says the LORD.

> Make Moab drunk—he has defied the LORD—                    26
> until he overflows with his vomit
> and even he becomes a butt for derision.
> But was Israel ever your butt?                    27
> Was he ever in company with thieves,
> that whenever you spoke of him you should shake your head?
> Leave your cities, you inhabitants of Moab,                    28
> and find a home among the crags;
> become like a dove which nests
> in the rock-face at the mouth of a cavern.

> We have heard of Moab's pride, and proud indeed he is,                    29
> proud, presumptuous, overbearing, insolent.
> I know his arrogance, says the LORD;                    30
> his boasting is false, false are his deeds.
> Therefore I will howl over Moab                    31
> and cry in anguish at the fate of every soul in Moab;
> I will moan over the men of Kir-heres.
> I will weep for you more than I wept for Jazer,                    32
> O vine of Sibmah

> whose branches spread out to the sea
>> and stretch as far as Jazer.
> The despoiler has fallen on your fruit and on your vintage,
33      gladness and joy are taken away
>> from the meadows of Moab,
> and I have stopped the flow of wine from the vats;
> nor shall shout follow shout from the harvesters—not one shout.

34 Heshbon and*ᵃ* Elealeh utter cries of anguish which are heard in Jahaz; the sound carries from Zoar to Horonaim and Eglath-shelishiyah; for the
35 waters of Nimrim have become a desolate waste. In Moab I will stop their sacrificing at hill-shrines and burning of offerings to their gods, says the
36 LORD. Therefore my heart wails for Moab like a reed-pipe, wails like a pipe for the men of Kir-heres. Their hard-earned wealth has vanished.
37 Every man's head is shorn in mourning, every beard shaved, every hand
38 gashed, and every waist girded with sackcloth. On Moab's roofs and in her broad streets nothing is heard but lamentation; for I have broken Moab
39 like a useless thing.*ᵇ* Moab in her dismay has shamefully turned to flight. Moab has become a butt of derision and a cause of dismay to all her neighbours.

40 For the LORD has spoken:

> A vulture shall swoop down
>> and spread out his wings over Moab.
41    The towns are captured, the strongholds taken;
> on that day the spirit of Moab's warriors shall fail
>> like the spirit of a woman in childbirth.
42    Then Moab shall be destroyed, no more to be a nation;
>> for he defied the LORD.
43    The hunter's scare, the pit, and the trap
>> threaten all who dwell in Moab,
>>> says the LORD.
44    If a man runs from the scare
>> he will fall into the pit;
> if he climbs out of the pit
>> he will be caught in the trap.
> All this will I bring on Moab in the year of their reckoning.
>> This is the very word of the LORD.

45    In the shadow of Heshbon the fugitives stand helpless;
>> for fire has blazed out from Heshbon,
> flames have shot out from the palace of Sihon;
>> they devour the homeland of Moab
>> and the country of the sons of tumult.
46    Alas for you, Moab! the people of Kemosh have vanished,
>> for your sons are taken into captivity
>> and your daughters led away captive.

---

*ᵃ* and: *prob. rdg., cp. Isa. 15. 4; Heb.* as far as.      *ᵇ Prob. rdg.; Heb. adds* says the LORD.

Yet in days to come I will restore Moab's fortunes. 47
    This is the very word of the LORD.
Here ends the sentence on Moab.

Of the people of Ammon. Thus says the LORD: **49**

Has Israel no sons? Has he no heir?
Why has Milcom inherited the land of Gad,
    and why do his people live in the cities of Gad?
Look, therefore, a time is coming, 2
    says the LORD,
when I will make Rabbath Ammon hear the battle-cry,
    when it will become a desolate mound of ruins
and its villages will be burnt to ashes,
and Israel shall disinherit those who disinherited him,
    says the LORD.

Howl, Heshbon, for Ai is despoiled. 3
    Cry aloud, you villages round Rabbath Ammon,
put on sackcloth and beat your breast,
    and score your bodies with gashes.
For Milcom will go into exile,
    and with him his priests and officers.
Why do you boast of your resources, 4
    you whose resources are melting away,
you wayward people who trust in your arsenals,
    and say, 'Who will dare attack me?'
Beware, I am bringing fear upon you from every side,[a] 5
    and every one of you shall be driven headlong
    with no man to round up the stragglers.
Yet after this I will restore the fortunes of Ammon. 6
    This is the very word of the LORD.

Of Edom. The LORD of Hosts has said: 7

Is wisdom no longer to be found in Teman?
Have her sages no skill in counsel?
    Has their wisdom decayed?
The people of Dedan have turned and fled 8
    and taken refuge in remote places;
for I will bring Esau's calamity upon him
    when his day of reckoning comes.
When the vintagers come to you 9[b]
    they will surely leave gleanings;
and if thieves raid your early crop in the night,
    they will take only as much as they want.
But I have ransacked Esau's treasure, 10
    I have uncovered his hiding-places,
    and he has nowhere to conceal himself;

---

[a] *Prob. rdg.; Heb. adds* says the Lord GOD of Hosts.   [b] *Verses 9 and 10: cp. Obad. 5, 6.*

his children, his kinsfolk and his neighbours are despoiled;
 there is no one to help him.
11   What! am I to save alive your fatherless children?
  Are your widows to trust in me?

12  For the LORD has spoken: Those who were not doomed to drink the
cup shall drink it none the less. Are you alone to go unpunished? You
13 shall not go unpunished; you shall drink it. For by my life, says the LORD,
Bozrah shall become a horror and reproach, a byword and a thing of
ridicule; and all her towns shall be a byword for ever.

14*a*  When a herald was sent among the nations, crying,
  'Gather together and march against her,
   rouse yourselves for battle',
  I heard this message from the LORD:

15   Look, I make you the least of all nations,
   an object of all men's contempt.
16   Your overbearing arrogance and your insolent heart
   have led you astray,
  you who haunt the crannies among the rocks
  and keep your hold on the heights of the hills.
  Though you build your nest high as a vulture,
   thence I will bring you down.
  This is the very word of the LORD.
17   Edom shall become a scene of horror,
  all who pass that way shall be horror-struck
  and shall jeer in derision at the blows she has borne,
18   overthrown like Sodom and Gomorrah and their neighbours,*b*
   says the LORD.
  No man shall live there,
  no mortal make a home in her.
19   Look, like a lion coming up
  from Jordan's dense thickets to the perennial pastures,
  in a moment I will chase every one away
  and round up the choicest of*c* her rams.
  For who is like me? Who is my equal?
  What shepherd can stand his ground before me?

20  Therefore listen to the LORD's whole purpose against Edom and all his
plans against the people of Teman:

  The young ones of the flock shall be carried off,
  and their pasture shall be horrified at their fate.
21   At the sound of their fall the land quakes;
  it cries out, and the cry is heard at the Red Sea.*d*

22   A vulture shall soar and swoop down
   and spread out his wings over Bozrah,

---

*a*  *Verses 14–16: cp. Obad. 1–4.*  *b*  *Or* inhabitants.  *c*  the choicest of: *prob.*
*rdg.; Heb.* who is chosen?  *d*  *Or* the Sea of Reeds.

and on that day the spirit of Edom's warriors shall fail
    like the spirit of a woman in labour.

Of Damascus.                                                                 23

    Hamath and Arpad are in confusion,
        for they have heard news of disaster;
    they are tossed up and down in anxiety
        like the unresting sea.
Damascus has lost heart and turns to flight;                                 24
        trembling has seized her,
the pangs of childbirth have gripped her.
    How forlorn is the town of joyful song,                               25
        the city of gladness!
Therefore her young men shall fall in her streets                            26
and all her warriors lie still in death that day.
    This is the very word of the LORD of Hosts.
Then will I kindle a fire against the wall of Damascus                       27
    and it shall consume the palaces of Ben-hadad.

Of Kedar and the royal princes *a* of Hazer which Nebuchadrezzar king        28
of Babylon subdued. The LORD has said:

    Come, attack Kedar,
        despoil the Arabs of the east.
    Carry off their tents and their flocks,                               29
        their tent-hangings and all their vessels,
        drive off their camels too,
and a cry shall go up: 'Terror let loose!'
    Flee, flee; make haste,                                               30
        take refuge in remote places, O people of Hazer,
    for the king of Babylon has laid his plans
    and formed a design against you,
        says the LORD.
Come, let us attack a nation living at peace,                                31
        in fancied security,
    with neither gates nor bars,
        sufficient to themselves.
    Their camels shall be carried off as booty,                           32
        their vast herds of cattle as plunder;
I will scatter them before the wind to roam the fringes of the desert, *b*
and bring ruin upon them from every side.
    Hazer shall become a haunt of wolves,                                 33
        for ever desolate;
    no man shall live there,
    no mortal make a home in her.
    This is the very word of the LORD.

*a* royal princes: *or* kingdom.      *b* them . . . desert: *or* to the wind those who clip
the hair on their temples.

34  This came to the prophet Jeremiah as the word of the LORD concerning
35  Elam, at the beginning of the reign of Zedekiah king of Judah: Thus says
the LORD of Hosts:

> Listen, I will break the bow of Elam,
>     the chief weapon of their might;
36  I will bring four winds against Elam
>     from the four quarters of heaven;
> I will scatter them before these four winds,
>     and there shall be no nation
> to which the exiles from Elam shall not come.
37  I will break Elam before their foes,
>     before those who are bent on their destruction;
> I will vent my anger upon them in disaster;
> I will harry them with the sword
>     until I make an end of them.
38  Then I will set my throne in Elam,
> and there I will destroy the king and his officers.
>     This is the very word of the LORD.
39  Yet in days to come I will restore the fortunes of Elam.
>     This is the very word of the LORD.

**50**  The word which the LORD spoke concerning Babylon, concerning the
land of the Chaldaeans, through the prophet Jeremiah:

2  Declare and proclaim among the nations,
> keep nothing back, spread the news:
>     Babylon is taken,
> Bel is put to shame, Marduk is in despair;
>     the idols of Babylon are put to shame,
>     her false gods are in despair.
3  For a nation out of the north has fallen upon her;
>     they will make her land a desolate waste
>     where neither man nor beast shall live.

4  In those days, at that time, says the LORD, the people of Israel and the
people of Judah shall come together and go in tears to seek the LORD their
5  God; they shall ask after Zion, turning their faces towards her, and they
shall come and join themselves to the LORD in an everlasting covenant
which shall not be forgotten.
6  My people were lost sheep, whose shepherds let them stray and run
wild on the mountains; they went from mountain to hill and forgot their
7  fold. Whoever found them devoured them, and their enemies said, 'We
incur no guilt, because they have sinned against the LORD, the LORD who
is the true goal and the hope of all their fathers.'

8  Flee from Babylon, from the land of the Chaldaeans;
>     go forth, and be like he-goats leading the flock.
9  For I will stir up a host of mighty nations
>     and bring them against Babylon,
>     marshalled against her from a northern land;

and from the north she shall be captured.
Their arrows shall be like a practised warrior
  who never comes back empty-handed;
the Chaldaeans shall be plundered,        10
and all who plunder them shall take their fill.
  This is the very word of the Lord.
You ravaged my patrimony; but though you rejoice and exult,      11
though you run free like a heifer after threshing,
  though you neigh like a stallion,
your mother shall be cruelly disgraced,        12
  she who bore you shall be put to shame.
  Look at her, the mere rump of the nations,
a wilderness, parched and desert,
unpeopled through the wrath of the Lord,      13
nothing but a desolate waste;
all who pass by Babylon shall be horror-struck
  and jeer in derision at the sight of her wounds.

Marshal your forces against Babylon, on every side,      14
  you whose bows are ready strung;
shoot at her, spare no arrows.
Shout in triumph over her, she has thrown up her hands,      15
her bastions are down, her walls demolished;
  this is the vengeance of the Lord.
  Take vengeance on her;
as she has done, so do to her.
Destroy every sower in Babylon,        16
every reaper with his sickle at harvest-time.
Before the cruel sword every man will go back to his people,
  every man flee to his own land.

Israel is a scattered flock        17
  harried and chased by lions:
as the king of Assyria was the first to feed on him,
so the king of Babylon was the last to gnaw his bones.
Therefore the Lord of Hosts the God of Israel says this:      18

  I will punish the king of Babylon and his country
as I have punished the king of Assyria.
I will bring Israel back to his pasture,      19
  and he shall graze on Carmel and Bashan;
in the hills of Ephraim and Gilead he shall eat his fill.

In those days, says the Lord, when that time comes, search shall be    20
made for the iniquity of Israel but there shall be none, and for the sin of
Judah but it shall not be found; for those whom I leave as a remnant I will
forgive.

  Attack the land of Merathaim;        21
  attack it and the inhabitants of Pekod;

       put all to the sword and destroy them,
       and do whatever I bid you.
         This is the very word of the LORD.

22        Hark, the sound of war in the land
         and great destruction!
23        See how the hammer of all the earth
         is hacked and broken in pieces,
       how Babylon has become
         a horror among the nations.
24        O Babylon, you have laid a snare to be your own undoing;
       you have been trapped, all unawares;
       there you are, you are caught,
         because you have challenged the LORD.
25        The LORD has opened his arsenal
         and brought out the weapons of his wrath;
     for this is work for the Lord the GOD of Hosts
         in the land of the Chaldaeans.
26        Her harvest-time has come:
     throw open her granaries,*a* pile her in heaps;
     destroy her, let no survivor be left.
27        Put all her warriors to the sword;
         let them be led to the slaughter.
     Woe upon them! for their time has come,
         their day of reckoning.
28        I hear the fugitives escaping from the land of Babylon
     to proclaim in Zion the vengeance of the LORD our God.

29        Let your arrows be heard whistling against Babylon,
         all you whose bows are ready strung.
       Pitch your tents all around her
         so that no one escapes.
       Pay her back for all her misdeeds;
         as she has done, so do to her,
     for she has insulted the LORD the Holy One of Israel.
30        Therefore her young men shall fall in her streets,
     and all her warriors shall lie still in death that day.
         This is the very word of the LORD.

31        I am against you, insolent city;
     for your time has come, your day of reckoning.
         This is the very word of the Lord GOD of Hosts.
32        Insolence shall stumble and fall
         and no one shall lift her up,
     and I will kindle fire in the heath around her
         and it shall consume everything round about.

---

*a Or* cattle-pens.

The LORD of Hosts has said this:                                    33

> The peoples of Israel and Judah together are oppressed;
> their captors hold them firmly and refuse to release them.
> But they have a powerful advocate,                              34
> whose name is the LORD of Hosts;
> he himself will plead their cause,
> bringing distress on Babylon and turmoil on its people.

> A sword hangs over the Chaldaeans,                              35
> over the people of Babylon, her officers and her wise men,
> says the LORD.
> A sword over the false prophets, and they are made fools,       36
> a sword over her warriors, and they despair,
> a sword over her horses and her chariots                        37
> and over all the rabble within her,
> and they shall become like women;
> a sword over her treasures, and they shall be plundered,
> a sword over her waters, and they shall dry up;                 38
> for it is a land of idols
> that glories in its dreaded gods.[a]

Therefore marmots and jackals shall skulk in it, desert-owls shall haunt 39
it, nevermore shall it be inhabited by men and no one shall dwell in it
through all the ages. As when God overthrew Sodom and Gomorrah and 40
their neighbours,[b] says the LORD, no man shall live there, no mortal make
a home in her.

> See, a people is coming from the north, a great nation,        41
> mighty[c] kings rouse themselves from earth's farthest corners;
> armed with bow and sabre, they are cruel and pitiless;         42
> bestriding horses, they sound like the thunder of the sea;
> they are like men arrayed for battle against you, Babylon.
> The king of Babylon has heard news of them                     43
> and his hands hang limp;
> agony grips him, anguish as of a woman in labour.
> Look, like a lion coming up                                     44
> from Jordan's dense thickets to the perennial pastures,
> in a moment I will chase every one away
> and round up the choicest of[d] the rams.
> For who is like me? Who is my equal?
> What shepherd can stand his ground before me?

Therefore listen to the LORD's whole purpose against Babylon and all 45
his plans against the land of the Chaldaeans:

> The young ones of the flock shall be carried off
> and their pasture shall be horrified at their fate.
> At the sound of the capture of Babylon                          46
> the land quakes and her cry is heard among the nations.

[a] dreaded gods: *or* dire portents.       [b] *Or* inhabitants.       [c] *Or* many.
[d] the choicest of: *prob. rdg.; Heb.* who is chosen?

**51** For thus says the LORD:

> I will raise a destroying wind
> against Babylon and those who live in Kambul,<sup>a</sup>

2 and I will send winnowers to Babylon,
> who shall winnow her and empty her land;
> for they shall assail her on all sides on the day of disaster.

3 How shall the archer then string his bow
> or put on his coat of mail?

> Spare none of her young men, destroy all her host,

4 and let them fall dead in the land of the Chaldaeans,
> pierced through in her streets.

5 Israel and Judah are not left widowed
> by their God, by the LORD of Hosts;
> but the land of the Chaldaeans is full of guilt,
> condemned by the Holy One of Israel.

6 Flee out of Babylon, every man for himself,
> or you will be struck down for her sin;
> for this is the LORD's day of vengeance,
> and he is paying her full recompense.

7 Babylon has been a gold cup in the LORD's hand
> to make all the earth drunk;
> the nations have drunk of her wine,
> and that has made them mad.

8 Babylon falls suddenly and is broken.
> Howl over her,
> fetch balm for her wound;
> perhaps she will be healed.

9 We would have healed Babylon, but she would not be<sup>b</sup> healed.
> Leave her and let us be off, each to his own country;
> for her doom reaches to heaven
> and mounts up to the skies.

10 The LORD has made our innocence plain to see;
> come, let us proclaim in Zion
> what the LORD our God has done.

11 Sharpen the arrows, fill the quivers.
> The LORD has roused the spirit of the king of the Medes;
> for the LORD's purpose against Babylon is to destroy it,
> and his vengeance is the avenging of his temple.

12 Raise the standard against Babylon's walls,
> mount a strong guard, post a watch, set an ambush;
> for the LORD has both planned and carried out
> what he threatened to do to the people of Babylon.

13 O opulent city, standing beside great waters,
> your end has come, your destiny is certain.

---

<sup>a</sup> Kambul: *prob. rdg.; Heb.* the heart of my opponents.     <sup>b</sup> would not be: *or* was not.

The LORD of Hosts has sworn by himself, saying,    14
Once I filled you with men, countless as locusts,
  yet a song of triumph shall be chanted over you.

God made the earth by his power,    15*a*
fixed the world in place by his wisdom,
  unfurled the skies by his understanding.
At the thunder of his voice the waters in heaven are amazed;*b*    16
he brings up the mist from the ends of the earth,
he opens rifts*c* for the rain
  and brings the wind out of his storehouses.
All men are brutish and ignorant,    17
every goldsmith is discredited by his idol;
for the figures he casts are a sham,
  there is no breath in them.
They are worth nothing, mere mockeries,    18
  which perish when their day of reckoning comes.
God, Jacob's creator, is not like these;    19
  for he is the maker of all.
Israel is the people he claims as his own;
  the LORD of Hosts is his name.

You are my battle-axe, my weapon of war;    20
with you I will break nations in pieces,
  and with you I will destroy kingdoms.
With you I will break horse and rider,    21
with you I will break chariot and rider,
with you I will break man and woman,    22
with you I will break young and old,
with you I will break young man and maiden,
with you I will break shepherd and flock,    23
with you I will break ploughman and team,
  with you I will break viceroys and governors.
So will I repay Babylon and the people of Chaldaea    24
for all the wrong which they did in Zion in your sight.
  This is the very word of the LORD.

I am against you, O destroying mountain,*d*    25
  you who destroy the whole earth,
and I will stretch out my hand against you
  and send you tumbling from your terraces
  and make you a burnt-out mountain.
No stone of yours shall be used as a corner-stone,    26
  no stone for a foundation;
but you shall be desolate, for ever waste.
  This is the very word of the LORD.

---

*a* *Verses 15-19: cp. 10. 12-16.*    *b* At the thunder ... amazed: *prob. rdg.; Heb.* At the sound of his giving tumult of waters in heaven.    *c* rifts: *prob. rdg.; Heb.* lightnings.
*d* *Or* O Mount of the Destroyer.

27 Raise a standard in the land,[a]
blow the trumpet among the nations,
hallow the nations for war against her,
summon the kingdoms of Ararat, Minni, and Ashkenaz,
appoint a commander-in-chief against her,
bring up the horses like a dark swarm of locusts;[b]

28 hallow the nations for war against her,
the king of the Medes, his viceroys and governors,
and all the lands of his realm.

29 The earth quakes and writhes;
for the LORD's designs against Babylon are fulfilled,
to make the land of Babylon desolate and unpeopled.

30 Babylon's warriors have given up the fight,
they skulk in the forts;
their courage has failed, they have become like women.
Her buildings are set on fire, the bars of her gates broken.

31 Runner speeds to meet runner,
messenger to meet messenger,
bringing news to the king of Babylon
that every quarter of his city is taken,

32 the river-crossings are seized,
the guard-towers set on fire
and the garrison stricken with panic.

33 For the LORD of Hosts the God of Israel has spoken:
Babylon is like a threshing-floor when it is trodden;
soon, very soon, harvest-time will come.

34 'Nebuchadrezzar king of Babylon has devoured me
and sucked me dry,
he has set me aside like an empty jar.
Like a dragon he has gulped me down;
he has filled his maw with my delicate flesh
and spewed me up.

35 On Babylon be the violence done to me,
the vengeance taken upon me!',
Zion's people shall say.
'My blood be upon the Chaldaeans!',
Jerusalem shall say.

36 Therefore the LORD says:
I will plead your cause, I will avenge you;
I will dry up her sea[c] and make her waters fail;

37 and Babylon shall become a heap of ruins, a haunt of wolves,
a scene of horror and derision, with no inhabitant.

38 Together they roar like young lions,
they growl like the whelps of a lioness.

[a] *Or* earth.    [b] *Or* hoppers.    [c] *Possibly the Euphrates.*

I will cause their drinking bouts to end in fever      39
and make them so drunk that they will writhe and toss,
then sink into unending sleep, never to wake.
     This is the very word of the LORD.
I will bring them like lambs to the slaughter,      40
rams and he-goats together.
Sheshak*a* is captured,      41
the pride of the whole earth taken;
Babylon has become a horror amongst the nations!
The sea has surged over Babylon,      42
she is covered by its roaring waves.
Her cities have become waste places,      43
a land dried up and desert,
a land in whose cities no man lives
and through which no mortal travels.
I will punish Bel in Babylon      44
and make him bring up what he has swallowed;
nations shall never again come streaming to him.
The wall of Babylon has fallen;
come out of her, O my people,      45
and let every man save himself
from the anger of the LORD.
Then beware of losing heart,      46
fear no rumours spread abroad in the land,
as rumour follows rumour,
each year a new one:
violence on earth and ruler against ruler.
Therefore a time is coming      47
when I will punish Babylon's idols,
and all her land shall be put to shame,
and all her slain shall lie fallen in her midst.
Heaven and earth and all that is in them      48
shall sing in triumph over Babylon;
for marauders from the north shall overrun her.
     This is the very word of the LORD.
Babylon must fall for the sake of *b* Israel's slain,      49
as the slain of all the world fell for the sake of Babylon.
You who have escaped from her sword, off with you, do not linger.      50
Remember the LORD from afar
and call Jerusalem to mind.
We are put to shame by the reproaches we have heard,      51
and our faces are covered with confusion:
strangers have entered the sacred courts of the LORD's house.

A time is coming therefore, says the LORD,      52
when I will punish her idols,
and all through the land there shall be the groaning of the wounded.

---

*a*   *A name for Babylon.*      *b*   for the sake of: *prob. rdg.; Heb. om.*

53        Though Babylon should reach to the skies
        and make her high towers inaccessible,
     I will send marauders to overrun her.
         This is the very word of the LORD.

54        Hark, cries of agony from Babylon!
        Sounds of destruction from the land of the Chaldaeans!

55        For the LORD is despoiling Babylon
     and will silence the hum of the city,
     before the advancing wave that booms and roars
        like mighty waters.

56        For marauders march on Babylon herself,
     her warriors are captured and their bows are broken;
     for the LORD, a God of retribution, will repay in full.

57         I will make her princes and her wise men drunk,
       her viceroys and governors and warriors,
     and they shall sink into unending sleep, never to wake.
       This is the very word of the King,
        whose name is the LORD of Hosts.

58    The LORD of Hosts says:
     The walls of broad Babylon shall be razed to the ground,
       her lofty gates shall be set on fire.
     Worthless now is the thing for which the nations toiled;
     the peoples wore themselves out for a mere nothing.

59    The instructions given by the prophet Jeremiah to the quartermaster Seraiah son of Neriah and grandson of Mahseiah, when he went to Babylon with Zedekiah king of Judah in the fourth year of his reign.

60    Jeremiah, having written down in a[a] book[b] a full description of the
61 disaster which would come upon Babylon, said to Seraiah, 'When you
62 come to Babylon, look at this, read it all and then say, "Thou, O LORD, hast declared thy purpose to destroy this place and leave it with no one
63 living in it, man or beast; it shall be desolate, for ever waste." When you have finished reading the book, tie a stone to it and throw it into the
64 Euphrates, and then say, "So shall Babylon sink, never to rise again after the disaster which I shall bring upon her." '

Thus far are the collected sayings of Jeremiah.

## Historical note about the fall of Jerusalem

52 1[c]  ZEDEKIAH WAS TWENTY-ONE YEARS OLD when he came to the throne, and he reigned in Jerusalem for eleven years; his mother was
2 Hamutal daughter of Jeremiah of Libnah. He did what was wrong in the
3 eyes of the LORD, as Jehoiakim had done. Jerusalem and Judah so angered

---

[a] *Or* one.     [b] *Prob. rdg.; Heb. adds* all these things which are written concerning Babylon.     [c] *Verses 1–27 : cp. 39. 1–10 and 2 Kgs. 24. 18—25. 21.*

the LORD that in the end he banished them from his sight; and Zedekiah rebelled against the king of Babylon.

In the ninth year of his reign, in the tenth month, on the tenth day of 4 the month, Nebuchadrezzar king of Babylon advanced with all his army against Jerusalem, invested it and erected watch-towers against it on every side; the siege lasted till the eleventh year of King Zedekiah. In the 5 6 fourth month of that year, on the ninth day of the month, when famine was severe in the city and there was no food for the common people, the city 7 was thrown open. When Zedekiah king of Judah saw this, he and*a* all his armed escort left the city and fled by night through the gate called Between the Two Walls, near the king's garden. They escaped towards the Arabah, although the Chaldaeans were surrounding the city. But the Chaldaean 8 army pursued the king and overtook him in the lowlands of Jericho; and all his company was dispersed. The king was seized and brought before 9 the king of Babylon at Riblah in the land of Hamath, where he pleaded his case before him. The king of Babylon slew Zedekiah's sons before his 10 eyes; he also put to death all the princes of Judah in Riblah. Then the king 11 of Babylon put Zedekiah's eyes out, bound him with fetters of bronze, brought him to Babylon and committed him to prison till the day of his death.

In the fifth month, on the tenth day of the month, in the nineteenth year 12 of Nebuchadrezzar king of Babylon, Nebuzaradan, captain of the king's bodyguard,*b* came to Jerusalem and set fire to the house of the LORD and 13 the royal palace; all the houses in the city, including the mansion of Gedaliah,*c* were burnt down. The Chaldaean forces with the captain of 14 the guard pulled down the walls all round Jerusalem. *d*Nebuzaradan 15 captain of the guard deported the rest of the people left in the city, those who had deserted to the king of Babylon and any remaining artisans. The 16 captain of the guard left only the weakest class of people to be vine-dressers and labourers.

The Chaldaeans broke up the pillars of bronze in the house of the LORD, 17 the trolleys, and the sea of bronze, and took the metal to Babylon. They 18 took also the pots, shovels, snuffers, tossing-bowls, saucers, and all the vessels of bronze used in the service of the temple. The captain of the 19 guard took away the precious metal, whether gold or silver, of which the cups, firepans, tossing-bowls, pots, lamp-stands, saucers, and flagons were made. The bronze of the two pillars, of the one sea and of the twelve 20 oxen supporting it, which King Solomon had made for the house of the LORD, was beyond weighing. The one pillar was eighteen cubits high and 21 twelve cubits in circumference; it was hollow and the metal was four fingers thick. It had a capital of bronze, five cubits high, and a decoration of net- 22 work and pomegranates ran all round it, wholly of bronze. The other pillar, with its pomegranates, was exactly like it. Ninety-six pomegranates were 23 exposed to view and there were a hundred in all on the network all round.

---

*a* When Zedekiah . . . and: *prob. rdg., cp. 39. 4; Heb. om.*          *b* captain . . . body-guard: *prob. rdg., cp. 2 Kgs. 25. 8; Heb.* captain of the bodyguard stood before the king of Babylon.          *c* Gedaliah: *prob. rdg.; Heb.* the great man.          *d* *Prob. rdg., cp. 39. 9 and 2 Kgs. 25. 11; Heb. prefixes* The weakest class of the people (*cp. verse 16*).

24 The captain of the guard took Seraiah the chief priest and Zephaniah
25 the deputy chief priest and the three on duty at the entrance; he took also
from the city a eunuch who was in charge of the fighting men, seven of
those with right of access to the king who were still in the city, the adjutant-
general*a* whose duty was to muster the people for war, and sixty men of
26 the people who were still there. These Nebuzaradan captain of the guard
27 brought to the king of Babylon at Riblah. There, in the land of Hamath,
the king of Babylon had them flogged and put to death. So Judah went into
exile from their own land.

28 These were the people deported by Nebuchadrezzar in the seventeenth*b*
29 year: three thousand and twenty-three Judaeans. In his eighteenth year,
30 eight hundred and thirty-two people from Jerusalem; in his twenty-third
year, seven hundred and forty-five Judaeans were deported by Nebuzaradan the captain of the bodyguard: all together four thousand six
hundred people.

31*c* In the thirty-seventh year of the exile of Jehoiachin king of Judah, on
the twenty-fifth day of the twelfth month, Evil-merodach king of Babylon
in the year of his accession showed favour to Jehoiachin king of Judah. He
32 brought him out of prison, treated him kindly and gave him a seat at table
33 above the kings with him in Babylon. So Jehoiachin discarded his prison
34 clothes and lived as a pensioner of the king for the rest of his life. For his
maintenance a regular daily allowance was given him by the king of
Babylon as long as he lived, to the day of his death.

# LAMENTATIONS

## Sorrows of captive Zion

1 How solitary lies the city, once so full of people!
Once great among nations, now become a widow;
once queen among provinces, now put to forced labour!

2 Bitterly she weeps in the night,
tears run down her cheeks;
she has no one to bring her comfort
among all that love her;
all her friends turned traitor
and became her enemies.

3 Judah went into the misery of exile
and endless servitude.
Settled among the nations,
she found no resting-place;
all her persecutors fell upon her
in her sore straits.

---

*a* *Prob. rdg.; Heb. adds* commander-in-chief.    *b* *Prob. rdg.; Heb.* seventh.
*c* *Verses 31–34: cp. 2 Kgs. 25. 27–30.*

The paths to Zion mourn,                        4
    for none attend her sacred feasts;
all her gates are desolate.
    Her priests groan and sigh,
    her virgins are cruelly treated.
How bitter is her fate!
Her adversaries have become her masters,        5
    her enemies take their ease,
    for the LORD has cruelly punished her
because of misdeeds without number;
    her young children have gone,
driven away captive by the enemy.
All majesty has vanished                         6
    from the daughter of Zion.
Her princes have become like deer
    that can find no pasture
and run on, their strength all spent,
    pursued by the hunter.
    Jerusalem has remembered                     7
her days of misery and wandering,[a]
when her people fell into the power of the adversary
    and there was no one to help her.
The adversary saw and mocked
    at her fallen state.
Jerusalem had sinned greatly,                    8
and so she was treated like a filthy rag;
all those who had honoured her held her cheap,
    for they had seen her nakedness.
What could she do but sigh
    and turn away?
    Uncleanness clung to her skirts,             9
and she gave no thought to her fate.
    Her fall was beyond belief
and there was no one to comfort her.
Look, LORD, upon her misery,
    see how the enemy has triumphed.
The adversary stretched out his hand            10
    to seize all her treasures;
then it was that she saw Gentiles
    entering her sanctuary,
Gentiles forbidden by thee to enter
    the assembly, for it was thine.
    All her people groaned,                      11
    they begged for bread;
they sold their treasures for food
    to give them strength again.

[a] *Prob. rdg.; Heb. adds* all her treasures which have been from days of old.

993

Look, O Lord, and see
how cheap I am accounted.

12 Is it of no concern to you who pass by?
If only you would look and see:
is there any agony like mine,
like these my torments
with which the Lord has cruelly punished me
in the day of his anger?

13 He sent down fire from heaven,
it ran through my bones;
he spread out a net to catch my feet,
and turned me back;
he made me an example of desolation,
racked with sickness all day long.

14 My transgressions were bound<sup>a</sup> upon me,
his own hand knotted them round me;
his yoke was lifted on to my neck,
my strength failed beneath its weight;
the Lord abandoned me to its hold,<sup>b</sup>
and I could not stand.

15 The Lord treated with scorn
all the mighty men within my walls;
he marshalled rank on rank against me
to crush my young warriors.
The Lord trod down, like grapes in the press,
the virgin daughter of Judah.

16 For these things I weep over my plight,<sup>c</sup>
my eyes run with tears;
for any to comfort me and renew my strength
are far to seek;
my sons are an example of desolation,
for the enemy is victorious.

17 Zion lifted her hands in prayer,
but there was no one to comfort her;
the Lord gave Jacob's enemies the order
to beset him on every side.
Jerusalem became a filthy rag in their midst.

18 The Lord was in the right;
it was I who rebelled against his commands.
Listen, O listen, all you nations,
and look on my agony:
my virgins and my young men are gone into captivity.

19 I called to my lovers, they broke faith with me;
my priests and my elders in the city
went hungry and could find nothing,

---

<sup>a</sup> bound: *prob. rdg.; Heb. word unknown.*   <sup>b</sup> its hold: *prob. rdg.; Heb. obscure.*
<sup>c</sup> my plight: *prob. rdg.; Heb. my eye.*

although they sought food for themselves
    to renew their strength.
See, LORD, how sorely I am distressed.    20
    My bowels writhe in anguish
and my stomach turns within me,
    because I wantonly rebelled.
The sword makes orphans in the streets,
    as plague does within doors.
Hear me when I groan    21
    with no one to comfort me.
All my enemies, when they heard of my calamity,
rejoiced at what thou hadst done;
but hasten the day thou hast promised
    when they shall become like me.
Let all their evil deeds come before thee;    22
    torment them in their turn,
as thou hast tormented me
    for all my transgressions;
for my sighs are many and my heart is faint.

## *Zion's hope of relief after punishment*

What darkness the Lord in his anger    2
    has brought upon the daughter of Zion!
He hurled down from heaven to earth
    the glory of Israel,
and did not remember in the day of his anger
    that Zion was his footstool.
The Lord overwhelmed without pity    2
    all the dwellings of Jacob.
    In his wrath he tore down
the strongholds of the daughter of Judah;
he levelled with the ground and desecrated
    the kingdom and its rulers.
    In his anger he hacked down    3
the horn of Israel's pride,
he withdrew his helping hand
    when the enemy came on;
and he blazed in Jacob like flaming fire
    that rages far and wide.
In enmity he strung his bow;    4
    he took his stand like an adversary
    and with his strong arm he slew
all those who had been his delight;
he poured his fury out like fire
    on the tent of the daughter of Zion.
The Lord played an enemy's part    5
    and overwhelmed Israel.

He overwhelmed all their towered mansions
and brought down their strongholds in ruins;
sorrow upon sorrow he brought
to the daughter of Judah.

6 He stripped his tabernacle as a vine is stripped,
and made the place of assembly a ruin.
In Zion the LORD blotted out all memory
of festal assembly[a] and of sabbath;
king and priest alike he scorned
in the grimness of his anger.

7 The Lord spurned his own altar
and laid a curse upon his sanctuary.
He delivered the walls of her mansions
into the power of the enemy;
in the LORD's very house they raised shouts of victory
as on a day of festival.

8 The LORD was minded to bring down in ruins
the walls of the daughter of Zion;
he took their measure with his line
and did not scruple to demolish her;
he made rampart and wall lament,
and both together lay dejected.

9 Her gates are sunk into the earth,
he has shattered and broken their bars;
her king and her rulers are among the Gentiles,
and there is no law;
her prophets too have received
no vision from the LORD.

10 The elders of the daughter of Zion
sit on the ground and sigh;
they have cast dust on their heads
and clothed themselves in sackcloth;
the virgins of Jerusalem
bow their heads to the ground.

11 My eyes are blinded with tears,
my bowels writhe in anguish.
In my bitterness my bile is spilt on the earth
because of my people's wound,
when children and infants faint
in the streets of the town

12 and cry to their mothers,
'Where can we get corn and wine?'—
when they faint like wounded things
in the streets of the city,
gasping out their lives
in their mothers' bosom.

---

[a] festal assembly: *or* appointed seasons.

How can I cheer you? Whose plight is like yours,       13
    daughter of Jerusalem?
To what can I compare you for your comfort,
    virgin daughter of Zion?
For your wound gapes wide as the ocean;
    who can heal you?
The visions that your prophets saw for you       14
    were false and painted shams;
they did not bring home to you your guilt
    and so reverse your fortunes.
The visions that they saw for you were delusions,
    false and fraudulent.*a*
All those who pass by       15
    snap their fingers at you;
they hiss and wag their heads at you,
    daughter of Jerusalem:
'Is this the city once called Perfect in beauty,
    Joy of the whole earth?'
All your enemies       16
    make mouths and jeer at you;
they hiss and grind their teeth,
    saying, 'Here we are,
this is the day we have waited for;
    we have lived to see it.'

The Lord has done what he planned to do,       17
    he has fulfilled his threat,
all that he ordained from days of old.
    He has demolished without pity
and let the enemy rejoice over you,
    filling your adversaries with pride.
Cry with a full heart*b* to the Lord,       18
    O wall of the daughter of Zion;
let your tears run down like a torrent
    by day and by night.
Give yourself not a moment's rest,
    let your tears never cease.
Arise and cry aloud in the night;       19
    at the beginning of every watch
pour out your heart like water
    in the Lord's very presence.
Lift up your hands to him
    for the lives of your children.*c*
Look, Lord, and see:       20
    who is it that thou hast thus tormented?

---

*a* fraudulent: *or* causing banishment.       *b* Cry . . . heart: *prob. rdg.; Heb.* Their
heart cried.       *c* *Prob. rdg.; Heb. adds* who faint with hunger at every street-
corner.

Must women eat the fruit of their wombs,
    the children they have brought safely to birth?
Shall priest and prophet be slain
    in the sanctuary of the Lord?

21 There in the streets young men and old
    lie on the ground.
My virgins and my young men have fallen
    by sword and by famine;
thou hast slain them in the day of thy anger,
    slaughtered them without pity.

22 Thou didst summon my enemies against me from
    every side,
    like men assembling for a festival;
not a man escaped, not one survived
    in the day of the LORD's anger.
All whom I brought safely to birth and reared
    were destroyed by my enemies.

3 I am the man who has known affliction,
    I have felt the rod of his wrath.

2 It was I whom he led away and left to walk
    in darkness, where no light is.

3 Against me alone he has turned his hand,
    and so it is all day long.

4 He has wasted away my flesh and my skin
    and broken all my bones;

5 he has built up walls around me,
    behind and before,

6 and has cast me into a place of darkness
    like a man long dead.

7 He has walled me in so that I cannot escape,
    and weighed me down with fetters;

8 even when I cry out and call for help,
    he rejects my prayer.

9 He has barred my road with blocks of stone
    and tangled up my way.

10 He lies in wait for me like a bear
    or a lion lurking in a covert.

11 He has made my way refractory and lamed me
    and left me desolate.

12 He has strung his bow
and made me the target for his arrows;

13 he has pierced my kidneys with shafts
    drawn from his quiver.

14 I have become a laughing-stock to all nations,
    the target of their mocking songs all day.

15 He has given me my fill of bitter herbs
    and made me drunk with wormwood.

He has broken my teeth on gravel;                              16
    fed on ashes, I am racked with pain;
peace has gone out of my life,                                 17
    and I have forgotten what prosperity means.
Then I cry out that my strength has gone                       18
    and so has my hope in the LORD.

The memory of my distress and my wanderings                    19
    is*a* wormwood and gall.
Remember, O remember,                                          20
and stoop down to me.*b c*
All this I take to heart                                       21
    and therefore I will wait patiently:
the LORD's true love is surely not spent,*d*                   22
    nor has his compassion failed;
they are new every morning,                                    23
    so great is his constancy.
The LORD, I say, is all that I have;                           24
    therefore I will wait for him patiently.
The LORD is good to those who look for him,                    25
    to all who seek him;
it is good to wait in patience and sigh                        26
    for deliverance by the LORD.
    It is good, too, for a man                                 27
to carry the yoke in his youth.
Let him sit alone and sigh                                     28
    if it is heavy upon him;
let him lay his face in the dust,                              29
    and there may yet be hope.
Let him turn his cheek to the smiter                           30
    and endure full measure of abuse;
for the Lord will not cast off                                 31
    his servants*e* for ever.
He may punish cruelly, yet he will have compassion             32
    in the fullness of his love;
he does not willingly afflict                                  33
    or punish any mortal man.

To trample underfoot                                           34
    any prisoner in the land,
to deprive a man of his rights                                 35
    in defiance of the Most High,
to pervert justice in the courts—                              36
    such things the Lord has never approved.

---

*a* The memory . . . is: *or* Remember my distress and my wanderings, the . . .
*b* stoop down to me: *prob. original rdg., altered in Heb. to* I sink down.
*c* Remember . . . me: *or* I remember, I remember them and sink down.
*d* spent: *prob. rdg.; Heb. unintelligible.*      *e* his servants: *prob. rdg.; Heb. om.*

| | |
|---|---|
| 37 | Who can command and it is done, |
| | if the Lord has forbidden it? |
| 38 | Do not both bad and good proceed |
| | from the mouth of the Most High? |
| 39 | Why should any man living complain, |
| | any mortal who has sinned? |
| 40 | Let us examine our ways and put them to the test |
| | and turn back to the LORD; |
| 41 | let us lift up our hearts, not our hands, |
| | to God in heaven. |
| 42 | We ourselves have sinned and rebelled, |
| | and thou hast not forgiven. |
| 43 | In anger thou hast turned*a* and pursued us |
| | and slain without pity; |
| 44 | thou hast hidden thyself behind the clouds |
| | beyond reach of our prayers; |
| 45 | thou hast treated us as offscouring and refuse |
| | among the nations. |
| 46 | All our enemies make mouths |
| | and jeer at us. |
| 47 | Before us lie hunter's scare and pit, |
| | devastation and ruin. |
| 48 | My eyes run with streams of water |
| | because of my people's wound. |
| 49 | My eyes stream with unceasing tears |
| | and refuse all comfort, |
| 50 | while the LORD in heaven looks down |
| | and watches my affliction,*b* |
| 51 | while the LORD torments*c* me |
| | with the fate of all the daughters of my city. |
| | |
| 52 | Those who for no reason were my enemies |
| | drove me cruelly like a bird; |
| 53 | they thrust me alive into the silent pit, |
| | and they closed it over me with a stone; |
| 54 | the waters rose high above my head, |
| | and I said, 'My end has come.' |
| 55 | But I called on thy name, O LORD, |
| | from the depths of the pit; |
| 56 | thou heardest my voice; do not turn a deaf ear |
| | when I cry, 'Come to my relief.' |
| 57 | Thou wast near when I called to thee; |
| | thou didst say, 'Have no fear.' |
| 58 | Lord, thou didst plead my cause |
| | and ransom my life; |

*a* *Prob. rdg.; Heb.* hidden.
*b* my affliction: *prob. rdg.; Heb.* my eye.
*c* the LORD torments: *prob. rdg.; Heb.* tormenting.

thou sawest, LORD, the injustice done to me                    59
  and gavest judgement in my favour;
    thou sawest their vengeance,                        60
    all their plots against me.
Thou didst hear their bitter taunts, O LORD,                    61
  their many plots against me,
the whispering, the murmurs of my enemies                       62
  all the day long.
See how, whether they sit or stand,                             63
  they taunt me bitterly.
Pay them back for their deeds, O LORD,                          64
  pay them back what they deserve.
Show them how hard thy heart can be,                            65
  how little concern thou hast for them.
Pursue them in anger and exterminate them                       66
  from beneath thy heavens, O LORD.

How dulled is the gold,                                         **4**
how tarnished the fine gold!
The stones of the sanctuary[a] lie strewn
  at every street-corner.
See Zion's precious sons,                                       2
  once worth their weight in finest gold,
now counted as pitchers of earthenware
  made by any potter's hand.
Even whales[b] uncover the teat                                 3
  and suckle their young;
but the daughters of my people are cruel
  as ostriches in the desert.
The sucking infant's tongue                                     4
  cleaves to its palate from thirst;
young children beg for bread
  but no one offers them a crumb.
Those who once fed delicately                                   5
  are desolate in the streets,
and those nurtured in purple
  now grovel on dunghills.
The punishment[c] of my people is worse                         6
  than the penalty[d] of Sodom,
which was overthrown in a moment
  and no one wrung his hands.
Her crowned princes[e] were once purer than snow,               7
  whiter than milk;
they were ruddier than branching coral,[f]
  and their limbs were lapis lazuli.

[a] The stones of the sanctuary: *or* Bright gems.    [b] *Prob. rdg.; Heb.* jackals.
[c] *Or* iniquity.    [d] *Or* sin.    [e] crowned princes: *or* Nazirites.    [f] than . . .
coral: *prob. rdg.; Heb.* branch than coral.

8     But their faces turned blacker than soot,
      and no one knew them in the streets;
    the skin was drawn tight over their bones,
      dry as touchwood.

9     Those who died by the sword were more fortunate
      than those who died of hunger;
    these wasted away, deprived
      of the produce of the field.

10     Tender-hearted women with their own hands
      boiled their own children;
    their children became their food
      in the day of my people's wounding.

11     The LORD glutted his rage
      and poured forth his anger;
    he kindled a fire in Zion,
      and it consumed her foundations.

12     This no one believed, neither the kings of the earth
      nor anyone that dwelt in the world:
    that enemy or invader would enter
      the gates of Jerusalem.

13     It was for the sins of her prophets
      and for the iniquities of her priests,
    who shed within her walls
      the blood of the righteous.

14     They wandered blindly in the streets,
      so stained with blood
    that men would not touch
      even their garments.

15     'Away, away; unclean!' men cried to them.
      'Away, do not come near.'
    They hastened away, they wandered among the nations,[a]
      unable to find any resting-place.

16     The LORD himself scattered them,
      he thought of them no more;
    he showed no favour to priests,
      no pity for elders.


17     Still we strain our eyes,
      looking in vain for help.
    We have watched and watched
      for a nation powerless to save us.

18     When we go out, we take to by-ways
    to avoid the public streets;
    our days are all but finished,[b]
      our end has come.

---

[a] *Prob. rdg.; Heb. adds* they said.      [b] our . . . finished: *prob. rdg.; Heb.* our end
has drawn near, our days are complete.

Our pursuers have shown themselves swifter     19
    than vultures in the sky;
they are hot on our trail over the hills,
they lurk to catch us in the wilderness.
    The LORD's anointed, the breath of life to us,     20
    was caught in their machinations;
    although we had thought to live
among the nations, safe under his protection.

Rejoice and be glad, daughter of Edom,     21
    you who live in the land of Uz.
Yet the cup shall pass to you in your turn,
and when you are drunk you will expose yourself to shame.
The punishment for your sin, daughter of Zion, is now complete,     22
    and never again shall you be carried into exile.
    But you, daughter of Edom, your sin shall be punished,
    and your guilt revealed.

## A prayer for remembrance and restoration

Remember, O LORD, what has befallen us;     5
    look, and see how we are scorned.
    Our patrimony is turned over to strangers     2
    and our homes to foreigners.
    We are like orphans, without a father;     3
    our mothers are like widows.
    We must buy our own water to drink,     4
our own wood can only be had at a price.
    The yoke is on our necks, we are overdriven;     5
we are weary and are given no rest.
    We came to terms, now with the Egyptians,     6
now with the Assyrians, to provide us with food.
    Our fathers sinned and are no more,     7
and we bear the burden of their guilt.
    Slaves have become our rulers,     8
and there is no one to rescue us from them.
    We must bring in our food from the wilderness,     9
    risking our lives in the scorching heat.[a]
    Our skins are blackened as in a furnace     10
by the ravages of starvation.
    Women were raped in Zion,     11
    virgins raped in the cities of Judah.
    Princes were hung up by their hands,     12
and elders received no honour.
    Young men toil to grind corn,     13
and boys stumble under loads of wood.

[a] in the scorching heat: *or* by the sword.

14 Elders have left off their sessions in the gate,
and young men no longer pluck the strings.
15 Joy has fled from our hearts,
and our dances are turned to mourning.
16 The garlands have fallen from our heads;
woe betide us, sinners that we are.
17 For this we are sick at heart,
for all this our eyes grow dim:
18 because Mount Zion is desolate
and over it the jackals run wild.

19 O Lord, thou art enthroned for ever,
thy throne endures from one generation to another.
20 Why wilt thou quite forget us
and forsake us these many days?
21 O Lord, turn us back to thyself, and we will come back;
renew our days as in times long past.
22 For if thou hast utterly rejected us,
then great indeed has been thy anger against us.

# THE BOOK OF THE PROPHET
# EZEKIEL

### *Ezekiel's call to be a prophet*

ON THE FIFTH DAY OF THE FOURTH MONTH in 1
the thirtieth year, while I was among the exiles by the river Kebar,*a*
the heavens were opened and I saw a vision of God. On the fifth 2
day of the month in the fifth year of the exile of King Jehoiachin, the word 3
of the LORD came to Ezekiel son of Buzi the priest, in Chaldaea, by the
river Kebar, and there the hand of the LORD came upon him.

I saw a storm wind coming from the north, a vast cloud with flashes of 4
fire and brilliant light about it; and within was a radiance like brass, glowing in the heart of the flames. In the fire was the semblance of four living 5
creatures in human form. Each had four faces and each four wings; their 6 7
legs were straight, and their hooves were like the hooves of a calf, glittering
like a disc of bronze. Under the wings on each of the four sides were human 8
hands; all four creatures had faces and wings, and their wings touched one 9
another. They did not turn as they moved; each creature went straight
forward. Their faces were like this: all four had the face of a man and the 10
face of a lion on the right, on the left the face of an ox and the face of an
eagle. Their wings were spread; each living creature had one pair touching 11
its neighbours',*b* while one pair covered its body. They moved straight 12
forward in whatever direction the spirit*c* would go; they never swerved
in their course. The appearance of the creatures was as if fire from burning 13
coals or torches were darting to and fro among them; the fire was radiant,
and out of the fire came lightning.*d*

As I looked at the living creatures, I saw wheels on the ground, one 15
beside each of the four.*e* The wheels sparkled like topaz, and they were 16
all alike: in form and working they were like a wheel inside a wheel, and 17
when they moved in any of the four directions they never swerved in their
course. All four had hubs and each hub had a projection which had the 18
power of sight,*f* and the rims of the wheels were full of eyes all round.
When the living creatures moved, the wheels moved beside them; when 19
the creatures rose from the ground, the wheels rose; they moved in what- 20
ever direction the spirit*c* would go; and the wheels rose together with them,
for the spirit of the living creatures was in the wheels. When the one moved, 21
the other moved; when the one halted, the other halted; when the creatures

---

*a* Or the Kebar canal.    *b* its neighbours': *prob. rdg.; Heb. unintelligible.*
*c* Or wind.    *d* *Prob. rdg., cp. Sept.; Heb. adds* (14) *and the living creatures went
out (prob. rdg.; Heb. obscure) and in like rays of light.*    *e* one ... four: *prob. rdg.;
Heb. obscure.*    *f* the power of sight: *prob. rdg.; Heb. fear.*

rose from the ground, the wheels rose together with them, for the spirit of the creatures was in the wheels.

22 Above the heads of the living creatures was, as it were, a vault glittering like a sheet of ice, awe-inspiring, stretched over their heads above them.
23 Under the vault their wings were spread straight out, touching one
24 another, while one pair covered the body of each. I heard, too, the noise of their wings; when they moved it was like the noise of a great torrent or of a cloud-burst,*a* like the noise of a crowd or of an armed camp; when they
25 halted their wings dropped. A sound was heard above the vault over their
26 heads, as they halted with drooping wings. Above the vault over their heads there appeared, as it were, a sapphire*b* in the shape of a throne, and high
27 above all, upon the throne, a form in human likeness. I saw what might have been brass glowing like fire in a furnace from the waist upwards; and from the waist downwards I saw what looked like fire with encircling
28 radiance. Like a rainbow in the clouds on a rainy day was the sight of that encircling radiance; it was like the appearance of the glory of the LORD.

When I saw this I threw myself on my face, and heard a voice speaking
2 1 2 to me: Man, he said, stand up, and let me talk with you. As he spoke, a spirit came into me and stood me on my feet, and I listened to him speak-
3 ing. He said to me, Man, I am sending you to the Israelites, a nation of rebels who have rebelled against me. Past generations of them have been
4 in revolt against me to this very day, and this generation to which I am sending you is stubborn and obstinate. When you say to them, 'These are
5 the words of the Lord GOD', they will know that they have a prophet among them, whether they listen or whether they refuse to listen, because
6 they are rebels. But you, man, must not be afraid of them or of what they say, though they are rebels against you and renegades, and you find your-self sitting on scorpions. There is nothing to fear in what they say, and
7 nothing in their looks to terrify you, rebels though they are. You must speak my words to them, whether they listen or whether they refuse to
8 listen, rebels that they are. But you, man, must listen to what I say and not be rebellious like them. Open your mouth and eat what I give you.
9 10 Then I saw a hand stretched out to me, holding a scroll. He unrolled it before me, and it was written all over on both sides with dirges and laments
3 and words of woe. Then he said to me, 'Man, eat what is in front of you,
2 eat this scroll; then go and speak to the Israelites.' So I opened my mouth
3 and he gave me the scroll to eat. Then he said, 'Man, swallow this scroll I give you, and fill yourself full.' So I ate it, and it tasted as sweet as honey.
4 Man, he said, go and tell the Israelites what I have to say to them.
5 You are sent not to people whose speech is thick and difficult, but to
6 Israelites. No; I am not sending you to great nations whose speech is so thick and so difficult that you cannot make out what they say; if however I
7 had sent you to them they would have listened to you. But the Israelites will refuse to listen to you, for they refuse to listen to me, so brazen are
8 they all and stubborn. But I will make you a match for them. I will make
9 you as brazen as they are and as stubborn as they are. I will make your

*a Or* of the Almighty.          *b Or* lapis lazuli.

brow like adamant, harder than flint. Never fear them, never be terrified by them, rebels though they are. And he said to me, Listen carefully, man, 10 to all that I have to say to you, and take it to heart. Go to your fellow- 11 countrymen in exile and speak to them. Whether they listen or refuse to listen, say, 'These are the words of the Lord GOD.'

Then a spirit *a* lifted me up, and I heard behind me a fierce rushing sound 12 as the glory of the LORD rose *b* from his place. I heard the sound of the living 13 creatures' wings brushing against one another, the sound of the wheels beside them, and a fierce rushing sound. A spirit *a* lifted me and carried me 14 along, and I went full of exaltation, the hand of the LORD strong upon me. So I came to the exiles at Tel-abib who were settled by the river Kebar. 15 For seven days I stayed with them, dumbfounded.

At the end of seven days the word of the LORD came to me: Man, I have 16 17 made you a watchman for the Israelites; you will take messages from me and carry my warnings to them. It may be that I pronounce sentence of 18 death on a wicked man: *c* if you do not warn him to give up his wicked ways and so save his life, the guilt is his; because of his wickedness he shall die, but I will hold you answerable for his death. But if you have warned him 19 and he still continues in his wicked and evil ways, he shall die because of his wickedness, but you will have saved yourself. Or it may be that a 20 righteous man turns away and does wrong, and I let that be the cause of his downfall; he will die because you have not warned him. He will die for his sin; the righteous deeds he has done will not be taken into account, and I will hold you answerable for his death. But if you have warned the 21 righteous man not to sin and he has not sinned, then he will have saved his life because he has been warned, and you will have saved yourself.

## The impending ruin of Jerusalem

THE HAND OF THE LORD CAME UPON ME there, and he said to me, 22 Rise up; go out into the plain, and there I will speak to you. So I rose 23 and went out into the plain; the glory of the LORD was there, like the glory which I had seen by the river Kebar, and I threw myself down on my face. Then a spirit came into me and stood me on my feet, and spoke to me: Go, 24 he said, and shut yourself up in your house. You shall be tied and bound 25 with ropes, man, so that you cannot go out among the people. I will fasten 26 your tongue to the roof of your mouth and you will be unable to speak; you will not be the one to rebuke them, rebels though they are. But when 27 I have something to say to you, I will give you back the power of speech. Then you will say to them, 'These are the words of the Lord GOD.' If anyone will listen, he may listen, and, if he refuses to listen, he may refuse; for they are rebels.

Man, take a tile and set it before you. Draw a city on it, the city of **4** Jerusalem: lay siege to it, erect watch-towers against it, raise a siege-ramp, 2 put mantelets in position, and bring battering-rams against it all round.

*a* Or wind.     *b* rose: *prob. rdg.; Heb. obscure.*     *c Prob. rdg.; Heb. adds if you do not warn him.*

3 Then take an iron griddle, and put it as a wall of iron between you and the city. Keep your face turned towards the city; it will be the besieged and you the besieger. This will be a sign to the Israelites.

4 Now lie on your left side, and I will lay Israel's iniquity on you; you shall
5 bear their iniquity for as many days as you lie on that side. Allowing one day for every year of their iniquity, I ordain that you bear it for one hundred
6 and ninety days; thus you shall bear Israel's iniquity. When you have completed all this, lie down a second time on your right side, and bear
7 Judah's iniquity for forty days; I count one day for every year. Then turn your face towards the siege of Jerusalem and bare your arm, and prophesy
8 against it. See how I tie you with ropes so that you cannot turn over from one side to the other until you complete the days of your distress.

9 Then take wheat and barley, beans and lentils, millet and spelt. Mix them all in one bowl and make your bread out of them. You are to eat it during
10 the one hundred and ninety days you spend lying on your side. And you must weigh out your food; you may eat twenty shekels' weight a day,
11 taking it from time to time. Measure out your drinking water too; you
12 may drink a sixth of a hin a day, taking it from time to time. You are to eat your bread baked like barley cakes, using human dung as fuel, and you
13 must bake it where people can see you. Then the LORD said, 'This is the kind of bread, unclean bread, that the Israelites will eat in the foreign lands
14 into which I shall drive them.' But I said, 'O Lord GOD, I have never been made unclean, never in my life have I eaten what has died naturally or been
15 killed by wild beasts; no tainted meat has ever passed my lips.' So he allowed me to use cow-dung instead of human dung to bake my bread.

16 Then he said to me, Man, I am cutting short their daily bread in Jerusalem; people will weigh out anxiously the bread they eat, and measure
17 with dismay the water they drink. So their food and their water will run short until they are dismayed at the sight of one another; they will waste away because of their iniquity.

5 Man, take a sharp sword, take it like a barber's razor and run it over your
2 head and your chin. Then take scales and divide the hair into three. When the siege comes to an end, burn one third of the hair in a fire in the centre of the city; cut up one third with the sword all round the city; scatter one
3 third to the wind, and I will follow it with drawn sword. Take a few of these
4 hairs and tie them up in a fold of your robe. Then take others of them, throw them into the fire and burn them, and out of them fire will come upon all Israel.

5 These are the words of the Lord GOD: This city of Jerusalem I have set
6 among the nations, with other countries around her, and she has rebelled against my laws and my statutes more wickedly than those nations and countries; for her people have rejected my laws and refused to conform to my statutes.

7 Therefore the Lord GOD says: Since you have been more ungrateful than the nations around you and have not conformed to my statutes and have
8 not kept my laws or even the laws of the nations around you, therefore, says the Lord GOD, I, in my turn, will be against you; I will execute judge-
9 ments in your midst for the nations to see, such judgements as I have never

executed before nor ever will again, so abominable have your offences been. Therefore, O Jerusalem, fathers will eat their children and children 10 their fathers in your midst; I will execute judgements on you, and any who are left in you I will scatter to the four winds. As I live, says the Lord GOD, 11 because you have defiled my holy place with all your vile and abominable rites, I in my turn will consume you without pity; I in my turn will not spare you. One third of your people shall die by pestilence and perish by 12 famine in your midst; one third shall fall by the sword in the country round about; and one third I will scatter to the four winds and follow with drawn sword. Then my anger will be spent, I will abate my fury against 13 them and be calm; when my fury is spent they will know that it is I, the LORD, who spoke in jealous passion. I have made you a scandal[a] and a 14 reproach to the nations around you, and all who pass by will see it. You 15 will be an object of reproach and abuse, a terrible lesson to the nations around you, when I pass sentence on you and do judgement in anger and fury. I, the LORD, have spoken. When I shoot the deadly arrows of famine 16 against you,[b] arrows of destruction, I will shoot to destroy you. I will bring famine upon you and cut short your daily bread; I will unleash 17 famine and beasts of prey upon you, and they will leave you childless. Pestilence and slaughter will sweep through you, and I will bring the sword upon you. I, the LORD, have spoken.

These were the words of the LORD to me: Man, look towards the **6** 1 2 mountains of Israel, and prophesy to them: Mountains of Israel, hear the 3 word of the Lord GOD. This is his word to mountains and hills, water-courses and valleys: I am bringing a sword against you, and I will destroy your hill-shrines. Your altars will be made desolate, your incense-altars 4 shattered, and I will fling down your slain before your idols. I will strew 5 the corpses of the Israelites before their idols, and I will scatter your bones about your altars. In all your settlements the blood-spattered altars[c] shall 6 be laid waste and the hill-shrines made desolate. Your altars will be waste and desolate and your idols shattered and useless, your incense-altars hewn down, and all your works wiped out; with the slain falling about you, 7 you shall know that I am the LORD. But when they fall,[d] I will leave you, 8 among the nations, some who survive the sword. When you are scattered in foreign lands, these survivors, in captivity among the nations, will 9 remember how I was grieved because their hearts had turned wantonly from me and their eyes had gone roving wantonly after idols. Then they will loathe themselves for all the evil they have done with their abomina-tions. So they will know that I am the LORD, that I was uttering no vain 10 threat when I said that I would bring this evil upon them.

These are the words of the Lord GOD: Beat your hands together, stamp 11 with your foot, bemoan your vile abominations, people of Israel. Men will fall by sword, famine, and pestilence. Far away they will die by pestilence; 12 at home they will fall by the sword; any who survive or are spared will die by famine, and so at last my anger will be spent. You will know that I am 13 the LORD when their slain fall among the idols round their altars, on every

<hr />

[a] *Or* desolation.          [b] *Prob. rdg.; Heb.* them.          [c] blood-spattered altars: *or* cities.          [d] when they fall: *prob. rdg.; Heb. obscure.*

high hill, on all mountain-tops, under every spreading tree, under every leafy terebinth, wherever they have brought offerings of soothing odour
14  for their idols one and all. So I will stretch out my hand over them and make the land a desolate waste in all their settlements, more desolate than the desert of Riblah.*a* They shall know that I am the LORD.

7  1 2  The word of the LORD came to me: Man, the Lord GOD says this to the land of Israel: An end is coming, the end is coming upon the four corners
3  of the land.*b* The end is now upon you; I will unleash my anger against you; I will call you to account for your doings and bring your abominations
4  upon your own heads. I will neither pity nor spare you: I will make you suffer for your doings and the abominations that continue in your midst. So you shall know that I am the LORD.

5  These are the words of the Lord GOD: Behold, it comes, disasters one
6 7  upon another; the end, the end, it comes, it comes.*c* Doom is coming upon you, dweller in the land; the time is coming, the day is near, with confusion
8  and the crash of thunder.*d* Now, in an instant, I will vent my rage upon you and let my anger spend itself. I will call you to account for your doings
9  and bring your abominations upon your own heads. I will neither pity nor spare; I will make you suffer for your doings and the abominations that continue in your midst. So you shall know that it is I, the LORD, who strike the blow.

10  Behold, the day! the doom is here, it has burst upon them. Injustice
11  buds, insolence blossoms, violence shoots up into injustice and wickedness. And it is all their fault, the fault of their turmoil and tumult and
12  all their restless ways. The time has come, the day has arrived; the buyer has no reason to be glad, and the seller none for regret, for I am angry
13  at all their turmoil. The seller will never go back on his bargain while either of them lives; for the bargain will never be reversed because of the turmoil, and no man will exert himself, even in his iniquity, as long
14  as he lives. The trumpet has sounded and all is ready, but no one goes out to war.

15  Outside is the sword, inside are pestilence and famine; in the country men will die by the sword, in the city famine and pestilence will carry
16  them off. If any escape and take to the mountains, like moaning doves,
17  there will I slay them, each for his iniquity, while their hands hang limp
18  and their knees run with urine. They will go in sackcloth, shuddering from
19  head to foot, with faces downcast and heads close shaved. They shall fling their silver into the streets and cast aside their gold like filth; their silver and their gold will be powerless to save them on the day of the LORD's fury. Their hunger will not be satisfied nor their bellies filled; for their
20  iniquity will be the cause of their downfall. They have fed their pride on their beautiful jewels, which they made into vile and abominable images.
21  Therefore I will treat their jewels like filth, I will hand them over as plunder to foreigners and as booty to the most evil people on earth, and these will
22  defile them. I will turn my face from them and let my treasured land be profaned; brigands will come in and defile it.

*a Prob. rdg.; Heb.* Diblah.      *b Or* earth.      *c Prob. rdg.; Heb. adds* it wakes up, behold it comes.      *d* and the crash of thunder: *prob. rdg.; Heb. unintelligible.*

Clench your fists, for the land is full of bloodshed*a* and the city full of 23
violence. I will let in the scum of nations to take possession of their houses; 24
I will quell the pride of the strong, and their sanctuaries shall be profaned.
Shuddering will come over them, and they will look in vain for peace. 25
Tempest shall follow upon tempest and rumour upon rumour. Men will 26
go seeking a vision from a prophet; there will be no more guidance from
a priest, no counsel from elders. The king will mourn, the prince will be 27
clothed with horror, the hands of the common people will shake with
fright. I will deal with them as they deserve, and call them to account for
their doings; and so they shall know that I am the LORD.

## *Jerusalem's guilt and punishment*

O N THE FIFTH DAY OF THE SIXTH MONTH in the sixth year, I was 8
sitting at home and the elders of Judah were with me. Suddenly the
hand of the Lord GOD came upon me, and I saw what looked like a man. 2
He seemed to be all fire from the waist down and to shine and glitter like
brass from the waist up. He stretched out what seemed a hand and seized 3
me by the forelock. A spirit*b* lifted me up between heaven and earth,
carried me to Jerusalem in a vision of God and put me down at the entrance
to the inner gate facing north, where stands the image of Lust to rouse
lustful passion. The glory of the God of Israel was there, like the vision 4
I had seen in the plain. The LORD said to me, 'Man, look northwards.' 5
I did so, and there to the north of the altar gate, at the entrance, was that
image of Lust. 'Man,' he said, 'do you see what they are doing? The 6
monstrous abominations which the Israelites practise here are driving me
far from my sanctuary, and you will see even more such abominations.'
Then he brought me to the entrance of the court, and I looked and found 7
a hole in the wall. 'Man,' he said to me, 'dig through the wall.' I did so, 8
and it became an opening. 'Go in,' he said, 'and see the vile abominations 9
they practise here.' So I went in and saw figures of reptiles, beasts, and 10
vermin, and all the idols of the Israelites, carved round the walls. Seventy 11
elders of Israel were standing in front of them, with Jaazaniah son of
Shaphan in the middle, and each held a censer from which rose the fragrant
smoke of incense. 'Man,' he said to me, 'do you see what the elders of 12
Israel are doing in darkness, each at the shrine of his own carved image?
They think that the LORD does not see them, or that he has forsaken the
country. You will see', he said, 'yet more monstrous abominations which 13
they practise.'
Then he brought me to that gateway of the LORD's house which faces 14
north; and there I saw women sitting and wailing for Tammuz. 'Man, 15
do you see that?' he asked me. 'But you will see abominations more
monstrous than these.' So he took me to the inner court of the LORD's 16
house, and there, by the entrance to the sanctuary of the LORD, between
porch and altar, were some twenty-five men with their backs to the
sanctuary and their faces to the east, prostrating themselves to the rising

---

*a* bloodshed: *prob. rdg.; Heb.* the judgement of bloodshed.    *b* *Or* wind.

17 sun. He said to me, 'Man, do you see that? Is it because they think these abominations a trifle, that the Jews have filled the country with violence? They provoke me further to anger, even while they seek to appease me;

18 I will turn upon them in my rage; I will neither pity nor spare. Loudly as they may cry to me, I will not listen.'

**9** A loud voice rang in my ears: 'Here they come, those appointed to

2 punish the city, each carrying his weapon of destruction.' Then I saw six men approaching from the road that leads to the upper northern gate, each carrying a battle-axe, one man among them dressed in linen, with pen

3 and ink at his waist; and they halted by the altar of bronze. Then the glory of the God of Israel rose from above the cherubim. He came to the terrace of the temple and called to the man dressed in linen with pen and ink at

4 his waist. 'Go through the city, through Jerusalem,' said the LORD, 'and put a mark on the foreheads of those who groan and lament over the

5 abominations practised there.' Then I heard him say to the others, 'Follow

6 him through the city and kill without pity; spare no one. Kill and destroy them all, old men and young, girls, little children and women, but touch no one who bears the mark. Begin at my sanctuary.' So they began with

7 the elders in front of the temple. 'Defile the temple,' he said, 'and fill the courts with dead bodies; then go out into the city and kill.'

8 While they did their work, I was left alone; and I threw myself upon my face, crying out, 'O Lord GOD, must thou destroy all the Israelites who are

9 left, pouring out thy anger on Jerusalem?' He answered, 'The iniquity of Israel and Judah is great indeed; the land is full of murder, the city is filled with injustice. They think the LORD has forsaken this country; they think

10 he sees nothing. But I will neither pity nor spare them; I will make them

11 answer for all they have done.' Then the man dressed in linen with pen and ink at his waist came and made his report: 'I have done what thou hast commanded.'

**10** Then I saw, above the vault over the heads of the cherubim, as it were a

2 throne of sapphire*a* visible above them. The LORD said to the man dressed in linen, 'Come in between the circling wheels under the cherubim, and take a handful of the burning embers lying among the cherubim; then toss them over the city.' So he went in before my eyes.

3 The cherubim stood on the right side of the temple as a man enters, and

4 a cloud filled the inner court. The glory of the LORD rose high from above the cherubim and moved on to the terrace; and the temple was filled with

5 the cloud, while the radiance of the glory of the LORD filled the court. The sound of the wings of the cherubim could be heard as far as the outer

6 court, as loud as if God Almighty were speaking. Then he told the man dressed in linen to take fire from between the circling wheels and among

7 the cherubim; the man came and stood by a wheel, and a cherub from among the cherubim put its hand into the fire that lay among them, and, taking some fire, gave it to the man dressed in linen; and he received it and went out.

8 Under the wings of the cherubim there appeared what seemed a human

9 hand. And I saw four wheels beside the cherubim, one wheel beside each

*a Or* lapis lazuli.

cherub. They had the sparkle of topaz, and all four were alike, like a wheel  10
inside a wheel. When the cherubim moved in any of the four directions,  11
they never swerved in their course; they went straight on in the direction
in which their heads were turned, never swerving in their course. Their  12
whole bodies, their backs and hands and wings, as well as the wheels,
were full of eyes all round the four of them.[a] The whirring of the wheels  13
sounded in my ears. Each had four faces: the first was that of a cherub,  14
the second that of a man, the third that of a lion, and the fourth that of
an eagle.

Then the cherubim raised themselves up, those same living creatures I  15
had seen by the river Kebar. When the cherubim moved, the wheels moved  16
beside them; when the cherubim lifted their wings and rose from the
ground, the wheels did not turn away from them. When the one halted,  17
the other halted; when the one rose, the other rose; for the spirit of the
creatures was in the wheels. Then the glory of the LORD left the temple  18
terrace and halted above the cherubim. The cherubim lifted their wings  19
and raised themselves from the ground; I watched them go with the
wheels beside them. They halted at the eastern gateway of the LORD's
house, and the glory of the God of Israel was over them.

These were the living creatures I had seen beneath the God of Israel at  20
the river Kebar; I knew that they were cherubim. Each had four faces and  21
four wings and the semblance of human hands under their wings. Their  22
faces were like those I had seen in vision by the river Kebar;[b] they moved,
each one of them, straight forward.

A spirit[c] lifted me up and brought me to the eastern gate of the LORD's  **11**
house, the gate that faces east. By the doorway were twenty-five men, and
I saw among them two of high office, Jaazaniah son of Azzur and Pelatiah
son of Benaiah. The LORD said to me, Man, it is these who are planning  2
mischief and plotting trouble in this city, saying to themselves, 'There  3
will be no building of houses yet awhile; the city is a stewpot and we are
the meat in it.' Therefore, said he, prophesy against them, prophesy, O man.  4
Then the spirit of the LORD came suddenly upon me, and he told me to  5
say, These are the words of the LORD: This is what you are saying to yourselves, you men of Israel; well do I know the thoughts that rise in your
mind. You have killed and killed in this city and heaped the streets with  6
the slain. These, therefore, are the words of the Lord GOD: The bodies  7
of the slain that you have put there, it is they that are the meat. The city
is indeed the stewpot, but I will take you out of it. It is a sword that you  8
fear, and a sword I will bring upon you, says the Lord GOD. I will take you  9
out of it; I will give you over to a foreign power; I will bring you to justice.
You too shall fall by the sword when I judge you on the frontier of Israel;  10
thus you shall know that I am the LORD. So the city will not be your  11
stewpot, nor you the meat in it. On the frontier of Israel I will judge you;
thus you shall know that I am the LORD. You have not conformed to my  12
statutes nor kept my laws, but you have followed the laws of the nations
around you.

[a] *Prob. rdg.; Heb. adds* their wheels.          [b] *Prob. rdg.; Heb. adds* and them.
[c] *Or* wind.

13 While I was prophesying, Pelatiah son of Benaiah fell dead; and I threw myself upon my face, crying aloud, 'O Lord GOD, must thou make an end of all the Israelites who are left?'

14 15 The word of the LORD came to me: Man, they are your brothers, your brothers and your kinsmen, this whole people of Israel, to whom the men who now live in Jerusalem have said, 'Keep your distance from the LORD;

16 the land has been made over to us as our property.' Say therefore, These are the words of the Lord GOD: When I sent them far away among the nations and scattered them in many lands, for a while I became their

17 sanctuary in the countries to which they had gone. Say therefore, These are the words of the Lord GOD: I will gather them from among the nations and assemble them from the countries over which I have scattered them,

18 and I will give them the soil of Israel. When they come into it, they will

19 do away with all their vile and abominable practices. I will give them a different heart and put a new spirit into them; I will take the heart of stone

20 out of their bodies and give them a heart of flesh. Then they will conform to my statutes and keep my laws. They will become my people, and I will

21 become their God. But as for those whose heart is set upon*a* their vile and abominable practices, I will make them answer for all they have done. This is the very word of the Lord GOD.

22 Then the cherubim lifted their wings, with the wheels beside them and

23 the glory of the God of Israel above them. The glory of the LORD rose up

24 and left the city, and halted on the mountain to the east of it. And a spirit *b* lifted me up and brought me to the exiles in Chaldaea. All this came in a vision sent by the spirit of God, and then the vision that I had seen left me.

25 I told the exiles all that the LORD had revealed to me.

## *Jerusalem's downfall certain*

12 1 2 THE WORD OF THE LORD CAME TO ME: Man, you live among a rebellious people. Though they have eyes they will not see, though they

3 have ears they will not hear, because they are a rebellious people. Therefore, man, pack up what you need for a journey into exile, by day before their eyes; then set off on your journey. When you leave home and go off into exile before their eyes, it may be they will see that they are rebels.

4 Bring out your belongings, packed as for exile; do it by day, before their eyes, and then at evening, still before their eyes, leave home, as if you were

5 going into exile. Next, before their eyes, break a hole through the wall, and

6 carry your belongings out through it. When dusk falls, take your pack on your shoulder, before their eyes, and carry it out, with your face covered so that you cannot see the ground. I am making you a warning sign for the Israelites.

7 I did exactly as I had been told. By day I brought out my belongings, packed as for exile, and at evening I broke through the wall with my hands. When dusk fell, I shouldered my pack and carried it out before their eyes.

---

*a* *Prob. rdg.; Heb. adds* the heart of.      *b* *Or* wind.

Next morning, the word of the LORD came to me: Man, he said, have 8 9
not the Israelites, that rebellious people, asked you what you are doing?
Tell them that these are the words of the Lord GOD: This oracle concerns 10
the prince in Jerusalem, and all the Israelites therein.*a* Tell them that you 11
are a sign to warn them; what you have done will be done to them; they
will go into exile and captivity. Their prince will shoulder his pack in the 12
dusk and go through a hole made to let him out, with his face covered so
that he cannot be seen nor himself see the ground. But I will cast my net 13
over him, and he will be caught in the meshes. I will bring him to Babylon,
the land of the Chaldaeans, though he will not see it; and there he will die.
I will scatter his bodyguard and drive all his squadrons to the four winds; 14
I will follow them with drawn sword. Then they shall know that I am the 15
LORD, when I disperse them among the nations and scatter them through
many lands. But I will leave a few of them who will escape sword, famine, 16
and pestilence, to tell the whole story of their abominations to the peoples
among whom they go; and they shall know that I am the LORD.

And the word of the LORD came to me: Man, he said, as you eat you must 17 18
tremble, and as you drink you must shudder with dread. Say to the com- 19
mon people, These are the words of the Lord GOD about those who live in
Jerusalem and about the land of Israel: They will eat with dread and be
filled with horror as they drink; the land shall be filled with horror because
it is sated with the violence of all who live there. Inhabited cities shall be 20
deserted, and the land shall become a waste. Thus you shall know that
I am the LORD.

The word of the LORD came to me: Man, he said, what is this proverb 21 22
current in the land of Israel: 'Time runs on, visions die away'? Say to 23
them, These are the words of the Lord GOD: I have put an end to this
proverb; it shall never be heard in Israel again. Say rather to them, The
time, with all the vision means, is near. There will be no more false visions, 24
no specious divination among the Israelites, for I, the LORD, will say what 25
I will, and it shall be done. It shall be put off no longer: in your lifetime,
you rebellious people, I will speak, I will act. This is the very word of the
Lord GOD.

The word of the LORD came to me: Man, he said, the Israelites say that 26 27
the vision you now see is not to be fulfilled for many years: you are prophesying of a time far off. Say to them, These are the words of the Lord 28
GOD: No word of mine shall be delayed; even as I speak it shall be done.
This is the very word of the Lord GOD.

The LORD said to me, Man, prophesy of the prophets of Israel; prophesy, 13 1 2
and say to those who prophesy out of their own hearts, Hear what the LORD
says: These are the words of the Lord GOD: Oh, the wicked folly of the 3
prophets! Their inspiration comes from themselves; they have seen no
vision. Your prophets, Israel, have been like jackals among ruins. They have 4 5
not gone up into the breach to repair the broken wall round the Israelites,
that they may stand firm in battle on the day of the LORD. Oh, false vision 6
and lying divination! Oh, those prophets who say, 'It is the very word of
the LORD', when it is not the LORD who has sent them; yet they expect their

*a* therein: *prob. rdg.; Heb.* among them.

7 words to control the event. Is it not a false vision that you prophets have seen? Is not your divination a lie? You call it the very word of the LORD, but it is not I who have spoken.

8     These, then, are the words of the Lord GOD: Because your words are
9 false and your visions a lie, I am against you, says the Lord GOD. I will raise my hand against the prophets whose visions are false, whose divinations are a lie. They shall have no place in the counsels of my people; they shall not be entered in the roll of Israel nor set foot upon its soil. Thus
10 you shall know that I am the Lord GOD. Rightly, for they have misled my people by saying that all is well when all is not well. It is as if they were
11 building a wall and used whitewash for the daubing. Tell these daubers that it will fall; rain will pour down in torrents, and I will send hailstones
12 hard as rock streaming down and I will unleash a stormy wind. When the building falls, men will ask, 'Where is the plaster you should have used?'
13 So these are the words of the Lord GOD: In my rage I will unleash a stormy wind; rain will come in torrents in my anger, hailstones hard as rock in my
14 fury, until all is destroyed. I will demolish the building which you have daubed with whitewash and level it to the ground, so that its foundations are laid bare. It shall fall, and you shall be destroyed within it; thus you
15 shall know that I am the LORD. I will spend my rage on the building and on those who daubed it with wash; and people*a* will say, 'The building is
16 gone and the men who daubed it are gone, those prophets of Israel who prophesied to Jerusalem, who saw visions of prosperity when there was no prosperity.' This is the very word of the Lord GOD.

17     Now turn, man, to the women of your people who prophesy out of their
18 own hearts, and prophesy to them. Say to them, These are the words of the Lord GOD: I loathe you, you women who hunt men's lives by sewing magic bands upon the wrists and putting veils over the heads of persons of every age; are you to hunt the lives of my people and keep your own lives
19 safe? You have violated my sanctity before my people with handfuls of barley and scraps of bread. You bring death to those who should not die, and life to those who should not live, by lying to this people of mine who
20 listen to lies. So these are the words of the Lord GOD: I am against your magic bands with which you hunt men's lives for the excitement of it. I will tear them from your arms and set those lives at liberty, lives that you
21 hunt for the excitement of it. I will tear up your long veils and save my people from you; you shall no longer have power to hunt them. Thus you
22 shall know that I am the LORD. You discouraged the righteous man with lies, when I meant him no hurt; you so strengthened the wicked that he
23 would not abandon his evil ways and be saved; and therefore you shall never see your false visions again nor practise your divination any more. I will rescue my people from your power; and thus you shall know that I am the LORD.

**14**     Some of the elders of Israel came to visit me, and while they sat with me
2 3 the LORD said to me, Man, these people have set their hearts on their idols and keep their eyes fixed on the sinful things that cause their downfall.
4 Am I to let such men consult me? Speak to them and tell them that these

    *a Prob. rdg.; Heb.* I.

are the words of the Lord GOD: If any Israelite, with his heart set on his idols and his eyes fixed on the sinful things that cause his downfall, comes to a prophet, I, the LORD, in my own person, shall be constrained to answer him, despite his many idols. My answer will grip the hearts of the Israelites, 5 estranged from me as they are, one and all, through their idols. So tell the 6 Israelites that these are the words of the Lord GOD: Turn away, turn away from your idols; turn your backs on all your abominations. If any man, 7 Israelite or alien, renounces me, sets his heart upon idols and fixes his eyes upon the vile thing that is his downfall—if such a man comes to consult me through a prophet, I, the LORD, in my own person, shall be constrained to answer him. I will set my face against that man; I will make him an 8 example and a byword; I will rid my people of him. Thus you shall know that I am the LORD. If a prophet is seduced into making a prophecy, it is 9 I the LORD who have seduced him; I will stretch out my hand and rid my people Israel of him. Both shall be punished; the prophet and the man who 10 consults him alike are guilty. And never again will the Israelites stray from 11 their allegiance, never again defy my will and bring pollution upon themselves; they will become my people, and I will become their God. This is the very word of the Lord GOD.

These were the words of the LORD to me: Man, when a country sins by 12 13 breaking faith with me, I will stretch out my hand and cut short its daily bread. I will send famine upon it and destroy both men and cattle. Even if 14 those three men were living there, Noah, Danel*a* and Job, they would save none but themselves by their righteousness. This is the very word of the Lord GOD. If I should turn wild beasts loose in a country to destroy its 15 inhabitants, until it became a waste through which no man would pass for fear of the beasts, then, if those three men were living there, as I live, says 16 the Lord GOD, they would not save even their own sons and daughters; they would save themselves alone, and the country would become a waste. Or if I should bring the sword upon that country and command it to go 17 through the land and should destroy men and cattle, then, if those three 18 men were living there, as I live, says the Lord GOD, they could save neither son nor daughter; they would save themselves alone. Or if I should send 19 pestilence on that land and pour out my fury upon it in blood, to destroy men and cattle, then, if Noah, Danel and Job were living there, as I live, 20 says the Lord GOD, they would save neither son nor daughter; they would save themselves alone by their righteousness.

These were the words of the Lord GOD: How much less hope is there for 21 Jerusalem when I inflict on her these four punishments of mine, sword and famine, wild beasts and pestilence, to destroy both men and cattle! Some 22 will be left in her, some survivors to be brought out, both sons and daughters. Look at them as they come out to you, and see how they have behaved and what they have done. This will be some comfort to you for all the harm I have done to Jerusalem and all I have inflicted upon her. It will bring you 23 comfort when you see how they have behaved and what they have done; for you will know that it was not without reason that I dealt thus with her. This is the very word of the Lord GOD.

*a Or, as otherwise read,* Daniel.

**15** These were the words of the LORD to me:

2     Man, how is the vine better than any other tree,
       than a branch from a tree in the forest?

3       Is wood got from it
        fit to make anything useful?
      Can men make it into a peg
      and hang things on it?

4       If it is put on the fire for fuel,
      if its two ends are burnt by the fire
        and the middle is charred,
        is it fit for anything useful?

5     Nothing useful could be made of it even when whole;
    how much less, when it is burnt by the fire and charred,
      can it be made into anything useful!

6 So these are the words of the Lord GOD:

    I treat the vine, as against forest-trees,
      only as fuel for the fire,
    even so I treat the people of Jerusalem;

7       I set my face against them.
    Though they escape from the fire, fire shall burn them up.
      Thus you shall know that I am the LORD
      when I set my face against them,

8       making the land a waste
    because they have broken faith.
      This is the very word of the Lord GOD.

**16** 1 2     The word of the LORD came to me: Man, he said, make Jerusalem see
3 her abominable conduct. Tell her that these are the words of the Lord GOD
to her: Canaan is the land of your ancestry and there you were born; an
4 Amorite was your father and a Hittite your mother. This is how you were
treated at birth: when you were born, your navel-string was not tied, you
were not bathed in water ready for the rubbing, you were not salted as you
5 should have been nor wrapped in swaddling clothes. No one cared for
you enough to do any of these things or, indeed, to have any pity for you;
you were thrown out on the bare ground in your own filth on the day of
6 your birth. Then I came by and saw you kicking helplessly in your own
7 blood; I spoke to you, there in your blood, and bade you live. I tended you
like an evergreen plant, like something growing in the fields; you throve
and grew. You came to full womanhood; your breasts became firm and
your hair grew, but still you were naked and exposed.

8     Again I came by and saw that you were ripe for love. I spread the skirt
of my robe over you and covered your naked body. Then I plighted my
troth and entered into a covenant with you, says the Lord GOD, and you
9 became mine. Then I bathed you in water and washed off the blood and
10 anointed you with oil. I gave you robes of brocade and sandals of stout
11 hide; I fastened a linen girdle round you and dressed you in lawn. For
12 jewellery I put bracelets on your arms and a chain round your neck; I gave
you a nose-ring, I put pendants in your ears and a beautiful coronet on your

head. You had ornaments of gold and silver, your dresses were of linen, 13
lawn, and brocade. You had flour and honey and olive oil for food, and you
grew very beautiful, you grew into a queen. The fame of your beauty went 14
all over the world, for the splendour with which I decked you made it
perfect. This is the very word of the Lord GOD.

But you trusted to your beauty and prostituted your fame; you com- 15
mitted fornication, offering yourself freely to any passer-by for your
beauty to become his. You took some of your clothes and decked a platform 16
for yourself in gay colours and there you committed fornication; you had
intercourse with him for your beauty to become his.*a* You took the splen- 17
did ornaments of gold and silver which I had given you, and made for
yourself male images with which you committed fornication. You covered 18
them with your robes of brocade and offered up my oil and my incense
before them. You took the food I had given you, the flour, the oil, and the 19
honey, with which I had fed you, and set it before them as an offering of
soothing odour. This is the very word of the Lord GOD.

You took the sons and daughters whom you had borne to me, and 20
sacrificed them to these images for their food. Was this of less account than
your fornication? No! you slaughtered my children and handed them over, 21
you surrendered them to your images. With all your abominable fornica- 22
tion you forgot those early days when you lay naked and exposed, kicking
helplessly in your own blood.

After all the evil you had done (Oh! the pity of it, says the Lord GOD), 23
you built yourself a couch and constructed a high-stool in every open place. 24
You built up your high-stools at the top of every street and disgraced your 25
beauty, offering your body to any passer-by in countless acts of fornication.
You committed fornication with your gross neighbours, the Egyptians, 26
and you provoked me to anger by your countless acts of fornication.

I stretched out my hand against you and cut down your portion. Then 27
I gave you up to women who hated you, Philistine women, who were so
disgusted by your lewd ways. Not content with this, you committed 28
fornication with the Assyrians, led them into fornication and still were not
content. You committed countless acts of fornication in Chaldaea, the 29
land of commerce, and even with this you were not content.

How you anger me! says the Lord GOD. You have done all this like the 30
imperious whore you are. You have built your couch at the top of every 31
street and constructed your stool in every open place, but, unlike the common prostitute, you have scorned a fee. An adulterous wife who owes 32
obedience to her husband takes a fee from *b* strangers. The prostitute also 33
takes her fee; but you give presents to all your lovers, you bribe them to
come from all quarters to commit fornication with you. You are the very 34
opposite of other women in your fornication: no one runs after you, you
do not receive a fee, you give it. You are the very opposite.

Listen to the words of the LORD, whore that you are. These are the words 35 36
of the Lord GOD: You have been prodigal in your excesses, you have
exposed your naked body in fornication with your lovers. In return for

---

*a* you had intercourse . . . his: *prob. rdg.; Heb. obscure.*  *b* a fee from: *prob. rdg.;*
*Heb. om.*

your abominable idols and for the slaughter of the children you have
37 given them, I will gather all those lovers to whom you made advances,[a]
all whom you loved and all whom you hated. I will gather them in from all
quarters against you; I will strip you naked before them, and they shall
38 see your whole body naked. I will put you on trial for adultery and murder,
39 and I will charge you with[b] blood shed in jealousy and fury. Then I will
hand you over to them. They will demolish your couch and pull down
your high-stool; they will strip your clothes off, take away your splendid
40 ornaments, and leave you naked and exposed. They will bring up the mob
against you and stone you, they will hack you to pieces with their swords.
41 They will burn down your houses and execute judgement on you, and
many women shall see it. I will put an end to your fornication, and you
42 shall never again give a fee to your lovers. Then I will abate my fury, and
my jealousy will turn away from you. I will be calm and will no longer be
43 provoked to anger. For you had forgotten the days of your youth and
exasperated me with all your doings: so I in my turn brought retribution
upon you for your deeds. This is the very word of the Lord GOD.

Did you not commit these obscenities, as well as all your other abomina-
44 tions? Dealers in proverbs will say of you, 'Like mother, like daughter.'
45 You are a true daughter of a mother who loathed her husband and children.
You are a true sister of your sisters who loathed their husbands and children. You are all daughters of a Hittite mother and an Amorite father.
46 Your elder sister was Samaria, who lived with her daughters to the north
of you; your younger sister, who lived with her daughters to the south of
47 you, was Sodom. Did you not behave as they did and commit the same
48 abominations? You came very near to doing even worse than they. As I
live, says the Lord GOD, your sister Sodom and her daughters never be-
49 haved as you and your daughters have done. This was the iniquity of your
sister Sodom: she and her daughters had pride of wealth and food in
plenty, comfort and ease, and yet she never helped the poor and wretched.
50 They grew haughty and did deeds abominable in my sight, and I made
51 away with them, as you have seen. Samaria was never half the sinner you
have been; you have committed more abominations than she, abominations
52 which have made your sister seem innocent. You must bear the humiliation which you thought your sisters deserved. Your sins are so much more
abominable than theirs that they appear innocent in comparison with you;
and now you must bear your shame and humiliation and make your sisters
seem innocent.

53 But I will restore the fortunes of Sodom and her daughters and of
54 Samaria and her daughters, and I will restore yours at the same time. Even
though you bring them comfort, you will bear your shame, you will be
55 disgraced for all you have done; but when your sister Sodom and her
daughters become what they were of old, and when your sister Samaria
and her daughters become what they were of old, then you and your
56 daughters will be restored. Did you not hear and talk much of your sister
57 Sodom in the days of your pride, before your wickedness was exposed, in

---

[a] to whom . . . advances: *or* whom you charmed.    [b] charge you with: *prob.*
*mng.; Heb.* give you.

the days when the daughters of Aram with those about her were disgraced, and the daughters of the Philistines round about, who so despised you? Now you too must bear the consequences of your lewd and abominable 58 conduct. This is the very word of the LORD.

These are the words of the Lord GOD: I will treat you as you have 59 deserved, because you violated a covenant and made light of a solemn oath. But I will remember the covenant I made with you when you were young, 60 and I will establish with you a covenant which shall last for ever. And you 61 will remember your past ways and feel ashamed when you receive your sisters, the elder and the younger. For I will give them to you as daughters, and they shall not be outside your covenant.*a* Thus I will establish my 62 covenant with you, and you shall know that I am the LORD. You will 63 remember, and will be so ashamed and humiliated that you will never open your mouth again once I have accepted expiation for all you have done. This is the very word of the Lord GOD.

These were the words of the LORD to me: Man, speak to the Israelites **17** 1 2 in allegory and parable. Tell them that these are the words of the Lord 3 GOD:

> A great eagle
> with broad wings and long pinions,
> in full plumage, richly patterned,
>     came to Lebanon.
> He took the very top of a cedar-tree,
> he plucked its highest twig;
> he carried it off to a land of commerce, 4
>     and planted it in a city of merchants.
> Then he took a native seed
>     and put it in nursery-ground; 5
> he set it like a willow,
> a shoot beside abundant water.
> It sprouted and became a vine,
>     sprawling low along the ground 6
> and bending its trailing boughs towards him *b*
> with its roots growing beneath him.
> So it became a vine, it branched out
>     and put forth shoots.
> But there was another great eagle
> with broad wings and thick plumage; 7
> and this vine gave its roots
>     a twist towards him; *b*
> it pushed out its trailing boughs towards him,
> seeking drink from the bed where it was planted,
>     though it had been set 8
> in good ground beside abundant water
> that it might bear shoots and be fruitful
>     and become a noble vine.

*a* and they . . . covenant: *or* though not on the ground of your covenant.      *b* *Or* inwards.

9 Tell them that these are the words of the Lord GOD:

> Can such a vine flourish?
> Will not its roots be broken off
>     and its fruit be stripped,
> and all its fresh sprouting leaves wither,
> until it is uprooted and carried away
> with little effort and few hands?
10 If it is transplanted, can it flourish?
> Will it not be utterly shrivelled,
> as though by the touch of the east wind,
>     on the bed where it ought to sprout?

11 12 These were the words of the LORD to me: Say to that rebellious people, Do you not know what this means? The king of Babylon came to Jeru- salem, took its king and its officers and had them brought to him at Bab- 13 ylon. He took a prince of the royal line and made a treaty with him, putting 14 him on his oath. He took away the chief men of the country, so that it should become a humble kingdom unable to raise itself but ready to 15 observe the treaty and keep it in force. But the prince rebelled against him and sent messengers to Egypt, asking for horses and men in plenty. Can such a man prosper? Can he escape destruction if he acts in this way? Can 16 he violate a covenant and escape? As I live, says the Lord GOD, I swear that he shall die in the land of the king who put him on the throne; he made light of his oath and violated the covenant he made with him. He shall die 17 in Babylon. Pharaoh will send no large army, no great host, to protect him in battle; no siege-ramp will be raised, no watch-tower put up, nor will 18 the lives of many men be lost. He has violated a covenant and has made light of his oath. He had submitted, and yet he did all these things; he shall not escape.

19 These then are the words of the Lord GOD: As I live, he has made light of the oath he took by me and has violated the covenant I made with him. I will 20 bring retribution upon him; I will cast my net over him, and he shall be caught in its meshes. I will carry him to Babylon and bring him to judge- 21 ment there, because he has broken faith with me. In all his squadrons every commander shall fall by the sword; those who are left will be scattered to the four winds. Thus you shall know that it is I, the LORD, who have spoken.

22 These are the words of the Lord GOD:

> I, too, will take a slip
> from the lofty crown of the cedar
>     and set it in the soil;
> I will pluck a tender shoot from the topmost branch
>     and plant it.
23 I will plant it high on a lofty mountain,
>     the highest mountain in Israel.
> It will put out branches, bear its fruit,
>     and become a noble cedar.
> Winged birds of every kind will roost under it,
>     they will roost in the shelter of its sweeping boughs.

> All the trees of the country-side will know                    24
>     that it is I, the LORD,
>   who bring low the tall tree
>   and raise the low tree high,
>   who dry up the green tree
>   and make the dry tree put forth buds.
> I, the LORD, have spoken and will do it.

THESE WERE THE WORDS OF THE LORD TO ME: What do you all mean **18** 1 2
by repeating this proverb in the land of Israel:

> 'The fathers have eaten sour grapes,
>     and the children's teeth are set on edge'?

As I live, says the Lord GOD, this proverb shall never again be used in 3
Israel. Every living soul belongs to me; father and son alike are mine. The 4
soul that sins shall die.

Consider the man who is righteous and does what is just and right. He 5 6
never feasts at mountain-shrines, never lifts his eyes to the idols of Israel,
never dishonours another man's wife, never approaches a woman during
her periods. He oppresses no man, he returns the debtor's pledge, he never 7
robs. He gives bread to the hungry and clothes to those who have none.
He never lends either at discount or at interest. He shuns injustice 8
and deals fairly between man and man. He conforms to my statutes and 9
loyally observes my laws. Such a man is righteous: he shall live, says the
Lord GOD.

He may have a son who is a man of violence and a cut-throat who turns 10
his back on these rules.[a] He obeys none of them, he feasts at mountain- 11
shrines, he dishonours another man's wife, he oppresses the unfortunate 12
and the poor, he is a robber, he does not return the debtor's pledge,
he lifts his eyes to idols and joins in abominable rites; he lends both at 13
discount and at interest. Such a man shall not live. Because he has committed all these abominations he shall die, and his blood will be on his
own head.

This man in turn may have a son who sees all his father's sins; he sees, 14
but he commits none of them. He never feasts at mountain-shrines, never 15
lifts his eyes to the idols of Israel, never dishonours another man's wife.
He oppresses no man, takes no pledge, does not rob. He gives bread to the 16
hungry and clothes to those who have none. He shuns injustice, he never 17
lends either at discount or at interest. He keeps my laws and conforms
to my statutes. Such a man shall not die for his father's wrongdoing; he
shall live.

His father may have been guilty of oppression and robbery and may have 18
lived an evil life among his kinsfolk, and so has died because of his iniquity.
You may ask, 'Why is the son not punished for his father's iniquity?' 19
Because he has always done what is just and right and has been careful
to obey all my laws, therefore he shall live. It is the soul that sins, and no 20
other, that shall die; a son shall not share a father's guilt, nor a father his

---

[a] who turns . . . rules: *prob. rdg.; Heb. unintelligible.*

son's. The righteous man shall reap the fruit of his own righteousness, and the wicked man the fruit of his own wickedness.

21 It may be that a wicked man gives up his sinful ways and keeps all my laws, doing what is just and right. That man shall live; he shall not die.

22 None of the offences he has committed shall be remembered against him;

23 he shall live because of his righteous deeds. Have I any desire, says the Lord GOD, for the death of a wicked man? Would I not rather that he should mend his ways and live?

24 It may be that a righteous man turns back from his righteous ways and commits every kind of abomination that the wicked practise; shall he do this and live? No, none of his former righteousness will be remembered in

25 his favour; he has broken his faith, he has sinned, and he shall die. You say that the Lord acts without principle? Listen, you Israelites, it is you who

26 act without principle, not I. If a righteous man turns from his righteousness, takes to evil ways and dies,[a] it is because of these evil ways that he dies.

27 Again, if a wicked man turns from his wicked ways and does what is just

28 and right, he will save his life. If he sees his offences as they are and turns his back on them all, then he shall live; he shall not die.

29 'The Lord acts without principle', say the Israelites. No, Israelites, it

30 is you who act without principle, not I. Therefore, Israelites, says the Lord GOD, I will judge every man of you on his deeds. Turn, turn from

31 your offences, or your iniquity will be your downfall. Throw off the load of your past misdeeds; get yourselves a new heart and a new spirit. Why

32 should you die, you men of Israel? I have no desire for any man's death. This is the very word of the Lord GOD.

**19** 1 2 Raise a lament over the princes of Israel and say:

> Your mother was a lioness
>> among the lions!
> She made her lair among the young lions
>> and many were the cubs she bore.

3
> One of her cubs she raised,
>> and he grew into a young lion.
> He learnt to tear his prey,
>> he devoured men.

4
> Then the nations shouted at[b] him
>> and he was caught in their pit,
> and they dragged him with hooks to the land of Egypt.

5
> His case, she saw, was desperate, her hope was lost;
>> so she took another of her cubs
>> and made him a young lion.

6
> He prowled among the lions
>> and acted like a young lion.
> He learnt to tear his prey,
>> he devoured men;

7
> he broke down their palaces, laid their cities in ruins.

---

[a] *Prob. rdg.; Heb. adds* because of them.
[b] shouted at: *or* heard a report about.

> The land and all that was in it
> was aghast at the noise of his roaring.
>> From the provinces all round                                    8
> the nations raised the hue and cry;
> they cast their net over him
>> and he was caught in their pit.
> With hooks they drew him into a cage                             9
> and brought him to the king of Babylon,
>> who flung him into prison,
> that his voice might never again be heard
>> on the mountains of Israel.

> Your mother was a vine in a vineyard*a*                          10
>> planted by the waterside.
> It grew fruitful and luxuriant,
>> for there was water in plenty.
> It had stout branches,                                           11
>> fit to make sceptres for those who bear rule.
> It grew tall, finding its way through the foliage,
> and conspicuous for its height and many trailing boughs.
> But it was torn up in anger and thrown to the ground;           12
>> the east wind blighted it,
>>> its fruit was blown off,
>>> its strong branches were blighted,
>>> and fire burnt it.
> Now it is replanted in the wilderness,                          13
> in a dry and thirsty land;
> and fire bursts forth from its own branches                     14
>> and burns up its shoots.*b*
> It has no strong branch any more
>> to make a sceptre for those who bear rule.

This is the lament and as a lament it passed into use.

ON THE TENTH DAY OF THE FIFTH MONTH in the seventh year, some  **20**
of the elders of Israel came to consult the LORD and were sitting with me.
Then this word came to me from the LORD: Man, say to the elders of  2 3
Israel, This is the word of the Lord GOD: Do you come to consult me? As
I live, I will not be consulted by you. This is the very word of the Lord GOD.

Will you judge them? Will you judge them, O man? Then tell them of  4
the abominations of their forefathers and say to them, These are the words  5
of the Lord GOD: When I chose Israel, with uplifted hand I bound myself
by oath to the race of Jacob and revealed myself to them in Egypt; I lifted
up my hand and declared: I am the LORD your God. On that day I swore  6
with hand uplifted that I would bring them out of Egypt into the land I
had sought out for them, a land flowing with milk and honey, fairest of all
lands. I told them, every one, to cast away the loathsome things on which  7

---

*a* in a vineyard: *prob. rdg.; Heb. obscure in context.*    *b* *Prob. rdg.; Heb. adds* its fruit.

they feasted their eyes and not to defile themselves with the idols of Egypt. I am the LORD your God, I said.

8  But they rebelled against me, they refused to listen to me, and not one of them cast away the loathsome things on which he feasted his eyes or forsook the idols of Egypt. I had thought to pour out my wrath and exhaust

9  my anger on them in Egypt. I acted for the honour of my name, that it might not be profaned in the sight of the nations among whom Israel was

10  living: I revealed myself to them by bringing Israel out of Egypt. I brought

11  them out of Egypt and led them into the wilderness. There I gave my statutes to them and taught them my laws, so that by keeping them men

12  might have life. Further, I gave them my sabbaths as a sign between us, so that they should know that I, the LORD, was hallowing them for myself.

13  But the Israelites rebelled against me in the wilderness; they did not conform to my statutes, they rejected my laws, though by keeping them men might have life, and they utterly desecrated my sabbaths. So again I thought to pour out my wrath on them in the wilderness to destroy them.

14  I acted for the honour of my name, that it might not be profaned in the sight of the nations who had seen me bring them out.

15  Further, I swore to them in the wilderness with uplifted hand that I would not bring them into the land I had given them, that land flowing

16  with milk and honey, fairest of all lands. For they had rejected my laws, they would not conform to my statutes and they desecrated my sabbaths,

17  because they loved to follow idols of their own. Yet I pitied them too much

18  to destroy them and did not make an end of them in the wilderness. I commanded their sons in the wilderness not to conform to their fathers' statutes, nor observe their laws, nor defile themselves with their idols.

19  I said, I am the LORD your God, you must conform to my statutes; you

20  must observe my laws and act according to them. You must keep my sabbaths holy, and they will become a sign between us; so you will know that I am the LORD your God.

21  But the sons too rebelled against me. They did not conform to my statutes or observe my laws, though any who had done so would have had life through them, and they desecrated my sabbaths. Again I thought to pour out my wrath and exhaust my anger on them in the wilderness.

22  I acted for the honour of my name, that it might not be profaned in the

23  sight of the nations who had seen me bring them out. Yes, and in the wilderness I swore to them with uplifted hand that I would disperse them

24  among the nations and scatter them abroad, because they had disobeyed my laws, rejected my statutes, desecrated my sabbaths, and turned longing

25  eyes toward the idols of their forefathers. I did more; I imposed on them statutes that were not good statutes, and laws by which they could not win

26  life. I let them defile themselves with gifts to idols; I made them surrender their eldest sons to them so that I might fill them with horror. Thus they would know that I am the LORD.

27  Speak then, O man, to the Israelites and say to them, These are the words of the Lord GOD: Once again your forefathers insulted me and broke faith

28  with me: when I brought them into the land which I had sworn with uplifted hand to give them, they marked down every hill-top and every

leafy tree, and there they offered their sacrifices, they made the gifts which roused my anger, they set out their offerings of soothing odour and poured out their drink-offerings. I asked them, What is this hill-shrine to which 29 you are going up? And 'hill-shrine' has been its name ever since.

So tell the Israelites, These are the words of the Lord GOD: Are you 30 defiling yourselves as your forefathers did? Are you wantonly giving yourselves to their loathsome gods? When you bring your gifts, when you 31 pass your sons through the fire, you are still defiling yourselves in the service of your crowd of idols. How can I let you consult me, men of Israel? As I live, says the Lord GOD, I will not be consulted by you. When you 32 say to yourselves, 'Let us become like the nations and tribes of other lands and worship wood and stone', you are thinking of something that can never be. As I live, says the Lord GOD, I will reign over you with a strong 33 hand, with arm outstretched and wrath outpoured. I will bring you out 34 from the peoples and gather you from the lands over which you have been scattered by my strong hand, my outstretched arm and outpoured wrath. I will bring you into the wilderness of the peoples; there will I confront 35 you, and there will I state my case against you. Even as I did in the wilder- 36 ness of Egypt against your forefathers, so will I state my case against you. This is the very word of the Lord GOD.

I will pass you under the rod and bring you within the bond*a* of the 37 covenant. I will rid you of those who revolt and rebel against me. I will 38 take them out of the land where they are now living, but they shall not set foot on the soil of Israel. Thus shall you know that I am the LORD.

Now, men of Israel, these are the words of the Lord GOD: Go, sweep 39 away your idols, every man of you. So in days to come you will never be disobedient to me or desecrate my holy name with your gifts and your idolatries. But on my holy hill, the lofty hill of Israel, says the Lord GOD, 40 there shall the Israelites serve me in the land, every one of them. There will I receive them with favour; there will I demand your contribution and the best of your offerings, with all your consecrated gifts. I will receive 41 your offerings of soothing odour, when I have brought you out from the peoples and gathered you from the lands where you have been scattered. I, and only I, will have your worship, for all the nations to see.

You will know that I am the LORD, when I bring you home to the soil 42 of Israel, to the land which I swore with uplifted hand to give your fore- fathers. There you will remember your past ways and all the wanton deeds 43 with which you have defiled yourselves, and will loathe yourselves for all the evils you have done. You will know that I am the LORD, when I have 44 dealt with you, O men of Israel, not as your wicked ways and your vicious deeds deserve but for the honour of my name. This is the very word of the Lord GOD.

These were the words of the LORD to me: Man, turn and face towards 45 46 Teman*b* and pour out your words to the south; prophesy to the rough country of the Negeb. Say to it, Listen to the words of the LORD. These are 47 the words of the Lord GOD: I will set fire to you, and the fire will consume all the wood, green and dry alike. Its fiery flame shall not be put out, but

*a Or* muster.       *b Or* face southward.

48 from the Negeb northwards every face will be scorched by it. All men will see that it is I, the LORD, who have set it ablaze; it shall not be put out.

49 'Ah no! O Lord GOD,' I cried; 'they say of me, "He deals only in parables."'

21 1 2 These were the words of the LORD to me: Man, turn and face towards Jerusalem, and pour out your words against her sanctuary;*a* prophesy

3 against the land of Israel. Say to the land of Israel, These are the words of the LORD: I am against you; I will draw my sword from the scabbard and

4 cut off from you both righteous and wicked. It is because I would cut off your righteous and your wicked equally that my sword will be drawn from

5 the scabbard against all men, from the Negeb northwards. All men shall know that I the LORD have drawn my sword; it shall never again be sheathed.

6 Groan in their presence, man, groan bitterly until your lungs are bursting.

7 When they ask you why you are groaning, say to them, 'I groan at the thing I have heard; when it comes, all hearts melt, all courage fails, all hands fall limp, all men's knees run with urine. It is coming. It is here.' This is the very word of the Lord GOD.

8 9 These were the words of the LORD to me: Prophesy, man, and say, This is the word of the Lord:

<blockquote>
A sword, a sword is sharpened and burnished,

10     sharpened to kill and kill again,<br>
burnished to flash*b* like lightning.

Ah! the club is brandished, my son,<br>
    to defy all wooden idols!

11     The sword is given to be burnished<br>
    ready for the hand to grasp.<br>
The sword—it is sharpened,<br>
    it is burnished,<br>
ready to be put into the slayer's hand.
</blockquote>

12 Cry, man, and howl; for all this falls on my people, it falls on Israel's princes who are delivered over to the sword and are slain with my people.

13 Therefore beat your breast in remorse, for it is the test—and what if it is not in truth the club of defiance? This is the very word of the Lord GOD.

<blockquote>
14     But you, man, prophesy and clap your hands together;<br>
    swing the sword twice, thrice:<br>
      it is the sword of slaughter,<br>
the great sword of slaughter whirling about them.

15     That their hearts may be troubled and many stumble and fall,<br>
I have set the threat of the sword at all their gates,<br>
    the threat of the sword*c* made to flash like lightning<br>
    and drawn to kill.

16     Be sharpened, turn right; be unsheathed, turn left,<br>
    wherever your point is aimed.
</blockquote>

17 I, too, will clap my hands together and abate my anger. I, the LORD, have spoken.

---

*a* her sanctuary: *prob. rdg.; Heb.* sanctuaries.     *b* to flash: *prob. rdg.; Heb. unintelligible.*     *c* the threat of the sword: *prob. rdg.; Heb. obscure in context.*

These were the words of the LORD to me: Man, trace out two roads by 18 19
which the sword of the king of Babylon may come, starting both of them
from the same land. Then carve a signpost, carve it at the point where the
highway forks. Mark out a road for the sword to come to the Ammonite 20
city of Rabbah, to Judah, and to Jerusalem at the heart of it. For the king 21
of Babylon halts to take the omens at the parting of the ways, where the
road divides. He casts lots with arrows, consults teraphim *a* and inspects
the livers of beasts. The augur's arrow marked 'Jerusalem' falls at his right 22
hand: here, then, *b* he must raise a shout and sound the battle-cry, set
battering-rams against the gates, pile siege-ramps and build watch-towers.
It may well seem to the people that the auguries are false, whereas they 23
will put me in mind of their wrongdoing, and they will fall into the enemies'
hand. These therefore are the words of the Lord GOD: Because you have 24
kept me mindful of your wrongdoing by your open rebellion, and your
sins have been revealed in all your acts, because you have kept yourselves
in my mind, you will fall into the enemies' hand by force.

You, too, you impious and wicked prince of Israel, your fate has come 25
upon you in the hour of final punishment. These are the words of the Lord 26
GOD: Put off your diadem, lay aside your crown. All is changed; raise the
low and bring down the high. Ruin! Ruin! I will bring about such ruin as 27
never was before, until the rightful sovereign comes. Then I will give
him all.

Man, prophesy and say, These are the words of the Lord GOD to the 28
Ammonites and to their shameful god:

> A sword, a sword drawn for slaughter,
> > burnished for destruction, *c*
> > to flash like lightning!
> Your visions are false, your auguries a lie,　　　　　　　　　　29
> > which bid you bring it *d* down
> upon the necks of impious and wicked men,
> > whose fate has come upon them
> > in the hour of final punishment.
> > Sheathe it again.　　　　　　　　　　　　　　　　　　　30
> I will judge you in the place where you were born,
> > the land of your origin.
> I will pour out my rage upon you;　　　　　　　　　　　　31
> I will breathe out my blazing wrath over you.
> I will hand you over to brutal men,
> > skilled in destruction.
> You shall become fuel for fire,　　　　　　　　　　　　　32
> > your blood shall be shed within the land
> > and you shall leave no memory behind.

For I, the LORD, have spoken.

These were the words of the LORD to me: Man, will you judge her, will **22** 1 2
you judge the murderous city and bring home to her all her abominable

---

*a* Or household gods.　　　　　*b* *Prob. rdg.; Heb. adds* he must set battering-rams.
*c* for destruction: *prob. rdg.; Heb. obscure.*　　　*d* *Prob. rdg.; Heb.* you.

3  deeds? Say to her, These are the words of the Lord GOD: Alas for the city
   that sheds blood within her walls and brings her fate upon herself, the city
4  that makes herself idols and is defiled thereby! The guilt is yours for the
   blood you have shed, the pollution is on you for the idols you have made.
   You have shortened your days by this and brought the end of your years
   nearer. This is why I exposed you to the contempt of the nations and the
5  mockery of every country. Lands far and near will taunt you with your
6  infamy and gross disorder. In you the princes of Israel, one and all, have
7  used their power to shed blood; men have treated their fathers and mothers
   with contempt, they have oppressed the alien and ill-treated the orphan
8  and the widow. You have disdained what is sacred to me and desecrated
9  my sabbaths. In you, Jerusalem, informers have worked to procure bloodshed; in you are men who have feasted at mountain-shrines and have
10 committed lewdness. In you men have exposed their fathers' nakedness;
11 they have violated women during their periods; they have committed an
   outrage with their neighbours' wives and have lewdly defiled their
   daughters-in-law; they have ravished their sisters, their own fathers'
12 daughters. In you men have accepted bribes to shed blood, and they have
   exacted discount and interest on their loans. You have oppressed your
   fellows for gain, and you have forgotten me. This is the very word of the
   Lord GOD.

13     See, I strike with my clenched fist in anger at your ill-gotten gains and
14 at the bloodshed within your walls. Will your strength or courage stand
15 when I deal with you? I, the LORD, have spoken and I will act. I will disperse you among the nations and scatter you abroad; thus will I rid you
16 altogether of your defilement. I will sift you*a* in the sight of the nations,
   and you will know that I am the LORD.

17 18    These were the words of the LORD to me: Man, to me all Israelites are
19 an alloy, their silver alloyed with copper, tin, iron, and lead.*b* Therefore,
   these are the words of the Lord GOD: Because you have all become alloyed,
20 I will gather you together into Jerusalem, as a mass of silver, copper, iron,
   lead, and tin is gathered into a crucible for the fire to be blown to full heat
   to melt them. So will I gather you in my anger and wrath, set you there and
21 melt you; I will collect you and blow up the fire of my anger until you are
22 melted within it. You will be melted as silver is melted in a crucible, and
   you will know that I, the LORD, have poured out my anger upon you.

23 24    These were the words of the LORD to me: Man, say to Jerusalem, You
   are like a land on which no rain has fallen; no shower has come down upon
25 you*c* in the days of indignation. The princes within her are like lions
   growling as they tear their prey. They have devoured men, and seized their
   treasure and all their wealth; they have widowed many women within her
26 walls. Her priests have done violence to my law*d* and profaned what is
   sacred to me. They make no distinction between sacred and common, and
   lead men to see no difference between clean and unclean. They have dis-
27 regarded my sabbaths, and I am dishonoured among them. Her officers

---

*a*  I will sift you: *or* You will be profaned.          *b*  their silver . . . lead: *prob. rdg.; Heb.*
copper, tin, iron, and lead inside a crucible; they are an alloy, silver.          *c*  *Prob. rdg.;*
*Heb.* it.          *d*  *Or* instruction.

within her are like wolves tearing their prey, shedding blood and destroy- 
ing men's lives to acquire ill-gotten gain. Her prophets use whitewash 28
instead of plaster;<sup>*a*</sup> their vision is false and their divination a lie. They say, 
'This is the word of the Lord GOD', when the LORD has not spoken. The 29
common people are bullies and robbers; they ill-treat the unfortunate 
and the poor, they are unjust and cruel to the alien. I looked for a man among 30
them who could build up a barricade, who could stand before me in the 
breach to defend the land from ruin; but I found no such man. I poured 31
out my indignation upon them and utterly destroyed them in the fire of my 
wrath. Thus I brought on them the punishment they had deserved. This 
is the very word of the Lord GOD.

The word of the LORD came to me: Man, he said, there were once two **23** 1 2
women, daughters of the same mother. They played the whore in Egypt, 3
played the whore while they were still girls; for there they let their breasts 
be fondled and their virgin bosoms pressed. The elder was named Oholah, 4
her sister Oholibah. They became mine and bore me sons and daughters. 
'Oholah' is Samaria, 'Oholibah' Jerusalem. While she owed me obedience 5
Oholah played the whore and was infatuated with her Assyrian lovers, 
staff officers in blue,<sup>*b*</sup> viceroys and governors, handsome young cavaliers 6
all of them, riding on horseback. She played the whore with all of them, 7
the flower of the Assyrian youth; and she let herself be defiled with all their 
idols, wherever her lust led her. She never gave up the whorish ways she 8
had learnt in Egypt, where men had lain with her when young, had pressed 
her virgin bosom and overwhelmed her with their fornication. So I 9
abandoned her to her lovers, the Assyrians, with whom she was infatuated. 
They ravished her, they took her sons and daughters, and they killed her 10
with the sword. She became a byword among women, and judgement was 
passed upon her.

Oholibah, her sister, had watched her, and she gave herself up to lust 11
and played the whore worse than her sister. She, too, was infatuated with 12
Assyrians, viceroys, governors and staff officers, all handsome young 
cavaliers, in full dress, riding on horseback. I found that she too had let 13
herself be defiled; both had gone the same way; but she carried her fornica- 14
tion to greater lengths: she saw male figures carved on the wall, sculptured 
forms of Chaldaeans, picked out in vermilion. Belts were round their 15
waists, and on their heads turbans with dangling ends. All seemed to be 
high officers and looked like Babylonians, natives of Chaldaea. As she 16
looked she was infatuated with them, so she sent messengers to Chaldaea 
for them. And the Babylonians came to her to share her bed, and defiled her 17
with fornication; she was defiled by them until she was filled with revul- 
sion. She made no secret that she was a whore but let herself be ravished 18
until I was filled with revulsion against her as I was against her sister. She 19
played the whore again and again, remembering how in her youth she had 
played the whore in Egypt. She was infatuated with their male prostitutes, 20
whose members were like those of asses and whose seed came in floods like 
that of horses. So, Oholibah, you relived the lewdness of your girlhood in 21
Egypt when you let your bosom be pressed and your breasts fondled.<sup>*c*</sup>

<sup>*a*</sup> Cp. 13. 8–16.     <sup>*b*</sup> Or violet.     <sup>*c*</sup> fondled: *prob. rdg.; Heb. unintelligible.*

22 Therefore these are the words of the Lord GOD: I will rouse them against you, Oholibah, those lovers of yours who have filled you with revulsion,
23 and bring them upon you from every side, the Babylonians and all those Chaldaeans, men of Pekod, Shoa, and Koa, and all the Assyrians with them. Handsome young men they are, viceroys and governors, commanders and
24 staff officers,*a* riding on horseback. They will come against you with war-horses, with chariots and wagons, with a host drawn from the nations, armed with shield, buckler, and helmet; they will beset you on every side. I will give them authority to judge, and they will use that authority to judge
25 you. I will turn my jealous wrath loose on you, and they will make you feel their fury. They will cut off your nose and your ears, and in the end you*b*
26 will fall by the sword.*c* They will strip you of your clothes and take away
27 all your finery. So I will put a stop to your lewdness and the way in which you learnt to play the whore in Egypt. You will never cast longing eyes on such things again, never remember Egypt any more.
28 These are the words of the Lord GOD: I am handing you over to those
29 whom you hate, those who have filled you with revulsion; and they will make you feel their hatred. They will take all you have earned and leave you naked and exposed; that body with which you have played the whore
30 will be ravished. It is your lewdness and your fornication that have brought this upon you, it is because you have followed alien peoples and played
31 the whore and have allowed yourself to be defiled with their idols. You have followed in your sister's footsteps, and I will put her cup into your hand.
32 These are the words of the Lord GOD:

> You shall drink from your sister's cup,
>     a cup deep and wide,
> charged with mockery and scorn,
>     more than ever cup can hold.
33 It*d* will be full of drunkenness and grief,
>     a cup of ruin and desolation,
> the cup of your sister Samaria;
34 and you shall drink it to the dregs.
>     Then you will chew*e* it in pieces
>     and tear out your breasts.
> This is my verdict, says the Lord GOD.

35 Therefore, these are the words of the Lord GOD: Because you have forgotten me and flung me behind your back, you must bear the guilt of your lewdness and your fornication.
36 The LORD said to me, Man, will you judge Oholah and Oholibah? Then
37 tax them with their vile offences. They have committed adultery, and there is blood on their hands. They have committed adultery with their idols and offered my children to them for food, the children they had borne
38 me. This too they have done to me: they have polluted my sanctuary and

---

*a* staff officers: *prob. rdg., cp. verses 5 and 12; Heb. obscure.* *b* in the end you: *or* your successors. *c* *Prob. rdg.; Heb. adds* They will take your sons and daughters, and in the end you will be burnt. *d* *Prob. rdg.; Heb.* You. *e* *Or* dash.

desecrated my sabbaths. They came into my sanctuary and desecrated it  39
by slaughtering their sons as an offering to their idols; this they did in my
own house. They would send for men from a far-off country; and the men  40
came at the messenger's bidding. You bathed your body for these men, you
painted your eyes, decked yourself in your finery, you sat yourself upon a  41
bed of state and had a table put ready before it and laid my own incense
and my own oil on it. Loud were the voices of the light-hearted crowd;  42
and besides ordinary folk Sabaeans were there, brought from the wilderness; they put bracelets on the women's hands and beautiful garlands on
their heads. I thought: Ah that woman, grown old in adultery! Now they  43
will commit fornication with her—with her of all women! They resorted to  44
her as a prostitute; they resorted to Oholah and Oholibah, those lewd
women. Upright men will condemn them for their adultery and blood-  45
shed; for adulterous they are, and blood is on their hands.

These are the words of the Lord GOD: Summon the invading host;  46
abandon them to terror and rapine. Let the host stone them and hack them  47
to pieces with their swords, kill their sons and daughters and burn down
their houses. Thus I will put an end to lewdness in the land, and other  48
women shall be taught not to be as lewd as they. You shall pay the penalty  49
for your lewd conduct and be punished for your idolatries, and you will
know that I am the Lord GOD.

These were the words of the LORD, spoken to me on the tenth day of the  **24**
tenth month in the ninth year: Man, write down a name for this day, this  2
very day: This is the day the king of Babylon invested Jerusalem. Sing a  3
song of derision to this people of rebels; say to them, These are the words
of the Lord GOD:

> Set a cauldron on the fire,
> set it on and pour water into it.
> Into it collect the pieces,
> all the choice pieces,  4
> cram it with leg and shoulder and the best of the bones;
> take the best of the flock.  5
> Pack the logs*a* round it underneath;
> seethe the stew
> and boil the bones in it.
>
> O city running with blood,  6
> O pot green with corrosion,
> corrosion that will never be clean!

Therefore these are the words of the Lord GOD:

> Empty it, piece after piece,
> though no lot is cast for any of them.
> The city had blood in her midst  7
> and she poured it out on the gleaming rock,
> not on the ground: she did not pour it there
> for the dust to cover it.

---

*a* *Prob. rdg., cp. verse 10; Heb.* bones.

8    But I too have spilt blood on the gleaming white rock
         so that it cannot be covered,
     to make anger flare up and to call down vengeance.

9  Therefore these are the words of the Lord GOD:
         O city running with blood,
         I too will make a great fire-pit.
10       Fill it with logs, light the fire;
             make an end of the meat,
         pour out all the broth*a* and the bones with it.*b*
11       Then set the pot empty on the coals
     so that its copper may be heated red-hot,
         and then the impurities in it may be melted
             and its corrosion burnt off.
12           Try as you may,*c*
     the corrosion is so deep that it will not come off;
         only fire will rid it of corrosion for you.
13       Even so, when I cleansed you in your filthy lewdness,
         you did not become clean from it,
             and therefore you shall never again be clean
             until I have satisfied my anger against you.

14    I, the LORD, have spoken; the time is coming, I will act. I will not
refrain nor pity nor relent; I will judge you for your conduct and for all
that you have done. This is the very word of the Lord GOD.

15 16    These were the words of the LORD to me: Man, I am taking from you
at one blow the dearest thing you have, but you must not wail or weep
17 or give way to tears. Keep in good heart; be quiet, and make no mourning for the dead; cover your head as usual and put sandals on your
feet. You shall not cover your upper lip in mourning nor eat the bread of
despair.

18    I spoke to the people in the morning; and that very evening my wife
19 died. Next morning I did as I was told. The people asked me to say what
20 meaning my behaviour had for them. I answered, These were the words
21 of the LORD to me: Tell the Israelites, This is the word of the Lord GOD:
I will desecrate my sanctuary, which has been the pride of your strength,
the delight of your eyes and your heart's desire; and the sons and daughters
22 whom you have left behind shall fall by the sword. But, I said, you shall
do as I have done: you shall not cover your upper lip in mourning nor eat
23 the bread of despair. You shall cover your head and put sandals on your
feet; you shall not wail nor weep. Because of your wickedness you will
24 pine away and will lament to*d* one another. The LORD says, Ezekiel will
be a sign to warn you, and when it happens you will do as he has done,
and you will know that I am the Lord GOD.

25    And now, man, a word for you: I am taking from them that fortress
whose beauty so gladdened them, the delight of their eyes, their heart's
26 desire; I am taking their sons and their daughters. Soon fugitives will come

---

*a* pour . . . broth: *prob. rdg.; Heb.* mix ointment.    *b* with it: *prob. rdg.; Heb.* will
be scorched.    *c* Try as you may: *prob. rdg.; Heb.* obscure.    *d* Or for.

and tell you their news by word of mouth. At once you will recover the  27
power of speech and speak with the fugitives; you will no longer be
dumb. So will you be a portent to them, and they shall know that I am
the LORD.

## Prophecies against foreign nations

THESE WERE THE WORDS OF THE LORD TO ME: Man, look towards  25 1 2
the Ammonites and prophesy against them. Say to the Ammonites,  3
Listen to the word of the Lord GOD. These are his words: Because you
cried 'Aha!' when you saw my holy place desecrated, the soil of Israel laid
waste and the people of Judah sent into exile, I will hand you over as a  4
possession to the tribes of the east. They shall pitch their camps and put
up their dwellings among you; they shall eat your crops; they shall drink
your milk. I will make Rabbah a camel-pasture and Ammon a sheep-walk.  5
Thus you shall know that I am the LORD. These are the words of the Lord  6
GOD: Because you clapped your hands and stamped your feet, and exulted
over the land of Israel with single-minded scorn, I will stretch out my hand  7
over you and make you the prey of the nations and cut you off from all
other peoples; in every land I will exterminate you and bring you to utter
ruin. Thus you shall know that I am the LORD.

These are the words of the Lord GOD: Because Moab said, 'Judah is  8
like all the rest', I will expose the flank of Moab and lay open its cities,*a*  9
from one end to the other—the fairest of its cities: Beth-jeshimoth, Baal-
meon and Kiriathaim. I will hand over Moab and Ammon together to the  10
tribes of the east to be their possession, so that the Ammonites shall not
be remembered among the nations, and so that I may execute judgement  11
upon Moab. Thus they shall know that I am the LORD.

These are the words of the Lord GOD: Because Edom took deliberate  12
revenge on Judah and by so doing incurred lasting guilt, I will stretch  13
my hand out over Edom, says the Lord GOD, and destroy both man and
beast in it, laying waste the land from Teman as far as Dedan; they
shall fall by the sword. I will wreak my vengeance upon Edom through  14
my people Israel. They will deal with Edom as my anger and fury
demand, and it shall feel my vengeance. This is the very word of the
Lord GOD.

These are the words of the Lord GOD: Because the Philistines have  15
taken deliberate revenge and have avenged themselves with single-minded
scorn, giving vent to their age-long enmity in destruction, I will stretch  16
out my hand over the Philistines, says the Lord GOD, I will wipe out the
Kerethites and destroy all the rest of the dwellers by the sea. I will take  17
fearful vengeance upon them and punish them in my fury. When I take
my vengeance, they shall know that I am the LORD.

　　　*a* and lay . . . cities: *prob. rdg.; Heb.* from the cities, from its cities.

**26**     These were the words of the LORD to me on the first day of the first
2   month in the eleventh year: Man, Tyre has said of Jerusalem,

> Aha! she that was the gateway of the nations
>     is broken,
> her gates swing open to me;
> I grow rich, she lies in ruins.

3   Therefore these are the words of the Lord GOD:

> I am against you, Tyre,
> and will bring up many nations against you
>     as the sea brings up its waves;
4      they will destroy the walls of Tyre and pull down her towers.
>     I will scrape the soil off her
> and make her a gleaming rock,
5      she shall be an islet where men spread their nets;
>     I have spoken, says the Lord GOD.
> She shall become the prey of nations,
6      and her daughters[a] shall be slain by the sword in the open country.

> Thus they shall know that I am the LORD.

7     These are the words of the Lord GOD: I am bringing against Tyre from
the north Nebuchadrezzar king of Babylon, king of kings. He will come
with horses and chariots, with cavalry and a great army.

8        Your daughters in the open country
>     he will put to the sword.
> He will set up watch-towers against you,
> pile up siege-ramps against you
> and raise against you a screen of shields.
9        He will launch his battering-rams on your walls
>     and break down your towers with his axes.
10      He will cover you with dust from the thousands of his cavalry;
>     at the thunder of his horses
>     and of his chariot-wheels
> your walls will quake when he enters your gates
>     as men enter a city that is breached.
11      He will trample all your streets
>     with the hooves of his horses
> and put your people to the sword,
> and your strong pillars will fall to the ground.
12        Your wealth will become spoil,
>     your merchandise will be plundered,
>     your walls levelled,
> your pleasant houses pulled down,
> your stones, your timber and your rubble
>     will be dumped into the sea.
13      So I will silence the clamour of your songs,
> and the sound of your harps shall be heard no more.

*a Or* daughter-towns.

I will make you a gleaming rock,        14
a place for fishermen to spread their nets,
    and you shall never be rebuilt.
I, the LORD, have spoken.
    This is the very word of the Lord GOD.

These are the words of the Lord GOD to Tyre: How the coasts and   15
islands will shake at the sound of your downfall, while the wounded groan,
and the slaughter goes on in your midst! Then all the sea-kings will come   16
down from their thrones, and lay aside their cloaks, and strip off their
brocaded robes. They will wear coarse loin-cloths; they will sit on the
ground, shuddering at every moment, horror-struck at your fate. Then   17
they will raise this dirge over you:

How you are undone, swept from the sea,
    O famous city!
You whose strength lay in the sea,
    you and your inhabitants,
who spread their terror throughout the mainland.*a*
Now the coast-lands tremble on the day of your downfall,        18
and the isles of the sea are appalled at your passing.

For these are the words of the Lord GOD: When I make you a desolate   19
city, like a city where no man can live, when I bring up the primeval ocean
against you and the great waters cover you, I will thrust you down with   20
those that descend to the abyss, to the dead of all the ages. I will make you
dwell in the underworld as in places long desolate, with those that go down
to the abyss. So you will never again be inhabited or take your place in the
land of the living. I will bring you to a fearful end, and you shall be no more;   21
men may look for you but will never find you again. This is the very word
of the Lord GOD.

These were the words of the LORD to me: Man, raise a dirge over Tyre   27 1 2
and say, Tyre, throned above your harbours, you who carry the trade of   3
the nations to many coasts and islands, these are the words of the Lord GOD:

O Tyre, you said,
    'I am perfect in beauty.'
Your frontiers are on the high seas,        4
    your builders made your beauty perfect;
they fashioned all your timbers        5
    of pine from Senir;
they took a cedar from Lebanon
    to raise up a mast over you.
They made your oars of oaks from Bashan;        6
    they made your deck strong*b* with box-wood
        from the coasts of Kittim.
    Your canvas was linen,        7
patterned linen from Egypt
    to make your sails;

---

*a* the mainland: *prob. rdg.; Heb.* her inhabitants.        *b* strong: *prob. rdg.; Heb.* ivory.

your awnings were violet and purple
from the coasts of Elishah.

8  Men of Sidon and Arvad became your oarsmen;
you had skilled men within you, O Tyre,
who served as your helmsmen.

9  You had skilled veterans from Gebal
caulking your seams.
You had all sea-going ships and their sailors
to market your wares;

10  men of Pharas,*a* Lud,*b* and Put, served
as warriors in your army;
they hung shield and helmet around you,
and it was they who gave you your glory.

11  Men of Arvad and Cilicia manned all your walls,
men of Gammad were posted on your towers
and hung their shields around your battlements;
it was they who made your beauty perfect.

12  Tarshish was a source of your commerce, from its abundant resources
13  offering silver and iron, tin and lead, as your staple wares. Javan,*c* Tubal,
and Meshech dealt with you, offering slaves and vessels of bronze as your
14  imports. Men from Togarmah offered horses, mares, and mules as
15  your staple wares. Rhodians dealt with you, great islands were a source
of your commerce, paying what was due to you in ivory and ebony.
16  Edom was a source of your commerce, so many were your undertakings,
and offered purple garnets, brocade and fine linen, black coral and
17  red jasper,*d* for your staple wares. Judah and Israel dealt with you,
offering wheat from Minnith, and meal, syrup, oil, and balsam, as your
18  imports. Damascus was a source of your commerce, so many were your
undertakings, from its abundant resources offering wine of Helbon and
19  wool of Suhar, and casks of wine from Izalla,*e* for your staple wares;
20  wrought iron, cassia, and sweet cane were among your imports. Dedan
21  dealt with you in coarse woollens for saddle-cloths. Arabia and all the
chiefs of Kedar were the source of your commerce in lambs, rams,
22  and he-goats; this was your trade with them. Dealers from Sheba and
Raamah dealt with you, offering the choicest spices, every kind of precious
23  stone and gold, as your staple wares. Harran, Kanneh, and Eden, dealers
24  from Asshur and all Media, dealt with you; they were your dealers
in gorgeous stuffs, violet cloths and brocades, in stores of coloured
fabric rolled up and tied with cords; your dealings with them were in
these.

25  Ships of Tarshish were the caravans for your imports;
you were deeply laden with full cargoes
on the high seas.

26  Your oarsmen brought you into many waters,
but on the high seas an east wind wrecked you.

---

*a Or* Persia.        *b Or* Lydia.        *c Or* Ionia.        *d Or and* carbuncles.
*e* casks . . . Izalla: *prob. rdg.; Heb. obscure.*

Your wealth, your staple wares, your imports,                    27
   your sailors and your helmsmen,
your caulkers, your merchants, and your warriors,
   all your ship's company,
     all who were with you,
were flung into the sea on the day of your disaster;
at the cries of your helmsmen the troubled waters tossed.        28

When all the rowers disembark from their ships,                  29
when the sailors, the helmsmen all together, go ashore,
   they exclaim over your fate,                     30
     they cry out bitterly;
   they throw dust on their heads
     and sprinkle themselves with ashes.
   They tear out their hair at your plight          31
     and put on sackcloth;
   they weep bitterly over you,
     bitterly wailing.
In their lamentation they raise a dirge over you,                32
   and this is their dirge:
     Who was like Tyre,
   with her buildings piled*a* off shore?
When your wares were unloaded off the sea                        33
   you met the needs of many nations;
     with your vast resources and your imports
     you enriched the kings of the earth.
Now you are broken by the sea                                    34
   in deep water;
your wares and all your company are gone overboard.
All who dwell on the coasts and islands                          35
   are aghast at your fate;
   horror is written on the faces of their kings
     and their hair stands on end.
Among the nations the merchants jeer in derision at you;         36
you have come to a fearful end and shall be no more for ever.

These were the words of the LORD to me: Man, say to the prince of **28** 1 2
Tyre, This is the word of the Lord GOD:

   In your arrogance you say,
     'I am a god;
   I sit throned like a god on the high seas.'
     Though you are a man and no god,
     you try to think the thoughts of a god.
   What? are you wiser than Danel*b*?                    3
     Is no secret too dark for you?

---

*a* with her buildings piled: *prob. rdg.; Heb. obscure.*          *b* *Or, as otherwise read,*
Daniel; *cp. 14. 14, 20.*

4       Clever and shrewd as you are,
         you have amassed wealth for yourself,
         you have amassed gold and silver in your treasuries;
5       by great cleverness in your trading
         you have heaped up riches,
         and with your riches your arrogance has grown.

6  Therefore these are the words of the Lord GOD:

       Because you try to think the thoughts of a god
7         I will bring strangers against you,
         the most ruthless of nations,
       who will draw their swords against your fine wisdom
         and lay your pride in the dust,
8         sending you down to the pit[a] to die
         a death of disgrace on the high seas.
9       Will you dare to say that you are a god
         when you face your assailants,
         though you are a man and no god
         in the hands of those who lay you low?
10      You will die strengthless
         at the hands of strangers.

For I have spoken. This is the very word of the Lord GOD.

11 12    These were the words of the LORD to me: Man, raise this dirge over the
king of Tyre, and say to him, This is the word of the Lord GOD:

       You set the seal on perfection;
         full of wisdom you were and altogether beautiful.
13      You were in an Eden, a garden of God,
         adorned with gems of every kind:
         sardin and chrysolite and jade,
         topaz, cornelian and green jasper,
         lapis lazuli,[b] purple garnet and green felspar.
         Your jingling beads were of gold,
         and the spangles you wore were made for you
         on the day of your birth.
14      I set you with a towering cherub[c] as guardian;
         you were on God's holy hill
       and you walked proudly among stones that flashed with fire.
15      You were blameless in all your ways
         from the day of your birth
         until your iniquity came to light.
16         Your commerce grew so great,
       lawlessness filled your heart and you went wrong,
      so I brought you down in disgrace from the mountain of God,
         and the guardian cherub banished you[d]
         from among the stones that flashed like fire.

---

[a] *Or* to destruction.    [b] *Or* sapphire.    [c] I set . . . cherub: *prob. rdg.; Heb.*
You were a towering cherub whom I set.    [d] and the . . . you: *or* and I parted
you, O guardian cherub, . . .

> Your beauty made you arrogant, 17
> you misused your wisdom to increase your dignity.
> I flung you to the ground,
> I left you there, a sight for kings to see.
> So great was your sin in your wicked trading 18
> that you desecrated your sanctuaries.
> So I kindled a fire within you,
> and it devoured you.
> I left you as ashes on the ground
> for all to see.
> All among the nations who knew you were aghast: 19
> you came to a fearful end and shall be no more for ever.

These were the words of the LORD to me: Man, look towards Sidon and 20 21
prophesy against her. These are the words of the Lord GOD: 22

> Sidon, I am against you
> and I will show my glory in your midst.
>
> Men will know that I am the LORD
> when I execute judgement upon her
> and thereby prove my holiness.
> I will let loose pestilence upon her 23
> and bloodshed in her streets;
> the slain will fall in her streets,
> beset on all sides by the sword;
> then men will know that I am the LORD.

No longer shall the Israelites suffer from the scorn of their neighbours, 24
the pricking of briars and scratching of thorns, and they shall know that
I am the Lord GOD.

These are the words of the Lord GOD: When I gather the Israelites from 25
the peoples among whom they are scattered, I shall thereby prove my
holiness in the sight of all nations. They shall live on their native soil,
which I gave to my servant Jacob. They shall live there in peace of mind, 26
build houses and plant vineyards; they shall live there in peace of mind
when I execute judgement on all their scornful neighbours. Thus they
shall know that I am the LORD their God.

These were the words of the LORD to me on the twelfth day of the tenth **29**
month in the tenth year: Man, look towards Pharaoh king of Egypt and 2
prophesy against him and all his country. Say, These are the words of the 3
Lord GOD:

> I am against you,
> Pharaoh king of Egypt,
> you great monster,
> lurking in the streams of the Nile.
> You have said, 'My Nile is my own;
> it was I who made it.'

4

    I will put hooks in your jaws
    and make them cling<sup>a</sup> to your scales.
    I will hoist you out of its streams
    with all its fish clinging to your scales.

5

    I will fling you into the wilderness,
    you and all the fish in your streams;
    you will fall on the bare ground
    with none to pick you up and bury you;
    I will make you food
    for beasts and for birds.

6

    So all who live in Egypt will know
    that I am the LORD,
    for the support that you gave to the Israelites
    was no better than a reed,

7

    which splintered in the hand when they grasped you,
    and tore their armpits;
    when they leaned upon you, you snapped
    and their limbs gave way.

8     This therefore is the word of the Lord GOD: I am bringing a sword upon
9 you to destroy both man and beast. The land of Egypt shall become a
desolate waste, and they shall know that I am the LORD, because you said,
10 'The Nile is mine; it was I who made it.' I am against you therefore, you
and your Nile, and I will make Egypt desolate, wasted by drought, from
11 Migdol to Syene and up to the very frontier of Cush. No foot of man shall
pass through it, no foot of beast; it shall lie uninhabited for forty years.
12 I will make the land of Egypt the most desolate of desolate lands; her cities
shall lie derelict among the ruined cities. For forty years shall they lie
derelict, and I will scatter the Egyptians among the nations and disperse
them among the lands.

13     These are the words of the Lord GOD: At the end of forty years I will
gather the Egyptians from the peoples among whom they are scattered.
14 I will turn the fortunes of Egypt and bring them back to Pathros, the
15 land of their origin, where they shall become a petty kingdom. She shall
be the most paltry of kingdoms and never again exalt herself over the
16 nations, for I will make the Egyptians too few to rule over them. The
Israelites will never trust Egypt again; this will be a reminder to them
of their sin in turning to Egypt for help. They shall know that I am the
Lord GOD.

17     These were the words of the LORD to me on the first day of the first
18 month in the twenty-seventh year: Man, long did Nebuchadrezzar king
of Babylon keep his army in the field against Tyre, until every head was
rubbed bare and every shoulder chafed. But neither he nor his army gained
19 anything from Tyre for their long service against her. This, therefore, is
the word of the Lord GOD: I am giving the land of Egypt to Nebuchadrezzar king of Babylon. He shall carry off its wealth, he shall spoil and plunder
20 it, and so his army will be paid. I have given him the land of Egypt as the

---

<sup>a</sup> make them cling: *prob. rdg.; Heb.* make the fish of your streams cling.

wages for his service because they have disregarded me. This is the very word of the Lord GOD.

At that time I will make Israel put out fresh shoots, and give you 21 back the power to speak among them, and they will know that I am the LORD.

These were the words of the LORD to me: Man, prophesy and say, These **30** 1 2 are the words of the Lord GOD:

> Woe, woe for the day!
> for a day is near, 3
> a day of the LORD is near,
> a day of cloud, a day of reckoning for the nations.
> Then a sword will come upon Egypt, 4
> and there will be anguish in Cush,
> when the slain fall in Egypt,
> when its wealth is taken and its foundations are torn up.
> Cush and Put and Lud,*a* 5
> all the Arabs and Libyans and the peoples of allied lands,
> shall fall with them by the sword.

These are the words of the LORD: 6

> All who support Egypt shall fall
> and her boasted might be brought low;
> from Migdol to Syene men shall fall by the sword.
> This is the very word of the Lord GOD.

They shall be the most desolate of desolate lands, and their cities shall 7 lie derelict among the ruined cities. When I set Egypt on fire and all her 8 helpers are broken, they will know that I am the LORD. When that time 9 comes messengers shall go out in haste from my presence to alarm Cush, still without a care, and anguish shall come upon her in Egypt's hour. Even now it is on the way.

These are the words of the Lord GOD: 10

> I will make an end of Egypt's hordes
> by the hands of Nebuchadrezzar king of Babylon.
> He and his people with him, the most ruthless of nations, 11
> will be brought to ravage the land.
> They will draw their swords against Egypt
> and fill the land with the slain.
> I will make the streams of the Nile dry land 12
> and sell Egypt to evil men;
> I will lay waste the land and everything in it by foreign hands.
> I, the LORD, have spoken.

These are the words of the Lord GOD: 13

> I will make an end of the lordlings *b*
> and wipe out the princelings*c* of Noph;
> and never again shall a prince arise in Egypt.

---

*a Or* Lydia.     *b Or* idols.     *c Or* false gods.

Then I will put fear in that land,
14      I will lay Pathros waste and set fire to Zoan
and execute judgement on No.
15      I will pour out my rage upon Sin,
the bastion of Egypt,
and destroy the horde of Noph.
16      I will set Egypt on fire,
and Syene shall writhe in anguish;
the walls of No shall be breached
and flood-waters shall burst into it.
17      The young men of On and Pi-beseth*ᵃ* shall fall by the sword
and the cities themselves go into captivity.
18      Daylight shall fail in Tahpanhes
when I break the yoke of Egypt there;
then her boasted might shall be subdued;
a cloud shall cover her,
and her daughters*ᵇ* shall go into captivity.
19      Thus I will execute judgement on Egypt,
and they shall know that I am the LORD.

20 This was the word of the LORD to me on the seventh day of the first
21 month in the eleventh year: Man, I have broken the arm of Pharaoh king
of Egypt. See, it has not been bound up with dressings and bandage to
22 give it strength to wield a sword. These, therefore, are the words of the
Lord GOD: I am against Pharaoh king of Egypt; I will break both his arms,
23 the sound and the broken, and make the sword drop from his hand. I will
scatter the Egyptians among the nations and disperse them over many
24 lands. Then I will strengthen the arms of the king of Babylon and put my
sword in his hand; but I will break Pharaoh's arms, and he shall lie wounded
25 and groaning before him. I will give strength to the arms of the king of
Babylon, but the arms of Pharaoh will fall. Men will know that I am the
LORD, when I put my sword in the hand of the king of Babylon, and he
26 stretches it out over the land of Egypt. I will scatter the Egyptians among
the nations and disperse them over many lands, and they shall know that
I am the LORD.

31 On the first day of the third month in the eleventh year this word came
2 to me from the LORD: Man, say to Pharaoh king of Egypt and all his
horde:

What are you like in your greatness?

3      Look at Assyria: it was a cedar in Lebanon,
whose fair branches overshadowed the forest,
towering high with its crown finding a way through the foliage.
4      Springs nourished it, underground waters gave it height,
their streams washed the soil all round it
and sent forth their rills to every tree in the country.
5      So it grew taller than every other tree.

*ᵃ Or* Bubastis.      *ᵇ Or* daughter-towns.

Its boughs were many, its branches spread far;
  for water was abundant in the channels.
In its boughs all the birds of the air had their nests,          6
under its branches all wild creatures bore their young,
and in its shadow all great nations made their home.
A splendid great tree it was, with its long spreading boughs,          7
for its roots were beside abundant waters.
No cedar in God's garden overshadowed it,          8
no fir could compare with its boughs,
and no plane-tree had such branches;
  not a tree in God's garden
could rival its beauty.
I, the LORD, gave it beauty          9
  with its mass of spreading boughs,
the envy of all the trees in Eden,
  the garden of God.

Therefore these are the words of the Lord GOD: Because it grew so high    10
and pushed its crown up through the foliage, and its pride mounted as it
grew, therefore I handed it over to a prince of the nations to deal with it;    11
I made an example of it as its wickedness deserved. Strangers from the    12
most ruthless of nations hewed it down and flung it away. Its sweeping
boughs fell on the mountains and in all the valleys, and its branches lay
broken beside all the streams in the land. All nations of the earth came out
from under its shade and left it. All the birds of the air settled on its fallen    13
trunk; the wild creatures all stood by its branches. Never again, therefore,    14
shall the well-watered trees grow so high or push their crowns up through
the foliage. Nor shall the strongest of them, well watered though they be,
stand erect in their full height; for all have been given over to death, to the
world below, to share the common doom and go down to the abyss.

These are the words of the Lord GOD: When he went down to Sheol,    15
I closed the deep over him as a gate, I dammed its rivers, the great waters
were held back. I put Lebanon in mourning for him, and all the trees of
the country-side wilted. I made nations shake with the crash of his fall,    16
when I brought him down to Sheol with those who go down to the abyss.
From this all the trees of Eden, all the choicest and best of Lebanon, all
the well-watered trees, drew comfort in the world below. They too like him    17
had gone down to Sheol, to those slain with the sword; and those who had
lived in his shadow were scattered among the nations. Which among the    18
trees of Eden was like you in glory and greatness? Yet you will be brought
down with the trees of Eden to the world below; you will lie with those who
have been slain by the sword, in the company of the strengthless dead. This
stands for Pharaoh and all his horde. This is the very word of the Lord GOD.

On the first day of the twelfth month in the twelfth year the word of the    **32**
LORD came to me: Man, raise a dirge over Pharaoh king of Egypt and say    2
to him:

  Young lion of the nations, you are undone.
  You were like a monster in the waters of the Nile

scattering the water with its snout, <sup>a b</sup>
churning the water with its feet
and fouling the streams.

3    These are the words of the Lord GOD: When many nations are gathered together I will spread my net over you, and you will be dragged up in its
4 meshes. I will fling you on land, dashing you down on the bare ground. I will let all the birds of the air settle upon you and all the wild beasts gorge
5 themselves on your flesh. Your flesh I will lay on the mountains, and fill
6 the valleys with the worms that feed on it. I will drench the land with your discharge, drench it with your blood to the very mountain-tops, and the
7 watercourses shall be full of you. When I put out your light I will veil the sky and blacken its stars; I will veil the sun with a cloud, and the
8 moon shall not give its light. I will darken all the shining lights of the sky above you and bring darkness over your land. This is the very word of the Lord GOD.
9    I will disquiet many peoples when I bring your broken army among the
10 nations into lands you have never known. I will appal many peoples with your fate; when I brandish my sword in the faces of their kings, their hair shall stand on end. In the day of your downfall each shall tremble for his
11 own fate from moment to moment. For these are the words of the Lord
12 GOD: The sword of the king of Babylon shall come upon you. I will make the whole horde of you fall by the sword of warriors who are of all men the most ruthless. They shall make havoc of the pride of Egypt, and all its
13 horde shall be wiped out. I will destroy all their cattle beside many waters.
14 No foot of man, no hoof of beast, shall ever churn them up again. Then will I let their waters settle and their streams run smooth as oil. This is
15 the very word of the Lord GOD. When I have laid Egypt waste, and the whole land is devastated, when I strike down all who dwell there, they shall know that I am the LORD.
16    This is a dirge, and the women of the nations shall sing it as a dirge. They shall sing it as a dirge, as a dirge over Egypt and all its horde. This is the very word of the Lord GOD.
17    On the fifteenth day of the first month in the twelfth year, the word of the LORD came to me:

18       Man, raise a lament, you and the daughters of the nations,
        over the hordes of Egypt and her nobles,
     whom I will bring down<sup>c</sup> to the world below
     with those that go down to the abyss.

19       Are you better favoured than others?
   Go down and be laid to rest with the strengthless dead.

20    A sword stands ready. Those who marched with her, and all her horde,
21 shall fall into the midst of those slain by the sword. Warrior chieftains in Sheol speak to Pharaoh and those who aided him:
     The strengthless dead, slain by the sword, have come down and are

---

<sup>a</sup> snout: *prob. rdg.; Heb.* streams.     <sup>b</sup> scattering . . . snout: *or* heaving itself up in the streams.     <sup>c</sup> her nobles . . . down: *prob. rdg.; Heb. obscure.*

laid to rest. There is Assyria with all her company, her buried around her, 22
all of them slain and fallen by the sword. Her graves are set in the recesses 23
of the abyss, with her company buried around her, all of them slain, fallen
by the sword, men who once filled the land of the living with terror. There 24
is Elam, with all her hordes buried around her, all of them slain, fallen by
the sword; they have gone down strengthless to the world below, men who
struck terror into the land of the living but now share the disgrace of those
that go down to the abyss. In the midst of the slain a resting-place has been 25
made for her, with all her hordes buried around her; all of them strengthless, slain by the sword. For they who once struck terror into the land of
the living now share the disgrace of those that go down to the abyss; they
are assigned a place in the midst of the slain. There are Meshech and Tubal 26
with all their hordes, with their buried around them, all of them strengthless and slain by the sword, men who once struck terror into the land of
the living. Do they not rest with warriors fallen strengthless,*a* who have 27
gone down to Sheol with their weapons, their swords under their heads and
their shields over their bones,*b* though the terror of their prowess once lay
on the land of the living? You also, Pharaoh, shall lie broken in the company 28
of the strengthless dead, resting with those slain by the sword. There is 29
Edom, her kings and all her princes, who, for all their prowess, have been
lodged with those slain by the sword; they shall rest with the strengthless
dead and with those that go down to the abyss. There are all the princes 30
of the North and all the Sidonians, who have gone down in shame with the
slain, for all the terror they inspired by their prowess. They rest strengthless with those slain by the sword, and they share the disgrace of those that
go down to the abyss.

Pharaoh will see them and will take comfort for his lost hordes—Pharaoh 31
who, with all his army, is slain by the sword, says the Lord GOD; though 32
he spread*c* terror throughout the land of the living, yet he with all his
horde is laid to rest with those that are slain by the sword, in the company
of the strengthless dead. This is the very word of the Lord GOD.

## The remnant of Israel in the land

THESE WERE THE WORDS OF THE LORD TO ME: Man, say to your 33 1 2
fellow-countrymen, When I set armies in motion against a land, its
people choose one of themselves to be a watchman. When he sees the 3
enemy approaching and blows his trumpet to warn the people, then if 4
anyone does not heed the warning and is overtaken by the enemy, he is
responsible for his own fate. He is responsible because, when he heard the 5
alarm, he paid no heed to it; if he had heeded it, he would have escaped.
But if the watchman does not blow his trumpet or warn the people when 6
he sees the enemy approaching, then any man who is killed is caught with
all his sins upon him; but I will hold the watchman answerable for his
death.

*a Prob. rdg.; Heb.* from strengthless ones.  *b* and . . . bones: *prob. rdg.; Heb.*
*unintelligible.*  *c Prob. rdg.; Heb.* I have spread.

7   Man, I have appointed you a watchman for the Israelites. You will take
8   messages from me and carry my warnings to them. It may be that I pronounce sentence of death on a man because he is wicked; if you do not warn
him to give up his ways, the guilt is his and because of his wickedness he
9   shall die, but I will hold you answerable for his death. But if you have
warned him to give up his ways, and he has not given them up, he will die
because of his wickedness, but you will have saved yourself.

10  Man, say to the Israelites, You complain, 'We are burdened by our sins
11  and offences; we are pining away because of them; we despair of life.' So
tell them: As I live, says the Lord GOD, I have no desire for the death of
the wicked. I would rather that a wicked man should mend his ways and
live. Give up your evil ways, give them up; O Israelites, why should
you die?

12  Man, say to your fellow-countrymen, When a righteous man goes wrong,
his righteousness shall not save him. When a wicked man mends his ways,
his former wickedness shall not bring him down. When a righteous man
13  sins, all his righteousness cannot save his life. It may be that, when I tell
the righteous man that he will save his life, he presumes on his righteousness and does wrong; then none of his righteous acts will be remembered:
14  he will die for the wrong he has done. It may be that when I pronounce
sentence of death on the wicked, he mends his ways and does what is just
15  and right: if he then restores the pledges he has taken, repays what he has
stolen, and, doing no more wrong, follows the rules that ensure life, he
16  shall live and not die. None of the sins he has committed shall be remembered against him; he shall live, because he does what is just and right.

17  Your fellow-countrymen are saying, 'The Lord acts without principle',
18  but it is their ways that are unprincipled. When a righteous man gives up
19  his righteousness and does wrong, he shall die because of it; and when a
wicked man gives up his wickedness and does what is just and right, he
20  shall live. How, Israel, can you say that the Lord acts without principle,
when I judge every man of you on his deeds?

21  On the fifth day of the tenth month in the twelfth year of our captivity,
fugitives came to me from Jerusalem and told me that the city had fallen.
22  The evening before they arrived, the hand of the LORD had come upon me,
and by the time they reached me in the morning the LORD had given me
back my speech. My speech was restored and I was no longer dumb.

23 24   These were the words of the LORD to me: Man, the inhabitants of these
wastes on the soil of Israel say, 'When Abraham took possession of the
land he was but one; now we are many, and the land has been granted to
25  us in possession.' Tell them, therefore, that these are the words of the
Lord GOD: You eat meat with the blood in it, you lift up your eyes to idols,
26  you shed*a* blood; and yet you expect to possess the land! You trust to the
sword, you commit abominations, you defile one another's wives; and you
27  expect to possess the land! Tell them that these are the words of the Lord
GOD: As I live, among the ruins they shall fall by the sword; in the open
country I will give them for food to beasts; in dens and caves they shall die
28  by pestilence. I will make the land a desolate waste; her boasted might

*a Or* pour out.

1048

shall be brought to nothing, and the mountains of Israel shall be an untrodden desert. When I make the land a desolate waste because of all the   29
abominations they have committed, they will know that I am the LORD.

Man, your fellow-countrymen gather in groups and talk of you under   30
walls and in doorways and say to one another, 'Let us go and see what
message there is from the LORD.' So my people will come crowding in, as   31
people do, and sit down in front of you. They will hear what you have to
say, but they will not do it. 'Fine words*a*!' they will say, but their hearts
are set on selfish gain. You are no more to them than a singer of fine songs*b*   32
with a lovely voice, or a clever harpist; they will listen to what you say but
will certainly not do it. But when it comes, as come it will, they will know   33
that there has been a prophet in their midst.

These were the words of the LORD to me: Prophesy, man, against the   **34** 1 2
shepherds of Israel; prophesy and say to them, You shepherds, these are
the words of the Lord GOD: How I hate the shepherds of Israel who care
only for themselves! Should not the shepherd care for the sheep? You   3
consume the milk, wear the wool, and slaughter the fat beasts, but you do
not feed the sheep. You have not encouraged the weary, tended the sick,   4
bandaged the hurt, recovered the straggler, or searched for the lost; and
even the strong you have driven with ruthless severity. They are scattered,   5
they have no shepherd, they have become the prey of wild beasts. My   6
sheep go straying over the mountains and on every high hill, my flock is
dispersed over the whole country, with no one to ask after them or search
for them.

Therefore, you shepherds, hear the words of the LORD. As surely as I   7 8
live, says the Lord GOD, because my sheep are ravaged by wild beasts and
have become their prey for lack of a shepherd, because my shepherds have
not asked after the sheep but have cared only for themselves and not for
the sheep—therefore, you shepherds, hear the words of the LORD. These   9 10
are the words of the Lord GOD: I am against the shepherds and will demand
my sheep from them. I will dismiss those shepherds: they shall care only
for themselves no longer; I will rescue my sheep from their jaws, and they
shall feed on them no more.

For these are the words of the Lord GOD: Now I myself will ask after   11
my sheep and go in search of them. As a shepherd goes in search of his   12
sheep when his flock is dispersed all around him, so I will go in search of
my sheep and rescue them, no matter where they were scattered in dark
and cloudy days. I will bring them out from every nation, gather them in   13
from other lands, and lead them home to their own soil. I will graze them
on the mountains of Israel, by her streams and in all her green fields. I   14
will feed them on good grazing-ground, and their pasture shall be the high
mountains of Israel. There they will rest, there in good pasture, and find
rich grazing on the mountains of Israel. I myself will tend my flock, I   15
myself pen them in their fold, says the Lord GOD. I will search for the lost,   16
recover the straggler, bandage the hurt, strengthen the sick, leave the
healthy and strong to play, and give them their proper food.

As for you, my flock, these are the words of the Lord GOD: I will judge   17

---

*a* Fine words: *or* Love songs.       *b* fine songs: *or* love songs.

18 between one sheep and another. You rams and he-goats! Are you not
satisfied with grazing on good herbage, that you must trample down the
rest with your feet? Or with drinking clear water, that you must churn up
19 the rest with your feet? My flock has to eat what you have trampled and
20 drink what you have churned up. These, therefore, are the words of the
Lord GOD to them: Now I myself will judge between the fat sheep and the
21 lean. You hustle the weary with flank and shoulder, you butt them with
your horns until you have driven them away and scattered them abroad.
22 Therefore I will save my flock, and they shall be ravaged no more; I will
23 judge between one sheep and another. Then I will set over them one
shepherd to take care of them, my servant David; he shall care for them
24 and become their shepherd. I, the LORD, will become their God, and my
servant David shall be a prince among them. I, the LORD, have spoken.
25 I will make a covenant with them to ensure prosperity; I will rid the land
of wild beasts, and men shall live in peace of mind on the open pastures and
26 sleep in the woods. I will settle them in the neighbourhood of my hill and
27 send them rain in due season, blessed rain. Trees in the country-side shall
bear their fruit, the land shall yield its produce, and men shall live in peace
of mind on their own soil. They shall know that I am the LORD when I
break the bars of their yokes and rescue them from those who have en-
28 slaved them. They shall never be ravaged by the nations again nor shall
wild beasts devour them; they shall live in peace of mind, with no one to
29 alarm them. I will give prosperity to their plantations; they shall never
again be victims of famine in the land nor any longer bear the taunts of the
30 nations. They shall know that I, the LORD their God, am with them, and
31 that they are my people Israel, says the Lord GOD. You are my flock, my
people, the flock I feed, and I am your God. This is the very word of the
Lord GOD.

35 1 2     These were the words of the LORD to me: Man, look towards the hill-
3 country of Seir and prophesy against it. Say, These are the words of the
Lord GOD:

> O hill-country of Seir, I am against you:
> I will stretch out my hand over you
> and make you a desolate waste.

4
> I will lay your cities in ruins
> and you shall be made desolate;
> thus you shall know that I am the LORD.

5
> For you have maintained an immemorial feud
> and handed over the Israelites to the sword
> in the hour of their doom,
> at the time of their final punishment.

6
> Therefore, as I live, says the Lord GOD,
> I make blood your destiny, and blood shall pursue you;
> you are most surely guilty of blood,
> and blood shall pursue you.

7
> I will make the hill-country of Seir a desolate waste
> and put an end to all in it who pass to and fro;

I will fill your hills and your valleys with its slain,                 8
and those slain by the sword shall fall into your streams.
I will make you desolate for ever,                                      9
and your cities shall not be inhabited;
thus you shall know that I am the LORD.

You say, The two nations and the two countries shall be mine and I   10
will take possession of them, though the LORD is*a* there. Therefore, as   11
I live, says the Lord GOD, your anger and jealousy shall be requited, for
I will do to you what you have done in your hatred against them. I shall be
known among you when I judge you; you shall know that I am the LORD.   12
I have heard all your blasphemies; you have said, 'The mountains of
Israel are desolate and have been given to us to devour.' You have set   13
yourselves up against me and spoken recklessly against me. I myself have
heard you. These are the words of the Lord GOD: I will make you so   14
desolate that the whole world will gloat over you. I will do to you as you   15
did to Israel my own possession when you gloated over its desolation.
O hill-country of Seir, you will be desolate, and it will be the end of all
Edom. Thus men will know that I am the LORD.

And do you, man, prophesy to the mountains of Israel and say, Moun-   **36**
tains of Israel, hear the words of the LORD. These are the words of the Lord   2
GOD: The enemy has said, 'Aha! now the everlasting highlands are ours.'
Therefore prophesy and say, These are the words of the Lord GOD: You   3
mountains of Israel, all round you men gloated over you and trampled you
down when you were seized and occupied by the rest of the nations; your
name was bandied about in the common talk of men. Therefore, listen to   4
the words of the Lord GOD when he speaks to the mountains and hills, to
the streams and valleys, to the desolate palaces and deserted cities, all
plundered and despised by the rest of the nations round you. These are   5
the words of the Lord GOD: In the fire of my jealousy I have spoken plainly
against the rest of the nations, and against Edom above all. For Edom,
swollen with triumphant scorn, seized on my land to hold it up to public
contempt. Therefore prophesy over the soil of Israel and say to the moun-   6
tains and hills, the streams and valleys, These are the words of the Lord
GOD: I have spoken my mind in jealousy and anger because you have had
to endure the taunts of all nations. Therefore, says the Lord GOD, I have   7
sworn with uplifted hand that the nations round about shall be punished
for*b* their taunts. But you, mountains of Israel, you shall put forth your   8
branches and yield your fruit for my people Israel, for their home-coming
is near. See now, I am for you, I will turn to you, and you shall be tilled and   9
sown. I will plant many men upon you—the whole house of Israel. The   10
cities shall again be inhabited and the palaces rebuilt. I will plant many men   11
and beasts upon you; they shall increase and be fruitful. I will make you
populous as in days of old and more prosperous than you were at first.
Thus you will know that I am the LORD. I will make men—my people   12
Israel—tread your paths again. They shall settle in you, and you shall be
their possession; but you shall never again rob them of their children.

*a* *Or* has been.     *b* be punished for: *or* bear.

13 These are the words of the Lord GOD: People say that you are a land that
14 devours men and robs your tribes of their children. But you shall never
devour men any more nor rob your tribes of their children, says the Lord
15 GOD. I will never let you hear the taunts of the nations again nor shall you
have to endure the reproaches of the peoples. This is the very word of the
Lord GOD.

16 17 These were the words of the LORD to me: Man, when the Israelites lived
on their own soil they defiled it with their ways and deeds; their ways were
18 foul and disgusting in my sight. I poured out my fury upon them because
of the blood they had poured out upon the land, and the idols with which
19 they had defiled it. I scattered them among the nations, and they were
dispersed among different countries; I passed on them the sentence which
20 their ways and deeds deserved. When they came among those nations,
they caused my holy name to be profaned wherever they came: men said
of them, 'These are the people of the LORD, and it is from his land that they
21 have come.' And I spared them for the sake of my holy name which the
Israelites had profaned among the nations to whom they had gone.

22 Therefore tell the Israelites that these are the words of the Lord GOD:
It is not for your sake, you Israelites, that I am acting, but for the sake of
my holy name, which you have profaned among the peoples where you
23 have gone. I will hallow my great name, which has been profaned among
those nations. When they see that I reveal my holiness through you, the
24 nations will know that I am the LORD, says the Lord GOD. I will take you
out of the nations and gather you from every land and bring you to your
25 own soil. I will sprinkle clean water over you, and you shall be cleansed
from all that defiles you; I will cleanse you from the taint of all your idols.
26 I will give you a new heart and put a new spirit within you; I will take the
27 heart of stone from your body and give you a heart of flesh. I will put my
spirit into you and make you conform to my statutes, keep my laws and
28 live by them. You shall live in the land which I gave to your ancestors; you
29 shall become my people, and I will become your God. I will save you from
all that defiles you; I will call to the corn and make it plentiful; I will bring
30 no more famine upon you. I will make the trees bear abundant fruit and
the ground yield heavy crops, so that you will never again have to bear the
31 reproach of famine among the nations. You will recall your wicked ways
and evil deeds, and you will loathe yourselves because of your wickedness
32 and your abominations. It is not for your sake that I am acting; be sure of
that, says the Lord GOD. Feel, then, the shame and disgrace of your ways,
men of Israel.

33 These are the words of the Lord GOD: When I cleanse you of all your
wickedness, I will re-people the cities, and the palaces shall be rebuilt.
34 The land now desolate shall be tilled, instead of lying waste for every
35 passer-by to see. Men will say that this same land which was waste has
become like a garden of Eden, and people will make their homes in the
36 cities once ruined, wasted, and shattered, but now well fortified. The
nations still left around you will know that it is I, the LORD, who have
rebuilt the shattered cities and planted anew the waste land; I, the LORD,
have spoken and will do it.

These are the words of the Lord GOD: Yet again will I let the Israelites 37
ask me to act in their behalf. I will make their men numerous as sheep,
like the sheep offered as holy-gifts, like the sheep in Jerusalem at times of 38
festival. So shall their ruined cities be filled with human flocks, and they
shall know that I am the LORD.

The hand of the LORD came upon me, and he carried me out by his 37
spirit and put me down in a plain full of bones. He made me go to and fro 2
across them until I had been round them all;*[a]* they covered the plain,
countless numbers of them, and they were very dry. He said to me, 'Man, 3
can these bones live again?' I answered, 'Only thou knowest that, Lord
GOD.' He said to me, 'Prophesy over these bones and say to them, O dry 4
bones, hear the word of the LORD. This is the word of the Lord GOD to 5
these bones: I will put breath*[b]* into you, and you shall live. I will fasten 6
sinews on you, bring flesh upon you, overlay you with skin, and put breath
in you, and you shall live; and you shall know that I am the LORD.' I began 7
to prophesy as he had bidden me, and as I prophesied there was a rustling
sound and the bones fitted themselves together. As I looked, sinews 8
appeared upon them, flesh covered them, and they were overlaid with
skin, but there was no breath in them. Then he said to me, 'Prophesy to 9
the wind, prophesy, man, and say to it, These are the words of the Lord
GOD: Come, O wind, come from every quarter and breathe into these
slain, that they may come to life.' I began to prophesy as he had bidden me: 10
breath came into them; they came to life and rose to their feet, a mighty
host. He said to me, 'Man, these bones are the whole people of Israel. They 11
say, "Our bones are dry, our thread of life is snapped, our web is severed
from the loom."*[c]* Prophesy, therefore, and say to them, These are the 12
words of the Lord GOD: O my people, I will open your graves and bring
you up from them, and restore you to the land of Israel. You shall know 13
that I am the LORD when I open your graves and bring you up from them,
O my people. Then I will put my spirit*[d]* into you and you shall live, and I 14
will settle you on your own soil, and you shall know that I the LORD have
spoken and will act. This is the very word of the LORD.'

These were the words of the LORD to me: Man, take one leaf of a wooden 15 16
tablet and write on it, 'Judah and his associates of Israel.' Then take another
leaf and write on it, 'Joseph, the leaf of Ephraim and all his associates of
Israel.' Now bring the two together to form one tablet; then they will be a 17
folding tablet in your hand. When your fellow-countrymen ask you to tell 18
them what you mean by this, say to them, These are the words of the Lord 19
GOD: I am taking the leaf of Joseph, which belongs to Ephraim and his
associate tribes of Israel, and joining*[e]* to it the leaf of Judah. Thus I shall
make them one tablet, and they shall be one in my hand. The leaves on 20
which you write shall be visible in your hand for all to see.

Then say to them, These are the words of the Lord GOD: I am gathering 21
up the Israelites from their places of exile among the nations; I will
assemble them from every quarter and restore them to their own soil.

---

*a* He made . . . all: *or* He made me pass all round them.          *b* Or wind *or* spirit.
*c* our web . . . loom: *prob. rdg.; Heb.* we are completely cut off.          *d* Or breath.
*e* Prob. rdg.; Heb. adds them.

22 I will make them one single nation in the land, on the mountains of Israel, and they shall have one king; they shall no longer be two nations or divided
23 into two kingdoms. They shall never again be defiled with their idols, their loathsome ways and all their disloyal acts; I will rescue them from all their sinful backsliding and purify them. Thus they shall become my people,
24 and I will become their God. My servant David shall become king over them, and they shall have one shepherd. They shall conform to my laws,
25 they shall observe and carry out my statutes. They shall live in the land which I gave my servant Jacob, the land where your fathers lived. They and their descendants shall live there for ever, and my servant David shall
26 for ever be their prince. I will make a covenant with them to bring them prosperity; this covenant shall be theirs for ever.*a* I will greatly increase
27 their numbers, and I will put my sanctuary for ever in their midst. They shall live under the shelter of my dwelling; I will become their God and
28 they shall become my people. The nations shall know that I the LORD am keeping Israel sacred to myself, because my sanctuary is in the midst of them for ever.

## God's triumph over the world

**38** 1 2 THESE WERE THE WORDS OF THE LORD TO ME: Man, look towards Gog, the prince of Rosh, Meshech, and Tubal, in the land of Magog,
3 and prophesy against him. Say, These are the words of the Lord GOD:
4 I am against you, Gog, prince of Rosh, Meshech, and Tubal. I will turn you about, I will put hooks in your jaws. I will lead you out, you and your whole army, horses and horsemen, all fully equipped, a great host with
5 shield and buckler, every man wielding a sword, and with them the men
6 of Pharas, Cush, and Put, all with shield and helmet; Gomer and all its squadrons, Beth-togarmah with its squadrons from the far recesses of the
7 north—a great concourse of peoples with you. Be prepared; make ready, you and all the host which has gathered to join you, and hold yourselves
8 in reserve for me.*b* After many days you will be summoned; in years to come you will enter a land restored from ruin, whose people are gathered from many nations upon the mountains of Israel that have been desolate so long. The Israelites, brought out from the nations, will all be living
9 undisturbed; and you will come up, driving in like a hurricane; you will cover the land like a cloud, you and all your squadrons, a great concourse of peoples.
10 This is the word of the Lord GOD: At that time a thought will enter
11 your head and you will plan evil. You will say, 'I will attack a land of open villages, I will fall upon a people living quiet and undisturbed,
12 undefended by walls, with neither gates nor bars.' You will expect to come plundering, spoiling, and stripping bare the ruins where men now live again, a people gathered out of the nations, a people acquiring cattle
13 and goods, and making their home at the very centre of the world. Sheba

*a* Prob. rdg.; Heb. adds and I will put them.    *b* and hold . . . me: or and you shall be their rallying-point.

and Dedan, the traders of Tarshish and her leading merchants, will say to you, 'Is it for plunder that you have come? Have you gathered your host to get spoil, to carry off silver and gold, to seize cattle and goods, to collect rich spoil?'

Therefore, prophesy, man, and say to Gog, These are the words of the 14 Lord GOD: In that day when my people Israel is living undisturbed, will you not awake and come with many nations from your home in the far 15 recesses of the north, all riding on horses, a great host, a mighty army? You 16 will come up against my people Israel; and in those future days you will be like a cloud covering the earth. I will bring you against my land, that the nations may know me, when they see me prove my holiness at your expense, O Gog.

This is the word of the Lord GOD: When I spoke in days of old through 17 my servants the prophets, who prophesied in those days unceasingly, it was you whom I threatened to bring against Israel. On that day, when at 18 length Gog comes against the land of Israel, says the Lord GOD, my wrath will boil over. In my jealousy and in the heat of my anger I swear that on 19 that day there shall be a great earthquake throughout the land of Israel. The fish in the sea and the birds in the air, the wild animals and all reptiles 20 that move on the ground, all mankind on the face of the earth, all shall be shaken before me. Mountains shall be torn up, the terraced hills collapse, and every wall crash to the ground. I will summon universal terror against 21 Gog, says the Lord GOD, and his men shall turn their swords against one another. I will bring him to judgement with pestilence and bloodshed; I 22 will pour down teeming rain, hailstones hard as rock, and fire and brimstone, upon him, upon his squadrons, upon the whole concourse of peoples with him. Thus will I prove myself great and holy and make myself known 23 to many nations; they shall know that I am the LORD.

And you, man, prophesy against Gog and say, These are the words of **39** the Lord GOD: I am against you, Gog, prince of Rosh, Meshech, and Tubal. I will turn you about and drive you, I will fetch you up from the far recesses 2 of the north and bring you to the mountains of Israel. I will strike the bow 3 from your left hand and dash the arrows from your right hand. There on 4 the mountains of Israel you shall fall, you, all your squadrons, and your allies; I will give you as food to the birds of prey and the wild beasts. You 5 shall fall on the bare ground, for it is I who have spoken. This is the very word of the Lord GOD. I will send fire on Magog and on those who live 6 undisturbed in the coasts and islands, and they shall know that I am the LORD. My holy name I will make known in the midst of my people Israel 7 and will no longer let it be profaned; the nations shall know that in Israel I, the LORD, am holy.

Behold, it comes; it shall be, says the Lord GOD, the day of which I have 8 spoken. The dwellers in the cities of Israel shall come out and gather 9 weapons to light their fires, buckler and shield, bow and arrows, throwing-stick and lance, and they shall kindle fires with them for seven years. They 10 shall take no wood from the fields nor cut it from the forests but shall light their fires with the weapons. Thus they will plunder their plunderers and spoil their spoilers. This is the very word of the Lord GOD.

11 In that day I will give to Gog, instead of[a] a burial-ground in Israel, the valley of Abarim east of the Sea.[b] There they shall bury Gog and all his horde, and all Abarim will be blocked; and they shall call it the Valley of
12 Gog's Horde. For seven months the Israelites shall bury them and purify
13 the land; all the people shall take their share in the burying. The day that I win myself honour shall be a memorable day for them. This is the very word of the Lord God.
14 Men shall be picked for the regular duty of going through the country and searching for[c] any left above ground, to purify
15 the land; they shall begin their search at the end of the seven months. They shall go through the country, and whenever one of them sees a human bone he shall put a marker beside it, until it has been buried in the Valley of
16 Gog's Horde. So no more shall be heard of that great horde,[d] and the land will be purified.

17 Man, these are the words of the Lord God: Cry to every bird that flies and to all the wild beasts: Come, assemble, gather from every side to my sacrifice, the great sacrifice I am making for you on the mountains of
18 Israel; eat flesh and drink blood, eat the flesh of warriors and drink the blood of princes of the earth; all these are your rams and sheep, he-goats
19 and bulls, and buffaloes of Bashan. You shall cram yourselves with fat and drink yourselves drunk on blood at the sacrifice which I am preparing for
20 you. At my table you shall eat your fill of horses and riders, of warriors and all manner of fighting men. This is the very word of the Lord God.

21 I will show my glory among the nations; all shall see the judgement that
22 I execute and the heavy hand that I lay upon them. From that day for-
23 wards the Israelites shall know that I am the Lord their God. The nations shall know that the Israelites went into exile for their iniquity, because they were faithless to me. So I hid my face from them and handed them over
24 to their enemies, and they fell, every one of them, by the sword. I dealt with them as they deserved, defiled and rebellious as they were, and hid my face from them.

25 These, therefore, are the words of the Lord God: Now I will restore the fortunes of Jacob and show my affection for all Israel, and I will be jealous
26 for my holy name. They shall forget their shame and all their unfaithfulness to me, when they are at home again on their own soil, undisturbed, with
27 no one to alarm them. When I bring them home out of the nations and gather them from the lands of their enemies, I will make them an example
28 of my holiness, for many nations to see. They will know that I am the Lord their God, because I who sent them into exile among the nations will bring them together again on the soil of their own land and leave none of them
29 behind. No longer will I hide my face from them, I who have poured out my spirit upon Israel. This is the very word of the Lord God.

---

[a] *Prob. rdg.; Heb. adds* there.　　[b] *That is* the Dead Sea.　　[c] searching for: *prob. rdg.; Heb.* burying those who are passing through.　　[d] So . . . horde: *prob. rdg.; Heb. obscure.*

## The restored theocracy

A T THE BEGINNING OF THE YEAR, on the tenth day of the month, in **40**
the twenty-fifth year of our exile, that is fourteen years after the
destruction of the city, on that very day, the hand of the LORD came upon
me and he brought me there. In a vision God brought me to the land of 2
Israel and set me on a very high mountain, where I saw what seemed the
buildings of a city facing me. He led me towards it, and I saw a man like 3
a figure of bronze holding a cord of linen thread and a measuring-rod, and
standing at the gate. 'Man,' he said to me, 'look closely and listen care- 4
fully; mark well all that I show you, for this is why you have been brought
here. Tell the Israelites all that you see.'

Round the outside of the temple ran a wall. The length of the rod which 5
the man was holding was six cubits, reckoning by the long cubit which was
one cubit and a hand's breadth. He measured the thickness and the height
of the wall; each was one rod. He came to a gate which faced eastwards, 6
went up its steps and measured the threshold of the gateway; its depth
was one rod. Each cell was one rod long and one rod wide; the space between 7
the cells five cubits, and the threshold of the gateway at the end of the
vestibule on the side facing the temple one rod. He measured the vestibule 8
of the gate and found it eight cubits, with pilasters two cubits thick; the 9
vestibule of the gateway lay at the end near the temple. Now the cells of 10
the gateway, looking back eastwards, were three in number on each side;
all three of the same size, and their pilasters on each side of the same size
also. He measured the entrance into the gateway; it was ten cubits wide, 11
and the gateway itself throughout its length thirteen cubits wide. In front 12
of the cells on each side lay a kerb, one cubit wide; each cell was six cubits
by six. He measured the width of the gateway through the cell doors which 13
faced one another, from the back of one cell to the back of the opposite
cell; he made it twenty-five cubits, and the vestibule twenty cubits, across; 14
the gateway on every side projected into*a* the court. From the front of the 15
entrance-gate to the outer face of the vestibule of the inner gate the distance was fifty cubits. Both cells and pilasters had loopholes all round 16
inside the gateway, and the vestibule had windows all round within and
palms carved on each pilaster.

He brought me to the outer court, and I saw rooms and a pavement all 17
round the court: in all, thirty rooms on the pavement. The pavement ran 18
up to the side of the gateways, as wide as they were long; this was the lower
pavement. He measured the width of the court from the front of the lower 19
gateway to the outside of the inner gateway; it was a hundred cubits. He
led me round to the north and I saw a gateway facing northwards, belong- 20
ing to the outer court, and he measured its length and its breadth. Its cells, 21
three on each side, together with its pilasters and its vestibule, were the
same size as those of the first gateway, fifty cubits long by twenty-five wide.
So too its windows, and those of*b* its vestibule, and its palms were the same 22
size as those of the gateway which faced east; it was approached by seven

*a* *Prob. rdg., Heb. adds* pilaster.　　　*b* those of: *prob. rdg.; Heb. om.*

23 steps with its vestibule facing them. A gate like that on the east side led to
the inner court opposite the northern gateway; he measured from gateway
24 to gateway, and it was a hundred cubits. Then he led me round to the south,
and I found a gateway facing southwards. He measured its cells, its pilas-
25 ters, and its vestibule, and found it the same size as the others, fifty cubits
long by twenty-five wide. Both gateway and vestibule had windows all
26 round like the others. It was approached by seven steps with a vestibule
27 facing them and palms carved on each pilaster. The inner court had a gateway facing southwards, and he measured from gateway to gateway; it was
a hundred cubits.

28    He brought me into the inner court through the southern gateway,
29 measured it and found it the same size as the others. So were its cells,
pilasters, and vestibule, fifty cubits long by twenty-five wide. It and its
31 vestibule had windows all round.*a* Its vestibule faced the outer court; it
had palms carved on its pilasters, and eight steps led up to it.

32    Then he brought me into the inner court, towards the east, and measured
33 the gateway and found it the same size as the others. So too were its cells,
pilasters, and vestibule; it and its vestibule had windows all round, and it
34 was fifty cubits long by twenty-five wide. Its vestibule faced the outer
court and had a palm carved on each pilaster; eight steps led up to it.
35 Then he brought me to the north gateway and measured it and found it
36 the same size as the others. So were its cells, pilasters, and vestibule, and
37 it had windows all round; it was fifty cubits long by twenty-five wide. Its
vestibule faced the outer court and had palms carved on the pilaster at
each side; eight steps led up to it.

38    There was a room opening out from the vestibule of the gateway;*b* here
39 the whole-offerings were washed. In the vestibule of the gateway were two
tables on each side, at which to slaughter the whole-offering, the sin-
40 offering, and the guilt-offering. At the corner on the outside, as one goes
up to the opening of the northern gateway, stood two tables, and two more
41 at the other corner of the vestibule of the gateway. Another four stood on
each side at the corner of the gateway, eight tables in all at which slaughter-
42 ing was done. Four tables used for the whole-offering were of hewn stone,
each a cubit and a half long by a cubit and a half wide and a cubit high; and
on them they put the instruments used for the whole-offering and other
43 sacrifices. The flesh of the offerings was on the tables, and ledges a hand's
breadth in width were fixed all round facing inwards.

44    Then he brought me right into the inner court, and I saw two rooms in
the inner court, one at the corner of the northern gateway, facing south,
45 and one at the corner of the southern gateway, facing north. This room
facing south, he told me, is for the priests who have charge of the temple.
46 The room facing north is for the priests who have charge of the altar;
these are the sons of Zadok, who alone of the Levites may come near to
47 serve the LORD. He measured the court; it was square, a hundred cubits
each way, and the altar lay in front of the temple.

---

*a So some MSS.; others add* (30) It had vestibules all round, and it was twenty-five cubits
long by five wide.          *b* the vestibule of the gateway: *prob. rdg.; Heb.* pilasters,
the gates.

Then he brought me into the vestibule of the temple, and measured a 48
pilaster of the vestibule; it was five cubits on each side, the width of the
gateway fourteen cubits and that of the corners of the gateway three
cubits in each direction. The vestibule was twenty cubits long by twelve 49
wide; ten steps led up to it, and by the pilasters rose pillars, one on each
side.

Then he brought me into the sanctuary and measured the pilasters; **41**
they were six cubits wide on each side. The opening was ten cubits wide 2
and its corners five cubits wide in each direction. He measured its length;
it was forty cubits, and its width twenty. He went inside and measured the 3
pilasters at the opening: they were two cubits; the opening itself was six
cubits, and the corners of the opening were seven cubits in each direction.
Then he measured the room at the far end of the sanctuary; its length and 4
its breadth were each twenty cubits. He said to me, 'This is the Holy of
Holies.'

He measured the wall of the temple; it was six cubits high, and each 5
arcade all round the house was four cubits wide. The arcades were arranged 6
in three tiers, each tier in thirty sections. In the wall all round the temple
there were intakes for the arcades, so that they could be supported without
being fastened into the wall of the temple. The higher up the arcades were, 7
the broader they were all round by the addition of the intakes, one above
the other all round the temple; the temple itself had a ramp running upwards on a base, and in this way one went up from the lowest to the highest
tier by way of the middle tier.

Then I saw a raised pavement all round the temple, and the foundations 8
of the arcades were flush with it and measured a full rod, six cubits high.
The outer wall of the arcades was five cubits thick. There was an un- 9
occupied area beside the terrace[a] which was adjacent to the temple, and 11[b]
the arcades opened on to this area, one opening facing northwards and one
southwards; the unoccupied area was five cubits wide on all sides. There 10
was a free space[c] twenty cubits wide all round the temple. On the western 12
side, at the far end of the free space, stood a building seventy cubits wide;
its wall was five cubits thick all round, and its length ninety cubits.

He measured the temple; it was a hundred cubits long; and the free 13
space, the building, and its walls, a hundred cubits in all. The eastern front 14
of the temple and the free space was a hundred cubits wide. He measured 15
the length of the building at the far end of the free space to the west of the
temple, and its corridors on each side: a hundred cubits.

The sanctuary, the inner shrine and the outer vestibule were panelled;
the embrasures all round the three of them were framed with wood all 16
round. From the ground up to the windows and above the door, both in 17
the inner and outer chambers, round all the walls, inside and out, were 18
carved figures,[d] cherubim and palm-trees, a palm between every pair of
cherubim. Each cherub had two faces: one the face of a man, looking 19
towards one palm-tree, and the other the face of a lion, looking towards

[a] beside the terrace: *prob. rdg.*; *Heb.* between the arcades.       [b] *Verses 10 and 11
transposed.*       [c] There . . . space: *prob. rdg.*; *Heb.* Between the rooms.       [d] carved
figures: *prob. rdg.*; *Heb.* measures and carving.

another palm-tree. Such was the carving round the whole of the temple.
20 The cherubim and the palm-trees were carved from the ground up to the
21 top of the doorway and on the wall of the sanctuary. The door-posts of
the sanctuary were square.*a*
22    In front of*b* the Holy Place was what seemed an altar of wood, three
cubits high and two cubits long; it was fitted with corner-posts, and its
base and sides also were of wood. He told me that this was the table which
23 stood before the LORD. The sanctuary had a double door, and the Holy
24 Place also had a double door: the double doors had swinging leaves, a pair
25 for each door. Cherubim and palm-trees like those on the walls were
carved on them.*c* Outside there was a wooden cornice over the vestibule;
26 on both sides of the vestibule were loopholes, with palm-trees carved at
the corners.*d*

42    Then he took me to the outer court round by the north and brought me
to the rooms facing the free space and facing the buildings to the north.
2 The length along the northern side was a hundred cubits, and the breadth
3 fifty. Facing the free space measuring twenty cubits, which adjoined the
inner court, and facing the pavement of the outer court, were corridors at
4 three levels corresponding to each other. In front of the rooms a passage, ten
cubits wide and a hundred cubits long, ran towards the inner court; their
5 entrances faced northwards. The upper rooms were shorter than the lower
and middle rooms, because the corridors took building space from them.
6 For they were all at three levels and had no pillars as the courts had, so that
7 the lower and middle levels were recessed from the ground upwards. An
outside wall, fifty cubits long, ran parallel to the rooms and in front of them,
8 on the side of the outer court. The rooms adjacent to the outer court were
9 fifty cubits long, and those facing the sanctuary a hundred cubits. Below
these rooms was an entry from the east as one entered them from the outer
10 court where the wall of the court began.*e* On the south side, passing by the
11 free space and the building, were other rooms with a passage in front of
them. These rooms corresponded, in length and breadth and in general
12 character, to those facing north, to the south. As one*f* went eastwards, where the
passages began, there was an entrance in the face of the inner*g* wall. Then
13 he said to me, 'The northern and southern rooms facing the free space
are the consecrated rooms where the priests who approach the LORD may
eat the most sacred offerings. There they shall put these offerings as well
as the grain-offering, the sin-offering, and the guilt-offering; for the place
14 is holy. When the priests have entered the Holy Place they shall not go
into the outer court again without leaving here the garments they have
worn while performing their duties, for these are holy. They shall put on
other garments when they approach the place assigned to the people.'
15    When he had finished measuring the inner temple, he brought me out
towards the gateway which faces eastwards and measured the whole

---

*a* The door-posts . . . square: *prob. rdg.; Heb. unintelligible.*      *b* In front of: *prob.*
*rdg.; Heb.* The face of.        *c Prob. rdg.; Heb. adds* on the doors of the sanctuary.
*Prob. rdg.; Heb. adds* and the arcades of the temple and the cornices.      *e* began:
*lo.; Heb.* breadth.      *f Prob. rdg.; Heb.* they.      *g Prob. rdg.; Heb. word unknown.*

area. He measured the east side with the measuring-rod, and it was five   16
hundred cubits. He turned and measured the north side with his rod, and   17
it was five hundred cubits. He turned to the south side and measured it   18
with his rod; it was five hundred cubits. He turned to the west and measured   19
it with his rod; it was five hundred cubits. So he measured all four sides;   20
in each direction the surrounding wall measured five hundred cubits.
This marked off the sacred area from the profane.

He led me to the gate, the gate facing eastwards, and I beheld the glory   **43** 1 2
of the God of Israel coming from the east. His voice was like the sound of
a mighty torrent, and the earth shone with his glory. The form that I saw   3
was the same as that which I had seen when he came to destroy the city,
and as that which I had seen by the river Kebar,*a* and I fell on my face.
The glory of the LORD came up to the temple towards the gate which faced   4
eastwards. A spirit*b* lifted me up and brought me into the inner court, and   5
the glory of the LORD filled the temple. Then I heard one speaking to me   6
from the temple, and the man was standing at my side. He said, Man, do   7
you see the place of my throne, the place where I set my feet, where I will
dwell among the Israelites for ever? Neither they nor their kings shall
ever defile my holy name again with their wanton disloyalty, and with the
corpses*c* of their kings when they die. They set their threshold by mine   8
and their door-post beside mine, with a wall between me and them, and
they defiled my holy name with the abominations they committed, and
I destroyed them in my anger. But now they shall abandon their wanton   9
disloyalty and remove the corpses*c* of their kings far from me, and I will
dwell among them for ever. So tell the Israelites, man, about this temple,   10
its appearance and proportions, that they may be ashamed of their iniquities. If they are ashamed of all they have done, you shall describe to   11
them the temple and its fittings, its exits and entrances, all the details and
particulars of its elevation and plan; explain them and draw them before
their eyes, so that they may keep them in mind and carry them out. This   12
is the plan of the temple to be built on the top of the mountain; all its
precincts on every side shall be most holy.

These were the dimensions of the altar in cubits (the cubit that is a cubit   13
and a hand's breadth). This was the height of the altar: the base was a
cubit high*d* and projected a cubit; on its edge was a rim one span deep.
From the base to the cubit-wide ridge of the lower pedestal-block was two   14
cubits, and from this shorter pedestal-block to the cubit-wide ridge of the
taller pedestal-block was four cubits. The altar-hearth was four cubits   15
high and was surmounted by four horns a cubit high. The hearth was twelve   16
cubits long and twelve cubits wide, being a perfect square. The upper   17
pedestal-block was fourteen cubits long and fourteen cubits wide along
its four sides, and the rim round it was half a cubit deep. The base of the
altar projected a cubit, and there were steps facing eastwards.

He said to me, Man, these are the words of the Lord GOD: These are   18
the regulations for the altar when it has been made, for sacrificing whole-
offerings on it and flinging the blood against it. The levitical priests of the   19

---

*a Or* the Kebar canal.     *b Or* wind.     *c Or* effigies.     *d* the base ... high:
prob. rdg.; *Heb.* the base of the cubit.

family of Zadok, and they alone, may come near to me to serve me, says
20 the Lord GOD. You shall assign them a young bull for a sin-offering; you
shall take some of the blood and put it on the four horns of the altar, on the
four corners of the upper pedestal and all round the rim, and so purify it
21 and make expiation for it. Then take the bull assigned as the sin-offering,
and they shall destroy it by fire in the proper place within the precincts
22 but outside the Holy Place. On the second day you shall present a he-goat
without blemish as a sin-offering, and with it they shall purify the altar
23 as they did with the bull. When you have completely purified the altar,
you shall present a young bull without blemish and a ram without blemish
24 from the flock. You shall present them before the LORD; the priests shall
25 throw salt on them and sacrifice them as a whole-offering to the LORD. For
seven days you shall provide as a daily sin-offering a goat, a young bull,
and a ram from the flock; all of them shall be provided free from blemish.
26 For seven days they shall make expiation for the altar, and pronounce it
27 ritually clean, and consecrate it. At the end of that time, on the eighth day
and onwards, the priests shall sacrifice on the altar your whole-offerings
and your shared-offerings, and I will accept you. This is the very word of
the Lord GOD.

44 He again brought me round to the outer gate of the sanctuary facing
2 eastwards, and it was shut. The LORD said to me, This gate shall be kept
shut; it must not be opened. No man may enter by it, for the LORD the God
3 of Israel has entered by it. It shall be kept shut. The prince, however, when
he is here as prince, may sit there to eat food in the presence of the LORD;
he shall come in and go out by the vestibule of the gate.
4 He brought me round to the northern gate facing the temple, and I saw
5 the glory of the LORD filling the LORD's house, and I fell on my face. The
LORD said to me, Mark well, man, look closely, and listen carefully to all
that I say to you, to all the rules and regulations for the house of the LORD.
Mark well the entrance to the house of the LORD and all the exits from the
6 sanctuary. Say to that rebel people of Israel, These are the words of the
7 Lord GOD: Enough of all these abominations of yours, you Israelites! You
have added to them by bringing foreigners, uncircumcised in mind and
body, to stand in my sanctuary and defile my house when you present my
food to me, both fat and blood, and they have made my covenant void.
8 Instead of keeping charge of my holy things yourselves, you have chosen
to put these men in charge of my sanctuary.
9 These are the words of the Lord GOD: No foreigner, uncircumcised in
mind and body, shall enter my sanctuary, not even a foreigner living among
10 the Israelites. But the Levites, though they deserted me when the Israelites
went astray after their idols and had to bear the punishment of their in-
11 iquity, shall yet do service in my sanctuary. They shall take charge of the
gates of the temple and do service there. They shall slaughter the whole-
offering and the sacrifice for the people and shall be in attendance to serve
12 them. Because they served them in the presence of their idols and brought
Israel to the ground by their iniquity, says the Lord GOD, I have sworn
with uplifted hand that they shall bear the punishment of their iniquity.
13 They shall not have access to me, to serve me as priests; they shall not come

near to my holy things or to the Holy of Holies; they shall bear the shame
of the abominable deeds they have done. I will put them in charge of the 14
temple with all the service which must be performed there.

But the levitical priests of the family of Zadok remained in charge of my 15
sanctuary when the Israelites went astray from me; these shall approach
me to serve me. They shall be in attendance on me, presenting the fat and
the blood, says the Lord GOD. It is they who shall enter my sanctuary and 16
approach my table to serve me and observe my charge. When they come to 17
the gates of the inner court they shall dress in linen; they shall wear no wool
when they serve me at the gates of the inner court and within. They shall 18
wear linen turbans, and linen drawers on their loins; they shall not fasten
their clothes with a belt so that they sweat. When they go out to the people in 19
the outer court, they shall take off the clothes they have worn while serving,
leave them in the sacred rooms and put on other clothes; otherwise they
will transmit the sacred influence to the people through their clothing.

They shall neither shave their heads nor let their hair grow long; they shall 20
only clip their hair. No priest shall drink wine when he is to enter the inner 21
court. He may not marry a widow or a divorced woman; he may marry a 22
virgin of Israelite birth. He may, however, marry the widow of a priest.

They shall teach my people to distinguish the sacred from the profane, 23
and show them the difference between clean and unclean. When disputes 24
break out, they shall take their place in court, and settle the case according
to my rules. At all my appointed seasons they shall observe my laws and
statutes. They shall keep my sabbaths holy.

They shall not defile themselves by contact with any dead person, 25
except*a* father or mother, son or daughter, brother or unmarried sister.
After purification, they shall count seven days and then be clean. When 26 27
they enter the inner court to serve in the Holy Place, they shall present
their sin-offering, says the Lord GOD.

They shall own no patrimony in Israel; I am their patrimony. You shall 28
grant them no holding in Israel; I am their holding. The grain-offering, 29
the sin-offering, and the guilt-offering shall be eaten by them, and everything in Israel devoted to God shall be theirs. The first of all the first- 30
fruits and all your contributions of every kind shall belong wholly to the
priests. You shall give the first lump of your dough to the priests, that a
blessing may rest upon your home. The priests shall eat no carrion, bird 31
or beast, whether it has died naturally or been killed by a wild animal.

When you divide the land by lot among the tribes for their possession, **45**
you shall set apart from it a sacred reserve for the LORD, twenty-five
thousand cubits in length and twenty thousand in width; the whole en-
closure shall be sacred. Of this a square plot, five hundred cubits each way, 2
shall be devoted to the sanctuary, with fifty cubits of open land round it.
From this area you shall measure out a space twenty-five thousand by ten 3
thousand cubits, in which the sanctuary, the holiest place of all, shall stand.
This space is for the priests who serve in the sanctuary and who come 4
nearest in serving the LORD. It shall include space for their houses and a
sacred plot for the sanctuary. An area of twenty-five thousand by ten 5

*a* any ... except: *or* anyone else's dead, but only their own ...

thousand cubits shall belong to the Levites, the temple servants; on this
6 shall stand the towns in which they live. You shall give to each town an
area of five thousand by twenty-five thousand cubits alongside the sacred
7 reserve; this shall belong to all Israel. On either side of the sacred reserve
and of the city's holding the prince shall have a holding facing the sacred
reserve and the city's holding, running westwards on the west and eastwards
on the east. It shall run alongside one of the tribal portions, and stretch
8 to the western limit of the land and to the eastern. It shall be his holding
in Israel; the princes of Israel shall never oppress my people again but
shall give the land to Israel, tribe by tribe.

9 THESE ARE THE WORDS OF THE LORD GOD: Enough, princes of Israel!
Put an end to lawlessness and robbery; maintain law and justice; relieve
10 my people and stop your evictions, says the Lord GOD. Your scales shall
11 be honest, your bushel and your gallon shall be honest. There shall be one
standard for each, taking each as the tenth of a homer, and the homer shall
12 have its fixed standard. Your shekel weight shall contain twenty gerahs;
your mina shall contain weights of ten*a* and twenty-five and fifteen shekels.
13 These are the contributions you shall set aside: out of every homer of
14 wheat or of barley, one sixth of an ephah. For oil the rule is*b* one tenth of a
15 bath from every kor (at ten bath to the kor); one sheep in every flock of
two hundred is to be reserved by every Israelite clan. For a grain-offering,
a whole-offering, and a shared-offering, to make expiation for them, says
16 the Lord GOD, all the people of the land shall bring*c* this contribution to
17 the prince in Israel; and the prince shall be responsible for the whole-
offering, the grain-offering, and the drink-offering, at pilgrim-feasts, new
moons, sabbaths, and every sacred season observed by Israel. He himself
is to provide the sin-offering and the grain-offering, the whole-offering
and the shared-offering, needed to make expiation for Israel.
18 These are the words of the Lord GOD: On the first day of the first
month you shall take a young bull without blemish, and purify the sanctuary.
19 The priest shall take some of the blood from the sin-offering and put it on
the door-posts of the temple, on the four corners of the altar pedestal and
20 on the gate-posts of the inner court. You shall do the same on the seventh
day of the month;*d* in this way you shall make expiation for the temple.
21 On the fourteenth day of the first month you shall hold the Passover,
22 the pilgrim-feast of seven days; bread must be eaten unleavened. On that
day the prince shall provide a bull as a sin-offering for himself and for all
23 the people. During the seven days of the feast he shall offer daily as a
whole-offering to the LORD seven bulls and seven rams without blemish,
24 and a he-goat as a daily sin-offering. With every bull and ram he shall provide a grain-offering of one ephah, together with a hin of oil for each ephah.
25 He shall do the same thing also on the fifteenth day of the seventh month at
the pilgrim-feast; this also shall last seven days, and he shall provide the
same sin-offering and whole-offering and the same quantity of grain and oil.

---

*a* *Prob. rdg.; Heb.* twenty.          *b* *Prob. rdg.; Heb. adds* the bath, the oil.
*c* All . . . bring: *prob. rdg.; Heb. unintelligible.*          *d* *Prob. rdg.; Heb. adds* This
comes from a man who is wrong and foolish. *Cp. Lev. 23. 24; Num. 29. 1.*

These are the words of the Lord GOD: The eastern gate of the inner **46** court shall remain closed for the six working days; it may be opened only on the sabbath and at new moon. When the prince comes through the 2 porch of the gate from the outside, he shall halt at the door-post, and the priests shall sacrifice his whole-offering and shared-offerings. On the terrace he shall bow down at the gate and then go out, but the gate shall not be shut till the evening. On sabbaths and at new moons the people 3 also shall bow down before the LORD at the entrance to that gate.

The whole-offering which the prince sacrifices to the LORD shall be as 4 follows: on the sabbath, six sheep without blemish and a ram without blemish; the grain-offering shall be an ephah with the ram and as much 5 as he likes with the sheep, together with a hin of oil for every ephah. At 6 the new moon it shall be a young bull without blemish, six sheep and a ram, all without blemish. He shall provide as the grain-offering to go with the 7 bull one ephah and with the ram one ephah, with the sheep as much as he can afford, adding a hin of oil for every ephah.

When the prince comes in, he shall enter through the porch of the gate 8 and come out by the same way. But on festal days when the people come 9 before the LORD, a man who enters by the northern gate to bow down shall leave by the southern gate, and a man who enters by the southern gate shall leave by the northern gate. He shall not turn back and go out through the gate by which he came in but shall go straight on. The prince shall then be 10 among them, going in when they go in and coming out when they come out.

At pilgrim-feasts and on festal days the grain-offering shall be an ephah 11 with a bull, an ephah with a ram and as much as he likes with a sheep, together with a hin of oil for every ephah.

When the prince provides a whole-offering or shared-offerings as a 12 voluntary sacrifice to the LORD, the eastern gate shall be opened for him,[a] and he shall make his whole-offering and his shared-offerings as he does on the sabbath; when he goes out the gate shall be closed[b] behind him.

You shall provide a yearling sheep without blemish daily as a whole- 13 offering to the LORD; you shall provide it morning by morning. With it 14 every morning you shall provide as a grain-offering one sixth of an ephah with a third of a hin of oil to moisten the flour; the LORD's grain-offering is an observance prescribed for all time. Morning by morning, as a regular 15 whole-offering, they shall offer a sheep with the grain-offering and the oil.

These are the words of the Lord GOD: When the prince makes a gift 16 out of his property to any of his sons, it shall belong to his sons, since it is part of the family property. But when he makes such a gift to one of his 17 slaves, it shall be his only till the year of manumission, when it shall revert to the prince; it is the property of his sons and shall belong to them.

The prince shall not oppress the people by taking part of their holdings; 18 he shall give his sons an inheritance from his own holding of land, so that my people may not be scattered and separated from their holdings.

Then he brought me through the entrance by the side of the gate to the 19 rooms which face north (the sacred rooms reserved for the priests), and,

---

*a* the eastern . . . him: *or* he shall open the gate facing east.     *b* the gate . . . closed: *or* he shall close the gate.

20 pointing to a place on their western side, he said to me, 'This is the place where the priests shall boil the guilt-offering and the sin-offering and bake the grain-offering; they shall not take it into the outer court for fear they
21 transmit the sacred influence to the people.' Then he brought me into the outer court and took me across to the four corners of the court, at each of
22 which there was a further court. These four courts were vaulted and were
23 the same size, forty cubits long by thirty cubits wide. Round each of the four was a row of stones, with fire-places constructed close up against the
24 rows. He said to me, 'These are the kitchens where the attendants shall boil the people's sacrifices.'

47 He brought me back to the gate of the temple, and I saw a spring of water issuing from under the terrace of the temple towards the east; for the temple faced east. The water was running down along the right side,
2 to the south of the altar. He took me out through the northern gate and brought me round by an outside path to the eastern gate of the court, and
3 water was trickling from the right side. When the man went out eastwards he had a line in his hand. He measured a thousand cubits and made me
4 walk through the water; it came up to my ankles. He measured another thousand and made me walk through the water; it came up to my knees. He measured another thousand and made me walk through the water;
5 it was up to my waist. Another thousand, and it was a torrent I could not cross, for the water had risen and was now deep enough to swim in; it
6 had become a torrent that could not be crossed. 'Mark this, man', he said,
7 and led me back to the bank of the torrent. When we came back to the bank
8 I saw a great number of trees on each side. He said to me, 'This water flows out to the region lying east, and down to the Arabah; at last it will reach
9 that sea whose waters are foul, and they will be sweetened. When any one of the living creatures that swarm upon the earth comes where the torrent flows, it shall draw life from it. The fish shall be innumerable; for these waters come here so that the others may be sweetened, and where the tor-
10 rent flows everything shall live. From En-gedi as far as En-eglaim fisher-men shall stand on its shores, for nets shall be spread there. Every kind
11 of fish shall be there in shoals, like the fish of the Great Sea; but its swamps and pools shall not have their waters sweetened but shall be left as salt-
12 pans. Beside the torrent on either bank all trees good for food shall spring up. Their leaves shall not wither, their fruit shall not cease; they shall bear early every month. For their water comes from the sanctuary; their fruit is for food and their foliage for enjoyment.'

13 These are the words of the Lord GOD: These are the boundary lines within which the twelve tribes of Israel shall enter into possession of the
14 land, Joseph receiving two portions. The land which I swore with hand uplifted to give to your fathers you shall divide with each other; it shall be
15 assigned to you by lot as your patrimony. This is the frontier: on its northern side, from the Great Sea through Hethlon, Lebo-hamath,
16 Zedad, Berutha, and Sibraim, which are between the frontiers of Damascus
17 and Hamath, to Hazar-enan, near the frontier of Hauran. So the frontier shall run from the sea to Hazar-enan on the frontier of Damascus and
18 northwards; this is its northern side. The eastern side runs alongside the

territories of Hauran, Damascus, and Gilead, and alongside the territory of Israel; Jordan sets the boundary to the eastern sea, to Tamar. This is the eastern side. The southern side runs from Tamar to the waters of 19 Meribah-by-Kadesh; the region assigned to you reaches the Great Sea. This is the southern side towards the Negeb. The western side is the Great 20 Sea, which forms a boundary as far as a point opposite Lebo-hamath. This is the western side. You shall distribute this land among the tribes 21 of Israel and assign it by lot as a patrimony for yourselves and for any aliens 22 living in your midst who leave sons among you. They shall be treated as native-born in Israel and with you shall receive a patrimony by lot among the tribes of Israel. You shall give the alien his patrimony with the tribe 23 in which he is living. This is the very word of the Lord GOD.

These are the names of the tribes: In the extreme north, in the direction **48** of Hethlon, to Lebo-hamath and Hazar-enan, with Damascus on the northern frontier in the direction of Hamath, and so from the eastern side to the western, shall be Dan: one portion.

Bordering on Dan, from the eastern side to the western, shall be Asher: 2 one portion.

Bordering on Asher, from the eastern side to the western, shall be 3 Naphtali: one portion.

Bordering on Naphtali, from the eastern side to the western, shall be 4 Manasseh: one portion.

Bordering on Manasseh, from the eastern side to the western, shall be 5 Ephraim: one portion.

Bordering on Ephraim, from the eastern side to the western, shall be 6 Reuben: one portion.

Bordering on Reuben, from the eastern side to the western, shall be 7 Judah: one portion.

Bordering on Judah, from the eastern side to the western, shall be the 8 reserve which you shall set apart. Its breadth shall be twenty-five thousand cubits and its length the same as that of the other portions, from the eastern side to the western, and the sanctuary shall be in the middle of it.

The reserve which you shall set apart for the LORD shall measure twenty- 9 five thousand cubits by twenty*a* thousand. The reserve shall be appor- 10 tioned thus: the priests shall have an area measuring twenty-five thousand cubits on the north side, ten thousand on the west, ten thousand on the east, and twenty-five thousand on the south side; the sanctuary of the LORD shall be in the middle of it. It shall be for the consecrated priests, the sons 11 of Zadok, who kept my charge and did not follow the Israelites when they went astray, as the Levites did. The area set apart for the priests from 12 the reserved territory shall be most sacred, reaching the frontier of the Levites.

The Levites shall have a portion running parallel to the border of the 13 priests. It shall be twenty-five thousand cubits long by ten thousand wide; altogether, the length shall be twenty-five thousand cubits and the breadth ten thousand. They shall neither sell nor exchange any part of it, nor shall 14 the best of the land be alienated; for it is holy to the LORD.

*a Prob. rdg.; Heb. ten.*

15     The strip which is left, five thousand cubits in width by twenty-five
thousand, is the city's secular land for dwellings and common land, and
16 the city shall be in the middle of it. These shall be its dimensions: on the
northern side four thousand five hundred cubits, on the southern side
four thousand five hundred cubits, on the eastern side four thousand five
hundred cubits, on the western side four thousand five hundred cubits.
17 The common land belonging to the city shall be two hundred and fifty
cubits to the north, two hundred and fifty to the south, two hundred and
18 fifty to the east, and two hundred and fifty to the west. What is left parallel
to the reserve, ten thousand cubits to the east and ten thousand to the west,*a*
19 shall provide food for those who work in the city. Those who work in the
city shall cultivate it; they may be drawn from any of the tribes of Israel.
20     You shall set apart the whole reserve, twenty-five thousand cubits
21 square, as sacred, as far as the holding of the city. What is left over on each
side of the sacred reserve and the holding of the city shall be assigned to
the prince. Eastwards, what lies over against the reserved twenty-five
thousand cubits, as far as the eastern side, and westwards, what lies over
against the twenty-five thousand cubits to the western side, parallel to the
tribal portions, shall be assigned to the prince; the sacred reserve and the
22 sanctuary itself shall be in the centre. The*b* holding of the Levites and
the*b* holding of the city shall be in the middle of that which is assigned to
the prince; it shall be between the frontiers of Judah and Benjamin.
23     The rest of the tribes: from the eastern side to the western shall be
Benjamin: one portion.
24     Bordering on Benjamin, from the eastern side to the western, shall be
Simeon: one portion.
25     Bordering on Simeon, from the eastern side to the western, shall be
Issachar: one portion.
26     Bordering on Issachar, from the eastern side to the western, shall be
Zebulun: one portion.
27     Bordering on Zebulun, from the eastern side to the western, shall be
Gad: one portion.
28     Bordering on Gad, on the side of the Negeb, the border on the south
stretches from Tamar to the waters of Meribah-by-Kadesh, to the Brook
as far as the Great Sea.
29     This is the land which you shall allot as a patrimony to the tribes of
Israel, and these shall be their lots. This is the very word of the Lord GOD.
30–31     These are to be the ways out of the city, and they are to be named after
the tribes of Israel. The northern side, four thousand five hundred cubits
32 long, shall have three gates, those of Reuben, Judah, and Levi; the eastern
side, four thousand five hundred cubits long, three gates, those of Joseph,
33 Benjamin, and Dan; the southern side, four thousand five hundred cubits
34 long, three gates, those of Simeon, Issachar, and Zebulun; the western
side, four thousand five hundred cubits long, three gates, those of Gad,
35 Asher, and Naphtali. The perimeter of the city shall be eighteen thousand
cubits, and the city's name for ever after shall be Jehovah-shammah.*c*

*a* *Prob. rdg.; Heb. adds* and it shall be parallel to the sacred reserve.     *b* *Prob. rdg.;*
*Heb.* Some of the.     *c* *That is* the LORD is there.

# THE BOOK OF
# DANIEL

## *Jews at the court of Nebuchadnezzar*

IN THE THIRD YEAR OF THE REIGN OF JEHOIAKIM 1
king of Judah, Nebuchadnezzar king of Babylon came to Jerusalem
and laid siege to it. The Lord delivered Jehoiakim king of Judah into 2
his power, together with all that was left of the vessels of the house of God;
and he carried them off to the land of Shinar, to the temple of his god,
where he deposited the vessels in the treasury. Then the king ordered 3
Ashpenaz, his chief eunuch, to take certain of the Israelite exiles, of the
blood royal and of the nobility, who were to be young men of good looks 4
and bodily without fault, at home in all branches of knowledge, well-
informed, intelligent, and fit for service in the royal court; and he was to
instruct them in the literature and language of the Chaldaeans. The king 5
assigned them a daily allowance of food and wine from the royal table.
Their training was to last for three years, and at the end of that time they
would*a* enter the royal service.

Among them there were certain young men from Judah called Daniel, 6
Hananiah, Mishael and Azariah; but the master of the eunuchs gave them 7
new names: Daniel he called Belteshazzar, Hananiah Shadrach, Mishael
Meshach and Azariah Abed-nego. Now Daniel determined not to con- 8
taminate himself by touching the food and wine assigned to him by the
king, and he begged the master of the eunuchs not to make him do so.
God made the master show kindness and goodwill to Daniel, and he said 9 10
to him, 'I am afraid of my lord the king: he has assigned you your food and
drink, and if he sees you looking dejected, unlike the other young men of
your own age, it will cost me my head.' Then Daniel said to the guard 11
whom the master of the eunuchs had put in charge of Hananiah, Mishael,
Azariah and himself, 'Submit us to this test for ten days. Give us only 12
vegetables to eat and water to drink; then compare our looks with those of 13
the young men who have lived on the food assigned by the king, and be
guided in your treatment of us by what you see.'*b* The guard listened to 14
what they said and tested them for ten days. At the end of ten days they 15
looked healthier and were better nourished than all the young men who
had lived on the food assigned them by the king. So the guard took away 16
the assignment of food and the wine they were to drink, and gave them only
the vegetables.

To all four of these young men God had given knowledge and under- 17
standing of books and learning of every kind, while Daniel had a gift for

*a* at the end . . . would: *or* all of them were to.     *b* be guided . . . see: *or* treat
us as you see fit.

18 interpreting visions and dreams of every kind. The time came which the king had fixed for introducing the young men to court, and the master of
19 the eunuchs brought them into the presence of Nebuchadnezzar. The king talked with them and found none of them to compare with Daniel,
20 Hananiah, Mishael and Azariah; so they entered the royal service. Whenever the king consulted them on any matter calling for insight and judgement, he found them ten times better than all the magicians and exorcists
21 in his whole kingdom. Now Daniel was there till the first year of King Cyrus.

**2** In the second year of his reign Nebuchadnezzar had dreams, and his
2 mind was so troubled that he could not sleep. Then the king gave orders to summon the magicians, exorcists, sorcerers, and Chaldaeans to tell him
3 what he had dreamt. They came in and stood in the royal presence, and the king said to them, 'I have had a dream and my mind has been troubled
4 to know what my dream was.' The Chaldaeans, speaking in Aramaic, said, <sup>a</sup>'Long live the king! Tell us what you dreamt and we will tell you the
5 interpretation.' The king answered, 'This is my declared intention. If you do not tell me both dream and interpretation, you shall be torn in pieces
6 and your houses shall be forfeit.<sup>b</sup> But if you can tell me the dream and the interpretation, you will be richly rewarded and loaded with honours. Tell
7 me, therefore, the dream and its interpretation.' They answered a second time, 'Let the king tell his servants the dream, and we will tell him the
8 interpretation.' The king answered, 'It is clear to me that you are trying to
9 gain time, because you see that my intention has been declared. If you do not make known to me the dream, there is one law that applies to you, and one only. What is more, you have agreed among yourselves to tell me a pack of lies to my face in the hope that with time things may alter. Tell me the dream, therefore, and I shall know that you can give me the interpreta-
10 tion.' The Chaldaeans answered in the presence of the king, 'Nobody on earth can tell your majesty what you wish to know; no great king or prince
11 has ever made such a demand of magician, exorcist, or Chaldaean. What your majesty requires of us is too hard; there is no one but the gods, who
12 dwell remote from mortal men, who can give you the answer.' At this the king lost his temper and in a great rage ordered the death of all the wise men
13 of Babylon. A decree was issued that the wise men were to be executed, and accordingly men were sent to fetch Daniel and his companions for execution.

14 When Arioch, the captain of the king's bodyguard, was setting out to execute the wise men of Babylon, Daniel approached him cautiously and
15 with discretion and said, 'Sir, you represent the king; why has his majesty
16 issued such a peremptory decree?' Arioch explained everything; so Daniel went in to the king's presence and begged for a certain time by which he
17 would give the king the interpretation. Then Daniel went home and told
18 the whole story to his companions, Hananiah, Mishael and Azariah. They should ask the God of heaven in his mercy, he said, to disclose this secret, so that they and he with the rest of the wise men of Babylon should not be

*a The Aramaic text begins here and continues to the end of ch. 7.*  *b Or made into a dunghill (mng. of Aram. word uncertain).*

put to death. Then in a vision by night the secret was revealed to Daniel, 19 and he blessed the God of heaven in these words: 20

> Blessed be God's name from age to age,
> for all wisdom and power are his.
> He changes seasons and times; 21
> he deposes kings and sets them up;
> he gives wisdom to the wise
> and all their store of knowledge to the men who know;
> he reveals deep mysteries; 22
> he knows what lies in darkness,
> and light has its dwelling with him.
> To thee, God of my fathers, I give thanks and praise, 23
> for thou hast given me wisdom and power;
> thou hast now revealed to me what we asked,
> and told us what the king is concerned to know.

Daniel therefore went to Arioch who had been charged by the king to 24 put to death the wise men of Babylon and said to him, 'Do not put the wise men of Babylon to death. Take me into the king's presence, and I will now tell him the interpretation of the dream.' Arioch in great trepidation brought 25 Daniel before the king and said to him, 'I have found among the Jewish exiles a man who will make known to your majesty the interpretation of your dream.' Thereupon the king said to Daniel (who was also called Belteshaz- 26 zar), 'Can you tell me what I saw in my dream and interpret it?' Daniel 27 answered in the king's presence, 'The secret about which your majesty inquires no wise man, exorcist, magician, or diviner can disclose to you. But there is in heaven a god who reveals secrets, and he has told King 28 Nebuchadnezzar what is to be at the end of this age. This is the dream and these the visions that came into your head: the thoughts that came to 29 you, O king, as you lay on your bed, were thoughts of things to come, and the revealer of secrets has made known to you what is to be. This secret 30 has been revealed to me not because I am wise beyond all living men, but because your majesty is to know the interpretation and understand the thoughts which have entered your mind.

'As you watched, O king, you saw a great image. This image, huge and 31 dazzling, towered before you, fearful to behold. The head of the image was 32 of fine gold, its breast and arms of silver, its belly and thighs of bronze,*ª* its legs of iron, its feet part iron and part clay. While you looked, a stone 33 34 was hewn from a mountain, not by human hands; it struck the image on its feet of iron and clay and shattered them. Then the iron, the clay, the 35 bronze, the silver, and the gold, were all shattered to fragments and were swept away like chaff before the wind from a threshing-floor in summer, until no trace of them remained. But the stone which struck the image grew into a great mountain filling the whole earth. That was the dream. 36 We shall now tell your majesty the interpretation. You, O king, king of 37 kings, to whom the God of heaven has given the kingdom with all its power, authority, and honour; in whose hands he has placed men and beasts and 38

---

*ª Or* copper.

birds of the air, wherever they dwell, granting you sovereignty over them
39 all—you are that head of gold. After you there shall arise another kingdom,
inferior to yours, and yet a third kingdom, of bronze, which shall have
40 sovereignty over the whole world. And there shall be a fourth kingdom,
strong as iron; as iron shatters and destroys all things, it shall break and
41 shatter the whole earth.[a] As, in your vision, the feet and toes were part
potter's clay and part iron, it shall be a divided kingdom. Its core shall be
42 partly of iron just as you saw iron mixed with the common clay; as the toes
were part iron and part clay, the kingdom shall be partly strong and partly
43 brittle. As, in your vision, the iron was mixed with common clay, so shall
men mix with each other by intermarriage, but such alliances shall not be
44 stable: iron does not mix with clay. In the period of those kings the God
of heaven will establish a kingdom which shall never be destroyed; that
kingdom shall never pass to another people; it shall shatter and make an
45 end of all these kingdoms, while it shall itself endure for ever. This is the
meaning of your vision of the stone being hewn from a mountain, not by
human hands, and then shattering the iron, the bronze, the clay, the silver,
and the gold. The mighty God has made known to your majesty what is
to be hereafter. The dream is sure and the interpretation to be trusted.'
46    Then King Nebuchadnezzar prostrated himself and worshipped Daniel,
and gave orders that sacrifices and soothing offerings should be made to
47 him. 'Truly,' he said, 'your god is indeed God of gods and Lord over kings,
48 a revealer of secrets, since you have been able to reveal this secret.' Then
the king promoted Daniel, bestowed on him many rich gifts, and made him
regent over the whole province of Babylon and chief prefect over all the
49 wise men of Babylon. Moreover at Daniel's request the king put Shadrach,
Meshach and Abed-nego in charge of the administration of the province
of Babylon. Daniel himself, however, remained at court.

3  KING NEBUCHADNEZZAR MADE AN IMAGE OF GOLD, ninety feet high
and nine feet broad. He had it set up in the plain of Dura in the province of
2 Babylon. Then he sent out a summons to assemble the satraps, prefects,
viceroys, counsellors, treasurers, judges, chief constables, and all governors of provinces to attend the dedication of the image which he had set
3 up. So they assembled—the satraps, prefects, viceroys, counsellors,
treasurers, judges, chief constables, and all governors of provinces—for
the dedication of the image which King Nebuchadnezzar had set up; and
4 they stood before the image which Nebuchadnezzar had set up. Then the
herald loudly proclaimed, 'O peoples and nations of every language, you
5 are commanded, when you hear the sound of horn, pipe, zither, triangle,
dulcimer, music, and singing of every kind, to prostrate yourselves and
6 worship the golden image which King Nebuchadnezzar has set up. Whoever does not prostrate himself and worship shall forthwith be thrown into a
7 blazing furnace.' Accordingly, no sooner did all the peoples hear the sound
of horn, pipe, zither, triangle, dulcimer, music, and singing of every kind,
than all the peoples and nations of every language prostrated themselves
and worshipped the golden image which King Nebuchadnezzar had set up.

[a] the whole earth: *prob. rdg.; Aram.* and like iron which shatters all these.

It was then that certain Chaldaeans came forward and brought a charge 8
against the Jews. They said to King Nebuchadnezzar, 'Long live the king! 9
Your majesty has issued an order that every man who hears the sound of 10
horn, pipe, zither, triangle, dulcimer, music, and singing of every kind
shall fall down and worship the image of gold. Whoever does not do so shall 11
be thrown into a blazing furnace. There are certain Jews, Shadrach, Me- 12
shach and Abed-nego, whom you have put in charge of the administration of the province of Babylon. These men, your majesty, have taken
no notice of your command; they do not serve your god, nor do they worship the golden image which you have set up.' Then in rage and fury 13
Nebuchadnezzar ordered Shadrach, Meshach and Abed-nego to be fetched,
and they were brought into the king's presence. Nebuchadnezzar said to 14
them, 'Is it true, Shadrach, Meshach and Abed-nego, that you do not
serve my god or worship the golden image which I have set up? If you are 15
ready at once to prostrate yourselves when you hear the sound of horn,
pipe, zither, triangle, dulcimer, music, and singing of every kind, and to
worship the image that I have set up, well and good. But if you do not
worship it, you shall forthwith be thrown into the blazing furnace; and
what god is there that can save you from my power?' Shadrach, Meshach 16
and Abed-nego said to King Nebuchadnezzar, 'We have no need to answer
you on this matter. If there is a god who is able to save us from the blazing 17
furnace, it is our God whom we serve, and he will save us from your power,
O king; but if not, be it known to your majesty that we will neither serve 18
your god nor worship the golden image that you have set up.'

Then Nebuchadnezzar flew into a rage with Shadrach, Meshach and 19
Abed-nego, and his face was distorted with anger. He gave orders that the
furnace should be heated up to seven times its usual heat, and commanded 20
some of the strongest men in his army to bind Shadrach, Meshach and
Abed-nego and throw them into the blazing furnace. Then those men in 21
their trousers, their shirts, and their hats and all their other clothes, were
bound and thrown into the blazing furnace. Because the king's order was 22
urgent and the furnace exceedingly hot, the men who were carrying
Shadrach, Meshach and Abed-nego were killed by the flames that leapt out;
and those three men, Shadrach, Meshach and Abed-nego, fell bound into 23
the blazing furnace.

Then King Nebuchadnezzar was amazed and sprang to his feet in great 24
trepidation. He said to his courtiers, 'Was it not three men whom we threw
bound into the fire?' They answered the king, 'Assuredly, your majesty.'
He answered, 'Yet I see four men walking about in the fire free and un- 25
harmed; and the fourth looks like a god.' Nebuchadnezzar approached the 26
door of the blazing furnace and said to the men, 'Shadrach, Meshach and
Abed-nego, servants of the Most High God, come out, come here.' Then
Shadrach, Meshach and Abed-nego came out from the fire. And the satraps, 27
prefects, viceroys, and the king's courtiers gathered round and saw how
the fire had had no power to harm the bodies of these men; the hair of their
heads had not been singed, their trousers were untouched, and no smell of
fire lingered about them.

Then Nebuchadnezzar spoke out, 'Blessed is the God of Shadrach, 28

Meshach and Abed-nego. He has sent his angel to save his servants who put their trust in him, who disobeyed the royal command and were willing to yield themselves to the fire rather than to serve or worship any god other 29 than their own God. I therefore issue a decree that any man, to whatever people or nation he belongs, whatever his language, if he speaks blasphemy against the God of Shadrach, Meshach and Abed-nego, shall be torn to pieces and his house shall be forfeit;[a] for there is no other god who can 30 save men in this way.' Then the king advanced the fortunes of Shadrach, Meshach and Abed-nego in the province of Babylon.

4 KING NEBUCHADNEZZAR TO ALL PEOPLES AND NATIONS of every 2 language living in the whole world: May all prosperity be yours! It is my pleasure to recount the signs and marvels which the Most High God has worked for me:

3         How great are his signs,
        and his marvels overwhelming!
        His kingdom is an everlasting kingdom,
        his sovereignty stands to all generations.

4   I, Nebuchadnezzar, was living peacefully at home in the luxury of my 5 palace. As I lay on my bed, I saw a dream which terrified me; and fantasies 6 and visions which came into my head dismayed me. So I issued an order summoning into my presence all the wise men of Babylon to make known 7 to me the interpretation of the dream. Then the magicians, exorcists, Chaldaeans, and diviners came in, and in their presence I related my dream. 8 But they could not interpret it. And yet another came into my presence, Daniel, who is called Belteshazzar after the name of my god, a man possessed by the spirit of the holy gods. To him, too, I related the dream: 9 'Belteshazzar, chief of the magicians, whom I myself know to be possessed by the spirit of the holy gods, and whom no secret baffles, listen to the vision I saw in a dream, and tell me its interpretation.

10   'Here is the vision which came into my head as I was lying upon my bed:

        As I was looking,
        I saw a tree of great height at the centre of the earth;
11         the tree grew and became strong,
        reaching with its top to the sky
        and visible to earth's farthest bounds.
12         Its foliage was lovely,
        and its fruit abundant;
        and it yielded food for all.
        Beneath it the wild beasts found shelter,
        the birds lodged in its branches,
        and from it all living creatures fed.

13   'Here is another vision which came into my head as I was lying upon my bed:

        As I was watching, there was a Watcher,
        a Holy One coming down from heaven.

      [a] *Or* made into a dunghill (*mng. of Aram. word uncertain*).

He cried aloud and said,　　　　　　　　　　　　　14
"Hew down the tree, lop off the branches,
strip away the foliage, scatter the fruit.
　　Let the wild beasts flee from its shelter
　　　　and the birds from its branches,
but leave the stump with its roots in the ground.　15
　　So, tethered with an iron ring,
　　let him eat his fill of the lush grass;
　　let him be drenched with the dew of heaven
　　and share the lot of the beasts in their pasture;
　　let his mind cease to be a man's mind,　　　　16
　　and let him be given the mind of a beast.
　　Let seven times pass over him.
　　The issue has been determined by the Watchers　17
　　and the sentence pronounced by the Holy Ones.

Thereby the living will know that the Most High is sovereign in the kingdom of men: he gives the kingdom to whom he will and he may set over it the humblest of mankind."

'This is the dream which I, King Nebuchadnezzar, have dreamed; now, 18 Belteshazzar, tell me its interpretation; for, though all the wise men of my kingdom are unable to tell me what it means, you can tell me, since the spirit of the holy gods is in you.'

Daniel, who was called Belteshazzar, was dumbfounded for a moment, 19 dismayed by his thoughts; but the king said, 'Do not let the dream and its interpretation dismay you.' Belteshazzar answered, 'My lord, if only the dream were for those who hate you and its interpretation for your enemies! The tree which you saw grow and become strong, reaching with its top to 20 the sky and visible to earth's farthest bounds, its foliage lovely and its fruit 21 abundant, a tree which yielded food for all, beneath which the wild beasts dwelt and in whose branches the birds lodged, that tree, O king, is you. 22 You have grown and become strong. Your power has grown and reaches the sky; your sovereignty stretches to the ends of the earth. Also, O king, 23 you saw a Watcher, a Holy One, coming down from heaven and saying, "Hew down the tree and destroy it, but leave its stump with its roots in the ground. So, tethered with an iron ring, let him eat his fill of the lush grass; let him be drenched with the dew of heaven and share the lot of the beasts until seven times pass over him." This is the interpretation, 24 O king—it is a decree of the Most High which touches my lord the king. You will be banished from the society of men; you will have to live with 25 the wild beasts; you will feed on grass like oxen and you will be drenched with the dew of heaven. Seven times will pass over you until you have learnt that the Most High is sovereign over the kingdom of men and gives it to whom he will. The command was given to leave the stump of the tree with 26 its roots. By this you may know that from the time you acknowledge the sovereignty of heaven your rule will endure. Be advised by me, O king: 27 redeem your sins by charity and your iniquities by generosity to the wretched. So may you long enjoy peace of mind.'

28 29     All this befell King Nebuchadnezzar. At the end of twelve months
30   the king was walking on the roof of the royal palace at Babylon, and he
exclaimed, 'Is not this Babylon the great which I have built as a royal
residence by my own mighty power and for the honour of my majesty?'
31   The words were still on his lips, when a voice came down from heaven: 'To
you, King Nebuchadnezzar, the word is spoken: the kingdom has passed
32   from you. You are banished from the society of men and you shall live
with the wild beasts; you shall feed on grass like oxen, and seven times will
pass over you until you have learnt that the Most High is sovereign over
33   the kingdom of men and gives it to whom he will.' At that very moment
this judgement came upon Nebuchadnezzar. He was banished from the
society of men and ate grass like oxen; his body was drenched by the dew
of heaven, until his hair grew long like goats' hair and his nails like eagles'
talons.[a]
34   At the end of the appointed time, I, Nebuchadnezzar, raised my eyes
to heaven and I returned to my right mind. I blessed the Most High,
praising and glorifying the Ever-living One:

> His sovereignty is never-ending
> and his rule endures through all generations;
35     all dwellers upon earth count for nothing
> and he deals as he wishes with the host of heaven;[b]
> no one may lay hand upon him
> and ask him what he does.

36   At that very time I returned to my right mind and my majesty and royal
splendour were restored to me for the glory of my kingdom. My courtiers
and my nobles sought audience of me. I was established in my kingdom
37   and my power was greatly increased. Now I, Nebuchadnezzar, praise and
exalt and glorify the King of heaven; for all his acts are right and his ways
are just and those whose conduct is arrogant he can bring low.

## Belshazzar's feast

5   BELSHAZZAR THE KING GAVE A BANQUET for a thousand of his
2   nobles and was drinking wine in the presence of the thousand. Warmed
by the wine, he gave orders to fetch the vessels of gold and silver which his
father Nebuchadnezzar had taken from the sanctuary at Jerusalem, that
he and his nobles, his concubines and his courtesans, might drink from
3   them. So the vessels of gold and silver from the sanctuary in the house of
God at Jerusalem were brought in, and the king and his nobles, his con-
4   cubines and his courtesans, drank from them. They drank wine and praised
the gods of gold and silver, of bronze and iron, and of wood and stone.
5   Suddenly there appeared the fingers of a human hand writing on the plaster
of the palace wall opposite the lamp, and the king could see the back of
6   the hand as it wrote. At this the king's mind was filled with dismay and he
turned pale, he became limp in every limb and his knees knocked together.

---

[a] goats' hair . . . eagles' talons: *prob. rdg.; Aram.* eagles' and his nails like birds'.
[b] *Prob. rdg.; Aram. adds* and the dwellers upon earth.

He called loudly for the exorcists, Chaldaeans, and diviners to be brought 7
in; then, addressing the wise men of Babylon, he said, 'Whoever can read
this writing and tell me its interpretation shall be robed in purple and
honoured with a chain of gold round his neck and shall rank as third in the
kingdom.' Then all the king's wise men came in, but they could not read 8
the writing or interpret it to the king. King Belshazzar sat there pale and 9
utterly dismayed, while his nobles were perplexed.

The king and his nobles were talking when the queen entered the 10
banqueting-hall: 'Long live the king!' she said. 'Why this dismay, and
why do you look so pale? There is a man in your kingdom who has in him 11
the spirit of the holy gods, a man who was known in your father's time to
have a clear understanding and godlike wisdom. King Nebuchadnezzar,
your father, appointed him chief of the magicians, exorcists, Chaldaeans,
and diviners. This same Daniel, whom the king named Belteshazzar, is 12
known to have a notable spirit, with knowledge and understanding, and
the gift of interpreting dreams, explaining riddles and unbinding spells;*a*
let him be summoned now and he will give the interpretation.' Daniel was 13
then brought into the king's presence and the king said to him, 'So you are
Daniel, one of the Jewish exiles whom the king my father brought from
Judah. I have heard that you possess the spirit of the holy gods and that 14
you are a man of clear understanding and peculiar wisdom. The wise men, 15
the exorcists, have just been brought into my presence to read this writing
and tell me its interpretation, and they have been unable to interpret it.
But I have heard it said of you that you are able to give interpretations and 16
to unbind spells.*b* So now, if you are able to read the words and tell me what
they mean, you shall be robed in purple and honoured with a chain of gold
round your neck and shall rank as third in the kingdom.' Then Daniel 17
answered in the king's presence, 'Your gifts you may keep for yourself;
or else give your rewards to another. Nevertheless I will read the writing
to your majesty and tell you its interpretation. My lord king, the Most 18
High God gave your father Nebuchadnezzar a kingdom and power and
glory and majesty; and, because of this power which he gave him, all 19
peoples and nations of every language trembled before him and were afraid.
He put to death whom he would and spared whom he would, he promoted
them at will and at will degraded them. But, when he became haughty, 20
stubborn and presumptuous, he was deposed from his royal throne and
his glory was taken from him. He was banished from the society of men, 21
his mind became like that of a beast, he had to live with the wild asses and
to eat grass like oxen, and his body was drenched with the dew of heaven,
until he came to know that the Most High God is sovereign over the kingdom of men and sets up over it whom he will. But you, his son Belshazzar, 22
did not humble your heart, although you knew all this. You have set your- 23
self up against the Lord of heaven. The vessels of his temple have been
brought to your table; and you, your nobles, your concubines, and your
courtesans have drunk from them. You have praised the gods of silver and
gold, of bronze and iron, of wood and stone, which neither see nor hear
nor know, and you have not given glory to God, in whose charge is your

*a Or* and solving problems.      *b Or* and to solve problems.

24 very breath and in whose hands are all your ways. This is why that hand
25 was sent from his very presence and why it wrote this inscription. And
these are the words of the writing which was inscribed: *Mene mene tekel*
26 *u-pharsin.* Here is the interpretation: *mene:*[a] God has numbered the days
27 of your kingdom and brought it to an end; *tekel:*[b] you have been weighed
28 in the balance and found wanting; *u-pharsin:*[c] and your kingdom has
29 been divided and given to the Medes and Persians.' Then Belshazzar gave
the order and Daniel was robed in purple and honoured with a chain of
gold round his neck, and proclamation was made that he should rank as
third in the kingdom.

30 31   That very night Belshazzar king of the Chaldaeans was slain, and Darius
the Mede took the kingdom, being then sixty-two years old.

## *Daniel in the lions' pit*

6  IT PLEASED DARIUS TO APPOINT SATRAPS over the kingdom, a
2  hundred and twenty in number in charge of the whole kingdom, and
over them three chief ministers, to whom the satraps should send reports
so that the king's interests might not suffer; of these three, Daniel was one.
3 In the event Daniel outshone the other ministers and the satraps because
of his ability, and the king had it in mind to appoint him over the whole
4 kingdom. Then the chief ministers and the satraps began to look round for
some pretext to attack Daniel's administration of the kingdom, but they
failed to find any malpractice on his part; for he was faithful to his trust.
5 Since they could discover no neglect of duty or malpractice, they said,
'There will be no charge to bring against this Daniel unless we find one
6 in his religion.' These chief ministers and satraps watched for an oppor-
7 tunity to approach the king, and said to him, 'Long live King Darius! All
we, the ministers of the kingdom, prefects, satraps, courtiers, and viceroys, have taken counsel and agree that the king should issue a decree and
bring an ordinance into force, that whoever within the next thirty days shall
present a petition to any god or man other than the king shall be thrown
8 into the lions' pit. Now, O king, issue the ordinance and have it put in
writing, so that it may be unalterable, for the law of the Medes and Persians
9 stands for ever.' Accordingly King Darius issued the ordinance in written
form.
10   When Daniel learnt that this decree had been issued, he went into his
house. He had had windows made in his roof-chamber looking towards
Jerusalem; and there he knelt down three times a day and offered prayers
11 and praises to his God as his custom had always been. His enemies watched
for an opportunity to catch Daniel and found him at his prayers making
12 supplication to his God. Then they came into the king's presence and
reminded him of the ordinance. 'Your majesty,' they said, 'have you not
issued an ordinance that any person who, within the next thirty days, shall
present a petition to any god or man other than your majesty shall be

---

[a] *That is* numbered.      [b] *That is* shekel *or* weight.      [c] *Prob. rdg.; Aram.* pheres.
*There is a play on three possible meanings* halves *or* divisions *or* Persians.

thrown into the lions' pit?' The king answered, 'Yes, it is fixed. The law
of the Medes and Persians stands for ever.' So in the king's presence they 13
said, 'Daniel, one of the Jewish exiles, has ignored the ordinance issued by
your majesty, and is making petition to his god three times a day.' When 14
the king heard this, he was greatly distressed. He tried to think of a way to
save Daniel, and continued his efforts till sunset; then those same men 15
watched for an opportunity to approach the king, and said to him, 'Your
majesty must know that by the law of the Medes and Persians no ordinance
or decree issued by the king may be altered.' So the king gave orders and 16
Daniel was brought and thrown into the lions' pit; but he said to Daniel,
'Your own God, whom you serve continually, will save you.' A stone was 17
brought and put over the mouth of the pit, and the king sealed it with his
signet and with the signets of his nobles, so that no one might intervene
to rescue Daniel.

The king went back to his palace and spent the night fasting; no woman 18
was brought to him and sleep eluded him. At dawn, as soon as it was light, 19
he rose and went in fear and trembling to the pit. When the king reached 20
it, he called anxiously to Daniel, 'Daniel, servant of the living God, has
your God whom you serve continually been able to save you from the
lions?' Then Daniel answered, 'Long live the king! My God sent his angel 21 22
to shut the lions' mouths so that they have done me no injury, because in
his judgement I was found innocent;*a* and moreover, O king, I had done
you no injury.' The king was overjoyed and gave orders that Daniel should 23
be lifted out of the pit. So Daniel was lifted out and no trace of injury was
found on him, because he had put his faith in his God. By order of the king 24
Daniel's accusers were brought and thrown into the lions' pit with their
wives and children, and before they reached the floor of the pit the lions
were upon them and crunched them up, bones and all.

Then King Darius wrote to all peoples and nations of every language 25
throughout the whole world: 'May your prosperity increase! I have issued 26
a decree that in all my royal domains men shall fear and reverence the God
of Daniel;

> for he is the living God, the everlasting,
> whose kingly power shall not be weakened;
> whose sovereignty shall have no end—
> a saviour, a deliverer, a worker of signs and wonders 27
> in heaven and on earth,
> who has delivered Daniel from the power of the lions.'

So this Daniel prospered during the reigns of Darius and Cyrus the 28
Persian.

## Daniel's visions

IN THE FIRST YEAR OF BELSHAZZAR king of Babylon, as Daniel lay 7
on his bed, dreams and visions came into his head. Then he wrote down
the dream, and here his account begins:

*a* in his judgement . . . innocent: *or* before him success was granted me.

2   In my visions of the night I, Daniel, was gazing intently and I saw a
3 great sea churned up by the four winds of heaven, and four huge beasts
4 coming up out of the sea, each one different from the others. The first was
like a lion but had an eagle's wings. I watched until its wings were plucked
off and it was lifted from the ground and made to stand on two feet like
5 a man; it was also given the mind of a man. Then I saw another, a second
beast, like a bear. It was half crouching and had three ribs in its mouth,
between its teeth. The command was given: 'Up, gorge yourself with
6 flesh.' After this as I gazed I saw another, a beast like a leopard with four
bird's wings on its back; this creature had four heads, and it was invested
7 with sovereign power. Next in my visions of the night I saw a fourth beast,
dreadful and grisly, exceedingly strong, with great iron teeth and bronze
claws.*a* It crunched and devoured, and trampled underfoot all that was
left. It differed from all the beasts which preceded it in having ten horns.
8 While I was considering the horns I saw another horn, a little one, springing up among them, and three of the first horns were uprooted to make
room for it. And in that horn were eyes like the eyes of a man, and a mouth
9 that spoke proud words. I kept looking, and then

> thrones were set in place and one ancient in years took his seat,
> his robe was white as snow and the hair of his head like cleanest
>   wool.
> Flames of fire were his throne and its wheels blazing fire;
10  a flowing river of fire streamed out before him.*b*
> Thousands upon thousands served him
> and myriads upon myriads attended his presence.
> The court sat, and the books were opened.

11   Then because of the proud words that the horn was speaking, I went
on watching until the beast was killed and its carcass destroyed: it was given
12 to the flames. The rest of the beasts, though deprived of their sovereignty,
13 were allowed to remain alive for a time and a season. I was still watching
in visions of the night and I saw one like a man coming with the clouds of
heaven; he approached the Ancient in Years and was presented to him.
14 Sovereignty and glory and kingly power were given to him, so that all
people and nations of every language should serve him; his sovereignty
was to be an everlasting sovereignty which should not pass away, and his
kingly power such as should never be impaired.
15   My spirit within me was troubled, and, dismayed by the visions which
16 came into my head, I, Daniel, approached one of those who stood there
and inquired from him what all this meant; and he told me the interpreta-
17 tion. 'These great beasts, four in number,' he said, 'are four kingdoms
18 which shall rise from the ground. But the saints*c* of the Most High shall
receive the kingly power and shall retain it for ever, for ever and ever.'
19   Then I desired to know what the fourth beast meant, the beast that was
different from all the others, very dreadful with its iron teeth and bronze
claws, crunching and devouring and trampling underfoot all that was left.
20  I desired also to know about the ten horns on its head and the other horn

*a* and bronze claws: *prob. rdg., cp. verse 19; Aram. om.*    *b* Or it.    *c* Or holy one

which sprang up and at whose coming three of them fell—the horn that
had eyes and a mouth speaking proud words and appeared larger than the
others. As I still watched, that horn was waging war with the saints and  21
overcoming them until the Ancient in Years came. Then judgement was  22
given in favour of the saints of the Most High, and the time came when
the saints gained possession of the kingly power. He gave me this answer:  23
'The fourth beast signifies a fourth kingdom which shall appear upon earth.
It shall differ from the other kingdoms and shall devour the whole earth,
tread it down and crush it. The ten horns signify the appearance of ten  24
kings in this kingdom, after whom another king shall arise, differing from
his predecessors; and he shall bring low three kings. He shall hurl defiance  25
at the Most High and shall wear down the saints of the Most High. He
shall plan to alter the customary times and law; and the saints shall be
delivered into his power for a time and times and half a time. Then the  26
court shall sit, and he shall be deprived of his sovereignty, so that in the
end it may be destroyed and abolished. The kingly power, sovereignty, and  27
greatness of all the kingdoms under heaven shall be given to the people of
the saints of the Most High. Their kingly power is an everlasting power and
all sovereignties shall serve them and obey them.'

  Here the account ends. As for me, Daniel, my thoughts dismayed me  28
greatly and I turned pale; and I kept these things in my mind.

  *a* In the third year of the reign of King Belshazzar, while I was in Susa  **8** 1-2
the capital city of the province of Elam, a vision appeared to me, Daniel,
similar to my former vision. In this vision I was watching beside the stream
of the Ulai. I raised my eyes and there I saw a ram with two horns standing  3
between me and the stream. The two horns were long, the one longer than
the other, growing up behind. I watched the ram butting west and north  4
and south. No beasts could stand before it, no one could rescue from its
power. It did what it liked, making a display of its strength. While I  5
pondered this, suddenly a he-goat came from the west skimming over the
whole earth without touching the ground; it had a prominent horn between
its eyes. It approached the two-horned ram which I had seen standing  6
between me and the stream and rushed at it with impetuous force. I saw  7
it advance on the ram, working itself into a fury against it, then strike the
ram and break its two horns; the ram had no strength to resist. The he-
goat flung it to the ground and trampled on it, and there was no one to
save the ram.

  Then the he-goat made a great display of its strength. Powerful as it  8
was, its great horn snapped and in its place there sprang out towards the
four quarters of heaven four prominent horns. Out of one of them there  9
issued one small horn, which made a prodigious show of strength south
and east and towards the fairest of all lands. It aspired to be as great as the  10
host of heaven, and it cast down to the earth some of the host and some of
the stars and trod them underfoot. It aspired to be as great as the Prince  11
of the host, suppressed his regular offering and even threw down his
sanctuary. The heavenly hosts were delivered up, and it raised itself*b*  12

---

*a*  *Here the Hebrew text resumes (see note at 2. 4).*          *b*  and it raised itself: *prob.*
*rdg.; Heb. om.*

impiously against the regular offering and threw true religion to the ground;
13 in all that it did it succeeded. I heard a holy one speaking and another
holy one answering him, whoever he was. The one said, 'For how long
will the period of this vision last? How long will the regular offering be
suppressed, how long will impiety cause desolation,*a* and both the Holy
14 Place and the fairest of all lands*b* be given over to be trodden down?' The
answer came, 'For two thousand three hundred evenings and mornings;
then the Holy Place shall emerge victorious.'

15    All the while that I, Daniel, was seeing the vision, I was trying to understand it. Suddenly I saw standing before me one with the semblance of a
16 man; at the same time I heard a human voice calling to him across the bend
17 of the Ulai, 'Gabriel, explain the vision to this man.' He came up to where
I was standing; I was seized with terror at his approach and threw myself
on my face. But he said to me, 'Understand, O man: the vision points to
18 the time of the end.' When he spoke to me, I fell to the ground in a trance;
19 but he grasped me and made me stand up where I was. And he said, 'I
shall make known to you what is to happen at the end of the wrath; for
20 there is an end to the appointed time. The two-horned ram which you saw
21 signifies the kings of Media and Persia, the he-goat is the kingdom*c* of
22 the Greeks and the great horn on his forehead is the first king. As for the
horn which was snapped off and replaced by four horns: four kingdoms
shall rise out of that nation, but not with power comparable to his.

23           In the last days of those kingdoms,
              when their sin is at its height,
           a king shall appear, harsh and grim, a master of stratagem.
24           His power shall be great, he shall work havoc untold;
              he shall succeed in whatever he does.
           He shall work havoc among great nations and upon a holy people.
25           His mind shall be ever active,
           and he shall succeed in his crafty designs;
              he shall conjure up great plans
           and, when they least expect it, work havoc on many.
              He shall challenge even the Prince of princes
              and be broken, but not by human hands.
26           This revelation which has been given
           of the evenings and the mornings is true;
              but you must keep the vision secret,
              for it points to days far ahead.'

27    As for me, Daniel, my strength failed me and I lay sick for a while. Then
I rose and attended to the king's business. But I was perplexed by the
revelation and no one could explain it.

9  IN THE FIRST YEAR OF THE REIGN OF DARIUS son of Ahasuerus (a
Mede by birth, who was appointed king over the kingdom of the Chal-
2 daeans) I, Daniel, was reading the scriptures and reflecting on the seventy

---

*a* will impiety cause desolation: *prob. rdg.; Heb. obscure.*          *b* fairest of all lands:
*prob. rdg., cp. verse 9; Heb. host.*          *c* *Prob. rdg.; Heb.* king.

years which, according to the word of the LORD to the prophet Jeremiah, were to pass while Jerusalem lay in ruins. Then I turned to the Lord God 3 in earnest prayer and supplication with fasting and sackcloth and ashes. I prayed to the LORD my God, making confession thus: 4

'Lord, thou great and terrible God who faithfully keepest the covenant with those who love thee and observe thy commandments, we have sinned, 5 we have done what was wrong and wicked; we have rebelled, we have turned our backs on thy commandments and thy decrees. We have not 6 listened to thy servants the prophets, who spoke in thy name to our kings and princes, to our forefathers and to all the people of the land. O Lord, 7 the right is on thy side; the shame, now as ever, belongs to us, the men of Judah and the citizens of Jerusalem, and to all the Israelites near and far in every land to which thou hast banished them for their treachery towards thee. O LORD, the shame falls on us as on our kings, our princes and our 8 forefathers; we have all sinned against thee. Compassion and forgiveness 9 belong to the Lord our God, though we have rebelled against him. We 10 have not obeyed the LORD our God, we have not conformed to the laws which he laid down for us through his servants the prophets. All Israel 11 has broken thy law and not obeyed thee, so that the curses set out in the law of Moses thy servant in the adjuration and the oath have rained down upon us; for we have sinned against him. He has fulfilled all that he said 12 about us and about our rulers, by bringing upon us and upon Jerusalem a calamity greater than has ever happened in all the world. It was all fore- 13 shadowed in the law of Moses, this calamity which has come upon us; yet we have done nothing to propitiate the LORD our God; we have neither repented of our wrongful deeds nor remembered that thou art true to thy word. The LORD has been biding his time and has now brought this calam- 14 ity upon us. In all that he has done the LORD our God has been right; yet we have not obeyed him.

'And now, O Lord our God who didst bring thy people out of Egypt by 15 a strong hand, winning for thyself a name that lives on to this day, we have sinned, we have done wrong. O Lord, by all thy saving deeds we beg that 16 thy wrath and anger may depart from Jerusalem, thy city, thy holy hill; through our own sins and our fathers' guilty deeds Jerusalem and thy people have become a byword among all our neighbours. And now, our 17 God, listen to thy servant's prayer and supplication; for thy own sake, O Lord, make thy face shine upon thy desolate sanctuary. Lend thy 18 ear, O God, and hear, open thine eyes and look upon our desolation and upon the city that bears thy name; it is not by virtue of our own saving acts but by thy great mercy that we present our supplications before thee. O Lord, hear; O Lord, forgive; O Lord, listen and act; for thy own sake 19 do not delay, O God, for thy city and thy people bear thy name.'

Thus I was speaking and praying, confessing my own sin and my people 20 Israel's sin, and presenting my supplication before the LORD my God on behalf of his holy hill. While I was praying, the man Gabriel, whom I had 21 already seen in the vision, came close to*ᵃ* me at the hour of the evening sacrifice, flying swiftly.*ᵇ* He spoke clearly to me and said, 'Daniel, I have 22

_____
*ᵃ Or* touched.          *ᵇ* flying swiftly: *prob. rdg.; Heb.* thoroughly wearied.

23 now come to enlighten your understanding. As you were beginning your supplications a word went forth; this I have come to pass on to you, for you are a man greatly beloved. Consider well the word, consider the vision:

24 Seventy weeks are marked out for your people and your holy city; then rebellion shall be stopped,*a* sin brought to an end,*b* iniquity expiated, everlasting right ushered in, vision and prophecy sealed, and the Most

25 Holy Place anointed. Know then and understand: from the time that the word went forth that Jerusalem should be restored and rebuilt, seven weeks shall pass till the appearance of one anointed, a prince; then for sixty-two weeks it shall remain restored, rebuilt with streets and conduits.

26 At the critical time, after the sixty-two weeks, one who is anointed shall be removed with no one to take his part; and the horde of an invading prince shall work havoc on city and sanctuary. The end of it shall be a

27 deluge, inevitable war with all its horrors. He shall make a firm league with the mighty*c* for one week; and, the week half spent, he shall put a stop to sacrifice and offering. And in the train of these abominations shall come an author of desolation; then, in the end, what has been decreed concerning the desolation will be poured out.'

**10** IN THE THIRD YEAR OF CYRUS king of Persia a word was revealed to Daniel who had been given the name Belteshazzar. Though this word was true, it cost him*d* much toil to understand it; nevertheless understanding came to him in the course of the vision.

2 3   In those days I, Daniel, mourned for three whole weeks. I refrained from all choice food; no meat or wine passed my lips, and I did not anoint myself

4 until the three weeks had gone by. On the twenty-fourth day of the first month, I found myself on the bank of the great river, that is the Tigris;

5 I looked up and saw a man clothed in linen with a belt of gold from Ophir

6 round his waist. His body gleamed like topaz, his face shone like lightning, his eyes flamed like torches, his arms and feet sparkled like a disc of bronze;

7 and when he spoke his voice sounded like the voice of a multitude. I, Daniel, alone saw the vision, while those who were near me did not see it,

8 but great fear fell upon them and they stole away, and I was left alone gazing at this great vision. But my strength left me; I became a sorry figure

9 of a man, and retained no strength. I heard the sound of his words and,

10 when I did so, I fell prone on the ground in a trance. Suddenly a hand

11 grasped me and pulled me up on to my hands and knees. He said to me, 'Daniel, man greatly beloved, attend to the words I am speaking to you and stand up where you are, for I am now sent to you.' When he addressed

12 me, I stood up trembling and he said, 'Do not be afraid, Daniel, for from the very first day that you applied your mind to understand and to mortify yourself before your God, your prayers have been heard, and I have come

13 in answer to them. But the angel prince of the kingdom of Persia resisted me for twenty-one days, and then, seeing that I had held out there, Michael, one of the chief princes, came to help me against the prince of the kingdom

14 of Persia. And I have come to explain to you what will happen to your people in days to come; for this too is a vision for those days.'

*a Or* restrained.        *b Or* sealed.        *c Or* many.        *d* him: *prob. rdg.; Heb. om.*

While he spoke to me I hung my head and was struck dumb. Suddenly 15 16
one like a man touched my lips. Then I opened my mouth to speak and
addressed him as he stood before me: 'Sir, this has pierced me to the heart,
and I retain no strength. How can my lord's servant presume to talk with 17
such as my lord, since my strength has failed me and no breath is left in
me?' Then the figure touched me again and restored my strength. He said, 18 19
'Do not be afraid, man greatly beloved; all will be well with you. Be strong,
be strong.' When he had spoken to me, I recovered strength and said,
'Speak, sir, for you have given me strength.' He said, 'Do you know why 20
I have come to you? I am first going back to fight with the prince of Persia,
and, as soon as I have left, the prince of Greece will appear: I have no ally 21-11 1
on my side to help and support me, except Michael your prince.*a* However
I will tell you what is written in the Book of Truth. Here and now I will 2
tell you what is true:

'Three more kings will appear in Persia, and the fourth will far surpass
all the others in wealth; and when he has extended his power through his
wealth, he will rouse the whole world against the kingdom of Greece. Then 3
there will appear a warrior king. He will rule a vast kingdom and will do
what he chooses. But as soon as he is established, his kingdom will be 4
shattered and split up north, south, east and west. It will not pass to his
descendants, nor will any of his successors have an empire like his; his
kingdom will be torn up by the roots and given to others as well as to them.
Then the king of the south will become strong; but another of the captains 5
will surpass him in strength and win a greater kingdom. In due course the 6
two will enter into a friendly alliance; to redress the balance the daughter
of the king of the south will be given in marriage to the king of the north,
but she will not maintain her influence and their line will not last. She and
her escort, her child, and also her lord and master, will all be the victims
of foul play. Then another shoot from the same stock as hers will appear 7
in his father's place, will penetrate the defences of the king of the north
and enter his fortress, and will win a decisive victory over his people. He 8
will take back as booty to Egypt even the images of their gods cast in metal
and their precious vessels of silver and gold. Then for some years he will
refrain from attacking the king of the north. After that the king of the 9
north will overrun the southern kingdom but will retreat to his own land.

'His sons will press on to assemble a great armed horde. One of them 10
will sweep on and on like an irresistible flood. And after that he will press
on as far as his enemy's stronghold. The king of the south, his anger roused, 11
will march out to do battle with the king of the north who, in turn, will raise
a great horde, but it will be delivered into the hands of his enemy. When 12
this horde has been captured, the victor will be elated and he will slaughter
tens of thousands, yet he will not maintain his advantage. Then the king 13
of the north will once more raise a horde even greater than the last and,
when the years come round, will advance with a great army and a large
baggage-train. During these times many will resist the king of the south, 14
but some hotheads among your own people will rashly attempt to give
substance to a vision and will come to disaster. Then the king of the north 15

---

*a Prob. rdg.; Heb. adds and as for me, in the first year of Darius the Mede.*

will come and throw up siege-ramps and capture a fortified town, and the
forces of the south will not stand up to him; even the flower of their army
16 will not be able to hold their ground. And so his adversary will do as he
pleases and meet with no opposition. He will establish himself in the fairest
17 of all lands and it will come wholly into his power. He will resolve to sub-
jugate all the dominions of the king of the south; and he will come to fair
terms with him,*a* and he will give him a young woman in marriage, for the
destruction of the kingdom; but she will not persist nor serve his purpose.
18 Then he will turn to the coasts and islands and take many prisoners, but
a foreign commander *b* will put an end to his challenge by wearing him
19 down;*c* thus he will throw back his challenge on to him. He will fall back
upon his own strongholds; there he will come to disaster and be overthrown
and be seen no more.

20    'He will be succeeded by one who will send out an officer with a royal
escort to extort tribute; after a short time this king too will meet his end,
yet neither openly nor in battle.

21    'A contemptible creature will succeed but will not be given recognition
as king; yet he will seize the kingdom by dissimulation and intrigue in
22 time of peace. He will sweep away all forces of opposition as he advances,
23 and even the Prince of the Covenant will be broken. He will enter into
fraudulent alliances and, although the people behind him are but few, he
24 will rise to power and establish himself in time of peace. He will overrun
the richest districts of the province and succeed in doing what his fathers
and forefathers failed to do, distributing spoil, booty, and property to his
followers. He will lay his plans against fortresses, but only for a time.

25    'He will rouse himself in all his strength and courage and lead a great
army against the king of the south, but the king of the south will press the
campaign against him with a very great and numerous army; yet the king
26 of the south will not persist, for traitors will lay their plots. Those who eat
at his board will be his undoing; his army will be swept away, and many
27 will fall on the field of battle. The two kings will be bent on mischief and,
sitting at the same table, they will lie to each other with advantage to
28 neither. Yet there will still be an end to the appointed time. Then one will
return home with a long baggage-train, and with anger in his heart against
the Holy Covenant; he will work his will and return to his own land.

29    'At the appointed time he will once more overrun the south, but he will
30 not succeed as he did before. Ships from the west will sail against him,
and he will receive a rebuff. He will turn and vent his fury against the Holy
Covenant; on his way back he will take due note of those who have for-
31 saken it. Armed forces dispatched by him will desecrate the sanctuary and
the citadel and do away with the regular offering. And there they will set
32 up "the abominable thing that causes desolation". He will win over by
plausible promises those who are ready to condemn the covenant, but the
33 people who are faithful to their God will hold firm and fight back. Wise
leaders of the nation will give guidance to the common people; yet for a
34 while they will fall victims to fire and sword, to captivity and pillage. But

---

*a* and he . . . with him: *prob. rdg.; Heb. obscure.*          *b Or* consul *or* legate.
*c* by wearing him down: *prob. rdg.; Heb. obscure.*

these victims will not want for help, though small, even if many who join
them are insincere. Some of these leaders will themselves fall victims for a   35
time so that they may be tested, refined and made shining white. Yet there
will still be an end*ᵃ* to the appointed time. The king will do what he chooses;   36
he will exalt and magnify himself above every god and against the God of
gods he will utter monstrous blasphemies. All will go well for him until
the time of wrath ends, for what is determined must be done. He will   37
ignore his ancestral gods, and the god beloved of women; to no god will
he pay heed but will exalt himself above them all. Instead he will honour   38
the god of the citadel, a god unknown to his ancestors, with gold and silver,
gems and costly gifts. He will garrison his strongest fortresses with aliens,   39
the people of a foreign god. Those whom he favours he will load with
honour, putting them in office over the common people and distributing
land at a price.

'At the time of the end, he and the king of the south will make feints at   40
one another, and the king of the north will come storming against him with
chariots and cavalry and many ships. He will overrun land after land,
sweeping over them like a flood, amongst them the fairest of all lands, and   41
tens of thousands shall fall victims. Yet all these lands [including Edom
and Moab and the remnant of the Ammonites] will survive his attack. He   42
will reach out to land after land, and Egypt will not escape. He will gain   43
control of her hidden stores of gold and silver and of all her treasures;
Libyans and Cushites will follow in his train. Then rumours from east and   44
north will alarm him, and he will depart in a great rage to destroy and to
exterminate many. He will pitch his royal pavilion between the sea and   45
the holy hill, the fairest of all hills; and he will meet his end with no one
to help him.

> At that moment Michael shall appear,                      **12**
>     Michael the great captain,
>     who stands guard over your fellow-countrymen;
>     and there will be a time of distress
>     such as has never been
>     since they became a nation till that moment.
> But at that moment your people will be delivered,*ᵇ*
>     every one who is written in the book:
> many of those who sleep in the dust of the earth will wake,       2
>     some to everlasting life
>     and some to the reproach of eternal abhorrence.
> The wise leaders shall shine like the bright vault of heaven,       3
>     and those who have guided the people in the true path
>     shall be like the stars for ever and ever.

But you, Daniel, keep the words secret and seal the book till the time of   4
the end. Many will be at their wits' end, and punishment will be heavy.'

And I, Daniel, looked and saw two others standing, one on this bank of   5
the river and the other on the opposite bank. And I said to the man clothed   6
in linen who was above the waters of the river, 'How long will it be before

---

*ᵃ* Yet . . . end: *prob. rdg.; Heb. has different word order.*      *ᵇ Or* will escape.

7 these portents cease?' The man clothed in linen above the waters lifted to heaven his right hand and his left, and I heard him swear by him who lives for ever: 'It shall be for a time, times, and a half. When the power of the holy people ceases to be dispersed, all these things shall come to an end.'

8 I heard but I did not understand, and so I said, 'Sir, what will the issue of

9 these things be?' He replied, 'Go your way, Daniel, for the words are kept

10 secret and sealed till the time of the end. Many shall purify themselves and be refined, making themselves shining white, but the wicked shall continue in wickedness and none of them shall understand; only the wise

11 leaders shall understand. From the time when the regular offering is abolished and "the abomination of desolation" is set up, there shall be

12 an interval of one thousand two hundred and ninety days. Happy the man who waits and lives to see the completion of one thousand three hundred

13 and thirty-five days! But go your way to the end and rest, and you shall arise to your destiny at the end of the age.'

# HOSEA

T HE WORD OF THE LORD which came to Hosea son of Beeri 1
during the reigns of Uzziah, Jotham, Ahaz, and Hezekiah, kings
of Judah, and during the reign of Jeroboam son of Jehoash king
of Israel.

## Hosea's unfaithful wife

T HIS IS THE BEGINNING of the LORD's message by Hosea. He said, 2
Go, take a wanton for your wife and get children of her wantonness;
for like a wanton this land is unfaithful to the LORD. So he went and took 3
Gomer, a worthless woman;*a* and she conceived and bore him a son. And 4
the LORD said to him,

> Call him Jezreel;*b* for in a little while
> I will punish the line of Jehu for the blood shed in Jezreel
>  and put an end to the kingdom of Israel.
>   On that day 5
> I will break Israel's bow in the Vale of Jezreel.

She conceived again and bore a daughter, and the LORD said to him, 6

> Call her Lo-ruhamah;*c*
> for I will never again show love to Israel,
>  never again forgive them.*d*

After weaning Lo-ruhamah, she conceived and bore a son; and the LORD 8 9
said,

> Call him Lo-ammi;*e*
>  for you are not my people,
>  and I will not be your God.
> The Israelites shall become countless as the sands of the sea 10
>  which can neither be measured nor numbered;
> it shall no longer be said, 'They are not my people',
>  they shall be called Sons of the Living God.
> Then the people of Judah and of Israel shall be reunited 11
>  and shall choose for themselves a single head,
>   and they shall become masters of the earth;
>   for great shall be the day of Jezreel.

---

*a* a worthless woman: *or* daughter of Diblaim.          *b* *That is* God shall sow.
*c* *That is* Not loved.          *d* *Prob. rdg.; Heb. adds* (7) Then I will love Judah and will
save them. I will save them not by bow or sword or weapon of war, by horses or by horsemen, but by the LORD their God.          *e* *That is* Not my people.

**2**    Then you will say to your brothers, 'You are my people',
and to your sisters, 'You are loved.'

**2**      Plead my cause with your mother;
is she not my wife and I her husband?*a*
Plead with her to forswear those wanton looks,
to banish the lovers from her bosom.

**3**        Or I will strip her and expose her
naked as the day she was born;
I will make her bare as the wilderness,
parched as the desert,
and leave her to die of thirst.

**4**        I will show no love for her children;
they are the offspring of wantonness,

**5**        and their mother is a wanton.
She who conceived them is shameless;
she says, 'I will go after my lovers;
they give me my food and drink,
my wool and flax, my oil and my perfumes.'

**6**      Therefore I will block her road with thorn-bushes
and obstruct her path with a wall,
so that she can no longer follow her old ways.

**7**      When she pursues her lovers she will not overtake them,
when she looks for them she will not find them;
then she will say,
'I will go back to my husband again;
I was better off with him than I am now.'

**8**      For she does not know that it is I who gave her
corn, new wine, and oil,
I who lavished upon her silver and gold
which they spent on the Baal.

**9**        Therefore I will take back
my corn at the harvest and my new wine at the vintage,
and I will take away the wool and the flax
which I gave her to cover her naked body;

**10**      so I will show her up for the lewd thing she is,
and no lover will want to steal her from me.

**12*b***      I will ravage the vines and the fig-trees,
which she says are the fee
with which her lovers have hired her,
and turn them into jungle where wild beasts shall feed.

**11**        I will put a stop to her merrymaking,
her pilgrimages and new moons, her sabbaths*c* and festivals.

**13**        I will punish her for the holy days
when she burnt sacrifices to the Baalim,

---

*a* is she . . . husband?: *or for she is no longer my wife nor I her husband.*
*b* *Verses 11 and 12 transposed.*
*c* *Or her full moons.*

when she decked herself with earrings and necklaces,
ran after her lovers and forgot me.
This is the very word of the LORD.

But now listen,                                          14
I will woo her, I will go with her into the wilderness
and comfort her:
there I will restore her vineyards,                      15
turning the Vale of Trouble into the Gate of Hope,[a]
and there she will answer as in her youth,
when she came up out of Egypt.
On that day she shall call me 'My husband'               16
and shall no more call me 'My Baal';[b]
and I will wipe from her lips the very names of the Baalim;   17
never again shall their names be heard.
This is the very word of the LORD.[c]

Then I will make a covenant on behalf of Israel with the wild beasts,   18
the birds of the air, and the things that creep on the earth, and I will break
bow and sword and weapon of war and sweep them off the earth, so that
all living creatures may lie down without fear. I will betroth you to myself   19
for ever, betroth you in lawful wedlock with unfailing devotion and love;
I will betroth you to myself to have and to hold, and you shall know the   20
LORD. At that time I will give answer, says the LORD, I will answer for the   21
heavens and they will answer for the earth, and the earth will answer for   22
the corn, the new wine, and the oil, and they will answer for Jezreel.
Israel shall be my new sowing in the land, and I will show love to Lo-   23
ruhamah and say to Lo-ammi, 'You are my people', and he will say, 'Thou
art my God.'
The LORD said to me,                                     3

Go again and love a woman
loved by another man, an adulteress,
and love her as I, the LORD, love the Israelites
although they resort to other gods
and love the raisin-cakes offered to their idols.

So I got her back[d] for fifteen pieces of silver, a homer of barley and a   2
measure of wine; and I said to her,                      3

Many a long day you shall live in my house
and not play the wanton,
and have no intercourse with a man, nor I with you.

For the Israelites shall live many a long day            4
without king or prince,
without sacrifice or sacred pillar,
without image or household gods;

---

[a] turning ... Hope: *or* Emek-achor to Pethah-tikvah.      [b] *Also means* My husband.
[c] This ... LORD: *transposed from after* On that day *in verse 16.*      [d] got her back·
*or* bought her.

5     but after that they will again seek
      the LORD their God and David their king,
      and turn anxiously to the LORD for his bounty in days to come.


## God's case against Israel

**4**      Hear the word of the LORD, O Israel;
      for the LORD has a charge to bring against the people of the land:
          There is no good faith or mutual trust,
          no knowledge of God in the land,
2     oaths are imposed and broken, they kill and rob;
          there is nothing but adultery and licence,*a*
          one deed of blood after another.
3     Therefore the land shall be dried up,
      and all who live in it shall pine away,
      and with them the wild beasts and the birds of the air;
      even the fish shall be swept from the sea.
4         But it is not for any man to bring a charge,
          it is not for him to prove a case;
      the quarrel with you, false priest, is mine.

5     Priest?*b* By day and by night you blunder on,
          you and the prophet with you.
6     My people are ruined for lack of knowledge;
          your own countrymen are brought to ruin.*c*
      You have rejected knowledge,
      and I will reject you from serving me as priest.
          You have forgotten the teaching of God,
      and I, your God, will forget your sons.

7     The more priests there are, the more they sin against me;
          their dignity I will turn into dishonour.
8             They feed on the sin of my people
      and batten on their iniquity.
9     But people and priest shall be treated alike.
      I will punish them for their conduct
      and repay them for their deeds:
10            they shall eat but never be satisfied,
      behave wantonly but their lust will never be overtaxed,
          for they have forsaken the LORD
11            to give themselves to sacred prostitution.
12    New wine and old steal my people's wits:*d*
          they ask advice from a block of wood
          and take their orders from a fetish;

---

*a* and licence: *prob. rdg.; Heb.* they exceed.      *b* the quarrel . . . Priest?: *prob. rdg.;*
*Heb.* and your people are like those who quarrel with a priest.      *c* My people . . .
ruin: *or* Your mother (Israel) is destroyed, my people destroyed for lack of knowledge.
*d* steal . . . wits: *or* embolden my people.

for a spirit of wantonness has led them astray
and in their lusts they are unfaithful to their God.
Your men sacrifice on mountain-tops                          13
  and burn offerings on the hills,
    under oak and poplar
and the terebinth's pleasant shade.
Therefore your daughters play the wanton
  and your sons' brides commit adultery.
I will not punish your daughters for playing the wanton      14
  nor your sons' brides for their adultery,
because your men resort to wanton women
  and sacrifice with temple-prostitutes.
A people without understanding comes to grief;
  they are a mother turned wanton.                         15
Bring no guilt-offering,*a* Israel;
  do not come to Gilgal, Judah,
do not go up to Beth-aven to swear by the life of the LORD,
since Israel has run wild, wild as a heifer;                 16
  and will the LORD now feed this people
    like lambs in a broad meadow?
Ephraim, keeping company with idols,                         17
  has held a drunken orgy,*b*                              18
  they have practised sacred prostitution,
they have preferred dishonour to glory.
The wind shall sweep them away, wrapped in its wings,        19
  and they will find their sacrifices a delusion.

Hear this, you priests,                                       **5**
and listen, all Israel; let the royal house mark my words.
  Sentence is passed on you;
  for you have been a snare at Mizpah,
and a net spread out on Tabor.
The rebels! they have shown base ingratitude,                2
  but I will punish them all.
I have cared for Ephraim                                      3
  and I have not neglected Israel;
  but now Ephraim has played the wanton
    and Israel has defiled himself.
Their misdeeds have barred their way back to their God;      4
  for a wanton spirit is in them,
    and they care nothing for the LORD.
Israel's arrogance cries out against him;                    5
 *c*Ephraim's guilt is his undoing,
  and Judah no less is undone.
They go with sacrifices of sheep and cattle                  6
  to seek the LORD, but do not find him.

---

*a* Bring no guilt-offering: *prob. rdg.; Heb.* Let him not be guilty.    *b* a drunken
orgy: *prob. rdg.; Heb. unintelligible.*    *c Prob. rdg.; Heb. prefixes* Israel.

He has withdrawn himself from them;
7     for they have been unfaithful to him,
and their sons are bastards.
Now an invader shall devour their fields.
8     Blow the trumpet in Gibeah,
    the horn in Ramah,
    raise the battle-cry in Beth-aven:
    'Benjamin, we are with you!'
9 On the tribes of Israel I have proclaimed this unalterable doom:
on the day of punishment Ephraim shall be laid waste.
10 The rulers of Judah act like men who move their neighbour's boundary;
on them will I pour out my wrath like a flood.
11     Ephraim is an oppressor trampling on justice,
    doggedly pursuing what is worthless.
12     But I am a festering sore to Ephraim,
    a canker to the house of Judah.
13     So when Ephraim found that he was sick,
    Judah that he was covered with sores,
    Ephraim went to Assyria,
    he went in haste to the Great King;
    but he has no power to cure you
    or to heal your sores.
14     Yes indeed, I will be fierce as a panther to Ephraim,
    fierce as a lion to Judah—
    I will maul the prey and go,
    carry it off beyond hope of rescue—I, the LORD.
15     I will go away and return to my place
until in their horror they seek me,
    and look earnestly for me in their distress.

6     Come, let us return to the LORD;
    for he has torn us and will heal us,
    he has struck us and he will bind up our wounds;
2     after two days he will revive us,
    on the third day he will restore us,
    that in his presence we may live.
3 Let us humble ourselves, let us strive to know the LORD,
    whose justice dawns like morning light,[a]
    and its dawning is as sure as the sunrise.
    It will come to us like a shower,
    like spring rains that water the earth.

4     O Ephraim, how shall I deal with you?
    How shall I deal with you, Judah?
    Your loyalty to me is like the morning mist,
    like dew that vanishes early.
5     Therefore have I lashed you through the prophets
    and torn you[b] to shreds with my words;

    [a] *Line transposed from end of verse 5.*     [b] *Prob. rdg.; Heb.* them.

loyalty is my desire, not sacrifice,                                         6
  not whole-offerings but the knowledge of God.

At Admah*ᵃ* they have broken my covenant,                                    7
  there they have played me false.
Gilead is a haunt of evildoers,                                              8
  marked by a trail of blood;
like robbers lying in wait for a man,                                        9
  priests are banded together
  to do murder on the road to Shechem;
  their deeds are outrageous.
At Israel's sanctuary I have seen a horrible thing:                         10
  there Ephraim played the wanton
  and Israel defiled himself.
And for you, too, Judah, comes a harvest of reckoning.                      11

When I would reverse the fortunes of my people,
  when I would heal Israel,                                                   7
  then the guilt of Ephraim stands revealed,
  and all the wickedness of Samaria;
  they have not kept faith.
They are thieves, they break into houses;*ᵇ*
  they are robbers, they strip people in the street,
little thinking that I have their wickedness ever in mind.
  Now their misdeeds beset them                                              2
  and stare me in the face.
They win over the king with their wickedness                                 3
  and princes with their treachery,
lecherous all of them, hot as an oven over the fire                         4
  which the baker does not stir
  after kneading the dough until it is proved.
On their king's festal day the officers                                      5
  begin to be inflamed with wine,
  and he joins in the orgies of arrogant men;
  for their hearts are heated by it*ᶜ* like an oven.                         6
    While they are relaxed all night long
    their passion slumbers,
  but in the morning it flares up
    like a blazing fire;
  they all grow feverish, hot as an oven,                                    7
    and devour their rulers.
King after king falls from power,
  but not one of them calls upon me.
Ephraim and his aliens make a sorry mixture;                                 8
Ephraim has become a cake half-baked.
  Foreigners fed on his strength,                                            9
    but he was unaware;

---

*ᵃ* At Admah: *prob. rdg.; Heb.* Like Adam.    *ᵇ* houses: *prob. rdg.; Heb. om.*
*ᶜ* are heated by it: *prob. rdg.; Heb.* draw near.

even his grey hairs turned white,
    but he was unaware.
10 So Israel's arrogance cries out against them;
    but they do not return to the LORD their God
      nor seek him, in spite of it all.
11 Ephraim is a silly senseless pigeon,
    now calling upon Egypt, now turning to Assyria for help.
12 Wherever they turn, I will cast my net over them
    and will bring them down like birds on the wing;
      I will take them captive as soon as I hear them flocking.
13 Woe betide them, for they have strayed from me!
May disaster befall them for rebelling against me!
    I long to deliver them,
but they tell lies about me.
14     There is no sincerity in their cry to me;
    for all their howling on their pallets
      and gashing of themselves over corn and new wine,
        they are turning away from me.
15 Though I support them, though I give them strength of arm,
    they plot evil against me.
16     Like a bow gone slack,
    they relapse into the worship of their high god;[a]
    their talk is all lies,[b]
and so their princes shall fall by the sword.

8     Put the trumpet to your lips!
A[c] vulture hovers over the sanctuary of the LORD:
    they have broken my covenant
    and rebelled against my instruction.
2     They cry to me for help:
'We know thee, God of Israel.'[d]
3 But Israel is utterly loathsome;
    and therefore he shall run before the enemy.
4 They make kings, but not by my will;
    they set up officers, but without my knowledge;
they have made themselves idols of their silver and gold.[e]

5     Your calf-gods stink, O Samaria;
my anger flares up against them.
Long will it be before they prove innocent.
6     For what sort of a god is this bull?
    It is no god,
a craftsman made it;
the calf of Samaria will be broken in fragments.

---

[a] they relapse . . . god: *prob. rdg.; Heb. obscure.*    [b] *Prob. rdg.; Heb. adds* that is
their stammering speech in Egypt.    [c] *Prob. rdg.; Heb. Like a.*    [d] We . . .
Israel: *prob. rdg.; Heb.* O my God, we know thee, Israel.    [e] *Prob. rdg.; Heb.
adds* so that he may be cut off.

Israel sows the wind and reaps the whirlwind;                    7
there are no heads on the standing corn, it yields no grain;
and, if it yielded any, strangers would swallow it up.
  Israel is now swallowed up,                                    8
  lost among the nations,
  a worthless nothing.
For, like a wild ass that has left the herd,                     9
  they have run to Assyria.
Ephraim has bargained for lovers;
and, because they have bargained among the nations,             10
  I will now round them up,
  and then they will soon abandon
this setting up of kings and princes.
For Ephraim in his sin has multiplied altars,                   11
altars have become his sin.
Though I give him countless rules in writing,                   12
  they are treated as invalid.
Though they sacrifice flesh as offerings to me and eat them,    13
  I,*a* the LORD, will not accept them.
Their guilt will be remembered
  and their sins punished.
They shall go back to Egypt,
or in Assyria they shall eat unclean food.

  Israel has forgotten his Maker                                 14
  and built palaces,
Judah has multiplied walled cities;
  but I will set fire to his cities,
  and it shall devour his castles.

Do not rejoice, Israel, do not exult like other peoples;         **9**
  for like a wanton you have forsaken your God,
  you have loved an idol*b*
on every threshing-floor heaped with corn.
Threshing-floor and winepress shall know them no more,           2
  new wine shall disown*c* them.
  They shall not dwell in the LORD's land;                       3
Ephraim shall go back to Egypt,
or in Assyria they shall eat unclean food.
They shall pour out no wine to the LORD,                         4
they shall not bring their sacrifices to him;
  that would be mourners' fare for them,
  and all who ate it would be polluted.
  For their food shall only stay their hunger;
  it shall not be offered in the house of the LORD.
  What will you do for the festal day,                           5
  the day of the LORD's pilgrim-feast?

---

*a* *Prob. rdg.; Heb.* he.   *b* an idol: *or* a harlot's fee.   *c* *Or* fail.

6          For look, they have fled from a scene of devastation:
               Egypt shall receive them,
               Memphis shall be their grave;
               the sands of Syrtes shall wreck them,
               weeds shall inherit their land,
               thorns shall grow in their dwellings.
7          The days of punishment are come,
               the days of vengeance are come
               when Israel shall be humbled.
               Then the prophet shall be made a fool
               and the inspired seer a madman
               by your great guilt.
8      With great enmity Ephraim lies in wait for God's people
           while the prophet is a fowler's trap by all their paths,
               a snare in the very temple of God.
9          They lead them deep into sin as at the time of Gibeah.
           Their guilt will be remembered and their sins punished.

10         I came upon Israel like grapes in the wilderness,
               I looked on their forefathers
               with joy like the first ripe figs;
               but they resorted to Baal-peor
               and consecrated themselves to a thing of shame,
11         and Ephraim became as loathsome as the thing he loved.
               Their honour shall fly away like a bird:
               no childbirth, no fruitful womb, no conceiving;
12             even if they rear their children,
               I will make them childless, without posterity.
           Woe to them indeed when I turn away from them!

13         As lion-cubs emerge only to be hunted,*a*
           so must Ephraim bring out his children for slaughter.
14             Give them, O Lord—what wilt thou give them?
           Give them a womb that miscarries and dry breasts.

15         All their wickedness was seen at Gilgal; there did I hate them.
           For their evil deeds I will drive them from my house,
           I will love them no more: all their princes are in revolt.
16             Ephraim is struck down:
           their root is withered, and they yield no fruit;
               if ever they give birth,
           I will slay the dearest offspring of their womb.

17             My God shall reject them,
               because they have not listened to him,
           and they shall become wanderers among the nations.

---

               *a* As lion-cubs . . . hunted: *prob. rdg.; Heb. unintelligible.*

## *God's judgement on Israel*

**10**

Israel is like a rank vine
    ripening its fruit:
his fruit grows more and more, and more and more his altars;
the fairer his land becomes, the fairer he makes his sacred pillars.
They are crazy now, they are mad.    2
    God himself will hack down their altars
    and wreck their sacred pillars.
Well may they say, 'We have no king,    3
    for we do not fear the LORD;
    and what can the king do for us?'
    There is nothing but talk,    4
imposing of oaths and making of treaties, all to no purpose;
    and litigation spreads like a poisonous weed
    along the furrows of the fields.
The inhabitants of Samaria tremble for the calf-god of Beth-aven;    5
the people mourn over it*ᵃ* and its priestlings howl,
    distressed for their image, their glory,
    which is carried away into exile.
It shall be carried to Assyria    6
as tribute to the Great King;
disgrace shall overtake Ephraim
and Israel shall feel the shame of their disobedience.
Samaria and her king are swept away    7
    like flotsam on the water;
    the hill-shrines of Aven are wiped out,    8
    the shrines where Israel sinned;
thorns and thistles grow over her altars.
    So they will say to the mountains, 'Cover us',
    and to the hills, 'Fall on us.'

Since the day of Gibeah Israel has sinned;    9
there they took their stand in rebellion.
Shall not war overtake them in Gibeah?
I have come against the rebels to chastise them,    10
and the peoples shall mass against them
    in hordes for their two deeds of shame.
Ephraim is like a heifer broken in,    11
    which loves to thresh corn,
across whose fair neck I have laid a yoke;*ᵇ*
    I have harnessed Ephraim to the pole that he*ᶜ* may plough,
    that Jacob may harrow his land.
Sow for yourselves in justice,    12
    and you will reap what loyalty deserves.
    Break up your fallow;

*ᵃ* the people mourn over it: *or* the high god and his people mourn.
*prob. rdg.; Heb. om.*    *ᶜ* he: *prob. rdg.; Heb.* Judah.    *ᵇ* a yoke:

for it is time to seek the LORD,
seeking him till he comes and gives you just measure of rain.

13 You have ploughed wickedness into your soil,
and the crop is mischief;
you have eaten the fruit of treachery.

Because you have trusted in your chariots,
in the number of your warriors,

14 the tumult of war shall arise against your people,
and all your fortresses shall be razed
as Shalman razed Beth-arbel in the day of battle,
dashing the mother to the ground with her babes.

15 So it shall be done to you, Bethel,
because of your evil scheming;
as sure as day dawns, the king of Israel shall be swept away.

11 When Israel was a boy, I loved him;
I called my son out of Egypt;

2 but the more I called, the further they went from me;
they must needs sacrifice to the Baalim
and burn offerings before carved images.

3 It was I who taught Ephraim to walk,
I who had taken them in my arms;

4 but they did not know that I harnessed them in leading-strings[a]
and led them with bonds of love[b]—
that I had lifted them like a little child[c] to my cheek,
that I had bent down to feed them.

5 Back they shall go to Egypt,
the Assyrian shall be their king;
for they have refused to return to me.

6 The sword shall be swung over their blood-spattered altars
and put an end to their prattling priests

7 and devour my people in return for all their schemings,
bent on rebellion as they are.
Though they call on their high god,
even then he will not reinstate them.

8 How can I give you up, Ephraim,
how surrender you, Israel?
How can I make you like Admah
or treat you as Zeboyim?
My heart is changed within me,
my remorse kindles already.

9 I will not let loose my fury,
I will not turn round and destroy Ephraim;
for I am God and not a man,
the Holy One in your midst;

[a] leading-strings: *or* cords of leather.  [b] bonds of love: *or* reins of hide.
[c] I had . . . child: *prob. rdg.; Heb.* like those who lift up a yoke.

I will not come with threats*a* like a roaring lion.                            10
   No; when I roar, I who am God,
my sons shall come with speed out of the west.
They will come speedily, flying like birds out of Egypt,            11
   like pigeons from Assyria,
and I will settle them in their own homes.
   This is the very word of the LORD.
Ephraim besets me with treachery,                                          12
   the house of Israel besets me with deceit;
and Judah is still restive under God,
   still loyal to the idols he counts holy.
Ephraim is a shepherd whose flock is but*b* wind,               **12**
a hunter chasing the east wind all day;*c*
he makes a treaty with Assyria
and carries tribute of oil to Egypt.

The LORD has a charge to bring against Judah                      2
and is resolved to punish Jacob for his conduct;
   he will requite him for his misdeeds.
Even in the womb Jacob overreached his brother,                 3
   and in manhood he strove with God.
The divine angel stood firm and held his own;*d*                   4
   Jacob wept and begged favour for himself.
   Then God met him at Bethel
and there spoke with him.
The LORD the God of Hosts, the LORD is his name.             5

Turn back all of you by God's help;                                          6
   practise loyalty and justice
and wait always upon your God.
False scales are in merchants' hands,                                        7
   and they love to cheat;
   so Ephraim says,                                                        8
'Surely I have become a rich man, I have made my fortune';
   but all his gains will not pay
   for the guilt*e* of his sins.
Yet I have been the LORD your God since your days in Egypt;   9
I will make you live in tents yet again, as in the old days.

   I spoke to the prophets,                                              10
it was I who gave vision after vision;
   I spoke through the prophets in parables.
Was there idolatry in Gilead?                                                   11
   Yes: they were worthless
and sacrificed to bull-gods in Gilgal;
their altars were common as heaps of stones beside a ploughed field.

---

*a Prob. rdg.; Heb. adds* they shall go after the LORD.   *b* is a . . . but: *or* feeds on.
*c Prob. rdg.; Heb. adds* piling up treachery and havoc.   *d* The divine . . . own: *or*
He stood firm against an angel, but flagged.   *e* for the guilt: *prob. rdg.; Heb.*
for me, guilt.

12      Jacob fled to the land of Aram;
        Israel did service to win a wife,
            to win a wife he tended sheep.

13      By a prophet the LORD brought up Israel out of Egypt
            and by a prophet he was tended.

14      Ephraim has given bitter provocation;
        therefore his Lord will make him answerable
            for his own death
        and bring down upon his own head the blame
            for all that he has done.

**13**      When the Ephraimites mumbled their prayers,
        God himself denounced Israel;
            they were guilty of Baal-worship and died.
2       Yet now they sin more and more;
        they have made themselves an image of cast metal,
        they have fashioned their silver into idols,
            nothing but the work of craftsmen;
            men say of them,
        'Those who kiss calf-images offer human sacrifice.'

3       Therefore they shall be like the morning mist
            or like dew that vanishes early,
        like chaff blown from the threshing-floor
            or smoke from a chimney.
4       But I have been the LORD your God since your days in Egypt,
            when you knew no other saviour than me,
                no god but me.
5           I cared for you in the wilderness,
6       in a land of burning heat, as if you were in pasture.
            So they were filled,
        and, being filled, grew proud;
            and so they forgot me.
7       So now I will be like a panther to them,
        I will prowl like a leopard by the wayside;
8       I will meet them like a she-bear robbed of her cubs
            and tear their ribs apart,
        like a lioness I will devour them on the spot,
            I will rip them up like a wild beast.
9       I have destroyed you, O Israel; who is there to help you?
10      Where now is your king that he may save you,
            or the rulers in all your cities
            for whom you asked me,
        begging for king and princes?
11      I gave you a king in my anger,
            and in my fury took him away.

Ephraim's guilt is tied up in a scroll, 12
his sins are kept on record.
When the pangs of his birth came over his mother, 13
he showed himself a senseless child;
for at the proper time he could not present himself
at the mouth of the womb.
Shall I redeem him from Sheol? 14
Shall I ransom him from death?
Oh, for your plagues, O death! Oh, for your sting, Sheol!
I will put compassion out of my sight.
Though he flourishes among the reeds,*a* 15
an east wind shall come, a blast from the LORD,
rising over the desert;
Ephraim's spring will fail and his fountain run dry.
It will carry away as spoil
his whole store of costly treasures.
Samaria will become desolate because she has rebelled against her God; 16
her babes will fall by the sword and be dashed to the ground,
her women with child shall be ripped up.

## Repentance, forgiveness, and restoration

Return, O Israel, to the LORD your God; **14**
for you have stumbled in your evil courses.
Come with your words ready, 2
come back to the LORD;
say to him, 'Thou dost not endure iniquity.*b*
Accept our plea,
and we will pay our vows with cattle from our pens.
Assyria shall not save us, nor will we seek horses to ride; 3
what we have made with our own hands
we will never again call gods;
for in thee the fatherless find a father's love.'

I will heal their apostasy; of my own bounty will I love them; 4
for my anger is turned away from them.
I will be as dew to Israel 5
that he may flower like the lily,
strike root like the poplar*c* 6
and put out fresh shoots,
that he may be as fair as the olive
and fragrant as Lebanon.
Israel shall again dwell in my*d* shadow 7
and grow corn in abundance;

*a* among the reeds: *prob. rdg.; Heb.* between (*or* a son of) brothers.   *b* Thou . . .
iniquity: *or* Thou wilt surely take away iniquity.   *c Prob. rdg.; Heb.* like Lebanon.
*d Prob. rdg.; Heb.* its.

> they shall flourish like a vine
> and be famous as the wine of Lebanon.

8    What has Ephraim any more to do with idols?
> I have spoken and I affirm it:
> I am the pine-tree that shelters you;
> to me you owe your fruit.

9    Let the wise consider these things and let him who considers take note; for the LORD's ways are straight and the righteous walk in them, while sinners stumble.

# JOEL

1    The word of the LORD which came to Joel son of Pethuel.

## *The day of the LORD*

2    Listen, you elders;
> hear me, all you who live in the land:
> has the like of this happened in all your days
> or in your fathers' days?

3    Tell it to your sons and they may tell theirs;
> let them pass it on from generation to generation.

4    What the locust has left the swarm eats,
> what the swarm has left the hopper eats,
> and what the hopper has left the grub eats.

5    Wake up, you drunkards, and lament your fate;
> mourn for the fresh wine, all you wine-drinkers,
> because it is lost to you.

6    For a horde has overrun my land,
> mighty and past counting;
> their teeth are a lion's teeth;
> they have the fangs of a lioness.

7    They have ruined my vines
> and left my fig-trees broken and leafless,
> they have plucked them bare
> and stripped them of their bark;
> they have left the branches white.

8    Wail like a virgin wife in sackcloth,
> wailing over the bridegroom of her youth:

9    the drink-offering and grain-offering are lost
> to the house of the LORD.
> Mourn, you priests, ministers of the LORD,

10    the fields are ruined, the parched earth mourns;

for the corn is ruined, the new wine is desperate,
  the oil has failed.
Despair, you husbandmen; you vinedressers, lament,                11
  because the wheat and the barley,
  the harvest of the field, is lost.
The vintage is desperate, and the fig-tree has failed;           12
  pomegranate, palm, and apple,
  all the trees of the country-side are parched,
  and none make merry over harvest.

Priests, put on sackcloth and beat your breasts;                 13
  lament, you ministers of the altar;
come, lie in sackcloth all night long, you ministers of my God;
  for grain-offering and drink-offering
  are withheld from the house of your God.
Proclaim a solemn fast, appoint a day of abstinence.             14
  You elders, summon all that live in the land
    to come together in the house of your God,
    and cry to the Lord.
    Alas! the day is near,                                       15
  the day of the Lord: it comes,
  a mighty destruction from the Almighty.
Look! it stares us in the face;                                  16
  the house of our God has lost its food,
    lost all its joy and gladness.
    The soil is parched,                                         17
    the dykes are dry,
    the granaries are deserted,
    the barns ruinous;
  for the rains have failed.
    The cattle are exhausted,                                    18
    the herds of oxen distressed
  because they have no pasture;
  the flocks of sheep waste away.
To thee I cry, O Lord;                                           19
  for fire has devoured the open pastures
and the flames have burnt up all the trees of the country-side.
The very cattle in the field look up to thee;                    20
  for the water-channels are dried up,
  and fire has devoured the open pastures.

Blow the trumpet in Zion,                                         2
  sound the alarm upon my holy hill;
  let all that live in the land tremble,
    for the day of the Lord has come,
  surely a day of darkness and gloom is upon us,                  2
    a day of cloud and dense fog;
  like a blackness spread over the mountains
  a mighty, countless host appears;

their like has never been known,
nor ever shall be in ages to come;
3   their vanguard a devouring fire,
their rearguard leaping flame;
before them the land is a garden of Eden,
behind them a wasted wilderness;
nothing survives their march.
4   On they come, like squadrons of horse,
like war-horses they charge;
5 bounding over the peaks they advance with the rattle of chariots,
like flames of fire burning up the stubble,
like a countless host in battle array.
6   Before them nations tremble,
every face turns pale.
7      Like warriors they charge,
they mount the walls like men at arms,
each marching in line,
no confusion in the ranks,
8   none jostling his neighbour,
none breaking line.
They plunge through streams without halting their advance;
9 they burst into the city, leap on to the wall,
climb into the houses,
entering like thieves through the windows.
10   Before them the earth shakes,
the heavens shudder,
sun and moon are darkened,
and the stars forbear to shine.
11   The LORD thunders before his host;
his is a mighty army,
countless are those who do his bidding.
Great is the day of the LORD and terrible,
who can endure it?
12   And yet, the LORD says, even now
turn back to me with your whole heart,
fast, and weep, and beat your breasts.
13   Rend your hearts and not your garments;
turn back to the LORD your God;
for he is gracious and compassionate,
long-suffering and ever constant,
always ready to repent of the threatened evil.
14   It may be he will turn back and repent
and leave a blessing behind him,
blessing enough for grain-offering and drink-offering
for the LORD your God.

15     Blow the trumpet in Zion,
proclaim a solemn fast, appoint a day of abstinence;

gather the people together, proclaim a solemn assembly;     16
    summon the elders,
gather the children, yes, babes at the breast;
    bid the bridegroom leave his chamber
    and the bride her bower.
    Let the priests, the ministers of the LORD,     17
    stand weeping between the porch and the altar
and say, 'Spare thy people, O LORD, thy own people,
    expose them not to reproach,
    lest other nations make them a byword
    and everywhere men ask,
      "Where is their God?" '

## Israel forgiven and restored

    Then the LORD's love burned with zeal for his land,     18
    and he was moved with compassion for his people.
He answered their appeal and said,     19
I will send you corn, and new wine, and oil,
    and you shall have your fill;
    I will expose you no longer
    to the reproach of other nations.
    I will remove the northern peril far away from you     20
and banish them into a land parched and waste,
    their vanguard into the eastern sea
    and their rear into the western,
and the stench shall rise from their rotting corpses
    because of their proud deeds!
Earth, be not afraid, rejoice and be glad;     21
    for the LORD himself has done a proud deed.
    Be not afraid, you cattle in the field;     22
    for the pastures shall be green,
    the trees shall bear fruit,
the fig and the vine yield their harvest.
    O people of Zion,     23
    rejoice and be glad in the LORD your God,
who gives you good food in due measure*a*
    and sends down rain*b* as of old.
    The threshing-floors shall be heaped with grain,     24
the vats shall overflow with new wine and oil.
    So I will make good the years     25
    that the swarm has eaten,
    hopper and grub and locust,
my great army which I sent against you;

---

*a* *Or* gives you a sign pointing to prosperity.      *b* *Prob. rdg.; Heb. adds* spring rain and autumn rain.

26 and you shall eat, you shall eat your fill
and praise the name of the LORD your God
who has done wonders for you,[a]
27 and you shall know that I am present in Israel,
that I and no other am the LORD your God;
and my people shall not again be brought to shame.
28 Thereafter the day shall come
when I will pour out my spirit on all mankind;
your sons and your daughters shall prophesy,
your old men shall dream dreams
and your young men see visions;
29 I will pour out my spirit in those days
even upon slaves and slave-girls.
30 I will show portents in the sky and on earth,
blood and fire and columns of smoke;
31 the sun shall be turned into darkness
and the moon into blood
before the great and terrible day of the LORD comes.
32 Then everyone who invokes the LORD by name
shall be saved:
for when the LORD gives the word
there shall yet be survivors on Mount Zion
and in Jerusalem a remnant[b]
whom the LORD will call.[c]

3 When that time comes, on that day
when I reverse the fortunes of Judah and Jerusalem,
2 I will gather all the nations together
and lead them down to the Valley of the LORD's Judgement
and there bring them to judgement
on behalf of Israel, my own possession;
for they have scattered my people
throughout their own countries,
have taken each their portion of my land
3 and shared out my people by lot,
bartered a boy for a whore,
and sold a girl for wine and drunk it down.

4 What are you to me, Tyre and Sidon and all the districts of Philistia?
Can you pay me back for anything I have done? Is there anything that
you can do to me? Swiftly and speedily I will make your deeds recoil upon
5 your own heads; for you have taken my silver and my gold and carried off
6 my costly treasures into your temples; you have sold the people of Judah
and Jerusalem to the Greeks, and removed them far beyond their own
7 frontiers. But I will rouse them to leave the places to which you have sold
8 them. I will make your deeds recoil upon your own heads: I will sell your

[a] *Prob. rdg.; Heb. adds* and my people shall not again be brought to shame (*cp. verse 27*).
[b] a remnant: *prob. rdg.; Heb.* among the remnant. [c] *Or* when the LORD calls.

sons and your daughters to the people of Judah, and they shall sell them to
the Sabaeans, a nation far away. The LORD has spoken.

Proclaim this amongst the nations:                                          9-12*a*
Declare a holy war, call your troops to arms!
    Beat your mattocks into swords
      and your pruning-hooks into spears.*b*
Rally to each other's help, all you nations round about.
Let the weakling say, 'I am strong',
    and let the coward show himself brave.*c*
Let all the nations hear the call to arms
    and come to the Valley of the LORD's Judgement;
let all the warriors come and draw near
    and muster there;
    for there I will take my seat
and judge all the nations round about.

Ply the sickle, for the harvest is ripe;                                          13
    come, tread the grapes,
for the press is full and the vats overflow;
    great is the wickedness of the nations.
The roar of multitudes, multitudes, in the Valley of Decision!                    14
    The day of the LORD is at hand
    in the Valley of Decision;
    sun and moon are darkened                                             15
and the stars forbear to shine.
    The LORD roars from Zion                                               16
and thunders from Jerusalem;
heaven and earth shudder,
but the LORD is a refuge for his people
    and the defence of Israel.

Thus you shall know that I am the LORD your God,                                  17
    dwelling in Zion my holy mountain;
Jerusalem shall be holy,
and no one without the right shall pass through her again.
    When that day comes,                                                   18
    the mountains shall run with fresh wine
and the hills flow with milk.
All the streams of Judah shall be full of water,
    and a fountain shall spring from the LORD's house
    and water the gorge of Shittim,
but Egypt shall become a desert                                                   19
and Edom a deserted waste,
    because of the violence done to Judah
    and the innocent blood shed in her land;

*a The order of lines in verses 9-12 has been re-arranged in several places.*    *b Beat . . .*
spears: *cp. Isa. 2. 4; Mic. 4. 3.*          *c and let . . . brave: prob. rdg.; Heb.* O LORD
bring down thy warriors.

20-21
> and I will spill their blood,
> the blood I have not yet spilt.
> Then there shall be people living in Judah for ever,
> in Jerusalem generation after generation;
> and the LORD will dwell in Zion.

# AMOS

1 THE WORDS OF AMOS, one of the sheep-farmers of Tekoa, which he received in visions concerning Israel during the reigns of Uzziah king of Judah and Jeroboam son of Jehoash king of Israel, 2 two years before the earthquake. He said,

> The LORD roars from Zion
> and thunders from Jerusalem;
> the shepherds' pastures are scorched
> and the top of Carmel*ᵃ* is dried up.

## The sins of Israel and her neighbours

3 These are the words of the LORD:

> For crime after crime of Damascus
>   I will grant them no reprieve,
> because they threshed Gilead under threshing-sledges spiked with iron.
4 > Therefore will I send fire upon the house of Hazael,
> fire that shall eat up Ben-hadad's palaces;
5 >   I will crush the great men of Damascus
> and wipe out those who live in the Vale of Aven
>   and the sceptred ruler of Beth-eden;
> the people of Aram shall be exiled to Kir.
> It is the word of the LORD.

6 These are the words of the LORD:

> For crime after crime of Gaza
>   I will grant them no reprieve,
> because they deported a whole band of exiles
>   and delivered them up to Edom.
7 > Therefore will I send fire upon the walls of Gaza,
> fire that shall consume its palaces.
8 > I will wipe out those who live in Ashdod
>   and the sceptred ruler of Ashkelon;
> I will turn my hand against Ekron,
>   and the remnant of the Philistines shall perish.
> It is the word of the Lord GOD.

---

*ᵃ* top of Carmel: *or* choicest farmland.

These are the words of the LORD:                                              9
   For crime after crime of Tyre
   I will grant them no reprieve,
   because, forgetting the ties of kinship,
they delivered a whole band of exiles to Edom.
   Therefore will I send fire upon the walls of Tyre,            10
   fire that shall consume its palaces.

These are the words of the LORD:                                             11
   For crime after crime of Edom
   I will grant them no reprieve,
   because, sword in hand, they hunted their kinsmen down,
   stifling their natural affections.
   Their anger raged unceasing,
   their fury stormed unchecked.
   Therefore will I send fire upon Teman,                       12
   fire that shall consume the palaces of Bozrah.

These are the words of the LORD:                                             13
   For crime after crime of the Ammonites
   I will grant them no reprieve,
   because in their greed for land
   they invaded the ploughlands of Gilead.
   Therefore will I set fire to the walls of Rabbah,            14
   fire that shall consume its palaces
   amid war-cries on the day of battle,
   with a whirlwind on the day of tempest;
   then their king shall be carried into exile,                 15
   he and his officers with him.
   It is the word of the LORD.

These are the words of the LORD:                                             **2**
   For crime after crime of Moab
   I will grant them no reprieve,
because they burnt the bones of the king of Edom to ash.*a*
   Therefore will I send fire upon Moab,                         2
   fire that shall consume the palaces in their towns;
   Moab shall perish in uproar,
   with war-cries and the sound of trumpets,
   and I will cut off the ruler from among them                 3
   and kill all their officers with him.
   It is the word of the LORD.

These are the words of the LORD:                                             4
   For crime after crime of Judah
   I will grant them no reprieve,
   because they have spurned the law of the LORD
   and have not observed his decrees,

*a* to ash: *or* for lime.

and have been led astray by the false gods
   that their fathers followed.
5      Therefore will I send fire upon Judah,
   fire that shall consume the palaces of Jerusalem.

6 These are the words of the LORD:

     For crime after crime of Israel
      I will grant them no reprieve,
     because they sell the innocent for silver
      and the destitute for a pair of shoes.
7     They grind the heads of the poor into the earth
      and thrust the humble out of their way.
     Father and son resort to the same girl,
      to the profanation of my holy name.
8     Men lie down beside every altar
      on garments seized in pledge,
     and in the house of their God[a] they drink liquor
      got by way of fines.

9     Yet it was I who destroyed the Amorites before them,
      though they were tall as cedars,
      though they were sturdy as oaks,
      I who destroyed their fruit above
      and their roots below.
10    It was I who brought you up from the land of Egypt,
     I who led you in the wilderness forty years,
      to take possession of the land of the Amorites;
11    I raised up prophets from your sons,
      Nazirites from your young men.
     Was it not so indeed, you men of Israel?
      says the LORD.
12    But you made the Nazirites drink wine,
    and said to the prophets, 'You shall not prophesy.'
13    Listen, I groan under the burden of you,
     as a wagon creaks under a full load.
14    Flight shall not save the swift,
     the strong man shall not rally his strength.
     The warrior shall not save himself,
15     the archer shall not stand his ground;
     the swift of foot shall not be saved,
     nor the horseman escape;
16    on that day the bravest of warriors
    shall be stripped of his arms and run away.
     This is the very word of the LORD.

[a] *Or* gods.

## Israel's sins and threatened punishment

LISTEN, ISRAELITES, to these words that the LORD addresses to you, **3**
to the whole nation which he brought up from Egypt:

> For you alone have I cared      2
> among all the nations of the world;
> therefore will I punish you
>     for all your iniquities.
> Do two men travel together      3
>     unless they have agreed?
> Does a lion roar in the forest      4
>     if he has no prey?
> Does a young lion growl in his den
>     if he has caught nothing?
> Does a bird fall into a trap on the ground      5
>     if the striker is not set for it?
> Does a trap spring from the ground
>     and take nothing?
> If a trumpet sounds the alarm,      6
>     are not the people scared?
> If disaster falls on a city,
>     has not the LORD been at work? [a]

For the Lord GOD does nothing      7
without giving to his servants the prophets knowledge of his plans.
> The lion has roared; who is not terrified?      8
The Lord GOD has spoken; who will not prophesy?

> Stand upon the palaces in Ashdod      9
>     and upon the palaces of Egypt,
>     and proclaim aloud:
> 'Assemble on the hills of Samaria,
> look at the tumult seething among her people
>     and at the oppression in her midst;
>     what do they care for honesty      10
> who hoard in their palaces the gains of crime and violence?'
> This is the very word of the LORD.

Therefore these are the words of the Lord GOD:      11

> An enemy shall surround[b] the land;
> your stronghold shall be thrown down
>     and your palaces sacked.

These are the words of the LORD:      12

> As a shepherd rescues out of the jaws of a lion
>     two shin bones or the tip of an ear,
> so shall the Israelites who live in Samaria be rescued
> like a corner of a couch or a chip from the leg of a bed. [c]

---

[a] If disaster . . . work?: *or* If there is evil in a city, will not the LORD act?    [b] shall
surround: *prob. rdg.; Heb.* and round.    [c] or a chip . . . bed: *prob. rdg.; Heb. obscure.*

13     Listen and testify against the family of Jacob.
This is the very word of the Lord God, the God of Hosts.

14     On the day when I deal with Israel
      for all their crimes,
        I will most surely deal with the altars of Bethel:
      the horns of the altar shall be hacked off
        and shall fall to the ground.

15     I will break down both winter-house and summer-house;
      houses of ivory shall perish,
      and great houses be demolished.
      This is the very word of the Lord.

**4**      Listen to this,
   you cows of Bashan who live on the hill of Samaria,
   you who oppress the poor and crush the destitute,
   who say to your lords, 'Bring us drink':

2    the Lord God has sworn by his holiness
   that your time is coming
      when men shall carry you away on their shields[a]
      and your children in fish-baskets.

3    You shall each be carried straight out
      through the breaches in the walls
      and pitched on a dunghill.[b]
      This is the very word of the Lord.

4    Come to Bethel—and rebel!
   Come to Gilgal—and rebel the more!
   Bring your sacrifices for the morning,
   your tithes within three days.

5    Burn your thank-offering without leaven;
   announce, proclaim your freewill offerings;
   for you love to do what is proper, you men of Israel!
      This is the very word of the Lord God.

6    It was I who kept teeth idle
      in all your cities,
   who brought famine on all your settlements;
      yet you did not come back to me.
      This is the very word of the Lord.

7    It was I who withheld the showers from you
   while there were still three months to harvest.
      I would send rain on one city
      and no rain on another;
      rain would fall on one field,
   and another would be parched for lack of it.

8    From this city and that, men would stagger to another
   for water to drink, but would not find enough;

---

[a] *Or* baskets.      [b] a dunghill: *prob. rdg.; Heb.* the Harmon.

yet you did not come back to me.
This is the very word of the LORD.

I blasted you with black blight and red;                    9
    I laid waste*ᵃ* your gardens and vineyards;
the locust devoured your fig-trees and your olives;
    yet you did not come back to me.
    This is the very word of the LORD.

I sent plague upon you like the plagues of Egypt;          10
    I killed with the sword
        your young men and your troops of horses.
    I made your camps stink in your nostrils;
        yet you did not come back to me.
        This is the very word of the LORD.

    I brought destruction amongst you                      11
as God destroyed Sodom and Gomorrah;
you were like a brand snatched from the fire;
    yet you did not come back to me.
    This is the very word of the LORD.

Therefore, Israel, this is what I will do to you;          12
and, because this is what I will do to you,
    Israel, prepare to meet your God.
It is he who forges the thunder and creates the wind,      13
    who showers abundant rain on the earth,*ᵇ*
who darkens the dawn with thick clouds
    and marches over the heights of the earth—
    his name is the LORD the God of Hosts.

Listen to these words; I raise a dirge over you, O Israel: **5**
    She has fallen to rise no more,                          2
        the virgin Israel,
    prostrate on her own soil, with no one to lift her up.

These are the words of the Lord GOD:                        3
        The city that marched out to war a thousand strong
            shall have but a hundred left,
            that which marched out a hundred strong
        shall have but ten men of Israel left.

These are the words of the LORD to the people of Israel:    4
    Resort to me, if you would live, not to Bethel;         5
go not to Gilgal, nor pass on to Beersheba;
    for Gilgal shall be swept away
    and Bethel brought to nothing.
    If you would live, resort to the LORD,                  6
    or he will break out against Joseph like fire,
    fire which will devour Israel with no one to quench it;

---

*ᵃ* I laid waste: *prob. rdg.; Heb.* to increase.        *ᵇ* who showers . . . earth: *prob. rdg.;*
*Heb.* who tells his thoughts to mankind.

8 [a]
> he who made the Pleiades and Orion,
> who turned darkness into morning
> and darkened day into night,
>> who summoned the waters of the sea
>> and poured them over the earth,

9
> who makes Taurus rise after Capella
> and Taurus set hard on the rising of the Vintager [b]—
>> he who does this, his name is the LORD. [c]

7
> You that turn justice upside down [d]
> and bring righteousness to the ground,

10
> you that hate a man who brings the wrongdoer to court
> and loathe him who speaks the whole truth:

11
> for all this, because you levy taxes on the poor
> and extort a tribute of grain from them,
> though you have built houses of hewn stone,
>> you shall not live in them,
> though you have planted pleasant vineyards,
>> you shall not drink wine from them.

12
> For I know how many your crimes are
>> and how countless your sins,
> you who persecute the guiltless, hold men to ransom
> and thrust the destitute out of court.

13
> At that time, therefore, a prudent man will stay quiet,
> for it will be an evil time.

14
> Seek good and not evil,
>> that you may live,
> that the LORD the God of Hosts may be firmly on your side,
>> as you say he is.

15
> Hate evil and love good;
>> enthrone justice in the courts;
> it may be that the LORD the God of Hosts
> will be gracious to the survivors of Joseph.

16
Therefore these are the words of the LORD the God of Hosts:

> There shall be wailing in every street,
> and in all open places cries of woe.
> The farmer shall be called to mourning,
> and those skilled in the dirge to [e] wailing;

17
> there shall be lamentation in every vineyard;
> for I will pass through the midst of you,
>> says the LORD.

18
> Fools who long for the day of the LORD,
> what will the day of the LORD mean to you?
> It will be darkness, not light.

---

[a] *Verse 7 transposed to follow verse 9.*     [b] who makes . . . Vintager: *prob. rdg.; Heb.* who smiles destruction on the strong, and destruction comes on the fortified city.     [c] his . . . LORD: *transposed from end of verse 8.*     [d] upside down: *prob. rdg.; Heb.* poison.     [e] *Prob. rdg.; Heb.* places *to before* those skilled.

It will be as when a man runs from a lion,                    19
   and a bear meets him,
or turns into a house and leans his hand on the wall,
   and a snake bites him.
The day of the LORD is indeed darkness, not light,           20
   a day of gloom with no dawn.

I hate, I spurn your pilgrim-feasts;                          21
   I will not delight in your sacred ceremonies.
When you present your sacrifices and offerings               22
   I will not accept them,
nor look on the buffaloes of your shared-offerings.
Spare me the sound of your songs;                            23
   I cannot endure the music of your lutes.
Let justice roll on like a river                             24
and righteousness like an ever-flowing stream.
Did you bring me sacrifices and gifts,                      25
you people of Israel, those forty years in the wilderness?
   No! but now you shall take up                  26
   the shrine of your idol king
   and the pedestals of your images,*a*
   which you have made for yourselves,
and I will drive you into exile beyond Damascus.            27
So says the LORD; the God of Hosts is his name.

Shame on you who live at ease in Zion,                       **6**
and you, untroubled on the hill of Samaria,
   men of mark in the first of nations,
you to whom the people of Israel resort!
Go, look at Calneh,                                          2
travel on to Hamath the great,
   then go down to Gath of the Philistines—
are you better than these kingdoms?
Or is your*b* territory greater than theirs*c*?
You who thrust the evil day aside                            3
and make haste to establish violence.*d*
You who loll on beds inlaid with ivory                       4
   and sprawl over your couches,
feasting on lambs from the flock
   and fatted calves,
   you who pluck the strings of the lute          5
and invent musical instruments like David,
   you who drink wine by the bowlful            6
   and lard yourselves with the richest of oils,
but are not grieved at the ruin of Joseph—

---

*a Prob. rdg.; Heb. adds* the star of your gods.      *b Prob. rdg.; Heb.* their.      *c Prob. rdg.; Heb.* yours.      *d* You . . . violence: *or* You who invoke the day of wrong-doing and bring near the sabbath of violence.

7        now, therefore,
        you shall head the column of exiles;
        that will be the end of sprawling and revelry.

8   The Lord GOD has sworn by himself:
        I loathe the arrogance of Jacob,
          I loathe his palaces;
        city and all in it I will abandon to their fate.

9        If ten men are left in one house,
          they shall die,
10      and a man's uncle and the embalmer shall take him up
        to carry his body out of the house for burial,
    and they shall call to someone in a corner of the house,
    'Any more there?', and he shall answer, 'No.'
        Then he will add, 'Hush!'—
    for the name of the LORD must not be mentioned.
11      For the LORD will command,
    and at the shock the great house will be rubble
        and the cottage matchwood.

12      Can horses gallop over rocks?
        Can the sea be ploughed with oxen?
        Yet you have turned into venom the process of law
        and justice itself into poison,
13       you who are jubilant over a nothing*a* and boast,
    'Have we not won power *a* by our own strength?'
14     O Israel, I am raising a nation against you,
          and they shall harry your land
        from Lebo-hamath to the gorge of the Arabah.
    This is the very word of the LORD the God of Hosts.

## *Visions foretelling doom upon Israel*

7  THIS WAS WHAT THE LORD GOD SHOWED ME: a swarm of locusts
    hatched out when the late corn, which comes after the king's early
2  crop, was beginning to sprout. As they were devouring the last of the
herbage in the land, I said, 'O Lord GOD, forgive; what will Jacob be after
3  this? He is so small.' Then the LORD relented and said, 'This shall not
happen.'
4    This was what the Lord GOD showed me: the Lord GOD was summoning a flame of fire *b* to devour the great abyss, and to devour all creation.
5  I said, 'O Lord GOD, I pray thee, cease; what will Jacob be after this? He
6  is so small.' The LORD relented and said, 'This also shall not happen.'

*a* a nothing *and* power: *Heb.* Lo-debar *and* Karnaim, *making a word-play on the two place-names.*    *b* a flame of fire: *prob. rdg.; Heb.* to contend with fire.

This was what the LORD showed me: there was a man standing by a 7
wall *a* with a plumb-line in his hand. The LORD said to me, 'What do you 8
see, Amos?' 'A plumb-line', I answered, and the Lord said, 'I am setting
a plumb-line to the heart of my people Israel; never again will I pass them
by. The hill-shrines of Isaac shall be desolated and the sanctuaries of 9
Israel laid waste; I will rise, sword in hand, against the house of Jeroboam.'

Amaziah, the priest of Bethel, reported to Jeroboam king of Israel: 10
'Amos is conspiring against you in Israel; the country cannot tolerate what
he is saying. He says, "Jeroboam shall die by the sword, and Israel shall 11
be deported far from their native land."' To Amos himself Amaziah said, 12
'Be off, you seer! Off with you to Judah! You can earn your living and do
your prophesying there. But never prophesy again at Bethel, for this is 13
the king's sanctuary, a royal palace.' 'I am *b* no prophet,' Amos replied to 14
Amaziah, 'nor am I a prophet's son; I am *b* a herdsman and a dresser of
sycomore-figs. But the LORD took me as I followed the flock and said to 15
me, "Go and prophesy to my people Israel." So now listen to the word of 16
the LORD. You tell me I am not to prophesy against Israel or go drivelling
on against the people of Isaac. Now these are the words of the LORD: Your 17
wife shall become a city strumpet *c* and your sons and daughters shall fall
by the sword. Your land shall be divided up with a measuring-line, you
yourself shall die in a heathen country, and Israel shall be deported far
from their native land and go into exile.'

This was what the Lord GOD showed me: there was a basket of summer 8
fruit, and he said, 'What are you looking at, Amos?' I answered, 'A basket 2
of ripe summer *d* fruit.' Then the LORD said to me, 'The time is ripe *d* for
my people Israel. Never again will I pass them by. In that day, says the 3
Lord GOD, the singing women in the palace shall howl, "So many dead men,
flung out everywhere! Silence!"'

Listen to this, you who grind the destitute and plunder *e* the humble, 4
you who say, 'When will the new moon be over so that we may sell corn? 5
When will the sabbath be past so that we may open our wheat again, giving
short measure in the bushel and taking overweight in the silver, tilting the
scales fraudulently, and selling the dust of the wheat; that we may buy the 6
poor for silver and the destitute for a pair of shoes?' The LORD has sworn 7
by the pride of Jacob: I will never forget any of their doings.

> Shall not the earth shake for this? 8
> Shall not all who live on it grieve?
> All earth shall surge and seethe like the Nile
> and subside like the river of Egypt.

> On that day, says the Lord GOD, 9
> I will make the sun go down at noon
> and darken the earth in broad daylight.
> I will turn your pilgrim-feasts into mourning 10
> and all your songs into lamentation.

---

*a* *Prob. rdg.; Heb. adds* of a plumb-line.     *b* *Or* was.     *c* become . . . strumpet: *or*
be carried off as a prostitute in a raid.     *d* ripe summer *and* ripe: *a play on the Heb.*
qais (summer) *and* qes (end).     *e* and plunder: *prob. rdg.; Heb.* to destroy.

I will make you all put sackcloth round your waists
and have all your heads shaved.
I will make it like mourning for an only son
and the end of it a bitter day.

11    The time is coming, says the Lord GOD,
when I will send famine on the land,
not hunger for bread or thirst for water,
but for hearing the word of the LORD.

12    Men shall stagger from north to south,[a]
they shall range from east to west,
seeking the word of the LORD,
but they shall not find it.

13    On that day fair maidens and young men
shall faint from thirst;

14    all who take their oath by Ashimah, goddess of Samaria,
all who swear, 'By the life of your god, O Dan',
and, 'By the sacred way to Beersheba',
shall fall to rise no more.

9    I saw the LORD standing by the altar, and he said:

Strike the capitals so that the whole porch is shaken;
I will smash them all into pieces[b]
and I will kill them to the last man[c] with the sword.
No fugitive shall escape,
no survivor find safety;

2    if they dig down to Sheol,
thence shall my hand take them;
if they climb up to heaven,
thence will I bring them down.

3    If they hide on the top of Carmel,
there will I search out and take them;
if they conceal themselves from me in the depths of the sea,
there will I bid the sea-serpent bite them.

4    If they are herded into captivity by their enemies,
there will I bid the sword slay them,
and I will fix my eye on them
for evil and not for good.

5    The Lord the GOD of Hosts,
at whose touch the earth heaves,
and all who dwell on it wither,[d]
it surges like the Nile,
and subsides like the river of Egypt,

6    who builds his stair up to the heavens
and arches his ceiling over the earth,

---

[a] south: *prob. rdg.; Heb.* west.   [b] I will . . . pieces: *prob. rdg.; Heb.* I will hack them on the heads of them all.   [c] them to the last man: *or* their children.   [d] *Or* mourn.

who summons the waters of the sea
and pours them over the land—
his name is the LORD.

Are not you Israelites like Cushites to me?                    7
says the LORD.
Did I not bring Israel up from Egypt,
the Philistines from Caphtor, the Aramaeans from Kir?
Behold, I, the Lord GOD,                                       8
have my eyes on this sinful kingdom,
and I will wipe it off the face of the earth.

## A remnant spared and restored

Yet I will not wipe out the family of Jacob root and branch,
says the LORD.
No; I will give my orders,                                     9
I will shake Israel to and fro through all the nations
as a sieve is shaken to and fro
and not one pebble falls to the ground.
They shall die by the sword, all the sinners of my people,    10
who say, 'Thou wilt not let disaster come near us
or overtake us.'
On that day I will restore                                     11
David's fallen house;
I will repair its gaping walls and restore its ruins;
I will rebuild it as it was long ago,
that they may possess what is left of Edom                     12
and all the nations who were once named mine.
This is the very word of the LORD, who will do this.

A time is coming, says the LORD,                              13
when the ploughman shall follow hard on the vintager, *a*
and he who treads the grapes after him who sows the seed.
The mountains shall run with fresh wine,
and every hill shall wave with corn.
I will restore the fortunes of my people Israel;             14
they shall rebuild deserted cities and live in them,
they shall plant vineyards and drink their wine,
make gardens and eat the fruit.
Once more I will plant them on their own soil,               15
and they shall never again be uprooted
from the soil I have given them.
It is the word of the LORD your God.

*a Or* reaper.

# OBADIAH

### *Edom's pride and downfall*

1[a] The vision of Obadiah: what the Lord GOD has said concerning Edom.

> When a herald was sent out among the nations, crying,
> 'Rouse yourselves;
> let us rouse ourselves to battle against Edom',
> I heard this message from the LORD:

2
> Look, I make you the least of all nations,
> an object of contempt.

3
> Your proud, insolent heart has led you astray;
> you who haunt the crannies among the rocks,
> making your home on the heights,
> you say to yourself, 'Who can bring me to the ground?'

4
> Though you soar as high as a vulture
> and your nest is set among the stars,
> thence I will bring you down.
> This is the very word of the LORD.

5[b]
> If thieves or robbers come to you by night,
> though your loss be heavy,
> they will steal only what they want;
> if vintagers come to you,
> will they not leave gleanings?

6
> But see how Esau's treasure is ransacked,
> his secret wealth hunted out!

7
> All your former allies march you to the frontier,
> your confederates mislead you and bring you low,
> your own kith and kin lay a snare for your feet,
> a snare that works blindly, without wisdom.

8
> And on that very day
> I will destroy all the sages of Edom
> and leave no wisdom on the mount of Esau.
> This is the very word of the LORD.

9
> Then shall your warriors, O Teman, be so enfeebled,
> that every man shall be cut down on the mount of Esau.

10
> For the murderous violence done to your brother Jacob
> you shall be covered with shame and cut off for ever.

---

[a] *Verses 1-4: cp. Jer. 49. 14-16.*     [b] *Verses 5 and 6: cp. Jer. 49. 9, 10.*

On the day when you stood aloof, 11
on the day when strangers carried off his wealth,
when foreigners trooped in by his gates
and parcelled out Jerusalem by lot,
you yourselves were of one mind with them.
Do not gloat over your brother on the day of his misfortune, 12
nor rejoice over Judah on his day of ruin;
do not boast on the day of distress,
nor enter my people's gates on the day of his downfall. 13
Do not gloat over his fall on the day of his downfall
nor seize his treasure on the day of his downfall.
Do not wait at the cross-roads to cut off his fugitives 14
nor betray the survivors on the day of distress.

For soon the day of the LORD will come on all the nations: 15
you shall be treated as you have treated others,
and your deeds will recoil on your own head.
The draught that you have drunk on my holy mountain 16
all the nations shall drink continually;
they shall drink and gulp down
and shall be as though they had never been;
but on Mount Zion there shall be those that escape, 17
and it shall be holy,
and Jacob shall dispossess those that dispossessed them.
Then shall the house of Jacob be fire, 18
the house of Joseph flame,
and the house of Esau shall be chaff;
they shall blaze through it and consume it,
and the house of Esau shall have no survivor.
The LORD has spoken.
Then they shall possess the Negeb, the mount of Esau, 19
and the Shephelah of the Philistines;
they shall possess the country-side of Ephraim and Samaria,
and Benjamin shall possess Gilead.
Exiles of Israel*a* shall possess*b* Canaan as far as Zarephath, 20
exiles of Jerusalem*c* shall possess the cities of the Negeb.
Those who find safety on Mount Zion shall go up 21
to hold sway over the mount of Esau,
and dominion shall belong to the LORD.

*a* *Prob. rdg.; Heb. adds* this army.     *b* shall possess: *prob. rdg.; Heb.* which.
*c* *Prob. rdg.; Heb. adds* who are in Sepharad.

# JONAH

## *Jonah's mission to Nineveh*

1
2
3
THE WORD OF THE LORD CAME TO JONAH son of Amittai: 'Go to the great city of Nineveh, go now and denounce it, for its wickedness stares me in the face.' But Jonah set out for Tarshish to escape from the LORD. He went down to Joppa, where he found a ship bound for Tarshish. He paid his fare and went on board, meaning
4 to travel by it to Tarshish out of reach of the LORD. But the LORD let loose a hurricane, and the sea ran so high in the storm that the ship threatened
5 to break up. The sailors were afraid, and each cried out to his god for help. Then they threw things overboard to lighten the ship. Jonah had gone
6 down into a corner of the ship and was lying sound asleep when the captain came upon him. 'What, sound asleep?' he said. 'Get up, and call on your god; perhaps he will spare us a thought and we shall not perish.'
7 At last the sailors said to each other, 'Come and let us cast lots to find out who is to blame for this bad luck.' So they cast lots, and the lot fell on
8 Jonah. 'Now then,' they said to him, 'what is your business? Where do
9 you come from? What is your country? Of what nation are you?' 'I am a Hebrew,' he answered, 'and I worship the LORD the God of heaven, who
10 made both sea and land.' At this the sailors were even more afraid. 'What can you have done wrong?' they asked. They already knew that he was
11 trying to escape from the LORD, for he had told them so. 'What shall we do with you', they asked, 'to make the sea go down?' For the storm grew
12 worse and worse. 'Take me and throw me overboard,' he said, 'and the sea will go down. I know it is my fault that this great storm has struck
13 you.' The crew rowed hard to put back to land but in vain, for the sea ran
14 higher and higher. At last they called on the LORD and said, 'O LORD, do not let us perish at the price of this man's life; do not charge us with the
15 death of an innocent man. All this, O LORD, is thy set purpose.' Then they took Jonah and threw him overboard, and the sea stopped raging.
16 So the crew were filled with the fear of the LORD and offered sacrifice
17 and made vows to him. But the LORD ordained that a great fish should swallow Jonah, and for three days and three nights he remained in its belly.

2   Jonah prayed to the LORD his God from the belly of the fish:

2
> I called to the LORD in my distress,
>     and he answered me;
> out of the belly of Sheol I cried for help,
>     and thou hast heard my cry.

3
> Thou didst cast me into the depths, far out at sea,
>     and the flood closed round me;
> all thy waves, all thy billows, passed over me.

I thought I was banished from thy sight                               4
and should never see thy holy temple again.
  The water about me rose up to my neck;                             5
    the ocean was closing over me.
  Weeds twined about my head
    in the troughs of the mountains;                                6
    I was sinking into a world
    whose bars would hold me fast for ever.
But thou didst bring me up alive from the pit, O LORD my God.
As my senses failed me I remembered the LORD,                       7
and my prayer reached thee in thy holy temple.
Men who worship false gods may abandon their loyalty,               8
but I will offer thee sacrifice with words of praise;               9
I will pay my vows; victory is the LORD's.

Then the LORD spoke to the fish and it spewed Jonah out on to the dry land.  10

The word of the LORD came to Jonah a second time: 'Go to the great **3** 1 2
city of Nineveh, go now and denounce it in the words I give you.' Jonah 3-4
obeyed at once and went to Nineveh. He began by going a day's journey
into the city, a vast city, three days' journey across, and then proclaimed:
'In forty days Nineveh shall be overthrown!' The people of Nineveh 5
believed God's word. They ordered a public fast and put on sackcloth,
high and low alike. When the news reached the king of Nineveh he rose 6
from his throne, stripped off his robes of state, put on sackcloth and sat
in ashes. Then he had a proclamation made in Nineveh: 'This is a decree 7
of the king and his nobles. No man or beast, herd or flock, is to taste food,
to graze or to drink water. They are to clothe themselves in sackcloth and 8
call on God with all their might. Let every man abandon his wicked ways
and his habitual violence. It may be that God will repent and turn away 9
from his anger: and so we shall not perish.' God saw what they did, and 10
how they abandoned their wicked ways, and he repented and did not bring
upon them the disaster he had threatened.

Jonah was greatly displeased and angry, and he prayed to the LORD: **4** 1 2
'This, O LORD, is what I feared when I was in my own country, and to
forestall it I tried to escape to Tarshish; I knew that thou art "a god
gracious and compassionate, long-suffering and ever constant, and always
willing to repent of the disaster".[a] And now, LORD, take my life: I should 3
be better dead than alive.' 'Are you so angry?' said the LORD. Jonah went 4 5
out and sat down on the east of the city. There he made himself a shelter
and sat in its shade, waiting to see what would happen in the city. Then the 6
LORD God ordained that a climbing gourd[b] should grow up over his head
to throw its shade over him and relieve his distress, and Jonah was grateful
for the gourd. But at dawn the next day God ordained that a worm should 7
attack the gourd, and it withered; and at sunrise God ordained that a scorch- 8
ing wind should blow up from the east. The sun beat down on Jonah's head
till he grew faint. Then he prayed for death and said, 'I should be better
dead than alive.' At this God said to Jonah, 'Are you so angry over the 9

---

[a] *a god . . . disaster: cp. Exod. 34. 6.*          [b] *a climbing gourd: or a castor-oil plant.*

10 gourd?' 'Yes,' he answered, 'mortally angry.' The LORD said, 'You are sorry
for the gourd, though you did not have the trouble of growing it, a plant
11 which came up in a night and withered in a night. And should not I be sorry
for the great city of Nineveh, with its hundred and twenty thousand who
cannot tell their right hand from their left, and cattle without number?'

# MICAH

1   THIS IS THE WORD OF THE LORD which came to Micah
of Moresheth during the reigns of Jotham, Ahaz, and Hezekiah, kings
of Judah; which he received in visions concerning Samaria and
Jerusalem.

## The rulers of Israel and Judah denounced

2     Listen, you peoples, all together;
    attend, O earth and all who are in it,
that the Lord GOD, the Lord from his holy temple,
    may bear witness against you.
3     For look, the LORD is leaving his dwelling-place;
    down he comes and walks on the heights of the earth.
4     Beneath him mountains dissolve
      like wax before the fire,
      valleys are torn open,
    as when torrents pour down the hill-side—
5   and all for the crime of Jacob and the sin of Israel.
What is the crime of Jacob? Is it not Samaria?
What is the hill-shrine of Judah? Is it not Jerusalem?
6     So I will make Samaria
a heap of ruins in open country,
    a place for planting vines;
I will pour her stones down into the valley
and lay her foundations bare.
7     All her carved figures shall be shattered,
her images burnt one and all;
I will make a waste heap of all her idols.
    She amassed them out of fees for harlotry,
    and a harlot's fee shall they become once more.
8     Therefore I must howl and wail,
    go naked and distraught;
I must howl like a wolf, mourn like a desert-owl.
9     Her wound cannot be healed;
    for the stroke has bitten deep into Judah,
    it has fallen on the gate of my people,
    upon Jerusalem itself.

Will you not weep your fill, weep your eyes out in Gath?          10
In Beth-aphrah sprinkle yourselves with dust;
    take the road, you that dwell in Shaphir;          11
have not the people of Zaanan gone out in shame from their city?
    Beth-ezel is a place of lamentation,
    she can lend you support no longer.
    The people of Maroth are greatly alarmed,          12
    for disaster has come down from the LORD
        to the very gate of Jerusalem.
Harness the steeds to the chariot, O people of Lachish,          13
for you first led the daughter of Zion into sin;
    to you must the crimes of Israel be traced.
Let Moresheth-gath be given her dismissal.          14
    Beth-achzib has*a* disappointed*b* the kings of Israel.
And you too, O people of Mareshah,          15
    I will send others to take your place;
and the glory of Israel shall hide in the cave of Adullam.
    Shave the hair from your head in mourning          16
    for the children of your delight;
    make yourself bald as a vulture,
    for they have left you and gone into exile.

Shame on those who lie in bed planning evil and wicked deeds          **2**
    and rise at daybreak to do them,
    knowing that they have the power!
They covet land and take it by force;          2
    if they want a house they seize it;
    they rob a man of his home
    and steal every man's inheritance.
Therefore these are the words of the LORD:          3

    Listen, for this whole brood I am planning disaster,
    whose yoke you cannot shake from your necks
and walk upright; it shall be your hour of disaster.

    On that day          4
    they shall take up a poem about you
    and raise a lament thrice told,
    saying, 'We are utterly despoiled:
the land of the LORD's*c* people changes hands.
    How shall a man have power *d*
to restore our fields, now parcelled out*e*?'
Therefore there shall be no one to assign to you          5
    any portion by lot in the LORD's assembly.

---

*a* Beth-achzib has: *prob. rdg.; Heb.* The houses of Achzib have.    *b* *Heb.* achzab.
*c* the LORD's: *prob. rdg.; Heb.* my.    *d* have power: *prob. rdg.; Heb.* remove from me.
*e* now parcelled out: *prob. rdg.; Heb.* he will parcel out.

6      How they rant! They may say, 'Do not rant';
     but this ranting is all their own,
     these insults are their *a* own invention.

7      Can one ask, O house of Jacob,
     'Is the LORD's patience truly at an end?
       Are these his deeds?
     Does not good come of the LORD's words?
       He is the upright man's best friend.'

8      But you are no *b* people for me,
     rising up as my enemy to my *c* face,
     to strip the cloak from him that was safe *d*
     and take away the confidence of returning warriors,

9      to drive the women of my people from their pleasant homes
     and rob the children of my glory for ever.

10      Up and be gone; this is no resting-place for you,
     you that to defile yourselves would commit any mischief,
       mischief however cruel.

11 If anyone had gone about in a spirit of falsehood and lies, saying, 'I will rant to you of wine and strong drink', his ranting would be what this people like.

12      I will assemble you, the whole house of Jacob;
      I will gather together those that are left in Israel.
     I will herd them like sheep in a fold,
     like a grazing flock which stampedes at the sight of a man.

13       So their leader breaks out before them,
     and they all break through the gate and escape,
      and their king goes before them,
       and the LORD leads the way.

**3** And I said:

     Listen, you leaders of Jacob, rulers of Israel,
     should you not know what is right?

2       You hate good and love evil,
     you flay men alive and tear the very flesh from their bones;

3       you devour the flesh of my people,
      strip off their skin,
       splinter their bones;
     you shred them like flesh into a pot,
      like meat into a cauldron.

4      Then they will call to the LORD, and he will give them no answer;
     when that time comes he will hide his face from them,
      so wicked are their deeds.

5    These are the words of the LORD concerning the prophets who lead

---

*a Prob. rdg.; Heb.* his.    *b* But . . . no: *prob. rdg.; Heb.* But yesterday.    *c* my: *prob. rdg.; Heb. om.*      *d* the cloak . . . safe: *prob. rdg.; Heb.* mantle, cloak.

my people astray, who promise prosperity in return for a morsel of food,
who proclaim a holy war against them if they put nothing into their
mouths:

> Therefore night shall bring you no vision,　　　　　　6
> 　darkness no divination;
> 　the sun shall go down on the prophets,
> 　the day itself shall be black above them.
> Seers and diviners alike shall blush for shame;　　　　7
> 　they shall all put their hands over their mouths,
> 　because there is no answer from God.

> But I am full of strength,*a* of justice and power,　　　8
> 　to denounce his crime to Jacob
> 　　and his sin to Israel.
> Listen to this, leaders of Jacob,　　　　　　　　9
> 　rulers of Israel,
> you who make justice hateful
> and wrest it from its straight course,
> building Zion in bloodshed　　　　　　　　　　10
> 　and Jerusalem in iniquity.
> Her rulers sell justice,　　　　　　　　　　　11
> her priests give direction in return for a bribe,
> her prophets take money for their divination,
> 　and yet men rely on the LORD.
> 'Is not the LORD among us?' they say;
> 'then no disaster can befall us.'
> 　Therefore, on your account　　　　　　　　12
> Zion shall become a ploughed field,
> Jerusalem a heap of ruins,
> and the temple hill rough heath.

## A remnant restored in an age of peace

> In days to come　　　　　　　　　　　　4 1*b*
> the mountain of the LORD's house
> shall be set over all other mountains,
> lifted high above the hills.
> Peoples shall come streaming to it,
> and many nations shall come and say,　　　　　　2
> 'Come, let us climb up on to the mountain of the LORD,
> 　to the house of the God of Jacob,
> 　that he may teach us his ways
> 　and we may walk in his paths.'
> For instruction issues from Zion,
> 　and out of Jerusalem comes the word of the LORD;

---

*a* *Prob. rdg.; Heb. adds* the spirit of the LORD.　　　　*b* *Verses 1–3: cp. Isa. 2. 2–4.*

3    he will be judge between many peoples
and arbiter among mighty nations afar.
    They shall beat their swords into mattocks
        and their spears into pruning-knives;
nation shall not lift sword against nation
    nor ever again be trained for war,
4        and each man shall dwell under his own vine,
        under his own fig-tree, undisturbed.
    For the LORD of Hosts himself has spoken.

5    All peoples may walk, each in the name of his god,
but we will walk in the name of the LORD our God
        for ever and ever.

6        On that day, says the LORD,
        I will gather those who are lost;
I will assemble the exiles and I will strengthen the weaklings.
7        I will preserve the lost as a remnant
        and turn the derelict into a mighty nation.
    The LORD shall be their king on Mount Zion
        now and for ever.
8    And you, rocky bastion, hill of Zion's daughter,
        the promises to you shall be fulfilled;
        and your former sovereignty shall come again,
        the dominion of the daughter of Jerusalem.

9        Why are you now filled with alarm?
            Have you no king?
            Have you no counsellor left,
        that you are seized with writhing like a woman in labour?
10    Lie writhing on the ground like a woman in childbirth,
            O daughter of Zion;
        for now you must leave the city
            and camp in the open country;
            and so you will come to Babylon.
            There you shall be saved,
        there the LORD will deliver you from your enemies.
11    But now many nations are massed against you;
            they say, 'Let her suffer outrage,
                let us gloat over Zion.'
12        But they do not know the LORD's thoughts
            nor understand his purpose;
        for he has gathered them like sheaves to the threshing-floor.
13        Start your threshing, daughter of Zion;
        for I will make your horns of iron,
        your hooves will I make of bronze,
        and you shall crush many peoples.
        You shall devote their ill-gotten gain to the LORD,
            their wealth to the Lord of all the earth.

Get you behind your walls, you people of a walled city; 5
 the siege is pressed home against you:
Israel's ruler shall be struck on the cheek with a rod.
 But you, Bethlehem in Ephrathah, 2
 small as you are to be among Judah's clans,
out of you shall come forth a governor for Israel,
 one whose roots are far back in the past, in days gone by.
 Therefore only so long as a woman is in labour 3
  shall he give up Israel;
  and then those that survive of his race
  shall rejoin their brethren.
 He shall appear and be their shepherd 4
  in the strength of the LORD,
 in the majesty of the name of the LORD his God.
And they shall continue, for now his greatness shall reach
  to the ends of the earth;
 and he shall be a man of peace. 5

 When the Assyrian comes into our land,
  when he tramples our castles,
we will raise against him seven men or eight
  to be shepherds and princes.
 They shall shepherd Assyria with the sword 6
 and the land of Nimrod with bare blades;
they shall deliver us from the Assyrians
 when they come into our land,
  when they trample our frontiers.

All that are left of Jacob, surrounded by many peoples, 7
  shall be like dew from the LORD,
  like copious showers on the grass,
  which do not wait for man's command
  or linger for any man's bidding.
All that are left of Jacob among the nations, 8
  surrounded by many peoples,
 shall be like a lion among the beasts of the forest,
  like a young lion loose in a flock of sheep;
 as he prowls he will trample and tear them,
  with no rescuer in sight.
Your hand shall be raised high over your foes, 9
and all who hate you shall be destroyed.

On that day, says the LORD, 10
I will destroy all your horses among you
  and make away with your chariots.
I will destroy the cities of your land 11
  and raze your fortresses.
I will destroy all your sorcerers, 12
  and there shall be no more soothsayers among you.

13    I will destroy your images and all the sacred pillars in your land;
      you shall no longer bow in reverence before things your own hands made.

14    I will pull down the sacred poles in your land,
          and demolish your blood-spattered altars.

15    In anger and fury will I take vengeance
          on all nations who disobey me.

## *Israel denounced for her people's sins*

6  Hear now what the LORD is saying:

       Up, state your case to the mountains;
       let the hills hear your plea.

2      Hear the LORD's case, you mountains,
           you everlasting pillars that bear up the earth;
       for the LORD has a case against his people,
           and will argue it with Israel.

3      O my people, what have I done to you?
       Tell me how I have wearied you; answer me this.

4          I brought you up from Egypt,
           I ransomed you from the land of slavery,
       I sent Moses and Aaron and Miriam to lead you.

5          Remember, my people,
       what Balak king of Moab schemed against you,
   and how Balaam son of Beor answered him;
       consider the journey*a* from Shittim to Gilgal,
       in order that you may know the triumph of the LORD.

6      What shall I bring when I approach the LORD?
       How shall I stoop before God on high?
   Am I to approach him with whole-offerings or yearling calves?

7      Will the LORD accept thousands of rams
           or ten thousand rivers of oil?
       Shall I offer my eldest son for my own wrongdoing,
           my children for my own sin?

8  God*b* has told you what is good;
       and what is it that the LORD asks of you?
       Only to act justly, to love loyalty,
       to walk wisely before your God.

9      Hark, the LORD, the fear of whose name brings success,
           the LORD calls to the city.

10     Listen, O tribe of Judah and citizens in assembly,*c*
       can I overlook*d* the infamous false measure,*e*
           the accursed short bushel?

---

*a* consider the journey: *prob. rdg.; Heb. om.*        *b* God: *prob. rdg.; Heb. obscure.*
*c* citizens in assembly: *prob. rdg.; Heb. unintelligible.*        *d* can I overlook: *prob.*
*rdg.; Heb. obscure.*        *e* *Prob. rdg.; Heb. adds* infamous treasures.

Can I connive at false scales or a bag of light weights?                    11
Your rich men are steeped in violence,                                     12
    your townsmen are all liars,
and their tongues frame deceit.
But now I will inflict a signal punishment on you                          13
    to lay you waste for your sins:
you shall eat but not be satisfied,                                        14
    your food shall lie heavy on your stomach;
    you shall come to labour but not bring forth,
    and even if you bear a child
    I will give it to the sword;
you shall sow but not reap,                                                15
you shall press the olives but not use the oil,
    you shall tread the grapes but not drink the wine.
        You have kept the precepts of Omri;                               16
        what the house of Ahab did, you have done;
        you have followed all their ways.
So I will lay you utterly waste;
    the nations shall jeer at your citizens,
    and their insults you shall bear.

## Disappointment turned to hope

Alas! I am now like the last gatherings of summer fruit,                    7
    the last gleanings of the vintage,
        when there are no grapes left to eat,
    none of those early figs that I love.
Loyal men have vanished from the earth,                                     2
    there is not one upright man.
All lie in wait to do murder,
each man drives his own kinsman like a hunter into the net.
They are bent eagerly on wrongdoing,                                        3
    the officer who presents the requests,*a*
the judge who gives judgement *b* for reward,
and the nobleman who harps on his desires.
Thus their goodness is twisted *c* like rank weeds                          4
and their honesty like briars.*d*
As soon as thine eye sees, thy punishment falls;
    at that moment bewilderment seizes them.
Trust no neighbour, put no confidence in your closest friend;              5
    seal your lips even from the wife of your bosom.
For son maligns father,                                                     6
    daughter rebels against mother,
        daughter-in-law against mother-in-law,
        and a man's enemies are his own household.

*a* the requests: *prob. rdg.; Heb. om.*        *b* who gives judgement: *prob. rdg.; Heb. om.*
*c* twisted: *prob. rdg.; Heb. obscure.*          *d* their honesty like briars: *prob. rdg.;*
*Heb. obscure.*

7 But I will look for the LORD,
I will wait for God my saviour; my God will hear me.
8 O my enemies, do not exult over me;
I have fallen, but shall rise again;
though I dwell in darkness, the LORD is my light.
9 I will bear the anger of the LORD, for I have sinned against him,
until he takes up my cause and gives judgement for me,
until he brings me out into light, and I see his justice.
10 Then may my enemies see and be abashed,
those who said to me, 'Where is he, the LORD your God?'
Then shall they be trampled like mud in the streets;
I shall gloat over them;
11 that will be a day for rebuilding your walls,
a day when your frontiers will be extended,
12 a day when men will come seeking you
from Assyria to Egypt
and from Egypt to the Euphrates,
from every sea and every mountain;
13 and the earth with its inhabitants shall be waste.
This shall be the fruit of their deeds.

14 Shepherd thy people with thy crook,
the flock that is thy very own,
that dwells by itself on the heath and in the meadows;
let them graze in Bashan and Gilead, as in days gone by.
15 Show us *a* miracles as in the days when thou camest out of Egypt;
16 let the nations see and be taken aback for all their might,
let them keep their mouths shut,
make their ears deaf,
17 let them lick the dust like snakes,
like creatures that crawl upon the ground.
Let them come trembling and fearful from their strongholds,
let them fear thee, O LORD our God.

18 Who is a god like thee? Thou takest away guilt,
thou passest over the sin of the remnant of thy own people,
thou dost not let thy anger rage for ever
but delightest in love that will not change.
19 Once more thou wilt show us tender affection
and wash out our guilt,
casting all our sins into the depths of the sea.
20 Thou wilt show good faith to Jacob,
unchanging love to Abraham,
as thou didst swear to our fathers in days gone by.

*a* *Prob. rdg.; Heb.* I will show him.

# NAHUM

An oracle about Nineveh: the book of the vision of Nahum the Elkoshite.  1

## *The vengeance of the LORD on his enemies*

The LORD is a jealous god, a god of vengeance;  2*ᵃ*
the LORD takes vengeance and is quick to anger.*ᵇ*
*ᶜ* In whirlwind and storm he goes on his way,  3
   and the clouds are the dust beneath his feet.
He rebukes the sea and dries it up  4
   and makes all the streams fail.
Bashan and Carmel languish,
   and on Lebanon the young shoots wither.
The mountains quake before him,  5
   the hills heave and swell,
and the earth, the world and all that lives in it,
   are in tumult at his presence.
Who can stand before his wrath?  6
   Who can resist his fury?
His anger pours out*ᵈ* like a stream of fire,
and the rocks melt*ᵉ* before him.
The LORD is a sure refuge  7
for those who look to him in time of distress;
he cares for all who seek his protection
and brings them safely*ᶠ* through the sweeping flood;  8
he makes a final end of all who oppose him
and pursues his enemies into darkness.
No adversaries dare oppose him twice;  9-11
all are burnt up*ᵍ* like tangled briars.
Why do you make plots against the LORD?
He himself will make an end of you all.
From you has come forth a wicked counsellor,
plotting evil against the LORD.
The LORD takes vengeance on his adversaries,
against his enemies he directs his wrath;
with skin scorched black, they are consumed
like stubble that is parched and dry.

---

*ᵃ* *Verses 2-14 are an incomplete alphabetic acrostic poem; some parts have been re-arranged accordingly.*  *ᵇ* *The rest of verse 2,* The LORD takes . . . wrath, *transposed to verse 11.*  *ᶜ* *Prob. rdg.; Heb. inserts two lines* The LORD is long-suffering and of great might, but the LORD does not sweep clean away.  *ᵈ* pours out: *or* fuses *or* melts.  *ᵉ* *Prob. rdg.; Heb.* are torn down.  *ᶠ* brings them safely: *prob. rdg.; Heb. om.*  *ᵍ* all are burnt up: *prob. rdg.; Heb.* for until.

## *Israel and Judah rid of the invaders*

These are the words of the LORD:

13        Now I will break his yoke from your necks
         and snap the cords that bind you.
14      Image and idol will I hew down in the house of your God.
       This is what the LORD has ordained for you:
       never again shall your offspring be scattered;
       and I will grant you burial, fickle though you have been.
12        Has the punishment been so great?
       Yes, but it has passed away and is gone.
       I have afflicted you, but I will not afflict you again.

15        See on the mountains the feet of the herald
         who brings good news.
       Make your pilgrimages, O Judah,
         and pay your vows.
       For wicked men shall never again overrun you;
         they are totally destroyed.
2 2*ᵃ*   The LORD will restore the pride of Jacob and Israel alike,
       although plundering hordes have stripped them bare
       and pillaged their vines.

## *Nineveh's enemies triumphant*

1        The battering-ram is mounted against your bastions,
         the siege is closing in.
     Watch the road and brace yourselves;
         put forth all your strength.
3        The shields of their warriors are gleaming red,
         their soldiers are all in scarlet;
         their chariots, when the line is formed,
         are like flickering*ᵇ* fire;
4      squadrons of horse advance on the city in mad frenzy;*ᶜ*
     they jostle one another in the outskirts, like waving torches;
5          the leaders display their prowess*ᵈ*
         as they dash to and fro like lightning,
         rushing*ᵉ* in headlong career;
     they hasten to the wall, and mantelets are set in position.
6      The sluices of the rivers are opened, the palace topples down;
7          the train of captives goes into exile,
         their slave-girls are carried off,
        moaning like doves and beating their breasts;

---

*ᵃ* *Verses 1 and 2 transposed.*          *ᵇ* flickering: *prob. rdg.; Heb. obscure.*
*ᶜ* *Prob. rdg.; Heb. adds* chariots.    *ᵈ* display their prowess: *or* shout their own names.
*ᵉ* *Prob. rdg.; Heb.* stumbling.

and Nineveh has become like a pool of water,     8
like the waters round her, which are ebbing away.
'Stop! Stop!' they cry; but none turns back.

Spoil is taken, spoil of silver and gold;     9
    there is no end to the store,
treasure beyond the costliest that man can desire.
    Plundered, pillaged, stripped bare!     10
Courage melting and knees giving way,
writhing limbs, and faces drained of colour!
        Where now is the lions' den,     11
    the cave*a* where the lion cubs lurked,
where the lion and*b* lioness and young cubs
        went unafraid,
    the lion which killed to satisfy its whelps     12
and for its mate broke the neck of the kill,
mauling its prey to fill its lair,
        filling its den with the mauled prey?

I am against you, says the LORD of Hosts,     13
    I will smoke out your pride,*c*
and a sword shall devour your cubs.
    I will leave you no more prey on the earth,
and the sound of your feeding*d* shall no more be heard.

Ah! blood-stained city, steeped in deceit,     **3**
full of pillage, never empty of prey!
        Hark to the crack of the whip,     2
    the rattle of wheels and stamping of horses,
bounding chariots, chargers rearing,     3
        swords gleaming, flash of spears!
    The dead are past counting, their bodies lie in heaps,
corpses innumerable, men stumbling over corpses—
all for a wanton's monstrous wantonness,     4
        fair-seeming, a mistress of sorcery,
    who beguiled nations and tribes
        by her wantonness and her sorceries.
I am against you, says the LORD of Hosts,     5
    I will uncover your breasts to your disgrace
and expose your naked body to every nation,
        to every kingdom your shame.
    I will cast loathsome filth over you,     6
    I will count you obscene and treat you like excrement.

Then all who see you will shrink from you and say,     7
'Nineveh is laid waste; who will console her?'
Where shall I look for anyone to comfort you?

---

*a* *Prob. rdg.; Heb.* pasture.     *b* and: *prob. rdg.; Heb. om.*     *c* your pride: *prob.*
*rdg.; Heb.* her chariot.     *d* your feeding: *prob. rdg.; Heb.* your messenger.

8       Will you fare better than No-amon?—
           she that lay by the streams of the Nile,
           surrounded by water,
      whose rampart was the Nile, waters her wall;
9       Cush and Egypt were her strength, and it was boundless,
      Put and the Libyans brought her help.
10     She too became an exile and went into captivity,
      her infants too were dashed to the ground at every street-corner,
           her nobles were shared out by lot,
           all her great men were thrown into chains.
11     You too shall hire yourself out, flaunting your sex;
      you too shall seek refuge from the enemy.
12     Your fortifications are like figs when they ripen:
      if they are shaken, they fall into the mouth of the eater.
13     The troops*a* in your midst are a pack of women,
      the gates of your country stand open to the enemy,
           and fire consumes their bars.
14          Draw yourselves water for the siege,
           strengthen your fortifications;
      down into the clay, trample the mortar,
           repair the brickwork.
15          Even then the fire will consume you,
           and the sword will cut you down.*b*
           Make yourselves many as the locusts,
           make yourselves many as the hoppers,
16     a swarm which spreads out and then flies away.
      You have spies as numerous as the stars in the sky;
17          your secret agents are like locusts,
           your commanders like the hoppers
      which lie dormant in the walls on a cold day;
      but when the sun rises, they scurry off,
      and no one knows where they have gone.
18          Your shepherds slumber, O king of Assyria,
           your flock-masters lie down to rest;
      your troops*a* are scattered over the hills,
           and no one rounds them up.
19     Your wounds cannot be assuaged, your injury is mortal;
      all who have heard of your fate clap their hands in joy.
      Are there any whom your ceaseless cruelty has not borne down?

---

*a Or* people.    *b Prob. rdg.; Heb. adds* and consume you like the locust (*or* hopper).

# HABAKKUK

An oracle which the prophet Habakkuk received in a vision.     1

## *Divine justice*

How long, O LORD, have I cried to thee, unanswered?     2
I cry, 'Violence!', but thou dost not save.
    Why dost thou let me see such misery,     3
    why countenance *a* wrongdoing?

    Devastation and violence confront me;
strife breaks out, discord raises its head,
    and so law grows effete;     4
    justice does not come forth victorious;
    for the wicked outwit the righteous,
    and so justice comes out perverted.

    Look, you treacherous people, look:     5
        here is what will astonish you and stun you,
    for there is work afoot in your days
    which you will not believe when it is told you.
It is this: I am raising up the Chaldaeans,     6
    that savage and impetuous nation,
        who cross the wide tracts of the earth
    to take possession of homes not theirs.
    Terror and awe go with them;     7
their justice and judgement are of their own making.
Their horses are swifter than hunting-leopards,     8
    keener than wolves of the plain; *b*
    their cavalry wait ready, they spring forward,
    they come flying from afar
    like vultures swooping to devour the prey.
Their whole army advances, violence in their hearts;     9
    a sea of faces rolls on;
    they bring in captives countless as the sand.
    Kings they hold in derision,     10
    rulers they despise;
    they despise every fortress,
    they raise siege-works and capture it.
    Then they pass on like the wind and are gone;     11
and dismayed are all those whose strength was their god.

*a* *Or* dost thou let me see.    *b* *Or* evening.

12         Art thou not from of old, O Lord?—
          my God, the holy, the immortal.[a]
       O Lord, it is thou who hast appointed them to execute judgement;
       O mighty God, thou who hast destined them to chastise,
13          thou whose eyes are too pure to look upon evil,
          and who canst not countenance wrongdoing,
          why dost thou countenance the treachery of the wicked?
      Why keep silent when they devour men more righteous than they?
14          Why dost thou make men like the fish of the sea,
          like gliding creatures that obey no ruler?
15          They haul them up with hooks, one and all,
            they catch them in nets
            and drag them in their trawls;
          then they make merry and rejoice,
16          sacrificing to their nets
            and burning offerings[b] to their trawls;
          for by these they live sumptuously
            and enjoy rich fare.
17        Are they then to unsheathe the sword every day,
         to slaughter the nations without pity?

2            I will stand at my post,
          I will take up my position on the watch-tower,
          I will watch to learn what he will say through me,
            and what I shall reply when I am challenged.[c]
2        Then the Lord made answer:
      Write down the vision, inscribe it on tablets,
         ready for a herald to carry it with speed;[d]
3          for there is still a vision for the appointed time.
        At the destined hour it will come in breathless haste,
           it will not fail.
           If it delays, wait for it;
          for when it comes will be no time to linger.

4        The reckless will be unsure of himself,
         while the righteous man will live by being faithful;[e]
5        as for the traitor in his over-confidence,
         still less will he ride out the storm, for all his bragging.
        Though he opens his mouth as wide as Sheol
        and is insatiable as Death,
         gathering in all the nations,
         making all peoples his own harvest,
6        surely they will all turn upon him
        with insults and abuse, and say,

---

[a] the immortal: *prob. original rdg., altered in Heb. to* we shall not die.    [b] *Or* incense.
[c] when I am challenged: *or* concerning my complaint.    [d] ready . . . speed:
*or* so that a man may read it easily.    [e] *Or* by his faithfulness (*cp. Romans 1. 17;
Galatians 3. 11*).

'Woe betide you who heap up wealth that is not yours *a*
and enrich yourself with goods taken in pledge!'
Will not your creditors suddenly start up,                                    7
   will not all awake who would shake you till you are empty,
and will you not fall a victim to them?
Because you yourself have plundered mighty *b* nations,                         8
   all the rest of the world will plunder you,
      because of bloodshed and violence done in the land,
      to the city and all its inhabitants.

   · Woe betide you who seek unjust gain for your house,                       9
   to build your nest on a height,
   to save yourself from the grasp of wicked men!
Your schemes to overthrow mighty *b* nations                                  10
   will bring dishonour to your house
   and put your own life in jeopardy.
The very stones will cry out from the wall,                                   11
and from the timbers a beam will answer them.

Woe betide you who have built a town with bloodshed                          12
   and founded a city on fraud,
      so that nations toil for a pittance,                                    13
      and peoples weary themselves for a mere nothing!
Is not all this the doing of the LORD of Hosts?
For the earth shall be full of the knowledge of the glory of the LORD   14
as the waters fill the sea.

Woe betide you who make your *c* companions drink the outpouring of 15
      your wrath,
   making them drunk, that you may watch their naked orgies!
Drink deep draughts of shame, not of glory;                                  16
you too shall drink until you stagger.
The cup in the LORD's right hand is passed to you,
and your shame will exceed *d* your glory.
      The violence done to Lebanon shall sweep over you,                     17
      the havoc done to its beasts shall break your own spirit,
      because of bloodshed and violence done in the land,
      to the city and all its inhabitants.

What use is an idol when its maker has shaped it?—                           18
      it is only an image, a source of lies;
or when the maker trusts what he has made?—
      he is only making dumb idols.
   Woe betide him who says to the wood, 'Wake up',                           19
   to the dead stone, 'Bestir yourself'!*e*

---

*a Prob. rdg.; Heb. adds till when.*          *b Or many.*          *c Prob. rdg.; Heb. his.*
*d will exceed: prob. rdg.; Heb. unintelligible.*          *e Prob. rdg.; Heb. adds he will*
teach.

Why, it is firmly encased in gold and silver
and has no breath in it.
20     But the LORD is in his holy temple;
let all the earth be hushed in his presence.

## A prayer for mercy

3  A prayer of the prophet Habakkuk.

2     O LORD, I have heard tell of thy deeds;
I have seen, O LORD, thy work.[a]
In the midst of the years thou didst make thyself known,
and in thy wrath thou didst remember mercy.

3     God comes from Teman,
the Holy One from Mount Paran;
his radiance overspreads the skies,
and his splendour fills the earth.

4     He rises like the dawn,
with twin rays starting forth at his side;
the skies are[b] the hiding-place of his majesty,
and the everlasting[c] ways are for[d] his swift flight.[e]

5     Pestilence stalks before him,
and plague comes forth behind.

6     He stands still and shakes the earth,
he looks and makes the nations tremble;
the eternal mountains are riven,
the everlasting[c] hills subside,

7     the tents of Cushan are snatched away,[f]
the tent-curtains of Midian flutter.

8     Art thou angry with the streams?
Is thy wrath against the sea, O LORD?
When thou dost mount thy horses,
thy riding is to victory.

9     Thou dost draw thy bow from its case[g]
and charge thy quiver with shafts.
Thou cleavest the earth with rivers;

10-11     the mountains see thee and writhe with fear.
The torrent of water rushes by,
and the deep sea thunders aloud.
The sun forgets to turn in his course,[h]
and the moon stands still at her zenith,
at the gleam of thy speeding arrows
and the glance of thy flashing spear.

---

[a] *Prob. rdg.; Heb. adds* in the midst of the years quicken it.     [b] the skies are:
*prob. rdg.; Heb.* there is.     [c] *Or* ancient.     [d] and . . . are for: *transposed from
end of verse 6.*     [e] his swift flight: *transposed, with slight change, from verse 7.*
[f] are snatched away: *prob. rdg.; Heb.* under wickedness.     [g] Thou . . . case:
*prob. rdg.; Heb.* Thy bow was quite bared.     [h] The sun . . . course: *prob. rdg.;
Heb.* The sun raised the height of his hands.

With threats thou dost bestride the earth    12
and trample down the nations in anger.
>Thou goest forth to save thy people,    13
>thou comest to save thy anointed;
thou dost shatter the wicked man's house from the roof down,[a]
uncovering its foundations to the bare rock.[b]
Thou piercest their[c] chiefs with thy[d] shafts,    14
and their leaders are torn from them by the whirlwind,
>as they open[e] their jaws
to devour their wretched victims in secret.

When thou dost tread the sea with thy horses    15
>the mighty waters boil.
I hear, and my belly quakes;    16
my lips quiver at the sound;
trembling comes over my bones,
and my feet totter in their tracks;
>I sigh for the day of distress
to dawn over my assailants.
>Although the fig-tree does not burgeon,    17
>the vines bear no fruit,
>the olive-crop fails,
the orchards yield no food,
the fold is bereft of its flock
>and there are no cattle in the stalls,
yet I will exult in the LORD    18
>and rejoice in the God of my deliverance.
The LORD God is my strength,    19
who makes my feet nimble as a hind's
>and sets me to range the heights.

# ZEPHANIAH

THIS IS THE WORD OF THE LORD which came to 1
Zephaniah son of Cushi, son of Gedaliah, son of Amariah, son of
Hezekiah, in the time of Josiah son of Amon king of Judah.

## *Doom on Judah and her neighbours*

I will sweep the earth clean of all that is on it,    2
>says the LORD.
I will sweep away both man and beast,    3
I will sweep the birds from the air and the fish from the sea,

---

[a] the wicked . . . down: *prob. rdg.; Heb.* a head from the house of the wicked.    [b] bare
rock: *prob. rdg.; Heb.* neck.    [c] their: *prob. rdg.; Heb. om.*    [d] *Prob. rdg.;*
*Heb.* his.    [e] from them . . . open: *prob. rdg.; Heb. obscure.*

and I will bring the wicked to their knees [a]
and wipe out mankind from the earth.
This is the very word of the LORD.

4    I will stretch my hand over Judah
and all who live in Jerusalem;
I will wipe out from this place the last remnant of Baal
and the very name of the heathen priests,
5         those who bow down upon the house-tops
to worship the host of heaven
and who swear by Milcom,
6         those who have turned their backs on the LORD,
who have not sought the LORD or consulted him.

7    Silence before the Lord GOD!
for the day of the LORD is near.
The LORD has prepared a sacrifice
and has hallowed his guests.
8    On the day of the LORD's sacrifice
I will punish the royal house and its chief officers
and all who ape outlandish fashions.
9         On that day
I will punish all who dance on the temple terrace,
who fill their master's [b] house with crimes of violence and fraud.

10        On that day, says the LORD,
an outcry shall be heard from the Fish Gate,
wailing from the second quarter of the city,
a loud crash from the hills;
11        and [c] those who live in the Lower Town shall wail.
For it is all over with the merchants,
and all the dealers in silver are wiped out.

12        At that time
I will search Jerusalem with a lantern
and punish all who sit in stupor over the dregs of their wine,
who say to themselves,
'The LORD will do nothing, good or bad.'
13        Their wealth shall be plundered,
their houses laid waste;
they shall build houses but not live in them,
they shall plant vineyards but not drink the wine from them.
14        The great day of the LORD is near,
it comes with speed;
no runner so fast as that day,
no raiding band so swift. [d]

---

[a] I will bring ... knees: *prob. rdg.; Heb.* the ruins with the wicked.     [b] *Or* their Lord's.
[c] and: *prob. rdg.; Heb. om.*          [d] no runner ... swift: *prob. rdg.; Heb.* hark, the
day of the LORD is bitter, there the warrior cries aloud.

That day is a day of wrath,      15
a day of anguish and affliction,
a day of destruction and devastation,
a day of murk and gloom,
a day of cloud and dense fog,
a day of trumpet and battle-cry      16
over fortified cities and lofty battlements.
    I will bring dire distress upon men;      17
they shall walk like blind men for their sin against the LORD.
    Their blood shall be spilt like dust
      and their bowels like dung;
    neither their silver nor their gold      18
      shall avail to save them.
On the day of the LORD's wrath, by the fire of his jealousy
    the whole land shall be consumed;
for he will make an end, a swift end,
    of all who live in the land.

Gather together, you unruly nation, gather together,      **2**
before you are sent far away and vanish*a* like chaff,      2
before the burning anger of the LORD comes upon you,
before the day of the LORD's anger comes upon you.
    Seek the LORD,      3
all in the land who live humbly by his laws,
seek righteousness, seek a humble heart;
    it may be that you will find shelter
    in the day of the LORD's anger.
    For Gaza shall be deserted,      4
    Ashkelon left desolate,
the people of Ashdod shall be driven out*b* at noonday
    and Ekron uprooted.

Listen, you who live by the coast, you Kerethite settlers.      5
    The word of the LORD is spoken against you;
    I will subdue you,*c* land of the Philistines,
    I will lay you waste and leave you without inhabitants,
and you, Kereth, shall be all shepherds' huts*d* and sheepfolds;      6
and the coastland shall belong to the survivors of Judah.      7
    They shall pasture their flocks by the sea*e*
    and lie down at evening in the houses of Ashkelon,
    for the LORD their God will turn to them
      and restore their fortunes.

I have heard the insults of Moab, the taunts of Ammon,      8
    how they have insulted my people
    and encroached on their frontiers.

---

*a* you are . . . vanish: *prob. rdg.; Heb. obscure.*      *b* the people . . . out: *or* Ashdod
shall be made an example.    *c* I . . . you: *prob. rdg.; Heb.* Canaan.    *d* you . . .
huts: *Heb. has these words in a different order.*    *e* by the sea: *prob. rdg.; Heb.* upon them.

9
Therefore, by my life,
says the LORD of Hosts, the God of Israel,
Moab shall be like Sodom,
Ammon like Gomorrah,
a pile of weeds, a rotting heap of saltwort,
waste land for evermore.
The survivors of my people shall plunder them,
the remnant of my nation shall possess their land.

10
11
This will be retribution for their pride, because they have insulted the
people of the LORD of Hosts and encroached upon their rights. The LORD
will appear against them with all his terrors; for he will reduce to beggary
all the gods of the earth, and all the coasts and islands of the nations will
worship him, every man in his own home.

12
You Cushites also shall be killed
by the sword of the LORD.[a]

13
So let him stretch out his hand over the north
and destroy Assyria,
make Nineveh desolate,
arid as the wilderness.

14
Flocks shall couch there,
and all the beasts of the wild.
Horned owl and ruffed bustard shall roost on her capitals;
the tawny owl shall hoot in the window,
and the bustard stand in the porch.[b]

15
This is the city that exulted in fancied security,
saying to herself, 'I am, and I alone.'
And what is she now? A waste, a haunt for wild beasts,
at which every passer-by shall hiss and shake his fist.

3
Shame on the tyrant city, filthy and foul!

2
No warning voice did she heed, she took no rebuke to heart,
she did not trust in the LORD or come near to her God.

3
Her officers were lions roaring in her midst,
her rulers wolves of the plain[c]
that did not wait[d] till morning,

4
her prophets were reckless, no true prophets.
Her priests profaned the sanctuary
and did violence to the law.

5
But the LORD in her midst is just;
he does no wrong;
morning by morning he gives judgement,
without fail at daybreak.[e]

6
I have wiped out the proud;
their battlements are laid in ruin.

[a] the sword of the LORD: *prob. rdg.; Heb.* my sword.   [b] *Prob. rdg.; Heb. adds an
unintelligible phrase.*   [c] *Or* evening.   [d] *Or* carry off.   [e] *Prob. rdg.; Heb.
adds* but the wrongdoer knows no shame.

I have made their streets a desert where no one passes.
Their cities are laid waste, deserted, unpeopled.
In the hope that she would remember all my instructions,   7
    I said, 'Do but fear me
        and take my rebuke to heart';
but they were up betimes and went about their evil deeds.

Wait for me, therefore, says the LORD,   8
    wait for the day when I stand up to accuse you;
for mine it is to gather nations
    and assemble kingdoms,
to pour out on them my indignation,
    all the heat of my anger;
the whole earth shall be consumed by the fire of my jealousy.
    I will give all peoples once again pure lips,   9
    that they may invoke the LORD by name
and serve him with one consent.
    From beyond the rivers of Cush   10
my suppliants of the Dispersion shall bring me tribute.

## A remnant preserved

On that day, Jerusalem,   11
you shall not be put to shame for all your deeds
    by which you have rebelled against me;
for then I will rid you
    of your proud and arrogant citizens,
and never again shall you flaunt your pride
    on my holy hill.
But I will leave in you a people   12
    afflicted and poor.
The survivors in Israel shall find refuge in the name of the LORD;   13
they shall no longer do wrong or speak lies,
    no words of deceit shall pass their lips;
    for they shall feed and lie down
        with no one to terrify them.

Zion, cry out for joy;   14
    raise the shout of triumph, Israel;
    be glad, rejoice with all your heart,
        daughter of Jerusalem.
The LORD has rid you of your adversaries,   15
    he has swept away your foes;
the LORD is among you as king, O Israel;
    never again shall you fear disaster.

On that day this shall be the message to Jerusalem:   16
Fear not, O Zion; let not your hands fall slack.

17     The LORD your God is in your midst,
           like a warrior, to keep you safe;
       he will rejoice over you and be glad;
           he will show you his love once more;
       he will exult over you with a shout of joy
18         as in days long ago.*a*

       I will take your cries of woe *b* away from you;
       and you shall no longer endure reproach for her.
19     When that time comes, see,
       I will deal with all your oppressors.
       I will rescue the lost and gather the dispersed;
       I will win my people praise and renown
           in all the world where once they were despised.
20     When the time comes for me to gather you, *c*
       I will bring you home.
   I will win you renown and praise
       among all the peoples of the earth,
       when I bring back your prosperity; and you shall see it.
       It is the LORD who speaks.

# HAGGAI

### *Zerubbabel restorer of the temple*

1  IN THE SECOND YEAR OF KING DARIUS, on the first
   day of the sixth month, the word of the LORD came through the prophet
   Haggai to Zerubbabel son of Shealtiel, governor of Judah, and to
2  Joshua son of Jehozadak, the high priest: These are the words of the LORD
   of Hosts: This nation says to itself that it is not yet time for the house of
3  the LORD to be rebuilt. Then this word came through Haggai the prophet:
4  Is it a time for you to live in your own well-roofed houses, while this house
5  lies in ruins? Now these are the words of the LORD of Hosts: Consider your
6  way of life. You have sown much but reaped little; you eat but never as
   much as you wish, you drink but never more than you need, you are clothed
   but never warm, and the labourer puts his wages into a purse with a hole in
7  it. These are the words of the LORD of Hosts: Consider your way of life.
8  Go up into the hills, fetch timber, and build a house acceptable to me,
9  where I can show my glory,*d* says the LORD. You look for much and get
   little. At the moment when you would bring home the harvest, I blast it.
   Why? says the LORD of Hosts. Because my house lies in ruins, while
10 each of you has a house that he can run to. It is your fault that the heavens

*a* as . . . ago: *prob. rdg.; Heb. obscure.*      *b* cries of woe: *prob. rdg.; Heb. obscure.*
*c* When . . . you: *prob. rdg.; Heb. and in the time, my gathering you.*      *d* show my
glory: *or* be honoured.

withhold their dew and the earth its produce. So I have proclaimed a  11
drought against land and mountain, against corn, new wine, and oil, and
all that the ground yields, against man and cattle and all the products of
man's labour.

Zerubbabel son of Shealtiel, Joshua son of Jehozadak, the high priest,  12
and the rest of the people listened to what the LORD their God had said
and what the prophet Haggai said when the LORD their God sent him, and
they were filled with fear because of the LORD. So Haggai the LORD's  13
messenger, as the LORD had commissioned him, said to the people: I am
with you, says the LORD. Then the LORD stirred up the spirit of Zerubbabel  14
son of Shealtiel, governor of Judah, of Joshua son of Jehozadak, the high
priest, and of the rest of the people; they came and began work on the
house of the LORD of Hosts their God on the twenty-fourth day of the sixth  15
month.

In the second year of King Darius, on the twenty-first day of the seventh  **2**
month, these words came from the LORD through the prophet Haggai:
Say to Zerubbabel son of Shealtiel, governor of Judah, to Joshua son of  2
Jehozadak, the high priest, and to the rest of the people: Is there anyone  3
still among you who saw this house in its former glory? How does it appear
to you now? Does it not seem to you as if it were not there? But now,  4
Zerubbabel, take heart, says the LORD; take heart, Joshua son of Jehozadak,
high priest. Take heart, all you people, says the LORD. Begin the work, for
I am with you, says the LORD of Hosts, and my spirit is present among you.  5
Have no fear. For these are the words of the LORD of Hosts: One thing  6
more: I will shake heaven and earth, sea and land, I will shake all nations;  7
the treasure of all nations shall come hither, and I will fill this house with
glory;*a* so says the LORD of Hosts. Mine is the silver and mine the gold,  8
says the LORD of Hosts, and the glory*a* of this latter house shall surpass  9
the glory*a* of the former, says the LORD of Hosts. In this place will I grant
prosperity and peace. This is the very word of the LORD of Hosts.

In the second year of Darius, on the twenty-fourth day of the ninth  10
month, this word came from the LORD to the prophet Haggai: These are  11
the words of the LORD of Hosts: Ask the priests to give their ruling: If a  12
man is carrying consecrated flesh in a fold of his robe, and he lets the fold
touch bread or broth or wine or oil or any other kind of food, will that also
become consecrated? And the priests answered, 'No.' Haggai went on,  13
But if a person defiled by contact with a corpse touches any one of these
things, will that also become defiled? 'It will', answered the priests. Haggai  14
replied, So it is with this people and nation and all that they do, says the
LORD; whatever offering they make here is defiled in my sight. And now  15
look back over recent times down to this day: before one stone was laid
on another in the LORD's temple, what was your plight? If a man came to a  16
heap of corn expecting twenty measures, he found but ten; if he came to
a wine-vat to draw fifty measures, he found but twenty. I blasted you  17
and all your harvest with black blight and red and with hail, and yet you
had no mind to return to me, says the LORD. Consider, from this day  18
onwards, from this twenty-fourth day of the ninth month, the day when the

*a Or* wealth.

19 foundations of the temple of the LORD are laid, consider: will the seed still
be diminished*ᵃ* in the barn? Will the vine and the fig, the pomegranate and
the olive, still bear no fruit? Not so, from this day I will bless you.
20     On that day, the twenty-fourth day of the month, the word of the LORD
21 came to Haggai a second time: Tell Zerubbabel, governor of Judah, I will
22 shake heaven and earth; I will overthrow the thrones of kings, break the
power of heathen realms, overturn chariots and their riders; horses and
23 riders shall fall by the sword of their comrades. On that day, says the LORD
of Hosts, I will take you, Zerubbabel son of Shealtiel, my servant, and will
wear you as a signet-ring; for you it is that I have chosen. This is the very
word of the LORD of Hosts.

# ZECHARIAH

## Zechariah's commission

1 IN THE EIGHTH MONTH of the second year of Darius, the
word of the LORD came to the prophet Zechariah son of Berechiah,
2 3 son of Iddo: The LORD was very angry with your forefathers. Say to
the people, These are the words of the LORD of Hosts: Come back to me,
4 and I will come back to you, says the LORD of Hosts. Do not be like your
forefathers. They heard the prophets of old proclaim, 'These are the words
of the LORD of Hosts: Turn back from your evil ways and your evil deeds.'
5 But they did not listen or pay heed to me, says the LORD. And where are
6 your forefathers now? And the prophets, do they live for ever? But the
warnings and the decrees with which I charged my servants the prophets
—did not these overtake your forefathers? Did they not then repent and
say, 'The LORD of Hosts has treated us as he purposed; as our lives and
as our deeds deserved, so has he treated us'?

## Eight visions with their interpretations

7 ON THE TWENTY-FOURTH DAY of the eleventh month, the month
Shebat, in the second year of Darius, the word of the LORD came to
the prophet Zechariah son of Berechiah, son of Iddo.
8     Last night I had a vision. I saw a man on a bay horse standing among the
myrtles in a hollow; and behind him were other horses, black, dappled,
9 and white. 'What are these, sir?' I asked, and the angel who talked with me
10 answered, 'I will show you what they are.' Then the man standing among
the myrtles said, 'They are those whom the LORD has sent to range through
11 the world.' They reported to the angel of the LORD as he stood among the
myrtles: 'We have ranged through the world; the whole world is still and
12 at peace.' Thereupon the angel of the LORD said, 'How long, O LORD of
Hosts, wilt thou withhold thy compassion from Jerusalem and the cities

ᵃ diminished: *prob. rdg.; Heb. om.*

of Judah, upon whom thou hast vented thy wrath these seventy years?'
Then the LORD spoke kind and comforting words to the angel who talked 13
with me, and the angel said to me, Proclaim, These are the words of the 14
LORD of Hosts: I am very jealous for Jerusalem and Zion. I am full of 15
anger against the nations that enjoy their ease, because, while my anger
was but mild, they heaped evil on evil. Therefore these are the words of 16
the LORD: I have come back to Jerusalem with compassion, and my house
shall be rebuilt in her, says the LORD of Hosts, and the measuring-line shall
be stretched over Jerusalem. Proclaim once more, These are the words of 17
the LORD of Hosts: My cities shall again overflow with good things; once
again the LORD will comfort Zion, once again he will make Jerusalem the
city of his choice.

I lifted my eyes and there I saw four horns. I asked the angel who talked 18 19
with me what they were, and he answered, 'These are the horns which
scattered Judah*a* and Jerusalem.' Then the LORD showed me four smiths. 20
I asked what they were coming to do, and he said, 'Those horns scattered 21
Judah and Jerusalem so completely that no man could lift his head. But
these smiths have come to reunite them and to throw down the horns of
the nations which had raised them against the land of Judah and scattered
its people.'

I lifted my eyes and there I saw a man carrying a measuring-line. I **2** 1 2
asked him where he was going, and he said, 'To measure Jerusalem and
see what should be its breadth and length.' Then, as the angel who talked 3
with me was going away, another angel came out to meet him and said 4
to him, Run to the young man there and tell him that Jerusalem shall
be a city without walls, so numerous shall be the men and cattle within
it. I will be a wall of fire round her, says the LORD, and a glory in the midst 5
of her.

Away, away; flee from the land of the north, says the LORD, for I will 6
make you spread your wings like the four winds of heaven, says the LORD.
Away, escape, you people of Zion who live in Babylon. 7

For these are the words of the LORD of Hosts, spoken when he sent me 8
on a glorious mission*b* to the nations who have plundered you, for whoever
touches you touches the apple of his eye: I raise*c* my hand against them; 9
they shall be plunder for their own slaves. So you shall know that the LORD
of Hosts has sent me. Shout aloud and rejoice, daughter of Zion; I am 10
coming, I will make my dwelling among you, says the LORD. Many nations 11
shall come over to the LORD on that day and become his people, and he will
make his dwelling with you. Then you shall know that the LORD of Hosts
has sent me to you. The LORD will once again claim Judah as his own 12
possession in the holy land, and make Jerusalem the city of his choice.

Silence, all mankind, in the presence of the LORD! For he has bestirred 13
himself out of his holy dwelling-place.

The angel who talked with me came back and roused me as a man is **4** 1*d*
roused from sleep. He asked me what I saw, and I answered, 'A lamp- 2
stand all of gold with a bowl on it; it holds seven lamps, and there are seven

*a* *Prob. rdg.; Heb. adds* Israel.     *b* on a glorious mission: *prob. rdg.; Heb. after glory.*
*c* *Or* wave.     *d* *3. 1–10 transposed to follow 4. 14.*

3 pipes for the lamps on top of it, with two olive-trees standing by it, one on
11[a] the right of the bowl and another on the left.' I asked him, 'What are these
two olive-trees, the one on the right and the other on the left of the lamp-
12 stand?' I asked also another question, 'What are the two sprays of olive
beside the golden pipes which discharge the golden oil from their bowls?'
13 14 He said, 'Do you not know what these mean?' 'No, sir', I answered. 'These
two', he said, 'are the two consecrated with oil who attend the Lord of all
the earth.'

3 1    Then he showed me Joshua the high priest standing before the angel of
the LORD, with the Adversary[b] standing at his right hand to accuse him.
2 The LORD said to the Adversary, 'The LORD rebuke you, Satan, the LORD
rebuke you who are venting your spite on Jerusalem.[c] Is not this man a
3 brand snatched from the fire?' Now Joshua was wearing filthy clothes as
4 he stood before the angel; and the angel turned and said to those in attendance on him, 'Take off his filthy clothes.' Then he turned to him and said,
'See how I have taken away your guilt from you; I will clothe you in fine
5 vestments'; and he added, 'Let a clean turban be put on his head.' So they
put a clean turban on his head and clothed him in clean garments, while
6 the angel of the LORD stood by. Then the angel of the LORD gave Joshua
7 this solemn charge: These are the words of the LORD of Hosts: If you will
conform to my ways and carry out your duties, you shall administer my
house and be in control of my courts, and I grant you the right to come and
8 go amongst these in attendance here. Listen, Joshua the high priest, you
and your colleagues seated here before you, all you who are an omen of
9-10 things to come: I will now bring my servant, the Branch. In one day I will
wipe away the guilt of the land. On that day, says the LORD of Hosts, you
shall all of you invite one another to come and sit each under his vine and
his fig-tree.

    Here is the stone that I set before Joshua, a stone in which are seven
4 4[d] eyes. I will reveal its meaning to you, says the LORD of Hosts. Then I
asked the angel of the LORD who talked with me, 'Sir, what are these?'
5 And he answered, 'Do you not know what these mean?' 'No, sir', I
answered. 'These seven', he said, 'are the eyes of the LORD ranging over the
whole earth.'[e]

6    Then he turned and said to me, This is the word of the LORD concerning
Zerubbabel: Neither by force of arms nor by brute strength, but by my
7 spirit! says the LORD of Hosts. How does a mountain, the greatest mountain, compare with Zerubbabel? It is no higher than a plain. He shall bring
8 out the stone called Possession[f] while men acclaim its beauty. This word
9 came to me from the LORD: Zerubbabel with his own hands laid the foundation of this house and with his own hands he shall finish it. So shall you
10 know that the LORD of Hosts has sent me to you. Who has despised the
day of small things? He shall rejoice when he sees Zerubbabel holding the
stone called Separation.[f]

---

[a] *4. 4–10 transposed to follow 3. 10.*      [b] *Heb.* the Satan.      [c] *the*
LORD . . . Jerusalem: *or the* LORD *who has chosen Jerusalem rebuke you.*    [d] *See note*
*on 4. 11 above.*                  [e] These seven . . . earth: *transposed from verse 10.*
[f] *Cp. Lev. 20. 24–26.*

I looked up again and saw a flying scroll. He asked me what I saw, and **5** 1 2
I answered, 'A flying scroll, twenty cubits long and ten cubits wide.' This, 3
he told me, is the curse which goes out over the whole land; for by the
writing on one side every thief shall be swept clean away, and by the writing
on the other every perjurer shall be swept clean away. I have sent it out, 4
the LORD of Hosts has said, and it shall enter the house of the thief and the
house of the man who has perjured himself in my name; it shall stay inside
that house and demolish it, timbers and stones and all.

The angel who talked with me came out and said to me, 'Raise your 5
eyes and look at this thing that comes forth.' I asked what it was, and he 6
said, 'It is a great barrel coming forth,' and he added, 'so great is their guilt
in all the land.' Then a round slab of lead was lifted, and a woman was 7
sitting there inside the barrel. He said, 'This is Wickedness', and he thrust 8
her down into the barrel and rammed the leaden weight upon its mouth.
I looked up again and saw two women coming forth with the wind in their 9
wings (for they had wings like a stork's), and they carried the barrel between earth and sky. I asked the angel who talked with me where they 10
were taking the barrel, and he answered, 'To build a house for it *a* in the 11
land of Shinar; when the house is ready, it *b* shall be set on the place prepared for it *a* there.'

I looked up again and saw four chariots coming out between two moun- **6**
tains, and the mountains were made of copper. *c* The first chariot had bay 2
horses, the second black, the third white, and the fourth dappled. I asked 3 4
the angel who talked with me, 'Sir, what are these?' He answered, 'These 5
are the four winds of heaven which have been attending the Lord of the
whole earth, and they are now going forth. The chariot with the black 6
horses is going to the land of the north, that with the white to the far west, *d*
that with the dappled to the south, and that with the roan to the land of the 7
east.' *e* They were eager to go and range over the whole earth; so he said,
'Go and range over the earth', and the chariots did so. Then he called me 8
to look and said, 'Those going to the land of the north have given my spirit
rest in the land of the north.'

The word of the LORD came to me: Take silver and gold from the exiles, 9 10
from Heldai, Tobiah, Jedaiah, and *f* Josiah son of Zephaniah, who have
come back from Babylon. Take it and make a crown; put the crown on the 11
head of Joshua son of Jehozadak, the high priest, *g* and say to him, These 12
are the words of the LORD of Hosts: Here is a man named the Branch;
he will shoot up from the ground where he is and will build the temple of
the LORD. It is he who will build the temple of the LORD, he who will 13
assume royal dignity, will be seated on his throne and govern, with a priest
at his right side, and concord shall prevail between them. The crown shall 14
be in the charge of Heldai, Tobiah, Jedaiah, and Josiah son of Zephaniah,
as a memorial in the temple of the LORD.

---

*a* Or her.     *b* Or she.     *c* Or bronze.     *d* to the far west: *prob.*
*rdg.; Heb.* behind them.     *e* to the land of the east: *prob. rdg.;*
*Heb.* om.     *f* and: *prob. rdg.; Heb.* and go on that day yourself and go to
the house of ...     *g* Joshua ... priest: *possibly an error for* Zerubbabel son of
Shealtiel, *cp. 3. 5; 4. 9.*

15 Men from far away shall come and work on the building of the temple of the LORD; so shall you know that the LORD of Hosts has sent me to you. If only you will obey the LORD your God!

## *Joy and gladness in the coming age*

7 THE WORD OF THE LORD CAME TO ZECHARIAH in the fourth year of the reign of King Darius, on the fourth day of Kislev, the ninth month.
2 Bethel-sharezer sent Regem-melech with his men to seek the favour of
3 the LORD. They were to say to the priests in the house of the LORD of Hosts and to the prophets, 'Am I to lament and abstain in the fifth month as I
4 have done for so many years?' Then the word of the LORD of Hosts came
5 to me: Say to all the people of the land and to the priests, When you fasted and lamented in the fifth and seventh months these seventy years, was it
6 indeed in my honour that you fasted? And when you ate and drank, was
7 it not to please yourselves? Was it not this that the LORD proclaimed through the prophets of old, while Jerusalem was populous and peaceful, as were the cities round her, and the Negeb and the Shephelah?
8 9 The word of the LORD came to Zechariah: These are the words of the LORD of Hosts: Administer true justice, show loyalty and compassion to
10 one another, do not oppress the orphan and the widow, the alien and the
11 poor, do not contrive any evil one against another. But they refused to listen, they turned their backs on me in defiance, they stopped their ears
12 and would not hear. Their hearts were adamant; they refused to accept instruction and all that the LORD of Hosts had taught them by his spirit through the prophets of old; and they suffered under the anger of the LORD
13 of Hosts. As they did not listen when I *a* called, so I did not listen when
14 they called, says the LORD of Hosts, and I drove them out among all the nations to whom they were strangers, leaving their land a waste behind them, so that no one came and went. Thus they made their pleasant land a waste.
8 1 2 The word of the LORD of Hosts came to me: These are the words of the LORD of Hosts: I have been very jealous for Zion, fiercely jealous for her.
3 Now, says the LORD, I have come back to Zion and I will dwell in Jerusalem. Jerusalem shall be called the City of Truth, and the mountain of the LORD
4 of Hosts shall be called the Holy Mountain. These are the words of the LORD of Hosts: Once again shall old men and old women sit in the streets
5 of Jerusalem, each leaning on a stick because of their great age; and the streets of the city shall be full of boys and girls, playing in the streets.
6 These are the words of the LORD of Hosts: Even if it may seem impossible *b* to the survivors of this nation on that day, will it also seem impossible to
7 me? *c* This is the very word of the LORD of Hosts. These are the words of the LORD of Hosts: See, I will rescue my people from the countries of the
8 east and the west, and bring them back to live in Jerusalem. They shall be my people, and I will be their God, in truth and justice.

*a* Prob. rdg.; Heb. he.    *b* Or wonderful.    *c* will ... me?: or it will seem wonderful also to me.

These are the words of the LORD of Hosts: Take courage, you who in 9
these days hear, from the prophets who were present when the foundations were laid for the house of the LORD of Hosts, their promise that the
temple is to be rebuilt. Till that time there was no hiring either of man or 10
of beast, no one could safely go about his business because of his enemies,
and I set all men one against another. But now I am not the same towards 11
the survivors of this people as I was in former days, says the LORD of Hosts.
For they shall sow in safety; the vine shall yield its fruit and the soil its 12
produce, the heavens shall give their dew; with all these things I will
endow the survivors of this people. You, house of Judah and house of 13
Israel, have been the very symbol of a curse to all the nations; and now I
will save you, and you shall become the symbol of a blessing. Courage!
Do not be afraid.

For these are the words of the LORD of Hosts: Whereas I resolved to 14
ruin you because your ancestors roused me to anger, says the LORD of
Hosts, and I did not relent, so in these days I have once more*a* resolved to 15
do good to Jerusalem and to the house of Judah; do not be afraid. This is 16
what you shall do: speak the truth to each other, administer true and sound
justice in the city gate. Do not contrive any evil one against another, and 17
do not love perjury, for all this I hate. This is the very word of the LORD.

The word of the LORD of Hosts came to me: These are the words of the 18 19
LORD of Hosts: The fasts of the fourth month and of the fifth, the seventh,
and the tenth, shall become festivals of joy and gladness for the house of
Judah. Love truth and peace.

These are the words of the LORD of Hosts: Nations and dwellers in great 20
cities shall yet come; people of one city shall come to those of another and 21
say, 'Let us go and entreat the favour of the LORD, and resort to the LORD
of Hosts; and I will come too.' So great nations and mighty peoples shall 22
resort to the LORD of Hosts in Jerusalem and entreat his favour. These are 23
the words of the LORD of Hosts: In those days, when ten men from nations
of every language pluck up courage, they shall pluck the robe of a Jew and
say, 'We will go with you because we have heard that God is with you.'

## *Judah's triumph over her enemies*

An oracle: the word of the LORD.                                              9

> He has come to the land of Hadrach
> and*b* established himself in Damascus;
>> for the capital city*c* of Aram is the LORD's,
>> as are all the tribes of Israel.
> *d* Sidon has closed her frontier against Hamath,                          2
>> for she is very wary.
> Tyre has built herself a rampart;                                           3
> she has heaped up silver like dust
>> and gold like mud in the streets.

*a* once more: *or* changed my mind and.          *b* He has come . . . and: *prob. rdg.;*
*Heb.* In the land of Hadrach he has . . .          *c* capital city: *or* chief part.          *d Prob.*
*rdg.; Heb. prefixes* Tyre and.

4    But wait, the Lord will dispossess her
     and strike down the power of her ships,
     and the city itself will be destroyed by fire.

5    Let Ashkelon see it and be afraid;
     Gaza shall writhe in terror,
     and Ekron's hope shall be extinguished;
     kings shall vanish from Gaza,
         and Ashkelon shall be unpeopled;

6    half-breeds shall settle in Ashdod,
     and I will uproot the pride of the Philistine.

7    I will dash the blood of sacrifices from his mouth
     and his loathsome offerings from his teeth;
     and his survivors shall belong*a* to our God
     and become like a clan in Judah,
         and Ekron like a Jebusite.

8    And I will post a garrison for my house
         so that no one may pass in or out,
     and no oppressor shall ever overrun them.
     [This I have lived to see with my own eyes.]

9    Rejoice, rejoice, daughter of Zion,
     shout aloud, daughter of Jerusalem;
     for see, your king is coming to you,
     his cause won, his victory gained,
     humble and mounted on an ass,
     on a foal, the young of a she-ass.

10   He shall banish chariots from Ephraim
         and war-horses from Jerusalem;
     the warrior's bow shall be banished.
     He shall speak peaceably to every nation,
     and his rule shall extend from sea to sea,
     from the River to the ends of the earth.

11   And as for you, by your covenant with me sealed in blood
     I release your prisoners from the dungeon.*b*

12   (Come back to the stronghold, you prisoners who wait in hope.)
     Now is the day announced
     when I will grant you twofold*c* reparation.

13   For my bow is strung, O Judah;
     I have laid the arrow to it, O Ephraim;
     I have roused your sons, O Zion, *d*
     and made you into the sword of a warrior.

14   The LORD shall appear above them,
     and his arrow shall flash like lightning;
     the Lord GOD shall blow a blast on the horn
     and march with the storm-winds of the south.

---

*a* his survivors shall belong: *or* he shall become kin.    *b* *Prob. rdg.; Heb. adds* no water
in it.    *c* *Or* equal.    *d* *Prob. rdg.; Heb. adds* against your sons, O Javan (*or* Greece).

The LORD of Hosts will be their shield; 15
they shall prevail, they shall trample on the sling-stones;
they shall be roaring drunk as if with wine,
brimful as a bowl, drenched like the corners of the altar.
So on that day the LORD their God 16
will save them, his own people, like sheep,
 setting them all about his land,
 like<sup>a</sup> jewels set to sparkle in a crown.

What wealth, what beauty, is theirs: 17
corn to strengthen young men,
 and new wine for maidens!
Ask of the LORD rain in the autumn, **10**
ask him for rain in the spring,
the LORD who makes the storm-clouds,
and he will give you showers of rain
and to every man grass in his field;
for the household gods make mischievous promises; 2
diviners see false signs,
they tell lying dreams<sup>b</sup>
 and talk raving nonsense.
Men wander about like sheep
in distress for lack of a shepherd.
My anger is turned against the shepherds, 3
 and I will visit with punishment the leaders of the flock;
but the LORD of Hosts will visit his flock,
 the house of Judah,
and make them his royal war-horses.
They shall be corner-stone and tent-peg, 4
they shall be the bow ready for battle,
and from them shall come every commander.
Together they shall be like warriors 5
who tramp the muddy ways in battle,
and they will fight because the LORD is with them;
they will put horsemen shamefully to rout.
And I will give strength to the house of Judah 6
and grant victory to<sup>c</sup> the house of Joseph;
I will restore them, for I have pitied them,
and they shall be as though I had never cast them off;
for I am the LORD their God and I will answer them.
So Ephraim shall be like warriors, 7
glad like men cheerful with wine,
and their sons shall see and be glad;
so let their hearts exult in the LORD.
I will whistle to call them in, for I have redeemed them; 8
 and they shall be as many as once they were.

---

<sup>a</sup> like: *prob. rdg.; Heb.* for.    <sup>b</sup> they ... dreams: *or* dreaming women make empty
promises.    <sup>c</sup> grant victory to: *or* expand.

9   If I disperse them[a] among the nations,
    in far-off lands they will remember me
    and will rear their sons and then return.
10   Then will I fetch them home from Egypt
    and gather them in from Assyria;
    I will lead them into Gilead and Lebanon
    until there is no more room for them.
11   Dire distress[b] shall come upon the Euphrates
    and shall beat down its turbulent waters;
    all the depths of the Nile shall run dry.
    The pride of Assyria shall be brought down,
    and the sceptre of Egypt shall pass away;
12   but Israel's strength shall be in the LORD,
    and they shall march proudly in his name.
    This is the very word of the LORD.

**11**   Throw open your gates, O Lebanon,
    that fire may feed on your cedars.
2   Howl, every pine-tree; for the cedars have fallen,
    mighty trees are ravaged.
    Howl, every oak of Bashan;
    for the impenetrable forest is laid low.
3   Hark to the howling of the shepherds,
    for their rich pastures are ravaged.
    Hark to the roar of the young lions,
    for Jordan's dense thickets are ravaged.

4   These were the words of the LORD my God: Fatten the flock for slaughter.
5   Those who buy will slaughter it and incur no guilt; those who sell will say,
'Blessed be the LORD, I am rich!' Its shepherds will have no pity for it.
6   For I will never again pity the inhabitants of the earth, says the LORD.
I will put every man in the power of his neighbour and his king, and as
each country is crushed I will not rescue him from their hands.
7   So I fattened the flock for slaughter for the dealers. I took two staves: one
8   I called Favour and the other Union, and so I fattened the flock. In one
month I got rid of the three shepherds, for I had lost patience with them
9   and they had come to abhor me. Then I said to the flock, 'I will not fatten
you any more. Any that are to die, let them die; any that stray, let them
10   stray; and the rest can devour one another.' I took my staff called Favour
and snapped it in two, annulling the covenant which the LORD[c] had made
11   with all nations. So it was annulled that day, and the dealers who were
12   watching me knew that all this was the word of the LORD. I said to
them, 'If it suits you, give me my wages; otherwise keep them.' Then
13   they weighed out my wages, thirty pieces of silver. The LORD said to me,
'Throw it into the treasury.' I took the thirty pieces of silver—that noble
sum at which I was valued and rejected by them!—and threw them into
14   the house of the LORD, into the treasury. Then I snapped in two my

---

[a] *Or* scatter them like seed.     [b] Dire distress: *or* An enemy.     [c] the LORD:
prob. rdg.; *Heb*. I.

second staff called Union, annulling the brotherhood between Judah and Israel.

Then the LORD said to me, Equip yourself again as a shepherd, a worth- 15
less one; for I am about to install a shepherd in the land who will neither 16
miss any that are lost nor search for those that have gone astray nor heal
the injured nor nurse the sickly, but will eat the flesh of the fat beasts and
throw away their broken bones.

> Alas for the worthless shepherd who abandons the sheep! 17
> A sword shall fall on his arm and on his right eye;
>> his arm shall be shrivelled
>> and his right eye blinded.
>
>> This is the very word of the LORD of Hosts: 13 7 *a*
> O sword, awake against my shepherd
>> and against him who works with me.
> Strike the shepherd, and the sheep will be scattered,
>> and I will turn my hand against the shepherd boys.
>> This also is the very word of the LORD: 8
>> It shall happen throughout the land
> that two thirds of the people shall be struck down and die,
>> while one third of them shall be left there.
> Then I will pass this third through the fire 9
> and I will refine them as silver is refined,
>> and assay them as gold is assayed.
> Then they will invoke me by my name,
>> and I myself will answer them;
>> I will say, 'They are my people',
> and they shall say, 'The LORD is our God.'

## *Jerusalem a centre of worship for all men*

AN ORACLE. This is the word of the LORD concerning Israel, the very 12
word of the LORD who stretched out the heavens and founded the
earth, and who formed the spirit of man within him: I am making the 2
steep approaches to Jerusalem slippery for all the nations pressing round
her; and Judah will be caught up in the siege of Jerusalem. On that day, 3
when all the nations of the earth will be gathered against her, I will make
Jerusalem a rock too heavy for any people to remove, and all who try to
lift it shall injure themselves. On that day, says the LORD, I will strike 4
every horse with panic and its rider with madness; I will keep watch over
Judah, but I will strike all the horses of the other nations with blindness.
Then the clans of Judah shall say to themselves, 'The inhabitants of 5
Jerusalem find their strength*b* in the LORD of Hosts their God.'

On that day I will make the clans of Judah like a brazier in woodland, 6
like a torch blazing among sheaves of corn. They shall devour all the nations
round them, right and left, while the people of Jerusalem remain safe in

---

*a* *13. 7-9 transposed to this point.*     *b* The . . . strength: *prob. rdg.; Heb.* O inhabitants of Jerusalem, I am strong.

7  their city. The LORD will first set free all the families[a] of Judah, so that the glory of David's line and of the inhabitants of Jerusalem may not surpass that of Judah.

8  On that day the LORD will shield the inhabitants of Jerusalem; on that day the very weakest of them shall be like David, and the line of David like God, like the angel of the LORD going before them.

9  On that day I will set about destroying all the nations that come against
10  Jerusalem, but I will pour a spirit of pity and compassion into the line of David and the inhabitants of Jerusalem. Then

They shall look on me, on him whom they have pierced,

and shall wail over him as over an only child, and shall grieve for him bitterly as for a first-born son.

11  On that day the mourning in Jerusalem shall be as great as the mourning
12  over Hadad-rimmon in the vale of Megiddo. The land shall wail, each family by itself: the family of David by itself and its women by themselves;
13  the family of Nathan by itself and its women by themselves; the family of Levi by itself and its women by themselves; the family of Shimei by itself
14  and its women by themselves; all the remaining families by themselves and their women by themselves.

13  On that day a fountain shall be opened for the line of David and for the inhabitants of Jerusalem, to remove all sin and impurity.

2  On that day, says the LORD of Hosts, I will erase the names of the idols from the land, and they shall be remembered no longer; I will also remove
3  the prophets and the spirit of uncleanness from the land. Thereafter, if a man continues to prophesy, his parents, his own father and mother, will say to him, 'You shall live no longer, for you have spoken falsely in the name of the LORD.' His own father and mother will pierce him through
4  because he has prophesied. On that day every prophet shall be ashamed of his vision when he prophesies, nor shall he wear a robe of coarse hair in
5  order to deceive. He will say, 'I am no prophet, I am a tiller of the soil who
6  has been schooled in lust from boyhood.' 'What', someone will ask, 'are these scars on your chest?' And he will answer, 'I got them in the house of my lovers.'[b]

14  A day is coming for the LORD to act, and the plunder taken from you
2  shall be shared out while you stand by. I will gather all the peoples to fight against Jerusalem; the city shall be taken, the houses plundered and the women raped. Half the city shall go into exile, but the rest of the nation in
3  the city shall not be wiped out. The LORD will come out and fight against
4  those peoples, as in the days of his prowess on the field of battle. On that day his feet will stand on the Mount of Olives, which is opposite Jeru-salem to the east, and the mountain shall be cleft in two by an immense valley running east and west; half the mountain shall move northwards
5  and half southwards. The valley between the hills[c] shall be blocked, for the new valley between them will reach as far as Asal. Blocked it shall be as it was blocked by the earthquake in the time of Uzziah king of Judah, and the LORD my God will appear with all the holy ones.

---

*a Or* tents.    *b Verses 7-9 transposed to follow 11. 17.*    *c Prob. rdg.; Heb.* my hills.

On that day there shall be neither heat nor cold nor frost. It shall be all 6 7 one day, whose coming is known only to the LORD, without distinction of day or night, and at evening-time there shall be light.

On that day living water shall issue from Jerusalem, half flowing to the 8 eastern sea and half to the western, in summer and winter alike. Then the 9 LORD shall become king over all the earth; on that day the LORD shall be one LORD and his name the one name. The whole land shall be levelled, 10 flat as the Arabah from Geba to Rimmon southwards; but Jerusalem shall stand high in her place, and shall be full of people from the Benjamin Gate [to the point where the former gate stood,] to the Corner Gate, and from the Tower of Hananel to the king's wine-vats. Men shall live in 11 Jerusalem, and never again shall a solemn ban be laid upon her; men shall live there in peace. The LORD will strike down all the nations who warred 12 against Jerusalem, and the plague shall be this: their flesh shall rot while they stand on their feet, their eyes shall rot in their sockets, and their tongues shall rot in their mouths.

On that day a great panic, sent by the LORD, shall fall on them. At the 13 very moment when a man would encourage his comrade his hand shall be raised to strike him down. Judah too shall join in the fray in Jerusalem, and 14 the wealth of the surrounding nations will be swept away—gold and silver and apparel in great abundance. And slaughter shall be the fate of horse and 15 mule, camel and ass, the fate of every beast in those armies.

All who survive of the nations which attacked Jerusalem shall come up 16 year by year to worship the King, the LORD of Hosts, and to keep the pilgrim-feast of Tabernacles. If any of the families of the earth do not go 17 up to Jerusalem to worship the King, the LORD of Hosts, no rain shall fall upon them. If any family of Egypt does not go up and enter the city, then 18 the same disaster shall overtake it as that which the LORD will inflict on any nation which does not go up to keep the feast. This shall be the punish- 19 ment of Egypt and of any nation which does not go up to keep the feast of Tabernacles.

On that day, not a bell on a war-horse but shall be inscribed 'Holy to 20 the LORD', and the pots in the house of the LORD shall be like the bowls before the altar. Every pot in Jerusalem and Judah shall be holy to the 21 LORD of Hosts, and all who sacrifice shall come and shall take some of them and boil the flesh in them. So when that time comes, no trader shall again be seen in the house of the LORD of Hosts.

# MALACHI

1 An oracle. The word of the LORD to Israel through Malachi.[a]

## Religious decline and hope of recovery

2 I LOVE YOU, says the LORD. You ask, 'How hast thou shown love to us?'
3 Is not Esau Jacob's brother? the LORD answers. I love Jacob, but I
hate Esau; I have turned his mountains into a waste and his ancestral home
4 into a lodging in the wilderness. When Edom says, 'We are beaten down;
let us rebuild our ruined homes', these are the words of the LORD of Hosts:
If they rebuild, I will pull down. They shall be called a realm of wicked-
5 ness, a people whom the LORD has cursed for ever. You yourselves will
see it with your own eyes; you yourselves will say, 'The LORD's greatness
reaches beyond the realm of Israel.'
6    A son honours his father, and a slave goes in fear of his master. If I am
a father, where is the honour due to me? If I am a master, where is the fear
due to me? So says the LORD of Hosts to you, you priests who despise my
7 name. You ask, 'How have we despised thy name?' Because you have
offered defiled food on my altar. You ask, 'How have we defiled thee?'
Because you have thought that the table of the LORD may be despised,
8 that if you offer a blind victim, there is nothing wrong, and if you offer a
victim lame or diseased, there is nothing wrong. If you brought such a
gift to the governor, would he receive you or show you favour? says the
9 LORD of Hosts. But now, if you placate God, he may show you mercy; if
you do this, will he withhold his favour from you? So the LORD of Hosts
10 has spoken. Better far that one of you should close the great door altogether,
so that the light might not fall thus all in vain upon my altar! I have no
pleasure in you, says the LORD of Hosts; I will accept no offering from you.
11 From furthest east to furthest west my name is great among the nations.
Everywhere fragrant sacrifice and pure gifts are offered in my name; for
12 my name is great among the nations, says the LORD of Hosts. But you
profane it by thinking that the table of the LORD may be defiled, and that
13 you can offer on it food you yourselves despise. You sniff at it, says the LORD
of Hosts, and say, 'How irksome!' If you bring as your offering victims that
are mutilated, lame, or diseased, shall I accept them from you? says the
14 LORD. A curse on the cheat who pays his vows by sacrificing a damaged
victim to the Lord, though he has a sound ram in his flock! I am the great
king, says the LORD of Hosts, and my name is held in awe among the
nations.
2 1 2    And now, you priests, this decree is for you: if you will not listen to me
and pay heed to the honouring of my name, says the LORD of Hosts, then
I will lay a curse upon you. I will turn your blessings into a curse; yes, into

---

a Malachi: or my messenger.

a curse, because you pay no heed. I will cut off your arm,*a* fling offal in 3
your faces, the offal of your pilgrim-feasts, and I will banish you from my
presence. Then you will know that I have issued this decree against you: 4
my covenant with Levi falls to the ground, says the LORD of Hosts. My 5
covenant was with him: I bestowed life and prosperity on him; I laid on
him the duty of reverence, he revered me and lived in awe of my name.
The instruction he gave was true, and no word of injustice fell from his 6
lips; he walked in harmony with me and in uprightness, and he turned
many back from sin. For men hang upon the words of the priest and seek 7
knowledge and instruction from him, because he is the messenger of the
LORD of Hosts. But you have turned away from that course; you have made 8
many stumble with your instruction; you have set at nought the covenant
with the Levites, says the LORD of Hosts. So I, in my turn, have made you 9
despicable and mean in the eyes of the people, in so far as you disregard
my ways and show partiality in your instruction.

Have we not all one father? Did not one God create us? Why do we 10
violate the covenant of our forefathers by being faithless to one another?
Judah is faithless, and abominable things are done in Israel and in Jeru- 11
salem; Judah has violated the holiness of the LORD by loving and marrying
daughters of a foreign god. May the LORD banish any who do this from the 12
dwellings of Jacob, nomads or settlers, even though they bring offerings
to the LORD of Hosts.

Here is another thing that you do: you weep and moan, and you drown 13
the altar of the LORD with tears, but he still refuses to look at the offering
or receive an acceptable gift from you. You ask why. It is because the LORD 14
has borne witness against you on behalf of the wife of your youth. You have
been unfaithful to her, though she is your partner and your wife by solemn
covenant. Did not the one God make her, both flesh and spirit? And what 15
does the one God require but godly children? Keep watch on your spirit,
and do not be unfaithful to the wife of your youth. If a man divorces 16
or puts away his spouse, he overwhelms her with cruelty, says the LORD
of Hosts the God of Israel. Keep watch on your spirit, and do not be
unfaithful.

You have wearied the LORD with your talk. You ask, 'How have we 17
wearied him?' By saying that all evildoers are good in the eyes of the LORD,
that he is pleased with them, or by asking, 'Where is the God of justice?'
Look, I am sending my messenger *b* who will clear a path before me. 3
Suddenly the Lord whom you seek will come to his temple; the messenger
of the covenant in whom you delight is here, here already, says the LORD
of Hosts. Who can endure the day of his coming? Who can stand firm when 2
he appears? He is like a refiner's fire, like fuller's soap; he will take his seat, 3
refining and purifying;*c* he will purify the Levites and cleanse them like
gold and silver, and so they shall be fit to bring offerings to the LORD. Thus 4
the offerings of Judah and Jerusalem shall be pleasing to the LORD as they
were in days of old, in years long past. I will appear before you in court, 5
prompt to testify against sorcerers, adulterers, and perjurers, against those

---

*a Or* posterity.          *b my messenger: Heb.* Malachi.          *c Prob. rdg.; Heb. adds*
silver.

who wrong[a] the hired labourer, the widow, and the orphan, who thrust the alien aside and have no fear of me, says the LORD of Hosts.

6  I am the LORD, unchanging; and you, too, have not ceased to be sons of
7  Jacob. From the days of your forefathers you have been wayward and have not kept my laws. If you will return to me, I will return to you, says the
8  LORD of Hosts. You ask, 'How can we return?' May man defraud God, that you defraud me? You ask, 'How have we defrauded thee?' Why, in
9  tithes and contributions. There is a curse, a curse on you all, the whole
10  nation of you, because you defraud me. Bring the tithes into the treasury, all of them; let there be food in my house. Put me to the proof, says the LORD of Hosts, and see if I do not open windows in the sky and pour a
11  blessing on you as long as there is need. I will forbid pests to destroy the produce of your soil or make your vines barren, says the LORD of Hosts.
12  All nations shall count you happy, for yours shall be a favoured land, says the LORD of Hosts.

## *Murmurers warned, the righteous triumphant*

13  YOU HAVE USED HARD WORDS ABOUT ME, says the LORD, and then
14  you ask, 'How have we spoken against thee?' You have said, 'It is useless to serve God; what do we gain from the LORD of Hosts by observing
15  his rules and behaving with deference? We ourselves count the arrogant happy; it is evildoers who are successful; they have put God to the proof and come to no harm.'
16  Then those who feared the LORD talked together, and the LORD paid heed and listened. A record was written before him of those who feared
17  him and kept his name in mind. They shall be mine, says the LORD of Hosts, my own possession against the day that I appoint, and I will spare
18  them as a man spares the son who serves him. You will again tell good men from bad, the servant of God from the man who does not serve him.
4  The day comes, glowing like a furnace; all the arrogant and the evildoers shall be chaff, and that day when it comes shall set them ablaze, says
2  the LORD of Hosts, it shall leave them neither root nor branch. But for you who fear my name, the sun of righteousness shall rise with healing in
3  his wings, and you shall break loose like calves released from the stall. On the day that I act, you shall trample down the wicked, for they will be ashes under the soles of your feet, says the LORD of Hosts.
4  Remember the law of Moses my servant, the rules and precepts which I bade him deliver to all Israel at Horeb.
5  Look, I will send you the prophet Elijah before the great and terrible
6  day of the LORD comes. He will reconcile fathers to sons and sons to fathers, lest I come and put the land under a ban to destroy it.

[a] *Prob. rdg.; Heb. adds* the wages of.

# APPENDIX

## MEASURES OF LENGTH

|       | span | cubit | rod[a] |
|-------|------|-------|--------|
| span  | 1    | ..    | ..     |
| cubit | 2    | 1     | ..     |
| rod[a]| 12   | 6     | 1      |

The 'short cubit' was traditionally the measure from the elbow to the knuckles of the closed fist; and what seems to be intended as a 'long cubit' measured a 'cubit and a hand-breadth', i.e. 7 instead of 6 hand-breadths (Ezek. 40. 5). What is meant by cubits 'according to the old standard of measurement' (2 Chr. 3. 3) is presumably this pre-exilic cubit of 7 hand-breadths. Modern estimates of the Hebrew cubit range from 12 to 25·2 inches, without allowing for varying local standards.

## MEASURES OF CAPACITY

| liquid measures | equivalences | dry measures |
|-----------------|--------------|--------------|
| 'log'           | 1 'log'      | ..           |
| ..              | 4 'log'      | 'kab'        |
| ..              | 7⅕ 'log'     | 'omer'       |
| 'hin'           | 12 'log'     | ..           |
| 'bath'          | 72 'log'     | 'ephah'      |
| 'kor'           | 720 'log'    | 'homer' or 'kor' |

According to ancient authorities the Hebrew 'log' was of the same capacity as the Roman *sextarius*; this according to the best available evidence was equivalent to 0·99 pint of the English standard.

## WEIGHTS AND COINS

|        | heavy (Phoenician) standard | | | light (Babylonian) standard | | |
|--------|--------|------|--------|--------|------|--------|
|        | shekel | mina | talent | shekel | mina | talent |
| shekel | 1      | ..   | ..     | 1      | ..   | ..     |
| mina   | 50     | 1    | ..     | 60     | 1    | ..     |
| talent | 3,000  | 60   | 1      | 3,600  | 60   | 1      |

The 'gerah' was 1/20 of the sacred or heavy shekel and probably 1/24 of the light shekel.

The 'sacred shekel' according to tradition was identical with the heavy shekel;

[a] Hebrew literally 'reed', the length of Ezekiel's measuring-rod.

# APPENDIX

while the 'shekel of the standard recognized by merchants' (Gen. 23. 16) was perhaps a weight stamped with its value as distinct from one not so stamped and requiring to be weighed on the spot.

The weight and value of the shekel varied so greatly according to the district and with the passing centuries that its evaluation in modern terms is impossible. Recent discoveries suggest that it may have weighed approximately 11·5 grammes.

Coins are not mentioned before the Exile. Only the 'daric' (1 Chr. 29. 7) and the 'drachma' (Ezra 2. 69; Neh. 7. 70–72), if this is a distinct coin, are found in the Old Testament; the former is said to have been a month's pay for a soldier in the Persian army, while the latter will have been the Greek silver drachma, estimated at approximately 4·4 grammes. The 'shekel' of this period (Neh. 5. 15) as a coin was probably the Graeco-Persian *siglos* weighing 5·6 grammes.

# THE NEW
# ENGLISH BIBLE

## THE APOCRYPHA

# CONTENTS

# INTRODUCTION

## TO THE APOCRYPHA

THE TERM 'APOCRYPHA', a Greek word meaning 'hidden (things)', was early used in different senses. It was applied to writings which were regarded as so important and precious that they must be hidden from the general public and reserved for the initiates, the inner circle of believers. It came to be applied to writings which were hidden not because they were too good but because they were not good enough, because, that is, they were secondary or questionable or heretical. A third usage may be traced to Jerome. He was familiar with the Scriptures in their Hebrew as well as their Greek form, and for him apocryphal books were those outside the Hebrew canon.

The generally accepted modern usage is based on that of Jerome. The Apocrypha as here translated consists of fifteen books or parts of books. They are:

(1) The First Book of Esdras
(2) The Second Book of Esdras
(3) Tobit
(4) Judith
(5) The Rest of the Chapters of the Book of Esther
(6) The Wisdom of Solomon
(7) Ecclesiasticus or the Wisdom of Jesus son of Sirach
(8) Baruch
(9) A Letter of Jeremiah
(10) The Song of the Three
(11) Daniel and Susanna
(12) Daniel, Bel, and the Snake
(13) The Prayer of Manasseh
(14) The First Book of the Maccabees
(15) The Second Book of the Maccabees

These works are outside the Palestinian canon; that is, they form no part of the Hebrew Scriptures, although the original language of some of them was Hebrew. With the exception, however, of the Second Book of Esdras, they are all in the Greek version of the Old Testament made for the Greek-speaking Jews in Egypt. As such they were accepted as biblical by the early Church and were quoted as Scripture by many early Christian writers, for their Bible was the Greek Bible.

In Greek and Latin manuscripts of the Old Testament these books are dispersed throughout the Old Testament, generally in the places most in accord with their contents. The practice of collecting them into a separate unit, a practice which dates back no farther than A.D. 1520, explains why certain of the items are but fragments; they are passages not found in the Hebrew Bible, and so have been removed from the books in which they occur in the Greek version. To help the reader over this disunity and lack of context the present translators have resorted to various devices. We have added the name Daniel to the titles of the stories of Susanna and of Bel and the Snake as a reminder that these tales are to be read with the Book of Daniel. A note we have inserted after the title, The Song of the Three, indicates that this item is to be found in the third chapter of the Greek form of Daniel. And the six additions to the Book of Esther are so disjointed and unintelligible as they stand in most editions of the Apocrypha that we have provided them with a context by rendering the whole of the Greek version of Esther.

The text used in this translation of the Apocrypha is that edited by H. B. Swete in *The Old Testament in Greek according to the Septuagint*. In places Swete includes two texts, and we have chosen to translate the Codex Sinaiticus text of Tobit and Theodotion's version of the additions to the Book of Daniel, namely, The Song of the Three, Daniel and Susanna, and Daniel, Bel, and the Snake. For Ecclesiasticus we have used, in addition to Codex Vaticanus as printed in Swete's edition, the text edited by J. H. A. Hart in *Ecclesiasticus : the Greek Text of Codex 248*, and constant reference has been made to the various forms of the Hebrew text. For the Second Book of Esdras, which apart from a few verses is not extant in a Greek form, we have based our translation on the Latin text of R. L. Bensly's *The Fourth Book of Ezra*. Throughout we have consulted the variant. readings given in critical editions of the Greek, the texts of the versions, and the suggestions of editors and commentators.

Alternative readings cited from Greek manuscripts (referred to as *witnesses*) and the evidence of early translations (*Vss.*, that is Versions) are given, as footnotes, only when they are significant either for text or for meaning. In a few places where the text seems to have suffered in the course of transmission and in its present form is obscure or unintelligible we have made a slight change in the text and marked our rendering of it *probable reading*, and we have indicated any evidence other than the evidence afforded by the context. Where an alternative interpretation seemed to deserve serious consideration it has been recorded as a footnote with *Or* as indicator.

In order to preserve the verse numbering of the Authorized (King James) Version of 1611 we have, when necessary, added at the foot of the page those passages which are found in the manuscripts on which the Authorized Version ultimately rests but which are absent from the earlier manuscripts now available.

We have not sought to achieve consistency in the treatment of proper names any more than did our predecessors. We have continued to use familiar English forms, especially when the reference is to well-known Old Testament characters or places. Sometimes as an aid to the correct pronunciation we have had recourse to such expedients as the affixing of an acute accent to the word Sidé or the introduction of a diphthong, as in our Soud for Sud. In general it may be said that Greek spellings have been

Latinized, but the Greek forms of place-names have not been brought into line with the Hebrew.

We have not aimed at consistency in our treatment of weights and measures. We have rendered terms into the nearest English equivalents only when these seemed suitable and natural in the context.

In the text of the First and Second Books of the Maccabees the dates given are reckoned according to the Greek or Seleucid era. As a help to the reader we have added at the foot of the page the nearest dates according to the Christian era.

This translation of the Apocrypha shares with other parts of The New English Bible the aim of providing a rendering which will be both faithful to the text translated and genuinely English in idiom. The translators have endeavoured to convey the meaning of the original in language which will be the closest natural equivalent. They have tried to avoid free paraphrase on the one hand and, on the other, formal fidelity resulting in a translation which would read like a translation. It is their hope that by their labours these documents, valuable in themselves and indispensable for the study of the background of the New Testament, have been made more intelligible and more readily accessible.

W. D. McH.

# MARGINAL NUMBERS

THE conventional verse divisions in the Apocrypha date only from editions printed in the sixteenth century and have no basis in the manuscripts. Any system of division into numbered verses is foreign to the spirit of this translation, which is intended to convey the meaning in continuous natural English.

For purposes of reference, verse numbers are placed in the margin opposite the line in which the first word belonging to the verse in question appears. Sometimes, however, successive verses are combined in a continuous translation, so that the precise point where a new verse begins cannot be fixed; in these cases the verse numbers, joined by a hyphen, are placed at the point where the passage begins.

# THE FIRST BOOK OF
# ESDRAS

## *Exile and return*

JOSIAH KEPT the Passover at Jerusalem in honour of his Lord 1
and sacrificed the Passover victims on the fourteenth day of the first
month. The priests, duly robed in their vestments, he stationed in the 2
temple of the Lord according to the order of daily service. He commanded 3
the Levites, who served the temple in Israel, to purify themselves for the
Lord, in order to place the holy Ark of the Lord in the house which was
built by King Solomon, son of David. Josiah said to them, 'You are no 4
longer to carry it on your shoulders. Make yourselves ready now, family
by family and clan by clan, to do service to the Lord your God and to
minister to his people Israel in the manner prescribed by King David and 5
provided for so magnificently by his son Solomon. Take your places in the
temple as Levites in the prescribed order of your families in the presence
of your brother Israelites; sacrifice the Passover victims, and prepare the 6
sacrifices for your brothers. Observe the Passover according to the ordinance of the Lord which was given to Moses.'

To those who were present Josiah made a gift of thirty thousand lambs 7
and kids and three thousand calves. These he gave from the royal estates in
fulfilment of his promise to the people and to the priests and Levites. The 8
temple-wardens, Chelkias, Zacharias, and Esyelus, gave the priests two
thousand six hundred sheep and three hundred calves for the Passover.
Jechonias, Samaeas, his brother Nathanael, Sabias, Ozielus, and Joram, 9
army officers of high rank, gave the Levites five thousand sheep and seven
hundred calves for the Passover.

This was the procedure. The priests and the Levites, bearing the un- 10
leavened bread, stood in all their splendour before the people, in the order
of their clans and families, to make offerings to the Lord as is laid down in 11
the book of Moses. This took place in the morning. They roasted the Pass- 12
over victims over the fire in the prescribed way and boiled the sacrifices in
the vessels and cauldrons, and a pleasant smell went up; then they carried 13
portions round to the whole assembly. After this they made preparations
both for themselves and for their brothers the priests, the sons of Aaron.
The priests went on offering the fat until nightfall, while the Levites made 14
the preparations both for themselves and for their brothers the priests, the
sons of Aaron. The sons of Asaph, the temple singers, with Asaph, Zacha- 15-16
rias, and Eddinous of the royal court, and the door-keepers at each gateway
remained at their station according to the ordinances of David, which pre-
scribe that no one may lawfully default in his daily duty; their brothers

17 the Levites made the preparations for them. All that pertained to the Lord's
18 sacrifice was completed that day: the keeping of the Passover and the offering of the sacrifices on the altar of the Lord according to the command of
19 King Josiah. The Israelites who were present on this occasion kept the
20 Passover and the Feast of Unleavened Bread for seven days. Such a Passover had not been kept in Israel since the time of the prophet Samuel;
21 none of the kings of Israel had kept such a Passover as was kept by Josiah,
the priests and the Levites, the men of Judah, and those Israelites who
22 happened to be resident in Jerusalem. It was in the eighteenth year of
Josiah's reign that this Passover was celebrated.

23 All that Josiah did he did rightly and in whole-hearted devotion to his
24 Lord. The events of his reign are to be found in ancient records which tell
a story of sin and rebellion against the Lord graver than that of any other
nation or kingdom, and of offences against him which brought down his
judgement upon Israel.

25 After all these doings of Josiah's it happened that Pharaoh king of Egypt
was advancing to attack Carchemish on the Euphrates, and Josiah took
26 the field against him. The king of Egypt sent him this message: 'What is
27 your business with me, king of Judah? It is not against you that the Lord
God has sent me to fight; my campaign is on the Euphrates. The Lord is
with me, the Lord, I say, is with me, driving me on. Withdraw, and do not
28 oppose the Lord.' Josiah did not turn his chariot but went forward to the
attack. He disregarded what the Lord had said through the prophet Jere-
29 miah and joined battle with Pharaoh in the plain of Megiddo. Pharaoh's
30 captains swept down upon King Josiah. The king said to his servants, 'Take
me out of the battle, for I am badly hurt.' At once his servants took him out
31 of the line and lifted him into his second chariot. He was brought back to
Jerusalem, and there he died and was buried in his ancestral tomb.

32 All Judah mourned Josiah, and the prophet Jeremiah lamented him.
The lamentation for Josiah has been observed by the chief men and their
wives from that day to this; it was proclaimed that it should be a custom
33 for ever for the whole people of Israel. These things are recorded in the
book of the histories of the kings of Judah; every deed that Josiah did which
won him fame and showed his understanding of the law of the Lord, both
what he did earlier and what is told of him here, is related in the book of the
kings of Israel and Judah.

34 His compatriots took Joachaz the son of Josiah and made him king in
35 succession to his father. He was twenty-three years old, and he reigned over
Judah and Jerusalem for three months. Then the king of Egypt deposed
36 37 him, fined the nation a hundred talents of silver and one talent of gold, and
38 appointed his brother Joakim king of Judah and Jerusalem. Joakim imprisoned the leading men and had his brother Zarius arrested and brought
back from Egypt.

39 Joakim was twenty-five years old when he became king of Judah and
40 Jerusalem; he did what was wrong in the eyes of the Lord. Nebuchadnezzar
king of Babylon marched against him; he put him in chains of bronze and
41 took him to Babylon. Nebuchadnezzar also took some of the sacred vessels
42 of the Lord, carried them off, and put them in his temple in Babylon. The

2

stories about Joakim, his sacrilegious and godless conduct, are recorded in the chronicles of the kings.

Joakim was succeeded on the throne by his eighteen-year-old son 43 Joakim. He reigned in Jerusalem for three months and ten days, and did 44 what was wrong in the eyes of the Lord.

A year later Nebuchadnezzar had him deported to Babylon together 45 with the sacred vessels of the Lord. He made Zedekiah king of Judah and 46 Jerusalem.•Zedekiah was twenty-one years old and reigned eleven years. He did what was wrong in the eyes of the Lord and disregarded what the 47 Lord had said through the prophet Jeremiah. King Nebuchadnezzar had 48 made him take an oath of allegiance by the Lord, but he broke it and revolted. He was stubborn and defiant, and transgressed the commandments of the Lord, the God of Israel.

The leaders of the people and the chief priests committed many wicked 49 and lawless acts, outdoing even the heathen in sacrilege, and they defiled the holy temple of the Lord in Jerusalem. The God of their fathers sent his 50 messenger to reclaim them, because he wished to spare them and his dwelling-place. But they derided his messengers, and on the very day 51 when the Lord spoke they were scoffing at his prophets. At last he was 52 roused to fury against his people for their impieties, and ordained that the kings of the Chaldaeans should attack them. These put their young men 53 to the sword all round the holy temple, sparing neither old nor young, neither boy nor girl; the Lord handed them all over to their enemies. All 54 the sacred vessels of the Lord, large and small, the furnishings of the Ark of the Lord, and the royal treasures were carried off to Babylon. The house 55 of the Lord was set on fire, the walls of Jerusalem destroyed, its towers burnt, and all its splendours ruined. Nebuchadnezzar carried off to Babylon the 56 survivors from the slaughter, and they remained slaves to him and his sons 57 until the Persians took his empire. This fulfilled the word of the Lord spoken by Jeremiah: 'Until the land has run the full term of its sabbaths, it shall 58 keep sabbath all the time of its desolation till the end of the seventy years.'

DURING THE FIRST YEAR of Cyrus king of Persia, the Lord, in order 2 1-2 to fulfil his word spoken through Jeremiah, moved Cyrus king of Persia to make a proclamation throughout his empire, which he also put in writing: 'This is the decree of Cyrus king of Persia: The Lord of Israel, the most 3 high Lord, has made me king of the world and has directed me to build 4 him a house at Jerusalem in Judaea. Whoever among you belongs to his 5 people, may his Lord be with him; let him go up to Jerusalem in Judaea and build the house of the Lord of Israel, the Lord who dwells in Jerusalem. Wherever each man lives let his neighbours help him with gold and 6 silver and other gifts, with horses and pack-animals, together with other 7 things set aside as votive offerings for the Lord's temple in Jerusalem.'

Then the chiefs of the clans of the tribe of Judah and of Benjamin, the 8 priests, the Levites, came forward, and all whose spirit the Lord had moved to go up to build the Lord's temple in Jerusalem. Their neighbours helped 9 with everything, with silver and gold, horses and pack-animals; and many were also moved to help with votive offerings in great quantity. King Cyrus 10

brought out the sacred vessels of the Lord which Nebuchadnezzar had
11 taken away from Jerusalem and set up in his idolatrous temple. Cyrus
king of Persia brought them out and delivered them to Mithradates his
12 treasurer, by whom they were delivered to Sanabassar, the governor of
13 Judaea. This is the inventory: a thousand gold cups, a thousand silver cups,
twenty-nine silver censers, thirty gold bowls, two thousand four hundred
14 and ten silver bowls, and a thousand other articles. In all, five thousand
15 four hundred and sixty-nine gold and silver vessels were returned, and
taken from Babylon to Jerusalem by Sanabassar together with the exiles.
16    In the time of Artaxerxes king of Persia, Belemus, Mithradates, Tabel-
lius, Rathymus, Beeltethmus, Semellius the secretary, and their colleagues
in office in Samaria and other places, wrote him a letter denouncing the
inhabitants of Judaea and Jerusalem in the following terms:

17        To our Sovereign Lord Artaxerxes your servants Rathymus the
recorder, Semellius the secretary, the other members of their council,
and the magistrates in Coele-syria and Phoenicia:
18        This is to inform Your Majesty that the Jews who left you to come here
have arrived in Jerusalem and are rebuilding that wicked and rebellious
city. They are repairing its streets and walls and laying the foundation of
19        the temple. If this city is rebuilt and the walls completed, they will cease
20    paying tribute and will rebel against the royal house. Since work on the
temple is in hand, we have thought it well not to neglect this important
21    matter but to bring it to Your Majesty's notice, in order that, if it is Your
Majesty's pleasure, search may be made in the records left by your prede-
22    cessors. You will find in the archives evidence about these matters and will
learn that this is a city that has resisted authority and given trouble to
23    kings and to other states, and has been a centre of armed rebellion by the
24    Jews from the earliest times. That is why it was laid in ruins. Now we submit to Your Majesty that, if this city be rebuilt and its walls rise again,
you will no longer have access to Coele-syria and Phoenicia.

25        Then the king wrote to Rathymus the recorder, Beeltethmus, Semellius
the secretary, and their colleagues in office in Samaria, Syria, and Phoenicia
this reply:

26        I have read your letter. I ordered search to be made and it was dis-
27    covered that this city has always been opposed to its overlords, and its
inhabitants have raised rebellions and made wars. There were kings in
Jerusalem, powerful and ruthless men, who in their time controlled
28    Coele-syria and Phoenicia and exacted tribute from them. I therefore
command that the men you mention be prevented from rebuilding the
29    city, and that measures be taken to enforce this order and to check the
spread of an evil likely to be a nuisance to the royal house.

30        When the letter from King Artaxerxes had been read, Rathymus,
Semellius the secretary, and their colleagues set out at once for Jerusalem
with cavalry and a large body of other troops and stopped the builders.
The building of the temple was broken off until the second year of the reign
of Darius king of Persia.

## A debate at the Persian court

KING DARIUS held a great feast for all those under him, his household, 3 the chief men of Media and Persia, and the satraps and commanders 2 and governors of his empire in the hundred and twenty-seven satrapies from India to Ethiopia. When they had eaten and drunk their fill, they 3 went away, and King Darius withdrew to his bedchamber; he went to sleep but woke up again. Then the three young men of the king's personal 4 bodyguard said to each other: 'Let each one of us name the thing which he 5 judges the strongest; and to the one whose opinion seems wisest King Darius will give rich gifts and prizes: he shall be clothed in purple, drink 6 from gold vessels, and sleep on a golden bed; and he shall have a chariot with gold-studded bridles, and a fine linen turban, and a chain about his neck. His wisdom shall give him the right to sit next to Darius and to be 7 given the title Kinsman of Darius.' Then each wrote down his own state- 8 ment, sealed it, and put it under the king's pillow. 'When the king wakes 9 again,' they said, 'the writing will be given him. The king and the three chief men of Persia shall judge whose statement is wisest, and the award will be made on the merits of the written statement.'

One wrote 'Wine is strongest', the second wrote 'The king is strongest', 10 11 and the third wrote 'Women are strongest, but truth conquers all'. When 12 13 the king got up he was presented with what they had written. He read it, and summoned all the chief men of Persia and Media, satraps, commanders, 14 governors, and chief officers. Then he took his seat in the council chamber, 15 and what they had written was read out before them. He said, 'Call the 16 young men and let them expound their statements.' They were called and came in. They were asked, 'Tell us about what you have written.' 17

The first, who spoke about the strength of wine, began. 'Sirs,' he said, 18 'how true it is that wine is strongest! It sends astray the wits of all who drink it; king and orphan, slave and free, rich and poor, it has the same 19 effect on them all. It turns all thoughts to revelry and mirth; it brings for- 20 getfulness of grief and debt. It makes all feel rich, cares nothing for king or 21 satrap, and makes men always talk in millions. When they are in their 22 cups, they forget to be friendly to friends and relations, and are quick to draw their swords; when they have recovered from their wine, they cannot 23 remember what they have done. Sirs, is not wine the strongest, seeing that 24 it forces men to behave in this way?' With this he ended.

Then the second, the one who spoke of the strength of the king, began 4 his speech: 'Sirs, is not man the strongest, man who masters the earth and 2 the sea and all that is in them? But the strongest of men is the king; he is 3 their lord and master, and they obey all his commands. If he bids them 4 make war upon one another they do it; if he dispatches them against his enemies, they march and level mountains and walls and towers. They kill 5 and are killed; they do not disobey the king's order. If they are victorious they bring everything to the king, their spoils and everything else. Or take 6 those who do not serve as soldiers or go to war, but work the land: they sow and reap, and bring their produce to the king. They compel each other to bring him their tribute. Though he is no more than one man, if he orders 7

5

8 them to kill, they kill; if he orders them to release, they release; he orders
them to attack and they attack, to lay waste and they lay waste, to build
9 and they build, to cut down and they cut down, to plant and they plant.
10 So all his people and his troops obey him. Besides this, while he himself
11 sits at table, eats and drinks, and goes to sleep, they stand in attendance
round about him and none can leave and see to his own affairs; they never
12 disobey him in anything. Sirs, of course the king must be strongest when
he commands such obedience!' So he stopped speaking.

13 The third, who spoke about women and truth—and this was Zerub-
14 babel—said: 'Sirs, it is true the king is great, men are many, and wine is
strong, but who rules over them? Who is the sovereign power? Women,
15 surely! The king and all his people who rule land and sea were born of
16 women, and from them they came. Women brought up the men who
17 planted the vineyards which yield the wine. They make clothes for men
18 and they bring honour to men; men cannot do without women. If they
have amassed gold and silver and all kinds of beautiful things, and then
19 see a woman with a lovely face and figure, they leave all these things to gape
and stare at her with open mouth, and all choose her in preference to gold
20 or silver or beautiful things. A man will desert his father who brought him
21 up, desert even his country, and become one with his wife. He forgets
father, mother, and country, and stays with his wife to the end of his days.
22 Here is the proof that women are your masters: do you not toil and sweat
23 and then bring all you earn and give it to your wives? A man will take his
24 sword and sally forth to plunder and rob, to sail on sea and river; he faces
lions, he travels in the dark; and when he has robbed and plundered he
brings the spoil home to his beloved.               ·

25 26 'A man loves his wife more than his father or mother. For women's sakes
many men have been driven out of their minds, many have been sold into
27 28 slavery, many have died or come to grief or ruined their lives. Do you
believe me now? Certainly the king wields great authority; no country
29 dare lift a finger against him. Yet I watched him with Apame, his favourite
concubine, daughter of the famous Bartacus. She was sitting on the king's
30 right; she took the diadem off his head and put it on her own, and slapped
31 his face with her left hand; and the king only gazed at her open-mouthed.
When she laughed at him he laughed; when she was cross with him he
32 coaxed her to make it up. Sirs, if women do as well as this, how can their
33 strength be denied?' The king and the chief men looked at one another.

34 He then went on to speak about truth: 'Sirs, we have seen that women
are strong. The earth is vast, the sky is lofty, the sun swift in his course,
for he moves through the circle of the sky and speeds home in a single day.
35 How great is he who does all this! But truth too is great and stronger than
36 all else. The whole earth calls on truth; the sky praises her. All created
37 things shake and tremble; with her there is no injustice. There is injustice
in wine, in kings, in women, in all men, and in all their works, and so forth.
38 There is no truth in them; they shall perish in their injustice. But truth
39 abides and is strong for ever; she lives and rules for ever and ever. With her
there is no favouritism or partiality; she chooses to do justice rather than
40 what is unjust and evil. All approve her works; in her judgements there is

no injustice. Hers are strength and royalty, the authority and majesty of all ages. Praise be to the God of truth!'

So he ended his speech, and all the people shouted and said, 'Great 41 is truth: truth is strongest!' Then the king said to him, 'Ask what you 42 will, even beyond what is in the writing, and I will grant it you. For you have been proved the wisest; and you shall sit by me and be called my Kinsman.'

Then he said to the king: 'Remember the vow you made on the day when 43 you came to the throne. You promised to rebuild Jerusalem and to send 44 back all the vessels taken from it which Cyrus set aside. When he vowed to destroy Babylon he also vowed to restore these vessels; and you too made 45 a vow to rebuild the temple which the Edomites burnt when Judaea was ravaged by the Chaldaeans. This is the favour that I now beg of you, my 46 lord king, this is the magnanimity I request: that you should perform the vow which you made to the King of heaven.'

King Darius stood up and kissed him, and wrote letters for him to all 47 the treasurers, governors, commanders, and satraps instructing them to give safe conduct to him and to all those who were going up with him to rebuild Jerusalem. To all the governors in Coele-syria and Phoenicia and 48 in Lebanon he wrote letters ordering them to transport cedar-wood from Lebanon to Jerusalem and join with Zerubbabel in building the city. He 49 gave all Jews going up from the kingdom to Judaea letters assuring their liberties: that no officer, satrap, governor, or treasurer should interfere with them, that all land which they should acquire should be immune 50 from taxation, and that the Edomites should surrender the villages they had seized from the Jews. Each year twenty talents were to be contributed 51 to the building of the temple until it was finished, and a further ten talents 52 annually for*ᵃ* burnt-offerings to be sacrificed daily upon the altar in accordance with their law. All those who were going from Babylonia to build 53-54 the city were to enjoy freedom, and their descendants after them. He gave written orders that all the priests going there should also receive maintenance and the vestments in which they would officiate; that the Levites too 55 should receive maintenance, until the day when the building of the temple and Jerusalem was completed; and that all who guarded the city should be 56 given land and pay. He sent back all the vessels from Babylon which Cyrus 57 had set aside. All that Cyrus had commanded, he reaffirmed, ordering everything to be restored to Jerusalem.

When the young man, Zerubbabel, went out, he turned his face toward 58 Jerusalem, looked up to heaven, and praised the King of heaven. 'From 59 thee comes victory,' he said, 'from thee comes wisdom; thine is the glory and I am thy servant. All praise to thee who hast given me wisdom; to thee 60 I give thanks, O Lord of our fathers.'

He took the letters and set off for Babylon, where he told his fellow-Jews. 61 They praised the God of their fathers because he had given them full free- 62 dom to go and rebuild Jerusalem and the temple called by his name, and 63 they feasted for a week with music and rejoicing.

*ᵃ Some witnesses add* seventeen.

## The temple rebuilt

5 AFTER THIS the heads of families, tribe by tribe, were chosen to go to
Jerusalem, with their wives, their sons and daughters, their male and
2 female slaves, and their pack-animals. Darius sent a thousand horsemen
to accompany them until they had brought them safely back to Jerusalem,
3 with a band of drums and flutes, and all their brothers dancing. So he sent
them off with their escort.

4 These are the names of the men who went to Jerusalem, according to their
5 families, tribes, and allotted duties. The priests, the sons of Phineas son of
Aaron, with Jeshua son of Josedek son of Saraeas, and Joakim his son; and [a]
Zerubbabel son of Salathiel of the house of David of the line of Phares
6 of the tribe of Judah, who spoke wise words before Darius king of Persia.
They went in the second year of his reign, in Nisan the first month.

7 Now these are the men of Judah who came up from amongst the captive
exiles, those whom Nebuchadnezzar king of Babylon had transported to
8 Babylon. They returned to Jerusalem and the rest of Judaea, each to his own
city: they came with Zerubbabel and Jeshua, Nehemiah, Zaraeas, Resaeas,
Enenius, Mardochaeus, Beelsarus, Aspharasus, Reelias, Romelius, and
9 Baana, their leaders. The numbers of those from the nation who returned
with their leaders were: the line of Phoros two thousand one hundred and
10 seventy-two; the line of Saphat four hundred and seventy-two; the line of
11 Ares seven hundred and fifty-six; the line of Phaath-moab, deriving from
12 the line of Jeshua and Joab, two thousand eight hundred and twelve; the
line of Elam one thousand two hundred and fifty-four; the line of Zathui
nine hundred and forty-five; the line of Chorbe seven hundred and five;
13 the line of Banei six hundred and forty-eight; the line of Bebae six hundred
and twenty-three; the line of Astaa one thousand three hundred and
14 twenty-two. The line of Adonikam six hundred and sixty-seven; the line
of Bagoi two thousand and sixty-six; the line of Adinus four hundred and
15 fifty-four; the line of Ater son of Hezekias ninety-two; the line of Keilan
and Azetas sixty-seven; the line of Azurus four hundred and thirty-two;
16 the line of Annias one hundred and one; the line of Arom and the line of
Bassa three hundred and twenty-three; the line of Arsiphurith one hundred
17 and twelve; the line of Baeterus three thousand and five. The line of
18 Bethlomon one hundred and twenty-three; the men of Netophae fifty-five;
the men of Anathoth one hundred and fifty-eight; the men of Bethasmoth
19 forty-two; the men of Cariathiarius twenty-five; the men of Caphira
20 and Beroth seven hundred and forty-three; the Chadasians and Ammi-
daeans four hundred and twenty-two; the men of Kirama and Gabbes six
21 hundred and twenty-one; the men of Macalon one hundred and twenty-
two; the men of Betolio fifty-two; the line of Phinis one hundred and fifty-
22 six; the line of Calamolalus and Onus seven hundred and twenty-five; the
23 line of Jerechus three hundred and forty-five; the line of Sanaas three
thousand three hundred and thirty.

24 The priests: the line of Jeddu son of Jeshua, deriving from the line of
Anasib, nine hundred and seventy-two. The line of Emmeruth one

---

[a] his son; and: *probable reading* (*compare Nehemiah 12. 10*)

thousand and fifty-two. The line of Phassurus one thousand two hundred 25
and forty-seven. The line of Charme one thousand and seventeen.

The Levites: the line of Jesue, Cadmielus, Bannus, and Sudius seventy- 26
four. The temple singers: the line of Asaph one hundred and twenty- 27
eight.

The door-keepers: the line of Salum, of Atar, of Tolman, of Dacubi, of 28
Ateta, of Sabi, in all one hundred and thirty-nine.

The temple-servitors: the line of Esau, of Asipha, of Taboth, of Keras, 29
of Susa, of Phaleas, of Labana, of Aggaba, of Acud, of Uta, of Ketab, of 30
Gaba, of Subai, of Anan, of Cathua, of Geddur, of Jairus, of Desan, of 31
Noeba, of Chaseba, of Gazera, of Ozius, of Phinoe, of Asara, of Basthae,
of Asana, of Maani, of Naphisi, of Acum, of Achipha, of Asur, of Pharakim,
of Baaloth, of Meedda, of Coutha, of Charea, of Barchue, of Serar, of 32
Thomi, of Nasith, of Atepha. The descendants of Solomon's servants: 33
the line of Asapphioth, of Pharida, of Jeeli, of Lozon, of Isdael, of Saphythi,
of Hagia, of Phacareth, of Sabie, of Sarothie, of Masias, of Gas, of Addus, 34
of Subas, of Apherra, of Barodis, of Saphat, of Adlon. All the temple- 35
servitors and the descendants of Solomon's servants numbered three
hundred and seventy-two.

The following came from Thermeleth and Thelsas with their leaders 36
Charaathalar and Alar, and could not prove by their families and 37
genealogies that they were Israelites: the line of Dalan, the line of Ban,
and the line of Necodan six hundred and fifty-two.

From among the priests the claimants to the priesthood whose record 38
could not be traced: the line of Obdia, of Accos, of Joddus, who married
Augia one of the daughters of Zorzelleas, and took his name; when search 39
was made for their family record in the register it could not be traced, and
so they were excluded from priestly service. Nehemiah the governor[a] told 40
them that they should not participate in the sacred offerings until a high
priest arose wearing the breast-piece of Revelation and Truth.

They were in all: Israelites from twelve years old, not counting slaves 41
male and female, forty-two thousand three hundred and sixty; their slaves 42
seven thousand three hundred and thirty-seven; musicians and singers
two hundred and forty-five; camels four hundred and thirty-five, horses 43
seven thousand and thirty-six, mules two hundred and forty-five, donkeys
five thousand five hundred and twenty-five.

Some of the heads of families, when they arrived at the temple of God 44
in Jerusalem, made a vow to erect the house again on its site as best they
could, and to give to the sacred treasury for the fabric fund one thousand 45
minas of gold and five thousand minas of silver and one hundred vestments.

The priests, the Levites, and some of the people settled in Jerusalem 46
and the neighbourhood, with the temple musicians and the door-keepers;
and all Israel settled in their villages.

WHEN THE SEVENTH MONTH came and the Israelites were in their 47
homes they gathered as one man in the broad square of the first gateway

---

[a] the governor: *probable meaning*; Gk. and Attharias.

9

48 toward the east. Jeshua son of Josedek and his brother priests and Zerubbabel son of Salathiel and his colleagues came forward and made ready
49 the altar of the God of Israel, to offer on it whole burnt-offerings according
50 to the directions in the book of Moses the man of God. They were joined <sup>a</sup>
by men from the other peoples of the land and they set up the altar on its
site (for the peoples in the land as a whole were hostile to them and were
too strong for them); and they offered sacrifices to the Lord at the proper
51 time, and whole burnt-offerings morning and evening. They observed the
Feast of Tabernacles as enjoined in the law, and the proper sacrifices day
52 by day; and thereafter the continual offerings, and sacrifices on sabbaths,
53 at new moons, and on all solemn feasts. All who had made a vow to God
offered sacrifices to God from the new moon of the seventh month,
54-55 although the temple of God was not yet built. Money was paid to the stonemasons and carpenters; the Sidonians and Tyrians were supplied with
food and drink, and with carts to bring cedar-trees from Lebanon, floating
them down as rafts to the anchorage at Joppa, as decreed by Cyrus king
of Persia.
56   In the second month of the second year, Zerubbabel son of Salathiel
came to the temple of God in Jerusalem and started the work. There were
with him Jeshua son of Josedek, their kinsmen, the levitical priests, and all
57 who had come to Jerusalem from the exile; and they laid the foundation
of the temple of God. This was at the new moon, in the second month of
58 the second year after they had returned to Judaea and Jerusalem. The
Levites from the age of twenty and upwards were set over the works of the
Lord. Jeshua, his sons, his brothers, his brother Cadoel, the sons of Jeshua
Emadabun, and the sons of Joda son of Iliadun with their sons and brothers,
all the Levites, supervisors of the work, were active as one man on the
works in the house of God. While the builders built the temple of the Lord,
59 the priests in their vestments with musical instruments and trumpets, and
60 the Levites the sons of Asaph with their cymbals, stood singing to the Lord
61 and praising him as David king of Israel had appointed. They sang psalms
praising the Lord, 'for his goodness and glory is for ever toward all Israel'.
62 All the people blew their trumpets and gave a loud shout, singing to the
Lord as the building rose.
63   The priests, the Levites, and heads of families, the older men who had
seen the former house, came to the building of this one with cries of
64 lamentation; and so, while many were sounding the trumpets loudly for
65 joy—so loudly as to be heard far away—the people could not hear the
trumpets for the noise of lamentation.
66   The enemies of Judah and Benjamin heard the noise of the trumpets
67 and came to see what it meant. They found the returned exiles building the
68 temple for the Lord God of Israel; they came to Zerubbabel and Jeshua
69 and the leaders of the families, and said: 'We will build with you; for like
you we obey your Lord and have sacrificed to him from the time of Asba-
70 sareth king of Assyria who transported us here.' But Zerubbabel and Jeshua
and the leaders of the families of Israel replied: 'You can have no share in
71 building the house for the Lord our God; we alone will build for the Lord

---

<sup>a</sup> Or attacked; *the clauses are perhaps in a confused order.*

of Israel, as Cyrus king of Persia decreed.' But the peoples of the land 72
harassed[a] the men of Judaea, blockaded them, and interrupted the building. Their plots, agitations, and riots held up the completion of the building 73
all the lifetime of King Cyrus. They were prevented from building for two
years until Darius became king.

In the second year of the reign of Darius, the prophets Haggai and Zecha- 6
riah son of Addo prophesied to the Jews in Judaea and Jerusalem in the
name of the Lord the God of Israel. Then Zerubbabel son of Salathiel and 2
Jeshua son of Josedek began to rebuild the house of the Lord in Jerusalem.
The prophets of the Lord were at their side to help them. At that time 3
Sisinnes, the governor-general of Syria and Phoenicia, with Sathrabuzanes
and their colleagues, came to them and said: 'Who has authorized you to 4
put up this building, complete with roof and everything else? Who are
the builders carrying out this work?' But, thanks to the Lord who protected 5
the returned exiles, the elders of the Jews were not prevented from build- 6
ing during the time that Darius was being informed and directions issued.

Here is a copy of the letter written to Darius, and sent by Sisinnes, the 7
governor-general of Syria and Phoenicia, with Sathrabuzanes and their
colleagues the authorities in Syria and Phoenicia:

To King Darius our humble duty. Be it known to our lord the king: 8
we visited the district of Judaea and entered the city of Jerusalem, and
there we found the elders of the Jews returned from exile building a 9
great new house for the Lord with costly hewn stone and with beams
set in the walls. This work was being done with all speed and the under- 10
taking was making good progress; it was being executed in great splendour
and with the utmost care. We then inquired of these elders by whose 11
authority they were building this house and laying such foundations.
We questioned them so that we could inform you in writing who their 12
leaders were, and asked for a list of their names. They answered as 13
follows: 'We are servants of the Lord who made heaven and earth. This 14
house was built and completed many years ago by a great and powerful
king of Israel. When our fathers sinned against the heavenly Lord of 15
Israel and provoked him, he delivered them over to Nebuchadnezzar,
king of Babylon, king of the Chaldaeans; and they pulled down the house, 16
set it on fire, and took the people into exile in Babylon. In the first year 17
of the reign of King Cyrus over Babylonia, the king decreed that this
house should be rebuilt. The sacred vessels of gold and silver which 18
Nebuchadnezzar had taken from the house in Jerusalem, and set up in
his own temple, he brought back out of the temple in Babylon and
delivered to Zerubbabel and Sanabassar the governor, with orders to 19
take all these vessels and to put them in the temple at Jerusalem, and
to rebuild this temple of the Lord on the same site as before. Then 20
Sanabassar came and laid the foundations of the house of the Lord in
Jerusalem. From then till now the building has continued and is still un-
finished.' Therefore, if it is Your Majesty's pleasure, let search be made 21
in the royal archives in Babylon, and if it is found that the building of the 22

---

[a] *Probable reading; Gk. obscure.*

house of the Lord in Jerusalem took place with the approval of King Cyrus, and if our lord the king so decide, let directions be issued to us on this subject.

23  Then King Darius ordered the archives in Babylon to be searched, and a scroll was found in the castle at Ecbatana in the province of Media which contained the following record:

24      In the first year of his reign King Cyrus ordered that the house of the Lord in Jerusalem, where they sacrifice with fire continually, should be
25  rebuilt. Its height should be sixty cubits and its breadth sixty cubits, with three courses of hewn stone to one of new local timber; the expenses
26  to be met from the royal treasury. The sacred gold and silver vessels of the house of the Lord which Nebuchadnezzar removed from the house in Jerusalem, and took to Babylon, should be restored to the house in Jerusalem and replaced where they formerly were.

27  Darius therefore instructed Sisinnes, the governor-general of Syria and Phoenicia, with Sathrabuzanes, their colleagues, and the governors in office in Syria and Phoenicia, to be careful not to interfere with the place, but to allow the servant of the Lord, Zerubbabel, governor of Judaea, and
28  the elders of the Jews to build the house of the Lord on its old site. 'I have also given instructions', he continued, 'that it should be completely rebuilt, and that they should not fail to co-operate with the returned exiles in
29  Judaea until the house of the Lord is finished. From the tribute of Coele-syria and Phoenicia let a contribution be duly given to these men for sacrifices to the Lord, payable to Zerubbabel the governor, for bulls, rams,
30  and lambs; and similarly wheat, salt, wine, and oil are to be provided regularly each year without question, as the priests in Jerusalem may
31  require day by day. Let all this be expended in order that sacrifices and libations may be offered to the Most High God for the king and his children,
32  and that intercession may be made on their behalf.' He also gave these orders: 'If anyone disobeys or neglects any of these orders written above or here set down, let a beam be taken from his own house and let him be
33  hanged on it and his estate forfeited to the king. May the Lord himself, therefore, to whom this temple is dedicated, destroy any king or people who shall lift a finger to delay or damage the Lord's house in Jerusalem.
34  I, Darius the king, decree that these orders be obeyed to the letter.'
7   Then, in accordance with the orders of King Darius, Sisinnes, governor-general of Coele-syria and Phoenicia, with Sathrabuzanes and their col-
2   leagues, carefully supervised the sacred works, co-operating with the
3   elders of the Jews and the temple officers. With the encouragement of the prophets Haggai and Zechariah, good progress was made with the sacred
4   works, and they were finished by the ordinance of the Lord God of Israel and with the approval of Cyrus, Darius, and Artaxerxes, kings of Persia.
5   It was on the twenty-third of Adar in the sixth year of King Darius that
6   the house was completed. The Israelites, the priests, the Levites, and the rest of the former exiles who had joined them carried out the directions
7   in the book of Moses. For the dedication of the temple of the Lord they
8   offered a hundred bulls, two hundred rams, four hundred lambs, and

twelve goats for the sin of all Israel corresponding to the twelve patriarchs of Israel. The priests and the Levites in their vestments stood family by 9 family to preside over the services of the Lord God of Israel according to the book of Moses. The door-keepers took their stand at every gateway.

The Israelites who had returned from exile kept the Passover on the 10 fourteenth day of the first month. The priests and the Levites were purified together; not all the returned exiles were purified with the priests, but*[a]* 11 the Levites were. They slaughtered the Passover victims for all the returned 12 exiles and for their brother priests and for themselves. All those Israelites 13 participated who had returned from exile and had segregated themselves from the abominations of the peoples of the land to seek the Lord. They 14 kept the Feast of Unleavened Bread for seven days, rejoicing before the Lord; for he had changed the policy of the Assyrian king towards them and 15 strengthened them for the service of the Lord the God of Israel.

## Ezra in Jerusalem

A FTER THESE EVENTS, in the reign of Artaxerxes king of Persia, came 8 Ezra, son of Saraeas, son of Ezerias, son of Chelkias, son of Salemus, son of Zadok, son of Ahitub, son of Amarias, son of Ezias, son of Ma- 2 reroth, son of Zaraeas, son of Savia, son of Bocca, son of Abishua, son of Phineas, son of Eleazar, son of Aaron the chief priest. This Ezra came from 3 Babylon as a talented scholar in the law of Moses which had been given by the God of Israel. The king held him in high regard and looked with favour 4 upon all the requests he made. He was accompanied to Jerusalem by some 5 Israelites, priests, Levites, temple singers, door-keepers, and temple-servitors, in the fifth month of the seventh year of Artaxerxes' reign.*[b]* 6 They left Babylon at the new moon in the first month and reached Jeru-salem at the new moon in the fifth month; for the Lord gave them a safe journey. Ezra's knowledge of the law of the Lord and the commandments 7 was exact in every detail, so that he could teach all Israel the ordinances and judgements.

The following is a copy of the mandate from King Artaxerxes to Ezra 8 the priest, doctor of the law of the Lord:

King Artaxerxes to Ezra the priest, doctor of the law of the Lord, 9 greeting.

I have graciously decided, and now command, that those of the 10 Jewish nation and of the priests and Levites, in our kingdom, who so choose, shall go with you to Jerusalem. I and my council of seven 11 Friends have decided that all who so desire may accompany you. Let 12 them look to the affairs of Judaea and Jerusalem in pursuance of the law of the Lord, and bring to Jerusalem for the Lord of Israel the gifts which 13 I and my Friends have vowed, all the gold and silver in Babylonia that may be found to belong to the Lord in Jerusalem, together with what 14 has been given by the nation for the temple of the Lord their God in

*[a]* not all . . . but: *probable meaning; Gk. obscure; some witnesses omit* not.     *[b]* *Probable reading; one witness adds* this was the king's second year.

15 Jerusalem. Let the gold and silver be expended upon[a] bulls, rams, lambs,
and so forth, so that sacrifices may be offered upon the altar of the Lord
16 their God in Jerusalem. Make use of the gold and silver in whatever
ways you and your colleagues desire, according to the will of your God,
17 and deliver the sacred vessels of the Lord which have been given you
for the use of the temple of your God in Jerusalem.

18 Any other expenses that you may incur for the needs of the temple of
19 your God you shall defray from the royal treasury. I, Artaxerxes the
king, direct the treasurers of Syria and Phoenicia to give without fail
to Ezra the priest, doctor of the law of the Most High God, whatever he
20 may request up to a hundred talents of silver, and similarly up to a
hundred sacks of wheat and a hundred casks of wine, and salt without
21 limit. Let him diligently fulfil in honour of the Most High God all the
requirements of God's law, so that divine displeasure may not befall the
22 kingdom of the king and of his descendants. You are also informed that
no tax or other impost is to be laid on the priests, the Levites, the temple
singers, the door-keepers, the temple-servitors, and the lay officers of this
23 temple; no one is permitted to impose any burden on them. You, Ezra,
under God's guidance, are to appoint judges and magistrates to judge all
who know the law of your God in all Syria and Phoenicia; you yourself
24 shall see to the instruction of those who do not know it. All who trans-
gress the law of your God and of the king shall be duly punished with
death, degradation, fine, or exile.

25 Then Ezra said: All praise to the Lord alone, who put this into the king's
26 mind, to glorify his house in Jerusalem. He singled me out for honour
27 before the king, his counsellors, and all his Friends and dignitaries. I took
courage from the help of the Lord my God and gathered men of Israel to
go up with me.

28 These are the leaders according to clans and divisions who went with me
29 from Babylon to Jerusalem in the reign of King Artaxerxes: from the line
of Phineas, Gershom; from the line of Ithamar, Gamael; from the line of
30 David, Attus son of Sechenias; from the line of Phoros, Zacharias and a
31 hundred and fifty men with him according to the register; from the line of
Phaath-moab, Eliaonias son of Zaraeas and with him two hundred men;
32 from the line of Zathoe, Sechenias son of Jezelus and with him three
hundred men; from the line of Adin, Obeth son of Jonathan and with him
33 two hundred and fifty men; from the line of Elam, Jessias son of Gotholias
34 and with him seventy men; from the line of Sophotias, Zaraeas son of
35 Michael and with him seventy men; from the line of Joab, Abadias son of
36 Jezelus and with him two hundred and twelve men; from the line of Bani,
37 Assalimoth son of Josaphias and with him a hundred and sixty men; from
the line of Babi, Zacharias son of Bebae and with him twenty-eight men;
38 from the line of Astath, Joannes son of Hacatan and with him a hundred
39 and ten men; last came those from the line of Adonikam, by name Eli-
40 phalatus, Jeuel, and Samaeas, and with them seventy men; from the line
of Bago, Uthi son of Istalcurus and with him seventy men.

[a] *Or* collected for.

14

I assembled them at the river called Theras, where we encamped for 41
three days, and I inspected them. As I found no one there who was of 42
priestly or levitical descent, I sent to Eleazar, Iduelus, Maasmas, Elnathan, 43 44
Samaeas, Joribus, Nathan, Ennatas, Zacharias, and Mosollamus, who
were prominent and discerning men. I told them to go to Doldaeus the 45
chief man at the treasury. I instructed them to speak with Doldaeus, his 46
colleagues, and the treasurers there, and ask them to send us priests to
officiate in the house of our Lord. Under the providence of God they 47
brought us discerning men from the line of Mooli son of Levi son of Israel,
Asebebias and his sons and brothers, eighteen men in all, also Asebias and 48
Annunus and Hosaeas his brother. Those of the line of Chanunaeus and
their sons amounted to twenty men; and those of the temple-servitors 49
whom David and the leading men appointed for the service of the Levites
amounted to two hundred and twenty. A register of all these names was
compiled.

There I made a vow that the young men should fast before our Lord 50
to beg him to give us a safe journey for ourselves, our children who accompanied us, and our pack-animals. I was ashamed to ask the king for an 51
escort of infantry and cavalry against our enemies; for we had told the 52
king that the strength of our Lord would ensure success for those who
looked to him. So once more we laid all these things before our Lord in 53
prayer and found him gracious.

I set apart twelve men from among the heads of the priestly families, 54
and with them Sarabias and Asamias and ten of their brother priests. I 55
weighed out for them the silver, the gold, and the sacred vessels of the
house of our Lord; these had been presented by the king himself, his
counsellors, the chief men, and all Israel. When I had weighed it all I 56
handed over to them six hundred and fifty talents of silver, and vessels of
silver weighing a hundred talents, a hundred talents of gold, and twenty 57
pieces of gold plate, and twelve vessels of brass so fine that it gleamed like
gold. I said to them: 'You are consecrated to the Lord, and so are the vessels; 58
the silver and the gold are vowed to the Lord, the Lord of our fathers. Be 59
vigilant and keep guard until you hand them over at Jerusalem, in the
priests' rooms in the house of our Lord, to the heads of the priestly and
levitical families and to the leaders of the clans of Israel.' The priests and 60
the Levites who received the silver, the gold, and the vessels in Jerusalem
brought them to the temple of the Lord.

We left the river Theras on the twelfth day of the first month, and under 61
the powerful protection which our Lord gave us we reached Jerusalem.
He guarded us against every enemy on our journey, and so we arrived at
Jerusalem. Three days passed, and on the fourth the silver and gold were 62
weighed and handed over in the house of our Lord to the priest Marmathi
son of Uri, with whom was Eleazar son of Phineas. With them also were 63
the Levites Josabdus son of Jeshua and Moeth son of Sabannus. Everything was numbered and weighed and every weight recorded there and 64
then. The returned exiles offered sacrifices to the Lord the God of Israel, 65
twelve bulls for all Israel, with ninety-six rams and seventy-two lambs, and 66
also twelve goats for a peace-offering, the whole as a sacrifice to the Lord.

67 They delivered the king's orders to the royal treasurers and the governors of Coele-syria and Phoenicia, and so added lustre to the nation and the temple of the Lord.

68 WHEN THESE MATTERS had been settled the leaders came to me and
69 said: 'The nation of Israel, the rulers, the priests, and the Levites, have not kept themselves apart from the alien population of the land with all their pollutions, that is to say the Canaanites, Hittites, Perizzites, Jebusites,
70 Moabites, Egyptians, and Edomites. For they and their sons have inter-married with the daughters of these peoples, and the holy race has been mingled with the alien population of the land; and the leaders and principal men have shared in this violation of the law from the very beginning.'
71 As soon as I heard of this I tore my clothes and sacred vestment, plucked out the hair of my head and my beard, and sat down perplexed and miser-
72 able. Those who at that time were moved by the word of the Lord of Israel gathered round me, while I grieved over this disregard of the law, and sat
73 in my misery until the evening sacrifice. Then I rose from my fast with my clothes and sacred vestment torn, and knelt down and, stretching out my
74 hands to the Lord, said:
75-76 'O Lord, I am covered with shame and confusion in thy presence. Our sins tower above our heads; from the time of our fathers our offences have
77 reached the sky, and today we are as deep in sin as ever. Because of our sins and the sins of our fathers, we and our brothers, our kings and our priests, were given over to the kings of the earth to be killed, taken prisoner,
78 plundered, and humiliated down to this very day. And now, Lord, how great is the mercy thou hast shown us! We still have a root and a name in the
79 place of thy sanctuary, and thou hast rekindled our light in the house of
80 our Lord, and given us food in the time of our servitude. Even when we were slaves we were not deserted by our Lord; for he secured for us the
81 favour of the kings of Persia, who have provided our food and added lustre to the temple of our Lord and restored the ruins of Zion, giving us a firm
82 foothold in Judaea and Jerusalem. And now, Lord, what are we to say, we who have received all this? For we have broken thy commandments given
83 us through thy servants the prophets. Thou didst say: "The land which you are to occupy is a land defiled with the pollution of its heathen peoples;
84 they have filled it with their impurities. Do not marry your daughters to
85 their sons nor take their daughters for your sons; never try to make peace with them if you want to be strong and enjoy the good things of the land
86 and take possession of it for your children for ever." All our misfortunes have come upon us through our evil deeds and our great sins. Although
87 thou, Lord, hast lightened the burden of our sins and given us so firm a root, yet we have fallen away again and broken thy law by sharing in the
88 impurities of the heathen peoples of this land. But thou wast not so angry
89 with us, Lord, as to destroy us, root, seed, and name; thou keepest faith,
90 O Lord of Israel; the root is left, we are here today. Behold us, now before thee in our sins; because of all we have done we can no longer hold up our heads before thee.'

While Ezra prayed and made confession, weeping prostrate on the ground 91 before the temple, a very large crowd gathered, men, women, and youths of Jerusalem, and there was widespread lamentation among the people. Jechonias son of Jeel, one of the Israelites, called out to Ezra: 'We have 92 sinned against the Lord in taking alien wives from the heathen population of this land; and yet there is still hope for Israel. Let us take an oath to the 93 Lord to expel all our wives of alien race with their children, in accordance 94 with your judgement and the judgement of all who are obedient to the law of the Lord. Come now, set about it, it is in your hands; take strong action 95 and we are with you.' Ezra got up and laid an oath upon the principal 96 priests and Levites of all Israel that they would act in this way, and they swore to it.

Ezra left the court of the temple and entered the room of the priest **9** Joanan son of Eliasibus. There he stayed, eating no food and drinking no 2 water, while he mourned over the serious violations of the law by the community. A proclamation was made throughout Judaea and in Jerusalem to 3 all the returned exiles that they should assemble at Jerusalem; those who 4 failed to arrive within two or three days, according to the decision of the elders in office, were to have their cattle confiscated for temple use and would themselves be excluded from the community of the returned exiles.

Three days later all Judah and Benjamin had assembled in Jerusalem; 5 the date was the twentieth of the ninth month. They all sat together in the 6 open space before the temple, shivering because winter had set in. Ezra 7 stood up and said to them: 'You have broken the law and married alien wives, bringing a fresh burden of guilt on Israel. Now make confession to 8 the Lord God of our fathers; do his will and separate yourselves from the 9 heathen population of this land and from your alien wives.'

The whole company answered with a shout: 'We will do as you have 10 said!' 'But', they said, 'our numbers are great, and we cannot stay here in 11 the open in this wintry weather. Nor is this the work of a day or two only; the offence is widespread among us. Let the leaders of the community stay 12 here, and let all members of our settlements who have alien wives attend at an appointed time along with the elders and judges of each place, until 13 we turn away the Lord's anger at what has been done.'

Jonathan son of Azael and Hezekias son of Thocanus took charge on 14 these terms, and Mosollamus, Levi, and Sabbataeus were their assessors. The returned exiles duly carried all this out.                                      15

Ezra the priest selected men by name, all chiefs of their clans, and on the 16 new moon of the tenth month they sat to investigate the matter. This affair 17 of the men who had alien wives was settled by the new moon of the first month.

Among the priests some of those who had come together were found to 18 have alien wives; these were Mathelas, Eleazar, Joribus, and Joadanus of 19 the line of Jeshua son of Josedek and his brothers, who undertook to send 20 away their wives and to offer rams in expiation of their error. Of the line of 21 Emmer: Ananias, Zabdaeus, Manes, Samaeus, Jereel, and Azarias; of the 22 line of Phaesus: Elionas, Massias, Ishmael, Nathanael, Okidelus, and

23 Saloas. Of the Levites: Jozabadus, Semis, Colius (this is Calitas), Phathaeus,
24 25 Judah, and Jonas. Of the temple singers: Eliasibus, Bacchurus. Of the door-keepers: Sallumus and Tolbanes.
26 Of the people of Israel there were, of the line of Phoros: Jermas, Jeddias,
27 Melchias, Maelus, Eleazar, Asibias, and Bannaeas. Of the line of Ela:
28 Matthanias, Zacharias, Jezrielus, Oabdius, Jeremoth, and Aedias. Of the line of Zamoth: Eliadas, Eliasimus, Othonias, Jarimoth, Sabathus, and
29 Zardaeas. Of the line of Bebae: Joannes, Ananias, Ozabadus, and Emathis.
30 Of the line of Mani: Olamus, Mamuchus, Jedaeus, Jasubus, Asaelus, and
31 Jeremoth. Of the line of Addi: Naathus, Moossias, Laccunus, Naidus,
32 Matthanias, Sesthel, Balnuus, and Manasseas. Of the line of Annas:
33 Elionas, Asaeas, Melchias, Sabbaeas, and Simon Chosomaeus. Of the line of Asom: Altannaeus, Mattathias, Bannaeus, Eliphalat, Manasses, and
34 Semi. Of the line of Baani: Jeremias, Momdis, Ismaerus, Juel, Mandae, Paedias, Anos, Carabasion, Enasibus, Mamnitanaemus, Eliasis, Bannus, Eliali, Somis, Selemias, and Nathanias. Of the line of Ezora: Sessis, Ezril,
35 Azael, Samatus, Zambris, and Josephus. Of the line of Nooma: Mazitias,
36 Zabadaeas, Edaes, Juel, and Banaeas. All these had married alien wives; they sent them away with their children.

37 THE PRIESTS, the Levites, and such Israelites as were in Jerusalem and its vicinity, settled down there on the new moon of the seventh month;
38 the other Israelites remained in their settlements. The entire body assembled as one in the open space before the east gateway of the temple
39 and asked Ezra the high priest and doctor of the law to bring the law of
40 Moses given by the Lord God of Israel. On the new moon of the seventh month he brought the law to all the multitude of men and women alike, and
41 to the priests, for them to hear. He read it in the open space before the temple gateway from daybreak until noon, in the presence of both men and
42 women, and the whole body listened intently. Ezra the priest and doctor of the law stood upon the wooden platform which had been prepared.
43 There stood with him, on his right, Mattathias, Sammus, Ananias,
44 Azarias, Urias, Hezekias, and Baalsamus, and on his left, Phaldaeus,
45 Misael, Melchias, Lothasubus, Nabarias, and Zacharias. Ezra took up the book of the law; everyone could see him, for he was seated in a con-
46 spicuous place in front of them all, and when he opened it they all stood up. Ezra praised the Lord God the Most High God of hosts, the Almighty.
47 All the multitude cried 'Amen, Amen', and lifting up their hands fell to
48 the ground and worshipped the Lord. Jeshua, Annus, Sarabias, Jadinus, Jacubus, Sabbataeas, Autaeas, Maeannas, Calitas, Azarias, Jozabdus, Ananias, and Phiathas, the Levites, taught the law of the Lord; they read the law of the Lord to the whole company, at the same time instilling into their minds what was read.
49 Then the governor*a* said to Ezra the high priest and doctor of the law
50 and to each of the Levites who taught the multitude: 'This day is holy to
51 the Lord.' All were weeping as they heard the law. 'Go then, refresh your-selves with rich food and sweet wine, and send shares to those who have

*a   Gk.* Attharates.

none; for the day is holy to the Lord. Let there be no sadness; for the Lord 52
will give you glory.' The Levites issued the command to all the people: 53
'This day is holy, do not be sad.' So they all departed to eat and drink and 54
make merry, and to send shares to those who had none, and to hold a great
celebration; because the teaching given them had been instilled into their 55
minds.

They gathered together. *a*

# THE SECOND BOOK OF
# ESDRAS

## *Israel's rejection and glory to come*

THE SECOND BOOK of the prophet Ezra, son of Seraiah, son 1
of Azariah, son of Hilkiah, son of Shallum, son of Zadok, son of
Ahitub, son of Ahijah, son of Phinehas, son of Eli, son of Amariah, 2
son of Aziah, son of Marimoth, son of Arna, son of Uzzi, son of Borith, son
of Abishua, son of Phinehas, son of Eleazar, son of Aaron, of the tribe 3
of Levi.

I, EZRA, was a captive in Media in the reign of Artaxerxes, king of Persia,
when the word of the Lord came to me: 'Go to my people and proclaim 4 5
their crimes; tell their children how they have sinned against me, and let
them tell their children's children. They have sinned even more than their 6
fathers; they have forgotten me and sacrificed to alien gods. Was it not I 7
who rescued them from Egypt, the country where they were slaves? And
yet they have provoked me to anger and ignored my warnings.

'Now, Ezra, pluck out your hair and let calamities loose upon these people 8
who have disobeyed my law. They are beyond correction. How much 9
longer shall I endure them, I who have lavished on them such benefits?
Many are the kings I have overthrown for their sake; I struck down Pharaoh 10
with his court and all his army. I destroyed every nation that stood in their 11
way, and in the east I routed the peoples of two provinces, Tyre and Sidon,
and killed all the enemies of Israel.

'Say to them, "These are the words of the Lord: Was it not I who brought 12 13
you through the sea, and made safe roads for you where no road had been?
I gave you Moses as your leader, and Aaron as your priest; I gave you light 14
from a pillar of fire, and performed great miracles among you. And yet
you have forgotten me, says the Lord.

' "These are the words of the Lord Almighty: I gave you the quails as 15
a sign; I gave you a camp for your protection. But all you did there was to
grumble and complain—instead of celebrating the victory I had given you 16

---

*a* *Probably the text originally carried on from this point; compare Nehemiah 8. 13.*

when I destroyed your enemies. From that day to this you have never
17 stopped complaining. Have you forgotten what benefits I conferred on
you? When you were hungry and thirsty in your journey through the
18 desert, you cried out to me, 'Why have you brought us into this desert to
kill us? Better to have remained in Egypt as slaves than to die here in the
19 desert!' I was grieved by your complaints, and gave you manna for food;
20 you ate the bread of angels. When you were thirsty, I split open the rock,
and out flowed water in plenty. Against the summer heat I gave you the
21 shelter of leafy trees. I gave you fertile lands to divide among your tribes,
expelling the Canaanites, Perizzites, and Philistines who opposed you.
What more could I do for you? says the Lord.
22   ' "These are the words of the Lord Almighty: When you were in the
23 desert, suffering thirst by the stream of bitter water and cursing me, I did
not bring down fire upon you for your blasphemy; I cast a tree into the
24 stream and made the water sweet. What am I to do with you, Jacob?
Judah, you have refused to obey me. I will turn to other nations; I will
25 give them my name, and they will keep my statutes. Because you have
deserted me, I will desert you; when you cry for mercy, I will show you
26 none; when you pray to me, I will not listen. You have stained your hands
27 with blood; you run hot-foot to commit murder. It is not I whom you have
deserted, but yourselves, says the Lord.
28   ' "These are the words of the Lord Almighty: Have I not pleaded with
you as a father with his sons, as a mother with her daughters or a nurse with
29 her children? Have I not said, 'Be my people, and I will be your God; be
30 my sons, and I will be your father'? I gathered you as a hen gathers her
chickens under her wings. But now what am I to do with you? I will toss
31 you away. When you offer me sacrifice, I will turn from you; I have rejected
32 your feasts, your new moons, and your circumcisions. I sent you my servants the prophets, but you took them and killed them, and mutilated
their dead bodies. For their murder I will call you to account, says the
Lord.
33   ' "These are the words of the Lord Almighty: Your house is abandoned.
34 I will toss you away like straw before the wind. Your children shall have
no posterity, because like you they have ignored my commandments and
35 done what I have condemned. I will hand over your home to a people soon
to come; a people who will trust me, though they have not known me;
36 who will do my bidding, though I gave them no signs; who never saw the
37 prophets, and yet will keep in mind what the prophets taught of old. I vow
that this people yet to come shall have my favour. Their little ones shall
jump for joy. They have not seen me with their eyes, but they shall perceive by the spirit and believe all that I have said."
38   'Now, father Ezra, look with triumph at the nation coming from the east.
39 The leaders I shall give them are Abraham, Isaac, and Jacob, Hosea and
40 Amos, Micah and Joel, Obadiah and Jonah, Nahum, Habakkuk, and
Zephaniah, Haggai and Zechariah, and Malachi, who is also called the
Lord's Messenger.
2   'These are the words of the Lord: I freed this people from slavery, and
gave them commandments through my servants the prophets; but they

shut their ears to the prophets, and let my precepts become a dead letter. The mother who bore them says to them: "Go, my sons; I am widowed 2 and deserted. Joyfully I brought you up; I have lost you with grief and 3 sorrow, because you have sinned against the Lord God and done what I know to be wrong. What can I do for you now, widowed and deserted as 4 I am? Go, my sons, ask the Lord for mercy." Now I call upon you, father 5 Ezra, to add your testimony to hers, that her children have refused to keep my covenant; and let your words bring confusion on them. May their 6 mother be despoiled, and may they themselves have no posterity. Con- 7 demn them to be scattered among the nations, and their name to vanish from the earth, because they have spurned my covenant.

'Woe to you, Assyria, for harbouring sinners! Remember, you wicked 8 nation, what I did to Sodom and Gomorrah: their land lies buried under 9 lumps of pitch and heaps of ashes. That is how I will deal with those who have disobeyed me, says the Lord Almighty.

'These are the words of the Lord to Ezra: Tell my people that I will 10 give to them the kingdom of Jerusalem which once I offered to Israel. I 11 will withdraw the splendour of my presence from Israel, and the home that was to be theirs for ever I will give to my own people. The tree of life 12 shall spread its fragrance over them; they shall not toil or grow weary. Ask, and you shall receive; so pray that your short time of waiting may be 13 made shorter still. The kingdom is ready for you now; be on the watch! Call heaven, call earth, to witness: I have cancelled the evil and brought 14 the good into being; for I am the Living One, says the Lord.

'Mother, cherish your sons. Rear them joyfully as a dove rears her 15 nestlings; teach them to walk without stumbling. You are my chosen one, says the Lord. I will raise up the dead from their resting-places, and bring 16 them out of their tombs, for I have acknowledged that they bear my name. Have no fear, mother of many sons; I have chosen you, says the Lord. 17

'I will send my servants Isaiah and Jeremiah to help you. As they pro- 18 phesied, I have set you apart to be my people. I have made ready for you twelve trees laden with different kinds of fruit, twelve fountains flowing 19 with milk and honey, and seven great mountains covered with roses and lilies. There will I fill your sons with joy. Champion the widow, defend 20 the cause of the fatherless, give to the poor, protect the orphan, clothe the naked. Care for the weak and the helpless, and do not mock at the cripple; 21 watch over the disabled, and bring the blind to the vision of my brightness. Keep safe within your walls both old and young. 22

'When you find the dead unburied, mark them with the sign and commit 23 them to the tomb; and then, when I cause the dead to rise, I will give you the chief place. Be calm, my people; for your time of rest shall come. Care 24 25 for your children like a good nurse, and train them to walk without falling. Of my servants whom I have given you not one shall be lost; I will demand 26 them back from among your number. Do not be anxious when the time of 27 trouble and hardship comes; others shall lament and be sad, but you shall have happiness and plenty. All nations shall envy you, but shall be power- 28 less against you, says the Lord.

'My power shall protect you, and save your sons from hell. Be joyful, 29 30

31 mother, you and your sons, for I will come to your rescue. Remember your children who sleep in the grave; I will bring them up from the depths of the earth, and show mercy to them; for I am merciful, says the Lord
32 Almighty. Cherish your children until I come, and proclaim my mercy to them; for my favour flows abundantly from springs that will never run dry.'

33 I, EZRA, received on Mount Horeb a commission from the Lord to go to Israel; but when I came, they scorned me and rejected the Lord's com-
34 mandment. Therefore I say to you Gentiles, you who hear and understand: 'Look forward to the coming of your shepherd, and he will give you everlasting rest; for he who is to come at the end of the world is close at
35 hand. Be ready to receive the rewards of the kingdom; for light perpetual
36 will shine upon you for ever and ever. Flee from the shadow of this world, and receive the joy and splendour that await you. I bear witness openly to
37 my Saviour. It is he whom the Lord has appointed; receive him and be joyful, giving thanks to the One who has summoned you to the heavenly
38 realms. Rise, stand up, and see the whole company of those who bear the
39 Lord's mark and sit at his table. They have moved out of the shadow of this
40 world and have received shining robes from the Lord. Receive, O Zion, your full number, and close the roll of those arrayed in white who have
41 faithfully kept the law of the Lord. The number of your sons whom you so long desired is now complete. Pray that the Lord's kingdom may come, so that your people, whom he summoned when the world began, may be set apart as his own.'

42 I, Ezra, saw on Mount Zion a crowd too large to count, all singing hymns
43 of praise to the Lord. In the middle stood a very tall young man, taller than all the rest, who was setting a crown on the head of each one of them; he
44 stood out above them all. I was enthralled at the sight, and asked the angel,
45 'Sir, who are these?' He replied, 'They are those who have laid aside their mortal dress and put on the immortal, those who acknowledged the name
46 of God. Now they are being given crowns and palms.' And I asked again, 'Who is the young man setting crowns on their heads and giving them
47 palms?', and the angel replied, 'He is the Son of God, whom they acknowledged in this mortal life.' I began to praise those who had stood so valiantly
48 for the Lord's name. Then the angel said to me: 'Go and tell my people all the great and wonderful acts of the Lord God that you have seen.'

## The mystery of human destiny

3 IN THE THIRTIETH YEAR after the fall of Jerusalem, I, Salathiel (who am also Ezra), was in Babylon. As I lay on my bed I was troubled; my
2 mind was filled with perplexity, as I considered the desolation of Zion and
3 the prosperity of those who lived in Babylon. My spirit was deeply dis-
4 turbed; and I uttered my fears to the Most High. 'My Lord, my Master,' I said, 'was it not you, and you alone, who in the beginning spoke the word
5 that formed the world? You commanded the dust, and Adam appeared. His body was lifeless; but yours were the hands that had moulded it, and

22

into it you breathed the breath of life. So you made him a living person.
You led him into paradise, which you yourself had planted before the 6
earth came into being. You gave him your one commandment to obey; he 7
disobeyed it, and thereupon you made him subject to death, him and his
descendants.

'From him were born nations and tribes, peoples and families, too
numerous to count. Each nation went its own way, sinning against you 8
and scorning you; and you did not stop them. But then again, in due time, 9
you brought the flood upon the inhabitants of the earth and destroyed
them. The same doom came upon all: death upon Adam, and the flood 10
upon that generation. One man you spared—Noah, with his household, 11
and all his righteous descendants.

'The population of the earth increased; families and peoples multiplied, 12
nation upon nation. But then once again they began to sin, more wickedly
than those before them. When they sinned, you chose for yourself one of 13
them, whose name was Abraham; him you loved, and to him alone, 14
secretly, at dead of night, you showed how the world would end. You 15
made an everlasting covenant with him and promised never to abandon
his descendants. You gave him Isaac, and to Isaac you gave Jacob and 16
Esau; of these you chose Jacob for yourself and rejected Esau; and Jacob
grew to be a great nation.

'You rescued his descendants from Egypt and brought them to Mount 17
Sinai. There you bent the sky, shook *a* the earth, moved the round world, 18
made the depths shudder, and turned creation upside down. Your glory 19
passed through the four gates of fire and earthquake, wind and frost; and
you gave the commandments of the law to the Israelites, the race of Jacob.
But you did not take away their wicked heart and enable your law to bear 20
fruit in them. For the first man, Adam, was burdened with a wicked heart; 21
he sinned and was overcome, and not only he but all his descendants. So 22
the weakness became inveterate. Although your law was in your people's
hearts, a rooted wickedness was there too; so that the good came to nothing,
and what was bad persisted.

'Years went by, and when the time came you raised up a servant for 23
yourself, whose name was David. You told him to build the city that bears 24
your name and there offer to you in sacrifice what was already your own.
This was done for many years; until the inhabitants of the city went astray, 25
behaving just like Adam and all his line; for they had the same wicked 26
heart. And so you gave your own city over to your enemies. 27

'I said to myself: "Perhaps those in Babylon lead better lives, and that is 28
why they have conquered Zion." But when I arrived here, I saw more 29
wickedness than I could reckon, and these thirty years I have seen many
evil-doers with my own eyes. My heart sank, because I saw how you 30
tolerate sinners and spare the godless; how you have destroyed your own
people, but protected your enemies. You have given no hint whatever to 31
anyone how to understand your ways.*b* Is Babylon more virtuous than
Zion? Has any nation except Israel ever known you? What tribes have put 32
their trust in your covenants as the tribes of Jacob have? But they have seen 33

*a So some Vss.; Lat.* fixed.          *b* how . . . ways: *so some Vss.; Lat. obscure.*

no reward, no fruit for their pains. I have travelled up and down among the nations, and have seen how they prosper, heedless though they are of
34 your commandments. So weigh our sins in the balance against the sins of
35 the rest of the world; and it will be clear which way the scale tips. Has there ever been a time when the inhabitants of the earth did not sin against you?
36 Has any nation ever kept your commandments like Israel? You may find one man here, one there; but nowhere a whole nation.'

4 1 2 The angel who was sent to me, whose name was Uriel, replied: 'You are at a loss to explain this world; do you then expect to understand the ways
3 of the Most High?' 'Yes, my lord', I replied.

'I have been sent to propound to you three of the ways of this world,'
4 he continued, 'to give you three illustrations. If you can explain to me any one of them, then I will answer your question about the way of the Most High, and teach you why the heart is wicked.'
5 I said, 'Speak, my lord.' 'Come then,' he said, 'weigh me a pound of fire, measure me a bushel*a* of wind, or call back a day that has passed.'
6 'How can you ask me to do that?' I replied; 'no man on earth can do it.'
7 He said: 'Suppose I had asked you, "How many dwellings are there in the heart of the sea? or how many streams to feed the deep? or how many watercourses above the vault of heaven? Where are the paths out of the
8 grave, and the roads into*b* paradise?", you might then have replied, "I have never been down into the deep, I have not yet gone down into the
9 grave, I have never gone up into heaven." But, as it is, I have only asked you about fire, about wind, and about yesterday, things you are bound to have met; and yet you have failed to tell me the answers.
10 'If then', he went on, 'you cannot understand things you have grown
11 up with, how can your small capacity comprehend the ways of the Most High? A man corrupted by the corrupt world can never know the way of the incorruptible.'*c*
12 When I heard that, I fell*d* prostrate and exclaimed: 'Better never to have come into existence than be born into a world of wickedness and
13 suffering which we cannot explain!' He replied, 'I went out into a wood,
14 and the trees of the forest were making a plan. They said, "Come, let us make war on the sea, force it to retreat, and win ground for more woods."
15 The waves of the sea made a similar plan: they said, "Come, let us attack
16 the trees of the forest, conquer them, and annex their territory." The plan made by the trees came to nothing, for fire came and burnt them down.
17 The plan made by the waves failed just as badly, for the sand stood its
18 ground and blocked their way. If you had to judge between the two, which would you pronounce right, and which wrong?'
19 I answered, 'Both were wrong; their plans were impossible, for the land is assigned to the trees, and to the sea is allotted a place for its waves.'
20 'Yes,' he replied, 'you have judged rightly. Why then have you failed to
21 do so with your own question? Just as the land belongs to the trees and the sea to the waves, so men on earth can understand earthly things and

*a So some Vss.; Lat. the blast.*            *b the grave . . . into: so some Vss.; Lat. omits.*
*c A man . . . incorruptible: reading based on other Vss.; Lat. obscure.*          *d When . . .*
*fell: so some Vss.; Lat. defective.*

nothing else; only those who live *a* above the skies can understand the things above the skies.'

'But tell me, my lord,' I said, 'why then have I been given the faculty of 22 understanding? My question is not about the distant heavens, but about the 23 things which happen every day before our eyes. Why has Israel been made a byword among the Gentiles; why has the people you loved been put at the mercy of godless nations? Why has the law of our fathers been brought to nothing, and the written covenants made a dead letter? We 24 pass like a flight of locusts, our life is but a vapour, and we are not worth the Lord's pity, though we bear his name; what then will he do for us? These 25 are my questions.'

He answered: 'If you survive, you will see; if you live long enough, you 26 will marvel. *b* For this present age is quickly passing away; it is full of 27 sorrow and frailties, too full to enjoy what is promised in due time for the godly. The evil about which you ask me has been sown, but its reaping has 28 not yet come. Until the crop of evil has been reaped as well as sown, until 29 the ground where it was sown has vanished, there will be no room for the field which has been sown with the good. A grain of the evil seed was sown 30 in the heart of Adam from the first; how much godlessness has it produced already! How much more will it produce before the harvest! Reckon this 31 up: if one grain of evil seed has produced so great a crop of godlessness, how 32 vast a harvest will there be when good seeds beyond number have been sown!'

I asked, 'But when? How long have we to wait? Why are our lives so 33 short and so miserable?' He replied, 'Do not be in a greater hurry than the 34 Most High himself. You are in a hurry for yourself alone; the Most High for many. Are not these the very questions which were asked by the 35 righteous in the storehouse of souls: "How long must we stay here? When will the harvest begin, the time when we get our reward?" And the arch- 36 angel Jeremiel gave them this answer: "As soon as the number of those like yourselves is complete. For the Lord has weighed the world in a balance, he has measured and numbered the ages; he will move nothing, 37 alter nothing, until the appointed number is achieved." '

'But, my lord, my master,' I replied, 'we are all of us sinners through and 38 through. Can it be that because of us, because of the sins of mankind, the 39 harvest and the reward of the just are delayed?' 'Go,' he said, 'ask a pregnant 40 woman whether she can keep the child in her womb any longer after the nine months are complete.' 'No, my lord,' I said, 'she cannot.' He went 41 on: 'The storehouses of souls in the world below are like the womb. As a 42 woman in travail is impatient to see the end of her labour, so they are impatient to give back all the souls committed to them since time began. Then all your questions will be answered.'                                                43

I said, 'If it is possible for you to tell and for me to understand, will you 44 be gracious enough to disclose one thing more: which is the longer—the 45 future still to come, or the past that has gone by? What is past I know, but 46 not what is still to be.' 'Come and stand on my right,' he said; 'you shall 47 see a vision, and I will explain what it means.'

---

*a* Or he who lives.          *b* So one Vs.; Lat. live, you will often marvel.

48 So I stood and watched, and there passed before my eyes a blazing fire; when the flames had disappeared from sight, there was still some smoke
49 left. After that a dark rain-cloud passed before me; there was a heavy storm,
50 and when it had gone over, there were still some raindrops left. 'Reflect on this', said the angel. 'The shower of rain filled a far greater space than the drops of water, and the fire more than the smoke. In the same way, the past far exceeds the future in length; what remains is but raindrops and smoke.'

51 'Pray tell me,' I said, 'do you think that I shall live to see those days?
52 Or in whose lifetime will they come?' 'If you ask me what signs will herald them,' he said, 'I can tell you in part. But the length of your own life I am not commissioned to tell you; of that I know nothing.

5 'But now to speak of the signs: there will come a time when the inhabitants of the earth will be seized with panic. *a* The way of truth will be hidden
2 from sight, and the land will be barren of faith. There will be a great increase in wickedness, worse than anything you now see or have ever
3 heard of. The country you now see governing the world will become a
4 trackless desert, laid waste for all to see. After the third period (if the Most High grants you a long enough life) you will see confusion everywhere. The sun will suddenly begin to shine in the middle of the night, and the
5 moon in the day-time. Trees will drip blood, stones will speak, nations
6 will be in confusion, and the courses of the stars will be changed. A king unwelcome to the inhabitants of earth will succeed to the throne; even the
7 birds will all fly away. The Dead Sea will cast up fish, and at night a voice
8 will sound, unknown to the many but heard by all.*b* Chasms*c* will open in many places and spurt out flames incessantly. Wild beasts will range far
9 afield, women will give birth to monsters, fresh springs will run with salt water, and everywhere friends will become enemies. Then understanding
10 will be hidden, and reason withdraw to her secret chamber. Many will seek her, but not find her; the earth will overflow with vice and wickedness.
11 One country will ask another, "Has justice passed your way, or any just
12 man?", and it will answer, "No." In those days men will hope, but hope in vain; they will strive, but never succeed.

13 'These are the signs I am allowed to tell you. But turn again to prayer, continue to weep and fast for seven days; and then you shall hear further signs, even greater than these.'

14 I awoke with a start, shuddering; my spirit faltered, and I was near to
15 fainting. But the angel who had come and talked to me gave me support and strength, and set me on my feet.

16 The next night Phaltiel, the leader of the people, came to me. 'Where
17 have you been?' he asked, 'and why that sad look? Have you forgotten that
18 Israel in exile has been entrusted to your care? Rouse yourself, take nourishment. Do not abandon us like a shepherd abandoning his flock to
19 savage wolves.' I replied: 'Leave me; for seven days do not come near me, then you may come again.' When he heard this, he left me.

*a So some Vss.; Lat. corrupt.*          *b Some Vss. read* and at night one whom the many do not know will utter his voice, and all will hear it.          *c So one Vs.; Lat.* Chaos.

FOR SEVEN DAYS I fasted, with tears and lamentations, as the angel 20
Uriel had told me to do. By the end of the seven days my mind was again 21
deeply disturbed, but I recovered the power of thought and spoke once 22
more to the Most High.

'My Lord, my Master,' I said, 'out of all the forests of the earth, and all 23
their trees, you have chosen one vine; from all the lands in the whole world 24
you have chosen one plot; and out of all the flowers in the whole world you
have chosen one lily. From all the depths of the sea you have filled one 25
stream for yourself, and of all the cities ever built you have set Zion apart
as your own. From all the birds that were created you have named one 26
dove, and from all the animals that were fashioned you have taken one
sheep. Out of all the countless nations, you have adopted one for your own, 27
and to this chosen people you have given the law which all men have
approved. Why then, Lord, have you put this one people at the mercy of 28
so many? Why have you humiliated*ª* this one stock more than all others,
and scattered your own people among the hordes of heathen? Those who 29
reject your promises have trampled on the people who trust your covenants.
If you so hate your people, they should be punished by your own hand.' 30

When I had finished speaking, the angel who had visited me that previous 31
night was sent to me again. 'Listen to me,' he said, 'and I will give you 32
instruction. Attend carefully, and I will tell you more.' 'Speak on, my 33
lord', I replied.

He said to me, 'You are in great sorrow of heart for Israel's sake. Do you
love Israel more than Israel's Maker does?' 'No, my lord,' I said, 'but 34
sorrow has forced me to speak; my heart is tortured every hour as I try to
understand the ways of the Most High and to fathom some part of his
judgements.'

He said to me, 'You cannot.' 'Why not, my lord?' I asked. 'Why then 35
was I born? Why could not my mother's womb have been my grave? Then
I should never have seen Jacob's trials and the weariness of the race of
Israel.'

He said to me, 'Count me those who are not yet born, collect the scattered 36
drops of rain, and make the withered flowers bloom again; unlock me the 37
storehouses and let loose the winds shut up there; or make visible the shape
of a voice. Then I will answer your question about Israel's trials.'

'My lord, my master,' I said, 'how can there be anyone with such know- 38
ledge except the One whose home is not among men? I am only a fool; 39
how then can I answer your questions?'

He said to me, 'Just as you cannot do any of the things I have put to 40
you, so you will not be able to find out my judgements or the ultimate
purpose of the love I have promised to my people.'

I said, 'But surely, lord, your promise*ᵇ* is to those who are alive at the 41
end. What is to be the fate of those who lived before us, or of ourselves, or
of those who come after us?'

He said to me, 'I will compare the judgement to a circle: the latest will 42
not be too late, nor the earliest too early.'

To this I replied, 'Could you not have made all men, past, present, and 43

_____
ª *So some Vss.; Lat.* prepared.     ᵇ *So one Vs.; Lat. obscure.*

future, at one and the same time? Then you could have held your assize
44 with less delay.' But he answered, 'The creation may not go faster than the
Creator, nor could the world support at the same time all those created to
live on it.'

45   'But, my lord,' I said, 'you have told me that you will at one and the
same time restore to life every creature you have made; how can that be?
If it is going to be possible for all of them to be alive at the same time and
for the world to support them all, then it could support all of them together
46 now.' 'Put your question in terms of a woman's womb', he replied. 'Say
to a woman, "If you give birth to ten children, why do you do so at intervals?
47 Why not give birth to ten at one and the same time?"' 'No, my lord, she
48 cannot do that,' I said; 'the births must take place at intervals.' 'True,'
he answered; 'and I have made the earth's womb to bring forth at intervals
49 those conceived in it. An infant cannot give birth, nor can a woman who is
too old; and I have made the same rule for the world I have created.'

50   I continued my questions. 'Since you have opened the way,' I said, 'may
I now ask: is our mother that you speak of still young, or is she already
51 52 growing old?' He replied, 'Ask any mother why the children she has lately
53 borne are not like those born earlier, but smaller. And she will tell you,
"Those who were born in the vigour of my youth are very different from
54 those born in my old age, when my womb is beginning to fail." Think of it
55 then like this: if you are smaller than those born before you, and those who
follow you are smaller still, the reason is that creation is growing old and
losing the strength of youth.'

56   I said to him, 'If I have won your favour, my lord, show me through
6 whom you will visit your creation.' He said to me, 'Think of the beginning
of this earth: the gates of the world had not yet been set up; no winds
2 gathered and blew, no thunder pealed, no lightning flashed; the founda-
3 tions of paradise were not yet laid, nor were its fair flowers there to see; the
powers that move the stars were not established, nor the countless hosts of
4 angels assembled, nor the vast tracts of air set up on high; the divisions of
the firmaments had not received their names. Zion had not yet been chosen
5 as God's own footstool; the present age had not been planned; the schemes
of its sinners had not yet been outlawed, nor had God's seal yet been set on
6 those who have stored up a treasure of fidelity. Then did I think my
thought; and the whole world was created through me and through me
alone. In the same way, through me and through me alone the end shall
come.'

7   'Tell me', I went on, 'about the interval that divides the ages. When will
8 the first age end and the next age begin?' He said, 'The interval will be no
bigger than that between Abraham and Abraham; for Jacob and Esau
were his descendants, and Jacob's hand was grasping Esau's heel at the
9 moment of their birth. Esau represents the end of the first age, and Jacob
10 the beginning of the next age. The beginning of a man is his hand, and the
end of a man is his heel.[a] Between the heel and the hand, Ezra, do not look
for any interval.'

11 12   'My lord, my master,' I said, 'if I have won your favour, make known
    [a] The beginning of a man . . . heel: *reading based on other Vss.; Lat. defective.*

28

to me the last of your signs, of which you showed me a part that former night.'

'Rise to your feet,' he replied, 'and you will hear a loud resounding voice. 13
When it speaks, do not be frightened if the place where you stand trembles 14–15
and shakes; it speaks of the end, and the earth's foundations will understand that it is speaking of them. They will tremble and shake; for they 16
know that at the end they must be transformed.' On hearing this I rose 17
to my feet and listened; and a voice began to speak. Its sound was like the
sound of rushing waters. The voice said: 18

'The time draws near when I shall come to judge those who live on the
earth, the time when I shall inquire into the wickedness of wrong-doers, 19
the time when Zion's humiliation will be over, the time when a seal will be 20
set on the age about to pass away. Then I will perform these signs: the
books shall be opened in the sight of heaven, and all shall see them at the
same moment. Children only one year old shall be able to talk, and preg- 21
nant women shall give birth to premature babes of three and four months,
who shall live and leap about. Fields that were sown shall suddenly prove 22
unsown, and barns that were full shall suddenly be found empty. There 23
shall be a loud trumpet-blast and it shall strike terror into all who hear it.
At that time friends shall make war on friends as though they were enemies, 24
and the earth and all its inhabitants shall be terrified. Running streams shall
stand still; for three hours they shall cease to flow.

'Whoever is left after all that I have foretold, he shall be preserved, and 25
shall see the deliverance that I bring and the end of this world of mine.
They shall all see the men who were taken up into heaven without ever 26
knowing death. Then shall men on earth feel a change of heart and come to
a better mind. Wickedness shall be blotted out and deceit destroyed, but 27 28
fidelity shall flourish, corruption be overcome, and truth, so long un-
fruitful, be brought to light.'

While the voice was speaking to me, the ground under me began to 29
quake.*ᵃ* Then the angel said to me, 'These, then, are the revelations I have 30
brought you this night.*ᵇ* If once again you pray and fast for seven days, 31
then I will return to tell you even greater things.*ᶜ* For be sure your voice 32
has been heard by the Most High. The Mighty God has seen your integrity
and the chastity you have observed all your life. That is why he has sent 33
me to you with all these revelations, and with this message: "Be confident,
and have no fear. Do not rush too quickly into unprofitable thoughts now 34
in the present age; then you will not act hastily when the last age comes."'

THEREUPON I WEPT and fasted again for seven days in the same way as 35
before, thus completing the three weeks enjoined on me. On the eighth 36
night I was again disturbed at heart, and spoke to the Most High. With 37
spirit aflame and in great agony of mind I said: 38

'O Lord, at the beginning of creation you spoke the word. On the first
day you said, "Let heaven and earth be made!", and your word carried
out its work. At that time the hovering spirit was there, and darkness 39

---

*ᵃ* the ground . . . quake: *reading based on other Vss.; Lat. obscure.*       *ᵇ* *So one Vs.;*
*Lat.* this coming night.       *ᶜ* *So other Vss.; Lat. adds* in the day-time.

40 circled round; there was silence, no sound as yet of human voice. *a* Then
you commanded a ray of light to be brought out of your store-chambers,
41 to make your works visible from that time onwards. On the second day you
created the angel *b* of the firmament, and commanded him to make a dividing barrier between the waters, one part withdrawing upwards and the other
42 remaining below. On the third day you ordered the waters to collect in a
seventh part of the earth; the other six parts you made into dry land, and
43 from it kept some to be sown and tilled for your service. Your word went
44 forth, and at once the work was done. A vast profusion of fruits appeared
instantly, of every kind and taste that can be desired, with flowers of the
most subtle colours and mysterious scents. These were made on the third
45 day. On the fourth day by your command you created the splendour of the
46 sun, the light of the moon, and the stars in their appointed places; and you
ordered them to be at the service of man, whose creation was about to take
47 place. On the fifth day you commanded the seventh part, where the water
48 was collected, to bring forth living things, birds and fishes. And so, at your
command, dumb lifeless water brought forth living creatures, and gave the
49 nations cause to tell of your wonders. Then you set apart two creatures:
50 one you called Behemoth and the other Leviathan. You put them in
separate places, for the seventh part where the water was collected was not
51 big enough to hold them both. A part of the land which was made dry on
the third day you gave to Behemoth as his territory, a country of a thousand
52 hills. To Leviathan you gave the seventh part, the water. You have kept
53 them to be food for whom you will and when you will. On the sixth day
you ordered the earth to produce for you cattle, wild beasts, and creeping
54 things. To crown your work you created Adam, and gave him sovereignty
over everything you had made. It is from Adam that we, your chosen
people, are all descended.
55 'I have recited the whole story of the creation, O Lord, because you have
56 said that you made this first world for our sake, and that all the rest of the
nations descended from Adam are nothing, that they are no better than
57 spittle, and, for all their numbers, no more than a drop from a bucket. And
yet, O Lord, those nations which count for nothing are today ruling over
58 us and devouring us; and we, your people, have been put into their power
—your people, whom you have called your first-born, your only son, your
59 champion, and your best beloved. Was the world really made for us? Why,
then, may we not take possession of our world? How much longer shall
it be so?'
7 When I had finished speaking, the same angel was sent to me as on the
2 previous nights. He said to me, 'Rise to your feet, Ezra, and listen to the
3 message I have come to give you.' 'Speak, my lord', I said.
He said to me: 'Imagine a sea set in a vast open space, spreading far *c*
4 5 and wide, but the entrance to it narrow like the gorge of a river. If anyone
is determined to reach this sea, whether to set eyes on it or to gain command
of it, he cannot arrive at its open waters except through the narrow gorge.
6 Or again, imagine a city built in a plain, a city full of everything you can

---

*a* *So some Vss.; Lat. adds* from you.    *b* *Literally* spirit.    *c* spreading
far: *reading based on other Vss.; Lat.* deep.

desire, but the entrance to it narrow and steep, with fire to the right and 7
deep water to the left. There is only the one path, between the fire and the 8
water; and that is only wide enough for one man at a time. If some man has 9
been given this city as a legacy, how can he take possession of his inheritance except by passing through these dangerous approaches?' 'That is 10
the only way, my lord', I agreed.

He said to me: 'Such is the lot of Israel. It was for Israel that I made the 11
world, and when Adam transgressed my decrees the creation came under
judgement. The entrances to this world were made narrow, painful, and 12
arduous, few and evil, full of perils and grinding hardship. But the entrances 13
to the greater world are broad and safe, and lead to immortality. All men 14
must therefore enter this narrow and futile existence; otherwise they can
never attain the blessings in store. Why then, Ezra, are you so deeply dis- 15
turbed at the thought that you are mortal and must die? Why have you not 16
turned your mind to the future instead of the present?'

'My lord, my master,' I replied, 'in your law you have laid it down that 17
the just shall come to enjoy these blessings but the ungodly shall be lost.
The just, therefore, can endure this narrow life and look for the spacious 18
life hereafter; but those who have lived a wicked life will have gone
through the narrows without ever reaching the open spaces.'

He said to me: 'You are not a better judge than God, nor wiser than the 19
Most High. Better that many now living should be lost, than that the law 20
God has set before them should be despised! God has given clear instruc- 21
tions for all men when they come into this world, telling them how to
attain life and how to escape punishment. But the ungodly have refused to 22
obey him; they have set up their own empty ideas, and planned deceit 23
and wickedness; they have even denied the existence of the Most High
and have not acknowledged his ways. They have rejected his law and 24
refused his promises, have neither put faith in his decrees nor done what
he commands. Therefore, Ezra, emptiness for the empty, fullness for 25
the full!

'Listen! The time shall come when the signs I have foretold will be 26
seen; the city which is now invisible *a* shall appear and the country now
concealed be made visible. Everyone who has been delivered from the evils 27
I have foretold shall see for himself my marvellous acts. My son the 28
Messiah *b* shall appear with his companions and bring four hundred years
of happiness to all who survive. At the end of that time, my son the 29
Messiah shall die, and so shall all mankind who draw breath. Then the 30
world shall return to its original silence for seven days as at the beginning
of creation, and no one shall be left alive. After seven days the age which is 31
not yet awake shall be roused and the age which is corruptible shall die.
The earth shall give up those who sleep in it, and the dust those who rest 32
there in silence; and the storehouses shall give back the souls entrusted to
them. Then the Most High shall be seen on the judgement-seat, and there 33
shall be an end of all pity and patience. Judgement alone shall remain; 34
truth shall stand firm and faithfulness be strong; requital *c* shall at once 35

*a So some Vss.; Lat.* the city, the bride, which is now seen . . .          *b So some
Vss.; Lat.* My son Jesus.          *c Probable meaning; literally* work.

begin and open payment be made; good deeds shall awake and wicked
[36] deeds shall not be allowed to sleep.*a* Then the place of torment shall appear,
and over against it the place of rest; the furnace of hell shall be displayed,
and on the opposite side the paradise of delight.

[37] 'Then the Most High shall say to the nations that have been raised from
the dead: "Look and understand who it is you have denied and refused to
[38] serve, and whose commandment you have despised. Look on this side,
then on that: here are rest and delight, there fire and torments." That is
what he will say to them on the day of judgement.

[39] [40] 'That day will be a day without sun, moon, or stars; without cloud,
thunder, or lightning; wind, water, or air; darkness, evening, or morning;
[41] without summer, spring, or winter; without heat, frost, or cold; without
[42] hail, rain, or dew; without noonday, night, or dawn; without brightness,
glow, or light. There shall be only the radiant glory of the Most High, by
[43] which all men will see everything that lies before them. It shall last as it
[44] were for a week of years. Such is the order that I have appointed for the
Judgement. I have given this revelation to you alone.'

[45] I replied: 'My lord, I repeat what I said before: "How blest are the
[46] living who obey the decrees you have laid down!" But as for those for
whom I have been praying, is there any man alive who has never sinned,
[47] any man who has never transgressed your covenant? I see now that there
are few to whom the world to come will bring happiness, and many to
[48] whom it will bring torment. For the wicked heart has grown up in us,
which has estranged us from God's ways,*b* brought us into corruption and
the way of death, opened out to us the paths of ruin, and carried us far
away from life. It has done this, not merely to a few, but to almost all who
have been created.'

[49] The angel replied: 'Listen to me and I will give you further instruction
[50] and correction. It is for this reason that the Most High has created not one
[51] world but two. There are, you say, not many who are just, but only a few,
[52] whereas the wicked are very numerous; well then, hear the answer. Suppose you had a very few precious stones; would you add to their number
[53] by putting common lead and clay among them*c*?' 'No,' I said, 'no one
[54] would do that.' 'Look at it also in this way,' he continued; 'speak to the
[55] earth and humbly ask her; she will give you the answer. Say to her: "You
[56] produce gold, silver, and copper, iron, lead, and clay. There is more silver
than gold, more copper than silver, more iron than copper, more lead than
[57] iron, more clay than lead." Then judge for yourself which things are
valuable and desirable—those that are common, or those that are rare.'
[58] 'My lord, my master,' I said, 'the common things are cheaper, and the
[59] rarer are more valuable.' He replied, 'Consider then what follows from
that: the owner of something hard to get has more cause to be pleased than
[60] the owner of what is common. In the same way, at my promised judgement,*d* I shall have joy in the few who are saved, because it is they who have

---

*a The passage from verse [36] to verse [105], missing from the text of the Authorized Version,
but found in ancient witnesses, has been restored.*      *b Literally from these things.*
*c by putting . . . them: probable reading, based on other Vss.; Lat. obscure.*      *d Reading
based on other Vss.; Lat. creation.*

made my glory prevail, and through them that my name has been made
known. But I shall not grieve for the many who are lost; for they are no [61]
more than a vapour, they are like flame or smoke; they catch fire, blaze up,
and then die out.'

Then I said: 'Mother Earth, what have you brought forth! Is the mind [62]
of man, like the rest of creation, a product of the dust? Far better then if the [63]
very dust had never been created, and so had never produced man's mind!
But, as it is, we grow up with the power of thought and are tortured by it; [64]
we are doomed to die and we know it. What sorrow for mankind; what [65]
happiness for the wild beasts! What sorrow for every mother's son; what
gladness for the cattle and flocks! How much better their lot than ours! [66]
They have no judgement to expect, no knowledge of torment or salvation
after death. What good to us is the promise of a future life if it is going [67]
to be one of torment? For every man alive is burdened and defiled [68]
with wickedness, a sinner through and through. Would it not have [69]
been better for us if there had been no judgement awaiting us after
death?'

The angel replied: 'When the Most High was creating the world and [70]
Adam and his descendants, he first of all planned the judgement and what
goes with it. Your own words, when you said that man grows up with the [71]
power of thought, will give you the answer. It was with conscious know- [72]
ledge that the people of this world sinned, and that is why torment awaits
them; they received the commandments but did not keep them, they
accepted the law but violated it. What defence will they be able to make [73]
at the judgement, what answer at the last day? How patient the Most High [74]
has been with the men of this world, and for how long!—not for their own
sake, but for the sake of the destined age to be.'

Then I said: 'If I have won your favour, my lord, make this plain to me: [75]
at death, when every one of us gives back his soul, shall we be kept at rest
until the time when you begin to create your new world, or does our torment begin at once?' 'I will tell you that also', he replied. 'But do not [76]
include yourself among those who have despised my law; do not count
yourself with those who are to be tormented. For you have a treasure of [77]
good works stored up with the Most High, though you will not be shown
it until the last days. But now to speak of death: when the Most High has [78]
given final sentence for a man to die, the spirit leaves the body to return
to the One who gave it, and first of all to adore the glory of the Most High.
But as for those who have rejected the ways of the Most High and despised [79]
his law, and who hate all that fear God, their spirits enter no settled abode, [80]
but roam thenceforward in torment, grief, and sorrow. And this for seven
reasons. First, they have despised the law of the Most High. Secondly, [81] [82]
they have lost their last chance of making a good repentance and so gaining
life. Thirdly, they can see the reward in store for those who have trusted [83]
the covenants of the Most High. Fourthly, they begin to think of the tor- [84]
ment that awaits them at the end. Fifthly, they see that angels are guarding [85]
the abode of the other souls in deep silence. Sixthly, they see that they are [86]
soon*a* to enter into torment. The seventh cause for grief, the strongest [87]

---

*a So some Vss.; Lat. obscure.*

cause of all, is this: at the sight of the Most High in his glory, they break down in shame, waste away in remorse, and shrivel with fear remembering how they sinned against him in their lifetime, and how they are soon to be brought before him for judgement on the last day.

[88] 'As for those who have kept to the way laid down by the Most High, this is what is appointed for them when their time comes to leave their mortal

[89] bodies. During their stay on earth they served the Most High in spite of constant hardship and danger, and kept to the last letter the law given

[90] [91] them by the lawgiver. Their reward is this: first they shall exult to see the glory of God who will receive them as his own, and then they shall enter

[92] into rest in seven appointed stages of joy. Their first joy is their victory in the long fight against their inborn impulses to evil, which have failed to

[93] lead them astray from life into death. Their second joy is to see the souls of the wicked wandering ceaselessly, and the punishment in store for

[94] them. Their third joy is the good report given of them by their Maker, that throughout their life they kept the law with which they were entrusted.

[95] Their fourth joy is to understand the rest which they are now to share in the storehouses, guarded by angels in deep silence, and the glory waiting for

[96] them in the next age. Their fifth joy is the contrast between the corruptible world they have escaped and the future life that is to be their possession, between the cramped laborious *a* life from which they have been set free and the spacious life which will soon be theirs to enjoy for ever and ever.

[97] Their sixth joy will be the revelation that they are to shine like stars, never

[98] to fade or die, with faces radiant as the sun. Their seventh joy, the greatest joy of all, will be the confident and exultant assurance which will be theirs, free from all fear and shame, as they press forward to see face to face the One whom they served in their lifetime, and from whom they are now to receive their reward in glory.

[99] 'The joys I have been declaring are the appointed destiny for the souls of the just; the torments I described before are the sufferings appointed for the rebellious.'

[100] Then I asked: 'When souls are separated from their bodies, will they

[101] be given the opportunity to see what you have described to me?' 'They will be allowed seven days,' he replied; 'for seven days they will be permitted to see the things I have told you, and after that they will join the other souls in their abodes.'

[102] Then I asked: 'If I have won your favour, my lord, tell me more. On the day of judgement will the just be able to win pardon for the wicked, or

[103] pray for them to the Most High? Can fathers do so for their sons, or sons for their parents? Can brothers pray for brothers, relatives and friends *b* for their nearest and dearest?'

[104] 'You have won my favour,' he replied, 'and I will tell you. The day of judgement is decisive, *c* and sets its seal on the truth for all to see. In the present age a father cannot send his son in his place, nor a son his father, a master his slave, nor a man his best friend, to be ill *d* for him, or sleep, or

[105] eat, or be cured for him. In the same way no one shall ever ask pardon for

---

*a So some Vss.; Lat. obscure.*        *b friends: so some Vss.; Lat. the faithful.*
*c So one Vs.; Lat. stern.*     *d So some Vss.; Lat. to understand.*

another; when that day comes, every individual will be held responsible for his own wickedness or goodness.'

To this I replied: 'But how is it, then, that we read of intercessions in scripture? First, there is Abraham, who prayed for the people of Sodom; then Moses, who prayed for our ancestors when they sinned in the desert. Next, there is Joshua, who prayed for the Israelites in the time of Achan, then Samuel in the time of Saul,*a* David during the plague,*b* and Solomon at the dedication of the temple. Elijah prayed for rain for the people, and for a dead man that he might be brought back to life. Hezekiah prayed for the nation in the time of Sennacherib; and there are many more besides. If, then, in the time when corruption grew and wickedness increased, the just asked pardon for the wicked, why cannot it be the same on the day of judgement?' 36 [106]
37 [107]
38 [108]
39 [109]
40 [110]
41 [111]

The angel gave me this answer: 'The present world is not the end, and the glory of God does not stay in it continually.*c* That is why the strong have prayed for the weak. But the day of judgement will be the end of the present world and the beginning of the eternal world to come, a world in which corruption will be over, all excess abolished, and unbelief uprooted, in which justice will be full-grown, and truth will have risen like the sun. On the day of judgement, therefore, there can be no mercy for the man who has lost his case, no reversal for the man who has won it.' 42 [112]
43 [113]
44 [114]
45 [115]

I replied, 'But this is my point, my first point and my last: how much better it would have been if the earth had never produced Adam at all, or, since it has done so, if he had been restrained from sinning! For what good does it do us all to live in misery now and have nothing but punishment to expect after death? O Adam, what have you done? Your sin was not your fall alone; it was ours also, the fall of all your descendants. What good is the promise of immortality to us, when we have committed mortal sins; or the hope of eternity, in the wretched and futile state to which we have come; or the prospect of dwelling in health and safety, when we have lived such evil lives? The glory of the Most High will guard those who have led a life of purity; but what help is that to us whose conduct has been so wicked? What good is the revelation of paradise and its imperishable fruit, the source of perfect satisfaction and healing? For we shall never enter it, since we have made depravity our home. Those who have practised self-discipline shall shine with faces brighter than the stars; but what good is that to us whose faces are darker than the night? For during a lifetime of wickedness we have never given a thought to the sufferings awaiting us after death.' 46 [116]
47 [117]
48 [118]
49 [119]
50 [120]
51 [121]
52 [122]
53 [123]
54 [124]
55 [125]
56 [126]

The angel replied, 'This is the thought for every man to keep in mind during his earthly contest: if he loses, he must accept the sufferings you have mentioned, but if he wins, the rewards I have been describing will be his. For that was the way which Moses in his time urged the people to take, when he said, "Choose life and live!" But they did not believe him, nor the prophets after him, nor me when I spoke to them. Over their 57 [127]
58 [128]
59 [129]
60 [130]
61 [131]

---

*a* in the time of Saul: *so some Vss.; Lat. omits.*  *b* during the plague: *so some Vss.; Lat. for the destruction.*  *c* does ... continually: *so some Vss.; Lat. regularly stays in it.*

damnation there will be no sorrow; there will only be joy for the salvation of those who have believed.'[a]

[132] 62 'My lord,' I replied, 'I know that the Most High is called "compas-
[133] 63 sionate", because he has compassion on those yet unborn; and called "merciful", because he shows mercy to those who repent and live by his
[134] 64 law; and "patient", because he shows patience to those who have sinned,
[135] 65 his own creatures as they are; and "benefactor", because he prefers giving
[136] 66 to taking; and "rich in forgiveness", because again and again he forgives
[137] 67 sinners, past, present, and to come. For without his continued forgiveness
[138] 68 there could be no hope of life for the world and its inhabitants. And he is called "generous", because without his generosity in releasing sinners from their sins, not one ten-thousandth part of mankind could hope to be
[139] 69 given life; and he is also called "judge", for unless he grants pardon to those who have been created by his word, and blots out their countless
[140] 70 offences, I suppose that of the entire human race only very few would be spared.'

8   The angel said to me in reply: 'The Most High has made this world for
2 many, but the next world for only a few. Let me give you an illustration, Ezra. Ask the earth, and it will tell you that it can produce plenty of clay for making earthenware, but very little gold-dust. The same holds good
3 for the present world: many have been created, but only a few will be saved.'

4 I SAID: 'My soul, drink deep of understanding and eat your fill of wisdom!
5 Without your consent[b] you came here, and unwillingly you go away; only
6 a brief span of life is given you. O Lord above, if I may be allowed to approach you in prayer, plant a seed in our hearts and minds, and make it
7 grow until it bears fruit, so that fallen man may obtain life. For you alone are God, and we are all shaped by you in one mould, as your word declares.
8 The body moulded in the womb receives from you both life and limbs; that which you create is kept safe amid fire and water; for nine months the
9 body moulded by you bears what you have created in it. Both the womb which holds safely and that which is safely held will be safe only because you keep them so. And after the womb has delivered up what has been
10 created in it, then from the human body itself, that is from the breasts,
11 milk, the fruit of the breasts, is supplied by your command. For a certain time what has been made is nourished in that way; and afterwards it is still
12 cared for by your mercy. You bring it up to know your justice, train it in
13 your law, and correct it by your wisdom. It is your creature and you made
14 it; you can put it to death or give it life, as you please. But if you should lightly destroy one who was fashioned by your command with so much labour, what was the purpose of creating him?

15   'And now let me say this: about mankind at large, you know best; but
16 it is for your own people that I grieve, for your inheritance that I mourn;
17 my sorrow is for Israel and my distress for the race of Jacob. For them and for myself, therefore, I will address my prayer to you, since I perceive how

_____

[a] *So some Vss.; Lat.* for those who are convinced of salvation.     [b] Without your consent: *so one Vs.; Lat.* To obey.

low we have fallen, we dwellers on earth; and I know well how quickly 18
your judgement will follow. Hear my words then, and consider the prayer 19
which I make to you.'

Here begins the prayer which Ezra made, before he was taken up to
heaven.

'O Lord, who dost inhabit eternity, to whom the sky and the highest 20
heavens belong; whose throne is beyond imagining, and whose glory is 21
past conceiving; who art attended by the host of angels trembling as they 22
turn themselves into wind and fire at thy bidding; whose word is true and
constant; whose commands are mighty and terrible; whose glance dries 23
up the deeps, whose anger melts the mountains, and whose truth stands
for ever:*a* hear thy servant's prayer, O Lord, listen to my petition, for 24
thou hast fashioned me, and consider my words. While I live I will speak; 25
while understanding lasts, I will answer.

'Do not look upon thy people's offences, look on those who have served 26
thee faithfully; pay no heed to the godless and their pursuits, but to those 27
who have observed thy covenant and suffered for it. Do not think of those 28
who all their life have been untrue to thee, but remember those who have
acknowledged and feared thee from the heart. Do not destroy those who 29
have lived like animals, but take account of those who have borne shining
witness to thy law. Do not be angry with those judged to be worse than 30
beasts; but show love to those who have put unfailing trust in thy glory.
For we and our fathers have lived in mortal sin,*b* yet it is on our account 31
that thou art called merciful; for if it is thy desire to have mercy on us 32
sinners, who have no just deeds to our credit, then indeed thou shalt be
called merciful. For the reward which will be given to the just, who have 33
many good works stored up with thee, will be no more than their own
deeds have earned.

'What is man, that thou shouldst be angry with him? or the race of 34
mortals, that thou shouldst treat them so harshly? The truth is, no man 35
was ever born who did not sin; no man alive is innocent of offence. It is 36
through thy mercy towards those with no store of good deeds to their name
that thy justice and kindness, O Lord, will be made known.'

The angel said to me in reply: 'Much of what you have said is just, and 37
it will be as you say. Be sure that I shall not give any thought to sinners, to 38
their creation, death, judgement, or damnation; but I shall take delight 39
in the just, in their creation, their departure from this world, their salvation, and their final reward. So I have said, and so it is. The farmer sows 40 41
many seeds in the ground and plants many plants, but not all the seeds
sown come up safely in season, nor do all the plants strike root. So too in
the world of men: not all who are sown will be preserved.'

To that I replied: 'If I have won your favour, let me speak. The farmer's 42 43
seed may never come up because it is given no rain at the right time, or it
may rot because of too much rain. But man, who was formed by your hands 44
and made in your image, and for whose sake you made everything—will you
compare him with seed sown by a farmer? Surely not, O Lord above! Spare 45
your own people and pity them, for you will be pitying your own creation.'

---

*a*  *So some Vss.; Lat.* bears witness.          *b*  in mortal sin: *so some Vss.; Lat. obscure.*

46 He answered: 'The present is for those now alive, the future for those
47 yet to come. You cannot love my creation with a love greater than mine—
far from it! But never again rank yourself among the unjust, as you have
48 49 so often done. Yet the Most High approves of the modesty you have rightly
shown; you have not sought great glory by including yourself among the
50 godly. In the last days, then, the inhabitants of the world will be punished
51 for their arrogant lives by bitter sufferings. But you, Ezra, should direct
52 your thoughts to yourself and the glory awaiting those like you. For all of
you, paradise lies open, the tree of life is planted, the age to come is made
ready, and rich abundance is in store; the city is already built, rest from
53 toil is assured, goodness and wisdom are brought to perfection. The root
of evil has been sealed off from you; for you there is no more illness, death[a]
54 is abolished, hell has fled, and decay is quite forgotten. All sorrows are at
55 an end, and the treasure of immortality has been finally revealed. Ask no
56 more questions, therefore, about the many who are lost. For they were
given freedom and used it to despise the Most High, to treat his law with
57 contempt and abandon his ways. Yes, and they trampled on his just ser-
58 vants; they said to themselves, "There is no God", though well aware that
59 they must die. Yours, then, will be the joys I have predicted; theirs the
thirst and torments which are prepared. It is not that the Most High has
60 wanted any man to be lost, but that those he created have themselves
brought dishonour on their Creator's name, and shown ingratitude to the
61 One who had put life within their reach. My day of judgement is now
62 close at hand, but I have not made this known to all; only to you and a few
like you.'

63    'My lord,' I replied, 'you have now revealed to me the many signs which
you are going to perform in the last days; but you have not told me when
that will be.'

**9**    The angel answered: 'Keep a careful count yourself; when you see that
2 some of the signs predicted have already happened, then you will understand that the time has come when the Most High will judge the world he
3 has created. When the world becomes the scene of earthquakes, insurrections, plots among the nations, unstable government, and panic among
4 rulers, then you will recognize these as the events which the Most High
5 has foretold since first the world began. Just as everything that is done on
6 earth has its beginning and end clearly marked,[b] so it is with the times
which the Most High has determined: their beginning is marked by portents and miracles, their end by manifestations of power.

7    'Whoever comes safely through and escapes destruction, thanks to his
8 good deeds or the faith he has shown, will survive all the dangers I have
foretold and witness the salvation that I shall bring to my land, the country
9 I have marked out from all eternity as my own. Then those who have mis-
used my law will be taken by surprise; their contempt for it will bring
10 them continual torment. All who in their lifetime failed to acknowledge me
11 in spite of all the good things I had given them, all who disdained my law
while freedom still was theirs, who scornfully dismissed the thought of
12 penitence while the way was still open—all these will have to learn the

[a] death: *so some Vss.; Lat. omits.*        [b] has ... marked: *so one Vs.; Lat. defective.*

truth through torments after death. Do not be curious any more, Ezra, to 13
know how the godless will be tormented, but only how and when the just
will be saved; the world is theirs and it exists for their sake.'

I answered, 'I repeat what I have said again and again: the lost out- 14 15
number the saved as a wave exceeds a drop of water.'

The angel replied: 'The seed to be sown depends on the soil, the colour 16 17
on the flower, the product on the workman, and the harvest on the farmer.
There was once a time before the world had been created for men to dwell 18
in; at that time I was planning it for the sake of those who now exist. No
one then disputed my plan, for no one existed. I supplied this world with 19
unfailing food and a mysterious law; but those whom I created turned to a
life of corruption. I looked at my world, and there it lay spoilt, at my earth 20
in danger from men's wicked thoughts; and at the sight I could scarcely 21
bring myself to spare them. One grape I saved out of a cluster, one tree
out of a forest.*a* So then let it be: destruction for the many who were born 22
in vain, and salvation for my grape and my tree, which have cost me such
labour to bring to perfection.

'You, Ezra, must wait one more week. Do not fast this time, but go to a 23 24
flowery field where no house stands, and eat only what grows there—no
meat or wine—and pray unceasingly to the Most High. Then I will come 25
and talk to you again.'

## Visions of the last days

SO I WENT OUT, as the angel told me, to a field called Ardat. There I 26
sat among the flowers; my food was what grew in the field, and I ate
to my heart's content. The week ended, and I was lying on the grass, 27
troubled again in mind with all the same perplexities. I broke my silence 28
and addressed the Most High. 'O Lord,' I said, 'you showed yourself to 29
our fathers in the desert at the time of the exodus from Egypt, when they
were travelling through the barren and untrodden waste. You said, "Hear 30
me, Israel; listen to my words, race of Jacob. This is my law, which I sow 31
among you to bear fruit and bring you glory for ever." But our fathers who 32
received your law did not keep it; they did not observe your commandments. Not that the fruit of the law perished; that was impossible, for it
was yours. Those who received it perished, because they failed to keep 33
safe the good seed that had been sown in them. Now the usual way of 34
things is that when seed is put into the earth, or a ship on the sea, or food
or drink into a jar, then if the seed, or the ship, or the contents of the jar 35
should be destroyed, what held or contained them does not perish with
them. But with us sinners it is different. Destruction will come upon us, 36
the recipients of the law, and upon our hearts, the vessel that held the law.
The law itself is not destroyed, but survives in all its glory.' 37

While these thoughts were in my mind, I looked round, and on my right 38
I saw a woman in great distress, mourning and loudly lamenting; her dress
was torn, and she had ashes on her head. Abandoning my meditations, I 39

---

*a So some Vss.; Lat.* tribe.

40  turned to her, and said: 'Why are you weeping? What is troubling you?'
41  'Sir,' she replied, 'please leave me to my tears and my grief; great is my
42  bitterness of heart, great my distress.' 'Tell me,' I asked, 'what has hap-
43  pened to you?' 'Sir,' she replied, 'I was barren and childless through thirty
44  years of marriage. Every hour of every day during those thirty years, day
45  and night alike, I prayed to the Most High. Then after thirty years, my
God answered my prayer and had mercy on my distress; he took note of
my sorrow and granted me a son. What happiness he brought to my
husband and myself and to all our neighbours! What praise we gave to the
46 47  Mighty God! I took great pains over his upbringing. When he came of age,
I chose a wife for him, and fixed the date of the wedding.

**10**   'But when my son entered his wedding-chamber, he fell down dead.
2  So we all put out our lamps, and all my neighbours came to comfort me;
3  I controlled my grief till the evening of the following day. When they had
all ceased urging me to take comfort and control my grief, I rose and
4  stole away in the night, and came here, as you can see, to this field. I have
made up my mind never to go back to the town, but to stay here eating
nothing and drinking nothing, and to continue my mourning and fasting
unbroken till I die.'

5  At that I interrupted the train of my thoughts, and I spoke sternly to
6  the woman: 'You are the most foolish woman in the world,' I said; 'are
7  you blind to the grief and sufferings of our nation? It is for the sorrow and
humiliation of Zion, the mother of us all, that you should mourn so deeply;
8  you should share in our common mourning and sorrow. But you are deep
9  in sorrow for your one son. Ask the earth and she will tell you; she must
mourn for the thousands and thousands who come to birth upon her.
10  From her we all originally sprang, and there are more to come. Almost all
11  her children go to perdition, and their vast numbers are wiped out. Who
then has the better right to be in mourning—the earth, who has lost such
12  vast numbers, or you, whose sorrow is for one alone? You may say to me,
"But my grief is very different from the earth's grief; I have lost the fruit
13  of my own womb, which I brought to birth with pain and travail, but it is
only in the course of nature that the vast numbers now alive on earth should
14  depart in the same way as they have come." My answer to that is: at the
cost of pain you have been a mother, but in the same way the earth has
always been the mother of mankind, bearing fruit to earth's creator.

15  'Keep your sorrow to yourself, therefore, and bear your misfortunes
16  bravely. If you will accept God's decree as just, then in due time you will
receive your son back again, and win an honoured name among women.
17  So go back to the town and to your husband.'

18  'No, I will not,' she replied; 'I will not go back to the town; I will stay
here to die.'

19 20  But I continued to argue with her. 'Do not do what you say,' I urged;
'be persuaded because of Zion's misfortunes, and take comfort to yourself
21  from the sorrow of Jerusalem. You see how our sanctuary has been laid
22  waste, our altar demolished, and our temple destroyed. Our harps are un-
strung, our hymns silenced, our shouts of joy cut short; the light of the
sacred lamp is out, and the ark of our covenant has been taken as spoil;

the holy vessels are defiled, and the name which God has conferred on us is disgraced; our leading men *a* have been treated shamefully, our priests burnt alive, and the Levites taken off into captivity; our virgins have been raped and our wives ravished, our godfearing men carried off, and our children abandoned; our youths have been enslaved, and our strong warriors reduced to weakness. Worst of all, Zion, once sealed with God's 23 own seal, has forfeited its glory and is in the hands of our enemies. Then 24 throw off your own heavy grief, and lay all your sorrows aside; may the Mighty God restore you to his favour, may the Most High give you rest and peace after your troubles!'

Suddenly, while I was still speaking to the woman, I saw her face begin 25 to shine; her countenance flashed like lightning, and I shrank from her in terror. While I wondered what this meant, she suddenly uttered a loud and 26 terrible cry, which shook the earth. I looked up and saw no longer a woman 27 but a complete city, built *b* on massive foundations. I cried aloud in terror, 'Where is the angel Uriel, who visited me before? It is his doing that I have 28 fallen into this bewilderment, that all my hopes are shattered,*c* and all my prayers in vain.'

I was still speaking when the angel appeared who had visited me before. 29 When he saw me lying in a dead faint, unconscious on the ground, he 30 grasped me by my right hand, put strength into me, and raised me to my feet. 'What is the matter?' he asked. 'Why are you overcome? What was it 31 that disturbed your mind and made you faint?' 'It was because you 32 deserted me', I replied. 'I did what you told me: I came out to the field; and what I have seen here and can still see is beyond my power to relate.'

'Stand up like a man,' he said, 'and I will explain it to you.' 33

'Speak, my lord,' I replied; 'only do not abandon me and leave me to die 34 unsatisfied. For I have seen and I hear things beyond my understanding— 35 unless this is all an illusion and a dream. I beg you to tell me, my lord, the 36 37 meaning of my vision.'

'Listen to me,' replied the angel, 'while I explain to you the meaning of 38 the things that terrify you; for the Most High has revealed many secrets to you. He has seen your blameless life, your unceasing grief for your 39 people, and your deep mourning over Zion. Here then is the meaning of 40 the vision. A little while ago you saw a woman in mourning, and tried to 41 give her comfort; now you no longer see that woman, but a whole city. She 42 43 told you she had lost her son, and this is the explanation. The woman you 44 saw is Zion, which you now see as a city with all its buildings. She told you 45 she was childless for thirty years; that was because there were three thousand years in which sacrifices were not yet offered in Zion. But then, 46 after the three thousand years, Solomon built the city and offered the sacrifices; that was the time when the barren woman bore her son. She 47 took great pains, she said, over his upbringing; that was the period when Jerusalem was inhabited. Then she told you of the great loss she suffered, 48 how her son died on the day he entered his wedding-chamber; that was the destruction which overtook Jerusalem. Such then was the vision that you 49

---

*a* So some Vss.; Lat. our children.      *b* *Probable meaning, based on other Vss.; Lat.* but a city was being built . . .      *c* *Or that my destiny turns out to be corruption.*

50 saw—the woman mourning for her son—and you tried to comfort her in her sufferings; this was the revelation you had to receive. Seeing your sincere grief and heartfelt sympathy for the woman, the Most High is now
51 showing you her radiant glory and her beauty. That was why I told you to
52 stay in a field where no house stood, for I knew that the Most High intended
53 to send you this revelation. I told you to come to this field, where no
54 foundation had been laid for any building; for in the place where the city of the Most High was to be revealed, no building made by man could stand.
55 'Have no fear then, Ezra, and set your trembling heart at rest; go into the city, and see the magnificence of the buildings, so far as your eyes have
56 power to see it all. Then, after that, you shall hear as much as your ears
57 have power to hear. You are more blessed than most other men, and few
58 have such a name with the Most High as you have. Stay here till tomorrow
59 night, when the Most High will show you in dreams and visions what he intends to do to the inhabitants of earth in the last days.' I did as I was told and slept there that night and the next.

**11** ON THE SECOND NIGHT I had a vision in a dream; I saw, rising from
2 the sea, an eagle with twelve wings and three heads. I saw it spread its wings over the whole earth; and all the winds blew on it, and the clouds[a]
3 gathered. Out of its wings I saw rival wings sprout, which proved to be
4 only small and stunted. Its heads lay still; even the middle head, which was
5 bigger than the others, lay still between them. As I watched, the eagle rose
6 on its wings to set itself up as ruler over the earth and its inhabitants. I saw it bring into subjection everything under heaven; it met with no
7 opposition at all from any creature on earth. I saw the eagle stand erect on
8 its talons, and it spoke aloud to its wings: 'Do not all wake at once,' it said;
9 'sleep in your places, and each wake up in turn; the heads are to be kept till
10 the last.' I saw that the sound was not coming from its heads, but from the
11 middle of its body. I counted its rival wings, and saw that there were eight of them.
12 As I watched, one of the wings on its right side rose and became ruler
13 over the whole earth. After a time, its reign came to an end, and it disappeared from sight completely. Then the next one arose and established
14 its rule, which it held for a long time. When its reign was coming to an
15 end and it was about to disappear like the first one, a voice could be heard
16 saying to it: 'You have ruled the world for so long; now listen to my mes-
17 sage before your time comes to disappear. None of your successors will
18 achieve a reign as long as yours, nor even half as long.' Then the third wing arose, ruled the world for a time like its predecessors, and like them dis-
19 appeared. In the same way all the wings came to power in succession, and in turn disappeared from sight.
20 As time went on, I saw the wings on the left[b] side also raise themselves up to seize power. Some of them did so, and passed immediately from
21 22 sight, while others arose but never came to power. At this point I noticed that two of the little wings were, like the twelve, no longer to be seen.

a the clouds: *so some Vss.; Lat.* omits.     b *So one Vs.; Lat.* right.

Nothing was now left of the eagle's body except the three motionless heads 23
and six little wings. As I watched, two of the six little wings separated from 24
the rest and took up a place under the head on the right. The other four
remained where they were; and I saw them planning to rise up and seize 25
power. One rose, but disappeared immediately; so too did the second, 26 27
vanishing even more quickly than the first. I saw the last two planning to 28
seize the kingship for themselves. But while they were still plotting, 29
suddenly one of the heads woke from sleep, the one in the middle, the
biggest of the three. I saw how it joined with the other two heads, and along 30 31
with them turned and devoured the two little wings which were planning
to seize power. This head got the whole earth into its grasp, establishing an 32
oppressive rule over all its inhabitants and a world-wide kingdom mightier
than any of the wings had ruled. But after that I saw the middle head vanish 33
just as suddenly as the wings had done. There were two heads left, and they 34
also seized power over the earth and its inhabitants, but as I watched, the 35
head on the right devoured the head on the left.

Then I heard a voice which said to me: 'Look carefully at what you see 36
before you.' I looked, and saw what seemed to be a lion roused from the 37
forest; it roared as it came, and I heard it address the eagle in a human
voice. 'Listen to what I tell you', it said. 'The Most High says to you: Are 38 39
you not the only survivor of the four beasts to which I gave the rule over
my world, intending through them to bring my ages to their end? You 40-41
are the fourth beast, and you have conquered all who went before, ruling
over the whole world and holding it in the grip of fear and harsh oppression.
You have lived*ᵃ* long in the world, governing it with deceit and with no
regard for truth. You have oppressed the gentle and injured the peaceful, 42
hating the truthful and loving liars; you have destroyed the homes of the
prosperous, and razed to the ground the walls of those who had done you
no harm. Your insolence is known to the Most High, and your pride to the 43
Mighty One. The Most High has surveyed the periods he has fixed: they 44
are now at an end, and his ages have reached their completion. So you, 45
eagle, must now disappear and be seen no more, you and your terrible
great wings, your evil small wings, your cruel heads, your grim talons, and
your whole worthless body. Then all the earth will feel relief at its deliver- 46
ance from your violence, and look forward hopefully to the judgement and
mercy of its Creator.'

While the lion was still addressing the eagle, I looked and saw the one 12 1 2
remaining head disappear. Then the two*ᵇ* wings which had gone over to
him arose and set themselves up as rulers. Their reign was short and
troubled, and when I looked at them they were already vanishing. Then 3
the eagle's entire body burst into flames, and the earth was struck with
terror.

So great was my alarm and fear that I awoke, and said to myself: 'See 4
the result of your attempt to discover the ways of the Most High! My mind 5
is weary; I am utterly exhausted. The terrors of this night have completely
drained my strength. So I will now pray to the Most High for strength to 6

*ᵃ* You are the fourth . . . lived: *so some Vss.; Lat.* The fourth beast came and conquered . . . It has lived . . .     *ᵇ So other Vss.; Lat. corrupt.*

7 hold out to the end.' Then I said: 'My Master and Lord, if I have won your favour and stand higher in your approval than most men, if it is true that
8 my prayers have reached your presence, then give me strength; reveal to me, my Lord, the exact interpretation of this terrifying vision, and so
9 bring full consolation to my soul. For you have already judged me worthy to be shown the end of the present age.'

10 11 He said to me: 'Here is the interpretation of your vision. The eagle you saw rising from the sea represents the fourth kingdom in the vision seen
12 by your brother Daniel. But he was not given the interpretation which I am
13 now giving you or have already given you. The days are coming when the
14 earth will be under an empire more terrible than any before. It will be ruled
15 by twelve kings, one after another. The second to come to the throne will
16 have the longest reign of all the twelve. That is the meaning of the twelve wings you saw.

17 'As for the voice which you heard speaking from the middle of the
18 eagle's body, and not from its heads, this is what it means: After this second king's reign, great conflicts will arise, which will bring the empire into danger of falling; and yet it will not fall then, but will be restored to its original strength.

19 'As for the eight lesser wings which you saw growing from the eagle's
20 wings, this is what they mean: The empire will come under eight kings
21 whose reigns will be trivial and short-lived; two of them will come and go just before the middle of the period, four will be kept back until shortly before its end, and two will be left until the end itself.

22 'As for the three heads which you saw sleeping, this is what they mean:
23 In the last years of the empire, the Most High will bring to the throne three
24 kings, who will restore much of its strength, and rule *a* over the earth and its inhabitants more oppressively than anyone before. They are called the
25 eagle's heads, because they will complete and bring to a head its long series
26 of wicked deeds. As for the greatest head, which you saw disappear, it
27 signifies one of the kings, who will die in his bed, but in great agony. The
28 two that survived will be destroyed by the sword; one of them will fall by the sword of the other, who will himself fall by the sword in the last days.

29 'As for the two little wings that went over to the head on the right side,
30 this is what they mean: They are the ones whom the Most High has reserved until the last days, and their reign, as you saw, was short and troubled.

31 'As for the lion which you saw coming from the forest, roused from sleep and roaring, which you heard addressing the eagle, taxing it with its
32 wicked deeds and words, this is the Messiah whom the Most High has kept back until the end. He will address *b* those rulers, taxing them openly with their sins, their crimes, and their defiance. He will bring them alive
33 to judgement; he will convict them and then destroy them. But he will be
34 merciful to those of my people that remain, all who have been kept safe in my land; he will set them free and give them gladness, until the final day of judgement comes, about which I told you at the beginning.

*a* who . . . rule: *so some Vss.; Lat.* and he will restore . . . and they will rule . . .
*b* He will address: *probable reading; Lat. defective.*

44

'That, then, is the vision which you saw, and its meaning. It is the secret  35 36
of the Most High, which no one except yourself has proved worthy to be
told. What you have seen you must therefore write in a book and deposit  37
it in a hiding-place. You must also disclose these secrets to those of your  38
people whom you know to be wise enough to understand them and to keep
them safe. But stay here yourself for seven more days, to receive whatever  39
revelation the Most High thinks fit to send you.' Then the angel left me.

When all the people heard that seven days had passed without my  40
returning to the town, they assembled and came to me. 'What wrong or  41
injury have we done you,' they asked me, 'that you have deserted us and
settled here? Out of all the prophets you are the only one left to us. You  42
are like the last cluster in a vineyard, like a lamp in the darkness, or a safe
harbour for a ship in a storm. Have we not suffered enough? If you desert  43 44
us, we had far better have been destroyed in the fire that burnt up Zion.
We are no better than those who perished there.' Then they raised a loud  45
lamentation.

I replied: 'Take courage, Israel; house of Jacob, lay aside your grief.  46
The Most High bears you in mind, and the Mighty One has not for ever *a*  47
forgotten you. I have not left you, nor abandoned you; I came here to pray  48
for Zion in her distress, and to beg for mercy for your sanctuary that has
fallen so low. Go to your homes now, every one of you; and in a few days'  49
time I will come back to you.'

So the people returned to the town as I told them, while I remained in  50 51
the field. I stayed there for seven days in obedience to the angel, eating
nothing but what grew in the field, and living on that for the whole of
the time.

THE SEVEN DAYS PASSED; and the next night I had a dream. In my  **13** 1 2
dream, a wind came up out of the sea and set the waves in turmoil. And  3
this wind brought a human figure rising from the depths, *b* and as I watched,
this man came flying *c* with the clouds of heaven. Wherever he turned his
eyes, everything that they fell on was seized with terror; and wherever the  4
sound of his voice reached, all who heard it melted like wax at the touch
of fire.

Next I saw an innumerable host of men gathering from the four winds  5
of heaven to wage war on the man who had risen from the sea. I saw that  6
the man hewed out a vast mountain for himself, and flew up on to it. I tried  7
to see from what quarter or place the mountain had been taken, but I
could not. Then I saw that all who had gathered to wage war against the  8
man were filled with fear, and yet they dared to fight against him. When  9
he saw the hordes advancing to attack, he did not so much as lift a finger
against them. He had no spear in his hand, no weapon at all; only, as I  10
watched, he poured what seemed like a stream of fire out of his mouth, a
breath of flame from his lips, and a storm of sparks from his tongue. All  11
of them combined into one mass—the stream of fire, the breath of flame,
and the great storm. It fell on the host advancing to join battle, and burnt

---

*a*  So one Vs.; Lat. in strife.                    *b*  And . . . depths: *so other Vss.; Lat. defective.*
*c*  *So other Vss.; Lat.* grew strong.

up every man of them; suddenly all that enormous multitude had disappeared, leaving nothing but dust and ashes and a reek of smoke. I was dumbfounded at the sight.

12 After that, I saw the man coming down from the mountain and calling
13 to himself a different company, a peaceful one. He was joined by great numbers of men, some with joy on their faces, others with sorrow. Some came from captivity; some brought others to him as an offering. I woke up
14 in terror, and prayed to the Most High. I said, 'You have revealed these marvels to me, your servant, all the way through; you have judged me
15 worthy to have my prayers answered. Now show me the meaning of this
16 dream also. How terrible, to my thinking, it will be for all who survive to
17 those days! But how much worse for those who do not survive! Those who
18 do not survive will have the sorrow of knowing what is in store in the last
19 days and yet missing it. Those who do survive are to be pitied for the terrible
20 dangers and trials which, as these visions show, they will have to face. But perhaps after all it is better to endure the dangers and reach the goal than to vanish out of the world like a cloud and never see the events of the last days.'

21 'Yes,' he replied, 'I will explain the meaning of this vision, and tell you
22 all that you ask. As for your question about those who survive, this is the
23 answer: the very person from whom the danger will then come will protect in danger those who have works and fidelity laid up to their credit with
24 the Most High. You may be assured that those who survive are more highly blessed than those who die.

25 'This is what the vision means: The man you saw rising from the depths
26 of the sea is he whom the Most High has held in readiness through many ages; he will himself deliver the world he has made, and determine the lot
27 of those who survive. As for the breath, fire, and storm which you saw
28 pouring from the mouth of the man, so that without a spear or any weapon in his hand he destroyed the hordes advancing to wage war against him,
29 this is the meaning: The day is near when the Most High will begin to
30 bring deliverance to those on earth. Then men will all be filled with great
31 alarm; they will plot to make war on one another, city on city, region on
32 region, nation on nation, kingdom on kingdom. When this happens, and all the signs that I have shown you come to pass, then my son will be
33 revealed, whom you saw as a man rising from the sea. On hearing his voice,
34 all the nations will leave their own territories and their separate wars, and unite in a countless host, as you saw in your vision, with a common intent
35 to go and wage war against him. He will take his stand on the summit of
36 Mount Zion, and Zion will come into sight before all men, complete and fully built. This corresponds to the mountain which you saw hewn out,
37 not by the hand of man. Then my son will convict of their godless deeds the nations that confront him. This will correspond to the storm you saw.
38 He will taunt them with their evil plottings and the tortures they are soon to endure. This corresponds to the flame. And he will destroy them without effort by means of *a* the law—and that is like the fire.

39 40 'Then you saw him collecting a different company, a peaceful one. They are the ten tribes which were taken off into exile in the time of King Hoshea,

*a* by means of: *so one Vs.; Lat.* and.

whom Shalmaneser king of Assyria took prisoner. He deported them
beyond the River, and they were taken away into a strange country. But 41
then they resolved to leave the country populated by the Gentiles and go
to a distant land never yet inhabited by man, and there at last to be obedient 42
to their laws, which in their own country they had failed to keep. As they 43
passed through the narrow passages of the Euphrates, the Most High per- 44
formed miracles for them, stopping up the channels of the river until they
had crossed over. Their journey through that region, which is called 45
Arzareth, was long, and took a year and a half. They have lived there ever 46
since, until this final age. Now they are on their way back, and once more 47
the Most High will stop the channels of the river to let them cross.

'That is the meaning of the peaceful assembly that you saw. With them 48
too are the survivors of your own people, all who are found inside my sacred
boundary. So then, when the time comes for him to destroy the nations 49
assembled against him, he will protect his people who are left, and show 50
them many prodigies.'

'My lord, my master,' I asked, 'explain to me why the man that I saw 51
rose up out of the depths of the sea.' He replied: 'It is beyond the power of 52
any man to explore the deep sea and discover what is in it; in the same way
no one on earth can see my son and his company until the appointed day.
Such then is the meaning of your vision. The revelation has been given to 53
you, and to you alone, because you have given up your own affairs, and 54
devoted yourself entirely to mine, and to the study of my law. You have 55
taken wisdom as your guide in everything, and called understanding your
mother. That is why I have given this revelation to you; there is a reward 56
in store for you with the Most High. In three days' time I will speak with
you again, and tell you some momentous and wonderful things.'

So I went away to the field, giving worship and praise to the Most High 57
for the wonders he performed from time to time and for his providential 58
control of the passing ages and what happens in them. There I remained
for three days.

## The writing of the sacred books

ON THE THIRD DAY I was sitting under an oak-tree, when a voice **14**
came to me from a bush, saying, 'Ezra, Ezra!' 'Here I am, Lord', I 2
answered, and rose to my feet. The voice went on: 'I revealed myself in the 3
bush, and spoke to Moses, when my people Israel was in slavery in Egypt,
and sent him to lead my people out of Egypt. I brought him up on to Mount 4
Sinai, and kept him with me for many days. I told him of many wonders, 5
showing him the secrets of the ages and the end of time, and instructed him
what to make known and what to conceal. So too I now give this order to 6 7
you: commit to memory the signs I have shown you, the visions you have 8
seen, and the explanations you have been given. You yourself are about to 9
be taken away from the world of men, and thereafter you will remain with
my son and with those like you, until the end of time. The world has lost 10
its youth, and time is growing old. For the whole of time is in twelve 11

12 divisions; nine<sup>a</sup> divisions and half the tenth have already passed, and only
13 two and a half still remain. Set your house in order, therefore; give warnings to your nation, and comfort to those in need of it; and take your leave
14 of mortal life. Put away your earthly cares, and lay down your human
15 burdens; strip off your weak nature, set aside the anxieties that vex you,
16 and be ready to depart quickly from this life. However great the evils you
17 have witnessed, there are worse to come. As this ageing world grows
18 weaker and weaker, so will evils increase for its inhabitants. Truth will move farther away, and falsehood come nearer. The eagle that you saw in your vision is already on the wing.'

19 20   'May I speak<sup>b</sup> in your presence, Lord?' I replied. 'I am to depart, by your command, after giving warning to those of my people who are now alive. But who will give warning to those born hereafter? The world is
21 shrouded in darkness, and its inhabitants are without light. For your law was destroyed in the fire, and so no one can know about the deeds you have
22 done or intend to do. If I have won your favour, fill me with your holy spirit, so that I may write down the whole story of the world from the very beginning, everything that is contained in your law; then men will have the chance to find the right path, and, if they choose, gain life in the last days.'

23   'Go,' he replied, 'call the people together, and tell them not to look for
24 you for forty days. Have a large number of writing-tablets ready, and take with you Seraiah and Dibri, Shelemiah, Ethan, and Asiel, five men all
25 trained to write quickly. Then return here, and I will light a lamp of understanding in your mind, which will not go out until you have finished all
26 that you are to write. When your work is complete, some of it you must make public; the rest you must give to wise men to keep secret. Tomorrow at this time you shall begin to write.'

27 28   I went as I was ordered and summoned all the people, and said: 'Israel,
29 listen to what I say. Our ancestors lived originally in Egypt as foreigners.
30 They were rescued from that land, and were given the law which offers life.
31 But they disobeyed it, and you have followed their example. Then you were given a land of your own, the land of Zion; but you, like your ancestors, sinned and abandoned the way laid down for you by the Most High.
32 Because he is a just judge he took away from you in due time what he had
33 given. And so you are now here in exile, and your fellow-countrymen are
34 still farther away. If then you will direct your understanding and instruct your minds, you shall be kept safe in life and meet with mercy after you
35 die. For after death will come the judgement; we shall be restored to life, and then the names of the just will be known and the deeds of the godless
36 exposed. From this moment no one must come to talk to me, nor look for me for the next forty days.'

37   I took with me the five men as I had been told, and we went away to the
38 field, and there we stayed. On the next day I heard a voice calling me, which
39 said: 'Ezra, open your mouth and drink what I give you.' So I opened my mouth, and was handed a cup full of what seemed like water, except that
40 its colour was the colour of fire. I took it and drank, and as soon as I had

---

<sup>a</sup> *Probable reading; Lat.* ten.     <sup>b</sup> May I speak: *so other Vss.; Lat. omits.*

48

done so my mind began to pour forth a flood of understanding, and wisdom grew greater and greater within me, for I retained my memory unimpaired. I opened my mouth to speak, and I continued to speak unceasingly. The 41 42 Most High gave understanding to the five men, who took turns at writing down what was said, using characters *a* which they had not known before. They remained at work through the forty days, writing all day, and taking food only at night. But as for me, I spoke all through the day; even at night 43 I was not silent. In the forty days, ninety-four *b* books were written. At 44 45 the end of the forty days the Most High spoke to me. 'Make public the books you wrote first,' he said, 'to be read by good and bad alike. But the 46 last seventy books are to be kept back, and given to none but the wise among your people. They contain a stream of understanding, a fountain 47 of wisdom, a flood of knowledge.' And I did so. 48

## Prophecies of doom

PROCLAIM TO MY PEOPLE the words of prophecy which I give you to 15 speak, says the Lord; and have them written down, because they are 2 trustworthy and true. Have no fear of plots against you, and do not be 3 troubled by the unbelief of those who oppose you. For everyone who does 4 not believe will die because of his unbelief. *c*

Beware, says the Lord, I am letting loose terrible evils on the world, 5 sword and famine, death and destruction, because wickedness has spread 6 over the whole earth and there is no room for further deeds of violence. Therefore the Lord says, I will not keep silence about their godless sins; 7 8 I will not tolerate their wicked deeds. See how the blood of innocent victims cries to me for vengeance, and the souls of the just never cease to plead with me! I will most surely avenge them, says the Lord, and will hear 9 the plea of all the innocent blood that has been shed. My people are being 10 led to the slaughter like sheep. I will no longer allow them to remain in Egypt, but will use all my power to rescue them; I will strike the Egyptians 11 with plagues, as I did before, and destroy their whole land. How Egypt will 12 mourn, shaken to its very foundations, when it is scourged and chastised by the Lord! How the tillers of the soil will mourn, when the seed fails to 13 grow, and when their trees are devastated by blight and hail and terrible storm! *d* Alas for the world and its inhabitants! The sword that will destroy 14 15 them is not far away. Nation will draw sword against nation and go to war. Stable government will be at an end; one faction will prevail over another, 16 caring nothing in their day of power for king or leading man of rank. A man 17 may want to visit a city, but will not be able to do so; for ambition and rivalry 18 will have reduced cities to chaos, destroyed houses, and filled men with panic. A man will violently assault his neighbour's house and plunder his 19 goods; no pity will restrain him, when he is in the grip of famine and grinding misery.

See how I summon before me all the kings of the earth, says God, from 20

---

*a* *Probable reading, based on other Vss.; Lat. corrupt.*          *b* *So other Vss.; Lat. corrupt.*          *c* *Or in his unbelief.*          *d* *Probable meaning; Lat. obscure.*

sunrise and south wind, from east and south,[a] to turn back and repay what
21 they have been given. I will do to them as they are doing to my chosen
people even to this day; I will pay them back in their own coin.

22      These are the words of the Lord God: I will show sinners no pity; the
sword will not spare those murderers who stain the ground with innocent
23 blood. The Lord's anger has overflowed in fire to scorch the earth to its
24 foundations and consume sinners like burning straw. Alas for sinners who
25 flout my commands! says the Lord; I will show them no mercy. Away from
26 me, you rebels! Do not bring your pollution near my holiness. The Lord
well knows all who sin against him, and has consigned them to death and
27 destruction. Already disaster has fallen upon the world, and you will never
escape it; God will refuse to rescue you, because you have sinned against
him.

28 29    How terrible the sight of what is coming from the east! Hordes of
dragons from Arabia will sally forth with countless chariots, and from the
first day of their advance their hissing will spread across the land, to fill all
30 who hear them with fear and consternation. The Carmanians, mad with
rage, will rush like wild boars out of the forest, advancing in full force to
join battle with them, and will devastate whole tracts of Assyria with their
31 tusks. But then the dragons will summon up their native fury, and will
prove the stronger. They will rally and join forces, and fall on them with
32 overwhelming might until they are routed, until their power is silenced,
33 and every one of them turns to flight. Then their way will be blocked by a
lurking enemy from Assyria, who will destroy one of them. Fear and panic
will spread in their army, and wavering among their kings.

34      See the clouds stretching from east and north to south! Their appearance
35 is hideous, full of fury and tempest. They will clash together, they will
pour over the land a vast storm;[b] blood, shed by the sword, will reach as
36 37 high as a horse's belly, a man's thigh, or a camel's hock. Terror and trembling will cover the earth; all who see the raging fury will shudder and be
38 stricken with panic. Then vast storm-clouds will approach from north and
39 south, and others from the west. But the winds from the east will be
stronger still, and will hold in check the raging cloud and its leader; and the
storm[b] which was bent on destruction will be fiercely driven back to the
40 south and west by the winds from the east. Huge mighty clouds, full of
fury, will mount up and ravage the whole land and its inhabitants; a
41 terrible storm[b] will sweep over the great and the powerful, with fire and
hail and flying swords; and a deluge of water will flood all the fields and
42 rivers. They will flatten to the ground cities and walls, mountains and hills,
43 trees in the woods and crops in the fields. They will advance all the way to
44 Babylon, and blot it out. When they reach it, they will surround it, and let
loose a storm[b] in all its fury. The dust and smoke will reach the sky, and all
45 her neighbours will mourn for Babylon. Any of her survivors will be
enslaved by her destroyers.

46      And you, Asia, who have shared the beauty and the splendour of
47 Babylon, alas for you, poor wretch! Like her you have dressed up your
daughters as whores, to attract and catch your lovers who have always

---

[a] south: *probable reading; Lat.* Lebanon.          [b] storm: *probable meaning; Lat. obscure.*

lusted for you. You have copied all the schemes and practices of that vile 48
harlot. Therefore God says, I will bring upon you terrible evils: widow- 49
hood and poverty, famine, sword, and plague, bringing ruin to your homes,
bringing violence and death. Your strength and splendour will wither like 50
a flower, when that scorching heat bears down upon you. Then you will be 51
a poor weak woman, bruised, beaten, and wounded, unable to receive your
wealthy lovers any more. Should I be so fierce with you, says the Lord, if 52 53
you had not killed my chosen ones continually, gloating over the blows you
struck them, and hurling your drunken taunts at their corpses?

Paint your face; make yourself beautiful! The harlot's pay shall be yours; 54 55
you will get what you have earned. What you do to my chosen people, God 56
will do to you, says the Lord; he will consign you to a terrible fate. Your 57
children will die of hunger; you will fall by the sword, your cities will be
blotted out, and all your people will fall on the field of battle. Those who 58
are up on the mountains will be dying of hunger, and their hunger and
thirst will force them to gnaw their own flesh and drink their own blood.
You will be foremost in misery, and still there will be more to come. As 59 60
the victors go past on their way home from the sack of Babylon, they will
smash your peaceful city, destroy a great part of your territory, and bring
much of your splendour to an end. They will destroy you—you will be 61
stubble, and they the fire. They will completely devour you and your 62
cities, your land and your mountains, and will burn all your forests and
your fruit-trees. They will make your children prisoners and plunder your 63
property; and not a trace will be left of your splendid beauty.

Alas for you, Babylon and Asia! Alas for you, Egypt and Syria! Put on **16** 1 2
sackcloth and hair-shirt, and raise a howl of lamentation for your sons;
your doom is close at hand. The sword is let loose against you, and who will 3
turn it aside? Fire is let loose upon you, and who will put it out? Cala- 4 5
mities have been let loose against you, and who is there to stop them?
Can any man stop a hungry lion in a forest, or put out a fire among the 6
stubble once it has begun to blaze? Can any man stop an arrow shot by a 7
strong archer? When the Lord God sends calamities, who can stop them? 8
When his anger overflows in fire, who can put it out? When the lightning 9 10
flashes, who will not tremble? When it thunders, who will not shake with
dread? When it is the Lord who utters his threats, is there any man who 11
will not be crushed to the ground at his approach? The earth is shaken to 12
its very foundations, and the sea is churned up from its depths; the waves
and all the fish with them are in turmoil before the presence of the Lord
and the majesty of his strength. For strong is his arm which bends the 13
bow, and sharp the arrows which he shoots; once they are on their way, they
will not stop before they reach the ends of the earth. Calamities are let loose, 14
and will not turn back before they strike the earth. The fire is alight and 15
will not be put out until it has burnt up earth's foundations. An arrow shot 16
by a powerful archer does not turn back; no more will the calamities be
recalled which are let loose against the earth.

Alas, alas for me! Who will rescue me on that day? When troubles come, 17 18
many will groan; when famine strikes, many will die; when wars break
out, empires will tremble; when the calamities come, all will be filled with

19 terror. What will men do then, in the face of calamity? Famine and plague,
20 suffering and hardship, are scourges sent to teach men better ways. But even so they will not abandon their crimes, nor keep in mind their scourg-
21 ing. A time will come when food grows cheap, so cheap that they will imagine they have been sent peace and prosperity. But at that very moment the earth will become a hotbed of disasters—sword, famine, and anarchy.
22 Most of its inhabitants will die in the famine; and those who survive the
23 famine will be destroyed by the sword. The dead will be tossed out like dung, and there will be no one to offer any comfort. For the earth will be
24 left empty, and its cities a ruin. None will be left to till the ground and sow
25 26 it. The trees will bear their fruits, but who will pick them? The grapes will ripen, but who will tread them? There will be vast desolation everywhere.
27 28 A man will long to see a human face or hear a human voice. For out of a whole city, only ten will survive; in the country-side, only two will be left,
29 hiding in the forest or in holes in the rocks. Just as in an olive-grove three
30 or four olives might be left on each tree, or as a few grapes in a vineyard
31 might be overlooked by the sharp-eyed pickers, so also in those days three
32 or four will be overlooked by those who search the houses to kill. The earth will be left a desert, and the fields will be overrun with briers; thorns will grow over all the roads and paths, because there will be no sheep to
33 tread them. Girls will live in mourning with none to marry them, women will mourn because they have no husbands, their daughters will mourn
34 because they have no one to support them. The young men who should have married them will be killed in the war, and the husbands wiped out by the famine.

35 BUT LISTEN TO ME, you who are the Lord's servants, and take my
36 words to heart. This is the word of the Lord. Receive it, and do not dis-
37 believe what he says. Calamities are here, close at hand, and will not delay.
38 When a pregnant woman is in the ninth month, and the moment of her child's birth is drawing near, there will be two or three hours in which her womb will suffer pangs of agony, and then the child will come from the
39 womb without a moment's delay; in the same way calamities will come on the earth without delay, and the world will groan under the pangs that grip it.
40 Listen to my words, my people; get ready for battle, and when the
41 calamities surround you, be as though you were strangers on earth. The seller must expect to have to run for his life, the buyer to lose what he buys;
42 the merchant must expect to make no profit, the builder never to live in
43 the house he builds. The sower must not expect to reap, nor the pruner to
44 gather his grapes. Those who marry must expect no children; the un-
45 married must think of themselves as widowed. For all labour is labour in
46 vain. Their fruits will be gathered by foreigners, who will plunder their goods, pull down their houses, and take their children captive. If they
47 have children, they will have been bred only for captivity and famine; any who make money do so only to have it plundered. The more care they
48 lavish on their cities, houses, and property, and on their own persons, the
49 fiercer will be my indignation against their sins, says the Lord. Like the

indignation of a virtuous woman towards a prostitute, so will be the 50
indignation of justice towards wickedness with all her finery; she will
accuse her to her face, when the champion arrives to expose all sin upon
earth. Do not imitate wickedness, therefore, and her actions. For in a very 51 52
short time she will be swept from the earth, and the reign of justice over
us will begin.

The sinner must not deny that he has sinned; he will only bring burn- 53
ing coals on to his own head if he says, 'I have committed no sin against
the majesty of God.' For the Lord knows all that men do; he knows their 54
plans, their schemes, and their inmost thoughts. He said, 'Let the earth 55
be made', and it was made; and 'Let the heavens be made', and they were
made. It was by the Lord's word that the stars were fixed in their places; 56
the number of the stars is known to him. He looks into the depths with their 57
treasures; he has measured the sea and everything it contains. By his word 58
he confined the sea within the bounds of the waters, and above the water he
suspended the land. He spread out the sky like a vault, and made it secure 59
upon the waters. He provided springs in the desert, and pools on the 60
mountain-tops as the source of rivers flowing down to water the earth. He 61
created man, and placed a heart in the middle of his body; he gave him
spirit, life, and understanding, the very breath of Almighty God who 62
created the whole world and searches out secret things in secret places.
He knows well your plans and all your inward thoughts. Alas for sinners 63
who try to hide their sins! The Lord will scrutinize all their deeds; he will 64
call you all to account. You will be covered with confusion, when your sins 65
are brought into the open, and your wicked deeds stand up to accuse you
on that day. What can you do? How can you hide your sins from God and 66
his angels? God is your judge: fear him! Abandon your sins, and have 67
done with your wicked deeds for ever! Then God will set you free from
all distress.

Fierce flames are being kindled to burn you. A great horde will descend 68
on you; they will seize some of you and make you eat pagan sacrifices.
Those who give in to them will be derided, taunted, and trampled on. In 69 70
place after place *a* and in all the neighbourhood there will be a violent
attack on those who fear the Lord. Their enemies will be like madmen, 71
plundering and destroying without mercy all who still fear the Lord. They 72
will destroy and plunder their property, and throw them out of their homes.
Then it will be seen that my chosen people have stood the test like gold in 73
the assayer's fire.

Listen, you whom I have chosen, says the Lord; the days of harsh suffer- 74
ing are close at hand, but I will rescue you from them. Away with your 75
fears and doubts! For God is your leader. You who follow my command- 76
ments and instructions, says the Lord God, must not let your sins weigh
you down, nor your wicked deeds get the better of you. Alas for those who 77
are entangled in their sins, and overrun with their wicked deeds! They
are like a field overrun by bushes, with brambles across the path and no
way through, completely shut off and doomed to destruction by fire. 78

*a* In place after place: *possible meaning; Lat. obscure.*

# TOBIT

## *The troubles of Tobit*

1 THIS IS THE STORY of Tobit, son of Tobiel, son of Hananiel, son of Aduel, son of Gabael, son of Raphael, son of Raguel, of the
2 family of Asiel, of the tribe of Naphtali. He was taken captive in the time of Shalmaneser *a* king of Assyria, from Thisbe which is south of Kedesh Naphtali in Upper Galilee above Hazor, behind the road to the west, north of Peor.

3 I, TOBIT, made truth and righteousness my lifelong guide; I did many acts of charity for my kinsmen, those of my nation who had gone into
4 captivity with me at Nineveh in Assyria. When I was quite young in my own country, Israel, the whole tribe of Naphtali my ancestor broke away from the dynasty of David, *b* and from Jerusalem, the city chosen out of all the tribes of Israel as the one place of sacrifice. It was there that God's dwelling-place, the temple, had been consecrated, built to last for all
5 generations. All my kinsmen, the whole house of Naphtali my ancestor, sacrificed on the mountains of Galilee to the calf which Jeroboam, king of
6 Israel, had made in Dan; at the festivals I was the only one to make the frequent journey to Jerusalem prescribed for all Israel as an eternal commandment. I used to hurry off to Jerusalem with the firstfruits of crops and herds, the tithes of the cattle, and the first shearings of the sheep; and
7 I gave them to the priests of Aaron's line for the altar, and the tithe of wine, corn, olive oil, pomegranates and other fruits to the Levites ministering in Jerusalem. The second tithe for the six years I converted into money,
8 and I went and distributed it in Jerusalem year by year among the orphans and widows, and the converts who had attached themselves to Israel. Every third year when I brought it and gave it to them, we held a feast according to the rule laid down in the law of Moses and the instructions given by Deborah the mother of Hananiel our grandfather; for my father had died leaving me an orphan.

9 When I came of age I took a wife from our kindred, and had a son by her
10 whom I called Tobias. After the deportation to Assyria when I was taken captive and came to Nineveh, everyone of my kindred and nation ate
11 12 gentile food; but I myself scrupulously avoided doing so. Since I was
13 whole-heartedly mindful of my God, the Most High endowed me with a presence which won me the favour of Shalmaneser, and I became his
14 buyer of supplies. As long as he lived I used to travel to Media and buy for him there. I deposited bags of money to the value of ten talents of
15 silver with my kinsman Gabael son of Gabri in Media. When Shalmaneser died and was succeeded by his son Sennacherib, the roads to

*a* Gk. Enemessaros.     *b* Gk. adds my ancestor.

54

Media passed out of Assyrian control and I could no longer make the journey.

In the time of Shalmaneser, I did many acts of charity for my fellow- 16
countrymen: I shared my food with the hungry and provided clothes for 17
the naked. If I saw the dead body of any man of my race lying outside the
wall of Nineveh, I buried it. I buried all those who fell victim to Senna- 18
cherib after his flight from Judaea, when the King of heaven executed
judgement on him for all his blasphemies, and in his rage he killed many
of the Israelites. I stole their bodies away and buried them, and Sennacherib looked for them but could not find them. One of the Ninevites 19
informed the king that I was giving burial to his victims; so I went into
hiding. When I learnt that the king knew about me and that I was wanted
for execution, I took fright and ran away. All my property was seized and 20
put into the royal treasury; I was left with nothing but Anna my wife and
my son Tobias. However, less than forty days afterwards, the king was 21
murdered by two of his sons. They took refuge in the mountains of Ararat,
and his son Esarhaddon succeeded him. He appointed Ahikar son of my
brother Anael to supervise all the finances of his kingdom; he had control
of the entire administration. Then Ahikar interceded on my behalf and I 22
came back to Nineveh. For he had been chief cupbearer, keeper of the
privy seal, comptroller, and treasurer when Sennacherib was king of
Assyria; and Esarhaddon renewed the appointments. Ahikar was my
nephew and so one of my kinsmen.

DURING THE REIGN of Esarhaddon, I returned to my house, and my 2
wife Anna and my son Tobias were restored to me. At our festival of Pentecost, that is the Feast of Weeks, a good dinner was prepared for me and I
sat down to eat. The table was laid and a lavish meal was put before me. 2
I said to my son Tobias: 'Go, my boy, and if you can find any poor man of
our captive people in Nineveh who is whole-heartedly mindful of God,
bring him and he shall share my dinner. I will wait for you until you return.'
Tobias went to look for a poor man of our people, but he came back ˙ud 3
said, 'Father!' 'Yes, my son?' I replied. He answered, 'Father, one of our
nation has been murdered and his body is lying in the market-place. He
was strangled only a moment ago.' I jumped up and left my dinner un- 4
tasted. I took the body from the square and put it in one of the outbuildings
until sunset when I could bury it; then I went home, duly bathed myself, 5
and ate my food in sorrow. I recalled the saying of the prophet Amos in 6
the passage about Bethel:

> 'Your feasts shall be turned into mourning,
>    and all your songs[a] into lamentation',

and I wept. After sunset I went and dug a grave and buried the body. The 7 8
neighbours jeered at me and said: 'Is he no longer afraid? He ran away last
time, when they were hunting for him to put him to death for this very
offence; and here he is burying the dead again!' That night I bathed my- 9
self and went into my courtyard. I lay down to sleep by the courtyard wall,

_____

[a] *So one Vs. (compare Amos 8. 10); Gk. ways.*

10 leaving my face uncovered because of the heat. I did not know that there were sparrows in the wall above me; and their droppings fell, still warm, right into my eyes and produced white patches. I went to the doctors to be cured, but the more they treated me with their ointments, the more my eyes were blinded by the white patches, until I lost my sight. For four years I was blind. All my kinsmen grieved for me, and Ahikar looked after me for two years until he moved to Elymais.

11 During that time my wife Anna used to earn money by women's work.
12 When she took what she had done to her employers they would pay her wages. One day, the seventh of Dystrus, when she had cut off the piece she had woven and delivered it, the owners not only paid her in full, but also
13 gave her a kid from their herd of goats to take home. When my wife came in to me the kid began to bleat. I called out to her: 'Where does that kid come from? I hope it was not stolen? Give it back to its owners; we have no right
14 to eat anything stolen.' She assured me: 'It was given me as a present, over and above my wages.' I did not believe her and insisted that she should give it back to its owners, and I blushed with shame for what she had done. She retorted: 'So much for all your good works and acts of charity! Now we can see what you are!'

3 1 2 In deep distress I groaned and wept, and as I groaned I prayed: 'Thou art just, O Lord, and all thy acts are just; in all thy ways thou art merciful
3 and true; thou art judge of the world. Remember me now, Lord, and look upon me. Do not punish me for the sins and errors which I and my fathers
4 have committed. We have sinned against thee and disobeyed thy commandments, and thou hast given us up to plunder, captivity, and death, until we have become a byword, a proverb, and a taunt to all the nations among
5 whom thou hast scattered us. I acknowledge the justice of thy many judgements, the due penalty for my sins, for we have not obeyed thy
6 commandments and have not lived in loyal obedience before thee. And now deal with me at thy pleasure, and command that my life be taken away, so that I may be removed from the face of the earth and turned to earth. I should be better dead than alive, for I have had to hear undeserved reproaches and am in deep grief. Lord, command that I may be released from this misery; let me go to my long home; do not turn thy face from me, O Lord. It is better for me to die than to live in such misery and to hear such reproaches.'

7 On that same day it happened that Sarah, the daughter of Raguel who lived at Ecbatana in Media, also had to listen to reproaches from one of her
8 father's maidservants, because she had been given in marriage to seven husbands, and before the marriage could be regularly consummated they had all been killed by the wicked demon Asmodaeus. The maidservant said to her: 'It is you who kill your husbands! You have already been given in marriage to seven, and you have not borne the name of any one of them.
9 Why punish us because they are dead? Go and join your husbands! I hope we never see son or daughter of yours!'

10 She was sad at heart that day, and went in tears up to the attic in her father's house meaning to hang herself. But she had second thoughts and said to herself: 'Perhaps they will reproach my father and say to him, "You

had one dear daughter and she hanged herself because of her troubles",
and so I shall bring my aged father in sorrow to the grave. No, I will not
hang myself; it would be better to beg the Lord to let me die and not live
on to hear such reproaches.' Then at once she spread out her hands towards 11
the window in prayer and said: 'Praise to thee, merciful God, praise to thy
name for ever; let all thy works praise thee for evermore. Now I lift up my 12
eyes and look to thee. Command me to be removed from this earth so that 13
I may no longer hear such reproaches. Thou knowest, Lord, that I am a 14
virgin, guiltless of intercourse with any man; I have not disgraced my 15
name nor my father's name in the land of my exile. I am my father's only
child; he has no other to be his heir, nor has he any near kinsman or relative who might marry me, and for whom I should stay alive. Already seven
husbands of mine have died. What have I to live for any longer? If it is not
thy will, O Lord, to let me die, listen now to my complaint.'

At that very time the prayers of both of them were heard in the glorious 16
presence of God. His angel Raphael was sent to cure them both of their 17
troubles: Tobit, by removing the white patches from his eyes so that he
might see God's light again, and Sarah daughter of Raguel by giving her in
marriage to Tobias son of Tobit and by setting her free from the wicked
demon Asmodaeus; for it was the destiny of Tobias and not of any other
suitor to possess her. At the moment when Tobit went back from the
courtyard into his house, Sarah daughter of Raguel came down from the
attic.

## The adventures of Tobias

THAT SAME DAY Tobit remembered the silver that he had deposited 4
with Gabael at Rages in Media, and he said to himself, 'I have asked 2
for death; before I die ought I not to send for my son Tobias and explain
to him about this money?' So he sent for Tobias, and when he came he 3
said to him: 'Give me decent burial. Show proper respect to your mother,
and do not leave her in the lurch as long as she lives; do what will please
her, and never grieve her heart in any way. Remember, my son, all the 4
dangers she faced for your sake while you were in her womb. When she
dies, bury her beside me in the same grave. And remember the Lord every 5
day of your life. Never deliberately do what is wrong or break his commandments. As long as you live do what is right. Do not fall into evil ways; for 6
an honest life leads to prosperity. To all who keep the law, the Lord gives 19
good guidance, and as he chooses he humbles men to the grave below.[a]

---

[a] To all . . . below: *in place of these words some witnesses have* To all who keep the law
(7) give alms from what you possess and never give with a grudging eye. Do not turn
your face away from any poor man, and God will not turn away his face from you. (8) Let
your almsgiving match your means. If you have little, do not be ashamed to give the little
you can afford; (9) you will be laying up a sound insurance against the day of adversity.
(10) Almsgiving saves the giver from death and keeps him from going down into darkness.
(11) All who give alms are making an offering acceptable to the Most High.
　(12) 'Beware, my son, of fornication; above all choose your wife from the race of your
ancestors. Do not take a foreign wife who is not of your father's tribe, because we are

Now, my son, remember these commands; let them never be effaced from your mind.

20  'Well now, my boy, let me tell you that I have ten talents of silver on
21  deposit with Gabael son of Gabri, at Rages in Media. Do not be anxious because we have become poor; there is great wealth waiting for you, if only you fear God and avoid all wickedness and do what is good in the sight of the Lord your God.'

5 12  Then Tobias said: 'I will do all that you have told me, father. But how shall I be able to get this money from him, since he does not know me and I do not know him? What proof of identity shall I give him to make him believe me and give me this money? Also I do not know the roads to Media
3  or how to get there.' To this Tobit replied: 'He gave me his note of hand, and I gave him mine, which I divided in two. We took one part each, and I put mine with the money. It is twenty years since I made this deposit. And now, my boy, find someone reliable to go with you, and we will pay him up to the time of your return; then go and recover the money from Gabael.'

4  Tobias went out to find a man who knew the way and would accompany
5  him to Media, and found himself face to face with the angel Raphael. Not knowing he was an angel of God, he questioned him: 'Where do you come from, young man?' 'I am an Israelite,' he replied, 'one of your fellow-countrymen, and I have come here to find work.' Tobias asked, 'Do you
6  know the road to Media?' 'Yes,' he said, 'I have often been there; I am familiar with all the routes and know them well. I have often travelled into Media and used to lodge with Gabael our fellow-countryman who lives there in Rages.[a] It is two full days' journey from Ecbatana to Rages; for
7  Rages is in the hills, and Ecbatana is in the middle of the plain.' Tobias said: 'Wait for me, young man, while I go in and tell my father. I need you
8  to go with me and will pay you your wages.' 'All right, I will wait,' he said; 'only do not be too long.'

Tobias went in and told his father. 'I have found a fellow-Israelite to accompany me', he said. His father replied, 'Call the man in, my son. I

descendants of the prophets. Remember, my son, that Noah, Abraham, Isaac, and Jacob, our ancestors, back to the earliest days, all chose wives from their kindred. They were blessed in their children, and their descendants shall possess the earth. (13) And you like them, my son, must love your kindred. Do not be too proud to take a wife from among the women of your own nation. Pride breeds ruin and anarchy, and the waster declines into poverty; waste is the mother of starvation.

(14) 'Pay your workmen their wages the same day; do not make any man wait for his money. If you serve God you will be repaid. Be circumspect, my son, in all that you do, and show yourself well-bred in all your behaviour. (15) Do not do to anyone what you yourself would hate. Do not drink to excess and so let drunkenness become a habit. (16) Give food to the hungry and clothes to the naked. Whatever you have beyond your own needs, give away to the poor, and do not give grudgingly. (17) Pour out your wine and offer your bread on the tombs of the righteous; but give nothing to sinners. (18) Ask any sensible man for his advice; do not despise any advice that may help you. (19) Praise the Lord God at all times and ask him to guide your course. Then all you do and all you plan will turn out well. The heathen all lack such guidance; it is the Lord himself who gives all good things, or humbles men at will, as he chooses.

[a] *Probable reading (compare 4. 1); Gk.* Ecbatana.

want to find out his family and tribe and make sure that he will be a trust-worthy companion for you.'

Tobias went out and called him: 'Young man, my father is asking for 9 you.' He went in, and Tobit greeted him first. To Raphael's reply, 'May all be well with you!', Tobit retorted: 'How can anything be well with me now? I am a blind man; I cannot see the light of heaven, but lie in darkness like the dead who cannot see the light. Though still alive, I am as good as dead. I hear men's voices, but the men I do not see.' Raphael answered: 'Take heart; in God's design your cure is at hand. Take heart.' Tobit went on: 'My son Tobias wishes to travel to Media. Can you go with him as his guide? I will pay you, my friend.' 'Yes,' he said, 'I can go with him; I know all the roads. I have often been to Media; I have travelled over all the plains and mountains there, and am familiar with all its roads.' Tobit 10 said to him, 'Tell me, my friend, what family and tribe you belong to.' He asked, 'Why need you know my tribe?' Tobit said, 'I do indeed wish to 11 know whose son you are, my friend, and what your name is.' 'I am Azarias,' 12 he replied, 'son of the older Ananias, one of your kinsmen.'

Tobit said to him: 'Good luck and a safe journey to you! Do not be angry 13 with me, my friend, because I wished to know the facts of your descent. It turns out that you are a kinsman, and a man of good family. I knew Ananias and Nathan the two sons of the older Semelias. They used to go with me to Jerusalem and worship with me there; they never went astray. Your kinsmen are worthy men; you come of a sound stock. Good luck go with you.' Tobit added: 'I will pay you a drachma a day and allow you 14 the same expenses as my son. Keep him company on his travels, and I will 15 add something to your wages.' Raphael answered: 'I will go with him. 16 Never fear; we shall travel there and back without mishap, because the road is safe.' Tobit replied, 'God bless you, my friend.' He called his son and said to him: 'My boy, get ready what you need for the journey, and set off with your kinsman. May God in heaven keep both of you safe on your journey there and restore you to me unharmed. May his angel safely escort you both.' Before setting out Tobias kissed his father and mother, and Tobit said to him, 'Goodbye, and a safe journey!'

Then his mother burst into tears. 'Why have you sent my boy away?' 17 she said to Tobit. 'Is he not our prop and stay? Has he not always been at home with us? Why send money after money? Write it off for the sake of 18 our boy! Let us be content to live the life the Lord has appointed for us.' 19 Tobit said to her: 'Do not worry; our son will go safely and come back 20 safely, and you will see him with your own eyes on the day of his safe return. Do not worry or be anxious about them, my dear. A good angel will 21 go with him, and his journey will prosper, and he will come back safe and sound.' At that she stopped crying. 22

THE BOY AND THE ANGEL left the house together, and the dog came 6 out with him and accompanied them. They travelled until night overtook them, and then camped by the river Tigris. Tobias went down to bathe his 2 feet in the river, and a huge fish leapt out of the water and tried to swallow the boy's foot. He cried out, and the angel said to him, 'Seize the fish and 3

4  hold it fast.' So Tobias seized it and hauled it on to the bank. The angel
said to him: 'Split the fish open and take out its gall, heart, and liver; keep
them by you, but throw the guts away; the gall, heart, and liver can be
5  used as medicine.' Tobias split the fish open, and put together its gall,
heart, and liver. He cooked and ate part of the fish; the rest he salted
and kept.

They continued the journey together until they came near Media.
6  Then the boy asked the angel: 'Azarias, my friend, what medicine is there
7  in the fish's heart, liver, and gall?' He said: 'You can use the heart and
liver as a fumigation for any man or woman attacked by a demon or evil
8  spirit; the attack will cease, and it will give no further trouble. The gall is
for anointing a man's eyes when white patches have spread over them, or
for blowing on the white patches in the eyes; the eyes will then recover.'
9      When he had entered Media and was now approaching Ecbatana,
10 Raphael said to the boy, 'Tobias, my friend.' 'Yes?' he replied. Raphael
said: 'We must stay the night with Raguel. He is your kinsman and he has
a daughter named Sarah. Apart from Sarah he has neither son nor daughter.
11 You are her next of kin and have the right to marry her and inherit her
12 father's property. The girl is sensible, brave, and very beautiful, and her
father is an honourable man.' He went on: 'It is right that you should
marry her. Be guided by me, my friend; I will speak to her father about the
girl this very night and ask for her hand as your bride, and on our return
from Rages we will celebrate her marriage. I know that Raguel cannot
withhold her from you or betroth her to another man without incurring
the death penalty according to the ordinance in the book of Moses; and he
is aware that his daughter belongs by right to you rather than to any other
man. Now be guided by me, my friend; we will talk about the girl tonight
and will betroth her to you, and when we return from Rages we shall take
her back with us to your home.'
13     Then Tobias answered Raphael: 'Azarias, my friend, I have heard that
she has already been given to seven husbands and they died the very night
14 they went into the bridal chamber to her. I have been told that it is a demon
who kills them. And now it is my turn to be afraid; he does her no harm,
but kills any man who tries to come near her. I am my father's only child;
I am afraid that if I die I shall bring my father and mother to the grave
15 with grief for me. They have no other son to bury them.' Raphael said to
him: 'Have you forgotten the orders your father gave you? He told you to
take a wife from your father's kindred. Now be guided by me, my friend:
do not worry about the demon, but marry her. I am sure that this night she
16 shall be given you as your wife. When you enter the bridal chamber, take
some of the fish's liver and its heart, and put them on the smoking incense.
17 The smell will spread, and when the demon smells it he will make off and
never be seen near her any more. When you are about to go to bed with her,
both of you must first stand up and pray, beseeching the Lord of heaven to
grant you mercy and deliverance. Have no fear; she was destined for you
before the world was made. You shall rescue her and she shall go with you.
No doubt you will have children by her and they will be very dear to you. *a*

*a Literally* be like brothers to you.

So do not worry!' When Tobias heard what Raphael said, and learnt that she was his kinswoman and of his father's house, he was filled with love for her and set his heart on her.

WHEN THEY REACHED ECBATANA, Tobias said, 'Azarias, my friend, 7 take me straight to our kinsman Raguel.' So Azarias brought him to Raguel's house, and they found him sitting by the courtyard door. They greeted him first, and he replied, 'A hearty welcome to you, friends. I am glad to see you well after your journey.' He took them into his house and 2 said to Edna his wife, 'Is not this young man like my kinsman Tobit?' Edna asked them, 'Where do you come from, friends?' 'We belong to the 3 tribe of Naphtali,' they answered, 'now in captivity at Nineveh.' 'Do you 4 know our kinsman Tobit?' she asked, and they replied, 'Yes, we do.' 'Is he well?' she said. 'He is alive and well', they answered, and Tobias added, 5 'He is my father.' Raguel jumped up and, with tears in his eyes, he kissed 6 him and said, 'God bless you, my boy, son of a good and noble father. But 7 what grievous news that so good and charitable a man has gone blind!' He embraced Tobias his kinsman and wept; and Edna his wife and their 8 daughter Sarah also wept for Tobit. Then Raguel slaughtered a ram from the flock and made them warmly welcome.

After they had taken a bath and washed their hands, and had sat down to dinner, Tobias said to Raphael, 'Azarias, my friend, ask Raguel to give me Sarah my kinswoman.' Raguel overheard and said to the young man: 9 'Eat, drink, and be happy tonight. There is no one but yourself who should 10 have my daughter Sarah; indeed I have no right to give her to anyone else, since you are my nearest kinsman. But I must tell you the truth, my son: I have given her in marriage to seven of our kinsmen, and they all died on 11 their wedding night. My son, eat now and drink, and may the Lord deal kindly with you both.' Tobias answered, 'I will not eat or drink anything here until you have disposed of this business of mine.' Raguel said to him, 12 'I will do so: I give her to you as the ordinance in the book of Moses prescribes. Heaven has ordained that she shall be yours. Take your kinswoman. From now on, you belong to her and she to you; she is yours for ever from this day. The Lord of heaven prosper you both this night, my son, and grant you mercy and peace.'

Raguel sent for his daughter Sarah, and when she came he took her hand 13 and gave her to Tobias, saying: 'Take her to be your wedded wife in accordance with the law and the ordinance written in the book of Moses. Keep her and take her home to your father; and may the God of heaven keep you safe and give you peace and prosperity.' Then he sent for her 14 mother and told her to bring paper, and he wrote out a marriage contract granting Sarah to Tobias as his wife, as the law of Moses ordains. After 15 that they began to eat and drink.

Raguel called his wife and said, 'My dear, get the spare room ready and 16 take her in there.' Edna went and prepared the room as he had told her, 17 and took Sarah into it. Edna cried over her, then dried her tears and said: 'Courage, dear daughter; the Lord of heaven give you joy instead of sorrow. 18 Courage, daughter!' Then she went out.

**8** When they had finished eating and drinking and were ready for bed,
2 they escorted the young man to the bridal chamber. Tobias recalled what
Raphael had told him; he took the fish's liver and heart out of the bag in
3 which he kept them, and put them on the smoking incense. The smell from
the fish held the demon off, and he took flight into Upper Egypt; and
Raphael instantly followed him there and bound him hand and foot.

4 When they were left alone and the door was shut, Tobias rose from the
bed and said to Sarah, 'Get up, my love; let us pray and beseech our Lord
5 to show us mercy and keep us safe.' She got up and they began to pray that
they might be kept safe. Tobias said: 'We praise thee, O God of our
fathers, we praise thy name for ever and ever. Let the heavens and all thy
6 creation praise thee for ever. Thou madest Adam, and Eve his wife to be
his helper and support; and those two were the parents of the human race.
This was thy word: "It is not good for the man to be alone; let us make him
7 a helper like him." I now take this my beloved to wife, not out of lust but
in true marriage. Grant that she and I may find mercy and grow old
8 9 together.' They both said 'Amen', and slept through the night.

Raguel got up and summoned his servants, and they went out and dug
10 a grave. For he said, 'He may have been killed, and then we shall have to
11 face scorn and disgrace.' When they had finished digging the grave, Raguel
12 went into the house and called his wife: 'Send one of the maidservants',
he said, 'to go in and see if he is alive. If he is dead, let us bury
13 him so that no one may know.' They lit a lamp, opened the door, and sent
14 a maidservant in; and she found them sound asleep together. She came
out and told them: 'He is alive and has come to no harm.'

15 Then they praised the God of heaven: 'We praise thee, O God, we
praise thee with all our heart. Let men praise thee throughout all ages.
16 Praise to thee for the joy thou hast given me; the thing I feared has not
17 happened, but thou hast shown us thy great mercy. Praise to thee for the
mercy thou hast shown to these two, these only children. Lord, show them
mercy, keep them safe, and grant them a long life of happiness and affec-
18 tion.' Then he ordered his servants to fill in the grave before dawn came.

19 He told his wife to bake a great batch of bread; he went to the herd and
brought two oxen and four rams and told his servants to get them ready;
20 so they set about the preparations. He then called Tobias and said: 'You
shall not stir from here for two weeks. Stay with us; let us eat and drink
21 together and cheer my daughter's heart after all her suffering. Here and
now take half of all I have, and go home to your father safe and sound; and
the other half will come to you both when my wife and I die. Be reassured,
my son, I am your father and Edna is your mother; we are as close to you
as to your wife, now and always. You have nothing to fear, my son.'

**9** 1 2 Tobias called Raphael and said to him: 'Azarias, my friend, take four
servants with you, and two camels, and make your way to Rages. Go to
Gabael's house, give him the bond and collect the money, and bring him
4 with you to the wedding-feast. You know that my father will be counting
3 the days and, if I am even one day late, it will distress him. You see what
5 Raguel has sworn, and I cannot go against his oath.' Raphael went with the
four servants and the two camels to Rages in Media and lodged there with

Gabael. He gave him his bond and informed him that Tobit's son Tobias had taken a wife and was inviting him to the wedding-feast. At once Gabael counted out the bags to him with their seals intact, and they put them together. They all made an early start and came to the wedding. 6 When they entered Raguel's house and found Tobias at the feast, he jumped up and greeted Gabael. With tears in his eyes Gabael blessed him and said: 'Good sir, worthy son of a worthy father, that upright and charitable man, may the Lord give Heaven's blessing to you and your wife, your father and your mother-in-law. Praise be to God that I have seen my cousin Tobias, so like his father.'

## Tobias's homecoming

NOW DAY BY DAY Tobit was keeping count of the time Tobias would 10 take for his journey there and back. When the days had passed and his son had not returned, Tobit said: 'Perhaps he has been detained there. 2 Or perhaps Gabael is dead and there is no one to give him the money.' And he grew anxious. Anna his wife said: 'My child has perished. He is 3 4 no longer in the land of the living.' She began to weep and lament for her son: 'O my child, the light of my eyes, why did I let you go?' Tobit said to 5 6 her: 'Hush, do not worry, my dear; he is all right. Something has happened there to distract them. The man who went with him is one of our kinsmen and can be trusted. Do not grieve for him, my dear; he will soon be back.' But she answered: 'Be quiet! Leave me alone! Do not try to deceive me. 7 My boy is dead.' Each day she would rush out and look down the road her son had taken, and would listen to no one; and when she came indoors at sunset she could never sleep, but wept and lamented the whole night long.

The two weeks of wedding celebrations which Raguel had sworn to hold for his daughter came to an end, and Tobias went up to him and said: 'Let me be off on my journey; for I am sure that my parents are thinking they will never see me again. I beg you, father, let me go home now to my father Tobit. I have already told you how I left him.' Raguel said to Tobias: 8 'Stay, my son. Stay with me, and I will send news of you to your father.' But Tobias answered: 'No; please let me go home to my father.' Then 9 10 without further delay Raguel handed over to Tobias Sarah his bride and half of all that he possessed, male and female slaves, sheep and cattle, donkeys and camels, clothes, money, and furniture. He saw them safely 11 off and embraced Tobias, saying: 'Goodbye, my son; a safe journey to you! May the Lord of heaven give prosperity to you and Sarah your wife; and may I live to see your children.' To his daughter Sarah he said: 'Go 12 to your father-in-law's house; they are now your parents as much as if you were their own daughter. Go in peace, my child; I hope to hear good news of you as long as I live.' He bade them both goodbye and sent them on their way. Edna said to Tobias: 'Child and beloved cousin, may the Lord bring you safely home, you and my daughter Sarah, and may I live long enough to see your children. In the sight of the Lord I entrust my daughter to you; do nothing to hurt her as long as you live. Go in peace, my son. From

now on I am your mother and Sarah is your beloved wife. May we all be blessed with prosperity to the end of our days!' She kissed them both and
11 saw them safely off. Tobias parted from Raguel in good health and spirits, thankful to the Lord of heaven and earth, the king of all, for the success of his journey. Raguel's last words to him were: 'May the Lord give you the means to honour your parents all their lives.'
2 When they reached Caserin close to Nineveh, Raphael said: 'You know
3 how your father was when we left him; let us hurry on ahead of your wife
4 and see that the house is ready before the others arrive.' As the two of them went on together Raphael said: 'Take the fish-gall in your hand.' The dog went with the angel and Tobias, following at their heels.
5 6 Anna sat watching the road by which her son would return. She saw him coming and exclaimed to his father, 'Here he comes, your son and the
7 man who went with him!' Before Tobias reached his father's house
8 Raphael said: 'I know for certain that his eyes will be opened. Spread the fish-gall on his eyes, and the medicine will make the white patches shrink and peel off. Your father will get his sight back and see the light of day.'
9 Anna ran forward and flung her arms round her son. 'Here you are, my boy; now I can die happy!' she cried out with tears in her eyes.
10 Tobit rose to his feet and came stumbling out through the courtyard door.
11 Tobias went up to him with the fish-gall in his hand and blew it into his father's eyes, and took him by the arm and said: 'It will be all right, father.'
12 13 Then when he had put the medicine on and applied it, using both hands he peeled off the patches from the corners of Tobit's eyes. Tobit flung his arms
14 round him and burst into tears. 'I can see you, my son, the light of my eyes!' he cried. 'Praise be to God, and praise to his great name, and to all his holy angels. May his great name rest upon us. Praised be all the angels for ever.
15 He laid his scourge on me, and now, look, I see my son Tobias!'
Tobias went in, rejoicing and praising God with all his strength. He told his father about the success of his journey, how he had brought the money with him and had married Sarah daughter of Raguel. 'She is on her
16 way,' he said, 'quite close to the city gate.' Tobit went out joyfully to meet his daughter-in-law at the gate, praising God as he went. At the sight of him passing through the city in full vigour and walking without a guide,
17 the people of Nineveh were astonished; and Tobit gave thanks to God before them all for his mercy in opening his eyes. When he met Sarah, the wife of his son Tobias, he blessed her and said to her: 'Come in, my daughter, and welcome. Praise be to your God who has brought you to us, my daughter. Blessings on your father, and on my son Tobias, and blessings on you, my daughter. Come into your home, and may health, blessings, and joy be yours; come in, my daughter.' It was a day of joy for all the Jews
18 in Nineveh; and Ahikar and Nadab, Tobit's cousins, came to share his happiness.
12 When the marriage-feast was over, Tobit called Tobias and said, 'My son, see that you pay the man who went with you, and give him some-
2 thing extra, over and above his wages.' Tobias said: 'Father, how much shall I pay him? It would not hurt me to give him half the money he and
3 I brought back. He has kept me safe, cured my wife, helped me bring the

money, and healed you. How much extra shall I pay him?' Tobit replied, 4
'It is right, my son, for him to be given half of all that he has brought with
him.' So Tobias sent for him and said, 'Half of all that you have brought 5
with you is yours for your wages; take it, and fare you well.'

Then Raphael called them both aside and said to them: 'Praise God and 6
thank him before all men living for the good he has done you, so that they
may sing hymns of praise to his name. Proclaim to all the world what God
has done, and pay him honour; do not be slow to give him thanks. A 7
king's secret ought to be kept, but the works of God should be acknowledged publicly. Acknowledge them, therefore, and pay him honour. Do
good, and evil shall not touch you. Better prayer with sincerity, and alms- 8
giving with righteousness, than wealth with wickedness. Better give alms
than hoard up gold. Almsgiving preserves a man from death and wipes out 9
all sin. Givers of alms will enjoy long life; but sinners and wrong-doers are 10
their own worst enemies.

'I will tell you the whole truth; I will hide nothing from you. Indeed I 11
told you just now when I said, "A king's secret ought to be kept, but the
works of God should be publicly honoured." When you and Sarah prayed, 12
it was I who brought your prayers into the glorious presence of the Lord;
and so too whenever you buried the dead. That day when you got up from 13
your dinner without hesitation to go and bury the corpse, I was sent to test
you; and again God sent me to cure both you and Sarah your daughter-in- 14
law at the same time. I am Raphael, one of the seven angels who stand in 15
attendance on the Lord and enter his glorious presence.'

The two men were shaken, and prostrated themselves in awe. But he 16 17
said to them: 'Do not be afraid, all is well; praise God for ever. It is no 18
thanks to me that I have been with you; it was the will of God. Worship
him all your life long, sing his praise. Take note that I ate no food; what 19
appeared to you was a vision. And now praise the Lord, give thanks to God 20
here on earth; I am ascending to him who sent me. Write down all these
things that have happened to you.' He then ascended, and when they rose 21
to their feet, he was no longer to be seen. They sang hymns of praise to God, 22
giving him thanks for these great deeds he had done when his angel
appeared to them.

Tᴏʙɪᴛ said:                                                                          **13**

　'Praise to the ever-living God and to his kingdom.
　He punishes and he shows mercy;                                          2
　he brings men down to the grave below,
　and up from the great destruction.
　Nothing can escape his power.
　Give him thanks, men of Israel, in the presence of the nations,    3
　for he has scattered you among them;
　there he has shown you his greatness.                                    4
　Exalt him in the sight of every living creature,
　for he is our Lord and God;
　he is our Father and our God for ever.

5    He will punish you for your wickedness,
and he will show mercy to you all,
gathering you from among all the nations
wherever you have been scattered.

6    When you turn to him with all your heart and soul
and act in loyal obedience to him,
then he will turn to you
and hide his face from you no longer.
Consider now the deeds he has done for you,
and give him thanks with full voice;
praise the righteous Lord
and exalt the King of ages. *a*

10    'Your sanctuary *b* shall be rebuilt for you with rejoicing.
May he give happiness to all your exiles
and cherish all who mourn and your descendants for ever.

11    Your light shall shine brightly to all the ends of the earth.
Many nations shall come to you from afar,
from all the corners of the earth to your holy name;
they shall bring gifts in their hands for the King of heaven.
In you endless generations shall utter their joy;
the name of the chosen city shall endure for ever and ever.

12    There shall be a curse upon all who speak harshly to you,
upon all who destroy you and pull down your walls,
upon all who demolish your towers and burn your houses;
but blessings shall be for evermore upon those who hold you in
reverence.

13    Come then, be joyful for the righteous,
for they shall all be gathered together
and shall praise the eternal Lord.

14    How happy shall they be who love you and rejoice in your prosperity,
happy all who grieve for you in your afflictions;
they shall rejoice over you and for ever be witness of your joy.

15    My soul, praise the Lord, the great king,
16    for Jerusalem shall be built as a city for him to dwell in for ever.

---

*a*  *Some witnesses add*

        In the land of my exile I give thanks to him
and declare his might and greatness to a sinful nation.
Turn, you sinners, and do what is right in his eyes;
who knows whether he may not welcome you and show you mercy?

7        I will exalt my God
and rejoice in the King of heaven.

8        Let all men tell of his majesty
and give him thanks in Jerusalem.

9        O Jerusalem, the holy city,
he will punish you for what your sons have done,
but he will again show mercy on the righteous.

10        Thank the good Lord and praise the King of ages.

*b*  *Or* home.

How happy I shall be when the remnant of my descendants shall see
your splendour
and give thanks to the King of heaven.
The gates of Jerusalem shall be built of sapphire and emerald,
and all your walls of precious stones.
The towers of Jerusalem shall be built of gold,
their battlements of the finest gold.
The streets of Jerusalem shall be paved with garnets and jewels of 17
Ophir.
The gates of Jerusalem shall sing hymns of joy 18
and all her houses shall say Alleluia,
praise to the God of Israel!
Blessed by him, they shall bless his holy name for ever and ever.'

So ENDED Tobit's thanksgiving. He died peacefully at the age of a 14
hundred and twelve, and was given honourable burial in Nineveh. He was 2
sixty-two years old when his eyes were injured, and after he recovered his
sight he lived in prosperity, doing his acts of charity and never ceasing to
praise God and proclaim his majesty.

When he was dying he sent for his son Tobias, and gave him these 3
instructions: 'My son, you must take your children and make your escape 4
to Media, for I believe God's word against Nineveh spoken by Nahum.
It will all come true; everything will happen to Asshur and Nineveh that
was spoken by the prophets of Israel whom God sent. Not a word of it will
fall short; everything will be fulfilled when the time comes. It will be safer
in Media than in Assyria and Babylon; I know, I am convinced, that all
God's words will be fulfilled. It will be so; not one of them will fail. Our
countrymen who live in Israel will all be scattered and carried off into
captivity out of that good land, and the whole territory of Israel laid waste.
Samaria and Jerusalem will lie waste, and for a time the house of God will
be in mourning; it will be burnt to the ground.

'Then God will have mercy on them again and will bring them back to 5
the land of Israel. They will rebuild the house of God, but not as it was
before, not until the time of fulfilment comes. Then they will all return
from their captivity and rebuild Jerusalem gloriously; then indeed the
house will be built in her as the prophets of Israel foretold. All the nations 6
of the world will be converted to the true worship of God; they will
abandon their idols which led them astray into falsehood, and praise the 7
eternal God according to his law. All the Israelites who survive at that
time and are firm in their loyalty to God will be brought together; they
will come to Jerusalem to take possession of the land of Abraham, and live
there for ever in safety. Those who love God in truth will rejoice; and
sinners and wrong-doers will disappear from the earth. Now, my children, 8
I give you this command: serve God in truth and do what pleases him.
Train your children to do what is right and give alms, to keep God in mind 9
at all times and praise his name in sincerity with all their strength.

'And now, my son, you must leave Nineveh. Do not stay here; once 10
you have laid your mother in the grave with me, do not spend another

night within the city boundaries. For I see that the place is full of wickedness and shameless dishonesty. My son, think what Nadab did to Ahikar who brought him up: he forced him to hide in a living grave. Ahikar survived to see God requite the dishonour done to him; he came out into the light of day, but Nadab passed into eternal darkness for his attempt to kill Ahikar. Because I gave alms, Ahikar escaped from the fatal trap Nadab

11 set for him, and Nadab fell into the trap himself and was destroyed. So, my children, see what comes of almsgiving, and see what comes of wickedness—death. But now my strength is failing.'

Then they laid him on his bed, and he died; and they gave him honour-

12 able burial. When his mother died, Tobias buried her beside his father. He and his wife went away to Media and settled at Ecbatana with his father-

13 in-law Raguel. He honoured and cared for his wife's parents in their old age. He buried them at Ecbatana in Media, and he inherited the estate of

14 Raguel as well as that of his father Tobit. He died greatly respected at the

15 age of one hundred and seventeen. He lived long enough to hear of the destruction of Nineveh by Ahasuerus king of Media and to see his prisoners of war brought from there into Media. So he praised God for all that he had done to the people of Nineveh and Asshur; and before he died he rejoiced over the fate of Nineveh and praised the Lord God who lives for ever and ever.

Amen.

# JUDITH

## *The Assyrian invasion*

1 IN THE TWELFTH YEAR of the reign of Nebuchadnezzar, who reigned over the Assyrians from his capital, Nineveh, Arphaxad

2 was ruling the Medes from Ecbatana. He it was who encircled Ecbatana with a wall built of hewn stones which were four and a half feet thick and nine feet long.[a] He made the wall a hundred and five feet high and seventy-

3 five feet thick, and at the city gates he set up towers a hundred and fifty feet

4 high with foundations ninety feet thick; and he made the gates a hundred and five feet high and sixty feet wide to allow his army to march out in full

5 force with his infantry in formation. It was in those days, then, that King Nebuchadnezzar waged war against King Arphaxad in the great plain on

6 the borders of Ragau. Nebuchadnezzar was opposed by all the inhabitants of the hill-country, by all those who lived along the Euphrates, the Tigris, and the Hydaspes; and, on the plain, by Arioch king of Elam; and many tribes of the Chelodites joined forces with them.

7 Then Nebuchadnezzar king of Assyria sent a summons to all the inhabitants of Persia, and to all who lived in the west: the inhabitants of Cilicia and Damascus, Lebanon and Antilebanon, all who lived near the coast,

a *In verses 2–4 the measurements are given in cubits in the Greek.*

the peoples in Carmel and Gilead, Upper Galilee, and the great plain 8
of Esdraelon, all who were in Samaria and its towns, and on the west of 9
Jordan as far as Jerusalem, Betane, Chelus, Cadesh, and the frontier *a*
of Egypt, those who lived in Tahpanhes, Rameses, and the whole land of
Goshen as far as Tanis and Memphis, and all the inhabitants of Egypt 10
as far as the borders of Ethiopia. But the entire region disregarded the 11
summons of Nebuchadnezzar king of Assyria and did not join him in the
war. They were not afraid of him, for he seemed to them to stand alone *b*
and unsupported; and they treated his envoys with contempt and sent
them back empty-handed.

This roused Nebuchadnezzar to fury against the whole region, and he 12
swore by his throne and his kingdom that he would have his revenge on all
the territories of Cilicia, Damascus, and Syria, and put their inhabitants
to the sword, along with the Moabites, the Ammonites, and the people in
all Judaea and in Egypt as far as the shores of the two seas.

In the seventeenth year of his reign he marshalled his forces against King 13
Arphaxad and defeated him in battle, routing his entire army, cavalry,
chariots, and all. He occupied his towns; and when he reached Ecbatana 14
he captured its towers, looted its bazaars, and turned its splendour to
abject ruin. He caught Arphaxad in the mountains of Ragau, speared him 15
through, and so made an end of him. Then he returned with his spoils to 16
Nineveh, he and his combined forces, an immense host of warriors. There
he rested and feasted with his army for four months.

In the eighteenth year, on the twenty-second day of the first month, a 2
proposal was made in the palace of Nebuchadnezzar king of Assyria to
carry out his threat of vengeance on the whole region. Assembling all his 2
officers and nobles, the king laid before them his personal decision about
the region and declared his intention of putting an end to its disaffection.
They resolved that everyone who had not obeyed his summons should be 3
put to death.

When his plans were completed, *c* Nebuchadnezzar king of Assyria 4
summoned Holophernes, his commander-in-chief, who was second only
to himself, and said to him, 'This is the decree of the Great King, lord of 5
all the earth: Directly you leave my presence, you are to take under your
command an army of seasoned troops, a hundred and twenty thousand
infantry with a force of twelve thousand cavalry, and march out against all 6
the peoples of the west who have dared to disobey my command. Tell 7
them to have ready their offering of earth and water, for I am coming to
vent my wrath on them. Their whole land will be smothered by my army,
and I will give them up to be plundered by my troops. Their dead will fill 8
the valleys, and every stream and river will be choked with corpses; and I 9
will send them into captivity to the ends of the whole earth. Now go and 10
occupy all their territory for me. If they surrender to you, hold them for me
until the time comes to punish them. But show no mercy to those who 11
resist; let them be slaughtered and plundered throughout the whole region.
By my life and my royal power I swear: I have spoken and I will be as good 12

*a Literally* river.              *b One witness reads* to be no more than their equal . . .
*c Or* When he had finished stating his purpose . . .

13 as my word. As for you, do not disobey a single one of my orders, but see
that you carry them out exactly as I your sovereign have commanded you.
Do this without delay.'

14  After leaving his sovereign's presence, Holophernes assembled all the
15 marshals, generals, and officers of the Assyrian army, and mustered picked
men, as the king had commanded, a hundred and twenty thousand infantry
16 and twelve thousand mounted archers, drawing them up in battle order.
17 He took an immense number of camels, asses, and mules for their baggage,
18 innumerable sheep, oxen, and goats for provisions, and ample rations for
every man, as well as a great quantity of gold and silver from the royal
19 palace. Then he set out with all his army to go ahead of King Nebuchadnezzar and to overrun the entire region to the west with chariots, cavalry,
20 and picked infantry. Along with them went a motley host like a swarm of
locusts, countless as the dust of the earth.

21  From Nineveh they marched for three days towards the plain of Bectileth, and encamped beside Bectileth near the mountain north of Upper
22 Cilicia. From there, Holophernes advanced into the hill-country with his
23 whole army, infantry, cavalry, and chariots. He devastated Put and Lud,
and plundered all the people of Rassis, and the Ishmaelites on the edge of
24 the desert south of the land of the Cheleans. Then he followed*a* the
' Euphrates and traversed Mesopotamia, destroying all the fortified towns
25 along the river Abron as far as the sea. He occupied the territory of Cilicia
and cut down all who resisted him. Then he came south to the borders of
26 Japheth fronting Arabia. He surrounded the Midianites, burnt their
27 encampments, and plundered their sheepfolds. At the time of wheat
harvest he went down to the plain of Damascus, burnt their crops,
exterminated their flocks and herds, sacked their towns, laid waste their
28 fields, and put all their young men to the sword. Fear and dread of him fell
on all the inhabitants of the coast at Tyre and Sidon, of Sur and Okina,
and of Jemnaan; the people of Azotus and Ascalon were terrified of him.

3 1 2   They sent envoys to sue for peace, who said: 'We are servants of the
Great King Nebuchadnezzar, we lie prostrate before you; do with us as
3 you please. Our buildings, our territory, our wheat fields, our flocks and
herds and every sheepfold in our encampments, all are yours to do with as
4 you wish. Our towns and their inhabitants are subject to you; come and
deal with them as you think fit.'

5 6   When the envoys came to Holophernes with this message, he went down
to the coast with his army and garrisoned all the fortified towns, taking
7 from them picked men as auxiliaries. Both there and in all the surrounding
8 country he was welcomed with garlands, dancing, and tambourines. He
demolished all their sanctuaries*b* and cut down their sacred groves, for he
had been commissioned to destroy all the gods of the land, so that
Nebuchadnezzar alone should be worshipped by every nation and invoked
as a god by men of every tribe and tongue.

9  Holophernes then advanced towards Esdraelon, near Dothan, which
10 faces the great ridge of Judaea, and encamped between Geba and Scythopolis, where he remained for a whole month to collect supplies for his army.

*a* Or crossed.      *b* So one Vs.; Gk. borders.

WHEN THE ISRAELITES who lived in Judaea heard of all that had been 4
done to the nations by Holophernes, the commander-in-chief of Nebuchadnezzar king of Assyria, and how he had plundered and totally destroyed
all their temples, they were terrified at his approach. They were in great 2
alarm for Jerusalem and for the temple of the Lord their God. For they 3
had just returned from captivity, and it was only recently that the people
had been re-united in Judaea, and the sacred vessels, the temple, and the
altar sanctified after their profanation. So they sent out a warning to the 4
whole of Samaria, Cona, Beth-horon, Belmain and Jericho, Choba and
Aesora and the valley of Salem, and occupied the tops of all the high hills. 5
They fortified the villages on them and laid up stores of food in preparation
for war; for their fields had just been harvested. Joakim, who was high 6
priest in Jerusalem at the time, wrote to the people of Bethulia and Bethomesthaim, which is opposite Esdraelon facing the plain near Dothan. He 7
ordered them to occupy the passes into the hill-country, because they controlled access to Judaea, and it was easy to hold up an advancing army, for
the approach was only wide enough for two men. The Israelites obeyed 8
the orders of the high priest Joakim and the senate of all Israel in Jerusalem. Fervently they sent up a cry to God, every man of Israel, and 9
fervently they humbled themselves before him. They put on sackcloth— 10
they themselves, their wives, their children, their livestock, and every
resident foreigner, hired labourer, and slave—and all the inhabitants of 11
Jerusalem, men, women, and children, prostrated themselves in front of
the sanctuary, and, with ashes on their heads, spread out their sackcloth
before the Lord. They draped the altar in sackcloth, and with one voice 12
they earnestly implored the God of Israel not to allow their children to be
captured, their wives carried off, their ancestral cities destroyed, and the
temple profaned and dishonoured, to the delight of the heathen. The Lord 13
heard their prayer and pitied their distress.

For many days the whole population of Judaea and Jerusalem fasted
before the sanctuary of the Lord Almighty. Joakim the high priest and the 14
priests who stood in the presence of the Lord, and all who served in the
temple, wore sackcloth when they offered the regular burnt-offering and
the votive and freewill offerings of the people; and with ashes on their 15
turbans they cried aloud to the Lord to look favourably on the whole
house of Israel.

When it was reported to Holophernes, the Assyrian commander-in- 5
chief, that the Israelites had prepared for war, and that they had closed
the passes in the hill-country, fortified all the heights, and dug pitfalls in
the plains, he was furious. He summoned all the rulers of Moab, the 2
Ammonite commanders, and all the governors of the coastal region, and 3
said to them, 'Tell me, you Canaanites, what nation is this that lives in the
hill-country? What towns do they inhabit? How big is their army? What
gives them their power and strength? Who is the king that commands
their forces? Why are they the only people of the west who have refused to 4
come and meet me?'

Then Achior, the leader of all the Ammonites, said to him, 'My lord, 5
if you will allow your servant to speak, I will tell you the truth about this

nation that lives in the hill-country near here; and no lie shall pass my lips.
6 7 They are descended from the Chaldaeans; and at one time they settled in Mesopotamia, because they refused to worship the gods their fathers
8 had worshipped in Chaldaea. They abandoned the ways of their ancestors and worshipped the God of Heaven, the god whom they now acknowledged. When the Chaldaeans drove them out from the presence of their gods, they
9 fled to Mesopotamia, where they lived for a long time. Then their god told them to leave their new home and go on to Canaan. They settled there and acquired great wealth in gold, silver, and livestock.

10    'Because of a famine which spread over the whole of Canaan, they went down to Egypt and lived there as long as they were supplied with food. While in Egypt, they multiplied so greatly that their numbers could not be
11 reckoned, and the king of Egypt turned against them. He exploited them by setting them to hard labour making bricks, and he reduced them to
12 abject slavery. They cried out to their god, and he inflicted incurable
13 plagues on the whole of Egypt. So the Egyptians turned them out; and
14 their god dried up the Red Sea for them and led them on to Sinai and Cadesh-barnea. Then they drove out all the inhabitants of the wilderness
15 and settled in the land of the Amorites, and they destroyed all the people of Heshbon by force of arms. After that they crossed the Jordan and occu-
16 pied all the hill-country, driving out the Canaanites, the Perizzites, the Jebusites, the Shechemites, and all the Girgashites. There they settled for a long time.

17    'As long as they did not sin against their god, they prospered; for theirs
18 is a god who hates wickedness. But when they left the path he had laid down for them, they suffered heavy losses in many wars and were carried captive to a foreign country; the temple of their god was razed to the
19 ground, and their towns were occupied by their enemies. But now that they have returned to their god, they have come back from the places where they had been dispersed, and have taken possession of Jerusalem, where their sanctuary is, and have settled in the hill-country, because it was uninhabited.

20    'Now, my lord and master, if these people are guilty of an error and are sinning against their god, and if we find out that they have committed this
21 offence, then we may go and make war on them. But if these people have committed no wickedness, leave them alone, my lord, for fear the god they serve should protect them and we become the laughing-stock of the
22 world.' When Achior stopped speaking there were protests from all those who stood round the tent. Holophernes' officers and all the people from the coastal region and from Moab demanded that Achior should be cut to
23 pieces. 'We are not going to be afraid of the Israelites,' they said, 'a people
24 quite incapable of putting an effective army in the field. Let us go ahead, Lord Holophernes; your great army will swallow them whole.'

6    When the hubbub among the men around the council had subsided, Holophernes, the Assyrian commander-in-chief, said to Achior and all the
2 Ammonites, in the presence of the assembled foreigners: 'And who are you, Achior, you and your Ammonite mercenaries, to play the prophet among us as you have done today, telling us not to make war against the

people of Israel because their god will protect them? What god is there but
Nebuchadnezzar? He will exert his power and wipe them off the face of ₃
the earth; and their god will not rescue them. We who serve Nebuchadnezzar will strike them all down as if they were only one man. They will not
be able to stand up to the weight of our cavalry; we shall overwhelm them. ₄
Their mountains will be drenched with blood, and their plains filled with
their dead. They cannot stand their ground against us; they will be completely wiped out. This is the decree of King Nebuchadnezzar, lord of the
whole earth. He has spoken; and what he has said will be made good. As ₅
for you, Achior, you Ammonite mercenary, the words you have spoken
today are treason, so from today you shall not see my face again until I
have taken vengeance on this brood of runaways from Egypt. But when I ₆
come back, the warriors of my bodyguard will run you through and add
you to their victims. My men are going to take you away now to the hill- ₇
country and leave you in one of the towns in the passes. You will not die ₈
until you share their fate. If you are so confident that they will not fall into ₉
our hands, you need not look downcast. I have spoken; and nothing that
I have said will fail to come true.'

Then Holophernes ordered his men, who were standing by in his tent, ₁₀
to seize Achior, take him off to Bethulia, and hand him over to the Israelites.
So they seized him and took him outside the camp to the plain, and from ₁₁
there into the hill-country, until they arrived at the springs below Bethulia.
When the men of the town saw them, they picked up their weapons and ₁₂
came out of the town to the top of the hill; then all the slingers pelted the
enemy with stones to prevent them from coming up. But they slipped ₁₃
through under cover of the hill, tied Achior up and left him lying at the foot
of it, and went back to their master. When the Israelites came down from ₁₄
the town and found him there, they untied him and took him into Bethulia,
where they brought him before the town magistrates then in office, Ozias ₁₅
son of Mica, of the tribe of Simeon, and Chabris son of Gothoniel, and
Charmis son of Melchiel. The magistrates summoned all the elders of the ₁₆
town; and all the young men and women came running to the assembly.
When Achior had been brought before the people, Ozias asked him what
had happened. He answered by telling them all that had taken place in ₁₇
Holophernes' council, what he himself had said in the presence of the
Assyrian commanders, and how Holophernes had boasted of what he
would do to Israel. Then the people prostrated themselves in worship and ₁₈
cried out to God: 'O Lord, God of heaven, mark their arrogance; pity our ₁₉
people in their humiliation; show favour this day to those who are thy
own.' Then they reassured Achior and commended him warmly. Ozias ₂₀ ₂₁
took him from the assembly to his own house, and gave a feast for the elders;
and all that night they invoked the help of the God of Israel.

THE NEXT DAY Holophernes ordered his whole army and all his allies ₇
to strike camp and march on Bethulia, seize the passes into the hill-country,
and make war on the Israelites. So the whole force set out that day, an ₂
army of a hundred and seventy thousand infantry and twelve thousand
cavalry, not counting the baggage train of the infantry, an immense host.

3 They encamped in the valley near Bethulia, beside the spring; and their camp extended in breadth towards Dothan as far as Belbaim, and in length
4 from Bethulia to Cyamon which faces Esdraelon. When the Israelites saw their numbers they said to each other in great alarm, 'These men will strip the whole country bare; the high mountains, the valleys, and the hills will
5 never be able to bear the burden of them.' Then each man stood to arms; and they lit the beacons on the towers and remained on guard all that night.
6 On the following day Holophernes led out all his cavalry in full view of
7 the Israelites in Bethulia, and reconnoitred the approaches to their town. He inspected the springs and seized them; and when he had stationed
8 detachments of soldiers there, he returned to his army. Then all the rulers of the Edomites and all the leaders of Moab and the commanders from the
9 coastal region came to him and said, 'Listen to our advice, Lord Holo-
10 phernes, and save your army from a crushing defeat. These Israelites do not trust in their spears but in the height of the mountains where they live; for it is no easy task to get up to the tops of these mountains of theirs.
11 Now, Lord Holophernes, avoid fighting a pitched battle with them, and
12 you will not lose a single man. Remain in your camp and keep your men in their quarters; but let your servants take possession of the spring at the
13 foot of the hill, for that is where all the townspeople of Bethulia get their water. When they are dying of thirst they will surrender the town. Mean-while, we and all our people will go up to the tops of the neighbouring hills
14 and camp there to see that not a man gets away from the town. They and their wives and children will waste away with famine; and before the sword
15 reaches them, their streets will be strewn with their corpses. So you will make them pay heavily for rebelling against you, instead of receiving you
16 peaceably.' Holophernes and all his staff approved this plan; and he gave
17 orders that it should be carried out. The Moabite force moved forward in company with five thousand Assyrians and encamped in the valley, where
18 they seized the springs which were the Israelites' water-supply. Then the Edomites and Ammonites went up and encamped in the hill-country opposite Dothan, and sent some of their number south-east*a* in the direction of Egrebel, which is near Chus on the Mochmur ravine. The rest of the Assyrian army encamped on the plain. They filled the entire country-side, their tents and baggage train forming an immense encampment, for they were a vast host.
19 Then the Israelites cried out to the Lord their God. Their courage failed, because all their enemies had surrounded them and there was no
20 way of escape. The whole Assyrian army, infantry, cavalry, and chariots, kept them blockaded for thirty-four days. The citizens of Bethulia came
21 to the end of their household supplies of water. The cisterns too were running dry; drinking-water was so strictly rationed that there was never
22 a day when their needs were satisfied. The children were lifeless, the women and young men faint with thirst. They collapsed in the streets and gateways from sheer exhaustion.
23 Then all the people, young men, women, and children, gathered round

*a Or* south and east.

74

Ozias and the magistrates of the town, shouting loudly. In the presence of
the elders they said: 'May God judge between us, for you have done us a 24
great wrong in not coming to terms with the Assyrians. Now we have no 25
one to help us. God has sold us into their power; they will find us dead of
thirst, and the ground strewn with our corpses. Surrender to them; let 26
Holophernes' people and his army sack the town. It is better for us to be 27
taken prisoner; for even as slaves we shall still be alive, and shall not have
to watch our babies dying before our eyes, and our wives and children at
their last gasp. We call heaven and earth to witness, we call our God, the 28
Lord of our fathers, to witness against you—the God who is punishing us
for our sins and for the sins of our fathers. We pray that he may not let our
forebodings come true this day.' Then the whole assembly broke into loud 29
lamentation and cried to the Lord God. Ozias said to them, 'Courage, my 30
friends! Let us hold out for five more days; by that time the Lord our God
may show us his mercy again. Surely he will not finally desert us. But if by 31
the end of that time no help has reached us, then I will do what you ask.'
Then he dismissed the men to their various posts; and they went off to the 32
walls and towers of the town. The women and children he sent indoors.
Throughout the town there was deep dejection.

## *Judith kills Holophernes*

NEWS OF WHAT WAS HAPPENING reached Judith, daughter of 8
Merari, son of Ox, son of Joseph, son of Oziel, son of Helkias, son
of Elias, son of Chelkias, son of Eliab, son of Nathanael, son of Salamiel,
son of Sarasadae, son of Israel. Her husband Manasses, who belonged to 2
her own tribe and clan, had died at the time of barley harvest. While he 3
was out in the fields supervising the binding of the sheaves, he got sun-
stroke, took to his bed, and died in Bethulia his native town; and they
buried him beside his ancestors in the field between Dothan and Balamon.
For three years and four months Judith had lived at home as a widow; she 4 5
had a shelter erected on the roof of her house; she put on sackcloth and
always wore mourning. After she became a widow she fasted every day 6
except sabbath eve, the sabbath itself, the eve of the new moon, the new
moon, and the Israelite feasts and days of public rejoicing. She was a very 7
beautiful and attractive woman. Her husband Manasses had left her gold
and silver, male and female slaves, livestock and land, and she lived on her
estate. No one spoke ill of her, for she was a very devout woman. 8
    When Judith heard of the shameful attack which the people had made 9
upon Ozias the magistrate, because they were demoralized by the shortage
of water, and how he had sworn to surrender the town to the Assyrians
after five days, she sent her maid who had charge of all her property to ask 10
Ozias, Chabris, and Charmis, the elders of the town, to come and see her.
When they arrived she said to them: 'Listen to me, magistrates of Bethulia. 11
You had no right to speak as you did to the people today, and to bind yourselves by oath before God to surrender the town to our enemies if the Lord
sends no relief within so many days. Who are you to test God at a time like 12

13 this, and openly set yourselves above him? You are putting the Lord
14 Almighty to the proof. You will never understand! You cannot plumb the
depths of the human heart or understand the way a man's mind works;
how then can you fathom man's Maker? How can you know God's mind,
and grasp his thought? No, my friends, do not rouse the anger of the Lord
15 our God. For even if he does not choose to help us within the five days, he
is free to come to our rescue at any time he pleases, or equally to let us be
16 destroyed by our enemies. It is not for you to impose conditions on the
Lord our God; God will not yield to threats or be bargained with like a
17 mere man. So we must wait for him to deliver us, and in the mean time
appeal to him for help. If he sees fit he will hear us.
18    'There is not one of our tribes or clans, districts or towns, that worships
man-made gods today, or has done so within living memory. This did
19 happen in days gone by, and that was why our ancestors were abandoned
to their enemies to be slaughtered and pillaged, and great was their down-
20 fall. But we acknowledge no god but the Lord, and so we are confident
21 that he will not spurn us or any of our race. For our capture will mean the
loss of all Judaea, and our temple will be looted; and God will hold us
22 responsible for its desecration. The slaughter and deportation of our fellow-
countrymen, and the laying waste of the land we inherited, will bring his
judgement upon us wherever we become slaves among the Gentiles. Our
23 masters will regard us with disgust and contempt. There will be no happy
ending to our servitude, no return to favour; the Lord our God will use
it to dishonour us.
24    'So then, my friends, let us set an example to our fellow-countrymen;
for their lives depend on us, and the fate of the sanctuary, the temple, and
25 the altar rests with us. We have every reason to give thanks to the Lord our
26 God; he is putting us to the test as he did our ancestors. Remember how he
dealt with Abraham and how he tested Isaac, and what happened to Jacob
in Syrian Mesopotamia when he was working as a shepherd for his uncle
27 Laban. He is not subjecting us to the fiery ordeal by which he tested their
loyalty, or taking vengeance on us: it is for discipline that the Lord scourges
his worshippers.'
28    Ozias replied, 'You are quite right; everything you say is true, and no
29 one can deny it. This is not the first time that you have given proof of your
wisdom. Throughout your life we have all recognized your good sense and
30 the soundness of your judgement. But the people were desperate with
thirst and compelled us to make this promise and to pledge ourselves by an
31 oath we may not break. Now, you are a devout woman; pray for us and
ask the Lord to send rain to fill our cisterns, and then we shall no longer
faint for lack of water.'
32    'Hear what I have to say', replied Judith. 'I am going to do a deed which
33 will be remembered among our people for all generations. Be at the gate
tonight yourselves, and I will go out with my maid. Before the day on
which you have promised to surrender the town to our enemies, the Lord
34 will deliver Israel by my hand. But do not try to find out my plan; I will
35 not tell you until I have accomplished what I mean to do.' Ozias and the
magistrates said to her, 'Go with our blessing, and may God be with you

to take vengeance on our enemies.' So they left the roof-shelter and 36
returned to their posts.

Then Judith prostrated herself, put ashes on her head, and uncovered 9
the sackcloth she was wearing; and at the time when the evening incense
was being offered in the temple in Jerusalem, she cried to the Lord: 'O 2
Lord, the God of my forefather Simeon! Thou didst put in his hand a
sword to take vengeance on those foreigners who had stripped off a virgin's
veil to defile her, uncovered her thighs to shame her, and polluted her
womb to dishonour her. Thou didst say, "It shall not be done"; yet they
did it. So thou didst give up their rulers to be slain, and their bed, which 3
blushed for their treachery, to be stained with blood; beneath thy stroke
slaves fell dead upon the bodies of princes, and princes upon their thrones.
Thou didst give up their wives as booty, and their daughters as captives, 4
and all their spoils to be divided among thy beloved sons, who, aflame with
zeal for thy cause and aghast at the pollution of their blood, called on thee
to help them. O God, thou art my God, hear now a widow's prayer. All 5
that happened then, and all that happened before and after, thou didst
accomplish. The things that are now, and are yet to be, thou hast designed;
and what thou didst design has come to pass. The things thou hast fore- 6
ordained present themselves and say, "We are here." Thy ways are prepared beforehand: foreknowledge determines thy judgement.

'Thou seest the Assyrians assembled in their strength, proud of their 7
horses and riders, boasting of the power of their infantry, and putting their
faith in shield and javelin, bow and sling. They do not know that thou art
the Lord who stamps out wars; the Lord is thy name. Shatter their strength 8
by thy power and crush their might in thy anger. For they have planned
to desecrate thy sanctuary, to pollute the dwelling-place of thy glorious
name, and to strike down the horns of thy altar with the sword. Mark 9
their arrogance, pour thy wrath on their heads, and give to me, widow as
I am, the strength to achieve my end. Use the deceit upon my lips to strike 10
them dead, the slave with the ruler, the ruler with the servant; shatter their
pride by a woman's hand. For thy might lies not in numbers nor thy 11
sovereign power in strong men; but thou art the God of the humble, the
help of the poor, the support of the weak, the protector of the desperate,
the deliverer of the hopeless. Hear, O hear, thou God of my forefather, 12
God of Israel's heritage, ruler of heaven and earth, creator of the waters,
king of all thy creation, hear thou my prayer. Grant that my deceitful words 13
may wound and bruise them; for they have cruel designs against thy covenant, thy sacred house, the summit of Zion, and thy children's home,
their own possession. Give thy whole nation and every tribe the knowledge 14
that thou alone art God, God of all power and might, and that thou and
thou alone art Israel's shield.'

When Judith had ended her prayer, prostrate before the God of Israel, 10 1-2
she rose, called her maid, and went down into the house, where she was
accustomed to spend her sabbaths and festivals. She removed the sack- 3
cloth she was wearing and took off her widow's weeds; then she washed,
and anointed herself with rich perfume. She did her hair, put on a head-
band, and dressed in her gayest clothes, which she used to wear when her

4 husband Manasses was alive. She put on sandals and anklets, bracelets
and rings, her ear-rings and all her ornaments, and made herself very
5 attractive, so as to catch the eye of any man who might see her. She gave
her maid a skin of wine and a flask of oil; then she filled a bag with roasted
grain, cakes of dried figs, and the finest bread, packed everything up, and
gave it all to her maid to carry.
6    They went out towards the gate of Bethulia and found Ozias standing
7 there, with Chabris and Charmis the elders of the town. When they saw
Judith transformed in appearance and quite differently dressed, they were
8 filled with admiration of her beauty, and said to her, 'The God of our
fathers grant you favour and fulfil your plans, so that Israel may triumph
9 and Jerusalem may be exalted!' Judith bowed to God in worship. Then
she said to them, 'Order the gate to be opened for me, and I will go out to
accomplish all that you say.' They ordered the young men to open the
10 gate as she had asked. When they had done so, Judith went out, accompanied by her maid; and the men of the town watched her until she had
gone down the hill-side and crossed the valley, and then they lost sight
of her.
11    The women went straight across the valley and were met by an Assyrian
12 outpost; they seized Judith and questioned her: 'What is your nationality?
Where have you come from? Where are you going?' 'I am a Hebrew,' she
replied; 'but I am running away from my people, because they are going to
13 fall into your hands and be devoured. I am on my way to Holophernes,
your commander-in-chief, with reliable information. I will show him a
route by which he can gain command of the entire hill-country without
losing a single man.'
14    As the men listened to her story they looked at her face and were amazed
15 at her beauty. 'You have saved your life', they said, 'by coming down at
once to see our master. Go to his tent straight away. Some of us will escort
16 you and hand you over to him. When you are in his presence, do not be
afraid; just tell him what you have told us, and he will treat you kindly.'
17 They detailed a hundred of their number to accompany her and her maid,
and they brought the two women to Holophernes' tent.

18 AS THE NEWS of her arrival spread from tent to tent, men came running
from all parts of the camp. They gathered round her as she stood outside
19 Holophernes' tent waiting until he had been told about her. Her wonderful
beauty made them think that the Israelites must be a wonderful people.
They said to each other, 'Who can despise a nation which has such women
as this? We had better not leave a man of them alive, for if they get away
they will be able to outwit the whole world.'
20    Then Holophernes' bodyguard and all his attendants came out and took
21 her into the tent. He was resting on his bed under a mosquito-net of purple
22 interwoven with gold, emeralds, and precious stones. When Judith was
announced he came out into the front part of the tent, with silver lamps
23 carried before him. He and his attendants were all amazed at the beauty
of her face as she stood before them. She prostrated herself and did obeisance to him; but his slaves raised her up.

'Take heart, madam,' said Holophernes; 'do not be afraid. I have never 11
harmed anyone who chose to serve Nebuchadnezzar, king of all the earth.
I should never have raised my spear against your people in the hill- 2
country if they had not insulted me; they brought it on themselves. Now 3
tell me why you have run away from them and joined us. By coming here
you have saved your life. Take heart! You are in no danger tonight or in
the future; no one will harm you. You will enjoy the good treatment which 4
is given to the subjects of my master King Nebuchadnezzar.'

Judith replied, 'My lord, grant your slave a hearing and listen to what I 5
have to say to you. The information I am giving you tonight is the truth.
If you follow my advice, God will do some great thing through you, and my 6
lord will not fail to attain his ends. By the life of Nebuchadnezzar, king 7
of all the earth, and by the living might of him who sent you to bring order
to all creatures, I swear: not only do men serve him, thanks to you, but wild
animals also, cattle, and birds, will owe their lives to your power as long
as Nebuchadnezzar and his dynasty reign.*a* We have heard how wise 8
and clever you are. You are known throughout the world as the man of
ability unrivalled in the whole empire, of powerful intelligence and amazing
skill in the art of war. We know about the speech that Achior made in your 9
council, because the men of Bethulia rescued him, and he told them what
he had said to you. Do not disregard what he said, my lord and master, 10
but give full weight to his words. They are true. No punishment ever falls
on our race and the sword does not subdue them, except when they sin
against their God. But now, my lord, you are not to be thwarted and cheated 11
of success, for they are doomed to die. Sin has them in its power, and
when they do wrong they will arouse their God's anger. Because they have 12
run out of food and their water-supply is low, they have decided to lay
hands on their cattle; they mean to consume everything that God by his
laws has prohibited as food; and they have resolved to use up the first- 13
fruits of the grain and the tithes of wine and oil, although these are dedicated and reserved for the priests who stand in attendance before our God
in Jerusalem, and no layman may so much as handle them. They have sent 14
men to Jerusalem to get permission from the senate, because even the
people there have done this. As soon as ever word reaches them and they 15
act on it, on that very day they will be given up to you to be destroyed.

'So, my lord, when I learnt all this, I ran away from them; and God 16
has sent me to do with you things that will be the wonder of the world,
wherever men hear about them. For I, your servant, am a religious woman: 17
day and night I worship the God of heaven. I will stay with you now, my
lord; and each night I shall go out into the valley and pray to God, and he
will tell me when they have committed their sins. Then, when I return and 18
bring you word, you may lead out your whole army, and you will meet
with no resistance from any of them. I will guide you across Judaea until 19
you reach Jerusalem, and I will set up your throne in the heart of the city.
They will follow you like sheep that have lost their shepherd, and not a

---

*a* not only . . . reign: *or* thanks to you and to your power, not only do men serve him,
but wild animals also, cattle, and birds, will live at the disposal of Nebuchadnezzar and
his household; *the text and meaning are uncertain.*

dog will so much as growl at you. I have been given foreknowledge of this. It has been revealed to me, and I have been sent to announce it to you.'

20 Judith's words delighted Holophernes and all his attendants, and they
21 were amazed at her wisdom. 'In the whole wide world', they said, 'there is not a woman to compare with her for beauty of face or shrewdness of
22 speech.' Holophernes said to her, 'Thank God for sending you out from your people, to bring strength to us and destruction to those who have
23 insulted my lord! You are a beautiful woman and your words are good. If you do as you have promised, your God shall be my God, and you shall live in King Nebuchadnezzar's palace and be renowned throughout the world.'

12 Holophernes then commanded them to bring her in where his silver was set out, and he ordered a meal to be served for her from his own food and
2 wine. But Judith said, 'I will not eat any of it, in case I should be breaking
3 our law. What I have brought with me will meet my needs.' Holophernes said to her, 'But if you use up all you have with you, where can we get you a fresh supply of the same kind? There is no one of your race here among
4 us.' Judith replied, 'As sure as you live, my lord, I shall not finish what I have brought with me before the Lord accomplishes through me what he has planned.'

5 Holophernes' attendants brought her into the tent; and she slept until
6 midnight. Shortly before the morning watch she got up and sent this message to Holophernes: 'My lord, will you give orders for me to be
7 allowed to go out and pray?' Holophernes ordered his bodyguard to let her pass. She remained in the camp for three days, going out each night
8 into the valley of Bethulia and bathing in the spring. When she came up from the spring, she prayed the Lord, the God of Israel, to prosper her
9 undertaking to restore her people. Then she returned to the camp purified, and remained in the tent until she took her meal towards evening.

10 ON THE FOURTH DAY Holophernes gave a banquet for his personal
11 servants only, and did not invite any of the army officers. He said to Bagoas, the eunuch in charge of all his affairs: 'Go to the Hebrew woman who is in
12 your care, and persuade her to join us and to eat and drink with us. It would be a disgrace if we let such a woman go without enjoying her
13 company. If we do not win her favours she will laugh at us.' Bagoas left Holophernes' presence, and went to Judith and said, 'Now, my beauty, do not be bashful; come along to my master and give yourself the honour of his company. Drink with us and enjoy yourself, and behave today like one of the Assyrian women in attendance at Nebuchadnezzar's palace.'
14 'Who am I to refuse my master?' said Judith. 'I am eager to do whatever
15 pleases him; and it will be something to boast of till my dying day.' She proceeded to dress herself up and put on all her feminine finery. Her maid went ahead of her, and spread on the ground in front of Holophernes the fleeces which she had received from Bagoas for her daily use, so that she
16 might recline on them when she ate. When Judith came in and took her place, Holophernes was beside himself with desire for her. He shook with passion and was filled with an ardent longing to possess her; indeed he had been looking for an opportunity to seduce her ever since he first set eyes on

her. So he said to her, 'Drink and enjoy yourself with us.' 'Indeed I will, my 17 18 lord,' said Judith; 'today is the greatest day of my whole life.' Then she 19 took what her servant had prepared, and ate and drank in his presence. Holophernes was delighted with her, and drank a great deal of wine, more, 20 indeed, than he had ever drunk on any single day since he was born.

When it grew late, Holophernes' servants quickly withdrew. Bagoas 13 closed the tent from outside, shutting out all the attendants from his master's presence, and they went to bed; the banquet had lasted so long that they were all worn out. Judith was left alone in the tent, with Holo- 2 phernes lying sprawled on his bed, dead drunk.

Judith had told her maid to stand outside the sleeping-apartment and 3 wait for her mistress to go out, as she did every day; she had said that she would be going out to pray, and had explained this to Bagoas also. When 4 they had all gone and not a soul was left, Judith stood beside Holophernes' bed and prayed silently: 'O Lord, God of all power, look favourably now on what I am about to do to bring glory to Jerusalem, for now is the time 5 to help thy heritage and to give success to my plan for crushing the enemies who have risen up against us.' She went to the bed-rail beside Holophernes' 6 head and took down his sword, and stepping close to the bed she grasped 7 his hair. 'Now give me strength, O Lord, God of Israel', she said; then 8 she struck at his neck twice with all her might, and cut off his head. She 9 rolled the body off the bed and took the mosquito-net from its posts; a moment later she went out and gave Holophernes' head to the maid, who 10 put it in her food-bag. The two of them went out together, as they had usually done for prayer. Through the camp they went, and round that valley, and up the hill to Bethulia till they reached the gates.

From a distance Judith called to the sentries at the gates: 'Open! Open 11 the gate! God, our God, is with us, still showing his strength in Israel and his might against our enemies. He has shown it today!' When the 12 citizens heard her voice, they hurried down to the gate and summoned the elders of the town. Everyone high and low came running, hardly able to 13 believe that Judith had returned. They opened the gate and let the two women in; they lit a fire to see by, and gathered round them. Then Judith 14 raised her voice and cried, 'Praise God! O praise him! Praise God, who has not withdrawn his mercy from the house of Israel, but has crushed our enemies by my hand this very night!' Then she took the head from the bag 15 and showed it to them. 'Look!' she said. 'The head of Holophernes, the Assyrian commander-in-chief! And here is the net under which he lay drunk! The Lord has struck him down by the hand of a woman! And I 16 swear by the Lord who has brought me safely along the way I have travelled that, though my face lured him to destruction, he committed no sin with me, and my honour is unblemished.'

The people were all astounded; and bowing down in worship to God, 17 they said with one voice, 'Praise be to thee, O Lord our God, who hast humiliated the enemies of thy people this day.' And Ozias said to Judith, 18 'My daughter, the blessing of God Most High is upon you, you more than all other women on earth; praise be to the Lord, the God who created heaven and earth, and guided you when you struck off the head of the

19 enemy commander. The sure hope which inspired you*a* will never fade
20 from men's minds while they commemorate the power of God. May God
make your deed redound to your honour for ever, and shower blessings
upon you! You risked your life for our country when it was faced with
humiliation. You went boldly to meet the disaster that threatened us, and
held firmly to God's straight road.' All the people responded: 'Amen!
Amen!'

## The triumph of Israel

**14** THEN JUDITH SAID TO THEM, 'Listen to me, my friends; take this
2        head and hang it out on the battlements of your wall. As soon as dawn
breaks and the sun rises, take up your weapons, every able-bodied man of
you, and march out of the town. You must set a commander at your head,
as if you were going down to the plain to attack the Assyrian outpost; but
3 do not go down. The Assyrians will take up their weapons and make for
their camp, and rouse the commanders, who will run to Holophernes' tent
but will not find him. They will all be seized with panic and will flee from
4 you; then pursue them, you and all who live within Israel's borders, and cut
5 them down in their tracks. But first of all summon Achior the Ammonite
to me, so that he may see and recognize the man who treated Israel with
contempt and sent him to us as if to his death.'
6    They summoned Achior from Ozias's house. When he came and saw
Holophernes' head held by one of the men in the assembly of the people,
7 he fainted and fell down. They lifted him up, and he threw himself at
Judith's feet and did obeisance to her, and said, 'Your praises will be sung
in every camp in Judah and among all nations. They will tremble when
8 they hear your name. Tell me now the whole story of what you have done
during these days.' Then Judith, in the hearing of the people, told him
9 everything from the day she left until that very moment. As she ended her
story, the people raised a great shout and made the town ring with their
10 cheers. And when Achior realized all that the God of Israel had done, he
came to full belief in God, and was circumcised, and admitted as a member
of the community of Israel, as his descendants still are.
11    When dawn came they hung Holophernes' head on the wall; then they
all took their weapons and went out in companies into the approaches to
12 the town. When the Assyrians saw them, they sent word to their leaders,
13 who then went to the generals, captains, and all the other officers. They
came to Holophernes' tent and said to his steward: 'Wake our master.
These slaves have had the audacity to offer us battle; they are asking to be
14 utterly wiped out.' Bagoas went in and knocked at the screen of the inner
15 tent, supposing that Holophernes was sleeping with Judith. When there
was no reply, he drew aside the screen, went into the sleeping-apartment,
16 and found the dead body sprawling over a footstool, and the head gone. He
17 gave a great cry, wailing and groaning aloud, and tore his clothes. Then
he went into the tent which Judith had occupied; and not finding her he
18 rushed out to the people shouting, 'The slaves have played us false. One
          *a Or* which you inspire.

Hebrew woman has brought shame on Nebuchadnezzar's kingdom. Look! Holophernes is lying on the ground, and his head is gone!' His words filled 19 the officers of the Assyrian army with dismay; they tore their clothes, and the camp rang with their shouts and cries.

When the news spread to the men in the camp, they were thrown into **15** consternation at what had happened. In terror and panic they all scattered 2 at once, with no attempt to keep together, and fled by every path across the plain and the hill-country. Those who were encamped in the hills round 3 Bethulia also took to flight. Then all the Israelites of military age sallied out after them. Ozias sent men to Bethomesthaim, Choba, and Chola, and the 4 whole territory of Israel, to give news of what had happened and to tell them to sally out against the enemy and destroy them. When the news reached 5 them, every man in Israel joined the attack and cut them down, going as far as Choba. The men from Jerusalem and all the hill-country also joined in, for they had been told what had happened in the enemy camp. The men of Gilead and Galilee outflanked the Assyrians and inflicted heavy losses on them, continuing beyond Damascus and the district round it. The rest of 6 the inhabitants of Bethulia fell upon the camp and made themselves rich with the spoils. When the Israelites returned from the slaughter, they took 7 possession of what remained. The villages and hamlets in the hill-country and in the plain got masses of booty, for there was a huge quantity of it.

Joakim the high priest and the senate of Israel came from Jerusalem to 8 see for themselves the great things the Lord had done for his people, and to meet Judith and wish her well. When they arrived they praised her with 9 one voice and said, 'You are the glory of Jerusalem, the heroine of Israel, the proud boast of our people! With your own hand you have done all this, 10 you have restored the fortunes of Israel, and God has shown his approval. Blessings on you from the Lord Almighty, for all time to come!' And all the people responded, 'Amen!'

The looting of the camp went on for thirty days. They gave Judith 11 Holophernes' tent, with all his silver, and his couches, bowls, and furniture. She took them and loaded her mule, then got her wagons ready and piled the goods on them. All the Israelite women came running to see her; 12 they sang her praises, and some of them performed a dance in her honour. She took garlanded wands in her hands and gave some also to the women who accompanied her; and she and those who were with her crowned 13 themselves with olive leaves. Then, at the head of all the people, she led the women in the dance; and the men of Israel, in full armour and with garlands on their heads, followed them singing hymns.

IN THE PRESENCE of all Israel, Judith struck up this hymn of praise **16** and thanksgiving, in which all the people joined lustily:

> 'Strike up a song to my God with tambourines;                    2
> sing to the Lord with cymbals;
> raise a psalm of praise *a* to him;
> honour him and invoke his name.

> *a Some witnesses read* a new psalm.

83

3    The Lord is a God who stamps out wars;
     he has brought me safe from my pursuers
     into his camp among his people.

4    The Assyrian came from the mountains of the north;
     his armies came in such myriads
     that his troops choked the valleys,
     his cavalry covered the hills.

5    He threatened to set fire to my land,
     put my young men to the sword,
     dash my infants to the ground,
     take my children as booty,
     and my maidens as spoil.

6    The Lord Almighty has thwarted them by a woman's hand.

7    It was no young man that brought their champion low;
     no Titan struck him down,
     no tall giant set upon him;
     but Judith daughter of Merari disarmed him by the beauty of her face.

8    She put off her widow's weeds
     to raise up the afflicted in Israel;
     she anointed her face with perfume,
     and bound her hair with a headband,
     and put on a linen gown to beguile him.

9    Her sandal entranced his eye,
     her beauty took his heart captive;
     and the sword cut through his neck.

10   The Persians shuddered at her daring,
     the Medes were daunted by her boldness.

11   Then my oppressed people shouted in triumph, and the enemy were
          afraid;
     my weak ones shouted, and the enemy cowered in fear;
     they raised their voices, and the enemy took to flight.

12   The sons of servant girls ran them through,
     wounding them like runaway slaves;
     they were destroyed by the army of my Lord.

13   'I will sing a new hymn to my God.
     O Lord, thou art great and glorious,
     thou art marvellous in thy strength, invincible.

14   Let thy whole creation serve thee;
     for thou didst speak and all things came to be;
     thou didst send out thy spirit and it formed them.
     No one can resist thy voice;

15   mountains and seas are stirred to their depths,
     rocks melt like wax at thy presence;
     but to those who revere thee
     thou dost still show mercy.

16   For no sacrifice is sufficient to please thee with its fragrance,
     and all the fat in the world is not enough for a burnt-offering,

but he who fears the Lord is always great.
Woe to the nations which rise up against my people!    17
The Lord Almighty will punish them on the day of judgement;
he will consign their bodies to fire and worms;
they will weep in pain for ever.'

When they arrived at Jerusalem they worshipped God. As soon as the   18
people were purified, they offered their burnt-offerings, freewill offerings,
and gifts. Judith dedicated to God all Holophernes' possessions, which the   19
people had given to her; and the net, which she had taken for herself from
the sleeping-apartment, she presented as a votive offering. For three   20
months the people continued their celebrations in Jerusalem in front of the
sanctuary; and Judith remained with them.

At the end of that time they all returned to their own homes. Judith went   21
back to Bethulia and lived on her estate. In her time she was famous
throughout the whole country. She had many suitors; but she remained   22
unmarried all her life after her husband Manasses died and was gathered
to his fathers. Her fame continued to increase; and she lived on in her   23
husband's house until she was a hundred and five years old. She gave her
maid her liberty. She died in Bethulia and was buried in the same tomb as
her husband Manasses, and Israel observed mourning for her for seven   24
days. Before her death she divided her property among all those who were
most closely related to her husband Manasses, and among her own nearest
relations.

No one dared to threaten the Israelites again in Judith's lifetime, or for   25
a long time after her death.

# THE REST OF THE CHAPTERS
# OF THE BOOK OF
# ESTHER

## WHICH ARE FOUND NEITHER IN THE HEBREW
## NOR IN THE SYRIAC

NOTE. *The portions of the Book of Esther commonly included in the Apocrypha are extracts from the Greek version of the book, which differs substantially from the Hebrew text (translated in* The New English Bible: Old Testament). *In order that they may be read in their original sequence, the whole of the Greek version is here translated, those portions which are not normally printed in the Apocrypha being enclosed in square brackets, with the chapter and verse numbers in italic figures. The order followed is that of the Greek text, but the chapter and verse numbers are made to conform to those of the Authorized Version. Proper names are given in the form in which they occur in the Greek version.*

**11** *2* IN THE SECOND YEAR of the reign of Artaxerxes the Great King, on the first day of Nisan, Mardochaeus son of Jairus, son of Semeius,
*3* son of Kisaeus, of the tribe of Benjamin, had a dream. Mardochaeus was a Jew living in the city of Susa, a man of high standing, who was
*4* in the royal service; he came of those whom Nebuchadnezzar king of Babylon had taken into exile from Jerusalem with Jechonias king of
*5* Judah. This was his dream: din and tumult, peals of thunder and an earth-
*6* quake, confusion upon the earth. Then appeared two great dragons, ready
*7* to grapple with each other, and the noise they made was terrible. Every nation was roused by it to prepare for war, to fight against the righteous
*8* nation. It was a day of darkness and gloom, with distress and anguish,
*9* oppression and great confusion upon the earth. And the whole righteous nation was troubled, dreading the evils in store for them, and they pre-
*10* pared for death. They cried aloud to God; and in answer to their cry there
*11* came as though from a little spring a great river brimming with water. It grew light, and the sun rose; the humble were exalted and they devoured
*12* the great. After he had had this dream and had seen what God had resolved to do, Mardochaeus woke; he kept it before his mind, seeking in every way to understand it, until nightfall.

**12** Now when Mardochaeus was resting in the royal courtyard with
*2* Gabatha and Tharra, the two eunuchs who guarded the courtyard, he heard them deep in discussion. He listened carefully to discover what was

on their minds, and found that they were plotting violence against King
Artaxerxes. He denounced them to the king, who had the two eunuchs 3
interrogated. They confessed and were led away to execution. Then the 4
king wrote an account of the affair, to have it on record; Mardochaeus also
wrote an account of it. The king gave Mardochaeus an appointment at 5
court, and rewarded him for his services. But Haman, the son of Hama- 6
dathus, a Bugaean, who enjoyed the king's favour, sought to injure Mardochaeus and his people because of the two eunuchs.

## A Jewess becomes queen in Persia

THOSE EVENTS HAPPENED in the days of Artaxerxes, the Artaxerxes 1
who ruled from India to Ethiopia, a hundred and twenty-seven provinces. At this time he sat on his royal throne in the city of Susa. Then in 2 3
the third year of his reign he gave a banquet for the King's Friends and
persons of various races, the Persian and Median nobles and the leading
provincial governors. And afterwards, after displaying to them the wealth 4
of his empire and the splendour of his rich festivities for a hundred and
eighty days, when these days of feasting were over, the king gave a banquet 5
for all the people of various races present in the city of Susa; it was held in
the court of the king's palace and lasted six days. The court was decorated 6
with white curtains of linen and cotton stretched on cords of purple, and
these were attached to blocks of gold and silver resting on stone and
marble columns. There were couches of gold and silver set on a pavement
of malachite, marble, and mother-of-pearl. There were mats of transparent
weave elaborately embroidered with roses arranged in a circle. The cups 7
were of gold and silver, and there was displayed a miniature cup made of
carbuncle worth thirty thousand talents. The wine was abundant and
sweet, from the king's own cellar. The drinking was not according to a 8
fixed rule, but the king had laid it down that all the stewards of his palace
should respect his will and that of the guests. In addition, Queen Astin 9
gave a banquet for the women in the same palace where King
Artaxerxes was.

On the seventh day, when he was in high good humour, the king ordered 10
Haman, Mazan, Tharra, Borazes, Zatholtha, Abataza, and Tharaba, the
seven eunuchs who were in attendance on the king's person, to bring the 11
queen before him, so that he might place the royal diadem on her head and
let her display her beauty to the officers and people of various races; for
she was indeed a beautiful woman. But Queen Astin refused to obey him 12
and come with the eunuchs. This offended the king and made him angry.

Then the king said to his courtiers, 'You hear what Astin said. Give your 13
ruling and judgement in the matter.' Then the nobles of Persia and Media 14
who were closest to the king—Harkesaeus, Sarsathaeus, and Malesear,
who sat next him in the chief seats—approached him and declared what 15
should be done according to the law to Queen Astin for disobeying the
order which the king sent her by the eunuchs. Then Muchaeus said to 16
the king and the nobles: 'Queen Astin has done wrong, and not to the

17 king alone, but to all his nobles and officers as well.' (For he had repeated
18 to them what the queen had said and how she had defied the king.) 'And just as she defied King Artaxerxes, so now the nobles of Persia and Media will find that all their ladies are bold enough to treat their husbands with
19 contempt, when they hear what she said to the king. If it please your majesty, let a royal decree go out from you, and let it be inscribed among the laws of the Medes and Persians, that Astin shall not again appear before the king; this is the only course. And let the king give her place as queen to
20 another woman who is more worthy of it than she. Let whatever law the king makes be proclaimed throughout his empire, and then all women will give
21 due honour to their husbands, rich and poor alike.' The advice pleased the
22 king and the princes, and the king did as Muchaeus had proposed. Letters were sent to all the provinces of the empire, to each province in its own language, in order that every man might be respected in his own house.

**2** Later, when the anger of King Artaxerxes had died down, he remembered Astin and what she had done, and how he had given judgement against her.
2 So the king's attendants said: 'Let beautiful girls of unblemished virtue
3 be sought out for your majesty. Let your majesty appoint commissioners in all the provinces of the empire to select these beautiful virgins and bring them to the city of Susa, into the women's quarters. There let them be committed to the care of the king's eunuch in charge of the women, and let
4 them be provided with cosmetics and everything else they need. Then the one who is most acceptable to the king shall become queen in place of Astin.' The advice pleased the king, and he acted on it.
5 Now there was a Jew in the city of Susa named Mardochaeus, son of
6 Jairus, son of Semeius, son of Kisaeus, of the tribe of Benjamin; he had been carried into exile from Jerusalem when it was taken by Nebuchad-
7 nezzar king of Babylon. He had a foster-child named Esther, the daughter of his father's brother Aminadab. She had lost her parents, and he had
8 brought her up to womanhood. She was a very beautiful girl. When the king's edict was proclaimed, many girls were brought to Susa to be entrusted to Gai, who had charge of the women, and among them was
9 Esther. She attracted his notice and received his special favour: he readily provided her with her cosmetics and allowance of food, and also with seven maids assigned to her from the king's palace. He gave her and her maids honourable treatment in the women's quarters.
10 Esther had not disclosed her race or country, because Mardochaeus had
11 forbidden her to do so. Every day Mardochaeus passed along by the forecourt of the women's quarters to keep an eye on Esther and see what would happen to her.
12 The period after which a girl was to go to the king was twelve months. This was for the completion of the required treatment—six months with
13 oil and myrrh and six months with perfumes and cosmetics. Then the girl went to the king. She was handed to the person appointed, and accompanied
14 him from the women's quarters to the king's palace. She entered the palace in the evening and returned in the morning to Gai, the king's eunuch in charge of the women, in another part of the women's quarters. She did not go to the king again unless summoned by name.

When the time came for Esther, daughter of Aminadab the uncle of  *15*
Mardochaeus, to go to the king, she neglected none of the instructions of
Gai the king's eunuch in charge of the women; for Esther charmed all who
saw her. She was taken to King Artaxerxes in the twelfth month, that is,  *16*
the month Adar, in the seventh year of his reign. The king fell in love with  *17*
her, finding her more acceptable than any of the other girls, and crowned
her with the queen's diadem. Then the king gave a banquet lasting seven  *18*
days for all the King's Friends and the officers, to celebrate Esther's
marriage. He also granted a remission of taxation to all subjects of his
empire.

Mardochaeus was in attendance in the courtyard. But Esther had not  *19 20*
disclosed her country—such were the instructions of Mardochaeus; but
she was to fear God and keep his commandments just as she had done
when she was with him. So Esther made no change in her way of life.

Two of the king's eunuchs, officers of the bodyguard, were offended at  *21*
the advancement of Mardochaeus and plotted to kill King Artaxerxes.
This became known to Mardochaeus, who told Esther, and she revealed  *22*
the plot to the king. The king interrogated the two eunuchs and had them  *23*
hanged, and he ordered that the service Mardochaeus had rendered should
be recorded in the royal archives to his honour.

## *A plot against the Jews*

Aftер тнis King Artaxerxes promoted Haman son of Hamadathus  **3**
the Bugaean, advancing him and giving him precedence above all the
King's Friends. So all who were at court did obeisance to Haman, for so  *2*
the king had commanded; but Mardochaeus did not do obeisance. Then  *3*
the king's courtiers said to him, 'Mardochaeus, why do you flout the king's
command?' Day by day they challenged him, but he refused to listen to  *4*
them. Then they informed Haman that Mardochaeus was resisting the
king's command. Mardochaeus had told them that he was a Jew. So when  *5*
Haman learnt that Mardochaeus was not doing obeisance to him, he was
infuriated and plotted to exterminate all the Jews under Artaxerxes' rule.  *6*

In the twelfth year of King Artaxerxes he arrived at a decision by casting  *7*
lots, taking the days and the months one by one, to decide on one day for
the destruction of the whole race of Mardochaeus. The lot fell on the
thirteenth*a* day of the month Adar.

Then Haman said to King Artaxerxes: 'There is a certain nation dis-  *8*
persed among the other nations of your empire. Their laws are different
from those of every other nation; they do not keep your majesty's laws. It
is not to your majesty's advantage to tolerate them. If it please your  *9*
majesty, let an order be made for their destruction; and I will contribute
ten thousand talents of silver to the royal treasury.' So the king took off his  *10*
signet-ring and gave it to Haman to seal the decree against the Jews. 'Keep  *11*
the money, and deal with these people as you will', he said.

On the thirteenth day of the first month the king's secretaries were  *12*

*a  So some witnesses, and compare 8. 12 (page 95); other witnesses read* fourteenth.

summoned, and in accordance with Haman's instructions, they wrote in the name of King Artaxerxes to his army commanders and governors in every province from India to Ethiopia. There were a hundred and twenty-seven
*13* provinces in all, and each was addressed in its own language. Instructions were dispatched by courier to all the empire of Artaxerxes to exterminate the Jewish race, on a given day of the twelfth month, Adar, and to plunder their possessions.]

**13** THIS IS A COPY of the letter:

Artaxerxes the Great King to the governors of the one hundred and twenty-seven provinces, from India to Ethiopia, and to the subordinate officials.
2    Ruler as I am over many nations and master of all the world, it is my will—not in the arrogance of power, but because my rule is mild and equitable—to ensure to my subjects a life permanently free from disturbance, to pacify my empire and make it safe for travel to its farthest
3    limits, and to restore the peace that all men long for. I asked my counsellors how this object might be achieved and received a reply from Haman. Haman is eminent among us for sound judgement, one whose worth is proved by his constant goodwill and steadfast loyalty, and who has
4    gained the honour of the second place at our court. He represented to us that scattered among all the races of the empire is a disaffected people, opposed in its laws to every nation, and continually ignoring the royal ordinances, so that our irreproachable plans for the unified administra-
5    tion of the empire cannot be made effective. We understand that this nation stands alone in its continual opposition to all men, that it evades the laws by its strange manner of life, and in disloyalty to our government commits grievous offences, thus undermining the security of our
6    empire. We therefore order that those who are designated to you in the indictments drawn up by Haman, our vicegerent and second father, shall all, together with their wives and children, be utterly destroyed by the sword of their enemies, without mercy or pity, on the thirteenth[a] day of
7    Adar, the twelfth month, of the present year. Those persons who have long been disaffected shall meet a violent death in one day so that our government may henceforth be stable and untroubled.

**3** *14*    [Copies of the document were posted up in every province, and all
*15* nations of the empire were ordered to be ready by that day. The matter was expedited also in Susa. While the king and Haman caroused together, the city of Susa was thrown into confusion.

**4** WHEN MARDOCHAEUS LEARNT all that was being done, he tore his clothes, put on sackcloth and sprinkled himself with ashes; and he rushed through the city, crying loudly: 'An innocent nation is being destroyed.'
2 He went as far as the king's gate, and there he halted, because no one was
3 allowed to enter the courtyard clothed with sackcloth and ashes. In every province where the king's decree was posted up, there was a great cry of

---

[a] *Gk.* fourteenth; *see note on 3. 7 (page 89).*

mourning and lamentation among the Jews, and they put on sackcloth and
ashes. When the queen's maids and eunuchs came and told her, she was 　4
distraught at the news, and sent clothes for Mardochaeus, urging him to
take off his sackcloth; but he would not consent. Then Esther summoned 　5
Hachrathaeus, the eunuch who waited upon her, and ordered him to obtain
accurate information for her from Mardochaeus.[a] So Mardochaeus told 　7
him all that had happened, and how Haman had promised to pay ten
thousand talents into the royal treasury to bring about the destruction of
the Jews. He also gave him a copy of the written decree for their destruc- 　8
tion which had been posted up in Susa, to show to Esther; and he gave him
a message for her, that she should go to the king and plead for his favour
and entreat him for her people. 'Remember', he said, 'those days when
you were brought up in my humble home; for Haman, who stands next
to the king, has spoken against us and demanded our death. Call upon the
Lord, and then speak for us to the king and save our lives.' Hachrathaeus 　9
returned and told her what Mardochaeus had said. She sent him back 　*10*
with this message: 'All nations of the empire know that if any person, man 　*11*
or woman, enters the king's presence in the inner court unbidden, there is
no escape for him. Only one to whom the king stretches out the golden
sceptre is safe; and it is now thirty days since I myself was called to go to
the king.'

When Hachrathaeus delivered her message, Mardochaeus told him to 　*12 13*
go back and say: 'Do not imagine, Esther, that you alone of all the Jews in
the empire will escape alive. For if you remain silent at such a time as this, 　*14*
the Jews will somewhere find relief and deliverance, but you and your
father's family will perish. Who knows whether it is not for such a time as
this that you have been made a queen?' Esther gave the messenger this 　*15*
answer to take back to Mardochaeus: 'Go and assemble all the Jews who 　*16*
are in Susa and fast for me; for three days take neither food nor drink,
night or day, and I and my maids will also go without food. Then in defiance
of the law I will enter the king's presence, even if it costs me my life.' So 　*17*
Mardochaeus went away and did as Esther had bidden him.]

AND MARDOCHAEUS PRAYED to the Lord, calling to mind all the works **13** 8
of the Lord. He said, 'O Lord, Lord and King who rulest over all, because 　9
the whole world is under thy authority, and when it is thy will to save
Israel there is no one who can stand against thee: thou didst make heaven 　*10*
and earth and every wonderful thing under heaven; thou art Lord of all, 　*11*
and there is no one who can resist thee, the Lord. Thou knowest all things; 　*12*
thou knowest, Lord, that it was not from insolence or arrogance or vainglory that I refused to bow before proud Haman, for I could gladly have 　*13*
kissed the soles of his feet to save Israel; no, I did it so that I might not 　*14*
hold a man in greater honour than God; I will not bow before any but thee,
my Lord, and it is not from arrogance that I refuse this homage. And now 　*15*
Lord, God and King, God of Abraham, spare thy people; for our enemies
are watching us to bring us to ruin, and they have set their hearts upon the

[a] *Some witnesses add* (6) So he went out to Mardochaeus in the street opposite the
city gate.

16 destruction of thy chosen people, thine from the beginning. Do not disdain thy own possession which thou didst ransom for thyself out of
17 Egypt. Hear my prayer, and have mercy on thy heritage, and turn our mourning into feasting, that we may live and sing of thy name, Lord; do
18 not put to silence the lips that give thee praise.' And all Israel cried aloud with all their might, for death stared them in the face.

**14**     Then Queen Esther, caught up in this deadly conflict,[a] took refuge in
2 the Lord. She stripped off her splendid attire and put on the garb of mourning and distress. Instead of proud perfumes she strewed ashes and dung over her head. She abased her body, and every part that she had
3 delightfully adorned she covered with her dishevelled hair. And so she prayed to the Lord God of Israel:

    'O my Lord, thou alone art our king; help me who am alone, with no
4 5 helper but thee; for I am taking my life in my hands. Ever since I was born I have been taught by my father's family and tribe that thou, O Lord, didst choose Israel out of all the nations, and out of all the founders of our race didst choose our fathers for an everlasting possession, and that what
6 thou didst promise them, thou didst perform. But now we have sinned
7 against thee, and thou hast handed us over to our enemies because we
8 honoured their gods; thou art just, O Lord. But they are not content with
9 our bitter servitude; they have now pledged themselves to their idols to annul thy decree and to destroy thy possession, silencing those who praise thee, extinguishing the glory of thy house, and casting down thy altar.
10 They would give the heathen cause to sing the praises of their worthless gods, and would have a mortal king held in everlasting honour.

11     'Yield not thy sceptre, O Lord, to gods that are nothing; let not our enemies mock at our ruin, but turn their plot against themselves, and make
12 an example of the man who planned it. Remember us, O Lord, make thy power known in the time of our distress, and give me courage, O King of
13 gods, almighty Lord. Give me the apt word to say when I enter the lion's den. Divert his hatred to our enemy, so that there may be an end of him and his confederates.

14     'Save us by thy power, and help me who am alone and have no helper
15 but thee, Lord. Thou knowest all; thou knowest that I hate the splendour of the heathen, I abhor the bed of the uncircumcised or of any Gentile.
16 Thou knowest in what straits I am: I loathe that symbol of pride, the headdress that I wear when I show myself abroad, I loathe it as one loathes a
17 filthy rag; in private I refuse to wear it. I, thy servant, have not eaten at Haman's table; I have not graced a banquet of the king or touched the wine
18 of his drink-offerings; I have not known festive joy from the time that I
19 was brought here until now except in thee, Lord God of Abraham. O God who dost prevail against all, give heed to the cry of the despairing: rescue us from the power of wicked men, and rescue me from what I dread.'

**15** ON THE THIRD DAY Esther brought her prayers to an end. She took off the clothes she had worn while she worshipped and put on all her splendour.
2 When she was in her royal robes and had invoked the all-seeing God, her

    *a* caught . . . conflict: *or* seized by mortal anxiety.

preserver, she took two maids with her; on one she leaned for support, as 3
befitted a fine lady, while the other followed, bearing her train. She was 4 5
blushing and in the height of her beauty; her face was as cheerful as it was
lovely, but her heart was in the grip of fear. She passed through all the doors 6
and reached the royal presence. The king was seated on his throne, in the
full array of his majesty. He was all gold and precious stones, an awe-
inspiring figure. He looked up, his face glowing with regal dignity, and 7
glanced at her in towering anger. The queen fell, changing colour in a faint,
and swooning on the shoulder of the maid who went before her.

Then God changed the spirit of the king to gentleness, and in deep con- 8
cern he leapt from his throne and took her in his arms until she came to herself. He soothed her with reassuring words: 'Esther, what is it? Have no 9
fear of me, your loving husband; you shall not die, for our order is only for 10
our subjects. Come to me.' And the king lifted his golden sceptre and laid 11
it upon her neck; then he kissed her and said, 'You may speak to me.' She 12 13
answered, 'I saw you, my lord, looking like an angel of God, and I was
awestruck at your glorious appearance; your countenance is so full of 14
grace, my lord, that I look on you in wonder.' But while she was speaking 15
she fell down in a faint; the king was distressed, and all his attendants com- 16
forted her.

[Then the king said, 'What is your wish, Queen Esther? What is your **5** 3
request? Up to half my empire, it shall be given you.' 'Today is a special 4
day for me', said Esther. 'If it please your majesty, will you come, and
Haman with you, to a banquet which I shall give today?' The king ordered 5
Haman to be sent for in haste, so that Esther's wish might be fulfilled; and
they both went to the banquet to which Esther had invited them. Over the 6
wine the king said to her, 'What is it, Queen Esther? Whatever you ask for
shall be yours.' Esther said, 'This is my humble request: if I have won your 7 8
majesty's favour, will your majesty and Haman come again tomorrow to
the banquet which I shall give for you both, and tomorrow I will do as I
have done today.'

So Haman went out from the royal presence in good spirits and well 9
pleased with himself. But when he saw Mardochaeus the Jew in the king's
courtyard, he was filled with rage. He went home, and called for his friends 10
and his wife Zosara, and held forth to them about his wealth and the 11
honours with which the king had invested him, how he had made him first
man in the empire. 'Queen Esther', he said, 'invited no one but myself 12
to accompany the king to her banquet; and I am invited again for tomorrow.
Yet all this is no pleasure to me so long as I see that Jew Mardochaeus in 13
the courtyard.' Then his wife Zosara and his friends said to him: 'Have a 14
gallows put up, seventy-five feet *a* high, and in the morning speak to the
king and have Mardochaeus hanged upon it. Then you can go with the
king to the banquet and enjoy yourself.' Haman thought this an excellent
plan, and the gallows was made ready.

*a* *Gk.* fifty cubits.

## *The triumph of the Jews*

**6** THAT NIGHT the Lord kept sleep from the king, so he ordered his
**2** private secretary to bring the court chronicle and read it to him. He
found written there the record about Mardochaeus, how he had given
information about the two royal eunuchs who, while they were on guard,
**3** had plotted violence against King Artaxerxes. Whereupon the king said,
'What honour or favour did we confer on Mardochaeus for this?' The
king's courtiers who were in attendance replied, 'You have done nothing
**4** for him.' While the king was inquiring about the service that Mardochaeus
had rendered, Haman appeared in the courtyard. 'Who is that in the court?'
asked the king. Now Haman had just come in to recommend to the king
that Mardochaeus should be hanged on the gallows which he had pre-
**5** pared; so the king's servants said, 'It is Haman standing in the court.'
**6** 'Call him', said the king. Then the king said to Haman, 'What shall I do
for the man I wish to honour?' Haman said to himself, 'Whom would the
**7** king wish to honour but me?' So he said to the king, 'For the man whom the
**8** king wishes to honour, let the king's attendants bring a robe of fine linen
**9** from the king's own wardrobe and a horse from the king's own stable. Let
both be delivered to one of the king's most honourable Friends, and let
him robe the man whom the king loves and mount him on the horse, and
let him proclaim through the city: "This shall be the lot of any man whom
**10** the king honours."' Then the king said to Haman, 'An excellent sug-
gestion! Do all this for Mardochaeus the Jew who serves in the courtyard.
**11** Let nothing that you have said be omitted.' So Haman took the robe and
put it on Mardochaeus, and mounted him on the horse; then he went
through the city, proclaiming: 'This shall be the lot of any man whom the
king wishes to honour.'

**12** Then Mardochaeus returned to the courtyard, and Haman hurried
**13** off home with head veiled in mourning. He told his wife Zosara
and his friends what had happened to him. They replied, 'If Mardochaeus is a Jew, and you have been humiliated before him, you are a
lost man. You cannot get the better of him, because the living God is on
his side.'

**14** While they were still talking with Haman, the king's eunuchs arrived
and hurried him away to the banquet which Esther had prepared.

**7** **1 2** So the king and Haman went to the queen's banquet. Again on that
second day, over the wine, the king said, 'What is it, Queen Esther? What
is your request? What is your petition? You shall have it, up to half my
**3** empire.' Queen Esther answered: 'If I have won your majesty's favour,
**4** my request is for my life, my petition is for my people. For it has come
to my ears that we have been sold, I and my people, to be destroyed,
plundered, and enslaved, we and our children, male and female. Our
**5** adversary is a disgrace to the king's court.' The king said, 'Who is it that
**6** has dared to do such a thing?' 'Our enemy', said Esther, 'is this wicked
**7** Haman.' Haman stood dumbfounded before the king and the queen. The
king rose from the banquet and went into the garden, and Haman began
to plead with the queen, for he saw that things were going badly for him.

When the king returned to the banqueting hall from the garden, Haman 8
in his entreaties had flung himself across the queen's couch. The king
exclaimed, 'What! You assault the queen in my own house?' At those
words Haman turned away in despair. Then Bugathan, one of the 9
eunuchs, said to the king, 'Look! Haman has even prepared a gallows
for Mardochaeus, the man who reported the plot against the king, and
there it stands, seventy-five feet*a* high, in Haman's compound.' 'Have
Haman hanged on it', said the king. So Haman was hanged on the gallows 10
that he himself had prepared for Mardochaeus. After that the king's
rage died down.

That day King Artaxerxes gave Esther all that had belonged to Haman 8
the persecutor; and Mardochaeus was called into the king's presence,
for Esther had told him how he was related to her. Then the king took 2
off his signet-ring, which he had taken back from Haman, and gave it
to Mardochaeus. And Esther put Mardochaeus in charge of Haman's
estate.

Once again Esther spoke before the king, falling at his feet and pleading 3
with him to avert the calamity planned by Haman and to frustrate his plot
against the Jews. The king stretched out the golden sceptre to Esther, and 4
she rose and stood before the king. 'May it please your majesty,' she said; 5
'if I have won your favour, let an order be issued recalling the letters which
Haman sent in pursuance of his plan to destroy the Jews in your empire.
How can I bear to see the downfall of my people? How escape myself 6
when my country is destroyed?' Then the king said to Esther: 'I have 7
given Haman's property to you, and hanged him on the gallows because
he threatened the lives of the Jews. If you want anything further, you may 8
draw up an order in my name, in whatever terms you think fit, and seal it
with my signet. An order written at the king's direction and sealed with the
royal signet cannot be contravened.'

And so, on the twenty-third day of the first month, Nisan, in the same 9
year, the king's secretaries were summoned; and the Jews were informed in
writing of the instructions given to the administrators and chief governors
in the provinces, from India to Ethiopia, a hundred and twenty-seven provinces, to each province in its own language. The orders were written as 10
from the king and sealed with his signet, and dispatched by courier. By 11
these documents the king granted permission to the Jews in every city to
observe their own laws and to defend themselves, and to deal as they would
with their opponents and enemies, throughout the empire of Artaxerxes, 12
on a given day, the thirteenth of the twelfth month, Adar.]

THE FOLLOWING IS A COPY of this letter:                                16

Artaxerxes the Great King to the governors of the one hundred and
twenty-seven provinces, from India to Ethiopia, and to those who are
of our allegiance, greeting.

Many who have been honoured only too often by the lavish generosity 2
of their benefactors have grown arrogant and not only attempt to 3

---

*a  Gk.* fifty cubits.

ill-treat our subjects but, unable to carry the favours heaped upon them-
4 selves, even plot mischief against those who grant them. Not content
with destroying gratitude in men, they are carried away by the insolence
of those who are strangers to good breeding; they even suppose that they
will escape the justice of all-seeing God, who is no friend to evil-doers.
5 And often, when the king's business has been entrusted to those he
counts his friends, they have, by their plausibility, made those in
supreme authority partners in shedding innocent blood and involved
6 them in irreparable misfortunes, for their malevolence with its misleading sophistries has imposed upon the sincere goodwill of their rulers.
7 The evil brought about by those who wield power unworthily you can
observe, not only in records of tradition and history but also in your
8 familiar experience, and apply the lesson to the future. Thus we shall
9 peacefully free this realm from disturbance for the benefit of all, making
no changes but always deciding matters which come under our notice
10 with firmness and equity. Now Haman son of Hamadathus, a Macedonian, an alien in fact with no Persian blood, a man with nothing of our
11 kindly nature,*a* was accepted by us and enjoyed*b* so fully the benevolence
with which we treat every nation that he was proclaimed our Father,
and all along received obeisance from everyone as second only to our
12 royal throne. But this man in his unbridled arrogance planned to deprive
13 us of our empire and our life by using fraud and tortuous cunning to
bring about the destruction of Mardochaeus, our constant benefactor
who had saved our life, and of Esther, our blameless consort, together
14 with their whole nation. For he thought that by these methods he would
catch us defenceless and would transfer to the Macedonians the sove-
15 reignty now held by the Persians. But we find that the Jews, whom this
triple-dyed villain had consigned to extinction, are no evil-doers; they
16 order their lives by the most just of laws, and are children of the living
God, most high, most mighty, who maintains the empire in most
wonderful order, for us as for our ancestors.
17 You will therefore disregard the letters sent by Haman son of Hama-
18 dathus, because he, the contriver of all this, has been hanged aloft at
the gate of Susa with his whole household, God who is Lord of all having
19 speedily brought upon him the punishment that he deserved. Copies of
this letter are to be posted up in all public places. Permit the Jews to
20 live under their own laws, and give them every assistance so that on the
thirteenth day of Adar, the twelfth month, on that very day, they may
avenge themselves on those who were ranged against them*c* in the time
21 of their oppression. For God, who has all things in his power, has made
22 this a day not of ruin, but of joy, for his chosen people. Therefore you
also must keep it with all good cheer, as a notable day among your feasts
23 of commemoration, so that henceforth it may be a standing symbol of
deliverance to us and our loyal Persians, but a reminder of destruction to
24 those who plot against us. Any city or country whatsoever which does
not act upon these orders shall incur our wrath and be wiped out with

*a* Or *a man fallen away greatly from our favour.*     *b* Or *won.*     *c* Or *may*
*defend themselves against their assailants.*

fire and sword. No man shall set foot in it and even the beasts and birds shall shun it for all time.

[Let copies be posted up conspicuously throughout the empire, so **8** *13* that the Jews may be prepared by that day to fight against their enemies.

Mounted messengers set out with all speed to do what the king com- *14* manded; and the decree was posted up also in Susa.

Mardochaeus left the king's presence in royal robes, wearing a golden *15* crown and a turban of fine linen dyed purple, and all in Susa rejoiced to see him. For the Jews there was light and gladness in every province and every *16 17* city. Wherever the decree was posted up there was joy and gladness for the Jews, feasting and merriment. And many of the Gentiles were circumcised and professed Judaism, because they were afraid of the Jews.

ON THE THIRTEENTH DAY of the twelfth month, Adar, the decree **9** drawn up by the king arrived. On that very day the enemies of the Jews perished. No one offered resistance, because they were afraid of them. The *2 3* leading provincial governors, the princes, and the royal secretaries paid all respect to the Jews, because fear of Mardochaeus weighed upon them. For they had received the king's decree that his name should be honoured *4* throughout the empire.*a b* In the city itself the Jews slaughtered five *6* hundred men, including Pharsanestan, Delphon, Phasga, Pharadatha, *7 8* Barsa, Sarbacha, Marmasima, Ruphaeus, Arsaeus, and Zabuthaeus, the *9 10* ten sons of Haman son of Hamadathus, the Bugaean, the Jews' great enemy; and that day they took plunder.

When the number of those killed in Susa was reported to the king, he *11 12* said to Esther, 'In the city of Susa the Jews have killed five hundred men. What do you suppose they have done in the surrounding country? What-ever further request you have will be granted.' Esther answered him, 'Let *13* the Jews be allowed to do the same tomorrow, and hang up the bodies of Haman's ten sons.' The king consented; he handed over the bodies of *14* Haman's sons to the Jews of the city to be hung up. The Jews in Susa *15* assembled on the fourteenth day of Adar also, and killed three hundred, but they took no plunder.

The rest of the Jews in the empire rallied together in self-defence, and *16-17* so were quit of their enemies; for they slaughtered fifteen thousand of them on the thirteenth of Adar; but they took no plunder. On the four-teenth they rested, and made that day a day of rest, with rejoicing and merriment. The Jews in the city of Susa had assembled also on the four- *18* teenth day of the month; they did not rest on that day, but they kept the fifteenth day with rejoicing and merriment. That is why Jews who are dis- *19* persed over the remoter parts keep the fourteenth day of Adar as a holiday with rejoicing and merriment, sending presents of food to one another; but those who live in the principal cities keep the fifteenth of Adar as a holiday, sending presents of food to one another.

*a* For they . . . empire: *probable reading; Gk. obscure.*      *b* *Some witnesses add from the Heb.* (5) So the Jews put their enemies to the sword with great slaughter and destruc-tion; they worked their will on those who hated them.

20 Then Mardochaeus wrote down the whole story in a book and sent it
21 to all the Jews in the empire of Artaxerxes, far and near, ordering them to
establish these holidays, and to keep the fourteenth and fifteenth of Adar,
22 because these were the days on which the Jews were quit of their enemies,
and to keep the whole month of Adar, in which came the great change
from sorrow to joy and from mourning to holiday, as a time for feasting and merriment, days for sending presents of food to friends and to
the poor.
23 So the Jews formally accepted the account which Mardochaeus wrote:
24 how Haman son of Hamadathus, the Bugaean,*a* fought against them; how
25 he cast lots to decide the date of their destruction; how he came before the
king with a proposal to hang Mardochaeus; and how all the evils which he
had plotted against the Jews recoiled on his own head, and he and his sons
26 were hanged. This is why these days were named 'Purim', which in the
Jews' language means 'lots'. Because of all that was recorded in this letter
—all that they had experienced, all that had happened—Mardochaeus
27 directed that this festival should be observed, and the Jews undertook, on
behalf of themselves, their descendants, and all who should join them, to
28 do so without fail. These were to be days of commemoration, duly celebrated age after age in every town, family, and province. These days of
Purim were to be kept for all time, and the commemoration was never to
cease throughout all ages.
29 Queen Esther daughter of Aminadab, and Mardochaeus the Jew,
recorded in writing all that they had done, and confirmed the regulations
30-31 for Purim. They made themselves responsible for this decision and staked
32 their life upon the plan.*b* Esther established it for all time by her decree,
and it was put on record.
**10** 1 2 The king made decrees for the empire by land and sea. His strength and
courage, his wealth and the splendour of his empire, are recorded in the
3 annals of the kings of the Persians and Medes. Mardochaeus acted for
King Artaxerxes; he was a great man in the empire and honoured by the
Jews. His way of life won him the affection of his whole nation.]

4 5 MARDOCHAEUS SAID, 'All this is God's doing. For I have been
reminded of the dream I had about these things; not one of the visions I saw
6 proved meaningless. There was the little spring which became a river, and
there was light and sun and water in abundance. The river is Esther, whom
7 the king married and made queen; the two dragons are Haman and myself;
8 9 the nations are those who gathered to wipe out the Jews; my nation is
Israel, which cried aloud to God and was delivered. The Lord has delivered
his people, he has rescued us from all these evils. God performed great
10 miracles and signs such as have not occurred among the nations. He made
11 ready two lots, one for the people of God and one for all the nations; then
came the hour and the time for these two lots to be cast, the day of decision
12 by God before *c* all the nations; he remembered his people and gave the
verdict for his heritage.

*a Some witnesses read* the Macedonian.     *b* They made . . . plan: *possible meaning;*
Gk. *obscure.*     *c Or* the day of judgement by God upon . . .

'So they shall keep these days in the month of Adar, the fourteenth and 13
fifteenth of that month, by gathering with joy and gladness before God
from one generation of his people to another, for ever.'

IN THE FOURTH YEAR of the reign of Ptolemy and Cleopatra, Dositheus, 11 1
who said that he was a levitical priest, and Ptolemaeus his son, brought the
foregoing letter about Purim, which they said was authentic and had been
translated by Lysimachus son of Ptolemaeus, a resident in Jerusalem.

# THE WISDOM OF
# SOLOMON

## *The promise of immortality*

LOVE JUSTICE, you rulers of the earth; set your mind upon the 1
Lord, as is your duty, and seek him in simplicity of heart; for he is 2
found by those who trust him without question, and makes himself
known to those who never doubt him. Dishonest thinking cuts men off 3
from God, and if fools will take liberties with his power, he shows them
up for what they are. Wisdom will not enter a shifty soul, nor make her 4
home in a body that is mortgaged to sin. This holy spirit of discipline will 5
have nothing to do with falsehood; she cannot stay in the presence of unreason, and will throw up her case at the approach of injustice. Wisdom is 6
a spirit devoted to man's good, and she will not hold a blasphemer blameless for his words, because God is a witness of his inmost being, who sees
clear into his heart and hears every word he says. For the spirit of the Lord 7
fills the whole earth, and that which holds all things together is well aware
of what men say. Hence no man can utter injustice and not be found out, 8
nor will justice overlook him when she passes sentence. The devices of a 9
godless man will be brought to account, and a report of his words will come
before the Lord as proof of his iniquity; no muttered syllable escapes that 10
vigilant ear. Beware, then, of futile grumbling, and avoid all bitter words; 11
for even a secret whisper will not go unheeded, and a lying tongue is a
man's destruction. Do not stray from the path of life and so court death; 12
do not draw disaster on yourselves by your own actions. For God did not 13
make death, and takes no pleasure in the destruction of any living thing;
he created all things that they might have being. The creative forces of the 14
world make for life; there is no deadly poison in them. Death is not king on
earth, for justice is immortal; but godless men by their words and deeds 15 16
have asked death for his company. Thinking him their friend, they have
made a pact with him because they are fit members of his party; and so
they have wasted away.

2 They said to themselves in their deluded way: 'Our life is short and full of trouble, and when a man comes to his end there is no remedy; no
2 man was ever known to return from the grave. By mere chance were we born, and afterwards we shall be as though we had never been, for the breath in our nostrils is but a wisp of smoke; our reason is a mere spark
3 kept alive by the beating of our hearts, and when that goes out, our body
4 will turn to ashes and the breath of our life disperse like empty air. Our names will be forgotten with the passing of time, and no one will remember anything we did. Our life will blow over like the last vestige of a cloud; and as a mist is chased away by the sun's rays and overborne by its heat,
5 so will it too be dispersed. A passing shadow—such is our life, and there is
6 no postponement of our end; man's fate is sealed, and none returns. Come then, let us enjoy the good things while we can, and make full use of the
7 creation, with all the eagerness of youth. Let us have costly wines and per-
8 fumes to our heart's content, and let no flower of spring escape us. Let us
9 crown ourselves with rosebuds before they can wither. Let none of us miss his share of the good things that are ours; who cares what traces our revelry leaves behind? This is the life for us; it is our birthright.
10 'Down with the poor and honest man! Let us tread him under foot; let us show no mercy to the widow and no reverence to the grey hairs of old
11 age. For us let might be right! Weakness is proved to be good for nothing.
12 Let us lay a trap for the just man; he stands in our way, a check to us at every turn; he girds at us as law-breakers, and calls us traitors to our up-
13 bringing. He knows God, so he says; he styles himself "the servant *a* of the
14 15 Lord". He is a living condemnation of all our ideas. The very sight of him is an affliction to us, because his life is not like other people's, and his ways
16 are different. He rejects us like base coin, and avoids us and our ways as if we were filth; he says that the just die happy, and boasts that God is his
17 father. Let us test the truth of his words, let us see what will happen to
18 him in the end; for if the just man is God's son, God will stretch out a hand
19 to him and save him from the clutches of his enemies. Outrage and torment are the means to try him with, to measure his forbearance and learn
20 how long his patience lasts. Let us condemn him to a shameful death, for on his own showing he will have a protector.'
21 So they argued, and very wrong they were; blinded by their own male-
22 volence, they did not understand God's hidden plan; they never expected that holiness of life would have its recompense; they thought that inno-
23 cence had no reward. But God created man for immortality, and made him
24 the image of his own eternal self; it was the devil's spite that brought death into the world, and the experience of it is reserved for those who take his side.
3 But the souls of the just are in God's hand, and torment shall not touch
2 them. In the eyes of foolish men they seemed to be dead; their departure
3 was reckoned as defeat, and their going from us as disaster. But they are at
4 peace, for though in the sight of men they may be punished, they have a
5 sure hope of immortality; and after a little chastisement they will receive great blessings, because God has tested them and found them worthy to

*a Or* child.

be his. Like gold in a crucible he put them to the proof, and found them 6
acceptable like an offering burnt whole upon the altar. In the moment of 7
God's coming to them they will kindle into flame, like sparks that sweep
through stubble; they will be judges and rulers over the nations of the 8
world, and the Lord shall be their king for ever and ever. Those who have 9
put their trust in him shall understand that he is true, and the faithful
shall attend upon him in love; they are his chosen, and grace and mercy
shall be theirs.

But the godless shall meet with the punishment their evil thoughts 10
deserve, because they took no account of justice and rebelled against the
Lord. Wretched indeed is he who thinks nothing of wisdom and discipline; 11
such men's hopes are void, their labours unprofitable, their actions futile;
their wives are frivolous, their children criminal, their parenthood is under 12 13
a curse. No, blessed is the childless woman if she is innocent, if she has
never slept with a man in sin; at the great assize of souls she shall find a
fruitfulness of her own. Blessed is the eunuch, if he has never done any- 14
thing against the law and never harboured a wicked thought against the
Lord; he shall receive special favour in return for his faith, and a place in
the Lord's temple to delight his heart the more. Honest work bears 15
glorious fruit, and wisdom grows from roots that are imperishable. But 16
the children of adultery are like fruit that never ripens; they have sprung
from a lawless union, and will come to nothing. Even if they attain length 17
of life, they will be of no account, and at the end their old age will be without honour. If they die young, they will have no hope, no consolation in 18
the hour of judgement; the unjust generation has a hard fate in store for it. 19

It is better to be childless, provided one is virtuous; for virtue held in **4**
remembrance is a kind of immortality, because it wins recognition from
God, and from men too. They follow the good man's example while it is 2
with them, and when it is gone they mourn its loss; and through all time
virtue makes its triumphal progress, crowned with victory in the contest
for prizes that nothing can tarnish. But the swarming progeny of the wicked 3
will come to no good; none of their bastard offshoots will strike deep root
or take firm hold. For a time their branches may flourish, but as they have 4
no sure footing they will be shaken by the wind, and by the violence of the
winds uprooted. Their boughs will be snapped off half-grown, and their 5
fruit will be worthless, unripe, uneatable, and good for nothing. Children 6
engendered in unlawful union are living evidence of their parents' sin
when God brings them to account.

But the good man, even if he dies an untimely death, will be at rest. For 7 8
it is not length of life and number of years which bring the honour due to
age; if men have understanding, they have grey hairs enough, and an un- 9
spotted life is the true ripeness of age. There was once such a man who 10
pleased God, and God accepted him and took him while still living from
among sinful men. He was snatched away before his mind could be per- 11
verted by wickedness or his soul deceived by falsehood (because evil is 12
like witchcraft: it dims the radiance of good, and the waywardness of
desire unsettles an innocent mind); in a short time he came to the per- 13
fection of a full span of years. His soul was pleasing to the Lord, who 14

15 removed him early from a wicked world. The mass of men see this and give it no thought; they do not lay to heart this truth, that those whom God has chosen enjoy his grace and mercy, and that he comes to the help of his
16 holy people. Even after his death the just man will shame the godless who are still alive; youth come quickly to perfection will shame the man
17 grown old in sin. Men will see the wise man's end, without understanding what the Lord had purposed for him and why he took him into safe keep-
18 ing; they will see it and make light of him, but it is they whom the Lord will laugh to scorn. In death their bodies will be dishonoured, and among
19 the dead they will be an object of contempt for ever; for he shall strike them speechless, fling them headlong, shake them from their foundations, and make an utter desert of them; they shall be full of anguish, and all
20 memory of them shall perish. So in the day of reckoning for their sins, they will come cringing, convicted to their face by their lawless doings.

5   Then the just man shall take his stand, full of assurance, to confront
2 those who oppressed him and made light of all his sufferings; at the sight of him there will be terror and confusion, and they will be beside them-
3 selves to see him so unexpectedly safe home. Filled with remorse, groaning and gasping for breath, they will say among themselves: 'Was not this the
4 man who was once our butt, a target for our contempt? Fools that we were,
5 we held his way of life to be madness and his end dishonourable. To think that he is now counted one of the sons of God and assigned a place of his
6 own among God's people! How far we strayed from the road of truth!
7 The lamp of justice never gave us light, the sun never rose upon us. We roamed to our heart's content along the paths of wickedness and ruin, wandering through trackless deserts and ignoring the Lord's highway.
8 What good has our pride done us? What can we show for all our wealth and
9 arrogance? All those things have passed by like a shadow, like a messenger
10 galloping by; like a ship that runs through the surging sea, and when she has passed, not a trace is to be found, no track of her keel among the waves;
11 or as when a bird flies through the air, there is no sign of her passing, but with the stroke of her pinions she lashes the insubstantial breeze and parts it with the whirr and the rush of her beating wings, and so she passes
12 through it, and thereafter it bears no mark of her assault; or as when an arrow is shot at a target, the air is parted and instantly closes up again and
13 no one can tell where it passed through. So we too ceased to be, as soon as we were born; we left no token of virtue behind, and in our wickedness we
14 frittered our lives away.' The hope of a godless man is like down flying on the wind, like spindrift swept before a storm and smoke which the wind whirls away, or like the memory of a guest who stayed for one day and passed on.

15   But the just live for ever; their reward is in the Lord's keeping, and the
16 Most High has them in his care. Therefore royal splendour shall be theirs, and a fair diadem from the Lord himself; he will protect them with his right
17 hand and shield them with his arm. He will put on from head to foot the armour of his wrath, and make all creation his weapon against his enemies.
18 With the cuirass of justice on his breast, and on his head the helmet of doom
19 20 inflexible, he will take holiness for his impenetrable shield and sharpen

his relentless anger for a sword; and his whole world shall join him in the fight against his frenzied foes. The bolts of his lightning shall fly straight 21 on the mark, they shall leap upon the target as if his bow in the clouds were drawn in its full arc, and the artillery of his resentment shall let fly a fury 22 of hail. The waters of the sea shall rage over them, and the rivers wash them relentlessly away; a great tempest will arise against them, and blow 23 them away like chaff before a whirlwind. So lawlessness will make the whole world desolate, and active wickedness will overturn the thrones of princes.

## In praise of wisdom

HEAR THEN, YOU KINGS, take this to heart; learn your lesson, lords 6 of the wide world; lend your ears, you rulers of the multitude, whose 2 pride is in the myriads of your people. It is the Lord who gave you your 3 authority; your power comes from the Most High. He will put your actions to the test and scrutinize your intentions. Though you are viceroys of his 4 kingly power, you have not been upright judges; you do not stand up for the law or guide your steps by the will of God. Swiftly and terribly will he 5 descend upon you, for judgement falls relentlessly upon those in high place. The small man may find pity and forgiveness, but the powerful will 6 be called powerfully to account; for he who is all men's master is obse- 7 quious to none, and is not overawed by greatness. Small and great alike are of his making, and all are under his providence equally, but it is the 8 powerful for whom he reserves the sternest inquisition. To you then who 9 have absolute power I speak, in hope that you may learn wisdom and not go astray; those who in holiness have kept a holy course, will be accounted 10 holy, and those who have learnt that lesson will be able to make their defence. Be eager then to hear me, and long for my teaching; so you will 11 learn.

Wisdom shines bright and never fades; she is easily discerned by those 12 who love her, and by those who seek her she is found. She is quick to make 13 herself known to those who desire knowledge of her; the man who rises 14 early in search of her will not grow weary in the quest, for he will find her seated at his door. To set all one's thoughts on her is prudence in its perfect 15 shape, and to lie wakeful in her cause is the short way to peace of mind. For 16 she herself ranges in search of those who are worthy of her; on their daily path she appears to them with kindly intent, and in all their purposes meets them half-way. The true beginning of wisdom is the desire to learn, and a 17 concern for learning means love towards her; the love of her means the 18 keeping of her laws; to keep her laws is a warrant of immortality; and 19 immortality brings a man near to God. Thus the desire of wisdom leads to 20 kingly stature. If, therefore, you value your thrones and your sceptres, 21 you rulers of the nations, you must honour wisdom, so that you may reign for ever.

What wisdom is, and how she came into being, I will tell you; I will hide 22 no secret from you. From her first beginnings I will trace out her course, and bring the knowledge of her into the light of day; I will not leave the

23 truth untold. Pale envy shall not travel in my company, for the spiteful
24 man will have no share in wisdom. Wise men in plenty are the world's
25 salvation, and a prudent king is the sheet-anchor of his people. Learn what
I have to teach you, therefore, and it will be for your good.

7 I too am a mortal man like all the rest, descended from the first man,
2 who was made of dust, and in my mother's womb I was wrought into flesh
during a ten-months space, compacted in blood from the seed of her
3 husband and the pleasure that is joined with sleep. When I was born, I
breathed the common air and was laid on the earth that all men tread; and
4 the first sound I uttered, as all do, was a cry; they wrapped me up and
5 6 nursed me and cared for me. No king begins life in any other way; for all
come into life by a single path, and by a single path go out again.

7 Therefore I prayed, and prudence was given to me; I called for help,
8 and there came to me a spirit of wisdom. I valued her above sceptre and
9 throne, and reckoned riches as nothing beside her; I counted no precious
stone her equal, because all the gold in the world compared with her is but
10 a little sand, and silver worth no more than clay. I loved her more than
health and beauty; I preferred her to the light of day; for her radiance is
11 unsleeping. So all good things together came to me with her, and in her
12 hands was wealth past counting; and all was mine to enjoy, for all follows
where wisdom leads, and I was in ignorance before, that she is the begin-
13 ning of it all. What I learnt with pure intention I now share without
14 grudging, nor do I hoard for myself the wealth that comes from her. She
is an inexhaustible treasure for mankind, and those who profit by it become God's friends, commended to him by the gifts they derive from her
instruction.

15 God grant that I may speak according to his will, and that my own
thoughts may be worthy of his gifts; for even wisdom is under God's
16 direction and he corrects the wise; we and our words, prudence and know-
17 ledge and craftsmanship, all are in his hand. He himself gave me true
understanding of things as they are: a knowledge of the structure of the
18 world and the operation of the elements; the beginning and end of epochs
and their middle course; the alternating solstices and changing seasons;
19 20 the cycles of the years and the constellations; the nature of living creatures
and behaviour of wild beasts; the violent force of winds and the thoughts of
21 men; the varieties of plants and the virtues of roots. I learnt it all, hidden
22 or manifest, for I was taught by her whose skill made all things, wisdom.

For in wisdom there is a spirit intelligent and holy, unique in its kind
yet made up of many parts, subtle, free-moving, lucid, spotless, clear,
23 invulnerable,*a* loving what is good, eager, unhindered, beneficent, kindly
towards men, steadfast, unerring, untouched by care, all-powerful, all-
24 surveying, and permeating all intelligent, pure, and delicate spirits. For
wisdom moves more easily than motion itself, she pervades and permeates
25 all things because she is so pure. Like a fine mist she rises from the power
of God, a pure effluence from the glory of the Almighty; so nothing defiled
26 can enter into her by stealth. She is the brightness that streams from*b* everlasting light, the flawless mirror of the active power of God and the image

*a* invulnerable: *or* working no harm.     *b* *Or* She is the reflection of . . .

of his goodness. She is but one, yet can do everything; herself unchanging, 27
she makes all things new; age after age she enters into holy souls, and makes
them God's friends and prophets, for nothing is acceptable to God but the 28
man who makes his home with wisdom. She is more radiant than the sun, 29
and surpasses every constellation; compared with the light of day, she is
found to excel; for day gives place to night, but against wisdom no evil can 30
prevail. She spans the world in power from end to end, and orders all 8
things benignly.

Wisdom I loved; I sought her out when I was young and longed to win 2
her for my bride, and I fell in love with her beauty. She adds lustre to her 3
noble birth, because it is given her to live with God, and the Lord of all
things has accepted her. She is initiated into the knowledge that belongs 4
to God, and she decides for him what he shall do. If riches are a prize to 5
be desired in life, what is richer than wisdom, the active cause of all
things? If prudence shows itself in action, who more than wisdom is the 6
artificer of all that is? If virtue is the object of a man's affections, the fruits 7
of wisdom's labours are the virtues; temperance and prudence, justice and
fortitude, these are her teaching, and in the life of men there is nothing of
more value than these. If a man longs, perhaps, for great experience, she 8
knows the past, she can infer what is to come; she understands the subtleties
of argument and the solving of problems, she can read signs and portents,
and can foretell the outcome of events and periods. So I determined to 9
bring her home to live with me, knowing that she would be my counsellor
in prosperity and my comfort in anxiety and grief. Through her, I thought, 10
I shall win fame in the eyes of the people and honour among older men,
young though I am. When I sit in judgement, I shall prove myself acute, 11
and the great men will admire me; when I say nothing, they will wait for 12
me to speak; when I speak they will attend, and though I hold forth at
length, they will lay a finger to their lips and listen. Through her I shall 13
have immortality, and shall leave an undying memory to those who come
after me. I shall rule over many peoples, and nations will become my sub- 14
jects. Grim tyrants will be frightened when they hear of me; among my 15
own people I shall show myself a good king, and on the battlefield a brave
one. When I come home, I shall find rest with her; for there is no bitterness 16
in her company, no pain in life with her, only gladness and joy.

I thought this over in my mind, and I perceived that in kinship with 17
wisdom lies immortality and in her friendship is pure delight; that in 18
doing her work is wealth that cannot fail, to be taught in her school gives
understanding, and an honourable name is won by converse with her. So
I went about in search of some way to win her for my own. As a child I was 19
born to excellence, and a noble soul fell to my lot; or rather, I myself was 20
noble, and I entered into an unblemished body; but I saw that there 21
was no way to gain possession of her except by gift of God—and it was a
mark of understanding to know from whom that gift must come. So I
pleaded with the Lord, and from the depths of my heart I prayed to him
in these words:

God of our fathers, merciful Lord, who hast made all things by thy word, 9
and in thy wisdom hast fashioned man, to be the master of thy whole 2

3 creation, and to be steward of the world in holiness and righteousness, and
4 to administer justice with an upright heart, give me wisdom, who sits
5 beside thy throne, and do not refuse me a place among thy servants. I am
thy slave, thy slave-girl's son, a weak ephemeral man, too feeble to under-
6 stand justice and law; for let a man be ever so perfect in the eyes of his
fellow-men, if the wisdom that comes from thee is wanting, he will be of
7 no account. Thou didst choose me to be king of thy own people, and
8 judge over thy sons and daughters; thou didst tell me to build a temple on
thy sacred mountain and an altar in the city which is thy dwelling-place,
9 a copy of the sacred tabernacle prepared by thee from the beginning. And
with thee is wisdom, who is familiar with thy works and was present at the
making of the world by thee, who knows what is acceptable to thee and in
10 line with thy commandments. Send her forth from the holy heavens, and
from thy glorious throne bid her come down, so that she may labour at my
11 side and I may learn what pleases thee. For she knows and understands all
things, and will guide me prudently in all I do, and guard me in her glory.
12 So shall my life's work be acceptable, and I shall judge thy people justly,
13 and be worthy of my father's throne. For how can any man learn what is
14 God's plan? How can he apprehend what the Lord's will is? The reasoning
15 of men is feeble, and our plans are fallible; because a perishable body
weighs down the soul, and its frame of clay burdens the mind so full of
16 thoughts. With difficulty we guess even at things on earth, and laboriously
find out what lies before our feet; and who has ever traced out what is in
17 heaven? Who ever learnt to know thy purposes, unless thou hadst given
18 him wisdom and sent thy holy spirit down from heaven on high? Thus
it was that those on earth were set upon the right path, and men were
taught what pleases thee; thus were they preserved by wisdom.

## Divine wisdom in history

10 WISDOM IT WAS who kept guard over the first father of the human
race, when he alone had yet been made; she saved him after his fall,
2 3 and gave him the strength to master all things. It was because a wicked
man forsook her in his anger that he murdered his brother in a fit of rage,
4 and so destroyed himself. Through his fault the earth was covered with a
deluge, and again wisdom came to the rescue, and taught the one good man
5 to pilot his plain wooden hulk. It was she, when heathen nations leagued in
wickedness were thrown into confusion, who picked out one good man and
kept him blameless in the sight of God, giving him strength to resist his
6 pity for his child. She saved a good man from the destruction of the godless,
7 and he escaped the fire that came down on the Five Cities, cities whose
wickedness is still attested by a smoking waste, by plants whose fruit can
never ripen, and a pillar of salt standing there as a memorial of an un-
8 believing soul. Wisdom they ignored, and they suffered for it, losing the
power to recognize what is good and leaving by their lives a monument of
9 folly, such that their enormities can never be forgotten. But wisdom
10 brought her servants safely out of their troubles. It was she, when a good

man was a fugitive from his brother's anger, who guided him on the straight path; she showed him that God is king, and gave him knowledge of his holiness;[a] she prospered his labours and made his toil productive. When men in their rapacity tried to exploit him, she stood by him and made 11 him rich. She kept him safe from his enemies, and preserved him from 12 treacherous attacks; she gave him victory after a hard struggle, and taught him that godliness is the greatest power of all. It was she who refused to 13 desert a good man when he was sold as a slave; she preserved him from sin and went down into the dungeon with him, nor did she leave him when he 14 was in chains until she had brought him sceptre and kingdom and authority over his persecutors; she gave the lie to his accusers, and brought him undying fame. It was she who rescued a godfearing people, a blameless race, 15 from a nation of oppressors; she inspired a servant of the Lord, and with 16 his signs and wonders he defied formidable kings. She rewarded the labours 17 of godfearing men, she guided them on a marvellous journey and became a covering for them by day and a blaze of stars by night. She brought them 18 over the Red Sea and guided them through its deep waters; but their 19 enemies she engulfed, and cast them up again out of the fathomless deep. So good men plundered the ungodly; they sang the glories of thy holy 20 name, O Lord, and praised with one accord thy power, their champion; for wisdom taught the dumb to speak, and made the tongues of infants 21 eloquent.

Wisdom, working through a holy prophet, brought them success in all **11** they did. They made their way across an unpeopled desert and pitched 2 camp in untrodden wastes; they resisted every enemy, and beat off hostile 3 assaults. When they were thirsty they called upon thee, and water to slake 4 their thirst was given them out of the hard stone of a rocky cliff. The self- 5 same means by which their oppressors had been punished were used to help them in their hour of need: those others found their river no unfail- 6 ing stream of water, but putrid and befouled with blood, in punishment 7 for their order that all the infants should be killed, while to these thou gavest abundant water unexpectedly. So from the thirst they then endured, 8 they learnt how thou hadst punished their enemies; when they themselves 9 were put to the test, though discipline was tempered with mercy, they understood the tortures of the godless who were sentenced in anger. Thy 10 own people thou didst subject to an ordeal, warning them like a father; those others thou didst put to the torture, like a stern king passing sentence. At home and abroad, they were equally in distress, for a double misery had 11 12 come upon them, and they groaned as they recalled the past. When they 13 heard that the means of their own punishment had been used to benefit thy people, they saw thy hand in it, O Lord. The man who long ago had 14 been abandoned and exposed, whom they had rejected with contumely, became in the event the object of their wonder and admiration; their thirst was such as the godly never knew.

In return for the insensate imagination of those wicked men, which 15 deluded them into worshipping reptiles devoid of reason, and mere vermin,

[a] showed . . . holiness: *or* gave him a vision of God's realm, and knowledge of his holy angels.

16 thou didst send upon them a swarm of creatures devoid of reason to chastise them, and to teach them that the instruments of a man's sin are
17 the instruments of his punishment. For thy almighty hand, which created the world out of formless matter, was not without other resource: it could
18 have let loose upon them a host of bears or ravening lions or unknown ferocious monsters newly created, either breathing out blasts of fire, or roaring and belching smoke, or flashing terrible sparks like lightning from
19 their eyes, with power not only to exterminate them by the wounds they
20 inflicted, but by their mere appearance to kill them with fright. Even without these, a single breath would have sufficed to lay them low, with justice in pursuit and the breath of thy power to blow them away; but thou hast ordered all things by measure and number and weight.
21 Great strength is thine to exert at any moment, and the power of thy
22 arm no man can resist, for in thy sight the whole world is like a grain that
23 just tips the scale or a drop of dew alighting on the ground at dawn. But thou art merciful to all men because thou canst do all things; thou dost
24 overlook the sins of men to bring them to repentance; for all existing things are dear to thee and thou hatest nothing that thou hast created—
25 why else wouldst thou have made it? How could anything have continued in existence, had it not been thy will? How could it have endured unless
26 called into being by thee? Thou sparest all things because they are thine,
12 our lord and master who lovest all that lives; for thy imperishable breath is in them all.
2 For this reason thou dost correct offenders little by little, admonishing them and reminding them of their sins, in order that they may leave their
3 evil ways and put their trust, O Lord, in thee. For example, the ancient
4 inhabitants of thy holy land were hateful to thee for their loathsome
5 practices, their sorcery and unholy rites, ruthless murders of children,
6 cannibal feasts of human flesh and blood; they were initiates of a secret ritual in which parents slaughtered their defenceless children. Therefore
7 it was thy will to destroy them at the hand of our forefathers, so that the land which is of all lands most precious in thine eyes could receive in God's
8 children settlers worthy of it. And yet thou didst spare their lives because even they were men, sending hornets as the advance-guard of thy army
9 to exterminate them gradually. It was well within thy power to let the godly overwhelm the godless in a pitched battle, or to wipe them out in an
10 instant with cruel beasts or by one stern word. But thou didst carry out their sentence gradually to give them space for repentance, knowing well enough that they came of evil stock, their wickedness ingrained, and that
11 their way of thinking would not change to the end of time, for there was a curse on their race from the beginning.
Nor was it out of deference to anyone else that thou gavest them an
12 amnesty for their misdeeds; for to thee no one can say 'What hast thou done?' or dispute thy verdict. Who shall bring a charge against thee for destroying nations which were of thy own making? Who shall appear
13 against thee in court to plead the cause of guilty men? For there is no other god but thee; all the world is thy concern, and there is none to whom thou
14 must prove the justice of thy sentence. There is no king or other ruler who

can outface thee on behalf of those whom thou hast punished. But thou art 15
just and orderest all things justly, counting it alien to thy power to condemn a man who ought not to be punished. For thy strength is the source 16
of justice, and it is because thou art master of all that thou sparest all. Thou 17
showest thy strength when men doubt the perfection of thy power; it is
when they know it and yet are insolent that thou dost punish them. But 18
thou, with strength at thy command, judgest in mercy and rulest us in
great forbearance; for the power is thine to use when thou wilt.

By acts like these thou didst teach thy people that the just man must also 19
be kind-hearted, and thou hast filled thy sons with hope by the offer of
repentance for their sins. If thou didst use such care and such indulgence 20
even in punishing thy children's enemies, who deserved to die, granting
them time and space to get free of their wickedness, with what discrimina- 21
tion thou didst pass judgement on thy sons, to whose fathers thou hast
given sworn covenants full of the promise of good!

So we are chastened by thee, but our enemies thou dost scourge ten 22
thousand times more, so that we may lay thy goodness to heart when we sit
in judgement, and may hope for mercy when we ourselves are judged.
This is why the wicked who had lived their lives in heedless folly were 23
tormented by thee with their own abominations. They had strayed far 24
down the paths of error, taking for gods the most contemptible and hideous
creatures, deluded like thoughtless children. And so, as though they were 25
mere babes who have not learnt reason, thou didst visit on them a sentence
that made them ridiculous; but those who do not take warning from such 26
derisive correction will experience the full weight of divine judgement.
They were indignant at their own sufferings, but finding themselves 27
chastised through the very creatures they had taken to be gods, they
recognized that the true God was he whom they had long ago refused to
know. Thus the full rigour of condemnation descended on them.

## The evils of idolatry

WHAT BORN FOOLS all men were who lived in ignorance of God, 13
who from the good things before their eyes could not learn to know
him who really is, and failed to recognize the artificer though they observed
his works! Fire, wind, swift air, the circle of the starry signs, rushing water, 2
or the great lights in heaven that rule the world—these they accounted
gods. If it was through delight in the beauty of these things that men sup- 3
posed them gods, they ought to have understood how much better is the
Lord and Master of it all; for it was by the prime author of all beauty that
they were created. If it was through astonishment at their power and 4
influence, men should have learnt from these how much more powerful is
he who made them. For the greatness and beauty of created things give us 5
a corresponding idea of their Creator. Yet these men are not greatly to be 6
blamed, for when they go astray they may be seeking God and really wishing to find him. Passing their lives among his works and making a close 7
study of them, they are persuaded by appearances because what they see is

8 9 so beautiful. Yet even so they do not deserve to be excused, for with enough understanding to speculate about the universe, why did they not sooner discover the Lord and Master of it all?

10     The really degraded ones are those whose hopes are set on dead things, who give the name of gods to the work of human hands, to gold and silver fashioned by art into images of living creatures, or to a useless stone carved

11 by a craftsman long ago. Suppose some skilled woodworker fells with his saw a convenient tree and deftly strips off all the bark, then works it up

12 elegantly into some vessel suitable for everyday use; and the pieces left

13 over from his work he uses to cook his food, and eats his fill. But among the waste there is one useless piece, crooked and full of knots, and this he takes and carves to occupy his idle moments, and shapes it with leisurely skill

14 into the image of a human being; or else he gives it the form of some contemptible creature, painting it with vermilion and raddling its surface with

15 red paint, so that every flaw in it is painted over. Then he makes a suitable

16 shrine for it and fixes it on the wall, securing it with iron nails. It is he who has to take the precautions on its behalf to save it from falling, for he knows

17 that it cannot fend for itself : it is only an image, and needs help. Yet he prays to it about his possessions and his wife and children, and feels no

18 shame in addressing this lifeless object; for health he appeals to a thing that is feeble, for life he prays to a dead thing, for aid he implores something utterly incapable, for a prosperous journey something that has not even

19 the use of its legs; in matters of earnings and business and success in handicraft he asks effectual help from a thing whose hands are entirely ineffectual.

**14**     The man, again, who gets ready for a voyage, and plans to set his course through the wild waves, cries to a piece of wood more fragile than the ship

2 which carries him. Desire for gain invented the ship, and the shipwright

3 with his wisdom built it;[a] but it is thy providence, O Father, that is its pilot, for thou hast given it a pathway through the sea and a safe course

4 among the waves, showing that thou canst save from every danger, so that

5 even a man without skill can put to sea. It is thy will that the things made by thy wisdom should not lie idle; and therefore men trust their lives even to the frailest spar, and passing through the billows on a mere raft come

6 safe to land. Even in the beginning, when the proud race of giants was being brought to an end, the hope of mankind escaped on a raft and,

7 piloted by thy hand, bequeathed to the world a new breed of men. For a

8 blessing is on the wooden vessel through which right has prevailed; but the wooden idol made by human hands is accursed, and so is its maker—he because he made it, and the perishable thing because it was called a god.

9 10 Equally hateful to God are the godless man and his ungodliness; the doer and the deed shall both be punished.

11     And so retribution shall fall upon the idols of the heathen, because though part of God's creation they have been made into an abomination,

12 to make men stumble and to catch the feet of fools. The invention of idols is the root of immorality; they are a contrivance which has blighted human

13 life. They did not exist from the beginning, nor will they be with us for

    *a Other witnesses read* and wisdom was the shipwright that built it.

ever; superstition brought them into the world, and for good reason a 14
short sharp end is in store for them.

Some father, overwhelmed with untimely grief for the child suddenly 15
taken from him, made an image of the child and honoured thenceforth as
a god what was once a dead human being, handing on to his household the
observance of rites and ceremonies. Then this impious custom, established 16
by the passage of time, was observed as a law. Or again graven images came
to be worshipped at the command of despotic princes. When men could 17
not do honour to such a prince before his face because he lived far away,
they made a likeness of that distant face, and produced a visible image of the
king they sought to honour, eager to pay court to the absent prince as
though he were present. Then the cult grows in fervour as those to whom 18
the king is unknown are spurred on by ambitious craftsmen. In his desire, 19
it may be, to please the monarch, a craftsman skilfully distorts the likeness
into an ideal form, and the common people, beguiled by the beauty of the 20
workmanship, take for an object of worship him whom lately they honoured
as a man. So this becomes a trap for living men: enslaved by mischance or 21
misgovernment, men confer on stocks and stones the name that none
may share.

Then, not content with gross error in their knowledge of God, men live 22
in the constant warfare of ignorance and call this monstrous evil peace.
They perform ritual murders of children and secret ceremonies and the 23
frenzied orgies of unnatural cults; the purity of life and marriage is 24
abandoned; and a man treacherously murders his neighbour or corrupts
his wife and breaks his heart. All is in chaos—bloody murder, theft and 25
fraud, corruption, treachery, riot, perjury, honest men driven to dis- 26
traction; ingratitude, moral corruption, sexual perversion, breakdown of
marriage, adultery, debauchery. For the worship of idols, whose names it 27
is wrong even to mention, is the beginning, cause, and end of every evil.
Men either indulge themselves to the point of madness, or produce 28
inspired utterance which is all lies, or live dishonest lives, or break their
oath without scruple. They perjure themselves and expect no harm be- 29
cause the idols they trust in are lifeless. On two counts judgement will over- 30
take them: because in their devotion to idols they have thought wrongly
about God, and because, in their contempt for religion, they have deliberately perjured themselves. It is not any power in what they swear by, but 31
the nemesis of sin, that always pursues the transgression of the wicked.

But thou, our God, art kind and true and patient, a merciful ruler of all **15**
that is. For even if we sin, we are thine; we acknowledge thy power. But 2
we will not sin, because we know that we are accounted thine. To know 3
thee is the whole of righteousness, and to acknowledge thy power is the
root of immortality. We have not been led astray by the perverted inven- 4
tions of human skill or the barren labour of painters, by some gaudy painted
shape, the sight of which arouses in fools a passionate desire for a mere 5
image without life or breath. They are in love with evil and deserve to 6
trust in nothing better, those who do these evil things or hanker after
them or worship them.

For a potter kneading his clay laboriously moulds every vessel for our 7

use, but out of the self-same clay he fashions without distinction the pots that are to serve for honourable uses and the opposite; and what the pur-
8 pose of each one is to be, the moulder of the clay decides. And then with ill-directed toil he makes a false god out of the same clay, this man who not long before was himself fashioned out of earth and soon returns to the place whence he was taken, when the living soul that was lent to him must be
9 repaid. His concern is not that he must one day fall sick or that his span of life is short; but he must vie with goldsmiths and silversmiths and copy the bronze-workers, and he thinks it does him credit to make counterfeits.
10 His heart is ashes, his hope worth less than common earth, and his life
11 cheaper than his own clay, because he did not recognize by whom he him-self was moulded, or who it was that inspired him with an active soul and
12 breathed into him the breath of life. No, he reckons our life a game, and our existence a market where money can be made; 'one must get a living',
13 he says, 'by fair means or foul'. But this man knows better than anyone that he is doing wrong, this maker of fragile pots and idols from the same earthy stuff.
14    The greatest fools of all, and worse than infantile, were the enemies and
15 oppressors of thy people, for they supposed all their heathen idols to be gods, although they have eyes that cannot see, nostrils that cannot draw breath, ears that cannot hear, fingers that cannot feel, and feet that are
16 useless for walking. It was a man who made them; one who draws borrowed breath gave them their shape. But no human being has the power to shape
17 a god like himself: he is only mortal, but what he makes with his impious hands is dead; and so he is better than the objects of his worship, for he is at least alive—they never can be.
18    Moreover, these men worship animals, the most revolting animals. Com-pared with the rest of the brute creation, their divinities are the least intel-
19 ligent. Even as animals they have no beauty to make them desirable; when God approved and blessed his work, they were left out.

## The pattern of divine justice

16 AND SO THE OPPRESSORS were fittingly chastised by creatures like
2 these: they were tormented by swarms of vermin. But while they were punished, thou didst make provision for thy people, sending quails for
3 them to eat, an unwonted food to satisfy their hunger; for thy purpose was that whereas those others, hungry as they were, should turn in loathing even from necessary food because the creatures sent upon them were so disgusting, thy people after a short spell of scarcity should enjoy unwonted
4 delicacies. It was right that the scarcity falling on the oppressors should be inexorable, and that thy people should learn by brief experience how their
5 enemies were tormented. Even when fierce and furious snakes attacked thy people and the bites of writhing serpents were spreading death, thy
6 anger did not continue to the bitter end; their short trouble was sent them as a lesson, and they were given a symbol *a* of salvation to remind them of

*a* Or pledge.

the requirements of thy law. For any man who turned towards it was 7
saved, not by the thing he looked upon but by thee, the saviour of all. In 8
this way thou didst convince our enemies that thou art the deliverer from
every evil. Those other men died from the bite of locusts and flies, and no 9
remedy was found to save their lives, because it was fitting for them to be
chastised by such creatures. But thy sons did not succumb to the fangs of 10
snakes, however venomous, because thy mercy came to their aid and healed
them. It was to remind them of thy utterances that they were bitten and 11
quickly recovered; it was for fear they might fall into deep forgetfulness
and become unresponsive to thy kindness. For it was neither herb nor 12
poultice that cured them, but thy all-healing word, O Lord. Thou hast 13
the power of life and death, thou bringest a man down to the gates of death
and up again. Man in his wickedness may kill, but he cannot bring back 14
the breath of life that has gone forth nor release a soul that death has
arrested.

But from thy hand there is no escape; for godless men who refused to 15 16
acknowledge thee were scourged by thy mighty arm, pursued by extraordinary storms of rain and hail in relentless torrents, and utterly destroyed
by fire. Strangest of all, in water, that quenches everything, the fire burned 17
more fiercely; creation itself fights to defend the godly. At one time the 18
flame was moderated, so that it should not burn up the living creatures
inflicted on the godless, who were to learn from this that it was by God's
justice that they were pursued; at another time it blazed even under water 19
with more than the natural power of fire, to destroy the produce of a sinful
land. By contrast, thy own people were given angels' food, and thou didst 20
send them from heaven, without labour of their own, bread ready to eat,
rich in delight of every kind and suited to every taste. The sustenance thou 21
didst supply showed thy sweetness towards thy children, and the bread,
serving the desire of each man who ate it, was changed into what he wished.
Its snow and ice resisted fire and did not melt, to teach them that whereas 22
their enemies' crops had been destroyed by fire that blazed in the hail and
flashed through the teeming rain, that same fire had now forgotten its own 23
power, in order that the godly might be fed.

For creation, serving thee its maker, exerts its power to punish the godless 24
and relaxes into benevolence towards those who trust in thee. And so it was 25
at that time too: it adapted itself endlessly in the service of thy universal
bounty, according to the desire of thy suppliants. So thy sons, O Lord, 26
whom thou hast chosen, were to learn that it is not the growing of crops by
which mankind is nourished, but it is thy word that sustains those who
trust in thee. That substance, which fire did not destroy, simply melted 27
away when warmed by the sun's first rays, to teach us that we must rise 28
before the sun to give thee thanks and pray to thee as daylight dawns. The 29
hope of an ungrateful man will melt like the hoar-frost of winter, and drain
away like water that runs to waste.

Great are thy judgements and hard to expound; and thus it was that un- **17**
instructed souls went astray. Thus heathen men imagined that they could 2
lord it over thy holy people; but, prisoners of darkness and captives of
unending night, they lay each immured under his own roof, fugitives from

3 eternal providence. Thinking that their secret sins might escape detection beneath a dark pall of oblivion, they lay in disorder, dreadfully afraid,
4 terrified by apparitions. For the dark corner that held them offered no refuge from fear, but loud unnerving noises roared around them, and
5 phantoms with downcast unsmiling faces passed before their eyes. No fire, however great, had force enough to give them light, nor had the
6 brilliant flaming stars strength to illuminate that hideous darkness. There shone upon them only a blaze, of no man's making, that terrified them, and in their panic they thought the real world even worse than that imagin-
7 ary sight. The tricks of the sorcerers' art failed, and all their boasted wisdom
8 was exposed and put to shame; for the very men who profess to drive away fear and trouble from sick souls were themselves sick with dread
9 that made them ridiculous. Even if nothing frightful was there to terrify them, yet having once been scared by the advancing vermin and the hiss-
10 ing serpents, they collapsed in terror, refusing even to look upon the air
11 from which there can be no escape.*a* For wickedness proves a cowardly thing when condemned by an inner witness, and in the grip of conscience
12 gives way to forebodings of disaster. Fear is nothing but an abandonment
13 of the aid that comes from reason; and hope, defeated by this inward weakness, capitulates before ignorance of the cause by which the torment comes.

14 So all that night, which really had no power against them because it came upon them from the powerless depths of hell, they slept the same
15 haunted sleep, now harried by portentous spectres, now paralysed by the treachery of their own souls; sudden and unforeseen, fear came upon them.
16 Thus a man would fall down where he stood and be held in durance,
17 locked in a prison that had no bars. Farmer or shepherd or labourer toiling in the wilds, he was caught, and awaited the inescapable doom; the same
18 chain of darkness bound all alike. The whispering breeze, the sweet melody of birds in spreading branches, the steady beat of water that rushes
19 by, the headlong crash of rocks falling, the racing of creatures as they bound along unseen, the roar of fierce wild beasts, or echo reverberating from
20 hollows in the hills—all these sounds paralysed them with fear. The whole world was bathed in the bright light of day, and went about its tasks un-
21 hindered; those men alone were overspread with heavy night, fit image of the darkness that awaited them; and heavier than the darkness was the burden each was to himself.

**18** But for thy holy ones there shone a great light. And so their enemies, hearing their voices but not seeing them, counted them happy because
2 they had not suffered like themselves, gave thanks for their forbearance under provocation, and begged as a favour that they should part company.
3 Accordingly, thy gift was a pillar of fire to be the guide of their uncharted journey, a sun that would not scorch them on their glorious expedition.
4 Their enemies did indeed deserve to lose the light of day and be kept prisoners in darkness, for they had kept in durance thy sons, through whom the imperishable light of the law was to be given to the world.
5 They planned to kill the infant children of thy holy people, but when one

*a Or there is no need to escape.*

child had been exposed to death and rescued, thou didst deprive them of all their children in requital, and drown them all together in the swelling waves. Of that night our forefathers were given warning in advance, so 6 that, having sure knowledge, they might be heartened by the promises which they trusted. Thy people were looking for the deliverance of the 7 godly and the destruction of their enemies; for thou didst use the same 8 means to punish our enemies and to make us glorious when we heard thy call. The devout children of a virtuous race were offering sacrifices in 9 secret, and covenanted with one consent to keep the law of God and to share alike in the same blessings and the same dangers, and they were already singing their sacred ancestral songs of praise. In discordant con- 10 trast there came an outcry from their enemies, as piteous lamentation for their children spread abroad. Master and slave were punished together 11 with the same penalty; king and common man suffered the same fate. All 12 alike had their dead, past counting, struck down by one common form of death; there were not enough living even to bury the dead; at one stroke the most precious of their offspring had perished. Relying on their magic 13 arts, they had scouted all warnings; but when they saw their first-born dead, they confessed that thy people have God as their father.

All things were lying in peace and silence, and night in her swift course 14 was half spent, when thy almighty Word leapt from thy royal throne in 15 heaven into the midst of that doomed land like a relentless warrior, bear- 16 ing the sharp sword of thy inflexible decree, and stood and filled it all with death, his head touching the heavens, his feet on earth. At once night- 17 mare phantoms appalled them, and unlooked-for fears set upon them; and as they flung themselves to the ground half dead, one here, one there, 18 they confessed the reason for their deaths; for the dreams that tormented 19 them had taught them before they died, so that they should not die ignorant of the reason why they suffered.

The godly also had a taste of death when a multitude were struck down 20 in the wilderness; but the divine wrath did not long continue. A blameless 21 man was quick to be their champion, bearing the weapons of his priestly ministry, prayer and the incense that propitiates; he withstood the divine anger and set a limit to the disaster, thus showing that he was thy servant. He overcame the avenging fury not by bodily strength or force of arms; by 22 words he subdued the avenger, appealing to the sworn covenants made with our forefathers. When the dead had already fallen in heaps one on 23 another, he interposed himself and beat back the divine wrath, barring its line of attack upon the living. On his long-skirted robe the whole world 24 was represented; the glories of the fathers were engraved on his four rows of precious stones; and thy majesty was in the diadem upon his head. To 25 these the destroyer yielded, for these made him afraid; only to taste his wrath had been enough.

But the godless were pursued by pitiless anger to the bitter end, for **19** God knew their future also: how after allowing thy people to depart, and 2 even urging their departure, they would change their minds and set out in pursuit. While they were still mourning, still lamenting at the graves of 3 their dead, they rushed into another foolish decision, and pursued as

4 fugitives those whom they had begged to leave. For the fate they had merited was drawing them on to this conclusion and made them forget what had happened, so that they might suffer the torments still needed to
5 complete their punishment, and that thy people might achieve an incredible journey, and that their enemies might meet an outlandish death.
6 The whole creation, with all its elements, was refashioned in subservience
7 to thy commands, so that thy servants might be preserved unscathed. Men gazed at the cloud that overshadowed the camp, at dry land emerging where before was only water, at an open road leading out of the Red Sea,
8 and a grassy plain in place of stormy waves, across which the whole nation passed, under the shelter of thy hand, after all the marvels they had seen.
9 They were like horses at pasture, like skipping lambs, as they praised thee,
10 O Lord, by whom they were rescued. For they still remembered their life in a foreign land: how instead of cattle the earth bred lice, and instead of
11 fish the river spewed up swarms of frogs; and how, after that, they had seen a new sort of bird when, driven by greed, they had begged for delicacies to
12 eat, and for their relief quails came up from the sea.
13 So punishment came upon those sinners, not unheralded by violent thunderbolts. They suffered justly for their own wickedness, for they had
14 raised bitter hatred of strangers to a new pitch. There had been others who refused to welcome strangers when they came to them, but these made
15 slaves of guests who were their benefactors. There is indeed a judgement
16 awaiting those who treated foreigners as enemies; but these, after a festal welcome, oppressed with hard labour men who had earlier shared their
17 rights. They were struck with blindness also, like the men at the door of the one good man, when yawning darkness fell upon them and each went groping for his own doorway.
18 For as the notes of a lute can make various tunes with different names though each retains its own pitch, so the elements combined among themselves in different ways, as can be accurately inferred from the observa-
19 tion of what happened. Land animals took to the water and things that
20 swim migrated to dry land; fire retained its normal power even in water,
21 and water forgot its quenching properties. Flames on the other hand failed to consume the flesh of perishable creatures that walked in them, and the substance of heavenly food, like ice and prone to melt, no longer melted.
22 In everything, O Lord, thou hast made thy people great and glorious and hast not neglected in every time and place to be their helper.

# ECCLESIASTICUS

## OR

### THE WISDOM OF JESUS SON OF SIRACH

## Preface

A LEGACY OF GREAT VALUE has come to us through the law, the prophets, and the writers who followed in their steps, and for this Israel's traditions of discipline and wisdom deserve recognition. It is the duty of those who study the scriptures not only to become expert themselves, but also to use their scholarship for the benefit of the outside world through both the spoken and the written word. So my grandfather Jesus, who had applied himself industriously to the study of the law, the prophets, and the other writings of our ancestors, and had gained a considerable proficiency in them, was moved to compile a book of his own on the themes of discipline and wisdom, so that, with this further help, scholars might make greater progress in their studies by living as the law directs.

You are asked then to read with sympathetic attention, and make allowances if, in spite of all the devoted work I have put into the translation, some of the expressions appear inadequate. For it is impossible for a translator to find precise equivalents for the original Hebrew in another language. Not only with this book, but with the law, the prophets, and the rest of the writings, it makes no small difference to read them in the original.

When I came to Egypt and settled there in the thirty-eighth year of[a] the reign of King Euergetes, I found great scope for education; and I thought it very necessary to spend some energy and labour on the translation of this book. Ever since then I have been applying my skill night and day to complete it, and to publish it for the use of those who have made their home in a foreign land, and wish to become scholars by training themselves to live according to the law.

---

[a] *Or* there at the age of thirty-eight in . . .

## The ways of wisdom

1 ALL WISDOM is from the Lord;
   wisdom is with him for ever.

2 Who can count the sand of the sea,
   the drops of rain, or the days of unending time?

3 Who can measure the height of the sky,
   the breadth of the earth, or the depth of the abyss[a]?

4 Wisdom was first of all created things;
   intelligent purpose has been there from the beginning.[b]

6 Who has laid bare the root of wisdom?
   Who has understood her subtlety?[c]

8 One alone is wise, the Lord most terrible,
   seated upon his throne.

9 It is he who created her, surveyed and measured her,
   and infused her into all his works.

10 To all mankind he has given her in some measure,
   but in plenty to those who love him.


11 THE FEAR OF THE LORD brings honour and pride,
   cheerfulness and a garland of joy.

12 The fear of the Lord gladdens the heart;
   it brings cheerfulness and joy and long life.

13 Whoever fears the Lord will be prosperous at the last;
   blessings will be his on the day of his death.

14 The essence of wisdom is the fear of the Lord;
   she is created with the faithful in their mother's womb,

15 she has built an everlasting home among men,
   and will keep faith with their descendants.

16 Those who fear the Lord have their fill of wisdom;
   she gives them deep draughts of her wine.

17 She stocks her home with all that the heart can desire
   and her storehouses with her produce.

18 Wisdom's garland is the fear of the Lord,
   flowering with peace and health.

19 She showers down knowledge and ability,
   and bestows high honour on those who hold fast to her.

20 Wisdom is rooted in the fear of the Lord,
   and long life grows on her branches.[d]

22 Unjust rage can never be excused;
   when anger tips the scale it is a man's downfall.

[a] *Some witnesses add* or wisdom.   [b] *Some witnesses add* (5) The fountain of wisdom is God's word on high, and her ways are the eternal commandments.   [c] *Some witnesses add* (7) Who has discovered all that wisdom knows, or understood her wealth of experience?   [d] *Some witnesses add* (21) The fear of the Lord drives away sins, and wherever it dwells it averts his anger.

Until the right time comes, a patient man restrains himself,            23
and afterwards cheerfulness breaks through again;
until the right moment he keeps his thoughts to himself,            24
and later his good sense is on everyone's lips.
In wisdom's store are wise proverbs,            25
but godliness is detestable to a sinner.
If you long for wisdom, keep the commandments,            26
and the Lord will give it you in plenty.
For the fear of the Lord is wisdom and discipline;            27
fidelity and gentleness are his delight.
Do not disregard the fear of the Lord            28
or approach him without sincerity.
Do not act a part before the eyes of the world;            29
keep guard over your lips.
Never be arrogant, for fear you fall            30
and bring disgrace on yourself;
the Lord will reveal your secrets
and humble you before the assembly,
because it was not the fear of the Lord that prompted you, *a*
but your heart was full of hypocrisy.


MY SON, if you aspire to be a servant of the Lord,            **2**
prepare yourself for testing.
Set a straight course, be resolute,            2
and do not lose your head in time of disaster.
Hold fast to him, never desert him,            3
if you would end your days in prosperity.
Bear every hardship that is sent you;            4
be patient under humiliation, whatever the cost.
For gold is assayed by fire,            5
and the Lord proves men in the furnace of humiliation.
Trust him and he will help you;            6
steer a straight course and set your hope on him.

You who fear the Lord, wait for his mercy;            7
do not stray or you will fall.
You who fear the Lord, trust in him,            8
and you shall not miss your reward.
You who fear the Lord, expect prosperity,            9
lasting happiness and favour.
Consider the past generations and see:            10
was anyone who trusted the Lord ever disappointed?
was anyone who stood firm in the fear of him ever deserted?
did he ever neglect anyone who prayed to him?
For the Lord is compassionate and merciful;            11
he forgives sins and comes to the rescue in time of trouble.

> *a* Or because you had no concern for the fear of the Lord.

12 Woe to faint hearts and nerveless hands
and to the sinner who leads a double life!

13 Woe to the feeble-hearted! they have no faith,
and therefore shall go unprotected.

14 Woe to you who have given up the struggle!
What will you do when the Lord's reckoning comes?

15 Those who fear the Lord never disobey his words;
and all who love him keep to his ways.

16 Those who fear the Lord try to do his will;
and all who love him steep themselves in the law.

17 Those who fear the Lord are always prepared;
they humble themselves before him and say:

18 'We will fall into the hands of the Lord, not into the hands of
men,
for his majesty is equalled by his mercy.'

3 CHILDREN, LISTEN TO ME, for I am your father;
do what I tell you, if you wish to be safe.

2 It is the Lord's will that a father should be honoured by his children,
and a mother's rights recognized by her sons.

3 Respect for a father atones for sins,

4 and to honour your mother is to lay up a fortune.

5 A son who respects his father will be made happy by his own children;
when he prays, he will be heard.

6 He who honours his father will have a long life,
and he who obeys the Lord comforts his mother;

7 he obeys his parents as though he were their slave.

8 My son, honour your father by word and deed,
so that you may receive his blessing.

9 For a father's blessing strengthens his children's houses,
but a mother's curse uproots their foundations.

10 Never seek honour at the cost of discredit to your father;
how can his discredit bring honour to you?

11 A man is honoured if his father is honoured,
and neglect of a mother is a disgrace to children.

12 My son, look after your father in his old age;
do nothing to vex him as long as he lives.

13 Even if his mind fails, make allowances for him,
and do not despise him because you are in your prime.

14 If you support your father it will never be forgotten,
but be put to your credit against your sins;

15 when you are in trouble, it will be remembered in your favour,
and your sins will melt away like frost in the sunshine.

16 To leave your father in the lurch is like blasphemy,
and to provoke your mother's anger is to call down the Lord's curse.

My son, be unassuming in all you do,                          17
and those the Lord approves will love you.
The greater you are, the humbler you must be,                 18
and the Lord will show you favour.[a]
For his power is great,                                       20
and he is honoured by the humble.
Do not pry into things too hard for you                       21
or examine what is beyond your reach.
Meditate on the commandments you have been given;            22
what the Lord keeps secret is no concern of yours.
Do not busy yourself with matters that are beyond you;       23
even what has been shown you is above man's grasp.
Many have been led astray by their speculations,             24
and false conjectures have impaired their judgement.[b]

Stubbornness will come to a bad end,                          26
and the man who flirts with danger will lose his life.
Stubbornness brings a load of troubles;                      27
the sinner piles sin on sin.
When calamity befalls the arrogant, there is no cure;        28
wickedness is too deėply rooted in him.

A sensible man will take a proverb to heart;                 29
an attentive ear is the desire of the wise.
As water quenches a blazing fire,                            30
so almsgiving atones for sin.
He who repays a good turn is mindful of the future;          31
when he falls he will find support.

My son, do not cheat a poor man of his livelihood            **4**
or keep him waiting with hungry eyes.
Do not tantalize a starving man                               2
or drive him to desperation in his need.
If a man is desperate, do not add to his troubles            3
or keep him waiting for the charity he asks.
Do not reject the appeal of a man in distress                4
or turn your back on the poor;
when he begs for alms, do not look the other way              5
and so give him reason to curse you,
for if he curses you in his bitterness,                       6
his Maker will listen to his prayer.
Make yourself popular in the assembly,                        7
and show deference to the great.
When a poor man speaks to you, give him your attention        8
and answer his greeting politely.

[a] *Some witnesses add* (19) Many are high and mighty; but he reveals his secrets to the modest.      [b] *Some witnesses add* (25) Without eyes you will be deprived of light; if you have no knowledge, do not lay claim to it.

9 Rescue the downtrodden from the oppressor,
and be firm when giving a verdict.
10 Be a father to orphans
and like a husband to their mother;
then the Most High will call you his son,
and his love for you will be greater than a mother's.

11 WISDOM RAISES her sons to greatness
and cares for those who seek her.
12 To love her is to love life;
to rise early for her sake is to be filled with joy.
13 The man who attains her will win recognition;
the Lord's blessing rests upon every place she enters.
14 To serve her is to serve the Holy One,
and the Lord loves those who love her.
15 Her dutiful servant will give laws to the heathen,
and because he listens to her, his home will be secure.
16 If he trusts her, he will possess her
and bequeath her to his descendants.
17 At first she will lead him by devious ways,
filling him with craven fears.
Her discipline will be a torment to him,
and her decrees a hard test
until he trusts her with all his heart.[a]
18 Then she will come straight back to him again and gladden him,
and reveal her secrets to him.
19 But if he strays from her, she will desert him
and abandon him to his fate.

20 WATCH YOUR CHANCE and defend yourself against wrong,
and do not be over-modest in your own cause;
21 for there is a modesty that leads to sin,
as well as a modesty that brings honour and favour.
22 Do not be untrue to yourself in deference to another,
or so diffident that you fail in your duty.
23 Never remain silent when a word might put things right,
24 for wisdom shows itself by speech,
and a man's education must find expression in words.
25 Do not argue against the truth,
but have a proper sense of your own ignorance.
26 Never be ashamed to admit your mistakes,
nor try to swim against the current.
27 Do not let yourself be a doormat to a fool
or curry favour with the powerful.
28 Fight to the death for truth,
and the Lord God will fight on your side.

[a] *Or* until she can trust him.

Do not be forward in your speech  29
but slack and neglectful in your work.
Do not play the lion in your home  30
or swagger *a* among your servants.
Do not keep your hand open to receive  31
and close it when it is your turn to give.

Do not rely upon your money  **5**
and say, 'I am independent.'
Do not yield to every impulse you can gratify  2
or follow the desires of your heart.
Do not say, 'I am my own master';  3
you may be sure the Lord will call you to account.
Do not say, 'I sinned, yet nothing happened to me';  4
it is only that the Lord is very patient.
Do not be so confident of pardon  5
that you sin again and again.
Do not say, 'His mercy is so great,  6
he will pardon my sins, however many.'
To him belong both mercy and wrath,
and sinners feel the weight of his retribution.
Come back to the Lord without delay;  7
do not put it off from one day to the next,
or suddenly the Lord's wrath will be upon you,
and you will perish at the time of reckoning.

Do not rely upon ill-gotten gains,  8
for they will not avail in time of calamity.
Do not winnow in every wind  9
or walk along every path. *b*
Stand firmly by what you know  10
and be consistent in what you say.
Be quick to listen,  11
but take time over your answer.
Answer a man if you know what to say,  12
but if not, hold your tongue.
Honour or shame can come through speaking,  13
and a man's tongue may be his downfall.
Do not get a name for being a gossip  14
or lay traps with your tongue;
for as there is shame in store for the thief,
so there is harsh censure for duplicity.
Avoid the little faults as well as the great.  15
Do not change from a friend into an enemy,  **6**
for a bad name brings shame and disgrace,
and this is the mark of duplicity.

*a Possible meaning; Gk. obscure.*  *b Gk. adds* this is the mark of duplicity (*from 6. 1*).

2   Never be roused by violent passions;
    they will tear you apart like a bull,[a]

3   they will eat up your leaves, destroy your fruit,
    and leave you a withered tree.

4   Evil passion ruins the man who harbours it,
    to the delight of his gloating enemies.

5   Pleasant words win many friends,
    and an affable manner makes acquaintance easy.

6   Accept a greeting from everyone,
    but advice from only one in a thousand.

7   When you make a friend, begin by testing him,
    and be in no hurry to trust him.

8   Some friends are loyal when it suits them
    but desert you in time of trouble.

9   Some friends turn into enemies
    and shame you by making the quarrel public.

10  Another sits at your table,
    but is nowhere to be found in time of trouble;

11  when you are prosperous, he will be your second self
    and make free with your servants,

12  but if you come down in the world, he will turn against you
    and you will not see him again.

13  Hold your enemies at a distance,
    and keep a wary eye on your friends.

14  A faithful friend is a secure shelter;
    whoever finds one has found a treasure.

15  A faithful friend is beyond price;
    his worth is more than money can buy.

16  A faithful friend is an elixir of life,
    found only by those who fear the Lord.

17  The man who fears the Lord keeps his friendships in repair,
    for he treats his neighbour as himself.


18  MY SON, seek wisdom's discipline while you are young,
    and when your hair is white, you will find her still.

19  Come to her like a farmer ploughing and sowing;
    then wait for her plentiful harvest.
    If you cultivate her, you will labour for a little while,
    but soon you will be eating her crops.

20  How harsh she seems to the undisciplined!
    The fool cannot abide her;

21  like a stone she is a burden that tests his strength,
    but he is quick to toss her aside.

22  Wisdom well deserves her name,
    for she is not accessible to many.

[a]  they . . . bull: *probable meaning; Gk. and Heb. both obscure.*

Listen, my son, accept my judgement; 23
do not reject my advice.
Put your feet in wisdom's fetters 24
and your neck into her collar.
Stoop to carry her on your shoulders 25
and do not chafe at her bonds.
Come to her whole-heartedly, 26
and keep to her ways with all your might.
Follow her track, and she will make herself known to you; 27
once you have grasped her, never let her go.
In the end you will find the relief she offers; 28
she will transform herself into joy for you.
Her fetters will become your strong defence 29
and her collar a gorgeous robe.
Her yoke*a* is a golden ornament 30
and her bonds a purple cord.
You shall put her on like a gorgeous robe 31
and wear her like a splendid crown.

If it is your wish, my son, you can be trained; 32
if you give your mind to it, you can become clever;
if you enjoy listening, you will learn; 33
if you are attentive, you will grow wise.
When you stand among your elders, 34
decide who is wise and join him.
Listen gladly to every godly argument 35
and see that no wise proverb escapes you.
If you discover a wise man, rise early to visit him; 36
let your feet wear out his doorstep.
Ponder the decrees of the Lord 37
and study his commandments at all times.
He will strengthen your mind
and grant your desire for wisdom.
Do no evil, and evil will not come upon you; 7
turn away from wrong, and it will avoid you. 2
Do not sow in the furrows of injustice, 3
for fear of reaping a sevenfold crop.

Do not ask the Lord for high office 4
or the king for preferment.
Do not pose as a righteous man before the Lord 5
or play the sage in the king's presence.
Do not aspire to be a judge, 6
unless you have the strength to put an end to injustice;
for you may be intimidated by a man of rank
and so compromise your integrity.
Do not commit an offence against the community 7
and so incur a public disgrace.

*a So Heb.; Gk.* Upon her.

8    Do not pile sin upon sin,
for even one is enough to make you guilty.

9    Do not say, 'My liberality will be taken into account;
when I make an offering to God Most High he will accept it.'

10   Do not grow weary of praying
or neglect the giving of charity.

11   Never laugh at a man in his bitter humiliation,
for there is One who both humbles and exalts.

12   Do not plot to deceive your brother
or pay back a friend in his own coin.

13   Refuse ever to tell a lie;
it is a habit from which no good comes.

14   Never be garrulous among your elders
or repeat yourself when you pray.

15   Do not resent manual labour or farm-work,
for it was ordained by the Most High.

16   Do not enlist in the ranks of sinners;
remember that retribution will not delay.

17   Humble yourself to the uttermost,
for the doom of the impious is fire and worms.

18   Do not part with a friend for gain,[a]
or a true brother for all the gold of Ophir.

19   Do not lose the chance of a wise and good wife,
for her attractions are worth more than gold.

20   Do not ill-treat a slave who works honestly
or a hired servant whose heart is in his work.

21   Love a good slave from the bottom of your heart
and do not grudge him his freedom.

22   Have you cattle? Take care of them,
and if they bring you profit, keep them.

23   Have you sons? Discipline them
and break them in from their earliest years.

24   Have you daughters? See that they are chaste,
and do not be too lenient with them.

25   Marry your daughter, and a great load will be off your hands;
but give her to a sensible husband.

26   If you have a wife after your own heart, do not divorce her;
but do not trust yourself to one you cannot love.

27   Honour your father with all your heart
and do not forget your mother's birth-pangs;

28   remember that your parents brought you into the world;
how can you repay what they have done for you?

29   Fear the Lord with all your heart
and reverence his priests.

30   Love your Maker with all your might
and do not leave his ministers without support.

[a] *Probable reading (compare 27. 1), supported by Vss.; Gk. for a trifle.*

Fear the Lord and honour the priest                              31
and give him his dues, as you have been commanded,
the firstfruits, the guilt-offering, and the shoulder of the victim,
the dedication sacrifice, and the firstfruits of holy things.
Be open-handed also with the poor,                               32
so that your own well-being may be complete.
Every living man appreciates generosity;                         33
do not withhold your kindness even when a man is dead.
Do not turn your back on those who weep,                         34
but mourn with those who mourn.
Do not hesitate to visit the sick,                               35
for by such visits you will win their affection.
Whatever you are doing, remember the end that awaits you;        36
then all your life you will never go wrong.

Do not pit yourself against a great man,                         **8**
for fear of falling into his power.
Do not quarrel with a rich man;                                  2
you may be sure he will outbid you.
For money has been the ruin of many
and has misled the minds of kings.
Do not argue with a long-winded man,                             3
and so add fuel to his fire.
Never make fun of an ill-mannered man,                           4
or you may hear your ancestors insulted.
Do not rebuke a man who is already penitent;                     5
remember that we are all guilty.
Despise no man for being old;                                    6
some of us are growing old as well.
Do not be smug over another man's death;                         7
remember that we must all die.

Do not neglect the studies of the learned,                       8
but apply yourself to their maxims;
from these you will learn discipline,
and how to be the servant of princes.
Do not ignore the discourse of your elders,                      9
for they themselves learned from their fathers;
they can teach you to understand
and to have an answer ready in time of need.

Do not kindle a sinner's coals,                                  10
for fear of being burnt in the flames of his fire.
Do not let a man's insolence bring you to your feet;             11
he will only sit waiting to trap you with your own words.
Do not lend to a man with more influence than yourself,          12
or, if you do, write off the loan as a loss.
Do not stand surety beyond your means,                           13
and, when you do stand surety, be prepared to pay.

14     Do not go to law with a judge,
    for in deference to his position they will give him the verdict.
15     Do not go travelling with a reckless man:
    you may find him a burden on you.
    He will do as he fancies,
    and his folly will bring death on you as well.
16     Do not fall out with a hot-tempered man
    or walk with him in unfrequented places;
    he thinks nothing of bloodshed,
    and where no help is at hand he will set upon you.
17     Never discuss your plans with a fool,
    for he cannot keep a secret.
18     Do nothing private in the presence of a stranger;
    you do not know what use he will make of it.
19     Do not tell what is in your mind to all comers
    or accept favours from them.

**9**     Do not be jealous over the wife you cherish,
    and so put into her head the idea of wronging you.
2     Do not surrender yourself to a woman
    and let her trample down your strength.
3     Do not go near a loose woman,
    for fear of falling into her snares.
4     Do not keep company with a dancing-girl,
    or you may be caught by her tricks.
5     Do not let your mind dwell on a virgin,
    or you may be trapped into paying damages for her.
6     Never surrender yourself to prostitutes,
    for fear of losing all you possess,
7     nor gaze about you in the city streets
    or saunter in deserted corners.
8     Do not let your eye linger on a woman's figure
    or your thoughts dwell on beauty not yours to possess.
    Many have been seduced by the beauty of a woman,
    which kindles passion like fire.
9     Never sit at table with another man's wife
    or join her in a drinking party,
    for fear of succumbing to her charms
    and slipping into fatal disaster.

10     Do not desert an old friend;
    a new one is not worth as much.
    A new friend is like new wine;
    you do not enjoy drinking it until it has matured.
11     Do not envy a bad man his success;
    you do not know what fate is in store for him.
12     Take no pleasure in the pleasures of the wicked;
    remember that they will not go scot-free all their lives.

Keep clear of a man who has power to kill,                          13
and you will not be haunted by the fear of death.
If you do approach him, make no false step
or you will risk losing your life.
Tell yourself that you are making your way among pitfalls,
or walking on the battlements of the city.
Take the measure of your neighbours as best you can,                14
and accept advice from those who are wise.
Let your discussion be with intelligent men                         15
and all your talk about the law of the Most High.
Choose the company of good men at table,                            16
and take pride in fearing the Lord.

A craftsman is recognized by his skilful hand                       17
and a councillor by his words of wisdom.
A gossip is the terror of his town,                                 18
detested for his unguarded talk.
A wise ruler trains his people,                                     **10**
and gives them sound and orderly government.
Like ruler, like ministers;                                         2
like sovereign, like subjects;
a king untutored is the people's ruin,                              3
but wise rulers make a city fit to live in.

## Man's life under divine providence

THE GOVERNMENT of the world is in the hand of the Lord;            4
at the right time he appoints the right man to rule it.
In the Lord's hand is all human success;                            5
it is he who confers honour on the legislator.

Do not nurse a grievance against your neighbour for every offence,  6
and do not resort to acts of insolence.
Arrogance is hateful to God and man,                                7
and injustice is offensive to both.
Empire passes from nation to nation                                 8
because of injustice, insolence, and greed.
What has man to be so proud of? He is only dust and ashes,          9
subject even in life to bodily decay.[a]
A long illness mocks the doctor's skill;                            10
today's king is tomorrow's corpse.
When a man dies, he comes into an inheritance                       11
of maggots and vermin and worms.
The origin of pride is to forsake the Lord,                         12
man's heart revolting against his Maker;

[a] subject . . . decay: *probable meaning, based on Heb.; Gk. obscure.*

13  as its origin is sin,
    so persistence in it brings on a deluge of depravity.
    Therefore the Lord sends upon them signal punishments
    and brings them to utter disaster.

14  The Lord overturns the thrones of princes
    and enthrones the gentle in their place.
15  The Lord pulls up nations by the roots
    and plants the humble instead.
16  The Lord lays waste the territory of nations,
    destroying them to the very foundations of the earth.
17  Some he shrivels away to nothing,
    so that all memory of them vanishes from the earth.
18  Pride was not the Creator's design for man
    nor violent anger for those born of woman.

19  What creature is worthy of honour? Man.
    What men? Those who fear the Lord.
    What creature is worthy of contempt? Man.
    What men? Those who break the commandments.
20  As the members of the family honour their head,
    so the Lord honours those who fear him. *a*
22  The rich, the famous, and the poor—
    their only boast is the fear of the Lord.
23  It is unjust to despise a poor man who is intelligent,
    and wrong to honour a man who is a sinner.
24  The prince, the judge, and the ruler win high honours,
    but none of them is as great as the godfearing man.
25  The wise slave will have free men to wait on him,
    and a man of sense will not grumble at it.

26  DO NOT BE TOO CLEVER to do a day's work
    or boast when you have nothing to live on.
27  It is better to work and have more than enough
    than to boast and go hungry.
28  My son, in all modesty, keep your self-respect
    and value yourself at your true worth.
29  Who will speak up for a man who is his own enemy,
    or respect one who disparages himself?
30  A poor man may be honoured for his wisdom,
    a rich man for his wealth;
31  if a man is honoured in poverty, how much more in wealth!
    And if he is depised in wealth, how much more in poverty!
11  A poor man with wisdom can hold his head high
    and take his seat among the great.

*a Some witnesses add* (21) Fear the Lord, and you will be accepted; be obstinate and proud, and you will be rejected.

Do not overrate one man for his good looks             2
or be repelled by another man's appearance.
The bee is small among winged creatures,             3
yet her produce takes first place for sweetness.
Do not pride yourself on your fine clothes             4
or be haughty when honours come to you;
for the Lord can perform marvels
which are hidden from the eyes of men.
Many kings have been reduced to sitting on the ground,             5
while a mere nobody has worn the crown.
Many rulers have been stripped of their honours,             6
and great men have found themselves at the mercy of others.

Do not find fault before examining the evidence;             7
think first, and criticize afterwards.
Do not answer without first listening,             8
and do not interrupt when another is speaking.
Never take sides in a quarrel not your own             9
or become involved in the disputes of rascals.

My son, do not engage in too many transactions;             10
if you attempt too much, you will come to grief.
When you are in pursuit, you will not overtake;
when you are in flight, you will not escape.
One man slaves and strains and hurries             11
and is all the farther behind.
Another is slow-witted and in need of help,             12
lacking in strength and abounding in poverty;
but the Lord turns a kindly eye upon him
and lifts him up out of his miserable plight.
He raises him to dignity             13
to the amazement of all.

Good fortune and bad, life and death,             14
poverty and wealth, all come from the Lord. *a*
His gifts to the devout are lasting;             17
his approval brings unending success.
A man may grow rich by stinting and sparing,             18
but what does he get for his pains?
When he says, 'I have earned my rest,             19
now I can live on my savings',
he does not know how long it will be
before he must die and leave his wealth to others.

Stand by your contract and give your mind to it;             20
grow old at your work.

*a* *Some witnesses add* (15) From the Lord come wisdom, understanding, and love, knowledge of the law, and the doing of good works. (16) Error and darkness have been with
sinners from their birth, and evil grows old along with those who take delight in it.

21 Do not envy a rogue his success;
trust the Lord and stick to your job.
It is no difficult thing for the Lord
to make a poor man rich in a moment.

22 The Lord's blessing is the reward of piety,
which blossoms in one short hour.

23 Do not say, 'What use am I?
What good*a* can the future hold for me?'

24 And do not say, 'I am independent;
nothing can ever go wrong for me.'

25 Hardship is forgotten in time of success,
and success in time of hardship.

26 Even on the day a man dies it is easy for the Lord
to give him his deserts.

27 One hour's misery wipes out all memory of delight,
and a man's end reveals his true character.

28 Call no man happy before he dies,
for not until death is a man known for what he is.*b*


29 DO NOT INVITE all comers into your home;
dishonesty has many disguises.

30 A proud man's mind is like a decoy-partridge in its cage,
or like a spy watching for a false step.

31 He waits for a chance to twist good into evil
or to cast blame on innocent actions.

32 A small spark kindles many coals,
and the insinuations of a bad man end in bloodshed.

33 Beware of a scoundrel and his evil plots,
or he may ruin your reputation for ever.

34 Admit a stranger to your home and he will stir up trouble for you
and make you a stranger to your own flesh and blood.

12 If you do a good deed, make sure to whom you are doing it;
then you will have credit for your kindness.

2 A good turn done to a godfearing man will be rewarded,
if not by him, then by the Most High.

3 No good comes to the persistent wrong-doer
or to the man who never gives alms;*c*

5 refuse him bread; give him nothing at all;
he will only use your gifts to get the better of you,
and you will suffer a double wrong
in return for the favours you have done him.

*a* Or 'What more do I need? What greater success . . .    *b* not . . . he is: *so Heb.;*
*Gk.* a man is known by his children.    *c* *The order of the following verses has*
*been disturbed in all versions; Gk. reads . . . gives alms;* (4) *give to a godfearing man, but*
*never help a sinner;* (5) *keep your good works for the humble, not the insolent; refuse*
*him . . .* (*compare verse 7*).

The Most High himself hates sinners                                          6
and sends bad men what they deserve.
Give to a good man, but never help a sinner;                                 7
keep your good works for the humble, not the insolent.*a*

Prosperity does not reveal your friends;                                     8
adversity does not conceal your enemies.
When all goes well a man's enemies are friendly,*b*                          9
but in hard times even his friend will desert him.
Never trust your enemy;                                                     10
he will turn vicious as sure as metal rusts.
If he appears humble and obsequious,                                        11
take care! Be on your guard against him!
Behave towards him like a man who polishes a mirror
to make sure that it does not corrode away.
Do not have him at your side,                                               12
or he will trip you up and supplant you.
Do not let him sit at your right hand,
or he will soon be wanting your own seat;
and in the end you will see the force of my words
and recall my warning with regret.
Who sympathizes with a snake-charmer when he is bitten,                     13
or with a tamer of wild animals?
No more does anyone pity the man who keeps bad company                      14
and involves himself in another's wickedness.
He may stand by you for a while,                                            15
but, if you falter, his friendship will not last.

An enemy has honey on his lips,                                             16
but in his heart he plans to trip you into the ditch.
He may have tears in his eyes,
but give him a chance and he will not stop at bloodshed.
If disaster overtakes you, you will find him there ahead of you,           17
ready, with a pretence of help, to pull your feet from under you.
Then he will nod his head and rub his hands                                18
and spread gossip, showing his true colours.
Handle pitch and it will make you dirty;                                    **13**
keep company with an arrogant man and you will grow like him

Do not lift a weight too heavy for you,                                      2
keeping company with a man greater and richer than yourself.
How can a jug be friends with a kettle?
If they knock together, the one will be smashed.
A rich man does wrong, and adds insult to injury;                           3
a poor man is wronged, and must apologize into the bargain.
If you can serve his turn, a rich man will exploit you,                     4
but if you are in need, he will leave you alone.

---

*a* keep ... insolent: *this is the beginning of verse 5 in Gk.*     *b* *So Heb.; Gk.* grieve.

5 If you are in funds, he will be your constant companion,
and drain you dry without a twinge of remorse.
6 He may need you; and then he will deceive you,
and will be all smiles and encouragement,
paying you compliments and asking, 'What can I do for you?',
7 embarrassing you with his hospitality,
until he has drained you two or three times over;
but in the end he will laugh at you.
Afterwards, when he sees you, he will pass you by,
nodding his head over you.

8 Take care not to be led astray
and humiliated when you are enjoying yourself.
9 If a great man invites you, be slow to accept,
and he will be the more pressing in his invitation.
10 Do not be forward, for fear of a rebuff,
but do not keep aloof, or you may be forgotten.
11 Do not presume to converse with him as an equal
or be over-confident if he holds you long in talk.
The more he speaks, the more he is testing you,
examining you even while he smiles.
12 The man who cannot keep your secrets is without compunction
and will not spare you harm or imprisonment;
13 so keep your secrets to yourself and be very careful,
for you are walking on the brink of ruin. *a*

15 Every animal loves its like,
and every man his neighbour.
16 All creatures flock together with their kind,
and men form attachments with their own sort.
17 What has a wolf in common with a lamb,
or a sinner with a man of piety?
18 What peace can there be between hyena and dog,
what peace between rich man and pauper?
19 As lions prey on the wild asses of the desert,
so the rich batten on the poor.
20 As humility disgusts the proud,
so is the rich man disgusted by the poor.

21 If a rich man staggers, he is held up by his friends;
a poor man falls, and his friends disown him as well.
22 When a rich man slips, many come to his rescue;
if he says something outrageous, they make excuses for him.
A poor man makes a slip, and they all criticize him;
even if he talks sense, he is not given a hearing.

*a Some witnesses add* When you hear this in your sleep, wake up. (14) Love the Lord all
your life and appeal to him for salvation.

A rich man speaks, and all are silent;                    23
then they praise his speech to the skies.
A poor man speaks, and they say, 'Who is this?',
and if he stumbles, they give him an extra push.


WEALTH IS GOOD, if sin has not tainted it;               24
poverty is a crime only to the ungodly.
It is a man's heart that changes the look on his face     25
either for better or worse.
The sign of a happy heart is a cheerful face,             26
but the invention of proverbs involves wearisome thought.
Happy the man who has never let slip a careless word,    **14**
who has never felt the sting of remorse!
Happy the man whose conscience does not accuse him,       2
whose hope has never been disappointed!


It is not proper for a mean man to be rich:               3
what use is money to a miser?
He deprives himself only to hoard for other men;          4
others will live in luxury on his riches.
How can a man be hard on himself and kind to others?      5
His possessions bring him no enjoyment.
No one is worse than the man who is grudging to himself:  6
his niggardliness is its own punishment.
If ever he does good, it is by mistake,                   7
and then in the end he reveals his meanness.
It is a hard man who has a grudging eye;                  8
he turns his back on need and looks the other way.
A covetous man's eye is not satisfied with his share;     9
greedy injustice shrivels the soul.
A miser grudges bread                                     10
and keeps an empty table.


My son, if you can afford it, do yourself well,           11
always offering to the Lord the sacrifice due to him.
Remember that death is not to be postponed;               12
the hour of your appointment with the grave is undisclosed.
Before you die, do good to your friend;                   13
reach out as far as you can to help him.
Do not miss a day's enjoyment                             14
or forgo your share of innocent pleasure.
Are you to leave to others all you have laboured for      15
and let them draw lots for your hard-earned wealth?
Give and receive; indulge yourself;                       16
you need not expect luxuries in the grave.
Man's body wears out like a garment;                      17
for the ancient sentence stands: You shall die.

18  In the thick foliage of a growing tree
one crop of leaves falls and another grows instead;
so the generations of flesh and blood pass
with the death of one and the birth of another.

19  All man's works decay and vanish,
and the workman follows them into oblivion.

20  HAPPY THE MAN who fixes his thoughts on wisdom
and uses his brains to think,

21  the man who contemplates her ways
and ponders her secrets.

22  Stalk her like a hunter
and lie in wait beside her path!

23  The man who peers in at her windows
and listens at her keyhole,

24  who camps beside her house,
driving his tent-peg into her wall,

25  who pitches his tent close by her,
where it is best for men to live—

26  he will put his children in her shade
and camp beneath her branches,

27  sheltered by her from the heat,
and dwelling in the light of her presence.

**15**  The man who fears the Lord will do all this,
and if he masters the law, wisdom will be his.

2  She will come out to meet him like a mother;
she will receive him like a young bride.

3  For food she will give him the bread of understanding
and for drink the water of knowledge.

4  He will lean on her and not fall;
he will rely on her to save him from disgrace.

5  She will promote him above his neighbours,
and find words for him when he speaks in the assembly.

6  He shall be crowned with joy and exultation;
lasting honour shall be his heritage.

7  Fools shall never possess wisdom;
sinners shall catch no glimpse of her.

8  She holds aloof from arrogance,
far from the thoughts of liars.

9  Worship is out of place on the lips of a sinner,
unprompted as he is by the Lord.

10  Worship is the outward expression of wisdom,
and the Lord himself inspires it.

11  Do not say, 'The Lord is to blame for my failure';
it is for you to avoid doing what he hates.

Do not say, 'It was he who led me astray';     12
he has no use for sinful men.
The Lord hates every kind of vice;     13
you cannot love it and still fear him.
When he made man in the beginning,     14
he left him free to take his own decisions;
if you choose, you can keep the commandments;     15
whether or not you keep faith is yours to decide.
He has set before you fire and water;     16
reach out and take which you choose;
before man lie life and death,     17
and whichever he prefers is his.
For in his great wisdom and mighty power     18
the Lord sees everything.
He keeps watch over those who fear him;     19
no human act escapes his notice.
But he has commanded no man to be wicked,     20
nor has he given licence to commit sin.

DO NOT SET YOUR HEART on a large family of ne'er-do-wells     16
or be content if your sons are godless.
However many they are, do not think yourself happy,     2
unless the fear of the Lord is in them.
Do not count on their living to be old     3
or rely on their numbers;
for one son can be better than a thousand;
better indeed to die childless than to have godless children.
Thanks to one man of good sense a city may be populous,     4
while a tribe of lawless men becomes a desert.
Many a time have I seen this with my own eyes,     5
and still weightier examples have come to my ears.

Where sinners gather, the fire breaks out;     6
retribution blazes up in a rebellious nation.
There was no pardon for the giants of old,     7
who revolted in all their strength.
There was no reprieve for Lot's adopted home,     8
abhorrent in its arrogance.
There was no mercy for the doomed nation,     9
exterminated for their sins—
those six hundred thousand warriors     10
marshalled in stubborn defiance.
Even if only one man were obstinate,     11
it would be a miracle for him to escape punishment.
For mercy and anger belong to the Lord;
he shows his power in forgiveness, or in the flood of his wrath.

12 His mercy is great, but great also is his condemnation;
he judges a man by what he has done.

13 He does not let the sinner escape with his loot
or try the patience of the godly too long.

14 He opens a way for every work of mercy,
and everyone is treated according to his own deserts.*ᵃ*

17 Do not say, 'I am hidden from the Lord;
who is there in heaven to give a thought to me?
Among so many I shall not be noticed;
what is my life compared with the measureless creation?

18 Heaven itself, the highest heaven,
the abyss and the earth are shaken at his coming;

19 the very mountains and the foundations of the world
tremble when he looks upon them.

20 What human mind can grasp this,
or comprehend his ways?

21 As a squall takes men unawares,
so most of his works are done in secret.

22 Who is to declare his acts of justice
or wait for his remote decree?'

23 These are the thoughts of a small mind,
the absurdities of a senseless and misguided man.

24 LISTEN TO ME, MY SON, and learn sense;
pay close attention to what I say;

25 I will show you exact discipline
and teach you accurate knowledge.

26 When the Lord created his works in the beginning,
and after making them defined*ᵇ* their boundaries,

27 he disposed them in an eternal order
and fixed their influences for all time.
They do not grow hungry or weary,
or abandon their tasks;

28 one does not jostle another;
they never disobey his word.

29 The Lord then looked at the earth
and filled it with his good things.

30 With every kind of living creature he covered the ground,
into which they must all return.

17 The Lord created man from the earth
and sent him back to it again.

---

*ᵃ Some witnesses add* (15) The Lord made Pharaoh too stubborn to acknowledge him, so
that his deeds might be published to the world. (16) He displays his mercy to the whole
creation, and has separated light from darkness with a plumb-line. *ᵇ* When . . .
defined: *probable reading, based on Heb.; Gk.* The works of the Lord have been under
his judgement from the beginning, . . . he defined . . .

He set a fixed span of life for men 2
and granted them authority over everything on earth.
He clothed them with strength like his own, *a* 3
forming them in his own image.
He put the fear of man into all creatures 4
and gave him lordship over beasts and birds. *b*
He gave men tongue and eyes and ears, 6
the power of choice and a mind for thinking.
He filled them with discernment 7
and showed them good and evil.
He kept watch over their hearts, 8
to display to them the majesty of his works. *c*
They shall praise his holy name, 10
proclaiming the grandeur of his works.
He gave them knowledge as well 11
and endowed them with the life-giving law.
He established a perpetual covenant with them 12
and revealed to them his decrees.
Their eyes saw his glorious majesty, 13
and their ears heard the glory of his voice.
He said to them, 'Guard against all wrongdoing', 14
and taught each man his duty towards his neighbour.

Their conduct always lies open before him, 15
never hidden from his scrutiny. *d*
For every nation he appointed a ruler, 17
but chose Israel to be his own possession. *e*
So whatever they do is clear to him as daylight; 19
he keeps constant watch over their lives.
Their wrongdoing is not hidden from the Lord; 20
he observes all their sins. *f*
A man's good deeds he treasures like a signet-ring, 22
and his kindness like the apple of his eye.
In the end he will rise up and give the wicked their deserts, 23
bringing down their recompense on their own heads.
Yet he leaves a way open for the penitent to return to him, 24
and gives the waverer strength to endure.

Turn to the Lord and have done with sin; 25
make your prayer in his presence, and so lessen your offence.

*a So one Vs.; Gk. their own.*       *b Some witnesses add* (5) The Lord gave them the use of the five faculties; as a sixth gift he distributed to them mind, and as a seventh, reason, the interpreter of those faculties.       *c Some witnesses add* (9) He has given them the right to boast for ever of his marvels.       *d Some witnesses read* ... scrutiny. (16) Every man from his youth tended towards evil; they could not make themselves hearts of flesh in place of their hearts of stone. (17) When he distributed the nations over all the earth, for every ...       *e Some witnesses add* (18) He rears them with discipline as his first-born, imparting to them the light of love and never neglecting them.       *f Some witnesses add* (21) The Lord who is gracious and knows what they are made of has neither rejected nor deserted them, but spared them.

26 Come back to the Most High, renounce wrongdoing,
and hate intensely what he abhors.

27 Who will praise the Most High in the grave
in place of the living who give him thanks?

28 When a man is dead and ceases to be, his gratitude dies with him;
it is when he is alive and well that he praises the Lord.

29 How great is the Lord's mercy
and his pardon to those who turn to him!

30 Not everything is within man's reach,
for the human race is not immortal.

31 Is anything brighter than the sun? Yet the sun suffers eclipse.
So flesh and blood have evil thoughts.

32 The Lord marshals the armies of high heaven,
but all men are dust and ashes.

**18** He who lives for ever is the Creator of the whole universe;

2 right belongs to the Lord alone. *a*

4 To no man is it given to unfold the story of his works;
who can trace his marvels to their source?

5 No one can measure his majestic power,
still less, tell the full tale of all his mercies.

6 Man can neither increase nor diminish them,
nor fathom the wonders of the Lord.

7 When a man comes to the end of them he is still at the beginning,
and when he has finished he will still be perplexed.

8 What is man and what use is he?
What do his good or evil deeds signify?

9 His span of life is at the most a hundred years;
10 compared with endless time, his few years
are like one drop of sea-water or a single grain of sand.

11 This is why the Lord is patient with them,
lavishing his mercy upon them.

12 He sees and knows the harsh fate in store for them,
and therefore gives full play to his forgiveness.

13 Man's compassion is only for his neighbour,
but the Lord's compassion is for every living thing.
He corrects and trains and teaches
and brings them back as a shepherd his flock.

14 He has compassion on those who accept discipline
and are eager to obey his decrees.

15 My son, do good without scolding;
do not spoil your generosity with hard words.

16 Does not the dew give respite from the sweltering heat?
So a word can do more than a gift.

*a* *Some witnesses add* and there is none beside him, (3) who can steer the world with his little finger, so that all things obey his will; as king of the universe, he has power to fix the bounds between what is holy and what is profane.

A kind word counts for more than a rich present;                    17
with a gracious man you will find both.
A fool cannot refrain from tactless criticism,                      18
and a grudging giver makes no eyes sparkle.

Before you speak, learn;                                            19
and before you fall sick, consult a doctor.
Before judgement comes, examine yourself,                           20
and you will find pardon in the hour of scrutiny.
Before you fall ill, humble yourself;                               21
show your penitence as soon as you sin.
Let nothing hinder the prompt discharge of your vows;              22
do not wait till death to be absolved.
Before you make a vow, give it due thought;                        23
do not be like those who try the Lord's patience.
Think of the wrath you must face in the hour of death,            24
when the time of reckoning comes, and he turns away his face.
In time of plenty remember the time of famine,                     25
poverty and need in days of wealth.
Between dawn and dusk times may alter;                             26
all change comes quickly, when the Lord wills it.
A wise man is always on his guard;                                 27
when sin is rife, he will beware of negligence.
Every man of sense makes acquaintance with wisdom,                28
and to him who finds her she gives cause for thankfulness.
Skilled speakers display their special wisdom                      29
by a flow of apt proverbs.

## Maxims of prudence and self-discipline

DO NOT LET your passions be your guide,                            30
but restrain your desires.
If you indulge yourself with all that passion fancies,            31
it will make you the butt of your enemies.
Do not revel in great luxury,                                      32
or the expense of it may ruin you.
Do not beggar yourself by feasting on borrowed money,             33
when there is nothing in your purse.
A drunken workman never grows rich;                              **19**
carelessness in small things leads little by little to ruin.
Wine and women rob the wise of their wits,                          2
and a frequenter of prostitutes becomes more and more reckless,
till sores*a* and worms take possession of him,                    3
and his recklessness becomes his undoing.

To trust a man hastily shows a shallow mind,                        4
and to sin is to do an injury to yourself.

             *a  Or* decay.

141

5  To delight in wickedness is to court condemnation,
6  but evil loses its hold on the man who hates gossip.
7  Never repeat what you hear,
   and you will never be the loser.
8  Tell no tales about friend or foe;
   unless silence makes you an accomplice, never betray a man's secret.
9  Suppose he has heard you and learnt to distrust you,
   he will seize the first chance to show his hatred.
10 Have you heard a rumour? Let it die with you.
   Never fear, it will not make you burst.
11 A fool with a secret goes through agony
   like a woman in childbirth.
12 As painful as an arrow through the thigh
   is a rumour in the heart of a fool.
13 Confront your friend with the gossip about him; he may not have
      done it;
   or if he did it, he will know not to do it again.
14 Confront your neighbour; he may not have said it;
   or if he did say it, he will know not to say it again.
15 Confront your friend; it will often turn out to be slander;
   do not believe everything you hear.
16 A man may let slip more than he intends;
   whose tongue is always free from guilt?
17 Confront your neighbour before you threaten him,
   and let the law of the Most High take its course. *a*

20 All wisdom is the fear of the Lord
   and includes the fulfilling of the law. *b*
22 The knowledge of wickedness is not wisdom,
   nor is there good sense in the advice of sinners.
23 There is a cleverness that is loathsome,
   and some fools are merely ignorant.
24 Better to be godfearing and lack brains
   than to have great intelligence and break the law.
25 A meticulous cleverness may lead to injustice,
   and a man may make himself offensive in order that right may prevail.
26 There is a scoundrel who stoops and wears mourning,
   but who is a fraud at heart.
27 He covers his face and pretends to be deaf,
   but when nobody is looking, he will steal a march on you;
28 and if lack of strength prevents him from doing wrong,
   he will still harm you at the first opportunity.

*a Some witnesses add* without giving way to anger. (18) The fear of the Lord is the way
towards acceptance, and wisdom wins love from him. (19) The knowledge of the Lord's
commandments is life-giving discipline, and those who do what pleases him eat from the
tree of immortality.        *b Some witnesses add* and a knowledge of his omnipotence.
(21) A servant who says, 'I will not do as you wish', even if he does it later,
angers the man who feeds him.

Yet you can tell a man by his looks                                    29
and recognize good sense at first sight.
A man's clothes, and the way he laughs,                                30
and his gait, reveal his character.

A reproof may be untimely,                                             **20**
and silence may show a man's good sense.
Yet how much better it is to complain than to nurse a grudge,          2
and confession saves a man from disgrace.[a]
Like a eunuch longing to seduce a girl                                 4
is the man who tries to do right by violence.
One man is silent and is found to be wise;                             5
another is hated for his endless chatter.
One man is silent, at a loss for an answer;                            6
another is silent, biding his time.
The wise man is silent until the right moment,                         7
but a swaggering fool is always speaking out of turn.
A garrulous man makes himself detested,                                8
and one who abuses his position arouses hatred.

A MAN SOMETIMES FINDS profit in adversity,                             9
and a windfall may result in loss.
Sometimes liberality does not benefit the giver,                       10
sometimes it brings a double return.
The quest for honour may lead to disgrace,                             11
but there are those who have risen from obscurity to eminence.
A man may make a good bargain,                                         12
but pay for it seven times over.
A wise man endears himself when he speaks,                             13
but fools scatter compliments in vain.
A gift from a fool will bring you no benefit;                          14
it looks bigger to him than it does to you.
He gives small gifts accompanied by long lectures,                     15
and opens his mouth as wide as the town crier.
He gives a loan today and asks it back tomorrow,
obnoxious fellow that he is!
The fool says, 'I have no friends,                                      16
I get no thanks for my kindnesses;
though they eat my bread, they speak ill of me.'
How everyone will laugh at him—and how often!                          17

Better a slip on the stone floor than a slip of the tongue;            18
and the fall of the wicked comes just as suddenly.
An ill-mannered man is like an unseasonable story,                     19
continually on the lips of the ill-bred.

[a] *Some witnesses add* (3) How good it is to respond to reproof with repentance, and so
escape deliberate sin!

20    A proverb will fall flat when uttered by a fool,
      for he will produce it at the wrong time.

21    Poverty may keep a man from doing wrong;
      when the day's work is over, conscience will not trouble him.

22    A man's diffidence may be his undoing,
      or the foolish figure he cuts in the eyes of the world.

23    A man may be shamed into making promises to a friend
      and needlessly turn him into an enemy.

24    A lie is an ugly blot on a man's name,
      and is continually on the lips of those who know no better.

25    It is better to be a thief than a habitual liar,
      but both will come to the same bad end.

26    A lying disposition brings disgrace;
      the shame of it can never be shaken off.

27    A wise man advances himself when he speaks,
      and a man of sense makes himself pleasant to the great.

28    The man who tills his land heaps up a harvest,
      and he who pleases the great reaps pardon for his wrongdoing.

29    Hospitality and presents make wise men blind;
      like a gag in the mouth they silence criticism.

30    Hidden wisdom and buried treasure,
      what use is there in either?

31    Better a man who hides his folly
      than one who hides his wisdom! *a*

21    Have you done wrong, my son? Do it no more,
      but ask pardon for your past wrongdoing.

2     Avoid wrong as you would a viper,
      for if you go near, it will bite you;
      its teeth are like a lion's teeth
      and can destroy the lives of men.

3     Every breach of the law is like a two-edged sword;
      it inflicts an incurable wound.

4     By intimidation and insolence a man forfeits his wealth;
      thus a proud man will be stripped of his possessions.

5     The Lord listens to the poor man's appeal,
      and his verdict follows without delay.

6     To hate reproof is to go the way of sinners,
      but whoever fears the Lord will repent whole-heartedly.

7     A great talker is known far and wide,
      but a sensible man is aware of his failings.

8     To build a house with borrowed money
      is like collecting stones for your own tomb. *b*

---

*a* *Some witnesses add* (32) Better to seek the Lord with unremitting patience than to be the masterless charioteer of one's own life.    *b* *Some witnesses read* like harvesting stones against the winter.

A gathering of lawless men is like a bundle of tow,   9
which ends by going up in flames.
The road of sinners is smoothly paved,   10
but it leads straight down to the grave.
Whoever keeps the law keeps his thoughts under control;   11
the fear of the Lord has its outcome in wisdom.


A MAN WHO IS NOT CLEVER cannot be taught,   12
but there is a cleverness which only breeds bitterness.
A wise man's knowledge is like a river in full spate,   13
and his advice is a life-giving spring.
A fool's mind is a leaky bucket:   14
it cannot hold anything it learns.
If an instructed man hears a wise saying,   15
he applauds it and improves on it.
If a rake hears it, he is annoyed
and throws it behind his back.
Listening to a fool is like travelling with a heavy pack,   16
but there is delight to be found in intelligent conversation.
The assembly welcomes a word from the wise man,   17
and thinks over what he says.


A fool's wisdom is like a tumbledown house;   18
his knowledge is a string of ill-digested sayings.
To fools education is like fetters,   19
like a handcuff on the wrist.
To the wise education is a golden ornament   21
like a bracelet on the arm.
A fool laughs out loud;   20
a clever man smiles quietly, if at all.


A fool rushes into a house,   22
while a man of experience hangs back politely.
A boor peers into the house from the doorstep,   23
while a well-bred man stands outside.
It is bad manners to listen at doors;   24
a man of sense would think it a crushing disgrace.
The glib only repeat what others have said,   25
but the wise weigh every word.
Fools speak before they think;   26
wise men think first and speak afterwards.
When a bad man curses his adversary,*a*   27
he is cursing himself.
A tale-bearer blackens his own character   28
and makes himself hated throughout the neighbourhood.

*a Or* curses Satan.

**22** An idler is like a filthy stone;
everyone jeers at his disgrace.
2 An idler is like a lump of dung;
whoever picks it up shakes it off his hand.

3 There is shame in being father to a spoilt son,
and the birth of a daughter means loss.
4 A sensible daughter wins a husband,
but an immodest one is a grief to her father.
5 A brazen daughter disgraces both father and husband
and is despised by both.
6 Unseasonable talk is like music in time of mourning,
but the lash of wisdom's discipline is always in season.

7 Teaching a fool is like mending pottery with glue,
or like rousing a sleeper from heavy sleep.
8 As well reason with a drowsy man as with a fool;
when you have finished, he will say, 'What was that?' *a*
11 Mourn over the dead for the eclipse of his light;
mourn over the fool for the eclipse of his wits.
Mourn less bitterly for the dead, for he is at rest;
but the fool's life is worse than death.
12 Mourning for the dead lasts seven days,
but for a godless fool it lasts all his life.
13 Do not talk long with a fool
or visit a stupid man.
Beware of him, or you may be in trouble
and find yourself bespattered when he shakes himself.
Avoid him, if you are looking for peace,
and you will not be worn out by his folly.
14 What is heavier than lead?
What is its name but 'Fool'?
15 Sand, salt, and a lump of iron
are less of a burden than a stupid man.

16 A tie-beam fixed firmly into a building
is not shaken loose by an earthquake;
so a mind kept firm by intelligent advice
will not be daunted in a crisis.
17 A mind solidly backed by intelligent thought
is like the stucco that decorates a smooth wall.
18 As a fence set on a hill-top
cannot stand against the wind,
so a mind made timid by foolish fancies
is not proof against any terror.

*a Some witnesses add* (9) Children well brought up reveal no trace of any humble origin.
(10) But those who run riot, haughty and undisciplined, sully the nobility of their
parentage.

Hurt the eye and tears will flow;                                                  19
hurt the mind and you will find it sensitive.
Throw a stone at the birds and you scare them away;               20
abuse a friend and you break off your friendship.
If you have drawn your sword on a friend,                              21
do not give up hope, there is still a way back.
If you have quarrelled with your friend,                                 22
never fear, there can still be a reconciliation.
But abuse, scorn, a secret betrayed, a stab in the back—
these will make any friend keep his distance.
Win your neighbour's confidence while he is poor,                 23
and you will share the joy of his prosperity;
stand by him in time of trouble,
and you will be his partner when he comes into a fortune.
As furnace-fumes and smoke come before the flame,            24
so insults come before bloodshed.
I will not be afraid to protect my friend                                  25
nor will I turn my back on him.
If harm should befall me on his account,                                26
everyone who hears of it will beware of him.


OH FOR A SENTRY to guard my mouth                              27
and a seal of discretion to close my lips,
to keep them from being my downfall,
and to keep my tongue from causing my ruin!
Lord, Father, and Ruler of my life,                                       **23**
do not abandon me to the tongue's control
or allow me to fall on its account.
Oh for wisdom's lash to curb my thoughts                          2
and to discipline my mind,
without overlooking my mistakes
or condoning my sins!
Then my mistakes would not multiply                                 3
nor my sins increase,
humiliating me before my opponents
and giving my enemy cause to gloat.
Lord, Father, and God of my life,                                       4
do not let me have a supercilious eye.
Protect me from the onslaught of desire;                             5
let neither gluttony nor lust take hold of me,                       6
nor give me over to the power of shameless passion.

Hear, my sons, how to discipline the mouth,                       7
take warning, and you will never be caught out.
It is by his own words that the sinner is ensnared;             8
he is tripped up by his own scurrility and pride.
Do not inure your mouth to oaths                                      9
or make a habit of naming the Holy One.

10 As a slave constantly under the lash
is never free from weals,
so the man who has oaths and the sacred name for ever on his lips
will never be clear of guilt.

11 A man given to swearing is lawless to the core;
the scourge will never be far from his house.
If he goes back on his word, he must bear the blame;
if he wilfully neglects it, he sins twice over;
if his oath itself was insincere, he cannot be acquitted;
his house will be filled with trouble.

12 There is a kind of speech that is the counterpart of death;
may it never be found among Jacob's descendants!
The pious keep clear of such conduct
and do not wallow in sin.

13 Do not make a habit of coarse, vulgar talk,
or you will be bound to say something sinful.

14 Remember your father and mother
when you take your seat among the great,
or you may forget yourself in their presence
and make a fool of yourself through bad habit;
then you will wish you had never been born,
and curse the day of your birth.

15 A man addicted to scurrilous talk
will never learn better as long as he lives.

16 TWO KINDS OF MEN add sin to sin,
and a third brings retribution on himself.
Hot lust that blazes like a fire
can never be quenched till life is destroyed.
A man whose whole body is given to sensuality
never stops till the fire consumes him.

17 To a seducer every loaf is as sweet as the last,
and he does not weary until he dies.

18 The man who strays from his own bed
says to himself, 'Who can see me?
All around is dark and the walls hide me;
nobody can see me, why need I worry?
The Most High will not take note of my sins.'

19 The eyes of men are all he fears;
he forgets that the eyes of the Lord
are ten thousand times brighter than the sun,
observing every step men take
and penetrating every secret.

20 Before the universe was created, it was known to him,
and so it is since its completion.

21 This man will pay the penalty in the public street,
caught where he least expected it.

So too with the woman who is unfaithful to her husband,    22
presenting him with an heir by a different father:
first, she disobeys the law of the Most High;    23
secondly, she commits an offence against her husband;
thirdly, she has prostituted herself
by bearing bastard children.
She shall be disgraced before the assembly,    24
and the consequences will fall on her children.
Her children will not take root,    25
nor will fruit grow on her branches.
A curse will rest on her memory,    26
and her shame will never be blotted out.
All who survive her will learn    27
that nothing is better than the fear of the Lord
or sweeter than obeying his commandments. *a*

## The praise of wisdom

HEAR THE PRAISE of wisdom from her own mouth,    **24**
as she speaks with pride among her people,
before the assembly of the Most High    2
and in the presence of the heavenly host:
'I am the word which was spoken by the Most High;    3
it was I who covered the earth like a mist.
My dwelling-place was in high heaven;    4
my throne was in a pillar of cloud.
Alone I made a circuit of the sky    5
and traversed the depth of the abyss.
The waves of the sea, the whole earth,    6
every people and nation were under my sway.
Among them all I looked for a home:    7
in whose territory was I to settle?
Then the Creator of the universe laid a command upon me;    8
my Creator decreed where I should dwell.
He said, "Make your home in Jacob;
find your heritage in Israel."
Before time began he created me,    9
and I shall remain for ever.
In the sacred tent I ministered in his presence,    10
and so I came to be established in Zion.
Thus he settled me in the city he loved    11
and gave me authority in Jerusalem.
I took root among the people whom the Lord had honoured    12
by choosing them to be his special possession.

---

*a* *Some witnesses add* (28) To follow God brings great honour; to win his approval means
long life.

13 'There I grew like a cedar of Lebanon,
   like a cypress on the slopes of Hermon,
14 like a date-palm at Engedi,
   like roses at Jericho.
   I grew like a fair olive-tree in the vale,
   or like a plane-tree planted beside the water.
15 Like cassia or camel-thorn I was redolent of spices;
   I spread my fragrance like choice myrrh,
   like galban, aromatic shell, and gum resin;
   I was like the smoke of incense in the sacred tent.
16 Like a terebinth I spread out my branches,
   laden with honour and grace.
17 I put forth lovely shoots like the vine,
   and my blossoms were a harvest of wealth and honour. *a*

19 'Come to me, you who desire me,
   and eat your fill of my fruit.
20 The memory of me is sweeter than syrup,
   the possession of me sweeter than honey dripping from the comb.
21 Whoever feeds on me will be hungry for more,
   and whoever drinks from me will thirst for more.
22 To obey me is to be safe from disgrace;
   those who work in wisdom will not go astray.'

23 All this is the covenant-book of God Most High,
   the law which Moses enacted to be the heritage of the assemblies of Jacob. *b*
25 He sends out wisdom in full flood like the river Pishon
   or like the Tigris at the time of firstfruits;
26 he overflows with understanding like the Euphrates
   or like Jordan at the time of harvest.
27 He pours forth instruction like the Nile, *c*
   like the Gihon at the time of vintage.
28 No man has ever fully known wisdom;
   from first to last no one has fathomed her;
29 for her thoughts are vaster than the ocean
   and her purpose deeper than the great abyss.

30 As for me, I was like a canal leading from a river,
   a watercourse into a pleasure-garden.
31 I said, 'I will water my garden,
   drenching its flower-beds';
   and at once my canal became a river
   and my river a sea.

---

*a* *Some witnesses add* (18) I give birth to noble love, reverence, knowledge, and holy hope;
   and I give all these my eternal progeny to God's elect (*probable meaning; Gk. obscure*).
*b* *Some witnesses add* (24) Never fail to be strong in the Lord; hold fast to him, so that he
   may strengthen you; the Lord Almighty is God alone; beside him there is no saviour.
*c* *So one Vs.; Gk.* He makes instruction shine like light.

I will again make discipline shine like the dawn,                    32
so that its light may be seen from afar.
I will again pour out doctrine like prophecy                          33
and bequeath it to future generations.
Truly, my labour has not been for myself alone                       34
but for all seekers of wisdom.


THERE ARE THREE SIGHTS which warm my heart[a]        **25**
and are beautiful in the eyes of the Lord and of men:
concord among brothers, friendship among neighbours,
and a man and wife who are inseparable.
There are three kinds of men who arouse my hatred,                    2
who disgust me by their manner of life:
a poor man who boasts, a rich man who lies,
and an old fool who commits adultery.


If you have not gathered wisdom in your youth,                        3
how will you find it when you are old?
Sound judgement sits well on grey hairs                               4
and wise advice comes well from older men.
Wisdom is fitting in the aged,                                        5
and ripe counsel in men of eminence.
Long experience is the old man's crown,                               6
and his pride is the fear of the Lord.


I can think of nine men I count happy,                                7
and I can tell you of a tenth:
a man who can take delight in his children,
and one who lives to see his enemy's downfall;
happy the husband of a sensible wife,                                 8
the farmer who does not plough with ox and ass together,[b]
the man whose tongue never betrays him,
and the servant who has never worked for an inferior!
Happy the man who has found a friend,[c]                              9
and the speaker who has an attentive audience!
How great is the man who finds wisdom!                                10
But no greater than he who fears the Lord.
The fear of the Lord excels all other gifts;                         11
to what can we compare the man who has it?[d]

[a] *So Vss.; Gk.* which make me beautiful.          [b] the farmer . . . together: *so Heb.;*
*Gk. omits.*          [c] *So Vss.; Gk.* found good sense.          [d] *Some witnesses add*
(12) The fear of the Lord is the source of love for him, and faith is the source of loyalty
to him.

## *Counsels upon social behaviour*

13 ANY WOUND but a wound in the heart!
Any spite but a woman's!

14 Any disaster but one caused by hate!
Any vengeance but the vengeance of an enemy!

15 There is no venom *a* worse than a snake's,
and no anger worse than an enemy's.

16 I would sooner share a home with a lion or a snake
than keep house with a spiteful wife.

17 Her spite changes her expression,
making her look as surly as a bear.

18 Her husband goes to a neighbour for his meals
and cannot repress a bitter sigh.

19 There is nothing so bad as a bad wife;
may the fate of the wicked overtake her! *b*

20 It is as easy for an old man to climb a sand-dune
as for a quiet husband to live with a nagging wife.

21 Do not be enticed by a woman's beauty
or set your heart on possessing her.

22 If a man is supported by his wife
he must expect tantrums, shamelessness, and outrage.

23 A bad wife brings humiliation,
downcast looks, and a wounded heart.
Slack of hand and weak of knee
is the man whose wife fails to make him happy.

24 Woman is the origin of sin,
and it is through her that we all die.

25 Do not leave a leaky cistern to drip
or allow a bad wife to say what she likes.

26 If she does not accept your control,
divorce her and send her away.

**26** A good wife makes a happy husband;
she doubles the length of his life.

2 A staunch wife is her husband's joy;
he will live out his days in peace.

3 A good wife means a good life;
she is one of the Lord's gifts to those who fear him.

4 Rich or poor, they are light-hearted,
and always have a smile on their faces.

5 Three things there are that alarm me,
and a fourth I am afraid to face:
the scandal of the town, the gathering of a mob,
and calumny—all harder to bear than death;

*a Probable meaning, based on one Vs.; Gk. head.*      *b Or may it fall to her lot to marry a scoundrel!*

but it is heart-ache and grief when a wife is jealous of a rival,          6
and everyone alike feels the lash of her tongue.
A bad wife is a chafing yoke;          7
controlling her is like clutching a scorpion.
A drunken wife is a great provocation;          8
she cannot keep her excesses secret.

A loose woman betrays herself by her bold looks;          9
you can tell her by her glance.
Keep close watch over a headstrong daughter;          10
if she finds you off your guard, she will take her chance.
Beware of her impudent looks          11
and do not be surprised if she disobeys you.
As a parched traveller with his tongue hanging out          12
drinks from any spring that offers,
she will open her arms to every embrace,
and her quiver to the arrow.

A wife's charm is the delight of her husband,          13
and her womanly skill puts flesh on his bones.
A silent wife is a gift from the Lord;          14
her restraint is more than money can buy.
A modest wife has charm upon charm;          15
no scales can weigh the worth of her chastity.
As beautiful as the sunrise in the Lord's heaven          16
is a good wife in a well-ordered home.
As bright as the light on the sacred lamp-stand          17
is a beautiful face in the settled prime of life.
Like a golden pillar on a silver base          18
is a shapely leg with a firm foot. *a b*

*a*  is . . . foot: *probable meaning; Gk. obscure.*
*b*  *Some witnesses add*

My son, guard your health in the bloom of your youth,          19
and do not waste your vigour on what belongs to others.
Search the whole plain for a fertile plot;          20
sow your own seed, trusting in your pedigree.
Then the children you leave behind          21
will prosper, confident in their parentage.
A woman of the streets counts as mere spittle,          22
a married woman as a mortuary for her lovers.
A godless woman is a good match for a lawless husband,          23
a pious one for a man who fears the Lord.
A brazen woman courts disgrace,          24
but a virtuous one is modest even before her husband.
A wilful woman is a shameless bitch,          25
but a modest one fears the Lord.
A woman who honours her husband is accounted wise by all,          26
but if she despises him, all know her as proud and godless.
A good wife makes a happy husband;
she doubles the length of his life.
A strident, garrulous wife is like a trumpet sounding the charge;          27
in a home like hers a man lives in the tumult of war.

28    TWO THINGS GRIEVE my heart,
and a third excites my anger:
a soldier in distress through poverty,
wise men treated with contempt,
and a man deserting right conduct for wrong—
the Lord will bring him to the scaffold.

29    How hard it is for a merchant to keep clear of wrong
or for a shopkeeper to be innocent of dishonesty!

**27**   Many have cheated for gain; *a*
a money-grubber will always turn a blind eye.

2    As a peg is held fast in the joint between stones,
so dishonesty squeezes in between selling and buying.

3    Unless a man holds resolutely to the fear of the Lord,
his house will soon be in ruins.

4    Shake a sieve, and the rubbish remains;
start an argument, and discover a man's faults.

5    As the work of a potter is tested in the furnace,
so a man is tried in debate.

6    As the fruit of the tree reveals the skill of its grower,
so the expression of a man's thought reveals his character.

7    Do not praise a man till you hear him in discussion,
for this is the test.

8    If justice is what you seek, you will succeed,
and wear it like a splendid robe.

9    Birds of a feather roost together,
and honesty comes home to those who practise it.

10    A lion lies in wait for its prey,
and so do sins for those who do wrong.

11    The conversation of the pious is constantly wise,
but a fool is as changeable as the moon.

12    Grudge every minute spent among fools,
but linger among the thoughtful.

13    The conversation of fools is repulsive;
they make a joke of unbridled vice.

14    Their cursing and swearing make the hair stand on end;
when such men quarrel, others stop their ears.

15    The quarrels of the proud lead to bloodshed;
their abuse offends the ear.

16    The betrayer of secrets loses his credit
and can never find an intimate friend.

17    Love your friend and keep faith with him,
but if you betray his secrets, keep out of his way;

*a Some witnesses read* for a trifle.

as a man kills his enemy, 18
so you have killed your neighbour's friendship.
As a bird that is allowed to escape your hand, 19
your neighbour, once lost, will not be caught again.
He has gone too far for you to pursue him, 20
and escaped like a gazelle from a trap.
A wound may be bandaged, an insult pardoned, 21
but the betrayer of secrets has nothing to hope for.

A man who winks is plotting mischief; 22
those who know him will keep their distance.
He speaks sweetly enough to your face 23
and admires whatever you say,
but later he will change his tune
and use your own words to trip you.
There are many things I hate, but him above all; 24
the Lord will hate him too.

Whoever throws a stone up in the air is throwing it at his own head, 25
and a treacherous blow means wounds all round.
Dig a pit and you will fall into it; 26
set a trap and you will be caught by it.
The wrong a man does recoils on him, 27
and he does not know where it has come from.
An arrogant man deals in mockery and insults, 28
but retribution lies in wait for him like a lion.
Those who rejoice at the downfall of good men will be trapped 29
and consumed with pain before they die.

Rage and anger, these also I abhor, 30
but a sinner has them ready at hand.
The vengeful man will face the vengeance of the Lord, **28**
who keeps strict account of his sins.
Forgive your neighbour his wrongdoing; 2
then, when you pray, your sins will be forgiven.
If a man harbours a grudge against another, 3
is he to expect healing from the Lord?
If he has no mercy on his fellow-man, 4
is he still to ask forgiveness for his own sins?
If a mere mortal cherishes rage, 5
where is he to look for pardon?
Think of the end that awaits you, and have done with hate; 6
think of mortality and death, and be true to the commandments;
think of the commandments, and do not be enraged at your neighbour; 7
think of the covenant of the Most High, and overlook faults.

To avoid a quarrel is a setback for sin, 8
for it is a hot temper that kindles quarrels.
A sinner sows trouble between friends 9
and spreads scandal where before there was peace.

10 A fire is kept hot by stoking
and a quarrel by persistence.
A man's rage is in proportion to his strength,
and his anger in proportion to his wealth.

11 A hasty argument kindles a fire,
and a hasty quarrel leads to bloodshed.

12 Blow on a spark to make it glow, or spit on it to put it out;
both results come from the one mouth.

13 Curses on the gossip and the tale-bearer!
For they have been the ruin of many peaceable men.

14 The talk of a third party has wrecked the lives of many
and driven them from country to country;
it has destroyed fortified towns
and demolished the houses of the great.

15 The talk of a third party has brought divorce on staunch wives
and deprived them of all they have laboured for.

16 Whoever pays heed to it will never again find rest
or live in peace of mind.

17 The lash of a whip raises weals,
but the lash of a tongue breaks bones.

18 Many have been killed by the sword,
but not so many as by the tongue.

19 Happy the man who is sheltered from its onslaught,
who has not been exposed to its fury,
who has not borne its yoke,
or been chained with its fetters!

20 For its yoke is of iron,
its fetters of bronze.

21 The death it brings is an evil death;
better the grave than the tongue!

22 But it has no power over the godfearing;
they cannot be burned in its flames.

23 Those who desert the Lord fall victim to it;
among them it will burn like fire and not be quenched.
It will launch itself against them like a lion
and tear them like a leopard.

24 As you enclose your garden with a thorn hedge,
and lock up your silver and gold,

25 so weigh your words and measure them,
and make a door and a bolt for your mouth.

26 Beware of being tripped by your tongue
and falling into the power of a lurking enemy.

**29** A DEVOUT MAN lends to his neighbour;
by supporting him he keeps the commandments.

2 Lend to your neighbour in his time of need;
repay your neighbour punctually.

Be as good as your word and keep faith with him,    3
and your needs will always be met.
Many treat a loan as a windfall    4
and bring trouble on those who helped them.
Until he gets a loan, a man kisses his neighbour's hand    5
and talks with bated breath about his money;
but when it is time to repay, he postpones it,
pays back only perfunctory promises,
and alleges that the time is too short. [a]
If he can pay, his creditor will scarcely get back half,    6
and will count himself lucky at that;
if he cannot pay, he has defrauded the other of his money,
and gratuitously made an enemy of him; [b]
he will pay him back in curses and insults
and with shame instead of honour.
Because of such dishonesty many refuse to lend,    7
for fear of being needlessly defrauded.

Nevertheless be patient with the penniless,    8
and do not keep him waiting for your charity;
for the commandment's sake help the poor,    9
and in his need do not send him away empty-handed.
Be ready to lose money for a brother or a friend;    10
do not leave it to rust away under a stone.
Store up for yourself the treasure which the Most High has commanded,    11
and it will benefit you more than gold.
Let almsgiving be the treasure in your strong-room,    12
and it will rescue you from every misfortune.
It will arm you against the enemy    13
better than stout shield or strong spear.

A good man will stand surety for his neighbour;    14
only a man who has lost all sense of shame will fail him.
If a man stands surety for you, do not forget his kindness,    15
for he has staked his very self for you.
A sinner wastes the property of his surety,    16
and an ungrateful man fails his rescuer.    17
Suretyship has ruined the prosperity of many    18
and wrecked them like a storm at sea;
it has driven men of influence into exile,
and set them wandering in foreign countries.
When a sinner commits himself to suretyship,    19
his pursuit of gain will involve him in lawsuits.
Help your neighbour to the best of your ability,    20
but beware of becoming too deeply involved.

[a] *Or* that times are hard.      [b] and . . . him: *some witnesses read* and the other has
won himself an enemy at his own expense.

21 The necessities of life are water, bread, and clothes,
and a home with its decent privacy;

22 better the life of a poor man in his own hut
than a sumptuous banquet in another man's house.

23 Be content with whatever you have,
and do not get a name for living on hospitality.[a]

24 It is a poor life going from house to house,
keeping your mouth shut because you are a visitor.

25 You receive the guests and hand the drinks without being thanked for it,
and into the bargain must listen to words that rankle:

26 'Come here, stranger, and lay the table;
whatever you have there, hand it to me.'

27 'Be off, stranger! Make way for a more important guest;
my brother has come to stay, and I need the guest-room.'

28 How hard it is for a sensible man to bear
criticism from the household or abuse from his creditor!

30 A MAN WHO LOVES HIS SON will whip him often
so that when he grows up he may be a joy to him.

2 He who disciplines his son will find profit in him
and take pride in him among his acquaintances.

3 He who gives his son a good education will make his enemy jealous
and will boast of him among his friends.

4 When the father dies, it is as if he were still alive,
for he has left a copy of himself behind him.

5 While he lived he saw and rejoiced,
and when he died he had no regrets.

6 He has left an heir to take vengeance on his enemies
and to repay the kindness of his friends.

7 A man who spoils his son will bandage every wound
and will be on tenterhooks at every cry.

8 An unbroken horse turns out stubborn,
and an unchecked son turns out headstrong.

9 Pamper a boy and he will shock you;
play with him and he will grieve you.

10 Do not share his laughter, for fear of sharing his pain;
you will only end by grinding your teeth.

11 Do not give him freedom while he is young
or overlook his errors.

12 Break him in while he is young,
beat him soundly while he is still a child,
or he may grow stubborn and disobey you
and cause you vexation.

13 Discipline your son and take pains with him
or he may offend you by some disgraceful act.

[a] *Reading based on one Vs.; Gk.* and do not hear reproaches from your family.

BETTER A POOR MAN who is healthy and fit                    14
than a rich man racked by disease.
Health and fitness are better than any gold,                15
and bodily vigour than boundless prosperity.
There is no wealth to compare with health of body,          16
no festivity to equal a joyful heart.
Better death than a life of misery,                         17
eternal rest than a long illness.
Good things spread before a man without appetite            18
are like offerings of food placed on a tomb.
What use is a sacrifice to an idol                          19
which can neither taste nor smell?
So it is with the man afflicted by the Lord.
He gazes at the food before him and sighs                   20
as a eunuch sighs when he embraces a girl.

Do not give yourself over to sorrow                         21
or distress yourself deliberately.
A merry heart keeps a man alive,                            22
and joy lengthens his span of days.
Indulge yourself, take comfort,                             23
and banish sorrow;
for sorrow has been the death of many,
and no advantage ever came of it.
Envy and anger shorten a man's life,                        24
and anxiety brings premature old age.
A man with a gay heart has a good appetite                  25
and relishes the food he eats.

A rich man loses weight by wakeful nights,                  **31**
when the cares of wealth drive sleep away;
sleepless worry keeps him wide awake,                       2
just as serious illness banishes*a* sleep.
A rich man toils to amass a fortune,                        3
and when he relaxes he enjoys every luxury.
A poor man toils to make a slender living,                  4
and when he relaxes he finds himself in need.

Passion for gold can never be right;                        5
the pursuit of money leads a man astray.*b*
Many a man has come to ruin for the sake of gold            6
and found disaster staring him in the face.
Gold is a pitfall to those who are infatuated with it,      7
and every fool is caught by it.
Happy the rich man who has remained free of its taint       8
and has not made gold his aim!

*a* banishes: *probable meaning, based on Heb.; Gk. obscure.*        *b* the pursuit . . .
astray: *so Heb.; Gk.* the man who pursues destruction shall have his fill of it.

9   Show us that man, and we will congratulate him;
    he has performed a miracle among his people.
10  Has anyone ever come through this test unscathed?
    Then he has good cause to be proud.
    Has anyone ever had it in his power to sin and refrained,
    or to do wrong and has not done it?
11  Then he shall be confirmed in his prosperity,
    and the whole people will hail him as a benefactor.


12  IF YOU ARE SITTING at a grand table,
    do not lick your lips and exclaim, 'What a spread!'
13  Remember, it is a vice to have a greedy eye.
    There is no greater evil in creation than the eye;
    that is why it must shed tears at every turn.
14  Do not reach for everything you see,
    or jostle your fellow-guest at the dish;
15  judge his feelings by your own
    and always behave considerately.
16  Eat what is set before you like a gentleman;
    do not munch and make yourself objectionable.
17  Be the first to stop for good manners' sake
    and do not be insatiable, or you will give offence.
18  If you are dining in a large company,
    do not reach out your hand before others.
19  A man of good upbringing is content with little,
    and he is not short of breath when he goes to bed.
20  The moderate eater enjoys healthy sleep;
    he rises early, feeling refreshed.
    But sleeplessness, indigestion, and colic
    are the lot of the glutton.
21  If you cannot avoid overeating at a feast,
    leave the table and find relief by vomiting.


22  Listen to me, my son; do not disregard me,
    and in the end my words will come home to you.
    Whatever you do, do it shrewdly,
    and no illness will come your way.
23  Everyone has a good word for a liberal host,
    and the evidence of his generosity is convincing.
24  The whole town grumbles at a mean host,
    and there is precise evidence of his meanness.


25  Do not try to prove your manhood by drinking,
    for wine has been the ruin of many.
26  As the furnace tests iron when it is being tempered,
    so wine tests character when boastful men are wrangling.

Wine puts life into a man, 27
if he drinks it in moderation.
What is life to a man deprived of wine?
Was it not created to warm men's hearts?
Wine brings gaiety and high spirits, 28
if a man knows when to drink and when to stop;
but wine in excess makes for bitter feelings 29
and leads to offence and retaliation.
Drunkenness inflames a fool's anger to his own hurt; 30
it saps his strength and exposes him to injury.
At a banquet do not rebuke your fellow-guest 31
or make him feel small while he is enjoying himself.
This is no time to take up a quarrel with him
or pester him to pay his debts.

If they choose you to preside at a feast, do not put on airs; **32**
behave to them as one of themselves.
Look after the others before you sit down;
do not take your place until you have discharged all your duties. 2
Let their enjoyment be your pleasure,
and you will win the prize for good manners.

Speak, if you are old—it is your privilege— 3
but come to the point and do not interrupt the music.
Where entertainment is provided, do not keep up a stream of talk; 4
it is the wrong time to show off your wisdom.
Like a signet of ruby in a gold ring 5
is a concert of music at a banquet.
Like a signet of emerald in a gold setting 6
is tuneful music with good wine.

Speak, if you are young, when the need arises, 7
but twice at the most, and only when asked.
Be brief, say much in few words, 8
like a man who knows and can still hold his tongue.
Among the great do not act as their equal 9
or go on chattering when another is speaking.
As lightning travels ahead of thunder, 10
so popularity goes before a modest man.
Leave in good time and do not be the last to go; 11
go straight home without lingering.
There you may amuse yourself to your heart's content, 12
and run no risk of arrogant talk.
And one thing more: give praise to your Maker, 13
who has filled your cup with his blessings.


THE MAN WHO FEARS THE LORD will accept his discipline, 14
and the diligent will receive his approval.

15     The genuine student will find satisfaction in the law,
        but it will prove a stumbling-block to the insincere.
16     Those who fear the Lord will discover what is right,
        and will make his decrees*a* shine out like a lamp.
17     A sinner will not accept criticism;
        he will find precedents to justify his choice.

18     A sensible man can always take a hint;
        but an arrogant heathen does not know the meaning of diffidence.
19     Never do anything without deliberation,
        and afterwards you will have no regrets.*b*
20     Do not travel by a road full of obstacles
        and stumble along through its boulders.
21     Do not be careless on a clear road
22     but watch where you are going.*c*
23     Whatever you are doing, rely on yourself,
        for this too is a way of keeping the commandments.
24     To rely on the law is to heed its commandments,
        and to trust the Lord is to want for nothing.

**33**     Disaster never comes the way of the man who fears the Lord:
        in times of trial he will be rescued again and again.
2     A wise man never hates the law,
        but the man who is insincere about it is like a boat in a squall.
3     A sensible man trusts the law
        and finds it as reliable as the divine oracle.

4     Prepare what you have to say, if you want a hearing;
        marshal your learning and then give your answer.
5     The feelings of a fool turn like a cart-wheel,
        and his thoughts spin like an axle.
6     A sarcastic friend is like a stallion
        which neighs no matter who is on its back.

7     Why is one day more important than another,
        when every day in the year has its light from the sun?
8     It was by the Lord's decision that they were distinguished;
        he appointed the various seasons and festivals:
9     some days he made high and holy,
        and others he assigned to the common run of days.
10     All men alike come from the ground;
        Adam was created out of earth.
11     Yet in his great wisdom the Lord distinguished them
        and made them go various ways:

*a* *Or* their good conduct.         *b* you . . . regrets: *or* do not change your mind.
*c* but . . . going: *so Heb.; Gk.* and keep an eye on your children.

some he blessed and lifted high,                                    12
some he hallowed and brought near to himself,
some he cursed and humbled
and removed from their place.
As clay is in the potter's hands,                                   13
to be moulded just as he chooses,
so are men in the hands of their Maker,
to be dealt with as he decides.
Good is the opposite of evil, and life of death;                    14
yes, and the sinner is the opposite of the godly.
Look at all the works of the Most High:                             15
they go in pairs, one the opposite of the other.

I was the last to wake up,                                          16
I was like a gleaner following the grape-pickers;
by the Lord's blessing I arrived in time
to fill my winepress as full as any of them.
Remember that I did not toil for myself alone,                      17
but for all who seek learning.
Listen to me, you dignitaries;                                      18
leaders of the assembly, give me your attention.

As long as you live, give no one power over yourself—               19
son or wife, brother or friend.
Do not give your property to another,
in case you change your mind and want it back.
As long as you have life and breath,                                20
never change places with anyone.
It is better for your children to ask from you                      21
than for you to be dependent on them.
Whatever you are doing, keep the upper hand,                        22
and allow no blot on your reputation.
Let your life run its full course,                                  23
and then, at the hour of death, distribute your estate.

Fodder, and stick, and burdens for the donkey;                      24
bread, and discipline, and work for the servant!
Make your slave work, if you want rest for yourself;                25
if you leave him idle, he will be looking for his liberty.
The ox is tamed by yoke and harness,                                26
the bad servant by racks and tortures.
Put him to work to keep him from being idle,                        27
for idleness is a great teacher of mischief.
Set him to work, for that is what he is for,                        28
and if he disobeys you, load him with fetters.

Do not be too exacting towards anyone                               29
or do anything contrary to justice.

30 If you have a servant, treat him as an equal,
because you bought him with blood.

31 If you have a servant, treat him like a brother;
you will need him as much as you need yourself.
If you ill-treat him and he takes to his heels,
where will you go to look for him?

**34** Vain hopes delude the senseless,
and dreams give wings to a fool's fancy.

2 It is like clutching a shadow, or chasing the wind,
to take notice of dreams.

3 What you see in a dream is nothing but a reflection,
like the image of a face in a mirror.

4 Purity cannot come out of filth;
how then can truth issue from falsehood?

5 Divination, omens, and dreams are all futile,
mere fantasies, like those of a woman in labour.

6 Unless they are sent by intervention from the Most High,
pay no attention to them.

7 Dreams have led many astray
and ruined those who built their hopes on them.

8 Such delusions can add nothing to the completeness of the law;
the wisdom spoken by the faithful is complete in itself.

9 An educated man knows many things,
and a man of experience understands what he is talking about.

10 An inexperienced man knows little,
but a man who travels grows in ability.

11 I have seen many things in the course of my travels,
and understand more than I can tell.

12 I have often been in deadly danger
and escaped, thanks to the experience I had gained.

## True piety and the mercy of God

13 THOSE WHO FEAR the Lord shall live,
for their trust is in one who can keep them safe.

14 The man who fears the Lord will have nothing else to fear;
he will never be a coward, because his trust is in the Lord.

15 How blest is the man who fears the Lord!
He knows where to look for support.

16 The Lord keeps watch over those who love him,
their strong shield and firm support,
a shelter from scorching wind and midday heat,
a safeguard against stumbles and falls.

17 He raises the spirits and makes the eyes sparkle,
giving health, and life, and blessing.

A sacrifice derived from ill-gotten gains is contaminated,    18
a lawless mockery that cannot win approval.
The Most High is not pleased with the offering of the godless,    19
nor do endless sacrifices win his forgiveness.
To offer a sacrifice from the possessions of the poor    20
is like killing a son before his father's eyes.
Bread is life to the destitute,    21
and it is murder to deprive them of it.
To rob your neighbour of his livelihood is to kill him,    22
and the man who cheats a worker of his wages sheds blood.
When one builds and another pulls down,    23
what have they gained except hard work?
When one prays and another curses,    24
which is the Lord to listen to?
Wash after touching a corpse and then touch it again,    25
and what have you gained by your washing?
So it is with the man who fasts for his sins    26
and goes and does the same again;
who will listen to his prayer?
what has he gained by his penance?

Keeping the law is worth many offerings;    **35**
to heed the commandments is to sacrifice a thank-offering.
A kindness repaid is an offering of flour,    2
and to give alms is a praise-offering.
The way to please the Lord is to renounce evil;    3
and to renounce wrongdoing is to make atonement.
Yet do not appear before the Lord empty-handed;    4
perform these sacrifices because they are commanded.    5
When the just man brings his offering of fat to the altar,    6
its fragrance rises to the presence of the Most High.
The just man's sacrifice is acceptable;    7
it will never be forgotten.
Be generous in your worship of the Lord    8
and present the firstfruits of your labour in full measure.
Give all your gifts cheerfully    9
and be glad to dedicate your tithe.
Give to the Most High as he has given to you,    10
as generously as you can afford.
For the Lord always repays;    11
you will be repaid seven times over.

Do not offer him a bribe, for he will not accept it,    12
and do not rely on a dishonest sacrifice;
for the Lord is a judge
who knows no partiality.
He has no favourites at the poor man's expense,    13
but listens to his prayer when he is wronged.

14    He never ignores the appeal of the orphan
      or the widow when she pours out her complaint.
15    How the tears run down the widow's cheeks,
      and her cries accuse the man who caused them!
16    To be accepted a man must serve the Lord as he requires,
      and then his prayer will reach the clouds.
17    The prayer of the humble pierces the clouds,
      but he is not consoled until it reaches its destination.
      He does not desist until the Most High intervenes,
      gives the just their rights, and sees justice done.
18    The Lord will not be slow,
      neither will he be patient with the wicked,
      until he crushes the sinews of the merciless
      and sends retribution on the heathen;
      until he blots out the insolent, one and all,
      and breaks the power of the unjust;
19    until he gives all men their deserts,
      judging their actions by their intentions;
      until he gives his people their rights
      and gladdens them with his mercy.
20    His mercy is as timely in days of trouble
      as rain-clouds in days of drought.


36    HAVE PITY ON US, O LORD, thou God of all; look down,
2     and send thy terror upon all nations.
3     Raise thy hand against the heathen,
      and let them see thy power.
4     As they have seen thy holiness displayed among us,
      so let us see thy greatness displayed among them.
5     Let them learn, as we also have learned,
      that there is no God but only thou, O Lord.
6     Renew thy signs, repeat thy miracles,
      win glory for thy hand, for thy right arm.
7     Rouse thy wrath, pour out thy fury,
      destroy the adversary, wipe out the enemy.
8     Remember the day thou hast appointed and hasten it, *a*
      and give men cause to recount thy wonders.
9     Let fiery anger devour the survivors,
      and let the oppressors of thy people meet their doom.
10    Crush the heads of hostile princes,
      who say, 'There is no one to match us.'
11·   Gather all the tribes of Jacob,
      and grant them their inheritance, *b* as thou didst long ago.
12    Have pity, O Lord, on the people called by thy name,
      Israel, whom thou hast named thy first-born.

*a* Remember . . . it: *some witnesses read* Hasten the day and remember thy oath.
*b* Or and take them to be thy own.

Show mercy to the city of thy sanctuary,     13
Jerusalem, the city of thy rest.
Fill Zion with the praise of thy triumph;     14
fill thy people with thy glory.
Thou didst create them at the beginning; acknowledge them now     15
and fulfil the prophecies spoken in thy name.
Reward those who wait for thee;     16
prove thy prophets trustworthy.
Listen, O Lord, to the prayer of thy servants,     17
who claim Aaron's blessing upon thy people.
Let all who live on earth acknowledge
that thou art the Lord, the eternal God.


## Man in society

ALL IS FOOD for the stomach,     18
but one food is better than another.
As the palate identifies game by its taste,     19
so the discerning mind detects lies.
A warped mind makes trouble,     20
but a man of experience can pay it back.

A woman will take any man for husband,     21
but a man may prefer one girl to another.
A woman's beauty makes a man happy,     22
and there is nothing he desires more.
If she has a kind and gentle tongue,     23
then her husband is luckier than most men.
The man who wins a wife has the beginnings of a fortune,     24
a helper to match his needs and a pillar to support him.
Where there is no hedge, property is plundered;     25
and where there is no wife, the wanderer sighs for a home.
Does anyone trust a roving bandit     26
who swoops on town after town?
No more will they trust a homeless man
who lodges wherever night overtakes him.

Every friend says, 'I too am your friend';     **37**
but some are friends in name only.
What a mortal grief it is     2
when a dear friend turns into an enemy!
Oh this propensity to evil, how did it creep in     3
to cover the earth with treachery?
A friend may be all smiles when you are happy,     4
but turn against you when trouble comes.
Another shares your toil for the sake of a meal,     5
and yet may protect you against an enemy.

6      Never forget a friend
or neglect him when prosperity comes your way.


7      Every counsellor says his own advice is best,
but some have their own advantage in view.

8      Beware of the man who offers advice,
and find out beforehand where his interest lies.
His advice will be weighted in his own favour
and may tip the scales against you.

9      He may say, 'Your road is clear',
and stand aside to see what happens.

10      Do not consult a man who is suspicious of you
or reveal your intentions to those who envy you.

11      Never consult a woman about her rival
or a coward about war,
a merchant about a bargain
or a buyer about a sale,
a skinflint about gratitude
or a hard-hearted man about a kind action,
an idler about work of any sort,
a casual labourer about finishing the job,
or a lazy servant about an exacting task—
do not turn to them for any advice.

12      Rely rather on a godfearing man
whom you know to be a keeper of the commandments,
whose interests are like your own,
who will sympathize if you have a setback.

13      But also trust your own judgement,
for it is your most reliable counsellor.

14      A man's own mind has sometimes a way of telling him more
than seven watchmen posted high on a tower.

15      But above all pray to the Most High
to keep you on the straight road of truth.


16      Every undertaking begins in discussion,
and consultation precedes every action.

17      Here you can trace the mind's variety.

18      Four kinds of destiny are offered to men,
good and evil, life and death;
and always it is the tongue that decides the issue.

19      A man may be clever enough to teach others
and yet be useless to himself.

20      A brilliant speaker may make enemies
and end by dying of hunger,

21      if the Lord has withheld the gift of popular appeal,
because he is devoid of wisdom.

22      If a man is wise in the conduct of his own life,
his good sense can be trusted when he speaks.

If a man is wise and instructs his people,      23
then his good sense can be trusted.
A wise man will have praise heaped on him,      24
and all who see him will count him happy.
The days of a man's life can be numbered,      25
but the days of Israel are countless.
A wise man will possess the confidence of his people,      26
and his name will live for ever.

MY SON, TEST YOURSELF all your life long;      27
take note of what is bad for you and do not indulge in it.
For not everything is good for everyone;      28
we do not all enjoy the same things.
Do not be greedy for every delicacy      29
or eat without restraint.
For illness is a sure result of overeating,      30
and gluttony is next door to colic.
Gluttony has been the death of many;      31
be on your guard and prolong your life.

Honour the doctor for his services,      **38**
for the Lord created him.
His skill comes from the Most High,      2
and he is rewarded by kings.
The doctor's knowledge gives him high standing      3
and wins him the admiration of the great.
The Lord has created medicines from the earth,      4
and a sensible man will not disparage them.
Was it not a tree that sweetened water      5
and so disclosed its properties[a]?
The Lord has imparted knowledge to men,      6
that by their use of his marvels he may win praise;
by using them the doctor[b] relieves pain      7
and from them the pharmacist makes up his mixture.      8
There is no end to the works of the Lord,
who spreads health over the whole world.

My son, if you have an illness, do not neglect it,      9
but pray to the Lord, and he will heal you.
Renounce your faults, amend your ways,      10
and cleanse your heart from all sin.
Bring a savoury offering and bring flour for a token      11
and pour oil on the sacrifice; be as generous as you can.[c]
Then call in the doctor, for the Lord created him;      12
do not let him leave you, for you need him.

[a] *Or* and revealed the power of the Lord.      [b] the doctor: *so Heb.; Gk.* he heals
and ...      [c] be ... can: *so Heb.; Gk. obscure.*

13　There may come a time when your recovery is in their hands;
14　then they too will pray to the Lord
　　to give them success in relieving pain
　　and finding a cure to save their patient's life.
15　When a man has sinned against his Maker,
　　let him put himself in the doctor's hands.


16　My son, shed tears for the dead;
　　raise a lament for your grievous loss.
　　Shroud his body with proper ceremony,
　　and do not neglect his burial.
17　With bitter weeping and passionate lament
　　make your mourning worthy of him.
　　Mourn for a few days as propriety demands,
　　and then take comfort for your grief.
18　For grief may lead to death,
　　and a sorrowful heart saps the strength.
19　When a man is taken away, suffering is over,
　　but to live on in poverty goes against the grain.
20　Do not abandon yourself to grief;
　　put it from you and think of your own end.
21　Never forget! there is no return;
　　you cannot help him and can only injure yourself.
22　Remember that his fate will also be yours:
　　'Mine today and yours tomorrow.'
23　When the dead is at rest, let his memory rest too;
　　take comfort as soon as he has breathed his last.


24　A SCHOLAR'S WISDOM comes of ample leisure;
　　if a man is to be wise he must be relieved of other tasks.
25　How can a man become wise who guides the plough,
　　whose pride is in wielding his goad,
　　who is absorbed in the task of driving oxen,
　　and talks only about cattle?
26　He concentrates on ploughing his furrows,
　　and works late to give the heifers their fodder.
27　So it is with every craftsman or designer
　　who works by night as well as by day,
　　such as those who make engravings on signets,
　　and patiently vary the design;
　　they concentrate on making an exact representation,
　　and sit up late to finish their task.
28　So it is with the smith, sitting by his anvil,
　　intent on his iron-work.
　　The smoke of the fire shrivels his flesh,
　　as he wrestles in the heat of the furnace.

The hammer rings again and again in his ears,
and his eyes are on the pattern he is copying.
He concentrates on completing the task,
and stays up late to give it a perfect finish.
So it is with the potter, sitting at his work,      29
turning the wheel with his feet,
always engrossed in the task
of making up his tally;
he moulds the clay with his arm,      30
crouching forward to apply his strength.
He concentrates on finishing the glazing,
and stays awake to clean out the furnace.

All these rely on their hands,      31
and each is skilful at his own craft.
Without them a city would have no inhabitants;      32
no settlers or travellers would come to it.
Yet they are not in demand at public discussions      33
or prominent in the assembly.
They do not sit on the judge's bench
or understand the decisions of the courts.
They cannot expound moral or legal principles
and are not ready with maxims.
But they maintain the fabric of this world,      34
and their prayers are about their daily work. *a*

How different it is with the man who devotes himself      **39**
to studying the law of the Most High,
who investigates all the wisdom of the past,
and spends his time studying the prophecies!
He preserves the sayings of famous men      2
and penetrates the intricacies of parables.
He investigates the hidden meaning of proverbs      3
and knows his way among riddles.
The great avail themselves of his services,      4
and he is seen in the presence of rulers.
He travels in foreign countries
and learns at first hand the good or evil of man's lot.
He makes a point of rising early      5
to pray to the Lord, his Maker,
and prays aloud to the Most High,
asking pardon for his sins.
If it is the will of the great Lord,      6
he will be filled with a spirit of intelligence;
then he will pour forth wise sayings of his own
and give thanks to the Lord in prayer.

*a   Or and their daily work is their prayer.*

7    He will have sound advice and knowledge to offer,
     and his thoughts will dwell on the mysteries he has studied.
8    He will disclose what he has learnt from his own education,
     and will take pride in the law of the Lord's covenant.
9    Many will praise his intelligence;
     it will never sink into oblivion.
     The memory of him will not die
     but will live on from generation to generation;
10   the nations will talk of his wisdom,
     and his praises will be sung in the assembly.
11   If he lives long, he will leave a name in a thousand,
     and if he goes to his rest, his reputation is secure.[a]


12   I HAVE STILL MORE in my mind to express;
     I am full like the moon at mid-month.
13   Listen to me, my devout sons, and blossom
     like a rose planted by a stream.
14   Spread your fragrance like incense,
     and bloom like a lily.
     Scatter your fragrance; lift your voices in song,
     praising the Lord for all his works.
15   Ascribe majesty to his name
     and give thanks to him with praise,
     with songs on your lips, and with harps;
     let these be your words of thanksgiving:
16   'All that the Lord has made is very good;
     all that he commands will happen in due time.'
17   No one should ask, 'What is this?' or 'Why is that?'
     At the proper time all such questions will be answered.
     When he spoke the water stood up like a heap,
     and his word created reservoirs for it.
18   When he commands, his purpose is fulfilled,
     and no one can thwart his saving power.
19   He sees the deeds of all mankind;
     there is no hiding from his gaze.
20   From the beginning to the end of time he keeps watch,
     and nothing is too marvellous for him.
21   No one should ask, 'What is this?' or 'Why is that?'
     Everything has been created for its own purpose.
22   His blessing is like a river in flood
     which inundates the parched ground.
23   But the doom he assigns the heathen is his wrath,
     as when he turned a watered plain into a salt desert.
24   For the devout his paths are straight,
     but full of pitfalls for the wicked.

[a] his reputation is secure: *possible reading; Gk. obscure.*

From the beginning good things were created for the good,    25
and evils for sinners.
The chief necessities of human life    26
are water, fire, iron, and salt,
flour, honey, and milk,
the juice of the grape, oil, and clothing.
All these are good for the godfearing,    27
but turn to evil for sinners.

There are winds created to be agents of retribution,    28
with great whips to give play to their fury;
on the day of reckoning, they exert their force
and give full vent to the anger of their Maker.
Fire and hail, famine and deadly disease,    29
all these were created for retribution;
beasts of prey, scorpions and vipers,    30
and the avenging sword that destroys the wicked.
They delight in carrying out his orders,    31
always standing ready for his service on the earth;
and when their time comes, they never disobey.

I have been convinced of all this from the beginning;    32
I have thought it over and left it in writing:
all the works of the Lord are good,    33
and he supplies every need as it occurs.
No one should say, 'This is less good than that',    34
for all things prove good at their proper time.
Come then, sing with heart and voice,    35
and praise the name of the Lord.

HARD WORK IS THE LOT of every man,    **40**
and a heavy yoke is laid on the sons of Adam,
from the day when they come from their mothers' womb
until the day of their return to the mother of all;
troubled thoughts and fears are theirs,    2
and anxious expectation of the day of their death.
Whether a man sits in royal splendour on a throne    3
or grovels in dust and ashes,
whether he wears the purple and a crown    4
or is clothed in sackcloth,
his life is nothing but anger and jealousy, worry and perplexity,    5
fear of death, and guilt, and rivalry.
Even when he goes to bed at night,
sleep only brings to mind the same things in a new form.
His rest is little or nothing;    6
he begins to struggle as hard in his sleep as in the day.*a*

     *a* he begins . . . day: *possible meaning; Gk. obscure.*

Disturbed by nightmares,
he fancies himself a fugitive from the battlefield;

7  and at the moment when he reaches safety, he wakes up,
astonished to find his fears groundless.

8  To all living creatures, man and beast—
and seven times over to sinners—

9  come death and bloodshed, quarrel and sword,
disaster, famine, ruin, and plague.

10  All these were created for the wicked,
and on their account the flood happened.

11  All that is of earth returns to earth again,
and all that is of water finds its way back to the sea.

12  Bribery and injustice will all vanish,
but good faith will last for ever.

13  The wealth of the wicked will dry up like a torrent
and die away like a great roll of thunder in a storm.

14  As a generous man will have cause for rejoicing,
so law-breakers will come to utter ruin.

15  The shoots of an impious stock put out few branches;
their tainted roots are planted on sheer rock.

16  The rush that grows on every river-bank
is pulled up before any other grass,

17  but kindness is like a luxuriant garden,
and almsgiving lasts for ever.

18  To be employed and to be one's own master, both are sweet,
but it is better still to find a treasure.

19  Offspring and the founding of a city perpetuate a man's name,
but better still is a perfect wife.

20  Wine and music gladden the heart,
but better still is the love of wisdom.

21  Flute and harp make pleasant melody,
but better still is a pleasant voice.

22  A man likes to see grace and beauty,
but better still the green shoots in a cornfield.

23  A friend or companion is always welcome,
but better still to be man and wife.

24  Brothers and helpers are a stand-by in time of trouble,
but better still is almsgiving.

25  Gold and silver make a man stand firm,
but better still is good advice.

26  Wealth and strength make for confidence,
but better still is the fear of the Lord.
To fear the Lord is to lack nothing
and never to be in need of support.

27  The fear of the Lord is like a luxuriant garden;
it shelters a man better than any riches.

My son, do not live the life of a beggar;     28
it is better to die than to beg.
When a man starts looking to another man's table,     29
his existence is not worth calling life.
It is demoralizing to live on another man's food,
and a wise, well-disciplined man will guard against it.
When a man has lost all shame, he speaks as if begging were sweet,     30
but inside him there is a blazing fire.

Death, how bitter is the thought of you     **41**
to a man living at ease among his possessions,
free from anxiety, prosperous in all things,
and still vigorous enough to enjoy a good meal!
Death, how welcome is your sentence     2
to a destitute man whose strength is failing,
worn down by age and endless anxiety,
resentful and at the end of his patience!
Do not be afraid of death's summons;     3
remember those who have gone before you, and those who will come after.
This is the Lord's decree for all living men;     4
why try to argue with the will of the Most High?
Whether life lasts ten years, or a hundred, or a thousand,
there will be no questions asked in the grave.

What a loathsome brood are the children of sinners,     5
brought up in haunts of vice!
Their inheritance dwindles away,     6
and their descendants suffer a lasting disgrace.
A godless father is blamed by his children     7
for the disgrace they endure on his account.
Woe to you, godless men     8
who have abandoned the law of God Most High!
When you are born, you are born to a curse,     9
and when you die, a curse is your lot.
Whatever comes from earth returns to earth;     10
so too the godless go from curse to ruin.
Men grieve over the death of the body,     11
but sinners have no good name to survive them.
Take thought for your name, for it will outlive you     12
longer than a thousand hoards of gold.
The days of a good life are numbered,     13
but a good name lasts for ever.

MY CHILDREN, BE TRUE to your training and live in peace.     14
Wisdom concealed and treasure hidden—
what is the use of either?
Better a man who hides his folly     15
than one who hides his wisdom!

16 Show deference then to my teaching:
shame is not always to be encouraged,
or given unqualified approval in all circumstances.

17 Be ashamed to be found guilty of fornication by your parents,
or of lies by a ruler or prince;

18 of crime by a judge or magistrate,
or of a breach of the law by the assembly and people;
of dishonesty by a partner or friend,

19 or of theft by the neighbourhood;
be ashamed before the truth of God and his covenant.
Be ashamed of bad manners at table,
of giving or receiving with a sneer,

20 of refusing to return a greeting,
or of ogling a prostitute.

21 Be ashamed of turning away a relative,
of robbing someone of his rightful share,
or of eyeing another man's wife.

22 Be ashamed of meddling with his slave-girl,
and keep away from her bed.
Be ashamed of reproaching your friends,
or following up your charity with a lecture.

23 Be ashamed of repeating what you have heard
and of betraying a secret.

24 Then you will be showing a proper shame
and will be popular with everyone.

**42** But at other times you must not be ashamed,
or you will do wrong out of deference to others.

2 Do not be ashamed of the law and covenant of the Most High,
or of justice, for fear you acquit the guilty;

3 of settling accounts with a partner or a travelling-companion,
or of sharing an inheritance with the other heirs;

4 of using accurate weights and measures,
or of business dealings, large or small,

5 and making a profit out of trade;
of frequent disciplining of children,
or of drawing blood from the back of a worthless servant.

6 If your wife is untrustworthy, or where many hands are at work,
it is well to keep things under lock and key.

7 When you make a deposit, see that it is counted and weighed,
and when you give or receive, have it all in writing.

8 Do not be ashamed to correct the ignorant and foolish,
or a greybeard guilty of fornication.
Then you will be showing your sound upbringing
and will win everyone's approval.

9 A daughter is a secret anxiety to her father,
and the worry of her keeps him awake at night;

when she is young, for fear she may grow too old to marry,
and when she is married, for fear she may lose her husband's love;
when she is a virgin, for fear she may be seduced                    10
and become pregnant in her father's house,
when she has a husband, for fear she may misbehave,
and after marriage, for fear she may be barren.
Keep close watch over a headstrong daughter,                    11
or she may give your enemies cause to gloat,
making you the talk of the town and a byword*a* among the people,
and shaming you in the eyes of the world.
Do not let her display her beauty to any man,                    12
or gossip in the women's quarters.*b*
For out of clothes comes the moth,                    13
and out of woman comes woman's wickedness.
Better a man's wickedness than a woman's goodness;                    14
it is woman who brings shame and disgrace.

## The wonders of creation

NOW I WILL CALL to mind the works of the Lord                    15
and describe what I have seen;
by the words of the Lord his works are made.
As the sun in its brilliance looks down on everything,                    16
so the glory of the Lord fills his creation.
Even to his angels the Lord has not given the power                    17
to tell the full story of his marvels,
which the Lord Almighty has established
so that the universe may stand firm in his glory.
He fathoms the abyss and the heart of man,                    18
he is versed in their intricate secrets;
for the Lord possesses all knowledge
and observes the signs of all time.
He discloses the past and the future,                    19
and uncovers the traces of the world's mysteries.
No thought escapes his notice,                    20
and not a word is hidden from him.
He has set in order the masterpieces of his wisdom,                    21
he who is from eternity to eternity;
nothing can be added, nothing taken away,
and he needs no one to give him advice.
How beautiful is all that he has made,                    22
down to the smallest spark that can be seen!
His works endure, all of them active for ever                    23
and all responsive to their various purposes.
All things go in pairs, one the opposite of the other;                    24
he has made nothing incomplete.

*a* a byword: *so Heb.; Gk. obscure.*        *b* Do not ... quarters: *so Heb.; Gk. obscure.*

25   One thing supplements the virtues of another.
Who could ever contemplate his glory enough?

**43**   What a masterpiece is the clear vault of the sky!
How glorious is the spectacle of the heavens!

2   The sun comes into view proclaiming as it rises
how marvellous a thing it is, made by the Most High.

3   At noon it parches the earth,
and no one can endure its blazing heat.

4   The stoker of a furnace works in the heat,
but three times as hot is the sun scorching the hills.
It breathes out fiery vapours,
and its glare blinds the eyes.

5   Great is the Lord who made it,
whose word speeds it on its course.

6   He made the moon also to serve in its turn,
a perpetual sign to mark the divisions of time.

7   From the moon, feast-days are reckoned;
it is a light that wanes as it completes its course.

8   The moon gives its name to the month;
it waxes marvellously as its phases change,
a beacon to the armies of heaven,
shining in the vault of the sky.

9   The brilliant stars are the beauty of the sky,
a glittering array in the heights of the Lord.

10   At the command of the Holy One they stand in their appointed place;
they never default at their post.

11   Look at the rainbow and praise its Maker;
it shines with a supreme beauty,

12   rounding the sky with its gleaming arc,
a bow bent by the hands of the Most High.

13   His command speeds the snow-storm
and sends the swift lightning to execute his sentence.

14   To that end the storehouses are opened,
and the clouds fly out like birds.

15   By his mighty power the clouds are piled up
and the hailstones broken small.

16-17   The crash of his thunder makes the earth writhe,
and, when he appears, an earthquake shakes the hills.
At his will the south wind blows,
the squall from the north and the hurricane.
He scatters the snow-flakes like birds alighting;
they settle like a swarm of locusts.

18   The eye is dazzled by their beautiful whiteness,
and as they fall the mind is entranced.

He spreads frost on the earth like salt,                                      19
and icicles form like pointed stakes.
A cold blast from the north,                                                  20
and ice grows hard on the water,
settling on every pool,
as though the water were putting on a breastplate.
He consumes the hills, scorches the wilderness,                               21
and withers the grass like fire.
Cloudy weather quickly puts all to rights,                                    22
and dew brings welcome relief after heat.

By the power of his thought he tamed the deep                                 23
and planted it with islands.
Those who sail the sea tell stories of its dangers,                           24
which astonish all who hear them;
in it are strange and wonderful creatures,                                    25
all kinds of living things and huge sea-monsters.
By his own action he achieves his end,                                        26
and by his word all things are held together.

However much we say, we cannot exhaust our theme;                             27
to put it in a word: he is all.
Where can we find the skill to sing his praises?                              28
For he is greater than all his works.
The Lord is terrible and very great,                                          29
and marvellous is his power.
Honour the Lord to the best of your ability,                                  30
and he will still be high above all praise.
Summon all your strength to declare his greatness,
and be untiring, for the most you can do will fall short.
Has anyone ever seen him, to be able to describe him?                         31
Can anyone praise him as he truly is?
We have seen but a small part of his works,                                   32
and there remain many mysteries greater still.
The Lord has made everything                                                  33
and has given wisdom to the godly.

## Heroes of Israel's past

L ET US NOW SING the praises of famous men,                                   **44**
    the heroes of our nation's history,
through whom the Lord established his renown,                                 2
and revealed his majesty in each succeeding age.
Some held sway over kingdoms                                                  3
and made themselves a name by their exploits.
Others were sage counsellors,
who spoke out with prophetic power.

4 Some led the people by their counsels
and by their knowledge of the nation's law;
out of their fund of wisdom they gave instruction.

5 Some were composers of music or writers of poetry.

6 Others were endowed with wealth and strength,
living peacefully in their homes.

7 All these won fame in their own generation
and were the pride of their times.

8 Some there are who have left a name behind them
to be commemorated in story.

9 There are others who are unremembered;
they are dead, and it is as though they had never existed,
as though they had never been born
or left children to succeed them.

10 Not so our forefathers; they were men of loyalty,
whose good deeds have never been forgotten.

11 Their prosperity is handed on to their descendants,
and their inheritance to future generations.[a]

12 Thanks to them their children are within the covenants—
the whole race of their descendants.

13 Their line will endure for all time,
and their fame will never be blotted out.

14 Their bodies are buried in peace,
but their name lives for ever.

15 Nations will recount their wisdom,
and God's people will sing their praises.

16 Enoch pleased the Lord and was carried off to heaven,
an example of repentance to future generations.

17 Noah was found perfect and righteous,
and thus he made amends in the time of retribution;
therefore a remnant survived on the earth,
when the flood came.

18 A perpetual covenant was established with him,
that never again should all life be swept away by a flood.

19 Great Abraham was the father of many nations;
no one has ever been found to equal him in fame.

20 He kept the law of the Most High;
he entered into covenant with him,
setting upon his body the mark of the covenant;
and, when he was tested, he proved faithful.

21 Therefore the Lord swore an oath to him,
that nations should find blessing through his descendants,
that his family should be countless as the dust of the earth
and be raised as high as the stars,
and that their possessions should reach from sea to sea,
from the Great River to the ends of the earth.

[a] Their prosperity ... generations: *probable meaning, based on other Vss.; Gk. obscure.*

To Isaac he made the same promise                                    22
for the sake of his father Abraham,
a blessing for all mankind and a covenant;
and so he transmitted them to Jacob.                                  23
He confirmed him in the blessings he had received
and gave him the land he was to inherit,
dividing it into portions,
which he allotted to the twelve tribes.

From Jacob's stock the Lord raised up a loyal servant,           **45**
who won the approval of all mankind,
beloved by God and men,
Moses of blessed memory.
The Lord made him equal in glory to the angels                        2
and gave him power to strike terror into his enemies.
At his request he put an end to the portents,                         3
and enhanced his reputation with kings.
He gave him commandments for his people
and showed him a vision of his own glory.
For his loyalty and humility he consecrated him,                      4
choosing him out of all mankind.
He let him hear his voice                                             5
and led him into the dark cloud.
Face to face, he gave him the commandments,
a law that brings life and knowledge,
so that he might teach Jacob the covenant
and Israel his decrees.

He raised to a like holy office                                       6
Moses' brother Aaron from the tribe of Levi.
He made a perpetual covenant with him,                                7
conferring on him the priesthood of the nation.
He honoured him with splendid ornaments
and clothed him in gorgeous vestments.
He robed him in perfect splendour                                     8
and armed him with the emblems of power,
the breeches, the mantle, and the tunic.
Round his robe he placed pomegranates                                 9
and a circle of many golden bells,
to make music as he walked,
ringing aloud throughout the temple
as a reminder to his people.
He gave him the sacred vestment adorned by an embroiderer           10
with gold and violet and purple;
the oracle of judgement with the tokens of truth; [a]
the scarlet thread spun with a craftsman's art;                     11

_____
[a] the oracle . . . truth: *or* the breast-piece of judgement with the Urim and Thummim
(*Exodus 28. 30*).

the precious stones, engraved like seals,
and placed by the jeweller in a gold setting,
with inscriptions to serve as reminders,
one for each of the tribes of Israel;

12  the gold crown upon his turban,
engraved like a seal with 'Holy to the Lord'. *a*
What rich adornments to feast the eyes!
What a miracle of art! What a proud honour!

13  Before him no such splendour existed,
and no one outside his family has ever put them on,
no one except his sons
and his descendants in perpetuity.

14  Twice every day without fail
they present his sacrifice of a whole-offering.

15  It was Moses who ordained him
and anointed him with sacred oil,
in token of the perpetual covenant made with him
and with his descendants as long as the heavens endure,
that he should be the Lord's minister in the priestly office
and bless his people in his name.

16  He chose him out of all mankind
to bring offerings to the Lord,
incense and the fragrance of memorial sacrifice,
to make atonement for the people.

17  He entrusted to him his commandments,
with authority to pronounce legal decisions,
to teach Jacob his decrees
and enlighten Israel about his law.

18  Upstarts grew jealous of him
and conspired against him in the desert,
Dathan and Abiram with their supporters
and Korah's band in their violent anger.

19  The Lord saw and refused his sanction;
he destroyed them in the heat of his wrath,
and worked a miracle against them
by consuming them in a blazing fire.

20  But he added fresh honours to Aaron
and gave him a special privilege,
allotting to the priests the choicest firstfruits,
to ensure that they above all should have bread in plenty.

21  For they eat the sacrifices of the Lord,
which he gave to Aaron and his descendants.

22  But he was to have no inheritance in the land of his people,
no portion allotted to him among them;
for the Lord himself is his portion, his inheritance.

*a Compare Exodus 28. 36; literally a seal of holiness.*

Phinehas son of Eleazar ranks third in renown    23
for being zealous in his reverence for the Lord,
and for standing firm with noble courage,
when the people were in revolt;
by so doing he made atonement for Israel.
Therefore a covenant was established with him,    24
assuring him command of the sanctuary and of the nation,
conferring on him and his descendants
the high-priesthood for ever.
Just as a covenant was made with David son of Jesse of the tribe of Judah,   25
that the royal succession should always pass from father to son,
so the succession was to pass from Aaron to his descendants.
May the Lord grant you a wise mind    26
to judge his people with justice,
so that their prosperity may never vanish
and their glory may be handed on to future generations!

Joshua son of Nun was a mighty warrior,    **46**
who succeeded Moses in the prophetic office.
He lived up to his name
as a great liberator of the Lord's chosen people,
able to take reprisals on the enemies who attacked them,
and to put Israel in possession of their territory.
How glorious he was when he raised his hand    2
and brandished his sword against cities!
Never before had a man made such a stand,    3
for he was fighting the Lord's battles.
Was it not through him that the sun stood still    4
and made one day as long as two?
He called on the Most High, the Mighty One,    5
when the enemy was pressing him on every side,
and the great Lord answered his prayer
with a violent storm of hail.    6
He overwhelmed that nation in battle
and crushed his assailants as they fled down the pass,
to make the nations recognize his strength in arms
and teach them that he fought under the very eyes of the Lord,
for he followed the lead of the Mighty One.

In the time of Moses he had proved his loyalty,    7
he and Caleb son of Jephunneh:
they stood their ground against the whole assembly,
restrained the people from sin,
and silenced their wicked grumbling.
Out of six hundred thousand warriors    8
these two alone escaped with their lives
to enter the land and take possession of it,
the land flowing with milk and honey.

9 The Lord gave Caleb strength,
which still remained with him in his old age,
so that he was able to invade the hill-country
and win possession of it for his descendants.

10 So all Israel could see
how good it is to be a loyal follower of the Lord.

11 Then there are the judges, name after famous name,
all of them men who rejected idolatry
and never rebelled against the Lord:
blessings be on their memory!

12 May their bones send forth new life from the ground where they lie!
May the fame of the honoured dead be matched by their sons!

13 Samuel was beloved by his Lord;
as prophet of the Lord he established the monarchy
and anointed rulers over his people.

14 As long as he dispensed justice according to the law of the Lord,
the Lord kept watch over Jacob.

15 Because of his fidelity he proved to be an accurate prophet;
the truth of his vision was shown by his utterances.

16 He called on the Mighty Lord,
when enemies were pressing him on every side,
and offered a sucking-lamb in sacrifice;

17 then the Lord thundered from heaven,
making his voice heard in a mighty crash,

18 and routed the leaders of the enemy, *a*
all the rulers of the Philistines.

19 Before the time came for his eternal sleep,
Samuel called the Lord and his anointed to witness:
'I never took any man's property,
not so much as a pair of shoes';
and no man accused him.

20 Even after he had gone to his rest he prophesied
and foretold to the king his death,
lifting up his voice in prophecy from the ground
to wipe out the people's guilt.

47 After him Nathan came forward
to be prophet in the reign of David.

2 As the fat is separated from the sacrifice,
so David was chosen out of all Israel.

3 He played with lions as though they were kids,
with bears as though they were lambs.

4 In his youth did he not kill a giant
and restore the honour of his people,
when he whirled his sling with its stone
and brought down boastful Goliath?

*a* the enemy: *so Heb.; Gk.* Tyre.

For he called on the Lord Most High,                                    5
who gave strength to his right arm
to strike down that mighty warrior
and win victory for his people.
So they hailed him as conqueror of tens of thousands,                   6
they sang his praises for the blessings bestowed by the Lord,
when he was offered the royal diadem.
For he subdued their enemies on every side                              7
and crushed the resistance of the Philistines,
whose power remains broken to this day.
In all he did he gave thanks,                                           8
ascribing glory to the Holy One, the Most High.
With his whole heart he sang hymns of praise,
to show his love for his Maker.
He appointed musicians to stand before the altar                        9
and sing sweet music to the harp.
So he gave splendour to the festivals                                   10
and fixed for all time the round of sacred seasons,
when men praise the holy name of the Lord
and the sanctuary resounds from morning to night.
The Lord pardoned his sins                                              11
and endowed him with great power for ever:
he gave him a covenant of kingship
and the glorious throne of Israel.

He was succeeded by a wise son, Solomon,                                12
who, thanks to his father David, lived in spacious days.
He reigned in an age of peace,                                          13
because God made all his frontiers quiet,
and so he was able to build a house in God's honour,
a sanctuary founded to last for ever.
How wise you were, Solomon, in your youth!                              14
Your mind was like a brimming river;
your influence spread throughout the world,                             15
which you filled with your proverbs and riddles.
Your fame reached to distant islands,                                   16
and you were beloved for your peaceful reign.
Your songs, your proverbs, your parables,                               17
and the answers you gave were the admiration of the world.
In the name of the Lord God,                                            18
who is known as the God of Israel,
you amassed gold and silver
as though they were tin and lead.
But you took women to lie at your side                                  19
and gave yourself up to their control.
You stained your reputation                                             20
and tainted your line.

You brought retribution on your children
and made them grieve over your folly,
21 because it divided the sovereignty
and produced out of Ephraim a rebel kingdom.
22 But the Lord never ceases to be merciful;
he does not destroy what he himself has made;
he will not wipe out the children of his chosen servant
or cut short the line of the man who has loved him.
So he granted a remnant to Jacob
and let one scion of David survive.

23 So Solomon died like his forefathers
and left one of his sons to succeed him,
a man of weak intelligence, the fool of the nation,
Rehoboam, whose policy drove the people to revolt.
Then Jeroboam son of Nebat led Israel into sin
and started Ephraim on its wicked course.
24 Their sins increased beyond measure,
until they were driven into exile from their native land;
25 for they had explored every kind of wickedness,
until retribution came upon them.

**48** Then Elijah appeared, a prophet like fire,
whose word flamed like a torch.
2 He brought famine upon them,
and his zeal made their numbers small.
3 By the word of the Lord he shut up the sky
and three times called down fire.
4 How glorious you were, Elijah, in your miracles!
Who else can boast such deeds?
5 You raised a corpse from death
and from the grave, by the word of the Most High.
6 You sent kings and famous men
from their sick-beds down to their deaths.
7 You heard a denunciation at Sinai,
a sentence of doom at Horeb.
8 So you anointed kings for vengeance,
and prophets to succeed you.
9 You were taken up to heaven in a fiery whirlwind,
in a chariot drawn by horses of fire.
10 It is written that you are to come at the appointed time with warnings,
to allay the divine wrath before its final fury,
to reconcile father and son,
and to restore the tribes of Jacob.
11 Happy are those who saw you
and were honoured with your love! *a*

*a* honoured . . . love: *probable meaning; Gk. adds* for we also shall certainly live.

When Elijah had vanished in a whirlwind,                    12
Elisha was filled with his spirit.
Throughout his life no ruler made him tremble;
no one could make him subservient.
Nothing was too difficult for him;                         13
even in the grave his body kept its prophetic power.
In life he worked miracles,                                14
and in death his deeds were marvellous.

In spite of all this the people did not repent             15
or renounce their sins,
until they were carried off as plunder from their land
and scattered over the whole earth.
Only a tiny nation was left,
with a ruler from the house of David;
and of these some did what was pleasing to the Lord,       16
but others heaped sin upon sin.

Hezekiah fortified his city,                               17
bringing water within its walls;
he drilled through the rock with tools of iron
and made cisterns for the water.
In his reign Sennacherib invaded the country.             18
He sent Rab-shakeh from Lachish, *a*
who made threats against Zion
and grew arrogant in his boasting.
Then they were unnerved in heart and hand;                19
they suffered the anguish of a woman in labour.
So they called on the merciful Lord,                      20
spreading out their hands in supplication to him.
The Holy One quickly answered their prayer from heaven
by sending Isaiah to the rescue;
he struck down the Assyrian camp,                         21
and his angel wiped them out.
For Hezekiah did what was pleasing to the Lord,           22
and kept firmly to the ways of his ancestor David,
as he was instructed by Isaiah,
the great prophet whose vision could be trusted.
In his time the sun went back,                            23
and he added many years to the king's life.
With inspired power he saw the future                     24
and comforted the mourners in Zion.
He revealed things to come before they happened,          25
the secrets of the future to the end of time.

The memory of Josiah is fragrant as incense               **49**
blended by the skill of the perfumer,
sweet as honey to every palate
or as music at a banquet.

    *a* from Lachish: *other witnesses read* and went away.

2 He did what was right: he reformed the nation
and rooted out their loathsome and lawless practices.
3 He was whole-heartedly loyal to the Lord
and in lawless times made godliness prevail.

4 Except David, Hezekiah, and Josiah,
all were guilty of wrongdoing,
for they deserted the law of the Most High;
and so the royal line of Judah came to an end.
5 They surrendered their power to others
and their glory to a foreign nation,
6 who set fire to the chosen city, the city of the sanctuary,
and left its streets deserted, as Jeremiah prophesied;
7 for they had ill-treated him,
a prophet consecrated even before his birth
to uproot, to destroy, and to demolish,
but also to build and to plant.

8 Ezekiel had a vision of the Glory,
which was revealed enthroned on the chariot of the cherubim.
9 The Lord remembered his enemies and sent a storm,
but he did good to those who kept to the straight path.
10 May the bones of the twelve prophets also
send forth new life from the ground where they lie!
For they put new heart into Jacob,
and rescued the people by their confident hope.

11 How can we tell the greatness of Zerubbabel,
who was like a signet-ring on the Lord's right hand?
12 With him was Joshua son of Jehozadak;
in their days they built the house,
raising a holy temple to the Lord,
destined for eternal glory.
13 Great is the memory of Nehemiah,
who raised our fallen walls,
constructed gates and bars,
and rebuilt our ruined homes.

14 No one on earth has been created to equal Enoch,
for he was taken up from the earth.
15 No man has been born to be Joseph's peer,
the ruler of his brothers and the strength of his people;
and the Lord kept watch over his body.
16 Shem and Seth were given distinction among men,
but Adam holds pre-eminence over all creation.

**50** It was the high priest Simon son of Onias
in whose lifetime the house was repaired,
in whose days the temple was fortified.

He laid the foundation for the high double wall,                    2
the high retaining wall of the temple precinct.
In his day they dug*a* the reservoir,                               3
a cistern broad as the sea.
He applied his mind to protecting his people from ruin             4
and strengthened the city against siege.
How glorious he was, surrounded by the people,                    5
when he came from behind the temple curtain!
He was like the morning star appearing through the clouds         6
or the moon at the full;
like the sun shining on the temple of the Most High               7
or the light of the rainbow on the gleaming clouds;
like a rose in spring                                             8
or lilies by a fountain of water;
like a green shoot upon Lebanon on a summer's day
or burning incense in the censer;                                 9
like a cup of beaten gold,
decorated with every kind of precious stone;
like an olive-tree laden with fruit                               10
or a cypress with its top in the clouds.
When he put on his gorgeous vestments,                            11
robed himself in perfect splendour,
and went up to the holy altar,
he added lustre to the court of the sanctuary.
When the priests were handing him the portions of the sacrifice,  12
as he stood by the altar hearth
with his brothers round him like a garland,
he was like a young cedar of Lebanon
in the midst of a circle of palms.
All the sons of Aaron in their magnificence                       13
stood with the Lord's offering in their hands
before the whole congregation of Israel.
To complete the ceremonies at the altar                           14
and adorn the offering of the Most High, the Almighty,
he held out his hand for the libation cup                         15
and poured out the blood of the grape,
poured its fragrance at the foot of the altar
to the Most High, the King of all.
Then the sons of Aaron shouted                                    16
and blew their trumpets of beaten silver;
they sounded a mighty fanfare
as a reminder before the Lord.
Instantly the people as one man fell on their faces               17
to worship the Lord their God, the Almighty, the Most High.
Then the choir broke into praise,                                 18
in the full sweet strains of resounding song,

*a* they dug: *so Heb.; Gk. obscure.*

19    while the people of the Most High
      were making their petitions to the merciful Lord,
      until the liturgy of the Lord was finished
      and the ritual complete.
20    Then Simon came down and raised his hands
      over the whole congregation of Israel,
      to pronounce the Lord's blessing,
      proud to take his name on his lips;
21    and a second time they bowed in worship
      to receive the blessing from the Most High.


22    COME THEN, PRAISE the God of the universe,
      who everywhere works great wonders,
      who from our birth ennobles our life *a*
      and deals with us in mercy.
23    May he grant us a joyful heart,
      and in our time send Israel lasting peace.
24    May he confirm his mercy towards us,
      and in his own good time grant us deliverance.


25    Two nations I detest,
      and a third is no nation at all:
26    the inhabitants of Mount Seir,*b* the Philistines,
      and the senseless folk that live at Shechem.


27    In this book I have written
      lessons of good sense and understanding,
      I, Jesus son of Sirach,*c* of Jerusalem,
      whose mind was a fountain of wisdom.
28    Happy the man who occupies himself with these lessons,
      who lays them to heart and grows wise!
29    If he lives by them, he will be equal to anything,
      with the light of the Lord shining on his path.


## Epilogue

51    I THANK THEE, my Lord and King,
      I praise thee, my God and Saviour,
      I give thee thanks,
2     because thou hast been my protector and helper,
      rescuing me from death,
      from the trap laid by a slanderous tongue
      and from lips that utter lies.
      In the face of my assailants thou didst come to my help;

---

*a* ennobles our life: *or* brings us up.       *b* Mount Seir: *so Heb.; Gk.* the mountain
of Samaria.        *c* Sirach: *some witnesses read* Sirach Eleazar.

in the fullness of thy mercy and glory thou didst rescue me          3
from grinding teeth which waited to devour me,
from hands that threatened my life,
from the many troubles I endured,
from the choking fire around me,                                     4
from the flames I had not kindled,
from the deep recesses of the grave,                                 5
from the foul tongue and its lies—
a wicked slander spoken in the king's presence.                      6
I came near to death;
I was on the brink of the grave.
They surrounded me on every side,                                    7
and there was no one to help me.
I looked for human aid and there was none.
Then I remembered thy mercy, Lord,                                   8
thy deeds in bygone days;
thou dost deliver those who patiently trust thee
and free them from the power of their enemies.
So I sent up a prayer from the earth                                 9
and begged for rescue from death.
I cried, 'Lord, thou art my Father; [a]                             10
do not desert me in time of trouble,
when I am helpless in the face of arrogance.
I will praise thee continually,                                     11
I will sing hymns of thanksgiving.'
And my prayer was granted;
for thou didst save me from death                                   12
and rescue me from my desperate plight.
Therefore I will thank thee and praise thee
and bless thee, O Lord.


When I was still young, before I set out on my travels,             13
I asked openly for wisdom in my prayers.
In the forecourt of the sanctuary I laid claim to her,              14
and I shall seek her out to the end.
From the first blossom to the ripening of the grape                 15
she has been the delight of my heart.
From my youth my steps have followed her without swerving.
I had hardly begun to listen when I was rewarded,                   16
and I gained for myself much instruction.
I made progress in my studies;                                      17
all honour to him who gives me wisdom!
I determined to practise what I had learnt;                         18
I pursued goodness, and shall never regret it.
I strove for wisdom with all my might,                              19
and was scrupulous in whatever I did.

    *a* thou . . . Father: *so Heb.; Gk.* Father of my lord.

I spread out my hands to heaven above,
   deploring my ignorance;
20 I set my heart on possessing wisdom,
   and by keeping myself pure I found her.
   With her I gained understanding from the first;
   therefore I shall never be at a loss.
21 Because I passionately yearned to discover her,
   I won a noble prize.
22 The Lord gave me eloquence as my reward,
   and with it I will praise him.

23 Come to me, you who need instruction,
   and lodge in my house of learning.
24 Why do you admit to a lack of these things,
   yet leave your great thirst unslaked?
25 I have made my proclamation:
   'Buy for yourselves without money,
26 bend your neck to the yoke,
   be ready to accept discipline;
   you need not go far to find it.'
27 See for yourselves how little were my labours
   compared with the great peace I have found.
28 Your share of instruction may cost you a large sum of silver,
   but it will bring you a large return in gold.
29 May you take delight in the Lord's mercy
   and never be ashamed of praising him.
30 Do your duty in good time,
   and in his own time he will reward you.

# BARUCH

*A message to a conquered people*

1 THIS IS THE BOOK OF BARUCH, son of Neriah, son of
   Mahseiah, son of Zedekiah, son of Hasadiah, son of Hilkiah, written
2 in Babylon, on the seventh day of the month, in the fifth year after
   the Chaldaeans had captured and burnt Jerusalem.
3 Baruch read the book aloud to Jeconiah son of Jehoiakim, king of Judah,
4 and to all the people who had assembled to hear it: the nobles, the princes
   of the royal blood, the elders, and the whole community, high and low—
5 in short, all who lived in Babylon, by the river Soud. Then they prayed
6 to the Lord with tears and fasting; and each of them collected as much
7 money as he could, and they sent it to Jerusalem, to Jehoiakim the high
   priest, son of Hilkiah, son of Shallum, and to the priests and all the people
8 who were with him. This was the time when he took the vessels belonging

to the house of the Lord which had been looted from the temple, and returned them to the land of Judah, on the tenth of the month Sivan. These were the silver vessels made by Zedekiah son of Josiah, king of Judah, after Nebuchadnezzar king of Babylon had deported Jeconiah, the rulers, 9 the captives, the nobles, and the common people from Jerusalem and taken them to Babylon.

They said: We are sending you money to buy whole-offerings, sin- 10 offerings, and incense; provide a grain-offering, and offer them all upon the altar of the Lord our God; and pray for Nebuchadnezzar king of 11 Babylon, and for his son Belshazzar, that their life on earth may last as long as the heavens. So the Lord will give us strength, and light to walk by, 12 and we shall live under the protection of Nebuchadnezzar king of Babylon, and of Belshazzar his son; we shall give them long service and gain their favour. Pray also for us to the Lord our God, because we have sinned 13 against him, and to this day the Lord's anger and wrath have not been averted from us.

You are to read this book that we are sending you, and make your con- 14 fession in the house of the Lord on the feast day and during the festal season, and say: The Lord our God is in the right; but on us the shame 15 rests to this very day—on the men of Judah, the citizens of Jerusalem, on 16 our kings and rulers, on our priests and prophets, and on our fathers. We 17 have sinned against the Lord and disobeyed him; we did not listen to the 18 Lord our God or follow the precepts he gave us. From the day when the 19 Lord brought our fathers out of Egypt until now, we have been disobedient to the Lord our God and have heedlessly disregarded his voice. So here we 20 are today in the grip of adversity, suffering under the curse which the Lord commanded his servant Moses to pronounce, when he led our fathers out of Egypt to give us a land flowing with milk and honey. Moreover we 21 refused to hear the Lord our God speaking in all the words of the prophets he sent us; we went our own way, each following the promptings of his 22 own wicked heart, serving other gods, doing what was evil in the sight of the Lord our God.

So the Lord made good the warning he had given to us, to our magis- **2** trates in Israel, our kings and our rulers, and the men of Israel and Judah. Nowhere under heaven have such deeds been done as were done in Jeru- 2 salem, thus fulfilling what was foretold in the law of Moses, that we should 3 eat the flesh of our children, one his own son and another his own daughter. The Lord made our nation subject to all the kingdoms round us, our land 4 a waste, our name a byword to all the nations among whom he had scattered our people. Instead of rising to the top, they sank to the bottom, because 5 we sinned against the Lord our God and did not listen to his voice. The 6 Lord our God is in the right; but on us and our fathers the shame rests to this very day. All these evils of which the Lord warned us have come about. 7 Yet we did not entreat the Lord that we might all turn away from the 8 thoughts of our wicked hearts. The Lord kept strict watch and brought 9 these evils on our heads, because he is just; he laid all these command- ments upon us, but we did not listen to his voice or follow the precepts 10 which he gave us.

11 And now, Lord God of Israel, who didst bring thy people out of Egypt
with a mighty hand, with signs and portents, with great power and arm
12 uplifted, winning for thyself a renown that lives on to this day: by our sin,
our godlessness, and our injustice we have broken all thy commandments,
13 O Lord our God. Be angry with us no longer, for we are left a mere hand-
14 ful among the heathen where thou hast scattered us. Listen, O Lord, to
our prayer and our entreaty, deliver us for thy own sake, and grant us
15 favour with those who have taken us into exile, so that the whole earth
may know that thou art the Lord our God, who hast named Israel and his
posterity as thy own.

16 O Lord, look down from thy holy dwelling and think of us. Turn thy
17 ear to us, Lord, and hear us; open thine eyes and see. The dead are in
their graves, the breath is gone from their bodies; it is not they who can
18 sing the Lord's praises or applaud his justice; it is living men, mourning
their fall from greatness, walking the earth bent and feeble, blind and
famished—it is these who will sing thy praises, O Lord, and applaud thy
justice.

19 Not for any just deeds of our fathers and our kings do we lay before thee
20 our plea for pity, O Lord our God. Thou hast vented upon us that wrath
and anger of which thou didst warn us through thy servants the prophets
21 who said: 'These are the words of the Lord: Bow your shoulders and
serve the king of Babylon and you shall remain in the land that I gave
22 to your fathers; but if you do not listen to the Lord and serve the king of
23 Babylon, then I will banish from Jerusalem and the cities of Judah all
sounds of joy and merriment, the voice of bride and bridegroom; the whole
24 land shall lie waste and uninhabited.' But we did not obey thy command to
serve the king of Babylon. And so thou didst make good the warning given
through thy servants the prophets: the bones of our kings and of our fathers
25 have been taken from their resting-place; and there they lie, exposed to the
heat by day and the frost by night. They died a painful death by famine,
26 sword, and disease.*a* And because of the wickedness of Israel and Judah
the house that was named as thine has become what it is today.

27 Yet thou hast shown us, O Lord our God, all thy wonted forbearance
28 and great mercy. For this is what thou didst promise through thy servant
Moses, on the day thou didst command him to write thy law in the presence
29 of the Israelites: 'If you will not listen to my voice, this great swarming
multitude will be reduced to a tiny remnant among the heathen where I
30 will scatter them. I know they will not hear me, this stubborn people, but
31 in the land of their exile they will come to their senses and know that I am
the Lord their God. I will give them a mind to understand and ears to hear.
32 Then they will praise me in the land of their exile and will turn their
33 thoughts to me; they will repent of their stubbornness and their wicked
34 deeds, for they will recall how their fathers sinned against the Lord. Then
I will restore them to the land that I swore to give to their forefathers,
Abraham, Isaac, and Jacob, and they shall rule over it. And I will increase
35 their number: they shall never dwindle away. I will enter into an eternal
covenant with them, that I will become their God and they shall become

*a* disease: *probable meaning (compare Jeremiah 32. 36); Gk. obscure.*

my people. Never again will I remove my people Israel from the land that I have given them.'

O Lord Almighty, God of Israel, the soul in anguish and the fainting 3 spirit cry out to thee. Listen, Lord, and have mercy, for we have sinned 2 against thee. Thou art enthroned for ever; we are for ever passing away. 3 Now, Almighty Lord, God of Israel, hear the prayer of Israel's dead and 4 of the sons of those who sinned against thee. They did not heed the voice of their God, and so we are in the grip of adversity. Do not recall the mis- 5 deeds of our fathers, but remember now thy power and thy name, for thou 6 art the Lord our God, and we will praise thee, O Lord. It is for this that 7 thou hast put the fear of thee in our hearts, to make us call upon thy name. And we will praise thee in our exile, for we have put away from us all the wrongdoing of our fathers who sinned against thee. Today we are in exile; 8 thou hast scattered us and made us a byword and a curse, to be punished for all the sins of our fathers, who rebelled against the Lord our God.

LISTEN, ISRAEL, to the commandments of life; hear, and learn wisdom. 9 Why is it, Israel, that you are in your enemies' country, that you have 10 grown old in an alien land? Why have you shared the defilement of the dead and been numbered with those that lie in the grave? It is because you 11 12 have forsaken the fountain of wisdom. If you had walked in the way of God, 13 you would have lived in peace for ever. Where is understanding, where is 14 strength, where is intelligence? Learn that, and then you will know where to find life and light to walk by, long life and peace. Has any man dis- 15 covered the dwelling-place of wisdom or entered her storehouse? Where 16 are the rulers of the nations now? Where are those who have hunted wild beasts or the birds of the air for sport? Where are those who have hoarded 17 the silver and gold men trust in, never satisfied with their gains? Where 18 are the silversmiths with their patient skill and the secrets of their craft? They have all vanished and gone down to the grave, and others have risen 19 to take their place. A younger generation saw the light of day and dwelt in 20 the land. But they did not learn the way of knowledge, or discover its paths; 21 they did not lay hold of it; their sons went far astray. Wisdom was not heard 22 of in Canaan, nor seen in Teman. The sons of Hagar who sought for 23 understanding on earth, the merchants of Merran and Teman, the myth-makers, the seekers after knowledge, none of them discovered the way of wisdom, or remembered her paths.

How great, O Israel, is God's dwelling-place, how vast the extent of his 24 domain! Great it is, and boundless, lofty, and immeasurable. There in 25 26 ancient time the giants were born, a famous race, great in stature, skilled in war. But these men were not chosen by God, nor shown the way of 27 knowledge. So their race died out because they had no understanding; they 28 lacked the wit to survive. Has any man gone up to heaven to gain wisdom 29 and brought her down from the clouds? Has any man crossed the sea to 30 find her or bought her for fine gold? No one can know the path or conceive 31 the way that will lead to her. Only the One who knows all things knows her: 32 his understanding discovered her. He who established the earth for all time filled it with four-footed beasts. He sends forth the light, and it goes on its 33

34 way; he called it, it feared him and obeyed. The stars shone at their appointed stations and rejoiced; he called them and they answered, 'We are
35 here!' Joyfully they shone for their Maker. This is our God; there is none
36 to compare with him. The whole way of knowledge he found out and gave
37 to Jacob his servant, and to Israel, whom he loved. Thereupon wisdom
4 appeared on earth and lived among men. She is the book of the commandments of God, the law that stands for ever. All who hold fast to her shall
2 live, but those who forsake her shall die. Return, Jacob, and lay hold of her;
3 set your course towards her radiance, and face her beacon light. Do not give
4 up your glory to another or your privileges to an alien people. Happy are
we, Israel, because we know what is pleasing to God!

5 6     Take heart, my people, you who keep Israel's name alive. You were sold
to the heathen, but not to be destroyed; it was because you roused God's
7 anger that you were handed over to your enemies. You provoked your
8 Maker by sacrificing to demons and to that which is not God. You forgot
the Everlasting God who nurtured you, and you grieved Jerusalem who
9 fostered you; for she saw how God's anger had come upon you, and she
said: Listen, you neighbours of Zion, God has brought great grief upon
10 me. I have seen the captivity of my sons and daughters which the Ever-
11 lasting has inflicted upon them; I nursed them in delight, but with tears
12 and mourning I saw them go. Let no one exult over me in my widowhood,
bereaved of so many. I have been left desolate through the sins of my
13 children, through their turning away from the law of God. They would
not learn his statutes, or follow his commandments, or let God guide and
train them in his righteousness.

14     Come then, neighbours of Zion, remember the captivity of my sons and
15 daughters which the Everlasting has inflicted upon them. For he brought
down on them a nation from far away, a ruthless nation speaking a strange
16 language and without reverence for age or pity for children. They carried
off the widow's beloved sons, and left her in loneliness, deprived of her
17 18 daughters. But I, how can I help you? Only the One who brought these
19 evils upon you can deliver you from your enemies. Go your way, my
20 children, go, for I am left desolate. I have put off the robes of peaceful days,
and put on the sackcloth of a suppliant. I will cry out to the Everlasting as
long as I live.

21     Take heart, my children! Cry out to God, and he will rescue you from
22 tyranny and from the power of your enemies. For I have set my hope of your
deliverance on the Everlasting; the Holy One, your everlasting saviour, has
23 filled me with joy over the mercy soon to be granted you. I saw you go with
mourning and tears, but God will give you back to me with joy and glad-
24 ness for ever. For as the neighbours of Zion have now seen your captivity,
so they will soon see your deliverance coming upon you from your God
25 with the great glory and splendour of the Everlasting. My children, endure
in patience the wrath God has brought upon you; your enemy has hunted
you down, but soon you will see him destroyed, and will put your foot upon
26 his neck. My pampered children have trodden rough paths; they have been
carried off like a flock seized by raiders.

27     Take heart, my children! Cry out to God, for he who afflicted you will

not forget you. You once resolved to go astray from God; now with tenfold 28
zeal you must turn about and seek him. He who brought these calamities 29
upon you will bring you everlasting joy when he delivers you.

Take heart, Jerusalem! He who called you by name will comfort you. 30
Wretched shall they be who despoiled you and gloated over your fall; 31
wretched the cities where your children were slaves; wretched the city that 32
received your sons! The same city that rejoiced at your downfall and made 33
merry over your ruin shall grieve over her own desolation. I will strip her 34
of the multitudes that were her boast, and turn her pride to mourning.
Fire from the Everlasting shall be her doom for many a day, and long shall 35
she be a haunt of demons.

Jerusalem, look eastwards and see the joy that is coming to you from 36
God. They come, the sons from whom you parted, they come, gathered 37
together at the word of the Holy One from east to west, rejoicing in the
glory of God.

Jerusalem, strip off the garment of your sorrow and affliction, and put 5
on for ever the glorious majesty that is the gift of God. Wrap about you his 2
robe of righteousness; set on your head for diadem the splendour of the
Everlasting; for God will show your radiance to every land under heaven. 3
You shall receive from God for ever the name Righteous Peace, Godly 4
Splendour.

Jerusalem, arise and stand upon the height; look eastwards and see 5
from west to east your children gathered together at the word of the Holy
One, rejoicing that God has remembered them. They went away from you 6
on foot, led off by their enemies, but God is bringing them home to you
borne aloft in glory, like a king on his throne. For God has commanded 7
every high mountain and the everlasting hills to be made low, and the
valleys to be filled and levelled, so that Israel may walk safely in the glory
of God. And woods and every fragrant tree shall give Israel shade by God's 8
command. For God shall lead Israel with joy in the light of his glory, grant- 9
ing them his mercy and his righteousness.

# A LETTER OF
# JEREMIAH

## *The folly of idolatry*

6<sup>a</sup>  A COPY OF A LETTER sent by Jeremiah to the captives who were to be taken to Babylon by the king of Babylon, conveying a message entrusted to him by God.

2  The sins you have committed in the sight of God are the cause of your being led away captive to Babylon by Nebuchadnezzar king of Babylon.

3  Once you are in Babylon, your stay there will be long; it will last for many years, up to seven generations; but afterwards I will lead you out in peace and prosperity.

4  Now in Babylon you will see carried on men's shoulders gods made of
5  silver, gold, and wood, which fill the heathen with awe. Be careful, then, never to imitate these Gentiles; do not be overawed by their gods when you
6  see them in the midst of a procession of worshippers. But say in your hearts,
7  'To thee alone, Lord, is worship due.' For my angel is with you; your lives are in his care.

8  The idols are plated with gold and silver, they have tongues fashioned
9  by a craftsman, but they are a fraud and cannot speak. And the people take gold and make crowns for the heads of their gods, as one might for a girl
10  fond of finery. Sometimes also the priests filch gold and silver from their
11  gods and spend it on themselves; they will even give some of it to the prostitutes in the inner chamber. They dress up the idols in clothes like
12  human beings, these gods of silver, gold, and wood. But the gods, decked in purple though they are, cannot protect themselves against rust and moth.
13  The dust in the temple, too, lies thick upon them, so that their faces have to
14  be wiped clean. Like a human judge the god holds a sceptre, yet he cannot
15  put to death anyone who offends him. In his right hand he has a dagger and
16  an axe, yet he cannot deliver himself from war and pillage. This shows they are not gods, so have no fear of them.

17  Their gods are no more use than a broken tool, sitting there in their temples. Their eyes get filled with dust from the feet of those who come in.
18  And just as the palace-court is barricaded to secure a traitor awaiting execution, so the priests secure their temples with doors and bolts and bars to
19  guard against plundering by robbers. They light lamps, more than they
20-21  need for themselves—yet the idols can see none of them. They are like one of the beams of the temple; their hearts are eaten out, as the saying is, for creatures crawl out of the ground and devour them and their clothing.

---

<sup>a</sup> *The chapter and verse numbering is that of the Authorized Version, in which this forms chapter 6 of Baruch.*

198

When their faces are blackened by the smoke of the temple they are quite unaware of it. Bats and swallows and birds of all kinds perch on their heads 22 and bodies, and cats do the same. From all this you may be sure that they 23 are not gods, so have no fear of them.

Though plated with gold for ornament, the idols will not shine, unless 24 someone rubs off the tarnish. Even when they were being cast they did not feel it. They were bought at great cost, but there is no breath in them. As 25 26 they have no real feet they are carried on men's shoulders, which shows how worthless they are. Even those who serve them are ashamed, because if ever 27 an idol falls on the ground, it does not get up by itself; nor, if anyone sets it up again, can it move by its own effort, and if it is tilted it cannot straighten itself. To set offerings before them is like setting them before the dead. The sacrifices made to gods are sold by the priests, who spend the proceeds 28 on themselves. Their wives are no better; they take portions of these sacrifices and cure the meat, and give no share to the poor or helpless. Their offerings are touched by women who are menstruating or by mothers 29 fresh from childbed. Be assured by all this that they are not gods, and have no fear of them.

Why should they be called gods? These gods of silver, gold, and wood 30 have food served to them by women. In their temples the priests sit shaven 31 and shorn, with their clothes rent, and their heads uncovered. They shout 32 and howl before these gods of theirs, like mourners at a funeral feast. The 33 priests strip vestments from the gods to clothe their own wives and children. Should anyone do these gods either injury or service they will 34 not be able to repay it. They cannot set up or depose a king. So also they are 35 incapable of bestowing wealth or money; if someone makes a vow to them and does not honour it, they will never exact payment. They will never 36 save any man from death, never rescue the weak from the strong. They 37 cannot restore the blind man's sight or give relief to the needy. They do 38 not pity the widow or befriend the orphan. They are like blocks from the 39 quarry, these wooden things plated with gold and silver, and their worshippers will be humiliated. How then can anyone suppose them to be 40 gods or call them so?

Besides, even the Chaldaeans themselves bring these idols of theirs into disrepute; for, when they see a dumb man without the power of articulate 41 speech, they bring him into the temple and make him call upon Bel, as if Bel could understand him. They cannot see the folly of it and abandon the 42 idols, because they themselves have no understanding. The women too sit 43 in the street with cords round them, burning bran for incense. And when a passer-by has pulled one of them to him and she has lain with him, she taunts her neighbour, because she has not been thought as attractive as herself and her cord has not been broken. Everything to do with these idols 44 is fraud and delusion. How then can anyone suppose them to be gods or call them so?

They are things manufactured by carpenters and goldsmiths; they can 45 be nothing but what the craftsmen wish them to be. Even their makers' 46 lives cannot be prolonged; what, then, can the things they make expect? It is simply a scandalous fraud that they have bequeathed to posterity. 47

48 When war and disasters befall the gods, it is the priests who discuss
49 amongst themselves where they and their gods can hide. How then can
men fail to see that these are not gods, when they cannot save themselves
50 from war and disaster? Since they are nothing but wood plated with gold
51 and silver, they will in time be recognized for the frauds they are. All the
heathen and their kings will plainly see that they are not gods but the work
52 of men's hands, with no divine power in them at all. Can there still be anyone who does not realize that they are not gods?
53     They cannot set up a king over a country, and they cannot give men rain.
54 They cannot decide a case or redress a wrong.[a] They are as helpless as
55 crows tossed about in mid air. When fire breaks out in a temple belonging
to those wooden gods all gilded and silvered, their priests will run away to
56 safety, but the gods will be burnt up in the flames like timbers. They cannot resist king or enemy. How then can anyone allow or believe that they
are gods?
57     They cannot save themselves from thieves and robbers, these wooden
58 gods, plated with silver and gold. Anyone who can will strip away their gold
and silver and make off with the clothing they wear, and the gods can do
59 nothing to help themselves. It is better to be a king who proves his courage
than such a sham god, better a household vessel that serves its owner's
purpose, better even the door of a house that keeps the contents safe, or a
60 wooden pillar in a palace. Sun and moon and the stars that shine so brightly
61 are sent to serve a purpose, and they obey. So too, when the lightning
flashes, it is seen far and wide. It is the same with the wind; it blows in
62 every land. And when God orders the clouds to travel over all the world
63 they carry out their task, and so does fire when it is sent down from above
to consume mountains and forests. But idols are not to be compared with
64 any of these, in appearance or in power. It follows that they are not to be
considered gods or called by that name, seeing that they are incapable of
65 pronouncing judgement or of conferring benefits on mankind. Recognize,
therefore, that they are not gods, and have no fear of them.
66     They wield no power over kings, either to curse them or to bless them;
67 and they cannot provide heavenly signs for the nations, either by shining
68 like the sun or by giving light like the moon. They are more helpless than
69 wild beasts, which can at least save themselves by taking cover. There is
no evidence at all that they are gods, so have no fear of them.
70     These wooden gods of theirs, plated with gold and silver, give no better
71 protection than a scarecrow in a plot of cucumbers. They are like a thorn-
bush in a garden, a perch for every bird, like a corpse cast out in the dark.
72 Such are their wooden gods, with their plating of gold and silver. The
purple and fine linen[b] rotting on them proves that they are not gods; in
the end they will themselves be eaten away, held in contempt throughout
the land.
73     Better, then, is an upright man who has no idols; he will be in no danger
of contempt.

[a] *Some witnesses read* cannot judge in their own cause, or redress a wrong done them.
[b] fine linen: *probable meaning;* Gk. marble.

# THE SONG OF
# THE THREE

## AN ADDITION IN THE GREEK VERSION
## OF DANIEL BETWEEN 3. 23 AND 3. 24

THEY WALKED IN THE HEART of the fire, praising God 1
and blessing the Lord. Azariah stood still among the flames and 2
began to pray aloud: 'Blessed art thou, O Lord, the God of our 3
fathers, thy name is worthy of praise and glorious for ever: thou art just 4
in all thy deeds and true in all thy works; straight are thy paths, and all thy
judgements just. Just sentence hast thou passed in all that thou hast 5
brought upon us and upon Jerusalem the holy city of our fathers: yes, just
sentence thou hast passed upon our sins. For indeed we sinned and broke 6
thy law in rebellion against thee, in all we did we sinned; we did not heed 7
thy commandments, we did not keep them, we did not do what thou hadst
commanded us for our good. In all the punishments thou hast sent upon 8
us thy judgements have been just. Thou hast handed us over to our 9
bitterest enemies, rebels against thy law, and to a wicked king, the vilest in
the world. And so now we are speechless for shame: contempt has fallen 10
on thy servants and thy worshippers. For thy honour's sake do not 11
abandon us for ever; do not annul thy covenant. Do not withdraw thy 12
mercy from us, for the sake of Abraham, thy beloved, for the sake of Isaac,
thy servant, and Israel, thy holy one. Thou didst promise to multiply their 13
descendants as the stars in the sky and the sand on the sea-shore. But now, 14
Lord, we have been made the smallest of all nations; for our sins we are
today the most abject in the world. We have no ruler, no prophet, no leader 15
now; there is no burnt-offering, no sacrifice, no oblation, no incense, no
place to make an offering before thee and find mercy. But because we come 16
with contrite heart and humbled spirit, accept us. As though we came with 17
burnt-offerings of rams and bullocks and with thousands of fat lambs, so
let our sacrifice be made before thee this day. Accept our pledge of loyalty
to thee,[a] for no shame shall come to those who put their trust in thee. Now 18
we will follow thee with our whole heart and fear thee. We seek thy presence; do not put us to shame, but deal with us in thy forbearance and in the 19
greatness of thy mercy. Grant us again thy marvellous deliverance, and win 20
glory for thy name, O Lord. Let all who do thy servants harm be humbled;
may they be put to shame and stripped of all their power, and may their 21
strength be crushed; let them know that thou alone art the Lord God, and 22
glorious over all the world.'

[a] Accept our . . . thee: *possible meaning; Gk. obscure.*

23  The servants of the king who threw them in kept on feeding the furnace
24  with naphtha, pitch, tow, and faggots, and the flames poured out above it to
25  a height of seventy-five feet.*a* They spread out and burnt those Chal-
26  daeans who were caught near the furnace. But the angel of the Lord came
     down into the furnace to join Azariah and his companions; he scattered the
27  flames out of the furnace and made the heart of it as if a moist wind were
     whistling through. The fire did not touch them at all and neither hurt nor
     distressed them.

## *The praises of creation*

28  THEN THE THREE with one voice praised and glorified and blessed
     God in the furnace:

29           'Blessed art thou, O Lord, the God of our fathers;
                 worthy of praise, highly exalted for ever.
30           Blessed is thy holy and glorious name;
                 highly to be praised, highly exalted for ever.
31           Blessed art thou in thy holy and glorious temple;
                 most worthy to be hymned and glorified for ever.
32           Blessed art thou who dost behold the depths from thy seat upon
                 the cherubim;
                 worthy of praise, highly exalted for ever.
33           Blessed art thou on thy royal throne;
                 most worthy to be hymned, highly exalted for ever.
34           Blessed art thou in the dome of heaven;
                 worthy to be hymned and glorified for ever.

35           'Let the whole creation bless the Lord,
                 sing his praise and exalt him for ever.
36           Bless the Lord, you heavens;
                 sing his praise and exalt him for ever.
37           Bless the Lord, you angels of the Lord;
                 sing his praise and exalt him for ever.
38           Bless the Lord, all you waters above the heavens;
                 sing his praise and exalt him for ever.
39           Bless the Lord, all you his hosts;
                 sing his praise and exalt him for ever.
40           Bless the Lord, sun and moon;
                 sing his praise and exalt him for ever.
41           Bless the Lord, stars of heaven;
                 sing his praise and exalt him for ever.
42           Bless the Lord, all rain and dew;
                 sing his praise and exalt him for ever.
43           Bless the Lord, all winds that blow;
                 sing his praise and exalt him for ever.

*a* *Gk*. forty-nine cubits.

Bless the Lord, fire and heat; 44
  sing his praise and exalt him for ever.
Bless the Lord, scorching blast and bitter cold; 45
  sing his praise and exalt him for ever.
Bless the Lord, dews and falling snow; 46
  sing his praise and exalt him for ever.
Bless the Lord, nights and days; 47
  sing his praise and exalt him for ever.
Bless the Lord, light and darkness; 48
  sing his praise and exalt him for ever.
Bless the Lord, frost and cold; 49
  sing his praise and exalt him for ever.
Bless the Lord, rime and snow; 50
  sing his praise and exalt him for ever.
Bless the Lord, lightnings and clouds; 51
  sing his praise and exalt him for ever.

'O earth, bless the Lord; 52
  sing his praise and exalt him for ever.
Bless the Lord, mountains and hills; 53
  sing his praise and exalt him for ever.
Bless the Lord, all that grows in the ground; 54
  sing his praise and exalt him for ever.
Bless the Lord, seas and rivers; 56
  sing his praise and exalt him for ever.
Bless the Lord, you springs; 55
  sing his praise and exalt him for ever.
Bless the Lord, you whales and all that swim in the waters; 57
  sing his praise and exalt him for ever.
Bless the Lord, all birds of the air; 58
  sing his praise and exalt him for ever.
Bless the Lord, you cattle and wild beasts; 59
  sing his praise and exalt him for ever.

'All men on earth, bless the Lord; 60
  sing his praise and exalt him for ever.
Bless the Lord, O Israel; 61
  sing his praise and exalt him for ever.
Bless the Lord, you priests of the Lord; 62
  sing his praise and exalt him for ever.
Bless the Lord, you servants of the Lord; 63
  sing his praise and exalt him for ever.
Bless the Lord, all men of upright spirit; 64
  sing his praise and exalt him for ever.
Bless the Lord, you that are holy and humble in heart; 65
  sing his praise and exalt him for ever.
Bless the Lord, Hananiah, Azariah, and Mishael; 66
  sing his praise and exalt him for ever.

For he has rescued us from the grave and from the power of death:
    he has saved us from the furnace of burning flame;
    he has rescued us from the heart of the fire.
67  Give thanks to the Lord, for he is good;
    for his mercy endures for ever.
68  All who worship the Lord, bless the God of gods;
    sing his praise and give him thanks,
    for his mercy endures for ever.'

# DANIEL AND SUSANNA

## *Innocence vindicated*

1 2 THERE ONCE LIVED in Babylon a man named Joakim. He
    married Susanna daughter of Hilkiah, a very beautiful and devout
3   woman. Her parents, religious people, had brought up their daughter
4   according to the law of Moses. Joakim was very rich and his house had a
fine garden adjoining it, which was a regular meeting-place for the Jews,
because he was the man of greatest distinction among them.
5   Now two elders of the community were appointed that year as judges.
It was of them that the Lord had said, 'Wickedness came forth from
Babylon from elders who were judges and were supposed to govern my
6   people.' These men were constantly at Joakim's house, and everyone who
had a case to be tried came to them there.
7   When the people went away at noon, Susanna used to go and walk in her
8   husband's garden. Every day the two elders saw her entering the garden
9   and taking her walk, and they were obsessed with lust for her. They no
longer prayed to God, but let their thoughts stray from him and forgot the
10  claims of morality. They were both infatuated with her; but they did not
11  tell each other what pangs they suffered, because they were ashamed to
12  confess that they wanted to seduce her. Day after day they watched eagerly
to see her.
13 14 One day they said, 'Let us go home; it is time for lunch.' So they went
off in different directions, but soon retraced their steps and found themselves face to face. When they questioned one another, each confessed his
passion. Then they agreed on a time when they might find her alone.
15  And while they were watching for an opportune day, she went into the
garden as usual with only her two maids; it was very hot, and she wished
16  to bathe there. No one else was in the garden except the two elders, who
17  had hidden and were spying on her. She said to her maids, 'Bring me soap
18  and olive oil, and shut the garden doors so that I can bathe.' They did as
she told them: they closed the garden doors and went out by the side door
to fetch the things they had been ordered to bring; they did not see the
19  elders because they were hiding. As soon as the maids had gone, the two

elders started up and ran to Susanna. 'Look!' they said, 'the garden doors   20
are shut, and no one can see us. We are burning with desire for you, so
consent and yield to us. If you refuse, we shall give evidence against you   21
that there was a young man with you and that was why you sent your maids
away.' Susanna groaned and said: 'I see no way out. If I do this thing, the   22
penalty is death; if I do not, you will have me at your mercy. My choice   23
is made: I will not do it. It is better to be at your mercy than to sin against
the Lord.'

With that Susanna gave a loud shout, but the two elders shouted her   24
down. One of them ran and opened the garden door. The household, hear-   25 26
ing the uproar in the garden, rushed in through the side door to see what
had happened to her. And when the elders had told their story, the ser-   27
vants were deeply shocked, for no such allegation had ever been made
against Susanna.

Next day, when the people gathered at her husband Joakim's house, the   28
two elders came, full of their criminal design to put Susanna to death. In   29
the presence of the people they said, 'Send for Susanna daughter of
Hilkiah, Joakim's wife.' So they sent for her, and she came with her parents   30
and children and all her relatives. Now Susanna was a woman of great   31
beauty and delicate feeling. She was closely veiled, but those scoundrels   32
ordered her to be unveiled so that they might feast their eyes on her beauty.
Her family and all who saw her were in tears. Then the two elders stood   33 34
up before the people and put their hands on her head. She looked up to   35
heaven through her tears, for she trusted in the Lord. The elders said: 'As   36
we were walking alone in the garden, this woman came in with two maids.
She shut the garden doors and dismissed her maids. Then a young man,   37
who had been in hiding, came and lay down with her. We were in a corner   38
of the garden, and when we saw this wickedness we ran up to them. Though   39
we saw them in the act, we could not hold the man; he was too strong for us,
and he opened the door and forced his way out. We seized the woman and   40
asked who the young man was, but she would not tell us. That is our
evidence.'

As they were elders of the people and judges, the assembly believed them   41
and condemned her to death. Then Susanna cried out loudly: 'Eternal   42
God, who dost know all secrets and foresee all things, thou knowest that   43
their evidence against me was false. And now I am to die, guiltless though
I am of all the wicked things these men have said against me.'

The Lord heard her cry. Just as she was being led off to execution, God   44 45
inspired a devout young man named Daniel to protest, and he shouted out,   46
'I will not have this woman's blood on my head.' All the people turned and   47
asked him, 'What do you mean by that?' He came forward and said: 'Are   48
you such fools, you Israelites, as to condemn a woman of Israel, without
making careful inquiry and finding out the truth? Re-open the trial; the   49
evidence these men have brought against her is false.'

So the people all hurried back, and the rest of the elders said to him,   50
'Come, take your place among us and state your case, for God has given
you the standing of an elder.' Daniel said to them, 'Separate these men   51
and keep them at a distance from each other, and I will examine them.'

52 When they had been separated Daniel summoned one of them. 'You
hardened sinner,' he said, 'the sins of your past have now come home to
53 you. You gave unjust decisions, condemning the innocent, and acquitting
the guilty, although the Lord has said, "You shall not put to death an
54 innocent and guiltless man." Now then, if you saw this woman, tell us,
under what tree did you see them together?' He answered, 'Under a
55 clove-tree.'*a* Then Daniel retorted, 'Very good: this lie has cost you your
56 life, for already God's angel has received your sentence from God, and he
will cleave *b* you in two.' And he told him to stand aside, and ordered them
to bring in the other.

He said to him: 'Spawn of Canaan, no son of Judah, beauty has been
57 your undoing, and lust has corrupted your heart! Now we know how you
have been treating the women of Israel, frightening them into consorting
with you; but here is a woman of Judah who would not submit to your
58 villainy. Now then, tell me, under what tree did you surprise them
59 together?' 'Under a yew-tree',*c* he replied. Daniel said to him, 'Very good:
this lie has cost you your life, for the angel of God is waiting with his sword
to hew *d* you down and destroy you both.'

60 Then the whole assembly gave a great shout and praised God, the
61 saviour of those who trust in him. They turned on the two elders, for out
of their own mouths Daniel had convicted them of giving false evidence;
62 they dealt with them according to the law of Moses, and put them to death,
as they in their wickedness had tried to do to their neighbour. And so an
63 innocent life was saved that day. Then Hilkiah and his wife gave praise for
their daughter Susanna, because she was found innocent of a shameful
64 deed, and so did her husband Joakim and all her relatives. And from that
day forward Daniel was a great man among his people.

# DANIEL, BEL, AND THE SNAKE

## The destruction of Bel

1 WHEN KING ASTYAGES was gathered to his fathers
2 he was succeeded on the throne by Cyrus the Persian. Daniel
was a confidant of the king, the most honoured of all the
King's Friends.
3 Now the Babylonians had an idol called Bel, for which they provided
every day twelve bushels of fine flour, forty sheep, and fifty gallons of wine.
4 The king held it to be divine and went daily to worship it, but Daniel

---

*a* clove: *literally* mastic.　　　*b* clove . . . cleave: *there is a play on words in the Gk.*
*c* yew: *literally* oak.　　*d* yew . . . hew: *there is a play on words in the Gk.*

worshipped his God. So the king said to him, 'Why do you not worship
Bel?' He replied, 'Because I do not believe in man-made idols, but in the 5
living God who created heaven and earth and is sovereign over all mankind.' The king said, 'Do you think that Bel is not a living god? Do you not 6
see how much he eats and drinks each day?' Daniel laughed and said, 'Do 7
not be deceived, your majesty; this Bel of yours is only clay inside and
bronze outside, and has never eaten anything.'

Then the king was angry, and summoned the priests of Bel and said to 8
them, 'If you cannot tell me who it is that eats up all these provisions, you
shall die; but if you can show that it is Bel that eats them, then Daniel shall 9
die for blasphemy against Bel.' Daniel said to the king, 'Let it be as you
command.' (There were seventy priests of Bel, not counting their wives 10
and children.) Then the king went with Daniel into the temple of Bel. The 11
priests said, 'We are now going outside; set out the food yourself, your
majesty, and mix the wine; then shut the door and seal it with your signet.
When you come back in the morning, if you do not find that Bel has eaten it 12
all, let us be put to death; but if Daniel's charges against us turn out to be
false, then he shall die.' They treated the whole affair with contempt, 13
because they had made a hidden entrance under the table, and they
regularly went in by it and ate everything up.

So when the priests had gone, the king set out the food for Bel; and 14
Daniel ordered his servants to bring ashes and sift them over the whole
temple in the presence of the king alone. Then they left the temple, closed
the door, sealed it with the king's signet, and went away. During the night 15
the priests, with their wives and children, came as usual and ate and drank
everything. Early in the morning the king came, and Daniel with him. The 16 17
king said, 'Are the seals intact, Daniel?' He answered, 'They are intact,
your majesty.' As soon as he opened the door, the king looked at the table 18
and cried aloud, 'Great art thou, O Bel! In thee there is no deceit at all.'
But Daniel laughed and held back the king from going in. 'Just look at the 19
floor,' he said, 'and judge whose footprints these are.' The king said, 'I see 20
the footprints of men, women, and children.' In a rage he put the priests 21
under arrest, with their wives and children. Then they showed him the
secret doors through which they used to go in and consume what was on
the table. So the king put them to death, and handed Bel over to Daniel, 22
who destroyed the idol and its temple.

## The destruction of the snake

NOW THERE WAS A HUGE SNAKE, which the Babylonians held to be 23
divine. The king said to Daniel, 'You cannot say that this is not a 24
living god; so worship him.' Daniel answered, 'I will worship the Lord my 25
God, for he is the living God. But give me authority, your majesty, and 26
without sword or staff I will kill the snake.' 'I give it you', said the king.
So Daniel took pitch and fat and hair, boiled them together, and made 27
them into cakes, which he put into the mouth of the snake. When the snake
ate them, it burst. Then Daniel said, 'See what things you worship!'

28 When the Babylonians heard of this they gathered in an angry crowd to oppose the king. 'The king has turned Jew!' they cried. 'He has pulled
29 down Bel, killed the snake, and put the priests to the sword.' So they went to the king and said, 'Hand Daniel over to us, or else we will kill you and
30 your family.' The king, finding himself hard pressed, was compelled to
31 give Daniel up to them. They threw him into the lion-pit, and he was there
32 for six days. There were seven lions in the pit, and every day two men and two sheep were fed to them; but now they were given nothing, to make sure that they would devour Daniel.

33 Now the prophet Habakkuk was in Judaea; he had made a stew and crumbled bread into the bowl, and he was on the way to his field, carrying
34 it to the reapers, when an angel of the Lord said, 'Habakkuk, carry the meal you have with you to Babylon, for Daniel, who is in the lion-pit.'
35 Habakkuk said, 'My lord, I have never been to Babylon. I do not know
36 where the lion-pit is.' Then the angel took the prophet by the crown of his head, and carrying him by his hair, he swept him to Babylon with the blast
37 of his breath and put him down above the pit. Habakkuk called out,
38 'Daniel, Daniel, take the meal that God has sent you!' Daniel said, 'O God, thou dost indeed remember me; thou dost never forsake those who love
39 thee.' Then he got up and ate; and God's angel returned Habakkuk at
40 once to his home. On the seventh day the king went to mourn for Daniel,
41 but when he arrived at the pit and looked in, there sat Daniel! Then the king cried aloud, 'Great art thou, O Lord, the God of Daniel, and there is
42 no God but thou alone.' So the king drew Daniel up; and the men who had planned to destroy him he flung into the pit, and then and there they were eaten up before his eyes.

# THE PRAYER OF MANASSEH

## *Repentance*

1 LORD ALMIGHTY,
   God of our fathers,
      of Abraham, Isaac, and Jacob,
      and of their righteous offspring;
2 who hast made heaven and earth in their manifold array;
3 who hast confined the ocean by thy word of command,
   who hast shut up the abyss and sealed it with thy fearful and glorious
      name;
4 all things tremble and quake in the face of thy power.
5 For the majesty of thy glory is more than man can bear,
   and none can endure thy menacing wrath against sinners;

the mercy in thy promise is beyond measure: none can fathom it.                    6
For thou art Lord Most High,                    7
compassionate, patient, and of great mercy,
relenting when men suffer for their sins.
For out of thy great goodness thou, O God,
hast promised repentance and remission to those who sin against thee,
and in thy boundless mercy thou hast appointed repentance for sinners as
    the way to salvation.[a]
So thou, Lord God of the righteous,                    8
didst not appoint repentance for Abraham, Isaac, and Jacob,
who were righteous and did not sin against thee,
but for me, a sinner,
whose sins are more in number than the sands of the sea.                    9
My transgressions abound, O Lord, my transgressions abound,
and I am not worthy to look up and gaze at the height of heaven
because of the number of my wrongdoings.
Bowed down with a heavy chain of iron,                    10
I grieve over my sins and find no relief,
because I have provoked thy anger
and done what is evil in thine eyes,
setting up idols and so piling sin on sin.
Now I humble my heart, imploring thy great goodness.                    11
I have sinned, O Lord, I have sinned,                    12
and I acknowledge my transgressions.
I pray and beseech thee,                    13
spare me, O Lord, spare me,
destroy me not with my transgressions on my head,
do not be angry with me for ever, nor store up evil for me.
Do not condemn me to the grave,
for thou, Lord, art the God of the penitent.
Thou wilt show thy goodness towards me,                    14
for unworthy as I am thou wilt save me in thy great mercy;
and so I shall praise thee continually all the days of my life.                    15
For all the host of heaven sings thy praise,
and thy glory is for ever and ever. Amen.

[a] *Some witnesses omit* For out of . . . salvation.

# THE FIRST BOOK OF THE
# MACCABEES

## *Antiochus and the Jewish revolt*

1 LEXANDER OF MACEDON, the son of Philip, marched
from the land of Kittim, defeated Darius, king of Persia and
2 Media, and seized his throne, being already king of Greece.*a* In
the course of many campaigns he captured fortified towns, slaughtered
3 kings, traversed the earth to its remotest bounds, and plundered innumerable nations. When at last the world lay quiet under his rule, his
4 pride knew no limits; he built up an extremely powerful army, and ruled
over countries, nations, and dominions; all paid him tribute.

5 6    The time came when he fell ill, and, knowing that he was dying, he
summoned his generals, nobles who had been brought up with him from
childhood, and divided his empire among them while he was still alive.
7 8 Alexander had reigned twelve years when he died. His generals took over
9 the government, each in his own province. On his death they were all
crowned as kings, and their descendants succeeded them for many years.
They brought untold miseries upon the world. ·

10    A scion of this stock was that wicked man, Antiochus Epiphanes, son of
King Antiochus. He had been a hostage in Rome before he succeeded to
the throne in the year 137 of the Greek era.*b*

11    At that time there appeared in Israel a group of renegade Jews, who
incited the people. 'Let us enter into a covenant with the Gentiles round
about,' they said, 'because disaster upon disaster has overtaken us since
12 we segregated ourselves from them.' The people thought this a good argu-
13 ment, and some of them in their enthusiasm went to the king and received
14 authority to introduce non-Jewish laws and customs. They built a sports-
15 stadium in the gentile style in Jerusalem. They removed their marks of
circumcision and repudiated the holy covenant. They intermarried with
Gentiles, and abandoned themselves to evil ways.

16    When he was firmly established on his throne, Antiochus made up his
17 mind to become king of Egypt and so to rule over both kingdoms. He
assembled a powerful force of chariots, elephants, and cavalry, and a great
18 fleet, and invaded Egypt. When battle was joined, Ptolemy king of Egypt
19 was seized with panic and took to flight, leaving many dead. The fortified
towns were captured and the land pillaged.

20    On his return from the conquest of Egypt, in the year 143,*c* Antiochus
21 marched with a strong force against Israel and Jerusalem. In his arrogance

---

*a* being . . . Greece: *probable meaning; Gk. obscure.*          *b* *That is* 175 B.C.
*c* *That is* 169 B.C.

he entered the temple and carried off the golden altar, the lamp-stand with
all its equipment, the table for the Bread of the Presence, the sacred cups    22
and bowls, the golden censers, the curtain, and the crowns. He stripped off
all the gold plating from the temple front. He seized the silver, gold, and    23
precious vessels, and whatever secret treasures he found, and took them    24
all with him when he left for his own country. He had caused much bloodshed, and he gloated over all he had done.

> Great was the lamentation throughout Israel;    25
> rulers and elders groaned in bitter grief.    26
> Girls and young men languished;
> the beauty of our women was disfigured.
> Every bridegroom took up the lament,    27
> and every bride sat grieving in her chamber.
> The land trembled for its inhabitants,    28
> and all the house of Jacob was wrapped in shame.

Two years later, the king sent to the towns of Judaea a high revenue    29
official, who arrived at Jerusalem with a powerful force. His language was    30
friendly, but full of guile. For, once he had gained the city's confidence, he
suddenly attacked it. He dealt it a heavy blow, and killed many Israelites,
plundering the city and setting it ablaze. He pulled down houses and walls    31
on every side; women and children were made prisoners, and the cattle    32
seized.

The city of David was turned into a citadel, enclosed by a high, stout    33
wall with strong towers, and garrisoned by impious foreigners and rene-    34
gades. Having made themselves secure, they accumulated arms and pro-    35
visions, and deposited there the massed plunder of Jerusalem. There they
lay in ambush, a lurking threat to the temple and a perpetual menace to    36
Israel.

> They shed the blood of the innocent round the temple;    37
> they defiled the holy place.
> The citizens of Jerusalem fled for fear of them;    38
> she became the abode of aliens,
> and alien herself to her offspring:
> her children deserted her.
> Her temple lay desolate as a wilderness;    39
> her feasts were turned to mourning,
> her sabbaths to a reproach,
> her honour to contempt.
> The shame of her fall matched the greatness of her renown,    40
> and her pride was bowed low in grief.

The king then issued a decree throughout his empire: his subjects were    41
all to become one people and abandon their own laws and religion. The    42
nations everywhere complied with the royal command, and many in Israel    43
accepted the foreign worship, sacrificing to idols and profaning the sabbath.
Moreover, the king sent agents with written orders to Jerusalem and the    44
towns of Judaea. Ways and customs foreign to the country were to be

45 introduced. Burnt-offerings, sacrifices, and libations in the temple were
46 forbidden; sabbaths and feast-days were to be profaned; the temple and
47 its ministers to be defiled. Altars, idols, and sacred precincts were to be
48 established; swine and other unclean beasts to be offered in sacrifice. They
must leave their sons uncircumcised; they must make themselves in every
49 way abominable, unclean, and profane, and so forget the law and change all
50 their statutes. The penalty for disobedience was death.
51     Such was the decree which the king issued to all his subjects. He appointed superintendents over all the people, and instructed the towns of
52 Judaea to offer sacrifice, town by town. People thronged to their side in
large numbers, every one of them a traitor to the law. Their wicked conduct
53 throughout the land drove Israel into hiding in every possible place of
refuge.
54     On the fifteenth day of the month Kislev in the year 145,[a] 'the abomination of desolation' was set up on the altar. Pagan altars were built through-
55 out the towns of Judaea; incense was offered at the doors of houses and in
56 the streets. All scrolls of the law which were found were torn up and burnt.
57 Anyone discovered in possession of a Book of the Covenant, or conform-
58 ing to the law, was put to death by the king's sentence. Thus month after
month these wicked men used their power against the Israelites whom they
found in their towns.
59     On the twenty-fifth day of the month they offered sacrifice on the pagan
60 altar which was on top of the altar of the Lord. In accordance with the royal
decree, they put to death women who had had their children circumcised.
61 Their babies, their families, and those who had circumcised them, they
62 hanged by the neck. Yet many in Israel found strength to resist, taking a
63 determined stand against eating any unclean food. They welcomed death
rather than defile themselves and profane the holy covenant, and so they
64 died. The divine wrath raged against Israel.[b]


2   AT THIS TIME a certain Mattathias, son of John, son of Symeon, appeared
on the scene. He was a priest of the Joarib family from Jerusalem, who had
2 3 settled at Modin. Mattathias had five sons, John called Gaddis, Simon
4 5 called Thassis, Judas called Maccabaeus, Eleazar called Avaran, and
Jonathan called Apphus.
6     When Mattathias saw the sacrilegious acts committed in Judaea and
7 Jerusalem, he said:

> 'Oh! Why was I born to see this,
> the crushing of my people, the ruin of the holy city?
> They sat idly by when it was surrendered,
> when the holy place was given up to the alien.
8 Her temple is like a man robbed of honour;
9 its glorious vessels are carried off as spoil.
> Her infants are slain in the street,
> her young men by the sword of the foe.

---

[a] *That is* 167 B.C.     [b] The divine . . . Israel: *or* Israel lived under a reign
of terror.

Is there a nation that has not usurped her sovereignty,*a*          10
a people that has not plundered her?
She has been stripped of all her adornment,          11
no longer free, but a slave.

Now that we have seen our temple with all its beauty and splendour laid          12
waste and profaned by the Gentiles, why should we live any longer?' So          13 14
Mattathias and his sons tore their garments, put on sackcloth, and mourned
bitterly.

The king's officers who were enforcing apostasy came to the town of          15
Modin to see that sacrifice was offered, and many Israelites went over to          16
them. Mattathias and his sons stood in a group. The king's officers spoke          17
to Mattathias: 'You are a leader here,' they said, 'a man of mark and
influence in this town, with your sons and brothers at your back. You be          18
the first now to come forward and carry out the king's order. All the nations
have done so, as well as the leading men in Judaea and the people left in
Jerusalem. Then you and your sons will be enrolled among the King's
Friends; you will all receive high honours, rich rewards of silver and gold,
and many further benefits.'

To this Mattathias replied in a ringing voice: 'Though all the nations          19
within the king's dominions obey him and forsake their ancestral worship,
though they have chosen to submit to his commands, yet I and my sons          20
and brothers will follow the covenant of our fathers. Heaven forbid we          21
should ever abandon the law and its statutes. We will not obey the          22
command of the king, nor will we deviate one step from our forms of
worship.'

As soon as he had finished, a Jew stepped forward in full view of all to          23
offer sacrifice on the pagan altar at Modin, in obedience to the royal command. The sight stirred Mattathias to indignation; he shook with passion,          24
and in a fury of righteous anger rushed forward and slaughtered the traitor
on the very altar. At the same time he killed the officer sent by the king to          25
enforce sacrifice, and pulled the pagan altar down. Thus Mattathias showed          26
his fervent zeal for the law, just as Phinehas had done by killing Zimri son
of Salu. 'Follow me,' he shouted through the town, 'every one of you who is          27
zealous for the law and strives to maintain the covenant.' He and his sons          28
took to the hills, leaving all their belongings behind in the town.

At that time many who wanted to maintain their religion and law went          29
down to the wilds to live there. They took their sons, their wives, and their          30
cattle with them, for their miseries were more than they could bear. Word          31
soon reached the king's officers and the forces in Jerusalem, the city of
David, that men who had defied the king's order had gone down into
hiding-places in the wilds. A large body of men went quickly after them,          32
came up with them, and occupied positions opposite. They prepared to
attack them on the sabbath. 'There is still time,' they shouted; 'come out,          33
obey the king's command, and your lives will be spared.' 'We will not come          34
out,' the Jews replied; 'we will not obey the king's command or profane the
sabbath.' Without more ado the attack was launched; but the Israelites did          35 36

*a* *Or* occupied her palaces.

nothing in reply; they neither hurled stones, nor barricaded their caves.
37 'Let us all meet death with a clear conscience,' they said; 'we call heaven
38 and earth to testify that there is no justice in this slaughter.' So they were
attacked and massacred on the sabbath, men, women, and children, up
to a thousand in all, and their cattle with them.

39 Great was the grief of Mattathias and his friends when they heard the
40 news. They said to one another, 'If we all do as our brothers have done, if
we refuse to fight the Gentiles for our lives as well as for our laws and
41 customs, then they will soon wipe us off the face of the earth.' That day
they decided that, if anyone came to fight against them on the sabbath,
they would fight back, rather than all die as their brothers in the caves
had done.

42 It was then that they were joined by a company of Hasidaeans, stalwarts
43 of Israel, every one of them a volunteer in the cause of the law; and all who
were refugees from the troubles came to swell their numbers, and so add
44 to their strength. Now that they had an organized force, they turned their
wrath on the guilty men and renegades. Those who escaped their fierce
attacks took refuge with the Gentiles.

45 Mattathias and his friends then swept through the country, pulling down
46 the pagan altars, and forcibly circumcising all the uncircumcised boys
47 found within the frontiers of Israel. They hunted down their arrogant
48 enemies, and the cause prospered in their hands. Thus they saved the law
from the Gentiles and their kings, and broke the power of the tyrant.

49 The time came for Mattathias to die, and he said to his sons: 'Arrogance
now stands secure and gives judgement against us; it is a time of calamity
50 and raging fury. But now, my sons, be zealous for the law, and give your
51 lives for the covenant of your fathers. Remember the deeds they did in
52 their generations, and great glory and eternal fame shall be yours. Did not
Abraham prove steadfast under trial, and so gain credit as a righteous man?
53 Joseph kept the commandments, hard-pressed though he was, and became
54 lord of Egypt. Phinehas, our father, never flagged in his zeal, and his was the
55 covenant of an everlasting priesthood. Joshua kept the law, and he became
56 a judge in Israel. Caleb bore witness before the congregation, and a share
57 in the land was his reward. David was a man of loyalty, and he was granted
58 the throne of an everlasting kingdom. Elijah never flagged in his zeal for
59 the law, and he was taken up to heaven. Hananiah, Azariah, and Mishael
60 had faith, and they were saved from the blazing furnace. Daniel was a man
61 of integrity, and he was rescued from the lions' jaws. As generation succeeds
generation, follow their example; for no one who trusts in Heaven shall
62 ever lack strength. Do not fear a wicked man's words; all his success will
63 end in filth and worms. Today he may be high in honour, but tomorrow
there will be no trace of him, because he will have returned to the dust and
64 all his schemes come to nothing. But you, my sons, draw your courage and
strength from the law, for by it you will win great glory.

65 'Now here is Symeon, your brother; I know him to be wise in counsel:
66 always listen to him, for he shall be a father to you. Judas Maccabaeus has
been strong and brave from boyhood; he shall be your commander in the
67 field, and fight his people's battles. Gather to your side all who observe the

law, and avenge your people's wrongs. Repay the Gentiles in their own 68
coin, and always heed the law's commands.'
    Then Mattathias blessed them, and was gathered to his fathers. He died 69 70
in the year 146,<sup>a</sup> and was buried by his sons in the family tomb at Modin.
All Israel raised a loud lament for him.

## The war under Judas and Jonathan

THEN JUDAS MACCABAEUS came forward in his father's place. He 3 1 2
had the support of all his brothers and his father's followers, and they
carried on the fight for Israel with zest.

> He enhanced his people's glory. 3
> He put on his breastplate like a giant,
> and girt himself with weapons of war.
> He fought battle on battle;
> he guarded his army with his sword.
> He was like a lion in his exploits, 4
> like a lion's whelp roaring for prey.
> He hunted and tracked down the lawless; 5
> he blasted the troublers of his people.
> The lawless cowered in fear of him; 6
> all evil-doers were confounded.
> The cause of freedom prospered in his hands;
> he provoked many kings to anger. 7
> But he made Jacob glad by his deeds;
> he is remembered for ever in blessing.
> He passed through the towns of Judaea; 8
> he destroyed the godless there.
> He turned wrath away from Israel;
> his fame spread to the ends of the earth, 9
> and he rallied a people near to destruction.

Apollonius now collected a gentile force and a large contingent from 10
Samaria, to fight against Israel. When Judas heard of it, he marched out to 11
meet him, and defeated and killed him. Many of the Gentiles fell, and the
rest took to flight. From the arms they captured, Judas took the sword of 12
Apollonius, and used it in his campaigns for the rest of his life.
    When Seron, who commanded the army in Syria, heard that Judas had 13
mustered a large force, consisting of all his loyal followers of military age,
he said to himself, 'I will win a glorious reputation in the empire by making 14
war on Judas and his followers, who defy the royal edict.' Seron was re- 15
inforced by a strong contingent of renegade Jews, who marched up to help
him take vengeance on Israel. When he reached the pass of Beth-horon, 16
Judas advanced to meet him with a handful of men. When his followers 17
saw the host coming against them, they said to Judas, 'How can so few of
us fight against so many? Besides, we have had nothing to eat all day, and
we are exhausted.'

<sup>a</sup> *That is* 166 B.C.

18 Judas replied: 'Many can easily be overpowered by a few; it makes no
19 difference to Heaven to save by many or by few. Victory does not depend
20 on numbers; strength comes from Heaven alone. Our enemies come filled
with insolence and lawlessness to plunder and to kill us and our wives and
21 22 children. But we are fighting for our lives and our religion. Heaven will
crush them before our eyes. You need not be afraid of them.'

23 When he had finished speaking, he launched a sudden attack, and Seron
24 and his army broke before him. They pursued them down the pass of Beth-
horon as far as the plain; some eight hundred of the enemy fell, and the rest
fled to Philistia.

25 Thus Judas and his brothers began to be feared, and alarm spread to the
26 Gentiles all round. His fame reached the ears of the king, and the story of
27 his battles was told in every nation. When King Antiochus heard this news,
he flew into a rage and ordered all the forces of his empire to be assembled,
28 an immensely powerful army. He opened his treasury and gave a year's pay
29 to his troops, ordering them to be prepared for any duty. But he found that
his resources were running low; his tribute, too, had dwindled as a result
of the disaffection and violence he had brought upon the world by abolish-
30 ing traditional laws and customs. He now saw with alarm that he might be
short of money, as had happened once or twice before, both for his normal
expenses and for the gifts he had been accustomed to distribute with an
even more lavish hand than any of his predecessors on the throne.

31 For a time he was much perplexed; then he decided to go to Persia,
collect the tribute due from the provinces, and raise a large sum of ready
32 money. He left Lysias, a distinguished member of the royal family, as
viceroy of the territories between the Euphrates and the Egyptian frontier.
33 34 He also appointed him guardian of his son Antiochus until his return. He
transferred to Lysias half the armed forces, together with the elephants,
and told him all that he wanted done, especially to the population of Judaea
35 and Jerusalem. Against these Lysias was to send a force, and break and
destroy the strength of Israel and those who were left in Jerusalem, to blot
36 out all memory of them from the place. He was to settle foreigners in all
37 their territory, and allot the land to the settlers. The other half of the
forces the king took with him, and set out from Antioch, his capital, in
the year 147.*a* He crossed the Euphrates and marched through the upper
provinces.

38 Lysias chose Ptolemaeus son of Dorymenes, with Nicanor and Gorgias,
39 all three powerful members of the order of King's Friends, and sent with
them forty thousand infantry and seven thousand cavalry to invade Judaea
40 and devastate the country as the king had commanded. They set out with
41 all their forces and encamped near Emmaus in the lowlands. The merchants of the region, impressed by what they heard of the army, took a large
quantity of silver and gold, with a supply of fetters, and came into the camp
to buy the Israelites for slaves. The army was also reinforced by troops
from Syria and Philistia.

42 Judas and his brothers saw that their plight had become grave, with the
enemy encamped inside their frontiers. They learnt, too, of the commands

*a* *That is* 165 B.C.

which the king had given for the complete destruction of the nation. So 43
they said to one another, 'Let us restore the shattered fortunes of our nation;
let us fight for our nation and for the holy place.' They gathered in full 44
assembly to prepare for battle, and to pray and seek divine mercy and
compassion.

Jerusalem lay deserted like a wilderness; 45
none of her children went in or out.
Her holy place was trampled down;
aliens and heathen lodged in her citadel.
Joy had been banished from Jacob;
and flute and harp were dumb.

They assembled at Mizpah, opposite Jerusalem, for in former times 46
Israel had a place of worship at Mizpah. That day they fasted, put on sack- 47
cloth, sprinkled ashes on their heads, and tore their garments. They un- 48
rolled the scroll of the law, seeking the guidance which Gentiles seek from
the images of their gods. They brought the priestly vestments, the first- 49
fruits, and the tithes; they presented Nazirites who had completed their
vows, and they cried to Heaven: 'What shall we do with these Nazirites, 50
and where shall we take them? Thy holy place is trodden down and defiled, 51
and sorrow and humiliation have come upon thy priests. And see, the 52
Gentiles have gathered against us to destroy us. Thou knowest the fate
they plan for us; how can we withstand them unless thou help us?' Then 53 54
the trumpets sounded, and a great shout went up.

Judas then appointed leaders of the people, officers over thousands, 55
hundreds, fifties, and tens. As the law commands, he ordered back to their 56
homes those who were building their houses or were newly wed or who were
planting vineyards, or who were faint-hearted. Thereupon the army moved 57
and took up their positions to the south of Emmaus, where Judas thus 58
addressed them: 'Prepare for action and show yourselves men. Be ready
at dawn to fight these Gentiles who are massed against us to destroy us and
our holy place. Better die fighting than look on while calamity overwhelms 59
our people and the holy place. But it will be as Heaven wills.' 60

Gorgias, taking a detachment of five thousand men and a thousand 4
picked cavalry, set out by night to attack the Jewish army and fall upon 2
them unawares; his guides were men from the citadel. But Judas had word 3
of this, and he and his soldiers moved out to attack the king's army in
Emmaus, while its forces were still divided. Gorgias reached the camp of 4 5
Judas during the night, but found no one there. He set out to search for
them in the hills, thinking, 'These Jews are running away from us.'

At daybreak, there was Judas in the plain with three thousand men, 6
though they had not all the armour and the swords they wanted. They saw 7
the Gentiles' camp strongly fortified with breastworks, while mounted
guards, seasoned troops, patrolled round it.

Judas said to his men: 'Do not be afraid of their great numbers or panic 8
when they charge. Remember how our fathers were saved at the Red Sea, 9
when Pharaoh and his army were pursuing them. Let us cry now to Heaven 10
to favour our cause, to remember the covenant made with our fathers, and

11 to crush this army before us today. Then all the Gentiles will know that there is One who saves and liberates Israel.'

12 When the foreigners looked up and saw them advancing to the attack,
13 they marched out of their camp to give battle. Judas and his men sounded
14 their trumpets and closed with them. The Gentiles broke, and fled to the
15 plain. All the rearmost fell by the sword. The pursuit was pressed as far as Gazara and the lowlands of Idumaea, Azotus and Jamnia; about three thousand of the enemy were killed.

16 17 Judas and his force then broke off the pursuit and returned. He said to the people: 'Curb your greed for spoil; there is more fighting before us;
18 Gorgias and his force are in the hills near by. Stand firm now against our enemies and fight; after that, plunder as you please.'

19 Before Judas had finished speaking, an enemy patrol appeared, recon-
20 noitring from the hills. They saw that their army was in flight, and that their camp was being set on fire; the smoke that met their gaze showed
21 what had happened. They were filled with panic as they took in the scene,
22 and when they saw the army of Judas in the plain, ready for battle, they all fled to Philistia.

23 Then Judas turned back to plunder the camp, and there they got much
24 gold and silver, violet and purple stuffs, and great riches. On their return they sang songs of thanksgiving and praised Heaven, 'for it is right, because
25 his mercy endures for ever'. That day saw a great deliverance for Israel.

26 Those of the Gentiles who escaped with their lives went and reported
27 to Lysias all that had happened. On hearing the news he was overwhelmed with disappointment, because Israel had not suffered the disaster he had hoped for, and the issue was not what the king had ordered.

28 In the following year he gathered sixty thousand picked infantry and
29 five thousand cavalry to make war on the Jews. They marched into Idumaea, and encamped at Bethsura, where Judas met them with ten
30 thousand men. When he saw the strength of the enemy's army, he prayed: 'All praise to thee, the Saviour of Israel, who didst break the attack of the giant by thy servant David. Thou didst deliver the army of the Philistines
31 into the power of Saul's son, Jonathan, and of his armour-bearer. In like manner put this army into the power of thy people Israel. Humble their
32 pride in their forces and their mounted men. Strike them with panic, turn their insolent strength to water, make them reel under a crushing defeat.
33 Overthrow them by the sword of those who love thee, and let all who know thy name praise thee with songs of thanksgiving.'

34 So they joined battle, and Lysias lost about five thousand men in the
35 close fighting. When he saw his own army routed and Judas's army full of daring, ready to live or die nobly, he departed for Antioch, and there collected a force of mercenaries, in order to return to Judaea with a much larger army than before.*a*

36 But Judas and his brothers said: 'Now that our enemies have been crushed, let us go up to Jerusalem to cleanse the temple and rededicate it.'
37 38 So the whole army was assembled and went up to Mount Zion. There they found the temple laid waste, the altar profaned, the gates burnt down, the

*a* in order . . . before: *probable meaning; Gk. obscure.*

courts overgrown like a thicket or wooded hill-side, and the priests' rooms
in ruin. They tore their garments, wailed loudly, put ashes on their heads, 39
and fell on their faces to the ground. They sounded the ceremonial 40
trumpets, and cried aloud to Heaven.

Then Judas detailed troops to engage the garrison of the citadel while 41
he cleansed the temple. He selected priests without blemish, devoted to 42
the law, and they purified the temple, removing to an unclean place the 43
stones which defiled it. They discussed what to do with the altar of burnt- 44
offering, which was profaned, and rightly decided to demolish it, for fear 45
it might become a standing reproach to them because it had been defiled
by the Gentiles. They therefore pulled down the altar, and stored away the 46
stones in a fitting place on the temple hill, until a prophet should arise who
could be consulted about them. They took unhewn stones, as the law com- 47
mands, and built a new altar on the model of the previous one. They 48
rebuilt the temple and restored its interior, and consecrated the temple
courts. They renewed the sacred vessels and the lamp-stand, and brought 49
the altar of incense and the table into the temple. They burnt incense on the 50
altar and lit the lamps on the lamp-stand to shine within the temple. When 51
they had put the Bread of the Presence on the table and hung the curtains,
all their work was completed.

Then, early on the twenty-fifth day of the ninth month, the month 52
Kislev, in the year 148,[a] sacrifice was offered as the law commands on the 53
newly made altar of burnt-offering. On the anniversary of the day when the 54
Gentiles had profaned it, on that very day, it was rededicated, with hymns
of thanksgiving, to the music of harps and lutes and cymbals. All the people 55
prostrated themselves, worshipping and praising Heaven that their cause
had prospered.

They celebrated the rededication of the altar for eight days; there was 56
great rejoicing as they brought burnt-offerings and sacrificed peace-
offerings and thank-offerings. They decorated the front of the temple with 57
golden wreaths and ornamental shields. They renewed the gates and the
priests' rooms, and fitted them with doors. There was great merry-making 58
among the people, and the disgrace brought on them by the Gentiles was
removed.

Then Judas, his brothers, and the whole congregation of Israel decreed 59
that the rededication of the altar should be observed with joy and gladness
at the same season each year, for eight days, beginning on the twenty-fifth
of Kislev.

At that time they encircled Mount Zion with high walls and strong 60
towers to prevent the Gentiles from coming and trampling it down as they
had done before. Judas set a garrison there; he also fortified Bethsura, so 61
that the people should have a fortress facing Idumaea.

WHEN THE GENTILES round about heard that the altar had been re-- 5
built and the temple rededicated, they were furious, and determined to 2
wipe out all those of the race of Jacob who lived among them. Thus began
the work of massacre and extermination among the people.

[a] *That is* 164 B.C.

3 Judas then made war on the descendants of Esau in Idumaea and attacked Acrabattene, because they had hemmed Israel in. There he inflicted on them a severe and humiliating defeat, and took spoils from
4 them. He remembered also the wrong done by the Baeanites, who with their traps and road-blocks were continually ambushing the Israelites.
5 He first confined them to their forts and took up positions against them; then he solemnly committed them to destruction and set the forts ablaze
6 with all their occupants. He crossed over to the Ammonites, and came upon a strong and numerous force under the command of a certain Timotheus.
7 He fought many battles with them, and they broke before him and were
8 crushed. After capturing Jazer and its dependent villages, he returned to Judaea.
9 Then the Gentiles in Gilead gathered against the Israelites within their territory, intending to destroy them; but they took refuge in the fortress of
10 Dathema, and sent this letter to Judas and his brothers:

11 The Gentiles round us have gathered to wipe us out. They are preparing to come and seize the fortress where we have taken refuge;
12 Timotheus is in command of their army. So come at once and rescue us
13 from their clutches, for many of our number have already fallen. All our fellow-Jews in the region of Tubias have been massacred, their wives and their children taken captive, and their property carried off. About a thousand men there have lost their lives.

14 While the letter was being read, other messengers with their garments
15 torn arrived from Galilee. 'Ptolemais, Tyre and Sidon,' they said, 'and all heathen Galilee have mustered their forces to make an end of us.'
16 When Judas and the people heard this, a full assembly was called to decide what they should do for their fellow-countrymen in distress and
17 under enemy attack. Judas said to Simon his brother, 'Choose your men, and go and rescue your countrymen in Galilee, while I and my brother
18 Jonathan march into Gilead.' The rest of his forces he left for the defences of Judaea, with Josephus son of Zacharias, and Azarias, leading citizens,
19 and gave them this order: 'Take charge of the people of Jerusalem, but
20 on no account join battle with the Gentiles until we return.' Simon was allotted three thousand men for the march on Galilee, and Judas eight thousand for the march on Gilead.
21 Simon invaded Galilee and, after many battles, broke the resistance of
22 the Gentiles. He pursued them as far as the gate of Ptolemais, killed nearly
23 three thousand of them, and stripped their corpses. He took back with him the Jews from Galilee and Arbatta, their wives and children, and all their property, and brought them to Judaea with great jubilation.
24 Meanwhile Judas Maccabaeus and his brother Jonathan crossed the
25 Jordan and made a three days' march through the desert. They came upon some Nabataeans, who met them peacefully, and gave them an account of
26 all that had happened to their fellow-Jews in Gilead: many of them were held prisoner in Bozrah and Bezer, in Alema, Casphor, Maked, and
27 Carnaim—all large fortified towns; some in the other towns of Gilead. 'Your enemies', they told them, 'are marshalling their forces to storm your

fortresses tomorrow so as to capture them and destroy all the Jews in them in a single day.'

Then Judas and his army suddenly turned aside to Bozrah by way of the 28 desert, captured the town, and put all the males to the sword. He plundered all their property and set fire to the town. From there he made a night- 29 march and came within reach of the fortress of Dathema. When dawn 30 broke they saw in front of them an innumerable host, bringing up scaling-ladders and siege-engines and engaging the defenders, to capture the fortress. Judas saw that battle was already joined, and a cry went up to 31 heaven from the town, with trumpeting and loud shouting. Judas said to 32 his men: 'Now is the time to fight for our brothers.'

They marched out in three columns to take the enemy in the rear. Then 33 they sounded the trumpets and cried aloud in prayer, and the army of 34 Timotheus recognized that it was Maccabaeus and took to flight before him. He inflicted a severe defeat on them, and nearly eight thousand of the enemy fell that day.

Judas then turned aside to Alema,*ᵃ* attacked and captured it, and killed 35 all the males. He plundered the town and set it on fire. From there he moved 36 on and occupied Casphor, Maked, Bezer, and the other towns of Gilead.

After these events, Timotheus gathered another army, and took up 37 position opposite Raphon, on the other side of the ravine. Judas sent spies 38 to their camp, and they reported that all the Gentiles in the neighbourhood had rallied in very great strength to Timotheus, who had also hired Arab 39 mercenaries to help them; they were encamped on the far side of the ravine, ready to engage him in battle. So Judas marched to meet them.

As Judas and his army were approaching the flooded ravine, Timotheus 40 said to his officers: 'If Judas crosses over to our side first, we shall not be able to stand up to him; he will certainly get the better of us. If, however, 41 his courage fails him and he takes up a position on the other side of the river, then we will cross over and get the better of him.' When Judas 42 reached the ravine, he stationed the officers of the muster on its bank, with instructions that no one should be allowed to take up a fixed position, but that all should advance to battle. Thus Judas forestalled the enemy by 43 crossing to attack them, with all his people following. The Gentiles broke before him; they all threw away their arms and took refuge in the temple at Carnaim. Judas captured the town and burnt the temple together with all 44 its occupants: Carnaim was completely subdued and could no longer withstand him.

Then Judas gathered together all the Israelites in Gilead to escort them 45 to Judaea. They amounted to an immense host, small and great, women and children, with their property. They came as far as Ephron, a large and 46 strongly fortified town on the road: it was impossible to pass by it on either side; the only route was through the town. But the townsmen kept 47 them out, barricading their gates with boulders. Judas sent them a con- 48 ciliatory message: 'We have to pass through your territory to reach our own. No one shall do you any harm: we shall only march through.' But they refused to open their gates to him.

---

*ᵃ Some witnesses read* Maapha.

49 Judas issued orders to the whole host for everyone to halt where he was.
50 Then the fighting men took up battle positions and attacked the town all
51 that day and all the night, until it fell into their hands. They put every male
to the sword, razed the town to the ground and plundered it, and then
52 marched through it over the bodies of the dead. They crossed the Jordan
53 to the great plain opposite Bethshan, while Judas brought up the stragglers
and encouraged the people all along the road till he arrived in Judaea.
54 They went up to Mount Zion with gladness and jubilation, and offered
burnt-offerings, because they had returned in safety without the loss of
a single man.

55 Now while Judas and Jonathan were in Gilead, and Simon their brother
56 in Galilee was besieging Ptolemais, the two commanders, Josephus son of
57 Zacharias, and Azarias, heard of their exploits in battle. 'We too', they
said, 'must make a name for ourselves: let us go and fight the Gentiles in
58 our neighbourhood.' So they gave orders to their forces and marched
59 against Jamnia. Gorgias came out of the town with his men to meet them
60 in battle; and Josephus and Azarias were routed and pursued to the
61 frontier of Judaea. Some two thousand of the people fell that day. So the
Israelites suffered a heavy defeat, because their commanders, thinking to
62 play the hero themselves, had not obeyed Judas and his brothers. They
were not, however, of that family to whom it was granted to bring deliverance to Israel.

63 Judas and his brothers won a great reputation in all Israel and among
64 the Gentiles, wherever their fame was heard, and crowds flocked to
acclaim them.

65 After this, Judas marched out with his brothers and made war on the
descendants of Esau to the south. He struck at Hebron and its villages,
66 demolished its fortifications, and burnt down its forts on all sides. He then
67 set out to invade Philistine territory, marching through Marisa. On that
day several priests, who had ill-advisedly gone into action wishing to dis-
68 tinguish themselves, fell in battle. Then Judas turned aside to Azotus in
Philistia. He pulled down their altars, burnt the images of their gods,
carried off the spoil from their towns, and returned to Judaea.

6 As King Antiochus marched through the upper provinces he heard that
there was a city in Persia called Elymais, famous for its wealth in silver and
2 gold. Its temple was very rich, full of gold shields, coats of mail, and arms,
left there by Alexander son of Philip, king of Macedon and the first to be
3 king over the Greeks. Antiochus came and tried to capture and plunder
the city, but failed because his plan had become known to the citizens.
4 They gave battle and put him to flight, and he withdrew to Babylon in
bitter disappointment.

5 A messenger met him in Persia with the news that the armies which had
6 invaded Judaea were in full retreat. Lysias had marched up with an excep-
tionally strong force, only to be flung back before the enemy, and the
strength of the Jews had grown by the capture of arms, equipment, and
7 spoils from the Syrian armies they had defeated. They had pulled down the
abomination he had built on the altar in Jerusalem, and surrounded their
temple with high walls as before, and had even fortified Bethsura.

When the king heard this news, he was thrown into such deep dismay 8
that he took to his bed, ill with grief at the miscarriage of his plans. There 9
he lay for many days, his bitter grief breaking out again and again, and he
realized that he was dying. So he summoned all his Friends and said to 10
them: 'Sleep has deserted me; the weight of care has broken my heart.
At first I said to myself, "Why am I overwhelmed by this flood of trouble, 11
I who was kind and well-loved in the day of my power?" But now I 12
remember the wrong I did in Jerusalem, when I took all her vessels of silver
and gold, and when I made an unjustified attempt to wipe out the inhabitants of Judaea. It is for this, I know, that these misfortunes have come 13
upon me; and here I am, dying of grief in a foreign land.'

He summoned Philip, one of his Friends, and appointed him regent 14
over his whole empire, giving him the crown, the royal robe, and the signet- 15
ring, with authority to take his son Antiochus and bring him up to be king.
King Antiochus died there in the year 149.[a] 16
When Lysias learnt that the king was dead, he placed the young Antio- 17
chus, whom he had brought up from boyhood, on the throne in succession
to his father, and gave him the name of Eupator.

MEANWHILE THE GARRISON of the citadel were confining the 18
Israelites to the neighbourhood of the temple, and giving continual support to the Gentiles by their harassing tactics. Judas therefore determined 19
to make an end of them. He gathered all the people together to lay siege to
the citadel in the year 150,[b] erecting emplacements and siege-engines 20
against the enemy.

Now some of the besieged garrison escaped and were joined by a number 21
of renegade Israelites. They went to the king and said: 'How long must we 22
wait for you to do justice and avenge our comrades? We were willing to 23
serve your father, to follow his instructions and to obey his decrees, and 24
what was the result? Our own countrymen became our enemies. They
actually killed as many of us as they could find, and robbed us of our property. Nor are we the only ones to suffer at their hands. They have attacked 25
all their neighbours as well. At this very moment they are besieging the 26
citadel in Jerusalem and mean to capture it; and they have fortified both the
temple and Bethsura. Unless your majesty quickly overpowers them they 27
will go to yet greater lengths, and you will not be able to keep them in
check.'

When the king heard this he was furious. He assembled all his Friends, 28
the commanders of his army, and his cavalry officers. He was joined by 29
mercenary troops from other kingdoms and from the islands. His forces 30
numbered one hundred thousand infantry, twenty thousand cavalry, and
thirty-two war-elephants. They passed through Idumaea and laid siege 31
to Bethsura. They kept up the attack for a long time and erected siege-
engines, but the defenders made a sortie and set fire to them, and fought
back manfully.

Judas now withdrew from the citadel and encamped at Bethzacharia, 32
opposite the camp of the king. Early next morning the king broke camp 33

a   *That is* 163 B.C.      b   *That is* 162 B.C.

and rushed his army along the road to Bethzacharia; there his forces were
34 drawn up for battle and the trumpets were sounded. The elephants were
35 roused for battle with the juice of grapes and of mulberries. The great
beasts were distributed among the phalanxes; by each were stationed a
thousand men, equipped with coats of chain-mail and bronze helmets.
36 Five hundred picked horsemen were also assigned to each animal. These
had been stationed beforehand where the beast was; and wherever it went,
37 they went with it, never leaving it. Each animal had a strong wooden turret
fastened on its back with a special harness, by way of protection, and
38 carried four *a* fighting men as well as an Indian driver. The rest of the
cavalry Lysias stationed on either flank of the army, to harass the enemy
39 while themselves protected by the phalanxes. When the sun shone on the
gold and bronze shields, they lit up the hills, which flashed like torches.
40 Part of the king's army was deployed over the heights, and part over the
41 low ground. They advanced confidently and in good order. All who heard
the din of this marching multitude and its clashing arms shook with fear.
It was a very great and powerful array indeed.
42 Judas advanced with his army and gave battle, and six hundred of the
43 king's men were killed. Eleazar Avaran, seeing that one of the elephants
wore royal armour and stood out above all the rest, thought that the king
44 was riding on it. So he gave his life to save his people and win everlasting
45 renown for himself. He ran boldly towards it, into the middle of the
phalanx, dealing death right and left, while they fell back on either side
46 before him. He got in underneath the elephant, and thrust at it from below
and killed it. It fell to the ground on top of him, and there he died.
47 When the Jews saw the strength and impetus of the imperial forces,
48 they fell back before them. Part of the king's army marched up to Jerusalem to renew the engagement, and the king put Judaea and Mount Zion
49 into a state of siege. He made peace with the people of Bethsura, who
abandoned the town, having no more food there to withstand a siege, as it
50 was a sabbatical year when the land was left fallow. Thus the king occupied
Bethsura and detailed a garrison to hold it.
51 He then attacked the temple and subjected it to a long siege; he set up
emplacements and siege-engines, with flame-throwers, catapults for dis-
52 charging stones and barbed missiles, and slings. But the defenders too
constructed engines to counter his engines, and put up a prolonged
53 resistance. There was no food, however, in the stores *b* because of the sabbatical year; those who from time to time had arrived in Judaea as refugees
54 from the Gentiles had eaten up all that remained of the provisions. There
were only a few men left in the temple, because the famine had been too
severe for them, and they had scattered to their own homes.
55 Lysias heard that Philip, whom King Antiochus had appointed before
56 he died to educate his son Antiochus for the kingship, had returned from
Persia and Media with the late king's expeditionary force, and that he was
57 seeking to take over the government. So he hastily gave orders for
departure, saying to the king, his commanders, and his troops: 'Every day

---

*a Probable reading; Gk.* thirty-two *(compare verse 30).*        *b Some witnesses read*
in the temple.

we are growing weaker, provisions are low, the place we are besieging is strong, and the affairs of the empire are pressing. So let us offer these men 58 terms and make peace with them and their whole nation. Let us guarantee 59 their right to follow their laws and customs as they used to do, for it was our abolition of these very customs and laws that roused their resentment, and produced all these consequences.'

The proposal met with the approval of the king and the commanders, 60 and an offer of peace was sent and accepted. The king and his commanders 61 bound themselves by oath, and on the agreed terms the besieged emerged from their stronghold. But when the king entered Mount Zion and saw 62 how strongly the place was fortified, he went back on the oath he had sworn, and gave orders for the surrounding wall to be demolished. He then 63 set off at top speed for Antioch, where he found Philip in possession; a battle ensued, and the city was taken by storm.

IN THE YEAR 151,[a] Demetrius son of Seleucus left Rome, landed with a 7 handful of men at a town on the coast, and there made himself king. While 2 he was travelling to the royal seat of his ancestors, the army seized Antiochus and Lysias, intending to hand them over to him. When this was 3 reported to him, he said, 'Do not let me set eyes on them.' The soldiers 4 accordingly put them to death, and Demetrius ascended the throne.

All the godless renegades from Israel, led by Alcimus, who aspired to 5 be high priest, came to the king and brought charges against their people. 6 They said to him: 'Judas and his brothers have killed all your supporters, and have driven us from our country. Be pleased now to send a man whom 7 you trust, to go and see what devastation they have brought upon us and upon the king's territory, and to punish them and all their supporters.' The king chose Bacchides, one of the royal Friends, who was governor 8 beyond the Euphrates, a man of high standing in the empire and loyal to the king. He sent him and the godless Alcimus, on whom he had con- 9 ferred the high-priesthood, with orders to take vengeance on Israel.

They set out with a large army and entered Judaea. Bacchides sent 10 envoys to Judas and his brothers to make false offers of friendship; but 11 when they saw what a large force he had brought with him, they took no notice of these offers.

A deputation of doctors of the law came before Alcimus and Bacchides, 12 asking for justice. The Hasidaeans were in fact the first group in Israel to 13 make overtures to them; for they said to themselves, 'A priest of the family 14 of Aaron has come with their forces, and he will do us no harm.' The 15 language of Alcimus was conciliatory; he assured them on oath that no harm was intended to them or their friends. But once he had gained their 16 confidence, he arrested sixty of them and put them to death in a single day; as Scripture says:

> 'The bodies of thy saints were scattered,                17
>     their blood was shed round Jerusalem,
>     and there was none to bury them.'

[a] *That is* 161 B.C.

18 This put all the people in fear and terror of them, and they said to each other, 'There is neither truth nor justice among them; they have broken
19 their pledge and the oath they swore.' Then Bacchides left Jerusalem and camped in Bethzaith; and he ordered the arrest of many of those who had deserted to him, together with some of the people, and had them slaughtered
20 and thrown into a great pit. He assigned the whole district to Alcimus, detailed some troops to assist him, and returned to the king.
21 22 Alcimus fought hard for his high-priesthood. All the trouble-makers rallied to him; they gained control over Judaea, and did terrible damage in
23 Israel. When Judas saw all the mischief which Alcimus and his followers had brought upon the Israelites, far worse than anything the Gentiles had
24 done, he marched through all the territory of Judaea and its environs, punishing deserters and debarring them from access to the country dis-
25 tricts. When Alcimus saw that Judas and his band had grown powerful, and recognized that he was unable to withstand them, he returned to the king and accused them of atrocities.
26 Then the king sent Nicanor, one of his distinguished commanders and
27 a bitter enemy of Israel, with orders to wipe them out. Nicanor arrived at Jerusalem with a large force, and sent envoys to Judas and his brothers
28 to make false offers of friendship: 'Let there be no quarrel between us,' he said; 'I propose to come with a few men for a friendly personal meeting.'
29 He came to Judas and they greeted one another as friends, yet the enemy
30 were preparing to kidnap Judas. When Judas discovered that Nicanor's
31 visit was a trick, he took alarm and refused to meet him again. Nicanor, realizing that his plan had been detected, marched out to engage Judas
32 near Capharsalama. About five hundred of Nicanor's army were killed, and the rest escaped to the city of David.
33 After these events, Nicanor went up to Mount Zion, and some of the priests and members of the senate came out from the temple to give him a friendly welcome, and to show him the burnt-offering which was being
34 sacrificed for the king. But he mocked them, jeered at them, and spat on
35 them,*a* boasting and swearing angrily: 'Unless Judas and his army are surrendered to me at once, when I return victorious I will burn down this
36 house.' And he went off in a rage. Thereupon the priests went in, and stood
37 facing the altar and the temple. They wept and said: 'Thou didst choose this house to bear thy name, to be a house of prayer and supplication for thy
38 people; take vengeance on this man and his army, and make them fall by the sword. Remember all their blasphemy, and grant them no reprieve.'
39 Nicanor moved from Jerusalem and encamped at Beth-horon, where he
40 was joined by an army from Syria. Judas encamped at Adasa with three
41 thousand men; there he prayed in these words: 'There was a king whose followers blasphemed, and thy angel came forth and struck down one
42 hundred and eighty-five thousand of them. So do thou crush this army before us today, and let all men know that Nicanor has reviled thy holy place; judge him as his wickedness deserves.'
43 The armies joined battle on the thirteenth of the month Adar, and the army of Nicanor suffered a crushing defeat, he himself being the first to

*a Literally* and polluted them.

fall in the battle. When his army saw that Nicanor had fallen, they threw 44
away their arms and took to flight. The Jews, sounding the signal trumpets 45
in the enemy's rear, pursued them as far as Gazara, a day's journey from
Adasa. From all the villages of Judaea round about, the inhabitants came 46
out and attacked their flanks, forcing them back upon their pursuers. They
all fell by the sword; there were no survivors. The Jews seized spoil and 47
booty; they cut off Nicanor's head and that right hand which he had
stretched out so arrogantly, and brought them to be displayed at Jerusalem.
There was great public rejoicing and that day was kept as a special day of 48
jubilation. It was ordained that the day should be observed annually, on 49
the thirteenth of Adar. Thus Judaea entered upon a short period of peace. 50

NOW JUDAS HAD HEARD about the Romans: they were renowned for 8
their military power and for the welcome they gave to those who became
their allies; any who joined them could be sure of their firm friendship.
He was told about the wars they had fought, and the valour they had shown 2
in their conquest of the Gauls, whom they had laid under tribute. He heard 3
of their successes in Spain, where they had seized silver-mines and gold-
mines, maintaining their hold on the entire country—distant as it was from 4
their own land—by their patience and good judgement. There were kings
from far and near who had marched against them, but they had been
beaten off after crushing defeats; others paid them annual tribute.
They had crushed in battle and conquered Philip, and Perseus king of 5
Kittim, and all who had attacked them. Antiochus the Great, king of Asia, 6
had marched against them with one hundred and twenty elephants, with
cavalry and chariots and an immense force, but they had totally defeated
him. They had taken the king alive, and had required that he and his suc- 7
cessors should pay them a large annual tribute, give hostages, and cede the 8
territories of India, Media, and Lydia, together with some of their finest
provinces. These they had taken from him and given to King Eumenes.
When the Greeks planned to attack and destroy them, they heard of it 9 10
and sent a single general against them. Battle was joined, and many of the
Greeks fell; the Romans took their women and children prisoner, plundered
their territory and annexed it, razed their fortifications, and made them
slaves, as they are to this day. The remaining kingdoms, the islands, and all 11
who had ever opposed them, they destroyed or reduced to slavery. With 12
their friends, however, and all who put themselves under their protection,
they maintained firm friendship. They thus conquered kings near and far,
and all who heard their fame went in fear of them. Those whom they wished 13
to help and to appoint as kings, became kings, and those they wished to
depose, they deposed; and thus they rose to great heights of power. For all 14
this, not one of them made any personal claim to greatness by wearing the
crown or donning the purple. They had established a senate where three 15
hundred and twenty senators met daily to deliberate, giving constant
thought to the proper ordering of the affairs of the common people. They 16
entrusted their government and the ruling of all their territory to one of
their number every year, all obeying this one man without envy or jealousy
among themselves.

17 Judas accordingly chose Eupolemus son of John son of Accos, and Jason son of Eleazar, and sent them to Rome to conclude a treaty of friend-
18 ship and alliance, so that the Romans might rid them of tyranny, for it was
19 clear that the Greek empire was reducing Israel to slavery. They made the long journey to Rome and entered the Senate, where they spoke as follows:
20 'Judas, known as Maccabaeus, his brothers, and the Jewish people have sent us to you to conclude a treaty of friendly alliance with you, so that we
21 may be enrolled as your allies and friends.' The Romans found the pro-
22 posal acceptable, and the following is a copy of the reply which they inscribed on tablets of bronze and sent to Jerusalem, so that the Jews there might have a record of the treaty of alliance:

23 Success to the Romans and the Jewish nation by sea and land for ever!
24 May sword and foe be far from them! But if war breaks out first against
25 Rome or any of her allies throughout her dominion, then the Jewish
26 nation shall support them whole-heartedly as occasion may require. To the enemies of Rome or of her allies the Jews shall neither give nor supply provisions, arms, money, or ships; so Rome has decided; and they shall observe their commitments, without compensation.

27 Similarly, if war breaks out first against the Jewish nation, then the
28 Romans shall give them hearty support as occasion may require. To their enemies there shall be given neither provisions, arms, money, nor ships; so Rome has decided. These commitments shall be kept without breach of faith.

29 These are the terms of the agreement which the Romans have made
30 with the Jewish people. But if, hereafter, both parties shall agree to add or to rescind anything, then they shall do as they decide; any such addition or rescindment shall be valid.

31 To this the Romans added: As for the misdeeds which King Demetrius is perpetrating against the Jews, we have written to him as follows: 'Why
32 have you oppressed our friends and allies the Jews so harshly? If they make any further complaint against you, then we will see that justice is done them, and will make war upon you by sea and by land.'

9 When Demetrius heard that Nicanor and his forces had fallen in battle, he sent Bacchides and Alcimus a second time into Judaea, with the right
2 wing of his army. They marched along the Gilgal road, laid siege to Messaloth in Arbela, and captured it, inflicting heavy loss of life.

3 4 In the first month of the year 152,*ᵃ* they moved camp to Jerusalem. From there they marched to Berea with twenty thousand infantry and two
5 thousand cavalry. Now Judas was in camp at Alasa, with three thousand
6 picked men. But when they saw the size of the enemy forces, their courage failed, and many deserted, leaving a mere eight hundred men in the field.
7 When Judas saw that with the campaign going against him his army had melted away, his heart sank, for there was no time to rally them. Though
8 much discouraged, he said to those who were left, 'Let us move to the attack
9 and see if we can defeat them.' But his men tried to dissuade him: 'Impossible!' they said. 'No; let us save our lives now and come back later with our

ᵃ *That is* 160 B.C.

comrades to fight them. Now we are too few.' But Judas replied: 'Heaven 10
forbid that I should do such a thing as run away! If our time is come, let us
die bravely for our fellow-countrymen, and leave no stain on our honour.'

The Syrian army left its camp and took up position to meet the Jews. 11
The cavalry*a* was divided into two detachments; the slingers and the
archers went ahead of the main force, and the picked troops were in the
front line. Bacchides was on the right. The phalanx came on in two divi- 12
sions with trumpets sounding; Judas's men also sounded their trumpets. 13
The earth shook at the din of the armies as battle was joined, and they
fought from dawn until evening.

When Judas saw that Bacchides and the main strength of his army was 14
on the right flank, all his stout-hearted men rallied to him, and they broke 15
the Syrian right; then he pursued them as far as Mount Azotus. When the 16
Syrians on the left wing saw that their right had been broken, they turned
about and followed on the heels of Judas and his men, attacking them in the
rear. The fighting became very heavy, and many fell on both sides. Judas 17 18
himself fell, and the rest of the Jews took to flight. Jonathan and Simon 19
carried off Judas their brother; they buried him in the family tomb at
Modin, and wept over him. Great was the grief in Israel, and they mourned 20
him for many days, saying,

> 'How is our champion fallen, 21
> the saviour of Israel!'

The rest of the history of Judas, his wars, exploits, and achievements—all 22
these were so numerous that they have not been written down.

AFTER THE DEATH OF JUDAS the renegades raised their heads in every 23
part of Israel, and all the evil-doers reappeared. In those days a terrible 24
famine broke out, and the country went over to their side. Bacchides chose 25
apostates to be in control of the country. These men set inquiries on foot, 26
and tracked down the friends of Judas and brought them before Bacchides,
who took vengeance on them, loading them with indignities. It was a time 27
of great affliction for Israel, worse than any since the day when prophets
ceased to appear among them. Then all the friends of Judas assembled 28
and said to Jonathan: 'Since your brother Judas died, there has not been a 29
man like him to take the lead against our enemies, Bacchides and those of
our own nation who are hostile to us. Today, therefore, we choose you to 30
succeed him as our ruler and leader and to fight our battles.' So Jonathan 31
took over the leadership at that time in place of his brother Judas.

The news reached Bacchides, and he set himself to kill Jonathan. When 32 33
Jonathan and his brother Simon and all their men learnt of this, they took
refuge in the desert of Tekoa, encamping by the pool of Asphar. Bacchides 34
discovered this on the sabbath, and crossed the Jordan with his whole
army. So Jonathan sent his brother John to take the camp followers and 35
appeal to his friends the Nabataeans to look after their baggage train, which

*a* The Syrian army . . . cavalry: *or* The Jewish army left its camp and stood to meet the
enemy. The Syrian cavalry . . .

36  was of some size. But the Jambrites appeared from Medaba and kidnapped
37  John; they seized the baggage and made off with it. Some time afterwards, news was brought to Jonathan and his brother Simon that the Jambrites were celebrating an important wedding, and bringing the bride, the daughter of one of the great nobles of Canaan, from Nadabath with a large
38  retinue. Remembering how their brother John had been killed, Jonathan
39  and his men set out and hid themselves under cover of a hill. They looked out and there they saw the bridegroom, in the middle of a bustling crowd and a train of baggage, coming to meet the bridal party, escorted by his friends and kinsmen fully armed, to the sound of drums and instruments of
40  music. Emerging from ambush, Jonathan attacked and cut them down; many fell, while others made off into the hills and the Jews took all their
41  goods as spoil. So the wedding was turned into mourning, and the sound of
42  music to lamentation. The blood of their brother was fully avenged, and Jonathan returned to the marshes of Jordan.
43      Bacchides heard this and came to the banks of Jordan on the sabbath
44  with a powerful force. Jonathan said to his men: 'Now is the time to fight
45  for our lives; we are today in worse plight than ever: the enemy in front, the water of Jordan behind, to right and left marsh and thicket; there is
46 47  no escape. Cry to Heaven to save you from the hands of the enemy.' Battle was joined, and Jonathan had raised his hand to strike down Bacchides,
48  when he fell back and evaded him. Then Jonathan and his men leapt into the Jordan and swam over to the other side; but the enemy did not cross
49  the river in pursuit. The army of Bacchides lost about a thousand men that day.
50      Bacchides returned to Jerusalem and fortified with high walls, gates, and bars a number of places in Judaea: the fortress at Jericho, Emmaus and
51  Beth-horon, Bethel, Timnath-pharathon, and Tephon; in all of these he
52  placed garrisons to harass Israel. He fortified the towns of Bethsura and
53  Gazara and the citadel, placing forces and stores of provisions there. He took the sons of the leading men of the country as hostages and put them under guard in the citadel at Jerusalem.
54      In the second month of the year 153,[a] Alcimus gave orders for the wall of the inner court of the temple to be demolished, thereby destroying the
55  work of the prophets. But at the moment when he began demolition, Alcimus had a stroke, which put a stop to his activities. Paralysed and with his speech impaired, he could not utter a word or give final instructions
56 57  about his property. Thus he died in great torment. On learning that Alcimus was dead, Bacchides returned to the king, and for two years Judaea had peace.
58      Then the renegades put their heads together: 'Look!' they said, 'Jonathan and his people are living in peace and security. Let us bring
59  Bacchides here; he will capture them all in a single night.' They went and
60  conferred with Bacchides, and he set out with a large force, sending letters secretly to all his supporters in Judaea, with instructions to seize Jonathan and his men. But they were unable to do so, because their plan leaked out.
61  About fifty of the ringleaders of this villainy in Judaea were seized and

[a] *That is* 159 B.C.

put to death. Jonathan, Simon, and their men then made their way out to Bethbasi in the desert, built up its ruined fortifications, and strengthened it. 62
When Bacchides learnt of this, he gathered together all his army and sent 63
word to those in Judaea. He came and took up position against Bethbasi, 64
and attacked it for a long time, erecting siege-engines. Jonathan left his 65
brother Simon in the town and slipped out into the country with a few men.
He attacked Odomera and his people and the Phasirites in their encamp- 66
ment; he began to get the better of them and to advance towards Bethbasi 67
with his forces.

Simon and his men made a sally out of the town and set fire to the siege-engines. They fought Bacchides and defeated him. They kept up heavy 68
pressure upon him, and so his plan and his expedition proved fruitless.
There was great anger against the renegades at whose instance he had 69
invaded the land, and many of them were put to death. Bacchides then
decided to return to his own country.

When Jonathan learnt of this, he sent envoys to Bacchides to arrange 70
terms of peace with him and a return of the Jewish prisoners. Bacchides 71
agreed and did as Jonathan proposed, swearing to do him no harm for the
rest of his life. He sent him back the prisoners he had taken previously from 72
Judaea, and returned to his own country; never again did he enter their
territory. So the war came to an end in Israel. Jonathan took up residence 73
in Michmash and began to govern the people, rooting the godless out
of Israel.

## Jonathan rules the nation

IN THE YEAR 160,[a] Alexander Epiphanes son of Antiochus came and 10
took possession of Ptolemais, where he was welcomed and proclaimed
king. When King Demetrius heard of this, he raised a huge army and 2
marched out to meet him in battle. At the same time Demetrius sent 3
Jonathan a letter in friendly and flattering terms; for he said to himself, 4
'Let us forestall Alexander by making peace with the Jews before Jonathan
comes to terms with him against us, for he will remember all the harm we 5
have done him by our treatment of his brothers and of his nation.' He gave 6
Jonathan authority to collect and equip an army, conferred on him the
title of ally, and ordered the hostages in the citadel to be handed over to
him. Jonathan came to Jerusalem and read the letter aloud before all the 7
people and the garrison of the citadel, who were filled with apprehension 8
when they heard that the king had given Jonathan authority to raise an
army. They surrendered the hostages to him, and he restored them to their 9
parents.

Jonathan took up his quarters in Jerusalem and began to repair and 10
rebuild the city. He gave orders to those engaged on the work to build the 11
walls and surround Mount Zion with a fortification of squared stones, and
this was done. The foreigners in the strongholds which Bacchides had 12
built made their escape, each man leaving his post and returning to his own 13

[a] *That is* 152 B.C.

14 country; however, in Bethsura there were still left some of those who had abandoned the law and ordinances, and had found asylum there.

15 King Alexander heard of the promises which Demetrius had sent to Jonathan, and was told of the battles and heroic deeds of Jonathan and his

16 brothers, and the hardships they had endured. 'Where shall we ever find another man like this?' he exclaimed. 'Let us make him our friend and ally.'

17 He therefore wrote a letter to Jonathan to this effect:

18     King Alexander to his brother Jonathan, greeting.

19     We have heard about you, what a valiant man you are and how fit to

20 be our friend. Now therefore we do appoint you this day to be High Priest of your nation with the title of King's Friend, to support our cause and to keep friendship with us.

He sent him a purple robe and a gold crown.

21 Jonathan assumed the vestments of the high priest in the seventh month of the year 160*ᵃ* at the Feast of Tabernacles, and he gathered an army together and prepared a large supply of arms.

22 23 When this news reached Demetrius he was mortified. 'How did we come to let Alexander forestall us', he asked, 'in gaining the friendship and sup-

24 port of the Jews? I too will send them cordial messages and offer honours

25 and gifts to keep them on my side.' So he sent a message to the Jews to this effect:

    King Demetrius to the Jewish nation, greeting.

26     We have heard with great pleasure that you have kept your agreements and remained in friendship with us and have not gone over to our

27 enemies. Continue, then, to keep faith with us, and we shall reward you

28 well for all that you do in our cause, both by granting you numerous exemptions and making you gifts.

29     I hereby release and exempt you and all Jews whatsoever from

30 tribute, from the tax on salt, and from the crown-money. From today and hereafter I release you from the one-third of the grain-harvest and the half of the fruit-harvest due to me. From today and for all time, I will no longer exact them from Judaea or from the three administrative districts, formerly part of Samaria and Galilee, which I now attach to Judaea.

31 Jerusalem and its environs, with its tithes and tolls, shall be sacred and

32 tax free. I also surrender authority over the citadel in Jerusalem and grant the High Priest the right to garrison it with men of his own choice.

33 All Jewish prisoners of war taken from Judaea into any part of my kingdom, I set at liberty without ransom. No man shall exact any levy what-

34 soever on the cattle of the Jews. All their festivals, sabbaths, new moons, and appointed days, and three days preceding and following each festival, shall be days of exemption and release for all the Jews in my

35 kingdom; no one shall have authority to impose any exaction or burden on a Jew in any respect.

36     Jews shall be enlisted in the forces of the King to the number of thirty

37 thousand men; they shall receive the usual army pay. Some of them shall

*ᵃ That is* 152 B.C.

be stationed in the great royal fortresses, others put in positions of trust in the kingdom. Their commanders and officers shall be of their own race, and they shall follow their own customs, just as the King has ordered for Judaea.

The three districts added to Judaea from the territory of Samaria 38 shall be attached to Judaea so as to be under one authority, and subject to the High Priest alone.

Ptolemais and the lands belonging to it I make over to the temple in 39 Jerusalem, to meet the expenses proper to it. I give fifteen thousand silver 40 shekels annually, charged on my own royal accounts, to be drawn from such places as may prove convenient. And the arrears of the subsidy, 41 in so far as it has not been paid by the revenue officials, as it formerly was, shall henceforth be paid in for the needs of the temple. In addition, the 42 five thousand silver shekels which used to be taken from the annual income of the temple are also released, because they belong to the ministering priests. Whoever shall take sanctuary in the temple at 43 Jerusalem, or in any part of its precincts, because of a debt to the crown or any other debt, shall be free from distraint on his person or on his property within my kingdom. The cost of the rebuilding 44 and repair of the temple shall be borne by the royal revenue; also the 45 repair of the walls of Jerusalem and its surrounding fortification, as well as of the fortresses in Judaea, shall be at the expense of the royal revenue.

When Jonathan and the people heard these proposals, they did not 46 believe or accept them, for they recalled the terrible calamity the king had brought upon Israel, and his harsh oppression. They favoured Alexander, 47 because it was he who had been the initiator of peaceful overtures; so they remained his allies to the end.

King Alexander mustered powerful forces and took up position against 48 Demetrius, and the two kings joined battle. The army of Alexander took to 49 flight, and Demetrius pursued him and got the better of them. He fought 50 hard till sunset, but on that day Demetrius fell.

Thereupon Alexander sent ambassadors to Ptolemy king of Egypt, with 51 a message to this effect: 'I have returned to my kingdom and sit on the 52 throne of my ancestors. I have assumed the government, defeated Demetrius, and made myself master of our country; for I gave him battle, and he 53 and his army were crushed by us, and we sit on the throne of his kingdom. Let us now form an alliance; make me your son-in-law by giving me your 54 daughter in marriage, and I will give presents to you and her worthy of your royal state.'

King Ptolemy replied: 'It was a happy day when you returned to the land 55 of your ancestors and ascended the throne of their realm. I will now do as 56 you ask; only come to Ptolemais so that we may meet, and I will become your father-in-law as you propose.'

In the year 162,[a] Ptolemy set out from Egypt, with his daughter Cleo- 57 patra, and arrived at Ptolemais, where King Alexander met him, and 58

[a] *That is* 150 B.C.

Ptolemy gave him his daughter in marriage. The wedding was celebrated in royal style, with great pomp.

59 60    King Alexander wrote to Jonathan to come and meet him. Jonathan went in state to Ptolemais, where he met the two kings; he gave them silver and gold, and also made many gifts to their Friends; and so he won their favour.

61    There were some scoundrelly Jewish renegades who conspired to lodge complaints against Jonathan. The king, however, paid no attention to
62 them, but gave orders for Jonathan to be divested of the garment he wore
63 and robed in purple, and this was done. The king made him sit at his side, and told his officers to go with Jonathan into the centre of the city and proclaim that no one should bring any complaint against him or make trouble
64 for him for any reason whatsoever. When this proclamation was made and those who planned to lodge complaints saw Jonathan's splendour, and the
65 purple robe he wore, they all made off. Thus the king honoured him, enrolling him in the first class of the order of King's Friends, and making
66 him a general and a provincial governor. Jonathan returned to Jerusalem well pleased with his success.

67 IN THE YEAR 165,[a] Demetrius, the son of King Demetrius, arrived in
68 the land of his fathers from Crete. King Alexander was greatly upset by
69 this news, and returned to Antioch. Demetrius appointed as his commander Apollonius the governor of Coele-syria, who raised a powerful force and encamped at Jamnia. From there he sent this message to Jonathan
70 the high priest: 'You are all alone in resisting us, and you are making me
71 look ridiculous and absurd. Why do you defy us up there in the hills? If you have confidence in your forces, come down to meet us on the plain, and let us try conclusions with each other there, for I have the power of
72 cities behind me. Make inquiries; find out who I am and who are our allies; you will be told that you cannot stand your ground against us, for your pre-
73 decessors have twice been routed in their own territory, and now you will not be able to resist my cavalry, and such a force as mine, on the plain, where there is not so much as a stone or a pebble to give you cover, or any place to which you can escape.'

74    Jonathan was provoked by this message from Apollonius. He took ten thousand men and marched out from Jerusalem, and was joined by his
75 brother Simon with reinforcements. He laid siege to Joppa, whose gates the citizens had closed against him because Apollonius had a garrison there.
76 But when fighting started, the citizens took fright and opened the gates;
77 thus Jonathan became master of Joppa. When Apollonius heard of it he took three thousand cavalry and a large force of infantry, and marched to Azotus as if to pass through it, but at the same time, relying on his numerous
78 cavalry, he advanced into the plain. Jonathan went in pursuit as far as
79 Azotus, where the armies joined battle. But Apollonius had left a thousand
80 cavalry in hiding in their rear, and Jonathan discovered that there was an ambush behind him. The enemy surrounded his army, showering arrows
81 on our people from dawn till dusk. But they stood fast as Jonathan had

*a. That is* 147 B.C.

ordered them, and the enemy cavalry grew weary. At that point Simon 82
led out his troops and joined battle with the enemy phalanx, now
that the cavalry was exhausted. They were routed by him and took to
flight. The horsemen scattered across the plain and took refuge in Azotus, 83
where they sought asylum in the temple of Dagon their idol. But Jonathan 84
set fire to Azotus and its surrounding villages, and plundered them; the
temple of Dagon, and those who had taken refuge there, he destroyed with
fire. The numbers of those who fell by the sword, together with those who 85
lost their lives in the fire, reached eight thousand. Jonathan marched away 86
from Azotus, and encamped at Ascalon, where the citizens came out to meet
him with great pomp. Then he and his men returned to Jerusalem loaded 87
with spoil.

When King Alexander heard of all this, he did Jonathan still greater 88
honour, sending him the gold clasp which it is the custom to give to the 89
King's Kinsmen. He also presented him with Accaron and all its districts.

The king of Egypt collected a huge army, countless as the sand on the 11
sea-shore, and a great fleet of ships, meaning to make himself master of
Alexander's kingdom by treachery and add it to his own. He set out for 2
Syria with professions of peace, and the people of the towns proceeded to
open their gates to him and went to meet him; King Alexander had ordered
them to do this, because Ptolemy was his father-in-law.

As he went on his progress from town to town, Ptolemy left a detach- 3
ment of troops in each of them as a garrison. When he reached Azotus, he 4
was shown the burnt-out temple of Dagon, the city itself and its ruined
suburbs strewn with corpses, and, piled up along his way, the bodies of
those who had been burned in the course of the fighting. They told the 5
king that it was Jonathan's doing, hoping that he would reprimand him;
but the king said nothing. Jonathan met him in state at Joppa, where they 6
exchanged greetings and passed the night. Jonathan accompanied the king 7
as far as the river Eleutherus and then returned to Jerusalem. King Ptolemy 8
made himself master of the coast towns as far as Seleucia-by-the-sea. He
was harbouring malicious designs against Alexander.

He sent ambassadors to King Demetrius with the following message: 9
'I propose that you and I should make a pact: I will give you my daughter,
now Alexander's wife, and you shall reign over the kingdom of your father.
I now regret having given my daughter to him, for he has tried to kill me.' 10
He maligned Alexander in this way because he coveted his kingdom, and 11 12
he took his daughter away and gave her to Demetrius. This led to a breach
between him and Alexander, and to open enmity.

Ptolemy now entered Antioch, where he assumed the crown of Asia; 13
thus he wore two crowns, that of Egypt and that of Asia.

King Alexander was at this time in Cilicia, because the inhabitants of that 14
region were in revolt. But when he heard the news he marched against 15
Ptolemy, who came to meet him with a powerful army and routed him.
Alexander fled to Arabia for protection, and King Ptolemy was triumphant. 16
Zabdiel the Arab chieftain cut off Alexander's head and sent it to Ptolemy. 17
But two days later King Ptolemy died, and his garrisons in the fortresses 18

19 were killed by the inhabitants. So in the year 167 *a* Demetrius became king.

20 At this time Jonathan gathered together the Judaeans to assault the citadel in Jerusalem, and they brought up many siege-engines against it.
21 But a number of renegades, enemies of their own people, went to the king
22 and reported that Jonathan was besieging the citadel. The king was furious at the news and immediately moved his quarters to Ptolemais. He wrote to Jonathan ordering him to raise the siege, and to meet him for conference at Ptolemais with all speed.

23 When Jonathan received this letter, he gave orders for the siege to be continued. Then, selecting elders of Israel and priests to accompany him,
24 he set out on his dangerous mission. He took with him silver and gold, and robes, and many other gifts, and went to meet the king at Ptolemais.

25 He won the favour of Demetrius, although some renegade Jews tried
26 to lodge complaints against him. But the king treated him just as his pre-
27 decessors had done, honouring him in the presence of all his Friends. He confirmed him in the high-priesthood and in all his former dignities, and appointed him head of the first class of the King's Friends.

28 Jonathan requested the king to exempt Judaea and the three Samaritan districts *b* from tribute, promising him in return three hundred talents.
29 King Demetrius consented, writing to Jonathan on all these affairs as follows:

30 King Demetrius to his brother Jonathan, and to the Jewish nation, greeting.

31 This is a copy of our letter written to our kinsman Lasthenes about you, which we have had made for your information:

32 'King Demetrius to his respected kinsman Lasthenes, greeting.

33 'Because our friends the Jewish nation show us goodwill, and observe
34 their obligations to us, we are resolved to become their benefactor. We have therefore settled on them the lands of Judaea and the three districts, Apherema, Lydda, and Ramathaim, which are now transferred from Samaria to Judaea, together with all the lands adjacent thereto, for the benefit of the priesthood at Jerusalem. This is a transfer of the annual dues which the King formerly received from these territories, from the
35 produce of the soil and of the orchards. Other of our revenues, the tithes and tolls now pertaining to us, the salt-pans, and the crown-money, all
36 these we shall cede to them. These provisions are irrevocable from now
37 for all future time. See to it then that you make a copy of them to be given to Jonathan and set by him in a conspicuous position on the holy mountain.'

38 When King Demetrius saw that the country was quiet under his rule and resistance was at an end, he disbanded all his forces, sending every man home, with the exception of the foreign mercenaries he had hired from the islands of the Gentiles. Then all the troops enlisted under his pre-
39 decessors turned against the king. A certain Trypho, formerly of the party

*a* *That is* 145 B.C.          *b* three . . . districts: *probable reading ; Gk.* three districts and Samaria.

236

of Alexander, aware of the disaffection of all the forces towards Demetrius, went to Imalcue, the Arab chieftain, who had charge of the child Antiochus, Alexander's son, and kept pressing him to hand the boy over to him to be made king in succession to his father. He also informed Imalcue of all the measures Demetrius was taking and of his unpopularity with his troops. There he remained for some time. 40

Meanwhile Jonathan sent to King Demetrius requesting him to withdraw, from the citadel in Jerusalem and from the fortresses, the garrisons which were constantly harassing Israel. Demetrius sent Jonathan this reply: 'I will not only meet your request, but when opportunity arises I will do you and your people the highest honour. And now be so good as to send men to support me, for all my troops are in revolt.' 41 42 43

Jonathan dispatched three thousand fighting men to Antioch, and the king was much relieved at their arrival. The citizens poured into the centre of the city, a hundred and twenty thousand strong, bent on killing the king. He took refuge in the palace, while the citizens seized control of the streets and fighting broke out. King Demetrius called the Jews to his assistance, and they rallied to him at once. They then dispersed all over the city and slaughtered that day as many as a hundred thousand, setting the city on fire and taking much booty. And thus they saved the king's life. 44 45 46 47 48

When the citizens saw that the Jews had the city completely at their mercy, their courage failed them and they clamoured to the king to accept their surrender and to stop the Jews fighting against them and the city. They threw down their arms and made peace; and the Jews, now in high repute with the king and all his subjects, returned to Jerusalem loaded with booty. But when King Demetrius was secure upon his throne, with the country quiet under him, he went back on all his promises and broke off relations with Jonathan; instead of repaying the benefits he had received, he put severe pressure upon him. 49 50 51 52 53

After this, Trypho returned, and with him Antiochus, a mere lad. Antiochus was crowned, and all the forces Demetrius had so contemptuously discharged rallied to the king. These fought against Demetrius, and he was utterly routed. Trypho brought up his elephants and made himself master of Antioch. The young Antiochus wrote to Jonathan confirming him in the high-priesthood, with authority over the four districts, and making him one of the King's Friends. He also sent him a service of gold plate, and gave him the right to drink from a gold cup, to be robed in purple, and to wear the gold clasp. He appointed Jonathan's brother Simon as officer commanding the area from the Ladder of Tyre to the borders of Egypt. 54 55 56 57 58 59

Jonathan made a tour through the country on the far side of the river and the towns there; and all the forces of Syria gathered to his support. 60

He went to Ascalon, where he was received with great honour by the citizens. From there he went on to Gaza, but the inhabitants closed the gates against him; so he blockaded the city, set fire to its suburbs, and plundered them. The citizens of Gaza then sought peace, and he made terms with them, taking the sons of their magistrates as hostages and 61 62

237

sending them off to Jerusalem; he himself continued his progress through the country in the direction of Damascus.

63 Jonathan heard that Demetrius's officers had arrived at Kedesh-in-
64 Galilee with a large force to prevent him from reaching his objective. He
65 went to meet them, leaving his brother Simon in Judaea. Simon took up position against Bethsura and, after prolonged fighting, blockaded it.
66 Finally the citizens sued for terms of peace and Simon consented; he evicted them, took over the town, and installed a garrison there.

67 Jonathan, who had encamped with his army by the Lake of Gennesaret,
68 marched out early in the morning into the plain of Asor. There in the plain the gentile army was advancing to meet him; they had set an ambush for
69 him in the hills, while they themselves confronted him. When the men from the ambush emerged and joined in the fighting, all Jonathan's men
70 took to flight; not one remained except Mattathias son of Absalom, and
71 Judas son of Chalphi, officers in the army. Jonathan tore his clothes, put
72 dust upon his head, and prayed. Then he turned upon the enemy and
73 routed them in headlong flight. When the fugitives of Jonathan's army saw this, they rallied to him and joined in the pursuit as far as the enemy base
74 at Kedesh; there they encamped. That day about three thousand of the Gentiles fell. Jonathan then returned to Jerusalem.

12 JONATHAN NOW SAW his opportunity and sent picked men on a mission to Rome to confirm and renew the treaty of friendship with that city.
2 3 He sent letters to the same effect to Sparta and to other places. The envoys travelled to Rome and went to the Senate House to deliver their message: 'Jonathan the High Priest and the Jewish people have sent us to renew their
4 former pact of friendship and alliance.' The Romans gave them letters requiring the authorities in each place to give them safe conduct to Judaea.
5 Here follows a transcript of the letter which Jonathan wrote to the Spartans:

6 Jonathan the High Priest, the Senate of the Jews, the priests, and the rest of the Jewish people, to our brothers of Sparta, greeting.

7 On a previous occasion a letter was sent to Onias the High Priest from Arius your king, acknowledging our kinship; a copy is given below.
8 Onias welcomed your envoy with full honours and received the letter in
9 which the terms of the alliance and friendship were set forth. We do not regard ourselves as needing such alliances, since our support is the holy
10 books in our possession. Nevertheless, we now venture to send and renew our pact of brotherhood and friendship with you, so that we may
11 not become estranged, for it is many years since you wrote to us. We never lose any opportunity, on festal and other appropriate days, of remembering you at our sacrifices and in our prayers, as it is right and
12 13 proper to remember kinsmen; and we rejoice at your fame. We ourselves have been under the pressure of hostile attacks on every side; all
14 the surrounding kings have made war upon us. In the course of these wars we had no wish to trouble you or the rest of our allies and friends:
15 we have the aid of Heaven to support us, and so we have been saved

from our enemies, and they have been humbled. Accordingly, we chose 16
Numenius son of Antiochus, and Antipater son of Jason, and have sent
them to the Romans to renew our former friendship and alliance with
them. We instructed them to go to you also with our greetings, and to 17
deliver this letter about the renewal of our pact of brotherhood. And now 18
we pray you to send us a reply to this letter.

This is a copy of the letter sent by the Spartans to Onias: 19

> Arius, King of Sparta, to Onias the High Priest, greeting. 20
> A document has come to light which shows that Spartans and Jews 21
> are kinsmen, descended alike from Abraham. Now that we have learnt 22
> this, we beg you to write and tell us how your affairs prosper. The 23
> message we return to you is, 'What is yours, your cattle and every kind
> of property, is ours, and what is ours is yours', and we have therefore
> instructed our envoys to report to you in these terms.

Jonathan heard that Demetrius's generals had returned to attack him 24
with larger forces than before. He marched from Jerusalem and met them 25
in the region of Hamath, giving them no chance to set foot in his territory.
He sent spies to their camp, who on their return reported that preparations 26
were being made for a night attack. At sunset Jonathan gave orders to his 27
men to stay awake and stand to arms all night, ready for battle; and he
stationed outposts all round the camp. When the enemy heard that 28
Jonathan and his men were ready for battle, they were alarmed; their
courage failed, and they withdrew, first lighting watch-fires in their camp.
Jonathan and his men, seeing the watch-fires burning, did not realize 29
what had happened until morning. Then Jonathan set out in pursuit, 30
but failed to overtake them, for they had crossed the river Eleutherus.
So Jonathan turned aside against the Arabs called Zabadaeans, and 31
he dealt them a severe blow and plundered them. He struck camp 32
and came to Damascus, and then made a march through the whole
country.

Simon set out and marched as far as Ascalon and the neighbouring 33-34
fortresses. He then turned towards Joppa; he had heard that the citizens
intended to hand it over to the supporters of Demetrius, but before they
could do so, he occupied the town and placed a garrison there to defend it.

When Jonathan returned he convened the senate. With their agreement 35
he decided to build fortresses in Judaea, to heighten the walls of Jerusalem, 36
and to erect a high barrier to separate the citadel from the city and so to
isolate it that the garrison could not buy or sell. They assembled to rebuild 37
the city, for the wall along the ravine to the east had partly collapsed, and
he repaired the section of the wall called Chaphenatha. Simon also rebuilt 38
and fortified Adida in the Shephelah, erecting gates and bars.

Trypho now aspired to be king of Asia; he meant to rebel against King 39
Antiochus and assume the crown himself. But he was afraid that Jonathan 40
would fight to prevent this, so he cast about for some means of capturing
and killing him. He set off and reached Bethshan. Jonathan marched out to 41
meet him with forty thousand picked troops, and he also reached Bethshan.

42 Trypho, seeing that Jonathan had a large force with him, was afraid to
43 attack. So he received him honourably and commended him to all his
Friends, gave him presents, and ordered his Friends and his troops to obey
44 Jonathan as they would himself. He said to Jonathan: 'Why have you put
45 all these men to so much trouble, when we are not at war? Send them home
now and choose a few to accompany you, and come with me to Ptolemais.
I will hand it over to you with all the other fortresses, the rest of the troops,
and all the officials, and then I will leave the country. This is the only pur-
46 pose of my coming.' Jonathan took him at his word and did as he said: he
47 dismissed his forces and they returned to Judaea. He kept back three
thousand men, of whom he left two thousand in Galilee, while a thousand
48 accompanied him. But when Jonathan entered Ptolemais, the citizens
closed the gates, seized him, and put to the sword all who had entered
with him.
49 Trypho sent a force of infantry and cavalry into Galilee to the great
50 plain, to wipe out all Jonathan's men. They now learnt that Jonathan had
been seized and was lost, along with his escort, but they put heart into one
51 another and marched in close formation, ready for battle. When their pur-
52 suers saw that they would fight to the death, they turned back. So all came
safely home to Judaea, mourning for Jonathan and his followers, and filled
53 with alarm. All Israel was plunged in grief. The surrounding Gentiles
were now bent on destroying them root and branch, saying to themselves,
'The Jews have no leader or champion, so now is the time to attack, and
we shall blot out all memory of them among men.'

## The high-priesthood of Simon

13 THE NEWS REACHED SIMON that Trypho had mustered a large force
2 for the invasion and destruction of Judaea, and it threw the people into
a state of panic. When Simon saw this, he went up to Jerusalem, called an
3 assembly, and encouraged them in these words: 'I need not remind you
of all that my brothers and I and my father's house have done for the laws
and the holy place, what battles we have fought, what hardships we have
4 endured. My brothers have all fallen in this cause, fighting for Israel, and
5 I am the only one left. Now Heaven forbid that I should grudge my own
life in any moment of danger, for I am not worth more than my brothers.
6 No! I will take up the cause of my nation and the holy place, of your wives
and children, since all the Gentiles in their hatred have gathered to destroy
7 8 us.' At these words the people plucked up courage, and they shouted in
answer: 'You shall be our leader in place of Judas and your brother
9 10 Jonathan. Fight our battles, and we will do whatever you tell us.' So Simon
mustered all the fighting men and hurried on the completion of the walls
11 of Jerusalem until it was fortified on all sides. He sent Jonathan son of
Absalom with a considerable force to Joppa; he expelled its inhabitants
and remained in possession of the town.
12 Trypho marched out from Ptolemais with a large force to invade Judaea,
13 taking Jonathan with him as a prisoner. Simon encamped at Adida on the

edge of the plain. When Trypho learnt that Simon had come forward to 14
take the place of his brother Jonathan, and that he was about to join battle
with him, he sent envoys to Simon with the following message: 'We are 15
detaining your brother Jonathan because of certain monies which he owed
to the royal treasury in connection with the offices he held. To ensure that he 16
will not again revolt if we release him, send one hundred talents of silver
and two of his sons as hostages, and we will let him go.' Simon himself 17
realized that this was a trick, but he had the money and the children brought
to him, fearing that otherwise he might arouse deep animosity among the
people, who would say, 'It was because you did not send the money and the 18
children that Jonathan lost his life.' So he sent the children and the hundred 19
talents, but Trypho broke his word and did not release Jonathan.

After this, Trypho set out to invade the country and ravage it, taking a 20
roundabout way through Adora. Simon and his army marched parallel
with him everywhere he went. Meanwhile the garrison of the citadel were 21
sending emissaries to Trypho, urging him to come to them by way of the
desert, and to send them provisions. Trypho prepared to send all his 22
cavalry, but that night there was a severe snow-storm, which prevented
their arrival; so he withdrew into Gilead. When he reached Bascama, he 23
had Jonathan put to death, and there he was buried. Trypho then turned 24
and went back to his own country.

Simon had the body of his brother Jonathan brought to Modin, and 25
buried in the town of their fathers; and all Israel made a great lamentation 26
and mourned him for many days. Simon built a high monument over the 27
tomb of his father and his brothers, visible at a great distance, faced back
and front with polished stone. He erected seven pyramids, those for his 28
father and mother and his four brothers arranged in pairs. For the pyramids 29
he contrived an elaborate setting: he surrounded them with great columns
surmounted with trophies of armour for a perpetual memorial, and between
the trophies carved ships, plainly visible to all at sea. This mausoleum 30
which he made at Modin stands to this day.

Trypho now plotted against the young King Antiochus and murdered 31
him. He usurped his throne and assumed the crown of Asia. This was a 32
disaster for the country.

Simon rebuilt the fortresses of Judaea, furnishing them with high towers 33
and great walls with gates and bars; he also provisioned the fortresses. He 34
sent representatives to King Demetrius to negotiate a remission of taxes
for the country, on the ground that all Trypho's exactions had been exorbi-
tant. Demetrius replied favourably to this request and wrote him a letter 35
in the following terms:

King Demetrius to Simon the High Priest and friend of kings, and 36
to the Senate and nation of the Jews, greeting.

We have received the golden crown and the palm branch which you 37
sent, and we are ready to make a lasting peace with you and to instruct
the revenue officers to grant you immunities. All our agreements with 38
you stand, and the strongholds which you built shall remain yours. We 39
give a free pardon for any errors of omission or commission, to take effect

from the date of this letter. We remit the crown-money which you owed us, and every other tax formerly exacted in Jerusalem is henceforth

40 cancelled. All those of you who are suitable for enrolment in our retinue shall be so enrolled. Let there be peace between us.

41 42 In the year 170,[a] Israel was released from the gentile yoke. The people began to write on their contracts and agreements, 'In the first year of Simon, the great high priest, general and leader of the Jews'.

43 Then Simon invested Gazara,[b] and surrounded it with his forces. He constructed a siege-engine and brought it up to the town, made a breach

44 in one of the towers and captured it. The men on the siege-engine leapt

45 out of it into the town, and there was a great commotion. The townspeople and their wives and children climbed up on to the city wall with their

46 garments torn, clamouring to Simon to offer them terms. 'Do not treat us as our wickedness deserves,' they cried, 'but as your mercy prompts you.'

47 Simon came to terms with them, and brought the war to an end. But he expelled them from the town, and after purifying the houses in which the

48 idols stood, he made his entry with songs of thanksgiving and praise. He removed every pollution from it and settled men in it who would keep the law. He strengthened its fortifications and built a residence there for himself.

49 The men in the citadel in Jerusalem were prevented from going in and out to buy and sell in the country; famine set in and many of them died of

50 starvation. They clamoured to Simon to accept their surrender, and he agreed: he expelled them from the citadel and cleansed it from its pollu-

51 tions. It was on the twenty-third day of the second month in the year 171[c] that he made his entry, with a chorus of praise and the waving of palm branches, with lutes, cymbals, and zithers, with hymns and songs, to

52 celebrate Israel's final riddance of a formidable enemy. Simon decreed that this day should be observed as an annual festival. He fortified the temple hill opposite the citadel, and he and his men took up residence

53 there. When Simon saw that his son John had become a man, he made him commander of all the forces, with Gazara as his headquarters.

**14** In the year 172,[d] King Demetrius mustered his army and went into

2 Media to recruit additional forces for his war against Trypho. When Arsakes king of Persia and Media heard that Demetrius had entered his

3 territories, he sent one of his generals to capture him alive. The general marched out and defeated Demetrius, captured him and brought him to Arsakes, who put him in prison.

4 As long as Simon lived, Judaea was at peace. He promoted his people's welfare, and they lived happily all through the glorious days of his reign.

5 Among other notable achievements he captured the port of Joppa to secure

6 his communications overseas. He extended his nation's territories and

7 made himself master of the whole land. He repatriated a large number of prisoners of war. Without meeting any resistance he gained control over Gazara and Bethsura and over the citadel, and removed their pollution.

[a] *That is* 142 B.C.  [b] *Probable reading; Gk.* Gaza.  [c] *That is* 141 B.C.
[d] *That is* 140 B.C.

They farmed their land in peace, and the land produced its crops, and 8
the trees in the plains their fruit. Old men sat in the streets, talking together 9
of their blessings; and the young men dressed themselves in splendid
military style. Simon supplied the towns with food in plenty and equipped 10
them with weapons for defence. His renown reached the ends of the earth.
He restored peace to the land, and there were great rejoicings throughout 11
Israel. Each man sat under his own vine and fig-tree, and they had no one 12
to fear. Those were days when every enemy vanished from the land and 13
every hostile king was crushed. Simon gave his protection to the poor 14
among the people; he paid close attention to the law and rid the country of
lawless and wicked men. He gave new splendour to the temple and 15
furnished it with a wealth of sacred vessels.

THE REPORT OF JONATHAN'S DEATH reached Rome, and Sparta 16
too, and they were deeply grieved. When they heard, however, that 17
his brother Simon had become high priest in his place, and was in firm
control of the country and the towns in it, they inscribed on bronze 18
tablets a renewal of the treaty of friendship and alliance which they had
established with his brothers Judas and Jonathan. This was read before 19
the assembly in Jerusalem. The following is a copy of the letter from 20
Sparta:

The rulers and city of Sparta to the High Priest Simon, to the
Senate, the priests, and the rest of the Jewish people, our brothers,
greeting.
The envoys you sent to our people have told us about your fame and 21
honour; their visit has given us great pleasure. We have entered a tran- 22
script of the message they brought in the minutes of the public assembly:
'Numenius son of Antiochus, and Antipater son of Jason, envoys of the
Jews, visited us to renew their treaty of friendship with us. It was 23
resolved by the public assembly to receive these men with honour and to
place a copy of their address in the public archives, so that the Spartans
might have it on permanent record. A copy of this document has been
made for Simon the High Priest.'

After this, Simon sent Numenius to Rome with a large gold shield, 24
worth a thousand minas, to confirm the alliance with the Romans.
When the people heard of these events they asked themselves how they 25
could show their gratitude to Simon and his sons. For he, with his brothers 26
and his father's family, had stood firm, fought off the enemies of Israel, and
ensured his nation's freedom. So an inscription was engraved on tablets of 27
bronze and placed on a monument on Mount Zion. A copy of the inscription follows:

On the eighteenth day of the month Elul, in the year 172,[a] the third
year of Simon's high-priesthood, at Asaramel, in a large assembly of 28
priests, people, rulers of the nation, and elders of the land, the following

---

[a] *That is* 140 B.C.

243

29 facts were placed on record. Whereas our land had been subject to frequent wars, Simon son of Mattathias, a priest of the Joarib family, and his brothers, risked their lives in resisting the enemies of their people, in order that the temple and law might be preserved, and they brought

30 great glory to their nation. Jonathan rallied the nation, became their high

31 priest, and then was gathered to his fathers. Their enemies resolved to

32 invade their land and destroy it, and to attack the temple. Then Simon came forward and fought for his nation. He spent large sums of his own

33 money to arm the soldiers of his nation and to provide their pay. He fortified the towns of Judaea, and Bethsura on the boundaries of Judaea,

34 formerly an enemy arsenal, and stationed a garrison of Jews there. He fortified Joppa by the sea, and Gazara near Azotus, formerly occupied by the enemy. There he settled Jews, and provided these towns with

35 everything needful for their welfare. When the people saw Simon's patriotism and his resolution to win fame for his nation, they made him their leader and high priest, in recognition of all that he had done, of his just conduct, his loyalty to his nation, and his constant efforts to enhance

36 its renown. His leadership was crowned with success, and the Gentiles were expelled from the land, as were also the troops in Jerusalem who had built themselves a citadel in the city of David, from which they sallied forth to bring defilement upon the whole precinct of the temple

37 and do violence to its purity. He settled Jews in it and fortified it for the security of the land and of the city, and he raised the height of the

38 walls of Jerusalem. King Demetrius confirmed him in the office of

39 high priest, made him one of his Friends, and granted him the highest

40 honours; for he had heard that the Romans were naming the Jews friends, allies, and brothers, and had gone in state to meet Simon's envoys.

41 The Jews and their priests confirmed Simon as their leader and high

42 priest in perpetuity until a true prophet should appear. He was to be their general, and to have full charge of the temple; and in addition to this the supervision of their labour, of the country, and of the arms and

43 fortifications was to be entrusted to him. He was to be obeyed by all; all contracts in the country were to be drawn up in his name. He was to wear the purple robe and the gold clasp.

44 None of the people or the priests shall have authority to abrogate any of these decrees, to oppose commands issued by Simon or convene any assembly in the land without his consent, to be robed in purple, or to wear

45 the gold clasp. Whoever shall contravene these provisions or neglect

46 any of them shall be liable to punishment. It is the unanimous decision

47 of the people that Simon shall officiate in the ways here laid down. Simon has agreed and consented to be high priest, general and ethnarch of the Jews and the priests, and to be the protector of them all.

48 This inscription, it was declared, should be engraved on bronze tablets

49 and set up within the precincts of the temple in a conspicuous position, and copies should be placed in the treasury, in the keeping of Simon and his sons.

Antiochus son of King Demetrius sent a letter from overseas to Simon 15
the high priest and ethnarch of the Jews, and to the whole nation. The 2
contents were as follows:

King Antiochus to Simon, High Priest and Ethnarch, and to the
Jewish nation, greeting.

Whereas certain traitors have seized my ancestral kingdom, I have 3
now decided to assert my claim to it, so that I may restore it to its former
condition. I have raised a large body of mercenaries and fitted out ships
of war. I intend to land in my country and to attack those who have 4
ravaged my kingdom and destroyed many of its cities. Now therefore I 5
confirm all the tax remissions which my royal predecessors granted you,
and all their other remissions of tribute. I permit you to mint your own 6
coinage as currency for your country. Jerusalem and the temple shall be 7
free. All the arms you have prepared, and the fortifications which you
have built and now hold, shall remain yours. All debts now owing to the 8
royal treasury and all future liabilities thereto shall be cancelled from
this time on for ever. When we have re-established our kingdom, we 9
shall confer the highest honours upon you, your nation and temple, to
make your country's greatness apparent to the whole world.

In the year 174,[a] Antiochus marched into his ancestral domain, and all 10
the armed forces came over to him, leaving very few with Trypho. Antio- 11
chus pursued him, and Trypho came as a fugitive to Dor by the sea. He 12
knew that his position was desperate now that all his troops had deserted.
Antiochus, at the head of a hundred and twenty thousand trained soldiers 13
and eight thousand horsemen, laid siege to Dor. He encircled the town, and 14
his ships joined in the blockade from the sea. He thus exerted heavy pressure on it from both land and sea, and prevented anyone from leaving or
entering.

NUMENIUS AND HIS PARTY arrived from Rome with a letter to the 15
various kings and countries, which read as follows:

Lucius, Consul of the Romans, to King Ptolemy, greeting. 16
Envoys have come to us from our friends and allies the Jews, sent by 17
Simon the High Priest and the Jewish people, to renew their original
treaty of friendship and alliance. They brought a gold shield worth a 18
thousand minas. We have decided, therefore, to write to the kings and 19
countries, requiring them to do no harm to the Jews, nor make war on
them or their cities or their country, nor ally themselves with those who
so make war. And we have decided to accept the shield from them. If 20 21
therefore any traitors have escaped from their country to you, hand
them over to Simon the High Priest to be punished by him according to
the law of the Jews.

The same message was sent to King Demetrius, to Attalus, Ariarathes, 22
Arsakes, Sampsakes, and the Spartans, and also to the following places: 23

[a] *That is* 138 B.C.

Delos, Myndos, Sicyon, Caria, Samos, Pamphylia, Lycia, Halicarnassus, Rhodes, Phaselis, Cos, Sidé, Aradus, Gortyna, Cnidus, Cyprus, and
24 Cyrene. A copy was sent to Simon the high priest.

25 KING ANTIOCHUS LAID SIEGE to Dor for the second time,[a] and launched repeated attacks against it; he had siege-engines constructed, and blockaded Trypho, preventing all movement in or out of the town.
26 Simon sent Antiochus two thousand picked men to assist him, with
27 silver and gold and much equipment; but he refused the offer. He repu-
28 diated all his previous agreements with Simon and broke off relations. He sent Athenobius, one of the Friends, to parley with him. This was his message: 'You are occupying Joppa and Gazara and the citadel in Jeru-
29 salem, cities that belong to my kingdom. You have laid waste their terri-tories, and done great damage to the country, and have made yourselves
30 masters of many places in my kingdom. I demand the return of the cities you have captured and the surrender of the tribute exacted from places beyond the frontiers of Judaea over which you have assumed control.
31 Otherwise, you must pay five hundred talents of silver on their account, and another five hundred as compensation for the destruction you have caused and for the loss of tribute from the cities. Failing this, we shall go to war with you.'
32 Athenobius, the King's Friend, came to Jerusalem, and when he saw the splendour of Simon's establishment, the gold and silver vessels on his sideboard, and his display of wealth, he was amazed. He delivered the
33 king's message, to which Simon replied: 'We have not occupied other people's land or taken other people's property, but only the inheritance of
34 our ancestors, unjustly seized for a time by our enemies. We have grasped
35 our opportunity and have claimed our patrimony. With regard to Joppa and Gazara, which you demand, these towns were doing a great deal of damage among our people and in our land. For these we offer one hundred talents.'
36 Athenobius answered not a word, but went off in a rage to the king; he reported what Simon had said, and described Simon's splendour and all the things he had seen. The king was furious.
37 Meanwhile Trypho boarded a ship and made good his escape to Orthosia.
38 The king appointed Kendebaeus as commander-in-chief of the coastal
39 zone, and gave him infantry and cavalry. He instructed him to blockade Judaea, to rebuild Kedron and strengthen its gates, and to make war on
40 our people, while he himself continued the pursuit of Trypho. Kendebaeus arrived in Jamnia and began to harass our people by invading Judaea, and
41 by capturing and killing the inhabitants. He rebuilt Kedron, stationing cavalry and troops there to sally out and patrol the roads of Judaea, in accordance with the king's instructions.

16 John came from Gazara and reported to his father Simon the results of
2 Kendebaeus's campaign. Simon summoned his two eldest sons Judas and John, and said to them: 'My brothers and I and my father's family have fought Israel's battles from our youth until this day, and many a time we

    _a Some witnesses read on the second day._

have been successful in rescuing Israel. Now I am old, but mercifully 3
you are in the prime of life. Take my place and my brother's and go out
and fight for our nation. And may help from on high be with you.'

He then levied from the country twenty thousand picked warriors and 4
cavalry, and they marched against Kendebaeus. After passing the night at
Modin they rose early and proceeded to the plain, where a large force of 5
infantry and cavalry stood ready to meet them on the far side of a gully.
When his army had taken up a position opposite, John saw that his men 6
were afraid to cross the gully. So he crossed first himself; his men saw him
and followed. John drew up his army with the cavalry in the centre of the 7
infantry, for the enemy cavalry were very numerous. The trumpets were 8
sounded, and Kendebaeus and his army were routed; many of them fell,
and the remainder took refuge in the fortress. It was in this engagement that 9
John's brother Judas was wounded. John kept up the pursuit until Kendebaeus reached Kedron, which he had rebuilt. The enemy took refuge in the 10
towers in the open country round Azotus, whereupon John set fire to
Azotus. Some two thousand of the enemy fell in the fighting, and John
returned to Judaea in safety.

Now Ptolemaeus son of Abubus had been appointed commander for 11
the plain of Jericho. He had great wealth, for he was the high priest's son- 12
in-law. But he became over-ambitious; he proposed to make himself 13
master of the country and plotted to put Simon and his sons out of the way.
In the course of a tour to inspect the towns in that region and to attend to 14
their needs, Simon came to Jericho with his sons Mattathias and Judas in
the year 177,*a* in the eleventh month, the month of Shebat. The son of 15
Abubus, with treachery in his heart, received them at the small fort called
Dok which he had built, and entertained them lavishly. But he had men in
concealment there, and when Simon and his sons had drunk freely, 16
Ptolemaeus and his accomplices jumped up, seized their weapons, and
rushed in to the banquet. They attacked Simon and killed him, along with
his two sons and some of his servants. It was an act of base treachery in 17
which evil was returned for good.

Ptolemaeus sent news of this in a dispatch to the king, asking him to send 18
troops to his assistance and to give him authority over the country and its
towns. He sent some of his men to Gazara to kill John, and wrote to the 19
army officers urging them to join him, and offering them silver and gold
and presents. Other troops he sent to take Jerusalem and the temple hill. 20
But someone ran ahead and reported to John at Gazara that his father and 21
brothers had been murdered, and that Ptolemaeus had sent men to kill
him as well. When John heard this he was beside himself; he arrested the 22
men who came to kill him, and put them to death, because he had discovered their plot against his life.

The rest of the story of John, his wars and the deeds of valour he per- 23
formed, the walls he built, and his exploits, are written in the annals of his 24
high-priesthood from the time when he succeeded his father.

*a That is* 134 B.C.

# THE SECOND BOOK OF THE

# MACCABEES

## Foreword : letters to the Jews in Egypt

1 TO THEIR JEWISH KINSMEN in Egypt, the Jews who are in Jerusalem and those in the country of Judaea send brotherly greeting.

2 May God give you peace and prosperity and remember his covenant
3 with Abraham, Isaac, and Jacob, his faithful servants. May he give to you all a will to worship him, to fulfil his purposes eagerly with heart and
4 soul. May he give you a mind open to his law and precepts. May he make
5 peace and answer your prayers, and be reconciled to you and not forsake
6 you in an evil hour. Here and now we are praying for you.

7 In the reign of Demetrius, in the year 169,[a] we the Jews wrote to you during the persecution and the crisis that came upon us in those years since the time when Jason and his partisans revolted from the holy land and
8 the kingdom. They set the porch of the temple on fire and shed innocent blood. Then we prayed to the Lord and were answered. We offered a sacrifice and fine flour, we lit the lamps, and set out the Bread of the
9 Presence. And now, you are to observe the celebration of a Feast of Tabernacles in the month Kislev.
10 Written in the year 188.[b]

FROM THE PEOPLE of Jerusalem and Judaea, from the Senate, and from Judas, to Aristobulus, the teacher of King Ptolemy and a member of the high-priestly family, and to the Jews in Egypt, greeting and good health.

11 We have been saved by God from great dangers, and give him all thanks,
12 as men standing ready to resist the king. It was God who drove out the enemy force in the holy city.
13 For when the king went into Persia with an army that seemed invincible, they were cut to pieces in the temple of Nanaea through a stratagem
14 employed by Nanaea's priests. Antiochus, along with his Companions, arrived at the temple to marry the goddess, in order to secure the consider-
15 able treasure by way of dowry. After this had been laid out by the priests, he went into the temple precinct with a small retinue. When Antiochus
16 entered, the priests shut the sanctuary, opened a secret door in the panelling, and hurled stones at them. The king fell, as if struck by a thunderbolt.
17 They hacked off limbs and heads and threw them to those outside. Blessed in all things be our God, who handed over the evil-doers to death!

[a] That is 143 B.C.    [b] That is 124 B.C.

248

We are about to celebrate the purification of the temple on the twenty-   18
fifth of Kislev, and think it right to inform you, so that you also for your
part may celebrate a Feast of Tabernacles, in honour of the fire which
appeared when Nehemiah offered sacrifices, after he had built the temple
and the altar. When our fathers were carried off to Persia, the pious priests   19
of those days secretly took fire from the altar and concealed it in a dry well.
It proved a safe hiding-place and remained undiscovered. After many   20
years had passed, in God's good time, Nehemiah was sent back by the king
of Persia. He then dispatched the descendants of the priests who had
hidden it to get the fire, and they informed our people that they found,
not fire, but a thick liquid. Nehemiah ordered them to draw some out and   21
bring it to him. When the materials of the sacrifice had been presented, he
ordered the priests to sprinkle this liquid over the wood and the things laid
upon it, and this was done. Some time passed; then the sun, which earlier   22
had been hidden by clouds, shone out and the altar burst into a great blaze,
so that everyone marvelled. As the sacrifice was burning, the priests   23
offered prayer, they and all those present: Jonathan began and the rest
responded, led by Nehemiah.

The prayer was in this style: 'O Lord God, creator of all things, thou the   24
terrible, the mighty, the just, and the merciful, the only King, the only
gracious one, the only giver, the only just, omnipotent, and everlasting one,   25
who dost deliver Israel from every evil, who didst choose the patriarchs and
set them apart: accept this sacrifice on behalf of thy whole people Israel;   26
they are thy own, watch over them and sanctify them. Gather the dis-   27
persed, free those who are in slavery among the heathen, look favourably
on the despised and detested; let the heathen know that thou art our God.
Punish our oppressors for their insolent brutality and make them suffer   28
torment; but plant thy people in thy holy place, as Moses said.'   29

Then the priests chanted the hymns. After the materials of the sacrifice   30 31
had been consumed, Nehemiah further ordered what remained of the
liquid to be poured over some great stones.*a* At this a flame shot up, but   32
burnt itself out as soon as the fire on the altar outshone it.*b*

These events became widely known. The king of Persia was told that,   33
in the place where the priests who were deported had hidden the fire, a
liquid had appeared, and that Nehemiah and his companions had used it
to burn up the materials of the sacrifice. When he had verified the fact,   34
the king enclosed the site and made it sacred. The custodians he appointed   35
received a share of the very substantial revenue that the king derived from
it. Nehemiah and his companions called the liquid 'nephthar', which means   36
'purification'; but most people call it 'naphtha'.

The records show that it was the prophet Jeremiah who ordered the   **2**
exiles to hide the fire, as has been mentioned; also that, having given them   2
the law, he charged them not to neglect the ordinances of the Lord, or be
led astray by the sight of images of gold and silver with all their finery. In   3
similar words he appealed to them not to abandon the law.

*a* what remained . . . stones: *so some witnesses; others read* that great stones should enclose
what remained of the liquid.          *b Or* but hardly had the light been reflected from
the altar, when it burnt itself out.

4   Further, this document records that, prompted by a divine message, the prophet gave orders that the Tent of Meeting and the ark should go with him. Then he went away to the mountain from the top of which Moses saw
5 God's promised land. When he reached the mountain, Jeremiah found a cave-dwelling; he carried the tent, the ark, and the incense-altar into it,
6 then blocked up the entrance. Some of his companions came to mark out
7 the way, but were unable to find it. When Jeremiah learnt of this he reprimanded them. 'The place shall remain unknown', he said, 'until God finally
8 gathers his people together and shows mercy to them. Then the Lord will bring these things to light again, and the glory of the Lord will appear with the cloud, as it was seen both in the time of Moses and when Solomon prayed that the shrine might be worthily consecrated.'
9   It was also related that Solomon, having the gift of wisdom, offered the
10 dedication sacrifice at the completion of the temple; and that, just as Moses prayed to the Lord and fire came down from heaven and burnt up the sacrificial offerings, so Solomon prayed and the fire came down and con-
11 sumed the whole-offerings. (Moses said: 'The sin-offering was burnt up
12 in the same way because it was not eaten.') Solomon celebrated the feast for eight days.
13   These same facts are set out in the official records and in the memoirs of Nehemiah. Just as Nehemiah collected the chronicles of the kings, the writings of prophets, the works of David, and royal letters about sacred
14 offerings, to found his library, so Judas also has collected all the books that had been scattered as a result of our recent conflict. These are in our pos-
15 session, and if you need any of them, send messengers for them.
16   As, then, we are about to celebrate the purification of the temple, we are
17 writing to impress upon you the duty of celebrating this festival. God has saved his whole people and granted to all of us the holy land, the kingship,
18 the priesthood, and the consecration, as he promised by the law; and in him we have confidence that he will soon be merciful to us and gather us from every part of the world to the holy temple. For he has delivered us from great evils and purified the temple.

## Preface to this abridgement

19 IN FIVE BOOKS Jason of Cyrene has set out the history of Judas Macca-baeus and his brothers, the purification of the great temple, and the
20 dedication of the altar. He has described the battles with Antiochus
21 Epiphanes and with his son Eupator, and the apparitions from heaven which appeared to those who vied with one another in fighting manfully for Judaism. Few though they were, they ravaged the whole country and
22 routed the foreign hordes; they restored the world-renowned temple, freed the city of Jerusalem, and reaffirmed the laws which were in danger of being abolished. All this they achieved because the Lord was merciful and gracious to them.
23 24   These five books of Jason I shall try to summarize in a single work; for I was struck by the mass of statistics and the difficulty which the bulk of the

material causes to those wishing to grasp the narratives of this history. I 25
have tried to provide for the entertainment of those who read for pleasure,
the convenience of students who must commit the facts to memory, and the
profit of even the casual reader. The task which I have taken upon myself 26
in making this summary is no easy one. It means toil and late nights, just 27
as it is no light task for the man who plans a dinner-party and aims to satisfy
his guests. Nevertheless, I will gladly undergo this hard labour for the
benefit of *a* readers in general. I shall leave to the original author the minute 28
discussion of every detail, and concentrate on the main points of my outline. As the architect of a new house must concern himself with the whole 29
of the structure, while the man who paints in encaustic on the walls needs
to discover only what is necessary for the ornamentation, so, I judge, it is
with me also. It is the province of the original author of a history to take 30
possession of the field, to spread himself in discussion, and to inquire
closely into particular questions. The man who makes a paraphrase must 31
be allowed to aim at conciseness of expression and to omit a full treatment
of the subject-matter.

Here, then, without adding anything further, I begin my narrative. It 32
would be absurd to make a lengthy introduction to the history and cut
short the history itself.

## Syrian oppression of the Jews

DURING THE RULE of the high priest Onias, the holy city enjoyed 3
complete peace and prosperity, and the laws were still observed most
scrupulously, because he was a pious man and hated wickedness. The 2
kings themselves held the sanctuary in honour and used to embellish the
temple with the most splendid gifts; even Seleucus, king of Asia, bore all 3
the expenses of the sacrificial worship from his own revenues.

But a certain Simon, of the clan Bilgah,*b* who had been appointed 4
administrator of the temple, quarrelled with the high priest about the
regulation of the city market. Unable to get the better of Onias, he went to 5
Apollonius son of Thrasaeus, then governor of Coele-syria and Phoenicia,
and alleged that the treasury at Jerusalem was full of untold riches— 6
indeed the total of the accumulated balances was incalculable and did not
correspond with the account for the sacrifices; he suggested that these
balances might be brought under the control of the king. When Apollonius 7
met the king, he reported what he had been told about the riches. The king
selected Heliodorus, his chief minister, and sent him with orders to remove
these treasures.

Heliodorus set off at once, ostensibly to make a tour of inspection of the 8
cities of Coele-syria and Phoenicia, but in fact to carry out the purpose of
the king. When he arrived at Jerusalem and had been courteously received 9
by the high priest and the citizens, he explained why he had come: he told
them about the allegations and asked if they were in fact true. The high 10

---

*a* for . . . of: *so some witnesses; others read* to win the gratitude of . . .　　　*b* *So some*
*witnesses (compare Nehemiah 12. 5, 18); others read* Benjamin.

priest intimated that the deposits were held in trust for widows and
11 orphans, apart from what belonged to Hyrcanus son of Tobias, a man of
very high standing; the matter was being misrepresented by the impious
Simon. In all there were four hundred talents of silver and two hundred of
12 gold. It was unthinkable, he said, that wrong should be done to those who
had relied on the sanctity of the place, on the dignity and inviolability of
13 the world-famous temple. But Heliodorus, in virtue of the king's orders,
replied that these deposits must without question be handed over to the
royal treasury.

14 ⸤He fixed a day and went into the temple to make an inventory. At this
15 there was great distress throughout the whole city. The priests, prostrating
themselves in their vestments before the altar, prayed to Heaven, to the
Lawgiver who had made deposits sacred, to keep them intact for their
16 rightful owners. The high priest's looks pierced every beholder to the
heart, for his face and its changing colour betrayed the anguish of his soul.
17 Alarm and shuddering gripped him, and the pain he felt was clearly ap-
18 parent to the onlookers. The people rushed pell-mell from their houses
to join together in supplication because of the dishonour which threatened
19 the holy place. Women in sackcloth, their breasts bare, filled the streets;
unmarried girls who were kept in seclusion ran to the gates or walls of their
20 houses, while others leaned out from the windows; all with outstretched
21 hands made solemn entreaty to Heaven. It was pitiful to see the crowd all
lying prostrate in utter confusion, and the high priest in an agony of
apprehension.

22 While the people were calling upon the Lord Almighty to keep the
23 deposits intact and safe for those who had deposited them, Heliodorus pro-
24 ceeded to carry out his decision. But at the very moment when he arrived
with his bodyguard at the treasury, the Ruler of spirits and of all powers
produced a mighty apparition, so that all who had the audacity to accompany Heliodorus were faint with terror, stricken with panic at the
25 power of God. They saw a horse, splendidly caparisoned, with a rider of
terrible aspect; it rushed fiercely at Heliodorus and, rearing up, attacked
26 him with its hooves. The rider was wearing golden armour. There also
appeared to Heliodorus two young men of surpassing strength and
glorious beauty, splendidly dressed. They stood on either side of him and
27 scourged him, raining ceaseless blows upon him. He fell suddenly to the
ground, overwhelmed by a great darkness, and his men snatched him up
28 and put him on a litter. This man, who so recently had entered the treasury
with a great throng and his whole bodyguard, was now borne off by them
quite helpless, publicly compelled to acknowledge the sovereignty of God.[a]

29 While he lay speechless, deprived by this divine act of all hope of
30 recovery, the Jews were praising the Lord for the miracle he had performed
in his own house. The temple, which a short time before was full of alarm
and confusion, now overflowed with joy and festivity, because the Lord
Almighty had appeared.

31 Some of Heliodorus's companions hastily begged Onias to pray to the

[a] *was now ... of God:* so some witnesses; *others read* they, recognizing the sovereignty of
God, now bore off quite helpless.

Most High, and so to spare the life of their master now lying at his very last gasp. The high priest, fearing that the king might suspect that Heliodorus 32 had met with foul play at the hands of the Jews, brought a sacrifice for the man's recovery. As the high priest was making the expiation, the same 33 young men, dressed as before, again appeared to Heliodorus. They stood over him and said: 'Be very grateful to Onias the high priest; for his sake the Lord has spared your life. You have been scourged by God; now tell all 34 men of his mighty power.' When they had said this, they vanished.

Heliodorus offered a sacrifice and made lavish vows to the Lord who had 35 spared his life; then, after taking friendly leave of Onias, he led his troops back to the king. He bore witness to everyone of the miracles of the supreme 36 God which he had seen with his own eyes.

When the king asked him what sort of man would be suitable to send to 37 Jerusalem another time, Heliodorus replied: 'If you have an enemy or 38 someone plotting against your government, that is the place to send him; you will receive him back soundly flogged, if he survives at all, for beyond doubt there is a divine power surrounding the temple. He whose habitation 39 is in heaven watches over it himself and gives it his aid; those who approach the place with evil intent he strikes and destroys.'

So runs the story of Heliodorus and the preservation of the treasury.    40

BUT THE SIMON MENTIONED EARLIER, the man who had made allega- **4** tions against his country about the money, slandered Onias, alleging that he had attacked Heliodorus and had been the author of these troubles. He 2 had the effrontery to accuse him of conspiracy against the government— this benefactor of the holy city, this protector of his fellow-Jews, this zealot for the laws. The enmity grew so great that one of Simon's trusted 3 followers even resorted to murder. Onias, realizing that Simon's rivalry 4 was dangerous and that Apollonius son of Menestheus, governor of Coele-syria and Phoenicia, was encouraging his evil ways, paid a visit to the king. 5 He did not appear as an accuser of his fellow-citizens, but as concerned for the interests of all the Jews, both as a nation and as individuals. For he saw 6 that unless the king intervened there could not possibly be peace in public affairs, nor could Simon be stopped in his mad course.

But when Seleucus was dead and had been succeeded by Antiochus, 7 known as Epiphanes, Jason, Onias's brother, obtained the high-priesthood by corrupt means. He petitioned the king and promised him three hundred 8 and sixty talents in silver coin immediately, and eighty talents from future revenue. In addition he undertook to pay another hundred and fifty 9 talents for the authority to institute a sports-stadium, to arrange for the education of young men there, and to enrol in Jerusalem a group to be known as the 'Antiochenes'.*a* The king agreed, and, as soon as he had 10 seized the high-priesthood, Jason made the Jews conform to the Greek way of life.

He set aside the royal privileges established for the Jews through the 11 agency of John, the father of that Eupolemus who negotiated a treaty of friendship and alliance with the Romans. He abolished the lawful way of

*a* Or enrol the inhabitants of Jerusalem as citizens of Antioch.

12  life and introduced practices which were against the law. He lost no time in establishing a sports-stadium at the foot of the citadel itself, and he made
13  the most outstanding of the young men assume the Greek athlete's hat. So Hellenism reached a high point with the introduction of foreign customs through the boundless wickedness of the impious Jason, no true high
14  priest. As a result, the priests no longer had any enthusiasm for their duties at the altar, but despised the temple and neglected the sacrifices; and in defiance of the law they eagerly contributed to the expenses of the wrestling-
15  school whenever the opening gong called them. They placed no value on their hereditary dignities, but cared above everything for Hellenic honours.
16  Because of this, grievous misfortunes beset them, and the very men whose way of life they strove after, and tried so hard to imitate, turned out to be
17  their vindictive enemies. To act profanely against God's laws is no light matter, as will become clear in due time.
18      When the quinquennial games were being held at Tyre in the presence
19  of the king, the blackguard Jason sent, as envoys to represent Jerusalem, Antiochenes carrying three hundred drachmas in cash for the sacrifice to Hercules. Even the bearers thought it improper that this money should be
20  used for a sacrifice, and considered that it should be spent otherwise. So, thanks to the bearers, the money designed by the sender for the sacrifice to Hercules went to fit out the triremes.
21      When Apollonius son of Menestheus was sent to Egypt for the enthrone-ment of King Philometor, Antiochus learnt that Philometor was now hostile to his state, and became anxious for his own security. So he went to Joppa,
22  and then on to Jerusalem, where he was lavishly welcomed by Jason and the city and received with torch-light and ovations. After this, he quartered his army in Phoenicia.
23      Three years later, Jason sent Menelaus, brother of the Simon mentioned above, to convey money to the king and to carry out his directions about
24  urgent business. But Menelaus established his position with the king by acting as if he were a person of great authority, outbid Jason by three hundred talents in silver, and so diverted the high-priesthood to himself.
25  He arrived back with the royal mandate, but with nothing else to make him worthy of the high-priesthood; he still had the temper of a cruel tyrant
26  and the fury of a savage beast. Jason, who had supplanted his own brother, was now supplanted in his turn and forced to flee to Ammonite territory.
27  As for Menelaus, he continued to hold the high-priesthood but without ever paying any of the money he had promised the king, although it was
28  demanded by Sostratus, the commander of the citadel, who was responsible for collecting the revenues. In consequence they were both summoned by
29  the king. As their deputies, Menelaus left his brother Lysimachus, and Sostratus left Crates, the commander of the Cypriots.
30      It was at this point that the inhabitants of Tarsus and Mallus revolted, because their cities had been handed over as a gift to the king's concubine
31  Antiochis. The king hastened off to restore order, leaving as regent
32  Andronicus, one of his ministers. Menelaus, thinking he had obtained a favourable opportunity, made a present to Andronicus of some of the gold plate belonging to the temple which he had appropriated. He had already

sold some of it to Tyre and to the neighbouring cities. When Onias heard 33
this on good authority, he withdrew to sanctuary at Daphne near Antioch
and denounced him. As a result, Menelaus approached Andronicus 34
privately and urged him to kill Onias. The regent went to Onias bent on
treachery; he greeted him, gave him assurances on oath, and persuaded
him, though still suspicious, to leave the sanctuary. Then at once, with no
respect for justice, he made away with him.

His murder filled not only Jews, but many from other nations as well, 35
with alarm and anger. So when the king returned from Cilicia, the Jews of 36
Antioch sent him a petition about the senseless killing of Onias, the Gentiles
sharing in their detestation of the crime. Antiochus was deeply grieved, and 37
was moved to pity and tears as he thought of the prudence and disciplined
habits of the dead man. In a burning fury, he immediately stripped 38
Andronicus of the purple, tore off his clothes, led him round the whole city
to that very place where he had committed sacrilege against Onias, and
there disposed of the murderer. Thus the Lord repaid him with the retribution he deserved.

Lysimachus committed many acts of sacrilegious plunder in Jerusalem 39
with the connivance of Menelaus. When the news of them became public
and the people heard that much of the gold plate had been disposed of,
they banded together against Lysimachus. Since the crowds were seething 40
with rage and getting out of hand, Lysimachus armed some three thousand
men and began to launch a vicious attack, led by a certain Auranus, a
man advanced in years and no less in folly. Realizing that the attack came 41
from Lysimachus, some of the crowd seized stones and others blocks of
wood, while others again took handfuls of the ashes that were lying round,
and there was complete confusion as they all hurled them at Lysimachus
and his men. As a result, they wounded many, killed some, and routed them 42
all; the sacrilegious man himself they dispatched near the treasury.

An action was brought against Menelaus in connection with this inci- 43
dent. When the king came to Tyre, the three men sent by the Jewish senate 44
pleaded the case before him. Menelaus's cause was as good as lost; but he 45
promised a large sum of money to Ptolemaeus son of Dorymenes to win
over the king. So Ptolemaeus led the king aside into a colonnade, as if to 46
take the air, and persuaded him to change his mind. The king acquitted 47
Menelaus, the cause of all the mischief, dismissed the charges brought
against him, and condemned his unfortunate accusers to death, men who
would have been discharged as entirely innocent had they appeared even
before Scythians. Without more ado those who had pleaded for their city, 48
their people, and their sacred vessels, suffered the unjust penalty. At this, 49
even some of the Tyrians showed their detestation of the crime by providing
a splendid funeral for the victims. Menelaus, thanks to the greed of those 50
in power, remained in office. He went from bad to worse, this arch-plotter
against his own fellow-citizens.

About this time Antiochus undertook his second invasion of Egypt. 5
Apparitions were seen in the sky all over Jerusalem for nearly forty days: 2
galloping horsemen in golden armour, companies of spearmen standing to
arms, swords unsheathed, cavalry divisions in battle order. Charges and 3

countercharges were made on each side, shields were shaken, spears massed and javelins hurled; breastplates and golden ornaments of every kind
4 shone brightly. All men prayed that this apparition might portend good.
5 Upon a false report of Antiochus's death, Jason collected no less than a thousand men and made a surprise attack on Jerusalem. The defenders on the wall were driven back and the city was finally taken; Menelaus took
6 refuge in the citadel, and Jason continued to massacre his fellow-citizens without pity. He little knew that success against one's own kindred is the greatest of failures, and he imagined that the trophies he raised marked the
7 defeat of enemies, not of fellow-countrymen. He did not, however, gain control of the government; he gained only dishonour as the result of his
8 plot, and returned again as a fugitive to Ammonite territory. His career came to a miserable end; for, after being imprisoned by Aretas the ruler of the Arabs, he fled from city to city, hunted by all, hated as a rebel against the laws, and detested as the executioner of his country and his fellow-
9 citizens, and finally was driven to take refuge in Egypt. In the end the man who had banished so many from their native land himself died in exile after setting sail for Sparta, where he had hoped to obtain shelter because
10 of the Spartans' kinship with the Jews. He who had cast out many to lie unburied was himself unmourned; he had no funeral of any kind, no resting-place in the grave of his ancestors.
11 When news of this reached the king, it became clear to him that Judaea was in a state of rebellion. So he set out from Egypt in savage mood, took
12 Jerusalem by storm, and ordered his troops to cut down without mercy everyone they met and to slaughter those who took refuge in the houses.
13 Young and old were murdered, women and children massacred, girls and
14 infants butchered. At the end of three days their losses had amounted to eighty thousand: forty thousand killed in action, and as many sold into slavery.
15 Not satisfied with this, the king had the audacity to enter the holiest temple on earth, guided by Menelaus, who had turned traitor both to his
16 religion and his country. He laid impious hands on the sacred vessels; his desecrating hands swept together the votive offerings which other kings had set up to enhance the splendour and fame of the shrine.
17 The pride of Antiochus passed all bounds. He did not understand that the sins of the people of Jerusalem had angered the Lord for a short time,
18 and that this was why he left the temple to its fate. If they had not already been guilty of many sinful acts, Antiochus would have fared like Heliodorus who was sent by King Seleucus to inspect the treasury; like him he
19 would have been scourged and his insolent plan foiled at once. But the Lord did not choose the nation for the sake of the sanctuary; he chose the
20 sanctuary for the sake of the nation. Therefore even the sanctuary itself first had its part in the misfortunes that overtook the nation, and afterwards shared its good fortune. It was abandoned when the Lord Almighty was angry, but restored again in all its splendour when he became reconciled.
21 Antiochus, then, carried off eighteen hundred talents from the temple and hastened back to Antioch. In his arrogance he was rash enough to think

that he could make ships sail on dry land and men walk over the sea. He 22
left commissioners behind to oppress the Hebrews: in Jerusalem Philip,
by race a Phrygian, by disposition more barbarous than his master, and in 23
Mount Gerizim, Andronicus, to say nothing of Menelaus, who was more
brutally overbearing to the citizens than the others. Such was the king's
hostility towards the Jews that he sent Apollonius, the general of the 24
Mysian mercenaries, with an army of twenty-two thousand men, and
ordered him to kill all the adult males and to sell the women and boys into
slavery. When Apollonius arrived at Jerusalem, he posed as a man of peace; 25
he waited until the holy sabbath day and, finding the Jews abstaining from
work, he ordered a review of his troops. All who came out to see the parade 26
he put to the sword; then, charging into the city with his soldiers, he killed
a great number of people.

BUT JUDAS, also called Maccabaeus, with about nine others, escaped 27
into the desert, where he and his companions lived in the mountains, fend-
ing for themselves like the wild animals. They remained there living on
what vegetation they found, so as to have no share in the pollution.

Shortly afterwards King Antiochus sent an elderly Athenian to force **6**
the Jews to abandon their ancestral customs and no longer regulate their
lives according to the laws of God. He was also commissioned to pollute 2
the temple at Jerusalem and dedicate it to Olympian Zeus, and to dedicate
the sanctuary on Mount Gerizim to Zeus God of Hospitality, following the
practice of the local inhabitants.

This evil hit them hard and was a severe trial. The Gentiles filled the 3 4
temple with licentious revelry: they took their pleasure with prostitutes
and had intercourse with women in the sacred precincts. They also brought
forbidden things inside, and heaped the altar with impure offerings pro- 5
hibited by the law. It was forbidden either to observe the sabbath or to 6
keep the traditional festivals, or to admit to being a Jew at all. On the 7
monthly celebration of the king's birthday, the Jews were driven by brute
force to eat the entrails of the sacrificial victims; and on the feast of Dionysus they were forced to wear ivy-wreaths and join the procession in his
honour. At the instigation of the inhabitants of Ptolemais[a] an order was 8
published in the neighbouring Greek cities to the effect that they should
adopt the same policy of compelling the Jews to eat the entrails and should 9
kill those who refused to change over to Greek ways.

Their miserable fate was there for all to see. For instance, two women 10
were brought to trial for having had their children circumcised. They were
paraded through the city, with their babies hanging at their breasts, and
then flung down from the fortifications. Other Jews had assembled in 11
caves near Jerusalem to keep the sabbath in secret; they were denounced
to Philip and were burnt alive, since they scrupled to defend themselves
out of regard for the holiness of the day.

Now I beg my readers not to be disheartened by these calamities, but to 12
reflect that such penalties were inflicted for the discipline of our race and
not for its destruction. It is a sign of great kindness that acts of impiety 13

[a] *Some witnesses read* At the instigation of Ptolemaeus . . .

should not be let alone for long but meet their due recompense at once.
14 The Lord did not see fit to deal with us as he does with the other nations:
with them he patiently holds his hand until they have reached the full
15 extent of their sins, but upon us he inflicted retribution before our sins
16 reached their height. So he never withdraws his mercy from us; though he
17 disciplines his people by calamity, he never deserts them. Let it be enough
for me to have recalled this truth; after this short digression, I must continue with my story.
18    There was Eleazar, one of the leading teachers of the law, a man of great
age and distinguished bearing. He was being forced to open his mouth and
19 eat pork, but preferring an honourable death to an unclean life, he spat it
20 out and voluntarily submitted to the flogging, as indeed men should act
who have the courage to refuse to eat forbidden food even for love of life.
21 For old acquaintance' sake, the officials in charge of this sacrilegious feast
had a word with Eleazar in private; they urged him to bring meat which he
was permitted to eat and had himself prepared, and only pretend to be eat-
22 ing the sacrificial meat as the king had ordered. In that way he would escape
death and take advantage of the clemency which their long-standing friend-
23 ship merited. But Eleazar made an honourable decision, one worthy of his
years and the authority of old age, worthy of the grey hairs he had attained
to and wore with such distinction, worthy of his perfect conduct from childhood up, but above all, worthy of the holy and God-given law. So he
24 answered at once: 'Send me quickly to my grave. If I went through with this
pretence at my time of life, many of the young might believe that at the age
25 of ninety Eleazar had turned apostate. If I practised deceit for the sake of a
brief moment of life, I should lead them astray and bring stain and pollu-
26 tion on my old age. I might for the present avoid man's punishment, but,
27 alive or dead, I shall never escape from the hand of the Almighty. So if I
28 now die bravely, I shall show that I have deserved my long life and leave the
young a fine example, to teach them how to die a good death, gladly and
nobly, for our revered and holy laws.'
    When he had finished speaking, he was immediately dragged away to be
29 flogged. Those who a little while before had shown him friendship now
became his enemies because, in their view, what he had said was madness.
30 When he was almost dead from the blows, Eleazar sighed deeply and said:
'To the Lord belongs all holy knowledge. He knows what terrible agony I
endure in my body from this flogging, though I could have escaped death;
yet he knows also that in my soul I suffer gladly, because I stand in awe
of him.'
31    So he died; and by his death he left a heroic example and a glorious
memory, not only for the young but also for the great body of the nation.
7    Again, seven brothers with their mother had been arrested, and were
being tortured by the king with whips and thongs to force them to eat pork,
2 when one of them, speaking for all, said: 'What do you expect to learn by
interrogating us? We are ready to die rather than break the laws of our
3 fathers.' The king was enraged and ordered great pans and cauldrons to be
4 heated up, and this was done at once. Then he gave orders that the spokesman's tongue should be cut out and that he should be scalped and mutilated

before the eyes of his mother and his six brothers. This wreck of a man the  5
king ordered to be taken, still breathing, to the fire and roasted in one of the
pans. As the smoke from it streamed out far and wide, the mother and her
sons encouraged each other to die nobly. 'The Lord God is watching', they  6
said, 'and without doubt has compassion on us. Did not Moses tell Israel
to their faces in the song denouncing apostasy: "He will have compassion
on his servants"?'

After the first brother had died in this way, the second was subjected to  7
the same brutality. The skin and hair of his head were torn off, and he was
asked: 'Will you eat, before we tear you limb from limb?' He replied in his  8
native language, 'Never!', and so he in turn underwent the torture. With  9
his last breath, he said: 'Fiend though you are, you are setting us free from
this present life, and, since we die for his laws, the King of the universe will
raise us up to a life everlastingly made new.'

After him the third was tortured. When the question was put to him, he  10
at once showed his tongue, boldly held out his hands, and said courage-  11
ously: 'The God of heaven gave me these. His laws mean far more to me
than they do, and it is from him that I trust to receive them back.' When  12
they heard this, the king and his followers were amazed at the young man's
spirit and his utter disregard for suffering.

When he too was dead, they tortured the fourth in the same cruel way.  13
At the point of death, he said to the king: 'Better to be killed by men and  14
cherish God's promise to raise us again. There will be no resurrection to
life for you!'

Then the fifth was dragged forward for torture. Looking at the king, he  15 16
said: 'You have authority over men, mortal as you are, and can do as you
please. But do not imagine that God has abandoned our race. Wait and see  17
how his great power will torment you and your descendants.'

Next the sixth was brought and said with his dying breath: 'Do not  18
delude yourself. It is our own fault that we suffer these things; we have
sinned against our God and brought these appalling disasters upon ourselves. But do not suppose you will escape the consequences of trying to  19
fight against God.'

The mother was the most remarkable of all, and deserves to be remem-  20
bered with special honour. She watched her seven sons all die in the space
of a single day, yet she bore it bravely because she put her trust in the Lord.
She encouraged each in turn in her native language. Filled with noble  21
resolution, her woman's thoughts fired by a manly spirit, she said to them:
'You appeared in my womb, I know not how; it was not I who gave you life  22
and breath and set in order your bodily frames. It is the Creator of the  23
universe who moulds man at his birth and plans the origin of all things.
Therefore he, in his mercy, will give you back life and breath again, since
now you put his laws above all thought of self.'

Antiochus felt that he was being treated with contempt and suspected  24
an insult in her words. The youngest brother was still left, and the king, not
content with appealing to him, even assured him on oath that the moment
he abandoned his ancestral customs he would make him rich and prosperous, by enrolling him as a King's Friend and entrusting him with high

25  office. Since the young man paid no attention to him, the king summoned
26  the mother and urged her to advise the lad to save his life. After much
27  urging from the king, she agreed to persuade her son. She leaned towards
    him, and flouting the cruel tyrant, she said in their native language: 'My
    son, take pity on me. I carried you nine months in the womb, suckled you
28  three years, reared you and brought you up to your present age. I beg you,
    child, look at the sky and the earth; see all that is in them and realize that
    God made them out of nothing, and that man comes into being in the
29  same way. Do not be afraid of this butcher; accept death and prove your-
    self worthy of your brothers, so that by God's mercy I may receive you
    back again along with them.'
30      She had barely finished when the young man spoke out: 'What are you
    all waiting for? I will not submit to the king's command; I obey the com-
31  mand of the law given by Moses to our ancestors. And you, King Antio-
    chus, who have devised all kinds of harm for the Hebrews, you will not
32 33 escape God's hand. We are suffering for our own sins, and though to cor-
    rect and discipline us our living Lord is angry for a short time, yet he will
34  again be reconciled to his servants. But you, impious man, foulest of the
    human race, do not indulge vain hopes or be carried away by delusions of
35  greatness, you who lay hands on God's servants. You are not yet safe from
36  the judgement of the almighty, all-seeing God. My brothers have now fallen
    in loyalty to God's covenant, after brief pain leading to eternal life;*a* but
37  you will pay the just penalty of your insolence by the verdict of God. I, like
    my brothers, surrender my body and my life for the laws of our fathers. I
    appeal to God to show mercy speedily to his people and by whips and
38  scourges to bring you to admit that he alone is God. With me and my
    brothers may the Almighty's anger, which has justly fallen on all our race,
    be ended!'
39      The king, exasperated by these scornful words, was beside himself with
40  rage. So he treated him worse than the others, and the young man died,
    putting his whole trust in the Lord, without having incurred defilement.
41  Then finally, after her sons, the mother died.
42      This, then, must conclude our account of the eating of the entrails and
    the monstrous outrages that accompanied it.

## The revolt of Judas Maccabaeus

8   MEANWHILE JUDAS, also called Maccabaeus, and his companions
    were making their way into the villages unobserved. They summoned
    their kinsmen and enlisted others who had remained faithful to Judaism,
2   until they had collected about six thousand men. They invoked the Lord
    to look down and help his people, whom all were trampling under foot, to
3   take pity on the temple profaned by impious men, and to have mercy on
    Jerusalem, which was being destroyed and would soon be levelled to the

*a* in loyalty . . . life: *or* after a brief time of pain, in loyalty to God's covenant of everlasting life.

ground. They prayed him also to give ear to the blood that cried to him for vengeance, to remember the infamous massacre of innocent children and 4 the deeds of blasphemy against his name, and to show his hatred of wickedness.

Once his band of partisans was organized, Maccabaeus proved invincible 5 to the Gentiles, for the Lord's anger had changed to mercy. He came on 6 towns and villages without warning and burnt them; he occupied the key positions, and inflicted many severe reverses on the enemy, choosing the 7 night-time as being especially favourable for these attacks. His heroism*a* was talked about everywhere. When Philip realized that the small gains 8 made by Judas were occurring with growing frequency, he wrote to Ptolemaeus, the governor of Coele-syria and Phoenicia, asking for his help in protecting the royal interests. Ptolemaeus immediately selected Nicanor, 9 son of Patroclus, a member of the highest order of King's Friends, and sent him at the head of at least twenty thousand troops of various nationalities to exterminate the entire Jewish race. With him Ptolemaeus associated Gorgias, a general of wide experience. Nicanor determined to pay off the 10 two thousand talents due from the king as tribute to the Romans, by the sale of the Jews he would take prisoner; and he at once made an offer of 11 Jewish slaves to the coastal towns, undertaking to deliver them at the price of ninety to the talent. But he did not expect the vengeance of the Almighty, which was soon to be at his heels.

Word of Nicanor's advance reached Judas, and he informed his men that 12 the enemy was at hand. The cowards who doubted God's justice took them- 13 selves off and fled. But the rest disposed of their remaining possessions, 14 and they prayed together to the Lord to save them from the impious Nicanor, who had sold them even before they met in battle; and if they 15 could not ask this for their own merits, they did so on the ground of the covenants God had made with their ancestors, and of his holy and majestic Name which they bore. Maccabaeus assembled his followers, six thousand 16 in number, and appealed to them not to flee in panic before the enemy nor to be afraid of the great host which was attacking them without just cause. Rather they should fight nobly, having before their eyes the wicked crimes 17 of the Gentiles against the temple, their callous outrage upon Jerusalem, and, further, their suppression of the traditional Jewish way of life. 'They 18 rely on their weapons and their audacity,' he said, 'but we rely on God Almighty, who is able to overthrow with a nod our present assailants and, if need be, the whole world.' He went on to recount to them the occasions 19 when God had helped their ancestors: how, in Sennacherib's time, one hundred and eighty-five thousand of the enemy had perished, and also how, 20 on the occasion of the battle against the Galatians in Babylonia, all the Jews engaged in the combat had numbered no more than eight thousand, with four thousand Macedonians, yet, when the Macedonians were hard pressed, the eight thousand through heaven's aid had destroyed one hundred and twenty thousand and taken much booty.

His words put them in good heart and made them ready to die for their 21 laws and for their country. He then divided the army into four and gave 22

---

*a Or His numerous force.*

each of his brothers, Simon, Josephus, and Jonathan, command of a
23 division of fifteen hundred men. Besides this, he appointed Eleazar to read
the holy book aloud,[a] and giving the signal for battle with the cry 'God is
our help', and taking command of the leading division in person, he
24 engaged Nicanor. The Almighty fought on their side, and they slaughtered
over nine thousand of the enemy, wounded and disabled the greater part of
25 Nicanor's forces, and routed them completely. They seized the money of
those who had come to buy them as slaves. After chasing the enemy a con-
26 siderable distance, they were forced to break off because it was late; for it
was the day before the sabbath, and for that reason they called off the pur-
27 suit. When they had collected the enemy's weapons and stripped the dead,
they turned to keep the sabbath. They offered thanks and praises loud and
long to the Lord who had kept the first drops of his mercy to shed on them
28 that day.[b] After the sabbath was over, they distributed some of the spoils
among the victims of persecution and the widows and orphans; the
29 remainder they divided among themselves. This done, all together made
supplication to the merciful Lord, praying him to be fully reconciled with
his servants.
30 The Jews now engaged the forces of Timotheus and Bacchides and
killed over twenty thousand of them. They gained complete control of
some high strongholds, and divided the immense booty, giving shares
equal to their own to the victims of persecution, to the widows and
31 orphans, and to the old men as well. They carefully collected all the
enemy's weapons and stored them at strategic points; the remainder of
32 the spoils they brought into Jerusalem. They killed the officer commanding
the forces of Timotheus, an utterly godless man who had caused the Jews
33 great suffering. During the victory celebrations in their capital, they burnt
alive the men who had set fire to the sacred gates, including Callisthenes,
who had taken refuge in a small house; he thus received the due reward of
his impiety.
34-35 Thus, by the Lord's help, Nicanor, that double-dyed villain who had
brought the thousand merchants to buy the Jewish captives, was humiliated
by the very people whom he despised above all others. He threw off his
magnificent uniform, and all alone like a runaway slave made his escape
through the interior, and was, indeed, very lucky to reach Antioch after
36 losing his whole army. So the man who had undertaken to secure tribute
for the Romans by taking prisoner the inhabitants of Jerusalem showed the
world that the Jews had a champion and were therefore invulnerable,
because they kept the laws he had given them.
9 It so happened that, about this time, Antiochus had returned in dis-
2 order from Persia. He had entered the city of Persepolis and attempted to
plunder its temples and assume control. But the populace rose and rushed
to arms in their defence, with the result that Antiochus was routed by
3 civilians and forced to beat a humiliating retreat. When he was near
Ecbatana, news reached him of what had happened to Nicanor and the

---

[a] Besides . . . aloud: *probable reading; Gk. obscure.*    [b] kept . . . day: *so some witnesses; others read* brought them safely to that day and had appointed it as the beginning of mercy for them.

forces of Timotheus. Transported with fury, he conceived the idea of 4
making the Jews pay for the injury inflicted by those who had put him to
flight, and so he ordered his charioteer to drive without stopping until the
journey was finished.

But riding with him was the divine judgement! For in his arrogance he
said: 'When I reach Jerusalem, I will make it a common graveyard for the
Jews.' But the all-seeing Lord, the God of Israel, struck him a fatal and 5
invisible blow. As soon as he had said the words, he was seized with
incurable pain in his bowels and with sharp internal torments—a punish- 6
ment entirely fitting for one who had inflicted many unheard-of torments
on the bowels of others. Still he did not in the least abate his insolence; 7
more arrogant than ever, he breathed fiery threats against the Jews. After
he had given orders to speed up the journey, it happened that he fell out
of his chariot as it hurtled along, and so violent was his fall that every joint
in his body was dislocated. He, who in his pretension to be more than man 8
had just been thinking that he could command the waves of the sea and
weigh high mountains on the scales, was brought to the ground and had
to be carried in a litter, thus making God's power*a* manifest to all. Worms 9
swarmed even from the eyes of this godless man and, while he was still
alive and in agony, his flesh rotted off, and the whole army was disgusted
by the stench of his decay. It was so unbearably offensive that nobody could 10
escort the man who only a short time before had seemed to touch the stars
in the sky.

In this broken state, Antiochus began to abate his great arrogance. 11
Under God's lash, and racked with continual pain, he began to see things
in their true light. He could not endure his own stench and said, 'It is right 12
to submit oneself to God and, being mortal, not to think oneself equal to
him.' Then the villain made a solemn promise to the Lord, who had no 13
intention of sparing him any longer, and it was to this effect: Jerusalem the 14
holy city, which he had been hurrying to level to the ground and to transform into a graveyard, he would now declare a free city; to all the Jews, 15
whom he had not considered worthy of burial but only fit to be thrown out
with their children as prey for birds and beasts, he would give privileges
equal to those enjoyed by the citizens of Athens. The holy temple which he 16
had earlier plundered he would adorn with the most splendid gifts; he
would replace all the sacred utensils on a much more lavish scale; he would
meet the cost of the sacrifices from his own revenues. In addition to all 17
this, he would even turn Jew and visit every inhabited place to proclaim
God's might.

When his pains in no way abated, because the just judgement of God 18
had fallen on him, he was in despair and, as a kind of olive branch, wrote to
the Jews the letter here copied:

To my worthy citizens, the Jews, warm greetings and good wishes 19
for their health and prosperity from Antiochus, King and Chief Magistrate.

May you and your children flourish and your affairs go as you wish. 20

---

*a Some witnesses read* litter. God made his power . . .

263

21 Having my hope in heaven, I keep an affectionate remembrance of your regards and goodwill.

As I was returning from Persia, I suffered a tiresome illness, and so I have judged it necessary to provide for the general safety of you all.
22 Not that I despair of my condition—on the contrary I have good hopes
23 of recovery—but I observed that my father, whenever he made an
24 expedition east of the Euphrates, appointed a successor, so that, if anything unexpected should happen or if some tiresome report should spread, his subjects would not be disturbed, since they would know to
25 whom the empire had been left. Further, I know well that the neighbouring princes on the frontiers of my kingdom are watching for an opportunity and waiting on events. So I have designated as king my son Antiochus, whom I frequently entrusted and recommended to most of you during my regular visits to the satrapies beyond the Euphrates. I
26 have written to him what is here copied. Wherefore I pray and entreat each one of you to maintain your existing goodwill towards myself and my son, remembering the services I have rendered to you both as a com-
27 munity and as individuals. For I am sure my son will follow my own policy of moderation and benevolence and will accommodate himself to your wishes.

28 Thus this murderer and blasphemer, suffering the worst of agonies, such as he had made others suffer, met a pitiable end in the mountains of a
29 foreign land. His body was brought back by Philip, his intimate friend; but he was afraid of Antiochus's son and went over to Ptolemy Philometor in Egypt.

**10** Maccabaeus with his men, led by the Lord, recovered the temple and
2 city of Jerusalem. He demolished the altars erected by the heathen in the
3 public square, and their sacred precincts as well. When they had purified the sanctuary, they constructed another altar; then, striking fire from flints, they offered a sacrifice for the first time for two whole years, and
4 restored the incense, the lights, and the Bread of the Presence. This done, they prostrated themselves and prayed the Lord not to let them fall any more into such disasters, but, should they ever happen to sin, to discipline them himself with clemency and not hand them over to blasphemous and
5 barbarous Gentiles. The sanctuary was purified on the twenty-fifth of Kislev, the same day of the same month as that on which foreigners had
6 profaned it. The joyful celebration lasted for eight days; it was like the Feast of Tabernacles, for they recalled how, only a short time before, they had kept that feast while they were living like wild animals in the mountains
7 and caves; and so they carried garlanded wands and branches with their fruits, as well as palm-fronds, and they chanted hymns to the One who had
8 so triumphantly achieved the purification of his own temple. A measure was passed by the public assembly to the effect that the entire Jewish race should keep these days every year.

## The campaign against Eupator

W E HAVE ALREADY RECOUNTED the end of Antiochus called 9
Epiphanes. Now we will describe what happened under that god- 10
less man's son, Antiochus Eupator, in a brief summary of the principal
evils brought about by his wars. At his accession, Eupator appointed as 11
vicegerent a man called Lysias who had succeeded Ptolemaeus Macron
as governor-general of Coele-syria and Phoenicia. For Ptolemaeus had 12
taken the lead in reversing the former unjust treatment of the Jews and had
attempted to maintain peaceful relations with them, and as a result he was 13
denounced by the King's Friends to Eupator. On every side he was called
traitor, because he had already abandoned Cyprus, entrusted to him by
Philometor, and had gone over to Antiochus Epiphanes. He still enjoyed
power, but no longer respect, and in despair he ended his life by poison.

When Gorgias became governor, he engaged mercenaries and took every 14
opportunity of attacking the Jews. At the same time the Idumaeans, who 15
were in control of strategic fortresses, were also harassing them; they
harboured the fugitives from Jerusalem and tried to carry on the war.
Maccabaeus and his men made public supplication and prayed God to 16
fight on their side. They made an assault on the Idumaean fortresses,
pressed the attack vigorously, and captured them; they drove off all who 17
were manning the walls, and killed all they met, to the number of at least
twenty thousand.

Nine thousand or more of the enemy took refuge in two towers, very 18
strongly fortified and fully equipped against a siege. Maccabaeus himself 19
set out for the places which were being hard pressed, but left Simon and
Josephus behind, with Zacchaeus and his men, enough to prosecute the
siege. But Simon's men were too fond of money, and when they were 20
bribed with seventy thousand drachmas by some of those in the towers,
they let them slip through their lines. When Maccabaeus was informed of 21
this, he assembled the leaders of the army and denounced these men for
having sold their brothers for money by letting their enemies escape. Then 22
he executed the men who had turned traitor, and immediately the two
towers fell to him. His military operations were completely successful; in 23
the two fortresses he destroyed over twenty thousand of the enemy.

After his previous defeat by the Jews, Timotheus collected a huge force 24
of mercenaries and Asian cavalry, and advanced to take Judaea by storm.
As he approached, Maccabaeus and his men made their prayer to God. 25
They sprinkled dust on their heads and put sackcloth round their waists;
they prostrated themselves on the altar-step and begged God to favour 26
them, 'to be an enemy of their enemies and an opponent of their opponents',
as the law clearly states.

When they had finished their prayer, they took up their weapons, 27
advanced a good distance from Jerusalem, and halted near the enemy. At 28
first light the two armies joined battle. For the Jews, success and victory
were guaranteed not only because of their bravery but even more because
the Lord was their refuge, whereas the Gentiles had only their own fury
to lead them into battle. As the fighting grew hot, the enemy saw in the sky 29

five magnificent figures riding horses with golden bridles, who placed
30 themselves at the head of the Jews, formed a circle round Maccabaeus, and
kept him invulnerable under the protection of their armour. They launched
arrows and thunderbolts at the enemy, who, confused and blinded, broke
31 up in complete disorder. Twenty thousand five hundred of the infantry,
as well as six hundred cavalry, were slaughtered.
32    Timotheus himself fled to a fortress called Gazara, commanded by
33 Chaereas and strongly garrisoned. Maccabaeus and his men welcomed this,
34 and for four days they laid siege to the place. The garrison, confident in the
strength of their position, hurled horrible and impious blasphemies at
35 them, until, at dawn on the fifth day, twenty young men from the force of
Maccabaeus, burning with rage at the blasphemy, courageously stormed
36 the wall and in savage anger cut down all they met. Under cover of this distraction others got up the same way, attacked the defenders, set light to the
towers, and started fires on which they burnt the blasphemers alive.
Others broke down the gates and let in the rest of the army, and thus the
37 city was occupied. Timotheus had hidden himself in a cistern, but he was
38 killed along with his brother Chaereas and Apollophanes. To celebrate
their achievement, the Jews praised with hymns and thanksgivings the
Lord who showers blessings on Israel and gives them the victory.

11    Very shortly afterwards, Lysias the vicegerent, the king's guardian and
2 relative, angered by these events, collected about eighty thousand troops,
in addition to his entire cavalry, and advanced on the Jews. He reckoned
3 on making Jerusalem a settlement for Gentiles, subjecting the temple to
taxation like all gentile shrines, and putting up the high-priesthood for sale
4 annually. He reckoned not at all with the might of God, but was elated with
his myriads of infantry, his thousands of cavalry, his eighty elephants.
5 Penetrating into Judaea, he approached Bethsura, a fortified place about
twenty miles from Jerusalem, and closely invested it.
6    When Maccabaeus and his men learnt that Lysias was besieging their
fortresses, they and all the people, wailing and weeping, prayed the Lord
7 to send a good angel to deliver Israel. Maccabaeus was the first to arm himself, and he urged the rest to share his danger and come to the help of their
8 brothers. One and all, they set out eagerly. They were still in the neighbourhood of Jerusalem when there appeared at their head a horseman arrayed
9 in white, brandishing his golden weapons. Then with one voice they
praised their merciful God and felt so strong in spirit that they could have
attacked not only men but also the most savage animals, and even walls of
10 iron. They came on fully armed, with their heavenly ally, under the mercy
11 of the Lord. They hurled themselves like lions against the enemy, cut
down eleven thousand of them, as well as sixteen hundred cavalry, and
12 put all the rest to flight. Most of those who escaped lost their weapons and
were wounded, and Lysias saved his life only by running away.
13    Lysias was no fool, and as he took stock of the defeat he had suffered
he realized that the Hebrews were invincible, because the mighty God
14 fought on their side. So he proposed a settlement on terms entirely acceptable, promising also to win the king over by putting pressure on him to
15 show friendship to the Jews. Maccabaeus agreed to all the proposals of

Lysias out of regard for the general welfare, for the king had accepted all the proposals from the Jewish side which Maccabaeus had forwarded to Lysias in writing.

The letter of Lysias to the Jews ran as follows:     16

Lysias to the Jewish community, greeting.

Your representatives John and Absalom have handed to me the docu- 17 ment here copied and have asked me to ratify what is contained in it. Whatever needed to be brought to the king's knowledge, I have communi- 18 cated to him, and what was within my own competence, I have granted. If, 19 therefore, you maintain your goodwill towards the empire, I for my part will endeavour to promote your welfare for the future. I have ordered your 20 representatives and mine to confer with you about the details. Farewell. 21

The twenty-fourth of Dioscorus in the year 148.*ᵃ*

The king's letter ran as follows:     22

King Antiochus to his brother Lysias, greeting.

Now that our royal father has gone to join the gods, we desire that our 23 subjects be undisturbed in the conduct of their own affairs. We have 24 learnt that the Jews do not consent to adopt Greek ways, as our father wished, but prefer their own mode of life and request that they be allowed to observe their own laws. We choose, therefore, that this nation 25 like the rest should be left undisturbed, and decree that their temple be restored to them and that they shall regulate their lives in accordance with their ancestral customs. Have the goodness, therefore, to inform 26 them of this and ratify it, so that, knowing what our intentions are, they may settle down confidently and quietly to manage their own affairs.

To the people the king's letter ran thus:     27

King Antiochus to the Jewish Senate and people, greeting.

We hope that you prosper. We too are in good health. Menelaus has 28 29 informed us of your desire to return to your own homes. Therefore we 30 declare an amnesty for all who return before the thirtieth of Xanthicus. The Jews may follow their own food-laws as heretofore, and none of them 31 shall be charged with any previous infringement. I am sending Menelaus 32 to reassure you. Farewell. 33

The fifteenth of Xanthicus in the year 148.*ᵃ*

The Romans also sent the Jews the following letter:     34

Quintus Memmius and Titus Manius, Roman legates, to the Jewish people, greeting.

We give our assent to all that Lysias, the king's relative, has granted 35 you. But examine carefully the questions which he reserved for reference 36 to the king; then send someone immediately, so that we may make suit- able proposals, for we are proceeding to Antioch. Send messengers 37 therefore without delay, so that we also may know what your opinion is. Farewell. 38

The fifteenth of Xanthicus in the year 148.*ᵃ*

---

*ᵃ That is* 164 B.C.

**12** When these agreements had been concluded, Lysias went off to the king,
2 and the Jews returned to their farming. But some of the governors in the
region, Timotheus and Apollonius son of Gennaeus and also Hieronymus
and Demophon, and in addition Nicanor, chief of the Cypriot mercenaries,
would not allow them to enjoy security and live in quiet.

3 I MUST NOW DESCRIBE an atrocity committed by the inhabitants of
Joppa. They invited the Jews living in the town to embark with their wives
and children in boats which they provided, with no indication of any ill
4 will towards them. As it was a public decision by the whole town, and
because they wished to live in peace and suspected nothing, they accepted;
but when they were out at sea, the people of Joppa sank the boats, drowning
5 no fewer than two hundred of them. When Judas learnt of this brutal
6 treatment of his fellow-countrymen, he alerted his troops, invoked God,
the just judge, and fell upon their murderers. He set the harbour of Joppa
on fire by night, burnt the shipping, and put to the sword those who had
7 taken refuge there. But finding the town gates closed, he withdrew, mean-
8 ing however to return and root out the entire community. When he learnt
that the people of Jamnia intended to do the same to the Jews who lived
9 among them, he attacked Jamnia by night and set fire to its harbour and
fleet; the light of the flames was visible in Jerusalem thirty miles away.
10 When they had marched more than a mile further in their advance
against Timotheus, they were set upon by not less than five thousand Arabs,
11 with five hundred cavalry. A violent combat ensued, in which by divine
help Judas and his men were victorious. The defeated nomads begged
Judas to make an alliance with them, and promised to supply him with
12 cattle and to give the Jews every other kind of help. Judas realized that they
could indeed be useful in many ways; so he agreed to make peace with
them, and, after receiving assurances from him, they went back to their
tents.
13 Judas also attacked Caspin, a walled town, strongly fortified and
14 inhabited by a motley crew of Gentiles. Confident in the strength of their
walls and in their store of provisions, the defenders behaved provocatively
towards Judas and his men, abusing them and also uttering the most
15 wicked blasphemies. But they invoked the world's great Sovereign who in
the days of Joshua threw down the walls of Jericho without battering-rams
16 or siege-engines. They attacked the wall fiercely and, by the will of God,
captured the town. The carnage was indescribable; the adjacent lake, a
quarter of a mile wide, appeared to be overflowing with blood.
17 Advancing about ninety-five miles from there, they reached Charax,
18 which is inhabited by the Tubian Jews, as they are called. They did not
find Timotheus there; he had by that time left the district, having had no
success, but in one place he had left behind an extremely strong garrison.
19 Dositheus and Sosipater, Maccabaeus's generals, set out and destroyed
20 the garrison, which consisted of over ten thousand men. Maccabaeus for
his part grouped his army in several divisions, appointed commanders for
them,[a] and hurried after Timotheus, whose forces numbered a hundred

---

[a] *Probable meaning, based on one Vs.; Gk.* appointed them to command the divisions.

and twenty thousand infantry and two thousand five hundred cavalry. When he learnt of Judas's approach, Timotheus sent off the women and 21 children with all the baggage to a town called Carnaim, this being an inaccessible place, hard to storm because all the approaches to it were narrow. But when Judas's first division appeared, terror and panic seized the enemy 22 at the manifestation of the all-seeing One. In their flight they rushed headlong in every direction, so that frequently they were injured by their comrades and were run through by the points of their swords. Judas pressed 23 the pursuit vigorously and put thirty thousand of these criminals to the sword. Timotheus himself was taken prisoner by the troops of Dositheus 24 and Sosipater. With much cunning, he begged them to let him go in safety, pointing out that most of them had parents, and some of them brothers, who were in his hands, and might never be heard of again. He pledged him- 25 self over and over again to restore these hostages safe and sound; and so they let him go in order to save their relatives.

Judas moved on Carnaim and the sanctuary of Atargatis, and killed 26 twenty-five thousand people there. After this victory and destruction he 27 next marched on Ephron, a fortified town inhabited by a mixed population.[a] Stalwart young men took up their position in front of the walls and fought vigorously, while inside there was a great supply of engines of war and ammunition. But the Jews invoked the Sovereign whose might 28 shatters all the strength of the enemy. They made themselves masters of the town and killed twenty-five thousand of the defenders. Leaving that 29 place, they advanced to Scythopolis, some seventy-five miles from Jerusalem. The Jews who lived there testified to the goodwill shown them by 30 the people of Scythopolis and the kindness with which they had treated them in their bad times; so Judas and his men thanked them, and charged 31 them to be equally friendly to the Jewish race for the future. They returned to Jerusalem in time for the Feast of Weeks.

After celebrating Pentecost, as it is called, they advanced to attack 32 Gorgias, the general in charge of Idumaea, who met them with three 33 thousand infantry and four hundred cavalry. When the ranks joined battle, 34 a small number of the Jews fell. But a cavalryman of great strength called 35 Dositheus, one of the Tubian Jews, had hold of Gorgias by his cloak and was dragging the villain off by main force, with the object of taking him alive, when a Thracian horseman bore down on him and chopped off his arm; so Gorgias escaped to Marisa.

Esdrias and his men had been fighting for a long time and were exhausted. 36 But Judas invoked the Lord to show himself their ally and leader in battle. Striking up hymns in his native language as a battle-cry, he put the forces 37 of Gorgias to flight by a surprise attack.

Regrouping his forces, he led them to the town of Adullam. The seventh 38 day was coming on, so they purified themselves, as custom dictated, and kept the sabbath there. Next day they went, as had by now become neces- 39 sary, to collect the bodies of the fallen in order to bury them with their relatives in the ancestral graves. But on every one of the dead, they found, 40 under the tunic, amulets sacred to the idols of Jamnia, objects which the law

[a] *Some witnesses add* where Lysias had his headquarters.

forbids to Jews. It was evident to all that here was the reason why these
41 men had fallen. Therefore they praised the work of the Lord, the just
42 judge, who reveals what is hidden; and, turning to prayer, they asked that
this sin might be entirely blotted out. The noble Judas called on the people
to keep themselves free from sin, for they had seen with their own eyes
43 what had happened to the fallen because of their sin. He levied a contribution from each man, and sent the total of two thousand silver drachmas
to Jerusalem for a sin-offering—a fit and proper act in which he took due
44 account of the resurrection. For if he had not been expecting the fallen to
rise again, it would have been foolish and superfluous to pray for the dead.
45 But since he had in view the wonderful reward reserved for those who die
a godly death, his purpose was a holy and pious one. And this was why he
offered an atoning sacrifice to free the dead from their sin.

13   In the year 149,[a] information reached Judas and his men that Antiochus
2 Eupator was advancing on Judaea with a large army; he was accompanied
by Lysias, his guardian and vicegerent, bringing in addition a Greek force,
consisting of one hundred and ten thousand infantry, five thousand three
hundred cavalry, twenty-two elephants, and three hundred chariots armed
with scythes.
3   Menelaus also joined them and urged Antiochus on; this he did most
disingenuously, not for his country's good, but because he believed he
4 would be maintained in office. However, the King of kings aroused the
rage of Antiochus against Menelaus: Lysias produced evidence that this
criminal was responsible for all Antiochus's troubles, and so the king
ordered him to be taken to Beroea and there to be executed in the manner
5 customary at that place. Now in Beroea there is a tower some seventy-five
feet[b] high, filled with ashes; it has a circular device sloping down sheer on
6 all sides into the ashes. This is where the citizens take anyone guilty of
7 sacrilege or any other notorious crime, and thrust him to his doom; and
such was the fate of the law-breaker Menelaus, who was not even allowed
8 burial—a fate he richly deserved. Many a time he had desecrated the
hallowed ashes of the altar-fire, and by ashes he met his death.
9   So the king came on with the barbarous intention of inflicting on the
10 Jews sufferings far worse than his father had inflicted. When Judas heard
this he ordered the people to invoke the Lord day and night and pray that
now more than ever he would come to their aid, since they were on the
11 point of losing law, country, and temple; and that he would not allow
them, just when they had begun to breathe again, to fall into the hands of
12 blaspheming Gentiles. They all obeyed his orders: for three days without
respite they prayed to their merciful Lord, they wailed, they fasted, they
prostrated themselves. Then Judas urged them to action and called upon
them to stand by him.
13   After holding a council of war with the elders, he decided not to wait until
the royal army invaded Judaea and took Jerusalem, but to march out and
14 with God's help to bring things to a decision. He entrusted the outcome to
the Creator of the world; his troops he charged to fight bravely to the
death for the law, for the temple and for Jerusalem, for their country and

*a* *That is* 163 B.C.        *b* some . . . feet: *Gk.* fifty cubits.

270

their way of life. He pitched camp near Modin, and giving his men the 15
signal for battle with the cry 'God's victory!', he made a night attack on
the royal pavilion with a picked force of the bravest young men. He killed
as many as two thousand in the enemy camp, and his men stabbed to death[a]
the leading elephant and its driver. In the end they reduced the whole 16
camp to panic and confusion, and withdrew victorious. It was all over by 17
daybreak, through the help and protection which Judas had received from
the Lord.

Now that he had had a taste of Jewish daring, the king tried stratagems 18
in attacking their strong-points. He advanced on Bethsura, one of their 19
powerful forts; he was repulsed; he attacked, he was beaten. Judas sent in 20
supplies to the garrison, but a soldier in the Jewish ranks, Rhodocus by 21
name, betrayed their secrets to the enemy. However, he was tracked down,
arrested, and put away. The king parleyed for the second time with the 22
inhabitants of Bethsura, and, when he had given and received guarantees,
he withdrew; he then attacked Judas and his men, but had the worst of it.
He now received news that Philip, whom he had left in charge of state 23
affairs in Antioch, had gone out of his mind. In dismay he summoned the
Jews, agreed to their terms, took an oath to respect all their rights, and,
after this settlement, offered a sacrifice, paid honour to the sanctuary and
its precincts, and received Maccabaeus graciously. He left behind Hege- 24
monides as governor of the region from Ptolemais to Gerra, and went him- 25
self to Ptolemais. Its inhabitants were furious at the treaty he had made,
and in their alarm wanted to repudiate it. Lysias mounted the rostrum, 26
made the best defence he could, won the people over, calmed them down,
and, having thus gained their support, left for Antioch.

Such was the course of the king's offensive and retreat.

## The victory of Maccabaeus over Nicanor

AFTER AN INTERVAL of three years, information reached Judas and 14
his men that Demetrius son of Seleucus had sailed into the harbour
of Tripolis with a powerful army and fleet, and, after disposing of Antio- 2
chus and his guardian Lysias, had taken possession of the country.

There was a man called Alcimus, who had formerly been high priest 3
but had submitted voluntarily to pollutions at the time of the secession.
This man, realizing that there was not now the slightest guarantee of his
safety, or any possibility of access to the holy altar, came to King Demetrius, 4
about the year 151,[b] and presented him with a gold crown and palm, and
also some of the customary olive branches from the temple. On that particular occasion he kept quiet; but he found a chance of forwarding his own 5
mad scheme when Demetrius summoned him to his council and questioned
him about the attitude and plans of the Jews. He replied: 'Those of the 6
Jews who are called Hasidaeans and are led by Judas Maccabaeus are keeping the war alive and fomenting sedition, refusing to leave the kingdom in
peace. Thus, although I have been deprived of my hereditary dignity—I 7

---

[a] stabbed to death: *probable reading, based on one Vs.*          [b] *That is* 161 B.C.

8 mean the high-priesthood—I am here today from two motives: first, a genuine concern for the king's rights; and secondly, a regard for my fellow-citizens, since our whole race is suffering considerable hardship as
9 a result of the folly of the people I have just mentioned. I would advise your majesty to acquaint yourself with every one of these matters and then make provision for our country and our beleaguered nation, as befits your
10 universal kindness and goodwill. For the empire will enjoy no peace so long as Judas remains alive.'
11   When he had spoken to this effect, the other Friends, who were hostile
12 to Judas, immediately inflamed Demetrius still more. The king at once selected Nicanor, commander of the elephant corps, gave him command
13 of Judaea, and sent him off with a commission to dispose of Judas himself and disperse his forces, and to install Alcimus as high priest of the great
14 temple. The gentile population of Judaea, refugees from the attacks of Judas, now flocked to Nicanor, thinking that defeat and misfortune for the Jews would mean prosperity for themselves.
15   When they learnt of Nicanor's offensive and the gentile attack, the Jews sprinkled dust over themselves and prayed to the One who established his people for ever, who never fails to manifest himself when his chosen are in
16 need of help. At their leader's command, they immediately struck camp
17 and joined battle with the enemy at the village of Adasa.*a* Simon, the brother of Judas, had fought an engagement with Nicanor, but, because
18 the enemy came up*b* unexpectedly, he had suffered a slight reverse. In spite of this, when Nicanor learnt how brave Judas and his troops were and how courageously they fought for their country, he shrank from
19 deciding the issue in battle. So he sent Posidonius, Theodotus, and Mattathias to negotiate a settlement.
20   After a lengthy consideration of the proposals, Judas informed his men
21 of them; they were unanimous in agreeing to make peace. A day was fixed for a private meeting of the leaders. A chariot advanced from each of the
22 two lines, and seats were placed for them; but Judas posted armed men at strategic points ready to deal with any unforeseen treachery on the enemy's
23 part. The discussion between the two leaders was harmonious. Nicanor stayed some time in Jerusalem and behaved correctly; he dismissed the
24 crowds that had flocked round him, and kept Judas always close to himself.
25 He had acquired a real affection for him, and urged him to marry and start a family. So Judas married and settled down to the quiet life of an ordinary citizen.
26   Alcimus noticed their friendliness and got hold of a copy of the agreement they had concluded. He went to Demetrius and said that Nicanor was pursuing a policy detrimental to the interests of the empire, by ap-
27 pointing that traitor Judas King's Friend designate. The king was furious and was provoked by these villainous slanders to write to Nicanor expressing his dissatisfaction with the agreement and ordering him to arrest
28 Maccabaeus and send him at once to Antioch. This message filled Nicanor with dismay; he took it hard that he should have to break his agreement

*a* Adasa: *probable reading; compare 1 Macc. 7. 40.*    *b* came up: *probable reading, based on one Vs.*

although the man had committed no offence, but since there was no going 29
against the king, he watched for a favourable opportunity of carrying out
the order by means of some stratagem. Maccabaeus, however, observed 30
that Nicanor had become less friendly towards him and no longer showed
him the same civility. He realized that this unfriendliness boded no good,
so he collected a large number of his followers and went into hiding from
Nicanor.

When Nicanor recognized that he had been outmanœuvred by the 31
resolute action of Judas, he went to the great and holy temple at the time
when the priests were offering the regular sacrifices, and ordered them to
surrender Judas to him. The priests declared on oath that they did not 32
know the whereabouts of the wanted man. But Nicanor stretched out his 33
right hand towards the shrine and swore this oath: 'Unless you surrender
Judas into my custody, I will raze God's sanctuary to the ground, I will
destroy the altar, and on this spot I will build a temple to Dionysus for all
the world to see.' With these words he left; but the priests with out- 34
stretched hands prayed to Heaven, the constant champion of our race:
'Lord, thou hast no need of anything in the world, yet it was thy pleasure 35
that among us there should be a shrine for thy dwelling-place. Now, Lord, 36
who alone art holy, keep this house, so newly purified, for ever free from
defilement.'

A man called Razis, a member of the Jerusalem senate, was denounced 37
to Nicanor. He was very highly spoken of, a patriot who for his loyalty was
known as 'Father of the Jews'. In the early days of the secession he had 38
stood his trial for practising Judaism, and with the utmost eagerness had
risked life and limb for that cause. Nicanor wished to give clear proof of 39
his hostility towards the Jews, and sent more than five hundred soldiers to
arrest Razis; he reckoned that his arrest would be a severe blow to the Jews. 40
The troops were on the point of capturing the tower where Razis was, 41
and were trying to force the outer door. Then an order was given to set the
door on fire, and Razis, hemmed in on all sides, turned his sword on himself. He preferred to die nobly rather than fall into the hands of criminals 42
and be subjected to gross humiliation. In his haste and anxiety he mis- 43
judged the blow, and with the troops pouring through the doors he ran
without hesitation on to the wall and heroically threw himself down into the
crowd. The crowd hurriedly gave way and he fell in the space they left. 44
He was still breathing, still on fire with courage; so, streaming with blood 45
and severely wounded, he picked himself up and dashed through the
crowd. Finally, standing on a sheer rock, and now completely drained of 46
blood, he took his entrails in both hands and flung them at the crowd. And
thus, invoking the Lord of life and breath to give these entrails back to him
again, he died.

Nicanor received information that Judas and his men were in the region **15**
of Samaria, and he determined to attack them on their day of rest, when it
could be done without any danger. Those Jews who were forced to ac- 2
company his army said, 'Do not carry out such a savage and barbarous
massacre, but respect the day singled out and made holy by the all-seeing
One.' The double-dyed villain retorted, 'Is there a ruler in the sky who has 3

4 ordered the sabbath day to be observed?' The Jews declared, 'The living Lord himself is ruler in the sky, and he ordered the seventh day to be kept
5 holy.' 'But I', replied Nicanor, 'am a ruler on earth, and I order you to take your arms and do your duty to the king.' However, he did not succeed in carrying out his cruel plan.
6   Now Nicanor, in his pretentious and extravagant conceit, had resolved
7 upon erecting a public trophy from the spoils of Judas's forces. But Maccabaeus's confidence never wavered, and he had not the least doubt that he
8 would obtain help from the Lord. He urged his men not to be afraid of the gentile attack, but to bear in mind the aid they had received from heaven in the past and so look to the Almighty for the victory which he would send
9 this time also. He drew encouragement for them from the law and the prophets and, by reminding them of the struggles they had already come
10 through, filled them with a fresh enthusiasm. When he had roused their courage, he gave them their orders, reminding them at the same time of the
11 Gentiles' broken faith and perjury. He armed each one of them, not so much with the security of shield and spear, as with the encouragement that brave words bring; and he also told them of a trustworthy dream he had had, a sort of waking vision, which put them all in good heart.
12   What he had seen was this: the former high priest Onias appeared to him, that great gentleman of modest bearing and mild disposition, apt speaker, and exponent from childhood of the good life. With outstretched
13 hands he was praying earnestly for the whole Jewish community. Next there appeared in the same attitude a figure of great age and dignity, whose wonderful air of authority marked him as a man of the utmost distinction.
14 Then Onias said, 'This is God's prophet Jeremiah, who loves his fellow-
15 Jews and offers many prayers for our people and for the holy city.' Jeremiah extended his right hand and delivered to Judas a golden sword, saying as
16 he did so, 'Take this holy sword, the gift of God, and with it crush your enemies.'
17   The eloquent words of Judas had the power of stimulating everyone to bravery and making men out of boys. Encouraged by them, the Jews made up their minds not to remain in camp, but to take the offensive manfully and fight hand to hand with all their strength until the issue was decided. This they did because Jerusalem, their religion, and their temple were in
18 danger. Their fear was not chiefly for their wives and children, not to mention brothers and relatives, but first and foremost for the sacred shrine.
19 The distress of those shut up in Jerusalem was no less, for they were anxious at the prospect of a battle on open ground.
20   All were waiting for the decisive struggle which lay ahead. The enemy had already concentrated his forces; his army was drawn up in order of battle, the elephants stationed in a favourable position and the cavalry
21 ranged on the flank. When Maccabaeus observed the deployment of the troops, the variety of their equipment, and the ferocity of the elephants, with hands upraised he invoked the Lord, the worker of miracles; for he knew that God grants victory to those who deserve it, not because of their
22 military strength but as he himself decides. This was his prayer: 'Master, thou didst send thy angel in the days of Hezekiah king of Judah, and he

killed as many as a hundred and eighty-five thousand men in Sennacherib's
camp. Now, Ruler of heaven, send once again a good angel to go in front 23
of us spreading fear and panic. May they be struck down by thy strong 24
arm, these blasphemers who are coming to attack thy holy people!' Thus
he ended.

Nicanor and his forces advanced with trumpets and war-songs, but Judas 25 26
and his men joined battle with invocations and prayers. Fighting with their 27
hands and praying to God in their hearts, they killed no fewer than thirty-
five thousand men, and were greatly cheered by the divine intervention.

The action was over, and they were joyfully disbanding, when they recog- 28
nized Nicanor lying dead in his armour. Then with tumultuous shouts they 29
praised their Master in their native language. Judas their leader, who had 30
always fought body and soul on behalf of his fellow-Jews, never losing his
youthful patriotism, now ordered Nicanor's head to be cut off, also his
hand and arm, and taken to Jerusalem. On arrival there he summoned all 31
the people and stationed the priests before the altar. Then he sent for the
men in the citadel, and showed them the head of the blackguardly Nicanor 32
and the hand which this bragging blasphemer had extended against the
Almighty's holy temple. He cut out the tongue of the impious Nicanor, and 33
said he would give it to the birds bit by bit; and he gave orders that the
evidence of what Nicanor's folly had brought upon him should be hung up
opposite the shrine. They all made the sky ring with the praises of the Lord 34
who had shown his power: 'Praise to him who has preserved his own
sanctuary from defilement!' Judas hung Nicanor's head from the citadel, 35
a clear proof of the Lord's help, for all to see. It was unanimously decreed 36
that this day should never pass unnoticed but be regularly celebrated. It
is the thirteenth of the twelfth month, called Adar in Aramaic, the day
before Mordecai's Day. Such, then, was the fate of Nicanor, and from that 37
time Jerusalem has remained in the possession of the Hebrews.

AT THIS POINT I will bring my work to an end. If it is found well written 38
and aptly composed, that is what I myself hoped for; if cheap and mediocre,
I could only do my best. For, just as it is disagreeable to drink wine alone 39
or water alone, whereas the mixing of the two gives a pleasant and delightful taste, so too variety of style in a literary work charms the ear of the
reader. Let this then be my final word.

# THE NEW
# ENGLISH BIBLE

## THE NEW TESTAMENT

# CONTENTS

# INTRODUCTION

## TO THE NEW TESTAMENT

THIS TRANSLATION of the New Testament was undertaken with the object of providing English readers, whether familiar with the Bible or not, with a faithful rendering of the best available Greek text into the current speech of our own time, and a rendering which should harvest the gains of recent biblical scholarship.

It is now some three centuries and a half since King James's men put out what we have come to know as the Authorized Version. Two hundred and seventy years later the New Testament was revised. The Revised Version of the New Testament, which appeared in 1881, marked a new departure especially in that it abandoned the so-called Received Text, which had reigned ever since printed editions of the New Testament began, but which the advance of textual criticism had antiquated. The Revisers no longer followed (as their predecessors had done) the text of the majority of manuscripts, which, being for the most part of late date, had been exposed not only to the accidental corruptions of long-continued copying, but also in part to deliberate correction and 'improvement'. Instead, they followed a very small group of manuscripts, the earliest, and in their judgement the best, of those which had survived. During the years which have passed since their time, textual criticism has not stood still. Manuscripts have been discovered of substantially earlier date than any which the Revisers knew. Other important sources of evidence have been either freshly discovered or made more fully available. Meanwhile the methods of textual criticism have themselves been refined and estimates of the value of particular manuscripts have sometimes been reconsidered. The problem of restoring a form of text as near as possible to the vanished autographs now appears less simple than it did to our predecessors. There is not at the present time any critical text which would command the same degree of general acceptance as the Revisers' text did in its day. Nor has the time come, in the judgement of most scholars, to construct such a text, since new material constantly comes to light, and the debate continues. The present translators therefore could do no other than consider variant readings on their merits, and, having weighed the evidence for themselves, select for translation in each passage the reading which to the best of their judgement seemed most likely to represent what the author wrote. Where other readings seemed to deserve serious consideration they have been recorded in footnotes. In assessing the evidence, the translators have taken into account (a) ancient manuscripts of the New Testament in Greek, (b) manuscripts of early translations into other languages, and (c) quotations from the New Testament by early Christian writers. These three sources of evidence are collectively referred to as 'witnesses'. A large number of variants, however, are such as could make no appreciable difference to the meaning so far as it could be represented in translation, and these have been passed over in silence. The translators are well aware that their judgement is at best provisional, but they believe the text they have followed to be an improvement on that underlying the earlier translations. This text can now be read in *The Greek New Testament*, edited by R. V. G. Tasker (Oxford and Cambridge University Presses, 1964).

So much for the text. The next step was the effort to understand the original as accurately as possible, as a preliminary to turning it into English. The Revisers of 1881 believed that a better knowledge of the Greek language made it possible to correct a number of mistranslations in the older version, though in doing so they were somewhat limited by the instruction 'to introduce as few alterations as possible . . . consistently with faithfulness'. Since their time the study of the Greek language has no more stood still than has textual criticism. In particular, our knowledge of the kind of Greek used by most of the New Testament writers has been greatly enriched since 1881 by the discovery of many thousands of papyrus documents in popular or non-literary Greek of about the same period as the New Testament. It would be wrong to suggest that they lead to any far-reaching change in our understanding of the Greek of the New Testament period, but they have often made possible a better appreciation of the finer shades of idiom, which sometimes clarifies the meaning of passages in the New Testament. Its language is indeed in many respects more flexible and easy-going than the Revisers were ready to allow, and invites the translator to use a larger freedom.

Our task, however, differed in an important respect from that of the Revisers of 1881. They were instructed not only to introduce as few alterations as possible, but also 'to limit, as far as possible, the expression of such alterations to the language of the Authorised and earlier English Versions'. The present translators were subject to no such limitation. In accordance with the original decision of the Joint Committee they were to make the attempt to use consistently the idiom of contemporary English to convey the meaning of the Greek.

The older translators, on the whole, considered that fidelity to the original demanded that they should reproduce, as far as possible, characteristic features of the language in which it was written, such as the syntactical order of words, the structure and division of sentences, and even such irregularities of grammar as were indeed natural enough to authors writing in the easy idiom of popular Hellenistic Greek, but less natural when turned into English. The present translators were enjoined to replace Greek constructions and idioms by those of contemporary English.

This meant a different theory and practice of translation, and one which laid a heavier burden on the translators. Fidelity in translation was not to mean keeping the general framework of the original intact while replacing Greek words by English words more or less equivalent. A word, indeed, in one language is seldom the exact equivalent of a word in a different language. Each word is the centre of a whole cluster of meanings and associations, and in different languages these clusters overlap but do not often coincide. The place of a word in the clause or sentence, or even in a larger unit of thought, will determine what aspect of its total meaning is in the foreground. The translator can hardly hope to convey in another language every shade of meaning that attaches to the word in the original, but if he is free to exploit a wide range of English words covering a similar area of meaning and association he may hope to carry over the meaning of the sentence as a whole. Thus we have not felt obliged (as did the Revisers of 1881) to make an effort to render the same Greek word everywhere by the same English word. We have in this respect returned to the wholesome practice of King James's men, who (as they expressly state in their preface) recognized no such obligation.

We have conceived our task to be that of understanding the original as precisely as we could (using all available aids), and then saying again in our own native idiom what we believed the author to be saying in his. We have found that in practice this frequently compelled us to make decisions where the older method of translation allowed a comfortable ambiguity. In such places we have been aware that we take a risk, but we have thought it our duty to take the risk rather than remain on the fence.

In doing our work, we have constantly striven to follow our instructions and render the Greek, as we understood it, into the English of the present day, that is, into the natural vocabulary, constructions, and rhythms of contemporary speech. We have sought to avoid archaism, jargon, and all that is either stilted or slipshod.

It should be said that our intention has been to offer a translation in the strict sense, and not a paraphrase, and we have not wished to encroach on the field of the commentator. But if the best commentary is a good translation, it is also true that every intelligent translation is in a sense a paraphrase. The line between translation and paraphrase is a fine one. But we have had recourse to deliberate paraphrase with great caution, and only in a few passages where without it we could see no way to attain our aim of making the meaning as clear as it could be made. Taken as a whole, our version claims to be a translation, free, it may be, rather than literal, but a faithful translation nevertheless, so far as we could compass it.

For this edition, the translation of the New Testament has been given a careful revision, in which account has been taken of numerous criticisms and suggestions which have come in from various quarters. It is hoped that the modifications introduced, mostly in minor details and seldom reflecting any substantial change of view about the meaning of a passage, will be found to be in the direction of improvement.

In the course of revision, consideration has been given to passages from the Old Testament quoted in the New. These have now been harmonized with the present version of the Old Testament, where this seemed desirable, and practicable. But the quotations are in Greek, and the Greek is by no means always an exact equivalent of the Hebrew. Where it is not, we have deemed it our duty to render the Greek as it lay before us, and not to attempt to reproduce the underlying Hebrew. On this point there has been consultation between representatives of the Old and the New Testament panels.

The translators are as conscious as anyone can be of the limitations and imperfections of their work. No one who has not tried it can know how impossible an art translation is. Only those who have meditated long upon the Greek original are aware of the richness and subtlety of meaning that may lie even within the most apparently simple sentence, or know the despair that attends all efforts to bring it out through the medium of a different language. Yet we may hope that we have been able to convey to our readers something at least of what the New Testament has said to us during these years of work, and trust that under the providence of Almighty God this translation may open the truth of the Scriptures to many who have been hindered in their approach to it by barriers of language.

C. H. D.

# MARGINAL NUMBERS

THE conventional verse divisions in the New Testament date only from 1551 and have no basis in the manuscripts. Any system of division into numbered verses is foreign to the spirit of this translation, which is intended to convey the meaning in continuous natural English rather than to correspond sentence by sentence with the Greek.

For purposes of reference, and of comparison with other translations, verse numbers are placed in the margin opposite the line in which the first word belonging to the verse in question appears. Sometimes, however, successive verses are combined in a continuous English sentence, so that the precise point where a new verse begins cannot be fixed; occasionally in the interests of clarity the order of successive verses is reversed (e.g. at John 4. 7, 8).

# THE GOSPEL

# THE GOSPEL ACCORDING TO
# MATTHEW

### *The coming of Christ*

A TABLE OF THE DESCENT of Jesus Christ, son of David, 1
son of Abraham.
    Abraham was the father of Isaac, Isaac of Jacob, Jacob of Judah 2
and his brothers, Judah of Perez and Zarah (their mother was Tamar), 3
Perez of Hezron, Hezron of Ram, Ram of Amminadab, Amminadab of 4
Nahshon, Nahshon of Salma, Salma of Boaz (his mother was Rahab), 5
Boaz of Obed (his mother was Ruth), Obed of Jesse; and Jesse was the 6
father of King David.
    David was the father of Solomon (his mother had been the wife of
Uriah), Solomon of Rehoboam, Rehoboam of Abijah, Abijah of Asa, 7
Asa of Jehoshaphat, Jehoshaphat of Joram, Joram of Azariah, Azariah of 8 9
Jotham, Jotham of Ahaz, Ahaz of Hezekiah, Hezekiah of Manasseh, 10
Manasseh of Amon, Amon of Josiah; and Josiah was the father of Jeconiah 11
and his brothers at the time of the deportation to Babylon.
    After the deportation Jeconiah was the father of Shealtiel, Shealtiel of 12
Zerubbabel, Zerubbabel of Abiud, Abiud of Eliakim, Eliakim of Azor, 13
Azor of Zadok, Zadok of Achim, Achim of Eliud, Eliud of Eleazar, Eleazar 14 15
of Matthan, Matthan of Jacob, Jacob of Joseph, the husband of Mary, who 16
gave birth to*a* Jesus called Messiah.
    There were thus fourteen generations in all from Abraham to David, 17
fourteen from David until the deportation to Babylon, and fourteen from
the deportation until the Messiah.

THIS IS THE STORY of the birth of the Messiah. Mary his mother was 18
betrothed to Joseph; before their marriage she found that she was with
child by the Holy Spirit. Being a man of principle, and at the same time 19
wanting to save her from exposure, Joseph desired to have the marriage
contract set aside quietly. He had resolved on this, when an angel of the 20
Lord appeared to him in a dream. 'Joseph son of David,' said the angel,
'do not be afraid to take Mary home with you as your wife. It is by the
Holy Spirit that she has conceived this child. She will bear a son; and you 21
shall give him the name Jesus (Saviour), for he will save his people from
their sins.' All this happened in order to fulfil what the Lord declared 22
through the prophet: 'The virgin will conceive and bear a son, and he 23

---

*a Some witnesses read* Joseph, to whom was betrothed Mary, a virgin, who gave birth
to . . .; *one witness has* Joseph, and Joseph, to whom Mary, a virgin, was betrothed, was
the father of . . .

24 shall be called Emmanuel', a name which means 'God is with us'. Rising from sleep Joseph did as the angel had directed him; he took Mary home
25 to be his wife, but had no intercourse with her until her son was born. And he named the child Jesus.

2 JESUS WAS BORN at Bethlehem in Judaea during the reign of Herod.
2 After his birth astrologers from the east arrived in Jerusalem, asking, 'Where is the child who is born to be king of the Jews?*a* We observed the rising of
3 his star, and we have come to pay him homage.' King Herod was greatly
4 perturbed when he heard this; and so was the whole of Jerusalem. He called a meeting of the chief priests and lawyers of the Jewish people, and put before them the question: 'Where is it that the Messiah is to be born?'
5 'At Bethlehem in Judaea', they replied; and they referred him to the
6 prophecy which reads: 'Bethlehem in the land of Judah, you are far from least in the eyes of*b* the rulers of Judah; for out of you shall come a leader to be the shepherd of my people Israel.'
7     Herod next called the astrologers to meet him in private, and ascertained
8 from them the time when the star had appeared. He then sent them on to Bethlehem, and said, 'Go and make a careful inquiry for the child. When you have found him, report to me, so that I may go myself and pay him homage.'
9     They set out at the king's bidding; and the star which they had seen at its rising went ahead of them until it stopped above the place where the
10 11 child lay. At the sight of the star they were overjoyed. Entering the house, they saw the child with Mary his mother, and bowed to the ground in homage to him; then they opened their treasures and offered him gifts:
12 gold, frankincense, and myrrh. And being warned in a dream not to go back to Herod, they returned home another way.
13     After they had gone, an angel of the Lord appeared to Joseph in a dream, and said to him, 'Rise up, take the child and his mother and escape with them to Egypt, and stay there until I tell you; for Herod
14 is going to search for the child to do away with him.' So Joseph rose from sleep, and taking mother and child by night he went away with
15 them to Egypt, and there he stayed till Herod's death. This was to fulfil what the Lord had declared through the prophet: 'I called my son out of Egypt.'
16     When Herod saw how the astrologers had tricked him he fell into a passion, and gave orders for the massacre of all children in Bethlehem and its neighbourhood, of the age of two years or less, corresponding with
17 the time he had ascertained from the astrologers. So the words spoken
18 through Jeremiah the prophet were fulfilled: 'A voice was heard in Rama, wailing and loud laments; it was Rachel weeping for her children, and refusing all consolation, because they were no more.'
19     The time came that Herod died; and an angel of the Lord appeared in
20 a dream to Joseph in Egypt and said to him, 'Rise up, take the child and his mother, and go with them to the land of Israel, for the men who threatened
21 the child's life are dead.' So he rose, took mother and child with him, and

*a Or* Where is the king of the Jews who has just been born?          *b Or* least among.

4

came to the land of Israel. Hearing, however, that Archelaus had succeeded 22
his father Herod as king of Judaea, he was afraid to go there. And being
warned by a dream, he withdrew to the region of Galilee; there he settled in 23
a town called Nazareth. This was to fulfil the words spoken through the
prophets: 'He shall be called a Nazarene.'

ABOUT THAT TIME John the Baptist appeared as a preacher in the 3
Judaean wilderness; his theme was: 'Repent; for the kingdom of Heaven 2
is upon you!' It is of him that the prophet Isaiah spoke when he said, 3
'A voice crying aloud in the wilderness, "Prepare a way for the Lord; clear
a straight path for him."'

John's clothing was a rough coat of camel's hair, with a leather belt 4
round his waist, and his food was locusts and wild honey. They flocked to 5
him from Jerusalem, from all Judaea, and the whole Jordan valley, and 6
were baptized by him in the River Jordan, confessing their sins.

When he saw many of the Pharisees and Sadducees coming for baptism 7
he said to them: 'You vipers' brood! Who warned you to escape from the
coming retribution? Then prove your repentance by the fruit it bears; 8
and do not presume to say to yourselves, "We have Abraham for our 9
father." I tell you that God can make children for Abraham out of these
stones here. Already the axe is laid to the roots of the trees; and every tree 10
that fails to produce good fruit is cut down and thrown on the fire. I baptize 11
you with water, for repentance; but the one who comes after me is mightier
than I. I am not fit to take off his shoes. He will baptize you with the Holy
Spirit and with fire. His shovel is ready in his hand and he will winnow his 12
threshing-floor; the wheat he will gather into his granary, but he will burn
the chaff on a fire that can never go out.'

Then Jesus arrived at the Jordan from Galilee, and came to John to be 13
baptized by him. John tried to dissuade him. 'Do you come to me?' he 14
said; 'I need rather to be baptized by you.' Jesus replied, 'Let it be so for the 15
present; we do well to conform in this way with all that God requires.'
John then allowed him to come. After baptism Jesus came up out of the 16
water at once, and at that moment heaven opened; he saw the Spirit of
God descending like a dove to alight upon him; and a voice from heaven 17
was heard saying, 'This is my Son, my Beloved,*a* on whom my favour
rests.'

JESUS WAS THEN LED AWAY by the Spirit into the wilderness, to be 4
tempted by the devil.

For forty days and nights he fasted, and at the end of them he was 2
famished. The tempter approached him and said, 'If you are the Son of 3
God, tell these stones to become bread.' Jesus answered, 'Scripture says, 4
"Man cannot live on bread alone; he lives on every word that God utters."'

The devil then took him to the Holy City and set him on the parapet of 5
the temple. 'If you are the Son of God,' he said, 'throw yourself down; for 6
Scripture says, "He will put his angels in charge of you, and they will
support you in their arms, for fear you should strike your foot against

*a Or* This is my only Son.

7  a stone." ' Jesus answered him, 'Scripture says again, "You are not to put the Lord your God to the test." '

8  Once again, the devil took him to a very high mountain, and showed him
9  all the kingdoms of the world in their glory. 'All these', he said, 'I will give
10  you, if you will only fall down and do me homage.' But Jesus said, 'Begone, Satan! Scripture says, "You shall do homage to the Lord your God and worship him alone." '

11  Then the devil left him; and angels appeared and waited on him.

12  When he heard that John had been arrested, Jesus withdrew to Galilee;
13  and leaving Nazareth he went and settled at Capernaum on the Sea of
14  Galilee, in the district of Zebulun and Naphtali. This was to fulfil the pas-
15  sage in the prophet Isaiah which tells of 'the land of Zebulun, the land of Naphtali, the Way of the Sea, the land beyond Jordan, heathen Galilee', and says:

16  'The people that lived in darkness saw a great light;
    light dawned on the dwellers in the land of death's dark shadow.'

17  From that day Jesus began to proclaim the message: 'Repent; for [a] the kingdom of Heaven is upon you.'

18  JESUS WAS WALKING by the Sea of Galilee when he saw two brothers, Simon called Peter and his brother Andrew, casting a net into the lake;
19  for they were fishermen. Jesus said to them, 'Come with me, and I will
20  make you fishers of men.' And at once they left their nets and followed him.
21  He went on, and saw another pair of brothers, James son of Zebedee and his brother John; they were in the boat with their father Zebedee,
22  overhauling their nets. He called them, and at once they left the boat and their father, and followed him.
23  He went round the whole of Galilee, teaching in the synagogues, preach-ing the gospel of the Kingdom, and curing whatever illness or infirmity
24  there was among the people. His fame reached the whole of Syria; and sufferers from every kind of illness, racked with pain, possessed by devils,
25  epileptic, or paralysed, were all brought to him, and he cured them. Great crowds also followed him, from Galilee and the Ten Towns, [b] from Jerusalem and Judaea, and from Transjordan.

## The Sermon on the Mount

5  WHEN HE SAW the crowds he went up the hill. There he took his seat,
2  and when his disciples had gathered round him he began to address them. And this is the teaching he gave:

3  'How blest are those who know their need of God;
    the kingdom of Heaven is theirs.
4  How blest are the sorrowful;
    they shall find consolation.

---

[a] *Some witnesses omit* Repent; for.          [b] *Greek* Decapolis.

How blest are those of a gentle spirit;                                       5
    they shall have the earth for their possession.
How blest are those who hunger and thirst to see right prevail; [a]           6
    they shall be satisfied.
How blest are those who show mercy;                                           7
    mercy shall be shown to them.
How blest are those whose hearts are pure;                                    8
    they shall see God.
How blest are the peacemakers;                                               9
    God shall call them his sons.
How blest are those who have suffered persecution for the cause of right;   10
    the kingdom of Heaven is theirs.

'How blest you are, when you suffer insults and persecution and every       11
kind of calumny for my sake. Accept it with gladness and exultation, for    12
you have a rich reward in heaven; in the same way they persecuted the
prophets before you.

'You are salt to the world. And if salt becomes tasteless, how is its salt-  13
ness to be restored? It is now good for nothing but to be thrown away and
trodden underfoot.

'You are light for all the world. A town that stands on a hill cannot be     14
hidden. When a lamp is lit, it is not put under the meal-tub, but on the     15
lamp-stand, where it gives light to everyone in the house. And you, like     16
the lamp, must shed light among your fellows, so that, when they see the
good you do, they may give praise to your Father in heaven.

'DO NOT SUPPOSE that I have come to abolish the Law and the prophets;        17
I did not come to abolish, but to complete. I tell you this: so long as heaven 18
and earth endure, not a letter, not a stroke, will disappear from the Law
until all that must happen has happened.[b] If any man therefore sets aside   19
even the least of the Law's demands, and teaches others to do the same, he
will have the lowest place in the kingdom of Heaven, whereas anyone who
keeps the Law, and teaches others so, will stand high in the kingdom of
Heaven. I tell you, unless you show yourselves far better men than the       20
Pharisees and the doctors of the law, you can never enter the kingdom of
Heaven.

'You have learned that our forefathers were told, "Do not commit            21
murder; anyone who commits murder must be brought to judgement."
But what I tell you is this: Anyone who nurses anger against his brother [c]   22
must be brought to judgement. If he abuses his brother he must answer
for it to the court; if he sneers at him he will have to answer for it in the
fires of hell.

'If, when you are bringing your gift to the altar, you suddenly remember     23
that your brother has a grievance against you, leave your gift where it is   24
before the altar. First go and make your peace with your brother, and only
then come back and offer your gift.

---

[a] *Or* to do what is right.    [b] *Or* before all that it stands for is achieved.    [c] *Some*
*witnesses insert* without good cause.

25 'If someone sues you, come to terms with him promptly while you are both on your way to court; otherwise he may hand you over to the judge,
26 and the judge to the constable, and you will be put in jail. I tell you, once you are there you will not be let out till you have paid the last farthing.

27 'You have learned that they were told, "Do not commit adultery."
28 But what I tell you is this: If a man looks on a woman with a lustful eye, he has already committed adultery with her in his heart.

29 'If your right eye is your undoing, tear it out and fling it away; it is better for you to lose one part of your body than for the whole of it to be thrown
30 into hell. And if your right hand is your undoing, cut it off and fling it away; it is better for you to lose one part of your body than for the whole of it to go to hell.

31 'They were told, "A man who divorces his wife must give her a note of
32 dismissal." But what I tell you is this: If a man divorces his wife for any cause other than unchastity he involves her in adultery; and anyone who marries a divorced woman commits adultery.

33 'Again, you have learned that our forefathers were told, "Do not break
34 your oath", and, "Oaths sworn to the Lord must be kept." But what I tell you is this: You are not to swear at all—not by heaven, for it is God's
35 throne, nor by earth, for it is his footstool, nor by Jerusalem, for it is the
36 city of the great King, nor by your own head, because you cannot turn
37 one hair of it white or black. Plain "Yes" or "No" is all you need to say; anything beyond that comes from the devil.

38 'You have learned that they were told, "Eye for eye, tooth for tooth."
39 But what I tell you is this: Do not set yourself against the man who wrongs you. If someone slaps you on the right cheek, turn and offer him your left.
40 If a man wants to sue you for your shirt, let him have your coat as well.
41 42 If a man in authority makes you go one mile, go with him two. Give when you are asked to give; and do not turn your back on a man who wants to borrow.

43 'You have learned that they were told, "Love your neighbour, hate your
44 enemy." But what I tell you is this: Love your enemies *a* and pray for your
45 persecutors; *b* only so can you be children of your heavenly Father, who makes his sun rise on good and bad alike, and sends the rain on the honest
46 and the dishonest. If you love only those who love you, what reward can
47 you expect? Surely the tax-gatherers do as much as that. And if you greet only your brothers, what is there extraordinary about that? Even the
48 heathen do as much. There must be no limit to your goodness, as your heavenly Father's goodness knows no bounds.

6 'BE CAREFUL not to make a show of your religion before men; if you do, no reward awaits you in your Father's house in heaven.
2 'Thus, when you do some act of charity, do not announce it with a flourish of trumpets, as the hypocrites do in synagogue and in the streets to win
3 admiration from men. I tell you this: they have their reward already. No; when you do some act of charity, do not let your left hand know what your

---

*a* *Some witnesses insert* bless those who curse you, do good to those who hate you.
*b* *Some witnesses insert* and those who treat you spitefully.

right is doing; your good deed must be secret, and your Father who sees  4
what is done in secret will reward you. *a*

'Again, when you pray, do not be like the hypocrites; they love to say  5
their prayers standing up in synagogue and at the street-corners, for
everyone to see them. I tell you this: they have their reward already. But  6
when you pray, go into a room by yourself, shut the door, and pray to your
Father who is there in the secret place; and your Father who sees what is
secret will reward you.*a*

'In your prayers do not go babbling on like the heathen, who imagine  7
that the more they say the more likely they are to be heard. Do not imitate  8
them. Your Father knows what your needs are before you ask him.

'This is how you should pray:                                             9

> "Our Father in heaven,
> thy name be hallowed;
> thy kingdom come,                                                      10
> thy will be done,
> on earth as in heaven.
> Give us today our daily bread.*b*                                      11
> Forgive us the wrong we have done,                                     12
> as we have forgiven those who have wronged us.
> And do not bring us to the test,                                       13
> but save us from the evil one." *c d*

For if you forgive others the wrongs they have done, your heavenly Father  14
will also forgive you; but if you do not forgive others, then the wrongs you  15
have done will not be forgiven by your Father.

'So too when you fast, do not look gloomy like the hypocrites: they make  16
their faces unsightly so that other people may see that they are fasting.
I tell you this: they have their reward already. But when you fast, anoint  17
your head and wash your face, so that men may not see that you are fasting,  18
but only your Father who is in the secret place; and your Father who sees
what is secret will give you your reward.

'DO NOT STORE UP for yourselves treasure on earth, where it grows rusty  19
and moth-eaten, and thieves break in to steal it. Store up treasure in  20
heaven, where there is no moth and no rust to spoil it, no thieves to break
in and steal. For where your treasure is, there will your heart be also.  21

'The lamp of the body is the eye. If your eyes are sound, you will have  22
light for your whole body; if the eyes are bad, your whole body will be in  23
darkness. If then the only light you have is darkness, the darkness is
doubly dark.

'No servant can be the slave of two masters; for either he will hate the  24
first and love the second, or he will be devoted to the first and think
nothing of the second. You cannot serve God and Money.

'Therefore I bid you put away anxious thoughts about food and drink  25

---

*a Some witnesses add* openly.        *b Or* our bread for the morrow.        *c Or* from evil.
*d Some witnesses add* For thine is the kingdom and the power and the glory, for ever.
Amen.

to keep you alive, and clothes to cover your body. Surely life is more than
26 food, the body more than clothes. Look at the birds of the air; they do not
sow and reap and store in barns, yet your heavenly Father feeds them. You
27 are worth more than the birds! Is there a man of you who by anxious
28 thought can add a foot to his height *a*? And why be anxious about clothes?
Consider how the lilies grow in the fields; they do not work, they do not
29 spin; *b* and yet, I tell you, even Solomon in all his splendour was not
30 attired like one of these. But if that is how God clothes the grass in the
fields, which is there today, and tomorrow is thrown on the stove, will he
31 not all the more clothe you? How little faith you have! No, do not ask
anxiously, "What are we to eat? What are we to drink? What shall we
32 wear?" All these are things for the heathen to run after, not for you,
33 because your heavenly Father knows that you need them all. Set your
mind on God's kingdom and his justice before everything else, and all the
34 rest will come to you as well. So do not be anxious about tomorrow;
tomorrow will look after itself. Each day has troubles enough of its own.

7 1 2 'PASS NO JUDGEMENT, and you will not be judged. For as you judge
others, so you will yourselves be judged, and whatever measure you deal
3 out to others will be dealt back to you. Why do you look at the speck of
sawdust in your brother's eye, with never a thought for the great plank in
4 your own? Or how can you say to your brother, "Let me take the speck out
5 of your eye", when all the time there is that plank in your own? You hypocrite! First take the plank out of your own eye, and then you will see clearly
to take the speck out of your brother's.

6    'Do not give dogs what is holy; do not throw your pearls to the pigs:
they will only trample on them, and turn and tear you to pieces.

7    'Ask, and you will receive; seek, and you will find; knock, and the door
8 will be opened. For everyone who asks receives, he who seeks finds, and
to him who knocks, the door will be opened.

9    'Is there a man among you who will offer his son a stone when he asks
10 11 for bread, or a snake when he asks for fish? If you, then, bad as you are,
know how to give your children what is good for them, how much more will
your heavenly Father give good things to those who ask him!

12    'Always treat others as you would like them to treat you: that is the Law
and the prophets.

13    'Enter by the narrow gate. The gate is wide that leads to perdition,
14 there is plenty of room on the road, *c* and many go that way; but the gate
that leads to life is small and the road is narrow, *d* and those who find it
are few.

15    'Beware of false prophets, men who come to you dressed up as sheep
16 while underneath they are savage wolves. You will recognize them by the
fruits they bear. Can grapes be picked from briars, or figs from thistles?
17 In the same way, a good tree always yields good fruit, and a poor tree bad

---

*a Or* a day to his life.
*b One witness reads* Consider the lilies: they neither card nor spin, nor labour.
*c Some witnesses read* The road that leads to perdition is wide with plenty of room.
*d Some witnesses read* but the road that leads to life is small and narrow.

fruit. A good tree cannot bear bad fruit, or a poor tree good fruit. And when 18 19 a tree does not yield good fruit it is cut down and burnt. That is why I say 20 you will recognize them by their fruits.

'Not everyone who calls me "Lord, Lord" will enter the kingdom of 21 Heaven, but only those who do the will of my heavenly Father. When that 22 day comes, many will say to me, "Lord, Lord, did we not prophesy in your name, cast out devils in your name, and in your name perform many miracles?" Then I will tell them to their face, "I never knew you; out of my 23 sight, you and your wicked ways!"

'What then of the man who hears these words of mine and acts upon 24 them? He is like a man who had the sense to build his house on rock. The 25 rain came down, the floods rose, the wind blew, and beat upon that house; but it did not fall, because its foundations were on rock. But what of the 26 man who hears these words of mine and does not act upon them? He is like a man who was foolish enough to build his house on sand. The rain 27 came down, the floods rose, the wind blew, and beat upon that house; down it fell with a great crash.'

When Jesus had finished this discourse the people were astounded at 28 his teaching; unlike their own teachers he taught with a note of authority. 29

## Teaching and healing

A<small>FTER HE HAD COME DOWN</small> from the hill he was followed by a great 8 crowd. And now a leper*a* approached him, bowed low, and said, 2 'Sir, if only you will, you can cleanse me.' Jesus stretched out his hand, 3 touched him, and said, 'Indeed I will; be clean again.' And his leprosy was cured immediately. Then Jesus said to him, 'Be sure you tell nobody; 4 but go and show yourself to the priest, and make the offering laid down by Moses for your cleansing; that will certify the cure.'

When he had entered Capernaum a centurion came up to ask his help. 5 'Sir,' he said, 'a boy of mine lies at home paralysed and racked with pain.' 6 Jesus said, 'I will come and cure him.'*b* But the centurion replied, 'Sir, 7 8 who am I to have you under my roof? You need only say the word and the boy will be cured. I know, for I am myself under orders, with soldiers under 9 me. I say to one, "Go", and he goes; to another, "Come here", and he comes; and to my servant, "Do this", and he does it.' Jesus heard him with 10 astonishment, and said to the people who were following him, 'I tell you this: nowhere, even in Israel, have I found such faith.

'Many, I tell you, will come from east and west to feast with Abraham, 11 Isaac, and Jacob in the kingdom of Heaven. But those who were born to 12 the kingdom will be driven out into the dark, the place of wailing and grinding of teeth.'

Then Jesus said to the centurion, 'Go home now; because of your faith, 13 so let it be.' At that moment the boy recovered.

*a The words* leper, leprosy, *as used in this translation, refer to some disfiguring skin disease which entailed ceremonial defilement. It is different from what is now called leprosy.*
*b Or Am I to come and cure him?*

14 Jesus then went to Peter's house and found Peter's mother-in-law in bed
15 with fever. So he took her by the hand; the fever left her, and she got up and waited on him.
16 When evening fell, they brought to him many who were possessed by devils; and he drove the spirits out with a word and healed all who were
17 sick, to fulfil the prophecy of Isaiah: 'He took away our illnesses and lifted our diseases from us.' *a*

18 AT THE SIGHT of the crowds surrounding him Jesus gave word to cross
19 to the other shore. A doctor of the law came up, and said, 'Master, I will
20 follow you wherever you go.' Jesus replied, 'Foxes have their holes, the birds their roosts; but the Son of Man has nowhere to lay his head.'
21 Another man, one of his disciples, said to him, 'Lord, let me go and bury
22 my father first.' Jesus replied, 'Follow me, and leave the dead to bury their dead.'
23 24 Jesus then got into the boat, and his disciples followed. All at once a great storm arose on the lake, till the waves were breaking right over the
25 boat; but he went on sleeping. So they came and woke him up, crying:
26 'Save us, Lord; we are sinking!' 'Why are you such cowards?' he said; 'how little faith you have!' Then he stood up and rebuked the wind and the
27 sea, and there was a dead calm. The men were astonished at what had happened, and exclaimed, 'What sort of man is this? Even the wind and the sea obey him.'
28 When he reached the other side, in the country of the Gadarenes, he was met by two men who came out from the tombs; they were possessed
29 by devils, and so violent that no one dared pass that way. 'You son of God,' they shouted, 'what do you want with us? Have you come here to torment
30 us before our time?' In the distance a large herd of pigs was feeding;
31 and the devils begged him: 'If you drive us out, send us into that herd
32 of pigs.' 'Begone!' he said. Then they came out and went into the pigs; the whole herd rushed over the edge into the lake, and perished in the water.
33 The men in charge of them took to their heels, and made for the town, where they told the whole story, and what had happened to the madmen.
34 Thereupon all the town came out to meet Jesus; and when they saw him
9 they begged him to leave the district and go. So he got into the boat and crossed over, and came to his own town.
2 And now some men brought him a paralysed man lying on a bed. Seeing their faith Jesus said to the man, 'Take heart, my son; your sins are for-
3 given.' At this some of the lawyers said to themselves, 'This is blasphemous
4 talk.' Jesus knew what they were thinking, and said, 'Why do you harbour
5 these evil thoughts? Is it easier to say, "Your sins are forgiven", or to say,
6 "Stand up and walk"? But to convince you that the Son of Man has the right on earth to forgive sins'—he turned to the paralysed man—'stand up, take
7 your bed, and go home.' Thereupon the man got up, and went off home.
8 The people were filled with awe at the sight, and praised God for granting such authority to men.

*a* Or *and bore the burden of our diseases.*

AS HE PASSED ON from there Jesus saw a man named Matthew at his seat 9
in the custom-house, and said to him, 'Follow me'; and Matthew rose and
followed him.

When Jesus was at table in the house, many bad characters—tax- 10
gatherers and others—were seated with him and his disciples. The 11
Pharisees noticed this, and said to his disciples, 'Why is it that your master
eats with tax-gatherers and sinners?' Jesus heard it and said, 'It is not the 12
healthy that need a doctor, but the sick. Go and learn what that text means, 13
"I require mercy, not sacrifice." I did not come to invite virtuous people,
but sinners.'

Then John's disciples came to him with the question: 'Why do we and 14
the Pharisees fast, but your disciples do not?' Jesus replied, 'Can you 15
expect the bridegroom's friends to go mourning while the bridegroom is
with them? The time will come when the bridegroom will be taken away
from them; that will be the time for them to fast.

'No one sews a patch of unshrunk cloth on to an old coat; for then the 16
patch tears away from the coat, and leaves a bigger hole. Neither do you 17
put new wine into old wine-skins; if you do, the skins burst, and then the
wine runs out and the skins are spoilt. No, you put new wine into fresh
skins; then both are preserved.'

EVEN AS HE SPOKE, there came a president of the synagogue, who bowed 18
low before him and said, 'My daughter has just died; but come and lay
your hand on her, and she will live.' Jesus rose and went with him, and so 19
did his disciples.

Then a woman who had suffered from haemorrhages for twelve years 20
came up from behind, and touched the edge of his cloak; for she said to 21
herself, 'If I can only touch his cloak, I shall be cured.' But Jesus turned and 22
saw her, and said, 'Take heart, my daughter; your faith has cured you.'
And from that moment she recovered.

When Jesus arrived at the president's house and saw the flute-players 23
and the general commotion, he said, 'Be off! The girl is not dead: she is 24
asleep'; and they only laughed at him. But, when everyone had been turned 25
out, he went into the room and took the girl by the hand, and she got up.
This story became the talk of all the country round. 26

As he passed on Jesus was followed by two blind men, who cried out, 27
'Son of David, have pity on us!' And when he had gone indoors they came 28
to him. Jesus asked, 'Do you believe that I have the power to do what you
want?' 'Yes, sir', they said. Then he touched their eyes, and said, 'As you 29
have believed, so let it be'; and their sight was restored. Jesus said to them 30
sternly, 'See that no one hears about this.' But as soon as they had gone out 31
they talked about him all over the country-side.

They were on their way out when a man was brought to him, who was 32
dumb and possessed by a devil; the devil was cast out and the patient 33
recovered his speech. Filled with amazement the onlookers said, 'Nothing
like this has ever been seen in Israel.' *a*

*a Some witnesses add* (34) But the Pharisees said, 'He casts out devils by the prince of
devils.'

35 SO JESUS WENT ROUND all the towns and villages teaching in their synagogues, announcing the good news of the Kingdom, and curing every kind

36 of ailment and disease. The sight of the people moved him to pity: they

37 were like sheep without a shepherd, harassed and helpless; and he said to

38 his disciples, 'The crop is heavy, but labourers are scarce; you must therefore beg the owner to send labourers to harvest his crop.'

**10** Then he called his twelve disciples to him and gave them authority to cast out unclean spirits and to cure every kind of ailment and disease.

2 These are the names of the twelve apostles: first Simon, also called Peter, and his brother Andrew; James son of Zebedee, and his brother

3 John; Philip and Bartholomew, Thomas and Matthew the tax-gatherer,

4 James son of Alphaeus, Lebbaeus,*a* Simon, a member of the Zealot party, and Judas Iscariot, the man who betrayed him.

5 These twelve Jesus sent out with the following instructions: 'Do not

6 take the road to gentile lands, and do not enter any Samaritan town; but

7 go rather to the lost sheep of the house of Israel. And as you go proclaim

8 the message: "The kingdom of Heaven is upon you." Heal the sick, raise the dead, cleanse lepers, cast out devils. You received without cost; give without charge.

9 10 'Provide no gold, silver, or copper to fill your purse, no pack for the road, no second coat, no shoes, no stick; the worker earns his keep.

11 'When you come to any town or village, look for some worthy person in it,

12 and make your home there until you leave. Wish the house peace as you

13 enter it, so that, if it is worthy, your peace may descend on it; if it is not

14 worthy, your peace can come back to you. If anyone will not receive you or listen to what you say, then as you leave that house or that town shake

15 the dust of it off your feet. I tell you this: on the day of judgement it will be more bearable for the land of Sodom and Gomorrah than for that town.

16 'Look, I send you out like sheep among wolves; be wary as serpents, innocent as doves.

17 'And be on your guard, for men will hand you over to their courts, they

18 will flog you in the synagogues, and you will be brought before governors

19 and kings, for my sake, to testify before them and the heathen. But when you are arrested, do not worry about what you are to say; when the time

20 comes, the words you need will be given you; for it is not you who will be speaking: it will be the Spirit of your Father speaking in you.

21 'Brother will betray brother to death, and the father his child; children

22 will turn against their parents and send them to their death. All will hate you for your allegiance to me; but the man who holds out to the end will be

23 saved. When you are persecuted in one town, take refuge in another; I tell you this: before you have gone through all the towns of Israel the Son of Man will have come.

24 'A pupil does not rank above his teacher, or a servant above his master.

25 The pupil should be content to share his teacher's lot, the servant to share his master's. If the master has been called Beelzebub, how much more his household!

26 'So do not be afraid of them. There is nothing covered up that will not

*a Some witnesses read* Thaddaeus.

be uncovered, nothing hidden that will not be made known. What I say 27
to you in the dark you must. repeat in broad daylight; what you hear
whispered you must shout from the house-tops. Do not fear those who kill 28
the body, but cannot kill the soul. Fear him rather who is able to destroy
both soul and body in hell.

'Are not sparrows two a penny? Yet without your Father's leave not 29
one of them can fall to the ground. As for you, even the hairs of your head 30
have all been counted. So have no fear; you are worth more than any 31
number of sparrows.

'Whoever then will acknowledge me before men, I will acknowledge 32
him before my Father in heaven; and whoever disowns me before men, 33
I will disown him before my Father in heaven.

'You must not think that I have come to bring peace to the earth; I have 34
not come to bring peace, but a sword. I have come to set a man against his 35
father, a daughter against her mother, a son's wife against her mother-in-
law; and a man will find his enemies under his own roof. 36

'No man is worthy of me who cares more for father or mother than for 37
me; no man is worthy of me who cares more for son or daughter; no man 38
is worthy of me who does not take up his cross and walk in my footsteps.
By gaining his life a man will lose it; by losing his life for my sake, he will 39
gain it.

'To receive you is to receive me, and to receive me is to receive the One 40
who sent me. Whoever receives a prophet as a prophet will be given a 41
prophet's reward, and whoever receives a good man because he is a good
man will be given a good man's reward. And if anyone gives so much as a cup 42
of cold water to one of these little ones, because he is a disciple of mine,
I tell you this: that man will assuredly not go unrewarded.'

When Jesus had finished giving his twelve disciples their instructions, **11**
he left that place and went to teach and preach in the neighbouring
towns.

JOHN, WHO WAS IN PRISON, heard what Christ was doing, and sent his 2
own disciples to him with this message: 'Are you the one who is to come, or 3
are we to expect some other?' Jesus answered, 'Go and tell John what you 4
hear and see: the blind recover their sight, the lame walk, the lepers are 5
made clean, the deaf hear, the dead are raised to life, the poor are hearing
the good news—and happy is the man who does not find me a stumbling- 6
block.'

When the messengers were on their way back, Jesus began to speak to 7
the people about John: 'What was the spectacle that drew you to the
wilderness? A reed-bed swept by the wind? No? Then what did you go 8
out to see? A man dressed in silks and satins? Surely you must look in
palaces for that. But why did you go out? To see a prophet? Yes indeed, 9
and far more than a prophet. He is the man of whom Scripture says, 10

"Here is my herald, whom I send on ahead of you,
and he will prepare your way before you."

I tell you this: never has there appeared on earth a mother's son greater 11 than John the Baptist, and yet the least in the kingdom of Heaven is greater than he.

12 'Ever since the coming of John the Baptist the kingdom of Heaven has
13 been subjected to violence and violent men*a* are seizing it. For all the
14 prophets and the Law foretold things to come until John appeared, and
15 John is the destined Elijah, if you will but accept it. If you have ears, then hear.

16 'How can I describe this generation? They are like children sitting in the market-place and shouting at each other,

17         "We piped for you and you would not dance."
        "We wept and wailed, and you would not mourn."

18 For John came, neither eating nor drinking, and they say, "He is pos-
19 sessed." The Son of Man came eating and drinking, and they say, "Look at him! a glutton and a drinker, a friend of tax-gatherers and sinners!" And yet God's wisdom is proved right by its results.'

20 THEN HE SPOKE of the towns in which most of his miracles had been
21 performed, and denounced them for their impenitence. 'Alas for you, Chorazin!' he said; 'alas for you, Bethsaida! If the miracles that were performed in you had been performed in Tyre and Sidon, they would have
22 repented long ago in sackcloth and ashes. But it will be more bearable,
23 I tell you, for Tyre and Sidon on the day of judgement than for you. And as for you, Capernaum, will you be exalted to the skies? No, brought down to the depths! For if the miracles had been performed in Sodom which
24 were performed in you, Sodom would be standing to this day. But it will be more bearable, I tell you, for the land of Sodom on the day of judgement than for you.'

25 At that time Jesus spoke these words: 'I thank thee, Father, Lord of heaven and earth, for hiding these things from the learned and wise, and
26 27 revealing them to the simple. Yes, Father, such*b* was thy choice. Everything is entrusted to me by my Father; and no one knows the Son but the Father, and no one knows the Father but the Son and those to whom the Son may choose to reveal him.

28 'Come to me, all whose work is hard, whose load is heavy; and I will give
29 you relief. Bend your necks to my yoke, and learn from me, for I am gentle
30 and humble-hearted; and your souls will find relief. For my yoke is good to bear, my load is light.'

## Controversy

12 ONCE ABOUT THAT TIME Jesus went through the cornfields on the
Sabbath; and his disciples, feeling hungry, began to pluck some ears
2 of corn and eat them. The Pharisees noticed this, and said to him, 'Look, your disciples are doing something which is forbidden on the Sabbath.'

*a Or* has been forcing its way forward, and men of force . . .    *b Or* Yes, I thank thee, Father, that such . . .

He answered, 'Have you not read what David did when he and his men 3
were hungry? He went into the House of God and ate the sacred bread, 4
though neither he nor his men had a right to eat it, but only the priests.
Or have you not read in the Law that on the Sabbath the priests in the 5
temple break the Sabbath and it is not held against them? I tell you, there 6
is something greater than the temple here. If you had known what that text 7
means, "I require mercy, not sacrifice", you would not have condemned
the innocent. For the Son of Man is sovereign over the Sabbath.'          8

He went on to another place, and entered their synagogue. A man was 9 10
there with a withered arm, and they asked Jesus, 'Is it permitted to heal on
the Sabbath?' (They wanted to frame a charge against him.) But he said to 11
them, 'Suppose you had one sheep, which fell into a ditch on the Sabbath;
is there one of you who would not catch hold of it and lift it out? And surely 12
a man is worth far more than a sheep! It is therefore permitted to do good
on the Sabbath.' Turning to the man he said, 'Stretch out your arm.' He 13
stretched it out, and it was made sound again like the other. But the 14
Pharisees, on leaving the synagogue, laid a plot to do away with him.

Jesus was aware of it and withdrew. Many followed, and he cured all 15
who were ill; and he gave strict injunctions that they were not to make 16
him known. This was to fulfil Isaiah's prophecy:                          17

> 'Here is my servant, whom I have chosen,                                18
>     my beloved, on whom my favour rests;
> I will put my Spirit upon him,
>     and he will proclaim judgement among the nations.
> He will not strive, he will not shout,                                  19
>     nor will his voice be heard in the streets.
> He will not snap off the broken reed,                                   20
>     nor snuff out the smouldering wick,
>     until he leads justice on to victory.
> In him the nations shall place their hope.'                             21

THEN THEY BROUGHT HIM a man who was possessed; he was blind and 22
dumb; and Jesus cured him, restoring both speech and sight. The by- 23
standers were all amazed, and the word went round: 'Can this be the Son of
David?' But when the Pharisees heard it they said, 'It is only by Beelzebub 24
prince of devils that this man drives the devils out.'

He knew what was in their minds; so he said to them, 'Every kingdom 25
divided against itself goes to ruin; and no town, no household, that is
divided against itself can stand. And if it is Satan who casts out Satan, Satan 26
is divided against himself; how then can his kingdom stand? And if it is 27
by Beelzebub that I cast out devils, by whom do your own people drive
them out? If this is your argument, they themselves will refute you. But 28
if it is by the Spirit of God that I drive out the devils, then be sure the
kingdom of God has already come upon you.

'Or again, how can anyone break into a strong man's house and make off 29
with his goods, unless he has first tied the strong man up before ransacking
the house?

30 'He who is not with me is against me, and he who does not gather with me scatters.

31 'And so I tell you this: no sin, no slander, is beyond forgiveness for men, except slander spoken against the Spirit, and that will not be forgiven.

32 Any man who speaks a word against the Son of Man will be forgiven; but if anyone speaks against the Holy Spirit, for him there is no forgiveness, either in this age or in the age to come.

33 'Either make the tree good and its fruit good, or make the tree bad and
34 its fruit bad; you can tell a tree by its fruit. You vipers' brood! How can your words be good when you yourselves are evil? For the words that the
35 mouth utters come from the overflowing of the heart. A good man produces good from the store of good within himself; and an evil man from evil within produces evil.

36 'I tell you this: there is not a thoughtless word that comes from men's
37 lips but they will have to account for it on the day of judgement. For out of your own mouth you will be acquitted; out of your own mouth you will be condemned.'

38 At this some of the doctors of the law and the Pharisees said, 'Master,
39 we should like you to show us a sign.' He answered: 'It is a wicked, godless generation that asks for a sign; and the only sign that will be given it is
40 the sign of the prophet Jonah. Jonah was in the sea-monster's belly for three days and three nights, and in the same way the Son of Man will be
41 three days and three nights in the bowels of the earth. At the Judgement, when this generation is on trial, the men of Nineveh will appear against it *a* and ensure its condemnation, for they repented at the preaching of Jonah;
42 and what is here is greater than Jonah. The Queen of the South will appear at the Judgement when this generation is on trial,*b* and ensure its condemnation, for she came from the ends of the earth to hear the wisdom of Solomon; and what is here is greater than Solomon.

43 'When an unclean spirit comes out of a man it wanders over the deserts
44 seeking a resting-place, and finds none. Then it says, "I will go back to the home I left." So it returns and finds the house unoccupied, swept clean,
45 and tidy. Off it goes and collects seven other spirits more wicked than itself, and they all come in and settle down; and in the end the man's plight is worse than before. That is how it will be with this wicked generation.'

46 He was still speaking to the crowd when his mother and brothers
47 appeared; they stood outside, wanting to speak to him. Someone said, 'Your mother and your brothers are here outside; they want to speak to
48 you.' Jesus turned to the man who brought the message, and said, 'Who
49 is my mother? Who are my brothers?'; and pointing to the disciples, he
50 said, 'Here are my mother and my brothers. Whoever does the will of my heavenly Father is my brother, my sister, my mother.'

13 1 2 THAT SAME DAY Jesus went out and sat by the lake-side, where so many people gathered round him that he had to get into a boat. He sat there, and

---

*a Or* will rise again together with it.     *b Or* At the Judgement the Queen of the South will be raised to life together with this generation.

all the people stood on the shore. He spoke to them in parables, at some 3
length.

He said: 'A sower went out to sow. And as he sowed, some seed fell along 4
the footpath; and the birds came and ate it up. Some seed fell on rocky 5
ground, where it had little soil, and it sprouted quickly because it had no
depth of earth; but when the sun rose the young corn was scorched, and 6
as it had no root it withered away. Some seed fell among thistles; and the 7
thistles shot up, and choked the corn. And some of the seed fell into good 8
soil, where it bore fruit, yielding a hundredfold or, it might be, sixtyfold
or thirtyfold. If you have ears, then hear.' 9

The disciples went up to him and asked, 'Why do you speak to them in 10
parables?' He replied, 'It has been granted to you to know the secrets of 11
the kingdom of Heaven; but to those others it has not been granted. For 12
the man who has will be given more, till he has enough and to spare; and the
man who has not will forfeit even what he has. That is why I speak to 13
them in parables; for they look without seeing, and listen without hearing
or understanding. There is a prophecy of Isaiah which is being fulfilled 14
for them: "You may hear and hear, but you will never understand; you
may look and look, but you will never see. For this people's mind has 15
become gross; their ears are dulled, and their eyes are closed. Otherwise,
their eyes might see, their ears hear, and their mind understand, and then
they might turn again, and I would heal them."

'But happy are your eyes because they see, and your ears because they 16
hear! Many prophets and saints, I tell you, desired to see what you now see, 17
yet never saw it; to hear what you hear, yet never heard it.

'You, then, may hear the parable of the sower. When a man hears the 18 19
word that tells of the Kingdom but fails to understand it, the evil one comes
and carries off what has been sown in his heart. There you have the seed
sown along the footpath. The seed sown on rocky ground stands for the 20
man who, on hearing the word, accepts it at once with joy; but as it strikes 21
no root in him he has no staying-power, and when there is trouble or
persecution on account of the word he falls away at once. The seed sown 22
among thistles represents the man who hears the word, but worldly cares
and the false glamour of wealth choke it, and it proves barren. But the seed 23
that fell into good soil is the man who hears the word and understands it,
who accordingly bears fruit, and yields a hundredfold or, it may be, sixtyfold or thirtyfold.'

Here is another parable that he put before them: 'The kingdom of 24
Heaven is like this. A man sowed his field with good seed; but while every- 25
one was asleep his enemy came, sowed darnel among the wheat, and made
off. When the corn sprouted and began to fill out, the darnel could be seen 26
among it. The farmer's men went to their master and said, "Sir, was it not 27
good seed that you sowed in your field? Then where has the darnel come
from?" "This is an enemy's doing", he replied. "Well then," they said, 28
"shall we go and gather the darnel?" "No," he answered; "in gathering it you 29
might pull up the wheat at the same time. Let them both grow together till 30
harvest; and at harvest-time I will tell the reapers, 'Gather the darnel first,
and tie it in bundles for burning; then collect the wheat into my barn.'"'

31 And this is another parable that he put before them: 'The kingdom of Heaven is like a mustard-seed, which a man took and sowed in his field.
32 As a seed, mustard is smaller than any other; but when it has grown it is bigger than any garden-plant; it becomes a tree, big enough for the birds to come and roost among its branches.'
33 He told them also this parable: 'The kingdom of Heaven is like yeast, which a woman took and mixed with half a hundredweight of flour till it was all leavened.'
34 In all this teaching to the crowds Jesus spoke in parables; in fact he never
35 spoke to them without a parable. This was to fulfil the prophecy of Isaiah: *a*

'I will open my mouth in parables;
I will utter things kept secret since the world was made.'

36 He then dismissed the people, and went into the house, where his disciples came to him and said, 'Explain to us the parable of the darnel in
37 the field.' And this was his answer: 'The sower of the good seed is the Son
38 of Man. The field is the world; the good seed stands for the children of the
39 Kingdom, the darnel for the children of the evil one. The enemy who sowed the darnel is the devil. The harvest is the end of time. The reapers are
40 angels. As the darnel, then, is gathered up and burnt, so at the end of time
41 the Son of Man will send out his angels, who will gather out of his kingdom
42 whatever makes men stumble, and all whose deeds are evil, and these will be thrown into the blazing furnace, the place of wailing and grinding of
43 teeth. And then the righteous will shine as brightly as the sun in the kingdom of their Father. If you have ears, then hear.
44 'The kingdom of Heaven is like treasure lying buried in a field. The man who found it, buried it again; and for sheer joy went and sold everything he had, and bought that field.
45 'Here is another picture of the kingdom of Heaven. A merchant looking
46 out for fine pearls found one of very special value; so he went and sold everything he had, and bought it.
47 'Again the kingdom of Heaven is like a net let down into the sea, where
48 fish of every kind were caught in it. When it was full, it was dragged ashore. Then the men sat down and collected the good fish into pails and threw the
49 worthless away. That is how it will be at the end of time. The angels will
50 go forth, and they will separate the wicked from the good, and throw them into the blazing furnace, the place of wailing and grinding of teeth.
51 'Have you understood all this?' he asked; and they answered, 'Yes.'
52 He said to them, 'When, therefore, a teacher of the law has become a learner in the kingdom of Heaven, he is like a householder who can produce from his store both the new and the old.'

53 54 WHEN HE HAD FINISHED these parables Jesus left that place, and came to his home town, where he taught the people in their synagogue. In amazement they asked, 'Where does he get this wisdom from, and these
55 miraculous powers? Is he not the carpenter's son? Is not his mother called
56 Mary, his brothers James, Joseph, Simon, and Judas? And are not all his

*a Some witnesses omit* of Isaiah.

sisters here with us? Where then has he got all this from?' So they fell 57
foul of him, and this led him to say, 'A prophet will always be held in
honour, except in his home town, and in his own family.' And he did not 58
work many miracles there: such was their want of faith.

It was at that time that reports about Jesus reached the ears of Prince 14
Herod. 'This is John the Baptist,' he said to his attendants; 'John has been 2
raised to life, and that is why these miraculous powers are at work in him.'

NOW HEROD had arrested John, put him in chains, and thrown him into 3
prison, on account of Herodias, his brother Philip's wife; for John had told 4
him: 'You have no right to her.' Herod would have liked to put him to 5
death, but he was afraid of the people, in whose eyes John was a prophet.
But at his birthday celebrations the daughter of Herodias danced before the 6
guests, and Herod was so delighted that he took an oath to give her any- 7
thing she cared to ask. Prompted by her mother, she said, 'Give me here 8
on a dish the head of John the Baptist.' The king was distressed when he 9
heard it; but out of regard for his oath and for his guests, he ordered the
request to be granted, and had John beheaded in prison. The head was 10 11
brought in on a dish and given to the girl; and she carried it to her mother.
Then John's disciples came and took away the body, and buried it; and 12
they went and told Jesus.

WHEN HE HEARD what had happened Jesus withdrew privately by boat 13
to a lonely place; but people heard of it, and came after him in crowds by
land from the towns. When he came ashore, he saw a great crowd; his 14
heart went out to them, and he cured those of them who were sick. When 15
it grew late the disciples came up to him and said, 'This is a lonely place,
and the day has gone; send the people off to the villages to buy themselves
food.' He answered, 'There is no need for them to go; give them something 16
to eat yourselves.' 'All we have here', they said, 'is five loaves and two 17
fishes.' 'Let me have them', he replied. So he told the people to sit down on 18 19
the grass; then, taking the five loaves and the two fishes, he looked up to
heaven, said the blessing, broke the loaves, and gave them to the disciples;
and the disciples gave them to the people. They all ate to their hearts' 20
content; and the scraps left over, which they picked up, were enough to
fill twelve great baskets. Some five thousand men shared in this meal, to 21
say nothing of women and children.

Then he made the disciples embark and go on ahead to the other side, 22
while he sent the people away; after doing that, he went up the hill-side to 23
pray alone. It grew late, and he was there by himself. The boat was already 24
some furlongs from the shore,[a] battling with a head-wind and a rough sea.
Between three and six in the morning he came to them, walking over the 25
lake. When the disciples saw him walking on the lake they were so shaken 26
that they cried out in terror: 'It is a ghost!' But at once he spoke to them: 27
'Take heart! It is I; do not be afraid.'

Peter called to him: 'Lord, if it is you, tell me to come to you over the 28
water.' 'Come', said Jesus. Peter stepped down from the boat, and walked 29

[a] *Some witnesses read* already well out on the water.

30 over the water towards Jesus. But when he saw the strength of the gale he was seized with fear; and beginning to sink, he cried, 'Save me, Lord.'
31 Jesus at once reached out and caught hold of him, and said, 'Why did you
32 hesitate? How little faith you have!' They then climbed into the boat;
33 and the wind dropped. And the men in the boat fell at his feet, exclaiming, 'Truly you are the Son of God.'
34 35 So they finished the crossing and came to land at Gennesaret. There Jesus was recognized by the people of the place, who sent out word to all
36 the country round. And all who were ill were brought to him, and he was begged to allow them simply to touch the edge of his cloak. And everyone who touched it was completely cured.

**15** THEN JESUS WAS APPROACHED by a group of Pharisees and lawyers
2 from Jerusalem, with the question: 'Why do your disciples break the
3 ancient tradition? They do not wash their hands before meals.' He answered them: 'And what of you? Why do you break God's commandment in the
4 interest of your tradition? For God said, "Honour your father and mother",
5 and, "The man who curses his father or mother must suffer death." But you say, "If a man says to his father or mother, 'Anything of mine which might
6 have been used for your benefit is set apart for God', then he must not honour his father or his mother." You have made God's law null and void
7 out of respect for your tradition. What hypocrisy! Isaiah was right when he
8 prophesied about you: "This people pays me lip-service, but their heart
9 is far from me; their worship of me is in vain, for they teach as doctrines the commandments of men."'
10 He called the crowd and said to them, 'Listen to me, and understand
11 this: a man is not defiled by what goes into his mouth, but by what comes out of it.'
12 Then the disciples came to him and said, 'Do you know that the Phari-
13 sees have taken great offence at what you have been saying?' His answer was: 'Any plant that is not of my heavenly Father's planting will be rooted
14 up. Leave them alone; they are blind guides,*a* and if one blind man guides another they will both fall into the ditch.'
15 16 Then Peter said, 'Tell us what that parable means.' Jesus answered,
17 'Are you still as dull as the rest? Do you not see that whatever goes in by the mouth passes into the stomach and so is discharged into the drain?
18 But what comes out of the mouth has its origins in the heart; and that is
19 what defiles a man. Wicked thoughts, murder, adultery, fornication, theft,
20 perjury, slander—these all proceed from the heart; and these are the things that defile a man; but to eat without first washing his hands, that cannot defile him.'

*a Some witnesses insert* of blind men.

## *Jesus and his disciples*

JESUS THEN LEFT that place and withdrew to the region of Tyre and 21 Sidon. And a Canaanite woman from those parts came crying out, 'Sir! 22 have pity on me, Son of David; my daughter is tormented by a devil.' But 23 he said not a word in reply. His disciples came and urged him: 'Send her away; see how she comes shouting after us.' Jesus replied, 'I was sent to the 24 lost sheep of the house of Israel, and to them alone.' But the woman came 25 and fell at his feet and cried, 'Help me, sir.' To this Jesus replied, 'It is not 26 right to take the children's bread and throw it to the dogs.' 'True, sir,' she 27 answered; 'and yet the dogs eat the scraps that fall from their masters' table.' Hearing this Jesus replied, 'Woman, what faith you have! Be it 28 as you wish!' And from that moment her daughter was restored to health.

After leaving that region Jesus took the road by the Sea of Galilee and 29 went up to the hills. When he was seated there, crowds flocked to him, 30 bringing with them the lame, blind, dumb, and crippled, and many other sufferers; they threw them down at his feet, and he healed them. Great 31 was the amazement of the people when they saw the dumb speaking, the crippled strong, the lame walking, and sight restored to the blind; and they gave praise to the God of Israel.

Jesus called his disciples and said to them, 'I feel sorry for all these 32 people; they have been with me now for three days and have nothing to eat. I do not want to send them away unfed; they might turn faint on the way.' The disciples replied, 'Where in this lonely place can we find bread enough 33 to feed such a crowd?' 'How many loaves have you?' Jesus asked. 'Seven,' 34 they replied; 'and there are a few small fishes.' So he ordered the people 35 to sit down on the ground; then he took the seven loaves and the fishes, 36 and after giving thanks to God he broke them and gave to the disciples, and the disciples gave to the people. They all ate to their hearts' content; and 37 the scraps left over, which they picked up, were enough to fill seven baskets. Four thousand men shared in this meal, to say nothing of women 38 and children. He then dismissed the crowds, got into a boat, and went to 39 the neighbourhood of Magadan.

The Pharisees and Sadducees came, and to test him they asked him to **16** show them a sign from heaven. His answer was: *a* 'It is a wicked generation 2 4 that asks for a sign; and the only sign that will be given it is the sign of Jonah.' So he went off and left them.

In crossing to the other side the disciples had forgotten to take bread 5 with them. So, when Jesus said to them, 'Beware, be on your guard against 6 the leaven of the Pharisees and Sadducees', they began to say among them- 7 selves, 'It is because we have brought no bread!' Knowing what was in their 8 minds, Jesus said to them: 'Why do you talk about bringing no bread? Where is your faith? Do you not understand even yet? Do you not remem- 9 ber the five loaves for the five thousand, and how many basketfuls you

*a Some witnesses here insert* 'In the evening you say, "It will be fine weather, for the sky is red"; (3) and in the morning you say, "It will be stormy today; the sky is red and lowering." You know how to interpret the appearance of the sky; can you not interpret the signs of the times?'

10 picked up? Or the seven loaves for the four thousand, and how many
11 basketfuls you picked up? How can you fail to see that I was not speaking
about bread? Be on your guard, I said, against the leaven of the Pharisees
12 and Sadducees.' Then they understood: they were to be on their guard,
not against baker's leaven, but against the teaching of the Pharisees and
Sadducees.

13 WHEN HE CAME to the territory of Caesarea Philippi, Jesus asked his
14 disciples, 'Who do men say that the Son of Man is*a*?' They answered,
'Some say John the Baptist, others Elijah, others Jeremiah, or one of the
15 16 prophets.' 'And you,' he asked, 'who do you say I am?' Simon Peter
17 answered: 'You are the Messiah, the Son of the living God.' Then Jesus
said: 'Simon son of Jonah, you are favoured indeed! You did not learn
18 that from mortal man; it was revealed to you by my heavenly Father. And
I say this to you: You are Peter, the Rock; and on this rock I will build my
19 church, and the powers of death shall never conquer it.*b* I will give you
the keys of the kingdom of Heaven; what you forbid on earth shall be forbidden in heaven, and what you allow on earth shall be allowed in heaven.'
20 He then gave his disciples strict orders not to tell anyone that he was the
Messiah.

21 From that time Jesus began to make it clear to his disciples that he had
to go to Jerusalem, and there to suffer much from the elders, chief priests,
and doctors of the law; to be put to death and to be raised again on the third
22 day. At this Peter took him by the arm and began to rebuke him: 'Heaven
23 forbid!' he said. 'No, Lord, this shall never happen to you.' Then Jesus
turned and said to Peter, 'Away with you, Satan; you are a stumbling-
block to me. You think as men think, not as God thinks.'

24 Jesus then said to his disciples, 'If anyone wishes to be a follower of mine,
he must leave self behind; he must take up his cross and come with me.
25 Whoever cares for his own safety is lost; but if a man will let himself be lost
26 for my sake, he will find his true self. What will a man gain by winning
the whole world, at the cost of his true self? Or what can he give that will
27 buy that self back? For the Son of Man is to come in the glory of his Father
with his angels, and then he will give each man the due reward for what
28 he has done. I tell you this: there are some of those standing here who
will not taste death before they have seen the Son of Man coming in his
kingdom.'

17 SIX DAYS LATER Jesus took Peter, James, and John the brother of James,
2 and led them up a high mountain where they were alone; and in their
presence he was transfigured; his face shone like the sun, and his clothes
3 became white as the light. And they saw Moses and Elijah appear, con-
4 versing with him. Then Peter spoke: 'Lord,' he said, 'how good it is that
we are here! If you wish it, I will make three shelters here, one for you,
5 one for Moses, and one for Elijah.' While he was still speaking, a bright
cloud suddenly overshadowed them, and a voice called from the cloud:

*a Some witnesses read* that I, the Son of Man, am.　　　*b Or* the gates of death shall
never close upon it.

'This is my Son, my Beloved,[a] on whom my favour rests; listen to him.'
At the sound of the voice the disciples fell on their faces in terror. Jesus then  6 7
came up to them, touched them, and said, 'Stand up; do not be afraid.'
And when they raised their eyes they saw no one, but only Jesus.  8

On their way down the mountain, Jesus enjoined them not to tell anyone  9
of the vision until the Son of Man had been raised from the dead. The  10
disciples put a question to him: 'Why then do our teachers say that Elijah
must come first?' He replied, 'Yes, Elijah will come and set everything  11
right. But I tell you that Elijah has already come, and they failed to recog-  12
nize him, and worked their will upon him; and in the same way the Son of
Man is to suffer at their hands.' Then the disciples understood that he  13
meant John the Baptist.

When they returned to the crowd, a man came up to Jesus, fell on his  14
knees before him, and said, 'Have pity, sir, on my son: he is an epileptic  15
and has bad fits, and he keeps falling about, often into the fire, often into
water. I brought him to your disciples, but they could not cure him.' Jesus  16 17
answered, 'What an unbelieving and perverse generation! How long shall
I be with you? How long must I endure you? Bring him here to me.' Jesus  18
then spoke sternly to the boy; the devil left him, and from that moment he
was cured.

Afterwards the disciples came to Jesus and asked him privately, 'Why  19
could not we cast it out?' He answered, 'Your faith is too small. I tell you  20
this: if you have faith no bigger even than a mustard-seed, you will say to
this mountain, "Move from here to there!", and it will move; nothing will
prove impossible for you.'[b]

THEY WERE GOING about together in Galilee when Jesus said to them,  22
'The Son of Man is to be given up into the power of men, and they will kill  23
him; then on the third day he will be raised again.' And they were filled
with grief.

On their arrival at Capernaum the collectors of the temple-tax came up  24
to Peter and asked, 'Does your master not pay temple-tax?' 'He does',  25
said Peter. When he went indoors Jesus forestalled him by asking, 'What
do you think about this, Simon? From whom do earthly monarchs collect
tax or toll? From their own people, or from aliens?' 'From aliens', said  26
Peter. 'Why then,' said Jesus, 'their own people are exempt! But as we do  27
not want to cause offence, go and cast a line in the lake; take the first fish
that comes to the hook, open its mouth, and you will find a silver coin;
take that and pay it in; it will meet the tax for us both.'

At that time the disciples came to Jesus and asked, 'Who is the greatest  **18**
in the kingdom of Heaven?' He called a child, set him in front of them,  2
and said, 'I tell you this: unless you turn round and become like children,  3
you will never enter the kingdom of Heaven. Let a man humble himself  4
till he is like this child, and he will be the greatest in the kingdom of Heaven.
Whoever receives one such child in my name receives me. But if a man is  5 6
a cause of stumbling to one of these little ones who have faith in me, it

[a] *Or* This is my only Son.          [b] *Some witnesses add* (21) But there is no means of
casting out this sort but prayer and fasting.

would be better for him to have a millstone hung round his neck and be
7 drowned in the depths of the sea. Alas for the world that such causes of
stumbling arise! Come they must, but woe betide the man through whom
they come!

8 'If your hand or your foot is your undoing, cut it off and fling it away;
it is better for you to enter into life maimed or lame, than to keep two hands
9 or two feet and be thrown into the eternal fire. If it is your eye that is your
undoing, tear it out and fling it away; it is better to enter into life with one
eye than to keep both eyes and be thrown into the fires of hell.

10 'Never despise one of these little ones; I tell you, they have their guardian
angels in heaven, who look continually on the face of my heavenly Father. *a*
12 'What do you think? Suppose a man has a hundred sheep. If one of them
strays, does he not leave the other ninety-nine on the hillside and go in
13 search of the one that strayed? And if he should find it, I tell you this: he
is more delighted over that sheep than over the ninety-nine that never
14 strayed. In the same way, it is not your heavenly Father's will that one of
these little ones should be lost.

15 'If your brother commits a sin,*b* go and take the matter up with him,
strictly between yourselves, and if he listens to you, you have won your
16 brother over. If he will not listen, take one or two others with you, so that
all facts may be duly established on the evidence of two or three witnesses.
17 If he refuses to listen to them, report the matter to the congregation; and
if he will not listen even to the congregation, you must then treat him as you
would a pagan or a tax-gatherer.

18 'I tell you this: whatever you forbid on earth shall be forbidden in heaven,
and whatever you allow on earth shall be allowed in heaven.

19 'Again I tell you this: if two of you agree on earth about any request you
20 have to make, that request will be granted by my heavenly Father. For
where two or three have met together in my name, I am there among them.'

21 Then Peter came up and asked him, 'Lord, how often am I to forgive
22 my brother if he goes on wronging me? As many as seven times?' Jesus
replied, 'I do not say seven times; I say seventy times seven. *c*

23 'The kingdom of Heaven, therefore, should be thought of in this way:
There was once a king who decided to settle accounts with the men who
24 served him. At the outset there appeared before him a man whose debt
25 ran into millions.*d* Since he had no means of paying, his master ordered him
to be sold to meet the debt, with his wife, his children, and everything he
26 had. The man fell prostrate at his master's feet. "Be patient with me," he
27 said, "and I will pay in full"; and the master was so moved with pity that
28 he let the man go and remitted the debt. But no sooner had the man gone
out than he met a fellow-servant who owed him a few pounds;*e* and catching
hold of him he gripped him by the throat and said, "Pay me what you owe."
29 The man fell at his fellow-servant's feet, and begged him, "Be patient with
30 me, and I will pay you"; but he refused, and had him jailed until he should
31 pay the debt. The other servants were deeply distressed when they saw

---

*a Some witnesses add* (11) For the Son of Man came to save the lost. *b Some witnesses insert* against you. *c Or* seventy-seven times. *d Literally* who owed 10,000 talents. *e Literally* owed him 100 denarii.

what had happened, and they went to their master and told him the whole
story. He accordingly sent for the man. "You scoundrel!" he said to him; 32
"I remitted the whole of your debt when you appealed to me; were you 33
not bound to show your fellow-servant the same pity as I showed you?"
And so angry was the master that he condemned the man to torture until 34
he should pay the debt in full. And that is how my heavenly Father will 35
deal with you, unless you each forgive your brother from your hearts.'

WHEN JESUS HAD FINISHED this discourse he left Galilee and came into 19
the region of Judaea across Jordan. Great crowds followed him, and he 2
healed them there.

Some Pharisees came and tested him by asking, 'Is it lawful for a man to 3
divorce his wife on any and every ground?'ᵃ He asked in return, 'Have you 4
never read that the Creator made them from the beginning male and
female?'; and he added, 'For this reason a man shall leave his father and 5
mother, and be made one with his wife; and the two shall become one flesh.
It follows that they are no longer two individuals: they are one flesh. What 6
God has joined together, man must not separate.' 'Why then', they ob- 7
jected, 'did Moses lay it down that a man might divorce his wife by note of
dismissal?' He answered, 'It was because your minds were closed that 8
Moses gave you permission to divorce your wives; but it was not like that
when all began. I tell you, if a man divorces his wife for any cause other 9
than unchastity, and marries another, he commits adultery.'ᵇ

The disciples said to him, 'If that is the position with husband and wife, 10
it is better not to marry.' To this he replied, 'That is something which not 11
everyone can accept, but only those for whom God has appointed it. For 12
while some are incapable of marriage because they were born so, or were
made so by men, there are others who have themselves renounced marriage
for the sake of the kingdom of Heaven. Let those accept it who can.'

They brought children for him to lay his hands on them with prayer. 13
The disciples rebuked them, but Jesus said to them, 'Let the children come 14
to me; do not try to stop them; for the kingdom of Heaven belongs to such
as these.' And he laid his hands on the children, and went his way. 15

And now a man came up and asked him, 'Master, what good must I do 16
to gain eternal life?' 'Good?' said Jesus. 'Why do you ask me about that? 17
One alone is good. But if you wish to enter into life, keep the commandments.' 'Which commandments?' he asked. Jesus answered, 'Do not 18
murder; do not commit adultery; do not steal; do not give false evidence;
honour your father and mother; and love your neighbour as yourself.' 19
The young man answered, 'I have kept all these. Where do I still fall short?' 20
Jesus said to him, 'If you wish to go the whole way, go, sell your possessions, 21
and give to the poor, and then you will have riches in heaven; and come,
follow me.' When the young man heard this, he went away with a heavy 22
heart; for he was a man of great wealth.

Jesus said to his disciples, 'I tell you this: a rich man will find it hard to 23
enter the kingdom of Heaven. I repeat, it is easier for a camel to pass through 24

ᵃ *Or* Is there any ground on which it is lawful for a man to divorce his wife?
ᵇ *Some witnesses add* And the man who marries a woman so divorced commits adultery.

the eye of a needle than for a rich man to enter the kingdom of God.'
25 The disciples were amazed to hear this. 'Then who can be saved?' they
26 asked. Jesus looked at them, and said, 'For men this is impossible; but
everything is possible for God.'
27 At this Peter said, 'We here have left everything to become your fol-
28 lowers. What will there be for us?' Jesus replied, 'I tell you this: in the world
that is to be, when the Son of Man is seated on his throne in heavenly splendour, you my followers will have thrones of your own, where you will sit
29 as judges of the twelve tribes of Israel. And anyone who has left brothers
or sisters, father, mother, or children, land or houses for the sake of my
30 name will be repaid many times over, and gain eternal life. But many who
are first will be last, and the last first.

20 'The kingdom of Heaven is like this. There was once a landowner who
2 went out early one morning to hire labourers for his vineyard; and after
3 agreeing to pay them the usual day's wage *a* he sent them off to work. Going
out three hours later he saw some more men standing idle in the market-
4 place. "Go and join the others in the vineyard," he said, "and I will pay
5 you a fair wage"; so off they went. At midday he went out again, and at
6 three in the afternoon, and made the same arrangement as before. An hour
before sunset he went out and found another group standing there; so he
said to them, "Why are you standing about like this all day with nothing
7 to do?" "Because no one has hired us", they replied; so he told them, "Go
8 and join the others in the vineyard." When evening fell, the owner of the
9 vineyard said to his steward, "Call the labourers and give them their pay,
beginning with those who came last and ending with the first." Those who
had started work an hour before sunset came forward, and were paid the
10 full day's wage.*b* When it was the turn of the men who had come first,
they expected something extra, but were paid the same amount as the
11 12 others. As they took it, they grumbled at their employer: "These late-
comers have done only one hour's work, yet you have put them on a level
13 with us, who have sweated the whole day long in the blazing sun!" The
owner turned to one of them and said, "My friend, I am not being unfair
14 to you. You agreed on the usual wage for the day,*c* did you not? Take your
15 pay and go home. I choose to pay the last man the same as you. Surely I am
free to do what I like with my own money. Why be jealous because I am
16 kind?" Thus will the last be first, and the first last.'

## Challenge to Jerusalem

17 JESUS WAS JOURNEYING towards Jerusalem, and on the way he took
18 the Twelve aside, and said to them, 'We are now going to Jerusalem, and
the Son of Man will be given up to the chief priests and the doctors of the
19 law; they will condemn him to death and hand him over to the foreign
power, to be mocked and flogged and crucified, and on the third day he
will be raised to life again.'

*a Literally* one denarius for the day.          *b Literally* one denarius each.
*c Literally* You agreed on a denarius.

28

The mother of Zebedee's sons then came before him, with her sons. She 20
bowed low and begged a favour. 'What is it you wish?' asked Jesus. 'I want 21
you', she said, 'to give orders that in your kingdom my two sons here may
sit next to you, one at your right, and the other at your left.' Jesus turned 22
to the brothers and said, 'You do not understand what you are asking.
Can you drink the cup that I am to drink?' 'We can', they replied. Then he 23
said to them, 'You shall indeed share my cup; but to sit at my right or left
is not for me to grant; it is for those to whom it has already been assigned
by my Father.'

When the other ten heard this, they were indignant with the two 24
brothers. So Jesus called them to him and said, 'You know that in the world, 25
rulers lord it over their subjects, and their great men make them feel the
weight of authority; but it shall not be so with you. Among you, whoever 26
wants to be great must be your servant, and whoever wants to be first must 27
be the willing slave of all—like the Son of Man; he did not come to be 28
served, but to serve, and to give up his life as a ransom for many.'

As they were leaving Jericho he was followed by a great crowd of people. 29
At the roadside sat two blind men. When they heard it said that Jesus was 30
passing they shouted, 'Have pity on us, Son of David.' The people told 31
them sharply to be quiet. But they shouted all the more, 'Sir, have pity on
us; have pity on us, Son of David.' Jesus stopped and called the men. 32
'What do you want me to do for you?' he asked. 'Sir,' they answered, 'we 33
want our sight.' Jesus was deeply moved, and touched their eyes. At once 34
their sight came back, and they followed him.

THEY WERE NOW nearing Jerusalem; and when they reached Bethphage **21**
at the Mount of Olives, Jesus sent two disciples with these instructions: 2
'Go to the village opposite, where you will at once find a donkey tethered
with her foal beside her; untie them, and bring them to me. If anyone speaks 3
to you, say, "Our Master needs them"; and he will let you take them at
once.'[a] This was to fulfil the prophecy which says, 'Tell the daughter of 4 5
Zion, "Here is your king, who comes to you in gentleness, riding on an ass,
riding on the foal of a beast of burden." '

The disciples went and did as Jesus had directed, and brought the donkey 6 7
and her foal; they laid their cloaks on them and Jesus mounted. Crowds of 8
people carpeted the road with their cloaks, and some cut branches from the
trees to spread in his path. Then the crowd that went ahead and the others 9
that came behind raised the shout: 'Hosanna to the Son of David! Blessings
on him who comes in the name of the Lord! Hosanna in the heavens!'

When he entered Jerusalem the whole city went wild with excitement. 10
'Who is this?' people asked, and the crowd replied, 'This is the prophet 11
Jesus, from Nazareth in Galilee.'

Jesus then went into the temple and drove out all who were buying and 12
selling in the temple precincts; he upset the tables of the money-changers
and the seats of the dealers in pigeons; and said to them, 'Scripture says, 13
"My house shall be called a house of prayer"; but you are making it a
robbers' cave.'

[a] *Or* "Our Master needs them and will send them back straight away."

14 In the temple blind men and cripples came to him, and he healed them.

15 The chief priests and doctors of the law saw the wonderful things he did, and heard the boys in the temple shouting, 'Hosanna to the Son of David!',

16 and they asked him indignantly, 'Do you hear what they are saying?' Jesus answered, 'I do; have you never read that text, "Thou hast made

17 children and babes at the breast sound aloud thy praise"?' Then he left them and went out of the city to Bethany, where he spent the night.

18 19 Next morning on his way to the city he felt hungry; and seeing a fig-tree at the roadside he went up to it, but found nothing on it but leaves. He said to the tree, 'You shall never bear fruit any more!'; and the tree withered

20 away at once. The disciples were amazed at the sight. 'How is it', they asked,

21 'that the tree has withered so suddenly?' Jesus answered them, 'I tell you this: if only you have faith and have no doubts, you will do what has been done to the fig-tree; and more than that, you need only say to this mountain, "Be lifted from your place and hurled into the sea", and what you

22 say will be done. And whatever you pray for in faith you will receive.'

23 He entered the temple, and the chief priests and elders of the nation came to him with the question: 'By what authority are you acting like this?

24 Who gave you this authority?' Jesus replied, 'I have a question to ask you

25 too; answer it, and I will tell you by what authority I act. The baptism of John: was it from God, or from men?' This set them arguing among themselves: 'If we say, "from God", he will say, "Then why did you not

26 believe him?" But if we say, "from men", we are afraid of the people, for

27 they all take John for a prophet.' So they answered, 'We do not know.' And Jesus said: 'Then neither will I tell you by what authority I act.

28 'But what do you think about this? A man had two sons. He went to the

29 first, and said, "My boy, go and work today in the vineyard." "I will, sir",

30 the boy replied; but he never went. The father came to the second and said the same. "I will not", he replied, but afterwards he changed his mind

31 and went. Which of these two did as his father wished?' 'The second', they said. Then Jesus answered, 'I tell you this: tax-gatherers and prostitutes

32 are entering the kingdom of God ahead of you. For when John came to show you the right way to live, you did not believe him, but the tax-gatherers and prostitutes did; and even when you had seen that, you did not change your minds and believe him.

33 'Listen to another parable. There was a landowner who planted a vineyard: he put a wall round it, hewed out a winepress, and built a watch-

34 tower; then he let it out to vine-growers and went abroad. When the vintage season approached, he sent his servants to the tenants to collect

35 the produce due to him. But they took his servants and thrashed one,

36 killed another, and stoned a third. Again, he sent other servants, this time

37 a larger number; and they did the same to them. At last he sent to them his

38 son. "They will respect my son", he said. But when they saw the son the tenants said to one another, "This is the heir; come on, let us kill him, and

39 get his inheritance." And they took him, flung him out of the vineyard,

40 and killed him. When the owner of the vineyard comes, how do you think

41 he will deal with those tenants?' 'He will bring those bad men to a bad end', they answered, 'and hand the vineyard over to other tenants, who will let

him have his share of the crop when the season comes.' Then Jesus said 42 to them, 'Have you never read in the scriptures: "The stone which the builders rejected has become the main corner-stone. This is the Lord's doing, and it is wonderful in our eyes"? Therefore, I tell you, the kingdom 43 of God will be taken away from you, and given to a nation that yields the proper fruit.'*a*

When the chief priests and Pharisees heard his parables, they saw that 45 he was referring to them; they wanted to arrest him, but they were afraid 46 of the people, who looked on Jesus as a prophet.

THEN JESUS SPOKE to them again in parables: 'The kingdom of Heaven **22** 1 2 is like this. There was a king who prepared a feast for his son's wedding; but when he sent his servants to summon the guests he had invited, they 3 would not come. He sent others again, telling them to say to the guests, 4 "See now! I have prepared this feast for you. I have had my bullocks and fatted beasts slaughtered; everything is ready; come to the wedding at once." But they took no notice; one went off to his farm, another to his 5 business, and the others seized the servants, attacked them brutally, and 6 killed them. The king was furious; he sent troops to kill those murderers 7 and set their town on fire. Then he said to his servants, "The wedding-feast 8 is ready; but the guests I invited did not deserve the honour. Go out to the 9 main thoroughfares, and invite everyone you can find to the wedding." The servants went out into the streets, and collected all they could find, 10 good and bad alike. So the hall was packed with guests.

'When the king came in to see the company at table, he observed one 11 man who was not dressed for a wedding. "My friend," said the king, "how 12 do you come to be here without your wedding clothes?" He had nothing to say. The king then said to his attendants, "Bind him hand and foot; 13 turn him out into the dark, the place of wailing and grinding of teeth." For 14 though many are invited, few are chosen.'

THEN THE PHARISEES went away and agreed on a plan to trap him in his 15 own words. Some of their followers were sent to him in company with men 16 of Herod's party. They said, 'Master, you are an honest man, we know; you teach in all honesty the way of life that God requires, truckling to no man, whoever he may be. Give us your ruling on this: are we or are we not per- 17 mitted to pay taxes to the Roman Emperor?' Jesus was aware of their 18 malicious intention and said to them, 'You hypocrites! Why are you trying to catch me out? Show me the money in which the tax is paid.' They 19 handed him a silver piece. Jesus asked, 'Whose head is this, and whose 20 inscription?' 'Caesar's', they replied. He said to them, 'Then pay Caesar 21 what is due to Caesar, and pay God what is due to God.' This answer took 22 them by surprise, and they went away and left him alone.

The same day Sadducees came to him, maintaining that there is no 23 resurrection. Their question was this: 'Master, Moses said, "If a man 24 should die childless, his brother shall marry the widow and carry on his

*a Some witnesses add* (44) Any man who falls on this stone will be dashed to pieces; and if it falls on a man he will be crushed by it.

25 brother's family." Now we knew of seven brothers. The first married and
26 died, and as he was without issue his wife was left to his brother. The same
thing happened with the second, and the third, and so on with all seven.
27 28 Last of all the woman died. At the resurrection, then, whose wife will she
29 be, for they had all married her?' Jesus answered: 'You are mistaken,
30 because you know neither the scriptures nor the power of God. At the
resurrection men and women do not marry; they are like angels in heaven.

31 'But about the resurrection of the dead, have you never read what God
32 himself said to you: "I am the God of Abraham, the God of Isaac, and the
33 God of Jacob"? He is not God of the dead but of the living.' The people
heard what he said, and were astounded at his teaching.

34 Hearing that he had silenced the Sadducees, the Pharisees met together;
35 36 and one of their number *a* tested him with this question: 'Master, which is
37 the greatest commandment in the Law?' He answered, ' "Love the Lord
38 your God with all your heart, with all your soul, with all your mind." That
39 is the greatest commandment. It comes first. The second is like it: "Love
40 your neighbour as yourself." Everything in the Law and the prophets
hangs on these two commandments.'

41 42 Turning to the assembled Pharisees Jesus asked them, 'What is your
opinion about the Messiah? Whose son is he?' 'The son of David', they
43 replied. 'How then is it', he asked, 'that David by inspiration calls him
44 "Lord"? For he says, "The Lord said to my Lord, 'Sit at my right hand
45 until I put your enemies under your feet.' " If David calls him "Lord",
46 how can he be David's son?' Not a man could say a word in reply; and from
that day forward no one dared ask him another question.

23 1 2 JESUS THEN ADDRESSED the people and his disciples in these words:
3 'The doctors of the law and the Pharisees sit in the chair of Moses; therefore
do what they tell you; pay attention to their words. But do not follow their
4 practice; for they say one thing and do another. They make up heavy packs
and pile them on men's shoulders, but will not raise a finger to lift the load
5 themselves. Whatever they do is done for show. They go about with broad
6 phylacteries *b* and with large tassels on their robes; they like to have places
7 of honour at feasts and the chief seats in synagogues, to be greeted respect-
fully in the street, and to be addressed as "rabbi".

8 'But you must not be called "rabbi"; for you have one Rabbi, and you are
9 all brothers. Do not call any man on earth "father"; for you have one Father,
10 and he is in heaven. Nor must you be called "teacher"; you have one
11 12 Teacher, the Messiah. The greatest among you must be your servant. For
whoever exalts himself will be humbled; and whoever humbles himself
will be exalted.

13 'Alas, alas for you, lawyers and Pharisees, hypocrites that you are! You
shut the door of the kingdom of Heaven in men's faces; you do not enter
yourselves, and when others are entering, you stop them. *c*

---

*a* *Some witnesses insert* a lawyer.          *b* *See Deuteronomy 6. 8–9 and Exodus 13. 9.*
*c* *Some witnesses add* (14) Alas for you, lawyers and Pharisees, hypocrites! You eat up
the property of widows, while you say long prayers for appearance' sake. You will receive
the severest sentence.

'Alas for you, lawyers and Pharisees, hypocrites! You travel over sea 15 and land to win one convert; and when you have won him you make him twice as fit for hell as you are yourselves.

'Alas for you, blind guides! You say, "If a man swears by the sanctuary, 16 that is nothing; but if he swears by the gold in the sanctuary, he is bound by his oath." Blind fools! Which is the more important, the gold, or the 17 sanctuary which sanctifies the gold? Or you say, "If a man swears by the 18 altar, that is nothing; but if he swears by the offering that lies on the altar, he is bound by his oath." What blindness! Which is the more important, the 19 offering, or the altar which sanctifies it? To swear by the altar, then, is to 20 swear both by the altar and by whatever lies on it; to swear by the sanctuary 21 is to swear both by the sanctuary and by him who dwells there; and to swear 22 by heaven is to swear both by the throne of God and by him who sits upon it.

'Alas for you, lawyers and Pharisees, hypocrites! You pay tithes of mint 23 and dill and cummin; but you have overlooked the weightier demands of the Law, justice, mercy, and good faith. It is these you should have practised, without neglecting the others. Blind guides! You strain off a midge, 24 yet gulp down a camel!

'Alas for you, lawyers and Pharisees, hypocrites! You clean the outside of 25 cup and dish, which you have filled inside by robbery and self-indulgence! Blind Pharisee! Clean the inside of the cup first; then the outside will be 26 clean also.

'Alas for you, lawyers and Pharisees, hypocrites! You are like tombs 27 covered with whitewash; they look well from outside, but inside they are full of dead men's bones and all kinds of filth. So it is with you: outside you 28 look like honest men, but inside you are brim-full of hypocrisy and crime.

'Alas for you, lawyers and Pharisees, hypocrites! You build up the tombs 29 of the prophets and embellish the monuments of the saints, and you say, 30 "If we had been alive in our fathers' time, we should never have taken part with them in the murder of the prophets." So you acknowledge that you 31 are the sons of the men who killed the prophets. Go on then, finish off what 32 your fathers began! *a*

'You snakes, you vipers' brood, how can you escape being condemned 33 to hell? I send you therefore prophets, sages, and teachers; some of them 34 you will kill and crucify, others you will flog in your synagogues and hound from city to city. And so, on you will fall the guilt of all the innocent blood 35 spilt on the ground, from innocent Abel to Zechariah son of Berachiah, whom you murdered between the sanctuary and the altar. Believe me, this 36 generation will bear the guilt of it all.

'O Jerusalem, Jerusalem, the city that murders the prophets and stones 37 the messengers sent to her! How often have I longed to gather your children, as a hen gathers her brood under her wings; but you would not let me. Look, look! there is your temple, forsaken by God.*b c* And I tell 38 39 you, you shall never see me until the time when you say, "Blessings on him who comes in the name of the Lord." '

*a Or* You too must come up to your fathers' standards.   *b Or* Look, your home is desolate.   *c Some witnesses add* and laid waste.

33

## Prophecies and warnings

**24** JESUS WAS LEAVING the temple when his disciples came and pointed to
2 the temple buildings. He answered, 'Yes, look at it all. I tell you this:
not one stone will be left upon another; all will be thrown down.'

3 When he was sitting on the Mount of Olives the disciples came to speak
to him privately. 'Tell us,' they said, 'when will this happen? And what will
be the signal for your coming and the end of the age?'

4 5 Jesus replied: 'Take care that no one misleads you. For many will come
claiming my name and saying, "I am the Messiah"; and many will be
6 misled by them. The time is coming when you will hear the noise of battle
near at hand and the news of battles far away; see that you are not alarmed.
7 Such things are bound to happen; but the end is still to come. For nation
will make war upon nation, kingdom upon kingdom; there will be famines
8 and earthquakes in many places. With all these things the birth-pangs of
the new age begin.

9 'You will then be handed over for punishment and execution; and men
10 of all nations will hate you for your allegiance to me. Many will fall from
11 their faith; they will betray one another and hate one another. Many false
12 prophets will arise, and will mislead many; and as lawlessness spreads,
13 men's love for one another will grow cold. But the man who holds out to the
14 end will be saved. And this gospel of the Kingdom will be proclaimed
throughout the earth as a testimony to all nations; and then the end will
come.

15 'So when you see "the abomination of desolation", of which the prophet
16 Daniel spoke, standing in the holy place (let the reader understand), then
17 those who are in Judaea must take to the hills. If a man is on the roof, he
18 must not come down to fetch his goods from the house; if in the field, he
19 must not turn back for his coat. Alas for women with child in those days,
20 and for those who have children at the breast! Pray that it may not be
21 winter when you have to make your escape, or Sabbath. It will be a time of
great distress; there has never been such a time from the beginning of the
22 world until now, and will never be again. If that time of troubles were not
cut short, no living thing could survive; but for the sake of God's chosen it
will be cut short.

23 'Then, if anyone says to you, "Look, here is the Messiah", or, "There he
24 is", do not believe it. Impostors will come claiming to be messiahs or
prophets, and they will produce great signs and wonders to mislead even
25 God's chosen, if such a thing were possible. See, I have forewarned you.
26 If they tell you, "He is there in the wilderness", do not go out; or if they
27 say, "He is there in the inner room", do not believe it. Like lightning
from the east, flashing as far as the west, will be the coming of the Son
of Man.

28 'Wherever the corpse is, there the vultures will gather.

29 'As soon as the distress of those days has passed, the sun will be darkened,
the moon will not give her light, the stars will fall from the sky, the celestial
30 powers will be shaken. Then will appear in heaven the sign that heralds

the Son of Man. All the peoples of the world will make lamentation, and
they will see the Son of Man coming on the clouds of heaven with great
power and glory. With a trumpet blast he will send out his angels, and they 31
will gather his chosen from the four winds, from the farthest bounds of
heaven on every side.

'Learn a lesson from the fig-tree. When its tender shoots appear and 32
are breaking into leaf, you know that summer is near. In the same way, 33
when you see all these things, you may know that the end is near,*a* at the
very door. I tell you this: the present generation will live to see it all. Heaven 34 35
and earth will pass away; my words will never pass away.

'But about that day and hour no one knows, not even the angels in 36
heaven, not even the Son; only the Father.

'As things were in Noah's days, so will they be when the Son of Man 37
comes. In the days before the flood they ate and drank and married, until 38
the day that Noah went into the ark, and they knew nothing until the flood 39
came and swept them all away. That is how it will be when the Son of Man
comes. Then there will be two men in the field; one will be taken, the other 40
left; two women grinding at the mill; one will be taken, the other left. 41

'Keep awake, then; for you do not know on what day your Lord is to 42
come. Remember, if the householder had known at what time of night the 43
burglar was coming, he would have kept awake and not have let his house
be broken into. Hold yourselves ready, therefore, because the Son of Man 44
will come at the time you least expect him.

'Who is the trusty servant, the sensible man charged by his master to 45
manage his household staff and issue their rations at the proper time?
Happy that servant who is found at his task when his master comes! I tell 46 47
you this: he will be put in charge of all his master's property. But if he is 48
a bad servant and says to himself, "The master is a long time coming", and 49
begins to bully the other servants and to eat and drink with his drunken
friends, then the master will arrive on a day that servant does not expect, 50
at a time he does not know, and will cut him in pieces. Thus he will find his 51
place among the hypocrites, where there is wailing and grinding of teeth.

'When that day comes, the kingdom of Heaven will be like this. There **25**
were ten girls, who took their lamps and went out to meet the bridegroom.
Five of them were foolish, and five prudent; when the foolish ones took 2 3
their lamps, they took no oil with them, but the others took flasks of oil 4
with their lamps. As the bridegroom was late in coming they all dozed off 5
to sleep. But at midnight a cry was heard: "Here is the bridegroom! Come 6
out to meet him." With that the girls all got up and trimmed their lamps. 7
The foolish said to the prudent, "Our lamps are going out; give us some of 8
your oil." "No," they said; "there will never be enough for all of us. You 9
had better go to the shop and buy some for yourselves." While they were 10
away the bridegroom arrived; those who were ready went in with him to
the wedding; and the door was shut. And then the other five came back. 11
"Sir, sir," they cried, "open the door for us." But he answered, "I declare, 12
I do not know you." Keep awake then; for you never know the day or the 13
hour.

*a Or* that he is near.

35

14 'It is like a man going abroad, who called his servants and put his capital
15 in their hands; to one he gave five bags of gold, to another two, to another
16 one, each according to his capacity. Then he left the country. The man who
had the five bags went at once and employed them in business, and made
17 18 a profit of five bags, and the man who had the two bags made two. But the
man who had been given one bag of gold went off and dug a hole in the
19 ground, and hid his master's money. A long time afterwards their master
20 returned, and proceeded to settle accounts with them. The man who had
been given the five bags of gold came and produced the five he had made:
"Master," he said, "you left five bags with me; look, I have made five more."
21 "Well done, my good and trusty servant!" said the master. "You have
proved trustworthy in a small way; I will now put you in charge of some-
22 thing big. Come and share your master's delight." The man with the two
bags then came and said, "Master, you left two bags with me; look, I have
23 made two more." "Well done, my good and trusty servant!" said the
master. "You have proved trustworthy in a small way; I will now put you
24 in charge of something big. Come and share your master's delight." Then
the man who had been given one bag came and said, "Master, I knew you
to be a hard man: you reap where you have not sown, you gather where you
25 have not scattered; so I was afraid, and I went and hid your gold in the
26 ground. Here it is—you have what belongs to you." "You lazy rascal!"
said the master. "You knew that I reap where I have not sown, and gather
27 where I have not scattered? Then you ought to have put my money on
28 deposit, and on my return I should have got it back with interest. Take the
29 bag of gold from him, and give it to the one with the ten bags. For the man
who has will always be given more, till he has enough and to spare; and
30 the man who has not will forfeit even what he has. Fling the useless servant
out into the dark, the place of wailing and grinding of teeth!"

31 'When the Son of Man comes in his glory and all the angels with him,
32 he will sit in state on his throne, with all the nations gathered before him.
He will separate men into two groups, as a shepherd separates the sheep
33 from the goats, and he will place the sheep on his right hand and the goats
34 on his left. Then the king will say to those on his right hand, "You have my
Father's blessing; come, enter and possess the kingdom that has been
35 ready for you since the world was made. For when I was hungry, you gave
me food; when thirsty, you gave me drink; when I was a stranger you took
36 me into your home, when naked you clothed me; when I was ill you came
37 to my help, when in prison you visited me." Then the righteous will reply,
"Lord, when was it that we saw you hungry and fed you, or thirsty and
38 gave you drink, a stranger and took you home, or naked and clothed you?
39 40 When did we see you ill or in prison, and come to visit you?" And the king
will answer, "I tell you this: anything you did for one of my brothers here,
41 however humble, you did for me." Then he will say to those on his left
hand, "The curse is upon you; go from my sight to the eternal fire that is
42 ready for the devil and his angels. For when I was hungry you gave me
43 nothing to eat, when thirsty nothing to drink; when I was a stranger you
gave me no home, when naked you did not clothe me; when I was ill and in
44 prison you did not come to my help." And they too will reply, "Lord, when

36

was it that we saw you hungry or thirsty or a stranger or naked or ill or in prison, and did nothing for you?" And he will answer, "I tell you this: 45 anything you did not do for one of these, however humble, you did not do for me." And they will go away to eternal punishment, but the righteous 46 will enter eternal life.'

## The final conflict

WHEN JESUS HAD FINISHED this discourse he said to his disciples, 26 'You know that in two days' time it will be Passover, and the Son 2 of Man is to be handed over for crucifixion.'

Then the chief priests and the elders of the nation met in the palace of the 3 High Priest, Caiaphas; and there they conferred together on a scheme to 4 have Jesus arrested by some trick and put to death. 'It must not be during 5 the festival,' they said, 'or there may be rioting among the people.'

JESUS WAS AT BETHANY in the house of Simon the leper, when a woman 6 7 came to him with a small bottle of fragrant oil, very costly; and as he sat at table she began to pour it over his head. The disciples were indignant 8 when they saw it. 'Why this waste?' they said; 'it could have been sold for 9 a good sum and the money given to the poor.' Jesus was aware of this, and 10 said to them, 'Why must you make trouble for the woman? It is a fine thing she has done for me. You have the poor among you always; but you will 11 not always have me. When she poured this oil on my body it was her way of 12 preparing me for burial. I tell you this: wherever in all the world this gospel 13 is proclaimed, what she has done will be told as her memorial.'

THEN ONE OF THE TWELVE, the man called Judas Iscariot, went to the 14 chief priests and said, 'What will you give me to betray him to you?' 15 They weighed him out*a* thirty silver pieces. From that moment he began 16 to look out for an opportunity to betray him.

On the first day of Unleavened Bread the disciples came to ask Jesus, 17 'Where would you like us to prepare for your Passover supper?' He 18 answered, 'Go to a certain man in the city, and tell him, "The Master says, 'My appointed time is near; I am to keep Passover with my disciples at your house.'"' The disciples did as Jesus directed them and prepared for 19 Passover.

In the evening he sat down with the twelve disciples; and during supper 20 21 he said, 'I tell you this: one of you will betray me.' In great distress they 22 exclaimed one after the other, 'Can you mean me, Lord?' He answered, 23 'One who has dipped his hand into this bowl with me will betray me. The 24 Son of Man is going the way appointed for him in the scriptures; but alas for that man by whom the Son of Man is betrayed! It would be better for that man if he had never been born.' Then Judas spoke, the one who was 25 to betray him: 'Rabbi, can you mean me?' Jesus replied, 'The words are yours.'*b*

*a Or* agreed to pay him . . .      *b Or* It is as you say.

26  During supper Jesus took bread, and having said the blessing he broke it
and gave it to the disciples with the words: 'Take this and eat; this is my
27  body.' Then he took a cup, and having offered thanks to God he gave it to
28  them with the words: 'Drink from it, all of you. For this is my blood, the
29  blood of the covenant, shed for many for the forgiveness of sins. I tell you,
never again shall I drink from the fruit of the vine until that day when I
drink it new with you in the kingdom of my Father.'

30  After singing the Passover Hymn, they went out to the Mount of Olives.
31  Then Jesus said to them, 'Tonight you will all fall from your faith on my
account; for it stands written: "I will strike the shepherd down and the
32  sheep of his flock will be scattered." But after I am raised again, I will go on
33  before you into Galilee.' Peter replied, 'Everyone else may fall away on
34  your account, but I never will.' Jesus said to him, 'I tell you, tonight before
35  the cock crows you will disown me three times.' Peter said, 'Even if I must
die with you, I will never disown you.' And all the disciples said the same.

36  JESUS THEN CAME with his disciples to a place called Gethsemane. He
37  said to them, 'Sit here while I go over there to pray.' He took with him
Peter and the two sons of Zebedee. Anguish and dismay came over him,
38  and he said to them, 'My heart is ready to break with grief. Stop here, and
39  stay awake with me.' He went on a little, fell on his face in prayer, and said,
'My Father, if it is possible, let this cup pass me by. Yet not as I will, but
as thou wilt.'

40  He came to the disciples and found them asleep; and he said to Peter,
41  'What! Could none of you stay awake with me one hour? Stay awake, and
pray that you may be spared the test. The spirit is willing, but the flesh is
weak.'

42  He went away a second time, and prayed: 'My Father, if it is not possible
43  for this cup to pass me by without my drinking it, thy will be done.' He came
44  again and found them asleep, for their eyes were heavy. So he left them
and went away again; and he prayed the third time, using the same words
as before.

45  Then he came to the disciples and said to them, 'Still sleeping? Still
taking your ease? The hour has come! The Son of Man is betrayed to
46  sinful men. Up, let us go forward; the traitor is upon us.'

47  While he was still speaking, Judas, one of the Twelve, appeared; with
him was a great crowd armed with swords and cudgels, sent by the chief
48  priests and the elders of the nation. The traitor gave them this sign: 'The
49  one I kiss is your man; seize him'; and stepping forward at once, he said,
50  'Hail, Rabbi!', and kissed him. Jesus replied, 'Friend, do what you are here
to do.'ᵃ They then came forward, seized Jesus, and held him fast.

51  At that moment one of those with Jesus reached for his sword and drew
52  it, and he struck at the High Priest's servant and cut off his ear. But Jesus
said to him, 'Put up your sword. All who take the sword die by the sword.
53  Do you suppose that I cannot appeal to my Father, who would at once
54  send to my aid more than twelve legions of angels? But how then could the
scriptures be fulfilled, which say that this must be?'

ᵃ *Or* Friend, what are you here for?

At the same time Jesus spoke to the crowd: 'Do you take me for a bandit, 55 that you have come out with swords and cudgels to arrest me? Day after day I sat teaching in the temple, and you did not lay hands on me. But this 56 has all happened to fulfil what the prophets wrote.'
Then the disciples all deserted him and ran away.

JESUS WAS LED OFF under arrest to the house of Caiaphas the High Priest, 57 where the lawyers and elders were assembled. Peter followed him at a 58 distance till he came to the High Priest's courtyard, and going in he sat down there among the attendants, meaning to see the end of it all.

The chief priests and the whole Council tried to find some allegation 59 against Jesus on which a death-sentence could be based; but they failed 60 to find one, though many came forward with false evidence. Finally two men alleged that he had said, 'I can pull down the temple of God, and 61 rebuild it in three days.' At this the High Priest rose and said to him, 'Have 62 you no answer to the charge that these witnesses bring against you?' But 63 Jesus kept silence. The High Priest then said, 'By the living God I charge you to tell us: Are you the Messiah, the Son of God?' Jesus replied, 'The 64 words are yours.*a* But I tell you this: from now on, you will see the Son of Man seated at the right hand of God*b* and coming on the clouds of heaven.' At these words the High Priest tore his robes and exclaimed, 'Blasphemy! 65 Need we call further witnesses? You have heard the blasphemy. What is 66 your opinion?' 'He is guilty,' they answered; 'he should die.'

Then they spat in his face and struck him with their fists; and others 67 said, as they beat him, 'Now, Messiah, if you are a prophet, tell us who 68 hit you.'

Meanwhile Peter was sitting outside in the courtyard when a serving- 69 maid accosted him and said, 'You were there too with Jesus the Galilean.' Peter denied it in face of them all. 'I do not know what you mean', he said. 70 He then went out to the gateway, where another girl, seeing him, said to 71 the people there, 'This fellow was with Jesus of Nazareth.' Once again he 72 denied it, saying with an oath, 'I do not know the man.' Shortly afterwards 73 the bystanders came up and said to Peter, 'Surely you are another of them; your accent gives you away!' At this he broke into curses and declared 74 with an oath: 'I do not know the man.' At that moment a cock crew; and 75 Peter remembered how Jesus had said, 'Before the cock crows you will disown me three times.' He went outside, and wept bitterly.

WHEN MORNING CAME, the chief priests and the elders of the nation met **27** in conference to plan the death of Jesus. They then put him in chains and 2 led him away, to hand him over to Pilate, the Roman Governor.

When Judas the traitor saw that Jesus had been condemned, he was 3 seized with remorse, and returned the thirty silver pieces to the chief priests and elders. 'I have sinned,' he said; 'I have brought an innocent 4 man to his death.' But they said, 'What is that to us? See to that yourself.' So he threw the money down in the temple and left them, and went and 5 hanged himself.

*a Or* It is as you say.      *b Literally* of the Power.

6    Taking up the money, the chief priests argued: 'This cannot be put into
7  the temple fund; it is blood-money.' So after conferring they used it to
8  buy the Potter's Field, as a burial-place for foreigners. This explains the
9  name 'Blood Acre', by which that field has been known ever since; and in
   this way fulfilment was given to the prophetic utterance of Jeremiah:
   'They took*a* the thirty silver pieces, the price set on a man's head (for that
10 was his price among the Israelites), and gave the money for the potter's field,
   as the Lord directed me.'

11    Jesus was now brought before the Governor; and as he stood there the
   Governor asked him, 'Are you the king of the Jews?' 'The words are
12 yours',*b* said Jesus; and to the charges laid against him by the chief priests
13 and elders he made no reply. Then Pilate said to him, 'Do you not hear all
14 this evidence that is brought against you?'; but he still refused to answer
   one word, to the Governor's great astonishment.

15    At the festival season it was the Governor's custom to release one
16 prisoner chosen by the people. There was then in custody a man of some
17 notoriety, called Jesus*c* Bar-Abbas. When they were assembled Pilate
   said to them, 'Which would you like me to release to you—Jesus*c* Bar-
18 Abbas, or Jesus called Messiah?' For he knew that it was out of malice
   that they had brought Jesus before him.

19    While Pilate was sitting in court a message came to him from his wife:
   'Have nothing to do with that innocent man; I was much troubled on his
   account in my dreams last night.'

20    Meanwhile the chief priests and elders had persuaded the crowd to ask
21 for the release of Bar-Abbas and to have Jesus put to death. So when the
   Governor asked, 'Which of the two do you wish me to release to you?',
22 they said, 'Bar-Abbas.' 'Then what am I to do with Jesus called Messiah?'
23 asked Pilate; and with one voice they answered, 'Crucify him!' 'Why,
   what harm has he done?' Pilate asked; but they shouted all the louder,
   'Crucify him!'

24    Pilate could see that nothing was being gained, and a riot was starting;
   so he took water and washed his hands in full view of the people, saying,
25 'My hands are clean of this man's blood; see to that yourselves.' And with
26 one voice the people cried, 'His blood be on us, and on our children.' He
   then released Bar-Abbas to them; but he had Jesus flogged, and handed
   him over to be crucified.

27 PILATE'S SOLDIERS then took Jesus into the Governor's headquarters,
28 where they collected the whole company round him. They stripped him
29 and dressed him in a scarlet mantle; and plaiting a crown of thorns they
   placed it on his head, with a cane in his right hand. Falling on their knees
30 before him they jeered at him: 'Hail, King of the Jews!' They spat on him,
31 and used the cane to beat him about the head. When they had finished their
   mockery, they took off the mantle and dressed him in his own clothes.

32    Then they led him away to be crucified. On their way out they met a man
   from Cyrene, Simon by name, and pressed him into service to carry his
   cross.

   *a* Or I took.      *b* Or It is as you say.      *c* *Some witnesses omit* Jesus.

So they came to a place called Golgotha (which means 'Place of a skull') 33
and there he was offered a draught of wine mixed with gall; but when he 34
had tasted it he would not drink.

After fastening him to the cross they divided his clothes among them by 35
casting lots, and then sat down there to keep watch. Over his head was 36 37
placed the inscription giving the charge: 'This is Jesus the king of the Jews.'

Two bandits were crucified with him, one on his right and the other on 38
his left.

The passers-by hurled abuse at him: they wagged their heads and cried, 39 40
'You would pull the temple down, would you, and build it in three days?
Come down from the cross and save yourself, if you are indeed the Son of
God.' So too the chief priests with the lawyers and elders mocked at him: 41
'He saved others,' they said, 'but he cannot save himself. King of Israel, 42
indeed! Let him come down now from the cross, and then we will believe
him. Did he trust in God? Let God rescue him, if he wants him—for he 43
said he was God's Son.' Even the bandits who were crucified with him 44
taunted him in the same way.

From midday a darkness fell over the whole land, which lasted until 45
three in the afternoon; and about three Jesus cried aloud, '*Eli, Eli, lema* 46
*sabachthani?*', which means, 'My God, my God, why hast thou forsaken
me?' Some of the bystanders, on hearing this, said, 'He is calling Elijah.' 47
One of them ran at once and fetched a sponge, which he soaked in sour 48
wine, and held it to his lips on the end of a cane. But the others said, 49
'Let us see if Elijah will come to save him.'

Jesus again gave a loud cry, and breathed his last. At that moment the 50 51
curtain of the temple was torn in two from top to bottom. There was an
earthquake, the rocks split and the graves opened, and many of God's 52
saints were raised from sleep; and coming out of their graves after his 53
resurrection they entered the Holy City, where many saw them. And when 54
the centurion and his men who were keeping watch over Jesus saw the
earthquake and all that was happening, they were filled with awe, and they
said, 'Truly this man was a son of God.'[a]

A NUMBER OF WOMEN were also present, watching from a distance; they 55
had followed Jesus from Galilee and waited on him. Among them were 56
Mary of Magdala, Mary the mother of James and Joseph, and the mother
of the sons of Zebedee.

When evening fell, there came a man of Arimathaea, Joseph by name, 57
who was a man of means, and had himself become a disciple of Jesus. He 58
approached Pilate, and asked for the body of Jesus; and Pilate gave orders
that he should have it. Joseph took the body, wrapped it in a clean linen 59
sheet, and laid it in his own unused tomb, which he had cut out of the rock; 60
he then rolled a large stone against the entrance, and went away. Mary of 61
Magdala was there, and the other Mary, sitting opposite the grave.

Next day, the morning after that Friday, the chief priests and the 62
Pharisees came in a body to Pilate. 'Your Excellency,' they said, 'we recall 63
how that impostor said while he was still alive, "I am to be raised again

___
[a] *Or* the Son of God.

64 after three days." So will you give orders for the grave to be made secure until the third day? Otherwise his disciples may come, steal the body, and then tell the people that he has been raised from the dead; and the final 65 deception will be worse than the first.' 'You may have your guard,' said 66 Pilate; 'go and make it secure as best you can.' So they went and made the grave secure; they sealed the stone, and left the guard in charge.

28 THE SABBATH WAS OVER, and it was about daybreak on Sunday, when 2 Mary of Magdala and the other Mary came to look at the grave. Suddenly there was a violent earthquake; an angel of the Lord descended from heaven; he came to the stone and rolled it away, and sat himself down on it. 3 4 His face shone like lightning; his garments were white as snow. At the sight of him the guards shook with fear and lay like the dead.

5 The angel then addressed the women: 'You', he said, 'have nothing to 6 fear. I know you are looking for Jesus who was crucified. He is not here; he has been raised again, as he said he would be. Come and see the place where 7 he was laid, and then go quickly and tell his disciples: "He has been raised from the dead and is going on before you into Galilee; there you will see him." That is what I had to tell you.'

8 They hurried away from the tomb in awe and great joy, and ran to tell 9 the disciples. Suddenly Jesus was there in their path. He gave them his greeting, and they came up and clasped his feet, falling prostrate before 10 him. Then Jesus said to them, 'Do not be afraid. Go and take word to my brothers that they are to leave for Galilee. They will see me there.'

11 The women had started on their way when some of the guard went into the city and reported to the chief priests everything that had happened. 12 After meeting with the elders and conferring together, the chief priests 13 offered the soldiers a substantial bribe and told them to say, 'His disciples 14 came by night and stole the body while we were asleep.' They added, 'If this should reach the Governor's ears, we will put matters right with him 15 and see that you do not suffer.' So they took the money and did as they were told. This story became widely known, and is current in Jewish circles to this day.

16 The eleven disciples made their way to Galilee, to the mountain where 17 Jesus had told them to meet him. When they saw him, they fell prostrate 18 before him, though some were doubtful. Jesus then came up and spoke to them. He said: 'Full authority in heaven and on earth has been committed 19 to me. Go forth therefore and make all nations my disciples; baptize men everywhere in the name of the Father and the Son and the Holy Spirit, 20 and teach them to observe all that I have commanded you. And be assured, I am with you always, to the end of time.'

# THE GOSPEL ACCORDING TO
# MARK

## The coming of Christ

HERE BEGINS THE GOSPEL of Jesus Christ the Son 1
of God.*a* In the prophet Isaiah it stands written: 'Here is my herald 2
whom I send on ahead of you, and he will prepare your way. A voice crying 3
aloud in the wilderness, "Prepare a way for the Lord; clear a straight path
for him."' And so it was that John the Baptist appeared in the wilderness 4
proclaiming a baptism in token of repentance, for the forgiveness of sins;
and they flocked to him from the whole Judaean country-side and the city 5
of Jerusalem, and were baptized by him in the River Jordan, confessing
their sins.

John was dressed in a rough coat of camel's hair, with a leather belt 6
round his waist, and he fed on locusts and wild honey. His proclamation 7
ran: 'After me comes one who is mightier than I. I am not fit to unfasten
his shoes. I have baptized you with water; he will baptize you with the 8
Holy Spirit.'

It happened at this time that Jesus came from Nazareth in Galilee and 9
was baptized in the Jordan by John. At the moment when he came up out 10
of the water, he saw the heavens torn open and the Spirit, like a dove,
descending upon him. And a voice spoke from heaven: 'Thou art my Son, 11
my Beloved;*b* on thee my favour rests.'

Thereupon the Spirit sent him away into the wilderness, and there he 12 13
remained for forty days tempted by Satan. He was among the wild beasts;
and the angels waited on him.

## In Galilee : success and opposition

AFTER JOHN HAD BEEN ARRESTED, Jesus came into Galilee proclaim- 14
ing the Gospel of God: 'The time has come; the kingdom of God is 15
upon you; repent, and believe the Gospel.'

Jesus was walking by the Sea of Galilee when he saw Simon and his 16
brother Andrew on the lake at work with a casting-net; for they were
fishermen. Jesus said to them, 'Come with me, and I will make you fishers 17
of men.' And at once they left their nets and followed him. 18

When he had gone a little further he saw James son of Zebedee and his 19
brother John, who were in the boat overhauling their nets. He called them; 20

---

*a Some witnesses omit* the Son of God.     *b Or* Thou art my only Son.

43

and, leaving their father Zebedee in the boat with the hired men, they went off to follow him.

21 They came to Capernaum, and on the Sabbath he went to synagogue and
22 began to teach. The people were astounded at his teaching, for, unlike the
23 doctors of the law, he taught with a note of authority. Now there was a man
24 in the synagogue possessed by an unclean spirit. He shrieked: 'What do you want with us, Jesus of Nazareth? Have you [a] come to destroy us?
25 I know who you are—the Holy One of God.' Jesus rebuked him: 'Be silent',
26 he said, 'and come out of him.' And the unclean spirit threw the man into
27 convulsions and with a loud cry left him. They were all dumbfounded and began to ask one another, 'What is this? A new kind of teaching! He speaks with authority. When he gives orders, even the unclean spirits submit.'
28 The news spread rapidly, and he was soon spoken of all over the district of Galilee.

29 On leaving the synagogue they went straight to the house of Simon and
30 Andrew; and James and John went with them. Simon's mother-in-law
31 was ill in bed with fever. They told him about her at once. He came forward, took her by the hand, and helped her to her feet. The fever left her and she waited upon them.

32 That evening after sunset they brought to him all who were ill or pos-
33 34 sessed by devils; and the whole town was there, gathered at the door. He healed many who suffered from various diseases, and drove out many devils. He would not let the devils speak, because they knew who he was.

35 Very early next morning he got up and went out. He went away to a lonely
36 spot and remained there in prayer. But Simon and his companions searched
37 38 him out, found him, and said, 'They are all looking for you.' He answered, 'Let us move on to the country towns in the neighbourhood; I have to
39 proclaim my message there also; that is what I came out to do.' So all through Galilee he went, preaching in the synagogues and casting out the devils.

40 Once he was approached by a leper, who knelt before him begging his
41 help. 'If only you will,' said the man, 'you can cleanse me.' In warm indignation Jesus stretched out his hand,[b] touched him, and said, 'Indeed
42 I will; be clean again.' The leprosy left him immediately, and he was clean.
43 44 Then he dismissed him with this stern warning: 'Be sure you say nothing to anybody. Go and show yourself to the priest, and make the offering
45 laid down by Moses for your cleansing; that will certify the cure.' But the man went out and made the whole story public; he spread it far and wide, until Jesus could no longer show himself in any town, but stayed outside in the open country. Even so, people kept coming to him from all quarters.

2 When after some days he returned to Capernaum, the news went round
2 that he was at home; and such a crowd collected that the space in front of the door was not big enough to hold them. And while he was proclaiming
3 the message to them, a man was brought who was paralysed. Four men
4 were carrying him, but because of the crowd they could not get him near. So they opened up the roof over the place where Jesus was, and when they

*a Or* You have.        *b Some witnesses read* Jesus was sorry for him and stretched out his hand; *one witness has simply* He stretched out his hand.

had broken through they lowered the stretcher on which the paralysed man was lying. When Jesus saw their faith, he said to the paralysed man, 'My 5 son, your sins are forgiven.'

Now there were some lawyers sitting there and they thought to them- 6 selves, 'Why does the fellow talk like that? This is blasphemy! Who but 7 God alone can forgive sins?' Jesus knew in his own mind that this was 8 what they were thinking, and said to them: 'Why do you harbour thoughts like these? Is it easier to say to this paralysed man, "Your sins are forgiven", 9 or to say, "Stand up, take your bed, and walk"? But to convince you that 10 the Son of Man has the right on earth to forgive sins'—he turned to the paralysed man—'I say to you, stand up, take your bed, and go home.' 11 And he got up, and at once took his stretcher and went out in full view of 12 them all, so that they were astounded and praised God. 'Never before', they said, 'have we seen the like.'

Once more he went away to the lake-side. All the crowd came to him, 13 and he taught them there. As he went along, he saw Levi son of Alphaeus 14 at his seat in the custom-house, and said to him, 'Follow me'; and Levi rose and followed him.

When Jesus was at table in his house, many bad characters—tax- 15 gatherers and others—were seated with him and his disciples; for there were many who followed him. Some doctors of the law who were Pharisees 16 noticed him eating in this bad company, and said to his disciples, 'He eats with tax-gatherers and sinners!' Jesus heard it and said to them, 'It is not 17 the healthy that need a doctor, but the sick; I did not come to invite virtuous people, but sinners.'

Once, when John's disciples and the Pharisees were keeping a fast, some 18 people came to him and said, 'Why is it that John's disciples and the disciples of the Pharisees are fasting, but yours are not?' Jesus said to them, 19 'Can you expect the bridegroom's friends to fast while the bridegroom is with them? As long as they have the bridegroom with them, there can be no fasting. But the time will come when the bridegroom will be taken 20 away from them, and on that day they will fast.

'No one sews a patch of unshrunk cloth on to an old coat; if he does, the 21 patch tears away from it, the new from the old, and leaves a bigger hole. No one puts new wine into old wine-skins; if he does, the wine will burst 22 the skins, and then wine and skins are both lost. Fresh skins for new wine!'

One Sabbath he was going through the cornfields; and his disciples, as 23 they went, began to pluck ears of corn. The Pharisees said to him, 'Look, 24 why are they doing what is forbidden on the Sabbath?' He answered, 'Have 25 you never read what David did when he and his men were hungry and had nothing to eat? He went into the House of God, in the time of Abiathar 26 the High Priest, and ate the sacred bread, though no one but a priest is allowed to eat it, and even gave it to his men.'

He also said to them, 'The Sabbath was made for the sake of man and 27 not man for the Sabbath: therefore the Son of Man is sovereign even over 28 the Sabbath.'

On another occasion when he went to synagogue, there was a man in the 3 congregation who had a withered arm; and they were watching to see 2

45

whether Jesus would cure him on the Sabbath, so that they could bring
3 a charge against him. He said to the man with the withered arm, 'Come and
4 stand out here.' Then he turned to them: 'Is it permitted to do good or to
do evil on the Sabbath, to save life or to kill?' They had nothing to say;
5 and, looking round at them with anger and sorrow at their obstinate
stupidity, he said to the man, 'Stretch out your arm.' He stretched it out
6 and his arm was restored. But the Pharisees, on leaving the synagogue,
began plotting against him with the partisans of Herod to see how they
could make away with him.

7 JESUS WENT AWAY to the lake-side with his disciples. Great numbers
8 from Galilee, Judaea and Jerusalem, Idumaea and Transjordan, and the
neighbourhood of Tyre and Sidon, heard what he was doing and came to
9 see him. So he told his disciples to have a boat ready for him, to save him
10 from being crushed by the crowd. For he cured so many that sick people of
11 all kinds came crowding in upon him to touch him. The unclean spirits too,
when they saw him, would fall at his feet and cry aloud, 'You are the Son of
12 God'; but he insisted that they should not make him known.
13 He then went up into the hill-country and called the men he wanted;
14 and they went and joined him. He appointed twelve as his companions,
15 whom he would send out to proclaim the Gospel, with a commission to
16 drive out devils. So he appointed the Twelve: to Simon he gave the name
17 Peter; then came the sons of Zebedee, James and his brother John, to whom
18 he gave the name Boanerges, Sons of Thunder; then Andrew and Philip and
Bartholomew and Matthew and Thomas and James the son of Alphaeus
19 and Thaddaeus and Simon, a member of the Zealot party, and Judas
Iscariot, the man who betrayed him.
20 He entered a house; and once more such a crowd collected round them
21 that they had no chance to eat. When his family heard of this, they set out
to take charge of him; for people were saying that he was out of his mind.[a]
22 The doctors of the law, too, who had come down from Jerusalem, said,
'He is possessed by Beelzebub', and, 'He drives out devils by the prince of
23 devils.' So he called them to come forward, and spoke to them in parables:
24 'How can Satan drive out Satan? If a kingdom is divided against itself,
25 that kingdom cannot stand; if a household is divided against itself, that
26 house will never stand; and if Satan is in rebellion against himself, he is
divided and cannot stand; and that is the end of him.
27 'On the other hand, no one can break into a strong man's house and
make off with his goods unless he has first tied the strong man up; then he
can ransack the house.
28 29 'I tell you this: no sin, no slander, is beyond forgiveness for men; but
whoever slanders the Holy Spirit can never be forgiven; he is guilty of
30 eternal sin.' He said this because they had declared that he was possessed
by an unclean spirit.
31 Then his mother and his brothers arrived, and remaining outside sent
32 in a message asking him to come out to them. A crowd was sitting round
and word was brought to him: 'Your mother and your brothers are outside

[a] *Or* of him. 'He is out of his mind', they said.

46

asking for you.' He replied, 'Who is my mother? Who are my brothers?' 33
And looking round at those who were sitting in the circle about him he said, 34
'Here are my mother and my brothers. Whoever does the will of God is 35
my brother, my sister, my mother.'

ON ANOTHER OCCASION he began to teach by the lake-side. The crowd 4
that gathered round him was so large that he had to get into a boat on the
lake, and there he sat, with the whole crowd on the beach right down
to the water's edge. And he taught them many things by parables. 2
  As he taught he said:
'Listen! A sower went out to sow. And it happened that as he sowed, 3 4
some seed fell along the footpath; and the birds came and ate it up. Some 5
seed fell on rocky ground, where it had little soil, and it sprouted quickly
because it had no depth of earth; but when the sun rose the young corn was 6
scorched, and as it had no root it withered away. Some seed fell among 7
thistles; and the thistles shot up and choked the corn, and it yielded no
crop. And some of the seed fell into good soil, where it came up and grew, 8
and bore fruit; and the yield was thirtyfold, sixtyfold, even a hundredfold.'
He added, 'If you have ears to hear, then hear.' 9
  When he was alone, the Twelve and others who were round him ques- 10
tioned him about the parables. He replied, 'To you the secret of the 11
kingdom of God has been given; but to those who are outside everything
comes by way of parables, so that (as Scripture says) they may look and 12
look, but see nothing; they may hear and hear, but understand nothing;
otherwise they might turn to God and be forgiven.'
  So he said, 'You do not understand this parable? How then are you to 13
understand any parable? The sower sows the word. Those along the foot- 14 15
path are people in whom the word is sown, but no sooner have they heard
it than Satan comes and carries off the word which has been sown in them.
It is the same with those who receive the seed on rocky ground; as soon as 16
they hear the word, they accept it with joy, but it strikes no root in them; 17
they have no staying-power; then, when there is trouble or persecution on
account of the word, they fall away at once. Others again receive the seed 18
among thistles; they hear the word, but worldly cares and the false glamour 19
of wealth and all kinds of evil desire come in and choke the word, and it
proves barren. And there are those who receive the seed in good soil; they 20
hear the word and welcome it; and they bear fruit thirtyfold, sixtyfold,
or a hundredfold.'
  He said to them, 'Do you bring in the lamp to put it under the meal-tub, 21
or under the bed? Surely it is brought to be set on the lamp-stand. For 22
nothing is hidden unless it is to be disclosed, and nothing put under cover
unless it is to come into the open. If you have ears to hear, then hear.' 23
  He also said, 'Take note of what you hear; the measure you give is the 24
measure you will receive, with something more besides. For the man who 25
has will be given more, and the man who has not will forfeit even what
he has.'
  He said, 'The kingdom of God is like this. A man scatters seed on the land; 26
he goes to bed at night and gets up in the morning, and the seed sprouts 27

28 and grows—how, he does not know. The ground produces a crop by itself,
29 first the blade, then the ear, then full-grown corn in the ear; but as soon
as the crop is ripe, he plies the sickle, because harvest-time has come.'

30 He said also, 'How shall we picture the kingdom of God, or by what
31 parable shall we describe it? It is like the mustard-seed, which is smaller
32 than any seed in the ground at its sowing. But once sown, it springs up
and grows taller than any other plant, and forms branches so large that the
birds can settle in its shade.'

33 With many such parables he would give them his message, so far as they
34 were able to receive it. He never spoke to them except in parables; but
privately to his disciples he explained everything.

## *Miracles of Christ*

35 THAT DAY, in the evening, he said to them, 'Let us cross over to the other
36 side of the lake.' So they left the crowd and took him with them in the
boat where he had been sitting; and there were other boats accompanying
37 him. A heavy squall came on and the waves broke over the boat until it
38 was all but swamped. Now he was in the stern asleep on a cushion; they
39 roused him and said, 'Master, we are sinking! Do you not care?' He awoke,
rebuked the wind, and said to the sea, 'Hush! Be still!' The wind dropped
40 and there was a dead calm. He said to them, 'Why are you such cowards?
41 Have you no faith even now?' They were awestruck and said to one
another, 'Who can this be? Even the wind and the sea obey him.'

5 So they came to the other side of the lake, into the country of the Gera-
2 senes. As he stepped ashore, a man possessed by an unclean spirit came up
3 to him from among the tombs where he had his dwelling. He could no
4 longer be controlled; even chains were useless; he had often been fettered
and chained up, but he had snapped his chains and broken the fetters. No
5 one was strong enough to master him. And so, unceasingly, night and day,
he would cry aloud among the tombs and on the hill-sides and cut himself
6 with stones. When he saw Jesus in the distance, he ran and flung himself
7 down before him, shouting loudly, 'What do you want with me, Jesus, son
8 of the Most High God? In God's name do not torment me.' (For Jesus was
9 already saying to him, 'Out, unclean spirit, come out of this man!') Jesus
asked him, 'What is your name?' 'My name is Legion,' he said, 'there are
10 so many of us.' And he begged hard that Jesus would not send them out
of the country.

11 Now there happened to be a large herd of pigs feeding on the hill-side,
12 and the spirits begged him, 'Send us among the pigs and let us go into
13 them.' He gave them leave; and the unclean spirits came out and went
into the pigs; and the herd, of about two thousand, rushed over the edge into
the lake and were drowned.

14 The men in charge of them took to their heels and carried the news to the
town and country-side; and the people came out to see what had happened.
15 They came to Jesus and saw the madman who had been possessed by the
legion of devils, sitting there clothed and in his right mind; and they were

afraid. The spectators told them how the madman had been cured and   16
what had happened to the pigs. Then they begged Jesus to leave the district.   17

As he was stepping into the boat, the man who had been possessed begged   18
to go with him. Jesus would not allow it, but said to him, 'Go home to   19
your own folk and tell them what the Lord in his mercy has done for you.'
The man went off and spread the news in the Ten Towns *a* of all that Jesus   20
had done for him; and they were all amazed.

As soon as Jesus had returned by boat to the other shore, a great crowd   21
once more gathered round him. While he was by the lake-side, the president   22
of one of the synagogues came up, Jairus by name, and, when he saw him,
threw himself down at his feet and pleaded with him. 'My little daughter',   23
he said, 'is at death's door. I beg you to come and lay your hands on her to
cure her and save her life.' So Jesus went with him, accompanied by a great   24
crowd which pressed upon him.

Among them was a woman who had suffered from haemorrhages for   25
twelve years; and in spite of long treatment by many doctors, on which   26
she had spent all she had, there had been no improvement; on the contrary,
she had grown worse. She had heard what people were saying about Jesus,   27
so she came up from behind in the crowd and touched his cloak; for she said   28
to herself, 'If I touch even his clothes, I shall be cured.' And there and then   29
the source of her haemorrhages dried up and she knew in herself that she
was cured of her trouble. At the same time Jesus, aware that power had gone   30
out of him, turned round in the crowd and asked, 'Who touched my
clothes?' His disciples said to him, 'You see the crowd pressing upon you   31
and yet you ask, "Who touched me?"' Meanwhile he was looking round   32
to see who had done it. And the woman, trembling with fear when she   33
grasped what had happened to her, came and fell at his feet and told him
the whole truth. He said to her, 'My daughter, your faith has cured you.   34
Go in peace, free for ever from this trouble.'

While he was still speaking, a message came from the president's house,   35
'Your daughter is dead; why trouble the Rabbi further?' But Jesus, over-   36
hearing the message as it was delivered, said to the president of the synagogue, 'Do not be afraid; only have faith.' After this he allowed no one to   37
accompany him except Peter and James and James's brother John. They   38
came to the president's house, where he found a great commotion, with
loud crying and wailing. So he went in and said to them, 'Why this crying   39
and commotion? The child is not dead: she is asleep'; and they only   40
laughed at him. But after turning all the others out, he took the child's
father and mother and his own companions and went in where the child was
lying. Then, taking hold of her hand, he said to her, '*Talitha cum*', which   41
means, 'Get up, my child.' Immediately the girl got up and walked about—   42
she was twelve years old. At that they were beside themselves with amazement. He gave them strict orders to let no one hear about it, and told them   43
to give her something to eat.

He left that place and went to his home town accompanied by his   6
disciples. When the Sabbath came he began to teach in the synagogue;   2
and the large congregation who heard him were amazed and said, 'Where

*a Greek* Decapolis.

does he get it from?', and, 'What wisdom is this that has been given him?',
3 and, 'How does he work such miracles? Is not this the carpenter, the son
of Mary,*a* the brother of James and Joseph and Judas and Simon? And
4 are not his sisters here with us?' So they fell foul of him. Jesus said to them,
'A prophet will always be held in honour except in his home town, and
5 among his kinsmen and family.' He could work no miracle there, except
6 that he put his hands on a few sick people and healed them; and he was
taken aback by their want of faith.

7 ON ONE OF HIS TEACHING JOURNEYS round the villages he summoned
the Twelve and sent them out in pairs on a mission. He gave them authority
8 over unclean spirits, and instructed them to take nothing for the journey
9 beyond a stick: no bread, no pack, no money in their belts. They might wear
10 sandals, but not a second coat. 'When you are admitted to a house', he
11 added, 'stay there until you leave those parts. At any place where they will
not receive you or listen to you, shake the dust off your feet as you leave,
12 as a warning to them.' So they set out and called publicly for repentance.
13 They drove out many devils, and many sick people they anointed with
oil and cured.

14 Now King Herod heard of it, for the fame of Jesus had spread; and
people were saying,*b* 'John the Baptist has been raised to life, and that is
15 why these miraculous powers are at work in him.' Others said, 'It is Elijah.'
16 Others again, 'He is a prophet like one of the old prophets.' But Herod,
when he heard of it, said, 'This is John, whom I beheaded, raised from
the dead.'

17 For this same Herod had sent and arrested John and put him in prison
on account of his brother Philip's wife, Herodias, whom he had married.
18 19 John had told Herod, 'You have no right to your brother's wife.' Thus
Herodias nursed a grudge against him and would willingly have killed him,
20 but she could not; for Herod went in awe of John, knowing him to be a good
and holy man; so he kept him in custody. He liked to listen to him, although
the listening left him greatly perplexed.
21 Herodias found her opportunity when Herod on his birthday gave a
banquet to his chief officials and commanders and the leading men of
22 Galilee. Her daughter came in*c* and danced, and so delighted Herod and
his guests that the king said to the girl, 'Ask what you like and I will give it
23 you.' And he swore an oath to her: 'Whatever you ask I will give you, up
24 to half my kingdom.' She went out and said to her mother, 'What shall I ask
25 for?' She replied, 'The head of John the Baptist.' The girl hastened back
at once to the king with her request: 'I want you to give me here and now, on
26 a dish, the head of John the Baptist.' The king was greatly distressed, but
out of regard for his oath and for his guests he could not bring himself to
27 refuse her. So the king sent a soldier of the guard with orders to bring
28 John's head. The soldier went off and beheaded him in the prison, brought
the head on a dish, and gave it to the girl; and she gave it to her mother.

*a Some witnesses read* Is not this the son of the carpenter and Mary ...     *b Some
witnesses read* and he said ...     *c Or* A festive occasion came when Herod on his
birthday gave ... of Galilee. The daughter of Herodias came in ...

When John's disciples heard the news, they came and took his body  29
away and laid it in a tomb.

The apostles now rejoined Jesus and reported to him all that they had  30
done and taught. He said to them, 'Come with me, by yourselves, to some  31
lonely place where you can rest quietly.' (For they had no leisure even to
eat, so many were coming and going.) Accordingly, they set off privately by  32
boat for a lonely place. But many saw them leave and recognized them,  33
and came round by land, hurrying from all the towns towards the place,
and arrived there first. When he came ashore, he saw a great crowd; and his  34
heart went out to them, because they were like sheep without a shepherd;
and he had much to teach them. As the day wore on, his disciples came up to  35
him and said, 'This is a lonely place and it is getting very late; send the  36
people off to the farms and villages round about, to buy themselves something to eat.' 'Give them something to eat yourselves', he answered. They  37
replied, 'Are we to go and spend twenty pounds *a* on bread to give them a
meal?' 'How many loaves have you?' he asked; 'go and see.' They found  38
out and told him, 'Five, and two fishes also.' He ordered them to make the  39
people sit down in groups on the green grass, and they sat down in rows,  40
a hundred rows of fifty each. Then, taking the five loaves and the two fishes,  41
he looked up to heaven, said the blessing, broke the loaves, and gave them
to the disciples to distribute. He also divided the two fishes among them.
They all ate to their hearts' content; and twelve great basketfuls of scraps  42 43
were picked up, with what was left of the fish. Those who ate the loaves  44
numbered five thousand men.

As soon as it was over he made his disciples embark and cross to Bethsaida  45
ahead of him, while he himself sent the people away. After taking leave of  46
them, he went up the hill-side to pray. It grew late and the boat was already  47
well out on the water, while he was alone on the land. Somewhere between  48
three and six in the morning, seeing them labouring at the oars against a
head-wind, he came towards them, walking on the lake. He was going to
pass them by; but when they saw him walking on the lake, they thought  49
it was a ghost and cried out; for they all saw him and were terrified. But  50
at once he spoke to them: 'Take heart! It is I; do not be afraid.' Then he  51
climbed into the boat beside them, and the wind dropped. At this they were
completely dumbfounded, for they had not understood the incident of  52
the loaves; their minds were closed.

So they finished the crossing and came to land at Gennesaret, where they  53
made fast. When they came ashore, he was immediately recognized; and  54 55
the people scoured that whole country-side and brought the sick on
stretchers to any place where he was reported to be. Wherever he went, to  56
farmsteads, villages, or towns, they laid out the sick in the market-places
and begged him to let them simply touch the edge of his cloak; and all who
touched him were cured.

*a Literally* 200 denarii.

## Growing tension

**7**
**2** A GROUP OF PHARISEES, with some doctors of the law who had come from Jerusalem, met him and noticed that some of his disciples were eating their food with 'defiled' hands—in other words, without washing
**3** them. (For the Pharisees and the Jews in general never eat without washing
**4** the hands,[a] in obedience to an old-established tradition; and on coming from the market-place they never eat without first washing. And there are many other points on which they have a traditional rule to maintain, for
**5** example, washing of cups and jugs and copper bowls.) Accordingly, these Pharisees and the lawyers asked him, 'Why do your disciples not conform
**6** to the ancient tradition, but eat their food with defiled hands?' He answered, 'Isaiah was right when he prophesied about you hypocrites in these words:
**7** "This people pays me lip-service, but their heart is far from me: their worship of me is in vain, for they teach as doctrines the commandments of
**8** men." You neglect the commandment of God, in order to maintain the tradition of men.'
**9** He also said to them, 'How well you set aside the commandment of God
**10** in order to maintain[b] your tradition! Moses said, "Honour your father and your mother", and, "The man who curses his father or mother must
**11** suffer death." But you hold that if a man says to his father or mother, "Anything of mine which might have been used for your benefit is Cor-
**12** ban"' (meaning, set apart for God), 'he is no longer permitted to do any-
**13** thing for his father or mother. Thus by your own tradition, handed down among you, you make God's word null and void. And many other things that you do are just like that.'
**14** On another occasion he called the people and said to them, 'Listen to
**15** me, all of you, and understand this: nothing that goes into a man from outside can defile him; no, it is the things that come out of him that defile a man.'[c]
**17** When he had left the people and gone indoors, his disciples questioned
**18** him about the parable. He said to them, 'Are you as dull as the rest? Do you not see that nothing that goes from outside into a man can defile him,
**19** because it does not enter into his heart but into his stomach, and so passes
**20** out into the drain?' Thus he declared all foods clean. He went on, 'It is
**21** what comes out of a man that defiles him. For from inside, out of a man's
**22** heart, come evil thoughts, acts of fornication, of theft, murder, adultery, ruthless greed, and malice; fraud, indecency, envy, slander, arrogance, and
**23** folly; these evil things all come from inside, and they defile the man.'
**24** Then he left that place and went away into the territory of Tyre. He found a house to stay in, and he would have liked to remain unrecognized,
**25** but this was impossible. Almost at once a woman whose young daughter was possessed by an unclean spirit heard of him, came in, and fell at his
**26** feet. (She was a Gentile, a Phoenician of Syria by nationality.) She begged
**27** him to drive the spirit out of her daughter. He said to her, 'Let the children

---

[a] *Some witnesses insert* with the fist; *others insert* frequently, *or* thoroughly.    [b] *Some witnesses read* establish.    [c] *Some witnesses here add* (16) If you have ears to hear, then hear.

be satisfied first; it is not fair to take the children's bread and throw it to the dogs.' 'Sir,' she answered, 'even the dogs under the table eat the children's 28 scraps.' He said to her, 'For saying that, you may go home content; the 29 unclean spirit has gone out of your daughter.' And when she returned 30 home, she found the child lying in bed; the spirit had left her.

On his return journey from Tyrian territory he went by way of Sidon to 31 the Sea of Galilee through the territory of the Ten Towns.*a* They brought 32 to him a man who was deaf and had an impediment in his speech, with the request that he would lay his hand on him. He took the man aside, away 33 from the crowd, put his fingers into his ears, spat, and touched his tongue. Then, looking up to heaven, he sighed, and said to him, '*Ephphatha*', 34 which means 'Be opened.' With that his ears were opened, and at the same 35 time the impediment was removed and he spoke plainly. Jesus forbade them 36 to tell anyone; but the more he forbade them, the more they published it. Their astonishment knew no bounds: 'All that he does, he does well,' they 37 said; 'he even makes the deaf hear and the dumb speak.'

THERE WAS ANOTHER OCCASION about this time when a huge crowd **8** had collected, and, as they had no food, Jesus called his disciples and said to them, 'I feel sorry for all these people; they have been with me now 2 for three days and have nothing to eat. If I send them home unfed, they 3 will turn faint on the way; some of them have come from a distance.' The 4 disciples answered, 'How can anyone provide all these people with bread in this lonely place?' 'How many loaves have you?' he asked; and they 5 answered, 'Seven.' So he ordered the people to sit down on the ground; 6 then he took the seven loaves, and, after giving thanks to God, he broke the bread and gave it to his disciples to distribute; and they served it out to the people. They had also a few small fishes, which he blessed and ordered 7 them to distribute. They all ate to their hearts' content, and seven baskets 8 were filled with the scraps that were left. The people numbered about four 9 thousand. Then he dismissed them; and, without delay, got into the boat 10 with his disciples and went to the district of Dalmanutha.*b*

Then the Pharisees came out and engaged him in discussion. To test 11 him they asked him for a sign from heaven. He sighed deeply to himself 12 and said, 'Why does this generation ask for a sign? I tell you this: no sign shall be given to this generation.' With that he left them, re-embarked, and 13 went off to the other side of the lake.

Now they had forgotten to take bread with them; they had no more than 14 one loaf in the boat. He began to warn them: 'Beware,' he said, 'be on your 15 guard against the leaven of the Pharisees and the leaven of Herod.' They 16 said among themselves, 'It is because we have no bread.' Knowing what 17 was in their minds, he asked them, 'Why do you talk about having no bread? Have you no inkling yet? Do you still not understand? Are your minds closed? You have eyes: can you not see? You have ears: can you 18 not hear? Have you forgotten? When I broke the five loaves among five 19 thousand, how many basketfuls of scraps did you pick up?' 'Twelve', they said. 'And how many when I broke the seven loaves among four 20

*a Greek* Decapolis.          *b Some witnesses give* Magedan; *others give* Magdala.

21 thousand?' They answered, 'Seven.' He said, 'Do you still not understand?'

22 They arrived at Bethsaida. There the people brought a blind man to
23 Jesus and begged him to touch him. He took the blind man by the hand and led him away out of the village. Then he spat on his eyes, laid his
24 hands upon him, and asked whether he could see anything. The man's sight began to come back, and he said, 'I see men; they look like trees, but
25 they are walking about.' Jesus laid his hands on his eyes again; he looked
26 hard, and now he was cured so that he saw everything clearly. Then Jesus sent him home, saying, 'Do not tell anyone in the village.' *a*

27 JESUS AND HIS DISCIPLES set out for the villages of Caesarea Philippi.
28 On the way he asked his disciples, 'Who do men say I am?' They answered, 'Some say John the Baptist, others Elijah, others one of the prophets.'
29 'And you,' he asked, 'who do you say I am?' Peter replied: 'You are the
30 Messiah.' Then he gave them strict orders not to tell anyone about him;
31 and he began to teach them that the Son of Man had to undergo great sufferings, and to be rejected by the elders, chief priests, and doctors of
32 the law; to be put to death, and to rise again three days afterwards. He spoke about it plainly. At this Peter took him by the arm and began to rebuke him.
33 But Jesus turned round, and, looking at his disciples, rebuked Peter. 'Away with you, Satan,' he said; 'you think as men think, not as God thinks.'

34 Then he called the people to him, as well as his disciples, and said to them, 'Anyone who wishes to be a follower of mine must leave self behind;
35 he must take up his cross, and come with me. Whoever cares for his own safety is lost; but if a man will let himself be lost for my sake and for the
36 Gospel, that man is safe. What does a man gain by winning the whole world
37 38 at the cost of his true self? What can he give to buy that self back? If anyone is ashamed of me and mine *b* in this wicked and godless age, the Son of Man will be ashamed of him, when he comes in the glory of his Father and of the holy angels.' *c*

9 He also said, 'I tell you this: there are some of those standing here who will not taste death before they have seen the kingdom of God already come in power.'

2 Six days later Jesus took Peter, James, and John with him and led them up a high mountain where they were alone; and in their presence he was
3 transfigured; his clothes became dazzling white, with a whiteness no
4 bleacher on earth could equal. They saw Elijah appear, and Moses with
5 him, and there they were, conversing with Jesus. Then Peter spoke: 'Rabbi,' he said, 'how good it is that we are here! Shall we make three
6 shelters, one for you, one for Moses, and one for Elijah?' (For he did not
7 know what to say; they were so terrified.) Then a cloud appeared, casting its shadow over them, and out of the cloud came a voice: 'This is my Son,
8 my Beloved;*d* listen to him.' And now suddenly, when they looked around, there was nobody to be seen but Jesus alone with themselves.

*a Some witnesses read* Do not go into the village.      *b Some witnesses read* me and my words.      *c Some witnesses read* Father with the holy angels.      *d Or* This is my only Son.

On their way down the mountain, he enjoined them not to tell anyone 9 what they had seen until the Son of Man had risen from the dead. They 10 seized upon those words, and discussed among themselves what this 'rising from the dead' could mean. And they put a question to him: 'Why 11 do our teachers say that Elijah must come first?' He replied, 'Yes, Elijah 12 does come first to set everything right. Yet how is it *a* that the scriptures say of the Son of Man that he is to endure great sufferings and to be treated with contempt? However, I tell you, Elijah has already come and they have 13 worked their will upon him, as the scriptures say of him.'

When they came back to the disciples they saw a large crowd surrounding 14 them and lawyers arguing with them. As soon as they saw Jesus the whole 15 crowd were overcome with awe, and they ran forward to welcome him. He asked them, 'What is this argument about?' A man in the crowd spoke 16 17 up: 'Master, I brought my son to you. He is possessed by a spirit which makes him speechless. Whenever it attacks him, it dashes him to the 18 ground, and he foams at the mouth, grinds his teeth, and goes rigid. I asked your disciples to cast it out, but they failed.' Jesus answered: 'What an 19 unbelieving and perverse generation! How long shall I be with you? How long must I endure you? Bring him to me.' So they brought the boy to him; 20 and as soon as the spirit saw him it threw the boy into convulsions, and he fell on the ground and rolled about foaming at the mouth. Jesus asked his 21 father, 'How long has he been like this?' 'From childhood,' he replied; 'often it has tried to make an end of him by throwing him into the fire or 22 into water. But if it is at all possible for you, take pity upon us and help us.' 'If it is possible!' said Jesus. 'Everything is possible to one who has 23 faith.' 'I have faith,' cried the boy's father; 'help me where faith falls 24 short.' Jesus saw then that the crowd was closing in upon them, so he 25 rebuked the unclean spirit. 'Deaf and dumb spirit,' he said, 'I command you, come out of him and never go back!' After crying aloud and racking 26 him fiercely, it came out; and the boy looked like a corpse; in fact, many said, 'He is dead.' But Jesus took his hand and raised him to his feet, and 27 he stood up.

Then Jesus went indoors, and his disciples asked him privately, 'Why 28 could not we cast it out?' He said, 'There is no means of casting out this 29 sort but prayer.' *b*

THEY NOW LEFT that district and made a journey through Galilee. Jesus 30 wished it to be kept secret; for he was teaching his disciples, and telling 31 them, 'The Son of Man is now to be given up into the power of men, and they will kill him, and three days after being killed, he will rise again.' But they did not understand what he said, and were afraid to ask. 32

So they came to Capernaum; and when he was indoors, he asked them, 33 'What were you arguing about on the way?' They were silent, because on 34 the way they had been discussing who was the greatest. He sat down, 35 called the Twelve, and said to them, 'If anyone wants to be first, he must make himself last of all and servant of all.' Then he took a child, set him 36

---

*a Or* Elijah, you say, comes first to set everything right: then how is it . . .     *b Some witnesses add* and fasting.

37  in front of them, and put his arm round him. 'Whoever receives one of
these children in my name', he said, 'receives me; and whoever receives
me, receives not me but the One who sent me.'

38      John said to him, 'Master, we saw a man driving out devils in your name,
39  and as he was not one of us, we tried to stop him.' Jesus said, 'Do not stop
him; no one who does a work of divine power in my name will be able the
40  next moment to speak evil of me. For he who is not against us is on our side.
41  I tell you this: if anyone gives you a cup of water to drink because you are
followers of the Messiah, that man assuredly will not go unrewarded.

42      'As for the man who is a cause of stumbling to one of these little ones
who have faith, it would be better for him to be thrown into the sea with
43  a millstone round his neck. If your hand is your undoing, cut it off; it
is better for you to enter into life maimed than to keep both hands and
45  go to hell and the unquenchable fire.*a* And if your foot is your undoing,
cut it off; it is better to enter into life a cripple than to keep both your feet
47  and be thrown into hell.*b* And if it is your eye, tear it out; it is better to enter
into the kingdom of God with one eye than to keep both eyes and be thrown
48  into hell, where the devouring worm never dies and the fire is not quenched.
49  'For everyone will be salted with fire.
50  'Salt is a good thing; but if the salt loses its saltness, what will you season
it with?
'Have salt in yourselves; and be*c* at peace with one another.'

**10**  ON LEAVING THOSE PARTS he came into the regions of Judaea and Transjordan; and when a crowd gathered round him once again, he followed his
2  usual practice and taught them. The question was put to him:*d* 'Is it
3  lawful for a man to divorce his wife?' This was to test him. He asked in
4  return, 'What did Moses command you?' They answered, 'Moses per-
5  mitted a man to divorce his wife by note of dismissal.' Jesus said to them,
'It was because your minds were closed that he made this rule for you;
6  but in the beginning, at the creation, God made them male and female.
7  For this reason a man shall leave his father and mother, and be made one
8  with his wife;*e* and the two shall become one flesh. It follows that they
9  are no longer two individuals: they are one flesh. What God has joined
together, man must not separate.'

10      When they were indoors again the disciples questioned him about this
11  matter; he said to them, 'Whoever divorces his wife and marries another
12  commits adultery against her: so too, if she divorces her husband and
marries another, she commits adultery.'

13      They brought children for him to touch. The disciples rebuked them,
14  but when Jesus saw this he was indignant, and said to them, 'Let the
children come to me; do not try to stop them; for the kingdom of God

*a Some witnesses add* (44) *where the devouring worm never dies and the fire is not
quenched.*        *b Some witnesses add* (46) *where the devouring worm never dies and
the fire is not quenched.*        *c Or* Have the salt of fellowship and be . . .; *or* You have
the salt of fellowship between you; then be . . .        *d Some witnesses read* The Pharisees came forward and asked him the question . . .        *e Some witnesses omit* and be
made . . . wife.

belongs to such as these. I tell you, whoever does not accept the kingdom  15
of God like a child will never enter it.' And he put his arms round them,  16
laid his hands upon them, and blessed them.

As he was starting out on a journey, a stranger ran up, and, kneeling  17
before him, asked, 'Good Master, what must I do to win eternal life?'
Jesus said to him, 'Why do you call me good? No one is good except God  18
alone. You know the commandments: "Do not murder; do not commit  19
adultery; do not steal; do not give false evidence; do not defraud; honour
your father and mother."' 'But, Master,' he replied, 'I have kept all these  20
since I was a boy.' Jesus looked straight at him; his heart warmed to him,  21
and he said, 'One thing you lack: go, sell everything you have, and give to
the poor, and you will have riches in heaven; and come, follow me.' At  22
these words his face fell and he went away with a heavy heart; for he was a
man of great wealth.

Jesus looked round at his disciples and said to them, 'How hard it will  23
be for the wealthy to enter the kingdom of God!' They were amazed that  24
he should say this, but Jesus insisted, 'Children, how hard it is *a* to enter
the kingdom of God! It is easier for a camel to pass through the eye of  25
a needle than for a rich man to enter the kingdom of God.' They were more  26
astonished than ever, and said to one another, 'Then who can be saved?'
Jesus looked at them and said, 'For men it is impossible, but not for God;  27
everything is possible for God.'

At this Peter spoke. 'We here', he said, 'have left everything to become  28
your followers.' Jesus said, 'I tell you this: there is no one who has given  29
up home, brothers or sisters, mother, father or children, or land, for my
sake and for the Gospel, who will not receive in this age a hundred times as  30
much—houses, brothers and sisters, mothers and children, and land—
and persecutions besides; and in the age to come eternal life. But many  31
who are first will be last and the last first.'

## Challenge to Jerusalem

THEY WERE ON THE ROAD, going up to Jerusalem, Jesus leading the  32
way; and the disciples were filled with awe, while those who followed
behind were afraid. He took the Twelve aside and began to tell them
what was to happen to him. 'We are now going to Jerusalem,' he said;  33
'and the Son of Man will be given up to the chief priests and the doctors
of the law; they will condemn him to death and hand him over to the foreign
power. He will be mocked and spat upon, flogged and killed; and three days  34
afterwards, he will rise again.'

James and John, the sons of Zebedee, approached him and said, 'Master,  35
we should like you to do us a favour.' 'What is it you want me to do?' he  36
asked. They answered, 'Grant us the right to sit in state with you, one at  37
your right and the other at your left.' Jesus said to them, 'You do not under-  38
stand what you are asking. Can you drink the cup that I drink, or be baptized with the baptism I am baptized with?' 'We can', they answered. Jesus  39

*a Some witnesses insert* for those who trust in riches.

said, 'The cup that I drink you shall drink, and the baptism I am baptized
40 with shall be your baptism; but to sit at my right or left is not for me to
grant; it is for those to whom it has already been assigned.' *a*
41     When the other ten heard this, they were indignant with James and
42 John. Jesus called them to him and said, 'You know that in the world
the recognized rulers lord it over their subjects, and their great men make
43 them feel the weight of authority. That is not the way with you; among you,
44 whoever wants to be great must be your servant, and whoever wants to be
45 first must be the willing slave of all. For even the Son of Man did not come
to be served but to serve, and to give up his life as a ransom for many.'
46     They came to Jericho; and as he was leaving the town, with his disciples
and a large crowd, Bartimaeus son of Timaeus, a blind beggar, was seated
47 at the roadside. Hearing that it was Jesus of Nazareth, he began to shout,
48 'Son of David, Jesus, have pity on me!' Many of the people told him to hold
his tongue; but he shouted all the more, 'Son of David, have pity on me.'
49 Jesus stopped and said, 'Call him'; so they called the blind man and said,
50 'Take heart; stand up; he is calling you.' At that he threw off his cloak,
51 sprang up, and came to Jesus. Jesus said to him, 'What do you want me to
do for you?' 'Master,' the blind man answered, 'I want my sight back.'
52 Jesus said to him, 'Go; your faith has cured you.' And at once he recovered
his sight and followed him on the road.

11  THEY WERE NOW APPROACHING Jerusalem, and when they reached
Bethphage and Bethany, at the Mount of Olives, he sent two of his disciples
2 with these instructions: 'Go to the village opposite, and, just as you enter,
you will find tethered there a colt which no one has yet ridden. Untie it
3 and bring it here. If anyone asks, "Why are you doing that?", say, "Our
4 Master *b* needs it, and will send it back here without delay." ' So they went
off, and found the colt tethered at a door outside in the street. They were
5 untying it when some of the bystanders asked, 'What are you doing, un-
6 tying that colt?' They answered as Jesus had told them, and were then
7 allowed to take it. So they brought the colt to Jesus and spread their cloaks
8 on it, and he mounted. And people carpeted the road with their cloaks,
9 while others spread brushwood which they had cut in the fields; and those
who went ahead and the others who came behind shouted, 'Hosanna!
10 Blessings on him who comes in the name of the Lord! Blessings on the
coming kingdom of our father David! Hosanna in the heavens!'
11     He entered Jerusalem and went into the temple, where he looked at the
whole scene; but, as it was now late, he went out to Bethany with the
Twelve.
12 13   On the following day, after they had left Bethany, he felt hungry, and,
noticing in the distance a fig-tree in leaf, he went to see if he could find
anything on it. But when he came there he found nothing but leaves; for
14 it was not the season for figs. He said to the tree, 'May no one ever again
eat fruit from you!' And his disciples were listening.
15     So they came to Jerusalem, and he went into the temple and began
driving out those who bought and sold in the temple. He upset the tables

*a Some witnesses add* by my Father.          *b Or* Its owner.

58

of the money-changers and the seats of the dealers in pigeons; and he 16
would not allow anyone to use the temple court as a thoroughfare for
carrying goods. Then he began to teach them, and said, 'Does not Scripture 17
say, "My house shall be called a house of prayer for all the nations"? But
you have made it a robbers' cave.' The chief priests and the doctors of the 18
law heard of this and sought some means of making away with him; for
they were afraid of him, because the whole crowd was spellbound by his
teaching. And when evening came he went out of the city.                 19

Early next morning, as they passed by, they saw that the fig-tree had 20
withered from the roots up; and Peter, recalling what had happened, said 21
to him, 'Rabbi, look, the fig-tree which you cursed has withered.' Jesus 22
answered them, 'Have faith in God. I tell you this: if anyone says to this 23
mountain, "Be lifted from your place and hurled into the sea", and has no
inward doubts, but believes that what he says is happening, it will be done
for him. I tell you, then, whatever you ask for in prayer, believe that you 24
have received it and it will be yours.

'And when you stand praying, if you have a grievance against anyone, 25
forgive him, so that your Father in heaven may forgive you the wrongs
you have done.' *a*

THEY CAME ONCE MORE to Jerusalem. And as he was walking in the 27
temple court the chief priests, lawyers, and elders came to him and said, 28
'By what authority are you acting like this? Who gave you authority to
act in this way?' Jesus said to them, 'I have a question to ask you too; 29
and if you give me an answer, I will tell you by what authority I act. The 30
baptism of John: was it from God, or from men? Answer me.' This set 31
them arguing among themselves: 'What shall we say? If we say, "from
God", he will say, "Then why did you not believe him?" Shall we say, 32
"from men"?'—but they were afraid of the people, for all held that John
was in fact a prophet. So they answered, 'We do not know.' And Jesus said 33
to them, 'Then neither will I tell you by what authority I act.'

He went on to speak to them in parables: 'A man planted a vineyard 12
and put a wall round it, hewed out a winepress, and built a watch-tower;
then he let it out to vine-growers and went abroad. When the season came, 2
he sent a servant to the tenants to collect from them his share of the produce.
But they took him, thrashed him, and sent him away empty-handed. Again, 3 4
he sent them another servant, whom they beat about the head and treated
outrageously. So he sent another, and that one they killed; and many more 5
besides, of whom they beat some, and killed others. He had now only one 6
left to send, his own dear son. *b* In the end he sent him. "They will respect
my son", he said. But the tenants said to one another, "This is the heir; 7
come on, let us kill him, and the property will be ours." So they seized him 8
and killed him, and flung his body out of the vineyard. What will the owner 9
of the vineyard do? He will come and put the tenants to death and give the
vineyard to others.

'Can it be that you have never read this text: "The stone which the 10

---

*a Some witnesses add* (26) But if you do not forgive others, then the wrongs you have
done will not be forgiven by your Father in heaven.        *b Or* his only son.

11 builders rejected has become the main corner-stone. This is the Lord's
doing, and it is wonderful in our eyes"?'

12 Then they began to look for a way to arrest him, for they saw that the
parable was aimed at them; but they were afraid of the people, so they left
him alone and went away.

13 A NUMBER OF PHARISEES and men of Herod's party were sent to trap
14 him with a question. They came and said, 'Master, you are an honest man,
we know, and truckle to no one, whoever he may be; you teach in all
honesty the way of life that God requires. Are we or are we not permitted
15 to pay taxes to the Roman Emperor? Shall we pay or not?' He saw how
crafty their question was, and said, 'Why are you trying to catch me out?
16 Fetch me a silver piece, and let me look at it.' They brought one, and he
said to them, 'Whose head is this, and whose inscription?' 'Caesar's', they
17 replied. Then Jesus said, 'Pay Caesar what is due to Caesar, and pay God
what is due to God.' And they heard him with astonishment.

18 Next Sadducees came to him. (It is they who say that there is no resur-
19 rection.) Their question was this: 'Master, Moses laid it down for us that
if there are brothers, and one dies leaving a wife but no child, then the next
20 should marry the widow and carry on his brother's family. Now there were
21 seven brothers. The first took a wife and died without issue. Then the
second married her, and he too died without issue. So did the third.
22 Eventually the seven of them died, all without issue. Finally the woman
23 died. At the resurrection, when they come back to life, whose wife will she
24 be, since all seven had married her?' Jesus said to them, 'You are mistaken,
and surely this is the reason: you do not know either the scriptures or the
25 power of God. When they rise from the dead, men and women do not
marry; they are like angels in heaven.

26 'But about the resurrection of the dead, have you never read in the Book
of Moses, in the story of the burning bush, how God spoke to him and said,
"I am the God of Abraham, the God of Isaac, and the God of Jacob"?
27 God is not God of the dead but of the living. You are greatly mistaken.'

28 Then one of the lawyers, who had been listening to these discussions and
had noted how well he answered, came forward and asked him, 'Which
29 commandment is first of all?' Jesus answered, 'The first is, "Hear, O
30 Israel: the Lord our God is the only Lord; love the Lord your God with
all your heart, with all your soul, with all your mind, and with all your
31 strength." The second is this: "Love your neighbour as yourself." There is
32 no other commandment greater than these.' The lawyer said to him, 'Well
said, Master. You are right in saying that God is one and beside him there
33 is no other. And to love him with all your heart, all your understanding,
and all your strength, and to love your neighbour as yourself—that is far
34 more than any burnt offerings or sacrifices.' When Jesus saw how sensibly
he answered, he said to him, 'You are not far from the kingdom of God.'

35 After that nobody ventured to put any more questions to him; and Jesus
went on to say, as he taught in the temple, 'How can the teachers of the law
36 maintain that the Messiah is "Son of David"? David himself said, when
inspired by the Holy Spirit, "The Lord said to my Lord, 'Sit at my right

hand until I put your enemies under your feet.'" David himself calls him 37
"Lord"; how can he also be David's son?'

There was a great crowd and they listened eagerly.*a* He said as he taught 38
them, 'Beware of the doctors of the law, who love to walk up and down in
long robes, receiving respectful greetings in the street; and to have the 39
chief seats in synagogues, and places of honour at feasts. These are the men 40
who eat up the property of widows, while they say long prayers for appearance' sake, and they will receive the severest sentence.'*b*

Once he was standing opposite the temple treasury, watching as people 41
dropped their money into the chest. Many rich people were giving large
sums. Presently there came a poor widow who dropped in two tiny coins, 42
together worth a farthing. He called his disciples to him. 'I tell you this,' 43
he said: 'this poor widow has given more than any of the others; for those 44
others who have given had more than enough, but she, with less than
enough, has given all that she had to live on.'

A S  H E  W A S  L E A V I N G  the temple, one of his disciples exclaimed, 'Look, **13**
Master, what huge stones! What fine buildings!' Jesus said to him, 'You 2
see these great buildings? Not one stone will be left upon another; all will
be thrown down.'

When he was sitting on the Mount of Olives facing the temple he was 3
questioned privately by Peter, James, John, and Andrew. 'Tell us,' they 4
said, 'when will this happen? What will be the sign when the fulfilment of
all this is at hand?'

Jesus began: 'Take care that no one misleads you. Many will come 5 6
claiming my name, and saying, "I am he"; and many will be misled by
them.

'When you hear the noise of battle near at hand and the news of battles 7
far away, do not be alarmed. Such things are bound to happen; but the end
is still to come. For nation will make war upon nation, kingdom upon 8
kingdom; there will be earthquakes in many places; there will be famines.
With these things the birth-pangs of the new age begin.

'As for you, be on your guard. You will be handed over to the courts. 9
You will be flogged in synagogues. You will be summoned to appear before
governors and kings on my account to testify in their presence. But before 10
the end the Gospel must be proclaimed to all nations. So when you are 11
arrested and taken away, do not worry beforehand about what you will say,
but when the time comes say whatever is given you to say; for it is not you
who will be speaking, but the Holy Spirit. Brother will betray brother to 12
death, and the father his child; children will turn against their parents
and send them to their death. All will hate you for your allegiance to me; 13
but the man who holds out to the end will be saved.

'But when you see "the abomination of desolation" usurping a place 14
which is not his (let the reader understand), then those who are in Judaea
must take to the hills. If a man is on the roof, he must not come down into 15

*a Or* The mass of the people listened eagerly.        *b Or* As for those who eat up the
property of widows, while they say long prayers for appearance' sake, they will have an
even sterner judgement to face.

16   the house to fetch anything out; if in the field, he must not turn back for his
17   coat. Alas for women with child in those days, and for those who have
18 19  children at the breast! Pray that it may not come in winter. For those days
      will bring distress such as never has been until now since the beginning
20    of the world which God created—and will never be again. If the Lord had
      not cut short that time of troubles, no living thing could survive. However,
      for the sake of his own, whom he has chosen, he has cut short the time.

21    'Then, if anyone says to you, "Look, here is the Messiah", or, "Look,
22    there he is", do not believe it. Impostors will come claiming to be messiahs
      or prophets, and they will produce signs and wonders to mislead God's
23    chosen, if such a thing were possible. But you be on your guard; I have
      forewarned you of it all.

24    'But in those days, after that distress, the sun will be darkened, the moon
25    will not give her light; the stars will come falling from the sky, the celestial
26    powers will be shaken. Then they will see the Son of Man coming in the
27    clouds with great power and glory, and he will send out the angels and
      gather his chosen from the four winds, from the farthest bounds of earth
      to the farthest bounds of heaven.

28    'Learn a lesson from the fig-tree. When its tender shoots appear and are
29    breaking into leaf, you know that summer is near. In the same way, when
      you see all this happening, you may know that the end is near,[a] at the very
30 31  door. I tell you this: the present generation will live to see it all. Heaven
      and earth will pass away; my words will never pass away.

32    'But about that day or that hour no one knows, not even the angels in
      heaven, not even the Son; only the Father.

33 34  'Be alert, be wakeful.[b] You do not know when the moment comes. It is
      like a man away from home: he has left his house and put his servants in
      charge, each with his own work to do, and he has ordered the door-keeper
35    to stay awake. Keep awake, then, for you do not know when the master
      of the house is coming. Evening or midnight, cock-crow or early dawn—
36 37  if he comes suddenly, he must not find you asleep. And what I say to you,
      I say to everyone: Keep awake.'

## The final conflict

14    NOW THE FESTIVAL of Passover and Unleavened Bread was only two
      days off; and the chief priests and the doctors of the law were trying
2     to devise some cunning plan to seize him and put him to death. 'It must not
      be during the festival,' they said, 'or we should have rioting among the
      people.'

3     Jesus was at Bethany, in the house of Simon the leper. As he sat at table,
      a woman came in carrying a small bottle of very costly perfume, pure oil
4     of nard. She broke it open and poured the oil over his head. Some of those
5     present said to one another angrily, 'Why this waste? The perfume might
      have been sold for thirty pounds[c] and the money given to the poor'; and

---

[a] *Or* that he is near.     [b] *Some witnesses add* and pray.     [c] *Literally* 300 denarii;
*some witnesses read* more than 300 denarii.

they turned upon her with fury. But Jesus said, 'Let her alone. Why must 6
you make trouble for her? It is a fine thing she has done for me. You have 7
the poor among you always, and you can help them whenever you like;
but you will not always have me. She has done what lay in her power; she 8
is beforehand with anointing my body for burial. I tell you this: wherever 9
in all the world the Gospel is proclaimed, what she has done will be told as
her memorial.'

Then Judas Iscariot, one of the Twelve, went to the chief priests to 10
betray him to them. When they heard what he had come for, they were 11
greatly pleased, and promised him money; and he began to look for a good
opportunity to betray him.

NOW ON THE FIRST DAY of Unleavened Bread, when the Passover lambs 12
were being slaughtered, his disciples said to him, 'Where would you like
us to go and prepare for your Passover supper?' So he sent out two of his 13
disciples with these instructions: 'Go into the city, and a man will meet
you carrying a jar of water. Follow him, and when he enters a house give 14
this message to the householder: "The Master says, 'Where is the room
reserved for me to eat the Passover with my disciples?'" He will show you 15
a large room upstairs, set out in readiness. Make the preparations for us
there.' Then the disciples went off, and when they came into the city 16
they found everything just as he had told them. So they prepared for
Passover.

In the evening he came to the house with the Twelve. As they sat at 17 18
supper Jesus said, 'I tell you this: one of you will betray me—one who is
eating with me.' At this they were dismayed; and one by one they said to 19
him, 'Not I, surely?' 'It is one of the Twelve', he said, 'who is dipping into 20
the same bowl with me. The Son of Man is going the way appointed for him 21
in the scriptures; but alas for that man by whom the Son of Man is betrayed!
It would be better for that man if he had never been born.'

During supper he took bread, and having said the blessing he broke it 22
and gave it to them, with the words: 'Take this; this is my body.' Then he 23
took a cup, and having offered thanks to God he gave it to them; and they
all drank from it. And he said, 'This is my blood, the blood of the covenant, 24
shed for many. I tell you this: never again shall I drink from the fruit of 25
the vine until that day when I drink it new in the kingdom of God.'

After singing the Passover Hymn, they went out to the Mount of Olives. 26
And Jesus said, 'You will all fall from your faith; for it stands written: 27
"I will strike the shepherd down and the sheep will be scattered." Never- 28
theless, after I am raised again I will go on before you into Galilee.' Peter 29
answered, 'Everyone else may fall away, but I will not.' Jesus said, 'I tell 30
you this: today, this very night, before the cock crows twice, you yourself
will disown me three times.' But he insisted and repeated: 'Even if I must 31
die with you, I will never disown you.' And they all said the same.

WHEN THEY REACHED a place called Gethsemane, he said to his disciples, 32
'Sit here while I pray.' And he took Peter and James and John with him. 33
Horror and dismay came over him, and he said to them, 'My heart is ready 34

35 to break with grief; stop here, and stay awake.' Then he went forward a
little, threw himself on the ground, and prayed that, if it were possible,
36 this hour might pass him by. 'Abba, Father,' he said, 'all things are possible to thee; take this cup away from me. Yet not what I will, but what
thou wilt.'

37     He came back and found them asleep; and he said to Peter, 'Asleep,
38 Simon? Were you not able to stay awake for one hour? Stay awake, all of
you; and pray that you may be spared the test. The spirit is willing, but the
39 40 flesh is weak.' Once more he went away and prayed.*a* On his return he
found them asleep again, for their eyes were heavy; and they did not know
how to answer him.

41     The third time he came and said to them, 'Still sleeping? Still taking your
ease? Enough!*b* The hour has come. The Son of Man is betrayed to sinful
42 men. Up, let us go forward! My betrayer is upon us.'

43     Suddenly, while he was still speaking, Judas, one of the Twelve, appeared,
and with him was a crowd armed with swords and cudgels, sent by the
44 chief priests, lawyers, and elders. Now the traitor had agreed with them
upon a signal: 'The one I kiss is your man; seize him and get him safely
45 away.' When he reached the spot, he stepped forward at once and said to
46 Jesus, 'Rabbi', and kissed him. Then they seized him and held him fast.
47     One of the party *c* drew his sword, and struck at the High Priest's servant,
48 cutting off his ear. Then Jesus spoke: 'Do you take me for a bandit, that
49 you have come out with swords and cudgels to arrest me? Day after day
I was within your reach as I taught in the temple, and you did not lay hands
50 on me. But let the scriptures be fulfilled.' Then the disciples all deserted
him and ran away.

51     Among those following was a young man with nothing on but a linen
52 cloth. They tried to seize him; but he slipped out of the linen cloth and ran
away naked.

53 THEN THEY LED Jesus away to the High Priest's house, where the chief
54 priests, elders, and doctors of the law were all assembling. Peter followed
him at a distance right into the High Priest's courtyard; and there he
remained, sitting among the attendants, warming himself at the fire.

55     The chief priests and the whole Council tried to find some evidence
56 against Jesus to warrant a death-sentence, but failed to find any. Many
57 gave false evidence against him, but their statements did not tally. Some
58 stood up and gave false evidence against him to this effect: 'We heard him
say, "I will pull down this temple, made with human hands, and in three
59 days I will build another, not made with hands."' But even on this point
their evidence did not agree.

60     Then the High Priest stood up in his place and questioned Jesus: 'Have
61 you no answer to the charges that these witnesses bring against you?' But
he kept silence; he made no reply.

Again the High Priest questioned him: 'Are you the Messiah, the Son
62 of the Blessed One?' Jesus said, 'I am; and you will see the Son of Man

*a Some witnesses add* using the same words.        *b The Greek is obscure; a possible mean-*
*ing is* 'The money has been paid', 'The account is settled.'        *c Or of the bystanders.*

seated at the right hand of God *a* and coming with the clouds of heaven.'
Then the High Priest tore his robes and said, 'Need we call further wit- 63
nesses? You have heard the blasphemy. What is your opinion?' Their 64
judgement was unanimous: that he was guilty and should be put to death.

Some began to spit on him, blindfolded him, and struck him with their 65
fists, crying out, 'Prophesy!' *b* And the High Priest's men set upon him
with blows.

Meanwhile Peter was still below in the courtyard. One of the High 66
Priest's serving-maids came by and saw him there warming himself. She 67
looked into his face and said, 'You were there too, with this man from
Nazareth, this Jesus.' But he denied it: 'I know nothing,' he said; 'I do 68
not understand what you mean.' Then he went outside into the porch; *c*
and the maid saw him there again and began to say to the bystanders, 'He 69
is one of them'; and again he denied it. 70

Again, a little later, the bystanders said to Peter, 'Surely you are one of
them. You must be; you are a Galilean.' At this he broke out into curses, 71
and with an oath he said, 'I do not know this man you speak of.' Then the 72
cock crew a second time; and Peter remembered how Jesus had said to
him, 'Before the cock crows twice you will disown me three times.' And he
burst into tears.

AS SOON AS MORNING CAME, the chief priests, having made their plan 15
with the elders and lawyers in full council, put Jesus in chains; then they
led him away and handed him over to Pilate. Pilate asked him, 'Are you the 2
king of the Jews?' He replied, 'The words are yours.' *d* And the chief priests 3
brought many charges against him. Pilate questioned him again: 'Have you 4
nothing to say in your defence? You see how many charges they are
bringing against you.' But, to Pilate's astonishment, Jesus made no 5
further reply.

At the festival season the Governor used to release one prisoner at the 6
people's request. As it happened, the man known as Barabbas was then in 7
custody with the rebels who had committed murder in the rising. When 8
the crowd appeared *e* asking for the usual favour, Pilate replied, 'Do you 9
wish me to release for you the king of the Jews?' For he knew it was out of 10
malice that they had brought Jesus before him. But the chief priests incited 11
the crowd to ask him to release Barabbas rather than Jesus. Pilate spoke 12
to them again: 'Then what shall I do with the man you call king of the
Jews?' They shouted back, 'Crucify him!' 'Why, what harm has he done?' 13 14
Pilate asked; but they shouted all the louder, 'Crucify him!' So Pilate, in 15
his desire to satisfy the mob, released Barabbas to them; and he had Jesus
flogged and handed him over to be crucified.

Then the soldiers took him inside the courtyard (the Governor's head- 16
quarters *f* ) and called together the whole company. They dressed him in 17
purple, and plaiting a crown of thorns, placed it on his head. Then they 18
began to salute him with, 'Hail, King of the Jews!' They beat him about the 19

*a* *Literally* of the Power.     *b* *Some witnesses add* Who hit you? *as in Matthew and*
*Luke.*     *c* *Some witnesses insert* and a cock crew.     *d* *Or* It is as you say.
*e* *Some witnesses read* shouted.     *f* *Greek* praetorium.

head with a cane and spat upon him, and then knelt and paid mock homage
20 to him. When they had finished their mockery, they stripped him of the
purple and dressed him in his own clothes.

21 THEN THEY TOOK HIM OUT to crucify him. A man called Simon, from
Cyrene, the father of Alexander and Rufus, was passing by on his way in
from the country, and they pressed him into service to carry his cross.
22 They brought him to the place called Golgotha, which means 'Place
23 24 of a skull'. He was offered drugged wine, but he would not take it. Then
they fastened him to the cross. They divided his clothes among them,
casting lots to decide what each should have.
25 26 The hour of the crucifixion was nine in the morning, and the inscription
27 giving the charge against him read, 'The king of the Jews.' Two bandits
were crucified with him, one on his right and the other on his left.*a*
29 The passers-by hurled abuse at him: 'Aha!' they cried, wagging their
heads, 'you would pull the temple down, would you, and build it in three
30 31 days? Come down from the cross and save yourself!' So too the chief
priests and lawyers jested with one another: 'He saved others,' they said,
32 'but he cannot save himself. Let the Messiah, the king of Israel, come down
now from the cross. If we see that, we shall believe.' Even those who were
crucified with him taunted him.
33 At midday a darkness fell over the whole land, which lasted till three in
34 the afternoon; and at three Jesus cried aloud, '*Eli, Eli, lema sabachthani?*',
35 which means, 'My God, my God, why hast thou forsaken me?'*b* Some of
36 the bystanders, on hearing this, said, 'Hark, he is calling Elijah.' A man
ran and soaked a sponge in sour wine and held it to his lips on the end of
37 a cane. 'Let us see', he said, 'if Elijah will come to take him down.' Then
38 Jesus gave a loud cry and died. And the curtain of the temple was torn in
39 two from top to bottom. And when the centurion who was standing opposite
him saw how he died,*c* he said, 'Truly this man was a son of God.'*d*

40 A NUMBER OF WOMEN were also present, watching from a distance.
Among them were Mary of Magdala, Mary the mother of James the
41 younger and of Joseph, and Salome, who had all followed him and waited
on him when he was in Galilee, and there were several others who had come
up to Jerusalem with him.
42 By this time evening had come; and as it was Preparation-day (that is,
43 the day before the Sabbath), Joseph of Arimathaea, a respected member of
the Council, a man who looked forward to the kingdom of God, bravely
44 went in to Pilate and asked for the body of Jesus. Pilate was surprised to
hear that he was already dead; so he sent for the centurion and asked him
45 whether it was long since he died. And when he heard the centurion's
46 report, he gave Joseph leave to take the dead body. So Joseph bought a
linen sheet, took him down from the cross, and wrapped him in the sheet.

*a Some witnesses add* (28) Thus that text of Scripture came true which says, 'He was
reckoned among criminals.'      *b Some witnesses read* My God, my God, why hast thou
shamed me?      *c Some witnesses read* saw that he died with a cry.      *d Or* the
Son of God.

Then he laid him in a tomb cut out of the rock, and rolled a stone against the entrance. And Mary of Magdala and Mary the mother of Joseph were 47 watching and saw where he was laid.

When the Sabbath was over, Mary of Magdala, Mary the mother of **16** James, and Salome bought *a* aromatic oils intending to go and anoint him; and very early on the Sunday morning, just after sunrise, they came to the 2 tomb. They were wondering among themselves who would roll away the 3 stone for them from the entrance to the tomb, when they looked up and 4 saw that the stone, huge as it was, had been rolled back already. They 5 went into the tomb, where they saw a youth sitting on the right-hand side, wearing a white robe; and they were dumbfounded. But he said to them, 6 'Fear nothing; you are looking for Jesus of Nazareth, who was crucified. He has been raised again; he is not here; look, there is the place where they laid him. But go and give this message to his disciples and Peter: "He is 7 going on before you into Galilee; there you will see him, as he told you."' Then they went out and ran away from the tomb, beside themselves with 8 terror. They said nothing to anybody, for they were afraid. *b*

And they delivered all these instructions briefly to Peter and his companions. Afterwards Jesus himself sent out by them from east to west the sacred and imperishable message of eternal salvation. *c*

When he had risen from the dead early on Sunday morning he appeared 9 first to Mary of Magdala, from whom he had formerly cast out seven devils. She went and carried the news to his mourning and sorrowful 10 followers, but when they were told that he was alive and that she had seen 11 him they did not believe it.

Later he appeared in a different guise to two of them as they were 12 walking, on their way into the country. These also went and took the news 13 to the others, but again no one believed them.

Afterwards while the Eleven were at table he appeared to them and 14 reproached them for their incredulity and dullness, because they had not believed those who had seen him after he was raised from the dead. Then he 15 said to them: 'Go forth to every part of the world, and proclaim the Good News to the whole creation. Those who believe it and receive baptism will 16 find salvation; those who do not believe will be condemned. Faith will bring 17 with it these miracles: believers will cast out devils in my name and speak in strange tongues; if they handle snakes or drink any deadly poison, they will 18 come to no harm; and the sick on whom they lay their hands will recover.'

So after talking with them the Lord Jesus was taken up into heaven, and 19 he took his seat at the right hand of God; but they went out to make their 20 proclamation everywhere, and the Lord worked with them and confirmed their words by the miracles that followed. *d*

*a Some witnesses omit* When the Sabbath . . . Salome, *reading* And they went and bought . . .
*b At this point some of the most ancient witnesses bring the book to a close.*     *c Some witnesses add this paragraph, which in one of them is the conclusion of the book.*     *d Some witnesses give verses 9–20 either instead of, or in addition to, the paragraph* And they delivered . . . eternal salvation (*here printed before verse 9*), *and so bring the book to a close. Others insert further additional matter.*

# THE GOSPEL ACCORDING TO
# LUKE

1 THE AUTHOR TO THEOPHILUS: Many writers have undertaken to draw up an account of the events that have hap-
2 pened among us, following the traditions handed down to us by
3 the original eyewitnesses and servants of the Gospel. And so I in my turn, your Excellency, as one who has gone over the whole course of these events
4 in detail, have decided to write a connected narrative for you, so as to give you authentic knowledge about the matters of which you have been informed.

## The coming of Christ

5 IN THE DAYS of Herod king of Judaea there was a priest named Zechariah, of the division of the priesthood called after Abijah. His wife also was of
6 priestly descent; her name was Elizabeth. Both of them were upright and devout, blamelessly observing all the commandments and ordinances of
7 the Lord. But they had no children, for Elizabeth was barren, and both were well on in years.
8 Once, when it was the turn of his division and he was there to take part
9 in divine service, it fell to his lot, by priestly custom, to enter the sanctuary
10 of the Lord and offer the incense; and the whole congregation was at
11 prayer outside. It was the hour of the incense-offering. There appeared to
12 him an angel of the Lord, standing on the right of the altar of incense. At
13 this sight, Zechariah was startled, and fear overcame him. But the angel said to him, 'Do not be afraid, Zechariah; your prayer has been heard:
14 your wife Elizabeth will bear you a son, and you shall name him John. Your
15 heart will thrill with joy and many will be glad that he was born; for he will be great in the eyes of the Lord. He shall never touch wine or strong drink.
16 From his very birth he will be filled with the Holy Spirit; and he will bring
17 back many Israelites to the Lord their God. He will go before him as forerunner,*a* possessed by the spirit and power of Elijah, to reconcile father and child, to convert the rebellious to the ways of the righteous, to prepare a people that shall be fit for the Lord.'
18 Zechariah said to the angel, 'How can I be sure of this? I am an old man and my wife is well on in years.'
19 The angel replied, 'I am Gabriel; I stand in attendance upon God, and
20 I have been sent to speak to you and bring you this good news. But now listen: you will lose your power of speech, and remain silent until the day

*a Or In his sight he will go forth.*

when these things happen to you, because you have not believed me, though at their proper time my words will be proved true.'

Meanwhile the people were waiting for Zechariah, surprised that he was 21 staying so long inside. When he did come out he could not speak to them, 22 and they realized that he had had a vision in the sanctuary. He stood there making signs to them, and remained dumb.

When his period of duty was completed Zechariah returned home. After 23 24 this his wife Elizabeth conceived, and for five months she lived in seclusion, thinking, 'This is the Lord's doing; now at last he has deigned to take away 25 my reproach among men.'

In the sixth month the angel Gabriel was sent from God to a town in 26 Galilee called Nazareth, with a message for a girl betrothed to a man named 27 Joseph, a descendant of David; the girl's name was Mary. The angel went 28 in and said to her, 'Greetings, most favoured one! The Lord is with you.' But she was deeply troubled by what he said and wondered what this greet- 29 ing might mean. Then the angel said to her, 'Do not be afraid, Mary, for 30 God has been gracious to you; you shall conceive and bear a son, and you 31 shall give him the name Jesus. He will be great; he will bear the title "Son of 32 the Most High"; the Lord God will give him the throne of his ancestor David, and he will be king over Israel*ª* for ever; his reign shall never end.' 33 'How can this be?' said Mary; 'I am still a virgin.' The angel answered, 'The 34 35 Holy Spirit will come upon you, and the power of the Most High will over- shadow you; and for that reason the holy child to be born will be called "Son of God".*ᵇ* Moreover your kinswoman Elizabeth has herself conceived a son 36 in her old age; and she who is reputed barren is now in her sixth month, for 37 God's promises can never fail.'*ᶜ* 'Here am I,' said Mary; 'I am the Lord's 38 servant; as you have spoken, so be it.' Then the angel left her.

About this time Mary set out and went straight to a town in the uplands 39 of Judah. She went into Zechariah's house and greeted Elizabeth. And 40 41 when Elizabeth heard Mary's greeting, the baby stirred in her womb. Then Elizabeth was filled with the Holy Spirit and cried aloud, 'God's blessing 42 is on you above all women, and his blessing is on the fruit of your womb. Who am I, that the mother of my Lord should visit me? I tell you, when 43 44 your greeting sounded in my ears, the baby in my womb leapt for joy. How 45 happy is she who has had faith that the Lord's promise would be fulfilled!' And Mary*ᵈ* said:                                                            46

> 'Tell out, my soul, the greatness of the Lord,
>      rejoice, rejoice, my spirit, in God my saviour;                    47
>      so tenderly has he looked upon his servant,                        48
>           humble as she is.
> For, from this day forth,
>      all generations will count me blessed,
>      so wonderfully has he dealt with me,                               49
>           the Lord, the Mighty One.

*ª Literally* the house of Jacob.          *ᵇ Or* the child to be born will be called holy, "Son of God".          *ᶜ Some witnesses read* for with God nothing will prove impossible.
*ᵈ So the majority of witnesses; some read* Elizabeth; *the original may have had no name.*

His name is Holy;
50    his mercy sure from generation to generation
          toward those who fear him;
51    the deeds his own right arm has done
          disclose his might:
      the arrogant of heart and mind he has put to rout,
52    he has brought down monarchs from their thrones,
          but the humble have been lifted high.
53    The hungry he has satisfied with good things,
          the rich sent empty away.

54    He has ranged himself at the side of Israel his servant;
55        firm in his promise to our forefathers,
      he has not forgotten to show mercy to Abraham
          and his children's children, for ever.'

56    Mary stayed with her about three months and then returned home.

57  NOW THE TIME CAME for Elizabeth's child to be born, and she gave birth
58  to a son. When her neighbours and relatives heard what great favour the
59  Lord had shown her, they were as delighted as she was. Then on the eighth
     day they came to circumcise the child; and they were going to name him
60  Zechariah after his father. But his mother spoke up and said, 'No! he is to
61  be called John.' 'But', they said, 'there is nobody in your family who has
62  that name.' They inquired of his father by signs what he would like him to
63  be called. He asked for a writing-tablet and to the astonishment of all wrote
64  down, 'His name is John.' Immediately his lips and tongue were freed and
65  he began to speak, praising God. All the neighbours were struck with awe,
     and everywhere in the uplands of Judaea the whole story became common
66  talk. All who heard it were deeply impressed and said, 'What will this child
     become?' For indeed the hand of the Lord was upon him. *a*
67      And Zechariah his father was filled with the Holy Spirit and uttered this
     prophecy:

68        'Praise to the God of Israel!
      For he has turned to his people, saved them and set them free,
69        and has raised up a deliverer of victorious power
          from the house of his servant David.

70        So he promised: age after age he proclaimed
          by the lips of his holy prophets,
71        that he would deliver us from our enemies,
          out of the hands of all who hate us;
72        that he would deal mercifully with our fathers,
          calling to mind his solemn covenant.

73        Such was the oath he swore to our father Abraham,
74            to rescue us from enemy hands,

*a Some witnesses read* 'What will this child become, for indeed the hand of the Lord is
upon him?'

and grant us, free from fear, to worship him
    with a holy worship, with uprightness of heart,          75
    in his presence, our whole life long.

And you, my child, you shall be called Prophet of the Highest,    76
for you will be the Lord's forerunner, to prepare his way
    and lead his people to salvation through knowledge of him,    77
    by the forgiveness of their sins:
for in the tender compassion of our God                            78
    the morning sun from heaven will rise *a* upon us,
to shine on those who live in darkness, under the cloud of death,  79
    and to guide our feet into the way of peace.'

As the child grew up he became strong in spirit; he lived out in the wilds  80
until the day when he appeared publicly before Israel.

IN THOSE DAYS a decree was issued by the Emperor Augustus for a  **2**
registration to be made throughout the Roman world. This was the first  2
registration of its kind; it took place when Quirinius *b* was governor of
Syria. For this purpose everyone made his way to his own town; and so  3 4
Joseph went up to Judaea from the town of Nazareth in Galilee, to register  5
at the city of David, called Bethlehem, because he was of the house of
David by descent; and with him went Mary who was betrothed to him.
She was expecting a child, and while they were there the time came for her  6
baby to be born, and she gave birth to a son, her first-born. She wrapped  7
him in his swaddling clothes, and laid him in a manger, because there was
no room for them to lodge in the house.
    Now in this same district there were shepherds out in the fields, keeping  8
watch through the night over their flock, when suddenly there stood before  9
them an angel of the Lord, and the splendour of the Lord shone round
them. They were terror-stricken, but the angel said, 'Do not be afraid;  10
I have good news for you: there is great joy coming to the whole people.
Today in the city of David a deliverer has been born to you—the Messiah,  11
the Lord. *c* And this is your sign: you will find a baby lying wrapped in  12
his swaddling clothes, in a manger.' All at once there was with the angel  13
a great company of the heavenly host, singing the praises of God:

      'Glory to God in highest heaven,                                  14
    and on earth his peace for men on whom his favour rests.' *d*

After the angels had left them and gone into heaven the shepherds said  15
to one another, 'Come, we must go straight to Bethlehem and see this thing
that has happened, which the Lord has made known to us.' So they went  16
with all speed and found their way to Mary and Joseph; and the baby was
lying in the manger. When they saw him, they recounted what they had  17
been told about this child; and all who heard were astonished at what the  18
shepherds said. But Mary treasured up all these things and pondered over  19

*a Some witnesses read* has risen.    *b Or* This was the first registration carried out
while Quirinius . . .   *c Some witnesses read* to you—the Lord's Messiah.   *d Some
witnesses read* and on earth his peace, his favour towards men.

20 them. Meanwhile the shepherds returned glorifying and praising God for what they had heard and seen; it had all happened as they had been told.

21 Eight days later the time came to circumcise him, and he was given the name Jesus, the name given by the angel before he was conceived.

22 Then, after their purification had been completed in accordance with the Law of Moses, they brought him up to Jerusalem to present him to the
23 Lord (as prescribed in the law of the Lord: 'Every first-born male shall be
24 deemed to belong to the Lord'), and also to make the offering as stated in the law: 'A pair of turtle doves or two young pigeons.'

25 There was at that time in Jerusalem a man called Simeon. This man was upright and devout, one who watched and waited for the restoration of
26 Israel, and the Holy Spirit was upon him. It had been disclosed to him by the Holy Spirit that he would not see death until he had seen the Lord's
27 Messiah. Guided by the Spirit he came into the temple; and when the parents brought in the child Jesus to do for him what was customary under
28 the Law, he took him in his arms, praised God, and said:

29 'This day, Master, thou givest thy servant his discharge in peace;
    now thy promise is fulfilled.
30 For I have seen with my own eyes
31 the deliverance which thou hast made ready in full view of all the nations:
32 a light that will be a revelation to the heathen,
    and glory to thy people Israel.'

33 The child's father and mother were full of wonder at what was being
34 said about him. Simeon blessed them and said to Mary his mother, 'This
35 child is destined to be a sign which men reject; and you too shall be pierced to the heart. Many in Israel will stand or fall *a* because of him, and thus the secret thoughts of many will be laid bare.'

36 There was also a prophetess, Anna the daughter of Phanuel, of the tribe of Asher. She was a very old woman, who had lived seven years with her
37 husband after she was first married, and then alone as a widow to the age of eighty-four. *b* She never left the temple, but worshipped day and night,
38 fasting and praying. Coming up at that very moment, she returned thanks to God; and she talked about the child to all who were looking for the liberation of Jerusalem.

39 When they had done everything prescribed in the law of the Lord, they
40 returned to Galilee to their own town of Nazareth. The child grew big and strong and full of wisdom; and God's favour was upon him.

41 Now it was the practice of his parents to go to Jerusalem every year for
42 the Passover festival; and when he was twelve, they made the pilgrimage
43 as usual. When the festive season was over and they started for home, the boy Jesus stayed behind in Jerusalem. His parents did not know of this;
44 but thinking that he was with the party they journeyed on for a whole day, and only then did they begin looking for him among their friends and
45 relations. As they could not find him they returned to Jerusalem to look for
46 him; and after three days they found him sitting in the temple surrounded

---

*a* Or Many in Israel will fall and rise again . . .
*b* Or widow for another eighty-four years.

by the teachers, listening to them and putting questions; and all who heard 47
him were amazed at his intelligence and the answers he gave. His parents 48
were astonished to see him there, and his mother said to him, 'My son, why
have you treated us like this? Your father and I have been searching for you
in great anxiety.' 'What made you search?' he said. 'Did you not know that 49
I was bound to be in my Father's house?' But they did not understand what 50
he meant. Then he went back with them to Nazareth, and continued to be 51
under their authority; his mother treasured up all these things in her heart.
As Jesus grew up he advanced in wisdom and in favour with God and men. 52

IN THE FIFTEENTH YEAR of the Emperor Tiberius, when Pontius Pilate 3
was governor of Judaea, when Herod was prince of Galilee, his brother
Philip prince of Ituraea and Trachonitis, and Lysanias prince of Abilene,
during the high-priesthood of Annas and Caiaphas, the word of God came 2
to John son of Zechariah in the wilderness. And he went all over the Jordan 3
valley proclaiming a baptism in token of repentance for the forgiveness of
sins, as it is written in the book of the prophecies of Isaiah: 4

'A voice crying aloud in the wilderness,
"Prepare a way for the Lord;
clear a straight path for him.
Every ravine shall be filled in, 5
and every mountain and hill levelled;
the corners shall be straightened,
and the rugged ways made smooth;
and all mankind shall see God's deliverance."' 6

Crowds of people came out to be baptized by him, and he said to them: 7
'You vipers' brood! Who warned you to escape from the coming retribution? Then prove your repentance by the fruit it bears; and do not begin 8
saying to yourselves, "We have Abraham for our father." I tell you that
God can make children for Abraham out of these stones here. Already the 9
axe is laid to the roots of the trees; and every tree that fails to produce good
fruit is cut down and thrown on the fire.'

The people asked him, 'Then what are we to do?' He replied, 'The man 10 11
with two shirts must share with him who has none, and anyone who has food
must do the same.' Among those who came to be baptized were tax- 12
gatherers, and they said to him, 'Master, what are we to do?' He told them, 13
'Exact no more than the assessment.' Soldiers on service also asked him, 14
'And what of us?' To them he said, 'No bullying; no blackmail; make do
with your pay!'

The people were on the tiptoe of expectation, all wondering about John, 15
whether perhaps he was the Messiah, but he spoke out and said to them 16
all: 'I baptize you with water; but there is one to come who is mightier
than I. I am not fit to unfasten his shoes. He will baptize you with the Holy
Spirit and with fire. His shovel is ready in his hand, to winnow his threshing- 17
floor and gather the wheat into his granary; but he will burn the chaff on
a fire that can never go out.'

In this and many other ways he made his appeal to the people and 18

19 announced the good news. But Prince Herod, when he was rebuked by him over the affair of his brother's wife Herodias and for his other misdeeds,
20 crowned them all by shutting John up in prison.

21 DURING A GENERAL BAPTISM of the people, when Jesus too had been
22 baptized and was praying, heaven opened and the Holy Spirit descended on him in bodily form like a dove; and there came a voice from heaven, 'Thou art my Son, my Beloved;*a* on thee my favour rests.'*b*
23     When Jesus began his work he was about thirty years old, the son, as
24 people thought, of Joseph, son of Heli, son of Matthat, son of Levi, son of
25 Melchi, son of Jannai, son of Joseph, son of Mattathiah, son of Amos,
26 son of Nahum, son of Esli, son of Naggai, son of Maath, son of Mattathiah,
27 son of Semein, son of Josech, son of Joda, son of Johanan, son of Rhesa, son
28 of Zerubbabel, son of Shealtiel, son of Neri, son of Melchi, son of Addi,
29 son of Cosam, son of Elmadam, son of Er, son of Joshua, son of Eliezer, son
30 of Jorim, son of Matthat, son of Levi, son of Symeon, son of Judah, son of
31 Joseph, son of Jonam, son of Eliakim, son of Melea, son of Menna, son
32 of Mattatha, son of Nathan, son of David, son of Jesse, son of Obed, son of
33 Boaz, son of Salmon, son of Nahshon, son of Amminadab,*c* son of Arni,*d*
34 son of Hezron, son of Perez, son of Judah, son of Jacob, son of Isaac, son of
35 Abraham, son of Terah, son of Nahor, son of Serug, son of Reu, son of
36 Peleg, son of Eber, son of Shelah, son of Cainan, son of Arpachshad, son
37 of Shem, son of Noah, son of Lamech, son of Methuselah, son of Enoch,
38 son of Jared, son of Mahalaleel, son of Cainan, son of Enosh, son of Seth, son of Adam, son of God.

**4** 1 2   Full of the Holy Spirit, Jesus returned from the Jordan, and for forty days was led by the Spirit up and down the wilderness and tempted by the devil. All that time he had nothing to eat, and at the end of it he was famished.
3     The devil said to him, 'If you are the Son of God, tell this stone to become
4 bread.' Jesus answered, 'Scripture says, "Man cannot live on bread alone."'
5     Next the devil led him up and showed him in a flash all the kingdoms of
6 the world. 'All this dominion will I give to you,' he said, 'and the glory that goes with it; for it has been put in my hands and I can give it to anyone
7 8 I choose. You have only to do homage to me and it shall all be yours.' Jesus answered him, 'Scripture says, "You shall do homage to the Lord your God and worship him alone."'
9     The devil took him to Jerusalem and set him on the parapet of the temple.
10 'If you are the Son of God,' he said, 'throw yourself down; for Scripture
11 says, "He will give his angels orders to take care of you", and again, "They will support you in their arms for fear you should strike your foot against
12 a stone."' Jesus answered him, 'It has been said, "You are not to put the Lord your God to the test."'
13     So, having come to the end of all his temptations, the devil departed, biding his time.

*a Or* Thou art my only Son.      *b Some witnesses read* My Son art thou; this day I have begotten thee.      *c Some witnesses add* son of Admin.      *d Some witnesses read* Aram; *Ruth 4. 19 and 1 Chronicles 2. 9 have* Ram.

## In Galilee : success and opposition

THEN JESUS, armed with the power of the Spirit, returned to Galilee; 14
and reports about him spread through the whole country-side. He 15
taught in their synagogues and all men sang his praises.

So he came to Nazareth, where he had been brought up, and went to 16
synagogue on the Sabbath day as he regularly did. He stood up to read the 17
lesson and was handed the scroll of the prophet Isaiah. He opened the scroll
and found the passage which says,

'The spirit of the Lord is upon me because he has anointed me; 18
he has sent me to announce good news to the poor,
to proclaim release for prisoners and recovery of sight for the blind;
to let the broken victims go free,
to proclaim the year of the Lord's favour.' 19

He rolled up the scroll, gave it back to the attendant, and sat down; and all 20
eyes in the synagogue were fixed on him.

He began to speak: 'Today', he said, 'in your very hearing this text has 21
come true.'*a* There was a general stir of admiration; they were surprised 22
that words of such grace should fall from his lips. 'Is not this Joseph's
son?' they asked. Then Jesus said, 'No doubt you will quote the proverb 23
to me, "Physician, heal yourself!", and say, "We have heard of all your
doings at Capernaum; do the same here in your own home town." I tell 24
you this,' he went on: 'no prophet is recognized in his own country. There 25
were many widows in Israel, you may be sure, in Elijah's time, when for
three years and six months the skies never opened, and famine lay hard
over the whole country; yet it was to none of those that Elijah was sent, 26
but to a widow at Sarepta in the territory of Sidon. Again, in the time 27
of the prophet Elisha there were many lepers in Israel, and not one of
them was healed, but only Naaman, the Syrian.' At these words the whole 28
congregation were infuriated. They leapt up, threw him out of the town, 29
and took him to the brow of the hill on which it was built, meaning to
hurl him over the edge. But he walked straight through them all, and went 30
away.

Coming down to Capernaum, a town in Galilee, he taught the people on 31
the Sabbath, and they were astounded at his teaching, for what he said had 32
the note of authority. Now there was a man in the synagogue possessed by 33
a devil, an unclean spirit. He shrieked at the top of his voice, 'What do you 34
want with us, Jesus of Nazareth? Have you*b* come to destroy us? I know
who you are—the Holy One of God.' Jesus rebuked him: 'Be silent', he 35
said, 'and come out of him.' Then the devil, after throwing the man down
in front of the people, left him without doing him any injury. Amazement 36
fell on them all and they said to one another: 'What is there in this man's
words? He gives orders to the unclean spirits with authority and power,
and out they go.' So the news spread, and he was the talk of the whole 37
district.

*a* Or 'Today', he said, 'this text which you have just heard has come true.'
*b* Or You have.

75

38　On leaving the synagogue he went to Simon's house. Simon's mother-
39　in-law was in the grip of a high fever; and they asked him to help her. He
came and stood over her and rebuked the fever. It left her, and she got up
at once and waited on them.

40　At sunset all who had friends suffering from one disease or another
brought them to him; and he laid his hands on them one by one and cured
41　them. Devils also came out of many of them, shouting, 'You are the Son of
God.' But he rebuked them and forbade them to speak, because they knew
that he was the Messiah.

42　When day broke he went out and made his way to a lonely spot. But the
people went in search of him, and when they came to where he was they
43　pressed him not to leave them. But he said, 'I must give the good news
of the kingdom of God to the other towns also, for that is what I was sent
44　to do.' So he proclaimed the Gospel in the synagogues of Judaea.[a]

5　One day as he stood by the Lake of Gennesaret, and the people crowded
2　upon him to listen to the word of God, he noticed two boats lying at the
water's edge; the fishermen had come ashore and were washing their nets.
3　He got into one of the boats, which belonged to Simon, and asked him to
put out a little way from the shore; then he went on teaching the crowds
4　from his seat in the boat. When he had finished speaking, he said to Simon,
5　'Put out into deep water and let down your nets for a catch.' Simon
answered, 'Master, we were hard at work all night and caught nothing at all;
6　but if you say so, I will let down the nets.' They did so and made a big haul
7　of fish; and their nets began to split. So they signalled to their partners in
the other boat to come and help them. This they did, and loaded both boats
8　to the point of sinking. When Simon saw what had happened he fell at
9　Jesus's knees and said, 'Go, Lord, leave me, sinner that I am!' For he and
10　all his companions were amazed at the catch they had made; so too were his
partners James and John, Zebedee's sons. 'Do not be afraid,' said Jesus to
11　Simon; 'from now on you will be catching men.' As soon as they had
brought the boats to land, they left everything and followed him.

12　He was once in a certain town where there happened to be a man covered
with leprosy; seeing Jesus, he bowed to the ground and begged his help.
13　'Sir,' he said, 'if only you will, you can cleanse me.' Jesus stretched out his
hand, touched him, and said, 'Indeed I will; be clean again.' The leprosy
14　left him immediately. Jesus then ordered him not to tell anybody. 'But go,'
he said, 'show yourself to the priest, and make the offering laid down by
15　Moses for your cleansing; that will certify the cure.' But the talk about him
spread all the more; great crowds gathered to hear him and to be cured of
16　their ailments. And from time to time he would withdraw to lonely places
for prayer.

17　One day he was teaching, and Pharisees and teachers of the law were
sitting round. People had come from every village of Galilee and from
Judaea and Jerusalem,[b] and the power of the Lord was with him to heal the
18　sick. Some men appeared carrying a paralysed man on a bed. They tried

[a] *Or* the Jewish synagogues; *some witnesses read* the synagogues of Galilee.
[b] *Some witnesses read* and Pharisees and teachers of the law, who had come from every
village of Galilee and from Judaea and Jerusalem, were sitting round.

to bring him in and set him down in front of Jesus, but finding no way to 19
do so because of the crowd, they went up on to the roof and let him down
through the tiling, bed and all, into the middle of the company in front of
Jesus. When Jesus saw their faith, he said, 'Man, your sins are forgiven you.' 20

The lawyers and the Pharisees began saying to themselves, 'Who is this 21
fellow with his blasphemous talk? Who but God alone can forgive sins?'
But Jesus knew what they were thinking and answered them: 'Why do you 22
harbour thoughts like these? Is it easier to say, "Your sins are forgiven 23
you", or to say, "Stand up and walk"? But to convince you that the Son of 24
Man has the right on earth to forgive sins'—he turned to the paralysed
man—'I say to you, stand up, take your bed, and go home.' And at once 25
he rose to his feet before their eyes, took up the bed he had been lying on,
and went home praising God. They were all lost in amazement and praised 26
God; filled with awe they said, 'You would never believe the things we
have seen today.'

Later, when he went out, he saw a tax-gatherer, Levi by name, at his seat 27
in the custom-house, and said to him, 'Follow me'; and he rose to his feet, 28
left everything behind, and followed him.

Afterwards Levi held a big reception in his house for Jesus; among the 29
guests was a large party of tax-gatherers and others. The Pharisees and the 30
lawyers of their sect complained to his disciples: 'Why do you eat and
drink', they said, 'with tax-gatherers and sinners?' Jesus answered them: 31
'It is not the healthy that need a doctor, but the sick; I have not come to 32
invite virtuous people, but to call sinners to repentance.'

Then they said to him, 'John's disciples are much given to fasting and the 33
practice of prayer, and so are the disciples of the Pharisees; but yours eat
and drink.' Jesus replied, 'Can you make the bridegroom's friends fast 34
while the bridegroom is with them? But a time will come: the bridegroom 35
will be taken away from them, and that will be the time for them to fast.'

He told them this parable also: 'No one tears a piece from a new cloak 36
to patch an old one; if he does, he will have made a hole in the new cloak,
and the patch from the new will not match the old. Nor does anyone put 37
new wine into old wine-skins; if he does, the new wine will burst the skins,
the wine will be wasted, and the skins ruined. Fresh skins for new wine! 38
And no one after drinking old wine wants new; for he says, "The old wine 39
is good." '

One Sabbath he was going through the cornfields, and his disciples were **6**
plucking the ears of corn, rubbing them in their hands, and eating them.
Some of the Pharisees said, 'Why are you doing what is forbidden on the 2
Sabbath?' Jesus answered, 'So you have not read what David did when he 3
and his men were hungry? He went into the House of God and took the 4
sacred bread to eat and gave it to his men, though priests alone are allowed
to eat it, and no one else.' He also said, 'The Son of Man is sovereign even 5
over the Sabbath.'

On another Sabbath he had gone to synagogue and was teaching. There 6
happened to be a man in the congregation whose right arm was withered;
and the lawyers and the Pharisees were on the watch to see whether Jesus 7
would cure him on the Sabbath, so that they could find a charge to bring

8 against him. But he knew what was in their minds and said to the man with the withered arm, 'Get up and stand out here.' So he got up and stood there.
9 Then Jesus said to them, 'I put the question to you: is it permitted to do
10 good or to do evil on the Sabbath, to save life or to destroy it?' He looked round at them all and then said to the man, 'Stretch out your arm.' He
11 did so, and his arm was restored. But they were beside themselves with anger, and began to discuss among themselves what they could do to Jesus.

12 During this time he went out one day into the hills to pray, and spent the
13 night in prayer to God. When day broke he called his disciples to him, and
14 from among them he chose twelve and named them Apostles: Simon, to whom he gave the name of Peter, and Andrew his brother, James and
15 John, Philip and Bartholomew, Matthew and Thomas, James son of
16 Alphaeus, and Simon who was called the Zealot, Judas son of James, and Judas Iscariot who turned traitor.

17 He came down the hill with them and took his stand on level ground. There was a large concourse of his disciples and great numbers of people from Jerusalem and Judaea and from the seaboard of Tyre and Sidon,
18 who had come to listen to him, and to be cured of their diseases. Those who
19 were troubled with unclean spirits were cured; and everyone in the crowd was trying to touch him, because power went out from him and cured them all.

20 THEN TURNING TO HIS DISCIPLES he began to speak:
   'How blest are you who are in need; the kingdom of God is yours.
21    'How blest are you who now go hungry; your hunger shall be satisfied.
   'How blest are you who weep now; you shall laugh.
22    'How blest you are when men hate you, when they outlaw you and insult you, and ban your very name as infamous, because of the Son of Man.
23 On that day be glad and dance for joy; for assuredly you have a rich reward in heaven; in just the same way did their fathers treat the prophets.
24    'But alas for you who are rich; you have had your time of happiness.
25    'Alas for you who are well-fed now; you shall go hungry.
   'Alas for you who laugh now; you shall mourn and weep.
26    'Alas for you when all speak well of you; just so did their fathers treat the false prophets.
27    'But to you who hear me I say:
28    'Love your enemies; do good to those who hate you; bless those who
29 curse you; pray for those who treat you spitefully. When a man hits you on the cheek, offer him the other cheek too; when a man takes your coat, let
30 him have your shirt as well. Give to everyone who asks you; when a man
31 takes what is yours, do not demand it back. Treat others as you would like them to treat you.
32    'If you love only those who love you, what credit is that to you? Even
33 sinners love those who love them. Again, if you do good only to those who
34 do good to you, what credit is that to you? Even sinners do as much. And if you lend only where you expect to be repaid, what credit is that to you?
35 Even sinners lend to each other to be repaid in full. But you must love your

enemies and do good; and lend without expecting any return;[a] and you will have a rich reward: you will be sons of the Most High, because he himself is kind to the ungrateful and wicked. Be compassionate as your 36 Father is compassionate.

'Pass no judgement, and you will not be judged; do not condemn, and 37 you will not be condemned; acquit, and you will be acquitted; give, and 38 gifts will be given you. Good measure, pressed down, shaken together, and running over, will be poured into your lap; for whatever measure you deal out to others will be dealt to you in return.'

He also offered them a parable: 'Can one blind man be guide to another? 39 Will they not both fall into the ditch? A pupil is not superior to his teacher; 40 but everyone, when his training is complete, will reach his teacher's level.

'Why do you look at the speck of sawdust in your brother's eye, with 41 never a thought for the great plank in your own? How can you say to your 42 brother, "My dear brother, let me take the speck out of your eye", when you are blind to the plank in your own? You hypocrite! First take the plank out of your own eye, and then you will see clearly to take the speck out of your brother's.

'There is no such thing as a good tree producing worthless fruit, nor 43 yet a worthless tree producing good fruit. For each tree is known by its own 44 fruit: you do not gather figs from thistles, and you do not pick grapes from brambles. A good man produces good from the store of good within 45 himself; and an evil man from evil within produces evil. For the words that the mouth utters come from the overflowing of the heart.

'Why do you keep calling me "Lord, Lord"—and never do what I tell 46 you? Everyone who comes to me and hears what I say, and acts upon it— 47 I will show you what he is like. He is like a man who, in building his house, 48 dug deep and laid the foundations on rock. When the flood came, the river burst upon that house, but could not shift it, because it had been soundly built. But he who hears and does not act is like a man who built his house 49 on the soil without foundations. As soon as the river burst upon it, the house collapsed, and fell with a great crash.'

WHEN HE HAD FINISHED addressing the people, he went to Capernaum. 7 A centurion there had a servant whom he valued highly; this servant was 2 ill and near to death. Hearing about Jesus, he sent some Jewish elders with 3 the request that he would come and save his servant's life. They approached 4 Jesus and pressed their petition earnestly: 'He deserves this favour from you,' they said, 'for he is a friend of our nation and it is he who built us our 5 synagogue.' Jesus went with them; but when he was not far from the 6 house, the centurion sent friends with this message: 'Do not trouble further, sir; it is not for me to have you under my roof, and that is why I 7 did not presume to approach you in person. But say the word and my servant will be cured. I know, for in my position I am myself under orders, 8 with soldiers under me. I say to one, "Go", and he goes; to another, "Come here", and he comes; and to my servant, "Do this", and he does it.' When 9 Jesus heard this, he admired the man, and, turning to the crowd that was

[a] *Or* without ever giving up hope; *some witnesses read* without giving up hope of anyone.

following him, he said, 'I tell you, nowhere, even in Israel, have I found
10 faith like this.' And the messengers returned to the house and found the
servant in good health.

11    Afterwards[a] Jesus went to a town called Nain, accompanied by his
12 disciples and a large crowd. As he approached the gate of the town he met
a funeral. The dead man was the only son of his widowed mother; and
13 many of the townspeople were there with her. When the Lord saw her his
14 heart went out to her, and he said, 'Weep no more.' With that he stepped
forward and laid his hand on the bier; and the bearers halted. Then he
15 spoke: 'Young man, rise up!' The dead man sat up and began to speak;
16 and Jesus gave him back to his mother. Deep awe fell upon them all, and
they praised God. 'A great prophet has arisen among us', they said, and
17 again, 'God has shown his care for his people.' The story of what he had
done ran through all parts of Judaea and the whole neighbourhood.

18 19    John too was informed of all this by his disciples. Summoning two of
their number he sent them to the Lord with this message: 'Are you the one
20 who is to come, or are we to expect some other?' The messengers made
their way to Jesus and said, 'John the Baptist has sent us to you: he asks,
21 "Are you the one who is to come, or are we to expect some other?"' There
and then he cured many sufferers from diseases, plagues, and evil spirits;
22 and on many blind people he bestowed sight. Then he gave them his answer:
'Go', he said, 'and tell John what you have seen and heard: how the blind
recover their sight, the lame walk, the lepers are made clean, the deaf hear,
23 the dead are raised to life, the poor are hearing the good news—and happy
is the man who does not find me a stumbling-block.'

24    After John's messengers had left, Jesus began to speak about him to the
crowds: 'What was the spectacle that drew you to the wilderness? A reed-
25 bed swept by the wind? No? Then what did you go out to see? A man
dressed in silks and satins? Surely you must look in palaces for grand
26 clothes and luxury. But what did you go out to see? A prophet? Yes indeed,
27 and far more than a prophet. He is the man of whom Scripture says,

"Here is my herald, whom I send on ahead of you,
and he will prepare your way before you."

28 I tell you, there is not a mother's son greater than John, and yet the least
in the kingdom of God is greater than he.'

29    When they heard him, all the people, including the tax-gatherers,
30 praised God, for they had accepted John's baptism; but the Pharisees and
lawyers, who refused his baptism, had rejected[b] God's purpose for
themselves.

31    'How can I describe the people of this generation? What are they like?
32 They are like children sitting in the market-place and shouting at each other,

"We piped for you and you would not dance."
"We wept and wailed, and you would not mourn."

---

[a] *Some witnesses read* On the next day.        [b] *Or* '. . . greater than he. And all the
people, including the tax-gatherers, when they heard him, accepted John's baptism and
acknowledged the righteous dealing of God; but the Pharisees and lawyers, by refusing
his baptism, rejected . . .'

For John the Baptist came neither eating bread nor drinking wine, and 33
you say, "He is possessed." The Son of Man came eating and drinking, 34
and you say, "Look at him! a glutton and a drinker, a friend of tax-gatherers
and sinners!" And yet God's wisdom is proved right by all who are her 35
children.'

One of the Pharisees invited him to eat with him; he went to the Pharisee's 36
house and took his place at table. A woman who was living an immoral life 37
in the town had learned that Jesus was at table in the Pharisee's house and
had brought oil of myrrh in a small flask. She took her place behind him, 38
by his feet, weeping. His feet were wetted with her tears and she wiped
them with her hair, kissing them and anointing them with the myrrh.
When his host the Pharisee saw this he said to himself, 'If this fellow were 39
a real prophet, he would know who this woman is that touches him, and
what sort of woman she is, a sinner.' Jesus took him up and said, 'Simon, 40
I have something to say to you.' 'Speak on, Master', said he. 'Two men were 41
in debt to a money-lender: one owed him five hundred silver pieces, the
other fifty. As neither had anything to pay with he let them both off. Now, 42
which will love him most?' Simon replied, 'I should think the one that was 43
let off most.' 'You are right', said Jesus. Then turning to the woman, he 44
said to Simon, 'You see this woman? I came to your house: you provided
no water for my feet; but this woman has made my feet wet with her tears
and wiped them with her hair. You gave me no kiss; but she has been kissing 45
my feet ever since I came in. You did not anoint my head with oil; but she 46
has anointed my feet with myrrh. And so, I tell you, her great love proves 47
that her many sins have been forgiven; where little has been forgiven, little
love is shown.' Then he said to her, 'Your sins are forgiven.' The other 48 49
guests began to ask themselves, 'Who is this, that he can forgive sins?' But 50
he said to the woman, 'Your faith has saved you; go in peace.'

AFTER THIS he went journeying from town to town and village to village, 8
proclaiming the good news of the kingdom of God. With him were the
Twelve and a number of women who had been set free from evil spirits 2
and infirmities: Mary, known as Mary of Magdala, from whom seven
devils had come out, Joanna, the wife of Chuza a steward of Herod's, 3
Susanna, and many others. These women provided for them out of their
own resources.

People were now gathering in large numbers, and as they made their 4
way to him from one town after another, he said in a parable: 'A sower 5
went out to sow his seed. And as he sowed, some seed fell along the footpath, where it was trampled on, and the birds ate it up. Some seed fell on 6
rock and, after coming up, withered for lack of moisture. Some seed fell 7
in among thistles, and the thistles grew up with it and choked it. And some 8
of the seed fell into good soil, and grew, and yielded a hundredfold.' As
he said this he called out, 'If you have ears to hear, then hear.'

His disciples asked him what this parable meant, and he said, 'It has been 9 10
granted to you to know the secrets of the kingdom of God; but the others
have only parables, so that they may look but see nothing, hear but understand nothing.

11 12   'This is what the parable means. The seed is the word of God. Those
        along the footpath are the men who hear it, and then the devil comes and
        carries off the word from their hearts for fear they should believe and be
13      saved. The seed sown on rock stands for those who receive the word with
        joy when they hear it, but have no root; they are believers for a while, but
14      in the time of testing they desert. That which fell among thistles represents
        those who hear, but their further growth is choked by cares and wealth
15      and the pleasures of life, and they bring nothing to maturity. But the seed
        in good soil represents those who bring a good and honest heart to the
        hearing of the word, hold it fast, and by their perseverance yield a harvest.
16          'Nobody lights a lamp and then covers it with a basin or puts it under the
        bed. On the contrary, he puts it on a lamp-stand so that those who come in
17      may see the light. For there is nothing hidden that will not become public,
        nothing under cover that will not be made known and brought into the
        open.
18          'Take care, then, how you listen; for the man who has will be given more,
        and the man who has not will forfeit even what he thinks he has.'
19          His mother and his brothers arrived but could not get to him for the
20      crowd. He was told, 'Your mother and brothers are standing outside, and
21      they want to see you.' He replied, 'My mother and my brothers—they are
        those who hear the word of God and act upon it.'
22          One day he got into a boat with his disciples and said to them, 'Let us
23      cross over to the other side of the lake.' So they put out; and as they sailed
        along he went to sleep. Then a heavy squall struck the lake; they began to
24      ship water and were in grave danger. They went to him, and roused him,
        crying, 'Master, Master, we are sinking!' He awoke, and rebuked the
        wind and the turbulent waters. The storm subsided and all was calm.
25      'Where is your faith?' he asked. In fear and astonishment they said to one
        another, 'Who can this be? He gives his orders to wind and waves, and
        they obey him.'
26          So they landed in the country of the Gergesenes,[a] which is opposite
27      Galilee. As he stepped ashore he was met by a man from the town who was
        possessed by devils. For a long time he had neither worn clothes nor lived
28      in a house, but stayed among the tombs. When he saw Jesus he cried out,
        and fell at his feet shouting, 'What do you want with me, Jesus, son of the
        Most High God? I implore you, do not torment me.'
29          For Jesus was already ordering the unclean spirit to come out of the man.
        Many a time it had seized him, and then, for safety's sake, they would
        secure him with chains and fetters; but each time he broke loose, and with
        the devil in charge made off to the solitary places.
30          Jesus asked him, 'What is your name?' 'Legion', he replied. This was
31      because so many devils had taken possession of him. And they begged him
        not to banish them to the Abyss.
32          There happened to be a large herd of pigs nearby, feeding on the hill;
        and the spirits begged him to let them go into these pigs. He gave them
33      leave; the devils came out of the man and went into the pigs, and the herd
        rushed over the edge into the lake and were drowned.

        *a Some witnesses read* Gerasenes; *others read* Gadarenes.

The men in charge of them saw what had happened, and, taking to their 34
heels, they carried the news to the town and country-side; and the people
came out to see for themselves. When they came to Jesus, and found the 35
man from whom the devils had gone out sitting at his feet clothed and in
his right mind, they were afraid. The spectators told them how the madman 36
had been cured. Then the whole population of the Gergesene *a* district 37
asked him to go, for they were in the grip of a great fear. So he got into the
boat and returned. The man from whom the devils had gone out begged 38
leave to go with him; but Jesus sent him away: 'Go back home,' he said, 39
'and tell them everything that God has done for you.' The man went all over
the town spreading the news of what Jesus had done for him.

When Jesus returned, the people welcomed him, for they were all 40
expecting him. Then a man appeared—Jairus was his name and he was 41
president of the synagogue. Throwing himself down at Jesus's feet he
begged him to come to his house, because he had an only daughter, about 42
twelve years old, who was dying. And while Jesus was on his way he could
hardly breathe for the crowds.

Among them was a woman who had suffered from haemorrhages for 43
twelve years; and *b* nobody had been able to cure her. She came up from 44
behind and touched the edge of *c* his cloak, and at once her haemorrhage
stopped. Jesus said, 'Who was it that touched me?' All disclaimed it, and 45
Peter and his companions said, 'Master, the crowds are hemming you in
and pressing upon you!' But Jesus said, 'Someone did touch me, for I felt 46
that power had gone out from me.' Then the woman, seeing that she was 47
detected, came trembling and fell at his feet. Before all the people she
explained why she had touched him and how she had been instantly cured.
He said to her, 'My daughter, your faith has cured you. Go in peace.' 48

While he was still speaking, a man came from the president's house with 49
the message, 'Your daughter is dead; trouble the Rabbi no further.' But 50
Jesus heard, and interposed. 'Do not be afraid,' he said; 'only show faith
and she will be well again.' On arrival at the house he allowed no one to go 51
in with him except Peter, John, and James, and the child's father and
mother. And all were weeping and lamenting for her. He said, 'Weep no 52
more; she is not dead: she is asleep'; and they only laughed at him, well 53
knowing that she was dead. But Jesus took hold of her hand and called her: 54
'Get up, my child.' Her spirit returned, she stood up immediately, and 55
he told them to give her something to eat. Her parents were astounded; 56
but he forbade them to tell anyone what had happened.

HE NOW CALLED the Twelve together and gave them power and authority 9
to overcome all the devils and to cure diseases, and sent them to proclaim 2
the kingdom of God and to heal. 'Take nothing for the journey,' he told 3
them, 'neither stick nor pack, neither bread nor money; nor are you each
to have a second coat. When you are admitted to a house, stay there, 4
and go on from there. As for those who will not receive you, when you leave 5
their town shake the dust off your feet as a warning to them.' So they set 6

*a Some witnesses read* Gergesene; *others read* Gadarene.  *b Some witnesses add*
though she had spent all she had on doctors.  *c Some witnesses omit* the edge of.

out and travelled from village to village, and everywhere they told the good news and healed the sick.

7    Now Prince Herod heard of all that was happening, and did not know what to make of it; for some were saying that John had been raised from
8    the dead, others that Elijah had appeared, others again that one of the old
9    prophets had come back to life. Herod said, 'As for John, I beheaded him myself; but who is this I hear such talk about?' And he was anxious to see him.

10    On their return the apostles told Jesus all they had done; and he took
11    them with him and withdrew privately to a town called Bethsaida. But the crowds found out and followed him. He welcomed them, and spoke to them about the kingdom of God, and cured those who were in need of
12    healing. When evening was drawing on, the Twelve came up to him and said, 'Send these people away; then they can go into the villages and farms round about to find food and lodging; for we are in a lonely place here.'
13    'Give them something to eat yourselves', he replied. But they said, 'All we have is five loaves and two fishes, nothing more—unless perhaps we
14    ourselves are to go and buy provisions for all this company.' (There were about five thousand men.) He said to his disciples, 'Make them sit down
15 16    in groups of fifty or so.' They did so and got them all seated. Then, taking the five loaves and the two fishes, he looked up to heaven, said the blessing over them, broke them, and gave them to the disciples to distribute to the
17    people. They all ate to their hearts' content; and when the scraps they left were picked up, they filled twelve great baskets.

18    One day when he was praying alone in the presence of his disciples, he
19    asked them, 'Who do the people say I am?' They answered, 'Some say John the Baptist, others Elijah, others that one of the old prophets has come
20    back to life.' 'And you,' he said, 'who do you say I am?' Peter answered,
21    'God's Messiah.' Then he gave them strict orders not to tell this to anyone.
22    And he said, 'The Son of Man has to undergo great sufferings, and to be rejected by the elders, chief priests, and doctors of the law, to be put to death and to be raised again on the third day.'

23    And to all he said, 'If anyone wishes to be a follower of mine, he must leave self behind; day after day he must take up his cross, and come with me.
24    Whoever cares for his own safety is lost; but if a man will let himself be lost
25    for my sake, that man is safe. What will a man gain by winning the whole
26    world, at the cost of his true self? For whoever is ashamed of me and mine, *a* the Son of Man will be ashamed of him, when he comes in his glory and
27    the glory of the Father and the holy angels. And I tell you this: there are some of those standing here who will not taste death before they have seen the kingdom of God.'

28    About eight days after this conversation he took Peter, John, and James
29    with him and went up into the hills to pray. And while he was praying the appearance of his face changed and his clothes became dazzling white.
30    Suddenly there were two men talking with him; these were Moses and
31    Elijah, who appeared in glory and spoke of his departure, the destiny he
32    was to fulfil in Jerusalem. Meanwhile Peter and his companions had been

*a Some witnesses read* me and my words.

in a deep sleep; but when they awoke, they saw his glory and the two men who stood beside him. And as these were moving away from Jesus, Peter 33 said to him, 'Master, how good it is that we are here! Shall we make three shelters, one for you, one for Moses, and one for Elijah?'; but he spoke without knowing what he was saying. The words were still on his lips, 34 when there came a cloud which cast a shadow over them; they were afraid as they entered the cloud, and from it came a voice: 'This is my Son, my 35 Chosen; listen to him.' When the voice had spoken, Jesus was seen to be 36 alone. The disciples kept silence and at that time told nobody anything of what they had seen.

Next day when they came down from the hills he was met by a large 37 crowd. All at once there was a shout from a man in the crowd: 'Master, look 38 at my son, I implore you, my only child. From time to time a spirit seizes 39 him, gives a sudden scream, and throws him into convulsions with foaming at the mouth, and it keeps on mauling him and will hardly let him go. I 40 asked your disciples to cast it out, but they could not.' Jesus answered, 41 'What an unbelieving and perverse generation! How long shall I be with you and endure you all? Bring your son here.' But before the boy could 42 reach him the devil dashed him to the ground and threw him into convulsions. Jesus rebuked the unclean spirit, cured the boy, and gave him back to his father. And they were all struck with awe at the majesty of God. 43

Amid the general wonder and admiration at all he was doing, Jesus said to his disciples, 'What I now say is for you: ponder my words. The Son of 44 Man is to be given up into the power of men.' But they did not understand 45 this saying; it had been hidden from them, so that they should not*a* grasp its meaning, and they were afraid to ask him about it.

A dispute arose among them: which of them was the greatest? Jesus 46 47 knew what was passing in their minds, so he took a child by the hand and stood him at his side, and said, 'Whoever receives this child in my name 48 receives me; and whoever receives me receives the One who sent me. For the least among you all—he is the greatest.'

'Master,' said John, 'we saw a man driving out devils in your name, but 49 as he is not one of us we tried to stop him.' Jesus said to him, 'Do not stop 50 him, for he who is not against you is on your side.'

## *Journeys and encounters*

AS THE TIME APPROACHED when he was to be taken up to heaven, he 51 set his face resolutely towards Jerusalem, and sent messengers ahead. 52 They set out and went into a Samaritan village to make arrangements for him; but the villagers would not have him because he was making for 53 Jerusalem. When the disciples James and John saw this they said, 'Lord, 54 may we call down fire from heaven to burn them up*b*?' But he turned and 55 rebuked them,*c* and they went on to another village. 56

*a Or* it was so obscure to them that they could not . . .          *b Some witnesses add* as Elijah did.          *c Some witnesses insert* 'You do not know', he said, 'to what spirit you belong; (56) for the Son of Man did not come to destroy men's lives but to save them.'

57 As they were going along the road a man said to him, 'I will follow you
58 wherever you go.' Jesus answered, 'Foxes have their holes, the birds their
59 roosts; but the Son of Man has nowhere to lay his head.' To another he
said, 'Follow me', but the man replied, 'Let me go and bury my father
60 first.' Jesus said, 'Leave the dead to bury their dead; you must go and
announce the kingdom of God.'

61 Yet another said, 'I will follow you, sir; but let me first say good-bye to my
62 people at home.' To him Jesus said, 'No one who sets his hand to the plough
and then keeps looking back *a* is fit for the kingdom of God.'

**10** After this the Lord appointed a further seventy-two *b* and sent them on
2 ahead in pairs to every town and place he was going to visit himself. He
said to them: 'The crop is heavy, but labourers are scarce; you must there-
3 fore beg the owner to send labourers to harvest his crop. Be on your way.
4 And look, I am sending you like lambs among wolves. Carry no purse or
5 pack, and travel barefoot. Exchange no greetings on the road. When you
6 go into a house, let your first words be, "Peace to this house." If there is a
man of peace there, your peace will rest upon him; if not, it will return and
7 rest upon you. Stay in that one house, sharing their food and drink; for the
8 worker earns his pay. Do not move from house to house. When you come
into a town and they make you welcome, eat the food provided for you;
9 heal the sick there, and say, "The kingdom of God has come close to you."
10 When you enter a town and they do not make you welcome, go out into its
11 streets and say, "The very dust of your town that clings to our feet we wipe
off to your shame. Only take note of this: the kingdom of God has come
12 close." I tell you, it will be more bearable for Sodom on the great Day than
for that town.

13 'Alas for you, Chorazin! Alas for you, Bethsaida! If the miracles that
were performed in you had been performed in Tyre and Sidon, they would
14 have repented long ago, sitting in sackcloth and ashes. But it will be more
15 bearable for Tyre and Sidon at the Judgement than for you. And as for you,
Capernaum, will you be exalted to the skies? No, brought down to the
depths!

16 'Whoever listens to you listens to me; whoever rejects you rejects me.
And whoever rejects me rejects the One who sent me.'

17 The seventy-two *b* came back jubilant. 'In your name, Lord,' they said,
18 'even the devils submit to us.' He replied, 'I watched how Satan fell, like
19 lightning, out of the sky. And now you see that I have given you the power
to tread underfoot snakes and scorpions and all the forces of the enemy,
20 and nothing will ever harm you. *c* Nevertheless, what you should rejoice
over is not that the spirits submit to you, but that your names are enrolled
in heaven.'

21 At that moment Jesus exulted in the Holy *d* Spirit and said, 'I thank thee,
Father, Lord of heaven and earth, for hiding these things from the learned
and wise, and revealing them to the simple. Yes, Father, such *e* was thy

---

*a Some witnesses read* No one who looks back as he sets hand to the plough . . .
*b Some witnesses read* seventy.        *c Or* and he will have no way at all to harm
you.        *d Some witnesses omit* Holy.        *e Or* Yes, I thank thee, Father,
that such . . .

choice.' Then turning to his disciples he said,[a] 'Everything is entrusted to 22
me by my Father; and no one knows who the Son is but the Father, or who
the Father is but the Son, and those to whom the Son may choose to
reveal him.'

Turning to his disciples in private he said, 'Happy the eyes that see what 23
you are seeing! I tell you, many prophets and kings wished to see what you 24
now see, yet never saw it; to hear what you hear, yet never heard it.'

ON ONE OCCASION a lawyer came forward to put this test question to 25
him: 'Master, what must I do to inherit eternal life?' Jesus said, 'What is 26
written in the Law? What is your reading of it?' He replied, 'Love the 27
Lord your God with all your heart, with all your soul, with all your strength,
and with all your mind; and your neighbour as yourself.' 'That is the right 28
answer,' said Jesus; 'do that and you will live.'

But he wanted to vindicate himself, so he said to Jesus, 'And who is my 29
neighbour?' Jesus replied, 'A man was on his way from Jerusalem down to 30
Jericho when he fell in with robbers, who stripped him, beat him, and
went off leaving him half dead. It so happened that a priest was going down 31
by the same road; but when he saw him, he went past on the other side.
So too a Levite came to the place, and when he saw him went past on the 32
other side. But a Samaritan who was making the journey came upon him, 33
and when he saw him was moved to pity. He went up and bandaged his 34
wounds, bathing them with oil and wine. Then he lifted him on to his own
beast, brought him to an inn, and looked after him there. Next day he pro- 35
duced two silver pieces and gave them to the innkeeper, and said, "Look
after him; and if you spend any more, I will repay you on my way back."
Which of these three do you think was neighbour to the man who fell into 36
the hands of the robbers?' He answered, 'The one who showed him kind- 37
ness.' Jesus said, 'Go and do as he did.'

While they were on their way Jesus came to a village where a woman 38
named Martha made him welcome in her home. She had a sister, Mary, 39
who seated herself at the Lord's feet and stayed there listening to his words.
Now Martha was distracted by her many tasks, so she came to him and said, 40
'Lord, do you not care that my sister has left me to get on with the work by
myself? Tell her to come and lend a hand.' But the Lord answered, 41
'Martha, Martha, you are fretting and fussing about so many things; but 42
one thing is necessary.[b] The part that Mary has chosen is best; and it shall
not be taken away from her.'

Once, in a certain place, Jesus was at prayer. When he ceased, one of his **11**
disciples said, 'Lord, teach us to pray, as John taught his disciples.' He 2
answered, 'When you pray, say,

> "Father,[c] thy name be hallowed;
> thy kingdom come.[d]

[a] *Some witnesses omit* Then . . . he said.　　　[b] *Some witnesses read* but few things are
necessary, or rather, one alone; *others omit* you are fretting . . . necessary.　　　[c] *Some*
*witnesses read* Our Father in heaven.　　　[d] *One witness reads* thy kingdom come upon us;
*some others have* thy Holy Spirit come upon us and cleanse us; *some insert* thy will be
done, on earth as in heaven.

3　　　　　　　Give us each day our daily bread. *a*

4　　　　　　　And forgive us our sins,
　　　　　　　　for we too forgive all who have done us wrong.
　　　　　　　　And do not bring us to the test." ' *b*

5　　　Then he said to them, 'Suppose one of you has a friend who comes to
6　him in the middle of the night and says, "My friend, lend me three loaves,
7　for a friend of mine on a journey has turned up at my house, and I have
　　nothing to offer him"; and he replies from inside, "Do not bother me. The
　　door is shut for the night; my children and I have gone to bed; and I can-
8　not get up and give you what you want." I tell you that even if he will not
9　provide for him out of friendship, the very shamelessness of the request
　　will make him get up and give him all he needs. And so I say to you, ask,
　　and you will receive; seek, and you will find; knock, and the door will be
10　opened. For everyone who asks receives, he who seeks finds, and to him
　　who knocks, the door will be opened.

11　　　'Is there a father among you who will offer his son *c* a snake when he asks
12 13　for fish, or a scorpion when he asks for an egg? If you, then, bad as you are,
　　know how to give your children what is good for them, how much more will
　　the heavenly Father give the Holy Spirit *d* to those who ask him!'

14　H E  W A S  D R I V I N G  O U T a devil which was dumb; and when the devil had
　　come out, the dumb man began to speak. The people were astonished,
15　but some of them said, 'It is by Beelzebub prince of devils that he drives
16　the devils out.' Others, by way of a test, demanded of him a sign from
17　heaven. But he knew what was in their minds, and said, 'Every kingdom
18　divided against itself goes to ruin, and a divided household falls. Equally
　　if Satan is divided against himself, how can his kingdom stand?—since,
19　as you would have it, I drive out the devils by Beelzebub. If it is by Beelze-
　　bub that I cast out devils, by whom do your own people drive them out?
20　If this is your argument, they themselves will refute you. But if it is by the
　　finger of God that I drive out the devils, then be sure the kingdom of God
　　has already come upon you.

21　　　'When a strong man fully armed is on guard over his castle his posses-
22　sions are safe. But when someone stronger comes upon him and over-
　　powers him, he carries off the arms and armour on which the man had
　　relied and divides the plunder.

23　　　'He who is not with me is against me, and he who does not gather with
　　me scatters. *e*

24　　　'When an unclean spirit comes out of a man it wanders over the deserts
　　seeking a resting-place; and if it finds none, it says, "I will go back to the
25 26　home I left." So it returns and finds the house *f* swept clean, and tidy. Off
　　it goes and collects seven other spirits more wicked than itself, and they all
　　come in and settle down; and in the end the man's plight is worse than
　　before.'

*a* Or our bread for the morrow.　　　　　*b* Some witnesses add but save us from the evil
one (or from evil).　　　　　　　　*c* Some witnesses insert a stone when he asks for bread,
or . . .　　　　　　　*d* Some witnesses read a good gift; some others read good things.
*e* Some witnesses add me.　　　*f* Some witnesses insert unoccupied.

While he was speaking thus, a woman in the crowd called out, 'Happy 27
the womb that carried you and the breasts that suckled you!' He rejoined, 28
'No, happy are those who hear the word of God and keep it.'

With the crowds swarming round him he went on to say: 'This is a 29
wicked generation. It demands a sign, and the only sign that will be given
it is the sign of Jonah. For just as Jonah was a sign to the Ninevites, so will 30
the Son of Man be to this generation. At the Judgement, when the men of 31
this generation are on trial, the Queen of the South will appear against *a*
them and ensure their condemnation, for she came from the ends of the
earth to hear the wisdom of Solomon; and what is here is greater than
Solomon. The men of Nineveh will appear at the Judgement when this 32
generation is on trial, and ensure *b* its condemnation, for they repented at
the preaching of Jonah; and what is here is greater than Jonah.

'No one lights a lamp and puts it in a cellar, *c* but rather on the lamp- 33
stand so that those who enter may see the light. The lamp of your body is 34
the eye. When your eyes are sound, you have light for your whole body;
but when the eyes are bad, you are in darkness. See to it then that the light 35
you have is not darkness. If you have light for your whole body with no 36
trace of darkness, it will all be as bright as when a lamp flashes its rays
upon you.'

WHEN HE HAD FINISHED SPEAKING, a Pharisee invited him to a meal. 37
He came in and sat down. The Pharisee noticed with surprise that he had 38
not begun by washing before the meal. But the Lord said to him, 'You 39
Pharisees! You clean the outside of cup and plate; but inside you there is
nothing but greed and wickedness. You fools! Did not he who made the 40
outside make the inside too? But let what is in the cup *d* be given in charity, 41
and all is clean.

'Alas for you Pharisees! You pay tithes of mint and rue and every 42
garden-herb, but have no care for justice and the love of God. It is these
you should have practised, without neglecting the others. *e*

'Alas for you Pharisees! You love the seats of honour in synagogues, and 43
salutations in the market-places.

'Alas, alas, you are like unmarked graves over which men may walk with- 44
out knowing it.'

In reply to this one of the lawyers said, 'Master, when you say things 45
like this you are insulting us too.' Jesus rejoined: 'Yes, you lawyers, it is 46
no better with you! For you load men with intolerable burdens, and will
not put a single finger to the load.

'Alas, you build the tombs of the prophets whom your fathers murdered, 47
and so testify that you approve of the deeds your fathers did; they com- 48
mitted the murders and you provide the tombs.

'This is why the Wisdom of God said, "I will send them prophets and 49
messengers; and some of these they will persecute and kill"; so that this 50

---

*a Or* will be raised to life together with . . .        *b Or* At the Judgement the men of
Nineveh will rise again together with this generation and will ensure . . .        *c Some*
*witnesses insert* or under the meal-tub.        *d Or* what you can afford.        *e Some wit-*
*nesses omit* It is . . . others.

generation will have to answer for the blood of all the prophets shed since
51 the foundation of the world; from the blood of Abel to the blood of Zechariah who perished between the altar and the sanctuary. I tell you, this
generation will have to answer for it all.

52 'Alas for you lawyers! You have taken away the key of knowledge. You
did not go in yourselves, and those who were on their way in, you stopped.'

53 After he had left the house, the lawyers and Pharisees began to assail
54 him fiercely and to ply him with a host of questions, laying snares to catch
him with his own words.

12 MEANWHILE, WHEN A CROWD of many thousands had gathered,
packed so close that they were treading on one another, he began to speak
first to his disciples: 'Beware of the leaven of the Pharisees; I mean their
2 hypocrisy. There is nothing covered up that will not be uncovered,
3 nothing hidden that will not be made known. You may take it, then, that
everything you have said in the dark will be heard in broad daylight, and
what you have whispered behind closed doors will be shouted from the
house-tops.

4 'To you who are my friends I say: Do not fear those who kill the body and
5 after that have nothing more they can do. I will warn you whom to fear:
fear him who, after he has killed, has authority to cast into hell. Believe me,
he is the one to fear.

6 'Are not sparrows five for twopence? And yet not one of them is over-
7 looked by God. More than that, even the hairs of your head have all been
counted. Have no fear; you are worth more than any number of sparrows.

8 'I tell you this: everyone who acknowledges me before men, the Son of
9 Man will acknowledge before the angels of God; but he who disowns me
before men will be disowned before the angels of God.

10 'Anyone who speaks a word against the Son of Man will receive forgiveness; but for him who slanders the Holy Spirit there will be no forgiveness.

11 'When you are brought before synagogues and state authorities, do
not begin worrying about how you will conduct your defence or what you
12 will say. For when the time comes the Holy Spirit will instruct you what
to say.'

13 A man in the crowd said to him, 'Master, tell my brother to divide the
14 family property with me.' He replied, 'My good man, who set me over you
15 to judge or arbitrate?'*a* Then he said to the people, 'Beware! Be on your
guard against greed of every kind, for even when a man has more than
16 enough, his wealth does not give him life.' And he told them this parable:
17 'There was a rich man whose land yielded heavy crops. He debated with
18 himself: "What am I to do? I have not the space to store my produce. This
is what I will do," said he: "I will pull down my storehouses and build them
19 bigger. I will collect in them all my corn and other goods, and then say to
myself, 'Man, you have plenty of good things laid by, enough for many
20 years: take life easy, eat, drink, and enjoy yourself.'" But God said to
him, "You fool, this very night you must surrender your life; you have
21 made your money—who will get it now?" That is how it is with the

*a Some witnesses omit* or arbitrate.

man who amasses wealth for himself and remains a pauper in the sight of God.*a*

'Therefore', he said to his disciples, 'I bid you put away anxious thoughts 22 about food to keep you alive and clothes to cover your body. Life is more 23 than food, the body more than clothes. Think of the ravens: they neither 24 sow nor reap; they have no storehouse or barn; yet God feeds them. You are worth far more than the birds! Is there a man among you who by 25 anxious thought can add a foot to his height*b*? If, then, you cannot do even 26 a very little thing, why are you anxious about the rest?

'Think of the lilies: they neither spin nor weave;*c* yet I tell you, even 27 Solomon in all his splendour was not attired like one of these. But if that is 28 how God clothes the grass, which is growing in the field today, and to-morrow is thrown on the stove, how much more will he clothe you! How little faith you have! And so you are not to set your mind on food and drink; 29 you are not to worry. For all these are things for the heathen to run after; 30 but you have a Father who knows that you need them. No, set your mind 31 upon his kingdom, and all the rest will come to you as well.

'Have no fear, little flock; for your Father has chosen to give you the 32 Kingdom. Sell your possessions and give in charity. Provide for yourselves 33 purses that do not wear out, and never-failing treasure in heaven, where no thief can get near it, no moth destroy it. For where your treasure is, there 34 will your heart be also.

'Be ready for action, with belts fastened and lamps alight. Be like men 35 36 who wait for their master's return from a wedding-party, ready to let him in the moment he arrives and knocks. Happy are those servants whom the 37 master finds on the alert when he comes. I tell you this: he will fasten his belt, seat them at table, and come and wait on them. Even if it is the middle 38 of the night or before dawn when he comes, happy they if he finds them alert. And remember, if the householder had known what time the burglar 39 was coming he would not have let his house be broken into. Hold your-40 selves ready, then, because the Son of Man will come at the time you least expect him.'

Peter said, 'Lord, do you intend this parable specially for us or is it for 41 everyone?' The Lord said, 'Well, who is the trusty and sensible man whom 42 his master will appoint as his steward, to manage his servants and issue their rations at the proper time? Happy that servant who is found at his 43 task when his master comes! I tell you this: he will be put in charge of all 44 his master's property. But if that servant says to himself, "The master is a 45 long time coming", and begins to bully the menservants and maids, and eat and drink and get drunk; then the master will arrive on a day that 46 servant does not expect, at a time he does not know, and will cut him in pieces. Thus he will find his place among the faithless.

'The servant who knew his master's wishes, yet made no attempt to 47 carry them out, will be flogged severely. But one who did not know them and 48 earned a beating will be flogged less severely. Where a man has been given

---

*a Some witnesses omit* That . . . God; *others add at the end* When he said this he cried out, 'If you have ears to hear, then hear.'    *b Or* a day to his life.    *c Some witnesses read* they grow, they do not toil or spin.

much, much will be expected of him; and the more a man has had entrusted to him the more he will be required to repay.

49 'I have come to set fire to the earth, and how I wish it were already
50 kindled! I have a baptism to undergo, and what constraint I am under until
51 the ordeal is over! Do you suppose I came to establish peace on earth? No
52 indeed, I have come to bring division. For from now on, five members of a
53 family will be divided, three against two and two against three; father against son and son against father, mother against daughter and daughter against mother, mother against son's wife and son's wife against her mother-in-law.'

54 He also said to the people, 'When you see cloud banking up in the west,
55 you say at once, "It is going to rain", and rain it does. And when the wind is
56 from the south, you say, "There will be a heat-wave", and there is. What hypocrites you are! You know how to interpret the appearance of earth and sky; how is it you cannot interpret this fateful hour?

57 'And why can you not judge for yourselves what is the right course?
58 When you are going with your opponent to court, make an effort to settle with him while you are still on the way; otherwise he may drag you before the judge, and the judge hand you over to the constable, and the constable
59 put you in jail. I tell you, you will not come out till you have paid the last farthing.'

13 AT THAT VERY TIME there were some people present who told him about
2 the Galileans whose blood Pilate had mixed with their sacrifices. He answered them: 'Do you imagine that, because these Galileans suffered this fate, they must have been greater sinners than anyone else in Galilee?
3 I tell you they were not; but unless you repent, you will all of you come to
4 the same end. Or the eighteen people who were killed when the tower fell on them at Siloam—do you imagine they were more guilty than all the
5 other people living in Jerusalem? I tell you they were not; but unless you repent, you will all of you come to the same end.'

6 He told them this parable: 'A man had a fig-tree growing in his vineyard;
7 and he came looking for fruit on it, but found none. So he said to the vine-dresser, "Look here! For the last three years I have come looking for fruit on this fig-tree without finding any. Cut it down. Why should it go on
8 using up the soil?" But he replied, "Leave it, sir, this one year while I dig
9 round it and manure it. And if it bears next season, well and good; if not, you shall have it down."'

10 11 One Sabbath he was teaching in a synagogue, and there was a woman there possessed by a spirit that had crippled her for eighteen years. She
12 was bent double and quite unable to stand up straight. When Jesus saw her
13 he called her and said, 'You are rid of your trouble.' Then he laid his hands
14 on her, and at once she straightened up and began to praise God. But the president of the synagogue, indignant with Jesus for healing on the Sabbath, intervened and said to the congregation, 'There are six working-
15 days: come and be cured on one of them, and not on the Sabbath.' The Lord gave him his answer: 'What hypocrites you are!' he said. 'Is there a single one of you who does not loose his ox or his donkey from the manger

and take it out to water on the Sabbath? And here is this woman, a daughter 16
of Abraham, who has been kept prisoner by Satan for eighteen long years:
was it wrong for her to be freed from her bonds on the Sabbath?' At these 17
words all his opponents were covered with confusion, while the mass of
the people were delighted at all the wonderful things he was doing.

'What is the kingdom of God like?' he continued. 'What shall I compare 18
it with? It is like a mustard-seed which a man took and sowed in his 19
garden; and it grew to be a tree and the birds came to roost among its
branches.'

Again he said, 'The kingdom of God, what shall I compare it with? It is 20 21
like yeast which a woman took and mixed with half a hundredweight of
flour till it was all leavened.'

HE CONTINUED HIS JOURNEY through towns and villages, teaching as 22
he made his way towards Jerusalem. Someone asked him, 'Sir, are only a 23
few to be saved?' His answer was: 'Struggle to get in through the narrow 24
door; for I tell you that many will try to enter and not be able.

'When once the master of the house has got up and locked the door, you 25
may stand outside and knock, and say, "Sir, let us in!", but he will only
answer, "I do not know where you come from." Then you will begin to say, 26
"We sat at table with you and you taught in our streets." But he will repeat, 27
"I tell you, I do not know where you come from. Out of my sight, all of
you, you and your wicked ways!" There will be wailing and grinding of 28
teeth there, when you see Abraham, Isaac, and Jacob, and all the prophets,
in the kingdom of God, and yourselves thrown out. From east and west 29
people will come, from north and south, for the feast in the kingdom of
God. Yes, and some who are now last will be first, and some who are first 30
will be last.'

At that time a number of Pharisees came to him and said, 'You should 31
leave this place and go on your way; Herod is out to kill you.' He replied, 32
'Go and tell that fox, "Listen: today and tomorrow I shall be casting out
devils and working cures; on the third day I reach my goal." However, 33
I must be on my way today and tomorrow and the next day, because it is
unthinkable for a prophet to meet his death anywhere but in Jerusalem.

'O Jerusalem, Jerusalem, the city that murders the prophets and stones 34
the messengers sent to her! How often have I longed to gather your children, as a hen gathers her brood under her wings; but you would not let
me. Look, look! there is your temple, forsaken by God. And I tell you, 35
you shall never see me until the time comes when you say, "Blessings on
him who comes in the name of the Lord!"'

ONE SABBATH he went to have a meal in the house of a leading Pharisee; **14**
and they were watching him closely. There, in front of him, was a man 2
suffering from dropsy. Jesus asked the lawyers and the Pharisees: 'Is it 3
permitted to cure people on the Sabbath or not?' They said nothing. So 4
he took the man, cured him, and sent him away. Then he turned to them 5
and said, 'If one of you has a donkey *a* or an ox and it falls into a well, will

*a Some witnesses read* son.

6 he hesitate to haul it up on the Sabbath day?' To this they could find no reply.

7 When he noticed how the guests were trying to secure the places of
8 honour, he spoke to them in a parable: 'When you are asked by someone to a wedding-feast, do not sit down in the place of honour. It may be that some
9 person more distinguished than yourself has been invited; and the host will come and say to you, "Give this man your seat." Then you will look
10 foolish as you begin to take the lowest place. No, when you receive an invitation, go and sit down in the lowest place, so that when your host comes he will say, "Come up higher, my friend." Then all your fellow-
11 guests will see the respect in which you are held. For everyone who exalts himself will be humbled; and whoever humbles himself will be exalted.'

12 Then he said to his host, 'When you are having a party for lunch or supper, do not invite your friends, your brothers or other relations, or your rich neighbours; they will only ask you back again and so you will
13 be repaid. But when you give a party, ask the poor, the crippled, the lame,
14 and the blind; and so find happiness. For they have no means of repaying you; but you will be repaid on the day when good men rise from the dead.'

15 One of the company, after hearing all this, said to him, 'Happy the man
16 who shall sit at the feast in the kingdom of God!' Jesus answered, 'A man
17 was giving a big dinner party and had sent out many invitations. At dinner-time he sent his servant with a message for his guests, "Please come, every-
18 thing is now ready." They began one and all to excuse themselves. The first said, "I have bought a piece of land, and I must go and look over it; please
19 accept my apologies." The second said, "I have bought five yoke of oxen,
20 and I am on my way to try them out; please accept my apologies." The next said, "I have just got married and for that reason I cannot come."
21 When the servant came back he reported this to his master. The master of the house was angry and said to him, "Go out quickly into the streets and alleys of the town, and bring me in the poor, the crippled, the blind, and the
22 lame." The servant said, "Sir, your orders have been carried out and there
23 is still room." The master replied, "Go out on to the highways and along
24 the hedgerows and make them come in; I want my house to be full. I tell you that not one of those who were invited shall taste my banquet."'

25 Once when great crowds were accompanying him, he turned to them
26 and said: 'If anyone comes to me and does not hate his father and mother, wife and children, brothers and sisters, even his own life, he cannot be a
27 disciple of mine. No one who does not carry his cross and come with me
28 can be a disciple of mine. Would any of you think of building a tower with-out first sitting down and calculating the cost, to see whether he could
29 afford to finish it? Otherwise, if he has laid its foundation and then is not
30 able to complete it, all the onlookers will laugh at him. "There is the man",
31 they will say, "who started to build and could not finish." Or what king will march to battle against another king, without first sitting down to con-sider whether with ten thousand men he can face an enemy coming to meet
32 him with twenty thousand? If he cannot, then, long before the enemy
33 approaches, he sends envoys, and asks for terms. So also none of you can be a disciple of mine without parting with all his possessions.

'Salt is a good thing; but if salt itself becomes tasteless, what will you 34
use to season it? It is useless either on the land or on the dung-heap: it can 35
only be thrown away. If you have ears to hear, then hear.'

ANOTHER TIME, the tax-gatherers and other bad characters were all **15**
crowding in to listen to him; and the Pharisees and the doctors of the law 2
began grumbling among themselves: 'This fellow', they said, 'welcomes
sinners and eats with them.' He answered them with this parable: 'If one 3 4
of you has a hundred sheep and loses one of them, does he not leave the
ninety-nine in the open pasture and go after the missing one until he has
found it? How delighted he is then! He lifts it on to his shoulders, and home 5 6
he goes to call his friends and neighbours together. "Rejoice with me!"
he cries. "I have found my lost sheep." In the same way, I tell you, there 7
will be greater joy in heaven over one sinner who repents than over ninety-
nine righteous people who do not need to repent.

'Or again, if a woman has ten silver pieces and loses one of them, does 8
she not light the lamp, sweep out the house, and look in every corner till
she has found it? And when she has, she calls her friends and neighbours 9
together, and says, "Rejoice with me! I have found the piece that I lost."
In the same way, I tell you, there is joy among the angels of God over one 10
sinner who repents.'

Again he said: 'There was once a man who had two sons; and the 11 12
younger said to his father, "Father, give me my share of the property." So
he divided his estate between them. A few days later the younger son 13
turned the whole of his share into cash and left home for a distant country,
where he squandered it in reckless living. He had spent it all, when a severe 14
famine fell upon that country and he began to feel the pinch. So he went 15
and attached himself to one of the local landowners, who sent him on to his
farm to mind the pigs. He would have been glad to fill his belly with[a] the 16
pods that the pigs were eating; and no one gave him anything. Then he 17
came to his senses and said, "How many of my father's paid servants have
more food than they can eat, and here am I, starving to death! I will set 18
off and go to my father, and say to him, 'Father, I have sinned, against
God and against you; I am no longer fit to be called your son; treat me as 19
one of your paid servants.'" So he set out for his father's house. But while 20
he was still a long way off his father saw him, and his heart went out to him.
He ran to meet him, flung his arms round him, and kissed him. The son 21
said, "Father, I have sinned, against God and against you; I am no longer
fit to be called your son."[b] But the father said to his servants, "Quick! 22
fetch a robe, my best one, and put it on him; put a ring on his finger and
shoes on his feet. Bring the fatted calf and kill it, and let us have a feast to 23
celebrate the day. For this son of mine was dead and has come back to life; 24
he was lost and is found." And the festivities began.

'Now the elder son was out on the farm; and on his way back, as he 25
approached the house, he heard music and dancing. He called one of the 26
servants and asked what it meant. The servant told him, "Your brother 27

[a] *Some witnesses read* to have his fill of ...    [b] *Some witnesses add* treat me as one of
your paid servants.

has come home, and your father has killed the fatted calf because he has
28  him back safe and sound." But he was angry and refused to go in. His
29  father came out and pleaded with him; but he retorted, "You know how
I have slaved for you all these years; I never once disobeyed your orders;
30  and you never gave me so much as a kid, for a feast with my friends. But
now that this son of yours turns up, after running through your money
31  with his women, you kill the fatted calf for him." "My boy," said the father,
32  "you are always with me, and everything I have is yours. How could we
help celebrating this happy day? Your brother here was dead and has come
back to life, was lost and is found."'

**16**  He said to his disciples, 'There was a rich man who had a steward, and he
2  received complaints that this man was squandering the property. So he
sent for him, and said, "What is this that I hear? Produce your accounts,
3  for you cannot be manager here any longer." The steward said to himself,
"What am I to do now that my employer is dismissing me? I am not strong
4  enough to dig, and too proud to beg. I know what I must do, to make sure
that, when I have to leave, there will be people to give me house and home."
5  He summoned his master's debtors one by one. To the first he said, "How
6  much do you owe my master?" He replied, "A thousand gallons of olive
oil." He said, "Here is your account. Sit down and make it five hundred;
7  and be quick about it." Then he said to another, "And you, how much do
you owe?" He said, "A thousand bushels of wheat", and was told, "Take
8  your account and make it eight hundred." And the master applauded the
dishonest steward for acting so astutely. For the worldly are more astute
than the other-worldly in dealing with their own kind.
9    'So I say to you, use your worldly wealth to win friends for yourselves,
so that when money is a thing of the past you may be received into an
eternal home.
10    'The man who can be trusted in little things can be trusted also in great;
and the man who is dishonest in little things is dishonest also in great
11  things. If, then, you have not proved trustworthy with the wealth of this
12  world, who will trust you with the wealth that is real? And if you have
proved untrustworthy with what belongs to another, who will give you
what is your own?
13    'No servant can be the slave of two masters; for either he will hate the
first and love the second, or he will be devoted to the first and think nothing
of the second. You cannot serve God and Money.'
14 15    The Pharisees, who loved money, heard all this and scoffed at him. He
said to them, 'You are the people who impress your fellow-men with your
righteousness; but God sees through you; for what sets itself up to be
admired by men is detestable in the sight of God.
16    'Until John, it was the Law and the prophets: since then, there is the
good news of the kingdom of God, and everyone forces his way in.
17    'It is easier for heaven and earth to come to an end than for one dot or
stroke of the Law to lose its force.
18    'A man who divorces his wife and marries another commits adultery;
and anyone who marries a woman divorced from her husband commits
adultery.

'There was once a rich man, who dressed in purple and the finest linen, 19
and feasted in great magnificence every day. At his gate, covered with sores, 20
lay a poor man named Lazarus, who would have been glad to satisfy his 21
hunger with the scraps from the rich man's table. Even the dogs used to  ·
come and lick his sores. One day the poor man died and was carried away 22
by the angels to be with Abraham. The rich man also died and was buried,
and in Hades, where he was in torment, he looked up; and there, far away, 23
was Abraham with Lazarus close beside him. "Abraham, my father," he 24
called out, "take pity on me! Send Lazarus to dip the tip of his finger in
water, to cool my tongue, for I am in agony in this fire." But Abraham said, 25
"Remember, my child, that all the good things fell to you while you were
alive, and all the bad to Lazarus; now he has his consolation here and it is
you who are in agony. But that is not all: there is a great chasm fixed be- 26
tween us; no one from our side who wants to reach you can cross it, and
none may pass from your side to us." "Then, father," he replied, "will 27
you send him to my father's house, where I have five brothers, to warn 28
them, so that they too may not come to this place of torment?" But Abraham 29
said, "They have Moses and the prophets; let them listen to them." "No, 30
father Abraham," he replied, "but if someone from the dead visits them,
they will repent." Abraham answered, "If they do not listen to Moses and 31
the prophets they will pay no heed even if someone should rise from the
dead."'

HE SAID TO HIS DISCIPLES, 'Causes of stumbling are bound to arise; **17**
but woe betide the man through whom they come. It would be better for 2
him to be thrown into the sea with a millstone round his neck than to cause
one of these little ones to stumble. Keep watch on yourselves. 3
'If your brother wrongs you, reprove him; and if he repents, forgive
him. Even if he wrongs you seven times in a day and comes back to you 4
seven times saying, "I am sorry", you are to forgive him.'
The apostles said to the Lord, 'Increase our faith'; and the Lord 5 6
replied, 'If you had faith no bigger even than a mustard-seed, you could
say to this mulberry-tree, "Be rooted up and replanted in the sea"; and it
would at once obey you.
'Suppose one of you has a servant ploughing or minding sheep. When 7
he comes back from the fields, will the master say, "Come along at once
and sit down"? Will he not rather say, "Prepare my supper, fasten your 8
belt, and then wait on me while I have my meal; you can have yours afterwards"? Is he grateful to the servant for carrying out his orders? So with 9 10
you: when you have carried out all your orders, you should say, "We are
servants and deserve no credit; we have only done our duty."'
In the course of his journey to Jerusalem he was travelling through the 11
borderlands of Samaria and Galilee. As he was entering a village he was 12
met by ten men with leprosy. They stood some way off and called out to 13
him, 'Jesus, Master, take pity on us.' When he saw them he said, 'Go and 14
show yourselves to the priests'; and while they were on their way, they
were made clean. One of them, finding himself cured, turned back praising 15
God aloud. He threw himself down at Jesus's feet and thanked him. And 16

17 he was a Samaritan. At this Jesus said: 'Were not all ten cleansed? The
18 other nine, where are they? Could none be found to come back and give
19 praise to God except this foreigner?' And he said to the man, 'Stand up
· and go on your way; your faith has cured you.'

20 THE PHARISEES ASKED HIM, 'When will the kingdom of God come?'
He said, 'You cannot tell by observation when the kingdom of God comes.
21 There will be no saying, "Look, here it is!" or "there it is!"; for in fact the
kingdom of God is among you.'<sup>a</sup>

22 He said to the disciples, 'The time will come when you will long to see
23 one of the days of the Son of Man, but you will not see it. They will say to
you, "Look! There!" and "Look! Here!" Do not go running off in pursuit.
24 For like the lightning-flash that lights up the earth from end to end, will
25 the Son of Man be when his day comes. But first he must endure much
suffering and be repudiated by this generation.

26 'As things were in Noah's days, so will they be in the days of the Son of
27 Man. They ate and drank and married, until the day that Noah went into
28 the ark and the flood came and made an end of them all. As things were in
Lot's days, also: they ate and drank; they bought and sold; they planted
29 and built; but the day that Lot went out from Sodom, it rained fire and
30 sulphur from the sky and made an end of them all—it will be like that on the
day when the Son of Man is revealed.

31 'On that day the man who is on the roof and his belongings in the house
must not come down to pick them up; he, too, who is in the fields must not
32 33 go back. Remember Lot's wife. Whoever seeks to save his life will lose it;
and whoever loses it will save it, and live.

34 'I tell you, on that night there will be two men in one bed: one will be
35 taken, the other left. There will be two women together grinding corn: one
37 will be taken, the other left.'<sup>b</sup> When they heard this they asked, 'Where,
Lord?' He said, 'Where the corpse is, there the vultures will gather.'

**18** HE SPOKE TO THEM in a parable to show that they should keep on praying
2 and never lose heart: 'There was once a judge who cared nothing for God
3 or man, and in the same town there was a widow who constantly came
4 before him demanding justice against her opponent. For a long time he
refused; but in the end he said to himself, "True, I care nothing for God
5 or man; but this widow is so great a nuisance that I will see her righted
6 before she wears me out with her persistence."' The Lord said, 'You
7 hear what the unjust judge says; and will not God vindicate his chosen,
who cry out to him day and night, while he listens patiently to them<sup>c</sup>?
8 I tell you, he will vindicate them soon enough. But when the Son of Man
comes, will he find faith on earth?'

9 And here is another parable that he told. It was aimed at those who were
10 sure of their own goodness and looked down on everyone else. 'Two men

---

<sup>a</sup> *Or* for in fact the kingdom of God is within you, *or* for in fact the kingdom of God is
within your grasp, *or* for suddenly the kingdom of God will be among you.
<sup>b</sup> *Some witnesses add* (36) two men in the fields: one will be taken, the other left.
<sup>c</sup> *Or* delays to help them.

went up to the temple to pray, one a Pharisee and the other a tax-gatherer. The Pharisee stood up and prayed thus:[a] "I thank thee, O God, that I am 11 not like the rest of men, greedy, dishonest, adulterous; or, for that matter, like this tax-gatherer. I fast twice a week; I pay tithes on all that I get." 12 But the other kept his distance and would not even raise his eyes to heaven, 13 but beat upon his breast, saying, "O God, have mercy on me, sinner that I am." It was this man, I tell you, and not the other, who went home 14 acquitted of his sins. For everyone who exalts himself will be humbled; and whoever humbles himself will be exalted.'

They even brought babies for him to touch. When the disciples saw 15 them they rebuked them, but Jesus called for the children and said, 'Let 16 the little ones come to me; do not try to stop them; for the kingdom of God belongs to such as these. I tell you that whoever does not accept the king- 17 dom of God like a child will never enter it.'

A man of the ruling class put this question to him: 'Good Master, what 18 must I do to win eternal life?' Jesus said to him, 'Why do you call me good? 19 No one is good except God alone. You know the commandments: "Do not 20 commit adultery; do not murder; do not steal; do not give false evidence; honour your father and mother."' The man answered, 'I have kept all 21 these since I was a boy.' On hearing this Jesus said, 'There is still one 22 thing lacking: sell everything you have and distribute to the poor, and you will have riches in heaven; and come, follow me.' At these words his heart 23 sank; for he was a very rich man. When Jesus saw it he said, 'How hard it 24 is for the wealthy to enter the kingdom of God! It is easier for a camel to go 25 through the eye of a needle than for a rich man to enter the kingdom of God.' Those who heard asked, 'Then who can be saved?' He answered, 26 27 'What is impossible for men is possible for God.'

Peter said, 'We here have left our belongings to become your followers.' 28 Jesus said, 'I tell you this: there is no one who has given up home, or wife, 29 brothers, parents, or children, for the sake of the kingdom of God, who 30 will not be repaid many times over in this age, and in the age to come have eternal life.'

## Challenge to Jerusalem

HE TOOK THE TWELVE ASIDE and said, 'We are now going up to 31 Jerusalem; and all that was written by the prophets will come true for the Son of Man. He will be handed over to the foreign power. He will be 32 mocked, maltreated, and spat upon. They will flog him and kill him. And 33 on the third day he will rise again.' But they understood nothing of all this; 34 they did not grasp what he was talking about; its meaning was concealed from them.

As he approached Jericho a blind man sat at the roadside begging. Hear- 35 36 ing a crowd going past, he asked what was happening. They told him, 37 'Jesus of Nazareth is passing by.' Then he shouted out, 'Jesus, Son of 38

[a] *Some witnesses read* stood up by himself and prayed thus; *others read* stood up and prayed thus privately.

39 David, have pity on me.' The people in front told him to hold his tongue;
40 but he called out all the more, 'Son of David, have pity on me.' Jesus
stopped and ordered the man to be brought to him. When he came up he
41 asked him, 'What do you want me to do for you?' 'Sir, I want my sight
42 back', he answered. Jesus said to him, 'Have back your sight; your faith
43 has cured you.' He recovered his sight instantly; and he followed Jesus,
praising God. And all the people gave praise to God for what they had
seen.

**19** 1 2    Entering Jericho he made his way through the city. There was a man
3 there named Zacchaeus; he was superintendent of taxes and very rich. He
was eager to see what Jesus looked like; but, being a little man, he could
4 not see him for the crowd. So he ran on ahead and climbed a sycamore-
5 tree in order to see him, for he was to pass that way. When Jesus came to the
place, he looked up and said, 'Zacchaeus, be quick and come down; I
6 must come and stay with you today.' He climbed down as fast as he could
7 and welcomed him gladly. At this there was a general murmur of dis-
8 approval. 'He has gone in', they said, 'to be the guest of a sinner.' But
Zacchaeus stood there and said to the Lord, 'Here and now, sir, I give half
my possessions to charity; and if I have cheated anyone, I am ready to
9 repay him four times over.' Jesus said to him, 'Salvation has come to this
10 house today!—for this man too is a son of Abraham, and the Son of Man
has come to seek and save what is lost.'

11    While they were listening to this, he went on to tell them a parable,
because he was now close to Jerusalem and they thought the reign of God
12 might dawn at any moment. He said, 'A man of noble birth went on a long
13 journey abroad, to be appointed king and then return. But first he called
ten of his servants and gave them a pound each, saying, "Trade with this
14 while I am away." His fellow-citizens hated him, and they sent a delega-
15 tion on his heels to say, "We do not want this man as our king." However,
back he came as king, and sent for the servants to whom he had given the
16 money, to see what profit each had made. The first came and said, "Your
17 pound, sir, has made ten more." "Well done," he replied; "you are a good
servant. You have shown yourself trustworthy in a very small matter, and
18 you shall have charge of ten cities." The second came and said, "Your
19 pound, sir, has made five more"; and he also was told, "You too, take
20 charge of five cities." The third came and said, "Here is your pound, sir;
21 I kept it put away in a handkerchief. I was afraid of you, because you are a
hard man: you draw out what you never put in and reap what you did not
22 sow." "You rascal!" he replied; "I will judge you by your own words.
You knew, did you, that I am a hard man, that I draw out what I never put
23 in, and reap what I did not sow? Then why did you not put my money on
deposit, and I could have claimed it with interest when I came back?"
24 Turning to his attendants he said, "Take the pound from him and give it
25 26 to the man with ten." "But, sir," they replied, "he has ten already." "I tell
you," he went on, "the man who has will always be given more; but the
27 man who has not will forfeit even what he has. But as for those enemies of
mine who did not want me for their king, bring them here and slaughter
them in my presence." '

WITH THAT JESUS WENT FORWARD and began the ascent to Jerusalem. 28
As he approached Bethphage and Bethany at the hill called Olivet, he sent 29
two of the disciples with these instructions: 'Go to the village opposite; 30
as you enter it you will find tethered there a colt which no one has yet
ridden. Untie it and bring it here. If anyone asks why you are untying it, 31
say, "Our Master needs it." ' The two went on their errand and found it 32
as he had told them; and while they were untying the colt, its owners asked, 33
'Why are you untying that colt?' They answered, 'Our Master needs it.' 34
So they brought the colt to Jesus.
                                                                          35
    Then they threw their cloaks on the colt, for Jesus to mount, and 36
they carpeted the road with them as he went on his way. And now, as he 37
approached the descent from the Mount of Olives, the whole company
of his disciples in their joy began to sing aloud the praises of God for all
the great things they had seen:

> 'Blessings on him who comes as king in the name of the Lord! 38
> Peace in heaven, glory in highest heaven!'

Some Pharisees who were in the crowd said to him, 'Master, reprimand 39
your disciples.' He answered, 'I tell you, if my disciples keep silence the 40
stones will shout aloud.'

When he came in sight of the city, he wept over it and said, 'If only you 41 42
had known, on this great day, the way that leads to peace! But no; it is
hidden from your sight. For a time will come upon you, when your enemies 43
will set up siege-works against you; they will encircle you and hem you in
at every point; they will bring you to the ground, you and your children 44
within your walls, and not leave you one stone standing on another,
because you did not recognize God's moment when it came.'

Then he went into the temple and began driving out the traders, with 45 46
these words: 'Scripture says, "My house shall be a house of prayer"; but
you have made it a robbers' cave.'

Day by day he taught in the temple. And the chief priests and lawyers 47
were bent on making an end of him, with the support of the leading
citizens, but found they were helpless, because the people all hung upon 48
his words.


ONE DAY, as he was teaching the people in the temple and telling them **20**
the good news, the priests and lawyers, and the elders with them, came
upon him and accosted him. 'Tell us', they said, 'by what authority you are 2
acting like this; who gave you this authority?' He answered them, 'I have 3
a question to ask you too: tell me, was the baptism of John from God or 4
from men?' This set them arguing among themselves: 'If we say, "from 5
God", he will say, "Why did you not believe him?" And if we say, "from 6
men", the people will all stone us, for they are convinced that John was a
prophet.' So they replied that they could not tell. And Jesus said to them, 7 8
'Then neither will I tell you by what authority I act.'

He went on to tell the people this parable: 'A man planted a vineyard, 9
let it out to vine-growers, and went abroad for a long time. When the 10
season came, he sent a servant to the tenants to collect from them his share

of the produce; but the tenants thrashed him and sent him away empty-
11 handed. He tried again and sent a second servant; but he also was thrashed,
12 outrageously treated, and sent away empty-handed. He tried once more
13 with a third; this one too they wounded and flung out. Then the owner of
the vineyard said, "What am I to do? I will send my own dear son;*a*
14 perhaps they will respect him." But when the tenants saw him they talked
it over together. "This is the heir," they said; "let us kill him so that the
15 property may come to us." So they flung him out of the vineyard and killed
16 him. What then will the owner of the vineyard do to them? He will come
and put these tenants to death and let the vineyard to others.'

17     When they heard this, they said, 'God forbid!' But he looked straight
at them and said, 'Then what does this text of Scripture mean: "The stone
18 which the builders rejected has become the main corner-stone"? Any
man who falls on that stone will be dashed to pieces; and if it falls on a man
he will be crushed by it.'

19     The lawyers and chief priests wanted to lay hands on him there and then,
for they saw that this parable was aimed at them; but they were afraid of
20 the people. So they watched their opportunity and sent secret agents in the
guise of honest men, to seize upon some word of his as a pretext for hand-
21 ing him over to the authority and jurisdiction of the Governor. They put
a question to him: 'Master,' they said, 'we know that what you speak and
teach is sound; you pay deference to no one, but teach in all honesty the
22 way of life that God requires. Are we or are we not permitted to pay taxes
23 24 to the Roman Emperor?' He saw through their trick and said, 'Show me a
silver piece. Whose head does it bear, and whose inscription?' 'Caesar's',
25 they replied. 'Very well then,' he said, 'pay Caesar what is due to Caesar,
26 and pay God what is due to God.' Thus their attempt to catch him out in
public failed, and, astonished by his reply, they fell silent.

27     Then some Sadducees came forward. They are the people who deny
28 that there is a resurrection. Their question was this: 'Master, Moses laid
it down for us that if there are brothers, and one dies leaving a wife but no
child, then the next should marry the widow and carry on his brother's
29 family. Now, there were seven brothers: the first took a wife and died child-
30 31 less; then the second married her, then the third. In this way the seven of
32 33 them died leaving no children. Afterwards the woman also died. At the
resurrection whose wife is she to be, since all seven had married her?'
34 35 Jesus said to them, 'The men and women of this world marry; but those
who have been judged worthy of a place in the other world and of the
36 resurrection from the dead, do not marry, for they are not subject to death
any longer. They are like angels; they are sons of God, because they share
37 in the resurrection. That the dead are raised to life again is shown by Moses
himself in the story of the burning bush, when he calls the Lord, "the God
38 of Abraham, Isaac, and Jacob". God is not God of the dead but of the living;
for him all are *b* alive.'

39 40     At this some of the lawyers said, 'Well spoken, Master.' For there was
no further question that they ventured to put to him.

41     He said to them, 'How can they say that the Messiah is son of David?
*a Or* my only son.          *b Or* they are all.

For David himself says in the Book of Psalms: "The Lord said to my 42
Lord, 'Sit at my right hand until I make your enemies your footstool.'" 43
Thus David calls him "Lord"; how then can he be David's son?' 44

In the hearing of all the people Jesus said to his disciples: 'Beware of the 45 46
doctors of the law who love to walk up and down in long robes, and have
a great liking for respectful greetings in the street, the chief seats in our
synagogues, and places of honour at feasts. These are the men who eat up 47
the property of widows, while they say long prayers for appearance' sake;
and they will receive the severest sentence.'

He looked up and saw the rich people dropping their gifts into the chest **21**
of the temple treasury; and he noticed a poor widow putting in two tiny 2
coins. 'I tell you this,' he said: 'this poor widow has given more than any 3
of them; for those others who have given had more than enough, but she, 4
with less than enough, has given all she had to live on.'

SOME PEOPLE WERE TALKING about the temple and the fine stones 5
and votive offerings with which it was adorned. He said, 'These things 6
which you are gazing at—the time will come when not one stone of them
will be left upon another; all will be thrown down.' 'Master,' they asked, 7
'when will it all come about? What will be the sign when it is due to
happen?'

He said, 'Take care that you are not misled. For many will come claim- 8
ing my name and saying, "I am he", and, "The Day is upon us." Do not
follow them. And when you hear of wars and insurrections, do not fall into 9
a panic. These things are bound to happen first; but the end does not follow
immediately.' Then he added, 'Nation will make war upon nation, kingdom 10
upon kingdom; there will be great earthquakes, and famines and plagues 11
in many places; in the sky terrors and great portents.

'But before all this happens they will set upon you and persecute you. 12
You will be brought before synagogues and put in prison; you will be haled
before kings and governors for your allegiance to me. This will be your 13
opportunity to testify; so make up your minds not to prepare your defence 14
beforehand, because I myself will give you power of utterance and a 15
wisdom which no opponent will be able to resist or refute. Even your 16
parents and brothers, your relations and friends, will betray you. Some of
you will be put to death; and all will hate you for your allegiance to me. 17
But not a hair of your head shall be lost. By standing firm you will win true 18 19
life for yourselves.

'But when you see Jerusalem encircled by armies, then you may be sure 20
that her destruction is near. Then those who are in Judaea must take to the 21
hills; those who are in the city itself must leave it, and those who are out
in the country must not enter; because this is the time of retribution, when 22
all that stands written is to be fulfilled. Alas for women who are with child 23
in those days, or have children at the breast! For there will be great distress
in the land and a terrible judgement upon this people. They will fall at the 24
sword's point; they will be carried captive into all countries; and Jerusalem will be trampled down by foreigners until their day has run its
course.

25 'Portents will appear in sun, moon, and stars. On earth nations will stand helpless, not knowing which way to turn from the roar and surge of
26 the sea; men will faint with terror at the thought of all that is coming
27 upon the world; for the celestial powers will be shaken. And then they will see the Son of Man coming on a cloud with great power and glory.
28 When all this begins to happen, stand upright and hold your heads high, because your liberation is near.'

29 30 He told them this parable: 'Look at the fig-tree, or any other tree. As
31 soon as it buds, you can see for yourselves that summer is near. In the same way, when you see all this happening, you may know that the kingdom of God is near.

32 33 'I tell you this: the present generation will live to see it all. Heaven and earth will pass away; my words will never pass away.

34 'Keep a watch on yourselves; do not let your minds be dulled by dissipation and drunkenness and worldly cares so that the great Day closes upon
35 you suddenly like a trap; for that day will come on all men, wherever they
36 are, the whole world over. Be on the alert, praying at all times for strength to pass safely through all these imminent troubles and to stand in the presence of the Son of Man.'

37 His days were given to teaching in the temple; and then he would leave
38 the city and spend the night on the hill called Olivet. And in the early morning the people flocked to listen to him in the temple. [a]

## *The final conflict*

22 NOW THE FESTIVAL of Unleavened Bread, known as Passover, was
2 approaching, and the chief priests and the doctors of the law were trying to devise some means of doing away with him; for they were afraid of the people.
3 Then Satan entered into Judas Iscariot, who was one of the Twelve;
4 and Judas went to the chief priests and officers of the temple police to
5 discuss ways and means of putting Jesus into their power. They were
6 greatly pleased and undertook to pay him a sum of money. He agreed, and began to look out for an opportunity to betray him to them without collecting a crowd.
7 Then came the day of Unleavened Bread, on which the Passover victim
8 had to be slaughtered, and Jesus sent Peter and John with these instruc-
9 tions: 'Go and prepare for our Passover supper.' 'Where would you like
10 us to make the preparations?' they asked. He replied, 'As soon as you set foot in the city a man will meet you carrying a jar of water. Follow him into
11 the house that he enters and give this message to the householder: "The Master says, 'Where is the room in which I may eat the Passover with my
12 disciples?'" He will show you a large room upstairs all set out: make the
13 preparations there.' They went and found everything as he had said. So they prepared for Passover.
14 When the time came he took his place at table, and the apostles with him;

[a] *Some witnesses here insert the passage printed on p. 143.*

and he said to them, 'How I have longed*a* to eat this Passover with you 15
before my death! For I tell you, never again shall I *b* eat it until the time 16
when it finds its fulfilment in the kingdom of God.'

Then he took a cup, and after giving thanks he said, 'Take this and share 17
it among yourselves; for I tell you, from this moment I shall drink from the 18
fruit of the vine no more until the time when the kingdom of God comes.'
And he took bread, gave thanks, and broke it; and he gave it to them, with 19
the words: 'This is my body.'*c*

'But mark this—my betrayer is here, his hand with mine on the table. 21
For the Son of Man is going his appointed way; but alas for that man by 22
whom he is betrayed!' At this they began to ask among themselves which of 23
them it could possibly be who was to do this thing.

Then a jealous dispute broke out: who among them should rank highest? 24
But he said, 'In the world, kings lord it over their subjects; and those in 25
authority are called their country's "Benefactors". Not so with you: on the 26
contrary, the highest among you must bear himself like the youngest, the
chief of you like a servant. For who is greater—the one who sits at table or 27
the servant who waits on him? Surely the one who sits at table. Yet here
am I among you like a servant.

'You are the men who have stood firmly by me in my times of trial; and 28 29
now I vest in you the kingship which my Father vested in me; you shall eat 30
and drink at my table in my kingdom and sit *d* on thrones as judges of the
twelve tribes of Israel.

'Simon, Simon, take heed: Satan has been given leave to sift all of you 31
like wheat; but for you I have prayed that your faith may not fail; and when 32
you have come to yourself, you must lend strength to your brothers.'
'Lord,' he replied, 'I am ready to go with you to prison and death.' Jesus 33 34
said, 'I tell you, Peter, the cock will not crow tonight until you have three
times over denied that you know me.'

He said to them, 'When I sent you out barefoot without purse or pack, 35
were you ever short of anything?' 'No', they answered. 'It is different now,' 36
he said; 'whoever has a purse had better take it with him, and his pack too;
and if he has no sword, let him sell his cloak to buy one. For Scripture says, 37
"And he was counted among the outlaws", and these words, I tell you,
must find fulfilment in me; indeed, all that is written of me is being fulfilled.' 'Look, Lord,' they said, 'we have two swords here.' 'Enough, 38
enough!' he replied.


THEN HE WENT OUT and made his way as usual to the Mount of Olives, 39
accompanied by the disciples. When he reached the place he said to them, 40
'Pray that you may be spared the hour of testing.' He himself withdrew 41
from them about a stone's throw, knelt down, and began to pray: 'Father, 42

---

*a Or said to them, 'I longed . . .'*          *b Some witnesses read* For I tell you, I shall not . . .
*c Some witnesses add, in whole or in part, and with various arrangements, the following :*
'which is given for you; do this as a memorial of me.' (20) In the same way he took the
cup after supper, and said, 'This cup, poured out for you, is the new covenant sealed by
my blood.'          *d Or* trial; and as my Father gave me the right to reign, so I give you
the right to eat and to drink . . . and to sit . . .

if it be thy will, take this cup away from me. Yet not my will but thine be done.'

43 And now there appeared to him an angel from heaven bringing him
44 strength, and in anguish of spirit he prayed the more urgently; and his sweat was like clots of blood falling to the ground. *a*

45 When he rose from prayer and came to the disciples he found them
46 asleep, worn out by grief. 'Why are you sleeping?' he said. 'Rise and pray that you may be spared the test.'

47 WHILE HE WAS STILL SPEAKING a crowd appeared with the man called Judas, one of the Twelve, at their head. He came up to Jesus to
48 kiss him; but Jesus said, 'Judas, would you betray the Son of Man with a kiss?'

49 When his followers saw what was coming, they said, 'Lord, shall we use
50 our swords?' And one of them struck at the High Priest's servant, cutting
51 off his right ear. But Jesus answered, 'Let them have their way.' Then he touched the man's ear and healed him. *b*

52 Turning to the chief priests, the officers of the temple police, and the elders, who had come to seize him, he said, 'Do you take me for a bandit,
53 that you have come out with swords and cudgels to arrest me? Day after day, when I was in the temple with you, you kept your hands off me. But this is your moment—the hour when darkness reigns.'

54 Then they arrested him and led him away. They brought him to the
55 High Priest's house, and Peter followed at a distance. They lit a fire in the
56 middle of the courtyard and sat round it, and Peter sat among them. A serving-maid who saw him sitting in the firelight stared at him and said,
57 'This man was with him too.' But he denied it: 'Woman,' he said, 'I do
58 not know him.' A little later someone else noticed him and said, 'You also
59 are one of them.' But Peter said to him, 'No, I am not.' About an hour passed and another spoke more strongly still: 'Of course this fellow was
60 with him. He must have been; he is a Galilean.' But Peter said, 'Man, I do not know what you are talking about.' At that moment, while he was still
61 speaking, a cock crew; and the Lord turned and looked at Peter. And Peter remembered the Lord's words, 'Tonight before the cock crows you will disown me three times.' *c*

63 64 The men who were guarding Jesus mocked at him. They beat him, they blindfolded him, and they kept asking him, 'Now, prophet, who hit you?
65 Tell us that.' And so they went on heaping insults upon him.

66 WHEN DAY BROKE, the elders of the nation, chief priests, and doctors
67 of the law assembled, and he was brought before their Council. 'Tell us,' they said, 'are you the Messiah?' 'If I tell you,' he replied, 'you will not
68 69 believe me; and if I ask questions, you will not answer. But from now on,
70 the Son of Man will be seated at the right hand of Almighty God.' *d* 'You are the Son of God, then?' they all said, and he replied, 'It is you who say I

---

*a Some witnesses omit* And now . . . ground.        *b Or* 'Let me do as much as this', and touching the man's ear, he healed him.        *c Some witnesses add* (62) He went outside, and wept bitterly, *as in Matthew 26. 75.*        *d Literally* of the Power of God.

am.'*a* They said, 'Need we call further witnesses? We have heard it our- 71
selves from his own lips.'

With that the whole assembly rose, and they brought him before Pilate. **23**
They opened the case against him by saying, 'We found this man subvert- 2
ing our nation, opposing the payment of taxes to Caesar, and claiming to be
Messiah, a king.'*b* Pilate asked him, 'Are you the king of the Jews?' He 3
replied, 'The words are yours.'*c* Pilate then said to the chief priests and 4
the crowd, 'I find no case for this man to answer.' But they insisted: 'His 5
teaching is causing disaffection among the people all through Judaea. It
started from Galilee and has spread as far as this city.'

When Pilate heard this, he asked if the man was a Galilean, and on 6 7
learning that he belonged to Herod's jurisdiction he remitted the case to
him, for Herod was also in Jerusalem at that time. When Herod saw Jesus 8
he was greatly pleased; having heard about him, he had long been wanting
to see him, and had been hoping to see some miracle performed by him.
He questioned him at some length without getting any reply; but the chief 9 10
priests and lawyers appeared and pressed the case against him vigorously.
Then Herod and his troops treated him with contempt and ridicule, and 11
sent him back to Pilate dressed in a gorgeous robe. That same day Herod 12
and Pilate became friends; till then there had been a standing feud between
them.

Pilate now called together the chief priests, councillors, and people, and 13 14
said to them, 'You brought this man before me on a charge of subversion.
But, as you see, I have myself examined him in your presence and found
nothing in him to support your charges. No more did Herod, for he has 15
referred him back to us. Clearly he has done nothing to deserve death. I 16
therefore propose to let him off with a flogging.' But*d* there was a general 18
outcry, 'Away with him! Give us Barabbas.' (This man had been put in 19
prison for a rising that had taken place in the city, and for murder.) Pilate 20
addressed them again, in his desire to release Jesus, but they shouted back, 21
'Crucify him, crucify him!' For the third time he spoke to them: 'Why, 22
what wrong has he done? I have not found him guilty of any capital offence.
I will therefore let him off with a flogging.' But they insisted on their 23
demand, shouting that Jesus should be crucified. Their shouts prevailed
and Pilate decided that they should have their way. He released the man 24 25
they asked for, the man who had been put in prison for insurrection and
murder, and gave Jesus up to their will.

As THEY LED HIM AWAY to execution they seized upon a man called 26
Simon, from Cyrene, on his way in from the country, put the cross on his
back, and made him walk behind Jesus carrying it.

Great numbers of people followed, many women among them, who 27
mourned and lamented over him. Jesus turned to them and said, 'Daugh- 28
ters of Jerusalem, do not weep for me; no, weep for yourselves and your
children. For the days are surely coming when they will say, "Happy are 29

*a Or* You are right, for I am.     *b Or* to be an anointed king.     *c Or* It is as
you say.     *d Some witnesses read* (17) At festival time he was obliged to release one
person for them; (18) and now . . .

the barren, the wombs that never bore a child, the breasts that never fed
30 one." Then they will start saying to the mountains, "Fall on us", and to the
31 hills, "Cover us." For if these things are done when the wood is green,
what will happen when it is dry?'

32    There were two others with him, criminals who were being led away to
33 execution; and when they reached the place called The Skull, they crucified
him there, and the criminals with him, one on his right and the other on his
34 left. Jesus said, 'Father, forgive them; they do not know what they are
doing.' *a*

35    They divided his clothes among them by casting lots. The people stood
looking on, and their rulers jeered at him: 'He saved others: now let him
36 save himself, if this is God's Messiah, his Chosen.' The soldiers joined in
37 the mockery and came forward offering him their sour wine. 'If you are
38 the king of the Jews,' they said, 'save yourself.' There was an inscription
above his head which ran: 'This is the king of the Jews.'

39    One of the criminals who hung there with him taunted him: 'Are not
40 you the Messiah? Save yourself, and us.' But the other rebuked him:
41 'Have you no fear of God? You are under the same sentence as he. For us
it is plain justice; we are paying the price for our misdeeds; but this man has
42 done nothing wrong.' And he said, 'Jesus, remember me when you come
43 to your throne.' *b* He answered, 'I tell you this: today you shall be with me
in Paradise.'

44    By now it was about midday and a darkness fell over the whole land,
45 which lasted until three in the afternoon; the sun's light failed. And the
46 curtain of the temple was torn in two. Then Jesus gave a loud cry and
said, 'Father, into thy hands I commit my spirit'; and with these words he
47 died. The centurion saw it all, and gave praise to God. 'Beyond all doubt',
he said, 'this man was innocent.'

48    The crowd who had assembled for the spectacle, when they saw what
had happened, went home beating their breasts.

49  HIS FRIENDS had all been standing at a distance; the women who had
accompanied him from Galilee stood with them and watched it all.

50    Now there was a man called Joseph, a member of the Council, a good,
51 upright man, who had dissented from their policy and the action they had
taken. He came from the Judaean town of Arimathaea, and he was one
52 who looked forward to the kingdom of God. This man now approached
53 Pilate and asked for the body of Jesus. Taking it down from the cross, he
wrapped it in a linen sheet, and laid it in a tomb cut out of the rock, in which
54 no one had been laid before. It was Friday, and the Sabbath was about to
begin.

55    The women who had accompanied him from Galilee followed; they took
56 note of the tomb and observed how his body was laid. Then they went home
and prepared spices and perfumes; and on the Sabbath they rested in
24 obedience to the commandment. But on the Sunday morning very early
2 they came to the tomb bringing the spices they had prepared. Finding that

*a Some witnesses omit* Jesus said, 'Father . . . doing.'        *b Some witnesses read* come
in royal power.

the stone had been rolled away from the tomb, they went inside; but the 3
body was not to be found. While they stood utterly at a loss, all of a sudden 4
two men in dazzling garments were at their side. They were terrified, and 5
stood with eyes cast down, but the men said, 'Why search among the dead
for one who lives?ᵃ Remember what he told you while he was still in 6
Galilee, about the Son of Man: how he must be given up into the power of 7
sinful men and be crucified, and must rise again on the third day.' Then 8
they recalled his words and, returning from the tomb, they reported all this 9
to the Eleven and all the others.

The women were Mary of Magdala, Joanna, and Mary the motherᵇ of 10
James, and they, with the other women, told the apostles. But the story 11
appeared to them to be nonsense, and they would not believe them. ᶜ

THAT SAME DAY two of them were on their way to a village called Emmaus, 13
which lay about seven miles from Jerusalem, and they were talking 14
together about all these happenings. As they talked and discussed it with 15
one another, Jesus himself came up and walked along with them; but 16
something kept them from seeing who it was. He asked them, 'What is it 17
you are debating as you walk?' They halted, their faces full of gloom, and 18
one, called Cleopas, answered, 'Are you the only person staying in Jerusalem not to knowᵈ what has happened there in the last few days?' 'What 19
do you mean?' he said. 'All this about Jesus of Nazareth,' they replied,
'a prophet powerful in speech and action before God and the whole people;
how our chief priests and rulers handed him over to be sentenced to death, 20
and crucified him. But we had been hoping that he was the man to liberate 21
Israel. What is more, this is the third day since it happened, and now some 22
women of our company have astounded us: they went early to the tomb,
but failed to find his body, and returned with a story that they had seen a 23
vision of angels who told them he was alive. So some of our people went to 24
the tomb and found things just as the women had said; but him they did
not see.'

'How dull you are!' he answered. 'How slow to believe all that the 25
prophets said! Was the Messiah not bound to suffer thus before entering 26
upon his glory?' Then he began with Moses and all the prophets, and 27
explained to them the passages which referred to himself in every part of
the scriptures.

By this time they had reached the village to which they were going, and 28
he made as if to continue his journey, but they pressed him: 'Stay with us, 29
for evening draws on, and the day is almost over.' So he went in to stay with
them. And when he had sat down with them at table, he took bread and 30
said the blessing; he broke the bread, and offered it to them. Then their 31
eyes were opened, and they recognized him; and he vanished from their
sight. They said to one another, 'Did we not feel our hearts on fire as he 32
talked with us on the road and explained the scriptures to us?'

ᵃ *Some witnesses insert* He is not here: he has been raised.     ᵇ *Or* wife, *or* daughter.
ᶜ *Some witnesses add* (12) Peter, however, got up and ran to the tomb, and, peering in, saw
the wrappings and nothing more; and he went home amazed at what had happened.
ᵈ *Or* Have you been staying by yourself in Jerusalem, that you do not know . . .

33 Without a moment's delay they set out and returned to Jerusalem. There
34 they found that the Eleven and the rest of the company had assembled, and
were saying, 'It is true: the Lord has risen; he has appeared to Simon.'
35 Then they gave their account of the events of their journey and told how
he had been recognized by them at the breaking of the bread.

36 As they were talking about all this, there he was, standing among them. *a*
37 38 Startled and terrified, they thought they were seeing a ghost. But he said,
'Why are you so perturbed? Why do questionings arise in your minds?
39 Look at my hands and feet. It is I myself. Touch me and see; no ghost has
41 flesh and bones as you can see that I have. *b* They were still unconvinced,
still wondering, for it seemed too good to be true. So he asked them, 'Have
42 you anything here to eat?' They offered him a piece of fish they had cooked,
43 which he took and ate before their eyes.

44 And he said to them, 'This is what I meant by saying, while I was still
with you, that everything written about me in the Law of Moses and in the
45 prophets and psalms was bound to be fulfilled.' Then he opened their
46 minds to understand the scriptures. 'This', he said, 'is what is written:
that the Messiah is to suffer death and to rise from the dead on the third
47 day, and that in his name repentance bringing the forgiveness of sins is to
48 be proclaimed to all nations. Begin from Jerusalem; it is you who are the
49 witnesses to it all. And mark this: I am sending upon you my Father's
promised gift; so stay here in this city until you are armed with the power
from above.'

50 Then he led them out as far as Bethany, and blessed them with uplifted
51 52 hands; and in the act of blessing he parted from them. *c* And they *d* returned
53 to Jerusalem with great joy, and spent all their time in the temple praising God.

# THE GOSPEL ACCORDING TO

# JOHN

## *The coming of Christ*

1 WHEN ALL THINGS BEGAN, the Word already was. *e*
The Word dwelt with God, and what God was, the Word was.
2 3 The Word, then, was with God at the beginning, and through
him all things came to be; no single thing was created without him. All
4 that came to be was alive with his life, *f* and that life was the light of men.
5 The light shines on in the dark, and the darkness has never mastered it.

*a Some witnesses insert* And he said to them, 'Peace be with you!'    *b Some witnesses*
*insert* (40) After saying this he showed them his hands and feet.    *c Some witnesses*
*add* and was carried up into heaven.    *d Some witnesses insert* worshipped
him and . . .    *e Or* The Word was at the creation.    *f Or* no single created
thing came into being without him. There was life in him . . .

There appeared a man named John, sent from God; he came as a wit- 6 7
ness to testify to the light, that all might become believers through him.
He was not himself the light; he came to bear witness to the light. The real 8 9
light which enlightens every man was even then coming into the world.*a*

He was in the world;*b* but the world, though it owed its being to him, 10
did not recognize him. He entered his own realm, and his own would not 11
receive him. But to all who did receive him, to those who have yielded him 12
their allegiance, he gave the right to become children of God, not born of 13
any human stock, or by the fleshly desire of a human father, but the offspring of God himself. So the Word became flesh; he came to dwell 14
among us, and we saw his glory, such glory as befits the Father's only Son,
full of grace and truth.

Here is John's testimony to him: he cried aloud, 'This is the man I 15
meant when I said, "He comes after me, but takes rank before me"; for
before I was born, he already was.'

Out of his full store we have all received grace upon grace; for while the 16 17
Law was given through Moses, grace and truth came through Jesus Christ.
No one has ever seen God; but God's only Son, he who is nearest to the 18
Father's heart, he has made him known.*c*

THIS IS THE TESTIMONY which John gave when the Jews of Jerusalem 19
sent a deputation of priests and Levites to ask him who he was. He con- 20
fessed without reserve and avowed, 'I am not the Messiah.' 'What then? 21
Are you Elijah?' 'No', he replied. 'Are you the prophet we await?' He
answered 'No.' 'Then who are you?' they asked. 'We must give an answer 22
to those who sent us. What account do you give of yourself?' He answered 23
in the words of the prophet Isaiah: 'I am a voice crying aloud in the wilderness, "Make the Lord's highway straight."'

Some Pharisees who were in the deputation asked him, 'If you are not 24 25
the Messiah, nor Elijah, nor the prophet, why then are you baptizing?'
'I baptize in water,' John replied, 'but among you, though you do not know 26
him, stands the one who is to come after me. I am not good enough to un- 27
fasten his shoes.' This took place at Bethany beyond Jordan, where John 28
was baptizing.

The next day he saw Jesus coming towards him. 'Look,' he said, 'there 29
is the Lamb of God; it is he who takes away the sin of the world. This is he 30
of whom I spoke when I said, "After me a man is coming who takes rank
before me"; for before I was born, he already was. I myself did not know 31
who he was; but the very reason why I came, baptizing in water, was that
he might be revealed to Israel.'

John testified further: 'I saw the Spirit coming down from heaven like 32
a dove and resting upon him. I did not know him, but he who sent me to 33
baptize in water had told me, "When you see the Spirit coming down upon
someone and resting upon him, you will know that this is he who is to

---

*a* Or The light was in being, light absolute, enlightening every man born into the world.
*b* Or The Word, then, was in the world.    *c* Some witnesses read but the only one,
the one nearest to the Father's heart, has made him known; *others read* but the only one,
himself God, the nearest to the Father's heart, has made him known.

34 baptize in Holy Spirit." I saw it myself, and I have borne witness. This is God's Chosen One.'ᵃ

35 36 The next day again John was standing with two of his disciples when Jesus passed by. John looked towards him and said, 'There is the Lamb

37 38 of God.' The two disciples heard him say this, and followed Jesus. When he turned and saw them following him, he asked, 'What are you looking for?' They said, 'Rabbi' (which means a teacher), 'where are you staying?'

39 'Come and see', he replied. So they went and saw where he was staying, and spent the rest of the day with him. It was then about four in the afternoon.

40 One of the two who followed Jesus after hearing what John said was

41 Andrew, Simon Peter's brother. The first thing he did was to findᵇ his brother Simon. He said to him, 'We have found the Messiah' (which is the

42 Hebrew for 'Christ'). He brought Simon to Jesus, who looked at him and said, 'You are Simon son of John. You shall be called Cephas' (that is, Peter, the Rock).

43 44 The next day Jesus decided to leave for Galilee. He met Philip, who, like Andrew and Peter, came from Bethsaida, and said to him, 'Follow me.'

45 Philip went to find Nathanael, and told him, 'We have met the man spoken of by Moses in the Law, and by the prophets: it is Jesus son of Joseph, from

46 Nazareth.' 'Nazareth!' Nathanael exclaimed; 'can anything good come

47 from Nazareth?' Philip said, 'Come and see.' When Jesus saw Nathanael coming, he said, 'Here is an Israelite worthy of the name; there is nothing

48 false in him.' Nathanael asked him, 'How do you come to know me?' Jesus

49 replied, 'I saw you under the fig-tree before Philip spoke to you.' 'Rabbi,'

50 said Nathanael, 'you are the Son of God; you are king of Israel.' Jesus answered, 'Is this the ground of your faith, that I told you I saw you under

51 the fig-tree? You shall see greater things than that.' Then he added, 'In truth, in very truth I tell you all, you shall see heaven wide open, and God's angels ascending and descending upon the Son of Man.'

## Christ the giver of life

2
2 ON THE THIRD DAY there was a wedding at Cana-in-Galilee. The mother of Jesus was there, and Jesus and his disciples were guests

3 also. The wine gave out, so Jesus's mother said to him, 'They have no wine

4 left.' He answered, 'Your concern, mother, is not mine. My hour has not

5 yet come.' His mother said to the servants, 'Do whatever he tells you.'

6 There were six stone water-jars standing near, of the kind used for Jewish

7 rites of purification; each held from twenty to thirty gallons. Jesus said to the servants, 'Fill the jars with water', and they filled them to the brim.

8 'Now draw some off', he ordered, 'and take it to the steward of the feast';

9 and they did so. The steward tasted the water now turned into wine, not knowing its source; though the servants who had drawn the water knew.

10 He hailed the bridegroom and said, 'Everyone serves the best wine first,

ᵃ *Some witnesses read* This is the Son of God.          ᵇ *Some witnesses read* In the morning he found . . .

and waits until the guests have drunk freely before serving the poorer sort;
but you have kept the best wine till now.'

This deed at Cana-in-Galilee is the first of the signs by which Jesus 11
revealed his glory and led his disciples to believe in him.

AFTER THIS he went down to Capernaum in company with his mother, 12
his brothers, and his disciples, but they did not stay there long. As it was 13
near the time of the Jewish Passover, Jesus went up to Jerusalem. There 14
he found in the temple the dealers in cattle, sheep, and pigeons, and the
money-changers seated at their tables. Jesus made a whip of cords and 15
drove them out of the temple, sheep, cattle, and all. He upset the tables of
the money-changers, scattering their coins. Then he turned on the dealers 16
in pigeons: 'Take them out,' he said; 'you must not turn my Father's house
into a market.' His disciples recalled the words of Scripture, 'Zeal for thy 17
house will destroy me.' The Jews challenged Jesus: 'What sign', they 18
asked, 'can you show as authority for your action?' 'Destroy this temple,' 19
Jesus replied, 'and in three days I will raise it again.' They said, 'It has 20
taken forty-six years to build this temple. Are you going to raise it again
in three days?' But the temple he was speaking of was his body. After his 21 22
resurrection his disciples recalled what he had said, and they believed the
Scripture and the words that Jesus had spoken.

WHILE HE WAS in Jerusalem for Passover many gave their allegiance to 23
him when they saw the signs that he performed. But Jesus for his part 24
would not trust himself to them. He knew men so well, all of them, that he 25
needed no evidence from others about a man, for he himself could tell what
was in a man.

THERE WAS ONE of the Pharisees named Nicodemus, a member of the 3
Jewish Council, who came to Jesus by night. 'Rabbi,' he said, 'we know 2
that you are a teacher sent by God; no one could perform these signs of
yours unless God were with him.' Jesus answered, 'In truth, in very truth 3
I tell you, unless a man has been born over again he cannot see the kingdom
of God.' 'But how is it possible', said Nicodemus, 'for a man to be born 4
when he is old? Can he enter his mother's womb a second time and be
born?' Jesus answered, 'In truth I tell you, no one can enter the kingdom 5
of God without being born from water and spirit. Flesh can give birth only 6
to flesh; it is spirit that gives birth to spirit. You ought not to be astonished, 7
then, when I tell you that you must be born over again. The wind *a* blows 8
where it wills; you hear the sound of it, but you do not know where it
comes from, or where it is going. So with everyone who is born from spirit *a*.'

Nicodemus replied, 'How is this possible?' 'What!' said Jesus. 'Is this 9 10
famous teacher of Israel ignorant of such things? In very truth I tell you, 11
we speak of what we know, and testify to what we have seen, and yet you
all reject our testimony. If you disbelieve me when I talk to you about 12
things on earth, how are you to believe if I should talk about the things of
heaven?

*a* wind *and* spirit *are translations of the same Greek word, which has both meanings.*

13 'No one ever went up into heaven except the one who came down from
14 heaven, the Son of Man whose home is in heaven. *a* This Son of Man must
15 be lifted up as the serpent was lifted up by Moses in the wilderness, so that
everyone who has faith in him may in him possess eternal life.

16 'God loved the world so much that he gave his only Son, that everyone
17 who has faith in him may not die but have eternal life. It was not to judge
the world that God sent his Son into the world, but that through him the
world might be saved.

18 'The man who puts his faith in him does not come under judgement;
but the unbeliever has already been judged in that he has not given his
19 allegiance to God's only Son. Here lies the test: the light has come into the
world, but men preferred darkness to light because their deeds were evil.
20 Bad men all hate the light and avoid it, for fear their practices should be
21 shown up. The honest man comes to the light so that it may be clearly seen
that God is in all he does.'

22 AFTER THIS, Jesus went into Judaea with his disciples, stayed there with
23 them, and baptized. John too was baptizing at Aenon, near to Salim,
because water was plentiful in that region; and people were constantly
24 coming for baptism. This was before John's imprisonment.
25 Some of John's disciples had fallen into a dispute with Jews about puri-
26 fication; so they came to him and said, 'Rabbi, there was a man with you
on the other side of the Jordan, to whom you bore your witness. Here he is,
27 baptizing, and crowds are flocking to him.' John's answer was: 'A man
28 can have only what God gives him. You yourselves can testify that I said,
29 "I am not the Messiah; I have been sent as his forerunner." It is the bridegroom to whom the bride belongs. The bridegroom's friend, who stands
by and listens to him, is overjoyed at hearing the bridegroom's voice. This
30 joy, this perfect joy, is now mine. As he grows greater, I must grow less.'
31 He who comes from above is above all others; he who is from the earth
belongs to the earth and uses earthly speech. He who comes from heaven *b*
32 bears witness to what he has seen and heard, yet no one accepts his witness.
33 34 To accept his witness is to attest that God speaks the truth; for he whom
God sent utters the words of God, so measureless is God's gift of the Spirit.
35 36 The Father loves the Son and has entrusted him with all authority. He who
puts his faith in the Son has hold of eternal life, but he who disobeys the
Son shall not see that life; God's wrath rests upon him.

4 A REPORT NOW REACHED the Pharisees: 'Jesus is winning and baptizing
2 more disciples than John'; although, in fact, it was only the disciples who
3 were baptizing and not Jesus himself. When Jesus learned this, he left
4 Judaea and set out once more for Galilee. He had to pass through Samaria,
5 and on his way came to a Samaritan town called Sychar, near the plot of
6 ground which Jacob gave to his son Joseph and the spring called Jacob's
well. It was about noon, and Jesus, tired after his journey, sat down by
the well.

*a Some witnesses omit* whose home is in heaven.    *b Some witnesses insert* is above
all and . . .

The disciples had gone away to the town to buy food. Meanwhile a 8 7
Samaritan woman came to draw water. Jesus said to her, 'Give me a drink.'
The Samaritan woman said, 'What! You, a Jew, ask a drink of me, a 9
Samaritan woman?' (Jews and Samaritans, it should be noted, do not use
vessels in common.<sup>a</sup>) Jesus answered her, 'If only you knew what God 10
gives, and who it is that is asking you for a drink, you would have asked
him and he would have given you living water.' 'Sir,' the woman said, 11
'you have no bucket and this well is deep. How can you give me "living
water"? Are you a greater man than Jacob our ancestor, who gave us the 12
well, and drank from it himself, he and his sons, and his cattle too?' Jesus 13
said, 'Everyone who drinks this water will be thirsty again, but whoever 14
drinks the water that I shall give him will never suffer thirst any more.
The water that I shall give him will be an inner spring always welling up
for eternal life.' 'Sir,' said the woman, 'give me that water, and then I shall 15
not be thirsty, nor have to come all this way to draw.'

Jesus replied, 'Go home, call your husband and come back.' She 16 17
answered, 'I have no husband.' 'You are right', said Jesus, 'in saying that
you have no husband, for, although you have had five husbands, the man 18
with whom you are now living is not your husband; you told me the truth
there.' 'Sir,' she replied, 'I can see that you are a prophet. Our fathers 19 20
worshipped on this mountain, but you Jews say that the temple where God
should be worshipped is in Jerusalem.' 'Believe me,' said Jesus, 'the time 21
is coming when you will worship the Father neither on this mountain, nor
in Jerusalem. You Samaritans worship without knowing what you worship, 22
while we worship what we know. It is from the Jews that salvation comes.
But the time approaches, indeed it is already here, when those who are 23
real worshippers will worship the Father in spirit and in truth. Such are the
worshippers whom the Father wants. God is spirit, and those who worship 24
him must worship in spirit and in truth.' The woman answered, 'I know 25
that Messiah' (that is Christ) 'is coming. When he comes he will tell us
everything.' Jesus said, 'I am he, I who am speaking to you now.' 26

At that moment his disciples returned, and were astonished to find him 27
talking with a woman; but none of them said, 'What do you want?' or,
'Why are you talking with her?' The woman put down her water-jar and 28
went away to the town, where she said to the people, 'Come and see a man 29
who has told me everything I ever did. Could this be the Messiah?' They 30
came out of the town and made their way towards him.

Meanwhile the disciples were urging him, 'Rabbi, have something to 31
eat.' But he said, 'I have food to eat of which you know nothing.' At this 32 33
the disciples said to one another, 'Can someone have brought him food?'
But Jesus said, 'It is meat and drink for me to do the will of him who sent 34
me until I have finished his work.

'Do you not say, "Four months more and then comes harvest"? But 35
look, I tell you, look round on the fields; they are already white, ripe for
harvest. The reaper is drawing his pay and gathering a crop for eternal life, 36
so that sower and reaper may rejoice together. That is how the saying comes 37

<sup>a</sup> *Or* Jews, it should be noted, are not on familiar terms with Samaritans; *some witnesses
omit these words.*

38 true: "One sows, and another reaps." I sent you to reap a crop for which you have not toiled. Others toiled and you have come in for the harvest of their toil.'

39 Many Samaritans of that town came to believe in him because of the
40 woman's testimony: 'He told me everything I ever did.' So when these Samaritans had come to him they pressed him to stay with them; and he
41 stayed there two days. Many more became believers because of what they
42 heard from his own lips. They told the woman, 'It is no longer because of what you said that we believe, for we have heard him ourselves; and we know that this is in truth the Saviour of the world.'

43 44 WHEN THE TWO DAYS were over he set out for Galilee; for Jesus himself
45 declared that a prophet is without honour in his own country. On his arrival in Galilee the Galileans gave him a welcome, because they had seen all that he did at the festival in Jerusalem; they had been at the festival themselves.

46 Once again he visited Cana-in-Galilee, where he had turned the water into wine. An officer in the royal service was there, whose son was lying ill
47 at Capernaum. When he heard that Jesus had come from Judaea into Galilee, he came to him and begged him to go down and cure his son, who
48 was at the point of death. Jesus said to him, 'Will none of you ever believe
49 without seeing signs and portents?' The officer pleaded with him, 'Sir,
50 come down before my boy dies.' Then Jesus said, 'Return home; your son
51 will live.' The man believed what Jesus said and started for home. When he was on his way down his servants met him with the news, 'Your boy is
52 going to live.' So he asked them what time it was when he began to recover.
53 They said, 'Yesterday at one in the afternoon the fever left him.' The father noted that this was the exact time when Jesus had said to him, 'Your son will live', and he and all his household became believers.

54 This was now the second sign which Jesus performed after coming down from Judaea into Galilee.

5 LATER ON Jesus went up to Jerusalem for one of the Jewish festivals. *a*
2 Now at the Sheep-Pool in Jerusalem there is a place with five colonnades.
3 Its name in the language of the Jews is Bethesda. In these colonnades there
5 lay a crowd of sick people, blind, lame, and paralysed. *b* Among them was
6 a man who had been crippled for thirty-eight years. When Jesus saw him lying there and was aware that he had been ill a long time, he asked him,
7 'Do you want to recover?' 'Sir,' he replied, 'I have no one to put me in the pool when the water is disturbed, but while I am moving, someone else
8 is in the pool before me.' Jesus answered, 'Rise to your feet, take up your
9 bed and walk.' The man recovered instantly, took up his stretcher, and began to walk.

10 That day was a Sabbath. So the Jews said to the man who had been

*a Some witnesses read* for the Jewish festival. *b Some witnesses add* waiting for the disturbance of the water; *some further insert* (4) for from time to time an angel came down into the pool and stirred up the water. The first to plunge in after this disturbance recovered from whatever disease had afflicted him.

cured, 'It is the Sabbath. You are not allowed to carry your bed on the Sabbath.' He answered, 'The man who cured me said, "Take up your bed 11 and walk."' They asked him, 'Who is the man who told you to take up 12 your bed and walk?' But the cripple who had been cured did not know; for 13 the place was crowded and Jesus had slipped away. A little later Jesus found 14 him in the temple and said to him, 'Now that you are well again, leave your sinful ways, or you may suffer something worse.' The man went away and 15 told the Jews that it was Jesus who had cured him.

It was works of this kind done on the Sabbath that stirred the Jews to 16 persecute Jesus. He defended himself by saying, 'My Father has never 17 yet ceased his work, and I am working too.' This made the Jews still more 18 determined to kill him, because he was not only breaking the Sabbath, but, by calling God his own Father, he claimed equality with God.

To this charge Jesus replied, 'In truth, in very truth I tell you, the Son 19 can do nothing by himself; he does only what he sees the Father doing: what the Father does, the Son does. For the Father loves the Son and shows 20 him all his works, and will show greater yet, to fill you with wonder. As 21 the Father raises the dead and gives them life, so the Son gives life to men, as he determines. And again, the Father does not judge anyone, but has 22 given full jurisdiction to the Son; it is his will that all should pay the same 23 honour to the Son as to the Father. To deny honour to the Son is to deny it to the Father who sent him.

'In very truth, anyone who gives heed to what I say and puts his trust in 24 him who sent me has hold of eternal life, and does not come up for judgement, but has already passed from death to life. In truth, in very truth I 25 tell you, a time is coming, indeed it is already here, when the dead shall hear the voice of the Son of God, and all who hear shall come to life. For 26 as the Father has life-giving power in himself, so has the Son, by the Father's gift.

'As Son of Man, he has also been given the right to pass judgement. Do 27 28 not wonder at this, because the time is coming when all who are in the grave shall hear his voice and come out: those who have done right will rise 29 to life; those who have done wrong will rise to hear their doom. I cannot 30 act by myself; I judge as I am bidden, and my sentence is just, because my aim is not my own will, but the will of him who sent me.

'If I testify on my own behalf, that testimony does not hold good. There 31 32 is another who bears witness for me, and I know that his testimony holds. Your messengers have been to John; you have his testimony to the truth. 33 Not that I rely on human testimony, but I remind you of it for your own 34 salvation. John was a lamp, burning brightly, and for a time you were 35 ready to exult in his light. But I rely on a testimony higher than John's. 36 There is enough to testify that the Father has sent me, in the works my Father gave me to do and to finish—the very works I have in hand. This 37 testimony to me was given by the Father who sent me, although you never heard his voice, or saw his form. But his word has found no home in you, 38 for you do not believe the one whom he sent. You study the scriptures 39 diligently, supposing that in having them you have eternal life; yet, although their testimony points to me, you refuse to come to me for that life. 40

41 42  'I do not look to men for honour. But with you it is different, as I know
43  well, for you have no love for God in you. I have come accredited by my
Father, and you have no welcome for me; if another comes self-accredited
44  you will welcome him. How can you have faith so long as you receive
honour from one another, and care nothing for the honour that comes from
45  him who alone is God? Do not imagine that I shall be your accuser at the
Father's tribunal. Your accuser is Moses, the very Moses on whom you
46  have set your hope. If you believed Moses you would believe what I tell
47  you, for it was about me that he wrote. But if you do not believe what he
wrote, how are you to believe what I say?'

6  SOME TIME LATER Jesus withdrew to the farther shore of the Sea of
2  Galilee (or Tiberias), and a large crowd of people followed who had seen
3  the signs he performed in healing the sick. Then Jesus went up the hill-
4  side and sat down with his disciples. It was near the time of Passover, the
5  great Jewish festival. Raising his eyes and seeing a large crowd coming
towards him, Jesus said to Philip, 'Where are we to buy bread to feed these
6  people?' This he said to test him; Jesus himself knew what he meant to do.
7  Philip replied, 'Twenty pounds *a* would not buy enough bread for every
8  one of them to have a little.' One of his disciples, Andrew, the brother of
9  Simon Peter, said to him, 'There is a boy here who has five barley loaves
10  and two fishes; but what is that among so many?' Jesus said, 'Make the
people sit down.' There was plenty of grass there, so the men sat down,
11  about five thousand of them. Then Jesus took the loaves, gave thanks, and
distributed them to the people as they sat there. He did the same with the
12  fishes, and they had as much as they wanted. When everyone had had
enough, he said to his disciples, 'Collect the pieces left over, so that nothing
13  may be lost.' This they did, and filled twelve baskets with the pieces left
uneaten of the five barley loaves.
14  When the people saw the sign Jesus had performed, the word went
round, 'Surely this must be the prophet that was to come into the world.'
15  Jesus, aware that they meant to come and seize him to proclaim him king,
withdrew again to the hills by himself.
16 17  At nightfall his disciples went down to the sea, got into their boat, and
pushed off to cross the water to Capernaum. Darkness had already fallen,
18  and Jesus had not yet joined them. By now a strong wind was blowing and
19  the sea grew rough. When they had rowed about three or four miles they saw
20  Jesus walking on the sea and approaching the boat. They were terrified, but
21  he called out, 'It is I; do not be afraid.' Then they were ready to take him
aboard, and immediately the boat reached the land they were making for.

22  NEXT MORNING the crowd was standing on the opposite shore. They
had seen only one boat there, and Jesus, they knew, had not embarked
23  with his disciples, who had gone away without him. Boats from Tiberias,
however, came ashore *b* near the place where the people had eaten the
24  bread over which the Lord gave thanks. *c* When the people saw that neither

*a Literally* 200 denarii.      *b Some witnesses read* Other boats from Tiberias came
ashore . . .      *c. Some witnesses omit* over which . . . thanks.

Jesus nor his disciples were any longer there, they themselves went aboard
these boats and made for Capernaum in search of Jesus. They found him 25
on the other side. 'Rabbi,' they said, 'when did you come here?' Jesus 26
replied, 'In very truth I know that you have not come looking for me
because you saw signs, but because you ate the bread and your hunger was
satisfied. You must work, not for this perishable food, but for the food that 27
lasts, the food of eternal life.

'This food the Son of Man will give you, for he it is upon whom God
the Father has set the seal of his authority.' 'Then what must we do', they 28
asked him, 'if we are to work as God would have us work?' Jesus replied, 29
'This is the work that God requires: believe in the one whom he has sent.'

They said, 'What sign can you give us to see, so that we may believe you? 30
What is the work you do? Our ancestors had manna to eat in the desert; as 31
Scripture says, "He gave them bread from heaven to eat."' Jesus answered, 32
'I tell you this: the truth is, not that Moses gave you the bread from heaven,
but that my Father gives you the real bread from heaven. The bread that 33
God gives comes down *a* from heaven and brings life to the world.' They 34
said to him, 'Sir, give us this bread now and always.' Jesus said to them, 35
'I am the bread of life. Whoever comes to me shall never be hungry, and
whoever believes in me shall never be thirsty. But you, as I said, do not 36
believe although you have seen. *b* All that the Father gives me will come to 37
me, and the man who comes to me I will never turn away. I have come down 38
from heaven, not to do my own will, but the will of him who sent me. It is 39
his will that I should not lose even one of all that he has given me, but raise
them all up on the last day. For it is my Father's will that everyone who 40
looks upon the Son and puts his faith in him shall possess eternal life; and
I will raise him up on the last day.'

At this the Jews began to murmur disapprovingly because he said, 'I am 41
the bread which came down from heaven.' They said, 'Surely this is Jesus 42
son of Joseph; we know his father and mother. How can he now say, "I
have come down from heaven"?' Jesus answered, 'Stop murmuring among 43
yourselves. No man can come to me unless he is drawn by the Father who 44
sent me; and I will raise him up on the last day. It is written in the prophets: 45
"And they shall all be taught by God." Everyone who has listened to the
Father and learned from him comes to me.

'I do not mean that anyone has seen the Father. He who has come from 46
God has seen the Father, and he alone. In truth, in very truth I tell you, the 47
believer possesses eternal life. I am the bread of life. Your forefathers ate 48 49
the manna in the desert and they are dead. I am speaking of the bread that 50
comes down from heaven, which a man may eat, and never die. I am that 51
living bread which has come down from heaven; if anyone eats this bread
he shall live for ever. Moreover, the bread which I will give is my own
flesh; I give it for the life of the world.'

This led to a fierce dispute among the Jews. 'How can this man give us 52
his flesh to eat?' they said. Jesus replied, 'In truth, in very truth I tell you, 53
unless you eat the flesh of the Son of Man and drink his blood you can have
no life in you. Whoever eats my flesh and drinks my blood possesses eternal 54

*a Or is he who comes down . . .*      *b Some witnesses add me.*

55 life, and I will raise him up on the last day. My flesh is real food; my blood
56 is real drink. Whoever eats my flesh and drinks my blood dwells continually
57 in me and I dwell in him. As the living Father sent me, and I live because
58 of the Father, so he who eats me shall live because of me. This is the
bread which came down from heaven; and it is not like the bread which
our fathers ate: they are dead, but whoever eats this bread shall live for
ever.'

59 THIS WAS SPOKEN in synagogue when Jesus was teaching in Capernaum.
60 Many of his disciples on hearing it exclaimed, 'This is more than we can
61 stomach! Why listen to such talk?' Jesus was aware that his disciples were
62 murmuring about it and asked them, 'Does this shock you? What if you
63 see the Son of Man ascending to the place where he was before? The spirit
alone gives life; the flesh is of no avail; the words which I have spoken to
64 you are both spirit and life. And yet there are some of you who have no
faith.' For Jesus knew all along who were without faith and who was to
65 betray him. So he said, 'This is why I told you that no one can come to me
unless it has been granted to him by the Father.'
66     From that time on, many of his disciples withdrew and no longer went
67 about with him. So Jesus asked the Twelve, 'Do you also want to leave me?'
68 Simon Peter answered him, 'Lord, to whom shall we go? Your words are
69 words of eternal life. We have faith, and we know that you are the Holy
70 One of God.' Jesus answered, 'Have I not chosen you, all twelve? Yet one
71 of you is a devil.' He meant Judas, son of Simon Iscariot. He it was who
would betray him, and he was one of the Twelve.

## The great controversy

7 AFTERWARDS JESUS went about in Galilee. He wished to avoid Judaea
2 because the Jews were looking for a chance to kill him. As the Jewish
3 Feast of Tabernacles was close at hand, his brothers said to him, 'You
should leave this district and go into Judaea, so that your disciples there
4 may see the great things you are doing. Surely no one can hope to be in the
public eye if he works in seclusion. If you really are doing such things as
5 these, show yourself to the world.' For even his brothers had no faith in
6 him. Jesus said to them, 'The right time for me has not yet come, but any
7 time is right for you. The world cannot hate you; but it hates me for
8 exposing the wickedness of its ways. Go to the festival yourselves. I am
not *a* going up to this festival because the right time for me has not yet
9 come.' With this answer he stayed behind in Galilee.
10     Later, when his brothers had gone to the festival, he went up himself,
11 not publicly, but almost in secret. The Jews were looking for him at the
12 festival and asking, 'Where is he?', and there was much whispering about
him in the crowds. 'He is a good man', said some. 'No,' said others, 'he is
13 leading the people astray.' However, no one talked about him openly, for
fear of the Jews.

---

*a Some witnesses read* not yet.

WHEN THE FESTIVAL was already half over, Jesus went up to the temple   14
and began to teach. The Jews were astonished: 'How is it', they said, 'that   15
this untrained man has such learning?' Jesus replied, 'The teaching that I   16
give is not my own; it is the teaching of him who sent me. Whoever has the   17
will to do the will of God shall know whether my teaching comes from him
or is merely my own. Anyone whose teaching is merely his own, aims at   18
honour for himself. But if a man aims at the honour of him who sent him
he is sincere, and there is nothing false in him.

'Did not Moses give you the Law? Yet you all break it. Why are you try-   19
ing to kill me?' The crowd answered, 'You are possessed! Who wants to   20
kill you?' Jesus replied, 'Once only have I done work on the Sabbath, and   21
you are all taken aback. But consider: Moses gave you the law of cir-   22
cumcision (not that it originated with Moses but with the patriarchs) and
you circumcise on the Sabbath. Well then, if a child is circumcised on the   23
Sabbath to avoid breaking the Law of Moses, why are you indignant with
me for giving health on the Sabbath to the whole of a man's body? Do not   24
judge superficially, but be just in your judgements.'

At this some of the people of Jerusalem began to say, 'Is not this the man   25
they want to put to death? And here he is, speaking openly, and they have   26
not a word to say to him. Can it be that our rulers have actually decided
that this is the Messiah? And yet we know where this man comes from,   27
but when the Messiah appears no one is to know where he comes from.'
Thereupon Jesus cried aloud as he taught in the temple, 'No doubt you   28
know me; no doubt you know where I come from.*a* Yet I have not come of
my own accord. I was sent by the One who truly is, and him you do not
know. I know him because I come from him and he it is who sent me.' At   29 30
this they tried to seize him, but no one laid a hand on him because his
appointed hour had not yet come. Yet among the people many believed in   31
him. 'When the Messiah comes,' they said, 'is it likely that he will perform
more signs than this man?'

The Pharisees overheard these mutterings of the people about him, so   32
the chief priests and the Pharisees sent temple police to arrest him. Then   33
Jesus said, 'For a little longer I shall be with you; then I am going away to
him who sent me. You will look for me, but you will not find me. Where   34
I am, you cannot come.' So the Jews said to one another, 'Where does he   35
intend to go, that we should not be able to find him? Will he go to the
Dispersion among the Greeks, and teach the Greeks? What did he mean   36
by saying, "You will look for me, but you will not find me. Where I am,
you cannot come"?'*b*

ON THE LAST and greatest day of the festival Jesus stood and cried aloud,   37
'If anyone is thirsty let him come to me; whoever believes in me, let him   38
drink.' As Scripture says, 'Streams of living water shall flow out from
within him.'*c* He was speaking of the Spirit which believers in him would   39

*a* Or Do you know me? And do you know where I come from?          *b* *Some witnesses*
*here insert the passage printed on p. 143.*          *c* Or 'If any man is thirsty let him come
to me and drink. He who believes in me, as Scripture says, streams of living water shall
flow out from within him.'

receive later; for the Spirit had not yet been given, because Jesus had not yet been glorified.

40 On hearing this some of the people said, 'This must certainly be the
41 expected prophet.' Others said, 'This is the Messiah.' Others again, 'Surely
42 the Messiah is not to come from Galilee? Does not Scripture say that the Messiah is to be of the family of David, from David's village of Bethlehem?'
43 44 Thus he caused a split among the people. Some were for seizing him, but no one laid hands on him.

45 The temple police came back to the chief priests and Pharisees, who
46 asked, 'Why have you not brought him?' 'No man', they answered, 'ever
47 spoke as this man speaks.' The Pharisees retorted, 'Have you too been
48 misled? Is there a single one of our rulers who has believed in him, or of
49 the Pharisees? As for this rabble, which cares nothing for the Law, a curse
50 is on them.' Then one of their number, Nicodemus (the man who had
51 once visited Jesus), intervened. 'Does our law', he asked them, 'permit us to pass judgement on a man unless we have first given him a hearing and
52 learned the facts?' 'Are you a Galilean too?' they retorted. 'Study the scriptures and you will find that prophets do not come from Galilee.' *a*

8 12 ONCE AGAIN JESUS addressed the people: 'I am the light of the world. No follower of mine shall wander in the dark; he shall have the light of life.'
13 The Pharisees said to him, 'You are witness in your own cause; your
14 testimony is not valid.' Jesus replied, 'My testimony is valid, even though I do bear witness about myself; because I know where I come from, and where I am going. You do not know either where I come from or where I
15 am going. You judge by worldly standards. I pass judgement on no man,
16 but if I do judge, my judgement is valid because it is not I alone who
17 judge, but I and he who sent me. In your own law it is written that the
18 testimony of two witnesses is valid. Here am I, a witness in my own cause,
19 and my other witness is the Father who sent me.' They asked, 'Where is your father?' Jesus replied, 'You know neither me nor my Father; if you knew me you would know my Father as well.'

20 These words were spoken by Jesus in the treasury as he taught in the temple. Yet no one arrested him, because his hour had not yet come.

21 Again he said to them, 'I am going away. You will look for me, but you
22 will die in your sin; where I am going you cannot come.' The Jews then said, 'Perhaps he will kill himself: is that what he means when he says,
23 "Where I am going you cannot come"?' So Jesus continued, 'You belong to this world below, I to the world above. Your home is in this world, mine
24 is not. That is why I told you that you would die in your sins. If you do not
25 believe that I am what I am, you will die in your sins.' They asked him,
26 'Who are you?' Jesus answered, 'Why should I speak to you at all? *b* I have much to say about you—and in judgement. But he who sent me speaks the truth, and what I heard from him I report to the world.'

27 They did not understand that he was speaking to them about the Father.
28 So Jesus said to them, 'When you have lifted up the Son of Man you will

---

*a Some witnesses here insert the passage 7. 53–8. 11, which is printed on p. 143.*
*b Or What I have told you all along.*

know that I am what I am. I do nothing on my own authority, but in all
that I say, I have been taught by my Father. He who sent me is present   29
with me, and has not left me alone; for I always do what is acceptable to
him.' As he said this, many put their faith in him.                      30

Turning to the Jews who had believed him, Jesus said, 'If you dwell     31
within the revelation I have brought, you are indeed my disciples; you   32
shall know the truth, and the truth will set you free.' They replied, 'We  33
are Abraham's descendants; we have never been in slavery to any man.
What do you mean by saying, "You will become free men"?' 'In very truth  34
I tell you', said Jesus, 'that everyone who commits sin is a slave. The slave  35
has no permanent standing in the household, but the son belongs to it for
ever. If then the Son sets you free, you will indeed be free.            36

'I know that you are descended from Abraham, but you are bent on         37
killing me because my teaching makes no headway with you. I am revealing  38
in words what I saw in my Father's presence; and you are revealing in
action what you learned from your father.' They retorted, 'Abraham is our  39
father.' 'If you were Abraham's children', Jesus replied, 'you would do as
Abraham did.$^a$ As it is, you are bent on killing me, a man who told you the  40
truth, as I heard it from God. That is not how Abraham acted. You are    41
doing your own father's work.'

They said, 'We are not base-born; God is our father, and God alone.'
Jesus said, 'If God were your father, you would love me, for God is the  42
source of my being, and from him I come. I have not come of my own
accord; he sent me. Why do you not understand my language? It is        43
because my revelation is beyond your grasp.

'Your father is the devil and you choose to carry out your father's desires.  44
He was a murderer from the beginning, and is not rooted in the truth;
there is no truth in him. When he tells a lie he is speaking his own language,
for he is a liar and the father of lies. But I speak the truth and therefore you  45
do not believe me. Which of you can prove me in the wrong?$^b$ If what I say  46
is true, why do you not believe me? He who has God for his father listens  47
to the words of God. You are not God's children; that is why you do not
listen.'

The Jews answered, 'Are we not right in saying that you are a Samaritan,  48
and that you are possessed?' 'I am not possessed,' said Jesus; 'I am honour-  49
ing my Father, but you dishonour me. I do not care about my own glory;   50
there is one who does care, and he is judge. In very truth I tell you, if any-  51
one obeys my teaching he shall never know what it is to die.'

The Jews said, 'Now we are certain that you are possessed. Abraham is   52
dead; the prophets are dead; and yet you say, "If anyone obeys my teaching he shall not know what it is to die." Are you greater than our father  53
Abraham, who is dead? The prophets are dead too. What do you claim
to be?'

Jesus replied, 'If I glorify myself, that glory of mine is worthless. It is  54
the Father who glorifies me, he of whom you say, "He is our God",
though you do not know him. But I know him; if I said that I did not   55

---

$^a$ *Some witnesses read* 'If you are Abraham's children', Jesus replied, 'do as Abraham did.'
$^b$ *Or* Which of you convicts me of sin?

know him I should be a liar like you. But in truth I know him and obey his word.

56 'Your father Abraham was overjoyed to see my day; he saw it and was
57 glad.' The Jews protested, 'You are not yet fifty years old. How can you
58 have seen Abraham?'*a* Jesus said, 'In very truth I tell you, before Abraham was born, I am.'

59 They picked up stones to throw at him, but Jesus was not to be seen; and he left the temple.*b*

**9** 1 2 AS HE WENT on his way Jesus saw a man blind from his birth. His disciples put the question, 'Rabbi, who sinned, this man or his parents? Why was
3 he born blind?' 'It is not that this man or his parents sinned,' Jesus answered; 'he was born blind so that God's power might be displayed in
4 curing him. While daylight lasts we*c* must carry on the work of him who
5 sent me; night comes, when no one can work. While I am in the world I am the light of the world.'

6 With these words he spat on the ground and made a paste with the
7 spittle; he spread it on the man's eyes, and said to him, 'Go and wash in the pool of Siloam.' (The name means 'sent'.) The man went away and washed, and when he returned he could see.

8 His neighbours and those who were accustomed to see him begging said,
9 'Is not this the man who used to sit and beg?' Others said, 'Yes, this is the man.' Others again said, 'No, but it is someone like him.' The man himself
10 11 said, 'I am the man.' They asked him, 'How were your eyes opened?' He replied, 'The man called Jesus made a paste and smeared my eyes with it, and told me to go to Siloam and wash. I went and washed, and gained my
12 sight.' 'Where is he?' they asked. He answered, 'I do not know.'

13 14 THE MAN who had been blind was brought before the Pharisees. As it was
15 a Sabbath day when Jesus made the paste and opened his eyes, the Pharisees now asked him by what means he had gained his sight. The man told them,
16 'He spread a paste on my eyes; then I washed, and now I can see.' Some of the Pharisees said, 'This fellow is no man of God; he does not keep the Sabbath.' Others said, 'How could such signs come from a sinful man?'
17 So they took different sides. Then they continued to question him: 'What have you to say about him? It was your eyes he opened.' He answered, 'He is a prophet.'

18 The Jews would not believe that the man had been blind and had gained
19 his sight, until they had summoned his parents and questioned them: 'Is this man your son? Do you say that he was born blind? How is it that he
20 can see now?' The parents replied, 'We know that he is our son, and that
21 he was born blind. But how it is that he can now see, or who opened his eyes, we do not know. Ask him; he is of age; he will speak for himself.'
22 His parents gave this answer because they were afraid of the Jews; for the Jewish authorities had already agreed that anyone who acknowledged Jesus

---

*a Some witnesses read* How can Abraham have seen you?      *b Or the division may be made after the words* was not to be seen; *the paragraph following would then begin* Then Jesus left the temple, and as he went . . .      *c Some witnesses read* I.

as Messiah should be banned from the synagogue. That is why the parents 23
said, 'He is of age; ask him.'

So for the second time they summoned the man who had been blind, 24
and said, 'Speak the truth before God. We know that this fellow is a sinner.'
'Whether or not he is a sinner, I do not know', the man replied. 'All I know 25
is this: once I was blind, now I can see.' 'What did he do to you?' they asked. 26
'How did he open your eyes?' 'I have told you already,' he retorted, 'but 27
you took no notice. Why do you want to hear it again? Do you also want to
become his disciples?' Then they became abusive. 'You are that man's 28
disciple,' they said, 'but we are disciples of Moses. We know that God 29
spoke to Moses, but as for this fellow, we do not know where he comes
from.'

The man replied, 'What an extraordinary thing! Here is a man who has 30
opened my eyes, yet you do not know where he comes from! It is common 31
knowledge that God does not listen to sinners; he listens to anyone who is
devout and obeys his will. To open the eyes of a man born blind—it is un- 32
heard of since time began. If that man had not come from God he could 33
have done nothing.' 'Who are you to give us lessons,' they retorted, 'born 34
and bred in sin as you are?' Then they expelled him from the synagogue.

Jesus heard that they had expelled him. When he found him he asked, 35
'Have you faith in the Son of Man[a]?' The man answered, 'Tell me who he 36
is, sir, that I should put my faith in him.' 'You have seen him,' said Jesus; 37
'indeed, it is he who is speaking to you.' 'Lord, I believe', he said, and 38
bowed before him.

Jesus said, 'It is for judgement that I have come into this world—to give 39
sight to the sightless and to make blind those who see.' Some Pharisees in 40
his company asked, 'Do you mean that we are blind?' 'If you were blind,' 41
said Jesus, 'you would not be guilty, but because you say "We see", your
guilt remains.

'IN TRUTH I tell you, in very truth, the man who does not enter the sheep- 10
fold by the door, but climbs in some other way, is nothing but a thief or a
robber. The man who enters by the door is the shepherd in charge of the 2
sheep. The door-keeper admits him, and the sheep hear his voice; he calls 3
his own sheep by name, and leads them out. When he has brought them all 4
out, he goes ahead and the sheep follow, because they know his voice. They 5
will not follow a stranger; they will run away from him, because they do not
recognize the voice of strangers.'

This was a parable that Jesus told them, but they did not understand 6
what he meant by it.

So Jesus spoke again: 'In truth, in very truth I tell you, I am the door of 7
the sheepfold. The sheep paid no heed to any who came before me, for 8
these were all thieves and robbers. I am the door; anyone who comes into 9
the fold through me shall be safe. He shall go in and out and shall find
pasturage.

'The thief comes only to steal, to kill, to destroy; I have come that men 10
may have life, and may have it in all its fullness. I am the good shepherd; 11
    [a] *Some witnesses read* Son of God.

12 the good shepherd lays down his life for the sheep. The hireling, when he sees the wolf coming, abandons the sheep and runs away, because he is no shepherd and the sheep are not his. Then the wolf harries the flock and
13 scatters the sheep. The man runs away because he is a hireling and cares nothing for the sheep.

14 'I am the good shepherd; I know my own sheep and my sheep know me—
15 as the Father knows me and I know the Father—and I lay down my life for
16 the sheep. But there are other sheep of mine, not belonging to this fold, whom I must bring in; and they too will listen to my voice. There will then
17 be one flock, one shepherd. The Father loves me because I lay down my
18 life, to receive it back again. No one has robbed me of it; I am laying it down of my own free will. I have the right to lay it down, and I have the right to receive it back again; this charge I have received from my Father.'

19 20 These words once again caused a split among the Jews. Many of them
21 said, 'He is possessed, he is raving. Why listen to him?' Others said, 'No one possessed by an evil spirit could speak like this. Could an evil spirit open blind men's eyes?'

22 IT WAS WINTER, and the festival of the Dedication was being held in
23 Jerusalem. Jesus was walking in the temple precincts, in Solomon's
24 Portico. The Jews gathered round him and asked: 'How long must you
25 keep us in suspense? If you are the Messiah say so plainly.' 'I have told you,' said Jesus, 'but you do not believe. My deeds done in my Father's
26 name are my credentials, but because you are not sheep of my flock you
27 do not believe. My own sheep listen to my voice; I know them and they
28 follow me. I give them eternal life and they shall never perish; no one shall
29 snatch them from my care. My Father who has given them to me is greater
30 than all, and no one can snatch them *a* out of the Father's care. My Father and I are one.'

31 32 Once again the Jews picked up stones to stone him. At this Jesus said to them, 'I have set before you many good deeds, done by my Father's
33 power; for which of these would you stone me?' The Jews replied, 'We are not going to stone you for any good deed, but for your blasphemy. You,
34 a mere man, claim to be a god.'*b* Jesus answered, 'Is it not written in your
35 own Law, "I said: You are gods"? Those are called gods to whom the word
36 of God was delivered—and Scripture cannot be set aside. Then why do you charge me with blasphemy because I, consecrated and sent into the world by the Father, said, "I am God's son"?

37 38 'If I am not acting as my Father would, do not believe me. But if I am, accept the evidence of my deeds, even if you do not believe me, so that you may recognize and know that the Father is in me, and I in the Father.'

39 This provoked them to one more attempt to seize him. But he escaped from their clutches.

*a Some witnesses read* My Father is greater than all, and that which he has given me no one can snatch . . .; *others read* That which my Father has given me is greater than all, and no one can snatch it . . .      *b Or* claim to be God.

## Victory over death

JESUS WITHDREW AGAIN across the Jordan, to the place where John 40
had been baptizing earlier. There he stayed, while crowds came to him. 41
They said, 'John gave us no miraculous sign, but all that he said about this
man was true.' Many came to believe in him there. 42

There was a man named Lazarus who had fallen ill. His home was at 11
Bethany, the village of Mary and her sister Martha. (This Mary, whose 2
brother Lazarus had fallen ill, was the woman who anointed the Lord with
ointment and wiped his feet with her hair.) The sisters sent a message to 3
him: 'Sir, you should know that your friend lies ill.' When Jesus heard 4
this he said, 'This illness will not end in death; it has come for the glory of
God, to bring glory to the Son of God.' And therefore, though he loved 5
Martha and her sister and Lazarus, after hearing of his illness Jesus waited 6
for two days in the place where he was.

After this, he said to his disciples, 'Let us go back to Judaea.' 'Rabbi,' 7 8
his disciples said, 'it is not long since the Jews there were wanting to stone
you. Are you going there again?' Jesus replied, 'Are there not twelve hours 9
of daylight? Anyone can walk in day-time without stumbling, because he
sees the light of this world. But if he walks after nightfall he stumbles, 10
because the light fails him.'

After saying this he added, 'Our friend Lazarus has fallen asleep, but I 11
shall go and wake him.' The disciples said, 'Master, if he has fallen asleep 12
he will recover.' Jesus, however, had been speaking of his death, but they 13
thought that he meant natural sleep. Then Jesus spoke out plainly: 14
'Lazarus is dead. I am glad not to have been there; it will be for your good 15
and for the good of your faith. But let us go to him.' Thomas, called 'the 16
Twin', said to his fellow-disciples, 'Let us also go, that we may die with
him.'

ON HIS ARRIVAL Jesus found that Lazarus had already been four days 17
in the tomb. Bethany was just under two miles from Jerusalem, and many 18 19
of the people had come from the city to Martha and Mary to condole with
them on their brother's death. As soon as she heard that Jesus was on his 20
way, Martha went to meet him, while Mary stayed at home.

Martha said to Jesus, 'If you had been here, sir, my brother would not 21
have died. Even now I know that whatever you ask of God, God will grant 22
you.' Jesus said, 'Your brother will rise again.' 'I know that he will rise 23 24
again', said Martha, 'at the resurrection on the last day.' Jesus said, 'I am 25
the resurrection and I am life.*a* If a man has faith in me, even though he die,
he shall come to life; and no one who is alive and has faith shall ever die. 26
Do you believe this?' 'Lord, I do,' she answered; 'I now believe that you 27
are the Messiah, the Son of God who was to come into the world.'

With these words she went to call her sister Mary, and taking her aside, 28
she said, 'The Master is here; he is asking for you.' When Mary heard this 29
she rose up quickly and went to him. Jesus had not yet reached the village, 30
but was still at the place where Martha had met him. The Jews who were in 31

*a Some witnesses omit* and I am life.

the house condoling with Mary, when they saw her start up and leave the house, went after her, for they supposed that she was going to the tomb to weep there.

32 So Mary came to the place where Jesus was. As soon as she caught sight of him she fell at his feet and said, 'O sir, if you had only been here my
33 brother would not have died.' When Jesus saw her weeping and the Jews
34 her companions weeping, he sighed heavily and was deeply moved. 'Where
35 have you laid him?' he asked. They replied, 'Come and see, sir.' Jesus wept.
36 37 The Jews said, 'How dearly he must have loved him!' But some of them said, 'Could not this man, who opened the blind man's eyes, have done something to keep Lazarus from dying?'
38 Jesus again sighed deeply; then he went over to the tomb. It was a cave,
39 with a stone placed against it. Jesus said, 'Take away the stone.' Martha, the dead man's sister, said to him, 'Sir, by now there will be a stench; he
40 has been there four days.' Jesus said, 'Did I not tell you that if you have
41 faith you will see the glory of God?' So they removed the stone.

Then Jesus looked upwards and said, 'Father, I thank thee; thou hast
42 heard me. I knew already that thou always hearest me, but I spoke for the sake of the people standing round, that they might believe that thou didst send me.'
43 44 Then he raised his voice in a great cry: 'Lazarus, come forth.' The dead man came out, his hands and feet swathed in linen bands, his face wrapped in a cloth. Jesus said, 'Loose him; let him go.'

45 NOW MANY of the Jews who had come to visit Mary and had seen what
46 Jesus did, put their faith in him. But some of them went off to the Pharisees and reported what he had done.
47 Thereupon the chief priests and the Pharisees convened a meeting of the Council. 'What action are we taking?' they said. 'This man is performing
48 many signs. If we leave him alone like this the whole populace will believe in him. Then the Romans will come and sweep away our temple and our
49 nation.' But one of them, Caiaphas, who was High Priest that year, said,
50 'You know nothing whatever; you do not use your judgement; it is more to your interest that one man should die for the people, than that the whole
51 nation should be destroyed.' He did not say this of his own accord, but as the High Priest in office that year, he was prophesying that Jesus would
52 die for the nation—would die not for the nation alone but to gather
53 together the scattered children of God. So from that day on they plotted his death.
54 Accordingly Jesus no longer went about publicly in Judaea, but left that region for the country bordering on the desert, and came to a town called Ephraim, where he stayed with his disciples.

55 THE JEWISH PASSOVER was now at hand, and many people went up from the country to Jerusalem to purify themselves before the festival.
56 They looked out for Jesus, and as they stood in the temple they asked one another, 'What do you think? Perhaps he is not coming to the festival.'
57 Now the chief priests and the Pharisees had given orders that anyone

who knew where he was should give information, so that they might arrest him.

SIX DAYS BEFORE the Passover festival Jesus came to Bethany, where 12 Lazarus lived whom he had raised from the dead. There a supper was 2 given in his honour, at which Martha served, and Lazarus sat among the guests with Jesus. Then Mary brought a pound of very costly perfume, 3 pure oil of nard, and anointed the feet of Jesus and wiped them with her hair, till the house was filled with the fragrance. At this, Judas Iscariot, a 4 disciple of his—the one who was to betray him—said, 'Why was this per- 5 fume not sold for thirty pounds *a* and given to the poor?' He said this, not 6 out of any care for the poor, but because he was a thief; he used to pilfer the money put into the common purse, which was in his charge. 'Leave her 7 alone', said Jesus. 'Let her keep it till the day when she prepares for my burial; for you have the poor among you always, but you will not always 8 have me.' *b*

A great number of the Jews heard that he was there, and came not only 9 to see Jesus but also Lazarus whom he had raised from the dead. The chief 10 priests then resolved to do away with Lazarus as well, since on his account 11 many Jews were going over to Jesus and putting their faith in him.

THE NEXT DAY the great body of pilgrims who had come to the festival, 12 hearing that Jesus was on the way to Jerusalem, took palm branches and 13 went out to meet him, shouting, 'Hosanna! Blessings on him who comes in the name of the Lord! God bless the king of Israel!' Jesus found a 14 donkey and mounted it, in accordance with the text of Scripture: 'Fear no 15 more, daughter of Zion; see, your king is coming, mounted on an ass's colt.'

At the time his disciples did not understand this, but after Jesus had 16 been glorified they remembered that this had been written about him, and that this had happened to him. The people who were present when he 17 called Lazarus out of the tomb and raised him from the dead told what they had seen and heard. That is why the crowd went to meet him; they had 18 heard of this sign that he had performed. The Pharisees said to one 19 another, 'You see you are doing no good at all; why, all the world has gone after him!'

AMONG THOSE who went up to worship at the festival were some Greeks. 20 They came to Philip, who was from Bethsaida in Galilee, and said to him, 21 'Sir, we should like to see Jesus.' So Philip went and told Andrew, and the 22 two of them went to tell Jesus. Then Jesus replied: 'The hour has come for 23 the Son of Man to be glorified. In truth, in very truth I tell you, a grain of 24 wheat remains a solitary grain unless it falls into the ground and dies; but if it dies, it bears a rich harvest. The man who loves himself is lost, but he 25 who hates himself in this world will be kept safe for eternal life. If anyone 26 serves me, he must follow me; where I am, my servant will be. Whoever serves me will be honoured by my Father.

'Now my soul is in turmoil, and what am I to say? Father, save me from 27

---

*a* Literally for 300 denarii.　　　*b* *Some witnesses omit* for you have . . . have me.

28 this hour.*a* No, it was for this that I came to this hour. Father, glorify thy
name.' A voice sounded from heaven: 'I have glorified it, and I will glorify

29 it again.' The crowd standing by said it was thunder, while others said,

30 'An angel has spoken to him.' Jesus replied, 'This voice spoke for your sake,

31 not mine. Now is the hour of judgement for this world; now shall the Prince

32 of this world be driven out. And I shall draw all men to myself, when I am

33 lifted up from the earth.' This he said to indicate the kind of death he was
to die.

34    The people answered, 'Our Law teaches us that the Messiah continues
for ever. What do you mean by saying that the Son of Man must be lifted

35 up? What Son of Man is this?' Jesus answered them: 'The light is among
you still, but not for long. Go on your way while you have the light, so that
darkness may not overtake you. He who journeys in the dark does not know

36 where he is going. While you have the light, trust to the light, so that you
may become men of light.' After these words Jesus went away from them
into hiding.

37 IN SPITE OF the many signs which Jesus had performed in their presence

38 they would not believe in him, for the prophet Isaiah's utterance had to be
fulfilled: 'Lord, who has believed what we reported, and to whom has the

39 Lord's power been revealed?' So it was that they could not believe, for

40 there is another saying of Isaiah's: 'He has blinded their eyes and dulled
their minds, lest they should see with their eyes, and perceive with their

41 minds, and turn to me to heal them.' Isaiah said this because *b* he saw his
glory and spoke about him.

42    For all that, even among those in authority a number believed in him,
but would not acknowledge him on account of the Pharisees, for fear of

43 being banned from the synagogue. For they valued their reputation with
men rather than the honour which comes from God.

44 SO JESUS CRIED ALOUD: 'When a man believes in me, he believes in him

45 46 who sent me rather than in me; seeing me, he sees him who sent me. I have
come into the world as light, so that no one who has faith in me should

47 remain in darkness. But if anyone hears my words and pays no regard to
them, I am not his judge; I have not come to judge the world, but to save the

48 world. There is a judge for the man who rejects me and does not accept my

49 words; the word that I spoke will be his judge on the last day. I do not speak
on my own authority, but the Father who sent me has himself commanded

50 me what to say and how to speak. I know that his commands are eternal life.
What the Father has said to me, therefore—that is what I speak.'

---

*a Or* ... turmoil. Shall I say, "Father, save me from this hour"?        *b Some witnesses
read* when.

## Farewell discourses

IT WAS BEFORE the Passover festival. Jesus knew that his hour had come 13 and he must leave this world and go to the Father. He had always loved his own who were in the world, and now he was to show the full extent of his love.

The devil had already put it into the mind of Judas son of Simon Iscariot 2 to betray him. During supper, Jesus, well aware that the Father had 3 entrusted everything to him, and that he had come from God and was going back to God, rose from table, laid aside his garments, and taking a 4 towel, tied it round him. Then he poured water into a basin, and began to 5 wash his disciples' feet and to wipe them with the towel.

When it was Simon Peter's turn, Peter said to him, 'You, Lord, washing 6 my feet?' Jesus replied, 'You do not understand now what I am doing, but 7 one day you will.' Peter said, 'I will never let you wash my feet.' 'If I do 8 not wash you,' Jesus replied, 'you are not in fellowship with me.' 'Then, 9 Lord,' said Simon Peter, 'not my feet only; wash my hands and head as well!'

Jesus said, 'A man who has bathed needs no further washing;*a* he is 10 altogether clean; and you are clean, though not every one of you.' He 11 added the words 'not every one of you' because he knew who was going to betray him.

After washing their feet and taking his garments again, he sat down. 12 'Do you understand what I have done for you?' he asked. 'You call me 13 "Master" and "Lord", and rightly so, for that is what I am. Then if I, 14 your Lord and Master, have washed your feet, you also ought to wash one another's feet. I have set you an example: you are to do as I have done for 15 you. In very truth I tell you, a servant is not greater than his master, nor 16 a messenger than the one who sent him. If you know this, happy are you 17 if you act upon it.

'I am not speaking about all of you; I know whom I have chosen. But 18 there is a text of Scripture to be fulfilled: "He who eats bread with me has turned against me."*b* I tell you this now, before the event, so that when it 19 happens you may believe that I am what I am. In very truth I tell you, he 20 who receives any messenger of mine receives me; receiving me, he receives the One who sent me.'

After saying this, Jesus exclaimed in deep agitation of spirit, 'In truth, 21 in very truth I tell you, one of you is going to betray me.' The disciples 22 looked at one another in bewilderment: whom could he be speaking of? One of them, the disciple he loved, was reclining close beside Jesus. So 23 24 Simon Peter nodded to him and said, 'Ask who it is he means.' That 25 disciple, as he reclined, leaned back close to Jesus and asked, 'Lord, who is it?' Jesus replied, 'It is the man to whom I give this piece of bread when 26 I have dipped it in the dish.' Then, after dipping it in the dish, he took it out and gave it to Judas son of Simon Iscariot. As soon as Judas had received 27 it Satan entered him. Jesus said to him, 'Do quickly what you have to do.'

*a Some witnesses read* needs only to wash his feet. *b Literally* has lifted his heel against me.

28 29 No one at the table understood what he meant by this. Some supposed that, as Judas was in charge of the common purse, Jesus was telling him to buy what was needed for the festival, or to make some gift to the poor.
30 As soon as Judas had received the bread he went out. It was night.

31 WHEN HE HAD GONE OUT Jesus said, 'Now the Son of Man is glorified,
32 and in him God is glorified. If God is glorified in him,[a] God will also
33 glorify him in himself; and he will glorify him now. My children, for a little longer I am with you; then you will look for me, and, as I told the
34 Jews, I tell you now, where I am going you cannot come. I give you a new commandment: love one another; as I have loved you, so you are to love
35 one another. If there is this love among you, then all will know that you are my disciples.'

36 Simon Peter said to him, 'Lord, where are you going?' Jesus replied, 'Where I am going you cannot follow me now, but one day you will.'
37 Peter said, 'Lord, why cannot I follow you now? I will lay down my life
38 for you.' Jesus answered, 'Will you indeed lay down your life for me? I tell you in very truth, before the cock crows you will have denied me three times.

14 'Set your troubled hearts at rest. Trust in God always; trust also in me.
2 There are many dwelling-places in my Father's house; if it were not so I should have told you; for I am going there on purpose to prepare a place
3 for you.[b] And if I go and prepare a place for you, I shall come again and
4 receive you to myself, so that where I am you may be also; and my way
5 there is known to you.'[c] Thomas said, 'Lord, we do not know where you
6 are going, so how can we know the way?' Jesus replied, 'I am the way; I am the truth and I am life; no one comes to the Father except by me.

7 'If you knew me you would know my Father too.[d] From now on you do
8 know him; you have seen him.' Philip said to him, 'Lord, show us the
9 Father and we ask no more.' Jesus answered, 'Have I been all this time with you, Philip, and you still do not know me? Anyone who has seen me
10 has seen the Father. Then how can you say, "Show us the Father"? Do you not believe that I am in the Father, and the Father in me? I am not myself the source of the words I speak to you: it is the Father who dwells
11 in me doing his own work. Believe me when I say that I am in the Father and the Father in me; or else accept the evidence of the deeds themselves.
12 In truth, in very truth I tell you, he who has faith in me will do what I am doing; and he will do greater things still because I am going to the Father.
13 Indeed anything you ask in my name I will do, so that the Father may be
14 glorified in the Son. If you ask[e] anything in my name I will do it.

15 16 'If you love me you will obey my commands; and I will ask the Father, and he will give you another to be your Advocate, who will be with you for
17 ever—the Spirit of truth. The world cannot receive him, because the world neither sees nor knows him; but you know him, because he dwells with you

---

[a] *Some witnesses omit* If God . . . in him.    [b] *Or if it were not so, should I have told* you that I am going to prepare a place for you?    [c] *Some witnesses read* also. You know where I am going and you know the way.    [d] *Some witnesses read* If you know me you will know my Father too.    [e] *Some witnesses insert* me.

and is*a* in you. I will not leave you bereft; I am coming back to you. In a   18 19
little while the world will see me no longer, but you will see me; because
I live, you too will live; then you will know that I am in my Father, and you   20
in me and I in you. The man who has received my commands and obeys   21
them—he it is who loves me; and he who loves me will be loved by my
Father; and I will love him and disclose myself to him.'

Judas asked him—the other Judas, not Iscariot—'Lord, what can have   22
happened, that you mean to disclose yourself to us alone and not to the
world?' Jesus replied, 'Anyone who loves me will heed what I say; then   23
my Father will love him, and we will come to him and make our dwelling
with him; but he who does not love me does not heed what I say. And the   24
word you hear is not mine: it is the word of the Father who sent me. I have   25
told you all this while I am still here with you; but your Advocate, the Holy   26
Spirit whom the Father will send in my name, will teach you everything,
and will call to mind all that I have told you.

'Peace is my parting gift to you, my own peace, such as the world cannot   27
give. Set your troubled hearts at rest, and banish your fears. You heard me   28
say, "I am going away, and coming back to you." If you loved me you would
have been glad to hear that I was going to the Father; for the Father is
greater than I. I have told you now, beforehand, so that when it happens you   29
may have faith.

'I shall not talk much longer with you, for the Prince of this world   30
approaches. He has no rights over me; but the world must be shown that   31
I love the Father, and do exactly as he commands; so up, let us go forward!*b*

'I AM THE REAL VINE, and my Father is the gardener. Every barren branch   **15**  1 2
of mine he cuts away; and every fruiting branch he cleans, to make it more
fruitful still. You have already been cleansed by the word that I spoke to   3
you. Dwell in me, as I in you. No branch can bear fruit by itself, but only   4
if it remains united with the vine; no more can you bear fruit, unless you
remain united with me.

'I am the vine, and you the branches. He who dwells in me, as I dwell in   5
him, bears much fruit; for apart from me you can do nothing. He who does   6
not dwell in me is thrown away like a withered branch. The withered
branches are heaped together, thrown on the fire, and burnt.

'If you dwell in me, and my words dwell in you, ask what you will, and   7
you shall have it. This is my Father's glory, that you may bear fruit in   8
plenty and so be my disciples.*c* As the Father has loved me, so I have loved   9
you. Dwell in my love. If you heed my commands, you will dwell in my   10
love, as I have heeded my Father's commands and dwell in his love.

'I have spoken thus to you, so that my joy may be in you, and your joy   11
complete.*d* This is my commandment: love one another, as I have loved   12
you. There is no greater love than this, that a man should lay down his life   13

---

*a Some witnesses read* shall be.     *b Or* for the Prince of this world is coming, though he
has nothing in common with me. But he is coming so that the world may recognize that
I love the Father, and do exactly as he commands. Up, and let us go forward to meet
him!     *c Some witnesses read* that you may bear fruit in plenty. Thus you will be my
disciples.        *d Or* so that I may have joy in you and your joy may be complete.

14 15 for his friends. You are my friends, if you do what I command you. I call you servants no longer; a servant does not know what his master is about. I have called you friends, because I have disclosed to you everything that I
16 heard from my Father. You did not choose me: I chose you. I appointed you to go on and bear fruit, fruit that shall last; so that the Father may give
17 you all that you ask in my name. This is my commandment to you: love one another.

18 19 'If the world hates you, it hated me first, as you know well.*a* If you belonged to the world, the world would love its own; but because you do not belong to the world, because I have chosen you out of the world, for that
20 reason the world hates you. Remember what I said: "A servant is not greater than his master." As they persecuted me, they will persecute you;
21 they will follow your teaching as little as they have followed mine. It is on my account that they will treat you thus, because they do not know the One who sent me.

22 'If I had not come and spoken to them, they would not be guilty of sin;
23 but now they have no excuse for their sin: he who hates me, hates my
24 Father. If I had not worked among them and accomplished what no other man has done, they would not be guilty of sin; but now they have both
25 seen and hated both me and my Father.*b* However, this text in their Law had to come true:*c* "They hated me without reason."

26 'But when your Advocate has come, whom I will send you from the Father—the Spirit of truth that issues from the Father—he will bear
27 witness to me. And you also are my witnesses, because you have been with me from the first.

16 'I have told you all this to guard you against the breakdown of your
2 faith. They will ban you from the synagogue; indeed, the time is coming when anyone who kills you will suppose that he is performing a religious
3 duty. They will do these things because they do not know either the Father
4 or me. I have told you all this so that when the time comes for it to happen you may remember my warning. I did not tell you this at first, because
5 then I was with you; but now I am going away to him who sent me. None
6 of you asks me "Where are you going?" Yet you are plunged into grief
7 because of what I have told you. Nevertheless I tell you the truth: it is for your good that I am leaving you. If I do not go, your Advocate will not
8 come, whereas if I go, I will send him to you. When he comes, he will con-
9 fute the world, and show where wrong and right and judgement lie. He will
10 convict them of wrong, by their refusal to believe in me; he will convince them that right is on my side, by showing that I go to the Father when I
11 pass from your sight; and he will convince them of divine judgement, by showing that the Prince of this world stands condemned.

12 'There is still much that I could say to you, but the burden would be too
13 great for you now. However, when he comes who is the Spirit of truth, he will guide you into all the truth; for he will not speak on his own authority, but will tell only what he hears; and he will make known to you the things

*a Or* bear in mind that it hated me first.      *b Or* but now they have indeed seen my
work and yet have hated both me and my Father.      *c Or* let this text in their Law
come true.

that are coming. He will glorify me, for everything that he makes known to 14
you he will draw from what is mine. All that the Father has is mine, and that 15
is why I said, "Everything that he makes known to you he will draw from
what is mine."

'A LITTLE WHILE, and you see me no more; again a little while, and you 16
will see me.' Some of his disciples said to one another, 'What does he mean 17
by this: "A little while, and you will not see me, and again a little while,
and you will see me", and by this: "Because I am going to my Father"?'
So they asked, 'What is this "little while" that he speaks of? We do not 18
know what he means.'

Jesus knew that they were wanting to question him, and said, 'Are you 19
discussing what I said: "A little while, and you will not see me, and again
a little while, and you will see me"? In very truth I tell you, you will weep 20
and mourn, but the world will be glad. But though you will be plunged in
grief, your grief will be turned to joy. A woman in labour is in pain because 21
her time has come; but when the child is born she forgets the anguish in
her joy that a man has been born into the world. So it is with you: for the 22
moment you are sad at heart; but I shall see you again, and then you will be
joyful, and no one shall rob you of your joy. When that day comes you will 23
ask nothing of me. In very truth I tell you, if you ask the Father for anything in my name, he will give it you.ᵃ So far you have asked nothing in my 24
name. Ask and you will receive, that your joy may be complete.

'Till now I have been using figures of speech; a time is coming when I 25
shall no longer use figures, but tell you of the Father in plain words. When 26
that day comes you will make your request in my name, and I do not say
that I shall pray to the Father for you, for the Father loves you himself, 27
because you have loved me and believed that I came from God. I came from 28
the Father and have come into the world. Now I am leaving the world
again and going to the Father.' His disciples said, 'Why, this is plain speak- 29
ing; this is no figure of speech. We are certain now that you know every- 30
thing, and do not need to be questioned; because of this we believe that you
have come from God.'

Jesus answered, 'Do you now believe? Look,ᵇ the hour is coming, has 31 32
indeed already come, when you are all to be scattered, each to his home,
leaving me alone. Yet I am not alone, because the Father is with me. I have 33
told you all this so that in me you may find peace. In the world you will
have trouble. But courage! The victory is mine; I have conquered the
world.'

AFTER THESE WORDS Jesus looked up to heaven and said:                    **17**
'Father, the hour has come. Glorify thy Son, that the Son may glorify
thee. For thou hast made him sovereign over all mankind, to give eternal 2
life to all whom thou hast given him. This is eternal life: to know thee who 3
alone art truly God, and Jesus Christ whom thou hast sent.

'I have glorified thee on earth by completing the work which thou gavest 4

ᵃ *Some witnesses read* if you ask the Father for anything, he will give it you in my name.
ᵇ *Or* At the moment you believe; but look . . .

5 me to do; and now, Father, glorify me in thy own presence with the glory which I had with thee before the world began.

6 'I have made thy name known to the men whom thou didst give me out of the world. They were thine, thou gavest them to me, and they have

7 obeyed thy command. Now they know that all thy gifts have come to me

8 from thee; for I have taught them all that I learned from thee, and they have received it: they know with certainty that I came from thee; they have had faith to believe that thou didst send me.

9 'I pray for them; I am not praying for the world but for those whom

10 thou hast given me, because they belong to thee. All that is mine is thine, and what is thine is mine; and through them has my glory shone.

11 'I am to stay no longer in the world, but they are still in the world, and I am on my way to thee. Holy Father, protect by the power of thy name those

12 whom thou hast given me,[a] that they may be one, as we are one. When I was with them, I protected by the power of thy name those whom thou hast given me,[b] and kept them safe. Not one of them is lost except the man who must be lost, for Scripture has to be fulfilled.

13 'And now I am coming to thee; but while I am still in the world I speak these words, so that they may have my joy within them in full measure.

14 I have delivered thy word to them, and the world hates them because they

15 are strangers in the world, as I am. I pray thee, not to take them out of the

16 world, but to keep them from the evil one. They are strangers in the world,

17 18 as I am. Consecrate them by the truth;[c] thy word is truth. As thou hast

19 sent me into the world, I have sent them into the world, and for their sake I now consecrate myself, that they too may be consecrated by the truth.[c]

20 'But it is not for these alone that I pray, but for those also who through

21 their words put their faith in me; may they all be one: as thou, Father, art in me, and I in thee, so also may they be in us, that the world may believe

22 that thou didst send me. The glory which thou gavest me I have given to

23 them, that they may be one, as we are one; I in them and thou in me, may they be perfectly one. Then the world will learn that thou didst send me, that thou didst love them as thou didst me.

24 'Father, I desire that these men, who are thy gift to me, may be with me where I am, so that they may look upon my glory, which thou hast given me

25 because thou didst love me before the world began. O righteous Father, although the world does not know thee, I know thee, and these men know

26 that thou didst send me. I made thy name known to them, and will make it known, so that the love thou hadst for me may be in them, and I may be in them.'

[a] *Or* keep in loyalty to thee those whom thou hast given me; *some witnesses read* protect them by the power of thy name which thou hast given me.      [b] *Or* kept in loyalty to thee those whom thou hast given me; *some witnesses read* protected them by the power of thy name which thou hast given me.      [c] *Or* in truth.

## The final conflict

AFTER THESE WORDS, Jesus went out with his disciples, and crossed **18**
the Kedron ravine. There was a garden there, and he and his disciples
went into it. The place was known to Judas, his betrayer, because Jesus **2**
had often met there with his disciples. So Judas took a detachment of **3**
soldiers, and police provided by the chief priests and the Pharisees,
equipped with lanterns, torches, and weapons, and made his way to the
garden. Jesus, knowing all that was coming upon him, went out to them **4**
and asked, 'Who is it you want?' 'Jesus of Nazareth', they answered. Jesus **5**
said, 'I am he.' And there stood Judas the traitor with them. When he said, **6**
'I am he', they drew back and fell to the ground. Again Jesus asked, 'Who **7**
is it you want?' 'Jesus of Nazareth', they answered. Then Jesus said, 'I have **8**
told you that I am he. If I am the man you want, let these others go.' (This **9**
was to make good his words, 'I have not lost one of those whom thou gavest
me.') Thereupon Simon Peter drew the sword he was wearing and struck **10**
at the High Priest's servant, cutting off his right ear. (The servant's name
was Malchus.) Jesus said to Peter, 'Sheathe your sword. This is the cup **11**
the Father has given me; shall I not drink it?'

THE TROOPS with their commander, and the Jewish police, now arrested **12**
Jesus and secured him. They took him first to Annas.[a] Annas was father- **13**
in-law of Caiaphas, the High Priest for that year[a]—the same Caiaphas **14**
who had advised the Jews that it would be to their interest if one man
died for the whole people. Jesus was followed by Simon Peter and an- **15**
other disciple. This disciple, who was acquainted with the High Priest,
went with Jesus into the High Priest's courtyard, but Peter halted at **16**
the door outside. So the other disciple, the High Priest's acquaintance,
went out again and spoke to the woman at the door, and brought Peter
in. The maid on duty at the door said to Peter, 'Are you another of this **17**
man's disciples?' 'I am not', he said. The servants and the police had **18**
made a charcoal fire, because it was cold, and were standing round it
warming themselves. And Peter too was standing with them, sharing the
warmth.

The High Priest questioned Jesus about his disciples and about what **19**
he taught. Jesus replied, 'I have spoken openly to all the world; I have **20**
always taught in synagogue and in the temple, where all Jews congregate;
I have said nothing in secret. Why question me? Ask my hearers what I **21**
told them; they know what I said.' When he said this, one of the police **22**
who was standing next to him struck him on the face, exclaiming, 'Is that
the way to answer the High Priest?' Jesus replied, 'If I spoke amiss, state **23**
it in evidence; if I spoke well, why strike me?'

So Annas sent him bound to Caiaphas the High Priest. [b] **24**

Meanwhile Simon Peter stood warming himself. The others asked, 'Are **25**
you another of his disciples?' But he denied it: 'I am not', he said. One of **26**
the High Priest's servants, a relation of the man whose ear Peter had cut

[a] *See note on verse 24.*　　[b] *Some witnesses give this verse after* first to Annas *in verse
13; others at the end of verse 13.*

27 off, insisted, 'Did I not see you with him in the garden?' Peter denied again; and just then a cock crew.

28 FROM CAIAPHAS Jesus was led into the Governor's headquarters. It was now early morning, and the Jews themselves stayed outside the head-
29 quarters to avoid defilement, so that they could eat the Passover meal.[a] So Pilate went out to them and asked, 'What charge do you bring against this
30 man?' 'If he were not a criminal,' they replied, 'we should not have brought
31 him before you.' Pilate said, 'Take him away and try him by your own law.'
32 The Jews answered, 'We are not allowed to put any man to death.' Thus they ensured the fulfilment of the words by which Jesus had indicated the manner of his death.

33 Pilate then went back into his headquarters and summoned Jesus. 'Are
34 you the king of the Jews?' he asked.[b] Jesus said, 'Is that your own idea, or
35 have others suggested it to you?' 'What! am I a Jew?' said Pilate. 'Your own nation and their chief priests have brought you before me. What have
36 you done?' Jesus replied, 'My kingdom does not belong to this world. If it did, my followers would be fighting to save me from arrest by the Jews.
37 My kingly authority comes from elsewhere.' 'You are a king, then?' said Pilate. Jesus answered, ' "King" is your word. My task is to bear witness to the truth. For this was I born; for this I came into the world, and all
38 who are not deaf to truth listen to my voice.' Pilate said, 'What is truth?', and with those words went out again to the Jews. 'For my part,' he said,
39 'I find no case against him. But you have a custom that I release one prisoner for you at Passover. Would you like me to release the king of the
40 Jews?' Again the clamour rose: 'Not him; we want Barabbas!' (Barabbas was a bandit.)

**19** 1 2 Pilate now took Jesus and had him flogged; and the soldiers plaited a crown of thorns and placed it on his head, and robed him in a purple cloak.
3 Then time after time they came up to him, crying, 'Hail, King of the Jews!', and struck him on the face.

4 Once more Pilate came out and said to the Jews, 'Here he is; I am bring-
5 ing him out to let you know that I find no case against him'; and Jesus came out, wearing the crown of thorns and the purple cloak. 'Behold the
6 Man!' said Pilate. The chief priests and their henchmen saw him and shouted, 'Crucify! crucify!' 'Take him and crucify him yourselves,' said
7 Pilate; 'for my part I find no case against him.' The Jews answered, 'We have a law; and by that law he ought to die, because he has claimed to be Son of God.'

8 9 When Pilate heard that, he was more afraid than ever, and going back into his headquarters he asked Jesus, 'Where have you come from?' But
10 Jesus gave him no answer. 'Do you refuse to speak to me?' said Pilate. 'Surely you know that I have authority to release you, and I have authority
11 to crucify you?' 'You would have no authority at all over me', Jesus replied, 'if it had not been granted you from above; and therefore the deeper guilt lies with the man who handed me over to you.'

[a] Or could share in the offerings of the Passover season. [b] Or 'You are king of the Jews, I take it', he said.

From that moment Pilate tried hard to release him; but the Jews kept 12
shouting, 'If you let this man go, you are no friend to Caesar; any man who
claims to be a king is defying Caesar.' When Pilate heard what they were 13
saying, he brought Jesus out and took his seat on the tribunal at the place
known as 'The Pavement' ('Gabbatha' in the language of the Jews). It was 14
the eve of Passover,[a] about noon. Pilate said to the Jews, 'Here is your king.'
They shouted, 'Away with him! Away with him! Crucify him!' 'Crucify 15
your king?' said Pilate. 'We have no king but Caesar', the Jews replied.
Then at last, to satisfy them, he handed Jesus over to be crucified. 16

JESUS WAS NOW TAKEN in charge and, carrying his own cross, went out 17
to the Place of the Skull, as it is called (or, in the Jews' language, 'Golgotha'),
where they crucified him, and with him two others, one on the right, one 18
on the left, and Jesus between them.

And Pilate wrote an inscription to be fastened to the cross; it read, 'Jesus 19
of Nazareth King of the Jews.' This inscription was read by many Jews, 20
because the place where Jesus was crucified was not far from the city, and
the inscription was in Hebrew, Latin, and Greek. Then the Jewish chief 21
priests said to Pilate, 'You should not write "King of the Jews"; write, "He
claimed to be king of the Jews."' Pilate replied, 'What I have written, I 22
have written.'

The soldiers, having crucified Jesus, took possession of his clothes, and 23
divided them into four parts, one for each soldier, leaving out the tunic.
The tunic was seamless, woven in one piece throughout; so they said to 24
one another, 'We must not tear this; let us toss for it'; and thus the text of
Scripture came true: 'They shared my garments among them, and cast
lots for my clothing.'

That is what the soldiers did. But meanwhile near the cross where Jesus 25
hung stood his mother, with her sister, Mary wife of Clopas, and Mary of
Magdala. Jesus saw his mother, with the disciple whom he loved standing 26
beside her. He said to her, 'Mother, there is your son'; and to the disciple, 27
'There is your mother'; and from that moment the disciple took her into
his home.

After that, Jesus, aware that all had now come to its appointed end, said 28
in fulfilment of Scripture, 'I thirst.' A jar stood there full of sour wine; so 29
they soaked a sponge with the wine, fixed it on a javelin,[b] and held it up to
his lips. Having received the wine, he said, 'It is accomplished!' He bowed 30
his head and gave up his spirit.[c]

Because it was the eve of Passover,[d] the Jews were anxious that the 31
bodies should not remain on the cross for the coming Sabbath, since that
Sabbath was a day of great solemnity; so they requested Pilate to have
the legs broken and the bodies taken down. The soldiers accordingly came 32
to the first of his fellow-victims and to the second, and broke their legs;
but when they came to Jesus, they found that he was already dead, so they 33
did not break his legs. But one of the soldiers stabbed his side with a lance, 34
and at once there was a flow of blood and water. This is vouched for by an 35

[a] *Or* It was Friday in Passover.     [b] *So one witness; the others read* on marjoram.
[c] *Or* breathed out his life.     [d] *Or* Because it was Friday in Passover . . .

eyewitness, whose evidence is to be trusted. He knows that he speaks the
36 truth, so that you too may believe; for this happened in fulfilment of the
37 text of Scripture: 'No bone of his shall be broken.' And another text says,
'They shall look on him whom they pierced.'

38 AFTER THAT, PILATE was approached by Joseph of Arimathaea, a disciple
of Jesus, but a secret disciple for fear of the Jews, who *a* asked to be allowed
to remove the body of Jesus. Pilate gave the permission; so Joseph came
39 and took the body away. He was joined by Nicodemus (the man who had
first visited Jesus by night), who brought with him a mixture of myrrh
40 and aloes, more than half a hundredweight. They took the body of Jesus
and wrapped it, with the spices, in strips of linen cloth according to Jewish
41 burial-customs. Now at the place where he had been crucified there was a
42 garden, and in the garden a new tomb, not yet used for burial. There,
because the tomb was near at hand and it was the eve of the Jewish Sabbath,
they laid Jesus.

**20** EARLY ON THE SUNDAY MORNING, while it was still dark, Mary of
Magdala came to the tomb. She saw that the stone had been moved away
2 from the entrance, and ran to Simon Peter and the other disciple, the one
whom Jesus loved. 'They have taken the Lord out of his tomb,' she cried,
3 'and we do not know where they have laid him.' So Peter and the other set
4 out and made their way to the tomb. They were running side by side, but
5 the other disciple outran Peter and reached the tomb first. He peered in
6 and saw the linen wrappings lying there, but did not enter. Then Simon
Peter came up, following him, and he went into the tomb. He saw the linen
7 wrappings lying, and the napkin which had been over his head, not lying
8 with the wrappings but rolled together in a place by itself. Then the
disciple who had reached the tomb first went in too, and he saw and
9 believed; until then they had not understood the scriptures, which showed
that he must rise from the dead.

10 11     So the disciples went home again; but Mary stood at the tomb outside,
12 weeping. As she wept, she peered into the tomb; and she saw two angels in
white sitting there, one at the head, and one at the feet, where the body of
13 Jesus had lain. They said to her, 'Why are you weeping?' She answered,
'They have taken my Lord away, and I do not know where they have laid
14 him.' With these words she turned round and saw Jesus standing there,
15 but did not recognize him. Jesus said to her, 'Why are you weeping? Who
is it you are looking for?' Thinking it was the gardener, she said, 'If it is
you, sir, who removed him, tell me where you have laid him, and I will
16 take him away.' Jesus said, 'Mary!' She turned to him and said, 'Rabbuni!'
17 (which is Hebrew for 'My Master'). Jesus said, 'Do not cling to me,*b* for
I have not yet ascended to the Father. But go to my brothers, and tell them
that I am now ascending *c* to my Father and your Father, my God and your
18 God.' Mary of Magdala went to the disciples with her news: 'I have seen
the Lord!' she said, and gave them his message.

*a* Or of Arimathaea. He was a disciple of Jesus, but had gone into hiding for fear of the
Jews. He now . . .        *b* Or Touch me no more.        *c* Or I am going to ascend . . .

Late that Sunday evening, when the disciples were together behind 19
locked doors, for fear of the Jews, Jesus came and stood among them. 'Peace
be with you!' he said, and then showed them his hands and his side. So 20
when the disciples saw the Lord, they were filled with joy. Jesus repeated, 21
'Peace be with you!', and said, 'As the Father sent me, so I send you.'
Then he breathed on them, saying, 'Receive the Holy Spirit! If you 22 23
forgive any man's sins, they stand forgiven; if you pronounce them
unforgiven, unforgiven they remain.'

One of the Twelve, Thomas, that is 'the Twin', was not with the rest 24
when Jesus came. So the disciples told him, 'We have seen the Lord.' 25
He said, 'Unless I see the mark of the nails on his hands, unless I put my
finger into the place where the nails were, and my hand into his side, I will
not believe it.'

A week later his disciples were again in the room, and Thomas was with 26
them. Although the doors were locked, Jesus came and stood among them,
saying, 'Peace be with you!' Then he said to Thomas, 'Reach your finger 27
here; see my hands. Reach your hand here and put it into my side. Be
unbelieving no longer, but believe.' Thomas said, 'My Lord and my 28
God!' Jesus said, 'Because you have seen me you have found faith. Happy 29
are they who never saw me and yet have found faith.'

There were indeed many other signs that Jesus performed in the pre- 30
sence of his disciples, which are not recorded in this book. Those here 31
written have been recorded in order that you may hold the faith*a* that Jesus
is the Christ, the Son of God, and that through this faith you may possess
life by his name.

SOME TIME LATER, Jesus showed himself to his disciples once again, by **21**
the Sea of Tiberias; and in this way. Simon Peter and Thomas 'the Twin' 2
were together with Nathanael of Cana-in-Galilee. The sons of Zebedee
and two other disciples were also there. Simon Peter said, 'I am going out 3
fishing.' 'We will go with you', said the others. So they started and got into
the boat. But that night they caught nothing.

Morning came, and there stood Jesus on the beach, but the disciples 4
did not know that it was Jesus. He called out to them, 'Friends, have you 5
caught anything?' They answered 'No.' He said, 'Shoot the net to star- 6
board, and you will make a catch.' They did so, and found they could
not haul the net aboard, there were so many fish in it. Then the disciple 7
whom Jesus loved said to Peter, 'It is the Lord!' When Simon Peter
heard that, he wrapped his coat about him (for he had stripped) and
plunged into the sea. The rest of them came on in the boat, towing the 8
net full of fish; for they were not far from land, only about a hundred
yards.

When they came ashore, they saw a charcoal fire there, with fish laid on 9
it, and some bread. Jesus said, 'Bring some of your catch.' Simon Peter 10 11
went aboard and dragged the net to land, full of big fish, a hundred and
fifty-three of them; and yet, many as they were, the net was not torn. Jesus 12
said, 'Come and have breakfast.' None of the disciples dared to ask 'Who

*a Some witnesses read* that you may come to believe . . .

13  are you?' They knew it was the Lord. Jesus now came up, took the bread, and gave it to them, and the fish in the same way.

14      This makes the third time that Jesus appeared to his disciples after his resurrection from the dead.

15      After breakfast, Jesus said to Simon Peter, 'Simon son of John, do you love me more than all else[a]?' 'Yes, Lord,' he answered, 'you know that I
16  love you.'[b] 'Then feed my lambs', he said. A second time he asked, 'Simon son of John, do you love me?' 'Yes, Lord, you know I love you.'[b] 'Then
17  tend my sheep.' A third time he said, 'Simon son of John, do you love me[c]?' Peter was hurt that he asked him a third time, 'Do you love me?'[d] 'Lord,' he said, 'you know everything; you know I love you.'[b] Jesus said, 'Feed my sheep.

18      'And further, I tell you this in very truth: when you were young you fastened your belt about you and walked where you chose; but when you are old you will stretch out your arms, and a stranger will bind you fast,
19  and carry you where you have no wish to go.' He said this to indicate the manner of death by which Peter was to glorify God. Then he added, 'Follow me.'

20      Peter looked round, and saw the disciple whom Jesus loved following— the one who at supper had leaned back close to him to ask the question,
21  'Lord, who is it that will betray you?' When he caught sight of him, Peter
22  asked, 'Lord, what will happen to him?' Jesus said, 'If it should be my will that he wait until I come, what is it to you? Follow me.'

23      That saying of Jesus became current in the brotherhood, and was taken to mean that that disciple would not die. But in fact Jesus did not say that he would not die; he only said, 'If it should be my will that he wait until I come, what is it to you?'

24.     It is this same disciple who attests what has here been written. It is in fact he who wrote it, and we know that his testimony is true.[e]

25      There is much else that Jesus did. If it were all to be recorded in detail, I suppose the whole world could not hold the books that would be written.

[a] *Or* more than they do.    [b] *Or* that I am your friend.    [c] *Or* are you my friend.
[d] *Or* that at the third asking he should have said, 'Are you my friend?'    [e] *Some witnesses here insert the passage printed on p. 143.*

## An incident in the temple*

AND THEY WENT each to his home, and Jesus to the Mount of Olives. 53 1*
At daybreak he appeared again in the temple, and all the people 2
gathered round him. He had taken his seat and was engaged in teaching
them when the doctors of the law and the Pharisees brought in a woman 3
caught committing adultery. Making her stand out in the middle they said 4
to him, 'Master, this woman was caught in the very act of adultery. In the 5
Law Moses has laid down that such women are to be stoned. What do you
say about it?' They put the question as a test, hoping to frame a charge 6
against him. Jesus bent down and wrote with his finger on the ground.
When they continued to press their question he sat up straight and said, 7
'That one of you who is faultless shall throw the first stone.' Then once 8
again he bent down and wrote on the ground. When they heard what he 9
said, one by one they went away,*a* the eldest first; and Jesus was left alone,
with the woman still standing there. Jesus again sat up and *b* said to the 10
woman, 'Where are they? Has no one condemned you?' She answered, 'No 11
one, sir.' Jesus said, 'Nor do I condemn you. You may go; do not sin
again.'

* *This passage, which in the most widely received editions of the New Testament is printed
in the text of John, 7. 53—8. 11, has no fixed place in our witnesses. Some of them do not
contain it at all. Some place it after Luke 21. 38, others after John 7. 36, or 7. 52, or 21. 24.*

*a* *Some witnesses insert* convicted by their conscience.     *b* *Some witnesses insert*
seeing no one but the woman.

# ACTS OF THE
# APOSTLES

# ACTS OF THE APOSTLES

## *The beginnings of the church*

IN THE FIRST PART of my work, Theophilus, I wrote of all that 1
Jesus did and taught from the beginning until the day when, after 2
giving instructions through the Holy Spirit to the apostles whom he
had chosen, he was taken up to heaven. He showed himself to these men 3
after his death, and gave ample proof that he was alive: over a period of
forty days he appeared to them and taught them about the kingdom of
God. While he was in their company he told them not to leave Jerusalem. 4
'You must wait', he said, 'for the promise made by my Father, about which
you have heard me speak: John, as you know, baptized with water, but you 5
will be baptized with the Holy Spirit, and within the next few days.'

So, when they were all together, they asked him, 'Lord, is this the time 6
when you are to establish once again the sovereignty of Israel?' He 7
answered, 'It is not for you to know about dates or times, which the Father
has set within his own control. But you will receive power when the Holy 8
Spirit comes upon you; and you will bear witness for me in Jerusalem, and
all over Judaea and Samaria, and away to the ends of the earth.'

When he had said this, as they watched, he was lifted up, and a cloud 9
removed him from their sight. As he was going, and as they were gazing 10
intently into the sky, all at once there stood beside them two men in white
who said, 'Men of Galilee, why stand there looking up into the sky? This 11
Jesus, who has been taken away from you up to heaven, will come in the
same way as you have seen him go.'

Then they returned to Jerusalem from the hill called Olivet, which is 12
near Jerusalem, no farther than a Sabbath day's journey. Entering the city 13
they went to the room upstairs where they were lodging: Peter and John
and James and Andrew, Philip and Thomas, Bartholomew and Matthew,
James son of Alphaeus and Simon the Zealot, and Judas son of James. All 14
these were constantly at prayer together, and with them a group of women,
including Mary the mother of Jesus, and his brothers.

It was during this time that Peter stood up before the assembled brother- 15
hood, about one hundred and twenty in all, and said: 'My friends, the 16
prophecy in Scripture was bound to come true, which the Holy Spirit,
through the mouth of David, uttered about Judas who acted as guide to
those who arrested Jesus. For he was one of our number and had his place 17
in this ministry.' (This Judas, be it noted, after buying a plot of land with 18
the price of his villainy, fell forward on the ground, and burst open, so that
his entrails poured out. This became known to everyone in Jerusalem, and 19

they named the property in their own language Akeldama, which means
20 'Blood Acre'.) 'The text I have in mind', Peter continued, 'is in the Book of
Psalms: "Let his homestead fall desolate; let there be none to inhabit it";
21 and again, "Let another take over his charge." Therefore one of those
who bore us company all the while we had the Lord Jesus with us, coming
22 and going, from John's ministry of baptism until the day when he was
taken up from us—one of those must now join us as a witness to his
resurrection.'

23   Two names were put forward: Joseph, who was known as Barsabbas,
24 and bore the added name of Justus; and Matthias. Then they prayed and
said, 'Thou, Lord, who knowest the hearts of all men, declare which of
25 these two thou hast chosen to receive this office of ministry and apostleship
26 which Judas abandoned to go where he belonged.' They drew lots and the
lot fell on Matthias, who was then assigned a place among the twelve
apostles.*a*

2  WHILE THE DAY of Pentecost was running its course they were all
2 together in one place, when suddenly there came from the sky a noise like
that of a strong driving wind, which filled the whole house where they were
3 sitting. And there appeared to them tongues like flames of fire, dispersed
4 among them and resting on each one. And they were all filled with the Holy
Spirit and began to talk in other tongues, as the Spirit gave them power of
utterance.

5   Now there were living in Jerusalem devout Jews*b* drawn from every
6 nation under heaven; and at this sound the crowd gathered, all bewildered
7 because each one heard his own language spoken. They were amazed and
in their astonishment exclaimed, 'Why, they are all Galileans, are they not,
8 these men who are speaking? How is it then that we hear them, each of us
9 in his own native language? Parthians, Medes, Elamites; inhabitants of
10 Mesopotamia, of Judaea and Cappadocia, of Pontus and Asia, of Phrygia
and Pamphylia, of Egypt and the districts of Libya around Cyrene; visitors
11 from Rome, both Jews and proselytes, Cretans and Arabs, we hear them
12 telling in our own tongues the great things God has done.' And they were
all amazed and perplexed, saying to one another, 'What can this mean?'
13 Others said contemptuously, 'They have been drinking!'

14   But Peter stood up with the Eleven, raised his voice, and addressed them:
'Fellow Jews, and all you who live in Jerusalem, mark this and give me a
15 hearing. These men are not drunk, as you imagine; for it is only nine in the
16 17 morning. No, this is what the prophet spoke of: "God says, 'This will
happen in the last days: I will pour out upon everyone a portion of my
spirit; and your sons and daughters shall prophesy; your young men shall
18 see visions, and your old men shall dream dreams. Yes, I will endue even
my slaves, both men and women, with a portion of my spirit, and they shall
19 prophesy. And I will show portents in the sky above, and signs on the earth
20 below—blood and fire and drifting smoke. The sun shall be turned to darkness, and the moon to blood, before that great, resplendent day, the day of

---

*a* *Some witnesses read* was then appointed a colleague of the eleven apostles.
*b* *Some witnesses read* devout men.

the Lord, shall come. And then, everyone who invokes the name of the 21
Lord shall be saved.'"

'Men of Israel, listen to me: I speak of Jesus of Nazareth, a man singled 22
out by God and made known to you through miracles, portents, and signs,
which God worked among you through him, as you well know. When he 23
had been given up to you, by the deliberate will and plan of God, you used
heathen men to crucify and kill him. But God raised him to life again, 24
setting him free from the pangs of death, because it could not be that death
should keep him in its grip.

'For David says of him: 25

"I foresaw that the presence of the Lord would be with me always,
    for he is at my right hand so that I may not be shaken;
therefore my heart was glad and my tongue spoke my joy; 26
moreover, my flesh shall dwell in hope,
for thou wilt not abandon my soul to death, 27
    nor let thy loyal servant suffer corruption.
Thou hast shown me the ways of life, 28
thou wilt fill me with gladness by thy presence."

'Let me tell you plainly, my friends, that the patriarch David died and 29
was buried, and his tomb is here to this very day. It is clear therefore that 30
he spoke as a prophet, who knew that God had sworn to him that one of
his own direct descendants should sit on his throne; and when he said he 31
was not abandoned to death, and his flesh never suffered corruption, he
spoke with foreknowledge of the resurrection of the Messiah. The Jesus we 32
speak of has been raised by God, as we can all bear witness. Exalted thus 33
with[a] God's right hand, he received the Holy Spirit from the Father, as
was promised, and all that you now see and hear flows from him. For it was 34
not David who went up to heaven; his own words are: "The Lord said to
my Lord, 'Sit at my right hand until I make your enemies your footstool.'" 35
Let all Israel then accept as certain that God has made this Jesus, whom 36
you crucified, both Lord and Messiah.'

When they heard this they were cut to the heart, and said to Peter and 37
the apostles,[b] 'Friends, what are we to do?' 'Repent,' said Peter, 'repent 38
and be baptized, every one of you, in the name of Jesus the Messiah for the
forgiveness of your sins; and you will receive the gift of the Holy Spirit.
For the promise is to you, and to your children, and to all who are far away, 39
everyone whom the Lord our God may call.'

In these and many other words he pressed his case and pleaded with 40
them: 'Save yourselves', he said, 'from this crooked age.' Then those who 41
accepted his word were baptized, and some three thousand were added to
their number that day.

They met constantly to hear the apostles teach, and to share the common 42
life, to break bread, and to pray. A sense of awe was everywhere, and many 43
marvels and signs were brought about through the apostles. All whose 44
faith had drawn them together held everything in common:[c] they would 45

---

[a] *Or at.*    [b] *Some witnesses read the rest of the apostles.*    [c] *Or All who had become believers held everything together in common.*

sell their property and possessions and make a general distribution as the
46 need of each required. With one mind they kept up their daily attendance
at the temple, and, breaking bread in private houses, shared their meals
47 with unaffected joy, as they praised God and enjoyed the favour of the
whole people. And day by day the Lord added to their number those
whom he was saving.

3 ONE DAY at three in the afternoon, the hour of prayer, Peter and John
2 were on their way up to the temple. Now a man who had been a cripple
from birth used to be carried there and laid every day by the gate of the
3 temple called 'Beautiful Gate', to beg from people as they went in. When
he saw Peter and John on their way into the temple he asked for charity.
4 But Peter fixed his eyes on him, as John did also, and said, 'Look at us.'
5 6 Expecting a gift from them, the man was all attention. And Peter said, 'I
have no silver or gold; but what I have I give you: in the name of Jesus
7 Christ of Nazareth, walk.' Then he grasped him by the right hand and
8 pulled him up; and at once his feet and ankles grew strong; he sprang up,
stood on his feet, and started to walk. He entered the temple with them,
9 leaping and praising God as he went. Everyone saw him walking and
10 praising God, and when they recognized him as the man who used to sit
begging at Beautiful Gate, they were filled with wonder and amazement at
what had happened to him.

11 And as he was clutching Peter and John all the people came running in
12 astonishment towards them in Solomon's Portico, as it is called. Peter saw
them coming and met them with these words: 'Men of Israel, why be
surprised at this? Why stare at us as if we had made this man walk by some
13 power or godliness of our own? The God of Abraham, Isaac, and Jacob,
the God of our fathers, has given the highest honour to his servant Jesus,
14 whom you committed for trial and repudiated in Pilate's court—repudiated
the one who was holy and righteous when Pilate had decided to release him.
15 You begged as a favour the release of a murderer, and killed him who has
led the way to life. But God raised him from the dead; of that we are
16 witnesses. And the name of Jesus, by awakening faith, has strengthened
this man, whom you see and know, and this faith has made him completely
well, as you can all see for yourselves.

17 'And now, my friends, I know quite well that you acted in ignorance,
18 and so did your rulers; but this is how God fulfilled what he had foretold
in the utterances of all the prophets: that his Messiah should suffer.
19 Repent then and turn to God, so that your sins may be wiped out. Then
20 the Lord may grant you a time of recovery and send you the Messiah he
21 has already appointed, that is, Jesus. He must be received into heaven until
the time of universal restoration comes, of which God spoke by his holy
22 prophets.*a* Moses said, "The Lord God will raise up a prophet for you
from among yourselves as he raised me;*b* you shall listen to everything
23 he says to you, and anyone who refuses to listen to that prophet must
24 be extirpated from Israel." And so said all the prophets, from Samuel
onwards; with one voice they all predicted this present time.

*a Some witnesses add* from the beginning of the world.     *b Or* like me.

'You are the heirs of the prophets; you are within the covenant which 25
God made with your fathers, when he said to Abraham, "And in your offspring all the families on earth shall find blessing." When God raised up 26
his Servant, he sent him to you first, to bring you blessing by turning
every one of you from your wicked ways.'

They were still addressing the people when the chief *a* priests came upon **4**
them, together with the Controller of the Temple and the Sadducees,
exasperated at their teaching the people and proclaiming the resurrection 2
from the dead—the resurrection of Jesus. They were arrested and put in 3
prison for the night, as it was already evening. But many of those who had 4
heard the message became believers. The number of men now reached
about five thousand.

Next day the Jewish rulers, elders, and doctors of the law met in Jeru- 5
salem. There were present Annas the High Priest, Caiaphas, Jonathan, *b* 6
Alexander, and all who were of the high-priestly family. They brought the 7
apostles before the court and began the examination. 'By what power', 
they asked, 'or by what name have such men as you done this?' Then 8
Peter, filled with the Holy Spirit, answered, 'Rulers of the people and
elders, if the question put to us today is about help given to a sick man, and 9
we are asked by what means he was cured, here is the answer, for all of you 10
and for all the people of Israel: it was by the name of Jesus Christ of
Nazareth, whom you crucified, whom God raised from the dead; it is by
his name *c* that this man stands here before you fit and well. This Jesus is 11
the stone rejected by the builders which has become the keystone—and
you are the builders. There is no salvation in anyone else at all, *d* for there 12
is no other name under heaven granted to men, by which we may receive
salvation.'

Now as they observed the boldness of Peter and John, and noted that 13
they were untrained laymen, they began to wonder, then recognized them
as former companions of Jesus. And when they saw the man who had been 14
cured standing with them, they had nothing to say in reply. So they ordered 15
them to leave the court, and then discussed the matter among themselves.
'What are we to do with these men?' they said; 'for it is common knowledge 16
in Jerusalem that a notable miracle has come about through them; and we
cannot deny it. But to stop this from spreading further among the people, 17
we had better caution them never again to speak to anyone in this name.'
They then called them in and ordered them to refrain from all public 18
speaking and teaching in the name of Jesus.

But Peter and John said to them in reply: 'Is it right in God's eyes for us 19
to obey you rather than God? Judge for yourselves. We cannot possibly 20
give up speaking of things we have seen and heard.'

The court repeated the caution and discharged them. They could not 21
see how they were to punish them, because the people were all giving glory
to God for what had happened. The man upon whom this miracle of heal- 22
ing had been performed was over forty years old.

As soon as they were discharged they went back to their friends and 23

---

*a Some witnesses omit* chief.       *b Some witnesses read* John.       *c Some witnesses
insert* and no other.       *d Some witnesses omit* There is no . . . at all.

24 told them everything that the chief priests and elders had said. When they heard it, they raised their voices as one man and called upon God:

'Sovereign Lord, maker of heaven and earth and sea and of everything
25 in them, who by the Holy Spirit,*a* through the mouth of David thy servant, didst say,

> "Why did the Gentiles rage and the peoples lay their plots in vain?
> 26    The kings of the earth took their stand and the rulers made common cause
> against the Lord and against his Messiah."

27 They did indeed make common cause in this very city against thy holy servant Jesus whom thou didst anoint as Messiah. Herod and Pontius
28 Pilate conspired with the Gentiles and peoples of Israel to do all the things
29 which, under thy hand and by thy decree, were foreordained. And now, O Lord, mark their threats, and enable thy servants to speak thy word with
30 all boldness. Stretch out thy hand to heal and cause signs and wonders to be done through the name of thy holy servant Jesus.'
31    When they had ended their prayer, the building where they were assembled rocked, and all were filled with the Holy Spirit and spoke the word of God with boldness.

32 THE WHOLE BODY of believers was united in heart and soul. Not a man of them claimed any of his possessions as his own, but everything was held
33 in common, while the apostles bore witness with great power to the resur-
34 rection of the Lord Jesus. They were all held in high esteem; for they had never a needy person among them, because all who had property in land
35 or houses sold it, brought the proceeds of the sale, and laid the money at the feet of the apostles; it was then distributed to any who stood in need.
36    For instance, Joseph, surnamed by the apostles Barnabas (which means
37 'Son of Exhortation'), a Levite, by birth a Cypriot, owned an estate, which he sold; he brought the money, and laid it at the apostles' feet.

5    But there was another man, called Ananias, with his wife Sapphira, who
2 sold a property. With the full knowledge of his wife he kept back part of the
3 purchase-money, and part he brought and laid at the apostles' feet. But Peter said, 'Ananias, how was it that Satan so possessed your mind that you
4 lied to the Holy Spirit, and kept back part of the price of the land? While it remained, did it not remain yours? When it was turned into money, was it not still at your own disposal? What made you think of doing this thing?
5 You have lied not to men but to God.' When Ananias heard these words he
6 dropped dead; and all the others who heard were awestruck. The younger men rose and covered his body, then carried him out and buried him.
7    About three hours passed, and then his wife came in, unaware of what
8 had happened. Peter turned to her and said, 'Tell me, were you paid such
9 and such a price for the land?' 'Yes,' she said, 'that was the price.' Then Peter said, 'Why did you both conspire to put the Spirit of the Lord to the test? Hark! there at the door are the footsteps of those who buried your
10 husband; and they will carry you away.' And suddenly she dropped dead

---

*a Some witnesses omit* by the Holy Spirit.

at his feet. When the young men came in, they found her dead; and they
carried her out and buried her beside her husband. And a great awe fell 11
upon the whole church, and upon all who heard of these events; and many 12
remarkable and wonderful things took place among the people at the hands
of the apostles.

THEY USED TO MEET by common consent in Solomon's Portico, no one 13
from outside their number venturing to join with them. But people in
general spoke highly of them,*a* and more than that, numbers of men and 14
women were added to their ranks as believers in the Lord.*b* In the end the 15
sick were actually carried out into the streets and laid there on beds and
stretchers, so that even the shadow of Peter might fall on one or another as
he passed by; and the people from the towns round Jerusalem flocked in, 16
bringing those who were ill or harassed by unclean spirits, and all of them
were cured.

Then the High Priest and his colleagues, the Sadducean party as it then 17
was, were goaded into action by jealousy. They proceeded to arrest the 18
apostles, and put them in official custody. But an angel of the Lord opened 19
the prison doors during the night, brought them out, and said, 'Go, take 20
your place in the temple and speak to the people, and tell them about this
new life and all it means.' Accordingly they entered the temple at day- 21
break and went on with their teaching.

When the High Priest arrived with his colleagues they summoned the
'Sanhedrin', that is, the full senate of the Israelite nation, and sent to the
jail to fetch the prisoners. But the police who went to the prison failed to 22
find them there, so they returned and reported, 'We found the jail securely 23
locked at every point, with the warders at their posts by the doors, but when
we opened them we found no one inside.' When they heard this, the Con- 24
troller of the Temple and the chief priests were wondering what could have
become of them,*c* and then a man arrived with the report, 'Look! the men 25
you put in prison are there in the temple teaching the people.' At that the 26
Controller went off with the police and fetched them, but without using
force for fear of being stoned by the people.

So they brought them and stood them before the Council; and the High 27
Priest began his examination. 'We expressly ordered you', he said, 'to 28
desist from teaching in that name; and what has happened? You have filled
Jerusalem with your teaching, and you are trying to make us responsible
for that man's death.' Peter replied for himself and the apostles: 'We must 29
obey God rather than men. The God of our fathers raised up Jesus whom 30
you had done to death*d* by hanging him on a gibbet. He it is whom God has 31
exalted with his own right hand*e* as leader and saviour, to grant Israel
repentance and forgiveness of sins. And we are witnesses to all this, and so 32
is the Holy Spirit given by God to those who are obedient to him.'

*a Or* . . . Portico. Although others did not venture to join them, the common people
spoke highly of them.          *b Or* and an ever-increasing number of believers, both
men and women, were added to the Lord.          *c Or* wondering about them, what
this could possibly mean.          *d Or* . . . Jesus, and you did him to death . . .
*e Or* at his right hand.

33 This touched them on the raw, and they wanted to put them to death.
34 But a member of the Council rose to his feet, a Pharisee called Gamaliel, a
teacher of the law held in high regard by all the people. He moved that the
35 men be put outside for a while. Then he said, 'Men of Israel, be cautious in
36 deciding what to do with these men. Some time ago Theudas came forward, claiming to be somebody, and a number of men, about four hundred,
joined him. But he was killed and his whole following was broken up and
37 disappeared. After him came Judas the Galilean at the time of the census;
he induced some people to revolt under his leadership, but he too perished
38 and his whole following was scattered. And so now: keep clear of these men,
I tell you; leave them alone. For if this idea of theirs or its execution is of
39 human origin, it will collapse; but if it is from God, you will never be able
to put them down, and you risk finding yourselves at war with God.'
40 They took his advice. They sent for the apostles and had them flogged;
then they ordered them to give up speaking in the name of Jesus, and dis-
41 charged them. So the apostles went out from the Council rejoicing that they
42 had been found worthy to suffer indignity for the sake of the Name. And
every day they went steadily on with their teaching in the temple and in
private houses, telling the good news of Jesus the Messiah. *a*

## The church moves outwards

6 DURING THIS PERIOD, when disciples were growing in number,
there was disagreement between those of them who spoke Greek *b*
and those who spoke the language of the Jews. *c* The former party complained that their widows were being overlooked in the daily distribution.
2 So the Twelve called the whole body of disciples together and said, 'It
would be a grave mistake for us to neglect the word of God in order to wait
3 at table. Therefore, friends, look out seven men of good reputation from
your number, men full of the Spirit and of wisdom, and we will appoint
4 them to deal with these matters, while we devote ourselves to prayer and
5 to the ministry of the Word.' This proposal proved acceptable to the whole
body. They elected Stephen, a man full of faith and of the Holy Spirit,
Philip, Prochorus, Nicanor, Timon, Parmenas, and Nicolas of Antioch,
6 a former convert to Judaism. These they presented to the apostles, who
prayed and laid their hands on them.
7 The word of God now spread more and more widely; the number of
disciples in Jerusalem went on increasing rapidly, and very many of the
priests adhered to the Faith.
8 Stephen, who was full of grace and power, began to work great miracles
9 and signs among the people. But some members of the synagogue called
the Synagogue of Freedmen, comprising Cyrenians and Alexandrians
and people from Cilicia and Asia, came forward and argued with Stephen,
10 but could not hold their own against the inspired wisdom with which he
11 spoke. They then put up men who alleged that they had heard him make

*a* Or the good news that the Messiah was Jesus.   *b* Literally the Hellenists.
*c* Literally the Hebrews.

blasphemous statements against Moses and against God. They stirred up 12
the people and the elders and doctors of the law, set upon him and seized
him, and brought him before the Council. They produced false witnesses 13
who said, 'This man is for ever saying things against this holy place and
against the Law. For we have heard him say that Jesus of Nazareth will 14
destroy this place and alter the customs handed down to us by Moses.' And 15
all who were sitting in the Council fixed their eyes on him, and his face
appeared to them like the face of an angel.

Then the High Priest asked, 'Is this so?' And he said, 'My brothers, 7 1 2
fathers of this nation, listen to me. The God of glory appeared to Abraham
our ancestor while he was in Mesopotamia, before he had settled in Harran,
and said: "Leave your country and your kinsfolk and come away to a land 3
that I will show you." Thereupon he left the land of the Chaldaeans and 4
settled in Harran. From there, after his father's death, God led him to
migrate to this land where you now live. He gave him nothing in it to call 5
his own, not one yard; but promised to give it in possession to him and his
descendants after him, though he was then childless. God spoke in these 6
terms: "Abraham's descendants shall live as aliens in a foreign land, held
in slavery and oppression for four hundred years. And I will pass judge- 7
ment", said God, "on the nation whose slaves they are; and after that they
shall come out free, and worship me in this place." He then gave him the 8
covenant of circumcision, and so, after Isaac was born, he circumcised him
on the eighth day; and Isaac begot Jacob, and Jacob the twelve patriarchs.

'The patriarchs out of jealousy sold Joseph into slavery in Egypt, but 9
God was with him and rescued him from all his troubles. He also gave him 10
a presence and powers of mind which so commended him to Pharaoh king
of Egypt, that he appointed him chief administrator for Egypt and the whole
of the royal household.

'But famine struck all Egypt and Canaan, and caused great hardship; 11
and our ancestors could find nothing to eat. But Jacob heard that there was 12
food in Egypt and sent our fathers there. This was their first visit. On the 13
second visit Joseph was recognized by his brothers, and his family con-
nections were disclosed to Pharaoh. So Joseph sent an invitation to his father 14
Jacob and all his relatives, seventy-five persons altogether; and Jacob went 15
down into Egypt. There he ended his days, as also our forefathers did.
Their remains were later removed to Shechem and buried in the tomb 16
which Abraham had bought and paid for from the clan of Emmor at
Shechem.

'Now as the time approached for God to fulfil the promise he had made 17
to Abraham, our nation in Egypt grew and increased in numbers. At length 18
another king, who knew nothing of Joseph, ascended the throne of Egypt.
He made a crafty attack on our race, and cruelly forced our ancestors to 19
expose their children so that they should not survive. At this time Moses 20
was born. He was a fine child, and pleasing to God. For three months he
was nursed in his father's house, and when he was exposed, Pharaoh's 21
daughter herself adopted him and brought him up as her own son. So 22
Moses was trained in all the wisdom of the Egyptians, a powerful speaker
and a man of action.

23   'He was approaching the age of forty, when it occurred to him to look
24   into the conditions of his fellow-countrymen the Israelites. He saw one of
     them being ill-treated, so he went to his aid, and avenged the victim by
25   striking down the Egyptian. He thought his fellow-countrymen would
     understand that God was offering them deliverance through him, but they
26   did not understand. The next day he came upon two of them fighting, and
     tried to bring them to make up their quarrel. "My men," he said, "you are
27   brothers; why are you ill-treating one another?" But the man who was at
     fault pushed him away. "Who set you up as a ruler and judge over us?"
28   he said. "Are you going to kill me as you killed the Egyptian yesterday?"
29   At this Moses fled the country and settled in Midianite territory. There
     two sons were born to him.

30      'After forty years had passed, an angel appeared to him in the flame of a
31   burning bush in the desert near Mount Sinai. Moses was amazed at the
     sight. But as he approached to look closely, the voice of the Lord was heard:
32   "I am the God of your fathers, the God of Abraham, Isaac, and Jacob."
33   Moses was terrified and dared not look. Then the Lord said to him, "Take
34   off your shoes; the place where you are standing is holy ground. I have
     indeed seen how my people are oppressed in Egypt and have heard their
     groans; and I have come down to rescue them. Up, then; let me send you
     to Egypt."

35      'This Moses, whom they had rejected with the words, "Who made you
     ruler and judge?"—this very man was commissioned as ruler and liberator
     by God himself, speaking through the angel who appeared to him in the
36   bush. It was Moses who led them out, working miracles and signs in Egypt,
37   at the Red Sea, and for forty years in the desert. It was he again who said to
     the Israelites, "God will raise up a prophet for you from among yourselves
38   as he raised me."[a] He it was who, when they were assembled there in the
     desert, conversed with the angel who spoke to him on Mount Sinai, and
     with our forefathers; he received the living utterances of God, to pass
     on to us.

39      'But our forefathers would not accept his leadership. They thrust him
40   aside. They wished themselves back in Egypt, and said to Aaron, "Make
     us gods to go before us. As for that Moses, who brought us out of Egypt,
41   we do not know what has become of him." That was when they made the
     bull-calf, and offered sacrifice to the idol, and held a feast in honour of the
42   thing their hands had made. But God turned away from them and gave
     them over to the worship of the host of heaven, as it stands written in the
     book of the prophets: "Did you bring me victims and offerings those forty
43   years in the desert, you house of Israel? No, you carried aloft the shrine of
     Moloch and the star of the god Rephan, the images which you had made
     for your adoration. I will banish you beyond Babylon."

44      'Our forefathers had the Tent of the Testimony in the desert, as God
     commanded when he told Moses to make it after the pattern which he had
45   seen. Our fathers of the next generation, with Joshua, brought it with them
     when they dispossessed the nations whom God drove out before them, and
46   there it was until the time of David. David found favour with God and

----

[a]  *Or* like me.

asked to be allowed to provide a dwelling-place for the God of Jacob;[a] but it was Solomon who built him a house. However, the Most High does 47 48 not live in houses made by men: as the prophet says, "Heaven is my throne 49 and earth my footstool. What kind of house will you build for me, says the Lord; where is my resting-place? Are not all these things of my own 50 making?"

'How stubborn you are, heathen still at heart and deaf to the truth! You 51 always fight against the Holy Spirit. Like fathers, like sons. Was there ever 52 a prophet whom your fathers did not persecute? They killed those who foretold the coming of the Righteous One; and now you have betrayed him and murdered him, you who received the Law as God's angels gave it to 53 you, and yet have not kept it.'

This touched them on the raw and they ground their teeth with fury. 54 But Stephen, filled with the Holy Spirit, and gazing intently up to heaven, 55 saw the glory of God, and Jesus standing at God's right hand. 'Look,' he 56 said, 'there is a rift in the sky; I can see the Son of Man standing at God's right hand!' At this they gave a great shout and stopped their ears. Then 57 they made one rush at him and, flinging him out of the city, set about 58 stoning him. The witnesses laid their coats at the feet of a young man named Saul. So they stoned Stephen, and as they did so, he called out, 'Lord Jesus, 59 receive my spirit.' Then he fell on his knees and cried aloud, 'Lord, do not 60 hold this sin against them', and with that he died. And Saul was among 8 those who approved of his murder.

THIS WAS THE BEGINNING of a time of violent persecution for the church in Jerusalem; and all except the apostles were scattered over the country districts of Judaea and Samaria. Stephen was given burial by 2 certain devout men, who made a great lamentation for him. Saul, mean- 3 while, was harrying the church; he entered house after house, seizing men and women, and sending them to prison.

As for those who had been scattered, they went through the country 4 preaching the Word. Philip came down to a city in Samaria and began pro- 5 claiming the Messiah to them. The crowds, to a man, listened eagerly to 6 what Philip said, when they heard him and saw the miracles that he per- formed. For in many cases of possession the unclean spirits came out with 7 a loud cry; and many paralysed and crippled folk were cured; and there was 8 great joy in that city.

A man named Simon had been in the city for some time, and had swept 9 the Samaritans off their feet with his magical arts, claiming to be someone great. All of them, high and low, listened eagerly to him. 'This man', they 10 said, 'is that power of God which is called "The Great Power".' They 11 listened because they had for so long been carried away by his magic. But 12 when they came to believe Philip with his good news about the kingdom of God and the name of Jesus Christ, they were baptized, men and women alike. Even Simon himself believed, and was baptized, and thereupon was 13 constantly in Philip's company. He was carried away when he saw the powerful signs and miracles that were taking place.

---

[a] *Some witnesses read* for the house of Jacob.

14 The apostles in Jerusalem now heard that Samaria had accepted the
15 word of God. They sent off Peter and John, who went down there and
prayed for the converts, asking that they might receive the Holy Spirit.
16 For until then the Spirit had not come upon any of them. They had been
17 baptized into the name of the Lord Jesus, that and nothing more. So Peter
and John laid their hands on them and they received the Holy Spirit.

18 When Simon saw that the Spirit was bestowed through the laying on of
19 the apostles' hands, he offered them money and said, 'Give me the same
power too, so that when I lay my hands on anyone, he will receive the Holy
20 Spirit.' Peter replied, 'Your money go with you to damnation, because you
21 thought God's gift was for sale! You have no part nor lot in this, for you
22 are dishonest with God. Repent of this wickedness and pray the Lord to
23 forgive you for imagining such a thing. I can see that you are doomed to
24 taste the bitter fruit and wear the fetters of sin.'*a* Simon answered, 'Pray
to the Lord for me yourselves and ask that none of the things you have
spoken of may fall upon me.'

25 So, after giving their testimony and speaking the word of the Lord, they
took the road back to Jerusalem, bringing the good news to many Samaritan
villages on the way.

26 Then the angel of the Lord said to Philip, 'Start out and go south to the
road that leads down from Jerusalem to Gaza.' (This is the desert road.)
27 So he set out and was on his way when he caught sight of an Ethiopian.
This man was a eunuch, a high official of the Kandake, or Queen, of
Ethiopia, in charge of all her treasure. He had been to Jerusalem on a
28 pilgrimage and was now on his way home, sitting in his carriage and read-
29 ing aloud the prophet Isaiah. The Spirit said to Philip, 'Go and join the
30 carriage.' When Philip ran up he heard him reading the prophet Isaiah
31 and said, 'Do you understand what you are reading?' He said, 'How can I
understand unless someone will give me the clue?' So he asked Philip to
get in and sit beside him.

32 The passage he was reading was this: 'He was led like a sheep to be
slaughtered; and like a lamb that is dumb before the shearer, he does
33 not open his mouth. He has been humiliated and has no redress. Who
will be able to speak of his posterity? For he is cut off from the world of
living men.'

34 'Now', said the eunuch to Philip, 'tell me, please, who it is that the
35 prophet is speaking about here: himself or someone else?' Then Philip
36 began. Starting from this passage, he told him the good news of Jesus. As
they were going along the road, they came to some water. 'Look,' said the
eunuch, 'here is water: what is there to prevent my being baptized?';*b*
38 and he ordered the carriage to stop. Then they both went down into the
39 water, Philip and the eunuch; and he baptized him. When they came up
out of the water the Spirit snatched Philip away, and the eunuch saw no
40 more of him, but went happily on his way. Philip appeared at Azotus, and
toured the country, preaching in all the towns till he reached Caesarea.

*a Literally* you are for gall of bitterness and a fetter of unrighteousness.
*b Some witnesses insert* (37) Philip said, 'If you whole-heartedly believe, it is permitted.'
He replied, 'I believe that Jesus Christ is the Son of God.'

MEANWHILE SAUL was still breathing murderous threats against the 9
disciples of the Lord. He went to the High Priest and applied for letters to 2
the synagogues at Damascus authorizing him to arrest anyone he found,
men or women, who followed the new way, and bring them to Jerusalem.
While he was still on the road and nearing Damascus, suddenly a light 3
flashed from the sky all around him. He fell to the ground and heard a voice 4
saying, 'Saul, Saul, why do you persecute me?' 'Tell me, Lord,' he said, 5
'who you are.' The voice answered, 'I am Jesus, whom you are persecuting.
But get up and go into the city, and you will be told what you have to do.' 6
Meanwhile the men who were travelling with him stood speechless; they 7
heard the voice but could see no one. Saul got up from the ground, but 8
when he opened his eyes he could not see; so they led him by the hand and
brought him into Damascus. He was blind for three days, and took no 9
food or drink.

There was a disciple in Damascus named Ananias. He had a vision in 10
which he heard the voice of the Lord: 'Ananias!' 'Here I am, Lord', he
answered. The Lord said to him, 'Go at once to Straight Street, to the 11
house of Judas, and ask for a man from Tarsus named Saul. You will find
him at prayer; he has had a vision of a man named Ananias coming in and 12
laying his hands on him to restore his sight.' Ananias answered, 'Lord, I 13
have often heard about this man and all the harm he has done to thy people
in Jerusalem. And he is here with authority from the chief priests to arrest 14
all who invoke thy name.' But the Lord said to him, 'You must go, for this 15
man is my chosen instrument to bring my name before the nations and
their kings, and before the people of Israel. I myself will show him all that 16
he must go through for my name's sake.'

So Ananias went. He entered the house, laid his hands on him and said, 17
'Saul, my brother, the Lord Jesus, who appeared to you on your way here,
has sent me to you so that you may recover your sight, and be filled with the
Holy Spirit.' And immediately it seemed that scales fell from his eyes, and 18
he regained his sight. Thereupon he was baptized, and afterwards he took 19
food and his strength returned.

He stayed some time with the disciples in Damascus. Soon he was pro- 20
claiming Jesus publicly in the synagogues: 'This', he said, 'is the Son of
God.' All who heard were astounded. 'Is not this the man', they said, 'who 21
was in Jerusalem trying to destroy those who invoke this name? Did he not
come here for the sole purpose of arresting them and taking them to the
chief priests?' But Saul grew more and more forceful, and silenced the 22
Jews of Damascus with his cogent proofs that Jesus was the Messiah.

As the days mounted up, the Jews hatched a plot against his life; but 23 24
their plans became known to Saul. They kept watch on the city gates day
and night so that they might murder him; but his converts took him one 25
night and let him down by the wall, lowering him in a basket.

When he reached Jerusalem he tried to join the body of disciples there; 26
but they were all afraid of him, because they did not believe that he was
really a convert. Barnabas, however, took him by the hand and introduced 27
him to the apostles. He described to them how Saul had seen the Lord on
his journey, and heard his voice, and how he had spoken out boldly in the

28 name of Jesus at Damascus. Saul now stayed with them, moving about
29 freely in Jerusalem. He spoke out boldly and openly in the name of the
Lord, talking and debating with the Greek-speaking Jews.*a* But they
30 planned to murder him, and when the brethren learned of this they
escorted him to Caesarea and saw him off to Tarsus.

31 MEANWHILE THE CHURCH, throughout Judaea, Galilee, and Samaria,
was left in peace to build up its strength. In the fear of the Lord, upheld by
the Holy Spirit, it held on its way and grew in numbers.
32      Peter was making a general tour, in the course of which he went down to
33 visit God's people at Lydda. There he found a man named Aeneas who had
34 been bed-ridden with paralysis for eight years. Peter said to him, 'Aeneas,
Jesus Christ cures you; get up and make your bed', and immediately he
35 stood up. All who lived in Lydda and Sharon saw him; and they turned
to the Lord.
36      In Joppa there was a disciple named Tabitha (in Greek, Dorcas, mean-
37 ing a gazelle), who filled her days with acts of kindness and charity. At that
time she fell ill and died; and they washed her body and laid it in a room
38 upstairs. As Lydda was near Joppa, the disciples, who had heard that Peter
was there, sent two men to him with the urgent request, 'Please come over
39 to us without delay.' Peter thereupon went off with them. When he arrived
they took him upstairs to the room, where all the widows came and stood
round him in tears, showing him the shirts and coats that Dorcas used to
40 make while she was with them. Peter sent them all outside, and knelt down
and prayed. Then, turning towards the body, he said, 'Get up, Tabitha.'
41 She opened her eyes, saw Peter, and sat up. He gave her his hand and
helped her to her feet. Then he called the members of the congregation
42 and the widows and showed her to them alive. The news spread all over
43 Joppa, and many came to believe in the Lord. Peter stayed on in Joppa for
some time with one Simon, a tanner.

10  At Caesarea there was a man named Cornelius, a centurion in the Italian
2 Cohort, as it was called. He was a religious man, and he and his whole
family joined in the worship of God. He gave generously to help the Jewish
3 people, and was regular in his prayers to God. One day about three in the
afternoon he had a vision in which he clearly saw an angel of God, who
4 came into his room and said, 'Cornelius!' He stared at him in terror. 'What
is it, my lord?' he asked. The angel said, 'Your prayers and acts of charity
5 have gone up to heaven to speak for you before God. And now send to
6 Joppa for a man named Simon, also called Peter: he is lodging with another
7 Simon, a tanner, whose house is by the sea.' So when the angel who was
speaking to him had gone, he summoned two of his servants and a military
8 orderly who was a religious man, told them the whole story, and sent them
to Joppa.
9      Next day, while they were still on their way and approaching the city,
10 about noon Peter went up on the roof to pray. He grew hungry and wanted
something to eat. While they were getting it ready, he fell into a trance.
11 He saw a rift in the sky, and a thing coming down that looked like a great

*a Literally the Hellenists.*

sheet of sail-cloth. It was slung by the four corners, and was being lowered
to the ground. In it he saw creatures of every kind, whatever walks or 12
crawls or flies. Then there was a voice which said to him, 'Up, Peter, kill 13
and eat.' But Peter said, 'No, Lord, no: I have never eaten anything pro- 14
fane or unclean.' The voice came again a second time: 'It is not for you to 15
call profane what God counts clean.' This happened three times; and then 16
the thing was taken up again into the sky.

While Peter was still puzzling over the meaning of the vision he had 17
seen, the messengers of Cornelius had been asking the way to Simon's
house, and now arrived at the entrance. They called out and asked if 18
Simon Peter was lodging there. But Peter was thinking over the vision, 19
when the Spirit said to him, 'Some *a* men are here looking for you; make 20
haste and go downstairs. You may go with them without any misgiving,
for it was I who sent them.' Peter came down to the men and said, 'You 21
are looking for me? Here I am. What brings you here?' 'We are from the 22
centurion Cornelius,' they replied, 'a good and religious man, acknowledged as such by the whole Jewish nation. He was directed by a holy angel
to send for you to his house and to listen to what you have to say.' So Peter 23
asked them in and gave them a night's lodging. Next day he set out with
them, accompanied by some members of the congregation at Joppa.

The day after that, he arrived at Caesarea. Cornelius was expecting them 24
and had called together his relatives and close friends. When Peter arrived, 25
Cornelius came to meet him, and bowed to the ground in deep reverence.
But Peter raised him to his feet and said, 'Stand up; I am a man like any- 26
one else.' Still talking with him he went in and found a large gathering. 27
He said to them, 'I need not tell you that a Jew is forbidden by his religion 28
to visit or associate with a man of another race; yet God has shown me
clearly that I must not call any man profane or unclean. That is why I 29
came here without demur when you sent for me. May I ask what was your
reason for sending?'

Cornelius said, 'Four days ago, just about this time, I was in the house 30
here saying the afternoon prayers, when suddenly a man in shining robes
stood before me. He said: "Cornelius, your prayer has been heard and your 31
acts of charity remembered before God. Send to Joppa, then, to Simon 32
Peter, and ask him to come. He is lodging in the house of Simon the tanner,
by the sea." So I sent to you there and then; it was kind of you to come. 33
And now we are all met here before God, to hear all that the Lord has
ordered you to say.'

Peter began: 'I now see how true it is that God has no favourites, but 34 35
that in every nation the man who is godfearing and does what is right is
acceptable to him. He sent his word to the Israelites and gave the good 36
news of peace through Jesus Christ, who is Lord of all. I need not tell you 37
what happened lately all over the land of the Jews, starting from Galilee
after the baptism proclaimed by John. You know about Jesus of Nazareth, 38
how God anointed him with the Holy Spirit and with power. He went
about doing good and healing all who were oppressed by the devil, for God
was with him. And we can bear witness to all that he did in the Jewish 39

*a* *One witness reads* Two; *others read* Three.

country-side and in Jerusalem. He was put to death by hanging on a
40 gibbet; but God raised him to life on the third day, and allowed him to
41 appear, not to the whole people, but to witnesses whom God had chosen
in advance—to us, who ate and drank with him after he rose from the dead.
42 He commanded us to proclaim him to the people, and affirm that he is the
one who has been designated by God as judge of the living and the dead.
43 It is to him that all the prophets testify, declaring that everyone who trusts
in him receives forgiveness of sins through his name.'

44     Peter was still speaking when the Holy Spirit came upon all who were
45 listening to the message. The believers who had come with Peter, men of
Jewish birth, were astonished that the gift of the Holy Spirit should have
46 been poured out even on Gentiles. For they could hear them speaking in
tongues of ecstasy and acclaiming the greatness of God. Then Peter spoke:
47 'Is anyone prepared to withhold the water for baptism from these persons,
48 who have received the Holy Spirit just as we did ourselves?' Then he
ordered them to be baptized in the name of Jesus Christ. After that they
asked him to stay on with them for a time.

**11**     News came to the apostles and the members of the church in Judaea
2 that Gentiles too had accepted the word of God; and when Peter came up
to Jerusalem those who were of Jewish birth raised the question with him.
3 'You have been visiting men who are uncircumcised,' they said, 'and sitting
4 at table with them!' Peter began by laying before them the facts as they had
happened.

5     'I was in the city of Joppa', he said, 'at prayer; and while in a trance I
had a vision: a thing was coming down that looked like a great sheet of sail-
cloth, slung by the four corners and lowered from the sky till it reached me.
6 I looked intently to make out what was in it and I saw four-footed creatures
7 of the earth, wild beasts, and things that crawl or fly. Then I heard a voice
8 saying to me, "Up, Peter, kill and eat." But I said, "No, Lord, no: nothing
9 profane or unclean has ever entered my mouth." A voice from heaven
answered a second time, "It is not for you to call profane what God counts
10 clean." This happened three times, and then they were all drawn up again
11 into the sky. At that moment three men, who had been sent to me from
12 Caesarea, arrived at the house where I was*a* staying; and the Spirit told
me to go with them.*b* My six companions here came with me and we went
13 into the man's house. He told us how he had seen an angel standing in his
14 house who said, "Send to Joppa for Simon also called Peter. He will speak
15 words that will bring salvation to you and all your household." Hardly had
I begun speaking, when the Holy Spirit came upon them, just as upon us
16 at the beginning. Then I recalled what the Lord had said: "John baptized
17 with water, but you will be baptized with the Holy Spirit." God gave them
no less a gift than he gave us when we put our trust in the Lord Jesus
Christ; then how could I possibly stand in God's way?'
18     When they heard this their doubts were silenced. They gave praise to
God and said, 'This means that God has granted life-giving repentance to
the Gentiles also.'

---

*a Some witnesses read* we were.          *b Some witnesses add* making no distinctions;
*others add* without any misgiving, *as in 10. 20.*

MEANWHILE THOSE who had been scattered after the persecution that 19
arose over Stephen made their way to Phoenicia, Cyprus, and Antioch,
bringing the message to Jews only and to no others. But there were some 20
natives of Cyprus and Cyrene among them, and these, when they arrived
at Antioch, began to speak to Gentiles as well, telling them the good news
of the Lord Jesus. The power of the Lord was with them, and a great many 21
became believers, and turned to the Lord.

The news reached the ears of the church in Jerusalem; and they sent 22
Barnabas to Antioch. When he arrived and saw the divine grace at work, 23
he rejoiced, and encouraged them all to hold fast to the Lord with resolute
hearts; for he was a good man, full of the Holy Spirit and of faith. And 24
large numbers were won over to the Lord.

He then went off to Tarsus to look for Saul; and when he had found 25 26
him, he brought him to Antioch. For a whole year the two of them lived
in fellowship with the congregation there, and gave instruction to large
numbers. It was in Antioch that the disciples first got the name of
Christians.

During this period some prophets came down from Jerusalem to Antioch. 27
One of them, Agabus by name, was inspired to stand up and predict a 28
severe and world-wide famine, which in fact occurred in the reign of
Claudius. So the disciples agreed to make a contribution, each according 29
to his means, for the relief of their fellow-Christians in Judaea. This they 30
did, and sent it off to the elders, in the charge of Barnabas and Saul.

IT WAS ABOUT THIS TIME that King Herod attacked certain members **12**
of the church. He beheaded James, the brother of John, and then, when 2 3
he saw that the Jews approved, proceeded to arrest Peter also. This
happened during the festival of Unleavened Bread. Having secured him, 4
he put him in prison under a military guard, four squads of four men each,
meaning to produce him in public after Passover. So Peter was kept in 5
prison under constant watch, while the church kept praying fervently for
him to God.

On the very night before Herod had planned to bring him forward, 6
Peter was asleep between two soldiers, secured by two chains, while outside the doors sentries kept guard over the prison. All at once an angel of 7
the Lord stood there, and the cell was ablaze with light. He tapped Peter
on the shoulder and woke him. 'Quick! Get up', he said, and the chains fell
away from his wrists. The angel then said to him, 'Do up your belt and put 8
your sandals on.' He did so. 'Now wrap your cloak round you and follow
me.' He followed him out, with no idea that the angel's intervention was 9
real: he thought it was just a vision. But they passed the first guard-post, 10
then the second, and reached the iron gate leading out into the city, which
opened for them of its own accord. And so they came out and walked the
length of one street; and the angel left him.

Then Peter came to himself. 'Now I know it is true,' he said; 'the Lord 11
has sent his angel and rescued me from Herod's clutches and from all that
the Jewish people were expecting.' When he realized how things stood, 12
he made for the house of Mary, the mother of John Mark, where a large

13 company was at prayer. He knocked at the outer door and a maid called
14 Rhoda came to answer it. She recognized Peter's voice and was so overjoyed
that instead of opening the door she ran in and announced that Peter was
15 standing outside. 'You are crazy', they told her; but she insisted that it was
so. Then they said, 'It must be his guardian angel.'
16   Meanwhile Peter went on knocking, and when they opened the door and
17 saw him, they were astounded. With a movement of the hand he signed to
them to keep quiet, and told them how the Lord had brought him out of
prison. 'Report this to James and the members of the church', he said.
Then he left the house and went off elsewhere.
18   When morning came, there was consternation among the soldiers: what
19 could have become of Peter? Herod made close search, but failed to find
him, so he interrogated the guards and ordered their execution.
20   Afterwards he left Judaea to reside for a time at Caesarea. He had for some
time been furiously angry with the people of Tyre and Sidon, who now by
common agreement presented themselves at his court. There they won
over Blastus the royal chamberlain, and sued for peace, because their
21 country drew its supplies from the king's territory. So, on an appointed
day, attired in his royal robes and seated on the rostrum, Herod harangued
22 them; and the populace shouted back, 'It is a god speaking, not a man!'
23 Instantly an angel of the Lord struck him down, because he had usurped
the honour due to God; he was eaten up with worms and died.
24   Meanwhile the word of God continued to grow and spread.
25   Barnabas and Saul, their task fulfilled, returned from Jerusalem,[a] taking
John Mark with them.

## The church breaks barriers

13 THERE WERE AT ANTIOCH, in the congregation there, certain prophets
and teachers: Barnabas, Simeon called Niger, Lucius of Cyrene,
2 Manaen, who had been at the court of Prince Herod, and Saul. While they
were keeping a fast and offering worship to the Lord, the Holy Spirit said,
'Set Barnabas and Saul apart for me, to do the work to which I have called
3 them.' Then, after further fasting and prayer, they laid their hands on
them and let them go.
4   So these two, sent out on their mission by the Holy Spirit, came down to
5 Seleucia, and from there sailed to Cyprus. Arriving at Salamis, they
declared the word of God in the Jewish synagogues. They had John with
6 them as their assistant. They went through the whole island as far as
Paphos, and there they came upon a sorcerer, a Jew who posed as a prophet,
7 Bar-Jesus by name. He was in the retinue of the Governor, Sergius Paulus,
an intelligent man, who had sent for Barnabas and Saul and wanted to
8 hear the word of God. This Elymas the sorcerer (so his name may be
translated) opposed them, trying to turn the Governor away from the
9 Faith. But Saul, also known as Paul, filled with the Holy Spirit, fixed his

[a] *Some witnesses read* their task fulfilled, returned to Jerusalem; *or, as it might be rendered,*
their task at Jerusalem fulfilled, returned.

eyes on him and said, 'You swindler, you rascal, son of the devil and enemy   10
of all goodness, will you never stop falsifying the straight ways of the Lord?
Look now, the hand of the Lord strikes: you shall be blind, and for a time   11
you shall not see the sunlight.' Instantly mist and darkness came over him
and he groped about for someone to lead him by the hand. When the   12
Governor saw what had happened he became a believer, deeply impressed
by what he learned about the Lord.

'Leaving Paphos, Paul and his companions went by sea to Perga in Pam-   13
phylia; John, however, left them and returned to Jerusalem. From Perga   14
they continued their journey as far as Pisidian Antioch. On the Sabbath
they went to synagogue and took their seats; and after the readings from   15
the Law and the prophets, the officials of the synagogue sent this message to
them: 'Friends, if you have anything to say to the people by way of exhortation, let us hear it.' Paul rose, made a gesture with his hand, and began:   16

'Men of Israel and you who worship our God, listen to me! The God   17
of this people of Israel chose our fathers. When they were still living as
aliens in Egypt he made them into a nation and brought them out of that
country with arm outstretched. For some forty years he bore with their   18
conduct*a* in the desert. Then in the Canaanite country he overthrew seven   19
nations, whose lands he gave them to be their heritage for some four   20
hundred and fifty years, and afterwards appointed judges for them until
the time of the prophet Samuel.

'Then they asked for a king and God gave them Saul the son of Kish,   21
a man of the tribe of Benjamin, who reigned for forty years. Then he   22
removed him and set up David as their king, giving him his approval in
these words: "I have found David son of Jesse to be a man after my own
heart, who will carry out all my purposes." This is the man from whose   23
posterity God, as he promised, has brought Israel a saviour, Jesus. John   24
made ready for his coming by proclaiming baptism as a token of repentance to the whole people of Israel. And when John was nearing the end of   25
his course, he said, "I am not what you think I am. No, after me comes one
whose shoes I am not fit to unfasten."

'My brothers, you who come of the stock of Abraham, and others   26
among you who revere our God, we are the people to whom the message
of this salvation has been sent. The people of Jerusalem and their rulers   27
did not recognize him, or understand the words of the prophets which are
read Sabbath by Sabbath; indeed they fulfilled them by condemning him.
Though they failed to find grounds for the sentence of death, they asked   28
Pilate to have him executed. And when they had carried out all that the   29
scriptures said about him, they took him down from the gibbet and laid
him in a tomb. But God raised him from the dead; and there was a period   30 31
of many days during which he appeared to those who had come up with
him from Galilee to Jerusalem.

'They are now his witnesses before our nation; and we are here to give   32
you the good news that God, who made the promise to the fathers, has   33
fulfilled it for the children*b* by raising Jesus from the dead, as indeed it

---

*a Some witnesses read* he sustained them.       *b Some witnesses read* our children; *others
read* us their children.

stands written, in the second *a* Psalm: "You are my son; this day I have
34 begotten you." Again, that he raised him from the dead, never again to
revert to corruption, he declares in these words: "I will give you the bless-
35 ings promised to David, holy and sure." This is borne out by another
36 passage: "Thou wilt not let thy loyal servant suffer corruption." As for
David, when he had served the purpose of God in his own generation, he
37 died, and was gathered to his fathers, and suffered corruption; but the one
38 whom God raised up did not suffer corruption; and you must understand,
my brothers, that it is through him that forgiveness of sins is now being
39 proclaimed to you. It is through him that everyone who has faith is acquitted
of everything for which there was no acquittal under the Law of Moses.
40 Beware, then, lest you bring down upon yourselves the doom proclaimed
41 by the prophets: "See this, you scoffers, wonder, and begone; for I am
doing a deed in your days, a deed which you will never believe when you
are told of it." '

42    As they were leaving the synagogue they were asked to come again and
43 speak on these subjects next Sabbath; and after the congregation had dispersed, many Jews and gentile worshippers went along with Paul and
Barnabas, who spoke to them and urged them to hold fast to the grace
of God.

44    On the following Sabbath almost the whole city gathered to hear the
45 word of God. When the Jews saw the crowds, they were filled with jealous
46 resentment, and contradicted what Paul said, with violent abuse. But Paul
and Barnabas were outspoken in their reply. 'It was necessary', they said,
'that the word of God should be declared to you first. But since you reject
it and thus condemn yourselves as unworthy of eternal life, we now turn
47 to the Gentiles. For these are our instructions from the Lord: "I have
appointed you to be a light for the Gentiles, and a means of salvation to
48 earth's farthest bounds." ' When the Gentiles heard this, they were overjoyed and thankfully acclaimed the word of the Lord, and those who were
49 marked out for eternal life became believers. So the word of the Lord
50 spread far and wide through the region. But the Jews stirred up feeling
among the women of standing who were worshippers, and among the
leading men of the city; a persecution was started against Paul and
51 Barnabas, and they were expelled from the district. So they shook the dust
52 off their feet in protest against them and went to Iconium. And the converts were filled with joy and with the Holy Spirit.

**14**   At Iconium similarly they went *b* into the Jewish synagogue and spoke to
such purpose that a large body both of Jews and Gentiles became believers.
2 But the unconverted Jews stirred up the Gentiles and poisoned their minds
3 against the Christians. For some time Paul and Barnabas stayed on and
spoke boldly and openly in reliance on the Lord; and he confirmed the
message of his grace by causing signs and miracles to be worked at their
4 hands. The mass of the townspeople were divided, some siding with the
5 Jews, others with the apostles. But when a move was made by Gentiles and
Jews together, with the connivance of the city authorities, to maltreat
6 them and stone them, they got wind of it and made their escape to the

---

*a Some witnesses read* first.         *b Or* At Iconium they went together . . .

Lycaonian cities of Lystra and Derbe and the surrounding country, where 7
they continued to spread the good news.

At Lystra sat a crippled man, lame from birth, who had never walked in 8
his life. This man listened while Paul was speaking. Paul fixed his eyes on 9
him and saw that he had the faith to be cured, so he said to him in a loud 10
voice, 'Stand up straight on your feet'; and he sprang up and started to
walk. When the crowds saw what Paul had done, they shouted, in their 11
native Lycaonian, 'The gods have come down to us in human form.' And 12
they called Barnabas Jupiter, and Paul they called Mercury, because he
was the spokesman. And the priest of Jupiter, whose temple was just out- 13
side the city, brought oxen and garlands to the gates, and he and all the
people were about to offer sacrifice.

But when the apostles Barnabas and Paul heard of it, they tore their 14
clothes and rushed into the crowd shouting, 'Men, what is this that you 15
are doing? We are only human beings, no less mortal than you. The good
news we bring tells you to turn from these follies to the living God, who
made heaven and earth and sea and everything in them. In past ages he 16
allowed all nations to go their own way; and yet he has not left you without 17
some clue to his nature, in the kindness he shows: he sends you rain from
heaven and crops in their seasons, and gives you food and good cheer in
plenty.'

With these words they barely managed to prevent the crowd from offer- 18
ing sacrifice to them.

Then Jews from Antioch and Iconium came on the scene and won over 19
the crowds. They stoned Paul, and dragged him out of the city, thinking
him dead. The converts formed a ring round him, and he got to his feet 20
and went into the city. Next day he left with Barnabas for Derbe.

After bringing the good news to that town, where they gained many 21
converts, they returned to Lystra, then to Iconium, and then to Antioch,
heartening the converts and encouraging them to be true to their religion. 22
They warned them that to enter the kingdom of God we must pass through
many hardships. They also appointed elders for them in each congrega- 23
tion, and with prayer and fasting committed them to the Lord in whom
they had put their faith.

Then they passed through Pisidia and came into Pamphylia. When they 24 25
had given the message at Perga, they went down to Attalia, and from there 26
set sail for Antioch, where they had originally been commended to the grace
of God for the task which they had now completed. When they arrived 27
and had called the congregation together, they reported all that God had
done through them, and how he had thrown open the gates of faith to the
Gentiles. And they stayed for some time with the disciples there. 28

NOW CERTAIN PERSONS who had come down from Judaea began to 15
teach the brotherhood that those who were not circumcised in accordance
with Mosaic practice could not be saved. That brought them into fierce 2
dissension and controversy with Paul and Barnabas. And so it was arranged
that these two and some others from Antioch should go up to Jerusalem
to see the apostles and elders about this question.

3    They were sent on their way by the congregation, and travelled through
Phoenicia and Samaria, telling the full story of the conversion of the
Gentiles. The news caused great rejoicing among all the Christians there.
4  ' When they reached Jerusalem they were welcomed by the church and
the apostles and elders, and reported all that God had done through them.
5  Then some of the Pharisaic party who had become believers came forward
and said, 'They must be circumcised and told to keep the Law of Moses.'
6 7  The apostles and elders held a meeting to look into this matter; and,
after a long debate, Peter rose and addressed them. 'My friends,' he said,
'in the early days, as you yourselves know, God made his choice among
you and ordained that from my lips the Gentiles should hear and believe
8  the message of the Gospel. And God, who can read men's minds, showed
his approval of them by giving the Holy Spirit to them, as he did to us.
9  He made no difference between them and us; for he purified their hearts
10  by faith. Then why do you now provoke God by laying on the shoulders
of these converts a yoke which neither we nor our fathers were able to
11  bear? No, we believe that it is by the grace of the Lord Jesus that we are
saved, and so are they.'
12   At that the whole company fell silent and listened to Barnabas and Paul
as they told of all the signs and miracles that God had worked among the
Gentiles through them.
13   When they had finished speaking, James summed up: 'My friends,' he
14  said, 'listen to me. Simeon has told how it first happened that God took
notice of the Gentiles, to choose from among them a people to bear his
15  name; and this agrees with the words of the prophets, as Scripture has it:

16    "Thereafter I will return and rebuild the fallen house of David;
even from its ruins I will rebuild it, and set it up again,
17    that they may seek the Lord—all the rest of mankind,
and the Gentiles, whom I have claimed for my own.
Thus says the Lord, whose work it is,
18    made known long ago."

19   'My judgement therefore is that we should impose no irksome restric-
20  tions on those of the Gentiles who are turning to God, but instruct them
by letter to abstain from things polluted by contact with idols, from fornica-
21  tion, from anything that has been strangled, and from blood.*a* Moses,
after all, has never lacked spokesmen in every town for generations past;
he is read in the synagogues Sabbath by Sabbath.'
22   Then the apostles and elders, with the agreement of the whole church,
resolved to choose representatives and send them to Antioch with Paul and
Barnabas. They chose two leading men in the community, Judas Barsabbas
23  and Silas, and gave them this letter to deliver:
'We, the apostles and elders, send greetings as brothers to our brothers
24  of gentile origin in Antioch, Syria, and Cilicia. Forasmuch as we have
heard that some of our number, without any instructions from us, have *b*

---

*a  Some witnesses omit* from fornication; *others omit* from anything that has been strangled;
*some add (after* blood) and to refrain from doing to others what they would not like done
to themselves.        *b  Some witnesses read* have gone out and . . .

disturbed you with their talk and unsettled your minds, we have resolved 25
unanimously to send to you our chosen representatives with our well-
beloved Barnabas and Paul, who have devoted themselves to the cause of 26
our Lord Jesus Christ. We are therefore sending Judas and Silas, who will 27
themselves confirm this by word of mouth. It is the decision of the Holy 28
Spirit, and our decision, to lay no further burden upon you beyond these
essentials: you are to abstain from meat that has been offered to idols, from 29
blood, from anything that has been strangled,*a* and from fornication.*b* If
you keep yourselves free from these things you will be doing right.
Farewell.'

So they were sent off on their journey and travelled down to Antioch, 30
where they called the congregation together, and delivered the letter.
When it was read, they all rejoiced at the encouragement it brought. Judas 31 32
and Silas, who were prophets themselves, said much to encourage and
strengthen the members, and, after spending some time there, were dis- 33
missed with the good wishes of the brethren, to return to those who had
sent them.*c* But Paul and Barnabas stayed on at Antioch, and there, along 35
with many others, they taught and preached the word of the Lord.

## *Paul leads the advance*

AFTER A WHILE Paul said to Barnabas, 'Ought we not to go back now 36
to see how our brothers are faring in the various towns where we
proclaimed the word of the Lord?' Barnabas wanted to take John Mark 37
with them; but Paul judged that the man who had deserted them in 38
Pamphylia and had not gone on to share in their work was not the man to
take with them now. The dispute was so sharp that they parted company. 39
Barnabas took Mark with him and sailed for Cyprus, while Paul chose Silas. 40
He started on his journey, commended by the brothers to the grace of the
Lord, and travelled through Syria and Cilicia bringing new strength to the 41
congregations.

He went on to Derbe and to Lystra, and there he found a disciple named 16
Timothy, the son of a Jewish Christian mother and a Gentile father. He 2
was well spoken of by the Christians at Lystra and Iconium, and Paul 3
wanted to have him in his company when he left the place. So he took him
and circumcised him, out of consideration for the Jews who lived in those
parts; for they all knew that his father was a Gentile. As they made their 4
way from town to town they handed on the decisions taken by the apostles
and elders in Jerusalem and enjoined their observance. And so, day by day, 5
the congregations grew stronger in faith and increased in numbers.

They travelled through the Phrygian and Galatian region,*d* because 6
they were prevented by the Holy Spirit from delivering the message in
the province of Asia; and when they approached the Mysian border they 7

*a Some witnesses omit* from anything that has been strangled.        *b Some witnesses
omit* and from fornication; *and some add* and refrain from doing to others what you would
not like done to yourselves.        *c Some witnesses add* (34) But Silas decided to
remain there.        *d Or* through Phrygia and the Galatian region.

8   tried to enter Bithynia; but the Spirit of Jesus would not allow them, so
9   they skirted*ᵃ* Mysia and reached the coast at Troas. During the night a
    vision came to Paul: a Macedonian stood there appealing to him and say-
10  ing, 'Come across to Macedonia and help us.' After he had seen this vision
    we at once set about getting a passage to Macedonia, concluding that God
    had called us to bring them the good news.

11      So we sailed from Troas and made a straight run to Samothrace, the
12  next day to Neapolis, and from there to Philippi, a city of the first rank in
    that district of Macedonia, and a Roman colony. Here we stayed for some
13  days, and on the Sabbath day we went outside the city gate by the river-
    side, where we thought there would be a place of prayer,*ᵇ* and sat down and
14  talked to the women who had gathered there. One of them named Lydia,
    a dealer in purple fabric from the city of Thyatira, who was a worshipper
    of God, was listening, and the Lord opened her heart to respond to what
15  Paul said. She was baptized, and her household with her, and then she said
    to us, 'If you have judged me to be a believer in the Lord, I beg you to come
    and stay in my house.' And she insisted on our going.

16      Once, when we were on our way to the place of prayer, we met a slave-
    girl who was possessed by an oracular spirit and brought large profits to
17  her owners by telling fortunes. She followed Paul and the rest of us, shout-
    ing, 'These men are servants of the Supreme God, and are declaring to you
18  a way of salvation.' She did this day after day, until Paul could bear it no
    longer. Rounding on the spirit he said, 'I command you in the name of
    Jesus Christ to come out of her', and it went out there and then.

19      When the girl's owners saw that their hope of gain had gone, they seized
    Paul and Silas and dragged them to the city authorities in the main square;
20  and bringing them before the magistrates, they said, 'These men are
21  causing a disturbance in our city; they are Jews; they are advocating
22  customs which it is illegal for us Romans to adopt and follow.' The mob
    joined in the attack; and the magistrates tore off the prisoners' clothes and
23  ordered them to be flogged. After giving them a severe beating they flung
    them into prison and ordered the jailer to keep them under close guard.
24  In view of these orders, he put them in the inner prison and secured their
    feet in the stocks.

25      About midnight Paul and Silas, at their prayers, were singing praises to
26  God, and the other prisoners were listening, when suddenly there was such
    a violent earthquake that the foundations of the jail were shaken; all the
27  doors burst open and all the prisoners found their fetters unfastened. The
    jailer woke up to see the prison doors wide open, and assuming that the
28  prisoners had escaped, drew his sword intending to kill himself. But Paul
29  shouted, 'Do yourself no harm; we are all here.' The jailer called for lights,
    rushed in and threw himself down before Paul and Silas, trembling with
30  fear. He then escorted them out and said, 'Masters, what must I do to be
31  saved?' They said, 'Put your trust in the Lord Jesus, and you will be saved,
32  you and your household.' Then they spoke the word of the Lord*ᶜ* to him
33  and to everyone in his house. At that late hour of the night he took them

---

*ᵃ Possibly* traversed.          *ᵇ Some witnesses read* where there was a recognized place
of prayer.     *ᶜ Some witnesses read* of God.

and washed their wounds; and immediately afterwards he and his whole
family were baptized. He brought them into his house, set out a meal, and 34
rejoiced with his whole household in his new-found faith in God.

When daylight came the magistrates sent their officers with instructions 35
to release the men. The jailer reported the message to Paul: 'The magistrates 36
have sent word that you are to be released. So now you may go free, and
blessings on your journey.'[a] But Paul said to the officers: 'They gave us a 37
public flogging, though we are Roman citizens and have not been found
guilty; they threw us into prison, and are they now to smuggle us out
privately? No indeed! Let them come in person and escort us out.' The 38
officers reported his words. The magistrates were alarmed to hear that they
were Roman citizens, and came and apologized to them. Then they 39
escorted them out and requested them to go away from the city. On leaving 40
the prison, they went to Lydia's house, where they met their fellow-
Christians, and spoke words of encouragement to them; then they departed.

THEY NOW TRAVELLED by way of Amphipolis and Apollonia and **17**
came to Thessalonica, where there was a Jewish synagogue. Following his 2
usual practice Paul went to their meetings; and for the next three Sabbaths
he argued with them, quoting texts of Scripture which he expounded and 3
applied to show that the Messiah had to suffer and rise from the dead.
'And this Jesus,' he said, 'whom I am proclaiming to you, is the Messiah.'
Some of them were convinced and joined Paul and Silas; so did a great 4
number of godfearing Gentiles and a good many influential women.[b]

But the Jews in their jealousy recruited some low fellows from the dregs 5
of the populace, roused the rabble, and had the city in an uproar. They
mobbed Jason's house, with the intention of bringing Paul and Silas before
the town assembly. Failing to find them, they dragged Jason himself and 6
some members of the congregation before the magistrates, shouting, 'The
men who have made trouble all over the world have now come here; and 7
Jason has harboured them. They all flout the Emperor's laws, and assert
that there is a rival king, Jesus.' These words caused a great commotion in 8
the mob, which affected the magistrates also. They bound over Jason and 9
the others, and let them go.

As soon as darkness fell, the members of the congregation sent Paul and 10
Silas off to Beroea. On arrival, they made their way to the synagogue. The 11
Jews here were more civil than those at Thessalonica: they received the
message with great eagerness, studying the scriptures every day to see
whether it was as they said. Many of them therefore became believers, 12
and so did a fair number of Gentiles, women of standing as well as men.
But when the Thessalonian Jews learned that the word of God had now 13
been proclaimed by Paul in Beroea, they came on here to stir up trouble
and rouse the rabble. Thereupon the members of the congregation sent 14
Paul off at once to go down to the coast, while Silas and Timothy both
stayed behind. Paul's escort brought him as far as Athens, and came away 15
with instructions for Silas and Timothy to rejoin him with all speed.

*a Some witnesses read . . .* free and take your journey.　　　*b Some witnesses read* a good
many wives of leading men.

16 Now while Paul was waiting for them at Athens he was exasperated to see
17 how the city was full of idols. So he argued in the synagogue with the Jews
and gentile worshippers, and also in the city square every day with casual
18 passers-by. And some of the Epicurean and Stoic philosophers joined
issue with him. Some said, 'What can this charlatan be trying to say?';
others, 'He would appear to be a propagandist for foreign deities'—this
19 because he was preaching about Jesus and Resurrection. So they took him
and brought him before the Court of Areopagus*a* and said, 'May we know
20 what this new doctrine is that you propound? You are introducing ideas
that sound strange to us, and we should like to know what they mean.'
21 (Now the Athenians in general and the foreigners there had no time for
anything but talking or hearing about the latest novelty.)

22 Then Paul stood up before the Court of Areopagus*b* and said: 'Men of
Athens, I see that in everything that concerns religion you are uncommonly
23 scrupulous. For as I was going round looking at the objects of your worship,
I noticed among other things an altar bearing the inscription "To an Unknown God". What you worship but do not know—this is what I now
proclaim.

24 'The God who created the world and everything in it, and who is Lord
25 of heaven and earth, does not live in shrines made by men. It is not because
he lacks anything that he accepts service at men's hands, for he is himself
26 the universal giver of life and breath and all else. He created every race of
men of one stock, to inhabit the whole earth's surface. He fixed the epochs
27 of their history*c* and the limits of their territory. They were to seek God,
and, it might be, touch and find him; though indeed he is not far from each
28 one of us, for in him we live and move, in him we exist; as some of your own
29 poets*d* have said, "We are also his offspring." As God's offspring, then,
we ought not to suppose that the deity is like an image in gold or silver or
30 stone, shaped by human craftsmanship and design. As for the times of
ignorance, God has overlooked them; but now he commands mankind, all
31 men everywhere, to repent, because he has fixed the day on which he will
have the world judged, and justly judged, by a man of his choosing; of this
he has given assurance to all by raising him from the dead.'

32 When they heard about the raising of the dead, some scoffed; and others
33 said, 'We will hear you on this subject some other time.' And so Paul left
34 the assembly. However, some men joined him and became believers,
including Dionysius, a member of the Court of Areopagus; also a woman
named Damaris, and others besides.

18 1 2 After this he left Athens and went to Corinth. There he fell in with a Jew
named Aquila, a native of Pontus, and his wife Priscilla; he had recently
arrived from Italy because Claudius had issued an edict that all Jews should
3 leave Rome. Paul approached them and, because he was of the same trade,
he made his home with them, and they carried on business together; they
4 were tent-makers. He also held discussions in the synagogue Sabbath by
Sabbath, trying to convince both Jews and Gentiles.
5 Then Silas and Timothy came down from Macedonia, and Paul devoted

---

*a Or* brought him to Mars' Hill.    *b Or* in the middle of Mars' Hill.    *c Or* fixed
the ordered seasons . . .    *d Some witnesses read* some among you.

himself entirely to preaching, affirming before the Jews that the Messiah was Jesus. But when they opposed him and resorted to abuse, he shook out 6 the skirts of his cloak and said to them, 'Your blood be on your own heads! My conscience is clear; now I shall go to the Gentiles.' With that he left, 7 and went to the house of a worshipper of God named Titius Justus, who lived next door to the synagogue. Crispus, who held office in the synagogue, 8 now became a believer in the Lord, with all his household; and a number of Corinthians listened and believed, and were baptized. One night in a 9 vision the Lord said to Paul, 'Have no fear: go on with your preaching and do not be silenced, for I am with you and no one shall attempt to do you 10 harm;*a* and there are many in this city who are my people.' So he settled 11 down for eighteen months, teaching the word of God among them.

But when Gallio was proconsul of Achaia, the Jews set upon Paul in a 12 body and brought him into court. 'This man', they said, 'is inducing people 13 to worship God in ways that are against the law.' Paul was just about to 14 speak when Gallio said to them, 'If it had been a question of crime or grave misdemeanour, I should, of course, have given you Jews a patient hearing, but if it is some bickering about words and names and your Jewish law, 15 you may see to it yourselves; I have no mind to be a judge of these matters.' And he had them ejected from the court. Then there was a general attack 16 17 on Sosthenes, who held office in the synagogue, and they gave him a beating in full view of the bench. But all this left Gallio quite unconcerned.

Paul stayed on for some time, and then took leave of the brotherhood 18 and set sail for Syria, accompanied by Priscilla and Aquila. At Cenchreae he had his hair cut off, because he was under a vow. When they reached 19 Ephesus he parted from them and went himself into the synagogue, where he held a discussion with the Jews. He was asked to stay longer, but declined 20 and set out from Ephesus, saying, as he took leave of them, 'I shall come 21 back to you if it is God's will.' On landing at Caesarea, he went up and 22 paid his respects to the church, and then went down to Antioch. After 23 spending some time there, he set out again and made a journey through the Galatian country and on through Phrygia, bringing new strength to all the converts.

NOW THERE ARRIVED at Ephesus a Jew named Apollos, an Alexandrian 24 by birth, an eloquent man,*b* powerful in his use of the scriptures. He had 25 been instructed in the way of the Lord and was full of spiritual fervour; and in his discourses he taught accurately the facts about Jesus,*c* though he knew only John's baptism. He now began to speak boldly in the syna- 26 gogue, where Priscilla and Aquila heard him; they took him in hand and expounded the new way*d* to him in greater detail. Finding that he wished 27 to go across to Achaia, the brotherhood gave him their support, and wrote to the congregation there to make him welcome. From the time of his arrival, he was very helpful to those who had by God's grace become believers; for he strenuously confuted the Jews, demonstrating publicly 28 from the scriptures that the Messiah is Jesus.

*a*   *Or* and you will not be harmed by anyone's attacks.      *b*   *Or* a learned man.
*c*   *Some witnesses read* about the Lord.     *d*   *Some witnesses read* the way of God.

**19** While Apollos was at Corinth, Paul travelled through the inland regions
2 till he came to Ephesus. There he found a number of converts, to whom he
said, 'Did you receive the Holy Spirit when you became believers?' 'No,'
3 they replied, 'we have not even heard that there is a Holy Spirit.' He said,
'Then what baptism were you given?' 'John's baptism', they answered.
4 Paul then said, 'The baptism that John gave was a baptism in token of
repentance, and he told the people to put their trust in one who was to
5 come after him, that is, in Jesus.' On hearing this they were baptized into
6 the name of the Lord Jesus; and when Paul had laid his hands on them, the
Holy Spirit came upon them and they spoke in tongues of ecstasy and
7 prophesied. Altogether they were about a dozen men.

8   During the next three months he attended the synagogue and, using
argument and persuasion, spoke boldly and freely about the kingdom of
9 God. But when some proved obdurate and would not believe, speaking
evil of the new way before the whole congregation, he left them, withdrew
his converts, and continued to hold discussions daily in the lecture-hall
10 of Tyrannus. This went on for two years, with the result that the whole
population of the province of Asia, both Jews and Gentiles, heard the word
11 12 of the Lord. And through Paul God worked singular miracles: when
handkerchiefs and scarves which had been in contact with his skin were
carried to the sick, they were rid of their diseases and the evil spirits came
out of them.

13   But some strolling Jewish exorcists tried their hand at using the name
of the Lord Jesus on those possessed by evil spirits; they would say, 'I
14 adjure you by Jesus whom Paul proclaims.' There were seven sons of
15 Sceva, a Jewish chief priest, who were using this method, when the evil
spirit answered back and said, 'Jesus I acknowledge, and I know about
16 Paul, but who are you?' And the man with the evil spirit flew at them, overpowered them all, and handled them with such violence that they ran out
17 of the house stripped and battered. This became known to everybody in
Ephesus, whether Jew or Gentile; they were all awestruck, and the name
18 of the Lord Jesus gained in honour. Moreover many of those who had
become believers came and openly confessed that they had been using
19 magical spells. And a good many of those who formerly practised magic
collected their books and burnt them publicly. The total value was reckoned
20 up and it came to fifty thousand pieces of silver. In such ways the word of
the Lord showed its power, spreading more and more widely and effec-
tively.

21   When things had reached this stage, Paul made up his mind*a* to visit
Macedonia and Achaia and then go on to Jerusalem; and he said, 'After I
22 have been there, I must see Rome also.' So he sent two of his assistants,
Timothy and Erastus, to Macedonia, while he himself stayed some time
longer in the province of Asia.

23   Now about that time, the Christian movement gave rise to a serious dis-
24 turbance. There was a man named Demetrius, a silversmith who made
silver shrines of Diana and provided a great deal of employment for the
25 craftsmen. He called a meeting of these men and the workers in allied

---

*a* Or Paul, led by the Spirit, resolved . . .

trades, and addressed them. 'Men,' he said, 'you know that our high standard of living depends on this industry. And you see and hear how this 26 fellow Paul with his propaganda has perverted crowds of people, not only at Ephesus but also in practically the whole of the province of Asia. He is telling them that gods made by human hands are not gods at all. There is 27 danger for us here; it is not only that our line of business will be discredited, but also that the sanctuary of the great goddess Diana will cease to command respect; and then it will not be long before she who is worshipped by all Asia and the civilized world is brought down from her divine pre-eminence.'

When they heard this they were roused to fury and shouted, 'Great is 28 Diana of the Ephesians!' The whole city was in confusion; they seized 29 Paul's travelling-companions, the Macedonians Gaius and Aristarchus, and made a concerted rush with them into the theatre. Paul wanted to 30 appear before the assembly but the other Christians would not let him. Even some of the dignitaries of the province, who were friendly towards 31 him, sent and urged him not to venture into the theatre. Meanwhile some 32 were shouting one thing, some another; for the assembly was in confusion and most of them did not know what they had all come for. But some of the 33 crowd explained the trouble to Alexander, whom the Jews had pushed to the front, and he, motioning for silence, attempted to make a defence before the assembly. But when they recognized that he was a Jew, a single 34 cry arose from them all: for about two hours they kept on shouting, 'Great is Diana of the Ephesians!'

The town clerk, however, quieted the crowd. 'Men of Ephesus,' he said, 35 'all the world knows that our city of Ephesus is temple-warden of the great Diana and of that symbol of her which fell from heaven. Since these facts 36 are beyond dispute, your proper course is to keep quiet and do nothing rash. These men whom you have brought here as culprits have committed 37 no sacrilege and uttered no blasphemy against our goddess. If therefore 38 Demetrius and his craftsmen have a case against anyone, assizes are held and there are such people as proconsuls; let the parties bring their charges and countercharges. If, on the other hand, you have some further question 39 to raise, it will be dealt with in the statutory assembly. We certainly run the 40 risk of being charged with riot for this day's work. There is no justification for it, and if the issue is raised we shall be unable to give any explanation of this uproar.' With that he dismissed the assembly. 41

WHEN THE DISTURBANCE had ceased, Paul sent for the disciples and, **20** after encouraging them, said good-bye and set out on his journey to Macedonia. He travelled through those parts of the country, often speaking 2 words of encouragement to the Christians there, and so came into Greece. When he had spent three months there and was on the point of embarking 3 for Syria, a plot was laid against him by the Jews, so he decided to return by way of Macedonia. He was accompanied by Sopater son of Pyrrhus, 4 from Beroea, the Thessalonians Aristarchus and Secundus, Gaius the Doberian[a] and Timothy, and the Asians Tychicus and Trophimus. These 5

---

[a] *Some witnesses read* the Derbaean.

6   went ahead and waited for us at Troas; we ourselves set sail from Philippi after the Passover season,*a* and in five days reached them at Troas, where we spent a week.

7   On the Saturday night, in our assembly for the breaking of bread, Paul, who was to leave next day, addressed them, and went on speaking until mid-
8   night. Now there were many lamps in the upper room where we were
9   assembled; and a youth named Eutychus, who was sitting on the window-ledge, grew more and more sleepy as Paul went on talking. At last he was completely overcome by sleep, fell from the third storey to the ground,
10  and was picked up for dead. Paul went down, threw himself upon him, seizing him in his arms, and said to them, 'Stop this commotion; there is
11  still life in him.' He then went upstairs, broke bread and ate, and after
12  much conversation, which lasted until dawn, he departed. And they took the boy away alive and were immensely comforted.

13  We went ahead to the ship and sailed for Assos, where we were to take Paul aboard. He had made this arrangement, as he was going to travel by
14  road. When he met us at Assos, we took him aboard and went on to Mity-
15  lene. Next day we sailed from there and arrived opposite Chios, and on the second day we made Samos. On the following day*b* we reached Miletus.
16  For Paul had decided to pass by Ephesus and so avoid having to spend time in the province of Asia; he was eager to be in Jerusalem, if he possibly
17  could, on the day of Pentecost. He did, however, send from Miletus to
18  Ephesus and summon the elders of the congregation; and when they joined him, he spoke as follows:

'You know how, from the day that I first set foot in the province of Asia,
19  for the whole time that I was with you, I served the Lord in all humility amid the sorrows and trials that came upon me through the machinations
20  of the Jews. You know that I kept back nothing that was for your good: I delivered the message to you; I taught you, in public and in your homes;
21  with Jews and Gentiles alike I insisted on repentance before God and
22  trust in our Lord Jesus. And now, as you see, I am on my way to Jerusalem, under the constraint of the Spirit.*c* Of what will befall me there I know
23  nothing, except that in city after city the Holy Spirit assures me that
24  imprisonment and hardships await me. For myself, I set no store by life; I only want to finish the race, and complete the task which the Lord Jesus assigned to me, of bearing my testimony to the gospel of God's grace.

25  'One word more: I have gone about among you proclaiming the King-
26  dom, but now I know that none of you will see my face again. That being
27  so, I here and now declare that no man's fate can be laid at my door; for I have kept back nothing; I have disclosed to you the whole purpose of
28  God. Keep watch over yourselves and over all the flock of which the Holy Spirit has given you charge, as shepherds of the church of the Lord,*d*
29  which he won for himself by his own blood.*e* I know that when I am gone,
30  savage wolves will come in among you and will not spare the flock. Even

---

*a Literally* after the days of Unleavened Bread.       *b Some witnesses read* . . . Samos, and, after stopping at Trogyllium, on the following day . . .       *c Or* under an inner compulsion.       *d Some witnesses read* of God.       *e Or, according to some witnesses,* by the blood of his Own.

from your own body there will be men coming forward who will distort
the truth to induce the disciples to break away and follow them. So be on 31
the alert; remember how for three years, night and day, I never ceased to
counsel each of you, and how I wept over you.

'And now I commend you to God and to his gracious word, which has 32
power to build you up and give you your heritage among all who are
dedicated to him. I have not wanted anyone's money or clothes for myself; 33
you all know that these hands of mine earned enough for the needs of my- 34
self and my companions. I showed you that it is our duty to help the weak 35
in this way, by hard work, and that we should keep in mind the words of
the Lord Jesus, who himself said, "Happiness lies more in giving than in
receiving."'

As he finished speaking, he knelt down with them all and prayed. Then 36 37
there were loud cries of sorrow from them all, as they folded Paul in their
arms and kissed him. What distressed them most was his saying that they 38
would never see his face again. So they escorted him to his ship.

When we had parted from them and set sail, we made a straight run and **21**
came to Cos; next day to Rhodes, and thence to Patara.*a* There we found 2
a ship bound for Phoenicia, so we went aboard and sailed in her. We came 3
in sight of Cyprus, and leaving it to port, we continued our voyage to Syria,
and put in at Tyre, for there the ship was to unload her cargo. We went and 4
found the disciples and stayed there a week; and they, warned by the
Spirit, urged Paul to abandon his visit to Jerusalem. But when our time 5
ashore was ended, we left and continued our journey; and they and their
wives and children all escorted us out of the city. We knelt down on the
beach and prayed, then bade each other good-bye; we went aboard, and 6
they returned home.

We made the passage from Tyre and reached Ptolemais, where we 7
greeted the brotherhood and spent one day with them. Next day we left 8
and came to Caesarea. We went to the home of Philip the evangelist, who
was one of the Seven, and stayed with him. He had four unmarried 9
daughters, who possessed the gift of prophecy. When we had been there 10
several days, a prophet named Agabus arrived from Judaea. He came to us, 11
took Paul's belt, bound his own feet and hands with it, and said, 'These
are the words of the Holy Spirit: Thus will the Jews in Jerusalem bind the
man to whom this belt belongs, and hand him over to the Gentiles.' When 12
we heard this, we and the local people begged and implored Paul to
abandon his visit to Jerusalem. Then Paul gave his answer: 'Why all these 13
tears? Why are you trying to weaken my resolution? For my part I am
ready not merely to be bound but even to die at Jerusalem for the name of
the Lord Jesus.' So, as he would not be persuaded, we gave up and said, 14
'The Lord's will be done.'

At the end of our stay we packed our baggage and took the road up to 15
Jerusalem. Some of the disciples from Caesarea came along with us, bring- 16
ing a certain Mnason of Cyprus, a Christian from the early days, with
whom we were to lodge. So we reached Jerusalem, where the brotherhood 17
welcomed us gladly.

*a Some witnesses add* and Myra.

18    Next day Paul paid a visit to James; we were with him, and all the elders
19    attended. He greeted them, and then described in detail all that God had
20    done among the Gentiles through his ministry. When they heard this,
      they gave praise to God. Then they said to Paul: 'You see, brother, how
      many thousands of converts we have among the Jews, all of them staunch
21`   upholders of the Law. Now they have been given certain information
      about you: it is said that you teach all the Jews in the gentile world to turn
      their backs on Moses, telling them to give up circumcising their children
22    and following our way of life. What is the position, then? They are sure to
23    hear that you have arrived. You must therefore do as we tell you. We have
24    four men here who are under a vow; take them with you and go through the
      ritual of purification with them, paying their expenses, after which they
      may shave their heads. Then everyone will know that there is nothing in
      the stories they were told about you, but that you are a practising Jew
25    and keep the Law yourself. As for the gentile converts, we sent them our
      decision that they must abstain from meat that has been offered to idols,
      from blood, from anything that has been strangled,*a* and from fornication.'
26    So Paul took the four men, and next day, after going through the ritual of
      purification with them, he went into the temple to give notice of the date
      when the period of purification would end and the offering be made for
      each one of them.

## From Jerusalem to Rome

27    BUT JUST BEFORE the seven days were up, the Jews from the province
      of Asia saw him in the temple. They stirred up the whole crowd, and
28    seized him, shouting, 'Men of Israel, help, help! This is the fellow who
      spreads his doctrine all over the world, attacking our people, our law, and
      this sanctuary. On top of all this he has brought Gentiles into the temple
29    and profaned this holy place.' For they had previously seen Trophimus
      the Ephesian with him in the city, and assumed that Paul had brought him
      into the temple.
30       The whole city was in a turmoil, and people came running from all
      directions. They seized Paul and dragged him out of the temple; and at
31    once the doors were shut. While they were clamouring for his death, a
      report reached the officer commanding the cohort, that all Jerusalem was in
32    an uproar. He immediately took a force of soldiers with their centurions
      and came down on the rioters at the double. As soon as they saw the
33    commandant and his troops, they stopped beating Paul. The commandant
      stepped forward, arrested him, and ordered him to be shackled with two
34    chains; he then asked who the man was and what he had been doing. Some
      in the crowd shouted one thing, some another. As he could not get at the
      truth because of the hubbub, he ordered him to be taken into barracks.
35    When Paul reached the steps, he had to be carried by the soldiers because
36    of the violence of the mob. For the whole crowd were at their heels yelling,
      'Kill him!'

      *a Some witnesses omit* from anything that has been strangled.

Just before Paul was taken into the barracks he said to the commandant, 37
'May I have a word with you?' The commandant said, 'So you speak
Greek, do you? Then you are not the Egyptian who started a revolt some 38
time ago and led a force of four thousand terrorists out into the wilds?'
Paul replied, 'I am a Jew, a Tarsian from Cilicia, a citizen of no mean city. 39
I ask your permission to speak to the people.' When permission had been 40
given, Paul stood on the steps and with a gesture called for the attention of
the people. As soon as quiet was restored, he addressed them in the Jewish
language:

'Brothers and fathers, give me a hearing while I make my defence before **22**
you.' When they heard him speaking to them in their own language, they 2
listened the more quietly. 'I am a true-born Jew,' he said, 'a native of 3
Tarsus in Cilicia. I was brought up in this city, and as a pupil of Gamaliel
I was thoroughly trained in every point of our ancestral law. I have always
been ardent in God's service, as you all are today. And so I began to per- 4
secute this movement to the death, arresting its followers, men and
women alike, and putting them in chains. For this I have as witnesses the 5
High Priest and the whole Council of Elders. I was given letters from them
to our fellow-Jews at Damascus, and had started out to bring the Christians
there to Jerusalem as prisoners for punishment; and this is what happened. 6
I was on the road and nearing Damascus, when suddenly about midday a
great light flashed from the sky all around me, and I fell to the ground. 7
Then I heard a voice saying to me, "Saul, Saul, why do you persecute me?"
I answered, "Tell me, Lord, who you are." "I am Jesus of Nazareth," he 8
said, "whom you are persecuting." My companions saw the light, but did 9
not hear the voice that spoke to me. "What shall I do, Lord?" I said, and 10
the Lord replied, "Get up and continue your journey to Damascus; there
you will be told of all the tasks that are laid upon you." As I had been 11
blinded by the brilliance of that light, my companions led me by the hand,
and so I came to Damascus.

'There, a man called Ananias, a devout observer of the Law and well 12
spoken of by all the Jews of that place, came and stood beside me and said, 13
"Saul, my brother, recover your sight." Instantly I recovered my sight and
saw him. He went on: "The God of our fathers appointed you to know his 14
will and to see the Righteous One and to hear his very voice, because you 15
are to be his witness before the world, and testify to what you have seen
and heard. And now why delay? Be baptized at once, with invocation of 16
his name, and wash away your sins."

'After my return to Jerusalem, I was praying in the temple when I fell 17
into a trance and saw him there, speaking to me. "Make haste", he said, 18
"and leave Jerusalem without delay, for they will not accept your testimony
about me." "Lord," I said, "they know that I imprisoned those who believe 19
in thee, and flogged them in every synagogue; and when the blood of 20
Stephen thy witness was shed I stood by, approving, and I looked after
the clothes of those who killed him." But he said to me, "Go, for I am send- 21
ing you far away to the Gentiles." '

Up to this point they had given him a hearing; but now they began 22
shouting, 'Down with him! A scoundrel like that is better dead!' And as 23

24 they were yelling and waving their cloaks and flinging dust in the air, the commandant ordered him to be brought into the barracks and gave instructions to examine him by flogging, and find out what reason there
25 was for such an outcry against him. But when they tied him up for the lash,*a* Paul said to the centurion who was standing there, 'Can you legally flog a man who is a Roman citizen, and moreover has not been found
26 guilty?' When the centurion heard this, he went and reported it to the commandant. 'What do you mean to do?' he said. 'This man is a Roman
27 citizen.' The commandant came to Paul. 'Tell me, are you a Roman
28 citizen?' he asked. 'Yes', said he. The commandant rejoined, 'It cost me a large sum to acquire this citizenship.' Paul said, 'But it was mine by birth.'
29 Then those who were about to examine him withdrew hastily, and the commandant himself was alarmed when he realized that Paul was a Roman citizen and that he had put him in irons.

30 THE FOLLOWING DAY, wishing to be quite sure what charge the Jews were bringing against Paul, he released him and ordered the chief priests and the entire Council to assemble. He then took Paul down and stood him before them.

**23** Paul fixed his eyes on the Council and said, 'My brothers, I have lived all my life, and still live today, with a perfectly clear conscience before God.'
2 At this the High Priest Ananias ordered his attendants to strike him on the
3 mouth. Paul retorted, 'God will strike you, you whitewashed wall! You sit there to judge me in accordance with the Law; and then in defiance of
4 the Law you order me to be struck!' The attendants said, 'Would you insult
5 God's High Priest?' 'My brothers,' said Paul, 'I had no idea that he was High Priest; Scripture, I know, says: "You must not abuse the ruler of your people."'
6 Now Paul was well aware that one section of them were Sadducees and the other Pharisees, so he called out in the Council, 'My brothers, I am a Pharisee, a Pharisee born and bred; and the true issue in this trial is our
7 hope of the resurrection of the dead.' At these words the Pharisees and Sadducees fell out among themselves, and the assembly was divided.
8 (The Sadducees deny that there is any resurrection, or angel, or spirit, but
9 the Pharisees accept them.) So a great uproar broke out; and some of the doctors of the law belonging to the Pharisaic party openly took sides and declared, 'We can find no fault with this man; perhaps an angel or spirit
10 has spoken to him.' The dissension was mounting, and the commandant was afraid that Paul would be torn in pieces, so he ordered the troops to go down, pull him out of the crowd, and bring him into the barracks.
11 The following night the Lord appeared to him and said, 'Keep up your courage; you have affirmed the truth about me in Jerusalem, and you must do the same in Rome.'
12 When day broke, the Jews banded together and took an oath not to eat
13 or drink until they had killed Paul. There were more than forty in this
14 conspiracy. They came to the chief priests and elders and said, 'We have bound ourselves by a solemn oath not to taste food until we have killed

*a Or* tied him up with thongs.

Paul. It is now for you, acting with the Council, to apply to the com- 15
mandant to bring him down to you, on the pretext of a closer investigation
of his case; and we have arranged to do away with him before he arrives.'

But the son of Paul's sister heard of the ambush; he went to the barracks, 16
obtained entry, and reported it to Paul. Paul called one of the centurions 17
and said, 'Take this young man to the commandant; he has something to
report.' The centurion took him and brought him to the commandant. 18
'The prisoner Paul', he said, 'sent for me and asked me to bring this young
man to you; he has something to tell you.' The commandant took him by 19
the arm, drew him aside, and asked him, 'What is it you have to report?'
He said, 'The Jews have made a plan among themselves and will request 20
you to bring Paul down to the Council tomorrow, on the pretext of obtain-
ing more precise information about him. Do not listen to them; for a party 21
more than forty strong are lying in wait for him. They have sworn not to
eat or drink until they have done away with him; they are now ready, and
wait only for your consent.' So the commandant dismissed the young man, 22
with orders not to let anyone know that he had given him this information.

Then he called a couple of his centurions and issued these orders: 'Get 23
ready two hundred infantry to proceed to Caesarea, together with seventy
cavalrymen and two hundred light-armed troops;[a] parade three hours
after sunset. Provide also mounts for Paul so that he may ride through under 24
safe escort to Felix the Governor.' And he wrote a letter to this effect: 25
'Claudius Lysias to His Excellency the Governor Felix. Your Excel- 26
lency: This man was seized by the Jews and was on the point of being 27
murdered when I intervened with the troops and removed him, because
I discovered that he was a Roman citizen. As I wished to ascertain the 28
charge on which they were accusing him, I took him down to their Council.
I found that the accusation had to do with controversial matters in their 29
law, but there was no charge against him meriting death or imprisonment.
However, I have now been informed of an attempt to be made on the man's 30
life, so I am sending him to you at once, and have also instructed his
accusers to state their case against him before you.'[b]

Acting on their orders, the infantry took Paul and brought him by night 31
to Antipatris. Next day they returned to their barracks, leaving the cavalry 32
to escort him the rest of the way. The cavalry entered Caesarea, delivered 33
the letter to the Governor, and handed Paul over to him. He read the letter, 34
asked him what province he was from, and learned that he was from Cilicia.
'I will hear your case', he said, 'when your accusers arrive.' He then 35
ordered him to be held in custody at his headquarters in Herod's palace.

FIVE DAYS LATER the High Priest Ananias came down, accompanied by **24**
some of the elders and an advocate named Tertullus, and they laid an
information against Paul before the Governor. When the prisoner was 2
called, Tertullus opened the case.

'Your Excellency,' he said, 'we owe it to you that we enjoy unbroken
peace. It is due to your provident care that, in all kinds of ways and in all

---

[a] Or two hundred spearmen (*the meaning of the Greek word is uncertain*).
[b] *Some witnesses read* '. . . before you. Farewell.'

sorts of places, improvements are being made for the good of this province.
3 4 We welcome this, sir, most gratefully. And now, not to take up too much
5 of your time, I crave your indulgence for a brief statement of our case. We
have found this man to be a perfect pest, a fomenter of discord among the
6 Jews all over the world, a ringleader of the sect of the Nazarenes. He even
8 made an attempt to profane the temple; and then we arrested him. *a* If you
will examine him yourself you can ascertain from him the truth of all the
9 charges we bring.' The Jews supported the attack, alleging that the facts
were as he stated.
10    Then the Governor motioned to Paul to speak, and he began his reply:
'Knowing as I do that for many years you have administered justice in this
11 province, I make my defence with confidence. You can ascertain the facts
for yourself. It is not more than twelve days since I went up to Jerusalem
12 on a pilgrimage. They did not find me arguing with anyone, or collecting
a crowd, either in the temple or in the synagogues or up and down the city;
13 14 and they cannot make good the charges they bring against me. But this
much I will admit: I am a follower of the new way (the "sect" they speak of),
and it is in that manner that I worship the God of our fathers; for I believe
15 all that is written in the Law and the prophets, and in reliance on God I
hold the hope, which my accusers too accept, that there is to be a resur-
16 rection of good and wicked alike. Accordingly I, no less than they, train
myself to keep at all times a clear conscience before God and man.
17    'After an absence of several years I came to bring charitable gifts to my
18 nation and to offer sacrifices. They found me in the temple ritually purified
and engaged in this service. I had no crowd with me, and there was no
19 disturbance. But some Jews from the province of Asia were there, and if
they had any charge against me it is they who ought to have been in court
20 to state it. Failing that, it is for these persons here present to say what
21 crime they discovered when I was brought before the Council, apart from
this one open assertion which I made as I stood there: "The true issue in
my trial before you today is the resurrection of the dead."'
22    Then Felix, who happened to be well informed about the Christian
movement, adjourned the hearing. 'When Lysias the commanding officer
23 comes down', he said, 'I will go into your case.' He gave orders to the
centurion to keep Paul under open arrest and not to prevent any of his
friends from making themselves useful to him.
24    Some days later Felix came with his wife Drusilla, who was a Jewess,
and sending for Paul he let him talk to him about faith in Christ Jesus.
25 But when the discourse turned to questions of morals, self-control, and
the coming judgement, Felix became alarmed and exclaimed, 'That will
do for the present; when I find it convenient I will send for you again.'
26 At the same time he had hopes of a bribe from Paul; and for this reason he
27 sent for him very often and talked with him. When two years had passed,
Felix was succeeded by Porcius Festus. Wishing to curry favour with the
Jews, Felix left Paul in custody.

*a Some witnesses insert* It was our intention to try him under our law; (7) but Lysias the
commandant intervened and took him by force out of our hands, (8) ordering his accusers
to come before you.

THREE DAYS AFTER taking up his appointment Festus went up from **25**
Caesarea to Jerusalem, where the chief priests and the Jewish leaders 2
brought before him the case against Paul. They asked Festus to favour 3
them against him, and pressed for him to be brought up to Jerusalem, for
they were planning an ambush to kill him on the way. Festus, however, 4
replied, 'Paul is in safe custody at Caesarea, and I shall be leaving Jerusalem shortly myself; so let your leading men come down with me, and if 5
there is anything wrong, let them prosecute him.'

After spending eight or ten days at most in Jerusalem, he went down to 6
Caesarea, and next day he took his seat in court and ordered Paul to be
brought up. When he appeared, the Jews who had come down from 7
Jerusalem stood round bringing many grave charges, which they were
unable to prove. Paul's plea was: 'I have committed no offence, either 8
against the Jewish law, or against the temple, or against the Emperor.'
Festus, anxious to ingratiate himself with the Jews, turned to Paul and 9
asked, 'Are you willing to go up to Jerusalem and stand trial on these
charges before me there?' But Paul said, 'I am now standing before the 10
Emperor's tribunal, and that is where I must be tried. Against the Jews I
have committed no offence, as you very well know. If I am guilty of any 11
capital crime, I do not ask to escape the death penalty; but if there is no
substance in the charges which these men bring against me, it is not open
to anyone to hand me over as a sop to them. I appeal to Caesar!' Then 12
Festus, after conferring with his advisers, replied, 'You have appealed to
Caesar: to Caesar you shall go.'

After an interval of some days King Agrippa and Bernice arrived at 13
Caesarea on a courtesy visit to Festus. They spent several days there, and 14
during this time Festus laid Paul's case before the king. 'We have a man',
he said, 'left in custody by Felix; and when I was in Jerusalem the chief 15
priests and elders of the Jews laid an information against him, demanding
his condemnation. I answered them, "It is not Roman practice to hand over 16
any accused man before he is confronted with his accusers and given an
opportunity of answering the charge." So when they had come here with 17
me I lost no time; the very next day I took my seat in court and ordered the
man to be brought up. But when his accusers rose to speak, they brought 18
none of the charges I was expecting; they merely had certain points of dis- 19
agreement with him about their peculiar religion, and about someone
called Jesus, a dead man whom Paul alleged to be alive. Finding myself 20
out of my depth in such discussions, I asked if he was willing to go to
Jerusalem and stand his trial there on these issues. But Paul appealed to be 21
remanded in custody for His Imperial Majesty's decision, and I ordered
him to be detained until I could send him to the Emperor.' Agrippa said to 22
Festus, 'I should rather like to hear the man myself.' 'Tomorrow', he
answered, 'you shall hear him.'

So next day Agrippa and Bernice came in full state and entered the 23
audience-chamber accompanied by high-ranking officers and prominent
citizens; and on the orders of Festus Paul was brought up. Then Festus 24
said, 'King Agrippa, and all you gentlemen here present with us, you see
this man: the whole body of the Jews approached me both in Jerusalem

25 and here, loudly insisting that he had no right to remain alive. But it was
clear to me that he had committed no capital crime, and when he himself
26 appealed to His Imperial Majesty, I decided to send him. But I have
nothing definite about him to put in writing for our Sovereign. Accordingly I have brought him up before you all and particularly before you,
King Agrippa, so that as a result of this preliminary inquiry I may have
27 something to report. There is no sense, it seems to me, in sending on a
prisoner without indicating the charges against him.'

**26**      Agrippa said to Paul, 'You have our permission to speak for yourself.'
Then Paul stretched out his hand and began his defence:

2      'I consider myself fortunate, King Agrippa, that it is before you that I
am to make my defence today upon all the charges brought against me by
3 the Jews, particularly as you are expert in all Jewish matters, both our
customs and our disputes. And therefore I beg you to give me a patient
hearing.

4      'My life from my youth up, the life I led from the beginning among my
5 people and in Jerusalem, is familiar to all Jews. Indeed they have known me
long enough and could testify, if they only would, that I belonged to the
6 strictest group in our religion: I lived as a Pharisee. And it is for a hope
kindled by God's promise to our forefathers that I stand in the dock today.
7 Our twelve tribes hope to see the fulfilment of that promise, worshipping
with intense devotion day and night; and for this very hope I am im-
8 peached, and impeached by Jews, Your Majesty. Why is it considered
incredible among you that God should raise dead men to life?

9      'I myself once thought it my duty to work actively against the name of
10 Jesus of Nazareth; and I did so in Jerusalem. It was I who imprisoned many
of God's people by authority obtained from the chief priests; and when they
11 were condemned to death, my vote was cast against them. In all the synagogues I tried by repeated punishment to make them renounce their faith;
indeed my fury rose to such a pitch that I extended my persecution to
foreign cities.

12      'On one such occasion I was travelling to Damascus with authority and
13 commission from the chief priests; and as I was on my way, Your Majesty,
in the middle of the day I saw a light from the sky, more brilliant than the
14 sun, shining all around me and my travelling-companions. We all fell to
the ground, and then I heard a voice saying to me in the Jewish language,
"Saul, Saul, why do you persecute me? It is hard for you, this kicking
15 against the goad." I said, "Tell me, Lord, who you are"; and the Lord
16 replied, "I am Jesus, whom you are persecuting. But now, rise to your feet
and stand upright. I have appeared to you for a purpose: to appoint you
my servant and witness, to testify both to what you have seen and to what
17 you shall yet see of me. I will rescue you from this people and from the
18 Gentiles to whom I am sending you. I send you to open their eyes and turn
them from darkness to light, from the dominion of Satan to God, so that,
by trust in me, they may obtain forgiveness of sins, and a place with those
whom God has made his own."

19 20      'And so, King Agrippa, I did not disobey the heavenly vision. I turned
first to the inhabitants of Damascus, and then to Jerusalem and all the

country of Judaea, and to the Gentiles, and sounded the call to repent
and turn to God, and to prove their repentance by deeds. That is why the  21
Jews seized me in the temple and tried to do away with me. But I had God's  22
help, and so to this very day I stand and testify to great and small alike. I
assert nothing beyond what was foretold by the prophets and by Moses:
that the Messiah must suffer, and that he, the first to rise from the dead,  23
would announce the dawn to Israel and to the Gentiles.'

While Paul was thus making his defence, Festus shouted at the top of his  24
voice, 'Paul, you are raving; too much study is driving you mad.' 'I am  25
not mad, Your Excellency,' said Paul; 'what I am saying is sober truth.
The king is well versed in these matters, and to him I can speak freely.  26
I do not believe that he can be unaware of any of these facts, for this has
been no hole-and-corner business. King Agrippa, do you believe the  27
prophets? I know you do.' Agrippa said to Paul, 'You think it will not take  28
much to win me over and make a Christian of me.' 'Much or little,' said  29
Paul, 'I wish to God that not only you, but all those also who are listening
to me today, might become what I am, apart from these chains.'

With that the king rose, and with him the Governor, Bernice, and the  30
rest of the company, and after they had withdrawn they talked it over.  31
'This man', they said, 'is doing nothing that deserves death or imprisonment.' Agrippa said to Festus, 'The fellow could have been discharged, if  32
he had not appealed to the Emperor.'

WHEN IT WAS DECIDED that we should sail for Italy, Paul and some  **27**
other prisoners were handed over to a centurion named Julius, of the
Augustan Cohort. We embarked in a ship of Adramyttium, bound for  2
ports in the province of Asia, and put out to sea. In our party was Aristarchus, a Macedonian from Thessalonica. Next day we landed at Sidon;  3
and Julius very considerately allowed Paul to go to his friends to be cared
for. Leaving Sidon we sailed under the lee of Cyprus because of the head-  4
winds, then across the open sea off the coast of Cilicia and Pamphylia, and  5
so reached Myra in Lycia.

There the centurion found an Alexandrian vessel bound for Italy and  6
put us aboard. For a good many days we made little headway, and we were  7
hard put to it to reach Cnidus. Then, as the wind continued against us, off
Salmone we began to sail under the lee of Crete, and, hugging the coast,  8
struggled on to a place called Fair Havens, not far from the town of Lasea.

By now much time had been lost, the Fast was already over, and it was  9
risky to go on with the voyage. Paul therefore gave them this advice: 'I can  10
see, gentlemen,' he said, 'that this voyage will be disastrous: it will mean
grave loss, loss not only of ship and cargo but also of life.' But the centurion  11
paid more attention to the captain and to the owner of the ship than to
what Paul said; and as the harbour was unsuitable for wintering, the  12
majority were in favour of putting out to sea, hoping, if they could get so
far, to winter at Phoenix, a Cretan harbour exposed south-west and north-
west. So when a southerly breeze sprang up, they thought that their pur-  13
pose was as good as achieved, and, weighing anchor, they sailed along the
coast of Crete hugging the land. But before very long a fierce wind, the  14

15 'North-easter' as they call it, tore down from the landward side. It caught
the ship and, as it was impossible to keep head to wind, we had to give way
16 and run before it. We ran under the lee of a small island called Cauda, and
17 with a struggle managed to get the ship's boat under control. When they
had hoisted it aboard, they made use of tackle and undergirded the ship.
Then, because they were afraid of running on to the shallows of Syrtis,
18 they lowered the mainsail and let her drive. Next day, as we were making
19 very heavy weather, they began to lighten the ship; and on the third day
20 they jettisoned the ship's gear with their own hands. For days on end there
was no sign of either sun or stars, a great storm was raging, and our last
hopes of coming through alive began to fade.

21   When they had gone for a long time without food, Paul stood up among
them and said, 'You should have taken my advice, gentlemen, not to sail
22 from Crete; then you would have avoided this damage and loss. But now
23 I urge you not to lose heart; not a single life will be lost, only the ship. For
last night there stood by me an angel of the God whose I am and whom I
24 worship. "Do not be afraid, Paul," he said; "it is ordained that you shall
appear before the Emperor; and, be assured, God has granted you the
25 lives of all who are sailing with you." So keep up your courage: I trust in
26 God that it will turn out as I have been told; though we have to be cast
ashore on some island.'

27   The fourteenth night came and we were still drifting in the Sea of Adria.
In the middle of the night the sailors felt that land was getting nearer.
28 They sounded and found twenty fathoms. Sounding again after a short
29 interval they found fifteen fathoms; and fearing that we might be cast
ashore on a rugged coast they dropped four anchors from the stern and
30 prayed for daylight to come. The sailors tried to abandon ship; they had
already lowered the ship's boat, pretending they were going to lay out
31 anchors from the bows, when Paul said to the centurion and the soldiers,
32 'Unless these men stay on board you can none of you come off safely.' So
the soldiers cut the ropes of the boat and let her drop away.

33   Shortly before daybreak Paul urged them all to take some food. 'For
the last fourteen days', he said, 'you have lived in suspense and gone
34 hungry; you have eaten nothing whatever. So I beg you to have something
to eat; your lives depend on it. Remember, not a hair of your heads will be
35 lost.' With these words, he took bread, gave thanks to God in front of them
36 all, broke it, and began eating. Then they all plucked up courage, and took
37 food themselves. There were on board two hundred and seventy-six of us
38 in all. When they had eaten as much as they wanted they lightened the ship
by dumping the corn in the sea.

39   When day broke they could not recognize the land, but they noticed
a bay with a sandy beach, on which they planned, if possible, to run the
40 ship ashore. So they slipped the anchors and let them go; at the same time
they loosened the lashings of the steering-paddles, set the foresail to the
41 wind, and let her drive to the beach. But they found themselves caught
between cross-currents and ran the ship aground, so that the bow stuck
fast and remained immovable, while the stern was being pounded to pieces
42 by the breakers. The soldiers thought they had better kill the prisoners for

fear that any should swim away and escape; but the centurion wanted to  43
bring Paul safely through and prevented them from carrying out their plan.
He gave orders that those who could swim should jump overboard first
and get to land; the rest were to follow, some on planks, some on parts of  44
the ship. And thus it was that all came safely to land.

Once we had made our way to safety we identified the island as Malta. **28**
The rough islanders treated us with uncommon kindness: because it was  2
cold and had started to rain, they lit a bonfire and made us all welcome.
Paul had got together an armful of sticks and put them on the fire, when a  3
viper, driven out by the heat, fastened on his hand. The islanders, seeing  4
the snake hanging on to his hand, said to one another, 'The man must be
a murderer; he may have escaped from the sea, but divine justice has not
let him live.' Paul, however, shook off the snake into the fire and was none  5
the worse. They still expected that any moment he would swell up or drop  6
down dead, but after waiting a long time without seeing anything extraordinary happen to him, they changed their minds and now said, 'He is
a god.'

In the neighbourhood of that place there were lands belonging to the  7
chief magistrate of the island, whose name was Publius. He took us in and
entertained us hospitably for three days. It so happened that this man's  8
father was in bed suffering from recurrent bouts of fever and dysentery.
Paul visited him and, after prayer, laid his hands upon him and healed
him; whereupon the other sick people on the island came also and were  9
cured. They honoured us with many marks of respect, and when we were  10
leaving they put on board provision for our needs.

Three months had passed when we set sail in a ship which had wintered  11
in the island; she was the *Castor and Pollux* of Alexandria. We put in at  12
Syracuse and spent three days there; then we sailed round and arrived at  13
Rhegium. After one day a south wind sprang up and we reached Puteoli
in two days. There we found fellow-Christians and were invited to stay a  14
week with them. And so to Rome. The Christians there had had news of  15
us and came out to meet us as far as Appii Forum and Tres Tabernae, and
when Paul saw them, he gave thanks to God and took courage.

WHEN WE ENTERED ROME Paul was allowed to lodge by himself with a  16
soldier in charge of him. Three days later he called together the local  17
Jewish leaders; and when they were assembled, he said to them: 'My
brothers, I, who never did anything against our people or the customs of
our forefathers, am here as a prisoner; I was handed over to the Romans
at Jerusalem. They examined me and would have liked to release me be-  18
cause there was no capital charge against me; but the Jews objected, and  19
I had no option but to appeal to the Emperor; not that I had any accusation to bring against my own people. That is why I have asked to see you  20
and talk to you, because it is for the sake of the hope of Israel that I am in
chains, as you see.' They replied, 'We have had no communication from  21
Judaea, nor has any countryman of ours arrived with any report or gossip
to your discredit. We should like to hear from you what your views are;  22
all we know about this sect is that no one has a good word to say for it.'

23    So they fixed a day, and came in large numbers as his guests. He dealt at length with the whole matter; he spoke urgently of the kingdom of God and sought to convince them about Jesus by appealing to the Law of Moses
24  and the prophets. This went on from dawn to dusk. Some were won over
25  by his arguments; others remained sceptical. Without reaching any agreement among themselves they began to disperse, but not before Paul had said one thing more: 'How well the Holy Spirit spoke to your fathers
26  through the prophet Isaiah when he said, "Go to this people and say: You may hear and hear, but you will never understand; you may look and look,
27  but you will never see. For this people's mind has become gross; their ears are dulled, and their eyes are closed. Otherwise, their eyes might see, their ears hear, and their mind understand, and then they might turn again, and
28  I would heal them." Therefore take notice that this salvation of God has been sent to the Gentiles; the Gentiles will listen.'*a*
30    He stayed there two full years at his own expense, with a welcome for all
31  who came to him, proclaiming the kingdom of God and teaching the facts about the Lord Jesus Christ quite openly and without hindrance.

*a Some witnesses add* (29) After he had spoken, the Jews went away, arguing vigorously among themselves.

# LETTERS

# THE LETTER OF PAUL

# TO THE

# ROMANS

*The Gospel according to Paul*

FROM PAUL, SERVANT of Christ Jesus, apostle by God's call, 1
set apart for the service of the Gospel.

This gospel God announced beforehand in sacred scriptures 2
through his prophets. It is about his Son: on the human level he was born 3
of David's stock, but on the level of the spirit—the Holy Spirit—he was 4
declared Son of God by a mighty act in that he rose from the dead:[a] it is
about Jesus Christ our Lord. Through him I received the privilege of a 5
commission in his name to lead to faith and obedience men in all nations,
yourselves among them, you who have heard the call and belong to Jesus 6
Christ.

I send greetings to all of you in Rome whom God loves and has called 7
to be his dedicated people. Grace and peace to you from God our Father
and the Lord Jesus Christ.

Let me begin by thanking my God, through Jesus Christ, for you all, 8
because all over the world they are telling the story of your faith. God is 9
my witness, the God to whom I offer the humble service of my spirit by
preaching the gospel of his Son: God knows how continually I make
mention of you in my prayers, and am always asking that by his will I may, 10
somehow or other, succeed at long last in coming to visit you. For I long to 11
see you; I want to bring you some spiritual gift to make you strong; or 12
rather, I want to be among you to be myself encouraged by your faith as
well as you by mine.

But I should like you to know,[b] my brothers, that I have often planned 13
to come, though so far without success, in the hope of achieving something
among you, as I have in other parts of the world. I am under obligation to 14
Greek and non-Greek, to learned and simple; hence my eagerness to 15
declare the Gospel to you in Rome as well as to others. For I am not 16
ashamed of the Gospel. It is the saving power of God for everyone who
has faith—the Jew first, but the Greek also—because here is revealed 17
God's way of righting wrong, a way that starts from faith and ends
in faith;[c] as Scripture says, 'he shall gain life who is justified through
faith'.

[a] *Or* declared Son of God with full powers from the time when he rose from the dead.
[b] *Some witnesses read* I believe you know.　　　　[c] *Or* . . . wrong. It is based on faith
and addressed to faith.

18 FOR WE SEE divine retribution revealed from heaven and falling upon all
the godless wickedness of men. In their wickedness they are stifling the
19 truth. For all that may be known of God by men lies plain before their eyes;
20 indeed God himself has disclosed it to them. His invisible attributes, that
is to say his everlasting power and deity, have been visible, ever since the
world began, to the eye of reason, in the things he has made. There is
21 therefore no possible defence for their conduct; knowing God, they have
refused to honour him as God, or to render him thanks. Hence all their
thinking has ended in futility, and their misguided minds are plunged in
22 darkness. They boast of their wisdom, but they have made fools of them-
23 selves, exchanging the splendour of immortal God for an image shaped
like mortal man, even for images like birds, beasts, and creeping things.
24    For this reason God has given them up to the vileness of their own
25 desires, and the consequent degradation of their bodies, because they have
bartered away the true God for a false one,*ᵃ* and have offered reverence and
worship to created things instead of to the Creator, who is blessed for
ever; amen.
26    In consequence, I say, God has given them up to shameful passions.
27 Their women have exchanged natural intercourse for unnatural, and their
men in turn, giving up natural relations with women, burn with lust for
one another; males behave indecently with males, and are paid in their
own persons the fitting wage of such perversion.
28    Thus, because they have not seen fit to acknowledge God, he has given
them up to their own depraved reason. This leads them to break all rules
29 of conduct. They are filled with every kind of injustice, mischief, rapacity,
and malice; they are one mass of envy, murder, rivalry, treachery, and
30 malevolence; whisperers and scandal-mongers, hateful to God, insolent,
arrogant, and boastful; they invent new kinds of mischief, they show no
31 loyalty to parents, no conscience, no fidelity to their plighted word; they
32 are without natural affection and without pity. They know well enough the
just decree of God, that those who behave like this deserve to die, and yet
they do it; not only so, they actually applaud such practices.
2    You therefore have no defence—you who sit in judgement, whoever
you may be—for in judging your fellow-man you condemn yourself, since
2 you, the judge, are equally guilty. It is admitted that God's judgement is
3 rightly passed upon all who commit such crimes as these; and do you
imagine—you who pass judgement on the guilty while committing the
same crimes yourself—do you imagine that you, any more than they, will
4 escape the judgement of God? Or do you think lightly of his wealth of
kindness, of tolerance, and of patience, without recognizing that God's
5 kindness is meant to lead you to a change of heart? In the rigid obstinacy
of your heart you are laying up for yourself a store of retribution for the
6 day of retribution, when God's just judgement will be revealed, and he will
7 pay every man for what he has done. To those who pursue glory, honour,
and immortality by steady persistence in well-doing, he will give eternal
8 life; but for those who are governed by selfish ambition, who refuse
obedience to the truth and take the wrong for their guide, there will be

*ᵃ Or the truth of God for the lie.*

the fury of retribution. There will be trouble and distress for every human 9
being who is an evil-doer, for the Jew first and for the Greek also; and for 10
every well-doer there will be glory, honour, and peace, for the Jew first
and also for the Greek.

For God has no favourites: those who have sinned outside the pale of 11 12
the Law of Moses will perish outside its pale, and all who have sinned
under that law will be judged by the law. It is not by hearing the law, but 13
by doing it, that men will be justified before God. When Gentiles who do 14
not possess the law carry out its precepts by the light of nature, then,
although they have no law, they are their own law, for they display the 15
effect of the law inscribed on their hearts. Their conscience is called as
witness, and their own thoughts argue the case on either side, against them
or even for them, on the day when God judges the secrets of human hearts 16
through Christ Jesus. So my gospel declares.

But as for you—you may bear the name of Jew; you rely upon the law 17
and are proud of your God; you know his will; instructed by the law, you 18
know right from wrong; you are confident that you are the one to guide 19
the blind, to enlighten the benighted, to train the stupid, and to teach the 20
immature, because in the law you see the very shape of knowledge and
truth. You, then, who teach your fellow-man, do you fail to teach your- 21
self? You proclaim, 'Do not steal'; but are you yourself a thief? You say, 22
'Do not commit adultery'; but are you an adulterer? You abominate false
gods; but do you rob their shrines? While you take pride in the law, you 23
dishonour God by breaking it. For, as Scripture says, 'Because of you the 24
name of God is dishonoured among the Gentiles.'

Circumcision has value, provided you keep the law; but if you break the 25
law, then your circumcision is as if it had never been. Equally, if an un- 26
circumcised man keeps the precepts of the law, will he not count as circumcised? He may be uncircumcised in his natural state, but by fulfilling 27
the law he will pass judgement on you who break it, for all your written
code and your circumcision. The true Jew is not he who is such in externals, 28
neither is the true circumcision the external mark in the flesh. The true 29
Jew is he who is such inwardly, and the true circumcision is of the heart,
directed not by written precepts but by the Spirit; such a man receives his
commendation not from men but from God.

Then what advantage has the Jew? What is the value of circumcision? **3**
Great, in every way. In the first place, the Jews were entrusted with the 2
oracles of God. What if some of them were unfaithful? Will their faithless- 3
ness cancel the faithfulness of God? Certainly not! God must be true 4
though every man living were a liar; for we read in Scripture, 'When thou
speakest thou shalt be vindicated, and win the verdict when thou art
on trial.'

Another question: if our injustice serves to bring out God's justice, what 5
are we to say? Is it unjust of God (I speak of him in human terms) to bring
retribution upon us? Certainly not! If God were unjust, how could he 6
judge the world?

Again, if the truth of God brings him all the greater honour because of 7
my falsehood, why should I any longer be condemned as a sinner? Why 8

not indeed 'do evil that good may come', as some libellously report me as saying? To condemn such men as these is surely no injustice.

9 What then? Are we Jews any better off?[a] No, not at all![b] For we have already drawn up the accusation that Jews and Greeks alike are all under
10 the power of sin. This has scriptural warrant:

'There is no just man, not one;
11 no one who understands, no one who seeks God.
12 All have swerved aside, all alike have become debased;
there is no one to show kindness; no, not one.

13 Their throat is an open grave,
they use their tongues for treachery,
adders' venom is on their lips,
14 and their mouth is full of bitter curses.

15 Their feet hasten to shed blood,
16 ruin and misery lie along their paths,
17 they are strangers to the high-road of peace,
18 and reverence for God does not enter their thoughts.'

19 Now all the words of the law are addressed, as we know, to those who are within the pale of the law, so that no one may have anything to say in self-defence, but the whole world may be exposed to the judgement of
20 God. For (again from Scripture) 'no human being can be justified in the sight of God' for having kept the law: law brings only the consciousness of sin.

21 BUT NOW, quite independently of law, God's justice has been brought to
22 light. The Law and the prophets both bear witness to it: it is God's way of righting wrong, effective through faith in Christ for all who have such
23 faith—all, without distinction. For all alike have sinned, and are deprived
24 of the divine splendour, and all are justified by God's free grace alone,
25 through his act of liberation in the person of Christ Jesus. For God designed him to be the means of expiating sin by his sacrificial death, effective through faith. God meant by this to demonstrate his justice,
26 because in his forbearance he had overlooked the sins of the past—to demonstrate his justice now in the present, showing that he is himself just and also justifies any man who puts his faith in Jesus.
27 What room then is left for human pride? It is excluded. And on what principle? The keeping of the law would not exclude it, but faith does.
28 For our argument is that a man is justified by faith quite apart from success in keeping the law.
29 Do you suppose God is the God of the Jews alone? Is he not the God of
30 Gentiles also? Certainly, of Gentiles also, if it be true that God is one. And he will therefore justify both the circumcised in virtue of their faith, and
31 the uncircumcised through their faith. Does this mean that we are using faith to undermine law? By no means: we are placing law itself on a firmer footing.

[a] *Or* Are we Jews any worse off?    [b] *Or* Not in all respects.

WHAT, THEN, are we to say about Abraham, our ancestor in the natural **4** line? If Abraham was justified by anything he had done, then he has a 2 ground for pride. But he has no such ground before God; for what does 3 Scripture say? 'Abraham put his faith in God, and that faith was counted to him as righteousness.' Now if a man does a piece of work, his wages are 4 not 'counted' as a favour; they are paid as debt. But if without any work to 5 his credit he simply puts his faith in him who acquits the guilty, then his faith is indeed 'counted as righteousness'. In the same sense David speaks 6 of the happiness of the man whom God 'counts' as just, apart from any specific acts of justice: 'Happy are they', he says, 'whose lawless deeds are 7 forgiven, whose sins are buried away; happy is the man whose sins the 8 Lord does not count against him.' Is this happiness confined to the 9 circumcised, or is it for the uncircumcised also? Consider: we say, 'Abraham's faith was counted as righteousness'; in what circumstances was it so 10 counted? Was he circumcised at the time, or not? He was not yet circumcised, but uncircumcised; and he later received the symbolic rite of 11 circumcision as the hall-mark of the righteousness which faith had given him when he was still uncircumcised. Consequently, he is the father of all who have faith when uncircumcised, so that righteousness is 'counted' to them; and at the same time he is the father of such of the circumcised as 12 do not rely upon their circumcision alone, but also walk in the footprints of the faith which our father Abraham had while he was yet uncircumcised.

For it was not through law that Abraham, or his posterity, was given the 13 promise that the world should be his inheritance, but through the righteousness that came from faith. For if those who hold by the law, and they alone, 14 are heirs, then faith is empty and the promise goes for nothing, because 15 law can bring only retribution; but where there is no law there can be no breach of law. The promise was made on the ground of faith, in order that 16 it might be a matter of sheer grace, and that it might be valid for all Abraham's posterity, not only for those who hold by the law, but for those also who have the faith of Abraham. For he is the father of us all, as Scripture 17 says: 'I have appointed you to be father of many nations.' This promise, then, was valid before God, the God in whom he put his faith, the God who makes the dead live and summons things that are not yet in existence as if they already were. When hope seemed hopeless, his faith was such 18 that he became 'father of many nations', in agreement with the words which had been spoken to him: 'Thus shall your descendants be.' With- 19 out any weakening of faith he contemplated his own body, as good as dead (for he was about a hundred years old), and the deadness of Sarah's womb, and never doubted God's promise in unbelief, but, strong in faith, gave 20 honour to God, in the firm conviction of his power to do what he had 21 promised. And that is why Abraham's faith was 'counted to him as 22 righteousness'.

Those words were written, not for Abraham's sake alone, but for our 23 24 sake too: it is to be 'counted' in the same way to us who have faith in the God who raised Jesus our Lord from the dead; for he was given up to 25 death for our misdeeds, and raised to life to justify us. *a*

*a* Or *raised to life because we were now justified.*

**5** THEREFORE, NOW THAT we have been justified through faith, let us
2 continue at peace *a* with God through our Lord Jesus Christ, through
whom we have been allowed to enter the sphere of God's grace, where we
now stand. Let us exult *b* in the hope of the divine splendour that is to be
3 ours. More than this: let us even exult *c* in our present sufferings, because
4 we know that suffering trains us to endure, and endurance brings proof
5 that we have stood the test, and this proof is the ground of hope. Such a
hope is no mockery, because God's love has flooded our inmost heart
through the Holy Spirit he has given us.

6 For at the very time when we were still powerless, then Christ died for
7 the wicked. Even for a just man one of us would hardly die, though perhaps
8 for a good man one might actually brave death; but Christ died for us while
we were yet sinners, and that is God's own proof of his love towards us.
9 And so, since we have now been justified by Christ's sacrificial death, we
shall all the more certainly be saved through him from final retribution.
10 For if, when we were God's enemies, we were reconciled to him through
the death of his Son, how much more, now that we are reconciled, shall
11 we be saved by his life! But that is not all: we also exult in God through our
Lord Jesus, through whom we have now been granted reconciliation.

12 Mark what follows. It was through one man that sin entered the world,
and through sin death, and thus death pervaded the whole human race,
13 inasmuch as all men have sinned. For sin was already in the world before
there was law, though in the absence of law no reckoning is kept of sin.
14 But death held sway from Adam to Moses, even over those who had not
sinned as Adam did, by disobeying a direct command—and Adam fore-
shadows the Man who was to come.

15 But God's act of grace is out of all proportion to Adam's wrongdoing.
For if the wrongdoing of that one man brought death upon so many, its
effect is vastly exceeded by the grace of God and the gift that came to so
16 many by the grace of the one man, Jesus Christ. And again, the gift of God
is not to be compared in its effect with that one man's sin; for the judicial
action, following upon the one offence, issued in a verdict of condemnation, but the act of grace, following upon so many misdeeds, issued in a
17 verdict of acquittal. For if by the wrongdoing of that one man death
established its reign, through a single sinner, much more shall those who
receive in far greater measure God's grace, and his gift of righteousness,
live and reign through the one man, Jesus Christ.

18 It follows, then, that as the issue of one misdeed was condemnation for
19 all men, so the issue of one just act is acquittal and life for all men. For as
through the disobedience of the one man the many were made sinners, so
through the obedience of the one man the many will be made righteous.

20 Law intruded into this process to multiply law-breaking. But where sin
21 was thus multiplied, grace immeasurably exceeded it, in order that, as sin
established its reign by way of death, so God's grace might establish its
reign in righteousness, and issue in eternal life through Jesus Christ
our Lord.

*a Some witnesses read* we are at peace.          *b Or* We exult.          *c Or* we even
exult.

What are we to say, then? Shall we persist in sin, so that there may be 6
all the more grace? No, no! We died to sin: how can we live in it any 2
longer? Have you forgotten that when we were baptized into union with 3
Christ Jesus we were baptized into his death? By baptism we were buried 4
with him, and lay dead, in order that, as Christ was raised from the dead
in the splendour of the Father, so also we might set our feet upon the new
path of life.

For if we have become incorporate with him in a death like his, we shall 5
also be one with him in a resurrection like his. We know that the man we 6
once were has been crucified with Christ, for the destruction of the sinful
self, so that we may no longer be the slaves of sin, since a dead man is no 7
longer answerable for his sin. But if we thus died with Christ, we believe 8
that we shall also come to life with him. We know that Christ, once raised 9
from the dead, is never to die again: he is no longer under the dominion of
death. For in dying as he died, he died to sin, once for all, and in living as 10
he lives, he lives to God. In the same way you must regard yourselves as 11
dead to sin and alive to God, in union with Christ Jesus.

So sin must no longer reign in your mortal body, exacting obedience to 12
the body's desires. You must no longer put its several parts at sin's disposal, 13
as implements for doing wrong. No: put yourselves at the disposal of God,
as dead men raised to life; yield your bodies to him as implements for doing
right; for sin shall no longer be your master, because you are no longer 14
under law, but under the grace of God.

What then? Are we to sin, because we are not under law but under 15
grace? Of course not. You know well enough that if you put yourselves at 16
the disposal of a master, to obey him, you are slaves of the master whom
you obey; and this is true whether you serve sin, with death as its result;
or obedience, with righteousness as its result. But God be thanked, you, 17
who once were slaves of sin, have yielded whole-hearted obedience to the
pattern of teaching to which you were made subject,[a] and, emancipated 18
from sin, have become slaves of righteousness (to use words that suit your 19
human weakness)—I mean, as you once yielded your bodies to the service
of impurity and lawlessness, making for moral anarchy, so now you must
yield them to the service of righteousness, making for a holy life.

When you were slaves of sin, you were free from the control of righteous- 20
ness; and what was the gain? Nothing but what now makes you ashamed, 21
for the end of that is death. But now, freed from the commands of sin, and 22
bound to the service of God, your gains are such as make for holiness, and
the end is eternal life. For sin pays a wage, and the wage is death, but God 23
gives freely, and his gift is eternal life, in union with Christ Jesus our
Lord.

You cannot be unaware, my friends—I am speaking to those who have 7
some knowledge of law—that a person is subject to the law so long as he is
alive, and no longer. For example, a married woman is by law bound to her 2
husband while he lives; but if her husband dies, she is discharged from the
obligations of the marriage-law. If, therefore, in her husband's lifetime 3
she consorts with another man, she will incur the charge of adultery; but

*a Or* which was handed on to you.

if her husband dies she is free of the law, and she does not commit adultery
4 by consorting with another man. So you, my friends, have died to the law
by becoming identified with the body of Christ, and accordingly you have
found another husband in him who rose from the dead, so that we may
5 bear fruit for God. While we lived on the level of our lower nature, the sinful passions evoked by the law worked in our bodies, to bear fruit for death.
6 But now, having died to that which held us bound, we are discharged from
the law, to serve God in a new way, the way of the spirit, in contrast to the
old way, the way of a written code.

7 What follows? Is the law identical with sin? Of course not. But except
through law I should never have become acquainted with sin. For example,
I should never have known what it was to covet, if the law had not said,
8 'Thou shalt not covet.' Through that commandment sin found its opportunity, and produced in me all kinds of wrong desires. In the absence of
9 law, sin is a dead thing. There was a time when, in the absence of law, I
was fully alive; but when the commandment came, sin sprang to life and
10 I died. The commandment which should have led to life proved in my
11 experience to lead to death, because sin found its opportunity in the commandment, seduced me, and through the commandment killed me.
12 Therefore the law is in itself holy, and the commandment is holy and
13 just and good. Are we to say then that this good thing was the death of me?
By no means. It was sin that killed me, and thereby sin exposed its true
character: it used a good thing to bring about my death, and so, through the
commandment, sin became more sinful than ever.

14 We know that the law is spiritual; but I am not: I am unspiritual, the
15 purchased slave of sin. I do not even acknowledge my own actions as mine,
16 for what I do is not what I want to do, but what I detest. But if what I do
is against my will, it means that I agree with the law and hold it to be
17 admirable. But as things are, it is no longer I who perform the action, but
18 sin that lodges in me. For I know that nothing good lodges in me—in my
unspiritual nature, I mean—for though the will to do good is there, the
19 deed is not. The good which I want to do, I fail to do; but what I do is the
20 wrong which is against my will; and if what I do is against my will, clearly
it is no longer I who am the agent, but sin that has its lodging in me.

21 I discover this principle, then: that when I want to do the right, only
22 the wrong is within my reach. In my inmost self I delight in the law of God,
23 but I perceive that there is in my bodily members a different law, fighting
against the law that my reason approves and making me a prisoner under
24 the law *a* that is in my members, the law of sin. Miserable creature that I
25 am, who is there to rescue me out of this body doomed to death *b*? God
alone, through Jesus Christ our Lord! Thanks be to God! In a word then,
I myself, subject to God's law as a rational being, am yet,*c* in my unspiritual nature, a slave to the law of sin.

8 The conclusion of the matter is this: there is no condemnation for those
2 who are united with Christ Jesus, because in Christ Jesus the life-giving
3 law of the Spirit has set you free from the law of sin and death. What the

*a* Or by means of the law.          *b* Or out of the body doomed to this death.
*c* Or Thus, left to myself, while subject . . . rational being, I am yet . . .

law could never do, because our lower nature robbed it of all potency, God has done: by sending his own Son in a form like that of our own sinful nature, and as a sacrifice for sin,*a* he has passed judgement against sin within that very nature, so that the commandment of the law may find 4 fulfilment in us, whose conduct, no longer under the control of our lower nature, is directed by the Spirit.

Those who live on the level of our lower nature have their outlook 5 formed by it, and that spells death; but those who live on the level of the 6 spirit have the spiritual outlook, and that is life and peace. For the outlook 7 of the lower nature is enmity with God; it is not subject to the law of God; indeed it cannot be: those who live on such a level cannot possibly please 8 God.

But that is not how you live. You are on the spiritual level, if only God's 9 Spirit dwells within you; and if a man does not possess the Spirit of Christ, he is no Christian. But if Christ is dwelling within you, then although the 10 body is a dead thing because you sinned, yet the spirit is life itself because you have been justified.*b* Moreover, if the Spirit of him who raised Jesus 11 from the dead dwells within you, then the God who raised Christ Jesus from the dead will also give new life to your mortal bodies through his indwelling Spirit.

It follows, my friends, that our lower nature has no claim upon us; 12 we are not obliged to live on that level. If you do so, you must die. But 13 if by the Spirit you put to death all the base pursuits of the body, then you will live.

For all who are moved by the Spirit of God are sons of God. The Spirit 14 15 you have received is not a spirit of slavery leading you back into a life of fear, but a Spirit that makes us sons, enabling us to cry 'Abba! Father!' In that cry the Spirit of God joins with our spirit in testifying that we are 16 God's children; and if children, then heirs. We are God's heirs and Christ's 17 fellow-heirs, if we share his sufferings now in order to share his splendour hereafter.

For I reckon that the sufferings we now endure bear no comparison with 18 the splendour, as yet unrevealed, which is in store for us. For the created 19 universe waits with eager expectation for God's sons to be revealed. It was 20 made the victim of frustration, not by its own choice, but because of him who made it so;*c* yet always there was hope, because*d* the universe itself 21 is to be freed from the shackles of mortality and enter upon the liberty and splendour of the children of God. Up to the present, we know, the whole 22 created universe groans in all its parts as if in the pangs of childbirth. Not 23 only so, but even we, to whom the Spirit is given as firstfruits of the harvest to come, are groaning inwardly while we wait for God to make us his sons and*e* set our whole body free. For we have been saved, though only in 24 hope. Now to see is no longer to hope: why should a man endure and wait*f* for what he already sees? But if we hope for something we do not yet 25 see, then, in waiting for it, we show our endurance.

---

*a* *Or* and to deal with sin.     *b* *Or* so that you may live rightly.     *c* *Or* because God subjected it.     *d* *Or* with the hope that . . .     *e* *Some witnesses omit* make us his sons and.     *f* *Some witnesses read* why should a man hope . . .

26 In the same way the Spirit comes to the aid of our weakness. We do not
even know how we ought to pray,[a] but through our inarticulate groans the
27 Spirit himself is pleading for us, and God who searches our inmost being
knows what the Spirit means, because he pleads for God's people in God's
28 own way; and in everything, as we know, he co-operates for good with those
29 who love God[b] and are called according to his purpose. For God knew his
own before ever they were, and also ordained that they should be shaped
to the likeness of his Son, that he might be the eldest among a large family
30 of brothers; and it is these, so fore-ordained, whom he has also called. And
those whom he called he has justified, and to those whom he justified he
has also given his splendour.

31 With all this in mind, what are we to say? If God is on our side, who is
32 against us? He did not spare his own Son, but gave him up for us all; and
33 with this gift how can he fail to lavish upon us all he has to give? Who will
be the accuser of God's chosen ones? It is God who pronounces acquittal;
34 then who can condemn? It is Christ—Christ who died, and, more than that,
was raised from the dead—who is at God's right hand, and indeed pleads
35 our cause.[c] Then what can separate us from the love of Christ? Can
affliction or hardship? Can persecution, hunger, nakedness, peril, or the
36 sword? 'We are being done to death for thy sake all day long,' as Scripture
37 says; 'we have been treated like sheep for slaughter'—and yet, in spite of
38 all, overwhelming victory is ours through him who loved us. For I am
convinced that there is nothing in death or life, in the realm of spirits or
superhuman powers, in the world as it is or the world as it shall be, in the
39 forces of the universe, in heights or depths—nothing in all creation that can
separate us from the love of God in Christ Jesus our Lord.

## The purpose of God in history

9 I AM SPEAKING the truth as a Christian, and my own conscience,
2 enlightened by the Holy Spirit, assures me it is no lie: in my heart there
3 is great grief and unceasing sorrow. For I could even pray to be outcast
4 from Christ myself for the sake of my brothers, my natural kinsfolk. They
are Israelites: they were made God's sons; theirs is the splendour of the
divine presence, theirs the covenants, the law, the temple worship, and the
5 promises. Theirs are the patriarchs, and from them, in natural descent,
sprang the Messiah.[d] May God, supreme above all, be blessed for ever![e]
Amen.

6 It is impossible that the word of God should have proved false. For not
7 all descendants of Israel are truly Israel, nor, because they are Abraham's

[a] Or what it is right to pray for.  [b] Or and, as we know, all things work together
for good for those who love God; *some witnesses read* and we know God himself co-
operates for good with those who love God.  [c] Or Who will be the accuser
of God's chosen ones? Will it be God himself? No, he it is who pronounces acquittal.
Who will be the judge to condemn? Will it be Christ—he who died, and, more than
that, . . . right hand? No, he it is who pleads our cause.  [d] Greek Christ.
[e] Or sprang the Messiah, supreme above all, God blessed for ever; or sprang the Messiah,
who is supreme above all. Blessed be God for ever!

offspring, are they all his true children; [a] but, in the words of Scripture, 'Through the line of Isaac your descendants shall be traced.' [b] That is to 8 say, it is not those born in the course of nature who are children of God; it is the children born through God's promise who are reckoned as Abraham's descendants. For the promise runs: 'At the time fixed I will come, 9 and Sarah shall have a son.'

But that is not all, for Rebekah's children had one and the same father, 10 our ancestor Isaac; and yet, in order that God's selective purpose might 11 stand, based not upon men's deeds but upon the call of God, she was told, 12 even before they were born, when they had as yet done nothing, good or ill, 'The elder shall be servant to the younger'; and that accords with the 13 text of Scripture, 'Jacob I loved and Esau I hated.'

What shall we say to that? Is God to be charged with injustice? By no 14 means. For he says to Moses, 'Where I show mercy, I will show mercy, 15 and where I pity, I will pity.' Thus it does not depend on man's will or 16 effort, but on God's mercy. For Scripture says to Pharaoh, 'I have raised 17 you up for this very purpose, to exhibit my power in my dealings with you, and to spread my fame over all the world.' Thus he not only shows mercy 18 as he chooses, but also makes men stubborn as he chooses.

You will say, 'Then why does God blame a man? For who can resist his 19 will?' Who are you, sir, to answer God back? Can the pot speak to the 20 potter and say, 'Why did you make me like this?'? Surely the potter can 21 do what he likes with the clay. Is he not free to make out of the same lump two vessels, one to be treasured, the other for common use?

But what if God, desiring to exhibit [c] his retribution at work and to make 22 his power known, tolerated very patiently those vessels which were objects of retribution due for destruction, and did so in order to make known the 23 full wealth of his splendour upon vessels which were objects of mercy, and which from the first had been prepared for this splendour?

Such vessels are we, whom he has called from among Gentiles as well 24 as Jews, as it says in the Book of Hosea: 'Those who were not my people 25 I will call My People, and the unloved nation I will call My Beloved. For 26 in the very place where they were told "you are no people of mine", they shall be called Sons of the living God.' But Isaiah makes this proclamation 27 about Israel: 'Though the Israelites be countless as the sands of the sea, only a remnant shall be saved; for the Lord's sentence on the land will be 28 summary and final'; as also he said previously, 'If the Lord of Hosts had 29 not left us the mere germ of a nation, we should have become like Sodom, and no better than Gomorrah.'

Then what are we to say? That Gentiles, who made no effort after 30 righteousness, nevertheless achieved it, a righteousness based on faith; whereas Israel made great efforts after a law of righteousness, but never 31 attained to it. Why was this? Because their efforts were not based on faith, 32 but (as they supposed) on deeds. They fell over the 'stone' mentioned in 33 Scripture: 'Here I lay in Zion a stone to trip over, a rock to stumble against; but he who has faith in him will not be put to shame.'

[a] *Or* all children of God.       [b] *Or* God's call shall be for your descendants in the line of Isaac.       [c] *Or* although he had the will to exhibit . . .

**10** BROTHERS, MY DEEPEST DESIRE and my prayer to God is for their
2 salvation. To their zeal for God I can testify; but it is an ill-informed zeal.
3 For they ignore God's way of righteousness, and try to set up their own, and
4 therefore they have not submitted themselves to God's righteousness. For
Christ ends the law and brings righteousness for everyone who has faith. *a*
5 Of legal righteousness Moses writes, 'The man who does this shall gain
6 life by it.' But the righteousness that comes by faith says, 'Do not say to
yourself, "Who can go up to heaven?"' (that is to bring Christ down),
7 'or, "Who can go down to the abyss?"' (to bring Christ up from the dead).
8 But what does it say? 'The word is near you: it is upon your lips and in your
9 heart.' This means the word of faith which we proclaim. If on your lips is
the confession, 'Jesus is Lord', and in your heart the faith that God raised
10 him from the dead, then you will find salvation. For the faith that leads to
righteousness is in the heart, and the confession that leads to salvation is
upon the lips.
11 Scripture says, 'Everyone who has faith in him will be saved from shame'
12 —everyone: there is no distinction between Jew and Greek, because the
same Lord is Lord of all, and is rich enough for the need of all who invoke
13 him. For everyone, as it says again—'everyone who invokes the name of the
14 Lord will be saved'. How could they invoke one in whom they had no faith?
And how could they have faith in one they had never heard of? And how
15 hear without someone to spread the news? And how could anyone spread
the news without a commission to do so? And that is what Scripture
affirms: 'How welcome are the feet of the messengers of good news!'
16 But not all have responded to the good news. For Isaiah says, 'Lord,
17 who has believed our message?' We conclude that faith is awakened by the
message, and the message that awakens it comes through the word of
Christ.
18 But, I ask, can it be that they never heard it? Of course they did: 'Their
voice has sounded all over the earth, and their words to the bounds of the
19 inhabited world.' But, I ask again, can it be that Israel failed to recognize
the message? In reply, I first cite Moses, who says, 'I will use a nation that
is no nation to stir your envy, and a foolish nation to rouse your anger.'
20 But Isaiah is still more daring: 'I was found', he says, 'by those who were
not looking for me; I was clearly shown to those who never asked about me';
21 while to Israel he says, 'All day long I have stretched out my hands to an
unruly and defiant people.'

**11** I ASK THEN, has God rejected his people? I cannot believe it! I am an
2 Israelite myself, of the stock of Abraham, of the tribe of Benjamin. No!
God has not rejected the people which he acknowledged of old as his own.
You know (do you not?) what Scripture says in the story of Elijah—how
3 Elijah pleads with God against Israel: 'Lord, they have killed thy prophets,
they have torn down thine altars, and I alone am left, and they are seeking
4 my life.' But what does the divine voice say to him? 'I have left myself
5 seven thousand men who have not knelt to Baal.' In just the same way at
the present time a 'remnant' has come into being, selected by the grace of

*a Or* Christ is the end of the law as a way to righteousness for everyone who has faith.

God. But if it is by grace, then it does not rest on deeds done, or grace 6
would cease to be grace.

What follows? What Israel sought, Israel has not achieved, but the 7
selected few have achieved it. The rest were made blind to the truth,
exactly as it stands written: 'God brought upon them a numbness of 8
spirit; he gave them blind eyes and deaf ears, and so it is still.' Similarly 9
David says:

> 'May their table be a snare and a trap,
> both stumbling-block and retribution!
> May their eyes become so dim that they lose their sight!          10
> Bow down their backs unceasingly!'

I now ask, did their failure mean complete downfall? Far from it! 11
Because they offended, salvation has come to the Gentiles, to stir Israel
to emulation. But if their offence means the enrichment of the world, and 12
if their falling-off means the enrichment of the Gentiles, how much more
their coming to full strength!

But I have something to say to you Gentiles. I am a missionary to the 13
Gentiles, and as such I give all honour to that ministry when I try to stir 14
emulation in the men of my own race, and so to save some of them. For if 15
their rejection has meant the reconciliation of the world, what will their
acceptance mean? Nothing less than life from the dead! If the first portion 16
of dough is consecrated, so is the whole lump. If the root is consecrated, so
are the branches. But if some of the branches have been lopped off, and 17
you, a wild olive, have been grafted in among them, and have come to
share the same root and sap as the olive, do not make yourself superior to 18
the branches. If you do so, remember that it is not you who sustain the
root: the root sustains you.

You will say, 'Branches were lopped off so that I might be grafted in.' 19
Very well: they were lopped off for lack of faith, and by faith you hold your 20
place. Put away your pride, and be on your guard; for if God did not spare 21
the native branches, no more will he spare you. Observe the kindness and 22
the severity of God—severity to those who fell away, divine kindness to
you, if only you remain within its scope; otherwise you too will be cut off,
whereas they, if they do not continue faithless, will be grafted in; for it is 23
in God's power to graft them in again. For if you were cut from your native 24
wild olive and against all nature grafted into the cultivated olive, how much
more readily will they, the natural olive-branches, be grafted into their
native stock!

For there is a deep truth here, my brothers, of which I want you to take 25
account, so that you may not be complacent about your own discernment:
this partial blindness has come upon Israel only until the Gentiles have
been admitted in full strength; when that has happened, the whole of 26
Israel will be saved, in agreement with the text of Scripture:

> 'From Zion shall come the Deliverer;
> he shall remove wickedness from Jacob.
> And this is the covenant I will grant them,                        27
> when I take away their sins.'

28 In the spreading of the Gospel they are treated as God's enemies for your sake; but God's choice stands, and they are his friends for the sake of the
29 patriarchs. For the gracious gifts of God and his calling are irrevocable.
30 Just as formerly you were disobedient to God, but now have received mercy
31 in the time of their disobedience, so now, when you receive mercy, they have proved disobedient, but only in order that they too may receive mercy.
32 For in making all mankind prisoners to disobedience, God's purpose was to show mercy to all mankind.

33   O depth of wealth, wisdom, and knowledge in God! How unsearchable
34 his judgements, how untraceable his ways! Who knows the mind of the
35 Lord? Who has been his counsellor? Who has ever made a gift to him, to
36 receive a gift in return? Source, Guide, and Goal of all that is—to him be glory for ever! Amen.

## *Christian behaviour*

12 THEREFORE, MY BROTHERS, I implore you by God's mercy to offer your very selves to him: a living sacrifice, dedicated and fit for his
2 acceptance, the worship offered by mind and heart.*a* Adapt yourselves no longer to the pattern of this present world, but let your minds be remade and your whole nature thus transformed. Then you will be able to discern the will of God, and to know what is good, acceptable, and perfect.

3   In virtue of the gift that God in his grace has given me I say to everyone among you: do not be conceited or think too highly of yourself; but think your way to a sober estimate based on the measure of faith that God has dealt
4 to each of you. For just as in a single human body there are many limbs and
5 organs, all with different functions, so all of us, united with Christ, form one body, serving individually as limbs and organs to one another.

6   The gifts we possess differ as they are allotted to us by God's grace, and must be exercised accordingly: the gift of inspired utterance, for
7 example, in proportion to a man's faith; or the gift of administration, in
8 administration. A teacher should employ his gift in teaching, and one who has the gift of stirring speech should use it to stir his hearers. If you give to charity, give with all your heart; if you are a leader, exert yourself to lead; if you are helping others in distress, do it cheerfully.

9 10   Love in all sincerity, loathing evil and clinging to the good. Let love for our brotherhood breed warmth of mutual affection. Give pride of place to one another in esteem.
11   With unflagging energy, in ardour of spirit, serve the Lord.*b*
12   Let hope keep you joyful; in trouble stand firm; persist in prayer.
13   Contribute to the needs of God's people, and practise hospitality.
14   Call down blessings on your persecutors—blessings, not curses.
15   With the joyful be joyful, and mourn with the mourners.
16   Care as much about each other as about yourselves. Do not be haughty, but go about with humble folk. Do not keep thinking how wise you are.

*a* *Or . . . acceptance, for such is the worship which you, as rational creatures, should offer.*
*b* *Some witnesses read* meet the demands of the hour.

Never pay back evil for evil. Let your aims be such as all men count 17
honourable. If possible, so far as it lies with you, live at peace with all men. 18
My dear friends, do not seek revenge, but leave a place for divine retribu- 19
tion; for there is a text which reads, 'Justice is mine, says the Lord, I will
repay.' But there is another text: 'If your enemy is hungry, feed him; if he 20
is thirsty, give him a drink; by doing this you will heap live coals on his
head.' Do not let evil conquer you, but use good to defeat evil.               21

Every person must submit to the supreme authorities. There is no 13
authority but by act of God, and the existing authorities are instituted by
him; consequently anyone who rebels against authority is resisting a divine 2
institution, and those who so resist have themselves to thank for the
punishment they will receive. For government, a terror to crime, has no 3
terrors for good behaviour. You wish to have no fear of the authorities?
Then continue to do right and you will have their approval, for they are 4
God's agents working for your good. But if you are doing wrong, then you
will have cause to fear them; it is not for nothing that they hold the power
of the sword, for they are God's agents of punishment, for retribution on
the offender. That is why you are obliged to submit. It is an obligation 5
imposed not merely by fear of retribution but by conscience. That is also 6
why you pay taxes. The authorities are in God's service and to these duties
they devote their energies.

Discharge your obligations to all men; pay tax and toll, reverence and 7
respect, to those to whom they are due. Leave no claim outstanding against 8
you, except that of mutual love. He who loves his neighbour has satisfied
every claim of the law. For the commandments, 'Thou shalt not commit 9
adultery, thou shalt not kill, thou shalt not steal, thou shalt not covet',
and any other commandment there may be, are all summed up in the one
rule, 'Love your neighbour as yourself.' Love cannot wrong a neighbour; 10
therefore the whole law is summed up in love.[a]

In all this, remember how critical the moment is. It is time for you to 11
wake out of sleep, for deliverance is nearer to us now than it was when first
we believed. It is far on in the night; day is near. Let us therefore throw off 12
the deeds of darkness and put on our armour as soldiers of the light. Let us 13
behave with decency as befits the day: no revelling or drunkenness, no
debauchery or vice, no quarrels or jealousies! Let Christ Jesus himself be 14
the armour that you wear; give no more thought to satisfying the bodily
appetites.

IF A MAN IS WEAK in his faith you must accept him without attempting 14
to settle doubtful points. For instance, one man will have faith enough to 2
eat all kinds of food, while a weaker man eats only vegetables. The man who 3
eats must not hold in contempt the man who does not, and he who does
not eat must not pass judgement on the one who does; for God has accepted
him. Who are you to pass judgement on someone else's servant? Whether 4
he stands or falls is his own Master's business; and stand he will, because
his Master has power to enable him to stand.

Again, this man regards one day more highly than another, while that 5

[a] *Or* the whole law is fulfilled by love.

man regards all days alike. On such a point everyone should have reached
6 conviction in his own mind. He who respects the day has the Lord in mind
in doing so, and he who eats meat has the Lord in mind when he eats, since
he gives thanks to God; and he who abstains has the Lord in mind no less,
since he too gives thanks to God.

7 For no one of us lives, and equally no one of us dies, for himself alone.
8 If we live, we live for the Lord; and if we die, we die for the Lord. Whether
9 therefore we live or die, we belong to the Lord. This is why Christ died
10 and came to life again, to establish his lordship over dead and living. You,
sir, why do you pass judgement on your brother? And you, sir, why do you
hold your brother in contempt? We shall all stand before God's tribunal.
11 For Scripture says, 'As I live, says the Lord, to me every knee shall bow and
12 every tongue acknowledge God.' So, you see, each of us will have to answer
for himself.

13 Let us therefore cease judging one another, but rather make this simple
judgement: that no obstacle or stumbling-block be placed in a brother's
14 way. I am absolutely convinced, as a Christian,*a* that nothing is impure in
itself; only, if a man considers a particular thing impure, then to him it is
15 impure. If your brother is outraged by what you eat, then your conduct is
no longer guided by love. Do not by your eating bring disaster to a man for
16 whom Christ died! What for you is a good thing must not become an occa-
17 sion for slanderous talk; for the kingdom of God is not eating and drink-
18 ing, but justice, peace, and joy, inspired by the Holy Spirit. He who thus
shows himself a servant of Christ is acceptable to God and approved
by men.

19 Let us then pursue the things that make for peace and build up the
20 common life. Do not ruin the work of God for the sake of food. Everything
is pure in itself, but anything is bad for the man who by his eating causes
21 another to fall. It is a fine thing to abstain from eating meat or drinking
22 wine, or doing anything which causes your brother's downfall. If you have
a clear conviction, apply it to yourself in the sight of God. Happy is the
23 man who can make his decision with a clear conscience!*b* But a man who
has doubts is guilty if he eats, because his action does not arise from his
conviction, and anything which does not arise from conviction is sin. *c*

15 Those of us who have a robust conscience must accept as our own burden
2 the tender scruples of weaker men, and not consider ourselves. Each of us
must consider his neighbour and think what is for his good and will build
3 up the common life. For Christ too did not consider himself, but might
have said, in the words of Scripture, 'The reproaches of those who re-
4 proached thee fell upon me.' For all the ancient scriptures were written
for our own instruction, in order that through the encouragement they give
5 us we may maintain our hope with fortitude. And may God, the source of
all fortitude and all encouragement, grant that you may agree with one
6 another after the manner of Christ Jesus, so that with one mind and one
voice you may praise the God and Father of our Lord Jesus Christ.

7 In a word, accept one another as Christ accepted us, to the glory of God.

*a* Or on the authority of the Lord Jesus.　　　　*b* Or who does not bring judgement
upon himself by what he approves!　　　*c* See p. 209, note c.

I mean that Christ became a servant of the Jewish people to maintain the 8
truth of God by making good his promises to the patriarchs, and at the 9
same time to give the Gentiles cause to glorify God for his mercy. As
Scripture says, 'Therefore I will praise thee among the Gentiles and sing
hymns to thy name'; and again, 'Gentiles, make merry together with his 10
own people'; and yet again, 'All Gentiles, praise the Lord; let all peoples 11
praise him.' Once again, Isaiah says, 'There shall be the Scion of Jesse, 12
the one raised up to govern the Gentiles; on him the Gentiles shall set their
hope.' And may the God of hope fill you with all joy and peace by your 13
faith in him, until, by the power of the Holy Spirit, you overflow with hope.

MY FRIENDS, I have no doubt in my own mind that you yourselves are 14
quite full of goodness and equipped with knowledge of every kind, well
able to give advice to one another; nevertheless I have written to refresh 15
your memory, and written somewhat boldly at times, in virtue of the gift
I have from God. His grace has made me a minister of Christ Jesus to the 16
Gentiles; my priestly service is the preaching of the gospel of God, and
it falls to me to offer the Gentiles to him as *a* an acceptable sacrifice, consecrated by the Holy Spirit.

Thus in the fellowship of Christ Jesus I have ground for pride in the 17
service of God. I will venture to speak of those things alone in which I have 18
been Christ's instrument to bring the Gentiles into his allegiance, by word
and deed, by the force of miraculous signs and by the power of the Holy 19
Spirit. As a result I have completed the preaching of the gospel of Christ
from Jerusalem as far round as Illyricum. It is my ambition to bring the 20
Gospel to places where the very name of Christ has not been heard, for I
do not want to build on another man's foundation; but, as Scripture says, 21

'They who had no news of him shall see,
and they who never heard of him shall understand.'

That is why I have been prevented all this time from coming to you. 22
But now I have no further scope in these parts, and I have been longing for 23
many years to visit you on my way to Spain; for I hope to see you as I 24
travel through, and to be sent there with your support after having enjoyed
your company for a while. But at the moment I am on my way to Jerusalem, 25
on an errand to God's people there. For Macedonia and Achaia have 26
resolved to raise a common fund for the benefit of the poor among God's
people at Jerusalem. They have resolved to do so, and indeed they are under 27
an obligation to them. For if the Jewish Christians shared their spiritual
treasures with the Gentiles, the Gentiles have a clear duty to contribute to
their material needs. So when I have finished this business and delivered 28
the proceeds under my own seal, I shall set out for Spain by way of your
city, and I am sure that when I arrive I shall come to you with a full 29
measure of the blessing of Christ.

I implore you by our Lord Jesus Christ and by the love that the Spirit 30
inspires, be my allies in the fight; pray to God for me that I may be saved 31
from unbelievers in Judaea and that my errand to Jerusalem may find

*a Or* . . . of God, so that the worship which the Gentiles offer may be . . .

32 acceptance with God's people, so that by his will I may come to you in a
33 happy frame of mind and enjoy a time of rest with you. The God of peace
be with you all. Amen.*ᵃ*

**16** I COMMEND TO YOU PHOEBE, a fellow-Christian who holds office in the
2 congregation at Cenchreae. Give her, in the fellowship of the Lord, a
welcome worthy of God's people, and stand by her in any business in
which she may need your help, for she has herself been a good friend to
many, including myself.

3    Give my greetings to Prisca and Aquila, my fellow-workers in Christ
4 Jesus. They risked their necks to save my life, and not I alone but all the
5 gentile congregations are grateful to them. Greet also the congregation at
their house.

Give my greetings to my dear friend Epaenetus, the first convert to
6 7 Christ in Asia, and to Mary, who toiled hard for you. Greet Andronicus
and Junias*ᵇ* my fellow-countrymen and comrades in captivity. They are
eminent among the apostles, and they were Christians before I was.

8 9    Greetings to Ampliatus, my dear friend in the fellowship of the Lord, to
10 Urban my comrade in Christ, and to my dear Stachys. My greetings to
Apelles, well proved in Christ's service, to the household of Aristobulus,
11 and my countryman Herodion, and to those of the household of Narcissus
12 who are in the Lord's fellowship. Greet Tryphaena and Tryphosa, who
toil in the Lord's service, and dear Persis who has toiled in his service so
13 long. Give my greetings to Rufus, an outstanding follower of the Lord,
14 and to his mother, whom I call mother too. Greet Asyncritus, Phlegon,
15 Hermes, Patrobas, Hermas, and all friends in their company. Greet
Philologus and Julia,*ᶜ* Nereus and his sister, and Olympas, and all God's
people associated with them.

16    Greet one another with the kiss of peace. All Christ's congregations
send you their greetings.

17    I implore you, my friends, keep your eye on those who stir up quarrels
and lead others astray, contrary to the teaching you received. Avoid them,
18 for such people are servants not of Christ our Lord but of their own
appetites, and they seduce the minds of innocent people with smooth and
19 specious words. The fame of your obedience has spread everywhere. This
makes me happy about you; yet I should wish you to be experts in goodness
20 but simpletons in evil; and the God of peace will soon crush Satan beneath
your feet. The grace of our Lord Jesus be with you!*ᵈ*

21    Greetings to you from my colleague Timothy, and from Lucius, Jason,
22 and Sosipater my fellow-countrymen. (I Tertius, who took this letter
23 down, add my Christian greetings.) Greetings also from Gaius, my host
and host of the whole congregation, and from Erastus, treasurer of this
city, and our brother Quartus. *ᵉ*

*ᵃ See p. 209, note c.*                    *ᵇ Or* Junia; *some witnesses read* Julia, *or* Julias.
*ᶜ Or* Julias; *some witnesses read* Junia, *or* Junias.        *ᵈ The words* The grace . . . with
you *are omitted at this point in some witnesses; in some, these or similar words are given as
verse 24, and in some others after verse 27 (see note on verse 23).*        *ᵉ Some witnesses
add* (24) The grace of our Lord Jesus Christ be with you all! Amen.

TO HIM who has power to make your standing sure, according to the  25
Gospel I brought you and the proclamation of Jesus Christ, according to
the revelation of that divine secret kept in silence for long ages but now  26
disclosed, and through prophetic scriptures by eternal God's command
made known to all nations, to bring them to faith and obedience—to God  27
who alone is wise, through Jesus Christ,*a* be glory for endless ages! Amen.*b c*

# THE FIRST LETTER OF PAUL
# TO THE
# CORINTHIANS

## Unity and order in the church

FROM PAUL, APOSTLE of Jesus Christ at God's call and by  1
God's will, together with our colleague Sosthenes, to the congrega-  2
tion of God's people at Corinth, dedicated to him in Christ Jesus,
claimed by him as his own, along with all men everywhere who invoke the
name of our Lord Jesus Christ—their Lord as well as ours.

Grace and peace to you from God our Father and the Lord Jesus Christ.  3
I am always thanking God for you. I thank him for his grace given to  4
you in Christ Jesus. I thank him for all the enrichment that has come to  5
you in Christ. You possess full knowledge and you can give full expression
to it, because in you the evidence for the truth of Christ has found con-  6
firmation. There is indeed no single gift you lack, while you wait expec-  7
tantly for our Lord Jesus Christ to reveal himself. He will keep you firm  8
to the end, without reproach on the Day of our Lord Jesus. It is God him-  9
self who called you to share in the life of his Son Jesus Christ our Lord;
and God keeps faith.

I appeal to you, my brothers, in the name of our Lord Jesus Christ:  10
agree among yourselves, and avoid divisions; be firmly joined in unity of
mind and thought. I have been told, my brothers, by Chloe's people that  11
there are quarrels among you. What I mean is this: each of you is saying,  12
'I am Paul's man', or 'I am for Apollos'; 'I follow Cephas', or 'I am
Christ's.' Surely Christ has not been divided among you! Was it Paul who  13
was crucified for you? Was it in the name of Paul that you were baptized?
Thank God, I never baptized one of you—except Crispus and Gaius. So  14 15
no one can say you were baptized in my name.—Yes, I did baptize the  16

*a Some witnesses insert* to whom.          *b Here some witnesses add* The grace of our
Lord Jesus Christ be with you!          *c Some witnesses place verses 25–27 at
the end of chapter 14, one other places them at the end of chapter 15, and others omit them
altogether.*

17 household of Stephanas; I cannot think of anyone else. Christ did not send me to baptize, but to proclaim the Gospel; and to do it without relying on the language of worldly wisdom, so that the fact of Christ on his cross might have its full weight.

18 This doctrine of the cross is sheer folly to those on their way to ruin,
19 but to us who are on the way to salvation it is the power of God. Scripture says, 'I will destroy the wisdom of the wise, and bring to nothing the
20 cleverness of the clever.' Where is your wise man now, your man of learning, or your subtle debater—limited, all of them, to this passing age?
21 God has made the wisdom of this world look foolish. As God in his wisdom ordained, the world failed to find him by its wisdom, and he chose to save
22 those who have faith by the folly of the Gospel. Jews call for miracles,
23 Greeks look for wisdom; but we proclaim Christ—yes, Christ nailed to the cross; and though this is a stumbling-block to Jews and folly to Greeks,
24 yet to those who have heard his call, Jews and Greeks alike, he is the power of God and the wisdom of God.

25 Divine folly is wiser than the wisdom of man, and divine weakness
26 stronger than man's strength. My brothers, think what sort of people you are, whom God has called. Few of you are men of wisdom, by any human
27 standard; few are powerful or highly born. Yet, to shame the wise, God has chosen what the world counts folly, and to shame what is strong, God
28 has chosen what the world counts weakness. He has chosen things low and
29 contemptible, mere nothings, to overthrow the existing order. And so
30 there is no place for human pride in the presence of God. You are in Christ Jesus by God's act, for God has made him our wisdom; he is our righteous-
31 ness; in him we are consecrated and set free. And so (in the words of Scripture), 'If a man must boast, let him boast of the Lord.'

2 As for me, brothers, when I came to you, I declared the attested truth of
2 God*a* without display of fine words or wisdom. I resolved that while I was with you I would think of nothing but Jesus Christ—Christ nailed to the
3 4 cross. I came before you weak, nervous, and shaking with fear. The word I spoke, the gospel I proclaimed, did not sway you with subtle arguments;
5 it carried conviction by spiritual power, so that your faith might be built not upon human wisdom but upon the power of God.

6 And yet I do speak words of wisdom to those who are ripe for it, not a wisdom belonging to this passing age, nor to any of its governing powers,
7 which are declining to their end; I speak God's hidden wisdom, his secret
8 purpose framed from the very beginning to bring us to our full glory. The powers that rule the world have never known it; if they had, they would
9 not have crucified the Lord of glory. But, in the words of Scripture, 'Things beyond our seeing, things beyond our hearing, things beyond our
10 imagining, all prepared by God for those who love him', these it is that God has revealed to us through the Spirit.

For the Spirit explores everything, even the depths of God's own
11 nature. Among men, who knows what a man is but the man's own spirit within him? In the same way, only the Spirit of God knows what God is.
12 This is the Spirit that we have received from God, and not the spirit of

*a Some witnesses read* I declared God's secret purpose . . .

the world, so that we may know all that God of his own grace has given us; and, because we are interpreting spiritual truths to those who have the 13 Spirit, we speak of these gifts of God in words found for us not by our human wisdom but by the Spirit. A man who is unspiritual refuses what 14 belongs to the Spirit of God; it is folly to him; he cannot grasp it, because it needs to be judged in the light of the Spirit. A man gifted with the Spirit 15 can judge the worth of everything, but is not himself subject to judgement by his fellow-men. For (in the words of Scripture) 'who knows the mind of 16 the Lord? Who can advise him?' We, however, possess the mind of Christ.

FOR MY PART, my brothers, I could not speak to you as I should speak 3 to people who have the Spirit. I had to deal with you on the merely natural plane, as infants in Christ. And so I gave you milk to drink, instead of solid 2 food, for which you were not yet ready. Indeed, you are still not ready for it, for you are still on the merely natural plane. Can you not see that while 3 there is jealousy and strife among you, you are living on the purely human level of your lower nature? When one says, 'I am Paul's man', and another, 4 'I am for Apollos', are you not all too human?

After all, what is Apollos? What is Paul? We are simply God's agents 5 in bringing you to the faith. Each of us performed the task which the Lord allotted to him: I planted the seed, and Apollos watered it; but God made 6 it grow. Thus it is not the gardeners with their planting and watering who 7 count, but God, who makes it grow. Whether they plant or water, they work 8 as a team,[a] though each will get his own pay for his own labour. We are 9 God's fellow-workers;[b] and you are God's garden.

Or again, you are God's building. I am like a skilled master-builder 10 who by God's grace laid the foundation, and someone else is putting up the building. Let each take care how he builds. There can be no other 11 foundation beyond that which is already laid; I mean Jesus Christ himself. If anyone builds on that foundation with gold, silver, and fine stone, or 12 with wood, hay, and straw, the work that each man does will at last be 13 brought to light; the day of judgement will expose it. For that day dawns in fire, and the fire will test the worth of each man's work. If a man's build- 14 ing stands, he will be rewarded; if it burns, he will have to bear the loss; 15 and yet he will escape with his life, as one might from a fire. Surely you 16 know that you are God's temple, where the Spirit of God dwells. Anyone 17 who destroys God's temple will himself be destroyed[c] by God, because the temple of God is holy; and that temple you are.

Make no mistake about this: if there is anyone among you who fancies 18 himself wise—wise, I mean, by the standards of this passing age—he must become a fool to gain true wisdom. For the wisdom of this world is folly in 19 God's sight. Scripture says, 'He traps the wise in their own cunning', and 20 again, 'The Lord knows that the arguments of the wise are futile.' So never 21 make mere men a cause for pride. For though everything belongs to you— Paul, Apollos, and Cephas, the world, life, and death, the present and the 22

---

[a] *Or* Whether they plant or water, it is all the same.     [b] *Or* We are fellow-workers in God's service.     [c] *Some witnesses read* is himself destroyed.

23 future, all of them belong to you—yet you belong to Christ, and Christ to God.

4 We must be regarded as Christ's subordinates and as stewards of the 2 secrets of God. Well then, stewards are expected to show themselves trust- 3 worthy. For my part, if I am called to account by you or by any human court of judgement, it does not matter to me in the least. Why, I do not even pass 4 judgement on myself, for I have nothing on my conscience; but that does 5 not mean I stand acquitted. My judge is the Lord. So pass no premature judgement; wait until the Lord comes. For he will bring to light what darkness hides, and disclose men's inward motives; then will be the time for each to receive from God such praise as he deserves.

6 Into this general picture, my friends, I have brought Apollos and myself on your account, so that you may take our case as an example, and learn to 'keep within the rules', as they say, and may not be inflated with pride 7 as you patronize one and flout the other. Who makes you, my friend, so important? What do you possess that was not given you? If then you really received it all as a gift, why take the credit to yourself?

8 All of you, no doubt, have everything you could desire. You have come into your fortune already. You have come into your kingdom—and left us out. How I wish you had indeed won your kingdom; then you might 9 share it with us! For it seems to me God has made us apostles the most abject of mankind. We are like men condemned to death in the arena, a 10 spectacle to the whole universe—angels as well as men. We are fools for Christ's sake, while you are such sensible Christians. We are weak; you 11 are so powerful. We are in disgrace; you are honoured. To this day we go hungry and thirsty and in rags; we are roughly handled; we wander from 12 place to place; we wear ourselves out working with our own hands. They 13 curse us, and we bless; they persecute us, and we submit to it; they slander us, and we humbly make our appeal. We are treated as the scum of the earth, the dregs of humanity, to this very day.

14 I am not writing thus to shame you, but to bring you to reason; for you 15 are my dear children. You may have ten thousand tutors in Christ, but you have only one father. For in Christ Jesus you are my offspring, and 16 mine alone, through the preaching of the Gospel. I appeal to you there- 17 fore to follow my example. That is the very reason why I have sent Timothy, who is a dear son to me and a most trustworthy Christian; he will remind you of the way of life in Christ which I follow, and which I teach every- 18 where in all our congregations. There are certain persons who are filled 19 with self-importance because they think I am not coming to Corinth. I shall come very soon, if the Lord will; and then I shall take the measure of these self-important people, not by what they say, but by what power is in them. 20 21 The kingdom of God is not a matter of talk, but of power. Choose, then: am I to come to you with a rod in my hand, or in love and a gentle spirit?

5 I ACTUALLY HEAR REPORTS of sexual immorality among you, im- morality such as even pagans do not tolerate: the union of a man with his 2 father's wife. And you can still be proud of yourselves! You ought to have gone into mourning; a man who has done such a deed should have been

rooted out of your company. For my part, though I am absent in body, I 3
am present in spirit, and my judgement upon the man who did this thing is
already given, as if I were indeed present: you all being assembled in the 4
name of our Lord Jesus, and I with you in spirit, with the power of our
Lord Jesus over us, this man is to be consigned to Satan for the destruction 5
of the body, so that his spirit may be saved on the Day of the Lord.

Your self-satisfaction ill becomes you. Have you never heard the saying, 6
'A little leaven leavens all the dough'? The old leaven of corruption is work- 7
ing among you. Purge it out, and then you will be bread of a new baking.
As Christians you are unleavened Passover bread; for indeed our Passover
has begun; the sacrifice is offered—Christ himself. So we who observe the 8
festival must not use the old leaven, the leaven of corruption and wickedness, but only the unleavened bread which is sincerity and truth.

In my letter I wrote that you must have nothing to do with loose livers. 9
I was not, of course, referring to pagans who lead loose lives or are grabbers 10
and swindlers or idolaters. To avoid them you would have to get out of the
world altogether. I now write that you must have nothing to do with any 11
so-called Christian who leads a loose life, or is grasping, or idolatrous, a
slanderer, a drunkard, or a swindler. You should not even eat with any
such person. What business of mine is it to judge outsiders? God is their 12 13
judge. You are judges within the fellowship. Root out the evil-doer from
your community.

IF ONE OF YOUR NUMBER has a dispute with another, has he the face to **6**
take it to pagan law-courts instead of to the community of God's people?
It is God's people who are to judge the world; surely you know that. And 2
if the world is to come before you for judgement, are you incompetent to
deal with these trifling cases? Are you not aware that we are to judge angels? 3
How much more, mere matters of business! If therefore you have such 4
business disputes, how can you entrust jurisdiction to outsiders, men
who count for nothing in our community? I write this to shame you. Can 5
it be that there is not a single wise man among you able to give a decision
in a brother-Christian's cause? Must brother go to law with brother—and 6
before unbelievers? Indeed, you already fall below your standard in going 7
to law with one another at all. Why not rather suffer injury? Why not
rather let yourself be robbed? So far from this, you actually injure and 8
rob—injure and rob your brothers! Surely you know that the unjust will 9
never come into possession of the kingdom of God. Make no mistake: no
fornicator or idolater, none who are guilty either of adultery or of homo-
sexual perversion, no thieves or grabbers or drunkards or slanderers or 10
swindlers, will possess the kingdom of God. Such were some of you. But 11
you have been through the purifying waters; you have been dedicated to
God and justified through the name of the Lord Jesus and the Spirit of
our God.

'I am free to do anything', you say. Yes, but not everything is for my 12
good. No doubt I am free to do anything, but I for one will not let anything
make free with me. 'Food is for the belly and the belly for food', you say. 13
True; and one day God will put an end to both. But it is not true that the

14 body is for lust; it is for the Lord—and the Lord for the body. God not
15 only raised our Lord from the dead; he will also raise us by his power. Do
you not know that your bodies are limbs and organs of Christ? Shall I then
take from Christ his bodily parts and make them over to a harlot? Never!
16 You surely know that anyone who links himself with a harlot becomes
physically one with her (for Scripture says, 'The pair shall become one
17 flesh'); but he who links himself with Christ is one with him, spiritually.
18 Shun fornication. Every other sin that a man can commit is outside the
19 body; but the fornicator sins against his own body. Do you not know that
your body is a shrine of the indwelling Holy Spirit, and the Spirit is God's
20 gift to you? You do not belong to yourselves; you were bought at a price.
Then honour God in your body.

## The Christian in a pagan society

7 AND NOW for the matters you wrote about.
It is a good thing for a man to have nothing to do with women;[a]
2 but because there is so much immorality, let each man have his own wife
3 and each woman her own husband. The husband must give the wife what
4 is due to her, and the wife equally must give the husband his due. The wife
cannot claim her body as her own; it is her husband's. Equally, the husband
5 cannot claim his body as his own; it is his wife's. Do not deny yourselves to
one another, except when you agree upon a temporary abstinence in order
to devote yourselves to prayer; afterwards you may come together again;
otherwise, for lack of self-control, you may be tempted by Satan.

6 7 All this I say by way of concession, not command. I should like you all to
be as I am myself; but everyone has the gift God has granted him, one this
gift and another that.

8 To the unmarried and to widows I say this: it is a good thing if they stay
9 as I am myself; but if they cannot control themselves, they should marry.
Better be married than burn with vain desire.

10 To the married I give this ruling, which is not mine but the Lord's: a
11 wife must not separate herself from her husband; if she does, she must
either remain unmarried or be reconciled to her husband; and the husband
must not divorce his wife.

12 To the rest I say this, as my own word, not as the Lord's: if a Christian
has a heathen wife, and she is willing to live with him, he must not divorce
13 her; and a woman who has a heathen husband willing to live with her must
14 not divorce her husband. For the heathen husband now belongs to God
through his Christian wife, and the heathen wife through her Christian
husband. Otherwise your children would not belong to God, whereas in
15 fact they do. If on the other hand the heathen partner wishes for a separation, let him have it. In such cases the Christian husband or wife is under
16 no compulsion; but God's call is a call to live in peace. Think of it: as a wife
you may be your husband's salvation; as a husband you may be your wife's
salvation.

[a] *Or* You say, 'It is a good thing . . . women'; . . .

However that may be, each one must order his life according to the gift 17
the Lord has granted him and his condition when God called him. That is
what I teach in all our congregations. Was a man called with the marks of 18
circumcision on him? Let him not remove them. Was he uncircumcised
when he was called? Let him not be circumcised. Circumcision or un- 19
circumcision is neither here nor there; what matters is to keep God's commands. Every man should remain in the condition in which he was called. 20
Were you a slave when you were called? Do not let that trouble you; but if 21
a chance of liberty should come, take it.*a* For the man who as a slave 22
received the call to be a Christian is the Lord's freedman, and, equally,
the free man who received the call is a slave in the service of Christ. You 23
were bought at a price; do not become slaves of men. Thus each one, my 24
friends, is to remain before God in the condition in which he received
his call.

On the question of celibacy, I have no instructions from the Lord, but 25
I give my judgement as one who by God's mercy is fit to be trusted.

It is my opinion, then, that in a time of stress like the present this is the 26
best way for a man to live—it is best for a man to be as he is. Are you bound 27
in marriage? Do not seek a dissolution. Has your marriage been dissolved?
Do not seek a wife. If, however, you do marry, there is nothing wrong in 28
it; and if a virgin marries, she has done no wrong. But those who marry
will have pain and grief in this bodily life, and my aim is to spare you.

What I mean, my friends, is this. The time we live in will not last long. 29
While it lasts, married men should be as if they had no wives; mourners 30
should be as if they had nothing to grieve them, the joyful as if they did not
rejoice; buyers must not count on keeping what they buy, nor those who 31
use the world's wealth on using it to the full. For the whole frame of this
world is passing away.

I want you to be free from anxious care. The unmarried man cares for 32
the Lord's business; his aim is to please the Lord. But the married man 33
cares for worldly things; his aim is to please his wife; and he has a divided 34
mind. The unmarried or celibate woman cares*b* for the Lord's business;
her aim is to be dedicated to him in body as in spirit; but the married
woman cares for worldly things; her aim is to please her husband.

In saying this I have no wish to keep you on a tight rein. I am thinking 35
simply of your own good, of what is seemly, and of your freedom to wait
upon the Lord without distraction.

But if a man has a partner in celibacy *c* and feels that he is not behaving 36
properly towards her, if, that is, his instincts are too strong for him,*d* and
something must be done, he may do as he pleases; there is nothing wrong
in it; let them marry.*e* But if a man is steadfast in his purpose, being under 37
no compulsion, and has complete control of his own choice; and if he has
decided in his own mind to preserve his partner *f* in her virginity, he will

---

*a Or* but even if a chance of liberty should come, choose rather to make good use of your
servitude.          *b Some witnesses read* . . . his wife. And there is a difference between
the wife and the virgin. The unmarried woman cares . . .          *c Or* a virgin daughter
*(or* ward).          *d Or* if she is ripe for marriage.          *e Or* let the girl and her
lover marry.          *f Or* his daughter.

38  do well. Thus, he who marries his partner *a* does well, and he who does not will do better.

39  A wife is bound to her husband as long as he lives. But if the husband die, she is free to marry whom she will, provided the marriage is within the
40  Lord's fellowship. But she is better off as she is; that is my opinion, and I believe that I too have the Spirit of God.

8  NOW ABOUT FOOD consecrated to heathen deities.
Of course we all 'have knowledge', as you say. This 'knowledge' breeds
2  conceit; it is love that builds. If anyone fancies that he knows, he knows
3  nothing yet, in the true sense of knowing. But if a man loves, *b* he is acknowledged by God. *c*
4  Well then, about eating this consecrated food: of course, as you say, 'a false god has no existence in the real world. There is no god but one.'
5  For indeed, if there be so-called gods, whether in heaven or on earth—as
6  indeed there are many 'gods' and many 'lords'—yet for us there is one God, the Father, from whom all being comes, towards whom we move; and there is one Lord, Jesus Christ, through whom all things came to be, and we through him.
7  But not everyone knows this. There are some who have been so accustomed to idolatry *d* that even now they eat this food with a sense of its heathen consecration, and their conscience, being weak, is polluted by the
8  eating. Certainly food will not bring us into God's presence: if we do not
9  eat, we are none the worse, and if we eat, we are none the better. But be
10  careful that this liberty of yours does not become a pitfall for the weak. If a weak character sees you sitting down to a meal in a heathen temple—you, who 'have knowledge'—will not his conscience be emboldened to eat food
11  consecrated to the heathen deity? This 'knowledge' of yours is utter
12  disaster to the weak, the brother for whom Christ died. In thus sinning against your brothers and wounding their conscience, *e* you sin against
13  Christ. And therefore, if food be the downfall of my brother, I will never eat meat any more, for I will not be the cause of my brother's downfall.

9  AM I NOT A FREE MAN? Am I not an apostle? Did I not see Jesus our
2  Lord? Are not you my own handiwork, in the Lord? If others do not accept me as an apostle, you at least are bound to do so, for you are yourselves the very seal of my apostolate, in the Lord.
3 4  To those who put me in the dock this is my answer: Have I no right to
5  eat and drink? Have I no right to take a Christian wife about with me, like
6  the rest of the apostles and the Lord's brothers, and Cephas? Or are
7  Barnabas and I alone bound to work for our living? Did you ever hear of a man serving in the army at his own expense? or planting a vineyard with-
8  out eating the fruit of it? or tending a flock without using its milk? Do not
9  suppose I rely on these human analogies, for the law says the same; in the

---

*a Or* gives his daughter in marriage.                    *b Some witnesses read* loves God.
*c Or* he is recognized.                    *d Some witnesses read* in whom the consciousness
of the false god is so persistent . . .                    *e Some witnesses insert* weak as it is.

Law of Moses we read, 'You shall not muzzle a threshing ox.' Do you suppose God's concern is with oxen? Or is the reference clearly to ourselves? 10 Of course it refers to us, in the sense that the ploughman should plough and the thresher thresh in the hope of getting some of the produce. If we 11 have sown a spiritual crop for you, is it too much to expect from you a material harvest? If you allow others these rights, have not we a stronger 12 claim?

But I have availed myself of no such right. On the contrary, I put up with all that comes my way rather than offer any hindrance to the gospel of Christ. You know (do you not?) that those who perform the temple service 13 eat the temple offerings, and those who wait upon the altar claim their share of the sacrifice. In the same way the Lord gave instructions that those 14 who preach the Gospel should earn their living by the Gospel. But I have 15 never taken advantage of any such right, nor do I intend to claim it in this letter. I had rather die! No one shall make my boast an empty boast. Even 16 if I preach the Gospel, I can claim no credit for it; I cannot help myself; it would be misery to me not to preach. If I dìd it of my own choice, I should 17 be earning my pay; but since I do it apart from my own choice, I am simply discharging a trust.*a* Then what is my pay? The satisfaction of preaching 18 the Gospel without expense to anyone; in other words, of waiving the rights which my preaching gives me.

I am a free man and own no master; but I have made myself every man's 19 servant, to win over as many as possible. To Jews I became like a Jew, to 20 win Jews; as they are subject to the Law of Moses, I put myself under that law to win them, although I am not myself subject to it. To win Gentiles, 21 who are outside the Law, I made myself like one of them, although I am not in truth outside God's law, being under the law of Christ. To the weak 22 I became weak, to win the weak. Indeed, I have become everything in turn to men of every sort, so that in one way or another I may save some. All this I do for the sake of the Gospel, to bear my part in proclaiming it. 23

You know (do you not?) that at the sports all the runners run the race, 24 though only one wins the prize. Like them, run to win! But every athlete 25 goes into strict training. They do it to win a fading wreath; we, a wreath that never fades. For my part, I run with a clear goal before me; I am like 26 a boxer who does not beat the air; I bruise my own body and make it know 27 its master, for fear that after preaching to others I should find myself rejected.

You should understand, my brothers, that our ancestors were all under **10** the pillar of cloud, and all of them passed through the Red Sea; and so they 2 all received baptism into the fellowship of Moses in cloud and sea. They 3 all ate the same supernatural food, and all drank the same supernatural 4 drink; I mean, they all drank from the supernatural rock that accompanied their travels—and that rock was Christ. And yet, most of them were not 5 accepted by God, for the desert was strewn with their corpses.

These events happened as symbols to warn us not to set our desires on 6 evil things, as they did. Do not be idolaters, like some of them; as Scripture 7

*a* *Or* If I do it willingly I am earning my pay; if I did it unwillingly I should still have a trust laid upon me.

8  has it, 'the people sat down to feast and rose up to revel'. Let us not commit fornication, as some of them did—and twenty-three thousand died in
9  one day. Let us not put the power of the Lord*ᵃ* to the test, as some of them
10 did—and were destroyed by serpents. Do not grumble against God, as
   some of them did—and were destroyed by the Destroyer.

11    All these things that happened to them were symbolic, and were recorded
   for our benefit as a warning. For upon us the fulfilment of the ages has
12 come. If you feel sure that you are standing firm, beware! You may fall.
13 So far you have faced no trial beyond what man can bear. God keeps faith,
   and he will not allow you to be tested above your powers, but when the
   test comes he will at the same time provide a way out, by enabling you to
   sustain it.

14 15 So THEN, DEAR FRIENDS, shun idolatry. I speak to you as men of sense.
16 Form your own judgement on what I say. When we bless 'the cup of blessing', is it not a means of sharing in the blood of Christ? When we break
17 the bread, is it not a means of sharing in the body of Christ? Because there
   is one loaf, we, many as we are, are one body;*ᵇ* for it is one loaf of which we
   all partake.

18    Look at the Jewish people. Are not those who partake in the sacrificial
19 meal sharers in the altar? What do I imply by this? that an idol is anything
20 but an idol? or food offered to it anything more than food? No; but the
   sacrifices the heathen offer are offered (in the words of Scripture) 'to
   demons and to that which is not God'; and I will not have you become
21 partners with demons. You cannot drink the cup of the Lord and the cup
   of demons. You cannot partake of the Lord's table and the table of demons.
22 Can we defy the Lord? Are we stronger than he?

23    'We are free to do anything', you say. Yes, but is everything good for us?
   'We are free to do anything', but does everything help the building of the
24 community? Each of you must regard, not his own interests, but the other
   man's.

25    You may eat anything sold in the meat-market without raising questions
26 of conscience; for the earth is the Lord's and everything in it.

27    If an unbeliever invites you to a meal and you care to go, eat whatever is
28 put before you, without raising questions of conscience. But if somebody
   says to you, 'This food has been offered in sacrifice', then, out of con-
29 sideration for him, and for conscience' sake, do not eat it—not your conscience, I mean, but the other man's.

   'What?' you say, 'is my freedom to be called in question by another
30 man's conscience? If I partake with thankfulness, why am I blamed for
31 eating food over which I have said grace?' Well, whether you eat or drink,
32 or whatever you are doing, do all for the honour of God: give no offence
33 to Jews, or Greeks, or to the church of God. For my part I always try
   to meet everyone half-way, regarding not my own good but the good
11 of the many, so that they may be saved. Follow my example as I follow
   Christ's.

   *ᵃ Some witnesses read* of Christ.
   *ᵇ Or* For we, many as we are, are one loaf, one body.

I COMMEND YOU for always keeping me in mind, and maintaining the 2
tradition I handed on to you. But I wish you to understand that, while 3
every man has Christ for his Head, woman's head is man,*a* as Christ's
Head is God. A man who keeps his head covered when he prays or pro- 4
phesies brings shame on his head; a woman, on the contrary, brings shame 5
on her head if she prays or prophesies bare-headed; it is as bad as if her head
were shaved. If a woman is not to wear a veil she might as well have her 6
hair cut off; but if it is a disgrace for her to be cropped and shaved, then
she should wear a veil. A man has no need to cover his head, because man 7
is the image of God, and the mirror of his glory, whereas woman reflects
the glory of man.*b* For man did not originally spring from woman, but 8
woman was made out of man; and man was not created for woman's sake, 9
but woman for the sake of man; and therefore it is woman's duty to have a 10
sign of authority*c* on her head, out of regard for the angels.*d* And yet, in 11
Christ's fellowship woman is as essential to man as man to woman. If 12
woman was made out of man, it is through woman that man now comes to
be; and God is the source of all.

Judge for yourselves: is it fitting for a woman to pray to God bare- 13
headed? Does not Nature herself teach you that while flowing locks dis- 14
grace a man, they are a woman's glory? For her locks were given for 15
covering.

However, if you insist on arguing, let me tell you, there is no such 16
custom among us, or in any of the congregations of God's people.

In giving you these injunctions I must mention a practice which I can- 17
not commend: your meetings tend to do more harm than good. To begin 18
with, I am told that when you meet as a congregation you fall into sharply
divided groups; and I believe there is some truth in it (for dissensions are 19
necessary if only to show which of your members are sound). The result 20
is that when you meet as a congregation, it is impossible for you to eat the
Lord's Supper, because each of you is in such a hurry to eat his own, and 21
while one goes hungry another has too much to drink. Have you no homes 22
of your own to eat and drink in? Or are you so contemptuous of the church
of God that you shame its poorer members? What am I to say? Can I
commend you? On this point, certainly not!

For the tradition which I handed on to you came to me from the Lord 23
himself: that the Lord Jesus, on the night of his arrest, took bread and, 24
after giving thanks to God, broke it and said: 'This is my body, which is
for you; do this as a memorial of me.' In the same way, he took the cup 25
after supper, and said: 'This cup is the new covenant sealed by my blood.
Whenever you drink it, do this as a memorial of me.' For every time you 26
eat this bread and drink the cup, you proclaim the death of the Lord, until
he comes.

It follows that anyone who eats the bread or drinks the cup of the Lord 27
unworthily will be guilty of desecrating the body and blood of the Lord.
A man must test himself before eating his share of the bread and drinking 28

---

*a Or* a woman's head is her husband.     *b Or* a woman reflects her husband's glory.
*c Some witnesses read* to have a veil.     *d Or* and therefore a woman should keep
her dignity on her head, for fear of the angels.

29 from the cup. For he who eats and drinks eats and drinks judgement on
30 himself if he does not discern the Body. That is why many of you are feeble
31 and sick, and a number have died. But if we examined ourselves, we should
32 not thus fall under judgement. When, however, we do fall under the
Lord's judgement, he is disciplining us, to save us from being condemned
with the rest of the world.

33     Therefore, my brothers, when you meet for a meal, wait for one another.
34 If you are hungry, eat at home, so that in meeting together you may not
fall under judgement. The other matters I will arrange when I come.

## *Spiritual gifts*

12 ABOUT GIFTS OF THE SPIRIT, there are some things of which I do
not wish you to remain ignorant.

2     You know how, in the days when you were still pagan, you were swept
3 off to those dumb heathen gods, however you happened to be led.[a] For
this reason I must impress upon you that no one who says 'A curse on
Jesus!' can be speaking under the influence of the Spirit of God. And no
one can say 'Jesus is Lord!' except under the influence of the Holy Spirit.

4 5     There are varieties of gifts, but the same Spirit. There are varieties of
6 service, but the same Lord. There are many forms of work, but all of them,
7 in all men, are the work of the same God. In each of us the Spirit is mani-
8 fested in one particular way, for some useful purpose. One man, through
the Spirit, has the gift of wise speech, while another, by the power of the
9 same Spirit, can put the deepest knowledge into words. Another, by the
same Spirit, is granted faith; another, by the one Spirit, gifts of healing,
10 and another miraculous powers; another has the gift of prophecy, and
another ability to distinguish true spirits from false; yet another has the
gift of ecstatic utterance of different kinds, and another the ability to
11 interpret it. But all these gifts are the work of one and the same Spirit,
distributing them separately to each individual at will.

12     For Christ is like a single body with its many limbs and organs, which,
13 many as they are, together make up one body. For indeed we were all
brought into one body by baptism, in the one Spirit, whether we are Jews
or Greeks, whether slaves or free men, and that one Holy Spirit was poured
out for all of us to drink.

14 15     A body is not one single organ, but many. Suppose the foot should say,
'Because I am not a hand, I do not belong to the body', it does belong to the
16 body none the less. Suppose the ear were to say, 'Because I am not an eye,
17 I do not belong to the body', it does still belong to the body. If the body were
all eye, how could it hear? If the body were all ear, how could it smell?
18 But, in fact, God appointed each limb and organ to its own place in the
19 body, as he chose. If the whole were one single organ, there would not be
20 a body at all; in fact, however, there are many different organs, but one
21 body. The eye cannot say to the hand, 'I do not need you'; nor the head to

[a] *Or* . . . pagan, you would be seized by some power which drove you to those dumb
heathen gods.

the feet, 'I do not need you.' Quite the contrary: those organs of the body 22
which seem to be more frail than others are indispensable, and those parts 23
of the body which we regard as less honourable are treated with special
honour. To our unseemly parts is given a more than ordinary seemliness,
whereas our seemly parts need no adorning. But God has combined the 24
various parts of the body, giving special honour to the humbler parts, so 25
that there might be no sense of division in the body, but that all its organs
might feel the same concern for one another. If one organ suffers, they all 26
suffer together. If one flourishes, they all rejoice together.

Now you are Christ's body, and each of you a limb or organ of it. Within 27 28
our community God has appointed, in the first place apostles, in the second
place prophets, thirdly teachers; then miracle-workers, then those who
have gifts of healing, or ability to help others or power to guide them, or
the gift of ecstatic utterance of various kinds. Are all apostles? all prophets? 29
all teachers? Do all work miracles? Have all gifts of healing? Do all speak 30
in tongues of ecstasy? Can all interpret them? The higher gifts are those 31
you should aim at.

And now I will show you the best way of all.

I may speak in tongues of men or of angels, but if I am without love, I **13**
am a sounding gong or a clanging cymbal. I may have the gift of prophecy, 2
and know every hidden truth; I may have faith strong enough to move
mountains; but if I have no love, I am nothing. I may dole out all I possess, 3
or even give my body to be burnt,*a* but if I have no love, I am none the
better.

Love is patient; love is kind and envies no one. Love is never boastful, 4
nor conceited, nor rude; never selfish, not quick to take offence. Love keeps 5
no score of wrongs; does not gloat over other men's sins, but delights in the 6
truth. There is nothing love cannot face; there is no limit to its faith, its 7
hope, and its endurance.

Love will never come to an end. Are there prophets? their work will be 8
over. Are there tongues of ecstasy? they will cease. Is there knowledge?
it will vanish away; for our knowledge and our prophecy alike are partial, 9
and the partial vanishes when wholeness comes. When I was a child, my 10 11
speech, my outlook, and my thoughts were all childish. When I grew up,
I had finished with childish things. Now we see only puzzling reflections 12
in a mirror, but then we shall see face to face. My knowledge now is partial;
then it will be whole, like God's knowledge of me. In a word, there are three 13
things that last for ever: faith, hope, and love; but the greatest of them all
is love.

Put love first; but there are other gifts of the Spirit at which you should **14**
aim also, and above all prophecy. When a man is using the language of 2
ecstasy he is talking with God, not with men, for no man understands him;
he is no doubt inspired, but he speaks mysteries. On the other hand, when 3
a man prophesies, he is talking to men, and his words have power to build;
they stimulate and they encourage. The language of ecstasy is good for the 4
speaker himself, but it is prophecy that builds up a Christian community.
I should be pleased for you all to use the tongues of ecstasy, but better 5

     *a Some witnesses read* even seek glory by self-sacrifice.

pleased for you to prophesy. The prophet is worth more than the man of ecstatic speech—unless indeed he can explain its meaning, and so help to
6 build up the community. Suppose, my friends, that when I come to you I use ecstatic language: what good shall I do you, unless what I say contains something by way of revelation, or enlightenment, or prophecy, or instruction?

7    Even with inanimate things that produce sounds—a flute, say, or a lyre —unless their notes mark definite intervals, how can you tell what tune is
8 being played? Or again, if the trumpet-call is not clear, who will prepare
9 for battle? In the same way if your ecstatic utterance yields no precise meaning, how can anyone tell what you are saying? You will be talking into
10 the air. How many different kinds of sound there are, or may be, in the
11 world! Nothing is altogether soundless. Well then, if I do not know the meaning of the sound the speaker makes, his words will be gibberish to me,
12 and mine to him. You are, I know, eager for gifts of the Spirit; then aspire above all to excel in those which build up the church.

13    I say, then, that the man who falls into ecstatic utterance should pray
14 for the ability to interpret. If I use such language in my prayer, the Spirit
15 in me prays, but my intellect lies fallow. What then? I will pray as I am inspired to pray, but I will also pray intelligently. I will sing hymns as
16 I am inspired to sing, but I will sing intelligently too. Suppose you are praising God in the language of inspiration: how will the plain man who is present be able to say 'Amen' to your thanksgiving, when he does not know
17 what you are saying? Your prayer of thanksgiving may be all that could be
18 desired, but it is no help to the other man. Thank God, I am more gifted in
19 ecstatic utterance than any of you,*a* but in the congregation I would rather speak five intelligible words, for the benefit of others as well as myself, than thousands of words in the language of ecstasy.

20    Do not be childish, my friends. Be as innocent of evil as babes, but at
21 least be grown-up in your thinking. We read in the Law: 'I will speak to this nation through men of strange tongues, and by the lips of foreigners;
22 and even so they will not heed me, says the Lord.' Clearly then these 'strange tongues' are not intended as a sign for believers, but for un-believers, whereas prophecy is designed not for unbelievers but for those
23 who hold the faith. So if the whole congregation is assembled and all are using the 'strange tongues' of ecstasy, and some uninstructed persons or
24 unbelievers should enter, will they not think you are mad? But if all are uttering prophecies, the visitor, when he enters, hears from everyone
25 something that searches his conscience and brings conviction, and the secrets of his heart are laid bare. So he will fall down and worship God, crying, 'God is certainly among you!'

26    To sum up, my friends: when you meet for worship, each of you con-tributes a hymn, some instruction, a revelation, an ecstatic utterance, or the interpretation of such an utterance. All of these must aim at one thing:
27 to build up the church. If it is a matter of ecstatic utterance, only two should
28 speak, or at most three, one at a time, and someone must interpret. If there is no interpreter, the speaker had better not address the meeting at

*a Or* . . . man. I say the thanksgiving; I use ecstatic speech more than any of you.

all, but speak to himself and to God. Of the prophets, two or three may 29
speak, while the rest exercise their judgement upon what is said. If some- 30
one else, sitting in his place, receives a revelation, let the first speaker stop.
You can all prophesy, one at a time, so that the whole congregation may 31
receive instruction and encouragement. It is for prophets to control pro- 32
phetic inspiration, for the God who inspires them is not a God of disorder 33
but of peace.

As in all congregations of God's people, women*a* should not address the 34
meeting. They have no licence to speak, but should keep their place as the
law directs. If there is something they want to know, they can ask their 35
own husbands at home. It is a shocking thing that a woman should address
the congregation.

Did the word of God originate with you? Or are you the only people to 36
whom it came? If anyone claims to be inspired or a prophet, let him recog- 37
nize that what I write has the Lord's authority. If he does not acknowledge 38
this, God does not acknowledge him.*b*

In short, my friends, be eager to prophesy; do not forbid ecstatic utter- 39
ance; but let all be done decently and in order. 40

## Life after death

AND NOW, MY BROTHERS, I must remind you of the gospel that I 15
preached to you; the gospel which you received, on which you have
taken your stand, and which is now bringing you salvation. Do you still 2
hold fast the Gospel as I preached it to you? If not, your conversion was
in vain.*c*

First and foremost, I handed on to you the facts which had been im- 3
parted to me: that Christ died for our sins, in accordance with the scriptures; that he was buried; that he was raised to life on the third day, 4
according to the scriptures; and that he appeared to Cephas, and after- 5
wards to the Twelve. Then he appeared to over five hundred of our brothers 6
at once, most of whom are still alive, though some have died. Then he 7
appeared to James, and afterwards to all the apostles.

In the end he appeared even to me. It was like an abnormal birth; I had 8 9
persecuted the church of God and am therefore inferior to all other
apostles—indeed not fit to be called an apostle. However, by God's grace 10
I am what I am, nor has his grace been given to me in vain; on the contrary,
in my labours I have outdone them all—not I, indeed, but the grace of
God working with me. But what matter, I or they? This is what we all 11
proclaim, and this is what you believed.

Now if this is what we proclaim, that Christ was raised from the dead, 12
how can some of you say there is no resurrection of the dead? If there be 13
no resurrection, then Christ was not raised; and if Christ was not raised, 14

*a Or* of peace, as in all communities of God's people. Women . . .      *b Some
witnesses read* If he refuses to recognize this, let him refuse!     *c Or* Do you
remember the terms in which I preached the Gospel to you?—for I assume you did not
accept it thoughtlessly.

15 then our gospel is null and void, and so is your faith; and we turn out to be
16 lying witnesses for God, because we bore witness that he raised Christ to
17 life, whereas, if the dead are not raised, he did not raise him. For if the dead
are not raised, it follows that Christ was not raised; and if Christ was not
raised, your faith has nothing in it and you are still in your old state of sin.
18 It follows also that those who have died within Christ's fellowship are
19 utterly lost. If it is for this life only that Christ has given us hope,*a* we of all
men are most to be pitied.

20 But the truth is, Christ was raised to life—the firstfruits of the harvest
21 of the dead. For since it was a man who brought death into the world, a
22 man also brought resurrection of the dead. As in Adam all men die, so in
23 Christ all will be brought to life; but each in his own proper place: Christ
the firstfruits, and afterwards, at his coming, those who belong to Christ.
24 Then comes the end, when he delivers up the kingdom to God the Father,
25 after abolishing every kind of domination, authority, and power. For he is
26 destined to reign until God has put all enemies under his feet; and the last
27 enemy to be abolished is death.*b* Scripture says, 'He has put all things in
subjection under his feet.' But in saying 'all things', it clearly means to
28 exclude God who subordinates them; and when all things are thus subject
to him, then the Son himself will also be made subordinate to God who
made all things subject to him, and thus God will be all in all.

29 Again, there are those who receive baptism on behalf of the dead. Why
should they do this? If the dead are not raised to life at all, what do they
mean by being baptized on their behalf?

30 31 And we ourselves—why do we face these dangers hour by hour? Every
day I die: I swear it by my pride in you, my brothers—for in Christ Jesus
32 our Lord I am proud of you. If, as the saying is, I 'fought wild beasts' at
Ephesus, what have I gained by it?*c* If the dead are never raised to life, 'let
us eat and drink, for tomorrow we die'.

33 34 Make no mistake: 'Bad company is the ruin of a good character.' Come
back to a sober and upright life and leave your sinful ways. There are some
who know nothing of God; to your shame I say it.

35 But, you may ask, how are the dead raised? In what kind of body?
36 How foolish! The seed you sow does not come to life unless it has first
37 died; and what you sow is not the body that shall be, but a naked grain,
38 perhaps of wheat, or of some other kind; and God clothes it with the body of
39 his choice, each seed with its own particular body. All flesh is not the same
flesh: there is flesh of men, flesh of beasts, of birds, and of fishes—all dif-
40 ferent. There are heavenly bodies and earthly bodies; and the splendour of
41 the heavenly bodies is one thing, the splendour of the earthly, another. The
sun has a splendour of its own, the moon another splendour, and the stars
42 another, for star differs from star in brightness. So it is with the resurrection
of the dead. What is sown in the earth as a perishable thing is raised

*a Or* If it is only an uncertain hope that our life in Christ has given us . . .     *b Or*
Then at the end, when . . . power (for he . . . feet), the last enemy, death, will
be abolished.     *c Or* If, as men do, I had fought wild beasts at Ephesus, what good
would it be to me? *or* If I had been in no better case than one fighting beasts in
the arena at Ephesus, what good would it be to me?

imperishable. Sown in humiliation, it is raised in glory; sown in weakness, 43
it is raised in power; sown as an animal body, it is raised as a spiritual body. 44

If there is such a thing as an animal body, there is also a spiritual body.
It is in this sense that Scripture says, 'The first man, Adam, became an 45
animate being', whereas the last Adam has become a life-giving spirit.
Observe, the spiritual does not come first; the animal body comes first, and 46
then the spiritual. The first man was made 'of the dust of the earth': the 47
second man is from heaven. The man made of dust is the pattern of all 48
men of dust, and the heavenly man is the pattern of all the heavenly. As 49
we have worn the likeness of the man made of dust, so we shall wear the
likeness of the heavenly man.

What I mean, my brothers, is this: flesh and blood can never possess 50
the kingdom of God, and the perishable cannot possess immortality.
Listen! I will unfold a mystery: we shall not all die, but we shall all be 51
changed in a flash, in the twinkling of an eye, at the last trumpet-call. For 52
the trumpet will sound, and the dead will rise immortal, and we shall be
changed. This perishable being must be clothed with the imperishable, 53
and what is mortal must be clothed with immortality. And when *a* our 54
mortality has been clothed with immortality, then the saying of Scripture
will come true: 'Death is swallowed up; victory is won!' 'O Death, where 55
is your victory? O Death, where is your sting?' The sting of death is sin, 56
and sin gains its power from the law; but, God be praised, he gives us the 57
victory through our Lord Jesus Christ.

Therefore, my beloved brothers, stand firm and immovable, and work for 58
the Lord always, work without limit, since you know that in the Lord your
labour cannot be lost.

## *Christian giving*

AND NOW about the collection in aid of God's people: you should **16**
follow my directions to our congregations in Galatia. Every Sunday 2
each of you is to put aside and keep by him a sum in proportion to his gains,
so that there may be no collecting when I come. When I arrive, I will give 3
letters of introduction to persons approved by you, and send them to carry
your gift to Jerusalem. If it should seem worth while for me to go as well, 4
they shall go with me.

I shall come to Corinth after passing through Macedonia—for I am 5
travelling by way of Macedonia—and I may stay with you, perhaps even 6
for the whole winter, and then you can help me on my way wherever I go
next. I do not want this to be a flying visit; I hope to spend some time with 7
you, if the Lord permits. But I shall remain at Ephesus until Whitsuntide, 8
for a great opportunity has opened for effective work, and there is much 9
opposition.

If Timothy comes, see that you put him at his ease; for it is the Lord's 10
work that he is engaged upon, as I am myself; so no one must slight him. 11

*a Some witnesses insert* our perishable nature has been clothed with the imperishable,
and . . .

Send him happily on his way to join me, since I am waiting for him with
12 our friends. As for our friend Apollos, I urged him strongly to go to
Corinth with the others, but he was quite determined not to go*ᵃ* at present;
he will go when opportunity offers.

13 14 Be alert; stand firm in the faith; be valiant and strong. Let all you do be
done in love.

15 I have a request to make of you, my brothers. You know that the
Stephanas family were the first converts in Achaia, and have laid themselves
16 out to serve God's people. I wish you to give their due position to such
persons, and indeed to everyone who labours hard at our common task.
17 It is a great pleasure to me that Stephanas, Fortunatus, and Achaicus have
18 arrived, because they have done what you had no chance to do; they have
relieved my mind—and no doubt yours too. Such men deserve recognition.
19 Greetings from the congregations in Asia. Many greetings in the Lord
20 from Aquila and Prisca and the congregation at their house. Greetings from
all the brothers. Greet one another with the kiss of peace.

21 This greeting is in my own hand—PAUL.

22 If anyone does not love the Lord, let him be outcast.
*Marana tha*—Come, O Lord!
23 The grace of the Lord Jesus Christ be with you.
24 My love to you all in Christ Jesus. Amen.

# THE SECOND LETTER OF PAUL

# TO THE

# CORINTHIANS

## *Personal religion and the ministry*

1 FROM PAUL, APOSTLE of Christ Jesus by God's will, and
our colleague Timothy, to the congregation of God's people at
Corinth, together with all who are dedicated to him throughout the
whole of Achaia.
2 Grace and peace to you from God our Father and the Lord Jesus Christ.
3 Praise be to the God and Father of our Lord Jesus Christ, the all-
4 merciful Father, the God whose consolation never fails us! He comforts
us in all our troubles, so that we in turn may be able to comfort others in
any trouble of theirs and to share with them the consolation we ourselves
5 receive from God. As Christ's cup of suffering overflows, and we suffer
6 with him, so also through Christ our consolation overflows. If distress be
our lot, it is the price we pay for your consolation, for your salvation; if our

*ᵃ* *Or* but it was by no means the will of God that he should go . . .

lot be consolation, it is to help us to bring you comfort, and strength to face
with fortitude the same sufferings we now endure. And our hope for you is 7
firmly grounded;[a] for we know that if you have part in the suffering, you
have part also in the divine consolation.

In saying this, we should like you to know, dear friends, how serious 8
was the trouble that came upon us in the province of Asia. The burden of
it was far too heavy for us to bear, so heavy that we even despaired of life.
Indeed, we felt in our hearts that we had received a death-sentence. This 9
was meant to teach us not to place reliance on ourselves, but on God who
raises the dead. From such mortal peril God delivered us; and he will 10
deliver us again,[b] he on whom our hope is fixed. Yes, he will continue to
deliver us, if you will co-operate by praying for us. Then, with so many 11
people praying for our deliverance, there will be many to give thanks on
our behalf for the gracious favour God has shown towards us.

There is one thing we are proud of: our conscience assures us that in our 12
dealings with our fellow-men, and above all in our dealings with you, our
conduct has been governed by a devout and godly sincerity,[c] by the grace
of God and not by worldly wisdom. There is nothing in our letters to you 13
but what you can read for yourselves, and understand too. Partial as your 14
present knowledge of us is, you will I hope come to understand fully that
you have as much reason to be proud of us, as we of you, on the Day of our
Lord Jesus.

It was because I felt so confident about all this that I had intended to 15
come first of all to you[d] and give you the benefit of a double visit: I meant to 16
visit you on my way to Macedonia, and after leaving Macedonia, to return
to you, and you would then send me on my way to Judaea. That was my 17
intention; did I lightly change my mind?[e] Or do I, when I frame my plans,
frame them as a worldly man might, so that it should rest with me to say
'yes' and 'yes', or 'no' and 'no'? As God is true, the language in which we 18
address you is not an ambiguous blend of Yes and No. The Son of God, 19
Christ Jesus, proclaimed among you by us (by Silvanus and Timothy, I
mean, as well as myself), was never a blend of Yes and No. With him it
was, and is, Yes. He is the Yes pronounced upon God's promises, every one 20
of them. That is why, when we give glory to God, it is through Christ Jesus
that we say 'Amen'. And if you and we belong to Christ, guaranteed as his 21
and anointed, it is all God's doing; it is God also who has set his seal upon us, 22
and as a pledge of what is to come has given the Spirit to dwell in our hearts.

I appeal to God to witness what I am going to say; I stake my life upon it: 23
it was out of consideration for you that I did not after all come to Corinth.
Do not think we are dictating the terms of your faith; your hold on the 24
faith is secure enough. We are working with you for your own happiness.
So I made up my mind that my next visit to you must not be another pain- 2
ful one. If I cause pain to you, who is left to cheer me up, except you, whom 2
I have offended? This is precisely the point I made in my letter: I did not 3

---

[a] *Some witnesses give these clauses* If distress . . . firmly grounded *in different sequence.*
[b] *Some witnesses read* and he still delivers us.     [c] *Some witnesses read* by sincere
and godly singleness of mind.     [d] *Or* had originally intended to come to you . . .
[e] *Or* In forming this intention, did I act irresponsibly?

want, I said, to come and be made miserable by the very people who ought to have made me happy; and I had sufficient confidence in you all to know
4 that for me to be happy is for all of you to be happy. That letter I sent you came out of great distress and anxiety; how many tears I shed as I wrote it! But I never meant to cause you pain; I wanted you rather to know the love, the more than ordinary love, that I have for you.

5 Any injury that has been done, has not been done to me; to some extent,
6 not to labour the point, it has been done to you all. The penalty on which
7 the general meeting has agreed has met the offence well enough. Something very different is called for now: you must forgive the offender and put heart into him; the man's sorrow must not be made so severe as to
8 overwhelm him. I urge you therefore to assure him of your love for him
9 by a formal act. I wrote, I may say, to see how you stood the test, whether
10 you fully accepted my authority. But anyone who has your forgiveness has mine too; and when I speak of forgiving (so far as there is anything for me to forgive), I mean that as the representative of Christ I have forgiven him
11 for your sake.[a] For Satan must not be allowed to get the better of us; we know his wiles all too well.

12 Then when I came to Troas, where I was to preach the gospel of Christ,
13 and where an opening awaited me for the Lord's work, I still found no relief of mind, for my colleague Titus was not there to meet me; so I took
14 leave of the people there and went off to Macedonia. But thanks be to God, who continually leads us about, captives in Christ's triumphal procession, and everywhere uses us to reveal and spread abroad the fragrance of the
15 knowledge of himself! We are indeed the incense offered by Christ to God, both for those who are on the way to salvation, and for those who are on the
16 way to perdition: to the latter it is a deadly fume that kills, to the former a
17 vital fragrance that brings life. Who is equal to such a calling? At least we do not go hawking the word of God about, as so many do; when we declare the word we do it in sincerity, as from God and in God's sight, as members of Christ.

3 ARE WE BEGINNING all over again to produce our credentials? Do we,
2 like some people, need letters of introduction to you, or from you? No, you are all the letter we need, a letter written on our heart; any man can
3 see it for what it is and read it for himself. And as for you, it is plain that you are a letter that has come from Christ, given to us to deliver: a letter written not with ink but with the Spirit of the living God, written not on stone tablets but on the pages of the human heart.

4 It is in full reliance upon God, through Christ, that we make such claims.
5 There is no question of our being qualified in ourselves: we cannot claim
6 anything as our own. The qualification we have comes from God; it is he who has qualified us to dispense his new covenant—a covenant expressed not in a written document, but in a spiritual bond; for the written law condemns to death, but the Spirit gives life.

7 The law, then, engraved letter by letter upon stone, dispensed death, and yet it was inaugurated with divine splendour. That splendour, though

[a] *Or* that I have forgiven him for your sake, in the presence of Christ.

it was soon to fade, made the face of Moses so bright that the Israelites
could not gaze steadily at him. But if so, must not even greater splendour   8
rest upon the divine dispensation of the Spirit? If splendour accompanied   9
the dispensation under which we are condemned, how much richer in splendour must that one be under which we are acquitted! Indeed, the splendour   10
that once was is now no splendour at all; it is outshone by a splendour
greater still. For if that which was soon to fade had its moment of splen-   11
dour, how much greater is the splendour of that which endures!

With such a hope as this we speak out boldly; it is not for us to do as   12 13
Moses did: he put a veil over his face to keep the Israelites from gazing on
that fading splendour until it was gone. But in any case their minds had   14
been made insensitive, for that same veil is there to this very day when the
lesson is read from the old covenant; and it is never lifted, because only in
Christ is the old covenant abrogated.[a] But to this very day, every time the   15
Law of Moses is read, a veil lies over the minds of the hearers. However,   16
as Scripture says of Moses, 'whenever he turns to the Lord the veil is
removed'.[b] Now the Lord of whom this passage speaks is the Spirit; and   17
where the Spirit of the Lord is, there is liberty. And because for us there is   18
no veil over the face, we all reflect as in a mirror the splendour of the Lord;
thus we are transfigured into his likeness, from splendour to splendour;
such is the influence of the Lord who is Spirit.

SEEING THEN THAT WE have been entrusted with this commission, which   **4**
we owe entirely to God's mercy, we never lose heart. We have renounced   2
the deeds that men hide for very shame; we neither practise cunning nor
distort the word of God; only by declaring the truth openly do we recommend ourselves, and then it is to the common conscience of our fellow-
men and in the sight of God. And if indeed our gospel be found veiled,   3
the only people who find it so are those on the way to perdition. Their   4
unbelieving minds are so blinded by the god of this passing age, that the
gospel of the glory of Christ, who is the very image of God, cannot dawn
upon them and bring them light. It is not ourselves that we proclaim; we   5
proclaim Christ Jesus as Lord, and ourselves as your servants, for Jesus'
sake. For the same God who said, 'Out of darkness let light shine', has   6
caused his light to shine within us, to give the light of revelation—the
revelation of the glory of God in the face of Jesus Christ.

We are no better than pots of earthenware to contain this treasure, and   7
this proves that such transcendent power does not come from us, but is
God's alone. Hard-pressed on every side, we are never hemmed in;   8
bewildered, we are never at our wits' end; hunted, we are never abandoned   9
to our fate; struck down, we are not left to die. Wherever we go we carry   10
death with us in our body, the death that Jesus died, that in this body also
life may reveal itself, the life that Jesus lives. For continually, while still   11
alive, we are being surrendered into the hands of death, for Jesus' sake, so
that the life of Jesus also may be revealed in this mortal body of ours. Thus   12
death is at work in us, and life in you.

[a]  *Or* in Christ is it abolished.
[b]  *Or* as Scripture says, when one turns to the Lord the veil is removed.

13 But Scripture says, 'I believed, and therefore I spoke out', and we too,
14 in the same spirit of faith, believe and therefore speak out; for we know
that he who raised the Lord Jesus to life will with Jesus raise us too, and
15 bring us to his presence, and you with us. Indeed, it is for your sake that all
things are ordered, so that, as the abounding grace of God is shared by
more and more, the greater may be the chorus of thanksgiving that ascends
to the glory of God.

16 No wonder we do not lose heart! Though our outward humanity is in
17 decay, yet day by day we are inwardly renewed. Our troubles are slight
and short-lived; and their outcome an eternal glory which outweighs them
18 far. Meanwhile our eyes are fixed, not on the things that are seen, but on the
things that are unseen: for what is seen passes away; what is unseen is
5 eternal. For we know that if the earthly frame that houses us today should
be demolished, we possess a building which God has provided—a house
2 not made by human hands, eternal, and in heaven. In this present body we
do indeed groan; we yearn to have our heavenly habitation put on over this
3 one—in the hope that, being thus clothed, we shall not find ourselves naked.
4 We groan indeed, we who are enclosed within this earthly frame; we are
oppressed because we do not want to have the old body stripped off. Rather
our desire is to have the new body put on over it, so that our mortal part
5 may be absorbed into life immortal. God himself has shaped us for this
very end; and as a pledge of it he has given us the Spirit.

6 Therefore we never cease to be confident. We know that so long as we
7 are at home in the body we are exiles from the Lord; faith is our guide, we
8 do not see him.[a] We are confident, I repeat, and would rather leave our
9 home in the body and go to live with the Lord. We therefore make it our
10 ambition, wherever we are, here or there, to be acceptable to him. For we
must all have our lives laid open before the tribunal of Christ, where each
must receive what is due to him for his conduct in the body, good or bad.

11 WITH THIS FEAR of the Lord before our eyes we address our appeal to
men. To God our lives lie open, as I hope they also lie open to you in your
12 heart of hearts. This is not another attempt to recommend ourselves to you:
we are rather giving you a chance to show yourselves proud of us; then you
will have something to say to those whose pride is all in outward show and
13 not in inward worth. It may be we are beside ourselves, but it is for God;
14 if we are in our right mind, it is for you. For the love of Christ leaves us no
choice, when once we have reached the conclusion that one man died for
15 all and therefore all mankind has died. His purpose in dying for all was
that men, while still in life, should cease to live for themselves, and should
16 live for him who for their sake died and was raised to life. With us therefore
worldly standards have ceased to count in our estimate of any man; even if
once they counted in our understanding of Christ, they do so now no
17 longer. When anyone is united to Christ, there is a new world;[b] the old
order has gone, and a new order has already begun.[c]

[a] *Or* faith is our guide and not the things we see.     [b] *Or* a new act of creation.
[c] *Or* When anyone is united to Christ he is a new creature: his old life is over; a new life
has already begun.

From first to last this has been the work of God. He has reconciled us men 18 to himself through Christ, and he has enlisted us in this service of reconciliation. What I mean is, that God was in Christ reconciling the world to 19 himself, *a* no longer holding men's misdeeds against them, and that he has entrusted us with the message of reconciliation. We come therefore as 20 Christ's ambassadors. It is as if God were appealing to you through us: in Christ's name, we implore you, be reconciled to God! Christ was innocent 21 of sin, and yet for our sake God made him one with the sinfulness of men, *b* so that in him we might be made one with the goodness of God himself. Sharing in God's work, we urge this appeal upon you: you have received **6** the grace of God; do not let it go for nothing. God's own words are: 2

'In the hour of my favour I gave heed to you;
on the day of deliverance I came to your aid.'

The hour of favour has now come; now, I say, has the day of deliverance dawned.

In order that our service may not be brought into discredit, we avoid giving 3 offence in anything. As God's servants, we try to recommend ourselves 4 in all circumstances by our steadfast endurance: in distress, hardships, and dire straits; flogged, imprisoned, mobbed; overworked, sleepless, 5 starving. We recommend ourselves by the innocence of our behaviour, 6 our grasp of truth, our patience and kindliness; by gifts of the Holy Spirit, by sincere love, by declaring the truth, by the power of God. We wield the 7 weapons of righteousness in right hand and left. Honour and dishonour, 8 praise and blame, are alike our lot: we are the impostors who speak the truth, the unknown men whom all men know; dying we still live on; 9 disciplined by suffering, we are not done to death; in our sorrows we 10 have always cause for joy; poor ourselves, we bring wealth to many; penniless, we own the world.

Men of Corinth, we have spoken very frankly to you; we have opened 11 our heart wide to you all. On our part there is no constraint; any constraint 12 there may be is in yourselves. In fair exchange then (may a father speak so 13 to his children?) open wide your hearts to us.

## Problems of church life and discipline

D O NOT UNITE yourselves with unbelievers; they are no fit mates 14 for you. What has righteousness to do with wickedness? Can light consort with darkness? Can Christ agree with Belial, or a believer join 15 hands with an unbeliever? Can there be a compact between the temple of 16 God and the idols of the heathen? And the temple of the living God is what we are. God's own words are: 'I will live and move about among them; I will be their God, and they shall be my people.' And therefore, 17 'come away and leave them, separate yourselves, says the Lord; touch nothing unclean. Then I will accept you, says the Lord, the Ruler of all 18

*a* Or God was reconciling the world to himself by Christ.      *b* Or and yet God made him a sin-offering for us.

being; I will be a father to you, and you shall be my sons and daughters.'
7 Such are the promises that have been made to us, dear friends. Let us therefore cleanse ourselves from all that can defile flesh or spirit, and in the fear of God complete our consecration.

2 DO MAKE A PLACE for us in your hearts! We have wronged no one, ruined
3 no one, taken advantage of no one. I do not want to blame you. Why, as I have told you before, the place you have in our heart is such that, come
4 death, come life, we meet it together. I am perfectly frank with you. I have great pride in you. In all our many troubles my cup is full of consolation, and overflows with joy.
5 Even when we reached Macedonia there was still no relief for this poor body of ours; instead, there was trouble at every turn, quarrels all round
6 us, forebodings in our heart. But God, who brings comfort to the downcast,
7 has comforted us by the arrival of Titus, and not merely by his arrival, but by his being so greatly comforted about you. He has told us how you long for me, how sorry you are, and how eager to take my side; and that has made me happier still.
8 Even if I did wound you by the letter I sent, I do not now regret it. I may have been sorry for it when I saw that the letter had caused you pain,
9 even if only for a time; but now I am happy, not that your feelings were wounded but that the wound led to a change of heart. You bore the smart as God would have you bear it, and so you are no losers by what we did.
10 For the wound which is borne in God's way brings a change of heart too salutary to regret; but the hurt which is borne in the world's way brings
11 death. You bore your hurt in God's way, and see what its results have been! It made you take the matter seriously and vindicate yourselves. How angered you were, how apprehensive! How your longing for me awoke, yes, and your devotion and your eagerness to see justice done! At every
12 point you have cleared yourselves of blame in this trouble. And so, although I did send you that letter, it was not the offender or his victim that most concerned me. My aim in writing was to help to make plain to you, in the
13 sight of God, how truly you are devoted to us. That is why we have been so encouraged.
But besides being encouraged ourselves we have also been delighted beyond everything by seeing how happy Titus is: you have all helped to
14 set his mind completely at rest. Anything I may have said to him to show my pride in you has been justified. Every word we ever addressed to you bore the mark of truth; and the same holds of the proud boast we made in
15 the presence of Titus: that also has proved true. His heart warms all the more to you as he recalls how ready you all were to do what he asked, meet-
16 ing him as you did in fear and trembling. How happy I am now to have complete confidence in you!

8 WE MUST TELL YOU, friends, about the grace of generosity which God
2 has imparted to*a* our congregations in Macedonia. The troubles they have been through have tried them hard, yet in all this they have been so

*a Or* how gracious God has been to . . .

exuberantly happy that from the depths of their poverty they have shown themselves lavishly open-handed. Going to the limit of their resources, as 3 I can testify, and even beyond that limit, they begged us most insistently, 4 and on their own initiative, to be allowed to share in this generous service to their fellow-Christians. And their giving surpassed our expectations; 5 for they gave their very selves, offering them in the first instance to the Lord, but also, under God, to us. The upshot is that we have asked Titus, 6 who began it all, to visit you and bring this work of generosity also to completion. You are so rich in everything—in faith, speech, knowledge, and 7 zeal of every kind, as well as in the loving regard you have for us[a]—surely you should show yourselves equally lavish in this generous service! This 8 is not meant as an order; by telling you how keen others are I am putting your love to the test. For you know how generous our Lord Jesus Christ 9 has been: he was rich, yet for your sake he became poor, so that through his poverty you might become rich.

Here is my considered opinion on the matter. What I ask you to do is in 10 your own interests. You made a good beginning last year both in the work you did and in your willingness to undertake it. Now I want you to go on 11 and finish it: be as eager to complete the scheme as you were to adopt it, and give according to your means. Provided there is an eager desire to give, 12 God accepts what a man has; he does not ask for what he has not. There is 13 no question of relieving others at the cost of hardship to yourselves; it is a 14 question of equality. At the moment your surplus meets their need, but one day your need may be met from their surplus. The aim is equality; as Scripture has it, 'The man who got much had no more than enough, and 15 the man who got little did not go short.'

I thank God that he has made Titus as keen on your behalf as we are! 16 For Titus not only welcomed our request; he is so eager that by his own 17 desire he is now leaving to come to you. With him we are sending one of 18 our company whose reputation is high among our congregations everywhere for his services to the Gospel. Moreover they have duly appointed 19 him to travel with us and help in this beneficent work, by which we do honour to the Lord himself and show our own eagerness to serve. We want 20 to guard against any criticism of our handling of this generous gift; for 21 our aims are entirely honourable, not only in the Lord's eyes, but also in the eyes of men.

With these men we are sending another of our company whose enthu- 22 siasm we have had many opportunities of testing, and who is now all the more earnest because of the great confidence he has in you. If there is any 23 question about Titus, he is my partner and my associate in dealings with you; as for the others, they are delegates of our congregations, an honour to Christ.[b] Then give them clear expression of your love and justify our 24 pride in you; justify it to them, and through them to the congregations.

About the provision of aid for God's people, it is superfluous for me to **9** write to you. I know how eager you are to help; I speak of it with pride to 2 the Macedonians: I tell them that Achaia had everything ready last year;

---

[a] *Some witnesses read* the love we have for you, *or* the love which we have kindled in your hearts.     [b] *Or* they are . . . congregations; they reflect Christ.

3 and most of them have been fired by your zeal. My purpose in sending these friends is to ensure that what we have said about you in this matter should not prove to be an empty boast. By that I mean, I want you to be
4 prepared, as I told them you were; for if I bring with me men from Macedonia and they find you are not prepared, what a disgrace it will be to us,
5 let alone to you, after all the confidence we have shown! I have accordingly thought it necessary to ask these friends to go on ahead to Corinth, to see that your promised bounty is in order before I come; it will then be awaiting me as a bounty indeed, and not as an extortion.

6 Remember: sparse sowing, sparse reaping; sow bountifully, and you will
7 reap bountifully. Each person should give as he has decided for himself; there should be no reluctance, no sense of compulsion; God loves a cheer-
8 ful giver. And it is in God's power to provide you richly with every good gift; thus you will have ample means in yourselves to meet each and every
9 situation, with enough and to spare for every good cause. Scripture says of such a man: 'He has lavished his gifts on the needy, his benevolence stands
10 fast for ever.' Now he who provides seed for sowing and bread for food will provide the seed for you to sow; he will multiply it and swell the harvest of
11 your benevolence, and you will always be rich enough to be generous.
12 Through our action such generosity will issue in thanksgiving to God, for as a piece of willing service this is not only a contribution towards the needs of God's people; more than that, it overflows in a flood of thanksgiving to
13 God. For through the proof which this affords, many will give honour to God when they see how humbly you obey him and how faithfully you confess the gospel of Christ; and will thank him for your liberal contribu-
14 tion to their need and to the general good. And as they join in prayer on your behalf, their hearts will go out to you because of the richness of the
15 grace which God has imparted to you. Thanks be to God for his gift beyond words!

## Trials of a Christian missionary

10 BUT I, PAUL, appeal to you by the gentleness and magnanimity of Christ—I, so feeble (you say) when I am face to face with you, so
2 brave when I am away. Spare me, I beg you, the necessity of such bravery when I come, for I reckon I could put on as bold a face as you please against
3 those who charge us with moral weakness. Weak men we may be, but it is
4 not as such that we fight our battles. The weapons we wield are not merely
5 human,*a* but divinely potent to demolish strongholds; we demolish sophistries and all that rears its proud head against the knowledge of God;
6 we compel every human thought to surrender in obedience to Christ; and we are prepared to punish all rebellion when once you have put yourselves in our hands.

7 Look facts in the face.*b* Someone is convinced, is he, that he belongs to

*a Or* charge us with worldly standards. We live, no doubt, in the world; but it is not on that level that we fight our battles. The weapons we wield are not those of the world . . .
*b Or* You are looking only at what catches the eye.

Christ? Let him think again, and reflect that we belong to Christ as much as he does. Indeed, if I am somewhat over-boastful about our authority— an authority given by the Lord to build you up, not pull you down—I shall make my boast good. So you must not think of me as one who scares you by the letters he writes. 'His letters', so it is said, 'are weighty and powerful; but when he appears he has no presence, and as a speaker he is beneath contempt.' People who talk in that way should reckon with this: when I come, my actions will show the same man as my letters showed in my absence.

We should not dare to class ourselves or compare ourselves with any of those who put forward their own claims. What fools they are to measure themselves by themselves, to find in themselves their own standard of comparison!*a* With us there will be no attempt to boast beyond our proper sphere; and our sphere is determined by the limit God laid down for us, which permitted us to come as far as Corinth. We are not overstretching our commission, as we should be if it did not extend to you, for we were the first to reach Corinth in preaching the gospel of Christ. And we do not boast of work done where others have laboured, work beyond our proper sphere. Our hope is rather that, as your faith grows, we may attain a position among you greater than ever before, but still within the limits of our sphere. Then we can carry the Gospel to lands that lie beyond you, never priding ourselves on work already done in another man's sphere. If a man must boast, let him boast of the Lord. Not the man who recommends himself, but the man whom the Lord recommends—he and he alone is to be accepted.

I wish you would bear with me in a little of my folly; please do bear with me. I am jealous for you, with a divine jealousy; for I betrothed you to Christ, thinking to present you as a chaste virgin to her true and only husband. But as the serpent in his cunning seduced Eve, I am afraid that your thoughts may be corrupted and you may lose your *b* single-hearted devotion to Christ. For if someone comes who proclaims another Jesus, not the Jesus whom we proclaimed, or if you then receive a spirit different from the Spirit already given to you, or a gospel different from the gospel you have already accepted, you manage to put up with that well enough. Have I in any way come short of those superlative apostles? I think not. I may be no speaker, but knowledge I have; at all times we have made known to you the full truth.

Or was this my offence, that I made no charge for preaching the gospel of God, lowering myself to help in raising you? It is true that I took toll of other congregations, accepting *c* support from them to serve you. Then, while I was with you, if I ran short I sponged on no one; anything I needed was fully met by our friends who came from Macedonia; I made it a rule, as I always shall, never to be a burden to you. As surely as the truth of Christ is in me, I will preserve my pride in this matter throughout Achaia, and nothing shall stop me. Why? Is it that I do not love you? God knows I do.

---

*a* *Some witnesses read* On the contrary we measure ourselves by ourselves, by our own standard of comparison.        *b* *Some witnesses insert* purity and . . .        *c* *Or* Did I take toll of other congregations by accepting . . . ?

12  And I shall go on doing as I am doing now, to cut the ground from under
those who would seize any chance to put their vaunted apostleship on the
13  same level as ours. Such men are sham-apostles, crooked in all their
14  practices, masquerading as apostles of Christ. There is nothing surprising
15  about that; Satan himself masquerades as an angel of light. It is therefore
a simple thing for his agents to masquerade as agents of good. But they will
meet the end their deeds deserve.

16      I repeat: let no one take me for a fool; but if you must, then give me the
17  privilege of a fool, and let me have my little boast like others. I am not
18  speaking here as a Christian, but like a fool, if it comes to bragging. So
19  many people brag of their earthly distinctions that I shall do so too. How
20  gladly you bear with fools, being yourselves so wise! If a man tyrannizes
over you, exploits you, gets you in his clutches, puts on airs, and hits you
21  in the face, you put up with it. And we, you say, have been weak! I admit
the reproach.

But if there is to be bravado (and here I speak as a fool), I can indulge in
22  it too. Are they Hebrews? So am I. Israelites? So am I. Abraham's descen-
23  dants? So am I. Are they servants of Christ? I am mad to speak like this,
but I can outdo them. More overworked than they, scourged more severely,
24  more often imprisoned, many a time face to face with death. Five times the
25  Jews have given me the thirty-nine strokes; three times I have been beaten
with rods; once I was stoned; three times I have been shipwrecked, and for
26  twenty-four hours I was adrift on the open sea. I have been constantly on
the road; I have met dangers from rivers, dangers from robbers, dangers
from my fellow-countrymen, dangers from foreigners, dangers in towns,
27  dangers in the country, dangers at sea, dangers from false friends. I have
toiled and drudged, I have often gone without sleep; hungry and thirsty,
I have often gone fasting; and I have suffered from cold and exposure.

28      Apart from these external things,*a* there is the responsibility that weighs
29  on me every day, my anxious concern for all our congregations. If anyone
is weak, do I not share his weakness? If anyone is made to stumble, does
30  my heart not blaze with indignation? If boasting there must be, I will boast
31  of the things that show up my weakness. The God and Father of the Lord
32  Jesus (blessed be his name for ever!) knows that what I say is true. When
I was in Damascus, the commissioner of King Aretas kept the city under
33  observation so as to have me arrested; and I was let down in a basket,
through a window in the wall, and so escaped his clutches.

**12**  I AM OBLIGED TO BOAST. It does no good; but I shall go on to tell of
2  visions and revelations granted by the Lord. I know a Christian man who
fourteen years ago (whether in the body or out of it, I do not know—God
3  knows) was caught up as far as the third heaven. And I know that this same
4  man (whether in the body or out of it, I do not know—God knows) was
caught up into paradise, and heard words so secret that human lips may not
5  repeat them. About such a man as that I am ready to boast; but I will not
6  boast on my own account, except of my weaknesses. If I should choose to
boast, it would not be the boast of a fool, for I should be speaking the

*a Or* Apart from things which I omit.

truth. But I refrain, because I should not like anyone to form an estimate of me which goes beyond the evidence of his own eyes and ears. And so, 7 to keep me from being unduly elated by the magnificence of such revelations, I was given *a* a sharp physical pain *b* which came as Satan's messenger to bruise me; this was to save me from being unduly elated. Three 8 times I begged the Lord to rid me of it, but his answer was: 'My grace is 9 all you need; power comes to its full strength in weakness.' I shall therefore prefer to find my joy and pride in the very things that are my weakness; and then the power of Christ will come and rest upon me. Hence I am well 10 content, for Christ's sake, with weakness, contempt, persecution, hardship, and frustration; for when I am weak, then I am strong.

I AM BEING VERY FOOLISH, but it was you who drove me to it; my 11 credentials should have come from you. In no respect did I fall short of these superlative apostles, even if I am a nobody. The marks of a true 12 apostle were there, in the work I did among you, which called for such constant fortitude, and was attended by signs, marvels, and miracles. Is 13 there anything in which you were treated worse than the other congregations—except this, that I never sponged upon you? How unfair of me! I crave forgiveness.

Here am I preparing to pay you a third visit; and I am not going to 14 sponge upon you. It is you I want, not your money; parents should make provision for their children, not children for their parents. As for me, I 15 will gladly spend what I have for you—yes, and spend myself to the limit. If I love you overmuch, am I to be loved the less? But, granted that I did 16 not prove a burden to you, still I was unscrupulous enough, you say, to use a trick to catch you. Who, of the men I have sent to you, was used by me to 17 defraud you? I begged Titus to visit you, and I sent our friend with him. 18 Did Titus defraud you? Have we not both been guided by the same Spirit, and followed the same course?

Perhaps you think that all this time we have been addressing our defence 19 to you. No; we are speaking in God's sight, and as Christian men. Our whole aim, my own dear people, is to build you up. I fear that when I come 20 I may perhaps find you different from what I wish you to be, and that you may find me also different from what you wish. I fear I may find quarrelling and jealousy, angry tempers and personal rivalries, backbiting and gossip, arrogance and general disorder. I am afraid that, when I come again, my 21 God may humiliate me in your presence, that I may have tears to shed over many of those who have sinned in the past and have not repented of their unclean lives, their fornication and sensuality.

This will be my third visit to you; and all facts must be established by the 13 evidence of two or three witnesses. To those who have sinned in the past, 2 and to everyone else, I repeat the warning I gave before; I gave it in person on my second visit, and I give it now in absence. It is that when I come this time, I will show no leniency. Then you will have the proof you seek of the 3

*a Some witnesses read* . . . ears, and because of the magnificence of the revelations themselves. Therefore to keep me from being unduly elated I was given . . .  *b Or a* painful wound to my pride (*literally* a stake, *or* thorn, for the flesh).

Christ who speaks through me, the Christ who, far from being weak with
4 you, makes his power felt among you. True, he died on the cross in weakness, but he lives by the power of God; and we who share his weakness shall by the power of God live with him in your service.

5 Examine yourselves: are you living the life of faith? Put yourselves to the test. Surely you recognize that Jesus Christ is among you?—unless of
6 course you prove unequal to the test. I hope you will come to see that we
7 are not unequal to it. Our prayer to God is that you may do no wrong; we are not concerned to be vindicated ourselves; we want you to do what is
8 right, even if we should seem to be discredited. For we have no power to
9 act against the truth, but only for it. We are well content to be weak at any time if only you are strong. Indeed, my whole prayer is that all may be put
10 right with you. My purpose in writing this letter before I come, is to spare myself, when I come, any sharp exercise of authority—authority which the Lord gave me for building up and not for pulling down.

11 And now, my friends, farewell. Mend your ways; take our appeal to heart; agree with one another; live in peace; and the God of love and peace
12 13 will be with you. Greet one another with the kiss of peace. All God's people send you greetings.

14 The grace of the Lord Jesus Christ, and the love of God, and fellowship in the Holy Spirit, be with you all.

# THE LETTER OF PAUL
# TO THE
# GALATIANS

## *Faith and freedom*

1 FROM PAUL, AN APOSTLE, not by human appointment or human commission, but by commission from Jesus Christ and
2 from God the Father who raised him from the dead. I and the group of friends now with me send greetings to the Christian congregations of Galatia.

3 Grace and peace to you from God the Father and our Lord Jesus Christ, *a*
4 who sacrificed himself for our sins, to rescue us out of this present age of
5 wickedness, as our God and Father willed; to whom be glory for ever and ever. Amen.

6 I am astonished to find you turning so quickly away from him who
7 called you by grace, *b* and following a different gospel. Not that it is in fact

---

*a Some witnesses read* God our Father and the Lord Jesus Christ.          *b Some witnesses read* from Christ who called you by grace, *or* from him who called you by grace of Christ.

another gospel; only there are persons who unsettle your minds by trying
to distort the gospel of Christ. But if anyone, if we ourselves or an angel 8
from heaven, should preach a gospel at variance with the gospel we
preached to you, he shall be held outcast. I now repeat what I have said 9
before: if anyone preaches a gospel at variance with the gospel which you
received, let him be outcast!

Does my language now sound as if I were canvassing for men's support? 10
Whose support do I want but God's alone? Do you think I am currying
favour with men? If I still sought men's favour, I should be no servant of
Christ.

I must make it clear to you, my friends, that the gospel you heard me 11
preach is no human invention. I did not take it over from any man; no man 12
taught it me; I received it through a revelation of Jesus Christ.

You have heard what my manner of life was when I was still a practising 13
Jew: how savagely I persecuted the church of God, and tried to destroy it;
and how in the practice of our national religion I was outstripping many of 14
my Jewish contemporaries in my boundless devotion to the traditions of my
ancestors. But then in his good pleasure God, who had set me apart from 15
birth and called me through his grace, chose to reveal his Son to me and 16
through me, in order that I might proclaim him among the Gentiles. When
that happened, without consulting any human being, without going up to 17
Jerusalem to see those who were apostles before me, I went off at once to
Arabia, and afterwards returned to Damascus.

Three years later I did go up to Jerusalem to get to know Cephas. I 18
stayed with him for a fortnight, without seeing any other of the apostles, 19
except *a* James the Lord's brother. What I write is plain truth; before God 20
I am not lying.

Next I went to the regions of Syria and Cilicia, and remained unknown 21 22
by sight *b* to Christ's congregations in Judaea. They only heard it said, 'Our 23
former persecutor is preaching the good news of the faith which once he
tried to destroy'; and they praised God for me.                          24

Next, fourteen years later, I went again *c* to Jerusalem with Barnabas, **2**
taking Titus with us. I went up because it had been revealed by God that 2
I should do so. I laid before them—but at a private interview with the men
of repute—the gospel which I am accustomed to preach to the Gentiles,
to make sure that the race I had run, and was running, should not be run in
vain. Yet even my companion Titus, Greek though he is, was not compelled 3
to be circumcised. That course was urged only as a concession to certain *d* 4
sham-Christians, interlopers who had stolen in to spy upon the liberty we
enjoy in the fellowship of Christ Jesus. These men wanted to bring us into
bondage, but not for one moment did I yield to their dictation; I was deter- 5
mined that the full truth of the Gospel should be maintained for you. *e*

---

*a* Or but only.        *b* Or unknown personally.        *c* *Some witnesses omit* again.
*d* Or The question was later raised because of certain . . .        *e* *Or, following the*
*reading of some witnesses,* Yet even . . . is, was under no absolute compulsion to be circumcised, but for the sake of certain . . . of Christ Jesus, with the intention of bringing us into
bondage, I yielded to their demand for the moment, to ensure that gospel truth should
not be prevented from reaching you.

6   But as for the men of high reputation (not that their importance matters to me: God does not recognize these personal distinctions)—these men of

7   repute, I say, did not prolong the consultation,[a] but on the contrary acknowledged that I had been entrusted with the Gospel for Gentiles as

8   surely as Peter had been entrusted with the Gospel for Jews. For God whose action made Peter an apostle to the Jews, also made me an apostle to the Gentiles.

9   Recognizing, then, the favour thus bestowed upon me, those reputed pillars of our society, James, Cephas, and John, accepted Barnabas and myself as partners, and shook hands upon it, agreeing that we should go

10  to the Gentiles while they went to the Jews. All they asked was that we should keep their poor in mind, which was the very thing I made[b] it my business to do.

11  But when Cephas came to Antioch, I opposed him to his face, because

12  he was clearly in the wrong. For until certain persons[c] came from James he was taking his meals with gentile Christians; but when they[d] came he drew back and began to hold aloof, because he was afraid of the advocates

13  of circumcision. The other Jewish Christians showed the same lack of principle; even Barnabas was carried away and played false like the rest.

14  But when I saw that their conduct did not square with[e] the truth of the Gospel, I said to Cephas, before the whole congregation, 'If you, a Jew born and bred, live like a Gentile, and not like a Jew, how can you insist that Gentiles must live like Jews?'

15 16  We ourselves are Jews by birth, not Gentiles and sinners. But we know that no man is ever justified by doing what the law demands, but only through faith in Christ Jesus; so we too have put our faith in Jesus Christ, in order that we might be justified through this faith, and not through deeds dictated by law; for by such deeds, Scripture says, no mortal man shall be justified.

17  If now, in seeking to be justified in Christ, we ourselves no less than the Gentiles turn out to be sinners against the law,[f] does that mean that Christ

18  is an abettor of sin? No, never! No, if I start building up again a system which I have pulled down, then it is that I show myself up as a transgressor

19 20  of the law. For through the law I died to law—to live for God. I have been crucified with Christ: the life I now live is not my life, but the life which Christ lives in me; and my present bodily life is lived by faith in the Son of

21  God, who loved me and gave himself up for me. I will not nullify the grace of God; if righteousness comes by law, then Christ died for nothing.

3   YOU STUPID GALATIANS! You must have been bewitched—you before

2   whose eyes Jesus Christ was openly displayed upon his cross! Answer me one question: did you receive the Spirit by keeping the law or by believing

3   the gospel message[g]? Can it be that you are so stupid? You started with the

---

*a Or gave me no further instructions.      b Or had made, or have made.      c Some witnesses read a certain person.      d Some witnesses read he.      e Or I saw that they were not making progress towards . . .      f Or no less than the Gentiles have accepted the position of sinners against the law.      g Or or by the message of faith, or or by hearing and believing.*

spiritual; do you now look to the material to make you perfect? Have all   4
your great experiences been in vain—if vain indeed they should be? I ask   5
then: when God gives you the Spirit and works miracles among you, why
is this? Is it because you keep the law, or is it because you have faith in the
gospel message? Look at Abraham: he put his faith in God, and that faith   6
was counted to him as righteousness.

You may take it, then, that it is the men of faith who are Abraham's sons.   7
And Scripture, foreseeing that God would justify the Gentiles through   8
faith, declared the Gospel to Abraham beforehand: 'In you all nations shall
find blessing.' Thus it is the men of faith who share the blessing with faith-   9
ful Abraham.

On the other hand those who rely on obedience to the law are under a   10
curse; for Scripture says, 'A curse is on all who do not persevere in doing
everything that is written in the Book of the Law.' It is evident that no one   11
is ever justified before God in terms of law; because we read, 'he shall gain
life who is justified through faith'. Now law is not at all a matter of having   12
faith: we read, 'he who does this shall gain life by what he does'.

Christ bought us freedom from the curse of the law by becoming for our   13
sake an accursed thing; for Scripture says, 'A curse is on everyone who is
hanged on a gibbet.' And the purpose of it all was that the blessing of   14
Abraham should in Jesus Christ be extended to the Gentiles, so that we
might receive the promised Spirit through faith.

My brothers, let me give you an illustration. Even in ordinary life, when   15
a man's will and testament has been duly executed, no one else can set it
aside or add a codicil. Now the promises were pronounced to Abraham and   16
to his 'issue'. It does not say 'issues' in the plural, but in the singular, 'and
to your issue'; and the 'issue' intended is Christ. What I am saying is this:   17
a testament, or covenant, had already been validated by God; it cannot be
invalidated, and its promises rendered ineffective, by a law made four
hundred and thirty years later. If the inheritance is by legal right, then it is   18
not by promise; but it was by promise that God bestowed it as a free gift
on Abraham.

Then what of the law? It was added to make wrongdoing a legal offence. *a*   19
It was a temporary measure pending the arrival of the 'issue' to whom the
promise was made. It was promulgated through angels, and there was an
intermediary; but an intermediary is not needed for one party acting alone,   20
and God is one.

Does the law, then, contradict the promises? No, never! If a law had   21
been given which had power to bestow life, then indeed righteousness
would have come from keeping the law. But Scripture has declared the   22
whole world to be prisoners in subjection to sin, so that faith in Jesus Christ
may be the ground on which the promised blessing is given, and given to
those who have such faith.

Before this faith came, we were close prisoners in the custody of law,   23
pending the revelation of faith. Thus the law was a kind of tutor in charge   24
of us until Christ should come, *b* when we should be justified through faith;
and now that faith has come, the tutor's charge is at an end.   25

*a Or* added because of offences.        *b Or* a kind of tutor to conduct us to Christ.

26  For through faith you are all sons of God in union with Christ Jesus.
27  Baptized into union with him, you have all put on Christ as a garment.
28  There is no such thing as Jew and Greek, slave and freeman, male and
29  female; for you are all one person in Christ Jesus. But if you thus belong to
    Christ, you are the 'issue' of Abraham, and so heirs by promise.

4   This is what I mean: so long as the heir is a minor, he is no better off
2   than a slave, even though the whole estate is his; he is under guardians and
3   trustees until the date fixed by his father. And so it was with us. During
4   our minority we were slaves to the elemental spirits of the universe,*a* but
    when the term was completed, God sent his own Son, born of a woman,
5   born under the law, to purchase freedom for the subjects of the law, in
    order that we might attain the status of sons.

6   To prove that you are sons, God has sent into our hearts the Spirit of his
7   Son, crying 'Abba! Father!' You are therefore no longer a slave but a son,
    and if a son, then also by God's own act an heir.

8   Formerly, when you did not acknowledge God, you were the slaves of
9   beings which in their nature are no gods.*b* But now that you do acknow-
    ledge God—or rather, now that he has acknowledged you—how can you
    turn back to the mean and beggarly spirits of the elements?*c* Why do you
10  propose to enter their service all over again? You keep special days and
11  months and seasons and years. You make me fear that all the pains I spent
    on you may prove to be labour lost.

12  PUT YOURSELVES in my place, my brothers, I beg you, for I have put
13  myself in yours. It is not that you did me any wrong. As you know, it was
14  bodily illness that originally*d* led to my bringing you the Gospel, and you
    resisted any temptation to show scorn or disgust at the state of my poor
    body;*e* you welcomed me as if I were an angel of God, as you might have
15  welcomed Christ Jesus himself. Have you forgotten how happy you thought
    yourselves in having me with you? I can say this for you: you would have
16  torn out your very eyes, and given them to me, had that been possible! And
    have I now made myself your enemy by being frank with you?
17  The persons I have referred to are envious of you, but not with an
    honest envy:*f* what they really want is to bar the door to you so that you
18  may come to envy*g* them. It is always a fine thing to deserve an honest
19  envy*h*—always, and not only when I am present with you, dear children.
    For my children you are, and I am in travail with you over again until you
20  take the shape of Christ. I wish I could be with you now; then I could
    modify my tone;*i* as it is, I am at my wits' end about you.

21  TELL ME NOW, you who are so anxious to be under law, will you not listen
22  to what the Law says? It is written there that Abraham had two sons, one

---

*a* Or the elements of the natural world, *or* elementary ideas belonging to this world.
*b* Or were slaves to 'gods' which in reality do not exist.         *c See note on 4. 3.*
*d* Or formerly, *or* on the first of my two visits.         *e* Or you showed neither
scorn nor disgust at the trial my poor body was enduring.         *f* Or paying
court to you, but not with honest intentions.         *g* Or pay court to.         *h* Or to be
honourably wooed.         *i* Or now, and could exchange words with you.

by his slave and the other by his free-born wife. The slave-woman's son 23
was born in the course of nature, the free woman's through God's promise.
This is an allegory. The two women stand for two covenants. The one 24
bearing children into slavery is the covenant that comes from Mount Sinai:
that is Hagar. Sinai is a mountain in Arabia and it represents the Jerusalem 25
of today, for she and her children are in slavery. But the heavenly Jeru- 26
salem is the free woman; she is our mother. For Scripture says, 'Rejoice, 27
O barren woman who never bore child; break into a shout of joy, you who
never knew a mother's pangs; for the deserted wife shall have more children than she who lives with the husband.'

And you, my brothers, like Isaac, are children of God's promise. But 28 29
just as in those days the natural-born son persecuted the spiritual son, so
it is today. But what does Scripture say? 'Drive out the slave-woman and 30
her son, for the son of the slave shall not share the inheritance with the free
woman's son.' You see, then, my brothers, we are no slave-woman's 31
children; our mother is the free woman. Christ set us free, to be free men.*a* 5
Stand firm, then, and refuse to be tied to the yoke of slavery again.

Mark my words: I, Paul, say to you that if you receive circumcision 2
Christ will do you no good at all. Once again, you can take it from me that 3
every man who receives circumcision is under obligation to keep the entire
law. When you seek to be justified by way of law, your relation with Christ 4
is completely severed: you have fallen out of the domain of God's grace.
For to us, our hope of attaining that righteousness which we eagerly await 5
is the work of the Spirit through faith. If we are in union with Christ Jesus 6
circumcision makes no difference at all, nor does the want of it; the only
thing that counts is faith active in love.*b*

You were running well; who was it hindered you from following the 7
truth? Whatever persuasion he used, it did not come from God who is call- 8
ing you; 'a little leaven', remember, 'leavens all the dough'. United with 9 10
you in the Lord, I am confident that you will not take the wrong view; but
the man who is unsettling your minds, whoever he may be, must bear
God's judgement. And I, my friends, if I am still advocating circumcision, 11
why is it I am still persecuted? In that case, my preaching of the cross is a
stumbling-block no more. As for these agitators, they had better go the 12
whole way and make eunuchs of themselves!

YOU, MY FRIENDS, were called to be free men; only do not turn your 13
freedom into licence for your lower nature, but be servants to one another in
love. For the whole law can be summed up in a single commandment: 14
'Love your neighbour as yourself.' But if you go on fighting one another, 15
tooth and nail, all you can expect is mutual destruction.

I mean this: if you are guided by the Spirit you will not fulfil the desires 16
of your lower nature. That nature sets its desires against the Spirit, while 17
the Spirit fights against it. They are in conflict with one another so that
what you will to do you cannot do. But if you are led by the Spirit, you are 18
not under law.

Anyone can see the kind of behaviour that belongs to the lower nature: 19

*a Or* What Christ has done is to set us free.      *b Or* inspired by love.

20 fornication, impurity, and indecency; idolatry and sorcery; quarrels, a contentious temper, envy, fits of rage, selfish ambitions, dissensions, party
21 intrigues, and jealousies; drinking bouts, orgies, and the like. I warn you, as I warned you before, that those who behave in such ways will never inherit the kingdom of God.

22 But the harvest of the Spirit is love, joy, peace, patience, kindness, good-
23 ness, fidelity, gentleness, and self-control. There is no law dealing with such
24 things as these. And those who belong to Christ Jesus have crucified the
25 lower nature with its passions and desires. If the Spirit is the source of our life, let the Spirit also direct our course.

26 We must not be conceited, challenging one another to rivalry, jealous
**6** of one another. If a man should do something wrong, my brothers, on a sudden impulse,[a] you who are endowed with the Spirit must set him right again very gently. Look to yourself, each one of you: you may be tempted
2 too. Help one another to carry these heavy loads, and in this way you will fulfil the law of Christ.

3 For if a man imagines himself to be somebody, when he is nothing, he is
4 deluding himself. Each man should examine his own conduct for himself; then he can measure his achievement by comparing himself with himself
5 and not with anyone else. For everyone has his own proper burden to bear.
6 When anyone is under instruction in the faith, he should give his teacher a share of all good things he has.

7 Make no mistake about this: God is not to be fooled; a man reaps what
8 he sows. If he sows seed in the field of his lower nature, he will reap from it a harvest of corruption, but if he sows in the field of the Spirit, the Spirit
9 will bring him a harvest of eternal life. So let us never tire of doing good, for if we do not slacken our efforts we shall in due time reap our harvest.
10 Therefore, as opportunity offers, let us work for the good of all, especially members of the household of the faith.

11 12 YOU SEE these big letters? I am now writing to you in my own hand. It is all those who want to make a fair outward and bodily show who are trying to force circumcision upon you; their sole object is to escape persecution
13 for the cross of Christ. For even those who do receive circumcision are not thoroughly observers of the law; they only want you to be circumcised
14 in order to boast of your having submitted to that outward rite. But God forbid that I should boast of anything but the cross of our Lord Jesus Christ, through which[b] the world is crucified to me and I to the world!
15 Circumcision is nothing; uncircumcision is nothing; the only thing that
16 counts is new creation! Whoever they are who take this principle for their guide, peace and mercy be upon them, and upon the whole Israel of God!
17 In future let no one make trouble for me, for I bear the marks of Jesus branded on my body.
18 The grace of our Lord Jesus Christ be with your spirit, my brothers. Amen.

*a Or* If a man is caught doing something wrong, my brothers, . . .     *b Or* whom.

# THE LETTER OF PAUL
# TO THE
# EPHESIANS

## The glory of Christ in the church

FROM PAUL, APOSTLE of Christ Jesus, commissioned by the 1
will of God, to God's people at Ephesus,[a] believers incorporate in
Christ Jesus.

Grace to you and peace from God our Father and the Lord Jesus Christ. 2

Praise be to the God and Father of our Lord Jesus Christ, who has 3
bestowed on us in Christ every spiritual blessing in the heavenly realms.
In Christ he chose us before the world was founded, to be dedicated, to be 4
without blemish in his sight, to be full of love; and he[b] destined us—such 5
was his will and pleasure—to be accepted as his sons through Jesus Christ,
in order that the glory of his gracious gift, so graciously bestowed on us in 6
his Beloved, might redound to his praise. For in Christ our release is 7
secured and our sins are forgiven through the shedding of his blood.
Therein lies the richness of God's free grace lavished upon us, imparting 8
full wisdom and insight. He has made known to us his hidden purpose— 9
such was his will and pleasure determined beforehand in Christ—to be 10
put into effect when the time was ripe: namely, that the universe, all in
heaven and on earth, might be brought into a unity in Christ.

In Christ indeed we have been given our share in the heritage, as was 11
decreed in his design whose purpose is everywhere at work. For it was his
will that we, who were the first to set our hope on Christ,[c] should cause his 12
glory to be praised. And you too, when you had heard the message of the 13
truth, the good news of your salvation, and had believed it, became incorporate in Christ and received the seal of the promised Holy Spirit; and 14
that Spirit is the pledge that we shall enter upon our heritage, when God
has redeemed what is his own, to his praise and glory.

Because of all this, now that I have heard of the faith you have in the 15
Lord Jesus and of the love you bear towards all God's people, I never 16
cease to give thanks for you when I mention you in my prayers. I pray that 17
the God of our Lord Jesus Christ, the all-glorious Father, may give you the
spiritual powers of wisdom and vision, by which there comes the knowledge of him. I pray that your inward eyes may be illumined, so that you 18
may know what is the hope to which he calls you, what the wealth and

---

[a] *Some witnesses omit* at Ephesus.　　　　　[b] *Or* ... sight. In his love he ...
[c] *Or* who already enjoyed the hope of Christ, *or* whose expectation and hope are in
Christ.

19 glory of the share he offers you among his people in their heritage, and how vast the resources of his power open to us who trust in him. They are
20 measured by his strength and the might which he exerted in Christ when he raised him from the dead, when he enthroned him at his right hand in
21 the heavenly realms, far above all government and authority, all power and dominion, and any title of sovereignty that can be named, not only in this
22 age but in the age to come. He put everything in subjection beneath his feet,
23 and appointed him as supreme head to the church, which is his body and as such holds within it the fullness of him who himself receives the entire fullness of God. *a*

**2** 1 2 TIME WAS when you were dead in your sins and wickedness, when you followed the evil ways of this present age, when you obeyed the commander of the spiritual powers of the air, the spirit now at work among
3 God's rebel subjects. We too were once of their number: we all lived our lives in sensuality, and obeyed the promptings of our own instincts and notions. In our natural condition we, like the rest, lay under the dreadful
4 judgement of God. But God, rich in mercy, for the great love he bore us,
5 brought us to life with Christ even when we were dead in our sins; it is by
6 his grace you are saved. And in union with Christ Jesus he raised us up and
7 enthroned us with him in the heavenly realms, so that he might display in the ages to come how immense are the resources of his grace, and how great
8 his kindness to us in Christ Jesus. For it is by his grace you are saved,
9 through trusting him; it is not your own doing. It is God's gift, not a
10 reward for work done. There is nothing for anyone to boast of. For we are God's handiwork, created in Christ Jesus to devote ourselves to the good deeds for which God has designed us.

11    Remember then your former condition: you, Gentiles as you are outwardly, *b* you, 'the uncircumcised' so called by those who are called 'the
12 circumcised' (but only with reference to an outward rite)—you were at that time separate from Christ, strangers to the community of Israel, outside God's covenants and the promise that goes with them. Your world was a
13 world without hope and without God. But now in union with Christ Jesus you who once were far off have been brought near through the shedding of
14 Christ's blood. For he is himself our peace. Gentiles and Jews, he has made the two one, and in his own body of flesh and blood has broken down the
15 enmity which stood like a dividing wall between them; for he annulled the law with its rules and regulations, so as to create out of the two a single new
16 humanity in himself, thereby making peace. This was his purpose, to reconcile the two in a single body to God through the cross, on which he killed the enmity. *c*

17    So he came and proclaimed the good news: peace to you who were far
18 off, and peace to those who were near by; for through him we both alike
19 have access to the Father in the one Spirit. Thus you are no longer aliens in

*a Or* as supreme head to the church, which is his body and as such holds within it the fullness of him who fills the universe in all its parts; *or* as supreme head to the church which is his body, and to be all that he himself is who fills the universe in all its parts.
*b Or* by birth.      *c Or* . . . cross. Thus in his own person he put the enmity to death.

a foreign land, but fellow-citizens with God's people, members of God's household. You are built upon the foundation laid by the apostles and 20 prophets, and Christ Jesus himself is the foundation-stone.*a* In him the 21 whole building *b* is bonded together and grows into a holy temple in the Lord. In him you too are being built with all the rest into a spiritual dwell- 22 ing for God.

WITH THIS IN MIND I make my prayer, I, Paul, who in the cause of you 3 Gentiles am now the prisoner of Christ Jesus—for surely you have heard 2 how God has assigned the gift of his grace to me for your benefit. It was 3 by a revelation that his secret was made known to me. I have already written a brief account of this, and by reading it you may perceive that I under- 4 stand the secret of Christ. In former generations this was not disclosed to 5 the human race; but now it has been revealed by inspiration to his dedicated apostles and prophets, that through the Gospel the Gentiles are joint heirs 6 with the Jews, part of the same body, sharers together in the promise made in Christ Jesus. Such is the gospel of which I was made a minister, by 7 God's gift, bestowed unmerited on me in the working of his power. To 8 me, who am less than the least of all God's people, he has granted of his grace the privilege of proclaiming to the Gentiles the good news of the unfathomable riches of Christ, and of bringing to light how this hidden 9 purpose was to be put into effect. It was hidden for long ages in God the creator of the universe, in order that now, through the church, the wisdom 10 of God in all its varied forms might be made known to the rulers and authorities in the realms of heaven. This is in accord with his age-long pur- 11 pose, which he achieved in Christ Jesus our Lord. In him we have access to 12 God with freedom, in the confidence born of trust in him. I beg you, then, 13 not to lose heart over my sufferings for you; indeed, they are your glory.

With this in mind, then, I kneel in prayer to the Father, from whom 14 15 every family *c* in heaven and on earth takes its name, that out of the trea- 16 sures of his glory he may grant you strength and power through his Spirit in your inner being, that through faith Christ may dwell in your hearts in 17 love. With deep roots and firm foundations, may you be strong to grasp, 18 with all God's people, what is the breadth and length and height and depth of the love of Christ, and to know it, though it is beyond knowledge. So 19 may you attain to fullness of being, the fullness of God himself. *d*

Now to him who is able to do immeasurably more than all we can ask or 20 conceive, by the power which is at work among us, to him be glory in the 21 church and in Christ Jesus from generation to generation evermore! Amen.

I ENTREAT YOU, THEN—I, a prisoner for the Lord's sake: as God has 4 called you, live up to your calling. Be humble always and gentle, and patient 2 too. Be forbearing with one another and charitable. Spare no effort to 3 make fast with bonds of peace the unity which the Spirit gives. There is one 4

*a Or* built upon the foundation of the apostles and prophets, and Christ Jesus himself is the keystone.      *b Or* every structure.      *c Or* his whole family.
*d Or* the fullness which God requires.

5 6 body and one Spirit, as there is also one hope held out in God's call to you; one Lord, one faith, one baptism; one God and Father of all, who is over all and through all and in all.

7 But each of us has been given his gift, his due portion of Christ's bounty.

8 Therefore Scripture says:

'He ascended into the heights
with captives in his train;
he gave gifts to men.'

9 Now, the word 'ascended' implies that he also descended to the lowest
10 level, down to the very earth.*a* He who descended is no other than he who
11 ascended far above all heavens, so that he might fill the universe. And these were his gifts: some to be apostles, some prophets, some evangelists,
12 some pastors and teachers, to equip God's people for work in his service,
13 to the building up of the body of Christ. So shall we all at last attain to the unity inherent in our faith and our knowledge of the Son of God—to mature manhood, measured by nothing less than the full stature of Christ.
14 We are no longer to be children, tossed by the waves and whirled about by every fresh gust of teaching, dupes of crafty rogues and their deceitful
15 schemes. No, let us speak the truth in love; so shall we fully grow up into
16 Christ. He is the head, and on him the whole body depends. Bonded and knit together by every constituent joint, the whole frame grows through the due activity of each part, and builds itself up in love.

17 This then is my word to you, and I urge it upon you in the Lord's name.
18 Give up living like pagans with their good-for-nothing notions. Their wits are beclouded, they are strangers to the life that is in God, because ignor-
19 ance prevails among them and their minds have grown hard as stone. Dead to all feeling, they have abandoned themselves to vice, and stop at nothing
20 21 to satisfy their foul desires. But that is not how you learned Christ. For were you not told of him, were you not as Christians taught the truth as it
22 is in Jesus?—that, leaving your former way of life, you must lay aside that old human nature which, deluded by its lusts, is sinking towards death.
23 24 You must be made new in mind and spirit, and put on the new nature of God's creating, which shows itself in the just and devout life called for by the truth.

25 Then throw off falsehood; speak the truth to each other, for all of us are the parts of one body.

26 If you are angry, do not let anger lead you into sin; do not let sunset find
27 you still nursing it; leave no loop-hole for the devil.

28 The thief must give up stealing, and instead work hard and honestly with his own hands, so that he may have something to share with the needy.

29 No bad language must pass your lips, but only what is good and helpful
30 to the occasion, so that it brings a blessing to those who hear it. And do not grieve the Holy Spirit of God, for that Spirit is the seal with which you
31 were marked for the day of our final liberation. Have done with spite and passion, all angry shouting and cursing, and bad feeling of every kind.

*a Or* descended to the regions beneath the earth.

Be generous to one another, tender-hearted, forgiving one another as 32
God in Christ forgave you.

In a word, as God's dear children, try to be like him, and live in love as 5 1 2
Christ loved you, and gave himself up on your behalf as an offering and
sacrifice whose fragrance is pleasing to God.

Fornication and indecency of any kind, or ruthless greed, must not be so 3
much as mentioned among you, as befits the people of God. No coarse, 4
stupid, or flippant talk; these things are out of place; you should rather be
thanking God. For be very sure of this: no one given to fornication or 5
indecency, or the greed which makes an idol of gain, has any share in the
kingdom of Christ and of God.

Let no one deceive you with shallow arguments; it is for all these things 6
that God's dreadful judgement is coming upon his rebel subjects. Have no 7
part or lot with them. For though you were once all darkness, now as 8
Christians you are light. Live like men who are at home in daylight, for 9
where light is, there all goodness springs up, all justice and truth. Try to 10
find out what would please the Lord; take no part in the barren deeds of 11
darkness, but show them up for what they are. The things they do in secret 12
it would be shameful even to mention. But everything, when once the light 13
has shown it up, is illumined, and everything thus illumined is all light.
And so the hymn says: 14

> 'Awake, sleeper,
> rise from the dead,
> and Christ will shine upon you.'

Be most careful then how you conduct yourselves: like sensible men, 15
not like simpletons. Use the present opportunity to the full, for these are 16
evil days. So do not be fools, but try to understand what the will of the 17
Lord is. Do not give way to drunkenness and the dissipation that goes with 18
it, but let the Holy Spirit fill you: speak to one another in psalms, hymns, 19
and*a* songs; sing and make music in your hearts to the Lord; and in the 20
name of our Lord Jesus Christ give thanks every day for everything to our
God and Father.

Be subject to one another out of reverence for Christ. 21

Wives, be subject to your husbands as to the Lord; for the man is the 22 23
head of the woman, just as Christ also is the head of the church. Christ is,
indeed, the Saviour of the body; but just as the church is subject to Christ, 24
so must women be to their husbands in everything.

Husbands, love your wives, as Christ also loved the church and gave 25
himself up for it, to consecrate it, cleansing it by water and word, so that 26 27
he might present the church to himself all glorious, with no stain or wrinkle
or anything of the sort, but holy and without blemish. In the same way men 28
also are bound to love their wives, as they love their own bodies. In loving
his wife a man loves himself. For no one ever hated his own body: on the 29
contrary, he provides and cares for it; and that is how Christ treats the
church, because it is his body, of which we are living parts. Thus it is that 30 31
(in the words of Scripture) 'a man shall leave his father and mother and

*a Some witnesses insert* spiritual, *as in Colossians 3. 16.*

32 shall be joined to his wife, and the two shall become one flesh'. It is a great truth that is hidden here. I for my part refer it to Christ and to the church,

33 but it applies also individually: each of you must love his wife as his very self; and the woman must see to it that she pays her husband all respect.

**6** 1 2 Children, obey your parents, for it is right that you should. 'Honour your father and mother' is the first commandment with a promise attached,

3 in the words: 'that it may be well with you and that you may live long in the land'.

4 You fathers, again, must not goad your children to resentment, but give them the instruction, and the correction, which belong to a Christian upbringing.

5 Slaves, obey your earthly masters with fear and trembling, single-
6 mindedly, as serving Christ. Do not offer merely the outward show of service, to curry favour with men, but, as slaves of Christ, do whole-
7 heartedly the will of God. Give the cheerful service of those who serve the
8 Lord, not men. For you know that whatever good each man may do, slave or free, will be repaid him by the Lord.

9 You masters, also, must do the same by them. Give up using threats; remember you both have the same Master in heaven, and he has no favourites.

10 11 Finally then, find your strength in the Lord, in his mighty power. Put on all the armour which God provides, so that you may be able to stand
12 firm against the devices of the devil. For our fight is not against human foes, but against cosmic powers, against the authorities and potentates of this
13 dark world, against the superhuman forces of evil in the heavens. There-fore, take up God's armour; then you will be able to stand your ground when things are at their worst, to complete every task and still to stand.
14 Stand firm, I say. Fasten on the belt of truth; for coat of mail put on
15 integrity; let the shoes on your feet be the gospel of peace, to give you firm
16 footing; and, with all these, take up the great shield of faith, with which you
17 will be able to quench all the flaming arrows of the evil one. Take salvation for helmet; for sword, take that which the Spirit gives you—the words that
18 come from God. Give yourselves wholly to prayer and entreaty; pray on every occasion in the power of the Spirit. To this end keep watch and per-
19 severe, always interceding for all God's people; and pray for me, that I may be granted the right words when I open my mouth, and may boldly and
20 freely make known his hidden purpose, for which I am an ambassador— in chains. Pray that I may speak of it boldly, as it is my duty to speak.

21 You will want to know about my affairs, and how I am; Tychicus will give you all the news. He is our dear brother and trustworthy helper in the
22 Lord's work. I am sending him to you on purpose to let you know all about us, and to put fresh heart into you.

23 Peace to the brotherhood and love, with faith, from God the Father
24 and the Lord Jesus Christ. God's grace be with all who love our Lord Jesus Christ, grace and immortality. *a*

*a Or* who love . . . Christ with love imperishable.

# THE LETTER OF PAUL
## TO THE
# PHILIPPIANS

### *The apostle and his friends*

FROM PAUL AND TIMOTHY, servants of Christ Jesus, to all 1
those of God's people, incorporate in Christ Jesus, who live at
Philippi, including their bishops and deacons.

Grace to you and peace from God our Father and the Lord Jesus Christ. 2
I thank my God whenever I think of you; and when I pray for you all, 3 4
my prayers are always joyful, because of the part you have taken in the 5
work of the Gospel from the first day until now. Of one thing I am certain: 6
the One who started the good work in you will bring it to completion by
the Day of Christ Jesus. It is indeed only right that I should feel like this 7
about you all, because you hold me in such affection, and because, when I
lie in prison or appear in the dock to vouch for the truth of the Gospel, you
all share in the privilege that is mine.[a] God knows how I long for you all, 8
with the deep yearning of Christ Jesus himself. And this is my prayer, that 9
your love may grow ever richer and richer in knowledge and insight of
every kind, and may thus bring you the gift of true discrimination.[b] Then 10
on the Day of Christ you will be flawless and without blame, reaping the 11
full harvest of righteousness that comes through Jesus Christ, to the glory
and praise of God.

Friends, I want you to understand that the work of the Gospel has 12
been helped on, rather than hindered, by this business of mine. My im- 13
prisonment in Christ's cause has become common knowledge to all at
headquarters[c] here, and indeed among the public at large; and it has given 14
confidence to most of our fellow-Christians to speak the word of God fearlessly and with extraordinary courage.

Some, indeed, proclaim Christ in a jealous and quarrelsome spirit; 15
others proclaim him in true goodwill, and these are moved by love for me; 16
they know that it is to defend the Gospel that I am where I am. But the 17
others, moved by personal rivalry, present Christ from mixed motives,
meaning to stir up fresh trouble for me as I lie in prison.[d] What does it 18
matter? One way or another, in pretence or sincerity, Christ is set forth,
and for that I rejoice.

[a] *Or* I am justified in taking this view about you all, because I hold you in closest union,
as those who, when I lie . . . of the Gospel, all share in the privilege that is mine.
[b] *Or* may teach you by experience what things are most worth while. [c] *Or* to
all the imperial guard, *or* to all at the Residency (*Greek* Praetorium). [d] *Or* meaning
to make use of my imprisonment to stir up fresh trouble.

19 Yes, and rejoice I will, knowing well that the issue of it all will be my deliverance, because you are praying for me and the Spirit of Jesus Christ
20 is given me for support.*ᵃ* For, as I passionately hope, I shall have no cause to be ashamed, but shall speak so boldly that now as always the greatness of Christ will shine out clearly in my person, whether through my life or
21 22 through my death. For to me life is Christ, and death gain; but what if my living on in the body may serve some good purpose? Which then am I to
23 choose? I cannot tell. I am torn two ways: what I should like is to depart
24 and be with Christ; that is better by far; but for your sake there is greater
25 need for me to stay on in the body. This indeed I know for certain: I shall stay, and stand by you all to help you forward and to add joy to your faith,
26 so that when I am with you again, your pride in me may be unbounded in Christ Jesus.

27 Only, let your conduct be worthy of the gospel of Christ, so that whether I come and see you for myself or hear about you from a distance, I may know that you are standing firm, one in spirit, one in mind, contending as
28 one man for the gospel faith, meeting your opponents without so much as a tremor. This is a sure sign to them that their doom is sealed, but a sign
29 of your salvation, and one afforded by God himself; for you have been granted the privilege not only of believing in Christ but also of suffering
30 for him. You and I are engaged in the same contest; you saw me in it once, and, as you hear, I am in it still.

2 IF THEN our common life in Christ yields anything to stir the heart, any loving consolation, any sharing of the Spirit, any warmth of affection or
2 compassion, fill up my cup of happiness by thinking and feeling alike, with the same love for one another, the same turn of mind, and a common
3 care for unity. There must be no room for rivalry and personal vanity among you, but you must humbly reckon others better than yourselves.
4 Look to each other's interest and not merely to your own.
5 Let your bearing towards one another arise out of your life in Christ
6 Jesus.*ᵇ* For the divine nature was his from the first; yet he did not think
7 to snatch at equality with God,*ᶜ* but made himself nothing, assuming the
8 nature of a slave. Bearing the human likeness, revealed in human shape, he humbled himself, and in obedience accepted even death—death on a
9 cross. Therefore God raised him to the heights and bestowed on him the
10 name above all names, that at the name of Jesus every knee should bow—
11 in heaven, on earth, and in the depths—and every tongue confess, 'Jesus Christ is Lord', to the glory of God the Father.
12 So you too, my friends, must be obedient, as always; even more, now that I am away, than when I was with you. You must work out your own
13 salvation in fear and trembling; for it is God who works in you, inspiring both the will and the deed, for his own chosen purpose.
14 15 Do all you have to do without complaint or wrangling. Show yourselves guileless and above reproach, faultless children of God in a warped and

*ᵃ Or* supplies me with all I need. which was also found in Christ Jesus.   *ᵇ Or* Have that bearing towards one another   *ᶜ Or* yet he did not prize his equality with God.

crooked generation, in which you shine[a] like stars in a dark world[b] and 16
proffer the word of life.[c] Thus you will be my pride on the Day of Christ,
proof that I did not run my race in vain, or work in vain. But if my life- 17
blood is to crown that sacrifice which is the offering up of your faith, I am
glad of it, and I share my gladness with you all. Rejoice, you no less than 18
I, and let us share our joy.

I HOPE (under the Lord Jesus) to send Timothy to you soon; it will 19
cheer me to hear news of you. There is no one else here who sees things as 20
I do, and takes[d] a genuine interest in your concerns; they are all bent on 21
their own ends, not on the cause of Christ Jesus. But Timothy's record is 22
known to you: you know that he has been at my side in the service of the
Gospel like a son working under his father. Timothy, then, I hope to send 23
as soon as ever I can see how things are going with me; and I am confident, 24
under the Lord, that I shall myself be coming before long.

I feel also I must send our brother Epaphroditus, my fellow-worker and 25
comrade, whom you commissioned to minister to my needs. He has been 26
missing all of you sadly, and has been distressed that you heard he was ill.
(He was indeed dangerously ill, but God was merciful to him, and merciful 27
no less to me, to spare me sorrow upon sorrow.) For this reason I am all 28
the more eager to send him, to give you the happiness of seeing him again,
and to relieve my sorrow. Welcome him then in the fellowship of the Lord 29
with whole-hearted delight. You should honour men like him; in Christ's 30
cause he came near to death, risking his life to render me the service you
could not give.

And now, friends, farewell; I wish you joy in the Lord. 3

TO REPEAT what I have written to you before is no trouble to me, and it
is a safeguard for you. Beware of those dogs and their malpractices. Beware 2
of those who insist on mutilation—'circumcision' I will not call it; we are 3
the circumcised, we whose worship is spiritual,[e] whose pride is in Christ
Jesus, and who put no confidence in anything external. Not that I am with- 4
out grounds myself even for confidence of that kind. If anyone thinks to
base his claims on externals, I could make a stronger case for myself:
circumcised on my eighth day, Israelite by race, of the tribe of Benjamin, 5
a Hebrew born and bred;[f] in my attitude to the law, a Pharisee; in pious 6
zeal, a persecutor of the church; in legal rectitude, faultless. But all such 7
assets I have written off because of Christ. I would say more: I count 8
everything sheer loss, because all is far outweighed by the gain of knowing
Christ Jesus my Lord, for whose sake I did in fact lose everything. I count
it so much garbage,[g] for the sake of gaining Christ and finding myself 9
incorporate in him, with no righteousness of my own, no legal rectitude,

---

[a] *Or* . . . generation. Shine out among them . . .  [b] *Or* in the firmament.
[c] *Or* as the very principle of its life.  [d] *Or* no one else here like him, who
takes . . .  [e] *Some witnesses read* who worship God in the spirit; *others read* who
worship by the Spirit of God.  [f] *Or* a Hebrew-speaking Jew of a Hebrew-speaking
family.  [g] *Or* dung.

but the righteousness which comes *a* from faith in Christ, given by God in
10 response to faith. All I care for is to know Christ, to experience the power
of his resurrection, and to share his sufferings, in growing confor-
11 mity with his death, if only I may finally arrive at the resurrection from
the dead.

12     It is not to be thought that I have already achieved all this. I have not yet
reached perfection, but I press on, hoping to take hold of that for which
13 Christ once took hold of me. My friends, I do not reckon myself to have got
hold of it yet. All I can say is this: forgetting what is behind me, and reach-
14 ing out for that which lies ahead, I press towards the goal to win the prize
which is God's call to the life above, in Christ Jesus.

15     Let us then keep to this way of thinking, those of us who are mature. If
there is any point on which you think differently, this also God will make
16 plain to you. Only let our conduct be consistent with the level we have
already reached.

17     Agree together, my friends, to follow my example. You have us for a
18 model; watch those whose way of life conforms to it. For, as I have often
told you, and now tell you with tears in my eyes, there are many whose
19 way of life makes them enemies of the cross of Christ. They are heading for
destruction, appetite is their god, and they glory in their shame. Their
20 minds are set on earthly things. We, by contrast, are citizens of heaven,
and from heaven we expect our deliverer to come, the Lord Jesus Christ.
21 He will transfigure the body belonging to our humble state, and give it a
form like that of his own resplendent body, by the very power which
4 enables him to make all things subject to himself. Therefore, my friends,
beloved friends whom I long for, my joy, my crown, stand thus firm in the
Lord, my beloved!

2     I beg Euodia, and I beg Syntyche, to agree together in the Lord's fellow-
3 ship. Yes, and you too, my loyal comrade, I ask you to help these women,
who shared my struggles in the cause of the Gospel, with Clement and my
other fellow-workers, whose *b* names are in the roll of the living.

4     Farewell; I wish you all joy in the Lord. I will say it again: all joy be
yours.

5     Let your magnanimity be manifest to all.

6     The Lord is near; have no anxiety, but in everything make your requests
7 known to God in prayer and petition with thanksgiving. Then the peace of
God, which is beyond our utmost understanding, *c* will keep guard over
your hearts and your thoughts, in Christ Jesus.

8     And now, my friends, all that is true, all that is noble, all that is just and
pure, all that is lovable and gracious, *d* whatever is excellent and admirable
—fill all your thoughts with these things.

9     The lessons I taught you, the tradition I have passed on, all that you
heard me say or saw me do, put into practice; and the God of peace will
be with you.

*a* Or and in him finding that, though I have no righteousness of my own, no legal rectitude, I have the righteousness which comes . . .          *b* *Some witnesses read* my
fellow-workers, and the others whose . . .               *c* Or of far more worth than
human reasoning.          *d* Or of good repute.

IT IS A GREAT JOY to me, in the Lord, that after so long your care for me 10
has now blossomed afresh. You did care about me before for that matter;
it was opportunity that you lacked. Not that I am alluding to want, for I 11
have learned to find resources in myself whatever my circumstances. I 12
know what it is to be brought low, and I know what it is to have plenty.
I have been very thoroughly initiated into the human lot with all its ups
and downs—fullness and hunger, plenty and want. I have strength for any- 13
thing through him who gives me power. But it was kind of you to share the 14
burden of my troubles.

As you know yourselves, Philippians, in the early days of my mission, 15
when I set out from Macedonia, you alone of all our congregations were
my partners in payments and receipts; for even at Thessalonica you con- 16
tributed to my needs, not once but twice over. Do not think I set my heart 17
upon the gift; all I care for is the profit accruing to you. However, here I 18
give you my receipt for everything—for more than everything; I am paid
in full, now that I have received from Epaphroditus what you sent. It is a
fragrant offering, an acceptable sacrifice, pleasing to God. And my God 19
will supply all your wants out of the magnificence of his riches in Christ
Jesus. To our God and Father be glory for endless ages! Amen. 20

Give my greetings, in the fellowship of Christ Jesus, to each one of God's 21
people. The brothers who are now with me send their greetings to you,
and so do all God's people here, particularly those who belong to the 22
imperial establishment.

The grace of our Lord Jesus Christ be with your spirit. 23

# THE LETTER OF PAUL
# TO THE
# COLOSSIANS

## *The centre of Christian belief*

FROM PAUL, APOSTLE of Christ Jesus commissioned by the 1
will of God, and our colleague Timothy, to God's people at Colossae, 2
brothers in the faith, incorporate in Christ.
Grace to you and peace from God our Father.

In all our prayers to God, the Father of our Lord Jesus Christ, we 3
thank him for you, because we have heard of the faith you hold in Christ 4
Jesus, and the love you bear towards all God's people. Both spring from the 5
hope stored up for you in heaven—that hope of which you learned when the
message of the true Gospel first came to you. In the same way it is coming 6
to men the whole world over; everywhere it is growing and bearing fruit

as it does among you, and has done since the day when you heard of the
7 graciousness of God and recognized it for what in truth it is. You were
taught this by Epaphras, our dear fellow-servant, a trusted worker for
8 Christ on our*a* behalf, and it is he who has brought us the news of your
God-given love.*b*

9    For this reason, ever since the day we heard of it, we have not ceased to
pray for you. We ask God that you may receive from him all wisdom and
10 spiritual understanding for full insight into his will, so that your manner
of life may be worthy of the Lord and entirely pleasing to him. We pray
that you may bear fruit in active goodness of every kind, and grow in the
11 knowledge of God. May he strengthen you, in his glorious might, with
ample power to meet whatever comes with fortitude, patience, and joy;
12 and to give thanks*c* to the Father who has made you fit to share the heritage
of God's people in the realm of light.

13    He rescued us from the domain of darkness and brought us away into
14 the kingdom of his dear Son, in whom our release is secured and our sins
15 forgiven. He is the image of the invisible God; his is the primacy over*d* all
16 created things. In him everything in heaven and on earth was created, not
only things visible but also the invisible orders of thrones, sovereignties,
authorities, and powers: the whole universe has been created through him
17 and for him. And he exists before everything, and all things are held to-
18 gether in him. He is, moreover, the head of the body, the church. He is its
origin, the first to return from the dead, to be in all things alone supreme.
19 For in him the complete being of God, by God's own choice, came to dwell.
20 Through him God chose to reconcile the whole universe to himself, making
peace through the shedding of his blood upon the cross—to reconcile all
things, whether on earth or in heaven, through him alone.

21    Formerly you were yourselves estranged from God; you were his enemies
22 in heart and mind, and your deeds were evil. But now by Christ's death in
his body of flesh and blood God has reconciled you to himself, so that he
may present you before himself as dedicated men, without blemish and
23 innocent in his sight. Only you must continue in your faith, firm on your
foundations, never to be dislodged from the hope offered in the gospel
which you heard. This is the gospel which has been proclaimed in the whole
creation under heaven; and I, Paul, have become its minister.

24    It is now my happiness to suffer for you. This is my way of helping to
complete, in my poor human flesh, the full tale of Christ's afflictions still
25 to be endured, for the sake of his body which is the church. I became its
servant by virtue of the task assigned to me by God for your benefit: to
26 deliver his message in full; to announce the secret hidden for long ages and
27 through many generations, but now disclosed to God's people, to whom it
was his will to make it known—to make known how rich and glorious it is
among all nations. The secret is this: Christ in*e* you, the hope of a glory to
come.

28    He it is whom we proclaim. We admonish everyone without distinction,

---

*a Some witnesses read* your.        *b* Or your love within the fellowship of the Spirit.
*c Or* with fortitude and patience, and to give joyful thanks . . .        *d Or* image of
the invisible God, born before . . .        *e Or* among.

we instruct everyone in all the ways of wisdom, so as to present each one
of you as a mature member of Christ's body. To this end I am toiling   29
strenuously with all the energy and power of Christ at work in me. For I   2
want you to know how strenuous are my exertions for you and the Laodi-
ceans and all who have never set eyes on me. I want them to continue in   2
good heart and in the unity of love, and to come to the full wealth of conviction which understanding brings, and grasp God's secret. That secret is
Christ himself; in him lie hidden all God's treasures of wisdom and know-   3
ledge. I tell you this to save you from being talked *a* into error by specious   4
arguments. For though absent in body, I am with you in spirit, and rejoice   5
to see your orderly array and the firm front which your faith in Christ
presents.

THEREFORE, SINCE JESUS was delivered to you as Christ and Lord,   6
live your lives in union with him. Be rooted in him; be built in him; be con-   7
solidated in the faith you were taught; *b* let your hearts overflow with
thankfulness. Be on your guard; do not let your minds be captured by   8
hollow and delusive speculations, based on traditions of man-made teaching and centred on the elemental spirits of the universe *c* and not on Christ.
For it is in Christ that the complete being of the Godhead dwells   9
embodied, *d* and in him you have been brought to completion. Every power   10
and authority in the universe is subject to him as Head. In him also you were   11
circumcised, not in a physical sense, but by being divested of the lower
nature; this is Christ's way of circumcision. For in baptism *e* you were   12
buried with him, in baptism also you were raised to life with him through
your faith in the active power of God who raised him from the dead. And   13
although you were dead because of your sins and because you were morally
uncircumcised, he has made you alive with Christ. For he has forgiven us
all our sins; he has cancelled the bond which pledged us to the decrees of   14
the law. It stood against us, but he has set it aside, nailing it to the cross.
On that cross he discarded the cosmic powers and authorities like a gar-   15
ment; he made a public spectacle of them and led them *f* as captives in his
triumphal procession.

ALLOW NO ONE therefore to take you to task about what you eat or drink,   16
or over the observance of festival, new moon, or sabbath. These are no   17
more than a shadow of what was to come; the solid reality is Christ's. You   18
are not to be disqualified by the decision of people who go in for self-
mortification and angel-worship, and try to enter into some vision of their
own. Such people, bursting with the futile conceit of worldly minds, lose   19
hold upon the Head; yet it is from the Head that the whole body, with all

*a Or* What I mean is this: no one must talk you . . .          *b Or* by your faith, as you
were taught.          *c Or* the elements of the natural world, *or* elementary ideas
belonging to this world.          *d Or* corporately.          *e Or* . . . nature, in the
very circumcision of Christ himself; for in baptism . . .          *f Or* he stripped
himself of his physical body, and thereby boldly made a spectacle of the cosmic powers
and authorities, and led them . . .; *or* he despoiled the cosmic powers and authorities, and
boldly made a spectacle of them, leading them . . .

its joints and ligaments, receives its supplies, and thus knit together grows according to God's design.

20 Did you not die with Christ and pass beyond reach of the elemental spirits of the universe *a* ? Then why behave as though you were still living
21 the life of the world? Why let people dictate to you: 'Do not handle this,
22 do not taste that, do not touch the other'—all of them things that must perish as soon as they are used? That is to follow merely human injunctions
23 and teaching. True, it has an air of wisdom, with its forced piety, its self-mortification, and its severity to the body; but it is of no use at all in combating sensuality.

3 Were you not raised to life with Christ? Then aspire to the realm above,
2 where Christ is, seated at the right hand of God, and let your thoughts
3 dwell on that higher realm, not on this earthly life. I repeat, you died; and
4 now your life lies hidden with Christ in God. When Christ, who is our life, is manifested, then you too will be manifested with him in glory.

5 Then put to death those parts of you which belong to the earth—fornication, indecency, lust, foul cravings, and the ruthless greed which is
6 nothing less than idolatry. Because of these, God's dreadful judgement is
7 impending; and in the life you once lived these are the ways you yourselves
8 followed. But now you must yourselves lay aside all anger, passion, malice,
9 cursing, filthy talk—have done with them! Stop lying to one another, now
10 that you have discarded the old nature with its deeds and have put on the new nature, which is being constantly renewed in the image of its Creator
11 and brought to know God. There is no question here of Greek and Jew, circumcised and uncircumcised, barbarian, Scythian, slave and freeman; but Christ is all, and is in all.

12 Then put on the garments that suit God's chosen people, his own, his
13 beloved: compassion, kindness, humility, gentleness, patience. Be forbearing with one another, and forgiving, where any of you has cause for
14 complaint: you must forgive as the Lord forgave you. To crown all, there
15 must be love, to bind all together and complete the whole. Let Christ's peace be arbiter in your hearts; to this peace you were called as members of
16 a single body. And be filled with gratitude. Let the message of Christ dwell among you in all its richness. Instruct and admonish each other with the utmost wisdom. Sing thankfully in your hearts to God, *b* with psalms and
17 hymns and spiritual songs. Whatever you are doing, whether you speak or act, do everything in the name of the Lord Jesus, giving thanks to God the Father through him.

18 WIVES, BE SUBJECT to your husbands; that is your Christian duty.
19 20 Husbands, love your wives and do not be harsh with them. Children, obey your parents in everything, for that is pleasing to God and is the Christian
21 way. Fathers, do not exasperate your children, for fear they grow disheartened. Slaves, give entire obedience to your earthly masters, not merely
22 with an outward show of service, to curry favour with men, but with single-
23 mindedness, out of reverence for the Lord. Whatever you are doing, put

*a* *Or* the elements of the natural world, *or* elementary ideas belonging to this world.
*b* *Some witnesses read* the Lord.

your whole heart into it, as if you were doing it for the Lord and not for
men, knowing that there is a Master who will give you your heritage as a  24
reward for your service. Christ is the Master whose slaves you must be.
Dishonesty will be requited, and he has no favourites. Masters, be just and  25 **4** 1
fair to your slaves, knowing that you too have a Master in heaven.

Persevere in prayer, with mind awake and thankful heart; and include a  2 3
prayer for us, that God may give us an opening for preaching, to tell the
secret of Christ; that indeed is why I am now in prison. Pray that I may  4
make the secret plain, as it is my duty to do.

Behave wisely towards those outside your own number; use the present  5
opportunity to the full. Let your conversation be always gracious, and  6
never insipid; study how best to talk with each person you meet.

YOU WILL HEAR all about my affairs from Tychicus, our dear brother  7
and trustworthy helper and fellow-servant in the Lord's work. I am send-  8
ing him to you on purpose to let you know all about us and to put fresh
heart into you. With him comes Onesimus, our trustworthy and dear  9
brother, who is one of yourselves. They will tell you all the news here.

Aristarchus, Christ's captive like myself, sends his greetings; so does  10
Mark, the cousin of Barnabas (you have had instructions about him; if he
comes, make him welcome), and Jesus Justus. Of the Jewish Christians,  11
these are the only ones who work with me for the kingdom of God, and they
have been a great comfort to me. Greetings from Epaphras, servant of  12
Christ, who is one of yourselves. He prays hard for you all the time, that
you may stand fast, ripe in conviction*a* and wholly devoted to doing God's
will. For I can vouch for him, that he works tirelessly for you and the people  13
at Laodicea and Hierapolis. Greetings to you from our dear friend Luke,  14
the doctor, and from Demas. Give our greetings to the brothers at Laodicea,  15
and Nympha and the congregation at her house.*b* And when this letter is  16
read among you, see that it is also read to the congregation at Laodicea,
and that you in return read the one from Laodicea. This special word to  17
Archippus: 'Attend to the duty entrusted to you in the Lord's service,
and discharge it to the full.'

This greeting is in my own hand—PAUL. Remember I am in prison.  18
God's grace be with you.

---

*a Or* stand fast, mature and complete . . .          *b Some witnesses read* Nymphas and
the congregation at his house.

# THE FIRST LETTER OF PAUL
# TO THE
# THESSALONIANS

*Hope and discipline*

1 FROM PAUL, Silvanus, and Timothy to the congregation of Thessalonians who belong to God the Father and the Lord Jesus Christ. Grace to you and peace.

2 We always thank God for you all, and mention you in our prayers con-
3 tinually. We call to mind, before our God and Father, how your faith has shown itself in action, your love in labour, and your hope of our Lord Jesus
4 Christ in fortitude. We are certain, brothers beloved by God, that he has
5 chosen you and that *a* when we brought you the Gospel, we brought it not in mere words but in the power of the Holy Spirit, and with strong conviction, as you know well. That is the kind of men we were at Thessalonica, and it was for your sake.

6 And you, in your turn, followed the example set by us and by the Lord; the welcome you gave the message meant grave suffering for you, yet you
7 rejoiced in the Holy Spirit; thus you have become a model for all believers
8 in Macedonia and in Achaia. From Thessalonica the word of the Lord rang out; and not in Macedonia and Achaia alone, but everywhere your
9 faith in God has reached men's ears. No words of ours are needed, for they themselves spread the news of our visit to you and its effect: how you turned
10 from idols, to be servants of the living and true God, and to wait expectantly for the appearance from heaven of his Son Jesus, whom he raised from the dead, Jesus our deliverer from the terrors of judgement to come.

2 You know for yourselves, brothers, that our visit to you was not fruitless.
2 Far from it; after all the injury and outrage which to your knowledge we had suffered at Philippi, we declared the gospel of God to you frankly and
3 fearlessly, by the help of our God. A hard struggle it was. Indeed, the appeal we make never springs from error or base motive; there is no attempt to
4 deceive; but God has approved us as fit to be entrusted with the Gospel, and on those terms we speak. We do not curry favour with men; we seek
5 only the favour of God, who is continually testing our hearts. Our words have never been flattering words, as you have cause to know; nor, as God
6 is our witness, have they ever been a cloak for greed. We have never sought honour from men, from you or from anyone else, although as Christ's own
7 envoys we might have made our weight felt; but we were as gentle with you
8 as a nurse caring fondly for her children. With such yearning love we chose

*a* Or ... chosen you, because ...

260

to impart to you not only the gospel of God but our very selves, so dear had
you become to us. Remember, brothers, how we toiled and drudged. We 9
worked for a living night and day, rather than be a burden to anyone, while
we proclaimed before you the good news of God.

We call you to witness, yes and God himself, how devout and just and 10
blameless was our behaviour towards you who are believers. As you well 11
know, we dealt with you one by one, as a father deals with his children,
appealing to you by encouragement, as well as by solemn injunctions, to 12
live lives worthy of the God who calls you into his kingdom and glory.

This is why we thank God continually, because when we handed on 13
God's message, you received it, not as the word of men, but as what it truly
is, the very word of God at *a* work in you who hold the faith. You have 14
fared like the congregations in Judaea, God's people in Christ Jesus. You
have been treated by your countrymen as they are treated by the Jews,
who killed the Lord Jesus and the prophets *b* and drove us out, the Jews 15
who are heedless of God's will and enemies of their fellow-men, hindering 16
us from speaking to the Gentiles to lead them to salvation. All this time
they have been making up the full measure of their guilt, and now retribution has overtaken them for good and all. *c*

MY FRIENDS, when for a short spell you were lost to us—lost to sight, not 17
to our hearts—we were exceedingly anxious to see you again. So we did 18
propose to come to Thessalonica—I, Paul, more than once—but Satan
thwarted us. For after all, what hope or joy or crown of pride is there for 19
us, what indeed but you, when we stand before our Lord Jesus at his
coming? It is you who are indeed our glory and our joy. 20

So when we could bear it no longer, we decided to remain alone at 3
Athens, and sent Timothy, our brother and God's fellow-worker *d* in the 2
service of the gospel of Christ, to encourage you to stand firm for the faith
and, under all these hardships, not to be shaken; *e* for you know that this 3
is our appointed lot. When we were with you we warned you that we were 4
bound to suffer hardship; and so it has turned out, as you know. And thus 5
it was that when I could bear it no longer, I sent to find out about your faith,
fearing that the tempter might have tempted you and my labour might
be lost.

But now Timothy has just arrived from Thessalonica, bringing good 6
news of your faith and love. He tells us that you always think kindly of us,
and are as anxious to see us as we are to see you. And so in all our diffi- 7
culties and hardships your faith reassures us about you. It is the breath of 8
life to us that you stand firm in the Lord. What thanks can we return to 9
God for you? What thanks for all the joy you have brought us, making us
rejoice before our God while we pray most earnestly night and day to be 10
allowed to see you again and to mend your faith where it falls short?

May our God and Father himself, and our Lord Jesus, bring us direct to 11
you; and may the Lord make your love mount and overflow towards one 12

---

*a Or* word of God who is at . . .          *b Some witnesses read* their own prophets.
*c Or* now at last retribution has overtaken them.          *d Or* and fellow-worker for
God; *one witness has simply* and fellow-worker.          *e Or* beguiled away.

13 another and towards all, as our love does towards you. May he make your hearts firm, so that you may stand before our God and Father holy and faultless when our Lord Jesus comes with all those who are his own.

4 AND NOW, MY FRIENDS, we have one thing to beg and pray of you, by our fellowship with the Lord Jesus. We passed on to you the tradition of the way we must live to please God; you are indeed already following it, but we beg you to do so yet more thoroughly.

2 For you know what orders we gave you, in the name of the Lord Jesus.
3 This is the will of God, that you should be holy: you must abstain from
4 fornication; each one of you must learn to gain mastery over his body, to
5 hallow and honour it, not giving way to lust like the pagans who are
6 ignorant of God; and no man must do his brother wrong in this matter,[a]
or invade his rights, because, as we told you before with all emphasis, the
7 Lord punishes all such offences. For God called us to holiness, not to
8 impurity. Anyone therefore who flouts these rules is flouting, not man, but God who bestows upon you his Holy Spirit.

9 About love for our brotherhood you need no words of mine, for you are
10 yourselves taught by God to love one another, and you are in fact practising this rule of love towards all your fellow-Christians throughout Mace-
11 donia. Yet we appeal to you, brothers, to do better still. Let it be your ambition to keep calm and look after your own business, and to work with
12 your hands, as we ordered you, so that you may command the respect of those outside your own number, and at the same time may never be in want.

13 WE WISH YOU not to remain in ignorance, brothers, about those who sleep in death; you should not grieve like the rest of men, who have no
14 hope. We believe that Jesus died and rose again; and so it will be for those who died as Christians; God will bring them to life with Jesus.[b]
15 For this we tell you as the Lord's word: we who are left alive until the
16 Lord comes shall not forestall those who have died; because at the word of command, at the sound of the archangel's voice and God's trumpet-call, the Lord himself will descend from heaven; first the Christian dead will
17 rise, then we who are left alive shall join them, caught up in clouds to meet
18 the Lord in the air. Thus we shall always be with the Lord. Console one another, then, with these words.

5 1 2 About dates and times, my friends, we need not write to you, for you know perfectly well that the Day of the Lord comes like a thief in the night.
3 While they are talking of peace and security, all at once calamity is upon them, sudden as the pangs that come upon a woman with child; and there
4 will be no escape. But you, my friends, are not in the dark, that the day
5 should overtake you like a thief.[c] You are all children of light, children of
6 day. We do not belong to night or darkness, and we must not sleep like
7 the rest, but keep awake and sober. Sleepers sleep at night, and drunkards
8 are drunk at night, but we, who belong to daylight, must keep sober, armed with faith and love for coat of mail, and the hope of salvation for

---

[a] *Or* must overreach his brother in his business (*or* in lawsuits).          [b] *Or* will bring them in company with Jesus.          [c] *Some witnesses read* thieves.

helmet. For God has not destined us to the terrors of judgement, but to the  9
full attainment of salvation through our Lord Jesus Christ. He died for us  10
so that we, awake or asleep, might live in company with him. Therefore  11
hearten one another, fortify one another—as indeed you do.

WE BEG YOU, BROTHERS, to acknowledge those who are working so hard  12
among you, and in the Lord's fellowship are your leaders and counsellors.
Hold them in the highest possible esteem and affection for the work they do.  13
You must live at peace among yourselves. And we would urge you,  14
brothers, to admonish the careless, encourage the faint-hearted, support
the weak, and to be very patient with them all.
See to it that no one pays back wrong for wrong, but always aim at doing  15
the best you can for each other and for all men.
Be always joyful; pray continually; give thanks whatever happens; for  16 17 18
this is what God in Christ wills for you.
Do not stifle inspiration, and do not despise prophetic utterances, but  19 20 21
bring them all to the test and then keep what is good in them and avoid the  22
bad of whatever kind. *a*
May God himself, the God of peace, make you holy in every part, and  23
keep you sound in spirit, soul, and body, without fault when our Lord
Jesus Christ comes. He who calls you is to be trusted; he will do it.  24
Brothers, pray for us also.  25
Greet all our brothers with the kiss of peace.  26
I adjure you by the Lord to have this letter read to the whole brother-  27
hood.
The grace of our Lord Jesus Christ be with you!  28

# THE SECOND LETTER OF PAUL
# TO THE
# THESSALONIANS

## *Hope and discipline*

FROM PAUL, Silvanus, and Timothy to the congregation of Thes-  1
salonians who belong to God our Father and the Lord Jesus Christ.
Grace to you and peace from God the Father and the Lord Jesus  2
Christ.
Our thanks are always due to God for you, brothers. It is right that we  3
should thank him, because your faith increases mightily, and the love you

*a* Or ... utterances. Put everything to the test; keep hold of what is good and avoid every
kind of evil.

4 have, each for all and all for each, grows ever greater. Indeed we boast about you ourselves among the congregations of God's people, because your faith remains so steadfast under all your persecutions, and all the
5 troubles you endure. See how this brings out the justice of God's judgement. It will prove you worthy of the kingdom of God, for which indeed you are suffering.
6 It is surely just that God should balance the account by sending trouble
7 to those who trouble you, and relief to you who are troubled, and to us as well, when our Lord Jesus Christ is revealed from heaven with his
8 mighty angels in blazing fire. Then he will do justice upon those who refuse to acknowledge God and upon those who will not obey *a* the
9 gospel of our Lord Jesus. They will suffer the punishment of eternal ruin, cut off from the presence of the Lord and the splendour of his might,
10 when on that great Day he comes to be glorified among his own and adored among all believers; for you did indeed believe the testimony we brought you.
11 With this in mind we pray for you always, that our God may count you worthy of his calling, and mightily bring to fulfilment every good pur-
12 pose and every act inspired by faith, so that the name of our Lord Jesus may be glorified in you, and you in him, according to the grace of our God and the Lord Jesus Christ.

2 AND NOW, BROTHERS, about the coming of our Lord Jesus Christ and
2 his gathering of us to himself: I beg you, do not suddenly lose your heads or alarm yourselves, whether at some oracular utterance, or pronouncement, or some letter purporting to come from us, alleging that the Day of
3 the Lord is already here. Let no one deceive you in any way whatever. That day cannot come before the final rebellion against God, when wickedness
4 will be revealed in human form, the man doomed to perdition. He is the Enemy. He rises in his pride against every god, so called, every object of men's worship, and even takes his seat in the temple of God claiming to be a god himself.
5 You cannot but remember that I told you this while I was still with you;
6 you must now be aware of the restraining hand which ensures that he shall
7 be revealed only at the proper time. For already the secret power of wickedness is at work, secret only for the present until the Restrainer disappears
8 from the scene. And then he will be revealed, that wicked man whom the Lord Jesus will destroy with the breath of his mouth, and annihilate by the
9 radiance of his coming. But the coming of that wicked man is the work of Satan. It will be attended by all the powerful signs and miracles of the Lie,
10 and all the deception that sinfulness can impose on those doomed to destruction. Destroyed they shall be, because they did not open their
11 minds to love of the truth, so as to find salvation. Therefore God puts them
12 under a delusion, which works upon them to believe the lie, so that they may all be brought to judgement, all who do not believe the truth but make sinfulness their deliberate choice.

*a Or* justice upon those who refuse . . . and will not obey . . .

BUT WE ARE BOUND to thank God always for you, brothers beloved by 13
the Lord, because from the beginning of time God chose you[a] to find
salvation in the Spirit that consecrates you, and in the truth that you
believe. It was for this that he called you through the gospel we brought, 14
so that you might possess for your own the splendour of our Lord Jesus
Christ.

Stand firm, then, brothers, and hold fast to the traditions which you have 15
learned from us by word or by letter. And may our Lord Jesus Christ him- 16
self and God our Father, who has shown us such love, and in his grace has
given us such unfailing encouragement and such bright hopes, still 17
encourage and fortify you in every good deed and word!

And now, brothers, pray for us, that the word of the Lord may have 3
everywhere the swift and glorious course that it has had among you, and 2
that we may be rescued from wrong-headed and wicked men; for it is not
all who have faith. But the Lord is to be trusted, and he will fortify you and 3
guard you from the evil one. We feel perfect confidence about you, in the 4
Lord, that you are doing and will continue to do what we order. May the 5
Lord direct your hearts towards God's love and the steadfastness of Christ!

These are our orders to you, brothers, in the name of our Lord Jesus 6
Christ: hold aloof from every Christian brother who falls into idle habits,
and does not follow the tradition you received from us. You know your- 7
selves how you ought to copy our example: we were no idlers among you;
we did not accept board and lodging from anyone without paying for it; 8
we toiled and drudged, we worked for a living night and day, rather than
be a burden to any of you—not because we have not the right to main- 9
tenance, but to set an example for you to imitate. For even during our stay 10
with you we laid down the rule: the man who will not work shall not eat.
We mention this because we hear that some of your number are idling 11
their time away, minding everybody's business but their own. To all such 12
we give these orders, and we appeal to them in the name of the Lord Jesus
Christ to work quietly for their living.

But you, my friends, must never tire of doing right. If anyone disobeys 13 14
our instructions given by letter, mark him well, and have no dealings with
him until he is ashamed of himself. I do not mean treat him as an enemy, 15
but give him friendly advice, as one of the family. May the Lord of peace 16
himself give you peace at all times and in all ways.[b] The Lord be with
you all.

The greeting is in my own hand, signed with my name, PAUL; this 17
authenticates all my letters; this is how I write. The grace[c] of our Lord 18
Jesus Christ be with you all.

---

[a] *Some witnesses read* because God chose you as his firstfruits . . .        [b] *Some*
*witnesses read* at all times, wherever you may be.        [c] *Or* . . . letters. My message is
this: the grace . . .

# THE FIRST LETTER OF PAUL
# TO
# TIMOTHY

*Church order*

1, 2 FROM PAUL, APOSTLE of Christ Jesus by command of God our Saviour and Christ Jesus our hope, to Timothy his true-born son in the faith.

Grace, mercy, and peace to you from God the Father and Christ Jesus our Lord.

3 When I was starting for Macedonia, I urged you to stay on at Ephesus. You were to command certain persons to give up teaching erroneous 4 doctrines and studying those interminable myths and genealogies, which issue in mere speculation and cannot make known God's plan for us, which works through faith.[a]

5 The aim and object of this command is the love which springs from a clean heart, from a good conscience, and from faith that is genuine. 6 Through falling short of these, some people have gone astray into a wilder- 7 ness of words. They set out to be teachers of the moral law, without understanding either the words they use or the subjects about which they are so dogmatic.

8 We all know that the law is an excellent thing, provided we treat it as 9 law, recognizing that it is not aimed at good citizens, but at the lawless and unruly, the impious and sinful, the irreligious and worldly; at parricides 10 and matricides, murderers and fornicators, perverts, kidnappers, liars, 11 perjurers—in fact all whose behaviour flouts the wholesome teaching which conforms with the gospel entrusted to me, the gospel which tells of the glory of God in his eternal felicity.

12 I thank him who has made me equal to the task, Christ Jesus our Lord; I thank him for judging me worthy of this trust and appointing me to his 13 service—although in the past I had met him with abuse and persecution and outrage. But because I acted ignorantly in unbelief I was dealt with 14 mercifully; the grace of our Lord was lavished upon me, with the faith and love which are ours in Christ Jesus.

15 Here are words you may trust, words that merit full acceptance: 'Christ Jesus came into the world to save sinners'; and among them I stand first. 16 But I was mercifully dealt with for this very purpose, that Jesus Christ might find in me the first occasion for displaying all his patience, and that I might be typical of all who were in future to have faith in him and gain

[a] *Or* cannot promote the faithful discharge of God's stewardship.

eternal life. Now to the King of all worlds, immortal, invisible, the only 17
God, be honour and glory for ever and ever! Amen.

This charge, son Timothy, I lay upon you, following that prophetic 18
utterance which first pointed you out to me. So fight gallantly, armed with 19
faith and a good conscience. It was through spurning conscience that certain
persons made shipwreck of their faith, among them Hymenaeus and 20
Alexander, whom I consigned to Satan, in the hope that through this
discipline they might learn not to be blasphemous.

FIRST OF ALL, then, I urge that petitions, prayers, intercessions, and **2**
thanksgivings be offered for all men; for sovereigns and all in high office, 2
that we may lead a tranquil and quiet life in full observance of religion and
high standards of morality. Such prayer is right, and approved by God our 3
Saviour, whose will it is that all men should find salvation and come to 4
know the truth. For there is one God, and also one mediator between God 5
and men, Christ Jesus, himself man, who sacrificed himself to win freedom 6
for all mankind, so providing, at the fitting time, proof of the divine purpose; of this I was appointed herald and apostle (this is no lie, but the truth), 7
to instruct the nations in the true faith.

It is my desire, therefore, that everywhere prayers be said by the men 8
of the congregation, who shall lift up their hands with a pure intention,
excluding angry or quarrelsome thoughts. Women again must dress in 9
becoming manner, modestly and soberly, not with elaborate hair-styles,
not decked out with gold or pearls, or expensive clothes, but with good 10
deeds, as befits women who claim to be religious. A woman must be a 11
learner, listening quietly and with due submission. I do not permit a woman 12
to be a teacher, nor must woman domineer over man; she should be quiet.
For Adam was created first, and Eve afterwards; and it was not Adam who 13 14
was deceived; it was the woman who, yielding to deception, fell into sin.
Yet she will be saved through motherhood*a*—if only women continue in 15
faith,*b* love, and holiness, with a sober mind.

There is a popular saying:*c* 'To aspire to leadership is an honourable **3**
ambition.' Our leader, therefore, or bishop, must be above reproach, faith- 2
ful to his one wife,*d* sober, temperate, courteous, hospitable, and a good
teacher; he must not be given to drink, or a brawler, but of a forbearing 3
disposition, avoiding quarrels, and no lover of money. He must be one who 4
manages his own household well and wins obedience from his children,
and a man of the highest principles. If a man does not know how to control 5
his own family, how can he look after a congregation of God's people? He 6
must not be a convert newly baptized, for fear the sin of conceit should
bring upon him a judgement contrived by the devil.*e* He must moreover 7
have a good reputation with the non-Christian public, so that he may not be
exposed to scandal and get caught in the devil's snare.

*a Or* saved through the Birth of the Child, *or* brought safely through childbirth.
*b Or* if only husband and wife continue in mutual fidelity . . .     *c Some witnesses*
*read* Here are words you may trust, *which some interpreters attach to the end of the pre-*
*ceding paragraph.*     *d Or* married to one wife, *or* married only once.     *e Or the*
judgement once passed on the devil.

8 Deacons, likewise, must be men of high principle, not indulging in double talk, given neither to excessive drinking nor to money-grubbing.
9 They must be men who combine a clear conscience with a firm hold on the
10 deep truths of our faith. No less than bishops, they must first undergo a
11 scrutiny, and if there is no mark against them, they may serve. Their wives, *a* equally, must be women of high principle, who will not talk scandal, sober
12 and trustworthy in every way. A deacon must be faithful to his one wife, *b*
13 and good at managing his children and his own household. For deacons with a good record of service may claim a high standing and the right to speak openly on matters of the Christian faith.

14 15 I am hoping to come to you before long, but I write this in case I am delayed, to let you know how men ought to conduct themselves in God's household, that is, the church of the living God, the pillar and bulwark of
16 the truth. And great beyond all question is the mystery of our religion:

> 'He who was manifested in the body,
>    vindicated in the spirit,
>       seen by angels;
> who was proclaimed among the nations,
>    believed in throughout the world,
>       glorified in high heaven.'

4 THE SPIRIT SAYS expressly that in after times some will desert from the faith and give their minds to subversive doctrines inspired by devils,
2 through the specious falsehoods of men whose own conscience is branded
3 with the devil's sign. They forbid marriage and inculcate abstinence from certain foods, though God created them to be enjoyed with thanksgiving
4 by believers who have inward knowledge of the truth. For everything that God created is good, and nothing is to be rejected when it is taken with
5 thanksgiving, since it is hallowed by God's own word and by prayer.
6 By offering such advice as this to the brotherhood you will prove a good servant of Christ Jesus, bred in the precepts of our faith and of the sound
7 instruction which you have followed. Have nothing to do with those god-less myths, fit only for old women. Keep yourself in training for the practice
8 of religion. The training of the body does bring limited benefit, but the benefits of religion are without limit, since it holds promise not only for
9 this life but for the life to come. Here are words you may trust, words that
10 merit full acceptance: 'With this before us we labour and struggle, *c* because *d* we have set our hope on the living God, who is the Saviour of all men'—the Saviour, above all, of believers.

11 12 Pass on these orders and these teachings. Let no one slight you because you are young, but make yourself an example to believers in speech and
13 behaviour, in love, fidelity, and purity. Until I arrive devote your attention to the public reading of the scriptures, to exhortation, and to teaching.

*a Or . . .* serve. Deaconesses . . .   *b Or* married to one wife, *or* married only once.
*c Some witnesses read* suffer reproach.   *d Or* since 'It holds promise . . . to come.'
These are words . . . acceptance. For this is the aim of all our labour and struggle, since . . .

Do not neglect the spiritual endowment you possess, which was given you, 14
under the guidance of prophecy, through the laying on of the hands of the
elders as a body. *a*

Make these matters your business and your absorbing interest, so that 15
your progress may be plain to all. Persevere in them, keeping close watch 16
on yourself and your teaching; by doing so you will further the salvation
of yourself and your hearers.

Never be harsh with an elder; appeal to him as if he were your father. **5**
Treat the younger men as brothers, the older women as mothers, and the 2
younger as your sisters, in all purity.

The status of widow is to be granted only to widows who are such in the 3
full sense. But if a widow has children or grandchildren, then they should 4
learn as their first duty to show loyalty to the family and to repay what they
owe to their parents and grandparents; for this God approves. A widow, 5
however, in the full sense, one who is alone in the world, has all her hope
set on God, and regularly attends the meetings for prayer and worship
night and day. But a widow given over to self-indulgence is as good as 6
dead. Add these orders to the rest, so that the widows may be above 7
reproach. But if anyone does not make provision for his relations, and 8
especially for members of his own household, he has denied the faith and
is worse than an unbeliever.

A widow should not be put on the roll under sixty years of age. She must 9
have been faithful in marriage to one man, and must produce evidence of 10
good deeds performed, showing whether she has had the care of children,
or given hospitality, or washed the feet of God's people, or supported those
in distress—in short, whether she has taken every opportunity of doing
good.

Younger widows may not be placed on the roll. For when their passions 11
draw them away from Christ, they hanker after marriage and stand con- 12
demned for breaking their troth with him. Moreover, in going round from 13
house to house they learn to be idle, and worse than idle, gossips and busy-
bodies, speaking of things better left unspoken. It is my wish, therefore, 14
that young widows shall marry again, have children, and preside over a
home; then they will give no opponent occasion for slander. For there have 15
in fact been some who have taken the wrong turning and gone to the devil.

If a Christian man or woman has widows in the family, he must sup- 16
port them himself; *b* the congregation must be relieved of the burden, so
that it may be free to support those who are widows in the full sense of
the term.

Elders who do well as leaders should be reckoned worthy of a double 17
stipend, in particular those who labour at preaching and teaching. For 18
Scripture says, 'You shall not muzzle a threshing ox'; and besides, 'the
worker earns his pay'.

Do not entertain a charge against an elder unless it is supported by two 19
or three witnesses. Those who commit sins you must expose publicly, to 20
put fear into the others. Before God and Christ Jesus and the angels who 21

*a Or* through your ordination as an elder.      *b Some witnesses read* If a Christian
woman has widows in her family, she must support them herself.

22 are his chosen, I solemnly charge you, maintain these rules, and never pre-judge the issue, but act with strict impartiality. Do not be over-hasty in laying on hands in ordination,[a] or you may find yourself responsible for other people's misdeeds; keep your own hands clean.

23 Stop drinking nothing but water; take a little wine for your digestion, for your frequent ailments.

24 While there are people whose offences are so obvious that they run before them into court, there are others whose offences have not yet over-

25 taken them. Similarly, good deeds are obvious, or even if they are not, they cannot be concealed for ever.

6 All who wear the yoke of slavery must count their own masters worthy of all respect, so that the name of God and the Christian teaching are not

2 brought into disrepute. If the masters are believers, the slaves must not respect them any less for being their Christian brothers. Quite the contrary; they must be all the better servants because those who receive the benefit of their service are one with them in faith and love.

3 THIS IS WHAT you are to teach and preach. If anyone is teaching otherwise, and will not give his mind to wholesome precepts—I mean those of

4 our Lord Jesus Christ—and to good religious teaching, I call him a pompous ignoramus. He is morbidly keen on mere verbal questions and quibbles, which give rise to jealousy, quarrelling, slander, base suspicions,

5 and endless wrangles: all typical of men who have let their reasoning powers become atrophied and have lost grip of the truth. They think

6 religion should yield dividends; and of course religion does yield high

7 dividends, but only to the man whose resources are within him. We brought nothing into the world; for that matter we cannot take anything

8 with us when we leave, but if we have food and covering we may rest

9 content. Those who want to be rich fall into temptations and snares and many foolish harmful desires which plunge men into ruin and perdition.

10 The love of money is the root of all evil things, and there are some who in reaching for it have wandered from the faith and spiked themselves on many thorny griefs.

11 But you, man of God, must shun all this, and pursue justice, piety,

12 fidelity, love, fortitude, and gentleness. Run the great race of faith and take hold of eternal life. For to this you were called; and you confessed your

13 faith nobly before many witnesses. Now in the presence of God, who gives life to all things, and of Jesus Christ, who himself made the same noble confession and gave his testimony to it before Pontius Pilate, I charge you

14 to obey your orders irreproachably and without fault until our Lord Jesus

15 Christ appears. That appearance God will bring to pass in his own good time—God who in eternal felicity alone holds sway. He is King of kings and

16 Lord of lords; he alone possesses immortality, dwelling in unapproachable light. No man has ever seen or ever can see him. To him be honour and might for ever! Amen.

17 Instruct those who are rich in this world's goods not to be proud, and not to fix their hopes on so uncertain a thing as money, but upon God, who

---

[a] *Or* in restoring an offender by the laying on of hands.

endows us richly with all things to enjoy. Tell them to do good and to grow 18
rich in noble actions, to be ready to give away and to share, and so acquire 19
a treasure which will form a good foundation for the future. Thus they will
grasp the life which is life indeed.

Timothy, keep safe that which has been entrusted to you. Turn a deaf 20
ear to empty and worldly chatter, and the contradictions of so-called
'knowledge', for many who lay claim to it have shot far wide of the faith. 21
Grace be with you all!

# THE SECOND LETTER OF PAUL

## TO

# TIMOTHY

### *Character of a Christian minister*

FROM PAUL, APOSTLE of Jesus Christ by the will of God, 1
whose promise of life is fulfilled in Christ Jesus, to Timothy his 2
dear son.

Grace, mercy, and peace to you from God the Father and our Lord
Jesus Christ.

I thank God—whom I, like my forefathers, worship with a pure inten- 3
tion—when I mention you in my prayers; this I do constantly night and
day. And when I remember the tears you shed, I long to see you again to 4
make my happiness complete. I am reminded of the sincerity of your faith, 5
a faith which was alive in Lois your grandmother and Eunice your mother
before you, and which, I am confident, lives in you also.

That is why I now remind you to stir into flame the gift of God which is 6
within you through the laying on of my hands. For the spirit that God gave 7
us is no craven spirit, but one to inspire strength, love, and self-discipline.
So never be ashamed of your testimony to our Lord, nor of me his prisoner, 8
but take your share of suffering for the sake of the Gospel, in the strength
that comes from God. It is he who brought us salvation and called us to a 9
dedicated life, not for any merit of ours but of his own purpose and his own
grace, which was granted to us in Christ Jesus from all eternity, but has 10
now at length been brought fully into view by the appearance on earth of
our Saviour Jesus Christ. For he has broken the power of death and
brought life and immortality to light through the Gospel.

Of this Gospel I, by his appointment, am herald, apostle, and teacher. 11
That is the reason for my present plight; but I am not ashamed of it, 12
because I know who it is in whom[a] I have trusted, and am confident of his

*a Or* I know the one whom . . .

power to keep safe what he has put into my charge,[a] until the great Day.

13 Keep before you an outline of the sound teaching which[b] you heard from
14 me, living by the faith and love which are ours in Christ Jesus. Guard the treasure put into our charge, with the help of the Holy Spirit dwelling within us.

15 As you know, everyone in the province of Asia deserted me, including
16 Phygelus and Hermogenes. But may the Lord's mercy rest on the house of Onesiphorus! He has often relieved me in my troubles. He was not
17 ashamed to visit a prisoner, but took pains to search me out when he came
18 to Rome, and found me. I pray that the Lord may grant him to find mercy from the Lord on the great Day. The many services he rendered at Ephesus you know better than I could tell you.

2 Now therefore, my son, take strength from the grace of God which is ours
2 in Christ Jesus. You heard my teaching in the presence of many witnesses; put that teaching into the charge of men you can trust, such men as will be competent to teach others.

3 4 Take your share of hardship, like a good soldier of Christ Jesus. A soldier on active service will not let himself be involved in civilian affairs;
5 he must be wholly at his commanding officer's disposal. Again, no athlete
6 can win a prize unless he has kept the rules. The farmer who gives his
7 labour has first claim on the crop. Reflect on what I say, for the Lord will help you to full understanding.

8 Remember Jesus Christ, risen from the dead, born of David's line. This
9 is the theme of my gospel, in whose service I am exposed to hardship, even to the point of being shut up like a common criminal; but the word of God
10 is not shut up. And I endure it all for the sake of God's chosen ones, with this end in view, that they too may attain the glorious and eternal salvation which is in Christ Jesus.

11 Here are words you may trust:

'If we died with him, we shall live with him;
12 if we endure, we shall reign with him.
If we deny him, he will deny us.
13 If we are faithless, he keeps faith,
for he cannot deny himself.'

14 GO ON REMINDING people of this, and charge them solemnly before God to stop disputing about mere words; it does no good, and is the ruin
15 of those who listen. Try hard to show yourself worthy of God's approval, as a labourer who need not be ashamed; be straightforward in your pro-
16 clamation of the truth. Avoid empty and worldly chatter; those who
17 indulge in it will stray further and further into godless courses, and the infection of their teaching will spread like a gangrene. Such are Hymenaeus
18 and Philetus; they have shot wide of the truth in saying that our resurrection
19 has already taken place, and are upsetting people's faith. But God has laid a foundation, and it stands firm, with this inscription: 'The Lord knows his

[a] *Or* what I have put into his charge.  [b] *Or* Keep before you as a model of sound teaching that which . . .

own', and, 'Everyone who takes the Lord's name upon his lips must forsake wickedness.' Now in any great house there are not only utensils of 20 gold and silver, but also others of wood or earthenware; the former are valued, the latter held cheap. To be among those which are valued and 21 dedicated, a thing of use to the Master of the house, a man must cleanse himself from all those evil things;<sup>a</sup> then he will be fit for any honourable purpose.

Turn from the wayward impulses of youth, and pursue justice, integrity, 22 love, and peace with all who invoke the Lord in singleness of mind. Have 23 nothing to do with foolish and ignorant speculations. You know they breed quarrels, and the servant of the Lord must not be quarrelsome, but kindly 24 towards all. He should be a good teacher, tolerant, and gentle when 25 discipline is needed for the refractory. The Lord may grant them a change of heart and show them the truth, and thus they may come to their senses 26 and escape from the devil's snare, in which they have been caught and held at his will.<sup>b</sup>

You must face the fact: the final age of this world is to be a time of 3 troubles. Men will love nothing but money and self; they will be arrogant, 2 boastful, and abusive; with no respect for parents, no gratitude, no piety, no natural affection; they will be implacable in their hatreds, scandal-3 mongers, intemperate and fierce, strangers to all goodness, traitors, 4 adventurers, swollen with self-importance. They will be men who put pleasure in the place of God, men who preserve the outward form of 5 religion, but are a standing denial of its reality. Keep clear of men like these. They are the sort that insinuate themselves into private houses and there 6 get miserable women into their clutches, women burdened with a sinful past, and led on by all kinds of desires, who are always wanting to be taught, 7 but are incapable of reaching a knowledge of the truth. As Jannes and 8 Jambres defied Moses, so these men defy the truth; they have lost the power to reason, and they cannot pass the tests of faith. But their successes 9 will be short-lived, for, like those opponents of Moses, they will come to be recognized by everyone for the fools they are.

But you, my son, have followed, step by step, my teaching and my 10 manner of life, my resolution, my faith, patience, and spirit of love, and my fortitude under persecutions and sufferings—all that I went through at 11 Antioch, at Iconium, at Lystra, all the persecutions I endured; and the Lord rescued me out of them all. Yes, persecution will come to all who want 12 to live a godly life as Christians, whereas wicked men and charlatans will 13 make progress from bad to worse, deceiving and deceived. But for your 14 part, stand by the truths you have learned and are assured of. Remember from whom you learned them; remember that from early childhood you 15 have been familiar with the sacred writings which have power to make you wise and lead you to salvation through faith in Christ Jesus. Every inspired 16 scripture has its use for teaching the truth and refuting error, or for reformation of manners and discipline in right living, so that the man who 17 belongs to God may be efficient and equipped for good work of every kind.

<sup>a</sup> *Or* must separate himself from these persons.     <sup>b</sup> *Or* escape from the devil's snare, caught now by God and made subject to his will.

**4**    Before God, and before Christ Jesus who is to judge men living and
2 dead, I charge you solemnly by his coming appearance and his reign, proclaim the message, press it home on all occasions,[a] convenient or in-
convenient, use argument, reproof, and appeal, with all the patience that
3 the work of teaching requires. For the time will come when they will not
stand wholesome teaching, but will follow their own fancy and gather a
4 crowd of teachers to tickle their ears. They will stop their ears to the truth
5 and turn to mythology. But you yourself must keep calm and sane at all
times; face hardship, work to spread the Gospel, and do all the duties of
your calling.

6    As FOR ME, already my life is being poured out on the altar, and the hour
7 for my departure is upon me. I have run the great race, I have finished the
8 course, I have kept faith. And now the prize awaits me, the garland of
righteousness which the Lord, the all-just Judge, will award me on that
great Day; and it is not for me alone, but for all who have set their hearts
on his coming appearance.

9 10    Do your best to join me soon; for Demas has deserted me because his
heart was set on this world; he has gone to Thessalonica, Crescens to
11 Galatia,[b] Titus to Dalmatia; I have no one with me but Luke. Pick up
12 Mark and bring him with you, for I find him a useful assistant. Tychicus
13 I have sent to Ephesus. When you come, bring the cloak I left with Carpus
at Troas, and the books, above all my notebooks.

14    Alexander the copper-smith did me a great deal of harm. Retribution
15 will fall upon him from the Lord. You had better be on your guard against
16 him too, for he violently opposed everything I said. At the first hearing of
my case no one came into court to support me; they all left me in the lurch;
17 I pray that it may not be held against them. But the Lord stood by me and
lent me strength, so that I might be his instrument in making the full
proclamation of the Gospel for the whole pagan world to hear; and thus I
18 was rescued out of the lion's jaws. And the Lord will rescue me from every
attempt to do me harm, and keep me safe until his heavenly reign begins.[c]
Glory to him for ever and ever! Amen.

19    Greetings to Prisca and Aquila, and the household of Onesiphorus.
20    Erastus stayed behind at Corinth, and I left Trophimus ill at Miletus.
21 Do try to get here before winter.

   Greetings from Eubulus, Pudens, Linus, and Claudia, and from all the
brotherhood here.

22    The Lord be with your spirit. Grace be with you all!

---

[a] *Or* be on duty at all times.       [b] *Or* Gaul; *some witnesses read* Gallia.
[c] *Or* from all that evil can do, and bring me safely into his heavenly kingdom.

# THE LETTER OF PAUL TO

# TITUS

*Training for the Christian life*

FROM PAUL, SERVANT of God and apostle of Jesus Christ, 1
marked as such by faith and knowledge and hope—the faith of
God's chosen people, knowledge of the truth as our religion has it,
and the hope of eternal life.*a* Yes, it is eternal life that God, who cannot lie, 2
promised long ages ago, and now in his own good time he has openly 3
declared himself in the proclamation which was entrusted to me by
ordinance of God our Saviour.

To Titus, my true-born son in the faith which we share, grace and peace 4
from God our Father and Christ Jesus our Saviour.

My intention in leaving you behind in Crete was that you should set in 5
order what was left over, and in particular should institute elders in each
town. In doing so, observe the tests I prescribed: is he a man of un- 6
impeachable character, faithful to his one wife,*b* the father of children who
are believers, who are under no imputation of loose living, and are not out
of control? For as God's steward a bishop must be a man of unimpeachable 7
character. He must not be overbearing or short-tempered; he must be no
drinker, no brawler, no money-grubber, but hospitable, right-minded, 8
temperate, just, devout, and self-controlled. He must adhere to the true 9
doctrine, so that he may be well able both to move his hearers with wholesome teaching and to confute objectors.

There are all too many, especially among Jewish converts, who are out 10
of all control; they talk wildly and lead men's minds astray. Such men must 11
be curbed, because they are ruining whole families by teaching things they
should not, and all for sordid gain. It was a Cretan prophet, one of their 12
own countrymen, who said, 'Cretans were always liars, vicious brutes,
lazy gluttons'—and he told the truth! All the more reason why you should 13
pull them up sharply, so that they may come to a sane belief, instead of 14
lending their ears to Jewish myths and commandments of merely human
origin, the work of men who turn their backs upon the truth.

To the pure all things are pure; but nothing is pure to the tainted minds 15
of disbelievers, tainted alike in reason and conscience. They profess to 16
acknowledge God, but deny him by their actions. Their detestable obstinacy
disqualifies them for any good work.

For your own part, what you say must be in keeping with wholesome 2

---

*a* Or apostle of Jesus Christ, to bring God's chosen people to faith and to a knowledge of
the truth as our religion has it, with its hope for eternal life.    *b* See note on
*1 Timothy 3. 2.*

2 doctrine. Let the older men know that they should be sober, high-principled,
3 and temperate, sound in faith, in love, and in endurance. The older
women, similarly, should be reverent in their bearing, not scandal-
4 mongers or slaves to strong drink; they must set a high standard, and school
5 the younger women to be loving wives and mothers, temperate, chaste, and
kind, busy at home, respecting the authority of their own husbands. Thus
the Gospel will not be brought into disrepute.

6 7    Urge the younger men, similarly, to be temperate in all things, and set
them a good example yourself. In your teaching, you must show integrity
8 and high principle, and use wholesome speech to which none can take
exception. This will shame any opponent, when he finds not a word to say
to our discredit.

9    Tell slaves to respect their masters' authority in everything, and to
10 comply with their demands without answering back; not to pilfer, but to
show themselves strictly honest and trustworthy; for in all such ways they
will add lustre to the doctrine of God our Saviour.

11    For the grace of God has dawned upon the world with healing for all
12 mankind; and by it we are disciplined to renounce godless ways and
worldly desires, and to live a life of temperance, honesty, and godliness in
13 the present age, looking forward to the happy fulfilment of our hope when
14 the splendour of our great God and Saviour *a* Christ Jesus will appear. He
it is who sacrificed himself for us, to set us free from all wickedness and to
make us a pure people marked out for his own, eager to do good.

15    These, then, are your themes; urge them and argue them. And speak
with authority: let no one slight you.

3    Remind them to be submissive to the government and the authorities,
2 to obey them, and to be ready for any honourable form of work; *b* to
slander no one, not to pick quarrels, to show forbearance and a consistently gentle disposition towards all men.

3    For at one time we ourselves in our folly and obstinacy were all astray.
We were slaves to passions and pleasures of every kind. Our days were
passed in malice and envy; we were odious ourselves and we hated one
4 another. But when the kindness and generosity of God our Saviour dawned
5 upon the world, then, not for any good deeds of our own, but because he
was merciful, he saved us through the water of rebirth and the renewing
6 power of *c* the Holy Spirit. For he sent down the Spirit upon us plentifully
7 through Jesus Christ our Saviour, so that, justified by his grace, we might
8 in hope become heirs to eternal life. These are words you may trust.

Such are the points I should wish you to insist on. Those who have
come to believe in God should see that they engage in honourable occupa-
tions, which are not only honourable in themselves, but also useful to their
9 fellow-men. *d* But steer clear of foolish speculations, genealogies, quarrels,
and controversies over the Law; they are unprofitable and pointless.

10    A heretic should be warned once, and once again; after that, have done

---

*a* Or of the great God and our Saviour . . .          *b* Or ready always to do good.
*c* Or the water of rebirth and of renewal by . . .          *d* Or should make it their
business to practise virtue. These precepts are good in themselves and useful to
society.

with him, recognizing that a man of that sort has a distorted mind and 11
stands self-condemned in his sin.

When I send Artemas to you, or Tychicus, make haste to join me at 12
Nicopolis, for that is where I have determined to spend the winter. Do 13
your utmost to help Zenas the lawyer and Apollos on their travels, and see
that they are not short of anything. And our own people must be taught to 14
engage in honest employment to produce the necessities of life; they must
not be unproductive.

All who are with me send you greetings. My greetings to those who are 15
our friends in truth.*a* Grace be with you all!

> *a Or* our friends in the faith.

# THE LETTER OF PAUL TO
# PHILEMON

## *A runaway slave*

1 2 FROM PAUL, a prisoner of Christ Jesus, and our colleague Timothy, to Philemon our dear friend and fellow-worker, and Apphia our sister, and Archippus our comrade-in-arms, and the congregation at your house.

3 Grace to you and peace from God our Father and the Lord Jesus Christ.

4 5 I thank my God always when I mention you in my prayers, for I hear of your love and faith towards the Lord Jesus and towards all God's 6 people. My prayer is that your fellowship with us in our common faith may deepen the understanding of all the blessings that our union with Christ 7 brings us.*a* For I am delighted and encouraged by your love; through you, my brother, God's people have been much refreshed.

8 Accordingly, although in Christ I might make bold to point out your 9 duty, yet, because of that same love, I would rather appeal to you. Yes, I, 10 Paul, ambassador as I am of Christ Jesus—and now his prisoner—appeal to you about my child, whose father I have become in this prison.

11 I mean Onesimus, once so little use to you, but now useful indeed, both 12 to you and to me. I am sending him back to you, and in doing so I am send- 13 ing a part of myself. I should have liked to keep him with me, to look after 14 me as you would wish, here in prison for the Gospel. But I would rather do nothing without your consent, so that your kindness may be a matter not 15 of compulsion, but of your own free will. For perhaps this is why you lost 16 him for a time, that you might have him back for good, no longer as a slave, but as more than a slave—as a dear brother, very dear indeed to me and how much dearer to you, both as man and as Christian.

17 If, then, you count me partner in the faith, welcome him as you would 18 welcome me. And if he has done you any wrong or is in your debt, put that 19 down to my account. Here is my signature, PAUL; I undertake to repay— 20 not to mention that you owe your very self to me as well. Now brother, as a Christian, be generous with me, and relieve my anxiety; we are both in Christ!

21 I write to you confident that you will meet my wishes; I know that you 22 will in fact do better than I ask. And one thing more: have a room ready for me, for I hope that, in answer to your prayers, God will grant me to you.

23 24 Epaphras, Christ's captive like myself, sends you greetings. So do Mark, Aristarchus, Demas, and Luke, my fellow-workers.

25 The grace of the Lord Jesus Christ be with your spirit!

*a Or that bring us to Christ.*

278

# A LETTER TO
# HEBREWS

## *Christ divine and human*

WHEN IN FORMER TIMES God spoke to our forefathers, 1
he spoke in fragmentary and varied fashion through the prophets.
But in this the final age he has spoken to us in the Son whom 2
he has made heir to the whole universe, and through whom he created all
orders of existence: the Son who is the effulgence of God's splendour and 3
the stamp of God's very being, and sustains *a* the universe by his word of
power. When he had brought about the purgation of sins, he took his seat
at the right hand of Majesty on high, raised as far above the angels, as the 4
title he has inherited is superior to theirs.

For God never said to any angel, 'Thou art my Son; today I have be- 5
gotten thee', or again, 'I will be father to him, and he shall be my son.'
Again, when he presents the first-born to the world, he says, 'Let all the 6
angels of God pay him homage.' Of the angels he says, 7

> 'He who makes his angels winds,
> and his ministers a fiery flame';

but of the Son, 8

> 'Thy throne, O God, is for ever and ever,
> and the sceptre *b* of justice is the sceptre of his kingdom.
> Thou hast loved right and hated wrong; 9
> therefore, O God, thy God *c* has set thee above thy fellows,
> by anointing with the oil of exultation.'

And again, 10

> 'By thee, Lord, were earth's foundations laid of old,
> and the heavens are the work of thy hands.
> They shall pass away, but thou endurest; 11
> like clothes they shall all grow old;
> thou shalt fold them up like a cloak; 12
> yes, they shall be changed like any garment.
> But thou art the same, and thy years shall have no end.'

To which of the angels has he ever said, 'Sit at my right hand until I 13
make thy enemies thy footstool'? What are they all but ministrant 14
spirits, sent out to serve, for the sake of those who are to inherit salvation?

---

*a* *Or* bears along.     *b* *Or* God is thy throne for ever and ever, and thy sceptre . . .
*c* *Or* therefore God who is thy God . . .

2    Thus we are bound to pay all the more heed tö what we have been told,
2 for fear of drifting from our course. For if the word spoken through angels had such force that any transgression or disobedience met with due retribu-
3 tion, what escape can there be for us if we ignore a deliverance so great? For this deliverance was first announced through the lips of the Lord him-
4 self; those who heard him confirmed it to us, and God added his testimony by signs, by miracles, by manifold works of power, and by distributing the gifts of the Holy Spirit at his own will.
5    For it is not to angels that he has subjected the world to come, which is
6 our theme. But there is somewhere a solemn assurance which runs:

> 'What is man, that thou rememberest him,
> or the son of man, that thou hast regard to him?
>
> 7    Thou didst make him for a short while lower than the angels;
> thou didst crown him with glory and honour;
>
> 8    thou didst put all things in subjection beneath his feet.'

For in subjecting all things to him, he left nothing that is not subject. But
9 in fact we do not yet see all things in subjection to man. In Jesus, however, we do see one who[a] for a short while was made lower than the angels, crowned now with glory and honour because he suffered death, so that, by God's gracious will, in tasting death he should stand[b] for us all.
10    It was clearly fitting that God for whom and through whom all things exist should, in bringing many sons to glory, make the leader who delivers
11 them perfect through sufferings. For a consecrating priest and those whom he consecrates are all of one stock; and that is why the Son does not
12 shrink from calling men his brothers, when he says, 'I will proclaim thy
13 name to my brothers; in full assembly I will sing thy praise'; and again, 'I will keep my trust fixed on him'; and again, 'Here am I, and the children
14 whom God has given me.' The children of a family share the same flesh and blood; and so he too shared ours, so that through death he might break
15 the power of him who had death at his command, that is, the devil; and might liberate those who, through fear of death, had all their lifetime been
16 in servitude. It is not angels, mark you, that he takes to himself, but the
17 sons of Abraham. And therefore he had to be made like these brothers of his in every way, so that he might be merciful and faithful as their high
18 priest before God, to expiate the sins of the people. For since he himself has passed through the test of suffering, he is able to help those who are meeting their test now.

3    Therefore, brothers in the family of God, who share a heavenly calling,
2 think of the Apostle and High Priest of the religion we profess,[c] who was faithful to God who appointed him. Moses also was faithful in God's
3 household; and Jesus, of whom I speak, has been deemed worthy of greater honour than Moses, as the founder of a house enjoys more honour than
4 his household. For every house has its founder; and the founder of all is
5 God. Moses, then, was faithful as a servitor in God's whole household;

---

[a] *Or* in subjection to him. But we see Jesus, who . . .     [b] *Some witnesses read* so that apart from God he should taste death . . .     [c] *Or* of him whom we confess as God's Envoy and High Priest.

his task was to bear witness to the words that God would speak; but Christ 6 is faithful as a son, set over his household. And we are that household of his, if only we are fearless and keep our hope high.

'TODAY', THEREFORE, as the Holy Spirit says—  7

'Today if you hear his voice,
do not grow stubborn as in those days of rebellion,  8
at that time of testing in the desert,
where your forefathers tried me and tested me,  9
and saw*a* the things I did for forty years.
And so, I was indignant with that generation  10
and I said, Their hearts are for ever astray;
they would not discern my ways;
as I vowed in my anger, they shall never enter my rest.'  11

See to it, brothers, that no one among you has the wicked, faithless 12 heart of a deserter from the living God; but day by day, while that word 13 'Today' still sounds in your ears, encourage one another, so that no one of you is made stubborn by the wiles of sin. For we have become Christ's 14 partners*b* if only we keep our original confidence firm to the end.

When Scripture says, 'Today if you hear his voice, do not grow stubborn 15 as in those days of rebellion', who, I ask, were those who heard and rebelled? 16 All those, surely, whom Moses had led out of Egypt. And with whom was 17 God indignant for forty years? With those, surely, who had sinned, whose bodies lay where they fell in the desert. And to whom did he vow that they 18 should not enter his rest, if not to those who had refused to believe? We 19 perceive that it was unbelief which prevented their entering.

Therefore we must have before us the fear that while the promise of **4** entering his rest remains open, one or another among you should be found to have missed his chance. For indeed we have heard the good news, as 2 they did. But in them the message they heard did no good, because it met with no faith in those who heard it. It is we, we who have become believers, 3 who enter the rest referred to in the words, 'As I vowed in my anger, they shall never enter my rest.' Yet God's work has been finished ever since the world was created; for does not Scripture somewhere speak thus of the 4 seventh day: 'God rested from all his work on the seventh day'?—and 5 once again in the passage above we read, 'They shall never enter my rest.' The fact remains that someone must enter it, and since those who first 6 heard the good news failed to enter through unbelief, God fixes another 7 day. Speaking through the lips of David after many long years, he uses the words already quoted: 'Today if you hear his voice, do not grow stubborn.' If Joshua had given them rest, God would not thus have spoken of another 8 day after that. Therefore, a sabbath rest still awaits the people of God; for 9 10 anyone who enters God's rest, rests from his own work as God did from his. Let us then make every effort to enter that rest, so that no one may fall 11 by following this evil example of unbelief.

*a* Or though they saw . . .        *b* Or have been given a share in Christ.

12 For the word of God is alive and active. It cuts more keenly than any two-edged sword, piercing as far as the place where life and spirit, joints
13 and marrow, divide. It sifts the purposes and thoughts of the heart. There is nothing in creation that can hide from him; everything lies naked and exposed to the eyes of the One with whom we have to reckon.
14 Since therefore we have a great high priest who has passed through the heavens, Jesus the Son of God, let us hold fast to the religion we profess.
15 For ours is not a high priest unable to sympathize with our weaknesses, but one who, because of his likeness to us, has been tested every way,[a]
16 only without sin. Let us therefore boldly approach the throne of our gracious God, where we may receive mercy and in his grace find timely help.

## The shadow and the real

5 FOR EVERY HIGH PRIEST is taken from among men and appointed their representative before God, to offer gifts and sacrifices for sins.
2 He is able to bear patiently with the ignorant and erring, since he too is
3 beset by weakness; and because of this he is bound to make sin-offerings
4 for himself no less than for the people. And nobody arrogates the honour
5 to himself: he is called by God, as indeed Aaron was. So it is with Christ: he did not confer upon himself the glory of becoming high priest; it was granted by God, who said to him, 'Thou art my Son; today I have begotten
6 thee'; as also in another place he says, 'Thou art a priest for ever, in the
7 succession of Melchizedek.' In the days of his earthly life he offered up prayers and petitions, with loud cries and tears, to God who was able to deliver him from the grave. Because of his humble submission his prayer
8 was heard: son though he was, he learned obedience in the school of
9 suffering, and, once perfected, became the source of eternal salvation for
10 all who obey him, named by God high priest in the succession of Melchizedek.
11 About Melchizedek we have much to say, much that is difficult to
12 explain, now that you have grown so dull of hearing. For indeed, though by this time you ought to be teachers, you need someone to teach you the ABC of God's oracles over again; it has come to this, that you need milk
13 instead of solid food. Anyone who lives on milk, being an infant, does not
14 know[b] what is right. But grown men can take solid food; their perceptions are trained by long use to discriminate between good and evil.
6 Let us then stop discussing the rudiments of Christianity. We ought not to be laying over again the foundations of faith in God and of repen-
2 tance from the deadness of our former ways, by instruction[c] about cleansing rites and the laying-on-of-hands, about the resurrection of the dead
3 and eternal judgement. Instead, let us advance towards maturity; and so we shall, if God permits.
4 For when men have once been enlightened, when they have had a taste

[a] *Or* who has been tested every way, as we are.    [b] *Or* is incompetent to speak of . . .
[c] *Or, according to some witnesses,* laying the foundations over again: repentance from the deadness of our former ways and faith in God, instruction . . .

of the heavenly gift and a share in the Holy Spirit, when they have experi- 5
enced the goodness of God's word and the spiritual energies of the age to
come, and after all this have fallen away, it is impossible to bring them 6
again to repentance; for with their own hands they are crucifying*a* the
Son of God and making mock of his death. When the earth drinks in the 7
rain that falls upon it from time to time, and yields a useful crop to those
for whom it is cultivated, it is receiving its share of blessing from God; but 8
if it bears thorns and thistles, it is worthless and God's curse hangs over it;
the end of that is burning. But although we speak as we do, we are convinced 9
that you, my friends, are in the better case, and this makes for your salvation. For God would not be so unjust as to forget all that you did for love 10
of his name, when you rendered service to his people, as you still do. But 11
we long for every one of you to show the same eager concern, until your hope
is finally realized. We want you not to become lazy, but to imitate those 12
who, through faith and patience, are inheriting the promises.

When God made his promise to Abraham, he swore by himself, because 13
he had no one greater to swear by: 'I vow that I will bless you abundantly 14
and multiply your descendants.' Thus it was that Abraham, after patient 15
waiting, attained the promise. Men swear by a greater than themselves, 16
and the oath provides a confirmation to end all dispute; and so God, desir- 17
ing to show even more clearly to the heirs of his promise how unchanging
was his purpose, guaranteed it by oath. Here, then, are two irrevocable 18
acts in which God could not possibly play us false, to give powerful
encouragement to us, who have claimed his protection by grasping*b* the
hope set before us. That hope we hold. It is like an anchor for our lives, an 19
anchor safe and sure. It enters in through the veil, where Jesus has entered 20
on our behalf as forerunner, having become a high priest for ever in the
succession of Melchizedek.

THIS MELCHIZEDEK, king of Salem, priest of God Most High, met 7
Abraham returning from the rout of the kings and blessed him; and Abra- 2
ham gave him a tithe of everything as his portion. His name, in the first place,
means 'king of righteousness'; next he is king of Salem, that is, 'king of
peace'. He has no father, no mother, no lineage; his years have no beginning, 3
his life no end. He is like the Son of God: he remains a priest for all time.

Consider now how great he must be for Abraham the patriarch to give 4
him a tithe of the finest of the spoil. The descendants of Levi who take the 5
priestly office are commanded by the Law to tithe the people, that is, their
kinsmen, although they too are descendants of Abraham. But Melchizedek, 6
though he does not trace his descent from them, has tithed Abraham himself, and given his blessing to the man who received the promises; and 7
beyond all dispute the lesser is always blessed by the greater. Again, in the 8
one instance tithes are received by men who must die; but in the other, by
one whom Scripture affirms to be alive. It might even be said that Levi, 9
who receives tithes, has himself been tithed through Abraham; for he was 10
still in his ancestor's loins when Melchizedek met him.

*a* Or crucifying again.     *b* Or to give to us, who have claimed his protection, a powerful incentive to grasp . . .

11 Now if perfection had been attainable through the Levitical priesthood (for it is on this basis that the people were given the Law), what further need would there have been to speak of another priest arising, in the suc-
12 cession of Melchizedek, instead of the succession of Aaron? For a change of
13 priesthood must mean a change of law. And the one here spoken of belongs to a different tribe, no member of which has ever had anything to do with
14 the altar. For it is very evident that our Lord is sprung from Judah, a tribe to which Moses made no reference in speaking of priests.
15 The argument becomes still clearer, if the new priest who arises is one
16 like Melchizedek, owing his priesthood not to a system of earth-bound
17 rules but to the power of a life that cannot be destroyed. For here is the testimony: 'Thou art a priest for ever, in the succession of Melchizedek.'
18 19 The earlier rules are cancelled as impotent and useless, since the Law brought nothing to perfection; and a better hope is introduced, through which we draw near to God.
20 21 How great a difference it makes that an oath was sworn! There was no oath sworn when those others were made priests; but for this priest an oath was sworn, as Scripture says of him: 'The Lord has sworn and will
22 not go back on his word, "Thou art a priest for ever."' How far superior
23 must the covenant also be of which Jesus is the guarantor! Those other priests are appointed in numerous succession, because they are prevented
24 by death from continuing in office; but the priesthood which Jesus holds
25 is perpetual, because he remains for ever. That is why he is also able to save absolutely those who approach God through him; he is always living to plead on their behalf.
26 Such a high priest does indeed fit our condition—devout, guileless, un-
27 defiled, separated from sinners, raised high above the heavens. He has no need to offer sacrifices daily, as the high priests do, first for his own sins and then for those of the people; for this he did once and for all when he
28 offered up himself. The high priests made by the Law are men in all their frailty; but the priest appointed by the words of the oath which supersedes the Law is the Son, made perfect now for ever.

8 NOW THIS IS my main point: just such a high priest we have, and he has
2 taken his seat at the right hand of the throne of Majesty in the heavens, a ministrant in the real sanctuary, the tent pitched by the Lord and not by
3 man. Every high priest is appointed to offer gifts and sacrifices; hence, this
4 one too must have*a* something to offer. Now if he had been on earth, he would not even have been a priest, since there are already priests who offer
5 the gifts which the Law prescribes, though they minister in a sanctuary which is only a copy and shadow of the heavenly. This is implied when Moses, about to erect the tent, is instructed by God: 'See to it that you make everything according to the pattern shown you on the mountain.'
6 But in fact the ministry which has fallen to Jesus is as far superior to theirs as are the covenant he mediates and the promises upon which it is legally secured.
7 Had that first covenant been faultless, there would have been no need

*a Or* must have had.

284

to look for a second in its place. But God, finding fault with them, says, 8
'The days are coming, says the Lord, when I will conclude a new covenant
with the house of Israel and the house of Judah. It will not be like the 9
covenant I made with their forefathers when I took them by the hand to
lead them out of Egypt; because they did not abide by the terms of that
covenant, and I abandoned them, says the Lord. For the covenant I will 10
make with the house of Israel after those days, says the Lord, is this: I
will set my laws in their understanding and write them on their hearts;
and I will be their God, and they shall be my people. And they shall not 11
teach one another, saying to brother and fellow-citizen,*a* "Know the
Lord!" For all of them, high and low, shall know me; I will be merciful 12
to their wicked deeds, and I will remember their sins no more.' By speak- 13
ing of a new covenant, he has pronounced the first one old; and anything
that is growing old and ageing will shortly disappear.

THE FIRST COVENANT indeed had its ordinances of divine service and **9**
its sanctuary, but a material sanctuary. For a tent was prepared—the first 2
tent—in which was the lamp-stand, and the table with the bread of the
Presence; this is called the Holy Place. Beyond the second curtain was the 3
tent called the Most Holy Place. Here was a golden altar of incense, and 4
the ark of the covenant plated all over with gold, in which were a golden
jar containing the manna, and Aaron's staff which once budded, and the
tablets of the covenant; and above it the cherubim of God's glory, over- 5
shadowing the place of expiation. On these we cannot now enlarge.

Under this arrangement, the priests are always entering the first tent 6
in the discharge of their duties; but the second is entered only once a year, 7
and by the high priest alone, and even then he must take with him the
blood which he offers on his own behalf and for the people's sins of ignorance. By this the Holy Spirit signifies that so long as the earlier tent still 8
stands, the way into the sanctuary remains unrevealed. All this is symbolic, 9
pointing to the present time. The offerings and sacrifices there prescribed
cannot give the worshipper inward perfection. It is only a matter of food 10
and drink and various rites of cleansing—outward ordinances in force until
the time of reformation.

But now Christ has come, high priest of good things already in being.*b* 11
The tent of his priesthood is a greater and more perfect one, not made by
men's hands, that is, not belonging to this created world; the blood of his 12
sacrifice is his own blood, not the blood of goats and calves; and thus he
has entered the sanctuary once and for all and secured an eternal deliverance. For if the blood of goats and bulls and the sprinkled ashes of a heifer 13
have power to hallow those who have been defiled and restore their external
purity, how much greater is the power of the blood of Christ; he offered 14
himself without blemish to God, a spiritual and eternal sacrifice; and his
blood will cleanse our conscience from the deadness of our former ways
and fit us for the service of the living God.

And therefore he is the mediator of a new covenant, or testament, under 15

---

*a Some witnesses read* brother and neighbour.        *b Some witnesses read* good things
which were (*or* are) to be.

which, now that there has been a death to bring deliverance from sins committed under the former covenant, those whom God has called may receive

16 the promise of the eternal inheritance. For where there is a testament it is

17 necessary for the death of the testator to be established. A testament is operative only after a death: it cannot possibly have force while the testator

18 is alive. Thus we find that the former covenant itself was not inaugurated

19 without blood. For when, as the Law directed, Moses had recited all the commandments to the people, he took the blood of the calves, with water, scarlet wool, and marjoram, and sprinkled the law-book itself and all the

20 people, saying, 'This is the blood of the covenant which God has enjoined

21 upon you.' In the same way he also sprinkled the tent and all the vessels of

22 divine service with blood. Indeed, according to the Law, it might almost be said, everything is cleansed by blood and without the shedding of blood there is no forgiveness.

23 If, then, these sacrifices cleanse the copies of heavenly things, those

24 heavenly things themselves require better sacrifices to cleanse them. For Christ has entered, not that sanctuary made by men's hands which is only a symbol of the reality, but heaven itself, to appear now before God on our

25 behalf. Nor is he there to offer himself again and again, as the high priest

26 enters the sanctuary year by year with blood not his own. If that were so, he would have had to suffer many times since the world was made. But as it is, he has appeared once and for all at the climax of history to abolish sin

27 by the sacrifice of himself. And as it is the lot of men to die once, and after

28 death comes judgement, so Christ was offered once to bear the burden of men's sins,[a] and will appear a second time, sin done away, to bring salvation to those who are watching for him.

10 FOR THE LAW contains but a shadow, and no true image,[b] of the good things which were to come; it provides for the same sacrifices year after year, and with these it can never bring the worshippers to perfection for all

2 time.[c] If it could, these sacrifices would surely have ceased to be offered, because the worshippers, cleansed once for all, would no longer have any

3 sense of sin. But instead, in these sacrifices year after year sins are brought

4 to mind, because sins can never be removed by the blood of bulls and goats.

5 That is why, at his coming into the world, he says:

'Sacrifice and offering thou didst not desire,
but thou hast prepared a body for me.

6 Whole-offerings and sin-offerings thou didst not delight in.

7 Then I said, "Here am I: as it is written of me in the scroll,
I have come, O God, to do thy will."'

8 First he says, 'Sacrifices and offerings, whole-offerings and sin-offerings, thou didst not desire nor delight in'—although the Law prescribes them—

9 and then he says, 'I have come to do thy will.' He thus annuls the former

10 to establish the latter. And it is by the will of God that we have been

---

a *Or* to remove men's sins.     b *One witness reads* a shadow and likeness . . .
c *Or* bring to perfection the worshippers who come continually.

consecrated, through the offering of the body of Jesus Christ once and for all.

Every priest stands performing his service daily and offering time after 11 time the same sacrifices, which can never remove sins. But Christ offered 12 for all time one sacrifice for sins, and took his seat at the right hand of God, where he waits henceforth until his enemies are made his footstool. For 13 14 by one offering he has perfected for all time those who are thus consecrated. Here we have also the testimony of the Holy Spirit: he first says, 'This is 15 16 the covenant which I will make with them after those days, says the Lord: I will set my laws in their hearts and write them on their understanding'; then he adds, 'and their sins and wicked deeds I will remember no more 17 at all.' And where these have been forgiven, there are offerings for sin no 18 longer.

SO NOW, MY FRIENDS, the blood of Jesus makes us free to enter boldly 19 into the sanctuary by the new, living way which he has opened for us 20 through the curtain, the way of his flesh.*a* We have, moreover, a great 21 priest set over the household of God; so let us make our approach in 22 sincerity of heart and full assurance of faith, our guilty hearts sprinkled clean, our bodies washed with pure water. Let us be firm and unswerving 23 in the confession of our hope, for the Giver of the promise may be trusted. We ought to see how each of us may best arouse others to love and active 24 goodness, not staying away from our meetings, as some do, but rather 25 encouraging one another, all the more because you see the Day drawing near.

For if we wilfully persist in sin after receiving the knowledge of the 26 truth, no sacrifice for sins remains: only a terrifying expectation of judge- 27 ment and a fierce fire which will consume God's enemies. If a man dis- 28 regards the Law of Moses, he is put to death without pity on the evidence of two or three witnesses. Think how much more severe a penalty that man 29 will deserve who has trampled under foot the Son of God, profaned the blood of the covenant by which he was consecrated, and affronted God's gracious Spirit! For we know who it is that has said, 'Justice is mine: I will 30 repay'; and again, 'The Lord will judge his people.' It is a terrible thing to 31 fall into the hands of the living God.

Remember the days gone by, when, newly enlightened, you met the 32 challenge of great sufferings and held firm. Some of you were abused and 33 tormented to make a public show, while others stood loyally by those who were so treated. For indeed you shared the sufferings of the prisoners, and 34 you cheerfully accepted the seizure of your possessions, knowing that you possessed something better and more lasting. Do not then throw away 35 your confidence, for it carries a great reward. You need endurance, if you 36 are to do God's will and win what he has promised. For 'soon, very soon' 37 (in the words of Scripture), 'he who is to come will come; he will not delay; and by faith my righteous servant shall find life; but if a man shrinks back, 38 I take no pleasure in him.' But we are not among those who shrink back 39 and are lost; we have the faith to make life our own.

*a Or* through the curtain of his flesh.

## A call to faith

**11** AND WHAT IS FAITH? Faith gives substance*a* to our hopes, and makes us certain of realities we do not see.

2 It is for their faith that the men of old stand on record.

3 By faith we perceive that the universe was fashioned by the word of God, so that the visible came forth from the invisible.

4 By faith Abel offered a sacrifice greater than Cain's, and through faith his goodness was attested, for his offerings had God's approval; and through faith he continued to speak after his death.

5 By faith Enoch was carried away to another life without passing through death; he was not to be found, because God had taken him. For it is the testimony of Scripture that before he was taken he had pleased God, 6 and without faith it is impossible to please him; for anyone who comes to God must believe that he exists and that he rewards those who search for him.

7 By faith Noah, divinely warned about the unseen future, took good heed and built an ark to save his household. Through his faith he put the whole world in the wrong, and made good his own claim to the righteousness which comes of faith.

8 By faith Abraham obeyed the call to go out to a land destined for him-
9 self and his heirs, and left home without knowing where he was to go. By faith he settled as an alien in the land promised him, living in tents, as did 10 Isaac and Jacob, who were heirs to the same promise. For he was looking forward to the city with firm foundations, whose architect and builder is God.

11 By faith even Sarah herself received strength to conceive, though she was past the age, because she judged that he who had promised would keep 12 faith; and therefore from one man, and one as good as dead, there sprang descendants numerous as the stars or as the countless grains of sand on the sea-shore.

13 All these persons died in faith. They were not yet in possession of the things promised, but had seen them far ahead and hailed them, and con-fessed themselves no more than strangers or passing travellers on earth.
14 Those who use such language show plainly that they are looking for a
15 country of their own. If their hearts had been in the country they had left,
16 they could have found opportunity to return. Instead, we find them long-ing for a better country—I mean, the heavenly one. That is why God is not ashamed to be called their God; for he has a city ready for them.

17 By faith Abraham, when the test came, offered up Isaac: he had received
18 the promises, and yet he was on the point of offering his only son, of whom he had been told, 'Through the line of Isaac your descendants shall be
19 traced.'*b* For he reckoned that God had power even to raise from the dead —and from the dead, he did, in a sense, receive him back.

20 21 By faith Isaac blessed Jacob and Esau and spoke of things to come. By faith Jacob, as he was dying, blessed each of Joseph's sons, and worshipped

---

*a* Or *assurance.*     *b* Or *God's call shall be for your descendants in the line of Isaac.*

God, leaning on the top of his staff. By faith Joseph, at the end of his life, 22
spoke of the departure of Israel from Egypt, and instructed them what to
do with his bones.

By faith, when Moses was born, his parents hid him for three months, 23
because they saw what a fine child he was; they were not afraid of the king's
edict. By faith Moses, when he grew up, refused to be called the son of 24
Pharaoh's daughter, preferring to suffer hardship with the people of God 25
rather than enjoy the transient pleasures of sin. He considered the stigma 26
that rests on God's Anointed greater wealth than the treasures of Egypt,
for his eyes were fixed upon the coming day of recompense. By faith he left 27
Egypt, and not because he feared the king's anger; for he was resolute, as
one who saw the invisible God.

By faith he celebrated the Passover and sprinkled the blood, so that the 28
destroying angel might not touch the first-born of Israel. By faith they 29
crossed the Red Sea as though it were dry land, whereas the Egyptians,
when they attempted the crossing, were drowned.

By faith the walls of Jericho fell down after they had been encircled on 30
seven successive days. By faith the prostitute Rahab escaped the doom of 31
the unbelievers, because she had given the spies a kindly welcome.

Need I say more? Time is too short for me to tell the stories of Gideon, 32
Barak, Samson, and Jephthah, of David and Samuel and the prophets.
Through faith they overthrew kingdoms, established justice, saw God's 33
promises fulfilled. They muzzled ravening lions, quenched the fury of 34
fire, escaped death by the sword. Their weakness was turned to strength,
they grew powerful in war, they put foreign armies to rout. Women 35
received back their dead raised to life. Others were tortured to death, dis-
daining release, to win a better resurrection. Others, again, had to face jeers 36
and flogging, even fetters and prison bars. They were stoned,*a* they were 37
sawn in two, they were put to the sword, they went about dressed in skins
of sheep or goats, in poverty, distress, and misery. They were too good for 38
a world like this. They were refugees in deserts and on the hills, hiding in
caves and holes in the ground. These also, one and all, are commemorated 39
for their faith; and yet they did not enter upon the promised inheritance,
because, with us in mind, God had made a better plan, that only in com- 40
pany with us should they reach their perfection.

AND WHAT OF OURSELVES? With all these witnesses to faith around 12
us like a cloud, we must throw off every encumbrance, every sin to which
we cling,*b* and run with resolution the race for which we are entered, our 2
eyes fixed on Jesus, on whom faith depends from start to finish: Jesus who,
for the sake of the joy that lay ahead of him,*c* endured the cross, making
light of its disgrace, and has taken his seat at the right hand of the throne
of God.

Think of him who submitted to such opposition from sinners: that will 3
help you not to lose heart and grow faint. In your struggle against sin, you 4

---

*a Some witnesses insert* they were put to the question.        *b Or* every clinging sin;
*one witness reads* the sin which all too readily distracts us.        *c Or* who, in place of
the joy that was open to him, . . .

5 have not yet resisted to the point of shedding your blood. You have forgotten the text of Scripture which addresses you as sons and appeals to you in these words:

> 'My son, do not think lightly of the Lord's discipline,
> nor lose heart when he corrects you;
6 > for the Lord disciplines those whom he loves;
> he lays the rod on every son whom he acknowledges.'

7 You must endure it as discipline: God is treating you as sons. Can anyone
8 be a son, who is not disciplined by his father? If you escape the discipline
9 in which all sons share, you must be bastards and no true sons. Again, we paid due respect to the earthly fathers who disciplined us; should we not
10 submit even more readily to our spiritual Father, and so attain life? They disciplined us for this short life according to their lights; but he does so for
11 our true welfare, so that we may share his holiness. Discipline, no doubt, is never pleasant; at the time it seems painful, but in the end it yields for those who have been trained by it the peaceful harvest of an honest life.
12 13 Come, then, stiffen your drooping arms and shaking knees, and keep your steps from wavering. Then the disabled limb will not be put out of joint, but regain its former powers.

14 Aim at peace with all men, and a holy life, for without that no one will
15 see the Lord. Look to it that there is no one among you who forfeits the grace
16 of God, no bitter, noxious weed growing up to poison the whole, no immoral person, no one worldly-minded like Esau. He sold his birthright
17 for a single meal, and you know that although he wanted afterwards to claim the blessing, he was rejected; though he begged for it to the point of tears, he found no way open for second thoughts.

18 REMEMBER WHERE YOU STAND: not before the palpable, blazing fire of
19 Sinai, with the darkness, gloom, and whirlwind, the trumpet-blast and the
20 oracular voice, which they heard, and begged to hear no more; for they could not bear the command, 'If even an animal touches the mountain, it must be
21 stoned.' So appalling was the sight, that Moses said, 'I shudder with fear.'
22 No, you stand before Mount Zion and the city of the living God,
23 heavenly Jerusalem, before myriads of angels, the full concourse and assembly of the first-born citizens of heaven, and God the judge of all,
24 and the spirits of good men made perfect, and Jesus the mediator of a new covenant, whose sprinkled blood has better things to tell than the blood
25 of Abel. See that you do not refuse to hear the voice that speaks. Those who refused to hear the oracle speaking on earth found no escape; still less shall
26 we escape if we refuse to hear the One who speaks from heaven. Then indeed his voice shook the earth, but now he has promised, 'Yet once again
27 I will shake not earth alone, but the heavens also.' The words 'once again'—and only once—imply that the shaking of these created things means their
28 removal, and then what is not shaken will remain. The kingdom we are given is unshakable; let us therefore give thanks to God, and so worship
29 him as he would be worshipped, with reverence and awe; for our God is a devouring fire.

**13** NEVER CEASE TO LOVE your fellow-Christians.

Remember to show hospitality. There are some who, by so doing, have 2 entertained angels without knowing it.

Remember those in prison as if you were there with them; and those who 3 are being maltreated, for you like them are still in the world.

Marriage is honourable; let us all keep it so, and the marriage-bond 4 inviolate; for God's judgement will fall on fornicators and adulterers.

Do not live for money; be content with what you have; for God him- 5 self has said, 'I will never leave you or desert you'; and so we can take 6 courage and say, 'The Lord is my helper, I will not fear; what can man do to me?'

Remember your leaders, those who first spoke God's message to you; 7 and reflecting upon the outcome of their life and work, follow the example of their faith.

Jesus Christ is the same yesterday, today, and for ever. So do not be 8 9 swept off your course by all sorts of outlandish teachings; it is good that our souls should gain their strength from the grace of God, and not from scruples about what we eat, which have never done any good to those who were governed by them.

Our altar is one from which *a* the priests of the sacred tent have no right 10 to eat. As you know, those animals whose blood is brought as a sin-offering 11 by the high priest into the sanctuary, have their bodies burnt outside the camp, and therefore Jesus also suffered outside the gate, to consecrate the 12 people by his own blood. Let us then go to him outside the camp, bearing 13 the stigma that he bore. For here we have no permanent home, but we are 14 seekers after the city which is to come. Through Jesus, then, let us con- 15 tinually offer up to God the sacrifice of praise, that is, the tribute of lips which acknowledge his name, and never forget to show kindness and to 16 share what you have with others; for such are the sacrifices which God approves.

Obey your leaders and defer to them; for they are tireless in their con- 17 cern for you, as men who must render an account. Let it be a happy task for them, and not pain and grief, for that would bring you no advantage.

Pray for us; for we are convinced that our conscience is clear; our one 18 desire is always to do what is right. All the more earnestly I ask for your 19 prayers, that I may be restored to you the sooner.

May the God of peace, who brought up from the dead our Lord Jesus, 20 the great Shepherd of the sheep, by the blood of the eternal covenant, make 21 you perfect in all goodness so that you may do his will; and may he make of us what he would have us be through Jesus Christ, to whom be glory for ever and ever! Amen.

I beg you, brothers, bear with this exhortation; for it is after all a short 22 letter. I have news for you: our friend Timothy has been released; and if 23 he comes in time he will be with me when I see you.

Greet all your leaders and all God's people. Greetings to you from our 24 Italian friends.

God's grace be with you all! 25

*a Or* one like that from which . . .

# A LETTER OF

# JAMES

## *Practical religion*

1 FROM JAMES, a servant of God and the Lord Jesus Christ.
Greetings to the Twelve Tribes dispersed throughout the world.
2 My brothers, whenever you have to face trials of many kinds,
3 count yourselves supremely happy, in the knowledge that such testing of
4 your faith breeds fortitude, and if you give fortitude full play you will go
5 on to complete a balanced character that will fall short in nothing. If any
of you falls short in wisdom, he should ask God for it and it will be given
him, for God is a generous giver who neither refuses nor reproaches any-
6 one. But he must ask in faith, without a doubt in his mind; for the doubter
7 is like a heaving sea ruffled by the wind. A man of that kind must not expect
8 the Lord to give him anything; he is double-minded, and never can keep *a*
a steady course.

9 The brother in humble circumstances may well be proud that God lifts
10 him up; and the wealthy brother must find his pride in being brought low.
11 For the rich man will disappear like the flower of the field; once the sun is
up with its scorching heat the flower withers, its petals fall, and what was
lovely to look at is lost for ever. So shall the rich man wither away as he
goes about his business.

12 Happy the man who remains steadfast under trial, for having passed that
test he will receive for his prize the gift of life promised to those who love
13 God. No one under trial or temptation should say, 'I am being tempted by
God'; for God is untouched by evil, *b* and does not himself tempt anyone.
14 Temptation arises when a man is enticed and lured away by his own lust;
15 then lust conceives, and gives birth to sin; and sin full-grown breeds
death.

16 17 Make no mistake, my friends. All good giving, every perfect gift, comes *c*
from above, from the Father of the lights of heaven. With him there is no
18 variation, no play of passing shadows.*d* Of his set purpose, by declaring the
truth, he gave us birth to be a kind of firstfruits of his creatures.
19 Of that you may be certain, my friends. But each of you must be quick
20 to listen, slow to speak, and slow to be angry. For a man's anger cannot
21 promote the justice of God. Away then with all that is sordid, and the malice
that hurries to excess, and quietly accept the message planted in your hearts,
which can bring you salvation.

*a Or* anything; a double-minded man never keeps . . .          *b Or* God cannot be
tempted by evil.          *c Or* All giving is good, and every perfect gift comes . . .
*d Some witnesses read* no variation, or shadow caused by change.

Only be sure that you act on the message and do not merely listen; for 22
that would be to mislead yourselves. A man who listens to the message but 23
never acts upon it is like one who looks in a mirror at the face nature gave
him. He glances at himself and goes away, and at once forgets what he 24
looked like. But the man who looks closely into the perfect law, the law 25
that makes us free, and who lives in its company, does not forget what he
hears, but acts upon it; and that is the man who by acting will find
happiness.

A man may think he is religious, but if he has no control over his tongue, 26
he is deceiving himself; that man's religion is futile. The kind of religion 27
which is without stain or fault in the sight of God our Father is this: to
go to the help of orphans and widows in their distress and keep oneself
untarnished by the world.

MY BROTHERS, believing as you do in our Lord Jesus Christ, who reigns 2
in glory, you must never show snobbery. For instance, two visitors may 2
enter your place of worship, one a well-dressed man with gold rings, and
the other a poor man in shabby clothes. Suppose you pay special attention 3
to the well-dressed man and say to him, 'Please take this seat', while to the
poor man you say, 'You can stand; or you may sit here*a* on the floor by my
footstool', do you not see that you are inconsistent and judge by false 4
standards?

Listen, my friends. Has not God chosen those who are poor in the eyes 5
of the world to be rich in faith and to inherit the kingdom he has promised
to those who love him? And yet you have insulted the poor man. More- 6
over, are not the rich your oppressors? Is it not they who drag you into
court and pour contempt on the honoured name by which God has 7
claimed you?

If, however, you are observing the sovereign law laid down in Scripture, 8
'Love your neighbour as yourself', that is excellent. But if you show snob- 9
bery, you are committing a sin and you stand convicted by that law as
transgressors. For if a man keeps the whole law apart from one single 10
point, he is guilty of breaking all of it. For the One who said, 'Thou shalt 11
not commit adultery', said also, 'Thou shalt not commit murder.' You may
not be an adulterer, but if you commit murder you are a law-breaker all the
same. Always speak and act as men who are to be judged under a law of 12
freedom. In that judgement there will be no mercy for the man who has 13
shown no mercy. Mercy triumphs over judgement.

MY BROTHERS, what use is it for a man to say he has faith when he does 14
nothing to show it? Can that faith save him? Suppose a brother or a sister 15
is in rags with not enough food for the day, and one of you says, 'Good luck 16
to you, keep yourselves warm, and have plenty to eat', but does nothing to
supply their bodily needs, what is the good of that? So with faith; if it does 17
not lead to action, it is in itself a lifeless thing.

But someone may object: 'Here is one who claims to have faith and 18

*a Some witnesses read* Stand where you are or sit here . . .; *others read* Stand where you
are or sit . . .

another who points to his deeds.' To which I reply: 'Prove to me that this faith you speak of is real though not accompanied by deeds, and by my
19 deeds I will prove to you my faith.' You have faith enough to believe that there is one God. Excellent! The devils have faith like that, and it makes
20 them tremble. But can you not see, you quibbler, that faith divorced from
21 deeds is barren? Was it not by his action, in offering his son Isaac upon the
22 altar, that our father Abraham was justified? Surely you can see that faith was at work in his actions, and that by these actions the integrity of his
23 faith was fully proved. Here was fulfilment of the words of Scripture: 'Abraham put his faith in God, and that faith was counted to him as
24 righteousness'; and elsewhere he is called 'God's friend'. You see then that
25 a man is justified by deeds and not by faith in itself. The same is true of the prostitute Rahab also. Was not she justified by her action in welcoming the messengers into her house and sending them away by a different route?
26 As the body is dead when there is no breath left in it, so faith divorced from deeds is lifeless as a corpse.

3 MY BROTHERS, not many of you should become teachers, for you may be certain that we who teach shall ourselves be judged with greater strict-
2 ness. All of us often go wrong; the man who never says a wrong thing is a
3 perfect character, able to bridle his whole being. If we put bits into horses'
4 mouths to make them obey our will, we can direct their whole body. Or think of ships: large they may be, yet even when driven by strong gales they can be directed by a tiny rudder on whatever course the helmsman
5 chooses. So with the tongue. It is a small member but it can make huge claims.*a*

What an immense stack of timber*b* can be set ablaze by the tiniest spark!
6 And the tongue is in effect a fire. It represents among our members the world with all its wickedness; it pollutes our whole being; it keeps the
7 wheel of our existence red-hot, and its flames are fed by hell. Beasts and birds of every kind, creatures that crawl on the ground or swim in the sea,
8 can be subdued and have been subdued by mankind; but no man can sub-
9 due the tongue. It is an intractable evil, charged with deadly venom. We use it to sing the praises of our Lord and Father, and we use it to invoke
10 curses upon our fellow-men who are made in God's likeness. Out of the same mouth come praises and curses. My brothers, this should not be so.
11 Does a fountain gush with both fresh and brackish water from the same
12 opening? Can a fig-tree, my brothers, yield olives, or a vine figs? No more does salt water yield fresh.

13 WHO AMONG YOU is wise or clever? Let his right conduct give practical
14 proof of it, with the modesty that comes of wisdom. But if you are harbour-ing bitter jealousy and selfish ambition in your hearts, consider whether
15 your claims are not false, and a defiance of the truth. This is not the
16 wisdom that comes from above; it is earth-bound, sensual, demonic. For
17 with jealousy and ambition come disorder and evil of every kind. But the wisdom from above is in the first place pure; and then peace-loving,

*a Or it is a great boaster.*      *b Or What a huge forest . . .*

considerate, and open to reason; it is straightforward and sincere, rich in mercy and in the kindly deeds that are its fruit. True justice is the harvest 18 reaped by peacemakers from seeds sown in a spirit of peace.

What causes conflicts and quarrels among you? Do they not spring from 4 the aggressiveness of your bodily desires? You want something which you 2 cannot have, and so you are bent on murder; you are envious, and cannot attain your ambition, and so you quarrel and fight. You do not get what you want, because you do not pray for it. Or, if you do, your requests are not 3 granted because you pray from wrong motives, to spend what you get on your pleasures. You false, unfaithful creatures! Have you never learned 4 that love of the world is enmity to God? Whoever chooses to be the world's friend makes himself God's enemy. Or do you suppose that Scripture has 5 no meaning when it says that the spirit which God implanted in man turns towards envious desires? And yet the grace he gives is stronger. Thus 6 Scripture says, 'God opposes the arrogant and gives grace to the humble.' Be submissive then to God. Stand up to the devil and he will turn and run. 7 Come close to God, and he will come close to you. Sinners, make your 8 hands clean; you who are double-minded, see that your motives are pure. Be sorrowful, mourn and weep. Turn your laughter into mourning and 9 your gaiety into gloom. Humble yourselves before God and he will lift 10 you high.

Brothers, you must never disparage one another. He who disparages a 11 brother or passes judgement on his brother disparages the law and judges the law. But if you judge the law, you are not keeping it but sitting in judgement upon it. There is only one lawgiver and judge, the One who is 12 able to save life and destroy it. So who are you to judge your neighbour?

A WORD WITH YOU, you who say, 'Today or tomorrow we will go off 13 to such and such a town and spend a year there trading and making money.' Yet you have no idea what tomorrow will bring. Your life, what is it? You 14 are no more than a mist, seen for a little while and then dispersing. What 15 you ought to say is: 'If it be the Lord's will, we shall live to do this or that.' But instead, you boast and brag, and all such boasting is wrong. Well then, 16 17 the man who knows the good he ought to do and does not do it is a sinner.

Next a word to you who have great possessions. Weep and wail over the 5 miserable fate descending on you. Your riches have rotted; your fine clothes 2 are moth-eaten; your silver and gold have rusted away, and their very rust 3 will be evidence against you and consume your flesh like fire. You have piled up wealth in an age that is near its close. The wages you never paid to the 4 men who mowed your fields are loud against you, and the outcry of the reapers has reached the ears of the Lord of Hosts. You have lived on earth 5 in wanton luxury, fattening yourselves like cattle—and the day for slaughter has come. You have condemned the innocent and murdered him; he offers 6 no resistance.

Be patient, my brothers, until the Lord comes. The farmer looking for 7 the precious crop his land may yield can only wait in patience, until the autumn and spring rains have fallen. You too must be patient and stout- 8 hearted, for the coming of the Lord is near. My brothers, do not blame 9

your troubles on one another, or you will fall under judgement; and there
10 stands the Judge, at the door. If you want a pattern of patience under ill-
11 treatment, take the prophets who spoke in the name of the Lord; remember: 'We count those happy who stood firm.' You have all heard how Job stood firm, and you have seen how the Lord treated him in the end. For the Lord is full of pity and compassion.

12 ABOVE ALL THINGS, my brothers, do not use oaths, whether 'by heaven' or 'by earth' or by anything else. When you say yes or no, let it be plain 'Yes' or 'No', for fear that you expose yourselves to judgement.
13   Is anyone among you in trouble? He should turn to prayer. Is anyone
14 in good heart? He should sing praises. Is one of you ill? He should send for the elders of the congregation to pray over him and anoint him with oil
15 in the name of the Lord. The prayer offered in faith will save the sick man, the Lord will raise him from his bed, and any sins he may have committed
16 will be forgiven. Therefore confess your sins to one another, and pray for one another, and then you will be healed. A good man's prayer is powerful
17 and effective. Elijah was a man with human frailties like our own; and when he prayed earnestly that there should be no rain, not a drop fell on the land
18 for three years and a half; then he prayed again, and down came the rain and the land bore crops once more.
19   My brothers, if one of your number should stray from the truth and
20 another succeed in bringing him back, be sure of this: any man who brings a sinner back from his crooked ways will be rescuing his soul from death and cancelling innumerable sins.


# THE FIRST LETTER OF
# PETER

## *The calling of a Christian*

1 FROM PETER, APOSTLE of Jesus Christ, to those of God's scattered people who lodge for a while in Pontus, Galatia, Cappa-
2 docia, Asia, and Bithynia—chosen of old in the purpose of God the Father, hallowed to his service by the Spirit, and consecrated with the sprinkled blood of Jesus Christ.
   Grace and peace to you in fullest measure.
3   Praise be to the God and Father of our Lord Jesus Christ, who in his great mercy gave us new birth into a living hope by the resurrection of
4 Jesus Christ from the dead! The inheritance to which we are born is one
5 that nothing can destroy or spoil or wither. It is kept for you in heaven, and you, because you put your faith in God, are under the protection of his

power until salvation comes—the salvation which is even now in readiness and will be revealed at the end of time.

This is cause for great joy, even though now you smart for a little while, 6 if need be, under trials of many kinds. Even gold passes through the 7 assayer's fire, and more precious than perishable gold is faith which has stood the test. These trials come so that your faith may prove itself worthy of all praise, glory, and honour when Jesus Christ is revealed.

You have not seen him, yet you love him; and trusting in him now with- 8 out seeing him, you are transported with a joy too great for words, while 9 you reap the harvest of your faith, that is, salvation for your souls. This 10 salvation was the theme which the prophets pondered and explored, those who prophesied about the grace of God awaiting you. They tried to find 11 out what was the time,*a* and what the circumstances, to which the spirit of Christ in them pointed, foretelling the sufferings in store for Christ and the splendours to follow; and it was disclosed to them that the matter they 12 treated of was not for their time but for yours. And now it has been openly announced to you through preachers who brought you the Gospel in the power of the Holy Spirit sent from heaven. These are things that angels long to see into.

You must therefore be mentally stripped for action, perfectly self- 13 controlled. Fix your hopes on the gift of grace which is to be yours when Jesus Christ is revealed. As obedient children, do not let your characters 14 be shaped any longer by the desires you cherished in your days of ignorance. The One who called you is holy; like him, be holy in all your behaviour, 15 because Scripture says, 'You shall be holy, for I am holy.' 16

If you say 'our Father' to the One who judges every man impartially on 17 the record of his deeds, you must stand in awe of him while you live out your time on earth. Well you know that it was no perishable stuff, like gold 18 or silver, that bought your freedom from the empty folly of your traditional ways. The price was paid in precious blood, as it were of a lamb 19 without mark or blemish—the blood of Christ. Predestined before the 20 foundation of the world, he was made manifest in this last period of time for your sake. Through him you have come to trust in God who raised him 21 from the dead and gave him glory, and so your faith and hope are fixed on God.

Now that by obedience to the truth you have purified your souls until 22 you feel sincere affection towards your brother Christians, love one another whole-heartedly with all your strength. You have been born anew, not of 23 mortal parentage but of immortal, through the living and enduring word of God.*b* For (as Scripture says) 24

> 'All mortals are like grass;
> all their splendour like the flower of the field;
> the grass withers, the flower falls;
> but the word of the Lord endures for evermore.' 25

And this 'word' is the word of the Gospel preached to you.

---

*a Or* who was the person . . .        *b Or* through the word of the living and enduring God.

**2** Then away with all malice and deceit, away with all pretence and
**2** jealousy and recrimination of every kind! Like the new-born infants you
are, you must crave for pure milk (spiritual milk, I mean), so that you may
**3** thrive upon it to your souls' health. Surely you have tasted that the Lord
is good.

**4** So come to him, our living Stone—the stone rejected by men but
**5** choice and precious in the sight of God. Come, and let yourselves be built,
as living stones, into a spiritual temple; become a holy priesthood,*a* to offer
**6** spiritual sacrifices acceptable to God through Jesus Christ. For it stands
written:

> 'I lay in Zion a choice corner-stone of great worth.
> The man who has faith in it will not be put to shame.'

**7** The great worth of which it speaks is for you who have faith. For those
who have no faith, the stone which the builders rejected has become
**8** not only the corner-stone,*b* but also 'a stone to trip over, a rock to
stumble against'. They fall when they disbelieve the Word. Such was their
appointed lot!

**9** But you are a chosen race, a royal priesthood, a dedicated nation, and a
people claimed by God for his own, to proclaim the triumphs of him who
**10** has called you out of darkness into his marvellous light. You are now the
people of God, who once were not his people; outside his mercy once, you
have now received his mercy.

**11** DEAR FRIENDS, I beg you, as aliens in a foreign land, to abstain from
**12** the lusts of the flesh which are at war with the soul. Let all your behaviour
be such as even pagans can recognize as good, and then, whereas they
malign you as criminals now, they will come to see for themselves that you
live good lives, and will give glory to God on the day when he comes to
hold assize.

**13** Submit yourselves to every human institution for the sake of the Lord,
**14** whether to the sovereign as supreme, or to the governor as his deputy for
the punishment of criminals and the commendation of those who do right.
**15** For it is the will of God that by your good conduct you should put ignorance and stupidity to silence.

**16** Live as free men; not however as though your freedom were there to
**17** provide a screen for wrongdoing, but as slaves in God's service. Give due
honour to everyone: love to the brotherhood, reverence to God, honour to
the sovereign.

**18** Servants, accept the authority of your masters with all due submission,
not only when they are kind and considerate, but even when they are per-
**19** verse. For it is a fine*c* thing if a man endure the pain of undeserved suffer-
**20** ing because God is in his thoughts. What credit is there in fortitude when
you have done wrong and are beaten for it? But when you have behaved
**21** well and suffer for it, your fortitude is a fine thing*d* in the sight of God. To

---

*a Or* a spiritual temple for the holy work of priesthood.        *b Or* the apex of the
building.        *c Or* creditable.        *d Or* is creditable.

that you were called, because Christ suffered<sup>a</sup> on your behalf, and thereby left you an example; it is for you to follow in his steps. He committed no sin, 22 he was convicted of no falsehood; when he was abused he did not retort 23 with abuse, when he suffered he uttered no threats, but committed his cause to the One who judges justly. In his own person he carried our sins 24 to<sup>b</sup> the gibbet, so that we might cease to live for sin and begin to live for righteousness. By his wounds you have been healed. You were straying like 25 sheep, but now you have turned towards the Shepherd and Guardian of your souls.

In the same way you women must accept the authority of your husbands, 3 so that if there are any of them who disbelieve the Gospel they may be won over, without a word being said, by observing the chaste and reverent be- 2 haviour of their wives. Your beauty should reside, not in outward adorn- 3 ment—the braiding of the hair, or jewellery, or dress—but in the inmost 4 centre of your being, with its imperishable ornament, a gentle, quiet spirit, which is of high value in the sight of God. Thus it was among God's 5 people in days of old: the women who fixed their hopes on him adorned themselves by submission to their husbands. Such was Sarah, who obeyed 6 Abraham and called him 'my master'. Her children you have now become, if you do good and show no fear.

In the same way, you husbands must conduct your married life with 7 understanding: pay honour to the woman's body, not only because it is weaker, but also because you share together in the grace of God which gives you life. Then your prayers will not be hindered.

To sum up: be one in thought and feeling, all of you; be full of brotherly 8 affection, kindly and humble-minded. Do not repay wrong with wrong, or 9 abuse with abuse; on the contrary, retaliate with blessing, for a blessing is the inheritance to which you yourselves have been called.

'Whoever loves life and would see good days          10
   must restrain his tongue from evil
   and his lips from deceit;
   must turn from wrong and do good,          11
   seek peace and pursue it.
For the Lord's eyes are turned towards the righteous,     12
   his ears are open to their prayers;
   but the Lord's face is set against wrong-doers.'

WHO IS GOING to do you wrong if you are devoted to what is good? 13 And yet if you should suffer for your virtues, you may count yourselves 14 happy. Have no fear of them:<sup>c</sup> do not be perturbed, but hold the Lord 15 Christ in reverence in your hearts.<sup>d</sup> Be always ready with your defence whenever you are called to account for the hope that is in you, but make that defence with modesty and respect. Keep your conscience clear, so that 16 when you are abused, those who malign your Christian conduct may be put to shame. It is better to suffer for well-doing, if such should be the will 17

---

<sup>a</sup> *Some witnesses read* died.      <sup>b</sup> *Or* on.      <sup>c</sup> *Or* Do not fear what they fear.
<sup>d</sup> *Or* hold Christ in reverence in your hearts, as Lord.

18 of God, than for doing wrong. For Christ also died[a] for our sins[b] once and for all. He, the just, suffered for the unjust, to bring us to God.

19 In the body he was put to death; in the spirit he was brought to life. And in the spirit he went and made his proclamation to the imprisoned spirits.

20 They had refused obedience long ago, while God waited patiently in the days of Noah and the building of the ark, and in the ark a few persons, eight

21 in all, were brought to safety through the water. This water prefigured the water of baptism through which you are now brought to safety. Baptism is not the washing away of bodily pollution, but the appeal made to God by a good conscience; and it brings salvation through the resurrection of

22 Jesus Christ, who entered heaven after receiving the submission of angelic authorities and powers, and is now at the right hand of God.

**4** Remembering that Christ endured bodily suffering, you must arm your-selves with a temper of mind like his. When a man has thus endured bodily

2 suffering he has finished with sin, and for the rest of his days on earth he

3 may live, not for the things that men desire, but for what God wills. You had time enough in the past to do all the things that men want to do in the pagan world. Then you lived in licence and debauchery, drunkenness,

4 revelry, and tippling, and the forbidden worship of idols. Now, when you no longer plunge with them into all this reckless dissipation, they cannot

5 understand it, and they vilify you accordingly; but they shall answer for it to him who stands ready to pass judgement on the living and the dead.

6 Why was the Gospel preached to those who are dead? In order that, although in the body they received the sentence common to men, they might in the spirit be alive with the life of God.

7 The end of all things is upon us, so you must lead an ordered and sober

8 life, given to prayer. Above all, keep your love for one another at full

9 strength, because love cancels innumerable sins. Be hospitable to one

10 another without complaining. Whatever gift each of you may have received, use it in service to one another, like good stewards dispensing the grace of

11 God in its varied forms. Are you a speaker? Speak as if you uttered oracles of God. Do you give service? Give it as in the strength which God supplies. In all things so act that the glory may be God's through Jesus Christ; to him belong glory and power for ever and ever. Amen.

12 MY DEAR FRIENDS, do not be bewildered by the fiery ordeal that is

13 upon you, as though it were something extraordinary. It gives you a share in Christ's sufferings, and that is cause for joy; and when his glory is

14 revealed, your joy will be triumphant. If Christ's name is flung in your teeth as an insult, count yourselves happy, because then that glorious Spirit

15 which is the Spirit of God is resting upon you. If you suffer, it must not be

16 for murder, theft, or sorcery,[c] nor for infringing the rights of others. But if anyone suffers as a Christian, he should feel it no disgrace, but confess that name to the honour of God.

17 The time has come for the judgement to begin; it is beginning with God's own household. And if it is starting with you, how will it end for those who

---

[a] *Some witnesses read* suffered.     [b] *Some witnesses read* for sins; *others read* for sins on our behalf.     [c] *Or* other crime.

refuse to obey the gospel of God? It is hard enough for the righteous to be 18
saved; what then will become of the impious and sinful? So even those who 19
suffer, if it be according to God's will, should commit their souls to him—
by doing good; their Maker will not fail them.

And now I appeal to the elders of your community, as a fellow-elder and 5
a witness of Christ's sufferings, and also a partaker in the splendour that is
to be revealed. Tend that flock of God whose shepherds you are, and do it, 2
not under compulsion, but of your own free will, as God would have it;
not for gain but out of sheer devotion; not tyrannizing over those who are 3
allotted to your care, but setting an example to the flock. And then, when 4
the Head Shepherd appears, you will receive for your own the unfading
garland of glory.

In the same way you younger men must be subordinate to your elders. 5
Indeed, all of you should wrap yourselves in the garment of humility
towards each other, because God sets his face against the arrogant but
favours the humble. Humble yourselves then under God's mighty hand, 6
and he will lift you up in due time. Cast all your cares on him, for you are 7
his charge.

Awake! be on the alert! Your enemy the devil, like a roaring lion, prowls 8
round looking for someone to devour. Stand up to him, firm in faith, and 9
remember that your brother Christians are going through the same kinds
of suffering while they are in the world. And the God of all grace, who called 10
you into his eternal glory in Christ, will himself, after your brief suffering,
restore, establish, and strengthen you on a firm foundation. He holds 11
dominion for ever and ever. Amen.

I write you this brief appeal through Silvanus, our trusty brother as I 12
hold him, adding my testimony that this is the true grace of God. In this
stand fast.

Greetings from her who dwells in Babylon, chosen by God like you, 13
and from my son Mark. Greet one another with the kiss of love.         14

Peace to you all who belong to Christ!

# THE SECOND LETTER OF
# PETER

### *The remedy for doubt*

1 FROM SIMEON PETER, servant and apostle of Jesus Christ, to those who through the justice of our God and Saviour Jesus Christ share our faith and enjoy equal privilege with ourselves.

2 Grace and peace be yours in fullest measure, through the knowledge of God and Jesus our Lord.

3 His divine power has bestowed on us everything that makes for life and true religion, enabling us to know the One who called us by his own 4 splendour and might. Through this might and splendour he has given us his promises, great beyond all price, and through them you may escape the corruption with which lust has infected the world, and come to share in the very being of God.

5 With all this in view, you should try your hardest to supplement your 6 faith with virtue, virtue with knowledge, knowledge with self-control, 7 self-control with fortitude, fortitude with piety, piety with brotherly kindness, and brotherly kindness with love.

8 These are gifts which, if you possess and foster them, will keep you from being either useless or barren in the knowledge of our Lord Jesus Christ. 9 The man who lacks them is short-sighted and blind; he has forgotten how 10 he was cleansed from his former sins. All the more then, my friends, exert yourselves to clinch God's choice and calling of you. If you behave so, you 11 will never come to grief. Thus you will be afforded full and free admission into the eternal kingdom of our Lord and Saviour Jesus Christ.

12 And so I will not hesitate to remind you of this again and again, although you know it and are well grounded in the truth that has already reached 13 you. Yet I think it right to keep refreshing your memory so long as I still 14 lodge in this body. I know that very soon I must leave it; indeed our Lord 15 Jesus Christ has told me so.[a] But I will see to it that after I am gone you will have means of remembering these things at all times.

16 It was not on tales artfully spun that we relied when we told you of the power of our Lord Jesus Christ and his coming; we saw him with our own 17 eyes in majesty, when at the hands of God the Father he was invested with honour and glory, and there came to him from the sublime Presence a voice which said: 'This is my Son, my Beloved,[b] on whom my favour rests.' 18 This voice from heaven we ourselves heard; when it came, we were with him on the sacred mountain.

[a] *Or* I must leave it, as our Lord Jesus Christ told me.     [b] *Or* This is my only Son.

All this only confirms for us the message of the prophets,[a] to which you 19
will do well to attend, because it is like a lamp shining in a murky place,
until the day breaks and the morning star rises to illuminate your minds.

BUT FIRST NOTE THIS: no one can interpret any prophecy of Scrip- 20
ture by himself. For it was not through any human whim that men pro- 21
phesied of old; men they were, but, impelled by the Holy Spirit, they
spoke the words of God.

But Israel had false prophets as well as true; and you likewise will have 2
false teachers among you. They will import disastrous heresies, disowning
the very Master who bought them, and bringing swift disaster on their own
heads. They will gain many adherents to their dissolute practices, through 2
whom the true way will be brought into disrepute. In their greed for money 3
they will trade on your credulity with sheer fabrications.

But the judgement long decreed for them has not been idle; perdition
waits for them with unsleeping eyes. God did not spare the angels who 4
sinned, but consigned them to the dark pits of hell,[b] where they are
reserved for judgement. He did not spare the world of old (except for 5
Noah, preacher of righteousness, whom he preserved with seven others),
but brought the deluge upon that world of godless men. The cities of Sodom 6
and Gomorrah God burned to ashes, and condemned them to total destruction, making them an object-lesson for godless men in future days. But he 7
rescued Lot, who was a good man, shocked by the dissolute habits of the
lawless society in which he lived; day after day every sight, every sound, 8
of their evil courses tortured that good man's heart. Thus the Lord is well 9
able to rescue the godly out of trials, and to reserve the wicked under
punishment until the day of judgement.

Above all he will punish those who follow their abominable lusts. They 10
flout authority; reckless and headstrong, they are not afraid to insult
celestial beings, whereas angels, for all their superior strength and might, 11
employ no insults in seeking judgement against them before the Lord.

These men are like brute beasts, born in the course of nature to be 12
caught and killed. They pour abuse upon things they do not understand;
like the beasts they will perish, suffering hurt for the hurt they have 13
inflicted. To carouse in broad daylight is their idea of pleasure; while they
sit with you at table they are an ugly blot on your company, because they
revel in their own deceptions.[c]

They have eyes for nothing but women, eyes never at rest from sin. 14
They lure the unstable to their ruin; past masters in mercenary greed,
God's curse is on them! They have abandoned the straight road and lost 15
their way. They have followed in the steps of Balaam son of Beor, who
consented to take pay for doing wrong, but had his offence brought home 16
to him when the dumb beast spoke with a human voice and put a stop to
the prophet's madness.

These men are springs that give no water, mists driven by a storm; the 17

*a Or* And in the message of the prophets we have something still more certain.
*b Some witnesses read* consigned them to darkness and chains in hell.      *c Some
witnesses read* in their love-feasts.

18 place reserved for them is blackest darkness. They utter big, empty words, and make of sensual lusts and debauchery a bait to catch those who have
19 barely begun to escape from their heathen environment. They promise them freedom, but are themselves slaves of corruption; for a man is the
20 slave of whatever has mastered him. They had once escaped the world's defilements through the knowledge of our Lord and Saviour Jesus Christ; yet if they have entangled themselves in these all over again, and are
21 mastered by them, their plight in the end is worse than before. How much better never to have known the right way, than, having known it, to turn
22 back and abandon the sacred commandments delivered to them! For them the proverb has proved true: 'The dog returns to its own vomit', and, 'The sow after a wash rolls in the mud again.'

3 THIS IS NOW my second letter to you, my friends. In both of them I have been recalling to you what you already know, to rouse you to honest
2 thought. Remember the predictions made by God's own prophets, and the commands given by the Lord and Saviour through your apostles.
3    Note this first: in the last days there will come men who scoff at religion
4 and live self-indulgent lives, and they will say: 'Where now is the promise of his coming? Our fathers have been laid to their rest, but still everything continues exactly as it has always been since the world began.'
5    In taking this view they lose sight of the fact*a* that there were heavens and earth long ago, created by God's word out of water and with water;
6 7 and by water that first world was destroyed, the water of the deluge. And the present heavens and earth, again by God's word, have been kept in store for burning; they are being reserved until the day of judgement when the godless will be destroyed.
8    And here is one point, my friends, which you must not lose sight of: with the Lord one day is like a thousand years and a thousand years like
9 one day. It is not that the Lord is slow in fulfilling his promise, as some suppose, but that he is very patient with you, because it is not his will for any to be lost, but for all to come to repentance.
10    But the Day of the Lord will come; it will come, unexpected as a thief. On that day the heavens will disappear with a great rushing sound, the elements will disintegrate in flames, and the earth with all that is in it will be laid bare.*b*
11    Since the whole universe is to break up in this way, think what sort of people you ought to be, what devout and dedicated lives you should live!
12 Look eagerly for the coming of the Day of God and work to hasten it on; that day will set the heavens ablaze until they fall apart, and will melt the
13 elements in flames. But we have his promise, and look forward to new heavens and a new earth, the home of justice.
14    With this to look forward to, do your utmost to be found at peace with
15 him, unblemished and above reproach in his sight. Bear in mind that our Lord's patience with us is our salvation, as Paul, our friend and brother,
16 said when he wrote to you with his inspired wisdom. And so he does in all his other letters, wherever he speaks of this subject, though they contain

*a* Or They choose to overlook the fact . . .      *b* *Some witnesses read* will be burnt up.

some obscure passages, which the ignorant and unstable misinterpret to their own ruin, as they do the other scriptures. *a*

But you, my friends, are forewarned. Take care, then, not to let these 17 unprincipled men seduce you with their errors; do not lose your own safe foothold. But grow in the grace and in the knowledge of our Lord and 18 Saviour Jesus Christ. *b* To him be glory now and for all eternity!

# THE FIRST LETTER OF
# JOHN

## Recall to fundamentals

IT WAS THERE from the beginning; we have heard it; we have 1 seen it with our own eyes; we looked upon it, and felt it with our own hands; and it is of this we tell. Our theme is the word of life. This life 2 was made visible; we have seen it and bear our testimony; we here declare to you the eternal life which dwelt with the Father and was made visible to us. What we have seen and heard we declare to you, so that you and we 3 together may share in a common life, that life which we share with the Father and his Son Jesus Christ. And we write this in order that the joy of 4 us all may be complete.

Here is the message we heard from him and pass on to you: that God is 5 light, and in him there is no darkness at all. If we claim to be sharing in his 6 life while we walk in the dark, our words and our lives are a lie; but if we 7 walk in the light as he himself is in the light, then we share together a common life, and we are being cleansed from every sin by the blood of Jesus his Son.

If we claim to be sinless, we are self-deceived and strangers to the truth. 8 If we confess our sins, he is just, and may be trusted to forgive our sins and 9 cleanse us from every kind of wrong; but if we say we have committed no 10 sin, we make him out to be a liar, and then his word has no place in us.

My children, in writing thus to you my purpose is that you should not 2 commit sin. But should anyone commit a sin, we have one to plead our cause *c* with the Father, Jesus Christ, and he is just. He is himself the 2 remedy for the defilement of our sins, not our sins only but the sins of all the world.

Here is the test by which we can make sure that we know him: do we 3 keep his commands? The man who says, 'I know him', while he disobeys 4 his commands, is a liar and a stranger to the truth; but in the man who is 5 obedient to his word, the divine love has indeed come to its perfection.

*a* Or his other writings.        *b* Or But grow up, by the grace of our Lord and Saviour Jesus Christ, and by knowing him.        *c* Literally we have an advocate . . .

6 Here is the test by which we can make sure that we are in him: whoever claims to be dwelling in him, binds himself to live as Christ himself lived.
7 Dear friends, I give you no new command. It is the old command which you always had before you; the old command is the message which you
8 heard at the beginning. And yet again it is a new command that I am giving you—new in the sense that the darkness is passing and the real light already shines. Christ has made this true, and it is true in your own experience.
9 A man may say, 'I am in the light'; but if he hates his brother, he is still
10 in the dark. Only the man who loves his brother dwells in light: there is
11 nothing to make him stumble. But one who hates his brother is in darkness; he walks in the dark and has no idea where he is going, because the darkness has made him blind.

12 I write to you, my children, because your sins have been forgiven for his sake.[a]

13 I write to you, fathers, because you know him who is and has been from the beginning. [b]

I write to you, young men, because you have mastered the evil one.

14 To you, children, I have written because you know the Father.

To you, fathers, I have written because you know him who is and has been from the beginning.[b]

To you, young men, I have written because you are strong; God's word remains in you, and you have mastered the evil one.

15 Do not set your hearts on the godless world or anything in it. Anyone
16 who loves the world is a stranger to the Father's love. Everything the world affords, all that panders to the appetites or entices the eyes, all the glamour of its life, springs not from the Father but from the godless world.
17 And that world is passing away with all its allurements, but he who does God's will stands for evermore.

18 MY CHILDREN, this is the last hour! You were told that Antichrist was to come, and now many antichrists have appeared; which proves to us
19 that this is indeed the last hour. They went out from our company, but never really belonged to us; if they had, they would have stayed with us. They went out, so that it might be clear that not all in our company truly belong to it.[c]
20 You, no less than they, are among the initiated;[d] this is the gift of the
21 Holy One, and by it you all have knowledge.[e] It is not because you are ignorant of the truth that I have written to you, but because you know it, and because lies, one and all, are alien to the truth.
22 Who is the liar? Who but he that denies that Jesus is the Christ? He is
23 Antichrist, for he denies both the Father and the Son: to deny the Son is to be without the Father; to acknowledge the Son is to have the Father too.

---

[a] *Or* forgiven, since you bear his name. [b] *Or* him whom we have known from the beginning. [c] *Or* that none of them truly belong to us. [d] *Literally* have an anointing (*Greek* chrism). [e] *Some witnesses read* you have all knowledge.

You therefore must keep in your hearts that which you heard at the begin- 24
ning; if what you heard then still dwells in you, you will yourselves dwell
in the Son and also in the Father. And this is the promise that he himself 25
gave us, the promise of eternal life.

So much for those who would mislead you. But as for you, the initiation *a* 26 27
which you received from him stays with you; you need no other teacher,
but learn all you need to know from his initiation, which is real and no
illusion. As he taught you, then, dwell in him.

Even now, my children, dwell in him, so that when he appears we may 28
be confident and unashamed before him at his coming. If you know that he 29
is righteous, you must recognize that every man who does right is his child.
How great is the love that the Father has shown to us! We were called God's 3
children, and such we are; *b* and the reason why the godless world does not
recognize us is that it has not known him. Here and now, dear friends, we 2
are God's children; what we shall be has not yet been disclosed, but we
know that when it is disclosed *c* we shall be like him, *d* because we shall see
him as he is. Everyone who has this hope before him purifies himself, as 3
Christ is pure.

To commit sin is to break God's law: sin, in fact, is lawlessness. Christ 4 5
appeared, as you know, to do away with sins, and there is no sin in him.
No man therefore who dwells in him is a sinner; the sinner has not seen 6
him and does not know him.

My children, do not be misled: it is the man who does right who is 7
righteous, as God is righteous; the man who sins is a child of the devil, 8
for the devil has been a sinner from the first; and the Son of God appeared
for the very purpose of undoing the devil's work.

A child of God does not commit sin, because the divine seed remains 9
in him; he cannot be a sinner, because he is God's child. That is the dis- 10
tinction between the children of God and the children of the devil: no one
who does not do right is God's child, nor is anyone who does not love his
brother. For the message you have heard from the beginning is this: that 11
we should love one another; unlike Cain, who was a child of the evil one 12
and murdered his brother. And why did he murder him? Because his own
actions were wrong, and his brother's were right.

My brothers, do not be surprised if the world hates you. We for our part 13 14
have crossed over from death to life; this we know, because we love our
brothers. The man who does not love is still in the realm of death, for 15
everyone who hates his brother is a murderer, and no murderer, as you
know, has eternal life dwelling within him. It is by this that we know what 16
love is: that Christ laid down his life for us. And we in our turn are bound
to lay down our lives for our brothers. But if a man has enough to live on, 17
and yet when he sees his brother in need shuts up his heart against him,
how can it be said that the divine love *e* dwells in him?

My children, love must not be a matter of words or talk; it must be 18

---

*a Literally* the anointing.              *b Or* We are called children of God! Not only
called, we really are his children.        *c Or* when he appears.        *d Or* we
are God's children, though he has not yet appeared; what we shall be we know, for when
he does appear we shall be like him.        *e Or* that love for God . . .

19 genuine, and show itself in action. This is how we may know that we belong
20 to the realm of truth, and convince ourselves in his sight that even if our
conscience condemns us, God is greater than our conscience [a] and knows all.
21 Dear friends, if our conscience does not condemn us, then we can ap-
22 proach God with confidence, and obtain from him whatever we ask, because
23 we are keeping his commands and doing what he approves. This is his
command: to give our allegiance to his Son Jesus Christ and love one
24 another as he commanded. When we keep his commands we dwell in him
and he dwells in us. And this is how we can make sure that he dwells within
us: we know it from the Spirit he has given us.

**4** BUT DO NOT TRUST any and every spirit, my friends; test the spirits,
to see whether they are from God, for among those who have gone out into
2 the world there are many prophets falsely inspired. This is how we may
recognize the Spirit of God: every spirit which acknowledges that Jesus
3 Christ has come in the flesh is from God, and every spirit which does not
thus acknowledge Jesus is not from God. This is what is meant by 'Antichrist'; [b] you have been told that he was to come, and here he is, in the
world already!
4 But you, my children, are of God's family, and you have the mastery
over these false prophets, because he who inspires you is greater than he
5 who inspires the godless world. They are of that world, and so therefore is
6 their teaching; that is why the world listens to them. But we belong to
God, and a man who knows God listens to us, while he who does not belong
to God refuses us a hearing. That is how we distinguish the spirit of truth
from the spirit of error.
7 Dear friends, let us love one another, because love is from God. Every-
8 one who loves is a child of God and knows God, but the unloving know
9 nothing of God. For God is love; and his love was disclosed to us in this,
10 that he sent his only Son into the world to bring us life. The love I speak
of is not our love for God, but the love he showed to us in sending his Son
11 as the remedy for the defilement of our sins. If God thus loved us, dear
12 friends, we in turn are bound to love one another. Though God has never
been seen by any man, God himself dwells in us if we love one another; his
love is brought to perfection within us.
13 Here is the proof that we dwell in him and he dwells in us: he has im-
14 parted his Spirit to us. Moreover, we have seen for ourselves, and we attest,
15 that the Father sent the Son to be the saviour of the world, and if a man
acknowledges that Jesus is the Son of God, God dwells in him and he dwells
16 in God. Thus we have come to know and believe the love which God
has for us.
God is love; he who dwells in love is dwelling in God, and God in him.
17 This is for us the perfection of love, to have confidence on the day of judgement, and this we can have, because even in this world we are as he is.

[a] *Or* and reassure ourselves in his sight in matters where our conscience condemns us,
because God is greater than our conscience . . .; *or* and yet we shall do well to convince
ourselves that if even our own conscience condemns us, still more will God who is greater
than conscience . . .     [b] *Or* This is the spirit of Antichrist.

There is no room for fear in love; perfect love banishes fear. For fear brings 18 with it the pains of judgement, and anyone who is afraid has not attained to love in its perfection. We love because he loved us first. But if a man says, 19 20 'I love God', while hating his brother, he is a liar. If he does not love the brother whom he has seen, it cannot be that he loves God whom he has not seen. And indeed this command comes to us from Christ himself: that 21 he who loves God must also love his brother.

Everyone who believes that Jesus is the Christ is a child of God, and to 5 love the parent means to love his child; it follows that when we love God 2 and obey his commands we love his children too. For to love God is to 3 keep his commands; and they are not burdensome, because every child of 4 God is victor over the godless world. The victory that defeats the world is our faith, for who is victor over the world but he who believes that Jesus 5 is the Son of God?

This is he who came with water and blood: Jesus Christ. He came, not 6 by water alone, but by water and blood; and there is the Spirit to bear witness, because the Spirit is truth. For there are three witnesses, the Spirit, 7 8 the water, and the blood, and these three are in agreement. We accept 9 human testimony, but surely divine testimony is stronger, and this three-fold testimony is indeed that of God himself, the witness he has borne to his Son. He who believes in the Son of God has this testimony in his own 10 heart, but he who disbelieves God, makes him out to be a liar, by refusing to accept God's own witness to his Son. The witness is this: that God has 11 given us eternal life, and that this life is found in his Son. He who possesses 12 the Son has life indeed; he who does not possess the Son of God has not that life.

THIS LETTER is to assure you that you have eternal life. It is addressed 13 to those who give their allegiance to the Son of God.

We can approach God with confidence for this reason: if we make 14 requests which accord with his will he listens to us; and if we know that 15 our requests are heard, we know also that the things we ask for are ours.

If a man sees his brother committing a sin which is not a deadly sin, he 16 should pray to God for him, and he will grant him life—that is, when men are not guilty of deadly sin. There is such a thing as deadly sin, and I do not suggest that he should pray about that; but although all wrongdoing is 17 sin, not all sin is deadly sin.

We know that no child of God is a sinner; it is the Son of God who keeps 18 him safe, and the evil one cannot touch him.

We know that we are of God's family, while the whole godless world lies 19 in the power of the evil one.

We know that the Son of God has come and given us understanding to 20 know him who is real; indeed we are in him who is real, since we are in his Son Jesus Christ. This is the true God, this is eternal life. My children, be 21 on the watch against false gods.

# THE SECOND LETTER OF
# JOHN

*Truth and love*

1 THE ELDER to the Lady chosen by God, and her children, whom
2 I love in truth—and not I alone but all who know the truth—for
the sake of the truth that dwells among us and will be with us for ever.
3 Grace, mercy, and peace shall be with us from God the Father and from
Jesus Christ the Son of the Father, in truth and love.
4 I was delighted to find that some of your children are living by the truth,
5 as we were commanded by the Father. And now I have a request to make of
you. Do not think I am giving a new command; I am recalling the one we
6 have had before us from the beginning: let us love one another. And love
means following the commands of God. This is the command which was
given you from the beginning, to be your rule of life.
7 Many deceivers have gone out into the world, who do not acknowledge
Jesus Christ as coming in the flesh. These are the persons described as the
8 Antichrist, the arch-deceiver. Beware of them, so that you may not lose
all that we worked for, but receive your reward in full.
9 Anyone who runs ahead too far, and does not stand by the doctrine of
the Christ, is without God; he who stands by that doctrine possesses both
10 the Father and the Son. If anyone comes to you who does not bring this
11 doctrine, do not welcome him into your house or give him a greeting; for
anyone who gives him a greeting is an accomplice in his wicked deeds.
12 I have much to write to you, but I do not care to put it down in black and
white. But I hope to visit you and talk with you face to face, so that our joy
13 may be complete. The children of your Sister, chosen by God, send their
greetings.

# THE THIRD LETTER OF
# JOHN

## *Trouble in the church*

THE ELDER to dear Gaius, whom I love in truth. 1
My dear Gaius, I pray that you may enjoy good health, and that 2
all may go well with you, as I know it goes well with your soul. I was 3
delighted when friends came and told me how true you have been; indeed
you are true in your whole life. Nothing gives me greater joy than to hear 4
that my children are living by the truth.

My dear friend, you show a fine loyalty in everything that you do for these 5
our fellow-Christians, strangers though they are to you. They have spoken 6
of your kindness before the congregation here. Please help them on their
journey in a manner worthy of the God we serve. It was on Christ's work 7
that they went out; and they would accept nothing from pagans. We are 8
bound to support such men, and so play our part in spreading the truth.

I sent a letter to the congregation, but Diotrephes, their would-be 9
leader,[a] will have nothing to do with us. If I come, I will bring up the 10
things he is doing. He lays baseless and spiteful charges against us; not
satisfied with that, he refuses to receive our friends, and he interferes with
those who would do so, and tries to expel them from the congregation.

My dear friend, do not imitate bad examples, but good ones. The well- 11
doer is a child of God; the evil-doer has never seen God.

Demetrius gets a good testimonial from everybody—yes, and from the 12
truth itself. I add my testimony, and you know that my testimony is true.

I have much to write to you, but I do not care to set it down with pen 13
and ink. I hope to see you very soon, and we will talk face to face. Peace 14
be with you. Our friends send their greetings. Greet our friends one by one.

---

[a] *Or* who enjoys being their leader.

# A LETTER OF

# JUDE

## The danger of false belief

1 FROM JUDE, servant of Jesus Christ and brother of James, to those whom God has called, who live in the love of God the Father and in the safe keeping of Jesus Christ.

2 Mercy, peace, and love be yours in fullest measure.

3 My friends, I was fully engaged in writing to you about our salvation—which is yours no less than ours—when it became urgently necessary to write at once and appeal to you to join the struggle in defence of the faith,

4 the faith which God entrusted to his people once and for all. It is in danger from certain persons who have wormed their way in, the very men whom Scripture long ago marked down for the doom they have incurred. They are the enemies of religion; they pervert the free favour of our God into licentiousness, disowning Jesus Christ, our only Master and Lord.[a]

5 You already know it all, but let me remind you how the Lord,[b] having once delivered the people of Israel out of Egypt, next time destroyed those

6 who were guilty of unbelief. Remember too the angels, how some of them were not content to keep the dominion given to them but abandoned their proper home; and God has reserved them for judgement on the great Day,

7 bound beneath the darkness in everlasting chains. Remember Sodom and Gomorrah and the neighbouring towns; like the angels, they committed fornication and followed unnatural lusts; and they paid the penalty in eternal fire, an example for all to see.

8 So too with these men today. Their dreams lead them to defile the body,

9 to flout authority, and to insult celestial beings. In contrast, when the archangel Michael was in debate with the devil, disputing the possession of Moses's body, he did not presume to condemn him in insulting words,[c] but said, 'May the Lord rebuke you!'

10 But these men pour abuse upon things they do not understand; the things they do understand, by instinct like brute beasts, prove their un-

11 doing. Alas for them! They have gone the way of Cain; they have plunged into Balaam's error for pay; they have rebelled like Korah, and they share his doom.

12 These men are a blot on your love-feasts, where they eat and drink without reverence. They are shepherds who take care only of themselves. They are clouds carried away by the wind without giving rain, trees that in

---

[a] Or disowning our one and only Master, and Jesus Christ our Lord.    [b] Some witnesses read Jesus (which might be understood as Joshua).    [c] Or to charge him with blasphemy.

season bear no fruit, dead twice over and pulled up by the roots. They are 13
fierce waves of the sea, foaming shameful deeds; they are stars that have
wandered from their course, and the place for ever reserved for them is
blackest darkness.

It was to them that Enoch, the seventh in descent from Adam, directed 14
his prophecy when he said: 'I saw the Lord come with his myriads of
angels, to bring all men to judgement and to convict all the godless of all 15
the godless deeds they had committed, and of all the defiant words which
godless sinners had spoken against him.'

They are a set of grumblers and malcontents. They follow their lusts. 16
Big words come rolling from their lips, and they court favour to gain their
ends. But you, my friends, should remember the predictions made by the 17
apostles of our Lord Jesus Christ. This was the warning they gave you: 18
'In the final age there will be men who pour scorn on religion, and follow
their own godless lusts.'

These men draw a line between spiritual and unspiritual persons, 19
although they are themselves*a* wholly unspiritual. But you, my friends, 20
must fortify yourselves in your most sacred faith. Continue to pray in the
power of the Holy Spirit. Keep yourselves in the love of God, and look 21
forward to the day when our Lord Jesus Christ in his mercy will give
eternal life.

There are some doubting souls who need your pity;*b* snatch them from 22 23
the flames and save them.*c* There are others for whom your pity must be
mixed with fear; hate the very clothing that is contaminated with sensuality.

Now to the One who can keep you from falling and set you in the presence 24
of his glory, jubilant and above reproach, to the only God our Saviour, be 25
glory and majesty, might and authority, through Jesus Christ our Lord,
before all time, now, and for evermore. Amen.

*a* *Or* These men create divisions; they are . . .            *b* *Some witnesses read* There
are some who raise disputes; these you should refute.            *c* *So one witness; the rest*
*read* some you should snatch from the flames and save.

# THE REVELATION
# OF JOHN

# THE REVELATION
# OF JOHN

THIS IS THE REVELATION given by God to Jesus Christ. 1
It was given to him so that he might show his servants what must
shortly happen. He made it known by sending his angel to his servant
John, who, in telling all that he saw, has borne witness to the word of God 2
and to the testimony of Jesus Christ.<sup>a</sup>

Happy is the man who reads, and happy those who listen to the words of 3
this prophecy and heed what is written in it. For the hour of fulfilment
is near.

## A message from Christ to the churches

JOHN TO THE SEVEN CHURCHES in the province of Asia. 4
Grace be to you and peace, from him who is and who was and who is
to come, from the seven spirits before his throne, and from Jesus Christ, 5
the faithful witness, the first-born from the dead and ruler of the kings of
the earth.

To him who loves us and freed us from our sins with his life's blood,
who made of us a royal house, to serve as the priests of his God and Father 6
—to him be glory and dominion for ever and ever! Amen.

Behold, he is coming with the clouds! Every eye shall see him, and 7
among them those who pierced him; and all the peoples of the world shall
lament in remorse. So it shall be. Amen.

'I am the Alpha and the Omega', says the Lord God, who is and who 8
was and who is to come, the sovereign Lord of all.

I, John, your brother, who share with you in the suffering and the 9
sovereignty and the endurance which is ours in Jesus—I was on the island
called Patmos because I had preached God's word and borne my testimony
to Jesus. It was on the Lord's day, and I was caught up by the Spirit; and 10
behind me I heard a loud voice, like the sound of a trumpet, which said to 11
me, 'Write down what you see on a scroll and send it to the seven churches:
to Ephesus, Smyrna, Pergamum, Thyatira, Sardis, Philadelphia, and
Laodicea.' I turned to see whose voice it was that spoke to me; and when I 12
turned I saw seven standing lamps of gold, and among the lamps one like 13
a son of man, robed down to his feet, with a golden girdle round his breast.
The hair of his head was white as snow-white wool, and his eyes flamed like 14
fire; his feet gleamed like burnished brass refined in a furnace, and his 15
voice was like the sound of rushing waters. In his right hand he held seven 16

<sup>a</sup> Or has borne his testimony to the word of God and to Jesus Christ.

stars, and out of his mouth came a sharp two-edged sword; and his face shone like the sun in full strength.

17 When I saw him, I fell at his feet as though dead. But he laid his right
18 hand upon me and said, 'Do not be afraid. I am the first and the last, and I am the living one; for I was dead and now I am alive for evermore, and
19 I hold the keys of Death and Death's domain. Write down therefore what you have seen, what is now, and what will be hereafter.

20 'Here is the secret meaning of the seven stars which you saw in my right hand, and of the seven lamps of gold: the seven stars are the angels of the seven churches, and the seven lamps are the seven churches.

2 'TO THE ANGEL of the church at Ephesus write:
  ' "These are the words of the One who holds the seven stars in his right
2 hand and walks among the seven lamps of gold: I know all your ways, your toil and your fortitude. I know you cannot endure evil men; you have put to the proof those who claim to be apostles but are not, and have found
3 them false. Fortitude you have; you have borne up in my cause and never
4 5 flagged. But I have this against you: you have lost your early love. Think from what a height you have fallen; repent, and do as you once did. Otherwise, if you do not repent, I shall come to you and remove your lamp from
6 its place. Yet you have this in your favour: you hate the practices of the
7 Nicolaitans, as I do. Hear, you who have ears to hear, what the Spirit says to the churches! To him who is victorious I will give the right to eat from the tree of life that stands in the Garden of God."

8 'To the angel of the church at Smyrna write:
  ' "These are the words of the First and the Last, who was dead and
9 came to life again: I know how hard pressed you are, and poor—and yet you are rich; I know how you are slandered by those who claim to be Jews
10 but are not—they are Satan's synagogue. Do not be afraid of the suffering to come. The Devil will throw some of you into prison, to put you to the test; and for ten days you will suffer cruelly. Only be faithful till death,
11 and I will give you the crown of life. Hear, you who have ears to hear, what the Spirit says to the churches! He who is victorious cannot be harmed by the second death."

12 'To the angel of the church at Pergamum write:
  ' "These are the words of the One who has the sharp two-edged sword:
13 I know where you live; it is the place where Satan has his throne. And yet you are holding fast to my cause. You did not deny your faith in me even at the time when Antipas, my faithful witness, was killed in your city, the
14 home of Satan. But I have a few matters to bring against you: you have in Pergamum some that hold to the teaching of Balaam, who taught Balak to put temptation in the way of the Israelites. He encouraged them to eat
15 food sacrificed to idols and to commit fornication, and in the same way you
16 also have some who hold the doctrine of the Nicolaitans. So repent! If you do not, I shall come to you soon and make war upon them with the
17 sword that comes out of my mouth. Hear, you who have ears to hear, what the Spirit says to the churches! To him who is victorious I will give some of the hidden manna; I will give him also a white stone, and

on the stone will be written a new name, known to none but him that
receives it."

'To the angel of the church at Thyatira write:  18
' "These are the words of the Son of God, whose eyes flame like fire and
whose feet gleam like burnished brass: I know all your ways, your love and  19
faithfulness, your good service and your fortitude; and of late you have
done even better than at first. Yet I have this against you: you tolerate that  20
Jezebel, the woman who claims to be a prophetess, who by her teaching
lures my servants into fornication and into eating food sacrificed to idols.
I have given her time to repent, but she refuses to repent of her fornication.  21
So I will throw her on to a bed of pain,*a* and plunge her lovers into terrible  22
suffering, unless they forswear what she is doing; and her children I will  23
strike dead. This will teach all the churches that I am the searcher of men's
hearts and thoughts, and that I will reward each one of you according to
his deeds. And now I speak to you others in Thyatira, who do not accept  24
this teaching and have had no experience of what they like to call the deep
secrets of Satan; on you I will impose no further burden. Only hold fast to  25
what you have, until I come. To him who is victorious, to him who per-  26
severes in doing my will to the end, I will give authority over the nations—
that same authority which I received from my Father—and he shall rule  27
them with an iron rod, smashing them to bits like earthenware; and I will  28
give him also the star of dawn. Hear, you who have ears to hear, what the  29
Spirit says to the churches!"

'To the angel of the church at Sardis write:  **3**
' "These are the words of the One who holds the seven spirits of God,
the seven stars: I know all your ways; that though you have a name for
being alive, you are dead. Wake up, and put some strength into what is left,  2
which must otherwise die! For I have not found any work of yours completed in the eyes of my God. So remember the teaching you received;  3
observe it, and repent. If you do not wake up, I shall come upon you like a
thief, and you will not know the moment of my coming. Yet you have a few  4
persons in Sardis who have not polluted their clothing. They shall walk
with me in white, for so they deserve. He who is victorious shall thus be  5
robed all in white; his name I will never strike off the roll of the living, for
in the presence of my Father and his angels I will acknowledge him as mine.
Hear, you who have ears to hear, what the Spirit says to the churches!"  6

'To the angel of the church at Philadelphia write:  7
' "These are the words of the holy one, the true one, who holds the key
of David; when he opens none may shut, when he shuts none may open:
I know all your ways; and look, I have set before you an open door, which  8
no one can shut. Your strength, I know, is small, yet you have observed
my commands and have not disowned my name. So this is what I will do:  9
I will make those of Satan's synagogue, who claim to be Jews but are lying
frauds, come and fall down at your feet; and they shall know that you are my
beloved people. Because you have kept my command and stood fast, I will  10
also keep you from the ordeal that is to fall upon the whole world and test
its inhabitants. I am coming soon; hold fast what you have, and let no one  11

---

*a One witness reads* into a furnace.

12 rob you of your crown. He who is victorious—I will make him a pillar in the temple of my God; he shall never leave it. And I will write the name of my God upon him, and the name of the city of my God, that new Jerusalem which is coming down out of heaven from my God, and my own new
13 name. Hear, you who have ears to hear, what the Spirit says to the churches!"
14 'To the angel of the church at Laodicea write:
' "These are the words of the Amen, the faithful and true witness, the
15 prime source of all God's creation: I know all your ways; you are neither
16 hot nor cold. How I wish you were either hot or cold! But because you are
17 lukewarm, neither hot nor cold, I will spit you out of my mouth. You say, 'How rich I am! And how well I have done! I have everything I want.' In fact, though you do not know it, you are the most pitiful wretch, poor,
18 blind, and naked. So I advise you to buy from me gold refined in the fire, to make you truly rich, and white clothes to put on to hide the shame of your
19 nakedness, and ointment for your eyes so that you may see. All whom I love I reprove and discipline. Be on your mettle therefore and repent.
20 Here I stand knocking at the door; if anyone hears my voice and opens the
21 door, I will come in and sit down to supper with him and he with me. To him who is victorious I will grant a place on my throne, as I myself was
22 victorious and sat down with my Father on his throne. Hear, you who have ears to hear, what the Spirit says to the churches!" '

## *The opening of the sealed book*

4 AFTER THIS I LOOKED, and there before my eyes was a door opened in heaven; and the voice that I had first heard speaking to me like a trumpet said, 'Come up here, and I will show you what must happen here-
2 after.' At once I was caught up by the Spirit. There in heaven stood a
3 throne, and on the throne sat one whose appearance was like the gleam of jasper and cornelian; and round the throne was a rainbow, bright as an
4 emerald. In a circle about this throne were twenty-four other thrones, and on them sat twenty-four elders, robed in white and wearing crowns of gold.
5 From the throne went out flashes of lightning and peals of thunder. Burning before the throne were seven flaming torches, the seven spirits of God,
6 and in front of it stretched what seemed a sea of glass, like a sheet of ice.
In the centre, round the throne itself, were four living creatures, covered
7 with eyes, in front and behind. The first creature like a lion, the second like an ox, the third had a human face, the fourth was like an eagle in flight.
8 The four living creatures, each of them with six wings, had eyes all over, inside and out; and by day and by night without a pause they sang:

'Holy, holy, holy is God the sovereign Lord of all, who was, and is, and is to come!'

9 As often as the living creatures give glory and honour and thanks to the
10 One who sits on the throne, who lives for ever and ever, the twenty-four elders fall down before the One who sits on the throne and worship him

who lives for ever and ever; and as they lay their crowns before the throne they cry:

> 'Thou art worthy, O Lord our God, to receive glory and honour and 11 power, because thou didst create all things; by thy will they were created, and have their being!'

Then I saw in the right hand of the One who sat on the throne a scroll, 5 with writing inside and out, and it was sealed up with seven seals. And I 2 saw a mighty angel proclaiming in a loud voice, 'Who is worthy to open the scroll and to break its seals?' There was no one in heaven or on earth or 3 under the earth able to open the scroll or to look inside it. I was in tears 4 because no one was found who was worthy to open the scroll or to look inside it. But one of the elders said to me: 'Do not weep; for the Lion from 5 the tribe of Judah, the Scion of David, has won the right to open the scroll and break its seven seals.'

Then I saw standing in the very middle of the throne, inside the circle 6 of living creatures and the circle of elders,*a* a Lamb with the marks of slaughter upon him. He had seven horns and seven eyes, the eyes which are the seven spirits of God sent out over all the world. And the Lamb went 7 up and took the scroll from the right hand of the One who sat on the throne. When he took it, the four living creatures and the twenty-four elders fell 8 down before the Lamb. Each of the elders had a harp, and they held golden bowls full of incense, the prayers of God's people, and they were singing a 9 new song:

> 'Thou art worthy to take the scroll and to break its seals, for thou wast slain and by thy blood didst purchase for God men of every tribe and language, people and nation; thou hast made of them a royal house, to 10 serve our God as priests; and they shall reign upon earth.'

Then as I looked I heard the voices of countless angels. These were all 11 round the throne and the living creatures and the elders. Myriads upon myriads there were, thousands upon thousands, and they cried aloud: 12

> 'Worthy is the Lamb, the Lamb that was slain, to receive all power and wealth, wisdom and might, honour and glory and praise!'

Then I heard every created thing in heaven and on earth and under the 13 earth and in the sea, all that is in them, crying:

> 'Praise and honour, glory and might, to him who sits on the throne and to the Lamb for ever and ever!'

And the four living creatures said, 'Amen', and the elders fell down and 14 worshipped.


THEN I WATCHED as the Lamb broke the first of the seven seals; and I 6 heard one of the four living creatures say in a voice like thunder, 'Come!' And there before my eyes was a white horse, and its rider held a bow. He 2 was given a crown, and he rode forth, conquering and to conquer.

*a Or* standing between the throne, with the four living creatures, and the elders . . .

3 When the Lamb broke the second seal, I heard the second creature say,
4 'Come!' And out came another horse, all red. To its rider was given power
to take peace from the earth and make men slaughter one another; and he
was given a great sword.

5 When he broke the third seal, I heard the third creature say, 'Come!'
And there, as I looked, was a black horse; and its rider held in his hand a
6 pair of scales. And I heard what sounded like a voice from the midst of the
living creatures, which said, 'A whole day's wage for a quart of flour, a whole
day's wage for three quarts of barley-meal! But spare the olive and the
vine.'

7 When he broke the fourth seal, I heard the voice of the fourth creature
8 say, 'Come!' And there, as I looked, was another horse, sickly pale; and its
rider's name was Death, and Hades came close behind. To him was given
power over a quarter of the earth, with the right to kill by sword and by
famine, by pestilence and wild beasts.

9 When he broke the fifth seal, I saw underneath *a* the altar the souls of
those who had been slaughtered for God's word and for the testimony they
10 bore. They gave a great cry: 'How long, sovereign Lord, holy and true,
must it be before thou wilt vindicate us and avenge our blood on the
11 inhabitants of the earth?' Each of them was given a white robe; and they
were told to rest a little while longer, until the tally should be complete of
all their brothers in Christ's service who were to be killed as they had
been.

12 Then I watched as he broke the sixth seal. And there was a violent earthquake; the sun turned black as a funeral pall and the moon all red as blood;
13 14 the stars in the sky fell to the earth, like figs shaken down by a gale; the sky
vanished, as a scroll is rolled up, and every mountain and island was moved
15 from its place. Then the kings of the earth, magnates and marshals, the rich
and the powerful, and all men, slave or free, hid themselves in caves and
16 mountain crags; and they called out to the mountains and the crags, 'Fall
on us and hide us from the face of the One who sits on the throne and from
17 the vengeance of the Lamb.' For the great day of their vengeance has come,
and who will be able to stand?

7 After this I saw four angels stationed at the four corners of the earth,
holding back the four winds so that no wind should blow on sea or land
2 or on any tree. Then I saw another angel rising out of the east, carrying the
seal of the living God; and he called aloud to the four angels who had been
3 given the power to ravage land and sea: 'Do no damage to sea or land or
trees until we have set the seal of our God upon the foreheads of his
4 servants.' And I heard the number of those who had received the seal.
From all the tribes of Israel there were a hundred and forty-four thousand:
5 twelve thousand from the tribe of Judah, twelve thousand from the tribe
6 of Reuben, twelve thousand from the tribe of Gad, twelve thousand from
the tribe of Asher, twelve thousand from the tribe of Naphtali, twelve
7 thousand from the tribe of Manasseh, twelve thousand from the tribe of
Simeon, twelve thousand from the tribe of Levi, twelve thousand from
8 the tribe of Issachar, twelve thousand from the tribe of Zebulun, twelve

*a Or* at the foot of . . .

thousand from the tribe of Joseph, and twelve thousand from the tribe of Benjamin.

After this I looked and saw a vast throng, which no one could count, 9 from every nation, of all tribes, peoples, and languages, standing in front of the throne and before the Lamb. They were robed in white and had palms in their hands, and they shouted together: 10

'Victory to our God who sits on the throne, and to the Lamb!'

And all the angels stood round the throne and the elders and the four 11 living creatures, and they fell on their faces before the throne and worshipped God, crying: 12

'Amen! Praise and glory and wisdom, thanksgiving and honour, power and might, be to our God for ever and ever! Amen.'

Then one of the elders turned to me and said, 'These men that are robed 13 in white—who are they and from where do they come?' But I answered, 14 'My lord, you know, not I.' Then he said to me, 'These are the men who have passed through the great ordeal; they have washed their robes and made them white in the blood of the Lamb. That is why they stand before 15 the throne of God and minister to him day and night in his temple; and he who sits on the throne will dwell with them. They shall never again feel 16 hunger or thirst, the sun shall not beat on them nor any scorching heat, because the Lamb who is at the heart of the throne will be their shepherd 17 and will guide them to the springs of the water of life; and God will wipe all tears from their eyes.'

Now when the Lamb broke the seventh seal, there was silence in heaven 8 for what seemed half an hour. Then I looked, and the seven angels that 2 stand in the presence of God were given seven trumpets.

Then another angel came and stood at the altar, holding a golden censer; 3 and he was given a great quantity of incense to offer with the prayers of all God's people upon the golden altar in front of the throne. And from the 4 angel's hand the smoke of the incense went up before God with the prayers of his people. Then the angel took the censer, filled it from the altar fire, 5 and threw it down upon the earth; and there were peals of thunder, lightning, and an earthquake.

## *The powers of darkness conquered*

THEN THE SEVEN ANGELS that held the seven trumpets prepared to 6 blow them.

The first blew his trumpet; and there came hail and fire mingled with 7 blood, and this was hurled upon the earth. A third of the earth was burnt, a third of the trees were burnt, all the green grass was burnt.

The second angel blew his trumpet; and what looked like a great blazing 8 mountain was hurled into the sea. A third of the sea was turned to blood, a third of the living creatures in it died, and a third of the ships on it 9 foundered.

10     The third angel blew his trumpet; and a great star shot from the sky,
11 flaming like a torch; and it fell on a third of the rivers and springs. The name of the star was Wormwood; and a third of the water turned to wormwood, and men in great numbers died of the water because it had been poisoned.

12     The fourth angel blew his trumpet; and a third part of the sun was struck, a third of the moon, and a third of the stars, so that the third part went dark and a third of the light of the day failed, and of the night.

13     Then I looked, and I heard an eagle calling with a loud cry as it flew in mid-heaven: 'Woe, woe, woe to the inhabitants of the earth when the trumpets sound which the three last angels must now blow!'

**9**     Then the fifth angel blew his trumpet; and I saw a star that had fallen from heaven to earth, and the star was given the key of the shaft of the
2 abyss. With this he opened the shaft of the abyss; and from the shaft smoke rose like smoke from a great furnace, and the sun and the air were darkened
3 by the smoke from the shaft. Then over the earth, out of the smoke, came
4 locusts, and they were given the powers that earthly scorpions have. They were told to do no injury to the grass or to any plant or tree, but only to
5 those men who had not received the seal of God on their foreheads. These they were allowed to torment for five months, with torment like a scorpion's
6 sting; but they were not to kill them. During that time these men will seek death, but they will not find it; they will long to die, but death will elude them.

7     In appearance the locusts were like horses equipped for battle. On their heads were what looked like golden crowns; their faces were like human
8 9 faces and their hair like women's hair; they had teeth like lions' teeth, and wore breastplates like iron; the sound of their wings was like the noise of
10 horses and chariots rushing to battle; they had tails like scorpions, with stings in them, and in their tails lay their power to plague mankind for five
11 months. They had for their king the angel of the abyss, whose name, in Hebrew, is Abaddon, and in Greek, Apollyon, or the Destroyer.

12     The first woe has now passed. But there are still two more to come.

13     The sixth angel then blew his trumpet; and I heard a voice coming from between the horns of the golden altar that stood in the presence of God.
14 It said to the sixth angel, who held the trumpet: 'Release the four angels
15 held bound at the great river Euphrates!' So the four angels were let loose, to kill a third of mankind. They had been held ready for this moment, for
16 this very year and month, day and hour. And their squadrons of cavalry, whose count I heard, numbered two hundred million.

17     This was how I saw the horses and their riders in my vision: They wore breastplates, fiery red, blue, and sulphur-yellow; the horses had heads like lions' heads, and out of their mouths came fire, smoke, and sulphur.
18 By these three plagues, that is, by the fire, the smoke, and the sulphur that
19 came from their mouths, a third of mankind was killed. The power of the horses lay in their mouths, and in their tails also; for their tails were like snakes, with heads, and with them too they dealt injuries.

20     The rest of mankind who survived these plagues still did not abjure the gods their hands had fashioned, nor cease their worship of devils and of

idols made from gold, silver, bronze, stone, and wood, which cannot see or
hear or walk. Nor did they repent of their murders, their sorcery, their 21
fornication, or their robberies.

THEN I SAW another mighty angel coming down from heaven. He was **10**
wrapped in cloud, with the rainbow round his head; his face shone like
the sun and his legs were like pillars of fire. In his hand he held a little scroll 2
unrolled. His right foot he planted on the sea, and his left on the land. Then 3
he gave a great shout, like the roar of a lion; and when he shouted, the seven
thunders spoke. I was about to write down what the seven thunders had 4
said; but I heard a voice from heaven saying, 'Seal up what the seven
thunders have said; do not write it down.' Then the angel that I saw stand- 5
ing on the sea and the land raised his right hand to heaven and swore by him 6
who lives for ever and ever, who created heaven and earth and the sea and
everything in them: 'There shall be no more delay; but when the time 7
comes for the seventh angel to sound his trumpet, the hidden purpose of
God will have been fulfilled, as he promised to his servants the prophets.'

Then the voice which I heard from heaven was speaking to me again, 8
and it said, 'Go and take the open scroll in the hand of the angel that stands
on the sea and the land.' So I went to the angel and asked him to give me the 9
little scroll. He said to me, 'Take it, and eat it. It will turn your stomach sour,
although in your mouth it will taste sweet as honey.' So I took the little 10
scroll from the angel's hand and ate it, and in my mouth it did taste sweet
as honey; but when I swallowed it my stomach turned sour.

Then they said to me, 'Once again you must utter prophecies over 11
peoples and nations and languages and many kings.'

I was given a long cane, a kind of measuring-rod, and told: 'Now go and **11**
measure the temple of God, the altar, and the number of the worshippers.
But have nothing to do with the outer court of the temple; do not measure 2
that; for it has been given over to the Gentiles, and they will trample the
Holy City underfoot for forty-two months. And I have two witnesses, 3
whom I will appoint to prophesy, dressed in sackcloth, all through those
twelve hundred and sixty days.' These are the two olive-trees and the two 4
lamps that stand in the presence of the Lord of the earth. If anyone seeks 5
to do them harm, fire pours from their mouths and consumes their enemies;
and thus shall the man die who seeks to do them harm. These two have the 6
power to shut up the sky, so that no rain may fall during the time of their
prophesying; and they have the power to turn water to blood and to strike
the earth at will with every kind of plague. But when they have completed 7
their testimony, the beast that comes up from the abyss will wage war upon
them and will defeat and kill them. Their corpses will lie in the street of the 8
great city, whose name in allegory is Sodom, or Egypt, where also their
Lord was crucified. For three days and a half men from every people and 9
tribe, of every language and nation, gaze upon their corpses and refuse them
burial. All men on earth gloat over them, make merry, and exchange pre- 10
sents; for these two prophets were a torment to the whole earth. But at the 11
end of the three days and a half the breath of life from God came into them;
and they stood up on their feet to the terror of all who saw it. Then a loud 12

voice was heard speaking to them from heaven, which said, 'Come up here!' And they went up to heaven in a cloud, in full view of their enemies.

13 At that same moment there was a violent earthquake, and a tenth of the city fell. Seven thousand people were killed in the earthquake; the rest in terror did homage to the God of heaven.

14 The second woe has now passed. But the third is soon to come.

15 Then the seventh angel blew his trumpet; and voices were heard in heaven shouting:

'The sovereignty of the world has passed to our Lord and his Christ, and he shall reign for ever and ever!'

16 And the twenty-four elders, seated on their thrones before God, fell on
17 their faces and worshipped God, saying:

'We give thee thanks, O Lord God, sovereign over all, who art and who wast, because thou hast taken thy great power into thy hands and
18 entered upon thy reign. The nations raged, but thy day of retribution has come. Now is the time for the dead to be judged; now is the time for recompense to thy servants the prophets, to thy dedicated people, and all who honour thy name, both great and small, the time to destroy those who destroy the earth.'

19 Then God's temple in heaven was laid open, and within the temple was seen the ark of his covenant. There came flashes of lightning and peals of thunder, an earthquake, and a storm of hail.

12 NEXT APPEARED a great portent in heaven, a woman robed with the sun, beneath her feet the moon, and on her head a crown of twelve stars.
2 She was pregnant, and in the anguish of her labour she cried out to be
3 delivered. Then a second portent appeared in heaven: a great red dragon
4 with seven heads and ten horns; on his heads were seven diadems, and with his tail he swept down a third of the stars in the sky and flung them to the earth. The dragon stood in front of the woman who was about to give
5 birth, so that when her child was born he might devour it. She gave birth to a male child, who is destined to rule all nations with an iron rod. But her
6 child was snatched up to God and his throne; and the woman herself fled into the wilds, where she had a place prepared for her by God, there to be sustained for twelve hundred and sixty days.

7 Then war broke out in heaven. Michael and his angels waged war upon
8 the dragon. The dragon and his angels fought, but they had not the
9 strength to win, and no foothold was left them in heaven. So the great dragon was thrown down, that serpent of old that led the whole world astray, whose name is Satan, or the Devil—thrown down to the earth, and his angels with him.

10 Then I heard a voice in heaven proclaiming aloud: 'This is the hour of victory for our God, the hour of his sovereignty and power, when his Christ comes to his rightful rule! For the accuser of our brothers is overthrown,
11 who day and night accused them before our God. By the sacrifice of the

Lamb they have conquered him, and by the testimony which they uttered;*ᵃ*
for they did not hold their lives too dear to lay them down. Rejoice then,  12
you heavens and you that dwell in them! But woe to you, earth and sea, for
the Devil has come down to you in great fury, knowing that his time is
short!'

When the dragon found that he had been thrown down to the earth, he  13
went in pursuit of the woman who had given birth to the male child. But  14
the woman was given two great eagle's wings, to fly to the place in the wilds
where for three years and a half she was to be sustained, out of reach of the
serpent. From his mouth the serpent spewed a flood of water after the  15
woman to sweep her away with its spate. But the earth came to her rescue  16
and opened its mouth and swallowed the river which the dragon spewed
from his mouth. At this the dragon grew furious with the woman, and went  17
off to wage war on the rest of her offspring, that is, on those who keep God's
commandments and maintain their testimony to Jesus. He took his stand  **13**
on the sea-shore.

Then*ᵇ* out of the sea I saw a beast rising. It had ten horns and seven
heads. On its horns were ten diadems, and on each head a blasphemous
name. The beast I saw was like a leopard, but its feet were like a bear's and  2
its mouth like a lion's mouth. The dragon conferred upon it his power and
rule, and great authority. One of its heads appeared to have received a  3
death-blow; but the mortal wound was healed. The whole world went after
the beast in wondering admiration. Men worshipped the dragon because  4
he had conferred his authority upon the beast; they worshipped the beast
also, and chanted, 'Who is like the Beast? Who can fight against it?'

The beast was allowed to mouth bombast and blasphemy, and was given  5
the right to reign for forty-two months. It opened its mouth in blasphemy  6
against God, reviling his name and his heavenly dwelling.*ᶜ* It was also  7
allowed to wage war on God's people and to defeat them, and was granted*ᵈ*
authority over every tribe and people, language and nation. All on earth  8
will worship it, except those whose names the Lamb that was slain keeps
in his roll of the living, written there since the world was made.

Hear, you who have ears to hear! Whoever is to be made prisoner, a  9 10
prisoner he shall be. Whoever takes the sword to kill, by the sword he is
bound to be killed. This is where the fortitude and faithfulness of God's
people have their place.

Then I saw another beast, which came up out of the earth; it had two  11
horns like a lamb's, but spoke like a dragon. It wielded all the authority of  12
the first beast in its presence, and made the earth and its inhabitants
worship this first beast, whose mortal wound had been healed. It worked  13
great miracles, even making fire come down from heaven to earth before
men's eyes. By the miracles it was allowed to perform in the presence of  14
the beast it deluded the inhabitants of the earth, and made them erect an
image in honour of the beast that had been wounded by the sword and yet

*a  Or* the word of God to which they bore witness.                    *b  Some witnesses read* . . .
testimony to Jesus. Then I stood by the sea-shore and . . .      *c  Some witnesses*
*read* reviling his name and his dwelling-place, that is, those that live in heaven.
*d  Some witnesses read* It was granted . . . (*omitting the words* was also . . . them, and).

15 lived. It was allowed to give breath to the image of the beast, so that it could speak, and could cause all who would not worship the image to be put to
16 death. Moreover, it caused everyone, great and small, rich and poor, slave
17 and free, to be branded with a mark on his right hand or forehead, and no one was allowed to buy or sell unless he bore this beast's mark, either name
18 or number. (Here is the key; and anyone who has intelligence may work out the number of the beast. The number represents a man's name, and the numerical value of its letters is six hundred and sixty-six.)

## Visions of the end

14 THEN I LOOKED, and on Mount Zion stood the Lamb, and with him were a hundred and forty-four thousand who had his name and the
2 name of his Father written on their foreheads. I heard a sound from heaven like the noise of rushing water and the deep roar of thunder; it was the
3 sound of harpers playing on their harps. There before the throne, and the four living creatures and the elders, they were singing a new song. That song no one could learn except the hundred and forty-four thousand, who
4 alone from the whole world had been ransomed. These are men who did not defile themselves with women, for they have kept themselves chaste, and they follow the Lamb wherever he goes. They have been ransomed as
5 the firstfruits of humanity for God and the Lamb. No lie was found in their lips; they are faultless.
6     Then I saw an angel flying in mid-heaven, with an eternal gospel to proclaim to those on earth, to every nation and tribe, language and people.
7 He cried in a loud voice, 'Fear God and pay him homage; for the hour of his judgement has come! Worship him who made heaven and earth, the sea and the water-springs!'
8     Then another angel, a second, followed, and he cried, 'Fallen, fallen is Babylon the great, she who has made all nations drink the fierce wine of*a* her fornication!'
9     Yet a third angel followed, crying out loud, 'Whoever worships the
10 beast and its image and receives its mark on his forehead or hand, he shall drink the wine of God's wrath, poured undiluted into the cup of his vengeance. He shall be tormented in sulphurous flames before the holy
11 angels and before the Lamb. The smoke of their torment will rise for ever and ever, and there will be no respite day or night for those who worship
12 the beast and its image or receive the mark of its name.' This is where the fortitude of God's people has its place—in keeping God's commands and remaining loyal to Jesus.
13     Moreover, I heard a voice from heaven, saying, 'Write this: "Happy are the dead who die in the faith of Christ! Henceforth",*b* says the Spirit,*c* "they may rest from their labours; for they take with them the record of their deeds." '

*a* Or drink the wine of God's wrath upon . . .      *b* Or Assuredly.      *c* *Some witnesses read* ". . . the dead who henceforth die in the faith of Christ!" "Yes," says the Spirit . . .

*Visions of the end*  REVELATION 14-16

Then as I looked there appeared a white cloud, and on the cloud sat one 14
like a son of man. He had on his head a crown of gold and in his hand a
sharp sickle. Another angel came out of the temple and called in a loud 15
voice to him who sat on the cloud: 'Stretch out your sickle and reap; for
harvest-time has come, and earth's crop is over-ripe.' So he who sat on the 16
cloud put his sickle to the earth and its harvest was reaped.

Then another angel came out of the heavenly temple, and he also had a 17
sharp sickle. Then from the altar came yet another, the angel who has 18
authority over fire, and he shouted to the one with the sharp sickle:
'Stretch out your sickle, and gather in earth's grape-harvest, for its clusters
are ripe.' So the angel put his sickle to the earth and gathered in its grapes, 19
and threw them into the great winepress of God's wrath. The winepress 20
was trodden outside the city, and for two hundred miles around blood
flowed from the press to the height of the horses' bridles.

Then I saw another great and astonishing portent in heaven: seven angels 15
with seven plagues, the last plagues of all, for with them the wrath of God
is consummated.

I saw what seemed a sea of glass shot with fire, and beside the sea of 2
glass, holding the harps which God had given them, were those who had
won the victory over the beast and its image and the number of its name.

They were singing the song of Moses, the servant of God, and the song 3
of the Lamb, as they chanted:

'Great and marvellous are thy deeds, O Lord God, sovereign over all;
just and true are thy ways, thou king of the ages.*a* Who shall not revere 4
thee, Lord, and do homage to thy name? For thou alone art holy. All
nations shall come and worship in thy presence, for thy just dealings
stand revealed.'

After this, as I looked, the sanctuary of the heavenly Tent of Testimony 5
was thrown open, and out of it came the seven angels with the seven plagues. 6
They were robed in fine linen, clean and shining, and had golden girdles
round their breasts. Then one of the four living creatures gave the seven 7
angels seven golden bowls full of the wrath of God who lives for ever and
ever; and the sanctuary was filled with smoke from the glory of God and 8
his power, so that no one could enter it until the seven plagues of the seven
angels were completed.

Then from the sanctuary I heard a loud voice, and it said to the seven 16
angels, 'Go and pour out the seven bowls of God's wrath on the earth.'

So the first angel went and poured his bowl on the earth; and foul 2
malignant sores appeared on those men that wore the mark of the beast
and worshipped its image.

The second angel poured his bowl on the sea, and it turned to blood like 3
the blood from a corpse; and every living thing in the sea died.

The third angel poured his bowl on the rivers and springs, and they 4
turned to blood.

Then I heard the angel of the waters say, 'Just art thou in these thy 5
judgements, thou Holy One who art and wast; for they shed the blood of 6

*a Some witnesses read king of the nations.*

329

thy people and of thy prophets, and thou hast given them blood to drink.
7 They have their deserts!' And I heard the altar cry, 'Yes, Lord God, sovereign over all, true and just are thy judgements!'
8  The fourth angel poured his bowl on the sun; and it was allowed to burn
9 men with its flames. They were fearfully burned; but they only cursed the name of God who had the power to inflict such plagues, and they refused to repent or do him homage.
10  The fifth angel poured his bowl on the throne of the beast; and its kingdom was plunged in darkness. Men gnawed their tongues in agony,
11 but they only cursed the God of heaven for their sores and pains, and would not repent of what they had done.
12  The sixth angel poured his bowl on the great river Euphrates; and its water was dried up, to prepare the way for the kings from the east.
13  Then I saw coming from the mouth of the dragon, the mouth of the beast, and the mouth of the false prophet, three foul spirits like frogs.
14 These spirits were devils, with power to work miracles. They were sent out to muster all the kings of the world for the great day of battle of God
15 the sovereign Lord. ('That is the day when I come like a thief! Happy the man who stays awake and keeps on his clothes, so that he will not have to go
16 naked and ashamed for all to see!') So they assembled the kings at the place called in Hebrew Armageddon.
17  Then the seventh angel poured his bowl on the air; and out of the
18 sanctuary came a loud voice from the throne, which said, 'It is over!' And there followed flashes of lightning and peals of thunder, and a violent
19 earthquake, like none before it in human history, so violent it was. The great city was split in three; the cities of the world fell in ruin; and God did not forget Babylon the great, but made her drink the cup which was
20 filled with the fierce wine of his vengeance. Every island vanished; there
21 was not a mountain to be seen. Huge hailstones, weighing perhaps a hundredweight, fell on men from the sky; and they cursed God for the plague of hail, because that plague was so severe.

17 THEN ONE OF THE SEVEN ANGELS that held the seven bowls came and spoke to me and said, 'Come, and I will show you the judgement on the
2 great whore, enthroned above the ocean. The kings of the earth have committed fornication with her, and on the wine of her fornication men all over
3 the world have made themselves drunk.' In the Spirit he carried me away into the wilds, and there I saw a woman mounted on a scarlet beast which was covered with blasphemous names and had seven heads and ten horns.
4 The woman was clothed in purple and scarlet and bedizened with gold and jewels and pearls. In her hand she held a gold cup, full of obscenities and
5 the foulness of her fornication; and written on her forehead was a name with a secret meaning: 'Babylon the great, the mother of whores and of
6 every obscenity on earth.' The woman, I saw, was drunk with the blood of God's people and with the blood of those who had borne their testimony to Jesus.
7  As I looked at her I was greatly astonished. But the angel said to me, 'Why are you so astonished? I will tell you the secret of the woman and

330

of the beast she rides, with the seven heads and the ten horns. The beast 8
you have seen is he who once was alive, and is alive no longer, but has yet
to ascend out of the abyss before going to perdition. Those on earth whose
names have not been inscribed in the roll of the living ever since the world
was made will all be astonished to see the beast; for he once was alive, and
is alive no longer, and has still to appear.

'But here is the clue for those who can interpret it. The seven heads are 9
seven hills on which the woman sits. They represent also seven kings,*a* of 10
whom five have already fallen, one is now reigning, and the other has yet
to come; and when he does come he is only to last for a little while. As for 11
the beast that once was alive and is alive no longer, he is an eighth—and
yet he is one of the seven, and he is going to perdition. The ten horns you 12
saw are ten kings who have not yet begun to reign, but who for one hour are
to share with the beast the exercise of royal authority; for they have but a 13
single purpose among them and will confer their power and authority upon
the beast. They will wage war upon the Lamb, but the Lamb will defeat 14
them, for he is Lord of lords and King of kings, and his victory will be
shared by his followers, called and chosen and faithful.'*b*

Then he said to me, 'The ocean you saw, where the great whore sat, is 15
an ocean of peoples and populations, nations and languages. As for the ten 16
horns you saw, they together with the beast will come to hate the whore;
they will strip her naked and leave her desolate, they will batten on her
flesh and burn her to ashes. For God has put it into their heads to carry out 17
his purpose, by making common cause and conferring their sovereignty
upon the beast until all that God has spoken is fulfilled. The woman you 18
saw is the great city that holds sway over the kings of the earth.'

After this I saw another angel coming down from heaven; he came with **18**
great authority and the earth was lit up with his splendour. Then in a 2
mighty voice he proclaimed, 'Fallen, fallen is Babylon the great! She has
become a dwelling for demons, a haunt for every unclean spirit, for every
vile and loathsome bird. For all nations have drunk deep of*c* the fierce 3
wine of her fornication; the kings of the earth have committed fornication
with her, and merchants the world over have grown rich on her bloated
wealth.'

Then I heard another voice from heaven that said: 'Come out of her, 4
my people, lest you take part in her sins and share in her plagues. For her 5
sins are piled high as heaven, and God has not forgotten her crimes. Pay 6
her back in her own coin, repay her twice over for her deeds! Double for
her the strength of the potion she mixed! Mete out grief and torment to 7
match her voluptuous pomp! She says in her heart, "I am a queen on my
throne! No mourning for me, no widow's weeds!" Because of this her 8
plagues shall strike her in a single day—pestilence, bereavement, famine,
and burning—for mighty is the Lord God who has pronounced her
doom!'

The kings of the earth who committed fornication with her and wallowed 9
in her luxury will weep and wail over her, as they see the smoke of her

---

*a Or* emperors.　　　　　*b Or . . .* kings, and his followers are faithful men, called
and selected for service.　　　　　*c Other witnesses read* have been ruined by . . .

10 conflagration. They will stand at a distance, for horror at her torment, and
will say, 'Alas, alas for the great city, the mighty city of Babylon! In a single
hour your doom has struck!'

11    The merchants of the earth also will weep and mourn for her, because
12 no one any longer buys their cargoes, cargoes of gold and silver, jewels
and pearls, cloths of purple and scarlet, silks and fine linens; all kinds of
scented woods, ivories, and every sort of thing made of costly woods,
13 bronze, iron, or marble; cinnamon and spice, incense, perfumes and
frankincense; wine, oil, flour and wheat, sheep and cattle, horses, chariots,
14 slaves, and the lives of men. 'The fruit you longed for', they will say, 'is
gone from you; all the glitter and the glamour are lost, never to be yours
15 again!' The traders in all these wares, who gained their wealth from her,
will stand at a distance for horror at her torment, weeping and mourning
16 and saying, 'Alas, alas for the great city, that was clothed in fine linen and
17 purple and scarlet, bedizened with gold and jewels and pearls! Alas that
in one hour so much wealth should be laid waste!'

Then all the sea-captains and voyagers, the sailors and those who traded
18 by sea, stood at a distance and cried out as they saw the smoke of her con-
19 flagration: 'Was there ever a city like the great city?' They threw dust on
their heads, weeping and mourning and saying, 'Alas, alas for the great
city, where all who had ships at sea grew rich on her wealth! Alas that in a
single hour she should be laid waste!'

20    But let heaven exult over her; exult, apostles and prophets and people
of God; for in the judgement against her he has vindicated your cause!

21    Then a mighty angel took up a stone like a great millstone and hurled
it into the sea and said, 'Thus shall Babylon, the great city, be sent hurtling
22 down, never to be seen again! No more shall the sound of harpers and
minstrels, of flute-players and trumpeters, be heard in you; no more shall
craftsmen of any trade be found in you; no more shall the sound of the mill
23 be heard in you; no more shall the light of the lamp be seen in you; no
more shall the voice of the bride and bridegroom be heard in you! Your
traders were once the merchant princes of the world, and with your sorcery
you deceived all the nations.'

24    For the blood of the prophets and of God's people was found in her, the
blood of all who had been done to death on earth.

**19**    After this I heard what sounded like the roar of a vast throng in heaven;
and they were shouting:

2    'Alleluia! Victory and glory and power belong to our God, for true and
just are his judgements! He has condemned the great whore who corrupted the earth with her fornication, and has avenged upon her the
blood of his servants.'

3 Then once more they shouted:

'Alleluia! The smoke goes up from her for ever and ever!'

4 And the twenty-four elders and the four living creatures fell down and
worshipped God as he sat on the throne, and they too cried:

'Amen! Alleluia!'

Then a voice came from the throne which said: 'Praise our God, all you 5 his servants, you that fear him, both great and small!'

Again I heard what sounded like a vast crowd, like the noise of rushing 6 water and deep roars of thunder, and they cried:

'Alleluia! The Lord our God, sovereign over all, has entered on his reign! Exult and shout for joy and do him homage, for the wedding-day 7 of the Lamb has come! His bride has made herself ready, and for her 8 dress she has been given fine linen, clean and shining.'

(Now the fine linen signifies the righteous deeds of God's people.)

Then the angel said to me, 'Write this: "Happy are those who are 9 invited to the wedding-supper of the Lamb!"' And he added, 'These are the very words of God.' At this I fell at his feet to worship him. But he said 10 to me, 'No, not that! I am but a fellow-servant with you and your brothers who bear their testimony to Jesus. It is God you must worship. Those who bear testimony to Jesus are inspired like the prophets.'*a*

THEN I SAW heaven wide open, and there before me was a white horse; 11 and its rider's name was Faithful and True, for he is just in judgement and just in war. His eyes flamed like fire, and on his head were many diadems. 12 Written upon him was a name known to none but himself, and he was 13 robed in a garment drenched in blood.*b* He was called the Word of God, and the armies of heaven followed him on white horses, clothed in fine 14 linen, clean and shining. From his mouth there went a sharp sword with 15 which to smite the nations; for he it is who shall rule them with an iron rod, and tread the winepress of the wrath and retribution of God the sovereign Lord. And on his robe and on his thigh there was written the 16 name: 'King of kings and Lord of lords.'

Then I saw an angel standing in the sun, and he cried aloud to all the 17 birds flying in mid-heaven: 'Come and gather for God's great supper, to 18 eat the flesh of kings and commanders and fighting men, the flesh of horses and their riders, the flesh of all men, slave and free, great and small!' Then 19 I saw the beast and the kings of the earth and their armies mustered to do battle with the Rider and his army. The beast was taken prisoner, and so 20 was the false prophet who had worked miracles in its presence and deluded those that had received the mark of the beast and worshipped its image. The two of them were thrown alive into the lake of fire with its sulphurous flames. The rest were killed by the sword which went out of the Rider's 21 mouth; and all the birds gorged themselves on their flesh.

Then I saw an angel coming down from heaven with the key of the abyss **20** and a great chain in his hands. He seized the dragon, that serpent of old, 2 the Devil or Satan, and chained him up for a thousand years; he threw 3 him into the abyss, shutting and sealing it over him, so that he might seduce the nations no more till the thousand years were over. After that he must be let loose for a short while.

*a* *Or . . . worship. For testimony to Jesus is the spirit that inspires prophets.*
*b* *Some witnesses read* spattered with blood.

4    Then I saw thrones, and upon them sat those to whom judgement was committed. I could see the souls of those who had been beheaded for the sake of God's word and their testimony to Jesus, those who had not worshipped the beast and its image or received its mark on forehead or hand. These came to life again and reigned with Christ for a thousand years,

5    though the rest of the dead did not come to life until the thousand years

6    were over. This is the first resurrection. Happy indeed, and one of God's own people, is the man who shares in this first resurrection! Upon such the second death has no claim; but they shall be priests of God and of Christ, and shall reign with him for the thousand years.

7    When the thousand years are over, Satan will be let loose from his

8    dungeon; and he will come out to seduce the nations in the four quarters of the earth and to muster them for battle, yes, the hosts of Gog and Magog,

9    countless as the sands of the sea. So they marched over the breadth of the land and laid siege to the camp of God's people and the city that he loves.

10   But fire came down on them from heaven and consumed them; and the Devil, their seducer, was flung into the lake of fire and sulphur, where the beast and the false prophet had been flung, there to be tormented day and night for ever.

11   Then I saw a great white throne, and the One who sat upon it; from his presence earth and heaven vanished away, and no place was left for them.

12   I could see the dead, great and small, standing before the throne; and books were opened. Then another book was opened, the roll of the living. From what was written in these books the dead were judged upon the

13   record of their deeds. The sea gave up its dead, and Death and Hades gave up the dead in their keeping; they were judged, each man on the record of

14   his deeds. Then Death and Hades were flung into the lake of fire. This lake

15   of fire is the second death; and into it were flung any whose names were not to be found in the roll of the living.

21   THEN I SAW a new heaven and a new earth, for the first heaven and

2    the first earth had vanished, and there was no longer any sea. I saw the holy city, new Jerusalem, coming down out of heaven from God, made ready like

3    a bride adorned for her husband. I heard a loud voice proclaiming from the throne: 'Now at last God has his dwelling among men! He will dwell among them and they shall be his people, and God himself will be with them.*a*

4    He will wipe every tear from their eyes; there shall be an end to death, and to mourning and crying and pain; for the old order has passed away!'

5    Then he who sat on the throne said, 'Behold! I am making all things new!' (And he said to me, 'Write this down; for these words are trustworthy

6    and true. Indeed they are already fulfilled.') 'I am the Alpha and the Omega, the beginning and the end. A draught from the water-springs of life will be

7    my free gift to the thirsty. All this is the victor's heritage; and I will be his

8    God and he shall be my son. But as for the cowardly, the faithless, and the vile, murderers, fornicators, sorcerers, idolaters, and liars of every kind, their lot will be the second death, in the lake that burns with sulphurous flames.'

*a Some witnesses read* God-with-them shall himself be their God (*see Isaiah 7. 14; 8. 8*).

Then one of the seven angels that held the seven bowls full of the seven 9
last plagues came and spoke to me and said, 'Come, and I will show you the
bride, the wife of the Lamb.' So in the Spirit he carried me away to a great 10
high mountain, and showed me the holy city of Jerusalem coming down out
of heaven from God. It shone with the glory of God; it had the radiance 11
of some priceless jewel, like a jasper, clear as crystal. It had a great high 12
wall, with twelve gates, at which were twelve angels; and on the gates were
inscribed the names of the twelve tribes of Israel. There were three gates 13
to the east, three to the north, three to the south, and three to the west.
The city wall had twelve foundation-stones, and on them were the names 14
of the twelve apostles of the Lamb.

The angel who spoke with me carried a gold measuring-rod, to measure 15
the city, its wall, and its gates. The city was built as a square, and was as 16
wide as it was long. It measured by his rod twelve thousand furlongs, its
length and breadth and height being equal. Its wall was one hundred and 17
forty-four cubits high, that is, by human measurements, which the angel
was using. The wall was built of jasper, while the city itself was of pure gold, 18
bright as clear glass. The foundations of the city wall were adorned with 19
jewels of every kind, the first of the foundation-stones being jasper, the
second lapis lazuli, the third chalcedony, the fourth emerald, the fifth 20
sardonyx, the sixth cornelian, the seventh chrysolite, the eighth beryl,
the ninth topaz, the tenth chrysoprase, the eleventh turquoise, and the
twelfth amethyst. The twelve gates were twelve pearls, each gate being 21
made from a single pearl. The streets of the city were of pure gold, like
translucent glass.

I saw no temple in the city; for its temple was the sovereign Lord God 22
and the Lamb. And the city had no need of sun or moon to shine upon it; 23
for the glory of God gave it light, and its lamp was the Lamb. By its light 24
shall the nations walk, and the kings of the earth shall bring into it all their
splendour. The gates of the city shall never be shut by day—and there will 25
be no night. The wealth and splendour of the nations shall be brought into 26
it; but nothing unclean shall enter, nor anyone whose ways are false or 27
foul, but only those who are inscribed in the Lamb's roll of the living.

Then he showed me the river of the water of life, sparkling like crystal, **22**
flowing from the throne of God and of the Lamb down the middle of the 2
city's street. On either side of the river stood a tree of life, which yields
twelve crops of fruit, one for each month of the year; the leaves of the trees
serve for the healing of the nations. Every accursed thing shall disappear. 3
The throne of God and of the Lamb will be there, and his servants shall
worship him; they shall see him face to face, and bear his name on their 4
foreheads. There shall be no more night, nor will they need the light of 5
lamp or sun, for the Lord God will give them light; and they shall reign
for evermore.

THEN HE SAID to me, 'These words are trustworthy and true. The Lord 6
God who inspires the prophets has sent his angel to show his servants what
must shortly happen. And, remember, I am coming soon!' 7

Happy is the man who heeds the words of prophecy contained in this

8 book! It is I, John, who heard and saw these things. And when I had heard and seen them, I fell in worship at the feet of the angel who had shown
9 them to me. But he said to me, 'No, not that! I am but a fellow-servant with you and your brothers the prophets and those who heed the words of
10 this book. It is God you must worship.' Then he told me, 'Do not seal up
11 the words of prophecy in this book, for the hour of fulfilment is near. Meanwhile, let the evil-doer go on doing evil and the filthy-minded wallow in his filth, but let the good man persevere in his goodness and the dedicated man be true to his dedication.'

12 'Yes, I am coming soon, and bringing my recompense with me, to
13 requite everyone according to his deeds! I am the Alpha and the Omega, the first and the last, the beginning and the end.'

14 Happy are those who wash their robes clean! They will have the right
15 to the tree of life and will enter by the gates of the city. Outside are dogs, sorcerers and fornicators, murderers and idolaters, and all who love and practise deceit.

16 'I, Jesus, have sent my angel to you with this testimony for the churches. I am the scion and offspring of David, the bright star of dawn.'

17 'Come!' say the Spirit and the bride.
'Come!' let each hearer reply.
Come forward, you who are thirsty; accept the water of life, a free gift to all who desire it.

18 For my part, I give this warning to everyone who is listening to the words of prophecy in this book: should anyone add to them, God will add
19 to him the plagues described in this book; should anyone take away from the words in this book of prophecy, God will take away from him his share in the tree of life and the Holy City, described in this book.

20 He who gives this testimony speaks: 'Yes, I am coming soon!'
Amen. Come, Lord Jesus!

21 The grace of the Lord Jesus be with you all.*a*

*a* *Some witnesses read* with all; *others read* with all God's people; *others read* with God's people; *some add* Amen.